HAWAII
HANDBOOK

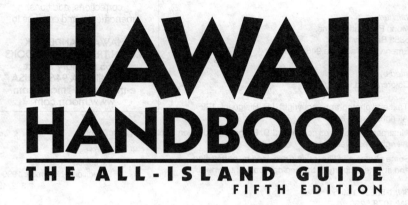

HAWAII HANDBOOK

THE ALL-ISLAND GUIDE
FIFTH EDITION

J.D. BISIGNANI

COMPILED AND REVISED BY
ROBERT NILSEN

MOON
TRAVEL
HANDBOOKS

HAWAII HANDBOOK
FIFTH EDITION

Published by
Moon Publications, Inc.
5855 Beaudry Street
Emeryville, California 94608, USA

Printed by
Colorcraft Ltd.

ISBN: 1-56691-160-5
ISSN: 1078-5299

Editors: Asha Johnson, Pauli Galin
Production & Design: David Hurst
Cartography: Eric Allan, Chris Folks, Allan Leech, Mike Morgenfeld
Index: Asha Johnson

Front cover photo: © John Elk, III; Mahalepu Beach, Kauai

All photos by J.D. Bisignani unless otherwise noted.
All illustrations by Bob Race unless otherwise noted.

Distributed in the United States and Canada by Publishers Group West

Printed in China

Please send all comments,
corrections, additions,
amendments, and critiques to:

**HAWAII HANDBOOK
MOON TRAVEL HANDBOOKS
5855 Beaudry Street
Emeryville, CA 94608, USA
e-mail: travel@moon.com
www.moon.com**

Printing History
1st edition—1987
5th edition—November 1999
5 4 3 2 1 0

To Sandy B.,
who from first glance
filled my life with aloha.
Love, Dad

CONTENTS

INTRODUCTION

BIG ISLAND

MAUI

OAHU

KAUAI

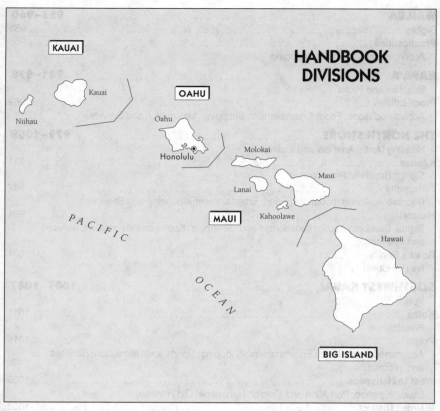

MAP SYMBOLS

═══ Superhighway	○ City	〰 Waterfall
══ Main Road	○ Town	▲ Mountain
── Other Road	▪ Sight	⊥⊤ Swamp/Marsh
┝┿┥ Railroad	● Accommodation	⣿ Lava
⋯⋯ Ferry	⌶ Golf Course	⁕ Cinder Cone
⋯⋯ Trail	✈ International Airport	▲ State Park
⬡ US Interstate	✘ Airfield/Airstrip	⚶ County Park
○ State Highway	△ Campground	Water
⊛ State Capital	🏯 Heiau	Reef
	🐟 Snorkeling	

MAPS

ACKNOWLEDGMENTS

Writing the acknowledgments for a book is supercharged with energy. It's a time when you look forward, hopefully, to a bright future for your work, and a time when you reflect on all that has gone into producing it. Mostly it's a time to say thank you. Thank you for the grace necessary to carry out the task, and thank you to all the wonderful people whose efforts have helped so much along the way. To the following people, I offer my most sincere thank you.

Firstly, to the Moon staff, professionals every one. As time has passed, and one book has followed another, they've become amazingly adept at their work, to the point where their mastery is a marvel to watch.

I would also like to thank the following people for their special help and consideration: Dr. Greg Leo, an adventurer and environmentalist who has done remarkable field research and provided me with invaluable information about the unique flora and fauna of Hawaii; Roger Rose of the Bishop Museum; Lee Wild, Hawaiian Mission Houses Museum; Marilyn Nicholson, State Foundation on Culture and the Arts; the Hawaii Visitors Bureau; Donna Jung, Donna Jung and Associates, who has shown confidence in me since day one; Haunani Vieira, Dollar Rent A Car; Keoni Wagner, Hawaiian Airlines; Jim and John Costello; Dr. Terry and Nancy Carolan; Aubrey Hawk, Bozelle Advertising; Constance Wright, Molokai Visitors Assoc.; Barbara Schonley, of Molokai; Elisa Josephsohn, Public Relations; Faith Ogawa, for helping me keep the faith; Joyce Matsumoto, Halekulani Hotel; Bernie Caalim-Polanzi, Hilton Hotels; Nancy Daniels, Outrigger Hotels; Donn Takahashi, Regional Manager Prince Hotels; Alvin Wong, Hawaii Prince Hotel Waikiki; Martin Kahn, Kahn Galleries; Allison Kneubuhl, Kahala Mandarin Oriental; Matt Bailey, Manele Bay Hotel; Kurt Matsumoto, Lodge at Koele; Stephanie Reid, Princeville Hotel; Margy Parker, Poipu Beach Resort Assoc.; Yvonne Landavazo, Ritz-Carlton Kapalua; Catherine Sharpe, Stryker Weiner; Adi Kohler, Percy Higashi, and Jon Fukuda, Mauna Kea Beach Hotel and Hapuna Prince Hotel; Donna Kimura, Orchid at Mauna Lani; Denise Anderson, Hawaiian Regent; Dennis Costa, Maui Hill; Kim Marshall, Grand Wailea Resort; Sheila Donnelly, of Sheila Donnelly and Associates; Sandi Kato-Klutke, Aston Kauai Beach Villa; Barbara Sheehan, Sheraton Moana Surfrider; Aston Hotels; Norm Manzione, Suntrips; Renee Cochran and Will Titus, Colony Resorts; Linda Darling-Mann, a helpful Kauai friend; Sonia Franzel, Public Relations; Alexander Doyle, Aston Wailea Resort. To all of you, my deepest *aloha*.

HELP MAKE THIS A BETTER BOOK

In today's world, things change so rapidly that it's impossible for one person to keep up with everything happening in any one place. This is particularly true in Hawaii, where situations are always in flux. Travel books are like automobiles: they require fine tuning and frequent overhauls to keep in shape. Help us keep this book in shape! We require input from our readers so that we can continue to provide the best, most current information available. Please write to let us know about any inaccuracies, new information, or misleading suggestions. Although we try to make our maps as accurate as possible, errors do occur. If you have any suggestions for improvement or places that should be included, please let us know about them.

We especially appreciate letters from female travelers, visiting expatriates, local residents, and hikers and outdoor enthusiasts. We also like hearing from experts in the field as well as from local hotel owners and individuals wishing to accommodate visitors from abroad.

If you take a photograph during your trip that you feel might be included in future editions, please send it to us. Send only good slide duplicates or glossy black-and-white prints. Drawings and other artwork are also appreciated. If we use your photo or drawing, you'll be mentioned in the credits and receive a free copy of the book. Keep in mind, however, that the publisher cannot return any materials unless you include a self-addressed, stamped envelope. Moon Publications will own the rights on all material submitted. Address your letter to:

Hawaii Handbook
Moon Travel Handbooks
P.O. Box 3040
Chico, CA 95927-3040 USA
e-mail: travel@moon.com

ABBREVIATIONS

AFB—Air Force Base
B&B—Bed and Breakfast
BYO—bring your own
4WD—Four-Wheel Drive
HVB—Hawaii Visitors Bureau
mph—miles per hour
NWR—National Wildlife Refuge
OHA—Office of Hawaiian Affairs
PADI—Professional Association of Dive Instructors
p/d—per day
pp—per person
p/w—per week
P.O.—Post Office
S.A.S.E.—Self-addressed stamped envelope
SRA—State Recreation Area
YH—Youth Hostel

ACCOMMODATIONS PRICE RANGES

Budget: under $35
Inexpensive: $35-60
Moderate: $60-85
Expensive: $85-100
Premium: $110-150
Luxury: $150 and up

INTRODUCTION

ÎLES SANDWICH, UN OFFICIER DU ROI EN GRAND COSTUME.

No alien land in all the world
has any deep, strong charm for me,
but that one;
no other land could
so longingly and beseechingly
haunt my sleeping and waking,
through half a lifetime,
as that one has done.
Other things leave me,
but it abides.

~Mark Twain, circa 1889

HAWAII STATE ARCHIVES

INTRODUCTION

The modern geological theory concerning the formation of the Hawaiian Islands is no less fanciful than the Polynesian legends sung about it. Science maintains that 30 million years ago, while the great continents were being geologically tortured into their rudimentary shapes, the Hawaiian Islands were a mere ooze of bubbling magma 20,000 feet below the surface of the primordial sea. For millions of years this molten rock flowed up through fissures in the sea floor. Slowly, layer upon layer of lava was deposited until an island rose above the surface of the sea. The island's great weight eventually sealed the fissures, whose own colossal forces progressively crept in a southwesterly direction, then burst out again and again to build the chain. At the same time, the entire Pacific plate, afloat on the giant sea of molten magma, was slowly gliding to the northwest, carrying the newly formed islands with it.

In the beginning the spewing crack formed Kure and Midway islands in the extreme northwestern sector of the Hawaiian chain. Today, more than 130 islands, islets, and shoals make up the Hawaiian Islands, stretching 1,600 miles across an expanse of the North Pacific. Some geologists maintain that the "hot spot" now primarily under the Big Island remains relatively stationary, and that the 1,600-mile spread of the Hawaiian archipelago is due to a northwestern drift of three to five inches per year. Still, with the center of activity under the Big Island, Mauna Loa and Kilauea volcanoes regularly add more land to the only state in the U.S. that is literally still growing. About 20 miles southeast of the Big Island is Loihi Seamount, waiting 3,000 feet below the waves. Frequent eruptions bring it closer and closer to the surface; one day it will emerge and become the newest Hawaiian island and later, perhaps, merge with the Big Island itself.

THE LAND

The Hawaiian Islands sit right in the middle of the North Pacific straddling the tropic of Cancer. They take up about as much room as a flower petal floating in a swimming pool. The sea makes life possible on the islands, and the Hawaiian sea is a mostly benign benefactor providing all the basics. It is also responsible for an endless assortment of pleasure, romance, and excitement, and a cultural link between Hawaii and its Polynesian counterparts. The slopes of the Hawaiian Islands rise dramatically from the sea floor, not gradually, but abruptly, like temple pillars rising straight up from Neptune's kingdom.

Physical Features

Hawaii is the southernmost state in the Union and the most westerly except for a few far-flung islands in the Alaskan Aleutians. The main islands lie just south of the tropic of Cancer at about the same latitude as Mexico City, Havana, Calcutta, and Hong Kong. Hawaii is the fourth smallest state, larger only than Connecticut, Rhode Island, and Delaware. Together, its 132 shoals, reefs, islets, and islands constitute 6,424 square miles of land. The eight *major* islands of Hawaii account for more than 99.9% of the total land area, and are home to 100% of the population (except for a staffed military installation here and there). They stretch over 400 miles of Pacific, and from southeast to northwest include: Hawaii (the Big Island), Maui, Kahoolawe (uninhabited), Lanai, Molokai, Oahu, Kauai, and Niihau. The little-known Northwestern Islands, less than one tenth of one percent of the state's total land mass, are dotted across the North Pacific for more than 1,100 miles running from Nihoa, about 150 miles off Kauai's north shore, to Kure in the far northwest. The state has 822 miles of coastline and just over 1,000 miles of tidal shoreline. It ranges in elevation from Mauna Kea's 13,796-foot summit to Maro Reef, which is often awash by the sea.

Volcanoes

The Hawaiians worshipped Pele, the fire goddess whose name translates equally well as "volcano," "fire pit," or "eruption of lava." When she was angry, Madame Pele spit fire and spewed lava that cooled and formed land. The Hawaiian Islands are perfect examples of **shield volcanoes.** These are formed by a succession of gentle submarine eruptions, which build an elongated dome much like a turtle shell. As the dome nears the surface of the sea, the eruptions combine with air and become extremely explosive due to the rapid temperature change and increased oxygen. Once above the surface they mellow again and steadily build upon themselves. As the island-mountain mushrooms, its weight seals off the spewing fissure below. Instead of forcing itself upward, the lava now finds less resistance by moving laterally. Eventually, the giant tube that carried lava to the top of the volcano sinks in upon itself and becomes a caldera. More eruptions occur periodically, but the lava is less dense and could be thought of as icing on a titanic cake. Then the relentless forces of wind and water take over to sculpt the raw lava into deep crevices and cuts that eventually become valleys. The smooth, once-single mountain is transformed into a miniature mountain range, while generations of coral polyps build reefs around the islands, and the rising and falling of the surrounding seas during episodic ice ages combine with eroded soil to add or destroy coastal plains.

Lava

The Hawaiian Islands are huge mounds of cooled **basaltic lava.** The main components of Hawaiian lava are silica, iron oxide, magnesium, and lime. Lava flows in two distinct types, for which the Hawaiian names have become universal geological terms: **a'a** and **pahoehoe.** They are easily distinguished by appearance, but chemically they're the same. Their appearance differs due to the amount of gases contained in the flow when the lava hardens. A'a lava is extremely rough and spiny, and will quickly tear up your shoes if you do much hiking over it. Also, if you have the misfortune to fall down on it, you'll immediately know why it's called a'a. Pahoehoe is a billowy, ropy lava that looks like burned pancake batter. Not nearly as dense as a'a, it can form fantastic shapes and designs.

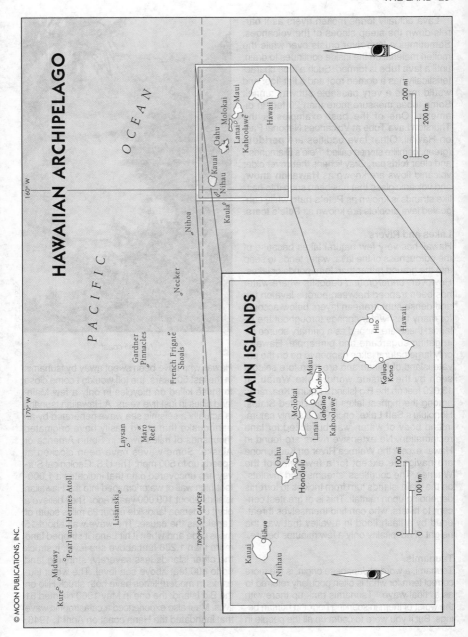

© MOON PUBLICATIONS, INC.

HAWAIIAN ARCHIPELAGO

PACIFIC OCEAN

Kure
Midway
Pearl and Hermes Atoll
Lisianski
Laysan
Maro Reef
Gardner Pinnacles
French Frigate Shoals
Necker
Nihoa

TROPIC OF CANCER

170° W
160° W

200 mi
200 km

MAIN ISLANDS

Kauai
Niihau
Lihue
Oahu
Honolulu
Molokai
Lanai
Kahoolawe
Maui
Lahaina
Kahului
Hawaii
Hilo
Kailua
Kona

100 mi
100 km

Kauai
Niihau
Kaula
Oahu
Molokai
Lanai
Kahoolawe
Maui
Hawaii

Lava actually forms molten rivers as it barrels down the steep slopes of the volcanoes. Sometimes a lava river crusts over while the molten material on the inside continues to drain, until a **lava tube** is formed. Such a tube characteristically has a domed roof and a flat floor and would make a very passable subway tunnel. Some tubes measure more than 20 feet in diameter. One of the best examples is the Thurston Lava Tube at Volcanoes National Park on Hawaii. Other lava oddities are **peridots** (green, gemlike stones called "Pele's Diamonds") and clear **feldspar.** Gray lichens that cover older volcanic flows are known as **Hawaiian snow,** and volcanic glass that has been spun into hairlike strands is known as **Pele's hair,** while congealed lava droplets are known as **Pele's tears.**

Lakes and Rivers

Hawaii has very few natural lakes because of the porousness of the lava: water tends to seep into the ground rather than form ponds or lakes. However, *underground* deposits where water has been trapped between porous lava on top and dense subterranean layers below account for many freshwater springs throughout the islands; these are tapped as a primary source for irrigating sugarcane and pineapple. Hawaii's only large natural lakes happen to be on the private island of Niihau and are therefore seldom seen by the outside world. **Lake Waiau,** at 13,020 feet on the Big Island's Mauna Kea, ranks among the highest lakes in the United States. Honolulu's **Salt Lake,** once Oahu's only natural inland body of water, was bulldozed for land reclamation. No extensive rivers are found in Hawaii except the **Waimea River** on Kauai; none are navigable except for a few miles of the Waimea. The countless "streams" and "rivulets" on the main islands turn from trickles to torrents depending upon rainfall. This is of greatest concern to hikers, who can find themselves threatened by a flash flood in a valley that was the height of hospitality only a few minutes before.

Tsunamis

Tsunami, a word of Japanese origin, is the more correct term for what is often popularly referred to as a "tidal wave." Tsunamis rank up there with the worst of them in sparking horror in human beings. But if you were to count up all the people in

Na Pali coast

Hawaii who have been swept away by tsunamis in the last 50 years, the toll wouldn't come close to those killed on bicycles in only a few Mainland cities in just five years. A Hawaiian tsunami is actually a seismic sea wave generated by an earthquake that could easily have originated thousands of miles away in South America or Alaska. Some waves have been clocked at speeds up to 500 mph. The U.S. Geological Survey has uncovered data that indicates a 1,000-foot-high wall of water crashed into the Hawaiian Islands about 100,000 years ago. They believe a giant undersea landslide about 25 miles south of Lanai was the cause. The wave was about 15 miles wide and when it hit Lanai it stripped land more than 1,200 feet above sea level. It struck the other islands less severely, stripping land up to 800 feet above sea level. The worst tsunamis in modern times have both struck Hilo on the Big Island: the one in May 1960 claimed 61 lives. Maui also experienced a catastrophic wave that inundated the Hana coast on April 1, 1946,

LAND STATISTICS

Area is expressed in square miles, coastline in miles, and highest point in feet.

Figures are approximate.

ISLAND	AREA	PERCENT OF STATE TOTAL	COASTLINE	HIGHEST POINT
Big Island	4,028	62.9	266	13,796
Maui	727	11.3	120	10,023
Lanai	140	2.2	47	3,370
Molokai	260	4	88	4,961
Kahoolawe	45	0.7	29	1,477
Oahu	597	9.3	112	4,020
Northwestern Islands	3		25	903
Kauai	552	8.6	90	5,243
Niihau	70	1	45	1,281
Total	6,423		822	

taking lives and destroying much property. Other waves have inexplicably claimed no lives. The Big Island's Waipio Valley, for example, was a place of royalty that, according to ancient Hawaiian beliefs, was protected by the gods. A giant tsunami inundated Waipio in the 1940s, catching hundreds of people in its watery grasp. Unbelievably, not one person was hurt. After the wave departed, many people rushed to the valley floor to gather thousands of fish that were washed ashore. Without warning, a second towering wave struck and grabbed the people again. Although giant trees and boulders were washed out to sea, not one person was harmed even the second time around. The safest place, besides high ground well away from beach areas, is out on the open ocean where an enormous wave is perceived only as a large swell. A tsunami is only dangerous when it is opposed by land.

Earthquakes

Earthquakes are also a concern in Hawaii and offer a double threat because they can generate tsunamis. If you ever feel a tremor and are close to a beach, evacuate as soon as possible. The Big Island, because of its active volcanoes, experiences hundreds of technical earthquakes every year, although 99% can only be felt on very delicate equipment. The last major quake occurred on the Big Island in late June 1989,

reaching 6.2 on the Richter scale and causing about a million dollars' worth of damage. Fortunately, since 1868 (when an earthquake and tsunami killed 81 people) only two lives have been lost.

Hawaii has an elaborate warning system against natural disasters. You will notice loudspeakers high atop poles along many beaches and coastal areas; these warn of tsunamis, hurricanes, and earthquakes. The loudspeakers are tested at 11 a.m. on the first working day of each month. All island telephone books contain a civil defense warning and procedures section—you should acquaint yourself with this information. Note the maps showing which areas traditionally have been inundated by tsunamis and what procedures to follow in case an emergency occurs.

Environmental Resource Groups

Anyone interested in Hawaii's environmental issues can contact the following for more information:

Earthjustice Legal Defense Fund (formerly Sierra Club Legal Defense Fund), 223 S. King St., 4th Fl., Honolulu, HI 96813, tel. (808) 599-2436, e-mail: eajushi@igc.apc.org.

Greenpeace, 1807 Waianuenue Ave., Hilo, HI 96720, tel. (808) 969-9910, website: www.greenpeace.org.

The Nature Conservancy, 1116 Smith St., Suite 201, Honolulu, HI 96817, tel. (808) 537-4508, e-mail: TNCH1@aol.com, website: www.tnc.org/hawaii.

Rainforest Action Network, 301 Broadway, Suite A, San Francisco, CA 94133, tel. (415) 398-4404, website: www.ran.org; e-mail: rainforest@ran.org.

Sierra Club Hawaii Chapter, 233 Merchant St., 2nd Fl., Honolulu, HI 96813, tel. (808) 538-6616, fax 537-9019, website: www.hi.sierraclub.org.

Earth Trust, 25 Kaneohe Bay Dr., Suite 205, Kailua, HI 96734, tel. (808) 254-2866, fax 254-6409, website: www.earthtrust.org.

A savvy monthly newsletter that focuses on environmental and political issues facing Hawaii today is *Environment Hawai'i,* 200 Kanoelehua Ave., Suite 103-325, Hilo, HI 96720, tel. (808) 934-0115, fax 934-8321, e-mail: pattum@aloha.net, individual subscription rate $35 per year. The well-researched and concisely written newsletter attempts to be fair to all parties concerned, explaining both sides to most controversies. Short on preaching and long on common sense, *Environment Hawai'i* is an excellent resource for anyone interested in sociopolitical and environmental issues.

CLIMATE

Of the wide variety of reasons for visiting Hawaii, most people have at least one in common: the weather! Nowhere on the face of the earth do human beings feel more physically comfortable than in Hawaii, and a happy body almost always means a happy mind and spirit too. Cooling trade winds, low humidity, high pressure, clear sunny days, negative ionization from the sea, and an almost total lack of industrial pollution combine to make Hawaii *the* most healthful spot in America.

"So Good" Weather

The ancient Hawaiians had words to describe climatic specifics such as rain, wind, fog, and even snow, but they didn't have a general word for "weather." The reason is that the weather is just about the same throughout the year and depends more on where you are on any given island than on what season it is. The Hawaiians did distinguish between *kau* (summer, May-Oct.)

and *hoo'ilo* (winter, Nov.-April), but this distinction included social, religious, and even navigational factors, far beyond a mere distinction of weather variations. The average daytime temperature throughout Hawaii is about 80° F, with the average winter day registering 78°, and the average summer day raising the thermometer only seven degrees to 85°. Nighttime temperatures drop less than 10°. Altitude, however, does drop temperatures about three degrees for every 1,000 feet; if you intend to visit the mountain peaks of Haleakala, Mauna Loa, or Mauna Kea (all more than 10,000 feet), expect the temperature to be at least 30° cooler than at sea level. The lowest temperatures ever recorded in Hawaii were atop Haleakala in January 1961 when the mercury dropped well below freezing to a mere 11°; the hottest day occurred in 1931 in the Puna District of the Big Island with a scorching (for Hawaii) 100°.

Precipitation

Hardly a day goes by when it isn't raining somewhere on *all* the main islands. If this amazes you, just consider each island to be a mini-continent: it would be the same as expecting no rain anywhere in North America on any given day. All islands have a windward (northeast, wet) and leeward (southwest, dry) side. It rains much more on the windward side, and much more often during winter than summer. (However, *kona* storms, because they come from the south, hit the islands' leeward sides most often.) Another important rain factor is the mountains, which act like water magnets. Moist winds gather around them and eventually build rain clouds. The ancient Hawaiians used these clouds—and the reflected green light on their underbellies—to spot land from great distances. Precipitation mostly occurs at or below the 3,000-foot level; thus, the upper slopes of taller mountains such as Haleakala are quite dry. The average annual rainfall on the seas surrounding Hawaii is only 25 inches, while a few miles inland around the windward slopes of mountains it can be 250 inches! A dramatic example of this phenomenon is seen by comparing Lahaina and Mt. Puu Kukui, only seven miles distant from each other on West Maui. Hot, arid Lahaina has an annual rainfall of only 15 inches; Puu Kukui can receive close to 40 *feet* of rainfall a year, rivaling Mt. Waialeale on

Kauai as the "wettest spot on earth." Another point to remember is where there's rain there's also an incredible explosion of colorful flowers like an overgrown natural hothouse. You'll find this effect mostly on the windward sides of the islands. Conversely, the best beach weather is on the leeward sides: Kaanapali, Waikiki, Kailua-Kona, Poipu. They all sit in the "rain shadows" of interior mountains, and if it happens to be raining at one leeward beach, just move down the road to the next. One more thing about Hawaiian rains—they aren't very nasty. Much of the time just a light drizzle, they hardly ever last all day. Because they are mostly localized, you can often spot them by looking for rainbows. Rain should never spoil your outings in Hawaii. Just "hang loose, brah," and go to the sunshine.

The Trade Winds

One reason Hawaiian temperatures are both constant and moderate is the trade winds, moderate breezes from the northeast blowing at about 5-15 miles per hour. These breezes are so prevailing that the northeast sides of the islands are always referred to as **windward,** regardless of where the wind happens to be blowing on any given day. You can count on the "trades" to be blowing an average of 300 days per year, hardly missing a day during summer, and occurring half the time in winter. While usually calm in the morning, they pick up during the heat of the afternoon, then weaken at night. Just when you need a cooling breeze, there they are, and when the temperature drops at night, it's as if someone turned down a giant fan.

The trade winds are also a factor in keeping down the humidity. They will suddenly disappear, however, usually in winter, and might not resume for a few weeks. The tropic of Cancer runs through the center of Hawaii, yet the latitude's famed oppressively hot and muggy weather is joyfully absent in the islands. Honolulu, on the same latitude as sweaty Hong Kong and Havana, has only a 50-60% daily humidity factor.

Kona Winds

Kona means "leeward" in Hawaiian, and when the trades stop blowing these southerly winds often take over. To anyone from Hawaii, *"kona wind"* is a euphemism for bad weather for it

HURRICANE FACTS

A **tropical depression** is a low-pressure system or cyclone with winds below 39 mph. A **tropical storm** is cyclone with winds 39-73 mph. A **hurricane** is a cyclone with winds over 74 mph. These winds are often accompanied by torrential rains, destructive waves, and storm surges.

The National Weather Service issues a **Hurricane Watch** if hurricane conditions are expected in the area within 36 hours. A **Hurricane Warning** is issued when a hurricane is expected to strike within 24 hours. The state of Hawaii has an elaborate warning system against natural disasters. You will notice loudspeakers high atop poles along many beaches and coastal areas; these warn of tsunamis, hurricanes, and earthquakes. As the figures below attest, property damage has been great but the loss of life has, thankfully, been minimal.

MAJOR HURRICANES SINCE 1950

NAME	DATE	ISLANDS AFFECTED	DAMAGES
Hiki	Aug. 1950	Kauai	1 death
Nina	Dec. 1957	Kauai	—
Dot	Aug. 1959	Kauai	$5.5 million
Fico	July 1978	Big Island	—
Iwa	Nov. 1982	Kauai, Oahu	1 death; $234 million
Estelle	July 1986	Maui, Big Island	$2 million
Iniki	Sept. 1992	Kauai, Oahu	8 deaths; $1.9 billion

brings in hot, sticky air. Luckily *kona* winds are most common Oct.-April when they appear roughly half the time. The temperatures drop slightly during the winter so these hot winds are tolerable, and even useful for moderating the thermometer. In the summer they are awful, but luckily again they hardly ever blow during this season.

A *kona* storm is another matter. These subtropical low-pressure storms develop west of the Hawaiian Islands, and as they move easterly draw winds up from the south. Usual only in winter, they can cause considerable damage to crops and real estate. There is no real pattern to *kona* storms—some years they come every few weeks while other years they don't appear at all.

Severe Weather
With all this talk of ideal weather it might seem like there isn't any bad. Read on. When a storm does hit an island, conditions can be bleak and miserable. The worst storms are in the fall and winter and often have the warped sense of humor to drop their heaviest rainfalls on areas that are normally quite dry. It's not infrequent for a storm to dump more than three inches of rain an hour; this can go as high as 10, making Hawaiian rainfalls some of the heaviest on earth.

Hawaii has also been hit with some walloping **hurricanes** in the last few decades. There haven't been many but they've been destructive. The vast majority of hurricanes originate far to the southeast off the Pacific coasts of Mexico and Latin America; some, particularly later in the season, start in the midst of the Pacific Ocean near the equator south of Hawaii. Hurricane season is generally considered June to November. Most hurricanes pass harmlessly south of Hawaii but some, swept along by *kona* winds, strike the islands. The most recent and destructive was Hurricane Iniki, which battered the islands in 1992, killing eight people and causing an estimated $2 billion in damage. It had its greatest effect on Niihau, the Poipu Beach area of Kauai, and on the leeward coast of Oahu.

FLORA AND FAUNA

Anyone who loves a mystery will be intrigued by the speculation about how plants and animals first came to Hawaii. Most people's idea of an island paradise includes swaying palms, dense mysterious jungles ablaze with wildflowers, and luscious fruits just waiting to be plucked. In fact, for millions of years the Hawaiian chain consisted of raw and barren islands where no plants grew and no birds sang. Why? Because they are geological orphans that spontaneously popped up in the middle of the Pacific Ocean. The islands, more than 2,000 miles from any continental landfall, were therefore isolated from the normal ecological spread of plants and animals. Even the most tenacious travelers of the flora and fauna kingdoms would be sorely tried in crossing the mighty Pacific. Those that made it by pure chance found a totally foreign ecosystem. They had to adapt or perish. The survivors evolved quickly, and many plants and birds became so specialized that they were not only limited to specific islands in the chain but to habitats that frequently encompassed a single isolated valley. It was as if after traveling so far and finding a niche, they never budged again. Luckily, the soil of Hawaii was virgin and rich, the competition from other plants or animals was nonexistent, and the climate was sufficiently varied and nearly perfect for most growing things.

The evolution of plants and animals on the isolated islands was astonishingly rapid. A tremendous change in environment, coupled with a limited gene pool, accelerated natural selection. For example, many plants lost their protective thorns and spines because there were no grazing animals or birds to destroy them. Before settlement, Hawaii had no fruits, vegetables, coconut palms, edible land animals, conifers, mangroves, or banyans. Tropical flowers, wild and vibrant as we know them today, were relatively few. In a land where thousands of orchids now brighten every corner, there were only four native varieties, the least in any of the 50 states. Today, the indigenous plants and animals have the highest rate of extinction anywhere on earth. By the beginning of this century, native plants growing below 1,500 feet in elevation were almost completely extinct or totally replaced by introduced species. The land and its living things have been greatly transformed by humans and their agriculture. This inexorable process began when Hawaii was the domain of its original Polynesian settlers, then greatly accelerated when the land was inundated by Western peoples.

The Greening of Hawaii

The first *deliberate* migrants to Hawaii were Polynesians from the Marquesas Islands. Many of their voyages were undertaken when life on their native islands became intolerable. They were prompted mostly by defeat in war, or by growing island populations that overtaxed the available food supply. Whatever the reasons, the migrations were deliberate and permanent. The first colonizers were known as "the land seekers" in the old Marquesan language—probably advance scouting parties who proved true the ancient chants, which sung of a land to the north. Once they discovered Hawaii, their return voyage to the southern homeland was relatively easy. They had the favorable trade winds at their backs, plus the certainty of sailing into familiar waters. Later both men and women would set out for the new land in canoes laden with seeds and plant cuttings necessary for survival, as well as animals for both consumption and sacrifice.

Not all the domesticated plants and animals came at once, but the colonizers brought enough to get started. The basic food plants included taro, banana, coconut, sugarcane, breadfruit, and yams. The Polynesians also brought the paper mulberry from which tapa was made, and the ti plant necessary for cooking and making offerings at *heiau*. Various gourds were grown to be used as bowls, containers, and even helmets for Hawaiian-style defensive armor. Arrowroot and turmeric were used in cooking and by the healing *kahuna* as medicines. *Awa* was brought by the high priests to be used in rituals; chewed, the resulting juice was spat into a bowl where it fermented and became a mild intoxicant. Bamboo, the natural wonder material, was planted and used for countless purposes. The only domesticated animals taken to the new land were pigs, dogs, and chickens. Rats also made the journey as stowaways.

In the new land the Polynesians soon found native plants that they incorporated and put to good use. Some included: *olona*, which made the best-known fiber cord anywhere in the world and later was eagerly accepted by sailing ships as new rigging and as a trade item; koa, an excellent hardwood used for the manufacture of highly prized calabashes and the hulls of magnificent seagoing canoes; *kukui* (candlenut), eaten as a tasty nut, strung to make lei, or burned as a source of light like a natural candle. For a thousand years a distinct Hawaiian culture formed in relative isolation. When the first whites came they found a people who had become intimately entwined with their environment. The relationship between Hawaiians and the *aina* (land) was spiritual, physical, and emotional: they were one.

PLANTS, FLOWERS, AND TREES

Much like the Polynesian settlers who followed, it was the drifters, castaways, and shanghaied of the plant and animal kingdom that were the first to reach Hawaii. Botanists say spores and seeds were carried aloft into the upper atmosphere by powerful winds, then made lucky landings on the islands. Some hardy seeds came with the tides and managed to sprout and grow once they hit land. Others were carried on the feathers and feet of migratory birds, while some made the trip in birds' digestive tracts and were ignominiously deposited with their droppings. This chance seeding of Hawaii obviously took a very long time: scientists estimate one plant arrival and establishment every 20,000-30,000 years. By latest count more than 1,700 distinct species of endemic (only Hawaiian) and indigenous (other islands of Polynesia) plants have been cataloged throughout the island chain. It is reasonably certain all of these plants were introduced by only 250 original immigrants; the 168 different Hawaiian ferns, for example, are the result of approximately 13 colonists. Most of the seeds and spores are believed to have come from Asia and Indonesia, and evidence of this spread can be seen in related plant species common to many Polynesian islands. Other endemic species such as the koa tree, which the Hawaiians put to great use in canoe building, have close relatives only in Australia. No other group of islands between Hawaii and Australia have such trees; the reason remains a mystery. Many plants and grasses came from North and South America and can be identified with common ancestors still there. Some species have become so totally Hawaiian that relatives are found nowhere else on earth. This last category has either evolved so dramatically they can no longer be recognized, or their common ancestors have long been extinct from the original environment. An outstanding example in this category is the silversword *(ahinahina),* found in numbers only atop Haleakala on Maui, with a few specimens extant on the volcanoes of the Big Island.

Hawaii's Flora

Hawaii's indigenous and endemic plants, flowers, and trees are both fascinating and beautiful, but unfortunately, like everything else that was native, they are quickly disappearing. The majority of flora considered exotic by visitors was introduced either by the original Polynesians or by later white settlers. The Polynesians who colonized Hawaii brought foodstuffs, gourds, *awa,* and the ti plant. Non-Hawaiian settlers over the years have brought mangos, papayas, passion fruit, pineapples, and many other tropical fruits and vegetables associated with the islands. Also, most of the flowers, including protea, plumeria, anthuriums, orchids, heliconia, ginger, and most hibiscus, have come from every continent on earth. Tropical America, Asia, Java, India, and China have contributed their most beautiful and delicate blooms. Hawaii is blessed with national and state parks, gardens, undisturbed rainforests, private reserves, and commercial nurseries that offer an exhaustive botanical survey of the island. The following is a sampling of the common native and introduced flora that add dazzling color and exotic tastes to the landscape.

Native Trees

Koa and ohia are two indigenous trees still seen on the main islands. Both have been greatly reduced by the foraging of introduced cattle and goats, and through logging and forest fires.

The koa, a form of acacia, is Hawaii's finest native tree. It can grow to more than 70 feet high and has a strong, straight trunk that can measure more than 10 feet in circumference. Koa is a quickly growing legume that fixes nitrogen in the soil. It is believed that the tree originated in Africa, where it was damp. It then migrated to Australia, where dry conditions caused the elimination of leaves, leaving only bare stems that could survive in the desert climate. When koa came to the Pacific Islands, instead of reverting to the true leaf, it just broadened its leaf stem into sickle-shaped, leaflike foliage that produces an inconspicuous, pale-yellow flower. When the tree is young or damaged it will revert to the original feathery, fernlike leaf that evolved in Africa millions of years ago. Koa does best in well-drained soil in deep forest areas, but scruffy specimens will grow in poorer soil. The Hawaiians used koa as the main log for their dugout canoes; elaborate ceremonies were performed when a log was cut and dragged to a canoe shed. Koa wood was also preferred for paddles, spears, even surfboards. Today it is still, unfortunately, considered an excellent furniture wood; and although fine specimens can be found in the reserve of Hawaii Volcanoes National Park on the Big Island, loggers elsewhere are harvesting the last of the big trees.

The ohia is a survivor and therefore the most abundant of all the native Hawaiian trees. Com-

ohia lehua tree

LOUISE FOOTE

koa tree

LOUISE FOOTE

ing in a variety of shapes and sizes, it grows as miniature trees in wet bogs or as 100-foot giants on cool, dark slopes at higher elevations. This tree is often the first life in new lava flows. The ohia produces a tuftlike flower—usually red, but occasionally orange, yellow, or white, the latter being very rare and elusive—that resembles a natural pompon. The flower was considered sacred to Pele; it was said she would cause a rainstorm if you picked ohia blossoms without the proper prayers. The flowers were fashioned into lei that resembled feather boas. The strong, hard wood was used to make canoes, poi bowls, and especially temple images. Ohia logs were also used as railroad ties and shipped to the Mainland from Pahoa. It's believed that the "golden spike" linking rail lines between the U.S. East and West coasts was driven into a Puna ohia log when the two railroads came together in Ogden, Utah.

Lobelia

More species of lobelia grow in Hawaii than anywhere else in the world. A common garden flower elsewhere, in Hawaii it grows to tree height. You'll see some unique species covered with hair or spikes. The lobelia flower is tiny and resembles a miniature orchid with curved and pointed ends, like the beak of the native 'i'iwi. This bird feeds on the flower's nectar; it's obvious that both evolved in Hawaii together and exhibit the strange phenomenon of nature mimicking nature.

Tropical Rainforests

When it comes to pure and diverse natural beauty, the U.S. is one of the finest pieces of real estate on earth. As if purple mountains' majesty and fruited plains weren't enough, it even contains tiny, living emeralds of tropical rainforest. A tropical rainforest is where the earth takes a

KUKUI (CANDLENUT)

Reaching heights of 80 feet, the *kukui* (candlenut) was a veritable department store to the Hawaiians, who made use of almost every part of this utilitarian giant. Its nuts, bark, or flowers were ground into potions and salves to be taken as a general tonic, applied to ulcers and cuts as an effective antibiotic, or administered internally as a cure for constipation or asthma attacks. The bark was mixed with water and the resulting juice was used as a dye in tattooing, tapa-cloth making, and canoe painting, and as a preservative for fishnets. The oily nuts were burned as a light source in stone holders, and ground and eaten as a condiment called *inamona*. Polished nuts took on a beautiful sheen and were strung as lei. Lastly, the wood itself was hollowed into canoes and used as fishnet floats.

LOUISE FOOTE

breath and exhales pure sweet oxygen through its vibrant green canopy. Located in the territories of Puerto Rico and the Virgin Islands, and in the state of Hawaii, these forests comprise only one-half of one percent of the world's total, and they must be preserved. The U.S. Congress passed two bills in 1986 designed to protect the unique biological diversity of its tropical areas, but their destruction has continued unabated. The lowland rainforests of Hawaii, populated mostly by native ohia, are being razed. Landowners slash, burn, and bulldoze them to create more land for cattle and agriculture, and, most distressingly, for wood chips to generate electricity! Introduced wild boar gouge the forest floor, exposing sensitive roots and leaving tiny fetid ponds where mosquito larvae thrive. Feral goats roam the forests like hoofed locusts and strip all vegetation within reach. Rainforests on the higher and steeper slopes of mountains have a better chance as they are harder for humans to reach. One unusual feature of Hawaii's rainforests is that they are "upside down." Most plant and animal species live on the forest floor, rather than in the canopy as in other forests.

Maui's Nature Conservancy Preserve in Waikamoi has managed to fence in a speck of this forest, keeping it safe from these animals for the time being. Almost half the birds classified in the U.S. as endangered live in Hawaii, and almost all of these make their homes in the rainforests. For example, Maui's rainforests have yielded the *poouli*, a new species of bird discovered only in 1974. Another forest survey in 1981 rediscovered the Bishop's *'o'o*, a bird thought to be extinct at the turn of the century. We can only lament the passing of the rainforests that have already fallen to ignorance, but if this ill-fated destruction continues on a global level, we will be lamenting our own passing. We must nurture the rainforests that remain, and with simple enlightenment, let them be.

BIRDLIFE

One of the great tragedies of natural history is the continuing demise of Hawaiian birdlife. Perhaps only 15 original species of birds remain of the more than 70 native families that thrived before the coming of humans. Experts believe that the ancient Hawaiians annihilated about 40 species, including seven species of geese, a rare one-legged owl, ibis, lovebirds, sea eagles, and hunting creepers. Since the arrival of Captain Cook in 1778, 23 species have become extinct, with 31 more in danger. Hawaii's endangered birds account for more than 40% of the birds officially listed by the U.S. Fish and Wildlife Service as endangered or threatened. In the last 200 years, more than four times as many birds have become extinct in Hawaii as in all of North America. These figures unfortunately suggest that a full 40% of Hawaii's endemic birds no longer exist. Almost all of Oahu's native birds are gone and few indigenous Hawaiian birds can be found on any island below the 3,000-foot level.

Native birds have been reduced in number because of multiple factors. The original Polynesians helped wipe out many species. They altered large areas for farming and used fire to destroy patches of pristine forests. Also, bird feathers were highly prized for the making of lei, for featherwork in capes and helmets, and for the large *kahili* fans that indicated rank among the *ali'i*. Introduced exotic birds and the new diseases they carried are another major reason for reduction of native bird numbers, along with predation by the mongoose and rat—especially upon ground-nesting birds. Bird malaria and bird pox were also devastating to the native species. Mosquitoes, unknown in Hawaii until they were accidently introduced at Lahaina in 1826, infected most native birds, causing a rapid reduction in birdlife. Feral pigs rooting deep in the rainforests knock over ferns and small trees, creating fetid pools in which mosquito larvae thrive. However, the most damaging factor by far is the assault upon native forests by agriculture and land developers. The vast majority of Hawaiian birds evolved into specialists. They lived in only one small area and ate a very limited number of plants or insects—if these were removed or altered, the birds died.

Preservation

Theodore Roosevelt established the Northwest Islands as a National Wildlife Reserve in the early 20th century, and efforts have continued since then to preserve Hawaii's unique avifauna. Many fine organizations are fighting the battle to preserve Hawaii's natural heritage, including:

Hawaii Audubon Society, University of Hawaii, U.S. Fish and Wildlife Service, World Wildlife Fund, and Hawaii Department of Natural Resources. While visiting Hawaii make sure to obey all rules regarding the natural environment. Never disturb nesting birds or their habitat while hiking. Be careful with fire and never cut living trees. If you spot an injured or dead bird do not pick it up, but report it to the local office of the U.S. Fish and Wildlife Service. Only through a conscientious effort of all concerned does Hawaii's wildlife stand a chance of surviving.

Hawaiian Honeycreepers

A most amazing family of all the birds on the face of earth is one known as Drepanididae, or Hawaiian honeycreepers. More than 40 distinct types of honeycreepers currently exist, although many more are suspected to have become extinct even before the arrival of Captain Cook, when a record was started. All are believed to have evolved from *a single* ancestral species. The honeycreepers have differing body types. Some look like finches, while others resemble warblers, thrushes, blackbirds, parrots, and even woodpeckers. Their bills range from long, pointed honeysuckers to tough, hooked nutcrackers. They are the most divergently evolved birds in the world. If Darwin, who studied the birds of the Galapagos Islands, had come to Hawaii, he would have found bird evolution that would make the Galapagos seem like child's play.

More Endangered Endemic Birds

Maui is the last home of the **crested honey-creeper** *(akohe'kohe),* that lives only on the windward slope of Haleakala from 4,500 to 6,500 feet. It once lived on Molokai but no longer. A rather large bird, it averages seven inches long and is predominantly black. Its throat and breast are tipped with gray feathers; bright orange decks its neck and underbelly. A distinctive fluff of feathers forms a crown. It primarily eats ohia flowers, and it's believed the crown feathers gather pollen and help propagate the ohia. The **Maui parrotbill** is another endangered bird found only on the slopes of Haleakala above 5,000 feet. It has an olive green back and yellow body. Its most distinctive feature is the parrotlike bill, which it uses to crack branches and pry out larvae.

The *poouli* is a dark brown, five-inch bird with a black mask and dark brown feet. It has a short tail and sports a conical bill. It was saved from extinction through efforts of the Sierra Club and Audubon Society, who successfully had it listed on the Federal List of Endangered Species. The bird has one remaining stronghold deep in the forests of Maui.

Two endangered waterbirds are the **Hawaiian stilt** *(ae'o)* and the **Hawaiian coot** *(alae ke'oke'o).* The stilt is a 16-inch, very thin wading bird. It is primarily black with a white belly, and long, pink sticklike legs. It lives on Maui at Kanaha and Kealia Ponds. The adults will pretend to be hurt, putting on an excellent "broken-wing" performance in order to lure predators away from their nests. The Hawaiian coot is a web-footed waterbird that resembles a duck. Found on all the main islands but mostly on Maui and Kauai, it has dull gray feathers, a white bill, and white tail feathers. It builds a large floating nest and vigorously defends its young. The **dark-rumped petrel** is slightly different from other petrels that are primarily marine birds. This petrel can usually be seen around the visitors center at Haleakala Crater about an hour after dusk May-October.

Survivors

The *amakihi* and the *'i'iwi* are endemic birds that aren't endangered at the moment. The *amakihi* is one of the most common native birds. Yellowish-green, it frequents the high branches of ohia, koa, and sandalwood looking for insects, nectar, or fruit. It's less specialized than most other Hawaiian birds, the main reason for its continued existence. The *'i'iwi* is a bright red bird with a salmon-colored hooked bill. It's found mainly on Maui, Hawaii, and Kauai in forests above 2,000 feet. It, too, feeds on a variety of insects and flowers. The *'i'iwi* is known for its harsh voice that sounds like a squeaking hinge, but is also capable of a melodious song.

The *elepaio* is found on several of the islands and is fairly common in the rainforest. This long-tailed, five-inch brown bird can be coaxed to come within touching distance of the observer. This bird was the special *aumakua* (personal spirit) of canoe builders in ancient lore. The *apapane,* the most common native bird, is the easiest to see. It's a chubby, red-bodied bird about five inches long with a black bill, legs, wingtips, and

HAWAII NATIONAL WILDLIFE REFUGES

BIG ISLAND

Hakalau Forest NWR

32 Kinoole St., Hilo, HI 96720, tel. (808) 933-6915. Located between the 3,900 and 7,200 foot elevation on the windward slope of Mauna Kea, it protects *akiapola'au*, Hawaiian *akepa*, Hawaiian creeper, Hawaiian hawk, *ou*, Hawaiian hoary bat, *amakihi*, Hawaiian thrush, *elepaio*, *'i'iwi*, and *apapane* in 11,000 acres of koa-ohia habitat. Instrumental in sustaining the naturally evolving mid-elevation rainforest. Entry is authorized for hiking on the last weekend of the month only, by special use permit. Contact manager.

MOLOKAI

Kakahai'a NWR

Hawaiian and Pacific Islands NWRs, 300 Ala Moana Blvd., P.O. Box 50167, Honolulu, HI 96850, tel. (808) 541-1201. Five miles east of Kaunakakai along Hwy. 450, it protects Hawaiian coot and Hawaiian stilt in 40 acres of freshwater pond and marsh with dense thickets of bulrush. Established 1976. Beach park on refuge land open to public.

OAHU

James C. Campbell NWR

Hawaiian and Pacific Islands NWRs, 300 Ala Moana Blvd., P.O. Box 50167, Honolulu, HI 96850, tel. (808) 541-1201. Near Kahuku on the northeastern shore of the island of Oahu, it protects Hawaiian gallinule *(alae'ula),* Hawaiian coot *(alae ke'oke'o),* Hawaiian stilt *(aeo),* Hawaiian duck *(koloa),* black-crowned night herons, introduced birds, migratory shorebirds, and waterfowl. Covers 142 acres in two units: Punamano Pond is a natural spring-fed marsh, the Kii Unit is a series of manmade ponds once used as sugarcane waste settling basins. Established in 1977. Open on specified weekends; contact manager for tours.

Pearl Harbor NWR

Hawaiian and Pacific Islands NWRs, 300 Ala Moana Blvd., P.O. Box 50167, Honolulu, HI 96850, tel. (808) 541-1201. Located within Pearl Harbor Naval Base, it protects Hawaiian gallinule, Hawaiian coot, Hawaiian stilt, *koloa* (Hawaiian duck), and black-crowned night herons on 40 acres of manmade wetlands. Established in 1977. Contact manager for tours.

KAUAI

Kilauea Point NWR

P.O. Box 87, Kilauea, HI 96754, tel. (808) 828-1413. One mile north of Kilauea on a paved road; headquarters and parking area on Kilauea Point. Protects red-footed boobies, shearwaters, great frigate birds, brown boobies, red-tailed and white-tailed tropic birds, and Laysan albatross; also green sea turtles, humpback whales, and dolphins. Covers 31 acres of cliffs and headlands with native coastal plants. Open Mon.-Fri., 10 a.m.-4 p.m.; admission. Binoculars are available to borrow.

Huleia NWR

P.O. Box 87, Kilauea, HI 96754, tel. (808) 828-1413. Viewing is best from the Menehune Fish Pond overlook along Hulemalu Rd. west of Puhi Road. Protects *koloa* (Hawaiian duck), Hawaiian coot, Hawaiian gallinule, and Hawaiian stilt. Covers 238 acres of seasonally flooded river bottomland and wooded slopes of the Huleia River Valley. Established in 1973. No general admittance.

Hanalei NWR

P.O. Box 87, Kilauea, HI 96754, tel. (808) 828-1413. On the north coast of Kauai, one and a half miles east of Hanalei on Hwy. 56. Observe wildlife from Ohiki Road, which begins at the west end of Hanalei River bridge, or from the highway overlook in Princeville. Protects *koloa* (Hawaiian duck), Hawaiian coot, Hawaiian gallinule, and Hawaiian stilt. Covers 917 acres of riverbottom land, taro farms, and wooded slopes in the Hanalei River Valley. Established in 1972.

ATOLLS

Hawaiian Islands NWR

c/o Hawaiian and Pacific Islands NWRs, 300 Ala Moana Blvd., P.O. Box 50167, Honolulu, HI 96850, tel. (808) 541-1202. Far-flung islands and atolls strung 1,000 miles from Nihoa Island to Pearl and Hermes Reef—rugged volcanic remnants and sparsely vegetated low sandy islands. Protects Laysan and black-footed albatrosses, sooty terns, white terns, brown and black noddies, shearwaters, petrels, red-tailed tropic birds, frigate birds, and boobies. Also protected are several land birds and ducks and the Hawaiian monk seal and the green sea turtle. Covers 1,800 acres of land and a quarter million acres of submerged reef and lagoons. Established in 1909. No general access.

Remote Pacific Refuges

Hawaiian and Pacific Islands NWRs, 300 Ala Moana Blvd., P.O. Box 50167, Honolulu, HI 96850, tel. (808) 541-1202. **Johnston Atoll NWR** is located about 825 miles southwest of Honolulu. Protects seabird nesting rookeries, sooty terns, gray-backed terns, shearwaters, red-footed boobies, brown boobies, masked boobies, lesser and great frigate birds, red-tailed tropic birds, and brown noddies. Refuge since 1926. Managed with the Defense Nuclear Agency.

Baker Island NWR, 340 acres, and **Howland**

Island NWR, 400 acres, are located about 1,600 miles southwest of Hawaii, just north of the equator. Each encompasses emerged and submerged land. Low islands covered in grasses, vines, and bush, that sustain various seabirds and migratory birds.

Jarvis Island NWR is about 1,300 miles south of Honolulu and includes 1,100 acres of nesting area for at least eight species of migratory birds.

Rose Atoll NWR is the easternmost point of the Samoan Archipelago and the southernmost U.S. national wildlife refuge. Covers 20 acres of islets, lagoon, and reef that support a dozen species of migratory birds. Administered jointly with the American Samoa government. Baker, Howland, Jarvis, and Rose NWRs were established in 1974.

tail feathers. It's quick and flitty and has a wide variety of calls and songs, from beautiful warbles to mechanical buzzes. Its feathers, like those of the *'i'iwi,* were sought by Hawaiians to produce distinctive capes and helmets for the *ali'i.*

Pueo

This Hawaiian owl is found on all of the main islands, but mostly on Maui, especially in Haleakala Crater. The *pueo* is one of the oldest examples of an *aumakua* in Hawaiian mythology. It was an especially benign and helpful guardian. Old Hawaiian stories abound in which a *pueo* came to the aid of a warrior in distress or a defeated army. Arriving at a tree in which a *pueo* had alighted, the soldiers are safe from their pursuers and are under the protection of "the wings of an owl." The many introduced barn owls in Hawaii are easily distinguished from a *pueo* by their heart-shaped faces. The *pueo* is about 15 inches tall with a mixture of brown and white feathers. The eyes are large, round, and yellow, and the legs are heavily feathered, unlike those of a barn owl. *Pueo* chicks are a distinct yellow color.

pueo

The *Nene*

The *nene,* or Hawaiian goose, deserves special mention because it is Hawaii's state bird and is making a comeback from the edge of extinction. The *nene* is found only on the slopes of Mauna Loa, Hualalai, and Mauna Kea on the Big Island, and in Haleakala Crater on Maui. It was extinct on Maui until a few birds were returned there in 1957, but some experts maintain the *nene* lived naturally only on the Big Island. *Nene* are raised at the Wildfowl Trust in Slimbridge, England, which placed the first birds at Haleakala, and at the Hawaiian Fish and Game Station at Pohakuloa, along the Saddle Road on Hawaii. By the 1940s, fewer than 50 birds lived in the wild. Now approximately 125 birds live on Haleakala and 500 on the Big Island. Although the birds can be raised successfully in captivity, their life in the wild is still in question.

The *nene* is believed to be a descendant of the Canada goose, which it resembles. Geese are migratory birds that form strong kinship ties, mating for life. It's speculated that a migrating goose became disabled, and along with its loyal mate, remained in Hawaii. The *nene* is smaller than its Canadian cousin, has lost a great deal of webbing in its feet, and is perfectly at home away from water, foraging and nesting on rugged and bleak lava flows. The nene is a perfect symbol of Hawaii: let it be, and it will live.

OTHER HAWAIIAN ANIMALS

Insects

No one knows for sure, but it's highly probable the first animal arrivals in Hawaii were insects. Again, the theory is that most were blown here by ancient hurricanes or drifted here imbedded in floating logs and other pieces of wood. Like the plants that preceded them, their success and rapid evolution were phenomenal. A pregnant female had to make the impossible journey, then happen upon a suitable medium in which to deposit her eggs. Here, at least, they would be free from predators and parasites with a good chance of developing to maturity. Again the gene pool was highly restricted and the environment so foreign that an amazing variety of evolutionary changes occurred. Biologists believe only 150 original insect species are responsible for the more than 10,000 species that occur in Hawaii today. Of these 10,000, nearly 98% are found nowhere else on earth. Many are restricted to only one island, and most are dependent on a single species of plant or fruit. For this reason, when Hawaiian plants become extinct, many insects disappear as well.

It's very probable there were no pests before humans arrived. The first Polynesians introduced flies, lice, and fleas. Westerners brought the indestructible cockroach, mosquito larvae in their ships' stores of water, termites, ants, and all the plant pests that could hitch a ride in the cuttings and fruits intended for planting. Today visitors will note the stringent agricultural controls at airports. Some complain about the inconvenience, but they should know that in the past 50 years more than 700 new insect species have become established in Hawaii. Many are innocent enough, while others cause great problems for Hawaii's agriculture.

Land Snails

People have the tendency to ignore snails until they step on one, and then they find them repulsive. But Hawaiian snails are some of the most remarkable and beautiful in the world. It's one thing to accept the possibility that a few insects or plant spores could have been driven to Hawaii by high winds or on birds' feet, given the fact of their uncountable billions. But how did the snails get here? Snails, after all, aren't known for their nimbleness or speed. Most Hawaiian snails never make it beyond the tree on which they're hatched. Yet more than 1,000 snail varieties are found in Hawaii and most are inexplicably found nowhere else. The Polynesians didn't bring them, seawater kills them, and it would have to be a mighty big bird that didn't notice one clinging to its foot. Biologists have puzzled over Hawaiian snails for years. One, J.T. Gulick, wrote in 1858, "These Achatinellinae [tree snails] never came from Noah's ark." Tree snails are found on Oahu, Maui, Molokai, and Lanai, but not on Kauai. Kauai has its own land dwellers, and the Big Island has land snails that have moved into the trees. Like all the other endemic species, Hawaiian land snails now face extinction. Of the estimated 1,000 species existing when the Europeans came, 600 are now gone forever, and many others are threatened. Agriculture, the demise of native flora, and the introduction of new species add up to a bleak future for the snails.

Drosophila, The Hawaiian Fly

Most people hardly pay attention to flies, unless one lands on their plate lunch. But geneticists from throughout the world, and especially from the University of Hawaii, make special pilgrimages to the volcano area of the Big Island and to Maui just to study the native Hawaiian drosophila. This critter is related to the fruit fly and housefly, but there are hundreds of native species that are singularly unique—more than one-third of the world's estimated total. The Hawaiian ecosystem is very simple and straightforward, so geneticists can trace the evolutionary changes from species to subspecies through mating behavior. The scientists compare the drosophila species between the two islands and chart the differences. Major discoveries in evolutionary genetics have been made through these studies.

Indigenous Land Animals

Before humans arrived, Hawaii had a paucity of higher forms of land animals. There were no amphibians and no reptiles, and except for a profusion of birdlife, insects, and snails, only two other animals were present: the **monk seal** and the **hoary bat,** both highly specialized mammals.

The monk seal has close relatives in the Caribbean and Mediterranean, although the Caribbean relatives are now believed to be extinct, making the monk seal one of the two tropical seals left on earth. It's believed that the monk seal's ancestors entered the Pacific about 200,000 years ago when the Isthmus of Panama was submerged. When the land rose, no more seals arrived, and the monk seal became indigenous to Hawaii. The main habitat for the Hawaiian monk seal is the outer islands, from the French Frigate Atolls north to Kure Island, but infrequently a seal is spotted on the shores of one of the main islands. Though the seals' existence was known to the native Hawaiians, who called them *'ilio-holo-i-ka-uaua* (dog running in the toughness), they didn't seem to play much of a role in their folklore or ecosystem. Whalers and traders certainly knew of their existence, hunting them for food and sometimes for skins. This kind of pressure almost wiped out the small seal population in the 18th century. Scientists were largely unaware of the monk seal until early this century. Finally, the seals were recognized as an endangered species and put under the protection of the Hawaiian Islands National Wildlife Refuge, where they remain in a touch-and-go battle against extinction. Today it's estimated that only 1,000 individuals are left.

The hoary bat *(pe'ape'a)* is a remarkable migratory animal that reached Hawaii from North and South America under its own power. The Hawaiian hoary bat no longer migrates, but its continental relatives still range far and wide. The Hawaiian bat has become somewhat smaller and reddish in color over the years, distinguishing it from its larger, darker brown cousins. Its tail has a whitish coloration, hence the name. The hoary bat has a 13-inch wingspan, gives birth to twins in early summer, and unlike other bats, is a solitary creature, roosting in trees. It doesn't live in caves like others of its species. The bats normally live at altitudes below 4,000 feet, but some have been observed on Mauna Loa and Mauna Kea above 6,000 feet. The main population is on the Big Island, with smaller breeding grounds on Maui and Kauai. Sometimes bats are spotted on the other main islands, but it remains uncertain whether they inhabit the islands or simply fly there from their established colonies. Recently, a second species of bat (now extinct) has been identified from bone fragments taken from caves on four of the Hawaiian islands.

Coral

Whether you're an avid scuba diver or novice snorkeler, you'll become aware of underwater coral gardens and grottoes whenever you peer at the fantastic seascapes below the waves. Although there is plenty of it, the coral in Hawaii doesn't do as well as in other more equatorial areas because the water is too wild and it's not quite as warm. Coral looks like a plant fashioned from colorful stone, but it's really the skeleton of tiny animals, zoophytes, that eat algae in order to live. Coral grows best on the west side of the islands where the water is quite still, the days more sunny, and the algae can thrive. Many of Hawaii's reefs have been dying in the last 20 years, and no one seems to know why. Pesticides, used in agriculture, have been pointed to as a possible cause.

WHALES

Perhaps it's their tremendous size and graceful power, coupled with a dancer's delicacy of movement, that render whales so esthetically and emotionally captivating. In fact, many people claim that they even feel a spirit-bond to these obviously intelligent mammals that at one time shared dry land with us and then re-evolved into creatures of the great seas. Experts often remark that whales exhibit behavior akin to the highest social virtues. For example, whales rely much more on learned behavior than on instinct, the sign of a highly evolved intelligence. Gentle mothers and protective "escort" males join to teach the young to survive. They display loyalty and bravery in times of distress, and innate gentleness and curiosity. Their "songs," especially those of the humpbacks, fascinate scientists and are considered a unique form of communication in the animal kingdom. Humpback whales migrate to Hawaii every year Nov.-May. Here, they winter, mate, give birth, and nurture their young until returning to food-rich northern waters in the spring. It's hoped that humankind can peacefully share the oceans with these magnificent giants forever. Then, perhaps, we will have taken the first steps toward saving ourselves.

Evolution and Socialization

Many millions of years ago, for an unknown reason, animals similar to cows—their closest land relative is the hippo—were genetically triggered to leave the land and readapt to the sea. Known as cetaceans, this order contains about 80 species of whales, porpoises, and dolphins. Being mammals, cetaceans are warm-blooded and maintain a body temperature of 96°, only 2.6 degrees less than humans. After a gestation period of about one year, whales give birth to fully formed young, which usually enter the world tail first. The mother whale spins quickly to snap the umbilical cord, then places herself under the newborn and lifts it to the surface to take its first breath. A whale must be taught to swim or it will drown like any other air-breathing mammal. The baby whale, nourished by its mother's rich milk, becomes a member of an extended family, or pod, through which it's cared for, socialized, and protected by many "nannies."

Physiology

The best way to spot a whale is to look for its "spout," a misty spray forced from a blowhole—really the whale's nostrils that have moved from its snout to just behind its head. The spray from the spout is not water, but highly compressed air heated by the whale's body and expelled with such force that it condenses into a fine mist. A whale's tail is called a fluke; unlike the vertical tail of fish, a whale's tail is horizontal. The fluke, a marvelous appendage for propelling the whale through the water, is a vestige of the pelvis. It's so powerful that a 40-ton humpback can lift itself completely out of the water with only three strokes of its fluke. A whale's flippers are used to guide it through the water. The bones in the flippers closely resemble those of the human arm and hand; small, delicate bones at the ends of the flippers look like fingers. On a humpback the flippers can be one-third as long as the body and supple enough to bend over its back, like a human reaching over the shoulder to scratch an itch.

A whale's eyes are functional but very small and not the primary sensors. Instead, the whale has developed keen hearing; the ears are small

holes about as big around as the lead of a pencil. They have protective wax plugs that build up over the years. Like the growth rings in a tree, the ear plugs can be counted to determine the age of a whale; its life span is about the same as that of a human being. Because of strong ocean currents, and because of the myriad dangers inherent in being at sea, whales enjoy a very light sleep, more like a rest similar to humans just awakening, a state that is not fully conscious but aware.

Types of Whales

Although all whales, dolphins, and porpoises are cetaceans, they are arbitrarily divided according to length. Whales are all those animals longer than 30 feet; dolphins range 6-30 feet; and porpoises are less than six feet long. There are basically two types of whales: toothed, which includes the sperm, killer, and pilot whales, as well as porpoises and dolphins; and baleen, including the blue, minke, right, fin, and humpback.

Toothed whales feed by capturing and tearing their prey with their teeth. The killer whale or orca is the best known of the toothed whales. With its distinctive black-and-white markings and propensity for aquabatics, it's a favorite at marine parks around the world. The orca hunts other cetaceans, oftentimes attacking in packs to overcome larger whales. A killer whale in the wild lives about four times as long as one in captivity, even if it is well cared for.

A baleen whale eats by gliding through the water with its mouth open, sucking in marine plankton and tiny shrimplike creatures called krill. The whale then expels the water and captures the food in row after row of a prickly, fingernail-like substance called baleen.

Hawaiian Whales and Dolphins

The role of whales and dolphins in Hawaiian culture seems quite limited. Unlike fish, which were intimately known and individually named, only two generic names described whales: kohola (whale), and palaoa (sperm whale). Dolphins were lumped together under one name, nai'a; Hawaiians were known to harvest dolphins on occasion by herding them onto a beach. Whale jewelry was worn by the ali'i. The most coveted ornament came from a sperm whale's tooth, called a lei niho palaoa, which was carved into one large curved pendant. Sperm whales have upward of 50 teeth, ranging in size 4-12 inches and weighing up to two pounds. One whale could provide numerous pendants. The most famous whale in Hawaiian waters is the humpback, but others often sighted include the sperm, killer, false killer, pilot, Cuvier's, Blainsville, and pygmy killer. There are technically no porpoises, but dolphins include the common, bottlenose, spinner, white-sided, broad- and slenderbeaked, and rough-toothed. The mahimahi, a favorite eating fish found on many menus, is commonly referred to as a dolphin but is unrelated and is a true fish, not a cetacean.

The Humpbacks of Maui

The humpback gets its name from its style of exposing its dorsal fin when diving, which gives it a humped appearance. This dorsal fin also puts it into the roqual family. There are about 10,000 humpback whales alive today, down from an estimated 100,000 at the turn of the century. The remaining whales are divided into three separate global populations: North Atlantic, North Pacific, and South Pacific groups. About 2,000 North Pacific humpbacks migrate from coastal Alaska beginning in November. Migration peaks in February, when humpbacks congregate mostly in the waters off Maui, with smaller groups heading for the waters off the other islands. In 1992, the **Hawaiian Islands Humpback Whale National Marine Sanctuary** was designated, encompassing waters off all six major islands. One hopes this will ensure a perpetual safe haven for the whales.

Adult humpbacks average 45 feet long and weigh in at a svelte 40 tons (80,000 pounds) or more. They come to Hawaii mainly to give birth to a single 2,000-pound, relatively blubberless calf, most of which are born by the end of January. The mother nurses her calf for about one year and becomes impregnated

again the next year. While in Hawaiian waters the humpbacks generally don't eat. They wait until returning to Alaska, where they gorge themselves on krill. It's estimated they can live off their blubber without peril for six months. They have enormous mouths stretching one-third the length of their bodies and filled with more than 600 rows of baleen. Humpbacks have been known to blow air underwater to create giant bubble-nets that help corral krill. They rush in with mouths agape and dine on their catch.

Like other baleen whales, humpbacks feed in relatively shallow waters and sound (dive) for periods lasting a maximum of about 25 minutes. In comparison, the sperm whale, a toothed bottom-feeder, can stay down for more than an hour. On the surface a humpback will breathe about once every two minutes. They also sleep on the surface or just below it.

A distinctive feature of the humpback is the 15-foot flipper that it can bend over its back. The flippers and tail flukes have white markings that differ between individuals, much as do human fingerprints. These markings are used to identify individual migrating humpbacks. Scientists photograph the distinctive tails and send prints to Seattle, Washington, a center of whale research. There a computer analysis is done to identify the individual or to record it as a new specimen. Thereafter, any sightings become part of its life history. The humpback is the most aquatic of all whales, and it is a thrilling sight to see one of these agile giants leap from the water and create a monumental splash.

The Humpback's Song

Unlike other whales, humpbacks have the special ability to sing. They create their melodies by grunting, shrieking, and moaning. No one knows exactly what the songs represent, but it's clear they're a definite form of communication. The singers appear to be "escort males" who tag along with, and seem to guard, a mother and her calf. Some scientists believe these are lone males and perhaps the song is territorial, or a mating call. The songs are exact renditions that last 20 minutes or longer and are repeated for hours. Amazingly, all the whales know and sing the same song, and the song

humpback whale

changes from year to year. The notes are so forceful they can be heard above and below the water for miles. Some of the deep bass notes carry underwater for 100 miles.

Good recordings of the humpbacks' songs can be heard aboard the *Carthaginian II,* a restored 19th-century square-rigged ship just to the right of the loading dock in Lahaina Harbor on Maui. It serves as a floating museum dedicated to whales and whaling. As you descend into the ship's hold and bright sunlight fades to cool shadow, you become a visitor in the watery world of the humpback whale. The mysterious songs of the humpback provide the background music and set the mood. Sit on comfortable captain's chairs and watch the excellent audiovisual display. The photos of whales are by Flip Nicklin, courtesy of the National Geographic Society. The *Carthaginian II* is a project of the Lahaina Restoration Foundation, P.O. Box 338, Lahaina, Maui HI 96761, tel. (808) 661-3262. The foundation is a nonprofit organization dedicated to educational and historical restoration in Lahaina.

Whaling History

Humans have known about whales for many thousands of years. A Minoan palace on the island of Crete depicts whales on a 5,000-year-old mural. The first whalers were probably Norwegians who used stone harpoon heads to capture their prey more than 4,000 years ago. Inuit have long engaged in whaling as a means of survival, and for centuries many peoples living along coastal waters have harpooned migrating whales that ventured close to shore. The Basques had a thriving medieval whaling industry in the 12th century centered in the Bay of Biscay, until they wiped out all the Biscayan right whales. The height of the classic whaling industry that inspired Melville's *Moby Dick* occurred 1820-1860. The international whaling capital perfectly situated in the center of the winter whaling grounds was Lahaina, Maui. At that time 900 sailing ships roamed the globe in search of whales. Of these, 700 were American, and they started the trend away from coastal to pelagic whaling by bringing their try-pots (blubber pots) aboard ship.

Although the killing was great during these years, every part of the whale was needed and used: blubber, meat, bone, teeth. Whale oil, the main product, was a superior lighting fuel and lubricant unmatched until petroleum came into general use in the mid-19th century. Today, every single whale by-product can be manufactured synthetically and there's absolutely no primary need to justify slaughtering whales.

During the great whaling days, the whales actually had a fighting chance. After all, they were hunted by men in wooden sailing ships that depended upon favorable winds. Once a whale was sighted by a sailor perched high in the rigging using a low-powered telescope, a small boat heaved off; after desperate rowing and dangerous maneuvering, the master harpooner threw his shaft by hand. When the whale was dead, it took every able-bodied man to haul it in.

Today, however, modern methods have wiped out every trace of daring and turned the hunt into technologically assisted slaughter. Low-flying aircraft radio the whales' locations to huge factory-ships that track them with radar and sonar. Once the pod is spotted, super-swift launches tear into them, firing cannon-propelled harpoons with lethal exploding tips. The killer launches keep firing until every whale in the pod is dead, and the huge factory-ship follows behind, merely scooping up the lifeless carcasses and hauling them aboard with diesel winches.

Many pirate whalers still roam the seas. The worst example perpetrated by these racketeers occurred in the Bahamas in 1971. A ship ironically carrying the name of *the* classic conservation group, *Sierra,* succeeded in wiping out every single humpback whale that wintered in Bahamian waters. Since 1971 not one whale has been sighted in the Bahamas, and whale-watchers lament that they will never return.

The Last Whalers

Thanks to world opinion and the efforts of benign but aggressive organizations such as Greenpeace and Earth Trust, the **International Whaling Commission** (IWC), a voluntary group of 17 nations, now sets standards and passes quotas on the number and species of whales that can be killed. Over the last 18 years the blue, right, gray, bowhead, and humpback have become totally protected. However, many great whales such as the sperm, minke, sei, and fin are still hunted. Also, the IWC has no power of enforcement except public opinion and possible voluntary economic sanction.

The Japanese and Norwegians still hunt for whales, their operations often thinly disguised as "research." Native American Inuit and a few other indigenous peoples of the world, like the villagers of Lamalera on Lembata in Indonesia, hunt whales but the number of whales taken by these groups is minuscule. The Japanese technically stay within their quotas, but they hire and outfit these and other nationals to hunt whales for them. Their main argument is that whaling is a traditional industry upon which they rely for food and jobs. This is patently false. Hardly more than 100 years old, pelagic whaling is a new industry to the Japanese. Much of the Japanese whale meat becomes pet food anyway, which is mainly exported.

Amazingly, a recent poll taken in Japan by the Whale and Dolphin Society of London found that 69% of the people opposed whaling. Finally, through the efforts of *ICEARCH* (International Cetacean Education And Research Conference), the first pillars of a bridge were laid between Japanese and Western scientists who are dedicated to finding a way for mankind and the great whales to live in harmony. In April 1993 these scientists came together on Maui for the first time to discuss the issue.

Whalewatching

If you're in Hawaii from late November to early May, you have an excellent chance of spotting a humpback. March is perhaps the best month. You can often see a whale from a vantage point on land, but this is nowhere near as thrilling as seeing them close up from a boat. Either way, binoculars are a must. Telephoto and zoom lenses are also useful, and you might even get a nifty photo in the bargain. But don't waste your film unless you have a fairly high-powered zoom: fixed-lens cameras give pictures with a lot of ocean and a tiny black speck. If you're lucky enough to see a whale breach (jump clear of the water), keep watching—they often repeat this a number of times. If a whale dives and lifts its fluke high in the air, expect it to be down for at least 15 minutes and not come up in the same spot. Other times they'll dive shallowly, then bob up and down quite often. If you time your arrival near sunset, even if you don't see a whale you'll enjoy a mind-boggling light show.

To learn more about whales and the Hawaiian Islands Humpback Whale National Marine Sanctuary, contact their office at 726 S. Kihei Rd., Kihei, HI 96753, tel. (800) 831-4888, website: www.t-link.net/~whale. The office is open Mon.-Fri. 9 a.m.-3 p.m.

HISTORY

THE ROAD FROM TAHITI

Until the 1820s, when New England missionaries began a phonetic rendering of the Hawaiian language, the past was kept vividly alive only by the sonorous voices of special *kahuna* who chanted the sacred *mele.* The chants were beautiful, flowing word pictures that captured the essence of every aspect of life. These *mele* praised the land *(mele aina),* royalty *(mele ali'i),* and life's tender aspects *(mele aloha).* Chants were dedicated to friendship, hardship, and favorite children. Entire villages sometimes joined together to compose a *mele*—every word was chosen carefully, and the wise old *kupuna* would decide if the words were lucky or unlucky. Some *mele* were bawdy or funny on the surface but contained secret meanings, often with biting sarcasm, that ridiculed an inept or cruel leader. But the most important chants took the listeners back into the dim past, even before people lived in Hawaii. From these genealogies *(ko'ihonua),* the *ali'i* derived the right to rule, since these chants went back to the gods Wakea and Papa from whom the *ali'i* were directly descended.

The Kumulipo
The great genealogies, finally compiled in the late 1800s by order of King Kalakaua, were collectively known as *The Kumulipo, A Hawaiian Creation Chant,* basically a Polynesian account of Genesis. Other chants related to the beginning of this world, but *The Kumulipo* sums it all up and is generally considered the best. The chant relates that after the beginning of time, there is a period of darkness. The darkness, however, mysteriously brims with spontaneous life; during this period plants and animals are born, as well as Kumulipo, the man, and Po'ele, the woman. In the eighth chant darkness gives way to light and the gods descend to earth. Wakea is "the sky father" and Papa is "the earth mother," whose union gives birth to the islands of Hawaii. First born is Hawaii, followed by Maui, then Kahoolawe. Apparently, Papa becomes bushed after three consecutive births and decides to va-

cation in Tahiti. While Papa is away recovering from postpartum depression and working on her tan, Wakea gets lonely and takes Kaula as his second wife; she bears him the island-child of Lanai. Not fully cheered up, but getting the hang of it, Wakea takes a third wife, Hina, who promptly bears the island of Molokai. Meanwhile, Papa gets wind of these shenanigans, returns from Polynesia, and retaliates by taking up with Lua, a young and virile god. She soon gives birth to the island of Oahu. Papa and Wakea finally decide that they really are meant for each other and reconcile to conceive Kauai, Niihau, Kaula, and Nihoa. These two progenitors are the source from which the *ali'i* ultimately traced their lineage, and from which they derived their god-ordained power to rule.

Basically, there are two major genealogical families: the **Nana'ulu,** who became the royal *ali'i* of Oahu and Kauai; and the **Ulu,** who provided the royalty of Maui and Hawaii. The best sources of information on Hawaiian myth and legend are Martha Beckwith's *Hawaiian Mythology* and the monumental three-volume opus *An Account of the Polynesian Race* compiled by Abraham Fornander 1878-1885. Fornander, after settling in Hawaii, married an *ali'i* from Molokai and had an illustrious career as a journalist, Maui circuit judge, and finally Supreme Court justice. For years Fornander sent scribes to every corner of the kingdom to listen to the elder *kupuna.* They returned with firsthand accounts, which he dutifully recorded.

Polynesians
Since prehistory, Polynesians have been seafaring people whose origins cannot be completely traced. They seem to have come from Southeast Asia mostly through the gateway of Indonesia, and their racial strain pulls features from all three dominant races: Caucasian, Negro, and Asian. They learned to navigate on tame narrow waterways along Indonesia and New Guinea, then fanned out eastward into the great Pacific. They sailed northeast to the low islands of Micronesia and southwest to Fiji, Vanuatu, and New Caledonia. Fiji is regarded as the "cra-

dle of Polynesian culture"; carbon dating places humans there as early as 3,500 B.C. Many races blended on Fiji, until finally the Negroid became dominant and the Polynesians moved on. Wandering, they discovered and settled Samoa and Tonga, then ranged far east to populate Tahiti, Easter Island, and the Marquesas. From the Marquesas, they eventually reached Hawaii. Ultimately, they became the masters of the "Polynesian Triangle," which measures more than 5,000 miles on each leg, stretching across both the North and South Pacific and studded with islands. The great Maori kingdom of New Zealand is the southern apex of the triangle, with Easter Island marking the point farthest

east; Hawaii, farthest north, was the last to be settled.

Migrations and Explorations

Ancient legends common throughout the South Pacific speak of a great Polynesian culture that existed on the island of Raiatea about 150 miles north of Tahiti. Here a powerful priesthood held sway in an enormous *heiau* in the Opoa district called Toputapuatea. Kings from throughout Polynesia came here to worship. Human sacrifice was common, as it was believed that the essence of the spirit could be utilized and controlled in this life; therefore the mana of Toputapuatea was great. Defeated warriors and com-

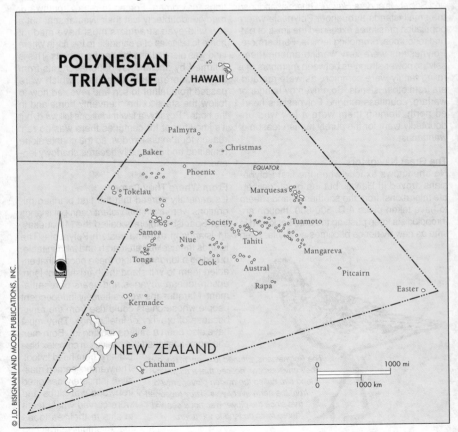

moners were used as living rollers to drag canoes up onto the beach, while corpses were dismembered and hung in trees. The power of the priests of Opoa lasted for many generations, evoking trembling fear in even the bravest warrior just by the mention of their names. Finally, their power waned and Polynesians lost their centralized culture, but the constant coming and going from Raiatea for centuries sharpened the Polynesians' already excellent sailing skills and convinced them that the world was vast and that unlimited opportunities existed to better their lot.

Many explorers left to look for the "heavenly homeland to the north." Samoans called it *Savai'i;* Tongans *Hawai;* Rarotongans *Avaiki;* and Society Islanders *Havai'i.* Others abandoned the small islands throughout Polynesia where population pressures exceeded the limits of natural resources, prompting famine. Furthermore, Polynesians were very warlike among themselves; power struggles between members of a ruling family were common, as were marauders from other islands. So, driven by hunger or warfare, countless refugee Polynesians headed north. Joining them were a few who undoubtedly went for the purely human reason of wanderlust.

The Great Navigators

No one knows exactly when the first Polynesians arrived in Hawaii, but the great "deliberate migrations" from the southern islands seem to have taken place A.D. 500-800, though anthropologists keep pushing the date backward in time as new evidence becomes available. Even

before that, however, it's reasonable to assume that the first people to set foot on Hawaii were probably fishermen, or perhaps defeated warriors whose canoes were blown hopelessly northward into unfamiliar waters. They arrived by a combination of extraordinary good luck and an uncanny ability to sail and navigate without instruments, using the sun by day and the moon and rising stars by night. They could feel the water and determine direction by swells, tides, and currents. Cloud formations and he movements of fish were also utilized to give direction. Since their arrival was probably an accident, they were unprepared to settle on the fertile but barren lands, having no stock animals, plant cuttings, or women. Forced to return southward, many undoubtedly lost their lives at sea, but a few wild-eyed stragglers must have made it home to tell tales of a paradise to the north where land was plentiful and the sea bounteous. This is affirmed by ancient navigational chants from Tahiti, Moorea, and Bora Bora, which were passed from father to son and revealed how to follow the stars to the "heavenly homeland in the north." Possibly a few migrations followed, but it's known that for centuries there was no real reason for a mass exodus, so the chants alone remained and eventually became shadowy legend.

From Where They Came

It's generally agreed that the first planned migrations were from the violent cannibal islands that Spanish explorers called the Marquesas, 11 islands in extreme eastern Polynesia. The islands themselves are harsh and inhospitable, breeding a toughness into these people that enabled them to withstand the hardships of long, unsure ocean voyages and years of resettlement. Marquesans were a fiercely independent people whose chiefs could rise from the ranks because of bravery or intelligence. They must have also been a savage-looking lot. Both men and women tattooed themselves in complex blue patterns from head to foot. The warriors carried massive, intricately designed ironwood war clubs and wore carved whale teeth in slits in their earlobes that eventually stretched

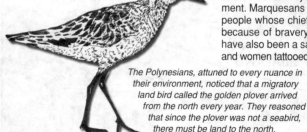

The Polynesians, attuned to every nuance in their environment, noticed that a migratory land bird called the golden plover arrived from the north every year. They reasoned that since the plover was not a seabird, there must be land to the north.

LOUISE FOOTE

to the shoulders. They shaved the sides of their heads with sharks' teeth, tied their hair in two topknots that looked like horns, and rubbed their heavily muscled and tattooed bodies with scented coconut oils. Their cults worshipped mummified ancestors; the bodies of warriors of defeated neighboring tribes were consumed.

They were masters at building great double-hulled canoes launched from huge canoe sheds. Two hulls were fastened together to form a catamaran, and a hut in the

The canoe hull was a log shaped by masterly stone adze work. The sides were planks drilled and sewn together with fiber cord.

center provided shelter in bad weather. The average voyaging canoe was 60-80 feet long and could comfortably hold an extended family of about 30 people. These small family bands carried all the staples they would need in the new lands.

The New Lands

For five centuries the Marquesans settled and lived peacefully on the new land, as if Hawaii's aloha spirit overcame most of their fierceness. The tribes coexisted in relative harmony, especially since there was no competition for land. Cannibalism died out. There was much coming and going between Hawaii and Polynesia as new people came to settle for hundreds of years. Then, it appears that in the 12th century a deliberate exodus of warlike Tahitians arrived and subjugated the settled islanders. They came to conquer. This incursion had a terrific significance on the Hawaiian religious and social system. Oral tradition relates that a Tahitian priest, Paao, found the mana of the Hawaiian chiefs to be low, signifying that their gods were weak. Paao built a *heiau* at Waha'ula on the Big Island, then introduced the warlike god Ku and the rigid *kapu* system through which the new rulers became dominant. Voyages between Tahiti and Hawaii continued for about 100 years and Tahitian customs, legends, and language became the Hawaiian way of life. Then suddenly, for no recorded or apparent reason, the voyages discontinued and Hawaii returned to total isolation.

The islands remained forgotten for almost 500 years until the indomitable English sailor, Capt. James Cook, sighted Oahu on January 18, 1778

and stepped ashore at Waimea on Kauai two days later. At that time Hawaii's isolation was so complete that even the Polynesians had forgotten about it. On an earlier voyage, Tupaia, a high priest from Raiatea, had accompanied Captain Cook as he sailed throughout Polynesia. Tupaia demonstrated his vast knowledge of existing archipelagos throughout the South Pacific by naming more than 130 islands and drawing a map that included the Tonga group, the Cook Islands, the Marquesas, even tiny Pitcairn, a rock in far eastern Polynesia where the mutinous crew of the *Bounty* found solace. In mentioning the Marquesas, Tupaia said, *"He ma'a te ka'ata,"* which means "Food is man" or simply "Cannibals!" But remarkably absent from Tupaia's vast knowledge was the existence of Easter Island, New Zealand, and Hawaii.

The next waves of people to Hawaii would be white, and the Hawaiian world would be changed quickly and forever.

THE WORLD DISCOVERS HAWAII

The late 18th century was an extraordinary time in Hawaiian history. Monumental changes seemed to happen all at once. First, Capt. James Cook, a Yorkshire farm boy fulfilling his destiny as the all-time greatest Pacific explorer, found Hawaii for the rest of the world. For better or worse, it could no longer be an isolated Polynesian homeland. For the first time in Hawaiian history, a charismatic leader—Kamehameha—emerged, and after a long civil war he united the islands into one centralized kingdom. The death of Captain Cook in Hawaii marked the beginning of a long series of tragic misunderstandings between whites and natives. When Kamehameha died, the old religious system of *kapu* came to an end, leaving the Hawaiians in a spiritual vortex. Many takers arrived to fill the void: missionaries after souls, whalers after their prey and a good time, traders and planters after profits and a home. The islands were opened and devoured like ripe fruit. Powerful nations,

LOUISE FOOTE

including Russia, Great Britain, France, and the United States, yearned to bring this strategic Pacific jewel under their influence. The 19th century brought the demise of the Hawaiian people as a dominant political force in their own land and with it the end of Hawaii as a sovereign monarchy. An almost bloodless yet bitter military coup followed by a brief Hawaiian Republic ended in annexation by the United States. As the U.S. became completely entrenched politically and militarily, a new social and economic order was founded on the plantation system. Amazingly rapid population growth occurred with the importation of plantation workers from Asia and Europe, which yielded a unique cosmopolitan blend of races like nowhere else on earth. By the dawning of the 20th century, the face of old Hawaii had been altered forever; the "sacred homeland in the north" was hurled into the modern age. The attack on Pearl Harbor saw a tremendous loss of life and brought Hawaii closer to the U.S. by a baptism of blood. Finally, on August 21, 1959, after 59 years as a "territory," Hawaii officially became the 50th state of the Union.

Captain Cook Sights Hawaii

In 1776 Capt. James Cook set sail for the Pacific from Plymouth, England, on his third and final expedition into this still vastly unexplored region of the world. On a fruitless quest for the fabled Northwest Passage across the North American continent, he sailed down the coast of Africa, rounded the Cape of Good Hope, crossed the Indian Ocean, and traveled past New Zealand, Tasmania, and the Friendly Islands (where an unsuccessful plot was hatched by the *friendly* natives to murder him). On January 18, 1778, Captain Cook's 100-foot flagship HMS *Resolution* and its 90-foot companion HMS *Discovery* sighted Oahu. Two days later, they sighted Kauai and went ashore at the village of Waimea. Though anxious to get on with his mission, Cook decided to make a quick sortie to investigate this new land and reprovision his ships. He did, however, take time to remark in his diary about the close resemblance of these newfound people to others he had encountered as far south as New Zealand, and he marveled at their widespread habitation across the Pacific.

The first trade was some brass medals for a mackerel. Cook also stated that he had never before met natives so astonished by a ship, and that they had an amazing fascination for iron, which they called *toe,* Hawaiian for "adze." There is even some conjecture that a Spanish ship under one Captain Gaetano had landed in Hawaii as early as the 16th century, trading a few scraps of iron that the Hawaiians valued even more than the Europeans valued gold. It was also noted that the Hawaiian women gave themselves freely to the sailors with the apparent good wishes of the island men. This was actually a ploy by the *kahuna* to test if the newcomers were gods or men—gods didn't need women. These sailors proved immediately mortal. Cook, who was also a physician, tried valiantly to keep the 66 men (out of 112) who had measurable cases of VD away from the women. The task proved impossible as women literally swarmed the ships; when Cook returned less than a year later, it was logged that signs of VD were already apparent on some natives' faces.

Cook was impressed with the Hawaiians' swimming ability and with their well-bred manners. They had happy dispositions and sticky fingers, stealing any object made of metal, especially nails. The first item stolen was a butcher's cleaver. An unidentified native grabbed it, plunged

HAWAII STATE ARCHIVES

Captain James Cook

overboard, swam to shore, and waved his booty in triumph. The Hawaiians didn't seem to care for beads and were not at all impressed with a mirror. Cook provisioned his ships by trading chisels for hogs, while common sailors gleefully traded nails for sex. Landing parties were sent inland to fill casks with fresh water. On one such excursion a Mr. Williamson, who was eventually drummed out of the Royal Navy for cowardice, unnecessarily shot and killed a native. After a brief stop on Niihau, the ships sailed away, but both groups were indelibly impressed with the memory of each other.

Cook Returns

Almost a year later, when winter weather forced Cook to return from the coast of Alaska, his discovery began to take on far-reaching significance. Cook had named Hawaii the Sandwich Islands, in honor of one of his patrons, John Montague, the Earl of Sandwich. On this return voyage, he spotted Maui on November 26, 1778. After eight weeks of seeking a suitable harbor, the ships bypassed it, but not before the coastline was duly drawn by Lt. William Bligh, one of Cook's finest and most trusted officers. (Bligh would find his own drama almost 10 years later as commander of the infamous HMS *Bounty*.) The *Discovery* and *Resolution* finally found safe anchorage at Kealakekua Bay on the Kona coast of the Big Island. It is very lucky for history that on board was Mr. Anderson, ship's chronicler, who left a handwritten record of the strange and tragic events that followed. Even more important were the drawings of John Webber, ship's artist, who rendered invaluable impressions in superb drawings and etchings. Other noteworthy men aboard were George Vancouver, who would lead the first British return to Hawaii after Cook's death and introduce many fruits, vegetables, cattle, sheep, and goats; and James Burney, who would become a long-standing leading authority on the Pacific.

The Great God Lono Returns

By all accounts Cook was a humane and just captain, greatly admired by his men. Unlike many other supremacists of that time, he was known to have a respectful attitude toward any people he discovered, treating them as equals and recognizing the significance of their cultures. Not known as a violent man, he would use his superior weapons against natives only in an absolute case of self-defense. His hardened crew had been at sea facing untold hardship for almost three years; returning to Hawaii was truly like reentering paradise.

A strange series of coincidences sailed with Cook into Kealakekua Bay on January 16, 1779. It was *makahiki* time, a period of rejoicing and festivity dedicated to the fertility god of the earth, Lono. Normal *kapu* days were suspended and willing partners freely enjoyed each other sexually. Dancing, feasting, and the islands' version of the Olympic games also took place. It was long held in Hawaiian legend that the great god Lono would return to earth. Lono's image was a small wooden figure perched on a tall, mastlike crossbeam; hanging from the crossbeam were long, white sheets of tapa. Who else could Cook be but Lono, and what else could his ships with their masts and white sails be but his sacred floating *heiau?* This explained the Hawaiians' previous fascination with his ships, but to add to the remarkable coincidence, Kealakekua Harbor happened to be considered Lono's private sacred harbor. Natives from throughout the land prostrated themselves and paid homage to the returning god. Cook was taken ashore and brought to Lono's sacred temple, where he was afforded the highest respect. The ships badly needed fresh supplies so the Hawaiians readily gave all they had, stretching their own provisions to the limit. To the sailors' delight, this included full measures of the aloha spirit.

The Fatal Misunderstandings

After an uproarious welcome and generous hospitality for more than a month, it became obvious that the newcomers were beginning to overstay their welcome. During the interim a seaman named William Watman died, convincing the Hawaiians that the *haole* were indeed mortals, not gods. Watman was buried at Hikiau Heiau, where a plaque commemorates the event to this day. Incidents of petty theft began to increase dramatically. The lesser chiefs indicated it was time to leave by "rubbing the Englishmen's bellies." Inadvertently many *kapu* were broken by the Englishmen, and once-friendly relations became strained. Finally, the ships sailed away on February 4, 1779.

After plying terrible seas for only a week, *Resolution's* foremast was badly damaged. Cook sailed back into Kealakekua Bay, dragging the mast ashore on February 13. The natives, now totally hostile, hurled rocks at the sailors. Orders were given to load muskets with ball; firearms had previously only been loaded with shot and a light charge. Confrontations increased when some Hawaiians stole a small boat and Cook's men set after them, capturing the fleeing canoe that held an *ali'i* named Palea. The Englishmen treated him roughly; to the Hawaiians' horror, they even smacked him on the head with a paddle. The Hawaiians then furiously attacked the marines, who abandoned the small boat.

Cook Goes Down

Next the Hawaiians stole a small cutter from the *Discovery* that had been moored to a buoy and partially sunk to protect it from the sun. For the first time Captain Cook became furious. He ordered Captain Clerk of the *Discovery* to sail to the southeast end of the bay and stop any canoe trying to leave Kealakekua. Cook then made a fatal error in judgment. He decided to take nine armed marines ashore in an attempt to convince the venerable King Kalaniopuu to accompany him back aboard ship, where he would hold him for ransom in exchange for the cutter. The old king agreed, but his wife prevailed upon him not to trust the *haole*. Kalaniopuu sat down on the beach to think while the tension steadily grew.

Meanwhile, a group of marines fired upon a canoe trying to leave the bay and a lesser chief, Nookemai, was killed. The crowd around Cook and his men reached an estimated 20,000, and warriors outraged by the killing of the chief armed themselves with clubs and protective straw-mat armor. One bold warrior advanced on Cook and struck him with his *pahoa* (dagger). In retaliation, Cook drew a tiny pistol lightly loaded with shot and fired at the warrior. His bullets spent themselves on the straw armor and fell harmlessly to the ground. The Hawaiians went wild. Lieutenant Molesworth Phillips, in charge of the nine marines, began a withering fire; Cook himself slew two natives.

Overpowered by sheer numbers, the marines headed for boats standing offshore, while Lieutenant Phillips lay wounded. It is believed that Captain Cook, the greatest Western sailor ever to enter the Pacific, stood helplessly in knee-deep water instead of making for the boats because he could not swim! Hopelessly surrounded, he was knocked on the head; countless then warriors passed a knife around and hacked and mutilated his lifeless body. A sad Lieutenant King lamented in his diary, "Thus fell our great and excellent commander."

The Death of Captain Cook *by John Webber, ship's artist on Cook's third Pacific exploration, circa 1779*

HAWAII STATE ARCHIVES

The Final Chapter

Captain Clerk, now in charge, settled his men and prevailed upon the Hawaiians to return Cook's body. On the morning of February 16 a grisly piece of charred meat was brought aboard: the Hawaiians, according to their custom, had afforded Cook the highest honor by baking his body in an underground oven to remove the flesh from the bones. On February 17, a group of Hawaiians in a canoe taunted the marines by brandishing Cook's hat. The English, strained to the limit and thinking that Cook was being desecrated, finally broke. Foaming with bloodlust, they leveled their cannons and muskets on shore and shot anything that moved. It is believed that Kamehameha the Great was wounded in this flurry, along with four *ali'i*; 25 *maka'ainana* (commoners) were killed. Finally, on February 21, 1779, the bones of Capt. James Cook's hands, skull, arms, and legs were returned and tearfully buried at sea. A common sailor, one Mr. Zimmerman, summed up the feelings of all who sailed under Cook when he wrote, ". . . he was our leading star." The English sailed next morning after dropping off their Hawaiian girlfriends who were still aboard.

Captain Clerk, in bad health, carried on with the fruitless search for the Northwest Passage. He died and was buried at the Siberian village of Petropavlovisk. England was at war with upstart colonists in America, so the return of the expedition warranted little fanfare. The *Resolution* was converted into an army transport to fight the pesky Americans; the once-proud *Discovery* was reduced to a convict ship ferrying inmates to Botany Bay, Australia. Mrs. Cook, the great captain's steadfast and chaste wife, lived to the age of 93, surviving all her children. She was given a stipend of 200 pounds per year and finished her days surrounded by Cook's mementos, observing the anniversary of his death to the very end by fasting and reading from the Bible.

THE UNIFICATION OF OLD HAWAII

Hawaii was already in a state of political turmoil and civil war when Cook arrived. In the 1780s the islands were roughly divided into three kingdoms: venerable Kalaniopuu ruled Hawaii and the Hana district of Maui; wily and ruthless warrior-king Kahekili ruled Maui, Kahoolawe, Lanai, and later Oahu; and Kaeo, Kahekili's brother, ruled Kauai. War ravaged the land until a remarkable chief, Kamehameha, rose and subjugated all the islands under one rule. Kamehameha initiated a dynasty that would last for about 100 years, until the independent monarchy of Hawaii forever ceased to be. To add a zing to this brewing political stew, Westerners and their technology were beginning to come in ever-increasing numbers. In 1786, Captain La Pérouse and his French exploration party landed in what's now La Perouse Bay near Lahaina, foreshadowing European attention to the islands. In 1786 two American captains, Portlock and Dixon, made landfall in Hawaii. Also, it was known that a fortune could be made on the fur trade between the Pacific Northwest and Canton, China; stopping in Hawaii could make it feasible. After this was reported, the fate of Hawaii was sealed.

Hawaii under Kamehameha was ready to enter its "golden age." The social order was medieval, with the *ali'i* as knights owing their military allegiance to the king, and the serflike *maka'ainana* paying tribute and working the lands. The priesthood of *kahuna* filled the posts of advisors, sorcerers, navigators, doctors, and historians. This was Polynesian Hawaii at its apex. But like the uniquely Hawaiian silversword, the old culture blossomed, and as soon as it did, began to wither. Ever since, all that was purely Hawaiian has been supplanted by the relentless foreign influences that began bearing down upon it.

Young Kamehameha

The greatest native son of Hawaii, Kamehameha, was born under mysterious circumstances in the Kohala District, probably in 1753. He was royal born to Keoua Kupuapaikalaninui, the chief of Kohala, and Kekuiapoiwa, a chieftess from Kona. Accounts vary, but one claims that before his birth, a *kahuna* prophesied that this child would grow to be a "killer of chiefs." Because of this, the local chiefs conspired to murder the infant. When Kekuiapoiwa's time came, she secretly went to the royal birthing stones near Mookini Heiau and delivered Kamehameha. She entrusted her baby to a manservant and instructed him to hide the child. He headed for the rugged and remote coast around Kapaau. Here Kamehameha was raised in the mountains, mostly by men. Always alone, he earned the nickname "The Lonely One."

Kamehameha was a man noticed by everyone; there was no doubt he was a force to be reckoned with. He had met Captain Cook when the *Discovery* unsuccessfully tried to land at Hana on Maui. While aboard, he made a lasting impression, distinguishing himself from the multitude of natives swarming the ships by his royal bearing. Lieutenant James King, in a diary entry, remarked that Kamehameha was a fierce-looking man, almost ugly, but that he was obviously intelligent, observant, and very good-natured. Kamehameha received his early military training from his uncle Kalaniopuu, the great king of Hawaii and Hana who fought fierce battles against Alapai, the usurper who stole his hereditary lands. After regaining Hawaii, Kalaniopuu returned to his Hana district and turned his attention to conquering all of Maui. During this period young Kamehameha distinguished himself as a ferocious warrior and earned the nickname of "The Hard-shelled Crab," even though old Kahekili, Maui's king, almost annihilated Kalaniopuu's army at the sand hills of Wailuku.

Kamehameha I as drawn by Louis Choris, ship's artist for the Von Kotzebue expedition, circa 1816. Supposedly it was the only time Kamehameha sat to have his portrait rendered.

When the old king neared death, he passed on the kingdom to his son Kiwalao. He also, however, empowered Kamehameha as the keeper of the family war god Kukailimoku: Ku of the Bloody Red Mouth, Ku the Destroyer. Oddly enough, Kamehameha had been born not 500 yards from Ku's great *heiau* at Kohala, and had heard the chanting and observed the ceremonies dedicated to this fierce god from his first breath. Soon after Kalaniopuu died, Kamehameha found himself in a bitter war that he did not seek against his two cousins, Kiwalao and his brother Keoua, with the island of Hawaii at stake. The skirmish lasted nine years until Kamehameha's armies met the two brothers at Mokuohai in an indecisive battle in which Kiwalao was killed. The result was a shaky truce with Keoua, a much-embittered enemy. During this fighting, Kahekili of Maui conquered Oahu, where he built a house of the skulls and bones of his adversaries as a reminder of his omnipotence. He also extended his will to Kauai by marrying his half-brother to a high-ranking chieftess of that island. A new factor would resolve this stalemate of power— the coming of the *haole*.

The Olowalu Massacre

In 1790 the American merchant ship *Ella Nora*, commanded by Yankee Capt. Simon Metcalfe, was looking for a harbor after its long voyage from the Pacific Northwest. Following a day behind was the *Fair American*, a tiny ship sailed by Metcalfe's son Thomas and a crew of five. Simon Metcalfe, perhaps by necessity, was a stern and humorless man who would tolerate no interference. While his ship was anchored at Olowalu, a beach area about five miles east of Lahaina, some natives slipped close in their canoes and stole a small boat, killing a sailor in the process. Metcalfe decided to trick the Hawaiians by first negotiating a truce and then unleashing full fury upon them. Signaling he was willing to trade, he invited canoes of innocent natives to visit his ship. In the meantime, he ordered that all cannons and muskets be readied with scatter shot. When the canoes were within hailing distance, he ordered his crew to fire at will. More than 100 people were slain; the Hawaiians remembered this killing as "the day of spilled brains." Metcalfe then sailed away to Kealakekua Bay and in an unrelated incident succeeded in insulting Kameiamoku, a ruling chief, who vowed to annihilate the next *haole* ship he saw.

Fate sent him the *Fair American* and young Thomas Metcalfe. The little ship was entirely overrun by superior forces. In the ensuing battle, the mate, Isaac Davis, so distinguished himself by open acts of bravery that his life alone was spared. Kameiamoku later turned over both Davis and the ship to Kamehameha. Meanwhile, while harbored at Kealakekua, the senior Metcalfe sent John Young to reconnoiter. Kamehameha, having learned of the capture of the *Fair American,* detained Young so he could not report, and Metcalfe, losing patience, marooned his own man and sailed off to Canton. (Metcalfe never learned of the fate of his son Thomas, and was later killed with another son while trading with the Native Americans along the Pacific coast of the Mainland.) Kamehameha quickly realized the significance of his two captives and the *Fair American* with its brace of small cannons. He appropriated the ship and made Davis and Young trusted advisors, eventually raising them to the rank of chief. They would all play a significant role in the unification of Hawaii.

Kamehameha the Great

Later in 1790, supported by the savvy of Davis and Young and the cannons from the *Fair American* (which he mounted on carts), Kamehameha invaded Maui, using Hana as his power base. The island's defenders under Kalaniekupule, son of Kahekili who was lingering on Oahu, were totally demoralized, then driven back into the death trap of Iao Valley. There, Kamehameha's forces annihilated them. No mercy was expected and none given, although mostly commoners were slain with no significant *ali'i* falling to the victors. So many were killed in this sheer-walled, inescapable valley that the battle was called *ka pani wai,* which means "the damming of the waters"—literally with dead bodies.

While Kamehameha was fighting on Maui, his old nemesis Keoua was busy running amok back on Hawaii, again pillaging Kamehameha's lands. The great warrior returned home flushed with victory, but in two battles could not subdue Keoua. Finally, Kamehameha was told that Ku would lead him to victory over all the lands of Hawaii if he would build a *heiau* to the war god at Kawaihae. Even before the temple was finished, old Kahekili attempted to invade Waipio, Kamehameha's stronghold. But Kamehameha summoned Davis and Young, and with the *Fair American* and an enormous fleet of war canoes

defeated Kahekili at Waimanu. Kahekili had no choice but to accept the indomitable Kamehameha as the king of Maui, although he himself remained the administrative head until his death in 1794.

Now only Keoua remained in the way and he would be defeated not by war, but by the great mana of Ku. While Keoua's armies were crossing the desert on the southern slopes of Kilauea, the fire goddess Pele trumpeted her disapproval and sent a huge cloud of poisonous gas and mud-ash into the air. It descended upon and instantly killed the middle legions of Keoua's armies and their families. The footprints of this ill-fated army remain to this day outlined in the mud-ash as clearly as if they were deliberately encased in wet cement. Keoua's intuition told him that the victorious mana of the gods had swung to Kamehameha and that his own fate was sealed. Kamehameha sent word that he wanted Keoua to meet with him at Ku's newly dedicated temple in Kawaihae. Both knew that Keoua must die. Riding proudly in his canoe, the old nemesis came gloriously outfitted in the red-and-gold feathered cape and helmet signifying his exalted rank, accompanied by a small band of warriors. When he stepped ashore he was killed by Keeaumoku and his warriors were slain by Kamehameha's. His body was ceremoniously laid upon the altar along with the others who were slaughtered and dedicated to Ku, of the Maggot-dripping Mouth.

Increasing Contact

By the time Kamehameha had won the Big Island, Hawaii was becoming a regular stopover for numerous ships seeking the lucrative sandalwood trade with China. In February 1791, Capt. George Vancouver, still seeking the Northwest Passage, returned to Kealakekua where he was greeted by a throng of 30,000. The captain at once recognized Kamehameha, who was wearing a Chinese dressing gown that he had received in tribute from another chief who in turn had received it directly from the hands of Cook himself. The diary of a crew member, Thomas Manby, relates that Kamehameha, missing his front teeth, was more fierce-looking than ever as he approached the ship in an elegant double-hulled canoe sporting 46 rowers. The king invited all to a great feast prepared for them on the beach. Kamehameha's appetite matched his tremendous size. It was noted that he ate two sizable fish, a king-size bowl of poi, a small pig, and an entire baked dog. Kamehameha personally entertained the English by putting on a mock battle in which he deftly avoided spears by rolling, tumbling, and catching them in midair, all the while hurling his own spear a great distance. The English reciprocated by firing cannon bursts into the air, creating an impromptu fireworks display. Kamehameha requested from Vancouver a full table setting with which he was provided, but his request for firearms was prudently denied. Captain Vancouver became a trusted advisor of Kamehameha and told him about the white people's form of worship. He even interceded for Kamehameha with his headstrong queen, Kaahumanu, and coaxed her from her hiding place under a rock when she sought refuge at Pu'uhonua O Honaunau. The captain gave gifts of beef cattle, fowl, and breeding stock of sheep and goats. The ship's naturalist, Archibald Menzies, was the first *haole* to climb Mauna Kea; he also introduced a large assortment of fruits and vegetables. The Hawaiians were cheerful and outgoing, and showed remorse when they indicated that the remainder of Cook's bones had been buried at a temple close to Kealakekua. John Young, by this time firmly entrenched into Hawaiian society, made no request to sail away with Vancouver. During the next two decades of Kamehameha's rule, the French, Russians, English, and Americans discovered the great whaling waters off Hawaii. Their increasing visits shook and finally tumbled the ancient religion and social order of *kapu*.

Finishing Touches

After Keoua was laid to rest, it was only a matter of time until Kamehameha consolidated his power over all of Hawaii. In 1794 the old warrior Kahekili of Maui died and gave Oahu to his son, Kalanikupule, while Kauai and Niihau went to his brother Kaeo. In wars between the two, Kalanikupule was victorious, though he did not possess the grit of his father nor the great mana of Kamehameha. He had previously murdered a Captain Brown, who had anchored at Honolulu, and seized his ship, the *Jackal*. With the aid of this ship, Kalanikupule now determined to attack Kamehameha. However, while en route,

the sailors regained control of their ship and cruised to the Big Island to inform and join with Kamehameha. An army of 16,000 was raised and sailed for Maui, where they met only token resistance. They destroyed Lahaina, pillaged the countryside, and subjugated Molokai in one bloody battle.

The war canoes sailed next for Oahu and the final showdown. The great army landed at Waikiki, and though defenders fought bravely, giving up Oahu by the inch, they were steadily driven into the surrounding mountains. The beleaguered army made its last stand at Nuuanu Pali, a great precipice in the mountains behind present-day Honolulu. Kamehameha's warriors mercilessly drove the enemy into the great abyss. Kalanikupule, who hid in the mountains, was captured after a few months and sacrificed to Ku, the Snatcher of Lands, thereby ending the struggle for power.

Kamehameha put down a revolt on Hawaii in 1796. The king of Kauai, Kaumuali, accepting the inevitable, recognized Kamehameha as supreme ruler without suffering the ravages of a needless war. Kamehameha, for the first time in Hawaiian history, was the undisputed ruler of all the islands of "the heavenly homeland in the north."

Kamehameha's Rule

Kamehameha was as gentle in victory as he was ferocious in battle. Under his rule, which lasted until his death on May 8, 1819, Hawaii enjoyed a peace unlike any the warring islands had ever known. The king moved his royal court to Lahaina, where in 1803 he built the "Brick Palace," Hawaii's first permanent building. The benevolent tyrant also enacted the "Law of the Splintered Paddle." This law, which protected the weak from the exploitation of the strong, had its origins in an incident of many years before. A brave defender of a small overwhelmed village had broken a paddle over Kamehameha's head and taught the chief—literally in one stroke—about the nobility of the commoner.

However, just as Old Hawaii reached its "golden age," its demise was at hand. The relentless waves of *haole* both innocently and determinedly battered the old ways into the ground. With the foreign ships came prosperity and fanciful new goods after which the *ali'i* lusted. The *maka'ai-*

nana were worked mercilessly to provide sandalwood for the China trade. This was the first "boom" economy to hit the islands, but it set the standard of exploitation that would follow. Kamehameha built an observation tower in Lahaina to watch for ships, many of which were his own returning laden with riches from the world at large. In the last years of his life Kamehameha returned to his beloved Kona coast, where he enjoyed the excellent fishing renowned to this day. He had taken Hawaii from the darkness of warfare into the light of peace. He died true to the religious and moral *kapu* of his youth, the only ones he had ever known, and with him died a unique way of life. Two loyal retainers buried his bones after the baked flesh had been ceremoniously stripped away. A secret burial cave was chosen so that no one could desecrate the remains of the great chief, thereby absorbing his mana. The tomb's location remains unknown, and disturbing the dead is still one of the strictest *kapu* to this day. The Lonely One's kingdom would pass to his son, Liholiho, but true power would be in the hands of his beloved and feisty wife Kaahumanu. As Kamehameha's spirit drifted from this earth, two forces sailing around Cape Horn would forever change Hawaii: the missionaries and the whalers.

MISSIONARIES AND WHALERS

The year 1819 was of the utmost significance in Hawaiian history. It marked the death of Kamehameha, the overthrow of the ancient *kapu* system, the arrival of the first "whaler" in Lahaina, and the departure from New England of Calvinist missionaries determined to convert the heathen islands. Great changes began to rattle the old order to its foundations. With the *kapu* system and the ancient gods abandoned (except for the fire goddess Pele of Kilauea), a great void permeated the souls of the Hawaiians. In the coming decades Hawaii, also coveted by Russia, France, and England, was finally consumed by America. The islands had the first American school, printing press, and newspaper (the *Polynesian*) west of the Mississippi. Lahaina, in its heyday, became the world's greatest whaling port, accommodating more than 500 ships during its peak years.

The Royal Family

Maui's Hana District provided Hawaii with one of its greatest queens, Kaahumanu, born in 1768 in a cave within walking distance of Hana Harbor. At the age of 17 she became the third of Kamehameha's 21 wives and eventually the love of his life. At first she proved to be totally independent and unmanageable and was known to openly defy her king by taking numerous lovers. Kamehameha placed a *kapu* on her body and even had her attended by horribly deformed hunchbacks in an effort to curb her carnal appetites, but she continued to flaunt his authority. Young Kaahumanu had no love for her great, lumbering, unattractive husband, but in time (even Captain Vancouver was pressed into service as a marriage counselor) she learned to love him dearly. She in turn became his favorite wife, although she remained childless throughout her life. Kamehameha's first wife was the supremely royal Keopuolani, who so outranked even him that the king himself had to approach her naked and crawling on his belly. Keopuolani produced the royal children Liholiho and Kauikeaouli, who became King Kamehameha II and III, respectively. Just before Kamehameha I died in 1819 he appointed Liholiho his successor, but he also had the wisdom to make Kaahumanu the *kuhina nui* or queen regent. Initially, Liholiho was weak and became a drunkard. Later he became a good ruler, but he was always supported by his royal mother Keopuolani and by the ever-formidable Kaahumanu.

Kapu Is *Pau*

Kaahumanu was greatly loved and respected by the people. On public occasions, she donned Kamehameha's royal cloak and spear: so attired and infused with the king's mana, she demonstrated that she was the real leader of Hawaii. For six months after Kamehameha's death, Kaahumanu counseled Liholiho on what he must do. The wise *kuhina nui* knew that the old ways were *pau* (finished) and that Hawaii could not hope to function in a rapidly changing world under the *kapu* system. In November 1819, Kaahumanu and Keopuolani prevailed upon Liholiho to break two of the oldest and most sacred *kapu* by eating with women and by allowing women to eat previously forbidden foods such as bananas and certain fish. Heavily fortified with strong drink and attended by other high-ranking chiefs and a handful of foreigners, Kaahumanu and Liholiho ate together in public. This feast became known as *Ai Noa* (Free Eating). As the first morsels passed Kaahumanu's lips, the ancient gods of Hawaii tumbled. Throughout the land, revered *heiau* were burned and abandoned and the idols knocked to the ground. Now the people had nothing to rely on but their weakened inner selves. Nothing and no one could answer their prayers; their spiritual lives were empty and in shambles.

Missionaries

Into this spiritual vortex sailed the brig *Thaddeus* on April 4, 1820. It had set sail from Boston on October 23, 1819, lured to the Big Island by Henry Opukahaia, a local boy born at Napoopoo in 1792. Coming ashore at Kailua-Kona, the Reverends Bingham and Thurston were granted a one-year trial missionary period by King Liholiho. They established themselves on the Big Island and Oahu and from there began the transformation of Hawaii. The missionaries were people of God, but also practical-minded Yankees. They brought education, enterprise, and most importantly, unlike the transient seafarers, a commitment to stay and build. By 1824 the new faith had such a foothold that Chieftess Keopuolani climbed to the fire pit atop Kilauea and defied Pele. This was even more striking than the previous breaking of the food *kapu* because the strength of Pele could actually be seen. Keopuolani ate forbidden *ohelo* berries and cried out, "Jehovah is my God." Over the next decades the governing of Hawaii slipped away from the Big Island and moved to the new port cities of Lahaina and later, Honolulu. In 1847, the Parker Ranch began with a two-acre grant given to John Parker. He coupled this with 360 acres given to his *ali'i* wife Kipikane by the land division known as the Great *Mahele*.

Rapid Conversions

The year 1824 also marked the death of Keopuolani, who was given a Christian burial. She had set the standard by accepting Christianity, and a number of the *ali'i* had followed the queen's lead. Liholiho had sailed off to England, where he and his wife contracted measles and died. Their bodies were returned by the British in 1825, on the HMS *Blonde* captained by Lord Byron, cousin of *the* Lord Byron. During these years, Kaahumanu allied herself with Rev. Richards, pastor of the first mission in the islands, and together they wrote Hawaii's first code of laws based upon the Ten Commandments. Foremost was the condemnation of murder, theft, brawling, and the desecration of the Sabbath by work or play. The early missionaries had the best of intentions, but like all zealots they were blinded by the singlemindedness that was also their greatest ally. They weren't surgically selective in their destruction of native beliefs. *Anything* native was felt to be inferior, and they set about wiping out all traces of the old ways. In their rampage they reduced the Hawaiian culture to ashes, plucking self-will and determination from the hearts of a once-proud people. More so than the whalers, they terminated the Hawaiian way of life.

The Early Seamen

A good portion of the common seamen of the early 19th century came from the dregs of the Western world. Many a whoremongering drunkard had awoken from a stupor and found himself on the pitching deck of a ship, discovering to his dismay that he had been "pressed into naval service." For the most part these sailors were a filthy, uneducated, lawless rabble. Their present situation was dim, their future hopeless, and they would live to be 30 if they were lucky and didn't die from scurvy or a thousand other miserable fates. They snatched brief pleasure in every port and jumped ship at every opportunity, especially in an easy berth like Lahaina. They displayed the worst elements of Western culture—which the Hawaiians naively mimicked. In exchange for *aloha* they gave drunkenness, sloth, and insidious death by disease. By the 1850s the population of native Hawaiians tumbled from the estimated 300,000 reported by Captain Cook in 1778 to barely 60,000. Common conditions such as colds, flu, venereal disease, and sometimes smallpox and cholera decimated the Hawaiians, who had no natural immunities to these foreign ailments. By the time the missionaries arrived, *hapa haole* children were common in Lahaina streets.

The earliest merchant ships to the islands were owned or skippered by lawless opportunists who had come seeking sandalwood after first filling their holds with furs from the Pacific Northwest. Aided by *ali'i* hungry for manufactured goods and Western finery, they raped Hawaiian forests of this fragrant wood so coveted in China. Next, droves of sailors came in search of whales. The whalers, decent men at home, left their morals back in the Atlantic and lived by the slogan "no conscience east of the Cape." The delights of Hawaii were just too tempting for most.

Two Worlds Tragically Collide

The 1820s were a time of confusion and soul-searching for the Hawaiians. When Kamehameha II died the kingdom passed to Kauikeaouli (Kamehameha III), who made his lifelong residence in Lahaina. The young king was only nine years old when the title passed to him, but his power was secure because Kaahumanu was still a vibrant *kuhina nui.* The young prince, more so than any other, was raised in the cultural confusion of the times. His childhood was spent during the very cusp of the change from old ways to new, and he was often pulled in two directions by vastly differing beliefs. Since he was royal born, he was bound by age-old Hawaiian tradition to mate and produce an heir with the highest-ranking *ali'i* in the kingdom. This mate happened to be his younger sister, the Princess Nahienaena. To the old Hawaiian advisors, this arrangement was perfectly acceptable and encouraged. To the increasingly influential missionaries, incest was an unimaginable abomination in the eyes of God. The problem was compounded by the fact that Kamehameha III and Nahienaena were drawn to each other and were deeply in love. The young king could not stand the mental pressure imposed by conflicting worlds. He became a teenage alcoholic too royal to be restrained by anyone in the kingdom, and his bouts of drunkenness and womanizing were both legendary and scandalous.

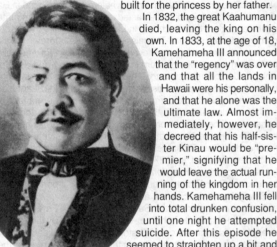

Kamehameha III

Meanwhile, Nahienaena was even more pressured because she was a favorite of the missionaries, baptized into the church at age 12. She too vacillated between the old and the new. At times a pious Christian, at others she drank all night and took numerous lovers. As the prince and princess grew into their late teens, they became even more attached to each other and hardly made an attempt to keep their relationship from the missionaries. Whenever possible, they lived together in a grass house built for the princess by her father.

In 1832, the great Kaahumanu died, leaving the king on his own. In 1833, at the age of 18, Kamehameha III announced that the "regency" was over and that all the lands in Hawaii were his personally, and that he alone was the ultimate law. Almost immediately, however, he decreed that his half-sister Kinau would be "premier," signifying that he would leave the actual running of the kingdom in her hands. Kamehameha III fell into total drunken confusion, until one night he attempted suicide. After this episode he seemed to straighten up a bit and mostly kept a low profile. In 1836, Princess Nahienaena was convinced by the missionaries to take a husband. She married Leleiohoku, a chief from the Big Island, but continued to sleep with her brother. It is uncertain who fathered the child, but Nahienaena gave birth to a baby boy in September 1836. The young prince survived for only a few hours, and Nahienaena never recovered from her convalescence. She died in December 1836 and was laid to rest in the mausoleum next to her mother, Keopuolani, on the royal island in Mokuhina Pond. After the death of his sister, Kamehameha III became a sober and righteous ruler. Often seen paying his respects at the royal mausoleum, he ruled longer than any other king until his death in 1854.

The Missionaries Prevail

In 1823, the first mission was established in Lahaina under the pastorage of Rev. Richards and his wife. Within a few years, many of the notable *ali'i* had been, at least in appearance, converted to Christianity. By 1828 the cornerstones for Wainee Church, the first stone church on the island, were laid just behind the palace of Kamehameha III. The struggle between missionaries and whalers centered around public drunkenness and the servicing of sailors by native women. The normally God-fearing whalers had signed on for perilous duty that lasted up to three years, and when they anchored in Lahaina they demanded their pleasure. The missionaries were instrumental in placing a curfew on sailors and prohibiting native women from boarding ships, which had become customary. These measures certainly did not stop the liaisons between sailor and *wahine,* but they did impose a modicum of social sanction and tolled the end of the wideopen days. The sailors were outraged; in 1825 the crew from the *Daniel* attacked the home of the meddler, Rev. Richards. A year later a similar incident occurred. In 1827, confined and lonely sailors from the whaler *John Palmer* fired their cannons at Rev. Richards' newly built home.

Slowly the tensions eased, and by 1836 many sailors were regulars at the Seamen's Chapel adjacent to the Baldwin home. Unfortunately, even the missionaries couldn't stop the pesky mosquito from entering the islands through the port of Lahaina. The mosquitoes arrived from Mexico in 1826 aboard the merchant ship *Wellington.* They were inadvertently carried as larvae in the water barrels and democratically pestered everyone in the islands from that day forward, regardless of race, religion, or creed.

Lahaina Becomes a Cultural Center

By 1831, Lahaina was firmly established as a seat of Western influence in Hawaii. That year marked the founding of Lahainaluna School, the first *real* American school west of the Rockies. Virtually a copy of a New England normal school, it attracted the best students, both native and nonnative, from throughout the kingdom. By 1834, Lahainaluna had an operating printing press publishing the islands' first newspaper, *The Torch of Hawaii,* starting a lucrative printing industry centered in Lahaina that dominated not only the islands but also California for many years.

An early native student was David Malo. He was brilliant and well educated, but more importantly, he remembered the "old ways." One of the first Hawaiians to realize his native land was being swallowed up by the newcomers, Malo compiled the first history of precontact Hawaii and the resulting book, *Hawaiian Antiquities,* became a reference masterpiece that has yet to be eclipsed. David Malo insisted that the printing be done in Hawaiian, not English. Malo is buried in the mountains above Lahainaluna where, by his own request, he is "high above the tide of foreign invasion." By the 1840s, Lahaina was firmly established as the "whaling capital of the world"; the peak year 1846 saw 395 whaling ships anchored here. A census in 1846 reported that Lahaina was home to 3,445 natives, 112 permanent *haole,* 600 sailors, and more than 500 dogs. The populace was housed in 882 grass houses, 155 adobe houses, and 59 relatively permanent stone and wooden framed structures. Lahaina would probably have remained the islands' capital, had Kamehameha III not moved the royal capital to the burgeoning port of Honolulu on the island of Oahu.

Foreign Influence

By the 1840s Honolulu was becoming the center of commerce in the islands; when Kamehameha III moved the royal court there from Lahaina, the ascendant fate of the new capital was guaranteed. In 1843, Lord Paulet, commander of the warship *Carysfort,* forced Kamehameha III to sign a treaty ceding Hawaii to the British. London, however, repudiated this act, and Hawaii's independence was restored within a few months when Queen Victoria sent Admiral Thomas as her personal agent of good intentions. The king memorialized the turn of events by a speech in which he uttered the phrase, *Ua mau ke ea o ka aina i ka pono* ("The life of the land is preserved in righteousness"), now Hawaii's motto. The French used similar bullying tactics to force an unfavorable treaty on the Hawaiians in 1839; as part of these heavy-handed negotiations they exacted a payment of $20,000 and the right of Catholics to enjoy religious freedom in the islands. In 1842 the U.S. recognized and guaranteed Hawaii's independence without a formal treaty, and by 1860 more than 80% of the islands' trade was with America.

The Great *Mahele*

In 1840 Kamehameha III ended his autocratic rule and instituted a constitutional monarchy. This brought about the Hawaiian Bill of Rights, but the most far-reaching change was the transition to private ownership of land. Formerly, all land belonged to the ruling chief, who gave wedge-shaped parcels called *ahupua'a* to lesser chiefs to be worked for him. The commoners did the real labor, their produce heavily taxed by the *ali'i*. The fortunes of war, the death of a chief, or the mere whim of a superior could force a commoner off the land. The Hawaiians, however, could not think in terms of "owning" land. No one could *possess* land; one could only *use* land, and its *ownership* was a strange and foreign concept. (As a result, naive Hawaiians gave up their lands for a song to unscrupulous traders, which remains an integral, unrectified problem to this day.)

In 1847 Kamehameha III and his advisors separated the lands of Hawaii into three groupings: crown land (belonging to the king), government land (belonging to the chiefs), and the people's land (the largest parcels). In 1848, 245 *ali'i* entered their land claims in the *Mahele Book*, assuring them ownership. In 1850 the commoners were given title in fee simple to the lands they cultivated and lived on as tenants, not including house lots in towns. Commoners without land could buy small *kuleana* (farms) from the government at 50 cents per acre. In 1850, foreigners were also allowed to purchase land in fee simple, and the ownership of Hawaii from that day forward slipped steadily from the hands of its indigenous people.

KING SUGAR

After attempts on Oahu and Kauai, the sugar industry burgeoned at Hana, Maui, in 1849. A whaler named George Wilfong hauled four blubber pots ashore and set them up on a rocky hill in the middle of 60 acres he had planted in sugar. A team of oxen turned "crushing rollers" and the cane juice flowed down an open trough into the pots, under which an attending native kept a roaring fire burning. Wilfong's methods of refining were crude but the resulting high-quality sugar turned a neat profit in Lahaina. The main problem was labor. The Hawaiians, who made excellent whalers, were basically indentured workers. They became extremely disillusioned with their contracts, which could last up to 10 years. Most of their wages were eaten up by manufactured commodities sold at the company store, and it didn't take long for them to realize that they were little more than slaves. At every opportunity they either left the area or just refused to work.

Imported Labor

The **Masters and Servants Act of 1850,** which allowed importation of laborers under the contract system, ostensibly guaranteed an endless supply of cheap labor for the plantations. Chinese laborers were imported, but were too enterprising to remain in the fields for a meager $3 per month. They left as soon as opportunity permitted, and went into business as small merchants and retailers. In the meantime, Wilfong had sold out, releasing most of the Hawaiians previously held under contract, and his plantation fell into disuse. In 1860 two Danish brothers, August and Oscar Unna, bought land at Hana to raise sugar. They solved the labor problem by importing Japanese laborers who were extremely hard-working and easily managed. The workday lasted 10 hours, six days a week, for a salary of $20 per month with housing and medical care thrown in. Plantation life was very structured, with stringent rules governing even bedtimes and lights out. A worker was fined for being late or for smoking on the job. Even the Japanese couldn't function under these circumstances, and improvements in benefits and housing were slowly gained.

Sugar Grows

The demand for "Sandwich Island Sugar" grew as California was populated during the gold rush, and increased dramatically when the American Civil War demanded a constant supply. The only sugar plantations on the Mainland were small plots confined to the Confederate states, whose products would hardly be bought by the Union and whose fields, later in the war, were destroyed. By the 1870s it was clear to the planters, still mainly New Englanders, that the U.S. was their market; they tried often to gain closer ties and favorable tariffs. The Americans also planted rumors that the British were interested in annexing Hawaii; this put pressure on the U.S. Congress to pass the long-desired **Reciprocity Act,** which would exempt sugar from import duty. It finally passed in 1875, in exchange for U.S. long-range rights to the strategic naval port of Pearl Harbor, among other concessions. These agreements gave increased political power to a small group of American planters whose outlooks were similar to those of the post-Civil War South, where a few powerful whites were the virtual masters of a multitude of dark-skinned laborers. Sugar was now big business and the Hana District alone exported almost 3,000 tons per year. All of Hawaii would have to reckon with the "sugar barons."

Changing Society
The sugar plantation system changed life in Hawaii physically, spiritually, politically, and economically. Now boatloads of workers came not only from Japan, but from Portugal, Germany, and even Russia. The white-skinned workers were most often the field foremen *(luna)*. With the immigrants came new religions, new animals and plants, unique cuisines, and a plantation language known as pidgin, or better yet, *da' kine*. Many Asians, and to a lesser extent the other groups including the white plantation owners, intermarried with Hawaiians. A new class of people properly termed "cosmopolitan" but more familiarly and aptly known as "locals" was emerging. These were the people of multiple racial backgrounds who couldn't exactly say *what* they were, but it was clear to all just *who* they were. The plantation owners became the new "chiefs" of Hawaii who could carve up the land and dispense favors. The Hawaiian monarchy was soon eliminated.

A KINGDOM PASSES

The Beginning of the End
Like the Hawaiian people themselves, the Kamehameha dynasty in the mid-1800s was dying from within. King Kamehameha IV (Alexander Liholiho) ruled 1854-63; his only child died in 1862. He was succeeded by his older brother Kamehameha V (Lot Kamehameha), who ruled until 1872. With his passing the Kamehameha line ended. William Lunalilo, elected king in 1873 by popular vote, was of royal, but not Kamehameha, lineage. He died after only a year in office, and being a bachelor, left no heirs. He was succeeded by David Kalakaua, known far and wide as "The Merrie Monarch," who made a world tour and was well received wherever he went. He built Iolani Palace in Honolulu and was personally in favor of closer ties with the U.S., helping push through the Reciprocity Act. Kalakaua died in 1891 and was replaced by his sister Lydia Liliuokalani, last of the Hawaiian monarchs.

The Revolution
When Liliuokalani took office in 1891, the native population was at a low of 40,000 and she felt that the U.S. had too much influence over her homeland. She was known to personally favor the English over the Americans. She attempted to replace the liberal constitution of 1887 (adopted by her pro-American brother) with an autocratic mandate in which she would have had much more political and economic control of the islands. When the McKinley Tariff of 1890 brought a decline in sugar profits, she made no attempt to improve the situation. Thus, the planters saw her as a political obstacle to their economic growth; most of Hawaii's American planters and merchants were in favor of a rebellion. She would have to go! A central spokesperson and firebrand was Lorrin Thurston, a Honolulu publisher who, with a central core of about 30 men, challenged the Hawaiian monarchy. Although Liliuokalani rallied some support and had a small military potential in her personal guard, the coup was ridiculously easy—it took only one casualty. Captain John Good shot a Hawaiian policeman in the arm and that did it. Naturally, the conspirators could not have succeeded without some solid assurances from a secret contingent in the U.S. Congress as well as outgoing president Benjamin Harrison, who favored Hawaii's annexation. Marines from the *Boston* went ashore to "protect American lives," and on January 17, 1893, the Hawaiian monarchy came to an end.

The provisional government was headed by Sanford B. Dole, who became president of the

HAWAII STATE ARCHIVES

Queen Liliuokalani

Hawaiian Republic. Liliuokalani surrendered not to the conspirators but to U.S. Ambassador John Stevens. She believed that the U.S. government, which had assured her of Hawaiian independence, would be outraged by the overthrow and would come to her aid. Incoming president Grover Cleveland *was* outraged and Hawaii wasn't immediately annexed as expected. When queried about what she would do with the conspirators if she were reinstated, Liliuokalani said that they would be hung as traitors. The racist press of the times, which portrayed the Hawaiians as half-civilized, bloodthirsty heathens, publicized this widely. Since the conspirators were the leading citizens of the land, the queen's words proved untimely. In January 1895 a small, ill-fated counterrevolution headed by Liliuokalani failed, and she was placed under house arrest in Iolani Palace. Officials of the republic insisted that she use her married name (Mrs. John Dominis) to sign the documents forcing her to abdicate her throne. She was also forced to swear allegiance to the new republic. Liliuokalani went on to write *Hawaii's Story* and the lyric ballad "Aloha O'e." She never forgave

the conspirators and remained "queen" to the Hawaiians until her death in 1917.

Annexation
The overwhelming majority of Hawaiians opposed annexation and desired to restore the monarchy. But they were prevented from voting by the new republic because they couldn't meet the imposed property and income qualifications—a transparent ruse by the planters to control the majority. Most *haole* were racist and believed that the "common people" could not be entrusted with the vote because they were childish and incapable of ruling themselves. The fact that the Hawaiians had existed quite well for a thousand years before white people even reached Hawaii was never considered. The Philippine theater of the Spanish-American War also prompted annexation. One of the strongest proponents was Alfred Mahon, a brilliant naval strategist who, with support from Theodore Roosevelt, argued that the U.S. military must have Hawaii in order to be a viable force in the Pacific. In addition, Japan, victorious in its recent war with China, protested the American intention to annex, and in so doing prompted even moderates to support annexation for fear that the Japanese themselves coveted the prize. On July 7, 1898, President McKinley signed the annexation agreement, and this "tropical fruit" was finally put into America's basket.

MODERN TIMES

Hawaii entered the 20th century totally transformed. The old Hawaiian language, religion, culture, and leadership were all gone; Western dress, values, education, and recreation were the norm. Native Hawaiians were now unseen citizens who lived in dwindling numbers in remote areas. The plantations, new centers of social order, had a strong Asian flavor; more than 75% of their workforce was Asian. There was a small white middle class, an all-powerful white elite, and a single political party ruled by that elite. Education, however, was always highly prized, and by the turn of the century all racial groups were encouraged to attend school. By 1900, almost 90% of Hawaiians were literate (far above the national norm) and schooling was mandatory for all children ages 6-15. Intermarriage was accepted, and there was a mixing of the races like nowhere else on earth. The military became increasingly important to Hawaii. It brought in money and jobs, dominating the island economy. The Japanese attack on Pearl Harbor, which began U.S. involvement in WW II, bound Hawaii to America forever. Once the islands had been baptized by blood, the average Mainlander felt that Hawaii was American soil. A movement among Hawaiians to become part of the United States began to grow. They wanted a real voice in Washington, not merely a voteless delegate as provided under their territory status. Hawaii became the 50th state in 1959, and the jumbo-jet revolution of the 1960s made it easily accessible to growing numbers of tourists from all over the world.

Military History

A few military strategists realized the importance of Hawaii early in the 19th century, but most didn't recognize the advantages until the Spanish-American War. It was clearly an unsinkable ship in the middle of the Pacific from which the U.S. could launch military operations. Troops were stationed at Camp McKinley, at the foot of Diamond Head, the main military compound until it became obsolete in 1907. Pearl Harbor was first surveyed in 1872 by General Schofield. Later, a military base named in his honor, Schofield Barracks, was a main military post in central Oahu. It housed the U.S. 5th Cavalry in 1909 and was heavily bombed by the Japanese at the outset of WW II. Pearl Harbor, first dredged in 1908, was officially opened on December 11, 1911. The first warship to enter was the cruiser *California*. Ever since, the military has been a mainstay of Island economy. Unfortunately, there has been long-standing bad blood between locals and military personnel. Each group has tended to look down upon the other.

Pearl Harbor Attack

On the morning of December 7, 1941, the Japanese carrier *Akagi,* flying the battle flag of the famed Admiral Togo of the Russo-Japanese War, received and broadcast over its PA system island music from Honolulu station KGMB. Deep in the bowels of the ship a radio man listened for a much different message, coming thousands of

The Honolulu Star Bulletin *banner headline announces the official beginning of U.S. involvement in WW II on Sunday, December 7, 1941*

miles from the Japanese mainland. When the ironically poetic message "east wind rain" was received, the attack was launched. At the end of the day, 2,325 U.S. servicemen and 57 civilians were dead; 188 planes were destroyed; 18 major warships were sunk or heavily damaged; and the U.S. was in the war. Japanese casualties were extremely light. The ignited conflict would rage for four years until Japan, through Nagasaki and Hiroshima, was vaporized into submission. At the end of hostilities, Hawaii would never again be considered separate from America.

Statehood

A number of economic and political reasons explain why the ruling elite of Hawaii desired statehood, but put simply, the vast majority of people who lived there, especially after WW II, considered themselves Americans. The first serious mention of making "The Sandwich Islands" a state was in the 1850s under President Franklin Pierce, but it wasn't taken seriously until the monarchy was overthrown in the 1890s. For the next 50 years statehood proposals were made repeatedly to Congress, but there was stiff opposition, especially from the southern states. With Hawaii a territory, an import quota system beneficial to Mainland producers could be enacted on produce, especially sugar. Also, there was prejudice against creating a state in a place where the majority of the populace was not white. This situation was illuminated by the infamous Massie Rape Case of 1931 (see **People,** below), which went down as one of the greatest miscarriages of justice in American history.

During WW II, Hawaii was placed under martial law, but no serious attempt was made to intern the Japanese population as it was in California. There were simply too many Japanese, who went on to gain the respect of the American people by their outstanding fighting record during the war. Hawaii's own 100th Battalion became the famous 442nd Regimental Combat Team, which gained notoriety by saving the Lost Texas Battalion during the Battle of the Bulge and went on to be *the* most decorated battalion in all of WW II. When these GIs returned home, *no one* was going to tell them that they were not loyal Americans. Many of these AJAs (Americans of Japanese Ancestry) took advantage of the GI Bill and received higher education. They were from the common people, not the elite, and they rallied grassroots support for statehood. When the vote finally occurred, approximately 132,900 voted in favor of statehood with only 7,800 votes against. Congress passed the Hawaii State Bill

on March 12, 1959, and on August 21, 1959, President Eisenhower announced that Hawaii was officially the 50th state.

GOVERNMENT

Being the newest state in America, Hawaii has had the chance to scrutinize the others, pick their best attributes, and learn from their past mistakes. The government of the state of Hawaii is in essence no different from that of any other state except that it is streamlined and, in theory, more efficient. With only two levels—state and county—the added bureaucracy of town or city governments is theoretically eliminated. Unfortunately, some of the state-run agencies, such as the centralized Board of Education, have become "red-tape" monsters. Hawaii, in anticipation of becoming a state, drafted a constitution in 1950 and was ready to go when statehood was ratified. Politics and government are taken seriously in the "Aloha State." For example, in the election to ratify statehood, hardly a ballot went uncast, with 95% of the voters opting for statehood. The bill carried every island of Hawaii except for Niihau, where, coincidentally, the majority of people (total population 250 or so) are of relatively pure Hawaiian blood. In the first state elections that followed, 173,000 of 180,000 registered voters voted. In recent years, the number

of votes cast in primary and general elections has slipped to unprecedented lows, as in the rest of the country.

State Government

Honolulu is the state capital of Hawaii and its seat of government. All major state-level executive, legislative, and judicial offices are located there. Hawaii's state legislature has 76 members, with 51 elected seats in the House of Representatives, and 25 in the State Senate. Members serve two- and four-year terms respectively. All officials come from 76 separate electorates based on population, which sometimes makes for strange political bedfellows. For example, Maui's split 7th Representative District encompasses much of West Maui and both the islands of Lanai and Molokai. This district combines one of Maui's richest tourist communities with Lanai, where many people are Filipino former field workers (now hotel staff), and with economically depressed Molokai, where the vast majority of the native Hawaiians live on welfare. Perhaps even stranger are the 12th Representative District, which takes in the eastern third of the island of Maui, and the 6th Senatorial District, which encompasses Kihei, Wailea, Makena, the half of Upcountry, and Hana. Both are paired with the north coast of Kauai, an area that has no traditional political or cultural bond with Maui. The last redrawing of district lines was done in 1991.

Oahu, which has the largest number of voters, elects 18 of 25 senators and 37 of 51 representatives, giving this island a majority in both houses. Kauai County, in comparison, elects 1.5 state senators and 2.5 representatives—the halves shared with Maui County.

The state of Hawaii has an overwhelming Democratic Party orientation. Of the 76 members of the legislature, 62 are Democrats. Although not exclusive, Republican strongholds are portions of the metropolitan areas of Honolulu, Kaneohe, and Kailua, on Oahu.

The state is divided into four administrative counties: the **County of Kauai,** covering Kauai and Niihau, with Lihue as the county seat; the **City and County of Honolulu,** which encompasses Oahu and includes all of the Northwestern Hawaiian Islands, with Honolulu as its county seat; the **County of Hawaii,** covering the Big Island, with Hilo as its county seat; and the **County of Maui,** administering the islands of Maui, Lanai, Molokai, and uninhabited Kahoolawe, with the county seat at Wailuku on Maui. Each county has an elected mayor—currently two Democrats and two Republicans. County councils are also elected to help administer each county. Honolulu, Hawaii, and Maui Counties each have nine council members, while Kauai has seven.

Branches of Government

The **State Legislature** is the collective body of the House of Representatives and the Senate. They meet during a once-yearly legislative session that begins on the third Wednesday of January and lasts for 60 working days. (These sessions are oftentimes extended and special sessions of up to 30 days are frequently called.) The Legislature primarily focuses on taxes, new laws, and appropriations. The **Executive Branch** is headed by the governor and lieutenant governor, both elected on a statewide basis for four years with a two-term maximum. The governor has the right to appoint the heads of 18 state departments outlined in the constitution. The department appointees must be approved by the Senate, and they usually hold office as long as the appointing administration. The present governor is Benjamin J. Cayetano, the second Hawaiian governor of the state and the first with any Filipino heritage. Mr. Cayetano has held this office since 1994. The **Judiciary** is headed by a state Supreme Court of five justices, an appeals court, and four circuit courts. All jurists are appointed by the governor and serve for 10 years with Senate approval. Twenty seven district courts have local jurisdiction; the judges are appointed for six-year terms by the chief justice of the Supreme Court.

Special Departments

The Department of Education is headed by a board of 13 nonpartisan representatives elected for four-year terms, 10 from Oahu and three from the other islands. The board has the right to appoint the Superintendent of Schools. Many praise the centralized board as a democratic body offering equal educational opportunity to all districts of Hawaii regardless of sociofinancial status. Detractors say that the centralized board provides "equal educational mediocrity" to all. The University of Hawaii is governed by a Board of Regents appointed by the governor. They choose the president of the university.

Federal Government Representatives

The state of Hawaii elects two senators and two representatives to the U.S. Congress. Currently, all four are Democrats. The senators are Daniel Inouye and Daniel Akaka. Neil Abercrombie and Patsy Mink are the representatives.

Political History

Before WW II Hawaii was run by a self-serving yet mostly benevolent oligarchy. The one real political party was Republican, controlled by the Hawaiian Sugar Planters Association. The planters felt that, having made Hawaii a paradise, they should rule because they had "right on their side." The Baldwin family of Maui *was* the government, with such supporters as the Rice family, which controlled Kauai, and William (Doc) Hill of Hawaii. These were the preeminent families of the islands; all were represented on the boards of the Big Five corporations that ruled

Hawaii economically by controlling sugar, transportation, and utilities. An early native politician was Prince Jonah Kuhio Kalanianaole, a brother to Liliuokalani, who joined with the Republicans to gain perks for himself and for his own people. Nepotism and political hoopla were the order of those days. The Republicans, in coalition with the native Hawaiians, maintained a majority over the large racial groups such as the Japanese and Filipinos who, left to their own devices, would have been Democrats. The Republicans also used unfair literacy laws, land ownership qualifications, and proof of birth in Hawaii to control the large numbers of immigrant workers who could threaten their ruling position. It was even alleged that during elections a pencil was hung on a string over the Republican ballot: if Hawaiians wanted to vote Democratic, they would have to pull the string to the other side of the voting booth. The telltale angle would be a giveaway. They would be unemployed the next day.

The Democrats Rise to Power

The Democrats were plagued with poor leadership and internal factionalism in the early years. Their first real rise to power began in 1935 when the International Longshoremen's and Warehousemen's Union (ILWU) formed a branch in Hilo on the Big Island. In 1937, an incident known as the "Hilo Massacre" occurred when policemen fired on and wounded 25 striking stevedores, which was the catalyst needed to bind labor together. Thereafter, the ILWU, under the leadership of Jack Hall, became a major factor in the Democratic party. Their relationship was strained in later years when the ILWU was linked to Communism, but during the early days, whomever the ILWU supported in the Democratic Party won.

The Democrats began to take over after WW II when returning Japanese servicemen become active in politics. The Japanese by this time were the largest ethnic group in Hawaii. A central character during the late 1940s and '50s was Jack Burns. Although a *haole,* this simple man was known to be for "the people" regardless of their ethnic background. During the war, as a police captain he made clear his view that he considered the Japanese exemplary Americans. The Japanese community never forgot this, and were instrumental in Burns's election as gover-

nor, both in 1962 and 1966. The majority of people in the Asian ethnic groups in Hawaii tended to remain Democrat even after they climbed the socioeconomic ladder. The first special election after statehood saw the governorship go to the previously appointed Republican Territorial Governor William Quinn, and the lieutenant governorship to another Republican, James Kealoha, of Hawaiian-Chinese ancestry. The first congressperson elected was Japanese-American, Democrat Daniel Inouye. Since then, every governor has been a Democrat and one out of every two political offices is held by a person of Japanese extraction. Former governor George Ariyoshi was the first governor of Japanese ancestry in the United States.

OFFICE OF HAWAIIAN AFFAIRS

In 1979, a constitutional mandate created the Office of Hawaiian Affairs (OHA). This remarkable piece of legislature recognized, for the first time since the fall of the monarchy in 1893, the special plight of native Hawaiians. For 75 years, no one in government was eager to face the "native question," but since 1979, OHA has opened a Pandora's box of litigation and accusation. For example, in 1983, a presidential commission investigated U.S. involvement in the overthrow of Hawaii's last queen, Liliuokalani, to decide if the federal government owed reparations to her Hawaiian people. After listening to testimony from thousands attesting to personal family loss of land and freedom, complete with old deeds documenting their claims, the commission concluded the U.S. was guiltless and native Hawaiians had nothing coming from Uncle Sam. Jaws dropped, and even those opposed to native Hawaiian rights couldn't believed this *white*wash. Then-governor George Ariyoshi said in a newspaper interview, "A recent congressional study did not accurately portray what went on here at the turn of the century. . . . To say that the monarchy was not overthrown . . . is something that I cannot accept. It is not historically true."

Trouble in Paradise

Since then, OHA, as the vanguard of native political activism, has focused on gaining moneys guaranteed in the state constitution as recently as 1959 for "ceded lands." It has also been instrumental in regaining disputed Hawaiian lands and has helped in the fight to save the sacred island of Kahoolawe, currently uninhabited and used as a bombing target from WW II until recently. To simply state a complex issue, native Hawaiians have been eligible for benefits from revenues accrued from ceded lands and haven't been receiving them. These lands (1.8 million acres) were crown and government lands belonging to the Hawaiian monarchy and, therefore, to its subjects. When the kingdom was overthrown, the lands passed on to the short-lived Republic, followed by the U.S. Protectorate, and then finally to the state in 1959. No one disputed these lands belonged to *the people,* who were entitled to money collected from rents and leases. Since statehood, however, these tens of millions of dollars have gone into a "general fund" used by various state agencies such as the Department of Transportation and the Department of Land and Natural Resources; the state is extremely reluctant to turn these funds over to what they derisively call an "unconstitutional special interest group." A Constitutional Convention in 1988 supposedly addressed this issue, but many problems still exist.

Native Hawaiian Rights

The question has always been, "Just what is a native Hawaiian?" The answer has always been ambiguous. The government has used the "blood quantum" as a measuring stick. This is simply the percentage of Hawaiian blood in a person's ancestry—customarily 50% qualifies a person as *Hawaiian.* The issue is compounded by the fact that no other group of people has been so racially intermarried for so many years. Even though many people have direct ancestry to pre-Republic Hawaiians, they don't have enough "Hawaiian-ness" to qualify. An overwhelming number of these people fall into the category of "locals": they "feel" Hawaiian, but blood-wise they're not. They suffer all of the negativity of second-class citizens and reap none of the benefits accorded Hawaiians. Those who do qualify according to blood quantum don't have the numbers or the political clout necessary to get re-

sults. In fact, many people involved with OHA would not qualify themselves, at least not according to the blood quantum! Strong factionalism within the native Hawaiian movement itself threatens its credibility. Many people who do qualify by the blood quantum view the others as impinging on their rightful claims. The most vocal activists point out that only a coalition of people who have Hawaiian blood, combined with those who "identify" with the movement, will get results. Political firebrands maintain "anti-Hawaiian rights" lobbyists such as the tourist industry, airlines, and large corporations are now stronger than the Hawaiians. They advise that the only way the Hawaiian rights movement can win is to become active "political warriors" and vote for legislators who will support their cause. The rhetoric of OHA is reminiscent of that of the equal rights movement of the 1960s.

Obviously compromise is necessary. Perhaps certain social entitlements (such as tuition grants) could be equal for all, whereas money and land entitlements could be granted by percentages equal to the claiming person's "blood quantum." OHA members appeal directly to the Hawaiian people and can build political constituencies at a grassroots level. Since they are elected by the people and not appointed by the government (the case with the Hawaiian Home Lands Department and the trustees of the Bishop Estate, two other *supposedly* Hawaiian institutions), the status quo political parties of Hawaii are wary of them. Their candidates may be opposed and defeated in the future. What makes the issue even more ludicrous is that some of the state's most powerful corporate families opposed to Hawaiian rights have direct lineage to not only pre-Republic Hawaiian ancestors, but to Hawaiian royalty. They themselves would receive "entitlements" from the ceded land according to blood quantum, but socioeconomically they are the natural enemies of OHA. The problem is difficult, and it is improbable that all concerned will get satisfaction. OHA maintains offices at 711 Kapiolani Blvd., Honolulu, HI 96813, tel. (808) 594-1980. They publish a newspaper entitled *Ka Wai Ola O OHA* (The Living Waters of OHA), which is available upon request. (Website: www.oha.org).

ECONOMY

Hawaii's mid-Pacific location makes it perfect for two primary sources of income: tourism and the military. Tourists come in anticipation of endless golden days on soothing beaches, while the military is provided with the strategic position of an unsinkable battleship. The tourism sector nets Hawaii about $11 billion annually, about one-third the state's revenue of $33.5 billion, while military spending comes in at just over $3 billion, money which should keep flowing smoothly and even increase in the foreseeable future. These revenues mostly remain aloof from the normal ups and downs of the Mainland economy, and both attract either gung-ho enthusiasts or rabidly negative detractors. The remaining 60% comes in descending proportions from construction, manufacturing, and agriculture (mainly sugar and pineapples). As long as the sun shines and the balance of global power requires a military presence, the economic stability of Hawaii is guaranteed.

TOURISM

"The earthly paradise! Don't you want to go to it? Why, of course!" This was the opening line of *The Hawaiian Guide Book* by Henry Whitney that appeared in 1875. In print for 25 years, it sold for 60 cents during a time when a roundtrip sea voyage between San Francisco and Honolulu cost $125. The technique is a bit dated, but the human desires remain the same: some of us seek paradise, all seek escape, some are drawn to play out a drama in a beautiful setting. Tourists have been coming to Hawaii ever since steamship service began in the 1860s. Until WW II, luxury liners carried the financial elite on exclusive voyages to the islands. By the 1920s 10,000 visitors a year were spending almost $5 million—cementing the bond between Hawaii and tourism.

A $25,000 prize offered by James Dole of pineapple fame sparked a trans-Pacific air race in 1927. The success of these aerial daredevils who answered the challenge proved that commercial air travel to Hawaii was feasible. Two years later, Hawaiian Air was offering regularly scheduled flights between the major islands. By 1950 airplanes had captured more than 50% of the transportation market, and ocean voyages were relegated to "specialty travel," catering to the elite. By 1960 the large airbuses made their debut; 300,000 tourists arrived on eight designated airlines. The Boeing 747 began operating in 1969. These enormous planes could carry hundreds of passengers at reasonable rates, so travel to Hawaii became possible for the average-income person. In 1970, two million arrived, and by 1990 close to six million passengers arrived on 22 international air carriers. In 1998, nearly seven million visitors chose Hawaii as their destination. The first hotel in Honolulu was the Hawaiian, built in 1872. It was pre-dated by Volcano House, which overlooks Kilauea Crater on the Big Island, and was built in 1866. The coral-pink Royal Hawaiian, built in 1927, is Waikiki's graciously aging grande dame, a symbol of days gone by. As late as the 1950s it had Waikiki Beach almost to itself. Only 10,000 hotel units were available in 1960; today there are more than 50,000 statewide and about 20,000 condo units as well.

Tourists: Who, When, and Where

Tourism-based income outstripped pineapples and sugar by the mid-'60s and the boom was on. Longtime residents could even feel a physical change in air temperature: many trees were removed from Honolulu to build parking lots, and reflected sunlight made Honolulu much hotter and at times unbearable. Even the trade winds, known to moderate temperatures, were not up to that task. So many people from the outlying farming communities were attracted to work in the hotels that there was a poi famine in 1967. But for the most part, islanders knew their economic future was tied to the "nonpolluting" industry of tourism. Most visitors (54%) are Americans, and by far the largest numbers come from the West Coast. Sun-seeking refugees from frigid Alaska, however, make up the greatest proportional number, according to population figures. The remaining arrivals are, in descending order of numbers, from Japan, Canada, Korea, Australia, Germany, England, and Taiwan. Europe, as a whole, sends proportionately fewer visitors than North America or Asia, while the fewest come from South America, the Middle East, and Africa.

The Japanese market grew constantly until 1995 when it reached two million Japanese visitors per year. Since then, and due largely to the Asian economic crisis, numbers have fallen off markedly, yet Japanese tourists still make up roughly 30% of the Hawaiian market. This is particularly beneficial to the tourist market because the average Western tourist spends about $135 per day, while a Japanese counterpart spends $340 per day. The average Japanese tourist, however, stays only about six days as opposed to 10 days for westbound travelers. Although still strong, there has been a slight decrease in numbers of Japanese tourists since 1997, principally due to the Asian economic malaise. Up until very recently the Japanese traveled only in groups and primarily stayed on Oahu. Now the trend is shifting to independent travel, or coming with a group and then peeling off, with a hefty percentage heading for the "Neighbor Islands" (all islands other than Oahu).

The typical visitor is slightly affluent, and female visitors outnumber males three to two. The average age (35) is a touch higher than in most vacation areas because it reflects an inflated proportion of retirees heading for Hawaii, especially Honolulu, to fulfill lifelong "dream" vacations. A typical stay lasts about 10 days, down from a month in the 1950s; a full 56% are repeat visitors. On any given day there are about 80,000 travelers on Oahu, 35,000 on Maui, 19,000 on Hawaii, and about 8,000 on Kauai. Molokai and Lanai get so few visitors, 1,400 and 1,000, respectively, that the figures are hardly counted.

In 1964 only 10% of the islands' hotel rooms were on the Neighbor Islands, but by 1966 the figure jumped to 25%, with more than 70% of tourists opting to visit the Neighbor Islands. Today four out of 10 hotel rooms are on the Neighbor Islands, with the figure steadily rising. The overwhelming number of tourists are on package tours, and the largest number of people congregate on Oahu in Waikiki, which has a 82% average hotel occupancy and attracts twice

as as many visitors as do the Neighbor Islands together. Obviously, Waikiki is still most people's idea of paradise. Those seeking a more intimate experience can have it with a 20-minute flight from Oahu to a Neighbor Island.

Joaquin Miller, the 19th-century poet of the Sierras, said, "I tell you my boy, the man who has not seen the Sandwich Islands, in this one great ocean's warm heart, has not seen the world." The times have certainly changed, but the sentiments of most visitors to Hawaii remain consistently the same.

Tourism-Related Problems

Tourism is both boon and blight to Hawaii. It is the root cause of two problems: one environmental, the other socioeconomic. The environmental impact is obvious, and is best described in the lament of singer Joni Mitchell's "Big Yellow Taxi": "They paved paradise and put up a parking lot." Put simply, tourism can draw too many people to an area and overburden it. In the process, it stresses the very land and destroys the natural beauty that attracted people in the first place. Tourists come to Hawaii for what has been called its "ambient resource": a balanced collage of indulgent climate, invigorating waters, intoxicating scenery, and exotic people all wrapped up neatly in one area that can both soothe and excite. It is in Hawaii's best interest to preserve this resource.

Most point to Waikiki as a prime example of development gone mad. It is super-saturated, and amazingly enough, hotel owners themselves are trying to keep development in check. Two prime examples of the best and the worst development can be found on Maui's south shore at Kihei and Wailea, less than five miles apart. Kihei looks like a high-rise, low-income, federally funded housing project. You can bet those who made a killing building here don't live here. Just down the road, Wailea is a model of what development could and should be. The architecture is tasteful, low-rise, unobtrusive, and done with people and the preservation of the scenery in mind. It's obviously more exclusive, but access points to the beaches are open to everyone and the view is still there for all to enjoy. It points the way for development standards of the future.

Changing Lifestyle

Like the land, humans are stressed by tourism. Local people, who once took the "Hawaiian lifestyle" for granted, became displaced and estranged in their own land. Some areas, predominantly along gorgeous beaches that were once average- to low-income communities, are now overdeveloped, with prices going through the roof. The locals are not only forced to move out, but often must come back as service personnel in the tourist industry and cater to the very people who displaced them. At one time the psychological blow was softened because, after all, the newcomers were merely benign tourists who would stay a short time, spend a wad of money, and leave.

Today, condos are being built and a different sort of visitor is arriving. Many condo owners are well-educated businesspeople and professionals in the above-average income brackets. The average condo owner is a Mainlander who purchases one as a second or retirement home. These people are not islanders and have a tough time relating to the locals, who naturally feel resentment. Moreover, since they don't *leave* like normal tourists, they use community facilities, find those special nooks and crannies for shopping or sunbathing that were once exclusively the domain of locals, and have a say as voters in community governments. The islanders become more and more disenfranchised. Many believe that the new order instigated by tourism is similar to what has always existed in Hawaii: a few from the privileged class being catered to by many from the working class. In a way it's an extension of the plantation system, but instead of carrying pineapples, most islanders find themselves carrying luggage, cocktails, or broiled fish. One argument, however, remains undeniable: whether it's people or pineapples, one has to make a living. The days of a little grass shack on a sunny beach aren't gone, but you need a steady job or a wallet full of credit cards to afford one.

THE MILITARY

Hawaii is the most militarized state in the U.S.: all five services are represented. Camp H.M. Smith, overlooking Pearl Harbor, is the headquarters of CINCPAC (Commander in Chief Pacific), which is responsible for 70% of the earth's surface, from California to the east coast of Africa and to both poles. The U.S. military presence dates back to 1887, when Pearl Harbor was given to the Navy as part of the Sugar Reciprocity Treaty. The sugar planters were given favorable duty-free treatment on their sugar, while the U.S. Navy was allowed exclusive rights to one of the best harbors in the Pacific. In 1894, when the monarchy was being overthrown by the sugar planters, the USS *Boston* sent a contingency of marines ashore to "keep order," which really amounted to a show of force, backing the

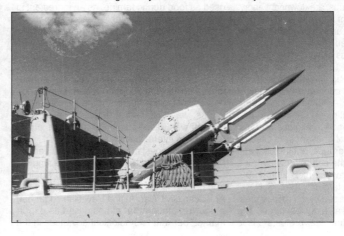

Missiles stand ready to defend the U.S. Battleship Hawaii.

revolution. The Spanish-American War saw U.S. troops billeted at Camp McKinley at the foot of Diamond Head, and Schofield Barracks opened to receive the 5th Cavalry in 1909. Pearl Harbor's flames ignited WW II and there has been no looking back since then.

About 44,000 military personnel are stationed in Hawaii (99% on Oahu), with more than 54,000 dependents. This number has slowly but steadily been decreasing since 1988, when the military was at its greatest strength in the state, and is now lower than at any time since the mid-'50s. The Army has the largest contingent with nearly 20,000, followed by the Navy at 11,000, Marine Corps at 7,000, Air Force at more than 5,000, and 1,500 or so with the Coast Guard. Besides this, 17,000 civilian support personnel account for 65% of all federal jobs in Hawaii. The combined services are one of the largest landholders with more than 210,000 acres, accounting for five percent of Hawaiian land. The two major holdings are the 100,000-acre Pohahuloa Training Area on Hawaii and 81,000 acres on Oahu, which is a full 22% of the entire island. The Army controls 58% of the military lands, followed by the Navy at 25%, and the remainder goes to the Air Force, Marines, and a few small installations to the Coast Guard.

The Military Has No *Aloha*

Not everyone is thrilled by the strong military presence in Hawaii. Two factions, native Hawaiians and antinuclear groups, are downright angry. Radical contingencies of native Hawaiian-rights groups consider Hawaii an independent country, besieged and "occupied" by the U.S. government. They date their loss of independence to Liliuokalani's overthrow in 1894. The vast majority of ethnic Hawaiians, though they consider themselves Americans, are concerned with loss of their rightful homelands—with no financial reparation—and about continuing destruction and disregard for their traditional religious and historical sites. A long list of grievances is cited by native Hawaiian action groups, but the best and clearest example was the controversy over the sacred island, Kahoolawe, which, until 1990, was used as a bombing target by the U.S. Navy.

A major controversy raised by the military presence focuses on Hawaii as a nuclear target. The ultimate goal of the antinuclear protesters is to see the Pacific, and the entire world, free from nuclear arms. They see Hawaii as a big target used by the international power merchants on the Mainland as both pawn and watchdog—if war breaks out, they say, the Hawaiian Islands will be reduced to cinders. The military naturally counters that a strong Hawaii is a deterrent to nuclear war and that Hawaii is not only a powerful offensive weapon, but one of the best-defended regions of the world. Unfortunately, when you are on an island there is no place to go: like a boxer in a ring, you can run, but you can't hide.

Also, the military has been cited for disposing of stockpiles of chemical weapons by incineration on Johnston Island, a military installation southwest of the Big Island. Because there was no environmental impact study, scientists fear that wind and currents could carry the pollutants to the main Hawaiian islands, destroying delicate coral reefs along the way.

SUGAR

Sugarcane *(ko)* was brought to Hawaii by its original settlers and was known throughout Polynesia. Its cultivation was well established and duly noted by Captain Cook when he first sighted the islands. The native Hawaiians used various strains of sugarcane for food, rituals, and medicine. It was never refined, but the stalk was chewed and juice was pressed from it. It was used as food during famine, as an ingredient in many otherwise unpalatable medicines, and especially as a love potion. Commercial growing started with a failure on Oahu in 1825, followed by a successful venture a decade later on Kauai. Until the mid-1990s, this original plantation was still productive. The industry received a technological boost in 1850 when a centrifuge, engineered by David Weston of the Honolulu Iron Works, was installed at a plantation on East Maui. It was used to spin the molasses out of the cooked syrup, leaving a crude crystal.

Hawaii's biggest market has always been the Mainland. Demand rose dramatically during the California gold rush of 1849-50, and again a decade later, for the Union Army during the American Civil War. At first Hawaiian sugar had a poor reputation that almost killed its export market, but with technological advances in the

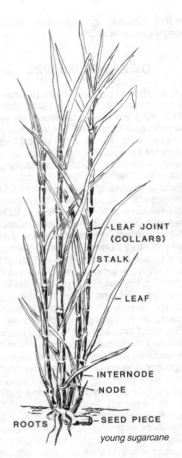

LEAF JOINT
(COLLARS)

STALK

LEAF

INTERNODE

NODE

ROOTS

SEED PIECE

LOUISE FOOTE

young sugarcane

barren land. The biggest hurdle to commercial sugarcane growing has always been water. One pound of sugar requires one ton of water, or about 250 gallons. A real breakthrough came when the growers reasoned that fresh water in the form of rain must seep through the lava and be stored underground. Fresh water will furthermore float atop heavier salt water and therefore be recoverable by a series of vertical wells and tunnels. By 1898, planters were tapping this underground supply of water, and sugar could be produced in earnest as an export crop.

The Plantation System

Sugarcane also produced the plantation system, which was in many ways socially comparable to that of the pre-Civil War South. It was the main cause of the cosmopolitan mixture of races found in Hawaii today. Workers were in great demand, and the sugar growers scoured the globe looking for likely sources. Importing plantation workers started with the liberalizing of the **The Masters and Servants Act,** which basically allowed the importation of conscripted workers. Even during its heyday, people with consciences felt that this system was no different from slavery. The first conscripts were Chinese, followed by Japanese, and then a myriad of people including other Polynesians, Germans, Norwegians, Spanish, Portuguese, Puerto Ricans, Filipinos, and even a few freed slaves from the southern U.S.

Today, with production down on Oahu and Maui (commercial production has ceased on Kauai and the Big Island), yearly sugar sales have fallen from those of a few years ago, when they were a hefty $500 million, to about $200 million currently. Nonetheless, the state's sugarcane-producing farms, and their attendant refineries, still employ a hefty amount of the islands' workforce. Newcomers, startled by what appear to be brush fires, are actually witnessing the burning of sugarcane prior to harvesting. Some sugar lands, such as those along Kaanapali on Maui, coexist side by side with a developed tourist area. Hawaii's sugarcane industry is still healthy and solvent, producing about five million tons of cane annually. If profits remain sweet, cane as a cash crop will flourish for many years to come.

last century it became the best-quality sugar available.

Irrigation and Profit Politics

In 1876 the **Reciprocity Treaty** freed Hawaiian sugar from import duty. Now a real fortune could be made. One entrepreneur, Claus Spreckels, a sugar-beet magnate from California, became the reigning Sugar King in Hawaii. His state-of-the-art refineries on Maui employed every modern convenience, including electric lighting; he was also instrumental in building marvelous irrigation ditches necessary to grow sugar on once-

PINEAPPLES

Next to cane, the majority of Hawaii's cultivated lands yield pineapples. The main farms are on Oahu, on the northwest tip of Maui, and on the lower slopes of Haleakala on Maui, with Lanai, once the world's largest pineapple plantation, now out of business. Pineapples were brought to the islands by Don Francisco Marin, an early Spanish agronomist, in the 1820s. Fresh pineapples were exported as early as 1850 to San Francisco, and a few cases of canned fruit appeared in 1876 at Hawaii's pavilion at the U.S. Centennial Exposition in Philadelphia. Old varieties of pineapples were pithier and pricklier than the modern variety. Today's large, luscious, golden fruits are the "smooth cayenne" variety from Jamaica, introduced by Captain Kidwell in 1886.

Dole

But Hawaiian pineapple, as we know it, is synonymous with one man, James Dole, who actually *made* the industry at the turn of this century. Jim Dole started growing pineapples on a 60-acre homestead in Wahiawa, Oahu. He felt that America was ready to add this fruit to its diet and that "canning" would be the conveyance. By 1903, he was shipping canned fruit from his Iwilei plant and by 1920 pineapples were a familiar item in most American homes. Hawaii was at that time the largest producer in the world. In 1922, Jim Dole bought the entire island of Lanai, whose permanent residents numbered only about 100, and started the world's largest pineapple plantation. By all accounts, Jim Dole was an exemplary human being, but he could never learn to "play ball" with the economic powers that ruled Hawaii, namely "The Big Five." They ruined him by 1932 and took control of his **Hawaiian Pineapple Company.** Today, the Hawaiian pineapple industry is beleaguered by competition from Asia, Central America, and the Philippines, resulting in the abandonment of many corporate farms. Hit especially hard was Molokai, where Del Monte shut down its operations in 1982, and Lanai, which stopped farming the prickly fruits in 1993. The other plantations are still reasonably strong, bringing in about $150 million dollars annually, but employment in the pineapple industry has dropped drastically in the last decade, and there are strong doubts these jobs will ever return.

OTHER AGRICULTURE

Every major food crop known can be grown in Hawaii because of its amazingly varied climates and rich soil. Farming ventures through the years have produced cotton, sisal, rice, and even rubber trees. Today, Hawaii is the world's largest producer of the Australian macadamia nut, considered by some the world's most useful and delicious nut. The islands' fresh exotic fruits are unsurpassed; juices and nectars made from papaya, passion fruit, and guava are becoming well known worldwide. Dazzling flowers such as protea, carnations, orchids, and anthuriums are also commercially grown. Hawaii has a very healthy livestock industry, headed by the Big Island's quarter-million-acre Parker Ranch, the largest singly owned cattle ranch in the United States. Poultry, dairy, and pork are also produced on many farms. The only coffee grown in the U.S. is grown in Hawaii on four islands. "Kona coffee" is of gourmet quality and well regarded for its aroma and rich flavor. Recently, chocolate manufacture was introduced to the Big Island, and production of this fine sweet is in full operation. *Pakalolo* (marijuana) is the most lucrative cash crop, but no official economic records exist. It's grown by enterprising gardeners on all the islands.

Hawaiian waters are alive with fish, but its commercial fleet is woefully small and obsolete. Fishing revenues amount to only $35 million per year, which is ludicrous in a land where fish is the obvious natural bounty. Native Hawaiians were masters of aquaculture, routinely building fishponds and living from their harvest. Where once there were hundreds of fishponds, only a handful are in use today. The main aquaculture is growing freshwater prawns; the state is considered the world leader, although there are fewer than 25 prawn farms operating at a yearly value of only $2.5 million. With all of these foodstuffs, unbelievable as it may sound, Hawaii must import much of its food. Hawaii can feed *itself*, but it cannot support the six million hungry tourists who come to sample its superb and diverse cuisine every year.

ECONOMIC POWER

The Big Five Corporations

Until statehood, Hawaii was ruled economically by a consortium of corporations known as the "Big Five": **C. Brewer and Co.,** sugar, ranching, and chemicals, founded in 1826; **Theo. H. Davies & Co.,** sugar, investments, insurance, and transportation, founded in 1845; **Amfac Inc.** (originally H. Hackfield Inc.—a German firm that changed its name and ownership during the anti-German sentiment of WW I to American Factors), sugar, insurance, and land development, founded in 1849; **Castle and Cooke Inc.,** (Dole) pineapple, food packing, and land development, founded in 1851; and **Alexander and Baldwin Inc.,** shipping, sugar, and pineapple, founded in 1895. This economic oligarchy ruled Hawaii with a steel grip in a velvet glove.

With members on every important corporate board, they controlled all major commerce, including banking, shipping, insurance, hotel development, agriculture, utilities, and wholesale and retail merchandising. Anyone trying to buck the system was ground to dust, finding it suddenly impossible to do business in the islands. The Big Five were made up of the islands' oldest and most well-established *haole* families; all included bloodlines from Hawaii's own nobility. They looked among themselves for suitable husbands and wives, so that breaking in from the outside even through marriage was hardly possible. The only time they were successfully challenged prior to statehood was when Sears, Roebuck and Co. opened a store on Oahu. Closing ranks, the Big Five decreed that their steamships would not carry Sears's freight. When Sears threatened to buy its own steamship line, the Big Five relented.

The land and industries of Hawaii are owned by old families and large corporations, and Hawaii is only so large.

~Jack London, circa 1916

Actually, statehood, and more to the point, tourism, broke their oligarchy. After 1960 too much money was at stake for Mainland-based corporations to ignore. Eventually the grip of the Big Five was loosened, but they are still enormously powerful and richer than ever. These days, however, they don't control everything; now their power is land. With only five other major landholders, they control 65% of the privately held land in Hawaii.

Land Ownership

Hawaii, landwise, is a small pie, and its slices are not at all well divided. Of the state's 6,423 square miles of land, the six main inhabited islands make up 98% of it. This figure does not include Niihau, which is privately owned by the Robinson family and inhabited by some of the last remaining pure-blooded Hawaiians; nor does it include uninhabited Kahoolawe. Of the 4,110,966 acres that make up the inhabited islands, 34% is owned by the state and 16% by the federal government; the remaining 50% is in private hands. While only 40 owners, with 5,000 or more acres each, own 75% of all private lands, the top seven control 46% of it. To be more specific, Castle and Cooke Inc. owns 99% of Lanai, while 40-60% of Maui, Oahu, Molokai, Kauai, and Hawaii is owned by fewer than a dozen private parties.

LAND OWNERSHIP

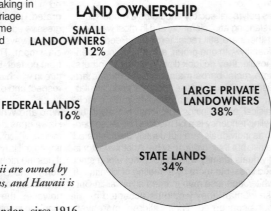

SMALL LANDOWNERS 12%

FEDERAL LANDS 16%

LARGE PRIVATE LANDOWNERS 38%

STATE LANDS 34%

The largest private landowner, with more than 336,000 acres or 8% of the total land area of the state, is the Kamehameha Schools/Bishop Estate, which recently lost a Supreme Court battle allowing the State of Hawaii to acquire privately owned land for "the public good." More than in any other state, Hawaiian landowners tend to lease land rather than sell it, and many private homes are on rented ground. This was the case with many homes rented from the Bishop Estate. The state acquired the land and resold it to long-term lease holders. These lands had previously earned a slow but steady profit for native Hawaiians. As land prices continue to rise, only the very rich land developers are able to purchase long-term leases, and the "people" of Hawaii continue to become even more land poor.

PEOPLE

Nowhere else on earth can you find such a kaleidoscopic mixture of people as in Hawaii. Every major race is accounted for, with more than 50 ethnic groups adding not only their genes, but their customs, traditions, and outlooks. The modern Hawaiian is the future's "everyman": a blending of all races. Interracial marriage has been long accepted in Hawaii, and people are so mixed it's already difficult to place them in a specific racial category. Besides the original Hawaiians, themselves a mixed race of Polynesians, people in the islands have multiple ancestor combinations. Hawaii is the most racially integrated state in the U.S., and although the newest, it epitomizes the time-honored American ideal of the melting-pot society.

THE ISSUE OF RACE

This polyracial society should be a model of understanding and tolerance, and in most ways it is, but there are still racial tensions. People tend to identify with one group, and though not openly hostile, they do look disparagingly on others. Some racial barbs maintain the Chinese are grasping, the Japanese too cold and calculating, the *haole* materialistic, Hawaiians lackadaisical, and Filipinos emotional. In Hawaii this labeling tendency is a bit modified because *people,* as individuals, are not usually discriminated against, but their *group* may be. Another factor is individuals identify with a group not along strict blood lines, but more by a "feeling of identity." If a white/Japanese man married a Hawaiian/Chinese woman, they would be accepted by all groups concerned. Their children, moreover, would be what they chose to be and, more to the point, what they "felt" like.

There are no ghettos as such, but there are traditional areas where people of similar racial strains live, and where outsiders are made to feel unwelcome. For example, the Waianae district of Oahu is considered a strong "Hawaiian" area where other people may meet with hostility, and the Kahala area of Oahu mostly attracts upwardly mobile whites. Some clubs make it difficult for nonwhites to become members; certain Japanese, Chinese, and Filipino organizations attract only members from these ethnic groups; and Hawaiian *ohana* would question any person seeking to join unless he or she had some Hawaiian blood. Generally, however, the vast majority of people get along with each other and mix with no discernible problems.

The real catalyst responsible for most racial acceptance is the Hawaiian public school system. Education has always been highly regarded in Hawaii; the classroom has long been integrated. Thanks to a standing tradition of progressive education, democracy and individualism have always been basic maxims taught in the classroom. The racial situation in Hawaii is far from perfect, but it does point the way to the future in which all people can live side by side with respect and dignity.

Who and Where

Hawaii has an approximate population of 1.2 million, which includes 100,000 permanently stationed military personnel and their dependents. It has the highest ratio of population to immigration in the U.S., and is the only state where whites are not the majority. White people are, however, the fastest growing group, due primarily to immigration from the U.S. West Coast. About 56% of Hawaiian residents were born in Hawaii; 26% were born on the Mainland U.S.;

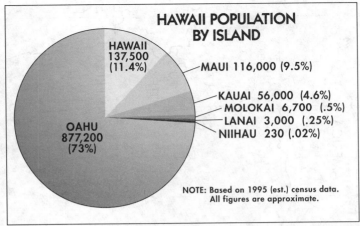

HAWAII POPULATION BY ISLAND

HAWAII 137,500 (11.4%)

MAUI 116,000 (9.5%)

KAUAI 56,000 (4.6%)

MOLOKAI 6,700 (.5%)

LANAI 3,000 (.25%)

NIIHAU 230 (.02%)

OAHU 877,200 (73%)

NOTE: Based on 1995 (est.) census data.
All figures are approximate.

and 18% are foreign-born. The average age is 29, and men slightly outnumber women. This is due to the large concentration of predominantly male military personnel, and to the substantial number of older bachelor plantation workers who came during the first part of this century and never found wives. The population has grown steadily in recent times, but has fluctuated wildly in the past. In 1876, it reached its lowest ebb, with only 55,000 permanent residents in the islands. This was the era of large sugar plantations; their constant demand for labor was the primary cause of importing various peoples from around the world, and led to Hawaii's racially integrated society. During WW II, Hawaii's population swelled from 400,000 just prior to the war to 900,000. These 500,000 were military personnel who left at war's end, but many returned to settle after getting a taste of island living.

Of the 1.2 million people in the islands today (1995 est.), 877,200 live on Oahu, with slightly less than half of these living in the Honolulu Metropolitan Area. The rest of the population is distributed as follows: 137,500 on Hawaii, with 47,000 living in Hilo; 116,000 on Maui, with the largest concentration, 53,000, in Wailuku/Kahului; 56,000 on Kauai, including 230 pure-blooded Hawaiians on Niihau; 6,700 on Molokai; and just under 3,000 on Lanai. The population density, statewide, is 186 people per square mile, approximately the same as California's. The population is not at all evenly distributed, with Oahu

claiming about 1,430 people per square mile, while the Big Island has barely 34 residents per square mile. Statewide, city dwellers outnumber those living in the country by nine to one. The average household size in Hawaii is 3.1 persons, down from 4.5 in 1940.

THE HAWAIIANS

The study of the native Hawaiians is ultimately a study in tragedy because it ends in their demise as a viable people. When Captain Cook first sighted Hawaii in 1778, an estimated 300,000 natives were living in harmony with their ecological surroundings; within 100 years a scant 50,000 demoralized and dejected Hawaiians existed almost as wards of the state. Today, although more than 210,000 people claim varying degrees of Hawaiian blood (some official surveys record 140,000), experts say fewer than 1,000 are pure Hawaiian, and this is stretching it. A resurgence of Hawaiian ethnic pride is sweeping the islands as many people trace their roots and attempt to absorb the finer aspects of their ancestral lifestyle. It's easy to see why they could be bitter over what they've lost, since they're now strangers in their own land, much like Native Americans. The overwhelming majority of "Hawaiians" are of mixed heritage, and the wisest take the best from all worlds. From the Hawaiian side comes simplicity, love of the land,

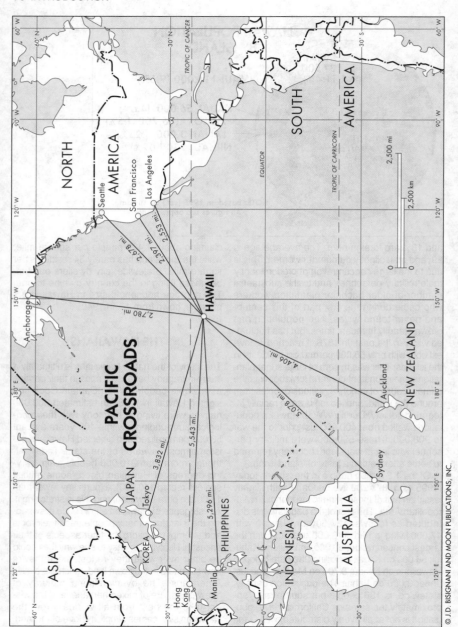

PACIFIC CROSSROADS

NORTH AMERICA

SOUTH AMERICA

ASIA

AUSTRALIA

INDONESIA

NEW ZEALAND

Seattle

San Francisco

Los Angeles

Anchorage

Tokyo

JAPAN

KOREA

Hong Kong

Manila

PHILIPPINES

Sydney

Auckland

HAWAII

TROPIC OF CANCER

EQUATOR

TROPIC OF CAPRICORN

2,678 mi.
2,553 mi.
2,397 mi.
2,780 mi.
3,832 mi.
5,296 mi.
5,543 mi.
5,078 mi.
4,406 mi.

2,500 mi

2,500 km

© J.D. BISIGNANI AND MOON PUBLICATIONS, INC.

Aloha *still shows.*

and acceptance of people. It is the Hawaiian legacy of *aloha* that remains immortal and adds the special elusive quality that *is* Hawaii.

Polynesian Roots

The Polynesians' original stock is muddled and remains an anthropological mystery, but it's believed they were nomads who migrated from both the Indian subcontinent and Southeast Asia through Indonesia, where they learned to sail and navigate on protected waterways. As they migrated, they honed their sailing skills until they could take on the Pacific, and as they moved, they absorbed people from other cultures and races until they had coalesced into what we now know as Polynesians.

Abraham Fornander, still considered a major authority on the subject, wrote in his 1885 *Account of the Polynesian Race* that he believed the Polynesians started as a white (Aryan) race that was heavily influenced by contact with the Cushite, Chaldeo-Arabian civilization. He estimated their arrival in Hawaii at A.D. 600 based on Hawaiian genealogical chants. Modern science seems to bear this date out, although it remains skeptical on his other surmises.

Thousands of years before Europeans even imagined the existence of a Pacific Ocean, Polynesians had populated the far-flung islands of the "Polynesian Triangle" stretching from New Zealand in the south, thousands of miles east to

Easter Island, and finally to Hawaii, the northern apex. Similar language, gods, foods, and crafts add credibility to this theory. Other more fanciful versions are all long on conjecture and short on evidence. For example, Atlantis, the most "found" lost continent in history, pops up again, with the Hawaiians the supposed remnants of this advanced civilization. The slim proof is the Hawaiian *kahuna,* so well versed in the curative arts they had to be Atlanteans. In fact, they not only made it to Hawaii, but also to the Philippines, where their secret powers have been passed on to the faith healers of today. That the Hawaiians are the "lost tribe of Israel" is another theory, but this too is wild conjecture.

The "Land Seekers"

The intrepid Polynesians who actually settled Hawaii are believed to have come from the Marquesas Islands, 1,000 miles southeast of Hawaii. The Marquesans were cannibals known for their tenacity and strength, attributes that would serve them well. They left their own islands because of war and famine; these migrations went on for centuries. Ships' logs mention Marquesan seagoing canoes setting sail in search of new land as late as the mid-19th century. The first navigator-explorers, advance scouting parties, were referred to as "land seekers." They were led northward by a few terse words sung in a chant that gave a general direction and promised some guiding stars (probably recounting the wild adventures of canoes blown far off course that somehow managed to return to the southern islands of Polynesia). The land seekers were familiar with the stars, currents, habits of land birds, and countless other subtle clues that are overlooked by "civilized" people.

After finding Hawaii, they were aided in their voyage home by favorable trade winds and familiar waters. They set sail again in canoes laden with hopeful families and all the foodstuffs necessary to colonize a new land, anticipating a one-way ride with no return. Over the centuries, the fierce Marquesans mellowed into Hawaiians, and formed a new benevolent culture based on the fertility god Lono. Then, in the 12th century, a ferocious army of Tahitians invaded Hawaii and supplanted not only the ruling chiefs but also the gentler gods with their war god Ku, who demanded human sacrifice. Abruptly, contact with Polynesia stopped. Some say the voyages, always fraught with danger, were no longer necessary. Hawaii was forgotten by the Polynesians, and the Hawaiians became the most rarefied race in the world. It was to these people that Captain Cook in 1778 brought the outside world. Finding Polynesians stretched so far and wide across the Pacific, he declared them "the most extensive nation upon earth."

The "Little People" of Hawaii

The Mu, Wa, Eepa, and Wao are all "little people" of Hawaii, but the most famous are the Menehune. As a group they resemble the trolls and leprechauns of Europe, but so many stories concern them that they appear to have actually existed in Hawaii at one time. Even in the late 18th century, an official census noted King Kaumualii of Kauai had 65 Menehune, who were said to live in Wainiha Valley. It's held that the Menehune drove out the Mu and the Wa. They also differed slightly in appearance. The Menehune are about two to three feet tall with hairy, well-muscled bodies. Their red faces have thick noses, protruding foreheads, and long eyebrows, and their hair is stringy. They love to frolic, especially by rolling down hills into the sea, and their favorite foods are shrimp and poi. They seldom speak, but their chatter sounds like the low growling of a dog. Nocturnal creatures, Menehune are frightened of owls and dogs.

The Mu are mute, while the Wa are noted for their loud blustering shouts. The Mu were thought to be black-skinned and to live deep in the forest on a diet of bananas. All had their specialties, but the Menehune were stonemasons par excellence. Many feats involving stonework are attributed to the Menehune. The most famous is the "Menehune Ditch" on Kauai. They finished their monumental tasks in one night, disappearing by daybreak. Even in the 1950s, masons building with stone near Diamond Head insisted their work was disturbed at night, and a *kahuna* had to be called in to appease the Menehune. After that, all went well.

In a more scientific vein, the Tahitian word for Menehune means "commoner." Many feel they were non-Polynesian aboriginals who somehow made it to the islands, and co-mingled with Hawaiians until their chiefs became alarmed tha their little race would vanish. (Mohikia and Analike are the respective names of a Menehune prince and princess who married Hawaiians and whose names have been preserved in legend.) The Menehune assembled en masse and supposedly floated away on an island descended from the heavens called "Kuaihelani." Some say they headed for the far-flung outer islands of Necker and Nihoa, where, oddly enough, stone gods found there are unlike any on the other Hawaiian islands. But there the trail grows cold. Today, island mothers warn their misbehaving toddlers that the Menehune will come and take them away, but in most stories they are actually pixielike and benign.

Fatal Flaws

When Captain Cook stepped ashore on Waimea, Kauai, on the morning of January 20, 1778, he discovered a population of 300,000 natives living in perfect harmony with their surroundings. Their agrarian society had flourished in the last thousand years. However, the ecological system of Hawaii has always been exceptionally fragile, its people included. White arrivals found a great people who were large, strong, and virile, but when it came to fighting even minor diseases they proved as delicate as hothouse flowers. To exacerbate the situation, the Hawaiians were totally uninhibited about sex between willing partners. Unfortunately, white sailors were laden with syphilis, gonorrhea, and all manner of other germs and common European diseases. Captain Cook tried desperately to keep sexually diseased members of his crew away from Hawaiian women, but it was impossible. The *hospitality* of Hawaiian women was legendary, and promises of "paradise" were actually used as a lure to get sailors for perilous cruises into the Pacific that could last for years. When Cook returned from the north in less than one year, there were already natives with telltale signs of venereal disease.

Hawaiian women brought venereal disease home, and it spread like wildfire. By the time the missionaries came in 1820 and halted the widespread fornication, the native population was only 140,000, less than half of what it had been only 40 years after initial contact. In 1804 alone, perhaps 100,000 died from *okuu* (either typhoid or cholera). In the next 50 years measles, mumps, influenza, and tuberculosis ravaged the people. In 1853 a smallpox epidemic ate further into the doomed and weakened Hawaiian race, and leprosy ranged far and wide in the land. In addition, during the whaling years, at least 25% of all able-bodied Hawaiian men sailed away, never to return. By 1880 King Kalakaua had only 48,000 Hawaiian subjects, a cataclysmic decrease of the original population. Wherever the king went, he would beseech his people, *"Hooulu lahui"* ("Increase the race"), but it was already too late. Nature itself had turned its back on these once-proud people. Many of their marriages were barren and in 1874 when only 1,400 children were born, a full 75% died in infancy. The final coup de grâce was intermarriage. With so many interracial marriages, the Hawaiians literally bred themselves out of existence.

Painful Adjustments

In the last century, the old paternalism inherent in the Hawaiian caste system was carried on by the ruling *haole* families. The remaining Hawaiians looked to the ruling class of whites as they had to their own *ali'i,* and for many years this attitude discouraged self help. Many Hawaiians fervently accepted the Christianity that had supplanted their own religion because it was a haven against a rapidly changing world in which they felt more and more alienated. Though Hawaiians were not favored as good plantation workers and were branded as lazy, they were actually hard and dedicated workers. Like all people attuned to their environment, they chose to work in the cool of the mornings and late afternoons, and could make no sense of laboring in the intense heat of the day. As fishermen they were unparalleled, and also made excellent cowboys on the ranches, preferring the open ranges to the constricting plantation fields.

Hawaiians readily engaged in politics and were impressed with all the hoopla and fanfare. They attended rallies, performed hula and songs, and in most instances sided with the whites against the Asians. They were known to accept money for their votes and almost considered it the obligation of the leader, whom they regarded as a sort of chief, to grease their palms. Educated Hawaiians tended to become lawyers, judges, policeman, and teachers, and there is still a disproportionate number of Hawaiians, population-wise, in these fields. Hawaiians were somewhat racist toward the Japanese and Chi-

nese. However, they would readily intermarry because, true to *aloha,* they accepted individual "people" even though they might be prejudiced against their group. In 1910, although the native population was greatly reduced, there are still twice as many full-blooded Hawaiians as mixed bloods. By 1940 mixed-blood Hawaiians were the fastest-growing group, and full bloods the fastest declining.

Hawaiians Today

Many of the Hawaiians who moved to the cities became more and more disenfranchised. Their folk society stressed openness and a giving nature, but downplayed the individual and the ownership of private property. These cultural traits made them easy targets for users and schemers until they finally became either apathetic or angry. About 140,000 people living in Hawaii have *some* Hawaiian blood. Most surveys reveal that although they number only 13% of the population, they account for almost 50% of the financially destitute families, arrests, and illegitimate births. Niihau, a privately owned island, is home to about 230 pure-blooded Hawaiians, the largest concentration per capita in the islands. The Robinson family, which owns the island, restricts visitors to invited guests only. The second largest concentration of people with Hawaiian blood is on Molokai, where 3,300 Hawaiians, living mostly on Hawaiian Homes lands, make up 48% of the population. The majority of part- or full-blooded Hawaiians, 92,000 or so, live on Oahu, where

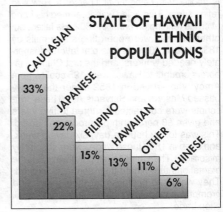

STATE OF HAWAII ETHNIC POPULATIONS

CAUCASIAN 33%
JAPANESE 22%
FILIPINO 15%
HAWAIIAN 13%
OTHER 11%
CHINESE 6%

they are particularly strong in the hotel and entertainment fields. People of Hawaiian extraction are a delight to meet, and visitors so lucky as to be befriended by one long regard this friendship as the highlight of their travels. The Hawaiians have always given their *aloha* freely and it is we who must accept it as a precious gift.

THE CHINESE

Next to Yankees from New England, the Chinese are the oldest migrant group in Hawaii, and their influence has far outshone their meager numbers. They have long been the backbone of the small, privately owned retail trade. They brought to Hawaii, along with their individuality, Confucianism, Taoism, and Buddhism, although many have long since become Christians. The Chinese population of about 68,000 makes up only six percent of the state's total, and the vast majority reside on Oahu. Their key to success has been indefatigable hard work, the shrewdness to seize a good opportunity, and above all, an almost fanatical desire to educate their children. As an ethnic group they account for the least amount of crime, the highest per capita income, and a disproportionate number of professionals. They are some of Hawaii's most prominent citizens.

The First Chinese

No one knows his name, but Chinese immigrant is credited with being the first person in Hawaii to refine sugar. This Asian wanderer tried his hand at crude refining on Lanai in 1802. He failed, but other Chinese were operating sugar mills by 1830. Within 20 years, the plantations desperately needed workers, and the first Chinese laborers brought to Hawaii were 195 coolies from Amoy who arrived in 1852 under the newly passed Masters and Servants Act. These conscripts were contracted for three to five years and given $3 per month plus room and board. This was for 12 hours a day, six days a week, and even in 1852 these wages were absolutely miserable. The Chinese almost always left the plantations the minute their contracts expired. They went into business for themselves and promptly monopolized the restaurant and small shop trade.

Bad Feelings

When they left the plantations, the Chinese were universally resented, due to prejudice, xenophobia, and their success in business. The first Chinese peddler in Honolulu was mentioned as early as 1823. The Chinese Consul in Hawaii was very conservative and sided with the plantation owners, giving his own people no support. When leprosy became epidemic in the islands, it was blamed on the Chinese. The Hawaiians called it *pake* disease, their derisive name for Chinese men, which, oddly enough, was an endearment in China meaning "uncle." Although leprosy cannot be blamed solely on the Chinese, a boatload of Chinese immigrants did bring smallpox in 1880. At the turn of the century, a smallpox epidemic broke out again in Honolulu's Chinatown (where half the residents were really Japanese) and was promptly burnt to the ground by the authorities.

Amidst all this negativity, some intrepid souls prospered. The greatest phenomenon was Chun Afong who, with little more than determination, became a millionaire by 1857, raised 16 children, and almost single-handedly created the Chinese bourgeoisie in Hawaii. The Chinese were also responsible for making rice Hawaii's second most important crop 1867-1872. It was another Chinese person, Ah In, who brought the first water buffalo used to cultivate rice during this period.

The Chinese Exclusion Act

Although reforms on the plantations were forthcoming, the Chinese preferred the retail trade. In 1880 half of all plantation workers were Chinese, by 1900 10% were, and by 1959, only 300 Chinese worked on plantations. When the "powers that were" decided Hawaii needed compliant laborers, not competitive businesspeople, the monarchy passed the Chinese Exclusion Act in 1886, forbidding any more Chinese contract laborers from entering Hawaii. Still, 15,000 more Chinese were contracted in the next few years. In 1900 there were about 25,000 Chinese in Hawaii, but because of the Exclusion Act and other prejudices, many sold out and moved away. By 1910 their numbers were reduced to 21,000.

The Chinese Niche

Although many people in Hawaii considered all Chinese ethnically the same, they were actually quite different. The majority came from Kwangtung Province in southern China. They were two distinct ethnic groups: the Punti made up 75% of the immigrants, and the Hakka made up the remainder. The Hakka had invaded Punti lands over a thousand years ago and lived in the hills overlooking Punti villages. In China, they remained separate from each other, never mixing; in Hawaii, they mixed out of necessity. Few Chinese women came at first, and the ones who followed were at a premium and gladly accepted as wives, regardless of ethnic background. The Chinese were also one of the first groups to willingly intermarry with the Hawaiians, from whom they gained a reputation for being exceptionally caring spouses.

By the 1930s, there was still resentment, the Chinese were firmly entrenched in the merchant class. Their thriftiness, hard work, and family solidarity had paid off. The Chinese accepted the social order and kept a low profile. During Hawaii's turbulent labor movements of the 1930s and '40s, the Chinese community produced not one labor leader, radical intellectual, or left-wing politician. When Hawaii became a state, one of the two first senators was Hiram Fong, a racially mixed Chinese. Since statehood, the Chinese community has carried on business as usual as they continue to rise even further both economically and socially.

THE JAPANESE

Most scholars believe that (inevitably) a few Japanese castaways floated to Hawaii long before Captain Cook arrived, and might have introduced iron, since the islanders seemed to be familiar with it before the white explorers arrived. Other scholars refute this claim and say Portuguese or Spanish ships lost in the Pacific introduced iron. Nevertheless, shipwrecked Japanese did make it to the islands. The most famous episode involved Jirokichi who, lost at sea for 10 months, was rescued by Captain Cathcart of Nantucket in 1839. Cathcart brought him to Hawaii, where Jirokichi boarded with prominent families. This adventure-filled episode is re-

counted in the Japanese classic *Ban Tan* (Stories of the Outside World) written by the scribe Yuten-sei. The first official arrivals from Japan were ambassadors sent by the Japanese shogun to negotiate with the U.S. in Washington. They stopped en route at Honolulu in March 1860, only seven years after Commodore Perry and his famous "Black Ships" had roused Japan from its self-imposed 200-year slumber.

A small group of Japanese plantation workers arrived in 1868, but mass migration was blocked for almost 20 years. King Kalakaua, among others, proposed that Japanese be brought in as contract laborers in 1881; it was thought that Japanese subsistence farmers held promise as an inexhaustible supply of hardworking, uncomplaining, inexpensive, resolute workers. In 1886, because of famine, the Japanese government allowed farmers mainly from southern Honshu, Kyushu, and Okinawa to emigrate. Among these were members of Japan's little-talked-about untouchable caste, called *eta* or *burakumin* in Japan and *chorinbo* in Hawaii. They gratefully seized this opportunity to better their lot, an impossibility in their homeland.

The Japanese Arrive

The first Japanese migrants were almost all men. Under Robert Irwin, the American agent for recruiting the Japanese, almost 27,000 Japanese came, for which he received a fee of $5 per head. The contract workers received $9 plus room and board, and an additional $6 for a working wife. This pay was for a 26-workday month at 10 hours per day in the fields or 12 hours in a factory. Between 1897 and 1908, migration was steady, with about 70% men and 30% women. Afterwards, immigration was nearly halted because of a "gentlemen's agreement," a euphemism for racism against the "yellow peril." By 1900, more than 60,000 Japanese had arrived in the islands, constituting the largest ethnic group.

Until 1907 most Japanese longed to return home and faithfully sent back part of their pay to help support their families. Eventually, a full 50% did return to Japan, but the others began to consider Hawaii their home and resolved to settle . . . if they could get wives! Between 1908 and 1924, "picture brides" arrived whose marriages had been arranged *(omiai)* by family members back home. These women clung to the old ways and reinforced the Japanese ethnic identity. Excellent plantation workers, they set about making their rude camps into model villages. They felt an obligation that extended from individual to family, village, and their new country. As peasants, they were imbued with a feeling of a natural social order that they readily accepted . . . if treated fairly.

Changing Attitudes

Unfortunately some plantation *luna* were brutal, and Japanese laborers were mistreated, exploited, and made to live in indecent conditions on the plantations. In unusual protest, they formed their first trade union under Yasutaro Soga in 1908 and gained better treatment and higher wages. In 1919 an unsuccessful statewide plantation strike headed by the Federation of Japanese Labor lasted seven bitter months, earning the lasting mistrust of the establishment. By the 1930s, the Japanese, frustrated at being passed over for advancement because they were nonwhite, began to move from the plantations, opening retail stores and small businesses. By WW II they owned 50% of retail stores and accounted for 56% of household domestics. Many became small farmers, especially in Kona, where they began to grow coffee. They also accounted for Hawaii's fledgling fishing fleet and would brave the deep waters in their small, seaworthy sampans. Like the Chinese, they were committed to bettering themselves and placed education above all else. Unlike the Chinese, they did not marry outside their ethnic group and remained, relatively, racially intact.

Americans of Japanese Ancestry (AJAs)

Parents of most Japanese children born in Hawaii before WW II were *issei* (first generation), who considered themselves apart from other Americans and clung to the notion of "we Japanese." They held traditional beliefs of unwavering family loyalty, and to propagate their values and customs they supported Japanese-language schools, which 80% of their children attended before the war. This group, who were never "disloyal," were, however, proud of being Japanese. Some diehards even refused to believe Japan lost WW II and were shamed by

their former homeland's unconditional surrender.

Their children, the *nissei* or second generation, were a different breed altogether. In one generation they had become Americans, and they put into practice the high Japanese virtues of obligation, duty, and loyalty to the homeland; that homeland was now unquestionably America. After Pearl Harbor was bombed, many people were terrified that the Hawaiian Japanese would be disloyal to America and would serve as spies and even as advance combatants for imperial Japan. The FBI kept close tabs on the Japanese community, and the menace of the "enemy within" prompted the decision to place Hawaii under martial law for the duration of the war. Because of their sheer numbers it was impossible to place the Hawaiian Japanese into concentration camps as was done in California, but prejudice and suspicion toward them, especially from Mainland military personnel, was fierce. It has since been noted that not a single charge of espionage or sabotage was ever reported against the Japanese community in Hawaii during the war.

AJAs As GIs

Although Japanese had formed a battalion during WW I, they were insulted by being considered unacceptable as American soldiers in WW II. Those already in the armed services were relieved of any duty involving weapons. People who knew better supported the AJAs. One was Jack Burns, a Honolulu policeman, who stated unequivocally that the AJAs were trustworthy. They never forgot his support, and thanks to a huge Japanese vote he was elected governor. Some Japanese-Americans volunteered to serve in labor battalions, and because of their flawless work and loyalty, it was decided to put out a call for a few hundred volunteers to form a combat unit. More than 10,000 signed up!

AJAs formed two distinguished units in WW II: the 100th Infantry Battalion and, later, the 442nd Regimental Combat Team. They landed in Italy at Salerno and even fought from Guadalcanal to Okinawa. The 442nd distinguished themselves as *the* most decorated unit in American military history. They made excellent newspaper copy; their exploits hit front pages around the nation. They were immortalized as the rescuers of a

Hawaii's former governor, George Ariyoshi, elected in 1974, was the country's first Japanese-American to reach such high office. Most Japanese, even as they climb the economic ladder, tend to remain Democrats.

Today, one out of every two political offices in Hawaii is held by a Japanese-American. In one of those weird quirks of fate, it is now the Hawaiian Japanese who are accused by other ethnic groups of engaging in unfair political practices—nepotism and discrimination. It's often heard that "if you're not Japanese, forget about getting a government job." Many of these accusations against AJAs are undoubtedly motivated by jealousy, but their record of social fairness is not without blemish, and true to their custom of family loyalty, they do stick together. Heavily into the "professions," they're committed to climbing the social ladder. The AJAs of Hawaii, now indistinguishable from "the establishment," enjoy a higher standard of living than most and are motivated to get the best education possible for their children. They are the least likely of any ethnic group to marry outside of their group—especially the men. There are now 250,000 people of Japanese ancestry in Hawaii, nearly one-quarter of the state's population.

The Japanese-American GIs returned as "our boys."

Texas company pinned down during the Battle of the Bulge. These Texans became known as "The Lost Battalion" and have periodic reunions with the AJA GIs who risked and lost so much to bring them to safety.

The AJAs Return

The AJAs returned home to a grateful country. In Hawaii, at first, they were accused of being cocky. Actually, they were refusing to revert to the pre-war status of second-class citizens and began to assert their rights as citizens who had defended their country. Many took advantage of the GI Bill and received college educations. The "Big Five" Corporations for the first time accepted former AJA officers as executives, and the old order began to wobble. Many Japanese became involved in Hawaiian politics, and the first elected member to Congress was Daniel Inouye, who had lost an arm fighting in the war.

CAUCASIANS

White people have a distinction separating them from all other ethnic groups in Hawaii: they are all lumped together as one. You can be anything from a Protestant Norwegian dock worker to a Greek Orthodox shipping tycoon, but if your skin is white, in Hawaii you're a *haole*. What's more, you could have arrived at Waikiki from Missoula, Montana, in the last 24 hours, or your *kama'aina* family can go back five generations, but again, if you're white, you're a *haole*.

The word *haole* has a floating connotation that depends upon the spirit in which it's used. It can mean anything from a derisive "honky" or "cracker" to nothing more than "white person." The exact Hawaiian meaning is clouded, but some say it meant "a man of no background," because white people couldn't chant a genealogical *kanaenae* telling the Hawaiians who they were. The word eventually evolved to mean "foreign white man" and today simply "white person."

White History

Next to Hawaiians themselves, white people have the oldest stake in Hawaii. They've been there as settlers in earnest since the missionaries of the 1820s, and were established long before any other migrant group. From last century until statehood, old *haole* families owned and controlled almost everything, and although they were generally benevolent, philanthropic, and paternalistic, they were also racist. They felt (not without certain justification) they had "made" Hawaii, and, consequently, that they had the right to rule. These established *kama'aina* families, many of whom made up the boards of the "Big Five" or owned huge plantations, formed an inner social circle closed to the outside except through marriage.

Their paternalism, which they accepted with grave responsibility, at first only extended to the Hawaiians, who saw them as replacing their own *ali'i*. Asians were primarily considered instruments of production. These supremacist attitudes tended to drag on in Hawaii until quite recent times. Today, they're responsible for the sometimes sour relations between white and nonwhite people in the islands. Since the *haole* had the power over other ethnic groups for so long, they have offended each group at one time or another. Today, all individual white people are resented to a certain degree because of these past acts, even though they personally were in no way involved.

White Plantation Workers

In the 1880s, the white landowners looked around and felt surrounded and outnumbered by Asians. Many figured these people would one day be a political force to be reckoned with, so they tried to import white people for plantation work. Some of the imported workers included: 600 Scandinavians in 1881; 1,400 Germans 1881-85; 400 Poles 1897-98; and 2,400 Russians 1909-12. None worked out. Europeans were accustomed to much higher wages and better living conditions than provided on the plantations. Although they were workers, not considered the equals of the ruling elite, they were expected to act like a special class and were treated preferentially, receiving higher wages for the same jobs performed by Asians. Even so, many proved troublesome to the landowners, unwilling to work

under the prevailing conditions; they were especially resentful of Hawaiian *luna*. Most moved quickly to the Mainland, and the Poles and Russians even staged strikes after only months on the job. A contingency of Scots, who first came as mule skinners and gained a reputation for hard work and frugality, became successful plantation managers and supervisors. There were so many on the Hamakua Coast of the Big Island that it was dubbed the "Scotch Coast." The Germans and Scandinavians were well received and climbed the social ladder rapidly, becoming professionals and skilled workers.

The Depression years, not as economically disastrous in Hawaii as in the continental U.S., brought many Mainland whites seeking opportunity, mostly from the South and the West. These new people tended to be even more racist toward brown-skinned people and Asians than the *kama'aina haole*. They made matters worse and competed intensely for jobs. The racial tension generated during this period came to a head in 1932 with the infamous "Massie Rape Case."

The Massie Rape Case

Thomas Massie, a naval officer, and his young wife Thalia attended a party at the Officers Club. After drinking and dancing all evening, they got into a row and Thalia rushed out in a huff. A few hours later, Thalia was at home, confused and hysterical, claiming to have been raped by some local men. On the most circumstantial evidence, Joseph Kahahawai and four friends of mixed ethnic background were accused. In a highly controversial trial rife with racial tensions, the verdict ended in a hung jury.

While a new trial was being set, Kahahawai and his friends were out on bail. Seeking revenge, Thomas Massie and Grace Fortescue, Thalia's mother, kidnapped Joseph Kahahawai with a plan of extracting a confession from him. They were aided by two enlisted men assigned to guard Thalia. While questioning Kahahawai, they killed him and attempted to dump his body in the sea but were apprehended. Another controversial trial—this time for Mrs. Fortescue, Massie, and the accomplices—followed. Clarence Darrow, the famous lawyer, sailed to Hawaii to defend them. For killing Kahahawai, these people served *one hour* of imprisonment in the judge's private chambers. The other four, acquitted with Joseph

Kahahawai, maintain innocence of the rape to this day. Later, the Massies divorced, and Thalia went on to become a depressed alcoholic who took her own life.

The Portuguese

The last time anyone looked, Portugal was still attached to the European continent, but for some anomalous reason the Portuguese weren't considered *haole* in Hawaii for the longest time. This was so because they weren't part of the ruling elite, but merely workers, showing that at one time the word *haole* implied social standing and not just skin color. About 12,000 arrived 1878-87 and another 6,000 came 1906-13. They were accompanied during the latter period by 8,000 Spanish, who were considered one and the same. Most of the Portuguese were illiterate peasants from Madeira and the Azores, while the Spanish hailed from Andalusia. The majority of Spanish and some Portuguese tended to leave for California as soon as they made passage money. Those who remained were well received because they were white, but not *haole,* making a perfect "buffer" ethnic group. Unlike other Europeans, they would take any job, worked hard, and accepted authority. Committed to staying in Hawaii, they rose to be skilled workers and the *luna* class on the plantations. However, the Portuguese did not invest as much in education and became very racist toward the upwardly mobile Asians, regarding them as a threat to their job security.

By 1920, the 27,000 Portuguese made up 11% of the population. After that they tended to blend with the other ethnic groups and weren't counted separately. Portuguese men tended to marry within their ethnic group, but a good portion of Portuguese women married other white men and became closer to the *haole* group, while another large portion chose Hawaiian mates and grew further away.

Although they didn't originate pidgin English (see **Language**), the unique melodious quality of their native tongue did give pidgin a certain lilt it has today. Also, the ukulele (jumping flea) was closely patterned after the *cavaquinho,* a Portuguese stringed folk instrument.

The White Population

Today Caucasians make up the largest racial group in the islands at 33% of the population, or about 370,000 individuals. They are spread evenly throughout Kauai, Oahu, Maui, and the Big Island, with much smaller percentages on Molokai and Lanai. Numerically, the vast majority (265,000) live on Oahu, in the more fashionable central valley and southeastern sections. Heavy white concentrations are also found on the Kihei and Kaanapali coasts of Maui and the north Kona coast of Hawaii. The white population is also the fastest growing in the islands because most people resettling in Hawaii are white Americans predominantly from the West Coast.

FILIPINOS AND OTHERS

The Filipinos who came to Hawaii brought high hopes of making personal fortunes and returning home as rich heroes; for most it was a dream that never came true. Filipinos were American nationals since the Spanish-American War of 1898, and as such weren't subject to immigration laws that curtailed the importation of other Asian workers at the turn of the century. The first to arrive were 15 families in 1906, but a large number came in 1924 as strikebreakers. The majority were illiterate Ilocano peasants from the northern Philippines with about 10% Visayans from the central cities. The Visayans were not as hardworking or thrifty, but were much more sophisticated. From the first, Filipinos were looked down upon by all the other immigrant groups, and were considered particularly uncouth by the Japanese. The value they placed on education was the least of any group, and even by 1930 only half could speak rudimentary English, while the majority remained illiterate. They were billeted in the worst housing, performed the most menial jobs, and were the last hired and first fired.

One big difference between Filipinos and other groups was that the men brought no Filipino women to marry, so they clung to the idea of returning home. In 1930 there were 30,000 men and only 360 women. This hopeless situation led to a great deal of prostitution and homosexuality. Many of these terribly lonely bachelors would feast and drink on weekends and engage in their gruesome but exciting pastime of cockfighting on Sunday. When some did manage to find wives, their mates were inevitably part

Hawaiian. Today, there are still plenty of old Filipino bachelors who never managed to get home, and the Sunday cockfight remains a way of life.

Filipinos constitute 15% of Hawaii's population, with nearly three-quarters living on Oahu. The largest concentration, however, is on Lanai, where they make up 60% of that island's population. Some of these men are new arrivals with the same dream held by their countrymen for more than 70 years. Many visitors to Hawaii mistake Filipinos for Hawaiians because of their dark skin, and this a minor irritant to both groups. Some streetwise Filipinos even claim to be Hawaiians, because being Hawaiian is "in," and goes over well with tourists, especially young women. For the most part, these people are hardworking, dependable laborers who do tough work for little recognition. They remain low on the social totem pole and have not yet organized politically to stand up for their rights.

Other Groups

About 11% of Hawaii's population is made up of a conglomerate of other ethnic groups. Of these, the largest and fastest growing is Korean, with 25,000 people. About 8,000 Koreans came to Hawaii 1903-1905, when their government halted emigration. During the same period about 6,000 Puerto Ricans arrived, but they have become so assimilated that only 4,000 people in Hawaii today consider themselves Puerto Rican. There were also two attempts made last century to import other Polynesians to strengthen the dying Hawaiian race, but they were failures. In 1869 only 126 central Polynesian natives could be lured to Hawaii, and 1878-1885, 2,500 Gilbert Islanders arrived. Both groups became immediately disenchanted with Hawaii. They pined for their own islands and departed for home as soon as possible.

Today, however, 15,000 Samoans have settled in Hawaii, and with more on the way they are the fastest growing minority. For inexplicable reasons, Samoans and native Hawaiians get along extremely poorly and have the worst racial tensions and animosity of any groups. The Samoans ostensibly should represent the archetypal Polynesians that the Hawaiians are seeking, but it doesn't work that way. Samoans are criticized by Hawaiians for their hot tempers, lingering feuds, and petty jealousies. They're clannish and are often the butt of "dumb" jokes. This racism seems especially ridiculous, but that's the way it is.

Just to add a bit more exotic spice to the stew, there are about 27,000 blacks, 5,000 Native Americans, and 6,000 Vietnamese refugees living on the islands.

LANGUAGE

Hawaii is part of America and people speak English there, but that's not the whole story. If you turn on the TV to catch the evening news, you'll hear "Walter Cronkite" English, unless of course you happen to tune in to a Japanese-language broadcast designed for tourists from that country. You can easily pick up a Chinese-language newspaper or groove to the music on a Filipino radio station, but let's not confuse the issue. All your needs and requests at airports, car-rental agencies, restaurants, hotels, or wherever you happen to travel will be completely understood, as well as answered, in English. However, when you happen to overhear islanders speaking, what they're saying will sound somewhat familiar but you won't be able to pick up all the words, and the beat and melody of the language will be noticeably different.

Hawaii—like New England, the Deep South, and the Midwest—has its own unmistakable linguistic regionalism. All the ethnic peoples who make up Hawaii have enriched the language with words, expressions, and subtle shades of meaning that are commonly used and understood throughout the islands. The greatest influence on English has come from the Hawaiian language itself, and words such as "aloha," "hula," and "muumuu" are familiarly used and understood by most Americans.

Other migrant peoples, especially the Chinese, Japanese, and Portuguese, influenced the local dialect to such an extent that the simplified plantation lingo they spoke has become known as "pidgin." A fun and enriching part of the "island experience" is picking up a few words of Hawaiian and pidgin. English is the official language of the state, business, education, and perhaps even the mind; but pidgin is the language of the people, the emotions, and life; while Hawaiian remains the language of the heart and the soul.

Note: Many Hawaiian words are commonly used in English, appear in English dictionaries, and therefore would ordinarily be subject to the rules of English grammar. The Hawaiian language, however, does not pluralize nouns by adding an "s"; the singular and plural are differ-entiated in context. For purposes of this book, and to highlight the Hawaiian culture, the Hawaiian style of pluralization will be followed for common Hawaiian words. The following are some examples of plural Hawaiian nouns treated this way in this book: *haole* (not *haoles*), hula, *kahuna*, lei, luau, and *nene*.

PIDGIN

The dictionary definition of pidgin is: a simplified language with a rudimentary grammar used as a means of communication between people speaking different languages. Hawaiian pidgin is a little more complicated than that. It had its roots during the plantation days of last century when white owners and *luna* (foremen) had to communicate with recently arrived Chinese, Japanese, and Portuguese laborers. It was designed as a simple language of the here and now, and was primarily concerned with the necessary functions of working, eating, and sleeping. It has an economical noun-verb-object structure (although not necessarily in that order).

Hawaiian words make up most of pidgin's non-English vocabulary. It includes a good smattering of Chinese, Japanese, and Samoan; the distinctive rising inflection is provided by the melodious Mediterranean lilt of the Portuguese. Pidgin is not a stagnant language. It's kept alive by hip new words introduced by people who are "so radical," or especially by slang words introduced by teenagers. It's a colorful English, like that spoken by American blacks, and it's as regionally unique as the speech of Cajuns from Louisiana's bayous. *Maka'ainana* of all socioethnic backgrounds can at least understand pidgin. Most islanders are proud of it, while some consider it low-class jargon. The Hawaiian House of Representatives has given pidgin an official sanction, and most people feel that it adds a real local style and should be preserved.

Pidgin Lives

Pidgin is first learned at school where all students, regardless of background, are exposed to it. The pidgin spoken by young people today is "fo' real" different from that of their parents. It's no longer only plantation talk but has moved to the streets and picked up some sophistication. At one time there was an academic movement to exterminate it, but that idea died away with the same thinking that insisted on making left-handed people write with their right hand. It is strange, however, that pidgin has become the unofficial language of Hawaii's grassroots movement, when it actually began as a white owners' language that was used to supplant Hawaiian and all other languages brought to the islands.

Although hip young *haole* use pidgin all the time, it has gained the connotation of being the language of the nonwhite locals, and is part of the "us against them" way of thinking. All local people, *haole* or not, consider pidgin their own island language, and don't really like it when it's used by *malihini* (newcomers). If you're in the islands long enough, you don't have to bother learning pidgin; it'll learn you. There's a book sold all over the islands called *Pidgin to da Max,* written by (you guessed it) a *haole* from Nebraska named Doug Simonson. You might not be able to understand what's being said by locals speaking pidgin (that's usually the idea), but you should be able to *feel* what's meant.

HAWAIIAN

The Hawaiian language sways like a palm tree in a gentle wind. Its words are as melodious as a love song. Linguists say that you can learn a lot about people through their language; when you hear Hawaiian you think of gentleness and love, and it's hard to imagine the ferocious side so evident in Hawaii's past. With its many Polynesian root words easily traced to Indonesian and Malay, Hawaiian is obviously from this same stock. The Hawaiian spoken today is very different from old Hawaiian. Its greatest metamorphosis occurred when the missionaries began to write it down in the 1820s. There is a movement to reestablish the Hawaiian language, and courses in it are offered at the University of Hawaii. Many scholars have put forth translations of Hawaiian, but there are endless, volatile disagreements in the academic sector about the real meanings of Hawaiian words. Hawaiian is no longer spoken as a language except on Niihau, and the closest tourists will come to it are in place-names, street names, and words that have become part of common usage, such as *aloha* and *mahalo.* A few old Hawaiians still speak it at home and there are sermons in Hawaiian at some local churches. Kawaiahao Church in downtown Honolulu is the most famous of these. (See the **Glossary** for a list of commonly used Hawaiian words.)

Wiki Wiki Hawaiian

Thanks to the missionaries, the Hawaiian language is rendered phonetically using only 12 letters. They are the five vowels, a-e-i-o-u, sounded as they are in Italian; and seven consonants, h-k-l-m-n-p-w, sounded exactly as they are in English. Sometimes "w" is pronounced as "v," but this only occurs in the middle of a word and always follows a vowel. A consonant is always followed by a vowel, forming two-letter syllables, but vowels are often found in pairs or even triplets. A slight oddity about Hawaiian is the glottal stop. This is an abrupt break in sound in the middle of a word, such as "oh-oh" in English and is denoted in this book by an apostrophe ('). A good example is *ali'i;* or even better, the Oahu town of Ha'iku, which actually means "abrupt break."

Pronunciation Key

For those unfamiliar with the sounds of Italian or other Romance languages, the vowels are sounded as follows:

A – in stressed syllables, pronounced as in "**ah**" (that feels good!). For example, Haleakala is pronounced "h**ah** le **ah** kah l**ah**." Unstressed syllables, pronounced as in "**a**gain" or "**a**bove." For example, Kamehameha "k**a** may h**a** may h**a.**

E – short "e" as in "p**e**n" or "d**e**nt" *(hal**e**.)* Long "e" sounded as "ay" as in "sw**ay**" or "d**ay**." For example, the Hawaiian goose *(nene)* is a "n**ay** n**ay**," not a "knee knee."

I – pronounced "ee" as in "s**ee**" or "w**e**" *(pali).*

O – pronounced as in "n**o**" or "**oh**" (k**o**a, or *on**o**).*

U—pronounced "oo" as in "d**o**" or "st**ew**" *(kap**u**,* or P**u**na).

Diphthongs

There are eight vowel pairs known as "diphthongs" (ae-ai-ao-au-ei-eu-oi-ou). These are the sounds made by gliding from one vowel to another within a syllable. The stress is placed on the first vowel. In English, examples would be s**oi**l and **eu**phoria. Common examples in Hawaiian are lei (lay) and *heiau* (hay-ow).

Stress

The best way to learn which syllables are stressed in Hawaiian is by listening closely. It becomes obvious after a while. Also, some vowel sounds are held longer than others; these can occur at the beginning of a word, such as the first "a" in *aina,* or in the middle of a word, like the first "a" in *lanai.* Again, it's a matter of tuning your ear and paying attention. No one is going to give you a hard time if you mispronounce a word. It's good, however, to pay close attention to the pronunciation of street and place-names, because many Hawaiian words sound alike and a misplaced vowel here or there could be the difference between getting where you want to go and getting lost.

RELIGION

The Lord saw fit to keep His island paradise secret from humans for a few million years, but once we finally arrived we were awfully thankful. Hawaii sometimes seems like a floating tabernacle; everywhere you look there's a church, temple, shrine, or *heiau.* The islands are either a very holy place, or there's a powerful lot of sinning going on that would require so many houses of prayer. Actually, it's just America's "right to worship" concept fully employed in microcosm. All the peoples who came to Hawaii brought their own forms of devotion. The Polynesian Hawaiians praised the primordial creators, Wakea and Papa, from whom their pantheon of animistically inspired gods sprang. Obviously, to a modern world these old gods would never do. There were simply too many, and belief in them was looked down upon as mere superstition, the folly of semicivilized pagans. So, the famous missionaries of the 1820s brought Congregational Christianity and the "true path to heaven."

Inconveniently, the Catholics, Mormons, Reformed Mormons, Adventists, Episcopalians, Unitarians, Christian Scientists, Lutherans, Baptists, Jehovah's Witnesses, Salvation Army, and every other major and minor denomination of Christianity that followed in their wake brought their own brands of enlightenment and never quite agreed with each other. The Chinese and Japanese immigrants established all the major sects of Buddhism, Confucianism, Taoism, and Shintoism. Allah is praised, the Torah is chanted in Jewish synagogues, and nirvana is available at a variety of Hindu temples. If the spirit moves you, a Hare Krishna devotee will be glad to point you in the right direction and give you a free flower for only a dollar or two. If the world is still too much with you, you might find peace at a Church of Scientology, or meditate at a Kundalini yoga institute, or perhaps find relief at a local assembly of Baha'i. Anyway, rejoice, because in Hawaii you'll not only find paradise, but might even find salvation.

HAWAIIAN BELIEFS

The Polynesian Hawaiians worshipped nature. They saw its forces manifested in a multiplicity of forms to which they ascribed godlike powers. Daily life was based on this animistic philosophy. Hand-picked and specially trained storytellers chanted the exploits of the gods. These ancient tales, kept alive in a special oral tradition called *moolelo,* were recited only by day. Entranced listeners encircled the chanter and, in respect for the gods and in fear of their wrath, were forbidden to move once the tale was begun. This was serious business during which a person's life could be at stake. It was not like the telling of *ka'ao,* which were simple fictions, tall tales, and yarns of ancient heroes, related for amusement and to pass the long nights. Any object, animate or inanimate, could be a god. All could be infused with mana, especially a dead body or a respected ancestor.

Ohana had personal family gods called *au-makua* on whom they called in times of danger or strife. There were children of gods, called *kupua*, who were thought to live among humans and were distinguished either for their beauty and strength or for their ugliness and terror. It was told that processions of dead *ali'i* called "Marchers of the Night" wandered through the land of the living, and unless you were properly protected it could mean death if they looked upon you. Simple ghosts known as *akua lapu* merely frightened people. Forests, waterfalls, trees, springs, and a thousand forms of nature were the manifestations of *akua li'i*, "little spirits" who could be invoked at any time for help or protection. It made no difference who or what you were in old Hawaii; the gods were ever-present and they took a direct and active role in your life.

Behind all of these beliefs was an innate sense of natural balance and order, and the idea that everything had its opposite—similar to the Asian idea of yin-yang. The time of darkness when only the gods lived was *po.* When the great gods descended to earth and created light, this was *ao*, and humanity was born. All of these *moolelo* are part of *The Kumulipo*, the great chant that records the Hawaiian version of creation. From the time the gods descended and touched earth at Ku Moku on Lanai, the genealogies were kept. Unlike in the Bible, these included the noble families of female as well as male *ali'i*.

Heiau and Idols

A *heiau* is a Hawaiian temple. The basic *heiau* was a masterfully built and fitted rectangular stone wall that varied in size from about as big as a basketball court to as broad as a football field. Once the restraining outer walls were built, the interior was backfilled with smaller stones, and the top dressing was expertly laid and then rolled, perhaps with a log, to form a pavementlike surface. All that remains of Hawaii's many *heiau* are the stone platforms. The buildings upon them, made from perishable wood, leaves, and grass, have long since disappeared.

Ku

Some *heiau* were dreaded temples where human sacrifices were made. Tradition says that this barbaric custom began at Waha'ula Heiau on the Big Island in the 12th century and was introduced by a ferocious Tahitian priest named Paao. Other *heiau,* such as Pu'uhonua O Honaunau, also on the Big Island, were temples of refuge where the weak, widowed, orphaned, and vanquished could find safety and sanctuary.

Within *heiau,* ceremonies were conducted by the priestly *kahuna*. Offerings of chickens, dogs, fish, fruit, and tapa were laid on the *lele,* a huge stone altar, in hopes the gods would act favorably toward the people. Some buildings held the bones of dead *ali'i,* infused with their mana. Other structures were god houses in which idols resided, while still others were oracle towers from which prophecies were made. The gods were honored by *ali'i* and *maka'ainana* alike, but the *kahuna* prayed for the *ali'i,* while the commoners represented themselves. There was a patron god for every aspect of life, especially farming and fishing, but gods could be invoked for everything from weaving to help for thieves! Men and women had their own gods, with rituals governing birth, cutting the umbilical cord, sickness, and death. Ceremonies, often lasting for many days, were conducted by *kahuna,* many of whom had highly specialized functions. Two of the most interesting were: *kahuna kilikilo,* who could see a person die in a dream and save his or her life through offerings of white dogs, chickens, tapa, and *awa;* and *kahuna kaula,* semi-hermits who could foretell the future.

The Hawaiian people worshipped gods who took the form of idols fashioned from wood, feathers, or stone. Some figures were more than six feet tall, and crowned with elaborate head pieces. Figures were often pointed at the end so they could be stuck into the ground. The eyes were made from shells and until these were inlaid, the idol was dormant. The hair used was often human hair, and the arms and legs were usually flexed. The mouth was either gaping or formed a wide figure-eight lying on its side, and more likely than not was lined with glistening dog teeth. Small figures were made of woven basketry, expertly covered with feathers. Red and yellow feathers were favorites taken from specific birds by men whose only work was to roam the forests in search of them.

GREAT GODS

Ku

The progenitors of the gods were Wakea, the "sky father," and Papa, the "earth mother," but the actual gods worshipped in Hawaii were Ku, Kane and Kanaloa, and Lono. Ku was a universal god who represented the male aspect of nature, and Hina, the moon goddess, was his female counterpart. Ku was prayed to at sunrise and Hina at sunset. Ku's maleness was represented by pointed stones, while flat ones symbolized Hina's womanhood. Ku ruled the forest, land, mountains, farming, and fishing—his benevolent side. But Ku was better known as the god of war. It was Ku who demanded human sacrifice, especially in times of calamity or in preparation for battle. At times, Ku was represented by an ohia log, and a human sacrifice was made in the forest where it was cut and also at the post hole that held it upright at the *heiau*. When Ku was invoked, the strict and serious ceremonies could go on for more than a week. The entire *aha* (assembly) kept complete silence and sat ramrod straight with the left leg and hand crossed over the right leg and hand in an attitude called *neepu*. At a precise command everyone simultaneously pointed their right hands heavenward. Anyone caught dozing or daydreaming, or who for some reason missed the command, instantly became the main course for Ku's lunch.

Kamehameha the Great carried a portable Ku into battle with him at all times, and this statue was known as Kukailimoku (the Snatcher of Lands). It was held that during battle this effigy, whose gaping mouth gleamed with canine incisors, would cry out in a loud voice and stir Kamehameha's warriors on to victory. After a battle, the slain enemies were taken to the *heiau* and placed upon Ku's altar with their arms encircling two pigs. Now Ku became Kuwahailo

(of the Dripping Maggot Mouth). With Ku's killing nature appeased, the people would pray for good crops, good fishing, and fertile wives. The scales were balanced and life went on.

Kane and Kanaloa

Kane is the Hawaiian word for "man" or "husband," and he was the leading god worshipped when the missionaries arrived. God of life, ancestor of all Hawaiians, Kane is the center of the Hawaiian creation myth, whose events are amazingly similar to those of Genesis. Kane comes forward from *po* (darkness) into *ao* (light), and with the help of Ku and Lono, fashions a man from clay gathered from the four cardinal points of the compass. Once the body is formed, the gods breathe (some say spit) into the mouth and nostrils and give it life. The man is placed upon a paradise island, *Kalani i hauola,* and a wife is fashioned for him out of his right side. Like Adam and Eve, these two break the law by eating from the forbidden tree and are driven from paradise by the sacred white albatross of Kane.

Kane is a forgiving god who demands no human sacrifice, because all life is sacred to him. He is a god of a higher order, not usually rendered as an idol. Instead he was symbolized as a single upright male stone splashed with oil and wrapped in white tapa. Kanaloa, the antithesis of Kane, was represented as a great squid, and often likened to the Christian devil. He warred with Kane and was driven out of heaven along with his minions. Kanaloa became the ruler of the dead, and was responsible for "black" sorcery and for poisonous things. However, these two gods were often linked together. For example, prayers would be offered to Kane when a canoe was built, and to Kanaloa to provide favorable winds. Farmers and diviners often prayed simultaneously to Kane and Kanaloa. Both gods were intimately connected to water and the intoxicating beverage *awa*.

Pele

The Hawaiian gods were toppled literally and figuratively in 1819, and began to fade from the minds of people. Two that remained prominent were Madame Pele, the fire goddess, who resides at Kilauea Volcano on Hawaii, and the demigod Maui, who is like Paul Bunyan and

Ulysses rolled into one. Many versions account for how Pele wound up living in Kilauea fire pit, but they all follow a general outline. It seems the beautiful young goddess, from a large family of gods, was struck by wanderlust. Tucking her young sister, in the convenient form of an egg, under her armpit, she set out to see the world. Fortune had its ups and downs in store for young Pele. For one, she was ravished by a real swine, Kamapua'a the pig god. Moreover, she fought desperately with her sister, Namaka o Kahai, over the love of a handsome young chief; Pele's sister stalked her and smashed her bones on the Hana coast of Maui at a spot called *Kaiwi o Pele* (the Bones of Pele).

Pulling herself back together, Pele set out to make a love nest for her lover and herself. She chose the fire pit at Kilauea Volcano and has long been held responsible for its lava flows along with anything else that deals with heat or fire. Pele can change her form from a withered old woman to a ravishing beauty; her moods can change from gentle to fiery hot. She is traditionally appeased with *ohelo* berries cast into her fire pit, but lately she prefers juniper berries in the form of gin. Pele's myth was shattered by the Hawaiian queen Keopuolani, one of the earliest and most fervent converts to Christianity. In the 1820s this brave queen made her way to Kilauea fire pit and defiantly ate the *ohelo* berries sacred to Pele. She then cast stones into the pit and cried in a loud voice, "Jehovah is my god . . . it is my God, not Pele, that kindled these fires."

Still, stories abound of Pele's continuing powers. Modern-day *kahuna* are always consulted and prayers offered over construction of an *imu,* which falls under Pele's fire domain. It's said by traditional Hawaiians and educated *haole* alike that when Kilauea erupts, the lava miraculously stops before or circles around a homestead over which proper prayers were made to the fire goddess. In addition, the rangers at Volcanoes National Park receive hundreds of stones every year that were taken as souvenirs and then returned by shaken tourists, who claim bad luck stalked them from the day they removed Pele's sacred stones from her volcano. And, no one who has lived in the islands for any length of time will carry pork over the volcano at night, lest they offend the goddess. She's perhaps still angry with that swine, Kamapua'a.

The Strifes of Maui

Of all the heroes and mythological figures of Polynesia, Maui is the best known. His "strifes" are like the great Greek epics, and they make excellent tales of daring that elders loved to relate to youngsters around the evening fire. Maui was abandoned by his mother Hina of Fire, when he was an infant. She wrapped him in her hair and cast him upon the sea where she expected him to die, but he lived and returned home to become her favorite. She knew then that he was a born hero and had strength far beyond that of ordinary mortals. His first exploit was to lift the sky. In those days the sky hung so low that humans had to crawl around on all fours. A seductive young woman approached Maui and asked him to use his great strength to lift the sky. In fine heroic fashion, this big boy agreed, if the beautiful woman would, euphemistically, "give him a drink from her gourd." He then obliged her by lifting the sky.

The territory of humankind was small at the time. Maui decided that more land was needed, so he conspired to "fish up islands." He descended into the land of the dead and petitioned an ancestress to fashion him a hook out of her jawbone. She obliged, and created the mythical hook *Manai ikalani.* Maui then secured a sacred *alae* bird that he intended to use for bait and bid his brothers to paddle him far out to sea. When he arrived at the deepest spot, he lowered *Manai ikalani* baited with the sacred bird, and his sister, Hina of the Sea, placed it into the mouth of "Old One Tooth," who held land fast to the bottom of the waters. Maui then exhorted his brothers to row, but warned them not to look back. They strained at the oars with all their might and slowly a great land mass rose. One brother, overcome by curiosity, looked back, and when he did so, the land shattered into all of the islands of Polynesia.

Maui desired to serve humankind further. People were without fire, the secret of which was held by the sacred *alae* birds, who had learned it from Maui's beneficent mother. Hina of Fire given Maui her burning fingernails, but he oafishly kept dropping them into streams until all had fizzled out, and he had totally irritated this generous progenitor. She pursued Maui, trying to burn him to a cinder, and Maui desperately chanted for rain to put out her scorching fires. When she saw her fires being quenched, Hina hid her fire in the barks of special trees and informed common mud hens where they could be found, but first made them promise never to tell humans. Maui learned of this and captured a mud hen, threatening to wring its scrawny, traitorous neck unless it gave up the secret. The bird tried trickery and told Maui first to rub together the stems of sugarcane, then of banana and even of taro. None worked, and Maui's determined rubbing is why these plants have hollow roots today. Finally, with Maui's hands tightening around the mud hen's neck, the bird confessed fire could be found in the *hau* tree and also the sandalwood, which Maui named *ili aha* (fire bark) in its honor. Maui then rubbed all the feathers of the mud hen's head for being so deceitful, which is why their crowns are featherless today.

Maui's greatest deed, however, was in snaring the sun and exacting a promise that it would go slower across the heavens. The people complained that there were not enough daylight hours to fish or farm. Maui's mother could not dry her tapa cloth because the sun rose and set so quickly. When she asked her son to help, Maui went to his blind grandmother for assistance. She lived on the slopes of Haleakala and was responsible for cooking the sun's bananas, which he ate every day in passing. Maui kept stealing his granny's bananas until she agreed to help. She told him to personally weave 16 strong ropes with nooses from his sister's hair. Some say these came from her head, but other versions insist that it was no doubt Hina's pubic hair that had the power to hold the sun god. Maui positioned himself, and as each of the 16 rays of the sun came across Haleakala, he snared them until the sun was defenseless and had to bargain for his life. Maui agreed to free him if he promised to go more slowly. The sun agreed, and from that time forward Haleakala (The House of the Sun) became Maui's home.

Lono and the Makahiki Festival

Lono was a benevolent god of clouds, harvest, and rain. In a fit of temper he killed his wife, whom he thought unfaithful. When he discovered his grave error, he roamed the countryside challenging everyone he met to a boxing match. Boxing later became an event of the Makahiki, the Harvest Festival, which was held in his honor.

Konane *(Hawaiian checkers) is often played during the Makahiki Festival.*

Lono decided to leave his island home, but promised one day to return on a floating island. Every year at the beginning of *ho'oilo* (winter), starting in October, the Makahiki was held. It was a jubilant time of harvest when taxes were collected and most *kapu* were lifted. It ended sometime in February, and then the new year began. During this time great sporting events included surfing, boxing, sledding, and a form of bowling. At night, people feasted at luau to the rhythm of drums and hula. Fertility was honored, and willing partners from throughout the land coupled and husbands and wives shared their mates in the tradition of *punalua.*

Lono's idol was an *akua loa,* a slender 15-foot pole with his small image perched atop. Another pole fastened at the top formed a cross. Hanging from the cross pole were long banners of white tapa cloth and it was festooned with the feathers and skins of seabirds. To this image the *kahuna* offered red and white fish, black coconut, and immature *awa.* This image, called "Long God," proceeded in a procession clockwise around the island. It was met at every *ahupua'a* (land division) by the chief of that region, and new tapa was offered by the chieftess along with roasted taro. The *maka'ainana* came and offered their produce from sea and land and so the taxes were collected. At the end of the festival a naked man representing the god Kohoali'i ate the eyeball of a fish and one of a human victim and proclaimed the New Year.

It was just during the Makahiki that Captain Cook sailed into Kealakekua Bay. *Kahuna* saw his great "floating islands" and proclaimed the return of Lono. Uncannily, the masts of the sailing ships draped in canvas looked remarkably like Lono's idol. Cook himself was particularly tall and white-skinned, and at the sight of him, many natives fell to their knees and worshipped him as "Lono returned."

THE CASTE AND *KAPU* SYSTEM

All was not heavenly in paradise due to horrible wars, but the people mainly lived quiet, ordered lives based on a strict caste society and the *kapu* system. Famine was contained to a regional level. The population was kept in check by herbal birth-control potions, crude abortions, and infanticide, especially of baby girls. The strict

caste system was determined by birth, which there was no chance of changing. The highest rank was the ***ali'i,*** the chiefs and royalty. The impeccable genealogies of the *ali'i* were traced back to the gods themselves, and recorded in chants *(mo'o ali'i)* memorized and sung by professionals called *ku'auhau.* Ranking passed from both father and mother, and custom dictated the first mating of an *ali'i* be with a person of equal rank. After a child was produced, the *ali'i* was free to mate with lesser *ali'i* or even with a commoner. The custom of *punalua,* the sharing of mates, was practiced throughout Hawaiian society. Moreover, incest was not only condoned but sanctioned among *ali'i.* To conceive an offspring of the highest rank, *ni'au pi'o* (coconut leaf looped back on itself), the parents were required to be full brothers and sisters. These offspring were so sacred they were considered *akua* (living gods), and people of all rank had to literally crawl on their stomachs in their presence. *Ali'i* who ran society's affairs were of lesser rank, and they were the real functionaries. The two most important were the land supervisors *(konohiki)* and caste priests *(kahuna).* The *konohiki* were in charge of the *ahupua'a,* pie-shaped land divisions running from mountain to sea. The common people came in contact with these *ali'i* as they also collected taxes and ruled as judges among the people.

Kahuna were highly skilled people whose advice was sought before any major undertaking, such as building a house, hollowing a canoe log, or even offering a prayer. The *mo'o kahuna* were the priests of Ku and Lono, in charge of praying and following rituals. These powerful *ali'i* kept strict secrets and laws concerning their various functions. The *kahuna* dedicated to Ku were severe: it was they who sought human sacrifice. The *kahuna* of Lono were more comforting to the people, but were of lesser rank

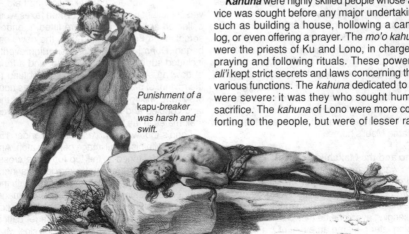

Punishment of a kapu-breaker was harsh and swift.

JACQUES ARAGO, HAWAII STATE ARCHIVES

than the Ku kahuna. Other kahuna were not ali'i but commoners. The two most important were the healers (kahuna lapa'au), and the black magicians (kahuna ana'ana), who could pray a person to death. The kahuna lapa'au had a pharmacopoeia of herbs and spices that could cure more than 250 diseases. They employed baths and massage and used various colored stones to outline the human body and accurately pinpoint not only the organs but the internal origins of illness. The kahuna ana'ana were given a wide berth by the people, who did everything possible to stay on their good side! The kahuna ana'ana could be hired to cast a love spell over a person or cause untimely death; they seldom had to send a reminder of payment.

The common people were called the **maka'ainana,** "people of the land." They were the farmers, craftspeople, and fishermen. Their land was owned by the ali'i, but they were not bound to it. If the local ali'i was cruel or unfair, the maka'ainana had the right to leave. Very unjust ali'i were even put to death by their own people, with no retribution if their accusations proved true. The maka'ainana mostly loved their local ali'i, and vice versa. Maka'ainana who lived close to the ali'i and could be counted on as warriors in times of trouble were called kanaka no lua kaua, "a man for the heat of battle." They were treated with greater favor than those who lived in the backcountry, kanaka no hii kua, whose lesser standing opened them up to discrimination and cruelty. All maka'ainana formed extended families (ohana) and usually lived on the same section of land (ahupua'a). Inland farmers would barter their produce with fishermen; thus all shared equally in the bounty of the land and sea.

A special group, **kauwa,** was a landless untouchable caste confined to living on reservations. Their origins were obviously Polynesian, but they appeared to be descendants of castaways who had survived and become perhaps the aboriginals of Hawaii before the main migrations. It was kapu for anyone to go onto kauwa lands; doing so meant instant death. A kauwa driven by necessity to leave his lands was required to cover his head with tapa cloth, his eyes focused on the ground in a humble manner. If a human sacrifice was needed, the kahuna simply summoned a kauwa, who had no recourse but to mutely comply. Through the years after discovery by Cook, the kauwa became obscured as a class and mingled with the remainder of the population. But even to this day, calling someone kauwa, which now supposedly only means servant, is still considered a fight-provoking insult.

Kapu and Daily Life

A strict division of labor existed between men and women. Only men were permitted to have anything to do with taro, a foodstuff so sacred it had a greater kapu than humans themselves. Men pounded poi and served it to women. Men were also the fishermen and builders of houses, canoes, irrigation ditches, and walls. Women tended gardens and were responsible for making tapa and tending to shoreline fishing. The entire family lived in the common house (hale noa). But certain things were kapu between the sexes. The primary kapu were entrance by a woman into the mua (men's house) and eating with men. Certain foods such as pork and bananas were forbidden to women. It was kapu for a man to have intercourse before going fishing, engaging in battle, or attending a religious ceremony. Young boys lived with the women until they underwent circumcision (pule ipu), after which they were required to keep the kapu of men.

Ali'i could also declare a kapu, and often did so. Certain lands or fishing areas were temporarily made kapu so they could revitalize. Even today, it is kapu for anyone to remove all the opihi (a type of limpet) from a rock. The great King Kamehameha I placed a kapu on the body of his notoriously unfaithful child bride, Kaahumanu. It didn't work! The greatest kapu (kapu moe) was afforded to the highest ranking ali'i: anyone coming into their presence had to prostrate themselves. Lesser ranking ali'i were afforded the kapu noho: lessers had to sit or kneel in their presence. Commoners could not let their shadows fall upon an ali'i or enter their houses except through a special door. Breaking a kapu meant immediate death.

Fun and Games

The native Hawaiians loved sports. A type of "Olympiad" was held each year during the Makahiki Festival. Events included boxing, swimming, diving, surfing, and running. A form of bowling used polished, wheel-shaped stones that tested for distance and accuracy. Hawaiians also enjoyed a more cerebral, chesslike game called *konane*. Intricately carved *konane* boards survive to this day. Hawaiians built special downhill courses for a runnered bobsled called a *holua*. They could coast over wet grasses or leaves for 200 yards. Strangely enough, the Hawaiians developed a bow and arrow but never employed it in warfare. It was merely a toy for shooting at targets or rats.

The greatest sport of all was surfing. **Surfing** originated with the Hawaiians, and many old records recount this singularly exhilarating activity. The boards, made of various woods, were greatly cared for, measuring up to 15 feet long and six inches thick. James King, a lieutenant with Cook, was "altogether astonished" by surfing, and Reverend Ellis wrote in 1826, ". . . to see fifty or a hundred persons riding on an immense billow . . . for a distance of several hundred yards together is one of the most novel and interesting sports a foreigner can witness in the islands."

Ghosts

The Hawaiians had countless superstitions and ghost legends, but two of the more interesting involve astral travel of the soul and the "Marchers of the Night." The soul, *uhane,* was considered by Hawaiians to be totally free and independent of its body, *kino.* The soul could separate, leaving the body asleep or very drowsy. This disincorporated soul *(hihi'o)* could visit people and was considered quite different from a *lapu,* an ordinary spirit of a dead person. A *kahuna* could immediately recognize if a person's *uhane* had left the body, and a special wreath was placed upon the head for protection and to facilitate reentry. A person confronted by an apparition could test to see if it was indeed dead or still alive by placing leaves of an *ape* plant upon the ground. If the leaves tore when they were walked upon, the spirit was human, but if they remained intact it was a ghost. Also,

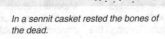

In a sennit casket rested the bones of the dead.

you could sneak up and startle the vision and if it disappeared it was a ghost. Also, if no reflection of the face appeared when it drank water from an offered calabash, it was a ghost. Unfortunately, there were no instructions to follow once you had determined you indeed had a ghost on your hands. Maybe it was better not to know! Some people would sprinkle salt and water around their houses, but this only kept away evil spirits, not ghosts.

There are also many stories of *kahuna* restoring souls to a dead bodies. First they had to catch one and keep it in a gourd. He then placed beautiful tapa and fragrant flowers and herbs about the body to make it more enticing. Slowly, the *kahuna* would coax the soul out of the gourd, and get it to reenter the body through the big toe.

Death Marchers

One inexplicable phenomenon that many people attest to is *ka huakai o ka po,* "Marchers of the Night." This march of the dead is fatal if you gaze upon it, unless one of the marchers happens to be a friendly ancestor who will protect you. The peak time for "the march" is 7:30 p.m.-2 a.m. The marchers can be dead *ali'i* and warriors, the gods themselves, or the lesser *aumakua.* When the *aumakua* march there is usually chanting and music. *Ali'i* marches are more somber. The entire procession, lit by torches, often stops at the house of a relative and might even carry him or her away. When the gods themselves march, there is often thunder, lightning, and heavy seas. The sky is lit with torches, and they walk six abreast, three gods and three goddesses. If you get in the way of a march, remove your clothing and prostrate yourself. If the marching gods or *aumakua* happen to be ones to which you pray, you might be spared. If it's a march of the *ali'i,* you might make it if you lie face upward and feign death. If you *do* see a death march, the last thing you'll worry about is lying naked on the ground and looking ridiculous.

LOUISE FOOTE

MISSIONARIES ONE AND ALL

In Hawaii when you say "missionaries," it taken for granted you're referring to the small, determined band of Congregationalists who arrived aboard the Brig *Thaddeus* in 1820 and the "companies" or "packets" that reinforced them over the next 40 years. They were sent from Boston by the American Board of Commissioners for Foreign Missions (ABCFM), who learned of the supposed sad and godless plight of the Hawaiian people from returning sailors and especially through the few Hawaiians who had come to America to study. The person most instrumental in bringing the missionaries to Hawaii was a young man named Henry Opukahaia. An orphan befriended by a captain and taken to New England, he studied theology and was obsessed with the desire to return home to save his people from sure damnation. His widely read accounts of life in Hawaii were the direct cause of the formation of the Pioneer Company to the Sandwich Islands Missions. Unfortunately, Opukahaia died in New England from typhus in 1819, the year before the missionaries sailed.

The first missionaries had the straightforward task of bringing the Hawaiians out of paganism and into Christianity and civilization. They met with extreme hostility—not from the natives, but from sea captains, sailors, and traders who were content with the open debauchery and wanton whoremongering that was the status quo in the Hawaii of 1820. The many direct confrontations between these two factions even included the cannonading of a missionary home by American sea captains who were denied the customary visits of island women, thanks to the meddlesome "do-gooders." The most memorable of these incidents involved "Mad Jack" Percival, the captain of the USS *Dolphin,* who bombed a church in Lahaina to show his rancor. In actuality, the truth of the situation was much closer to the sentiments of James Jarves, who wrote, "The missionary was a far more useful and agreeable man than his catechism would indicate; and the trader was not so bad a man as the missionary would make him out to be." The missionary's primary aim was conversion, but the most fortuitous by-product was education, which raised the consciousness of every Hawaiian regardless of religious affiliation. In 40 short years Hawaii was considered a civilized nation well on its way into the modern world, and the American Board of Missions officially ended its support in 1863.

Some of Hawaii's finest museums and grandest architecture are part of the missionary legacy. Some of the most notable are: Mokuaikaua Church in Kona, Hawaii, the first Christian church, founded in 1820; the Lyman House Museum of Hilo; Kawaiahao Church in Honolulu, founded 1821, and next door the superb Mission House Museum; Wainee Church, the first stone church in Hawaii, founded in Lahaina in 1828, and the Baldwin Home just down Front Street; and Lahainaluna High School and Printing House, the first American school and publishing house west of the Rockies. The churches, but especially the homes and museums, not only offer a glimpse of religious life, but are some of the finest "windows" into 19th-century America. Their collections of artifacts, utensils, and general memorabilia put the life and times of 19th-century Yankees in a setting that could hardly be more different than New England.

Bonanza for Missionaries

Although the missionaries were the first, they by no means had the field to themselves. Hot on the same religious trail came the Catholics—French Sacred Hearts led by Father Bachelot, who arrived in Honolulu in July 1827 aboard the *La Comete.* Immediately, Queen Kaahumanu, who had been converted by the Congregationalists, ordered them to leave. They refused. For the next 10 years the Catholic priests and their converts met with open hostility and persecution which, in true missionary fashion, only strengthened their resolve. The humiliation of a young convert, Juliana Keawahine, who was tied to a tree and scourged, became a religious rallying point. After this incident the persecutions stopped. Honolulu's Our Lady of Peace Cathedral was completed in 1843 and Ahuimanu Catholic School, Oahu's counterpart to Lahainaluna, opened for instruction in 1846. Today, Roman Catholicism, with 230,000 adherents, is the single largest religious group in Hawaii.

The Saints Come Marching In

A strange episode in Hawaii's history involved the Mormons. In 1850, the Latter-Day Saints arrived direct from missionary work in California gold fields. By 1852, George Cannon had already translated the *Book of Mormon* into Hawaiian. The five original Mormon missionaries spent every moment traveling and converting the Hawaiians. They had a grand plan of constructing a "City of Joseph" on Lanai, where they managed to gain a large tract of land. In 1858 the Mormon Wars broke out in Utah and the missionaries were called home. One of their band, Walter Murray Gibson, who stayed to manage the fledgling Mormon Church, became one of the most controversial and singularly strange fixtures in Hawaiian politics. When the Mormons returned in 1864, they found Gibson had indeed carried on the "City of Joseph," but had manipulated all of the deeds and land grants into his personal possession. Furthermore, he had set himself up as an omnipotent grand patriarch and openly denounced the polygamous beliefs of the Mormons of the day. Immediately excommunicated, Gibson was abandoned to his fate and the Mormons moved to Oahu where they founded a sugar plantation and temple in Laie.

The Mormon Church now has approximately 40,000 members, the largest Protestant denomination in Hawaii. Their settlement on Oahu at Laie is now home to an impressive Mormon Temple and an island branch of Brigham Young University. Close by, the Mormons also operate the Polynesian Cultural Center, which is one of the top tourist attractions in all of Hawaii.

As for Gibson, he was elected to the legislature in 1876 and became a private counselor to King Kalakaua. In 1882, he worked himself into the office of "Premier," which he ran like a petty dictator. One of his more visionary suggestions was to import Japanese labor. Two of his most ridiculous were to drive non-Hawaiians from the islands (excluding himself) and to gather Oceania into one Pacific nation with Hawaii at the forefront. By 1887 he and Kalakaua had so infuriated the sugar planters that Gibson was railroaded out of the islands and Kalakaua was forced to sign a constitution that greatly limited his power. Gibson died in 1888 and his daughter Talulah and her husband sold the lands on Lanai for a song, after they tried but failed to grow sugarcane.

Non-Christian

By the turn of this century, Shintoism and Buddhism, brought by the Japanese and Chinese, were firmly established in Hawaii. The first official Buddhist Temple was Hongpa Hongwanji, established on Oahu in 1889. All denominations of Buddhism account for 17% of the island's religious total, and there are about 50,000 Shintoists. The Hindu religion has perhaps 2,000 adherents, and roughly 7,000 Jewish people live throughout Hawaii. About 10,000 island residents are in new religious movements and lesser-known faiths such as Baha'i and Unitarianism. The largest number of people in Hawaii (300,000) remain unaffiliated.

DIANA LASICH HARPER

M.G.L. DOMENY DE RIENZI

ON THE ROAD
SPORTS AND RECREATION

Hawaii is a playground for young and old with sports, games, and activities galore. Everyone can find something they enjoy, and most activities are free, relatively cheap, or once-in-a-lifetime thrills that are worth the money. The sea is the ideal playground. You can swim, snorkel, scuba, surf, bodysurf, windsurf, fish, sail, canoe, kayak, parasail, cruise, or stroll along the shore picking up shells or exploring tidepools. Every island offers tennis and golf, along with plenty of horseback riding, hiking, biking, and hunting, with more limited freshwater fishing. Spectator sports such as baseball, basketball, polo, and especially football are popular, and the Kona coast of the Big Island is a mecca for world-class triathletes. Whatever your desire or physical abilities may be, there'll be some activity that strikes your fancy in Hawaii.

One of the best tonics for relaxation is to play hard at something you thoroughly enjoy, so you're deliciously tired and fulfilled at day's end. For you this might be hooking onto an 800-pound marlin that'll test you to the limit, or perhaps just giving yourself to the sea and floating on gentle

waves. Hawaii is guaranteed to thrill the young, invigorate the once young, put a twinkle in your eye, and add a bounce to your step.

Note
The following sports and recreation overview is designed to give you an idea of what's available. More in-depth information can be found in the travel chapters. There you'll also find specific entries for localized sports like horseback riding, jet skiing, water-skiing, snow skiing, parasailing, kayaking, and much more. Whatever else you may do in Hawaii, you owe it to yourself to do one thing: enjoy it!

CAMPING AND HIKING

A major aspect of the "Hawaii experience" is found in the simple beauty of nature and the outdoors. Some visitors come to Hawaii to luxuriate at resorts and dine in fine restaurants, but everyone heads for the sand and surf, and most are captivated by the lush mountainous interior. What better way to savor this natural beauty than by hiking slowly through it or pitching a tent in the middle of it? Hawaii offers a full range of hiking and camping, and what's more, most of it is easily accessible. Camping facilities are located near many choice beaches and amid some of the most scenic areas in the islands. They range in amenities from full housekeeping cabins to primitive "hike-in" sites. Camping permits can be obtained by walk-in application to the appropriate office, or by writing or phoning. Although there is usually no problem obtaining sites, when writing, request reservations well in advance, allowing a minimum of one month for letters to go back and forth.

Some restrictions to hiking apply because much of the land is privately owned, so advance permission to hike may be required. But plenty of public access trails along the coast and deep into the interior would fill the itineraries of even the most intrepid trekkers. If you enjoy the great outdoors on the Mainland, you'll be thrilled by these "mini-continents," where in one day you can go from the frosty summits of alpine wonderlands down into baking cactus-covered deserts and emerge through jungle foliage onto a sun-soaked subtropical shore.

Equipment

Like everything else you take to Hawaii, your camping and hiking equipment should be lightweight and durable. Camping equipment size and weight should not cause a problem with baggage requirements on airlines: if it does, it's a tip-off that you're hauling too much. One odd luggage consideration you might make is to bring along a small **styrofoam cooler** packed with equipment. Exchange the equipment for food items when you get to Hawaii. If you intend to car camp successfully and keep food prices down, you'll definitely need the cooler. You can also buy one on arrival for only a few dollars.

You'll need a lightweight **tent,** preferably with a rainfly and a sewn-in floor. This will save you from getting wet and miserable and will keep out mosquitoes, cockroaches, ants, and the islands' few stinging insects. **Sleeping bags** are a good idea, although you can get along at sea level with only a blanket. Down-filled bags are necessary for Haleakala, Mauna Kea, Mauna Loa, or any high-elevation camping—you'll freeze

without one. **Campstoves** are needed because there's very little wood in some volcanic areas, it's often wet in the deep forest, and open fires are often prohibited. If you'll be car-camping, take along a multiburner stove; for trekking, a backpacker's stove will be necessary. The grills found at some campgrounds are popular with many families who often go to the beach parks for open-air dinners. You can buy a very inexpensive charcoal grill at many variety stores throughout Hawaii. It's a great idea to take along a **lantern.** This will add safety for car-campers. Definitely take a **flashlight,** replacement batteries, and a few small **candles.** A complete **first-aid kit** can be the difference between life and death, and it's worth the extra bulk. Hikers, especially those leaving the coastal areas, should take **rain gear,** plastic ground cloth, utility knife, compass, safety whistle, mess kit, water purification tablets, canteen, nylon twine, and waterproof matches. You will find a limited number of stores that sell or rent camping and hiking equipment.

Safety

There are two things in Hawaii that you must keep your eye on in order to remain safe: humans and nature. The general rule is: the farther you get away from towns, the safer you'll be from human-induced hassles. If possible, don't hike or camp alone, especially if you're a woman. Don't leave your valuables in your tent, and always carry your money, papers, and camera with you. Don't tempt the locals by being overly friendly or unfriendly, and make yourself scarce if they're drinking. While hiking, remember that many trails are well maintained, but trailhead markers are often missing. The trails themselves can be muddy, which can make them treacherously slippery and often knee-deep. Always bring food because you cannot, in most cases, forage from the land. Water in most streams is biologically polluted and will give you bad stomach problems if you drink it without purifying it first by boiling, filtering, or adding purification tablets. For your part, please don't use the streams as a toilet.

Precautions

Always tell a ranger or official of your hiking intentions. Supply an itinerary and your expected route, then stick to it. Twilight is short in the islands, and night sets in rapidly. In June sunrise and sunset are around 6 a.m. and 7 p.m.; in December these occur at 7 a.m. and 6 p.m. If lost, walk on ridges and avoid the gulches, which have more obstacles and make it harder for rescuers to spot you. If you become lost at night, stay put, light a fire if possible, and keep as dry as you can. Hawaii is made of volcanic rock which is brittle and crumbly. Never attempt to climb steep *pali* (cliffs). Every year people are stranded and fatalities have occurred. Be careful of elevation sickness, especially on Haleakala, Mauna Loa, and Mauna Kea. The best cure is to head down as soon as possible. Be mindful of flash floods. Small creeks can turn into raging torrents with upland rains. Never camp in a dry creekbed. Fog is only encountered at elevations of 1,500-5,000 feet, but be careful of disorientation.

Heat can cause you to lose water and salt. If you become woozy or weak, rest, take salt, and drink water as you need it. Remember, it takes much more water to restore a dehydrated person than to keep hydrated; take small frequent sips. Generally, stay within your limits, be careful, and enjoy yourself.

Hiking Groups and Information

The **Department of Land and Natural Resources,** Division of Forestry and Wildlife, 1151 Punchbowl St., Honolulu, HI 96813, tel. (808) 587-0166, is helpful in providing trail maps, accessibility information, hunting and fishing regulations, and general forest rules. Although somewhat out of date, their "Recreation Maps" are excellent and free, and there is one for each of the four main islands.

The following organizations can provide general information on wildlife, conservation, and organized hiking trips: **Hawaiian Audubon Society,** P.O. Box 22832, Honolulu, HI 96822; and **Sierra Club, Hawaii Chapter** P.O. Box 2577, Honolulu, HI 96803, tel. (808) 538-6616. The Sierra Club organizes weekly hikes, $1 for members and $3 for nonmembers. Information about the organization and their hikes is listed in their newsletter and on their website: www.hi.sierra-club.org. They also sell the useful booklet *Hiking Softly in Hawai'i* ($5) that gives general information about hiking in Hawaii; preparation, etiquette, and precautions; a brief chart of major

trails on each island, along with their physical characteristics; information on obtaining maps and permits; and other sources of information.

Hiking and Camping Books

For a well-written and detailed hiking guide complete with maps, check out *Maui Trails, Kauai Trails, Oahu Trails* and *Hawaii Trails* by Kathy Morey. See also *Hawaiian Hiking Trails* by Craig Chisholm, and Robert Smith's *Hawaii's Best Hiking Trails,* and his *Hiking Maui, Hiking Oahu, Hiking Hawaii* and *Hiking Kauai.*

Two helpful camping books are *Hawaii: A Camping Guide* by George Cagala and Richard McMahon's *Camping Hawaii.*

Topographical Maps and Nautical Charts

For detailed topographical maps, write **U.S. Geological Survey, Information Services,** P.O. Box 25286, Denver, CO 80225; or call (800) USA-MAPS or (703) 648-4888. (Website: www.usgs.gov). Many types of maps are available at Borders Books throughout the islands. A wide range of topographical maps, nautical charts, and local maps can be purchased at independent shops like **Pacific Map Center,** 560 N. Nimitz Hwy., Suite 206A, Honolulu, HI, tel. (808) 545-3600 and **Basically Books,** 46 Waianuenue St., tel. (808) 961-0144, in downtown Hilo on the Big Island. Also useful, but not for hiking, are the University of Hawaii Press reference maps of each island.

For nautical charts, write **National Ocean Service,** Riverdale, MD 20737-1199, tel. (301) 436-6990 or (800) 638-8972.

NATIONAL PARKS

Hawaii's two National Parks sit atop volcanoes: **Haleakala National Park** on Maui, and **Hawaii Volcanoes National Park** centered around Kilauea Crater on the Big Island. Camping is free at both, and permits are not required except for the cabins and campgrounds inside Haleakala crater. See the travel chapters for detailed information. Get free information by writing to the individual park headquarters: Hawaii Volcanoes National Park, P.O. Box 52, Hawaii National Park, HI 96718, tel. (808) 985-6000, website: www.nps.gov/havo; Haleakala National Park,

P.O. Box 369, Makawao, HI 96768, tel. (808) 572-9306, website: www.nps.gov/hale; or from the Hawaii office of the **National Park Service,** 300 Ala Moana Blvd., Honolulu, HI 96850, tel. (808) 541-2693.

STATE PARKS

Hawaii's 54 state parks, which include historical parks, recreation areas, recreation piers, waysides, monuments, and underwater parks, are managed by the Department of Land and Natural Resources, through their Division of State Parks branch offices on each island. Some are for looking at, some are restricted to day use, and at 14 (which may change periodically without notice) there is overnight camping. At seven of these parks, A-frames, self-contained cabins, or group accommodations are available on a fee basis with reservations necessary. At the others, camping is free, but permits are required. RVs are technically not allowed.

Permits and Rules

Camping permits are good for a maximum stay of five consecutive nights at any one park, except for the Na Pali Coast State Park, which has one- and three-night limits at certain campsites. A permit to the same person for the same park is again available only after 30 days from the last day of previous use. Campgrounds are open every day on the Neighbor Islands, but closed Wednesday and Thursday on Oahu. Arrive after 2 p.m. and check out by 11 a.m., except again on Oahu where Wednesday checkout is 8 a.m. You must be 18 for park permits; anyone under that age must be accompanied by an adult. Alcoholic beverages are prohibited, along with nude sunbathing and swimming. Plants and wildlife are protected, but reasonable amounts of fruits and seeds may be gathered for personal consumption. Fires are allowed on cookstoves or in designated pits only. Dogs and other pets must be under control at all times (if allowed), and are not permitted to run around unleashed. Hunting and freshwater fishing are allowed in season with a license, and ocean fishing is permitted except when disallowed by posting. Permits are required for certain trails, pavilions, and remote camps, so check.

Cabins and Shelters

With one exception, housekeeping cabins, A-frames, and group lodges are available daily at seven state parks throughout the state; at Polipoli Spring on Maui, cabins are not available on Tuesday. See specific travel chapters for details. As with camping, permits are required and have the same five-day maximum-stay limitations. Reservations are necessary because of popularity, and a 50% deposit within two weeks of reservation is required. There is a 15-day cancellation requirement for refunds, with payment made in cash, money order, cashiers check, or certified check. If you pay by personal or business check, it must be received 30 days before arrival. The exact balance is due on arrival in cash; check in is 2 p.m., checkout 11 a.m.

State Park Permit-Issuing Offices

Permit applications can be made by mail, by phone, or in person at one of the issuing offices, not more than one year in advance (30 days in advance for Oahu). Reservations by letter must including your name, address, phone number, names and identification numbers of those over 18 years old in your party, type of permit requested, and duration of stay. Permits can be picked up from the issuing office on arrival with proof of identification. Office hours are Mon.-Fri. 8 a.m.-4 p.m. Usually, camping permits are no problem (Oahu excepted) to secure on the day you arrive, but reserving ensures you a space and alleviates anxiety. The permits are available from the following offices: **Oahu,** Division of State Parks, 1151 Punchbowl St., Honolulu, HI 96813, tel. (808) 587-0300; **Hawaii,** Division of State Parks, 75 Aupuni St., Hilo, HI 96720, tel. (808) 974-6200; **Maui and Molokai,** Division of State Parks, 54 S. High St., Wailuku, HI 96793, tel. (808) 984-8109; **Kauai,** Division of State Parks, 3060 Eiwa St., Lihue, HI 96766, tel. (808) 274-3444. For lodging at **Koke'e State Park,** Kauai, write Koke'e Lodge, P.O. Box 819, Waimea, HI 96796, tel. (808) 335-6061 (9 a.m.-3:45 p.m.); and for **Malaekahana SRA,** Oahu, write Friends of Malaekahana, P.O. Box 305, Laie, HI, 96762, tel. (808) 293-1736 (10 a.m.-3 p.m.).

COUNTY PARKS

The state of Hawaii is broken up into counties, and the counties control their own parks. Of the more than 600 county parks, more than 100 are scattered primarily along the coastlines, and are generally referred to as **beach parks.** Most are for day use only, where visitors fish, swim, snorkel, surf, picnic, and sunbathe, but more than 35 have overnight camping. The rules governing their use vary slightly from county to county, so check the individual travel chapters below, but most have about the same requirements as state parks. The main difference is that most county parks charge a fee for overnight use. Again, the differences between individual parks are too numerous to mention, but the majority have a central pavilion for cooking, restrooms, and cold-water showers (solar heated at a few). Some have individual fire pits, picnic tables, and electricity (usually only at the central pavilion). RVs are allowed to park in appropriate spaces.

Fees and Permits

The fees are quite reasonable at $1-3 per night, per person, children about 50 cents each. One safety point to consider is that beach parks are open to the general public and most are used with regularity. Quite a few people pass through, and your chances of encountering a hassle or rip-off are slightly higher than average (see **Theft and Hassles** later in this chapter for safety tips). To get a permit and pay your fees for use of a county park, either write in advance or visit one of the following issuing offices. Most will accept reservations months in advance, with offices generally open during normal working hours. Write or visit the Department of Parks and Recreation, County Parks: **Oahu,** 650 S. King St., Honolulu, HI 96813, tel. (808) 523-4525; **Maui,** War Memorial Gym, 1580-C Kaahumanu Ave., Wailuku, HI 96793, tel. (808) 243-7389; **Hawaii,** 25 Aupuni St., Hilo, HI 96720, tel. (808) 961-8311; **Kauai,** 4193 Hardy St., Lihue, HI 96766, tel. (808) 241-6670, or during off hours Lihue Police Station, 3060 Umi St., Lihue, HI 96766, tel. (808) 245-9711; **Molokai,** Mitchell Pauole Center, Kaunakakai, HI 96748, tel. (808) 553-3204.

SCUBA AND SNORKELING

If you think Hawaii is beautiful above the sea, wait until you explore below. The warm tropical waters and coral growth make it a fascinating haven for reef fish and aquatic plantlife. Snorkel and dive sites, varying in difficulty and challenge, are accessible from all islands. Sites can be totally hospitable ones where families snorkeling for the first time can have an exciting but safe frolic, or they can be accessible only to the experienced diver. Every island has dive shops where you can rent or buy equipment, and where dive boats and instruction on all levels can be arranged. You'll soon discover that Hawaiian waters are remarkably clear with excellent visibility. Below, fish in every fathomable color parade by. Lavender clusters of coral, red and gold coral trees, and more than 1,500 different types of shells carpet the ocean floor. In some spots (like Oahu's Hanauma Bay) the fish are so accustomed to humans they'll eat bread from your hand. In other spots, lurking moray eels add the zest of danger. Sharks and barracuda pose less danger than scraping your knee on the coral or being driven against the rocks by a heavy swell. There are enormous but harmless sea bass and a profusion of sea turtles. All this awaits you below Hawaii's waters.

Scuba

If you're a scuba diver you'll have to show your "C Card" before local shops will rent you gear, fill your tanks, or take you on a charter dive. Plenty of outstanding scuba instructors will give you lessons toward certification, and they're especially reasonable because of the stiff competition. Prices vary, but you can take a four- to five-day semiprivate (PADI) certification course including all equipment for about $375. Divers unaccustomed to Hawaiian waters should not dive alone regardless of their experience. Most opt for dive tours to special dive grounds guaranteed to please. These vary also, but an *accompanied* single-tank dive where no boat is involved goes for about $65. For a single-tank boat dive, expect to spend $65-85. There are charter dives, night dives, and photography dives. Most companies pick you up at your hotel, take you to the site, and return you home. Basic equipment rental costs

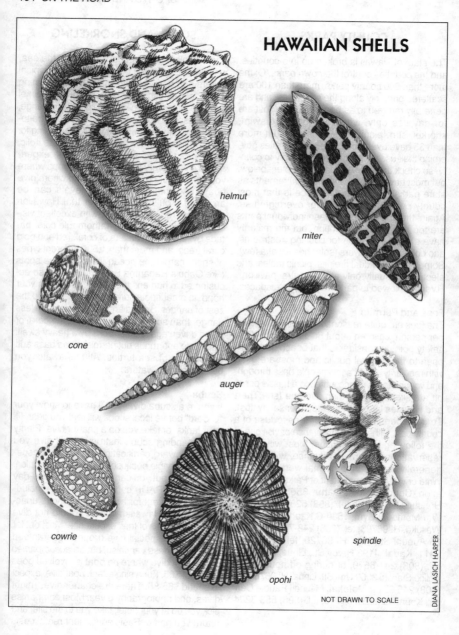

HAWAIIAN SHELLS

helmut

miter

cone

auger

cowrie

opohi

spindle

NOT DRAWN TO SCALE

DIANA LASICH HARPER

$25-35 for the day, and most times the water is so mild you'll only need the top of a wetsuit.

Snorkeling

Scuba diving takes expensive special equipment, skills, and athletic ability. Snorkeling in comparison is much simpler and enjoyable to anyone who can swim. In about 15 minutes you can be taught the fundamentals of snorkeling, so you're comfortable and confident in the water— you really don't need formal instructions. Other snorkelers or dive shop attendants can tell you enough to get you started. Because you can breathe without lifting your head, you get great propulsion from the fins and hardly ever need to use your arms. You can go for much greater distances and spend longer in the water than if you were swimming. Experienced snorkelers make an art of this sport and you too can see and do amazing things with a mask, snorkel, and flippers. Don't, however, get a false sense of invincibility and exceed your limitations.

Gear and Excursions

You can buy or rent equipment in dive shops and in department stores. Sometimes condos and hotels offer free snorkeling equipment for their guests, but if you have to rent it, don't do it at a hotel or condo; go to a dive shop where it's much cheaper. Expect to spend $7 a day for mask, fins, and snorkel. A special option is an underwater camera. Rental of camera, film included, runs about $15-20. Many boats will take you out snorkeling. Prices range from about $30 (half day, four hours) to $60 (full day, eight hours). Activities centers can also arrange these excursions for no extra charge.

Snuba

No that's not a typo. Snuba offers a hybrid sport that is half snorkeling and half scuba diving. You have a regulator, a weight belt, mask, and flippers, and you're tethered to scuba tanks that float 20 feet above you on a sea-sled. The unofficial motto of snuba is "secure but free." The idea is that many people become anxious diving under the waves encumbered by tanks and all the scuba apparatus. Snuba frees you. You would think that being tethered to the sled would slow you down, but actually you're sleeker and can make better time than a normal scuba diver.

The sled is made from industrial-strength polyethylene and is 2.5 feet wide by 7.5 feet long, consisting of a view window and a belly in the sled for location of the scuba tank. If you get tired, just surface and use it as a raft.

SURFING AND WINDSURFING

Surfing

Surfing is a sport indigenous to Hawaii. When the white man first arrived, he was astonished to see natives paddling out to meet the ships on long carved boards, then gracefully riding them in to shore on crests of waves. The Hawaiians called surfing *he'enalu* (to "slide on a wave"). The newcomers were fascinated by this sport, recording it in engravings and woodcuts, marveled at around the world. Meanwhile, the Polynesians left records of surfing in petroglyphs and in *mele* of past exploits. A Waikiki beachboy named Duke Kahanamoku won a treasure box full of gold medals for swimming at the 1912 Olympic Games. Thereafter, he became a celebrity, introducing surfing to California, Australia, and the rest of the world. Surfing later became a lifestyle, popularized far and wide by the songs of the Beach Boys in the '60s. Now surfing is a sport enjoyed around the world, complete with championships, movies, magazines, and advanced board technology.

It takes years of practice to become good, but with determination, good swimming ability, and a sense of balance you can learn the fundamentals in a short time. One of the safest places, offering ideal conditions to learn, is Waikiki. The sea is just right for the beginner, and legions of beachboys offer lessons. At surf shops on all islands you can rent a board for very reasonable prices. The boards of the ancient *ali'i* were up to 20 feet long and weighed more than 150 pounds, but today's board is made from ultralight foam plastic covered in fiberglass. They're about six feet long and weigh 12 pounds or so. Innovations occur every day in surfing, but one is the changeable "skeg" or rudder allowing you to surf in variable conditions.

The sport of surfing is still male-dominated, but women champions have been around for years. The most famous surfing beach in the

(continues on page 108)

REEF FISH

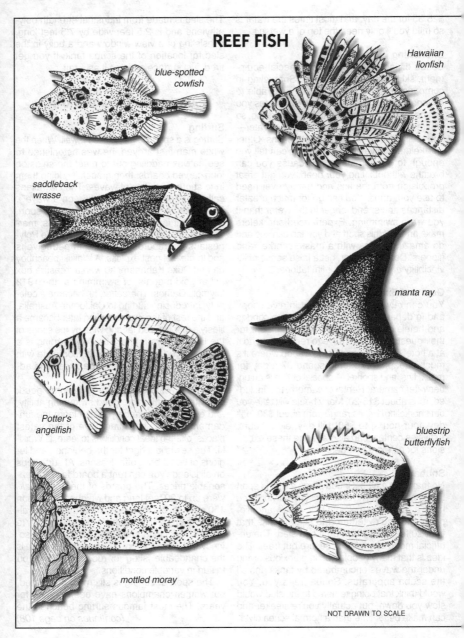

blue-spotted cowfish

Hawaiian lionfish

saddleback wrasse

manta ray

Potter's angelfish

bluestrip butterflyfish

mottled moray

NOT DRAWN TO SCALE

trumpetfish

manini

moorish idol

lagoon humu

threadfin butterflyfish

red-lipped parrotfish

uhu

Achilles tang

LOUISE FOOTE/DIANA LASICH HARPER

world is Sunset Beach and the Banzai Pipeline on North Shore Oahu. Every year the nationally televised pro-tour Triple Crown of Surfing is held here, usually in late November and December. It's only a matter of time before surfing becomes an Olympic sport. One of the most brilliant books ever written on surfing is *Surfing, the Ultimate Pleasure,* by Leonard Lueras. It can be found at almost every surf shop.

Sailboarding

One of the fastest growing water sports, both in Hawaii and around the world, is windsurfing. Technically called sailboarding, most people call this relatively new sport windsurfing, after the name of one of the most famous manufacturers of sailboards. A combination of surfing and sailing, the equipment is a rather large and stable surfboard mounted with a highly maneuverable sail. It may sound difficult, but most people find it slightly easier than surfing because you're mobilized by the wind and not at the mercy of the waves. You don't have to "read" the waves as well as a surfer, and like riding a bicycle, as long as you keep moving, you can hold your balance. Boards and lessons are available on all the major islands. Sailboards are slightly more expensive than surfboards to rent, but you should be in business for about $35.

Boogie Boards

If surfing or sailboarding are a bit too much for you, try a boogie board—a foam board about three feet long that you lie on from the waist up. With the help of flippers for maneuverability, you can get tremendous rides on boogie boards. You can learn to ride in minutes and it's much faster, easier, and more thrilling than bodysurfing. Boogie boards are for sale all over the islands and are relatively cheap. You can rent one from a dive or surf shop for $5-7, or buy your own for $80-350.

GOLF AND TENNIS

Golf

People addicted to chasing that little white ball around the links are going to be delighted with Hawaii. You can golf every day of the year on more than 80 golf courses scattered around the state. Many are open to the public and are built along some of the most spectacular scenery in the world, where pounding surf or flower-dappled mountains form the backdrop. You'll find everything from Lanai's nine-hole Cavendish Golf Course, where you put your money in an envelope on the honor system, to some of the most highly praised, exclusive, and exciting golf courses in the world. Master builders such as Robert Trent Jones and Jack Nicklaus have laid out links in the islands where major tournaments are yearly events. Fees range from as little as $10 for some little nine-holers up to $200 at the most exclusive resorts.

Municipal and public courses are open to everyone. Resort course cater to the public as well as to resort guests. Private courses are for members only and their guests, although some set aside a day or two a week for nonmembers. Military personnel and dependents, DOD personnel, and those who have access to military bases are welcome to golf at the military courses (only on Oahu). If you wish to golf at other than municipal or public courses, be sure to call ahead to verify accessibility. Many courses have pros and pro shops, most offer lessons. Many have driving ranges, some that are lighted. Virtually all have clubhouses with restaurants and lounges. Greens fees listed in the charts in the following island chapters are for non-Hawaii residents, and for civilians at military courses. Many courses offer reduced *kama'aina* rates, special time rates, and twilight hour rates, and summer specials. Be sure to ask about these rates as they often afford substantial savings. Some courses charge higher fees for non-U.S. residents. Military courses charge different greens fees for civilians than for military personnel, and the military fees differ depending upon rank.

Tennis

Tennis courts are found on every island of Hawaii and enjoyed by locals and visitors on a year-round basis. County courts, under the control and maintenance of Department of Parks and Recreation, are open to the public for free. Play is on a first-come, first-served basis, and limited to 45 minutes if there are people waiting. Weekends are often fairly busy, but it's relatively easy to get a court on weekdays. Court rules apply and only soft-sole shoes are allowed. Some hotel and private courts are also open to the public, where fees range from complimentary to about $12 for non-hotel guests. Most courts are of Laykold or plexi-pave asphalt. Many courts are lighted.

BICYCLING

Bicycling in Hawaii can be both fascinating and frustrating. The countryside is great, the weather is perfect, but for the most part, Hawaii is not as bicycle conscious as many places in the country. Few bicycle trails and bicycle lanes exist. Most roads are well paved and some have adequately wide shoulders. Others have no shoulders at all. While coastal roads are generally flat and offer suburb views, they are often heavily trafficked. Because of steep climbs, many mountain roads can challenge the most dedicated riders, but these offer grand vistas to those who persevere. Many roads are full of twists and turns and, while fun to bike, do not offer much sight distance for a vehicle coming up behind. Traffic in and around the Honolulu metropolitan area is heavy and riding a bicycle can be dicey. Traffic in small towns and out in the country is much less severe. Fortunately, there are many roads with little traffic, particularly on the Big Island, so bicycling can be very enjoyable and rewarding experience. Off road riders have some choice of trails but the number of trails is still small, with more found of the Big Island than anywhere else.

If you're planning on spending any length of time on a bicycle in Hawaii, you're probably better off bringing your own bike than renting. If you do rent a bicycle, instead of a delicate road bike, you might want to consider getting a **cruiser** or **mountain bike**, which will allow for the sometimes poor road conditions and open up the possibilities of off-road biking. Even experienced mountain bikers should be careful on off-road trails, which are often extremely muddy and rutted. While the roads are sometimes congested, peddling around is usually safe, and a fun way of seeing the sights. Always use a helmet, always lock your bike, and always take your bike bag.

You can take your bike with you interisland by plane, but it will cost about $20 one-way—just check it in as baggage. Bikes must be packed in a box or hard case, supplied by the owner. Handlebars must be turned sideways and the pedals removed or turned in. Bikes go space available only—usually not a problem, except, perhaps, during bicycle competitions. In addition, a release of liability for damage must be signed before the airline will accept the bike. If you plan ahead, you can send your bike the previous day by air freight. You can also take your bike on the interisland ferry between Maui and Lanai. It will cost you $10 each way, but you don't need to pack it.

Getting your bike to Hawaii from the Mainland will depend upon which airline you take. Some will accept bicycles as baggage traveling with you (approximate additional charge of $30) if the bikes are properly broken down and boxed in a bicycle box, while others will only take them as air freight, in which case the rates are exorbitant. Check with the airlines well before you plan to go or explore the possibility of shipping it by sea through a freight company.

For general information on biking in Hawaii, contact **Hawaii Bicycling League**, P.O. Box 4403, Honolulu, HI 96812-4403. This nonprofit organization promotes biking as recreation, sport, and transportation, encourages safe biking practices, conducts biking education, and advocates for biking issues. It publishes a monthly newsletter, *Spoke-n-Words,* filled with news of the organization's business, its bicycle safety program for kids, and rides that are open to the public, as well as current bicycle issues and sponsored bicycle competitions throughout the state. If you are a bicycle rider living in the islands or simply want a subscription to the newsletter, write for membership information. For mountain biking and trail information on all the major islands, pick up a copy of *Mountain Biking the Hawaiian Islands* by John Alford.

For additional information, have a look at the *Bicycle Regulations and Illustrated Safety Tips* booklet, put out by the Department of Transportation Services, City and County of Honolulu. Although written for the island of Oahu, the information is applicable to all the islands, except for a few minor details. On Oahu, pick up a copy at city hall or any satellite city hall and most bike shops. From the Neighbor Islands or if coming from outside the state, write or call for a copy: Bicycle Coordinator, City and County of Honolulu,

711 Kapiolani Blvd., Suite 1200, Honolulu, HI 96813, tel. (808) 527-5044. Also very informative for rules of the road and common sense biking tips is the *Rights and Responsibilities for Hawai'i's Bicyclists* booklet. This booklet and the *Bike Oahu* bicycle route map are available free from the State Bicycle/Pedestrian Coordinator, State Department of Transportation, 869 Punchbowl St., Honolulu, HI 96813, tel. (808) 587-2321, and may be available at city halls and tourist offices.

GONE FISHING

Hawaii has some of the most exciting and productive "blue waters" in all the world. You'll find a statewide "sport fishing fleet" made up of skippers and crews who are experienced professional anglers. You can also fish from jetties, piers, rocks, and the shore. If rod and reel don't strike your fancy, try the old-fashioned throw net, or take along a spear when you go snorkeling or scuba diving. There's nighttime torch fishing that requires special skills and equipment, and freshwater fishing in public areas. Streams and irrigation ditches yield introduced trout, bass, and catfish. While you're at it, you might want to try crabbing for Kona and Samoan crabs, or working low-tide areas after sundown hunting octopus, a tantalizing island delicacy.

Deep-Sea Fishing

Most game-fishing boats work the waters on the calmer leeward sides of the islands. Some skippers, carrying anglers who are accustomed to the sea, will also work the much rougher windward coasts and island channels where the fish bite just as well. Trolling is the preferred method of deep-sea fishing; this is usually done in waters of 1,000-2,000 fathoms (a fathom is six feet). The skipper will either "area fish," which means running in a crisscross pattern over a known productive area; or "ledge fish," which involves trolling over submerged ledges where game fish are known to feed. The most advanced marine technology, available on many boats, sends sonar bleeps searching for fish. On deck, the crew and anglers scan the horizon in the age-old Hawaiian tradition—searching for clusters of seabirds feeding on bait fish pursued to the surface by the huge and aggressive game fish. "Still fishing," or "bottom fishing" with hand lines, can yield some tremendous fish.

The Game Fish

The most thrilling game fish in Hawaiian waters is marlin, generically known as "billfish" or *a'u* to the locals. The king of them is the blue marlin, with record catches well over 1,000 pounds. There are also striped marlin and sailfish, which often go more than 200 pounds. The best times for marlin are during spring, summer, and fall. The fishing tapers off in January and picks up again by late February. "Blues" can be caught year-round, but, oddly enough, when they stop biting it seems as though the striped marlin pick up. Second to the marlin is tuna. *Ahi* (yellowfin tuna) is caught in Hawaiian waters at depths of 100-1,000 fathoms. It can weigh 300 pounds, but 25-100 pounds is common. There's also *aku* (skipjack tuna), and the delicious *ono*, which averages 20-40 pounds.

Mahimahi is another strong-fighting, deep-water game fish abundant in Hawaii. These delicious fish can weigh up to 70 pounds. Shore fishing and bait-casting yield *papio*, a jack tuna. *Akule*, a scad, (locally called *halalu*), is a smallish schooling fish that comes close to shore and is great to catch on light tackle. *Ulua* is a shore fish that can be found in tidepools. They're excellent eating, averaging two to three pounds, and are taken at night or with spears. *O'io* are bonefish that come close to shore to spawn. They're caught by bait-casting and bottom fishing with cut bait. Although bony, they're a favorite for fish cakes and *poki*. *Awa* is a schooling fish that loves brackish water. It can get up to three feet long and is a good fighter. A favorite for throw netters, it's even raised commercially in fishponds. Besides these there are plenty of goatfish, mullet, mackerel, snapper, sharks, and even salmon.

"Blue Water" Areas

One of the most famous fishing spots in Hawaii is the **Penguin Banks** off the west coast of Molokai and the south coast of Oahu. The "Chicken Farm" at the southern tip of the Penguin Banks has great trolling waters for marlin and mahimahi. The calm waters off the Waianae Coast of Oahu yield marlin and *ahi*. The Kona coast of the Big Island, with its crystal waters, is the most famous marlin grounds in Hawaii. Every year the **Hawaiian International Billfish Tournament** draws anglers from around the world to Kona. The marlin are found in 1,000 fathoms of water, but close in on the Kona coast you can hook *ono* and hand line for *onaga* and *kahala*. Maui fishermen usually head for the waters formed by the triangle of Maui, Lanai, and Kahoolawe where they troll for marlin, *mahi*, and *ono*, or bottom fish for snapper. Kauai has excellent fishing waters year-round, with *ono, ahi*, and marlin along the ledges. Large schools of *ahi* come to Kauai in the spring, and the fishing is fabulous with possible 200-pound catches.

Charter Boats

The charter boats of Hawaii come in all shapes and sizes, but all are staffed by professional, competent crews and captains with intimate knowledge of Hawaiian waters. Prices vary but expect to spend $85-150 on a share basis. The average number of fishermen per boat is six, and most boats rent all day for $750. You can also arrange half days, and bigger boats with more anglers can cost as little as $50 per person. Tackle weighing 30-130 pounds is carried on the boats and is part of the service. Oftentimes soft drinks are supplied, but usually you carry your own lunch. It is customary for the crew to be given any fish that are caught, but naturally this doesn't apply to trophy fish; the crew is also glad to cut off steaks and fillets for your personal use. Honolulu's Kewalo Basin, only a few minutes from Waikiki, has the largest fleet of charter boats. Pokai Bay also has a fleet, and many charter boats sail out of Kaneohe Bay. On the Big Island, Kailua-Kona has the largest concentration of charter boats, with some boats out of Kawaihae. Maui boats come out of Lahaina or Maalaea Bay. Molokai has a few boats berthed at Kaunakakai, and on Kauai most boats sail out of Nawiliwili Harbor.

Freshwater Fishing

Due to Hawaii's unique geology, only a handful of natural lakes and rivers and a few reservoirs are good for fishing. The state maintains four "Public Fishing Areas" spread over Kauai, Oahu, and Hawaii. None are found on Maui, Lanai, or Molokai. Public fishing areas include: on Oahu,

Wahiawa Public Fishing Area, a 300-acre irrigation reservoir primarily for sugarcane located near Wahiawa in central Oahu, and **Nuuanu Freshwater Fish Refuge: Reservoir no. 4,** located in the Koolau Mountains above Honolulu; on Kauai, **Koke'e Public Fishing Area,** located north of Kekaha, with 13 miles of stream, two miles of irrigation ditches, and a 15-acre reservoir offering only rainbow trout; and on Hawaii, **Waiakea Public Fishing Area,** a 26-acre estuarine pond within the city of Hilo.

Freshwater Fish and Rules

Hawaii has only one native freshwater game fish, the *'o'opu*. This gobie is an oddball with fused ventral fins. It grows to 12 inches and is found on all islands, especially Kauai. Introduced species include largemouth and smallmouth bass, bluegill, catfish, *tucunare*, oscar, carp, *pongee* (snakehead), and *tilapia*. The only trout to survive is the rainbow, found only in the streams of Kauai and the Big Island. The *tucunare* is a tough-fighting, good-tasting game fish introduced from South America, similar to the oscar, from the same region. Both have been compared to bass, but are of a different family. The *tilapia* is from Africa and has become common in Hawaii's irrigation ditches. It's a "mouth breeder" and the young will take refuge in their parents' protective jaws even a few weeks after hatching. The snakehead is an eel-like fish that inhabits reservoirs and is a great fighter. The channel catfish can grow to more than 20 pounds and bites best after sundown. There's also the carp, and with its broad tail and tremendous strength, it's the poor person's game fish. All of these species are best caught with light spinning tackle, or with a bamboo pole and a trusty old worm.

A license is needed for freshwater fishing only. A **Freshwater Game Fishing License** is good for one year, from July 1 to June 30. Licenses cost $7.50 for nonresidents, $3.50 for tourists (good for 30 days), $3.75 for residents over age 15 and military personnel and their dependents over age 15, $1.50 for children ages 9-15; they are free to senior citizens and children under age nine when accompanied by an adult with a license. You can pick up a license at sporting goods stores or at the Division of Aquatic Resources on each of the main islands. Be sure to ask for their *Hawaii Fishing Regulations* and *Freshwater Fishing in Hawaii* booklets. All game fish may be taken year-round, except trout. Trout, on Kauai only, may be taken for 16 days commencing on the first Saturday of August. Thereafter, for the remainder of August and September, trout can be taken only on Saturday, Sunday, and state holidays. Fishing is usually allowed in most State Forest Reserve Areas. Owners permission must be obtained to fish on private property.

HUNTING

Most people don't think of Hawaii as a place to hunt, but actually it's quite good. Seven species of introduced game animals and 15 species of game birds are regularly hunted. Not all species of game animals are open on all islands, but every island offers hunting. Please refer to the travel chapters for full details on hunting on particular islands.

General Hunting Rules

Hunting licenses are mandatory in order to hunt on public, private, or military land anywhere in Hawaii. They're good for one year beginning July 1 and cost $15 residents and servicemen, $95 nonresidents; free to senior citizens. Licenses are available from sporting goods stores and from the various offices of the Division of Forestry and Wildlife. This government organization also sets and enforces the rules, so contact them with any questions. Generally, hunting hours are from a half hour before sunrise to a half hour after sunset. Checking stations are maintained, where the hunter must check in before and after hunting.

Rifles must have a muzzle velocity greater than 1,200 foot-pounds. Shotguns larger than .20 gauge are allowed, and muzzleloaders must have a .45 caliber bore or larger. Bows must have a minimum draw of 40 pounds for straight bows, 35 pounds for a recurve, and 30 pounds for compounds. Arrows must be broadheads. The use of hunting dogs is permitted only for certain species of birds and game, and when dogs are permitted, only smaller caliber rifles and shotguns, along with spears and knives, may be used—no big bore guns/shotguns.

Hunters must wear orange safety cloth on front and back no smaller than a 12-inch square. Certain big game species are hunted only by lottery selection; contact the Division of Forestry and Wildlife two months in advance. Guide service is not mandatory, but is advised if you're unfamiliar with hunting in Hawaii. You can hunt on private land only with permission, and you must possess a valid hunting license. Guns and ammunition brought into Hawaii must be registered with the chief of police of the corresponding county within 48 hours of arrival.

Information

Hunting rules and regulations are always subject to change. Also, environmental considerations often change bag limits and seasons. Make sure to check with the State Division of Forestry and Wildlife for the most current information. Request *Rules Regulating Game Bird Hunting, Rules Regulating Game Mammal Hunting,* and *Hunting in Hawaii.* Direct inquiries to: Department of Land and Natural Resources, Division of Forestry and Wildlife Office, 1151 Punchbowl St., Honolulu, HI 96813, tel. (808) 587-0166; on Maui, 54 S. High St., Wailuku, HI 96793, tel. (808) 984-8100; on Hawaii, Box 4849, Hilo, HI 96720, tel. (808) 974-4221; on Lanai, P.O. Box 732, 911 Fraser Ave., Lanai City, HI 96763, tel. (808) 565-6688; on Kauai, 3060 Eiwa St., P.O. Box 1671, Lihue, HI 96766, tel. (808) 241-3444; on Molokai, P.O. Box 347, Kaunakakai, Molokai, HI 96748, tel. (808) 533-5019.

Game Animals

All game animals on Hawaii have been introduced. Some have adapted admirably and are becoming well entrenched, while the existence of others is still precarious. **Axis deer** originated in India and were brought to Lanai and Molokai, where they're doing well. The small herd on Maui is holding its own. Their unique flavor makes them one of the best wild meats. They're hunted on Lanai from mid-February to mid-May, by public lottery. **Feral pigs** are escaped domestic pigs that have gone wild and are found on all islands except Lanai. The stock is a mixture of original Polynesian pigs and subsequently introduced species. Hunted with dogs and usually killed with a spear or long knife, pig hunting is not recommended for the timid or tender-hearted. These beasts' four-inch tusks and fighting spirit make them tough and dangerous. **Feral goats** come in a variety of colors. Found on all islands except Lanai, they have been known to cause erosion and are considered a pest in some areas, especially on Haleakala. They're openly hunted on all islands, and when properly cooked, their meat is considered delicious. **Black-tailed deer** come from Oregon. Forty were released on Kauai in 1961; the herd is now stabilized at around 400 and they're hunted in October by public lottery. **Mouflon sheep** are native to Corsica and Sardinia. They do well on Lanai and on the windswept slopes of Mauna Loa and Mauna Kea, where they're hunted at various times, also by public lottery. **Feral sheep** haunt the slopes of Mauna Kea and Mauna Loa at 7,000-12,000 feet. They travel in flocks and destroy vegetation. It takes determination and a good set of lungs to bag one, especially with a bow and arrow. **Pronghorn antelope** on Lanai, **feral cattle** on the Big Island, and **rock walla-** **bies** from Australia, who now make their home on Oahu, are not hunted.

Game Birds

A number of game birds are found on most of the islands. Bag limits and hunting seasons vary, so check with the Division of Forestry and Wildlife for details. The **ring-necked pheasant** is one of the best game birds, and is found on all the islands. The **kalij pheasant** from Nepal is found only on the Big Island, where the **green pheasant** is also prevalent, with some found on Oahu, Maui, and Lanai. **Francolins,** gray and black birds from India and the Sudan, are similar to partridges. They are hunted with dogs on all islands and are great roasted. There are also **chukar** from Tibet, found on the slopes of all islands; a number of **quail,** including the Japanese and California varieties; **doves;** and the wild **Rio Grande turkey** found on all islands except Kauai and Oahu.

gray francolin

ARTS AND MUSIC

Referring to Hawaii as "paradise" is about as hackneyed as you can get, but when you combine it into "artists' paradise" it's the absolute truth. Something about the place evokes art (or at least personal expression) from most people. The islands are like a magnet: they not only draw artists to them, but they draw art *from* the artists. The list of literary figures who visited Hawaii and had something inspirational to say reads like a freshman survey in literature: William Henry Dana, Herman Melville, Mark Twain, Robert Louis Stevenson, Jack London, Somerset Maugham, Joaquin Miller, and of course, James Michener.

The inspiration comes from the astounding natural surroundings. The land is so beautiful yet so raw; the ocean's power and rhythm are primal and ever-present; the riotous colors of flowers and fruit leap from the deep-green jungle background. Crystal water beads and pale mists turn the mountains into mystic temples, while rainbows ride the crests of waves. The stunning variety of faces begging to be rendered suggests that all the world sent delegations to the islands. And in most cases it did! Inspiration is everywhere, as is art, good or bad.

Sometimes the artwork is overpowering in itself and in its sheer volume. Though geared to the tourist's market of cheap souvenirs, there is hardly a shop in Hawaii that doesn't sell some item that falls into the general category of "art." You can find everything from carved monkey-face coconut shells to true masterpieces. The Polynesian Hawaiians were master craftspeople, and their legacy still lives in a wide variety of woodcarvings, basketry, and weavings. The hula is art in swaying motion, and the true form is rigorously studied and taken very seriously. There is hardly a resort area that doesn't offer the "bump and grind" tourist's hula, but even these revues are accompanied by proficient local musicians. Nightclubs offer "slack key" balladeers; island music performed on ukuleles and on Hawaii's own steel guitars spills from many lounges.

Vibrant fabrics that catch the spirit of the islands are rendered into muumuu and aloha shirts at countless local factories. They're almost a mandatory purchase! Pottery, heavily influenced by the Japanese, is a well-developed craft at numerous kilns. Local artisans fashion delicate jewelry from coral and olivine, while some ply the whaler's craft of etching on ivory, called scrimshaw. There are fine traditions of quilting, flower art in lei, and street artists working in everything from airbrush to glass. The following is an overview; for local offerings please see **Shopping** in the travel chapters.

ARTS OF OLD HAWAII

Since everything in old Hawaii had to be fashioned by hand, almost every object was either a genuine work of art or the product of a highly refined craft. With the "civilizing" of the natives, most of the "old ways" disappeared, including the old arts and crafts. Most authentic Hawaiian art exists only in museums, but with the resurgence of Hawaiian roots, many old arts are being revitalized, and a few artists are becoming proficient in them.

Magnificent Canoes

The most respected artisans in old Hawaii were the canoe makers. With little more than a stone adze and a pump drill, they built canoes that could carry 200 people and last for generations—sleek, well proportioned, and infinitely seaworthy. The main hull was usually a gigantic koa log, and the gunwale planks were minutely drilled and sewn to the sides with sennit rope. Apprenticeships lasted for years, and a young man knew that he had graduated when one day he was nonchalantly asked to sit down and eat with the master builders. Small family-size canoes with outriggers were used for fishing and perhaps carried a spear rack; large oceangoing double-hulled canoes were used for migration and warfare. On these, the giant logs had been adzed to about two inches thick. A mainsail woven from pandanus was mounted on a central platform, and the boat was steered by two long paddles. The hull was dyed with plant juices and char-

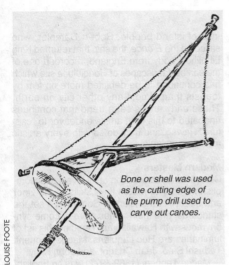

Bone or shell was used as the cutting edge of the pump drill used to carve out canoes.

LOUISE FOOTE

coal, and the entire village helped launch the canoe in a ceremony called "drinking the sea."

Carving and Weaving

Wood was a primary material used by Hawaiian craftsmen. They almost exclusively used koa because of its density, strength, and natural luster. It was turned into canoes, woodware, calabashes, and furniture used by the *ali'i*. Temple idols were also a major product of woodcarving. A variety of stone artifacts was turned out, including poi pounders, mirrors, fish sinkers, and small idols.

Hawaiians became the best basket makers and mat weavers in all of Polynesia. *Ulana* (mats) were made from *lau hala* (pandanus) leaves. Once split, the spine was removed and the leaves stored in large rolls. When needed they were soaked, pounded, and then fashioned into various floor coverings and sleeping mats. Intricate geometrical patterns were woven in, and the edges were rolled and well fashioned. Coconut palms were not used to make mats in old Hawaii, but a wide variety of basketry was made from the aerial root *'ie'ie*. The shapes varied according to use. Some baskets were tall and narrow, some were cones, others were flat like trays, while many were woven around gourds and calabashes.

A strong tradition of weaving and carving has survived in Hawaii, and the time-tested material

of *lau hala* is still the best, although much is now made from coconut fronds. You can purchase anything from beach mats to a woven hat, and all share the desirable qualities of strength, lightness, and ventilation.

Featherwork

This highly refined art was found only on the islands of Tahiti, New Zealand, and Hawaii, while the fashioning of feather helmets and idols was unique to Hawaii. Favorite colors were red and yellow, which came only in a very limited supply from a small number of birds such as the *'o'o*, *'i'iwi, mamo,* and *apapane*. Professional bird hunters in old Hawaii paid their taxes to *ali'i* in

The ali'i *wore magnificent feathered capes that signified their rank.*

prized feathers. The feathers were fastened to a woven net of *olona* cord and made into helmets, idols, and beautiful flowing capes and cloaks. These resplendent garments were made and worn only by men, especially during battle when a fine cloak became a great trophy of war. Featherwork was also employed in the making of *kahili* and lei which were highly prized by the noble *ali'i* women.

Tapa Cloth

Tapa, cloth made from tree bark, was common throughout Polynesia and was a woman's art. A few trees such as the *wauke* and *mamaki* produced the best cloth, but a variety of other types of bark could be utilized. First the raw bark was pounded into a feltlike pulp and beaten together to form strips (the beaters had distinctive patterns that also helped make the cloth supple). They were then decorated by stamping (using a form of block printing) and colored in shades of gray, purple, pink, and red with dyes made from plants and sea animals. They were even painted with natural brushes made from pandanus fruit, with an overall gray color made from charcoal. The tapa cloth was sewn together to make bed coverings, and fragrant flowers and herbs were either sewn or pounded in to produce a permanent fragrance. Tapa cloth is still available today, but the Hawaiian methods have been lost, and most comes from other areas of Polynesia.

First Western Artists

When Captain Cook made first contact in 1778, the ship's artists immediately began recording things Hawaiian. John Webber and James Clevely made etchings and pen-and-ink drawings of Hawaiian people, structures, *heiau*, and everyday occurrences that struck them as noteworthy or peculiar. William Ellis, ship's surgeon, also a fair hand at etching, was attracted to portraying native architecture. These three left a priceless and faithful record of what Hawaii was like at the moment of contact. Louis Choris, ship's artist with Otto Von Kotzebue in 1816, painted early portraits of King Kamehameha and Queen Kaahumanu, the two grandest figures in Hawaii's history. Jacques Arago, aboard the *Uranie* with the French Captain de Freycinet in 1819, recorded some gruesome customs of punishment of *kapu* breakers, and made many drawings of island people. Robert Dampier, who sailed on the *Blonde,* the ship that returned King Liholiho's body from England, recorded one of the earliest landscapes of Honolulu, a site which has continued to be depicted more on film by tourists than almost any other city on earth. These early artists set a trend that continues unabated to this day; artists endeavor to "capture" Hawaii, and they do so with every artistic medium available.

Modern Masters

Countless artists working at all levels of accomplishment try to match their skills to the vigor and beauty of the islands. Some have set the standards, and their names have become synonymous with Hawaiian art. Heading this list of luminaries are Huc Luquiens, Madge Tennent, Tadashi Sato, Jean Charlot, and John Kelly.

Madge Tennent (1889-1972) was an Englishwoman who came to Hawaii via Samoa after spending years in South Africa and New Zealand. She worked in oils that she applied liberally and in bold strokes. Enamored with the people of Hawaii, her portraits are of a race striking in appearance and noble in character. Her works, along with those of other island artists, are displayed at the Tennent Art Foundation, on the slopes of Punchbowl on Oahu.

Huc Luquiens, former chair of the art department at the University of Hawaii, was a master at etching, and was especially accomplished in drypoint. His works, mainly island landscapes, are displayed in the Hawaiiana Collection of the Honolulu Academy of Arts.

Maui-born Tadashi Sato, a superbly accomplished muralist, has produced such famous mosaics as the 30-foot *Aquarius* at the state capitol in Honolulu, and the 60-foot *Portals of Immortality* at the Maui Memorial Gymnasium in Lahaina.

Frenchman Jean Charlot perfected his mural art in Mexico before coming to Hawaii in 1949. He is renowned for his frescoes and became a well-known art critic and the grand old man of Hawaiian art. He died in 1979 at the ripe old age of 90. John M. Kelly was in love with Hawaiian women; his etchings of them are both inspired and technically flawless. Kelly was infinitely patient, rendering his subjects in the minutest detail.

These artists are the "Big Five of Hawaiian Art"; their accomplishments a gauge of what

Hawaii can inspire in an artist. By observing their works you can get an instant art course and a comparative view of the state of the arts in Hawaii.

Contemporary Artists

The crop of new artists making their marks always seems bounteous and their works, heavily influenced by the "feeling of Hawaii," continue to be superb. Every island has art galleries, co-ops, or unofficial art centers. One of the finest groups of island artists can be found along the "fence" of the Honolulu Zoo fronting Kapiolani Park. The following list of artists, with a short description of their work, is by no means exhaustive. It merely shows the wide range of artwork available.

Roy Tabora specializes in dramatic seascapes of windwhipped palm trees and crashing surf illuminated by glorious sunsets. His work is a dramatic crescendo of sea, surf, and spirit, entwined to capture the awesome power that is Hawaii.

James Hoyle, a longtime Kauai resident, captures the spirit of Hawaii through color and movement. His media are oil, pastel, and polymer that he applies on canvas in a distinctive style of macro-pointillism. The sense that permeates all of Hoyle's work is that in humankind cannot conquer nature, but must learn to live in harmony with the *aina*, which is very much alive.

Robert Nelson is a Maui artist who superbly transmits the integrated mystical life of land and sea. His watercolors are often diffused with the strange filtered light found beneath the waves. A conservationist, he has often depicted the gentle frolicking life of the whales that visit Hawaiian waters.

Bill Christian is a master of scrimshaw, which he renders on slate. He also produces fine oil paintings of the sea and old salts. A world-class artist, he has had his works displayed at art galleries on Maui as well as at the Smithsonian and at the New Bedford Massachusetts Whaling Museum.

Pegge Hopper is often compared with Madge Tennent. She works in bold colors and strokes. Her subject matter is islanders, especially the delicacy and inner strength of women. Her works are displayed at various galleries, particularly on Maui and Oahu, and are often available in limited-edition serigraphs.

Alapai Hanapi is a traditionalist sculptor who re-creates the motifs of his Hawaiian ancestors. He works in wood and stone with tools that he fashions himself. His driving force is cultural awareness and through his art he tells of the old ways. His work is known for its simplicity.

Al Furtado is a freelance artist working in Honolulu. He specializes in capturing the movement of Hawaiian dance. His depictions are often larger than life, with a strong sense of vitality and motion.

Daniel Wang was born in Shanghai, where he learned the art of Chinese watercolors. Although born deaf and mute, he speaks loudly, clearly, and beautifully through his art. Daniel has a special technique in which the palm of his hand becomes his artistic tool. He can transmit intense inner emotions directly from his body to the canvas.

The following is a potpourri of distinguished artists displayed at various galleries around the islands. Any work bearing their name is authentic island art considered superior by fellow artists. William Waterfall, photographer; Satoru Abe, sculptor; Ruthadell Anderson, weaver; Betty Tseng Yu-ho Ecke, *dsui* painter; Claude Horan, sculptor, ceramics; Erica Karawina, stained glass; Ron Kowalke, painter; Ben Norris, painter; Louis Pohl, printmaker; Mamoru Sato, sculptor; Reuben Tam, painter; Jean Williams, weaver; John Wisnosky, painter; and John Young, painter.

ARTS TO BUY

Wild Hawaiian shirts or bright muumuu, especially when worn on the Mainland, have the magical effect of making wearers "feel" like they're in Hawaii, while at the same time eliciting spontaneous smiles from passersby. Maybe it's the colors, or perhaps it's just the "vibe" that signifies "party time" or "hang loose," but nothing says Hawaii like alohawear does. More than a dozen fabric houses in Hawaii turn out distinctive patterns, and many dozens of factories creat their own personalized designs. These factories often have attached retail outlets, but in any case you can find hundreds of shops selling alohawear. Aloha shirts were the brilliant idea of a Chinese merchant in Honolulu, who used to hand-tailor them and then sell them to the tourists who arrived by ship in the glory days before WW II. They were an instant success. Muumuu or "Mother Hubbards" were the idea of missionaries, who were appalled by Hawaiian women running about au naturel and insisted on covering their new Christian converts from head to foot. Now the roles are reversed, and it's Mainlanders who come to Hawaii and immediately strip down to as little clothing as possible.

Alohawear

At one time alohawear was exclusively made of cotton or from manmade, natural fiber-based rayon, and these materials are still the best for any tropical clothing. Beware, however: polyester has slowly crept into the market. No material could possibly be worse for the island climate, so when buying your alohawear make sure to check the label for material content. Muumuu now come in a variety of styles and can be worn for the entire spectrum of social occasions in Hawaii. Aloha shirts are basically cut the same as always, but the patterns have undergone changes, and apart from the original flowers and ferns, modern shirts might depict an island scene in the manner of a silk-screen painting. A basic good-quality muumuu or aloha shirt starts at about $45 and is guaranteed to be worth its price in good times and happy smiles. The connoisseur might want to purchase *The Hawaiian Shirt, Its Art and History,* by R. Thomas Steele. It's illustrated with more than 150 shirts that are now considered works of art by collectors the world over.

Scrimshaw

This art of etching and carving on bone and ivory has become an island tradition handed down from the times of the old whaling ships. Although scrimshaw can be found throughout Hawaii, the

scrimshaw

center remains in the old whaling capital of Lahaina. Along Front Street are a few shops specializing in scrimshaw. Today, pieces are carved on fossilized walrus ivory that is gathered by Inuit and shipped to Hawaii. It comes in a variety of shades from pure white to mocha, depending upon the mineral content of the earth in which it was buried. Elephant ivory or whale bone is no longer used because of ecological considerations, but there is a "gray market" in Pacific walrus tusks. Inuit can legally hunt the walrus. They then make a few minimal scratches on the tusks, which technically qualifies them to be "Native American art" and free of most governmental restrictions. The tusks are then sent to Hawaii as art objects, but the superficial scratches are immediately removed and the ivory is reworked by artisans. Scrimshaw is made into everything from belt buckles to delicate earrings and even into coffee-table centerpieces. The prices can go from a few dollars up into the thousands.

Woodcarvings

One surviving Hawaiian art is woodcarving. Old Hawaiians used koa almost exclusively but koa is becoming increasingly scarce—though many items are still available—and costly. Milo and monkeypod are also excellent woods for carving and have largely replaced koa. You can buy tikis, bowls, and furniture at numerous shops. Countless inexpensive carved items such as hula dancers or salad servers are sold at variety stores, but most of these are imported from Asia or the Philippines and can be bought at any variety store.

Weaving

The minute you arrive in Hawaii you should shell out a few dollars for a woven beach mat. This is a necessity, not a frivolous purchase, but it definitely won't have been made in Hawaii. What is made in Hawaii is *lau hala.* This is traditional Hawaiian weaving from the leaves *(lau)* of the pandanus *(hala)* tree. These leaves vary greatly in length, with the largest more than six feet, and they have a thorny spine that must be removed before they can be worked. The color ranges from light tan to dark brown. The leaves are cut into strips from one-eighth- to one-inch wide and are then employed in weaving. Any variety of items can be made or at least covered in *lau hala*. It makes great purses, mats, baskets, and table mats.

Woven into a hat, it's absolutely superb but should not be confused with a palm-frond hat. A *lau hala* hat is amazingly supple and even when squashed will pop back into shape. A good one is expensive and with proper care will last for years. All *lau hala* should be given a light application of mineral oil on a monthly basis, especially if it's exposed to the sun. For flat items, iron over a damp cloth and keep purses and baskets stuffed with paper when not in use. Palm fronds also are widely used in weaving. They, too, are a great natural raw material, but not as good as *lau hala*. Almost any woven item, such as a beach bag, makes a good authentic yet inexpensive gift or souvenir. A wide selection is available in countless shops.

Gift Items
Jewelry is always an appreciated gift, especially if it's distinctive, and Hawaii has some of the most original. The sea provides the basic raw materials of pink, gold, and black corals that are as beautiful and fascinating as gemstones. Harvesting coral is very dangerous work. The Lahaina beds off Maui have one of the best black coral lodes in the islands, but unlike reef coral these trees grow at depths bordering the outer limits of a scuba diver's capabilities. Only the best can dive 180 feet after the black coral, and about one diver per year dies in pursuit of it. Conservationists have placed great pressure on the harvesters of these deep corals, and the State of Hawaii has created strict limits and guidelines on the firms and divers involved.

Pink coral has long been treasured by humans. The Greeks considered it a talisman for good health, and there's even evidence that it has been coveted since the Stone Age. Coral jewelry is on sale at many shops throughout Hawaii, its value determined by the color of the coral and the workmanship.

Puka shells (with small, naturally occurring holes) and *opihi* shells are also made into jewelry. Many times these items are very inexpensive, yet they are authentic and great purchases for the price. Hanging macrame planters festooned with seashells are usually quite affordable and sold at roadside stands along with shells.

Hawaii produces unique food items that are appreciated by many people. Various-size jars of macadamia nuts and butters are great gifts, as are tins of rich, gourmet-quality coffee, the only coffee produced in the United States. Guava, pineapple, passion fruit, and mango are often gift-boxed into assortments of jams, jellies, and spicy chutneys. And for that special person in your life, you can bring home perfumes and colognes in the exotic island fragrances of gardenia, plumeria, and even ginger. All of the above items are reasonably priced, lightweight, and easy to carry.

LANGUAGE OF THE LEI

The goddess Hiiaka is Pele's youngest sister, and although many gods are depicted wearing flower garlands, the lei is most associated with her. Perhaps this is because Hiiaka is the goddess of mercy and protection, qualities that the lei is deemed to symbolize. Hiiaka traveled throughout the islands destroying evil spirits wherever she found them. In the traditional translation of "The Song of the Islands" by Rev. Samuel Kapu, the last verses read, "We all call to you, answer us o Hiiaka, the woman who travels the seas. This is the conclusion of our song, o wreaths of Hawaii, respond to our call." A special day, May 1, is Lei Day in Hawaii. It started in 1928 as a project of Don Blanding, an island poet.

Hardly a more beautiful tradition exists anywhere in the world than placing a flower garland around the neck of someone special. The traditional time to give a lei is when someone is arriving or departing the islands, so every airport has lei sellers, mostly older women who have a little booth at the entrance to the airport. But lei are worn on every occasion, from marriages to funerals, and are equally apt to appear around the lovely neck of a hula dancer or as a floral hatband on the grizzled head of an old *paniolo*, or even draped around his horse's neck. In old Hawaii lei were given to the local *ali'i* as a sign of affection. When two warring chiefs sat together and wove a lei, it meant the end of hostilities and symbolized the circle of peace.

Lei Making
Any flower or blossom can be strung into a lei, but the most common are carnations or the love-

ly smelling plumeria. Lei, like babies, are all beautiful, but special lei are highly prized by those who know what to look for. Of the different stringing styles, the most common is *kui* —stringing the flower through the middle or side. Most "airport-quality" lei are of this type. The *humuhumu* style, reserved for making flat lei, is made by sewing flowers and ferns to a ti, banana, or sometimes *hala* leaf. A *humuhumu* lei makes an excellent hatband. *Wili* is the winding together of greenery, ferns, and flowers into short, bouquet-type lengths. The most traditional form is *hili*, which requires no stringing at all but involves braiding fragrant ferns and leaves such as *maile*. If flowers are interwoven, the *hili* becomes the *haku* style, the most difficult and most beautiful type of lei.

The Lei of the Land

Every major island is symbolized by its own lei made from a distinctive flower, shell, or fern. Each island has its own official color as well, though it doesn't necessarily correspond to the color of the island's lei.

The island of Hawaii's lei is made from the red (or rare creamy white or orange) *lehua* blossom. The *lehua* tree grows from sea level to 9,000 feet and produces an abundance of tufted flowers. The official color of Hawaii Island, like the lava from its active volcanoes, is red.

Kauai, oldest of the main islands, is represented by the *mokihana* lei and the regal color purple. The *mokihana* tree produces a small, cubelike fruit that smells like anise. Green when strung into Kauai's lei, the fruit turn a dark brown and keep their scent for months.

Maui is the pink island and its lei is the corresponding small pink rose called the *lokelani*. These flowers are not native, but were imported and widely cultivated at one time. In recent years they've fallen prey to a rose beetle and sometimes when they're scarce, a substitute *roselani* is used for Maui's lei.

Molokai is the silvery green island, and its lei is fashioned from the green leaves and small white flowers of the *kukui* tree. After it's shaped and polished, the *kukui* nut makes some of the most permanent and beautiful lei for sale in Hawaii. *Kukui* nut lei are quite common and make excellent gifts. Although not the official lei of any island, they could easily be the official lei representing all the islands.

Lanai has one of the most traditional forms of lei in Hawaii. Both its color and its lei are represented by the orange *kaunaoa*. This plant commonly grows along beaches and roadsides. Its orange, leafless stems are twisted into strands to form a lei.

Oahu, the color of the sun, is garlanded by the yellow *ilima*. This flower is reminiscent of the *'o'o* bird whose yellow feathers made the finest capes in Hawaii. The *ilima* often bears double yellow flowers and will infrequently produce a light red flower too rare to be used in lei.

Kahoolawe, the sacred island, is given the color gray and is represented by the silvery leaves and small, white, sweet-scented flowers of the *hinahina*. This heliotrope grows on sandy beaches just above the high-water mark, and is a very common plant throughout the Pacific.

Niihau, the Forbidden Island, is home to some of the last remaining pure-blooded Hawaiians, and takes the color white. The island's lei is the rare *pupu* shell. This white shell sometimes has brown spots and is less than one-half inch long. The shell was once the home of a mollusk that died on the offshore reef. These *pupu* lei, considered fine jewelry, fetch a handsome price. Very cheap facsimiles made of *pikake* shells are sold everywhere; most have been imported from the Cook and Society Islands of the South Pacific.

The last island is the semi-submerged volcano of Molokini, just off Maui's south shore. Molokini is represented by the very traditional lei made from *limu kala,* a brown, coarse seaweed with feathery spiny leaves that makes a boa-type lei.

Besides these island lei, two others must be mentioned. A lei made from *maile* is perhaps the most traditional of all. *Maile* is a green, leafy vine. Its stiff, bonelike inner stem is removed, leaving the leaves and pliable bark intact, which are then twisted into lei. They might be ordinary to look at, but they have a delicious smell that is Hawaii. *Maile* is often used in conjunction with flowers to make top-notch lei. *Lauae* is a common fern with large, coarse, shiny leaves. It is used to fluff out many lei and when bruised, the leaves have a mild scent of *maile*. Lei have one quality that is unsurpassed: they feel just as good to give as they do to receive.

HULA

The hula is more than an ethnic dance; it is the soul of Hawaii expressed in motion. It began as a form of worship during religious ceremonies and was only danced by highly trained men. It gradually evolved into a form of entertainment, but in no regard was it sexual. The hula was the opera, theater, and lecture hall of the islands all rolled into one. It was history portrayed in the performing arts. In the beginning an androgynous deity named Laka descended to earth and taught men how to dance the hula. In time the male aspect of Laka departed for the heavens, but the female aspect remained. The female Laka set up her own special hula *heiau* at Haena Point on the Na Pali coast of Kauai, where it still exists. As time went on women were allowed to learn the hula. Scholars surmise that men became too busy wresting a living from the land to maintain the art form. Most likely, it was the dance's swaying movements and primal rhythm that attracted the women. And once they began showing off what nature had bestowed upon them, what chief in his right mind was going to tell them to stop?!

Men did retain a type of hula for themselves called *lua*. This was a form of martial art employed in hand-to-hand combat that included paralyzing holds, bone-crunching punches, and thrusting with spears and clubs, which evolved into a ritualized warfare dance called *hula kui*. During the 19th century, the hula almost vanished because the missionaries considered it vile and heathen. King Kalakaua is generally regarded as saving it during the 1800s, when he formed his own troupe and encouraged the dancers to learn the old hula. Many of the original dances were forgotten, but some were retained and are performed to this day. Although professional dancers were highly trained, everyone took part in the hula. *Ali'i*, commoners, young, and old all danced. Early drawings by ships' artists like Arago, Choris, and Webber recorded hula scenes. Old folks even did it sitting down if their legs were too weak to perform some of the gyrations.

Hula Training

Only the most beautiful, graceful, and elegant girls were chosen to enter the hula *halau* (school). At one time, the *halau* was a temple in its own right and the girls who entered at the ages of four or five would emerge as accomplished dancers in their early teens to begin lifelong careers of the highest honor. In the *halau*, the *haumana* (pupils) were under the strict and total guidance of the *kumu* (teacher), and many *kapu* were placed upon them. The hula was a subordination of gross strength into a sublime coupling of grace and elegance. Once a woman became a proficient and accomplished dancer, her hula showed a personal, semi-spontaneous interpretation based upon past experiences. Today, *hula halau* are active on every island, teaching hula and keeping the old ways and culture alive. Performers still spend years perfecting their techniques. They show off their accomplishments during the fierce competition of the Merrie Monarch Festival in Hilo every April. The winning *halau* is praised and recognized throughout the islands.

The Special World of Hula

Hawaiian hula was never performed in grass skirts; tapa or ti-leaf skirts were worn. Grass skirts came to Hawaii from the Gilbert Islands, and if you see grass and cellophane skirts in a "hula revue," it's not traditional. Almost every major resort offering entertainment or a luau also offers a revue. Most times, young island beauties accompanied by local musicians put on a floor show for the tourists. It'll be fun, but it won't be traditional. A hula dancer has to learn how to control every part of her/his body, including facial expressions, which help set the mood. The hands are extremely important and provide instant background scenery. For example, if the hands are thrust outward in an aggressive manner, this can mean a battle; if they sway gently overhead, they refer to the gods or to creation; they can easily become rain, clouds, sun, sea, or moon. Watch the hands to get the gist of the story, though in the words of one wiseguy, "You watch the parts you like, and I'll watch the parts I like!" The motion of swaying hips can denote a long walk, a canoe ride, or sexual intercourse. Foot motion can portray a battle, a walk, or any kind of conveyance. The overall effect is multi-directional synchronized movement. The correct chanting of the *mele* is an integral part of the performance. These story chants, accompanied by musical instruments, make the hula very much like opera; it is especially similar in the way the tale unfolds.

Hula Music

Accompaniment is provided by chants called *mele* or *oli* and by a wide variety of instruments. The *ipu* is a primary hula instrument made of two gourds fastened together. It's thumped on a mat and slapped with the hand. In the background is the steady rhythm of the *pahu*, a large bass drum made from a hollowed coconut or breadfruit tree log, and covered with a sharkskin membrane. Hawaii's largest drum, it was sometimes placed on a pedestal and used in ceremonies at the *heiau*. The *uli uli* is a gourd or coconut filled with shells or pebbles and used like rattles, while *ili ili* are stones clicked together like castanets. The *punui* is a small drum made from a coconut shell half and beaten in counterpoint to the *ipu*. Oftentimes it was played by the hula dancer, who had it fastened to her body as a knee drum. The *puili* is a length of bamboo split at one end to look like a whisk, and struck against the body to make a rattling noise, while the *kaekaekee* and *kalau* are bamboo cut to various lengths and struck to make a rudimentary xylophonic sound. Two unique instruments are the *kupee niho ilio*, a dog's tooth rattle worn as an ankle bracelet by men only, now replaced by sea shells; and an *ohe hano ihu*, a nose flute of bamboo that accompanied chants. None of these instruments are actually necessary to perform a hula. All that's needed are a dancer and a chant.

THAT GOOD OLD ISLAND MUSIC

The missionaries usually take a beating when it's recounted how much Hawaiian culture they destroyed while "civilizing" the natives. However, they seem to have done one thing right. They introduced the Hawaiians to the diatonic musical scale and immediately opened a door to latent and superbly harmonious talent. Before the missionaries, the Hawaiians knew little about melody. Though sonorous, their *mele* were repetitive chants in which the emphasis was placed on historical accuracy and not on "making music." The Hawaiians, in short, didn't *sing*. But within a few years of the missionaries' arrival, they were belting out good old Christian hymns, and one of their favorite pastimes became group and individual singing.

Early in the 1800s, Spanish *vaqueros* from California were imported to teach the Hawaiians how to be cowboys. With them came guitars and moody ballads. The Hawaiian *paniolo* (cowboys) quickly learned how to punch cows and croon away the long lonely nights on the range. Immigrants who came along a little later in the 19th century, especially from Portugal, helped create a Hawaiian-style music. Their biggest influence was a small, four-stringed instrument called a *braga* or *cavaquinho*. One owned by Augusto Dias was the prototype of a homegrown Hawaiian instrument that became known as the ukulele. "Jumping flea," the translation of ukulele, is an appropriate name devised by the Hawaiians when they saw how nimble the fingers were as they "jumped" over the strings.

The Merry Monarch, King Kalakaua, and Queen Liliuokalani were both patrons of the arts who furthered the Hawaiian musical identity at the turn of the century. Kalakaua revived the hula and was also a gifted lyricist and balladeer. He wrote the words to "Hawaii Pono," which became the national anthem of Hawaii and later the state anthem. Liliuokalani wrote the hauntingly beautiful "Aloha Oe," which is often pointed to as the "spirit of Hawaii" in music. Detractors say that its melody is extremely close to the old Christian hymn, "Rock Beside the Sea," but the lyrics are so beautiful and perfectly fitted that this doesn't matter.

Just prior to Kalakaua's reign a Prussian bandmaster, Capt. Henri Berger, was invited to head the fledgling Royal Hawaiian Band, which he turned into a very respectable orchestra lauded by many visitors to the islands. Berger was open-minded and learned to love Hawaiian music. He collaborated with Kalakaua and other island musicians to incorporate their music into a Western format. He headed the band for 43 years until 1915, and was instrumental in making music a serious pursuit of talented Hawaiians.

Popular Hawaiian Music

Hawaiian music has a unique twang, a special feeling that says the same thing to everyone who hears it: "Relax, sit back in the moonlight, watch the swaying palms as the surf sings a lullaby." This special sound is epitomized by the bouncy ukulele, the falsettos of Hawaiian crooners, and the smooth ring of the "steel" or "Hawaiian" guitar. The steel guitar is a variation originated by Joseph Kekuku in the 1890s. Stories abound of how Joseph Kekuku devised this instrument; the most popular versions say that Joe dropped his comb or pocketknife on his guitar strings and liked what he heard. Driven by the faint rhythm of an inner sound, he went to the machine shop at the Kamehameha Schools and turned out a steel bar for sliding over the strings. To complete the sound he changed the cat-gut strings to steel and raised them so they wouldn't hit the frets. Voila!—Hawaiian music as the world knows it today.

The first melodious strains of **slack-key guitar** *(ki ho'alu)* can be traced back to the time of Kamehameha III and the *vaqueros* from California. The Spanish had their way of tuning the guitar, and played difficult and aggressive music that did not sit well with Hawaiians, who were much more gentle and casual in their manners.

Hawaiians soon became adept at making their own music. At first, one person played the melody, but it lacked fullness. There was no body to the sound. So, as one *paniolo* fooled with the melody, another soon learned to play bass, which added depth. But, a player was often alone, and by experimenting learned that he could get the right hand going with the melody, and at the same time could play the bass note with the thumb to improve the sound. Singers also learned that they could "open tune" the guitar to match their rich voices.

Hawaiians believed knowledge was sacred, and what is sacred should be treated with utmost respect—which meant keeping it secret, except from sincere apprentices. Guitar playing became a personal art form whose secrets were closely guarded, handed down only to family members, and only to those who showed ability and determination. When old-time slack-key guitar players were done strumming, they loosened all the strings so no one could figure out how they had them tuned. If they were playing, and some folks came by who were interested and weren't part of the family, the Hawaiians stopped what they were doing, put their guitars down, and put their feet across the strings to wait for the folks to go away. As time went on, more and more Hawaiians began to play slack key, and a common repertoire emerged.

An accomplished musician could easily figure out the simple songs, once they had figured out how the family had tuned the guitar. One of the most popular tunings was the "open G." Old Hawaiian folks called it the "taro patch tune." Different songs came out, and if you were in their family and were interested in the guitar, they took the time to sit down and teach you. The way they taught was straightforward—and a test of your sincerity at the same time. The old master would start to play. He just wanted you to listen and get a feel for the music—nothing more than that. You brought your guitar and *listened.* When you felt it, you played it, and the knowledge was transferred. Today, only a handful of slack-key guitar players know how to play the classic tunes classically. The best-known and perhaps greatest slack-key player was Gabby Pahinui, with The Sons of Hawaii. He passed away recently, but left many recordings behind. A slack-key master still singing and playing is Raymond Kane. Kane now teaches a handful of students his wonderful and haunting music. Not one of his students is from his own family, and most are *haole* musicians trying to preserve the classical method of playing.

Hawaiian music received its biggest boost from a remarkable radio program known as *Hawaii Calls.* This program sent out its music from the Banyan Court of the Moana Hotel from 1935 until 1975. At its peak in the mid-1950s, it was syndicated on more than 700 radio stations throughout the world. Ironically, Japanese pilots heading for Pearl Harbor tuned in island music as a signal beam. Some internationally famous classic tunes came out of the '40s and '50s. Jack Pitman composed "Beyond the Reef" in 1948; more than 300 artists have recorded it and it has sold well over 12 million records. Other million-sellers include: "Sweet Leilani," "Lovely Hula Hands," "The Crosseyed Mayor of Kaunakakai," and "The Hawaiian Wedding Song."

By the 1960s, Hawaiian music began to die. Just too corny and light for those turbulent years, it belonged to the older generation and the good times that followed WW II. One man was instrumental in keeping Hawaiian music alive during this period. Don Ho, with his "Tiny Bubbles," became the token Hawaiian musician of the '60s and early '70s. He's persevered long enough to become a legend in his own time, and his Polynesian Extravaganza at the Hilton Hawaiian Village packed visitors in until the early 1990s. He's now at the Waikiki Beachcomber. Al Harrington, "The South Pacific Man," until his recent retirement had another Honolulu "big revue" that drew large crowds. Of this type of entertainment, perhaps the most Hawaiian is Danny Kaleikini, still performing at the Kahala Mandarin, who entertains his audience with dances, Hawaiian anecdotes, and tunes on the traditional Hawaiian nose flute.

The Beat Goes On

Beginning in the mid-'70s islanders began to assert their cultural identity. One of the unifying factors was the coming of age of "Hawaiian" music. It graduated from the "little grass shack" novelty tune and began to include sophisticated jazz, rock, and contemporary rhythms. Accomplished musicians whose roots were in traditional island music began to highlight their tunes with this distinctive sound. The best embellish their arrangements with ukuleles, steel guitars, and traditional percussion and melodic instruments. Some excellent modern recording artists have become island institutions. The local people say that you know if the Hawaiian harmonies are good if they give you "chicken skin."

Each year special music awards, **Na Hoku Hanohano,** or Hoku for short, are given to distinguished island musicians. The following are recent Hoku winners considered by their contemporaries to be among the best in Hawaii. If they're playing while you're there, don't miss them. **Barney Isaacs and George Kuo** won Instrumental Album of the year for *Hawaiian Touch*. Na Leo Pilimihan *(Flying With Angels)* won Song of the Year, Album of the Year, Contemporary Album of the Year, and Group of the Year. **Robi Ka-**

ART AND CRAFT INFORMATION

Bishop Museum, 1525 Bernice St., Honolulu, HI 96817, tel. (808) 847-3511, is the world's *best* museum covering Hawaii and Polynesia. Features include exhibits, galleries, archives, demonstrations of Hawaiian crafts, and a planetarium. On the premises, Shop Pacifica has a complete selection of books and publications on all aspects of Hawaiian art and culture.

Hawaii Craftsmen, P.O. Box 22145, Honolulu, HI 96823, tel. (808) 596-8128, increases awareness of Hawaiian crafts through programs, exhibitions, workshops, lectures, and demonstrations.

Honolulu Academy of Arts, 900 S. Beretania St., Honolulu, HI 96814, tel. (808) 532-8700, collects, preserves, and exhibits works of fine art, as well as offering public art education programs related to its collections. Also offered are tours, classes, lectures, films, and a variety of publications.

Maui Arts and Cultural Center, P.O. Box 338, Kahului, HI 96733, tel. (808) 242-7469, website: www.maui.net/~macc, is a new center that focuses on the performing arts, presenting concerts, exhibitions, and educational programs.

Pacific Handcrafters Guild, P.O. Box 29389, Honolulu, HI 96820-1789, tel. (808) 254-6788, focuses on developing and preserving handicrafts and fine arts of all mediums. The guild sponsors four major crafts fairs annually.

State Foundation on Culture and the Arts, 44 Merchant St., Honolulu, HI 96813, tel. (808) 586-0300, website: state.hi.us/sfca, was begun by the State Legislature in 1965 to preserve and promote Hawaii's diverse cultural, artistic, and historical heritage. It manages grants and maintains programs in folk arts and art in public places.

hakalau's *Sistah Robi* earned Female Vocalist and Island Contemporary Album of the Year. "Friends in Me" won Single of the Year for **Brothers and Sister. Keali'i Reichel**'s *Lei Hali'a* was voted Popular Hawaiian Album of the Year (and the artist also won Male Vocalist of the Year and Favorite Entertainer of the Year). *Broken Hearts* earned **Darren Benitez** a Most Promising Artist of the Year award; **Sonny Kamahele** received a Lifetime Achievement Award; and **Ledward Ka'apana** is a Slack Key Award winner.

Past Hoku winners who have become renowned performers include: **Brothers Cazimero,** who are blessed with beautiful harmonic voices; **Krush,** who are highly regarded for their contemporary sounds; **The Peter Moon Band,** fantastic performers with a strong traditional sound; **Karen Keawehawai'i,** who has a sparkling voice and can be very funny when the mood strikes her; and **Henry Kapono,** formerly of Cecilio and Kapono, who keeps a low profile but is an incredible performer and excellent songwriter (his shows are noncommercial and very special). **Cecilio** is now teamed up with **Maggie Herron;** they are hot together and have a strong following in Honolulu. **The Beamer Brothers** are excellent performers, and can be seen at various nightspots. **Loyal Garner,** who was awarded Female Vocalist of the Year for *I Shall Sing,* is a truly wonderful artist. **Del Beazley** is a talented, energized performer. **Makaha Sons Of Niihau** are the best traditional Hawaiian band and shouldn't be missed. **Hawaiian Style Band** is known for *Vanishing Treasures,* a terrific album filled with contemporary music. **Bryan Kessler & Me No Hoa Aloha** perform songs like "Heiau," a haunting melody. **Susan Gillespie** and **Susi Hussong** are first-rate instrumentalists, and **Kealohi,** who recorded *Kealohi,* is very promising.

Other top-notch performers with strong followings are Ledward Kaapana; Mango; Oliver Kelly; Ka'eo; Freitas Brothers; Brickwood Galuteria, who won a double Hoku for Best Male Vocalist and Most Promising Artist; and Third Road Delite.

FESTIVALS, HOLIDAYS, AND EVENTS

In addition to all the American national holidays, Hawaii celebrates its own festivals, pageants, and ethnic fairs, and puts on a multitude of specialized exhibits. They occur throughout the year, some particular to only one island or locality, while others such as Aloha Week and Lei Day are celebrated on all the islands. Some of the smaller local happenings are semi-spontaneous, so there's no *exact* date when they're held. These are some of the most rewarding, because they provide the best times to have fun with the local people. At festival time, everyone is welcome. Check local newspapers and the free island magazines for exact dates of events. For additional events of all sorts throughout the state, visit the calendar of events listing on the HVB website: www.gohawaii.com.

Note: Island-specific festivals and events are listed in the individual island chapters below.

Statewide Events
Wesak or Buddha Day is on the closest Sunday to April 8, and celebrates the birthday of Gautama Buddha. Ornate offerings of tropical flowers are placed at temple altars throughout Hawaii. Enjoy the sunrise ceremonies at Kapiolani Park, Honolulu, with Japanese in their best *kimonos* along with flower festivals, pageants, and dance programs in many island temples.

May 1 is May Day to the communist world, but in Hawaii red is only one of the colors when everyone dons a lei for **Lei Day.** Festivities abound throughout Hawaii, but there are special goings-on at Kapiolani Park, Waikiki.

Agricultural exhibits, down-home cooking, entertainment, and fresh produce are presented for four weekends starting in late May at the **50th State Fair,** at Aloha Stadium, Honolulu.

King Kamehameha Day, June 11, is a state holiday honoring Kamehameha the Great, with festivities on all islands. Check local papers for times and particulars. The following are the main events: Oahu holds a lei-draping ceremony at the King Kamehameha statue at the Civic Center in downtown Honolulu, along with parades complete with floats and pageantry featuring a *ho'olaule'a* (street party) in Waikiki; Kailua-Kona on the Big Island is hospitable with a *ho'olaule'a,* parades, art demonstrations, entertainment, and contests; on Kauai enjoy parades, *ho'olaule'a*, arts, and crafts centered around the Kauai County Building; Maui's Lahaina and Kahului are decked out for parades and pageants.

The **Aloha Festival** is a two month long celebration (Sept.-Oct.) with more than 300 events on all of the islands, where everyone celebrates Hawaii's own "intangible quality," *aloha*. There are parades, luau, historical pageants, balls, and various entertainment. The spirit of *aloha* is infectious and all are welcomed to join in. The festival in 1998 was the 52nd year running. Check local papers and tourist literature for happenings near you. For information, call (800) 852-7690.

In order to promote cultural understanding and awareness among people of the different ethnic groups in the state, the **Hawaii International Film Festival,** screens some of the best films from the "East," "West," and Oceania at various theaters around the island during November. Seminars and workshops are also held. For information, call (808) 752-8193 or (800) 752-8193. (Website: www.hiff.org)

On **New Year's Eve** hold onto your hat, because they do it up big in Hawaii. Merriment and alcohol flow all over the islands. Firecrackers are illegal, but they go off everywhere. Beware of hangovers and "amateur" drunken drivers.

ACCOMMODATIONS

Hawaii's accommodations won't disappoint anyone. The state has an exceptionally wide range of places to stay with varieties both in style and in price. You can camp on a totally secluded beach three days down a hiking trail, have a dream vacation at one of the undisputed top resorts in the world, or get a package deal including a week's lodging in one of many island hotels for less than you would spend for a hotel at home. If you want to experience the islands as if you lived here, bed and breakfasts are becoming popular and easy to arrange. Condominiums are plentiful, and great for extended stays for families who want to set up home away from home, or for a group of friends who want to save money by sharing costs. There is a smattering of youth hostels, YM/WCAs, and home exchanges. If you're a student, a summer session at the University of Hawaii can mix education and fun.

Hawaii makes the greater part of its living from visitors, and all concerned desire to keep Hawaiian standards up and vacationers coming back. This means accommodations in Hawaii are operated by professionals who know the business of pleasing people. This adds up to benefits for you. Rooms in even the more moderate hotels are clean; the standard of services ranges from adequate to luxurious pampering. With the tips and advice given below, you should be able to find a place to stay that will match your taste and your pocketbook. For specifics, please refer to **Accommodations** in each of the travel chapters.

HOTELS

Even with the wide variety of other accommodations available, most visitors, at least first-timers, tend to stay in hotels. At one time, hotels were the only places to stay. Characters like Mark Twain were berthed at Kilauea's rude Volcano House, while millionaires and nobility sailed for Waikiki where they stayed in luxury at the Moana Hotel or Royal Hawaiian, which both still stand as vintage reminders of days past. Maui's Pioneer Inn dates from the turn of the century, and if you were Hawaii-bound, these and a handful that haven't survived were about all that was offered. Today, there are approximately 50,000 hotel rooms statewide, and every year more hotels are built and older ones renovated. They come in all shapes and sizes, from 10-room family-run affairs to high-rise giants. A trend turned some into condominiums, while the Neighbor Islands have learned an aesthetic lesson from Waikiki and built low-rise resorts that don't obstruct the view and that blend more readily with the surroundings. Whatever accommodation you want, you'll find it in Hawaii.

Types of Hotel Rooms

Most readily available and least expensive is a bedroom with bath, the latter sometimes shared in the more inexpensive hotels. Some hotels also offer a studio, a large sitting room that converts to a bedroom; a suite, a bedroom with sitting room; or an apartment with full kitchen plus at least one bedroom. Kitchenettes are often available and each contains a refrigerator, sink, and stove usually in a small corner nook or fitted together as one space-saving unit. Kitchenettes cost a bit more but save you a bundle by allowing you to prepare some of your own meals. To get that vacation feeling while keeping costs down, eat breakfast in, pack a lunch for the day, and go out to dinner. If you rent a kitchenette, make sure all the appliances work as soon as you arrive. If they don't, notify the front desk immediately, and if the hotel will not rectify the situation ask to be moved or for a reduced rate. Hawaii has cockroaches, so put all food away.

Amenities

All hotels have some of them, and some hotels have all of them. Air-conditioning is available in most, but under normal circumstances you won't need it. Balmy trade winds provide plenty of breezes, which flow through louvered windows and doors in many hotels. Casablanca-style room fans are better. TVs are often included in the rate, but not always. In-room phones are provided, but a service charge of up to 85 cents per call is often tacked on, even for local calls. Swimming pools are very common, even though the hotel may sit right on the beach. There is always a restaurant of some sort, a coffee shop or two, a bar, a cocktail lounge, and sometimes a sundries shop. Some hotels also offer tennis courts or golf courses either as part of the premises or affiliated with the hotel; usually an "activities desk" can book you into a variety of daily outings. Plenty of hotels offer laundromats on the premises, and hotel towels can be used at the beach. Bellhops get about $1 per bag, and

maid service is free, though maids are customarily tipped $1-2 per day, or a bit more if kitchenettes are involved. Parking is free and often valet parking is provided. Hotels can often arrange special services like baby-sitters, all kinds of lessons, and special entertainment activities. A few even have bicycles and snorkeling equipment to lend. They'll receive and send mail for you, cash your traveler's checks, and take messages. For your convenience, each room should be equipped with a directory of hotel service and information, and some hotels also include information about area sights, restaurants, and activities.

ACCOMMODATIONS PRICE RANGES
Budget: under $35
Inexpensive: $35-60
Moderate: $60-85
Expensive: $85-100
Premium: $110-150
Luxury: $150 and up

Hotel Rates: Add 10% Room Tax

Every year Hawaiian hotels welcome in the New Year by hiking their rates by about 10%. To give you an idea of price ranges (which don't change as quickly as actual prices) we've assigned categories to the accommodations listings: budget, under $35; inexpensive, $35-60; moderate, $60-85; expensive, $85-100; premium, $110-150, and luxury, $150 and up. Information on accommodations prices is meant to be a guide; the price you are quoted will depend on season and availability.

Hawaii, because of its gigantic tourist flow and tough competition, offers hotel rooms at universally lower rates than those at most developed resort areas around the world; so, even with the 10% room tax (six percent transient accommodations tax, plus four percent state excise tax), there are still many reasonable rates to be had. Package deals, especially to Waikiki, almost throw in a week's lodging for the price of an air ticket. The basic **daily rate** is geared toward double occupancy; singles are hit in the pocketbook. Single rates are cheaper than doubles, but never as low as half the double rate; the most you get off is 40%. **Weekly and monthly** rates will save you approximately 10% off the daily rate. Make sure to ask because this information won't be volunteered. Many hotels will charge for a double and then add an additional charge (often $12-40) for each extra person. Some hotels—not always the budget ones—let you cram in as many as can sleep on the floor for no additional charge, so again, ask. Others have a policy of **minimum stay,** usually three days, but their rates can be cheaper, and **business/ corporate rates** are usually offered to anyone who can at least produce a business card. Senior citizens are sometimes offered special discount rates of 10-20%. This information will usually not be offered so you must inquire.

Hawaii's **peak season** runs from just before Christmas until after Easter, and then again in early summer. Rooms are at a premium then, and peak-season rates are an extra 10% above the normal daily rate. Often, hotels will also suspend weekly and monthly rates during peak season. The **off-peak** season is in late summer and fall, when rooms are easy to come by and most hotels offer off-peak rates. Here, subtract about 10% from the normal rate.

In Hawaiian hotels you always pay more for a good view. Terms vary slightly, but usually "oceanfront" means your room faces the ocean and most of your view is unimpeded. "Ocean view" is slightly more vague. It could be a decent view, or it could require standing on the dresser and craning your neck to catch a tiny slice of the sea sandwiched between two skyscrapers. Rooms are also designated and priced upward as **standard, superior,** and **deluxe.** As you go up, this could mean larger rooms with more amenities or can merely signify a better view.

Plenty of hotels offer the **family plan,** which allows children under a certain age (often 17) to stay in their parents' room free, if they use the existing bedding. If another bed or crib is required, there is an additional charge. Only a limited number of hotels offer the **American plan,** in which breakfast and dinner are included with the night's lodging. Many hotels provide a mini-refrigerator and a coffee machine to make coffee and tea at no extra charge.

Paying, Deposits, and Reservations

The vast majority of Hawaiian hotels accept foreign and domestic traveler's checks, personal checks preapproved by the management, foreign cash, and most major credit cards. Reservations are always the best policy, and they're easily made through travel agents or by directly contacting the hotel. In all cases, bring documentation of your confirmed reservations with you in case of a mix-up.

Deposits are not always required to make reservations, but they do secure them. Some hotels require the first night's payment in advance. Reservations without a deposit can be legally released if the room is not claimed by 6 p.m. Remember, too, that letters "requesting reservations" are not the same as "confirmed reservations." In letters, include your dates of stay, type of room you want, and price. Once the hotel answers your letter, *confirm* your reservations with a phone call or follow-up letter and make sure that the hotel sends you a copy of the confirmation. All hotels and resorts have **cancellation requirements** for refunding deposits. The time limit on these can be as little as 24 hours before arrival, to a full 30 days. Some hotels require full **advance payment** for your length of stay, especially during peak season or during times of crowded special events. Be aware of the time required for a cancellation notice *before* making your reservation deposit, especially when dealing with advance payment. If you have confirmed reservations, especially with a deposit, and there is no room for you, or one that doesn't meet prearranged requirements, you should be given the option of accepting alternate accommodations. You are owed the difference in room rates if there is any. If there is no room whatsoever, the hotel is required to find you one at another comparable hotel and refund your deposit in full.

CONDOMINIUMS

Hawaii was one of the first states struck by the condominium phenomenon; it began in the 1950s and has increased ever since. Now condos are almost as common as hotels, and renting one is just about as easy. Condos, unlike hotel rooms, are privately owned apartments normally part of a complex or high-rise. The condo is usually an absentee owner's second or vacation home. An on-premises condo manager rents out vacant units and is responsible for maintenance and security.

Things to Know

Staying in a condo has advantages and disadvantages over staying in a hotel. The main qualitative difference between a condo and a hotel is amenities. At a condo, you're more on your own. You're temporarily renting an apartment, so there won't be any bellhops, and rarely a bar, restaurant, or lounge on the premises, though many times you'll find a sundries store. The main lobby, instead of having that grand entrance feel of many hotels, is more like an apartment house entrance, although there might be a front desk. A condo can be an efficiency (one big room), but most are one- or multiple-bedroom affairs with complete kitchens. Reasonable housekeeping items should be provided: linens, furniture, and a fully equipped kitchen. Most have TVs and phones, but remember the furnishings are provided by the owner. You can find brand-new furnishings that are top of the line, right down to "garage sale" bargains. Inquire about the furnishings when you make your reservations. Maid service might be included on a limited basis (for example, once weekly), or you might have to pay extra for it.

Condos usually require a minimum stay, although some will rent on a daily basis, like hotels. Minimum stays when applicable are often three days, but seven is also commonplace, and during peak season, two weeks isn't unheard of. Swimming pools are common, and depending on the "theme" of the condo, you can find saunas, weight rooms, jacuzzis, or tennis courts. Rates are about 10-15% higher than at comparable hotels. A nominal extra fee (usually $15-20) is charged for more than two people; condos can normally accommodate four to six guests. You can find clean, decent condos for as little as $200 per week, all the way up to exclusive apartments for well over $1,500. Their real advantage is for families, friends who want to share, and especially long-term stays for which you will always get a special rate. The kitchen facilities save a great deal on dining costs, and it's common to find units with their own washers and dryers. Parking space is ample for guests, and like hotels, plenty of stay/drive deals are offered. The method of paying for and reserving a condo is just about the same as for a hotel. However, requirements for deposits, final payments, and cancellation charges are much stiffer than in hotels. Make absolutely sure you understand these requirements when you make your reservations.

Hotel/Condominium Information

The best source of hotel/condo information is the Hawaii Visitors Bureau. While planning your trip, either visit one nearby or write to them in Hawaii. (Addresses are listed in the **Hawaii Visitors Bureau** section later in this chapter.) Request a copy of their free and current *Member Accommodation Guide*. This handy booklet lists all the hotel/condo members of the HVB, with addresses, phone numbers, facilities, rates, and general tips. Understand that these are not all of the hotels/condos in Hawaii, just members of HVB.

For condo booking agencies on the different islands, see the individual travel chapter introductions below.

BED AND BREAKFAST

Bed-and-breakfast (B&B) inns are hardly a new idea. The Bible talks of the hospitable hosts who opened the gates of their homes and invited the wayfarer in to spend the night. B&Bs have a long tradition in Europe and were commonplace in Revolutionary America. Nowadays, lodging in private homes called bed and breakfasts is fashionable throughout America, and Hawaii is no exception, with about 100,000 B&B guests yearly. Not only can you visit Hawaii, you can "live" there for a time with a host family and share an intimate experience of daily life.

Points to Consider

The primary feature of bed and breakfasts is that every one is privately owned, and therefore uniquely different from every other. The range of B&Bs is as wide as the living standards in America. You'll find everything from a semi-mansion in the most fashionable residential area to a little grass shack offered by a down-home fisherman and his family. This means that it's particularly important for the guest to choose a host family with whom his or her lifestyle is compatible.

Unlike at a hotel or a condo, you'll be living *with* a host (usually a family), although your room will be private, with private baths and separate entrances being quite common. You don't just "check in" at a B&B. You can make arrangements directly or you might want to go through agencies (listed below) which act as go-betweens, matching host and guest. Write to them and they'll send you a booklet with a complete description of the B&B, its general location, the fees charged, and a good idea of the lifestyle of your host family. With the reservations application they'll include a questionnaire that will basically determine your profile: Are you single? Do you have children? Smoker? etc., as well as arrival and departure dates and all pertinent particulars.

Since B&Bs are run by individual families, the times that they will accept guests can vary according to what's happening in their lives. This makes it imperative to write well in advance: three months is good; earlier is too long and too many things can change. Four weeks is about the minimum time required to make all necessary arrangements. Expect a minimum stay (three days is common) and a maximum stay. B&Bs are not long-term housing, although it's hoped that guest and host will develop a friendship and that future stays can be as long as both desire.

B&B Agencies

A top-notch B&B agency with more than 150 homes is **Bed and Breakfast Hawaii,** operated by Evelyn Warner and Al Davis. They've been running this service since 1978, and their reputation is excellent. B&B Hawaii has a membership fee of $10 yearly. For this they mail you their "Directory of Homes," a periodic "hot sheet" of new listings, and all pertinent guest applications; add $1 handling. Write Bed and Breakfast Hawaii, P.O. Box 449, Kapaa, HI 96746, tel. (808) 822-7771 or (800) 733-1632. (Website: www.planet-hawaii.com/bandb; e-mail: bandb @aloha .net).

One of the most experienced agencies, **Bed And Breakfast Honolulu Statewide,** at 3242 Kaohinanai Dr., Honolulu, HI 96817, tel. (808) 595-7533, 595-2030, or (800) 288-4666, owned and operated by Marylee and Gene Bridges, began in 1982. Since then, they've become masters at finding visitors the perfect accommodations to match their desires, needs, and pocketbooks. Their repertoire of guest homes offers more than 350 rooms, with half on Oahu and

the other half scattered around the state. When you phone, they'll match your needs to their computerized in-house guidelines. (Website: www.planet-hawaii.com/bnb-honolulu; e-mail: bnbshi@aloha.net).

Babson's Vacation Rentals and Reservation Service, 3371 Keha Dr., Kihei, Maui, HI 96753, tel. (808) 874-1166 or (800) 824-6409, is owned and operated by Ann and Bob Babson, a delightful couple who will try hard to match your stay with your budget. This is a statewide agency and accepts credit cards; car packages available.

Go Native Hawaii will send you a directory and all needed information if you write to them at 65 Halaulani Pl., P.O. Box 11418, Hilo, HI 96721, tel. (808) 935-4178 or (800) 662-8483.

All Island Bed and Breakfast, 463 Iliwahi Loop, Kailua, HI 96734, tel. (808) 263-2342 or (800) 542-0344, can match your needs up with about 700 homes throughout the state. (Website: planet-hawaii.com/all-island; e-mail: cac@aloha .net).

Run by Susan Campbell, **Hawaii's Best Bed and Breakfast,** P.O. Box 563, Kamuela, HI 96743, tel. (808) 885-4550 or (800) 262-9912, fax (808) 885-0559, is a smaller business but has listings all over the state. (Website: www.best-bnb.com; e-mail: bestbnb@aloha.net).

Hawaiian Islands Vacation Rentals, 1277 Mokulua Dr., Kailua, HI 96734, tel. (808) 261-7895 or (800) 258-7895, is owned and operated by Rick Maxey, who can arrange stays on all islands and help with inter-island flights and car rental.

Agencies specializing in beachfront villas, luxury condominiums, and exclusive estates are **Villas of Hawaii,** 4218 Waialae Ave., Suite 203, Honolulu, HI 96816, tel. (808) 735-9000; and **Vacation Locations Hawaii,** P.O. Box 1689, Kihei, HI 96753, tel. (808) 874-0077.

HOSTELS AND YM/WCA

While there are very few hostels in Hawaii, each of the four major islands has at least one, although only one is an official American Youth Hostel member. All are located in major towns and several are just a few blocks from the beach in Waikiki. These are basic accommodations that offer a common room, several bathrooms, bunk rooms, and a limited number of private rooms. Kitchens are usually available, as is long term storage. Each offers a number of other amenities that vary by place, that may include transportation to and/or from the airport, local excursions, low car rental rates, and free use of water equipment. European travelers, surfers, and backpackers make up the bulk of visitors. Generally, a bunk bed runs about $15 and private rooms $35-45.

YM/WCAs are quite limited in Hawaii—all with rooms are located in Honolulu. They vary as far as private room and bath are concerned, so each should be contacted individually. Prices vary too, but expect to pay $25 single. Men or women are accepted at respective Ys unless otherwise stated.

HOME EXCHANGES

One other method of staying in Hawaii, open to homeowners, is to offer the use of your home for use of a home in Hawaii. This is done by listing your home with an agency that facilitates the exchange and publishes a descriptive directory. To list your home and to find out what is available, contact one of the following agencies:

Vacation Exchange Club (Affiliate of Homelink, Int'l), P.O. Box 650, Key West, FL 33041, tel./fax (305) 294-1448 or (800) 638-3841. **Intervac U.S.,** P.O. Box 590504, San Francisco, CA 04159, tel. (415) 535-3497, fax (415) 435-7440. **Worldwide Home Exchange Club,** 806 Brantford Ave., Silver Spring, MD 20904, tel. (301) 680-8950.

FOOD AND DRINK

Hawaii is a gastronome's Shangri-La, a sumptuous smorgasbord in every sense of the word. The varied ethnic groups that have come to Hawaii in the last 200 years have each brought their own special enthusiasms and cultures—and lucky for all, they didn't forget their cookpots, hearty appetites, and taste buds.

The Polynesians who first arrived found a fertile but barren land. Immediately they set about growing taro, coconuts, and bananas, and raising chickens, pigs, fish, and dogs, though the latter were reserved for nobility. Harvests were bountiful and the islanders thanked the gods with the traditional feast called the luau. Most food was baked in the underground oven (imu). Participants were encouraged to feast while relaxing on straw mats and enjoying the hula and various entertainments. The luau is as popular as ever, and a treat that's guaranteed to delight anyone with a sense of eating adventure.

The missionaries and sailors came next and their ships' holds carried barrels of ingredients for puddings, pies, dumplings, gravies, and roasts—the sustaining "American foods" of New England farms. The mid-1800s saw the arrival of boatloads of Chinese and Japanese peasants, who wasted no time making rice instead of bread the staple of the islands. The Chinese added their exotic spices, creating complex Sichuan dishes as well as workers' basics like chop suey. The Japanese introduced shoyu (soy sauce), sashimi, boxed lunches (bento), delicate tempura, and rich, filling noodle soups. The Portuguese brought their luscious Mediterranean dishes of tomatoes and peppers and plump spicy sausages, nutritious bean soups, and mouthwatering sweet treats like malasadas (holeless donuts) and pao dolce (sweet bread). Koreans carried crocks of zesty kimchi and quickly fired up barbecue pits for pulgogi, a marinated beef cooked over a fire. Filipinos served up their delicious adobo stews—fish, meat, or chicken in a rich sauce of vinegar and garlic.

Recently, Thai and Vietnamese restaurants have been offering their irresistible dishes next door to restaurants offering fiery burritos from Mexico and elegant marsala cream sauces from France. The ocean breezes of Hawaii not only cool the skin but waft with them some of the most delectable aromas on earth, to make the taste buds thrill and the spirit soar.

Special Note

Nothing is sweeter to the appetite than reclining on a beach and deciding just what dish will make your taste buds laugh that night. Kick back, close your eyes, and let the smells and tastes of past meals drift into your consciousness. The following should help you decide exactly what you're in the mood for, and give you an idea of Hawaii's dishes and their ingredients. Particular restaurants and eateries will be covered in the travel chapters.

HAWAIIAN FOODS

Hawaiian cuisine, the oldest of the islands, consists of wholesome, well prepared, and delicious foods. All you have to do on arrival is notice the size of some of the local boys (and women) to know immediately that food to them is indeed a happy and serious business. An oft-heard island joke is that "local men don't eat until they're full, they eat until they're tired." Many Hawaiian dishes have become standard fare at a variety of restaurants, eaten at one time or another by anyone who spends time in the islands. Hawaiian food in general is called *kaukau,* cooked food is *kapahaki,* and something broiled is called *kaola.* All of these prefixes on a menu will let you know that Hawaiian food is served. Usually inexpensive, it will definitely fill you and keep you going.

Traditional Favorites
In old Hawaii, although the sea meant life, many more people were involved in cultivating beautifully tended garden plots of taro, sugarcane, breadfruit, and various sweet potatoes *(uala)* than with fishing. They husbanded pigs and barkless dogs *(ilio),* and prized *moa* (chicken) for their feathers and meat, but found eating the eggs repulsive. Their only farming implement was the *'o'o,* a sharpened hardwood digging stick. The Hawaiians were the best farmers of Polynesia, and the first thing they planted was taro, a tuberous root created by the gods at the same time as humans. This main staple of the old Hawaiians was pounded into poi. Every luau will have poi, a glutinous purple paste made from pounded taro root. It comes in liquid consistencies referred to as one-, two-, or three-finger poi. The fewer fingers you need to eat it, the thicker it is. Poi is one of the most nutritious carbohydrates known, but people unaccustomed to it find it bland and tasteless. Some of the best, fermented for a day or so, has an acidic bite. Poi is made to be eaten *with* something, but lo-

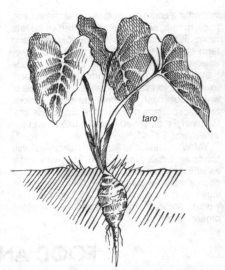

taro

cals who love it pop it in their mouths and smack their lips. Those unaccustomed to it will suffer constipation if they eat too much.

A favorite popular desert is *haupia,* a custard made from coconut. *Limu* is a generic term for edible seaweed, which many people still gather from the shoreline and eat as a salad, or mix with ground *kukui* nuts and salt as a relish. A favorite Hawaiian snack is *opihi,* small shellfish (limpets) that cling to rocks. Those who gather them always leave some on the rocks for the future. Cut from the shell and eaten raw by all peoples of Hawaii, *opihi* sell for $150 per gallon in Honolulu—a testament to their popularity. A general term that has come to mean "hors d'oeuvres" in Hawaii is *pu pu.* Originally the name of a small shellfish, it is now used for any finger food. A traditional liquor made from ti root is *okolehao.* It literally means "iron bottom," reminiscent of the iron blubber pots used to ferment it.

Pacific Rim (a.k.a. "Hawaiian Regional") Cuisine
At one time the "tourist food" in Hawaii was woeful. Of course, there has always been a handful of fine restaurants, but for the most part the food lacked soul, with even the fine hotels opting to offer second-rate renditions of food more ap-

propriate to large Mainland cities. Surrounded by some of the most fertile and pristine waters in the Pacific, you could hardly find a restaurant offering fresh fish, and it was an ill-conceived boast that even the fruits and vegetables lying limply on your table were "imported." Beginning with a handful of extremely creative and visionary chefs in the early 1980s, who took the chance of perhaps offending the perceived simple palates of visitors, a delightfully delicious new cuisine was born. Based upon the finest traditions of continental cuisine—including, to a high degree, its sauces, pastas, and presentations—the culinary magic of Pacific Rim boldly adds the pungent spices of Asia, the fantastic fresh vegetables, fruits, and fish of Hawaii, and, at times, the earthy cooking methods of the Southwest. The result is a cuisine of fantastic tastes, subtle yet robust, and satiating but health-conscious—the perfect marriage of fresh foods prepared in a fresh way. Now restaurants on every island proudly display menus labeled "Hawaiian Regional." As always, some are better than others, but the general result is that the "tourist food" has been vastly improved and everyone benefits. Many of these exemplary chefs left lucrative and prestigious positions at many of Hawaii's five-diamond hotels and opened signature restaurants of their own, making this fine food much more available and affordable.

Luau

Thick cookbooks are filled with common Hawaiian dishes, but you can get a good sampling at a well-done luau. The central feature is the *imu,* an underground oven. Basically, a shallow hole is dug and lined with stones upon which a roaring fire is kindled. Once the fire dies down and the stones are super-heated, the ashes are swept away and the *imu* is ready for cooking. At one time only men could cook in this fashion; it was *kapu* for women. These restrictions have long been lifted, but men still seem to do most of the pit cooking, while women primarily serve. The main dish at a luau is *kalua* pork. *Kalua* refers to any dish baked underground. A whole pig *(pua'a)* is wrapped in ti and banana leaves and placed in the pit's hot center. The pig's stomach cavity is filled with more hot stones; surrounding it are bundles of food wrapped in ti leaves. These savory bundles, *lau lau,* contain the side dishes:

fish, chicken, poi, sweet potatoes, breadfruit, and bananas. The entire contents are then covered with multiple layers of banana, ti, or sometimes ginger leaves, and a final coating of earth. A long tube of bamboo may stick from the *imu* so that water (for steam) can be added. In about four hours the coverings are removed and the luau begins. You are encouraged to recline on *lau hala* mats placed around the central dining area, although tables and chairs are usually provided. There are forks and plates, but traditionally it is proper to use your fingers and a sturdy banana leaf as a plate. Professional luau cooks pride themselves on their cooking methods and their food, and for a fixed price you can gorge yourself like an ancient *ali'i.* All luau supply entertainment, and exotic drinks flow like the tides. Your biggest problem after one of these extravaganzas will be finding the strength to rise from your *lau hala* mat.

Luau range in price but are generally about $55 per adult and half that for children. This price includes entertainment, and, when applicable, admission to the theme parks at which some are now presented. Most commercial luau are still put on by hotels, but many others are also very successful and well-regarded. Generally, luau run from about 5:30 to 8:30 p.m. On your luau day, eat a light breakfast, skip lunch, and do belly-stretching exercises! Luau food is usually served buffet-style, although some do it family-style. All luau have pretty much the same format, although the type of food and entertainment differ. The least expensive, most authentic, and best luau are often put on by local churches or community groups. They are not held on a regular basis, so make sure to peruse the free tourist literature where they advertise.

INTERNATIONAL DISHES

Chinese and Japanese cuisines have a strong influence on island cooking, and their well-known spices and ingredients are creatively used in many recipes. Other cuisines, such as Filipino, Korean, and Portuguese, are not as well known, but are now becoming standard island fare.

Chinese
Tens of thousands of fortune cookies yield their

little springs of wisdom every day to hungry diners throughout Hawaii. The Chinese, who came to Hawaii as plantation workers, soon discovered a brighter economic future by striking out on their own. Almost from the beginning, these immigrants opened restaurants. The tradition is still strong, and if the smallest town in Hawaii has a restaurant at all, it's probably Chinese. These restaurants are some of the least expensive, especially at lunchtime when prices are lower. In them, you'll find the familiar chop suey, chow mein, Peking duck, and fried rice. Takeout is common and makes a good, inexpensive picnic lunch.

Japanese
For the uninitiated, Japanese food is simple, aesthetically pleasing, and delicious. Sushi bars are plentiful, especially in Honolulu, using the freshest fish from local waters. Some common dishes include: teriyaki chicken, fish, or steak, which is grilled in a marinated *shoyu* (soy) sauce base; tempura, or mouth-size bites of fish and vegetables dipped in a flour and egg batter and deep fried; sukiyaki, or vegetables, meat, mushrooms, tofu, and vermicelli you cook at your table in a prepared stock kept boiling with a little burner, then dip the morsels into a mixture of egg and *shoyu; shabu shabu,* similar to sukiyaki though without noodles and with the emphasis on beef; *donburi,* (various ingredients on rice in a bowl), such as *ten donburi,* battered shrimp on rice; and various tofu dishes and miso soup, which provide some of the highest sources of nonmeat protein. Japanese restaurants span the entire economic range, from elegant and expensive to hole-in-the-wall eateries where the surroundings are basic but the food is fit for a samurai. Above all, cleanliness is guaranteed.

Filipino
Most people have never sampled Filipino food. This cuisine is spicy with plenty of exotic sauces. The following is a sampling found in most Filipino restaurants: *singang,* sour soup made from fish, shrimp, or vegetables, that has an acidic base from fruits like tamarind; *adobo,* a generic term for anything (chicken and pork are standards) stewed in vinegar and garlic; *lumpia,* a Filipino spring roll; *pancit,* many variations of noodles made into ravioli-like bundles stuffed

with pork or other meats; *lechon,* a whole suckling pig stuffed and roasted; *siopao,* a steam-heated dough ball filled with chicken or other tasty ingredients; and *halo halo,* a confection of shaved ice smothered in preserved fruits and canned milk.

Korean
Those who have never dined on Korean dishes are in for a sumptuous treat: *kalbitang,* a beef rib soup in a thin but tasty broth; *pulgogi,* marinated beef and vegetables grilled over an open flame; *pulkalbi,* beef ribs grilled over an open flame; *pibimbap,* a large bowl of rice smothered with beef, chicken, and vegetables that you mix together before eating; kimchi, fermented cabbage and hot spices made into a zesty "slaw"; *kimchi chigyae,* a stew of kimchi, pork, vegetables, and spices in a thick soup base.

TROPICAL FRUITS AND VEGETABLES

Some of the most memorable taste treats from the islands require no cooking at all: the luscious tropical and exotic fruits and vegetables sold in markets and roadside stands, or just found hanging on trees, waiting to be picked. Make sure to experience as many as possible. The general rule in Hawaii is that you are allowed to pick fruit on public lands, but the amount should be limited to personal consumption. The following is a sampling of some of Hawaii's best produce.

Bananas
No tropical island is complete without them. There are more than 70 species in Hawaii, with hundreds of variations. Some are for peeling and eating while others are cooked. A "hand" of bananas is great for munching, backpacking, or picnicking. Available everywhere—and cheap.

Avocados
Brought from South America, avocados were originally cultivated by the Aztecs. They have a buttery consistency and nutty flavor. Hundreds of varieties in all shapes and colors are available fresh year-round. They have the highest fat content of any fruit except the olive.

Coconuts

What tropical paradise would be complete without coconuts? Indeed, these were some of the first plants brought by the Polynesians. When a child was born, a coconut trees was planted to provide fruit for the child throughout his or her lifetime. Truly tropical fruits, coconuts know no season. Drinking nuts are large and green, and when shaken you can hear the milk inside. You get about a quart of fluid from each. It takes skill to open one, but a machete can handle anything. Cut the stem end flat so that it will stand, then bore a hole into the pointed end and put in a straw or hollow bamboo. Coconut water is slightly acidic and helps balance alkaline foods. Spoon meat is a custardlike gel on the inside of drinking nuts. Sprouted coconut meat is also an excellent food. Split open a sprouted nut, and inside is the yellow fruit, like a moist sponge cake. "Millionaire's salad" is made from the heart of a coconut palm. At one time an entire tree was cut down to get to the heart, which is just inside the trunk below the fronds and is like an artichoke heart except that it's about the size of a watermelon. In a downed tree, the heart stays good for about two weeks.

breadfruit

DIANA LASICH HARPER

Breadfruit

This island staple provides a great deal of carbohydrate, but many people find the baked, boiled, or fried fruit bland. It grows all over the islands and is really thousands of little fruits growing together to form a ball.

Mangos

These are some of the most delicious fruits known to humans. They grow wild all over the islands; the ones on the leeward sides of the islands ripen April-June, while the ones on the windward sides can last until October. They're found in the wild on trees up to 60 feet tall, and the problem is to stop eating them once you start!

Papaya

This truly tropical fruit has no real season but is mostly available in the summer. Papayas grow on branchless trees and are ready to pick as soon as any yellow appears. Of the many varieties, the "solo papaya," meant to be eaten by one person, is the best. Split them in half, scrape out the seeds and have at them with a spoon.

Passion Fruit

Known by their island name of *lilikoi,* passion fruit make excellent juice and pies. The small yellow fruit (similar to lemons but smooth-skinned) is mostly available in summer and fall. Many grow wild on vines, waiting to be picked. Slice off the stem end, scoop the seedy pulp out with your tongue, and you'll know why they're called "passion fruit."

Guavas

These small round yellow fruits are abundant in the wild, where they are ripe from early summer to late fall. They're considered a pest—so pick all you want. A good source of vitamin C, they're great for juice, jellies, and desserts.

Macadamia Nuts

The king of nuts was brought from Australia in 1882. Now it's the state's fourth largest agricultural product, producing 90% of the world's output. Available plain, roasted, candied, or buttered.

Litchi

Called nuts but really small fruit with thin red shells, litchi have sweet, juicy white flesh when fresh and appear nutlike when dried.

Other Fruit

Along with the above, you'll find pineapples, oranges, limes, kumquats, thimbleberries, and blackberries in Hawaii, as well as carambolas, wild cherry tomatoes, and tamarinds.

FISH AND SEAFOOD

Anyone who loves fresh fish and seafood has come to the right place. Island restaurants specialize in seafood, and it's available everywhere. Pound for pound, seafood is one of the best dining bargains in Hawaii. You'll find it served in every kind of restaurant, and often the fresh catch of the day is proudly displayed on ice in a glass case. The following is a sampling of the best.

Mahimahi

This excellent eating fish is one of the most common and least expensive in Hawaii. It's referred to as "dolphin," but is definitely a fish, not a mammal. Mahimahi can weigh 10-65 pounds; the flesh is light and moist. This fish is broadest at the head. When caught it's a dark olive color, but after a while the skin turns iridescent shades of blue, green, and yellow. It can be served as a main course, or as a patty in a fish sandwich.

A'u

This true island delicacy is a broadbill swordfish or marlin. It's expensive even in Hawaii because the damn thing's so hard to catch. The meat is moist and white—truly superb. If it's offered on the menu, order it. It'll cost a bit more, but you won't be disappointed.

Ono

Ono means "delicious" in Hawaiian so that should tip you off to the taste of this wahoo, or king mackerel. *Ono* is regarded as one of the finest eating fishes in the ocean, and its white, flaky meat lives up to its name.

Manini

These five-inch fish are some of the most abundant in Hawaii and live in about 10 feet of water. They school and won't bite a hook but are easily taken with spear or net. Not often on a menu, but they're favorites with local people who know best.

Ulua

This member of the crevalle jack family ranges 15-100 pounds. Its flesh is white and has a steaklike texture. Delicious and often found on menu.

Uku

This gray snapper is a favorite with local people. The meat is light and firm and grills well.

Ahi

A yellowfin tuna with distinctive pinkish meat, *ahi,* is a great favorite cooked or served raw in sushi bars.

Moi

This is the Hawaiian word for "king." This fish has large eyes and a sharklike head. Considered one of the finest eating fishes in Hawaii, it's best during the autumn months.

Seafood Potpourri

Other island seafood found on menus include *opihi,* a small shellfish (limpet) that clings to rocks and is considered one of the best island delicacies, eaten raw; *aloalo,* similar to tiny lobsters; crawfish, plentiful in taro fields and irrigation ditches; *ahipalaka,* albacore tuna; various octopuses and squid (calamari); and shark of various types.

A'ama are the ubiquitous little black crabs that you'll spot on rocks and around pier areas. They're everywhere. For fun, local fishermen try to catch them with poles, but the more efficient way is to throw a fish head into a plastic bucket and wait for the crabs to crawl in and trap themselves. The *a'ama* are about as big as two fingers and make delicious eating.

Limu is edible seaweed that has been gathered as a garnish since precontact times, and is frequently found on traditional island menus. There's no other seaweed except *limu* in Hawaii. Because of this, the heavy, fishy-ocean smell that people associate with the sea but which is actually that of seaweed is absent in Hawaii.

MUNCHIES AND ISLAND TREATS

Certain finger foods, fast foods, and island treats are unique to Hawaii. Some are meals in themselves, others are snacks. Here are some of the best and most popular.

Pu Pu

Pronounced as in "Winnie the Pooh Pooh," these are finger foods and hors d'oeuvres. They can be anything from crackers to cracked crab. Often, they're given free at lounges and bars and can even include chicken drumettes, fish kabobs, and tempura. At a good display of them you can have a free meal.

Crackseed
A sweet of Chinese origin, these are preserved and seasoned fruits and seeds. Favorites include coconut, watermelon, pumpkin seeds, mango, plum, and papaya. Distinctive in taste, they take some getting used to, but make great trail snacks. They are available in all island markets. Also look for dried fish (cuttlefish) on racks, usually near the crackseed. Nutritious and delicious, it makes a great snack.

Shave Ice
This real island institution makes the Mainland "snow cone" melt into insignificance. Special machines literally shave ice to a fluffy consistency. It's mounded into a paper cone and you choose from dozens of exotic island syrups is generously poured over it. Given a straw and a spoon, you just slurp away.

Malasadas and Pao Dolce
Two sweets from the Portuguese, *malasadas* are holeless doughnuts and *pao dolce* is sweet bread. Sold in island bakeries, they're great for breakfast or as treats.

Lomi Lomi Salmon
This salad of salmon, tomatoes, and onions with garnish and seasonings often accompanies "plate lunches" and is featured at buffets and luau.

MONEY-SAVERS

Only one thing is better than a great meal: a great meal at a reasonable price. The following are island institutions and favorites that will help you eat well and keep prices down.

Kaukau Wagons
These are lunch wagons, but instead of slick, stainless-steel jobs, most are old delivery trucks converted into portable kitchens. Some say they're a remnant of WW II, when workers had to be fed on the job; others say that the meals they

serve were inspired by the Japanese *bento,* a boxed lunch. You'll see these wagons parked along beaches, in city parking lots, or on busy streets. Usually a line of local people will be placing their orders, especially at lunchtime—a tip-off that the wagon serves delicious, nutritious island dishes for reasonable prices. They might have a few tables, but basically they serve food to go. Most of their filling meals are about $3.50, and they specialize in the "plate lunch."

Plate Lunch
One of the best island standards, these lunches give you a sampling of authentic island food that can include teriyaki chicken, mahimahi, *lau lau,* and *lomi* salmon among others. They're on paper or styrofoam plates, are packed to go, and usually cost less than $3.50. Standard with a plate lunch is "two scoop rice" and a generous dollop of macaroni or other salad. Full meals, they're great for keeping down food costs and for instant picnics. Available everywhere from *kaukau* wagons to restaurants.

Saimin
Special "saimin shops," as well as restaurants, serve this hearty, Japanese-inspired noodle soup. Saimin is a word unique to Hawaii. In Japan, these soups would be called *ramin* or *soba,* and it's as if the two were combined to saimin. A large bowls of noodles in broth, stirred with meat, chicken, fish, or vegetables, costs only a few dollars and is big enough for an evening meal. The best place to eat saimin is in a local hole-in-the-wall shop run by a family.

Buffets
Buffets are also quite common in Hawaii, and like luau are all-you-can-eat affairs. Offered at a variety of restaurants and hotels, they usually cost $12 and up. The food, however, ranges considerably from passable to quite good. At lunchtime, they're lower priced than dinner, and breakfast buffets are cheaper yet. Buffets are always advertised in free tourist literature, which often includes discount coupons.

Tips
Even some of the island's best restaurants in the fanciest hotels offer "early-bird specials"—the regular-menu dinners offered to diners who come

in before the usual dinner hour, which is approximately 6 p.m. You pay as little as half the normal price and can dine in luxury on some of the best foods. These specials are often advertised in free tourist booklets, which might also include coupons for two-for-one meals or limited dinners at much lower prices.

Many lounges and bars have a "happy hour," usually around sundown, where the price of drinks is reduced. Some also offer free *pu pu* during happy hour, and at the best, these *pu pu* could make a meal.

ISLAND DRINKS

To complement the fine dining in the islands, bartenders have been busy creating their own tasty concoctions. The full range of beers, wines, and standard drinks is served in Hawaii, but for a real treat you should try mixed drinks inspired by the islands. Most look very innocent because they come in pineapples, coconut shells, or tall

The coconut was very important to the Hawaiians and every part was used. A tree was planted when a child was born as a prayer for a good food supply throughout life. The trunks were used for building homes and heiau and carved into drums to accompany hula. The husks became bowls, utensils, and even jewelry. 'Aha, sennit rope braided from the husk fiber, was renowned as the most saltwater-resistant natural rope ever made.

frosted glasses. They're often garnished with little umbrellas or sparklers, and most have enough fruit in them to give you your vitamins for the day. Rum is used as the basis of many of them; it's been an island favorite since it was introduced by the whalers of last century. Here are some of the most famous: mai tai, a mixture of light and dark rum, orange curaçao, orange and almond flavoring, and lemon juice; chi chi, a simple concoction of vodka, pineapple juice, and coconut syrup—a real sleeper because it tastes like a milk shake; blue Hawaii, vodka and blue curaçao; planter's punch, light rum, grenadine, bitters, and lemon juice—a great thirst quencher; and Singapore sling, a sparkling mixture of gin and brandy with cherry and lemon juice.

Drinking Laws

There are no state-run liquor stores; all kinds of spirits, wines, and beers are available in markets and shops, generally open during normal business hours, seven days a week. The drinking age is 21, and no towns are "dry." Legal hours for serving drinks depend on the type of establishment. Hours generally are: hotels, 6 a.m.-4 a.m.; discos, and nightclubs where there is dancing, 10 a.m.-4 a.m.; bars and lounges where there is no dancing, 6 a.m.-2 a.m. Most restaurants serve alcohol, and in many that don't, you can bring your own.

Coffee

Kona coffee is the only coffee grown in the United States. It originates from the Kona District of the Big Island and it is a rich, aromatic, truly fine coffee. Within the past decade or so, coffee farms have been started on Maui, Molokai, and Kauai, and these operations have become large commercial concerns, surpassing in output the Big Island coffee companies.

DIANA LASICH HARPER

GETTING THERE

With the number of visitors each year more than six million—and double that number of travelers just passing through—the state of Hawaii is one of the easiest places in the world to get to . . . by plane. About half a dozen large U.S. airlines (and other small ones) fly to and from the islands. About the same number of foreign carriers, mostly from Asia and Oceania, also touch down on a daily basis. In 1978 airlines were "deregulated." In 1984, the reign of the Civil Aeronautics Board (CAB), which controlled exactly which airlines flew where and how much they could charge, ended. Routes, prices, and schedules were thrown open to free competition. Airlines that had previously monopolized preferred destinations found competitors prying loose their strangleholds. Thus, Hawaii is now one of the most hotly contested air markets in the world. The competition between carriers is fierce, and this makes for "sweet deals" and a wide choice of fares for the money-wise traveler. It also makes for pricing chaos. It's impossible to quote airline prices that will hold true for more than a month, if that long. But it's comforting to know that flights to Hawaii remain relatively cheap, and mile for mile are one of the best travel bargains in the industry. Familiarize yourself with the alternatives at your disposal so you can make an informed travel selection. Now more than ever, you should work with a sharp travel agent who's on your side.

When to Go

The prime tourist season starts two weeks before Christmas and lasts until Easter. It picks up again with summer vacation in early June and ends once more in late August. Everything is usually booked solid and prices are inflated. Hotel, airline, and car reservations, which are a must, are often hard to coordinate at this time of year. You can save 10-50% and a lot of hassling if you go in the artificially created "off-season," September to early December, and mid-April (after Easter) until early June. Recently, the reduction in numbers of tourist during the off-season has not been nearly as substantial as in years past, indicating the increasing popularity of the island at this time of year, but you'll still find the prices better and the beaches, trails, campgrounds, and even restaurants less crowded. The people will be happier to see you, too.

Airflight: The Early Years

On May 20-21, 1927, the people of the world were mesmerized by the heroic act of Charles Lindbergh, The Lone Eagle, as he safely piloted his sturdy craft, *The Spirit of St. Louis,* across the Atlantic. With the Atlantic barrier broken, it took only four days for Jim Dole, of pineapple fame, to announce an air race from the West Coast to Hawaii. He offered the same first prize of $25,000 that Lindbergh had claimed, and to sweeten the pot he offered $10,500 for second place. The **Dole Air Derby** applied only to civilian flights, though the military was already at work attempting the Pacific crossing.

In August 1925, a Navy flying boat took off from near San Francisco, piloted by Comdr. John Rodgers. The seaplane flew without difficulty across the wide Pacific's expanse, but ran out of gas just north of the Hawaiian Islands and had to put down in a stormy sea. Communication devices went dead and the mission was given up as lost. Heroically, Rodgers and his crew made crude sails from the wing's fabric and sailed the plane to within 12 miles of Kauai, where they were spotted by an incredulous submarine crew. On June 28, 1927, Army Lieutenants Maitland and Hegenberger successfully flew a Fokker trimotor land plane, *The Bird of Paradise,* from Oakland to Oahu in just under 26 hours.

On July 14, 1927, independent of the air derby, two indomitable pilots, Smith and Bronte, flew their *City of Oakland* from its namesake to a forced landing on the shoreline of Molokai. On August 16, 1927, eight planes lined up in Oakland to start the derby. The first to take off was the *Woolaroc,* piloted by Art Goebel and Bill Davis. It went on to win the race and claim the prize in just over 26 hours. Second place went to the appropriately named *Aloha,* crewed by Martin Jensen and Paul Schluter, coming in two hours behind the *Woolaroc.* Unfortunately, two planes were lost in the crossing and two more in the rescue attempt, which accounted for a total of 12 dead. However, the race proved that flying to Hawaii was indeed feasible.

WINGS TO HAWAII

There are two categories of airlines you can take to Hawaii: **domestic,** meaning American-owned, and **foreign**-owned. An American law, penned at the turn of the century to protect American shipping, says that "only" an American carrier can transport you to and from two American cities. In the airline industry, this law is still very much in effect. It means, for example, that if you want a roundtrip between San Francisco and Honolulu, you *must* fly on a domestic carrier, such as United or American. If, however, you are flying San Francisco to Tokyo, you are at liberty to fly a "foreign" airline such as Japan Air Lines, and you may even have a stopover in Hawaii, but you must continue to Tokyo or some other foreign city and cannot fly JAL back to San Francisco. Canadians have no problem flying Canadian Pacific roundtrip from Toronto to Honolulu because this route does not connect two American cities, and so it is with all foreign travel to and from Hawaii. Travel agents know this, but if you're planning your own trip be aware of this fact; if you're flying roundtrip it must be on a domestic carrier.

Kinds of Flights

The three kinds of flights are the "milk run," direct, and nonstop. Milk runs are the least convenient. On these, you board a carrier—say, in your home town—fly it to a gateway city, change planes and carriers, fly on to the West Coast, change again, and then fly to Hawaii. They're a hassle—your bags have a much better chance of getting lost, you waste time in airports, and to top it off, they're not any cheaper. Avoid them if you can.

On direct flights you fly from point A to point B without changing planes; it doesn't mean that you don't land in between. Direct flights do land usually once to board and deplane passengers, but you sit cozily on the plane along with your luggage and off you go again. Nonstop is just that, but can cost a bit more. You board and when the doors open again you're in Hawaii. All flights from the West Coast gateway cities are

nonstop, "God willing"—because there is only the Pacific in between!

Stopover Flights

All airlines that fly to Hawaii land at Honolulu, and a few fly nonstop to Maui, Kauai, and the Big Island. Major carriers have an interline agreement with island carriers, including Hawaiian Airlines and Aloha Airlines, for getting you to the Neighbor Islands from Honolulu, if one of those is your destination. This sometimes involves a plane change, but your baggage can be booked straight through.

Travel Agents

At one time people went to a travel agent the same way they went to a barber or beautician, loyally sticking with one. Most agents are reputable professionals who know what they're doing. They should be members of the American Society of Travel Agents (ASTA) and licensed by the Air Traffic Conference (ATC). Most have the inside track on the best deals, and they'll save you countless hours calling 800 numbers and listening to elevator music while on hold. Unless you require them to make very special arrangements, their services are free—they are paid a commission by the airlines and hotels that they book for you.

If you've done business with a travel agent in the past, and were satisfied with the services and prices, by all means stick with him or her. If no such positive rapport exists, then shop around. Ask friends or relatives for recommendations; if you can't get any endorsements go to the *Yellow Pages*. Call two or three travel agents to compare prices. Make sure to give all of them the same information and be as precise as possible. Tell them where and when you want to go, how long you want to stay, what class you want to travel, and any special requirements. Write down their information. It's amazing how confusing travel plans can be when you have to keep track of flight numbers, times, prices, and all the preparation information. When you compare, don't look only for the cheapest price. Check for convenience in flights, amenities of hotels, and any other fringe benefits that might be included. Then make your choice of agents, and if he or she is willing to give you individualized service, stick with that agent from then on.

Agents become accustomed to offering the same deals to many clients because they're familiar with the arrangements and because the deals have worked well in the past. Sometimes these are indeed the best, but if they don't suit you, don't be railroaded into accepting them. Any good agent will work with you. After all, it's your trip and your money.

Package Tours

For the independent traveler, practical package deals that include only flight, car, and lodging are okay. Agents put these together all the time and they just might be the best, but if they don't suit you, make arrangements separately. A package *tour* is totally different. On these you get your hand held by an escort, eat where they want you to eat, go where they want you to go, and watch Hawaii slide by your bus window. For some people, especially groups, this might be the way to do it, but everyone else should avoid the package tour. You'll see Hawaii best on your own, and if you want a tour you can arrange one there, often cheaper. Once arrangements have been made with your travel agent, make sure to take all receipts and letters of confirmation (hotel, car) with you to Hawaii. They probably won't be needed, but if they are, nothing will work better in getting results.

Mainland and International Fares

There are many categories of airline fares, but only three apply to the average traveler: first class, coach, and excursion (APEX). Traveling **first class** seats you in the front of the plane, gives you free drinks and movie headsets, a wider choice of meals, more leg room, and access to VIP lounges, if they exist. There are no restrictions, no penalties for advance-booking cancellations or rebooking of return flights, and no minimum-stay requirements.

Coach, the way that most people fly, is totally adequate. You sit in the plane's main compartment behind first class. Your seats are comfortable, but you don't have as much leg room or as wide a choice of meals. Movie headsets and drinks cost you a few dollars, but that's about it. Coach offers many of the same benefits of first class and costs about 30% less. You can buy tickets up until takeoff; you have no restrictions on minimum or maximum stays; you re-

ceive liberal stopover privileges; and you can cash in your return ticket or change your return date with no penalties.

Excursion or advance payment excursion (APEX) fares are the cheapest. You are accommodated on the plane exactly the same as if you were flying coach. There are, however, some restrictions. You must book and pay for your ticket in advance (usually 7-14 days). At the same time, you must book your return flight, and under most circumstances you can't change either without paying a penalty. Also, your stopovers are severely limited and you will have a minimum/maximum stay period. Only a limited number of seats on any one plane are set aside for APEX fares, so book as early as you can. Also, if you must change travel plans, you can go to the airport and get on as a standby passenger using a discounted ticket, even if the airline doesn't have an official standby policy. There's always the risk that you won't get on, but you do have a chance, as well as priority over an actual standby customer.

Standby is exactly what its name implies: you go to the airport and wait around to see if any flights going to Hawaii have an empty seat. You can save some money, but you cannot have a firm itinerary or limited time. Since Hawaii is such a popular destination, standbys can wait days before catching a plane.

Charters

Charter flights were at one time only for groups or organizations that had memberships in travel clubs. Now they're open to the general public. A charter flight is an entire plane or a block of seats purchased at a quantity discount by a charter company and then sold to customers. Because they are bought at wholesale prices, charter fares can be the cheapest available. As in package deals, only take a charter flight if it is a "fly only," or perhaps includes a car. You don't need one that includes a guide and a bus. Most importantly, make sure that the charter company is reputable. They should belong to the same organizations (ASTA and ATC) as most travel agents. If not, check them out at the local chamber of commerce.

More restrictions apply to charters than to any other flights. You must pay in advance. If you cancel after a designated time, you can be penalized severely or lose your money entirely. You cannot change departure or return dates and times. However, up to 10 days before departure the charter company is legally able to cancel, raise the price by 10%, or change time and dates. They must return your money if cancellation occurs, or if changed arrangements are unacceptable to you. Mostly they are on the up-and-up and flights go smoothly, but there are horror stories. Be careful. Be wise. Investigate!

Tips

Flights from the West Coast take about five hours; you gain two hours over Pacific standard time when you land in Hawaii. From the East Coast it takes about 11 hours and you gain five hours over eastern standard time. Flights from Japan take about seven hours and there is a five-hour difference between the time zones. Travel time between Sydney, Australia, or Auckland, New Zealand, and Hawaii is about nine hours. They are ahead of Hawaii time by 20 and 22 hours, respectively. Try to fly Mon.-Thurs., when flights are cheaper and easier to book. Pay for your ticket as soon as your plans are firm. If prices go up there is no charge is added, but merely booking doesn't guarantee the lowest price. Make sure the airlines, hotels, and car agencies get your phone number too—not only your travel agent's—in case any problems with availability arise (travel agents are often closed on weekends). It's not necessary, but it's a good idea to call and reconfirm flights 24-72 hours in advance.

First-row (bulkhead) seats are good for people who need more leg room, but bad for watching the movie. Airlines will give you special meals (vegetarian, kosher, low cal, low salt) often at no extra charge, but you must notify them in advance. If you're "bumped" from an overbooked flight, you're entitled to a comparable flight to your destination within one hour. If more than an hour elapses, you get denied-boarding compensation, which goes up proportionally with the amount of time you're held up. Sometimes this is cash or a voucher for another flight to be used in the future. You don't have to accept what an airline offers on the spot, if you feel they aren't being fair.

Traveling with Children

Fares for children ages 2-12 are 50% of the adult fare; children under two not occupying a seat travel free. If you're traveling with an infant or active toddler, book your flight well in advance and request the bulkhead seat or first row in any section and a bassinet if available. Many carriers have fold-down cribs with restraints for baby's safety and comfort. Toddlers appreciate the extra space provided by the front-row seats. Be sure to reconfirm, and arrive early to ensure this special seating. On long flights you'll be glad you took these extra pains.

Although most airlines have coloring books, puppets, etc., to keep your child busy, it's always a good idea to bring your own. These can make the difference between a pleasant flight and a harried ordeal. Also, remember to bring baby bottles, formula, diapers, and other necessities, as many airlines may not be equipped with exactly what you need. Make all inquiries ahead of time so you're not caught unprepared.

Baggage

You are allowed two free pieces of checked—one large, the other small—and a carry-on bag. The two checked pieces can weigh up to 70 pounds each; an extra charge is levied for extra weight. The larger bag can have an overall added dimension (height plus width plus length) of 62 inches; the smaller, 55 inches. Your carry-on must fit under your seat or in the overhead storage compartment. Purses and camera bags are not counted as carry-ons and may be taken aboard. Surfboards and bicycles are about $15 extra. Although they make great mementos, remove all previous baggage tags from your luggage; they can confuse handlers. Attach a sturdy holder with your name and address on the handle, or use a stick-on label on the bag itself. Put your name and address inside the bag, and the address where you'll be staying in Hawaii if possible. Carry your cosmetics, identification, money, prescriptions, tickets, reservations, change of underwear, camera equipment, and perhaps a change of shirt or blouse in your carry-on.

Visas

Entering Hawaii is like entering anywhere else in the U.S. Foreign nationals must have a current passport and proper visa, an ongoing or return air ticket, and sufficient funds for the proposed stay in Hawaii. Canadians do not need a visa or passport, but must have proper identification such as passport, driver's license, or birth certificate.

Agricultural Inspection

Everyone visiting Hawaii must fill out a "Plant and Animal Inspection Form" and present it to the appropriate official upon arrival in the state. Anyone carrying any of the listed items must have these items inspected by an agricultural inspection agent at the airport.

Remember that before you leave Hawaii for the Mainland, all of your bags are again subject to an agricultural inspection, a usually painless procedure taking only a minute or two. To facilitate your departure, leave all bags unlocked until after inspection. There are no restrictions on beach sand from below the high water line, coconuts, pre-packaged sugarcane, dried flower arrangements, fresh flower lei, pineapples, certified pest-free plants, seashells, seed lei, and wood roses. However, avocado, litchi, and papaya must be treated before departure. Some other restricted items are berries, fresh gardenias, roses, jade plants, live insects, snails, cotton, plants in soil, soil itself, and sugarcane. Raw sugarcane is okay, however, if it is cut between the nodes, has the outer covering peeled off, and is split into fourths. For any questions pertaining to plants that you want to take to the Mainland, call the Agricultural Quarantine Inspection office on any island before your planned departure.

DOMESTIC CARRIERS

The following are the major domestic carriers to and from Hawaii. The planes used are primarily DC-10s and 747s, with a smaller 727 flown now and again. A list of the "gateway cities" from which they fly direct and nonstop flights is given, but "connecting cities" are not. All flights, by all carriers, land at Honolulu International Airport except the limited direct flights to Maui, Hawaii, and Kauai. Only the established companies are listed. Entrepreneurial small airlines such as the defunct Hawaii Express pop up now and again and specialize in dirt-cheap fares. There is a hectic frenzy to buy their tickets, and business is great for a while, but then the established companies lower their fares and the gamblers fold.

Hawaiian Airlines

One of Hawaii's own domestic airlines has entered the Mainland market. They operate a daily flight from Los Angeles, San Francisco, Las Vegas, Seattle, and Portland to Honolulu; four weekly flights from San Francisco and Seattle to Kahului, Maui; with the addition of flights from Los Angeles to Maui and Los Angeles to Kona via Maui. The "common fare" ticket price includes an ongoing flight to any of the Neighbor Islands, and if you're leaving Hawaii, a free flight from a Neighbor Island to the link-up in Honolulu. Senior-citizen discounts for people age 60 or older are offered on trans-Pacific and interisland flights. Scheduled flights to the South Pacific run between Honolulu and Pago Pago twice a week and once a week to Papeete, Tahiti. Hawaiian Airlines offers special discount deals with Dollar rental cars and select major-island hotels. Contact Hawaiian Airlines at (800) 367-5320 Mainland and Canada, (800) 882-8811 in Hawaii.

United Airlines

Since their first island flight in 1947, United has become top dog in flights to Hawaii. Their Mainland routes connect more than 100 cities to Honolulu. The main gateway cities of San Francisco, Los Angeles, and Chicago have direct flights to Honolulu; flights from all other cities connect through these. They also offer direct flights to Maui from San Francisco and Los Angeles, from San Francisco and Los Angeles to Kona on the Big Island, and from Los Angeles to Lihue, Kauai. Continuing through Honolulu, United flights go to Tokyo, where connections can be made for other Asian cities. United offers a number of packages, including flight and hotel on Oahu, and flight, hotel, and car on the Neighbor Islands. They inter-line with Aloha Airlines and deal with Hertz rental cars. They're the "big guys" and they intend to stay that way—their packages are hard to beat. Call (800) 241-6522.

American Airlines

American offers direct flights to Honolulu from Los Angeles, San Francisco, Dallas/Fort Worth, and Chicago. They also fly daily from Los Angeles to Maui. Call (800) 433-7300.

Pan American Airlines, now out of business, opened Hawaii to mass air travel with this historic 19 hour and 48 minute flight on Wednesday, April 17, 1935.

Continental

Flights from all Mainland cities to Honolulu connect via Los Angeles, Newark, and Houston. Also available are direct flights from Guam to Honolulu. Call (800) 525-0280 or (800) 231-0856 for international information.

Northwest

Northwest flies to Honolulu from Los Angeles, San Francisco, Seattle, and Minneapolis. There are onward flights to Tokyo, Osaka, Nagoya, Manila, Guam, Bangkok, Singapore, Hong Kong, Taipei, and Seoul. Call (800) 225-2525.

Delta Air Lines

In 1985, Delta entered the Hawaiian market; when it bought out Western Airlines its share became even bigger. They have nonstop flights to Honolulu from Dallas/Fort Worth, Los Angeles, San Francisco, and Atlanta; and a direct flight to Kahului, Maui, from Los Angeles. Call (800) 221-1212.

FOREIGN CARRIERS

The following carriers operate throughout Asia and Oceania but have no U.S. flying rights. This means that in order for you to vacation in Hawaii using one of these carriers, your flight must originate or terminate in a foreign city. You can have a stopover in Honolulu with a connecting flight to

a Neighbor Island. For example, if you've purchased a flight on Japan Air Lines from San Francisco to Tokyo, you can stop in Hawaii, but you must then carry on to Tokyo. Failure to do so will result in a stiff fine, and the balance of your ticket will not be refunded.

Canadian Airlines International

Nonstop flights from Canada to Honolulu originate in Vancouver and Toronto. Canadian has an interisland agreement with Aloha Airlines for travel to the neighboring islands. Call (800) 426-7000 in the U.S. or (800) 665-7530 in Canada.

Air New Zealand

Flights link New Zealand, Australia, and numerous South Pacific islands to Honolulu, with continuing flights to Mainland cities. All flights run via Auckland, New Zealand. Call (800) 926-7255 or (800) 262-1234 in the U.S. and (800) 663-5494 in Canada for current information.

Japan Air Lines

The Japanese are the second-largest group, next to Americans, to visit Hawaii. JAL flights to Honolulu originate in Tokyo (Narita), Nagoya, and Osaka (Kansai), Hiroshima, Sapporo, Sendai, and Fukuoka. In addition, there are flights between Tokyo (Narita) and Kona on the Big Island. There are no JAL flights between the Mainland and Hawaii. Call (800) 525-3663.

Qantas

Daily flights connect Sydney with Honolulu; all other flights feed through this hub. Call (800) 227-4500.

China Airlines

Routes to Honolulu with China Airlines are from Taipei direct three times a week or through Tokyo five times a week, but all flights may not be available year-round. Connections in Taipei to most Asian capitals. Call (800) 227-5118.

Korean Air

Korean Air offers some of the least expensive flights to Asia. All flights to/from Honolulu go directly to Seoul. Connections to many Asian cities. Call (800) 438-5000.

Other Airlines

Aside from the above airlines, large volume charter operators book flights to the various island with such carriers as **Canada 3000, American Trans Air,** and **Rich International Air.**

TRAVEL BY SHIP

Some companies offering varied cruises include **P&O Lines,** which operates the *Sea Princess* through the South Pacific, making port at Honolulu on its way from the West Coast once a year.

Royal Cruise Line out of Los Angeles, or Auckland alternatively, sails the *Royal Odyssey,* which docks in Honolulu on its South Pacific and Orient cruise, $2,200-4,000.

The **Holland America Line** sails a year-long World Cruise, calling at Honolulu. Call (800) 426-0327.

Society Expeditions offers a 42-day cruise throughout the South Pacific departing from Honolulu. Fares range $3,000-9,000. Call (800) 426-7794.

Information

Most travel agents can provide information on the above cruise lines. If you're especially interested in traveling by freighter, contact **Freighter Travel Club of America,** P.O. Box 12693, Salem, OR 97309; or **Ford's Freighter Travel Guide,** P.O. Box 505, 22151 Clarendon St., Woodland Hills, CA 91367.

TOUR COMPANIES

Many tour companies advertise packages to Hawaii in large city newspapers every week. They offer very reasonable airfares, car rentals, and accommodations. Without trying, you can get roundtrip airfare from the West Coast and a week in Hawaii for $400-500 using one of these companies. The following companies offer great deals and have excellent reputations. This list is by no means exhaustive.

SunTrips

This California-based tour and charter company sells vacations all over the world. They're primarily a wholesale company, but will work with the general public. SunTrips often works with Rich International Air, tel. (305) 871-5113. When you receive your SunTrips tickets, you are given discount vouchers for places to stay that are convenient to the airport of departure. Many of these hotels have complimentary airport pick-up service, and will allow you to park your car, free of charge, for up to 14 days, which saves a considerable amount on airport parking fees. SunTrips does not offer assigned seating until you get to the airport. They recommend you get there two hours in advance, and they ain't kidding! This is the price you pay for getting such inexpensive air travel. SunTrips usually has a deal with a car-rental company. Remember that everyone on your incoming flight is offered the same deal, and all make a beeline for the rental car's shuttle van after landing and securing their baggage. If you have a traveling companion, work together to beat the rush by leaving your companion to fetch the baggage while you head directly for the van as soon as you arrive. Pick your car up, then return for your partner and the bags. Even if you're alone, you could zip over to the car-rental center and then return for your bags without having them sit very long on the carousel. Contact SunTrips, 2350 Paragon Dr., P.O. Box 18505, San Jose, CA 95158, tel. (800) 786-8747 in California, 941-2697 in Honolulu.

Council Travel Services

These full-service, budget-travel specialists are a subsidiary of the nonprofit Council on International Educational Exchange, and the official

U.S. representative to the International Student Travel Conference. They'll custom-design trips and programs for everyone from senior citizens to college students. Bona fide students have extra advantages, however, including eligibility for the International Student Identification Card (CISC), which often gets you discount fares and waived entrance fees. Groups and business travelers are also welcome. For full information, call (800) 226-8624, or write to Council Travel Services at one of these offices: 530 Bush St., San Francisco, CA 94108, tel. (415) 421-3473; or 205 E. 42nd St., New York, NY 10017, tel. (212) 661-1450. Other offices are in Austin, Berkeley, Boston, Davis, Long Beach, Los Angeles, Miami, Portland, San Diego, and Seattle.

Student Travel Network

STA Travel is a full-service travel agency specializing in student travel, regardless of age. Those under 26 do not have to be full-time students to get special fares. Older independent travelers can avail themselves of services, although they are ineligible for student fares. STA works hard to get you discounted or budget rates. STA's central office is at 7202 Melrose Ave., Los Angeles, CA 90046, tel. (213) 934-8722 or (800) 777-0112. STA maintains 39 offices throughout the U.S., Australasia, and Europe, along with **Travel Cuts,** a sister organization operating in Canada. Many tickets issued by STA are flexible, allowing changes with no penalty, and are open-ended for travel up to one year. STA also maintains **Travel Help,** a service available at all offices designed to solve all types of problems that may arise while traveling. STA is a well-established travel agency with an excellent and well-deserved reputation.

Nature Expeditions International

These quality tours have nature as the theme. Trips are 15-day, four-island, natural-history expeditions, with an emphasis on plants, birds, and geology. Their guides are experts in their fields and give personable and attentive service. Contact Nature Expeditions International at 6400 E. El Dorado, Suite 200, Tucson, AZ 85714, tel. (520) 721-6712 or (800) 869-0639.

Ocean Voyages

This unique company offers seven- and 10-day itineraries aboard a variety of yachts in the Hawaiian Islands. The yachts, equipped to carry 2-10 passengers, ensure individualized sail training. The vessels sail throughout the islands, exploring hidden bays and coves, and berth at different ports as they go. This opportunity is for anyone who wishes to see the islands in a timeless fashion, thrilling to sights experienced by the first Polynesian settlers and Western explorers. For rates and information contact Ocean Voyages, 1709 Bridgeway, Sausalito, CA 94965, tel. (415) 332-4681.

Pleasant Hawaiian Holidays

A California-based company specializing in Hawaii, Pleasant Hawaiian Holidays makes arrangements for flights, accommodations, and transportation only. For flights, they primarily use American Trans Air. At 2404 Townsgate Rd., Westlake Village, CA 91361, tel. (800) 242-9244.

Travelers with Disabilities

Accessible Vans of Hawaii (formerly Wheelers of Hawaii), 186 Mehani Circle, Kihei, HI 96753, tel. (808) 879-5521, fax 879-0649, (800) 303-3750 Hawaii or (888) AVAVANS Mainland, is a private company, owned and operated by Dave McKown, who has traveled the world with his paraplegic brother. Dave knows firsthand the obstacles faced by people with disabilities, and his disabled associate does as well. Accessible Vans of Hawaii provides a full service travel agency, booking rooms, flights, and activities for the physically disabled. Wheelchair lift equipped vans are rented on Oahu, Maui, and the Big Island for $109 a day or $560 a week, plus tax. If a van is needed on Kauai, it must be shipped at the renter's expense. Dave and his associate are good sources of information for any traveler with disablities.

EcoTours to Hawaii

Sierra Club Trips offers Hawaii trips for nature lovers who are interested in an outdoor experience. Various trips include hikes over Maui's Haleakala and, on Kauai, a kayak trip along the Na Pali Coast and a family camping spree in Kauai's Koke'e region. All trips are led by experienced guides and are open to Sierra Club members only ($35 per year to join). For information contact the Sierra Club Outing Department, 85 2nd St., 2nd Fl., San Francisco, CA 94105, tel. (415) 775-5500.

Earthwatch allows you to become part of an expeditionary team dedicated to conservation and the study of the natural environment. An expedition might include studying dolphins in Kewalo Basin Marine Mammal Laboratory or diving Maui's threatened reefs. If you become an assistant field researcher, your lodgings may be a dorm room at the University of Hawaii, and your meals may come from a remote camp kitchen. Fees vary and are tax deductible. If you are interested in this learning experience, contact Earthwatch, 680 Mt. Auburn St., P.O. Box 403-P, Watertown, MA 02272, tel. (617) 926-8200.

Backroads, 801 Cedar St., Berkeley, CA 94710, tel. (510) 527-1555, fax (510) 527-1444, or (800) 462-2848, arranges easy-on-the-envi-

ronment bicycle and hiking trips to the Big Island. Basic tours include a six-day hiking/camping tour ($698), a six-day hiking/inn tour ($1,295), and a five-day bicycle/camping tour ($649). Prices include hotel/inn accommodations or tent when applicable, most meals, and professional guide service. Airfare is not included, and bicycles and sleeping bags can be rented (BYO okay) for reasonable rates. (Website: www.back-roads.com.)

Crane Tours, 15101 Magnolia Blvd., Sherman Oaks, CA 91403, tel. (800) 653-2545, owned and operated by Bill Crane, has been taking people kayaking and backpacking to the Big Island, Maui, and Kauai since 1976. Basic prices for these eco-adventures start at $650, with the most expensive tour around $1,145 (airfare not included).

GETTING AROUND

BY AIR

Interisland air travel is highly developed, economical, and completely convenient. You can go almost anywhere at any time on everything from wide-bodied jets to single-engine air taxis. Hawaiians take flying for granted, using planes the way most people use buses. A shopping excursion to Honolulu from a Neighbor Island is commonplace, as is a trip from the city for a picnic at a quiet beach. Most interisland flights are

20-40 minutes long, with some shorter and a few longer. The moody sea can be uncooperative to mass transit, but the skies above Hawaii are generally clear and perfect for flying. Their infrequent gloomier moments can delay flights, but the major airlines of Hawaii have been flying nonstop ever since Hawaiian Air's maiden flight in 1929. The fares are competitive, the schedules convenient, and the service friendly.

Brief History

Little more than a motorized kite, the *Hawaiian Skylark* was the first plane to fly in Hawaii. On New Year's Day, 1911, it circled a Honolulu polo field, where 3,000 spectators, including Queen Liliuokalani, witnessed history. Hawaiians have been soaring above their lovely islands ever since. The first paying customer, Mrs. Newmann, took off on a $15 joyride in 1913 with a Chinese aviator named Tom Gunn. In February 1920, Charles Fern piloted the first interisland customer roundtrip from Honolulu to Maui for $150. He worked for Charles Stoffer, who started the first commercial airline the year before with one Curtiss biplane, affectionately known as "Charlie's Crate." For about 10 years sporadic attempts at interisland service amounted to little more than extended joyrides to deliver the day's newspaper from Honolulu. The James Dole Air

Race in 1927 proved trans-Pacific flight was possible, but interisland passenger service didn't really begin until Stanley C. Kennedy, a WW I flier and heir to Inter-Island Steam Navigation Co., began Inter-Island Airways in January 1929. For a dozen years he ran Sikorsky Amphibians, considered the epitome of safety. By 1941 he converted to the venerable workhorse, the DC-3, and changed the company name to **Hawaiian Air.**

By 1948, Hawaiian Air was unopposed in the interisland travel market, because regularly scheduled boats had already become obsolete. However, in 1946 a fledgling airline named Trans-Pacific opened for business. A nonscheduled airline with only one war surplus DC-3, they carried a hunting party of businessmen to Molokai on their maiden flight. By June 1952, they were a regularly scheduled airline in stiff competition with Hawaiian Air and had changed their name to **Aloha Airlines.** Both airlines had their financial glory days and woes over the next decade; by the end of the '60s both were flying interisland jets.

A healthy crop of small unscheduled airlines known as "air taxis" always darted about the wings of the large airlines, flying to minor airfields and performing flying services uneconomical for the bigger airlines. Most of these tiny, often one-plane air taxis were swatted from the air like gnats whenever the economy went sour or tourism went sluggish. They had names like Peacock and Rainbow, and after a brief flash of wings, they were gone.

INTERISLAND CARRIERS

The only effective way for most visitors to travel between the Hawaiian Islands is by air. Luckily, Hawaii has excellent air transportation that boasts one of the industry's safest flight records. The following airlines have competitive prices, with interisland flights about $90 each way, with substantial savings for state residents. With both Hawaiian and Aloha airlines, you can save about $7 per ticket by purchasing a booklet of six **flight coupons.** These are only available in state at any ticket office or airport counter, and are *transferable.* Just book a flight as normal and present the filled-in voucher to board the plane.

Perfect for families or groups of friends.

Note: Although every effort has been made for up-to-date accuracy, remember that schedules are constantly changing. The following should be used only as a point of reference. Please call the airlines listed below for their latest schedules.

Hawaiian Air, tel. (800) 367-5320 Mainland and Canada, (800) 882-8811 statewide, is not only the oldest airline in Hawaii, it is also the biggest. It flies more aircraft, to more airports, more times per day than any other airline in Hawaii. It services all islands, including Molokai and Lanai, and flies all jets. (Website: www.hawaiianair.com.)

Aloha Airlines, tel. (800) 367-5250 Mainland, (800) 235-0936 Canada, 244-9071 Maui, with its all-jet fleet of 737s, is also an old and venerable Hawaiian company with plenty of flights connecting Oahu to Kauai, Maui, and both Kona and Hilo on Hawaii. It offers more flights to Maui than any other island carrier. (Website: www.alohaair.com.)

Island Air (formerly Aloha Island Air), tel. (800) 323-3345 Mainland, (800) 652-6541 statewide, offers scheduled flights to and from Honolulu, Molokai, Lanai; Kahului, Kapalua, and Hana airports on Maui; and Kona on the Big Island. About half their flights are on jet aircraft and half on Dash-8 turboprop airplanes. (Website: alohaair.com.)

Charter Airlines and Air Tours

Hawaii has a good but dwindling selection of charter airlines offering some regularly scheduled flights, air tours, and special flights the big carriers don't service. They're so handy and personalized they might be considered "air taxis." All use smaller aircraft that seat 6-12 people and fly low enough that their normal interisland flights are like air tours. Stories abound of passengers being invited to ride co-pilot, or of a pilot going out of his way to show off a glimmering coastline or a beautiful waterfall. Many times you get the sense that it's "your" flight and the airline is doing everything possible to make it memorable. The commuter airlines are limited in plane size and routes serviced. Among themselves, prices are very competitive, but, except on their specialty runs, they tend to be more expensive than the three major interisland carriers. They're also not

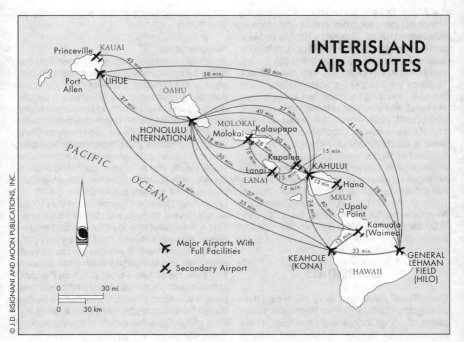

© J.D. BISIGNANI AND MOON PUBLICATIONS, INC.

INTERISLAND AIR ROUTES

Major Airports With Full Facilities

Secondary Airport

0   30 mi
0   30 km

as generous on baggage allowance. You'll be charged more for the extra bulk, or some of it may not be allowed to accompany you on the plane.

Companies include **Big Island Air,** tel. (808) 329-4868, or (800) 303-8868, operating out of Kailua-Kona, with charter service and flightseeing tours around the Big Island. **Paragon Air,** tel. (808) 244-3356, (800) 428-1231, has charter flights to all of Hawaii's airports, and flightseeing tours to Molokai and the Big Island. (Website: www .maui.net/~wings/index.htm). **Pacific Wings,** tel. (888) 575-4546, has regularly scheduled flights to Hana, Molokai, and Kamuela on the Big Island from Kahului, Maui, and Honolulu. (Website: www.pacificwings.com.)

Helicopters Tours

A growing number of helicopters fly in the islands, offering air tours and adventures. Waimea Canyon and the Na Pali coast, a night flight over Honolulu, Molokai's north shore, Haleakala, and Kilauea when it's spouting lava are some of the

more popular sightseeing tours. Some land in remote areas, so you can enjoy your own private waterfall and views. Look for listings under **Sightseeing Tours** in the various travel chapter introductions.

BY SHIP

American Hawaii Cruises

This American cruise ship company operates the 800-passenger SS *Independence.* This ship offers a seven-day itinerary that calls at five ports on the four main islands. For those who want just a taste of a cruise through the islands, three- and four-day trips are also offered. The seven-day fares start at $1,230 pp double occupancy, three- and four-day fares from $670 and $805, respectively. Fares go up from there according to the class and location of your cabin. Children under 18 are often given special rates and cruise free June-Sept. when they share a cabin with their parents. All cruises leave on Saturday from the Aloha Towers in Honolulu. After leaving Honolulu, the seven-day cruise first stops at Nawiliwili on Kauai, followed by Kahului on Maui, and Hilo and Kona on the Big Island, before returning to Honolulu. For the three-day cruise, you board in Honolulu and alight in Kahului. Those on the four-day trip board in Kahului and get off in Honolulu. Each ship is a luxury seagoing hotel and gourmet restaurant; swimming pools, health clubs, movies, and nightclubs are all part of the amenities. Onshore excursions are offered at each port of call. Airfare to Hawaii, interisland air flights, rental cars, and accommodation on any island after your cruise can be arranged for you by American Hawaii Cruises. For details contact: American Hawaii Cruises, Robin St. Wharf, 1380 Port of New Orleans Pl., New Orleans, LA 70130-1890, tel. (800) 765-7000, fax (504) 585-0690. (Website: www.cruise-hawaii.com.)

CAR RENTALS

Does Hawaii really have more rental cars than pineapples? Oahu's *Yellow Pages* has seven pages of listings for car rental agencies. There are more than 25 firms on Maui, and a dozen or so on the Big Island and Kauai. Molokai has three, and even Lanai has two. You can rent anything from a 60-passenger Scenic-cruiser to a 60cc moped, but sedans and other passenger cars are the most common. Gaining in popularity, however, especially for the more adventurous travelers on the Neighbor Islands, are Jeeps and other 4WD vehicles. Still, it's best to reserve your car well before your arrival in Hawaii. If you visit the islands during the peak tourist frenzy without reserving your wheels in advance, you may be marooned at the airport.

There is a tremendous field of cars and agencies from which to choose, and vehicles are cheaper than anywhere else in America. Special deals come and go like tropical rain showers; swashbuckling price slashings and come-ons are all over the rental car market. A little knowledge combined with some shrewd shopping around can save you a bundle. And renting a car is the best way to see the islands if you're going to be here for a limited time. Outside of Oahu, it simply isn't worthwhile to hassle with the poor public transportation system or rely on your thumb.

Requirements
A variety of requirements are imposed on the renter by car agencies, but the most important clauses are common. Some of the worst practices being challenged are: no rentals to people under 25 and over 70, and no rentals to military personnel or Hawaiian residents! Before renting, check that you fulfill the requirements. Generally, you must be 21, although some agencies rent to 18-year-olds, while others still require you to be 25. You must possess a valid driver's license, with licenses from most countries accepted, but if you are not American, get an International Driver's License to be safe. You should have a major credit card in your name. This is the easiest way to rent a car. Some companies will take a deposit, but it will be very stiff. It could easily be $50 per day on top of your rental fees and sometimes much more. In addition, they may require a credit check on the spot, complete with phone calls to your employer and bank. If you damage the car, charges will be deducted from your deposit, and the car company itself determines the extent of the damages. Some companies *will not* rent you a car without a major credit card in your name, no matter how much of a deposit you are willing to leave.

When to Rent
On this one, you'll have to make up your own mind, because it's a "bet" that you can either win or lose big. But it's always good to know the odds before you plop down your money. You can reserve your car in advance when you book your air ticket, or play the field when you get there. If you book in advance, you'll obviously have a car waiting for you, but the deal that you made is the deal that you'll get—it may or may not be the best around. On the other hand, if you wait, you can often take advantage of excellent on-the-spot deals. However, you're betting that cars are available. You might be totally disappointed and not able to rent a car at all, or you might make a honey of a deal.

If you're arriving during the peak seasons of Christmas, Easter, or late summer vacation, absolutely *book your car in advance*. They are all accounted for during this period, and even if you can find a junker from a fly-by-night, they'll price-gouge you mercilessly. If you're going off-peak, you stand a good chance of getting the car you want at the price you want. It's generally best to book ahead; the majority of car companies have toll-free 800 numbers. At least call them for an opinion of your chances of getting a car upon your intended arrival.

Rates

If you pick up a car rental brochure at a travel agency, notice that the prices for Hawaii rentals are about the lowest in the U.S. The two rate options for renting are mileage and flat rate. A third type, mileage/minimum, is generally a bad idea unless you plan to do some heavy-duty driving. Mileage rate costs less per day, but you are charged for every mile driven. Mileage rates are best if you drive less than 30 miles per day—but even on an island that isn't much! The flat rate is best, providing a fixed daily rate and unlimited mileage. With either rate, you buy the gas; don't buy the cheapest because the poor performance from low octane eats up your savings.

Discounts of about 10-15% for weekend, weekly, and monthly rates are available. It's sometimes cheaper to rent a car for the week even if you're only going to use it for five days. Both weekly and monthly rates can be split between Neighbor Islands.

The average price of a subcompact standard shift, without a/c, is $30 per day, $120 per week (add about $8 per day—$50 per week—for an automatic), but rates vary widely. Luxury cars are about $10 per day more, with a comparable weekly rate. Most of the car companies, local and national, offer special rates and deals. These deals fluctuate too rapidly to give any hard-and-fast information. They are common, however, so make sure to inquire. Also, peak periods have "black outs" where normally good deals no longer apply.

Warning: If you keep your car beyond your contract, you'll be charged the highest daily rate unless you notify the rental agency beforehand. *Don't keep your car longer than the contract without notifying the company.* Companies are *quick* to send out their repossession specialists. You might find yourself in a situation with your car gone, a warrant for your arrest, and an extra charge on your bill. A simple courtesy call noti-

fying them of your intentions saves a lot of headaches and hassle.

What Wheels to Rent

The super-cheap rates on the eye-catcher brochures refer to subcompact standard shifts. The price goes up with the size of the car and with an automatic transmission. As with options on a new car, the more luxury, the more you pay. If you can drive a standard shift, get one. They're cheaper to rent and operate and a standard shift gives you greater control. AM/FM radios are good to have for entertainment and for weather and surf conditions. If you have the choice, take a car with cloth seats instead of sticky vinyl.

Insurance

Before signing your car rental agreement, you'll be offered "insurance" for around $10 per day. Since insurance is already built into the contract (don't expect the rental agency to point this out), what you're really buying is a waiver on the deductible ($500-1,000), in case you crack up the car. If you have insurance at home, you will almost always have coverage on a rental car—including your normal deductible—although not all policies are the same, so check with your agent. Also, if you haven't bought their waiver, and you have a mishap, the rental agencies will put a claim against your major credit card on the spot for the amount of deductible, even if you can prove that your insurance will cover. They'll tell you to collect from your insurance company because they don't want to be left holding the bag on an across-the-waters claim. If you have a good policy with a small deductible, it's hardly worth paying the extra money for the waiver, but if your own policy is inadequate, buy the insurance. Also, most major credit cards offer complimentary car-rental insurance as an incentive for using their cards to rent the car. Simply call your credit card company to see if this service is included.

Driving Tips

Protect your children as you would at home with car seats. Their rental prices vary considerably: Alamo offers them free of charge; National charges $3 per day; Hertz needs 48 hours' notice; Dollar gives them free, but they're not always available at all locations. Almost every agency can make arrangements if you give them enough notice. Check before you go and if all else fails, bring one from home.

In most cases, you'll only get one key for your rental car. Don't lock it your car. If you do, call AAA (or other auto emergency service that you have) and ask for assistance. Failing that, a local locksmith can open your car for a fee or the rental car agency can send out a second key by taxi but both of these options can get quite pricey.

There are few differences between driving in Hawaii and on the Mainland. Just remember that many people on the roads are tourists and can be confused about where they're going. Since many drivers are from somewhere else, there's hardly a "regular style" of driving in the islands. A farmer from Iowa accustomed to poking along on back roads can be sandwiched between a frenetic New Yorker who's trying to drive over his roof and a super-polite but horribly confused Japanese tourist who normally drives on the left.

In Hawaii, drivers don't honk their horns except to say hello, or in an emergency. It's considered rude, and honking to hurry someone might earn you a knuckle sandwich. Hawaiian drivers reflect the climate: they're relaxed and polite. Often, they'll brake to let you turn left when they're coming at you. They may assume you'll do the same, so be ready, after a perfunctory turn signal from another driver, for him or her to turn across your lane. The more rural the area, the more apt this is to happen.

It may seem like common sense, but remember to slow down when you enter the little towns strung along the circle-island route. It's easy to bomb along on the highway and flash through these towns, missing some of Hawaii's best scenery. Also, rural children expect *you* to be watchful and will assume that you are going to stop for them when they dart onto the crosswalks.

Oahu's **H-1, H-2, and H-3 freeways** throw many Mainlanders a Polynesian "screwball." Accustomed to driving on superhighways, Main-

landers assume these are the same. They're not. Oahu's superhighways are generally much more convoluted than most Mainland counterparts. Subliminally they look like normal freeways, except they've been tied into Hawaiian knots. There are split-offs, crossroads, and exits in the middle of exits. Stay alert and don't be lulled into complacency.

The mile markers on back roads are great for pinpointing sites and beaches. The lower number on these signs is the highway number, so you can always make sure that you're on the right road.

BYO Car

If you want to bring your own car, write for information to: Director of Finance, Division of Licenses, 1455 S. Beretania St., Honolulu, HI 96814. However, unless you'll be in Hawaii for a bare minimum of six months and will spend all your time on one island, don't even think about it. It's an expensive proposition and takes time and plenty of arrangements. From California, the cost is at least $600 to Honolulu, and an additional $100 to any other island. To save on rental costs, it would be better to buy and sell a car in the islands, or to lease for an extended period.

Four-Wheel-Drives

For normal touring, it is unnecessary to rent 4WDs in Hawaii except on Lanai where they're a must, or if you really want to get off the beaten track on the other islands. They are expensive ($70-120 per day), and you simply don't need them. If you still want one, most car rental agencies have them, and some specialize in them. Because their numbers are limited, reservations are highly recommended.

CAR RENTAL AGENCIES

When you arrive at any of Hawaii's airports, you'll walk the gauntlet of car rental booths and courtesy phones. Of the two categories of car rental agencies in Hawaii, each has its advantage. In the first category are the big national firms like Dollar, National, Hertz, Avis, and Budget. These big guys are familiar and easy to work with, sometimes offer special fly/drive deals with airlines, and live up to their promises. If you want your rental experience to be hassle-free, they're the ones. Also, don't be prejudiced against them just because they're so well known; sometimes they offer the best deals.

Hawaii has spawned a good crop of local entrepreneurial rental agencies. Their deals and cars can range, like rummage-sale treasures, from great finds to pure junk. Local companies have the advantage of being able to cut deals on the spot. If nothing is moving from their lot on the day you arrive, you might get a real bargain. Unfortunately, mixed in this category is a hodge-podge of fly-by-nights. Some of these are small, but adequate, while others are a rip-off.

National Agencies

All of the following national companies are represented in Hawaii. Only the 800 numbers are given below. For local numbers and for other agencies, see the individual travel chapters.

One of the best firms with an excellent reputation for service and prices is **Dollar**, tel. (800) 342-7398 statewide and (800) 800-4000 worldwide, website: www.dollarcar.com. With an excellent reputation and very competitive prices, Dollar rents mostly Chrysler vehicles: sedans, jeeps, convertibles, and 4WDs. Great weekly rates, and all major credit cards accepted.

Alamo, tel. (800) 327-9633, website: www.goalamo.com, has good weekly rates. Mostly GM cars.

National Car Rental, tel. (800) 227-7368 worldwide, website: www.nationalcar.com, features GM and Nissan cars and accepts all major credit cards. They sometimes rent without a credit card if you leave a $100/day deposit—less if you take full insurance coverage.

Avis, tel. (800) 321-3712 nationwide, website: www.avis.com, features late model GM cars as well as most imports and convertibles.

Budget, tel. (800) 527-0700 worldwide, website: www.drivebudget.com, offers competitive rates on a variety of late model Ford and Lincoln-Mercury cars and specialty vehicles.

Hertz, tel. (800) 654-3011 worldwide, website: www.hertz.com, is competitively priced with many fly/drive deals. They feature Ford vehicles.

Thrifty, tel. (800) 367-2277 worldwide, website: www.thrifty.com, uses Chrysler Corp. vehicles.

Enterprise, tel. (800) 736-8222 in Honolulu or (800) 325-8007 elsewhere, website: www.pick-enterprise.com, handles mostly GM cars.

Car Pickup

The majority of agencies listed above have booths at all of the airport terminal buildings throughout Hawaii. If they don't, they have clearly marked courtesy phones in the lobbies. Just pick one up and they'll give directions on where to wait, then come fetch you in their shuttle. Some of the larger local agencies also have courtesy phones and booths at airport terminals, but many only work out of their lots.

MOTORCYCLES AND MOPEDS

Driving a motorcycle can be liberating and exhilarating, yet because they are unprotected, motorcycle drivers are more vulnerable than drivers of cars and trucks. Enjoy your ride, but be very aware of traffic conditions. Drive safely and defensively, and always wear a helmet. Mopeds fall into the same vehicle category as bicycles, so become aware of all appropriate rules and regulations regarding them before you rent and ride.

Most motorcycles for rent in Hawaii are the big Harley-Davidsons while some Japanese models are also available. Rates vary but run around $100 for half a day and $140-160 for 24 hours; longer rentals can be arranged. All drivers must be 21 years old, have a valid motorcycle license, and be in possession of a major credit card. Insurance is available. Companies want you to stay on good paved roads. Although it is not required by state law to wear them, helmets are available.

BY BOAT

Ironically, in the country's only island state complete with a long sailing history, modern shipping, and port towns, ferry service between the islands, except for that between Maui and Lanai, is nonexistent. The previous service between Maui and Molokai has stopped. Periodically, there is a cry to reinstate some sort of coastal and interisland boat or ferry service. Some say visitors and islanders alike would enjoy the experience and be able to travel more economically. Others argue that Hawaiian waters are as dangerous and unpredictable as ever, and no evidence of need or enough passengers exists.

A few skippers run pleasure craft between Maui-Molokai-Lanai and are willing to take on passengers, but this is a hit-and-miss situation based on space. For now, interisland travelers have to be content with seeing the islands from the air.

PUBLIC TRANSPORTATION

Public transportation is very limited in Hawaii, except for Oahu's exemplary **TheBus.** TheBus, tel. (808) 848-4500, can take you just about anywhere you want to go on Oahu for only $1 adult or 50 cents for students. Carrying more than a quarter million passengers per day, it's a model of what a bus system should be.

The MTS Line, popularly called the **Hele-On Bus,** tel. (808) 935-8241 or 961-8744, is a woefully slow, very local bus system that services the Big Island. It's cheap and okay for short hops, but infrequent and slow for long distances. Travelers say they consistently make better time hitchhiking between Hilo and Kona than waiting for Hele On to waddle by.

Bus service is not available on the other islands, but private, short-distance shuttle service seems to take up the slack in many tourist areas. There are a few remaining novelty pedicabs in Waikiki, and many hotel shuttles to and from airports. Check the travel chapter introductions below for details on what is available on each island.

HITCHHIKING

Hitchhiking varies from island to island, both in legality and method of thumbing a ride. On Oahu, hitchhiking is legal, and you use the tried-and-true style of facing traffic and waving your thumb—but you can only hitchhike from bus stops. Not many people hitchhike and the pickings are reasonably easy, but TheBus is only $1 for anywhere you want to go, and the paltry sum you save by hitchhiking is lost in "seeing time." It's legal to hitch on Kauai and the police don't bother you on Hawaii. Remember Hawaii is indeed a "big" island; be prepared to take some time getting from one end to the other. While hitching is illegal on Lanai and Molokai, hardly any policemen are to be seen. If they stop, it will probably be just to warn you, but note that the traffic is light on both islands. On Maui, thumbing a ride is now legal. As one of her last duties, former mayor Linda Lingle signed a bill in early 1999 to give the right to hitch a ride back to the people. Where once you had to play the game with no thumb, now you can solicit rides in that old tried-and-true method. You can get around quite well by thumb, if you're not on a schedule.

In general, you will get a ride, eventually, but in comparison to the amount of traffic going by, it isn't easy. Two things against you: many of the drivers are tourists and don't want to bother with hitchhikers, and many locals don't want to bother with nonlocal hitchhikers. When you do get a ride, most of the time it will be from a *haole* who is either a tourist on his or her own or a new island resident. If you are hitchhiking along a well-known beach area, perhaps in your bathing suit and obviously not going far, you can get a ride more easily. Women should exercise caution as they do everywhere else in the U.S. and avoid hitchhiking alone.

SIGHTSEEING TOURS

Tours offered on all the major islands will literally let you cover an individual island from top to bottom; you can walk it, drive it, sail around it, fly over it, or see it from below the water. Please refer to the travel chapters' **Sightseeing Tours** and **Sports and Recreation** sections for specific information on particular islands.

Ecotourism in Hawaii
Ecotourism is economically, culturally, socially, and environmentally sensitive and sustainable tourism that helps promote local communities and organizations and works in harmony with nature. Although small potatoes yet in the Hawaiian (and worldwide) tourism economy, ecotourism and its goals are growing in importance and will become a major factor in the economic vitality of tourism in the state. For more information on ecotourism in Hawaii, contact the Hawaii Ecotourism Association, P.O. Box 61435, Honolulu, HI 96839, tel. (808) 956-2866, website: www.planet-hawaii.com/hea; e-mail: hea@aloha.net. In addition, the following organizations also can provide related information and contacts:

Ecotourism Society International, P.O. Box 755, North Bennington, VT 05257, tel. (802) 447-2121, fax (802) 447-2122, website: www.ecotourism.org; e-mail: ecotsocy@iga.apc.org; and the Center For Responsible Travel, P.O. Box 827, San Anselmo, CA 94979, tel. (415) 258-6594.

The following is a partial list of organizations offering environmentally sound tours and outings throughout the Hawaiian Islands. See the following travel chapter introductions for other organizations on each specific island.

Hawaii Audubon Society, 212 Merchant St., Suite 320, Honolulu, HI 96813, tel. (808) 528-1432 (hiking and birding).

The Nature Conservancy, 1116 Smith St., Suite 201, Honolulu, HI 96817, tel. (808) 537-4508 (hikes).

Sierra Club, P.O. Box 2000, Kahului, HI 96732, www.hi.sierraclub.org (hikes and service trips).

HEALTH AND SAFETY

In a recent survey published by *Science Digest,* Hawaii was cited as the healthiest state in the U.S. in which to live. Indeed, Hawaiian citizens live longer than anywhere else in America: men to 76 years and women to 82. Lifestyle, heredity, and diet help with these figures, but Hawaii is still an oasis in the middle of the ocean, and germs just have a tougher time getting here. There are no cases of malaria, cholera, or yellow fever. Because of a strict quarantine law, rabies is also nonexistent. On the other hand, tooth decay, perhaps because of a wide use of sugar and the enzymes present in certain tropical fruits, is 30% above the national average. With the perfect weather, a multitude of fresh-air activities, soothing negative ionization from the sea, and a generally relaxed and carefree lifestyle, everyone feels better there. Hawaii is just what the doctor ordered: a beautiful, natural health spa. That's one of its main drawing cards. The food and water are perfectly safe, and the air quality is the best in the country.

Handling the Sun

Don't become a victim of your own exuberance. People can't wait to strip down and lie on the sand like beached whales, but the tropical sun will burn you to a cinder if you're silly. The burning rays come through more easily in Hawaii because of the sun's angle, and you don't feel them as much because there's always a cool breeze. The worst part of the day is 11 a.m.-3 p.m. You'll just have to force yourself to go slowly. Don't worry; you'll be able to flaunt your best souvenir, your golden Hawaiian tan, to your green-with-envy friends when you get home. It's better than showing them a boiled lobster body with peeling skin! If your skin is snowflake white, 15 minutes per side on the first day is plenty. Increase by 15-minute intervals every day, which will allow you a full hour per side by the fourth day. Have faith; this is enough to give you a deep golden, uniform tan.

Haole Rot

A peculiar condition caused by the sun is referred to locally as *haole* rot. It's called this because it supposedly affects only white people, but you'll notice some dark-skinned people with the same condition. Basically, the skin becomes mottled with white spots that refuse to tan. You get a blotchy effect, mostly on the shoulders and back. Dermatologists have a fancy name for it, and they'll give you a fancy prescription with a not-so-fancy price tag to cure it. It's common knowledge throughout the islands that Selsun Blue shampoo has some ingredient that stops the white mottling effect. Wash your hair with it and then make sure to rub the lather over the affected areas, and it should clear up.

Bugs

Everyone, in varying degrees, has an aversion to vermin and creepy crawlers. Hawaii isn't infested with a wide variety, but it does have its share. Mosquitoes were unknown in the islands until their larvae stowed away in the water barrels of the *Wellington* in 1826 and were introduced at Lahaina. They bred in the tropical climate and rapidly spread to all the islands. They are a particular nuisance in the rainforests. Be prepared, and bring a natural repellent like citronella oil, available in most health stores on the islands, or a commercial product available in all groceries or drugstores. Campers will be happy to have mosquito coils to burn at night as well.

Cockroaches are very democratic insects. They hassle all strata of society equally. They breed well in Hawaii, and most hotels are at war with them, trying desperately to keep them from being spotted by guests. One comforting thought is that in Hawaii they aren't a sign of filth or dirty housekeeping. They love the climate like everyone else, and it's a real problem keeping them under control.

Poisonous Plants

A number of plants in Hawaii, mostly imported, contain toxins. In almost every case you have to eat a quantity of them before they'll do you any real harm. The following is a partial list of the most common poisonous plants you'll encounter and the parts to avoid: poinsettia—leaves, stems, and sap; oleander—all parts; azalea—all parts; crown flower—juice; lantana—berries; castor bean—all parts; bird of paradise—seeds; coral plant—seeds.

Pollution in Paradise

Calling Hawaii the healthiest state in America doesn't mean that it has totally escaped pollution. It is the only state, however, in which all of the natural beauty is protected by state law, with a statewide zoning and a general development plan. For example, the absence of billboard advertising is due to the pioneering work of a women's club, "The Outdoor Circle," which was responsible for an anti-billboard law passed in 1927. It's strictly enforced, but unfortunately high-rise and ill-advised development have obscured some of the lovely views that these far-sighted women were trying to preserve. Numerous environmental controversies, including nuclear proliferation and the ill effects of rampant development, rage on the islands.

The most obvious infringements occur on Oahu, with 74% of the state's population, which places the greatest stress on the environment. An EPA study found that almost 20% of Oahu's wells have unacceptably high concentrations of DBCP and TCP. Because of Hawaii's unique water lenses (fresh water trapped by layers of lava), this fact is particularly onerous. The "Great Oahu Milk Crisis" of 1982 saw dairies shut down when their milk was found to have abnormally high concentrations of heptachlor, a chemical used in the pineapple industry. This was traced to the tops of pineapple plants sold as fodder, which tainted the milk.

Widespread concern existed over a 1,500-unit development on the Waianae coast known as West Beach. According to environmentalists, the recently completed development will not only put a major strain on diminishing water resources, but impinge on one of the last fruitful fishing areas near long-established homes of native Hawaiians. Oahu's H-3 Freeway was cut across an ecologically sensitive mountain range, and an alternative biomass energy plant is denuding the islands of its remaining indigenous ohia trees. On the Big Island, plans are always lurking for resort development on South Point and even in the magnificent Waipio Valley. Also on the Big Island, a thermal energy plant was bitterly challenged because its builders insisted on locating it in the middle of sensitive rainforest when other, more ecologically acceptable sites were readily available. And just to be pesky, the Mediterranean fruit fly made its appearance and Malathion had to be sprayed. Compared to those in many states, these conditions are small potatoes, but they lucidly point out the holistic global concept that no place on earth is immune to the ravages of pollution.

Environmental Resource Groups

Anyone interested in Hawaii's environmental issues can contact the following for more information:

Earthjustice Legal Defense Fund (formerly Sierra Club Legal Defense Fund), 223 S. King St., 4th Fl., Honolulu, HI 96813, tel. (808) 599-2436, e-mail: eajushi@igc.apc.org.

Greenpeace, 1807 Waianuenue Ave., Hilo, HI 96720, tel. (808) 969-9910, website: www.greenpeace.org.

The Nature Conservancy, 1116 Smith St., Suite 201, Honolulu, HI 96817, tel. (808) 537-4508, e-mail: TNCH1@aol.com, website: www.tnc.org/hawaii.

Rainforest Action Network, 301 Broadway, Suite A, San Francisco, CA 94133, tel. (415) 398-4404, e-mail: rainforest@ran.org, website: www.ran.org.

Sierra Club Hawaii Chapter, 233 Merchant St., 2nd Fl., Honolulu, HI 96813, tel. (808) 538-

6616, fax 537-9019, website: www.hi.sierra-club.org.

Earth Trust, 25 Kaneohe Bay Dr., Suite 205, Kailua, HI 96734, tel. (808) 254-2866, fax 254-6409, website: www.earthtrust.org.

A savvy monthly newsletter that focuses on environmental and political issues facing Hawaii today is *Environment Hawai'i,* 200 Kanoele-hua Ave., Suite 103-325, Hilo, HI 96720, tel. (808) 934-0115, fax 934-8321, e-mail: pattum @aloha.net, individual subscription rate $35 per year. The well-researched and concisely written newsletter attempts to be fair to all parties concerned, explaining both sides to most controversies. Short on preaching and long on common sense, *Environment Hawaii* is an excellent resource for anyone interested in sociopolitical and environmental issues.

WATER SAFETY

Hawaii has one very sad claim to fame: more people drown here than anywhere else in the world. Moreover, there are dozens of yearly swimming victims with broken necks and backs or with injuries from scuba and snorkeling accidents. These statistics shouldn't keep you out of the sea, because it is indeed beautiful—benevolent in most cases—and a major reason to go to Hawaii. But if you're foolish, the sea will bounce you like a basketball and suck you away for good. The best remedy is to avoid situations you can't handle. Don't let anyone dare you into a situation that makes you uncomfortable. "Macho men" who know nothing about the power of the sea will be tumbled into Cabbage Patch dolls in short order. Ask lifeguards or beach attendants about conditions, and follow their advice. If local people refuse to go in, there's a good reason. Even experts get in trouble in Hawaiian waters. Some beaches, such as Waiki-ki, are as gentle as lambs and you would have to tie an anchor around your neck to drown there. Others, especially on the north coasts during the winter months, are frothing giants.

While beachcombing, or especially when walking out on rocks, never turn your back on the sea. Be aware of undertows (the waves drawing back into the sea). They can knock you off your feet. Before entering the water, study it for rocks, breakers, reefs, and riptides. Riptides are powerful currents, like rivers in the sea, that can drag you out. Mostly they peter out not too far from shore, and you can often see their choppy waters on the surface. If caught in a "rip," don't fight to swim directly against it; you'll lose and only exhaust yourself. Swim diagonally across it, while going along with it, and try to stay parallel to the shore. Don't waste all your lung power yelling, and rest by floating.

When bodysurfing, never ride straight in; come to shore at a 45-degree angle. Remember, waves come in sets. Little ones can be followed

HOWARD LINDEMAN

This "denizen of the deep" is much more afraid of you than you are of it.

by giants, so watch the action awhile instead of plunging right in. Standard procedure is to duck under a breaking wave. You can survive even thunderous oceans using this technique. Don't try to swim through a heavy froth and never turn your back and let it smash you. Don't swim alone if possible, and obey all warning signs. Hawaiians want to entertain you and they don't put up signs just to waste money. The last rule is, "If in doubt, stay out."

Yikes!

Sharks live in all the oceans of the world. Most mind their own business and stay away from shore. Hawaiian sharks are well fed—on fish—and don't usually bother with unsavory humans. If you encounter a shark, don't panic. Never thrash around because this will trigger their attack instinct. If they come close, scream loudly.

Portuguese man-of-wars put out long, floating tentacles that sting if they touch you. Don't wash the sting off with fresh water, as this will only aggravate it. Hot salt water will take away the sting, as will alcohol (the drinking or the rubbing kind), after-shave lotion, and meat tenderizer (MSG), which can be found in any supermarket or Chinese restaurant.

Coral can give you a nasty cut, and it's known to cause infections because it's a living organism. Wash the cut immediately and apply an antiseptic. Keep the cut clean and covered, and watch for infection.

Poisonous sea urchins, such as the lacquer-black *wana*, can be beautiful creatures. They are found in shallow tidepools and will hurt you if you step on them. Their spines will break off, enter your foot, and burn like blazes. There are cures. Vinegar and wine poured on the wound will stop the burning. If those aren't available, the Hawaiian solution is urine. It might seem ignominious to have someone pee on your foot, but it'll put the fire out. The spines will disintegrate in a few days, and there are generally no long-term effects.

Hawaiian reefs also have their share of moray eels. These creatures are ferocious in appearance but will never initiate an attack. You'll have to poke around in their holes while snorkeling or scuba diving to get them to attack. Sometimes this is inadvertent on the diver's part, so be careful where you stick your hand while underwater.

HAWAIIAN FOLK MEDICINE AND CURES

Hawaiian folk medicine is well developed, and its cures for common ailments have been used effectively for centuries. Hawaiian *kahuna* were highly regarded for their medicinal skills, and Hawaiians were by far some of the healthiest people in the world until the coming of the Europeans. Many folk remedies and cures are used to this day and, what's more, they work. Many of the common plants and fruits that you'll encounter provide some of the best remedies. When roots and seeds and special exotic plants are used, the preparation of the medicine is as painstaking as in a modern pharmacy. These prescriptions are exact and take an expert to prepare. They should never be prepared or administered by an amateur.

Common Curative Plants

Arrowroot, for diarrhea, is a powerful narcotic used in rituals and medicines. The pepper plant *(Piper methisticum)* is chewed and the juice is spat into a container for fermenting into *awa*. Used as a medicine for urinary tract infections, rheumatism, and asthma, it also induces sleep and cures headaches. A poultice for wounds is made from the skins of ripe bananas. Peelings have a powerful antibiotic quality and contain vitamins A, B, and C, phosphorous, calcium, and iron. The nectar from the plant was fed to babies as a vitamin juice. Breadfruit sap is used for healing cuts and as a moisturizing lotion. Coconut is used to make moisturizing oil, and the juice was chewed, spat into the hand, and used as a shampoo. Guava is a source of vitamins A, B, and C. Hibiscus has been used as a laxative. *Kukui* nut oil makes a gargle for sore throats and a laxative, plus the flowers are used to cure diarrhea. *Noni,* an unappetizing hand-grenade-shaped fruit that you wouldn't want to eat unless you had to, reduces tumors, diabetes, and high blood pressure, and the juice is good for diarrhea. Sugarcane sweetens many concoctions, and the juice of toasted cane was a tonic for sick babies. Sweet potato is used as a tonic during pregnancy and juiced as a gargle for phlegm. Tamarind is a natural laxative and contains the most acid and sugar of any fruit on earth. Taro has been used for lung infections and thrush, and as a suppository. Yams are good for coughs, vomiting, constipation, and appendicitis.

Commonly Treated Ailments

For arthritis make a poultice of *koali* and Hawaiian salt; cover the area and keep warm. A bad-breath gargle is made from the *hapu'u* fern. The latex from inside the leaves of aloe is great for soothing burns and sunburn, as well as for innumerable skin problems. If you get chapped lips or windburned skin, use oil from the *hinu honu*. A headache is lessened with *awa* or *ape*. Calm nervousness with *awa* and *lomi lomi*, Hawaiian-style massage. To get rid of a raspy sore throat, chew the bark of the root of the *uhaloa*. A toothache is eased by the sticky narcotic juice from the *pua kala* seed, a prickly poppy.

Lomi Lomi

This traditional Hawaiian massage is of exceptional therapeutic value. It has been practiced since very early times and is especially useful in cases of fatigue, general body aches, preventive medicine, and sports injuries. When Otto Von Kotzebue arrived in 1824, he noted, ". . . Queen Nomahana, after feasting heartily, turned on her back, whereupon a tall fellow sprang upon her body and kneaded it unmercifully with his knees and fists as if it had been the dough of bread. Digestion was so assisted that the queen resumed her feasting." *Lomi lomi* practitioners must be accredited by the state.

MEDICAL SERVICES

Each major island has numerous hospitals that provide emergency room, long-term, and acute care facilities; clinics, for immediate care and first-aid treatment; and pharmacies, for drug prescriptions and other medical necessities. Island by island lists of these facilities are in the specific travel chapters below.

Alternative Medicine

Most ethnic groups who migrated to Hawaii brought along their own cures. The Chinese and Japanese are especially known for their unique and effective treatments, such as herbal medicine, acupuncture, and shiatsu. The time-honored Chinese therapy of acupuncture is available throughout the islands. On Oahu, contact the Hawaii Acupuncture Association, P.O. Box 11202, Honolulu, HI 96828, tel. (808) 538-6692, for referrals to state-licensed acupuncturists throughout the islands. Hawaii also has a huge selection of chiropractors. All types of massage are available throughout the islands, everything from shiatsu to Hawaii's own *lomi lomi* massage. The *Yellow Pages* on all islands lists holistic practitioners, herbalists, naturopaths, chiropractors, as well as "massage."

SERVICES FOR TRAVELERS WITH DISABLITIES

A person with disablities can have a wonderful time in Hawaii; all that's needed is a little pre-planning. The following general advice should help your planning.

Commission on Persons with Disabilities

This commission was designed with the express purpose of aiding handicapped people. It is a source of invaluable information and distributes self-help booklets free of charge. Any person with disabilities heading to Hawaii should write first or visit their offices on arrival. For the *Aloha Guide to Accessibility* ($3) write or visit the head office at: Commission on Persons with Disabilities, 500 Ala Moana Blvd., Honolulu, HI 96813, tel. (808) 586-8121; on Maui, 54 High St., Wailuku, Maui, HI 96793, tel. (808) 243-5441; on Kauai, 3060 Eiwa St. #207, Lihue, Kauai, HI 96766, tel. (808) 241-3308; on Hawaii, P.O. Box 1641, Hilo, HI 96820, tel. (808) 933-7747. Other printed pamphlets list accessibility to shopping centers, theaters, tourist attractions, parks, and hotels around the islands.

General Information

The key for a smooth trip is to make as many arrangements ahead of time as possible. Tell the transportation companies and hotels that you'll be dealing with the nature of your handicap in advance so that they can make arrangements to accommodate you. Bring your medical records and notify medical establishments of your arrival if you'll be needing their services. Travel with a friend or make arrangements for an aide on arrival. Bring your own wheelchair if possible and let airlines know if it is battery-powered; boarding interisland carriers requires steps. No problem: they'll board you early on special lifts, but they must know that you're coming. Many hotels and restaurants accommodate people with disabilities, but always call ahead just to make sure.

For specific services on each island, see the travel chapter introductions below.

PROSTITUTION

Though the small towns and villages are as safe as you can find anywhere in America, Hawaii isn't all good clean fun. Wherever there's constant tourist flow, a huge military presence, and high cost of living, there will be those people your mama warned you about. Most of the heavy night action occurs in Honolulu's Waikiki and Chinatown. Something about the *vibe* exudes sexuality. The land is raw and wild, and the settings are intoxicating. All those glistening bodies under the tropical sun and the carefree lifestyle are super-conducive to you know what! It's long been known as a great place for boy meets girl, or whomever, but there also exists "play for pay."

Prostitution—The Way It Was
Ever since the first ship arrived in 1778, Hawaii has known prostitution. At that time, a sailor paid for a night with a woman with one iron nail. Funny, today they'll take a plastic card. Prostitution, rampant until the missionaries arrived in 1819, was a major cause of the tragic population decline of the Hawaiian race. The tradition carried on into this century. Iwilei was a notorious redlight district in Honolulu at the turn of the century. The authorities, many of whom were clientele, not only turned a blind eye to this scene, but semilegalized it. A policeman was stationed inside the "stockade" and police rules were listed on the five entrances. The women were required to have a weekly VD checkup from the Board of Health, and without a current disease-free certificate they couldn't work. Iwilei was even considered by some to be an attraction: when Somerset Maugham passed through the islands in 1916 on his way to Russia as a spy for Eng-

land, he was taken there as if on a sightseeing tour. The long-established military presence in Hawaii has also helped keep prostitution a flourishing business. During WW II, troops were entertained by streetwalkers, houses of prostitution, and at dance halls. The consensus of the military commanders was that prostitution was a necessary evil, needed to keep up the morale of the troops.

The Scene Today
You can go two ways on the "sleaze" scene in Hawaii: ignore it or remain aloof and never see any; or look for and find it with no trouble. The following is neither a condemnation nor an endorsement of how you should act and what you should do. It's merely an interpretation and the choice is up to you.

The two areas notorious for prostitution today are in Honolulu: Kuhio and Kalakaua Avenues in Waikiki, which are geared toward the tourist, and Hotel Street in Chinatown, for servicemen and a much rougher trade. All sorts of women solicit—whites, blacks, and Asians—but the majority are young white women from the Mainland. They cruise along in the old-fashioned style, meeting eyes and giving the nod. As long as they keep walking, the police won't roust them.

Most hookers prefer Japanese clientele, followed by the general tourist, and lastly, the always-broke serviceman. In the terse words of one streetwalker queried about the preference for Japanese, she said, "They're small, clean, fast, and they pay a lot." If anyone in Waikiki can speak Japanese, a hooker can. Most are not "equal opportunity employees." Western guys, whether white or black, don't stand much of a chance. The prostitutes are after the Japanese in a sort of crazy payback. The Japanese fish American waters, and the "pros" of Waikiki hook big Japanese fish.

A Honolulu policeman on his Kuhio Avenue beat said, "I can't do anything if they keep walking. It's a free country. Besides, I'm not here to teach anyone morals. . . . Last week a john "fell" out of an eight-story window and a prostitute was found with her throat slit. . . . I'm just on the front lines fighting herpes and AIDS. Just fighting herpes and AIDS, man." Unlike during the days of Iwilei, there is absolutely no official control or testing for VD.

Then there is Chinatown; it's as rough as guts. The girls are shabby, the bars and strip joints are shabbier, and the vibe is heavy.

Women can find male prostitutes on most of the beaches of Honolulu and Waikiki. Mostly these transactions take place during the day. Although many men make a legitimate living as "beach boys" instructing in surfing and the like, some are really prostitutes. It's always up to the woman to decide how far the "lessons" proceed.

Massage Parlors, Etc.

Besides streetwalkers, Honolulu and some of the Neighbor Islands have their share of massage parlors, escort services, and exotic dance joints. For massage parlors and escort services you can let your fingers do the walking—through the *Yellow Pages*. Unfortunately, legitimate massage practitioners share the same listings with the other kind of massage parlors. If the *Yellow Pages* listing reads something like "Fifi's Playthings—We'll rub it day or night, wherever it is," this should tip you off. Such parlors usually offer escort services too, for both men and women.

Exotic dance clubs are basically strip joints with a twist. The dancers are attractive women brought over from the Mainland. They can easily make $150 per night dancing, and the majority are not prostitutes. An act lasts for three songs, and gets raunchier as it goes. If you invite a dancer to have a drink, it'll cost you, but it will be a real drink. This gets you nothing but conversation. Working the sexually agitated male crowd are women who can best be described as "lap sitters." They're almost always older Korean women who've been through the mill. They'll charge you double for a fake drink, and then try to entice you over to a dark corner table, where they'll chisel more money from you for all you can manage, or are brave enough to do, in a dark corner of a nightclub. Their chief allies are dim lights and booze.

ILLEGAL DRUGS

The use and availability of illegal, controlled, and recreational drugs are about the same in Hawaii as throughout the rest of America. Cocaine constitutes the fastest-growing recreational drug, and it's available on the streets of the main cities, especially Honolulu. Although most dealers are small-time, the drug is brought in by organized crime. The underworld here is mostly populated by men of Asian descent, and the Japanese *yakuza* is said to have heightened involvement in Hawaiian organized crime.

A newer drug menace hitting the streets is known as "ice." Ice is smokable methamphetamine that will wire a user for up to 24 hours. The high lasts longer, and is cheaper, than cocaine or its derivative, "crack." Users become quickly dependent, despondent, and violent because ice robs them of their sleep as well as their dignity. Its use is particularly prevalent among late-night workers. Many of the violent deaths in Honolulu have been linked to the growing use of ice.

However, the main drug available and commonly used in Hawaii is marijuana, which is locally called *pakalolo*. There are also three varieties of psychoactive mushrooms that contain the hallucinogen psilocybin. They grow wild but are considered illegal controlled substances.

Pakalolo Growing

About 25 years ago, mostly *haole* hippies from the Mainland began growing pot in the more remote sections of the islands, such as Puna on Hawaii and around Hana on Maui. They discovered what legitimate planters had known for 200 years: plant a broomstick in Hawaii, treat it right, and it'll grow. *Pakalolo*, after all, is a weed, and it grows in Hawaii like wildfire. The locals quickly got into the act when they realized that they, too, could grow a "money tree." As a matter of fact, they began resenting the *haole* usurpers, and a quiet and sometimes dangerous feud has been going on ever since. Much is made of the viciousness of the backcountry "growers" of Hawaii. There are tales of booby traps and armed patrols guarding their plants in the hills, but mostly it's a cat-and-mouse game between the authorities and the growers. If you, as a tourist, are tramping about in the forest and happen upon someone's "patch," don't touch anything. Just back off and you'll be okay. Pot has the largest monetary turnover of any crop in the islands, and as such, is now considered a major source of agricultural revenue. There are all kinds of local names and varieties of pot in Hawaii, the most potent being "Kona Gold," "Puna Butter," and "Maui Wowie." These names are all becoming passé.

THEFT AND HASSLES

Theft and minor assaults can be a problem, but they're usually not violent or vicious as in some Mainland cities. Mostly, it's a locals with a chip on his shoulder and few prospects, who will ransack your car or make off with your camera. A big Hawaiian or local guy will be obliged to flatten your nose if you look for trouble, but mostly it will be sneak thieves out to make a fast buck.

From the minute you sit behind the wheel of your rental car you'll be warned not to leave valuables unattended and to lock your car up tighter than a drum. Signs warning about theft at most major tourist attractions help fuel your paranoia. Many hotel rooms offer coin-operated safes so you can lock your valuables away and relax while getting sunburned. Stories abound about purse snatchings and surly locals just itching to give you a hard time. Well, they're all true to a degree, but Hawaii's reputation is much worse than the reality. In Hawaii you'll have to observe two golden laws: if you look for trouble, you'll find it; and a fool and his camera are soon parted.

Theft

The majority of theft in Hawaii is of the "sneak thief" variety. If you leave your hotel door unlocked, a camera sitting on the seat of your rental car, or valuables on your beach towel, you'll be inviting a very obliging thief to pad away with your stuff. You have to learn to take precautions, but they won't be anything like those employed in rougher areas like South America or Southeast Asia—just normal American precautions.

If you must walk alone at night, stay on the main streets in well-lit areas. Always lock your hotel door and windows and place valuable jewelry in the hotel safe. When you leave your hotel for the beach, there is absolutely no reason to carry all your traveler's checks and credit cards, or a big wad of money. Just take what you'll need for drinks and lunch. If you're uptight about leaving money in your beach bag, stick it in your bathing suit or bikini. American money is just as negotiable if it is damp. Don't leave your camera or portable stereo on the beach unattended. Ask a person nearby to watch it for you while you go for a dip. Most people won't mind at all, and you can repay the favor.

While sightseeing in your shiny new rental car, which immediately brands you as a tourist, again, don't take more than what you'll need for the day. Why people leave a camera sitting on the seat of their car is a mystery! Many people lock valuables in the trunk, but remember that most good car thieves can "jimmy" it open as quickly as you can open it with your key. If you must, for some reason, leave your camera or valuables in your car, lock them in the trunk, stash them under a seat back that's been reclined, or consider putting them under the hood. Thieves usually don't look there, and on most modern cars you can only pop the hood with a lever inside the car. It's not fail-safe, but it's worth a try.

Campers face special problems because their entire camp is open to thievery. Most campgrounds don't have any real security, but who, after all, wants to fence an old tent or a used sleeping bag? Many tents have zippers that can be secured with a small padlock. If you want to go trekking and are afraid to leave your gear in the campgrounds, take a large green garbage bag with you. Transport your gear down the trail and then walk off through some thick brush. Put your gear in the garbage bag and bury it under leaves and other light camouflage. That's about as safe as you can be. You can also use a variation on this technique instead of leaving your valuables in your rental car.

Hassles

Another self-perpetuating myth about Hawaii is that "the natives are restless." An undeniable animosity exists between locals (especially those with some Hawaiian blood) and *haole*. Fortunately, this prejudice is directed mostly at the group and not at the individual. The locals are resentful of those *haole* who came, took their land, and relegated them to second-class citizenship. They realize that this is not the average tourist and they can tell what you are at a glance. Tourists usually are treated with understanding and are given a type of immunity. Besides, Hawaiians are still among the most friendly, giving, and understanding people on earth.

Haole who live in Hawaii might tell you stories of their children having trouble at school. They could even mention an unhappy situation at some schools called "beat-up-a-*haole*" day, and you might hear that if you're a *haole* it's not a matter of "if" you'll be beaten up, but "when." Truthfully, most of this depends upon your attitude and your sensitivity. The locals feel infringed upon, so don't fuel these feelings. If you're at a beach park and there is a group of local people in one area, don't crowd them. If you go into a local bar and you're the only one of your ethnic group in sight, you shouldn't have to be told to leave. Much of the hassle involves drinking. Booze brings out the worst prejudice on all sides. If you're invited to a beach party, and the local guys start getting drunk, make this your exit call.

> *Some were rapacious exploiters, seeking to deceive, loot and leave. Hawaii has known them by the thousands through the years.*
> ~Edward Joesting

Don't wait until it's too late.

Most trouble seems to be directed toward white men. White women are mostly immune from being beaten up, but they have to beware of the violence of sexual abuse and rape. Although plenty of local women marry white men, it's not a good idea to try to pick up a local woman. If you're known in the area and have been properly introduced, that's another story. Also, women out for the night in bars or discos can be approached if they're not in the company of local guys. If you are with your bikini-clad girlfriend, and a bunch of local guys are, say, drinking beer at a beach park, don't go over and try to be friendly and ask, "What's up?" You, and especially your girlfriend, just might find out. Maintain your own dignity and self-respect by treating others with dignity and respect. Most times you'll reap what you sow.

WHAT TO TAKE

It's a snap to pack for a visit to Hawaii. Everything is on your side. The weather is moderate and uniform on the whole, and the style of dress is delightfully casual. The rule of thumb is to pack lightly: few items, and light clothing both in color and weight. What you'll need will depend largely on your itinerary and your desires. Are you drawn to the nightlife, the outdoors, or both? If you forget something at home, it won't be a disaster. You can buy everything you'll need in Hawaii. As a matter of fact, Hawaiian clothing, such as muumuu and aloha shirts, is one of the best purchases you can make, both in comfort and style. It's quite feasible to bring only one or two changes of clothing with the express purpose of outfitting yourself while here. Prices on bathing suits, bikinis, and summer wear in general are quite reasonable.

Matters of Taste

A grand conspiracy in Hawaii adhered to by

everyone—tourist, traveler, and resident—is to "hang loose" and dress casually. Best of all, alohawear is just about all you'll need for comfort and virtually every occasion. The classic muumuu is large and billowy, and aloha shirts are made to be worn outside the pants. The best of both are made of cool cotton. Rayon is a natural fiber that isn't too bad, but polyester is hot, sticky, and not authentic. Not all muumuu are of the "tent persuasion." Some are very fashionable and form-fitted with peek-a-boo slits up the side, down the front, or around the back. A *holomuu* is a muumuu fitted at the waist with a flowing skirt to the ankles. They are not only elegant, but perfect for "stepping out."

In the Cold and Rain

Two occasions for which you'll have to consider dressing warmly are visits to mountaintops and boat rides when wind and ocean sprays are a factor. You can conquer both with a jogging suit (sweat suit) and a featherweight, water-resistant windbreaker. If you intend to visit Mauna Kea, Mauna Loa, or Haleakala it'll be downright chilly. Your jogging suit with a hooded windbreaker/raincoat will do the trick for all occasions. If you're going to camp or trek, you should add another layer, a woolen sweater being one of the best. Wool is the only natural fiber that retains most of its warmth-giving properties even if it gets wet. Several varieties of "fleece" synthetics currently on the market also have this ability. If your hands get cold, put a pair of socks over them. Tropical rain showers can happen at any time so you might consider a fold-up umbrella, but the sun quickly breaks through and the warming winds blow.

Shoes

Dressing your feet is hardly a problem. You'll most often wear zoris (rubber thongs) for going to and from the beach, leather sandals for strolling and dining, and jogging shoes for trekking and sightseeing. A few discos require dress shoes, but it's hardly worth bringing them just for that. If you plan on heavy-duty trekking, you'll definitely want your hiking boots. Lava, especially a'a, is murderous on shoes. Most backcountry trails are rugged and muddy, and you'll need those good old lug soles for traction. If you plan moderate hikes, consider bringing rubberized ankle supports to complement your jogging shoes. Most drugstores sell them, and the best are a rubberized sock with toe and heel cut out.

Specialty Items

Following is a list of specialty items that you might consider bringing along. They're not necessities but most will definitely come in handy. A pair of binoculars really enhances sightseeing—great for viewing birds and sweeping panoramas, and almost a necessity if you're going whalewatching. A folding, Teflon-bottomed travel iron makes up for cotton's one major shortcoming, wrinkles; you can't always count on hotels to have irons. Nylon twine and miniature clothespins are handy for drying garments, especially bathing suits. Commercial and hotel laundromats abound, but many times you'll get by with hand-washing a few items in the sink. A transistor radio/tape recorder provides news, weather, and entertainment, and can be used

to record impressions, island music, and a running commentary for your slide show. Hair dryer: although the wind can be relied upon to dry wet hair, it leaves a bit to be desired in the styling department. An inflatable raft for riding waves, along with flippers, mask, and snorkel, can easily be bought in Hawaii but don't weigh much or take up much space in your luggage. If you'll be camping, trekking, or boating with only seawater available for bathing, take along the biodegradable "Camp Suds" or similar soap, available from good sporting goods stores.

For the Camper

If you don't want to take it with you, all necessary camping gear can be purchased or rented while in Hawaii. Besides the above, you should consider taking the following: framed backpack or a convertible pack that turns into a suitcase, daypack, matches in a waterproof container, all-purpose knife, mess kit, eating utensils, flashlight (remove batteries), candle, nylon cord, and sewing kit (dental floss works as thread). Take a first-aid kit containing Band-Aids, all-purpose antiseptic cream, alcohol swabs, tourniquet string, cotton balls, elastic bandage, razor blade, Telfa pads, and a small mirror for viewing private nooks and crannies. A light sleeping bag is good, although your fleecy jogging suit with a ground pad and light blanket or even your rain poncho will be sufficient. Definitely bring a down bag for Haleakala or mountainous areas. In a film container pack a few nails, safety pins, fishhooks, line, and bendable wire. Nothing else does what these do and they're all handy for a million and one uses.

Basic Necessities

As previously mentioned, you really have to consider only two "modes" of dressing in Hawaii: beachwear and casual clothing. The following list is designed for the mid-range traveler carrying one suitcase or a backpack. Remember that there are laundromats, and that you'll be spending a considerable amount of time in your bathing suit. Consider the following: one or two pairs of light cotton slacks for going out and about, and one pair of jeans for trekking, or better yet, corduroys which can serve both purposes; two or three casual sundresses—muumuu are great; three or four pairs of shorts for beachwear and for sightseeing; four to five short-sleeved shirts or blouses and one long-sleeved; three or four colored and printed T-shirts that can be worn anytime from trekking to strolling; a beach coverup—the short terry-cloth type is the best; a brimmed hat for rain and sun—the crushable floppy type is great for purse or daypack, or pick up a straw or woven hat here for about $10; two or three pairs of socks are sufficient, nylons you won't need; two bathing suits (nylon ones dry quickest); plastic bags to hold wet bathing suits and laundry; five to six pairs of underwear; towels (optional, because hotels provide them, even for the beach); a first-aid kit, pocket-size is sufficient; suntan lotion and insect repellent; a daypack or large beach bag. And don't forget your wind-breaker, perhaps a shawl for the evening, and an all-purpose jogging suit.

Pets and Quarantine
Hawaii has a very rigid pet quarantine policy designed to keep rabies and other Mainland diseases from reaching the state. All domestic pets are subject to **120 days' quarantine,** (a 30-day quarantine is allowed by meeting certain pre-arrival and post-arrival requirements—inquire). Unless you are contemplating a move to Hawaii, it is not feasible to take pets. For complete information, contact the Department of Agriculture, Animal Quarantine Division, 99-951 Halawa Valley St., Aiea, HI 96701, tel. (808) 483-7151.

INFORMATION AND SERVICES

HAWAII VISITORS BUREAU

In 1903 the Hawaiian Promotion Committee thought tourism could be the economic wave of the future. They began the "Hawaii Tourist Bureau," which became the Hawaii Visitors Bureau. The HVB is now a top-notch organization providing help and information to Hawaii's visitors. Anyone contemplating a trip to Hawaii should visit or write the HVB about any specific information that may be required. Their advice and excellent brochures on virtually every facet of living, visiting, or simply enjoying Hawaii are free. The materials offered are too voluminous to list, but for basics, request individual island brochures (including maps), individual island vacation planners (also on the web at www.hs hawaii.com), and ask for copies of their *Member Accommodation Guide* and *Member Restaurant Guide.* Allow two to three weeks for requests to be answered. (Website: www.gohawaii.com.)

HVB Offices Statewide
Statewide offices include: **HVB Administrative Office,** Waikiki Business Plaza, 2270 Kalakaua Ave., Suite 801, Honolulu, HI 96815, tel. (808) 923-1811; **Oahu Visitors Bureau,** 733 Bishop St., Suite 1872, Honolulu, HI 96813, tel. (877) 525-6248, website: www.visit-oahu.com; **Big Island HVB, Hilo Branch,** 250 Keawe St., Hilo, HI 96720, tel. (808) 961-5797, website: www.big-island.org; **Big Island, Kona Branch,** 75-5719 W. Ali'i Dr., Kailua-Kona, HI 96740, tel. (808) 329-7787; **Kauai HVB,** 3016 Umi St., Suite 207, Lihue, HI 96766, tel. (808) 245-3971, website: www.kauaivisitorsbureau.org; **Maui HVB,** 1727 Wili Pa Loop, Wailuku, HI 96793, tel. (808) 244-3530, website: www.visitmaui.com.

North American Offices
HVB New York, Empire State Bldg., 350 5th Ave., Suite 1827, New York, NY 10018, tel. (212) 947-0717.
   HVB Washington DC, 3975 University Dr., #335, Fairfax, VA 22030, tel. (703) 691-1800.

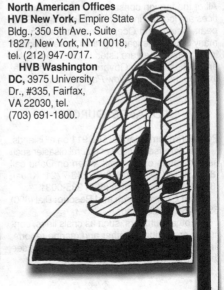

HVB San Diego, 11835 Carmel Mountain Rd., #1304-353, San Diego, CA 92128, tel. (619) 485-7278.

HVB Canada, c/o Comprehensive Travel, 1260 Hornby St., #104, Vancouver, B.C., Canada V6Z1W2, tel. (604) 669-6691.

European Office
HVB United Kingdom, P.O. Box 208, Sunbury on Thames, Middlesex, England, TW165RJ, tel. 44-181-941-4009.

Asia/Pacific Offices
HVB Japan, Kokusai Bldg., #2F, 1-1, Marunouchi 3-chome, Chiyoda-ku, Tokyo 100, tel. 011-81-3-3201-0430.

HVB Korea, c/o Travel Press, Inc., Samwon Bldg., 10th Fl., 112-5, Sokong-dong, Chung-gu, Seoul 100-070, tel. 82-2-773-6719.

HVB New Zealand, c/o Walshes World, 87 Queen St., 2nd Fl., Dingwall Bldg., Auckland, tel. 64-9-379-3708.

HVB Taiwan, c/o Federal Transportation Co., 8th Fl., 61 Nanking E. Rd., Section 3, Taipei, tel. 886-2-507-8133.

FOREIGN CONSULATES

All of the foreign consulates and diplomatic offices are located in Honolulu. Most major European, Asian, and Oceanic nations, along with many South American countries, have delegates in Honolulu. They are listed under "Consulates and Other Foreign Government Representatives" in the Oahu *Yellow Pages.*

LOCAL RESOURCES

Police, fire, ambulance: Dial **911** on all islands.

Civil defense: In case of natural disaster such as hurricanes or tsunamis when on Oahu call (808) 523-4121; Maui, (808) 243-7721; Kauai, (808) 241-6336; Hawaii, (808) 935-0031.

Coast Guard Search and Rescue: Dial (800) 552-6458 on all islands.

For other numbers, such as crisis lines, consumer protection, weather and marine reports, and the *Aloha Pages* information services, see the individual travel chapters below.

Post Offices
Post offices are located in all major towns and cities. Most larger hotels also offer limited postal services. Normal business hours are Mon.-Fri. 8 or 8:30 a.m. to 4 or 4:30 p.m., some offices are open Saturday 8 a.m.-noon. The first three zip code digits, 967, are the same for all of Hawaii, except Honolulu, where it's 968. The last two digits designate the particular post office.

The simplest way to receive mail is to have it sent to your lodgings if you'll be there long enough to receive it. Have it addressed to you in care of your hotel or condo, and include the room number if you know it. It'll be in your box at the front desk. If you plan frequent moves, or a multiple-island itinerary with short stays on each island, have mail sent "General Delivery" to a post office in a town you plan to visit. The post office will hold your mail in general delivery for 30 days. It takes about five days for a first-class letter to arrive in Hawaii from the Mainland. It's a good idea to notify the postmaster of the post office where you will be receiving mail of the dates you expect to pick it up.

OTHER INFORMATION

Telephone
The telephone system on the main islands is modern and comparable to any system on the Mainland. You can "direct dial" from Hawaii to the Mainland and more than 160 foreign countries. Undersea cables and satellite communications ensure top-quality phone service. Public telephones are found at hotels, street booths, restaurants, most public buildings, and some beach parks. It is common to have a phone in most hotel rooms and condominiums, though a service charge is usually collected, even on local calls. The **area code** for all islands is **808.**

Rates
Like everywhere else in the U.S., long-distance rates go down at 5 p.m. and again at 11 p.m. until 8 a.m. the next morning. From Friday at 5 p.m. until Monday morning at 8 a.m. rates are

The area code for all Hawaii is 808

cheapest. Local calls from public telephones (anywhere on the same island is a local call) cost 25 cents. Calling between islands is a toll call, and the price depends on when and from where you call and how long you speak. Emergency calls are always free. For directory assistance: local, 1-411; interisland, 1-555-1212; Mainland, 1-area code-555-1212; toll free, 1-800-555-1212.

Time Zones

There is no daylight saving time in Hawaii. When daylight saving time is not in effect on the Mainland, Hawaii is two hours behind the West Coast, four hours behind the Midwest, and five hours behind the East Coast, and 11 hours behind Germany. Hawaii, being just east of the international date line, is almost a full day behind most Asian and Oceanic cities. Hours behind these countries and cities are: Japan, 19 hours; Singapore, 18 hours; Sydney, 20 hours; New Zealand, 22 hours; Fiji, 22 hours.

Electricity

The same electrical current is in use in Hawaii as on the U.S. Mainland and is uniform throughout the islands. The system functions on 110 volts, 60 cycles of alternating current (AC). Appliances from Japan will work, but there is some danger of burn out, while those requiring the normal European current of 220 will not work.

Distance, Weights, and Measures

Hawaii, like all of the U.S., employs the "English method" of measuring weights and distances. Basically, dry weights are in ounces and pounds; liquid measures are in ounces, quarts, and gallons; and distances are measured in inches, feet, yards, and miles. The metric system, based on units of 10, is known but is not in general use. The conversion chart at the back of the book should be helpful.

MONEY AND FINANCES

Currency

U.S. currency is among the drabbest in the world. It's all the same size and color; those unfamiliar with it should spend some time getting acquainted so that they don't make costly mistakes. U.S. coins include one cent, five cents, 10 cents, 25 cents, 50 cents, and $1 (uncommon); paper currency is $1, $2, (uncommon), $5, $10, $20, $50, $100. Bills larger than $100 are not in common usage.

Banks

Full-service banks tend to open slightly earlier than Mainland banks, at 8:30 a.m. Mon.-Friday. Closing is at 3 p.m., except for late hours on Friday when most banks remain open until 6 p.m. Of most value to travelers, banks sell and cash traveler's checks, give cash advances on credit cards, exchange and sell foreign currency, and have 24-hour ATM machines.

Traveler's Checks

Traveler's checks are accepted throughout Hawaii at hotels, restaurants, car rental agencies, and most stores and shops. However, to be readily acceptable they should be in American currency. Some larger hotels that frequently have Japanese and Canadian guests will accept their currency. Banks accept foreign currency traveler's checks, but it'll mean an extra trip and inconvenience. It's best to get most of your traveler's checks in $20-50 denominations; anything larger will be hard to cash in smaller shops and boutiques, though not in hotels.

Credit Cards

More and more business is transacted in Hawaii using credit cards. Almost every form of accommodation, shop, restaurant, and amusement accepts them. For renting a car they're almost a must. With "credit card insurance" readily available, they're as safe as traveler's checks and sometimes even more convenient. Write down the numbers of your cards in case they're stolen. Don't rely on them completely because some establishments won't accept them, or perhaps won't accept the kind you carry.

NEWSPAPERS AND TOURIST PUBLICATIONS

Hawaii's two main English-language dailies are the *Honolulu Star Bulletin* and the *Honolulu Advertiser,* both with circulations around 100,000. The Japanese-English *Hawaii Hochi* has a circulation of 10,000, and the Chinese *United Chinese Press* sells 1,000 copies per day. All are published on Oahu and are available on the other islands.

Weeklies and Magazines

There's a stampede of weeklies in Hawaii; all major islands have at least one and Oahu has at least six. On Kauai look for the *Kauai Times* and the slightly smaller *Garden Island,* Maui has the *Maui News,* the Big Island offers the *Hawaii Tribune Herald* out of Hilo and *West Hawaii Today,* published in Kailua. All of these papers are great for what's happening and for money-saving coupons for restaurants, rentals, and amusements. A few military newspapers are printed on Oahu, as are a handful of foreign-language newspapers like the *Ashai Shinbun* from Japan and the *Korea Times.*

Aside from these newspapers, several dozen magazines are published in Hawaii, many on business, travel, and sports.

Free Tourist Publications

On every island, at airports, hotel lobbies, shopping malls, and main streets are racks filled with free magazines, pamphlets, and brochures. Sometimes the sheer volume is overwhelming, but most have up-to-the-minute information on what's happening and many money-saving coupons. They're also loaded with maps and directions to points of interest. The best, published in a convenient narrow format, are *This Week . . . Oahu, Maui, Kauai, Big Island,* published weekly. *Guide to . . .* all major islands is in normal magazine format, with good maps. Regional magazines such as *Maui Gold* and *Kona Coast,* are also well worth checking out, as is the weekly *Drive Guide* available from major car rental agencies.

TIDBITS: OFFICIAL AND UNOFFICIAL

Official Hawaii

The state flower is the yellow hibiscus. More than 5,000 species grow in Hawaii. The state tree is the *kukui.* The candlenut was one of the most useful trees of old Hawaii, providing food, medicine, and light. The state bird is the *nene,* a

ISLAND	CITY/TOWN	POP.
Big Island	Hilo	47,000
	Kailua-Kona	10,000
	Captain Cook	2,500
Maui	Kahului/Wailuku	53,000
	Kihei	11,000
	Lahaina	11,000
Lanai	Lanai City	2,800
Molokai	Kaunakakai	2,500
Oahu	Honolulu	400,000
	Kailua/Kaneohe	100,000
	Pearl City	40,000
	Waipahu	30,000
	Wahiawa	17,000

LARGEST CITIES/TOWNS

goose that came to Hawaii eons ago and adapted to the rugged terrain, becoming a permanent resident and losing its instinct for migration. The state fish, with a name bigger than itself, is the Humuhumunukunukuapua'a (humu, for short). Found in a few scattered beds at depths of up to 100 meters is black coral, the state gem. The humpback whale that visits Hawaii every year was made the official mammal in 1979.

Hawaii's nickname is "The Aloha State." The motto, *Ua mau ke ea o ka aina i ka pono* ("The life of the land is perpetuated in righteousness"), came from King Kamehameha III, when in 1843 Hawaii was restored to self-sovereignty after briefly being seized by the British. The anthem, "Hawaii Pono," was written by the "Merry Monarch," King Kalakaua, and put to music by the royal bandmaster, Henri Berger, in 1876. "Hawaii Pono" at one time was the anthem of the Kingdom of Hawaii and later of the Territory before becoming the official state anthem.

Little-Known Facts

The Hawaiian Islands, from Kure Atoll in the north to the Big Island in the south, stretch 1,600 miles. South Point *(Ka Lae)* on the Big Island is the southernmost point of the U.S. The islands are 25 million years old and were entirely created by volcanic activity. Haleakala on Maui is the world's largest inactive volcano, while Hawaii's

Mauna Loa is the world's largest active volcano, and Kilauea is *the* most active volcano in the world. Kauai's Mt. Waialeale is the wettest spot on earth, receiving about 450 inches of rain per year on average. Honolulu's Iolani Palace is the only "Royal Palace" in the United States. Hawaii had the first company (C. Brewer), American school (Lahainaluna), newspaper *(Sandwich Island Gazette),* bank (First Hawaiian), and church (Pukoo, Molokai) west of the Rocky Mountains.

Tidbits
American captains Shaler and Cleveland brought the first horses aboard the *Lydia Byrd,* and introduced them at Lahaina in 1803. Two were given to Kamehameha the Great, who was not impressed. Tattooing was common in old Hawaii; many people had the date of the death of a loved one tattooed on their body, and gouged their eyes and knocked out their own teeth as signs of mourning. The greatest insult was to inlay a spittoon with the teeth of a defeated enemy. The name of the channel between Maui and Kahoolawe, *Kealaikahiki,* means "the way to Tahiti." Voyagers got their bearings here for the long voyage south. "It will happen when Boki comes back" means something is impossible. Boki was a chief who sailed away in 1829 looking for sandalwood. He never returned. Only 20 of the 500 who sailed with him made it back to Hawaii.

BIG ISLAND

In what other land save this one is the commonest form of greeting not "Good Day," . . . but "Love?" . . . Aloha . . . It is the positive affirmation of one's own heart giving.

~Jack London, 1916

SHIP'S ARTIST, JOHN WEBBER

INTRODUCTION

The island of Hawaii is grand in so many ways. Its two nicknames, "The Orchid Island" and "The Volcano Island," are both excellent choices: the island produces more of the delicate blooms than anywhere else on earth; and Pele, the fire goddess who makes her mythological home here, regularly sends rivers of lava from the world's largest and most active volcanoes. However, to the people who live here, Hawaii has only one real nickname, "The Big Island." Big isn't necessarily better, but when you combine it with beautiful, uncrowded, traditional, and inexpensive, it's hard to beat.

The Big Island was the first to be inhabited by the Polynesian settlers, yet it's geologically the youngest of the Hawaiian Islands at barely a million years old. Like all the islands in the Hawaiian chain, it's a mini-continent whose geographical demarcations are much more apparent because of its size. There are parched deserts, steaming fissures, jet-black sand beaches, raw semi-cooled lava flows, snow-covered mountains, upland pastures, entire forests encased in hardened stone, and lush valleys where countless waterfalls break through the rock faces of 1,000-foot-tall chasms. There are small working villages that time has passed by, the state's most tropical city, and an arid coast stretching more than 90 miles where the sun is guaranteed to shine. You'll find some of the islands' least expensive accommodations as well as some of the world's most exclusive resorts.

Historically, the Big Island is loaded with religious upheavals, the births and deaths of great people, vintage missionary homes and churches, reconstructed *heiau,* and even a royal palace. Here is the country's largest privately owned ranch, where cowboy life is the norm; America's oldest and once the only coffee plantations; and enclaves of the counterculture, where people with alternative lifestyles are still trying to keep the faith of the '60s.

Sportspeople love it here, too. The Big Island is a mecca for triathletes and offers snow skiing in season, plenty of camping and hiking, and the best marlin waters in all the oceans of the world.

There are direct flights to the Big Island, where the fascination of perhaps not "old" Hawaii, but definitely "simple" Hawaii, still lingers.

OVERVIEW

Hilo on the east coast and Kailua-Kona on the west are the two ports of entry to the Big Island. At opposite ends of the island as well as of the cultural spectrum, the two have a friendly rivalry. It doesn't matter at which one you arrive, because a trip to the Big Island without visiting both is unthinkable. Better yet, split your stay and use each as a base while you tour. The Big Island is the only Hawaiian island big enough that you can't drive around it comfortably in one day, nor should you try. Each of the six districts is interesting enough to spend at least one day exploring.

Hilo and Vicinity

Hilo is the oldest port of entry, the most tropical town in Hawaii, and the only major city built on the island's windward coast. The city is one tremendous greenhouse where exotic flowers and tropical plants are a normal part of the landscape, and entire blocks canopied by adjoining banyans are taken for granted. The town, which hosts the yearly Merrie Monarch Festival, boasts an early morning fish market, Japanese gardens, the Lyman House Museum, and a profusion of natural phenomena, including Rainbow Falls and Boiling Pots. Plenty of rooms in Hilo are generally easily available, and its variety of restaurants will titillate anyone's taste buds. Both go easy on the pocketbook while maintaining high standards.

Saddle Road begins just outside of Hilo. It slices across the island through a most astonishing high valley or "saddle" separating the mountains of Mauna Loa and Mauna Kea. Passable, but the bane of car rental companies, it slides down the western slope of Mauna Kea meeting the Belt Road from where it's an easy drive to either Waimea or Kona. From the Saddle Road, a spur road heads up to the top of Mauna Kea at 13,796 feet, where a series of astronomical observatories peer into the heavens through the clearest air on earth.

Hamakua Coast

Hamakua refers to the entire northeast coast, where streams, wind, and pounding surf have chiseled the lava into towering cliffs and precipitous valleys known locally by the unromantic name of "gulches." Until recently, all the flatlands here were awash in a green sea of sugarcane; no commercial and few private fields remain. A spur road from the forgotten town of Honomu leads to Akaka Falls, whose waters tumble over a 442-foot cliff—the highest sheer drop of water in Hawaii. North along the coastal road is Honokaa, a one-street town of stores, restaurants, and crafts shops. The main road bears left here to the cowboy town of Waimea, but a smaller road inches farther north. It dead-ends at the top of Waipio Valley, cradled by cliffs on three sides with its mouth wide open to the sea. The valley is reachable only by foot, 4WD vehicle, or horseback. On its verdant floor a handful of families live simply by raising taro, a few head of cattle, and horses. Waipio was a burial ground of Hawaiian *ali'i,* where *kahuna* traditionally came to commune with spirits. The enchantment of this "power spot" remains.

Puna

Puna lies south of Hilo and makes up the majority of the southeast coast. Here are the greatest lava fields that have spewed from Kilauea, the heart of Volcanoes National Park. An ancient flow embraced a forest in its fiery grasp, entombing trees that stand like sentinels today in Lava Tree State Monument. Cape Kumukahi, a pointed lava flow that reached the ocean in 1868, is officially the easternmost point in Hawaii. Just below it is a string of beaches featuring ebony-black sand. Past the small village of Kalapana, the road skirts the coast before it dead-ends where it has been covered over by lava. Chain of Craters Road is now passable only *from* Hawaii Volcanoes National Park. This road spills off the mountain through a forbidding, yet vibrant, wasteland of old lava flows until it comes to the sea, where this living volcano fumes and throbs. Atop the volcano, miles of hiking trails crisscross the park and lead to the very summit of Mauna Loa. You can view the natural phenomena of steaming fissures, boiling mud, Devastation Trail, and Thurston Lava Tube, large enough to accommodate a subway train. Here, too, you can lodge or dine at Volcano House, a venerable inn carved into the rim of the crater.

Kau

Kau, the southern tip of the island, is primarily a

HAWAII (THE BIG ISLAND)

desert. On well-marked trails leading from the main road you'll discover ancient petroglyphs and an eerie set of footprints, the remnants of an ill-fated band of warriors who were smothered under the moist ash of a volcanic eruption and whose demise marked the ascendancy of Kamehameha the Great. Here are some lovely beaches and state parks you'll have virtually to yourself. A tiny road leads to **Ka Lae** (South Point), the most southerly piece of ground in the United States.

Kona

Kona, the west coast, is in every way the opposite of Hilo. It's dry, sunny, and brilliant, with large expanses of old barren lava flows. When watered, the rich soil blossoms, as in South Kona, renowned for its diminutive coffee plantations. The town of Captain Cook, named after the intrepid Pacific explorer, lies just above the very beach where he was slain because of a terrible miscommunication two centuries ago. Ironically, nearby is the restored Pu'uhonua o

Honaunau Heiau, where mercy and forgiveness were rendered to any *kapu*-breaker or vanquished warrior who made it into the confines of this safe refuge.

Kailua-Kona is the center of Kona. The airport is just north of town and here is a concentration of condos and hotels. The town itself boasts an array of art and designer shops; world-class triathletes come here to train, and charter boats depart in search of billfish and other denizens of the deep. Within Kailua is Mokuaikaua Church, a legacy of the very first packet of missionaries to arrive in the islands; and Hulihee Palace, vacation home of the Kamehameha line of kings. Dominating this entire coastline, Mt. Hualalai rises to the east, and northward, the Kona District offers a string of fine beaches.

Kohala

Up the coast in South Kohala is Hapuna Beach, best on the island. In 1965, Laurence Rockefeller opened the Mauna Kea Resort here. For the last three decades, this resort, along with its sculptured, coast-hugging golf course, has been considered one of the finest in the world. Just south is the Kona Village Resort, whose guests spend the night in a "simple" grass shack on the beach. Its serenity is broken only by the soothing music of the surf and by the not-so-melodious singing of "Kona nightingales," a pampered herd of wild donkeys that frequents this area. Over the years, other expansive resorts and golf courses have been added here, making this the island's luxury resort area, on a par with any in the state. Upcountry, at the base of the Kohala Mountains, is **Waimea** (Kamuela), center of the enormous Parker Ranch. Here in the cool mountains, cattle graze in chest-high grass and *paniolo,* astride their sturdy mounts, ride herd in time-honored tradition. Hunters range the slopes of Mauna Kea in search of wild goats and boars, and the Fourth of July is boisterously acknowledged by the wild whoops of cowboys at the world-class Parker Ranch Rodeo.

North Kohala is primarily the hilly peninsular thumb on the northern extremity of the island. Along the coast are beach parks, empty except for an occasional local family picnic. A series of *heiau* dot the coast, and on the northernmost tip a broad plain overlooking a sweeping panorama marks the birthplace of Kamehameha the Great. The main town up here is Hawi, holding on after the sugar companies pulled out a few years ago. Down the road is Kapaau, where Kamehameha's statue resides in fulfillment of a *kahuna* prophecy. Along this little-traveled road, a handful of artists offer their crafts in small shops. At road's end is the overlook of Pololu Valley, where a steep descent takes you to secluded beaches and camping in an area once frequented by some of the most powerful sorcerers in the land.

THE LAND

Science and *The Kumulipo* oral history differ sharply on the age of the Big Island. Scientists say that Hawaii is the youngest of the islands, being a little more than one million years old; the chanters claim that it was the first "island-child" of Wakea and Papa. It is, irrefutably, closest to the "hot spot" on the Pacific floor, evidenced by Kilauea's frequent eruptions and by Loihi Seamount. The geology, geography, and location of the Hawaiian Islands, and their ongoing drifting and building in the middle of the Pacific, make them among the most fascinating pieces of real estate on earth. The Big Island is the *most* fascinating of them all—it is truly unique.

Size

The Big Island dwarfs all the others in the Hawaiian chain at 4,028 square miles and growing. It accounts for about 63% of the state's total land mass; the other islands could fit within it two times over. With 266 miles of coastline, the island stretches about 95 miles from north to south and 80 miles from east to west. Cape Kumukahi is the easternmost point in the state, and Ka Lae (South Point) is the southernmost point in the country.

The Mountains

The tremendous volcanic peak of **Mauna Kea** (White Mountain), located in north-central Hawaii, has been extinct for more than 3,500 years. Its seasonal snowcap earns Mauna Kea its name and reputation as a good skiing area in winter. More than 18,000 feet of mountain below the surface rises straight up from the ocean floor—making Mauna Kea actually 31,796 feet tall, a substantial 2,768 feet taller than Mt. Everest; some consider it the tallest mountain in the world. At 13,796 feet above sea level, it is without doubt the tallest peak in the Pacific. Near its top, at 13,020 feet, is **Lake Waiau,** the highest lake in the state and third highest in the country. Mauna Kea was obviously a sacred mountain to the Hawaiians, and its white dome was a welcome beacon to seafarers. On its slope is the largest adze quarry in Polynesia, from which high-quality basalt was taken to be fashioned into prized tools. The atmosphere atop the mountain, which sits mid-Pacific far from pollutants, is the most rarefied and cleanest on earth. The clarity makes Mauna Kea a natural for astronomical observatories. The complex of telescopes on its summit is internationally staffed and provides data to scientists around the world.

The **Kohala Mountains** to the northwest are the oldest and rise only to 5,480 feet at Kaunu o Kaleiho'ohei peak. This section looks more like the other Hawaiian Islands, with deep gorges and valleys along the coast and a forested interior. As you head east toward Waimea from Kawaihae on Rt. 19, for every mile you travel you pick up about 10 inches of rainfall per year. This becomes obvious as you begin to pass little streams and rivulets running from the mountains.

Mount Hualalai at 8,271 feet is the backdrop to Kailua-Kona. It's home to many of the Big Island's endangered birds and supports many of the region's newest housing developments. Just a few years ago, Mt. Hualalai was thought to be extinct, since the last time it erupted was in 1801. It is now known that within the last thousand years, the mountain has erupted about every two or three centuries. In 1929 it suffered an earthquake swarm, which means that there was a large movement of lava inside the mountain that caused tremors. Now USGS scientists consider Mt. Hualalai only dormant and very likely to erupt at some point in the future. When it does, it's expected to produce a tremendous amount of lava that will pour rapidly down its steep sides.

From the side of this mountain has grown the cone Pu'u Wa'awa'a. At 3,967 feet, it's only slightly shorter than the very active Kilauea on the far side of Mauna Loa. Obsidian is found here and is one of the few places in Hawaii where this substance has been quarried in such quantities.

Even though **Mauna Loa** (Long Mountain) measures a respectable 13,679 feet, its height isn't its claim to fame. This active volcano, 60 miles long by 30 wide, is comprised of 10,000 cubic miles of iron-hard lava, making it the densest and most massive mountain on earth. In 1950, a tremendous lava flow belched from Mauna Loa's summit, reaching an astonishing rate of 6,750,000 cubic yards per hour. Seven lava rivers flowed for 23 days, emitting more than 600 million cubic yards of lava that covered 35 square miles. There were no injuries, but the villages of Kaapuna and Honokua were partially destroyed along with the Magoo Ranch. Its last eruption in 1984 was small by comparison yet created fountaining inside the summit crater and a "curtain of fire" along its eastern rift.

The lowest of the island's major peaks, **Kilauea** rises only to 4,078 feet. Its pragmatic name means "The Spewing," and is the world's most active volcano. In the last hundred years, it has erupted on the average once every 11 months. The Hawaiians believed that the goddess Pele inhabited every volcano in the Hawaiian chain, and that her home is now Halemaumau Crater in Kilauea Caldera. Kilauea is the most scientifically watched volcano in the world, with a permanent observatory built right into the crater rim. When it erupts, the flows are so predictable that observers run toward the mountain, not away from it! The flows, however, can burst from fissures far from the center of the crater in areas that don't seem "active." This occurs mainly in the Puna District. In 1959, Kilauea Iki Crater came to life after 91 years, and although the flow wasn't as massive as others, it did send blazing fountains of lava 1,900 feet into the air. Kilauea has been very active within the last few years, with eruptions occurring at least once a month and expected to continue. Most activity has been from a vent below Pu'u O'o crater. You might be lucky enough to see this phenomenon while visiting.

Tsunamis

Hilo has been struck with the two worst tsunamis in modern history. A giant wave smashed the islands on April 1, 1946, swept away 159 people and more than 1,300 homes; Hilo sustained most of these losses. Again, on May 23, 1960, Hilo took the brunt of a wave that rumbled through the business district killing 61 people. There is an elaborate warning system throughout the island; warning procedures and inundation maps are found in the front of the telephone directory.

Beaches and Ponds

The Big Island takes the rap for having poor beaches—this isn't true! They are certainly few and far between, but they are spectacular. Hawaii is big and young, so distances are greater than on other islands, and the wave action hasn't had enough time to grind new lava and coral into sand. The Kona and Kohala coast beaches, along with a few nooks and crannies around Hilo, are gorgeous. Puna's beaches are incredible black sand, and the southern part of the island has a string of hidden beaches enjoyed only by those intrepid enough to get to them. Full listings are found in the various travel chapters under **Beaches.**

Makalawena, just north of Kona airport on a rough coastal trail, has a beautiful white-sand beach. Inland is its associated wetland pond, probably the most important one on the Big Island. This fragile and archaeologically important area is managed by the Bishop Estate. Currently, entry is not allowed except with a U.S. Fish and Wildlife Service official or a state biologist. However, the Sierra Club and Audubon Society

are permitted to enter, and you can arrange to accompany them on a field trip. If you wish to visit this beautiful area, consider contacting these organizations long before your trip to the Big Island. Two other coastal ponds are located in Kaloko-Honokohau National Historical Park between the Kona airport and Kailua-Kona.

CLIMATE

The average temperature around the island varies between 72 and 78° F. Summers raise the temperature to the mid-80s and winters cool off to the low 70s. Both Kona and Hilo seem to maintain a year-round average of about 74°, and the South Kohala coast is a few degrees warmer. As usual, it's cooler in the higher elevations, and Waimea sees most days in the mid-60s to low 70s, while Volcano maintains a steady 60°. Atop Mauna Kea, the temperature rarely climbs above 50° F or dips below 30, while the summit of Mauna Loa is about 10° warmer. The lowest recorded temperature on the Big Island (and for the state) was 1° F inside the Mauna Kea summit crater in January 1970, while the highest ever recorded was in April 1931 at Pahala in Kau—a scorching (for Hawaii) 100° F.

Rainfall

Weatherwise, the Big Island's climate varies not so much in temperature but precipitation. Hawaii has some of the wettest and driest coastal areas in the islands. The line separating wet from dry can be dramatic. Waimea, for example, has an actual dry and wet side of town, as if a boundary line split the town in two! Houses on the dry side

BIG ISLAND TEMPERATURE AND RAINFALL

TOWN		JAN.	MARCH	MAY	JUNE	SEPT.	NOV.
Hilo	high	79	79	80	82	82	80
	low	62	62	61	70	70	65
	rain	11	15	7	10	10	15
Kona	high	80	81	81	82	82	81
	low	62	64	65	68	68	63
	rain	4	3	2	0	2	1

Note: Temperature is expressed in degrees Fahrenheit; rainfall in inches.

are at a premium. Kona and Hilo are opposites. The Kona Coast is almost guaranteed to be sunny and bright, receiving as little as 15 inches of rainfall per year but with an average of 28 inches. Both Kona and the Kau Desert to the south are in the rain shadow of Mauna Loa, and most rain clouds coming from east to west are pierced by its summit before they ever reach Kona. Hilo is wet, with predictable afternoon and evening showers—they make the entire town blossom. Though this reputation keeps many tourists away, the rain's predictability makes it easy to avoid a drenching while exploring the town. Hilo does get as much as 128 inches of rainfall per year, with a record of 153.93 inches set in 1971. It also holds the dubious honor of being the town with the most rainfall recorded by the National Weather Service in a 24-hour period—a drenching 22.3 inches in February 1979.

FLORA AND FAUNA

The indigenous plants and birds of the Big Island have suffered the same fate as those of the other Hawaiian Islands: they're among the most endangered species on earth and disappearing at an alarming rate. There are some sanctuaries on the Big Island where native species still live, but they must be vigorously protected. Do your bit to save them; enjoy but do not disturb.

COMMON FLORA

The Hawaiians called the **prickly pear cactus** *panini,* which translates as "very unfriendly," undoubtedly because of the sharp spines covering the flat, thick leaves. The cactus is typical of those found in Mexico and the southwestern United States. It was introduced to Hawaii before 1810 and established itself coincidentally with the cattle brought in at the time; *panini* is very common in North Kohala, especially on the Parker Ranch lands. It is assumed that Don Marin, a Spanish advisor to Kamehameha I, was responsible for importing the plant. Perhaps the early *paniolo* (cowboys) felt lonely without it. The *panini* can grow to heights of 15 feet and is now considered a pest, but nonetheless looks as if it belongs. It develops small, delicious, pear-shaped fruits. Hikers who decide to pick the fruit should be careful of small, yellowish bristles that can burrow under the skin and irritate. The beautiful yellow and orange flowers measure three inches across. An attempt is being made to control the cactus in *paniolo* country. *El cosano rojo,* the red worm found in the bottom of Mexican tequila, has been introduced to destroy the plant. It burrows into the cactus and eats the hardwood center, causing the plant to wither and die.

More species of **lobelia** grow in Hawaii than anywhere else in the world. A common garden flower elsewhere, in Hawaii it grows to tree height. You'll see some unique species covered with hair or with spikes. The lobelia flower is tiny and resembles a miniature orchid with curved and pointed ends, like the beak of the native *'i'iwi*. This bird feeds on the flower's nectar; it's obvious that both evolved in Hawaii together and exhibit the strange phenomenon of nature mimicking nature.

The Big Island has more species of **gesneriad,** the African violet family, than anywhere else on earth. Many don't have the showy flowers that you normally associate with African violets, but have evolved into strange species with huge, fuzzy leaves.

The *puahanui,* meaning "many flowers," is Hawaii's native hydrangea; it is common in the upland forests of the Big Island.

Ferns
If you travel to Volcanoes National Park you will find yourself deep in an amazing, high-altitude tropical rainforest. This unique forest exists because of the 120 inches of annual rainfall, which turns the raw lava into a lush forest. Besides stands of ohia and koa, you'll be treated to a primordial display of ferns. All new fronds on ferns are called "fiddleheads" because of the way they unfurl and resemble the scrolls of violin heads. Fiddleheads were eaten by Hawaiians during times of famine. The most common ferns are *hapu'u,* a rather large tree fern, and *amauamau,* a smaller type with a more simple frond. A soft, furry growth around the base of the stalks is

Fiddlehead ferns are prevalent along trails where the lava has weathered.

called *pulu*. At one time *pulu* was collected for stuffing mattresses, and a factory was located atop Volcanoes. But *pulu* breaks down and forms a very fine dust after a few years, so it never really became generally accepted for mattresses.

At high altitudes, young ferns and other plants will often produce new growth that turns bright red as protection against the sun's ultraviolet rays. You'll see it on new foliage before it hardens. Hawaiians called this new growth *liko*. Today, people still make lei from *liko* because it has so many subtle and beautiful colors. Ohia *liko* is a favorite for lei because it is so striking.

BIRDS

You'll spot birds all over the Big Island, from the coastal areas to the high mountain slopes. Some are found on other islands as well, but the ones listed below are found only or mainly on the Big

BIG ISLAND BOTANICAL GARDENS

Hilo Tropical Gardens, 1477 Kalanianaole Ave., Hilo, tel. (808) 935-4957. Open daily 9 a.m.-5 p.m.; admission $3 for self-guided tour. All plants, including plumeria, lipstick trees, anthuriums, orchids, birds of paradise, even pineapples, coconuts, and papayas, have been labeled.

The **Hilo Arboretum,** located along Kilauea Ave., between Lanikaula and Kawili Streets, is maintained by the Department of Natural Resources, Division of Forestry. Open Mon.-Fri. 7:45 a.m.-4:30 p.m., closed Saturday, Sunday, and holidays; free. This tree nursery contains most of the trees present in Hawaii, including indigenous and imported specimens. The site is used for the propagation of rare and endangered plant species, for research, and for experimental pursuits.

Nani Mau Gardens, 421 Makalika St., Hilo, tel. (808) 959-3541, is open daily 8 a.m.-5 p.m. Admission is $5, $2 pp for an optional tram tour, or $6 for a self-drive golf cart. The gardens feature separate areas: fruit orchards, heliconia garden, ginger garden, anthurium garden, orchid garden, orchid pavilion, gardenia garden, and bromeliad garden.

Hawaii Tropical Botanical Gardens, tel. (808) 964-5233, open daily 9 a.m.-5:30 p.m., is a few miles north of Hilo. Admission is $12, children under 16 free. Here you are in the middle of a tamed jungle, walking along manicured paths, among more than 2,000 different species of trees and plants.

Amy B. H. Greenwell Ethnobotanical Garden, tel. (808) 323-3318, along Rt. 11, just past mile marker 110, between the communities of Kealakekua and Captain Cook. The garden is open Mon.-Fri., 7 a.m.-3:30 p.m., guided tours on the second Saturday of every month at 10 a.m., but visitors are welcome any time during daylight hours; free. This 10-acre interpretive ethnobotanical garden has indigenous Hawaiian plants, Polynesian introduced plants, and Hawaiian medicinal plants. The garden has remnants of the Kona field system, which dates from precontact times.

Island. Every bird listed is either threatened or endangered.

Hawaii's Own

The *nene,* or Hawaiian goose, deserves special mention because it is Hawaii's state bird and is making a comeback from the edge of extinction. The *nene* is found only on the slopes of Mauna Loa, Hualalai, and Mauna Kea on the Big Island, and in Haleakala Crater on Maui. It was extinct on Maui until a few birds were returned there in 1957, but some experts maintain that the *nene* lived naturally only on the Big Island. Approximately 500 live on the Big Island.

Good places to view *nene* are in Volcanoes National Park at Kipuka Nene Campground, Summit Caldera, Devastation Trail, and at Volcanoes Golf Course, at dawn and dusk. They gather at the golf course because they love to feed on grasses. The places to view them on the Kona side are at Puulani, a housing development north of Kailua-Kona; or at Kaloka Mauka, another housing development on the slopes of Mt. Hualalai. At the top of the road up Mt. Hualalai is a trail, a good place to see the *nene.* Unfortunately, as the housing developments proliferate and the residents invariably acquire dogs and cats, the *nene* will disappear.

The **Hawaiian crow,** or *alala,* is reduced to fewer than 12 birds living on the slopes of Hualalai and Mauna Loa above the 3,000-foot level. It looks like the common raven but has a more melodious voice and sometimes dull brown

The nene, *the state bird, lives only on the slopes of Mauna Loa and Mauna Kea on the Big Island and in the crater of Haleakala, Maui.*

feathers. The *alala* breeds in early spring, and the greenish-blue, black-flecked eggs hatch from April to June. It is extremely nervous while nesting, and any disturbance will cause it to abandon its young.

The **Hawaiian hawk** (*'io*) primarily lives on the slopes of Mauna Loa and Mauna Kea below 9,000 feet. This noble bird, the royalty of the skies, symbolized the *ali'i.* The hawk exists only on the Big Island, for reasons that are not entirely clear. The *'io* population was once dwindling, and many scientists feared that the bird was headed for extinction. The good news is that the *'io* is making a dramatic comeback.

The **akiapola'au,** a honeycreeper, is a five-inch yellow bird hardly bigger than its name. It lives mainly on the eastern slopes in ohia and koa forests above 3,500 feet. It has a long, curved upper beak for probing and a smaller lower beak that it uses woodpecker-fashion. The *akiapola'au* opens its mouth wide, strikes the wood with its lower beak, and then uses the upper beak to scrape out any larvae or insects. Listen for the distinctive rapping sound to spot this melodious singer. The *akiapola'au* can be seen at the Hakalau Forest National Wildlife Refuge and along the Pu'u O'o Volcano Trail from Volcanoes National Park. It's estimated that only about 1,000 of these rare birds are left.

In addition, two other birds of the Big Island that are considered endangered are the *koloa maoli* duck, which resembles a mallard, and the slate gray or white *alae ke'oke'o* coot.

Marine Birds

Two coastal birds that breed on the high slopes of Hawaii's volcanoes and feed on the coast are the **Hawaiian dark-rumped petrel** (*'ua'u*) and the **Newell shearwater** (*'a'o*). The *'ua'u* lives on the barren high slopes and craters, where it nests in burrows or under stones. Breeding season lasts from mid-March to mid-October. Only one chick is born and is nurtured on regurgitated squid and fish. The *'ua'u* suffers heavily from predation. The *'a'o* prefers the forested slopes of the interior. It breeds April-Nov., and spends its days at sea and nights inland. Feral cats and dogs reduce its numbers considerably. In addition, the *ae'o,* Hawaiian black-necked stilt, has become endangered.

Forest Birds

The following birds are found in the upland forests of the Big Island. The *elepaio* is found on other islands but is also spotted in Volcanoes National Park. The *amakihi* and *'i'iwi* are endemic birds not endangered at the moment. The yellowish green *amakihi* is one of the most common native birds. It is less specialized than most other Hawaiian birds, the main reason for its continued existence. The *'i'iwi* is a bright red bird with a salmon-colored, hooked bill; it feeds on a variety of insects and flowers.

The *apapane* is abundant on Hawaii, especially atop Volcanoes, and being the most common native bird, is the easiest to see. It's a chubby, red-bodied bird about five inches long with a black bill, legs, wingtips, and tail feathers. It's quick and flitty and has a wide variety of calls and songs, from beautiful warbles to mechanical buzzes. Its feathers were sought by Hawaiians to produce distinctive capes and helmets for the *ali'i*.

The **Hawaiian thrush** *(oma'o)* is a fairly common bird found above 3,000 feet in the windward forests of Hawaii. This eight-inch gray bird is a good singer, often seen perching with distinctive drooping wings and a shivering body. The best place to look for it is at the Thurston Lava Tube, where you can see it doing its baby-bird shivering-and-shaking act. A great mimic, it can sound like a cat or even like an old-fashioned radio with stations changing as you turn the dial.

The *akepa* is a four- to five-inch bird. The male is a brilliant orange to red, the female a drab green and yellow. It is found mainly on Hualalai and in windward forests.

The six-inch, bright yellow *palila* is found only on Hawaii in the forests of Mauna Kea above 6,000 feet. It depends exclusively upon *mamane* trees for survival, eating its pods, buds, and flowers.

MAMMALS

Hawaii had only two indigenous mammals: the monk seal *('ilio-holu-i-ka-uaua)* (found throughout the islands) and the hoary bat (found mainly on the Big Island), both of which are threatened or endangered. The remainder of the Big Island's mammals are transplants. But like anything else, including people, that has been in the islands long enough, they have taken on characteristics that make them "local."

The following animals are found primarily on the Big Island. The **Hawaiian hoary bat** *(pe'ape'a)* is a cousin of the Mainland bat. Its tail has a whitish coloration, hence its name. The hoary bat has a 13-inch wingspan. Unlike other bats, it is a solitary creature, roosting in trees. It gives birth to twins in early summer and can often be spotted over Hilo and Kealakekua Bays just around sundown.

The **feral dog** *(ilio)* is found on all the islands but especially on the slopes of Mauna Kea, where packs chase feral sheep. Poisoned and shot by local ranchers, their numbers are diminishing. Black dogs, thought to be more tender, are still eaten in some Hawaiian and Filipino communities.

The **feral sheep** an escaped descendants of animals brought to the islands by Captain Vancouver in the 1790s, and of merinos brought to the island later and raised for their exceptional woolly fleece. These sheep exist only on the Big Island, on the upper slopes of Mauna Loa, Mauna Kea, and Hualalai. The fleece is a buff brown, and its two-foot-wide curved horns are often sought as hunting trophies. Feral sheep are responsible for the overgrazing of young *mamane* trees, necessary to the endangered *palila* bird. In 1979, a law was passed to exterminate or remove the sheep from Mauna Kea so that the native *palila* could survive.

The **mouflon sheep** was introduced to Lanai and Hawaii to cut down on overgrazing and serve as a trophy animal. This Mediterranean sheep can interbreed with feral sheep to produce a hybrid. It lives on the upper slopes of Mauna Loa and Mauna Kea. Unfortunately, its introduction has not been a success. No evidence concludes that the smaller family groups of mouflon cause less damage than the herding feral sheep, and hunters reportedly don't like the meat as much as feral mutton.

The **feral donkey**, better known as the "Kona nightingale," came to Hawaii as a beast of burden. Domesticated donkeys are found on all islands, but a few wild herds still roam the Big Island along the Kona Coast, especially near the exclusive Kona Village Resort at Kaupulehu.

Feral cattle were introduced by Captain Vancouver, who gave a few domesticated head to Kamehameha; immediately a *kapu* against killing them went into effect for 10 years. The lush grasses of Hawaii were perfect and the cattle flourished; by the early 1800s they were out of control and were hunted and exterminated. Finally, Mexican cowboys were brought to Hawaii to teach the locals how to be range hands. From this legacy sprang the Hawaiian *paniolo*.

MARINE LIFE

Humpback Whales

Humpback whales, known in Hawaii as *kohola,* migrate to Hawaiian waters yearly, arriving in late December and departing by mid-March. The best places to view them are along the South Kona Coast, especially at Kealakekua Bay and Ka Lae (South Point), with many sightings off the Puna coast around Isaac Hale Beach Park.

Hawksbill Turtle

Hawaii Volcanoes National Park stretches from the top of Mauna Kea all the way down to the sea. It is here, around Apua Point, that three of the last-known nesting sites of the very endangered hawksbill turtle *(honu 'ea)* are found. This creature has been ravished in the Pacific, where it is ruthlessly hunted for its shell, which is made into women's jewelry, especially combs. It is illegal to bring items made from turtle shell into the U.S., but the hunt goes on.

Billfish

Although these magnificent game fish occur in various South Sea and Hawaiian waters, catching them is easiest in the clear, calm waters off the Kona Coast. The billfish—swordfish, sailfish, marlin, and *a'u*—share two distinctive common features: a long, spearlike or swordlike snout and a prominent dorsal fin. The three main species of billfish caught are the blue, striped, and black marlin. Of these three, the **blue marlin** is the leading game fish in Kona waters. The blue has tipped the scales at well over 1,000 pounds, but the average fish weighs in at 300-400 pounds. When alive, this fish is a striking cobalt blue, but when dead, its color changes to slate blue. It feeds on skipjack tuna; throughout the summer, fishing boats look for schools of tuna as a tip-off to blues in the area. The **black marlin** is the largest and most coveted catch for blue-water anglers. This solitary fish is infrequently found off the banks of Kona. Granddaddies can weigh 1,800 pounds, but the average is a mere 200. The **striped marlin** is the most common commercial billfish, a highly prized food served in finer restaurants and often sliced into sashimi. Its coloration is a remarkable royal blue. Its spectacular leaps when caught give it a great reputation as a fighter. The striped marlin is smaller than the other marlins, so a 100-pounder is a very good catch.

THE HAKALAU FOREST NATIONAL WILDLIFE REFUGE

The Hakalau Forest National Wildlife Refuge, acquired with the help of the Nature Conservancy but administered solely by the U.S. Fish and Wildlife Service, is a large tract of land off the Saddle Road that goes all the way up to the Parker Ranch lands. It's upland forest and scrub that drifts down into solid rainforest. The U.S. Fish and Wildlife Service is working hard to reconvert this refuge into natural habitat and efforts include fencing, snaring, and hunting, ridding the area of feral pigs and cattle, and replanting with koa, ohia, opeka, pilo, and other native species while removing introduced and exotic foliage. It's a tremendous task that's mainly being shouldered by Dick Wass and Jack Jeffrey, rangers with the U.S. Fish and Wildlife Service. The refuge is not adequately staffed to accept visits by the general public at all times, but the Maulau Tract, the northernmost section of the refuge, is open for hiking and birding on the last weekend of every month. This area is a two hour drive from Hilo, one half of which is over a rugged dirt road traversable only by a 4WD vehicle. Additionally, the refuge is open the first three weekends of the month for public hunting of feral pigs. Numerous volunteer opportunities are available for various ongoing projects, either in the field or at the greenhouse, for a weekend or week-long stint. If you *truly* have a dedication to help and aren't afraid to get your hands dirty, contact Dick or Jack for a very rewarding experience. To enter the refuge for any reason, first contact the office, tel. (808) 933-6915 or fax 933-6917, and make arrangements. The refuge is very beautiful, a diamond in the rough, and en- compasses an incredible rainforest like few on the Big Island.

HISTORY

The Big Island plays a significant role in Hawaii's history. A long list of "firsts" have occurred here. Historians generally believe (backed up by oral tradition) that the Big Island was the first in the Hawaiian chain to be settled by the Polynesians. The dates now used are A.D. 600-700. Hawaii is geographically the closest island to Polynesia; Mauna Loa and especially Mauna Kea, with its white summit, present easily spotted landmarks. Psychologically, the Polynesian wayfarers would have been very attracted to Hawaii as a lost homeland. Compared to Tahiti and most other South Sea Islands (except Fiji's main islands), it's huge. It *looked* like the promised land. Some may wonder why the Polynesians chose to live atop an obviously active volcano and not by- pass it for a more congenial island. The volcan- ism of the Big Island is comparatively gentle; the lava flows follow predictable routes and rarely turn killer. The animistic Hawaiians would have been drawn to live where the godly forces of na- ture were so apparent. The mana (power) would be exceptionally strong, and therefore the *ali'i* would be great. Human sacrifice was introduced to Hawaii at Waha'ula Heiau in the Puna Dis- trict in the 13th century, and from there *luakini* (human-sacrifice temples) spread throughout the islands.

The Great One

The greatest native son of Hawaii, Kamehame- ha, was born under mysterious circumstances in the Kohala District, probably in 1753. Kame- hameha became a renowned warrior and a loyal retainer to his uncle, Kalaniopuu, the *moi* (ruler) of Hawaii. Before Kalaniopuu died, he made Kamehameha the keeper of the feathered fam- ily war god, Kukailimoku, or Ku the Land Snatch- er, while Kamehameha's cousins Kiwalao and Keoua engaged in a civil war over land rights. Kamehameha, aided by disgruntled chiefs from Kona, waged war on both, and at Mokuohai, Ki- walao was killed. Kamehameha went on to fight on Maui. By this time he had acquired a small

ship, the *Fair American,* and using cannon manned by two white sailors, Isaac Davis and John Young, he defeated the Maui warriors at Iao Valley. If he could defeat Keoua at home, he would be king of all Hawaii.

The Gods Speak

A great oracle from Kauai announced war would end on Hawaii only after a great *heiau* was built at Puukohola (Kawaihae), dedicated by the corpse of a great chief. Kamehameha instantly set about building this *heiau,* and through cun- ning, wisdom, and true belief placed the con- quest of Hawaii in the hands of the gods. Mean- while, a fleet of war canoes belonging to Ka- hekili of Maui attacked Kamehameha's forces at Waimanu, near Waipio. Aided again by the *Fair American* and Davis and Young, Kame- hameha won a decisive battle and subdued Ka- hekili once and for all. Keoua seized this oppor- tunity to ravage Kamehameha's lands all the way from Waipio to Hilo. He sent his armies south through Kau, but when the middle legions were passing the foot of Kilauea, it erupted and suffocated them with poisonous gas and a heavy deposit of ash. Footprints, encased in the ce- mentlike ash, still mark their last steps.

Kamehameha and Keoua both took this as a direct sign from the gods. Kamehameha returned to Puukohala and finished the *heiau.* Upon com- pletion he summoned Keoua, who came by canoe with a small band of warriors resplendent in feather helmet and cape. He knew the fate that awaited him, and when he stepped ashore he was slaughtered by Keeaumoku. Keoua's body was laid on the altar, and at that moment the islands of Hawaii were united under one supreme ruler, Kamehameha, The Lonely One. He ruled until his death in 1819, and his passing marked the beginning of the end for old Hawaii.

Great Changes

The great navigator and explorer, Captain Cook, was killed at Kealakekua Bay on February 14,

1779. Kalaniopuu was still alive at the time and Kamehameha was only a minor chief, although Cook had previously written about him in the ship's log when he came aboard off Maui. During Kamehameha's reign ships from the United States, England, and various European countries came to trade. Americans monopolized the lucrative sandalwood business with China, and New England whalers discovered the rich whaling waters. The Englishman, Captain Vancouver, became a trusted advisor of Kamehameha and told him about the white people's form of worship, while introducing plants and animals such as oranges, grapes, cows, goats, and sheep. He even interceded for Kamehameha with his headstrong queen, Kaahumanu, coaxing her out from her hiding place under a rock at Pu'uhonua o Honauanau, where she had sought refuge from Kamehameha's wrath.

When Kamehameha died in 1819, Hawaii was ripe for change. His two great queens, Kaahumanu and Keopuolani, realized the old ways were coming to an end. They encouraged Liholiho (Kamehameha II) to end the *kapu* system. Men and women were forbidden to eat together, and those who violated this principal *kapu* were immediately killed to placate the gods before they retaliated with grave destruction. Keopuolani defied this belief when she sat down with Kauikeaouli, the seven-year-old brother of Li-

holiho. The gods remained quiet. Encouraged, Liholiho called for a great *luau* at Kailua, and openly sat down to eat with his chiefs and chieftesses. Symbolically, the impotent gods were toppled with every bite, and *heiau* and idols were razed throughout the land.

Into this spiritual vortex sailed the brig *Thaddeus* on April 4, 1820. Those on board had set sail from Boston on October 23, 1819, lured to the Big Island by Henry Opukahaia, a local boy born at Napoopoo in 1792. Coming ashore at Kailua-Kona, the Reverends Bingham and Thurston were granted a one-year trial period by King Liholiho. Hawaii changed forever in those brief months. By 1824 the new faith had such a foothold that Chieftess Keopuolani climbed to the fire pit atop Kilauea and defied Pele. This was even more striking than the previous breaking of the food *kapu* because the strength of Pele could actually be seen. Keopuolani ate forbidden *ohelo* berries and cried out, "Jehovah is my God." Over the next decades the governing of Hawaii slipped away from the Big Island and moved to the new port cities of Lahaina, and later, Honolulu. In 1847, the Parker Ranch began with a two-acre grant given to John Parker. He coupled this with 360 acres given to his *ali'i* wife Kipikane by the land division known as the Great *Mahele*.

GOVERNMENT

The county of Hawaii is almost entirely Democratic and currently has only one Republican elected state legislative member. The current mayor is Stephen K. Yamashiro, a Democrat. The mayor is assisted by an elected county council consisting of nine members, one from each council district around the island.

Of the 25 State Senatorial Districts, Hawaii County is represented by three, all Democrats.

The First District takes in the whole northern section of the island: the Hamakua Coast, Mauna Kea, North and South Kohala, and part of North Kona. The Second District is mainly Hilo and its outlying area. The Third comprises Puna, Kau, South Kona, and most of North Kona. Hawaii County has six of 51 seats in the State House of Representatives.

ECONOMY

The Big Island's economy is the state's most agriculturally based. More than 6,000 farmlands, horticultural workers, and *paniolo* work the land to produce about one third of the state's vegetables and melons and more than three quarters of the fruit, especially papaya. The Big Island also produces 60 million pounds of macadamia nuts, the state's entire crop except for what's produced by small farms here and there on the other islands. Hawaii has the oldest commercial coffee plantations in the state. Each year, due to the increased interest in gourmet Kona coffee, its share in the economy of the island is increasing. The Big Island is the only place in the country where cocoa beans for making chocolate are grown commercially. About 300 or more horticultural farms produce the largest number of orchids and anthuriums in the state, leaving the Big Island awash in color and fragrance. In the hills, entrepreneurs raise *pakalolo* (marijuana), which has become the state's most productive cash crop. More than $400 million worth is confiscated every year by law enforcement agencies (two-thirds of the total taken in the state), so you can imagine how much remains to hit the street.

Sugar

Hawaii used to be the state's largest sugar grower, with more than 90,000 acres in cane. These commercial fields produced four million tons of refined sugar, 40% of the state's output. The ma-

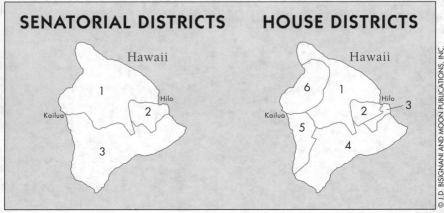

SENATORIAL DISTRICTS

HOUSE DISTRICTS

© J.D. BISIGNANI AND MOON PUBLICATIONS, INC.

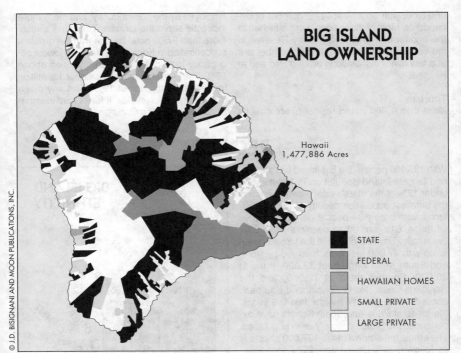

BIG ISLAND
LAND OWNERSHIP

Hawaii
1,477,886 Acres

STATE

FEDERAL

HAWAIIAN HOMES

SMALL PRIVATE

LARGE PRIVATE

© J.D. BISIGNANI AND MOON PUBLICATIONS, INC.

jority of sugar land was along the Hamakua Coast, long known for its abundant water supply. At one time, the cane was even transported to the mills by water flumes. Another large pocket of cane fields was found on the southern part of the island, mostly in Puna. With the closing of the last mill in 1996, sugar has no longer been grown commercially on the island on any large scale. Still, small entrepreneurial farms grow it on greatly reduced acreage. The big cane trucks have ceased to roll and the smokestacks stand in silent testimony to an era gone by.

Coffee

Coffee has been grown on the Big Island since 1828. The Kona District is a splendid area for raising coffee; it gives the beans a beautiful tan. Lying in Mauna Loa's rain shadow, it gets dewy mornings followed by sunshine and an afternoon cloud shadow. This coffee has long been accepted as gourmet quality, and is sold in the better restaurants throughout Hawaii and in fine coffee shops around the world. It's a dark, full-bodied coffee with a rich aroma. Approximately 650 small farms produce nearly $7 million a year in coffee revenue. Few, however, make it a full-time business. The production of Kona coffee makes up only about one tenth of one percent of the coffee grown around the world. As such a rare bean, it's often blended with other varieties. When sold unblended it is quite expensive.

Cattle

Hawaii's cattle ranches produce more than 5 million pounds of beef per year, 50% of the state's total. More than 400 independent ranches are located on the island, but they are dwarfed both in size and production by the massive Parker Ranch (now held as a public trust), which alone is three-quarters the size of Oahu.

The Military

On average, there are about 60 military personnel are stationed on the Big Island at any one time, with about the same number of dependents. Most of these people are attached to the enormous Pohakuloa Military Reserve in the center of the island; a lesser number are at a few minor installations around Hilo and at Kilauea.

Tourism

More than 4,000 island residents are directly employed by the hotel industry, and many more indirectly serve the tourists. There are slightly more than 9,500 hotel rooms, with the greatest concentration in Kona. They have the lowest occupancy rate in the state, rarely rising above 60%. The Big Island receives about 1.2 million tourists annually, about 19,500 on any given day. Of the major islands, it ranks third in annual visitors, following Oahu and Maui.

PEOPLE

With 137,000 people, the Big Island has the second-largest island population in Hawaii, just under 12% of the state's total. However, it has the smallest population density of the main islands, with barely 34 people per square mile. Of these, 61% are urban dwellers while 39% live rurally. The Hilo area has the largest population with 47,000 residents, followed by North and South Kona with about 33,000, Puna at 28,000, South Kohala at 12,000, and the Hamakua Coast, North Kohala, and Kau each about 5,000-6,000. Within the last five years, the areas of Puna and South Kohala have experienced the greatest increases in population. The ethnic breakdown of the 137,000 people is as follows: 34% Caucasian, 27% Japanese, 19% Hawaiian, 14% Filipino, 2% Chinese, 4% other.

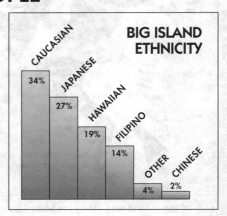

SPORTS AND RECREATION

You'll have no problem having fun on the Big Island. Everybody goes outside to play. You can camp and hike, drive golf balls over lagoons, smack tennis balls at private and public courts, ski, snorkel, windsurf, gallop a horse, bag a wild turkey, spy a rare bird, or latch on to a marlin that'll tail-walk across a windowpane sea. Choose your sport and have a ball.

CAMPING AND HIKING

The Big Island has the best camping in the state, with more facilities and less competition for campsites than on the other islands. More than three dozen parks fringe the coastline and sit deep in the interior; almost half offer camping. The others boast a combination of rugged hikes, easy strolls, self-guided nature walks, swimming, historical sites, and natural phenomena. The ones with campgrounds are state-, county-, and nationally operated, ranging from remote walk-in sites to housekeeping cabins. All require camping permits—inexpensive for the county and state parks, free for the national park. Camping permits can be obtained by walk-in application to the appropriate office or by writing. Although there is usually no problem obtaining sites, when writing, request reservations well in advance, allowing a minimum of one month for letters to go back and forth.

General Information

Most campgrounds have pavilions, fireplaces, toilets (sometimes pit), and running water, but usually no individual electrical hookups. Pavilions often have electric lights, but sometimes campers appropriate the bulbs, so it's wise to carry your own. Drinking water is available, but at times brackish water is used for flushing toilets and for showers, so read all signs regarding water. Backcountry shelters have catchment water, but never hike without an adequate supply of your own. Cooking fires are allowed in established fire pits, but no wood is provided. Charcoal is a good idea. When camping in the mountains, be prepared for cold and rainy weather. Women, especially, should never hike or camp alone, and everyone should exercise precaution against theft, though it's not as prevalent as on the other islands.

County Parks

The county-maintained parks are open to the public for day-use, and permits are only required for overnight camping (tents or RVs). For information write: Department of Parks and Recreation, County of Hawaii, 25 Aupuni St., Hilo, HI 96720, tel. (808) 961-8311. You can obtain a permit by mail or pick it up in person, 8 a.m.-4:30 p.m., Mon.-Friday. If you'll be arriving after hours or on a weekend, have the permits mailed to you. Branch offices (most with reduced hours) are located at Hale Halawai in Kailua-Kona, tel. (808) 329-5277; in Waimea Community Center in Waimea, tel. (808) 885-5454; in Yano Hall in Captain Cook, tel. (808) 323-3060; in Naalehu, tel. (808) 929-9166, and in Pahala, tel. (808) 928-6206. Fees are $1 per adult p/d; children 13-17 pay 50 cents p/d; youngsters camp free. Pavilions for exclusive use are $5 p/d with kitchen, $2 without. Camping is limited to one week for any one site June-Aug. and for two weeks at any one site for the rest of the year.

State Parks and Cabins

Day-use of state parks is free, with no permit required, but you will need one for tent camping and for cabins. Five consecutive nights is the limit for either camping or cabins at any one site. If you want a permit, at least one week's notice is required regardless of availability. You can pick up your permit at the state parks office 8 a.m.-4

Rainbow Falls

p.m. (applications accepted only 8 a.m.-noon), but again it saves time if you do it all by mail. Write: Department of Land and Natural Resources, Division of State Parks, Box 936 (75 Aupuni St.), Hilo, HI 96721, tel. (808) 974-6200.

Camping is permitted only at Kalopa and MacKenzie State Recreation Areas (SRA). Cabins are located at Mauna Kea SRA's Pohakuloa Camp, tel. (808) 935-7237 and Kalopa SRA, tel. (808) 775-7114. A-frames are located only at Hapuna Beach SRA, tel. (808) 882-7995. A-frames are a flat $20 per night. The housekeeping cabins at Mauna Kea SRA are $45 for up to four persons, and group cabins at Mauna Kea and Kalopa SRAs are $55 for up to eight people. When writing for permits, specify exactly which facility you require, for how long, and for how many people.

Hawaii Volcanoes National Park

The day use of campgrounds in Hawaii Volcanoes National Park is free but for overnight camping, permits are required and available through the park visitor center. The drive-in campgrounds throughout the park can be reserved, but usually operate on a first-come, first-served basis. Your stay is limited to seven days per campground per year. A-frame cabins are provided at Namakani Paio Campground, and arrangements are made through Volcano House, Hawaii Volcanoes National Park, HI 96718, tel. (808) 967-7321. There are free walk-in trail cabins and shelters throughout the park; you can't re-

serve them and you should expect to share them with other hikers. Coleman stoves and lanterns are sometimes provided (check), but you provide the fuel. Basic bedding and cooking utensils are also there for your convenience. Shelters, in the park along the coast, are three-sided, open affairs that offer only a partial covering against the elements. For information on camping and hiking in the park, write Hawaii Volcanoes National Park, P.O. Box 52, Hawaii National Park, HI 96718.

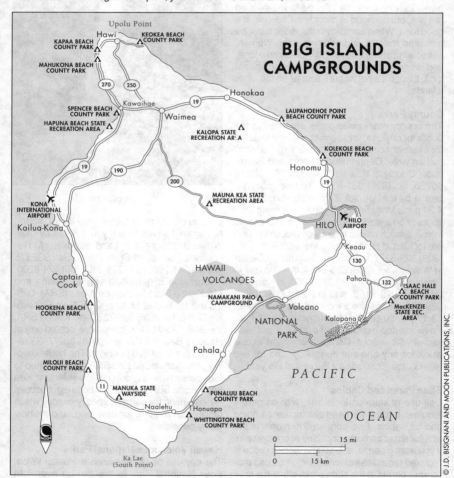

BIG ISLAND CAMPGROUNDS

© J.D. BISIGNANI AND MOON PUBLICATIONS, INC.

Hiking the Big Island

Hiking on the Big Island is stupendous. There's something for everyone, from civilized walks to the breathtaking Akaka Falls to huff-puff treks to the summit of Mauna Loa. The largest number of trails, and the most outstanding according to many, are laced across Volcanoes National Park. After all, this is the world's most active volcano. You can hike across the crater floor, spurred on by the knowledge that it can shake to life at any moment. Or dip down off the mountain and amble the lonely trails in the Kau Desert or remains of the King's Coastal Trail in Puna.

The most important thing to do before heading out in Volcanoes is to stop at Park Headquarters and inquire about trail conditions. Make absolutely sure to register, giving the rangers your hiking itinerary. In the event of an eruption, they will be able to locate you and send a helicopter if necessary. Follow this advice; your life may depend upon it! Everyone can enjoy vistas on Devastation Trail, Sulfur Bank, or at the Thurston Lava Tube without any danger whatsoever. In the north you'll find Waipio, Waimanu, and Pololu Valleys. All offer secluded hiking and camping where you can play Robinson Crusoe on your own beach and gather a variety of island fruits from once-cultivated trees gone wild.

Birdwatching and Hiking Tours

Hawaii has its fair share of birds. One type or other of the state's many species can be seen and heard wherever you are on the island, whether sunbathing along the shore, putting on a golf green, or hiking high on the mountainside. The most common will soon be obvious, but to see some of Hawaii's rare winged creatures you have to be adventurous, quiet, and willing to walk. Be sure to bring your binoculars. Anyone can appreciate birds where they are, but hardcore birders might want to go to spots where the chance of getting a fleeting glimpse of that "rare one" will be greater.

If you're not familiar with good birdwatching spots on Hawaii contact Rob or Cindy Pacheco at **Hawaii Forest & Trail,** tel. (808) 322-8881 or (800) 464-1993, (fax) 322-8883, P.O. Box 2975, Kailua-Kona, HI 96745, e-mail: hitrail @aloha.net, website: www.hawaii-forest. This well-established naturalist company uses 4WD vehicles to get you to where the less common

birds are. This company's two exclusive birdwatching tours take you to the rainforests of the Pu'u O'o Ranch and the Hakalau National Wildlife Refuge, both on the eastern slope of Mauna Kea. Their other tours include the Rainforest Discovery Adventure to the Pu'u O'o Ranch, the Palani Ranch Mountain Adventure on the slopes of Hualalai Volcano, the Valley Waterfall Adventure to the spectacular Pololu Valley of North Kohala, the Kohala Mule Trail Adventure into Pololu Valley, and a tour to the Hawaii Volcanoes National Park. Two new half-day tours are the Kahua Cloud Forest Adventure and the Kaupulehu Cave Adventure. Other birdwatching and custom tours can be arranged. All tours are kept to a maximum of 10 people, guided by knowledgeable naturalists, fully catered, provide the necessary equipment, and include pickup and drop-off from your accommodation in Kona or from the Kona airport. The birdwatching, rainforest, and volcano tours run $130 pp, the valley waterfall tour $110 ($79 for a half day), and the geologic and natural history Palani Ranch tour $110. The new mule ride into Pololu Valley runs $95 for adults and $85 for children ages 11-15. Children ages 5-12 are discounted 15%; kids below age five are free. The cloud forest hike and the cave scramble run $89 for adult and $79 for children 12 and below. Children under age eight are not allowed on the cave tour.

Birdwatching tours are also the specialty of **McCandless Ranch Ecotour,** tel. (808) 328-8246, on their 15,000 acre spread across the lower slopes on Mauna Loa. Many of Hawaii's endangered and threatened birds can be seen here. Tours last all day and run about $400 per couple. Early risers only, as the group heads out before 6 a.m. from their headquarters at 1,100 feet. For those who want to be close at hand, ask about their B&B accommodations.

The Big Island **Audubon Society** group also runs periodic bird watching excursions. For information, contact them at P.O. Box 1371, Kailua-Kona, HI 96745 or call (808) 329-9141.

A well-established and reputable hiking company that will help you stretch your legs in the great outdoors yet have minimal impact on the land is **Hawaiian Walkway,** P.O. Box 2193, Kamuela, Hawaii 96743, tel./fax (808) 885-7759 or (800) 457-7759. Not for the faint-hearted, hikes last 6-10 hours. Custom hikes and hiking/

camping tours can also be arranged. Six basic hikes are offered, which take you to Hawaii Volcanoes National Park, the north Kohala mountains and valleys, along the north Kona coast, and up on the slope of Mt. Hualalai. Scheduled day hikes run $110 for adults and $80 for children under age 13; custom hikes are $125 and $95, respectively. A small day pack, rain gear, lunch and drinks are provided.

The **Kona Hiking Club,** tel. (808) 328-8192, offers organized hikes on the island. Write them for information: P.O. Box 569, Captain Cook, HI 96704.

For a more educational, "guided geologic adventure" on one of the earth's most changeable pieces of real estate, try **Hawaii Volcano Geo-Ventures,** P.O. Box 794, Volcano, HI 96785, tel. (808) 985-8972, e-mail: jbabb@aloha.net; website: planet-hawaii.com/hea/volcano.

Precautions

Always tell a ranger or official of your hiking intentions. Supply an itinerary and your expected route, then stick to it. Be aware of current lava flows, and heed all posted advice. If lost, walk on ridges and avoid the gulches, which have more obstacles and make it harder for rescuers to spot you. Be careful of elevation sickness, especially on Mauna Loa and Mauna Kea. The best cure is to descend as soon as possible.

Heat can cause you to lose water and salt. If you become woozy or weak, rest, take salt, and drink water as you need it. Remember, it takes much more water to restore a dehydrated person than to keep hydrated; take small, frequent sips. Be mindful of flash floods. Small creeks can turn into raging torrents with upland rains. Never camp in a dry creekbed. Fog is only encountered at elevations of 1,500-5,000 feet, but be careful of disorientation. Generally, stay within your limits, be careful, and enjoy yourself.

Camping Equipment and Maps

You can find plenty of stores that sell, and a few stores that rent, camping equipment. Try **Hilo Surplus Store,** 148 Mamo Ave. in downtown Hilo, tel. (808) 935-6398; **Pacific Rent All,** 1080 Kilauea Ave., Hilo, tel. (808) 935-2974; **Kona Rent All,** tel. (808) 329-1644; and **C&S Cycle and Surf,** tel. (808) 885-5005, in Waimea

On the Big Island, **Basically Books,** in downtown Hilo at 46 Waianuenue St., tel. (808) 961-0144, has an unbeatable selection of maps. You can get anywhere you want to go with their nautical charts, road maps, and topographical maps, which include sectionals for serious hikers and trekkers. Their collection covers most of the Pacific. Also try **Big Island Marine, Inc.,** 73-4840 Kanalani St., #A-1, Kailua-Kona, HI 96740, tel. (808) 329-3719.

DEEP-SEA AND FRESHWATER FISHING

Fishing Boats and Charters

The fishing around the Big Island's Kona Coast ranges from excellent to outstanding! It's legendary for marlin fishing, but there are other fish in the sea. A large fleet of charter boats with skilled captains and tested crews is ready, willing, and competent to take you out. The vast majority are berthed at Honokohau Small Boat Harbor just north of Kailua-Kona. The best times of year for marlin are July-Sept. and Jan.-March (when the generally larger females arrive). August is the optimum month. Rough seas can keep boats in for a few days during December and early January, but by February all are generally out.

To charter a boat, contact the individual captains directly, check at your hotel activities desk, or book through one of the following agencies. **Charter Services Hawaii,** operated by Ed Barry, tel. (808) 334-1881 or (800) 567-5662, offers more than 50 boats in all sizes and price ranges from which to choose. Ed also offers complete packages including room, car, and boat along with a cash prize of $1 million if you book through his agency and top the world record. If you're after a company that's knowledgeable about getting you onto a boat that will bring you to waters where you'll have the opportunity to catch one of the twirling and gigantic "big blues," this is the place to come. (E-mail: fishing@aloha.com; website: www.aloha.com/~hdc/charter). Located on the dock at Honokohau Harbor, the **The Charter Desk,** tel. (808) 329-5735 or (800) 566-2487, is another reputable booking agency that tries to match you and your desire with the right boat and captain for best results. Other general booking agencies include: **Kona Activities Cen-**

ter in Kailua-Kona, tel. (808) 329-3171 and **Kona Charter Skippers Assoc.,** P.O. Box 806, Kailua-Kona, HI 96740, tel. (808) 329-3600.

Most of the island's 80 charter boats are berthed at Honokohau Harbor off Rt. 19, about midway between downtown Kailua and Kona Airport. Big fish are sometimes still weighed in at Kailua Pier, in front of King Kamehameha's Kona Beach Hotel for the benefit of the tourists. But Honokohau Harbor has eclipsed Kailua Pier, which is now tamed and primarily for swimmers, triathletes, and boogie boarders. Congestion makes it difficult for charter boats to get in and out so the majority of the trade has moved up to Honokohau.

An excellent publication listing boats and general deep-sea fishing information is **Fins and Fairways, Hawaii,** P.O. Box 9014, Kailua-Kona, HI 96745, tel. (808) 325-6171 or (800) 367-8014 from the Mainland, or fax (808) 325-6378, e-mail: fishkona@fishkona.com; website: www.fish-kona.com. This tabloid, published by Capt. Tom Armstrong and available free at newsstands and in hotel/condo lobbies, is filled with descriptions of boats, phone numbers, captains' names, maps, and photos of recent catches. Write for subscription rates. For general fishing information and a listing of tournaments throughout the islands, pick up a copy of the *Hawaii Fishing News* at a newsstands or supermarket.

You can also contact **The Hawaiian International Billfish Assoc.,** tel. (808) 329-6155, 74-381 Kealakehe Pkwy, Kailua-Kona, HI 96740, for details on upcoming tournaments and on "what's biting and when."

Coastal and Freshwater Fishing

You don't have to hire a boat to catch fish! The coastline is productive too. *Ulua* are caught all along the coast south of Hilo, and at South Point and Kealakekua Point. *Papio* and *halalu* are caught in bays around the island, while *manini* and *ama'ama* hit from Kawaihae to Puako. Hilo Bay is easily accessible to anyone, and the fishing is very exciting, especially at the mouth of the Wailuku River.

Licensed fishing is limited to the **Waiakea Public Fishing Area,** a state-operated facility in downtown Hilo. This 26-acre pond offers a variety of saltwater and brackish-water species. A license is required. You can pick one up at sport-

ing goods stores or at the Division of Conservation and Resources Enforcement Office, 75 Aupuni St., Hilo, HI 96720, tel. (808) 974-6201.

SNORKELING, SCUBA, AND OTHER WATER SPORTS

Scuba

Those in the know consider the deep diving along the steep drop-offs of Hawaii's geologically young coastline some of the best in the state. The ocean surrounding the Big Island has not had a chance to turn the relatively new lava to sand, which makes the visibility absolutely perfect, even to depths of 150 feet or more. There's also 60-70 miles of coral belt around the Big Island, which adds up to a magnificent diving experience. Only advanced divers should attempt deep-water dives, but beginners and snorkelers will have many visual thrills inside the protected bays and coves.

Companies and Equipment Rentals

More than two dozen companies on the Big Island, mostly in Kona, offer scuba instruction and escorted dives, and rent scuba and snuba equipment.

One of the best outfits to dive with on the Big Island is **Dive Makai** in Kona, tel. (808) 329-2025, operated by Tom Shockley and Lisa Choquette. These very experienced divers have run this service for years and have many dedicated customers. Both Tom and Lisa are conservationists who help preserve the fragile reef. They've worked very hard with the Diver's Council to protect dive sites from fish collectors and to protect the reef from destruction by anchors. Their motto, "We care," is not a trite saying, as they continue to preserve the reef for you and your children.

Another excellent diving outfit is **Jack's Diving Locker,** tel. (808) 329-7585, (800) 345-4807, 75-5819 Ali'i Dr.—a responsible outfit that does a good job of watching out for their customers and taking care of the reef. Owners, Teri and Jeff Leicher (Jeff logged his 10,000th dive in 1996), along with their crew, run diving and snorkeling excursions along the Kona Coast from Kealakekua Bay to Keahole Point, which takes in more than 50 dive sites (most of which have permanent moorings to protect the reef from damage by anchoring). Jack's also specializes in snorkel sales and rentals, scuba rentals, certification classes, and dive classes. You can do a five-hour snorkel/sail on the *Blue Dolphin* departing at 8:30 a.m., or on their larger *Na Pali Kai II.*

Hawaiian Divers in King Kamehameha's Kona Beach Hotel, Kailua-Kona, tel. (808) 329-5662, offers a daily boat charter that gives you a two-tank certified dive with your own gear for

$85, $95 with their gear. An introductory dive is $95, and snorkeling is $45. This includes continental breakfast, lunch, and soft drinks.

Big Island Divers, tel. (808) 329-6068, or (800) 488-6068, at 75-5467 Kaiwi St., departing from Honokohau Harbor on their custom built 35-foot dive boat, offers a very inexpensive scuba certification course that's given on four consecutive Saturdays or Wednesdays, so you must intend to stay on the Big Island for that length of time. The normal four-day course costs

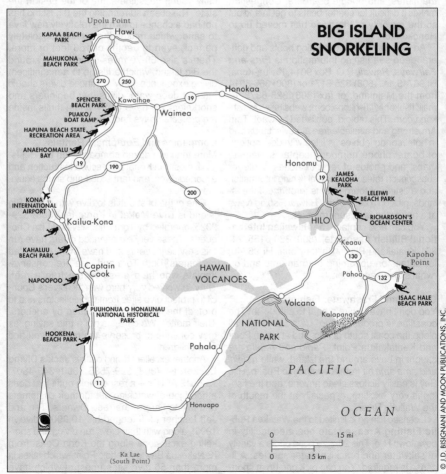

BIG ISLAND SNORKELING

© J.D. BISIGNANI AND MOON PUBLICATIONS, INC.

about $450. Dives range from a two-tank two-location dive for $69.95 to a three-tank three-location dive for $110. They also rent complete snorkel gear for only $6 for 24 hours and offer introductory and night dives.

Kohala Divers, located along Rt. 270 in the Kawaihae Shopping Center, open daily 8 a.m.-5 p.m., tel. (808) 882-7774, offers scuba certification for $300, snorkel rentals for $10 (24 hours), and scuba rentals for $22. They lead two-tank dives for $75, and will take snorkelers along if they have room on the boat ($15). It's a bit far to go from Kailua-Kona but it's a big savings, and they're the only dive company along the Kohala coast. (E-mail: theboss@kohaladivers.com, website: www.kohaladivers.com.)

Kona Coast Divers, 74-5614 Palani Rd., Kona, tel. (808) 329-8802, (800) 562-3483, is owned and operated by long-time Kona Coast diver, Jim Robertson. This outfit is efficient and to the point. Rates are: two tank boat dive $70; night dive $55; introductory dive $95; boat riders and snorkelers $30. Full underwater gear is sold and rented. (E-mail: divekona@ilhawaii.net; website: konacoastdivers.com.)

Snorkel Bob's, tel. (808) 329-0770, in the parking lot next to the Royal Kona Resort right in front of Huggo's Restaurant, offers snorkel gear for $15 per week for basic equipment. Upgrading to a comfortable surgical silicone mask with Italian fins is $27. Boogie boards are $9-15 p/d, $22-35 p/w depending on quality.

For those still dancing to the primordial tune of residual DNA left over from our one-celled ocean dwelling ancestors, *Kona Aggressor II,* is a "liveaboard" dive boat, tel. (808) 329-8182, or (800) 344-5662, departing Kona every Saturday for six days of diving along the Kona coast toward South Point. Passengers dive up to five times per day and night, as the Aggressor completely fulfills its motto to "Eat, Sleep, and Dive."

A Sea Paradise Scuba, tel. (808) 322-2500, offers introductory dives $80-90, and an array of morning and night dives priced $57-85. Owners and divers John and Roy have had well over a decade of experience off the Kona Coastline. They're reputable, fun, and well tested. A good choice.

Sandwich Isle Divers, 329-9188, is owned and operated by Steve and Larry, long-time Kona coast divers who know all the spots. They have

a custom six-passenger dive boat, great for small personalized trips for avid divers.

The **Nautilus Dive Center,** 382 Kamehameha Ave., Hilo, tel. (808) 935-6939, open Mon.-Sat. 9 a.m.-4 p.m., Sunday by appointment, owned and operated by certified instructor, William DeRooy, is one of the longest established dive companies on the Hilo side. This full-service dive center offers PADI certification (group session) at a very reasonable $125, new and used dive gear, shore and boat dives at $55 including transportation from Hilo, snorkeling excursions starting at $40, and snorkel gear rental at $5 for 24 hours. Mr. DeRooy is also willing to offer information over the phone for anyone coming to the Hilo side to dive or snorkel. He will update you on ocean conditions, suggest spots compatible with your ability, and even offers a free dive and snorkel map whether you're a customer or not. Bill is a font of information about the Big Island's water sports, and is willing to share in the true *aloha* spirit. Definitely stop in!

An alternative to boat dives is shore diving. *Shore Diving in Kona* is a great book listing sites, equipment, regulations, and suggestions for successful and safe dives. If your budget is limited and you're an experienced shore diver, it's a way to have a great outing at a reasonable price.

Snuba Tours of Kona, tel. (808) 326-7446, at King Kamehameha's Kona Beach Hotel, or **Snuba Big Island, Inc.,** tel. (808) 326-7446, can each set you up for this new adventure. Prices vary depending upon services provided such as an additional cruise and lunch, but a basic snuba experience costs about $60.

Snorkel, Scuba, and Snuba Boats

Snorkeling, scuba, and snuba excursions are also provided by the following: The **Fair Wind,** tel. (808) 322-2788 or (800) 677-9461 off island, is a well established company with a great reputation and is sure to please. Its 60-foot catamaran leaves daily from magnificent Keauhou Bay and stops at Kealakekua Bay in front of the Capt. Cook monument. **The Body Glove,** tel. (808) 326-7122, (800) 551-8911, a full fledged snorkel, scuba, and snuba company offering a bar, lunch, and plenty of other snorkelers, departs from the Kailua pier. **Kamanu Charters,** tel. (808) 329-2021, Kona's original snorkel sail in business more than 30 years provides a full day of fun with beer and snacks as part of the price. They sail Kona's only sailing catamaran, maximum of 24 passengers. Or try **Capt. Cook VI,** tel. (808) 329-6411, which sails a 79-foot glass-bottom boat twice a day

Scuba and snorkel cruises can also be booked through the various activity centers along the Kona and Kohala coasts and at your hotel travel desk.

Surfing and Sailboarding

The surfing off the Big Island is rather uninspiring compared to that off the other islands. The reefs are treacherous and the surf is lazy. Some surfers bob around off Hilo Bay, and sometimes in Kealakekua and Wailua Bays on the Kona side. Puna also attracts a few off Isaac Hale and Kaimu Beaches, and up north off Waipio Valley Beach. Generally, the north and west shores have better swells during the winter, the east and south shores in summer. Surfboards are for rent only on the Kona side. Try Honolua Surf Co., tel. (808) 329-1001, for starters. While surfing is not the best, the winds are great for sailboarding.

Parasailing, Etc.

UFO Parasailing, tel. (808) 325-5836, (800) 359-4836, offers boat platform take off and landing. Costs are: Early Bird Special $37; a 400 feet for seven minute standard ride for $42; and an 800 foot for 10 minute ride for $52.; and boat ride-alongs for $17. You too can dangle from a parachute and put your life in the hands of these fun filled Kona guys that will streak you through the air. For an alternative, try **Kona Water Sports,** tel. (808) 329-1593.

Kayaking

Kona Kai-Yaks owned and operated by David Johnson who claims to have been paddling so long that he actually entered this life by kayak directly from the womb, is located at Honokohau Harbor, tel. (808) 326-2922, open Mon.-Fri. 9 a.m.-5 p.m., Saturday 9 a.m.-1 p.m. David opened this shop in 1987, and from here rents kayaks and offers tours. Rental kayaks are of different types: "the Frenzy" (the name is a bit of a confidence buster, "The Water Couch" might be better for beginners); the Pro Prism; and the Malibu; that rent for $5-13 per hour, and $9.95-39.95 per day, depending upon the kayak cho-

sen (weekend and weekly discounts available). David offers guided day tours for around $80 per person. Overnight camping trips are also offered for the intrepid outdoor enthusiast, and are custom designed to fit group or individual needs. Overnight trips are $100 per person per night plus $100 per day for the guide (food included). A "liquid luxury" overnighter that pampers you with gourmet meals, night dives with manta rays, and even hot showers is another option. You paddle by day, trailed by the mother ship, *The Sun Seeker,* a 53-foot yacht upon which you spend the night; $250 per person per night, plus $100 per day for the guide. Try to tough it out!

A twist on the kayak business is offered by **Kohala Mountain Kayak Cruise,** tel. (808) 899-6922. On an outing with this company, you'll float several scenic miles of the Kohala irrigation canal flumes, over small ravines, and through several tunnels in the remote, private lands of the north Kohala coast. Completed in the early part of this century and considered a feat of engineering, this irrigation system supplied the Kohala Sugar mills with a steady supply of water until the plantation ceased business in the '70s. Guided by experts using the best equipment, you'll not only experience the beauty of the surrounding rainforest and rugged scenery but will also absorb a lesson in the history and culture of this area. No experience required. Bring an extra set of dry clothes.

SKIING

Bored with sun and surf? Strap the "boards" to your feet and hit the slopes of Mauna Kea. There are no lifts so you'll need a 4WD to get to the top, and someone willing to pick you up again at the bottom. You can rent 4WDs from the car rental agencies already mentioned, but if that seems like too much hassle just contact **Ski Guides Hawaii,** P.O. Box 1954, Kamuela, HI 96743, tel. (808) 885-4188 or 889-6747. Here you can rent skis and they'll provide the "lifts" to the top. Skis, boots, and poles rent for $20 a day, and the popular full-day ski tour with equipment, ride and driver, ski guide, and lunch costs $120. Other ski packages are available and priced on request. You can expect snow Dec.-May, but you can't always count on it.

GOLF

The Big Island has some of the most beautiful golf links in Hawaii. The Kohala area courses taken together are considered by some to be the crown jewel of the state's golf options. Robert Trent Jones Sr. and Jr. have both built exceptional courses here. Dad built the Mauna Kea Beach Hotel course, while the kid built his at the Waikoloa Beach Resort. The Mauna Kea course bedevils many as the ultimate challenge. If the Kohala courses are too rich for your blood, you can hit nine holes in Hilo for about $25. How

about golfing at Volcano Golf Course, where if you miss a short putt, you can blame it on an earthquake.

TENNIS

Many tennis courts dot the Big Island, and plenty of them are free. County courts are under the control of the Department of Parks and Recreation, which maintains a combination of lighted and unlighted courts around the island. Some private and hotel courts are open to the public for a fee, while others restrict play to guests only.

BIG ISLAND GOLF COURSES

COURSE	PAR	YARDS	FEES	CART	CLUB RENTAL
Discovery Harbor Golf and Country Club P.O. Box 62, Naalehu, HI 96772 tel. 929-7353	72	6326	$28	incl.	$12
Hamakua Country Club Box 344, Honokaa, HI 96727 tel. 775-7244	33	2520 (9 holes)	$10	(no carts)	(no club rental)
Hapuna Golf Course 62-100 Kauna'oa Dr., Kamuela, HI 96743 tel. 880-3000	72	6029	$130	incl.	$30
Hilo Municipal Golf Course 340 Haihai St., Hilo, HI 96720 tel. 959-7711	71	6006	$25	$14.50	$10
Hualalai Golf Club P.O. Box 1119, Kailua-Kona, HI 96745 tel. 325-8480	72	6032	$125 (Four Seasons Hotel guests only)	incl.	$40
Kona Country Club 78-7000 Ali'i Dr., Kailua-Kona, HI 96740 tel. 322-2595					
Ali'i Course	72	5841	$125	incl.	$25
Ocean Course	72	6155	$125	incl.	$25
Makalei Hawaii Country Club 72-3890 Hawaii Belt Rd. Kailua-Kona, HI 96740 tel. 325-6625	72	6161	$110	incl.	$25
Mauna Kea Beach Resort Golf Course 62-100 Mauna Kea Beach Dr., Kamuela, HI 96743 tel. 880-3480	72	6737	$150	incl.	$35

(continues on next page)

BIG ISLAND GOLF COURSES
(continued)

COURSE	PAR	YARDS	FEES	CART	CLUB RENTAL
Mauna Lani Resort					
Frances H. I'i Brown Golf Courses					
68-1310 Mauna Lani Dr.					
Kohala Coast, HI 96743					
tel. 885-6655					
South Course	72	5940	$170	incl.	$30
North Course	72	6086	$160	incl.	$30
Naniloa Country Club	35	2740	$30	$14	$19
120 Banyan Dr.		(9 holes)	(9 holes)		
Hilo, HI 96720			$40		
tel. 935-3000			(18 holes)		
Seamountain Golf Course	72	6492	$40	incl.	$15
P.O. Box 190, Pahala, HI 96777					
tel. 928-6222					
Volcano Golf and Country Club	72	6180	$60	incl.	$16
Box 46					
Hawaii Volcanoes National Park, HI 96718					
tel. 967-7331					
Waikoloa Beach Golf Club					
1020 Keana Place, Waikoloa, HI 96743					
tel. 885-6060					
Beach Course	70	5958	$120	incl.	$30
King's Course	72	6010	$120	incl.	$35
Waikoloa Village Golf Club	72	6230	$55	incl.	$25
P.O. Box 383910, Waikoloa, HI 96738					
tel. 883-9621					
Waimea Country Club	72	6210	$60	incl.	$25
Box 2155, Kamuela, HI 96743					
tel. 885-8777					

HORSEBACK RIDING

Waipio Na'alapa Trail Rides, operated by Sherri Hannum, tel. (808) 775-0419, offers the most unique rides on Hawaii. Sherri and her family have lived in Waipio Valley for more than 20 years and know its history, geology, and legends intimately. She offers pick up service from Kukuihaele for the 9:30 a.m. and 1 p.m. rides ($75). Sherri treats guests like family. If you have time, don't miss this wonderful adventure!

H.R.T. Waipio Tour Desk, tel. (808) 775-7291, located in the Hawaiian Holiday Macadamia Nut Factory in Honokaa, offers horseback riding through fabulous Waipio Valley. The rides start at 9:30 a.m. and 1:30 p.m., last two and a half hours, and cost $65, including transportation from Honokaa to Waipio. Make reservations 24 hours in advance.

Enjoyable rides are also offered by the **Mauna Kea Resort Stables** (for nonguests also), tel. (808) 882-4288. They have an arrangement with the Parker Ranch, which will supply a *paniolo* to guide you over the quarter-million acres of open range on the slopes of Mauna Kea, morning or afternoon. The stable is open Mon.-Sat., 9 a.m.-3 p.m. Rates are $40 pp for a one-hour

BIG ISLAND TENNIS COURTS

PUBLIC COURTS

Under jurisdiction of the County Department of Parks and Recreation, 25 Aupuni St., Hilo, HI 96720, tel. 961-8311.

TOWN	LOCATION	NO. OF COURTS	LIGHTED
Hilo	Ainaole Park	1	No
	Hakalau Park	2	No
	Hoolulu Park	8	Yes
	Lincoln Park	4	Yes
	Lokahi Park	2	Yes
	Malama Park	2	Yes
	Mohouli Park	2	No
	Panaewa Park	2	Yes
	Papaaloa Park	2	Yes
Honokaa	Honokaa Park	2	Yes
Puna	Kurtistown Park	1	No
Keaau	Keaau Park	2	No
Kau	Kau High School	2	Yes
	Naalehu Park	2	Yes
Kona	Greenwell Park	1	Yes
	Keauhou Park	1	No
	Kailua Park (Old Kona Airport)	4	Yes
	Kailua Playground	1	Yes
Waimea	Waimea Park	2	Yes
Kapaau	Kamehameha Park	2	Yes

HOTEL AND PRIVATE COURTS OPEN TO THE PUBLIC

TOWN	LOCATION	NO. OF COURTS	LIGHTED
Hilo	Hilo High School	1	No
	University of Hawaii-Hilo College	2	No
Pahala	Seamountain Tennis Center (fee)	4	No
Keauhou-Kona	Kona Surf Hotel Racket Club (fee)	7	Yes
	Keauhou Beach Hotel (fee)	6	Yes
Kona	Country Club Villas	2	No
Kailua-Kona	Royal Kona Resort	6	Yes
	King Kamehameha Kona Beach Hotel (fee)	2	Yes
Waikoloa	Waikoloa village (fee)	2	Yes
Waimea	Hawaii Prep Academy	4	Yes
	Waimea Park	2	Yes

ride and $70 for the two-hour ride; special trail rides available on request. Eight years old is the minimum age for riders and 210 pounds is the maximum weight. The stables are at Parker Ranch headquarters in Waimea.

Paniolo Riding Adventures, tel. (808) 889-5354, offers horseback riding on a working ranch in the Kohala Mountains. With your comfort in mind, they offer chaps, rain slickers, cowboy hats, and fleece saddle covers to keep you happy where the sun don't shine. Prices vary according to ride chosen, from novice to cowpoke.

Kohala Na'alapa Trail Rides, tel. (808) 889-0022, offers trail rides onto the historic Kahua, and Kohala Ranch, high in the Kohala Mountains. Rides are offered daily at 9 a.m. and 1:30 p.m., with prices $55-75 depending upon the ride.

Using horses from their own working ranch in Waimea, **Dahana Ranch,** tel. (808) 885-0057, gives riders free range trail rides on their property.

King's Trail Rides O'Kona, tel. (808) 323-2388, has offices along Rt. 11 at mile marker 111, high above the Kona Coast on the outskirts of Kealakekua. Their wranglers will lead you (4-6 people maximum) on a custom trail ride down to Captain Cook's Monument on the shores of Kealakekua Bay. This four-hour trip, departing at 9 a.m., (two hours of actual riding) includes snorkeling in the bay, along with a delicious picnic lunch, all for $95. The office doubles as a retail shop, open daily 7:30 a.m.-5 p.m., where you can purchase chocolate covered coffee beans, bottled salad dressings made in the area, honey, koa boxes, along with cowboy items like spurs

Sheri Hannum of Waipo Na'alapa Trail Rides

(honeymooners take note) western belts, and a full assortment of tack. Dave "Bones" Inkster, the owner and top hand, spent his life in the saddle and taught his twin daughters, Melissa and Nicole, to ride like the wind. The girls were chosen to represent Hawaii in 1996 at the National Finals held in Pueblo, Colorado on the Dally Team (heading, heeling, and roping), the first twin girls from Hawaii ever to do so. Ride 'em cowgirls! (E-mail: bones@interpac.net; website: interpac.net/~hit/ktr.hmtl.)

Rain Forest Trailrides, tel. (808) 322-7126, takes you on horseback across the face of the Hualalai Mountains. Open daily, 9 a.m.-5 p.m., rides vary from one to two and a half hours (latter with lunch included) for $45-80.

Also offering rides over the slopes of Hualalai between 1,500-3,000 feet are **Waiono Meadows Trail Rides,** tel. (808) 329-0888. A one-hour ride costs $15, a two-hour ride costs $28, and breakfast, lunch, and sunset rides are available.

Horse-drawn Wagon Rides
Waipio Valley Wagon Tour, tel. (808) 775-9518, owned and operated by Peter Tolin, is a mule-drawn tour of the magnificent Waipio Valley. The one and a half hour tours leave five times daily at 9 and 10:30 a.m. and 12:30 2, and 4 p.m. The cost is $35, children under 12 half price, children two and under free.

Wagon rides of a different sort are now also offered at the Parker Ranch in Waimea. A wonderful family outing, these tame, 45-minute rides leave weekdays from the Parker Ranch Visitors Center every hour 10 a.m.-3 p.m. and show you a portion of the working ranch up close. Children ages 3-12 ride for $12, while adults pay $15. Call the visitors center, tel. 885-7655, for reservations.

Mule Rides
The only commercial mule ride on the Big Island is offered by **Hawaii Forest & Trail,** tel. (808) 322-8881. This company, which also offers various hiking and birding tours, takes riders on these sure-footed beasts into Pololu Valley and the north end of the island, starting from the old Kohala Ditch Company mule station. The ride takes you about 400 feet down the valley side to the black sand beach of the valley mouth.

BICYCLING

Bicycle Shops

For rentals, try the following. **Hawaiian Pedals Ltd.,** tel. (808) 329-2294, in the Kona Inn Shopping Plaza, rents mountain bikes at $15 for five hours, $20 for 24 hours, $15 p/d for 2-3 days, $12 p/d for 4-5 days, $10 p/d for 6-7 days, and $9 p/d for more than one week. Performance bikes are slightly more expensive; tandems cost $35 all day. Bike racks and baby seats are also for rent. They deliver. Ask about their tours. **Island Cycle Rentals** is at Jack's Diving Locker at the Kona Inn Plaza, tel. (808) 329-7585.

Dave's Bike and Triathlon Shop, owned and pedaled by triathlete, Dave Bending, is located just a long stride or two from the beginning of the Ironman Triathlon across from King Kamehameha's Kona Beach Hotel in the Kona Square Shopping Center, at 75-5669 Ali'i Dr., tel. (808) 329-4522. Dave rents competition quality road bikes at $25 p/d, and Caloi mountain bikes at $15 first day, $12 second day, $10 third day, or at $60 p/w. Prices include a helmet, water bottles, a map, bicycle lock, and most importantly road advice. Dave knows his stuff, so pay heed!

In Waimea, try either **C&C Cycle and Surf,** tel. (808) 885-5005 or **Mauna Kea Mountain Bikes,** tel. (808) 883-0130, for wheels that will get up to the high country.

Teo's Safaris in Keaau, just south of Hilo, tel. (808) 982-5221, rents bicycles and leads mountain tours. Rentals for 21-speed mountain bikes are $10 p/d, $15 for 24 hours, $20 two days, or $50 for the week. Teo leads a 2-3 hour rainforest ride that includes bike and helmet for $20 (call 24 hours in advance). Teo also has panniers, bike racks, and camping equipment available for people renting his bikes (rates subject to length of rental). **Pacific United Rental** at 1080 Kilauea Ave., Hilo, tel. (808) 935-2974,

has rentals limited to the Hilo area at $10 p/d for single-speed bikes. Also in Hilo is **Mid Pacific Wheels,** tel. (808) 935-6211, at 1133C Manono Street.

Bicycle Tours

For those interested in bicycle touring, contact one of the following for their specialized bike trips. The owners and tour leaders of **Island Bicycle Adventures,** 569 Kapahulu Ave., Honolulu, HI 96815, tel. (808) 734-0700, or (800) 233-2226, are intimately familiar with bicycle touring and are members of the Hawaii Bicycling League. They offer tours to Maui, the Big Island, and Kauai. **Hawaiian Eyes Big Island Bicycle Tours,** P.O. Box 1500, Honokaa, HI 96727, tel. (808) 775-7335, offers a variety of guided rides including along the Hamakua Coast, down the Saddle Road, and a round-island journey. **Mauna Kea Mountain Bikes,** tel. (808) 883-0180, offers cross-country, downhill, and off-road guided tours. Customized tours can be arranged. **Backroads,** 1516 5th St., Suite PR, Berkeley, CA 94710, tel. (510) 527-1555, (800) 462-2848, goes easy on the environment with their bicycle and hiking trips to the Big Island.

HUNTING

Huge unpopulated expanses of grassland, forest, and scrubby mountainside are very good for hunting. The Big Island's game includes feral pig, sheep, and goats, plus a variety of pheasant, quail, dove, and wild turkey. Public game lands are located throughout the island; a license is required to take birds and game. For full information, write the Department of Land and Natural Resources, Division of Forestry and Wildlife Office, P.O. Box 4849, Hilo, HI 96720, tel. (808) 974-4221.

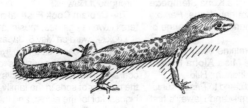

FESTIVALS, HOLIDAYS, AND EVENTS

The following events and celebrations are either particular to the Big Island, or they're celebrated here in a special way. Everyone is welcome to join in the fun, and most times the events are either free or nominally priced. There's no better way to enjoy yourself while vacationing than by joining in a local party or happening.

JANUARY

Thump in the New Year with a traditional Japanese **Mochi Pounding Festival** at Volcano Art Center, Volcanoes National Park.

The athletes gear up with the Big Island **Triathlon Invitational** held in late December or early January. This is a three-day event that ranges all over the island and includes an overnight stay at Volcanoes National Park.

FEBRUARY

February offers everything from the links to skiing at the **Mauna Kea Ski Meet** atop the Big Island's 13,000-foot volcano—weather and snow conditions dictate the exact time, which can vary from early January to March. Skiers from around the world compete in cup and cross-country skiing.

Enjoy the authentic western flavor of the **Great Waikoloa Horse Races and Rodeo** at Waikoloa Stables, Waikoloa. Major rodeo events draw skilled *paniolo* from around the islands.

MARCH

Mid-March rumbles in with the **Kona Stampede** at Honaunau Arena, Honaunau, Kona. *Paniolo* provide plenty of action during the full range of rodeo events.

Mid-month features feminine beauty, grace, and athletic ability at the **Miss Aloha Hawaii Pageant** at Hilo Civic Auditorium, Hilo.

The end of March is dedicated to Prince Kuhio, a member of the royal family and Hawaii's first delegate to the U.S. Congress. **Prince Kuhio**

Day is a state holiday honoring the prince, held on March 26, his birthday.

APRIL

Wesak, or **Buddha Day,** on the closest Sunday to April 8, celebrates the birthday of Gautama Buddha. Ornate offerings of tropical flowers are placed at temple altars throughout Hawaii.

The **Mo'ikeha Cup Hawaiian Sailing Canoe Race** honors the Hawaiian sailing traditions with a triangular race starting and ending at Kawaihae Harbor.

The **Paniolo Ski Meet** features exciting skiing atop the Big Island's Mauna Kea, conditions permitting.

The **Merrie Monarch Festival** in Hilo sways with the best hula dancers that the islands' *hula halau* have to offer. Gentle but stiff competition features hula in both its ancient *(kahiko)* and modern *(auana)* forms. The festival runs for a week on a variable schedule from year to year. It's immensely popular with islanders, so hotels, cars, and flights are booked solid. For information call the Hawaii Naniloa Hotel, tel. (808) 935-9168, or the HVB at (808) 961-5797.

The **Kona Sports Festival,** Kailua-Kona, is a solid week of sports entertainment and frivolity held toward the end of the month.

MAY

May 1 is May Day to the communist world, but in Hawaii red is only one of the colors when everyone dons a lei for Lei Day. Festivities abound throughout Hawaii.

The **Captain Cook Festival** at Kailua-Kona offers Hawaiian games, music, and fishing.

Look skyward on May 5, **Japanese Boys' Day,** and you'll see paper carp (koi) flying from rooftops. Carp symbolize the virtues of strength and courage. The number of koi kites corresponds to the number of sons in the family, with the largest, highest koi for the eldest, and then down the line.

Filipino Fiesta is a month-long celebration of

the islands' Filipino population. Food, various festivities, and a beauty contest are part of the fiesta.

Costumed riders from the annals of Hawaiian history ride again at **Hawaii on Horseback.** Horsemanship and a Western flair mark these days held in and around Waimea and the Parker Ranch.

Annual Western Week at Honokaa is a fun-filled week with a Western theme. It includes a cookout, parade, rodeo, and dance.

The **Annual Keauhou-Kona Triathlon** at Keauhou Bay is open to athletes unable to enter Ironman, and to anyone in good health. Each of its three events is half as long as in the Ironman, and it allows relay-team racing for each grueling segment. Call (808) 329-0601. (Website: ilhawaii.net/~kkt/).

JUNE

King Kamehameha Day, June 11, is a state holiday honoring Kamehameha the Great, a Big Island native son, with festivities on all islands. Check local papers for times and particulars. Kailua-Kona is hospitable with a *ho'olaule'a* (street party), parades, art demonstrations, entertainment, and contests.

The **Kamehameha Ski Meet** atop Mauna Kea takes place in early June, when bikini-clad contestants add a little extra spice on those bouncy moguls.

Hilo flashes its brilliant colors with the **Annual Hilo Orchid Society Show** at the Hilo Civic Auditorium, and the **Annual Big Island Bonsai Show,** Wailoa Center, Hilo (both sometimes scheduled for early July).

Bon Odori, the Japanese festival of departed souls, features dances and candle-lighting ceremonies held at numerous Buddhist temples throughout the island. These festivities change yearly and can be held anytime from late June to early August.

JULY

The week of the **Fourth of July** offers the all-American sport of rodeo along with parades. Don't miss the **July 4 Parker Ranch Rodeo and Horseraces,** Paniolo Park, Waimea. The epitome of rodeo by Hawaii's top cowboys is set at the Parker Ranch.

Annual Naalehu Rodeo, in Naalehu, includes rodeo events, motorcycle and dune buggy races, luaus, food booths and Hawaiian entertainment.

The **Big Island Marathon** in Hilo consists of a full and half marathon starting and ending at the Hilo Hawaiian Hotel.

Four-person teams of one pro and three amateurs compete in the 54-hole **Mauna Kea Beach Hotel's Annual Pro-Am Golf Tournament** held at the hotel links along the Kohala Coast.

The **International Festival of the Pacific** in mid-July features a "Pageant of Nations" in Hilo. Folk dances, complete with authentic costumes from throughout Asia and the Pacific, add a rare excitement to the festivities.

The beauty and grace of one of Hawaii's ethnic groups is apparent at the **Miss Hawaii Filipina Pageant,** Hawaii Naniloa Hotel, Hilo.

The annual **Kilauea Volcano Wilderness Run** is held over rough lava, in and out of volcanic craters, and through ohia and fern forests within the Hawaii Volcanoes National Park. A less grueling 10-mile race around the crater rim is also featured. For information, tel. (808) 982-7783.

AUGUST

The first August weekend is **Establishment Day.** Traditional hula and lei workshops are presented at the Puukohala Heiau in Kawaihae, where traditional artifacts are also on display.

The **Pro-Am Billfish Tournament** held in the waters off Kona, precedes and is a qualifying meet for the more famous **Annual Hawaiian International Billfish Tournament,** held about one week later. A world-renowned tournament and the Big Daddy of them all, the HIBT has been held every year since 1959. Since the beginning, the tournament organizer has been Peter Fithian. More than 90% of the fish caught are tagged and released. A percentage of the event's proceeds goes to the Pacific Ocean Research Foundation. For information, call (808) 329-6155.

The macadamia nut harvest is celebrated with sporting events, horse racing and a "Harvest Ball" at the **Macadamia Nut Harvest Festival,** Honokaa.

August 17 is **Admission Day,** a state holiday recognizing the day that Hawaii became a state.

Kailua-Kona hosts the annual **Queen Lili-uokalani Long Distance Canoe Race** every Labor Day weekend. Single-hull, double-hull, and one-person events are held over a two-day period.

The annual **Kona Marathon** is held along the route that Ironman participants take. Also half marathon and shorter runs and walks. Call (808) 325-0287 for information.

SEPTEMBER

In early September don't miss the **Parker Ranch Round-Up Rodeo** at Paniolo Park in Waimea.

The **Million Dollar Golden Marlin Fishing Tournament** catches plenty of fishermen at Kailua-Kona.

The **Hawaii County Fair** at Hilo is an old-time fair held on the grounds of Hilo Civic Auditorium.

Aloha Festivals celebrates Hawaii's own "intangible quality," *aloha*. This two-month-long series of several dozen individual festivals includes parades, luau, athletic competitions, historical pageants, balls, and various entertainment. The spirit of *aloha* is infectious and all are welcomed to join in. Check local papers and tourist literature for happenings near you.

OCTOBER

When they really "wanna have fun," super-athletes come to the **Ironman World Triathlon Championship** at Kailua-Kona. A 2.4-mile open-ocean swim, followed by a 112-mile bike ride, and topped off with a 26.2-mile full marathon, is their idea of a good day. First place winners receive $35,000; total prize purse is $250,000. This race was 20 years old in 1998. Ironman Office, tel. (808) 329-0063. (Website: www.iron-mantri.com.)

The **Big Island International Marathon and Ekiden Relay** traces a route through the old sugar towns near Hilo. Call (808) 961-6666.

NOVEMBER

Taste the best coffee commercially grown in the U.S. at the **Annual Kona Coffee Cultural Festival** in Kailua-Kona. Parades, arts and crafts, and ethnic foods and entertainment are part of the festivities. It's the oldest food festival in the state—the 28th was held 1998. For information, call (808) 326-7820. (Website: www.konacoffeefest.com)

The **Annual King Kalakaua Keiki Hula Festival** is for children from around the state who come to Kailua-Kona to perform their hula. Plenty of fun, but the competition is serious.

Honokaa Taro Festival takes place in Honokaa on the Hamakua Coast and includes a poi-eating contest, food and craft booths, entertainment, and exhibits. Call (808) 775-0043 for information.

November 11, **Veterans Day,** is a national holiday celebrated by parades.

Christmas in the Country, atop Hawaii's volcano, is a delight. Merrymakers frolic in the crisp air or relax around a blazing fire, drinking hot toddys. Also, plenty of arts and crafts, food, and Santa for the *keiki.* Contact the Volcano Art Center, Hawaii Volcanoes National Park, tel. (808) 967-8222.

DECEMBER

The **Hamakua Music Festival** held around the first week of December in Honokaa lasts for four days and attracts island musicians proficient in everything from Hawaiian music to jazz.

Christmas Fantasyland of Trees at Honokaa is an early showing of gaily decorated trees. The right Christmas spirit auctions them off for charity.

The people of Hilo celebrate a New England Christmas in memory of the missionaries with **A Christmas Tradition.** Held at the Lyman House Memorial Museum, Hilo, tel. (808) 935-5021.

Bodhi Day is ushered in with ceremonies at Buddhist temples to commemorate Buddha's day of enlightenment.

At the **Mauna Kea Beach Hotel's Annual Invitational Golf Tournament,** men and women play at this fabulous golf course on the Kohala Coast.

On **New Year's Eve** hold onto your hat, because they do it up big in Hawaii. The merriment and alcohol flow all over the islands. Firecrackers are illegal, but they go off everywhere. Beware of hangovers and "amateur" drunken drivers.

SHOPPING

The following is an overview of the main shopping areas and where their locations around the island. Almost every town has at least a gas station and market, and they will be listed in the travel chapters. Look under **Shopping** for directions to and descriptions of specific malls, art shops, and boutiques in the area. Supermarkets, health food stores, and local markets are listed in the individual travel chapters, generally in the **Food** sections.

SHOPPING CENTERS

General shopping centers are found in Hilo, Kailua-Kona, Waimea, and Captain Cook. Like most shopping malls, these have a variety of stores whose offerings include apparel, dry goods, sporting goods, food, photography supplies, or outdoor rentals.

Hilo Malls
The main shopping center in Hilo is the **Prince Kuhio Plaza** at 111 E. Puainako. This shoppers' paradise is Hilo's newest and the island's largest shopping mall. An older but still full-service shopping center is **Kaiko'o Mall** at 777 Kilauea Avenue. The **Hilo Shopping Center** is about one-half mile south on Kilauea Avenue at the corner of Kekuanoa Street. This smaller mall has only a handful of local shops. **Puainako Town Center** is located at 2100 Kanoelehua Avenue. **Waiakea Kai Shopping Plaza,** at 88 Kanoelehua Ave., has a small clutch of stores.

Kona Malls
Two commodities that you're guaranteed in Kailua-Kona are plenty of sunshine and plenty of shopping. **Kona Inn Shopping Village** is located in central Kailua at 75-5744 Ali'i Dr. and has more than 40 shops selling everything from fabrics to fruits. **World Square** is smaller and just across the road. **Kona Banyan Court,** also in central Kailua, has a dozen shops with a medley of goods and services. **Kailua Bay Inn Shopping Plaza** is along Ali'i Drive, **Akona Kai Mall** is across from Kailua Pier, while the **Kona Coast Shopping Plaza** and the **North Kona Shopping Center** are both along Palani Road. **Lanihau Center,** at 75-5595 Palani Rd., is one of Kailua-Kona's newest shopping additions. **King Kamehameha's Kona Beach Hotel Mall** is an exclusive shopping haven on the first floor of the hotel, while **Rawson Plaza,** at 74-5563 Kaiwi St., is in the industrial area and offers bargains. **Waterfront Row** is a new shopping and food complex at the south end of downtown Kailua-Kona that's done in period architecture with rough-cut lumber.

Keauhou Shopping Center is conveniently located at the corner of Ali'i Dr. and Kamehameha III Rd. at the far end of Kailua-Kona. Here you'll find everything from a post office to a supermarket. Continuing south on Rt. 11, you'll spot **Kainaliu Village Mall** along the main drag.

Kealakekua Ranch Center, in Captain Cook, is a two-story mall with fashions and general supplies.

Waimea (Kamuela) Malls
After the diversity of shopping malls in Kailua and Hilo, it's like a breath of fresh air to have fewer choices. In Waimea try the **Parker Ranch Shopping Center,** which has more than 30 shops, including a pharmacy, grocery, and general merchandise. A small herd of shops in this center also features ranch and Western-wear with a Hawaiian twist. **Parker Square Shopping Mall,** along Rt. 19, has a collection of fine boutiques and shops. **Waimea Shopping Center,** also along Rt. 19, is one of Waimea's newest shopping malls.

The "Martinizing" of the Big Island
The Big Island has been "martinized:" Wal-Mart is here, along with Kmart, the largest store in the Hawaii chain (oh joy), and Costco Warehouse, causing a bit of "spindling, mutilating, and unfortunately folding" of the local small retail shops. Although, to some, these shopping "meccas" have had a positive effect upon the island—sort of. These retail behemoths have definitely lowered prices and have made more goods available, and with an eye toward corporate gain

have put the squeeze on local "mom and pop" shops, the traditional retailers of The Big Island. Part of the enjoyment in purchasing a traditional Hawaiian craft was obtaining it either directly from the person who made it, or from the bare wood shelves of a local store that was very close to the source. Since the "marts" have entered the retail scene, plenty of locally owned stores and boutiques have gone under. Wal-Mart, Kmart, and Costco have stores in Kailua-Kona, and Wal-Mart also has one in Hilo.

FOOD STORES AND SUPERMARKETS

Groceries and supplies can be purchased in almost every town on the island. Many of the markets in the smaller towns also sell a limited supply of sundries and dry goods. The general rule is: the smaller the market, the higher the prices. The largest and least expensive stores with the biggest selections are found in Hilo and Kailua-Kona. The following is a sampling of what you'll find. More extensive listings are found in the individual district chapters.

Hilo and Kona
Supermarkets in Hilo include **Food Fair,** 194 Kilauea Ave.; **Safeway,** 333 Kilauea Ave.; **Sack 'n Save Foods** at Puainako Shopping Center; **Sure Save Supermarket** in Kaiko'o Mall; and **KTA Super Stores** at Puainako Shopping Center and along Kilauea Ave. downtown.

In Kona, **K. Tanaguchi Market** at Kona Coast Shopping Center and **Food for Less** in Lanihau Center, are two of the main supermarkets. **KTA Super Stores** are at both the Kona Coast Shopping Center and at the Keauhou Shopping Center, at the extreme south end of Ali'i Drive.

Around the Island
These smaller markets should meet your needs as you travel around the Big Island. Along the eastern Hamakua Coast you'll find **Ishigo's General Store** in Honomu Village en route to Akaka Falls. Further north along Rt. 24 in Honokaa are **T. Kaneshiro Store** and **K.K. Super-Mart.** In Kukuihaele, the last village before Waipio Valley, look for **The Last Chance Store.**

In Waimea, **Sure Save Supermarket** is at the Parker Ranch Shopping Center. Meat lovers can't go wrong at the **Kamuela Meat Market,** also at the center, selling Parker Ranch beef at home-town prices. On the Kohala Peninsula look for **Kohala Market** in Kawaihae, **M. Nakahara** for general supplies and liquor in Hawi, and Kapaau's **Union Market** for a good assortment of grains, nuts, fruit, and locally made pastries and breads.

South of Hilo you'll find in Pahoa Town **Pahoa Cash and Carry.** Along the Puna coast is the **Kalapana General Store.** In Volcano Village try **Kilauea General Store** along Rt. 11 just before entering Hawaii Volcanoes National Park.

Kamigaki Market and **Sure Save** are in Kealakekua. **Shimizu Market** is south on Rt. 11 in Honaunau. Farther south between mile markers 77 and 78 you'll find the very well-stocked **Ocean View General Store.** In the Kau District look for **Wong Yuen Store** in Waiohinu, and **Pick and Pay** in Naalehu, which bills itself as the southernmost market in the United States.

Health Food, Fruit Stores, and Farmers' Markets
Abundant Life Natural Foods is in downtown Hilo at 292 Kamehameha Avenue. Stay healthy in Kona with **Kona Healthways** in the Kona Coast Shopping Center. The **Aloha Village Store,** just next door to the Aloha Cafe in Kainaliu, sells gifts, sundries, and natural foods. In Kealakekua look for the well-stocked **Ohana O Ka Aina Food Co-op.** In Naalehu the **Naalehu Fruit Stand** is a favorite with local people for its fresh fruit, grains, minerals, vitamins, and health foods. While heading south from Hilo to Volcanoes, stop along Rt. 11 at **Keaau Natural Foods;** or in Pahoa at **Pahoa Natural Groceries,** which specializes in organic fruits and juices and is one of the finest health food stores on the Big Island.

On Wednesday and Saturday morning, check out the **Hilo Farmers' Market** (best produce and deals are early in the morning) at Kamehameha Ave. and Mamo St., fronting the bay in the center of the downtown area. For a real treat visit the early morning (over by 8 a.m.) **Suisan Fish Market** at 85 Lihiwai St. in Hilo. In Pahoa, the **"Caretakers of Our Land" Farmers' Market** puts out their wares on Saturday 7:30 a.m.-12 p.m. at the Sacred Heart Church. At the Cooper

BIG ISLAND MUSEUMS

Hilo Tsunami Museum, tel. (808) 935-0926, is housed in the art deco-style First Hawaiian Bank building near the bayfront in Hilo. It's dedicated to those who lost their lives in the destructive tsunamis that hit and virtually destroyed the city in 1946 and 1960. Open Wed.-Sat. 10 a.m.-4 p.m.

Hulihee Palace, a Victorian-style building in downtown Kailua-Kona, is one of two royal palaces in the state. Used by the Hawaiian monarchs until 1916, it now contains countless items owned and used by the royal families. It's a treasure house and well worth a look. Open Mon.-Fri. 9 a.m.-4 p.m. Admission is $5. Call (808) 329-1877 for information.

Kamuela Museum, tel. (808) 885-4724, is an eclectic private collection of Hawaiiana, items from upcountry *paniolo* life, Asian artifacts, and photos of the Parker family. Located west of downtown Waimea, it's open daily 8 a.m.-5 p.m.; $5 admission.

Kona Historical Society Museum, tel. (808) 323-3222, near Captain Cook, is open Mon.-Fri. 8 a.m.-4 p.m. and Saturday 10 a.m.-2 p.m.; $2 admission. Housed in a general store built in 1875 from native stone and lime mortar, this museum has a small collection of glassware and photographs. An archive of Kona-area historical items is housed in the basement and is open by appointment only.

Lyman House Memorial Museum first opened in 1932. The main building is a New England-style frame structure from 1839, the oldest wood frame house on the island. It contains furniture and household goods from Rev. and Mrs. Lyman and other missionary families on the island. In an annex are a collection of Hawaiian artifacts and items of daily use in the Island Heritage Gallery and a very fine collection of rocks and minerals in the Earth Heritage Gallery. Located at 276 Haile St. in Hilo, tel. (808) 935-5021, this museum is open Mon.-Sat. 9 a.m.-5 p.m. and Sunday 1-4 p.m.; $5 admission.

Onizuka Space Center, tel. (808) 329-3441, is at the Kona International Airport. Its hours are 8:30 a.m.-4:30 p.m. daily except Thanksgiving, Christmas, and New Year's Day; $2 admission. This center is a memorial to Hawaii's first astronaut and a space education facility for adults and children. It includes interactive and static exhibits, models, audiovisual displays, and lots of reading material.

Parker Ranch Historic Homes are located a few miles outside Waimea and are open daily 10 a.m.-5 p.m.; $7.50 admission. Puuopelu, the ranch home of the Parker family, is a structure to be appreciated in and of itself, but it also houses artwork of world-prominent artists collected by Richard Smart, the last of the Parker line. Reconstucted nearby is Mana House, the original Parker ranch home from 1847.

Center in Volcano, you'll find produce, flowers, and baked goods at the **Volcano Farmers' Market** every Sunday 8-10 a.m. For locally grown produce on the west side of the island try the **Kona Farmers' Market** every Saturday and Sunday 8 a.m.-2:30 p.m. at Kaiwi Square in Kona; the **Kailua Village Farmers' Market** across from Hale Kalawai on Wednesday, Friday, Saturday, and Sunday; or the **Kona Country Farmers' Market** every Saturday and Sunday along Hwy. 11 between mile markers 112 and 113 near Kealakekua. The **Hawaiian Homestead Market** held in Waimea every Saturday, 7 a.m.-noon, is where local farmers come to sell their produce, much of which is organic. Look for a dozen or so stalls in the parking lot of the Hawaiian Homelands Building located along Rt. 19, about two miles east of town center heading

toward Honokaa. Alternately in Waimea, shop at the **Kamuela Farmers' Market** every Saturday 8 a.m.-12 p.m. at the Parker School.

BOOKSTORES

Two aspects of a quality vacation are knowing what you're doing and thoroughly relaxing while doing it. Nothing helps you do this better than a good book. The following stores offer full selections.

Hilo has excellent bookstores. **Basically Books,** downtown at 46 Waianuenue St., has a good selection of Hawaiiana and out-of-print books, and an unbeatable selection of maps. You can get anywhere you want to go with their nautical charts, road maps, and topographical maps, which include sectionals for serious hikers and trekkers. Their collection covers most of the Pacific. They also feature a very good selection of travel books, and flags from countries throughout the world. The **Book Gallery**, at Prince Kuhio Plaza, is a full-selection bookstore featuring Hawaiiana, hardcovers, and paperbacks. **Waldenbooks,** also at Prince Kuhio Plaza, is the largest and best-stocked bookstore in the Hilo area. A fine selection of Hawaiiana along with its usual broad collection can also be found at **Borders Books** at the Waiakea Center on Maka'ala Street.

Kailua-Kona bookstores include **Waldenbooks** in Lanihau Center on Palani Rd.; **Middle Earth Bookshop** at 75-5719 Ali'i Dr., in the Kona Plaza Shopping Arcade; and **Keauhou Village Bookshop** at Keauhou Shopping Village.

Waimea offers books at the **Waimea General Store,** located at the Parker Square Shopping Mall, and **Pueo Bookshop,** at the Waimea Center.

SPECIALTY SHOPS, ART, AND NEAT THINGS

You can stroll in and out of flower shops, T-shirt factories, and a panoply of boutiques offering ceramics, paintings, carvings, and all manner of island handicrafts. Art and crafts shops are always a part of the Big Island's shopping malls, and in even the smallest village you can count on at least one local artist displaying his or her creations. The following list of artists and shops is by no means exhaustive, but for the most part, they are in out-of-the-way places and worth a visit. Art shops and boutiques in specific areas will be covered in the travel sections under **Shopping.**

In Hilo, **Hawaiian Handicrafts** specializes in woodcarvings. **Sugawara Lauhala and Gift Shop** is a virtually unknown Hilo institution making genuine *lau hala* weavings. **Old Town Printer and Stationers** has been in business for 35 years selling stationery, office supplies, postcards, note cards, and a terrific selection of calendars. They also have a fax and copy center for travelers. **Sig Zane Design** is one of the most unique and distinctive shops on the island, selling distinctive island wearables in 100% cotton.

While heading up the Hamakua Coast, make sure to visit **The Hawaiian Artifacks Shop** along

ipu, *a drum used to accompany hula*

the main drag in Honokaa. **Waipio Valley Artworks** in Kukuihaele showcases exclusive artwork of distinguished island artists.

If you are after an exquisite piece of art, a unique memento, or an inexpensive but distinctive souvenir, make sure to visit the **Volcano Art Center** in Hawaii Volcanoes National Park.

Collectors Fine Art in the Kona Inn Shopping Village is a perfect labyrinth of rooms and hallways showcasing fine art from around the world. **Kona Inn Jewelry,** for world treasures, is one of the oldest and best-known shops for a square deal in Kona. **Alapaki's,** at Keauhou Shopping Center, sells traditional island arts and craft, and **Showcase Gallery** here offers glasswork, beadwork, featherwork, enameling, and shell lei from the islands, with emphasis on the Big Island.

The mountain village of Holualoa has become an artists' haven. As you enter the village you'll spot **Kimura's Lauhala Shop,** which has been selling and producing its famous *lau hala* hats ever since local weavers began bartering their creations for groceries in 1915. In town you'll find a converted and brightly painted coffee mill that's the home of the **Kona Art Center,** a community art-cooperative since 1965. The premier shop in town, **Studio 7,** showcases the work of Hiroki Morinoue and his wife Setsuko, famous *raku* potter Chiu Leong, and numerous other island artists. A separate shop in the same building is **Goldsmithing by Sam Rosen,** featuring unusual, one-of-a-kind works mostly in gold, silver, and precious stones.

The Little Grass Shack is an institution in Kealakekua. It looks like a tourist trap, but don't let that stop you from going in and finding some authentic souvenirs, most of which come from the surrounding area. **Tropical Temptations** in Kealakekua turns the best available grade of local fruits, nuts, and coffee beans into delicious candies. In the nearby village of Kainaliu, look for **The Blue Ginger Gallery** displaying art of owners Jill and David Bever as well as artists' works from all over the island.

In the *paniolo* town of Waimea you can pick up down-home cowboy items or sophisticated artwork. One of the galleries in town, **Gallery of Great Things,** really is loaded with great things—everything from a carousel horse to koa hair sticks. Along the north shore in Kapaau across from the Kamehameha statue is **Ackerman Gallery,** where you'll find the work of artist Gary Ackerman along with displays of local pottery, carvings, and one-of-a-kind jewelry. Many other artists and galleries call Kohala home.

ACCOMMODATIONS

Finding suitable accommodations on the Big Island is never a problem. The 9,500-plus rooms available at the island's 170 properties have the lowest annual occupancy rate of any in the islands at only 60%. Except for during the height of the high seasons and during the Merrie Monarch Festival in Hilo, you can count on finding a room at a bargain. The highest concentration of rooms is strung along Ali'i Drive in Kailua-Kona—more than 5,000 in condos, apartment hotels, and standard hotels. Hilo has almost 2,000 rooms; many of its hotels have "gone condo," and you can get some great deals. The rest are scattered around the island in small villages from Naalehu in the south to Hawi in the north, where you can almost count on being the only off-island guest. You can comfortably stay in the cowboy town of Waimea, or perch above Kilauea Crater at one of the oldest hotel sites in the islands. There are also bed and breakfasts, and the camping is superb, with a campsite almost guaranteed at any time.

The Range

The Big Island has a tremendous range of accommodations. A concentration of the world's greatest luxury resorts are within minutes of each other on the Kohala coast: The Mauna Kea, Hapuna, Mauna Lani, Royal Waikoloa, and Kona Village Resort. The Mauna Kea, built by Laurence Rockefeller, has everything the name implies. The others are just as superb, with hideaway "grass shacks," exquisite art collections as an integral part of the grounds, world-ranked golf courses, and perfect crescent beaches.

Kona has fine hotels like the King Kamehameha's Kona Beach Hotel and Royal Kona Resort in downtown Kailua. Just south toward Keahou is a string of reasonably priced yet luxurious hotels like the Keauhou Beach Hotel. Interspersed among the big hotels are smaller hotels and condominiums with homey atmospheres and great rates. Hilo offers the best accommodations bargains. Luxury hotels such as the Hilo Hawaiian and Naniloa Surf are priced like midrange hotels on the other islands. There are also semi-fleabags in town that pass the basic cleanliness test, along with gems like the Dolphin Bay Hotel, which gives you so much for your money it's embarrassing. And for a real treat, head to Hawaii Volcanoes National Park and stay at one of the bed and breakfasts tucked away there, or at Volcano House where raw nature has thrilled kings, queens, and luminaries like humorist Mark Twain for more than a century.

If you want to get away from everybody else, it's no problem, and you don't have to be rich to do it. Pass-through towns like Captain Cook and

Waimea have accommodations at very reasonable prices. You can try a self-growth retreat in Puna at Kalani Honua Oceanside Eco-resort or at the Wood Valley Buddhist Temple above Pahala. Want ultimate seclusion? Head down to Tom Araki's Hotel in Waipio Valley.

Hotel/Condo Booking and Reservations

The following is a partial list of booking agents handling a number of properties on the Big Island.

Aston Hotels and Resorts, 2250 Kuhio Ave., Honolulu, HI 96815, tel. (808) 931-1400 or (800) 922-7886 Mainland, (800) 445-6633 Canada, or (800) 321-2558 in Hawaii.

Go Condo Hawaii, tel. (800) 452-3463, website: www.gocondohawaii.com.

Hawaii Resort Management, 75-5776 Kuakini Hwy., Suite 105C, Kailua-Kona, HI 96740, tel. (808) 329-9393, fax (808) 326-4136.

Homes and Villas in Paradise, 116 Hekili St., Suite 201, Kailua, HI 96734, tel. (808) 262-4663 or (800) 282-2736, website: planet-hawaii .com/homes-villas.

Keahou Property Management, 76-6225 Kuakini Hwy., Suite C105, Kailua-Kona, HI 96740, tel. (808) 326-9075, or (800) 745-5662, fax (808) 326-2055.

Marc Resorts Hawaii, 2155 Kalakaua Ave., Honolulu, HI 96815, tel. (808) 926-5900 or (800) 535-0085.

SunQuest Vacations, 77-6435 Kuakini Hwy., Kailua-Kona HI 96740, tel. (808) 329-6488, (800) 367-5168 Mainland, or (800) 800-5662 in Canada.

Hostels

The Big Island has two very reasonably priced hostels operating at this time. **Arnott's Lodge,** 98 Apapane Rd., Hilo, HI 96720, tel. (808) 969-7097, (800) 368-8752 Mainland, (800) 953-7773 Hawaii, offers a dormitory bunk for $17, and semiprivate rooms with a shared bath, kitchen and living room for $30 s, $40 d. Arnott's also offers inexpensive hiking and snorkeling excursions.

Patey's Place, 75-5731 Ala Hou St., Kailua-Kona, HI 96740, tel. (808) 326-7018, will set you up in a bunk for $15, a private room for $35, or a room with bath and kitchen for $45.

The **Hotel Honokaa Club,** P.O. Box 247, Honokaa, HI 96727, tel. (808) 775-0678, has three private ($20) and two communal ($15) rooms in its basement level. All rooms share a bath and kitchen facilities, and upstairs is a dining room.

FOOD

Luau

The following is a listing of the luau available on the Big Island at the present time. For full descriptions including prices, menus, and times, see the listings in the appropriate district chapters. **Tihati's Drums of Polynesia Luau** at the Royal Kona Resort, tel. (808) 329-3111; **Royal Luau** at the Royal Waikoloan Hotel, tel. (808) 885-6789; **Island Breeze Luau** at King Kamehameha's Kona Beach Hotel, tel. (808) 326-4969; **Hale Ho'okipa—Friday Night Luau** at Kona Village Resort, tel. (808) 325-5555; **Old Hawaiian Aha'aina Luau** at the Mauna Kea Beach Hotel, tel. (808) 822-7222; and **Kamehameha Court** at Hilton Waikoloa Village, tel. (808) 885-1234.

GETTING THERE

Almost all travelers to the Big Island arrive by air. A few lucky ones come by private yacht, or by the cruise ship SS *Independence*, which docks at Hilo on Thursday, then sails around the island to Kona on Friday. For the rest, the island's two major airports are at Hilo and Kona. Almost every flight to the Big Island has a stopover, mostly in Honolulu, but a few are flown nonstop to the island.

The Airports

The largest airport on the Big Island is **Hilo International Airport,** tel. (808) 935-0809, which services Hilo and the eastern half of the island. It's a modern facility with full amenities and its runways can handle all jumbo jets. Flights from here connect to Kona, Lihue, Kahului, and Honolulu. The two-story terminal has an information center, restaurant, a number of vendors (including lei shops), and lockers. Most major car rental agencies have booths outside the terminal; a taxi for the three-mile ride to town costs about $8. The airport features 20 acres of landscaped flowers and an assortment of fountains and waterfalls supplied by rainwater collected on the terminal's roof.

Kona International Airport, tel. (808) 329-2484, is nine miles north of Kailua-Kona and handles the air traffic for Kona, a much prettier town to fly into than Hilo. This airport handles a growing amount of air traffic from other island cities and all the Mainland and international flights, eclipsing Hilo as the island's major air transportation hub. Interisland flights arrive from Hilo, Honolulu, Kahului, and Lihue; Mainland and international flights arrive from San Francisco, Los Angeles, and Tokyo. The terminal is a series of open-sided, Polynesian-style buildings which, because of the increasing volume of traffic into Kona, is being expanded. Here too are lockers, food, visitor information, various vendors, and most car-rental agencies. A private cab to your hotel will be $15 or more.

Waimea-Kohala Airport, tel. (808) 885-4520, is just outside Waimea (Kamuela). There are few amenities and no public transportation to town. **Upolu Airport,** is a lonely strip on the extreme northern tip of the island, with no facilities whatsoever and no scheduled flights. Both are serviced only on request by small charter airlines.

Nonstop Flights

Most island flights in the past landed at Hilo International Airport. With the Kona Coast gaining popularity, domestic flights from the Mainland have shifted to that side of the island, and the only direct international connection to the Big Island lands there as well. United Airlines operates the only nonstop flights to the Big Island from the Mainland—daily flights from San Francisco and Los Angeles to Kona. In the past during peak season, United has run a flight to Hilo International Airport, but it's an on-and-off affair depending on the number of travelers. Japan Airlines offers daily flights from Tokyo to Kona.

Interisland Carriers

Getting to and from the Big Island via the other islands is easy and convenient.

Hawaiian Airlines, tel. (800) 367-5320 nationwide, (800) 882-8811 statewide, or tel. (808) 326-5615 on the Big Island, website: www.hawaiianair.com. From Honolulu to Kona, 11 flights (about 40 minutes) are spread throughout the day approximately 5:20 a.m.-7 p.m. From Kona to Honolulu, there are 14 daily flights, 6:25 a.m.-8:05 p.m., two of which stop in Kahului, Maui. A similar scheduling applies to Hilo, with a few flights stopping in either Kahului, Maui, or Kona on the way. Hawaiian Airlines offers fewer daily flights from Kauai and Maui to both Hilo and Kona (about one hour and 40 minutes).

Aloha Airlines, tel. (800) 367-5250 Mainland, (800) 235-0936 Canada, (808) 935-5771 Big Island, also services the Big Island with flights from the neighboring islands. Their 19 daily Honolulu-Kona runs start at 5:25 a.m., with the last at 7:20 p.m.; 16 Honolulu-to-Hilo flights depart throughout the day, 5:25 a.m.-7 p.m. There are the same number of flights in the reverse direction to both destinations, leaving 6:30 a.m.-8:25 p.m. Aloha also flies from both Kona and Hilo to Lihue with about a dozen or so flights from each spread throughout the day. Flight to/from Kahalui, Maui, are much fewer, with two from Hilo and three from Kona. Aloha also has one flight daily from Hilo to Kona. (Website: www.alohaair.com.)

Island Air (formerly Aloha Island Air), tel. (800) 323-3345 nationwide or (800) 652-6541 statewide runs two daily flights to Kona, one from Kapalua-West Maui Airport and the other from Lanai. (Website: www.alohaair.com.)

GETTING AROUND

The first thing to remember when traveling on the Big Island is that it *is* big, more than four times larger than Rhode Island. A complete range of vehicles is available for getting around, everything from helicopters to mopeds. Hawaii, like Oahu, has some public transportation. Choose the conveyance that fits your style, and you should have no trouble touring the Big Island.

CAR RENTALS

The best way to tour the island is in a rented car, but keep these tips in mind. Most car companies charge you a fee if you rent the car in Hilo and drop it off in Kona, and vice versa. The agencies are prejudiced against the Saddle Road and the spur road leading to South Point, both of which offer some of *the* most spectacular scenery on the island. Their prejudice is unfounded because both roads are paved, generally well maintained, and no problem if you take your time. They'll claim the insurance will not cover you if you have a mishap on these roads. A good automobile policy at home will cover you in a rental car, but definitely check this before you take off. It's even possible, but not recommended, to drive to the top of Mauna Kea if there is no snow. Plenty of signs to the summit say "4WD only"; heed them, not so much for going up, but for needed braking power coming down. Don't even hint of these intentions to the car rental agencies, or they won't rent you a car.

No way whatsoever should you attempt to drive down to Waipio Valley in a car! The grade is unbelievably steep, and only a 4WD compound first gear can make it. Put simply, you have a good chance of being killed if you try it in a car.

Gas stations are farther apart than on the other islands, and sometimes they close very early. As a rule, fill up whenever the gauge reads half full.

Both Hilo International Airport and Kona International Airport have a gauntlet of car-rental booths and courtesy phones outside the terminals.

Auto Rental Companies

The following are major firms that are represented at both the Hilo and Kona airports. Kona numbers begin with "329" and "327," Hilo with "961" or "935."

Dollar, tel. (808) 961-6059, 329-2744, (800) 342-7398 statewide, or (800) 800-4000 worldwide, website: www.dollarcar.com, has an excellent reputation and very competitive prices. Dollar rents mostly Chrysler vehicles: sedans, jeeps, convertibles, and 4WDs. Great weekly rates, and all major credit cards accepted.

Alamo, tel. (808) 961-3343, 329-8896, or (800) 327-9633, website: www.goalamo.com, has good weekly rates on mostly GM cars.

National, tel. (808) 935-0891, 329-1674, or (800) 227-7368 worldwide, website: www.nationalcar.com, features GM and Nissan cars and accepts all major credit cards. They sometimes rent without a credit card if you leave a $100/day deposit—less if you take full insurance coverage.

Avis, tel. (808) 935-1290, 327-3000, or (800) 321-3712 nationwide, website www.avis.com, features late model GM cars as well as most imports and convertibles.

Budget, tel. (808) 935-6878, 329-8511, or (800) 527-0700 nationwide, website: www.drivebudget.com, offers competitive rates on a variety of late model Ford and Lincoln-Mercury cars and specialty vehicles.

Hertz, tel. (808) 935-2896, 329-3566, (800) 654-3011 worldwide, ebsite: www.hertz.com, is competitively priced with many fly/drive deals. They feature Ford vehicles.

A few short years ago, local companies abounded, but today only two have survived.

As always, caveat emptor. The firms are: **Harper**, in Hilo at tel. (808) 969-1478 and in Kona at (808) 329-6688, where you can rent a car, truck, 7-15 passenger van, or 4WD; and **V/N Rental** at 75-5799 Ali'i Dr., tel. (808) 329-7328, that rents used but not too abused longer term cars.

Motorcycles and Mopeds

D.J.'s Rentals, tel. (808) 329-1700, open daily 7:30 a.m.-6 p.m., at 75-5663 Palani Rd., across from King Kamehameha's Hotel in an outdoor booth, rents mopeds, jogs (faster version of a moped but for only one person), scooters, and motorcycles. Costs are: mopeds $8 hourly, $24.95 daily, and $29.95 24 hours; jogs $12 hourly, $34.95 daily, and $39.95 24 hours; scooters (two person and will attain highway speeds) $15 hourly, $44.95 daily, $49.95 24 hours; Big Twin Harley-Davidson's motorcycles at $125 daily, or $80 half day; and all other motorcycles are $99 daily or $65 for half day. A half day is 7:30 a.m.-noon, and then again noon-6 p.m. A good deal is to rent it noon-6 p.m., and then pay an extra $10 to keep the cycle overnight. Weekly and three-day special rates are also available.

ALTERNATIVE TRAVEL

Buses

The county of Hawaii maintains the Mass Transportation System (MTS), known throughout the island as the **Hele-On Bus.** For information, schedules, and fares contact the Mass Transit Agency at 25 Aupuni St., Hilo 96720, tel. (808) 961-8744 or 935-8241. The main bus terminal is in downtown Hilo at Mooheau Park, just at the corner of Kamehameha Avenue and Mamo Street. Recently, it's been completely rebuilt and modernized. Like bus terminals everywhere, it has a local franchise of derelicts and down-and-outers, but they leave you alone. What the Hele-On Bus lacks in class, it more than makes up for in *color* and affordability. The Hele-On operates Mon.-Sat. approximately 6 a.m.-6 p.m., depending on the run, except for the routes to Kona and Kohala, which operate Saturday and/or Sunday. There are a number of intra-Hilo routes with additional intercity routes to points around the periphery of the island. If you're in a hurry definitely forget about taking it, but if you want to meet the people of Hawaii, there's no better way. The base fare is 75 cents, which increases whenever you go into another zone. Have exact change for fare when you board. You can also be charged an extra $1 for a large backpack or suitcase. Don't worry about that—the Hele-On is one of the best bargains in the country. There are five basic intercity routes connecting to Hilo. One goes from Kealia, south of Captain Cook, all the way to Hilo on the east coast via Kailua, Waimea, Honokaa, and Honomu. This journey (operating Mon.-Sat.) covers 110 miles in just over four hours and costs about $6, the most expensive fare in the system. From Kohala, a daily bus from the Hilton Waikoloa Village Resort makes its way through Waimea to Hilo. You can take the southern route from Ocean View Estates through Kau, passing through Naalehu and Volcano, and continuing on to Hilo. This trip takes just over two hours and costs $5.25. A fourth runs from Pahoa through Keaau to Hilo, while the fifth goes down the coast from Honokaa to Hilo. In the Kohala district a bus runs every weekday morning from Kapaau to Hilton Waikoloa Village and returns in the late afternoon.

The county also maintains the **Banyan Shuttle** in Hilo. This bus does five runs Mon.-Fri. 9 a.m.-2:55 p.m. The Shuttle costs 75 cents but you can buy a $2 pass for one-day's unlimited use. The Shuttle runs from the Hukilau Hotel at the end of Banyan Drive to the Mooheau Bus Terminal in downtown Hilo. En route it stops at the better hotels, Puainako Town Center, Hilo and Kaikoo malls, Lyman Museum, and Rainbow Falls, where you're allowed 10 minutes for a look.

Kailua-Kona has the **Ali'i Shuttle,** tel. (808) 775-7121, that cruises Ali'i Drive. This red, white, and blue bus runs every 30-45 minutes or so, 8:30 a.m.-10 p.m. Rides are $2 each way, $5 for a day pass, $20 for a weekly pass, or $40 for a monthly pass.

The newest of the island shuttles services the hotels and shops of South Kohala. The **Kohala Resort Shuttle,** tel. (808) 325-5448, runs on a continuous schedule between the Mauna Kea Hotel and Hilton Waikoloa Village, stopping at the Hapuna Beach Prince Hotel, The Orchid at Mauna Lani, and King's Shops on the way. Running from mid-morning until 9 p.m., it's $5 each way.

Taxis

Both the Hilo and Kona airports always have taxis waiting for fares. From Hilo's airport to downtown costs about $12, and from Kona to most hotels along Ali'i Drive in Kailua is $22. Obviously, a taxi is no way to get around if you're trying to save money. Most taxi companies, both in Kona and Hilo, run sightseeing services for fixed prices. In **Kona** try: Kona Taxi, tel. (808) 329-7779; Paradise Taxi, tel. (808) 329-1234; Marina Taxi, tel. (808) 329-2481. In **Hilo** try: Hilo Harry's Taxi, tel. (808) 935-7091; A-1 Bob's Taxi, tel. (808) 959-4800; ABC Taxi, tel. 9692076; Hawaii Taxi, tel. (808) 959-6359.

Note: Inquire from the County Transit Agency, tel. (808) 935-8241, about money-saving coupons for "shared-ride taxi service." They allow door-to-door taxi service within nine miles of the urbanized areas of Hilo and Kona. Service hours and other restrictions apply.

Hitchhiking

The old thumb works on the Big Island about as well as anywhere else. Some people hitchhike rather than take the Hele-On Bus not so much to save money as to save time! It's a good idea to check the bus schedule (and routes), and set out about 30 minutes before the scheduled departure. If you don't have good luck, just wait for the bus to come along and hail it. It'll stop.

SIGHTSEEING TOURS

Bus and Van Tours

Narrated and fairly tame island bus tours are operated by **Robert's Tours,** tel. (808) 329-1688 or 966-5483 and **Polynesian Adventure Tours,** tel. (808) 329-8008. Tours cost $40-60 pp, and either circle the island or have Kilauea Volcano as their main feature.

Four-wheel-drive van tours include: **Waipio Valley Shuttle,** tel. (808) 775-7121, offering a two-hour tour down to Waipio Valley ($25) and a Mauna Kea summit tour ($75), minimum four people; and **Hawaiian Resorts Transportation Company,** tel. (808) 775-7291, which also offers a trip into Waipio Valley ($26). In addition, Arnott's Lodge in Hilo, tel. (808) 969-7097, offers a Mauna Kea tour on Tuesday and Friday 10 a.m.-7 p.m. for $75. At other times, the van can be

Waipio Valley Shuttle

chartered for $300 for four people, $75 for each extra person.

Paradise Safaris, tel. (808) 322-2366 or (800) 545-5662, owned and operated by Pat Wright, has been taking visitors on high-adventure trips around the Big Island for the last 10 years. Pat, originally from New Mexico, is a professional guide who's plied his trade from the Rockies to New Zealand, and has taken people on trips ranging from mountaineering to white-water rafting. Your comfort and safety are ensured as you ride in sturdy GMC High Sierra vans with 4WD and a/c. The premier trip offered by Paradise Safaris is an eight-hour journey to the top of Mauna Kea. Pat not only fills your trip with stories, anecdotes, and fascinating facts during the ride, he tops off the safari by setting up an eight-inch telescope so you can get a personal view of the heavens through the rarefied atmosphere atop the great mountain. Pat will pick you up at your hotel in Kailua-Kona at about 4 p.m. If you're staying on the Hilo side, he will meet you at a predetermined spot along the Saddle Road. The price is $125, with hot savory drinks and good warm parkas included. Paradise Safaris will also tailor special trips for photography, hiking, astronomy, or shore fishing. (E-mail: parsaf@maunakea.com; website: www.maunakea.com.)

Tour Tapes and Brochures

For a unique concept, rent Tour Tapes, narrated by Russ Apple, Ph.D., a retired national-park ranger and 1987 winner of the *Historic Hawaii Foundation Award.* Russ dispenses his knowledge about the Big Island as you drive along prescribed routes, mostly in and around Hawaii Volcanoes National Park. Tapes and decks are available in Hilo from the Hilo Hawaiian Hotel, Aston Naniloa Resort, and Lyman House Museum. They are also available at the Volcano Art Center.

The Big Island chapter of the HVB puts out the free "Hawaii's Big Island Driving Tour" brochure. Maps, photos, and text detail one and multiple-day self-drive itineraries of major historical and cultural points of interest, scenic spots, and other highlights around the island. Cursory coverage, but it introduces all areas of the island. Pick one up at either the Hilo or Kona HVB office.

Helicopter and Air Tours

Air tours are a great way to see the Big Island, but they are expensive, especially when the volcano is putting on a mighty display. Expect to spend a minimum of $135-275 for a front-row seat to watch the amazing light show from the air. Kilauea volcano erupting is like winning the lottery for these small companies, and many will charge whatever the market will bear.

Tip: to get the best view of the volcanic activity, schedule your flight for the morning, and no later than 2 p.m. Later, clouds and fog can set in, obstructing your view.

Volcano Helitours, tel. (808) 967-7578, owned and operated by David Okita, is intimately familiar with the volcano area. Their heliport sits atop Kilauea and is located just off a fairway of the Volcano Golf and Country Club. Rates are extremely competitive, and because your flight originates atop the volcano, you waste no air time going to or from the eruption sites. The helicopter is a four-passenger (all seats have windows) Hughes 500D.

Helicopter flights from Hilo International Airport are very competitively priced, with savings over the companies operating out of Kailua-Kona.

Try **Io Aviation,** tel. (808) 935-3031, or **Kainoa Aviation,** tel. (808) 961-5591. **Safari Helicopters,** tel. (808) 969-1259 or (800) 326-3356 from other islands, also flies from Hilo. Its prices run $130-249. (E-mail: safari@safariair.com; website: www.safariair.com.)

Mauna Kea Helicopters, tel. (808) 885-6400, flies from the small Kamuela Airport in Waimea.

Helicopter tours also leave from the Kona side. One of the oldest and most knowledgeable helicopter companies on the Big Island is **Kenai Helicopters,** tel. (808) 329-7424 in Kona, (808) 969-3131 in Hilo, or (800) 622-3144 from the Mainland. They offer a "Creations of Pele and Hidden Treasures of Kohala" tour for $299, leaving from the Hapuna helipad. From Hilo are the "Fire and Rain Tour," which includes a rainforest and Puna Coast flyover for $160, "Formations of Pele" for $160, and "Hidden Treasures of Kohala" for $140. A ride with Kenai is a once-in-a-lifetime thrill. With its spotless safety record, **Blue Hawaiian Helicopters,** tel. (808) 961-5600 or (800) 745-2583, operates from the Waikoloa Heliport on the Kona side and from the Hilo airport. (Website: bluehawaiian.com; e-mail: blue@maui.net.) **Hawaii Helicopters,** tel. (808) 329-4700, flies from the Kona airport. (E-mail: pchild@pixi.com; website: www.hawaiiheli.com.)

For fixed-wing air tours try one of the following: **Big Island Air** offers small-plane flights from Kona Airport, two person minimum, tel. (808) 329-4868 or (800) 303-8868. They fly a volcano tour in an eight-passenger Cessna 402 for $199 pp or $119 for the early bird special. Every seat is a window seat. The plane can be chartered for $550 an hour from Kona or $660 and hour from Hilo. From either Kona or Hilo, **Classic Aviation,** tel. (808) 329-8687 or (800) 695-8100, offers a number of flying adventures from $125-250 pp in their open-cockpit biplane. (E-mail: biplane@ilhawaii.net; website: planet-hawaii.com/biplane.)

Ocean Tours

Whether its skimming across the ocean surface on a trim sloop, diving by submarine to view coral fields, or watching whales breach and play, there are many and various ocean tours to excite visitors to the Big Island. Some of the more popular options follow.

Captain Zodiac, tel. (808) 329-3199 or (800) 422-7824, 74-425 Kealakehe Pkwy., Suite 16, Kailua-Kona, 96740, will take you on a fantastic ocean odyssey beginning at Honokohau Small Boat Harbor just north of Kailua-Kona, from where you'll skirt the coast south all the way to Kealakekua Bay. A Zodiac is a very tough, motorized rubber raft. It looks like a big, horseshoe-shaped inner-tube that bends itself and undulates with the waves like a floating waterbed. These seaworthy craft, powered by twin Mercury 280s, have five separate air chambers for unsinkable safety. They'll take you for a thrilling ride down the Kona coast, pausing along the way to whisk you into sea caves, grottoes and caverns. The Kona coast is also marked with ancient ruins and the remains of villages, which the captains point out, and about which they relate historical anecdotes as you pass by. You stop at Kealakekua Bay, where you can swim and snorkel in this underwater conservation park. Roundtrips departing at 8 a.m., and again at 1 p.m., take about four hours and cost $62 adults, $52 children under 11. Captain Zodiac also provides a light tropical lunch of fresh exotic fruit, taro chips, fruit juice, iced tea, and sodas. All you need are a bathing suit, sun hat, towel, lotion, camera, and sense of adventure.

Atlantis Submarine, tel. (808) 329-6626 or (800) 548-6262, website: goatlantis.com, allows everyone to live out the fantasy of Captain Nemo on a silent cruise under the waves off Kailua-Kona. After checking in at their office in King Kamehameha's Kona Beach Hotel Mall, you board a launch at Kailua Pier that takes you on a 10-minute cruise to the waiting submarine tethered offshore. You're given all of your safety tips on the way there. The underwater portion last about one half hour. As you descend to 120 feet, notice that everything white, including teeth, turns pink, because the ultraviolet rays are filtered out. The only colors that you can see clearly beneath the waves are blues and greens because water is 800 times denser than air and filters out the reds and oranges. Everyone has an excellent seat with a viewing port; there's not a bad seat in this 48-passenger submarine, so you don't have to rush to get on. Don't worry about being claustrophobic either—the sub is amazingly airy and bright, with white space-age plastic on the inside walls, and aircraft-quality air blowers over your seat.

The Atlantis Sub is getting some competition from the **Nautilus II,** tel. (808) 326-2003, a semi-submersible very similar to the famous "ironsides" first used in the Civil War. This high-tech model offers a narrated one-hour tour in its spacious, air-conditioned lower deck. Departures are daily from Kailua Pier: adults $29.95, children under 12 $19.95.

The *Maile,* berthed at Kawaihae Harbor, P.O. Box 44335, Kamuela, HI 96743, tel. (808) 326-5174 or (800) 726-SAIL, is a 50-foot Gulfstar sloop available for luxury sailing charters and shorter-term whalewatching, snorkeling, and fishing expeditions. Skippered by Ralph Blancato, a U.S. Coast Guard-certified Master, the sloop offers competitive prices on half- or full-day charters, sunset sails, and long-term rental. Blantaco teaches his guests about marine life, reef ecology, and island environment. Aside from her commercial use, the *Maile* also functions as the research boat for both the Ocean Mammal Institute and the Oceanic Society.

For more conventional sailing and boating adventures, try one of the following. **Captain Beans',** tel. (808) 329-2955, is a Kona institution that will take you aboard its glass-bottom boat daily at 5:15 p.m. from Kailua Pier at $45 adults; only open to those age 21 and older. During the very tame cruise you'll spot fish, listen to island music, and enjoy a sunset dinner. **Captain Cook VII,** tel. (808) 329-6411, is also a glass-bottom boat. Its tour includes snorkeling and lunch for $25 adults.

Whalewatch Cruises

In season (Nov.-April), these fascinating adventures are provided by **Royal Hawaiian Cruises,** tel. (808) 329-6411. Morning and afternoon cruises usually last about three hours and cost $35 adults, $17 for children 5-12. Accompanied by naturalists from the University of Hawaii, the educational cruise advertises that you will "see a whale, or get a coupon for another whale watch free."

Three hour whalewatching tours on the 40-foot boat *Lady Ann* are offered by **Dan Mc-Sweeney's Whalewatching Adventures,** tel. (808) 322-0028 or (888) WHALES6, P.O. Box 139, Holualoa, HI 96725, e-mail: dmcswwa@interpac.net, website: www.ilovewhales.com. While many are interested in looking only for the humpback whale, Dan, a marine biologist and whale researcher, takes visitors year round so they can also learn about different kinds of whales and other ocean mammals that inhabit this coast.

For a day of snorkeling, sailing and whale-watching in season, contact **Kamanu Charters,** tel. (808) 329-2021. From Waikoloa, try **Ocean Sports,** tel. (808) 885-5555; they offer snorkeling and whalewatching cruises with five departures per day.

SPECIAL NEEDS

Hawaii Services
At Hilo Airport there are no facilities for deplaning nonambulatory people from propeller planes, only from jets and on the jetways. Interisland flights should be arranged only on jets. Ramps and a special elevator provide access in the bi-level terminal. Parking is convenient in designated areas. At Kona airport, boarding and deplaning is possible for the handicapped. Ramps make the terminal accessible. To get around, **Handi-Vans** are available in Hilo, tel. (808) 961-6722. **Kamealoha Unlimited** has specially equipped vans, tel. (808) 966-7244. **Parking permits** are available from the Department of Finance, tel. (808) 961-8231. Medical help, nurses, and companions can be arranged through **Big Island Center for Independent Living,** tel. (808) 935-3777. Doctors are referred by **Hilo Hospital,** tel. (808) 961-4211, and **Kona Hospital,** tel. (808) 322-9311. Medical equipment is available from **Kamealoha Unlimited,** tel. (808) 966-7244; **Medi-Home,** tel. (808) 969-1123; **Pacific Rent-All,** tel. (808) 935-2974.

INFORMATION AND SERVICES

For police, fire, and ambulance anywhere on the island, dial 911.

Civil Defense: In case of natural disaster such as hurricanes or tsunamis on the Big Island, call (808) 935-0031.

Coast Guard Search and Rescue; tel. (800) 552-6458.

Sexual Assault Crisis Line; tel. (808) 935-0677.

Time of day; tel. (808) 961-0212.

Aloha Pages, tel. (808) 935-1666, is a free 24-hour "talking telephone" information service on a variety of topics including weather, news, sports, community service, and entertainment. For specific information, dial the above number, followed by a four-digit code number as directed, or check your local Hawaiian phone book for a complete listing of available topics.

Weather, Marine, and Volcano Reports
For recorded information on local island weather, call (808) 961-5582; for the marine report, call (808) 935-9883; and for volcano activity, call (808) 967-7977.

Consumer Protection
If you encounter problems with accommodations, bad service, or downright rip-offs, try the following: the Chamber of Commerce in Hilo, tel. (808) 935-7178, or in Kailua-Kona, tel. (808) 329-1758; the Hawaii Hotel Association, tel. (808) 923-0407; the Office of Consumer Protection, tel. (808) 974-6230; or the Better Business Bureau, tel. (808) 941-5222.

Tourism Information
The best information on the Big Island is dispensed by the HVB Hilo Branch, 250 Keawe St., Hilo, HI 96720, tel. (808) 961-5797; or HVB Kona Branch, 75-5719 W. Ali'i Dr., Kailua-Kona, HI 96740, tel. (808) 329-7787. (Website: www.big-island.org).

For general information about the Big Island and specific accommodation and activities listings, ask for their official vacation planner, or check it on the web at www.hshawaii.com/bivp.

Other Tourism-Related Information Sources
The State Visitor Information centers at the airports, tel. (808) 934-5840 (Hilo) or (808) 329-3423 (Kona), are good sources of information available on arrival.

Post Office
Branch post offices are found in most major towns. Window service is offered Mon.-Fri. 8:30 a.m.-4 p.m.; some offices are open Saturday 10 a.m.-noon. The following are the main offices:

Hilo, tel. (808) 933-7090; Kailua, tel. (808) 329-1927; Captain Cook, tel. (808) 323-3663; Waimea/Kamuela, tel. (808) 885-4026; Volcano, tel. (808) 967-7611; Hawi, tel. (808) 889-5301.

Hospitals and Pharmacies
Medical help is available from Hilo Medical Center, tel. (808) 974-4700; Kona Community Hospital in Kealakekua, tel. (808) 322-9311; Honokaa Hospital, tel. (808) 775-7211; North Hawaii Community Hospital in Kamuela, tel. (808) 889-6211; and Kau Hospital in Pahala, tel. (808) 928-8331.

Of the numerous drug stores throughout the island, the following should meet your needs: Longs Drugs, Hilo, tel. (808) 935-3357, or Kona, tel. (808) 329-1380; Village Pharmacy, Waimea, tel. (808) 885-4418.

Reading Material
Make sure to pick up the following free literature. Besides maps and general information, they often include money-saving coupons. Available at most hotels/condos and at all tourist areas, the weekly publications include: *Guide: Big Island, Beach and Activity Guide: Big Island,* and *This Week: Big Island.* Island newspapers include: *Hawaii-Tribune Herald,* a Hilo publication; *West Hawaii Today,* published in Kona, and the *Ka'u Landing,* a monthly out of Ocean View.

Libraries are located in towns and schools all over the island. The main branch is at 300 Waianuenue Ave., Hilo, tel. (808) 933-4650. They provide all information regarding libraries. In Kailua-Kona, the library is at 75-140 Hualalai Rd., tel. (808) 327-3077. For bookstores, please refer to the **Shopping** section above.

Island Radio
More than a dozen radio stations broadcast on the Big Island. Among those that are popular are: K-BIG 106.1 FM in Kona and 97.9 FM in Hilo playing contemporary music; KIPA 620 AM Rainbow Radio out of Hilo with contemporary sounds and requests; KKOA 107.7 FM with hot country in Hilo; KKON 790 AM with contemporary songs from Kealakekua; KPUA 670 AM with news and sports broadcasting from Hilo; The WAVE at 97.1 FM broadcasting contemporary sound from Hilo, and Y101.5 FM for island rock.

Island Facts
Hawaii has three fitting nicknames: the Big Island, the Volcano Island, and the Orchid Island. It's the youngest, most southerly, and largest (4,028 square miles) island in the Hawaiian chain. Its color is red, the island flower is the red lehua (ohia), and the island lei is fashioned from the ohia-lehua blossom.

HILO

Hilo is a blind date. Everyone tells you what a beautiful personality she has, but . . . But? . . . it rains: 133 inches a year. Mostly the rains come in winter and are limited to predictable afternoon showers, but they do scare some tourists away, keeping Hilo reasonably priced and low key. In spite of, and because of, the rain, Hilo is gorgeous. It's one of the oldest permanently settled towns in Hawaii, and the largest on the windward coast of the island. Hilo's weather makes it a natural greenhouse. Twenty acres of exotic orchids and flowers line the runways at the airport! Botanical gardens and flower farms surround Hilo like a giant lei, and shoulder-to-shoulder banyans canopy entire city blocks. To counterpoint this tropical explosion, Mauna Kea's winter snows backdrop the town. The crescent of Hilo Bay blazes gold at sunrise, while a sculpted lagoon, Asian pagodas, rock gardens, and even a tiny island connected by a footbridge line its shores. Downtown's waterfront has the perfect false-front buildings that always need a paint

job. They lean on each other like "old salts" who've had one too many. Don't make the mistake of underestimating Hilo, or of counting it out because of its rainy reputation. For most, the blind date with this exotic beauty turns into a fun-filled love affair.

Hilo is a unique town in a unique state in America. You can walk down streets with names like Puueo and Keawe, and they could be streets in Anywhere, U.S.A., with neatly painted houses surrounded by white picket fences. Families live here. There are roots, and traditions, but the town is changing. Fishermen still come for the nightly ritual of soul-fishing and story-swapping from the bridge spanning the Wailuku River, while just down the street newly arrived chefs prepare Cajun blackened fish at a yuppie restaurant as midnight philosophers sip gourmet coffee and munch sweets next door. Hilo is a classic tropical town. Some preserved buildings, proud again after new face-lifts, are a few stories tall and date from the turn of the century when Hilo

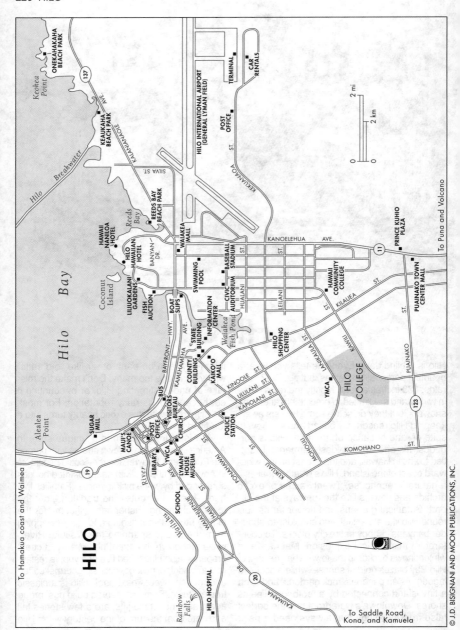

HILO

To Hamakua coast and Waimea

Alealea Point

Hilo Bay

Keokea Point

ONEKAHAKAHA BEACH PARK

137

Hilo Breakwater

KEAUKAHA BEACH PARK

SILVA ST.

KALANIANAOLE AVE.

Reeds Bay

REEDS BAY BEACH PARK

HAWAII NANILOA HOTEL

Coconut Island

HILO HAWAIIAN HOTEL

BANYAN DR.

LILIUOKALANI GARDENS

FISH AUCTION

BOAT SLIPS

SWIMMING POOL

WAIAKEA MALL

BASEBALL STADIUM

CIVIC AUDITORIUM

HUALANI

Waiakea Fish Pond

BAYFRONT HWY.

KAMEHAMEHA AVE.

STATE BUILDING

INFORMATION CENTER

KANOELEHUA AVE.

HILO INTERNATIONAL AIRPORT (GENERAL LYMAN FIELD)

POST OFFICE

CAR RENTALS

TERMINAL

KEKUANAOA ST.

KILAUEA

HAWAII COMMUNITY COLLEGE

LEILANI ST.

11

To Puna and Volcano

PRINCE KUHIO PLAZA

PUAINAKO TOWN CENTER MALL

HILO SHOPPING CENTER

KAWILI ST.

LANIKAULA ST.

HILO COLLEGE

PUAINAKO

123

SUGAR MILL

BUS

VISITORS BUREAU

COUNTY BUILDING

KAIKO'O MALL

KINOOLE ST.

ULULANI ST.

KAPIOLANI ST.

YMCA

MAUI'S CANOE

POST OFFICE

CHURCH

YWCA

LYMAN HOUSE MUSEUM

LIBRARY

SCHOOL

PONAHAWAI

POLICE STATION

KEAWE ST.

KINOOLE ST.

KUKUAU ST.

MOHOULI ST.

KOMOHANO ST.

River

Wailuku

WAIANUENUE AVE.

HAILI ST.

Rainbow Falls

HILO HOSPITAL

KAUMANA DR.

20

19

To Saddle Road, Kona, and Kamuela

2 mi

2 km

0   0

© J.D. BISIGNANI AND MOON PUBLICATIONS, INC.

was a major port of entry to Hawaii. Sidewalks in older sections are covered with awnings because of the rains and add a turn-of-the-century gentility. Because Hilo is a town, most Americans can relate to it: it's big enough to have one-way streets and malls, but not so big that it's a metropolis like Honolulu, or so small that it's a village like Hana. You can walk the central area comfortably in an afternoon, but the town does sprawl, and it's *happening*. Teenagers in "boom box" cars cruise the main strip, which is lined with fine restaurants, high-tech discos, and mom-and-pop shops. There's even a down-and-out section where guys hunker down in alleyways, smoking cigarettes and peering into the night. In the still night, there's the deep-throated sound of a ship's foghorn, a specter of times past when Hilo was a vibrant port. Hilo is the opposite of Kailua-Kona both spiritually and physically. There, everything runs super fast; it's a clone of Honolulu. In Hilo the old beat, the old music, that feeling of a tropical place where rhythms are slow and sensual, still exist. Hilo nights are alive with sounds of the tropics and the heady smell of fruits and flowering trees wafting on the breeze. Hilo remains what it always was—a town, a place where people live.

Hilo is the eastern hub of the island. Choose a direction, and an hour's driving puts you in a time-lost valley deep in *paniolo* country, or on the blackness of a recent lava flow, or above the steaming fumaroles of Hawaii Volcanoes National Park. In and around town are museums, riverbank fishing, cultural centers, plenty of gardens, waterfalls, a potholed riverbed, and lava caves. Hilo's beaches are small, rocky, and hard to find—perfect for keeping crowds away. Hilo is bite-size, but you'll need a rental car or the Banyan Shuttle to visit most of the sights around town.

The main thoroughfares through town are Kilauea Street, which merges into Keawe Street and runs one-way toward the Wailuku River; and Kinoole Street, which runs one-way away from the river. Basically they feed into each other and make a big loop through the downtown area. Kamehameha Avenue fronts the town area and runs along the bay.

SIGHTS AND BEACHES

SIGHTS

Lyman Mission House and Museum

The preserved New England-style homestead of David and Sarah Lyman, Congregationalist missionaries who built it in 1839, is the oldest frame building still standing on the Big Island. Lyman House, at 276 Haili St., Hilo, HI 96720, tel. (808) 935-5021, open Mon.-Sat. 9 a.m.-5 p.m., Sunday 1-4 p.m., admission $5 adults, $2.50 children 6-18, opened as a museum in 1932! In 1856, a second story was added, which provided more room and a perfect view of the harbor. In 1926, Haili Street was extended past the home, and at that time the Wilcox and Lyman families had the house turned parallel to the street so that it would front the entrance.

The furniture is authentic "Sandwich Isles" circa 1850, the best pieces fashioned from koa. Much of it has come from other missionary homes, although many pieces belonged to the original occupants.

The floors, mantels, and doors are deep, luxurious koa. The main door is a "Christian door," built by the Hilo Boys Boarding School. The top panels form a cross and the bottom depicts an open Bible. Many of the artifacts on the deep windowsills are tacked down because of earthquakes. One room was used as a schoolroom/dayroom where Mrs. Lyman taught arithmetic, mapmaking, and proper manners. The dining room holds an original family table that was set with the "Blue Willow" china seen in a nearby hutch. Some of the most interesting exhibits are of small personal items like a music box that still plays and a collection of New England autumn leaves that Mrs. Lyman had sent over to show her children what that season was like. Upstairs are bedrooms that were occupied by the parents and the eight children (six were boys). Their portraits hang in a row. Mrs. Lyman kept a diary and faithfully recorded eruptions, earthquakes, and tsunamis. Scientists still refer to it for some of the earliest recorded data on these natural disturbances. The master bedroom has a large bed with pineapples carved into the bedposts, crafted by a ship's carpenter who lived with the family for about eight months. The bedroom mirror is an original, in which many Hawaiians received their first surprised look at themselves. A nursery holds a cradle used by all eight children. It's obvious that the Lymans did not live luxuriously, but they were comfortable in their new island home.

Next door to the Lyman House, in a modern two-story building, is the museum. The first floor is designated the **Island Heritage Gallery.** The entry is a replica of a Hawaiian grass house, complete with thatched roof and floor mats. Nearby are Hawaiian tools: hammers of clinkstone, chisels of basalt, and state-of-the-art "stone age" polishing stones with varying textures used to rub bowls and canoes to a smooth finish. Hawaiian fiberwork, the best in Polynesia, is the next display. As well as coconut and pandanus, the Hawaiians used the pliable air root of the 'ie'ie. The material, dyed brown or black, was woven into intricate designs. You'll also see fishhooks, stone lamps, mortars and pestles, lomi lomi sticks, even a display on kahuna, with a fine text on the kapu system. Precontact displays give way to kimonos from Japan, a Chinese herbal medicine display, and a nook dedicated to Filipino heritage. Saying good-bye is a bust of Mark Twain, carved from a piece of the very monkeypod tree that he planted in Waiohinu in 1866.

Upstairs is the **Earth Heritage Gallery.** The mineral and rock collection here is rated one of the top 10 in the entire country, and by far the best in Polynesia. Marvel at thunder eggs, agates, jaspers, India blue mezolite, aquamarine lazurite from Afghanistan, and hunks of weirdly shaped lava. These displays are the lifelong collection of the great-grandson of the original Rev. Lyman. Anything coming from the earth can be exhibited here: shells named and categorized from around the world, petrified wood, glass paperweights, crystals, and Chinese artifacts. Other exhibits explain the geology and volcanology of Kilauea and Mauna Kea, and an entire section is dedicated to the vanishing flora and fauna of Hawaii. The museum is an educational delight.

Natural Sites and Walking Tour

Start your tour of Hilo by picking up a pamphlet/map entitled *Discover Downtown Hilo, A Walking Tour of Historic Sites,* free at most restaurants, hotels, and shops. This self-guiding pamphlet takes you down the main streets and back lanes where you discover the unique architecture of Hilo's glory days. The majority of the vintage buildings have been restored, and the architecture varies from the continental style of the Hawaiian Telephone Building to the Zen Buddhist Taishoji Shoto Mission.

A remarkable building is the old police station just across from Kalakaua Park. Behind it, in a classic plantation building, is the home of the **East Hawaii Cultural Center,** a nonprofit organization that supports local arts and hosts varying festivals, performances, and workshops throughout the year.

Hilo suffered a devastating tsunami in 1946 and again in 1960. Both times, most of the city was destroyed, but the 1930s First Hawaiian Bank building survived, owing to its structural integrity. Appropriately, the **Tsunami Museum** is now housed in this fine art deco structure and dedicated to those who lost their lives in the devastating waves that raked the island. Stop in Wed.-Sat. 10 a.m.-4 p.m. for a look; 130 Kamehameha Avenue.

After you leave the Lyman Museum, it's a short walk over to Hilo's library, 300 Waianuenue Avenue. Sitting at the entrance are two large stones. The larger is called the **Naha Stone,** known for its ability to detect any offspring of the ruling Naha clan. The test was simple: place a baby on the stone, and if the infant remained silent, he or she was Naha; if the baby cried, he or she wasn't. It is believed that this 7,000-pound monolith was brought from Kauai by canoe and placed near Pinao Temple in the immediate vicinity of what is now Wailuku Drive and Keawe Street. Kamehameha the Great supposedly fulfilled a prophecy of "moving a mountain" by budging this stone. The smaller stone is thought to be an entrance pillar of the Pinao Temple. Just behind the library is the Wailuku River. Pick any of its bridges for a panoramic view down to the sea. Often, local fishermen try their luck from the Wailuku's grassy banks. The massive boulder sitting in the river's mouth is known as Maui's Canoe.

A few miles out of town, heading west on Waianuenue Avenue, are two natural spectacles definitely worth a look. Just past Hilo High School a sign directs you to Wailuku River State Park. Here is **Rainbow Falls,** a most spectacular yet easily visited natural wonder. You'll look down on a circular pool in the river below that's almost 100 feet in diameter; cascading into it is a lovely waterfall. The 80-foot falls deserve their name because as they hit the water below, their mists throw flocks of rainbows into the air. Underneath the falls is a huge cavern, held by legend to be the abode of Hina, mother of the god Maui. Most people are content to look from the vantage point near the parking lot, but if you walk to the left, you can take a stone stairway leading to a private viewing area directly over the falls. Here the river, strewn with volcanic boulders, pours over the edge. Follow the path for a minute or so along the bank to a gigantic banyan tree and a different vantage point.

Follow Waianuenue Avenue for two more miles past Hilo Hospital to the heights above town. A sign to turn right onto Pe'epe'e Falls Street points to the **Boiling Pots.** Usually no one is here. At the parking lot is an emergency phone and toilets. Follow the path past No Swimming signs to an overlook. Indented into the riverbed below is a series of irregularly shaped holes that look as though a peg-legged giant left his peg prints in the hot lava. Seven or eight resemble naturally bubbling jacuzzis. Best after a heavy rain. Turn your head upriver to see **Pe'epe'e Falls,** a gorgeous, five-spouted waterfall. You'll have this area to yourself, and it's great for a quiet picnic lunch.

Around Banyan Drive

If your Hilo hotel isn't situated along Banyan Drive, go there. This bucolic road skirts the edge of the Waiakea Peninsula that sticks out into Hilo Bay. Lining the drive is an almost uninterrupted series of banyans forming a giant hedgerow, while the fairways and greens of the Banyan Golf Course take up the center of the tiny peninsula. Park your car at one end and take a 15-minute stroll through this parklike atmosphere; the banyans have been named for well-known American luminaries. Boutiques and a variety of restaurants sit in the coolness under the trees.

Liliuokalani Gardens are formal Japanese-style gardens located along the west end of Banyan Drive. Meditatively quiet, they offer a beautiful view of the bay. **Coconut Island** just offshore is connected by a footbridge leading from the gardens. Along the footpaths are pagodas designed for relaxing, torii gates, stone lanterns, and half-moon bridges spanning a series of ponds and streams. Few people visit, and if it weren't for the striking fingers of black lava and the coconut trees, you could easily be in Japan. The peninsula, now blanketed by the gardens and the adjacent hotels, was once a populated residential area, an offshoot of central Hilo.

Suisan Fish Market is at the corner of Banyan Dr. and Lihiwai St., which crosses Kamehameha Avenue. This fish auction draws island fishermen of every nationality. The auctioneer's staccato is pure pidgin. Restaurateurs, housewives, and a smattering of tourists gather by 7:30 a.m. to eyeball the catch of the day. Boats tie up and fishermen talk quietly about the prices. Next door, a small snack shop sells sandwiches and piping-hot coffee. Grab a cup and walk over to the gardens through a nearby entrance—you'll have them to yourself.

Cross Lihiwai Street heading south. **Waiakea Pond,** a brackish lagoon where people often fish, is on your right. To the left are **Hoolulu County Park, Civic Center Auditorium,** and a city nursery brimming with orchids. The **Culture Center Nihon** is here too, at 123 Lihiwai St.; it displays artwork and cultural exhibits from Japan. The center is also a restaurant and sushi bar, with a special room set aside for the "tea ceremony."

On the opposite side of Waiakea Fish Pond (drive down Kamehameha Avenue and make a left onto Pauahi Street since no bridges cross), you'll find **Wailoa Center,** dispensing all manner of brochures and pamphlets on Hilo and Big Island activities. The walls of this 10-sided building are used to display works of local artists and cultural/historic exhibits, changed on a monthly basis.

Hilo's Gardens

Hilo's greatest asset is its flowers. Its biggest cash crops are orchids and anthuriums. Flowers grow everywhere, but to see them in a more formalized way, visit one of the following nurseries in and around town. Most have excellent prices for floral arrangements sent back to the Mainland. They'll do a Hawaiian bouquet with heliconia, anthuriums, and orchids for around $25 including shipping. The flowers arrive neatly packaged but unassembled, with a picture of the arrangement so that you can put them together yourself. These hearty cut flowers will look fresh and vibrant for as long as two weeks, so a few days in the mail won't hurt them.

Hilo Tropical Gardens and Gallery (formerly Kong's Floraleigh), 1477 Kalanianaole Ave., Hilo, HI 96720, tel. (808) 935-4957, is open daily 9 a.m.-5 p.m. The admission price of $3 (children under 12 free) includes a free cup of Kona coffee. Here you can go on a self-guided tour through the gardens; all plants have been labeled. Everything's here: plumeria, lipstick trees, anthuriums, orchids, birds of paradise, even pineapples, coconuts, and papayas. You can purchase all manner of dried and fresh-cut flowers, seeds, packaged plants, seedlings, and corsages. The Gallery Gift Shop features art and local crafts

HISTORY OF THE ANTHURIUM

Originally a native of Central America, the anthurium was introduced into Hawaii in 1889 by Samuel M. Damon, an English missionary. Damon discovered that Hawaii's climate and volcanic soil made an ideal environment for this exotic flower. Over the years since then, anthurium production has turned into a million-dollar export industry with all the major growers located on the Big Island.

DIANA LASICH HARPER

of the Big Island, including prints, books, wood items, and pottery. The "no-pressure" salespeople are courteous and friendly. Shipping purchases is no problem.

Along Kilauea Ave., between Lanikaula and Kawili Streets, the Department of Natural Resources, Division of Forestry maintains the **Hilo Arboretum,** open Mon.-Fri. 7:45 a.m.-4:30 p.m., closed Saturday, Sunday, and holidays; free. This tree nursery contains most of the trees present in Hawaii, including indigenous and imported specimens. The office will provide you with a mimeographed sheet entitled "Hilo Nursery Arboretum." It's basically a self-guided tour, but the clerks will warn you that it's not very good. It attempts to name the trees by matching them with points on the map as you pass by, instead of referring to signs on each specimen. However, the trees are magnificent and you will have this quiet area virtually to yourself. Originally the site was an animal quarantine station operated by the Territory of Hawaii; the 19.4 acres of the arboretum were established in 1920 by Brother Mathias Newell. Brother Newell was a nurseryman employed by the Catholic boys' school in Hilo. At that time the Division of Forestry was already actively introducing plant species from all over the world. For the 40 years between 1921 and 1961 the department was engaged in the development and maintenance of arboretums consisting primarily of plant species from Australia and Africa. Arboretum sites ranged from sea level to Mauna Kea. Plant materials were exchanged and thousands of breadfruit cuttings were exported. Over 1,000 different tree species and 500 different fruit trees were field tested. Here at the Hilo Arboretum over 1,000 trees were planted. A few trees such as the paper bark and some pines are more than 50 years old. Presently a small number of timber species are grown for reforestation purposes. Essentially the Hilo site is utilized for the propagation of rare and endangered plant species, for research, and for experimental pursuits.

Nani Mau Gardens are some of the largest in and around Hilo, and touring these spectacular displays is well worth an afternoon. Located at 421 Makalika St. (off Rt. 11), Hilo, HI 96720, tel. (808) 959-3541, the gardens are open daily 8 a.m.-5 p.m. Admission is $10 adult, $5 child, 5 pp for an an optional tram tour, or $6 for a self-drive golf cart. The gardens consist of 20 sculpted acres; 33 more are being developed. More than a botanical garden, Nani Mau is a "floral theme park" designed as a tourist attraction. Walks throughout the garden are very tame but very beautiful; umbrellas are provided during rainy weather, which adds its own dripping, crystalline charm to the experience. Plants are labeled in English, Latin, and Japanese. The gardens are a huge but ordered display of flowers, flowering trees, and shrubbery. The wildly colored plumage of tropical birds here and there competes with the colors of the exotic blooms. The gardens are broken off into separate areas: fruit orchards, heliconia garden, ginger garden, anthurium garden, orchid garden, orchid pavilion, gardenia garden, and bromeliad garden. The new 33 acres include an annual garden, white-sand beach, small volcano, picture garden for photos, and orchids and more orchids. It also features floral sculptures, a small reflective pond, and an assortment of flowers and shrubs laid out in geometric patterns, hearts, mountains, and even "aloha" and "Hilo Hawaii" spelled out. The tourist shop and snack area is exactly like a Japanese *omiyagi* (souvenir) shop. No wonder, since it's owned by Japanese, and the tour buses coming here are all filled with Japanese. If you enjoy a clean outdoor experience surrounded by magnificent flowers, this is the place.

Tanaka's is an excellent nursery from which to buy and to send flowers. They call themselves Jewel Box Orchids and also The Orchidarium, Hawaii Inc., at 524 Manono St., Hilo, HI. It's off the main track. Follow Rt. 11 toward Volcano, make a right on Kekuanaoa St., and go down four blocks to Manono. Make a right and they're a few hundred yards down on the left. For beautiful orchids at unbeatable prices, search them out.

While in the neighborhood, visit **Paradise Plants** at 575 Hinano St., tel. (808) 935-4043, a complete garden center specializing in indoor-outdoor plants and tropical fruit trees. They send orchids and other live flowers to the Mainland. Also featured is a large gift area with gifts from around the world. While browsing, check out their free orchid garden, which ranks as Hilo's oldest.

Kualoa Farms is at the corner of Mamaki (off Rt. 11) and Kealakai Streets, tel. (808) 959-4565, open daily 8 a.m.-4 p.m. A guided tour takes you over some of the 62 acres planted in anthuriums, ti plants, torch gingers, and macadamia and papaya orchards.

Mauna Loa Macadamia Nut Factory is located along Mauna Loa Rd., eight miles out of Hilo on Rt. 11 heading towards Volcanoes National Park. Head down the drive until you come to the Visitors Center. Inside will be a free video explaining the development and processing of macadamia nuts in Hawaii. Take a self-guided tour through the orchards, where all trees and plants are identified. Then return to the snack shop for mac-nut goodies like ice cream and cookies. The gift shop has a wide assortment of mac-nut items at considerably lower prices than anywhere else on the island. Open daily 8:30 a.m.-5 p.m.; tel. (808) 966-8612.

Panaewa Rainforest Zoo

Not many travelers can visit a zoo in such a unique setting, where the animals virtually live in paradise. The road to the zoo is a trip in itself, getting you back into the country. Follow Rt. 11 toward Volcanoes National Park for a few miles until you see the sign pointing down Mamaki Street to the zoo. On a typical weekday, you'll have the place to yourself. The zoo, operated by the county Department of Parks and Recreation, is open daily 9 a.m.-4 p.m., closed Christmas and New Year's Day. Admission is free. For information, call (808) 959-7224.

Here you have the feeling that the animals are not "fenced in" so much as you are "fenced out." The collection of about 50 species includes ordinary and exotic animals from around the world. You'll see a giant anteater from Costa Rica, pygmy hippos from Africa, and a wide assortment of birds like pheasants and peacocks. The zoo is also a botanical garden with many of the trees, shrubs, and ferns labeled. The zoo hosts many endangered animals indigenous to Hawaii like the Laysan duck, Hawaiian coot, *pueo,* Hawaiian gallinule, and even a feral pig in his own stone minicondo. There are some great iguanas and mongooses, lemurs, and an aviary section with exotic birds like yellow-fronted parrots and blue and gold macaws. The central area is a tigers' playground; a tall fence marks this rather large area where tigers still rule their domain. It's got its own pond and tall grasses that make the tigers feel at home but also make them hard to spot.

VICINITY OF HILO

PACIFIC OCEAN

Cape Kumukahi

KUMUKAHI LIGHTHOUSE

137

HAWAIIAN BEACHES SUBDIVISION COUNTY PARK

HONOLULU LANDING

LAVA TREE STATE MONUMENT

HAWAIIAN PARADISE COUNTY PARK

Pahoa

LEHIA BEACH COUNTY PARK

Leleiwi Point

ANA PUKA (CAVE)

Papai

MACADAMIA FACTORY AND ORCHARDS

ONEKAHAKAHA BEACH CO. PARK

LELEIWI BEACH CO. PARK

Wainaku

Hilo Bay

KAOII RD

HAWAIIAN PARADISE PARK

To Kalapana Area (Lava Inundated)

HILO AIRPORT

KEAAU TOWN CENTER MALL

130

KOLEKOLE BEACH COUNTY PARK

Kohola Point

HONOMU COUNTY PARK

Pepeekoe Point

Pepeekoe Mill

PEPEEKEO SCENIC DRIVE

Onomea Bay

HAWAII TROPICAL BOTANICAL GARDENS

Papaikou

19

Honomu

220

HILO

Keaau

11

Kurtistown

AKAKA FALLS STATE PARK

To Honokaa

Waiemi Falls

PAPAIKOU COUNTY PARK

Waialae Falls

Paukaa

HONOLII BEACH COUNTY PARK LOOKOUT

Kaiwiki

PANAEWA ZOO AND COUNTY PARK

Kawainui Stream

Pahoehoe Stream

Wailoa Falls

KAIWIKI COUNTY PARK

Rainbow Falls

KAUMANA CAVES COUNTY PARK

Kawainui

Pohakupa Stream

Hawaii Falls

HILO GOLF COURSE

Mountain View

11

Glenwood

OLAA RAINFOREST

ROAD

STAINBACK

200

SADDLE

To Waimea and Kailua-Kona

0   5 mi

0   5 km

© J.D. BISIGNANI AND MOON PUBLICATIONS, INC.

A touching spot is the **Astronaut Grove,** in memory of the astronauts who were killed on the regrettable explosion of the space shuttle *Columbia.* All are remembered, especially Ellison Onizuka, a native son of the Big Island. The zoo makes a perfect side trip for families or for anyone wishing to get off the beaten track.

Kaumana Caves
In 1881 Mauna Loa's tremendous eruption discharged a huge flow of lava. The river of lava crusted over, forming a tube through which molten lava continued to flow. Once the eruption ceased, the lava inside siphoned out, leaving the tube now called Kaumana Caves. The caves are only five miles out of Hilo along Rt. 200, clearly marked next to the road. Oddly enough, they are posted as a fallout shelter. Follow a staircase down into a gray hole draped with green ferns and brightened by wildflowers. You can walk about 50 yards into the cave before you'll need a flashlight. It's a thrill to turn around and look at the entrance, where blazing sunlight shoots through the ferns and wildflowers. The floor of the cave is cemented over for easy walking. Another cave visible across the way is undeveloped and more rugged to explore.

Two miles past Kaumana Caves is **Hilo Municipal Golf Course,** a 6,006-yard, par-71 course where you can golf for $25.

Pepeekeo Scenic Drive
Route 19 heading north from Hilo toward Honokaa is a must, with magnificent inland and coastal views one after another. (See the **Hamakua Coast** chapter for full coverage of the northern section leading to Waipio.) Only five minutes from Hilo, you'll come to Papaikou town. Look for a small convenience store on the right. Just here is a road posted as a scenic drive, which dips down toward the coast. Take it. Almost immediately a sign says Narrow Winding Road, 20 MPH, letting you know what kind of area you're coming into. Start down this lane past some very modest homes and into the jungle that covers the road like a living green tunnel. Prepare for tiny bridges crossing tiny valleys. Stop, and you can almost hear the jungle growing. The Scenic Drive is like a mini-version of Maui's Hana Road.

In a few minutes you'll come to **Hawaii Tropical Botanical Gardens,** tel. (808) 964-5233, open daily 9 a.m.-5 p.m., with the last shuttle van departing for the garden from the registration area at 4 p.m.Admission is $15, children 6-16 $5, and kids five and under are free. Remember that the $12 entrance fee not only allows you to walk through the best-tamed tropical rainforest on the Big Island, but helps preserve the area in perpetuity. The gardens were established in 1978 when Dan and Pauline Lutkenhouse purchased the property in order to educate the public to the beauty of tropical plants in their natural setting. The gardens have been open for viewing since 1984. Mr. Lutkenhouse, a retired San Francisco businessman, purchased the 25-acre valley and personally performed the work that transformed it into one of the most exotic spots in all of Hawaii. The locality was amazingly beautiful but inaccessible because it was so rugged. Through a personal investment of nearly $1 million and six painstaking years of toil aided only by two helpers, he hand-cleared the land, built trails and bridges, developed an irrigation system, acquired more than 2,000 different species of trees and plants, and established one mile of scenic trails and a large water lily lake stocked with *koi* and tropical fish. A shuttle van takes you on a five-minute ride down to Onomea Bay where the gardens are located. Onomea was a favorite spot with the Hawaiians, who came to fish and camp for the night. The valley was a fishing village called Kahlili in the early 1800s. Later on it became a rough-water seaport used for shipping sugarcane and other tropical products. Recently, a remake of *Lord of the Flies* was filmed here, and it's easy to see why the area made the perfect movie set.

The van drops you off at a staging area in the garden where you'll find self-guiding maps, drinking water, restrooms, umbrellas for your convenience, and jungle perfume—better known as mosquito repellent! Plants from the four corners of the globe, including Iran, Central China, Japan, tropical Africa, India, Borneo, Brazil, East Indies, South Pacific Islands, tropical America, and the Philippines, are named with a full botanical description. Native plants from Hawaii are included. Listen for the songs of birds: the white-tailed tropic bird, black-crowned heron, Pacific golden plover, Hawaiian hawk, Japanese white eye, common mynah, and northern cardinal. Choose one of the aptly named trails like Ocean Trail or Waterfall Trail and lose yourself in the beauty of the surroundings. You are in the middle of a tamed jungle, walking along manicured paths. Stroll the Ocean Trail down to the sea, where the rugged coastline is dramatically pummeled by frothy waves. You can hear the waves entering submerged lava caves, where they blow in and out like a giant bellows. Away from the sea you'll encounter screened gazebos filled with exotic birds like cockatoos from Indonesia and blue-fronted Amazon parrots. Walk the inland trails past waterfalls, streams, a bamboo grove, and innumerable flowers. For at least a brief time you get to feel the power and beauty of a living Garden of Eden.

Hawaiian Artifacts, just a minute down Scenic Drive past the gardens, is a shop owned and operated by Paul Gephart, tel. (808) 964-1729, open Mon.-Sat. 9 a.m.-5 p.m. Paul creates wood sculptures mainly from koa and ohia that he turns into whales, dolphins, birds, and poi bowls. Here's also a small but tasteful collection of jewelry and seashells, all at very decent prices.

Continue for another two to three miles, and you'll come to a wooden bridge with a white railing overlooking a cascading mountain stream with a big swimming hole. Great for a freshwater dip, but always be careful: these streams can be torrential during a heavy rain. The side road rejoins Rt. 19 at Papeeko, a workers' village where you can get gas or supplies.

BEACHES

If you define a beach as a long expanse of white sand covered by a thousand sunbathers and their beach umbrellas, then Hilo doesn't have any. If a beach, to you, can be a smaller, more intimate affair where a good but not gigantic number of tourists and families can spend the day on pockets of sand between fingers of black lava, then Hilo has plenty. Hilo's best beaches all lie to the east of the city along Kalanianaole Avenue, an area also known as the Keaukaha Strip, which runs six miles from downtown Hilo to its dead end at Leleiwi Point. Not all beaches are clearly marked, but they are easily spotted by

cars parked along the road or in makeshift parking lots.

Hilo Bayfront Park is a thousand yards of black sand that narrows considerably as it runs west from the Wailoa River toward downtown. At one time it went all the way to the Wailuku River and was renowned throughout the islands for its beauty, but commercialism of the harbor has ruined it. By 1960, so much sewage and industrial waste had been pumped into the bay that it was considered a public menace, and then the great tsunami came. Reclamation projects created the Wailoa River State Recreation Area at the east end, and shorefront land became a buffer zone against future inundation. Few swimmers come to the beach because the water is cloudy and chilly, but the sharks don't seem to mind! The bay is terrific for fishing and picnicking, and the sails of small craft and windsurfers can always be seen. It's a perfect spot for canoe races, and many local teams come here to train. Notice the judging towers and canoe sheds. Toward the west end, near the mouth of the Wailuku River, surfers catch long rides during the winter months, entertaining spectators.

The **Wailoa River State Recreation Area** is a 134-acre preserve set along the spring-fed Wailoa River in downtown Hilo. City residents use the area for picnics, pleasure walks, informal get togethers, and launching boats. Stop at the Wailoa Center off Pauahi Street for information and cultural displays. Additional parking for this landscaped, parklike area is at the end of Pi'ilani Street.

Coconut Island Park is reached by footbridge from a spit of land just outside Liliuokalani Gardens. It was at one time a *pu'uhonua* (place of refuge) opposite a human sacrificial *heiau* on the peninsula side. Coconut Island has restrooms, a pavilion, and picnic tables shaded by tall coconut trees and ironwoods. A favorite picnic spot for decades, it has a diving tower and a sheltered natural pool area for children. The only decent place to swim in Hilo Bay, it also offers the best panorama of the city, bay, and Mauna Kea beyond.

Reeds Bay Beach Park is on the east side of the Waiakea Peninsula at the end of Banyan Drive. It too is technically part of Hilo Bay and offers good swimming, though the water is notoriously cold because of a constantly flowing freshwater spring. Most people just picnic here, and fishermen frequent the area.

Keaukaha Beach, located on Puhi Bay, is the first in a series of beaches as you head east on Kalanianaole Avenue. Look for Baker Avenue and pull off to the left into a parking area near an old pavilion. This is a favorite spot with local people, who swim at "Cold Water Pond," a spring-fed inlet at the head of the bay. A sewage treatment plant fronts the western side of Puhi Bay. Much nicer areas await you just up Kalanianaole Avenue.

Onekahakaha Beach Park has it all: safe swimming, white-sand beach, lifeguards, and all amenities. Turn left onto Machida Ln. and park in the lot of Hilo's favorite "family" beach, although very recently a number of local homeless people have been living in this area. Swim in the large, sandy-bottomed pool protected by the breakwater. Outside the breakwater the currents can be fierce and drownings have been recorded. Walk east along the shore to find an undeveloped area of the park with many small tidal pools. Beware of sea urchins.

James Kealoha Park, also known locally as "4 Mile," is next; people swim, snorkel, and fish here, and during winter months it's a favorite surfing spot. A large grassy area is shaded by trees and a picnic pavilion. Just offshore is an island known as Scout Island because local Boy Scouts often camp here. This entire area was known for its fishponds, and inland, just across Kalanianaole Avenue, is the 60-acre Loko'aka Pond. This site of ancient Hawaiian aquaculture is now a commercial operation that provides the best mullet on the island.

Leleiwi Beach Park lies along a lovely residential area carved into the rugged coastline. Part of the park is dedicated to the Richardson Ocean Center, and the entire area is locally called **Richardson's Beach.** Look for Uwau Street, just past the Mauna Loa Shores Condo, and park along the road here. Look for a fancy house surrounded by tall coconut trees and follow the pathway through the grove. Use a shower that's coming out of the retaining wall surrounding the house. Keep walking until you come to a seawall. A tiny cove with a black-sand beach is the first in a series. This is a terrific area for snorkeling, with plenty of marinelife, including *humu* (green sea turtles). Walk east to a natural lava breakwater. Behind it are pools filled and flushed by the surging tide. The water breaks over the top of the lava and rushes into the pools, making natural jacuzzis. This is one of the most picturesque swimming areas on the island. At Leleiwi Beach Park proper (three pavilions), the shore is open to the ocean and there are strong currents; it's best to head directly to Richardson's.

Lehia Park is the end of the road. When the pavement stops, follow the dirt track until you come to a large, grassy field shaded by a variety of trees. This unofficial camping area has no amenities whatsoever. A series of pools like those at Richardson's are small, sandy-bottomed, and safe. Outside of the natural lava breakwater, currents are treacherous. Winter often sends tides surging inland here, making Lehia unusable. This area is about as far away as you can get and still be within a few minutes of downtown Hilo.

PRACTICALITIES

ACCOMMODATIONS

Accommodations in Hilo are hardly ever booked up, and they're reasonably priced. Sounds great, but many hotels have "gone condo" to survive while others have simply shut their doors, so there aren't as many as there once were. During the Merrie Monarch Festival (late April), the entire town is booked solid! The best hotels are clustered along Banyan Drive, with a few gems tucked away on the city streets.

Hostel

Arnott's Lodge, 98 Apapane Rd., Hilo, HI 96720, tel. (808) 969-7097, fax 961-9638, is a very reasonably priced hostel, extremely well run, safe, clean, and friendly. Follow Kamehameha Avenue south until it turns into Kalanianaole Avenue; in about five minutes you'll see a white sign pointing to Arnott's. Those without private transportation can be picked up by a free shuttle service operating 8 a.m.-9 p.m., with outbound departures set at 8 a.m., 12:30 p.m., and 5:30 p.m. A ride downtown or to the airport costs only $1, and share-ride taxi service can be arranged for $5. Arnott's staff can also help with inexpensive interisland air tickets, along with an in-house eight-hour hiking and snorkeling excursions for $36 (gear included) that take you Volcano National Park, the Puna coast, South Point, or the Hilo waterfalls, depending upon the day; nonguests pay $50. The premier excursion, however, is the Mauna Kea Expedition, $75 including snacks, offered on Tuesday and Friday. Other services are bicycle rental at $10 p/d, snorkel gear at $5 p/d, coin laundry, telephones, and safe storage of valuables and backpacks at no cost. If you're traveling around the island but don't have your own transportation, ask about Arnott's "Big Island Experience," a van trip that circles the island stopping at various sights, parks, eateries, and accommodations on the way. Dormitory bunks—male, female, and coed—at $17 are spotlessly clean and cooled by cross ventilation and ceiling fans. Single rooms with bath, kitchen, and living room shared with

one other room are $30; a double room with the same setup is $40. A self-contained suite with two bedrooms, one with a double bed and the other with twins, includes a bathroom, kitchen, and living room for $105 for up to five people; each additional person $10. Check-in until 10 p.m. only. Tenting on the lawn with your own tent is now an option for $7 per person. Leisure time can be spent in a central courtyard or in a separate gazebo (for those who want to burn the midnight oil or watch one of a huge selection of videos). A backyard covered lanai has pink, blue, and green picnic tables so enormous that you feel like you're back in kindergarten, along with barbecue grills for your convenience, and a meditation platform built in a tree. To help keep prices down, Arnott's hosts an all-you-can-eat barbecue/mixer on Wednesday and Saturday from 7 p.m., where you can have teriyaki or veggie burgers, salsa and chips, fresh fruit salads, ice cream, and tossed salads for only $6. Arnott's is an excellent hostel offering a quality, hassle-free stay. Inexpensive.

Banyan Drive Hotels

The following hotels lie along Banyan Drive. They range from inexpensive to luxury and all are serviced by the Banyan Shuttle.

The **Country Club Condo Hotel,** 121 Banyan Dr., tel. (808) 935-7171, is a very basic hotel/condo with reasonable rates. Rates based on double occupancy are: standard with kitchenette $50, standard oceanfront $60, one-bedroom suite $100; extra person $10, daily rental deposit $20, weekly rental deposit $100. Monthly rates range from fully furnished standard studio for $400 ($440 with weekly maid service), up to a deluxe one-bedroom suite at $700 ($760 with weekly maid service). Since this is a condo hotel, the rooms vary from unit to unit, but most have either double beds or a queen-size bed. Inexpensive.

You can't miss the orange-and-black **Hilo Seaside Hotel,** 126 Banyan Dr., tel. (808) 935-0821 or (800) 367-7000. This is the budget hotel on Banyan Drive. It's island-owned by the Kimi family, and like the others in this small chain, it's clean and well kept and has Polynesian-inspired decor. Room prices are $50 standard, $60 superior, $70 deluxe, and $80 kitchenette. Add approximately $20 for a room/car package. Ask about off-season rates, and they will sometimes offer a better rate depending on the amount of business at the time. The grounds are laid out around a central courtyard and the pool is secluded and away from the street. At this family-style hotel with a motel atmosphere, the friendly staff goes out of its way to make you feel welcome. Moderate.

Uncle Billy's Hilo Bay Hotel is sandwiched between much larger hotels at 87 Banyan Dr., Hilo, HI 96720, tel. (808) 935-0861, (800) 367-5102 Mainland, (800) 442-5841 in Hawaii, website: aloha.net/~uncleb. Rooms here begin at $69 d, $79 including breakfast for two, and $95 for a room-and-car package. The Hilo Bay's blue metal roof and white louvered shutters make it look a bit like "Long John Silver's Meets Polynesia." The lobby's rattan furniture and thatched longhouse theme are pure '50s-kitsch Hawaii. Definitely have a look. There are parking and a pool, all rooms are clean and air-conditioned, and each room has a TV and phone. The hotel offers excellent value for the money. Uncle Billy's Polynesian Marketplace, where you can buy everything from beer to sundries, is part of the complex. Moderate.

Hawaii Naniloa Resort, 93 Banyan Dr., Hilo, HI 96720, tel. (808) 969-3333 or (800) 442-5845, is a massive, 317-room hotel offering deluxe accommodations. Rates start at $100 standard, $120 superior, $140-160 deluxe with private balcony. Private suites are available from $190. A third person costs $15 additional; children under 17 sharing with parents are free. They offer a/c, TV, hotel parking, restaurant, and a pool setting—just above the lava—that is the nicest in Hilo. The original hotel dates back more than 60 years and has built up a fine reputation for value and service. The Hawaii Naniloa has recently undergone extensive renovations and is now as beautiful as ever. Expensive.

Prices at the classy **Hilo Hawaiian Hotel,** 71 Banyan Dr., Hilo, HI 96720, tel. (808) 935-9361 or (800) 272-5275, are $104-325; all rooms have a/c, phone, and TV, plus there's a pool. The Hilo Hawaiian occupies the most beautiful grounds of any hotel in Hilo. From the vantage of the hotel's colonnaded veranda, you overlook formal gardens, Coconut Island, and Hilo Bay. Designed as a huge arc, the hotel's architecture blends well with its surroundings and expresses the theme set by Hilo Bay, that of a long, sweeping crescent. The hotel buffet, especially the Friday and Saturday seafood version, is absolutely out of this world. As a deluxe hotel, the Hilo Hawaiian is the best that Hilo has to offer. Expensive.

Downtown Accommodations

The following hotels are found along Hilo's downtown streets. Some are in quiet residential areas, while others are along busy thoroughfares. Prices are inexpensive to moderate.

The Wild Ginger Inn, at 100 Puueo St., Hilo, HI 96720, tel. (808) 935-5556, (800) 882-1887, is a refurbished plantation-style hotel, painted shocking pink and green, that bills itself as a bed-and-breakfast inn. An open-aired lobby leads to an encircling veranda overlooking the central courtyard area, with a view of the bay in the distance. Each of the 25 wainscoted rooms, very basic but very clean, has a refrigerator, private shower-bath, cross ventilation, and one double and one twin bed. A double hammock and vintage chairs in the lobby area are for your relaxation. Rates for standard rooms are $39, deluxe rooms with cable TV $50. Discounts are available for three nights or longer. The homestyle Hawaiian buffet is terrific. The inn is completely non-smoking, with a special area provided for smokers in the garden. The Wild Ginger Inn, with a friendly staff and good service, is an excellent choice for budget accommodations and gives more than full value for the money. Inexpensive.

Dolphin Bay Hotel is a sparkling little gem— simply the best hotel bargain in Hilo, one of those places where you get more than you pay for. It sits on a side street in the Puueo section of town at the north end of Hilo Bay: 333 Iliahi St., Hilo, HI 96720, tel. (808) 935-1466. John Alexander, the owner/manager, is at the front desk every day. He's a font of information about the Big Island and will happily dispense advice on how to make your day-trips fulfilling. The hotel was built by his father, who spent years in Japan, and you'll be happy to discover this influence when you sink deep into the *ofuro*-type tubs in every room. All 24 units have full modern kitchens. Rates are single studio apartment $59, superior $69, one bed-

John Alexander of the
Dolphin Bay Hotel

DOLPHIN BAY HOTEL

room $79, two-bedroom fully furnished unit $89, additional guest $10. Deluxe units upstairs have open-beam ceilings and lanai, and with three spacious rooms feel like apartments. No swimming pool or a/c, but there are color TVs and fans with excellent cross ventilation. The grounds and housekeeping are immaculate. Hotel guests can partake of free bananas, papayas, and other exotic fruits found in hanging baskets in the lobby, as well as free coffee. Weekly rates range from $325 for a studio to $550 for a two-bedroom deluxe. Make reservations, because everyone who has found the Dolphin Bay comes back again and again. Moderate.

B&Bs

Just four miles north of town is **Our Place Papaikou's B&B,** P.O. Box 469, Papaikou, HI 96781, tel. (808) 964-5250 or (800) 245-5250, e-mail: rplace@aloha.met; website: www.best.com/~ourplace. Set among thick vegetation, the four rooms of this cedar home open onto a large lanai that overlooks Kupua Stream. The Early American and Oriental Rooms run $55 a night, and the Master Bedroom and Treehouse Room are $80, two-night minimum. Inexpensive.

Also try the residence of John and Charlotte Holmes, **Holmes' Sweet Home B&B,** 107 Koula St., Hilo, HI 96720, tel. (808) 961-9089, e-mail: homswhom@gte.com, website: www.hawaii-bnb.com/holmes.html. On a quiet cul-de-sac with a view of Hilo Bay, the home provides two rooms priced $60-70 (no credit cards) that fea-

ture their own private entrances, baths, and guest refrigerator and microwave. A continental breakfast is included. Moderate.

Extra Special

A house can have presence, and, if it's brushed by magic like the Tin Man in *The Wizard of Oz,* it can even attain a heart. The home we're referring to was a purchase motivated by love and occupied by a large, dynamic family. The Shipman House, known locally as "the Castle," perched on five verdant acres high above Hilo, has such a heart.

After a quarter century on the Mainland, Barbara Ann Andersen, great-granddaughter of William H. "Willie" Shipman, the original owner, returned with her children and her husband Gary to restore to its former grandeur the residence where she spent her childhood Easters and Christmases. The house was figuratively stripped to its petticoats and outfitted in grand style.

Shipman House B&B Inn, 131 Ka'iulani St., Hilo, HI 96720, tel. (808) 934-3002, (800) 627-8447, e-mail: bighouse@bigisland.com, is the grandest B&B in all Hawaii, and to appreciate it fully, you must know its history, which goes back as far as the first tall ships that arrived from New England bearing the missionaries and their new faith to the old kingdom. The first members of the family to reside in Hawaii were The Rev. William C. Shipman and his wife Jane, who arrived in the 1850s. The Rev. Shipman died young, leaving Jane alone and in need of a means to support herself and their three children; she accomplished this by opening a Hawaiian girls' boarding school in Hilo. Later she met and married Mr. Reed, a famous engineer responsible for most of Hilo's bridges and for whom, by strange coincidence, "Reed's Island," the section of Hilo where the mansion sits, was named.

One of the boys, William H. "Willie" Shipman, married Mary Melekahuia Johnson, one of the young Hawaiian ladies at his mother's school. Mary was descended from the ruling *ali'i*, and her grandfather was a high chief and advisor to King Kamehameha. Willie originally determined to study medicine, but one day his stepfather, Mr. Reed, made him an offer he couldn't refuse, saying, "Son, if you will give up medicine and take up the study of business, I'll give you a ranch to run." Willie knew a good opportunity when he saw it, and over the years he became one of the largest landholders on the Big Island, founding W.H. Shipman, Ltd., which is today chaired by his grandson, Roy Blackshear—Barbara Ann's father.

Around the turn of the century, Mary often implored Willie to take her for a drive, which would invariably pass by a lovely home being built on Ka'iulani Street. Holding his hand and looking into his eyes she would ask, "Willie, won't you buy me that house?" and he would reply, " I can't. The Wilsons own it." Finally, one day as they passed the house, Mary asked once again, but this time Willie smiled, brandished his cigar, and said, "Yes, my dear. It's been ours for 30 days." They moved into the house in April 1903.

Mary was a dear friend of Hawaii's last queen, Liliuokalani, who would stay at the Shipman house whenever she was in Hilo. While there the queen would preside over simple but elegant "poi luncheons," always seated at the place of honor at the huge round koa dining room table, where she could look out the bay windows at Hilo below. After lunch, Liliuokalani would slip away to the "Library" to clandestinely savor a fine cigar, sheltered from the prying eyes of the press.

To arrive at the Castle, ascend Waianuenue Avenue until you come to the fourth bridge from the sea; cross it, turn left, and you'll see the Castle. Climb the steps to the wraparound lanai, a necessity even for well-to-do families, who, like all Hawaii residents, spend a great deal of time out-

doors. The broad landing provides a wonderful view of Hilo and the sea in the distance, with wild flowers and tangled greenery cascading into a tropical bowl at your feet. Two stained glass windows, encircled by a laurel wreath, the classic sign of a congenial home, greet you on entering. The Double Parlor, the first floor of the rounded three-story Tower that caps the home, is magnificent. Everywhere is glass—old-fashioned, handmade curved glass—its mottled and rippled texture giving a surrealistic twist to the panorama.

Pad along on the burnished fir flooring past koa-wainscoted walls to enter the Dining Room, where an enormous round dining table and *punee* are still very functional. The back area of the home is called the Conservatory, really the center of the home for day-to-day life where the family took their meals. Just off it is a Solarium and the Butler's Pantry, next to an "Otis in-home elevator," installed in the 1930s and probably Hilo's first. Here, too, is the back bedroom, formerly reserved for guests like Jack London and his wife Charmagne. The peaceful Library, waiting to engulf an afternoon reader within its impressive 12-foot ceilings, is warmed by a brick fireplace with a koa mantel, and is fringed by built-in floor-to-ceiling koa bookcases.

Take the ancient elevator or ascend the central staircase to the second floor, where once upon a time a ballroom adorned in white wallpaper with twinkling stars swayed with dancing and music; nowadays it's been converted into two bedrooms. Notice a window opening to a catwalk that leads to a small room built over the water tank. This served as great-grandfather Willie's "Office," his haven from the clamor of 10 children! Enter the circular second-floor section of the Tower, which contains the Master Bedroom; the four-poster koa bed is simply enormous, with the headboard about eight feet tall, and the mattress itself well above waist level. The bed's size and height served a practical purpose, placing the occupants at window level so that they could luxuriate and look out, while at the same time allowing the breeze to flow under the bed and help keep its occupants cool.

A spiral staircase ascends to the attic where a "canvas room" was the children's dormitory. A large, free-standing credenza holds hats and antique clothing still bearing labels like "extra quality A. J. White, hatter to the royal family, 74 German St., Saint James, and 10 Regent Street." Also in the attic is the entrance to the Tower, a wine barrel of a room with wraparound windows.

The main house offers one guest room with antique koa twin beds, mosquito netting, private bath, and doors that open to a 10-foot wide lanai. Other guests will lodge in the Cottage, a separate building on the grounds, originally built for the express purpose of accommodating visitors. The Cottage contains two spacious bedrooms, each with queen-size bed, window seats, and private bath. Both rooms have private entrances, ceiling fans, and a small refrigerator, with TVs available upon request. The rate is $130 d; $25 per extra person.

In the early afternoons, drinks and hors d'oeuvres are served on the main house's lanai. The Library is open to guests, along with use of the 1903 Steinway piano whose keys were once tinkled by Liliuokalani. A complete historical tour is offered daily. Breakfast, served 7:30-9 a.m. (earlier upon request, and special diets accommodated), is an expanded continental with homemade cereals, hot cereals on request, assorted local fruits (there are 20 varieties of fruit trees on the property), fruit juices, Kona coffee, yogurt, fruit bread, muffins, popovers, and cinnamon rolls. Check in is 3-6 p.m., and checkout is at 10 a.m. Shipman House is once again one of the finest homes in all Hawaii in which to spend a quiet and elegant visit. Premium.

FOOD

Inexpensive Dining

Lodged in a gray and white building with matching awning over four picnic tables, **Broke the Mouth** at 55 Mamo St., tel. (808) 934-7670, open Tuesday, Thursday and Friday 9 a.m.-2 p.m. and Wednesday and Saturday 7 a.m.-2 p.m., is owned and operated by organic farmers Tip and Penny Davis, who grow and then cook the food served at this all-natural vegetarian restaurant. Their philosophy is "Farm-fresh, organically grown, local food is the best." Since 1992 the couple has owned and worked 16 acres of the island's finest soil, growing a variety of herbs, greens, and veggies. They had dinner guests who said, "You guys should open up a restau-

rant," and voilà! Hearty plates include the Mamo, which is fresh greens, *ono* pesto pasta, and a "big aloha" vegetarian hot dog for $4.50; and The Bomboola-fresh greens, *ono* pesto pasta, and Hawaiian salad with summer roll for $5.50. All plates include *manapua* and a side of *kulolo*, a dessert that's a mixture of steamed and grated taro and coconut cream. The Hawaiian salad is a healthy bowl of taro root, sweet potato, and green onion with mac-gado-gado sauce, and the greens include basil, mizuna, kale, collards, red chard, sorrel, and edible flowers. *Manapua*, made with whole wheat, are stuffed with *kulolo*, sweet potato basil pesto, or tofu and dill, and sell for 75 cents each, or $4 for a half dozen. Beverages are coffee for 50 cents; smoothie (fresh fruit and juice) $2.50; teas including ginger and lemongrass, mint, or anise $1; and fresh-squeezed, lemon-lime-tangerinade. They also offer bottled sauces and dressings like "mac-gado," a sweet-and-sour dressing with macadamia nuts, ginger, and lemongrass. Broke The Mouth is *the* choice for anyone into hearty, nutritious, deliciously healthy food.

Named after the famous all-Japanese fighting battalion that predated even the famous "442," the **Cafe 100,** at 969 Kilauea Ave., open Mon.-Thurs. 6:45 a.m.-8:30 p.m., Fri.-Sat. until 9:30 p.m., is a Hilo institution. The Miyashiro family has been serving food at their indoor-outdoor restaurant here since the late '50s. Although the loco moco, a cholesterol atom bomb containing a hamburger and egg atop rice smothered in gravy, was invented at Hilo's Lincoln Grill, the Cafe 100, serving it since 1961, has actually patented this belly-buster and turned it into an art form. There are the regular loco moco, the teriyaki loco, the sukiyaki loco, the hot dog loco, the *oyako* loco, and for the health conscious, the mahi loco. With a few exceptions, they cost $2 or less. So, if your waistline, the surgeon general, and your arteries permit, this is *the* place to have one. Breakfast choices include everything from bacon and eggs to coffee and donuts, while lunches ($3.25-3.95) feature beef stew, mixed plate, and fried chicken, or an assortment of sandwiches from teri-beef to good old BLT for $2 or so. Make your selection and sit at one of the picnic tables under the veranda to watch the people of Hilo go by.

All trips to Hilo must include a brief stop at **Low's International Food,** long occupying the corner of Kilauea and Ponahawai Streets, tel. (808) 969-6652, open daily except Wednesday, 9 a.m.-8 p.m., where *everyone* comes for the unique bread. Some of the more fanciful loaves are made from taro, breadfruit, guava, mango, passion fruit, coconut, banana, pumpkin, and cinnamon. The so-you-want-to-taste-it-all rainbow bread is a combination of taro, guava, and sweet bread. Loaves cost $4.25-5.25, and arrangements can be made to ship them home by Federal Express. Lunches, most under $5, range from their famous pot-roast pork tail with black bean sauce to turkey plate to lamb curry stew. Choose a table under the pavilion and enjoy your picnic in downtown Hilo.

Open every day 7 a.m.-9 p.m., a place that's getting praise from local people is **Freddie's,** at 454 Manono St., tel. (808) 935-1108. The decor might be called upscale Formica, but Freddie's serves down-home food, all for under $6. Lunch and all entrees are served with two scoops of rice, fries, or mashed potatoes. Among the items on the menu are saimin, teri steak sandwich, chili dogs, and burgers.

If you want to eat anything but uninspired "American standard" in Hilo after 9 p.m., go to **Nori's Saimin and Snacks,** 688 Kinoole St., tel. (808) 935-9133, stuck away and hard to spot (but worth it) in a little alley across from the bowling alley. Here you can have a totally "island experience" in a humble but proud restaurant that specializes in authentic "local grinds." Inside, where the service is slow but friendly, are Formica tables and chairs, counter stools, and the "that's what you really look like" glow of fluorescent lighting. Boiling pots hold saimin of all sorts, ranging in price $2.80-5, that is generously ladled into steaming bowls and topped with fresh vegetables. Plate lunches like yakitori chicken with a scoop of rice or a scoop of macaroni salad are under $5. Two people can eat until they waddle at Nori's for about $15. There's no atmosphere, but the food is authentic and good.

Mun Cheong Lau is a cheap Chinese joint in downtown Hilo at 172 Kilauea Ave., tel. (808) 935-3040 (takeout too), open daily 11 a.m.-11 p.m., closed Tuesday. If you want to eat with "the people," this is the spot. Soups on the front of the menu are $3.50; those on the back are

$2.50 and are about the same except that they don't contain noodles. The servings are generous. Entrees like crispy chicken in oyster sauce for under $5 are delicious at any price. Seafoods include abalone with veggies, abalone with black mushrooms, and shrimp with corn. A variety of pork or beef dishes are all priced under $3.50, while pineapple spareribs are $2.70 and boneless chicken with mushrooms is $3.75. These are full plates served with steamed rice, 60 cents extra if you want fried rice. For under $4 you can fill up in this place. It's clean, service is friendly, and the dining experience, while certainly not fancy, is definitely authentic.

Owned and operated by Dotty and Rey Frasco, **Dotty's Coffee Shop and Restaurant,** at the Puainako Town Center, tel. (808) 959-6477, is open for breakfast daily 7-11 a.m., for lunch Mon.-Sat. 10:30 a.m.-2 p.m., and for dinner Mon.-Thurs. 5-8 p.m., Friday 5-9 p.m. Dotty's is an institution where local people come for the large and hearty portions. Breakfast favorites are corned beef hash and eggs or French toast made with thick slices of sweet bread from Punaluu covered with real maple or coconut syrup at $3.75. Lunch includes grilled chicken supreme with mushrooms and Swiss cheese for $4.65 or Dotty's ultimate steak sandwich with slices of sirloin, sautéed mushrooms, onions, and Swiss cheese on a grilled potato roll for $5.65. Those in the know come from around the island to dine on Dotty's famous oven-roasted turkey, fresh catch of the day, barbecued pork ribs with their own smoke-flavored sauce, and an amazing combination plate for $9.85 that gives you a choice of two: top sirloin, teriyaki steak, ribs, scampi, sautéed shrimp, or the catch of the day. Fresh vegetables, real mashed potatoes, and homemade soups (great chowder on Friday) come with all full meals. For a hearty Hawaiian meal, stop in on Friday when Ray does the cooking for this special offering, all for $7.29—a lot better deal than a $60 luau feast. The decor is "American standard" with a Formica counter and leatherette booths. Check out the black-and-white photos hanging on the walls.

Ting Hao Mandarin Kitchen is a family affair run by Alice Chang and her sister, also in the Puainako Town Center, tel. (808) 959-6288, open weekdays 11 a.m.-8:30 p.m., weekends 5-8:30 p.m. Seek them out for a mouth-watering, home-cooked meal. The two most expensive items on the menu are Seafood Treasure for $6, and half a tea-smoked duck for $7; all others are under $5. Service is slow due to individual-order cooking, and those in the know pick up a handout menu and call in their orders 30 minutes before arriving. Also at Puainako Town Center is **Five Spice** with an assortment of *bento* for under $4 and quick snacks like chili and rice ($1.90) and chili dogs ($1.95).

Bear's Coffee Shop, 106 Keawe, tel. (808) 935-0708, is an upscale coffee shop renowned for its breakfast, served daily 7-11:30 a.m. It features Belgian waffles (made from malted flour) and an assortment of egg dishes for $2.95. Lunch is hearty sandwiches of turkey, pastrami, chicken fillet, tuna, or ham for under $5, along with a small but zesty selection of Mexican food as well as salads. Beverages include Italian sodas, homemade lemonade, and a large selection of coffee, cappuccino, and caffe latte from their full espresso bar. All perfect with desserts like carrot cake, Bear's brownies, cheesecake, and pies. A great place to relax, read the morning paper, and watch Hilo life go by.

Kay's Lunch Center, at 684 Kilauea Ave., tel. (808) 969-1776, open Tues.-Sun. 5 a.m.-2 p.m. and 5-9 p.m., can't be beat for a good square meal of Asian, Hawaiian, or American standards. Sandwich favorites like hamburgers, fish burgers, grilled cheese, and tuna are all under $3. Large bowls of saimin and wonton soups are under $4. Their grilled plates, like Korean barbecued beef or *kalbi* (short ribs), are cooked over an open wood fire and are delicious. Combo plates of their grilled offerings are $5.95 for one choice, $6.95 for two choices, and $7.95 for three choices, and include rice, miso soup, four kinds of kimchi, and vegetables. Kay's isn't much to look at, with leatherette booths and Formica tables, but it's a winner.

The **Ichiban Deli,** at 415 Kilauea Ave., across from the Hilo Hongwanji Temple, open Tues.-Sat. 7 a.m.-2 p.m. and 5-8:30 p.m., takeout available, is a basic Japanese-Hawaiian-American restaurant with breakfast like eggs with bacon or link sausage or corned beef hash $3.35, and lunches like fried chicken or spareribs, each at $4.25. The Japanese meals are standards like *bento* or tempura for under $5. No decor at all, but the prices are very reasonable.

Satsuki's, along the 200 block of Keawe St., receives the highest recommendation because when local people want a good meal at an inexpensive price they head here. Open for lunch 10 a.m.-2 p.m., dinner 4:30-9 p.m., closed Tuesday. Specialties are oxtail soup, the lunch special for $4.25, and the Okinawa *soba* plate lunch for only $3.95. Dinner specials ($6-8) are beef teriyaki, *tonkatsu,* and fish teriyaki. Plenty of traditional favorites like *donburi* and *nabemono.* All meals come with miso soup, Japanese pickles and condiments, rice, and tea. No decor, but spotlessly clean and friendly. Excellent food at excellent value.

Sachi's Gourmet, only a few seconds away at 250 Keawe St., open Monday 8 a.m.-2 p.m. only, Tues.-Sat. 8 a.m.-2 p.m. and dinner 5-9 p.m., Sunday dinner only 5-9 p.m., is the same type of restaurant as Satsuki's, with its own loyal local clientele. The food is excellent here, too, and the prices are unbeatable. You'll walk away stuffed on traditional Japanese food for about $8 for a full meal.

Hukilau Restaurant at the Hilo Seaside Hotel, 136 Banyan Way, is open daily 7 a.m.-1 p.m. and 4-9 p.m. For breakfast you can have steak and eggs ($6.95), fish and eggs ($2.95), two eggs and toast ($1.85), ham omelette ($2.75), or a full choice of hotcakes and waffles at reasonable prices. The lunch menu offers a choice of Reuben sandwich, steak and rice, baked chicken, or hamburger deluxe; each choice comes with a buffet salad bar at a fixed price of $5.25. The dinner menu is reasonable ($9.95-14.95) with T-bone steak, steak and lobster, oven roast prime rib, or the captain's platter—fried fish, shrimp, scallops, and oysters. All dinners come with soup of the day and salad bar. The decor is orange Naugahyde booths and brown Formica tables. Some of the vegetables come out of a can, and the deep-fried offerings have enough grease to clog the Alaska pipeline, but the view of Hilo Bay is exceptional and helps digestion.

The **New China Restaurant,** at 510 Kilauea Ave., tel. (808) 961-5677, open daily 10 a.m.-10 p.m., serves basic Chinese combo plates of chicken, duck, pork, beef, and seafood. The most expensive seafood on the menu is $7 for abalone and Chinese mushrooms. Special plates include steamed chicken with ginger, onion sauce, and steamed rice for $3.80; beef broccoli and crispy chicken for $2.80. Not much class—almost like a McDonald's of Chinese food—but it's bright, shiny, and sparkly.

When Hilo residents want plate lunchs, they go to **Hilo Lunch Shop,** at the corner of Kalanikoa and Piilani, tel. (808) 935-8273, open daily except Sunday 6:15 a.m.-1:30 p.m. At this very basic restaurant, you pick and choose each separately priced item for your plate: tempura 90 cents; mahimahi 50 cents; vegetables 45 cents; for about $3 your plate will be huge.

Down Piilani, just at the Kentucky Fried Chicken, make a right onto Hinano St. and in a minute you'll see **Don's Grill,** tel. (808) 935-9099, open daily except Monday 10:30 a.m.-9 p.m., and to 10 p.m. on Friday. This American/Hawaiian restaurant is known for good food at reasonable prices. Inside find wood-trimmed blue Formica tables in a very modern yet functionally tasteful setting. Breakfast starts with two eggs and toast ($2.50), omelettes ($4.95), and on weekends only, sweet bread French toast for $2.75. Lunch ($5-6) can be taco salad, Philadelphia cheese steak, club sandwich, or your own burger creation. Entrees are barbecued ribs, pork chops, or fillet of fish, all priced under $6. There's homemade pie, cheesecake, and pudding to top off your meal. Don's is a basic American standard restaurant where you can get a good square meal for a good price.

Shooter's, 121 Banyan Dr., tel. (808) 969-7069, open 11 a.m.-2 a.m., is a bar and restaurant where you can dance seven nights a week, but you might not want to tell your mommy that you went there! DJ music ranges from reggae to rock to rap depending upon the crowd and the night. The cavernous interior is like a giant rumpus room with cement floors, neon beer signs, a graffiti wall, and TVs at every angle. The decor is industrial chic—the bar is galvanized metal, the liquor shelves are made from pipe, and the cement supporting pillars have been painted purple and gold to add a touch of tropical color. The mainly appetizer-and-burger menu ($2.50-7) offers a basket of grilled garlic bread buffalo wings, fried calamari, Thai chicken salad, and burgers with a variety of toppings. There's a small selection of pasta, from linguine with fresh basil pesto for $6.75 to seafood marinara at $11.75. Limited main dishes ($11.50-13.75) are New York steak, fresh *ahi,* and char-broiled chicken.

Don't be put off by the atmosphere, which can seem a bit stark and hard at first glance. Shooter's is friendly, has security, and boasts that "there hasn't been one confrontation since the day we opened." That's nice!

Fast Foods and Snacks

Okay! For those who must, **McDonald's** is at 88 Kanoelehua Ave. and 177 Ululani Street. **Pizza Hut,** which actually has a decent salad bar, is at 326 Kilauea Avenue. Fast-food junkies will be totally happy at the **Puainako Town Center,** where glass and Formica cubes hold an endless supply of munchies from **McDonald's, Pizza Hut, Subway Sandwiches,** and **Taco Bell.**

The Hilo Hawaiian Hotel, a landmark on Banyan Drive, has expensive and romantic dining, but for $2-3 you can get terrific snacks and *pu pu* at the hotel's **Wai'ole Lounge** after 11 a.m., with savory items like sautéed chicken with macadamia peanut sauce, toasted garlic bread topped with mozzarella and parmesan cheeses and served with marinara sauce on the side, and the chopped steak (real steak cut into bite-size pieces). The setting is congenial, overlooking Hilo Bay with palm trees and flowers right outside the windows. For a light lunch at unbelievable prices, try the Wai'ole Lounge.

On Banyan Drive just outside of the Hilo Hawaiian Hotel, get delicious scoops of ice cream in island flavors like macadamia nut at the **Ice Cream Factory.** Nearby is the **Banyan Snack Shop,** which dispenses whopping plate lunches like the loco moco—two scoops of rice and a hamburger covered in fried egg and gravy—for only $2.75. The breakfast specials here are very cheap too.

Two other places for a refreshing scoop of dessert are the **Hilo Homemade Ice Cream** at Hilo Tropical Gardens and **Tropical Dreams Ice Cream** at the refurbished Kress Building downtown.

Hilo Seeds and Snacks next to Lehua's Restaurant at 15 Waianuenue Ave. sells sandwiches and authentic crackseed. The **Kilauea Preserve Center,** at the corner of Kilauea and Ponahawai Streets, also sells authentic crackseed.

Lanky's Pastries and Deli, Hilo Shopping Center, tel. (808) 935-6381, open 6:30 a.m.-9 p.m., deli side from 6 a.m., is a perfect place to head if you have a sweet tooth that *must* be satisfied. The deli/bakery is especially known for its "long johns,"—long, thin sugar donuts filled with custard—but they also have all kinds of baked goods from bread to apple turnovers. Their deli case holds sandwiches priced under $3, along with an assortment of *bento,* perfect for a picnic lunch.

Cathy's Lunch Shop, at 270 Kamehameha Ave., is a tiny place with two tables, where only a few dollars will get you breakfast, a plate lunch, a hamburger, or even a taco.

Island Grinds serves plate lunches, burgers, a salad bar, and vegetarian entrees from its lunch wagon at the bayfront beach Mon.-Fri., 10 a.m.-2 p.m.

Moderately Priced

Restaurant Miwa, at Hilo Shopping Center, 1261 Kilauea Ave., tel. (808) 961-4454, is open daily 10 a.m.-9 p.m., sometimes until 10 p.m. for meals and until 2 a.m. at the bar. Very beautifully appointed, Miwa is a surprise, especially since it's stuck back in the corner of the shopping center. Enter to find traditional shoji screens and wooden tables adorned with fine linens, along with a classic sushi bar. The waitresses wear kimonos, though most are local women and not necessarily Japanese. The menu is excellent, with appetizers like sake-flavored steamed clams for $4.95 and crab *sunomono* (seaweed, cucumber slices, and crab meat) for $4.25. A specialty is *nabemono,* a hearty and zesty soup/stew prepared at your table with a two-order minimum. Traditional favorites popular with Westerners include beef sukiyaki and *shabu shabu* (each $14), and there's also a variety of combination dinners that give you a wider sampling of the menu at good value. Restaurant Miwa is an excellent choice for a gourmet meal at a reasonable price in a congenial setting.

Very clean and down-home proud, the **Royal Siam Thai Restaurant,** at 68 Mamo St., tel. (808) 961-6100, serves up tasty Thai treats Mon.-Sat. 11 a.m.-2:30 p.m. and 5-9 p.m. Appetizers include a crispy Thai noodle dish for $4.95 or fish patty for $5.95. Two of the several soups are coconut chicken soup for $4.95 and a seafood soup for $7.95. Entrees range from an inexpensive water chestnut fried rice dish for $4.95 through curries and meat dishes to a reasonable red snapper for $16.95.

Modern and chic with a checkerboard floor, gray-on-black tables and chairs, ceiling fans, and the calming effect of ferns and flowers, **Cafe Pesto,** at 308 Kamehameha Ave., tel. (808) 969-6640, is open Sun.-Thurs. 11 a.m.-9 p.m., Fri.-Sat. 11 a.m.-10 p.m. One of Hilo's established restaurants, it offers affordable gourmet food in an unpretentious and comfortable setting. The pizza from their ohia wood-fired oven can be anything from *quatro formaggio* (four cheeses) for $5.95 to Southwestern pizza with fresh cilantro, pesto, *chipolte,* barbecued chicken, and red onions for $9.95 small and $15.95 large. Another pizza that lets you know that you are in Hawaii is Pizza Luau, which is topped with *kalua* pork, local sweet onions, and fresh Hawaiian pineapple for $8.95 and $14.95. (Plenty of calzone choices, too, at $12.95.) Combined with dinner salads of "wild greens" at $3.50, the pizza or a calzone makes a great meal for two. Delectable yet inexpensive ($3-4) items are focaccia with rosemary and Gorgonzola, *crostini* (fresh bread with a creamy, fresh herb garlic butter), and soup of the day, or try the seared *poki,* sesame marinated with green onion, ginger, and tamarind honey vinaigrette on a bed of spinach with fresh baked bread at $8.95. Heartier appetites will be satisfied with chicken Lallo Rosa, a breast of chicken, greens, Maui onions, cherry tomatoes, and coriander dressing, *ceviche* pasta salad, smoked salmon with fettuccine, wild chicken and mushroom risotto, Island Seafood risotto with fresh fish, prawns, lobster, and corn served in a sweet chili risotto, and New York steak with wild mushrooms, grilled onions, and wasabi mashed potatoes (all $7.95-19.95). Cafe Pesto also has a brass-railed espresso bar where you can order caffe latte or iced cappuccino to top off your meal in one of the best "budget gourmet" restaurants on the Big Island.

Fiasco's, a good restaurant and nightspot, is at the Waiakea Shopping Center, 200 Kanoelehua St., tel. (808) 935-7666, open Sun.-Thurs. 11 a.m.-10 p.m., weekends to 11 p.m., with dancing 9 p.m. until closing on weekends (see **Entertainment**). Featuring a country inn flavor, Fiasco's has a cobblestoned entrance that leads you to the cozy, post-and-beam dining room appointed with stout wooden tables and captain's chairs, with semiprivate booths lining the walls. The mahogany bar, a classic with polished lion's-head brass rails, offers comfortable stools and black leather booths. The menu begins with appetizers ($3-7) like fried mozzarella, escargot, or a big plate of onion rings. Lighter appetites might enjoy the salad bar buffet ($6.50) or a taco salad with beef or chicken ($6.25). Sandwiches ($5-7) range from the croissant club to French dip to a classic burger. Entrees include Mexican fare like tacos for $6.25 and American standards like rib eye steak or prime rib for $14.95. Families can save money with a special children's menu.

Uncle Billy's at the Hilo Bay Hotel along Banyan Dr., tel. (808) 935-0861, is open for breakfast 7-8:30 a.m., dinner 5:30-8:30 p.m. Enjoy the free nightly hula show 6-7:30 p.m. The interior of the banquet hall-style restaurant is neo-Polynesian, and hanging from the open beam ceiling are thatched umbrella-type chandeliers and mobiles with cascading white shells. Chairs are comfortable bent bamboo and every table is brightened by an orchid. Breakfast ($3-5.50) can be the *wiki wiki*, which is a scrambled eggs, rice, and ham for a very reasonable $2.99, a chef's omelette, or Hawaiian French toast with sausage. Dinner can be fresh catch, charbroiled or sautéed, that includes a salad, vegetable of the day, and rice pilaf, at market price or golden fried shrimp dinner, shellfish sauté, lemon macadamia nut chicken, or broiled hibachi chicken and New York steak (all $11-16). Treat yourself by coming to Uncle Billy's Bar, open daily from 5:30 p.m., and order an exotic drink while you peer through the louvered windows into the central garden bursting with the magical colors of tropical plants and flowers.

Ken's House of Pancakes is one of a chain but you can have a good meal for a good price. Open 24 hours every day of the year, it's conveniently located on the way to the airport at 1730 Kamehameha Ave., tel. (808) 935-8711.

Nihon Culture Center, 123 Lihiwai St., tel. (808) 969-1133 (reservations required), presents authentic Japanese meals, an excellent sushi bar, and combination dinners along with cultural and artistic displays. Open daily for breakfast, lunch, and dinner until 9 p.m., sushi bar until 10 p.m.

Reuben's Mexican Restaurant, 336 Kamehameha Ave., tel. (808) 961-2552, open Mon.-Fri. 11 a.m.-9 p.m., Saturday 12-9 p.m., will en-

liven your palate with its zesty dishes. The interior has a Mexican flair and the menu is reasonable ($7-8), with selections like *carne asada,* steak tacos, chicken or beef tostadas, and vegetarian bean chili verde burrito. All are served with beans and rice. The bar has a large selection of *cerveza,* including Pacifico, Negra Modelo, and Carta Blanca for $3, and most domestics for $2. But Reuben's is most famous for their margaritas—more than one will get you acting like a human *chimichanga.* ¡Olé!

Expensive Restaurants
Queen's Court Restaurant at the Hilo Hawaiian Hotel on Banyan Dr., tel. (808) 935-9361, offers a nightly buffet that is *the* best in Hilo. Connoisseurs usually don't consider buffets to be gourmet quality, but the Queen's Court proves them wrong. Throughout the week, buffets ($19.95-22.50) include: Monday and Thursday, prime rib and crab buffet; Friday and Saturday, the legendary seafood buffet; Sunday, Hawaiian and seafood buffet. All are extraordinary and would give the finest restaurants anywhere a run for their money. The dining room is grand, with large archways and windows overlooking Hilo Bay. On buffet nights, a massive table is laden with fresh island vegetables and 15 different salads. For example, on seafood night, you choose from oysters, shrimp, crab, sushi, and sashimi. Then the chefs take over. Resplendent in white uniforms and chef's hats, they stand ready to sauté or broil your choice of fish, which always includes best selections like swordfish or *ono.* Beverages include white, rosé, and rich red wines, plus fresh-squeezed guava and orange juice. The dessert table entices you with fresh fruits and imported cheeses, and dares you to save room for cream pies, fresh-baked cookies, and éclairs. Sunday champagne brunch is more of the same quality at $19.95. A breakfast buffet is served daily 6:30 a.m.-9:30 a.m., with the continental breakfast buffet priced at $5.95, hot entrees for $6.95, and both (don't explode) for $8.25. You can also order from the menu items like two eggs any style with toast for $3.75; a short stack of griddle cakes for $3.75; an "Omelette by the Bay" with mushrooms, shrimp and mozzarella cheese for $7.50; or a local scramble with Portuguese sausage or green onions for $6.75. Lunch is reasonable

($4-7), with yakitori chicken sauté, saimin supreme, salads and sandwiches. Pricier entrees range from a stuffed crab salad sandwich for $9 to a New York steak for $14. For dinner, if you don't choose the buffet, try vegetarian linguine for $6, filet mignon for $16.50, seafood brochette for $16, or fresh catch, broiled, blackened or sautéed at market price. Make reservations, especially on seafood night, because the Hilo Hawaiian attracts many Hilo residents who love great food.

Sicilian fishermen would feel right at home at **Pescatore Ristorante,** 235 Keawe St., tel. (808) 969-9090, open daily for lunch 11 a.m.-2 p.m., dinner 5:30-9 p.m., and until 10 p.m. Friday and Saturday. The building housing Pescatore is part of the Main Street U.S.A. Project evident in downtown Hilo. The building has had multiple uses over the years, and as part of its colorful past, served as a house of ill repute. Completely redone, it has been transformed into a bright, cheery room with high-backed, red velvet armchairs and formally set tables with green linen tablecloths. Italian-style chandeliers, lace curtains, exposed beams, and koa trim add to the elegance. You can also request a "Portofino Room," a separate area for romance and privacy. Lunch fare begins with antipasto of marinated fish with olive oil, garlic, and vinegar, or of fresh clams, when available. Primo piati can be pollo marsala $8.95, or fresh steamed garden vegetables, plain or with extra virgin olive oil, served with marinara sauce and Romano cheese for $8.95. If your taste turns to pasta, go for the primavera with fresh vegetables in tomato sauce for a very reasonable $7.95. Or try the putanesca, a famous dish cooked by the Italian ladies of the evening for their clientele; it's made from garlic, anchovies, sun-dried tomatoes, black olives, capers, and olive oil and costs $7.95. For dinner, start with their special minestrone for $3.50, or with the ensalata of sliced tomatoes, mozzarella, and spinach with Italian vinaigrette dressing for $4.95. For a dinner antipasto try the hearts of artichokes sautéed with fresh basil, garlic, and tomatoes and sprinkled with Parmesan cheese for $5.95. Dinner entrees can be cioppino classico alla pescatore, swimming with morsels of lobster, mussels, clams, shrimp, fish, and scallops served with garlic bread for $24.95; gamberetti Alfredo, large shrimp sautéed in butter, garlic, fresh basil, and Parmesan cheese in a white-wine sauce; or vongole, steamed clams and choice of red or white clam sauce for $17.95. Also, a dinner special includes soup or salad, one dinner entree from the menu, coffee or tea, and dessert for $19.95. Pescatore's offers good food for reasonable prices.

Lehua's Bar and Restaurant, at 11 Waianuenue Ave., tel. (808) 935-8055, open for lunch 11 a.m.-4 p.m., dinner 5-9 p.m., is another upscale restaurant in a restored building. The mood is set with track lighting, Casablanca fans, and an excellent sound system. The decor is gray-on-gray with cane chairs and art deco silverware; the walls hold works of local artists. Owners Mark and Larry, transplanted from Oahu where they spent years in the nightclub business, have joined to create a restaurant inspired by island-style cuisine. Lunch offerings ($4-10) feature Lehua's homemade soup, Caesar salad (plain or with with chicken or shrimp), Lehua's chicken clubhouse sandwich, and a full salad bar for $7.95 (children under 10 pay $3.95). Lunch also brings pasta like linguine, fettuccine, or penne pasta smothered with a fresh tomato, basil, and garlic cream sauce for $7.50, or with charbroiled chicken and cilantro-pesto sauce for $8.95. Lighter appetites will enjoy yakitori sticks for $1.95; Lehua's quesadilla with cilantro pesto, cheese, and salsa fresca for $4.25; or juicy paniolo ribs for $5.95. Evening brings the dinner menu ($10.95-17.95), with selections like Thai coconut shrimp with sweet chili basil sauce, sautéed garlic shrimp with grilled sourdough bread, catch of the day, mixed grill (prawns, chicken, and teriyaki steak), and country pork spareribs. The dinner menu also includes a medley of stir-fried vegetables over white or brown rice with teriyaki or oyster sauce or a New York or rib eye steak charbroiled to order. Friday and Saturday nights bring live entertainment, mostly rock and blues. Lehua's is upbeat, with delicious food, and fun thrown in for free.

Sandalwood Room is the main restaurant of the Hawaii Naniloa Hotel on Banyan Dr., tel. (808) 935-0831. Here, in an elegant room overlooking the bay and lined with aromatic sandalwood, you can feast on dishes from around the world. Zesty curries, rich French sauces, chops done in wine, and Polynesian-inspired dishes are offered on this full and expensive menu.

KK Tei Restaurant, 1550 Kamehameha Ave., tel. (808) 961-3791, is a favored restaurant of many local people. The centerpiece is a bonsai garden complete with pagodas and arched moon bridges. Cook your own beef, chicken, or fish at your tableside hibachi and dip it into an array of savory sauces—or the chefs will prepare your selection from their full menu of Japanese dishes. Entrees cost about $10 in this unique Asian setting. Those in the know accord this restaurant gourmet status. The place is packed for the $1 draft beers and free *pu pu* 5 p.m.-8 p.m.

Harrington's, at 135 Kalanianaole St., tel. (808) 961-4966, is open nightly for dinner 5:30-10 p.m., Sunday 5:30-9 p.m.; lounge open 5:30-closing. The setting couldn't be more brilliant, as the restaurant overlooks the bay. A sunset cocktail or dinner is even more romantic with the melodic strains of live jazz, contemporary, or Hawaiian music playing softly in the background. The continental cuisine features appetizers ($3.50-7.50) like shrimp cocktail, seafood chowder, mushroom tempura, escargot in casserole, and a variety of salads. Special vegetarian dishes like eggplant parmigiana are $12.50, while seafood selections ($15.95-19.95) include prawns scampi, scallops chardonnay, and calamari meunière. Meat and fowl dishes (same price range) are tempting: Slavic steak, prime rib au jus, and chicken marsala.

ENTERTAINMENT

Hilo doesn't have a lot of nightlife, but it's not a morgue either. You can dance, disco, or listen to quiet piano music at a few lounges and hotels around town.

In a classic plantation building behind the old police station, on Kalakaua between Keawe and Kinoole Streets, is the East Hawaii Culture Center, a nonprofit organization that supports local art and culture by showcasing the works of different artists monthly on a revolving basis in the large entrance hall of the old police station and an annex building. They also host Shakespeare in the Park, a local repertory of performers who stage, direct, design, and enact Shakespearean plays under the large banyan in Kalakaua Park during the month of July. If you're in Hilo at this time, it shouldn't be missed.

The Big Island Arts Guild and the Dance Council also meet here. The bulletin board is always filled with announcements of happenings in the local art scene.

Lehua's Bar and Restaurant, 11 Waianuenue Ave., offers a mixed bag of jazz, Hawaiian, or contemporary music on weekends. Occasionally there is a comedy night. Upbeat vibes with good food as well.

Hilo has its own little sleaze bar, The Green Onion, at 885 Kilauea Ave., where exotic dancers can *sometimes* be coaxed on stage if the clientele takes up a collection and offers them a minimum amount of money. Sound good to you? Things *can't* be that bad!

Fiasco's at the Waiakea Shopping Mall, 200 Kanoelehua Ave., tel. (808) 935-7666, swings with a full venue of live music on weekends. Doors open at 9 p.m., with a cover and relaxed dress code.

If you're looking for a night out, you can't beat the Wai'oli Lounge at the Hilo Hawaiian Hotel, where there is live music every night ranging from contemporary Hawaiian to rock. Uncle Billy's Restaurant at the Hilo Bay Hotel has a free hula show nightly 6-7:30 p.m. Harrington's, one of Hilo's most romantic night spots, offers live jazz, contemporary, or Hawaiian music nightly. Perfect for dinner or just for relaxing.

Others

To catch a flick, try the Waiakea Theaters, at Waiakea Mall on Kanoelehua Ave., tel. (808) 935-9747; the Prince Kuhio Theaters, at the Prince Kuhio Plaza, tel. (808) 959-4595; or the newer Kress Cinemas downtown, tel. (808) 961-3456. You'll enjoy great listening on KIPA Rainbow Radio (AM 620). This station plays an excellent selection of contemporary music with few commercial interruptions. It sounds the way FM used to. K-BIG FM 106 is worth listening to, and the Wave at 97.1 FM sends out easy listening jazz and Hawaiian music.

SHOPPING

Shopping Malls

Hilo has the best general-purpose shopping on the island. Stock up on film and food before you do any touring or camping. Prince Kuhio Plaza, at 111 E. Puainako, open weekdays 9:30 a.m.-9 p.m., Saturday to 5:30 p.m., Sunday 10 a.m.-5 p.m., is the island's largest shopping mall. Restaurants, jewelry shops, shoe stores, supermarkets, and large department stores like Sears and Liberty House make it a one-stop shopper's paradise. Here too you'll find Longs Drugs for film and Waldenbooks for an extensive selection of reading material. An older but still full-service shopping center is **Kaiko'o Mall** at 777 Kilauea Avenue. **Hilo Shopping Center** is about one-half mile south on Kilauea Ave. at the corner of Kekuanaoa Street. This smaller mall has only a handful of local shops, but it does have some excellent inexpensive restaurants and a fine pastry shop. **Puainako Town Center** is located at 2100 Kanoelehua Ave. (Rt. 11 south toward Volcanoes), with lots of shops, Sack 'n' Save Market, and plenty of fast foods. Nearby are Wal-Mart, Denny's Restaurant, and a Barnes and Noble bookstore. **Waiakea Shopping Plaza,** handy to the airport at 100 Kanoelehua Ave., has a small clutch of stores.

Hilo's real treasures are its commercial flower gardens. The proprietors of these gardens are experts at preparing and shipping vibrant and colorful floral arrangements. Prices are reasonable and no other gift says Hawaii like a magnificent bouquet of exotic flowers.

Food Markets

For groceries and supplies try: **KTA Super Store,** 321 Kiawe Ave. or in the Puainako Town Center; **Safeway,** 111 E. Puainako; **Sack 'n' Save** at Puainako Town Center; or **Sure Save Supermarket** in Kaiko'o Mall. For a real treat visit the early morning **Suisan Fish Auction** at 85 Lihiwai St., one of only a few open-air fish auctions in the state. Their retail fresh-fish market is next door.

The **Macadamia Nut Factory Outlet** in front of Uncle Billy's Hotel on Banyan Dr., open daily 8 a.m.-9 p.m., is stocked with liquor, beer, pantry and deli items, and curios and gifts.

Health Food and Fruit Stores

Abundant Life Natural Foods, owned and operated by Leslie Miki since 1977, is in downtown Hilo at 292 Kamehameha Ave., open daily 8:30 a.m.-6 p.m., Saturday until 5 p.m., and Sunday 11 a.m.-3 p.m., tel. (808) 935-7411. The store's kitchen puts out daily specials of soup, salads,

sandwiches, and *bento,* all for well under $5, while the shelves are stocked with an excellent selection of fresh fruits and veggies, bulk foods, cosmetics, vitamins, and herbs. The bookshelves cosmically vibrate with a selection of tomes on metaphysics and new-age literature.

On Wednesday and Saturday morning, check out the **farmers' market** along Kamehameha Avenue fronting the bay in the center of the downtown area. Great for bargains and local color.

Bookstores

Hilo has excellent bookstores. **Basically Books,** downtown at 46 Waianuenue St., tel. (808) 961-0144, (800) 903-6277, has a good selection of Hawaiiana, out-of-print books, and an unbeatable selection of maps. You can get anywhere you want to go with their nautical charts, road maps, and topographical maps. The selection includes sectionals for serious hikers and trekkers. Their collection covers most of the Pacific. They also feature a very good selection of travel books, and flags from countries throughout the world. Owner and proprietress Christine Reed can help you with any of your literary needs.

The **Book Gallery** at Prince Kuhio Plaza, 111 E. Puainako, tel. (808) 959-7744, is a full-selection bookstore featuring Hawaiiana, hardcovers, and paperbacks.

Waldenbooks, also at Prince Kuhio Plaza, tel. (808) 959-6468, open daily 9 a.m.-9 p.m., is the largest and best-stocked bookstore in the Hilo area.

Barnes and Noble, at the Puainako Town Center, has a fine selection of material for the discriminating reader.

Gifts and Crafts

If you're looking for that special island memento or souvenirs to bring home to family and friends, Uncle Billy covers all the bases and along with everything else offers the **Polynesian Market Place,** adjacent to the Hilo Bay Hotel on Banyon Drive. Open daily 8 a.m.-8 p.m., the marketplace sells a lot of good junk, liquor, and resortwear. The **Hilo Hattie** store at Prince Kuhio Plaza, 111 E. Puainako, has all you need in island clothing, tourist style. **Hawaiian Handcrafts** at 760 Kilauea Ave., tel. (808) 935-5587, specializes in woodcarvings. Here, Dan DeLuz uses exotic woods to turn out bowls, boxes, and vases; he also sells shells from around the Pacific.

Sugawara Lauhala and Gift Shop at 59 Kalakaua St. is a virtually unknown Hilo institution operated by the Sugawara sisters, who have been in business for most of their 70-plus years. They make genuine *lau hala* weavings right on the premises of their character-laden shop. Their best hats sell for $75 and up, and they also have baskets from $15. If you are after the genuine article, made to last a lifetime, you'll find it here. One by one, the old-timers—the best weavers—are dying or losing their eyesight, so these unique woven products are becoming more and more scarce and will undoubtedly increase in value as time goes by.

Just down from Sugawara's at 38 Kalakala St., tel. (808) 935-4555, is **Hanahou.** Open Mon.-Sat. 10 a.m.-5 p.m., this wonderful little shop sells mostly vintage island treasures like *lau hala* weavings, baskets, pillows, hats, and sandals. Most of the items are made on the Big Island but some are imported from Niue, east of Tonga.

Old Town Printer and Stationers, at 201 Kinoole St., open weekdays 8 a.m.-5 p.m., has been in business for 35 years selling stationery, office supplies, postcards, notecards, and a terrific selection of calendars.

At 35 Waianuenue Ave. is the classy little shop called **Etsko's,** tel. (808) 961-3778. It's Ginza and Paris in Hilo. This eclectic little shop sells all sorts of arts and craft items, gifts, furniture, jewelry, and a small selection of silk and natural fiber clothing. Perhaps a hand-painted silk tie for him or a Japanese *tansu* chest for her is just the piece you're looking for. After you've shopped yourself into oblivion, head for the espresso bar at the back of the shop to rejuvenate yourself on coffee, Italian soda, or a wide variety of baked goods. Open Mon.-Fri. 9 a.m.-6 p.m. and until 4 p.m. on Saturday; closed Sunday.

Sig Zane Design, at 122 Kamehameha Ave., tel. (808) 935-7077, open Mon.-Sat. 9 a.m.-5 p.m., is one of the most unique and distinctive shops on the island. Here, owner and designer Sig Zane creates distinctive island wearables in 100% cotton. All designs are not only Hawaiian/tropical but also chronicle useful and medicinal Hawaiian plants and flowers. Sig's wife, Nalani, who helps in the shop, is a *kumu hula* who learned the intricate dance steps from her mother, Edith Kanakaole, a legendary dancer who has been memorialized with a local tennis stadium that bears her name. You can get shirts for $59, dresses for around $75, and pareus for $30, as well as affordable house slippers, sweatshirts, T-shirts, *hapi* coats, and even futon covers. The shelves also hold *lau hala* hats, handbound koa notebooks, and basketry made from natural fibers. Outfit yourself from head to toe at Sig's shop and be totally in style and comfort.

Dragon Mama, a lovely boutique at 266 Kamehameha Ave., features natural-fiber futons, fine bedding, wool, cotton fabrics, custom covers, meditation pillows, and Japanese rice paper.

Dreams of Paradise, at 308 Kamehameha Ave. (the restored S. Hata Building, erected in 1912), tel. (808) 935-5670 or (800) 935-5670, open Mon.-Sat. 10 a.m.-9 p.m., Sunday noon-7 p.m., shipping available, is a combination boutique and gallery owned and operated by Susan Starr, who is herself a talented artist capturing the heart of Hawaii's *aina* in oils, pastels, and textiles. Some artists showcased in Dreams of Paradise are: Andrew Plack, a nature artist specializing in the flora and fauna of Hawaii; Gerard Beauvalet, a multitalented artist producing fine koa furniture as well as distinctive acrylic paintings—mostly depicting Polynesian women in natural poses of meditation and serenity—that are also reproduced as distinctive T-shirt designs; Beverly Jackson, who catches the sun in her stained glass renditions of breadfruit, lotus blossoms, and various Hawaiian flowers; and Terry Taube, a sculptor producing lava sculptures and renditions of animal life, especially *honu,* the green sea turtle. Shelves also hold gourmet food items, incidental bags, distinctive cooking aprons, and plenty of inexpensive but tasteful souvenirs.

The **Rift Zone,** at 106 #1 Kamehameha Ave., tel. (808) 969-9976, is open Tues.-Sat. 9 a.m.-6 p.m. Owned and operated by the husband-and-wife team of Robert and Cathy Joiner (he the potter, she the glazier), this gallery features about 50 artists, predominantly from the Big Island. Works include paintings by Avi Kriaty, fantastic fiber-sculptured baskets by Mika McCann, gorgeous hand-painted silks by Kalalani, outrageous photographs of volcanoes and lava by Brad Lewis, a multitude of furniture made from island woods, and of course, pottery by the owners. If you care to have a look at the Rift Zone pottery studio, they are located at 13-3522 Kaupilai St. in Pahoa, tel. (808) 965-9509.

Watch as your T-shirt is screen-printed at **Hawaiian Arts,** 284 Kamehameha Ave., tel. (808) 935-1860, a functioning T-shirt factory. Most shirts are $12.99, and hanging on the wall is *the* biggest T-shirt in all of Hawaii.

Caravan Town at 194 Kamehameha Ave. is open daily except Sunday 8 a.m.-4:30 p.m., Friday until 5:30 p.m., and Saturday until 4 p.m. It is one of the most interesting junk stores in Hilo. The shelves hold an internationally eclectic mix of merchandise that includes pendulum clocks, plaster Greek goddesses, luggage, and paper lanterns. Also, the shop specializes in over-the-counter Chinese herbs and medicines purportedly effective for everything from constipation to impotence.

Big Island Estate Jewelry, at 300 Kamehameha Ave., open Mon.-Fri. 9 a.m.-6 p.m., Saturday 9 a.m.-4 p.m., is much more than its name implies, functioning as a pawn shop and discovery shop. Inside are antiques, collectibles, knickknacks, vases, musical instruments, and a good selection of used camera gear.

The Kipuka Smoke Shop, at 308 Kamehameha Ave., Suite 102, tel. (808) 961-5082, open Mon.-Thurs. 9 a.m.-6 p.m., Friday 9 a.m.-8 p.m., Saturday 9 a.m.-4 p.m., is a tiny, aromatic closet of a shop selling cigars, cigarettes, pipe tobacco, rolling papers, lighters, and even walking sticks.

The 100 block of Keawe Ave., between Shipman and Kalakaua Streets, is Hilo's **yuppie row.** Here are **The Most Irresistible Shop in Hilo,** with Ciao backpacks and bags; and **The Fire Place Store,** featuring coffeepots, Mexican *piñatas,* children's toys, greeting cards, pareus, T-shirts, and a good selection of cosmetics.

The other side of yuppie row is down-home Hilo. One downtown shop along Keawe Street is **Kodani's Florist,** for fresh-cut flowers and lei. Gift shops, antique stores, and used-book emporiums fill this area.

Hawaii Sales and Surplus, featuring raincoats, hats, military supplies, knives, backpacks, rubber rafts, and plenty of old and new military uniforms, can be found on Mamo Street. Also along this street at #64 is **Pacific Isle Pawn.** Open Mon.-Fri. 9:30 a.m.-5 p.m., Saturday 9:30 a.m.-2 p.m., this is one of those places where you might come across a treasure, especially old gold jewelry. **Northern Lights Antiques,** not far away on Ponahawai Street, is another treasure chest overflowing with antiques, curios, lamps, beads, and Asian heirlooms.

The **Modern Camera Center,** at 165 Kiawe St., tel. (808) 935-3279, is one of the few full-service camera shops in Hilo.

SERVICES AND INFORMATION

Emergencies and Health

When in need call: police, tel. (808) 935-3311, or Hilo Hospital at 1190 Waianuenue St., tel. (808) 974-4700.

Keiko Gibo has an office at 321 Kinoole St., where she practices the ancient healing arts of acupuncture and shiatsu and various therapeutic massages.

Also for massage, *lomi lomi,* and herbal and nutritional products, contact the Academy of Therapeutic Massage, tel. (808) 935-1405, at 180 Kinoole St.; it offers classes too.

The Hilo Pharmacy, tel. (808) 961-9267, in the 300 block of Kamehameha Ave., open Mon.-Fri. 8:30 a.m.-5:30 p.m., Saturday 8:30 a.m.-12:30 p.m., is a full-service pharmacy.

Information

Two good sources of maps and helpful brochures are Hawaii Visitors Bureau, at the corner of Keawe and Haili Streets, tel. (808) 961-5797, open Mon.-Fri. 8 a.m.-noon and 1-4:30 p.m.; and the Chamber of Commerce, 202 Kamehameha Ave., tel. (808) 935-7178. Also try the Hilo Public Library, 300 Waianuenue St., tel. (808) 933-4650; or the University of Hawaii at Hilo information, tel. (808) 974-7516.

Banks and Post Office

For your money needs try the following: City Bank at Kaiko'o Mall, tel. (808) 935-6844; Central Pacific, 525 Kilauea Ave., tel. (808) 935-5251; Bank of Hawaii, 120 Pauahi, tel. (808) 935-0084; or First Hawaiian Bank, 1205 Kilauea Ave., tel. (808) 969-2211.

The central post office, open weekdays 9 a.m.-4:30 p.m., Saturday 9 a.m.-12:30 p.m., is an efficiently run, modern post office, clearly marked on the access road to the airport. It is extremely convenient for mailings prior to departure.

HAWAII STATE ARCHIVES

THE SADDLE ROAD

Slicing west across the Hilo District with a northward list is Rt. 200, the Saddle Road. Everyone with a sense of adventure loves this bold cut across the Big Island along a high valley separating the two great mountains, Mauna Loa and Mauna Kea. Along it you pass explorable caves, a *nene* sanctuary, camping areas, and spur roads leading to the tops of Mauna Kea and Mauna Loa. Besides, it's a great adventure for anyone traveling between Hilo and Kona. Keep your eyes peeled for convoys of tanks and armored personnel carriers as they sometimes sally forth from Pohakuloa Military Camp.

Road Conditions
The car-rental companies cringe when you men-

tion the Saddle Road. Some even intimidate you by saying that their insurance won't cover you on this road. They're terrified you'll rattle their cars to death. For the most part these fears are groundless. For a few miles the Saddle Road is corrugated because of heavy use by the military but, by and large, it's a good road, no worse than many others around the island. However, it *is* isolated, and there are no facilities along the way. If you bypass it, you'll miss some of the best scenery on the Big Island. From Hilo, follow Waianuenue Avenue west past Rainbow Falls. Saddle Road (Rt. 200) splits left within a mile or two and is clearly marked. If you follow it across the island, you'll intersect Rt. 190 on which you can turn north to Waimea or south to Kona.

MAUNA KEA

The lava along both sides of the road is old as you approach Mauna Kea (White Mountain). The lowlands are covered with grass, ferns, small trees, and mossy rocks. Twenty-seven miles out of Hilo, a clearly marked road to your right leads to the summit of 13,796-foot Mauna

Kea. A sign warns you that this road is rough, unpaved, and narrow, with no water, food, fuel, restrooms, or shelters. Moreover, you can expect winds, rain, fog, hail, snow, and altitude sickness. Intrigued? Proceed: It's not as bad as it sounds. A 4WD vehicle is highly advised, and if there's snow, the road is impossible to drive without one. A normal rental car isn't powerful enough, mainly because you're gaining more than 8,000 feet of elevation in 15 miles, which plays havoc with carburetors. But the real problem is coming down. For a small car with not very good gearing you're going to be riding your brakes for 15 miles. If they fail, you'll stand a very good chance of becoming a resident spirit of the mountain!

Four miles up you pass **Hale Pohaku** (House of Stone), which looks like a ski resort; many of the scientists from the observatory atop the mountain live here. A sign says that you need a permit from the Department of Land and Natural Resources (in Hilo) and a 4WD vehicle to proceed. Actually, the road is graded, banked, and well maintained, with the upper four miles paved so that dust is kept to a minimum to protect the sensitive "eyes" of the telescopes. As you climb, you pass through the clouds to a barren world devoid of vegetation. The earth is a red, rolling series of volcanic cones. You get an incredible vista of Mauna Loa peeking through the clouds and what seems like the entire island lying at your feet. In the distance the lights of Maui flicker. **Lake Waiau,** which unbelievably translates as "Swim Water," is almost at the top at 13,020 feet, making it the third-highest lake in the U.S. For some reason, ladybugs love this area.

If the vistas aren't enough, bring a kite along and watch it soar in the winds of the earth's upper atmosphere. Off to your right is Pu'u Kahinahina, a small hill whose name means "hill of the silversword." It's one of the only places on the Big Island where you'll see this very rare plant. The mountaintop was at one time federal land, and funds were made available to eradicate feral goats, one of the worst destroyers of the silversword and many other native Hawaiian plants.

Mauna Kea is the only spot in the tropical Pacific that was glaciated. The entire summit of the mountain was covered in 500 feet of ice. Toward the summit, you may notice piles of rock—these are terminal moraines of these ancient glaciers. The snows atop Mauna Kea are unpredictable. Some years it is merely a dusting, while in other years, such as 1982, there was enough snow to ski from late November to late July. The ski run comes all the way down from the summit, giving you about a four-mile trail. For skiing guides, see **Skiing.**

Here and there around the summit are small caves, remnants of ancient quarries where Hawaiians came to dig a special kind of fired rock that is the hardest in all Hawaii. They hauled roughed-out tools down to the lowlands, where they refined them into excellent implements that became coveted trade items.

A natural phenomenon is the strange thermal properties manifested by the cinder cones that dot the top of the mountain. Only 10 feet or so under

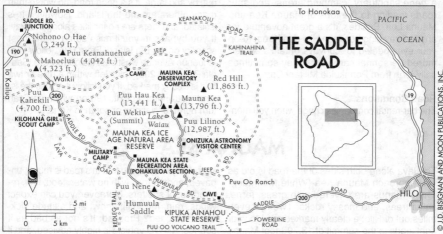

their surface is permafrost that dates back 10,000 years to the Pleistocene Epoch. If you drill into the cones for 10-20 feet and put a pipe in, during daylight hours air will be sucked into the pipe. At night, warm air comes out of the pipe with sufficient force to keep a hat levitating.

The Hawaiians were the finest adze makers in Polynesia. One of the best stone quarries was atop Mauna Kea.

Evening brings an incredibly clean and cool breeze that flows down the mountain. The Hawaiians called it the Keihau Wind, whose source, according to ancient legend, is the burning heart of the mountain. To the Hawaiians, this inspiring heavenly summit was the home of Poliahu, The Goddess of Snow and Ice, who vied with the fiery Pele across the way on Mauna Loa for the love of a man. He could throw himself into the never-ending embrace of a mythical ice queen or of a red-hot mama. Tough choice, poor fellow!

MAUNA KEA OBSERVATORY COMPLEX

Atop the mountain is a mushroom grove of astronomical observatories, as incongruously striking as a futuristic earth colony on a remote planet of a distant galaxy. The crystal-clear air and lack of dust and light pollution make the Mauna Kea Observatory site *the* best in the world. At close to 14,000 feet, it is above 40% of the earth's atmosphere and 98% of its water vapor. Although temperatures generally hover around freezing, there's only 9-11 inches of precipitation annually, mostly in the form of snow. The astronomers have come to expect an average of 325 crystal-clear nights per year, perfect for observation. The state of Hawaii leases the tops of the cinder cones, upon which various institutions from all over the world construct telescopes. These institutions in turn give the University of Hawaii up to 15% of their viewing time. The uni-

versity sells the excess viewing time for $5,000-10,000 a night, which supports the entire astronomy program and makes a little money on the side. Those who work up here must come down every four days because the thin air seems to make them forgetful and susceptible to making minor calculation errors.

Scientists from around the world book months in advance for a squint through one of these phenomenal telescopes. Teams from Great Britain, The Netherlands, Canada, France, and Japan as well as from the U.S. maintain permanent outposts here.

The first telescope that you see on your left is the U.K.'s **James Clerk Maxwell Telescope,** a radio telescope with a primary reflecting surface more than 15 meters in diameter. It was dedicated by Britain's Prince Philip, who rode all the way to the summit in a Rolls Royce. The **Canada-France-Hawaii Telescope,** built in 1977 for $33 million, was the first to spot Halley's comet in 1983.

A newer eye to the heavens atop Mauna Kea is the **W.M. Keck Observatory,** completed in March 1993 at a cost of $94 million. The Keck Foundation, a philanthropic organization from Los Angeles, funded the telescope, one of the world's most high tech, powerful, and expensive. Operated by the California Association for Research in Astronomy (CARA), a joint project of the University of California and Cal Tech, the telescope has an aperture of 400 inches and employs entirely new and unique types of technology. The primary reflector is fashioned from a mosaic of 36 hexagonal mirrors, each only three inches thick and six feet in diameter. These "small" mirrors have been very carefully joined together to form one incredibly huge, actively controlled light reflector surface. Each of the mirror segments is separately positionable to an accuracy of a millionth of an inch, and is computer-controlled to bring the heavenly objects into perfect focus. This titanic eyeball has already spotted both the most distant known galaxy and the most distant known object in the universe, 12 and 13 billion light years from earth, respectively. The light received from these objects today was emitted not long after the "Big Bang" that created the universe theoretically occurred. In a very real sense, these scientists are looking back toward the beginning of time! The Keck

LOUISE FOOTE

Observatory includes a public gallery. Keck II, Son of Cyclops, is an copy of Keck I and was operational in 1996. Scientists now have an immensely more powerful tool for their earthbound exploration of the heavens.

In addition to these are the following: The **NASA Infrared Telescope Facility** does only infrared viewing with its three-meter mirror. Also only with infrared capabilities, the **United Kingdom Infrared Telescope (UKIRT),** in operation since 1979, searches the sky with its 3.8-meter lens. The **California Institute of Technology 10.4-meter Submillimeter Telescope** has been looking into the sky since 1987. Completed in 1970, the **University of Hawaii 2.2-meter Telescope** is one of the smaller telescopes at the top. **Subaru (Japan National Large Telescope),** with a monolithic 8.3-meter mirror capable of both optical and infrared viewing, will come into operation in 1998. And the **Gemini Northern 8-meter Telescope,** also with both optical and infrared viewing, is run by a consortium from the U.S., U. K., Canada, Chile, Argentina, and Brazil, and should be completed around 1999. Also under construction is the **Submillimeter Array.** About two miles distant from the top is the **Hawaii Antenna of the Very Long Baseline Array,** a series of 25-meter-wide, centimeter wavelength, radio dishes.

The entire mountaintop complex, plus almost all of the land area above 12,000 feet, is managed by the University of Hawaii. Visitors are welcome to tour the complex and to have a look through the telescopes on weekends, starting at 1 p.m. Reservations are a must; arrangements can be made by calling the **Mauna Kea Support Services** in Hilo at (808) 935-3371 or the Visitors Center at (808) 961-2180. The **Onizuka Visitor Center** at the 9,200-foot level, named in honor of astronaut Ellison Onizuka who died in the *Challenger* tragedy, is a must-stop for stargazers. It allows visitors a chance to acclimatize to the thin, high-mountain air, another must. A stay of one hour here is recommended before you head up to the 13,796-foot summit. (Because of the high altitude and the remoteness of the mountaintop from emergency medical facilities, children under age 16 are prohibited from venturing to the summit. People with cardiopulmonary or respiratory problems or with physical infirmities or weakness, and those who are very obese, are also discouraged

from attempting the trip.) The Visitors Center provides the last public restrooms before the summit and is a good place to stock up on water, also unavailable higher up. The Visitors Center is open Fri.-Sun. 9 a.m.-noon and 1-4:30 p.m. The stargazing tours are offered Thurs.-Sun. 6:30-10 p.m. and an observatory tour every Saturday and Sunday at 1 p.m. (weather permitting). Call (808) 961-2180 for more information, or (808) 969-3218 for the weather report. For information on the Internet about the mountaintop observatory, the individual telescope installations, or the Visitors Center, log onto the Mauna Kea Observatory website (www.ifa.hawaii.edu/mko/) or the University of Hawaii Institute for Astronomy website (www.ifa.hawaii.edu/) and follow the links from there.

If you plan on continuing up to the summit, you must provide your own transportation. Observatory personnel suggest calling **Harper Car and Truck Rentals** in Hilo, tel. (808) 969-1478, or (808) 329-6688 in Kona, which offers 4WD rentals. Alternately, make arrangements for a guided tour to the top with **Paradise Safaris** of Kona, tel. (808) 322-2366 or (800) 545-5662, e-mail: parsaf@ilhawaii.net; or with Arnott's Lodge in Hilo, tel. (808) 969-7097. Take extra layers of warm clothing—it can snow up there any month of the year—and your camera. Photographers, using fast film, get some of the most dazzling shots *after* sunset. During the gloaming, the light show begins. Look down upon the clouds to see them filled with fire. This heavenly light is reflected off the mountain to the clouds and then back up like a celestial mirror in which you get a fleeting glimpse of the soul of the universe.

MAUNA KEA STATE RECREATION AREA

This area, known as Pohakuloa (Long Stone), is five miles west of the Mauna Kea Observatory Road (35 miles from Hilo). The altitude is 6,500 feet and the land begins to change into the rolling grasslands for which this *paniolo* country is famous. Here you'll find a cluster of seven cabins that can be rented (arrange in advance) from the Department of Land and Natural Resources, Division of State Parks, 75 Aupuni St., Hilo, HI 96720, tel. (808) 974-6200. The cabins are completely furnished with cooking facilities and hot showers. You'll need warm clothing, but the days and nights are unusually clear and dry with very little rain. The park is within the Pohakuloa Game Management Area, so expect hunting and shooting in season. A few minutes west is the Pohakuloa Military Camp, whose maneuvers can sometimes disturb the peace in this high mountain area.

Birdwatchers or nature enthusiasts should turn into Koa Kipuka, a bite-size hill just near mile marker 28. (A *kipuka* is a very special area, usual-

ly a hill or gully, in the middle of a lava flow that was never inundated by lava and therefore provides an old, original, and established ecosystem.) Look for Powerline Road and Pu'u O'o Volcano Trail. Follow either for a chance to see the very rare *akiapola'au* or *apapane,* and even wild turkeys.

Follow the Saddle Road about 20 miles west to intersect Rt. 190, on which you can turn right (north) to Waimea—seven miles—or left (south) to Kailua-33 miles.

HAWAII STAE ARCHIVES

HAMAKUA COAST

Along the shore, cobalt waves foam into razor-sharp valleys where cold mountain streams meet the sea at lonely pebbled beaches. Inland, the Hamakua Coast, once awash in a rolling green sea of sugarcane, has been put to other uses. Along a 50-mile stretch of the Belt Road (Rt. 19) from Hilo to Waipio, the Big Island grew its cane for 100 years or more. Water was needed for sugar, a ton to produce a pound, and this coast has plenty. Huge flumes once carried the cut cane to the mills. Last century so many Scots worked the plantations hereabouts that Hamakua was called the "Scotch Coast." Now most residents are a mixture of Scottish, Japanese, Filipino, and Portuguese ancestry. Side roads dip off Rt. 19 into one-family valleys where modest, weather-beaten homes of plantation workers sit surrounded by garden plots on tiny, hand-hewn terraces. These valleys, as they march up the coast, are unromantically referred to as "gulches." From the Belt Road's many bridges, you can trace silvery-ribboned streams that mark the valley floors as they open to the sea. Each valley is jungle—lush with wildflowers and fruit trees transforming the steep sides to emerald-green velvet.

HONOMU TO LAUPAHOEHOE

The ride alone, as you head north on the Belt Road, is gorgeous enough to be considered a sight. But there's more! You can pull off the road into sleepy one-horse towns where dogs are safe snoozing in the middle of the road. You can visit a plantation store in Honomu on your way to Akaka Falls, or take a cautious dip at one of the seaside beach parks. If you want solitude, you can go inland to a forest reserve and miles of trails. The largest town on the coast is Honokaa, with supplies, handmade mementos, and a macadamia nut factory. You can veer west to Waimea from Honokaa, but don't. Take the spur road, Rt. 240, to Waipio Valley, known as the "Valley of Kings," one of the most beautiful in all of Hawaii.

HONOMU AND VICINITY

During its heyday, Honomu (Silent Bay) was a bustling center of the sugar industry boasting saloons, a hotel/bordello, and a church or two for repentance. Now Honomu mainly serves as a stop as you head somewhere else, but definitely take the time to linger and soak in the feel of classic village life that still permeates its streets. Honomu is 10 miles north of Hilo and a mile or so inland on Rt. 220, which leads to Akaka Falls. On entering, you'll find a string of false-front buildings that are doing a great but unofficial rendition of a "living history museum." The town has recently awoken from a long nap and is now bustling—if that's possible in a two-block town—with wonderful art galleries, small gourmet cafes, and a B&B inn. At the south end of town, just at the turn to Akaka Falls, notice the **Odaishasan,** a beautifully preserved Buddhist Temple. Honomu is definitely worth a stop. It takes only minutes to walk the main street, but those minutes can give you a glimpse of history that will take you back 100 years.

Practicalities

Before entering town proper you'll spot **Jan's,** a convenience store selling cold beer and groceries.

As you enter town look for **Akaka Falls Flea Market,** tel. (808) 963-6171, open daily 9 a.m.-5 p.m., shipping available, where owner Dennis Sevilla claims "all new quality merchandise at reduced prices." Although the merchandise constantly changes, you might find Baltic amber necklaces for $85, Chinese hole-coins, Niihau shell lei, Czech crystals, batiks from Indonesia, wind chimes, plenty of furniture, and of course T-shirts. Can't forget those! Especially look for Hawaiian *pahu* (temple drums) made by master drum maker Tuifua (whose work is displayed at the prestigious Bishop Museum), hula instruments, a Polynesian *toere* (a split bamboo mouth drum), and a "can't live without" crocheted Budweiser beer can hat.

On the left as you drive along the main street is **Aloha Akaka Plate Lunch,** open daily except Wednesday 10 a.m.-5 p.m., where Nancy Tanemoto serves up charsiu (Chinese barbecued pork) for $5.50; miso with limpets for $4.50;

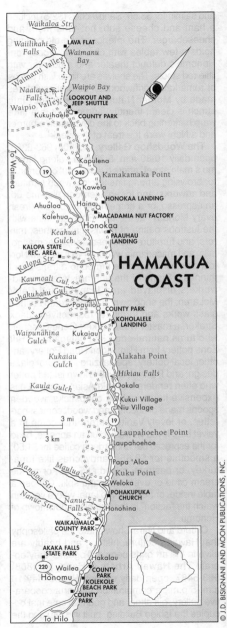

and saimin for $3.50. Sandwiches ($2-5) include a ham and cheese sub, hot tuna melt, and cheeseburger. The interior of the old building holds a few tables with chairs salvaged from Honomu's defunct theater and a counter with little red stools. The shelves are lined with pieces of remarkable driftwood, all natural sculptures made by Mother Nature. Aloha Akaka Plate Lunch is clean, friendly, and caught in a time warp harkening back to the days when a burger and a Nehi were the treat of the week!

The Woodshop Gallery, tel. (808) 963-6363, open daily 10:30 a.m.-5:30 p.m., along Honomu's main street, offers a wonderful opportunity for browsing among fine tropical wood furniture and artworks, and for an afternoon pick-me-up, an espresso, or a homemade ice cream (fresh every Monday) at the bar. Shelves shine with the lustrous patina of bowls, calabashes, mirrors, and furniture fashioned from koa, mango, milo, and macadamia wood, as well as from Norfolk pine, which can be turned to a translucent thinness. Some of the fine artists and woodworkers displayed are: Jeanette and Peter McLaren, the shop owners, who create stained glass works and furniture, respectively; Jack Straker, a master woodworker; Gene Buscher, who turns natural-edge koa calabashes; Rift Zone pottery from Hilo; Moon Road Pottery, another local pottery, specializing in a floral glaze design; and Pachini, a well-known island potter who often renders a simple Asian design. Less expensive items include chopsticks, wooden spoons made of coconut and wood, combs, barrettes, or lovely vanity mirrors that come in a velvet bag. If you've worked up an appetite, head for the espresso bar and order a coffee for $1.50, a smoothie for $2.65, sandwiches like tuna, turkey, or pastrami priced at $3.50, or an ice cream cone or even a banana split. Choose a table inside, or head for the lanai where you can watch the "action" in the two-block downtown of Honomu.

Clifford and Nara Chow share the philosophy that Hawaii's culture, history, and beauty are alive in the art of its people. Together they operate **The Hawaii Artists O'Hana,** tel. (808) 963-5467, open daily except Wednesday 10 a.m.-5 p.m., a combination fine arts cooperative gallery, gift shop, and gourmet cafe that occupies the Ishigo Building, built in 1880 and the oldest building in Honomu. Gracing the shelves and walls of the two-story gallery are works by some of the island's best artists, including: Avi Kiriaty, who uses bold colors to capture the emotions of Hawaii in the expressive faces of its women; Edward Kayton, who sees the "soul fire" of Hawaii in its ancient warriors; Raymond Helgeson, whose canoe paddlers match rippling muscle with rippling sea; Andrew Plack, who gives wings to color, offering bouquets of "birds of paradise"; Kathleen Kan, who travels in spirit with Polynesian voyagers and the animals of the sea; and Brad Lewis, a photographer who sees lava, colored like the ali'i feathered cape, as the red and yellow mana of Hawaii. Indigenous water gourds are grown from seed by Olivia Ling, who then carves them into beautifully functional art pieces; and paddles are expertly carved by Mal Pauole from curly koa and mango wood. The downstairs gallery offers more works and a clothing boutique with truly distinctive T-shirts by artist Bob Hackney, who prints them with a famous design titled Out Of Hand, along with geckos, petroglyph designs, and paddlers. There are handmade vests by Carolyn Ainsworth, aromatherapy care products, essential oils handmade by a local Hawaiian woman, an extensive collection of Niihau shells, and dark, naturally burnished kukui nut lei. All guess are treated to a glass of lemongrass iced tea, but if you're hungry head for the Bamboo Lanai, a covered and screened veranda appointed with lau hala weaving, where you can order specialties like fresh ahi (tuna) salad for $6.95, homemade meatloaf for $6.50, lasagna (vegetarian or with Italian sausage) with garlic bread and salad for $7.50, and a garden burger deluxe for $6.95. The Hawaii Artists O'Hana is a jewel of a shop where the spirit, heart, and vision of old Hawaii are very much alive.

You'd feel comfortable in your bowler hat or calico dress ordering up a root beer float in the **Akaka Falls Inn, Gift Gallery and Cafe,** 28-1676 Main St., P.O. Box 190, Honomu, HI 96728, tel. (808) 963-5468, a semiconverted 1920s ice cream parlor that still retains the original ambience with bent iron stools, a foot rail, a marble countertop, and a mirrored breakfront. The cafe section offers a turkey sandwich on potato bread with lettuce, tomato, and sprouts for $4.50; quiche for $2.50; curried veggies in puff pastry for $2.95;

DAVID STANLEY

Akaka Falls

the two guest rooms, as is the comfortable parlor—perfect for relaxing. Peer through the windows into the back yards of Honomu, and in a few short few days you will be absorbed in the life of this simple village. Inexpensive.

Another establishment worth a visit is **Glass of the Past,** with vintage bottles and collectibles.

Akaka Falls State Park
Follow Rt. 220 from Honomu past sugarcane fields for 3.5 miles to the parking lot of Akaka Falls. From here, walk counterclockwise along a paved "circle route" that takes you through everybody's idea of a pristine Hawaiian valley. For 40 minutes you're surrounded by heliconia, gingers, orchids, ferns, and bamboo groves as you cross bubbling streams on wooden footbridges. Many varieties of plants that would be in window pots anywhere else are giants here, almost trees. An overlook provides views of Kahuna Falls spilling into a lush green valley below. The trail becomes an enchanted tunnel through hanging orchids and bougainvillea. In a few moments you arrive at Akaka Falls. The mountain cooperates with the perfect setting, forming a semicircle from which the falls tumble 442 feet in one sheer drop, the tallest single-tier waterfall in the state. After heavy rains, expect a mad torrent of power; during dry periods marvel at liquid-silver threads forming mist and rainbows. The area, maintained by the Division of State Parks, is one of the most easily accessible forays into Hawaii's beautiful interior.

Kolekole Beach Park
Look for the first tall bridge (100 feet high) a few minutes past Honomu, where a sign points to a small road that snakes its way down the valley to the beach park below. Amenities include restrooms, grills, electricity, picnic tables, and a camping area (county permit). Kolekole is very popular with local people, who use its five pavilions for all manner of special occasions, usually on weekends. A black-sand beach fronts an extremely treacherous ocean. The entire valley was inundated with more than 30 feet of water during the great 1946 tsunami. The stream running through Kolekole comes from Akaka Falls, four miles inland. It forms a pool complete with waterfall that is safe for swimming but quite cold.

or a simple old-fashioned peanut butter and jelly sandwich for $1.75. Sides include potato or macaroni salad, apple and macadamia nut slaw, and Greek pasta—only 75 cents each. Shelves hold gourmet items like mango syrup and ginger mango dressing, and a small freezer is packed with various flavors of ice cream, sold by the cone. Two back rooms, serving as the gift gallery, are stuffed with quality souvenir items like koa bracelets, mirrors, beaded necklaces, calendars, cutting boards, earrings, books, and artwork. As you meander through, look for potions and lotions, candles, pareus, T-shirts, and real Hawaiian quilts made by "a lady from Hilo." Ascend a wainscoted stairway to the two-room bed-and-breakfast inn furnished in "plantation style" with hardwood floors, sash windows, and Casablanca fans. One guest room, at $55, features twin beds and a rollaway cot, while the other, at $65, holds a queen bed and a day bed; both are bright with Hawaiian quilts and rattan furniture. A large tiled bathroom, with tub and shower, is shared by

LAUPAHOEHOE

This wave-lashed peninsula is a finger of smooth pahoehoe lava that juts into the bay. Located about halfway between Honomu and Honokaa, the valley at one time supported farmers and fishermen who specialized in catching turtles. Laupahoehoe was the best boat landing along the coast, and for years canoes and, later, schooners would stop here. A plaque commemorates the tragic loss of 20 schoolchildren and their teacher who were taken by the great tsunami of 1946. Afterwards, the village was moved to the high ground overlooking the point. **Laupahoehoe Beach Park** now occupies the low peninsula; it has picnic tables, showers, electricity, and a county camping area. The sea is too rough to swim but many fishermen come here, along with some daring surfers. Laupahoehoe makes a beautiful rest stop along the Belt Road. At the Laupahoehoe scenic overlook is the new **Laupahoehoe Train Museum and Visitor Center,** tel. 962-2221. Open daily 9 a.m.-4:30 p.m., this museum treats you to a taste of the olden days when trains hauled sugar cane, people, and goods up and down this rugged coast.

Ten miles inland from Laupahoehoe Point along a very rugged jeep trail is **David Douglas Historical Monument.** This marks the spot where the naturalist, after whom the Douglas fir is named, lost his life under mysterious circumstances. Douglas, on a fact-gathering expedition on the rugged slopes of Mauna Kea, never returned. His body was found at the bottom of a deep pit that was used at the time to catch feral cattle. Douglas had spent the previous night at a cabin occupied by an Australian who had been a convict. Many suspected that the Australian had murdered Douglas in a robbery attempt and thrown his body into the pit to hide the deed. No hard evidence of murder could be found, and the death was officially termed accidental.

Practicalities

Just before Laupahoehoe on the Hilo side, look for a sign to **Papaaloa.** Turn here, and head down the road to the **Papaaloa Neighborhood Store,** where local people go to buy the area's *best* smoked meats and fish, including marlin, beef, pork, and *laulau* made right at the store; they'll also fix a plate lunch to go.

In Laupahoehoe along Rt. 19, look for **Sakado Store,** open 7:30 a.m.-5:30 p.m., an old-fashioned Hawaiian-style convenience store. They sell basic items like milk, bread, and soft drinks, enough for a picnic.

Keoki's Place, tel. (808) 962-0011, open Tues.-Sat. 10 a.m.-7 p.m., Sunday 10 a.m.-5 p.m., in a white and turquoise painted vintage building in Laupahoehoe Village, is a combination plate lunch restaurant and pizza parlor. Pizzas range $8-12 plus $1 for extra toppings; $2 by the slice. Deli sandwiches like ham, turkey, chicken, tuna, avocado, veggie, or eggplant parmigiana are all under $5, while a salami, meatball, sausage, or pastrami sandwich is $5.50, a hamburger $4.75, and a salmon burger $5.50. Plate lunches priced under $5 are the standards, from mahimahi to teriyaki beef. Desserts are homemade cheesecake $2.50, pies $1.75, and ice cream one scoop $1.75, two scoops $2.50. Keoki's also offers milk shakes and malteds at $3.10 and $3.95 respectively. The atmosphere is as local as you can get!

HONOKAA TO KUKUIHAELE

HONOKAA AND VICINITY

With a population of nearly 2,000, Honokaa (Crumbling Bay) is the major town on the Hamakua Coast. Here you can continue on Rt. 19 to Waimea, or take Rt. 240 through Honokaa and north to Waipio, which you should not miss. First, however, stroll the main street of Honokaa, Mamane Street, where a number of shops specialize in locally produced handicrafts. This is also the best place to stock up on supplies or gasoline. The surrounding area is the center of the macadamia nut industry. If you are proceeding north along Rt. 240, the coastal route heading to Waipio Valley, just past mile marker 6 on the left, keep an eye peeled for a lava-tube cave right along the roadway. This is just a tease of the amazing natural sights that follow.

Kalopa State Recreation Area

This spacious natural area is 12 miles north of Laupahoehoe (five miles southeast of Honokaa), three miles inland on a well-marked secondary road, and 2,000 feet in elevation. Little used by tourists, it's a great place to get away from it all. Hiking is terrific throughout the park on a series of nature trails where much of the flora has been identified. All trails are well marked and vary widely in difficulty. The park provides an excellent opportunity to explore some of the lush gulches of the Hamakua Coast, as well as tent camping and furnished cabins (state permit required) that can house up to eight people.

Hawaiian Holiday Macadamia Nut Factory

This factory, open 9 a.m.-6 p.m., is on a side road that leads from the middle of town down a steep hill toward the sea. A self-guided tour explains how John MacAdams discovered the delicious qualities of these nuts, and how they were named after him. The macadamia nut industry was started in Honokaa when W.H. Purvis, a British agriculturalist who had been working in Australia, brought the first trees to Honokaa in 1881, one of which is still bearing! In 1924, W. Pierre Naquin, then manager of the Honokaa Sugar Co., started the first commercial nut farm in the area. You can buy a large variety of macadamia items, from butters to candies. A delicious and nutritious munchie is a five-ounce, vacuum-packed can of nuts that make a great souvenir or add a special touch to a picnic lunch. The Nut Factory also has a small deli selection and ice cream. Inside the same facility is the **H.R.T. Waipio Tour Desk,** tel. (808) 775-7291, where you can arrange a van or horseback tour through fabulous Waipio.

Accommodations and Food

Centrally located along Rt. 240 in downtown Honokaa, is the **Hotel Honokaa Club,** P.O. Box 247, Honokaa, HI 96727, tel. (808) 775-0678 or (800) 808-0678. What it lacks in elegance it makes up for in cleanliness and friendliness. The hotel, mostly used by local people, is old and well used, but clean and comfortable. Follow a wainscoted hallway to the upstairs rooms, priced at $55; all are upgraded with carpeting and fluffy quilts; each features a view and TV. The more spartan but very clean downstairs rooms, with private

baths, go for $40. Hostel rooms, located in the basement, all with shared bath and kitchen facilities, are separated into three private rooms at $20 and two communal rooms (one sleeping three people and the other six people) that rent for $15. The basement hostel rooms—although a bit dungeonesque—are clean, with windows to catch the breeze. The hotel's dining room is open daily except Monday, serving breakfast 7:30-10:30 a.m., lunch 11 a.m.-1:30 p.m., and dinner 5-8:30 p.m., with all meals prepared in a new and much upgraded kitchen. The breakfast menu offers a low-cholesterol breakfast like Eggbeaters and turkey bacon for $5.50; local standards like two eggs and choice of Spam, bacon, Portuguese sausage, ham or Vienna sausage with homemade hashbrowns, toast, and coffee for only $4.70; and the hotel's famous pancakes and homemade corned beef hash patties. The "Sunrise Special," which is one egg, breakfast meat, and toast or rice for only $2.75, is served Mon.-Fri. 6:30-7:30 a.m. only. Lunch brings $6-7 entrées like hamburger steak, boneless and skinless chicken, and their famous pork chops with onions and gravy. You can also choose sandwiches, everything from a burger to a tuna melt or a mushroom cheeseburger, for around $5. The restaurant features dinner specials daily, but they always serve local cuisine like an authentic Japanese dinner with a choice of shrimp tempura, chicken *katsu,* mahimahi, or stir-fried vegetables for $9.25; 10-ounce teriyaki steak for $12.95; or chicken *katsu* for $8.75. The specialty is lobster that must be ordered by phone a day ahead and that sells at market price, usually around $25. The meals, although not gourmet, are wholesome, with plenty of well-prepared food. Budget.

Luana Ola B&B and Cottages, at P.O. Box 430, Honokaa, HI 96727, tel. (808) 775-7727 or (800) 357-7727, fax (808) 775-0949, owned by Tim and Jeannie Mann, is located on a side street in the residential area of Honokaa, overlooking lands once owned by Hamakua Sugar that slope directly to the sea. Each cottage (handicapped accessible) has a kitchen, laundry room, full bath, lanai, and private phone. The B&B rooms come with a full continental breakfast. Prices range from $75, with weekly discounts available. E-mail: luana@aloha.net; website: www.stayhawaii.com/luana.html. Moderate.

Local people thought that Jolene was such a

good cook, they talked her into opening **Jolene's Kau Kau Corner** in downtown Honokaa, tel. (808) 775-9498, open Mon.-Fri. 10 a.m.-8 p.m., Saturday 10 a.m.-3 p.m., closed Sunday. Most tried-and-true recipes were handed down by her extended family, who also lend a hand in running the restaurant. They currently serve only lunch and dinner, with breakfast a possibility in the near future. The restaurant, located in a vintage storefront, is trim and neat, and the menu includes a variety of plate lunches ($5-6) like beef tips teriyaki, shrimp plate, and a steaming bowl of beef stew. Saimin in two sizes is $2.50 and $3.95, while most burgers and fries are under $5. The dinner menu ($5-17) brings broiled mahimahi, shrimp tempura, shrimp and chicken baskets, a steak and seafood combination, and vegetarian stir-fry. Jolene's is as down-home and local as you can get, and what she lacks in atmosphere, she more than makes up for in friendly service, hearty dishes, and reasonable prices. This is one of the best places to eat along the northern Hamakua Coast!

Follow the comforting aroma of fresh-baked bread to **Mamane Street Bakery & Café,** tel. (808) 775-9478, open Mon.-Fri. 7 a.m.-5:30 p.m., Saturday 7 a.m.-4 p.m., closed Sunday, owned and operated by Eliahu "Ely" Pessah, and assisted by his fiancée Emma, who has a smile sweeter than the cupcakes on the shelves. Ely bakes goodies including coconut turnovers, Danish pastries, and *ensemada,* a special type of cinnamon roll, all priced $1-1.50, but what the local people come in for are the honey-nut bran muffins, crunchy with chunks of macadamia nuts. Ely's oven also turns out ham and cheese croissants, mozzarella or marinara focaccia, or three-cheese focaccia, all under $5.95. Eat in or take out while enjoying your purchase with a cup of steaming coffee or tea. Make sure to visit the "Gift Shop," constructed in free-form design with 52 different kinds of wood. Here, you'll discover painted fish, glass fish, wooden earrings, *lau hala* bracelets, carved elephants, a smattering of pottery, notecards, and Hawaiian dolls. Also ask to see the plaster of Paris "castings" of old lava flows, a very unique expression of "art."

"On a Wing and a Prayer" is part of the logo welcoming you to **Simply Natural Ice Cream Parlor, and More,** tel. (808) 775-0119, open Mon.-Sat. 9 a.m.-5 p.m., Sunday 11 a.m.-5 p.m., where the owner, Sharon, does the praying and Bernie the Cockatoo is the wing man and official greeter. Besides ice cream in tropical and standard flavors, which comes in cones, cups, or waffle cones, a board offers a full sandwich and burger menu with plenty of vegetarian items. Choose a garden salad sandwich or a garden burger for $4.25, or delicious bowl of Thai coconut curry soup with chicken or vegetarian. Other sandwiches are grilled mahimahi for $5.50, teriyaki chicken for $4.50, and the handmade and "old-fashioned real" Awesome Burger at $2.75-4.50 depending upon what you want on it. Sharon is also adding a full Mexican menu with everything from tacos to tostadas, available with beef or chicken, or vegetarian. Beverages include soft drinks, fresh squeezed carrot juice, Kona coffee, espresso, and cappuccino.

Genuine cowpokes as well as city slickers from the Mainland pretending to be *paniolo* will have the urge to fling their Stetsons in the air and yell "yuppie yi yo kai yea!" when their trail leads to the **Texas Drive-In and Restaurant,** open daily 5 a.m.-9 p.m., a little later on weekends. The long-established Hamakua restaurant is known for its fresh *malasadas.* Get some! Upon entering Honokaa along Rt. 240 coming from Hilo, look for the chain-link fence of the Honokaa High and Elementary School. Make a left where it ends up Pakalana Street and follow it to the top of the hill where you'll see the Texas Drive-In on your left, a plain cinder-block building with a yellow and red exterior. Basically a walk-up window restaurant, it has a few tables out front; a cavernous dining room in the back will remind you of a school cafeteria. They specialize in inexpensive local food like *kalua* pork, teriyaki chicken and beef, hamburgers, and fresh fish. No item costs more than $8; most dinners are priced around $5, and sandwiches are only $2-3. Local people and (an even better sign) the local police come here to chow down on good, easy-on-the-wallet food.

Herb's Place, in downtown Honokaa, is open for breakfast, lunch, and dinner Mon.-Fri. from 5:30 a.m., Saturday from 8:30 a.m., closed Sunday. You get basic meals and cocktails in this little roadside joint.

C.C. Jon's is a plate-lunch, local fast-food stand, just as you enter town. Most of their dishes are under $4.50.

Shopping

World-renowned art critic and author Amaury St. Giles just can't seem to get enough of volcanic islands. After residing in Japan for more than 30 years, where he became an expert in Japanese pottery—publishing *Earth and Fire,* an acclaimed book on the subject—and where he was a columnist appearing in the *Mainichi Shimbun,* an English-language daily, he decided to move to the Big Island. Luckily for us, he's continued his life-long love affair with art and now operates the **Amaury St. Giles Modern Art Gallery,** tel. (808) 775-9278, open daily except Wednesday 10 a.m.-5 p.m., major credit cards accepted, shipping available, located in a vintage building in downtown Honokaa that has been remodeled to display perfectly the personally chosen art that graces its walls. Some of the fine artists represented are: Phil Gallagher, who uses watercolors to capture the simple yet evocative figures in ancient petroglyphs; Wailehua Gray, a native Hawaiian whose spiritual heart sees the legends of old Hawaii, allowing him to render them on canvas; John Young, one of Hawaii's premier artists, who has tuned into the soul of Hawaii; Tom Adolf, a local Honokaa artist who has perfected painting in a series of panels depicting circular panoramas of places and things Hawaiian; Raymond Helgeson, who realistically paints the joy and power of Hawaiian canoe paddlers, creating an amazing correlation between the ripples in the sea and the ripples in their muscled arms and sinewy backs; Lauan Okano, a calligrapher who uses words to create what looks from a distance like a painted fan, koi, or rose, but on close inspection is revealed as fine calligraphy rendered repeatedly to form the simple but powerful images. Amaury St. Giles has a superb eye for art, honed to fine sharpness over the years. If he has chosen a work to appear in his gallery, you know that it is one of great merit.

If you are at all interested in the history of Hawaii, make sure to stop by the **The Hawaiian "Artifacks" Shop** along the main drag in downtown Honokaa. Just look for a carved mermaid and a strobe light blinking you into the shop. This amazing curio and art shop is owned and operated by Lokikamakahiki "Loki" Rice, who ran it for many years with her husband James; unfortunately, he passed away in the spring of 1996. Loki, elderly and in failing health, keeps no set hours, opening when she feels like it, usually for a few hours in the afternoon, but never before 2 p.m. At first glance the shop may look inauthentic, but once you're inside, that impression quickly melts away. Loki, a full-blooded Hawaiian, was born and raised in Waipio Valley, and James traveled the Pacific for years. The stories from the old days are almost endless. Notice a tiki that serves as a main beam, and two giant shields against the back wall. They belonged to Loki's father, a giant of a man just under seven feet tall and more than 450 pounds who had to have a special coffin made when he was buried on the island of Niihau. Local people bring in their carvings and handicrafts to sell, many of which are hula implements and instruments like drums and rattles. Some of the bric-a-brac is from the Philippines or other South Sea islands, but Loki will identify them for you. Mingled in with what seems to be junk are some real artifacts like poi pounders, adzes, and really good drums. Many have come from Loki's family, while others have been collected by the Rices over the years. But the real treasure is Loki, who will share her *aloha* as long as time and the call from above permits.

Hamakua Woodworks, tel. (808) 775-9910, open Mon.-Sat. 9 a.m.-5 p.m., Sunday 11 a.m.-4 p.m. in downtown Honokaa, offers custom koa woodwork by island artists, including the furniture of Dennis and Marie Smith, koa fans and lazy Susans for $125 by Kayong Walton, and lovely koa boxes for $125 by the proprietors Walker and Susan Sanders assisted by their daughter, Elizabeth. Simple items include koa mirrors for $35, candleholders for $4.50, chopsticks at $9.50, a koa napkin holder for $18, and barrettes for $18. A display case also holds glass earrings, sterling silver jewelry, and a smattering of beadwork.

Kanani Woods and Crafts, tel. (808) 775-0109, open Mon.-Sat. 10 a.m.-5 p.m., owned by Kanani Weller and Dave Moniz, showcases *lau hala* weavings and woodwork made on the Big Island. Dave does all the woodwork, creating everything from bowls to keychains using island woods that include koa, milo, mango, and ohia. A specialty item is a *makini,* the owl-eyed helmet with a *hau* headdress used by warriors in the ancient days. The people in Hawaii often dangle them from their rear view mirrors, but Mainlanders will appreciate them more as artpieces.

Kama'aina Woodworks, tel. (808) 775-7722, in Honokaa halfway down the hill leading to Hawaiian Holiday Macadamia Nut Factory, is usually open daily 9 a.m.-5 p.m. except Sunday but this depends on the weather, their inclination, and how the spirits are moving on any particular day. The shop is owned and operated by Bill Keb and Roy Mau, talented woodworkers who specialize in fabulous bowls turned from native woods like koa, milo, extremely rare *kou,* and a few introduced woods like mango and Norfolk Island pine. All of the wooden artpieces, priced at $20-1,000, are one-of-a-kind and utilitarian. Less expensive items are koa or milo bracelets $10-20, letter openers $5, and rice paddles $4. When you first enter the shop, don't be surprised if it looks like someone's home, with a TV on in the sitting room and glass cases filled with Hawaiian flora and fauna.

The Honokaa Trading Company, tel. (808) 775-0808, open daily 10 a.m.-5 p.m., is a discovery shop owned and operated by Denise Walker. Items come and go, but you can expect to find classic artwork from the Matson Steamship Lines, hula dolls, Japanese netsuke, poi bowls, costume jewelry, pots and pans, bottles, and old crockery. Denise has also filled this rambling building with a good selection of old books, Hawaiian instruments, Japanese fans, and vintage signs. Denise focuses not only on things *from* Hawaii, but on things *brought to* Hawaii. Much of the furniture and many of the antique items were brought to Hawaii by *kama'aina* and GI families.

At the south end of town, **Seconds To Go,** open daily except Sunday 9:30 a.m.-5 p.m., is owned and operated by Elaine Carlsmith. The collectibles-and-antique shop specializes in Hawaiian artifacts; it brims with classic Hawaiian ties and shirts from the '50s, dancing hula-doll lamps, antique hardware and building materials, clawfoot bathtubs, old books, Japanese bowls, a good collection of plates and saucers, and a ukulele. Elaine also sells used fishing gear in case you want to try your luck.

In town, **S. Hasegawa** has a few racks of local fashions and a few bolts of traditional Japanese cloth. Look for the very ethnic **Filipino Store** along the main drag to soak up a cultural experience and to find an array of exotic spices and food ingredients. You can pick up supplies and even a few health food items at **T. Kaneshiro Store** and **K.K. Super-Mart,** two well-stocked markets in town.

Other Practicalities

The once run-down and classic "Last Picture Show" **Honokaa Movie Theater,** along the main drag , is now renovated and showing slightly late, first-run movies for a mere $4.

You can take care of most of your banking needs at Bank of Hawaii, also located in the downtown area. Gas can be purchased at either a Union 76 or a Chevron, both well marked along the main drag.

The **Hamakua Music Festival,** held around the first week of December and lasting four days, attracts island musicians proficient in everything from Hawaiian to jazz. Contact Hamakua Music Festival, P.O. Box 1757, Honokaa, HI 96727 for a newsletter regarding the festivities and the performing artists.

KUKUIHAELE

For all of you looking for the "light at the end of the tunnel," Kukuihaele (Traveling Light) is it. On the main road, the **Last Chance** grocery and gas station, open daily 9 a.m.-6 p.m., stocks basic supplies plus a small assortment of handicrafts and gift items. The Last Chance has an excellent selection of domestic and imported beers, along with light snacks for a picnic lunch. The store attendants are friendly and don't mind answering a few questions about the Waipio area if they are not too busy.

Waipio Valley Artworks, tel. (808) 775-0958, open daily 9 a.m.-5 p.m., is an excellent shop in which to pick up an art object. There are plenty of offerings in wood by some of the island's best woodworkers that include carvings and bowls, but the shop also showcases various Hawaii-based artists working in different mediums. Definitely check out inspired prints by Sue Sweardlow, who has tuned in to the soul of Hawaii; paintings by Carli Oliver and Kim Starr; and the inspired art of Cathy Long and her mother, Mary Koskie. You'll also find tikis, earrings, basketry made from natural fibers, and ceramics by

Robert Joiner and Ann Rathbun. The shop features a snack window serving ice cream, sandwiches, and soft drinks. Out back, a small boutique offers designer T-shirts, alohawear, a smattering of souvenir items, and a fairly extensive collection of books mostly on Hawaiiana. Waipio Valley Artworks is also the meeting place for **Waipio Valley Shuttle,** tel. (808) 775-7121, which will take you down to Waipio Valley.

Accommodations
A vintage home of a one-time plantation manager, **Waipio Wayside,** P.O. Box 840, Honokaa, HI 96727, tel. (808) 775-0275 or (800) 833-8849, is now owned and operated by Jackie Horne as a congenial B&B. Look for the Waipio Wayside sign hung on a white picket fence exactly two miles toward Waipio from the Honokaa post office. You enter through double French doors, onto a rich wooden floor shining with a well-waxed patina. The walls are hand-laid vertical paneling, the prototype that modern paneling tries to emulate. The home contains five double bedrooms ranging in price $55-85 s, $65-95

d for multiple-night stays; $15 extra for single-night stays; $15 extra person. One large master bedroom is in its own little space out back, but attached to the house. The room, rich with knotty pine, is spacious and airy with plenty of windows. Every bedroom has beautiful Battenburg lace curtains. The back deck, where you will find hammocks in which to rock away your cares, overlooks manicured grounds that gently slope to a panoramic view of the coast. Jackie, whose meticulous and tastefully appointed home is straight from the pages of *Ladies' Home Journal,* is also a gourmet cook. Breakfast is sometimes waffles with strawberries and whipped cream, sometimes omelettes and biscuits, with fresh fruit from the property. Beverages are pure Hamakua coffee—grown no more than 12 miles away—or Kona and Jamaican Blue Mountain coffee, juices, and an assortment of 24 gourmet teas from around the world. A stay at Waipio Wayside is guaranteed to be civilized, relaxing, and affordable. E-mail: wayside@ilhawaii.net; website: www.stayhawaii.com/wayside.html. Moderate.

WAIPIO VALLEY

Waipio is the way the Lord would have liked to fashion the Garden of Eden, if he hadn't been on such a tight schedule. You can read about this incredible valley, but you really can't believe it until you see it for yourself. Route 240 ends a minute outside of Kukuihaele at an overlook, and 1,000 feet below is Waipio (Arching Water), the island's largest and most southerly valley of the many that slice the harsh Kohala Mountains. The valley is a mile across where it fronts the sea at a series of high sand dunes. It's vibrantly green, always watered by Waipio Stream and lesser streams that spout as waterfalls from the *pali* at the rear of the valley. The green is offset by a wide band of black-sand beach. The far side of the valley ends abruptly at a steep *pali* that is higher than the one on which you're standing. A six-mile trail leads over it to Waimanu Valley, smaller, more remote, and more luxuriant.

Travelers have long extolled the amazing abundance of Waipio. From the overlook you can make out the overgrown outlines of garden

terraces, taro patches, and fishponds in what was Hawaii's largest cultivated valley. Every foodstuff known to the Hawaiians once flourished here; even Waipio pigs were said to be bigger than anywhere else. In times of famine, the produce from Waipio could sustain the populace of the entire island (estimated at 100,000 people). On the valley floor and alongside the streams you'll still find avocados, bananas, coconuts, passion fruit, mountain apples, guavas, breadfruit, tapioca, lemons, limes, coffee, grapefruit, and pumpkins. The old fishponds and streams are alive with prawns, wild pigs roam the interior, and there are abundant fish in the sea.

But the lovingly tended order, most homes, and the lifestyle were washed away in the tsunami of 1946. Now Waipio is unkempt, a wild jungle of mutated abundance. The valley is a neglected maiden with a dirty face and disheveled, wind-blown hair. Only love and nurturing can refresh her lingering beauty.

HISTORY

Legend and Oral History

Waipio is a mystical place. Inhabited for more than 1,000 years, it figures prominently in old Hawaiian lore. In the primordial past, Wakea, progenitor of all the islands, favored the valley, and oral tradition holds that the great gods Kane and Kanaloa dallied in Waipio intoxicating themselves on *awa*. One oral chant relates that the demigod Maui, that wild prankster, met his untimely end here by trying to steal baked bananas from these two drunken heavyweights. Lono, god of the Makahiki, came to Waipio in search of a bride. He found Kaikilani, a beautiful maiden who lived in a breadfruit tree near **Hiilawe Waterfall,** which tumbles 1,300 feet to the valley below and is Hawaii's highest single falls.

Nenewe, a shark-man, lived near a pool at the bottom of another waterfall on the west side of Waipio that has been recently fenced so that access is no longer available. The pool was connected to the sea by an underwater tunnel. All went well for Nenewe until his grandfather disobeyed a warning never to feed his grandson meat. Once Nenewe tasted meat, he began eating Waipio residents after first warning them about sharks as they passed his sea-connected pool on their way to fish. His constant warnings roused suspicions. Finally, a cape he always wore was ripped from his shoulders, and there on his back was a shark's mouth! He dove into his pool and left Waipio to hunt the waters of the other islands.

Pupualenalena, a *kupua* (nature spirit), takes the form of a yellow dog who can change his size from tiny to huge. He was sent by the chiefs of Waipio to steal a conch shell that mischievous water sprites were constantly blowing, just to irritate the people. The shell was inherited by Kamehameha and is now in the Bishop Museum. Another dog-spirit lives in a rock embedded in the hillside halfway down the road to Waipio. In times of danger, he comes out of his rock to stand in the middle of the road as a warning that bad things are about to happen.

Finally, a secret section of Waipio Beach is called **Lua o milu,** the legendary doorway to the land of the dead. At certain times, it is believed, ghosts of great *ali'i* come back to earth as "Marchers of the Night," and their strong chants and torch-lit processions fill the darkness in Waipio. Many great kings were buried in Waipio, and it's felt that because of their mana, no harm will come to the people who live here. Oddly enough, the horrible tsunami of 1946 and a raging flood in 1979 filled the valley with wild torrents of water. In both cases, the devastation to homes and the land was tremendous, but not one life was lost. Everyone who still lives in Waipio will tell you that somehow, they feel protected.

The remains of **Paka'alana Heiau** is in a grove of trees on the right-hand side of the beach as you face the sea. It dates from the 12th century and was a "temple of refuge" where *kapu* breakers, vanquished warriors, and the weak and infirm could find sanctuary. The other restored and more famous temple of this type is Pu'uhonua O Honaunau in Kona. Paka'alana was a huge *heiau* with tremendous walls that were mostly intact until the tsunami of 1946. The tsunami sounded like an explosion when the waters hit the walls of Paka'alana, according to firsthand accounts. The rocks were scattered, and all was turned to ruins. Nearby, **Hanua'aloa** is another *heiau* that is in ruins. Archaeologists know even less about this *heiau,* but all agree that both were healing temples of body and spirit, and the local people feel that their positive mana is part of the protection in Waipio.

Recorded History

Great chiefs have dwelt in Waipio. King Umialiloa planted taro just like a commoner, and fished with his own hands. He went on to unite the island into one kingdom in the 15th century. Waipio was the traditional land of Kamehameha the Great and in many ways was the basis of his earthly and spiritual power. He came here to rest after heavy battles, and offshore was the scene of the first modern naval battle in Hawaii. Here, Kamehameha's war canoes faced those of his nemesis, Keoua. Both had recently acquired cannons bartered from passing sea captains. Kamehameha's artillery was manned by two white sailors, Davis and Young, who became trusted advisors. Kamehameha's forces won the engagement in what became known as the "Battle of the Red-Mouthed Gun."

When Captain Cook came to Hawaii, 4,000 natives lived in Waipio; a century later only 600

Waipio Valley

remained. At the turn of this century many Chinese and Japanese moved to Waipio and began raising rice and taro. People moved in and out of the valley by horse and mule and there were schools and a strong community spirit. Waipio was painstakingly tended. The undergrowth was kept trimmed and you could see clearly from the back of the valley all the way to the sea. WW II arrived and many people were lured away from the remoteness of the valley by a changing lifestyle and a desire for modernity. The tsunami in 1946 swept away most of the homes, and the majority of the people pulled up stakes and moved away. For 25 years the valley lay virtually abandoned. The Peace Corps considered it a perfect place to build a compound in which to train volunteers headed for Southeast Asia. This too was abandoned. Then in the late '60s and early '70s a few "back to nature" hippies started trickling in. Most only played "Tarzan and Jane" and moved on, especially after Waipio served them a "reality sandwich" in the form of the flood of 1979.

Waipio is still very unpredictable. In a three-week period from late March to early April of 1989, 47 inches of rain drenched the valley. Roads were turned to quagmires, houses washed away, and more people left. Part of the problem is the imported trees in Waipio. Until the 1940s, the valley was a manicured garden, but now it's very heavily forested. All of the trees that you will see are new; the oldest are mangroves and coconuts. The trees are both a boon and a blight. They give shade and fruit, but when there are floods, they fall into the river, creating logjams that increase the flooding dramatically. Waipio takes care of itself best when humans do not interfere. Now the taro farmers are having problems because the irrigation system for their crops was washed away in the last flood. But, with hope and a prayer to Waipio's spirits, they'll rebuild, knowing full well that there will be a next time. And so it goes.

Waipio Now

Waipio is at a crossroads. Many of the old people are dying off or moving topside (above the valley) with relatives. Those who live here learned to accept life in Waipio and genuinely come to love the valley, while others come only to exploit its beauty. Fortunately, the latter underestimate the raw power of Waipio. Developers have eyed the area for years as a magnificent spot in which to build a luxury resort. But even they are wise enough to realize that nature rules Waipio, not humankind. For now the valley is secure. A few gutsy families with a real commitment have stayed on and continue to revitalize Waipio. The valley now supports perhaps 50 residents. A handful of elderly Filipino bachelors who worked for the sugar plantation continue to live here. About 50 more people live topside but come down to Waipio to tend their gardens. On entering the valley, you'll see a lotus-flower pond, and if you're lucky enough to be there in December, it will be in bloom. It's tended by an 80-

year-old Chinese gentleman, Mr. Nelson Chun, who wades into the chest-deep water to harvest the sausage-linked lotus roots by clipping them with his toes! Margaret Loo comes to harvest wild ferns served at the exclusive banquets at the Mauna Kea Beach Resort. Seiko Kaneshiro is perhaps the most famous taro farmer because of his poi factory that produces "Ono Ono Waipio Brand Taro." Another old-timer is Charlie Kawashima, who still grows taro the old-fashioned way, as an art form passed from father to son. He harvests the taro with an o'o (digging stick) and after it's harvested cuts off the corm and sticks the huli (stalk) back into the ground, where it begins to sprout again in a week or so.

Harrison Kanakoa, deceased, mostly lived topside because of failing health in his later years. He was born in a house built in 1881 near Kauiki Heiau, one of the biggest and most powerful heiau in the valley. Harrison loved to "talk story," relating tales of when his family was the keeper of the heiau. When he was a small boy his grandfather took him to the heiau, where he rolled away an entrance stone to reveal a small tunnel that went deep inside. He followed his grandfather in a ways, but his child's courage failed, and he turned away and ran out. He said his grandfather yelled after him something in Hawaiian like "You coward," and refused to show him that place again. In 1952, C.H. Brewer, a very powerful sugarcane company in this area, bulldozed the heiau and planted macadamia nuts on top. The trees still bear nuts, but the heiau was obliterated.

ACTIVITIES

Driving
The road leading down to Waipio is outrageously steep and narrow. If you attempt it in a regular car, it'll eat you up and spit out your bones. More than 20 fatalities have occurred since people started driving it, and it has only been paved since the early 1970s. You'll definitely need 4WD, low range, to make it; downhill vehicles yield to those coming up. There is very little traffic on the road except when surfing conditions are good. Sometimes Waipio Beach has the first good waves of the season and this brings out the surfers en masse. **Waipio Valley Shuttle,** tel.

(808) 775-7121, has its office at Waipio Valley Artworks in Kukuihaele. They use comfortable air-conditioned 4WD vans for their 90-minute descent and tour. The tour costs $30. Buy your ticket at the Artworks, and then proceed to the Waipio Overlook from where the vans leave every hour on the hour. This is the tamest, but safest, way to enjoy the valley. If you decide to hike down or stay overnight, you can make arrangements for the van to pick you up or drop you off for an added cost. The same company also offers a trip to the top of Mauna Kea.

Hiking
If you have the energy, the hike down the paved section of the road is just over one mile, but it's a tough mile coming back up! Expect to take three to four hours down and back, adding more time to swim or look around.

The **Waipio Valley Aqueduct Trail,** which follows the clearly marked water system of the recently defunct Hamakua Sugar Plantation and skirts the rear of the valley where the natural flora is still thriving, has just been opened up to the public. It's not an overly vigorous hike, as the trail is rather flat (except for one spot that requires scrambling down a ladder). In some places, the sugar company followed an irrigation system laid by native Hawaiians more than 1,000 years ago that watered ancient terraces growing wetland taro.

Waipio Beach
Stretching over a mile, this is the longest black-sand beach on the island. The surf here can be very dangerous and there are many riptides. During the summer the sands drift to the western side of the valley; in winter they drift back east. If there is strong wave action, swimming is not advised. It is, however, a good place for surfing and fishing.

Horseback Riding
For a fun-filled experience guaranteed to please, try horseback riding with **Waipio Na'alapa Trail Rides,** tel. (808) 775-0419. Sherri Hannum, a young mother of three who moved to Waipio from Missouri almost 30 years ago, and her husband Mark, own and operate the trail rides. Both are enamored with the valley, and as fate would have it, have become the old-timers of Waipio.

They gladly accept the charge of keeping the ancient accounts and oral traditions alive. The adventure begins when Mark picks you up at 9:30 a.m. at Waipio Valley Artworks in Kukuihaele. You begin a 40-minute 4WD ride down to the ranch, which gives you an excellent tour of the valley in and of itself, since their spread is even deeper into the valley than the end of the line for the commercial valley tour! En route you cross three or four streams, as Mark tells you some of the history and lore of Waipio. When you arrive, Sherri has the horses ready to go. Sherri knows the trails of Waipio intimately. She puts you in the saddle of a sure-footed Waipio pony and spends all day telling you legends and stories while leading you to waterfalls, swimming holes, grave sites, and finally a *heiau.* The lineage of the horses of Waipio dates from the late 1700s. They were gifts to the *ali'i* from Capt. George Vancouver. Waipio was especially chosen because the horses were easy to corral and could not escape. Today, more than 150 semi-wild progeny of the original stock roam the valley floor. Technically, you should bring your own lunch for the ride, since you can't always count on the fruits of Waipio to be happening. But if they are, Sherri will point them out and you can munch to your heart's delight. Tours lasting 2.5 hours cost $75 and start at 9:30 a.m. and 1 p.m. Full-day tours can be arranged, but a minimum of two and a maximum of four riders is required. Sorry, no children under 12 or riders weighing more than 230 pounds. Go prepared with long pants, shoes, and swimsuit. A ride with Sherri isn't just an adventure; it's an experience with memories that will last a lifetime.

Wagon Tour
Waipio Valley Wagon Tour, P.O. Box 1340, Honokaa, HI 96727, tel. (808) 775-9518, owned and operated by Peter Tolin, is the newest and one of the most fun-filled ways of exploring Waipio. This surrey-type wagon, which can hold about a dozen people, is drawn by two Tennessee mules. The fascinating 1.5-hour tours depart five times daily at 9 a.m., 10:30 a.m., 12:30 p.m., 2 p.m., and 4 p.m. Cost is $35, children under 12 half price, children two and under free. To participate, make reservations 24 hours in advance. Then check in 30 minutes before departure at the Waipio Overlook, where a 4WD

vehicle will come to fetch you. The overlook also has a pay phone from which you can call the Wagon Tour to see if there is last-minute room for you, but a space is definitely not guaranteed. Lunch is not included, but if you bring your own, you can walk down to the beach and have a great picnic. The original wagon was built by Peter himself from parts that he ordered from the Mainland. Unfortunately, every part that he ordered broke down over a nine-month trial period. Peter had all new parts made at a local machine shop, only three times thicker than the originals! Now that the wagon has been *Waipionized,* the problems have ceased. The only high-tech aspect of the wagon ride is a set of small loudspeakers through which Peter narrates the history, biology, and myths of Waipio as you roll along.

Aloha Distress
In the summer of 1992, the Bishop Museum requested an environmental impact survey on Waipio Valley because the frequency of visitors to the valley had increased tremendously. Old-time residents were complaining not only about the overuse of the valley, but about the loss of their quiet and secluded lifestyle. Sherri Hannum of Waipio Na'alapa Trail Rides and Peter Tolin of Waipio Valley Wagon Tour cooperated fully, and did their best to help in the preservation and reasonable use of one of Hawaii's grandest valleys. They have complied with the regulations imposed by the Bishop Museum even when it meant a significant financial loss to themselves. Because of the impact study, the commercial tours are not allowed to go to the beach area, which is now open to foot traffic only, and the valley is **closed on Sunday** to commercial tours. Other tour operators, resentful of the Bishop Museum, were not as cooperative as Sherri and Peter, and apparently have put personal gain above the preservation of Waipio.

There also seems to be some kind of socioethnic battle evolving in the valley. Long-term residents, mostly but not exclusively of Hawaiian decent, are staking out the valley as their own and have largely withdrawn the spirit of *aloha* from the melanin-challenged visitors to their wonderful valley. Their dissatisfaction is not wholly without basis, as some who have come to the valley have been quite disrespectful, trespassing on private property, threatening to sue landowners for injuries caused by themselves, or finding themselves stuck in a river that no one in their right mind would try to cross in a vehicle. Many wonderful, open, and loving people still live in the valley, but don't be too surprised to get the *stink face* treatment from others. Be respectful and stay on public property. If the sign says *Kapu* or Keep Out, believe it. It is everyone's right to walk along the beach, the switchback that goes to Waimanu, and generally waterways. These are traditional free lands in Hawaii open to all people, and they remain so. It's really up to you. With proper treatment by visitors Waipio's mood will change again, and *aloha* will return.

STAYING IN THE VALLEY

Camping in Waipio

For camping in Waipio Valley you must get a permit from the Kamehameha Schools Bernice Pauahi Bishop Estate, Paauilo Office, tel. (808) 776-1104. The office is located about 15 minutes from the overlook in Paauilo. To get the permit, you must call well in advance, giving the dates requested (four day maximum) and number of people in your party. You will be faxed an application, and *all adult members* in your party must sign a "liability waiver" (parents or legal guardians must sign for any children) before the permit will be granted. Also, you must provide your own "Port-A-Potty" (yes it's true), that you must remove when you leave. A small "camper style" potty, available in Hawaii, is sufficient. Camping is allowed in designated areas only on the east side of Waipio Stream. Many hikers and campers have stayed in Waipio overnight without a permit and have had no problem, but it is illegal! Remember, however, that most of the land, except for the beach, *is* privately owned.

Accommodations

Waipio has a hotel! Owned and operated by Tom Araki, it was built by his dad to serve as a residence for teachers who came to teach at the local school, and was later used for instructors of a nearby, now defunct, Peace Corps training camp. You'll find eight basic but clean rooms. Light is provided by kerosene lamps, and you must bring your own food to prepare in a communal kitchen. Tom, well into his 80s, is a treasure house of information about Waipio, and a "character" who's more interested in tending his taro patch, telling stories, and drinking wine than he is in running a hotel. His philosophy, which has enabled him to get along with everyone from millionaires to hippies, is a simple "live and let live." The **Waipio Hotel** has become known and it's even fashionable to stay there. For reservations, write Tom Araki, 25 Malama Pl., Hilo, HI 96720, or call Tom down in Waipio Valley at tel. (808) 775-0368. Expect to pay about $20 per person. Budget.

Ever fantasized about running off to a tropical island and living a life of "high" adventure? *The* most secluded accommodation in all of Hawaii is **The Treehouse,** Box 5086, Honokaa, HI 96727, tel. (808) 775-7160, owned and operated by Linda Beech. The Treehouse is located deep in Waipio Valley on three acres of land completely surrounded by holdings of the Bishop Museum. To get there, Linda will fetch you from topside in a sturdy 4WD, and ferry you across at least five rivers until you come to her idyllic settlement at the foot of Papala Waterfall. Tumbling 2,000 feet over the towering *pali,* the falls provide the water for a hydroelectric power plant (solar backup) that runs everything from stereos to ceiling fans. Linda purchased the land about 30 years ago after returning to Hawaii, the place of her birth. She has had a most interesting life, traveling throughout the Orient. In Japan she was a famous personality starring in a very popular and long running TV sitcom entitled, *"Ao Mei No Tokyo Nikki"* (Blue Eyes Tokyo Diary).

After much deliberation, Linda selected master boatbuilders Eric Johnson and Steven Oldfather to build the Treehouse in 1972, and chose her 65-foot monkeypod tree as its perch. Using an ingenious "three pin anchoring system," the Treehouse gently sways like a moored boat, allowing the tree to grow without causing structural damage. It has survived 120 mph winds and has proven to be a most "seaworthy" treehouse. Eric Johnson came back some years ago to reroof the structure, and found it to be still square and level. Of this structure he says, "Here I pinnacled." Both men have given up professional boatbuilding and have become very famous on the Big Island as custom home builders.

The Treehouse is fascinating, but quite basic. As you climb the steps, the first landing holds a flushing toilet. Inside, the Treehouse is plain teak wood and screened windows, not much more. It's very comfortable with island-style furnishings and provides a full kitchen and all utensils, but it is not luxurious. The luxury is provided by Waipio itself, flooding the interior with golden light and the perfume of tropical flowers wafting on the breeze. All around, the melodious songs of indigenous birds and the ever-present wind and cascading waters serenades day and night. If you don't wish to perch high in a tree, Linda also offers **The Hale,** an earthbound but commodious structure where the walls of glass and screen open to the magnificent still-life surrounding you. All guests are invited to use a traditional Japanese *ofuro,* a hot tub, brought back by Linda from her 20-year residence in Japan. Remember, however, that The Treehouse is a vacation rental, not a B&B—you should bring all of your own food and do your own light housekeeping. Because The Treehouse is so remote, it is necessary to make reservations well in advance. The Treehouse can handle two "very friendly" couples; rates are $200 per day for two or more nights or $250 for one night, and $25 per additional person over 12 years old. Rates for The Hale, which can sleep up to six, are the same. A 50% deposit is requested with the reservation, and a six-week cancellation notice prior to arrival is necessary for a refund. Nature still rules Waipio, and about five days per year the streams are flooded, making it impossible to get either in or out. If you can't get in, a prompt refund will be made, and if you're lucky enough to be marooned, complimentary lodging and food will be cordially provided for the duration of your stay. Expensive.

WAIMAU VALLEY, CAMPING AND HIKING

The hike down to Waipio and over the *pali* to Waimanu Valley 12 miles away is one of the top three treks in Hawaii. You must be fully prepared for camping and in excellent condition to attempt this hike. Also, water from the streams and falls is not always good for drinking due to irrigation and cattle grazing topside; bring purification tablets or boil or filter it to be safe. To get to Waimanu Valley, a switchback trail leads over the *pali* about 100 yards inland from Waipio Beach.

The beginning of the switchback trail has a post with a painting that reads Warning Menehune. Waimanu was bought by the State of Hawaii about 12 years ago, and they are responsible for trail maintenance. The trail ahead is rough, as you go up and down about 14 gulches before reaching Waimanu. At the ninth gulch is a trail shelter. Finally, below is Waimanu Valley, half the size of Waipio but more verdant, and even wilder because it has been uninhabited for a longer time. Cross Waimanu Stream in the shallows where it meets the sea. For drinking water (remember to treat it), walk along the west side of the *pali* until you find a likely waterfall. To stay overnight in Waimanu Valley you must have a (free) camping permit available through the Division of Forestry and Wildlife, P.O. Box 4849, Hilo, HI 96721, tel. (808) 974-4221, open Tues.-Fri. 8 a.m.-4 p.m., Monday 10 a.m.-4 p.m. Your length of stay is limited to seven days and six nights. Each of the nine designated campsites has a fireplace and a composting outhouse. Carry out what you carry in!

Early this century, because of economic necessity brought on by the valley's remoteness, Waimanu was known for its *okolehau* (moonshine). Solomon, one of the elders of the community at the time, decided that Waimanu had to diversify for the good of its people. He decided to raise domesticated pigs introduced by the Chinese, who roasted them with spices in rock ovens as a great delicacy. Solomon began to raise and sell the pigs commercially, but when he died, out of respect, no one wanted to handle his pigs, so they let them run loose. The pigs began to interbreed with feral pigs, and after a while there were so many pigs in Waimanu that they ate all the taro, bananas, and breadfruit. The porkers' voracious appetites caused a famine that forced the last remaining families of Waimanu to leave in the late 1940s. Most of the trails that you will encounter are made by wild-pig hunters who still regularly go after Solomon's legacy.

According to oral tradition the first *kahuna lapa'au* (healing doctor) of Hawaii was from Waimanu Valley. His disciples crossed and recrossed Waipio Valley, greatly influencing the development of the area. Some of the *heiau* in Waipio are specifically dedicated to the healing of the human torso; their origins are traced to the healing *kahuna* of Waimanu.

M.G.L. DOMENY DE RIENZI

PUNA

The Puna District, south of Hilo on the southeast coast, was formed from rivers of lava spilling from Mauna Loa and Kilauea again and again over the last million years or so. The molten rivers stopped only when they hit the sea, where they fizzled and cooled, forming a chunk of semiraw land that bulges into the Pacific—marking the state's easternmost point at **Cape Kumukahi.** These titanic lava flows have left phenomenal reminders of their power. **Lava Tree State Monument** was once a rainforest whose giant trees were covered with lava, like hot dogs dipped in batter. The encased wood burned, leaving a hollow stone skeleton. You can stroll through this lichen-green rock forest before you head farther east into the brilliant sunshine of the coast. Little-traveled side roads take you past a multitude of orchid, anthurium, and papaya farms, oases of color in a desert of solid black lava. A lighthouse sits atop Cape Kumukahi, and to the north an ancient paved trail passes beaches where no one ever goes.

Southward is a string of popular beaches—some white, some black. You can camp, swim, surf, or just play in the water to your heart's delight. Villages have gas and food, and all along the coast you can visit natural areas where the sea tortured the hot lava into caves, tubes, arches, and even a natural bathtub whose waters are flushed and replenished by the sea. There are historical sites where petroglyphs tell vague stories from the past, and where generations of families placed the umbilical cords of their newborns into manmade holes in the rock. On Puna's south coast are remains of ancient villages, including Kamoamoa where you can camp. The park **Visitors Center** that used to stand just before the beginning of Chain of Craters Road burned down in the summer of 1989 when lava surged across the road, severing this eastern gateway to Volcanoes National Park. (The road is still closed, with no opening scheduled for the near future.) The **Hawaii Belt Road** (Rt. 11) is a corridor cutting through the center of Puna. It goes through the highlands to Volcanoes National Park, passing well-established villages and scattered housing developments as new as the lava on which they precariously sit. Back in these hills, new-wave gardeners grow "Puna Butter" *pakalolo,* as wild and raunchy as its name. On the border of Puna and the Kau District to the south is **Hawaii Volcanoes National Park.** Here the goddess Pele resides at Kilauea Caldera, center of one of the world's most active volcanoes.

ROUTE 130 AND THE SOUTHEAST COAST

The most enjoyable area in the Puna District is the southeast coast, with its beaches and points of natural and historical interest. If you take Rt. 130 south from Keaau, in about 12 miles you pass **Pahoa.** Like Keaau, Pahoa is primarily a crossroads. You can continue due south on Rt. 130 to the seaside villages of **Kaimu** and **Kalapana,** where Rt. 130 used to join coastal Rt. 137, feeding into Chain of Craters Road before much of this area was buried by lava flows. Along Rt. 130, about halfway between Pahoa and Kaimu, look for a small, unobtrusive sign that reads Scenic Overlook. Pull off and walk toward the sea until you find four hot steam vents. Many local people use them as natural saunas.

You might go directly east from Pahoa along Rt. 132. This lovely, tree-lined country road takes you past **Lava Tree State Monument,** which shouldn't be missed, and then branches northeast, intersecting Rt. 137 and terminating at **Cape Kumukahi.** If this seems *too* far out of the way, head down **Pohoiki Road,** just past Lava Tree. You bypass a controversial geothermal power station, then reach the coast at **Isaac Hale Beach Park.** From there, Rt. 137 heads southwest down the coast to Kalapana, passing the best Puna beaches en route. Fortunately for you, this area of Puna is one of those places where no matter which way you decide to go, you really can't go wrong.

KEAAU

Keaau, though technically not in Puna, is the first town south of Hilo (10 miles) on Rt. 11, and although pleasant enough, it's little more than a Y in the road. At the junction of Rt. 11 (Hawaii Belt Rd.) and Rt. 130 is **Keaau Town Center,** a small shopping mall with a handful of variety stores, a laundromat, a post office, restaurants, and a Bank of America. Here, the Sure Save Supermarket has not only groceries but plenty of sundries and a decent camera department, along with a public fax service.

Note

Route 11 (Hawaii Belt Rd.) splits in Keaau and passes through the high mountain villages of Kurtistown, Mountain View, Glenwood, and Volcano, then enters Hawaii Volcanoes National Park. For a description of these villages see below.

Food

The local **Dairy Queen,** in the Keaau Town Center, not only makes malts and sundaes but serves breakfast, lunch, and dinner. Plate specials, burgers, and sandwiches like a Reuben with french fries go for $4.95. For those who want to try an island treat like crackseed or shave ice, the center's **Kaeo Krack Seed** is open daily except Sunday 9 a.m.-5 p.m. Also in the shopping center is **Keaau Natural Foods,** tel. (808) 329-3111, with a large stock of organic food items, herbs, and grains but no juice or snack bar. However, pre-made sandwiches from the deli case are always available. Have a look at their bulletin board for information on alternative happenings in the community. Open Mon.-Fri. 9 a.m.-8 p.m., Saturday 9 a.m.-9 p.m., and Sunday 10 a.m.-5 p.m. Have a beer while you wait for your laundry to wash at the **Suds and Duds** laundromat. *Pu pu,* snacks, and simple meals are also available. The bar is open Mon.-Sat. 11 a.m.-9 p.m. with happy hour 3-6 p.m. weekdays and all day Saturday.

Keaau Cafe, tel. (808) 966-6758, is basically a walk-up window that offers a variety of meat and vegetable *bento,* with hardly anything more than $7.50. With only two little tables inside, the **Keaau Chop Suey House,** tel. (808) 966-7573, is next door with everything on their menu costing less than $6, including several vegetarian dishes.

A few hundred yards down Rt. 130 heading toward Pahoa, you'll see **Verna's Drive-In,** which serves plate lunches. Behind that is **Chief's Pizza.**

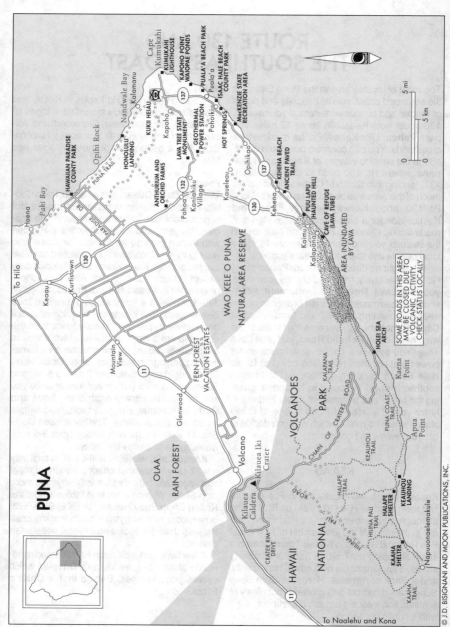

© J.D. BISIGNANI AND MOON PUBLICATIONS, INC.

PAHOA AND VICINITY

You can breeze through this "one-street" town, but you won't regret stopping if even for a few minutes. A raised wooden sidewalk passing false-front shops is fun to walk along to get a feeling of the last century. Most of the shops lining it are family-run fruit and vegetable stands supplied by local gardeners. Selections depend upon whether the old pickup truck started and made it to town that day. At one time Pahoa boasted *the* largest sawmill in America. Its buzz saw ripped ohia railway ties for the Santa Fe and other railroads. It was into one of these ties that the *golden spike* uniting the East and West coasts of the Mainland was driven. Many local people earned their livelihood from ohia charcoal that they made and sold all over the island until it was made obsolete by the widespread use of kerosene and gas introduced in the early 1950s. Pahoa's commercial heart went up in flames in 1955. Along the main street was a tofu factory that had a wood-fired furnace. The old fellow who owned the factory banked his fires as usual before he went home for the night. Somehow, they got out of control and burned all the way down to the main alley dividing the commercial district. The only reason the fire didn't jump the alley was because a papaya farmer happened to be around and had a load of water on the back of his truck, which he used to douse the buildings and save the town.

Pahoa is attempting to become part of the *Main Street U.S.A. Project,* which will protect and revitalize its commercial center and bring new life to vintage buildings like the Akebono Theater, where classic movies are once again being shown. Pahoa has one of the highest concentrations of old buildings still standing in Hawaii that are easily accessible. Although it has been bypassed by a new road, make sure to enter the town and stroll along the tiny back roads. The town is attempting to become the anthurium capital of the world, and they have a good start on it. In virtually every garden, surrounded by distinctive lava-rock walls, you'll see black shade mesh under which are magnificent specimens of the usually red flowers, plus plenty of white ones, a few green, and even black anthuriums.

Lava Tree State Monument

In 1790, slick, fast-flowing pahoehoe lava surged through this ohia forest, covering the tree trunks from the ground to about a 12-foot level. The moisture inside the trees cooled the lava, forming a hardened shell. At the same time, tremors and huge fissures cracked the earth in the area. When the eruption ended, the still-hot lava drained away through the fissures, leaving the encased tree trunks standing like sentinels. The floor of the forest is so smooth in some areas that the lava seems like asphalt. Each lava tree has its own personality; some resemble totem poles, and it doesn't take much imagination to see old, craggy faces staring back at you. The most spectacular part of the park is near the entrance. Immense trees loom over cavernous cracks *(puka)* in the earth and send their roots, like stilled waterfalls, tumbling down into them. To get to Lava Tree, take Rt. 132 east from Pahoa for three miles and look for the well-marked entrance on the left. Brochures are available as you enter. Drinking water is not available.

Cape Kumukahi

It's fitting that Kumukahi means "First Beginning" since it is the easternmost point of Hawaii and was recognized as such by the original Polynesian settlers. Follow Rt. 132 past Lava Tree for about 10 miles until it hits the coast, where a lighthouse sits like an exclamation point. Along the way, get an instant course in volcanology: you can easily chart the destructive and regenerative forces at work on Hawaii. At the five-mile marker an HVB Warrior points out the lava flow of 1955. Tiny plants give the lava a greenish cast, and shrubs are already eating into it, turning it to soil. Papaya orchards grow in the raw lava of an extensive flat basin. The contrast between the black, lifeless earth and the vibrant green trees is startling. In the center of the flatland rises a cinder cone, a caldera of a much older mini-volcano unscathed by the modern flows; it is gorgeous with lush vegetation. An HVB Warrior points out the lava flow of 1960, and you can see at a glance how different it was from the flow of five years earlier. When Rt. 132 intersects Rt. 137, go straight ahead east down a paved road for two miles to the Cape Kumukahi Lighthouse. People in these parts swear that on the fateful night in 1960 when the nearby village of Kapoho was consumed by the lava flow, an old woman (a favorite guise of Madame Pele) came to town begging for food and was turned away by everyone. She next went to the lighthouse asking for help, and was cordially treated by the lighthouse keeper. When the flow was at its strongest, it came within yards of the lighthouse and then miraculously split, completely encircling the structure but leaving it unharmed as the flow continued out to sea for a considerable distance.

Accommodations

Out behind the Paradise Cafe is the **Pahoa Inn,** tel. (808) 965-0066, a one-time house of ill repute. Japanese entertainment troupes used to lodge here while performing at one of three major theaters in town. The hotel has 14 rooms, a quiet courtyard filled with flowers and cacti, and a Japanese *ofuro* which is now an outside bath painted by a local artist to look like the inside of an aquarium. The classically designed redwood structure is in remarkably good shape. Monthly rates only are $250-300 including utilities. Shared bathrooms are clean and newly painted but basic. No reservations are accepted because of the limited number of rooms. Budget.

Right downtown, occupying the second floor of a building erected in 1910, is the **Village Inn,** tel. (808) 965-6444. A stairway with brass hand rail leads to the second floor; as you ascend imagine how many others have grasped that very rail. You're greeted at the top by Koko—the resident parrot and king of his big cage—your musical entertainment during your stay here. This small hotel has five rooms, all with cable TV, lace curtains, and white wicker furniture like grandma used to have on her porch. Other furniture is reminiscent of the '30s and '40s and ceiling fans help cool the rooms. While simple, everything is neat and clean. Rooms start at $30 and go up from there; some share a bathroom. Owner Bill Male runs the **Whimseys** gift shop on the first floor. It's more like an antique shop; his stock is always changing but you can find such items as vintage jewelry, Hawaiian artifacts and stoneware, glassware, and aloha shirts. Budget.

Pahoa Natural Groceries rents out **The Bamboo House,** $45 d first night, $35 three nights or more, with rates for four people, just a minute's walk from the store. Small, basic, and clean, it features a bedroom with a queen-size bed, foldout couch, private bath, and cable color TV. Write the Bamboo House, P.O. Box 1429, Pahoa, HI 96778; or phone the health food store at tel. (808) 965-8322. A 25% deposit is required. Inexpensive.

Whittaker's B&B, P.O. Box 1324, Pahoa, HI 96778, tel. (808) 965-7015, offers two bedrooms with private baths in a new home located in the Puna rainforest. Each room, large enough for a small family, rents for $50 double, children under 12 free. Inexpensive.

Food

At the Pahoa Village Center is a **Dairy Queen,** open daily 7 a.m.-8:30 p.m. for breakfast, lunch, and dinner. They serve everything from banana splits to chicken, pizza, and plate lunches. Just down the street is **Pahoa Chop Suey,** a down-home restaurant where you can eat cheaply; and farther down is **Luquin's Place,** open daily 11 a.m.-9 p.m., tel. (808) 965-9990, a reasonably priced Mexican restaurant that offers enchiladas, burritos, tacos, and combination platters for $5-7. It now serves drinks; margaritas are a house specialty.

A block away is **Mady's Cafe Makana,** tel. (808) 965-0608, open every day except Sunday 7:30 a.m.-3 p.m. Mady's is a full cafe and boutique. Pareus are one of the mainstays in the boutique and they run $7-35. Women's toiletries, candles, greeting cards, and carved wooden items are also sold. After shopping, stop in at the cafe for a bite to eat. Nearly everything is under $5. Fruit smoothies for $2.25, a bowl of hearty lentil soup for $3.95, a tamale for $1.75, a samosa for $3.35, or a veggie croissant for $2.75 are samplings from the menu. All choices are organic, healthy, and nutritious. Mady's also supplies baked goods and deli sandwiches to some of the health food stores in the area.

Try **Naung Mai Thai Food,** tel. (808) 965-8186, open daily for lunch and dinner, where you can dine on Thai spring rolls for $4.95; red, green, or yellow curried shrimp, chicken, or beef for $8.95; or a hearty bowl of Thai chicken-coconut soup for $6.95. A full vegetarian selection, including tofu and eggplant curry for $5.95 and rice and noodles for $7.95, completes the menu.

One of the best places to eat in Pahoa is **Paradise Cafe,** tel. (808) 965-0066, open daily 7 a.m.-2 p.m., breakfast until noon, owned and operated by Dave and Carrie Marry. Dave has a remarkable knowledge of Pahoa's history that he is willing to share if time permits. Breakfast is served with hash browns, rice, and buttermilk biscuits, and includes eggs with bacon for $5.50, two eggs with fresh catch priced daily, and their very famous hollandaise sauce that tops eggs Benedict. One of the best deals is *huevos rancheros* with tortillas, beans, and salsa for $5.95. The lunch menu is basic cheeseburgers, turkey sandwiches, and the like, all priced under $6.50. The menu changes daily, but you can count on fresh fish, tender steaks, and pasta for $8.95 that can be covered with sun-dried tomatoes, olive oil, parmesan, and fresh basil. They also take care of the vegetarians with tofu scramble and a daily veggie special.

Pahoa Sports Lounge, tel. (808) 964-7488, features theme nights like jam night on Wednesday, Hawaiian on Thursday, rock and roll on Friday, and country western on Saturday. There are TVs everywhere, as they try to cover all the big sporting events. A barbecue grill serves up complimentary *pu pu* on Friday and Saturday evenings. The main koa wood-topped bar is the heart of the lounge; the small back bar, looking out over the garden, opens when they are really busy. Out back is a tiny bamboo garden and a game room with regular and electronic darts, foosball, and a pool table. This place has been cleaned up and rejuvenated, creating a place where you can have a good time.

Next door is **Koho Okazuya,** open from 7 a.m., a window restaurant serving continental breakfast for $2.60 and a variety of lunches like pineapple chicken, beef stew, and hamburger patties. A minute farther down the elevated sidewalk is **Da Store,** with groceries, a deli case, beer, and liquor.

Let your mind and stomach be soothed with cosmic vibrations and libations at **Huna Ohana,** open daily 8 a.m.-5 p.m., Sunday 9 a.m.-1 p.m., tel. (808) 965-9661. The metaphysical bookstore (open until 6 p.m.) and cafe is owned and operated by Dawn Hurwitz. Vegetarian breakfast dishes include egg soufflé or tofu scramble served with cottage potatoes and multigrain toast at $3.95; bagels and cream cheese for $1.75;

and an assortment of croissants and blueberry muffins. Lunch brings veggie sandwiches for $3.50, filling garden burgers (a blend of mushrooms, onions, rolled oats, lowfat mozzarella, brown rice, cottage cheese, eggs, cheddar, bulgur wheat, walnuts, and spices) for $4.95, or filling tempeh burger made with ginger teriyaki sauce for $4.95. To get those cosmic vibes kicked into high gear, order a cup of espresso, mocha latte, or cappuccino, choose a likely tome from the bookstore section, and kick back on an overstuffed couch or outside in the garden area.

Yo Pizza, tel. (808) 965-7033, open daily except Monday 11 a.m.-10 p.m., uses homemade sauces and dough to make small, medium, and large traditional pizzas costing $4.90-14.90. They also have Italian Caesar salads ($4.50), garden salad ($2.75), garlic bread ($1.50), and hot, rich cappuccino and espresso, perfect with slices of homemade pie. Lunch can be sub sandwiches ($4.50), or you can dine on dinner specials like lasagna or spaghetti and meatballs for $6.50. The decor is "basic pizza parlor," redolent of olive oil and garlic.

A newer place in town is **Paolo's** Italian restaurant, open Tues.-Sun. 5:30-9 p.m. Dine inside at tables topped with blue and white checkered tablecloths, or have a seat in the patio outside. Start with an appetizer, like a bowl of minestrone soup for $2.95 or fresh mozzarella antipasto for $6.95, and follow that with pasta ravioli with spinach and ricotta for $7.95 or pasta with prawns for $12.95. Their special entrees, like chicken Marcella at $12.95, cioppino for $14.95, or pizza à la palios (gourmet pizza Italian style with capers, anchovies, tomato, oregano, and mozzarella) for $14.95, might be more to your taste. To round out the meal, have a cup of espresso or a caffe latte.

Shopping and Services

When you pull into Pahoa you are greeted by the **Pahoa Village Center,** a small shopping center where you'll find a laundromat, a video store, and the Dairy Queen. A minute down the road is the full-service **Pahoa Cash and Carry** grocery store, 7-Eleven, and the Pahoa Casherette, which are enough for any supplies or incidentals that you may need. Right next to the Pahoa Village Center is the **Pahoa flea market** for reasonably priced secondhand goods.

Pahoa Natural Groceries, tel. (808) 965-8322, open weekdays 9 a.m.-9 p.m., Sunday 9 a.m.-6 p.m., specializing in organic food items, is one of the finest health food stores on the Big Island. They have an excellent selection of fresh veggies, organic grains, herbs and minerals, deli items, and a very good bakery selection. There's a kitchen on premises, so what you get is not only healthful but very fresh.

Adjacent is **The Emporium,** tel. (808) 965-6634, open daily 10 a.m.-6 p.m., with a small but excellent selection of jewelry, Guatemalan clothing, Balinese batik, Yucatán hammocks, gifts, magazines, and cards. The Emporium also displays artwork, some by local artists, and a colorful selection of rugs. Their shirts and dresses, all cotton and rayon, cost $25-50. Some of the clothing is either designed or handmade here in Puna. The back room displays a profusion of these vibrant rainbow-colored clothes.

Hale Mana, tel. (808) 965-7783, open Mon.-Fri. 9 a.m.-5 p.m. or by appointment, adjacent to the health food store, is an acupuncture and massage clinic. The acupuncturists are Françoise Hesselink, Jocelyn Mayeux, and Rhonda Ashby. Relax as you lie on the table and breezes blow through the vintage rooms. Let one of these fine practitioners energize and revitalize your spirit and put spring back into your aching muscles.

For anyone interested in body art, **Kaleidoscope** tattoo parlor is a place to check out. Actually a club, the $10 entry fee allows you to hang out with others who have similarly adorned themselves and to attend their periodic parties. Joseph Gonsalves (a.k.a. TJ, a.k.a. Tattoo Joe) does only a few tattoos here but mostly makes house calls. Also in this shop you can pick up bullwhips, daggers, canes, handcarved chairs, and other such eccentric items.

If a permanent memento from the tattoo artist isn't what you had in mind, try next door at **Happily** antique shop for something more ordinary, like jewelry, wooden bowls, baskets, and hats. Open daily 10 a.m.-5 p.m. except Sunday, this shop has been around a long time and is almost an institution in town.

Along the elevated boardwalk, are numerous shops for gifts and other diversions. At **Pacific Mystics,** a new-age shop, you can consult the tarot while browsing among books, crystals, local crafts, surfboards, and a cosmic smattering of clothes and sunglasses. They now have a health food section as well.

BEACHES, PARKS, AND CAMPGROUNDS

All of Puna's beaches, parks, and campgrounds lie along coastal Rt. 137 stretching for 20 miles from Pohoiki to Kamoamoa (recently wiped out by lava flow). Surfers, families, transients, even nude-sunbathing "buffs" have their favorite beaches along this southeast coast. For the most part, swimming is possible, but be cautious during high tide. There is plenty of sun, snorkeling sites, and good fishing, and the campgrounds are almost always available.

Pohoiki a.k.a. Isaac Hale County Beach Park

You can't miss this beach park located on Pohoiki Bay, at the junction of Rt. 137 and Pohoiki Road. Just look for a jumble of boats and trailers parked under the palms. At one time Pohoiki Bay served the Hawaiians as a canoe landing, then later became the site of a commercial wharf for the Puna Sugar Company. It remains the only boat launching area for the entire Puna Coast, used by pleasure boaters and commercial fishermen. Due to this dual role, it's often very crowded. Amenities include pavilions, restrooms, and a picnic area; potable water is not available. Camping is permitted with a county permit. Experienced surfers dodge the rip-current in the center of the bay, and swimming is generally good when the sea is calm. Pohoiki Bay is also one of the best scuba and snorkel sites on the island. Within walking distance of the salt-and-pepper beach are hot springs that bubble into lava sinks surrounded by lush vegetation. They're popular with tourists and residents, and provide a unique and relaxing way to wash away sand and salt. To find them, face away from the sea and turn left, then look for a small but well-worn path that leads through the jungle. The pools are warm, small, and tranquil. Harmless, tiny brine shrimp nibble at your toes while you soak.

MacKenzie State Recreation Area

This popular state park was named for forest ranger A.J. MacKenzie, highly regarded through-

the Puna Coast

out the Puna District and killed in the area in 1938. The park's 13 acres sit among a cool grove of ironwoods originally planted by MacKenzie. A portion of the old King's Hwy., scratched out by prisoners last century as a form of community service, bisects the area. Many people who first arrive on the Big Island hang out at MacKenzie until they can get their start. Consequently, the park receives its share of hard-core types, which has earned it a reputation for rip-offs. Mostly it's safe, but if you're camping, take precautions with your valuables. The entire coastline along MacKenzie is bordered by rugged black-lava seacliffs. Swimming is dangerous, but the fishing is excellent. Be extremely careful when beach-walking, especially out on the fingers of lava; over the years, people have been swept away by freak waves. MacKenzie Park is located along Rt. 137, two miles south of Isaac Hale. Picnic facilities are available, but there is no drinking water. A state permit is required for overnight camping.

Puala'a Beach Park
Quietly opened by the County of Hawaii on July 4, 1993, this lovely, 1.3-acre beach park (short on parking) was an ancient fishing village on the boundary of the *ahupua'a* of Leapao'o and Puala'a. Located along the *red road* between Kapoho and Opihikao, the park features a pool thermally heated to a perfect temperature. Some people use the pond to do watsu, a type of in-water massage. The swimming is safe except during periods of very high surf, when ocean water washes in. The park is perfect for families with young children. The pond is now watched over by a lifeguard, and bathrooms have been set up for your convenience.

Kehena
Kehena is actually two pockets of black-sand beach below a low seacliff. Entrance to the beach is marked only by a scenic pulloff on Rt. 137, about five miles south of MacKenzie; usually a half-dozen cars are parked there. At one time Kehena was very popular, and a stone staircase led down to the beach. In 1975 a strong earthquake jolted the area, breaking up the stairway and lowering the beach by three feet. Now access is via a well-worn path, but make sure to wear sneakers because the lava is rough. The ocean here is dangerous, and often pebbles and rocks whisked along by the surf can injure legs. Once down on the beach, head north for the smaller patch of sand, because the larger patch is open to the sea and can often be awash in waves. The black sand is hot, but a row of coconut palms provides shade. The inaccessibility of Kehena makes it a favorite "no-hassle" nude beach with many "full" sunbathers congregating here.

Note: Unfortunately, recent lava flows have completely covered the very popular **Kaimu Beach Park,** also known as Black Sand Beach, and **Harry K. Brown Beach Park.** Now, raw and rugged lava meets the sea to be slowly turned into beach parks for future generations.

KAIMU AND KALAPANA

Special Note

Kaimu and Kalapana have been annihilated by the advancing lava flow. For a full description of **Chain of Craters Road** and recent volcanic activity, see the following chapter on Hawaii Volcanoes National Park. Parts of the road are still open, but only *from* the park.

The Painted Church

Star of the Sea Catholic Church is a small but famous structure better known as "The Painted Church." An effort to save the historic church from the lava was mounted, and it has been moved. A brief history of the area asserts that the now-inundated Kalapana was a spiritual magnet for Roman Catholic priests. Old Spanish documents support evidence that a Spanish priest, crossing the Pacific from Mexico, actually landed very near here in 1555. Father Damien, famous priest of the Molokai Leper Colony, established a grass church about two miles north and conducted a school when he first arrived in the islands in 1864. The present church dates from 1928, when Father Everest Gielen began its construction. Like an inspired but much less talented Michelangelo, this priest painted the ceiling of the church, working mostly at night by oil lamp. Father Everest was transferred to Lanai in 1941, and the work wasn't completed until 1964, when Mr. George Heidler, an artist from Atlanta, Georgia, came to Kalapana and decided to paint the unfinished lower panels in the altar section. The artwork itself can only be described as gaudy but sincere. The colors are wild blues, purples, and oranges. The ceiling is adorned with symbols, portraits of Christ, the angel Gabriel, and scenes from the Nativity. Behind the altar, a painted perspective gives the impression that you're looking down a long hallway at an altar that hangs suspended in air. The church is definitely worth a few minutes at least.

End of the Road

Just near the lava-inundated village of Kalapana, Routes 130 and 137 come to an abrupt halt where Madame Pele has repaved the road with lava. At the end of the line you come to a barricaded area. Volcanic activity has continued virtually unabated here since January 1983, when lava fountains soared 1,500 feet into the sky and produced a cone more than 800 feet tall. The initial lava flow was localized at Pu'u O'o vent, but after dozens of eruptive episodes it shifted to Kupaianaha, which has continuously produced about half a million cubic yards of lava per day. Today it is mostly erupting once again from flank vents on Pu'u O'o. The lava flows eight miles to the sea, mostly through lava tubes. It has inundated almost 36.5 square miles, caused $61 million worth of property damage, and added more than 500 acres of new land to the Puna Coast-and it's still growing.

A sign strongly warns you against walking out onto the lava. Some hazards that you may encounter are brushfires, smoke, ash, and methane gas, which is extremely explosive. You can also fall through the thin-crusted lava into a tube

inside the Painted Church

which will immediately reduce you to a burnt offering to Pele and unceremoniously deposit your ashes into the sea! New lava can cut like broken glass, and molten lava can be flung through the air by steam explosions, especially near the coastline. Seacliffs collapse frequently, and huge boulders can be tossed several hundred feet into the air. The steam clouds contain minerals that can cause burning eyes, throat and skin irritations, and difficulty breathing.

If you are still intrigued, realize that you are on the most unstable piece of real estate on the face of the earth. For those maniacs, fools, adventurers, and thrill-seekers who just can't stay away, the walk to the sea takes about 25 minutes. Give yourself up for dead, and proceed. Follow the old roadbed, up and down, over the lava. When you can no longer discern the road, look off to your left and you'll see a large steam cloud rising. Pick your way to it, but don't get too close. Observers say that every day, huge chunks fall off into the sea in this area. As you look back at the mountain you can see heat waves rising from the land upon which you are standing. A camera with a zoom lens or a pair of binoculars accentuates this phenomenon. The whole mountain waves in front of you. As you walk closer to the sea, the lava cools and you can see every type there is: rope lava, lava toes, lava fingers. The tortured flow, which crinkles as you walk over it, has created many imaginative shapes: gargoyles, medieval faces, dolphins, and mythical creatures. At the coast, the lava pours into the sea, creating a white spume of steam lifting 200-300 feet into the air. No other place in the world gives you the opportunity to be the first person to tread upon the earth's newest land.

Accommodations

Kalani Honua Oceanside Eco-Resort, RR 2 Box 4500, Kehena Beach, HI 96778, tel. (808) 965-7828 or (800) 800-6886, fax (808) 965-9613, is a nonprofit, international conference and retreat center, a haven where people come when they truly want to get away from it all. The entrance is located a few miles northeast of Kalapana on Rt. 137 between mile markers 17 and 18. Look for a large Visitors Welcome sign and proceed until you see the office area and a gift and sundries shop. Depending upon the yearly schedule, they offer a variety of activities that include holistic massage, hula, meditation, yoga, and lei-making, for men, women, couples, and families. Contact them to find out what's happening when you'll be on the Big Island. The grounds have a botanical atmosphere, with a rain-fed swimming pool, hot tub, jacuzzi, assembly studios, classrooms, cottages with views of the ocean and cedar lodges with kitchen facilities. It's the only place along the Puna Coast that offers lodging and vegetarian fare. Rates are $45 s for a dorm room with shared bath, $60 s and $70 d for a private room with shared bath, $75 s and $85 d for a private room with private bath, $85 s and $95 d for a guest cottage. You can also camp for $15 a night. A blown conch shell calls you to breakfast at 8 a.m., lunch at noon, and dinner at 6 p.m. (nonguests welcome). The meals cost $7, $8, and $12 respectively, with a meal ticket pre-purchased at the office; or guests can purchase a "meal plan" for $25 which entitles you to all three. Lights go out at 10:30 p.m., but candles are provided for night owls. Kalani Eco-Resort is not for everyone, but if you are looking for unpretentious peace and quiet and healthful food, there's no better place on the island. E-mail: kh@ILHawaii.net; website: www.randm.com/kh.html. Moderate.

THE HAWAII BELT ROAD FROM HILO

Route 11 (Hawaii Belt Road) splits in Keaau and passes through several high mountain villages before entering Hawaii Volcanoes National Park. The Belt Road, although only two lanes, is straight, well-surfaced, and scrupulously maintained. At approximately 10-mile intervals are Kurtistown, Mountain View, Glenwood, and Volcano.

Fuku Bonsai Center, at 17-631 Volcano Hwy. (Belt Road), in Kurtistown behind the Post Office and B.J.'s Service Station, tel. (808) 982-9880, open weekdays 8 a.m.-4 p.m. and by appointment, will sell you diminutive bonsai plants that are agriculturally inspected and mailable to the Mainland.

Mountain View is a village of nurseries specializing in anthuriums. Many of them sport signs inviting you to a free tour. Along Rt. 11 is a minimart and **Verna's Too Snack Shop** serving plate lunches, burgers, and shakes. As you pass through, take a minute to explore the short sideroad into the village itself. Every house has a garden of ferns, flowers, and native trees. In the village is **Mt. View Bakery,** home of the famous stone cookies; and the **Mt. View Village Store,** which is fairly well supplied.

Look for a vintage plantation house painted-blue between mile markers 12 and 13. This is **Tinny Fisher's Antique Shop,** owned and op-

erated by Charles and Dorothy Wittig. What started as "yard sale treasures" about 10 years ago has turned into a unique curio, antique, and collectibles shop. Open daily except Monday, noon-6 p.m., the shop has all kinds of antiques and collectibles from Asia and Hawaii, including glass balls, Asian furniture, jewelry, and glassware galore. Tinny's also features a good Hawaiiana collection, with artifacts from the ancient days like *kukui* nut lamps, poi pounders, and stone knives.

Glenwood, between mile markers 19 and 20, offers a gas station and **Hirano's General Store** for basic provisions. A few minutes down the road you pass **Akatsuka Tropical Orchids and Flower Gardens,** tel. (808) 967-8234, open daily 8:30 a.m.-5 p.m., except major holidays. They offer a complimentary orchid to all visitors. If tour buses don't overflow the parking lot, stop in for a look at how orchids are grown or to use the clean restrooms.

Just before you enter Volcanoes National Park, a sign points to the right down a short side road to **Volcano Village** where you will find accommodations, restaurants, and shopping (see below). The Hawaii Belt Road continues southwest through **Kau,** the southernmost district of the Big Island, eventually arriving in Kona.

M.G.L. DOMENY DE RIENZI

HAWAII VOLCANOES NATIONAL PARK
INTRODUCTION

Hawaii Volcanoes National Park (HVNP) is an unparalleled experience in geological grandeur. The western end of the park is the summit of stupendous **Mauna Loa,** the most massive mountain on earth. The park's heart is **Kilauea Caldera,** encircled by 11 miles of **Crater Rim Drive.** At the park visitor center you can give yourself a crash course in geology while picking up park maps and information. Nearby is **Volcano House,** Hawaii's oldest hotel, which has hosted a steady stream of adventurers, luminaries, royalty, and heads of state ever since it opened its doors in the 1860s. Amidst all the natural wonders is a golf course—for those who want to boast they've done it all after hitting a sand wedge from a volcanic fissure. Just down the road is one of Hawaii's last remaining indigenous forests, providing the perfect setting for a bird sanctuary. Mauna Loa Road branches off Crater Rim Dr. and ends at a foot trail for

the hale and hearty who trek to the 13,679-foot summit.

The rim drive continues past steam vents, sulfur springs, and tortured fault lines that always seem on the verge of gaping wide and swallowing. You can peer into the maw of **Halemaumau Crater,** home of the fire goddess, Pele, and you'll pass **Hawaiian Volcano Observatory** (not open to public), which has been monitoring geologic activity since the turn of the century. Nearby is the **Thomas A. Jaggar Museum,** an excellent facility where you can educate yourself on the past and present volcanology of the park. A fantastic walk is **Devastation Trail,** a paved path across a desolate black lava field where gray, lifeless trunks of a suffocated forest lean like old gravestones. Within minutes is **Thurston Lava Tube,** a magnificent natural tunnel *"leid"* by amazingly vibrant fern grottoes at the entrance and exit.

The indomitable power of Volcanoes National Park is apparent to all who come here. Mark Twain, enchanted by his sojourn through Volcanoes in the 1860s, quipped, "The smell of sulfur is strong, but not unpleasant to a sinner." Amen brother! Wherever you stop to gaze, realize that you are standing on a thin skin of cooled lava in an unstable earthquake zone atop one of the world's most active volcanoes.

Established in 1916 as the 13th U.S. national park, HVNP now covers 377 square miles. Based on its scientific and scenic value, the park was named an International Biosphere Reserve by UNESCO in 1980, giving it greater national and international prestige.

Admission to the park is $10 per vehicle (good for multiple entries over a seven-day period), $15 for an annual permit, $5 for bicycle traffic and hikers, and free to those 62 and over with a Golden Age Passport or Golden Eagle Passport. These "passports" are available at the park headquarters for a one-time fee of $10 and are good at any national park in the United States.

For information about the park, write or call HVNP, P.O. Box 52, HNP, HI 96718-0052, tel. (808) 985-6000. For up-to-the-minute reports on volcanic activity, go to the Volcano Watch website at http://hvo.wr.usgs.gov/volcanowatch. Related information is also available at www.soest.hawaii.edu/GG/HCV andhttp://hvo.wr.usgs.gov.

Geologic History: Science Versus Madame Pele

The goddess Pele is an irascible old dame. Perhaps it's because she had such a bad childhood. All she wanted was a home of her own where she could house her family and entertain her lover, a handsome chief from Kauai. But her sea goddess sister, Namakaokaha'i, flooded her out wherever she went after Pele seduced her husband, and the pig god, Kama Pu'a, ravished Pele for good measure. So Pele finally built her love nest at Halemaumau Crater at the south end of Kilauea Caldera. Being a goddess obviously isn't as heavenly as one would think, and whenever the pressures of life get too much for Pele, she blows her stack. These tempestuous outbursts made Pele one of the most revered gods in the Hawaiian pantheon because her presence and might were so easily felt.

For a thousand years Pele was appeased by offerings of pigs, dogs, sacred *ohelo* berries (her favorite) and now and again an outcast man or two (never women) who would hopefully turn her energy from destruction to more comfortable pursuits. Also, if Pele was your family's personal goddess, your remains were sometimes allowed to be thrown into the fire pit as a sign of great respect. In the early 1820s, the chieftess Kapiolani, an ardent convert to Christianity, officially challenged Pele in an attempt to topple her like the other gods of old. Kapiolani climbed down into Pele's crater and ate the sacred *ohelo* berries, flagrantly violating the ageless *kapu*. She then took large stones and defiantly hurled them into the fire pit below while bellowing, "Jehovah is my God. It is He, not Pele, that kindled these flames."

Yet today, most residents, regardless of background, have an inexplicable reverence for Pele. The goddess has modernized her tastes, switching from *ohelo* to juniper berries that she prefers in liquid form as bottles of gin! The Volcano Post Office receives an average of three packages a week containing lava rocks taken by tourists as souvenirs (sometimes 30 per day). Some hold that Pele looks upon these rocks as her children and taking them from her is kidnapping. The accompanying letters implore the officials to return the rocks because ever since the offender brought them home, luck has been bad. The officials take the requests very seriously, returning the rocks with the customary peace offering: a bottle of gin. Many follow-up "thank you" letters have been written to express relief that the bad luck has been lifted. There is no reference in Hawaiian folklore to this phenomenon, although Hawaiians did hold certain rocks sacred. Park rangers will tell you that the idea of "the bad-luck rocks" was initiated a few decades back by a tour bus driver who became sick and tired of tourists getting his bus dirty by piling aboard their souvenirs. *Voilà!* Another ancient Hawaiian myth! Know, however, that the rocks in Hawaii Volcanoes National Park are protected by federal law, much meaner and more vindictive than Pele ever imagined being.

Pele is believed to take human form. She customarily appears before an eruption as a ravishing beauty or a withered old hag, often accompanied by a little white dog. She expects to

river of lava from
a recent flow

be treated cordially, and it's said that she will stand by the roadside at night hitching a ride. After a brief encounter, she departs and seems to mysteriously evaporate into the ether. Kindness on your part is the key; if you come across a strange woman at night, treat her well—it might not help, but it definitely won't hurt.

Eruptions

The first white man atop Kilauea was Rev. William Ellis, who scaled it in 1823. Until the 1920s, the floor of the caldera was exactly what people thought a volcano would be: a burning lake of fire. Then the forces of nature changed, and the fiery lava subsided and hardened over. Today, Kilauea is called the only "drive-in" volcano in the world, and in recent years has been one of the most active, erupting almost continuously since 1983. When it begins gushing, the result is not a nightmare scene of people scrambling away for their lives, but just the opposite; people flock *to* the volcano. Most thrill-seekers are in much greater danger of being run over by a tour bus hustling to see the fireworks than of being entombed in lava. The volcanic action, while soul-shakingly powerful, is predictable and almost totally safe. The Hawaiian Volcano Observatory has been keeping watch since 1912, making Kilauea one of the best-understood volcanoes in the world. The vast volcanic field is creased by rift zones, or natural pressure valves. When the underground magma builds up, instead of *kaboom!* as in Mt. St. Helens, it bubbles to the surface like a spring and gushes out as a river of lava. Naturally, anyone or anything in its path would be burned to a cinder, but scientists routinely walk within a few feet of the still-flowing lava to take readings. In much the way canaries detect mine gas, longtime lava observers pay attention to their ears. When the skin on top begins to blister, they know that they are too close. The lava establishes a course that it follows much like an impromptu mountain stream caused by heavy rains.

This does not mean that the lava flows are entirely benign, or that anyone should visit the area during an eruption without prior approval by the park service. When anything is happening, the local radio stations give up-to-the-minute news, and the park service provides a recorded message at tel. (808) 985-6000. In 1790 a puff of noxious gases was emitted from Kilauea and descended on the Kau Desert, asphyxiating a rival army of Kamehameha's that just happened to be in the area. Eighty people died in their tracks. In 1881 a flow of lava spilled toward undeveloped Hilo and engulfed an area within today's city limits. In 1942, a heavy flow came within 12 miles of the city. Still, this was child's play in comparison with the unbelievable flow of 1950. Luckily, this went down the western rift zone where only scattered homes were in its path. It took no lives as it disgorged well over 600 million cubic yards of magma that covered 35 square miles! The flow continued for 23 days and produced seven huge torrents of lava that

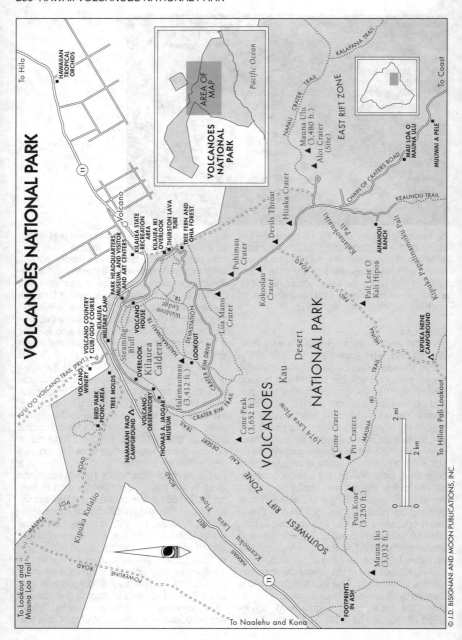

VOLCANOES NATIONAL PARK

sliced across the Belt Road in three different areas. At its height, the lava front traveled six miles per hour and put out enough material to pave an eight-lane freeway twice around the world. In 1960, a flow swallowed the town of Kapoho on the east coast. In 1975, an earthquake caused a tsunami to hit the southeast coast, killing two campers and sinking almost the entire Puna Coast by three feet.

The most recent, and very dramatic, series of eruptions that spectacularly began on January 3, 1983, have continued virtually unabated ever since, producing more than one cubic kilometer of lava. Magma bubbled to the surface about two miles away from Pu'u O'o. The gigantic fissure fountained lava and formed Pu'u O'o Cinder Cone that is now 830 feet high and almost 1,000 feet across. Over a three-and-a-half-year period, there were 47 eruptions from this vent. On July 20, 1986, a new fissure, composed of approximately two miles of fountaining lava, broke upon the surface at Kupaianaha, and has since formed a lava lake about one acre in size and 180 feet deep. At the end of April 1987 all activity suddenly stopped and the lava drained from the lake and tube system, allowing scientists to accurately gauge the depth. About a week later, it all started up again when lava poured back into the lake, went through the tube system, and flowed back down to the ocean. The output was estimated at 650,000 cubic yards per day, which is equal to 55,000 truckloads of cement, enough to cover a football field 38 miles high.

From that point, the flow turned destructive and started taking homes. It moved to the coast in tubes, wiping out Kapaahu, parts of Kalapana, and most of the Royal Gardens Subdivision, with more than 70 homes incinerated. In May 1989 it moved into the national park proper, and on June 22, it swallowed the park visitor center at Waha'ula. Since 1992, lava has been flowing into the ocean within the park. Unexpectedly, in January of 1997 the dramatic activity shifted two miles westward to the Napau Crater where lava erupted in spouts of fire and flows, and Pu'u O'o ceased spewing. From February of 1997, the majority of activity moved back to Pu'u O'o Cinder Cone where there has been a continual shift of vent locations on the west and southwestern flanks and constant renewed activity inside the crater. Until 1997, remote Waha'ula Heiau was

spared, but in August of that year lava inundated and buried the sacred spot. The destruction has caused more than $61 million worth of damage. Many of the homesteaders in the worst areas of the flow were rugged individualists and back-to-nature alternative types who lived in homes that generally had no electricity, running water, or telephones. The homes were wiped out. Some disreputable insurance companies with legitimate policy holders tried to wiggle out of paying premiums for lost homes, although the policies specifically stipulated loss by lava flow. The insurance companies whined that the 2,000° lava never really touched some of the homes, and therefore they were exonerated from paying the coverage. Their claims were resoundingly repudiated in the courts, and people were paid for their losses. One gentleman, however, has been forced to continue living in the middle of the lava flow. He's been there from the beginning because his insurance company will not pay if he leaves, claiming that the house was abandoned and therefore not covered. He sits in the middle of the lava plain with the flows all around him. For the last seven years, he's ridden a bicycle out from his house o the road. From there he goes to work and goes about his business, then goes back in on his bicycle. Sometimes in the middle of the night, or while he's gone, a lava flow occurs and he has to wait a couple of days for it to crust over before he can get in and out. Makes you want to rush right out and pay your premium to your caring friends in the insurance business. A prayer to Pele would easily be more effective. There is only one way to treat the power of Hawaii's magnificent volcanoes: not with fear, but with the utmost respect.

Mauna Loa

At 13,679 feet, this magnificent mountain is a mere 117 feet shorter than its neighbor Mauna Kea, which is the tallest peak in the Pacific, and by some accounts, tallest in the world. Measured from its base, 18,000 feet beneath the sea, it would top even Mt. Everest. Mauna Loa is the most massive mountain on earth, containing 10,000 cubic miles of solid, iron-hard lava. This titan weighs more than California's entire Sierra Nevada range! In fact, Mauna Loa (Long Mountain), at 60 miles long and 30 wide, occupies the entire southern half of the Big Island, with

Volcanoes National Park merely a section of its great expanse.

Special Note

Everything in the park—flora and fauna, rocks, buildings, trails, etc.—is protected by federal law. Be respectful! The *nene,* Hawaii's state bird, is endangered. By feeding these birds, visitors have taught them to stand in parking lots and by the roadside. What appears to be a humane and harmless practice actually helps kill these rare birds. Automobiles running them over has become the leading cause of death of adult birds in the park. Please look, but do not try to approach, feed, or harass the *nene* in any way.

Hiking

The slopes of Mauna Loa and HVNP are a trekker's paradise. You'll find trails that last for days or for an hour or two. Many have shelters, and those trails that require overnight stays provide cabins. Because of the possibility of an eruption or earthquake, it is *imperative* to check in at park headquarters, where you can also pick up current trail info and maps.

The 18-mile hike to the summit of **Mauna Loa** (13,679 feet) is the most grueling. The trailhead is at the lookout at the end of the pavement of Mauna Loa Road. Hikers in excellent condition can make the summit in three days roundtrip, but four would be more comfortable. There is a considerable elevation gain so expect freezing weather even in summer, and snow in winter. Altitude sickness can also be a problem. En route you pass through *nene* country, with a good chance to spot these lava-adapted geese.

Fences keep out feral goats, so remember to close gates after you. The first cabin is at Red Hill (10,035 feet) and the second is on the rim of Moku'aweoweo Crater (13,250 feet). Water is from roof catchment and should be boiled. The summit treats you to a sweeping panorama that includes Haleakala. Mauna Loa's Moku'aweoweo Caldera is more than three miles long and has vertical walls towering 600 feet. From November to May, if there is snow, steam rises from the caldera.

The **Crater Rim Loop Trail** begins at park headquarters and follows Crater Rim Dr., crossing back and forth a number of times. Hiking the entire 11 miles takes a full day, but you can take it in sections as time and energy permit. It's a well-marked and maintained trail; all you need are warm clothing, water, and determination. For your efforts, you'll get an up-close view of all of the sights outlined along Crater Rim Drive.

Kilauea Iki Trail begins at the Thurston Lava Tube, or at park headquarters via the Waldron Ledge Trail. This four-mile trail generally takes 3-4 hours as it passes through the center of Kilauea Iki Caldera. It's easy to link up with the Byron Ledge Trail or with the Halemaumau Trail. You can return north to park headquarters or continue on either of these two trails to the Halemaumau parking area directly south of park headquarters.

Halemaumau Trail provides the best scenery for the effort. It begins at park headquarters and descends into Kilauea Caldera, covering seven miles there and back (five hours). If possible, arrange to be picked up at the Halemaumau parking area due south of park headquarters.

KILAUEA CALDERA

The sights of Hawaii Volcanoes National Park are arranged one after another along **Crater Rim Drive.** Off the beaten track but worth a look are **Mauna Loa Road** (which takes you to places of special interest such as **Tree Molds** and **Bird Park**—10-minute detours) and **Kau Desert Trail,** about eight miles south of the visitor center on the Hawaii Belt Road, Hwy. 11. Most of the sights are the "drive-up" variety, but plenty of major and minor trails lead off here and there.

Tips

Expect to spend a long full day atop Kilauea to take in all the sights, and never forget that you're on a rumbling volcano where a misstep or loss of concentration at the wrong moment can lead to severe injury, or even loss of life. Try to arrive by 9 a.m. with a picnic lunch to save time and hassles. Kilauea Caldera, at 4,000 feet, is about 10° cooler than the coast. It's often overcast and there can be showers. Wear your walking shoes and bring a sweater and/or windbreaker. Binoculars, sunglasses, and a hat will also come in handy.

Warning! Small children, pregnant women, and people with respiratory ailments should note that the fumes from the volcano can cause problems. Just stay away from areas of sulfur vents and don't overdo it, and you should be fine.

A very dramatic way to experience the awesome power of the volcano is to take a **helicopter tour.** The choppers are perfectly suited for the up-close maneuverability necessary to get an intimate bird's-eye view. The pilots will fly you over the areas offering the most activity, often dipping low over lava pools, skimming still-glowing flows, and circling the towering steam clouds rising from where lava meets the sea. When activity is really happening, tours are jammed, and prices, like lava fountains, go sky-high. Remember, however, that there is growing resentment by hikers or anyone else trying to have a quiet experience, and that new regulations might limit flights over the lava area. Also, choppers do go down, and it is the park rangers and their rescue units who must go to their aid.

VISITORS CENTER AREA

The best place to start is at the Visitors Center/Park Headquarters. The turnoff is clearly marked off Belt Road (Hwy. 11). By midmorning it's jammed, so try to be an early bird. The center is well run by the National Park Service. They offer a free lecture and film about geology and volcanism, with tremendous highlights of past eruptions, and with plenty of detail on Hawaiian culture and natural history. It runs every hour on the hour starting at 9 a.m. Also, a self-guided natural history museum gives more information about the geology of the area, with plenty of exhibits of the flora and fauna. You will greatly enrich your visit if you take a half-hour tour of the museum. Actually, the visitor center has been eclipsed by the state-of-the-art information available at the **Thomas A. Jaggar Museum** a few minutes up the road.

For safety's sake, anyone trekking to the backcountry *must* register with the rangers at the visitor center, especially during times of eruption. Do not be foolhardy! There is no charge for camping, and the rangers can give you up-to-the-minute information on trails, backcountry shelters, and cabins. Trails routinely close due to lava flows, tremors, and rock slides. The rangers cannot help you if they don't know where you are. Many day trails leading into the caldera from the rim road are easy walks that need no special preparation. The backcountry trails can be very challenging, and detailed maps (highly recommended) are sold at the center along with special-interest geology and natural history publications prepared by the Hawaii Natural History Association. The visitor center is open daily 7:45 a.m.-5 p.m.; call (808) 985-6000 for trail, camping, or volcanic activity information.

Volcano House

Have you ever dreamed of sleeping with a goddess? Well, you can cuddle up with Pele by staying at Volcano House. If your plans don't include an overnight stop, go in for a look. Sometimes this is impossible, because not only do tour buses from the Big Island disgorge here, but tour groups are flown in from Honolulu as well. A stop at the bar provides refreshments and a tremendous view of the crater. Volcano House still has the feel of a country inn, although in reality it's a Sheraton Inn. This particular building dates from the 1940s, but the site has remained the same since a grass hut was perched on the rim of the crater by a sugar planter in 1846. He charged $1 a night. A steady stream of notable visitors have come ever since: almost all of Hawaii's kings and queens dating from the middle of last century, as well as royalty from Europe. Mark Twain was a guest, followed by Franklin Roosevelt. Most recently, a contingent of astronauts lodged here and used the crater floor to prepare for walking on the moon. In 1866 a large grass hut replaced the first, and in 1877 a wooden Victorian-style hotel was built. It is now the Volcano Art Center and has been moved just across the road. The longest owner/operator of Volcano House was George Lycurgus, who took over management of the hotel in the 1890s. His son, Nick, followed him and managed the hotel until the 1960s.

Volcano Art Center

Art and history buffs should walk across the street to the Volcano Art Center, tel. (808) 967-8222, which is the original 1877 Volcano House,

Hawaii's oldest hotel. You not only get to see some fine arts and crafts, you can take a self-guided tour of this minimuseum, open daily 9 a.m.-5 p.m. A new show featuring one of the many superlative island artists on display is presented monthly. Some prominent artists represented are Chiu Leong, who has a studio nearby where he turns out inspired *raku* pottery; Rick Mills, a master glass artist; Dietrich Varez, who makes affordable and distinctive wood block prints; Wilford Yamazawa, another amazing glassworker; Marion Burger, a young artist who lives in Volcano, known as one of the best naturalist painters around; George Allen, an oil painter whose themes are Hawaiian landscapes, flowers, and fish; Kathy Long, creator of insightful pencil drawings of local people; Pam Barton, who does whimsical fiber arts; woodworker Jack Straka, famous for his rich turned bowls; Kelly Dunn, who turns large bowls of Norfolk pine; Michael Riley, a Volcano resident who does rocking chairs in koa and other exotic woods in a style that follows the master woodworker Sam Maloof; and Boone Morrison, the center's founder, a photographer and architect who apprenticed under Ansel Adams. There is also a profusion of less expensive but distinctive items like posters, cards, and earthy basketry made from natural fibers collected locally. One of the functions of the art center is to provide interpretation for the national park. All of the 250-plus artists who exhibit here do works that in some way relate to Hawaii's environment and culture. Volcano Art Center is one of the finest art galleries in the entire state, boasting works from the best that the islands have to offer. A new facility on recently acquired land will soon allow the Volcano Art Center to expand and provide greater space for future projects.

CRATER RIM DRIVE

There are so many intriguing nooks and crannies to stop at along Crater Rim Drive that you'll have to force yourself to be picky if you intend to cover the park in one day. Crater Rim Drive is a circular route; it matters little which way you proceed. Take your choice, but the following sights are listed counterclockwise beginning from Kilauea Visitors Center. Your biggest problem will be timing your arrival at the "drive-in" sights to avoid the steady stream of tour buses.

Sulphur Banks

You can easily walk to Sulfur Banks from Volcano Art Center along a 10-minute trail. If you're driving, signs along Rim Drive direct you, and your nose will tell you when you're close. As you approach these fumaroles, the earth surrounding them turns a deep reddish-brown, covered over in yellowish-green sulfur. The rising steam is caused by surface water leaking into the cracks where it becomes heated and rises as vapor. Kilauea releases hundreds of tons of sulfur gases every day, with Sulfur Banks being an example. This gaseous activity stunts the growth of vegetation. And when atmospheric conditions create a low ceiling, the gases sometimes cause the eyes and nose to water. The area is best avoided by those with heart and lung conditions.

Steam Vents

Next you'll come to Steam Vents, which are also fumaroles, but without sulfur. The entire field behind the partitioned area steams. The feeling is like being in a sauna. There are no strong fumes to contend with here, just the tour buses. **Kilauea Military Camp** beyond the vent is not open to the public. The camp serves as an R&R facility for military personnel.

Hawaii Volcano Observatory

This observatory has been keeping tabs on the volcanic activity in the area since the turn of the century. The actual observatory is filled with delicate seismic equipment and is closed to the public, but a lookout nearby gives you a dentist's view into the mouth of Halemaumau Crater (House of Ferns), Pele's home. Steam rises and you can feel the power, but until 1924 the view was even more phenomenally spectacular: a lake of molten lava. The lava has since sunk below the surface, which is now crusted over. Scientists do not predict a recurrence in the near future, but no one knows Pele's mind. This is a major stop for the tour buses, but a two-minute saunter along the hiking trail gives you the view to yourself. Information plaques in the immediate area tell of the history and volcanology of the park. One points out a spot from which to observe the perfect shield volcano form of Mauna

Loa—most times too cloudy to see. Another reminds you that you're in the middle of the Pacific, an incredible detail you tend to forget when atop these mountains. Here too is Uwekahuna (Wailing Priest) Bluff, where the *kahuna* made offerings of appeasement to Pele. A Hawaiian prayer commemorates their religious rites.

Thomas A. Jaggar Museum

This newest addition to the national park is located next door to the Hawaiian Volcano Observatory, and offers a fantastic multimedia display of the amazing geology and volcanology of the area. The state-of-the-art museum, complete with a miniseries of spectacular photos on movable walls, topographical maps, inspired paintings, and TV videos, is open daily 8:30 a.m.-5 p.m., admission free. The expert staff constantly upgrades the displays to keep the public informed on the newest eruptions. The 30-45 minutes that it takes to explore the teaching museum will enhance your understanding of the volcanic area immeasurably. Do yourself a favor and visit this museum before setting out on any explorations.

Moon Walks

A string of interesting stops follows the observatory. One points out the **Kau Desert,** an inhospitable site of red-earth plains studded with a few scraggly plants. Next comes the **Southwest Rift,** a series of cracks running from Kilauea's summit to the sea. You can observe at a glance that you are standing directly over a major earthquake fault. Dated lava flows follow in rapid succession until you arrive at **Halemaumau Trail.** The well-maintained trail is only one-quarter mile long and gives an up-close view of the crater. The area is rife with fumaroles and should be avoided by those with respiratory problems. At the end you're treated to a full explanation of Halemaumau. Farther along the road, a roped-off area was once an observation point that caved in. You won't take the ground under your feet for granted! Close by is **Keanakakoi,** a prehistoric quarry from which superior stone was gathered to make tools. It was destroyed by a flow in 1877. If that seems in the remote past, realize that you are now on a section of road that was naturally paved over with lava from a "quickie" eruption in 1982!

Most visitors hike along **Devastation Trail,** which could aptly be renamed "Regeneration Trail." The half mile it covers is fascinating, one of the most-photographed areas in the park. It leads across a field devastated by a tremendous eruption from **Kilauea Iki** (Little Kilauea) in 1959, when fountains of lava shot 1,900 feet into the air. The area was once an ohia forest that was denuded of limbs and leaves, then choked by black pumice and ash. The vegetation has regenerated since then, and the recuperative power of the flora is part of an ongoing study. Blackberries, not indigenous to Hawaii, are slowly taking over. The good news is that you'll be able to pick and eat blackberries as you hike along the paved trail, but note that the rangers are waging a mighty war against them. Notice that many of the trees have sprouted aerial roots trailing down from the branches: this is total adaptation to the situation, as these roots don't normally appear. As you move farther along the trail, tufts of grass and bushes peek out of the pumice. Then the surroundings become totally barren and look like the nightmare of a nuclear holocaust.

Thurston Lava Tube

If the Devastation Trail produced a sense of melancholy, the Thurston Lava Tube makes you feel like Alice walking through the looking glass. Inside is a fairy kingdom. As you approach, the expected billboard gives you the lowdown on the geology and flora and fauna of the area. Take the five minutes to educate yourself. The paved trail starts as a steep incline which quickly enters a fern forest. All about you are fern trees, vibrantly green, with native birds flitting here and there. As you approach the lava tube, it seems almost manmade, like a perfectly formed tunnel leading into a mine. Ferns and moss hang from the entrance, and if you stand just inside the entrance looking out, it's as if the very air is tinged with green. If there were such things as elves and gnomes, they would surely live here. The walk through takes about 10 minutes, and the tube rolls and undulates through narrow passages and into large "rooms." At the other end, the fantasy world of ferns and moss reappears.

SMALL DETOURS

Volcano Village

You shouldn't miss taking a ride through the village of Volcano, a beautiful settlement with truly charming houses and cottages outlined in ferns. Tiny gravel roads lace the development, which sits virtually atop one of the world's undeniable "power spots." The area is so green and so vibrant that it appears surrealistic. With flowers, ferns, and trees everywhere, it is hard to imagine a more picturesque village in all of America. But even in this little parcel of paradise, things are changing, if slowly. The town now boasts two general stores, a TrueValue Hardware store, a small art gallery, a post office, a farmers' market, a winery, and several accommodations and restaurants along with the old standbys.

Volcano Golf and Country Club

What's most amazing about this course is where it is. Imagine! You're teeing off atop an active volcano surrounded by one of the last pristine forests in the state. At the right time of year, the surrounding ohia turn scarlet when they are in bloom. The fairways are carved from lava, while in the distance Mauna Loa looms. A poor shot, and you can watch your ball disappear down a steam vent. The course began about 70 years ago when a group of local golfers hand-cleared three "greens," placing stakes that served as holes. Later this was improved to sand greens with tin cans for holes, and after an eruption in 1924 blanketed the area with volcanic ash that served as excellent fertilizer, the grass grew and the course became a lush green. After WW II the course was extended to 18 holes, and a clubhouse was added. Finally, Jack Snyder, a well-known course architect, redesigned the course to its present par-72, 6,180-yard layout. Rates are $50 with shared cart. To beat the heavy lunch crowd at Volcano House, try the restaurant at the course. The course is located just north of the Belt Road, about two miles west of the park entrance. Phone (808) 967-7331 for more information.

Volcano Winery

About one mile beyond the golf course (after the road turns to dirt) and off to your left are the brown buildings of the Volcano Winery, tel. (808) 967-7479, owned by Dr. Lynn McKinney, a retired veterinarian from Honolulu. It's a hands-on winery where everything is done manually, even the bottling and corking. About 3.4 acres of this rough countryside are currently under cultivation, producing about three tons of grape per acre, yielding about 10,000 gallons a year. Because the land is at an elevation of about 4,000 feet, the patented Symphony grape is grown to take best advantage of the climatic conditions, which are similar to those in Oregon and Washington. Bottled are dry and semidry wines, guava/chablis and jaboticaba/chablis blends, a lehua honey wine, and a macadamia nut honey wine. A local favorite, the jaboticaba blend is made with a Brazilian fruit of that name. Although no tours of the winery are available, a tasting room is open daily 10 a.m.-5 p.m. Have a sip at the glass-covered koa bar and maybe you'll want to purchase a bottle for later in the evening or a 12-bottle case to share with friends when you get home. There also is a small boutique on the premises selling T-shirts, jewelry, *kukui* nut leis, postcards, and other gift items.

Mauna Loa Road

About 2.5 miles west of the park entrance on the Belt Road, Mauna Loa Road turns off to the north. This road will lead you to the Tree Molds and a bird sanctuary, as well as to the trailhead for the Mauna Loa summit trail. As an added incentive, a minute down this road leaves 90% of the tourists behind.

Tree Molds is an ordinary name for an extraordinary place. Turn off Mauna Loa Road soon after leaving the Belt Road and follow the signs for five minutes to a cul-de-sac. At the entrance, a billboard tries hard to dramatically explain what occurred here. In a moment, you realize that you're standing atop a lava flow, and that the scattered potholes are entombed tree trunks, most likely the remains of a once-giant koa forest. Unlike at Lava Tree State Monument, where the magma encased the tree and flowed away, the opposite action happened here. The lava stayed put while the tree trunk burned away, leaving 15-to 18-foot-deep holes.

Kipuka Puaulu is a sanctuary for birds and nature lovers who want to leave the crowds behind, just under two miles from Rt. 11 down Mauna Loa Road. The sanctuary is an island atop an island. A *kipuka* is a piece of land that is surrounded by lava but has not been inundated by it, leaving the original vegetation and land contour intact. A few hundred yards away, small scrub vegetation struggles, but in the sanctuary the trees form a towering canopy a hundred feet tall. The first sign for Bird Park takes you to an ideal picnic area; the second, 100 yards beyond, takes you to Kipuka Puaulu Loop Trail. As you enter the trail, a bulletin board describes the birds and plants, some of the last remaining indigenous fauna and flora in Hawaii. Please follow all rules. The trail is self guided, and pamphlets describing the stations along the way are dispensed from a box 50 feet down the path. The loop is only one mile long, but to really assimilate the area, especially if you plan to do any birdwatching, expect to spend an hour minimum. It doesn't take long to realize that you are privileged to see some of the world's rarest plants, such as a small, nondescript bush called *aalii*. In the branches of the towering ohia trees you might see an *elepaio* or an *apapana,* two birds native to Hawaii. Common finches and Japanese white eyes are imported birds that are here to stay. There's a fine example of a lava tube, and an explanation of how ash from eruptions provided soil and nutrients for the forest. Blue morning glories have taken over entire hillsides. Once considered a pest and aggressively eradicated, they have recently been given a reprieve and are now considered good ground cover—perhaps even indigenous. When you do come across a native Hawaiian plant, it seems somehow older, almost prehistoric. If a precontact Hawaiian could come back today, he or she would recognize only a few plants and trees even here in this preserve. More than four times as many plants and animals have become extinct in Hawaii in the last 200 years as on the entire North American continent. As you leave, listen for the melodies coming from the treetops, and hope the day never comes when no birds sing.

Mauna Loa Road continues westward and gains elevation for approximately 10 miles. At the end of the pavement, at 6,662 feet, you find a parking area and lookout. A trail leads from here to the summit of Mauna Loa. It takes three to four days to hike. Under no circumstances should it be attempted by novice hikers or those unprepared for cold alpine conditions.

Olaa Track

Off Rt. 11 close to Volcano village, turn on Wright Road (or County Rd. 148) heading toward Mauna Loa (on a clear morning you can see Mauna Kea). Continue for approximately three miles until you see a barbed-wire fence. The fence is distinctive because along it you'll see a profusion of *hapu'u* ferns that are in sharp contrast to the adjacent property. Here is an *ola'a* rainforest, part of the national park and open to the public, although park scientists like to keep it quiet. Be aware that the area is laced with lava tubes. Most are small ankle twisters, but others can open up under you like a glacial crevasse. Here is a true example of a quickly disappearing native forest. What's beautiful about an endemic forest is that virtually all species coexist wonderfully. The ground cover is a rich mulch of decomposing ferns and leaves, fragrant and amazingly soft. This walk is for the intrepid hiker or naturalist who is fascinated by Hawaii's unique foliage.

Remember, trails in this section of the park are poorly marked and quite confusing. You can get lost, and if no one knows that you're in there, it could be life threatening. Also, be aware that you may be trampling native species and could be inadvertently introducing alien species. The park service is trying to bring the area back to its native Hawaiian rainforest condition through eradication of alien plants and elimination of feral pigs.

Kau Desert Trail

Kau Desert Trail starts about eight miles south of the visitor center along Rt. 11, between mile markers 37 and 38. It's a short hike from the trailhead to the **Kau Desert Footprints.** People going to or from Kailua-Kona can see them en route, but those staying in Hilo should take the time to visit the footprints. The trek across the small section of desert is fascinating, and the history of the footprints makes the experience more evocative. The trail is only 1.6 miles roundtrip and can be hustled along in less than 30 minutes, but allow at least an hour, mostly for observation. The predominant foliage is a red bottlebrush that contrasts with the bleak surroundings—the feeling throughout the area is one of foreboding. You pass a wasteland of a'a and pahoehoe lava flows to arrive at the footprints. A metal fence in a sturdy pavilion surrounds the prints, that look as though they're cast in cement. Actually they're formed from pisolites: particles of ash stuck together with moisture, which formed mud that hardened like plaster.

In 1790 Kamehameha was waging war with Keoua over control of the Big Island. One of Keoua's warrior parties of approximately 80 people attempted to cross the desert while Kilauea was erupting. Toxic gases descended upon them and the warriors and their families were en-

veloped and suffocated. They literally died in their tracks, but the preserved footprints, although romanticism would wish otherwise, were probably made by a party of people who came well after the eruption. This unfortunate occurrence was regarded by the Hawaiians as a direct message from the gods proclaiming their support for Kamehameha. Keoua, who could not deny the sacred signs, felt abandoned and shortly thereafter became a human sacrifice at Puukohola Heiau, built by Kamehameha to honor his war god, Kukailimoku.

CHAIN OF CRATERS ROAD

The Chain of Craters Road that once linked Volcanoes National Park with Kalapana village on the east coast has been severed by an enormous lava flow, and can only be driven from Volcanoes down to where the flow crosses the road near the now-inundated and inaccessible Kamoamoa Campground. Remember that the volcanic activity in this area is unpredictable, and that the road can be closed at a moment's notice. Flying volcanic ash, mixed with the frequent drizzle, can be as slippery as ice. As you head down the road, every bend—and they are uncountable—offers a panoramic vista. There are dozens of pulloffs, many of which have names, like Naulu (Sea Orchards); plaques provide geological information about past eruptions and lava flows. The grandeur, power, and immensity of the forces that have been creating the earth from the beginning of time are right before your eyes. The lower part of the road is spectacular. Here, blacker-than-black seacliffs, covered by a thin layer of green, abruptly stop at the sea. The surf rolls in, sending up spumes of seawater. In the distance, steam billows into the air where the lava flows into the sea. At road's end you will find a barricade staffed by park rangers. Heed their warnings. The drive from atop the volcano to the barricade takes about 30 minutes. If you are going in the evening, when the spectacle is more apparent, bring a flashlight. When rangers are there, they will escort you onto the flow, giving an interpretive talk as you walk along. To experience the lava flow from the Kalapana side, see **Route 130 and the Southeast Coast.**

When the road almost reaches the coast, look for a roadside marker that indicates the **Kau Puna Trail.** Just across the road is the **Pu'u Loa Petroglyph Field.** The Kau Puna Trail leads you along the coast, where you can find shelters at Keauhou and Halape. Rain catchment tanks provide drinking water. All campers must register at the Kilauea Visitors Center. In 1975 an earthquake rocked the area, generating a tsunami that killed two campers; more than 30 others had to be helicoptered to safety. Only registering will alert authorities to your whereabouts in case of a disaster. A number of trails cross in this area and you can take them back up to Chain of Craters Road or continue on a real expedition through the Kau Desert. The Kau Puna Trail requires full trekking and camping gear.

Pu'u Loa Petroglyphs
The walk out to Pu'u Loa Petroglyphs is delightful and highly educational, and only takes one hour. The trail, although it traverses solid lava, is discernible. The tread of feet over the centuries has discolored the rock. As you walk along, note the *ahu,* traditional trail markers that are piles of stone shaped like little Christmas trees. Most of the lava field leading to the petroglyphs is undulating pahoehoe and looks like a frozen sea. You can climb bumps of lava, from eight to 10 feet high, to scout the immediate territory. Mountainside, the *pali* is quite visible and you can pick out the most recent lava flows—the blackest and least vegetated. As you approach the site, the lava changes dramatically and looks like long strands of braided rope.

DAVID STANLEY

petroglyphs

The petroglyphs are in an area about the size of a soccer field. A wooden walkway encircles them and ensures their protection. A common motif of the petroglyphs is a circle with a hole in the middle, like a donut; you'll also see designs of men with triangular-shaped heads. Some rocks are entirely covered with designs while others have only a symbolic scratch or two. If you stand on the walkway and trek off at the two o'clock position, you'll see a small hill. Go over and down it, and you will discover even better petroglyphs that include a sailing canoe about two feet high. At the back end of the walkway a sign proclaims that Pu'u Loa meant "Long Hill," which the Hawaiians turned into the euphemism "Long Life." For countless generations, fathers would come here to place pieces of their infants' umbilical cords into small holes as offerings to the gods to grant long life to their children. Concentric circles were surrounded by the holes that held the umbilical cords. The entire area, an obvious power spot, screams in utter silence, and the still-strong mana is easily felt. The Big Island has the largest concentration of this ancient art form in the state.

Waha'ula Heiau

Waha'ula Heiau (Temple of the Red Mouth) radically changed the rituals and practices of the relatively benign Hawaiian religion by introducing the idea of human sacrifice. The 13th century marked the end of the frequent comings and goings between Hawaii and the "Lands to the South" (Tahiti), and began the isolation that would last 500 years until Captain Cook arrived. Unfortunately, this last influx of Polynesians brought a rash of conquering warriors carrying ferocious gods who lusted for human blood before they would be appeased. Paao, a powerful Tahitian priest, supervised the building of Waha'ula and brought in a new chief, Pili, to strengthen the diminished mana of the Hawaiian chiefs due to their practice of intermarriage with commoners. Waha'ula became the foremost *luakini* (human sacrifice) temple in the island kingdom and held this position until the demise of the old ways in 1819. Not at all grandiose, the *heiau* was merely an elevated rock platform smoothed over with pebbles.

Note: This entire area is now completely inundated by recent lava flows. Until 1997, the *heiau* itself was a small island in a sea of black lava that miraculously escaped destruction, but in August of that year lava oozed over these 700-year-old walls and filled the compound. Madame Pele has taken back her own.

PRACTICALITIES

ACCOMMODATIONS

If you intend to spend the night atop Kilauea, your choices of accommodations are few and simple. Volcano House provides the only hotel, but cabins are available at the campgrounds, and there are plenty of tenting sites and a wonderful assortment of bed and breakfasts.

Campgrounds and Cabins

The main campground in Volcanoes, **Namakani Paio,** clearly marked off Rt. 11, is situated in a stately eucalyptus grove. There is no charge for tent camping and no reservations are required. A cooking pavilion has fireplaces, but no wood or drinking water are provided. Also, there are no shower facilities for those camping and hiking within the park, so make sure that you're with people who like you a whole bunch. Cabins are available through Volcano House. Each accommodates four people and costs $35 s/d, $8 additional person. A $10 refundable key deposit gives access to the shower and toilet; and a $5 refundable deposit gets you linens, soap, towels, and a blanket (extra sleeping bag recommended). Each cabin contains one double bed and two single bunk beds and an electric light, but no electrical outlets. Outside are a picnic table and barbecue grill but you must provide your own charcoal and cooking utensils. Check in at Volcano House at 3 p.m. and check out by noon.

For backcountry overnight camping, apply at the Kilauea Visitors Center (7:45 a.m.-4:45 p.m.) for a free permit no earlier than the day before you plan to hike

Hale Kilauea

Green pines and native ohia shade Hale Kilauea, P.O. Box 28, Volcano, HI 96785, tel. (808) 967-7591, owned and operated by Maurice Thomas. In the main lodge, a central common room is very comfortable with reading materials, fireplace, parlor games, and TV. The spacious and airy rooms in the main lodge, $65-85 d, $20 extra person, all with private baths, are comfortable but not luxurious. Upstairs rooms are more deluxe with plush carpeting, knotty pine trim, refrigerator, small divan, and private lanai. Ask for a room in the rear so that you can overlook the quiet green forest instead of the parking area. Two rooms across from the main building are warm and cozy, although quite small. They are private and the least expensive at $55. The best deal, however, is a refurbished plantation cottage that sits across the road. The rate is $85 d, with special weekly and monthly rates. The wainscoted cottage provides a small but serviceable kitchen, separate bedroom, and living room that can sleep a few more. Don't expect luxury, but a night in the cottage is a window into Hawaii's past of humble workers in humble homes. With all the rooms, including the cottage, a hearty breakfast of hot and cold cereals, various breads, cheeses, plump sausages, and occasionally quiche, waffles, or pancakes is provided. Inexpensive.

Volcano House

If you decide to lodge at Volcano House, P.O. Box 53, Hawaii Volcanoes National Park, HI 96718, tel. (808) 967-7321 or (800) 325-3535, don't be frightened away by the daytime crowds. They disappear with the sun. Then Volcano House metamorphoses into what it has always been: a quiet country inn. The 42 rooms are comfy but old-fashioned. Who needs a pool or TV when you can look out your window into a volcano caldera? To the left of the reception area indoors, a crackling fireplace warms you from the chill in the mountain air. In front of the fireplace are stuffed leather chairs and a wonderful wooden rocker. One wall in the inn displays paintings and vintage photographs of the Hawaiian kings and queens of the Kamehameha line, while another wall holds magnificent photos of eruptions of the mountain. The management problems that afflicted the hotel over the past several years seem to have abated with the new owner and operator, Ken Fujiama. Although privately owned, it is the park service that sets the standards and pricing for the rooms. Room rates are: main building with crater view $131, noncrater view $105, Ohia Wing noncrater view $79,

$10 additional person. No charge for children under 12 occupying the same room as their parents. Rooms include koa wood furniture, Hawaiian comforters, telephone, heater, and private bath and shower. Efficiently run, the hotel has a restaurant, lounge, shops, 24-hour front desk service, maid service, safe-deposit boxes, city bus service, and fax machines. Besides that, you could hardly get closer to the crater if you tried. Moderate.

Kilauea Military Camp
One mile west of the park entrance, within the park boundary, is the Kilauea Military Camp. Offering rooms and meals, this facility is only open to active duty and retired military personnel, civilian employees of the Department of Defense, and their families. Call (808) 967-7315 for information and availability.

Bonnie Goodell's Guest House
This very friendly hideaway, P.O. Box 6, Volcano, HI 96785, tel. (808) 967-7775, is on the back roads of Volcano Village. The fully furnished house is designed as a self-sufficient unit where the guests are guaranteed peace and quiet on a lovely six-acre homesite. Bonnie grew up in Hawaii and was for many years the education director for the Honolulu Botanic Gardens. She *knows* her plants and is willing to chat with her guests. The place is particularly good for families. Children have plenty of room to play, while their parents can roam the orchards on the property. Bonnie and her husband have cut a two-mile long path from here to the Thurston lava tube, and if she has time, Bonnie may give you an interpretive tour describing the flora and fauna of the area. The two-story guest home is bright and airy. Enter into a combo living room, kitchen, and dining area with a large bathroom off to the right. Upstairs is a sleeping area with two twin beds and a queen-size fold-out bed; downstairs is another fold-out bed. Futons can sleep even more. Another cottage, smaller but more luxurious and wheelchair-accessible, is designed for honeymoon couples who want to be alone. The rate is $60 d, $10 for each additional person (off-season rates available). Sometimes Bonnie will allow an emergency one-night stay if the house is not booked, but she charges $10 extra because the entire house has to be cleaned. Moderate.

Lokahi Lodge
Built in 1992 specifically as a B&B by Patrick Dixon and Danny DiCastro, Lokahi Lodge, P.O. Box 7, Volcano, HI 96785, tel. (808) 985-8647 (on Oahu, Maui and Kauai tel. 922-6597 or 800-457-6924), offers quiet country comfort. A rocking-chair veranda, perfect for keeping off sun and showers, completely surrounds the spacious ranch house. In the common sitting room (with 16-foot vaulted ceilings), you can relax on overstuffed couches and chairs while warming yourself in front of a red enameled free-standing stove. An old-fashioned, crank-handled telephone hangs on the wall, and an ensemble of organ, piano, and harp awaits anyone inclined to make their own music. A continental breakfast of homemade banana bread, fresh papaya and pineapple, fruit juices, jams, jellies, coffee, and tea assortment is offered at a huge banquet table surrounded by high-backed chairs. The stardust-speckled hallway is lined with vintage lei that have been collected by owner Danny DiCastro, a famous hula dancer. Rooms, $65 d, $15 extra person, are triple-insulated for guaranteed quiet, are fully carpeted, offer large closets, and have differing decor—for example, billowy paisley curtains and bedspreads with matching wallpaper. Comfortable furniture for private relaxation, tasteful oil prints, and bathrooms with tub, shower, and pedestal sink complete the rooms. For the most privacy request the "yellow or blue rooms" at the far end of the hallway. Each room has a private entrance leading onto the veranda, so that you may come and go without disturbing anyone. Lokahi Lodge definitely lives up to its name, which translates as "peace and harmony." Moderate.

Hale Ohia Cottages
Follow a private mountain lane for a few minutes into an enchanted clearing where the artwork of a meticulous Japanese garden surrounds a New England gabled-and-turreted home and its attendant cottages of red-on-brown rough-cut shingles. Once the hideaway of the Dillinghams, an old and influential *kama'aina* family, Hale Ohia, P.O. Box 758, Volcano Village, HI 96785, tel. (808) 967-7986 or (800) 455-3803, fax (808) 967-8610, e-mail: haleohia@bigisland.com, is now owned and operated by Michael D. Tuttle, who recently purchased the property after falling

Hale Ohia

hopelessly in love at first sight. The main house holds the Dillingham Suite ($85), with its own sitting room, bath, and glass-covered lanai. Simple and clean, with hardwood floors and wainscoted walls, the home is the epitome of country elegance, Hawaiian style.

Hale Ohia, once the gardener's cottage, has two stories, with the bottom floor occupied by the Iiwi ($60) and Camellia ($75) suites, which are wheelchair-accessible and can be combined for larger groups ($85). Stained-glass windows with a calla lily-and-poppy motif add a special touch, while the low ceilings are reminiscent of the captain's quarters on a sailing ship. The first floor has a full kitchen and a covered lanai complete with barbecue grill that makes it perfect for evening relaxation. Narrow stairs lead to a full bath located on the first landing, from where you get a sweeping view of the grounds while performing your morning meditation. Upstairs opens into a bright and airy parlor and adjacent bedrooms that can sleep five comfortably.

Hale Lehua, once a private study, is secluded down its own lava footpath. Enter to find a wall of windows framing the green-on-green grounds. The interior is cozy with its own fireplace, bamboo and wicker furniture, self-contained bathroom, covered lanai, and partial kitchen with microwave, toaster, and refrigerator. Hale Lehua features a skylight, fireplace, and leaded glass windows through which the surrounding fern forest will emit its emerald radiance.

To make your stay even more delightful, room rates include an "extended" continental breakfast, and guests are welcome to immerse themselves in the bubbling jacuzzi that awaits you under a canopy of Japanese cedars and glimmering stars. Moderate.

Carson's Volcano Cottages

Deep in the fern forest, Carson's Volcano Cottages, P.O. Box 503, Volcano, HI 96785, tel. (808) 967-7683 or (800) 845-LAVA, fax (808) 967-8094, owned and operated by Tom and Brenda Carson, offers four B&B rooms, one in its own studio cottage, and the others in a three-room cottage. The accommodations all have private baths, entrances, and decks, and on the deck of the main house is a hot tub for everyone to use. Two of the rooms have kitchens. The one-acre property is naturally landscaped with ohia and fern, while moss-covered sculptures of Balinese gods peek through the foliage. The studio cottage, $95 d, a miniature plantation house with corrugated roof, has a kitchen and a bath with a skylight. Appointed with fluffy pillows and downy quilts, this would be a perfect rendezvous for a "Victorian lady" and her paramour. The three-room cottage, $75-85 d per room, has vaulted ceilings, beds with wooden headboards, wicker furniture, and vintage photos on the walls. In one room, the crocheted bedspreads are helped by electric blankets, while a free-standing credenza from the '30s adds a touch of charm. Leaded glass windows open to a private porch.

Another room, all in pink, also with its own vaulted ceiling and free-standing wardrobe, is appointed with vintage kitsch bric-a-brac like hula dancer glasses and lamps. A retired "lady of the evening" could easily relive memories in this room. Finally, the Oriental Room, striking in black and white, features Balinese masks and a Japanese doll mural. Located at the side of the cottage, this room has a more private entrance and a tiny kitchenette. Tom and Brenda provide an extended continental breakfast that might include banana bread, French toast, passion fruit juice, bagels and lox, or strawberry crepes. The Carsons also rent out another home in the Volcano Village area called Koa Halei; it starts at $125. The house has two queen-size beds and is appointed in '30s and '40s vintage Hawaiian style. You'll be comfortable in front of the living room fireplace or enjoy the evening sky from the hot tub on the back porch. E-mail: carsons@aloha.net; website: www.carsonscottage.com. Moderate.

Other Moderate Lodging

A B&B with an excellent reputation is **My Island Bed and Breakfast Inn,** P.O. Box 100, Volcano, HI 96785, tel. (808) 967-7216, fax 967-7719. Rates range from a very reasonable $45 s with shared bath to $75 for a double with private bath. A private studio with bathroom and kitchenette runs $85 and a fully furnished vacation house goes for $120. E-mail: myisland@ilhawaii.net; website: www.stayhawaii.com/myhawaii/myisld.html.

Victoria Rose, a one-room B&B, tel. (808) 967-8026, owned and operated by Lisa Farmer, is a fancy jewelry box done in maroon, pink, and lace, lots of lace. A four-poster "pineapple" bed and a private bath ensure privacy and comfort.

Volcano Country Cottages, P.O. Box 545, Volcano, HI 96785, tel. (808) 967-7960 or (800) 967-7960, is another convenient place to try. Available are the Ohelo Berry studio cottage for $75 a night and the two-bedroom Artist's House for $120. Contact Kathleen Ing for information, reservations, and directions. E-mail: vccbnb@aloha.net.

Bed & Breakfast Mountain View, in the village of Mountain View, P.O. Box 963, Kurtistown, HI 96720, tel. (808) 968-6868, fax 968-7017, is owned by Jane and Linus Chao, both accomplished artists. They offer rooms priced $55-75, all with private bath, TV and VCR, along with a hearty breakfast prepared and served in the family art gallery. The couple's inspired artwork graces the home. E-mail: info@bbmtview.com; website: www.bbmtview.com.

Kilauea Lodge

A superb addition to the Volcano area, Kilauea Lodge, P.O. Box 116, Volcano Village, HI 96785, tel. (808) 967-7366, fax 967-7367, owned and operated by Lorna Larsen-Jeyte and Albert Jeyte, is the premier restaurant and lodge atop Volcano, as well as one of the very best on the island. The solid stone and timber structure was built in 1938 as a YMCA camp and functioned as such until 1962, when it became a "mom and pop operation," often failing and changing ownership. It faded into the ferns until Lorna and Albert revitalized it in 1987, opening in 1988. The lodge is a classic, with a vaulted, open-beamed ceiling. A warm and cozy "international fireplace" dating from the days of the YMCA camp is embedded with stones and plaques from all over the world, along with coins from countries such as Malaysia, Japan, Singapore, Australia, New Zealand, Finland, Germany, and Italy, to name a few.

Kilauea Lodge is an exquisite inn with an assortment of rooms ranging $105-195, including a complete breakfast for all guests. The architect, Virginia McDonald, a Volcano resident, worked magic in transforming the brooding rooms of the original section into bright, comfortable, and romantic suites. Each bathroom, with vaulted 18-foot ceilings, has a skylight. The sink and grooming area is one piece of Corian with a light built into it, so that the entire sink area glows. The rooms, all differently appointed, range in decor from Hawaiian-European to Asian with a motif of Japanese fans. Almost every room has original artwork by Gwendolyn O'Connor. Each has a working fireplace, queen-size bed, and swivel rocking chair. A separate one-bedroom cottage, set in the ferns at the back of the lodge, features a wood-burning stove (central heat too), wet bar, a queen-size bed, private bath with jacuzzi, and small living room with queen-size pull-out sofa. In 1991, Kilauea Lodge opened seven new units centered around a commodious common room where you can read and snooze by a crackling fire. All rooms in the new section are tastefully furnished with wicker furniture, white curtains, vaulted ceilings, oak trim, Japanese and Hawaiian art prints, and fluffy quilts to keep off the evening chill. The Kilauea Lodge provides one of the most *civilized* atmospheres in Hawaii in one of its most powerful natural areas. The combination is hard to beat. E-mail: k-lodge@aloha.net. Expensive.

Tutu's Place

Just up the road from the Kilauea Lodge is the cute little two-bedroom cottage, Tutu's Place. Built in 1929 by the Uncle Billy of hotel chain fame for "tutu" (grandma), it was bought several decades later by the Warner family. Mr. Warner was a minister and was involved in Hawaiian politics. His wife, Ruth Warner, lived in the cottage for 30 years until in was bought in 1995 by Lorna Larson-Jeyte, the owner of the Kilauea Lodge. Although it's been completely refurbished, people in the know say that the cottage is still imbued with the spirit of Ruth Warner. It's done in a theme of rattan and koa, with a fireplace in the living room, a full kitchen, and a wonderful little bathroom. The rate is $135 for two people, including breakfast at the Kilauea Lodge; $15 for each additional person. To make reservations, call the Kilauea Lodge, tel. (808) 967-7366, and ask for Tutu's Place. Premium.

Chalet Kilauea

Peeking from the *hapuu* fern forest in a manicured glen is Chalet Kilauea, P.O. Box 998, Volcano Village, HI 96785, tel. (808) 967-7786, (800) 937-7786, e-mail: bchawaii@aol.com, where you will be cordially accommodated by owners Lisha and Brian Crawford. Enter the second level of the main house to find a guest living room where you can while away the hours playing chess, listening to a large collection of CDs, or gazing from the wraparound windows at a treetop view of the surrounding forest, ferns, and impeccable grounds. Just out the door, a make-over of a one-time Japanese *ofuro* resulted in an ornamental plant holder. Downstairs is an outdoor lounge area, and a black-and-white checkerboard dining room where wrought-iron tables sit before a huge picture window. On the lawn, a free-standing gazebo houses an eight-person jacuzzi hot tub available 24-hours a day.

Breakfasts (changeable daily), friendly and relaxed but with formal table settings, are remarkable: lox and bagels, fresh Volcano onions and tomatoes, macadamia nut or banana pancakes with strawberry topping, fresh papaya and squeezed juices, and Brian's own house blend Kona coffee with a hint of cinnamon.

The main house holds three suites and two additional rooms, $135-295. The Oriental Jade Room is richly appointed with Chinese folding screens, samurai murals, Oriental carpet, and jade-green bedspread. The green marble bathroom embellishes the green theme of the surrounding vegetation. Plush terry cloth robes are available for all guests. The lanai outside is shared with the Out of Africa Room, which has a strong color theme of burgundy and brass. The Continental Lei Suite is fluff and lace, the bridal suite. Here the colors are white, gold, and pink; a wedding dress hangs in the corner to accentuate the theme. Located on the first floor, the Owners Suite is designed for up to three people. Pink carpet covers the floor and a green floral spread covers the bed. With two shower heads in the shower stall, you can be happy showering together. Connected by a deck to the main house is the Treehouse Suite, a two-story unit with bath, sitting room, wet bar, and kitchenette downstairs, and a large bedroom on the upper floor. The surrounding glass makes the living forest part of the decor. A private lanai overlooks the garden, and a handcrafted wooden circular staircase connects the two floors.

Brian and Lisha have six other properties in and around Volcano ranging $95-225, including the Hide-a-way Cottage, Ginger House, and the Lodge at Volcano (big enough for a small business group). Give them a call and they will provide all the details. They also own and operate **Volcano Reservations,** a B&B reservation service with guest homes available statewide. Premium.

The Inn at Kulaniapia

Located on 22 acres of macadamia nut and tropical fruit orchards, with views over Hilo and the ocean and the 120-foot Kulaniapia Waterfall on the property, is The Inn at Kulaniapia, P.O. Box 204, Kurtistown, HI 96762 tel. (808) 966-6373, e-mail: waterfalls@prodigy.net. This recently built B&B features large suites with private tiled baths and covered balconies. Private and serene, it's conveniently located near both Hilo and the lowlands and the upcountry volcano area. Rates are $135-165 d. Premium.

FOOD AND SHOPPING

Food
The **Kilauea Lodge Restaurant,** open for dinner 5:30-9 p.m. nightly, reservations a must, is an extraordinary restaurant serving gourmet continental cuisine at reasonable prices. Choose a seat below the neo-Victorian windows or at a table from which you can view the vibrant green ferns and manicured trees of the grounds. A very friendly and professional staff serves the excellent food prepared by Albert, and starts you off with a fresh "loafette" studded like their fireplace, but with sunflower and sesame seeds. Appetizers such as mushroom caps stuffed with crab and cheese will titillate your palate. Entrees, ranging $13-26, include soup, salad, and vegetables. Vegetarians will be delighted with a stew of Mediterranean vegetables served atop fettuccine at $13.50, while shrimp tempura at $18.50 adds an Asian touch. Dinner features seafood Mauna Kea (succulent pieces of seafood served atop a bed of fettuccine) and paupiettes of beef (prime rib slices rolled around herbs and mushrooms in a special sauce), both for under $20. Always a great choice, the catch of the day is baked, broiled, or sautéed with a savory sauce. Desserts are wonderful, and the meal is topped off with a cup of Irish or Italian coffee.

Volcano House Restaurant offers a breakfast buffet, $9.50 pp, $5.50 for children ages 2-11, daily 7-10:30 a.m., with hot and cold cereals, assorted juices, pancakes topped with fruit and macadamia nuts, sweet bread French toast, scrambled eggs, bacon, chili links, and Portuguese sausage. A lighter continental breakfast is $5.50. The lunch buffet ($12.50 adult, $7.50 child, served daily 11 a.m.-2 p.m.), often terribly crowded because of the tour buses, offers tossed greens and assorted vegetables, fresh fruit platters, stuffed mahimahi, teriyaki beef, pot roast, honey-dipped chicken, rolls and butter, soft drinks, coffee, and tea. Dinner nightly, 5:30-9 p.m., starts with appetizers like sautéed mush-

rooms ($6.50) and fruit platter ($8.50). It moves on to entrees like seafood linguine ($18.50), roast prime rib ($19.95), and Volcano House scampi ($17.50). For the vegetarian, a steamed vegetable platter goes for $9.50. A child's menu is also available with dishes under $7.50. The quality is fair and the prices reasonable; however, the lunchtime buffet is overwhelmingly crowded and should be avoided if possible.

You can get away from the crowds and have a satisfying meal at **Volcano Country Club Restaurant** at Volcano Golf Course. The green and white interior complements the fairways, which can be seen through the surrounding plate glass windows. The cuisine is quite good. Complete breakfast is served daily 7-10 a.m., a full lunch menu daily 10:30 a.m.-2:30 p.m., and light snacks and *pu pu* until 5 p.m. For breakfast choose from mahimahi and eggs for $6, Hawaiian stew with chunks of beef and vegetables for $7.25, or a short stack of pancakes for $4.75. Lunch selections include hearty ham, tuna, turkey, or chicken sandwiches for $6.25 and less ($7.75 with a bowl of soup); clubhouse sandwich for $8.50; or burgers with trimmings for around $7.50. There is also a good selection of local favorites like loco moco or chili with rice for $7.25 and less. The bar is well stocked, serving name-brand liquor, exotic drinks, and beer and wine. Next to the Kilauea Lodge, this is the best place for lunch in the area.

On the porch of Volcano Store in Volcano village, tel. (808) 967-7210, open 5 a.m.-7 p.m. daily, is a window-service restaurant called **Ali Bakery,** open Mon.-Thurs. 8 a.m.-4:30 p.m., Fri.-Sat. until 5 p.m., Sunday until 4 p.m., with seating available. Breakfasts are everything from coffee and a sweet roll to ham and eggs for $3.95 to pancake and link sausage for $5.50. Lunches are burgers and fries for around $3, an assortment of plate lunches for under $6, or beef stew and rice for $4.95.

Shopping and Services
If you are after an exquisite piece of art, a unique memento, or an inexpensive but distinctive souvenir, be sure to visit the **Volcano Art Center.**

A **farmers' market** open 8:30 a.m.-11 p.m. every Sunday of the month sells local produce, baked goods, used books, and other used items. It's located at the Cooper Center.

Volcano Store, in the middle of Volcano village, tel. (808) 967-7210, open 5 a.m.-7 p.m. daily, sells gasoline, film, a few camping supplies, and a good selection of basic foods. In front are a few telephone booths, and just next door is a full-service post office.

Just down the road, **Kilauea General Store,** open 6 a.m.-7:30 p.m., Sunday 6:30 a.m.-6:30 p.m., also sells gas, and although it is not as well stocked as a grocery, it does have a deli case, a good stock of beer and liquor, and an excellent community bulletin board.

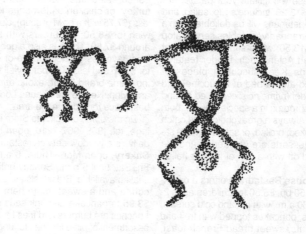

KAU

The Kau District is as simple and straightforward as the broad, open face of a country gentleman. It's not boring, and it does hold pleasant surprises for those willing to look. Formed entirely from the massive slopes of Mauna Loa, the district presents some of the most ecologically diverse land in the islands. The bulk of it stretches 50 miles from north to south and almost 40 miles from east to west, tumbling from the snowcapped mountain through the cool green canopy of highland forests. At lower elevations it becomes pastureland of belly-deep grass ending in blistering-hot black sands along the coast that are encircled by a necklace of foamy white sea. At the bottom of Kau is **Ka Lae** (South Point), the southernmost tip of Hawaii and the southernmost point in the U.S. It lies at a latitude 500 miles farther south than Miami and twice that below Los Angeles. Ka Lae was probably the first landfall made by the Polynesian explorers on the islands. A variety of archaeological remains supports this belief.

Most people dash through Kau on the Hawaii Belt Road, heading to or from Volcanoes National Park. Its main towns, **Pahala** and **Naalehu,** are little more than pit stops. The Belt Road follows the old Mamalahoa Trail where, for centuries, nothing moved faster than a contented man's stroll. Kau's beauties, mostly tucked away down secondary roads, are hardly given a look by most unknowing visitors. If you take the time and get off the beaten track, you'll discover black-and green-sand beaches, the world's largest macadamia nut farm, Wild West rodeos, and an electricity farm sprouting windmill generators. The upper slopes and broad pasturelands are the domain of hunters, hikers, and *paniolo,* who still ride the range on sure-footed horses. In Kau are sleepy plantation towns that don't even know how quaint they are, and beach parks where you can count on finding a secluded spot to pitch a tent. Time in Kau moves slowly, and *aloha* still forms the basis of day-to-day life.

The majority of Kau's pleasures are accessible by standard rental car, but many secluded coastal spots can be reached only by 4WD. For example, **Kailiki,** just west of Ka Lae, was an important fishing village in times past. A few archaeological remains are found here, and the beach has a green cast due to the lava's high olivine content. Few tourists ever visit; although hardy souls come to angle the coastal waters. Spots of this type abound, especially in Kau's remote sections. But civilization has found Kau as well: when you pass mile marker 63, look down to the coast and notice a stand of royal palms and a large brackish pond. This is Lua-hinivai Beach, one of the finest on the island, where country and western star Loretta Lynn has built a fabulous home. Those willing to abandon their cars and to hike the sparsely populated coast or interior of Kau are rewarded with areas unchanged and untouched for generations.

SIGHTS AND BEACHES

PAHALA

Some 22 miles west of Volcano is Pahala, clearly marked off Rt. 11. The Hawaii Belt Road flashes past this town, but if you drive into it, heading for the tall stack of the Kau Sugar Co., you'll find one of the best-preserved examples of a classic sugar town in the islands. It was once gospel that sugar would be "king" in these parts forever, but the huge stone stack of the sugar mill puffs no longer, while in the background the whir of a modern macadamia nut-processing plant breaks the stillness.

In Pahala you'll find the basics like a gas station, small shopping center, post office, Bank of Hawaii, Mizuno's Superette, and takeout plate lunch restaurant.

Wood Valley Temple

Also known as Nechung Dorje Drayang Ling, or Island of Melodious Sound, the Wood Valley Temple, P.O. Box 250, Pahala, HI 96777, tel. (808) 928-8539, is true to its name. This Tibetan Buddhist temple sits like a sparkling jewel surrounded by the emerald-green velvet of its manicured grounds that are scented by an aromatic stand of majestic eucalyptus trees. Here Marya and Miguel, the caretakers and administrators, will greet you if they are not off on one of their frequent trips to Asia.

Note: Recently, sightseers have been coming to the temple, and although most respect the fact that it functions as a spiritual retreat center, a few have not. Marya and Miguel are very warm and open-hearted people who welcome all guests, but they have requested that directions not be given to the general public. If you wish to spend time at Wood Valley Temple, please contact them at the above address or by phone, and they will direct you.

Buddha gave the world essentially 84,000 different teachings to pacify, purify, and develop the mind. In Tibetan Buddhism there are four major lineages, and this temple, founded by Tibetan master Nechung Rinpoche, is a classic synthesis of all four. Monks, lama, and scholars from different schools of Buddhism are periodically invited to come and lecture as resident teachers. The Dalai Lama came in 1980 to dedicate the temple, and graced the temple once again in 1994 when he addressed an audience here of more than 3,500 people. Two affiliate temples are located in Dharamsala, India, and in Lhasa, Tibet. Programs vary, but people genuinely interested in Buddhism come here for meditation and soul-searching as well as for peace, quiet, relaxation, and direction. Morning and evening services at 7 a.m. and 7 p.m. are led by Debala, the Tibetan monk in residence. Formal classes depend upon which invited teacher is in residence (write ahead for a schedule of programs).

The majority of the flowering and fruit trees on the premises are imports. Plenty of parishioners are into agriculture, and there is a strong movement by the temple members to slowly replant the grounds with native vegetation that they collect from various sites in and around Pahala. The grounds, like a botanical garden, vibrate with life and energy. Buddhists strive to become wise and compassionate people. The focus of the temple is to bring together all meditation and church groups in the community. Plenty of local Christian and Buddhist groups use the nonsectarian facilities. Any group that is spiritually, socially, and community oriented and that has a positive outlook is welcome. Wood Valley Temple can't promise nirvana, but they can point you to the path.

The retreat facility is called the **Tara Temple** and at one time housed a Japanese Shingon

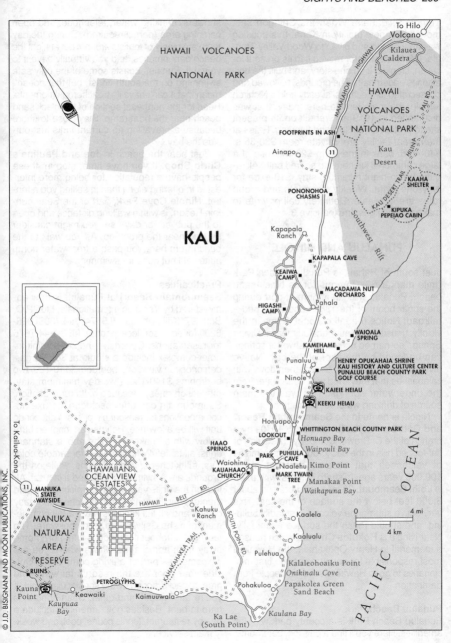

To Hilo
Volcano

Kilauea
Caldera

HAWAII VOLCANOES

NATIONAL PARK

HAWAII

VOLCANOES

NATIONAL PARK

Kau
Desert

FOOTPRINTS IN ASH

Ainapo

(11)

KAAHA
SHELTER

KIPUKA
PEPEIAO CABIN

Southwest Rift

PONONOHOA
CHASMS

KAU

Kapapala
Ranch

KAPAPALA CAVE

KEAIWA
CAMP

MACADAMIA NUT
ORCHARDS

HIGASHI
CAMP

Pahala

WAIOALA
SPRING

KAMEHAME
HILL

Punaluu

HENRY OPUKAHAIA SHRINE
KAU HISTORY AND CULTURE CENTER
PUNALUU BEACH COUNTY PARK
GOLF COURSE

Ninole

KAIEIE HEIAU

KEEKU HEIAU

Honuapo

WHITTINGTON BEACH COUTNY PARK

LOOKOUT

Honuapo Bay

HAAO
SPRINGS

Waipouli Bay

PARK

PUHIULA
CAVE

To Kailua-Kona

Waiohinu

KAUAHAAO
CHURCH

Naalehu

Kimo Point

MARK TWAIN
TREE

Manakaa Point

Waikapuna Bay

HAWAIIAN

OCEAN VIEW

ESTATES

(11)

MANUKA
STATE
WAYSIDE

HAWAII

BELT

RD.

Kahuku
Ranch

SOUTH POINT RD.

Kaalela

0   4 mi
0   4 km

MANUKA

NATURAL

AREA

RESERVE

KAHAKAHAKEA TRAIL

Kaalualu

Pulehua

RUINS

Kaunа
Point

PETROGLYPHS

Keawaiki

Kaimuuwala

Kalaleohoaiku Point

Onikinalu Cove

Papakolea Green
Sand Beach

Pohakuloa

*Kaupuaa
Bay*

Ka Lae
(South Point)

Kaulana Bay

PACIFIC

OCEAN

© J.D. BISIGNANI AND MOON PUBLICATIONS, INC.

Temple in Pahala. When the Shingon sect moved to a new facility in Kona, this building was abandoned and given to Wood Valley Temple. A local contractor moved it to its present location, cranked it up one story, and built the dormitories underneath. The grounds, hallowed and consecrated for decades, already held a Nichiren temple, the main temple here today, that was dismantled in 1919 and rebuilt on its present site to protect it from lowland flooding. Rates at the retreat facility are: private room $30-35 s, $40-45 d; bunk in the dorm $20 with use of a large communal kitchen and shared bath. All require a two-night minimum stay, $10 extra for only one night. Weekly discounts and group rates are available. Definitely call or write to make reservations. Inexpensive.3

PUNALUU AND NINOLE

Just south of Pahala is Punaluu Beach Park (mile marker 56), famous for its black-sand beach. Punaluu was an important port during the sugar boom of the 1880s and even had a railroad. Notice the tall coconut palms in the vicinity, unusual for Kau. Punaluu means "Diving Spring," so-named because freshwater springs can be found on the floor of the bay. Native divers once paddled out to sea, then dove with calabashes that they filled with fresh water from the underwater springs. This was the main source of drinking water for the region.

Ninole is home to the **Seamountain Resort and Golf Course,** built in the early 1970s by a branch of the C. Brewer Company. The string of flat-topped hills in the background is the remains of volcanoes that became dormant about 100,000 years ago. In sharp contrast with them is **Loihi Seamount,** 20 miles offshore and about 3,000 feet below the surface of the sea. This very active submarine volcano is steadily building, and should reach the surface eventually. Near Ninole is **Hokuloa Church,** which houses a memorial to Henry Opukahaia, the Hawaiian most responsible for encouraging the first missionaries to go to Hawaii to save his people from damnation.

Punaluu Beach Park

Punaluu Beach Park is a county park with full amenities. Here you'll find a pavilion, bathrooms, showers, drinking water, telephone, and open camping area (permit required). During the day there are plenty of tourists around, but at night the beach park empties, and you virtually have it to yourself. Punaluu boasts some of the only safe swimming on the south coast, but that doesn't mean that it can't have its treacherous moments. Head for the northeast section of the black sand beach near the boat ramp. Stay close to shore because a prevailing rip current lurks just outside the bay.

Just near the beach is **Joe and Pauline's Curio Shop.** If you have time, stop in; these people have a reputation for being more interested in offering *aloha* than in selling you a trinket. **Ninole Cove Park,** part of the Seamountain Resort, is within walking distance and open to the public. For day use, you might consider parking near the pro shop. As you walk to the beach from here you pass a freshwater pond, quite cold but good for swimming.

Practicalities

Seamountain Resort at Punaluu is now administered by Vacation Internationale, Ltd., P.O. Box 297, Kailua-Kona, HI 96745, tel. (808) 928-6200 (direct resort local phone), (800) 344-7675 for reservations. Options at the condominium/hotel complex include a studio at $85-95 garden or ocean view, one bedroom $110-120, two bedrooms $140-150, (two-day minimum stay, off-season rates). Because of its rural location, Seamountain can offer secluded, deluxe accommodations for reasonable prices. Your condo unit will be a low-rise, Polynesian-inspired bungalow with a shake roof. The above standard units, all tastefully furnished, offer remote color TVs, full kitchens, and full baths, while on the grounds are a swimming pool and a jacuzzi. Although the units vary, all are furnished in island theme, typically with rattan couches and easy chairs, and all full kitchens have a full complement of dishes, silverware, and cookware. The feeling throughout the resort is a friendly, home away from home atmosphere where you are welcomed as part of a living community. Outside your door are the resort's fairways and greens, backdropped by the spectacular coast. If you're after peace and quiet, Seamountain is hard to beat. Besides golf, amenities include a nearby restaurant, tennis courts, pool, and weekly maid service.

Seamountain Golf Course Club House, open daily 10 a.m.-2 p.m., serves a limited menu of sandwiches and *pu pu* and also offers a full bar and morning coffee available at 7 a.m. A *kaukau* wagon parks daily except Monday at Punaluu Beach, offering island sandwiches, cold drinks, and snacks.

The only organized sporting facility in Kau is at the Seamountain Resort. Here you'll find four unlit tennis courts and a 6,500-yard, 18-hole, par-72 course. Greens fees are $30 ($40 for a visitor), cart $20, and clubs $15. Range balls are $5 a bucket and golf lessons $25 an hour.

NAALEHU AND VICINITY

Whittington Beach Park

Three miles north of Naalehu is a county park with full amenities and camping. This park is tough to spot from the road because it's not clearly marked. As you're coming down a steep hill from Naalehu you'll see a bridge at the bottom. Turn right and you're there. The park is a bit run down, but never crowded. If you follow the dirt roads to its undeveloped sections you encounter many old ruins from the turn of the century when Honuapo Bay was an important sugar port.

Naalehu

Naalehu, the largest town in the area and the most southern town in the U.S., is lush. Check out the overhanging monkeypod trees. They form a magnificent living tunnel as you go down Rt. 11 through the center of town. Between Naalehu and Punaluu, the coastal area is majestic; stretching into the aqua-blue sea is a tableland of black lava with waves crashing against it in a surrealistic seascape that seems to go on forever. Every Fourth of July, a down-home rodeo is held in town for all the amateur riders of the district. Come and enjoy.

Waiohinu

A tall church steeple welcomes you to the small town of Waiohinu. There's nothing remarkable about this village, except that as you pass through you'll be seeing an example of the real Hawaiian lifestyle as it exists today. Just before the well-marked Shirakawa Motel on the *mauka* side of the road is the **Mark Twain Monkeypod**

Tree. Unfortunately, Waiohinu's only claim to fame except for its undisturbed peace and quiet blew down in a heavy windstorm in 1957. Part of the original trunk, carved into a bust of Twain, is on display at the Lyman House Museum in Hilo. Now, a few shoots have begun sprouting from the original trunk and in years to come the Monkeypod Tree will be an attraction again.

Accommodations

The **Shirakawa Motel,** P.O. Box 467, Naalehu, HI 96772, tel. (808) 929-7462, is a small, clean, comfortable, "hang loose bruddah" motel where your peace and quiet are guaranteed. It's been open since 1928; prices are a reasonable $30 s, $35 d, $42 with kitchen, $55 apartment complete with cardboard fireplace built by a man from Michigan who just couldn't forget the cold. There's a 10% discount for a one-week stay, 15% for longer, plus fees of $8 "roll away child," $10 "roll away adult" (if only it were that easy!).You'll be greeted by Kai, a golden Lab, who has given up aggression for the "hang loose, no worries" island lifestyle. Inexpensive.

Becky's Bed & Breakfast, P.O. Box 673, Naalehu, HI 96772, tel./fax (808) 929-9690 or (800) 235-1233, about 100 yards past the theater on the left, is owned and operated by Becky and Chuck McLinn. Available in this modest but cheery 60-year-old home are a spacious room with a queen bed and private bath for $50 s, $60 d; and a room with private entrance, two double beds, and private bath at $55 s, $65 d. There is no official policy, but if you stay four nights or longer, a discount can be arranged. To help you relax, the B&B features a backyard deck with a barbecue grill, inviting hammock, and hot tub to unjangle nerves. Becky serves a full breakfast of juice, fruit, and either Hawaiian French toast or hotcakes with bacon or sausage. Chuck serves as general handy man; he also takes a Polaroid photo of every guest and pastes it next to their comments in a guest book. Make sure to have a look at this ongoing account from visitors around the world. E-mail: beckys@interpac.net; website: hawaii-bnb.com/beckt.html. Moderate.

Margo Hobbs and Philip Shaw of **Margo's Corner,** P.O. Box 447, Naalehu, HI 96772, tel. (808) 929-9614, e-mail: margos.corner@mailcity.com, can accommodate you in a brightly painted pentagonal guesthouse for $50 s or $60 d, which includes two vegetarian meals with the family. The guesthouse, with a private bath and shower, has a queen-size bed. Two nights minimum preferred. Call for reservations and directions. Touring bicyclists and backpackers can camp ($25 pp) in the yard among Norfolk pines and an organic vegetable garden. A shower is available. No smoking and no excessive drinking, please. For your extra food needs, Margo's maintains a "small, but well-stocked health food store." Moderate.

Food

For homemade goodies and coffee, try **Cafe Ohia,** tel. (808) 929-8086, across from the Texaco gas station.

A mile farther south is **South Point Bar and Restaurant,** which is the best, albeit the "only" (which helps) restaurant and bar in the area. Actually, the bar and restaurant are separate establishments sharing the same roof. The restaurant is open daily noon-5 p.m. for lunch and 5-8 p.m. for dinner, with the bar open until 10 p.m. and live music on Friday night. Lunch ($5-9) can be sandwiches like ham and turkey for, clubhouse, garden burger, soup and small dinner salad, shrimp salad, mountainous chef salad, and a whopping one-third-pound burger with tomato, sprouts, and choice of fresh cut fries or potato salad. For dinner try a 16-oz. rib eye steak at $15.95, seafood platter for $14.95, or vegetable lasagna at $7.95. Sunday noon-2 p.m., the bar offers a barbecue out back that brings in the local people—always a good sign. The full bar serves wine, liquor, and draft and bottled beers, and there are pool tables and televised sports to pass the time. Most patrons are friendly local people.

In Waiohinu, about a mile west of Naalehu, look for **Mark Twain's Square Café and Gift Shop,** open Mon.-Fri. 8 a.m.-5 p.m., Saturday 8 a.m.-4 p.m., owned and operated by the Fujikawa family. The luscious smells will lead you to fresh-baked bread, *manapua,* and an assortment of sandwiches all under $4, as well as plate lunches and daily specials like barbecue pork with rice and salad for $5.50.

As you are entering the west side of town, a large, easily spotted sign on the left marks the **Punaluu Bake Shop and Visitor's Center,** tel. (808) 929-7343, open daily 9 a.m.-5 p.m. The bake shop, tempting with all kinds of pastries,

is especially known for its *pao dolce,* sweet bread. Park and follow daily busloads of tourists down a cement pathway to the retail shop for baked goods, sandwiches, coffee, cold drinks and a smattering of souvenirs.

For a quick sandwich or full meal try the **Naalehu Coffee Shop,** open daily, tel. (808) 929-7238. Many of the local people call this restaurant "Roy's," after the owner's first name. The menu is typical island cuisine with a Japanese flavor; the best item is the fresh fish from local waters. The restaurant is basic and clean, with most meals on the menu around $7. They also have a wide assortment of souvenirs and tourist junk, and a large koi pond outside. Look for the big yellow building just near the shopping center as you enter town.

Naalehu Fruit Stand, tel. (808) 929-9009, open Mon.-Thurs. 9 a.m.-6:30 p.m., Friday and Saturday till 7 p.m., Sunday till 5 p.m., is a favorite with local people, always a tip-off that the food is great. Along with fresh fruit, they sell submarines, hot dogs, pizza, salads, sodas, teas, coffee, fresh-baked goods, and a good selec-

a local favorite

tion of grains, minerals, vitamins, and health foods. The owners, John and Dorene Santangelo, are very friendly and willing to give advice about touring the Kau area (good bulletin board for local events). This is the best place on the south coast for a light meal or picnic lunch.

About 100 yards from the Naalehu Fruit Stand, notice the baseball park. Here **Kalaiki Plate Lunch,** open daily 5:30 a.m.-4 p.m., run by the Hanoa family, serves hearty sandwiches and island favorites ready to go. They are especially known for their full breakfasts, only $3-4.

Shopping and Supplies

In Naalehu you can gas yourself or your car at the **Luzon Liquor Store,** open daily 7 a.m.-9 p.m. You can also find basic groceries and supplies in this jam-packed, friendly local establishment (public telephone on porch).

Naalehu Shopping Center is along the road at the west end of town. In the small complex you'll find Food Mart and Ed's Laundromat.

The **Southern Star Theater** is a large building also at the west end of town. It's a classic old-time theater usually open on weekends, adults $3.25, children $1.75.

Kau Fishing Supply in Waiohinu offers fresh local fish that would make a perfect self-prepared meal for anyone heading out of town. Just down the road, you can pick up supplies at **Wong Yuen General Store and Gas Station,** open Mon.-Sat. 8:30 a.m.-5 p.m., Sunday to 3 p.m., tel. (808) 929-7223.

Turtle Cove Woods, open daily 10 a.m.-6 p.m., is a souvenir and neat tourist junk shop across from Whittington Beach. Inside, along with hula skirts, wooden boxes, *kukui* nut lei, wooden platters, straw hats, and tiki carvings (done by owner J.D.), you'll find Nalani Kona Coffee at only $10 per pound.

SOUTH POINT

The Hawaiians simply called this Ka Lae (The Point). Some scholars believe Polynesian sailors made landfall here as early as A.D. 150, and that their amazing exploits became navigating legend long before colonization began. A paved, narrow, but passable road branches off from Rt. 11 approximately six miles west of Naalehu, and drops directly south for 12 miles to land's end.

Luckily the shoulders are firm, so you can pull over to let another car go by. The car-rental agencies warn against using this road, but their fears are unfounded. You proceed through a flat, treeless area trimmed by free-ranging herds of cattle and horses: more road obstacles to be aware of. Suddenly, incongruously, huge mechanical windmills appear, beating their arms against the sky. This is the **Kamoa Wind Farm.** Notice that this futuristic experiment at America's most southern point uses windmills made in Japan by Mitsubishi! The trees here are bent over by the prevailing wind, demonstrating the obviously excellent wind-power potential of the area. Farther along, a road sign informs you that the surrounding countryside is controlled by the **Hawaiian Homeland Agency,** and that you are forbidden to enter. That means that you are not welcome on the land, but you do have right-of-way on the road.

Here the road splits left and right. Go right until road's end, where you'll find a parking area usually filled with the pickup trucks of local fishermen. Walk to the cliff and notice attached ladders that plummet straight down to where the fishing boats are anchored. Local skippers moor their boats here and bring supplies and their catch up and down the ladders. Proceed south along the coast for only five minutes and you'll see a tall white structure with a big square sign on it turned sideways like a diamond. It marks the true *South Point,* the southernmost tip of the United States. Proceed to the sea and notice the tidepools, a warning that the swells can come high onto the rocks and that you can be swept away if you turn your back on *moana.* Usually, a few people are line-fishing for crevalle or pompano. The rocks are covered with Hawaiian dental floss—monofilament fishing line that has been snapped. Survey the mighty Pacific and realize that the closest continental landfall is Antarctica, 7,500 miles to the south.

Back at the Hawaiian Homes sign, follow the road left and pass a series of WW II barracks being reclaimed by nature. This road, too, leads to a parking area and a boat ramp where a few seaworthy craft are bobbing away at their moorings. Walk toward the navigational marker and you may notice small holes drilled into the stone. These were used by Hawaiian fishermen to secure their canoes to shore by long ropes while the current carried them a short way offshore. In this manner, they could fish without being swept away. Today fishermen still use these holes, but instead of canoes they use floats or tiny boats to carry only their lines out to sea. The *ulua,* tuna, and *ahi* fishing is renowned throughout this area. The fishing grounds here have always been extremely fertile, and thousands of shell and bone fishhooks have been found throughout the area. Scuba divers say that the rocks off South Point are covered with broken fishing line that the currents have woven into wild macramé.

When the Kona winds blow out of the South Pacific, South Point takes it on the chin. The weather should always be a consideration when you visit. In times past, any canoe caught in the wicked currents was considered lost. Even today, only experienced boaters brave South Point, and only during fine weather.

There is no official camping or facilities of any kind at South Point, but plenty of boat owners bivouac for a night to get an early start in the morning. The lava flow in this area is quite old and grass-covered, and the constant winds act like a natural lawn mower.

The best **windsurfing** in the area is at Kaulana Bay. Head down South Point Road, and about a half mile before you get to the windmills is a passable dirt road to the left. You can only see about a half mile down it when you first start out, but keep going. Pass through cattle gates and make absolutely sure to close them behind you. When you get to the bay, go to the left-hand side for the best entry. Remember that down here, no help is available, and you are totally on your own!

Green Sand Beach

From the boat ramp, a footpath leads east toward Kaulana Bay. All along here are remnants of precontact habitation, including the remains of a *heiau* foundation. If you walk for three miles, you'll come to Papakolea, better known as Green Sand Beach. The lava in this area contains olivine, a green semiprecious stone that weathered into sandlike particles distributed along the beach. The road heading down to Green Sand Beach is incredible. It begins as a very rugged jeep trail, and disintegrates from there. Do not attempt this walk unless you have closed-toe shoes. Thongs will not make it. You're walking into the wind going down, but it's not a rough go—there's no elevation gain to speak of. The

lava in the area is a'a, weathered and overlaid by a rather thick ground cover. Follow the road, and after 10 minutes, the lava ends and rich, green pastureland begins. An ancient eruption deposited 15-18 feet of ash right here, and the grasses grew.

Continue for approximately 35 minutes, until you see what is obviously an eroded cinder cone at the edge of the sea. (About 15 minutes back, you'll have noticed an area where many 4WDs have pulled off at an overlook. That isn't it!) Peer over the edge to see the beach with its definite green tinge. This is the only *beach* along the way, so it's hard to mistake. Getting down to it is absolutely treacherous. You'll be scrambling over tough lava rock, and you'll have to make drops of four to five feet in certain spots. The best approach is to go over the edge as soon as you come to the cinder cone area; don't walk around to what would be the south point of the caldera where the sand is. Once you get over the lip of heavy-duty rock, the trail down is not so bad. When you begin your descent, notice overhangs, almost like caves, where rocks have been piled up to extend them. These rocked-in areas make great shelters, and you can see remnants of recent campfires in spots perfect for a night's bivouac.

Green Sand Beach definitely lives up to its name, but don't expect emerald green. It's more like an army green, a dullish khaki green. Down at the beach, be very aware of the wave action. Watch for at least 15 minutes to be sure breakers are not inundating the entire beach. Then you can walk across it, but stay close to the lava rock wall. The currents can be wicked here and you should only enter the water on very calm days. No one is around to save you, and you don't want to wind up as flotsam in Antarctica.

Manuka State Wayside

The Manuka State Wayside is 12 miles west of South Point Rd. and just inside the Kau District. This civilized scene has restrooms, pavilions, and trails through manicured gardens surrounded by an arboretum. Shelter camping (no tents) is allowed on the grounds. All plants are identified. This is an excellent rest or picnic stop. The forested slopes above Manuka provide ample habitat for introduced, and now totally successful, colonies of wild pigs, pheasants, and turkeys.

KONA

Kona is long and lean and takes its suntanned body for granted. This district *is* the west coast of the Big Island and lies in the rain shadows of both Mauna Loa and Mauna Kea. You can come here expecting brilliant sunny days and glorious sunsets, and you won't be disappointed; this reliable sunshine has earned Kona the nickname "The Gold Coast." Offshore, the fishing grounds are legendary, especially for marlin that lure game-fishing enthusiasts from around the world. There are actually two Konas, north and south, and both enjoy an upland interior of forests, ranches, and homesteads while most of the coastline is low, broad, and flat. If you've been fantasizing about swaying palms and tropical jungles dripping with wild orchids, you might be in for "Kona shock," especially if you fly directly into the Kona Airport. Around the airport the land is raw black lava that can appear as forbidding as the tailings from an old mining operation. Don't despair. Just north is one of the premier resorts in Hawaii, with a gorgeous white-sand beach lined with dancing coconut palms, and throughout Kona the lava has been transformed into beautiful gardens with just a little love and care.

The entire Kona District is both old and historic. This was the land of Lono, god of fertility and patron of the Makahiki Festival. It was also the spot where the first missionary packet landed and changed Hawaii forever, and it's been a resort since the 19th century. In and around **Kailua** are restored *heiau,* a landmark lava church, and a royal palace where the monarchs of Hawaii came to relax. The coastline is rife with historical sites: lesser *heiau,* petroglyph fields, and curious amusement rides dating from the days of the Makahiki. Below the town of Captain Cook is **Kealakekua Bay,** the first and main *haole* anchorage in the islands until the development of Honolulu Harbor. This bay's historical significance is overwhelming, alternately being a place of life, death, and hope from where the spirit of Hawaii was changed for all time. Here on the southern coast is a Hawaiian "temple of refuge," restored and made into a National Historical Park. The majority of Kona's sights are strung along Rt. 11. Except for Kailua-Kona, where a walking tour is perfect, you need a rental car to visit the sights; the Big Island's Hele-On Bus is too infrequent to be feasible. If you're walking, pick up a copy of the pamphlet *Walking Tour of Historic Kailua Village,* put out by the Kona Historical Society.

Kailua-Kona is the heart of North Kona, by far the most developed area in the district. Its **Ali'i Drive** is lined with shops, hotels, and condos, but for the most part the shoreline vista remains intact because most of the buildings are low-rise. To show just how fertile lava can be when tended, miles of multihued bougainvillea and poinsettias line Ali'i Dr. like a lei that leads to the flowerpot of the **Kona Gardens.** East of town is **Mount Hualalai** (8,271 feet), where local people still earn a living growing vegetables and taro on small truck farms high in the mountain coolness.

South Kona begins in the town of **Captain Cook.** Southward is a region of diminutive coffee plantations, the only ones in the U.S. The bushes grow to the shoulder of the road and the air is heady with the rich aroma of roasting coffee. Farther south, rough but passable roads branch from the main highway and tumble toward hidden beaches and tiny fishing villages where time just slips away. From north to south, Kona is awash in brilliant sunshine, and the rumble of surf and the plaintive cry of seabirds create the music of peace.

KAILUA-KONA AND VICINITY

SIGHTS

Mokuaikaua Church
Kailua is one of those towns that would love to contemplate its own navel if it could only find it. It doesn't really have a center, but if you had to pick one, it would be the 112-foot steeple of Mokuaikaua (The trees are felled, now let us eat) Church. This highest structure in town has been a landmark for travelers and seafarers ever since the church was completed in January 1838. The church claims to be the oldest house of Christian worship in Hawaii. The site was given by King Liholiho to the first Congregationalist missionaries who arrived on the brig *Thaddeus* in 1820. The actual construction was undertaken in 1836 by the Hawaiian congregation under the direction of Rev. Asa Thurston. Much thought was given to the orientation of the structure, designed so the prevailing winds blow through the entire length of the church to keep it cool and comfortable. The walls of the church are fashioned from massive, rough-hewn lava stone, mortared with plaster made from crushed and burned coral that was bound with *kukui* nut oil. The huge cornerstones are believed to have been salvaged from a *heiau* built in the 15th century by King Umi. The masonry is crude but effective—still sound after 150 years.

Inside, the church is extremely soothing, expressing a feeling of strength and simplicity. The resolute beams are native ohia, pegged together and closely resembling the fine beamwork used in barns throughout 19th-century New England. The pews, railings, pulpit, and trim are all fashioned from koa, a rich brown, lustrous wood that begs to be stroked. Although the church is still used as a house of worship, it also has the air of a museum, housing paintings of historical personages instrumental in Hawaii's Christian past. The crowning touch is an excellent model of the brig *Thaddeus,* painstakingly built by the men of the Pacific Fleet Command and presented to the church in 1934. The church is open daily from sunrise to sunset, and volunteer hostesses answer your questions 10 a.m.-noon and 1-3:30 p.m. Mokuaikaua Church is a few hundred yards south of Kailua Pier on the *mauka* side of Ali'i Drive.

Hulihee Palace
Go from the spiritual to the temporal by walking across the street from Mokuaikaua Church and entering Hulihee (Turning Point) Palace. This two-story Victorian structure commissioned by Hawaii's second governor, John Kuakini, also dates from 1838. A favorite summer getaway for all the Hawaiian monarchs who followed, especially King Kalakaua, it was used as such until 1916. At first glance, the outside is unimpressive, but the more you look the more you realize how simple and grand it is. The architectural lines are those of an English country manor, and indeed Great Britain was held in high esteem by the Hawaiian royalty. Inside, the palace is bright and airy. Most of the massive carved furniture is made from koa. The most magnificent pieces include a huge formal dining table, 70

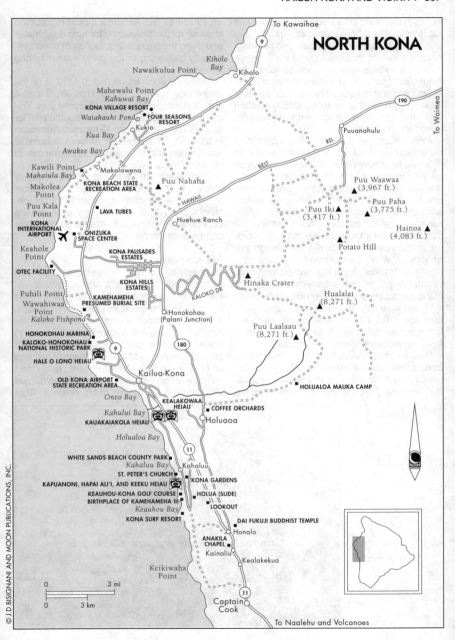

NORTH KONA

To Kawaihae

Kiholo Bay
Kiholo

Nawaikulua Point

190

To Waimea

Mahewalu Point
Kahuwai Bay
KONA VILLAGE RESORT
Waiakauhi Pond ● FOUR SEASONS RESORT
○ Kukio
Kua Bay

Puuanahulu

RD.

Awakee Bay

Kawili Point
Mahaiula Bay
■ Makalawena

KONA BEACH STATE RECREATION AREA
■ Puu Nahaha

BELT

Puu Waawaa ▲
(3,967 ft.)

Makolea Point

Puu Kala Point

■ LAVA TUBES

HAWAII

Huehue Ranch

Puu Iki ▲
(3,417 ft.)

Puu Paha ▲
(3,775 ft.)

Hainoa ▲
(4,083 ft.)

KONA INTERNATIONAL AIRPORT ✈

■ ONIZUKA SPACE CENTER

Keahole Point

■ KONA PALISADES ESTATES

Potato Hill ▲

■ OTEC FACILITY

Puhili Point

Wawahiwaa Point

Kaloko Fishpond

KALOKO DR.

KONA HILLS ESTATES ■

KAMEHAMEHA PRESUMED BURIAL SITE ■

○ Honokohau
(Palani Junction)

Hinaka Crater ▲

Hualalai ▲
(8,271 ft.)

HONOKOHAU MARINA ■

KALOKO-HONOKOHAU NATIONAL HISTORIC PARK

Puu Laalaau ▲
(8,271 ft.)

HALE O LONO HEIAU ■

9

180

OLD KONA AIRPORT ■ STATE RECREATION AREA

Kailua-Kona

Oneo Bay

KEALAKOWAA HEIAU

■ HOLUALOA MAUKA CAMP

Kahului Bay 🔱🔱

■ COFFEE ORCHARDS

KAUAKAIAKOLA HEIAU

Holuaoa

Holualoa Bay

WHITE SANDS BEACH COUNTY PARK ■

11

Kahaluu Bay

ST. PETER'S CHURCH ■
Kahaluu

■ KONA GARDENS

KAPUANONI, HAPAI ALI'I, AND KEEKU HEIAU 🔱

KEAUHOU-KONA GOLF COURSE ■
BIRTHPLACE OF KAMEHAMEHA III ■

■ HOLUA (SLIDE)

Keauhou Bay

■ LOOKOUT

KONA SURF RESORT ■

■ DAI FUKUJI BUDDHIST TEMPLE

Honalo

ANAKILA CHAPEL ■

Keikiwaha Point

Kainaliu

Kealakekua

11

Captain Cook

To Naalehu and Volcanoes

0   3 mi
0   3 km

© J.D BISIGNANI AND MOON PUBLICATIONS, INC.

inches in diameter, fashioned from one solid koa log. Upstairs is a tremendous four-poster bed that belonged to Queen Kapiolani, and two magnificent cabinets that were built by a Chinese convict who was serving a life sentence for smuggling opium. King Kalakaua heard of his talents and commissioned him to build the cabinets. They proved to be so wonderfully crafted that after they were completed the king pardoned the craftsman.

Prince Kuhio, who inherited the palace from his uncle, King Kalakaua, was the first Hawaiian delegate to Congress. He decided to auction off all the furniture and artifacts to raise money, supposedly for the benefit of the Hawaiian people. Providentially, the night before the auction each piece was painstakingly numbered by the royal ladies of the palace, and the name of the person bidding for the piece was dutifully recorded. In the years that followed, the **Daughters of Hawaii,** who now operate the palace as a museum, tracked down the owners and convinced many to return the items for display. Most of the pieces are privately owned, and because each is unique, the owners wish no duplicates to be made. It is for this reason, coupled with the fact that flashbulbs can fade the wood, that a strict *no photography* policy is enforced.

Delicate and priceless heirlooms on display include a tiger-claw necklace that belonged to Kapiolani. You'll also see a portrait gallery of Hawaiian monarchs. Personal and mundane items are on exhibit as well—there's an old report card showing a 68 in philosophy for King Kalakaua—and lining the stairs is a collection of spears reputedly belonging to the great Kamehameha himself.

Hulihee Palace, tel. (808) 329-1877, is on the *makai* side of Ali'i Dr., open Mon.-Fri. 9 a.m.-4 p.m., Saturday and Sunday 10 a.m.-4 p.m. You can look around on your own or ask the staff for a tour, which usually lasts 45 minutes. Admission is $5 adult, $4 seniors, $1 student. A hostess knowledgeable in Hawaiiana is usually on duty to answer most questions.

The **Palace Gift Shop,** small but with quality items, is on the grounds next door to the palace. It offers a fine selection of koa sculptures of fish, sharks, and even a turtle, along with Hawaiiana books and postcards. Just outside is a saltwater pond with tropical fish.

Ahuena Heiau

Directly behind King Kamehameha's Kona Beach Hotel, at the north end of "downtown" Kailua, is the restored Ahuena Heiau. Built around Kamakahonu (Eye of the Turtle) Beach, it's in a very important historical area. Kamehameha I, the great conqueror, came here to spend the last years of his life, settling down to a peaceful existence after many years of war and strife. The king, like all Hawaiians, reaffirmed his love of the *aina* and tended his own royal taro patch on the slopes of Mt. Hualalai. After

Ahuena Heiau

he died, his bones were prepared according to ancient ritual on a stone platform within the temple, then taken to a secret burial place just north of town which is believed to be somewhere near Wawahiwaa Point. It was Kamehameha who initiated the first rebuilding of Ahuena Heiau, a temple of peace and prosperity dedicated to Lono, god of fertility. The rituals held here were a far cry from the bloody human sacrifices dedicated to the god of war, Kukailimoku, that were held at Puukohola Heiau, which Kamehameha had built a few leagues north and a few decades earlier. At Ahuena, Kamehameha gathered the sage *kahuna* of the land to discourse in the Hale Mana (main prayer house) on topics concerning wise government and statesmanship. It was here that Liholiho, Kamehameha's son and heir, was educated, and it was here that as a grown man he sat down with the great queens, Keopuolani and Kaahumanu, and broke the ancient *kapu* of eating with women, thereby destroying the old order.

The tallest structure on the temple grounds is the *anuu* (oracle tower), where the chief priest, in deep trance, received messages from the gods. Throughout the grounds are superbly carved *kia akua* (temple images) in the distinctive Kona style, considered some of the finest of all Polynesian art forms. The spiritual focus of the *heiau* was humanity's higher nature, and the tallest figure, crowned with an image of the golden plover, was that of Koleamoku, a god of healing. Another interesting structure is a small thatched hut of sugarcane leaves, Hale Nana Mahina, which means "house from which to watch the farmland." Kamehameha would come here to meditate while a guard kept watch from a nearby shelter. The commanding view from the doorway affords a sweeping panorama from the sea to the king's plantations on the slopes of Mt. Hualalai. Though the temple grounds, reconstructed under the auspices of the Bishop Museum, are impressive, they are only one-third their original size. The *heiau* is open daily 9 a.m.-4 p.m., and admission is free. You can wander around following a self-guided tour, or take the free tour offered by King Kamehameha's Kona Beach Hotel, tel. (808) 329-2911, which includes a tour of their own hotel grounds as well. The hotel portion of the tour includes a walk through the lobby, where various artifacts are displayed, and features an extremely informative botanical tour that highlights the medicinal herbs of old Hawaii. The hotel tours begin at 1:30 p.m. weekdays. Don't miss this excellent educational opportunity, well worth the time and effort!

While in the area, make sure to visit the **Kailua Pier,** across the street from the *heiau*. Fishing boats are in and out all day, with most charters returning around 5 p.m. You'll have a chance to see some of the marlin for which Kona is noted, but if you have a sympathetic heart or weak stomach it might not be for you. This area is frantic with energy during the various "billfish tournaments" held throughout the year.

Honokohau Marina

Honokohau Harbor, three miles north of Kailua-Kona, is a small boat harbor and deep-sea fishing facility that has eclipsed the old Kailua Pier. The harbor area is full of fishing-oriented shops and is also home to the **Harbor House Restaurant,** where you can have a yarn with Kona's old salts. Primarily, this is where you come to see huge marlin caught that day, and to talk to the skippers of the deep-sea fishing boats that go after them. (For a description of deep-sea fishing see the **Sports and Recreation** section in the Out and About chapter) When you pull into the marina, you'll see a road that goes off to the left. Head that way toward the tan building with a Texaco sign, to where the pier and the weigh-station are located. The huge fish will be hoisted, measured, and photographed while the skippers and their crews clean and prepare the boats for the next day's outing. **Weigh in** is every day 11 a.m.-1 p.m., and 3-6 p.m., tel. (808) 334-1881 for information. If you are fascinated by deep-sea fishing, this is your chance to pick a likely boat and to get acquainted with the crew.

Natural Energy Laboratory of Hawaii Authority (NELHA), a.k.a. OTEC

The future is now at these amazing Ocean Technology facilities located just south of the airport between mile markers 95 and 94, where you'll find a turnoff heading toward the sea. Incredible things are being done here. For example, cold water from several thousand feet below the surface of the ocean is placed in a turbine with warm surface water, a process that generates electricity and also provides desalinated water. In

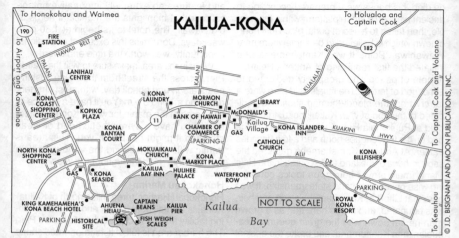

KAILUA-KONA

To Honokohau and Waimea

To Holualoa and Captain Cook

To Airport and Kawaihae

To Captain Cook and Volcano

To Keauhou

190 • FIRE STATION
HAWAII BELT RD.
PALANI RD.
LANIHAU CENTER
KONA COAST SHOPPING CENTER
KOPIKO PLAZA
KONA BANYAN COURT
NORTH KONA SHOPPING CENTER
GAS • KONA SEASIDE
KING KAMEHAMEHA'S KONA BEACH HOTEL
PARKING
HISTORICAL SITE
AHUENA HEIAU
CAPTAIN BEANS
KAILUA PIER
FISH WEIGH SCALES
KAILUA BAY INN
HULIHEE PALACE
MOKUAIKAUA CHURCH
KONA MARKET PLACE
WATERFRONT ROW
KONA LAUNDRY
MORMON CHURCH
BANK OF HAWAII
CHAMBER OF COMMERCE
PARKING
KALANI ST.
11
McDONALD'S
LIBRARY
Kailua Village
GAS
KONA ISLANDER INN
CATHOLIC CHURCH
KUAKINI HWY.
KUAKINI
ALII DR.
KONA BILLFISHER
182
KUAKINI RD.
PARKING
ROYAL KONA RESORT

Kailua Bay

NOT TO SCALE

© J.D. BISIGNANI AND MOON PUBLICATIONS, INC.

addition, the cold water is used for raising very un-Hawaiian things such as strawberries, lobsters, abalone, sea cucumbers, commercial black pearls, and Japanese flounder, as well as for raising *limu,* a local edible seaweed. Others use its alternative energy source to make fish jerky, to grow shiitake mushrooms, and even to raise tropical fish that will become living bouquets of color in fish tanks around the world. Cyanotech, a leading manufacturer of marine products for worldwide nutrition and pharmaceutical markets, uses the facilities to make spirulina, available in health food stores. Tours are offered Thursday at 10 a.m.; call (808) 329-7341 for reservations. If you choose to take a tour, don't be overwhelmed by the size of the complex; the products are brought to a central area for your viewing. Afterward, you can request a tour of the facility. No tasting is offered, so bring your own snacks. For those who want to walk around on their own, maps are available.

Onizuka Space Center

Dedicated to Hawaii's own Col. Ellison S. Onizuka and to the men and women who tragically perished aboard the spacecraft *Challenger* on January 28, 1986, the center is located at Kona International Airport, P.O. Box 833, Kailua-Kona, HI 96745, tel. (808) 329-3441, fax 326-9751, website: www.planet-hawaii.com/astronautonizuka. Hours are daily 8:30 a.m.-4:30 p.m. except Thanksgiving, Christmas, and New Year's Day; admission $3 adults, $1 children. From this tragedy, a living memorial and space education facility was erected. Inside the modern, well-appointed building children and adults alike can marvel at human exploration of space by viewing exhibits like a "moon rock," scale model of a space shuttle and space station, an interactive staffed maneuvering unit, and a space theater with educational showings throughout the day. There is a gift shop with plenty of fascinating reading material concerning the international effort to explore the heavens. Stop in before flying out.

Along Ali'i Drive

Ali'i Drive heads south from Kailua, passing the majority of Kona's resorts. On the mountain side of the road, a continuous flow of flowers drapes the shoulder like a femme fatale's seductive boa, while seaside the coastline slips along, rugged and bright, making Ali'i Drive a soothing sight.

At your first stop, near White Sands Beach, look for the historic **Ohana Congregational Church** built in 1855 by Rev. John D. Paris. Services are still held every Sunday at 8 a.m. The base of the church is mostly original lava rock topped with a new roof. The cemetery area is peaceful and quiet and offers a perfect meditative perch from which to scan the coast below. Back on the road, look for signs to Kahaluu Beach

Park; pull in and park here. On the rocky northern shore of this bay is **St. Peter's Catholic Church.** Its diminutive size, capped by a blue tin roof that winks at you from amidst the lava like a bright morning glory in an ebony vase, has earned it the nickname **Little Blue Church.** Built in 1889 on the site of an old, partially reclaimed *heiau,* the church is a favorite spot for snapshots. Inside, the epitome of simplicity reigns with bare wood walls and a simple crucifix. The only splash of color is a bouquet of fresh flowers on the altar. To the right of the church as you face it are the remains of **Kuemanu Heiau,** and within a 10-minute walk heading south from the church along the coast are strung the remains of **Kapuanoni, Hapai Ali'i,** and **Keeku** *heiau.* All are unrestored historical sites that still show signs of being used, and all offer fantastic vantage points from which to view the coast.

Do yourself a favor and visit the grounds of the **Kona Surf Resort,** which have graciously been opened to the public. You're free to stroll around on your own, and nonguests can take a tour on Sunday, Tuesday, or Thursday at 3 p.m. Here are 14 acres of ponds and gardens glorious with the perfumes and blooms of more than 30,000 plants, flowers, fruits, and shrubs gathered from throughout Polynesia. To complement the natural setting of the grounds, a profusion of Asian and Hawaiian artwork has been placed here and there. Inside, the main hallways of the hotel's four wings are resplendent with more than a million dollars' worth of wall hangings and tapestries. For a special treat, visit in the evening, when the hotel shines spotlights on the water, bringing tiny crustaceans to the surface. Often, huge manta rays will also surface in the light to feed on this delectable buffet. Some local dive shops offer night dives especially for this thrilling experience.

A short stroll or a minute's drive south brings you to **Keauhou Bay.** Here you'll find a cluster of historical sites, and the pier for the Fair Winds Snorkel Dive and Charter. Look for a monument marking the birthplace of Kamehameha III in 1814. Local people come to fish from the pier around 5 p.m. for *halalu,* a tough little fish to catch. Ask at the Keauhou Beach Resort for a free area map. Along the shoreline are a number of partially developed *heiau* sites. You'll also find a *holua,* grass-covered rocks that were slicked with water to form a slide. Hawaiians rode it on

St. Peter's Church

wooden sleds, especially during the Makahiki Festival. A small home stuck on a point of land on the edge of the bay is where John Wayne married his wife Pilar in 1954, and marks the site of the first modern house built on the bay.

BEACHES AND PARKS

If Kona is short on anything, it is beaches. The ones that it has are adequate and quite striking in their own way, but they tend to be small, few, and far between. Most people expecting a huge expanse of white sands will be disappointed. These beaches do exist on the Big Island's west coast, but they are north of Kailua-Kona in the Kohala District. Kona does, however, have beaches alive with marine life, providing excellent and safe snorkeling and top-notch tidepooling.

Note: The following are the main beaches in Kailua-Kona and North Kona. For descriptions of South Kona beaches see below.

Kamakahonu Beach

You couldn't be more centrally located than at "Eye of the Turtle" Beach. Find it in downtown Kailua-Kona near Kailua Pier and King Kamehameha's Kona Beach Hotel. Local people refer to it as "Kids' Beach" because it is so gentle and perfect for a refreshing dip. Big kids come here to play too, when every year world-class athletes churn the gentle waters into a fury at the start of the Ironman Triathlon. Rent snorkel gear, kayaks, and Hobie Cats for reasonable prices from the **Beach Shack**, located on the beach itself. Restrooms are on the pier.

Old Kona Airport State Recreation Area

In 1970 the old Kona Airport closed and the state of Hawaii turned it into a beach park. To get there, simply walk along the shoreline for a few hundred yards north of King Kamehameha's Kona Beach Hotel. If driving, follow Ali'i Drive to the junction just before the North Kona Shopping Center and turn left on the Kuakini Highway Extension. Facilities include showers, restrooms, and a picnic area. Parking is unlimited along the old runway, where you can also walk, bike, rollerblade, or jog. The park gate closes at 8 p.m. The white-sand beach is sandwiched between water's edge and the runway. You can enter the water at some shallow inlets, but the bottom is often rocky (be sure to wear water shoes) and the waters can be treacherous during high surf. The safest spot is a little sandy cove at the southern end of the beach. Snorkeling is good at the northern end of the beach, and offshore a break makes Old Airport popular with Kona surfers. There is no official camping at the park, but people often do camp at the north end. A heated controversy erupted when a developer purchased the land adjacent to the north end of the park, then closed it to camping. Local fishermen had camped here for years. Protesting in 1981, they raised a tent village named Kukai-limoku, which disbanded when the leaders were arrested for trespassing. It's also disputed whether the developer has claimed eight acres that actually belong to the state. The controversy goes on.

Honokohau Beach

All types of people come to Honokohau Beach, including fishermen, surfers, and snorkelers, but it's primarily known as a **clothing optional**

beach. This status has been drastically changing ever since the area officially became part of **Kaloko-Honokohau National Historical Park.** Follow Rt. 19 north from Kailua-Kona for three miles and turn left on the marked road leading to the Honokohau Small Boat Harbor. Stay to the right and park almost at the end of the access road near the "boat graveyard" in a dirt parking lot. Don't walk straight ahead onto land being claimed by the Pai 'ohana, a local Hawaiian family trying to establish a homestead within the "sovereign jurisdiction of the Kingdom of Hawaii." Instead clamber over the berm, follow the well-worn path into the vegetation, and keep walking for a few minutes to the beach.

This area, more toward Kaloko, was heavily populated during old Hawaiian days, and plenty of archaeological sites—mostly fishponds, ruins of houses, and a few petroglyphs—are found along the shoreline. Most of these sites are closed to protect them for posterity; if you come to an archaeological area, obey all posted signs and approach with great care and respect. Remember, it is imperative that you do not touch, disturb, or remove any historical artifacts. The coarse gray sand beach offers safe swimming in somewhat shallow water, and except for a composting toilet, there are no facilities.

The status of nudity along the beach is changing, and as part of the General Management Plan, the "proposed action" is to make nudity illegal. Camping and open fires, now illegal, are citable offenses under federal regulations. Walk to the north end of the beach, where a trail leads inland through thick vegetation. Follow it to the "Queen's Bath" (officially called the "Anchialine Bath" by the park service), a brackish pond surrounded by rock cairns. Because it is under consideration as a historical site, swimming in the pond is not recommended. There's sometimes a ranger back in here, and although the park is officially open, visitation is neither encouraged nor discouraged. On the way out, pause at the active small-boat harbor. Although shark signs are posted, snorkelers frequent the bay.

Kaloko Beach, about a 10-minute hike north of Queen's Bath, has great snorkeling in only 10-20 feet of water. Here, you can explore a series of sea arches. The entire area is a favorite with green sea turtles, who make their presence known mainly in the evenings.

Dedicated in 1978, the 1,160-acre Kaloko-Honokohau National Historical Park can be entered either from Honokohau Small Boat Harbor or via Kaloko Gate, just off Hwy. 19 across from the Kaloko New Industrial Park. For information, call (808) 329-6881.

North Kona Beaches
The first beach that you come to heading north from Kailua-Kona is the famous **Pine Trees** surfing beach, located near the OTEC facility just south of the airport between mile markers 95 and 94. Look for a well-worn dirt road leading to the left away from OTEC, and follow it to Pine Trees. Although famous with surfers and the site of many competitions, Pine Trees (none of which are in evidence) is not a good swimming beach. There are a few one-towel coves along the rocky shoreline where you can gain access to the water, but mostly it's a place from which to observe the action. You can also follow the road toward the OTEC facility until you find a large, sandy, public beach, fronted by rock and coral. Here are a few volleyball nets, a restroom, and some picnic tables. Next come the numerous secluded beaches of the **Kona Coast State Park** (see below).

Finally, just before you get to the luxury resorts of South Kohala, you'll find **Kiholo Bay** and **Luahinewai Pond,** considered yet another Queen's Bath. Look for a stand of royal palms marking the spot, and follow the rough but passable road down to the beach, where you will find a large round wooden house that once belonged to Loretta Lynn. Close by, a path leads over the lava to a tiny cove made more dramatic by a black-sand beach.

Kona Coast State Park
Recently opened and well marked, the Kona Coast State Park stretches north, encompassing several sandy secluded beaches. The first is about two miles north of the airport between mile markers 91 and 90. Follow the rugged but passable dirt road for about 1.5 miles to one of the closest beaches to Kailua-Kona. The semi-improved area has a lavatory and dilapidated picnic tables built around palm trees. The land rises before getting to the beach, and to the left are the remains of a concession stand. The swimming here is safe in season, but always be careful.

Before you get to the official parking area, notice a walking path off to the right. It is a five-minute walk to **Mahaiula Bay.** En route, you'll pass a portable toilet (clean), and about 200 yards further along is magnificent Mahaiula Beach. This crescent of white sand stretches for about 200 yards, with shade trees coming down almost to the water's edge. Completely unimproved and secluded, it's a great beach to "get away from it all" for the day.

Two miles further north, between mile markers 89 and 88, look for the Pu'u Ku'ili cinder cone whose vegetation has been given a crew cut by the trade winds. Turn here on a very rugged, 4WD-only dirt road that takes you down to **Makalawena Beach.** En route to this totally secluded area, you'll pass over rough lava and coral and eventually come to a gate, where you park. Proceed on foot, and you'll have your choice of three wonderful beaches ranging in size from 30 to 100 yards long; all are frequented by green sea turtles. Walk to the left past the biggest beach, and look for a path behind it that leads to a brackish but mostly freshwater pond where you can rinse off. Don't be alarmed by the harmless brine shrimp that nibble at your toes. They're much too small to do any real damage. If you do not have 4WD, you can still enjoy this area, but it means a hike of about 30 minutes. Be sure to bring water, especially if you intend to spend the day. From Mahaiula Beach, walk north along a path and in about five minutes you'll come to the remains of an abandoned estate that once belonged to the Magoon Family, longtime island residents and major stockholders in Hawaiian Airlines. The state has purchased this land—which was at one time being eyed by a Japanese firm that wished to build a luxury resort—and it is now, thankfully, in the public domain. After enjoying your short coastal hike, you will come to Makalawena, where you will be totally secluded. Remember not to take any chances during high surf, since there is no safety supervision whatsoever.

Alternatively, a few minutes farther north by car, just past the cinder cone, you'll find another road that starts off paved but almost immediately turns to lava and coral. If you have 4WD you can go to the end of the road and then walk to the beach, but you can also walk for about 15 minutes from the turnout near the highway.

The well-worn path leads you to **Kua Bay,** a famous swimming and boogie-boarding beach.

Ali'i Drive Beaches

The following beaches are strung one after the other along Kailua-Kona's Ali'i Drive. **White Sands Beach County Park** (a.k.a. **Magic Sands** or **Disappearing Sands**) is an excellent spot for a dip—if the sand is there. Every year, usually in March and April, the sands are stripped away by heavy seas and currents, exposing rough coral and making the area rugged for the average swimmer. People still come during those months because it's a good vantage point for observing migrating humpback whales. The sands always come back and when they do, the beach is terrific for all kinds of water sports, including bodysurfing and snorkeling. The annual **Magic Sands Bodysurfing Contest** is held during the winter months. The best board surfing is just north of the beach in a break the locals call "Banyans." White Sands' amenities include drinking water, showers, and restrooms, making the beach a favorite spot with local people and tourists.

Kahaluu Beach Park on Kahaluu Bay has always been a productive fishing area. Even today, fishermen come to "throw net." You'll occasionally see large family parties surrounding their favorite fish with a huge *hukilau* net, then sharing their bounty among all participants. Because of this age-old tradition, the area has not been designated a marine conservation district. Kahaluu became a beach park in 1966. This ensured that the people of Kona would always have access to this favorite spot, which quickly became surrounded by commercial development. Amenities include picnic tables, showers, restrooms, even a basketball court. The swimming is very good, but the real attraction is snorkeling. The waters are very gentle and Kahaluu is a perfect place for families or beginning snorkelers. However, stay *within* the bay because a powerful and dangerous rip current lurks outside, and more rescues are made on this beach than on any other in Kona. The shoreline waters are alive with tropical fish: angelfish, parrotfish, unicorn fish, the works. Bring bread or cheese with you, and in a minute you'll be surrounded by a living rainbow of colors. Some fish are even bold enough to nip your fingers. It's very curious that when these semitame fish spot a swimmer with a spear gun, they'll completely avoid him. They know the difference! Unfortunately, Kahaluu is often crowded, but it is still worth a visit.

ACCOMMODATIONS

Almost all of Kona's accommodations lie along the six miles of Ali'i Dr. from Kailua-Kona to Keauhou. Most hotels/condos fall in the moderate to expensive range, including one super-luxury hotel just north of Kailua-Kona. A few inexpensive hotels are scattered here and there along Ali'i Dr., and back up in the hills are a "sleeper" or two that are cheap but decent. The following list should provide you with a good cross section.

Camping Note

It's sad but true: except for the limited beach parks at Hookena and Milolii, south of Kailua-Kona, there is *no* official camping in all of the Kona District. Campers wishing to enjoy the Kona Coast must go north to the Kohala District to find a campground, or south to Kau. Some unofficial camping does exist in Kona, but as always, this generates certain insecurities. Bivouacking for a night or two in any of the unofficial camp spots should be hassle free. Good luck!

Budget

Patey's Place, 75-195 Ala Ona Ona St., Kailua-Kona, HI 96740, tel. (808) 326-7018, fax 326-7640, is a reasonably priced and traveler-friendly hostel. Upon arrival, it will appear as though a section of the living sea was taken from the coast, and moved whole into a residential area of Kona. You will be cohabiting with whales, mermaids, and dolphins, all rendered by airbrush *air*tist, Paul Fullbrook, a resident Aussie artist who was undoubtedly a green sea turtle in his past life. Robert Patey, manager/owner, is a long-time island resident, who has plenty of *aloha* and will point you in the right direction. He takes pride in his hostel, and it shows. Rates are: bunk room, $17.50; private room $31.50 s, $41.50 d; deluxe private with a/c and shared bath $70 at the Islander Inn (two private units owned by Patey's at this condo right on the beach). A $10 key and linen deposit is returned on departure. Patey's also provides free transportation *from* the airport if you stay two or more nights; airport drop-off for $5; various island tours for $40-55; body boards, fishing gear, and snorkel gear for a one-time fee of $5; lockers; safe deposit box; and free and invaluable information. The bunk rooms (maximum four people) are clean, lockable, and cooled by cross ventilation and ceiling fans. The hostel is also outfitted with four full bathrooms, three kitchens, a tanning deck, laundry facilities, gas barbecues, and an activities desk. Patey's is an excellent choice for the adventurer, budget traveler, or anyone else who enjoys a dynamic international setting. Website: www.hostels.com/patey's; e-mail: patey@mail.gte.net.

Inexpensive to Moderate

For a reasonable and homey hotel, try the **Kona Tiki,** 75-5968 Ali'i Dr., Kailua-Kona, HI 96745, tel. (808) 329-1425, fax 327-9402, featuring refrigerators in all rooms (some kitchen units) and complimentary continental breakfast daily. Island fruits and a few old fishing poles are also furnished for the guests. The hotel is close to the road so it's a bit noisy in the day but quiets down at night except for the lullaby of the rolling surf. Rooms are clean, with ceiling fans but no phones or TVs, and have been refurnished with new curtains and bedspreads of pastel tropical design. All units face the ocean so everyone gets a view. There's a lovely lanai, a pool, and a trim little garden of raked sand. Prices are $56 s/d, kitchenette unit $62, extra person $8, three-day minimum.

Kona Seaside Hotel is another basic but well-cared-for downtown hotel at 75-5646 Palani Rd., Kailua-Kona, HI 96740, tel. (808) 329-2455 or (800) 367-7000. It's part of the island-owned Sands, Seaside, and Hukilau chain. Most rooms have a/c, cross ventilation, and lanai, but no TV. There's a sun deck and central area with enclosed courtyard and lobby. Prices range from $70 standard to $100 deluxe, double occupancy (car package available).

The **Kona Bay Hotel,** at 75-5739 Ali'i Dr., Kailua-Kona, HI 96740, tel. (808) 329-1393 or (800) 367-5102, is a locally owned downtown hotel run by Uncle Billy and his Kona family. Its best feature is the friendly and warm staff. The hotel is a remaining wing of the old Kona Inn, the rest of which was torn down to accommodate the shopping center across the road. The Kona Bay is built around a central courtyard and garden containing the Banana Cafe, pool, and bar. As at Uncle Billy's Hilo Bay Hotel, the motif is "cellophane Polynesian," highlighted by some artificial palms. The rooms are a combination of basic and superior with a/c, TV, green carpeting, one wall papered and the other bare cinder block. Each room has a minifridge, and some can be outfitted with kitchenettes. Rates begin at $77-92, and $87-97 for a kitchenette; car-rental package available. E-mail: unclebilly@aloha.net; website: www.aloha.net/~uncleb.

A few reasonably priced and attractive condominium apartments include the following. **Kona Plaza,** tel. (808) 329-1132, downtown, has a swimming pool and sun decks and is wheelchair accessible. Daily rates are $55 d, $65 up to four. Weekly, monthly, and off-season rates available.

Kona Billfisher, tel. (808) 329-9277, near downtown, offers full kitchens, pool, barbecues, limited maid service, and gazebo. One-bedroom units cost $60 daily for up to four persons, two-bedroom units $80 for up to six guests. Weekly and monthly rates and discounts.

Ali'i Villas, oceanside just a half mile from Kailua-Kona, offers full kitchens, lanais, TVs, parking, a pool, and barbecues. Rates vary from one-bedroom units at $450-485 weekly (two to three guests) to two bedrooms (all units oceanfront) from $800-850 weekly (up to four guests). Additional guests cost extra. There is a 20% monthly discount during low season. For bookings, contact Norma C. Edens, Kona Sun Coast Properties, tel. (800) 326-4751.

Kona Mansion, a quarter mile from downtown, offers one-bedroom suites for up to four persons for $70. Each unit has a full kitchen. There's a swimming pool, parking, TV, and maid service on request, with a minimum stay of five nights. Contact Hawaiian Apartment Leasing, 1240 Cliff Dr., Laguna Beach, CA 92651, tel. (714) 497-4253, (800) 854-8843, (800) 472-8449 California.

Casa De Emdeko is a condominium that receives the best possible praise: people who have lodged there once always return. It's a quiet, low-rise condo surrounding a central courtyard with freshwater and saltwater pools and an on-site convenience store. All units have a/c, full kitchen, and lanai. Prices start at $75 d, $10 extra person, for a garden-view apartment with every seventh night free. Contact Casa De Emdeko at 75-6082 Ali'i Dr., Kailua-Kona, HI 96740, tel. (808) 329-2160 (resident manager); or the booking agent of SunQuest Vacations, tel. (808) 329-6488, (800) 367-5168 Mainland, (800) 800-5662 Canada. Office hours are weekdays only 8 a.m.-5 p.m.; check in is at 1 p.m., checkout at 11 a.m. The office is closed on weekends and holidays but special arrangements can be made to accommodate you, and there is a buzzer at the front desk that summons the resident manager.

Expensive

Kona Islander Inn condominium apartments are well appointed for a reasonable price. Conveniently located within walking distance of downtown Kailua-Kona, they're next door to the Spindrifter Restaurant. The style is "turn-of-the-century plantation" shaded by tall palms. All 22 rental units have phone, off-road parking, a/c, and TV. Rates run $99-129. For information write Kona Islander Inn, 75-5776 Kuakini Hwy., Kailua-Kona, HI 96740, tel. (808) 329-3181, or Marc Resorts, tel. (800) 535-0085.

The **Kona Surf Resort,** 78-128 Ehukai St., Kailua-Kona, HI 96740, tel. (808) 322-3411, (800) 367-8011, fax (808) 322-3245, is located at Keauhou Bay, six miles south of Kailua-Kona. The building, comprised of four wings and lined with more than $1 million worth of art, is architecturally superb. The impeccable hotel grounds are a magnificent match for the building and are open to the public. All 535 rooms have a/c, phones, and TVs. Prices begin at $99 and go to $365 for a suite. There are two swimming pools, lighted tennis courts, and the Keauhou-Kona Golf Course next door, with special rates and starting times for hotel guests. E-mail: konasurf@ilhawaii.net; website: www.ilhawaii.net/konasurf.

Premium

King Kamehameha's Kona Beach Hotel in downtown Kailua-Kona at 75-5660 Palani Rd., Kailua-Kona, HI 96740, tel. (808) 329-2911 or (800) 367-6060, is located on a spot favored by Hawaiian royalty; Kamehameha the Great spent the last days of his life here. It's one of the only Kona hotels that has its own beach, adjacent to the restored Ahuena Heiau. The walls of the lobby are lined with artifacts of ancient battles. Portraits of the Kamehameha royal family beginning with the great chief Kamehameha are displayed in the reception area, and two *kahili* stand nearby as signs of royalty. Hotel staff members give historical tours of the grounds. Rooms (each with a/c, TV, refrigerator, safe, and phone), are appointed in shades of blue with rattan furniture, each featuring a lanai with a sweeping panorama of the bay and Mt. Hualalai. Prices range from $110 for a standard room up to $500 for a three-bedroom suite, additional person $20, and children under 18 free when sharing their parents' room. The hotel features restaurants, a famous luau, cocktail lounges, tennis courts, shops, and a pool. (E-mail: reservations@hthcorp.com, website: konabeachhotel.com.)

The **Aston Keauhou Beach Resort,** 78-6740 Ali'i Dr., Kailua-Kona, HI 96740, tel. (808) 322-3441, (800) 922-7866 from the Mainland or (800) 321-2558 in Hawaii, is built on a historic site that includes the remains of a *heiau* and a reconstruction of King Kamehameha III's summer cottage. The hotel is famous for its bougainvillea that plummets over the seven-story face of the hotel. Kahaluu Beach Park is adjacent, and the entire area is known for fantastic tidepools. This famous Kona hotel has recently undergone an extensive $15 million renovation, and reopened in March of 1999. Rates range from $115 for a garden view up to $200 for deluxe oceanfront room, with suites to $350. Each room has a/c, TV, phone, private lanai, and small refrigerator. All the new restaurant and beverage services at the hotel are being directed by the island-famous chef, Sam Choy, which should be a real boon to its popularity. In keeping with the new outlook, the hotel is offering daily activities and presentations in Hawaiian dance, music, sports, arts and crafts. The hotel also offers a free shuttle service to local shopping, golfing, and dining.

The **Royal Kona Resort,** 75-5852 Ali'i Dr., Kailua-Kona, HI 96740, tel. (808) 322-3411, (800) 919-8333, has figuratively and literally become a Kona landmark. The rooms are spacious and each includes a lanai (so protected from public view that it easily serves as an outdoor room). The tennis facilities are superb, and an ocean-fed pool is sheltered from the force of the waves by huge black lava boulders. Standard rates run from $130 for a garden view to $160 for a partial ocean view, $180 for an ocean view, and $210 for an ocean front, with the ocean front corner king rooms costing $250. The hotel, built like rising steps with the floor below larger than the one above, commands a magnificent view from its perch atop a beautiful promontory of black lava. On the property, you can dine in the **Tropics Cafe Restaurant,** which has a lovely sun-soaked veranda with a sweeping view of the surrounding coastline. Executive chief Daniel Thiebaut has created a whole new menu for this establishment. The hotel also boasts a mini-shopping mall complete with a sundries store. The **Windjammer,** an open-air lounge, features entertainment several evenings each week. The hotel pool, completely refurbished, has an upper kiddies' pool and a lower re-tiled main pool adjacent to the rolling surf. Between the main building and the beach tower is the coconut grove. The *imu* is fired up every Monday, Friday, and Saturday evening, creating delectable morsels for the famous Kona sunset luau that comes complete with island entertainment that fills the grounds with music and laughter. Reservations are recommended (tel. 808-329-3111). The tennis courts, attended by a professional staff, are lit for nighttime play. Costs are a reasonable $6 hourly per court or $7 for all day; nonguests pay $7 and $9 respectively. Other full-service amenities include a laundry, free parking, beauty salon, baby-sitters, and no charge for children under 17 years of age sharing a room with their parents. The Royal Kona Resort keeps alive the tradition of quality service at a quality hotel. Website: www.royalkona.com.

Luxury

The **Aston Royal Sea Cliff Resort,** winner of an American Automobile Association Three Diamond Award, offers classy condo apartments. The white alabaster building features rooms fronting a central courtyard where you'll find the pool and spa. The unobstructed views of the coast from most rooms are glorious and a perfect day-ending activity is sunsets enjoyed on your private lanai. Amenities, such as free tennis,

daily maid service, two swimming pools, cable color TV, activities desk, jet spa and sauna, and sundries shop are offered but there are no restaurants or activities. Rates start with a studio at $150 and move to one bedroom $165-215, two bedrooms $195-505; there's a special 15% rate reduction during the off-season as well as a "family plan." Contact Royal Sea Cliff Resort, 75-6040 Ali'i Dr., Kailua-Kona, HI 96740, tel. (808) 329-8021 or (800) 922-7866.

Kanaloa at Kona, 78-261 Manukai St., Kailua-Kona, HI 96740, tel. (808) 322-9625 or (800) 688-7444, is situated in an upscale residential area at the southern end of Kailua-Kona and is one of those special places where you feel that you get more than what you pay for. The one- to three-bedroom units are enormous. Bigger isn't always better, but in this case it is. Each unit comes equipped with a complete and modern kitchen, two baths, a lanai with comfortable outdoor furniture, and a wet bar for entertaining. Rates for the tastefully furnished units range from $165 for one bedroom to $275 for two bedrooms; the rooms can accommodate four and six people respectively at no extra charge. A security officer is on duty, and on the grounds you'll find three pools, lighted tennis courts, jacuzzis, gas barbecues, an activities desk with free morning coffee, and even a restaurant and cocktail lounge overlooking the black-sand beach. The complex itself is made up of low-rise units around a central courtyard. If you would like to escape the hustle and bustle but stay near the action, the Kanaloa at Kona is the place.

Kona by the Sea, 75-6106 Ali'i Dr., Kailua-Kona, HI 96740, tel. (808) 327-2300 or (800) 922-7866 U.S. and Canada, (800) 321-2558 in Hawaii, is a rather new and beautifully situated condominium with extraordinary coastal views. Like many of Kona's properties, it has no beach, but there is a freshwater pool on the premises and a saltwater pool run by the state only a minute away. From the balcony of your suite overlooking a central courtyard, you can watch the aqua-blue surf crash onto the black lava rocks below. Each spacious one- or two-bedroom unit has two bathrooms, tiled lanai, modern kitchen complete with dishwasher and garbage disposal, living room with fold-out couch, dining room, color cable TV, and central air. Furniture differs slightly from unit to unit but is always tasteful and often includes rattan with plush cushions, and mauve and earth-toned rugs and walls. Prices are a reasonable $225-299 for one- and two-bedroom units. Kona by the Sea, like most properties managed by Aston Resorts, offers excellent value for a peaceful Kona vacation.

Bed and Breakfast

High above Kailua-Kona on the road to Holualoa, surrounded by lush tropical foliage that permeates the air with a sweet perfume, perches **Hale Maluhia Country Inn Bed and Breakfast,** 76-770 Hualalai Rd., Kailua-Kona, HI 96740, tel. (808) 329-5773, (800) 559-6627, fax (808) 326-5487, a hideaway lovingly tended by hosts Ken and Ann Smith. Built and furnished in rustic Hawaiian style with a Victorian twist, the B&B offers accommodations in the main house or the separate Banyan Cottage. The interiors of the central house and cottage feature open-beamed ceilings, plenty of natural wood trim, koa cabinets, and full kitchens. There's even a functional working office with a computer, laser printer, and fax machine for those forced to mix business with pleasure. On the property are an outdoor stone-and-tile Japanese *ofuro* (spa) with massage jets, and a massage table where your cares and aches will float away on the evening breeze. Two relaxing common areas are outfitted with board games, a pool table, a large library, and surround sound color TV/VCR (large video library), while five lanais present the natural drama of a Michaelangelo sunset nightly; all are wheelchair friendly. Ken spoils you every morning with a sumptuous home-cooked breakfast buffet laden with tropical fruits and juices, fresh bread and pastries, savory breakfast meats, herbal teas, and robust Kona coffee. In the evenings, Ken, a man of earth and spirit, will gladly converse with you on the wonders of the Big Island, offering suggestions on how to enrich your journey. All rooms, painted a soothing mauve and teal, are decorated with Hawaiian and provincial antique furniture, and feature private baths. Rates are $75-110 d for a guest room in the main house, and $145 for the Banyan Cottage. Discounts for longer stays. Hale Maluhia (House of Peace) is all that its name implies. E-mail: hawaii-inns@aloha.net; website: www.hawaii-bnb.com/halemal.html. Moderate.

FOOD

Inexpensive

"So, for the budget traveler," you've been asking yourself, "which is the best restaurant in town, with the most food at the lowest prices, with that down-home atmosphere?" **The Ocean View Inn,** tel. (808) 329-9998, is it! The gigantic menu of Chinese, American, Japanese, and Hawaiian food is like a minidirectory. Lunch and dinner range $6-12, and a huge breakfast goes for about $3.50. The most expensive dinner is T-bone steak at $12.95. They're open daily except Monday, 6:30 a.m.-2:45 p.m. and 5:15-9 p.m., with the bar open daily 6:30 a.m.-9 p.m. Located across from the seawall near King Kamehameha's Kona Beach Hotel, they're always crowded with local people, a sure sign that the food is good.

Stan's Restaurant, tel. (808) 329-4500, is an open-air establishment one notch up in both price and atmosphere from the Ocean View Inn next door. Here you have a cocktail lounge and a stab at atmosphere with some cozy lighting and rattan furniture. Breakfast is pleasing, with an assortment of island-inspired hotcakes and a special for $3.95; no lunch is served. Dinner specials ($8-12), starting at 5 p.m., are hibachi chicken or fillet of mahimahi, fresh island fish, the "daily special" ($7.95), and the captain's seafood dinner. All include salad, rice or whipped potatoes, fresh fruit, and dinner bread. However, the best items are their many Hawaiian foods like *kalua* pig and *lala poi* for under $6. The food is good, but not great, and you generally get a square meal for a very reasonable price.

The **Royal Jade Garden,** in the Lanihau Center, tel. (808) 326-7288, open Sun.-Thurs.10:30 a.m.-9:30 p.m., Fri.-Sat. until 10 p.m., is a Chinese restaurant where you can get an amazing amount of well-prepared food for a moderate price. They have the run-of-the-mill chow meins for $5.50-7.50, noodle soups under $6, and meat dishes of chicken, duck, pork, or beef for $5.95-7.50. More expensive items include lobster with black bean sauce for $18.95 and a variety of fresh fish and seafoods for $8 and up. But they have an unbeatable special every night: you choose three entrees plus fried rice or fried noodles for only $6.50 (fewer choices, less expensive). It's pre-prepared and placed on a hot table, but it's not cooked to death. You wind up with so much food that the most difficult part is keeping it on your plate. In the Royal Jade there's no decor, but if you are hungry and on a tight budget, this is one of the best values in town.

The **Big Island Bagel Company,** in the Kopiko Plaza along Palani Rd., open Mon.-Fri. 6 a.m.-7 p.m., Saturday 7 a.m.-4 p.m., is an upbeat bagelry with a Mediterranean touch achieved by overhanging porticos. The display case is filled with all kinds of bagels: chocolate chip, cinnamon, cinnamon raisin, banana nut, cinnamon apple. There are even bagel pastries, cheese bagels, pizza bagels, bagel sandwiches, and breakfast on a bagel. Pick one that looks yummy and enjoy it with a cup of Royal Kona coffee, iced latte, cafe mocha, or Italian soda. The food is inexpensive, freshly made, and delicious.

Kona's **old industrial area,** although it doesn't sound inviting, is a great place to find inexpensive food, along with stores where the *people* shop. To get to the industrial area, head for the airport, and about one minute north of the junction of Rt. 19 (the airport road) and Palani Road, make a left on Kaiwi Street. Or follow Kuakini Road, a major intersection off Palani Road just a minute from the seawall, to Kaiwi Street. The triangle formed by Kaiwi and Kuakini is primarily the old industrial area. The **French Bakery,** Kaahumanu Plaza, 74-5467 Kaiwi St., tel. (808) 326-2688, open weekdays 5:30 a.m.-3 p.m., Saturday 5:30 a.m.-2 p.m., is a budget gourmet deli/restaurant where the food is great and the prices are low. Not only does it have the full range of pastries you would expect, it has wonderful sandwiches like pizza roll with cheese for only $1.75 and with ham or bacon for $2. All of the sandwiches are under $5, and the European-style coffee is full-bodied and rich.

Su's Thai Kitchen, in the industrial area at 74-5588A Pawai Pl. (just off Kaiwi St.), tel. (808) 326-7808, open for lunch weekdays 11 a.m.-2:30 p.m. and for dinner nightly 5-9 p.m., is a semi-open-air restaurant with a distinctive touch of southeast Asia (also in Waimea at the Parker Ranch Shopping Plaza, tel. 808-885-8688). You can sit inside, but choose a spot on the veranda, where there is absolutely no view but where the breezes blow and bamboo curtains are dropped for a feeling of privacy. The extensive menu offers a *pu pu* platter (a combination of all the appetizers including spring roll, shrimp, and chicken sauté served with homemade plum sauce and peanut sauce) for $10.95. Other choices are lightly breaded and pan-fried shrimp combined with fresh mint, lime juice, garlic, and kafir for $8.95; savory Thai soups mostly with a coconut base, with morsels of fish, scallops, or pork ($6.95-9.95); salads ($4.95-9.95); and a full selection of curries ($7.95-9.95). Vegetarians will be happy with vegetable curry, vegetable stir-fry, or sweet-and-sour vegetables. The daily lunch special for $5.95 might be a mini *pu pu* platter; green curry with chicken and eggplant accompanied by a bowl of white rice; or yellow curry with chicken, potatoes, carrots, and onions with a bowl of white rice. The service is friendly, the portions large for the money. Su's is a favorite with local people—the highest recommendation.

Magic Sands Café, 74-5596 Pawai Pl., Bay Q, tel. (808) 334-1811, open Mon.-Fri. 11 a.m.-4 p.m., Saturday 11 a.m.-2 p.m., is out of the way—in the old industrial area not far from Su's Thai Kitchen—but is worth seeking out because it is inexpensive and gets the "thumbs-up" from local people, always a good sign. Both the decor and the food served are very basic, but portions are plentiful, inexpensive, and very good. The money-saving menu offers fresh catch for only $6.50, Big Island Garden Salad for $3.25, and a variety of plate lunches, vegetarian meals, and sandwiches, all reasonably priced.

A friendly gorilla greets you at the **Pot Belli Deli** (in the industrial area, see above) at 74-5543 Kaiwi St., tel. (808) 329-9454, open weekdays 6 a.m.-4 p.m. The refrigerated deli case holds chicken, ham, or tuna salad sandwiches for $2.65 (jumbo $4.25); spinach pie for $4.25; and bagels with cream cheese. The shelves hold all the condiments and extras you need for a terrific picnic lunch. You can get your order to go or eat at one of the few booths inside.

Tom Bombadill's menu takes its inspiration from Tolkien's Middle Earth, but its location is a lot noisier, perched over Ali'i Dr. and overlooking the Royal Kona Resort's tennis courts, open daily 11 a.m.-10 p.m., tel. (808) 329-1292. They talk about the ocean view, but your neck will have to stretch like the mozzarella on their pizza to see it. The bar pours domestic beers at $2.50, imports at $3.50, and pitchers for $8.50. The menu includes all sorts of hamburgers for under $6; soups ($3); soup and sandwich combination ($5.75); island salad ($4.25 small, $7.25 large); steak sandwich ($10.25); chicken teriyaki dinner ($11.95); shrimp plate ($10.25). All of these meals are good but the real specialty is pizza, priced from only $3.25. They also deliver 11:30 a.m.-2:30 p.m., and then again 5-9 p.m., all the way from Keauhou to Palisades. Bombadill's has been around long enough to become a Kona institution.

Harbor House, formerly Attilla's Bar and Grill, at the Honokohau Small Boat Harbor, tel. (808) 326-4166, open daily 10:30 a.m.-8:30 p.m., features Kona's longest bar. Harbor House is more or less an open-air pavilion, but it is actually quite picturesque as it overlooks the harbor. If you are interested in a charter fishing boat, this is the best place to come to spin a yarn with the local skippers who congregate here nightly at about 4:30 p.m. Over the bar hangs a gigantic 1,556-pound marlin, almost as big as the Budweiser sign. Strategically placed TVs make it a good sports bar, and the jukebox has a great selection of oldies and contemporary tunes. A variety of draft beers from Steinlager to Coors Light come in 16-ounce chilled schooners for only $2.50, with Heineken and Carlsburg $2.75. Sunday and Monday, the frothy schooners are only $2, with the same price daily during happy hour: 3-6 p.m. The bill of fare ($3-7) offers grilled bacon cheeseburgers with fries, shrimp and chips, crabsalad sandwich, clam chowder, and chili and rice. Try their delicious macadamia nut pie for $2.50. Harbor House is one of the truly *colorful* places in Kailua-Kona, and one of the best places to relax and have a hassle-free brew.

Giuseppe's, in the Kailua Bay Inn Shopping Plaza at 75-5699F Ali'i Dr. across from the Kona seawall, tel. (808) 329-7888, open daily 11:30 a.m.-9 p.m. and until 4:30 p.m. on Sunday, serves dishes of savory pasta in a tiny but tasteful restaurant where you can dine in or take out. Lunch specials served until 4 p.m. range from spaghetti marinara for $5.50 to fettuccine with artichoke hearts for $6.50. Dinner is *delisioso,* with choices like chicken marsala ($12.75) and scampi Mediterranean ($14.25), which includes pasta, dinner salad, and a choice of cheese bread. The minestrone soup served all day for $3.50 per bowl is excellent. The menu is rounded out with a small selection of sandwiches and various dishes from the children's menu for only $4.50 for lunch and $5.50 for dinner. During the triathlon, Giuseppe's offers all the pasta you can eat for $10.

Aki's Cafe, also in the Kailua Bay Inn Shopping Plaza, tel. (808) 329-0090, is a moderately priced Japanese/American restaurant offering breakfast, lunch, and dinner. Breakfast ($4-7) can be three-egg omelettes, egg Benedict scramble, pancakes or a Japanese breakfast with eggs, miso soup, rice, and choice of meat. Lunch ($5-7) can be California sushi, fried noodles to which you can add chicken or shrimp, or curry with rice. Or try the mahimahi burger, buffalo steak burger, or BLT or vegetarian sandwiches. The dinner menu offers marinated New York steak for $15.50, chicken teriyaki for $10.50, garlic pasta for only $6.50, and fish and chips for $6.99. There are also cold drinks, ice cream, and coffee, including espresso, cappuccino, and caffe latte. Aki's is a centrally located, simple restaurant that adds a decent touch to ordinary food.

If you look up into the Kona night sky and the moon hits your eye like a big pizza pie, you've probably consumed one too many mai tais and are actually looking into the window of **Basil's Pizzeria and Restaurant** in downtown Kailua-Kona at 75-5707 Ali'i Dr., tel. (808) 326-7836, open daily 11 a.m.-10 p.m., where they make their own pizza dough. Individual gourmet pizzas range $5.95-8.95, depending upon your choice of toppings; New York-style pizza, 14-inch and 16-inch, is $8.95-14.95. Besides pizza, Basil's offers soup of the day for $2.95, Italian antipasto ($6.95), angel hair primavera ($8.95), fettuccine Alfredo ($8.95), and spaghetti with marinara sauce ($6.95 with meatballs $7.95). There is also seafood: shrimp marinara ($12.95) and scallops scampi ($13.95). Or try eggplant parmigiana at $8.95. A nightly "fresh catch special" is priced around $13.95, or you can order any number of sandwiches and burgers for under $6. Basil's offers free delivery of any item on the menu all along Ali'i Drive. So go ahead, recline on your condo lanai and call Basil's, and they'll be over *molto rapido.*

King Yee Lau, in the Ali'i Sunset Plaza at 75-5799 Ali'i Dr. across from the seawall at the south end of town, tel. (808) 329-7100, open

Mon.-Sat. 11 a.m.-2 p.m., nightly 5-9 p.m., offers an all-you-can-eat lunch buffet and the usual Chinese dishes like pressed crisp duck, beef with ginger sauce, and shrimp with seasoned vegetables, all priced under $7.95. Vegetarians can dine on tofu with oyster sauce or a variety of chow mein for under $6.50.

Thai Rin, also in the Ali'i Sunset Plaza, tel. (808) 329-2929, open weekdays for lunch 11 a.m.-2:30 p.m., dinner 5-9:30 p.m., fills the air in the small plaza with the aromas of its savory Thai spices. The menu offers spring rolls for $4.95 and entrees ($7-9) such as fried noodles Chinese-style; vegetarian Thai fried rice; stir-fried chicken, beef, or pork; and Thai garlic shrimp or squid. Thai Rin also features a variety of lunch specials for about $5.95.

Mona's Barbecue, also in the Ali'i Plaza, tel. (808) 326-2532, open Mon.-Fri. 11 a.m.-9 p.m., Saturday 12-9 p.m., is an eat in or takeout plate lunch restaurant where $6-7 will get you teriyaki chicken, chicken *katsu,* spicy pork ribs, or a barbecued burger with a variety of trimmings. Mona's is basic, clean, local, and cheap.

Fast Foods, Coffee, Delis, and Snacks

You can't get "hotter" than **Lava Java** in the Ali'i Sunset Plaza at 75-5799 Ali'i Dr., across from the seawall at the south end of town, open daily 7 a.m.-10 p.m., Kona's popular coffeehouse/restaurant. Here, local people and tourists alike come to kick back, read the papers, and actually engage in the lost art of conversation. Sandwiches are served 9 a.m.-7 p.m. on white or whole wheat bread or a freshly baked baguette. Try the turkey and cranberry sandwich for $5.95, a garden burger for $4.50, Polish hot dog for $3.25, or croissants topped with hot ham and cheese. Or try the pastrami and cheese melt for under $5. Lava Java has a counter offering muffins, cookies, root beer floats, Kona coolers made with tropical fruit sorbet, Italian sodas, and ice cream. Bulk coffee by the pound (about $18) is also available.

A Piece of the Apple, also in the Ali'i Plaza, open Mon.-Sat. 8 a.m.-4 p.m., is a New York-style deli with a healthful twist. Offered are fresh carrot juice, fresh-squeezed orange juice, smoothies, and fresh baked bagels. The deli section has two-fisted sandwiches for $7.25 like the Reuben, New Yorker (pastrami with Swiss cheese), vegetarian, and "Seinfeld" (smoked turkey, roasted red peppers, mozzarella, and red onions). Light appetites will enjoy a California salad with smoked turkey, avocado, and Swiss cheese, a chef salad, or a garden salad (all $5.75), or house salad for $2.50. You can sit inside, but the best spot is outside at a picnic table shaded by dwarf palms.

At the Kona Inn Shopping Village, try one of the following. **Mrs. Barry's Cookies** are homemade yummies that include macadamia nut, chocolate chip, and peanut butter, gift boxed to send home. Follow your nose to the **Coffee Cantata** and drink a cup in the little courtyard. **Kona Kai Farms Coffee House** features a sampler cup of Kona coffee.

To get your motor revved up on an early Kona morning, order a mug of locally grown coffee from **Hawaiian Angel Brand Coffee,** located next door to the Ocean View Inn, along Ali'i Dr. just near the pier. They serve coffee by the cup for $1.25 and homemade lemonade for $1.75, along with cappuccino, double espressos for Dr. Kevorkian failures, and farmer-direct coffee at $6.50 per pound. They're under a yellow umbrella in the little nook with a few tables on the front porch.

Around town, the **Bartender's Ocean Breeze** serves up 12-ounce mugs of ice-cold beer for $1 and grill-your-own burgers for $2.75. Other snacks are available on Ali'i Dr. near the Royal Kona Resort tennis courts, tel. (808) 329-7622.

In the Kona Marketplace, **Chili by Max,** open Mon.-Sat. 10 a.m.-8 p.m., Sunday 11 a.m.-8 p.m., is famous for its award-winning oven-baked chili, made with beef or turkey. Also on the bill of fare are kosher hot dogs, chili dogs, chili nachos, baked potatoes, and ice cream.

Across Sarona Rd. from Kona Marketplace and down toward Kuakini Hwy. there's **Subway Sandwiches,** a chain selling double-fisted sandwiches to go. On Kuakini Hwy. next to **McDonald's** golden arches is a **7-Eleven,** open 24 hours; and along Palani Rd. is **Taco Bell,** next door to **Pizza Hut,** which is across the road from **Burger King.**

In the Lanihau Center along Palani Rd., you can snack at **Buns in the Sun,** open Mon.-Fri. 5 a.m.-5 p.m., Saturday until 4 p.m., Sunday until 3 p.m., a bakery-deli serving everything from croissants to apple turnovers, along with espresso, cappuccino, and latte. Breakfast specials include a fried egg on a Kaiser roll for $2; or deviled egg and ham and cheese on a Kaiser for $3.70. Also enjoy sandwiches priced around $5.50, or homemade soups like garden vegetable or cream of mushroom, served with a roll for only $1.99. Sit, eat, and enjoy at a wrought-iron table under their outdoor canopy. The center's **Kona Grill,** open Mon.-Thurs. 6 a.m.-8 p.m., Friday to 10 p.m., Saturday 8 a.m.-10 p.m., and Sunday 8 a.m.-4 p.m., is a counter restaurant serving standard breakfasts and plates like teriyaki beef, *kalbi* ribs, and shrimp platter for about $6.50. The Kona Grill is not special, but the food is acceptable and inexpensive. The center also houses **Kentucky Fried Chicken,** where you can pick up a bucket Mon.-Thurs. 10 a.m.-9:30 p.m., Fri.-Sat. 10 a.m.-10 p.m., Sunday 10 a.m.-9:30 p.m.; and **Baskin-Robbins,** open daily 11 a.m.-10 p.m., selling cones of their famous 31 flavors. For an island treat try **Island Snow,** a kiosk outside of Long's selling shave ice with plenty of flavors to choose from.

Rocky's Pizza, tel. (808) 322-3223, open daily 11 a.m.-9 p.m. at the Keauhou Shopping Village, offers whole pizzas for $9.95-14.95 or slices for $1.75 each. Rocky's also features delicious sub sandwiches like hot pastrami on crusty bread; they are favorites with the locals, who like good food at a good price.

In the Kopiko Plaza, along Palani Rd. and just down from the Lanihau Center, you'll find several places to eat: **Yuni's,** tel. (808) 329-1018, is open daily 10:30 a.m.-8 p.m. This basic saimin stand offer charsiu saimin, seafood *udon,* and a variety of other noodle dishes for under $6. **Domino's Pizza** offers eat in, takeout, or delivery; **Mask** is a bar and grill so new that it hasn't developed a personality yet; and **Kona Mix Plate** serves inexpensive plate lunches. The best, however, is **Big Island Bagel Company.**

The Kona Coast Shopping Center, also along Palani Rd., has a number of small local and ethnic restaurants in their "food court" where you can get inexpensive but savory meals. For the health-conscious, **Kona Health Ways,** open Mon.-Sat. 9 a.m.-8 p.m., Sunday to 7 p.m., is a full-service health food store that makes ready-to-eat sandwiches, salads, and soups geared toward the vegetarian. Other places are: **Poquito Mas,** a Mexican "window restaurant" with burri-

tos, quesadillas, nachos, enchiladas, and tacos all priced well under $5; and **Betty's Kitchen,** open Mon.-Sat. 10 a.m.-9 p.m., Sunday 10 a.m.-7 p.m., offering Chinese food with plenty of vegetarian selections—many priced under $6.50. Inside, the interior is black-and-white tile and there's a walk-up counter. Next door is the **Kamuela Deli,** open Mon.-Sun.10 a.m.-9 p.m., with plate lunches like teriyaki beef or breaded veal with "two scoop rice" and macaroni salad for around $6. They also offer sandwiches ranging from a BLT to a mahi burger for $2.45. Finally, for a quick snack, try **TCBY Yogurt,** open 11 a.m.-10 p.m.

You can perk up 24 hours a day at **Crusin Coffee Kona** at the King Kamehameha Mall, tucked away at the bottom of Pilani Road. The tasteful coffee shop is done in red, white, and black. Choose espresso, cappuccino, mocha, or just a good old cup of "joe" made from local Kahauloa coffee or SBC, a blend imported from Seattle. Also on the menu are Kona Natural Juices, ice cream, milk shakes, Italian cream sodas, cookies, cinnamon rolls, bagels, and sandwiches.

On your way to Pu'uhonua O Honaunau you might consider stopping at **Barry's Nut Farm** along Rt. 160. They'll give you a free tour of the gardens and nursery, or you can browse for pottery or buy sandwiches and drinks. Open daily 9 a.m.-5 p.m., tel. (808) 329-6055.

Moderate
Cafe Sibu, in the Kona Banyan Court, open daily 11:30 a.m.-3 p.m. for lunch and 5-9 p.m. for dinner, tel. (808) 329-1112, is an Indonesian restaurant serving savory marinated meats and vegetables spiced with zesty sauces and flame grilled. The restaurant, across from the seawall under the big banyan tree, has only a few outside tables and makes a light attempt at decor with a few antique Indonesian masks. They do, however, win the prize for the most ventilated restaurant in all of Hawaii, with nine ceiling fans whirring in a 10 by 10 foot room! To make the menu even more varied, the Italian owner offers a daily pasta dish, using recipes more than 100 years old that have been handed down by her grandmother. *Delisioso!* If you're hungry, go for the *gado gado* for $9.50, an Indonesian salad layered with spices and peanut sauce that can be

dinner for one or a salad entree for two or three. Stir-fried vegetables with chicken or tofu are $9.95; chicken and vegetable curries are $10.50 and $8 respectively; and Balinese chicken marinated in tarragon, garlic, and spices is $10.95. The combination plates are the best deals: you get a stir-fry, chicken curry, and choice of sauté for $11.95. Lunch prices on all of the above are about $2 cheaper. Cafe Sibu serves *the* best and *the* most interesting moderately priced food in Kailua-Kona.

Look for a bright *akachochin*, a red paper lantern, marking the entrance to **Restaurant Yokohama** in the Ali'i Sunset Plaza at 75-5799 Ali'i Dr., across from the seawall at the south end of town, tel. (808) 329-9661, open Tuesday, Friday, and Sunday for lunch 11 a.m.-2 p.m., and Tues.-Sun. 5:30-9 p.m. Inside is simplicity: Japanese kites, light wood furniture, and a few glowing lanterns. Their classic lunches include *soba sukiyaki* for $7; *teishoku* or fixed-plate lunch such as *tonkatsu* pork cutlets that includes an appetizer, salad, rice, and miso soup for $7; a sushi combination for $8.50; and *donburi,* "something" on rice, like grilled beef for around $7. Start dinner with appetizers like sashimi ($6.50), fried chicken ($5.50), or *tsukemono* ($4). Move on to traditional entrees cooked right at your table, like sukiyaki for $21.25, or *shabu shabu,* thin slices of beef and assorted vegetables boiled in stock for $23.50. Restaurant Yokohama also features sushi combination dinners costing $9.25-15.25. Although in a shopping plaza, both the atmosphere and cuisine are genuine.

The **Kona Ranch House** located two minutes from downtown at the corner of Kuakini Hwy. and Palani Rd., tel. (808) 329-7061, is a delightful restaurant with something for everyone. It has two rooms: the family-oriented Paniolo Room, where hearty appetites are filled family style; and the elegant Plantation Lanai, where both palate and sense of beauty are satiated. This restaurant, highlighted by copper drainpipes, brass ceiling fans, wicker furniture, and latticework, all against a natural wood-and-brick background, epitomizes plantation dining. The Kona Ranch House is a classy establishment where you get more than what you pay for. Prices range from reasonable to expensive, and the menus in the two separate rooms reflect this. Open daily 6:30 a.m.-10 p.m., and Sunday for

brunch. Reservations are needed for the Plantation Lanai.

The **Jolly Roger,** walking distance from downtown at 75-5776 Ali'i Dr., tel. (808) 329-1344, is another Kona restaurant with a remarkable seaside setting. The gently rolling surf lapping at the shore is like free dessert. Full breakfasts are served 6:30 a.m.-noon and start at $4, with waffles and pancakes cheaper. Lunch is served 11 a.m.-4 p.m., dinner 5:30-10 p.m. Sandwiches start at $3; assorted salads are $5; full salad bar is $5.95; and entrees of fresh fish, seafood, and beef are from $10. Happy hour daily, 11 a.m.-6 p.m., features an assortment of *pu pu.* A daily special of steak and eggs Benedict, available 6:30 a.m.-noon, costs $4.75. The decor is bent bamboo with puffy cushions, and the tile-floored veranda has marble-topped tables and white wrought-iron chairs.

Banana Bay Buffet, tel. (808) 329-1393, is located in the courtyard of Uncle Billy's downtown Kona Bay Hotel. Following in the semi-plastic Polynesian tradition of Uncle Billy, they serve a fair to passable buffet for $8.95. A stuffed marlin, seemingly too huge and colorful to be real, gazes down at everyone from the wall. Sometimes free hula shows are part of the bargain. Open daily at 6:30 a.m. (breakfast specials $4.95), this restaurant could be an "old reliable" with a touch more care in the food preparation.

Cassandra's Greek Taverna, tel. (808) 334-1066, open Mon.-Sat. 11 a.m.-10 p.m., Sunday 4:30-9 p.m., tucked away along Ali'i Dr. in the Kona Plaza Shopping Center, uses a predominant blue and white motif reminiscent of the Greek Isles. A full bar features liquors, wines, and beer, while the lunch menu ($6-9) offered 11 a.m.-4 p.m. serves up omelettes with pita bread and feta cheese, a Greek pita pizza with spinach and feta cheese, and *souvlaki* made with chicken, beef, or pork. Traditional appetizers ($5-8) include *dolmades* (grape leaves stuffed with meat and rice), *keftedes* (pan-fried Greek meatballs) with *satzikai,* or stuffed kalamari $7.95 (no "c" in Greek). Entrees ($13-22) are savory: a *gyro* plate, Greek-style baby pork ribs, *souvlaki* kabobs of beef, chicken, pork or shrimp, garlic prawns, or steak and lobster. Cassandra's also features stir-fry "à la George" with chicken, beef, prawns, or vegetables for $10.95-15.95, along with a sample platter for two for $38.95. The interior is quite comfortable with white captain's chairs or bent back bamboo chairs with armrests and fluffy pillows. The bar is tucked in the corner. Earthy, vibrant Greek music to stir the soul wafts through the air.

Don Drysdale's Club 53, overlooking the bay at the Kona Inn Shopping Village, tel. (808) 329-6651, open daily 10 a.m.-2 a.m., is owned by the famous Dodger pitcher and in the good sense of the word can best be described as a saloon. The amiable bar and grill serves reasonably priced beer, drinks, and sandwiches until 1 a.m. Sports fans away from home can always catch their favorite events on the bar's TV. Fare includes soup and salads from $2.50, a wide variety of *pu pu* from $4, sandwiches $3-5, plus the special peanut-butter cream pie at $2.35. Drysdale's is one of the most relaxing and casual bars in town.

Located on the second floor across from the pier, **Kona Galley,** tel. (808) 329-5550, open for lunch 11:30 a.m.-4 p.m. and for dinner 4-9 p.m., features bright paintings of sunsets, flowers, and ferns reflecting the island mood of the beach and bay below. Lunchtime begins with gourmet burgers, from the simple and unadorned at $5.95, a vegetarian sandwich for $6.50, a Cajun burger or chicken sandwich for $6.95, to a New York steak sandwich for $9.95. Dinner is more full-bodied, with dishes like chicken Jerusalem made with mushrooms, garlic, artichoke hearts, capers, and a Dijon dill sauce ($12.95); scallops or shrimp Bombay ($16.95); Pacific seafood medley, a mix of shrimp, scallops, and fresh fish, all sautéed with garlic and served with lemon butter ($18.95); or a New York steak and lobster tail ($32.95).

Quinn's, across from King Kamehameha's Kona Beach Hotel, tel. (808) 329-3822, is Kona's socially eclectic bar and grill where everyone from local bikers to pink-roasted tourists are welcomed. It's also a roost for night owls who come here to munch and have a beer when everything else in town is closed. Quinn's is open daily for lunch 11 a.m.-5:30 p.m. and dinner 5:30 p.m.-1 a.m. (Sunday until 10 p.m.). The local in-crowd comes to the patio for sandwiches, vegetarian specialties, and seafood. The inside bar is cozy, friendly, and sports oriented. For lunch, a gigantic mound of shrimp and crab salad for $8.95 is wonderful. The fresh catch-of-the-day

sandwiches with salad for $8.25 are a deal, but they're not always available. Reasonably priced specialties include tenderloin tips sautéed in brandy with onions for $8.95, shrimp and chips for $8.95, and fish and chips for $6.95. Dinner entrees are savory: sautéed scallops ($15.95), chicken stir-fry ($12.95), and fresh catch sautéed or baked for $18.50 up. All include soup or dinner salad, vegetable, rice, and Quinn's homefried potatoes.

Cool down with a frosty margarita and watch life go by as you perch on a stool at the upstairs location of **Pancho and Lefty's,** 75-5719 Ali'i Dr., tel. (808) 326-2171, open daily 11 a.m.-10 p.m., happy hour 3-6 p.m. offers 12-ounce drafts for $1 and big, potent 16-ounce margaritas for $2.75. Menu selections begin with appetizers ($6-8) such as buffalo wings, skinny dippers (potatoes covered with bacon and cheese or guacamole), and nachos. Full dinners include taco salad for $7.95; seafood salad with crisp greens for $9.95; or fajitas—steak, chicken or seafood (fresh catch)—for $15.95 (an order for two is $22.95). Specials are enchilada rancheros ($10.95), carne asada ($12.95), tostada ($8.95), or Mexican burger ($6.95). "Tight-Wad Tuesday" saves money with two entrees from the "Just Mexican Menu" for the price of one. Finish off your meal with ice cream, cheesecake, or cinnamon crisps. Pancho and Lefty's is a good-time place with satisfying food that's easy on the budget.

When you enter the Kaloko Industrial Park (not Kona's old industrial area near downtown), just past mile marker 97 and about three miles north from Kailua-Kona, the setting makes you think you're after plumbing supplies. What you'll find is terrific food prepared by one of Hawaii's greatest chefs at **Sam Choy's Restaurant,** tel. (808) 326-1545, open weekdays 6 a.m.-2 p.m. and Wed.-Sat. 5-9 p.m. for dinner, reservations suggested. To get there, make a right along the main road as soon as you enter the industrial park, and pass a gas station (a good place to fuel if you're returning your rental car to the airport). About 50 yards past the gas station, make a left and look for Sam's in a nondescript gray building halfway up the hill on the right. The atmosphere is pleasant enough, but those in the know who have dined on Sam's sumptuous creations, either here or at the old Kona Hilton

Chef Sam Choy (left) and assistant

(where he used to be executive chef), come for the food! Breakfasts like the ultimate stew omelette (a three-egg omelette filled with Sam's beef stew) for $6.95, steak and eggs for $8.95, or the local favorite of fried rice and egg for $4, will keep you going most of the day. The regular menu also includes fresh island fish prepared *poki* style and then flash-fried for $6.95; Kaloko steak marinated in teriyaki sauce with grilled onions for $8.95; and Kaloko noodle mania (chow mein noodles cooked with fresh vegetable and meat and served in a crispy wonton ball) for $6.75 Or try one of the specials, such as fresh *ahi* sauté ($9.95), or homemade beef stew ($6.50). For a gourmet dinner, choose oriental lamb chops with shiitake mushrooms ($19.95), vegetable pasta ($16.95), Sam Choy's Award Winning seafood *lau lau* made with fresh fish, assorted veggies, and Waipio Valley taro leaves for $23.95, or Chinese honey duck with Kau orange sauce for $17.95, all with soup and salad. Sam prepares wonderful food, and being a dad himself, he doesn't forget the kids—they have their own menu.

Under The Palms, tel. (808) 329-7366, is an open-air bar and restaurant owned and operated by Brian Anderson, who also owns the Palm Café, tel. (808) 329-7765, which is not only upscale, but literally upstairs. Their motto, "Please come in. If you don't we'll both starve," sets the tone for this much more casual and much less expensive yet good restaurant. Breakfast is traditional, with poached eggs on an English muffin

($6.95), or da kine waffle with maple syrup ($3.95), along with sticky bun pastries ($1.50) and Kona coffee, both regular and flavored. Lunch brings specialties like Hawaiian wild boar green chili with tortilla rojas and hapa tomato stuffs for $5.25; or shellfish antipasto marinated in white wine vinaigrette with sausage, olives, artichokes, assorted cheeses, and wild mushrooms for $12.95. Or try the full plate salads, like Kona mixed greens for $4.75 or *yaki soba* (fried noodle) salad with chicken, cucumbers, and Asian vegetables for $8.25. Sandwiches include roast beef ($7.95) and smoked turkey club ($9.25). They also have a full bar where you can get beers like Budweiser, Coors, or Pacific Golden Ale for $3, Fire Rock Pale Ale made here in Kona for $3.75, or old favorites like Anchor Steam and Guinness for $4.50. Under The Palms has a small wine selection, exotic drinks, and a cappuccino bar to finish off your meal. Sit back and enjoy the natural rhythm from the sea just across the road while local musicians blend their voices in lovely Hawaiian harmonies every night.

Calling **Bianelli's** "just a pizza shop" is like calling a Ferrari "just a car." Although they make pizza, and it is superb, they also have a full deli counter and plenty of delicious lunch and dinner entrees, all of which they deliver. Bianelli's has two locations, the main shop at the Pine Plaza at 75-240 Nani-Kailua between Hualalai Rd. and the Kona Belt Rd., tel. (808) 326-4800, open Mon.-Fri. 11 a.m.-10 p.m., and Sat.-Sun. 5-11 p.m., dinner only; and a more limited shop at The Club in Kona, a fitness center located at the Kona Center where you can get protein drinks, juices, pizza by the slice, and salads (made with organic local greens when possible). The full menu includes specialty sandwiches like a scrumptious Philly cheese steak served on fresh-baked French bread, and meals such as manicotti, a variety of spaghetti dishes, and lasagna, all well under $10. A great deal is "all you can eat" homemade pasta for only $7.45, or $9.20 with salad. Bianelli's makes their own pizza dough, and they offer pizza pies ranging from $7.95 for a hand-tossed, New York-style mini-pizza to $15.95 for an exotic pie smothered in garlic and herb sauce, layered with Parmesan and buffalo-milk-mozzarella cheeses, and topped with whole peeled tomatoes and fresh herbs. Vegetarian pizza topped with artichoke hearts, eggplant, sun-dried tomatoes, and Maui onions costs about $14. The wine cellar is outstanding, with more than 64 different selections ranging from California merlot to French pinot noir; prices range from about $14 to more than $200 per bottle. Bianelli's also has a tremendous selection of domestic and imported beers. The interior is tastefully decorated in Italian-American style with the mandatory red-checkered tablecloths, while the walls are covered with posters ranging from blues legend Lead Belly to bicycle great Greg Le Monde. The food and service at both are excellent. *Delisioso!*

Kona Amigos, across the seawall in downtown Kailua-Kona at 75-5669 Ali'i Dr., tel. (808) 326-2840, is open daily 11 a.m.-10 p.m. for food, with the bar open a little later. The cantina features special dishes like beef, chicken, fresh fish, or vegetarian fajitas priced $14-18 and enough for two; or enchilada rancheras for $10.50. Less expensive but savory items include a fiesta tostada $9.95, chiles rellenos or the Mauna Loa (roasted pork rolled in a flour tortilla) for $11.95. The Southwestern Caesar salad for $9.95 comes with either grilled chicken breast or grilled fresh fish. Happy hour is 3-6 p.m. daily with bargains on well drinks and margaritas, while Bud Light Drafts are $1.50. Free tostada bar Monday, Wednesday, and Friday, when you can have a snack whipped up before your eyes. Sit on the veranda to people-watch or to survey the entire harbor area. In season, the Kona Triathlon starts and finishes in front of this restaurant.

Kaminari's, in the Kopiko Plaza along Palani Rd. just near the Lanihau Center, tel. (808) 326-7799, open Mon.-Sat. 5:30-9 p.m., is an authentic and moderately priced Japanese restaurant. The decor is functional cafeteria style, and the menu includes tempura or *tonkatsu donburi* (deep-fried shrimp, vegetables, and pork cutlet atop rice) for $7; an assortment of *teishoku,* including soup, salad, pickles, and rice for $11.80; sashimi priced daily; Japanese-style steak for $13.80; and yakitori (grilled chicken) for $5.50.

Expensive

Oui oui monsieur, but of course we have zee restaurant *Français.* It is **La Bourgogne,** tel. (808) 329-6711, open Mon.-Sat. 6-10 p.m., located in Kuakini Plaza South, five minutes from downtown Kailua-Kona along Rt. 11. Guy Chatelard, the original owner of La Bourgogne, sold the restaurant to master chef Ron Gallagher and his manager wife Colleen Moore. Guy stayed on for a transition period, sharing his recipes and food philosophy with Ron and Colleen, who are dedicated to keeping up the fine service and cuisine. For those who just can't live without escargot, shrimp Provençal, or pheasant, you've been saved. How much? Plenty, *mon petit!* Cold and hot appetizers include *pâté du chef* for $6, jumbo shrimp cocktail for $12.50, and escargot d'Bourgogne for $7.50. Soups of the day are scrumptious: French onion $4.50 and homemade lobster soup (when available) for $6. For salads ($4-5), order greens with choice of homemade dressing, or Caesar or wilted spinach salad. Titillating seafood and poultry entrees ($16-25) feature fresh catch of the day; jumbo shrimp in butter, parsley, and garlic sauce; and breast of chicken filled with mousse of veal, ham, and morel mushrooms. Meat courses are delectable roast saddle of lamb with creamy mustard sauce or tenderloin of venison with dried cherries and pomegranate sauce, both for $28.50. Top off your gourmet meal with fresh, made-in-house desserts. This restaurant, small and slightly out of the way, is definitely worth a visit for those who enjoy exceptional food.

Jameson's-by-the-Sea, 77-6452 Ali'i Dr., tel. (808) 329-3195, is open for lunch weekdays 11 a.m.-2:30 p.m. and dinner every evening 5:30-10 p.m. Jameson's makes a good attempt at elegance with high-backed wicker chairs, crystal everywhere, white linen table settings, and a back-lit fish tank in the entry. The sea foams white and crashes on the shore just outside the restaurant's open windows. The quality of the food is very good, just shy of gourmet. The bar serves domestic beer ($3), imported beer ($3.75), well drinks ($4), and exotics ($5.50), which you can take to the veranda with some *pu pu* to enjoy the sunset. The lunch menu lists appetizers like sashimi, salmon pâté, fried calamari, and shrimp cocktail, all from $7.95. Lunch sandwiches are hearty fish of the day, grilled ham and cheese, or teriyaki steak for around $8. A number of seafood Louie salads made with crab, shrimp, or other seafood cost around $10. The dinner menu offers the same appetizers but adds a seafood platter with sashimi shrimp and fresh oysters for $10.50. The dinner entrees range from fresh catches like *opakapaka, ono,* and mahimahi at market price, to fried shrimp and scallops with oyster sauce and Chinese pea pods for $18.95. Other full meals ($18-23) include filet mignon with béarnaise sauce, baked stuffed shrimp, sesame chicken, and shrimp curry with mango chutney. For dessert save room for their assortment of homemade chiffon pies from $4.50.

At **Huggo's Restaurant,** on Ali'i Dr. next door to the Royal Kona Resort, tel. (808) 329-1493, it's difficult to concentrate on the food because the setting is so spectacular. If you were any closer to the sea, you'd be in it, and of course the sunset is great. Because it is built on a pier, you can actually feel the floor rock. When you are having dinner, ask the waitperson for some bread between courses so that you can feed the fish. Huggo's is open Mon.-Fri. 11:30 a.m.-2:30 p.m. for full lunch service, 2:30-5 p.m. for late-lunch sandwiches only served at the bar, and 5:30-10 p.m. for dinner, with entertainment most nights. Waiters and waitresses are outfitted in alohawear, and the heavy wooden tables are inlaid with maps of the Pacific. Huggo's executive chef, Mark Painter, and the head chef, Peter Bartsch from Switzerland, have created a combination of continental, Hawaiian, and Pacific Rim cuisine that is extraordinarily good and affordable. Lunch is reasonable, with tasties like Huggo's club; or try a gourmet Boboli pizza with your choice of toppings for around $8. Huggo's

burgers are around $8 and include the classic Huggo (with onions and mushrooms and your choice of Swiss or American cheese), the garden burger (a nonmeat patty with all the trimmings), the fresh-catch burger (priced daily), and the teriyaki chicken burger. Lunch salads include the Kona Caesar for $7.25 and the Chinese chicken salad for $8.95. Meat-lovers must try Huggo's "almost world famous" barbecued ribs with beans for $7.95—more on your plate than you can eat—served only on Tuesday and Thursday at lunchtime. The dinner menu is superb and starts with fresh *sashimi* (which can be seared on request) at market price; and seafood chowder made from clams and fresh fish and seasoned with sherry, cream sauce, and butter, a reasonable $3.50 per cup or $5.25 per bowl. The best entrees come from the sea just outside the door and are priced daily at around $22. A fantastic selection is the stuffed fish, delicious with an exotic blend of tender bay shrimp and dijonnaise sauce. Also worth trying is shrimp scampi for $21.95; or Kona paella made with fresh fish, Maine lobster claw, shrimp, and chicken all tossed with lemon and saffron and served with rice pilaf for $22.95. Huggo's has been in business for more than 30 years, and is consistently outstanding. Enjoy free *pu pu* Mon.-Fri. 4-6 p.m. while sipping a cocktail as the red Kona sun dips into the azure sea.

The Kona Inn Restaurant at the Kona Inn Shopping Village, tel. (808) 329-4455, open daily for lunch and dinner, is a lovely but lonely carryover from the venerable old Kona Inn. Part of the deal for tearing down the Kona Inn and putting up the Kona Inn Shopping Village was giving the restaurant a prime location. On entering, notice the marlin over the doorway and a huge piece of hung glass through which the sunset sometimes forms prismatic rainbows. The bar and dining area are richly appointed in native koa and made more elegant with a mixture of turn-of-the-century wooden chairs, high-backed peacock thrones, polished hardwood floors, and sturdy open-beam ceilings. If you want to enjoy the view, try a cocktail and some of the *pu pu* served all day, or try one of the light choices ($6-10) like guacamole and chips, pasta and chicken salad, or shrimp salad. Lunch is reasonable: steak sandwich for $11.95, or Hawaiian chicken sandwich on whole-wheat bun with pineapple and cheese for $6.95. The dinner menu starts with Boston chowder for $3.45 and mixed green salad of crisp romaine tossed with Caesar dressing and topped with bay shrimp for a very reasonable $4.95. The specialties are local fish like *ono, ahi, opakapaka,* or mahimahi for around $20; and seafood pasta topped with shrimp, scallops, and mussels for $18.95. Less expensive selections include stir-fried chicken for $13.95 and chicken chardonnay (chicken lightly sautéed with chardonnay, simmered in a Dijon cream sauce, and served over fettuccine with leeks and mushrooms) for $15.95. The Kona Inn Restaurant epitomizes Kona beachside dining and the view is simply superb.

Michelangelo's, in Waterfront Row at 75-5770 Ali'i Dr., tel. (808) 329-4436, is run by Mike Medeiros—a true *Meditarraneo* if there ever was one. It is open for lunch daily 11 a.m.-4 p.m., and for dinner until 10 p.m., with a limited late night supper menu until 1 a.m. Savory selections include antipasto for two at $6.95-11.95, clam chowder for $4.95, and specialty salads that could make a meal, like scallops, crab, and shrimp marinated in olive oil, garlic, and fresh herbs for $10.95. For lunch ($7-11), try seafood frutte d'mare, Kona crust pizza, Italian hamburger with feta cheese, risotto ala formagio, or fresh fish of the day sandwich sautéed or Cajun style. For pasta dishes choose penne or rigatoni, spaghetti and meatballs, or chicken parmesan. A great lunch special is chardonnay shrimp scampi for $11.95. A children's menu with items all priced around $4.95 offers a bambino burger and spaghetti marinara, among other dishes. The dinner menu ($9-19) brings angel leaf Caesar salad, spaghetti boulinnaise, chicken parmesan, Lava Fire Calamari, or Norwegian smoked salmon. The extensive wine list offers varietals from Italy, France, Australia, and California. The large room is appointed with open-beam ceilings joined by distinctive copper couplings, and with Casablanca fans. Weekends bring live music, with Hawaiian headliners like Willie K.

Also in Waterfront Row, the **Chart House,** tel. (808) 329-2451, open daily for dinner 5-10 p.m., is part of a small chain of restaurants that have built a good reputation for service, value, and well-prepared food. Primarily, they are a steak and seafood house with most meals costing $16-25. The location is very pleasant, away from the street noise and with a good view of the sea.

The Continent meets Asia on a Pacific island by way of the magnificent creations of master chef Daniel Thiebaut at the **Palm Cafe,** Coconut Grove Marketplace, 75-5819 Ali'i Dr., tel. (808) 329-7765, open daily 5:30-10 p.m., reservations suggested. Perched above Ali'i Dr., with the sea in the distance, the restaurant has an elegant interior comfortably done in a soothing green-on-green motif with high-backed chairs, linen tablecloths, large louvered windows, and subdued lighting. Start with seared *ahi* served on a bed of crisp leeks and jicama stir-fry for $7.50, or Chinese ravioli stuffed with ground pork, shiitake mushrooms, balsamic vinegar, and ginger butter sauce. Salads range from Big Island field greens with Portuguese sweet bread and croutons for $5.50 to the Palm Cafe Caesar for a very reasonable $4.50. Vegetarians will be pleased with vegetable and tofu tempura ($16.50), or timbale of vegetables with a Hawaiian chili curry sauce and brown rice ($15). The fresh fish dishes are the best, whether prepared with lemon and cilantro butter; Kona style, with ginger, green onions, shoyu, and hot peanut oil; or with an elegant vinaigrette of Kau orange and benishoga. The fish itself is grilled or steamed; daily quote about $22. Another specialty is baked *ono* with almond sesame crust, papaya, and Kona tomato relish, made piquant with ginger lime sauce. The wine selection is superb and can be counted on to complement the meal perfectly. To top off your meal, choose one of the devilish pastry selections, and end with the Earl Gray Tea liqueur.

The **Kona Beach Restaurant,** at King Kamehameha's Kona Beach Hotel, tel. (808) 329-2911, is open daily for breakfast, lunch, and dinner and is especially known for its Sunday brunch served 9 a.m.-1 p.m. Appetizers include crab cakes for $6.95 and sashimi medley $7.95, while entrées range from kiawe-smoked prime rib of beef at $17.95 to barbecued baby-back ribs for $13.95. More moderately priced pastas are made scrumptious with Cajun prawns or sautéed with herbs and spices. Fresh catch or broiled salmon combined with prime rib is $19.95. Hearty luncheon sandwiches are reasonably priced—served with french fries for under $8. The restaurant itself is tasteful, but the best feature is an unobstructed view of the hotel's beach, especially fine at sunset.

Luaus, Buffets, Etc.

Tihati's Drums of Polynesia Luau, at the Royal Kona Resort, tel. (808) 329-3111, held every Monday, Friday, and Saturday, offers an authentic evening of entertainment and feasting, Hawaiian style. The luau begins at 5:30 p.m. and is followed by an open bar, lavish buffet, and thrilling entertainment for three fun-filled hours. Many supposedly authentic luaus play-act with the *imu*-baked pig, but here it is carved and served to the guests. Prices are $49 adults, $18 children ages 6-12, free for children under age five. Reservations are strongly recommended.

A sumptuous feast is held at the **Kona Village Resort,** just north of Kailua-Kona. It's worth attending this luau just to visit and be pampered at this private hotel beach. Adults pay around $63, children 6-12 $35, children 2-5 $21. Held every Friday, by reservation only, tel. (808) 325-5555. The *imu* ceremony is at 6 p.m., followed by no-host cocktails; the luau and Hawaiian entertainment begin at 8 p.m. Also, limited reservations are accepted during the week for lunch, dinner, and special dinners and buffets.

The **Royal Waikoloan Hotel Luau,** tel. (808) 885-6789, is offered on Sunday and Wednesday with the *imu* ceremony beginning at 6 p.m. followed by an open bar. Hawaiian entertainment and dinner begin at 6:30 p.m. Prices are adults $52, children 6-12 $25, free for children five and under.

King Kamehameha's Kona Beach Hotel, tel. (808) 326-4969, sways with Hawaiian chants during its famous **Island Breeze Luau** held every Sunday, Tuesday, Wednesday, and Thursday on the beach and grounds of King Kamehameha's last residence, Ahuena. The pig is placed into the *imu* every morning at 10 a.m. and the festivities begin in the evening with a lei greeting at 5:30 p.m. and a torch-lighting *imu* pageant at 6 p.m. Cocktails flow 6-8 p.m.; the 22-course luau dinner is served 6:30-8:30 p.m. Prices are $52 adults, $19.50 children 6-12, free for children five and under. Reservations are required. Call (808) 326-4969 or stop by the luau desk in the lobby of the hotel. **Kona Beach Restaurant,** also at King Kamehameha's Kona Beach Hotel, tel. (808) 329-2911, features a breakfast buffet at $9.50, Mon.-Sat. 6:30-10 a.m., Sunday to 9:30 a.m. As good as the breakfast buffet may be, the restaurant is very famous for its **King's Brunch,** served Sunday 10 a.m.-1 p.m., $19.95 adults, $9.95 children 6-12. The long tables are laden with fruit, vegetables, pasta salad, peel-and-eat shrimp, omelettes, waffles, hot entrees from fresh catch to sashimi, and desserts so sinful you'll be glad that someone's on their knees praying at Sunday services. Friday and Saturday nights are very special because of the **Prime Rib & Seafood Buffet** at $18.95, which brings hungry people from around the island.

Captain Beans' Dinner Cruise departs Kailua Pier daily at 5 p.m. and returns at 8 p.m. You are entertained while the bar dispenses liberal drinks and the deck groans with all-you-can-eat food. And you get a terrific panorama of the Kona Coast from the sea. You can't help having a good time on this cruise, and if the boat sinks with all that food and booze in your belly, you're a goner—but what a way to go! Minimum age is 18 years, $30 includes tax and tip. Reservations suggested; call (808) 329-2955.

ENTERTAINMENT AND ACTIVITIES

Kona nights come alive mainly in the restaurants and dining rooms of the big hotels. The most memorable experience for most is free: watching the sunset from Kailua Pier, and taking a leisurely stroll along Ali'i Drive. All of the luaus previously mentioned have "Polynesian Revues" of one sort or another, which are generally good, clean, sexy fun, but of course these shows are limited only to the luau guests. For those who have "dancin' feet" or wish to spend the evening listening to live music, there's a small but varied selection from which to choose.

Around Town

Huggo's Restaurant, with its romantic waterfront setting along Ali'i Dr., features music 8:30 p.m.-12:30 a.m. The entertainment changes nightly; *karaoke* on Tuesday features Juni Maderas. Excellent local bands like Mango, Nightlife, and Kona Blend offer smooth Jahwaiian and other mellow contemporary sounds with a touch of rock now and again.

The **Aston Keauhou Beach Resort** soothes you with easy listening, Hawaiian style. Weekends bring live bands like Holua and Nightlife, who will rock you with everything from original

Enjoy the free spectacle as some of the island's best canoeists come to Kailua Bay to work out every evening.

tunes to classic Hawaiian numbers. Also, Uncle George Naope, a renowned *kumu hula,* delights audiences with members of his local dance troupe on the Kuakini Terrace, Friday 11 a.m.-1:30 p.m. and then again 5:30-9:30 p.m., Saturday 5:30-9 p.m., Sunday 10 a.m.-1 p.m. (usually!).

At the **Royal Kona Resort's Windjammer Lounge,** an open-air bar, sip a flavorful tropical concoction while watching the sun melt into the Pacific. Entertainment is offered several evenings a week, featuring jazz on Sunday afternoon. Call the resort at (808) 329-3111 for a schedule of entertainment.

In downtown Kailua-Kona you can pick your fun at King Kamehameha's Kona Beach Hotel. Here, the **Billfish Bar** has live entertainment on weekends 6-10:30 p.m., featuring mellow Hawaiian music by Pomaikai. The bar is open 10:30 a.m.-10:30 p.m. with happy hour 5-7 p.m.

Around town, the **Eclipse Restaurant** has dance music 10 p.m.-1:30 a.m. every night. **Jolly Roger Restaurant** offers a variety of live music throughout the week beginning at 8:30 p.m. At the **Keauhou-Kona Golf Course Restaurant** you can enjoy live contemporary Hawaiian music performed by local artists every evening from 7 p.m. For a quiet beer, sports talk, or just hanging out with the local people try **Quinn's, Drysdale's, Ocean View Inn,** or **Sam's Hideaway,** all in downtown Kailua-Kona.

At **Fisherman's Landing Restaurant,** *karaoke* is presented every Wednesday 9 p.m.-midnight. They also have live music and dancing

nightly to the tunes of Sugar Sugar, a local dance band; Fri.-Sat. 6-9 p.m. a solo musician plays a mixed bag of country, classic rock-and-roll, and Hawaiian music.

For movies try the **World Square Theater** in the Kona Marketplace or the **Hualalai Theater** in Kailua-Kona.

The **Aloha Theater** in Kainaliu has a semi-professional local repertory company, the Aloha Community Theater, that puts on plays about six times per year that run for about three weeks each. Showtime in the completely refurbished and well-appointed theater is usually 8 p.m., and admission is a very reasonable $8 (senior discount). Check the local newspaper or the HVB office, or look for posters here and there around town.

SHOPPING

Below is an overview of Kona-area malls, including a general idea of what they contain.

Kailua-Kona Malls

The Kailua-Kona area has an abundance of two commodities near and dear to a tourist's heart: sunshine and shopping malls.

One of the largest malls in Kailua is the **Kona Inn Shopping Village** at 75-5744 Ali'i Drive. This shopping village boasts more than 40 shops selling fabrics, fashions, art, fruits, gems and jewelry, photo and music needs, food, and even exotic skins.

Kona Banyan Court, in central Kailua-Kona, has a dozen shops with a medley of goods and services. Distinctive shops include: **Kona Fine Woods** for souvenir-quality woodcarvings; **Unison,** a surfing shop with T-shirts, sandals, hats, and boogie boards; and **Paradise Antiques,** filled with Hawaiian-style treasures and bric-a-brac. To gain control of your hair in the wild Kona breeze, put it in the hands of Darlene, who owns **Hair We Are,** open daily 9 a.m.-7 p.m., Sunday 10 a.m.-4 p.m. Men, women, and children are welcome. The most impressive shop in the complex is **Big Island Jewelers,** tel. (808) 329-8571, open Mon.-Sat. 9 a.m.-9 p.m., Sunday 10 a.m.-6 p.m., owned and operated by brothers Flint and Gale Carpenter, master goldsmiths. The shop motto, "Have your jewelry made by a Carpenter," applies to custom-made jewelry fashioned to their or your personal design. Big Island Jewelers, in business for more than 15 years, does repairs and also carries a full line of pearls and loose stones that they will mount into any setting you wish.

You'll also find **Kailua Bay Inn Shopping Plaza** along Ali'i Dr., with shops like **Mil-Rose** filled with sun and fun wear, swimwear, and accessories mostly for women; **Kona Jog and Gift,** with official Ironman Triathlon products along with running shorts, biking shorts, sweat shirts, T-shirts, waterproof watches, hats, incidental bags, and even some aloha shirts; **Waiting for the Sun Petroglyph Jewelry** specializing in glassware and gifts; and **Kona Arts and Crafts,** offering genuine Hawaiian gifts. The **Akona Kai Mall** lies across from Kailua Pier, and the **Kona Marketplace** in central Kailua-Kona offers a variety of shops selling everything from burgers to bathing suits.

King Kamehameha's Kona Beach Hotel Mall, fully air-conditioned, features a cluster of specialty shops and a **Liberty House.** Shops include: **Resort Sundries,** selling wine, liquor, and beer along with suntan lotions, gift items, magazines, novels, and T-shirts; **Jewel Palace,** sparkling with watches and fine jewelry fashioned from gold and silver; **Liberty House Kids,** featuring aloha and resort wear especially designed for children; **Silver Reef,** featuring Hawaiian-motif jewelry, glassware, Japanese dolls, and porcelain wear; **Ali'i Artwear,** specializing in distinctive resort and beach wear for women;

and **Kailua Village Artists,** hung with paintings and prints.

Catercorner to King Kamehameha's Hotel is the **Seaside Mall,** with most shops open daily 9 a.m.-6 p.m. Here you'll find **Neptune's Garden** creating rainbows with its display of stained glass art fashioned into lamps, creative hangings, vases, and a few paintings. Here, too, is **Tropical Tees,** where you can outfit yourself with distinctive T-shirts and sunglasses; and the **Sandal Stop,** where your tootsies will purr in a new pair of sandals, dress shoes, or Birkenstocks for men, women, or children. Across the way is **Eel Skin Liquidators;** no, they don't juice eels, but they do sell eelskin accessories like purses and belts, along with an assortment of souvenir-quality artifacts, jewelry, and knickknacks. Other shops are the **Kona Coast Sunglass Company,** who will help you protect your eyes from those harmful rays; **Gold Fish,** selling painted fish, necklaces, back scratchers, toe rings, bracelets, and hanging mobiles; **Starshine,** with its distinctive T-shirts; and **Bubi's Sportswear** for T-shirts, sweatshirts, towels, hats, and tourist niceties for beach, sun, and surf.

The **Kona Square Shopping Center,** next to the Seaside Mall with most shops open daily 9 a.m.-6 p.m., features **Mermaid's By The Sea,** a distinctive ladies' and children's clothing boutique bright with alohawear, pareus, sun and evening dresses, and a ceiling hung with cherubic angels if you're not sharing your Hawaii vacation with one of your own. Directly across from Mermaids is **Island Silversmiths,** Kona's oldest modern-day shop, in business since 1973, so you know they're doing something right. To complete your ensemble from Mermaids, peruse the display cases filled with bracelets, rings, and necklaces fashioned from silver and gold. Motifs are pure Hawaiian, with geckos, fish hooks, dolphins, whales, and the odd unicorn or scorpion thrown in just to be worldly. Here too is **Gems of the Sea,** displaying shoreline treasures—shells of all types from all over the world. Inside you can also choose from coral jewelry, fish hooks, necklaces of all kinds, troll dolls, sea urchin night lights, and wind chimes.

The **Lanihau Center,** tel. (808) 329-9333, at 75-5595 Palani Rd., is one of Kailua-Kona's newest shopping meccas. It offers **Longs Drugs** for sundries and photo supplies; an assortment of restaurants; apparel and shoe stores including **Feet First; Waldenbooks,** an excellent all-purpose bookstore; **Radio Shack** for electronic gizmos of all sorts; and **H2O Action Surf Shop** for jeans, surf boards, boogie boards, sporting goods, in-line skates, shirts, T-shirts, hats, and sunglasses.

Kopiko Plaza, along Palani Rd. just down from the Lanihau Center, is a small mall containing **Scott's Knife Center** for fine cutlery from carving knives to Swiss Army knives; **Action Sports** for the largest selection of sporting equipment in town; and, **Tempo Music,** where you can get all of your music needs, including plenty of island sounds. The mall also has a smattering of inexpensive restaurants, both for takeout and eat in.

Waterfront Row is a relatively new shopping and food complex at the south end of downtown Kailua-Kona. Built of rough-cut lumber, it's done in period architecture reminiscent of an outdoor promenade in a Boston shipyard at the turn of the century. **Pacific Vibrations,** a surf shop, sells everything from postcards to hats, backpacks, and aloha shirts. **Pleasant Hawaiian Holidays** maintains a booth here from where you can book a wide range of activities. **Crazy Shirts** sells unique island creations, and **Kona Jack's** offers distinctive unisex apparel featuring its logo. Restaurants include the **Chart House** for steaks and seafood, **Michelangelo's** for Italian cuisine, and **Jolly Roger** for American and Hawaiian cuisine.

Rawson Plaza, at 74-5563 Kaiwi St., is just past King Kamehameha's Kona Beach Hotel in the industrial area. This practical, no-frills area abounds in "no-name" shops selling everything you'll find in town but at substantial savings.

Kona Coast Shopping Center along Palani Rd. features **Pay 'n' Save** for sundries and everything from scuba gear to Styrofoam coolers; **KTA Market;** the **Undercover Shop,** with fine lingerie; **Hallmark Cards; Marshals,** open Mon.-Sat. 10 a.m.-9 p.m., Sunday 10 a.m.-6 p.m., a family oriented clothing store with decent prices; **Blockbuster Video,** where you can rent a movie for the evening, open daily 10 a.m.-midnight; **Men's Shop,** open Mon.-Sat. 9 a.m.-6 p.m., Sunday 10 a.m.-5 p.m., with alohawear, shirts, shorts, slacks, jackets, and big men's sizes; and **Fantastic Sams,** a hair salon open Mon.-Thurs.

9 a.m.-6 p.m., Fri.-Sat. 9 a.m.-7 p.m., Sunday 9 a.m.-5 p.m., no appointment necessary.

South of Kailua Malls

If, god forbid, you haven't found what you need in Kailua, or if you suddenly need a "shopping fix," even more malls are south on Rt. 11. **Keauhou Shopping Village** is at the corner of Ali'i Dr. and Kamehameha III Road. Look for flags waving in the breeze high on the hill marking the entrance. This mall houses apparel shops, restaurants, a post office, and photo-processing booths. You can find all your food and prescription needs at **KTA Supermarket,** the largest in the area. **Keauhou Village Bookshop** is a full-service bookstore. **Kona-kai Cafe,** an espresso and coffee shop open daily 8:30 a.m.-6 p.m., will take care of your sweet tooth and drooping energy; you can also buy a pound or two of fresh Kona coffee there. **Drysdale's** is an indoor/outdoor bar and grill where you can relax over a cold beer or choose from their extensive sandwich menu. Other shops include: the **Showcase Gallery,** for glassware, paintings, ceramics, and local crafts; **Long's Drugstore,** for everything from foot care products to photography; **Ace Hardware** for nuts and bolts; **Radio Shack** to tune in; **Liberty House** for family fashions; and **Alapaki's,** for island goods from black coral jewelry to colorful muumuu.

Continuing south on Rt. 11, you'll spot the **Kainaliu Village Mall** along the main drag.

Food Markets

KTA Supermarket, open daily 6 a.m.-midnight, is generally the cheapest market in town and is located at the Kona Coast Shopping Center along Palani Rd.; there's another one at the Keauhou Village Mall, at the extreme south end of Ali'i Dr. at its junction with Kamehameha III Road. They're well stocked with sundries; an excellent selection of Asian foods, fresh veggies, fish, and fruit; and a smattering of health food. The market also contains a full-service pharmacy.

The **Kailua Village Farmers Market** along Ali'i Dr. just across from Waterfront Row, open Wednesday, Friday, Saturday, and Sunday 6 a.m.-3 p.m., tel. (808) 329-1393, sells locally grown (some organic) fruits and vegetables, nuts, flowers, and coffee. Every Wednesday, Friday, Saturday, and Sunday 6 a.m.-2 p.m.

Uncle Billy's Farmers Market is held in the parking lot across the street from Uncle Billy's Kona Bay Hotel. Lots of local produce, flowers, and coffee.

Across the road, **Sack 'n' Save,** in the Lanihau Center, open 5 a.m.-midnight, is one of the main supermarkets in town.

Kona Wine Market, in the small King Kamehameha Mall, 75-5626 Kuakini Hwy., tel. (808) 329-9400, open daily 10 a.m.-8 p.m., Sunday noon-6 p.m., is the best wine shop on the Kona coast. They feature an impressive international selection of wine and varietals from California, Italy, Spain, France, Chile, and Australia. Prices range from $4.95 for a table wine to $200 for a bottle of select boutique wine. A large cooler holds a fine selection of beer, both domestic and imported, and the store shelves hold wonderful gourmet munchies like Indian chutney, Sicilian olives, mustards, dressings, marinades, smoked salmon, hearty cheeses, and even pasta imported from Italy. Cigar smokers will also appreciate the humidor filled with fine cigars from around the world.

Casa De Emdeko Liquor and Deli is south of town center at 75-6082 Ali'i Drive. It's well stocked with liquor and groceries, but at conveniencestore prices. Other markets include **King Kamehameha Pantry,** tel. (808) 329-9191, selling liquors, groceries, and sundries; and **Keauhou Pantry,** tel. (808) 322-3066, in Keauhou along Ali'i Dr., selling more of the same.

Health Food Stores

Kona keeps you healthy with **Kona Healthways** in the Kona Coast Shopping Center, tel. (808) 329-2296, open Mon.-Sat. 9 a.m.-8 p.m., Sunday to 7 p.m. Besides a good assortment of health foods, they have cosmetics, books, and dietary supplements. Vegetarians will like their ready-to-eat sandwiches, salads, and soups. Shelves are lined with teas and organic vitamins. They also have a cooler with organic juices, cheeses, and soy milk. A refrigerator holds organic produce, while bins are filled with bulk grains.

A **General Nutrition Center,** located in the Lanihau Center along Palani Rd., open Mon.-Fri. 10 a.m.-8 p.m., Sat.-Sun. 10 a.m.-6 p.m., is stocked with vitamins, food supplements, and minerals.

Bookstores

Waldenbooks, in the Lanihau Center on Palani Rd., tel. (808) 329-0015, open Mon.-Thurs. 9:30 a.m.-7 p.m., Friday 9:30 a.m.-9 p.m., Sunday 10 a.m.-5 p.m., not only has the well-stocked and far-ranging selection for which this national chain has become famous, but also features an in-depth Hawaiiana collection and even some Hawaiian music tapes.

In Kailua-Kona be sure to venture into **Middle Earth Bookshop** at 75-5719 Ali'i Dr., in the Kona Plaza Shopping Arcade, tel. (808) 329-2123, open Mon.-Sat. 9 a.m.-9 p.m., Sunday to 6 p.m. This jam-packed bookstore has shelves laden with fiction, nonfiction, paperbacks, hardbacks, travel books, maps, and Hawaiiana. A great place to browse.

Keauhou Village Bookshop at Keauhou Shopping Village, tel. (808) 322-8111, open Mon.-Sat. 9 a.m.-6 p.m., Sunday 9 a.m.-5 p.m., is a full-service bookstore with plenty of Hawaiiana selections, general reading material, a children's section, and a superb travel section, along with an excellent selection of maps, especially on Hawaii. They also sell CDs and cassettes.

Photo Needs

Zac's Photo, in the North Kona Shopping Center, at the corner of Palani Rd. and Kuakini Hwy., tel. (808) 329-0006, open daily 7 a.m.-9 p.m., develops prints in one hour and slides in two days. Zac, a native of Belgium, will even make minor camera repairs free of charge. Prices are very competitive and you can save more by clipping two-for-one and 20% discount coupons from the free tourist brochure, *This Week, Big Island.*

Longs Drugs, in the Lanihau Center along Palani Rd., tel. (808) 329-1380, also has excellent prices on film and camera supplies.

Kona Photo Arts, in the North Kona Shopping Plaza, tel. (808) 329-2566, is open Mon.-Sat. 8 a.m.-6 p.m. It is a *real* photography store where you can get lenses, cameras, filters, and even telescopes and binoculars. Their processing is competitive, and they also offer custom developing.

More Malls: Art and Specialty Shops

In King Kamehameha's Kona Beach Hotel, **The Shellery** lives up to its name with baubles, bangles, and beads made from shells, along with a selection of fine jewelry and pearls; and **Kailua Village Artists** displays paintings and prints for sale.

Island Togs is across from the Kona Beach Restaurant at King Kamehameha's Kona Beach Hotel, tel. (808) 329-2144. This long-established shop hidden from the main tourist gauntlet is known by the locals as one of the best places to purchase women's bathing suits and bikinis. They also feature very reasonable prices on resortwear, shorts, and an assortment of tops.

In the World Square Shopping Center visit **Coral Isle Art Shop** for modern versions of traditional Hawaiian carvings. You'll find everything from tikis to scrimshaw, with exceptionally good carvings of sharks and whales for a pricey $75 or so.

Enjoy the beauty of Hawaii with flowers from **Editha's Lei Stand,** a.k.a. Oriental Flower Decor, tel. (808) 334-1194, located in front of Huggo's Restaurant, open daily 10:30 a.m.-6 p.m., except Sunday with a slightly earlier closing. Editha creates lovely lei that run from $3.75 for a basic strand to $20 for a magnificent triple lei, along with a variety of fresh-cut flower arrangements. All of Editha's flowers are "certified" so if you want to take them home, you'll have no hassle with agricultural inspection. If you prefer direct shipping to the Mainland, that'll be no problem with a minimum cost of $37 including shipping.

Also in the parking lot in front of Huggo's Restaurant, along Ali'i Dr., look for a little truck business called **Nikki's** that sells Kona coffee at $8.49 per pound and macadamia nuts at $6.95 per pound, both decent prices.

At the **Kona Inn Shopping Village** you can buy custom jewelry at **Jim Bill's Gemfire.** Featured at the **T-shirt Company,** a.k.a. Island Salsa, are designer tee's that are some of the best in Kona. Prices are normally around $18, but they run specials all the time. You can pick up one-of-a-kind creations by Roberta, the owner/artist, for around $10. They also feature alohawear for the entire family, ladies' evening wear, swimwear, and dinner clothes. **Collectors Fine Art** is a perfect labyrinth of rooms and hallways showcasing the acclaimed works of international artists. Not a shop at which to buy trinkets; prices range from $300 to $250,000 for some of the finer paintings and sculptures by internationally acclaimed artists. **Hula Heaven,** open daily 9 a.m.-9 p.m., is situated in a stone tower dating from 1927 and specializes in vintage Hawaiian shirts and modern reproductions. Prices range from $50 for the "look alikes" to $1,000 for the rarest of the classics. Because many of the items on display date from the '40s and '50s, the shop is like a trip back in time. Other shops include: **Noa Noa,** featuring hand-painted, one-of-a-kind original clothing, mostly from Indonesia; **Kona Jewelry Factory,** featuring island-inspired jewelry; **Hawaiian Fruit and Flower Company** for sweets and sweet-smelling flowers; **Fare Tahiti Fabrics** for incidental travel bags, pareus, and fabrics; **Golden Orchid,** a women's resort wear and casual wear shop; **Kona Inn Children's Wear,** featuring Hawaiian fashions for the little ones; **Limited Editions Hawaii,** with original designs on T-shirts; and **Kona Inn General Store,** with sundries, beer, and liquor.

At **Kona Inn Flower and Lei** you can pick up flowers to add that perfect touch to a romantic evening. Nearby **Christel's Collectibles** has stuffed toys, stuffed pillows, and some clothing. **Kona Inn Jewelry,** for worldwide treasures, is one of the oldest and best-known shops for a square deal in Kona. Owned and operated by Joe Goldscharek and his family, they take time to help you choose just the right gift. Inside you'll find stained-glass hangings, jewelry, fine gemstones, and a collection of hand-painted fish. The family tries to pick unique items from around the world that can be found in no other Kona shop. Be aware that the shop is protected by Mama Cat, a sleeping ball of fur honored with her own postcard, who if you're not careful will purr you to death.

Other shops in the center include: **Flamingo's** for contemporary island clothing and evening wear mainly for women; **Big Island Hat Co.** for headgear ranging from pith helmets to sombreros; **The Treasury,** specializing in jewelry, T-shirts, beachwear, hats, sunglasses, backpacks, shoulder bags, and postcards; **Tahiti Fabrics,** offering bolts of cloth and a nice collection of Hawaiian shirts; **Alley Gecko's,** showcasing colorful gifts from around the world; and the **Old Hawaiian Gold Co.,** which can bedeck you in gold chains or pearl and coral jewelry.

At the **Kona Marketplace** in the downtown area, look for **Kona Jewelers,** specializing in fine jewelry and ceramics. The jam-packed **Aloha From Kona** specializes in baubles, bangles, postcards, handbags, and purses. In contrast is **Ali'i Nexus,** for fine jewelry, one of the nicest and most low-key shops in town. The **Kona Flea Market** stuck to the rear of the mall sells inexpensive travel bags, shells, beach mats, suntan lotion, and all the junk that you could want.

Kona Gold, tel. (808) 327-9373, in the Kailua Bay Inn Shopping Plaza, open daily except Sunday 9 a.m.-9 p.m., has excellent prices on custom-made jewelry by Harold Booton, the goldsmith and proprietor. Harold also imports jewelry from around the world, especially silver, and if it's not on sale, bargaining is definitely okay! The store stocks coral jewelry, a smattering of T-shirts, and lifelike wooden sculptures of whales and marine animals, many of which come from Indonesia. Kona Gold is a perfect shop in which to purchase a lifelong memento at a very reasonable price.

Alapaki's, at Keauhou Shopping Village, sells distinctive island arts and crafts. Inside you'll find pink, gold, and black coral jewelry; lei of shells and seeds; and *tutu* dolls bedecked in colorful muumuu. Distinctive items include koa bowls, each signed by the artist; and a replica of a Hawaiian double-hulled canoe made from coconut and cloth with traditional crab-claw sails. Original paintings by R.K. McGuire feature Hawaiian animals; basketry, fans, and jewelry made from ironwood needles are by local artist Barb Walls. Some of the finest artworks displayed are feather lei by Eloise Deshea and woodcarvings by Thomas Baboza.

For some practical purchases at wholesale prices, check **Liberty House Penthouse** at Keauhou Shopping Village; it will appeal to bargain hunters. This outlet store sells items that have been cleared and reduced from the famous Liberty House stores. You can save on everything from alohawear to formal dresses.

Kailua Candy Company, in the industrial section on the corner of Kurakini and Kiawi Streets, tel. (808) 329-2522 or (800) 622-2462, is open daily 8 a.m.-6 p.m. It was recognized as one of the "top 10 chocolate shops in the United States" in the February 1993 issue of *Bon Appetit*

magazine. All the chocolates are made of the finest ingredients available, and all would try the willpower of Gandhi, but the specialty is the macadamia nut *honu,* Hawaiian for turtle. The best sampler is the one-pound Kailua Candy Company Assortment, hand-packed with a quarter pound each of *honu,* the award-winning Kona coffee swirl, dark macadamia nut clusters, and white coconut Mauna Kea snowballs. It costs $17.10, or $21 shipped anywhere on the Mainland. Shipping of all the candy is available at the cost of postage plus $1 handling fee; shipments are guaranteed to be in perfect condition or they will be replaced free. Every day 8 a.m.-6 p.m., have a free look into the kitchen and nibble samples of their products.

Poor soul! If your lover's run off with an escaped felon, your life savings can fit into a change purse, a birthday party you threw for all your friends fit at a table for one, and you've already suffered the ultimate humiliation of hurling yourself off Kona Pier only to splat onto damp sand at low tide, perhaps you should head for **Ancient Wisdoms,** in the Ali'i Sunset Plaza at 75-5799 Ali'i Dr., across from the seawall at the south end of town, tel. (808) 329-9412, open Sun.-Mon. 10 a.m.-6 p.m., Tues.-Sat. 10 a.m.-9 p.m. On its shelves you will find metaphysical and "old-age" books, new-age music, basketry, aromatherapy, crystals, crystal balls, jewelry, incense, paintings from local artists, a Native American section, posters, postcards, and souvenirs. Saturday nights (call for details), Ancient Wisdoms shows foreign and classic films, free, at 7 p.m. You can also arrange a massage ranging from *lomi lomi* to Swedish in the shop's massage room. If this doesn't lift your spirits, try the last resort . . . whining and wishful thinking.

Along Ali'i Dr., diagonally across from Hulihee Palace, is **Hawaiian Wear Unlimited,** where you can pick up alohawear for a very reasonable price. Just up the road, across from the seawall along Likana Lane, is **Ululani Fresh Cut Flowers,** a reasonably priced lei stand. **Goodies** just up the alley has gift boxes of jams and jellies, Maui onion mustard, macadamia nuts, an assortment of coffees, and various perfumes and scents.

Real treasure hunters will love the **Kona Gardens Flea Market** held every Wednesday and Saturday 8 a.m.-2 p.m. in the parking lot next to St. Michael's Church along Ali'i Drive. Unfortunately, this formerly huge flea market is now only a shadow of its former self and is always tottering on the brink of closure.

The **Banyan Tree Bazaar** (not really the name, but no one has bothered to give it one yet) is along Ali'i Dr. next to Stan's Restaurant across from the seawall. Look for blue and white umbrellas under which local merchants sell handcrafted and locally made necklaces, earrings, and bracelets. Others sell various artworks like stuffed animals, along with an array of inexpensive but neat tourist junk.

SERVICES, INFORMATION, AND TRANSPORTATION

Emergencies and Health
For ambulance, fire, and police emergencies call 911. The Kona Hospital is in Kealakekua, tel. (808) 322-9311. The most convenient pharmacy is Longs Drugs, tel. (808) 329-1380. For alternative health care services and massage, both well established in Kailua-Kona, see the **Health and Conduct** section in the Out and About chapter.

Information
An information gazebo is open daily 7 a.m.-9 p.m. along the boardwalk in the Kona Inn Shopping Village. They can handle your questions about everything from dining to diving. The Hawaii Visitors Bureau maintains an office in the Kona Plaza Shopping Arcade, at 75-5719 Ali'i Dr., tel. (808) 329-7787, open Mon.-Fri. 8 a.m.-noon, then again 1-4:30 p.m. The staff is friendly, helpful, and extremely knowledgeable about touring the Big Island. The library is at 75-140 Hualalai Rd., tel. (808) 327-3077.

An excellent tourist map that highlights restaurants, accommodations, and businesses is available free at the HVB office and at many shops in Kona and throughout the Big Island. The map is published by the Island Map Company, 159 Kiawe St., Suite 1, Hilo, HI 96720, tel. (808) 934-9007.

Services
First Hawaiian Bank, in the Lanihau Center on Palani Rd., can be reached at tel. (808) 329-2461. Also in the center at Sack 'n' Save, Bank of America maintains a 24-hour Versatel machine. Bank of Hawaii maintains two area offices, one in Kailua, tel. (808) 326-3927, the other in Kealakekua, tel. (808) 322-9377. The main post office is on Palani Rd., tel. (808) 329-1927, just past the Lanihau Center. Mail Boxes Etc. at the Crossroads Shopping Center provides postal, shipping, and wrapping services. The Hele Mai Laundromat is near King Kamehameha's Kona Beach Hotel.

Ali'i Shuttle
If you want to concentrate on the scenery and not the driving, take the Ali'i Shuttle, tel. (808) 775-7121. Painted red, white, and blue, the bus runs daily every 30-45 minutes (more or less) along Ali'i Dr. 8:30 a.m.-10 p.m., and charges $2 each direction ($5 day pass, $20 weekly). The terminal points are Lanihau Shopping Center on the north end and Kona Surf Resort on the south end, with pickups at major hotels along the way. You can hail the bus and it will stop if possible.

CENTRAL AND SOUTH KONA

Kailua-Kona's Ali'i Dr. eventually turns up the mountainside and joins Rt. 11, which in its central section is called the **Kuakini Highway**. This road, heading south, quickly passes the towns of **Honalo, Kainaliu** (Bail the Bilge), **Kealakekua**, and **Captain Cook**. You'll have ample opportunity to stop along the way for gas, picnic supplies, or browsing. These towns have some terrific restaurants, specialty shops, and boutiques. At Captain Cook, you can dip down to the coast and visit a working coffee mill, or continue south to **Pu'uhonua O Honaunau,** a reconstructed temple of refuge, the best in the state. Farther south still, little-traveled side roads take you to the sleepy seaside villages of **Hookena** and **Milolii,** where traditional lifestyles are still the norm.

Or for an alternative, instead of heading directly south out of Kailua-Kona on Rt. 11, take Hualalai Rd. (Rt. 182) to Rt. 180, a high mountain road that parallels Rt. 11 and takes you to the artists' community of **Holualoa,** from where you get an expansive view of the coastline below. When leaving Holualoa for points south, stay on Rt. 180, the Mamalahoa Hwy., a gorgeous road with great views from the heights.

HOLUALOA

Holualoa (The Sledding Course) is an undisturbed mountain community perched high above the Kailua-Kona Coast with many of the island's most famous artists creating art in galleries that line paintbrush to easel along its vintage main street. Prior to its transformation to an art community, Holualoa had another history. In days past, general stores, hotels, restaurants, bars, and pool halls lined its streets. Before Hawaii found its potential for tourism and started to develop its coastal areas, rural Hawaii was primarily agricultural, and the farms, and consequently most of the people, were located on the mountainsides. Large agricultural areas sustained working communities and Holualoa was one such population center. While agriculture is still a part of the local economy, it has been eclipsed by tourism and the arts. Get there by

taking the spur Rt. 182, known as **Hualalai Road,** off Rt. 11 (Queen Kaahumanu Hwy.) from Kailua-Kona, or by taking Rt. 180 (Mamalahoa Hwy.) from Honalo in the south or from Honokohau in the north (junction with Rt. 190, Palani Rd. from Kailua-Kona). Climbing Hualalai Rd. (Rt. 182), the best route, affords glorious views of the coast below. Notice the immediate contrast of the lush foliage against the scant vegetation of the lowland area. On the mountainside, bathed in tropical mists, are tall forest trees interspersed with banana, papaya, and mango trees. Flowering trees pulsating in the green canopy explode in vibrant reds, yellows, oranges, and purples. If you want to get away from the Kona heat and dryness, head up to the well-watered coolness of Holualoa.

Note: Keep in mind that it is customary for most of the galleries to be *closed on Monday.*

Shops and Other Sights

After you wind your way up Rt. 182 through this verdant jungle area, you suddenly enter the village and are greeted by **Kimura's Lauhala Shop,** tel. (808) 324-0053, open daily 9 a.m.-5 p.m., closed Sunday. The shop, still tended by Mrs. Kimura and her daughters, Alfreida and Ella, has been in existence since 1915. In the beginning, Kimura's was a general store, but they always sold *lau hala* and became famous for their hats, which local people would make to barter for groceries. Famous, on and later off island, only *Kona-side* hats have a distinctive pullstring that makes the hat larger or smaller. Mrs. Kimura, and most of her friends who helped manufacture the hats, are getting on in age and can no longer keep up with the demand. Many hatmakers have passed away, and there are few young people interested in keeping the dying art alive. They still have hats, but the stock is dwindling. All *lau hala* weavings are done on the premises, while some of the other gift items are brought in. Choose from authentic baskets, floor mats, handbags, slippers, and of course an assortment of the classic sun hats that start at $35. A terrific purchase is a *lau hala* tote bag, lined with 100% cotton tapa style cloth. This specialty item, priced around $45, with two big pouches and a zippered pouch, works equally well as a day bag, beach bag, or picnic basket. Also for an authentic souvenir, look for a round basket with a strap, the original Kona coffee basket.

After Kimura's follow the road for a minute or so to enter the actual village, where the **post office** and a cross atop a white steeple welcome you to town. The tiny village, complete with its own elementary school, is well kept, with an obvious double helping of pride put into this artists' community by its citizens. Just here is **Paul's Place,** a well-stocked country store, open weekdays 7:30 a.m.-8 p.m., weekends 8 a.m.-8 p.m.

Along the main road is a converted coffee mill, gaily painted and decorated, and currently the home of the nonprofit **Kona Art Center,** open Tues.-Sat. 10 a.m.-4 p.m., which began as a labor of love by husband and wife artist team Robert and Carol Rogers. Uncle Bob, as he was affectionately known, passed away, but Aunt Carol is still creating art at the center. Both had an extensive background in art teaching. They moved from San Francisco to Holualoa in 1965 and began offering community workshop classes. Carol says, "I love Kona because we share, care, and love with our people here." Across the road is a restored building, a one-time country church rescued from the ravages of weather and termites, that now proudly displays the works of the center's members. In here you will find everything from hobby crafts to serious renderings that might include paintings, basketry, sculptures, and even tie-dyed shirts. The center is very friendly and welcomes guests with a cup of Kona coffee. The building is rickety and old, but it's obviously filled with good vibrations and love. However, time moves on and things change. The building has been sold, and the new owners—who tried to cooperate with the center by keeping it housed here—were advised by a number of outside architects that the building is beyond saving and must be torn down. The idea is to replace it with a new center that will house a restaurant and various shops and provide space for the art center in the rear. This is in the planning stage.

Across the road from the Kona Art Center is **Dahlia's Flower Shop,** tel. (808) 322-3189, open daily except Sunday 9:30 a.m.-3 p.m., specializing in tropical flower arrangements, mums, and fresh *maile* lei. The prices are excellent and Dahlia offers shipping to the Mainland and Canada. All of her flowers are "certified" so there is no hassle with agricultural inspection.

Opposite the Holualoa Library is the **Country Frame Shop,** tel. (808) 324-1590, open Mon.-Fri. 9:30 a.m.-4:30 p.m., Saturday 9:30 a.m.-1:30 p.m. It specializes in framing artwork in koa but also displays works by famous local artists including: Carla Sachi-Nifash, a watercolor artist who renders Hawaii in everything from still life to underwater scenes; furniture artist Mike Felig, who turns koa into contemporary and traditional pieces of furniture; Sue Swerdlow, who is a master at capturing color as it bursts from the jungle; Jennifer Pontz, who etches glass with Hawaiian motifs; and Tom Breeze and Mary Jo Lake, who create affordable, functional pieces, such as cutting boards, that you can use every day and will remind you of your trip to the Big Island. The owner, Chuck Hart, accepts credit cards and will ship anywhere. The Country Frame Shop is well worth a visit, if only just to browse.

"He's a potter, I'm a painter," is the understatement, uttered by Mary Lovein, the female half of the artistic husband and wife team of Mary and Matthew Lovein. They produce and display their lovely and inspired artwork at **Holualoa Gallery,** tel. (808) 322-8484, open Tues.-Sat., 10 a.m.-5 p.m., which is easily spotted along Holualoa's main thoroughfare. Mary uses her acrylics and airbrush to create large, bold, and bright seascapes and landscapes of Hawaii. Matthew specializes in *raku:* magnificent works of waist-high vases, classic Japanese-style ceramics glazed in deep rose, iridescent greens, crinkled gray, and deep periwinkle blue. Mary and Matthew collaborate on some of the larger pieces. Matt creates the vessel and, while it is still greenware, its underglaze is painted by Mary. Other artists featured in the shop are: Herb Kane, world renowned for his dream-reality paintings of Hawaii and its people; Cecilia Faith Black, who does delicate jewelry; Patricia Van Asperen-Hume, who creates fused glassworks; and Frances Dennis, who hand-paints romantic Hawaiian imagery on porcelain.

The flora and fauna of Hawaii, both aboveground and beneath the waves, come alive in the **White Garden Gallery,** open Tues.-Sat., 10

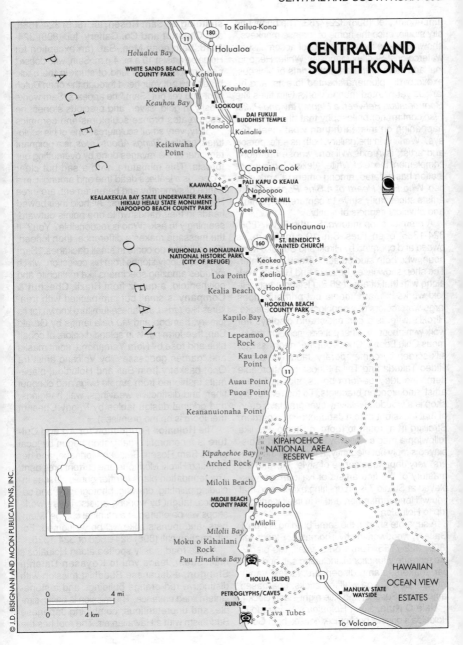

CENTRAL AND SOUTH KONA

To Kailua-Kona

180

11

Holualoa

Holualoa Bay

WHITE SANDS BEACH
COUNTY PARK

Kahaluu

KONA GARDENS

Keauhou

Keauhou Bay

LOOKOUT

DAI FUKUJI
BUDDHIST TEMPLE

Honalo

Kainaliu

Keikiwaha
Point

Kealakekua

Captain Cook

KAAWALOA

PALI KAPU O KEAUA

Napoopoo

KEALAKEKUA BAY STATE UNDERWATER PARK
HIKIAU HEIAU STATE MONUMENT
NAPOOPOO BEACH COUNTY PARK

COFFEE MILL

Keei

Honaunau

PUUHONUA O HONAUNAU
NATIONAL HISTORIC PARK
(CITY OF REFUGE)

ST. BENEDICT'S
PAINTED CHURCH

160

Keokea

Loa Point

Kealia

Kealia Beach

Hookena

HOOKENA BEACH
COUNTY PARK

Kapilo Bay

Lepeamoa
Rock

Kau Loa
Point

11

Auau Point

Puoa Point

Keananuionaha Point

Kipahoehoe Bay

KIPAHOEHOE
NATIONAL AREA
RESERVE

Arched Rock

Milolii Beach

MILOLII BEACH
COUNTY PARK

Hoopuloa

Milolii

Milolii Bay

Moku o Kahailani
Rock

Puu Hinahina Bay

HOLUA (SLIDE)

11

PETROGLYPHS/CAVES

MANUKA STATE
WAYSIDE

RUINS

Lava Tubes

HAWAIIAN
OCEAN VIEW
ESTATES

To Volcano

PACIFIC OCEAN

MOON

0   4 mi

0   4 km

a.m.-4 p.m., tel. (808) 322-7733. The bright and airy studio, once the home of "grease monkeys," showcases the fantastic works of accomplished watercolorist Shelley Maudsley-White. Her original and state-of-the art *giclé* prints of hibiscus, exotic birds, plumeria-scented forests, and hilarious yet pointed marine works with titles like *Confrontation Between a Manta Ray and Puffer Fish* confirm her philosophy that "there is more happening on this earth than what meets the eye." Working in the gallery, both as salesperson and artist, is Alexis Wilson, whose creations complement those of White. Alexis's fertile imagination has created, among others, a work entitled *Who Ever Heard of a Blue Papaya?* Both artists sucessfully strive to capture the spiritual and physical aspects of reality.

A premier shop in town, **Studio 7,** tel. (808) 324-1335, open Tues.-Sat. 10 a.m.-5 p.m., is owned and operated by Hiroki and Setsuko Morinoue, who both studied at the Kona Art Center. The shop showcases Setsuko and Hiroki's work along with that of about 20 Big Island artists. Hiroki works in many media but primarily does large watercolors or woodblock prints. Setsuko, Hiroki's wife, is a ceramicist and displays her work with about six other potters, including the famous Chiu Leong. Check out the "neoclassical" silk-screen by contemporary Japanese artists Hideo Takeda and Taika Kinoshita. Affordable items include free-form bowls, signed by the artist, and wooden bracelets. To the rear of the shop is a wooden walkway over gray lava gravel that looks out onto a Japanese-style garden. Strolling from room to room in Studio 7 is like following a magic walkway where the art is displayed simply but elegantly, a legacy of the owners' very Japanese sense of style. Viewing the mastery of the fine artists of Kailua-Kona displayed at Studio 7 is an uplifting experience that you will long remember, and is in itself worth the trip to Holualoa.

A separate shop in the same building is **Koa T Gallery,** woodworking by Thomas A. Stoudt, tel. (808) 322-7755. Tom works small. His pieces are extremely functional, including salt and pepper shakers, stamp dispensers, ladies' vanity mirrors, bowls, koa walking sticks, koa-based lamps, lazy Susans, and little night-stand clocks.

Hale O Kula, along Holualoa's main road in Holualoa's original post office, houses both **Gold**smithing by Sam Rosen,** tel. (808) 324-1688, and **Chesnut and Co. Gallery,** tel. (808) 324-1446, both open Mon.-Sat. (an exception for Holualoa artists) 10 a.m.-4 p.m. Sam, who doesn't need much room, is kind of stuck in the back. When you put your head through the open Dutch door and yell out "Sam," he appears. Sam works mostly in gold, silver, and precious stones; he also creates bronze sculptures and ceramics . . . very, very small sculptures. One of his sculptures, entitled *Things About Trees,* is a poignant reminder of the ravages done by overcutting our forests. This miniature, with a sad but clear "voice," is a leafless dead tree and around it, in a dance of sympathy and bereavement, are three Hawaiian "night marchers." All hold their bowed heads in their hands while one points outward, seemingly to ask, "Who is responsible? You?" If the message makes a difference, then indeed, "Good things do come in small packages." Sam can also supply stones from his collection, which includes amazing specimens like malachite and polyhedroid, a quartz from Brazil. **Chesnut & Company** is small but jam-packed with treasures like *tansu,* Japanese furniture known for its joinery; bamboo and *lau hala* lamps by Gerald Ben; free-form prints in splendid colors of cobalt blue and rose by Nora Yamanoha; spirit masks and "garden goddesses" by Volcano artist Ira Ono; basketry from Bali and Holualoa; placemats fashioned from supple twigs and coconut fiber; and distinctive weavings, wall hangings, and original design tables by Peggy Chesnut (her loom is on the premises).

The **Holualoa Foundation for Art and Culture** is a nonprofit organization begun by local artists Sam Rosen, Setsuko Morinoue, and her husband Hiroki Morinoue, the current president. The foundation plans to offer public classes including painting, drawing, photography, and ceramics, taught by working artists. These workshops will be offered at a nominal charge. Members, and tourists alike will be welcomed. For information call (808) 324-1688 or 324-1335.

A side road, easily spotted along Holualoa's main street, leads you to **Koyasan Daishiji Shingon,** a Japanese Buddhist mission with distinctive red-orange buildings and a stone-lantern lined entrance. The mission is basic, simple, and unpretentious, combining Japanese Buddhism with a Hawaiian air. The roof has the distinctive shape of a temple, but unlike those found in Japan, which are fashioned from wood, this is corrugated iron. Getting to the temple takes only a few minutes, and coming back down the road rewards you with an inspiring vista of Kona and the sea.

Practicalities

The enticing aroma of rich coffee has been wafting on the breeze in this mountain community ever since the **Holuakoa Cafe,** owned and operated by Meggi Worbach, opened its doors in mid-1992. Just up the hill from the Kona Hotel, the cafe, open Mon.-Sat. 6:30 a.m.-5 p.m., tel. (808) 322-2233, serves wonderful apple coffee cake, bagels, muffins, and coffee and espresso from mocha frappés to double cappuccinos. Other offerings include smoothies, juices, and herbal teas. The cafe also serves as a revolving art gallery for local artists who may include Bob Smith, known for carving koa canoe paddles in the ancient tradition. The cafe displays a few boutique and souvenir items, including jewelry from Indonesia, and a smattering of wooden art pieces. You can sit inside at a table, perch at the counter, or enjoy your coffee and pastry alfresco on the veranda, from where the two-block metropolis of Holualoa sprawls at your feet.

A wooden jewel box nestled in velvet greenery waits to be opened as it rests on the edge of Holualoa high above the wide, rippling, cerulean Pacific. **The Holualoa Inn Bed and Breakfast** at 76-5932 Mamalahoa Hwy., P.O. Box 222, Holualoa, HI 96725, tel. (808) 324-1121 or (800) 392-1812, fax (808) 322-2472, e-mail: holualoa@il-hawaii.net, is the retirement home of Thurston Twigg-Smith, CEO of the *Honolulu Advertiser* and member of an old *kama'aina* family. Mr. Twigg-Smith built the original home in 1978, but tragically, it burned to the ground. Undaunted, he rebuilt, exactly duplicating the original. After living here a few years Mr. Twigg-Smith decided it was too quiet and peaceful and went back to live in Honolulu. Following its conversion to a B&B in 1987, it is now operated by grandson, Michael Twigg-Smith, and his wife, Leia. The home is a marvel of taste and charm—light, airy, and open. Follow the serpentine drive from Holualoa's main road into the midst of vibrant foliage daubed with red hibiscus, manicured thickets of ripening green coffee, sun-yellow papaya, and wind-swirled palms. The home at the end of the drive pleasantly shocks the senses. Top to bottom, it is the natural burnished red of cedar and eucalyptus. Here the Hawaiian tradition of removing your shoes upon entering is made a pleasure. The floors, softly polished, cool, and smooth, massage your feet; the roof rides above the walls so that the air circulates easily. The front lanai is pure relaxation, with koa rocking chairs and a queen-size leather *punee;* stained glass puncturing the walls here and there creates swirls of rainbow light. Throughout the home are original artworks done by the Twigg-Smith family. A pool table holds king's court in the commodious games room, as doors open to a casual yet elegant sitting room where breakfast is served. A back staircase leads to a gazebo, floored with tile and brazenly open to the elements, while the back lanai is encircled by a roof made of copper. From here, Kailua-Kona glows with the imaginative mistiness of an impressionist painting, and, closer by, 40 acres are dotted with cattle raised by the family. Just below is the inn's pool, tiled in blue with a torch ginger motif. A plan is afoot to install a jacuzzi in the coffee grove. The six rooms cost $130-170 and all differ in size and decor. The Polynesian Room, on ground level, is a minisuite with sitting room, bedroom, and large bath. Another, the Bali Room, floored with reed mats, opens its windows to the splendid view. A few years back, Mr. Twigg-Smith was offered $7 million for the home. Much to our benefit, he said no. Premium.

The **Kona Hotel,** along Holualoa's main street, tel. (808) 324-1155, primarily rents its 11 units to local people who spend the work-week in Kailua-Kona's seaside resorts and then go home on weekends. They are more than happy, however, to rent to any visitor passing through, and are a particular favorite with Europeans. The Inaba family opened the hotel in 1926, and it is still owned and operated by Goro Inaba and his wife Yayoko, who will greet you at the front desk upon arrival. A clean room with bare wooden floors, a bed and dresser, and a shared bath down the hall goes for $20 s, $26 d, and $30 twin. Call ahead for reservations. No meals are served, but Mrs. Inaba will make coffee in the morning if you wish. The hotel is simple, clean, and safe. Budget.

SIGHTS FROM HONALO
TO CAPTAIN COOK AND VICINITY

The mountainside communities of Honalo, Kainaliu, Kealakekua, and Captain Cook lie along a five-mile strip of Rt. 11, and if it weren't for the road signs, it would be difficult for the itinerant traveler to know where one village ends and the next begins. If you are after budget accommodations, unique boutique shopping, inexpensive island cuisine, and some off-the-beaten-track sightseeing, you won't be disappointed. About five miles south of Captain Cook is the small community of Honaunau and the road leading down to Pu'uhonua O Honaunau Historical Park.

Honalo

This dot on the map is at the junction of Routes 11 and 180. Not much changes here, and the town is primarily known for **Dai Fukuji Buddhist Temple** along the road. It's open daily 9 a.m.-4:30 p.m., free. Inside are two ornate altars; feel free to take photos but please remember to remove your shoes.

Kona Historical Society Museum

The main building of the Kona Historical Society Museum was originally a general store built around 1875 by local landowner and businessman H.N. Greenwell using native stone and lime mortar made from burnt coral. Now on both the Hawaiian and national registers of historic places, the building served many uses, including the warehousing and packaging of sweet oranges raised by Greenwell, purported to be the largest, sweetest, and juiciest in the world. The Kona Museum, P.O. Box 398, Captain Cook, HI 96704, tel. (808) 323-3222 (for tour reservations call 808-323-2005), is open weekdays 8 a.m.-4 p.m. and Saturday 10 a.m.-2 p.m. if a guide is available; admission is $2. To get there, as you approach Kealakekua along Rt. 11, look on the right for a sign that reads "Kona Specialty Meat Co." Pull into this road and follow it around to the back of the meat market, where you will find the parking lot for the museum.

The main artifact is the building itself, but inside, you will find a few antiques like a surrey and glassware, and the usual photographic exhibit with themes like coffee-growing—part of the legacy of Kona. The basement of the building houses archives filled with birth and death records of local people, photographs both personal and official, home movies, books, and maps, most of which were donated by the families of Kona. The archives are open to the public by appointment only. According to the director, Jill Olson, the main purpose of the Historical Society is the preservation of Kona's history and the dissemination of historical information. Sometimes the society sponsors lectures and films (nominal charge), which are listed in the local newspapers. They also offer 4WD tours of the Kona area ($55) three times per year, usually in March, July, and November, and a historical boat tour in late January ($20) that takes you from Kailua-Kona south along the coast. There is no fixed schedule, but if you are in the area during those times of year, it would be well worth the trouble to contact the museum to find out if these excellent tours are being offered. However, historic walking tours of Kailua-Kona ($10), are regularly scheduled Tues.-Sat. at 9:30 a.m. The tours usually last about one hour at a leisurely pace, but they do have a tendency to take on a personality of their own, and may go longer.

Another excellent tour that gets to the heart of the area is the walking tour conducted at the historic **D. Uchida Coffee Farm** (listed on the National Register of Historic Places), begun by Japanese immigrants in 1925. Located in Mahukona, not far from Kealakekua, the 90-minute tour ($15) is offered Tuesday and Thursday at 9 a.m., with special tours by appointment; for reservations call (808) 323-2005.

Amy B.H. Greenwell
Ethnobotanical Garden

You can not only smell the flowers but feel the history of the region at the Amy B.H. Greenwell Ethnobotanical Garden, tel. (808) 323-3318, along Rt. 11 just past mile marker 110 and marked by an HVB Warrior between the communities of Kealakekua and Captain Cook. The garden is open Mon.-Fri., 7 a.m.-3:30 p.m., with guided tours on the second Saturday of every month at 10 a.m., but visitors are welcome anytime during daylight hours—free. Amy B.H. Greenwell died in 1974 and left her lands to the Bishop Museum, which then opened a 10-acre interpretive ethnobotanical garden, planting it with indigenous Hawaiian plants, Polynesian introduced plants, and Hawaiian medicinal plants.

When you step up to the office, take a fact sheet that describes the garden, complete with self-guiding map. The garden has remnants of the Kona field system, dating from precontact times when a fantastic network of stone ridges linked 50 square miles of intensive agriculture.

Royal Kona Coffee Mill and Museum

In the town of Captain Cook, Napoopoo Road branches off Rt. 11 and begins a roller-coaster ride down to the sea, where it ends at Kealakekua Bay. En route it passes the well-marked Royal Kona Coffee Mill. Along the way you can't help noticing the trim coffee bushes planted along the hillside. Many counterculture types have taken up residence in semi-abandoned "coffee shacks" throughout this hard-pressed economic area, but the cheap, idyllic, and convenience-free life isn't as easy to arrange as it once was. The area is being "rediscovered" and getting more popular. For those just visiting, the tantalizing smell of roasting coffee and the lure of a "free cup" are more than enough stimulus to make you stop. Mark Twain did! The museum is small, of the nontouchable variety with most exhibits behind glass. Mostly they're old black-and-white prints of the way Kona coffee country used to be. Some heavy machinery is displayed out on the back porch. The most interesting is a home-made husker built from an old automobile. While walking around be careful not to step on a couple of lazy old cats so lethargic they might as well be stuffed. Perhaps a cup of the local "java" in their milk bowl would put spring in their feline steps! Inside, more or less integrated into the museum, is a small gift shop. You can pick up the usual souvenirs, but the real treats are gourmet honeys, jellies, jams, candies, and of course coffee. Buy a pound of Royal Kona Blend for about $15, or 100% Royal Kona for around $27.89. Actually, it's cheaper at other retail outlets and supermarkets around the island, but you can't beat the freshness of getting it right from the source. Refill anyone? The museum is open for self-guided tours daily 8 a.m.-5 p.m., tel. (808) 328-2511.

Kealakekua Bay

Continue down Napoopoo Road through the once-thriving fishing village of Napoopoo (Holes), now just a circle on the map with a few houses fronted by neat gardens. At road's end, you arrive at Kealakekua (Road of the God) Bay. Relax a minute and tune in all your sensors because you're in for a treat. The bay is not only a **Marine Life Conservation District** with a fine beach and top-notch snorkeling, but it drips with history. *Mauka,* at the parking lot, is the well-preserved **Hikiau Heiau,** dedicated to the god Lono, who had long been prophesied to return from the heavens to this very bay to usher in a "new order." Perhaps the soothsaying *kahuna* were a bit vague on the points of the new order, but it is undeniable that at this spot of initial contact between Europeans and Hawaiians, great changes occurred that radically altered the course of Hawaiian history.

Royal Kona Coffee Mill and Museum

DAVID STANLEY

The *heiau* is carved into the steep *pali* that form a well-engineered wall. From these heights the temple priests had a panoramic view of the ocean to mark the approach of Lono's "floating island," heralded by tall white tapa banners. The *heiau* platform was meticulously backfilled with smooth, small stones; a series of stone footings, once the bases of grass and thatch houses used in the religious rites, is still very much intact. The *pali* above the bay is pocked with numerous burial caves that still hold the bones of the ancients.

Captain James Cook, leading his ships *Resolution* and *Discovery* under billowing white sails, entered the bay on the morning of January 17, 1778, during the height of the Makahiki Festival, and the awestruck natives were sure that Lono had returned. Immediately, traditional ways were challenged. An old crew member, William Watman, had just died, and Cook went ashore to perform a Christian burial atop the *heiau*. This was, of course, the first Christian ceremony in the islands, and a plaque at the *heiau* entrance commemorates the event. On February 4, 1778, a few weeks after open-armed welcome, the goodwill camaraderie that had developed between the English voyagers and their island hosts turned sour, due to terrible cultural misunderstandings. The sad result was the death of Captain Cook. During a final conflict, this magnificent man, who had resolutely sailed and explored the greatest sea on earth, stood helplessly in knee-deep water, unable to swim to rescue-boats sent from his waiting ships. Hawaiians, provoked to a furious frenzy because of an unintentional insult, beat, stabbed, and clubbed the great captain and four of his marines to death. (For a full accounting of these events, see **History** in the Introduction.) A 27-foot obelisk of white marble erected to Cook's memory in 1874 "by some of his fellow countrymen" is at the far northern end of the bay. Another plaque is dedicated to Henry Opukahaia, a young native boy taken to New England, where he was educated and converted to Christianity. Through impassioned speeches begging for salvation for his pagan countrymen, he convinced the first Congregationalist missionaries to come to the islands in 1820.

The land around the monument is actually under British rule, somewhat like the grounds of a foreign consulate. Once a year, an Australian ship comes to tend it, and sometimes local people are hired to clear the weeds. The monument fence is fashioned from old cannons topped with cannon balls. Here too is a bronze plaque often awash by the waves that marks the exact spot where Cook fell. You can see the marble obelisk from the *heiau,* but actually getting to it is tough. Expert snorkelers have braved the mile swim to the point, but be advised it's through open ocean, and Kealakekua Bay is known for sharks that come in during the evening to feed. A rugged jeep/foot trail leads down the *pali* to the monument, but it's poorly marked and starts way back near the town of Captain Cook, almost immediately after Napoopoo Rd. branches off from Rt. 11. If you opt for this route, you'll have to backtrack to visit the coffee museum and the *heiau* side of the bay.

Napoopoo Beach County Park

Kealakekua Bay has been known as a safe anchorage since long before the arrival of Captain Cook and still draws boats of all descriptions. The area, designated a **Marine Life Conservation District,** lives up to its title by being an excellent scuba and snorkeling site. Organized tours from Kailua-Kona often flood the area with boats and divers, but the ocean expanse is vast and you can generally find your own secluded spot to enjoy the underwater show. If you've just come for a quick dip or to enjoy the sunset, look for beautiful, yellow-tailed tropic birds that frequent the bay. Napoopoo Beach County Park has full amenities, including showers, picnic tables, and restrooms. Lifeguards are on duty during the weekends.

Heading for Pu'uhonua O Honaunau

This historical park, the main attraction in the area, shouldn't be missed. Though it was once known as City of Refuge Park, the official name is coming into more use in keeping with the emergence of Hawaiian heritage. The best way to get there is to bounce along the four miles of coastal road from Kealakekua Bay. En route, you pass a smaller, more rugged road to **Keei;** this side trip ends at a black-sand canoe launch area and a cozy white-sand beach good for swimming. A channel to an underwater grotto has been sliced through the coral. On the shore are the remains of **Kamaiko Heiau,** where humans were once sacrificed.

The other, more direct way to Pu'uhonua O Honaunau is Rt. 160 at Keokea, where it branches off Rt. 11 at mile marker 104, a short distance past Honaunau. Whether you are going or coming this way, make sure to take a five-minute side trip off Rt. 160 to **St. Benedict's Painted Church.** This small house of worship is fronted by latticework, and with its gothic-style belfry looks like a little castle. Inside, a Belgian priest, John Berchman Velghe, took house paint and, with a fair measure of talent and religious fervor, painted biblical scenes on the walls. His masterpiece is a painted illusion behind the altar that gives you the impression of being in the famous Spanish cathedral in Burgos. Father John was pastor here 1899-1904, during which time he did these paintings, similar to others that he did in small churches throughout Polynesia. Before leaving, visit the cemetery to see its petroglyphs and homemade pipe crosses.

Pu'uhonua O Honaunau National Historical Park

The setting of Pu'uhonua O Honaunau couldn't be more idyllic. It's a picture-perfect cove with many paths leading out onto the sea-washed lava flow. The tall royal palms surrounding this compound shimmer like neon against the black lava so prevalent in this part of Kona. Planted for this purpose, these beacons promised safety and salvation to the vanquished, weak, and war-tossed, as well as to the *kapu*-breakers of old Hawaii. If you made it to this "temple of refuge," scurrying frantically ahead of avenging warriors or leaping into the sea to swim the last desperate miles, the attendant *kahuna,* under pain of their own death, had to offer you sanctuary. *Kapu*-breakers were particularly pursued because their misdeeds could anger the always moody gods, who might send a lava flow or tsunami to punish all. Only the *kahuna* could perform the rituals that would bathe you in the sacred mana and thus absolve you from all wrongdoing. This *pu'uhonua* (temple of refuge) was the largest in all Hawaii, and be it fact or fancy, you can feel its power to this day.

The temple complex sits on a 20-acre finger of lava bordered by the sea on all sides. A massive, 1,000-foot-long mortarless wall, measuring 10 feet high and 17 feet thick, borders the site on the landward side and marks it as a temple of refuge. Archaeological evidence dates use of the temple from the mid-16th century, and some scholars argue that it was a well-known sacred spot as much as 200 years earlier. Actually, three separate *heiau* are within the enclosure. In the mid-16th century, Keawe, a great chief of Kona and the great-grandfather of Kamehameha, ruled here. After his death, he was entombed in *Hale O Keawe Heiau* at the end of the great wall, and his mana reinfused the temple with cleansing powers. For 250 years the *ali'i* of Kona continued to be buried here, making the spot more and more powerful. Even the great Queen Kaahumanu came here seeking sanctuary. As a 17-year-old bride, she refused to submit to the will of her husband, Kamehameha, and defied him openly, often wantonly giving herself to lesser chiefs. To escape Kamehameha's rampage, she made for the temple. Kaahumanu chose a large rock to hide under, and she couldn't be found until her pet dog barked and gave her away. Kaahumanu was coaxed out only after a lengthy intercession by Capt. George Vancouver, who had become a friend of the king. The last royal personage buried here was a son of Kamehameha who died in 1818. Soon afterwards, the "old religion" of Hawaii died and the temple grounds were abandoned but not entirely destroyed. The foundations of this largest city of refuge in the Hawaiian Islands were left intact.

In 1961, the National Park Service opened Pu'uhonua O Honaunau after a complete and faithful restoration was carried out. Careful consultation of old records and vintage sketches from early ships' artists gave the restoration a true sense of authenticity. Local artists used traditional tools and techniques to carve giant ohia logs into faithful renditions of the temple gods. They now stand again, protecting the *heiau* from evil. One of the most curious is a god-figure, with his maleness erect, glaring out to sea as if looking for some voluptuous mermaid. (Perhaps a sign of mermaid luck, good or bad, the erect member disappears from time to time, but more likely it just becomes the ill-gotten booty of weenie vandals . . . a sign reading "Hands Off" is a bit improprietous!) All the buildings are painstakingly lashed together in the Hawaiian fashion, but with nylon rope instead of traditional cordage, which would have added the perfect touch.

Stop at the visitor center to pick up a map and brochure for a self-guided tour. Exhibits line a wall, complete with murals done in heroic style.

Push a button and the recorded messages give you a brief history of Hawaiian beliefs and the system governing daily life—educate yourself. The visitor center, tel. (808) 328-2288, is open daily 7:30 a.m.-5:30 p.m. Entrance to the 180-acre park is $2 per person. The beach park section is open 6 a.m.-midnight. Follow the refuge wall toward the northwest to a large, flat rock perfect for lying back and watching the sunset.

Every year on the weekend closest to the 1st of July, a free three-day cultural festival is held here, featuring traditional Hawaiian arts, crafts, music, and dance. Be sure to stop by for a peek into the past if you are in the area during this time.

ACCOMMODATIONS

So you came to Kona for the sun, surf, and scenery and couldn't care less about your room so long as it's clean and the people running the hotel are friendly? Well, you can't go wrong with any of the following out-of-the-mainstream hotels. They're all basic, but not fleabags. At all of these inexpensive hotels, it is very important to get your rooms first thing in the morning, if you don't have reservations. They are very, very, tough to get into. People know about them, so the rooms are at a premium.

Budget to Inexpensive
Teshima's Inn, tel. (808) 322-9140, is a small, clean, family-run affair in Honalo. Operated by Mr. and Mrs. Harry Teshima and family, it's somewhat like a Japanese *minshuku* with all rooms fronting a Japanese garden. To be sure of getting a room, call three days to a week in advance, and to reserve you must send at least one night's deposit (no credit cards accepted). If you just turn up, you have a slim chance of getting one of the 11 rooms. Check in is at the restaurant section. The rooms, at $20 s, $30 d, $250-300 monthly, are spartan but very clean.

Manago Hotel, P.O. Box 145, Captain Cook, Kona, HI 96704, tel. (808) 323-2642, fax 323-3451, has been in the Manago family for 75 years, and anyone who puts his name on a place and keeps it there that long is doing something right. The old section of the hotel along the road is clean but a little worse for wear and doesn't impress much because it looks like a storefront.

The rooms in the old section are small with wooden floors, double beds, and utilitarian dressers. Walk in to find a bridgeway into a garden area that's open, bright, and secluded away from the road. The new section features rooms with wall-to-wall carpeting, new furniture, private bath, louvered windows, and private lanai. The rates are $35 shared bath, $41 new section, plus $3 for an extra person. There is also one Japanese room that goes for $52 s, $55 d; weekly and monthly discount on all rooms. The views of the Kona Coast from the hotel grounds are terrific. You can dine in a restaurant in the old section, open for breakfast Tues.-Thurs. 7-9 a.m., lunch 11 a.m.-2 p.m., dinner 5-7:30 p.m., Fri.-Sun. 5-7 p.m., closed Monday. People come from all over the island for the legendary pork chop dinners.

Moderate
Lion's Gate, owned by Diane and Bill Shriner, P.O. Box 761, Honaunau, HI 96726, tel./fax (808) 328-2335, offers rooms on a working macadamia nut and Kona coffee farm. Only minutes from the Pu'uhonua O Honaunau National Historical Park, Lion's Gate features a jacuzzi, refrigerator, and TV in all rooms, great views of the coast, a gazebo for relaxing, and, of course, complimentary Kona coffee and macadamia nuts. Rooms run $60-75. E-mail: liongate@aloha.net; website: www.stayhawaii.com/liongte.html.

RBR Farms Bed and Breakfast, P.O. Box 930, Captain Cook, HI 96704, tel./fax (808) 328-9212 or (800) 328-9212, can also accommodate you on a working coffee and macadamia nut farm. The cottage with fully equipped kitchen rents for $150 per couple ($175 holiday rate). Rooms are also available in the main house for $75-90. The upstairs rooms have the best view over the coast. All rooms have private entrance, TV, and ceiling fan. Everyone shares the pool and jacuzzi. E-mail: rbrfarms@gte.net; website: www.konaweb.com/rbr.

Merryman's Bed and Breakfast, owned by Don and Penny Merryman, P.O. Box 474, Kealakekua, HI 96750, tel. (808) 323-2276 or (800) 545-4390, is considered, even by others with B&Bs, to be one of the best on the island. The Merrymans, snow-birds from Alaska, came to the Big Island and built their cedar dream house, which they are willing to share with other people. The extra large knotty pine and glass rooms, always perfumed by fresh cut flowers and furnished with antiques, are made private with bamboo curtains. The bedspreads are thick, white quilts in a floral design, while the floors are covered with textured carpet. Your relaxation is ensured by rattan chairs with "Miss Muffet-like" puffed pillows into which you can sink with the setting sun. The outdoor jacuzzi and deck with comfortable lounging furniture is the premier spot on the property. Rates range $75-95. E-mail: merryman@ilhawaii.net; website: www.hawaii-bnb.com/merymn.html.

A Dragonfly Ranch, P.O. Box 675, Honaunau, HI 96762, tel. (808) 328-2159, (800) 487-2159, fax 328-9570, owned and operated by David and Barbara Link, offers "tropical fantasy lodging" at a country estate. Rooms are remarkable and range from the "Hale in the Trees" to the "Honeymoon Suite" featuring an outdoor water bed. All rooms include a wet bar and refrigerator, private outdoor shower, cable TV, stereo, and small Hawaiiana library. Rates run $70 for a suite in the main house, $120 for the Redwood Cottage and Writer's Studio, and $160 for the Honeymoon Suite (substantial discounts for longer stays). However, be aware that A Dragonfly Ranch is the epitome of the adage "beauty is in the eye of the beholder." To some, the touted tropical fantasy may be a "tropical nightmare." The hosts are very friendly and inviting, indeed, but definitely have an alternative philosophy. The "Honeymoon Suite," for example is almost "open air." Dragonfly Ranch is one of those places that people totally adore or else dash away from. E-mail: dfly@aloha.net.

FOOD

All of the restaurants in this section happen to fall in the inexpensive range. All are worth a stop if you're hungry when you go by. Some are great, especially for breakfast and brunch.

Teshima's Restaurant in Honalo, open daily 6:30 a.m.-1:45 p.m. and 5-9:30 p.m., is just like the homey Inn that adjoins it. Here, in unpretentious surroundings, you can enjoy a full American, Hawaiian, or Japanese lunch for about $7, a filling daily special for $7.50, and dinner at $7.50-11. Another specialty is a *bento,* a box lunch for $5.50 that includes rice balls, luncheon meat, fried fish, teriyaki beef, *kamaboku* (fish cake), and Japanese roll. If you're interested in a good square meal, you can't go wrong.

Aloha Theater Cafe, open daily 8 a.m.-9 p.m., Sunday for brunch only 9 a.m.-2 p.m., tel. (808) 322-3383, is part of the lobby of the Aloha Theater in Kainaliu. The enormous breakfasts ($5-8) feature locally grown eggs, homemade muffins, and potatoes. Lunchtime sandwiches, $6-8.50, are super-stuffed with varied morsels, from tofu and avocado to vegetarian tempeh burgers. There's also a variety of soups and salads and Mexican dishes like a quesadilla *especial* for $7.50. Full dinners like fresh *ahi* and *ono* are $15.95, filet mignon goes for $15.95, and pasta and shells are $12.95. For a snack choose from an assortment of homemade baked goods that you'll enjoy with an espresso or cappuccino. Order at the counter first (table service for dinner), and then sit on the lanai that overlooks a bucolic scene of cows at a watering trough, with the coast below. This is an excellent place to have breakfast or to pick up a picnic lunch on your way south. Also, check out the bulletin board for local happenings, sales, services, and the like.

The **Korner Pocket Bar and Grill,** tel. (808) 322-2994, serving lunch and dinner weekdays 11 a.m.-10 p.m., until midnight Friday and Saturday, is a family-oriented/friendly biker bar where you can get excellent food at very reasonable prices. To get there, turn left off Rt. 11 in Kealakekua onto Halekii St., a half block before McDonald's, and look for the Korner Pocket in the small shopping center on the left. Start with *pu pu* ($2.50-7) like twice-baked potato, calamari strips, chicken hot wings, and chilled shrimp cocktail. Grill selections ($5-8) are a poolroom burger, fresh catch, or scrumptious bistro burger of grilled beef on crusty sourdough topped with fresh mushrooms sautéed in wine garlic sauce. Dinners are tempting: garlic scampi for $12.95; chicken aiko accented with zesty Japanese sauce of lemon, apple, laurel, and spices; and prime rib eight ball, their encore entree at $11.95. The complete bar is well stocked with wines and spirits, or you can wash down your sandwich with an assortment of draft beers. The Pocket rocks with live music Friday night featuring various local rock bands, while Saturday usually brings jazz for quieter dining and dancing. The

Korner Pocket looks as ordinary as a Ford station wagon, both inside and out, but the food is surprisingly good, and the owners, Paul and Judy, are very friendly.

Just beyond McDonald's golden arches as you enter Kealakekua, look for the **Canaan Deli,** tel. (808) 323-2577, open Mon.-Fri. 7 a.m.-7 p.m. and Sat.-Sun. 7 a.m.-1 p.m., a luncheonette with an Italian flair. The owners, Geegee and Dawn Gambone, hail from Philadelphia and bring the "back East" deli tradition of a lot of food for little money along with them. You can't go wrong with a Philly cheese-steak sub for $5.50; or try a pizza smothered in cheese and delectables, ranging from a 10-inch cheese to a 17-inch Master for $28. All sauces, breads, and the pizza dough are homemade. Breakfast specials include a three-egg omelette for $5.50, toasted bagels for as little as $1.25, or steak and eggs for $6. Lunch is deli sandwiches (it is a *full* deli), from pastrami to a good old BLT costing $4-5.50, big fatso hoagies priced around $6-7, a meatball sandwich for $6, a loco moco for those a quart low on cholesterol, and various burgers. Free deliveries (minimum purchase $15) are provided from Keauhou to Honaunau in South Kona. Don't forget, you are dealing with an Italian guy from Philadelphia, so you have to treat him with respect, or you'll be swimming with the fishes all right . . . permanently!

There are very few places in Captain Cook where you can get a meal. On the right as you enter town is a takeout restaurant with barbecued ribs, chicken, hot biscuits, coleslaw, and salad. You can also try **Hong Kong Chop Suey** in the Ranch Center, which is as basic as can be, with most items at $5, including sides. Also, try the legendary pork chop dinner served at the **Manago Hotel** restaurant in downtown Captain Cook. Limited hours for breakfast, lunch, and dinner, Tues.-Sunday. Another place to try in Captain Cook is the **Kahauloa Coffee Company Coffee Shack,** offering bulk coffee, deli sandwiches, pastries, fresh baked bread, pizza, salad, and soup d'jour.

You'll be dancing like Zorba, singing like Caruso, and leisurely digesting like a *lomi lomi*ed Kamehameha after entering **The Kona Theater Cafe,** in Captain Cook just across from the post office, tel. (808) 328-2244, open daily 6 a.m.-6 p.m. Reopened and revitalized by Ted Georgakis, a half-Italian, half-Greek man with an island flair, the ethnic atmosphere allows you to casually yet passionately philosophize over a menu that offers breakfast all day, fresh baked sweets, hot lunches, deli sandwiches, full entrées, and espresso. The cafe is still in transition, figuratively; a brick is laid daily, as in Roma, to create an atmosphere of restaurant, deli, theater, and espresso bar. Ted offers steamed fritatta and toast for $4.25; a breakfast sandwich consisting of a bagel with egg, melted cheese, and Italian ham—a farmer's breakfast at $4.99; fresh waffles for $3.25; specialty Greek or Italian salads for $5.65; Hawaiian, Greek, or Italian chicken sandwiches on home-baked bread for $5.95; healthful tempeh burgers $4.99; and deli-style sandwiches ($5-6) such as hot pastrami on rye, Italian sausage and peppers, or turkey and Swiss (takeout available). Ted also handmakes fresh carrot juice, smoothies, and ginger lemonade, along with coffee selections from the espresso bar. He gets organic greens from a transplanted Florentine, Barbara Cappelli, a lady not only of innate beauty and artistry, but a woman with working hands that coax 18 different types of leafy edibles from the rich but tough local soil. Ted plans to revitalize the theater but will work on keeping it as close to original as possible. When it's complete (call to find out when), you will be able to enjoy art films, foreign films, community theater, and small concerts. Ted, being the Italian-Greek that he is, will feed not only your body, but your artistic soul as well. *Bravissimo!*

SHOPPING

Kainaliu

Next door to the Aloha Cafe, the **Aloha Store,** tel. (808) 322-1717, open daily Mon.-Sat. 9 a.m.-8 p.m., Sunday 10 a.m.-2 p.m., sells gifts and sundries. The store has a wonderful selection ranging from stuffed teddy bears to teapots, along with local clothing and jewelry. You can also find items like koa barrettes and bracelets, children's games and books, music tapes, necklaces, earrings, and sterling silver jewelry. There's a rack of aloha shirts, candle holders, pottery, a smattering of honey and fruit gift items, and lotions and potions locally made. The bulletin board is great for letting you know what's happening, especially alternatively, in the area.

The Blue Ginger Gallery, tel. (808) 322-3898, open Mon.-Sat. 9 a.m.-5 p.m., showcases the art of owners Jill and David Bever, as well as artists' works from all over the island. David creates art pieces in stained glass, fused glass, and wood. Jill paints on silk, creating fantasy works in strong primary colors. Using her creations as base art, she then designs one-of-a-kind clothing items that can be worn as living art pieces. The small but well-appointed shop brims over with paintings, ceramics, sculptures, woodworking, and jewelry. A section includes Asian artworks, including Polynesian masks, carved elephants, Buddha heads, and batiks from Indonesia. The Blue Ginger Gallery is a perfect place to find a memorable souvenir of Hawaii.

The Rainbow Path is in downtown Kainaliu in the Basque Bldg. at 79-7407 Hawaii Belt Rd., P.O. Box 2208, Kealakekua, HI 96750, tel. (808) 322-0651, open Mon.-Fri. 9 a.m.-6 p.m., Saturday 10 a.m.-6 p.m. Monday, Wednesday, and Saturday, metaphysical readings are given by appointment. The Rainbow Path specializes in books on Hawaii, metaphysics, self-help, personal discovery, and books for children. You can also find tapes and CDs that include Hawaiian chants, Native American Indian music, Celtic music, and music especially composed to induce relaxation and relieve stress. Your body is taken care of with Ayurvedic medicine, incense, beeswax candles, bath and body products made by the Island Massage Company, and natural perfumes of island scents. The soul will stir with crystal pendants, pyramids, beaded necklaces, and dream catchers. All who are on the path will find this bookstore an oasis.

Badass Coffee Company, tel. (808) 322-9196, open daily 7 a.m.-9 p.m., is a coffee and espresso bar where they roast their own beans on the premises in a Royal No. 4 Roaster manufactured in 1910, probably the last operational roaster of its type left in the state. Pure Kona coffee of the best grade sells for $29.95 per pound. After watching the roasting, take your cup of coffee and a homemade pastry to the rear of the shop, where you'll find an indoor stone grotto area away from the noise of the street.

Don't let the tourist junk piled outside **Hawaiian Crafts & Gifts,** in downtown Kainaliu across from the Bad Ass Coffee Co., tel. (808) 322-0642, stop you from going in. Owned by Jeffrey Matias and open Mon.-Sat. 9 a.m.-5 p.m., the shop has a very surprising interior, filled as it is with authentic jewelry, shells, and Jeff's own beadwork. Many of the items are purchased from local people and include hula instruments, *lau hala* weavings, Niihau shellwork, Hawaiian fishhook pendants, *kukui* nut lei, and even an assortment of Hawaiian food products like mustard and salad dressings. Hanging on the walls are carvings of tikis, dolphins, turtles, and owls, the *aumakua* of ancient Hawaii. For the children, there are Hawaiian dolls, and children of all ages will love a replica of a sea-going canoe with the distinctive crab claw sail. Jeff also imports unique jewelry from the Balkans! For those who can't live without another T-shirt, you'll find them as well as artificial flower lei.

At the south end of town, in the new Mango Court, is **Ohana O Ka Aina Food Co-op,** open 9 a.m.-6 p.m. weekdays, 10 a.m.-5 p.m. Saturday. This full-range health food store serves freshly made sandwiches from their deli. You can buy fresh orange and ginger lemonade made on the premises. The co-op, the last of its kind in Hawaii, has a large supply of herbs, plenty of vitamins and minerals, a smattering of fresh produce, and an excellent assortment of bulk grains. If you are a bona fide member of an organic foods co-op, and you have your card along with you, they will give you a reciprocal member discount.

This is one time that you'll enjoy an outbreak of **Pandamonium,** in downtown Kainaliu, open Mon.-Sat. 10 a.m.-6 p.m., tel. (808) 324-7799, a shop filled with locally handcrafted artwear and crafts. Racks also hold high quality hand-painted Indonesian clothing, a designer line of T-shirts by Dr. Bill, and, if you just happen to be feeling a bit peaked after a long day of shopping, Chinese herbs, vitamins, and minerals in a side concession room. Not only can you come here and dress your body, you can address what ails you as well.

As you are leaving the built-up area of Kainaliu, look to see a sign for **Island Books,** "Used Books Bought and Sold," owned by Jev and Jonathan Thompson, open Mon.-Sat. 10 a.m.-6 p.m., P.O. Box 645, Kealakekua, Hawaii 96750, tel. (808) 322-2006. They stock a general mix of titles, but history, geography, Hawaiiana, and a good selection of used travel books are the specialty. Here's a great place to purchase some casual reading material and save money at the same time.

Oshima's General Store is well stocked with cameras and film, drugs, fishing supplies, magazines, and some wines and spirits. Also in town is **Kimura's Market,** a general grocery store with some sundries.

Kealakekua

Right next door to the Kona Central Union Church is **Changing Hands,** a resale shop owned by Norma Hand that specializes in vintage clothing, glassware, and mostly Hawaiian antiques and bric-a-brac. It's open weekdays 10:30 a.m.-4:30 p.m., occasionally Saturday. You can pick up a treasure ranging in cost from a dollar or two to a few hundred.

The **Kahanahou Hawaiian Foundation,** tel. (808) 322-3901, deals in ancient Hawaiian handicrafts, including masks, hula drums, and hula accoutrements. This nonprofit organization serves as an apprenticeship school for native Hawaiians who are trying to revitalize traditional arts. Unfortunately, no one seems to be in attendance in the shop, and you are instructed to ring the buzzer. A sign says, If you're just here to browse and to kill time don't kill ours; we can't afford the luxury. That sets the tone of your greeting when someone finally appears to scowl at you. Obviously the foundation is not into preserving *aloha.*

The **Grass Shack,** a.k.a. Little Grass Shack, open Mon.-Sat. 9 a.m.-5 p.m., sometimes Sunday noon-5 p.m., tel. (808) 323-2877, is an institution in Kealakekua, owned and operated by *kama'aina* Lish Jens. It looks like a tourist trap, but don't let that stop you from going in and finding some authentic souvenirs, most of which come from the area or from Ms. Jens's many years of traveling and collecting. The items *not* from Hawaii are clearly marked with a big orange sign that says, Sorry These Items Were Not Made In Hawaii. But the price is right. There are plenty of trinkets and souvenir items, as well as a fine assortment of artistic pieces, especially wooden bowls, hula items, exquisite Niihau shellwork, and Hawaiian masks. A shop specialty is items made from curly koa. Each piece is signed with the craftsperson's name and the type of wood used. One of the artisans displayed

here is master woodworker Jack Straka. Items are also made from Norfolk pine and milo. A showcase holds jewelry and tapa cloth imported from Fiji, and a rack holds tapes of classic Hawaiian musicians from the '40s and '50s. The shop is famous for its distinctive *lau hala* hats, the best hat for the tropics.

Tropical Temptations, tel. (808) 323-3131, open Mon.-Sat. 10 a.m.-5 p.m., is housed in a gaily painted yellow and green building. Climb the steps to the porch, where you'll find a service buzzer that will summon owner and chief tempter Lance Dassance, who will smile a welcome into his candy kitchen. Remember, however, that most of the business is wholesale and not really set up for drop-in visitors. Lance turns the best available grade of local fruits, nuts, and coffee beans into delicious candies. The fresh-fruit process uses no preservatives, additives, waxes, or extenders and no sugars except in the chocolate, which is the best grade possible. A slow-drying process is used, so as few nutrients as possible are lost. A shop specialty is candy made from rare white pineapple, which grows for only eight weeks per year. Lance, if not too busy, will be happy to take you on a tour of the facility. He takes a personal pride in making the best candy possible and stresses that he uses only fruit ripened in the last 24 hours. Tropical Temptations, the healthiest candy store in Hawaii, has an outlet booth in Kailua-Kona at the Kona Inn Shopping Village.

Konakai Coffee Farms has a tasting room and restaurant at the south end of Kealakekua. They produce and serve cups of Kona coffee plain or as espresso, cappuccino, and caffe latte. Check the racks of fresh-roasted pure Kona coffee.

The **Kamigaki Market** is also in Kealakekua.

Captain Cook

The **Kealakekua Ranch Center,** in Captain Cook, is a two-story mall with fashions, food, general supplies, and a Sure Save Supermarket.

Honaunau

Bong Brothers, 84-5227 Mamalahoa Hwy., on the *makai* side of the road near mile marker 106, tel. (808) 328-9289, is open Mon.-Fri. 8:30 a.m.-6 p.m., Sunday 10 a.m.-6 p.m. It's housed in a coffee mill complex circa 1920, one of the oldest in Honaunau, and sells not only coffee but organic produce and health food deli items. Jay Koerner, the manager, is knowledgeable about both the area and about coffee and will show you around, time permitting. Ricardo, a local chef, makes pesto,"Ricardo's Revenge Salsa" with red hot habaneros, mango chutney, black bean and brown rice burritos and, on Thursdays, fresh pizza with a crust of five-grain flour, flax meal, or whole wheat; it's spiced with pesto made out of four kinds of basil and with a six-nut mix, and topped with a seven-cheese blend and all kinds of diced organic goodies. The shelves hold dried mango, candied ginger, bulk coffee, chocolate-covered coffee beans, Puna honey, Sam's Organic Gourmet salad dressings, dried pineapple, apples, and bananas, special sauces, and the "no shop is complete without them" T-shirts. Also look for a stack of burlap coffee bags, some bearing the Bong Brothers logo, that cost only $3 and make a nifty souvenir. Adjacent is **Gold Mountain Mill,** a functional roasting mill tended by Tom Bong and his dog Bear; if time permits they'll will show you around the operation. Coffee from the surrounding area comes in about three times per week to be roasted. The process that you will see includes pulping the bean, where the inside portion is squeezed out after soaking and then placed on the sun decks to dry. When nearly dry, the beans are placed in a large, turning drum, which blows hot air throughout to achieve the perfect moisture level. Next, a parchmentlike inner skin is removed from the beans; then they're ready for roasting in the still functional, vintage 1930s roaster.

Also in Honaunau is the **Shimizu Market.**

HOOKENA AND MILOLII

Hookena

If you want to see how the people of Kona still live, visit Hookena. A mile or two south of the Pu'uhonua O Honaunau turnoff, or 20 miles south of Kailua-Kona, take a well-marked spur road *makai* off Rt. 11 and follow it to the sea. The village is in a state of disrepair, but a number of homey cottages and some semipermanent tents are used mostly on weekends by local fishermen. Hookena also boasts the **Hookena**

secluded Hookena Beach

Beach County Park with pavilions, restrooms, and picnic tables, but no potable water. Camping is allowed with county permit. For drinking water, a tap is attached to the telephone pole near the beginning of your descent down the spur road. The black-sand (actually gray) beach is broad, long, and probably *the* best in South Kona for both swimming and bodysurfing. If the sun gets too hot, plenty of palms lining the beach provide not only shade but a picture-perfect setting. Until the road connecting Kona to Hilo was finally finished in the 1930s, Hookena shipped the produce of the surrounding area from its bustling wharf. At one time, Hookena was the main port in South Kona and even hosted Robert Louis Stevenson when he passed through the islands in 1889. Part of the wharf still remains, and nearby a fleet of outrigger fishing canoes is pulled up on shore. The surrounding cliffs are honeycombed with burial caves. If you walk a half mile north, you'll find the crumpled walls and steeple of Maria Lanakila Church, leveled in an earthquake in 1950. The church was another "painted church" done by Father John Velghe in the same style as St. Benedict's.

Milolii

This active fishing village is approximately 15 miles south of Pu'uhonua O Honaunau. Again, look for signs to a spur road off Rt. 11 heading *makai*. The road, leading through bleak lava flows, is extremely narrow but worth the detour. Milolii (Fine Twist) earned its name from times past when it was famous for producing *'aha,* a sennit made from coconut-husk fibers; and *olona,* a twine made from the *olona* plant and best for fishnets. This is one of the last villages in Hawaii where traditional fishing is the major source of income and where old-timers are heard speaking Hawaiian. Fishermen still use small outrigger canoes, now powered by outboards, to catch *opelu,* a type of mackerel that schools in these waters. The method of catching the *opelu* has remained unchanged for centuries. Boats gather and drop packets of chum made primarily from poi, sweet potatoes, or rice. No meat is used so sharks won't be attracted. The **Milolii Beach County Park** is a favorite with local people on the weekends; camping by permit. Tents are pitched in and around the parking lot, just under the ironwoods at road's end. Notice that a number of the tents appear to be semipermanent. There are flushing toilets, a basketball court, and a brackish pond in which to rinse off, but no drinking water, so bring some. Swimming is safe inside the reef and the tidepooling in the area is some of the best on the south coast. A 15-minute trail leads south to Honomalino Bay, where a white-sand beach is secluded and great for swimming. But always check with the local people first about conditions! In the village, a small, understocked store is operated by Willie Kaupiko, though the whole family pitches in.

Kula Kai Caverns

The newest and perhaps most curious offering of this region is the recently opened Kula Kai Caverns, one of the two lava tube caves in the state that are open to commercial tours (the other is the Ka'eleku Caverns in Hana, Maui). In contrast to the Ka'eleku Caverns on Maui, which are about 30,000 years old, the Kula Kai Cavern system is a mere baby at about 1,000 years old. A tour underground here gives you a look at the bowels of the largest mountain on the world, once used for shelter and as a place to collect water in this region of low rainfall. Like other lava tubes in the world, the Kula Kai Caverns shows fine examples of lava shelves, pillars, lava bombs, and other customary lava formations. As these interconnected tubes are so close to the surface in some spots, roots of *ohia* trees have penetrated the ceiling of the cave and hang like hairy tendrils. An easy one-hour ($12 for adults, $8 for kids) tour leads through the lighted section of the caverns. The more rigorous two-hour tour ($45 and $25) and half-day tour ($125, age 12 and up) take you deeper into the maze. Long pants and closed-toed shoes are required; gloves, knee pads, hard hats, and lights are provided. For information and reservations, contact Kula Kai Caverns, P.O. Box 6313, Ocean View, HI 96737, tel. (808) 937-3083.

Accommodations to the South
Bougainvillea Bed and Breakfast, P.O. Box 6045, Ocean View, HI 96737, tel./fax (808) 929-7089 or (800) 688-1763, has views of the ocean and South Point. The inn is quiet and romantic; each room has a private entrance and bath. Guests share the pool, hot tub, TV, and video library. Great stargazing. Rooms cost $59 s, $65 d. E-mail: peaceful@interpac.net; website: www.hawaii-bnb.com/bougvl.html. Moderate.

FRITZ KRAFT

SOUTH KOHALA

The Kohala District is the peninsular thumb in the northwestern portion of the Big Island. At its tip is Upolu Point, only 40 miles from Maui across the Alenuihaha Channel. Kohala was the first section of the Big Island to rise from beneath the sea. The long-extinct volcanoes of the Kohala Mountains running down its spine have been reduced by time and the elements from lofty, ragged peaks to rounded domes of 5,000 feet or so. Kohala is divided into North and South Kohala. South Kohala boasts *the* most beautiful swimming beaches on the Big Island, along with good camping and world-class hotels. Inland is Waimea (Kamuela), the *paniolo* town and center of the massive Parker Ranch.

THE COAST

The shoreline of South Kohala, from Anae-hoomalu Bay north to Kawaihae Bay, is rich in perhaps the finest super-deluxe resorts in the state. This coast's fabulous beaches are known not only for swimming and surfing, but for tide-pooling and awe-inspiring sunsets as well. Also, the two main beaches offer camping and even rental cabins. There are little-disturbed and rarely visited archaeological sites, expressive petro-glyph fields well off the beaten track, the edu-cational **Puukohola Heiau,** and even a rodeo. No "towns" lie along the coast, in the sense of a laid-out community with a main street and at-tendant businesses and services. The closest facsimile is Kawaihae, with a small cluster of restaurants, shops, and gas station. Waikoloa Village also provides some services, with exclu-sive boutique shopping.

SIGHTS AND NEARBY COMMUNITIES

The following sights and beaches are listed from south to north. All except for Waikoloa Village lie along coastal Rt. 19, which is posted with mile markers, so finding the spots where you want to stop is easy.

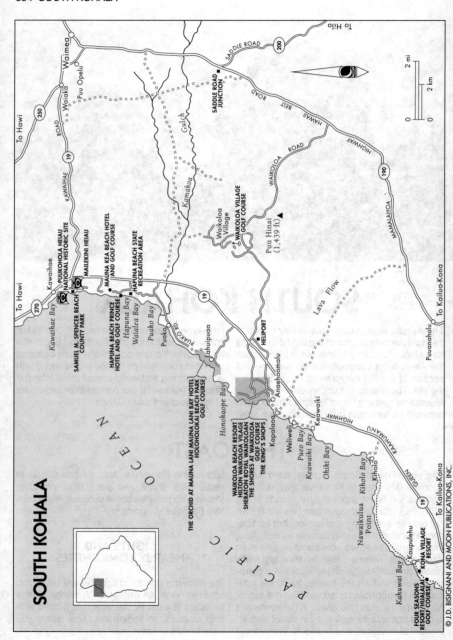

SOUTH KOHALA

To Hilo

SADDLE ROAD

200

2 mi

2 km

Waimea

Puu Opelu

To Hawi

250

Waiaka

ROAD

19

KAWAIHAE

Puukohola Heiau NATIONAL HISTORIC SITE

Mailekini Heiau

SADDLE ROAD JUNCTION

HAWAII BELT HIGHWAY

WAIKOLOA ROAD

190

MAMALAHOA

To Kailua-Kona

Kamakoa Gulch

Mauna Kea Beach Hotel and Golf Course

Hapuna Beach State Recreation Area

Kawaihae

270

To Hawi

Samuel M. Spencer Beach County Park

Kawaihae Bay

Hapuna Beach Prince Hotel and Golf Course

Hapuna Bay

Waialea Bay

Puako Bay

Waikoloa Village

Waikoloa Village Golf Course

Puu Hinai (1,439 ft)

Lava Flow

PUAKO RD.

19

Puako

Lahuipuaa

HELIPORT

Anaehoomalu

Kapalaoa

To Kailua-Kona

PACIFIC OCEAN

The Orchid at Mauna Lani

Mauna Lani Bay Hotel

Holoholokai Beach Park

Mauna Lani Bay Hotel Golf Course

Honokaope Bay

Waikoloa Beach Resort

Hilton Waikoloa Village

Sheraton Royal Waikoloan

The Shores at Waikoloa

Waikoloa Golf Course

The King's Shops

Weliweli

Puco Bay

Keawaiki Bay

Ohiki Bay

QUEEN KAAHUMANU HIGHWAY

Kiholo Bay

Kiholo

Nawaikulua Point

Kaupulehu

Kona Village Resort

Kahuwai Bay

19

To Kailua-Kona

Four Seasons Resort/Hualalai Golf Course

© J.D. BISIGNANI AND MOON PUBLICATIONS, INC.

Waikoloa Village

If you're interested in visiting Waimea (Kamuela) as well as seeing the South Kohala coast, you might consider turning right off Rt. 19 between mile markers 74 and 75 onto Waikoloa Road. This is a great deal of territory to cover in one day! This route cuts inland for 13 miles, connecting coastal Rt. 19 with inland Rt. 190, which leads to Waimea. About halfway, you pass the planned and quickly growing community of Waikoloa Village (about six miles inland from Waikoloa Resorts) that is unfortunately heralded by a condo complex of stark gray in neo-Alcatraz design, which could aptly be called "Prisoners of Paradise" but is misnamed "The Greens." Try to overlook them, and head for the village itself, which is low-rise and quite tasteful.

The village is serviced by the **Waikoloa Highlands Center,** a small but adequate shopping mall with a gas station, full-service supermarket, First Hawaiian Bank, postal service store, small medical center, and a few restaurants and shops. This is also the home of **Waikoloa Stables,** tel. (808) 883-9335, which hosts a number of rodeos and Wild West shows. They offer saddle horses and a variety of trail rides for the visitor. Here too is the **Waikoloa Village Golf Club,** tel. (808) 883-9621, a private course open to the public; **Roussels** restaurant is in the clubhouse.

Puako

This alluring area is located *makai* on a side road off Rt. 19 about four miles south of Kawaihae. Hawaiians lived here in times past, but a modern community has been building along the three miles of Puako Bay since the 1950s. A thin ribbon of white sand runs the length of the beach that provides fair swimming, good fishing and snorkeling, and terrific tidepooling. Sunsets here are magnificent and you'll usually have a large stretch of beach to yourself, but remember your flashlight for the walk back because there's no lighting. Near-shore scuba diving is excellent, with huge caverns and caves to explore, and a colorful concentration of coral and marine life.

Along Puako Road is **Hokuloa Church,** built by Rev. Lorenzo Lyons in 1859. This musically talented reverend mastered the Hawaiian language and composed lovely ballads such as "Hawaii Aloha," which has become the unofficial anthem of the islands.

Puako Petroglyphs

These rock carvings, approximately 3,000 individual designs, are considered some of the finest and oldest in Hawaii, but carvings of horses and cattle signify ongoing art that happened long after Westerners appeared. Circles outlined by a series of small holes belonged to families who placed the umbilical cords of their infants into these indentations to tie them to the *aina* and give them strength for a long and good life. State archaeologists and anthropologists have reported a deterioration of the site due to vandalism, so please look but don't deface, and stay on all established paths. Access is by a well-marked, self-guiding trail starting from Holoholo Kai Beach Park. Other nearby groupings are located near the Outrigger Waikoloa Beach Hotel. Any of the large Kohala hotels here offer brochures and information concerning the petroglyph field.

Organized tours of the nearby petroglyphs start daily at 8:30 a.m. from the food pavilion at the King's Shops. The Outrigger Waikoloa Beach Hotel also offers a free guided tour of petroglyphs near its property on Tuesday and Thursday at 8:15 a.m. Be sure to bring plenty of water and wear good walking shoes and a hat.

Puukohola Heiau

Don't miss this completely restored Hawaiian temple, a National Historical Site located one mile south of Kawaihae where coastal Rt. 19 turns into Rt. 270 heading into North Kohala. This site, covering 77 acres, includes **Mailekini Heiau** and the nearby **John Young House** site. Administered by the National Park Service, it is open daily 7:30 a.m.-4 p.m.; admission is free. As you enter, pick up a map highlighting the main points of interest. It's worthwhile checking out the visitor center (tel. 882-7218), where Ranger Benjamin Saldua and others provide excellent information. Puukohola (Whale Hill) received its name either because the hill itself resembles a whale, or because migrating whales pass very close offshore every year. It was fated to become a hill of destiny.

Kamehameha I built this *heiau* in 1790 on the advice of Kapoukahi, a prophet from Kauai who said that Kamehameha would unify all the islands only after he built a temple to his war-god Kukailimoku. Kamehameha complied, building this last of the great Hawaiian *heiau* from mortarless stone that when finished measured 100 by 224 feet. The dedication ceremony of the *heiau* is fascinating history. Kamehameha's last rival was his cousin, Keoua Kuahuula. This warlike chief realized that his mana had deserted him and that it was Kamehameha who would rise to be sovereign of all the islands. Kamehameha invited him to the dedication ceremony, but en route Keoua, in preparation for the inevitable outcome, performed a death purification ceremony by circumcising his own penis. When the canoes reached the beach, they were met by a hail of spears and musket balls. Keoua was killed and his body laid on Kukailimoku's altar. Kamehameha became the unopposed sovereign of the Big Island and, within a few years, of all of Hawaii.

Every August on the weekend closest to Establishment Day, a free two-day cultural festival is held on the *heiau* grounds, including arts and crafts exhibitions, games, hula demonstrations, music, and dance.

Near the *heiau* is the house site of John Young, an English seaman who became a close adviser to Kamehameha, who dubbed him Olohana, "All Hands." Young taught the Hawaiians how to use cannons and muskets and fought alongside Kamehameha in many battles. He turned Mailekini Heiau into a fort, and over a century later it was used during WW II by the U.S. Army as an observation area. Young became a respected Hawaiian chief and grandfather of Queen Emma. He's one of only two white men buried at the Royal Mausoleum in Nuuanu Valley on Oahu.

Kawaihae Town
The port marks the northern end of the South Kohala coast. Here Rt. 19 turns eastward toward Waimea, or turns into Rt. 270 heading up the coast into North Kohala. Kawaihae town is basically utilitarian, with wharves and fuel tanks. A service cluster has numerous shops and restaurants.

BEACHES, PARKS, AND CAMPGROUNDS

Anaehoomalu Bay
After almost 30 miles of the transfixing monochrome blackness of Kohala's lava flows, a green standout of palm trees beckons in the distance. Between mile markers 76 and 77, on the Waikoloa Resorts Road, another well-marked access road heads *makai* to the Outrigger Waikoloa Beach Hotel and historic Anaehoomalu Bay. The bay area, with its freshwater springs, coconut trees, blue lagoon, and white-sand beach, is a picture-perfect seaside oasis. Between the large coconut grove and the beach are two well-preserved fishponds where mullet was raised *only* for consumption by the royalty who lived nearby or were happening by in seagoing canoes. Throughout the area along well-marked trails are **petroglyphs,** a segment of the cobblestoned **King's Highway,** and numerous archaeological sites including house sites and some hard-to-find burial caves. The white-sand beach is open to the public, with access, parking, and beautiful lava stone showers/bathhouses. Although the sand is a bit grainy, the swimming, snorkeling, scuba, and windsurfing are fine. A walk north along the bay brings you to an area of excellent tidepools and waters heavily populated by marine life. The next beach north is at Puako Bay.

Holoholokai Beach Park
Located near the Orchid at Mauna Lani Hotel on a well-marked access road, the picturesque beach park, open to the public daily 6:30 a.m.-7 p.m., is improved with a bathroom, running water, picnic tables, and resort-quality landscaping. Unfortunately, the beach itself is mostly coral boulders with only tiny pockets offering very limited water access. However, the park is used very little and is perfect for relaxing under a palm tree or for a leisurely stroll to explore the many tidepools.

Hapuna Beach State Recreation Area
Approximately eight miles north of Anaehoomalu is the *second*-best, but most accessible, white-sand beach on the island. (The best, Kauna'oa, is listed next.) **Camping** is available in six A-frame screened shelters that rent for $20 per night and accommodate up to four. Provided are sleeping platforms (no bedding), electric outlets, cold-water showers, and toilets in separate comfort stations, plus a shared range and refrigerator in a central pavilion. Check in at 2 p.m., checkout at 10 a.m. The A-frames are very popu-

lar, so reservations and deposit are required. You can receive full information by contacting the Division of State Parks, P.O. Box 936 (75 Aupuni St.), Hilo, HI 96721, tel. (808) 974-6200. There is unofficial camping south along **Waialea Bay** that you can get to by walking or taking the turnoff at mile marker 69.

Hapuna Beach is wide and spacious, almost 700 yards long by 70 wide in summer, with a reduction by heavy surf in winter. A lava finger divides the beach into almost equal halves. During good weather the swimming is excellent and lifeguards are on duty. During heavy weather, usually in winter, the rips are fierce, and Hapuna has claimed more lives than any other beach park on all of Hawaii! At the north end is a small cove almost forming a pool that is always safe, a favorite with families and children. Many classes in beginning scuba and snorkeling are held in this area, and shore fishing is good throughout. At the south end, good breaks make for tremendous bodysurfing (no boards allowed), and those familiar with the area make spectacular leaps from the seacliffs.

Kauna'oa Beach
Better known as **Mauna Kea Beach** because of the nearby luxury hotel of the same name, Kauna'oa is less than a mile north of Hapuna Beach and is considered to be the best beach on the Big Island by not only the local population, but also by those who judge such things from a broader perspective. In 1997, the National Geographic Traveler magazine ranked it one of the five best beaches in the United States. In times past, it was a nesting and mating ground for green sea turtles, and although these activities no longer occur because of human pressure on the habitat, turtles still visit the south end of the beach. Mauna Kea Beach is long and wide, and the sandy bottom makes for excellent swimming. It is more sheltered than Hapuna, but can still be dangerous. Hotel beach boys, always in attendance, are unofficial lifeguards who have saved many unsuspecting tourists. During high surf, the shoreline is a favorite with surfers. All beaches in Hawaii are public, but *access* to this beach was won only by a lawsuit against the Mauna Kea Beach Hotel in 1973. The ruling forced the

hotel to open the beach to the public, which they did in the form of 10 parking spaces, a right of way, public shower, and toilet facilities. To keep the number of nonguests down, only 10 parking passes are handed out each day on a first-come, first-served basis. Pick them up at the guardhouse as you enter the hotel grounds. These entitle you to spend the day on the beach, but on weekends they're gone by 9:30 a.m. You can wait for someone to leave and then get the pass, but that's unreliable. The hotel also issues a pass for a one-hour visit to the hotel grounds (overstaying results in a $10 fine). You can use this pass to drop off family, friends, beach paraphernalia, and picnic supplies, then park at Hapuna and return via an easy mile-long **nature trail** connecting Hapuna and Mauna Kea Beaches, the route used by the majority of people unable to get a pass. Also, the hotel issues a "food and drink" pass that entitles you to stay as long as you wish, if you get it validated at one of the restaurants or snack bars. So as long as you're in there, you might as well use the beach for the price of a soft drink. In time the hotel will catch on, so test the waters before winding up with a fine.

Spencer Beach County Park
Look for the entrance a minute or two past Puukohola Heiau on Rt. 19 just before entering Kawaihae. Trails lead from the beach park up to the *heiau,* so you can combine a day at the beach with a cultural education. The park is named after Samuel Mahuka Spencer, a long-time island resident who was born in Waimea, served as county mayor for 20 years, and died in 1960 at Honokaa. The park provides pavilions, restrooms, cold-water showers, electricity, picnic facilities, and even tennis courts. Day use is free, but tent and trailer **camping** is by county permit only. Spencer Beach is protected from wind and heavy wave action by an offshore reef and by breakwaters built around Kawaihae Bay. These make it the safest and best swimming beach along South Kohala's shore and a favorite with local families with small children. The wide, shallow reef is home to a wide spectrum of marine life, making the snorkeling entertaining. The shoreline fishing is also excellent.

PRACTICALITIES

LUXURY RESORTS

Kona Village Resort

So you want to go "native," and you're dreaming of a "little grass shack" along a secluded beach? No problem! The Kona Village Resort is a once-in-a-lifetime dream experience. Located on Kahuwai Bay, a picture-perfect cove of white sand dotted with coconut palms, the village lies seven miles north of the Kona Airport, surrounded by 82 open acres promising seclusion. The accommodations are distinctive "hales," individual renditions of thatch-roofed huts found throughout Polynesia and Hawaii. They are simple but luxurious, and in keeping with the idea of getting away from it all, have no TVs, radios, or telephones. All, however, do have ceiling fans and louvered windows to let the tropical breezes blow through. Beds are covered with distinctive quilts and pillows. Each hut features a wet bar, fridge, coffee-making machine, and extra-large bathroom. Your Do Not Disturb sign is a coconut that you place upon your private lanai, and messages are hand-delivered and placed in a basket, also on the lanai. At one time you had to fly into the hotel's private airstrip, but today you can arrive by car. Almost exactly at mile marker 87 look for a sign reading "Hualalai" where you turn in, and then make a right within 100 yards; actually, Hualalai is the name of the mountain to your back, and the area down by the sea was called *Kaupulehu* (Roasted Breadfruit) by the native Hawaiians who lived in this once thriving village area.

Return guests will find the entrance changed from when the Kona Village was the only hotel in the area. You enter by an access road that leads through the coal black lava fields of South Kohala. Don't despair! Down by the sea you can see the shimmering green palm trees as they beckon you to the resort. Kona Village gives you your money's worth, with tennis, Ping-Pong, lei greetings, water sports, and a variety of cocktail parties and luau. Guided tours are also offered to the many historic sites in the area, along with classes in lei making, shoreline tidepool exploring, *lau hala* weaving, Hawaiian quilting, and even a botanical tour of the grounds complete with legends and explanations of the ancient medicinal uses of the plants. Rates start at $395 d, full American plan (three meals), and go up to $680 for oceanfront. Deduct $90 for single occupancy and add $25 for children under age two, $55 for children 2-5, $110 for children 6-12, and $160 for an extra adult. The hotel's "Keikis in Paradise" is a children's program included in the price of a room that will entertain and educate children ages six and up throughout the day. There is a strict reservations and refund policy, so check. For information, contact Kona Village Resort, P.O. Box 1299, Kailua-Kona, HI 96745, tel. (808) 325-5555, (800) 432-5450 from anywhere in the state, or (800) 367-5290 from the Mainland. E-mail: kvr@aloha.net; website: www.konavillage.com.

Meals are served in the Hale Moana, the main dining room; and at the Hale Moana Terrace, where a famous luncheon buffet is served daily 12:30-2 p.m. Hale Samoa is the fine dining restaurant, open daily except Wednesday and Friday, for dinner. Upon entering Hale Samoa, your spirits rise immediately with the sweep of cathedral ceiling. On the walls is an original painting by Herb Kane, Hawaii's foremost artist, that depicts *The Fair American*, a tiny ship commandeered by King Kamehameha that was instrumental in changing the history of old Hawaii. The walls also hold portraits of the hotel's original owner, Johnno Jackson, an oil driller from California, who in 1960 sailed in with his wife Helen, their Labrador dog, a monkey, and a parrot—all in a 42-foot schooner—landing on these shores and declaring, "This is the spot!" Also on the grounds are Hale H'ookipa "House of Hospitality," where a luau is held on Friday nights, and a steak-fry every Wednesday. Drinks and tropical libations are offered at the Hale Samoa Terrace, Shipwreck Bar, and Bora Bora Bar at the poolside.

A public tour is offered weekdays from 11 a.m. that includes a 15-acre petroglyph field on the property that you can inspect if you make prior arrangements. You will be instructed to meet a tour guide at the main gate at about

10:50 a.m. The hotel manager is Fred Duerr, who's been at the facility since 1966, along with most of his highly professional and seasoned personnel. They take pride in the hotel and do everything to help you have a rewarding, enjoyable, and relaxing stay at this premier resort. The Kona Village is a Hawaiian classic that deserves its well-earned reputation for excellence.

Four Seasons Resort

The Four Seasons Resort, Hualalai, at historic Ka'upulehu, opened in late 1996. Located at 8 Queen Kaahumanu Hwy., this 243-room resort is split into 36 low-rise bungalows in four crescent groups that front a half-mile beach just up from Kona Village Resort. Located in among old lava flows from the Hualalai volcano, 32 of these units have ocean access and four are located along the 18th green of the accompanying golf course. Polynesian in style, the units are a mixture of dark mahogany wood, light wall colors and carpeting, pleasing medium brown rattan furniture, and gray slate flooring. Authentic Hawaiian art pieces from the late 1700s to the present are displayed throughout the hotel. With all the greenery around, the lobby exudes a feeling of the outdoors. Plate glass windows behind the front desk allow the slope of Hualalai to sit unobstructed before you. Be sure to check out the interpretive center just downstairs from the lobby, where Mr. Kaleo will enlighten you about the surrounding waters, this area of Hawaii, and the life and lifestyle of ancient Hawaiians. A 1,200-gallon reef aquarium approximates the offshore ocean environment with live coral and fish from the local area. Before you snorkel, have a look in here to see what you'll encounter.

Rooms are more than 600 square feet and filled with furniture and decorations. King-size beds predominate and are accompanied by free-standing credenzas, desks, couches, walk-in closets, an entertainment center, a fax line, and a refrigerated wet bar. Large as well are the bathrooms, each of which looks out onto a private garden, lanai, or patio. The slate floors of the main rooms are covered with seagrass mats and the beds with material reminiscent of tapa cloth.

The resort's two restaurants will certainly fill your every culinary need for all three meals of the day. Both the elegant **Puhu I'a Restaurant** and the casual **Beach Tree Bar and Grill** are set at oceanside. The more formal Puhu I'a features Hawaiian, Western, and Asian cuisine and includes many fish dishes, vegetarian entrees, and plenty of desserts and wine.

Located near the tennis courts is the Sports Club and Spa, a full-service facility open 7 a.m.-7 p.m., seven days a week. Pick from tai chi or aerobics instruction, a 25-meter lap pool, or Nautilus machines for a workout, then soothe those muscles on the massage table. A half basketball court is available for all the aspiring Magic Johnsons, and mountain bikes are conveniently for rent. After your exercise, stop in at the Trading Company store a few steps away for munchable supplies to bring back to the room, or for a noontime picnic. Hualalai Tennis Club is open 7 a.m.-9 p.m. only for hotel guests; reservations are required. Court fees are $10 per person per day. Private lessons are available and ball machines can be rented. The Hualalai Golf Club offers an 18-hole, par-72 golf course designed by Jack Nicklaus that lies along the ocean. Green fees run $105 per person. The clubhouse holds the pro shop, locker rooms, cart and bag storage area and, for refreshment, the **Hualalai Club Grille and Bar.**

On the ocean side of the meeting room building is **Kids for all Seasons,** the hotel's service to take care of your children while you have fun yourself. Open 9 a.m.-5 p.m. for those 5-12 years old, the service provides a wide variety of fun-filled and supervised indoor and outdoor activities.

An exceptional place, Four Seasons is not cheap. Rooms run $450-550 a night, suites $550-750 a night; $90 for an extra adult. From December 20 through January 3, there is a seven-night minimum for all stays. For information and reservations, contact the resort at P.O. Box 1269, Kailua-Kona, HI 96745, tel. (808) 325-8000, (888) 340-5662, or (800) 332-3442, fax (808) 325-8100.

Outrigger Waikoloa Beach Hotel

The Sheraton chain wanted to enter the luxury hotel market with a splash, so in 1981 they opened the $70-million, 545-room Sheraton Royal Waikoloan Hotel. They found the perfect spot at Anaehoomalu Bay (between mile markers 77 and 78), and produced a class act. The hotel lobby is a spacious open-air affair, beautifully appointed in koa and objets d'art. All rooms are tastefully decorated and provide a/c, color TV, king-size beds, and private lanai. In early 1999, the hotel was sold to the Outrigger group and will undergo renovation until its reopening as the Outrigger Waikoloa Beach Hotel in the fall of 1999. For reservations and all the new information, contact: Outrigger Waikoloa Beach Hotel, 69-275 Waikoloa Beach Dr., Kamuela, HI 96743-9763, tel. (808) 885-6789, or (800) 688-7444.

On the superbly kept grounds are six tennis courts, numerous ponds, and a swimming pool. Special features include a small shopping arcade, (King's Shops a minute across the road) horseback riding (off property), and free shuttle service throughout Waikoloa. The focal points, however, are two marvelous golf courses. The Beach Course was designed by Robert Trent Jones Jr.; he learned his trade from his dad, whose masterpiece is just up the road at the Mauna Kea Resort. The King's Course is also known as the Weiskopf-Morrish Course after its designers, Tom Weiskopf and Jim Morrish.

You have a choice of dining facilities. The **Royal Terrace** opens its doors to the sea and features American cuisine daily for breakfast, lunch, and dinner. The atmosphere is relaxed and the prices are affordable for such a hotel. **The Tiare,** elegant dining in elegant surroundings for elegant prices, offers signature dishes such as Waikoloa seafood trio, a fisherman's stew made with fresh catch and fish from these wonderful Hawaiian waters just off Kona, fresh fish prepared in a variety of ways, and rack of lamb. Open daily except Wednesday and Sunday 6:30-9:30 p.m., tel. (808) 885-6789, reservations recommended.

For those interested in the wonderful petroglyphs that are found throughout the area, you are invited to come to the Royal Waikoloan on Tuesday and Thursday at 8:15 a.m., when a knowledgeable staff member will take you on a petroglyph tour that includes petroglyph rubbing. A Ku'uali'i Fish Pond Tour is also offered on a variable schedule throughout the week. A special fish called the Ku'uali'i still thrives in the ponds that were *kapu* except to the *ali'i*, and were raised for their consumption alone.

The Shores at Waikoloa

The Shores at Waikoloa are secluded luxury condominiums nestled away in the planned community of Waikoloa at 69-1035 Keana Place, P.O. Box 5460, Waikoloa, HI 96743, tel. (808) 885-5001; for reservations phone Aston Hotel and Resorts, tel. (800) 922-7866 Mainland, (800) 445-6633 Canada, (800) 321-2558 Hawaii. To get there, turn off Rt. 19 into well-marked Waikoloa at mile marker 76, and proceed straight ahead past the King's Shops, a small shopping area. Keep going for a few minutes and you will come to a sign that says Condominiums and another marker that points you to The Shores at Waikoloa. Enter through a security gate to see the peaceful and beautifully manicured grounds of the low-rise condominium. A few minutes away are the best beaches on Hawaii and all of the activities offered by the large luxury hotels, if you wish to participate. The condominium offers an "activities desk" where you can arrange a snorkeling or sailing excursion or hire a babysitter. A swimming pool and jacuzzi are open until 10 p.m., and two complimentary tennis courts (and a few rackets too) are available. The condos are decorated by the individual owners so each room is unique, but there are guidelines and standards so that every unit is tastefully and comfortably decorated, mostly in an island motif. All units are extremely spacious, with many boasting marble and terra-cotta floors; huge bathrooms with double tubs, showers, and sinks; full modern kitchens; and light and airy sitting rooms complete with state-of-the-art entertainment centers. Rates range $215 for a one-bedroom to $505 for a three-bedroom golf villa. Low season brings a 25% reduction, and The Shores offers an unbeatable low-season "golf package." If you are after a luxury vacation within a vacation where you can get away from it all after you've gotten away from it all, The Shores at Waikoloa is a superb choice.

Hilton Waikoloa Village

At the Hilton Waikoloa Village (formerly Hyatt Regency Waikoloa), 425 Waikoloa Beach Dr., Waikaloa, HI 96743, tel. (808) 885-1234 or (800) 445-8667, website: www.waikoloavillage.hilton .com, the idea was to create a reality so beautiful and naturally harmonious that anyone who came here, sinner and saint alike, would be guaranteed a glimpse of paradise.

From Kona airport, travel north on Rt. 19 for about 15 minutes. Look for mile marker 76, and turn beachside toward Waikoloa. Follow the

Artwork surrounds you at the Hilton Waikoloa Village.

roadway through the lava fields until you arrive at the hotel. Valets will park your car.

The architecture, "fantasy grand," is subdued and understated, not gaudy. The three main towers, each enclosing a miniature fern-filled botanical garden, are spread over the grounds almost a mile apart and are linked by pink flagstone walkways, canals navigated by hotel launches, and a quiet, space-age tram. Everywhere sculptures, art treasures, and brilliant flowers soothe the eyes. Songs of rare tropical birds and the wind whispering through a bamboo forest create the natural melody that surrounds you. You can swim in a private lagoon accompanied by dolphins, dine in magnificent restaurants, explore surrounding ranchlands, or just let your cares slip away as you lounge in perfect tranquillity.

Inside, attention to the smallest detail is immediately apparent. Elevators are done in rich woods and burnished brass. An alcove may hold a dozen superbly hand-carved puppets from Indonesia. Halls are bedecked with chandeliers, marble-topped tables, and immense floral displays. Even cigarette receptacles are artworks: large Asian pots or ceramic dolphins with mouths agape, filled with black sand.

A museum promenade displays a Hawaiiana collection of carved koa bowls and feather lei, along with carvings from Thailand, paintings from Japan, and porcelains from China. Fantastic pots, taller than a person, are topped with two handles of gold elephant faces and tusks. Look through archways at perfectly framed grottoes harboring koi ponds and waterfalls. Sit on royal thrones and benches next to intricately carved credenzas and tables and simply delight at the beauty.

The hotel's restaurants are culinary extravaganzas, and every taste is provided for. **Donatoni's** features classic Italian; **Cascades** presents a different theme nightly which includes Polynesian, Chinese, Italian, and Mexican; **Imari** serves traditional Japanese fare; **Kamuela Provision Co.** specializes in steak and seafood; and the hotel's bars, lounges, and casual poolside dining options are surprisingly moderately priced. In addition, try the evening **Kamehameha Court Luau** for food, dinner show, and dancing.

The beach fronting the property offers excellent snorkeling, while three gigantic pools and a series of lagoons are perfect for water activities and sunbathing.

Take the amazing "Behind the House" tour of the facility (free). You are led below ground, deep into the heart of the hotel, where you get to see how everything works. An underground service roadway, complete with stop signs and traffic cops, runs for more than a mile and is traveled by employees on bicycles and motorized utility carts. As you pass offices with signs that read Wildlife Director, Curator of Art, Astronomer, you come to realize how distinctive an undertaking the hotel is. Next come the florist shop, the butcher, the baker, the laundry (with more output than any other laundry in the state of Hawaii—22 pounds of linen go in each room) and wardrobe, responsible for outfitting the hotel's 2,000 employees. You're given staggering figures: 750,000 gallons of fresh water is needed for the pools; more than 18 million gallons of seawater is pumped through the canals daily; each motor launch costs $300,000; the 41 chandeliers weigh more than 24 tons; the hotel's 300 computers are linked by more than 28 miles of cable. On and on, the statistics match the magnificence of what you see.

With all this splendor, the most talked-about feature at the hotel is still **Dolphin Quest**. A specially constructed saltwater pond, 65 times larger than federal regulations require, is home to Atlantic bottlenose dolphins from Florida's Gulf Coast, where they're found in bays and lagoons living most of their lives in water 16-20 feet deep. Here, their pond is 22 feet deep in the center, measures 350 feet long, and contains 2.5 million gallons of naturally filtered seawater.

Daily, on a lottery basis for adults, but with "two months in advance reservations available to children up to 19 years of age" (arranged through your travel agent or by phoning the hotel), guests are allowed to "interact with the dolphins." Dolphin Quest is trying to steer the program away from the concept of "swimming with dolphins," and more toward an educational experience. The program was founded by two highly respected marine veterinarians, Drs. Jay Sweeney and Rae Stone, both prominent in their field for their efforts to protect and preserve marine mammal populations. It was their idea to bring a new experience to the public in which the interaction was from the dolphin's point of view. Instead of a typical stadium-type setting where the dolphins are performers and the people are spectators, they created something more natural.

Here you don't ride the dolphins and they don't do tricks for you. In the half-hour session, the guests wade in chest-deep water with the dolphins gliding by while a staff member imparts information concerning not only dolphins, but all marine life and human interdependence with it. If the dolphins want to be petted they stop, if not they move past like a torpedo. The experience is voluntary on the dolphins' part—*they* choose to swim with *you* as a guest in their domain.

Much of the proceeds from the program goes toward marine research. At one time, a team from the University of California at Santa Cruz was housed, funded, and provided with boats to investigate a way to save the more than 100,000 spinner dolphins that are caught in tuna nets every year. Pointing to success, four baby dolphins have been born on the property since the inception of Dolphin Quest. There are two male dolphins: one an immature "teenager" and the other a full-grown adult, Hobie, who keeps company with four female dolphins, dubbed "Hobie's Harem."

This futuristic and fantastic hotel complex has set a new standard against which all future resorts will be measured. Of course, as you would expect, all this luxury comes at a price; rates are $210-360 standard and $550-3,950 suites. Experience and time has matured the Hilton Waikoloa Village into one of the finest resorts in Kohala.

The Orchid at Mauna Lani

In a tortured field of coal-black lava made more dramatic by free-form pockets of jade-green lawn rises ivory-white The Orchid at Mauna Lani, a proud addition to Sheraton's Luxury Collection, at One N. Kaniku Dr., Kohala Coast, HI 96743, tel. (808) 885-2000, hotel direct at (800) 845-9905, or Sheraton Inns at (800) 325-3589, website: www.orchid-maunalani.com. A rolling drive lined with *haku lei* of flowering shrubs entwined with stately palms leads to the open-air porte cochere. Enter to find koa and marble reflecting the diffused and soothing light of the interior. Straight ahead, off the thrust-proscenium Sunset Terrace, a living blue-on-blue still-life of sea and sky is perfectly framed. Nature, powerful yet soothing, surrounds the hotel. Stroll the grounds, where gentle breezes always blow and where the ever-present surf is the back beat of a melody created by trickling rivulets and falling waters as they meander past a magnificent free-form pool and trimmed tropical gardens of ferns and flowers. The Orchid at Mauna Lani was formerly a Ritz-Carlton Hotel, and although "the body" has not changed, "the soul" has. The Orchid is now much more casually elegant, a place to relax in luxury "island style." Gone is the sense of formality, and in its place is warm *aloha*.

The hallways and lobbies open from the central area like the delicate ribs of a geisha's fan. Overhead hang magnificent cut-crystal chandeliers of differing designs. The walls are graced with Hawaiian quilts and exquisite art rendered by some of Hawaii's most famous artists, including Susan Hansen, Betty Freeland, Russell Lowrey, Fabienne Blanc, Nancy Poes, and Ken Bushnell. There are excellent artworks on view everywhere, from the walls of the superb Grill Restaurant to the Fitness Center. Elevators are koa-paneled, and every set of stairs boasts a velvety smooth koa banister carved with the pineapple motif, the Hawaiian symbol of hospitality.

Located in two six-story wings off the main reception hall, the 539 hotel rooms, each with private lanai and sensational view, are a mixture of kings, doubles, and suites. Done in neutral tones, the stylish and refined rooms feature handcrafted quilts, twice-daily room attendance, turndown service complete with a complimentary orchid and locally made chocolates, remote-control color TV, 24-hour room service, fully stocked honor bar, and in-room safe. Wardrobes, featuring automatic lighting, are hung with plush terry robes and plump satin hangers. The spacious marble bathrooms, with wide, deep tubs, separate commodes, and shower stalls are appointed with dressing and vanity mirrors, double sinks, hair dryers, and name-brand grooming products. Rates begin at $310 for a garden view to $440 for a deluxe oceanfront room. The Club Level, an exclusive floor with its own concierge, offers extra amenities—$510 will get you a room as well as continental breakfast, light lunch, cocktails, cordials, and a full spread of evening hors d'oeuvres. Suites range from an executive one-bedroom to the magnificent Presidential Suite and cost $495-2,800.

The hotel offers first-rate guest services, amenities, and activities that include a small shopping mall with everything from sundries to designer boutiques, complimentary shuttle to and from Mauna Lani's famous championship golf courses (to Waikoloa if time permits), bag storage, 11 tennis courts (with seven lit for evening play), complimentary use of fitness center and snorkel equipment, an enormous swimming pool and sun deck, bicycles for short tours, safe-deposit boxes, on-property car rental, and baby-sitting. **Keiki Aloha** is a special instructional day-camp program for children ages 5-12. Reasonably priced and offered half or full days, Keiki Aloha, in its secure and separate "children's room," includes lunch and lets kids engage in a variety of fascinating activities such as making shell jewelry, stringing lei, exploring petroglyphs, painting, and playing Hawaiian games and water sports.

Dining at the The Orchid can be everything from poolside casual (burgers and fries) to haute cuisine (fine delectables from around the world.)

Executive Chef David Reardon and his staff prepare island cuisine in various styles, using locally grown produce, herbs, meats, and seafood. The culinary results are not only mouth-watering, but healthy and wonderfully nutritious.

At **The Grill,** open for dinner 6:30-9:30 p.m., cocktails and dancing until closing, most dishes are either Hawaiian style or northern Mediterranean influenced. Whet your appetite with crab cakes, vegetable raviolis, or guava grilled pork tenderloin for $10-13, and move on to Maui onion soup gratiné, grilled corn and seafood chowder, or any of several salads for $7-10. Entrées include a selection of grilled fresh island fish, beef, poultry, and vegetarian dishes. Specialties include rack of lamb, pan-seared sea scallops, and roasted onaga with saffron linguine. Entrées range $26-36.

The **Orchid Court** is open daily for breakfast and dinner and also serves an extraordinary Sunday brunch. The Orchid Court is a casual restaurant featuring Pacific Rim and local fare, and including both a children's and a you-can-run-but-you-can't-hide fitness menu. Prices for standard complete breakfasts are $15-16, the fitness breakfast $13, and a complete breakfast buffet $19. À la carte dishes are also available. Dinner entrees include sesame crusted mahi-mahi and red miso and pineapple glazed chicken breast.

The poolside **Brown's Beach House,** open daily for lunch and dinner, is the hotel's most casual restaurant, where you dine alfresco in a garden setting. Lunch offerings range from American standards and healthful salads to pizza and pasta. The dinner menu includes entrées like pumpkin seed and coriander crusted onaga and Asian spiced roast rack of lamb. At your feet, a perfect crescent white-sand beach opens to the great Pacific.

Mauna Lani Bay Hotel

As soon as you turn off Rt. 19, the entrance road, trimmed in purple bougainvillea, sets the mood for this $70-million, 350-room hotel that opened in 1983. The per-unit cost of $200,000 was the most ever spent in Hawaii up to that time, and it shows in the oversize rooms emphasizing relaxation and luxury, the majority with an ocean view. The hotel has a tennis garden with 10 courts, a lovely beach and lagoon area, a health spa, exclusive shops, and swimming pools. Enter through a grand portico, whose blue tile floor, a mimic of the ever-present sea and sky, immediately creates a sense of sedate but beautiful grandeur. Below is a central courtyard, where full-size palms sway amidst a lava-rock water garden; cascading sheets of clear water splash through a series of koi ponds, making naturally soothing music. A short stroll leads you through a virtual botanical garden to a white-sand beach perfect for island relaxation.

Surrounding the hotel is the marvelous **Francis I'i Brown Golf Course** (North and South Courses), whose artistically laid-out fairways, greens, and sand traps make it a modern landscape sculpture. The courses are carved from lava, with striking ocean views in every direction; the 15th hole of the South Course requires a drive over a finger of ocean. Both are challenging, but not *too* much so, though they measure more than 6,300 yards each, par 72. Greens fees are expensive, with preferred starting times given to hotel guests. Terrific savings with special "Room and Golf Packages" are offered by the hotel. (Call the Pro Shop at 808-885-6655 for more information.)

The prestigious *Tennis Magazine* has also rated the Mauna Lani's 10 plexi-pave courts among the "top 50 greatest tennis courts in the U.S." Special "Tennis Packages" offer reduced room rates along with a can of balls per room per day, a round robin tournament daily, a one-hour usage of the ball machine, and complimentary unlimited court time daily.

For parents with young children who have come to the realization that "families who want to stay together, don't always play together," the hotel offers a break from those little bundles of joy with **Camp Mauna Lani Bay,** for children ages 5-12. Day camp, 9 a.m.-3 p.m., is $25 including lunch and snacks, with a reduction in fee for additional children from the same family. Evening camp, 5-10 p.m., which is more responsible for romance then even a bottle of fine wine, is $20 per child with dinner and snacks. Full day camp, 9 a.m.-10 p.m., is $40 with lunch, dinner, and snacks for the first child, discounted thereafter. In-room baby-sitters are available on a per-hour basis. Throughout the day, the children at camp learn about Hawaiiana with coconut frond weaving, nature walks, and Hawaiian games, and de-

velop their artistic skills with sand paintings, cookie decorating, and beadwork. Also, to work off some excess energy, there are lawn games, scavenger hunts, sand castle building and, for "couch potatoes in training," video games.

Don't forget about the teens. The hotel has initiated the **Eco-Teen Island Bound Adventures** program for kids 13-17 who want to explore ways to spend their time. Day-long activities include a hike along the Kohala coast, sea kayak trip, petroglyph tour, introduction to deep-sea fishing, volleyball tournaments, hula dancing, and more. This program is offered only from late March to late April, from mid-June to early September, and during Thanksgiving and Christmas vacation times.

The Mauna Lani's rooms begin at $415 ocean view to $520 oceanfront, with suites from $835 and royal bungalows for $3,200-4,100 (includes a personal chef, valet, live-in maid, and swimming pool). The hotel also offers one- to three-bedroom ocean villas, weekly and monthly rates available and three-night minimum required. Each room includes a private lanai, remote color TV and VCR, honor bar, in-room safe, make-up mirrors, and fluffy his/her robes. Guest privileges include complimentary use of the health spa (massage extra), snorkeling equipment, classes on Hawaiiana such as lei making and hula lessons, fish feeding, complimentary morning coffee and newspapers in the Bay Terrace Restaurant, and resort and historic tours. For full information, contact: Mauna Lani Bay Hotel, 68-1400 Mauna Lani Dr., Kohala Coast, HI 96743, tel. (808) 885-6622 or (800) 367-2323, (800) 992-7987 Hawaii. E-mail: maunalani@maunalani.com, website: www.maunalani.com.

The **Bay Terrace,** open daily for breakfast and dinner, offers the most casual but still superb dining. Daily offerings include everything from full-course breakfasts to dinner entrées like rack of lamb. Weekend nights feature a fabulous seafood buffet that shouldn't be missed, and the Sunday brunch served 9 a.m.-2 p.m. is legendary.

The oceanfront **Canoe House,** open daily for dinner, delights you with Pacific Rim cuisine. The koa menus (always changing with new items) feature special *pu pu* like nori-wrapped tempura *ahi* with soy-mustard sauce and tomato-ginger relish for $18.50 or fresh corn risotto for $10. A variety of soups and salads ($8-12) include creamy lobster leek and potato soup, miso-style avocado salad, or fresh asparagus and buffalo mozzarella with kalamata-olive vinaigrette dressing. Main dishes (around $30) tantalize you, with items like fresh seared mahimahi, pesto-seared scallops with roasted eggplant and kalamata olives, or grilled Korean-style chicken. Of course, there are also herb-crusted rack of lamb, and a wonderful Thai style seafood curry with lobster, shrimp, and Chinese vegetable stir-fry.

The **Ocean Grill,** where you'll be comfortable in bathing suit and cover-up, serves lunches and cocktails, while **The Gallery Restaurant and Knickers Bar,** at the Golf Pro Shop, serves lunch 11 a.m.-3 p.m. and dinner 5:30-9 p.m. (complimentary coffee and pastries for early tee times), closed Sun.-Monday. The award-winning restaurant is probably the least expensive fine-dining restaurant at the resort. Lunch ($7-11) can be Caesar salad with seared peppered *ahi,* smoked chicken salad, club house sandwich, roasted turkey sandwich, or specialties like curry *Indienne,* beef slowly cooked in spicy Madras curry and served with rice and condiments. Dinner ($20-30) starts with tomato and Maui onions with balsamic dressing, peppered *ahi,* and onion bisque with fontina croutons. "Wannabe Italians" (and who wouldn't) will enjoy ravioli with pesto sauce or the always popular spaghetti with clams, garlic, white wine, and Italian parsley. Other gourmet fare includes New York steak, rib eye, roasted rack of lamb with sweet potato purée on thyme juice, the fresh catch (which can be broiled with shrimp, grilled in a citrus five-spice butter sauce, or baked with a macadamia nut crust), and a one-pound, Kona-raised lobster served with shrimp and clams in a basil shellfish broth.

The **Honu Bar** is a perfect place to relax after a day of golf or tennis; there you will find a pool table and an excellent selection of liqueurs, wine, and fine cigars.

The Mauna Kea Beach Hotel

This hotel has set the standard of excellence along Kohala's coast ever since former Hawaii Governor William Quinn interested Laurence Rockefeller in the lucrative possibilities of building a luxury hideaway for the rich and famous. Beautiful coastal land was leased from the Parker Ranch, and the resort opened in 1965. The

Mauna Kea was the only one of its kind for a few years until other luxury hotels were built along this coast. It's getting a bit older, and getting stiff competition from newer nearby luxury resorts, but class is always class and the Mauna Kea receives very high accolades as a fine resort. After an extensive restoration, the Mauna Kea reopened with youthful enthusiasm in December 1995.

The hotel's classic, trend-setting **golf course** designed by the master, Robert Trent Jones, has been voted among America's 100 greatest courses and Hawaii's finest. Also, *Tennis Magazine* includes the hotel among the "50 greatest U.S. tennis resorts." The hotel itself is an eight-story terraced complex of simple, clean-cut design. The grounds and lobbies showcase more than 1,000 museum-quality art pieces from throughout the Pacific, and more than a half-million plants add greenery and beauty to the surroundings. The landings and lobbies, open and large enough to hold full-grown palm trees, also display beautiful tapestries, bird cages with their singing captives, and huge copper pots on polished brick floors. The Mauna Kea offers a modified American plan (breakfast and dinner), the best beach on the island, and its own dive boat for seagoing adventure. Million-dollar condos also grace the grounds. Guests tend to come back year after year. The beautifully appointed rooms, starting at $280, $45 extra person, feature an extra-large lanai and specially made wicker furniture. From there, rates go up to $1,050 for a suite. A television-free resort at its inception, the hotel now has TVs in most of the rooms as part of the recent restoration. For full information contact Mauna Kea Beach Hotel, One Mauna Kea Beach Dr., Kohala Coast, HI 96743, tel. (808) 882-7222 or (800) 882-6060, website: www.maunakeabeachhotel.com.

Sumptuous dining is presented in the **Batik Room,** dinner nightly 7-10 p.m., where the Sri Lankan-inspired decor adds a touch of Eastern mystery and romance. Intricate *batik* tapestries, brass liner plates, and regal *houdah* (elephant thrones) set the mood for the exotic menu. Begin your feast with whole roasted garlic and escargot with wild mushrooms for $14.50, or with island *ahi* tartar cake for $17. Soups ranging from a salmon broth with fresh vegetables to lobster bisque armagnac cost $7-8.50. Entrees, magnificent creations from around the world starting at $28, include roasted duck with sweet corn polenta; a variety of island fish grilled, steamed and sautéed; and zesty curries made from lamb, veal, chicken, or shrimp. A titillating dessert is chocolate soufflé topped with macadamia nuts, champagne sauce, Grand Marnier, or fresh blueberries.

The Garden, another of the hotel's fine dining restaurants, open nightly for dinner 6:30-9:30 p.m., set the standards in the mid-1980s when it was one of the first restaurants to offer Hawaiian regional cuisine. Now it serves authentic Italian cuisine in its garden setting. **The Terrace,** informal and alfresco, is well-known along this coast for its Sunday buffet, $32.The choices seem endless at the serving table and you come away feeling like you won't need to eat for a week. The Terrace also serves a daily lunch buffet for $24 and has an à la carte menu of appetizers, soups, and salads.

For breakfast, lunch, or dinner in an open-air setting, try the **Pavilion** restaurant. Breakfast can be à la carte, from a simple continental breakfast to a traditional American meal with eggs, potatoes, juice, and bacon; or choose a lavish buffet offering fresh fruits, cereals, French toast, Belgian waffles, the finest and most delectable breakfast meats, steaming pots of Kona coffee, pineapple crepes, and even *huevos rancheros.* Lunch can similarly be à la carte—club sandwich or Cobb salad, for example—or a magnificent buffet of chilled seafood, sashimi, salmon, steaks, chops, lox, a cornucopia of island fruits and vegetables, and a dessert bar. Dinner offers starters like sesame seed prawns with green papaya salad and Waimea spring vegetables and mushroom risotto, all under $12.50. Baked onion soup or egg noodle soup with braised duck and shiitake mushrooms are sure to please. Entrées are a variety of pasta, fish, and meat dishes, most for under $30.

For light fare and quick snacks try the hotel's beachside **Hau Tree Cafe,** serving lunch and cocktails 11:30 a.m.-3:30 p.m.; or try **The 19th Hole,** adjoining the pro shop, where you can snack on everything from burgers to sushi daily 11 a.m.-4:30 p.m. The Mauna Kea is also famous for its 6 p.m. Saturday-evening **clambake** at the Hau Tree Cafe, where you can feast on Maine lobster, garlic shrimp, and sumptuous steamed clams while the sun sets to the melodious strains of musician extraordinaire George Kahumoku and Friends. Tuesday is extra special, featuring the Mauna Kea's world-famous **Old Hawaiian Aha'aina Luau.** As the sun sends blazing shafts of red and gold over the Luau Gardens at North Pointe, you dine on island favorites like *laulau, hulihuli* pork, Korean short ribs, island-grown steaks, and snow crab claws. The evening entertainment includes a torch lighting ceremony, traditional hula presented by *kumu hula* Nani Lim, and the dramatic Samoan fire dance.

Hapuna Beach Prince Hotel

Opened in 1994, the low-slung Hapuna Beach Prince Hotel fronts Hapuna Beach about one mile down the coast from the Mauna Kea Hotel. These two hotels, owned and operated by the Westin Hotel chain, are separate entities but function as one resort, joined as if in marriage. The princess, Mauna Kea, has finally found her prince. Long and lean, this hotel steps down the hillside toward the beach in eight levels. A formal portico fronts the main entryway through which you have a splendid view of palm trees and the ocean. This entryway is simple in design yet welcoming in spirit. Chinese flagstone, stained reddish by iron oxide, paves the main entry floor. Walls are the color of sand, and the wood throughout is light brown or dark teak. Lines are simple and decoration subtle. An attempt has been made to simplify and let surrounding nature become part of the whole. As at the Mauna Kea, visitors are not overwhelmed by sensory overload. A shuttle connects the Hapuna Beach Hotel to the Mauna Kea and all services available at one are open to guests of the other.

Carpeted bedrooms are spacious, allowing for king-size beds, and the bathrooms have marble floors. Each well-appointed room has an entertainment center, comfy chairs, live plants, prints on the walls, and a lanai with table, chaise lounge, and rack to dry clothes. Although each room is air conditioned, they all have louvered doors, allowing you to keep out the sun while letting breezes flow through. Rates for the 350 guest rooms start at $325 and go up to $460 a night; suites run $900-6,000. For information and reservations, contact the hotel at 62-100 Kaunaoa Dr., Kohala Coast, HI 96743, tel. (808) 880-1111 or (800) 882-6060, website: www.hapunabeachprincehotel.com.

Of the hotel's four restaurants, the **Coast Grill** is its signature establishment. It specializes in fresh seafood and meat dishes and is only open for dinner; reservations are recommended. Starters, like Manila clam and Waimea corn chowder or smoked duck *lumpia*, generally run $6-12. Move on to snapper wrapped in ti leaves, tenderloin of beef and marinated jumbo shrimp, smoked baby back ribs, or any other entree for $23-35. **Ocean Terrace** serves breakfast and dinner in a casual, open-air setting. Breakfast is either the buffet or from the menu; most dinner entrees, either from the sea or from the range, are grilled. The **Hakone** serves not only a Japanese buffet—an unusual treat and perfect opportunity to sample a variety of Japanese foods at one sitting—but offers individual entrées and items from its sushi bar. Resort evening attire is required. Located in the clubhouse, **Arnie's** serves standard American and health-conscious food and caters mainly to the golfers. In addition, you can get drinks, lunch items, and afternoon snacks at the **Beach Bar** down by the pool. The resort's executive chef, Corey Waite, and his staff do a superb job in the preparation and presentation of each meal and pride themselves on the Hawaiian regional cuisine that they serve. All restaurants except Hakone have children's menus.

The **Westin Kids Club** ($20 half day, $40 full day) offers a reprieve to parents who desire some time away from their energetic kids. The kids' time is filled not only with fun activities but with educational projects. Staffed by accredited nannies, the kids' club accepts children 5-12 years old. A baby-sitting service is also available for infants.

The **Hapuna Golf Course** clubhouse on the premises has Arnie's restaurant and the hotel's physical fitness center. While the fitness center has weights, its main focus is on dance, yoga, stretching, and alignment techniques. Various massage therapies are available. The staff is certified and fully licensed. Massages are $80 an hour and $40 a half hour. Open to the public, the fitness center costs $15 a day, $20 a week, or $50 a month.

Kenai Helicopters has a heliport on the hotel grounds, so if Madame Pele decides to blow her stack again you can be the first in line to go up and see the spectacle. **Mauna Kea Stable,** the resort's private stables located up the hill in Waimea, offers various rides and is the only stable allowed to ride on the huge Parker Ranch. Guests are given priority for rides but nonguests can also make use of the services.

OTHER ACCOMMODATIONS

Puako Beach Condos
Puako village has the only reasonably priced accommodations in this diamond-studded neck of the woods. The units go for $100 a night; three-night minimum. All units have a kitchen, laundry facilities, lanai, and charged maid service. There are ample parking, TV, and a swimming pool. Write Puako Beach Condos, 3 Puako Beach Dr., Kamuela, HI 96743, tel. (808) 882-7711 or tel./fax (808) 965-9446. Expensive.

Waikoloa Villas
Up the hill in Waikoloa Village you'll find Waikoloa Villas, P.O. Box 385134, Waikoloa, HI 96738, tel. (808) 883-9144, or call Marc Resorts (800) 535-0085 for reservations. Rates for these condo units are one bedroom $159-169, two bedrooms $179-189, three bedrooms $229-239; two-night minimum stay. Amenities include swimming pool, nearby golf, and weekly maid service. All units are fully furnished with complete kitchens. The condo offers a money-saving condo/car package. Luxury.

FOOD

Except for a few community-oriented restaurants in Waikoloa Village and a few reasonably priced roadside restaurants in Kawaihae, all of the food in South Kohala is served in the elegant but expensive restaurants of the luxury hotels. These hotels also provide the **entertainment** along the coast, mostly in the form of quiet musical combos and dinner shows. The following is a list of the very limited food options in South Kohala, independent of that offered at the luxury resorts, hotels, and condominiums.

Restaurants at the King's Shops
Hama Yu Japanese Restaurant is open daily 11:30 a.m.-3 p.m. and 5:30-9 p.m. Choose appetizers ($4.50-7) like soft-shell crab, yakitori, and a variety of sashimi and sushi. Dinners ($20-

26) include tempura, Japanese steak, and *ton-katsu*.

For a smaller and more moderately priced meal try **Hawaiian Chili by Max,** a window restaurant where you can have a variety of chilis and hot dogs, all well prepared and health-conscious. A separate area called **The Food Pavilion** will satisfy anyone on the run with everything from a Subway Sandwich to pizza and espresso coffee.

The Grand Palace Chinese Restaurant, open daily 11 a.m.-9:30 p.m., serves appetizers ranging from $6.95 for deep fried chicken wings to $12.95 for a cold platter. Soups are from $7.50 for pork with mustard cabbage all the way up to $43 for shark's fin soup. Chicken and duck dishes range from $7.95 for sweet and sour chicken to $38 for a whole Peking duck. Seafood includes sautéed shrimp with asparagus for $12.95, steamed fresh oysters in the shell with black bean sauce for $14.95, and kung pao squid for $8.95. There are also your standard beef, pork, and vegetable dishes like egg fu yung for $5.95 or spinach with garlic sauce for $6.95. Specialties are clay pot dishes such as stewed beef brisket for $9.95 and the "house special" fried rice for $8.95.

The **Big Island Steakhouse,** featuring the Merry Wahine Bar, is open daily from 5 p.m., serving items like a *pu pu* platter with baby back ribs $8.95, sashimi at market price, and a variety of salads from simple onion and tomato $4.95, to aloha salads with fish, chicken, or beef $10.95-13.95. Entrees ($15-20) are prime rib, Thai pasta with stir-fry vegetables, and coconut prawns.

Golf Cart Vendor

You can actually buy a well-made sandwich, hot dog with all the trimmings, and a variety of soft drinks and beer from the strategically placed and gaily canopied Golf Cart Vendor at the Mauna Lani Resort Golf Course. Follow Kaniku Drive toward the hotel and look for the access road pointing to Holoholokai Beach Park. Follow it, and in about 100 yards just where the golf cart track crosses the road, look to the right for the cart. This makes a perfect stop if you're heading to the Puako Petroglyphs or to the beach park. The sandwiches, fairly hearty, are under $4, the hot dogs $2.50, and the beer, soda and snacks are priced amazingly right for this exclusive neck of the woods!

Blue Dolphin

In Kawaihae Village along Rt. 270 is the Blue Dolphin, run by husband-and-wife team Randy and Leona Roberts, tel. (808) 882-7771, open for lunch Mon.-Fri. 10:30 a.m.-2 p.m., for dinner Mon.-Sat. 5-9 p.m. Their menu features the house shrimp salad for $7.50, a variety of burgers ranging $5-8.50, and sandwiches like turkey with Swiss cheese for $4.95. They also serve plate lunches ($7-8) such as teriyaki beef or chicken and chicken luau. Dinner ($10-15) begins with the soup of the day for $1.95 a cup and appetizers like sautéed mushrooms for $5.95 and fresh ceviche for $3.95. Hawaiian entrées include *kalua* pork and mixed Hawaiian plate, with specialties like sautéed prawns and scallops, barbecued ribs, and a vegetarian mixed plate. If you're heading north and want to picnic along the way, the Blue Dolphin will be happy to pack things to go.

The Blue Dolphin Restaurant keeps the beat cool with jazz Friday nights from 7 p.m. and the first Tuesday of the month, when a local group, *Almost A Capella,* comes to perform its ensemble of oldies.

Cafe Pesto

Who'd expect a yuppie upscale restaurant in the sleepy village of Kawaihae? Cafe Pesto, tel. (808) 882-1071, open Sun.-Thurs. 11 a.m.-9 p.m., Fri.-Sat. 11 a.m.-10 p.m., has a chic interior design with black-and-white checkerboard flooring and black tables trimmed with wood, similar to its sister cafe in Hilo. The bold gourmet menu tantalizes you with starters like *crostini* (French bread with a fresh, creamy herb garlic butter) for $2.95 and freshly made soups from $3.25. Daily specials might be wild green salad ($3.50), bleu Caesar salad ($3.95), or Greek pasta salad ($6.95). Pasta dishes are scrumptious: smoked-salmon pasta with spinach, capers, and sun-dried tomatoes; and fettuccine in saffron cream sauce for $12.95. Lunch, served 11 a.m.-4 p.m., brings an assortment of hot sandwiches that includes everything from smoked ham to a chicken pita for under $8. Cafe Pesto also serves gourmet pizza with crust and sauces made fresh daily. Among their best pizzas are shiitake mushrooms and artichokes with rosemary and Gorgonzola sauce, seafood pesto pizza, and pizza luau, all ranging in price from $5.95 for a small to $16.95 for a large. Dinner entrees are wild, with North Kohala fresh catch which can be grilled, seared, or sautéed for $19-21.95, and seafood risotto sumptuous with morsels of Keahole lobster, tiger prawns, jumbo scallops, and Pahoa corn all seared with sweet chili for $18.95. Cafe Pesto is *the* perfect place to stop for a civilized meal as you explore the Kohala coast.

Kawaihae Harbor Grill

This restaurant in Kawaihae serves lunch daily 11:30 a.m.-2:30 p.m., and dinner 5:30-9:30 p.m. Climb the steps to the large veranda from where you have a bird's-eye view of Kawaihae and unfortunately an unobstructed view of the petrochemical tanks across the road. The lunch menu ($7-11) offers calamari, seared island *poki,* a steak sandwich, and chicken and chips. Light dining ($4-7.25) consists of a veggie *pu pu* platter, the house salad, and a chicken sandwich. In the evening, dinners include harbor grill *lau lau,* which is fresh catch, scallops, and crab steamed in ti leaves ($18.95), steak and seafood combo ($20.95), grilled chicken (half $9.95, whole $16.95), and charbroiled rib eye steak ($18.95). Inside, the one-time village store is quite tasteful, with *lau hala mats,* mood lamps, and a glass partition that has been etched with an octopus and tropical fish. Although not quite elegant, the Kawaihae Harbor Grill is tasteful and presented with pride.

Tres Hombres Beach Grill

Pancho Villa in aloha shirt and sombrero and riding a surfboard (!) would be instantly at home in Tres Hombres, tel. (808) 882-1031, located in the Kawaihae Center, open 11:30 a.m.-midnight, dinners to 9 p.m. on weekdays and to 10 p.m. weekends. Besides being a south-of-the-border restaurant run by *hombre* Rafael Cifuentes, Tres Hombres is an unofficial surfing museum filled with a fine collection of surfboards and surfing memorabilia donated by such legendary greats as Dewey Weber, Greg Knoll, and Jack Wise. Some of the tables are fashioned from wooden surfboards made of balsa wood with mahogany striping, others from green-and-white Mexican tiles. Bar stools are of provincial Mexican design topped with leather. The bamboo-appointed interior has a relaxed tropical effect. The extensive menu offers savories ($6-9) such as nachos, nachitos, calamari, and chimichangas. Substantial meals ($10-18) include Island Salad with boneless breast of chicken over greens with avocado and fresh papaya; tostada grande with beef, chicken, shrimp, or vegetarian black bean; and beef, chicken, or bean and cheese burritos. The beach grill also offers fish, filet mignon, crab enchiladas, and combination dinners made up from a choice of enchiladas, tacos, tostadas, and chiles rellenos. For dessert, try their deep-fried ice cream for $5.95. The full bar serves not only all the island favorites, but adds special concoctions like K-38s, Swamis, mango margaritas, Kawaihae Sunsets that will help you go down for the evening, and Mauna Kea Sunrises that, with a great deal of wishful thinking, will pop you back up. *Pu pu* are served 3-6 p.m. daily. Relax with an ice-cold margarita on the lanai of this tastefully casual restaurant, and experience an excellent change of pace from the luxury hotels just down the road.

Roussels Waikoloa Village

A few years ago, the well-respected Roussels Restaurant in Hilo closed its doors and some time later opened again in Waikoloa, to everyone's delight. Roussels, tel. (808) 883-9644, is open seven days a week; lunch 11 a.m.-2 p.m., appetizers 2-9:30 p.m., and dinner Tues.-Sat. only 5-9:30 p.m. Reservations recommended. For those wanting to stay along the coast, Roussels is a bit out of the way, but for those willing to venture inland, the restaurant lies like a pot of gold at the end of the rainbow. In Waikoloa Village, turn onto Malia St. and follow it to the golf course clubhouse where the old Roussels sign will direct you to the new restaurant.

Still in partnership with head chef Spencer Oliver, Roussels' niche is spicy Cajun food. It's the only restaurant on the island whose main emphasis is food from New Orleans and the Creole South. The shrimp and oyster gumbo at $4.95 a cup is outstanding, as is the shrimp Creole for $16.25. Whet your appetite with escargot in a garlic and tomato sauce ($6.75), blackened sashimi at market price, or crab and shrimp cocktail ($8.25). Delightful salads are Waimea greens *beaucoup* (local greens with crumbled blue cheese and a shallot vinaigrette), tempting avocado and seafood salad with a remoulade mayonnaise dressing for $12.85 as an entree, or a Creole Caesar salad for $3.95. Move on to the

Cajun entrees of chicken Pontalba (sautéed boneless chicken breast with béarnaise sauce) for $14.95, duck in orange sauce ($18.75), or prime rib seasoned and flash-cooked ($19.75). Seafood entrees include fresh local catch with your choice of preparation at market price, soft shell crab meunière also at market price, or prawns scampi for $21.95. All entrees are served with salad, vegetables, and fresh-baked bread. Complement the meal with a choice wine, choose from an assortment of cakes, pies, and mousses baked daily, and end with a wonderful liqueur. While the dinner menu hasn't changed much, lunches are now a bit faster and geared toward the local golf clientele. Salads, hamburgers, po'boy and other sandwiches, soups, gumbo, fish, chicken, and pasta are on the menu. This is upscale Cajun cooking in an upcountry island setting.

SHOPPING AND ACTIVITIES

The King's Shops
The Waikoloa Beach Resort community has its own small but adequate shopping center, The King's Shops, open daily 9:30 a.m.-9:30 p.m., which features more than 35 different shops and restaurants, along with entertainment, special events, and a **tourist information center.** A number of the shops feature Hawaiian artifacts, with museum-quality exhibits displayed here and there, and even some petroglyphs that offer a link to the mythology of ancient Hawaii. The shops include: **Benetton** and **Crazy Shirts** for distinctive tops, shirts, and tees; **Zac's** for your photo and copy needs; **Liberty House** for department-store merchandise; **Whaler's General Store** for light groceries and sundries; and **Noa Noa** for an excellent selection of imported fashions from throughout Southeast Asia, especially Indonesia. Fabrics range from rayon to silk; the batik prints were individually designed. Excellent prices. **Endangered Species** welcomes you with a python overhead. Most items, from T-shirts to sculptures, have an animal or floral motif. A portion of the proceeds from all sales goes to the World Wildlife Foundation. **Kunahs** mainly offers casual tropical wear for men, such as shorts, T-shirts, hats, aloha shirts, and classic aloha shirts for $40-78. **Dolphin Galleries Artwork** sails the high seas with marine art, lures the ladies with fine jewelry, and even offers a few distinctive 3D sculptures. **Island Shells** is hung with dolphins, fish, shellwork, and jewelry; **Pacific Rim Collections** is where you will find Hawaiian quilts, masks from throughout the South Pacific, and carved whales and dolphins; **Malia** offers fine women's wear; and **Under the Koa Tree** showcases Hawaiian artists who have turned their hands to koa woodwork and fine jewelry.

Free **entertainment** is offered at the King's Shops every Tuesday 6-8 p.m. when a local *hula halau* comes to perform, and Thursday 6-8 p.m. when local musicians come to perform contemporary Hawaiian music. The Outrigger Waikoloa Beach Hotel offers *pu pu* and refreshments at the event for a nominal charge. The evening is popular with both tourists and local people, and is an excellent chance to have fun Hawaiian style.

Organized tours of nearby **petroglyphs** start at 8:30 a.m. daily from in front of the food pavilion. Wear comfortable clothing and bring water for this hour to hour-and-a-half walk.

Kawaihae Center
The Kawaihae Shopping Center can take care of your rudimentary shopping needs. It sits at the Y-junction of Routes 19 and 270 and is situated so that the upper floors face Rt. 19 and the lower floors are along Rt. 270. There's a **7-Eleven** convenience store, the **Cactus Tree** for alohawear, and **Tropical Dreams** for homemade ice creams and sorbets. You'll also find the **Upstairs Gallery** featuring porcelain, paintings, and prints by Pegge Hopper. For a mid-day pick-me-up caffeine blast try the **Kawaihae Bad Ass Coffee Shack.** Restaurants are on both levels.

Across the road are a **76 gas station** and **Laau's Fish Market,** open Mon.-Sat. 6 a.m.-6 p.m., offering fresh fish from local waters.

An excellent art shop is **Kohala Collections,** tel. (808) 882-1510, open daily 11:30 a.m.-8:30 p.m. and on Tuesday in the evenings only 6-8:30 p.m. It displays mostly Big Island artists. The gallery's features include works by Jurgen Wilms, who does Big Island landscapes in oils; distinctive bamboo lamps by Cal Hashimoto; fine carvings of sea turtles done in milo wood by Greg Pontius; Hawaiian theme paintings in pastel by Jeremiah Cordero; folding screens by

Kalalani; koa frames by Tai Lake; distinctive furniture by master craftsman Don Wilkinson; oil paintings by Avi Kiriaty; fused glass by Patricia Van Aspern-Hume; bronze sculpture by Deborah Fellows; and the fine pottery of Matt Lovein. Less expensive items include petroglyph coasters, koa bookmarks, wooden turtles, and island jewelry. Kohala Collections is an excellent gallery featuring some of the very best artists on the Big Island today.

Kohala Divers

Located along Rt. 270 in Kawaihae, open daily 8 a.m.-5 p.m., tel. (808) 882-7774, Kohala Divers offers scuba certification for $350, snorkel rentals for $10 (24 hours), and scuba rentals for $22. They lead two-tank dives for $75, and will take snorkelers along if they have room on the boat ($25). Kohala Divers is also a retail shop where you can buy boogie boards, fins, masks, snorkels, and scuba equipment. If you are a scuba enthusiast, you can come here to get your tanks refilled for $4, or overhaul your diving gear for $35 plus parts. It's a bit far to go from Kailua-Kona, but they offer big savings, and they're the only dive company along the Kohala coast.

GETTING THERE

From Hilo

If you're approaching Kohala from Hilo or the east side of the island, you can take one of two routes. The Saddle Road (Rt. 200) comes directly west from Hilo and passes Mauna Kea and the Observatory Road. This very scenic road has the alluring distinction of being the least favorite route of the car-rental agencies. The Saddle Road intersects Rt. 190, where you can turn north for six miles to Waimea or south for 32 miles to Kailua-Kona. Route 19, the main artery connecting Hilo with the west coast, changes its "locally known" name quite often, but it's always posted as Rt. 19. Directly north from Hilo as it hugs the Hamakua Coast, it's called the Hawaii Belt Road. When it turns west in Honokaa, heading for Waimea, it's called the Mamalahoa Highway. From Waimea directly west to Waikui on the coast Rt. 19 becomes Kawaihae Road, and when it turns due south along the coast heading

for Kailua-Kona its moniker changes again to Queen Kaahumanu Highway.

From Kailua-Kona

As you begin heading north from Kailua-Kona on coastal Rt. 19 (Queen Kaahumanu Hwy.), you leave civilization behind. There won't be a house or any structures at all, and you'll understand why they call it the "Big Island." Perhaps to soften the shock of what's ahead, magnificent bushes loaded with pink and purple flowers line the roadway for a while. Notice too that friends and lovers have gathered and placed white coral rocks on the black lava, forming pleasant graffiti messages such as "Aloha Mary" and "Love Kevin."

Suddenly you're in the midst of enormous flows of old a'a and pahoehoe as you pass through a huge and desolate lava desert. At first it appears ugly and uninviting, but the subtle beauty begins to grow. On clear days you can see Maui floating on the horizon, and *mauka* looms the formidable presence of Mauna Kea streaked by sunlight filtering through its crown of clouds. Along the roadside, wisps of grass have broken through the lava. Their color, a shade of pinkish gold, is quite extraordinary, and made more striking juxtaposed against the inky-black lava. Caught by your headlights at night, or especially in the magical light of dusk, the grass wisps come alive, giving the illusion of wild-haired gnomes rising from the earth. In actuality, it's fountain grass imported from Africa.

Around mile marker 70, the land softens and changes. The lava is older, carpeted in rich green grass appearing as rolling hills of pastureland. No cows are in evidence, but be aware of "Kona nightingales," wild jackasses that roam throughout this area and can be road hazards. Also, these long, flat stretches of road can give you "lead foot." Be careful! The police patrol this strip heavily, using unmarked cars (high-performance Trans Ams and the like are favorites) and looking for unsuspecting tourists who have been "road hypnotized." From Kailua-Kona to the Outrigger Waikoloa Beach Hotel at Anaehoomalu is about 30 miles, with another 10 miles to the Mauna Kea Beach Hotel near Kawaihae. If you're day-tripping to the beaches, expect to spend an hour each way.

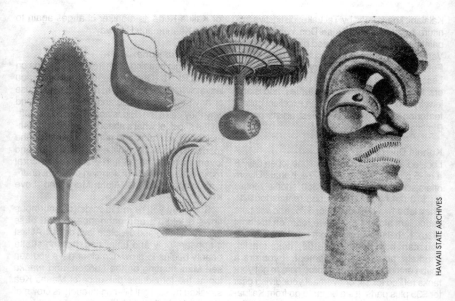

HAWAII STATE ARCHIVES

WAIMEA (KAMUELA)

Waimea is in the South Kohala District, but because of its inland topography of high mountain pasture, mostly covering Mauna Kea's western slopes, Waimea can be considered a district in its own right. It also has a unique culture inspired by the range-riding *paniolo* of the expansive **Parker Ranch.** This spread, founded early last century by John Palmer Parker, dominates the heart and soul of the region. Waimea revolves around ranch life and livestock. Herds of rodeos and "Wild West shows" are scheduled throughout the year. But a visit here isn't one-dimensional. In town are homey accommodations and inspired country dining. For fun and relaxation there's a visitor and ranch center; Puuopelu, the Parker mansion and art collection; a wonderful museum operated by John Parker's great-great granddaughter and her husband; a litany of historic shrines and churches; and an abundance of fresh-air and wide-open spaces, the latter not so easily found in the islands.

The town, elevation 2,670 feet, is split almost directly down the center—the east side is the wet side, and the west is the dry side. Houses on the east side are easy to find and reasonable to rent; houses on the dry side are expensive and usually unavailable. You can literally walk from verdant green fields and tall trees to dry desert in a matter of minutes. This imaginary line also demarcates the local social order: upper-class ranch managers (dry), and working-class *paniolo* (wet). However, the air of Waimea, refreshed and cooled by fine mists *(kipuupuu),* combines with only 20 inches of rainfall a year into the best mountain weather in Hawaii. Waimea is equally known as Kamuela, the Hawaiianized version of Samuel, after one of John Parker's grandsons. Kamuela is used as the post office address, so as not to confuse Waimea with a town of the same name on the island of Kauai. The village is experiencing a growth spurt. In 1980 it had no traffic lights and was home to about 2,000 people. Now the population has grown fivefold and there are traffic jams. Waimea is modernizing, and its cowboy backwoods character is rapidly changing.

HISTORY

John Palmer Parker was a seaman who left Newton, Massachusetts, on a trading vessel in 1809 and landed in Kealakekua, becoming a fast friend of Kamehameha the Great. Parker, then only 19, continued his voyages, returning in 1814. The Parker dynasty began when he jumped ship and married Kipikani, the granddaughter of King Kamehameha. Domesticated cattle, a present from Captain Vancouver to Kamehameha, had gone wild due to neglect and were becoming a dangerous nuisance all over the Big Island. Parker was hired to round up the best of them and to exterminate the rest. While doing so, he chose the finest head for his own herd. In 1847 King Kamehameha III divided the land by what was known as the Great *Mahele*, and John Parker was granted Royal Deed No. 7, for a two-acre parcel on the northeast slopes of Mauna Kea. His wife, being royal born, was entitled to 640 acres, and with these lands and tough determination, the mighty 225,000-acre Parker Ranch began.

Unfortunately, many members of the Parker family died young. The first-born, John Palmer Parker II, married Hanai. His brother, Ebenezer, married Kilea, a woman from Maui, who bore him four children. One of their boys was Samuel Parker, known in Hawaiian as Kamuela, the co-name of Waimea. Samuel married Napela, and together they had nine children. Samuel's father Ebenezer died at age 26 after swallowing the bone of a flubber (a bird the size of a pigeon) that punctured his intestine. Kilea could never get over his death and visited his grave daily.

Finally, she decided that she wanted to return to her family on Maui. She was advised by the people of the island not to go because of rough seas. Kilea did not heed the advice, and along with her entourage was lost at sea.

Meanwhile, John Palmer Parker II and Hanai gave birth to only one boy who died within 12 months. Childless, they adopted one of their nephew Samuel's nine children as a *hanai* child, in a practice that continues to this day. He was the fifth child, John, who became John Palmer Parker III and who later married Elizabeth Dowsick, known as Aunt Tootsie. They had on girl, Thelma Parker, before John III died of pneumonia at age 19. Aunt Tootsie raised Thelma as a single parent, and somehow managed to purchase Samuel Parker's and his eight children's half of the ranch. Thelma Parker married Gillian Smart. They had one boy, Mr. Richard Smart, before his mother Thelma died at age 20 of tuberculosis. Aunt Tootsie literally took the bull by the horns to keep the ranch going, and when she passed away in 1943, she left everything to her grandson Richard. The ranch prospered under his ownership and spread to its present 225,000 acres, the largest privately owned ranch in the U.S. with 1,000 horses and 50,000 head of cattle that supply fully one-third of the beef in the Hawaiian Islands. After his death, the ranch, although still producing cattle, has become a charitable trust called **The Parker Ranch Charitable Foundations** that benefits the people of Waimea and local communities long associated with its operation. The Parker Ranch is the second largest private landowner in the state, following the Bishop Estate.

SIGHTS

PARKER RANCH HISTORIC HOMES

Richard Smart, last heir to the fantastic Parker Ranch, opened **Puuopelu,** a century-old family mansion, to the public just a few years before he passed away on November 12, 1992. Inside this living museum, the works of prominent artists are displayed, but since his death, the artworks are being sold off and the collection is rapidly diminishing. On the grounds, original and re-

constructed Parker Ranch homes are also open to visitors. Puuopelu is located along Rt. 190 a few minutes southeast of town, tel. (808) 885-7655, and is open daily 10 a.m.-5 p.m., admission $7.50 adults, $5 children.

A formal drive lined with stately eucalyptus leads to the mansion. Enter an elegant sitting room illuminated by a crystal chandelier to begin your tour. The home was begun in 1852 by John Palmer Parker II. In 1910 Richard Smart's grandmother, Aunt Tootsie, added the living room,

WAIMEA

To Hilo

To Hawi

To Kawaihae and Hale Kea

To Kona

BELT RD.

19

MANA RD.

KUHIO HALE
HAWAIIAN HOMES
HALL

POLICE

FIRE
STATION

KUHIO VILLAGE

HAWAII KOHALA AIRPORT

IMIOLA
CHURCH

MEDICAL CENTER
STATE OFFICES

PARKER SCHOOL

WAIMEA
CENTER

POST OFFICE

NEW
KAHILU
THEATER

PARKER
RANCH
MALL

PARKER
RANCH
VISITOR
CENTER

TOWN
HALL

PARKER
RANCH
STABLES

KAMUELA
INN

WAIMEA
COUNTRY
LODGE

LIBRARY

GYM

KAMUELA OFFICE
CENTER

WAIMEA
SCHOOL

PARKER SQUARE
MALL

OPELO PLAZA

WAIMEA VISITOR
CENTER

PANIOLO PARK

RACE TRACK

MAMALAHOA

190

PARKER RANCH
HISTORIC HOMES

HAWAII PREP
ACADEMY

WALAKA BRIDGE

POWER
PLANT

DUMP

KAMUELA MUSEUM

250

19

Waimea Park

KAMAMALAHOA HWY.

LINDSEY RD.

KAWAILANI RD.

HOKUULA RD.

OPELU RD.

LAELAE RD.

Kohakohau Str.

Kawaihae Gulch

Haleaha

Waikoloa

Keanuiomano Str.

0   0.5 mi
0   0.5 km

© J.D. BISIGNANI AND MOON PUBLICATIONS, INC.

Ranch life still dominates Waimea.

kitchen, and fireplace. In 1969 Richard Smart, who inherited the ranch lands and home from Aunt Tootsie, gutted the home and raised the ceiling to 19 feet to accommodate his art collection. He added elegant French doors and skylights. Part of the kitchen was converted into a dining room, the Gold Room was created, and the koa doorways were raised to match. Richard Smart became a well-known actor. He studied at the Pasadena Playhouse in the late '20s, and appeared on Broadway with such famous names as Carol Channing and Nannette Fabray. Mr. Smart performed in plays all over the U.S., and recordings of him singing songs in Italian, French, and Spanish provide the background music as you tour the art collection. You've heard of actors becoming ranchers; well, he was a rancher who became an actor. Recently opened is Richard Smart's bedroom, which is loaded with memorabilia from his stage performances, and with mementos given by the people who he knew on Broadway. The tour is self guided with all art pieces named. Besides works of famous artists, there are magnificent pieces like a tall wooden cabinet with carved yellow Chinese Peiping glass from the 19th century, silver tea sets, decanters for pouring wine at elegant functions, large cut-crystal punch bowls, and magnificent chandeliers hung from the skylights overhead. Make sure to see the little side bedroom, called the Venetian Room, aptly decorated with paintings of gondolas and appointed with treasures from Venice. Lighting the room are two chandeliers,

one pink and the other turquoise. Here, the filigreed art-deco mirrors are also fabulous. The feeling is of genteel elegance, but notice that the walls are rather rough board-and-batten covered with beautiful artwork. You get feeling of class, but it's obvious that you are on a ranch. In the emerald-green kingdom that is the Parker Ranch, Puuopelu is the crowning jewel.

Just outside Puuopelu is the reconstructed **Mana Home** (admission included), the original Parker Ranch homestead. A knowledgeable tour guide, Judy Apo, leads you through and provides historical anecdotes about the Parker family. The home was built in 1847 by family patriarch John Palmer Parker from the durable native koa found at high elevations on the ranch lands. The sons, who were by then married, built two homes, and as children came, added more rooms in the sprawling New England tradition. They also built one large community kitchen, at which the entire family cooked and dined. A replica shows how the home grew over the years, and it is a good indicator of how the Parker fortunes grew along with it. As the children's children got older, they needed a schoolhouse, so they built one at the corner of the original site. It still stands and is maintained by a *paniolo* and his family who live there.

The exterior of the original home, covered by a heavy slate roof, was too brittle to move from its original site 12 miles away, but the interior was removed, numbered, and put back together again like a giant jigsaw puzzle in the reconstructed home. A model in the living room shows you what the original site looked like back in the 1800s. To preserve the rich wood interior of the home, all that's required is to wipe it down once a year with lemon oil. At first the home seems like a small cabin, just what you'd expect from the 1850s, but in actuality it's a two-story home with one bedroom downstairs and three upstairs.

SIGHTS IN TOWN

Parker Ranch Visitor Center and Museum

This is the first place to stop while in town. The visitor center, at the Parker Ranch Shopping Center, is open daily 9 a.m.-5 p.m., tel. (808) 885-7311, adults $5, children $3.75 (joint admission to Puuopelu available). After spending an hour at the center's two museums and taking in the slide presentation, you'll have a good overview of the history of the Parker Ranch and, by extension, Waimea. Exhibits at the John Palmer Parker Museum depict the history and genealogy of the six generations of Parkers who have owned the ranch. At the entrance is a photo of the founder, John Parker.

In the museum, old family photos include one of Rev. Elias Bond, who presided over the Christian marriage of Parker and his Hawaiian wife in 1820. Preserved also are old Bibles, clothing from the era, and an entire koa hut once occupied by woodcutters and range riders. There are fine examples of quilting, stuffed animals, an arsenal of old weapons, and even a vintage printing press. The 15-minute video in the comfortable **Thelma Parker Theater** begins whenever enough people have assembled after going through the museum. The video presents a thorough and professional rendition of the Parker Ranch history, along with sensitive glimpses of ranch life of the still very active *paniolo*.

There isn't much happening around the old town entertainment-wise, but **free hula lessons** are given at the Parker Ranch Visitor Center on Monday afternoons.

Imiola Church

Head east on Rt. 19 to "church row," a cluster of New England-style structures on the left, a few minutes past the Parker Ranch Shopping Center. Most famous among them is Imiola (Seeking Life) Church. It was built in 1855 by the Rev. Lorenzo Lyons, who mastered the Hawaiian language and translated some of the great old Christian hymns into Hawaiian, as well as melodic Hawaiian chants into English. The current minister is a friendly and urbane man, Rev. Bill Hawk, who is assisted by his wife Sandra. Restored in 1976, the yellow clapboard church with white trim would be at home along any New England village green. When you enter, you'll notice an oddity: the pulpit is at the near side and you walk around it to face the rear of the church. The walls and ceilings are of rich brown koa, but the pews, supposedly of the same lustrous wood, have been painted pink! The hymnals contain many of the songs translated by Father Lyons. Outside is a simple monument to Rev. Lyons, along with a number of his children's gravesites. A tour of the church is free, and definitely worth the time.

Kamuela Museum

The Kamuela Museum, largest privately owned museum in Hawaii, is a fantastic labor of love. For the octogenarian owners, founders, and curators, Albert and Harriet Solomon, it's a vocation that began in 1968 and fulfilled a prophecy of Albert's grandmother, who was pure Hawaiian and a renowned *kahuna* from Pololu Valley. When Albert was only eight years old, his grandmother foretold that he would build "a great longhouse near three mountains and that he would become famous, visited by people from all over the world." This prediction struck him so much that he wrote it down and kept it throughout his life. When grown, he married Harriet, the great-great granddaughter of John Palmer Parker, and the two lived in Honolulu for most of their adult lives, where Albert was a policeman. For 50 years the Solomons collected, collected, and collected! Harriet, being a Parker, was given heirlooms by family members, which are also on exhibit. The museum is west of town center on Rt. 19, 50 yards after the junction with Rt. 250 heading toward Hawi. The museum, dedicated to Mary Ann Parker, John Parker's only daughter, is open every day of the year 8 a.m.-5 p.m., tel. (808) 885-4724; admission $5, children under 12, $2. Plan on at least an hour.

As you enter, the screen door bangs like a shot to signal Albert and Harriet that another visitor has arrived. Although the tour is self guided, Mrs. Solomon directs you through the museum, almost like a stern "schoolmarm" who knows what's best for you, but actually she's a sweetheart who has plenty of time for her guests and is willing to "talk story." Inside it's easy to become overwhelmed as you're confronted with everything from sombreros to a stuffed albatross, moose head, and South American lizard. An extensive weapons collection includes Khyber rifles, Japanese machine guns, swords, and knives. If you enjoy Hawaiiana, check out the kahili and konane boards, poi pounders, stone sinkers and hooks, wooden surfboards, and a

very unique "canoe buster." The museum has a few extremely rare stone idols and a good collection of furniture from the Hawaiian nobility, including Prince Kuhio's council table. Antiques of every description include Japanese and Hawaiian feathered fans, carved Chinese furniture, a brass diving helmet, some of the first Hawaiian Bibles, and even buffalo robes used by the pioneers. Everywhere are old photos commemorating the lives of the Parkers down through the years. Before you leave, go into the front room, where the view through a huge picture window perfectly frames a pond and three round-topped mountains in paniolo country.

PRACTICALITIES

ACCOMMODATIONS

As far as staying in Waimea is concerned, you won't be plagued with indecision. Of the two hotels in town, both are basic and clean, with room rates ranging from inexpensive to luxury.

The **Kamuela Inn**, P.O. Box 1994, Kamuela, HI 96743, tel. (808) 885-4243, fax 885-8857, a one-time basic cinder-block motel with 19 units, has been transformed into a bright and airy 31-unit boutique hotel. It is located down a small cul-de-sac off Rt. 19 just before Opelu Road. Office hours are 7 a.m.-8 p.m., but a key and instructions will be left for late arrivals. The owner, Carolyn Cascavilla, takes personal pride in the hotel and offers each guest a complimentary continental breakfast. The small but pleasant grounds are appointed with flowers and manicured trees and you'll find a swing to lull you into relaxation. A new wing features the deluxe "Executive Suite" and a "Penthouse" where Governor John Waihee, among other dignitaries, has found peace and quiet. The new wing is comfortable and tasteful with hardwood floors, queen-size beds, a full kitchen, and a small anteroom that opens onto a private lanai, perfect for a quiet morning breakfast. The Penthouse is upstairs, and breaks into two joinable units that can accommodate up to five guests. The basic motel rooms are small, neat, and tidy with twin beds with wicker headboards, private bathrooms, and color TV, but no a/c (not needed) or phones.

About one third of the units have kitchens. Prices range from $59 for a basic room to $185 for the deluxe suites. Inexpensive.

The **Waimea Country Lodge**, P.O. Box 2559, Kamuela, HI 96743, tel. (808) 885-4100, is located along Lindsey Rd. in "downtown" Waimea, but don't let "downtown" fool you because it's very quiet. The rooms, most with kitchenettes and vaulted ceilings, have full baths, and are well appointed with rich brown carpeting, a pine credenza and writing desk, king-size bed (twins in some rooms) with turned pine lamps at each end, wicker easy chairs, phones, and TVs. The barn-red board-and-batten inn sits off by itself and lives up to being in paniolo country by giving the impression of a gentleman's bunkhouse. Rates are $80 standard, $84 superior (refrigerators), $93 with a kitchenette, $100 deluxe, $10 additional person. Moderate.

FOOD

Inexpensive/Moderate
Maha's, sharing space with Cook's Discovery in the vintage Spencer House at the Waimea Center, tel. (808) 885-0693, open daily except Tuesday 6 a.m.-4:30 p.m., offers island style food made fresh daily. Maha—a name given her by her three sons when they were children—learned to cook for her large Hawaiian family. Maha worked professionally for many years as a pastry chef and then cooked at Knickers at the

Mauna Lani Resort. From her diminutive kitchen comes breakfast of poi pancakes with coconut syrup $3.50, and an assortment of too tempting pastries including homestyle banana bread, papaya coffeecake, croissants, or pan biscuits $2.50, and always-fresh Kona coffee. Lunch can be Waipio Ways, a plate of broiled fresh fish with sliced and steamed Waipio taro and sweet potato on a bed of Kahua greens with ginger vinaigrette dressing for $9, smoked *ahi* with *lilikoi* salsa, or *ahi* marinated in a honey smoked sauce and baked in a flour tortilla with shredded cheese, both at $10.50. Kahala Harvest is a vegetarian delight mounded with vine-ripened tomatoes, Waimea broccoli, mushrooms, cucumbers, bell peppers, sweet onions, spinach, and clover sprouts for $7.50; or try one of the sandwiches, like roasted lamb with chutney on squaw bread. Aloha Ahiahi, a version of afternoon tea served 3-4:30 p.m., brings a sampler of Maha's pastries, including croissants, Cook's Discoveries jams, open faced finger sandwiches, shortbreads, or cobblers (assortment changes) for $12. This is an instance in which you can mix pleasure with pleasure, shopping at Cook's Discoveries and dining at Maha's.

Seek out **Kelei's Kama'aina Kitchen,** in the Holomua Center near the first stoplight, tel. (808) 885-0344, open Wed.-Sat. 10 a.m.-6 p.m., and sometimes on Sunday if they haven't decided to go fishing. This is where the people of Waimea go to get home-cooked food at down-home prices (primarily takeout, but you can eat there). Plate lunches include *kalua* plate with *kalua* pig, *lomi* salmon, and Waipio salad for $6.25; or the Waimea Special, which is *kalua* pig, *lau lau, lomi* salmon, fried fish, and poi for $7. Sandwiches are fresh *ahi* burger for an unbelievable $3.50, shrimp burger ($2.75), or a *kalua* pig sandwich ($3.50). Salads are Chinese chicken salad ($5), or Kelei's original crab sweet potato salad for only $1.25! *Lomi* salmon also sells for $6 per pound, and they make *poki* fresh daily, the variety depending upon the availability of local fish. But, what everyone really comes for is the *kiawe* barbecued chicken, available all day Saturday, and sold the moment it comes off the grill!

Su's Thai Kitchen, long known in Kailua-Kona for its delicious and moderately priced Thai cuisine, has opened a branch restaurant in the Parker Ranch Center, open daily 9 a.m.-9 p.m. American and island style breakfast, $2-6 and served until 11 a.m., can be two eggs over easy, hot oatmeal, cinnamon rolls, three-egg omelettes with a choice of three ingredients, and French toast with cinnamon and powdered sugar. For lunch, $6-7 and served 10 a.m.-3 p.m., Su's offers Japanese specials like a mini-tempura platter and sukiyaki, along with Hunan beef and an assortment of Thai lunch specials priced around $5.95. Dinner starts with an extra-large *pu pu* platter for $10.95, chicken wings ($4.95), shrimp toast ($4.95), and steaming bowls of different Thai soups for $6.95-9.95. Salads are Su's House Salad ($4.95), or *yumyai* shrimp and chicken with bean thread noodle ($9.95). Savory curries, red, yellow, or green, can be made with a with a combination of scallops, crab, fish, and shrimp for $16.95, with most priced around $9.95. A specialty is Volcano fish, flash-fried and then topped with Su's homemade sweet and sour sauce for $16.95. Su's, although very basic in its decor, continues to enjoy a well-deserved reputation for excellent food.

Also in the Parker Ranch Center is **Morelli's Pizza,** tel. (808) 885-6100, open Mon.-Sat. 11 a.m.-8 p.m., and Sunday 11 a.m.-7 p.m. Besides trays of pizza, their oven yields pizza by the slice for only $1.85, garlic bread ($1, with cheese $1.50), and oven baked sandwiches like turkey, pastrami, ham, or veggie for $6. The pizzas range from a small cheese pizza for $5.75 to a three-topping monster tray at $17.50. To round out your meal, you can also order garden and chef salads and homemade soup. A small dining room with picnic tables is provided if you choose to eat at the pizza parlor.

For mid-range fare try **Great Wall Chopsui** at the Waimea Center along the Mamalahoa Hwy. (Rt. 19), tel. (808) 885-7252, open daily except Wednesday 11 a.m.-8:30 p.m., lunch 11 a.m.-3 p.m. Its appealing selection of standard Chinese dishes includes a lunch special of one, two, or three choices for $4.95, $5.95, and $6.95, respectively. Dinner specials are an all-you-can-eat buffet at $6.95, and fresh *manapua* is made daily. For entrees try a variety of beef, chicken, and pork dishes all around $5.50, or lobster with black bean sauce at $12.50, the most expensive item on the menu. Karaoke nightly.

Also in the Waimea Center is **Young's Kalbi,** a Korean restaurant open daily except Monday,

10:30 a.m.-9 p.m., that serves dishes like *kalbi* chicken, shrimp tempura, oyster-sauce chicken, and spicy pork, all priced under $7. The most expensive item is three *kalbi* beef short ribs for $7.50. Young's is very basic but clean, and the food is good.

And for those who insist on taking their nourishment from portion-controlled frozen patties served in Styrofoam boxes, you'll find **McDonald's** clearly marked by its arches along the highway at the entrance to the Waimea Center. Here, too, are **Subway** and **TCBY Yogurt.** Also look for the cafeteria-style **Kamuela Deli,** offering sirloin steak, grilled ham steak, and boneless spicy chicken, all priced around $6.50. They also do breakfast like corned beef hash or hamburger patties with eggs and hash browns, both priced at $4.50. Deli sandwiches, priced $2-3, include teri beef, shrimp burgers, and ham sandwiches. Plate lunches are also available. **Leilani Bakery,** open weekdays 5:30 a.m.-6:30 p.m., Sunday 6 a.m.-6 p.m., tantalizes with fresh-baked rolls and breads, cookies, cakes, pies, and pastries.

Paniolo Country Inn, tel. (808) 885-4377, in the town center, open daily for breakfast 7-11 a.m., lunch 11 a.m.-5 p.m., dinner 5-8:45 p.m., specializes in full breakfasts, flame-broiled steaks, burgers, and plate lunches. Breakfast selections include omelettes with one item $3.75, and the *wikiwiki* breakfast of English muffin, banana bread or wheat toast, coffee, and small fruit juice for $3.25. Lunches can be the $5.95 Rodeo Special (a bun heaped with pepperoni, salami, bell peppers, mushrooms, and onions and smothered with pizza sauce and melted cheese), or the $6.50 Paniolo Country (a sandwich made with layers of spiced ham, turkey breast, bacon, tomato, onion, melted cheese, mayonnaise, and sprouts). Hamburgers range from $5.75 for a regular burger to $6.95 for the deluxe with the works. Soups and salads are $4.25, the *paniolo* taco salad is $6.25, and the tostada grande salad is $6.95. Plate lunches are standards like teriyaki short ribs for $7.25, while a dinner plate could be top sirloin for $12.50. The Paniolo Country Inn even has pizza and a children's menu to keep prices down. The food is wholesome, the atmosphere American standard, and the service prompt and friendly.

Don's Pake Kitchen, about two miles east of town on Rt. 19, open daily 10 a.m.-9 p.m., has a good reputation for food at reasonable prices even though most of their selections are of the steam-table variety. Chef's specials are ginger beef, oyster chicken, and shrimp-sauce pork all priced under $6. Steamed rice sold by the pint is $1.20. Don's also specializes in large pans of food that can feed entire families. Next door is **The Vegetable Stop,** open Monday, Wednesday, Saturday 9 a.m.-5 p.m. Most of the best veggies and fruits, homegrown but not necessarily organic, are gone by noon.

Waimea Coffee Company, in the Parker Square Shopping Mall, is open Mon.-Fri. 7 a.m.-5 p.m., Saturday 8 a.m.-4 p.m. Order coffee both in bulk and by the cup. Lunch is served 11 a.m.-3 p.m.: sandwiches of turkey, ham, or tuna; Caesar salad; quiche; and homemade soups. The pastries come from Kona's French Bakery, one of the very best on the island.

The **Hawaiian Style Café,** in a modest pink and blue building across from Parker Square, open Mon.-Fri. 6 a.m.-1 p.m., Sunday 7 a.m.-11 p.m., closed the last Sunday and Monday of each month, offers local and American standard food at very reasonable prices. Inside the blue painted interior, short diner stools line a counter where the menu offers breakfasts ($3-5) of two eggs with Spam or bacon, a three-egg omelette with a side of pancakes, Hawaiian-style loco moco, and Belgian waffles with whipped butter, strawberries, and maple syrup. Plate lunches (under $7) served with rice and potato or macaroni salad include broiled mahimahi, beef and tripe stew, or a steak plate. Daily specials include Friday's luau plate for $8.95. A little short on Martha Stewart panache but long on pride, the Hawaiian Style Cafe will fill you up while being easy on your wallet.

Perhaps slightly ignominiously located across from the Opelo Plaza along Rt. 19 at Waimea "Express Gas," **Aloha Luigi Restaurant,** open Mon.-Sat. 11 a.m.-8 p.m. and Sunday 1-7 p.m., serves inexpensive pasta, pizza, and salads.

Fine Dining

One of the best benefits of Waimea's coming of age is the number of excellent restaurants that have recently opened. The competition among gourmet-food establishments is stiff, so each one tries to find its culinary niche.

The Edelweiss on Rt. 19 across from the Kamuela Inn, tel. (808) 885-6800, is Waimea's established gourmet restaurant, where chef Hans-Peter Hager, formerly of the super-exclusive Mauna Kea Beach Hotel, serves gourmet food in rustic but elegant surroundings. The Edelweiss is open Tues.-Sat. for lunch 11:30 a.m.-1:30 p.m. and for dinner 5-9 p.m. Inside, heavy posts and beams exude that "country feeling," but fine crystal and pure white tablecloths let you know you're in for some superb dining. The wine cellar is quite extensive, with selections of domestic, French, Italian, and German wines. Affordable lunches include offerings like soup, turkey sandwiches, and chicken salad in papaya for under $8.50. Dinner starts with appetizers ($5-6.50) such as melon with prosciutto, escargot, onion soup, and Caesar salad. Some Edelweiss specialties are sautéed veal, lamb, beef, and bacon with pfefferling ($20.75); roast duck braised with a light orange sauce ($18.50); half spring chicken diablo ($16.50); and of course German favorites like Wiener schnitzel and roast pork and sauerkraut (both $16.50). The cooking is rich and delicious; the proof a loyal clientele who return again and again.

Merriman's, in the Opelo Plaza along Rt. 19, tel. (808) 885-6822, open for lunch weekdays 11:30 a.m.-1:30 p.m., dinner 5:30-9 p.m., has received a great deal of well-deserved praise from travelers and residents alike for its excellent food. The restaurant, resembling a small house from the outside, is stylish with pink and gray tablecloths, multicolored Fiestaware settings, and blue-green cushioned chairs of bent bamboo. Chef Sandra Rivera creates classical European and American haute cuisine from local ingredients like Kohala lamb, Ulupalakua Ranch beef, Waimea lettuce, Puna goat cheese, and vine-ripened tomatoes. The menu changes every few months, but perennial appetizer favorites ($5.95-7.95) are corn and Kahuku shrimp fritters, vine-ripened Lokelani tomatoes with Maui onions, and spinach salad with balsamic vinaigrette dressing. Lunch fare ($5.95-9.95) is coconut grilled chicken with peanut dipping sauce and rice; grilled eggplant with Puna goat cheese, basil, and hot sauce; and grilled shrimp on Asian linguine. Entrees ($15-25) are superb: Oahu

chicken ginger-grilled with Indonesian peanut sauce; seafood sausage, chicken, fish, and shellfish in a saffron sauce; and Thai-style shrimp curry. Vegetarians can graze on linguine with tomato capers and snow peas, or on stir-fried vegetables with spicy curry. Some of the most delicious offerings, however, are the fresh catch at market price, prepared in various gourmet styles including wrapped in nori and sautéed with wasabi, or herb-marinated and grilled with mango-lime sauce, banana, mango, and coconut relish. Merriman's is a Big Island classic. Enjoy!

The **Island Bistro,** along Rt. 19, tel. (808) 885-1222, open daily for lunch, dinner, and cocktails, is owned and operated by Stanley Monsef, an original founder of the highly acclaimed Merriman's, who presents through his talented chef, Michael Neff, wonderful dishes of Hawaiian regional cuisine. Pass through the covered lanai where you can choose to dine alfresco, and enter the intimate off-white and pastel appointed bistro shining with glass-topped tables and alive with the green of plants and the tinkling of a background piano. In the bar area, a rack holds bottles of vintage wines offered on the menu. Here you can order a pre-dinner cocktail or a frothy mug of draft beer from selected microbreweries. Lunch ($6-7) can be bistro sandwiches like herb roasted lamb, big bistro burger, a special half sandwich with small green salad, grilled fish of the day with lemon basil at market price, or grilled chicken breast. Dinner, always served with a special touch such as edible flowers or volcano-shaped rice cones, is excellent with choices like pu pu vegetable summer rolls ($5.75), kalua pork ribs ($6.95), grilled vegetable sauté ($5.50), five onion garlic soup ($3.95), Waimea field greens ($6.95), and Sichuan sesame Caesar salad ($7.50). Entrees are mouth-watering pork tenderloin (small plate $12.95, entrée $19.95), Thai marinated grilled chicken (small plate $10.95, entrée $17.95), fresh catch of the day at market price, nori-sautéed salmon ($14.95 and $22.95); and scampi ($13.95 and $21.95). The Island Bistro, with its combination of fine cuisine, tasteful decor, and the tutelage of a proven restaurateur, can't help becoming a Big Island classic.

SHOPPING

Waimea's accelerated growth can be measured by the shopping centers springing up around town. One new center across from the Parker Ranch Shopping Center has some people concerned as it will surround the Spencer House, a classical home from the ranch period. People were not thrilled when this area was denuded of its stately trees to accommodate the shopping center.

The Parker Ranch Shopping Center

This long-established mall has more than 30 specialty stores selling shoes, apparel, sporting goods, toys, and food. The **Parker Ranch Store** sells boots, cowboy hats, shirts, skirts, and buckles and bows. Many handcrafted items are made on the premises. Open daily. The **Big Island Coffee Company,** open daily 8 a.m.-5 p.m., offers samples of pure Kona coffee that you can then choose to purchase off the rack. Bulk coffee comes in tiny burlap bags holding eight ounces of whole beans, or in a gift pack for $10. Other savories include pineapple cookies, macadamia nuts, and chocolate-covered whole coffee beans that'll keep you zipping right along. Displays hold souvenirs like carved tikis, hula dancers, straw hats for men and women, T-shirts, and sweatshirts, with 90% from the Big Island, or at least from Hawaii. **Keep In Touch** offers distinctive T-shirts and resortwear; **Blue Sky** sells art and distinctive apparel; **Malia Kamuela** has racks of resortwear for women; **Ali'i Creations** shines with glassware and small gift items; and **Collectibles** has women's clothing along with art items like carved ivory and koa, and a display case holding locally made jewelry. **Setay,** a unique fine-jewelry shop, sells china, crystal, silver, and gold; and **Waimea Design Center and Art Gallery** tel. (808) 885-6171, has Asian handicrafts and Hawaiian koa bowls and furniture.

Waimea Center

Well marked along the Mamalahoa Hwy. near McDonald's is Waimea's newest mall. Most stores open weekdays 9 a.m.-5 p.m. and Saturday 10 a.m.-5 p.m. Among its shops you will find a **KTA Superstore** with everything from groceries to pharmaceuticals; **Zac's Photo** for

developing and all photo needs, open Mon.-Fri. 9 a.m.-6 p.m., Saturday 9 a.m.-5 p.m., Sunday 10 a.m.-4 p.m.; **Natural Foods,** open Mon.-Sat. 9:30 a.m.-6 p.m., Sunday 10 a.m.-4 p.m. (well stocked with natural canned and boxed items, bulk foods including grain, flour, and pasta, a good selection of organic vegetables and produce, a cold case holding drinks and cheeses, and an excellent supply of vitamins and minerals); the **Men's Shop,** whose name says it all; **Kamuela Kids** for children's clothing; **Mailboxes Etc.,** open Mon.-Fri. 9 a.m.-6 p.m., Saturday 9 a.m.-3 p.m., for all mailing and packaging needs including fax service; **Rhythm and Reading,** open Mon.-Thurs. and Saturday 9 a.m.-7 p.m., closing an hour later on Friday and an hour earlier on Sunday, selling tapes, CDs, records, videos, and gifts; **Pueo Book Shop,** open Mon.-Sat. 10 a.m.-5 p.m., and sometimes on Sunday 10 a.m.-3 p.m., small, but well stocked with new-age books, bestsellers, and a good selection of Hawaiiana; the **Kamuela Hat Company,** who will cover your dome with Stetson hats, straw hats, and planter's hats for both men and women (*paniolo* oriented, this store is excellent if you're after Western wear); and **Quality Discount Shoes** for men, women, and children. The Waimea Center also has some fast-food eateries and inexpensive restaurants.

The word *kama'aina* was invented with Patti Cook in mind. The proprietor of **Cook's Discoveries,** tel. (808) 885-3633, open daily 10 a.m.-6 p.m., Patti has filled her shop with personally chosen items displaying her impeccable taste and knowledge about all things relating to Hawaii. Cook's Discoveries fills the classic and restored **Spencer House,** the first frame house ever built in Waimea, in 1852. The house was once surrounded by the lush green grasses of *paniolo* country but is now in the middle of the black asphalt of the Waimea Center's parking lot! Everything inside, fashioned by craftspeople from throughout the state, says Hawaii. Shelves hold lustrous koa boxes, bracelets, cribbage boards, and pen sets, all easily transportable. Look for traditional pieces, including a carved ivory pendant (fossilized walrus tusk) representing a human tongue, the "voice of authority," traditionally worn only by the highest *ali'i,* and hung from a necklace of woven black silk (substituting for human hair); this ancient weaving process is known only to a handful of people in the entire state. Other traditional pieces are *lei o mano* (lei of sharks' teeth), a clublike war weapon yielded in battle or when absolute and immediate persuasion was necessary, *kukui* nut lei, distinctive warrior helmets with mushroomlike protuberances atop, poi bowls, and decorated gourds once used for food storage. Contemporary "made in Hawaii" articles include handmade coconut lotion soap, plenty of jewelry, carved tiki walking sticks, and brush and mirror sets. A room in the rear can best be described as the "fashion room." Here, you'll find muumuu; pareus in tropical designs and colors; T-shirts emblazoned with Nenewe, the shark god; exquisite Hawaiian quilts; and also decorator jars of jams, jellies, and sauces made from *lilikoi, ohelo* berries (Pele's favorite), and Waimea's famous strawberries. A nook on the front porch houses **Alice's Lei and Garden Shop,** where you'll find Alice using her nimble fingers to make fresh flower bouquets and lei. Along with her flower arrangements, Alice uses all natural ingredients to blend lotions and potions that include, among others, a gardener's hand cream made with macadamia nut oil, aloe, and Hawaiian beeswax; mosquito bite cream made with chickweed, citronella, and lemon balm; mango lip balm; and pure lavender oil, which is good for sunburn. Two front rooms in the Spencer House are filled with delicious aromas coming from the kitchen (about as big as your car's dashboard) of **Maha's,** where you can enjoy everything from smoked *ahi* to afternoon tea.

The Parker Square Shopping Mall

Located along Rt. 19, heading west from town center, this small mall has a collection of fine boutiques and shops. Here, the **Gallery of Great Things,** tel. (808) 885-7706, open Mon.-Sat. 9:30 a.m.-5:30 p.m., Sunday 10 a.m.-4 p.m., really is loaded with great things. Inside you'll find novelty items like a carousel horse, silk dresses—pricey at $200—straw hats, koa paddles for $700, Nihau shellwork priced $100-25,000, vintage kimonos, an antique water jar from the Chiang Mai area of northern Thailand for $925, Japanese woodblock prints, and less expensive items like shell earrings for $8 and koa hair sticks for $4. The Gallery of Great Things represents about 200 local artists on a revolving basis, and the

owner, Maria Brick, also travels throughout the Pacific collecting art. A recent trip yielded a rare and authentic "Palauan story board" priced at $3,500. With its museum-quality items, the Gallery of Great Things is definitely worth a browse. But remember, all items are one of a kind and "now you see them, now you don't."

Sweet Wind, tel. (808) 885-0562, open Mon.-Fri. 9:30 a.m.-5:30 p.m., Saturday 9 a.m.-4 p.m., Sunday 11 a.m.-4 p.m., owned and operated by Wendy Gilliam, is packed with books, beads, and unique gifts. This "alternative thought and resource center" also sells incense, aromatherapy tinctures, and crystals. The beads come from the world over and a display case holds Native American rattles, drums, and silver and amber jewelry. Visiting Wendy at Sweet Wind is soothing for body and soul.

The **Silk Road Gallery,** tel. (808) 885-7474, open Mon.-Sat. 9:30 a.m.-5:30 p.m., owned and operated by Geoffrey and Helena Orme, is resplendent with Asian antiques, specializing in ancient creations from Japan, China, and Korea. In this tasteful shop you will discover such treasures as carved ivory *netsuke,* a favorite of the well-dressed samurai; ornate silk kimonos; Sung Dynasty vases; and Satsumayaki painted pottery from Japan. As you look around you may spot lacquer tables and bowls, ornate *tansu* (chests), straw sandals, an actual water wheel, sacred scrolls that hang in a place of honor in Japanese homes, a Chinese jade bowl with elaborate dragon handles, and an 18th-century Chinese moghul lotus bowl. Geoffrey and Helena, experts in Asian antiques, make frequent trips to Asia, where they personally hand-pick all the items in their shop—at which the artistic wonders of the ancient Silk Road are still on display.

Other stores in the center include **Bentley's,** with crockery, glassware, books, *lau hala* bags, and ceramics; and **Imagination Toys,** hung with kites, Hawaiian dolls, stuffed gorillas, parrots, and puzzles.

Don't be fooled by the name: the **Waimea General Store** sells mostly sundries with plenty of stationery, children's games, stuffed toys, and books on Hawaiiana. Gadgets include porcelain coffeepots, corn-on-the-cob holders, crochet needles and yarn, garlic crushers, handheld food grinders, mugs, and incidental kitchenware.

The Opelo Plaza

Also along Rt. 19 heading west from town center is one of Waimea's newer shopping malls, the Opelo Plaza. **Waimea Booksellers,** tel. (808) 885-8616, open Tues.-Fri. 11 a.m.-7 p.m., Saturday 10 a.m.-5 p.m., Sunday 10 a.m.-2 p.m., primarily a "used" bookstore owned by Fred Fortin and Anita Gerhard, also stocks new books. The shelves hold mysteries, adventure novels, women's books, gay and lesbian books, travel guides, music, westerns (the largest selection on the Big Island), many books on oceanography and sailing ships, fiction, and fantasy. Choose a tome and enjoy your read while sitting on a comfy wooden bench facing a tiny garden bright with flowers. Waimea Booksellers hosts special events like author readings, publishes a newsletter with reviews of new books, will do special orders, and will also search for out-of-print books free of charge.

Here too are **Mean Cuisine** and **Merriman's,** two of Waimea's best restaurants in their categories.

Food Markets and Sundries

For food shopping at the Parker Ranch Shopping Center there's **Sure Save Supermarket** and **Kamuela Meat Market,** featuring fine cuts of Parker Ranch beef. At the Waimea Center, look for the **KTA Superstore,** with everything from groceries to pharmaceuticals.

A **farmers' market** is held in Waimea every Saturday 7:30 a.m.-noon, when local farmers come to sell their produce, much of which is organic. Look for a dozen or so stalls in the parking lot of the Hawaiian Homelands Building located along Rt. 19 about two miles east of town center heading toward Honokaa. In one of the first stalls is Marie McDonald, a Hawaiian woman (don't let the name fool you) who is an expert at fashioning *haku lei,* a beautiful and intricate form of lei-making with multiple strands of intertwined

DIANA LASICH HARPER

flowers and ferns. Ms. McDonald and her daughter, who often helps at the stand, will take time to "talk story" and to inform you about medicinal herbs and some of the unique produce found at the market.

SERVICES AND INFORMATION

Health

Physicians are available at Lucy Henriques Medical Center, tel. (808) 885-7921. Angela Longo, in the Kamuela Office Center, tel. (808) 885-7886, is a practitioner of acupuncture and a Chinese herbalist. Angela, who graduated from U.C. Berkeley with a Ph.D. in biochemistry, combines principles from both East and West into a holistic approach to health and well-being. Besides attending to her demanding practice, Angela is a devoted single parent and a classical Indian dancer who performs at special functions around the island. She is one of the most amazing health practitioners in the entire state.

Chiropractic care is available from Dr. Ken Williams at the Waimea Chiropractic Clinic, tel. (808) 885-7719. Stillpoint Therapies, tel. (808) 885-7383, in Waimea's Ironwood Bldg., in association with chiropractor J. Michael Beard, is a team made up of Wendy Rundell and John Worcester, who practice the healing arts of hypnotherapy, massage, trigger massage, and craniosacral massage.

Transpersonal psychologist Dr. Dominie Cappadona, Ph.D., tel. (808) 885-8446, specializes in solutions for mid-life crisis and menopause, employing various techniques including dream work, conceptual therapy, shamanistic practices, and psychological analysis.

Information/Services

The post office is located in the Parker Ranch Shopping Center. Mailing address for Waimea is Kamuela, so as not to confuse it with the Waimeas on Oahu and Kauai.

The Waimea visitor center is west of town along Rt. 19, almost directly across from the Opelo Shopping Center. They hand out free maps and brochures of the area and provide public restrooms.

TRANSPORTATION

Waimea is at the crossroads of the main east coast road (Rt. 19) from Hilo and Rt. 190 from Kailua-Kona. Route 19 also continues west, reaching the coast at Kawaihae then running south along the coast to Kailua-Kona.

The main artery connecting Waimea and Kailua-Kona is Rt. 190, also known as the Hawaii Belt Road. This stretch is locally called the Mamalahoa Highway. From Kailua-Kona, head out on Palani Road until it turns into Rt. 190. As you gain elevation heading into the interior, look left to see the broad and flat coastal lava flows. Seven miles before reaching Waimea, Saddle Road (Rt. 200) intersects the road from the right, and now the highlands, with grazing cattle amidst fields of cactus, look much more like Marlboro Country than the land of aloha. The **Waimea-Kohala Airport,** tel. (808) 885-4520, is along Rt. 190 just a mile or so before you enter town. Facilities amount to a basic restroom and waiting area with a few car-rental windows. Unless a flight is scheduled, even these are closed.

DIANA LASICH HARPER

NORTH KOHALA

In North Kohala, jungle trees with crocheted shawls of hanging vines stand in shadowed silence as tiny stores and humble homes abandoned by time melt slowly back into the muted earth. This secluded region changes very little, and very slowly. It also has an eastward list toward the wetter side of the island, so if you're suffering from "Kona shock" and want to see flowers, palms, banana trees, and Hawaiian jungle, head for the north coast. Here the island of Hawaii lives up to its reputation of being not only big, but bold and beautiful as well.

North Kohala was the home of Kamehameha the Great. From this fiefdom he launched his conquest of all the islands. The shores and lands of North Kohala are rife with historical significance, and with beach parks where only a few local people ever go. Here cattle were introduced to the islands in the 1790s by Captain Vancouver, an early explorer and friend of Kamehameha. Among North Kohala's cultural treasures is **Lapakahi State Historical Park,** a must-stop offering "touchable" exhibits that allow you to become actively involved in Hawaii's traditional past. Northward is **Kamehameha's birthplace**—the very spot—and within walking distance is **Mookini Heiau,** one of the oldest in Hawaii and still actively ministered by the current generation of a long line of *kahuna.*

Hawi was a sugar town whose economy turned sour when the sugar company drastically cut back its local operations. Hawi is making a comeback, along with this entire northern shore, which has seen an influx of small, boutiquelike businesses and art shops. In **Kapaau,** a statue of Kamehameha I peering over the chief's ancestral dominions fulfills an old *kahuna* prophecy. On a nearby side road stands historic **Kalahikiola Church,** established in 1855 by Rev. Elias Bond. On the same side road is the old **Bond Homestead,** the most authentic yet virtually unvisited missionary home in all of Hawaii. Financially strapped, but lovingly tended by the remaining members of the Bond family, it's on the National Historical Record. The main coastal road ends at **Pololu Valley Lookout,** where you can overlook one of the premier taro-growing valleys of old Hawaii. A walk down the steep *pali* into this valley is a walk into timelessness, with civilization disappearing like an ebbing tide.

Orientation

In Kawaihae, at the base of the North Kohala peninsula, Rt. 19 turns east and coastal Rt. 270, known as the Akoni Pule Hwy., heads north along the coast. It passes through both of North Kohala's two major towns, Hawi and Kapaau, and ends at the *pali* overlooking Pololu Valley. All the historical sites, beach parks, and towns in the following sections are along this route, listed from south to north.

Route 250, the back road to Hawi, is a delightful country lane that winds through gloriously green grazing lands for almost 20 miles along the leeward side of the Kohala Mountains. It begins in the western outskirts of Waimea and ends in Hawi on the far north coast. One of the most picturesque roads on the island, it's dot-

ted with mood-setting cactus and small "line shacks." Suddenly vistas open to your left, and far below are expansive panoramas of rolling hills tumbling to the sea. At mile marker 8 is **Von Holt Memorial Park,** a scenic overlook perfect for a high mountain picnic. Around mile marker 19, keep your eyes peeled for a herd of llamas on the left. At the coast, Rt. 250 splits. Right takes you to Kapaau, and left to Hawi. If you're coming along the coastal Rt. 270 from Kapaau toward Hawi, look for the H. Naito Store, and make a left there to go back over Rt. 250 to Waimea; you don't have to go all the way to Hawi to catch Rt. 250.

Upolu Airport, tel. (808) 889-9958, is a lonely strip at Upolu Point, the closest spot to Maui. A sign points the way at mile marker 20 along coastal Rt. 270. Here, you'll find only a bench and a public telephone. The strip is serviced only on request by the small propeller planes of charter and commuter airlines.

SIGHTS, BEACHES, AND TOWNS

KAWAIHAE COAST

Lapakahi State Historical Park

This 600-year-old reconstructed Hawaiian fishing village, combined with adjacent **Koai'e Cove Marine Conservation District,** is a standout hunk of coastline 12 miles north of Kawaihae. Gates are open daily except holidays 8 a.m.-4 p.m. for a self-guided tour, but the ranger's knowledgeable anecdotes make a guided tour much more educational.

The small grass shack near some *lau hala* trees at the entrance stocks annotated brochures and yellow water jugs. As you walk counterclockwise around the numbered stations, you pass canoe sheds and a fish shrine dedicated to Ku'ula, to whom the fishermen always dedicated a portion of their catch. A salt-making area demonstrates how the Hawaiians evaporated seawater by moving it into progressively smaller "pans" carved in the rock. There are numerous homesites along the wood-chip trail. Particularly interesting to children are exhibits of games like *konane* (Hawaiian checkers) and *ulimika* (a

form of bowling using stones) that the children are encouraged to try. Throughout the area, all trees, flowers, and shrubs are identified, and as an extra treat, migrating whales come close to shore Dec.-April. Don't leave without finding a shady spot and taking the time to look out to sea. For information write Lapakahi State Historical Park, P.O. Box 100, Kapaau, HI 96755, tel. (808) 889-5566.

Mahukona and Kapaa Beach County Parks

Mahukona Beach County Park is a few minutes north of Lapakahi down a well-marked side road. As you approach, notice a number of abandoned buildings and warehouses; Mahukona was once an important port from which the Kohala Sugar Co. shipped its goods. Still there is a pier with a hoist used by local fishermen to launch their boats. The harbor is filled with industrial debris, which makes for some good underwater exploring, and snorkeling the offshore reef rewards you with an abundance of sealife. Only 150 yards off shore (follow the anchor chain from the landing) in only 20 feet of water lie the remains of a wrecked steamboat, the only wreck in

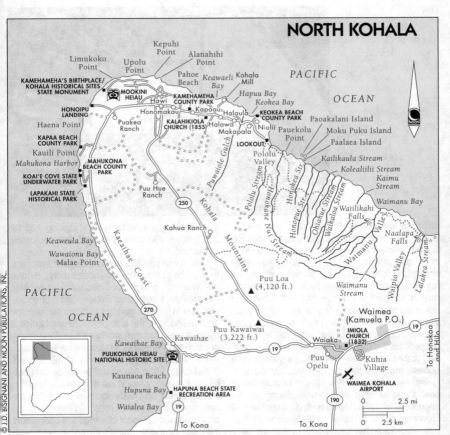

NORTH KOHALA

Hawaii that's accessible from shore. The wooden boat has almost completely deteriorated, but you will find a huge boiler, engine, shaft, and propeller. Swimming off the pier is also good, but all water activities are dangerous during winter months and high surf. Picnic facilities include a large pavilion and tables. There are also cold-water showers and restrooms, and electricity is available in the pavilion. Although numerous signs close to the pavilion say No Camping, both tent and trailer camping are allowed with a county permit near the parking lot.

Kapaa Beach County Park is five minutes farther north. Turn *makai* on a side road and cross a cattle grate as you head toward the sea. This

park is even less visited than Mahukona. The rocky beach makes water entry difficult. It's primarily for day use and fishing, but there are showers, a restroom, and a pavilion. Camping is allowed with a county permit. Neither of these two beaches is spectacular, but they are secluded and accessible. If you're interested in a very quiet spot to contemplate a lovely panorama of Maui in the distance, this is it.

Mookini Heiau and Kamehameha's Birthplace

At mile marker 20, turn down a one-lane road to Upolu Airport. Follow it until it reaches the dead end at the runway. Turn left here on a *very* rough

Mookini Heiau

dirt road to Mookini Heiau. This entire area is one of the most rugged and isolated on the Big Island, with wide, windswept fields; steep sea-cliffs; and pounding surf. Pull off at any likely spot along the road and keep your eyes peeled for signs of cavorting humpback whales that frequent this coast yearly Nov.-May. After bumping down the road for about two miles, look for a tall transmission tower pointing its bony metal finger skyward, which marks the road to the *heiau.* Sometimes the road is closed with a locked gate and you'll have to walk five minutes uphill to gain access, but if the gate is open, you can drive in.

Only *ali'i* came to the *heiau* to purify themselves and worship, sometimes offering human sacrifices. In 1963, Mookini Heiau was the first Hawaiian site to be listed in the National Historical Sites Registry. Legend says that the very first temple at Mookini was built as early as A.D. 480. This incredible date implies that Mookini must have been built immediately upon the arrival of the first Polynesian explorers, who many scholars maintain arrived in large numbers a full two centuries later. More believable oral history relates that the still-standing foundation of the temple was built by the Tahitian high priest Paao, who came with conquering warriors from the south in the 12th century, bringing the powerful mana of the fierce war-god Kukailimoku. The oral tale relates that the stones for the temple were fitted in a single night, passed hand to hand by a human chain of 18,000 warriors for a distance of 14 miles from Pololu Valley. They cre-

ated an irregular rectangle measuring 125 by 250 feet, with 30-foot-high and 15-foot-thick walls all around.

When you visit the *heiau,* pick up a brochure from a box at the entrance (often empty); if none are available, a signboard nearby gives general information. Notice that the leeward stones are covered in lichens, giving them a greenish cast and testifying to the age of the *heiau.* Notice a huge, flat stone near another embedded in the ground with the menacing atmosphere of a sacrificial altar. Nearby is a clone of the famous "Phallic Rock" on Molokai. Please be respectful as you walk around, as this temple is still in use, and stay on the designated paths that are cordoned off by woven rope. To the rear is an altar area where recent offerings are often seen; the floor of the temple is carpeted with well-placed stones and tiny green plants that give a natural mosaic effect. For at least eight and perhaps 15 centuries, members of the Mookini family have been the priests and priestesses of the temple. Today, the inherited title of *kahuna nui* rests with Leimomi Mookini Lum, a nearby resident. The entire *heiau* is surrounded by a wave-like hump, perhaps the remnant of an earlier structure, that resembles a castle moat. Be sure to visit the nearby "little grass shack," one of the best examples of this traditional Hawaiian architecture in the islands. Check how sturdy the walls are, and what excellent protection is provided by the grass-shingled roof. Also, be aware of the integration of its stone platform and how perfectly suited the shack is to provide comfort against the elements in Hawaii. Look through the door at a timeless panorama of the sea and surf.

A minute from the *heiau* along the dirt road, an HVB Warrior points to Kamehameha's birthplace, **Kamehameha Akahi Aina Hanau.** The entrance to the area is at the back side, away from the sea. Inside the low stone wall, which always seems to radiate heat, are some large boulders believed to be the actual "birthing stones" where the high chieftess Kekuiapoiwa, wife of the warrior *ali'i* Keoua Kupuapaikalananinui, gave birth to Kamehameha sometime around 1752. This male child, born as his father prepared a battle fleet to invade Maui, would grow to be the greatest of the Hawaiian chiefs— a brave, powerful, but lonely man, like the flat plateau upon which he drew his first breath. The temple's ritual drums and haunting chants dedicated to Ku were the infant's first lullabies. He would grow to accept Ku as his god, and together they would subjugate all of Hawaii. In this expansive North Kohala area, Kamehameha was confronted with unencumbered vistas and sweeping views of neighboring islands, unlike most Hawaiians, whose outlooks were held in check by the narrow, confining, but secure walls of steep-sided valleys. Only this man with this background could rise to become "The Lonely One," high chief of a unified kingdom.

Together, Mookini Heiau and King Kamehameha's birthplace make up the seven-acre **Kohala Historical Sites State Monument.**

HAWI

As you come into Hawi along Rt. 270, you'll see a line of false-front buildings leaning shoulder-to-shoulder like patient old men knowing that something *will* happen, and it has! One of the buildings is an ancient movie theater that still shows films. Introducing you to the town are Sacred Heart Church and Hawi Jodo Buddhist Mission, two lovely temples of worship and symbols of Hawaii's diversified spirituality. In the middle of town, Rt. 250, crossing the Kohala Mountains from Waimea, intersects the main road.

Hawi was once a bustling sugar town that boasted four movie theaters in its heyday. In the early 1970s, the Kohala Sugar Co. pulled up stakes, leaving the one-industry town high and dry. Still standing is the monumental stack of the sugarworks, a dormant reminder of what once was. The people of Hawi have always had grit, and instead of moving away they toughed it out and have revitalized their town. Spirit, elbow grease, and paint were their chief allies. Hawi has risen from its slumber and is now making a comeback with new restaurants, and shops opening their doors. Here, too, is a handful of local shops selling food and household goods, an information center, a hotel (the only functional one in North Kohala), and some remarkable crafts shops and boutiques.

Accommodation

The 18-room **Kohala Village Inn,** 55-514 Hawi Rd., Hawi, HI 96755, tel. (808) 889-0419, was long known as Luke's Hotel. The hotel has always catered to local working people or island families visiting the area, as well as passing tourists. Located in central Hawi, it has a quiet little courtyard, nearby restaurant, and in-room TVs (extra charge). Rooms are a reasonable $47-95. Clean and adequate, the hotel has a friendly, quiet atmosphere. Inexpensive.

Food

A glowing example of Hawi's modern restoration and revitalization is the **Bamboo Restaurant,** tel. (808) 889-5555, open Tues.-Sat. 11 a.m.-2 p.m. for lunch, 6-9 p.m. for dinner, and Sunday for breakfast from 11:30 until mid-afternoon. Recently opened by Jim and Joan Channon in the N. Takata Store, this venerable old building was built by the Harada Family between 1911-1915, serving as a hotel that housed contract workers brought to North Kohala by buckboard and later relocated to work camps. As the sugar trade took root, merchants came to town, and the hotel began catering to this more upscale clientele. These traveling salesmen were the epitome of the stereotype, and desired evening entertainment. "Ladies of the night" took up residence in a few back rooms, and, with the proximity to the cane fields, might aptly have been known as "sugar babies." The fortunes of the Harada family took a turn for the worse, and the building was bought in 1926 by the Takata family, who converted it to a grocery and dry goods store that served the community until 1991, when they moved, building a new store just down the road. The old building fell into disrepair until Jim and Joan purchased it, opening their restaurant after 16 months of restoration. Touches were added, like the old wicker chairs that once rocked wealthy vacationers into a light slumber at Waikiki's Moana Hotel, but they left the best alone, preserving the original feel of the building. Upon entering, notice the floor, heavily trodden over the decades, every nick marking a memory. The original wavy window glass is intact and still bears the original painted signs reading, "Fruits, Groceries, Cigars, Candy, Meats, and Coca Cola." The restaurant section, to the left, seats you in high-backed chairs with armrests, where you will feel very comfortable for an evening of dining. The tables themselves, although not technically made from bamboo, have bamboo inlaid under Plexiglas, and are bright with flowers. A mural ascends the central stairway; vintage photos hang on the walls and greenery hangs from an indoor awning. In the rear a dory hangs over rough wood tables that rest on the trunks of stout bamboo stalks; other tables are black bent-back bamboo set with floral tablecloths. Lunch can be a homemade soup of the day; or try one of the salads, like the Bamboo Salad, a Kohala tradition, with locally grown organic greens and spicy macadamia nuts and Maui onions at $3.50 and $5.50, or a Caesar classic at $3.25 and $4.95. More substantial dishes ($5-8) are *kalua* pork and cabbage, stir-fried noodles, calamari strips, Hawaiian tostada with vegetarian chili, or Kohala coconut chicken with lemongrass, garlic, ginger, and lime. There is also an assortment of sandwiches and burgers. Dinner begins with *pu pu* such as margarita prawns ($6.95) and *kalua* pork quesadilla ($5.25). From the ocean comes fresh catch at market price, broiled, sautéed, or baked in a sesame and nori crust, with a choice of sauce like Thai coconut or margarita. From the land comes flame-broiled New York steak at market price, or local favorites like teriyaki beef at a reasonable $9.95. Breakfast, offered on Sunday along with Sunday brunch, can be platters like eggs Bamboo—poached egg on toasted English muffin with a slice of smoked ham or vegetables and topped with *lilikoi* hollandaise sauce, $5.95 one egg, $7.95 two; or Mo Mona Palaoa

toast, a sweet bread dipped in special egg batter for $2.95; or two eggs with smoked ham or pork for $5.50. A limited lunch menu always features fresh fish.

You can also get a good, inexpensive meal at **Kohala Village Restaurant,** tel. (808) 889-0105, in the "food wing" of the Kohala Village Inn in downtown Hawi. It's open Monday 11 a.m.-2 p.m., Wed.-Sun. 8 a.m.-2 p.m., closed Tuesday; dinner is served Mon.-Sat. 5:30-9 p.m. Monday is "Family Night" with reduced prices on special menu items. Start the day with homemade buttermilk pancakes ($4.25); two eggs with bacon, ham, Spam, or Portuguese sausage, rice or home fries, coffee, tea, milk, or juice for a reasonable $5.50; a three-egg omelette from the omelette station with choice of ingredients ($5.25); or the breakfast sandwich ($3.95). Lunch brings you appetizers like fried wonton ($3.75), California BLT sandwiches ($5.50), or grilled ham and Swiss ($5.50). There are also salads, like an Oriental chicken salad for $6.50, and more substantial entrées such as red pesto pizza, veggie pasta, or chicken stir-fry, each $6.95. The dinner menu offers appetizers ($4-7) such as chips and salsa, quesadilla, or Cajun crab cakes with chili mayonnais, along with entrees ($10-14) like shrimp pasta, grilled chicken and Italian sausage over pasta, herb roasted chicken, and a chicken and ribs combo. The Kohala Village Restaurant is priced right and family-oriented.

Ohana Pizza & Beer Garden, tel. (808) 889-5888, also in downtown Hawi, features very good pizza for $5.50-10.75 depending upon size and toppings. This clean, friendly restaurant also offers hefty sandwiches for $2.95, and pasta dinners (like homemade lasagna) served with dinner salad and homemade garlic bread for $6. Salads are $1.50, and homemade garlic bread, $1. You can order wine or a chilled domestic beer for $1.75, or an import for $2.50. The staff of local people is friendly and hospitable. This is a great place to pick up a picnic lunch.

Sun, surf, and the trek to Hawi made you a bit droopy? Salvation is at hand at the **Kohala Coffee Mill** in downtown Hawi, open Mon.-Fri. 6:30 a.m.-4 p.m., Saturday 8 a.m.-4 p.m., and Sunday 8-?, according to the sign. Inside the remodeled vintage building, order Kona coffee, espresso, cappuccino, pastry, and soft drinks. Shelves hold T-shirts, herbal teas, fruit jelly and jam, and honey.

Matthew's Place, tel. (808) 889-5500 or 889-0630, open daily (one of the few open all day on Sunday in Hawi), operated by the Cerezo family, offers local food, seafood, and pizza. You can't go wrong at this simple, clean, good, and inexpensive restaurant.

Shopping

K. Takata is a well-stocked grocery store in Hawi, tel. (808) 889-5261. **Kohala Health Food,** in downtown Hawi, tel. (808) 889-0277, is open daily except Sunday 10:30 a.m.-6:30 p.m.; its shelves are filled with herbs, vitamins, minerals, and local organic produce when available. **Pumehana Flowers,** tel. (808) 889-5541, next to Kohala Health Food, is alive with flowers and plants. Inside are small gift items and a cooler holding lei, perfect for brightening the day for that "special person," and perhaps for brightening the evening prospects for you. **Kohala Trade Center,** a basic convenience store in downtown Hawi, is open Mon.-Fri. 10 a.m.-10 p.m., Saturday 11 a.m.-10 p.m., and Sunday 12 a.m.-8 p.m.

Proof that two establishments can occupy the same place at the same time, the **Kohala Koa Gallery,** tel. (808) 889-0055, open Monday 10 a.m.-5 p.m., Tues.-Sat. 10 a.m.-9 p.m., Sunday 10 a.m.-4 p.m., owned and operated by Michael and Robin Felig, is housed in the vintage N. Takata Building along with the Bamboo Restaurant. Living up to its name, the gallery is lustrous with all types of koa artwork: furniture, covered photo albums, jewelry boxes, and sculptures, representing the work of more than 70 island artists. The furniture is mainly by Michael Felig, who creates rocking chairs that beg to be sat in, and fine koa dining room tables, both of which carry price tags of more than $2,000. Works of other well-known artists on display: lazy Susans, cribbage boards, and lovely boxes by John Glasser; creamy white hand thrown crystalline glazed ceramics with flower or fish motifs by Jon and Pam Pacini; and smaller and less expensive items like tapa-covered notebooks, replicas of sailing canoes, a smattering of aloha shirts, hand-painted silkwares from Kalalani Studio, jewelry with an ocean motif, and bright prints.

Look for a brightly painted sign on the left, as you enter Hawi, marking the entrance to **Hawaii Moon** (no relation), tel. (808) 889-0880, open Mon.-Sat. 10 a.m.-5 p.m., Sunday 10 a.m.-4 p.m., owned and operated by Robin Fetig, co-owner of Kohala Koa Gallery, just next door. Small, but packed with arts, crafts, and clothing, the shop displays the artistic woman's touch. Racks hold sundresses, pareus, shoulder bags, aloha shirts, and shorts. Look for a shelf of chubby women dolls, their hair done in silver and red foil, that are as cute as . . . chubby little women dolls! Artists include: Omodt, a husband and wife team that creates very distinctive low-fired pottery pieces, primarily in black and white or blue, that includes paperweights, earrings, and clocks, all with an "island" motif; Himani, who does hand-tinted, original black-and-white photos of Hawaiian dancers; Pacini, another husband and wife ceramic artist team making vases and sculptures with Hawaiian themes; and Steven Hatland (how did he pass the one-name requirement?), a ceramic artist who employs a distinctive blue and blue-green glaze on everything from fruit bowls to water pitchers. Smaller souvenir items include: shell key chains, stuffed fish, leather bracelets, jewelry, and paperweights.

Hale Wood, tel. (808) 889-5075, (800) 664-5075, in Hawi across from the launderette, open Mon.-Fri. 9 a.m.-7 p.m., Saturday 10 a.m.-6 p.m., and Sunday 11 a.m.-5 p.m., is owned and operated by husband-and-wife team Buck and Juli, woodworker and finisher, respectively. They work mostly in koa, fashioning everything from hope chests to coat racks, along with curly koa chop sticks for only $5. Besides their work, you will also find pieces by Jane Haggardt, a Kau artist who fashions palm baskets, adorning them with protea, dried flowers, and shells; and Nalani, a creator of fiber baskets who uses twigs and bits of bark and fallen leaves. A small rack in the back room holds pareus, and a nearby case is filled with jewelry. Although quite small, Hale Koa is a great place to browse, and Buck and Juli are very friendly and helpful.

The last laugh won't be on you if you turn up a small alley in downtown Hawi (just near the Kohala Coffee Mill Espresso Bar) and seek out **First Laugh,** a name derived from a Navajo Indian legend (ask), tel. (808) 889-0183, open daily 9 a.m.-5 p.m. The shop is owned and operated by

Victoria Woollard, a mom herself, who sells new and used children's clothing (infants to 12 years), along with items like homemade soaps, toys, works of local artists, and children's books. The prices can't be beat.

Services and Information
The Kohala Visitor Center dispenses maps, information, and *aloha*. It's open daily and located just near the junction of Routes 270 and 250 in Hawi. Next door is the local laundromat, a semi-open-aired affair that can be used just about all the time. Police can be reached at (808) 889-6225, emergency fire and ambulance at (808) 961-6022. The area post office is a new and large facility on Rt. 270 between Hawi and Kapaau just near the H. Naito Store. The full-service Kamehameha Pharmacy is along Rt. 270 in downtown Kapaau.

KAPAAU

Kapaau is a sleepy community, the last town for any amenities on Rt. 270 before you reach the end of the line at Pololu Overlook. There's a gas station, grocery store, library, bank, and police station. Most young people have moved away seeking economic opportunity, but the old folks remain, and macadamia nuts are bringing some vitality back into the area. Here too, but on a smaller scale than in Hawi, local artists and some new folks are starting shops and businesses catering to tourists. The main attraction in town is **Kamehameha's Statue,** in front of the Kapaau Courthouse. The statue was commissioned by King Kalakaua in 1878, at which time an old *kahuna* said that the statue would feel at home only in the lands of Kamehameha's birth. Thomas Gould, an American sculptor living in Italy, was hired to do the statue, and he used John Baker, a part Hawaiian and close friend of Kalakaua, as the model. Gould was paid $10,000 to produce the remarkable and heroic sculpture, which was sent to Paris to be bronzed. It was freighted to Hawaii, but the ship carrying the original statue sank just off Port Stanley in the Falkland Islands, and the nine-ton statue was thought lost forever. With the insurance money, Gould was recommissioned and he produced another statue that arrived in Honolulu in 1883, where it still stands in front of the Judiciary Building. Within a few weeks, however, a British ship arrived in Honolulu, carrying the original statue that had somehow been salvaged and unceremoniously dumped in a Port Stanley junkyard. The English captain bought it there and sold it to King Kalakaua for $850. There was only one place where the statue could be sent: to the then-thriving town of Kapaau in the heart of Kamehameha's ancestral homelands. Every year, on the night before Kamehameha Day, the statue is freshly painted with a new coat of house paint; the bronze underneath remains as strong as the great king's will.

Kamehameha County Park, down a marked side road, has a full recreation area, including an Olympic pool open to the public, basketball courts, and weight rooms in the main building along with outside tennis courts with night lighting and a driving range. There are a kiddie area, restrooms, and picnic tables, all free.

Kalahikiola Church
A few minutes east of town an HVB Warrior points to a county lane leading to Kalahikiola Congregational Church. The road is delightfully lined with palm trees, pines, and macadamias like the formal driveway that it once was. Pass the weathering buildings of the Bond Estate and follow the road to the church on the hill. This church was built by Rev. Elias Bond and his wife Ellen, who arrived at Kohala in 1841 and dedicated the church in 1855. Rev. Bond and his parishioners were determined to overcome many formidable obstacles in building Kalahikiola (Life from the Sun) Church, so that they could "sit in a dry and decent house in Jehovah's presence." They hauled timber for miles, quarried and carried stone from distant gulches, raised lime from the sea floor, and brought sand by the jarful all the way from Kawaihae to mix their mortar. After two years of backbreaking work and $8,000, the church finally stood in God's praise, 85 feet long by 45 wide. The attached bell tower, oddly out of place, looks like a shoe box standing on end topped by four mean-looking spikes. Note that the doors don't swing, but slide—some visitors leave because they think it's locked. Inside, the church is dark and cool and, inexplicably, the same type of spikes as on the bell tower flank both sides of the altar. There is also a remarkable koa table. Pamphlets (25 cents) describe the history of the church.

The Bond Estate

The *most* remarkable and undisturbed missionary estate still extant in Hawaii (and one of two undisturbed mission districts in the world—the other is in Nepal) is the old Bond Homestead and its attendant buildings, including the now defunct but partially renovated Kohala Girl's School and the Kalahikiola Church. All three of these wonderful structures are on the National Historical Register. The community-based, nonprofit organization Ho'omau O Iole is working toward the restoration and preservation of this mission district, with the goal of eventually opening the home to public tours. Currently, only outside walking tours of the homestead grounds, the girl's school, and the church are conducted. One to one and a half-hour guided tours are offered Mon.-Sat. (Sunday on request) at 10 a.m., 11:30 a.m., 1 p.m., and 2:30 p.m. (with an additional summer tour at 4 p.m.). Reservations are requested, but those who just show up are not turned away. The tour costs $20 adult, $10 kids ages 6-13; ask about the cost of a family pass. A shortened (30- to 45-minute) guided tour is also available for $12 and $6, respectively. Self-guided tours run $8 and $4. For information, contact the Bond Historic Tours, tel. (808) 889-0883, 10 a.m.-5 p.m.; or (888) BOND888 from the Western U.S. or Canada.

When you enter the grounds, the clock turns back 100 years. The first buildings were completed in 1841 by Rev. Isaac Bliss, who preceded Elias and Ellen Bond. The main buildings, connected in New England farm fashion and made with barn-style peg and beam construction, have steep-pitched roofs designed to keep off the "back East" snows. They worked equally well here to keep rainwater out, as they were originally covered in thatch. The original furniture and family possessions are placed as if the residents are out for the afternoon, although the family has not lived in the house since 1925, when it was occupied by Dr. Benjamin Bond. In the majority of missionary homes and museums in Hawaii, suitable period furniture had to be purchased or replicas made to fill the houses, but here it is all original! The homey dining and writing room is dominated by a large table that can take six leaves because the Bonds never knew how many there would be for dinner—four, or 60 (who might have landed by schooner in the middle of the afternoon). A full set of dishes waits undisturbed in the sideboard. A cozy little parlor has comfortable wicker rocking chairs and a settee under a photo of Elias Bond himself. The reverend built the settee and most of the furniture in the house. His furniture from New England arrived on a ship after he did, but because it was the Sabbath, the reverend refused to have it unloaded. Unfortunately, the ship caught fire and all the Bond's personal possessions were lost. In the kitchen area a refrigerator dating from the '20s looks like a bank vault. It ran on electricity from a generator on the homestead that was frequently used by local plantation owners to recharge their batteries. Off in a side room, an old wooden bathtub is as sound as the day it was built. In Rev. Bond's bedroom is a crocheted "primer" dated 1817, made by his sister Eliza who died before he came to Hawaii; he brought it as a memento and it still hangs on the wall. Upstairs are two large rooms in disrepair, which contain treasure trove of antiques.

The small wing attached to the main house, called "The Cottage," was built when Dr. Benjamin Bond was first married. The family ate together in the main house, using the cottage as a Victorian bedroom and sitting room that now abounds with photos and antiques. The attached bathroom was once a summerhouse that was dragged to the present location by a steam tractor, then plumbed. As you look around, you'll feel that everything is here except for the people.

Keokea Beach County Park

Two miles past Kapaau toward Pololu you pass a small fruit stand and an access road heading *makai* to secluded Keokea Beach County Park. The park, on the side of the hill going down to the sea, is very picturesque and luxuriant. It is a favorite spot of North Kohala residents, especially on weekends, but it receives little use during the week. The rocky shoreline faces the open ocean, so swimming is not advised except during summer calm. There are a pavilion, restrooms, showers, and picnic tables. A county permit is required for tent and trailer camping.

Accommodation and Food

There are no established hotels in Kapaau but you can find a room at **Don's Tropical Valley Vacation Rentals,** P.O. Box 1333, Kapaau, HI

96755, tel. (808) 889-0369. Located in the quiet residential community of Makapala at mile marker no. 27, this hostel is walking distance from Keokea Beach and the Pololu Valley overlook. The house has two private bedrooms for one or two persons and a dorm room that sleeps up to four. Rates start at $15 a night. Reservations should be made three days in advance. Website: www.comevisit.com/tropical or e-mail: tropical@pacific-ocean.com. Budget.

Guest rentals and studio apartments are also available from the following individuals and families: D. Chapon, tel. (808) 889-6440 or 882-1510; Nani, tel. (808) 889-5606; or the Brown family, tel. (808) 884-5122.

Don's Family Deli, tel. (808) 889-5822, open daily for breakfast and lunch until 6 p.m., across the street from the Kamehameha Statue in Kapaau, is a taste of New York in North Kohala. How can a visit to tropical paradise be complete without bagels and lox, lasagna, or a thick slice of quiche? Don's features Dreyer's ice cream, coffee and cappuccino, and homemade biscotti filled with nuts and that zesty anisette flavor. Don Rich, a longtime Kohala resident, will also fix you up with a tofu or mahimahi burger, and offers a wide selection of meats and breads if you prefer to make your own picnic lunch.

Shopping

For food shopping in Kapaau try **Union Market,** along Rt. 270 coming into Kapaau, tel. (808) 889-6450, which sells not only general merchandise and meats, but also a hefty assortment of grains, nuts, fruits, and locally made pastries and breads. **H. Naito Store** is a general grocery, dry goods, and fishing supplies store in Kapaau, tel. (808) 889-6851.

David Gomes, tel. (808) 889-5100, is a local guitar and ukulele maker. He works in koa and other woods and does inlay in shell, abalone, and wood. His beautiful instruments take 4-6 months to complete. His small shop is located about a half mile on the Kapaau side of the junction of Routes 270 and 250.

In Kapaau, across from the Kamehameha statue, is **Ackerman Gallery,** open daily 9 a.m.-5:30 p.m., tel. (808) 889-5971, owned and operated by artist Gary Ackerman. Besides showcasing his own sensitive, island-inspired paintings, he displays local pottery, carvings, and one-of-a-kind jewelry. He also carries a smattering of artwork from throughout the Pacific. The artwork selections are tasteful, but expensive. You can also choose a reasonably priced gift item, especially from the handmade jewelry section. Make sure to check out the beautiful hand-blown glass display by a local artist named Yamazawa. The distinctive, iridescent glaze is achieved by using volcanic cinders—you can bring home a true island memento that includes a bit of Madame Pele herself. Gary has expanded and has opened another Ackerman Gallery in Kapaau. This lovely gallery, housed in a turn-of-the-century building, showcases the fine art of local island artists like Greg Pontius and Kelly Dunn as well as Gary.

Wo On Gallery, tel. (808) 889-5002, is owned and operated by Leslie Patten, P.O. Box 1065, Kapaau, HI 96755. This gallery, dedicated to local artists, occupies the historic Wo On (Harmony and Peace) General Store that served the Chinese community during plantation days. Next door is lovely and historically significant Tong Wo Cemetery and Temple, well worth a visit.

POLOLU VALLEY AND BEYOND

Finally you come to Pololu Valley Overlook. Off to the right is a small home belonging to Bill Sproat, a man of mixed Hawaiian ancestry and a longtime resident of Pololu. Bill, whose vim and vigor belie his 80-plus years, was a mule skinner throughout the area for 50 years. He is a treasure house of knowledge and homespun wisdom, and still speaks fluent Hawaiian. His mother was a Hawaiian who became a schoolteacher down in Pololu, and his dad was an adventurer who came to Hawaii in the 1890s. Bill's grandmother was a *kahuna* who lived in the valley and never converted to Christianity. Most of the folks feared her dark powers, but not Bill who, although a strong Christian, learned much about Hawaii and its ways from his grandmother. If Bill is in his yard, perhaps tending a mule, make sure to stop and talk with him.

It's about 12 miles from Pololu to Waipio Valley, with five U-shaped valleys in between, including Honokea and Waimanu, two of the largest. From the lookout it takes about 15 minutes to walk down to the floor of Pololu. The trail is well maintained as you pass through a heavy growth of *lau hala,* but it can be slippery when wet. At the bottom is a gate that keeps grazing animals in; make sure to close it after you! **Kohala Ditch,** a monument to labor-intensive engineering, is to the rear of these valleys. It carried precious water to the sugar plantations, and today carries adventurous kayakers for a very unusual thrill ride. Pololu and the other valleys were once inhabited and were among the richest wet taro plantations of old Hawaii. Today, abandoned and neglected, they have been taken over by introduced vegetation. The black-sand beach fronting Pololu is lined with sand dunes, with a

small sandbar offshore. The rip current here can be very dangerous, so enter the water only in summer months. The rip fortunately weakens not too far from shore; if you're caught, go with it and ride the waves back in. Many people hike into Pololu for seclusion and back-to-nature camping. Make sure to boil the stream water before drinking. Plenty of wild fruits can augment your food supply, and the shoreline fishing is excellent. The trails leading eastward to the other valleys are in disrepair and should not be attempted unless you are *totally* prepared, and better yet, accompanied by someone who knows the terrain.

DIANA LASICH HARPER

MAUI

How shall we account for this nation spreading itself so far over this vast ocean? We find them from New Zealand to the south, to these islands to the north and from Easter Island to the Hebrides; . . . how much farther is not known . . .

~Captain James Cook

HAWAII STATE ARCHIVES

INTRODUCTION

The Kumulipo, the ancient genealogical chant of the Hawaiians, sings of the demigod Maui, a half-human mythological sorcerer known and revered throughout Polynesia. Maui was a prankster on a grand scale who used guile and humor to create some of the most amazing feats of derring-do ever recorded. A Polynesian combination of Paul Bunyan and Hercules, Maui had adventures known as "strifes." He served humankind by fishing up the islands of Hawaii from the ocean floor, securing fire from a tricky mud hen, lifting the sky so humans could walk upright, and slowing down the sun-god by lassoing his genitals with a braided rope of his sister's pubic hair. Maui accomplished this last feat on the summit of the great mountain Haleakala (House of the Sun), thus securing more time in the day to fish and to dry tapa. Maui met his just but untimely end between the legs of the great goddess, Hina. This final prank, in which he attempted to crawl into the sleeping goddess's vagina, left his feet and legs dangling out, causing uproarious laughter among his comrades, a band of warrior birds. The noise awakened Hina, who saw no humor in the situation. She unceremoniously squeezed Maui to death. The island of Maui is the only island in Hawaii and throughout Polynesia named after a god. With such a legacy the island couldn't help but become known as *"Maui no ka oi"* ("Maui is the best").

AN OVERVIEW

In a land of superlatives, it's quite a claim to call your island *the* best, but Maui has a lot to back it up. Maui has more miles of swimmable beach than any of the other islands. Haleakala, the massive mountain that *is* East Maui, is the largest dormant volcano in the world, and its hardened lava rising more than 30,000 feet from the sea floor makes it one of the heaviest concentrated masses on the face of the earth. There are legitimate claims that Maui grows the best onions and potatoes, but the boast of the best *pakalolo* may only be a pipe dream, since all the islands have great soil and weather and many enterprising gardeners.

West Maui
If you look at the silhouette of Maui on a map, it looks like the head and torso of the mythical

demigod bent at the waist and contemplating the uninhabited island of Kahoolawe. The head is West Maui, and its profile is that of a wizened old man whose wrinkled brow and cheeks are the West Maui Mountains. The highest peak here is **Puu Kukui**, at 5,788 feet, located just about where the ear would be. If you go to the top of the head you'll be at Kapalua, a resort community recently carved from pineapple fields. Fleming Beach begins a string of beaches that continues down over the face, stopping at the chin, and picking up again on the chest, which is South Maui. Kaanapali is located at the forehead; its massive beach continues almost uninterrupted for four miles, an area that in comparison would take in all of Waikiki, from Diamond Head to Ala Moana. Sugarcane fields fringe the mountain side of the road, while condos are strung along the shore. The resorts here are cheek to jowl, but the best are tastefully done with uninterrupted panoramic views and easy and plentiful access to the beach.

Lahaina is located at the Hindu "third eye." This town is where it's "happening" on Maui, with concentrations of craftspeople, artists, museums, historical sites, restaurants, and nightspots. Used in times past by royal Hawaiian *ali'i* and then by Yankee whalers, Lahaina has always been somewhat of a playground, and the good-times mystique still lingers. At the tip of the nose is Olowalu, where a lunatic Yankee trader, Simon Metcalf, decided to slaughter hundreds of curious Hawaiians paddling toward his ship just to show them he was boss. From Olowalu you can see four islands: Molokai, Lanai, Kahoolawe, and a faint hint of Hawaii far to the south. The back of Maui's head is an adventurer's paradise. Back here are tremendous coastal views, bird sanctuaries, *heiau*, and Kahakuloa, a tiny fishing village reported to be a favorite stomping ground of great Maui himself.

The Isthmus

A low, flat isthmus planted primarily in sugarcane is the neck that connects the head of West Maui to the torso of East Maui, which is Haleakala. The Adam's apple is the little port of Maalaea, which has a good assortment of pleasure and fishing boats, hosts the new Maui Ocean Center, and provides an up-close look at a working port not nearly as frenetic as La-

haina. The nape of the neck is made up of the twin cities of Wailuku, the county seat, and Kahului, where visitors arrive at Maui's airport. These towns are where the "people" live. Some say the isthmus, dramatically separating east and west, is the reason Maui is called "The Valley Isle." Head into Iao Valley from Wailuku, where the West Maui Mountains have been worn into incredible peaked monolithic spires. This stunning valley area played a key role in Kamehameha's unification of the Hawaiian Islands, and geologically seems to be a more fitting reason for Maui's nickname.

East Maui/Haleakala

Once you cross the isthmus you're on the immensity of Haleakala, the one mountain that makes up the entire bulging, muscled torso of the island. A continent in microcosm, Haleakala's geology encompasses alpine terrain, baking desert, moonscape, blazing jungle, pastureland, and lava-encrusted wasteland. The temperature, determined by altitude, ranges from subfreezing to subtropical. If you head east along the spine, you'll find world-class sailboarding beaches, artist villages, last-picture-show towns, and a few remaining family farms planted in taro. Route 360, the only coastal road, rocks and rolls you over more than 600 curves and shows you more waterfalls and pristine pools than you can count. After crossing more than 50 bridges, you come to Hana. Here, the "dream" Hawaii that people seek still lives. Farther along is Kipahulu, and Oheo Gulch, known for its fantastic pools and waterfalls. Close by is where Charles Lindbergh is buried, and many celebrities have chosen the surrounding hillsides for their special retreats and hideaways.

On Haleakala's broad chest are macho cowboy towns complete with Wild West rodeos contrasting with the gentle but riotous colors of carnation and protea farms. Polipoli Spring State Park is here, a thick forest canopy with more varieties of imported trees than anywhere else in Oceania. A weird cosmic joke places Kihei just about where the armpit would be. Kihei is a mega-growth condo area ridiculed as an example of what developers shouldn't be allowed to do. Oddly enough, Wailea, just down the road, exemplifies a reasonable and aesthetic planned community and is highly touted as a "model" development area. Just at the belly button, close to the kundalini, is Makena, long renowned as Maui's "alternative beach," but rapidly losing its status as the island's last "free" beach.

Finally, when you pilgrimage to the summit of Haleakala, it'll be as if you've left the planet. It's another world: beautiful, mystical, raw, inspired, and freezing cold. When you're alone on the crater rim with the world below garlanded by the brilliance of sunrise or sunset, you'll know that you have come at last to great Maui's heart.

THE LAND

After the Big Island of Hawaii, Maui is the second largest and second youngest of the main Hawaiian Islands. The land was formed from two volcanoes: the **West Maui Mountains** and **Haleakala.** The West Maui Mountains are geologically much older than Haleakala, but the two were joined by subsequent lava flows that formed a connecting low, flat isthmus. **Puu Kukui,** at 5,788 feet, is the tallest peak of the West Maui Mountains. It's the lord of a mountain domain whose old weathered face has been scarred by a series of deep crags, verdant valleys, and inhospitable gorges. Rising more than 30,000 feet from the ocean floor, **Haleakala** is by comparison an adolescent with smooth, rounded features looming 10,023 feet above sea level, with a landmass four times larger than West Maui. The two parts of Maui combine to form 727 square miles of land with 120 linear miles of coastline. At its widest, Maui is 26 miles from north to south, and 48 miles east to west. The coastline has the largest number of swimmable beaches in Hawaii, and the interior is a miniature continent with almost every conceivable geological feature evident.

Rivers and Lakes
Maui has no navigable rivers but there are hundreds of streams. Two of the largest are **Palikea Stream,** which runs through Kipahulu Valley forming Oheo Gulch, and **Iao Stream,** which has sculpted the amazing monoliths in Iao Valley. The longest, at 18 miles, is Kalialinui-Waiale Stream that starts just below the summit of Haleakala, runs through Pukalani and empties into the ocean near the Kahului airport. A few reservoirs dot the island, but the two largest natural bodies of water are the 41-acre **Kanaha Pond,** on the outskirts of Kahului, and 500-acre **Kealia Pond,** on the southern shore of the isthmus, both major bird and wildlife sanctuaries. Hikers should be aware of the countless streams and rivulets that can quickly turn from trickles to torrents, causing flash floods in valleys that were the height of hospitality only minutes before.

West Maui Mountains

ROBERT NILSEN

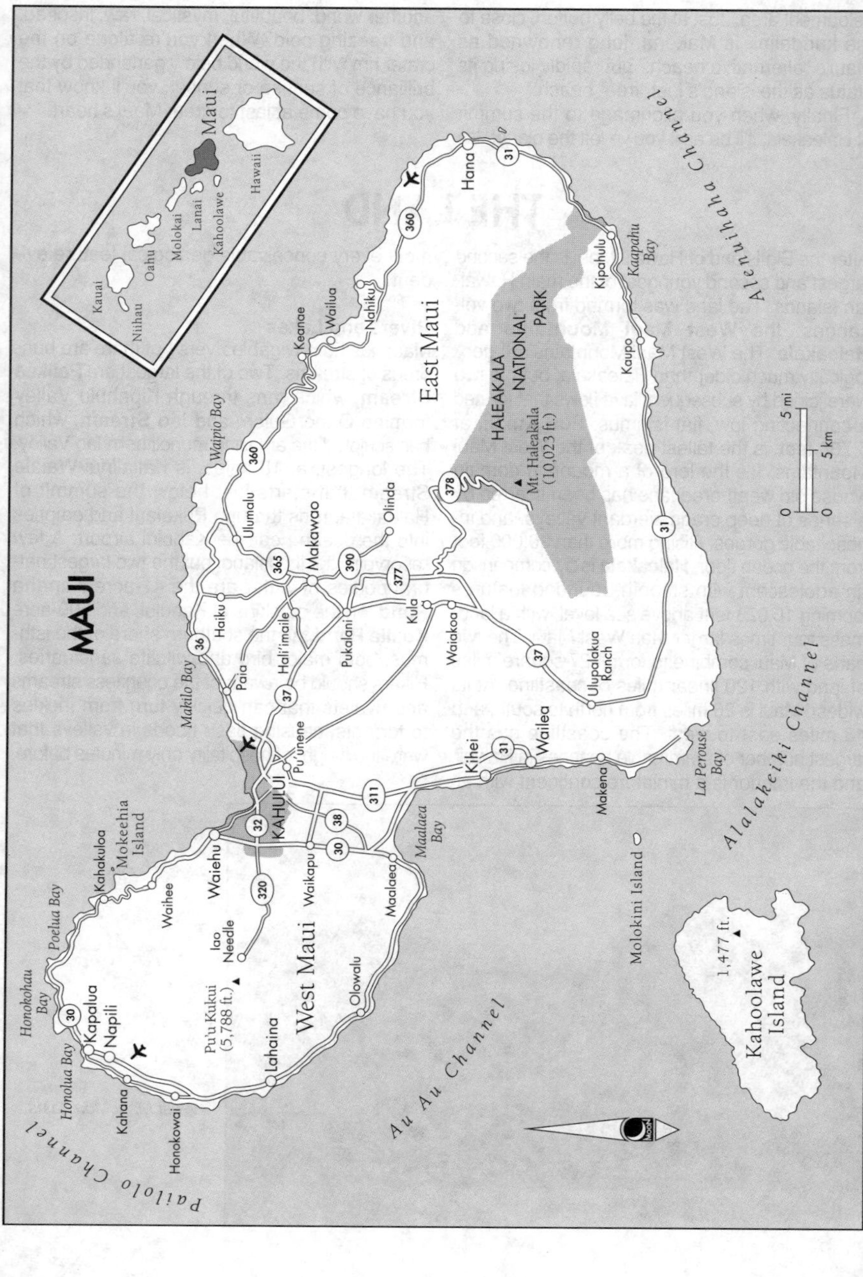

MAUI

Maui

Kauai
Niihau
Oahu
Molokai
Lanai
Kahoolawe
Hawaii

East Maui

HALEAKALA NATIONAL PARK

Mt. Haleakala (10,023 ft.)

Hana

Kipahulu

Kaupo

Kaapahu Bay

Keanae
Wailua
Nahiku
Waipio Bay

Ulumalu
Makawao
Olinda
Haiku
Hali'imaile
Pukalani
Kula
Waiakoa
Ulupalakua Ranch

Paia
Kahului
Pu'unene
Waikapu
Maalaea
Kihei
Wailea
Makena
La Perouse Bay

Waiehu
Waihee
Iao Needle

West Maui

Pu'u Kukui (5,788 ft.)

Kahakuloa
Mokeehia Island
Kapalua
Napili
Kahana
Honokowai
Lahaina
Olowalu

Honokohau Bay
Honolua Bay
Peelua Bay

Molokini Island

Kahoolawe Island
1,477 ft.

Alenuihaha Channel
Alalakeiki Channel
Au Au Channel
Pailolo Channel

5 mi
5 km

© J.D. BISIGNANI AND MOON PUBLICATIONS, INC.

31
360
360
365
390
377
378
37
31
37
36
32
30
38
311
320
30

MAUI TEMPERATURE AND RAINFALL

TOWN		JAN.	MARCH	MAY	JUNE	SEPT.	NOV.
Lahaina	high	80	81	82	83	84	82
	low	62	63	68	68	70	65
	rain	3	1	0	0	0	1
Hana	high	79	79	80	80	81	80
	low	60	60	62	63	65	61
	rain	9	7	2	3	5	7
Kahului	high	80	80	84	86	87	83
	low	64	64	67	69	70	68
	rain	4	3	1	0	0	2

Note: Temperature is expressed in degrees Fahrenheit; rainfall in inches.

CLIMATE

Maui has similar weather to the rest of the Hawaiian islands, though some aficionados claim that it gets the most sunshine of all. The weather on Maui depends more on where you are than on what season it is. The average daily temperature along the coast is about 78° F (25.5° C) in summer and during winter is about 72° F (22° C). On Haleakala summit, that average is 43-50° F (6-10° C). Nights are usually no more than 10° F cooler than days. Since Haleakala is a main feature on Maui, you should remember that altitude drastically affects the weather. Expect an average drop of three degrees for every 1,000 feet of elevation, so at the top, Haleakala is about 30 degrees cooler than at sea level. The lowest temperature ever recorded on Maui was atop Haleakala in 1961, when the mercury dropped well below freezing to a low, low 11° F. In contrast, sunny Kihei has recorded a blistering 98° F.

Precipitation

Rain on Maui is as much a factor as it is elsewhere in Hawaii. On any day, somewhere on Maui it's raining, while other areas experience drought. A dramatic example of this phenomenon is a comparison of Lahaina with Mount Puu Kukui, both on West Maui and separated by only seven miles. Lahaina, which translates as "Merciless Sun," is hot, arid, and gets only 15 inches of rainfall annually, while Puu Kukui can receive close to 500 inches (40 *feet!*) of precipitation but averages 375. This rivals Mt. Waialeale on Kauai as the wettest spot on earth. Other leeward towns get a comparable amount of rain to Lahaina, but as you move upcountry and around the north coast, the rains become greater. Finally, in Hana, rainfall is about five times as great as on the leeward side, averaging more than 80 inches a year. The windward (wet) side of Maui, outlined by the Hana Road, is the perfect natural hothouse. Here, valleys sweetened with blossoms house idyllic waterfalls and pools that visitors treasure when they happen upon them. On the leeward (dry) side are Maui's best beaches: Kapalua, Kaanapali, Kihei, Wailea, and Makena. They all sit in Haleakala's rain shadow. If it happens to be raining at one, just move a few miles down the road to the next. Anyway, the rains are mostly gentle, and the brooding sky—especially at sundown—is even more spectacular than usual.

FLORA AND FAUNA

Maui's indigenous and endemic plants, trees, and flowers are both fascinating and beautiful, but unfortunately, like everything else that was native, they are quickly disappearing. The majority of flora considered exotic by visitors was introduced either by the original Polynesians or by later white settlers. Maui is blessed with state parks, gardens, undisturbed rainforests, private reserves, and commercial nurseries, all of which offer brilliant and dazzling colors to the landscape.

Silversword

Maui's official flower is a tiny pink rose called a *lokelani*. The island's unofficial symbol, however, is the silversword. The Hawaiian name for silversword is *ahinahina*, which translates as "gray gray," and the English name derives from a silverfish, whose color the plant is said to resemble. The silversword belongs to a remarkable plant family that claims 28 members, with five in the specific silversword species. It's kin to the common sunflower, and botanists say the entire family evolved from a single ancestral species. Hypothetically, the members of the silversword family can interbreed and produce remarkable hybrids. Some plants are shrubs, while others are climbing vines, and some even become trees. They grow anywhere from desert conditions to steamy jungles. On Maui, the silversword is only found on Haleakala, above the 6,000-foot level, and is especially prolific in the crater. Each plant lives 5-20 years and ends its life by sprouting a gorgeous stalk of hundreds of purplish-red flowers. It then withers from a majestic six-foot plant to a flat gray skeleton. An endangered species, silverswords are totally protected. They protect themselves, too, from radiation and lack of moisture by growing fuzzy hairs all over their swordlike stalks. You can see them along the Haleakala Park Road at **Kalahaku Overlook,** or by hiking along **Silversword Loop** on the floor of the crater.

Protea

These exotic flowers are from Australia and South Africa. Because they come in almost limitless shapes, sizes, and colors, they captivate everyone who sees them. They are primitive, almost otherworldly in appearance, and they exude a life force more like an animal than a flower. The slopes of leeward Haleakala between 2,000 and 4,000 feet are heaven to protea—the growing conditions could not be more perfect. Here are found the hardiest, highest-quality protea in the world. The days are warm, the nights are cool, and the well-drained volcanic soil has the exact combination of minerals on which protea thrive. Haleakala's crater even helps by creating a natural air flow that produces cloud cover, filters the sun, and protects the flowers. Protea make excellent gifts that can be shipped anywhere. As fresh-cut flowers they are gorgeous, but they have the extra benefit of drying superbly. Just hang them in a dark, dry, well-ventilated area and they do the rest. You can see protea, along with other botanical specialties, at the gardens, flower farms, and gift shops in Kula.

Carnations

If protea aren't enough to dazzle you, how about fields of carnations? Most Mainlanders think of carnations stuck in a groom's lapel, or perhaps have seen a table dedicated to them in a hothouse, but not fields

silversword

DIANA LASICH HARPER

full of carnations! The Kula area produces carnations that grow outside nonchalantly, in rows, like cabbages. They fill the air with their unmistakable perfume, and they are without doubt a joy to behold. You can see family and commercial plots throughout the upper Kula area.

Prickly Pear Cactus
Interspersed in countless fields and pastures on the windward slope of Haleakala, adding that final nuance to cattle country, are clusters of prickly pear cactus. The Hawaiians call them *panini,* which translates as "very unfriendly," undoubtedly because of the sharp spines covering the flat, thick leaves. These cactus are typical

of those found in Mexico and the southwestern United States. They were introduced to Hawaii before 1810 and established themselves, coincidentally, in conjunction with the cattle being brought in at that time. It's assumed that Don Marin, a Spanish adviser to Kamehameha I, was responsible for importing the plant. Perhaps the early *paniolo* felt lonely without them. The *panini* can grow to heights of 15 feet and are now considered a pest, but nonetheless looks as if they belong. They develop small pear-shaped fruits that are quite delicious. Hikers who decide to pick them should be careful of small yellowish bristles that can burrow under the skin and become very irritating. Prickly pears also have

MAUI BOTANICAL GARDENS AND FOREST AREAS

Kula Botanical Gardens, tel. (808) 878-1715, has nearly 2,000 varieties of tropical and semitropical plants, including orchids, bromeliads, fuchsia, protea, *kukui* and sandalwood trees, and numerous ferns, on more than five acres. Located at 3,300 feet near the junction of Rt. 377 (Kekaulike Ave.) and Rt. 37 at the south end, this privately owned garden is open daily 9 a.m.-4 p.m. for self-guided tours; $4 entrance fee.

Enchanting Floral Gardens, tel. (808) 878-2531, is located along Rt. 37 just south of Pukalani at mile marker 10. This private garden features about 1,500 species of native Hawaiian plants as well as exotic plants from around the world on eight acres. Open 9 a.m.-5 p.m. for self-guided tours; admission $4.

University of Hawaii Experimental Station offers 20 acres of constantly changing, quite beautiful plants, although the grounds are uninspired, scientific, rectangular plots. Located on Mauna Place just off Copp Rd. above Rt. 37 in Kula, this garden is open Mon.-Thurs. 7:30 a.m.-3:30 p.m., closed for lunch. Although admission is free, visitors should check in with the station manager.

Keanae Arboretum, above Keanae Peninsula on the Hana Hwy. (Rt. 360), is always open. In a natural setting with walkways, many identifying markers, and mosquitoes, this six-acre arboretum is split into two sections: ornamental tropical plants and Hawaiian domestic plants. The native forest swaths the surrounding hillsides. No fee.

Kahanu Gardens, tel. (808) 284-8912, a branch of the Pacific Tropical Botanical Gardens, is located on the rugged lava coast east of Hana at the site of Piilanihale Heiau. In this 120-acre garden, you'll find stands of breadfruit and coconut trees, a pandanus grove, and numerous other tropical plants from throughout the world. Open for two-hour guided tours daily at 1 p.m. for $10 per person; call for reservations.

Polipoli Spring State Recreation Area is the finest Upcountry camping and trekking area on Maui. At the south end of Rt. 377, turn onto Waipoli Rd. for 10 miles of bad road. Overnight camping is recommended. Native and introduced birds, and magnificent stands of redwoods, eucalyptus, conifers, ash, cypress, cedar, *sugi* and other pines may be found here. This area is known for delicious methley plums, which ripen in early June. For camping information contact Division of State Parks in Wailuku, tel. (808) 984-8109.

Hosmer Grove, within Haleakala National Park at 6,800 feet in elevation, is an experimental forest project from the early 20th century. Here are fine examples of introduced trees like cedar, pine, fir, juniper, and *sugi* pine that were originally planted in hopes of finding a commercial, economically marketable wood for Hawaii. A short trail now winds through the no-longer-orderly stands of trees. Ranger-guided tours are offered periodically. For more information, contact the Haleakala National Park Headquarters, tel. (808) 572-9306.

beautiful yellow and orange flowers. An attempt is being made to control the cactus in *paniolo* country. *El cosano rojo,* the red worm found in the bottom of Mexican tequila, has been introduced to destroy the plant. It burrows into the cactus and eats the hardwood center, causing the plant to wither and die.

Maui's Endangered Birds and Others

Maui's native birds are disappearing. The island is the last home of the crested honeycreeper, *(akohe'kohe)* that lives only on the windward slope of Haleakala at 4,500-6,500 feet. It once lived on Molokai, but no longer. The Maui parrotbill is another endangered bird, found only on the slopes of Haleakala above 5,000 feet. The *poouli* is a very rare dark brown bird that was saved from extinction through efforts of the Sierra Club and Audubon Society, who successfully had it listed as the newest addition to the Federal List of Endangered Species. The bird has one remaining stronghold deep in the forests of Maui. Two waterbirds found on Maui are the Hawaiian stilt *(ae'o)* and the Hawaiian coot *(alae ke'oke'o).* The *amakihi,* and the *'i'iwi* are endemic birds that aren't endangered at the moment. One of the most common native birds, the *amakihi* is less specialized than most other Hawaiian birds, the main reason for its continued existence. The *'i'iwi* is found mainly on Maui, Hawaii, and Kauai in forests above 2,000 feet. Other indigenous birds found on Maui are the wedge-tailed shearwater, the white-tailed tropic bird, the black noddy, the American plover, and a large variety of escaped exotic birds.

Humpback Whales of Maui

Humpbacks get their name from their style of exposing their dorsal fin when they dive, which gives them a humped appearance. Their dorsal fin also puts them into the roqual family. There are about 10,000 humpback whales alive today, down from an estimated 100,000 at the turn of the century. The remaining whales are divided into three separate global populations: North Atlantic, North Pacific, and South Pacific groups. About 2,000 North Pacific humpbacks migrate from coastal Alaska beginning in November. Migration peaks in February, when humpbacks congregate mostly in the waters off Maui, with a smaller groups heading for the waters off the other islands. In 1992, the **Hawaiian Islands Humpback Whale National Marine Sanctuary** was designated, encompassing waters off all six major islands. This will hopefully ensure a perpetual safe haven for the whales.

Whalewatching

If you're in Hawaii from late November to early May, you have an excellent chance of spotting a humpback. March is perhaps the best month. You can often see a whale from a vantage point on land, but this is nowhere near as thrilling as seeing them close-up from a boat. From shore you're likely to see whales anywhere along Maui's south coast. If you're staying at any of the hotels or condos along Kaanapali or Kihei and have an ocean view, you can spot them from your lanai or window. Two good vantage spots are Papawai Point and McGregor Point along Rt. 30 just west of Maalaea. During whalewatching season, a Pacific Whale Foundation naturalist may be at one of these spots to help people locate whales and answer questions. In addition, a free talk on whales is sometimes conducted by a naturalist on the ocean observatory deck at the Kealia Beach Plaza weekdays around noon. Maalaea Bay is another favorite nursing ground for female whales and their calves; there you can also see a small working harbor up close. Another excellent viewpoint is Makena Beach, on the spit of land separating Little and Big Beaches. If you time your arrival near sunset, even if you don't see a whale you'll enjoy a mind-boggling light show.

To learn more about whales and the Hawaiian Islands Humpback Whale National Marine Sanctuary, stop by their office at 726 S. Kihei Rd., Kihei, HI 96753, tel. (800) 831-4888, website: www.t-link.net/~whale. The office is open Mon.-Fri. 9 a.m.-3 p.m., grounds open dawn to dusk.

Note: For whalewatching cruises see **whalewatching.**

HISTORY

The Kumulipo sings that Maui was the second island child of Wakea and Papa. Before the coming of white people and their written record, it's clear the island was a powerful kingdom. Wars raged throughout the land and kings ruled not only Maui, but the neighboring islands of Lanai and Kahoolawe. By the 16th century, a royal road called the *Alaloa* encircled the island and signified unity. Today, on West Maui, the road is entirely obliterated; only a few portions remain on East Maui. When white people began to arrive in the late 1700s, Maui became their focal point. Missionaries, whalers, and the new Hawaiian kings of the Kamehameha line all made Lahaina their seat of power. For about 50 years, until the mid-19th century, Maui blossomed. Missionaries built the first permanent stone structures in the islands. An exemplary New England-style school at Lahainaluna attracted students even from California cities. Here, too, a famous printing press brought not only revenue but refinement, through the written word. The commercially viable sugar industry began in secluded Hana and fortunes were made; a new social order under the Plantation System began. But by the turn of this century, the glory years were over. The whaling industry faded away and Oahu took over as the central power spot. Maui slipped into obscurity. It was revived in the 1960s when tourists rediscovered what others had known: Maui is a beauty among beauties.

Maui's Great Kings

Internal turmoil raged in Hawaii just before Captain Cook's arrival in 1778. Shortly after contact, the great Kamehameha would rise and consolidate all the islands under one rule, but in the 1770s a king named Kahekili ruled Maui. (Some contend Kahekili was Kamehameha's father.) The Hana District, however, was ruled by Kalaniopuu of Hawaii. He was the same king who caused the turmoil on the day Captain Cook was killed at Kealakekua.

In 1776, Kalaniopuu invaded Maui, but his forces were annihilated by Kahekili's warriors at Sand Hill near Wailuku, which means Bloody Waters. On November 26, 1778 Captain Cook spotted Maui, but bypassed it because he could find no suitable anchorage. It wasn't until May 28, 1786 that a French expedition led by Commander La Pérouse came ashore near Lahaina after finding safe anchorage at what became known as La Perouse Bay. Maui soon became a regular port of call. In 1790 Kamehameha finally defeated Kahekili's forces at Iao Needle and brought Maui under his domain. The great warrior Kahekili was absent from the battle, during which Kamehameha used a cannon from the *Fair American,* a small ship seized a few years before. Davis and Young, two marooned seamen, provided the technical advice for these horrible but effective new weapons.

Maui's Rise

The beginning of the 19th century brought amazing changes to Hawaii, many of which came through Maui—especially the port of Lahaina. In 1793, Captain Vancouver visited Lahaina and confirmed La Pérouse's report that it was a fine anchorage. In 1802 Kamehameha stopped with his enormous Pelelu fleet of war canoes on his way to conquer Oahu. He lingered for more than a year collecting taxes and building his Brick Palace at Lahaina. The bricks were poorly made, but marked the first Western-style structure in the islands. He also built a fabulous straw house for his daughter Princess Nahienaena that was so well constructed it was later used as the residence of the U.S. Consul. In 1819 the first whaler, *The Bellina,* stopped at Lahaina and marked Hawaii's ascendancy as the capital of the whaling industry, a position that lasted until the majority of the whaling fleet was lost in the Arctic in 1871. During Lahaina's heyday, more than 500 ships visited the port in one year. Also in 1819, the year of his death, Kamehameha built an observation tower in Lahaina so he could watch for returning ships, many of which held his precious cargo. In that prophetic year the French reappeared, with a warship this time, and the drama began. The great Western powers of the period maneuvered to upstage each other in the quest for dominance of this Pacific jewel.

The Missionaries

In 1823 the first Christian mission was built in Lahaina under the pastorage of Reverend Richards, and the conversion of Hawaii began in earnest. In that year Queen Keopuolani, the first great convert to Christianity, died. She was buried in Lahaina not according to the ancient customs accorded an *ali'i,* but as a reborn child of Christ.

The Reverend Richards and Queen Kaahumanu worked together to produce Hawaii's first Civil Code based on the Ten Commandments. The whalers fought the interference of the missionaries to the point where attempts were made on Reverend Richards's life, including a naval bombardment of his home. Over the next decade, the missionaries, ever hard at work, became reconciled with the sailors, who donated funds to build a Seaman's Chapel. This house of worship was located just next to The Baldwin Home, an early, permanent, New England-style house, which still stands on Front Street. The house originally belonged to the Spaulding family, but the Baldwins were such an influence that it was known by their name. Lahainaluna High School, situated in the cool of the mountains just north of Lahaina, became the paramount institution of secondary learning west of the Rocky Mountains. The newly wealthy of Hawaii and California sent their progeny here to be educated along with the nobility of the Kingdom of Hawaii.

Maui Fades

If the following 30 years of Maui's historical and sociological development were put on a graph, it would show a sharp rise followed by a crash. By mid-century, Maui boasted the first Constitution, Catholic Mass, Temperance Union, Royal Palace, and steamship service. A census was taken and a prison built to house reveling seamen. Kamehameha III moved the capital to Honolulu and the 1850s brought a smallpox epidemic, the destruction of Wainee Church by a "ghost wind," and the death of David Malo, a classic historian of precontact Hawaii. By the late 1860s, the whaling industry was dead, but sugar would rise to take its place. The first successful sugar plantation was started by George Wilfong in 1849 along the Hana coast, and the first great sugar mill was started by James Campbell in 1861. The 1870s saw the planting of Lahaina's famous Banyan Tree by Sheriff W.O. Smith, and the first telephone and telegraph cable linking Paia with Haiku.

The 20th Century

When the Pioneer Hotel was built in 1901, Lahaina was still important. Claus Spreckels, King Sugar himself, had large holdings on Maui and along with his own sugar town, Spreckelsville, built the Haiku Ditch in 1878. This 30-mile ditch brought 50 million gallons of water a day from Haiku to Puunene so the "green gold" could flourish. The entrepreneur was able to buy the land for his sugar plantation cheaply. The highly superstitious Hawaiians of the time didn't value this particular plot of land, believing that the souls of those who had not made the leap to heaven were condemned to wander the wasteland. To them it was obviously cursed, supporting only grasses and scrub bushes, and they felt that they were getting the bargain, off-loading it onto the unsuspecting *haole.* Moreover, Spreckels was a gambler. In a series of late-night poker games with Kamehameha III he was able to win the water rights to a dozen or so streams in the area, thereby creating the possibility for his Haiku Ditch. Sugar and Maui became one.

Then, because of sugar, Lahaina lost its dominance and Paia became *the* town on Maui during the 1930s, where it housed plantation workers in camps according to nationality. Maui slid more and more into obscurity. A few luminaries brought passing fame: Tandy MacKenzie, for example, born in Hana in 1892, was a gifted operatic star whose career lasted until 1954. In the 1960s, Maui, as well as all of Hawaii, became accessible to the average tourist. It was previously discovered by men like Sam Pryor, retired vice-president of Pan Am who made his home in Hana and invited Charles Lindbergh to visit, then to live and finally die in this idyllic spot. In the mid-'60s, the Lahaina Restoration Foundation was begun. It dedicated itself to the preservation of Old Lahaina and other historical sites on the island. It now attempts to preserve the flavor of what once was while looking to future growth. Today, Maui is once again in ascendancy, the second most visited island in Hawaii after Oahu.

GOVERNMENT

The political boundaries of Maui County are a bit oddball. Maui County encompasses Maui Island, as well as Lanai, Molokai, and the uninhabited island of Kahoolawe. One historical geographical oddity consisted of an arc on East Maui, from Makawao past Hana and along the south coast almost to Kihei, which was a "shared" political area, aligned culturally with the Kohala District of the Big Island since Polynesian times. As a traditional carryover, these two districts were joined with each other until political lines were redrawn in 1991, severing that political connection. The real strangeness occurs in Maui's 6th Senatorial District and the 7th and 12th Representative Districts. The 7th Representative District includes much of West Maui and the islands of Lanai and Molokai. The area of West Maui, with Kaanapali and Lahaina, is one of the most developed and financially sound areas in all of Hawaii. It's a favorite area with tourists, and is one of the darlings of developers. On the other hand, Lanai has a tiny population, a growing tourist industry and, in comparison, a minuscule economy. Molokai has the largest per capita concentration of native Hawaiians, a "busted economy" with a tremendous share of its population on welfare, and a grass-roots movement determined to preserve the historical integrity of the island and the dignity of the people. The 12th Representative District, which takes in the eastern third of the island of Maui, and 6th Senatorial District, which encompasses Kihei, Wailea, Makena, half of Upcountry, and Hana, are paired with the north coast of Kauai, from Kapaa through Hanalei to the Na Pali coast, an area that has no traditional political or cultural bond with Maui. You'd have to be a political magician to fairly represent all of the constituents in these widely differing districts.

The current mayor is James Apana. The mayor is assisted by an elected county council, one from each council district around the county. Like the rest of the state, Maui County is overwhelmingly Democratic and has only one Republican elected state legislative member. Of the 25 State Senatorial Districts, Maui County is represented by three, all Democrats. Maui County has six of 51 seats in the State House of Representatives, all Democrats, except for one Republican representing the area of Kihei, Wailea, and part of Upcountry.

ECONOMY

Maui's economy is a mirror image of the state's economy: it's based on tourism, agriculture, and government expenditures. The primary growth is in tourism, with Maui being the second most frequently chosen Hawaiian destination after Oahu. More than 17,000 rooms are available on Maui in all categories, and they're filled 75% of the time. On average, Maui attracts about two million tourists per year, and on any given day there are about 40,000 visitors enjoying the island. The majority of the rooms are in Kihei-Wailea and the Kaanapali to Kapalua strip. With tourists finding Maui more and more desirable every year, and with agriculture firmly entrenched, Maui's economic future is bright.

Tourism-related Problems

Two prime examples of the best and the worst development can be found on Maui's south shore at Kihei and Wailea, less than five miles apart. In the late '60s Kihei experienced a development-inspired "feeding frenzy" that made the real sharks offshore seem about as dangerous as Winnie the Pooh. Condos were slapped up as fast as cement can dry, their architecture reminiscent of a stack of shoeboxes. A coastline renowned for its beauty was overburdened, and the view was wiped out in the process. Anyone who had the bucks built, and now parts of Kihei look like a high-rise, low-income, federally funded housing project. You can bet that those who made a killing building here don't live here.

Conversely, just down the road is Wailea, a model of what development could (and should) be. The architecture is tasteful, low-rise, unobtrusive, and designed with people and the preservation of the scenery in mind . . . mostly. It's obviously more exclusive, but access points to the beaches are open to everyone, and the view is still there for all to enjoy. Wailea points the way for the development of the future.

Agriculture and Ranching

Maui generates revenue through cattle, sugar, pineapples, and flowers, along with a substantial subculture economy in *pakalolo*. **Cattle grazing** occurs on the western and southern slopes of Haleakala, where 35,000 acres are owned by the Haleakala Ranch, and more than 23,000 acres by the Ulupalakua Ranch. The upper slopes of Haleakala around Kula are a gardener's dream. Delicious onions, potatoes, and all sorts of garden vegetables are grown, but are secondary to large plots of gorgeous flowers, mainly carnations and the amazing protea.

Sugar, actually a member of the grass family, is still very important to Maui's economy, but without federal subsidies it wouldn't be a viable cash crop. The largest acreage is in the central

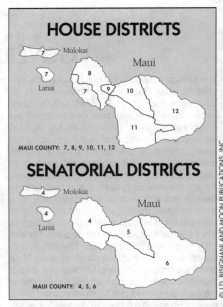

HOUSE DISTRICTS

Molokai 7

Lanai 7

Maui 8, 7, 9, 10, 11, 12

MAUI COUNTY: 7, 8, 9, 10, 11, 12

SENATORIAL DISTRICTS

Molokai 4

Lanai 4

Maui 4, 5, 6

MAUI COUNTY: 4, 5, 6

© J.D. BISIGNANI AND MOON PUBLICATIONS, INC.

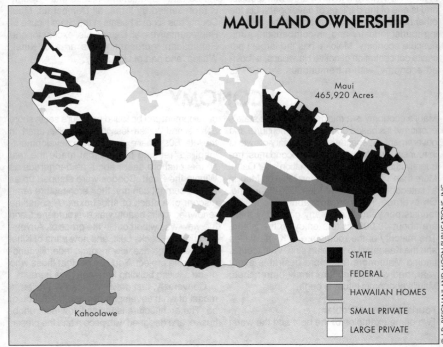

MAUI LAND OWNERSHIP

Maui
465,920 Acres

Kahoolawe

- STATE
- FEDERAL
- HAWAIIAN HOMES
- SMALL PRIVATE
- LARGE PRIVATE

© J.D. BISIGNANI AND MOON PUBLICATIONS, INC.

people of Lanai

isthmus area, which is virtually all owned by the Alexander and Baldwin Company. There are also large sugarcane tracts along Kaanapali and the west coast that are owned by Amfac and Maui Land and Pineapple. Those lodging in Kaanapali will become vividly aware of the cane fields when they're burned off just prior to harvesting. Making these unsightly burnings even worse is the fact that the plastic pipe used in the drip irrigation of the fields is left in place. Not cost-efficient to recover, it is burned along with the cane, adding its noxious fumes to the air.

Pineapples grow in central east Maui between Paia and Makawao, where Alexander and Baldwin own most of the land, and substantial acreage has been planted in Kapalua in the far northwest where Maui Land and Pineapple controls most of the holdings.

PEOPLE

With 116,000, Maui has the third-largest island population in Hawaii, about 9.5% of the state's total. Maui's population density is 158 people per square mile, and that for Molokai and Lanai is 26 and 20, respectively. The Kahului/Wailuku area has the island's greatest density of population, with at about 53,000 people. The Upcountry population is just over 33,000, while a little less than 20,000 live along the west coast. Hana district registers a handful over 2,000 people. The ethnic breakdown of Maui Island's 115,000 people is as follows: 42% Caucasian, 19% Filipino, 18% Japanese, 14% Hawaiian, 2% Chinese, and 5% other.

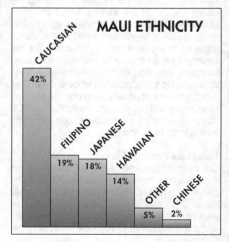

SPORTS AND RECREATION

Maui won't let you down when you want to go outside and play. More than just a giant sandbox for big kids, its beaches and surf are warm and inviting, and there are all sorts of water sports from scuba diving to parasailing. You can fish, hunt, camp, or indulge yourself in golf or tennis to your heart's content. The hiking is marvelous and the horseback riding on Haleakala is some of the most exciting in the world. The information offered in this chapter is merely an overview to let you know what's available. Have fun!

CAMPING

A major aspect of the "Maui experience" is found in the simple beauty of nature and the outdoors. Some visitors come to Maui to luxuriate at resorts and dine in fine restaurants, but everyone heads for the sand and surf, and most are captivated by the lush mountainous interior. What better way to savor this natural beauty than by hiking slowly through it or pitching a tent in the middle of it? Maui offers a full range of hiking but more limited camping, and most of it is easily accessible. Camping facilities are located both along the coast and amid the scenic forest areas of Haleakala. They range in amenities from housekeeping cabins to primitive "hike-in" sites. All require camping permits—inexpensive for the county, free for the state and national parks. Camping permits can be obtained by walk-in application to the appropriate office or by writing. Although there is usually no problem obtaining sites, when writing, request reservations well in advance, allowing a minimum of one month for letters to go back and forth.

Haleakala National Park
Camping at Haleakala National Park is free, but there is an automobile entrance fee of $10, $5 for bikers and hikers. Permits are not needed to camp at Hosmer Grove, just a short drive from park headquarters, or at Kipahulu Campground along the coastal road 10 miles south of Hana. Camping is on a first-come, first-served basis, and there's an official three-day stay limit, but

it's a loose count, especially at Kipahulu, which is almost always empty. The case is much different at the campsites located inside Haleakala Crater proper. On the floor of the crater are two primitive tenting campsites, one at Paliku on the east side and the other at Holua on the north rim. For these you'll need a wilderness permit from park headquarters. Because of ecological considerations, only 25 campers per night can stay at each site, and a three-night, four-day per month maximum stay is strictly enforced, with tenting allowed at any one site for only two consecutive nights. However, because of the strenuous hike involved, campsites are open most of the time. You must be totally self-sufficient and equipped for cold-weather camping to be comfortable at these two sites.

Also, Paliku, Holua, and another site at Kapalaoa on the south rim offer cabins. Fully self-contained with stoves, water, and nearby pit toilets, they can handle a maximum of 12 campers each. Bunks are provided, but you must have your own warm bedding. The same maximum-stay limits apply as in the campgrounds. Staying at these cabins is at a premium—they're popular with visitors and residents alike. Reservations for the cabins must be made at least 90 days in advance by mail using only a special cabin reservation request form. A lottery of the applicants chosen for sites keeps it fair for all. These cabins are geared toward groups, with rates of $40 for one to six people or $80 for up to the limit of 12. To have a chance at getting a cabin, write well in advance for complete information to: Haleakala National Park, P.O. Box 369, Makawao, HI 96768, or call (808) 572-9306, website: http://www.nps.gov/hale/.

State Parks
There are eight state parks on Maui, managed by the Department of Land and Natural Resources through their Division of State Parks. These facilities include everything from historical sites to wildland parks accessible only by trail. Some are only for looking at, some are restricted to day use, and two of them have overnight camping. Polipoli Spring and Wainapanapa offer free

Haleakala crater

Usually, tent camping permits are no problem to secure on the day you arrive, but reserving ensures you a space and alleviates anxiety. The permits are available from the Maui (Molokai also) Division of State Parks, 54 S. High St., Wailuku, HI 96793, tel. (808) 984-8109. Office hours are Mon.-Fri. 8 a.m.-4 p.m.

County Parks

There are 16 county parks scattered primarily along Maui's coastline, and because of their locations, they're generally referred to as **beach parks.** Most are for day use only, where visitors fish, swim, snorkel, surf, picnic, and sunbathe, but only Kanaha Beach Park in Kahului has overnight camping. Camping fees are quite reasonable at $3 per night per person, 50 cents for children, with no more than three consecutive nights at the park. To get a permit and pay your fees for use of a county beach park, either write in advance or visit the following issuing offices (Mon.-Fri. 9 a.m. to 5 p.m.): **Maui,** Dept. of Parks and Recreation, Permit Office, 1580-C Kaahumanu Ave., (in the War Memorial Gym) Wailuku, HI 96793, tel. (808) 243-7389; or **Molokai,** Mitchell Pauole Center, Kaunakakai, HI 96748, tel. (808) 553-3204.

HIKING

The hiking on Maui is excellent; most times you have the trails to yourself, and the wide possibility of hikes range from a family saunter to a strenuous trek. The trails are mostly on public lands although some cross private property. With the latter, the more-established routes cause no problems, but for others you'll need special permission. But plenty of public access trails along the coast and deep into the interior will fill the itineraries of even the most intrepid trekkers. If you enjoy the great outdoors on the Mainland, you'll be thrilled by these "mini-continents," where in one day you can go from the frosty summits of alpine wonderlands down into baking cactus-covered deserts and emerge through jungle foliage onto a sun-soaked subtropical shore.

Haleakala Hikes

The most spectacular hikes on Maui are through Haleakala Crater's 30 miles of trail. **Halemauu**

tenting, and housekeeping cabins are available; reservations highly necessary. Permits are required at each, and RVs technically are not allowed.

Housekeeping cabins are available. As with camping, permits are required with the same five-day maximum stay (Polipoli Spring cabin is closed on Tuesday night). Reservations are absolutely necessary, especially at Wainapanapa, and a 50% deposit at time of confirmation is required. There's a three-day cancellation requirement for refunds, and payment is to be made in cash, money order, certified check, or personal check, the latter only if it's received 30 days before arrival so that cashing procedures are possible. The balance is due on date of arrival. Cabins are $45 per night for up to four people, and $5 for each person up to the limit (six for Wainapanapa and 10 for Polipoli Spring). These are completely furnished down to the utensils, with heaters for cold weather and private baths.

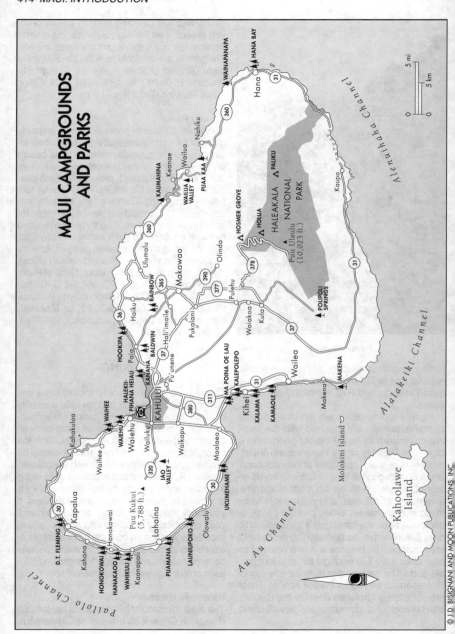

MAUI CAMPGROUNDS AND PARKS

© J.D. BISIGNANI AND MOON PUBLICATIONS, INC.

Trail is 10 miles long, beginning three miles up the mountain from park headquarters. It quickly winds down a switchback descending 1,400 feet to the crater floor. It passes Holua Cabin and goes six more miles to Paliku Cabin, offering expansive views of Koolau Gap along the way. A spur leads to Sliding Sands Trail and a short walk to the visitors center. This trail passes Silversword Loop and the Bottomless Pit, two attractions in the crater. **Sliding Sands Trail** might be considered the main trail, beginning from the visitors center at the summit and leading 10 miles over the crater floor to Paliku Cabin. It passes Kapalaoa Cabin en route and offers the best walk through the crater, with up-close views of cinder cones, lava flows, and unique vegetation. **Kaupo Gap Trail** begins at Paliku Cabin and descends rapidly through the Kaupo Gap, depositing you in the semi-ghost town of Kaupo. Below 4,000 feet the lava is rough and the vegetation thick. You pass through the private lands of the Kaupo Ranch along well-marked trails. Without a pickup arranged at the end, this is a tough one because the hitching is scanty.

West Maui Trails
The most frequented trails on West Maui are at Iao Needle. From the parking area you can follow the **Tableland Trail** for two miles, giving you beautiful panoramas of Iao Valley as you steadily climb to the tableland above, or you can descend to the valley floor and follow Iao Stream to a series of small but secluded swimming holes. **Waihee Ridge Trail** is a three-mile trek leading up the windward slopes of the West Maui Mountains. Follow Rt. 34 around the backside to Maluhia Road and turn up it to the Boy Scout camp. From here the trail rises swiftly to 2,560 feet. The views of Waihee Gorge are spectacular. The **Waihee Trail** runs into this narrow valley. North of the town of Waihee turn left at the Oki Place road sign. Proceed as far as you are able to drive, park your car, and walk up along the flume. This level track takes you over two suspension footbridges, through a bamboo forest, and under huge banyan trees until you reach the head dam. By crossing the river here, you can follow a smaller trail farther up the valley. **Kahakuloa Valley Trail** begins from the tiny fishing village of Kahakuloa on Maui's backside along Rt. 34. Start from the schoolhouse, passing burial caves and old terraced agricultural sites. Fruit trees line the way to trails ending two miles above the town.

Lahaina Pali Trail is a Na Ala Hele (Hawaii Trail and Access System) trail. Five miles long, it starts near mile marker 11, west of the Lahaina Tunnel, follows an old established trail that crosses the Kealaloloa Ridge at 1,600 feet, and descends to an access road that meets the highway near the junction of Highway 30 and 380. This trail is hot and dry so bring plenty of water.

Kula and Upcountry Trails
Most of these trails form a network through and around Polipoli Spring State Recreation Area, and are all accessible from the camping area at 6,200 feet. **Redwood Trail,** 1.7 miles, passes through a magnificent stand of redwoods, past the ranger station and down to an old Civilian Conservation Corps camp at 5,300 feet where there's a rough old shelter. **Tie Trail,** one-half mile, joins Redwood Trail with **Plum Trail,** so named because of its numerous plum trees, which bear during the summer. **Skyline Trail,** 6.5 miles, starts atop Haleakala at 9,750 feet, passing through the southwest rift and eventually joining the **Haleakala Ridge Trail,** 1.6 miles, at the 6,500-foot level, then descends through a series of switchbacks. You can join the Plum Trail or continue to the shelter at the end. Both the Skyline and Ridge trails offer superb vistas of Maui.

Others throughout the area include: **Polipoli,** 0.6 miles, passing through the famous forests of the area; **Boundary Trail,** four miles, leading from the Kula Forest Reserve to the ranger's cabin, passing numerous gulches still supporting native trees and shrubs; **Waiohuli Trail,** descending the mountain to join Boundary Trail and overlooking Keokea and Kihei with a shelter at the end; **Waiakoa Trail,** seven miles, beginning at the Kula Forest Reserve Access Road. It ascends Haleakala to the 7,800-foot level and then descends through a series of switchbacks, covering rugged territory and passing a natural cave shelter. It eventually meets up with the three-mile **Waiakoa Loop Trail.** All of these trails offer intimate forest views of native and introduced trees, and breathtaking views of the Maui coastline far below.

Coastal Trails

Along Maui's southernmost tip the **King's Highway Coastal Trail**, 5.5 miles, leads from La Perouse Bay through the rugged and desolate lava flow of 1790, the time of Maui's last volcanic eruption. This trail gets extremely rugged and should not be attempted by car, but is easy on foot. It leads over smooth stepping stones that were at one time trudged by royal tax collectors. The trail heads inland and passes many ancient Hawaiian stone walls and stone foundation sites. Spur trails lead down to the sea, including an overview of Cape Hanamanioa and its Coast Guard lighthouse. The trail eventually ends at private land.

Hana Wainapanapa Coastal Trail is on the opposite side of East Maui. You start from Wainapanapa State Park or from a gravel road near Hana Bay and again you follow the flat, laid stones of the "King's Highway." The trail is well maintained but fairly rugged due to lava and cinders. You pass natural arches, a string of *heiau*, blowholes, and caves. The vegetation is lush, and long fingers of black lava stretch out into cobalt-blue waters. This trail should take about three hours. The trail does continue beyond Wainapanapa along the coast to the Hana Airport, another two hours.

Hiking Tours

Hike Maui, P.O. Box 330969, Kahului, Maui, HI 96733, tel. (808) 879-5270, fax 876-0308, as its name implies, offers walking tours to Maui's best scenic areas accompanied by Ken Schmitt, a professional nature guide. Ken has dedicated years to hiking Maui and has accumulated an unbelievable amount of knowledge about this awesome island. He's proficient in Maui archaeology, botany, geology, anthropology, zoology, history, oceanography, and ancient Hawaiian cosmology. Moreover, he is a man of dynamic and gracious spirit who has tuned in to the soul of Maui. He hikes every day and is superbly fit, but will tailor his hikes for anyone, though good physical conditioning is essential. Ken's hikes are actually workshops in Maui's natural history. As you walk along, Ken imparts his knowledge but he never seems to intrude on the beauty of the site itself. Ken has finally expanded his operation to include a small hand-picked staff of assistants, each trained in the sciences, with the soul of an adventurer, and the heart of an environmentalist. His hikes require a minimum of four people and a maximum of eight. He offers gourmet breakfasts, lunches, and snacks with an emphasis on natural health foods. All special equipment is provided, but you are requested to wear comfortable walking/hiking shoes. His hikes take in sights from Hana to West Maui and to the summit of Haleakala, and range from the moderate to the hardy ability level. Half-day hikes last about five hours and all-day hikes go for eight hours or more. The rates vary from $75 ($55 for children) to $115 ($90 for children). A day with Ken Schmitt or one of his guides is a classic outdoor experience. You'll be in the hands of experts. Don't miss it! (E-mail: hike@hikemaui.com, website: www.hikemaui.com.)

Mango Mitch Ecotours is another well established company (since 1984) that offers half day, full day, and overnight hikes, as well as multiple day expeditions to other islands, for small groups. Half day hikes and snorkel trips run $48-58, the full day Hana area hike and swim is $88. An overnight in Haleakala crater runs $118. Call for information on multiple day trips. For Maui tours, refreshments and some gear are provided; all meals and equipment are provided on the overnight tours. Aside from the hiking experience itself, Mango Mitch wants to impart knowledge about Hawaii's natural history and culture to all his guests. Write or call: P.O. Box 2511, Wailuku, HI 96793, tel. (808) 875-9106, (800) 552-6541 or e-mail: mangopik@maui.net.

Maui Hiking Safaris, P.O. Box 11198, Lahaina, HI 96761, tel. (808) 573-0168, (888) 445-3963, fax (808) 572-3037, also offers organized group hike for $49 a half day or $89 a full day, all gear, snacks, and beverages provided. Various hikes are offered through valleys and forests, to waterfalls, up along ridges, and onto lava flows, and each hike is narrated with special attention to history, botany, and/or volcanology. Tours are led by Randy Weaver. (E-mail: mhs@maui.net, website: www.maui.net/~mhs.)

Paths in Paradise offers various hikes, easy to strenuous, from half day to full day, most on Haleakala and its slope, with an emphasis on natural history and birds. Fees run $75-115 with discounts for children. All food and necessary gear are provided. Hikes are lead by Renate

Gassmann-Duvall, Ph.D.; tours in German available. For information and reservations: P.O. Box 667, Makawao, HI 96768, tel. (808) 573-0094, fax 572-1584. (Website: www.maui.net/~corvusco; e-mail: corvusco@maui.net).

Soul Journeys to Paradise runs easy to challenging half day and full day hikes, $85-120, snacks and any equipment included. These hikes can be done in conjunction with rejuvenating retreats in Upcountry. Contact them at P.O. Box 612, Kula, HI 96790, tel. (808) 876-1629, e-mail: journeys@maui.net, website: www.maui.net/~journeys.

Or try **Eco Tours** for various hike, hike-swim, and overnight options costing $55-285, with family rates available. For information and reservations, call (808) 572-8331, e-mail: daniel@maui.net, website: www.maui.net/~daniel.

For hikes through tracts of Maui Land and Pineapple Company of West Maui, try **Kapalua Nature Society.** Two hikes are given, the private Maunalei Arboretum and Pu'u Ka'eo nature walk and the Manienie Ridge hike. Both $80, these hikes are moderate in endurance. All moneys go to the maintenance of Pu'u Kukui Preserve, on the mountainside above. Contact Kapalua Nature Society, 800 Kapalua Dr., Kapalua, HI 96761, tel. (808) 669-8088, website: www.kapaluamaui.com/nature.htm.

Equipment

You can find only a few stores that sell or rent camping and hiking equipment on Maui. For sales in Kahului, try **The Bike Shop** at the Triangle Square Mall in Kahului, open Tues.-Fri. 10 a.m.-6 p.m., and Saturday 9 a.m.-5 p.m. **Sports Authority, Costco,** and **K-Mart** also carry some equipment, but not usually as fine a quality. **Base Camp** across from the Steak House in Makawao, open 10 a.m.-6 p.m. Mon.-Fri., until 1 p.m. on Saturday, has a full range of camping and hiking equipment, more than you'll find anywhere else on the island. They also rent: exterior-frame backpacks at $35 a weekend, two-person tents at $35 a weekend, and sleeping bags, $25 the first night and $10 each night after that for a 20-degree bag for inside the crater, or $20 the first night and $5 additional nights for lighter-weight bags.

BEACHES AND PARKS

Since the island is blessed with 150 miles of coastline, more than 32 of which are wonderful beaches, your biggest problem is to choose which one you'll grace with your presence. The following should help you choose just where you'd like to romp about. But before you romp, pick up and read the brochures *Maui Beach Safety Tips* by the American Red Cross, and *Beach and Ocean Safety Information,* both found at most free information stands around the island.

West Maui Beaches

The most plentiful and best beaches for swimming and sunbathing are on West Maui, strung along 18 glorious miles from Kapalua to Olowalu. For an all-purpose beach you can't beat **D.T. Fleming Beach** or **Kapalua Beach** on Maui's western tip. It has everything: safe surf (except in winter), great swimming, snorkeling, and bodysurfing in a first-class, family-oriented area. Then come the **Kaanapali Beaches** along Rt. 30, bordered by the hotels and condos. These are open to the public, and "rights of way" pass just along hotel grounds. **Black Rock** at the Sheraton is the best for snorkeling. In Lahaina, **Lahaina Beach,** is convenient but not private and just so-so. **Puamana and Launiupoko Beaches** have only fair swimming, but great views and picnic areas. **Olowalu** has very good swimming beaches just across from the General Store, and **Papalaua Wayside** offers seclusion on a narrow beach fringed by *kiawe* trees that surround tiny patches of white sand.

Kihei and Wailea Beaches

The 10 miles stretching from Maalaea to Wailea are dotted with beaches that range from poor to excellent. **Maalaea** and **Kealia** beaches extend four miles from Maalaea to Kihei. These are excellent for walking, windsurfing, and enjoying the view, but little else. **Kamaole Beach I, II,** and **III** are at the south end of Kihei. Top-notch beaches, they have it all—swimming, snorkeling, and safety. **Keawakapu** is more of the same. Then come the great little beaches of Wailea that get more secluded as you head south: **Mokapu, Ulua, Wailea,** and **Polo.** All are surrounded by the picture-perfect hotels of Wailea and all have public access. **Makena Beach,** down the road from Wailea, is very special. It's one of the island's best beaches. At one time, alternative people made Makena a haven and it still attracts free-spirited souls. There's nude bathing here in secluded coves, unofficial camping, and freedom. It gets the highest compliment when locals, and those staying at hotels and condos around Maui, come here to enjoy themselves.

Wailuku and Kahului
Poor ugly ducklings! The beaches in town are shallow, unattractive beaches and no one spends any time there. However, **Kanaha Beach** near the airport isn't bad at all and it's a favorite of beginning windsurfers. **H.P. Baldwin Beach** has a reputation for hostile locals protecting their turf, but the beach is good and you won't be hassled if you "live and let live." **Hookipa Beach** just east of Paia isn't good for the average swimmer, but it is the "sailboarding capital" of Hawaii, and you should visit here just to see the exciting, colorful spectacle of people skipping over the ocean with bright sails.

Hana Beaches
Everything about Hana is heavenly, including its beaches. There's **Red Sand Beach,** small, but almost too pretty to be real. **Wainapanapa** black sand beach is surrounded by the state park and good for swimming and snorkeling, even providing a legendary cave whose waters turn blood red. **Hana Bay** is well protected and safe for swimming. Just south of town is the white sand **Hamoa Beach,** described by James Michener as looking like the South Pacific.

Freshwater Swimming
There are several places for freshwater swimming in various stream pools on the road to Hana. One of the very best is **Twin Falls,** up a short trail from Hoolawa Bridge. **Helio's Grave** is another good swimming spot between Hana and Oheo Gulch. Farther along at **Kipahulu** you'll find the paradise you've been searching for—gorgeous freshwater pools at the base of wispy waterfalls and fronted by a tremendous sea of pounding surf only a few yards away. Also, you can take a refreshing dip at **Iao Stream** when

you visit Iao Needle or in the next large valley north of there in **Waihee Stream.**

SNORKELING AND SCUBA

Maui is as beautiful under the waves as it is above. There is world-class snorkeling and diving at many coral reefs and beds surrounding the island. You'll find some of the best, coincidentally, just where the best beaches are: mainly from Kihei to Makena, up around Napili Bay and especially around Olowalu. Backside Maui is great (but mostly for experts), and for a total thrill, try diving Molokini, the submerged volcano, just peeking above the waves and designated a Marine Life Conservation District.

Great Underwater Spots
These are some of the best on Maui, but there are plenty more. Use the same caution when scuba diving or snorkeling as when swimming. Be mindful of currents. It's generally safer to enter the water in the center of a bay than at the sides where rips are more likely to occur. The following sites are suitable for beginners to intermediates: on Maui's western tip **Honolua Bay** and nearby **Mokuleia Bay,** known as "Slaughterhouse," but gentle, both part of a Marine Life Conservation District; **Napili Bay** for usually good and safe conditions; in Kaanapali you'll enjoy **Black Rock** at the Sheraton Hotel; at **Olowalu,** the ocean is very gentle with plenty to see; also try **Kamaole Parks II** and **III** in Kihei, and **Ulua, Polo,** and **Wailea** beaches in Wailea. On the windward side, **Baldwin Beach Park** in Paia and **Wainapanapa State Park** near Hana are both generally good. Under no circumstances should you miss taking a boat out to **Molokini.** It's worth every penny, even though it's getting rather crowded! Some boats also stop at **Turtle Town** off the south coast.

For scuba divers, there are underwater caves at **Nahuna** (Five Graves) **Point** just up from Makena landing, great diving at **Molokini,** magnificent caves out at the **Lanai Cathedrals,** and a **sunken Navy sub,** the USS *Bluegill,* to explore. Advanced divers *only* can attempt the backside of **West Maui,** the coast at **Kipahulu,** and beyond **Pu'uiki Island** in Hana Bay.

Equipment

Sometimes condos and hotels have snorkeling equipment free for their guests, but if you have to rent it, don't do it from a hotel or condo; go to a dive shop where it's much cheaper. Expect to spend $5-7 a day for mask, fins, and snorkel. One of the best snorkel deals is through **Snorkel Bob's,** tel. (808) 879-7449 Kihei, 661-4421 Lahaina (also in Napili and Kihei). Old Snorkel Bob will dispense information and full snorkel gear for only $14 weekly, which you can return on a neighbor island for a mere $3 charge, if you'll be heading that way before the week is up. More expensive custom snorkel equipment, hard bottom boogie boards, and flotation boards are also available for rent. **A & B Rentals and Sportswear,** in Honokowai in Da Rose Mall at 3481 Lower Honoapiilani Rd., tel. (808) 669-0027, open daily 9 a.m.-5 p.m., rents snorkel gear ($2.50 per day and $9 per week) and boogie boards. Numerous other shops on the island also rent snorkel gear at comparable but variable rates depending upon the quality of the equipment.

Scuba divers can rent gear for about $40 from most shops. All the shops listed below rent snorkel gear as well. In Lahaina rent from: **Lahaina Divers,** tel. (808) 667-7496, at 143 Dickenson St., one of the best all-around shops/schools on Maui; **Maui Dive Shop,** Lahaina Cannery Mall, tel. (808) 661-5388; **Capt. Nemo's Scuba Shack,** 150 Dickenson, tel. (808) 661-5555; and **Maui Diving,** in Anchor Square in Lahaina, tel. (808) 667-0633.

In Kihei-Wailea all-around dive shops are **Maui Dive Shop,** 1455 S. Kihei Rd., tel. (808) 879-3388; **Dive and Sea Maui,** 1975 S. Kihei Rd., tel. (808) 874-1952; and **Pacific Dive Maui,** at 1993 S. Kihei Rd., tel. (808) 874-5332. You might also consider renting an underwater camera. Expect to spend $15-20, including film.

With a name like Chuck Thorne, what else can you expect but a world-class athlete of some kind? Well, Chuck is a diver who lives on Maui and receives the highest accolades from other people. He's written *The Divers' Guide to Maui,* the definitive book on all the best dive/snorkel spots on the island. While he's no longer available as a guide, his book is still available at many scuba outlets and Amazon.com or you can write for it direct: Maui Dive Guide, P.O. Box 40, Hana,

HI 96713. This book is an invaluable resource, well worth the money and the effort to check it out.

Scuba Certification

A number of Maui companies take you from your first dive to PADI, NAUI, or NASDS certification. Prices range from $50 for a quickie refresher dive up to $300-400 for a four- to five-day certification course. Courses or arrangements can be made with any of the dive shops listed above, or with **Ocean Activities Center,** tel. (808) 879-4485; **Beach Activities of Maui,** tel. (808) 661-5500; **Ed Robinson's Diving Adventures,** tel. (808) 879-3584; or **Maui Diving,** tel. (808) 667-0633. Most major hotels also contract for scuba instruction for their guests, and most of these providers have booths on the hotel property.

Snorkel and Scuba Excursions

Many boats will take you out snorkeling or diving. Prices range from $30 (half day, four hours) to $60 (full day, eight hours) for a snorkeling adventure, and $50-100 for scuba diving. Some of these boats also do deep-sea fishing, moonlight cruises, and other charters. All "activities centers" on the island can arrange these excursions for no extra charge. Although there is some cross over, typically boats leaving from Lahaina harbor go to Lanai or to spots along the west and north Maui coast to dive; those out of Maalaea or Makena go to Molokini or along the south coast of Maui.

Mike Severns, tel. (808) 879-6596, is one of the most experienced and respected divers on Maui. As a marine scientist/explorer, he is extremely knowledgeable about Maui both above and below the waves. Mike has his own boat and accepts both beginning and advanced divers. He dives mostly along the south coast. Diving with Mike is an extraordinary educational experience.

Dive and Sea Maui, 1975 S. Kihei Rd., tel. (808) 874-1952, open daily 7 a.m.-5 p.m., until noon on Sunday, is a full-service dive shop offering scuba dives, certification classes, air refills, equipment rentals, and dive/snorkel trips to Molokini Crater on a six-passenger Mako boat so that you are given individual attention and full value for the money.

The **Maui Dive Shop,** at Azeka II Shopping Center along S. Kihei Rd., tel. (808) 891-0153 or (800) 542-3483 (with nine other locations on the island) is a full-service water sports store that also operates snorkel and scuba dives to Molokini Crater and the south shore, or to Lanai depending upon water conditions and harbor of departure. (Website: www.mauidiveshop.com.)

For a magnificent day of sailing, exploring, and snorkeling, you can't beat **Trilogy Excursions,** tel. (808) 661-4743 or (800) 874-2666, whose sleek catamarans leave Lahaina Harbor for a day-trip to Lanai and Maalaea Harbor for Molokini.

Capt. Nemo's Scuba Shack, 150 Dickenson St. (with two locations in Kihei), tel. (808) 661-5555 or (800) 367-8088, offers open-water certification classes, beach dives, and night dives. This full-service scuba/snorkel store does daily rentals on scuba and snorkel equipment, boogie boards and other water gear, and also has a complete repair facility and air fill station for those already certified. Nitrox available. Snorkel tours are also offered to South Maui locations.

Lahaina Divers, at 143 Dickenson St. next to Pacific Whale Foundation, tel. (808) 667-7496, (800) 998-3483, website: www.lahainadivers .com, offers a snorkeling experience, various scuba dives, and certification courses. Lahaina Divers uses its own boats for all of their excursions and offers beverages and snacks on all trips. This company is well regarded.

A great deal for those staying in South Maui is **Ed Robinson's Diving Adventures,** tel. (808) 879-3584 or (800) 635-1273 Mainland, e-mail: robinson@maui.net, website: www.mauiscuba.com. They operate a beach cabana at the Four Seasons Resort in Wailea and run tours from their fully equipped boat to spots all over the island and to Molokini and Lanai. Offered are free daily scuba clinics at the hotel, introductory and refresher shore and boat dives, Wailea reef dives, 007 underwater scooter dives, one-, two-, and three-tank dives, and night dives. PADI certification runs $485 and includes everything.

Among the many other companies check out: in South Maui: **Provider,** tel. (808) 875-4004; **Reef Watchers,** tel. (808) 874-3467; **Makena Coast Charters,** tel. (808) 874-1273 or (800) 833-6483; or **Boss Frog's,** tel. (808) 875-4477; or in West Maui: **Tropical Divers Maui,** tel. (808)

667-7709, website: www.scubamaui.com; **Happy Maui Diving and Tours,** tel. (808) 669-0123; or **Maui Diving,** tel. (808) 667-0633.

For a pure snorkeling adventure besides those offered by the dive shops and tour boats above, try **Island Explorations,** tel. (808) 572-8437, with Ann Fielding, the naturalist author of *Hawaiian Reefs and Tide Pools* and *Underwater Guide To Maui,* which details many of the invertebrates and reef fish that you will encounter on one of her fantastic dives. Ms. Fielding will instruct you in snorkeling and in the natural history and biology of what you'll be seeing below the waves. She tailors the dive to fit the participants, and does scuba as well. A basic snorkel dive, about two hours, costs $40.

Snuba

Try **The Four Winds,** tel. (808) 879-8188, a snorkel-dive boat that goes to Molokini Crater, or **Island Scuba,** tel. (808) 661-3369. Only a few others outfits are now starting to offer snuba on Maui.

MORE WATER SPORTS

Bodysurfing

All you need are the right waves, conditions, and ocean bottom to have a ball bodysurfing. Always check conditions first, as bodysurfing has led to some very serious neck and back injuries for the ill-prepared. The following are some decent areas: Ulua, Wailea, Polo, or Makena beaches; the north end of Kamaole Beach Park I in Kihei; Napili Bay; and Baldwin Park.

Surfing

While the north coast of Oahu is known as the best surfing area in Hawaii—and arguably the best in the world—Maui has a few decent spots for the enthusiast. For good surfing on Maui try: Honolua Bay, Napili Bay, Baldwin Park, and Hookipa beaches. Many beginners stay at the more gentle beaches between Lahaina and Olowalu, Maalaea Beach, and the beaches in Kihei. Maui does have one spot, however, that has gained worldwide notoriety over the last several years. This is "Jaws." Jaws is a place where, on a good day, waves rise to 30-50 feet high! The conventional method of catching a wave—

paddling belly down on your board until you gain enough speed and momentum to slip down the front of the wave—doesn't work here because the height and speed of these waves. Ingenious (and maybe a bit crazy) surfers have come up with a solution—use a jet ski to gain speed and tow the surfer to the right spot before dashing out of harm's way. Some surfers use the tow rope as a big slingshot to propel themselves even faster from behind the jet ski. Surf boards used at Jaws have straps for the feet similar to a sailboard. So far, no one has died in this highly risky endeavor, but it seems likely that over time someone will bite it big. Jaws is located about 10 minutes past Hookipa Beach on the road to Hana and then down a road toward the ocean. People are reluctant to give the exact location, although locals know the spot well. Some fear, and rightly so, that inexperienced surfers will give this monster a try, but home owners in the area just don't like the traffic and congestion. On a high surf day, there may be as many as 350 cars parked on the approach road.

Surfing Instruction and Gear

About three dozen shops on Maui rent surf boards and perhaps a dozen or more companies and individuals that teach the basics of surfing. Some are listed below. You can get surfing lessons in groups or individually. Lessons generally run in the vicinity of $55-65 for a group lesson that lasts about two hours and about $80 for a private lesson. Many lessons are taught directly to the south of Lahaina Harbor, while some instruction is done at the beach parks between Lahaina and Olowalu or in Kihei

The **Maui Surfing School** offers lessons at the beach just to the side of Lahaina Harbor, call (808) 875-0625 and ask for Andrea Thomas, website: www.mauisurf.com. Specializing in "beginners and cowards," they guarantee results after one lesson. Another "learn in one day" guarantee is offered by **Nancy Emerson School of Surfing,** tel. (808) 244-7873, website: www.maui .net/~ncesurf. Also in Lahaina are **Goofy Foot,** tel. (808) 244-9283; **Surf Dog Maui,** tel. (808) 250-7873; or **Maui Surf Camp,** tel. (808) 669-8940. Give **Maui Waveriders** a call in Kihei, tel. (808) 875-4761.

A good place to rent or buy surf boards and clothing in Lahaina is **Harbor Surf and Dive** at

113 Prison St., tel. (808) 667-6165. Also in Lahaina try **West Maui Cycles,** tel. (808) 661-9005; **Local Motion,** 661-7873; or **Maui Boardriders,** tel. (808) 667-7978. **A & B Rentals and Sportswear,** at the Da Rose Mall in Honokowai, tel. (808) 669-0027, open daily 9 a.m.-5 p.m., rents boogie boards, surfboards, and even fishing poles per day or week for reasonable rates. Kahului has at least three big shops where you can buy and rent surfing equipment: **Extreme Sports Maui,** tel. (808) 871-7953; **HI-Tech Surf Sports,** tel. (808) 877-2111; and **Hawaiian Island Surf and Sport,** tel. (808) 873-0689.

Sailboarding: Windsurfing

This is one of the world's newest sports, and unlike surfing, which tends to be male-dominated, women, too, are excellent at sailboarding. Hookipa Beach, just east of Paia, is the "sailboarding capital of the world," and the big-money O'Neill International Championship used to be held here every year in March and April. Today, the **Aloha Classic,** held in late October or early November, is as big as it gets, with prize money at $5,000-10,000. In addition, other windsurfing races are held annually during July and August, just down the coast at Kanaha Beach. During these events, hundreds of colorful boards fill the water to the delight of the shoreline crowd. Kanaha Beach Park, in nearby Kahului, has perfect, gentle winds and waves for learning the sport, and Kealia Beach in north Kihei is the choice of many. Summer is best for windsurfing because of the wind characteristics. Mornings are good for the novice as winds are lighter. As winds pick up in the afternoon the more advanced board riders hit the water. Any sailboard shop will point you in the right direction for location and gear according to your skill level.

To rent equipment or take instructions, try: **Maui Windsurf Company,** tel. (808) 877-4816 or (800) 872-0999, website: www.maui.net/~hst-cadiz. They have rentals from $45 a day to $395 for two weeks, and lessons for about $60-70. Remember—start with a big board and a small sail! Take lessons to save time and energy. Several others to try, with comparable rates for lessons and rentals are **Hi-Tech,** tel. (808) 877-2111; **Maui Sails,** tel. (808) 877-7443; **Hawaiian Island Surf and Sports,** tel. (808) 873-0827; **Hawaii Sail and Sport,** tel. (808) 879-0178;

Sailboards Maui, tel. (808) 871-7954; and **Windsurfing West Maui,** tel. (808) 871-8733.

For windsurfing race information and entry applications, contact **High Tech** at (808) 877-2111 or fax (808) 871-6943.

THRILL CRAFT

A recent controversy has focused on what has been called "thrill craft." Usually this refers to jet skis, water-skiing boats, speedboats, parasailing, and even sailboards. The feeling among conservationists is that these craft disturb humans, and during whale season disturb the whales that come to calve in the rather small Lahaina Roads. This is definitely a case of "one man's pleasure is another man's poison." On March 31, 1991 a law was passed that bans these types of craft from operating in west and south Maui waters during whale season: December 15-May 15. Although you might assume that this is due to the sound of the motors roaring through the waters—research has been done to determine if this is also a problem—the restriction was set in place because of the speed and unpredictable nature of these water craft.

Jet Skis

To try this exciting sport, contact **Pacific Jet Sport,** tel. (808) 667-2066, daily 9 a.m.-4 p.m., for use of jet skis and wave runners. Meet the shuttle boat on the beach in front of the Hyatt Hotel in Kaanapali and they will take you out to the pontoon boat and riding area where you'll get instruction on how to operate these water machines. Rates for either craft are $47 for a half hour or $68 an hour, and $10 extra for each additional person up to three for the wave runners.

Water-skiing

Maui Beach Activities, tel. (808) 667-1964, does water-skiing for $50 a half hour, one or two people, or $90 for an hour, for up to four people. They can pick up in the Kaanapali or Lahaina area. Visit their booth in the Whalers Village mall in Kaanapali.

Parasailing

If you've ever wanted to soar like an eagle, here's your chance with no prior experience neces-sary. Basically a parasail is a parachute tethered to a speedboat. And away we go! The most dangerous part seems to be getting in and out of the shuttle boat that takes you to the power boat from where you take off. On the power boat is a special harness attached to a parachute. You're put in a life vest, and strapped to the harness that forms a cradle upon which you sit while aloft. Make sure, once you're up, to pull the cradle as far under your thighs as you can. It's much more comfortable. Don't be afraid to loosen your steel grip on the guide ropes because that's not what's holding you anyway. In the air, you are as free as a bird and the unique view is phenomenal. You don't have time to fret about going up. The boat revs and you're airborne almost immediately. Once up, the feeling is very secure. The technology is simple, straightforward, and safe. Relax and have a ball. Cost is about $50 for a 10-minute joyride that lets out about 800 feet of line or $42 for a seven-minute ride where you are at the end of a 400-foot line. Boats leave from Mala wharf and off Kaanapali Beach. Try **West Maui Para-Sail,** tel. (808) 661-4060; **UFO Parasail,** tel. 661-7UFO; or **Para-Sail Kaanapali,** tel. (808) 669-6555.

Rental Boats

If you really want to drive one on your own, **SeaEscape U-Drive Boat Rental,** tel. (808) 879-3721, 1979 S. Kihei Rd., can rent you a boat. The inflatable seagoing Zodiac rafts go for $75/hour and the 17-foot mono-hull Boston Whaler for $95/hour. Both are Coast Guard approved for six persons and rent for a minimum of two hours.

You can also pilot a rigid-hull, inflatable Zodiac raft by contacting **H2O Tropical Tours,** tel. (808) 665-0488. Rates are $95 an hour, up to $495 for eight hours.

FISHING

Fishing Boats and Charters

The fishing around Maui ranges from very good to excellent. A sizable fleet of charter boats with skilled captains and tested crews is ready, willing, and competent to take you out. Most are berthed at Lahaina Harbor while others are at Maalaea Harbor. The best times of year for marlin are July-Sept. and Jan.-March (when the generally

the Salty Dog

larger females arrive). August is the optimum month. Rough seas can keep boats in for a few days during December and early January, but by February all are generally out.

Some of the best boats at Maalaea Harbor include: *Carol Ann,* tel. (808) 877-2181; *No Ka Oi III,* tel. (808) 879-4485, run by Ocean Activities Center; and **Makoa Kai,** tel. (808) 875-2251, captained by Dave Ventura who does only private fishing charters. In Lahaina you can't go wrong with the *Judy Ann,* tel. (808) 667-6672; **Aerial Sportfishing,** tel. (808) 667-9089; *The Finest Kind,* tel. (808) 661-0338; and *Reel Hooker,* tel. (808) 661-0338; or *Lucky Strike II,* tel. (808) 661-4606.

HORSEBACK RIDING

Those who love sightseeing from the back of a horse are in for a big treat on Maui. Stables dot the island, so you have a choice of terrain for your trail ride: a breathtaking ride through Hale-

akala Crater, across rangeland, or a backwoods ride into the rainforest. There is no riding on the beach. Choose the stable by area or type of ride offered. Unfortunately, none of this comes cheap, but you won't be disappointed by either the quality of trail hand or scenery. It's advisable to wear jeans (jogging suit bottoms will do) and a pair of closed toes shoes. Sunscreen and a hat are also recommended on most rides. All stables have age and weight restrictions, some also a height restriction, so be sure to check with them directly for all details.

Ironwood Ranch

You'll have your choice of rides: sunset, mountain, pineapple field, and extended rides for experienced riders. The West Maui Journey for all skill levels, $75 for 1.5 hours, runs through the foothills of the mountains. Also for all riders are the two-hour sunset ride for $100, and a two-hour Picnic in Paradise ride that also takes you on a short hike through a bamboo forest for $135. For the advanced rider, the Ironwood Odyssey takes you up the mountain for $125. No one over 220 pounds please. Horses are matched to the rider's experience level and all rides are escorted. Ironwood Ranch, 5095 Napilihau, Suite 308, Lahaina, HI 96761, tel. (808) 669-4991, is located at mile-marker 29 along Rt. 30 above Napili. As all rides are conducted on private ranch land, meet at the pickup point across the highway from Napili Plaza.

Makena Stables

Makena Stables, tel. (808) 879-0244, is located at the end of Makena Alanui on La Perouse Bay; owners Helaine and Pat Borge will take you on a two-hour introductory ride through low-elevation rangeland, lava flows, and along the mountain trails of Ulupalakua Ranch, three-hour morning or sunset rides, or on a five- to six-hour bay and lunch ride.

Haleakala and Environs

A few Upcountry companies offer trail rides through the crater or over the mountain. Wear *warm* clothes! **Charley's Trailride and Pack Trips** takes you on overnight camping to Haleakala, supplying all meals; in on Wednesday out on Thursday, or in on Saturday and out on Sunday. Run by Charles Aki, c/o Kaupo Store, Hana, HI 96713, tel. (808) 248-8209 (call before

ROBERT NILSEN

10 a.m. or in the evening), rates on rides of more than two people are: $250 per person per night, which includes food and camping equipment; $225 per night without food included. For only two people, the rate is $300 per person per day. Meet at Charley's residence in Kaupo for a 9 a.m. departure, early reservations required, along with $75 deposit well in advance. A hat, warm clothing, rain ponchos, and boots are recommended for all rides.

Pony Express Tours offers trail rides into Haleakala crater; full day $160, partial day $130, lunch provided. One- and two-hour rides ($40-88) are also offered across Haleakala Ranch land at the 4,000 foot elevation on this volcanic mountain. Riders must be at least 10 years old, under 65, and not more than 235 pounds. Contact Pony Express Tours, P.O. Box 535, Kula, HI 96791, tel. (808) 667-2200, e-mail: ponex@maui .net, website: www.maui.net/~ponex.

Thompson Ranch Riding Stables, a family-operated stable that will even mount up children under 10, guides you over the slopes of Haleakala on one of Maui's oldest cattle ranches. Located at 3,700 feet, just outside of Keokea. Contact Thompson Stables, Thompson Rd., Kula, HI 96790, tel. (808) 878-1910.

Adventures On Horseback offers waterfall rides along the north coast over lands of a private estate in Haiku taking a maximum of six riders, who must be at least 16 years old, more than five feet tall, and not over 225 pounds. Bring your own swimming suit and towel. For reservations and information, call (808) 242-7445, or write P.O. Box 1419, Makawao, Maui, HI 96768.

Maui Mule Ride offers two-, five-, and six-hour rides into Haleakala crater on these sure-footed beasts of burden, leaving from the visitor center parking lot near the top. Rates are $95, $155, and $190, per person, respectively. Long pants, shoes, and a jacket are a must, and it's best to bring sunglasses and a hat. A picnic lunch is provided on the longer rides, refreshments on all. For information and reservations call (808) 244-6853 or 878-1743.

Hana District

The hotel guests are given priority for use of the horses at the **Hana Ranch Stables,** but you can call ahead to arrange a trail ride on this truly magnificent end of the island. The one-hour easy guided rides (two rides in the morning and one in the afternoon) go either along the coast or into the upper pastureland; $35 per person and you must be at least seven years old. Private rides are given after 3 p.m. for $70 per person. For information, call (808) 248-8811.

In Kipahulu you'll find **Oheo Stables,** tel. (808) 667-2222. Two rides (10:30 and 11:30 a.m.) are given every day, both three hours on the trail, and the destination is the highland above Makahiku and Waimoku falls in Haleakala National Park. A maximum of six riders are taken per ride. Both rides include a continental breakfast, snacks, and drinks, while the later ride also includes lunch. The early ride is $119, the later ride $139.

Backside West Maui

Mendez Ranch and Trail Rides offer three-hour morning rides daily except Sunday over a small working ranch on the rugged north coast of Maui, $130 per person. You must be at least 11 years old and no more than 250 pounds. You'll have a look at the shoreline, pastureland, lush valleys, and waterfalls, and you round out the ride with a real *paniolo* barbecue picnic. This is a local experience lead by real cowboys. Located just past mile marker 6 on Rt. 330 north of Wailuku. For reservations, contact them at P.O. Box 150, Wailuku, HI 96793, tel. (808) 871-5222.

Past mile market 9 is **Seahorse Ranch,** which has three-hour trail rides over rangeland along the spectacular north coast. Lunch and drinks are served. Rides are $99, no one under 12. For reservations, call (808) 244-9862.

BICYCLING

Bicycles

Bicycle enthusiasts should be thrilled with Maui, but the few flaws might flatten your spirits as well as your tires. The countryside is great, the weather is perfect, but the roads are heavily trafficked and the most interesting ones are narrow and have bad shoulders. Peddling to Hana will give you an up-close personal experience, but for bicycle safety this road is one of the worst. Haleakala is stupendous, but with a rise of more than 10,000 feet in less than 40 miles it is considered one of the most grueling rides in the world. And a paved bike path runs from Lahaina to Kaanapali that's tame enough for everyone. Cycling on Maui as your primary means of transportation is not for the neophyte; because of safety considerations and the tough rides, only experienced riders should consider it.

Bicycle Rentals

Some bicycle rental shops will tell you that the Park Service does not allow you to take your bike up to Haleakala National Park—horse pucky! You *cannot* ride the bike on the hiking paths, but going up the road (40 miles uphill) is okay if you have the steam. You are given this misinformation because the bike rental shops don't want the wear and tear on their bikes, but for the prices they charge, they shouldn't squawk.

South Maui Bicycles, 1993 S. Kihei Rd., tel. (808) 874-0068, open daily 10 a.m.-6 p.m., Sunday until 2 p.m., is a rental and bike repair shop that boasts the largest fleet on Maui from which to choose. Rates are: street bikes $17 per day, $79 per week; mountain bikes $30 a day or $110 a week. Frank Hackett, the shop owner, will take time to give you tips including routes and the best times to travel.

West Maui Cycles, in Lahaina at 193 Lahainaluna Rd., tel. (808) 661-9005, and its sister store at the Kahana Manor Shops, tel. (808) 669-1169, is a full service bike sale and rental store that also carries other sporting equipment. The Lahaina store has mostly road bikes; the Kahana store, mostly mountain bikes. Standard road bike rates run from $19 a day to $79 a week; more for a high-end bike or a tandem. Mountain bikes vary from $19 a day to $200 a week, depending on suspension.

A & B Rentals and Sportswear, in Honokowai at 3481 Lower Honoapiilani Rd., tel. (808) 669-0027, open daily 9 a.m.-5 p.m., rents basic mountain bikes at $15 for 24 hours, $60 per week. Aside from running bike tours, **Haleakala Bike Company,** tel. (808) 572-2200, in Haiku also rents mountain bikes, all equipment, and a rack if you need one for $29 the first day, $20 after that, or $110 a week. Upgraded suspension increases the cost. **The Island Biker,** 415 Dairy Rd., tel. (808) 877-7744, in Kahului, rents bicycles along with their sales and repair services. Mostly mountain bikes, they go for $25 a day, $85 a week, or $250 a month.

Haleakala Bicycle Tours

An adventure on Maui that's become famous is riding a specially equipped bike from the summit of Mt. Haleakala for 40 miles to the bottom at Paia. These bikes are modified cruisers with padded seats, wide tires, and heavy-duty drum brakes, front and back. Typically, these tours take about eight hours with about three hours on the bike. Most offer a shuttle pickup and drop-off at your hotel. For tours that go to the top of the mountain for sunrise, expect to get picked up about 3 a.m.—get to bed early! Everyone who rides through the national park on these tours must wear a full motorcycle helmet. Other tours that start outside the park will provide you with a regular bicycle helmet. Warm, layered clothing is a must, long pants and closed toe shoes recommended. Most bike companies have some guidelines, like no pregnant women, minimum age of 12, must be at least five feet tall, but each company's requirements may be slightly different, so check directly with them.

A pioneer in this field is **Maui Downhill,** 199 Dairy Rd., Kahului, tel. (808) 871-2155, (800) 535-BIKE. Included in the bike ride for $115 you get two meals (continental breakfast, brunch, or a gourmet picnic lunch), windbreakers, gloves, and helmets. To drench yourself in the beauty of a Haleakala sunrise, you have to pay your dues. You arrive at the base yard in Kahului at about 3:30 a.m. after being picked up at your condo by the courtesy van. Here, you'll muster with other bleary-eyed but hopeful adventurers and munch donuts and coffee, which at this time of the morning is more like a transfusion. Up the mountain, in the van, through the chilly night air takes about one and one-half hours, with singing and storytelling along the way. Once atop, find your spot for the *best* natural light show in the world: the sun goes wild with colors as it paints the sky and drips into Haleakala Crater. This is your first reward. Next comes your bicycle environmental cruise down the mountain with vistas and thrills every inch of the way, with stops for sightseeing, food, and to let cars pass. For the not-so-early risers, other mountain descent tours are available for $50-80.

Maui Mountain Cruisers of Makawao, tel. (808) 871-6014, and **Mountain Riders,** tel. (808) 242-9739, the other two of the "big three" bike touring companies, offer pretty much the same guided bike services at competitive rates.

As twist to this convoy guided bike tour is offered by **Haleakala Bike Company,** tel. (808) 572-2200, in Haiku. With this outfit, you meet at the bike store and get fitted with your bike and given all necessary equipment. For the Sunrise tours, the van leaves at about 4:15 a.m. and brings you to the top of the mountain in the park for your sunrise experience. When the bike riders start down the mountain, the company van stays with them until they are comfortable with the bikes and route and then lets them go the rest of the way by themselves, taking their time or zipping down the hill as they like, stopping when they want and eating where they desire. All that it required is that they return by about 4 p.m. It's bike freedom. Later in the morning, another drop-off goes to the crater rim. These rides are $59. Also leaving later in the morning, drop-offs at the park entrance go for $39.

Two other companies that do a go-at-your-own-pace tour are: **Haleakala Bike Adventures,** tel. (808) 573-2888, that does a summit sunrise trip for $58 and a day-trip starting at the park entrance for $38; and **Aloha Bicycle Tours,** tel. (808) 249-0911, does a run south on Routes 37 and 377 to Ulupalakua.

Chris's Bike Adventures, tel. 871-BIKE, offers a variation on the theme, taking you on a mountain-bike adventure down Haleakala including a tour of the Tedeschi Winery, and a walk along the lava fields around La Perouse Bay, all for $99. Or you can take an afternoon ride, winding up at the winery where you can soothe your beaten bottom with a glass of *vino.*

Bicycle Touring

For those interested in bicycle touring, contact one of the following for their specialized bike trips. The owners and tour leaders of **Island Bicycle Adventures,** 569 Kapahulu Ave., Honolulu, HI 96815, tel. (808) 734-0700 or (800) 233-2226, are intimately familiar with bicycle touring and are members of the Hawaii Bicycling League. They offer tours to Maui, the Big Island, and Kauai. **Chris' Adventures** P.O. Box 869, Kula, HI 96790, tel. (808) 871-2453, runs two tours on Maui, one down Haleakala and the other on the backside of West Maui. Call for rates.

For those who like to strike out on their own, two routes are recommended. One takes you

for a 50-mile loop from Wailuku (or Lahaina) up the Kaanapali coast and around the head of Maui back to Wailuku. The road starts out in good repair, but the traffic will be heavy until you pass Kapalua. Here the road begins to wind along the north coast. Since this road has been paved, traffic around the north end has picked up, so the road will not be just yours anymore. Around the north end there is no place to get service. Go prepared, and be on the lookout for cars.

The second route is from Kahului up to Kula or Pukalani via Pulehu Road and back down the mountainside via Paia, Haiku, or Ulumalu, taking you through irrigated cane fields, the cool Upcountry region, the lush, sculpted north slope of Haleakala, and along the back of Maui.

GOLF

Maui has 10 golf courses with 16 links; all but one have 18 holes. These range from modest municipal courses to world-class private clubs. Some are set along the coast, while others back against the mountain with sweeping views of the lowlands. The high-class resort areas of Kaanapali, Kapalua, and Wailea are built around golf courses.

TENNIS

There are many tennis courts on Maui, and plenty of them are free. County courts are under the control of the Department of Parks and Recreation, which maintains a combination of lighted and unlit courts around the island. Also, some resort and private courts are open to the public for a fee, while others restrict play to members and guests only. The accompanying chart is a partial listing of what's available.

SPORTING CLAYS

An outgrowth of hunting, sporting clays is a sport that helps develop and maintain your hand-eye coordination. Shooting is done from different stations around a course, and the object is to hit a small round clay disk. Different than trap

MAUI GOLF COURSES

COURSE	PAR	YARDS	FEES	CART	CLUB RENTAL
Grand Waikapu Resort Country Club Wailuku, HI 96793 tel. (808) 244-7888	72	6,647	$200	Incl.	$30
Kaanapali Golf Courses Kaanapali, HI 96761 tel. (808) 661-3691					
North Course	71	6,136	$120	Incl.	$27
South Course	71	6,067	$120	Incl.	$27
Kapalua Golf Club Kapalua, HI 96791 tel. (808) 669-8044					
Bay Course	72	6,051	$140	Incl.	$35
Villa Course	71	6,001	$140	Incl.	$35
Plantation Course	73		$140	Incl.	$35
Makena Golf Courses Makena, HI 96753 tel. (808) 879-3344					
North Course	72	6,151	$140	Incl.	$35
South Course	36	6,168	$140	Incl.	$35
Maui Country Club Paia, HI 96779 tel. (808) 877-0616 (Monday only for visitors)	74	6,549	$45	Incl.	$10
Pukalani Country Club Pukalani, HI 96788 tel. (808) 572-1314	72	6,494	$55	Incl.	$20
Sandalwood Golf Course Wailuku, HI 96793 tel. (808) 242-4653	72	6,011	$75	Incl.	$30
Silversword Golf Club Kihei, HI 96753 tel. (808) 874-0777	71	6,404	$70	Incl.	$22
Waiehu Municipal Golf Course Waiehu, HI 96793 tel. (808) 243-7400	72	6,330	$25	$15	$25 (weekdays) $30 (weekends)
Wailea Golf Club Wailea, HI 96753 tel. (808) 875-5155, 875-5111					
Blue Course	72	6,152	$130	Incl.	$30
Gold Course	72	6,152	$115	Incl.	$30
Emerald Course	72	5,873	$140	Incl.	$30

MAUI TENNIS COURTS

COUNTY COURTS

Under jurisdiction of the Department of Parks & Recreation, 200 High St., Wailuku, Maui, tel. (808) 244-7750; there are three additional locations around the island. Courts listed are in or near visitor areas and open to the public.

TOWN	LOCATION	NO. OF COURTS	LIGHTED
Haliimaile	Haliimaile Park	1	Yes
Hana	Hana Ball Park	2	Yes
Kahului	Kahului Community Center	2	Yes
Kihei	Kalami Park	4	Yes
	Waipulani Park	6	No
Lahaina	Lahaina Civic Center	5	Yes
	Malu-ulu-olele Park	4	Yes
Makawao	Eddie Tam Memorial Center	2	Yes
Pukalani	Pukalani Park	2	Yes
Wailuku	Wailuku War Memorial Complex	4	Yes
	Wells Park	7	Yes

HOTEL AND PRIVATE COURTS OPEN TO THE PUBLIC (fees vary)

TOWN	LOCATION	TEL. (808)	NO. OF COURTS	LIGHTED
Kaanapali	Hyatt Regency	661-1234	5	Yes
	Maui Marriott Resort	667-1200	5	No
	Royal Lahaina Hotel	661-3611	10	6
	Sheraton Maui Hotel	661-0031	3	Yes
	Whaler	661-5552	5	No
Kapalua	Kapalua Tennis Center	669-6200	10	5
	Kapalua Tennis Garden	669-6200	10	4
Makena	Makena Tennis Club	874-1111	6	2
Napili Bay	Napili Kai Beach Club	669-6271	2	No
Wailea	Wailea Tennis Club	875-7767	11	3

or skeet shooting, sporting clays relies upon moving targets that mimic different animals and birds, hopping along the ground as a rabbit, springing off the ground like a teal, or flying high like a pheasant. Hawaii has about half dozen sporting clay grounds, two are on Maui and one is on Lanai. Each is designed differently but all provide the same basic service. Although a variety of options are available for the beginner to the advanced shooter, a typical round with a 20 gauge shotgun would take about an hour and cost around $100. Open daily 8:30 a.m.-dusk, **Papaka Sporting Clays** is located in Makena, tel. (808) 879-5649; call for reservations and directions. **Westside Sporting Clays** is 3.3 miles beyond Office Road in Kapalua, tel. (808) 669-7468. Reservations recommended.

FESTIVALS, HOLIDAYS, AND EVENTS

National holidays and Hawaiian state events are all celebrated and commemorated in Maui County, but several other unique happenings occur only on the Valley Isle, Molokai, and Lanai. If you happen to be visiting when any of the following are in progress, be sure to attend!

January

The **Makahiki Games,** ancient Hawaiian Olympics, plus food, arts, and crafts are held at Kaunakakai Park on Molokai, tel. (808) 533-3876.

Late January brings the college all-star **Hula Bowl** football game to the War Memorial Stadium in Kahului, tel. (808) 244-3530.

Maui Pro Surf Meet holds surfing competitions for men and women at Hookipa Beach and Honolua Bay with $40,000 in prize money; tel. (808) 575-9264.

March

The Valley Island Runners sponsor the **Maui Marathon** in early March from Kaahumanu Center in Kahului to Whalers Village in Kaanapali, tel. (808) 871-6441.

Mid-month features feminine beauty, grace, and athletic ability at the **Miss Maui Pageant** at Baldwin High School, Wailuku.

Community Kite Flying is held in Lanai City.

The **East Maui Taro Festival,** tel. (808) 248-8892, website: www.hookele.com/tarofest, is celebrated in Hana with traditional ceremonies, music, food markets, symposiums, demonstrations, and exhibitions to honor one of the island's most basic food sources and the resurgence of Hawaiian cultural traditions.

April

The **Da Kine Hawaiian Pro Am** professional windsailing competition for men and women is held at Hookipa Beach, tel. (808) 575-9264.

The "Ulupalakua Thing," otherwise known as the **Maui Agricultural Trade Show,** is the largest event for displaying and promoting Maui grown and manufactured products. Held at the Ulupalakua Ranch, admission; tel. (808) 572-7543.

May

Costumed pageants, canoe races, and a beard-judging contest commemorate times past at the **Lahaina Whaling Spree,** Lahaina.

A **May Day Program** is held at Lanai High, in Lanai City.

Maui's equestrians strut their stuff at the **Oskie Rice Polo Match** at Haleakala Ranch, Maui.

Music, song, and hula contests are the focus of the day at the **Molokai Ka Hula Piko,** held at Papahako Beach Park on the west end of Molokai. This event is held to honor the birth of hula. Craft and art demonstrations; tel. (808) 553-3876.

The annual **Molokai Challenge** is a kayak race from the west end of Molokai to Honolulu, 38 miles; tel. (808) 545-1149.

Ho'omanao Challenge is an outrigger canoe championship that starts at Kaanapali Beach and ends at Waikiki Beach on Oahu; tel. (808) 661-3271.

June

The **Annual Upcountry Fair** at the Eddie Tam Center, Makawao, is an old-fashioned farm fair right in the heart of Maui's *paniolo* country. Crafts, food, and competitions are part of the fair, tel. (808) 242-2278.

July

Head for the coolness of Upcountry Makawao for the annual **4th of July rodeo.** *Paniolo* are an old and very important tradition in Hawaiian life. Held at the Oskie Rice Arena, this old-time Upcountry rodeo can't be beat for fun and entertainment anywhere in the country.

Maui Onion Festival celebrates the island's most famous vegetable. All sorts of food and cooking related events. At Whalers Village in Kaanapali, tel. (808) 661-4567.

August

Late July or early August offers *the* most difficult marathon in the world. **The Run to the Sun** takes runners from sea level to the top of Haleakala (10,023 feet), over 37 long, grueling miles.

September
Labor Day weekend brings the well-respected **Maui Writers Conference,** usually held at one of the fancy hotel on the island; tel. (808) 879-0061.

Head back up to Makawao for another excellent **Maui County Rodeo** as well as plenty of good happenings during the statewide **Aloha Week.**

The **Molokai to Oahu Canoe Race** for women (men in October) takes off at the end of September in Hawaiian-style canoes from the remote Hale O Lono Beach on Molokai's west end to Fort DeRussy in Honolulu. In crossing, the teams must navigate the always-rough Kaiwi Channel.

October
The **Molokai Hoe Outrigger Canoe Race** for men (women in September).

Visit the **Maui County Fair** held at the fairgrounds in Kahului or the Wailuku War Memorial Complex. An old-fashioned fair with Western and homespun flavor. Ride, booths, games. Admission is $3; tel. (808) 875-0457.

Wild costumes and outlandish behavior set the mood island-wide for **Halloween** in Lahaina. The "Mardi Gras of the Pacific."

Lahaina's Pioneer Inn is headquarters for the **Lahaina Jackpot Fishing Tournament,** where the biggest marlin landed can bring big prize money.

The **Kaanapali Classic Senior PGA Golf Tournament** lures some of the game's living legends to the Kaanapali links.

November
The **Lincoln-Mercury Kapalua PGA Golf Tournament** brings golfers from around the world for this major event.

December
This month remembers Maui of old with the **Na Mele O Maui** festival in Lahaina and Kaanapali. Hawaiian music, dance, arts, and crafts are featured.

SHOPPING

This chapter will provide general information about shopping on Maui for general merchandise, arts and crafts, food, and specialty items. Specific shops are listed in the "Shopping" section of each travel chapter. Here, you should get an overview of what's available and where, with enough information to get your pockets twitching and your credit cards smoldering! Happy bargain hunting!

SHOPPING CENTERS

Those who enjoy one-stop shopping will be happy with the choices in Maui's various malls. You'll find regularly known department stores as well as small shops featuring island-made goods. The following are Maui's main shopping malls.

Kahului/Wailuku
Along Kaahumanu Avenue, you'll find **Kaahumanu Center,** the largest on the island. Here's everything from Sears and Liberty House to Sew Special, a tiny store featuring island fabrics. The mall is full-service with apparel stores, shoe stores, computer centers, art shops, music stores, gourmet coffee shop, and Waldenbooks. You can eat at numerous restaurants, buy ice cream cones, or enjoy a movie at Kaahumanu Theater.

Down the road is **Maui Mall,** featuring a photo center, Longs for everything from aspirin to film, another Waldenbooks, sports and swimwear shops, and numerous restaurants and food outlets. Sandwiched between these two modern facilities is **Kahului Shopping Center.** It's definitely "down-home" with old-timers sitting around outside. The shops here aren't fancy, but they are authentic and you can make some offbeat purchases by strolling through.

The past few years have seen a rapid expansion of mercantile outlets in Kahului. In the triangle by Kahana Pond is **Triangle Square** center, and many of its shops are dedicated to sports. Several small malls are strung along Dairy Road between Hana Highway and Hulilike Street. The newest and the second largest in

MAUI MUSEUMS AND HISTORICAL SOCIETIES

Alexander and Baldwin Sugar Mill Museum, at the corner of Puunene Ave. and Hanson Rd. in Puunene, tel. (808) 871-8058, is a small but highly informative museum on the history and culture of sugar and sugar production on the island, set next to a functioning sugar mill. Open Mon.-Sat. 9:30 a.m.-4:30 p.m.; $4 admission.

Baldwin Home, on Front St. across from the harbor in Lahaina, tel. (808) 661-3262, is the two-story home of medical missionary Rev. Dwight Baldwin. This showcase museum is the oldest stone structure on the island, and it portrays the early days of the missions on Maui. Open daily 10 a.m.-4 p.m.; $3 admission. Next door to the Baldwin Home is the Master's Reading Room, a storehouse turned officers' club from the whaling days.

Carthaginian II is a floating museum anchored at the Lahaina Harbor. This ship is a replica of a 19th-century brig, featuring whaling artifacts and exhibits on the humpback whale. Open daily 10 a.m.-4 p.m.; $4 admission.

Hale Pa'i is a printing house located on the grounds of Lahainaluna school on the hillside above Lahaina. It has an operational relic of an original printing press, original Lahainaluna press publications, and an exhibit of Lahainaluna school past and present. Open Mon.-Fri. 10 a.m.-3 p.m.

Lahaina Restoration Foundation was begun in 1962. This privately funded organization seeks to preserve and maintain the flavor and authenticity of Lahaina and its old buildings and artifacts. Its office is in the Master's Reading Room, tel. (808) 661-3262.

Bailey House Museum, at 2375 Main St., Wailuku, is a repository of Hawaiian historical objects, arfacts from the early days of the missionaries on Maui, and the paintings of Edward Bailey. Once Bailey's home, it also served at one time as a dormitory for the Wailuku Female Seminary boarding school. Open Mon.-Sat. 10 a.m.-4 p.m.; $4 admission.

Maui Historical Society is housed in the lower level of the Bailey House Museum. This society promotes interest in and knowledge of the history of Hawaii and Maui County. Free lectures during the year.

Hana Cultural Center, tel. (808) 248-8622, is located across from the entrance to Hana Bay. It preserves and restores historical artifacts, photos, and documents from the Hana area. On the grounds are a restored courthouse and jail. This cultural center also has four traditional-style buildings and maintains an ethnobotanical garden. Open daily 10 a.m.-4 p.m.; admission by donation.

Whalers Village Museum, at the Whalers Village mall in Kaanapali, displays whaling artifacts and portrays the history and culture of whaling in Hawaii. A second gallery seeks to explain the evolution and species of whale. In the courtyard is a 30-foot sperm whale skeleton. Self-guided learning experience while you shop. Open daily; free.

---

town is the **Maui Marketplace Mall** on the south side of Dairy Road, where you can find Sports Authority, Eagle Hardware, OfficeMax, several banks, clothing shops, jewelry stores, and a Borders Books outlet.

Lahaina
You can't beat Lahaina's Front Street for the best, worst, most artistic, and tackiest shopping on Maui. This is where the tourists are, so this is where the shops are . . . shoulder to shoulder. The list is endless, but you'll find art studios and galleries, T-shirts galore, scrimshaw, jewelry, silks, boutiques, leathers, souvenir junk, eel-skins, and even a permanent tattoo memory of Maui. No wimps allowed! Lahaina also has the best special-interest shopping on Maui in various little shops strung out along Front Street.

The following are the local malls: **The Wharf Cinema Center,** on Front St. has a multitude of eating establishments, as well as stores and boutiques in its multilevel shopping facility. Nearly across the street are the **Pioneer Inn Shops,** again with a multitude of clothing and gift shops, but all on street level. **Lahaina Market Place,** tucked down an alley off Front St. near Lahainaluna Road, features established shops along with open-air stalls. **Lahaina Square**

Shopping Center, Lahaina Shopping Center, and **Anchor Square,** all set between Rt. 30 and Front St., have various shops, and are the most *local* of the Lahaina malls. The **505 Front Street Mall,** is at the south end of Front St. and offers distinctive and quiet shopping away from the frenetic activity.

The **Lahaina Cannery Mall,** on Lahaina's north end, featuring restaurants, boutiques, specialty shops, fast food, and plenty of bargains. It's the largest mall on West Maui and has some of the best shopping under one roof on the island. The newest mall in town is the open-air **Lahaina Center,** located along Front St. at Papalaua Street. Stores include Hilo Hattie, Liberty House, Banana Republic, Wet Seal, Maui Dive Shop, Hard Rock Cafe, and the Front Street Theaters.

Kaanapali to Kapalua

Whaler's Village, the only mall in Kaanapali, is set right on the ocean and features a decent self-guided whaling museum. There are various eateries, upscale boutiques, art galleries, a bottle shop, film processing center, and a sundries store. It's a great place to stroll, buy, and learn a few things about Maui's past. The **Sheraton, Marriott, Westin Maui, Hyatt Regency,** and **Royal Lahaina** hotels all have shopping arcades. You'll need a suitcase stuffed with money to buy anything there, but it's a blast just walking around the grounds and checking out the big-ticket items.

Along Lower Honoapiilani Road, the villages of Honokowai, Kahana, and Napili all have small local shopping malls, mostly for everyday items. Two new and larger malls have opened on Honoapiilani Highway, however. At **Kahana Gateway Mall** is one of Maui's finest restaurants, a hardware store, a number of apparel shops, a laundromat, and even a sporting goods store. Farther along is the more recently opened **Napili Plaza** with restaurants, shops, and a food market.

Aside from the swanky arcade at the Ritz-Carlton, and **Honolua Store,** which has a mix of clothing, gifts, and deli foods, the only place to shop in Kapalua is at the **Kapalua Shops** attached to the Kapalua Bay Hotel. Here are high-end clothing retailers, an import store, art gallery, gift shop, and one restaurant.

Kihei and Wailea

Azeka Place, Azeka Place II, and **Longs Shopping Center** are all located in the center of Kihei along Kihei Road. Here there's food shopping, a multitude of clothing, gift, and specialty shops, with a few sporting goods store, dive shops, and activities centers thrown in. Strung south along Kihei Road, one after another, are **Kukui Mall, Kihei Town Center, Kalama Village Marketplace, Dolphin Shopping Center, Kamaole Beach Center, Rainbow Mall, Kamaole Shopping Center,** and **Kai Nani Kai Village Plaza** where restaurants, food outlets, boutiques, and all manner of gift shops can be found. Aside from these larger malls, there are numerous small arcades and individual shops throughout the area.

The exclusive **Wailea Shopping Village,** has an assortment of both chic and affordable boutiques and eateries near the Renaissance, Outrigger Wailea Resort, Grand Wailea, The Four Seasons, and Kea Lani hotels, all of which have ritzy shopping arcades of their own.

The "Martinizing" of Maui

Maui has been "martinized:" K-Mart is here in Kahului, along with Costco and OfficeMax, causing a bit of spindling, mutilating, and . . . folding of local small retail shops. But to some consumers, these shopping meccas have had a positive effect upon the island—sort of.

These retail behemoths have definitely lowered some prices and made more goods available, but with an eye toward corporate gain they've put the squeeze on local "mom and pop" shops, the island's traditional retailers. We have all been programmed to accept the dubious concept that "progress is our most important product," and in consequence the demise of the neighborhood store has been repeated countless times in towns and cities around the nation. However, in the encapsulated island economy of Hawaii, this brand of progress has been particularly devastating, since there is only a limited number of shoppers to go around, especially "tourist shoppers" whose dollars are the lifeblood of the small shops. In a free economy, all have the right to trade, and you may even feel that the coming of the "big boys" was inevitable. However, some of their business practices seem to be particularly aimed at crushing their small competitors. Since the "marts" have entered the retail scene, plenty of locally owned stores and boutiques have gone under. Keep this in mind when making that "special purchase," which can just as easily be bought from a local merchant tending his or her counter, as from a blue-smocked, name-tagged Assistant Manager in Training striding the antiseptic aisles.

FOOD MARKETS

If you're shopping for general food supplies and are not interested in gourmet, specialty items, or organic foods, you'll save money by shopping at the big-name supermarkets, located in Lahaina, Kahului, and Kihei, often in malls. Smaller towns have general stores, which are adequate but a bit more expensive. You can also find convenience items at commissaries in many condos and hotels, but these should be used only for snack foods or when absolutely necessary, because the prices are just too high.

Kahului and Wailuku
The greatest number of supermarkets is found in Kahului. Three are conveniently located along Kaahumanu Avenue in or adjacent to the three malls, one right after the other. **Foodland,** open daily until 10 p.m., is in the Kaahumanu Center. Just down the road in the Kahului Shopping Center is the ethnic **Ah Fooks** open daily until 7 p.m., closes early Saturday and Sunday, specializing in Japanese, Chinese, and Hawaiian foods. Farther along in the Maui Mall is **Star Market,** open every day until 9 p.m., except on Sunday until 7 p.m. Just behind the Maui Mall on E. Kamehameha Ave. is a **Safeway.** The biggest and most well-stocked in Wailuku is **Ooka Supermarket.** Along with the usual selection of items, it has a great ethnic food section. Open daily into the evening.

Kihei
In Kihei you've got your choice of **Foodland** in the Kihei Town Center, **Star Market** up the road, and **Azeka's Market.** Azeka's is an institution, and is very famous for its specially prepared (uncooked) ribs, perfect for a barbecue.

West Maui
In Lahaina you can shop at **Foodland** in the Lahaina Square Shopping Center. More interesting is **Nagasako's** across the street at the Lahaina Shopping Center. They've got all you need, plus a huge selection of Chinese and Japanese items. Nagasako's is open daily, 7 a.m.-9 p.m., till 7 p.m. Sunday. If you're staying at a condo and doing your own cooking, the largest and generally least expensive supermarket on West Maui is the **Safeway,** open 24 hours daily, in the Lahaina Cannery Mall. North of Lahaina are the smaller but full service **Food Pantry** in Honokowai and the **Napili Market** in Napili Plaza. All others are smaller convenience stores with more limited selection and higher prices.

Around and About
Other stores where you might pick up supplies are: **Komoda's** in Makawao. They're famous throughout Hawaii for their cream buns, which are sold out by 8 a.m. At **Pukalani Superette** in Pukalani, open seven days a week, you can pick up supplies and food to go, including sushi. Larger yet, with a greater selection, is **Foodland** in the Pukalani Terrace Center. In Paia try **Nagata's** or **Paia General Store** on the main drag. In Hana is the **Hana Store,** which carries all the necessities and even has a selection of health foods and imported beers. Open daily 7:30 a.m.-6:30 p.m.

HEALTH FOOD

Those into organic foods, fresh vegetables, natural vitamins, and take-out snack bars have it made on Maui. At the island's fine health food stores you can have most of your needs met. Try the following: in Kahului, **Down to Earth Natural Foods** is an excellent full-service health food store complete with vitamins, minerals, and supplements, bulk foods, canned and boxed goods, and fresh vegetables and fruit. This store also has a deli counter, salad bar, and bakery. Open Mon.-Sat. 7 a.m.-9 p.m., Sunday 8 a.m.-8 p.m. The smaller **Maui Natural Foods,** in the Maui Mall in Kahului is open daily and has a fair selection of fresh foods, refrigerated deli items, and a huge selection of vitamins, minerals, herbs, and supplements. **Westside Natural Food** in

Lahaina is located at the corner of Lahainaluna and Wainee Streets. Open daily, they're a full-service health food store, featuring bulk items, prepared goods, and a full selection of vitamins, minerals, and supplements. In Paia, at 49 Baldwin Ave., is **Mana Natural Foods,** open daily 8 a.m.-8 p.m. You can pick up here whatever you need for your trip to Hana. They have a full range of bulk and packaged items, supplements, drinks, a deli counter, and picnic foods.

Farmer's Markets

For the best and freshest fruits, veggies, baked goods, flowers, and sometimes crafts and clothing, search out the farmers markets. Gardeners from Kula bring their fresh vegetables to the Da Rose Mall in Honokowai on Monday and Thursday 6:30-11:30 a.m., also every Tuesday and Friday 1-5 p.m. in the parking lot of Suda's Store along the *mauka* side at 61 S. Kihei Road. Be early for the best selections. In Kihei, Longs Shopping Center also hosts a farmers market every Saturday 8 a.m.-noon. All along the road to Hana are family fruit and flower stands. Many times no one is in attendance and produce, at very reasonable prices, is paid for on the honor system.

SPECIALTY SHOPS AND NEAT THINGS

Some truly nifty and distinctive stores are wedged in among Maui's run-of-the-mill shopping centers; however, for real treasures you'll find the solitary little shop the best. Lahaina's Front Street has the greatest concentration of top-notch boutiques, but others are dotted here and there around the island. The following is only a sampling of the best; many more are listed in the individual chapters.

Tattered sails on a rotted mast, tattooed seadogs in wide-striped jerseys, grim-faced Yankee captains squinting at the horizon, exotic (probably extinct) birds on the wing, flowers and weather-bent trees, and the beautiful, simple faces of Polynesians staring out from ancient days are faithfully preserved at **Lahaina Printsellers Ltd.,** one of the most unusual purveyors of art on Maui. Their three shops, like mini-museums, are hung with original engravings, draw-ings, maps, charts, and naturalist sketches ranging in age from 150 to 400 years. Each, marked with an authenticity label, can come from anywhere in the world, but the Hawaiiana collection is amazing in its depth. Many works feature a nautical theme, reminiscent of the daring explorers who opened the Pacific. The Lahaina Printsellers have been collecting for years, and are the largest collectors of material relating to Captain Cook in the entire Pacific Basin. Prices range from $25 for the smallest antique print, up to $150,000 for a rare museum-quality work. The Lahaina Printsellers keep Maui's art alive by representing modern artists as well. The three shops are at the Whaler's Village in Kaanapali, the Lahaina Cannery Mall, and at the Grand Wailea Resort.

For a unique memento of Maui have your photo taken along Front Street in front of the Pioneer Inn Shops. Here, you'll become the human perch for macaws and cockatoos. The birds are very tame, natural hams, and the only thing on Maui guaranteed to be more colorful than your Hawaiian shirt. For about $25, they'll take your picture and deliver your developed photos the next day.

Paia is quickly becoming an unofficial art center of Maui, along with being the windsurfing capital of Hawaii. Lahaina has slicker galleries, but you come much closer to the source in Paia. The **Maui Crafts Guild** is an exemplary crafts shop that displays the best in local island art. All artists must be selected by active members before their works can be displayed. All materials used must be natural, with an emphasis on those found only in Hawaii. Artists and craftspeople also work in Haiku and the vicinity, many having studios is the old Haiku or Pauwela canneries.

Upcountry's Makawao is a wonderful and crazy combination of old-time *paniolo*, matured hippies who now worry about drugs and their kids, alternative health practitioners, and up and coming artists. This hodgepodge makes for a town with tack shops, hardware stores, exclusive boutiques, art galleries, health food stores, and oriental health clinics, all strung along two Dodge City-like streets.

Kahului Swap Meet at Maui County Fairgrounds in Kahului, off Puunene Ave. is open every Saturday 8 a.m.-1 p.m. Great junk! Wailuku is Maui's **antique attic** turned out on the street.

About half a dozen odd little shops on Market Street display every kind of knickknack, curio, art treasure, white elephant, grotesque and sublime piece of furniture, jewelry, stuffed toy, game, or oddity that ever floated, sailed, flew, or washed up on Maui's beaches.

Whalers General Store and **ABC Discount Stores** are good places to look for sundries, but they can hardly be beat for prices on such things as snacks, bottles of liquor, beach towels, straw mats, straw hats, zoris, gift items, Hawaiian made products, and postcards. Anywhere on the island, you can pick up ordinary postcards, 3-5 for $1. Large size postcards go for 50 cents or $1 each, and exotic cards for various rates.

ACCOMMODATIONS

With about 18,000 rooms available, in some 225 properties, Maui is second only to Oahu in the number of visitors it can accommodate. There's a tremendous concentration of condos on Maui, approximately 9,000 units, predominating in the Kihei, Honokowai, and Kahana areas; plenty of hotels, the majority in Kaanapali and Wailea; and a growing number of bed and breakfasts. Camping is limited to a handful of parks, but what it lacks in number it easily makes up for in quality.

The Range
More than 90 hotels and condos have sprouted on West Maui, from Lahaina to Kapalua. The most expensive are strung along some of Maui's best beaches in **Kaanapali** and **Kapalua** and include the Hyatt Regency, Westin Maui, Sheraton, Kapalua Bay, and Ritz-Carlton. The older condos in Honokowai are cheaper, with a mixture of expensive and moderate as you head north. **Lahaina** itself offers only a handful of places to stay: condos at both ends of town, three renovated old-style inns, and a handful of bed and breakfasts. Most people find the pace a little too hectic, but you couldn't get more in the middle of *it* if you tried. **Maalaea Bay,** between Lahaina and Kihei, has 11 quiet condos. Prices are reasonable, the beach is fair, and you're within striking distance of the action in either direction.

Kihei is "condo row," with close to 100 of them along the six miles of Kihei Road, plus a few hotels. This is where you'll find top-notch beaches and the best deals on Maui. **Wailea** just down the road is expensive, but the hotels here are world-class and the secluded beaches are gorgeous. **Kahului** often takes the rap for being an unattractive place to stay on Maui. It isn't all that bad. You're smack in the middle of striking out to the best of Maui's sights, and the airport is minutes

Relax and enjoy la dolce vita.

away for people staying only a short time. Prices are cheaper and Kanaha Beach is a sleeper, with great sand, surf, and few visitors. **Hana** is an experience in itself. You can camp, rent a cabin, or stay at an exclusive hotel. Always reserve in advance and consider splitting your stay on Maui, spending your last few nights in Hana. You can really soak up this wonderful area, and you won't have to worry about rushing back along the Hana Highway.

To round things out, there are numerous B&Bs located here and there around the island and on Molokai and Lanai, and two hostels in Wailuku to cater to the alternative traveler. For B&B agencies, see the main introduction.

Condo Booking and Reservations

The following is a partial list of booking agents handling a number of properties on Maui.

Aston Hotels and Resorts, 2250 Kuhio Ave., Honolulu, HI 96815, tel. (808) 931-1400 or (800) 922-7886 Mainland, (800) 445-6633 Canada, or (800) 321-2558 in Hawaii, website: aston-hotels.com.

Marc Resorts Hawaii, 2155 Kalakaua Ave., Honolulu, HI 96815, tel. (808) 926-5900 or (800) 535-0085, e-mail: marc@aloha.net, website: marcresorts.com.

Destination Resorts Hawaii, 3750 Wailea Alanui, Wailea, HI 96753, tel. (808) 879-1595, (800) 367-5246, fax (808) 874-3554, website: www.destinationresortshi.com, rents condos in six separate luxury villages in Wailea.

Go Condo Hawaii, tel. (800) 452-3463, website: www.gocondohawaii.com.

Maui Condominium and Home Realty, 2511 S. Kihei Rd., P.O. Box 1840 Kihei, Maui, HI 96753, tel. (808) 879-5445, (800) 822-4409 Mainland and Canada, website: www.mauicondo.com, has more than 300 listings in all price categories with most in the Kihei area.

Condo Rentals Hawaii, 362 Huku Li'i Place, #204, Kihei, HI 96753, tel. (800)367-5242 Mainland (800) 663-2101 Canada, e-mail: crh@maui .net, website: www.maui.net/~crh.

Maui Beachfront Rentals, 256 Papalaua St., Lahaina, HI 96761, tel. (808) 661-3500, (888) 661-5200, fax (808) 661-5200, website: www.maui .net/~beachfrt, has high-end homes and condo units on West Maui.

AA Oceanfront Condo Rentals, 2439 S. Kihei Rd., Kihei, HI 96753, tel. (808) 879-7288, (800) 488-6004, has more than three dozen units from Kihei to Makena.

Kihei Maui Vacations, P.O. Box 1055, Kihei, HI 96753, tel. (808) 879-7581, (800) 541-6284, website: www.kmvmaui.com/home.html.

Klahani Resorts, P.O. Box 11108, Lahaina, HI 96761, tel. (808) 667-2712, (800) 628-6731, fax (808) 661-5875, offers units in half a dozen properties from Lahaina to Kahana.

Maalaea Bay Rentals, tel. (808) 244-7012, (800) 367-6084, fax (808) 242-7476, handles more than 100 units in a majority of the condos in Maalaea.

Unique Island Homes, tel. (808) 875-8808, (800) 961-9196.

FOOD

Luau

The luau is an island institution. For a fixed price of about $55, you get to gorge yourself on a tremendous variety of island foods, sample a few island drinks, and have a night of entertainment as well. Generally, luau run from about 5:30-8:30 p.m. On your luau day, eat a light breakfast, skip lunch, and do belly-stretching exercises! Luau food is usually served buffet-style, although one or two do it family-style. All luau have pretty much the same format, although the type of food and entertainment differ. Following is a list of the luau presently available on Maui.

Old Lahaina Luau, on the beach at its new location near the Mala Wharf, tel. (808) 667-1998, has an excellent reputation because it is as close to authentic as you can get. Seating is Mon.-Sat. 5:30-8:30 p.m., but reserve at least three to six days in advance to avoid disappointment, especially during peak season. The luau, featuring a "local's favorite," all-you-can-eat buffet and all-you-can-drink bar, costs $57 adults, children 3-12 half price. The traditional hula dancers use ti-leaf skirts, and the music is *fo' real.* The Old Lahaina Luau is one of the oldest and best luau on the island.

Renaissance Wailea Beach Resort, tel. (808) 879-4900, recounts tales of old Hawaii with its very authentic and professional hula show and luau every Tuesday, Thursday, and Saturday at 5:30 p.m. Hawaiian music, hula, drumming, and a fire dancer entertain as you dine through the evening on a wonderful assortment of foods expertly prepared by the chefs. Price includes open bar at $57 adults, $28 children 5-12. Reservations are required.

The **Royal Lahaina Resort,** tel. (808) 661-9119, has been offering a nightly luau and entertainment for years in their Luau Gardens. The show is still spectacular and the food offered is authentic and good. Prices are $62 adults, children $28, reservations suggested.

Wailea's Finest Luau, tel. (808) 879-1922, at the Outrigger Wailea Resort has garnered awards for its luau fare and Polynesian show

and its fire/knife dancer has also won an international award for his skill three years in a row. Held Monday, Tuesday, Thursday, and Friday 5-8 p.m., $58 adults, $26 children 6-12.

Hyatt Regency Maui's **Drums of the Pacific,** tel. (808) 667-4720, is held every evening 5-8 p.m., $62 adults, $39 for ages 13-20, and $25 for kids 6-12.

Legends of Makena Luau, tel. (808) 874-1111, is put on every Sunday 5:30-8:30 p.m. at the Maui Prince Hotel in Makena, $55 adults and $27 children ages 6-12. Food here is served family style, not buffet style as at most.

The **Maui Marriott** also presents its version of the luau and Polynesian show, starting the night with some Polynesian games and activities. The evening starts at 5 p.m. and runs until 8 p.m., $60 adults, $28 children 6-12. Call (808) 661-5828 for reservations.

GETTING THERE

Almost all travelers to Maui arrive by air. A few lucky ones come by private yacht, the interisland ferry from Lanai, or the cruise ship SS *Independence* which docks at Kahului. Maui, the Hawaiian destination second only to Oahu, attracts more than two million visitors per year. A limited number of direct air flights from the Mainland U.S., Canada, and Japan are offered, but most airlines servicing Hawaii, both domestic and foreign, land at Honolulu International Airport and then carry on to Maui or offer connecting flights on "interisland carriers." In most cases the connecting flights are part of the original ticket price with no extra charge. Different airlines have "interline" agreements with different Hawaiian carriers so check with your travel agent. All major and most smaller interisland carriers service Maui from throughout Hawaii with more than 100 flights per day in and out of Kahului Airport and less than a dozen a day to Kapalua-West Maui airport.

Maui's Airports
There are three commercial airports on Maui, but the vast majority of travelers will be concerned with **Kahului Airport,** which accommodates 95% of the flights in and out of Maui. Kahului Airport is only minutes from Kahului city cen-

ter, on the north-central coast of Maui. A full-service facility with all amenities, it has a few gift and snack shops, a restaurant, two tourist information booths, a newsstand, display cases of Hawaiian arts and crafts, a lost and found office, luggage storage office, bathrooms, public telephones, car rental agencies, and limited private transportation. As you face the terminal building from the parking lot, the departure lounge is on your right, the arrival lounge is on your left, and splitting the two is an upper level courtyard with shops. For your entertainment, a hula and music show is performed here for two hours at mid-day. A few steps beyond the rental car booths at the front of the arrival building is the commuter terminal, and on the far side of the runway is the heliport. **Island Air, Paragon, Pacific Wings,** and **Scenic Air** operate flights from the commuter terminal. Public parking at the airport costs $1 for the first one half hour, $1 for each additional hour, or $7 maximum per day. The Kahului Airport has recently undergone a major expansion that allows it to land the biggest commercial planes and handle a great increase in traffic, including direct international flights. Major roads lead from Kahului Airport to all primary destinations on Maui.

Hawaiian Airlines opened the one-strip **Kapulua-West Maui Airport** in early 1987. You fly in over pineapple fields. This facility is conveniently located between Kaanapali and the Kapalua resort areas, on the *mauka* side of the Honoapiilani Highway at Mahinahina just a few minutes from the major Kaanapali hotels and condos of Honokowai and Kahana. As convenient as it is to this area of West Maui, it is not heavily used. Hawaiian Air no longer operates connecting flights to West Maui with the rest of Hawaii, and for now only Island Air schedules flights and has a booth here. The small terminal is user-friendly with a snack bar, sundries shop, and courtesy phones for car rental pickup, but there is only fee parking.

The third airstrip is **Hana Airport,** an isolated runway with a tiny terminal on the northeast coast just west of Hana. It has no amenities aside from a bathroom and telephone and transportation is available only to the Hotel Hana Maui via the hotel shuttle. People flying into Hana Airport generally plan to vacation in Hana for an extended period and have made prior arrangements for being picked up. The only rental cars available in Hana can be arranged by calling Dollar Rent A Car at (808) 248-8237—call before you come!

Nonstop Flights

Until recently, United Airlines was the only carrier that offered nonstop flights from the Mainland to Maui. United flies one daily nonstop to Maui from both San Francisco and Los Angeles. Now, Delta Airlines flies once daily from Los Angeles, with other flights originating in Los Angeles and San Francisco going through Honolulu at no extra charge. American Airlines also flies daily from Los Angeles nonstop to Kahului. Hawaiian Airlines offers four weekly flights from San Francisco and Seattle to Maui.

Interisland Carriers

Hawaiian Airlines can be contacted at tel. (800) 367-5320 Mainland and Canada, (800) 882-8811 statewide, or (808) 871-6132 on Maui, website: www.hawaiianair.com. Most flights are to and from Honolulu (average flight time 35 minutes), with about two dozen per day in each direction. Hawaiian Airlines flights to Kahului, Maui, from Honolulu begin at 5:30 a.m., with flights thereafter about every 30 minutes until 9 p.m. Flights from Kahului to Honolulu begin at 6:30 a.m. and go all day until 9 p.m. There are two flights to/from Hilo daily, one at mid-morning and one in the late afternoon. Kona, on the Big Island, is serviced with one daily morning flight from Kahului, and two from Kona to Kahului, one in the morning and one in the afternoon. Kahului and Lihue, Kauai, are connected by just over a dozen flights daily in each direction, beginning at 6:30 a.m. and going into the early evening. There is one daily direct flight between Maui and Molokai. Molokai and Lanai are connected by daily late afternoon flights.

Aloha Airline, tel. (800) 367-5250 Mainland, (800) 235-0936 Canada, (808) 244-9071 Maui, website: www.alohaair.com, with its all-jet fleet of 737s, offers more flights to Maui than any other interisland carrier. It flies from Honolulu to Maui about 30 times per day beginning at 5:15 a.m. with the last flight at 8 p.m.; to Honolulu at 6:12 a.m., last at 9 p.m. Multiple flights throughout the day from Kauai begin at 6:30 a.m. until 7 p.m.; to Kauai at 6:12 a.m. and throughout the day until 6:50 p.m. To/from Hilo, two flights daily, one at mid-morning and the second in the late afternoon. From Kona three flights leave 9:30 a.m.-5:37 p.m.; to Kona, 8:47 a.m. until 4:07 p.m.

Formerly Aloha Island Air but now known simply as **Island Air,** tel. (800) 323-3345 nationwide, (800) 652-6541 statewide, (808) 877-5755 Kahului, website: www.alohaair.com, this airlines offers daily flights connecting Maui with all the major islands. Along with the main airports of Honolulu and Kahului, they service the smaller and more out-of-the-way airports of Kapalua and Hana on Maui, Lanai City on Lanai, and Hoolehua and Kalaupapa on Molokai. About half their flights are on jet aircraft and half on Dash-8 turboprop airplanes. Seven flights a day connect Honolulu to Kahului, all making stops on either Molokai or Lanai, beginning at 7:25 a.m. (5:55 from Honolulu) and run until 6:35 p.m. (5:05 from Honolulu). Four daily flights run from Molokai to Kahului (6:55 a.m.-4:30 p.m.), with two of these carrying on to Hana. Direct flights to/from Honolulu and Kapalua West Maui Airport run nine times daily 7:20 a.m.-5:15 p.m. Their newest are a direct daily flights from Kapalua-West Maui Airport to Kona, on the Big Island, and from Lanai to Kona. There are regular twice-daily flights to Kalaupapa on Molokai from Hoolehua on Molokai and from Honolulu, but only with sponsorship from a resident or a reservation on one of the organized Damien Tours.

A local company operating eight-seat, twin engine Cessna 402C planes, **Pacific Wings**, tel. (888) 575-4546, website: www.pacificwings.com, flies out of Kahului for Hana (three a day), Molokai (four a day), and Kamuela on the Big Island (once a day), as well as from Honolulu to those three destinations, no more than twice daily.

Charter Airlines
If you've got the bucks or just need to go when there's no regularly scheduled flight, try **Paragon Air**, tel. (808) 244-3356 or (800) 428-1231, website: www.maui.net/~wings/index.htm, for islandwide service. **Pacific Wings** also offers charter service throughout the state.

GETTING AROUND

If it's your intention to *see* Maui when you visit, and not just to lie on the beach in front of your hotel, the only efficient way is to rent a car. Limited public transportation, a few free shuttles, taxis, and the good old thumb are available, but all these are flawed in one way or another. Other unique and fun-filled ways to tour the island include renting a bike or moped, or hopping on a helicopter, but these conveyances are highly specialized and are more in the realm of sports than touring.

RENTAL VEHICLES

Maui has about three dozen car rental agencies that can put you behind the wheel of anything from a Mercedes convertible to a used station wagon with chipped paint and torn upholstery. There are national companies, interisland firms, good local companies, and a few fly-by-nights that'll rent you a clunker. Eight companies are clustered in little booths at the Kahului Airport, a none at either Kapalua-West Maui Airport or Hana Airport, but the Hana Hotel can arrange a car for you or you can do it yourself by calling Dollar at (808) 248-8237 *before* you arrive. The rest are scattered around the island, with a heavy concentration in Kahului, at the Kaanapali Transportation Center, and along S. Kihei Road. Those without an airport booth either have a courtesy phone or a number to call; they'll pick you up and shuttle you to their lots. Stiff competition tends to keep the prices more or less reasonable. Good deals are offered off-season, with price wars flaring at anytime and making for real savings. Even with all these companies, it's best to book ahead. You might not save money, but you can save yourself headaches.

Auto Rental Companies
The following are major firms that have booths at Kahului Airport—exit the arrival terminal and go to your right. Many pre-booked cars are waiting at these booths, but if not, and if you want to rent a car upon arrival, you must take a company shuttle to the yard across the airport parking lot to arrange for your car.

Dollar, tel. (808) 877-6526, 667-2651 in Kahului, 248-8237 in Hana, or (800) 342-7398 statewide, (800) 800-4000 worldwide, website: www.dollar.com, has an excellent reputation and very competitive prices. Dollar rents all kinds of cars as well as jeeps and convertibles. Great weekly rates, and all major credit cards accepted.

Alamo has good weekly rates, tel. (808) 871-6235 in Kahului, 661-7181 in Kaanapali, or (800) 327-9633, website: www.goalamo.com.

National Car Rental, tel. (808) 871-8851, 667-9737 in Kaanapali, or (800) 227-7368 nationwide, website: www.nationalcar.com, has cars, vans, jeeps, and station wagons.

Avis, tel. (808) 871-7575, 661-4588 Kaanapali, (800) 831-8000 nationwide, website: www.avis.com, features late-model GM cars as well as most imports and convertibles.

Budget, tel. (808) 244-4721, (800) 451-3600 statewide, or (800) 527-0700 nationwide, website: www.drivebudget.com, offers competitive rates on a variety of late-model cars.

Hertz, tel. (808) 877-5167, (800) 654-3131 nationwide, website: www.hertz.com, perhaps the best known company, offers a wide variety of vehicles with some special weekly rates.

The following local companies are based in Hawaii and either have booths at the airport or pickup services through courtesy phones. **Word of Mouth Rent a Used Car,** at 150 Hana Hwy., tel. (808) 877-2436, (800) 533-5929, pickup van provided, offers some fantastic deals on their used, but not abused, cars. All cars, standard shift or automatic, can go for as little as $90 per week (good price for windsurfers) with a three-day minimum or $15.95 per day, but expect to spend $119 per week for a nice four-door a/c late model car. Office open 8 a.m.-5 p.m., but they will leave a car at the airport at earlier or later hours with prior arrangement. Others include: **Andres,** tel. (808) 877-5378; **Kihei Rent A Car,** tel. (808) 879-7257 or (800) 251-5288; **Regency,** tel. (808) 871-6147; **Wheels R Us,** tel. (808) 667-7751 or 871-6858; and **Maui Cruisers,** tel. (808) 249-2319, who will put you in a car that will make you "look local."

Four-Wheel Drive

Though much more expensive than cars, some people might feel safer in them for completely circling Maui or driving some roads in Upcountry. Also unlike cars, the rental companies offering 4WDs put no restrictions on driving past Oheo Gulch or around the backside of West Maui. Obtain 4WDs from **Maui Rent A Jeep,** tel. (808) 877-6626 or (800) 701-JEEP; **Wheels R Us, Kihei Rent A Car,** or **Island Riders,** tel. (808) 661-9966. **Dollar** and a few other of the "big boys" also rent 4WD Jeeps. Rates vary from company to company, but are mostly around $70 per day, dependent on availability and length of rental.

Vanity Vehicles

If you feel like steeping out in *style,* consider renting a flashy sports cars. **Island Riders,** tel. (808) 661-9966 in Lahaina or 874-0311 in Kihei rents a Dodge Viper, Ferrari 348TS and 328GTS, Cobra, Porsche, and Corvette. These cars are classy but they're not cheap. However, for that one night of luxury, it may be worth it to you. Rates run from $199 for five hours to $349 for 24 hours.

Motorcycles

A few companies also rent motorcycles for the intrepid traveler. Rental bikes are all Harley-David-son big hogs or sportsters. Rates vary but run around $100 for half a day and $140-160 for 24 hours; longer rentals can be arranged. All drivers must be 21 years old, have a valid motorcycle license, and be in possession of a major credit card. Insurance is available. Companies want you to stay on good paved roads and don't usually allow trips to Hana. Although it is not required by state law to wear them, helmets are available. For riding one of these big steeds, contact **Mavrik Motorcycles Maui,** 370 Dairy Rd. in Kahului, tel. (808) 871-7118; 1215 S. Kihei Rd. in Kihei, tel. (808) 891-2299; or 10-1 Halawai Dr. in Kaanapali, tel. (808) 661-3099. Also try **Island Riders,** tel. (808) 661-9966 in Lahaina or 874-0311 in Kihei.

Mopeds

Just for running around town or to the beach mopeds are great. Expect to pay about $15 for two hours, $25 for eight hours, or $125 for the week. Check with **A & B Rentals,** in Honokowai at the Da Rose Mall, tel. (808) 669-0027; **Kukui Activity Center** at 1819 S. Kihei Rd., tel. (808) 875-1151; or **Wheels R Us,** tel. (808) 667-7751 in Lahaina or 871-6858 in Kahului.

ALTERNATIVE TRANSPORTATION

Shuttle Service

There is no public bus service on Maui, but numerous shuttle services operate from the Kahului Airport to South Maui and West Maui, between South Maui and West Maui, and within the resort developments of Kaanapali and Wailea.

Speedi Shuttle, tel. (808) 875-8070, connects Kihei and Wailea to the Kahului Airport daily 5 a.m.-9 p.m. Pickup can be from any hotel or condo in the area. Use the telephone next to the information booth in the baggage claim area when at the airport. Rates are $16 for one up to $51 for 10 people.

Airporter Shuttle, tel. (808) 877-7308 or (800) 231-6984, operated by TransHawaiian, runs a regular service to/from Lahaina and Kaanapali, with pickup/drop-off in Honokowai and Kahana by reservation only. They operate 15 runs a day, starting from the Kahului Airport at 9 a.m., with the last run from West Maui at 5 p.m. A courtesy phone and ticket booth are available at Kahului Airport next to the tourist information booth in the baggage area. Fares are $19 roundtrip, $13.50 from the airport to West Maui, and $7 from West Maui to the airport.

The free **Kaanapali Trolley** runs along the Kaanapali strip about every half hour 9 a.m.-6 p.m., stopping at all major resorts, the golf course, and the Whaler's Village shopping complex. Look for the green jitneys. Pick up free printed tourist literature or ask at any hotel desk for the schedule.

Also free is the **Lahaina Express** shuttle, which runs 9 a.m.-10 p.m. connecting various stops in Lahaina to Kaanapali. The major pickup point in Lahaina is at the rear of the Wharf Cinema Center along Front Street.

The **Wailea Shuttle** is a complimentary jitney that stops at all major hotels and condos, the Wailea Shopping Village, and golf and tennis courts in Wailea about every 20-30 minutes. It operates 6:30 a.m.-8:30 p.m. Be sure to check with the driver about the last pickup times if you are out in the evening. For information on the schedule and stops, call (808) 879-2828.

The **West Maui Shopping Express** runs two routes, both from Lahaina, one to Kaanapali and the other to Kapalua. Stops include the hotels in Kapalua and Kaanapali, the Whalers Village shopping mall in Kaanapali, and the Wharf Shopping Center, Hilo Hattie, and the Lahaina Cannery Mall in Lahaina. Buses run about every hour from mid-morning until mid-evening. Cost is $1 per person each way.

The **Whalers Village Shuttle,** called Maui Shopping Express, makes three shopping runs each day from hotels and condos in Makena, Wailea, and Kihei to the Whalers Village shopping mall in Kaanapali. The one-way fare is $15 adult, $5 for a child, but the return is free with a receipt from one of the shops or restaurants. Call (808) 877-7308 for exact pick up times and locations.

The old-style trolley-like bus, **"Da Mall" Trolley,** connects Wailea and Kihei to Kaahumanu Center, the Maui Mall, and Maui Marketplace in Kahului for your shopping pleasure. This trolley operates every day except Tuesday and Wednesday, and makes three runs each way each day: 9 a.m., 11 a.m., and 2 p.m. from the south, and 10:15 a.m., 12:15 p.m., and 5 p.m.

from Kahului. The fare is $6 per person each way, but the return trip is free with a proof-of-purchase receipt from one of the stores in these malls. Call 873-7108 for information.

For those riding the Sugar Cane Train, free transportation aboard the **Sugar Cane Trolley** is available from Front Street and the Lahaina Harbor to the Lahaina Station. Another trolley connects the Whalers Village shopping mall to the Kaanapali platform.

To get to and from the Maui Ocean Center from either Whalers Village in Kaanapali or a number of the hotels and condos in the Kihei/Wailea area, ride the center shuttle, $7 roundtrip. Starting at the Maui Prince Hotel, this shuttle runs to the center three times a day each way, once at mid-morning, the second in late morning, and the last at mid-afternoon. Call (808) 270-7000 or talk to your hotel concierge for the exact schedule.

Taxis
About two dozen taxi companies on Maui more or less operate in a fixed area. Most, besides providing normal taxi service, also run tours all over the island. While sedans predominate, some minivans are being used as well. Taxis are expensive and metered by the distance traveled. For example, a ride from Kahului Airport to Kaanapali is $55, $70 to Kapalua, and about $40 to Wailea. Expect $5-10 in and around town. In the Kihei/Wailea area, try: **Yellow Cab of Maui,** tel. (808) 877-7000; **Wailea Taxi,** tel. (808) 874-5000; or **Kihei Taxi,** tel. (808) 879-3000; in Central Maui: **Kahului Taxi Service,** tel. (808) 877-5681; and in West Maui: **Alii Cab** tel. (808) 661-3688; **AB Taxi,** tel. (808) 667-7575; or **Island Taxi,** tel. (808) 667-5656.

Classy Taxi operates between Lahaina and Kapalua, using renovated old cars from the '20s and '30s. A ride from Lahaina to Kaanapali will run about $7 and from there to Kapalua about $14.

For those who desire private limo service, there are several companies on the island that can fill the bill. These are expensive rides, however, and will run, for example, more than $120 one way from the Kahului Airport to Kaanapali. Ask your hotel concierge for assistance in arranging for this service.

Hitchhiking

After 30 years as a criminal offense, hitchhiking is no longer illegal on Maui. As one of her last duties, former mayor Linda Lingle signed a bill in early 1999 to give the right to hitch a ride back to the people. Where once you had to play the game with no thumb, now you can solicit rides in that old tried-and-true method. You can get around quite well by thumb, if you're not on a schedule. The success rate of getting a ride to the number of cars that go by isn't that great, but you will get picked up. Locals and the average tourist with family will generally pass you by. Recent residents and single tourists will most often pick you up, and 90% of the time these will be white males. Hitching short hops along the resort beaches is easy. People can tell by the way you're dressed that you're not going far and will give you a lift. Catching longer rides to Hana or up to Haleakala can be done, but it'll be tougher because the driver will know that you'll be with him or her for the duration of the ride. Under no circumstances should women hitch alone.

BY INTERISLAND FERRY

Molokai-Maui Interisland Ferry

From time to time, ferry companies have operated in Hawaii, but very stiff competition generated by the airline industry and the notoriously rough waters of the Hawaiian channels have combined to scuttle their opportunity for success. During the mid-'90s, the 118-foot vessel, *Maui Princess,* had a regular schedule ferrying passengers between Lahaina and Kaunakakai, Molokai. Alas, it to has ceased this service, but now operates several day and overnight tours to Molokai, so you can still get there by boat. For information and reservations call (808) 661-8397 or (800) 833-5800. Perhaps someday this ferry or a state-funded operation will once again take passengers by water between these two islands.

Lanai-Maui Interisland Ferry

A passenger ferry, *Expeditions,* plies between Lahaina and Manele Bay on Lanai. This shuttle service is not luxury travel but offers a speedy, efficient, and convenient transportation alternative to the Pineapple Island. You are allowed to take luggage free of charge, but there's an extra $10 fee for a bicycle. The one-hour crossing leaves Lahaina's public launch pier daily at 6:45 a.m., 9:15 a.m., 12:45 p.m., 3:15 p.m., and 5:45 p.m.; from Manele Bay at 8 a.m., 10:30 a.m., 2 p.m., 4:30 p.m., and 6:45 p.m.; adults pay $25 one-way, and children under 2-11 pay $20. *Ka-ma'aina* rates available. It is best to reserve your place. For information and reservations contact Expeditions, tel. (800) 695-2624, 661-3756 or write P.O. Box 10, Lahaina, Maui, HI 96767.

SIGHTSEEING TOURS

Tours are offered that will let you cover Maui from head to foot; you can drive it, sail around it, fly over it, or see it from below the water. Almost every major hotel has a tour desk from which you can book, and there are many private booking agencies that will do the same. Some of these are listed below.

Note: For bicycling and hiking tours, see the **Sports and Recreation.**

Booking Agencies

Ocean Activities Center, tel. (808) 879-4485, is one of the biggest and perhaps the best agency for booking any and all kinds of activities on Maui. For many of the fun events like snorkeling, scuba diving, whalewatching, sunset cruises, and deep sea fishing, the center has its own facilities and equipment, which means they not only provide you with an excellent outing, but offer very competitive prices. Ocean Activities can also book you on helicopters, parasails, land tours, and they rent and sell boogie boards, snorkel equipment, sailboards, and surfboards. They have sun and surf store/booking agencies in the Kihei/Wailea area at the Kea Lani Hotel, Mana Kai Maui Resort, and Maui Hill Resort; the Lahaina Cannery Mall in Lahaina; and the Maui Marriott in Kaanapali. Ocean Activities also runs a boat from the beach at the Maui Prince Hotel to the underwater fantasy of Molokini Crater. Prices on all of their activities are very reasonable, and the service is excellent. If you had to choose one agency for all your fun needs, this would be a good bet.

Another very reputable outfit with two booking offices is **Barefoot's Cashback Tours,** which gives you up to a 10% discount on all your activities. They too can set you up with virtually any activity around the island. In Lahaina, they're at 834 Front St., tel. (808) 661-8889; and in Kihei, go to 2395 S. Kihei Rd. in the Dolphin Plaza, tel. (808) 879-4100, e-mail: barefoot@maui.net, website: www.tombarefoot.com.

Activity Warehouse can provide the same service, often with last minute reservations, and they also rent some ocean equipment. You can find them in Lahaina, tel. (808) 667-4000, and in Kihei, tel. (808) 875-4000.

In Lahaina along Front Street try any of the **Fantasy Island Activities and Tours** kiosks or call (808) 667-9740. Also try the **Activities Information Center** in the Wharf Shopping Complex, tel. (808) 662-3100 or at 888 Wainee St. in Anchor Square, tel. (808) 667-7777. These are legitimate venders with solid reputations. You will, however, find a horde of other activities desks up and down Front Street; you don't have to search for them—they'll find you, especially to make an exhausting high-pressured pitch for time shares! Avoid them—unless you want to listen to the rap in exchange for your reduced ticket price.

One of the easiest ways to book an activity and sightsee at the same time is to walk along the Lahaina Wharf—there's an information booth here operated by many of the companies who rent slips at the harbor. Check it out first, and then plan to be there when the tour boats return. Asking the passengers, right on the spot, if they've had a good time is about the best you can do. You can also check out the boats and do some comparative pricing of your own.

For boats and a full range of activities out of quiet Maalaea Harbor, contact the **Maalaea Activity Center**, tel. (808) 242-6982. They do it all, from helicopters to horseback, but specialize in the boats berthed at Maalaea.

Land Tours

It's easy to book tours to Maui's famous areas such as Lahaina, Hana, Iao Valley, and Haleakala. Normally they're run on either half- or full-day schedules (Hana is always a full day) and range anywhere from $30 to $110 with hotel pickup included. Big bus tours are run by **Roberts Hawaii,** tel. (808) 871-6226, (800) 831-5541 in Hawaii, or (888) 472-4729. These tours are quite antiseptic—you sit behind tinted glass in an air-conditioned bus. Smaller companies, with smaller tour buses and vans, also hit the high points but have specialty tours. Try **Ekahi Tours,** tel. (808) 572-9775; **Polynesian Adventure Tours,** tel. (808) 877-4242; and **Valley Isle Excursions,** tel. (808) 661-8687.

Temptation Tours, tel. (808) 887-8888, operates the ultimate in luxury van tours for the discriminating traveler. Their deluxe vans, more like limousines, seat each of the eight passengers in a comfortable captain's chair for their trips to Hana and Haleakala. This outfit offers two optional tours: one, either down to or back from Hana by helicopter, with the van making the connection for the reverse trip; and two, fly to and from Hana by small plane from where you tour the Hana area by van.

For those who desire a go-at-your-own pace alternative to van tours, yet want the convenience of an escort, **Best of Maui Cassette Tours** 333 Dairy Rd., Kahului, tel. (808) 871-1555, may be for you. Rent a quality tapes to the Hana Highway for $20. This rental comes with a cassette player, a small guidebook of sights, history, and legends, a route map, coupons for free water-equipment rental, and a discount lunch. For $25, you get all of the above plus a free tour video of the entire island. Pick up your cassettes 6 a.m.-1 p.m.; reservations are appreciated.

For a personalized tour down the Hana Highway where a guide drives your car and takes you to "local" places, try **Hana Road Adventures,** tel. (808) 877-4042.

The Sugar Cane Train

The old steam engine puffs along from Lahaina to Puukolii platform in Kaanapali, pulling old-style open-air passenger cars through cane fields and the Kaanapali golf course. The six miles of narrow-gauge track are covered in 25 minutes (each way) and the cost roundtrip is $14 adult and $7.50 for children 3-12. A free double-decker bus shuttles between Lahaina Station and the waterfront and from the Whalers Village Shopping Center to the Kaanapali Station to accommodate the most popular tour on Maui. The train runs throughout the day 8:55 a.m.-4:40 p.m. It's very popular so book in advance—more than 400,000 ride the train every year. All rides are narrated and there will be a singing conductor. It's not only great fun for children, everybody has a good time. All kinds of combination tours are offered as well: some feature lunch, a tour of Lahaina with admission into the Baldwin House and the *Carthaginian II,* and even a cruise on a glass-bottom boat. They're tame, touristy, and fun. The price is right. Call the Lahaina Kaanapali and Pacific Railroad at (808) 661-0089, website: www.maui.net/~choochoo/sugrcane.html.

Air Tours

Maui is a spectacular sight from the air. A few small charter airlines, a handful of helicopter companies, and one sailplane outfit swoop you around the island. These joyrides are literally the highlight of many people's experiences on Maui, but they are expensive. The excursions vary, but expect to spend at least $100 for a basic half-hour tour. The most spectacular ones take you over Haleakala Crater, or perhaps to the remote West Maui Mountains, where inaccessible gorges lie at your feet. Other tours are civilized; expect a champagne brunch after you visit Hana. Still others take you to nearby Molokai to view some of the world's most spectacular seacliffs and remote beaches. Know, however, that many hikers and trekkers have a beef with the air tours: after they've spent hours, or maybe days, hiking into remote valleys in search of peace and quiet, out of the sky comes the mechanical whir of a chopper to spoil the solitude.

For a Maui joyride out of Kahului Airport, contact **Paragon Air,** tel. (808) 244-3356. Paragon offers several different options, like their flight to Molokai with a tour of Kalaupapa for $199 or a flight to Molokai coupled with the mule ride down to Kalaupapa for $259. Others include a Big Island volcano tour for $275, and a six-island tour for $425.

Flying from both Kahului Airport and Kapalua West Maui Airport, **Volcano Air Tours,** tel. (808) 877-5500, offers two-hour air tours of Maui and the volcanoes of the Big Island. Using twin-engine Piper Navajo Chieftains, flights run several times a day, including one that catches the sunset, and all cost $219. (Website: www.maui.net/~mauisle.)

For hang gliding and motorized hang gliding, contact **Hang Gliding Maui,** at (808) 572-6557. The motorized flight runs $150, the tandem hang gliding flight $250.

Helicopter Tours

Most companies use a six-seat A-STAR helicopter. Each is air conditioned and has a window ventilation system. For all, tours are narrated over specially designed earphones, and some companies offer a video of your helicopter tour of Maui as a souvenir at the end of the flight for an extra $20. On certain flights the craft will touch down for a short interlude, and on some flights a complimentary lunch will be served. Most companies will make special arrangements to drop off

Alex Air helecopter

ROBERT NILSEN

and pick up campers in remote areas, or design a package especially for you. What is particularly attractive about helicopter rides is that you can sightsee from a perspective not possible from the ground and you can get close to areas not accessible by foot. There may be a tradeoff, however. Steep turns, quick descents, and unstable pockets of air can cause some riders to get air sick. Chopper companies are competitively priced, with tours of West or East Maui at around $100-125, with a Hana/Haleakala flight at about $135. Circle-island tours are approximately $200, but the best might be to include a trip to Molokai at approximately $180 in order to experience the world's tallest sea cliffs along the isolated windward coast.

All flights leave from the heliport at the back side of Kahului Airport—access off Haleakala Highway extension road. Each company has an office here where you check in, pay your money, and receive your pre-flight instructions. There is a fee parking lot here: free the first 15 minutes, $1 for 15-30 minutes, $1 each additional hour, maximum of $7 a day.

Alex Air, tel. (808) 871-0792 or (888) 418-8458, website: mauigateway.com/~alexair, is a small personable company that runs a tight ship. They offer a wide variety of flights on two types of helicopters, ranging from the West Maui special at $69 to the deluxe circle-island tour for $240.

Sunshine Helicopter, tel. (808) 871-0722, (800) 544-2520, website: www.sunshinehelicopters.com, is another local, family-run outfit. They fly the "Black Beauties." The seating is two-by-two, and owner and chief pilot, Ross Scott, goes out of his way to give you a great ride over Maui.

Air Maui, tel. (808) 877-7005, seem to be the "little guys" but they try hard. to please. A family-owned company, Air Maui offers all the standards and can customize a tour for you.

Hawaii Helicopter, tel. (808) 877-3900 or (800) 994-9099 in Hawaii, website: www.hawaii-iheli.com, is a state-wide company. Their helicopters have plush interiors for your comfort, but may squeeze four people in the back, so the two middle ones don't always get a good view. Their helicopters have two engines. This company now offers two longer tours using a Sikorsky S-76, one that covers the four islands that make up Maui County and the second that takes

you to the volcanoes of the Big Island; two- and three-hours, respectively, the shorter flight costs $220 and the longer $399.

Blue Hawaiian Helicopters, tel. (808) 871-8844, website: www.bluehawaiian.com, operates on Maui and the Big Island. It's a company that does lots of advertising, gets a lot of passengers, and has done work for film companies.

OCEAN TOURS

You haven't really seen Maui unless you've seen it from the sea. Tour boats operating out of Maui's Lahaina and Maalaea Harbors take you fishing, sailing, whalewatching, dining, diving, and snorkeling. You can find power boats, sailboats, catamarans, and Zodiac rafts that offer a combination of some or all of these options or just sail you around for pure pleasure—Maui presents one of the premier sailing venues in the Pacific. Many take day-trips to Lanai. Others visit Molokini, a submerged volcano with only half the crater rim above water, which has been designated a Marine Life Conservation District. The majority of Maui's pleasure boats are berthed in Lahaina Harbor and most have a booth right there on the wharf where you can sign up. A substantial number of other boats come out of Maalaea, and a few companies are based in Kihei. The following are basically limited to sailing/dining/touring activities, with snorkeling often part of the experience. Scuba and fishing excursions are listed in their respective sections.

Excursions/Dinner Sails

Sunset cruises are very romantic, and very popular. They last for about two hours and cost $40-70 for the basic cruise; but for a dinner sail expect to spend $70-90. Remember, too, that the larger established companies are usually on Maui to stay, but that smaller companies come and go with the tide! The following are general tour boats that offer a variety of cruises.

Trilogy Excursions, tel. (808) 661-4743 or (800) 874-2666, website: www.sailtrilogy.com, founded and operated by the Coon Family, is a success in every way; their Lanai Cruise is the best on Maui. Although the handpicked crews have made the journey countless times, they never forget that it's your first time. They run catamarans that carry up to 50 passengers to Lanai. Once aboard, you're served a mug of steaming Kona coffee, fresh juice, and Mama Coon's famous cinnamon rolls. Once at Lanai, you can frolic at Hulopoe Bay, which is great for swimming and renowned as an excellent snorkeling area. All gear is provided. While you play, the crew is busy at work preparing a delicious barbecue at the picnic facilities at Manele Harbor. You couldn't have a more memorable or enjoyable experience than sailing with Trilogy. But don't spoil your day; be sure to bring along (and use!) a wide-brim hat, sunglasses, sunscreen, a long-sleeve shirt, and a towel. For this full day's experience, adults pay $159, children (3-12) half price. Trilogy Excursions also runs a popular half-day trip to Molokini Crater, sailing daily from Maalaea Harbor at 6:30 a.m., adults $75, children half price, which includes breakfast, lunch, and all snorkeling gear; a five-hour mid-day picnic sail from Kaanapali Beach, and two-hour whale-watching sails during whale season, also from Kaanapali Beach.

If you've had enough of Front Street Lahaina, **Club Lanai,** tel. (808) 871-1144, (800) 531-5262, is a Maui-based company that runs day excursions to its developed facilities on the east side of Lanai (whalewatches and cocktail cruises, too). Besides Trilogy Excursions, Club Lanai is the only company with permission to land on Lanai. You board your catamaran at Lahaina Harbor, leaving at 7:30 a.m. and returning at around 3:30 p.m. after a full day. En route you're served breakfast. The boats cruise to Club Lanai's private beach just near old Halepaloa Landing, between the deserted villages of Keomuku and Naha, on Lanai's very secluded eastern shore. Awaiting you is an oasis of green landscaped beach. Palm trees provide shade over manmade lagoons, and hammocks wait for true relaxation. The club provides you with snorkel gear, wave skis, kayaks with instruction, bicycles for your personal exploration of the area, horseshoes, volleyball, and even a guided historic wagon tour. Scuba diving can also be arranged at an extra charge. On the grounds are a gift shop and a Hawaiian village where you can learn handicrafts from local or visiting artists. The bar serves exotic drinks and is open all day, and lunch is buffet style. The entire day including sail, meals, and use of facilities is reasonably priced at $89, with children and senior rates. Family oriented with plenty of activities for children of all ages, Club Lanai lets you set your own pace . . . do it all, or do nothing at all.

The **Navatek II,** a snow-white manta ray, has risen from Maui's waters and is prepared to instantly skim in effortless grace the frothing waves. This state-of-the-art marvel, built on Oahu and engineered expressly for use in Hawaii, is actually a SWATH vessel (Small Water Plane Area Twin Hull) of revolutionary design that features two submerged hulls, remote-controlled submarines, connected by two half-moon arching struts that support the above-water superstructure. The design means that the $5 million, 82 foot long and 36 foot wide cruise ship handles the waves with amazing dexterity since no part of the above-water decks come into actual contact with the waves. The result is the island's most steady, nimble, and comfortable craft. With the touch of a finger, ballast tanks in the submersibles can be either flooded or blown to balance the craft, while a joystick raises or lowers the bow, and a polished aluminum ship's wheel only the size of a hockey puck steers the agile SWATH. Fronting the pilothouse is stepped amphitheater seating, and behind is a tanning deck comfortable with lounge chairs, restrooms, and even hot showers, very welcome after a swim or snorkeling adventure. The glass-enclosed lower deck converts to a floating restaurant, with stage, dance floor, full table settings, kitchen, and complete bar. *The Navatek II* offers a Lanai snorkel and whalewatch for $125 adults, $95 juniors 12-17, and $75 children ages 5-11, leaving daily except Friday from Maalaea Harbor at 8 a.m. and returning at about 2 p.m. The cruise offers a delicious breakfast buffet, barbecue lunch, snorkeling and sail to and from the lightly visited island of Lanai. The Sunset Dinner Cruise, adults $87, children 2-11 $55, departs Maalaea harbor nightly around 5:30 p.m. returning at 7:30 p.m. and features, *pu pu,* cocktail hour, and a complete three-course dinner and dessert served at your table by a professional wait staff. The *Navatek II* also does a two-hour whalewatch tour daily except Friday from January through mid-April, after it returns from Lanai, $39 adults, $26.50 children 2-11. For complete details contact Navatek II, a division of Royal Hawaiian Cruises, tel. (808) 661-8787 or (800) 852-4183.

Scotch Mist, tel. (808) 661-0386, has one racing yacht, *The Scotch Mist II.* They are the oldest sailing charters on Maui (since 1970) and claim to be the fastest sailboats in the Lahaina Harbor: boasting the lightest boat, the biggest sail, and the best crew. They'll sail/snorkel to Lanai in the morning for $55 per person, West Maui in the afternoon, or take their 25 passengers on a sunset sail complete with champagne for $45 per person. When the time is right, a moonlight-starlight sail and a whalewatching sail are offered, for $40 each.

Other sailing ships that do a variety of snorkel, sunset, or sailing tours include the following. The **Lavengro,** tel. (808) 879-8188, a 60-foot "Roaring 20s" pleasure craft that even saw coastal duty during WW II, offers a lovely sail on this tall, two-masted wooden ship. This ship and its glass-bottom catamaran companion, **Four Winds,** make morning snorkel runs to Molokini; $59 for the *Lavengro* and $69 for the *Four Winds.* The sloops **Flexible Flyer,** tel. (808) 244-6655, and **Cinderella,** tel. (808) 244-0009, also leave from Maalaea Harbor. America's Cup contender, **America II,** tel. (808) 667-2195, sails out of Lahaina Harbor, and **World Class,** tel. (808) 667-7733, leaves from Kaanapali Beach.

One of the least expensive cruises is a cocktail sail aboard the 44-foot catamaran **Frogman,** tel. (808) 667-7622. It departs from Maalaea Harbor and serves *pu pu,* mai tais, and beer on its trade wind sail. Also, from Maalaea Harbor is the champagne sunset dinner sail offered by Ocean Activities Center, tel. (808) 879-4485, aboard their 65-foot catamaran **Wailea Kai.** They sail Tuesday, Thursday, Friday, and Saturday. Also out of Maalaea Harbor is the **Mahana Maia,** tel. (808) 871-8636, a 58-foot cat that'll carry 50 passengers out to Molokini.

The **Prince Kuhio,** tel. (800) 468-1287, (808) 242-8777 on Maui, offers a different kind of trip altogether. Comfort, luxury, and stability come with this 92-foot ship. Departing from Maalaea Harbor daily, the *Prince Kuhio* does a four-hour snorkel cruise to Molokini ($75 adult, $40 children under 12) including a continental breakfast, buffet lunch, open bar, and champagne on the return voyage; and in season, an afternoon whalewatching trip for $30

The quickest way to Molokini, which means more time in the water, is aboard the catamaran **Kai Kanani,** tel. (808) 879-7218, which departs from in front of the Maui Prince Hotel in Makena. Equipment and food are provided.

Pacific Whale Foundation's **The Manutea,** tel. (808) 879-8811, a 50-foot catamaran, offers a deluxe dinner sail for $69 from Maalaea Harbor. Pacific Whale Foundation has three other boats, one more leaving from Maalaea Harbor and two from Lahaina, that do whale, dolphin, and turtle sails. **Zip-Purr,** tel. (808) 667-2299, one of Maui's newest catamarans offers a morning snorkel sail, sunset sail, and whalewatch in season with an Earthtrust scientist aboard for interpretation (some money goes to Earthtrust)— this family operated, 41-foot catamaran was built in Hawaii expressly for Hawaiian waters. The **Maui Princess,** tel. (808) 667-6165, offers dinner cruises aboard its sleek 118-foot motor yacht for $75 ($35 children) that includes open bar, dinner, entertainment, and dancing; and **Windjammer,** tel. (808) 661-8600, also does a salmon and prime rib dinner cruise on its three-masted schooner; sailings daily at 5:30 and 7:30 p.m.

Some of the above companies offer a variety of cocktail sails and whalewatches for much cheaper prices, but many tend to pack people in so tightly that they're known derisively as "cattle boats." Don't expect the personal attention you'd receive on smaller boats, and always check number of passengers when booking. Some boats going to Lanai may take passengers for a one-way trip. You won't participate in the snorkeling or the food, but the price (negotiable) should be in line with the cost of a ferry ticket. This extra service is offered only if there's room. Talk to the individual captains.

Unique Ocean Tours
For a totally different experience, try a rafting trip. Several rafting companies have sprung up in the last few years so there's plenty of competition. These rafts are small rigid-bottom crafts with a sun shade; most seat 6-24 people. Their vessels are highly maneuverable, totally seaworthy, high-tech motorized rafts whose main features are their speed and ability to get intimate with the sea as the supple form bends with the undulations of the water. You're right on the water, so you'll get wet, and you often ride right on the inflatable rubber tubes. Like boat tours, these rafts do one or a combination of tours that involve whalewatching, snorkeling, sea caves, coastal cruises, or the circumnavigation of Lanai.

For half day rides, you can expect a charge of about $65. The first company in Maui waters was **Blue Water Rafting,** tel. (808) 879-7238, website: www.maui.net/~mark/BWR.html, which still departs from the Kihei Boat Ramp. **Ocean Riders,** tel. (808) 661-3586, departs from Mala Wharf in Lahaina for trips to Lanai and Molokai. Royal Hawaiian Cruises runs the *Maui Nui Explorer* out of Lahaina Harbor to Lanai. Other options are **Ocean Rafting,** tel. (808) 667-2191 or (888) 677-7238, website: www.maui.net/~ocnraftn; **Hawaiian Rafting Adventures,** tel. (808) 661-7333; and **Ultimate Rafting,** tel. (808) 667-5678, website: www.maui.net/~ecoraft.

Kayaking has also become quite popular over the last few years. Located in the Rainbow Mall at 2439 S. Kihei Rd., **South Pacific Kayaks,** tel. (808) 875-4848, (800) 776-2326, website: www.mauikayak.com, open daily 8 a.m.-5 p.m., offers a half-day introductory trip (with drinks and snacks) for $59, or an advanced explorer trip along the remote coastline of Southwest Maui (including drinks and full lunch) for $89. Both tours include lunch along with plenty of snorkeling opportunities as you glide in and out tiny bays fashioned from jutting lava rock fingers. South Pacific Kayaks offers rentals of single at $25-40 and double kayaks at $35-45, per day. **Kelii's Kayak Tours,** tel. (808) 874-7652 has several tours to various sites around the island ranging $55-99. See also **Pacific Whale Foundation** whalewatching tours, tel. (808) 879-8811, website: http://pacificwhale.org; or **Makena Kayak,** tel. (808) 879-8426.

Undersea adventures have also come to Maui. With *Atlantis,* tel. (800) 548-6262, you can dive to more than 100 feet to view the undersea world through glass windows. The basic tour starts at $69; you must be at least three feet tall to board. The *Reefrider,* tel. (808) 667-2133, and *Sea-View Adventures,* tel. (808) 661-5550, are both submersibles that let you view the underwater from the depth of no more than 10 feet. But it's a great view nonetheless. All tours leave from Lahaina Harbor.

Whalewatching

Anyone on Maui from November to April gets the added treat of watching humpback whales as they frolic just off Lahaina, one of the world's major wintering areas for the humpback. Almost every boat in the harbor runs a special whale-watch during this time of year.

Whales Alive Maui, tel. (808) 874-6855, is a fantastic organization of dedicated scientists and naturalists who have made a career of studying the magnificent humpback whale and who operate whalewatches every day in season. Whales Alive Maui operates two-hour whalewatches for a reasonable $30 through the **Ocean Activities Center,** tel. (808) 879-4485 or (800) 798-0652. Part of the proceeds are donated to further the research of this fine organization. Whales Alive Maui leaves Maalaea Harbor twice daily in the afternoon on the *Makakai,* and *Wailea Kai.* On each of these stable and seaworthy catamarans is a fully trained Whales Alive Maui naturalist who offers a very educational and entertaining interpretive narration. When one of these wonderful animals shows itself by breaching, spouting, or slapping a pectoral fin, the naturalist will make every effort to inform you of what's going on, and especially how it relates to the social pattern of whale life. By showing people these magnificent creatures and teaching them about their lives, Whales Alive staff hope everyone will become aware of the whale's delicate place in nature and learn to appreciate their significance as something to be protected. There is no better way to have a truly Hawaiian experience of sea, surf, and natural beauty than enjoying a whalewatch sail with Whales Alive Maui.

Another highly educational whalewatch is sponsored by the **Pacific Whale Foundation,** located at Kealia Beach Plaza, Suite 25, 101 N. Kihei Rd., Kihei, HI 96753, tel. (808) 879-8811, e-mail: staff@pacificwhale.org, website: http://pacificwhale.org, open daily 8 a.m.-5 p.m. A nonprofit organization founded in 1980, it is dedicated to research, education, and conservation and is one of the only research organizations that has been able to survive by generating its own funds through membership, donations, and excellent whalewatch cruises. They have one of the best whalewatches on the island aboard their own ships, berthed for your convenience at Maalaea and Lahaina Harbors. The scientists and researchers who make up the crew rotate shifts and come out on the whalewatch when they're not out in the Lahaina Roads getting up close to identify, and make scientific observations of, the whales. Most of the information that the other whalewatches dispense to the tourists is generated by the Pacific Whale Foundation.

Departures from Maalaea and Lahaina Harbors are several times daily. The foundation also offers an "Adopt-a-whale Program" and various reef and snorkel cruises that run throughout the year.

SPECIAL NEEDS

Maui Services

On arrival at Kahului Airport, parking spaces are directly in front of the main terminal. The restaurant here has steps, so food will be brought to you in the cocktail lounge. There are no special emergency medical services, but visitor information is available at (808) 872-3893. There is no centralized medical service, but Maui Memorial Hospital in Wailuku will refer, tel. (808) 244-9056. Getting around can be tough because there is virtually no public transportation on Maui, and most tour operators do not accommodate non-ambulatory persons. However, both Hertz and Avis rent cars that can be fitted with hand controls (both right and left), but some restrict these controls to certain size or type vehicles. They generally require prior arrangements, one or two days at least, preferably when making your advanced reservation. Rates are comparable with or the same as for standard rental cars. A private special shuttle company operating all over the island is **Hawaii Care Van Shuttle,** tel. (808) 669-2300 in Lahaina; they can accommodate people who use wheelchairs. **Accessible Vans of Hawaii,** tel. (808) 879-5521, fax 879-0649, or (800) 303-3750, rents wheelchair-lift equipped vans on Oahu, Maui, and the Big Island for $109 a day or $560 a week. This is a full service travel agency and a good source of information on traveling with disabilities. Valid, out-of-state, **handicapped parking placards** may be used throughout the state of Hawaii. A Hawaiian **handicapped parking permits** can be obtained from the county driver's licensing section at the War Memorial Complex in Wailuku, tel. (808) 243-7793.

For **medical support services,** contact: Maui Center for Independent Living, tel. (808) 242-4966; Action Medical Personnel, tel. (808) 875-8300; CareResourse Hawaii, tel. (808) 871-2115; or Interim Healthcare, tel. (808) 877-2676. Medical equipment is available Gammie Homecare, tel. (808) 877-4032.

INFORMATION AND SERVICES

For police, fire or ambulance anywhere on Maui, dial 911.

Civil Defense: In case of natural disaster such as hurricanes or tsunamis on Maui, call (808) 243-7721.

Coast Guard: tel. (800) 331-6176 or (800) 552-6458.

Sexual Assault Crisis Line: tel. (808) 242-4357. For time of day, call (808) 242-0212.

Aloha Pages, tel. (808) 244-8934, is a free 24-hour "talking telephone" information service on a variety of topics including weather, news, sports, community service, and entertainment. For specific information, dial the above number, followed by a four-digit code number as directed, or check your local Hawaiian phone book for a complete listing of available topics.

Weather and Marine Reports

For recorded information on local island weather, call (808) 877-5111; for the marine report, call (808) 877-3477; and for conditions on Haleakala, call (808) 571-5054.

Consumer Protection and Tourism Complaints

If you encounter problems with accommodations, bad service, or downright rip-offs, try the following: Maui Chamber of Commerce, 250 Ala Maha, Kahului, tel. (808) 871-7711; the Office of Consumer Protection, tel. (808) 984-8244; or the Better Business Bureau (Oahu), tel. (808) 941-5222. If you're hassled while on Maui or have a general tourism complaint, try the Office of the Mayor's Information and Complaint line, tel. (808) 243-7587.

Tourism Information

The best information on Maui is dispensed by the Maui HVB, 1727 Wili Pa Loop, Wailuku, HI 96793, tel. (808) 244-3530, website: www.visit-maui.com.

For general information about Maui and specific accommodation and activities listings, ask for their official vacation planner, or check it on the web at www.hshawaii.com/mvp.

Other Tourism-Related Information Sources

The state operates two visitors' kiosks at Kahului Airport, one in the center building upper level and the other in the baggage claim area of the arrival terminal. Open daily, 6:30 a.m.-10 p.m., tel. (808) 872-3892, they have plenty of practical brochures and helpful information. Also, scattered around the arrival terminal lower level are numerous racks of free brochures, magazines, and other tourist literature.

Post Offices

Branch post offices are found in most major towns. Window service is offered Mon.-Fri. 8:30 a.m.-4 p.m.; some offices are open Saturday 10 a.m.-noon. The following are the main offices: Wailuku, tel. (808) 244-4815; Kahului, tel. (808) 871-4710; Kihei, tel. (808) 879-2403; Lahaina at the Lahaina Shopping Center, tel. (808) 661-0550; Lahaina at the Civic Center, tel. (808) 667-6611.

Health Care

Maui Memorial Hospital, is located at 221 Mahalani St., Wailuku, tel. (808) 244-9056. Kihei-Wailea Medical Center, 41 E. Lipoa St., Kihei, tel. (808) 874-8100 (near Star Market) offers a number of physicians in varying specialties and a laboratory; open Mon.-Fri. 8 a.m.-8 p.m., Saturday and Sunday until 5 p.m.

There are several clinics around the island, including the following. Upstairs in the Dolphin Mall in Kihei are Kihei Clinic and Wailea Medical Services, tel. (808) 879-0114, open Mon.-Fri. 8 a.m.-7 p.m., Saturday until 6 p.m., and Sunday and holidays 9 a.m.-2 p.m. Kaiser Permanente has a clinic in Kihei in Azeka Place II, tel. (808) 891-3000, in Lahaina at 910 Wainee, tel. (808) 661-7400, and in Wailuku at 80 Mahalani St., tel. (808) 243-6000; open Mon.-Fri. 8 a.m.-5 p.m., closed 12-1 p.m., weekends, and holidays. In the center of Wailuku at 2180 Main St., try Maui Medical Group, tel. (808) 242-6464.

Of the numerous pharmacies throughout the island, the following should meet your needs: Longs Drug in Kihei, tel. (808) 879-2033; Lahaina, tel. (808) 667-4390; and Kahului, tel. (808) 877-0068.

Reading Material

Free tourist literature is well done and loaded with tips, discounts, maps, happenings, etc. Found in hotels, restaurants, and street stands, they include: *This Week Maui* and *Guide to Maui,* weekly; *Maui Gold* and *Maui Magazine,* one for each season; and the monthly *Today Magazine* and *Pleasant Hawaii Magazine.* The weekly *Drive Guide,* with excellent maps and tips, is given out free by all car rental agencies. Both *Menu* and *Maui Menus* are all about food.

Both the *Honolulu Advertiser* and *Honolulu Star Bulletin* are available on Maui for 75 cents apiece. Aside from these two big Honolulu newspapers, local papers available on Maui include the *Maui News,* published Mon.-Fri., which has a good "Datebook" listings of local events. *Lahaina News* is a community paper of news, feature stories, and entertainment listings, 25 cents. It's a daily, as is the free *Maui Times,* The *South Maui Weekly* and *Haleakala Times* are weeklies, and *Gold Coast* and *MauiAina* are seasonal.

The main branch library is at 251 High St., Wailuku, tel. (808) 243-5945, with other branches in Kahului, Lahaina, Makawao, Kihei, and Hana. They're open a hodgepodge of hours through the week, usually closed Friday or Saturday.

Island Radio

More than a dozen radio stations broadcast on Maui. KHPR 88.1 FM broadcasts from Honolulu and is the island's public radio station; KQMQ 93.1 FM plays Top-40 songs; KPOA 93.5 FM out of Lahaina does a mix of contemporary Hawaiian and standard rock; for easy listening tune to KUMU 94.7 FM; the format on KAOI 95.1 FM in Wailuku is mostly adult rock with a request line, and KAOI 1110 AM does news, talk, and sports; broadcasting from Honolulu, KRTR 96.3 FM and KPOI 97.5 FM both play rock and roll.

Maui Facts

Maui is the second youngest and second largest Hawaiian island after Hawaii. Its nickname is the Valley Island. Its color is pink and its flower is the *lokelani,* a small rose.

M.G.L. DOMENY DE RIENZI

CENTRAL MAUI: THE ISTHMUS

KAHULUI

It is generally believed that Kahului means "The Winning," but perhaps it should be "The Survivor." Kahului suffered attack by Kamehameha I in the 1790s, when he landed his war canoes here in preparation for battle at Iao Valley. In 1900 it was purposely burned to thwart the plague, then rebuilt. Combined with Wailuku, the county seat just down the road, this area is home to 53,000 Mauians, nearly one-half the island population. Here's where the people live. It's a practical, homey town, the only deep-water port from which Maui's sugar and pineapples are shipped. Although Kahului was an established sugar town by 1880, it's really only grown up in the last 20 years. In the 1960s, Hawaiian Commercial and Sugar Co. began building low-cost housing for its workers, which became a model development for the whole of the U.S. Most people land at the airport, blast through for Lahaina or Kihei, and never give Kahului a

second look. It's in no way a resort community, but it has the best general-purpose shopping on the island, a few noteworthy sites, and a convenient location to the airport.

SIGHTS

Kanaha Pond State Wildlife Sanctuary

This one-time royal fishpond is located between downtown and the airport at the junctions of Routes 36 and 38. It's on the migratory route of various ducks and Canada geese, but most importantly it's home to the endangered Hawaiian stilt (ae'o) and the Hawaiian coot (alae ke'oke'o). The stilt is a slender, 16-inch bird with a black back, white belly, and stick-like pink legs. The coot is a gray-black ducklike bird that builds large floating nests. An observation pavilion is maintained on the south edge of the pond, accessed by a short walkway from a small parking area. The observation stand is always open and free of charge. Bring binoculars.

Maui Community College

Just across the street from the Kaahumanu Center on Rt. 32, the college is a good place to check out the many bulletin boards for various activities, items for sale, and cheaper long-term housing. The **Student Center** is conspicuous as you drive in, and is a good place to get most information. The library is adequate.

War Memorial

At the corner of Kaahumanu and Kanaloa Avenues is **Wailuku War Memorial Park and Center.** Here you'll find a football stadium, baseball field, gymnasium, Olympic-size swimming pool, tennis courts, track, and free hot showers. After years of being played at the Aloha Stadium in Honolulu, the college all-star Hula Bowl now takes place at the War Memorial Stadium and is scheduled to be played there at least until 2002. To the left, at the entrance to the gym, you can pick up county camping permits.

Going up the hill from there you'll find Baldwin High School, followed by the Aloha Bowling Center and Stillwell's Bakery. Toward the ocean are the new and very large Keopuolani Park and the Maui Arts and Cultural Center, the new center of cultural activity, education, and entertainment for the island.

Alexander and Baldwin Sugar Mill Museum

The museum is located at the intersection of Puunene Ave. (Rt. 350) and Hanson Rd., about one-half mile from Dairy Road (Rt. 380), tel. (808) 871-8058. Hours are Mon.-Sat. 9:30 a.m.-4:30 p.m.; admission is $4 adults, $2 children, ages five and under admitted free. (Avoid the area around 3 p.m. when the still-working mill changes shifts.) This small but highly informative museum could easily be your first stop after arriving at Kahului Airport only 15 minutes away, especially if you're heading to Kihei. Once you get off the plane, you'll realize that you're in the midst of sugarcane fields. If you want to know the history of this crop and the people who worked and developed it, visit the museum. The vintage museum building was the home of the sugar mill supervisor, who literally lived surrounded by

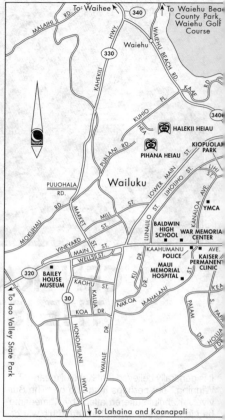

his work. Inside is a small but well-stocked bookstore and gift shop featuring Hawaiiana and handmade clothing and artifacts, with goodies like guava and coconut syrups and raw sugar.

As you begin your tour, notice the ancient refrigerator in the corner that the staff still uses. In the first room, you are given a brief description of the natural history of Maui, along with a rendition of the legends of the demigod Maui. Display cases explain Maui's rainfall and use of irrigation for a productive sugarcane yield. There is an old-fashioned copper rain gauge along with pragmatic artifacts from the building of the Haiku Ditch. A collection of vintage photos features the Baldwin and Alexander families, while a historical plaque recalls when workers lived in ethnic

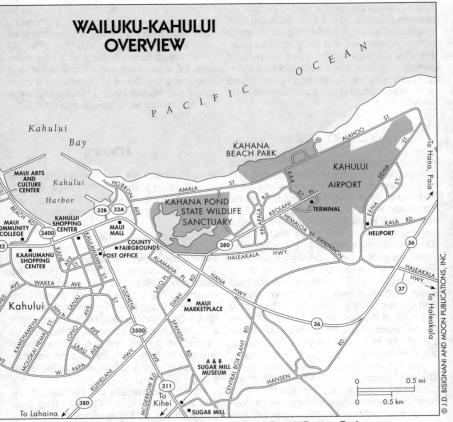

WAILUKU-KAHULUI OVERVIEW

PACIFIC OCEAN

Kahului Bay

Kahului Harbor

KAHANA BEACH PARK

KAHULUI AIRPORT

ALAHOO ST.

KAA ST. PL.

EEHIA ST.

To Hana, Paia →

MAUI ARTS AND CULTURE CENTER

HOBRON AVE.

AMALA ST.

KAHANA POND STATE WILDLIFE SANCTUARY

PAAPALA RD.

KEOLANI

TERMINAL

HEMALOA ST. EXTENSION

EENA ST.

KALA RD.

HELIPORT

36

MAUI COMMUNITY COLLEGE

BEACH RD.

32B 32A

KAHULUI SHOPPING CENTER

3400

MAUI MALL

KANE ST.

KAAHUMANU SHOPPING CENTER

KAUAHINE ST.

COUNTY FAIRGROUNDS

POST OFFICE

ALAMAHA PL.

380

HALEAKALA HWY.

HANA HWY.

36

HALEAKALA HWY.

37

To Haleakala →

32

WAKEA AVE.

KANE ST.

PUUNENE AVE.

DAIRY RD.

LAIO PL.

Kahului

HEE AVE.

KAMEHAMEHA ST.

JANAI AVE.

LONO AVE.

MOLOKAI ST.

HEMA ST.

LAAU AVE.

HINA AVE.

3500

SPANISH RD.

MAUI MARKETPLACE

W. PAPA AVE.

KUIHELANI HWY.

MCGERROW RD.

311

To Kihei

A & B SUGAR MILL MUSEUM

CENTRAL BOX PLANT RD.

HANSEN

0   0.5 mi

0   0.5 km

380

SUGAR MILL

← To Lahaina

© J.D. BISIGNANI AND MOON PUBLICATIONS, INC.

---

camps, each with its own euphemistic name (Chinese at Ah Fong, Japanese at Nashiwa, Portuguese at Cod Fish). This setup was designed to discourage competition (or cooperation) between the ethnic groups during labor disputes, and to ease the transition to the new land. These people are represented by everything from stuffed fighting cocks to baseball mitts from the '30s. Included is an educational video on the various methods of sugarcane production, and scale models show just how selected machinery works. The museum is in the shadow of the state's largest sugar mill, and you can hear the wheels turning and the mill grinding. It's not an antiseptic remembrance, but a vital one where the history still continues. No tours are given of the mill.

Kanaha Beach County Park

This is the only beach worth visiting in the area. Good for a swim and a picnic, the broad beach here is flanked by plenty of trees so you can get out of the sun. In this strip of trees are picnic tables, barbecue pits, bathrooms, and a pavilion. This beach is used by one of the outrigger canoe clubs on the island, and you'll see their canoes drawn up on shore when they're not out on the water practicing their strokes. It's also *the* best place to learn sailboarding. Rent your board in town. The wind is steady but not too strong, and the wave action is gentle. Many sailboard instructors bring their students here. From Kaahumanu Avenue or the Hana Highway, turn onto Hobron Avenue, and then immediately right onto

Amala Street, and follow the signs to the park. Alternately, follow Rt. 38 to the airport. Swing back around and turn right on Ka'a Street. Pass the rental car agencies and carry on to Hobron. There are two entrances to the park and plenty of parking. The only drawback might be the frequent and noisy arrivals and departures of aircraft at the airport, which is only a few hundred yards away.

ACCOMMODATIONS

Kahului features three motel/hotels because most people are short-term visitors, heading to or from the airport. These accommodations are all bunched together next to Hoaloha Park on the harbor side of Kaahumanu Avenue (Rt. 32). The **Maui Beach Hotel,** tel. (808) 877-0051, has a pool on the second floor, open 9 a.m.-9 p.m. daily, and its daily buffets at the Rainbow Dining Room are good value. Cocktails and *pu pu* are served at the Rainbow Lounge near the dining room from 5 p.m. On the lobby level of the Maui Beach are the front desk, small gift shop, and the Red Dragon Chinese restaurant. The central courtyard off the main foyer leads down to the narrow beach. Rates for the Maui Beach are $93-115 for its standard to oceanfront rooms, and $180 for an oceanfront suite. Expensive.

Just across a parking lot is its sister hotel, **The Maui Palms,** tel. (808) 877-0071; both are Castle Resort and Hotel properties. The Maui Beach is more like a standard hotel—with a Polynesian-style roof over its lobby—while the Maui Palms has more the feel of an economical motel. Both are low-rise affairs. At the Maui Palms, rates are $60-80 for the standard to deluxe rooms. Both offer the sixth night free or a free one-day rental car package. During a reconstruction phase at the Maui Palms, check-in will be handled at the Maui Beach Hotel. For reservations, call (800) 367-5004, interisland (800) 272-5275. These hotels offer a complimentary shuttle to the airport every half hour 6:30 a.m.-9 p.m.; reservations required. Moderate

The one other hotel, 100 yards to the east, is the **Maui Seaside,** tel. (808) 877-3311 or (800) 560-5552, e-mail: sandsea@aloha.net, website: www.sand-seaside.com, part of the Sand and Seaside Hotels, a small island-owned chain.

Friendly and economical, this too is a low-rise facility with a swimming pool in the central courtyard, access to the beach, a guest activities desk, a lobby lounge, and Vi's Restaurant. All rooms hold two double beds or a king, have color TV, a small refrigerator, ceiling fan, and air-conditioning. Some kitchenettes are available. Rates are $80-140 or $110-170 with rental car. For central reservations, call (800) 367-7000. Moderate.

FOOD

The Kahului area has some elegant dining spots as well as an assortment of inexpensive yet good eating establishments. Many are found in the shopping malls. Here are some of the best.

Inexpensive

Several basic restaurants and other food purveyors are located along Dairy Road. **Ma Chan's,** tel. (808) 877-7818, is a cement-floored, no-atmosphere restaurant at 199 Dairy Rd., located in the fading pink-on-green Maui Plantation Shops. Open daily for breakfast and lunch until 6 p.m., Ma Chan's has a variety of inexpensive sandwiches, burgers, and plate lunches, all with an island twist. The restaurant is a little worse for wear, but the staff is very friendly, and the food is very good.

Maui Bakery Bagelry and Deli, almost next door at 201 Dairy Rd., tel. (808) 871-4825, open daily 6:30 a.m.-5:30 p.m., makes fresh (preservative-, fat-, and cholesterol-free) rye, blueberry, whole wheat, garlic, poppy seed, sesame, and onion bagels. Choose a buttered bagel or one smothered with a layer of cream cheese and have it wrapped to go, or eat it at one of the tables. Or try a tasty deli sandwich, served on a bagel, French bread, or rye. The bakery also makes mouthwatering cinnamon and walnut coffee cake, fudge brownies, strudel, and loaves of French, rye, and whole wheat bread. A deli case also holds a variety of drinks and flavored cream cheese.

If you're looking for a wholesome, natural deli item, fresh salad, or freshly baked pastry try the deli counter at **Down to Earth Natural Foods,** 305 Dairy Rd., tel. (808) 877-2661. It's open daily; as it's a full-service grocery store, you can also shop for all your food items here.

At the Dairy Center just up the road, you'll find the inexpensive eateries **Local Boys** for Hawaiian plate lunches, **Koko Ichiban-ya** for Japanese-inspired plate lunches, and **Piñata's** Mexican restaurant.

At 444 Dairy Rd. is **Maui Coffee Roasters,** tel. (808) 877-2877, for those who want a hot brew now or want take-home beans. Other drinks, sandwiches, soups, salads, veggie burgers, and baked goods are also available in this good-time, upscale, yuppie-ish place. Right next door is **Connoisseur Food and Wine.** All that its name implies, it handles high-end wine, vinegar, cheese, pasta, spices, other foods, and a big selection of cigars.

Follow your nose in the Kaahumanu Shopping Center to **The Coffee Store,** tel. (808) 871-6860, open daily 7 a.m.-6 p.m., till 9 p.m. on Thursday and Friday, and Sunday 9 a.m.-3 p.m. Light lunches include savories like a hot croissant or a spinach roll pastry puff. Coffee by the cup is under $2.25, refills 35 cents. The coffees, roasted on the premises, are from more than 20 gourmet varieties handpicked in Africa, South America, Indonesia, and of course Hawaii, and include exotic beans like Jamaican Blue Mountain. Gifts and giftwear too!

The **Maui Mall,** off of Puunene Ave., has a terrific selection of inexpensive eateries. **Matsu Restaurant** is a fast-food Japanese restaurant with an assortment of daily specials for under $6, or a steaming bowl of various types of saimin for $5. Very authentic, like a *soba-ya* in Japan. Japanese standards include *katsu don buri,* tempura, or curry rice. Adjacent is **Siu's Chinese Kitchen,** where most of their typical Chinese dishes are under $5. **Stanton's,** tel. (808) 877-3711, is another gourmet coffee, food gift, and tobacco shop that offers a commodious setting for sipping fresh-brewed coffee and eating gourmet sandwiches. A good place for an inexpensive lunch with some atmosphere. **Luigi's Pasta and Pizzeria** serves up decent Italian food, and **SW Bar-B-Q** is a terrific indoor/outdoor fast-food restaurant with Korean favorites, plate lunches under $5, and a delicious grilled chicken sandwich.

Around back at the Maui Mall is the **Wayfinders Cafe,** tel. (808) 877-6670, where you can have health-conscious food and drinks while you spend time on the Internet, send e-mail, or just play on the computer.

Others worth trying include **Shirley's Drive In** and **Dairy Queen,** near each other on Lono Avenue. Both serve good and inexpensive lunches and sandwiches, and Shirley's is open early mornings.

Finally, for those who need their weekly fix of something fried and wrapped in Styrofoam, Kahului's streets behind Maui Mall are dotted with McDonald's, Pizza Hut, Burger King, Taco Bell, Jack-in-the-Box, KFC, and other fast-food restaurants. Other fast-food outlets can be found in the food courts at Maui Marketplace and Kaahumanu Center.

Moderate

The Maui Beach Hotel's **Rainbow Dining Room** serves food in the second-floor dining room. You can fill up here at the breakfast buffet 7-9:30 a.m. for $8.75 or at the lunch buffet 11 a.m.-2 p.m. for $10.75. Order off the menu for dinner or choose the Japanese Imperial dinner buffet 5:30-8:30 p.m. for $18.75. On the lobby level, dine Wed.-Sun. 5:30-8:30 p.m. at the **Red Dragon Restaurant.** Featured is an all-you-can-eat buffet, $16 per person, where many of the dishes change nightly.

Vi's Restaurant, tel. (808) 871-6494, at the Maui Seaside Hotel, serves a standard American fare breakfast 7-9 a.m. for $5 or less and dinner 6-8 p.m. for $8-12. Vi's offers more than 20 dinners, and breakfasts include omelettes, hotcakes, and other island favorites.

In the Kahului Shopping Center you'll find **Ichiban,** an authentic and inexpensive Japanese restaurant, tel. (808) 871-6977, open daily except Sunday 6:30 a.m.-2 p.m., dinner 5-9 p.m., featuring full and continental breakfast, along with Japanese, American, and local specialties. Much of the breakfast menu is typically American, like eggs and bacon, omelettes, and pancakes, most around $6. The lunch menu includes teriyaki chicken or shrimp tempura, chicken cutlet, *don buri* dishes, a variety of *udon,* and basic noodles, most under $7. Sandwiches are everything from a BLT to baked ham. Dinner features combination plates, with your choice of any two items like shrimp and vegetable tempura, sashimi, or teriyaki chicken for around $12, along with more expensive special combinations like steak

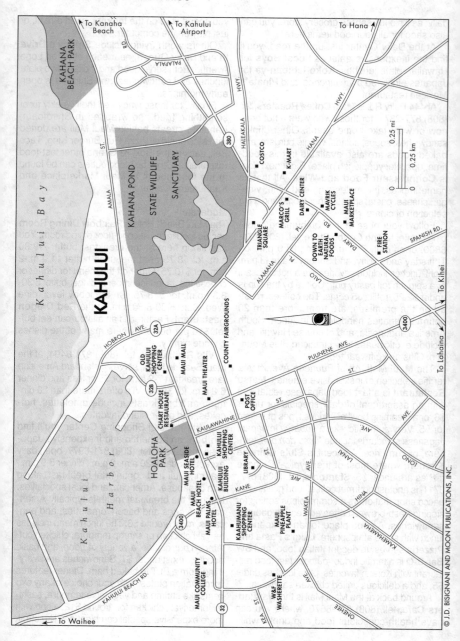

KAHULUI

Kahului Bay

KAHANA BEACH PARK

To Kanaha Beach

To Kahului Airport

To Hana

PAIAALA RD.

KAHANA POND STATE WILDLIFE SANCTUARY

AMALA ST.

HALEAKALA HWY.

HANA HWY.

380

COSTCO

K-MART

DAIRY CENTER

MAVRIK CYCLES

MAUI MARKETPLACE

MARCO'S GRILL

TRIANGLE SQUARE

DOWN TO EARTH NATURAL FOODS

FIRE STATION

SPANISH RD.

ALAMAHA

DAIRY RD.

LALO PL.

0.25 mi

0.25 km

To Kihei

HOBRON AVE.

32A

COUNTY FAIRGROUNDS

3400

OLD KAHULUI SHOPPING CENTER

32B

MAUI MALL

MAUI THEATER

PUUNENE AVE.

ST.

To Lahaina

CHART HOUSE RESTAURANT

POST OFFICE

KAULAWAHINE ST.

AVE.

HOALOHA PARK

Kahului Harbor

MAUI SEASIDE HOTEL

KAHULUI SHOPPING CENTER

KAHULUI BUILDING

LIBRARY

KANE ST.

LANAI AVE.

ONO AVE.

MAUI BEACH HOTEL

MAUI PALMS HOTEL

KAAHUMANU SHOPPING CENTER

MAUI PINEAPPLE PLANT

WAKEA AVE.

HINA AVE.

KAMEHAMEHA AVE.

3400

MAUI COMMUNITY COLLEGE

32

W&F WASHERETTE

KEA ST.

ONEHEE AVE.

To Waihee

© J.D. BISIGNANI AND MOON PUBLICATIONS, INC.

and lobster, the most expensive item on the menu. The interior is basic American with a pinch of Japanese.

At the back of Kahului Shopping Center is the **Asian Sports Bar,** tel. (808) 877-7776. Open for lunch and dinner, this place serves Japanese and Korean food. For lunch, try the lunch box for $5.95, or the tempura *soba* or Bul Go Ki plate, both for $5.50. The dinner menu is a bit more extensive with items from barbecued chicken at $6.95 to sukiyaki for $16.95.

Another sports bar of sorts is **Koho Grill and Bar,** tel. (808) 877-5588, at the Kaahumanu Shopping Center. Koho combines appetizers and salads with burgers, plate lunches, a few Mexican and Italian dishes, plus fish and standard American meat entrees. It's an easygoing, good-time place, but not necessarily quiet when the big games are broadcast on the large screen TV in the bar.

At the corner of Dairy Rd. and the Hana Hwy. is **Marco's Grill and Deli,** tel. (808) 877-4446, a casual place with tuck-and-roll leather booths and marble tabletops, and high-backed cane chairs set around tiled tables. White and black predominate and you might hear Tony Bennett being played as background music. It's very Italian. For breakfast try chocolate cinnamon French toast for $6.95, pancakes, omelettes, or pastries. A quick lunch might be one of the many deli sandwiches or a hot sandwich from the grill, most for under $10. Among the usual Italian fare are Italian sausage and linguine at $15.95 and veal parmesan for $18.95. Other specialties are vodka rigatoni or ravioli at $15.95 and seafood pasta at $20.95. Takeout is available for anything on the menu, or choose something from the deli case. A glass block wall separates the main dining area from the bar, so here too you can sit down and relax in the evening over a drink. Open 7:30 a.m.-10 p.m. daily.

Expensive
The **Chart House,** on Kahului Bay at 500 N. Puunene Ave., tel. (808) 877-2476, is a steak and seafood restaurant that's not too expensive. This is a favorite with businesspeople and island residents. The quality is good and the atmosphere is soothing. Set next to Hoaloha Park, the Chart House overlooks Kahului Bay, so you can eat in the dining room or out on the lanai overlooking the water. Dinners come with a salad, squash, bread, and rice pilaf. Most entrees run around $25. This Chart House is known for its salad bar. On Monday it has a prime rib special with salad bar for $19.95. Open for dinner only 5-10 p.m.

Sam Choy has opened another of his wonderful restaurants at the Kaahumanu Center. **Sam Choy's Kahului Restaurant,** tel. (808) 893-0366, serves breakfast 7-10:30 a.m., lunch 10:30 a.m.-3 p.m., and dinner 5-9 p.m. (Friday and Saturday to 9:30). Choose a table in the back or a stool at the counter and watch the cooks prepare your food in the open kitchen. For breakfast try Sam's plantation-style breakfast, which is two eggs, your choice of meat, rice, hash browns, or home fries, and toast and jelly for $5.75, or such things as Makawao steak and eggs for $9.50, or Paia veggie moco at $6.95. Lunch offerings include sandwiches, plate lunches, and rice and noodle dishes, most below $7. Dinners are more expensive, $18.95-31.95, with such items as oven-roasted duck, veal osso bucco, and vegetarian lasagna, with the most pricey being the Hawaiian-style seafood bouillabaisse. Although Sam Choy's is decorated in a very pleasing manner, people come for the food. There are always large portions, and the presentation is as fine as the taste. It's always busy, so come early for lunch; dinner reservations recommended.

On the first floor of the Kahului Building at 33 Lono Ave. you'll find **Papa's N Chiles,** tel. (808) 871-2074, an upscale restaurant serving authentic Mexican cuisine. Specials are in the $12-17 range, seafood up to $19, with salads, soups, appetizers, and combination plates. Closed Monday; open Tues.-Fri. 11 a.m.-10 p.m., Saturday and Sunday 5-10 p.m. only.

Groceries
For basic grocery items try any of the following in Kahului: **Star Market** at the Maui Mall, **Ah Fooks** at the Kahului Shopping Center, **Foodland** at the Kaahumanu Center, **Safeway** at 170 E. Kamehameha Ave. behind the Maui Mall, or **Down to Earth Natural Foods** at 305 Dairy Rd. across from the Maui Marketplace mall.

Liquor
Connoisseur Food and Wine, 444 Dairy Rd.,

open Mon.-Sat. 9 a.m.-7 p.m., is a good place for a high-end bottle of bubbly. For a quick stop at a basic bottle shop try **Ah Fooks** at the Kahului Shopping Center or **Star Market** at the Maui Mall.

ENTERTAINMENT

The six-plex **Kaahumanu Theater,** tel. (808) 873-3133, is at the Kaahumanu Center, and **The Maui Theater,** tel. (808) 877-3560, is to the side of the Kahului Shopping Center. In addition, live theater is offered by the **Maui Community Theater,** 68 N. Market St., Wailuku, tel. (808) 242-6969, in the remodeled Iao Theater building. Major productions occur four times a year.

Opened in 1994, the $32 million **Maui Arts and Cultural Center** is becoming a big draw for the island. Big-name concerts are held here, as well as local art exhibitions, educational programs, and films. Call (808) 242-7469 for information and tickets.

SHOPPING

Because of the three malls right in a row along Kaahumanu Avenue and the new Maui Marketplace on Dairy Road, Kahului has the best all-around shopping on the island. Here you can find absolutely everything you might need. Combine this with the smaller shopping plazas, Kmart, Costco, and individual shops around town and you're in general shopping heaven. For something different, don't miss the **Aloha Maui Swap Meet,** tel. (808) 877-3100, at the fairgrounds on Puunene Ave. every Saturday 7 a.m.-noon.

You can also shop almost the minute you arrive or just before you leave at two touristy but good shops along Keolani Place. Less than a half mile from the airport are the **T-shirt Factory,** with original Maui designs and custom T-shirts for $5-25, all cotton, as well as Aloha shirts, sarongs, and pareus; and **Coral Factory,** for pink and black coral and jewelry set with semiprecious stones—the Coral Factory seems to be set up largely to cater to Japanese tour groups. When Keolani Place turns into Dairy Road you'll find **Airport Flower and Fruits,** which can provide you with produce that's pre-inspected and admissible to the Mainland. It also has a large se-

lection of lei, which can be packed to go. On Dairy Road between Haleakala and Hana Highways are the two huge stores housing Kmart and Costco. Mainland American mercantilism has invaded.

The two-story **Kaahumanu Center** along Kaahumanu Avenue is Kahului's largest mall (third largest in the state) and has the widest selection of stores. There's lots of free parking. The mall's central courtyard is covered with a big skylight and a huge sail-like expanse of canvas—a good way to let the light and breezes through. You'll find the big stores like **Liberty House, Sears,** and **JCPenney** anchoring this mall, with smaller chains, like **Shirokiya** and **Ben Franklin,** here as well. Numerous other apparel, shoe, jewelry, and specialty stores and a half dozen restaurants fill this center, and a dozen inexpensive international fast-food eateries are located in the food court. Several of the specialty shops are **Waldenbooks,** tel. (808) 871-6112, for one of the best selections of books on Maui; **GNC** for nutritional supplements, and **Fox Photo** for all your camera needs. A great place for a relaxing cup of coffee or light lunch is **The Coffee Store. Maui Dive Shop** has a full range of snorkel and scuba equipment for rent and sale. On the upper level, you can relax in the cool dark comfort of the **Kaahumanu Theater** and catch a movie. Local musicians perform at the center 6-8 p.m. on the first and last Mondays of the month.

The low-rise, open-air Maui Mall is more pedestrian, yet it has a nice ambience as its buildings are set around courtyards filled with greenery. At the intersection of Hana Hwy. and Kaahumanu Ave., **Maui Mall** has **Longs** for everything from aspirin to film, **Star Market, Roy's Photo and Video,** another **Waldenbooks,** and other clothing and specialty shops.

At the **Kahului Shopping Center,** 47 Kaahumanu Ave., you will find **Ah Fooks,** specializing in Asian foods; **Burger King;** and the inexpensive but authentic **Ichiban Restaurant. Maui Organic Farmers Market** holds court here on Wednesday 8 a.m.-noon. This mall is less distinctive than the other two along Kaahumanu Avenue and seems to have suffered most because of the newer malls in town.

The **Old Kahului Shopping Center,** at 55 Kaahumanu Ave., just across from the Maui Mall, is just that, an old building from 1916 that held a bank and a series of shops that was modernized and brought back to life in the late '80s. Once full of boutiques and specialty shops, it's now mostly empty. Only two stores and a doctor's office remain. **Lightening Bolt** specializes in surfboards and surf attire, modern fashions, women's apparel, hats, and sunglasses. **Mannequin** carries women's clothes.

The newest mall in Kahului, with a style from Anywhere U.S.A., occupies a huge area along Dairy Road. This is the **Maui Marketplace Mall,** and here you'll find such stores as **Borders Books,** open until 10 p.m. daily; the **Sports Authority;** numerous clothing stores including **Hawaiian Island Creations;** the huge **Eagle Hardware and Garden** center for anything you might need for your house or yard; **OfficeMax** for your business needs; several jewelry stores; numerous other smaller shops; and a food court. For banking needs, try the **First Federal Savings Bank** or **Bank of Hawaii** along Dairy Road.

Also new is the **Triangle Square** mall, on Hwy. 36 across from Kahana Pond, where you'll find **Hi-Tech Surf Sports** and **Maui Sails** for all water sports equipment and information. For food, step into **Boomers** and order a burger, taco, or deli item.

On the corner across from Kmart is **Hawaiian Island Surf and Sport,** which also carries a multitude of water sports equipment, new and used, for sale and rental. Next door is **Island Bikery,** which sells and rents mountain bikes.

In **Dairy Center** on Dairy Road you'll find **Extreme Sports Maui, Piñata's** for reasonable Mexican food, **Koko Ichiban-ya** Japanese restaurant for inexpensive plate lunches and noodle and rice dishes, a **Local Boys** restaurant for local grind plate lunches, and **Kinko's.** If you need to check your e-mail while on Maui, you can stop at Kinko's and use a computer for a reasonable fee. Extreme Sports rents the usual water equipment, plus skateboards and bikes. It also has a small climbing wall.

Just down the street and across from the new Maui Marketplace is **Down to Earth Natural Foods,** open Mon.-Sat. 7 a.m.-9 p.m., Sunday 8 a.m.-8 p.m. A full-service grocery with bulk items, canned and boxed goods, fresh vegetables and fruit, and vitamins, minerals, and supplements, the store also has a deli counter, salad bar, and bakery, so stop in for a wholesome lunch for under $10.

SERVICES

Kahului has numerous banks, most with ATM machines. There is a Bank of Hawaii, tel. (808) 871-8220, at 11 S. Puunene Ave.; First Hawaiian Bank, tel. (808) 877-2311, at 20 W. Kaahumanu Ave. and another branch at 86 Kamehameha Ave.; and an American Savings Bank, tel. (808) 871-5501, and a City Bank, tel. (808) 871-7761, at the Kaahumanu Center.

The Kahului post office is on Puunene Ave. (Rt. 350) just across the street from the fairgrounds, tel. (808) 871-4710.

The library, at 90 School St., tel. (808) 873-3097, has irregular hours.

The W & F Washerette, 125 S. Wakea, tel. (808) 877-0353, features video games to while away the time as well as a little snack bar. Open daily 6 a.m.-9 p.m.

For medical emergencies, try Maui Memorial Hospital, tel. (808) 244-9056, at 221 Mahalani. Clinics include Kaiser Permanente, tel. (808) 243-6000, at 20 Mahalani.

WAILUKU

Often, historical towns maintain a certain aura long after their time of importance has passed. Wailuku is one of these. Maui's county seat since 1905, the town has the feel of one that has been important for a long time. Wailuku earned its name, "Bloody Waters," from a ferocious battle fought by Kamehameha I against Maui warriors just up the road in Iao Valley. The slaughter was so intense that more than four miles of the local stream literally ran red with blood. Last century the missionaries settled in Wailuku, and their architectural influences, such as a white-steepled church and the courthouse at the top of the main street, give an impression of a New England town. Later in the century, sugar came to town and this vast industry grew with muscle and pumped great vitality into the community. After the turn of the century, Wailuku strengthened its stance as the island's center of government, business, and industry, and the wealthy and influential built homes here. Wailuku maintained this strong position until the '60s when the sugar industry declined and the growth of tourism began to create other centers of population and industry on the island. Although still a vibrant government and population center, much of Wailuku's importance to the island's economy has been eclipsed.

While much of Wailuku is a pretty town, it's a mixed bag in the back streets. The historical town center lends it dignity, and much is being done to maintain and refurbish it. Comely rows of plantation-era bungalows are scattered here and there around town, yet fading sections past their prime also exist, not always too far from the new and modern developments. Built on the rolling foothills of the West Maui Mountains, this adds some character—unlike the often-flat layout of many other Hawaiian towns. You can "do" Wailuku in only an hour, though most people don't even give it that much time. They just pass through on their way to Iao Needle, where everyone goes, or through Happy Valley and on to Kahakuloa, around the back side.

You *can* see Wailuku's sights from the window of your car, but don't shortchange yourself this way. Definitely visit the Bailey House Muse-

um, and while you're out, walk the grounds of Kaahumanu Church. Clustered near these two are other historical buildings, several of which are listed on the Hawaii and national registers of historic places. These include the Circuit Courthouse (1907), Old County Building (1925), Territorial Building (1930), Wailuku Public Library (1928), Wailuku Union Church (1911), and the Wailuku Public School (1904). One block away is the Church of the Good Shepherd (1911), and beyond that the Iao Theater (1928). This theater is the last remaining of the 19 theaters that dotted the island in the era between the world wars. Market Street, between Main and Mill Streets, has a clutch of intriguing antique and curio shops that you can peek into while you're at it.

SIGHTS

Kaahumanu Church
It's fitting that Maui's oldest existing stone church is named after the resolute but loving Queen Kaahumanu. This rock-willed woman is the "Saint Peter" of Hawaii, upon whom Christianity in the islands was built. She was *the* most important early convert, often attending services in Kahului's humble grass-hut chapel. It is also worth noting that the church was erected on Maui king Kahekili's *heiau*—the squashing of one religion with the growing presence of another. In 1832 an adobe church was built on the same spot and named in her honor. Rain and time washed it away, to be replaced by the island's first stone structure in 1837. In 1876 the church went through its fourth metamorphosis, the church tower and clock being delayed until 1884, and what remains is the white and green structure we know today. Its construction was supervised by the missionary Edward Bailey, whose home stands to the rear. A three-year renovation project ended in 1976, bringing the church back to form. Oddly enough, the steeple was repaired in 1984 by Skyline Engineers, who hail from Massachusetts, the same place from which the missionaries came 150 years earlier! You can see the church sitting there on High

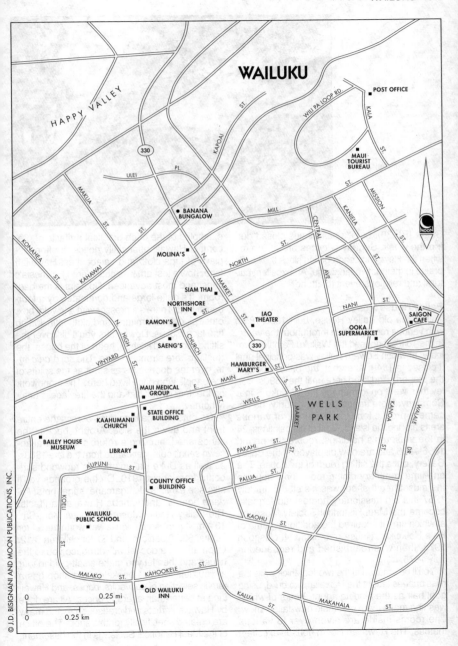

WAILUKU

HAPPY VALLEY

330

ULEI PL.

● BANANA BUNGALOW

MOLINA'S ■

SIAM THAI ■

NORTHSHORE INN ●

RAMON'S ■

SAENG'S ■

IAO THEATER ■

HAMBURGER MARY'S ■

MAUI MEDICAL GROUP ■

STATE OFFICE BUILDING ■

KAAHUMANU CHURCH ■

BAILEY HOUSE MUSEUM ■

LIBRARY ■

COUNTY OFFICE BUILDING ■

WAILUKU PUBLIC SCHOOL ■

OLD WAILUKU INN ●

POST OFFICE ■

WILI PA LOOP RD.

MAUI TOURIST BUREAU ■

A SAIGON CAFE ■

OOKA SUPERMARKET ■

WELLS PARK

MAKUA ST.

KONAHEA ST.

KAHAWAI ST.

N. HIGH ST.

VINYARD ST.

KAPOAI ST.

N. MARKET ST.

NORTH ST.

CHURCH ST.

MILL ST.

CENTRAL AVE.

KANIELA ST.

MISSION ST.

KALA ST.

NANI ST.

S. MARKET ST.

KANOA ST.

WALAIF DR.

E. MAIN ST.

WELLS ST.

PAKAHI ST.

PALUA ST.

KAOHU ST.

KAHOOKELE ST.

MALAKO ST.

KALUA ST.

MAKAHALA ST.

AUPUNI ST.

KOELI ST.

N

MOON

0   0.25 mi

0   0.25 km

© J.D. BISIGNANI AND MOON PUBLICATIONS, INC.

Bailey House

ROBERT NILSEN

Street (Rt. 30), but it's sometimes closed during the week. Sunday services are at 9 a.m., when the Hawaiian congregation sings the Lord's praise in their native language. An excellent cultural and religious event to attend!

Bailey House Museum

This is the old Bailey House, built 1833-1850, with various rooms added throughout the years. In the 1840s it housed the Wailuku Female Seminary, of which Edward Bailey was principal until it closed in 1849. After that, the Baileys bought the property and lived here until the 1890s. Bailey then went on to manage the Wailuku Sugar Company. More important for posterity, he became a prolific landscape painter of various areas around the island. Most of his paintings, 26 in the museum's holdings, record the period 1866-1896 and are now displayed in the Bailey Gallery, once the sitting room of the house. The one-time seminary dining room, now housing the museum gift shop, was his studio. In July 1957 this old missionary homestead formally became the Maui Historical Society Museum, at which time it acquired the additional name of Hale Hoikeike, "House of Display." It closed in 1973, then was refurbished and reopened in July 1975.

You'll be amazed at the two-foot-thick walls the missionaries taught the Hawaiians to build, using goat hair as the binding agent. Years of whitewashing make them resemble new-fallen snow. The rooms inside are given over to various themes. The Hawaiian Room houses excellent examples of the often practical artifacts of pre-contact Hawaii; especially notice the fine displays of tapa cloth and calabashes. Hawaiian tapa, now a lost art, was considered Polynesia's finest and most advanced. Upstairs is the bedroom. It's quite large and dominated by a four-poster bed. There's a dresser with a jewelry box, other pieces of furniture, and clothes including fine lace gloves. Downstairs you'll discover the sitting room and kitchen, heart of the house: the "feelings" are strongest here. The solid *ohio* lintel over the doorway is as stout as the spirits of the people who once lived here. The stonework on the floor is well laid and the fireplace is totally homey.

Go outside! The lanai runs across the entire front and down the side. Around back is the canoe shed, housing a refurbished Hawaiian-sewn sennit outrigger canoe from the late 1800s, as well as Duke Kahanamoku's redwood surfboard from about 1910. On the grounds you'll also see exhibits of sugarcane, sugar pots, *konane* boards, and various Hawaiian artifacts. The Bailey House Museum is open Mon.-Sat. 10 a.m.-4 p.m. Admission is well worth the $4 for adults, $3.50 seniors, and $1 for children 6-12. Upon arrival, a docent will introduce you to the house and then let you make a self-guided tour at your leisure. The bookstore/gift shop has a terrific selection of souvenirs, books, and Hawaiiana at better-than-average prices. All are done by Hawaiian artists and craftspeople, and many are created specifically for this shop. The office of the Maui Historical Society is in the basement, tel. (808) 244-3326. It seems appropriate that this society, which collects and preserves artifacts and disseminates information about the history and culture of Maui, should be located on the grounds where Kahekili, Maui's last king, had his compound.

Kepaniwai Park

As you head up Rt. 320 to Iao Valley, you're in for a real treat. Two miles after leaving Wailuku, you come across Kepaniwai Park and Heritage Gardens. Here the architect, Richard C. Tongg, envisioned and created a park dedicated to all of Hawaii's people. See the Portuguese villa and garden complete with an outdoor oven, a thatch-roofed Hawaiian grass shack, a New England "salt box," a Chinese pagoda, a Japanese tea-house with authentic garden, and a bamboo house—the little "sugar shack" that songs and dreams are made of. Admission is free and there are pavilions with picnic tables. This now-tranquil spot is where the Maui warriors fell to the invincible Kamehameha and his merciless patron war god, Ku. Kepaniwai means "Damming of the Waters"—literally with corpses. Kepaniwai is now a monument to man's higher nature: harmony and beauty.

Hawaii Nature Center

Located just above Kepaniwai Park is the Hawaii Nature Center, Iao Valley, a private, nonprofit educational and interactive science center—good for kids and grown-ups alike and highly recommended. Open 10 a.m.-4 p.m., $6 adults, $4 children, this center boasts 30 exhibits that will beg you to participate, challenge your mind, and teach you about all aspects of Hawaiian nature at the same time. This seems an appropriate spot for a nature center as the West Maui Mountains harbor 12 distinct plant communities, about 300 species of plants, of which 10 are endemic to this locale, and literally thousands of varieties of animals and insects. Daily nature walks are guided through the valley to bring you face to face with some of the wonders that this valley has to offer. Reservations are required for the walks; call (808) 244-6500.

The Changing Profile

Up the road toward Iao Valley you come to a scenic area long known as Pali Ele'ele, or Black Gorge. This stream-eroded amphitheater canyon has attracted attention for centuries. Amazingly, after President Kennedy was assassinated, people noticed his likeness portrayed there by a series of large boulders; mention of a profile had never been noted or recorded there before. A pipe stuck in the ground serves as a rudimentary sighting instrument. Squint through it and there he is, with eyes closed in deep repose. The likeness is uncanny, and easily seen, unlike most of these formations, where you have to stretch your imagination to the breaking point. Recently, however, the powers that be (a committee of the State Department of Land and Natural Resources) have pronounced that this image is really that of the late-15th-century kahuna Kauaka'iwai. Legend has it that he was turned to stone to protect the ali'i buried in this valley. Go figure. You obviously see what you want to in these stones anyway.

Iao Valley State Park

This valley has been a sacred spot and a place of pilgrimage since ancient times. Before Westerners arrived, the people of Maui, who came here to pay homage to the "Eternal Creator," named this valley Iao, "Supreme Light." Facing almost directly east, the valley catches the warming morning sunlight. According to legend, the gods Maui and Hina raised their daughter Iao in this valley. As Iao grew, she became entranced with a half-man, half-fish god, and they became lovers. This arrangement did not please her father, who, in revenge, turned Iao's lover into a stone pinnacle, the peak we know as Iao Needle.

Historically, Iao Valley was a place set aside and did not belong to the traditional ahupua'a land division system. No commoners were allowed into the valley except on special occasions, and royalty were buried here in secret graves. During the Battle of Kepaniwai in 1790, when King Kamehameha defeated Maui's King Kahekili, this valley was valiantly defended but overrun. Countless commoners perished while the ali'i escaped over the mountains to Olowalu.

In the center of this velvety green amphitheater-like valley is a pillar of stone rising more than 1,200 feet (actual height above sea level is 2,250 feet), its grassy plateau top at one time a natural altar and lookout for defense. Kuka'emoku, now commonly called "The Needle," is a tough basaltic ridge that remained after water

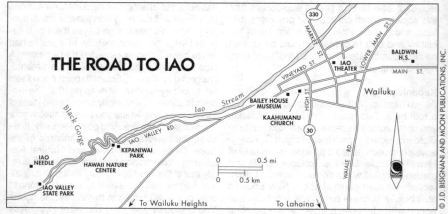

THE ROAD TO IAO

Black Gorge

Iao Stream

IAO NEEDLE

HAWAII NATURE CENTER

IAO VALLEY STATE PARK

KEPANIWAI PARK

IAO VALLEY RD.

BAILEY HOUSE MUSEUM

KAAHUMANU CHURCH

IAO THEATER

VINEYARD ST.

MARKET ST.

HIGH ST.

LOWER MAIN ST.

MAIN ST.

BALDWIN H.S.

Wailuku

WAIALE RD.

330

30

0   0.5 mi

0   0.5 km

← To Wailuku Heights

To Lahaina ↓

© J.D. BISIGNANI AND MOON PUBLICATIONS, INC.

swirled away the weaker stone surrounding it, leaving only a saddle that connects it to the valley wall, unseen from below. Iao Valley is actually the remnant of the volcanic caldera of the West Maui Mountains, whose grooved walls have been smoothed and enlarged by the restlessness of mountain streams. Robert Louis Stevenson had to stretch poetic license to create a word for Iao when he called it "viridescent."

The road ends in a parking lot. Signs point you to paths, tame and well maintained, some even paved, with plenty of vantage points for photographers. If you take the lower path to the river below, you'll find a good-size, popular swimming hole; but remember, these are the West Maui Mountains, and it can rain at any time. Puu Kukui, West Maui Mountains' tallest peak, lies on the western edge of this crater rim and gets about 400 inches of rain a year! You can escape the crowds even in this heavily touristed area by following a path up to the pavilion. As you head back, take the paved path that bears to the right. It soon becomes dirt, skirting the river, and the tourists magically disappear. Here are a number of pint-size pools where you can take a refreshing dip. No real path continues up this valley so you'll have to make your way up through the stream or along the banks. About a mile up is a fork in the stream, beyond which it is not recommended to go.

Iao is for day use only; hours are 7 a.m.-7 p.m. On your way back to Wailuku you might take a five-minute side excursion up to Wailuku Heights. Look for the road on your right. There's little here besides a mid- to upper-end residential area, but the view below is tops!

ROBERT NILSEN

Iao Needle

Maui Tropical Plantation and Country Store

This attraction is somewhat out of the ordinary. The 60-acre Maui Tropical Plantation presents a model of a working plantation that you can tour by small tram. Most interesting is an up-close look at Maui's agricultural abundance. Displays of each of these products are situated around the taro patches at the plantation village. A 40-minute tram ride (optional, as you can also walk) takes you through fields of cane, banana, guava, mango, papaya, pineapple, coffee, and macadamia nuts; flowers here and there add exotic color. Leaving every 45 minutes 10 a.m.-4 p.m., this tram runs $8.50 for adults and $3.50 for children. The plantation, with its restaurant, gift shop, and tropical flower nursery, is in Waikapu, a small village along Rt. 30 between Wailuku and Maalaea. If you visit over the noon hour, stop by the Plantation Cafe for lunch, open 10:30 a.m.-3 p.m. daily. The Country Store sells Maui-produced goods and can mail gift packages of fruits, nuts, and coffee, while the nursery will ship flowers to anywhere in the country. Look for the windmill! Open daily 9 a.m.-5 p.m., tel. (808) 244-7643.

ACCOMMODATIONS

Visitors to Wailuku mostly stay elsewhere on Maui because there really isn't any place to lodge in town except for a few very specialized and very humble hostels and one very comfortable and historic bed and breakfast inn.

The Bungalow

Tthe Bungalow, tel. (808) 244-3294, rents rooms for $18 s or $25 d, weekly at $120 s or $125 d, or monthly for $300 s and $350 d; monthly stays require a $200 deposit. All rooms share a common bathroom. Budget.

Northshore Inn

Two doors down from the Bungalow, this "hostel and hotel," 2080 Vineyard St., tel. (808) 242-8999, fax (808) 244-5004, website: http://mac-mouse.com/hostel/maui.html, is easily spotted with its row of international flags fluttering from the second-floor balcony. Enter via the alley sidewalk. With a capacity of about 45, this clean, light, and comfortable hostel caters mostly to young independent travelers and surfers. Skylights brighten the upstairs; potted plants add color to the walls; and the homey sitting room offers a place for the international guests to talk, listen to music, or watch television; the balcony is a fine place to catch the evening air; and a bulletin board is filled with helpful information about Maui and the other islands. Bunk rooms go for $13.65 a bed, single rooms $26.95, and double rooms $39.95, exclusive of tax; all rooms share four bathrooms. Not only is this an easygoing, well-cared-for place, the management is environmentally conscious. There are laundry facilities; a safe for valuables; storage facilities for sailboards, backpacks, and large items; free use of boogie boards and snorkel equipment; cheap moped, bicycle, and surfboard rental; a full communal kitchen, free morning coffee; inexpensive dinners nightly; free evening movies; reasonable Internet rates; and a small garden in the back with an 80-year-old banyan tree and tropical fruit trees. The Northshore Inn also has a shuttle van with delivery service to the airport and daily island excursions. Ask about the deal with Word of Mouth Rental Cars for low daily rates. The Northshore Inn won the respect of the community for transforming the former fleabag Wailuku Grand Hotel into a viable business and dealing equitably with the locals. Inexpensive.

Banana Bungalow

The Banana Bungalow is located only a few blocks away on the edge of Happy Valley at 310 N. Market St., Wailuku, HI 96793, tel. (808) 244-5090, (800) 846-7835, or (800) 746-7871, fax (808) 846-3678, e-mail: Bungalow@gte.net, website: home1.gte.net/bungalow; office hours are 7 a.m.-11 p.m. Until very recently, this too was a flophouse for locals who were down on their luck. Now it's a clean and spartan hostel, with a fresh coat of (yellow) paint, many new artistic decorations, and refurbished bathrooms up and down. Typically, you're liable to hear languages from a dozen countries, and if you're into sailboarding or just after a cross-cultural experience, this is the spot. The Banana offers basic accommodations, and if you care more about your experience than what your bedroom looks like, it's the place for you. Rates are $29 single, $35 double, or $14 ($10 the first night) for a bunk in a four- to six-person dorm. Extra services include a free and convenient airport/beach shuttle; low-cost adventure tours; free coffee, movies, and parties; laundry and storage facilities; a common room for conversation or TV; inexpensive morning and evening meals at the communal kitchen; a jacuzzi in the garden under tropical fruit trees; discounts on water equipment and lessons; and inexpensive car rental deals. Inexpensive.

Molina's

The name Molina's Tropical Hideaway conjures up a different image than reality. Molina's, tel. (808) 244-4100, at 197 Market St. on the periphery of downtown Wailuku, offers utilitarian rooms at $35 a night, $125 a week, or $460 a month. Other rooms go for $45 a night, and a bunk in the dorm runs $15 per person. All rooms have bathrooms, TVs, and small refrigerators. The $25 key deposit is returned on exit. Although cleaned up in the last few years, Bogart playing a character with a five-day-old beard and a hangover might still be comfortable waking up at this basic, clean, and friendly fleabag. Many renters are long-term, so be sure to call ahead to see if a room is available. Downstairs, Molina's Bar is a neighborhood joint with satellite TV and live jazz on Sunday evening. Inexpensive.

The Old Wailuku Inn at Ulupono

The first, best, and only fine place to stay in Wailuku is at the attentively renovated Old Wailuku Inn, now on the Hawaii Register of Historic Places. Built in 1924 for the son and daughter-in-law of Maui's first bank president, this was the queen of homes in one of Maui's poshest neighborhoods. Refurbished in 1997, this house was brought back to its early-century charm, lovingly detailed, filled with period furniture that evokes the feeling of grandma's house, and decorated with Hawaiian and Asian antiques and artwork. It's a gem. Yet no modern amenity is left out. Each room has a TV, VCR, telephone, private bath, ceiling fan, and gorgeous Hawaiian quilt on its spacious bed. A fax machine, photocopier, and computer are also available for use. The house has central air-conditioning, but the cooling trade winds are generally enough to moderate the temperature. Catching the morning

sun, the screened breakfast room looks out over the rear garden. The open-air front porch is a perfect spot for afternoon tea or reading a book from the extensive house library, and the living room a fine place to relax in the evening. Each of the seven guest rooms is named for a Hawaiian flower, and their color and design motifs follow. The four upstairs rooms are spacious and grand, with native hardwood floors and 10-foot ceilings. The downstairs rooms are cozier, and two have their own courtyards. A gourmet breakfast accompanies each night's stay and, no matter what the offering, is tasty, filling, nutritious, and well-presented. You'll be pampered. Born and raised on the island, the gracious and personable hosts, Tom and Janice Fairbanks, have intimate knowledge of what to do, what to see, and where to eat throughout the island and will gladly share their knowledge and recommendations with you. Rooms run $130-180 double occupancy, two nights minimum. Parking is on property. For information and reservations contact the Old Wailuku Inn at Ulupono, 2199 Kaho'okele St., Wailuku, HI 96793, tel. (800) 305-4899 or (808) 244-5897, fax (808)242-9600, e-mail: Mauibandb @aol.com, website: aitv.com/ulupono. Premium.

FOOD

Downtown

Wailuku has some of the best and the most inexpensive restaurants on Maui. The establishments listed below are all in the bargain or reasonable range. The decor in most is basic and homey, with the emphasis placed on the food. Even here in this nontouristy town, however, some of the restaurants are sprucing up and becoming a bit gentrified.

Saeng's, 2119 Vineyard, tel. (808) 244-1567, serves excellent Thai food at great prices. Dishes include appetizers like Thai crisp noodles for $4.95, green papaya salad for $6.50, and shrimp salad at $8.50. The savory soups, enough for two, include spicy coconut shrimp soup for $8.50 and *po teak,* a zesty seafood combination soup for $10.95. Thai specialties such as pad Thai vegetables, cashew chicken, and eggplant shrimp are all under $10, while vegetarian selections like stir-fry vegetables and Evil Prince tofu are under $7.50. The best seating, although the interior is quite tasteful with linen tablecloths and paisley booths, is outside in a garden area where a small waterfall gurgles pleasantly. Open Mon.-Sat. for lunch 11 a.m.-3 p.m. and dinner nightly 5-9:30 p.m. Saeng's and its friendly competitor Siam Thai are the two best reasonably priced restaurants in town.

Siam Thai is a small restaurant painted black and white at 123 N. Market, tel. (808) 244-3817, open Mon.-Sat. 11:30 a.m.-2:30 p.m., daily 5-9:30 p.m. It serves excellent Thai food with an emphasis on vegetarian cuisine, at prices that are comparable with Saeng's. Extensive menu.

Ramon's, 2101 Vineyard St., tel. (808) 244-7243, serves breakfast, lunch, and dinner; open 10 a.m.-9 p.m. daily (until 10 p.m. Friday and Saturday). It's one of the few places in town open for Sunday breakfast. As the name implies, its flavor is Mexican, but you can get many local dishes here as well. For breakfast, try an omelette, huevos rancheros, or a stack of pancakes. During the rest of the day, order burritos, tacos, enchiladas, tamales, chiles rellenos, or any number of combination plates on the Mexican side or various plate lunches from the Hawaiian side of the menu. No entree is more than $10. Dishes can be made vegetarian as no animal fat is used. Ramon's has a full-service bar, so you can accompany your meal with a frosty beer, glass of wine, or mixed drink. Fiesta Hour at the bar runs Mon.-Fri. 3-6 p.m.

Across the street at 2092 Vineyard St. is **Maui Bake Shop and Deli**, tel. (808) 242-0064, open weekdays 6 a.m.-5:30 p.m., Saturday 7 a.m.-3 p.m., closed Sunday. This establishment has a full selection of home-baked goods and sandwiches at very reasonable prices. Sandwich selections include turkey, ham, roast beef, pastrami, or veggie all for about $3.75, with soup du jour $5.95. Daily specials can be pizza, quiche, filled croissants, or even lox and bagels for under $5. Tantalizing baked goods include apple strudel, coconut macaroons, apricot twists, fruit tarts, homemade pies, and a menagerie of butter and cream pigs, rabbits, and frogs. Enjoy your selection with an espresso, cappuccino, or hot tea.

Underneath the Northshore Inn is **Restaurant Mushroom**, tel. (808) 244-7117, a clean and reasonably priced place serving local, American, and Japanese foods. You can get mostly soups and sandwiches here as well as saimin and other Asian noodle dishes. Lunch 10 a.m.-2 p.m., dinner 5-8:30 p.m. The **Applause Cafe** at the remodeled Iao Theater serves lunch daily and theme dinners on performance nights. About a block down Vineyard is the **Silk Road** restaurant, serving Chinese and Korean dishes. Open Mon.-Sat. 10 a.m.-9 p.m., tel. (808) 249-2399.

Hamburger Mary's, at the corner of N. Main and E. Market Streets, tel. (808) 244-7776, open Mon.-Sat. 10 a.m.-2 a.m., is a very friendly bar and restaurant, where people of all sexual lifestyles are welcome, and where you can have a quiet beer or boogie the night away to video rock music. There's a $5 cover for dancing when a DJ spins discs. Thursday, Friday, and Saturday nights there's food until midnight, every other night until 10 p.m. The interior, like the inside of a big kid's toy box, is brightened with Pee Wee Herman riding a sled, the man in the moon hanging from the ceiling, a mannequin riding a horse, a winged mermaid floating in celestial bliss, Japanese fans, Hawaiiana from the 1940s, surfboards, a small mirrored dance floor, and cherubic angels and fairies perched here and there about the room. Start your day with a breakfast of Portuguese sausage and eggs for $6, create-your-own omelettes for $6, or Mary's short stack for $4.50. The lunch menu has *pu pu* like home-fried melt for $4 and an assortment of fresh salads and homemade soups for under $6. Large two-fisted sandwiches and burgers include avocado burger for $6.75, meatless patty burger for $6.95, and the bird of paradise sandwich with cheddar cheese, sliced bacon, turkey, and avocado for $8.95. Hamburger Mary's claims to have the biggest burgers on the island and has been voted the best on a couple of occasions. You can also enjoy a gigantic charbroiled steak with salad for $11.25, or Mary's mahimahi or a breast of chicken for $10.25. Every day there's a lunch and dinner special. Happy hour, daily 3-6 p.m., features $2 well drinks and domestic beers, while Saturday special Bloody Marys are $3.

A little out of the way at 1792 Main St., but well worth the effort to find, is **A Saigon Cafe**, tel. (808) 243-9560. A great family place, clean but not fancy, this may be the best Vietnamese cuisine on the island. Although there's no large sign yet advertising its location, it's a favorite local stop, and you'll know why once you try. Start with spring rolls at $5.75 or shrimp pops for $7.25 and move on to one of the tasty soups like hot and sour fish soup for $9.20 or a green papaya salad for $5.50. Entrees, all under $10 except the Saigon fondue, which is cooked at your table, include a wide range of noodle, meat, fish, and vegetarian dishes, all with good portions. The menu is extensive. Open daily 10 a.m.-10 p.m. (Sunday until 9 p.m.), this restaurant is behind Ooka Supermarket, below the bridge.

Both **Wakamatsu** at 145 N. Market St. and **Nagasako Fish Market** on Lower Main offer a wide variety of fresh fish. For general grocery shopping, go to **Ooka Supermarket** at 1870 Main St., where you'll find not only the usual groceries but also many ethnic foods.

Food off the Main Drag

If you get out of downtown and take Mill Street and Lower Main, you'll be rewarded with some of the *most* local and *least* expensive restaurants on West Maui. They are totally unpretentious, and serve hefty portions of tasty, homemade local foods. If your aim is to *eat* like a local, search out one of these.

The **Tasty Crust Restaurant,** 1770 Mill St., tel. (808) 244-0845, opens daily 5:30 a.m.-11 p.m. (Friday and Saturday until midnight). Similar to a diner, with bar stools at the counter, booths, and a few tables, the welcome sign says "This is where old friends meet." If you have to carbo-load for a full day of sailing, snorkeling, or windsurfing, order the famous giant homemade hotcakes.

Sam Sato's, tel. (808) 244-7124, is at 1750 Wili Pa Loop Rd. in the Mill Yard. Sato's is famous for *manju*, a puff-like pastry from Japan usually filled with sweets, meats, or *adzuki* beans. One of those places that, if you are a local resident, you *must* bring Sato's *manju* when visiting friends or relatives off-island. Aside from the *manju* there are noodles, sandwiches, plate lunches, and side dishes. Most everything is under $6. Open Mon.-Sat. 7 a.m.-2 p.m., pickup until 4 p.m. A highly specialized place, but worth the effort.

Or try **Nazo's Restaurant,** 1063 Lower Main St., second floor of the Puuone Plaza, an older yellowish two-story building, tel. (808) 244-0529. Park underneath and walk upstairs. Daily specials cost under $8, but Nazo's is renowned for its

oxtail soup, a clear-consommé broth with peanuts and water chestnuts floating around, a delicious combination of East and West.

Tokyo Tei, in the same complex, tel. (808) 242-9630, open daily 11 a.m.-1:30 p.m. for lunch, 5-8:30 p.m. dinner, open Sunday for dinner only, is another institution that has been around for decades serving Japanese dishes to a devoted clientele. Eating here is as consistent as eating at grandma's kitchen, with traditional Japanese dishes like tempura, various *don buri*, and seafood platters. If you want to sample real Japanese food at affordable prices, come here!

Norm's Cafe, "Where food and people of good taste come together," is located at 740 Lower Main St., tel. (808) 242-1667. A place of local atmosphere in a no-nonsense part of town, the inside is pink, white, and yellow, with booths and a few tables. Breakfast starts at 5 a.m. and includes items like pancakes, omelettes, and loco moco. For lunch and dinner, try salads, sandwiches, or a more hardy dish like the bamboo-steamed *ono*. Nothing on the menu is more than $7. Norm's is an institution.

For a different taste treat, try the *mochi* made fresh daily at Wailuku's **Shishido Manju Shop,** 758 Lower Main Street.

On the edge of town toward Kahului near the underpass is **Stillwell's Bakery and Cafe,** 1740 Kaahumanu Ave., tel. (808) 243-2243. Having established a fine reputation with locals, it's now becoming known to visitors. The surroundings are nothing special, but the food is worthy of the reputation and the baked goods are delicious—and served at some fine restaurants on the island. Stop in for a pastry or a full lunch.

If you're out at Maui Tropical Plantation or coming up from Lahaina and need to stop for a quick bite to eat on the way, try **Waikapu Stop** in Waikapu, a few miles south of Wailuku. Choose from many plate lunches, hamburgers, and sandwiches, most for under $6; open Mon.-Sat. 6 a.m.-1:30 p.m.

SHOPPING

Most shopping in this area is done in Kahului at the big malls. But for an interesting diversion try one of these, all on or around Main or Market Street.

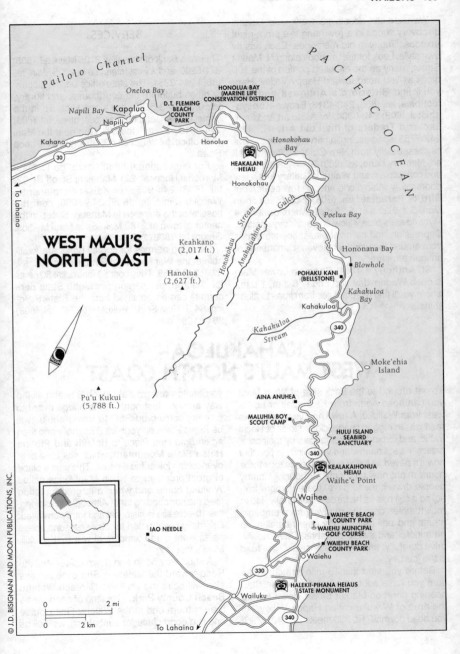

Pailolo Channel

PACIFIC OCEAN

Oneloa Bay
Napili Bay
Kapalua
Napili
Kahana

HONOLUA BAY
(MARINE LIFE
CONSERVATION DISTRICT)

D.T. FLEMING
BEACH
COUNTY PARK

Honolua

30

To Lahaina

Honokohau
Bay

HEAKALANI
HEIAU

Honokohau

Poelua Bay

Keahkano
(2,017 ft.)

WEST MAUI'S
NORTH COAST

Hanolua
(2,627 ft.)

Honokohau Stream

Anakaluahine Gulch

Hononana Bay

POHAKU KANI
(BELLSTONE)

Blowhole

Kahakuloa
Bay

Kahakuloa

Kahakuloa
Stream

340

Moke'ehia
Island

Pu'u Kukui
(5,788 ft.)

AINA ANUHEA

MALUHIA BOY
SCOUT CAMP

HULU ISLAND
SEABIRD
SANCTUARY

340

KEALAKAIHONUA
HEIAU

Waihe'e Point

Waihee

IAO NEEDLE

WAIHE'E BEACH
COUNTY PARK

WAIEHU MUNICIPAL
GOLF COURSE

WAIEHU BEACH
COUNTY PARK

Waiehu

330

HALEKII-PIHANA HEIAUS
STATE MONUMENT

Wailuku

340

To Lahaina

0   2 mi
0   2 km

© J.D. BISIGNANI AND MOON PUBLICATIONS, INC.

Wailuku's attic closets are overflowing. Several discovery shops in a row hang like prom-night tuxedos, limp with old memories. Each has its own style. Look for these shops along N. Market Street, many on the elevated portion of the 100 block as you head toward Happy Valley. Here you'll find **Bitterford's Antiques and Collectibles,** tel. (808) 242-4313; **Brown-Kobayashi,** tel. (808) 242-0804, for Asian art and furniture; and **Traders of the Lost Art,** tel. (808) 242-7753, specializing in carvings from the Pacific, especially from New Guinea. Here as well are **Memory Lane,** tel. (808) 244-4196, for curios and collectibles; and **Wailuku Gallery** just a few doors away. Also along antique row search out **Bird of Paradise,** tel. (808) 242-7699, open Mon.-Sat. 9:30 a.m.-5:30 p.m., where owner Joe Myhand sells blue willow china, vintage bottles, Depression and carnival glass, license plates from around the world, and even a smattering of antique furniture.

St. Anthony's Thrift Shop on Lower Main is open Wednesday and Friday 8 a.m.-1 p.m., where you'll find used articles from irons to aloha shirts.

SERVICES

There's a Bank of Hawaii at 2105 Main, tel. (808) 871-8200, and a First Interstate at 2005 Main, tel. (808) 244-3951. The state office building, county office building, old courthouse, and library, tel. (808) 243-5566, are along High St. in the center of town, and the new post office, tel. (808) 244-4815, is out in the Mill Yard near the Maui HVB office, tel. (808) 244-3530, on Wili Pa Loop Road.

For conventional health care, go to Maui Memorial Hospital, 221 Mahalani St. off Rt. 32, tel. (808) 244-9056, or Kaiser Permanente, Wailuku Clinic, tel. (808) 243-6000, near the hospital at the entrance to Mahalani Street. In the center of town at 2180 Main St. is Maui Medical Group, tel. (808) 242-6464.

Camping permits for county parks are available at the War Memorial Gym, Room 102, tel. (808) 243-7389. They cost $3 for adults, 50 cents for children, per person per night. State park permits can be obtained from the State Building, 54 S. High St., Wailuku, HI 96793, tel. (808) 984-8109.

KAHAKULOA~ WEST MAUI'S NORTH COAST

To get around to the back side of West Maui you can head north from Kaanapali or northwest from Wailuku. A few short years ago, this road was in rugged shape, closed to all but local traffic, and forbidden to rental cars by their companies. It's still narrow and very windy in part, but now it's paved all the way. What once took three hours might now take only an hour. As many people drive it these days, there is more traffic, so it still has its hazards. Additionally, loose rock tumbles onto the roadway from embankments and *pali* (particularly after rainfalls), so be mindful and aware of debris. Drive slowly, drive carefully, and drive defensively. The road is the journey.

Before you start this 18-mile stretch, make sure you have adequate gas and water. Start heading north on Market Street, down toward the area of Wailuku called Happy Valley. As you head downhill, Rt. 330 meets Rt. 340, which

you'll follow toward Kahakuloa Bay and all the way around. Just north of the bridge over Iao Stream, coming up Rt. 340 from Kahului, will be Kuhio Place on your left. Turn here and then again onto Hea Place to **Halekii and Pihana Heiau State Monument,** which sits on a bluff overlooking lower Iao Stream. This was a place of great prominence when Maui kings called Wailuku home and when a large population filled the surrounding land. Although uninspiring, this 10-acre site is historical and totally unvisited. Originally constructed for other reasons, these *heiau* were made temples of war by Kahekili, Maui's last king.

A short way north and down Lower Waiehu Road toward the water—a Shoreline Access sign will point the way—you'll reach **Waiehu Beach County Park.** This strip of sand meets the southern end of the Waiehu Golf Course and is a good place for sunbathing, as well as swimming when the water is calm.

Back on Rt. 340 you come shortly to **Waihee** (Slippery Water); there's a little store here. Turn at the Kiwanis Park (softball on Saturday) and follow the sign pointing you to **Waiehu Golf Course;** call (808) 243-7400 for tee times. Mostly local people golf here; it's full of kids and families on the weekend. The fairways, strung along the sea, are beautiful to play. **Waiehu Inn Restaurant** is an adequate little eatery at the golf course.

Like its sister on the south edge of the golf course, **Waiehu Beach County Park** is tucked into its northern corner. It too is secluded and frequented mostly by local people. Some come here to spear fish inside the reef. Although both parks are for day use only, they'd probably be okay for an unofficial overnight stay. To reach this park, go left and follow the fence just before the golf course parking lot.

At mile marker 11, the pavement begins to deteriorate. The road hugs the coastline and gains elevation quickly; the undisturbed valleys are resplendent. Here you pass the entrance to a Boy Scout camp and a trailhead leading up into the West Maui Mountains. With the paving of this road, several commercial establishments have been opened along this back route. One of these is **Aina Anuhea,** a private garden. While not spectacular, this garden is fine for a short stop. From here you're able to see not only the bay below but Haleakala off in the distance. Walkways take you through the diminutive gardens and a short path leads up to a small, quiet waterfall, a peaceful place for a picnic on the rocks or to sit in meditation for a few minutes.

Smitty will greet you as you come up the driveway, collect your $4 entrance fee, and set you on the right path.

In a few miles you skirt a tall headland—easily seen from Paia and points along the north shore—and enter the fishing village of **Kahakuloa** (Tall Hill), with its dozen weatherworn houses and tiny green church. Being on the north coast, the turbulent waters constantly wash the beach of round black stones. Although a tiny community (you are greeted with Aloha, Welcome, and Farewell all on one sign), each house is well kept with pride. To cater to the increased through traffic, several fruit stands have popped up along the road. Overlooking Kahakuloa on the western side is a pullout and promontory where you have good views over the rugged coast. Here the road is at its absolute narrowest. The valley is very steep-sided and beautiful. Supposedly, great Maui himself loved this area.

Two miles past Kahakuloa, you come to **Pohaku Kani,** the bell stone. It's about six feet tall and the same in diameter, but graffiti spoils it. The seascapes along this stretch are tremendous. The surf pounds along the coast below and sends spumes skyward, roaring through a natural blowhole. Nakalele blowhole sits near the Nakalele Lighthouse coast guard beacon site. From the road, it's a short walk down to the water—good for the family. Enjoy the spume close-up and explore the tide pools, but be aware that it's a rough coastline with occasional heavy surf, churning seas, and lots of wind and spray. The road becomes wider again but still curvy and you're soon at **D.T. Fleming Beach Park.** Civilization comes again too quickly.

M.G.L. DOMENY DE RIENZI

WEST MAUI
LAHAINA

Lahaina (Merciless Sun) is and always has been the premier town on Maui. It's the most energized town on the island as well, and you can feel it from the first moment you walk down Front Street. Maui's famed warrior-king Kahekili lived here and ruled until Kamehameha, with the help of newfound cannon power, subdued Kahekili's son in Iao Valley at the turn of the 19th century. When Kamehameha I consolidated the island kingdom, he chose Lahaina as his seat of power. It served as such until Kamehameha III moved to Honolulu in the 1840s. Lahaina is where the modern world of the West and the old world of Hawaii collided, for better or worse. The *ali'i* of Hawaii loved to be entertained here; the royal surf spot, mentioned numerous times as an area of revelry in old missionary diaries, is just south of the Small Boat Harbor. Kamehameha I built in Lahaina the islands' first Western structure in 1801, known as the Brick Palace; a small ruin still remains. Queens Keopuolani and Kaahumanu, the two most powerful wives of the great Kamehameha's harem of more than 20, were local Maui women who remained after their husband's death and helped to usher in the new order.

The whalers came preying for "sperms and humpbacks" in 1819 and set old Lahaina Town a-reelin'. Island girls, naked and willing, swam out to meet the ships, trading their favors for baubles from the modern world. Grog shops flourished, and drunken sailors with their brown-skinned doxies owned the debauched town. The missionaries, invited by Queen Keopuolani, came praying for souls in 1823. Led by the Reverends Stuart and Richards, they tried to harpoon moral chaos. In short order, there was a curfew, a *kapu* placed on the ships by wise but ineffectual old Governor Hoapili, and a jail and a fort to discourage the strong-arm tactics of unruly captains. The pagan Hawaiians transformed like willing children to the new order, but the Christian sailors damned the meddling missionaries. They even whistled a few cannonballs into the La- haina homestead of Reverend Richards, hoping to send him speedily to his eternal reward. Time, a new breed of sailor, and the slow death of the whaling industry eased the tension.

Meanwhile, the missionaries built the first school and printing press west of the Rockies at Lahainaluna, in the mountains just above the town, along with downtown's Wainee Church, the first stone church on the island. Lahaina's glory days slipped by and it became a sleepy "sugar town" dominated by the Pioneer Sugar Mill, which has operated since 1860. In 1901, the Pioneer Inn was built to accommodate interisland ferry passengers, but no one *came* to Lahaina. In the 1960s, Amfac Inc. had a brilliant idea. It turned Kaanapali, a magnificent stretch of beach just west, into one of the most beautifully planned and executed resorts in the world. The Pioneer Sugar Mill had long used the area as a refuse heap, but now the ugly duckling became a swan, and Lahaina flushed with new life. With superb farsightedness, the Lahaina Restoration Foundation was begun in those years and almost the entire town was made a national historical landmark. Lahaina, subdued but never tamed, throbs with its special energy once again.

Parking

Traffic congestion is a problem that needs to be addressed. Be parked and settled 4:30-5:30 p.m., when traffic is heaviest. While there still are no traffic lights on Front Street, a spree of construction in the last several years has increased the number of lights on the highway from two to more than half a dozen. The other thing to know to make your visit carefree is where to stash your car. The two lots along Dickenson Street are centrally located and charge a reasonable daily rate. A little more expensive but closer to Front Steet is the lot behind Burger King. There are two smallish lots along Luakini Street, small lots behind the Baldwin Home and the Lahaina Hotel, and an underground lot below the 505 Front Street Mall. These lots charge $3-8 a day; exact fee only, no attendants on duty. The large lot at Prison and Front Streets is free but has a three-hour limit. The lots at Maluuluolele and Kamehameha Iki parks are above free and ostensibly for use by park users only, but people do park and walk into town from there. Aside from these public parking lots, all shop-

ping centers in town have parking: some are free, some charge, and some offer reduced rates with validation. Most of the meters in town are a mere one hour, and the most efficient people on Maui are the "meter patrol!" ($15-20 per parking ticket). Your car will wind up in the pound if you're not careful! Those staying in Kaanapali should leave cars behind and take the Lahaina Express or West Maui Shopping Express shuttles for the day or hop on the Sugar Cane Train.

SIGHTS

In short, strolling around Lahaina offers the best of both worlds. It's busy, but it's bite-size. It's engrossing enough, but you can "see" it in half a day. The main attractions are mainly downtown within a few blocks of each other. Lahaina technically stretches, long and narrow, along the coast for about four miles, but you may only be interested in the central core, a mere mile or so. All along Front Street, the main drag, and the side streets running off it are innumerable shops, restaurants, and hideaways where you can browse, recoup your energy, or just wistfully watch the sun set. Go slowly and savor, and you'll feel the dynamism of Lahaina past and present all around you. Enjoy!

The Banyan Tree

The best place to start your tour of Lahaina is at this magnificent tree at the corner of Hotel and Front Streets. You can't miss it as it spreads its shading boughs over almost an entire acre. It is the largest banyan in the state. Use the benches to sit and reconnoiter while the sun, for which Lahaina is infamous, is kept at bay. Children love it, and it seems to bring out the Tarzan in everyone. Old-timers sit here chatting, and you might be lucky enough to hear Ben Victorino, a tour guide who comes here frequently, entertain people with his ukulele and endless repertoire of Hawaiian tunes. On Saturday and Sunday, members of the Lahaina Art Society gather here to display and sell their artwork under the tree's broad branches. This banyan was planted in April 1873 by Sheriff Bill Smith in commemoration of the Congregationalist Missions' golden anniversary. One hundred years later, a ceremony was held here and more than 500 people were accommodated under this natural canopy. Just left of the banyan, down the lane toward the harbor, was a canal and the Government Market. All kinds of commodities, manufactured and human, were sold here during the whaling days, and it was given the apt name of "Rotten Row."

The Courthouse

Behind the banyan on Wharf Street is the Courthouse. Built in the late 1850s from coral blocks recycled from Kamehameha III's ill-fated palace,

Hale Piula (House of Iron), it also served a post office, customs office, and the police station, complete with a jail in the basement. Until its most recent renovation, the jail was home to the **Lahaina Art Society,** where paintings and artifacts were kept behind bars, waiting for patrons to liberate them. Since its renovation in 1998, the Lahaina Visitors Center has occupied the old courthouse.

Adjacent is **The Fort,** built in the 1830s to show the sailors that they couldn't run amok in Lahaina. Even with its 20-foot-high walls, it was more for show than for force. When it was torn down, the blocks were hauled over to Prison Street to build the real jail, **Hale Pa'ahao.** A corner battlement of the fort was restored, but that's it, because restoring the entire structure would mean mutilating the banyan. The cannons, from a military vessel sunk in Honolulu harbor a few years prior and now set along the wharf in front of the courthouse, are in approximately the location that they had when they were fixtures on the fort wall.

Small Boat Harbor

Walking along the harbor stimulates the imagination and the senses. The boats waiting at anchor sway in confused syncopation. Hawser ropes groan and there's a feeling of anticipation and adventure in the air. Here you can board for all kinds of seagoing excursions. In the days of whaling there was no harbor; the boats tied up one to the other offshore in the "roads," at times forming an impromptu floating bridge. The whalers came ashore in their chase boats; with the winds always up, departure could be made at a moment's notice. The activity here is still dominated by the sea.

Just as today, the old commercial and whaling boats used a light to guide their way to port. Beyond the *Carthaginian II* anchored at the harbor's mouth is the site of the Lahaina's first lighthouse. In 1840, before any were built along what would later be the West Coast of the U.S., King Kamehameha III ordered a lighthouse to be constructed here. The original wooden nine-foot structure was rebuilt to 26 feet in 1869, and the present concrete structure installed in 1919. As might be expected, a whale oil lamp was first used for light, later to be supplanted by electricity.

The *Carthaginian II*

The masts and square rigging of this replica of the enterprising freighters that braved the Pacific tower over Lahaina Harbor. You'll be drawn to it . . . go! It's the only truly square-rigged ship left afloat on the seas. It replaced the *Carthaginian I* when that ship went aground in 1972 while being hauled to Honolulu for repairs. The Lahaina Restoration Foundation found this steel-hulled ship in Denmark; built in Germany in 1920 as a two-masted schooner, it tramped around the Baltic under converted diesel power. The foundation had it sailed 12,000 miles to Lahaina, where it underwent extensive conversion until it became the beautiful replica that you see today.

The *Carthaginian II* is a floating museum dedicated to whaling and to whales. It's open daily 10 a.m.-4 p.m., but arrive no later than 3:30 to see all the exhibits and videos. Admission is $4 adults, seniors $3, $5 for the whole family. Whale researchers Debra and Mark Ferrari narrate a video documenting the life of humpbacks. Belowdecks is the museum containing artifacts and implements from the whaling days. There's even a whaling boat that was found intact in Alaska in the 1970s. The light below decks is subdued, and while you sit in the little "captains' chairs" the humpbacks chant their peaceful hymns in the background. Flip Nicklin's sensitive photos adorn the bulkheads.

The Brick Palace

This rude structure was commissioned by Kamehameha I in 1801 and slapped together by two forgotten Australian exconvicts. It was the first Western structure in Hawaii, but unfortunately the substandard materials have for the most part disintegrated. Kamehameha never lived in it, but it was occupied and used as a storehouse until the 1850s. Just to the right of the Brick Palace site, as you face the harbor, is **Hauola Stone**. Formed like a chair, it was believed by the Hawaiians to have curative powers if you sat on it and let the ocean bathe you. Best view at low tide.

Pioneer Inn

This vintage inn, situated at the corner of Hotel and Wharf Streets, is just exactly where it belongs. Stand on its veranda and gaze out at the *Carthaginian II*. Presto . . . it's magic time! You'll

the Carthaginian II

see. It was even a favorite spot for actors like Errol Flynn and later Spencer Tracy, when he was in Lahaina filming *Devil at Four O'clock.* The green and white inn was built in 1901 to accommodate interisland ferry passengers, but its style seems much older. If ironwork had been used on the veranda, you'd think you were in New Orleans. A new wing was built behind it in 1965 and the two form a courtyard. Make sure to read the hilarious rules governing behavior that are posted in the main lobby. The inn is still functional and retains some character and atmosphere even though it has undergone a recent major remodeling.

Baldwin Home

One of the best attractions in Lahaina is the Baldwin Home, on the corner of Front and Dickenson Streets. It was occupied by Doctor/Reverend Dwight Baldwin, his wife Charlotte, and their eight children. He was a trained teacher, as well as the first doctor/dentist in Hawaii. The

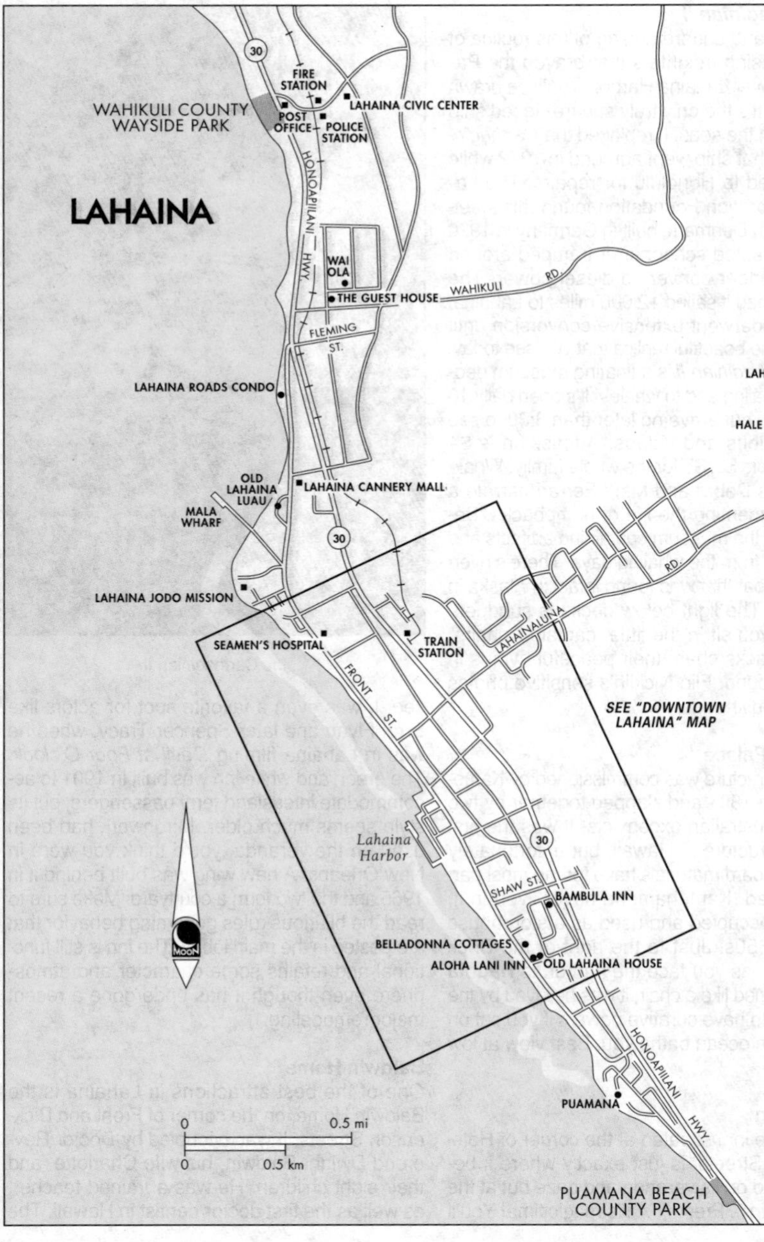

LAHAINA

WAHIKULI COUNTY WAYSIDE PARK

FIRE STATION
POST OFFICE
POLICE STATION
LAHAINA CIVIC CENTER

30

HONOAPIILANI HWY

WAI OLA
THE GUEST HOUSE

WAHIKULI RD

FLEMING ST

LAHAINA ROADS CONDO

LAHAINALUNA HIGH SCHOOL

HALE PA'I

OLD LAHAINA LUAU
LAHAINA CANNERY MALL

MALA WHARF

30

LAHAINA JODO MISSION

SEAMEN'S HOSPITAL

TRAIN STATION

LAHAINALUNA RD

SEE "DOWNTOWN LAHAINA" MAP

FRONT ST

Lahaina Harbor

30

SHAW ST
BAMBULA INN

BELLADONNA COTTAGES
ALOHA LANI INN   OLD LAHAINA HOUSE

MOON

0   0.5 mi
0   0.5 km

HONOAPIILANI HWY

PUAMANA

PUAMANA BEACH COUNTY PARK

© J.D. BISIGNANI AND MOON PUBLICATIONS, INC.

building served from the 1830s to 1868 as a dispensary, meeting room, and boarding home for anyone in need. The two-foot-thick walls are of cut lava, and the mortar made of crushed coral over which plaster was applied. As you enter, notice how low the doorway is, and that the doors inside are "Christian doors"—with a cross forming the upper panels and an open Bible at the bottom. The Steinway piano that dominates the entrance was built in 1859. In the bedroom to the right, along with all of the period furniture, is a wooden commode. Also notice the lack of closets; all items were kept in chests. Upstairs was a large dormitory where guests slept.

The doctor's fees are posted and are hilarious. Payment was by "size" of sickness: very big $50, diagnosis $3, refusal to pay $10! The Reverend Baldwin was 32 when he arrived in Hawaii from New England, and his wife was 25. She was supposedly sickly (eight children!), and he had heart trouble, so they moved to Honolulu in 1868 to receive better health care. The home became a community center, housing the library and meeting rooms. Today, the Baldwin Home is a showcase museum of the Lahaina Restoration Society. It's open daily 10 a.m.-4 p.m., admission $3 adult (or $5 for the Baldwin House and the *Carthaginian II*), $2 seniors, and $5 for the family.

The oldest coral-block house in Hawaii was built for Rev. William Richards and his family when they came to serve in Lahaina in the 1830s. Now gone, the house occupied the site of Campbell Park next door to the Baldwin Home.

Master's Reading Room

Originally a missionaries' storeroom, the Master's Reading Room was converted to an officers' club in 1834. Located next door to the Baldwin Home, these two venerable buildings constitute the oldest Western structures on Maui, and fittingly, this uniquely constructed coral-stone building is home to the Lahaina Restoration Foundation, tel. (808) 661-3262. The building is not really open to the public, but you can visit to pick up maps, brochures, and information about Lahaina; open weekdays 9 a.m.-4 p.m.

The **Lahaina Restoration Foundation,** begun in 1962 by Jim Luckey, a historian who knows a great deal about Lahaina and the whaling era, is now headed by Keoki Freeland, an old Maui resident and grandson of the builder of the Pioneer Inn. The main purpose of the foundation is to preserve the flavor and authenticity of Lahaina without stifling progress—especially tourism. The foundation is privately funded and has managed to purchase many of the important historical sites in Lahaina. It owns two of the buildings mentioned, the restored Wo Hing Temple, and the land under the U.S. Seamen's Hospital, and it will own the plantation house next door to it in a few years. The 42 people on the board of directors come from all socioeconomic backgrounds. You don't get on the board by how much money you give but by how much effort and time you are willing to invest in the foundation; the members are extremely dedicated. Merchants approach the foundation with new ideas for business and ask how they can best comply with the building codes. The townspeople know that their future is best served if they preserve the feeling of old Lahaina rather than rush headlong into frenzied growth. The historic village of Williamsburg, Virginia, is often cited as Lahaina's model, except that Lahaina wishes to remain a "real" living, working town.

Hale Pa'ahao

This is Lahaina's old prison, located midblock on Prison Street, and its name literally means "Stuck-in-Irons House." It was constructed by prisoners in the 1850s from blocks of stone salvaged from the old defunct Fort. It had a catwalk for an armed guard and cells complete with shackles for hardened criminals, but most were drunks who yahooed around town on the Sabbath, wildly spurring their horses. The cells were rebuilt in 1959, the gatehouse in 1988, and the structure is maintained by the Lahaina Restoration Foundation. The cells, curiously, are made of wood, which shows that the inmates weren't that interested in busting out. It's open daily; admission is free but donations are accepted.

Malu Ulu O Lele Park

"The Breadfruit Shelter of Lele" park—Lele was the former name of Lahaina—is a nondescript area at the corner of Shaw and Front that was at one time the most important spot in Lahaina. Here was a small pond with a diminutive island in the center. The pond, Mokuhinia, was home to a *mo'o,* a lizard spirit. The tiny island,

Mokuula, was the home of the Maui chiefs and the Kamehamehas when they were in residence. It became a royal mausoleum, but in the early years of the 20th century all the remains were taken away and the pond was filled and the ground leveled. King Kamehameha III and his sister Princess Nahienaena were raised together in Lahaina. They fell in love, but the new ways caused turmoil and tragedy. Instead of marrying and producing royal children, a favored practice only 20 years earlier, they were wrenched apart by the new religion. He, for a time, numbed himself with alcohol, while she died woefully from a broken heart. She was buried here, and for many years Kamehameha III could frequently be found at her grave, quietly sitting and meditating.

Kamehameha Iki Park

Across the street from Malu Ulu O Lele Park was the site of Hale Piula, a two-story royal stone palace built in the late 1830s for King Kamehameha III. Never finished, its stones were later used to construct the courthouse that now stands between the banyan tree and harbor. This mostly barren spot is now known as Kamehameha Iki Park. On this site the 62-foot double-hulled sailing canoe, Mo'o Kiha (Sacred Lizard), has been built by the cultural group Hui O Wa'a Kaulua, and is considered by them to be "Maui's flagship of Hawaiian culture and goodwill." Future plans for the park include additional canoes, canoe sheds, traditional-style buildings, landscaping, and educational and cultural training programs. Access to one of the two in-town beaches is here.

Wainee Church and Cemetery

The church itself is not impressive, but its history is. This is the spot where the first Christian services were held in Hawaii, in 1823. A church was built here in 1832 that could hold 3,000 people, but it was razed by a freak hurricane in 1858. Rebuilt, it survived until 1894, when it was deliberately burned by an angry mob, upset with the abolition of the monarchy in Hawaii and the islands' annexation by the United States. Another church was built, but it too was hit not only by a hurricane but by fire as well. The present structure was built in 1953. In the cemetery is a large part of Maui's history: buried here are Hawaiian

royalty. Lying near each other are Queen Keopuolani, her star-crossed daughter, Princess Nahienaena, and old Governor Hoapili, their royal tomb marked by two large headstones surrounded by a wrought-iron fence. Other graves hold missionaries such as William Richards and many infants and children.

Churches and Temples

You may wish to stop for a moment at Lahaina's churches and temples dotted around town. They are reminders of the mixture of faiths and peoples that populated this village and added their particular cultural styles. **Holy Innocents Episcopal Church,** built in 1927, is on Front St., near Kamehameha III school. Known for its "Hawaiian Madonna," its altar is resplendent with fruits, plants, and birds of the islands. Stop by on Sunday when the church is full and hear the sermon preached and hymns sung in Hawaiian. **The Episcopal Cemetery** on Wainee St. shows the English influence in the islands. Many of the royal family, including King Kalakaua, became Anglicans. This cemetery holds the remains of many early Maui families, and of Walter Murray Gibson, the notorious settler, politician, and firebrand of the 1880s. Just behind is **Hale Aloha,** "House of Love," a small structure built by Maui residents in thanksgiving for being saved from a terrible smallpox epidemic that ravaged Oahu but bypassed Maui in 1858. The structure was restored in 1974. Also on Wainee is **Maria Lanakila Church,** the site of the first Roman Catholic Mass in Lahaina, celebrated in 1841. The present structure dates from 1928. Next to the church's cemetery is the **Seamen's Cemetery** where many infirm from the ships that came to Lahaina were buried after failing to recover. Most stones have been obliterated by time, and only a few remain. Herman Melville came here to pay his last respects to a cousin buried in this yard. **Hongwanjii Temple** is also on Wainee, between Prison and Shaw. It's a Buddhist temple with the largest congregation in Lahaina and dates from 1910, though the present structure was raised in 1927. Down Luakini Street is the tall clapboard **Shingon Buddhist Temple,** a plantation-era structure.

The **Wo Hing Temple** on Front St. is the Lahaina Restoration Foundation's newest reconstruction. It was opened to the public in 1984 and shows the Chinese influence in Lahaina. Downstairs are displays, upstairs is the altar. In the cookhouse next door, you can see film clips of Hawaii taken by the Edison Company in 1899 and 1906. It's open daily 10 a.m.-4:15 p.m.; admission is by donation.

The **Lahaina Jodo Mission** is near Mala Wharf on Ala Moana Street. When heading west, you'll leave the main section of town and keep going until you see a sign over a building that reads "Jesus Coming Soon." Turn left toward the beach and you'll immediately spot the three-storied pagoda. Here the giant bronze Buddha sits exposed to the elements. The largest outside of Asia, it was dedicated in 1968 in commemoration of the centennial of the arrival of Japanese workers in Hawaii. The grounds are impeccable and serenely quiet. You may stroll around, but the buildings are closed to the public. If you climb the steps to peek into the temple, kindly remove your shoes. The entire area is quiet and a perfect spot for solitary meditation if you've had enough of frenetic Lahaina. The Puupia cemetery is across the street along the beach. It seems incongruous to see tombstones set in sand. There is beach access here between the temple and cemetery, at the end of Pu'unoa Place, and at the turnaround on Kai Pali Place, the next two streets in toward town.

Mala Wharf

Once an integral part of Lahaina commerce, the Mala Wharf now stands decaying at the northern end of town. It sports a boat launch ramp, which is used by some local fishermen and some ocean activities companies. There are restrooms here but no other amenities or services.

U.S. Seamen's Hospital

This notorious hospital was reconstructed by the Lahaina Restoration Foundation in 1982. Here is where sick seamen were cared for under the auspices of the U.S. State Department. Allegations during the late 1850s claimed that the care here extended past the grave! Unscrupulous medicos supposedly charged the U.S. government for care of seamen who had long since died. The hospital is located at Front and Baker, heading toward Kaanapali, near the Jodo Mission. While the stony exterior of this building has been maintained, the building now houses Paradise TV, a company that produces the visitor channel. In the front yard is a 10,000-pound, swivel-end Porter anchor, found off Black Rock in Kaanapali.

Lahainaluna

Head up the mountain behind Lahaina on Lahainaluna Road for approximately two miles. On your left you'll pass the **Pioneer Sugar Mill,** in operation since 1860. Once at Lahainaluna (Above Lahaina) you'll find the oldest school west of the Rockies, opened by the Congregationalist missionaries in 1831. Children from all over the islands, and many from California, came here if their parents could afford to send them

Hale Pa'i, printing house

away to boarding school. Today, the school is West Maui's public high school, but many children still come here to board. The first students were not only given a top-notch academic education, but a practical one as well. They built the school buildings, and many were also apprentices in the famous **Hale Pa'i** (Printing House), which turned out Hawaii's first newspaper and made Lahaina famous as a printing center.

One look at Hale Pa'i and you think of New England. It's a white stucco building with blue trim and a wood-shake roof. It houses a replica printing press and copies of documents once printed here. It was restored in 1982 and is open Mon.-Fri. 10 a.m.-3 p.m. If you visit the campus when school is in session, you may go to Hale Pa'i, but if you want to walk around, please sign in at the vice principal's office. Lahainaluna High School is still dedicated to the preservation of Hawaiian culture. Every year, in April, it celebrates the anniversary of the death of one of its most famous students, David Malo. Considered Hawaii's first scholar, he authored the definitive *Hawaiian Antiquities*. His final wish was to be buried "high above the tide of foreign invasion," and his grave is close to the giant "L" atop Mount Ball, behind Lahainaluna. At graduation, students from the school follow a decades-old tradition of surrounding the "L" with lighted tiki torches, making quite a sight from town. On the way back down to town, you get a wide, impressive panorama of the cane fields, port, Lahaina Roads, and Lanai, and realize that Lahaina is not a big place as you can see it all easily from end to end.

Heading East

Five miles east of Lahaina along the coastal road (Rt. 30) is the little village of **Olowalu**. Today, little more than the Olowalu General Store and Chez Paul French Restaurant are here. This was the place of the Olowalu Massacre perpetrated by Captain Metcalf, whose far-reaching results greatly influenced Hawaiian history. Two American seamen, Young and Davis, were connected with this incident, and with their help Kamehameha I subdued all of · Hawaii. Behind the general store a half-mile dirt track leads to **petroglyphs;** make sure you pass a water tower within the first few hundred yards because there are three similar roads here. You'll

come to the remains of a wooden stairway going up a hill. There once was an HVB Warrior here, but it might be gone. Claw your way up the hill to the petroglyphs, which are believed to be 300 years old.

If you continue east on Rt. 30, you'll pass **Papawai** and **McGregor Point,** both noted for their vistas and as excellent locations to spot whales in season. The road sign merely indicates a scenic lookout. Near mile marker 14 there is good snorkeling.

BEACHES

The best beaches around Lahaina are just west of town in Kaanapali, or just east toward Olowalu. A couple of adequate places to spread your towel are right in Lahaina, but they're not quite on a par with the beaches just a few miles away.

In-Town Beaches
One beach stretches east of the harbor starting at Kamehameha Iki Park. It's crowded at times and there's plenty of "wash up." It's cleaner and quieter at the east end down by Lahaina Shores Hotel. Close to the old royal compound, it was a favorite with the *ali'i*. There are restrooms, the swimming is fair, and the snorkeling acceptable past the reef. **Lahaina Beach** is at the west end of town near Mala Wharf. Follow Front to Pu'unoa Place and turn down to the beach. This is a good place for families with tots because the water is clear, safe, and shallow.

Puamana Beach County Park
About two miles before you enter Lahaina from the southeast along Rt. 30, you'll see signs for this beach park, a narrow strip between the road and the sea. The swimming and snorkeling are only fair. The setting, however, is quite nice with picnic tables shaded by ironwood trees. The views are terrific and this is a great spot to eat your plate lunch only minutes from town.

Launiupoko Wayside Park
A mile farther southeast, this park has restrooms and showers, but only a small enclosed kiddie beach that's best at high tide when it fills with water. This is more of a picnic area than anything else, although many come to sunbathe on

the grass below the coconut trees. Beginning surfers like this spot and some beginning surf lessons are taught here because the waves are gentle.

South of here you'll see lots of shore fishermen and others out for a quiet afternoon. Although not a designated park, the water is adequate for swimming. Find parking where you can under the trees.

East of Olowalu

Between Olowalu and the highway tunnel are **Ukumehame Beach County Park** and **Papalaua Wayside**. The first is a small park with picnic tables, barbecue pits, toilets, and a tiny lawn for sunbathing; swimming is okay. The second is an unimproved area with lots of ironwood trees for shade. This long narrow beach is a favorite of shore fishermen.

Wahikuli State Wayside

Along Rt. 30 between Lahaina and Kaanapali, this park is a favorite with local people and excellent for a picnic. With three parking areas, it's as if the park was split into three units. This wayside is very clean and well maintained. Tennis courts are located up across the street behind the main Lahaina post office.

Just up the highway, as if connected to this wayside park, is **Hanakaoo Beach County Park**. This beach runs north past some of the most exclusive hotels on the island. Often the local canoe club will put their canoes in the water here and at certain times of the year paddling events will be held at this beach.

ACCOMMODATIONS

Lodging in Lahaina is limited, surprisingly inexpensive, and an experience . . . of sorts. Most visitors head for Kaanapali, because Lahaina tends to be hot and hot to trot, especially at night. But you can find good bargains here, and if you want to be in the thick of the "action," you're in the right spot.

Pioneer Inn

This is the oldest hotel on Maui still accommodating guests. Located at 658 Wharf St., Lahaina, HI 96761, tel. (808) 661-3636 or (800)

This "old salt" guards the grog shop at the Pioneer Inn.

457-5457, it has undergone more than a facelift. The semi-seedy old-timey essence has now been spiffed up and yuppified. Now a Best Western hotel, the Pioneer had half a million dollars poured into it in 1997-98—with more to come. For decades, the Pioneer Inn had absolutely no luxury whatsoever, only a double scoop of atmosphere. It was the place to come if you wanted to save money and be the star of your own movie with the Pioneer Inn as the stage set. Creaky stairways, threadbare carpets, low-light hallways, shared baths, and questionable merrymakers and occupants—the place had it all. Now the stairway doesn't creak anymore, new carpet has been laid, TVs installed—baths have shiny new tiles and fixtures, bedrooms have new furniture, the queen-size beds are comfortable and covered in Hawaiian quilts, and you can even have a room with air conditioning, although fans and louvered windows are also available.

What does remain the same are the lanai, which, depending upon your room, look out over the banyan tree (nonsmoking rooms) or the hotel courtyard (smoking rooms) and the front desk with its many pigeonholes for keys, the posted house rules, and the old salt that stands at the front door. Rooms run $90-130; AAA and Best Western Gold Club discounts available. Expensive.

Maui Islander

Located a few blocks away from the hubbub, at 660 Wainee St., Lahaina, HI 96761, tel. (808) 667-9766 or (800) 367-5226, the Maui Islander is a very adequate hotel offering rooms with kitchenettes, studios, and one- and two-bedroom suites. All have daily maid service, a/c and TV, plus a swimming pool, lighted tennis courts (hotel guests only), and a barbecue and picnic area. There is a laundry facility on premise. Low-rise design in a garden setting lends a homey atmosphere; activities are planned daily. Basic hotel rooms start at $92, studios $105-114, and suites $125-182. Rates are $10 cheaper for singles. Studios and suites all have kitchens. Even if you don't stay here, take a botanical walk through the garden, where plants are numbered and identified. This fine little hideaway is now an Aston property. Expensive.

Lahaina Inn

Another reborn classic is the Lahaina Inn, 127 Lahainaluna Rd., Lahaina, HI 96761, tel. (808) 661-0577 or (800) 669-3444, fax (808) 667-9480, e-mail: inntown@aloha.net, website: www.lahainainn.com. Completely renovated and remodeled, this one-time dowdy orphan, the old, down-at-the-heels traveler's classic, Lahainaluna Hotel, emerged in 1989 as a lovely lady. Gone from this cockroach paradise are the weather-beaten linoleum floors, bare-bulbed musty rooms, and rusted dripping faucets. In their place are antique-stuffed, neo-Victorian, tastefully appointed rooms that transport you back to the late 1800s. Each room is individually decorated and nothing in any room is older than 1894. Period pieces include everything from wardrobes to nightstands, rugs, ceramic bowls, mirrors, pictures, lamps, and books. If you really fall in love with something and decide that you can't live without it, make the management an offer. All pieces are privately owned antiques and the owner has been known to part with some. The only deference to modernity are the bathrooms with their new-but-old-style fixtures, the air-conditioning, telephones, and safes—no TV. You can still peer from the balcony of this vintage hotel—each room has a lanai with two hardwood rocking chairs and a table—or observe the masses below from behind heavy drapes and lace curtains. The 12 units include three spacious suites. Rates are $99 for the rooms and $169 for the parlor suites, and include a complimentary continental breakfast, served every morning from about 7:30 a.m. at the sideboard at the end of the hall. For dinner, you might try downstairs at the renowned David Paul's Restaurant, which offers inn guests a discount. Children over 15 are welcome at the inn. The Lahaina Inn's only minor drawback is the lack of on-site parking. Hotel guests are charged $5 for 24 hours in an adjacent parking lot; this is much lower than regular rates. Expensive.

Lahaina Roads

This condo/apartment is at the far west end of town at 1403 Front St., Lahaina, HI 96761, tel. (808) 661-3166 or (800) 624-8203. All units have fully equipped kitchens, TV, and maid service on request. One-bedroom units (for two) run $100, two-bedroom units (for four) are $180. There is a three-night minimum stay and a deposit required to hold your reservation. Select credit cards are honored. There is no beach as it sits right along the seawall, but there is a freshwater pool, and you couldn't have a better view, as every unit faces the ocean. Parking is on ground level below the rooms. Rentals are handled through Klahani Resorts, P.O. Box 11108, Lahaina, HI 96761, tel. (808) 667-2712 or (800) 628-6731, fax (808) 661-5875. Expensive.

Puamana

A 28-acre private community of condos, located on the south edge of town along the ocean, Puamana is a quiet hideaway away from the hustle and bustle of town. The clubhouse (1923) here was the Pioneer Sugar Company's former plantation manager's residence, and it's a beauty. Surrounding it are broad lawns and the guesthouses. One-bedroom condo units run $100-175, two-bedroom units $140-250, and three-bedroom townhouses $300-350. Discounts are given for long stays. All units have fully equipped kitchens, all linens, TVs and VCRs, a/c, and outdoor barbecue grills. Puamana also features an oceanside swimming pool plus two others on property; a sauna, reading parlor, and lending library in the clubhouse; a guests-only tennis court; badminton and volleyball courts; and children's play areas. The only drawback is that it's wedged against the highway, but a thick hedge blocks out much of the noise. For rentals, contact Klahani Resorts, P.O. Box 11108, Lahaina, HI 96761, tel. (808) 667-2712 or (800) 628-6731, fax (808) 661-5875; or Whaler's Realty, tel. (808) 661-8777 or (800) 367-5632, fax (808) 661-8951. Expensive.

The Plantation Inn

If Agatha Christie were seeking inspiration for *the* perfect setting for one of her mysteries, this is where she would come. The neo-Victorian building is appointed with posted verandas, hardwood floors, natural wood wainscoting and trim counterpointed by floral wall coverings, bedspreads, and deep-cushioned furniture. Rays of sunlight stray through stained-glass windows and wide double doors. Each uniquely decorated room is comfortable, with four-poster beds and private tiled baths with bold porcelain and brass fixtures; most have sofas. The complete illusion is turn-of-the-century, but the modern amenities of a/c, remote TV and VCR, a fridge, daily maid service, and a soothing spa and pool are included. The back addition brings the total room count to 19. Most of the 12 new units have lanai overlooking the garden, pool, spa, and guest pavilion. Prices are a reasonable $135 standard, $155 superior, $175 deluxe, $215 suite (some with kitchenette and jacuzzi), and all include a filling breakfast buffet at poolside prepared by Gerard's, the fine French restaurant on the first floor. The Plantation Inn also has money-saving options for dinner at Gerard's, rental cars, and package deals. While now associated with the Kaanapali Beach Hotel in Kaanapali, it still maintains great autonomy. For full information contact the inn at 174 Lahainaluna Rd., Lahaina, HI 96761, tel. (808) 667-9225 or (800) 433-6815, fax (808) 667-9293, e-mail: inn@maui.net, website: www.maui.net/~inn. Set on a side street away from the bustle, it's

simply one of the best accommodations that Maui has to offer. Premium.

Lahaina Shores

This six-story condo was built before the Lahaina building code limited the height of new structures. Located at the south end of town, at 475 Front St., Lahaina, HI 96761, tel. (808) 661-4835 or (800) 628-6699, the condo has become a landmark for incoming craft. The Shores offers a swimming pool and spa and is the only accommodation in Lahaina located on a beach. From a distance, the Southern-mansion facade is striking; up close, though, it becomes painted cement blocks and false colonnades. The rooms, however, are good value for the money. The basic room contains a full bathroom, powder room, large color TV, and equipped kitchen. They're all light and airy, and the back side views of the harbor or front side of the mountains are the best in town. Studios are $130 mountain view and $165 ocean view; one-bedroom suites are $180 mountain view and $210 ocean view. The penthouse suites run $220 and $245 for mountain and ocean views, respectively. Reduced rates of about 20% are given during low season. Other amenities include daily maid service, laundry facilities, and an activities desk. Premium.

B&Bs and Guesthouses

Aloha Lani Inn, 13 Kauaula Rd., Lahaina, HI 96761, tel. (808) 661-8040 or (800) 572-5642, fax (808) 661-8045, e-mail: tony@maui.net, website: www.maui.net/~tony/index.html, off Front St., is a homey, cozy, and clean single-family home turned guesthouse. Located across from the neighborhood beach, this guest home is a few minutes' walk south of downtown Lahaina. The three guest rooms rent for $59 single, $69 double and share two baths; two nights minimum. Guests have use of the kitchen, the living room with its books, television, and sound system, laundry facilities, and the backyard lanai under a mango tree. Complimentary (strong) coffee is available all day, but no breakfast is served. For information and reservations, talk with Melinda. Moderate.

Next door is John and Sherry Barbier's **Old Lahaina House,** P.O. Box 10355, Lahaina, HI 96761, tel. (808) 667-4663 or (800) 847-0761, fax

(808) 667-5615, e-mail: olh@oldhouse.com, website: www.mauiweb.com/maui/olhouse. This big salmon-colored house, surrounded by a wall of the same color, has four rooms (two with private baths) that range $50-95. All rooms include a/c, telephone, TV, and access to the swimming pool, which occupies the front yard, and the garden; breakfast is included. Reduced rental car rates can be arranged. Old Lahaina House is a relaxing homey place, lived in by the family (so there are kids around). Moderate.

The **GuestHouse,** 1620 Ainakea Rd., Lahaina, HI 96761, tel. (808) 661-8085 or (800) 621-8942, fax (808) 661-1896, e-mail: Guest-House@compuserv.com, website: ourworld .compuserve.com/homepages/guesthouse, is a well-appointed B&B where the host will provide free snorkel gear, and even scuba lessons for a fee. The GuestHouse caters largely to honeymooners and scuba enthusiasts. All rooms have queen beds, a/c, ceiling fans, TV, refrigerators, phones, and private lanai, and all but one have private baths. Full breakfast is provided. Everyone shares the living room, kitchen, barbecue, and laundry facility. Rates for the honeymoon suites run $95 a couple, $85 single, and $15 each additional guest. The room with the shared bath is $65 a couple or $55 single. For all five rooms with two people a room is $395 a night. Moderate.

At 418 Front St. is **Belladona Cottages,** tel. (808) 661-0358 or (888) 889-7440, fax (808) 667-0394, e-mail: belladon@mauigate.com, website: www.mauigate.com/~belladon. Lush gardens surround this house, and a large swimming pool occupies the yard. Rooms have full baths, TV, a refrigerator and microwave. Rates are $82 a night per couple, $20 each additional person, $550 a week, or $2,000 a month. Moderate.

In the streets behind, you'll find the **Bambula Inn Bed and Breakfast,** 518 Ilikahi St., Lahaina, HI 96761, tel. (808) 667-6753 or (800) 544-5524, fax (808) 667-0979, e-mail: bambula@maui.net, website: www.maui.net/~bambula. Here, the two studios are separated at the back of the house so you're more independent from the family. Each unit has a kitchen, private bath, TV, phone, and lanai. The detached cottage ($95) has a/c while the attached unit ($85) has a ceiling fan; $10 less in low season. Three nights minimum.

Breakfast is brought to your room, and a complimentary sunset sail aboard the family sailboat *Bambula* is offered every evening, weather permitting. Contact Pierre or Irene for information and reservations. Expensive.

At 1565 Kuuipo is **Wai Ola Vacation Paradise,** tel./fax (808) 661-7901 or tel./fax (800) 4WAIOLA, e-mail: tai@maui.net, website: www .maui.net/~tai/WaiOla.html. This private home has three units. Located just off the pool, the large one-bedroom apartment is more than 1,000 square feet, with full kitchen and amenities. It runs $135 a couple and $15 each extra person up to four. Newly remodeled, the studio apartment is about half as big but also has a full kitchen and all amenities. Located in the garden, it runs $115 a couple. The newest is the honeymoon Kuuipo Room, with its own private lanai and larger king bed. It goes for $120 a night. Low season rates are $20 less. All units have a/c, TV, VCR, and phones, and everyone has use of the laundry facilities and the swimming pool. As a vacation rental, no food is served. Contact Julie Frank at P.O. Box 12580, Lahaina, HI 96761, for information and reservations. Premium.

FOOD

Lahaina's menu of restaurants is gigantic; all palates and pocketbooks can easily be satisfied: there's fast food, sandwiches, sushi, happy hours, vegetarian, and elegant cosmopolitan restaurants. Because Lahaina is a dynamic tourist spot, restaurants and eateries come and go with regularity. The following is not an exhaustive list of Lahaina's food spots—it couldn't be. But there is plenty listed here to feed everyone at breakfast, lunch, and dinner. *Bon appétit!*

Fast Food and Snacks
Fanatics can get their fix at: **Burger King** on Front St. near the banyan tree, **Pizza Hut** at 127 Hinau St. near the Sugar Cane Train depot, or at the Lahaina Shopping Center, which has **McDonald's** and **Kentucky Fried Chicken.**

Lappert's Ice Cream, at the Pioneer Inn Mall, not only has ice cream, shave ice, and cookies, but also serves fat- and sugar-free ice cream, about the only thing on Maui that is fat-free!

Down in front of the banyan tree, **Tropical Dreams Ice Cream** can also serve up your favorite flavor and probably others you're not familiar with.

A good one for a quick snack is **Mr. Sub** at 129 Lahainaluna Rd. It features double-fisted sandwiches and packed picnic lunches.

Planet Juice and Java in the Lahaina Square Shopping Center is a relaxing place to stop for fresh fruit juices, smoothies, and coffee drinks. Also served are nutritious wraps, pitas, garden burgers, pizza, sandwiches, and salads. Eat in or take out.

Take Home Maui at 121 Dickenson St., mail order tel. (800) 545-MAUI, is a food store and delicatessen that specializes in packaging agriculturally inspected Maui produce such as pineapples, papayas, Maui onions, protea, potato chips, macadamia nut products, and even Kona coffee, which they will deliver to you at the airport before your departing flight. For an on-the-spot treat they prepare deli sandwiches like roast beef or ham for under $5.50, a variety of quiches, and sides of macaroni and potato salad. Take Home Maui is famous for its fresh-fruit smoothies, homemade soups, and picnic lunches. Choose a shaded spot on the veranda and enjoy your lunch while taking a break from the jostle of Front Street.

Try **Athens Greek Restaurant** in the Lahaina Cannery Mall food court for gyros, shish kebabs, moussaka, pita, falafel, or tabbouleh, and other Mediterranean specialties. Vegetarian plates available, as are Greek salad and spanakopita.

Your sweet tooth will begin to sing the moment you walk into **The Bakery** at 911 Limahana, near the Sugar Cane Train. You can't beat the stuffed croissants for under $3, or the sandwiches for under $5! Coffee is cheap and the pastries, breads, and pasta are gooood! Open daily 7 a.m.-5 p.m., until noon on Sunday, tel. (808) 667-9062.

Inexpensive

Smokehouse BBQ, 1307 Front St., tel. (808) 667-7005, serves baby back ribs, chicken, and fish smoked over a kaiwe grill and smothered in special barbecue sauce. Also available for lunch are a variety of burgers and sandwiches, and always sides like rice, barbecued beans, and cole slaw. This is where local people and those in the know come for a very good but no-frills meal. If eating hearty without caring about the ambience (actually the sunset view couldn't be better) is your aim, come here. Takeout available.

The **Thai Chef,** tel. (808) 667-2814, will please any Thai food lover who wants a savory meal at a good price. Search for this restaurant stuck in a corner at the Lahaina Shopping Center, open Mon.-Fri. 11 a.m.-2:30 p.m. for lunch, dinner nightly 5-10 p.m. As in most Thai restaurants vegetarians are well taken care of with plenty of spicy tofu and vegetable dishes. The extensive menu offers everything from scrumptious Thai soups with ginger and coconut for $7.25 (enough for two) to curries and seafood. Most entrees are under $10 with a good selection under $8. It's not fancy, but food-wise you won't be disappointed. Takeout available. When in Kihei, visit Thai Chef's second restaurant in the Rainbow Mall.

Zushi's is a hole-in-the-wall, very reasonably priced Japanese restaurant selling sushi and various other Japanese dishes directly across the street from McDonald's on Wainee Street. Zushi's serves lunch (takeout too) 11 a.m.-2 p.m., dinner 5-9 p.m. Authentic with most items under $6. Also in the plaza next to the Activities Information Center is a small takeout window with the imaginative name of **Local Food,** which sells local food in the form of plate lunches. Basic, cheap, filling, and good.

The open-air **Cheeseburger in Paradise** at 811 Front St., tel. (808) 661-4855, open 10:30 a.m.-11 p.m., live music nightly, is a joint down by the sea overlooking the harbor out back. Served are a whole slew of burgers priced $6.95-7.95, the jumbo cheese dog covered with cheese and grilled onions for $5.95, or the Maui classic BLT for $5.95. Other selections include the aloha fish and seasoned fries at $9.95, a huge Upcountry salad for $6.95, or various sides for $3.50-6.50. Cheeseburger also has a full bar that sells a range of both imported and domestic beer, along with tropical concoctions. If you were going to pick one spot to have a beer, soak in the sights, and capture the flavor of old Lahaina, "the Burg" has all the trimmings.

Sunrise Cafe, open 6 a.m.-6 p.m. at 693 Front, tel. (808) 661-8558, is the kind of place that locals keep secret. It's a tiny little restaurant where you can have excellent coffee and a sandwich or more substantial gourmet food at down-home prices. The nutritious and wholesome food includes breakfast specials like freshly baked quiche or yogurt and cottage cheese $5.95, and lunch salads from Caesar to fresh island fruit all priced under $7. Heartier appetites can choose various hot or cold sandwiches for under $7, pasta, plate lunches, and a more substantial fish or seafood dinner meal for under $10. A deli case holds scrumptious award-winning pastries that are complemented by fine coffee selections always freshly brewed, and a good selection of herbal teas. Eat inside or out on the back patio and enjoy the nightly live entertainment.

The tiny yellow cinder block **Sushiya Deli** is a local plate lunch, *bento,* and saimin place on Prison St. just after you turn toward the mountains off Front Street. Look for it across the street from the public parking lot. Open weekdays 6 a.m.-4 p.m., they make their own sushi but are usually sold out by early afternoon. You can also choose from a full selection of plate lunches like beef teriyaki, or a hamburger plate. This is a very local restaurant with unbeatable prices.

Next door to the new Old Lahaina Luau venue near Mala Wharf is **Aloha Plate Lunch,** tel. (808) 661-3322, a great spot for a simple authentic meal and a cold drink. While noodle dishes, burgers, and sandwiches are on the menu, the specialties are the plate lunches. Available in three sizes, they run $2.95-9.95. Open 10:30 a.m.-10 p.m.; happy hour 3-7 p.m. Live Hawaiian music is performed on a regular schedule, with karaoke on Thursday, Friday, and Saturday 9 p.m.-1 a.m.

Also good for a filling local meal is **Local Boys** in the Lahaina Square Mall. Most items on the full menu are $6-7. Also in this shopping center is **Denny's,** which serves up standard American fare.

The Wharf Shopping Center at 658 Front St. includes the inexpensive **Blue Lagoon Tropical Bar and Grill** on the ground floor, open daily 9 a.m.-10 p.m. The surroundings in the courtyard are pleasant, and most everything on the menu is under $12. **Orange Julius** dispenses its famous drinks, along with hot dogs and sandwiches for a quick, cheap meal. To the rear on the opposite side is **Song's Oriental Kitchen.** This unpretentious restaurant is of the precooked hot plate variety, but you can stuff yourself on

meals like beef stew for $3.95 or barbecued chicken, $3.85, all with two-scoop rice and macaroni salad. **Chun's Chinese Barbecue** on the second level offers plate lunches, *bento,* a full selection of Chinese food, and some Korean favorites. Also in this center are **Nanny's Kitchen** for hearty German food and **Pancho and Lefty's** Mexican restaurant.

Located over the ABC Store at the Wharf Cinema Center is **Il Bucaniere,** tel. (808) 661-3966. Open for lunch 11 a.m.-2:30 p.m. and dinner from 5:30 p.m., Il Bucaniere offers live entertainment nightly 6-10 p.m. A casual place that overlooks the big banyan tree at Lahaina Harbor, lunch might be soup and salad, pasta, sandwiches, burgers, or pizza, most for under $10. Dinner includes more pizza, salads, and a wider selection of pasta, meat, and fish for under $15. *Pu pu* can be ordered after dinner until closing. Full bar.

The Hard Rock Café, at the Lahaina Shopping Center on the corner of Front and Papalaua Streets, tel. (808) 667-7400, open daily from 11:30 a.m., is a large breezy, screened restaurant keeping the rock and roll faith. Over the bar is a '59 Cadillac convertible woody, and on the walls are prints of rock stars and electric guitars including a Gibson autographed by The Grateful Dead. The floors have a shiny patina, and the raised stools and round-top tables give you a view of the street and the sea beyond. Menu prices are moderate, with homemade onion rings at $3.75, Caesar salad for $7.59, country club sandwich at $7.99, barbecued chicken for $8.95, and the natural veggie burger for $7.99. The bar serves house wine, champagne, domestic and imported beer, mixed drinks, soft drinks, and coffee. Sit inside at the bar or dining section or outside under the umbrellas. Food is served until 10 p.m. Sun.-Thurs., until 10:30 Friday and Saturday; the bar is open two hours longer every night.

Almost next door at 900 Front St. is **World Cafe,** tel. (808) 661-1515, basically a sports bar with pool and foosball tables. Food includes sandwiches, chicken wings, pizza, and burritos. Drinks are well prices and every night there is a special. Always music, but no dancing. The World Cafe is a good-time bar, a fine place for a little fun.

Aside from the full range of produce, vitamins, health foods, and bulk foods, the **Westside Nat-**

ural Foods and Deli on Lahainaluna St., tel. (808) 667-2855, has some reasonably priced and healthy prepared hot and cold foods and fruit drinks. Open daily until 9 p.m., 8 p.m. on Sunday.

Moderate

You won't be a pawn when you walk onto the black-and-white checkered floor at **Longhi's**, 888 Front St., tel. (808) 667-2288, open daily 7:30 a.m.-10 p.m. Longhi owns the joint and he's a character. He feels that his place has "healing vibes" and that man's basic food is air. Longhi's has been around since 1976 and it's many people's favorite. Prices at Longhi's may seem expensive but the portions are enormous and can easily fill two. Better yet, order a half-order. With all meals and salads comes a wonderful basket of jalapeño and pizza breads. Mornings you can order frittatas, like spinach, ham, and bacon, easily enough for two. A good lunch choice is pasta Siciliana with calamari, spicy with marinara sauce; for dinner, the prawns amaretto and shrimp Longhi are signature dishes. Save room for the fabulous desserts. It's hard not to have a fine meal here, and the wine list is a winner. There's always a line, reservations accepted, never a dress code, and always complimentary valet parking! Live music is provided only on Friday and Saturday evenings.

Kobe Japanese Steak House is at 136 Dickenson at the corner of Luakini, tel. (808) 667-5555, open daily for dinner from 5:30 p.m. Service is *teppan yaki*-style, which means that the chef comes to you. His sharp blade flashes through the air and thumps the table, keeping the culinary beat as it slices, dices, and minces faster than any Veg-o-matic you've ever seen. The delectables of marinated meat, chicken, and vegetables are then expertly flash-fried at your own grill, oftentimes with aplomb in a ball of sake-induced flame. The experience is fun, the food very good, and the interior authentic Japanese. *Teppan* meals come complete with rice, soup, and tea. Expect to spend at least $18 for an entree (less for the early bird specials), $10 for an appetizer, and $11 for four pieces of sushi. Complement your meal with a glass of sake or Japanese beer.

Pioneer Inn Grill and Bar, tel. (808) 661-3636, at the historic Pioneer Inn serves breakfast 6:30-11 a.m., offering buttermilk pancakes for $4.95, corned beef hash and eggs for $8.95, and a selection of side orders for under $1.50. Lunch, 11 a.m.-5:30 p.m., is a hearty bowl of Portuguese soup for $5.95, romaine Caesar salad for $8.95, a full selection of sandwiches for under $9, or a variety of burgers for less than $11. Pioneer Inn also has ice cream, shaved ice, and a host of desserts. Dinner is also served at the hotel 5:30-10 p.m. Try the baby back rib appetizers for under $10 or soup and salad. Select dinner entrees are grilled beef filet for $21.95, shellfish for around $20.95, and herbed chicken at $15.95. Since the Pioneer Inn is the oldest hotel in town, and a true landmark with a great lanai from which you can view the harbor, the experience is really the history and the atmosphere.

Kimo's, 845 Front St., tel. (808) 661-4811, is friendly and has great harbor and sunset views on the lower level. If you're in Lahaina around 6 p.m. and need a break, head here to relax with some "Kimo therapy." Popular, but no reservations taken. Kimo's offers seafood from $16.95, with most entrees $15-20, and is known for the catch of the day, usually the best offering on the menu; limited menu for children. Dine upstairs or down. The downstairs bar has top-notch well drinks featuring brand-name liquors.

Across the street, **Moose McGillycuddy's**, tel. (808) 667-7758, is almost an institution. A wild and zany place, there is music nightly (live on Friday and Saturday), daily specials, early bird specials (both breakfast and dinner), and a happy hour 3-6 p.m. The large portions are filling, and the menu reads like a book. Take a moment and have a look at all the stuff hanging on the walls.

Located at 839 Front St. is **Aloha Cantina**, tel. (808) 661-8788, with touches that might remind you of a Mexican restaurant or beach palapa. Serving breakfast, lunch, and dinner, the place is open 8 a.m.-10 p.m. (till 11:30 on Thursday and Friday), with live music most nights. Breakfast meals include omelettes and huevos rancheros for around $6.95, while a fajita lunch or sandwich costs a few dollars more. For dinner, it's especially known for the chicken, beef, or shrimp fajitas, which run about $15, but Aloha Cantina has most other items that you'd expect on the menu of a Mexican restaurant. To complement your entree, order a tropical drink or smoothie from the bar and watch the sunset off the back veranda.

The Lahaina Fish Company, 831 Front St., tel. (808) 661-3472, open daily from 11 a.m. for lunch and 5-10 p.m. for dinner, buys from local fishermen so the fish is guaranteed fresh. Belly up to the Hammerhead Bar, fashioned from glass and brass, or choose a table that looks directly out onto Lahaina Harbor. Notice the vintage Coca Cola vending machine and a display of knots that were tied by the old salts who visited Lahaina. Happy hour brings domestic beer, house wine, and well drinks for $2, while imports and exotic drinks are only $2.50. The limited lunch menu has burgers and other light foods, mostly for under $10. The evening dinner menu starts with dinner salads at $2.95, fried calamari at $8.95, or a bowl of fresh fish chowder for $3.95. Entrees can be island fish and chips at $8.95, fisherman's pasta with fish and vegetables for $12.95, or sautéed sea scallops for $16.95. Meat and poultry dishes include Hawaiian ginger chicken for $12.95, luau-style pork ribs for $15.95, or top sirloin steak for $12.95. The fresh fish, depending on what's caught that day, is grilled, oven broiled, or blackened Cajun style and offered at market price, and every day brings a chef's special that ranges $17.95-21.95.

The Old Lahaina Cafe is located at the 505 Front Street Mall and is famous for offering one of the best luau on Maui. The post-and-beam cafe, tel. (808) 661-3303, open daily 7:30 a.m.-10 p.m., happy hour noon-6 p.m., is blue-on-blue with shutters that open to the sea breezes. Breakfast entrees are served 7:30-11:30 a.m., with Sunday brunch 8 a.m.-3 p.m., and include the *paniolo* breakfast of two eggs, Portuguese sausage, pineapple sausage, bacon or papaya wedge, along with rice or home-fried potatoes for $6.95. You can build your own omelette from $5.95, or forget about your arteries and order a loco moco, two fried eggs over hamburger steak with gravy on a bed of rice for $6.95. Lunch, served noon-3:30 p.m., offers very reasonable selections like soup du jour for $3.75, a selection of sandwiches $6.95-9.95, and an assortment of plate lunches for under $7.95. Dinner entrees, served 5:30-10 p.m., include fresh island fish broiled over *kiawe* or sautéed in a papaya and ginger sauce, or the luau dinner (without the entertainment) that includes *kalbi* ribs, chicken long

rice, *lomi lomi* salmon, sweet potatoes, rice, and *kalua* pork. There's also broiled lobster tail and a selection of beef and chicken entrees that are priced $12.95-23.95. The Old Lahaina Cafe has very good food at reasonable prices in a congenial atmosphere and is worth the money.

Next door is **Hecock's,** tel. (808) 661-8810, open daily 7 a.m.-10 p.m. for food service, bar open until 2 a.m., owned and operated by Tom and Nancy, a husband and wife team who bring you good food at reasonable prices. Hecock's breakfast could be ranch eggs with a grilled New York steak for $8.95, or a three-egg scampi omelette for $8.95, along with the classics like French toast or buttermilk pancakes with the trimmings for under $8. The lunch menu offers a chef salad for $8.95, assorted burgers and sandwiches priced under $8.25, and pasta dishes like cheese tortellini or fettuccine Alfredo for under $8.95. The dinner bill of fare includes fettuccine Alfredo $14.95, scampi for $20.95, and rack of lamb at $21.95. A children's menu, happy hour, daily specials, and an early bird special offered 5-6 p.m. help to keep prices down.

Pacific'O Cafe, tel. (808) 667-4341, at 505 Front St., is a newcomer to the restaurant scene in Lahaina but has garnered a solid reputation. Foods and flavors from the West, the East, and the Pacific are blended together, using only the freshest ingredients from the islands, to create a very delectable Pacific Rim cuisine. Start with a fine Kula mixed green salad for $4.50 and move on to a more substantial Caesar with roasted bell peppers, macadamia nuts, and anchovies for $7.50. Lunch entrees, like the seared fish sandwich or the penne pasta with smoked shrimp, sautéed tomatoes, and fresh basil, are all reasonable at less than $11. Dinner entrees run $21-25 and might be fish tempura wrapped in wakame, mushroom ravioli, or sesame-crusted lamb. Comfortable seating, attentive servers, and the views out over the ocean might tempt you to linger over your meal and savor an excellent bottle of wine. Open daily for lunch 11 a.m.-4 p.m. and dinner 5:30-10 p.m.; there's live jazz Thurs.-Sat. evenings.

Lahaina Coolers on Dickenson St. presents quick easy meals throughout the day in an open-air setting. Try pancakes, omelettes, or eggs Benedict for breakfast; salads, sandwiches, and burgers for lunch; and pasta, tortillas, fresh fish, steak, and burgers for dinner. Nothing on the evening menu is over $16.95, with most in the $12-15 range. Coolers is a late-night place; you can get food until midnight.

B.J.'s Pizzeria, tel. (808) 661-0700, on the second floor overlooking the seawall, is one of the newer places in town. Along with pizza, try the pasta, sandwiches, and a sesame chicken salad. Eat in or take out. B.J.'s has a large beer selection and live entertainment in the evenings. Close by is **Planet Hollywood,** serving California cuisine with a Hawaiian twist, and up the street is the movie-inspired **Bubba Gump's** for shrimp off the old wooden boat.

For a little bit of New York in Lahaina, try **Scaroles** for pizza—its main focus—salads, sandwiches, and pasta dishes. Done with thick crusts, the pizzas run $12-25; salads are about $6, sandwiches are less than $9, and the pasta dishes vary $7-13. Even with something from the bar, you can have an inexpensive lunch or dinner. Scaroles is located at 930 Wainee St. in Lahaina, tel. (808) 661-4466.

Compadres Mexican Bar and Grill, tel. (808) 661-7189, at the Lahaina Cannery Mall, has a full menu ranging from nacho appetizers through soups, salads, and sandwiches to a complete list of entrees, most in the $9-18 range. Sit down, relax, have a beer or margarita, and enjoy your meal and the surroundings.

Gourmet Dining

When you feel like putting a major dent in your budget and satisfying your desire for gourmet food, you should be pleased with one of the following.

Whoever said "East is East and West is West" would have whistled a different tune if only they had had the pleasure of dining at the **Avalon,** tel. (808) 667-5559, in the courtyard at 844 Front St., open daily for lunch and dinner. Owner/chef Mark Ellman has put together a uniquely blended Hawaiian regional cuisine menu. Here are dishes from Sausalito to Saigon, and from Mexico City to Tokyo, with a bit of Nebraska and Hong Kong thrown in for good measure. Moreover, Avalon has spiced, herbed, and garnished its delectables by mixing and matching the finest and most refined tastes from all the geographical areas, creating a culinary extravaganza. If you're tired of the same old appetizers, try Maui onion

rings with tamarind-chipotle catsup, or don't resist the combination platter with a selection of the best appetizers for $16.95 (enough for two). Move on to mixed greens and crispy noodles tempting in a ginger sesame dressing, or *gado-gado* on a bed of brown rice turned sumptuous by a Balinese peanut sauce. Drift the Pacific through their grill selections like whole fresh *opakapaka* in Thai sauce. If you need more convincing, try the chili seared salmon, which is a layered dish of mashed potatoes, eggplant, salmon, greens, and island tomato salsa, or the mouthwatering Asian pasta like mama-*san* wished she could make. If only people could get along together as well as this food. Choose indoor seating where you dine in air-conditioned comfort, or dine alfresco in the courtyard. The Avalon boasts a fine wine list, or order one of its unique drinks, like the chocolate martini. The Avalon has only one dessert, caramel miranda, made fresh daily and sure to please. While here, have a look at the art on the walls.

Gerard's elegant restaurant is in the Plantation Inn, at 174 Lahainaluna Rd., tel. (808) 661-8939, open daily for dinner only 6-9 p.m., with validated free parking nearby. The epitome of neo-Victorian charm, the room is comfortable with puff-pillowed wicker chairs and always set with fine crystal atop starched linen. Fronting the building is a small dining garden, and inside the interior is rich with hardwood floors and oak bar. Chef Gerard Reversade, trained in the finest French culinary tradition since age 14, creates masterpieces. He feels that eating is *the* experience of life, around which everything else that is enjoyable revolves. Gerard insists that the restaurant's waiters and waitresses share his philosophy, so along with the excellent food comes excellent service. The menu changes, but it's always gourmet. Gerard's is not cheap but it's worth every penny as nothing on the menu is less than excellent. Appetizers range $8.50-18.50, entrees $26.50-32.50, and desserts are $7.50. Some superb salad choices are the island greens with Kiawe honey vinaigrette dressing, or spinach salad with grilled scallops, shaved parmesan cheese, and truffle sauce. Appetizers feature mouthwatering choices like shiitake and oyster mushrooms in a puff pastry. Full entrees like grilled rack of lamb with mint crust or savory stuffed breast of veal with spinach and herb sauce and glazed vegetables titillate the palate. Confit of duck with pommes frites served with mixed greens in a walnut-oil dressing is one of Gerard's superb signature dishes. Even if you possess great self control, you have less than an even chance of restraining yourself from choosing a luscious dessert like crème brûlée, chocolate mousse in cream puffs with raspberry sabayon, or even fresh strawberries glazed with suzette butter and macadamia nut cream.

David Paul's Lahaina Grill, 127 Lahainaluna Rd., tel. (808) 667-5117, open for dinner nightly 6-10 p.m., is one of Lahaina's finest gourmet restaurants. Here owner David Paul Johnson, famous for his sauces, presents "artwork on a plate." The dining room is quite lovely, with coved and molded ceilings from which hang punchbowl chandeliers illuminating the starched white table settings. The restaurant has expanded from its once-crowded confines to incorporate a much larger and also well-appointed room, and its new chairs are more comfortable, meant for a long romantic evening of salubrious relaxation. The waiters and waitresses, professional, friendly, and well-dressed in black pants, white shirts, and ties, definitely give you attentive service. The menu is wonderful. Start with rich white bean soup, with roasted ham hock broth and goat cheese tortellini for $8, a Kona lobster-crab cake for $15, or a heart of romaine Caesar salad for $12. Entrees include David Paul's signature dish, the "seafood painted desert"—a savory creation of grilled seafood served on a bed of chardonnay and Gorgonzola sauce, and three pepper-flavored butters that David uses to paint cacti and a red setting sun—available on request. Other wonderfully prepared dishes are tequila shrimp and firecracker rice, another signature entree, made from tiger prawns marinated in chili oil, lemons, cilantro, cumin, and brown sugar in a blend of vanilla bean and chili rice for $28, or Kona coffee roasted lamb for $37. Vegetarians will find at least one meatless entree on each menu, and other dietary restrictions can be accommodated by the masterful chefs. No matter what is on the changing menu, you can be assured that the ingredients are the freshest available. The very wicked dessert tray, with everything priced at $6, combined with a cup of rich roasted coffee, ends a wonderful meal.

Chez Paul, tel. (808) 661-3843, five miles east of Lahaina in Olowalu, is secluded, romantic, very popular, and French—what else! There are two seatings nightly at 6:30 and 8:30 p.m., by reservation only, credit cards accepted. Local folks into elegant dining give it two thumbs up. The wine list is tops, the desserts fantastic, and the food, *magnifique!* Start with luscious hors d'oeuvres like warm Maine lobster salad with a brandy cocktail sauce, homemade country pâté, or more simply with bay shrimp salad, and a bowl of soup du jour all priced $7-16. Entrees are delightful with fresh island fish poached in champagne, scampi smothered with fresh mushrooms, lobster in a cream bisque, veal in lemon butter, or a medley of island vegetables, all priced $22-34, except for *bloc de foie gras* at $36. Chez Paul is definitely worth the trip from Lahaina with a short stroll along the beach recommended as a perfect aperitif.

ENTERTAINMENT

Lahaina is one of those places where the real entertainment is the town itself. The best thing to do here is to stroll along Front Street and people-watch. As you walk along, it feels like a block party with the action going on all around you—as it does on Halloween. Some people duck into one of the many establishments along Front Street for a breather, a drink, or just to watch the sunset. It's all free, enjoyable, and safe.

Art Night

Friday night is Art Night in Lahaina. In keeping with its status as the cultural center of Maui, Lahaina opens the doors of its galleries, throws out the welcome mat, sets out food and drink, provides entertainment, and usually hosts a well-known artist or two for this weekly party. It's a fine social get-together where the emphasis is upon gathering people together to appreciate the arts and not necessarily on making sales. Take your time and stroll Front Street from one gallery to the next. Stop and chat with shopkeepers, munch the goodies, sip the wine, look at the pieces on display, corner the featured artist for comment on his/her work, soak in the music of the strolling musicians, and strike up a conversation with the person next to you who is eyeing that same piece of art with the same respect and admiration. It's a party. People dress up, but don't be afraid to come casually. Take your time and immerse yourself in the immense variety and high quality of art on display in Lahaina 6-10 p.m.

Halloween

This is one of the big nonofficial events of the year. It seems that everyone dresses in costume, strolls Front Street, parties around town, and gets into the spirit of the evening. It is a party in the street with lots of people, dancing, music, color, and activities. In fact, it's becoming so popular with some that they fly in from Honolulu just for the night.

Nightspots and Dancing

All of the evening musical entertainment in Lahaina is in restaurants and lounges, except for the acclaimed Old Lahaina Luau, now at its new venue near Mala Wharf.

There's piano music with the sound of water falling in the background at the **Blue Lagoon** in the lower courtyard of the Wharf Cinema Center. You, too, can be a disco king or queen on **Longhi's** black-and-white chessboard dance floor every weekend. Longhi's has live music on Friday and Saturday nights featuring island groups. **Moose McGillycuddy's** (just listen for the loud music on Front Street) is still a happening place with nightly music, though it's becoming more of a cruise joint for post-adolescents. Those who have been around Lahaina for a while usually give it a miss, but if you want to feast your eyes on prime American two-legged beef on the hoof, this place is for you.

The open-air **Cheeseburger in Paradise** rocks with live music nightly until 11 p.m. There's no cover charge, and you can sit upstairs or down listening to the tunes. Similarly, you can hear live rock music at **Il Bucaniere** at the Wharf Cinema Center across from the banyan tree, and at the **Pioneer Inn Grill and Bar** at the Pioneer Inn. Other restaurants also offer live music, particularly on the weekends.

Cinema

Lahaina Cinemas, once the only multiplex theater on West Maui, is located on the third floor of the Wharf Cinema Center. Showing only first-run features, movies start at about noon and run

throughout the day. Adults $7, kids 2-11 $3.50, seniors $3.75; all seats $4 until 5 p.m. Call (808) 661-3347 for what's showing. Lahaina's second cinema is **Front Street Theaters** at the Lahaina Center.

The Hawaii Experience Domed Theater, 824 Front St., tel. (808) 661-8314, has continuous showings on the hour daily 10 a.m.-10 p.m. (45-minute duration), for adults $6.95, children 4-12 $3.95. The idea is to give you a total sensory experience by means of the giant, specially designed concave screen. You sit surrounded by it. You will tour the islands as if you were sitting in a helicopter or diving below the waves. And you'll be amazed at how well the illusion works. You'll soar over Kauai's Waimea Canyon, dip low to frolic with humpbacks, and rise over Hawaii's active volcanoes. If you can't afford the real thing, this is about as close as you can get. The lobby of the theater doubles as a gift shop where you can pick up souvenirs like carved whales, T-shirts, and a variety of inexpensive mementos, including Maui chips.

Hula and Polynesian Shows

For a different type of entertainment, stop to see the free grown-up hula show, Wednesday and Friday at 2 p.m., or the *keiki* hula show, same days at 6 p.m., at Hale Kahiko in the parking lot of the Lahaina Shopping Center. Hale Kahiko is a reproduction Hawaiian village displaying implements and items of everyday use; open 9 a.m.-6 p.m. Various weekly shows are also offered at center stage at the Lahaina Cannery Mall. Tuesday and Thursday at 7 p.m. there's a free Polynesian show, and a *keiki* hula show is presented Saturday and Sunday 1-2 p.m.

SHOPPING

Once learned, everybody loves to do the "Lahaina Stroll." It's easy. Just act cool, nonchalant, and give it your best strut as you walk the gauntlet of Front Street's exclusive shops and boutiques. The fun is just in being here. If you begin in the evening, go to the south end of town and park down by Prison Street; it's much easier to find a spot and you walk uptown, catching the sunset.

The Lahaina Stroll

On Prison Street, check out **Dan's Green House,** tel. (808) 661-8412, open daily 9 a.m.-5 p.m., specializing in *fuku-bonsai,* miniature plants originated by David Fukumoto. They're mailable (except to Australia and Japan), and when you get them home, just plop them in water and presto . . . a great little plant (from $25). Dan's also specializes in exotic birds like African gray parrots, macaws from Australia, common cockatoos, and various cheeky parrots, and has a few other miniature animals. Dan's is a great place to browse, especially for families.

As you head up Front Street, the first group of shops includes **Sea Level Trading Company** with mostly women's alohawear and men's aloha shirts, and **Camellia** with a treasure chest laden with gifts and jewelry made from gold, silver, and ivory. Here as well is **Original Maui Divers,** which has some fancy jewelry including its specialty, black tree coral. Check out the jewelry design center on the second floor of the Wharf Cinema Center a few steps away. Visit the "pin and ink" artist upstairs at **Skin Deep Tattooing,** 626 Front St., tel. (808) 661-8531, open daily 10 a.m.-10 p.m., until 5 p.m. Sunday, where you can get a permanent memento of your trip to Maui. Skin Deep features "new-age primal, tribal tattoos," Japanese-style intricate beauties, with women artists available for shy women clientele. The walls are hung with sample tattoos that you can choose from. A sobriety test is necessary to get tattooed. No wimps allowed! This is a legitimate place where the artists know what they're doing; they've been in business now for more than 20 years.

Moving down the Line

The following shops are all located along Front Street. By no means exhaustive, this list just gives you an idea of some of the unique shops here.

Between the Pioneer Inn and the seawall, walk onto the sandy floor of the Polynesian-style **Gecko Store,** where all the items including shorts, T-shirts, bathing suits, and sweatshirts bear the bug-eyed sucker-footed logo of Hawaii's famous clicking geckos. Nearby is the **Lahaina Hat Co.,** where you can find the perfect chapeau to shield your head from the "merciless" Lahaina sun.

Noah himself would have been impressed with the **Endangered Species Store,** open daily 9 a.m.-10:30 p.m., where a life-size mountain gorilla, coiled python, flitting butterflies, and fluttering birds bid you welcome to this lovely jam-packed menagerie. The shelves hold world globes, maps, cuddly panda bears, posters of trumpeting elephants, sculptures of soaring eagles, parlor games, postcards, and memento flora- and fauna-inspired T-shirts of 100% cotton designed by local artists. A percentage of the profits from every purchase is set aside to advance environmental issues of all kinds. Moreover, the store tries to deal with vendors who also contribute to the well-being of endangered species and the environment.

Golden Reef, 695 Front St., is open daily 10 a.m.-10 p.m. Inside is all manner of jewelry from heirloom quality to costume baubles made from black, gold, red, and pink coral, malachite, lapis, and mother of pearl. All designs are created on the premises. Everyone will be happy shopping here because prices range from $1 to $1,000 and more. Golden Reef is also very happy to create an individual one-of-a-kind work for you and you alone.

Back on the mountain side of the street, **Tropical Blues,** 754 Front, presents the T-shirt art of Mark and Irene Ciaburri, who create all the designs for their cotton shirts. A display case holds the shimmering rhinestones and twinkling gold of costume jewelry. Next door at 752 Front, one of the three **Serendipity** shops on the island offers a unique collection of casual island wear, furniture, woodcarvings, and accouterments of an Asian and Hawaiian nature.

The **Whaler's Locker,** 780 Front St., open 9 a.m.-10 p.m., is a sea chest filled with hand-engraved scrimshaw on fossilized walrus and mammoth ivory. Lahaina, historically a premier whaling port, has long been known for this sailor's art etched on everything from pocketknives to whale-tooth pendants. Display cases also hold gold and amber jewelry, Niihau shellwork, Japanese netsuke, and even some coral necklaces. If you are looking for a distinctive folk-art gift that truly says Maui, the Whaler's Locker is an excellent store from which to make your choice.

Sharing the same address is **The South Seas Trading Post.** Open daily 8:30 a.m.-10 p.m., it is the second oldest shop in modern Lahaina, dating back to 1871. It indeed has artifacts from the South Pacific, like tapa cloth from Tonga, but also colorful rugs from India, primitive carvings from Papua New Guinea, and Burmese *kalaga* wall hangings with their beautiful and intricate stitching for $30-300. You can pick up a one-of-a-kind bead necklace for only a few dollars, or a real treasure that would adorn any home, for a decent price. Sold are antiques and reproductions; the bona fide antiques have authenticating dates on the back or bottom sides.

In the courtyard just off Front Street and Lahainaluna Rd. is **The Lahaina Market Place,** a collection of semi-open-air stalls and a handful of storefronts, open daily 9 a.m.-9 p.m. Some vendors have roll-up stands and sell trinkets and baubles. Some is junk, but it's neat junk. Four little gift shops here compete for your business as do **Captain Dave's,** which sells fish and chips and other snacks, and a **Häagen-Dazs Dessert Shop,** which has that cooling ice cream you've been looking for. **Maui Crystal Creations** has fine examples of Austrian crystal and pewterware and seems a mainstay of this alleyway market. Three art galleries, all facing Lahainaluna Road, back up against this courtyard.

The Far End

On both sides of Front Street beyond Lahainaluna Road the shops continue. The "sexually incorrect" will love **David's of Hawaii,** at 815 Front St., where you can find all kinds of lewd postcards, T-shirts, and souvenirs. If T-shirts bearing sexually implicit puns offend you, keep strolling—it's nasty in there. Funky and audacious. Open daily 9 a.m.-10:30 p.m.

In the **Old Poi Factory** at 819 Front St. is **Pacific Visions,** selling hand-painted local garments done at Haiku, art-deco items from Los Angeles, San Francisco, and New York, and lots of artifacts from Bali. Open daily. One of the oldest shops at the Poi Factory is **Valley Isle Promotions,** opened in 1974, which specializes in children's and women's clothing, along with 14-karat gold jewelry designed in Indonesia by Jeanette, the store's owner.

Lahaina Scrimshaw, 845 Front St. (across from Wo Hing temple), tel. (808) 661-8820, open daily 9 a.m.-10 p.m., boasts its own master scrimshander, John Lee, who works in the window every day from about 7:30 a.m.-noon, and

who is friendly and willing to answer questions about this seaman's art. Most of the scrimshaw is done on antique whale's teeth from the whaling era or on fossilized walrus and mastodon tusks. The scrimshaw offered is authentic, and made by about 40 artists, most of whom are from Hawaii.

Luana's features contemporary resortwear, hand-painted accessories, and jewelry. **Seabreeze Ltd.** is a souvenir store with fake lei and generic muumuu that are no better or worse than others you'll find along Front Street, but the prices are good, especially for film.

Crazy Shirts also has a great assortment of T-shirts and other clothes. Also in this store at 865 Front St. is the tiny but intriguing **Lahaina Whaling Museum** (free), displaying antiques, nautical instruments, scrimshaw, harpoons, and other whaling artifacts. Open Mon.-Sat. 9 a.m.-10 p.m., Sunday until 9 p.m.

Off the Main Drag

Fox Photo at 139 Lahainaluna Rd., tel. (808) 667-6255, open daily, is a full-service, one-hour-developing camera store. It's good in West Maui for any specialized photo needs. A second one-hour lab is down the street and around the corner at 820 Front Street.

Take Home Maui, at 121 Dickenson St., mail order tel. (800) 545-MAUI, is a food store and delicatessen that specializes in packaging "agriculturally inspected" Maui produce such as pineapples, papayas, Maui onions, protea, potato chips, macadamia nut products, and even Kona coffee that they will deliver to you at the airport before your departing flight.

Even if you haven't been out on a whale-watching tour, stop in at the **Pacific Whale Foundation** shop at 143 Dickenson St. for a look at all the clothing, posters, jewelry, and gift items relating to the whale and other sea creatures. It's almost an education having a look here, and the proceeds help support this worthy organization.

Up the street at Dickenson Square is a **Whalers General Store,** for sundries.

The **Salvation Army Thrift Shop** on Shaw St. just up from Front St. has the usual collection of inexpensive used goods but occasionally some great buys on older aloha shirts. Open Mon.-Sat., regular business hours.

505 Front Street Mall

The 505 Front Street Mall, with most shops open daily 9 a.m.-9 p.m., offers a barrel full of shops and restaurants at the south end of Front Street, away from the heavier foot traffic. The mall is like a New England village, and the shopping is good and unhurried with free underground parking for customers. Some shops include a **Whalers General Store; KPOA FM Music Shop,** where you can find the latest in cassettes and CDs, with an emphasis on local Hawaiian sounds; and **Mad About Art,** which handles mostly nostalgic alohawear, jewelry, and Hawaiian-made gifts, photos, and postcards. Several other art and clothing shops inhabit this mall, as do half a dozen restaurants.

The Wharf Cinema Center

The Wharf Cinema Center at 658 Front offers three floors of eateries, shops, and a movie theater. Playing first-run movies, the triplex **Lahaina Cinemas** occupies much of the third floor. Browse **Crazy Shirts** with its excellent selection of quality T-shirts, or **Gigi's Leather Boutique,** for everything from jackets to purses. **Hawaiian Styles and Creations** offers tropical sportswear, and **Island Swimwear** carries bathing suits for men and women. There's a coffee bar where you can relax and read. **Island Coins and Stamps** on the second floor is a shop as frayed as an old photo album. It specializes in philatelic supplies. For postal needs and gifts, stop by the **Lahaina Mail Depot** on the lower level at the rear; open weekdays 10 a.m.-4 p.m., Saturday until 1 p.m. Across the walk is a free exhibit about the lighthouses of Hawaii, a project of the Lahaina Restoration Foundation. The Fresnel lens on display was once in the lighthouse at Kalaupapa on Molokai. Next door to this display is **Island Sandals,** tel. (808) 661-5110, a small shop run in the honest old-style way that produces fully adjustable tie sandals, styled from the days of Solomon. As the gregarious sandalmaker says, he creates the right sandal for $135 ($115 women's) and gives you the left as a gift. Stop in and have him trace your feet for an order. As he works, he'll readily talk about political, social, or local island issues. Out front is an **ABC Discount Store.** For those coming from Kaanapali, both the West Maui Shopping Express and the free Lahaina Express shuttles stop at the Wharf Cinema Center.

Pioneer Inn Shops

Below Pioneer Inn is a clutch of shops that includes **Aloha Magnets** for a zillion of these colorful items to stick on your refrigerator, **Fox One-hour Photo, Products of Hawaii Too** for gift and craft items, **Watch-N-See** for timepieces and sunglasses, a **Lifestyle** alohawear clothing shop, and a **Whalers General Store.** Several other clothing stores are here as are **Waterfront Gallery** for jewelry, gifts, and artwork, **Häagen-Dazs** for ice cream treats, and an **Atlantis submarine** booth where you can arrange a memorable underwater Maui adventure. Most shops are open 9 a.m.-9 p.m.

The Lahaina Shopping Center

The Lahaina Shopping Center, just behind Longhi's, has a few inexpensive shops, **Ace Hardware,** and **Nagasako's Market,** known for its good selection of local and Oriental food. Here as well are the midtown **post office,** a **Bank of Hawaii,** and an **American Savings Bank.** In the back portion, you'll find **Nagasako General Store, Nagasako Variety,** and the **Lahaina Pharmacy,** along with several inexpensive restaurants.

Across Wainee Street is the **Lahaina Square Shopping Center,** with a big **Foodland** grocery store and more cheap eateries. Next door at **Anchor Square** is an activities center.

The Lahaina Center

Lahaina's newest shopping center, at the corner of Front and Papalaua Streets at the north edge of downtown, had the finishing touches put on it in early 1993. The signature establishments of this mall are the **Hard Rock Café,** filled with memorabilia of rock and roll greats and serving American standards and cold beer; the Hawaiian department store Liberty House; a Banana Republic for livable fashions; and **Hilo Hattie** for Hawaiian clothing and gifts. In the center you will also find **Local Motion Hawaii,** a hip clothing store selling tank tops, swimwear, and locally designed T-shirts that can be stenciled on the premises; **Wet Seal** for young women's clothing; several other fashion shops; an **ABC** store for sundries and inexpensive beach gear; a **Dive Maui** outlet for water activities and equipment; and a **Made in Hawaii** shop for a good selection of local products. With pool and foosball tables, the **World Cafe** is something of a sports bar and late-night entertainment spot that also serves food. Cool yourself down at the **Paniolo Coffee Company** with a shave ice or milk shake, or give yourself a pick-me-up with a steaming espresso. Lahaina's second cinema complex, the **Front Street Theaters,** occupies one of the center buildings. There is a pay parking lot here that's free with validation. The West Maui Shopping Express shuttle stops at the Hilo Hattie store more than 10 times a day on its route between Lahaina and Kaanapali; $1 per person each way.

After shopping, stop by **Hale Kahiko** and have a look at the traditional-style Hawaiian buildings and items of everyday use displayed as a cultural showcase in a landscaped enclosure to the side of the parking lot. Open daily 9 a.m.-6 p.m. While here enjoy the hula show at 2 p.m. on Wednesday and Friday or the *keiki* hula show at 6 p.m. on the same days.

Lahaina Cannery Mall

As practical looking as its name on the outside—it is a converted pineapple cannery, after all—the center's bright, well-appointed, and air-conditioned interior features some of the best and most convenient shopping on West Maui, open daily 9:30 a.m.-9 p.m. The mall is located at 1221 Honoapiilani Hwy., near Mala Wharf. If you'll be staying at a condo and doing your own cooking, the largest and generally least expensive supermarket on West Maui is **Safeway,** open daily 24 hours. To book any activities, from a whalewatch to a dinner cruise, you'll find the **Ocean Activities Center** kiosk offers the great activities on Maui for the right price. Sundries can be picked up at the **ABC Store,** and you can beat the sun's glare by stopping into **Shades of Hawaii.** Some of the clothing shops you'll find here are **Crazy Shirts, Maui Waterwear, Escape to Maui,** and **Reyn's.** Food is available at **Compadres Mexican Bar and Grill** and **Mango Cafe,** as well as other shops in the food court. Although the mall is relatively new, don't let that fool you because some of Lahaina's oldest and best shops, like **Lahaina Printsellers,** are here. **Waldenbooks** has one of its excellent,

well-stocked stores in the mall. One of the most unusual shops is **The Kite Fantasy,** featuring kites, windsocks, and toys for kids of all ages. You can buy kites like a six-foot flexifoil for more than $100 or a simple triangular plastic kite for only a few bucks. Cloth kites are made from nylon with nice designs for a reasonable $15.95. If you're into designer coffees and cigars come to **Sir Wilfred's.** It's one of the few places on this side of the island for such delicacies. If you're hungry, try the deli case for pastries and the like, or order up a cup of soup, quiche, lasagna, or a cool drink. A good assortment of gift items round out what's sold here. **Longs Drugs** is one of the cheapest places to buy and develop film. You can also find a selection of everything from aspirin to boogie boards. There's plenty of free parking at this mall, but the West Maui Shopping Express bus stops here a dozen times a day shuttling between Lahaina and Kaanapali; $1 per person each way.

Booths are set up in the mall Mon.-Fri. 10 a.m.-4 p.m., displaying and selling Hawaiian art and crafts. Also, a free **Polynesian Show** is presented every Tuesday and Thursday evening 7-8 p.m., and there's a **Keiki Hula Show** every Saturday and Sunday 1-2 p.m.

Arts

It's said that Lahaina is the world's third-largest art market. Who determined that to be so is a question unanswered, yet it is certain that you can view countless works of art here and spend a fortune acquiring it. Many artists on display at the galleries in Lahaina are local island artists and others from the state, although other Americans and numerous foreigners are also represented. Although not all, many of the galleries in town are open until 10 p.m.

Due to the renovation of the old Lahaina Courthouse in 1998, the **Lahaina Art Society Galleries** had to vacate its digs in the basement of the old jail. They've moved (at least temporarily) to a space in the Lahaina Center, where they still put on month-long exhibits and periodic individual exhibitions. Where its future home will be is still in question. For now stroll under the banyan tree every Saturday and Sunday 9 a.m.-5 p.m. to see these artists and craftspeople displaying their wares for sale at **Art in the Park.** The artists here are up and coming, and the prices for sometimes remarkable works are reasonable. These artists are trying to make a living by their skills, and most are not displayed at the well-known galleries in town.

The Village Galleries, with two locations at 120 Dickenson St., tel. (808) 661-4402 or (800) 346-0585, open daily 9 a.m.-9 p.m., and at 180 Dickenson St., tel. (808) 661-5559, were founded by Lynn Shue in 1970 and are among the oldest continuous galleries featuring original works of Maui artists. At the original gallery at 120 Dickenson, enter to find everything from *raku* pottery to hand-blown glass, and sculptures done in both wood and metal. Some of the accomplished painters on display are: George Allan, who works in oils; Joyce Clark, another oil painter noted for her seascapes; Betty Hay-Freeland, a landscape artist; Fred Kenknight, who uses watercolors to depict island scenes; Lowell Mapes, who also uses oil to render familiar landmarks like the Pioneer Inn. The galleries also have inexpensive items like postcards, posters, and limited edition prints, all perfect as mementos and souvenirs. The gallery at 180 Dickenson St. features more contemporary and abstract works that evoke a feeling more than an actual scene.

The Wyland Gallery, 711 Front St., tel. (808) 667-2285, showcases the works of Wyland, renowned worldwide for his "whaling wall" murals of cavorting whales. Wyland's visionary oil and watercolor paintings of marvelous aquatic scenes adorn the walls, while his compassionate bronze renderings of whales and dolphins sing their soul songs from white pedestals. Also displayed are the organic sculptures of Dale Joseph Evers, a pioneer in functional furnishings, who has turned bronze and acrylic into dolphin-shaped tables. Outside is a quiet lanai overlooking the harbor, where more aquatic-inspired glass sculptures are counterpointed against the actual living sea. At 697 Front St., a second Wyland Gallery, tel. (808) 661-7099, vibrates with fantastic colors and images created by Hawaii's premier artists. At 136 Dickenson is a third Wyland Gallery, tel. (808) 661-0590.

The two Galerie Lassen, at 700 and 844 Front St., tel. (808) 661-1101 and (808) 667-7707, showcase original and limited edition prints by Christian Reise Lassen, who boldly applies striking colors to bring to life his two-worlds perspective of sea and earth. Typical of his dynamic vision is a displayed painting entitled *Majestic Encounters,* which depicts a pond alive with whales and dolphins who are being observed by a fierce-eyed tiger, who in turn is espied by the fixed and ageless glare of a stony-eyed sphinx. Complementing the exaggerated hues of Lassen's works is the subtle patina of Richard Steirs' cast-iron sculptures of supple whales and dolphins. Mr. Steirs, an Upcountry resident, is among the most admired sculptors on Maui with his limited edition castings.

The Lahaina Galleries, 728 Front St., tel. (808) 667-2152 (a branch gallery at the Kapalua Shops), is one of the oldest galleries on the island. The gallery, with a central room and two in the rear, is hung with the works of Dario Campanile, Thomas Le Yung, Guy Buffet, and other widely acclaimed painters, and the mesmerizing acrylic sculptures of Fredrick Hart.

Robert Lynn Nelson Studio, 802 Front St. on the corner of Lahainaluna Rd., tel. (808) 667-9300, shows originals and prints only of Robert Lynn Nelson, the father of the modern marine art movement, which splits the canvas between land and undersea scenes.

Displaying idyllic home scenes, waterfalls, snowscapes, and the like by Thomas Kincade is the Thomas Kincade Gallery, 780 Front St., tel. (808) 667-7170.

Flowers, birds, and Chinese fans make up the majority of works displayed at the David Lee Galleries, 712 Front St., tel. (808) 667-7740. David Lee uses natural powder pigments to create his vivid colors and even grinds lapis, pearl, turquoise, and gold for their colors. Originals, lithographs, and posters.

Displaying works in the pop and contemporary vein is Madeline Michaels, 816 Front St., tel. (808) 661-3984. Showing more pop art with bright colors and other nontraditional works of art in many and various mediums is another gallery right on the corner of Front St. and Lahainaluna Road. Around the corner and up Lahainaluna Road are Island Art Collection and the well-established Sargents Fine Art gallery, both carrying more traditional works or art.

Lahaina Printsellers at the Lahaina Cannery Mall, open daily 9:30 a.m.-9 p.m., tel. (808) 667-7843 or (800) 669-7843, has walls festooned with beautiful prints of old Hawaii, including endangered birds and historical figures that featured prominently in Hawaii's past. Printsellers specializes in antique maps, especially those depicting the Pacific basin, and Captain Cook memorabilia. Original antique prints and maps, many from the beginning of last century, start at only $25 and can go all the way up to $100,000. Lahaina Printsellers also offers handrubbed koa frames and will be happy to send you a brochure of thitseir selections if you would like to choose your artwork at home. With its heavy use of dark wood, many tables, and frames everywhere, this shop has the feel of an old library just waiting to be explored.

Food/Liquor Stores

The following markets/supermarkets are in and around Lahaina. The larger ones also stock beer, wine, and liquor.

Safeway, at the Lahaina Cannery Mall, open 24 hours, is a large supermarket complete with deli, fish market, floral shop, and bakery.

Foodland, at the Lahaina Square Shopping center, is also a well-stocked supermarket.

Nagasako Supermarket, at the Lahaina Shopping Center, open daily 7 a.m.-9 p.m., Sunday until 7 p.m., is a local supermarket with plenty of ethnic Hawaiian, Japanese, Chinese, and Korean foods, along with liquor selections. The market is also known for its fresh fish and produce.

Mr. Wine, tel. (808) 661-5551, on the corner of Lahainaluna and Wainee St., not only has a huge selection of wines, and some beer, liquors, and liqueurs, but keeps the better wines and champagnes under cellar conditions in a climatically controlled room at 55° F and 70% humidity. Beat the hot Lahaina sun and stop in for a perfect bottle for the evening. Open Mon.-Sat. 11 a.m.-7 p.m.

For bulk foods, health food items, vitamins, minerals, and supplements, and hot and cold prepared foods, try the full-service **Westside Natural Foods and Deli,** tel. (808) 667-2855, at the corner of Lahainaluna and Wainee Street. Open daily, with shorter hours on Sunday.

The Olowalu General Store, tel. (808) 661-3774, located five miles east of Lahaina along Rt. 30, open Mon.-Fri. 6 a.m.-6:30 p.m., Saturday 7 a.m.-6:30 p.m., Sunday 7 a.m.-5 p.m., is fairly well stocked and the only place to pick up supplies in this area. It also has light snacks including sandwiches and hot dogs, a perfect stop if you are snorkeling or swimming on the nearby beaches.

Sports, Excursions, and Equipment

The **Maui Dive Shop,** at the Lahaina Cannery Mall, tel. (808) 661-5388, and a second store at the Lahaina Center are full-service dive shops offering tours, snorkel and scuba rentals, lessons, and equipment and clothing sales. **Lahaina Divers,** tel. (808) 667-7496, next to the Pacific Whale Foundation store at 143 Dickenson St., also rents snorkel equipment, offers scuba lessons, and arranges tours on its fleet of boats. Everyone gives this company a thumbs-up. **Capt. Nemo's Scuba Shack,** 150 Dickenson, tel. (808) 661-5555, has been around for many years and offers similar service and equipment, sales, rentals, and lessons.

Snorkel Bob's, at 161 Lahainaluna Rd., tel. (808) 661-4421, rents snorkel gear for $15 per week (daily rental also), which you can take to a neighboring island and return there for a small extra fee. Boogie boards are available at $13 per day or $26 per week, and Snorkel Bob's advice, whether you need it or not, is plentiful and free.

West Maui Cycles, 193 Lahainaluna Rd., tel. (808) 661-9005, rents snorkel gear, surfboards, and boogie boards, but its big thing is the sale, service, and rental of road and mountain bicycles. Stop here for all your cycling needs.

Companies that can set you up with most any activity offered on the island include **Barefoot's Cashback Tours,** tel. (808) 661-8889, 834 Front St.; **Ocean Activities Center,** tel. (808) 661-5309, at the Lahaina Cannery Mall; **Activity Warehouse,** tel. (808) 667-4000, across from Kamehameha III School along Front St.; and **Activity Information Center,** with two locations, one at the Anchor Square Center, tel. (808) 667-7777, and the other at the Wharf Cinema Center, tel. (808) 662-3100.

SERVICES AND INFORMATION

For fire, police, or ambulance, dial 911 throughout the Lahaina area. The police station, fire station, and Lahaina civic center are located above Wahikuli State Wayside Park between Lahaina and Kaanapali. In Lahaina during normal banking hours try the Bank of Hawaii, tel. (808) 661-8781, or the American Savings Bank, tel. (808) 667-9561, in the Lahaina Shopping Center; or First Hawaiian Bank, 215 Papalaua St., tel. (808) 661-3655.

Post Office
The post office is on the very northwest edge of town where Kaanapali begins, tel. (808) 667-6611. The in-town postal branch, tel. (808) 661-0550, is located at the Lahaina Shopping Center.

Lahaina Mail Depot is a post office contract station located at The Wharf Cinema Center, 658 Front St., tel. (808) 667-2000. It's open weekdays 10 a.m.-4 p.m. (Saturday until 1 p.m.), and along with the normal stamps, etc., it specializes in sending packages home. Mailing boxes, tape, and packaging materials are all available, as are souvenir packs of coffee, nuts, candies, and teas, which might serve as a last-minute purchase, but are expensive. In the Lahaina Shopping Center you'll find The Mail Room, tel. (808) 661-5788, for shipping and packaging services and supplies. Hours are Mon.-Fri. 9:30 a.m.-6 p.m., Saturday until 3:30 p.m.; closed for lunch.

Medical Treatment
A concentration of all types of specialists is found at the Maui Medical Group, 130 Prison St., tel. (808) 661-0051. Open Mon.-Fri. 8 a.m.-5 p.m. and Saturday 8 a.m.-noon; call for emergency hours. Professional medical care can also be found at the Kaiser Permanente clinic, 910 Wainee St., tel. (808) 661-7400. Alternatively, the Lahaina Health Center, 180 Dickenson St. at Dickenson Square, Suite 205, tel. (808) 667-6268, offers acupuncture, chiropractic, therapeutic massage, and podiatry.

Pharmacies in Lahaina include: Lahaina Pharmacy at the Lahaina Shopping Center, tel. (808) 661-3119; Longs Drugs at the Lahaina Cannery Mall, tel. (808) 667-4384; and Valley Isle Pharmacy, 130 Prison St., tel. (808) 661-4747.

Laundromat
For a self-service laundromat try Kwik N Kleen, tel. (808) 661-7949, at the Lahaina Shopping Center.

Information
The following groups and organizations should prove helpful: Lahaina Restoration Foundation, P.O. Box 338, Lahaina, HI 96761, tel. (808) 661-3262, or in the Master's Reading Room next to the Baldwin Home along Front Street. The foundation is a storehouse of information about historical Maui; be sure to pick up the brochure *Lahaina, A Walking Tour of Historic and Cultural Sites*. The Lahaina Town Action Commmittee, 120 Dickenson St., tel. (808) 667-9193, sponsors events in Lahaina and can provide information about what's happening in the area. The Lahaina Art Society, tel. (808) 661-3228, has information about the art scene and art events in town.

For popular events and activities happening in Lahaina, contact the Lahaina Visitors Center events line at (808) 667-9194. This center is operated by the Lahaina Town Action Committee, tel. (808) 667-9175, an organization that also sponsors cultural events and other activities throughout the year, including Art Night. The Visitors Center has an office in the Old Lahaina Courthouse fronting the pier.

The Lahaina Public Library is at 680 Wharf St., tel. (808) 662-3066, open Mon.-Fri., various hours.

KAANAPALI

Five lush valleys, nourished by streams from the West Maui Mountains, stretch luxuriously for 10 miles from Kaanapali north to Kapalua. All along the connecting **Honoapiilani Highway** (Rt. 30), the dazzle and glimmer of beaches is offset by black volcanic rock. Two sensitively planned and beautifully executed resorts are at each end of this drive. Kaanapali Resort is 500 acres of fun and relaxation at the south end. It houses six luxury hotels, a handful of beautifully appointed condos, a shopping mall and museum, 36 holes of world-class golf, tennis courts galore, and epicurean dining in a chef's salad of cuisines. Two of the hotels, the Hyatt Regency and Sheraton, are inspired architectural showcases that blend harmoniously with Maui's most beautiful seashore surroundings. At the northern end is another gem, the Kapalua Resort, 1,650 of Maui's most beautifully sculpted acres with its own showcases, the Kapalua Bay Hotel and the Ritz-Carlton. Here, too, is prime golf, Kapalua and Fleming Beaches, plus exclusive shopping, horseback riding, and tennis aplenty.

Kaanapali, with its four miles of glorious beach, is Maui's westernmost point. It begins where Lahaina ends and continues north along Rt. 30 until a mile or so before the village of Honokowai. From here to Kapalua are the villages of Honokowai, Kahana, and Napili, which service the condos tucked away here and there along the coast. All are practical stops where you can buy food, gas, and all necessary supplies to keep your vacation rolling. The accommodations are not as grand, but the beaches and vistas are. Along this entire shore, Maui flashes its most captivating pearly white smile. The sights here are either natural or manmade, but not historical. This is where you come to gaze from mountain to sea and bathe yourself in natural beauty. Then, after a day of surf and sunshine, you repair to one of the gorgeous hotels or restaurants for a drink or dining, or just to promenade around the grounds.

History

Western Maui was a mixture of scrub and precious *lo'i*, land, reserved for taro, the highest life-sustaining plant given by the gods. The farms stretched to Kapalua, skirting the numerous bays all along the way. The area was important enough for a "royal highway" to be built by Chief Piilani, and it still bears his name. Westerners used the lands surrounding Kaanapali to grow sugarcane, and **The Lahaina, Kaanapali, and Pacific Railroad,** known today as the "Sugar Cane Train," chugged to Kaanapali Beach to unburden itself onto barges that carried the cane to waiting ships. Kaanapali, until the 1960s, was a blemished beauty where the Pioneer Sugar Mill dumped its rubbish. Then Amfac, one of the "Big Five," decided to put the land to better use. In creating Hawaii's first planned resort, it outdid itself. Robert Trent Jones was hired to mold the golf course along this spectacular coast, while the Hyatt Regency and its grounds became an architectural marvel. The Sheraton-Maui was built atop, and integrated with, Puu Kekaa, "Black Rock." This area is a wave-eroded cinder cone, and the Sheraton architects used its sea cliffs as part of the walls of the resort. Here, on a deep underwater shelf, daring divers descend to harvest Maui's famous black coral trees. The Hawaiians believed that Puu Kekaa was a very holy place where the spirits of the dead left this earth and migrated into the spirit world. Kahekili, Maui's most famous 18th-century chief, often came here to leap into the sea below. This old-time daredevil was fond of the heart-stopping activity, and made famous "Kahekili's Leap," an even more treacherous sea cliff on nearby Lanai. Today, the Sheraton puts on a sunset show where this "leap" is reenacted.

Unfortunately, developers picked up on Amfac's great idea and built condos up the road starting in Honokowai. Interested in profit, not beauty, they earned that area the dubious title of "condo ghetto." Fortunately, the Maui Land and Pineapple Co. owned the land surrounding the idyllic Kapalua Bay. Colin Cameron, one of the heirs to this holding, had visions of developing 750 acres of the plantation's 23,000 into the extraordinary Kapalua Bay Resort. He teamed up with Laurence Rockefeller, and the complex was opened in 1979, later expanding to 1,650 acres.

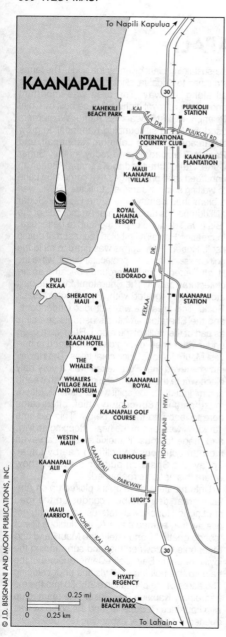

KAANAPALI

To Napili Kapulua

KAHEKILI
BEACH PARK

KAI ALA DR.

PUUKOLII
STATION

PUUKOLII RD.

INTERNATIONAL
COUNTRY CLUB

KAANAPALI
PLANTATION

MAUI
KAANAPALI
VILLAS

ROYAL
LAHAINA
RESORT

KEKAA DR.

MAUI
ELDORADO

KAANAPALI
STATION

PUU
KEKAA

SHERATON
MAUI

KAANAPALI
BEACH HOTEL

THE
WHALER

WHALERS
VILLAGE MALL
AND MUSEUM

KAANAPALI
ROYAL

KAANAPALI GOLF
COURSE

HONOAPIILANI HWY.

WESTIN
MAUI

KAANAPALI
ALII

CLUBHOUSE

KAANAPALI PARKWAY

LUIGI'S

MAUI
MARRIOT

NOHEA KAI DR.

HYATT
REGENCY

0   0.25 mi
0   0.25 km

HANAKAOO
BEACH PARK

To Lahaina

© J.D. BISIGNANI AND MOON PUBLICATIONS, INC.

Black Rock

One of the most easily accessible and visually engaging snorkeling spots on Maui is located at the Sheraton's Black Rock. Follow the main road past the Sheraton until it climbs the hill around back. Walk up the hill and through the hotel grounds until you come to a white metal fence. Follow the fence down toward the sea. You'll come to a spur of rock jutting out, and that's it. The entire area is like an underwater marine park. Enter at the beach area and snorkel west around the rock, staying close to the cinder cone. There are schools of reef fish, rays, and even a lonely turtle. There is limited free public parking in Kaanapali, so you may have to park in one of the few pay lots. Alternately, park at Kahekili Beach Park at the far north end of Kaanapali near the Maui Kaanapali Villas, from where it's only a 10-minute walk.

Whaling Museum

The free **Whalers Village Museum** at Whaler's Village shopping mall has a few outside displays, but most items are inside on the upper level of the mall. The most dramatic outside display is the skeleton of a 40-foot sperm whale. This big boy greets you at the entrance to the mall as you come up the steps. The compact display area upstairs on the mezzanine level is full of whaling history, photographs, drawings, artifacts from whaling ships, a reconstructed forecastle, a video on whaling, and many informative descriptions and stories about the whaling industry, whaling life, and the whalers themselves. After a walk through the museum, pick up a memento at the museum gift shop.

Across the walkway, **Hale Kohola** is set up to explain the evolution of the whale, describe the various species, display specimens of whale parts, and show a video on whales and dolphins. Engross yourself in these exhibit halls. They are a learning experience.

Sports

For a full listing of the sporting facilities and possibilities in the Kaanapali area, contact the information booth at Whalers Village or any of the activity desks at the hotels on the strip. **Golf** courses at the Kaanapali Golf Courses, tel. (808) 661-3691, are each par 71. Both the north and south courses share a clubhouse that sits at the entrance to Kaanapali along the Honoapiilani

Highway. For **tennis,** the most famous is the Royal Lahaina Tennis Ranch with 10 courts, tennis clinics, and tournaments. The Hyatt and Marriott have five courts each, the Sheraton three, and five are located at The Whaler. For **water sports,** catamarans are available from the Hyatt, Sheraton, and Westin Maui. Other water sport activitiesWhalers and equipment are available from each hotel. Contact any major hotel beach activities desk, or Beach Activities of Maui at the Whalers Village, tel. (808) 661-5552.

Kaanapali Extras

Two situations in and around Kaanapali mar its outstanding beauty—you might refer to them as "Kaanapali Perfumes." There are still plenty of sugarcane fields in the area, and when they're being burned off, the smoke is heavy in the air; the soot falling at this time is called "black snow" by locals. Also, the sewage treatment plant is inadequate, and even the constantly blowing trade winds are insufficient to push this stench out to sea.

Transportation

Kaanapali is serviced by the free **Kaanapali Trolley** within the resort area. The **West Maui Shopping Express** runs between Kaanapali and Lahaina, and the **Whalers Village Shuttle** runs to South Maui. Going as far as Maalaea is the **Maui Ocean Center Shuttle,** and the **Trans-Hawaiian** airporter shuttles make runs to the airport in Kahului. The **Sugar Cane Train** offers fun for the entire family on its route between Kaanapali and Lahaina. The Kapalua-West Maui Airport is the most convenient for air travel to this end of the island, but few airlines operate in and out of this airstrip. Most air traffic to Maui still goes via Kahului.

BEACHES

The four-mile stretch of pristine sand at Kaanapali is what people come to experience in Maui, and they are never disappointed.

Hanakaoo Beach Park

Just as you leave Lahaina and enter Kaanapali you'll find this beach park. It's a good swimming and sailboarding spot, with lifeguards, showers, and parking; and while so close, it's away from the hotel crowds of Kaanapali. The Kahana Canoe Club is based here and you can often see rowers out on the water practicing their strokes. Between the beach and the road is an old cemetery with mostly Chinese characters written on the headstones.

Hanakaoo Beach is an uninterrupted stretch of sand running from the park, past the Hyatt Regency to the Sheraton. A stretch of this beach, called "Dig Me Beach," is known for its people watching and those who come to be watched. Although these are some of the most exclusive hotels on the island, public access to the beach is guaranteed in the state's constitution. There are "rights of way," but parking your car is definitely a hassle. A good idea is to park at either Hanakaoo or Wahikuli park and walk northward along the beach. You can park (10 cars) in the Hyatt's lower lot and enter along a right of way. There's access between the Hyatt and the Marriott (pay parking ramp), between the Marriott and the Kaanapali Ali'i, which also has limited parking, and between the Kaanapali Ali'i and the Westin Maui. There is also some parking near the Sheraton and at the Whalers Shopping Center parking ramp, but you must pass through the gauntlet of shops.

Kahekili Park

A short stroll down the beach from Black Rock, this park is dedicated to Maui's King Kahekili. The newest beach park in the area, it's a commodious place with a broad lawn, palm trees, a pavilion for cooking, and tables for a picnic. The large shaded parking area can accommodate many cars, and you can count on always finding someone here. The beach, sometimes used for scuba lessons, runs uninterrupted to Black Rock.

Beach Walk

As in Wailea, a beach walkway has been created in Kaanapali that runs along the sand from the Hyatt Regency in the south to the Sheraton in the north. This walkway is a convenient way to pass from one property to another: peruse your neighbor hotel, try one of the restaurants down the line, or walk to shop. During the cool hours of the day and at sunset, this walkway is also used by joggers out for exercise and those who want the perfect location to watch the sun go down.

LUXURY HOTELS

The Kaanapali Resort offers hotels that are all in the luxury category—no budget accommodations here. The following should give you an idea of what's available.

Hyatt Regency Maui

The moment you enter the main lobby of this luxury hotel the magic begins. A multitiered architectural extravaganza opens to the sky, birds fly freely, and magnificent potted plants and full-size courtyard palm trees create the atmosphere of a modern Polynesian palace located at Kaanapali's southern extremity, at 200 Nohea Kai Dr., Lahaina, HI 96761, tel. (808) 661-1234 or (800) 233-1234, fax (808) 667-4498, website: www .hyatt.com. Nooks and crannies abound where you can lounge in kingly wicker thrones. Peacocks strut their regal stuff amid impeccable Japanese gardens, and ducks and swans are floating alabaster on landscaped ponds. The swimming pools are inspired by the islands: grottoes, caves, waterfalls, and a huge slide are all built in. A swinging wooden bridge connects the sections, and you can have an island drink at a sunken poolside bar. There are four fine restaurants on property, half a dozen lounges, and the Drums of the Pacific Luau. The "Elephant Walk" is a covey of specialty shops and boutiques. The little kids will love it here too. Camp Hyatt for children ages 3-12 runs daily 9 a.m.-3 p.m. for $50 a child and includes activities and excursions that change daily, arts and crafts, lunch, and snacks. An evening camp 6-10 p.m. is also available, so put those little kiddies in the care of professionals and have a romantic night out. All beach activities, equipment rentals, and lessons, including a sail/snorkel ride on the *Kiele V* catamaran, can be arranged through the beach activities center at oceanside, or expend some energy at the health club and tennis center. For those with less physical activity in mind, check out the daily Hawaiian demonstrations in the lobby, the hotel wildlife tour, the art and garden tour, or the nightly astronomy show on the hotel roof. Rates are $275 for terrace rooms, $345 for golf/mountain rooms, $375 for ocean-view rooms, and $415 for oceanfront rooms. Rates are higher for the special Regency floors. Suites

run $600-3,000. If you visit, valet parking is in front of the hotel, complimetary if you validate your ticket by dining at Spats or the Palm Court, or spend $25 in one of the shops. Or you can self-park out front or around in the back. From here, both the north end of Lahaina, pretty at night with its colored lights reflecting on the water, and Lanai, floating across the Lahaina Roads, are easily visible.

Sheraton Maui

The 510 rooms of the Sheraton Maui, 2605 Kaanapali Pkwy., Lahaina, HI 96761, tel. (808) 661-0031 or (800) 325-3535, fax (808) 661-0458, website: www.sheraton-maui.com, are built around Kaanapali's most conspicuous natural phenomenon, Puu Kekaa, "Black Rock." Originally opened in 1963, the Sheraton reopened in 1997 after a two-year complete renovation. Open, bright, and breezy, the lobby looks out over the finely landscaped gardens and an enticing meandering pool with a water slide. Three classy restaurants grace the hotel, and a bar is situated at poolside. The guest activities desk can arrange almost any activity that the island offers, and you can rent water equipment and have lessons from the beach activity booth. The snorkeling around Black Rock is the best in the area, and every evening there is a torch-lighting ceremony and cliff dives from the rock. As a guest, you can avail yourself of several daily catamaran rides aboard the *Teralani* or head for some sporting competition at the resort's tennis club. The north end of the Kaanapali beach walk ends at the Sheraton, so you can walk all the way to the Hyatt at the south end without leaving the oceanside. Most rooms at the Sheraton face the ocean, and all are air conditioned and have full amenities. Rates are $290-330 for garden and mountain views, $360-365 for ocean-view and oceanfront rooms, $575 for an Ohana family suite, and other suites from $750.

The Westin Maui

The newest in luxury hotels to spring up along Kaanapali, at 2365 Kaanapali Pkwy., Lahaina, HI 96761, tel. (808) 667-2525 or (800) 228-3000, fax (808) 661-5764, website: www.westinmaui.com, is actually a phoenix, risen from the old Maui Surf Hotel. True to the second life of that mythical bird, it is a beauty. Westin is known for its fabulous entranceways, lobbies, and quiet nooks. You won't be disappointed here. A series of strolling paths takes you through resplendent manicured grounds that surround an extensive multi-pool area. Waterfalls, water slides, and natural rock formations all blend to create civilized paradise. To the left of the main lobby is a collection of exclusive boutiques. You'll find just what you want to eat or drink at any time of day at one of the hotel's eight restaurants and lounges. The ocean activity center can set you up with all sorts of rentals on the beach, or a ride on *Gemini*, the hotel's catamaran. A business center is set up for the traveling businessperson, and kids are taken care of at the supervised daily Keiki Kamp. The daily kids' program runs 9 a.m.-3 p.m. at $45 a child, with evening programs also available. For the experience of all, each Friday 8:30 a.m.-5 p.m. brings Ho'olauna, a Hawaiian culture and arts program, which is put on at various spots around the hotel. If you just want to soak in some beauty, have a tour of the hotel's $2 million art collection. The Westin Maui has more than 750 guest rooms. Standard terrace rooms run $265, a garden-view room $295, golf/mountain-view $345, ocean-view $375-420, oceanfront $445-495, and suites go upward from there.

Royal Lahaina Resort

Twenty-seven idyllic acres surround 542 luxurious rooms of the Royal Lahaina Resort, the largest complex in Kaanapali, 2780 Kekaa Dr., Lahaina, HI 96761, tel. (808) 661-3611 or (800) 447-6925, fax (808) 661-6150, website: 2maui .com. Here the tropical landscaping leads directly to the sun-soaked beach. The Royal Lahaina, one of the first properties to be developed, is divided into cottages and towers. Rates range from a standard room at $215 to an oceanfront room at $335. Cottages rent for $295 and $385, suites $600-1,500; condo/car packages are available. The renovated rooms are decorated in a comfortable Hawaiian style with all amenities and private lanai; some of the cottages have kitchens. There are no less than three restaurants, a nightly luau, and three swimming pools on the well-maintained grounds. A score of shops are located in the main hotel for your convenience. The beach activities booth rents snorkel equipment, windsurfing boards,

and kayaks, and arranges scuba lessons. The resort is also home to the **Royal Lahaina Tennis Ranch,** boasting 10 courts and a 3,500-seat stadium along with special tennis packages for those inclined.

Maui Marriott

The fifth of the big five hotels on Kaanapali Beach is the Maui Marriott, 100 Nohea Kai Dr., Lahaina, 96761, tel. (808) 667-1200, (800) 228-9290, or (800) 542-6821 in Hawaii. With more than 700 rooms, two swimming pools, a beach recreation center, five tennis courts, two dozen shops, a half dozen restaurants and lounges, and indoor and outdoor parking, the Marriott is one of the largest properties on West Maui, but not as elegant as some others in Kaanapali. Open to the beach and facing the setting sun, the hotel is graced with cooling breezes that waft across its manicured courtyard and through the open atriums of both its buildings. Indoors, the many flowers and potted plants bring the outdoors inside. On the premises are Lokelani, an excellent seafood restaurant, Nikko Japanese Steak House, one of the best spots for Japanese cuisine on the island, the Makai Bar for excellent *pu pu* and evening entertainment, and the Marriott Luau. The hospitable staff orchestrates the numerous daily handicraft and recreational activities, and a kids' program is scheduled three times a week. There's plenty to keep every family busy. Snorkel sets, boogie boards, and kayaks can be rented at the beach activities center, and kayak tours are led from here. Room rates range from $280 for a standard room to $328 for a deluxe ocean view; $399 for suites. Special honeymoon, tennis, golf, and family plans are available, as well as optional meal plans.

Kaanapali Beach Hotel

Not as luxurious as its famous neighbors, but an excellent hotel nonetheless, the Kaanapali Beach Hotel is a bargain. Located at 2525 Kaanapali Pkwy., tel. (808) 661-0011, (800) 262-8450, or (800) 233-1014, e-mail: mauikbh@aloha.net, website: www.kaanapalibeachhotel.com, this is perhaps the most "Hawaiian" of the hotels in Kaanapali. There is no glitz here, just warm and friendly service, reasonably priced restaurants, and nearly as many activities and amenities as the big boys down the line. Guest service provides many activities and demonstrations including lei-making, hula lessons, *lau hala* weaving, and a free sunset hula show nightly; the tour desk can always hook you up with any activity on the island. Have a swim in the distinctive whale-shaped pool or check with the beach center for water equipment for rent. Standard rooms range from $160 to $250 for an ocean view, with suites priced $210-585; many special packages available.

CONDOS

Generally less expensive than the hotels, most condos offer full kitchens, TVs, some maid service, swimming pools, tennis courts, and often convenience stores and laundry facilities. Combinations of the above are too numerous to mention, so it's best to ask all pertinent questions when booking. Off-season rates and discounts for longer stays are usually offered. Not all condos accept credit cards, and a deposit is the norm when making reservations.

Located right on the strip along the water are the fancy high-rise Kaanapali Ali'i and The Whaler condos. Set amidst the golf links and following the lay of the land are the low-rise Kaanapali Royal and El Dorado. The International Colony Club is located in a more residential area up above the highway and are farther away from the water and golf courses. A short way north up the beach and off on a road by itself is Maui Kaanapali Villas.

International Colony Club

This condo, near the Sugar Cane Train rail line, is on the *mauka* side of Rt. 30 at 2759 Kalapu Dr., tel. (808) 661-4070. This hillside property with two pools and walkways connecting all units offers fully furnished one- and two-bedroom cottages that sleep from two to six people. One-bedroom units run $105, two-bedroom units $125; three-night minimum. For rental information, contact Maui Diversified Real Estate, tel. (800) 642-6098. Premium.

Aston Maui Kaanapali Villas

Enjoy the surroundings of 11 sculpted acres at this affordable condo at 45 Kai Ala Dr., tel. (808) 667-7791 or (800) 922-7866, fax (808) 667-

0366. The extensive grounds of cool swaying palms harbor three pools, a beach service booth, the Castaway Restaurant, and a sundries shop. Rates begin at $160 for a hotel room with refrigerator. Studios with kitchens run $200-230, and it's $245-280 for a one-bedroom suite with a/c, cable TV, full kitchen, plus maid service. This property, located at the far north end of the Kaanapali development, has an added bonus of peace and quiet along with the best of the Kaanapali beach, although you remain just minutes from the action and a short stroll from Black Rock, a superb snorkeling area. These units are very large with spacious bedrooms; even the studios are capable of handling four people. Luxury.

Outrigger Properties

Both the Kaanapali Royal and Maui Eldorado Resort are managed by Outrigger Hotels and Resorts. **Kaanapali Royal,** 2560 Keka'a Dr., tel. (808) 879-2205, fax 874-3497, a golfer's dream right on the course, has rooms for $195-250, with low-season and long-term discounts. Each suite has a full kitchen and a lanai that faces the fairway. Take advantage of the guest-only swimming pool, lighted tennis courts, and barbecue pit. The **Maui Eldorado Resort,** 2661 Keka'a Dr., tel. (808) 661-0021, fax 667-7039, website: www.outrigger.com, slides down the hill alongside a fairway culminating in beachfront cabanas. There are also three swimming pools and a sundries store on property. These studios and suites run $175-325 during the winter season but are discounted the rest of the year. For toll-free reservations and information, call Outrigger at (800) 688-7444. Some units here are also offered for rent directly by their owners or through independent agents like Whaler's Realty, tel. (800) 367-5632. Luxury.

The Whaler

The Whaler comprises two high-rise buildings set right on the beach next to Whalers Village shopping mall. Outwardly, it has less character than the Kaanapali Ali'i but offers numerous amenities. On property are a pool and spa, exercise room, and tennis courts. These units run from a 640-square-foot studio to a 1,950-square-foot two-bedroom two-bath suite. Rates are $195-470, slightly higher for some units during high season. There is a two-night minimum stay and several car/condo, honeymoon, and senior packages are available. The Whaler is located at 2481 Kaanapali Pkwy., Lahaina, HI 96761, tel. (808) 661-4861 or (800) 367-7052, website: tenio.com/vri. Luxury.

Kaanapali Ali'i

The Kaanapali Ali'i sits in a finely landscaped yard right on the ocean. The four high-rise towers are aesthetically pleasing and are set off by flowers and greenery hanging from many of the balconies. If you need space, try here as each of the large units runs 1,600-1,900 square feet. All have full kitchens, separate living and dining rooms, two full baths, and air conditioning. Free parking, a beach activity center, complimentary tennis, and room service from the Maui Marriott next door are extras. Many area activities and restaurant bills can be put on your room charge as a service. Room rates are $240-650, slightly higher during high season. For information and reservations, contact Kaanapali Ali'i, 50 Nohea Kai Dr., Lahaina, HI 96761, tel. (808) 667-1400 or (800) 642-6284, fax (808) 661-1025, e-mail: info @classicresorts.com, website: kaanapali-alii.com. Luxury.

FOOD

Every hotel in Kaanapali has at least one restaurant, with several others scattered throughout the area. Some of the most expensive and exquisite restaurants on Maui are found in these hotels, but surprisingly, at others you can dine very reasonably. The only cheap eats in the area are the few fast-food restaurants at Whalers Village shopping mall

Reilley's Steak House

This Irish restaurant and bar is located upstairs in the clubhouse at Kaanapali Golf Courses, tel. (808) 667-7477. Open for breakfast, lunch, and dinner, Reilley's is known for its Tuesday all-you-can-eat prime rib dinner for $16.95 and its Sunday full lobster dinner for $19.95. Other meat and seafood entrees are generally in the $20-25 range. Reilley's has a full bar, so come and have a drink after a round of golf or just to watch the sun set over the fairway.

Luigi's

This is one of two locations for Luigi's, located just off Honoapiilani Hwy. at the entrance to Kaanapali Resort. Pizza prices start at $10.99 for a regular cheese-only item to $27.99 for a large House Special, super combination pizza smothered with toppings, or you can nibble a salad for only $3.99. Pasta ranges from $10.99 for a marinara sauce to $15.99 for manicotti. Full-course meals include scallops Luigi for $16.99 and top sirloin Luigi-style for $19.99. Early bird specials on pasta 5:30-6:30 p.m. run $9.95. This is a pleasant, family-oriented restaurant. Don't expect food like mama used to make, but it's not bad for adopted Italians. For reservations call (808) 661-4500. Downstairs is **Kaanapali Pizza,** which also runs a bar.

Westin Maui

Cook's At The Beach is known especially for its nightly all-you-can-eat prime rib buffet for $27.95 ($19.95 before 6:30 p.m.). Regular menu selections are also available and include barbecued spare ribs, fresh island catch, and the chef's famous stir-fry. From 7:30 p.m., a hula show accompanies dinner. Starting at 6:30 a.m., a breakfast buffet is offered, with American and Japanese selections, along with an à la carte menu. Lunch is lighter fare with salads, sandwiches, and burgers.

Finer dining at the hotel is at **The Villa.** Set over the lagoon like floating islands, this restaurant serves the best of island fish and seafood. Open for dinner only 6-10 p.m., reservations are recommended and resort attire is expected. Appetizers include paper rice prawn spring rolls. Fish might be a ginger marinated snapper, and sake glazed salmon is one of the specialties; most entrees are priced $22-26. The chef's special prix fixe menu runs $28. To enjoy the flavors but save a little cash, have the early bird special 6-6:30 p.m. for $19.95.

Perhaps the most well-known dining at the Westin is the champagne Sunday brunch, $24.95, served 9 a.m.-1 p.m. at the **Sound of the Falls** restaurant. Here, you'll be treated to scrumptious delicacies, the waterfall will fill your ears, and your eyes will feast on pink flamingos with the blue ocean as a backdrop.

Royal Lahaina Resort

You have no less than three establishments from which to choose, plus a luau. Follow your nose nightly at 4:45 p.m. to the **Luau Gardens** for the banquet and show, where the biggest problem after the Polynesian Revue is standing up after eating mountains of traditional food. Reservations needed, tel. (808) 661-3611; adults $64, children under 12 $28. The **Royal Ocean Terrace,** the resort's best dining, is open daily for breakfast, lunch, and dinner, offering a breakfast buffet and better-than-average salad bar. Most evening entrees are in the $17-22 range. Sunday brunch 9 a.m.-2 p.m. is a winner. **Beachcombers** is a bit more casual with nightly specials and the flavors of Hawaii.

Located at the entrance to the Royal Lahaina Resort is **Basil Tomatoes,** tel. (808) 662-3210, an Italian grill that's open 5:30 p.m.-midnight—food served until 10 p.m.; reservations suggested. Start with an antipasto like fried green tomatoes at $7.95 or seafood-stuffed mushrooms at $8.95 and move on to a Caesar salad for $9.95 or another fine bowl of greens. The entrees cover the whole range of pastas, meats, poultry, and fish, and are generally in the $16-24 range. To complement any dinner selection, choose from a variety of beers, wine, or aperitifs, and round out your meal with cup of coffee and a sweet dessert.

Hyatt Regency

The **Swan Court** is the Hyatt's signature restaurant. Save this one for a very special evening. You don't come here to eat, you come here to dine, peasant! Anyone who has been enraptured by those old movies where couples regally glide down a central staircase to make their grand entrance will have his or her fantasies come true. Although expensive, with entrees $19-30, you get your money's worth not only with the many wonderful tastes but also with the attention to detail; prosciutto is served with papaya, ginger butter with the fresh catch of the day, and pineapple chutney with the oysters. The wine list is a connoisseur's delight. The Swan Court offers a sumptuous breakfast buffet daily. Dinner, 6-10 p.m., is grand; reservations are recommended, and resort attire is required. For reservations, call (808) 667-4727. The cocktail lounge is open 11 a.m.-11 p.m.

Also at the Hyatt, **Spats Trattoria** is open for dinner only. This restaurant is downstairs and decorated in heavy dark wood and carpets, premodern artwork, and low light. Spats specializes in "country homestyle" Italian food, with the average entree around $25. Casual attire, reservations recommended. Music at Spats piano bar entertains 7:30-11:30 p.m. nightly.

Sheraton

The **Coral Reef Restaurant** is the hotel's finest restaurant. Open for dinner only, the Coral Reef presents Pacific Rim cuisine and is reasonably priced with most entrees $14-26. Reservations are needed, tel. (808) 661-0031. Reservations are also necessary at the dinner-only **Teppan Yaki Dan,** where the Japanese food is prepared with a flourish at your table. Entrees here are a bit more expensive. Less expensive and less formal is the **Keka'a Terrace** restaurant where you can order all day long while surveying the gardens, pool, and Black Rock.

Maui Marriott

The signature restaurant at the Maui Marriott, the **Lokelani,** tel. (808) 667-1200, serves dinner only Wed.-Sun. 6-9 p.m. Seafood is the focus of this award-winning restaurant, but the menu changes monthly. Starters might include Maui onion soup and Big Island shrimp cocktail, and entrees could be seared jumbo tiger prawns, pepper-crusted grilled *ahi* steak, or *opakapaka* and rack of lamb. Expect to pay $20-25 per person. A special Hukilau Feast is offered nightly 6-6:45 for $20.

The **Nikko Japanese Steak House** is open for dinner nightly 6-9 p.m. No cheap imports here; prices are high, but the Japanese chef works right at your table slicing meats and vegetables quicker than you can say "samurai." Aside from *teppan yaki,* Nikko is known for its tempura and sushi. Western entrees are also available. An expensive but fun meal. The less expensive Samurai Sunset menu is offered 6-6:30 p.m. Serving breakfast, lunch, and dinner by the gardens is **The Moana Terrace.** This family-style restaurant is known for its buffets and is reasonably priced.

Kaanapali Beach Hotel

The restaurants here are down-to-earth, reasonably priced, and offer a native Hawaiian diet unlike any other restaurants in the area. The **Tiki Terrace** is the main food venue of the Kaanapali Beach Hotel and offers casual dining in an open-air setting. Breakfast can be à la carte or buffet style and consists mostly of American standards. It runs 7-11 a.m. daily, except for Sunday when it gives way to a Champagne Sunday Brunch that runs 9 a.m.-2 p.m. More Hawaiian-inspired dishes are on the table for this brunch, $20.95, and the whole affair is accompanied by Hawaiian music. Dinner in the Tiki Terrace runs 6-9 p.m. and reservations are recommended, tel. (808) 661-0011. Expect your meal to run around $20. Many Hawaiian dishes are on the menu, and on Friday the Tiki Terrace does a *huli huli* barbecue of whole pig. Aside from the eats, a free hula show is given nightly at 6:30 p.m.

Open daily 6 a.m.-9 p.m., the **Kaanapali Mixed Plate** restaurant serves all-you-can-eat meals and deli sandwiches 2-4 p.m. In the courtyard next to the whale-shaped pool, have a salad, sandwich, or burger from the **Tiki Bar and Grill**, 11:30 a.m.-6 p.m., or just stop for a drink when the *pu pu* are put out 3-6 p.m.

At Whalers Village

This shopping mall has a half dozen or so dining establishments. You can find everything from pizza and frozen yogurt to lobster tails. Prices range from bargain to moderate.

The well-established **Leilani's,** tel. (808) 661-4495, has a downstairs Beachside Grill open 11 a.m.-11 p.m., and the upstairs fine-dining section is open for dinner 5-10 p.m. A daily dinner special is featured 5-6:30 p.m. The Beachside Grill offers plate lunches of barbecued ribs, *paniolo* steak, or stir-fry chicken all priced around $10, along with appetizers like sashimi at a daily quote, and creamy seafood chowder for $3.50. The burgers range $5.95-7.95. Dinner from the upstairs broiler can be fresh fish of the day, filet mignon for $19.95 from the lava rock broiler, baby back pork ribs at $15.95 from the kiawe-wood smoker, or spinach, mushroom, and cheese raviolis for $10.95. A children's menu helps keep prices down, and cocktails are served until midnight.

Another favorite here is the partially indoors but mostly outdoors **Hula Grill and Barefoot Bar,** tel. (808) 667-6636. Open 11 a.m.-midnight, with dinner served 5-9:30 p.m. You can eat either in the casual Barefoot Bar under a thatch umbrella or in the more formal dining area. No matter where you sit, however, the sunsets are always great. At the Barefoot Bar, try burgers, salads, pizza, and fish. The dining room features seafood and steak in a style known as Hawaiian regional cuisine. Expect to pay about $25 for your meal. Music and hula dancing nightly.

The **Rusty Harpoon,** tel. (808) 661-3123, offers a completely new menu and pleasing atmosphere. It also has a bar that claims to serve the best daiquiris on Maui, along with a happy hour 2-6 p.m. Breakfast served 8-11 a.m. gets you started for the day with three-egg-create-your-own omelettes for $8.95, a homestyle breakfast with potatoes, eggs, and sausage links for $7.95, continental breakfast at $7.95, and a Belgian waffle bar with your choice of various fruit toppings and garnishes for $7.95. Lunch, 11 a.m.-4:30 p.m., is an extensive menu starting with appetizers like a house salad for $4.95, or crab-stuffed mushrooms for $9.95. Sandwiches are priced $8.95-9.95, burgers around the same. Dinner 5-10 p.m. offers entrees priced $16.95-24.95 including linguine Mediterranean, pineapple teriyaki chicken, and rack of lamb; only the Pacific lobster tail at $39.95 is pricier. Don't forget about the sushi and seafood bar, or the luscious desserts. To save money the Rusty Harpoon has a senior special 5-6 p.m. and a children's menu.

Castaway Cafe

The Maui Kaanapali Villas resort is the only Kaanapali condo that has a restaurant. The casual Castaway Cafe is located only steps from the beach and is open for breakfast, lunch, and dinner. Breakfast items include omelettes, items from the griddle, and fruit, all for under $7. Burgers, sandwiches, and salads are served for lunch, and for dinner, a variety of seafood, pasta, chicken, and steaks go for $13-18. Every day there are specials and the full bar can set you up with a drink any time of the day.

ENTERTAINMENT

The dinner shows accompanying the luau at the Hyatt Regency feature pure island entertainment. "Drums of the Pacific" is a musical extravaganza that you would expect from the Hyatt. There are torch-lit processions and excitingly choreographed production numbers, with all the hula-skirted *wahines* and *malo*-clad *kanes* that you could imagine. Flames add drama to the setting and the grand finale is a fire dance. Similarly, the luau at the Royal Lahaina Resort and Maui Marriott entertain you with music and dance while you stuff yourself on fine island cuisine. The Kaanapali Beach Hotel presents a free hula and music show nightly in its courtyard.

Spats at the Hyatt has a quiet piano bar, but if you are into livelier music try the **Hula Grill** or the **Makai Bar** at the Marriott. For Hawaiian music and song, check with the Kaanapali Beach Hotel.

SHOPPING

Kaanapali provides a varied shopping scene: the **Whalers Village** shopping complex, which is affordable; the **Maui Marriott** and **Royal Lahaina Resort** for some distinctive purchases; and the **Hyatt Regency, Westin Maui,** and **Sheraton** where most people get financial jitters even window-shopping.

Whalers Village
You can easily find anything at this shopping complex that you might need. Some of the shops are: **Reyn's,** for upscale tropical clothing; **Giorgiou** and others for expensive women's fashions; the exclusive **Louis Vuitton** for designer luggage; **Blue Ginger Designs,** for women's and children's resortwear and alohawear; **Dolphin Gallery,** with beautiful creations in glass, sculptures, paintings, and jewelry; **Lahaina Scrimshaw,** for fine scrimshaw pieces and other art objects ranging from affordable to expensive; **Endangered Species Store,** where you are greeted by a stuffed python and proceeds go to help endangered species; **Eyecatcher Sunglasses,** where you can take care of your eyes with shades from $150 Revos to $5 cheapies; **Jessica's Gems,** featuring the work of designer David Welty, along with coral jewelry and black Tahitian pearl rings; **Fox Photo** for film developing; **Whalers Fine Wine and Spirits,** a full-service bottle shop; and an **ABC Discount Store** for sundries. There are many other shops tucked away here and there. They come and go with regularity.

A fascinating shop is **Lahaina Printsellers,** featuring original engravings, drawings, maps, charts, and naturalist sketches ranging in age from 150 to 400 years, each with an authenticity label. The collection comes from all over the world, but the Hawaiiana collection is amazing in its depth, with many works featuring a nautical theme reminiscent of the amazing explorers who opened the Pacific. The Lahaina Printsellers have been collecting for more than 20 years and are the largest purveyor of material relating to Captain Cook in the entire Pacific Basin. Prices range from $25 for the smallest antique print up to $15,000 for rare museum-quality work.

The Whalers Village also has plenty of fast-food shops, three restaurants, West Maui Healthcare Center, a whaling museum, and a tourist information booth in the lower courtyard. The Kaanapali Shuttle, West Maui Shopping Express, and the Whalers Village Shuttle all stop at the mall.

Be sure to catch the free **hula show** at 7 p.m. Monday, Wednesday, and Sunday, and the periodic sand sculpture demonstration in front of the stage on the lower level. Contemporary Hawaiian music is also performed at the center on the last Sunday of every month.

SERVICES AND INFORMATION

Banks
There are no banks in Kaanapali; the closest are in Lahaina. Most larger hotels can help with some banking needs, especially with the cashing of traveler's checks. An ATM machine is located on the lower level of the Whalers Village mall.

Medical
The West Maui Healthcare Center maintains an office at the Whalers Village shopping mall, tel. (808) 667-9721; open 8 a.m.-10 p.m. daily. Doctors On Call, tel. (808) 667-7676, operates daily out of the Hyatt Regency and Westin Maui but makes house calls.

Information
Stop by the tourist information booth at Whalers Village mall. For a complete source of information on all aspects of the Kaanapali area, contact Kaanapali Beach Resort Association, tel. (808) 661-3271.

HONOKOWAI, KAHANA, AND NAPILI

You head for Honokowai, Kahana, and Napili if you want to enjoy Maui's west coast and not spend a bundle of money. They're not quite as pretty as Kaanapali or Kapalua, but proportionate to the money you'll save, you come out ahead. These areas are not clearly distinct from one another so you may have some trouble determining where one ends and the next begins, but generally they are separated by some stretch of residential neighborhood. Napili is at the far north end of this strip. It adjoins and in some ways is connected to Kapalua. However, because of the distinct difference between the condo setting and the manicured resort, Napili is included in this section. To get to this area, travel along Honoapiilani Highway past Kaanapali and then take Lower Honoapiilani Road through Honokowai, and continue on it to Kahana and Napili. Three short connector roads link the new highway with the old road.

Beaches

The whole strip here is rather rocky and full of coral, so not particularly good for swimming. However, there are two spots that might do and one that's a winner.

Honokowai Beach Park is right in Honokowai just across from the Food Pantry. Here you have a large lawn with palm trees and picnic tables, but a small beach. The water is shallow and tame—good for tots. The swimming is not as nice as at Kaanapali, but take a dip after shopping. Snorkeling is fair, and you can get through a break in the reef at the north end.

Kahana Beach is near the Kahana Beach Resort; park across the street. Nothing spectacular, but the protected small beach is good for catching some rays. There's a great view of Molokai and the beach is never crowded. Just south of there is **Pohaku Park**. It's a narrow strip with only a few parking stalls but is often used for picnics or by surfers.

By far the best beach in this area, and one of the best on the island, is that at **Napili Bay**. This gentle crescent slopes easily into the water, and its sandy bottom gives way to coral so snorkeling is good here as well. There are rights of

way to this perfect, but condo-lined, beach. Look for beach access signs along Napili Place and on Hui Drive. They're difficult to spot, but once on the beach there's better-than-average swimming, snorkeling, and a good place for beginning surfers and boogie boarders.

ACCOMMODATIONS

At last count there were well over three dozen condos and apartment complexes in the four miles encompassing Honokowai, Kahana, and Napili. There are plenty of private homes out here as well, which gives you a good cross-section of Hawaiian society. A multimillion-dollar spread may occupy a beach, while out in the bay is a local fisherman with his beat-up old boat trying to make a few bucks for the day. And his house may be up the street. Many of the condos built out here were controversial. Locals refused to work on some because they were on holy ground, and a few actually experienced bad luck jinxes as they were being built. The smarter owners called in *kahuna* to bless the ground and the disturbances ceased.

As usual, condos are more of a bargain the longer you stay, especially if you can share costs with a few people by renting a larger unit. And as always, you'll save money on food costs. The following should give you an idea of what's available in this area, starting from the south end moving north.

Mahana at Kaanapali

Aston's Mahana at Kaanapali is billed as an "all oceanfront resort," and in fact all apartments have an ocean view at no extra cost. The second that you walk into these reasonably priced condos and look through a large floor-to-ceiling window framing a swimming pool and the wide blue sea, your cares immediately begin to slip away. The condo sits on a point of beach at 110 Kaanapali Shore Pl., tel. (808) 661-8751 or (800) 922-7866, fax (808) 661-5510, and is one in the first group of condos north of Kaanapali. Enjoy a complete kitchen plus pool, sauna, tennis, maid service, activities desk, and a money-saving family plan. Rates begin with studios at $105-135 to one-bedroom suites at $265-300 and huge two-bedroom suites (up to six people) for $400-455. Expensive.

Embassy Vacation Resort

Open, airy, and with an atrium courtyard, this pink pyramid occupies a sliver of beach between the Mahana and Kaanapali Shores. Each suite has a kitchen, separate living area, large-screen TV, and lanai. Daily maid service is offered, as are a children's program, two restaurants, an ocean activities desk, and laundry facilities. Rates run $270-410 for a one-bedroom suite and $560 for a two-bedroom suite that sleeps six. A Marc Resort, the Embassy is located at 104 Kaanapali Shores Place, tel. (808) 661-2000 or (800) 669-3155. Luxury.

Aston Kaanapali Shores

The green tranquillity of this created oasis at 3445 Lower Honoapiilani Rd., tel. (808) 667-2211 or (800) 922-7866, fax (808) 661-0836, offers an unsurpassed view of sun-baked Lanai and Molokai just across the channel. You enter a spacious and airy open lobby, framing a living sculpture of palms and ferns. The grounds are a trimmed garden in large proportions dappled with sunlight and flowers. Soak away your cares in two whirlpools, one tucked away in a quiet corner of the central garden area for midnight romance, the other near the pool. Make use of the gift shop, fitness center, lighted tennis courts, and activities desk, or enroll the little ones in Camp Kaanapali, a program for children ages 3-8. Enjoy a romantic dinner at The Beach Club restaurant, which serves meals all day and offers entertainment in the evening. All studios and suites have been refurbished and include full kitchens, sweeping lanai, TV, a/c, and daily maid service. Prices range from an affordable studio at $195 to a two-bedroom oceanfront suite for $465. Several hotel rooms with refrigerators are also available at $165. The Aston Kaanapali Shores offers good value for the money. Luxury.

Paki Maui Resort

At 3615 Lower Honoapiilani Rd., tel. (808) 669-8235 or (800) 535-0085, this excellent-value condo presents airy and bright rooms with sweeping panoramas of the Lahaina Roads. Well-appointed studios for two begin at $179, to $299 for a two-bedroom oceanfront apartment for up to six people; additional guests $15. Amenities include maid service, a/c, cable TV, complete kitchens, pool with spa, and coin laundry facilities. Every unit has a private lanai overlooking a gem of a courtyard or the ocean. You can save money by getting a garden-view unit without sacrificing that delightful feeling that you are in the tropics. A complimentary mai tai party is held weekly for all guests. Although the Paki Maui is in town, it feels secluded the moment you walk onto this property, which forms a little oasis of tranquillity. There is no sand beach fronting the condo, but the snorkeling along the reef is excellent. A Marc Resort. Luxury.

Maui Park

On the *mauka* side of the road at 3626 Lower Honoapiilani Rd., tel. (808) 669-6622 or (800) 367-5004, this condo is a regular kind of place that offers excellent value. Rooms start at $99 for a hotel room with a refrigerator. Studios run $109-115, and suites $125-169. All studios and suites have full kitchens, and every room has a/c and a lanai. There is a large swimming pool on property, as well as a spa and barbecue area. Expensive.

Honokowai Palms

At 3666 Lower Honoapiilani Rd., tel. (808) 669-6130 or (800) 669-6284, this condo is an old standby for budget travelers. A basic two-story cinder block affair, originally used as housing for workers constructing the Sheraton down the road, it's basically a long-term place now with a few rental units. The Palms is older, but not run-down; no tinsel and glitter, but neat, clean, and adequate. There is no view. Fully furnished with kitchens, TV, full baths, and queen- or king-size beds. A swimming pool and coin laundry are on the premises. A one-bedroom unit runs $65, $75 for two bedrooms; three nights minimum. Contact the Klahani Resort for details and reservations, tel. (808) 667-2712 or (800) 628-6731. Moderate.

Hale Maui

This very reasonably priced apartment hotel, P.O. Box 516 Lahaina, HI, 96767, tel. (808) 669-6312, fax 669-1302, owned and operated by

Hans Zimmerman, offers one-bedroom apartments that can accommodate up to five people. All have a full kitchen, private lanai, color TV, and limited maid service, with washers and dryers and barbecue grills available to guests. Rates are $65-95, extra person $10, weekly and monthly discount rates available; three nights minimum. All units are bright, tasteful, and clean. The Hale Maui is an excellent choice for budget travelers who would rather spend money on having fun than on a luxurious hotel room. Moderate.

Hale Ono Loa

Four floors high with a pool in the garden, this place will give you a basic condo experience. Amenities include complete kitchens, separate living and dining areas, TV, lanai, partial maid service, and laundry facility. Hale Ono Loa, 3823 Lower Honoapiilani Rd., tel. (808) 669-0525 or (800) 300-5399, fax (808) 669-0631, has peak- and low-season rates with a $20 difference. High-season one-bedroom, ocean-view is $95, a two-bedroom ocean-view runs $185; three nights minimum, discounts for stays more than 28 days. Expensive.

Noelani

This AAA-approved condo located at 4095 Lower Honoapiilani Rd., tel. (808) 669-8374 or (800) 367-6030, fax (808) 669-7904, e-mail: noelani@maui.net, website: www.noelani-condo-resort.com, rents studios from $97, one bedrooms for $120, two and three bedrooms for $167 and $197; 10% discount offered after 28 days. Car/condo, senior, AAA, and honeymoon discounts are given. All units are oceanfront, with fully equipped kitchens, ceiling fans, color TVs, VCRs (video rental available), washer/dryers in the nonstudio units, and midweek maid service. On the grounds are two heated pools, a jacuzzi spa, and a barbecue area. You're welcomed on the first morning with a complimentary continental breakfast served poolside, where you are given an island orientation by the concierge. You'll find peace and quiet here; you can't go wrong. Expensive.

Blue Horizons B&B

True to its name, the Blue Horizons has good views of the blue Pacific looking to the west over Honokowai and Kahana. Set in a residential neighborhood below the Kapalua-West Maui Airport, this modern-style bed and breakfast offers three rooms. All have private bathrooms, one has a kitchenette, and two have refrigerators. The living room, kitchen, screened lanai, lap pool, barbecue grill, and washer/dryer are for everyone's use. Breakfast is included Mon.-Saturday. Room rates run $79-99 for two, $15 an additional person; two nights minimum. The Blue Horizon is located at 3894 Mahinahina St., perhaps the only B&B north of Lahaina on the west coast. Write or call: P.O. Box 10578, Lahaina, HI 96761, tel./fax (808) 669-1965, tel. (800) 669-1948, e-mail: chips@maui.net, website: www.maui.net/~chips. Expensive.

Sands of Kahana

You know you're in Kahana when you pass Pohaku Park and spot the distinctive blue tile roofs of this gracious complex, which forms a central courtyard area at 4299 Lower Honoapiilani Rd., tel. (808) 669-0400 or (888) 669-0400, e-mail: info@sands-of-kahana.com, website: www.sands-of-kahana.com. The condo boasts the poolside Kahana Terrace Restaurant, which serves breakfast, lunch, and dinner. The sandy-bottomed beach fronting the property is very safe and perfect for swimming and sunbathing. The Sands of Kahana gives you extraordinarily large units for the money, with lots of glass for great views, and to sweeten the pot, they're beautiful and well appointed, mostly in earth tones and colors of the islands. One-bedroom units from $185, two-bedroom units from $250, and three-bedroom units from $320 are massive with two lanai, two baths with a tub built for two, walk-in closets, and great ocean views. Each unit offers a gourmet kitchen, cable TV (free HBO), daily maid service, and washer/dryer units. The property, with pool, three tennis courts, putting green, barbecue area, fitness center, and spa, exudes a sense of peace and quiet, and although there are plenty of guests, you never feel crowded. This is where you come when you want to get away from it all, but still be within reach of the *action*. Luxury.

Kahana Villa Maui

Across the street from the Sands of Kahana, at 4242 Lower Honoapiilani Rd., tel. (808) 669-

5613 or (800) 535-0085, fax (808) 669-0397, this modern, five-story condo steps up the hillside and looks out over the channel to Lanai and Molokai. Pleasantly and casually attractive with contemporary designs and Hawaiian artwork, each of the large units features a complete kitchen, color TV, video equipment in some rooms, washer/dryer, and daily maid service. This is a suite-only condo. On the property are a pool, jacuzzi, barbecue grills, tennis and volleyball courts, an activities desk, and a sundries store. An added special feature is highly acclaimed Erik's Seafood Grotto restaurant, privately operated but located on the property. High-season rates start at $159 for a one-bedroom garden-view unit that sleeps four to $259 for a deluxe ocean-view two-bedroom suite that sleeps six. A Marc Resort. Luxury.

Kahana Village

Up the road at 4531 Lower Honoapiilani Rd., tel. (808) 669-5111 or (800) 824-3065, fax (808) 669-0974, website: www.maui.net/~village/kahana.html, this graceful vacation condominium is a group of low beach houses surrounded by well-manicured lawns on three acres. Each of the pleasantly comfortable units is individually owned, so all have a slightly different character. All are light and breezy, appointed in earth tones, and each has a complete kitchen, color TV, VCR, and large lanai. Ground-level apartments are large at 1,700 square feet and feature three bedrooms and two baths. The upper-level units are a bit smaller but still spacious at 1,200 square feet and have two bedrooms (one as a loft), two baths, and high open-beam ceilings. There is a narrow pebble beach out front, and the property has a swimming pool, jacuzzi, and barbecue grills. Rates are $195-235 for second-floor units and $255-320 for ground-level units, one to four persons, and $20 per night for each extra person; five nights minimum. Low season rates are abut 20% less; 10% discount for stays longer than 14 days. Luxury.

Kahana Sunset

This property has a superb spot on a wonderful little beach. Set alone on the small and protected Keoninue Bay, the finely sculpted gardens and trellised lanai set off the attractive and privately owned condo units that step down to the water.

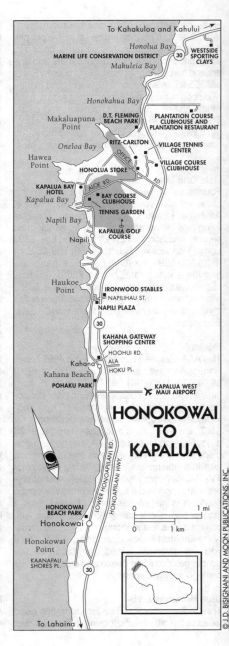

HONOKOWAI TO KAPALUA

© J.D. BISIGNANI AND MOON PUBLICATIONS, INC.

All units have full kitchens, private lanai, color TVs, washers and dryers, and daily maid service. Ceiling fans are used in each unit and louvered windows catch the cooling sea breezes. Rates are $160-180 for a one-bedroom unit, and two bedrooms run $165-265, with substantial off-season and monthly discounts. Some packages available. There is a two-night minimum, except during the year-end holidays when there's a 14-day minimum. Some credit cards accepted. At 4909 Lower Honoapiilani Road. Contact P.O. Box 10219, Lahaina, HI 96761, tel. (808) 669-8011 or (800) 669-1488, fax (808) 669-9170, website: www.kahanasunset.com. Luxury.

Napili Point Resort

Napili Point is one of the most beautifully situated complexes on Maui. This low-rise property sits on its own promontory of black lava separating Kahana and Napili, located at 5295 Honoapiilani Rd., tel. (808) 669-9222 or (800) 669-6252, fax (808) 669-7984, e-mail: napilipt@compuserve, website: www.napilipointresort.com. The reef fronting the condo is home to a colorful display of reef fish and coral, providing some of the best snorkeling on the west end. Not graced with a sand beach (it's 100 yards north along a path), nature, however, was generous in another way. Each room commands an unimpeded panorama with a breathtaking sunset view of Lanai and Molokai. You get a deluxe room for a standard price. Because of the unique setting, little development has occurred in the area, and the condo is very secluded though convenient to shops and stores. The two-story buildings offer fully furnished one- and two-bedroom units from a very affordable $184 to $279, less during regular season, with full kitchens, washers and dryers, walk-in closets, and large dressing and bath areas. Up to four people, rollaway $10, and this includes maid service, two pools, barbecue grills, and a family plan. Two-bedroom units on the second floor include a loft with its own sitting area. Floor-to-ceiling windows frame the living still life of sea and surf so you can enjoy the view from every part of the apartment. Luxury.

Napili Shores

Next door to Napili Point and overlooking Napili Bay from the lava-rock shoreline is the two-story Napili Shores condominium, 5315 Lower Honoapiilani Rd., tel. (808) 669-8061 or (800) 688-7444, fax (808) 669-5407. All units surround a tropical garden, fishpond, manicured lawn, jacuzzi, and swimming pool. Although not large nor ostentatious, each unit is comfortable and contains a full kitchen, color TV, and large lanai. Rates run $150-200 for studios, $210-245 for one-bedroom units, with an additional $15 for extra persons. Many packages available. There are three restaurants on the premises, including the Orient Express Thai Restaurant, Harry's Sushi and Pupu Bar, and the Gazebo; da Store for food items, gifts, and sundries; an activity desk; and a guest laundry. Luxury.

Napili Surf Beach Resort

Located at 50 Napili Pl., tel. (808) 669-8002 or (800) 541-0638, fax (808) 669-8004, website: www.napilisurf.com, these are reasonably priced full condo units at the south end of Napili Beach that attract mostly an older crowd with some younger families. Both the buildings and grounds have been upgraded recently. The grounds are not luxurious but nicely manicured, and have two pools and three shuffleboard lanes. Very clean rooms with full kitchens have ceiling fans, TVs, and their own lanai. Daily maid service is provided, and there's a laundry facility on premises. Garden-view studio units run $89 during regular season and $104 during high season. Ocean-view studio and one-bedroom units run $130-180, respectively, during low season and $142-199 during high season. Minimum stay is five nights, 10 during the Christmas holiday season; 10% discount for 30 days or longer. Car/condo packages and other special deals are offered. Premium.

Napili Sunset

At 46 Hui Dr., this newer AAA-approved condo has two buildings on the beach and one away from the water. All units have fully equipped kitchens, ceiling fans, color TVs, and daily maid service, and share the pool, the beachfront barbecue grill, and a laundry area. Studio apartments in the building away from the beach go for $95, one bedrooms $185, and two bedrooms $265; all have reduced rates during the low season. For additional information and reservations contact Napili Sunset at (808) 669-8083 or (800)

447-9229, fax (808) 669-2730, website: www
.napilisunset.com. Expensive.

The Mauian

Opened in 1959, this property is the oldest on the
bay and it couldn't have a better location. Don't
let the age fool you, however, as all 44 units
have been recently and attentively renovated
with new kitchens and bathrooms, pleasing period-style reproduction bamboo and hardwood
furniture, and Hawaiian artwork that helps conjure up the feeling of a slower, more hospitable
Hawaii. And you'll find hospitality here. Lots of it.
This is a gem. The '50s-era buildings blend well
with the garden, in which you'll find not only tropical flowers and bushes, but also taro and medicinal plants. The open central lawn holds a pool
and shuffleboard courts (join a tournament), and
every unit has a lanai with a view of the beach
and ocean. It's the kind of place where you might
expect to hear slack-key guitar wafting across the
garden, and you'll certainly hear the water lapping at the shore, lulling you to sleep at night.
Ceiling fans and louvered windows create air
flow; there is no air conditioning. There also are
no TVs or phones in the studios, but there is a TV
and a phone as well as video and book libraries
in the community Ohana Room, where a complimentary continental breakfast is served daily.
Because of the hospitality and sense of *ohana*
(family), many guests return year after year.
Based on double occupancy, rates for low and
high seasons are: $155/$175 for a beachfront
unit, $140/$160 for beach-view units, and
$125/$145 for garden units; $10 each extra per-
son. The Mauian is located at 5441 Lower
Honoapiilani Road. For information and reservations call (808) 669-6205 or (800) 367-5034,
fax (808) 669-0129, e-mail: info@mauian.com,
website: www.mauian.com. Premium.

Napili Kai Beach Club

At 5900 Honoapiilani Rd., tel. (808) 669-6271
or (800) 367-5030, fax (808) 669-5740, e-mail:
nkbc@maui.net, website: www.napilikai.com,
this accommodation is the last in Napili before
you enter the landscaped expanse of Kapalua.
The Napili Kai Beach Club, the dream-come-
true of now deceased Jack Millar, was built before regulations forced properties back from the
water. Jack Millar's ashes are buried near the

restaurant under a flagpole bearing the U.S. and
Canadian flags. The setting is idyllic, with the
beach a crescent moon with gentle wave action. The bay itself is a swim-only area with no
pleasure craft allowed. It's $170 for a garden-
view hotel room to $550 for an oceanfront luxu-
ry two-bedroom suite, but amenities include a
kitchenette, private lanai, air-conditioning in most
units, complimentary snorkel gear, daily tea
party, activities desk, and all the comforts of
home. Several special packages are available.
There are four pools, "Hawaii's largest whirlpool,"
an exercise room, a croquet lawn, putting greens,
and tennis courts on property, and the Kapalua
Bay Golf Course is just a nine-iron away. All
rooms have Japanese touches complete with
shoji screens. There's fine dining, dancing, and
entertainment at the Sea House Restaurant overlooking the beach. Luxury.

FOOD AND ENTERTAINMENT

The Beach Club

Whether you're a guest or not, a quiet and lovely restaurant in which to dine is The Beach Club
at the Aston Kaanapali Shores. One of Honokowai's best-kept secrets, the restaurant is centered in the condo's garden area and opens directly onto the sea. Request a table on the terrace overlooking the pool for an especially romantic setting. The restaurant changes throughout the day from a casual cafe in the morning to
a more formal candlelit room in the evening, but
always the service is friendly. Breakfast, served
7-11:30 a.m., with early bird specials until 9 a.m.,
can be *paniolo* French toast, scrambled eggs
and bacon, or a variety of gourmet omelettes.
Lunch, served 11:30 a.m.-3 p.m., offers sandwiches and lighter fare. The evening dinner
menu, served 5:30-9:30 p.m., whets your appetite with sautéed mushrooms or Cajun *ahi*
served with wasabi and *shoyu.* The soup of the
day and salads lead to main entrees like chicken
marsala, grilled scallops, or clams pesto with
linguine, with most in the $15-20 range. A chil-
dren's menu is also offered, and entertainment is
provided several nights a week.

A Pacific Cafe Honokowai

Building on a well-deserved reputation, Jean-

Marie Josselin has opened this new restaurant in the Honokowai Marketplace at 3350 Lower Honoapiilani Rd., tel. (808) 669-2724. Open daily 5-10 p.m.

Lourdes Kitchenette
At Da Rose Mall, 3481 Lower Honoapiilani Rd., tel. (808) 669-5725, just as you enter Honokowai proper, Lourdes offers takeout or delivery service along with a few red picnic tables out front where you can eat. Open daily until 4 p.m. They prepare plate lunches and simple Filipino food with everything under $6.50. Lourdes is small, simple, clean, and adequate.

Pizza and Deli
Pizza Hut, in 5-A Rent a Space at 3600 Lower Honoapiilani Rd., tel. (808) 669-6996, open Sun.-Thurs. 11 a.m.-11 p.m., weekends until midnight, offers carry-out and delivery pizza. For a quick bite, **Honokowai Okozuya Deli** is available for an amazing selection of Chinese, Japanese, Italian, Mexican, and vegetarian foods.

Erik's Seafood Grotto
At 4242 Lower Honoapiilani Rd., second floor of Kahana Villa, tel. (808) 669-4806, Erik's is open daily for lunch 11:30 a.m.-2 p.m. and dinner 5-10 p.m. It is decorated in an appropriately nautical theme, with fish tanks, divers' helmets, and mounted trophy fish. The early bird specials run 5-6 p.m. and cost $12-14. Bouillabaisse, cioppino, and baked stuffed prawns are among the chef's specialties. Shellfish, lobster, steak, and poultry are on the menu, but the real focus is the wide variety of fish that can be prepared in numerous ways. Most dinners run $17-25 with a good selection of appetizers. Erik's is known to have the *best* selection of fresh fish on Maui—up to nine selections nightly. This is a quality restaurant with excellent service. The food is delicious but the prices are not cheap.

Kahana Terrace Restaurant
Under the blue roof by the pool at the Sands of Kahana Resort, 4299 Lower Honoapiilani Rd., tel. (808) 669-5399, this open-air and moderately priced restaurant is good for sunsets. Breakfast offerings feature omelettes and items from the griddle; lunch is mostly sandwiches and burgers. Appetizers like coconut shrimp and

crab quesadilla and various salads precede entrees that can be fresh catch of the day at $16.95, New York steak for $17.95, or shrimp fettuccine at $14.95. A couple of early bird specials run $9.95. This is not fine cuisine, but is nutritious and satisfying. Live music nightly 5-7 p.m.

Dollie's
Located at 4310 Honoapiilani Hwy. in the Kahana Manor Shops, tel. (808) 669-0266, Dollie's is open daily 11 a.m.-midnight, with happy hour 4-6 p.m. Dollie's features several TVs with satellite hook-up for sporting events, cappuccino, and weekend entertainment. The good food and fair prices on Dollie's menu feature 20 sandwiches from which to choose, all priced around $7.50; plates of lasagna, fettuccine Alfredo, or linguine marinara for $9.95-13.95; pizza by the tray for $7.95-20 or by the slice during happy hour for $1.25; and plenty of finger foods. The sandwiches and other entrees are good, but the pizza is the best. The bar has a wide selection of domestic and imported beers, wines, and a daily exotic drink special. Dollie's, one of the few eateries in the area, is usually a laid-back pub/pizzeria but can get hopping on the weekend and is perhaps the most happening place for late night get-togethers in Kahana.

China Boat
The China Boat restaurant at 4474 Lower Honoapiilani Hwy. in Kahana, tel. (808) 669-5089, is open daily for lunch 11:30 a.m.-2 p.m. and dinner 5-10 p.m. It's almost elegant with its highly polished, black lacquer furniture, pink tablecloths, scroll paintings, and island-inspired prints, but the food quality is variable. A typically large MSG-free Chinese menu offers seafood, beef, chicken, vegetables, pork, and noodle dishes at a reasonable price.

Roy's Kahana Bar and Grill
Finally McDonald's has a culinary purpose—to landmark Roy's Kahana Bar and Grill, located at the new Kahana Gateway Mall, 4405 Honoapiilani Hwy., Kahana, tel. (808) 669-6999, open daily for dinner 5:30-10 p.m., where Roy Yamaguchi, the restaurant's founder and inspirational chef, and the executive chef work kitchen magic preparing the best in Pacific Rim cuisine. Roy has a penchant for locating his restaurants in

pragmatic shopping malls. At Roy's Kahana, the surroundings are strictly casual, like a very upscale cafeteria. The enormous room, reverberating with the clatter of plates and the low hum of dinner conversations, has 40-foot vaulted ceilings, a huge copper-clad preparation area, heavy koa tables and booths, track lighting, and windows all around. Roy's philosophy is to serve truly superb dishes post haste, but impeccably, focusing on the *food* as the dining experience, not the surroundings. Although part of the menu changes every night, you could start your culinary extravaganza with island-style pot stickers with a spicy almond sate peanut sauce for $5.75, wood-roasted Sichuan baby back pork ribs for $7.50, or treat yourself to penne pasta with grilled shrimp, or pesto and tomato sauce for $8.95. There are also individual *imu* pizzas for less than $7.50. Fresh salads include a crispy Upcountry romaine salad with a creamy parmesan garlic dressing for only $6.75, and savory fresh mahimahi with cilantro vinaigrette for $7.95. Move on to the entrees like hibachi-style chicken at $15.95, grilled filet mignon $24.95, or seared Tex-Mex grilled marlin with smoked scallops and risotto for $21.95. Desserts feature the chocolate macadamia tart or a fluffy dark chocolate soufflé at $6.50 (allow 20 minutes to prepare). The full bar serves beer, mixed drinks, and personally selected wine by the bottle or glass. Eating at Roy's "elegant cafeteria" is no place to linger over a romantic cocktail. It's more like sipping the world's finest champagne from a beer mug. But the best by any other name is still the best!

Roy's Nicolina Restaurant

Nicole Yamaguchi has a restaurant named in her honor, just next door to her dad's place at the Kahana Gateway, open daily from 5:30 p.m., tel. (808) 669-5000. The restaurant features Euro-Asian cuisine heavily spiced with California and Southwestern dishes. For example, try a gourmet pizza-like flatbread covered in red onions, tomatoes, and pesto; or Cajun shrimp and handmade sausage for under $6. Appetizers can be pan-fried calamari with anchovy mayonnaise, or seared goat cheese and eggplant with cilantro pesto and red pepper vinaigrette for under $9. Entrees are delicious and fascinating, offerings like roasted orange-ginger plum duck at $19.50, or Yankee pot roast with mashed pota-

toes and garlic spinach for only $11.95. While much of the menu at Nicolina's is the same across the hall at Roy's, about half is created only for this restaurant and it too changes nightly. If dad's place is filled up, you'll love the quieter Nicolina's, a "Sichuan-spiced taco chip off the old block."

Napili Plaza Restaurants

The following restaurants are all located at Napili Plaza, easily spotted just off the highway. **Koho's Grill and Bar,** an American standard comfortably appointed with booths and tables, ceiling fans, and wide-screen TVs with satellite feed, also has a full-service bar. The menu offers chili cheese fries for $5.95, soups and dinner salads for $2.45, and fish and chips for $6.25. A sandwich board offers everything from BLTs to a club sandwich, all for under $6.25, while full-dress burgers are priced around $6. Plate lunches, all around $6.50, include teriyaki beef or chicken and mahimahi, and some standard fajitas run about $8.50 More substantial entrees include rib plate at $11.95 and a strip steak for $14.95. Open 11 a.m.-11 p.m. daily, with early bird specials 4-7 p.m.

Maui Taco has reasonably priced, health-conscious fast food and a variety of drinks. Try a chimichanga for up to $5.95, a tostada for under $5, tacos for about $2, or a two-fisted burrito that will keep you full all day for $6.95. The salsa and guacamole are made fresh daily. No MSG or lard is used.

Subway Submarine, open daily 7 a.m.-10 p.m., Friday and Saturday to midnight, serves double-fisted fatso sandwiches.

Napili Shores Resort

Three restaurants are located at this resort, 5315 Honoapiilani Hwy., about one mile before Kapalua town. The **Orient Express,** tel. (808) 669-8077, is open daily for dinner only 5:30-10 p.m. The restaurant serves Thai and Chinese food with a flair for spices; duck salad and stuffed chicken wings are a specialty. The early bird special, served before 6:30 p.m., is a five-course dinner for $11.95. The full but not extensive menu of finely spiced foods includes Orient Express's well-known curry dishes; takeout available. Most entrees are in the $10-13 range. Overlooking the koi pond at the resort, this restaurant is a good choice. Sharing the same space with the Orient Express is **Harry's Sushi and Pupu Bar,** where everything is prepared before you at the counter. Nigiri sushi orders run $4-6, sashimi $9-15, with a few other items on the menu. Both Harry's and the Orient Express are associated with the fine dining restaurants Chez Paul in Olowalu and the Lobster Cove Restaurant in Wailea.

The **Gazebo,** tel. (808) 669-5621, open 7:30 a.m.-2 p.m., one of the best-kept secrets in the area, is a little brown gazebo with louvered windows next to the resort pool. Be prepared for a line. Locals in the know come here for a breakfast of the Gazebo's famous banana, pineapple, and especially the macadamia nut pancakes for $5.25. There are also eggs and omelettes of all sorts under $6.95. The lunch menu features a range of sandwiches from $4.75 to $6.95, along with burgers and lunch plates under $7.95. You can enjoy a world-class view sitting inside or outside the Gazebo for down-home prices.

The Sea House

At the Napili Kai Beach Club, tel. (808) 669-1500, the Sea House is open daily for breakfast 8-11 a.m., lunch 12-2 p.m., and dinner 5:30-9 p.m.; reservations suggested. Inside the semi-open-air restaurant, appetizers like lemongrass-crusted prawns range $8-12, and soups and salads are equally reasonable. Dinner choices, all served with almond flatbread, vegetables, and rice pilaf or potato, include fresh catch (priced daily); seared pork loin medallions for $17; seasoned and broiled rack of lamb for $24; and a special "lite" fare. Besides the normal menu, every night brings a special dinner menu, but the best is the lobster tail dinner on Thursday for $17.95. A full wine list includes selections from California and France. There is Hawaiian music nightly and a wonderful Friday night Napili Kai Foundation children's Polynesian show (dinner seating at 6 p.m., show at 7:30 p.m.; $35 adults, $20 children) put on by local children who have studied their heritage under the guidance of the foundation. If you just want to soak up the rays and gorgeous view of Napili Bay, you can wear your swimwear and have a cool drink or light fare on the **Whale Watcher's Bar.**

SHOPPING AND SERVICES

Da Rose Mall

Look for this tiny mall located at the south end of town at 3481 Lower Honoapiilani Rd., where you'll find **A & B Rentals and Sportswear,** tel. (808) 669-0027, open daily 9 a.m.-5 p.m., specializing in mopeds, bicycles, snorkel gear, boogie boards, and surfboards. Prices are: mopeds $13 for two hours or $150 per week; bicycles $15 for 24 hours, $60 per week; snorkeling gear $2.50 per day and $9 per week. Boogie boards, surfboards, and even fishing poles are rented by the day or week. The sportswear includes lycra mini dresses, tie-dyed dresses, sundresses, sarongs, T-shirts, and men's printed shirts. In front is **Lourdes Kitchenette,** and around the side are **One Hour Wiki Wiki Photo,** whose name says it all; **Blooming Rose Boutique** studio for women's fashions, and the **Macadamia Nut Shop,** selling gifts and souvenirs. Next door is **ABC Store,** hours 6:30 a.m.-11 p.m., a minimarket selling everything from resortwear to wine.

Every Monday and Thursday morning 6:30-11:30 a.m. a **farmers' market** is held in the parking lot of Da Rose Mall, with vendors selling mostly food items and some clothing and crafts.

5-A Rent a Space Mall

At 3600 Lower Honoapiilani Hwy., this mall is usually located by reference to the Pizza Hut here. Honokowai Okozuya Deli is the other eatery in this strip of shops. Here you'll find **Snorkels N' More,** tel. (808) 665-0804, open daily 8 a.m.-5 p.m., which has reasonable rates for sales and rental of snorkel gear, boogie boards, surfboards, and other water equipment. There are a usually a few bikes for rent as well, and same-day film processing. If you're staying at one of the condos in the area, **Kelly's Video,** tel. (808) 669-6004, can provide the evening's entertainment.

Honokowai Food Pantry

Aside from the Napili Supermarket in Napili Plaza, the only real place north of Lahaina that has a full selection of groceries, fruits, vegetables, meats, and sundries is the Food Pantry located at 3636 Lower Honoapiilani Rd., tel. (808) 669-6208, open daily 6:30 a.m.-11 p.m. The prices are just about right at this supermarket. Condo convenience stores in the area are good in a pinch but charge way too much. Stock up here; it's worth the drive.

The **Honokowai post office** is inside the Honokowai Food Pantry. Never busy, this full-service post office accepts packages.

Kahana Manor Shops

Aside from **Dollie's,** in the Kahana Manor Shops there is the **Kahana Manor Groceries,** a one-stop sundries and liquor store open Mon.-Sat. 7 a.m.-11 p.m.; the **Women Who Run With Wolves** boutique for beach and athletic wear and accessories for active women; and the **Wiki Wiki Photo II** for all your camera needs. **West Maui Cycles,** tel. (808) 669-1169, rents bikes by the day or week, so stop in for some good exercise and inexpensive fun. The sundry store at **The Kahana Villa** has most everything from beer to sunglasses, plus fresh fruits and vegetables.

Kahana Gateway Shopping Center

At this newest shopping addition to the Kahana area, easily spotted along Rt. 30 by **McDonald's** golden arches, you'll find a **gas station,** a **Whalers General Store, Bank of Hawaii,** and the **Koin-Op Laundromat.** However, the premier stop is **Roy's Kahana Bar and Grill,** one of the finest gourmet restaurants on Maui, and

Roy's Nicolina Restaurant next door. Also at the center is the **Maui Dive Shop,** tel. (808) 669-3800, a full-service water activities store where you can rent snorkel equipment, scuba gear, and beach accessories; **O'Rourke's Tourist Trap,** for a 99-cent beach mat, artificial lei, or postcards; **Gallerie Hawaii** for contemporary artwork; and **Kafe Kahana,** tel. (808) 669-6699, which not only has the sweetest buns in town, but also sandwiches and salads.

Napili Plaza

Napili's newest shopping center offers the full service **First Hawaiian Bank; Napili Supermarket,** open daily 6:30 a.m.-11 p.m., featuring fresh fish; **Mail Services Plus,** open daily 9 a.m.-6 p.m., Saturday until 1 p.m., closed Sunday, for all your postal and shipping needs; and several inexpensive eateries.

Napili Village Shopping Center

At 5425 Lower Honoapiilani Rd., the **Napili Village General Store,** tel. (808) 669-6773, is a well-stocked little store and known landmark, good for last-minute items, with fairly good prices for where it is. You can pick up picnic items and sandwiches, groceries, sundries, and liquor. Next door is **Snorkel Bob's,** tel. (808) 669-9603, where you can rent snorkel equipment (prescription masks available) and boogie boards for only $15 per week; **da Store** at Napili Shores is mainly a gift shop and convenience store, open 8 a.m.-9 p.m. daily

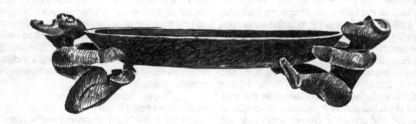

KAPALUA

Kapalua sits like a crown atop Maui's head. One of the newest areas on Maui to be developed, it's been nicely done. Out here are the Kapalua Bay and Ritz-Carlton luxury hotels, upscale condominium communities, exclusive shops, three championship golf courses, two tennis centers, horseback riding at the Ironwood Ranch stables, a sporting clays shooting range, sweeping vistas, and terrific beaches (website: Kapaluamaui.com). All of this has been carved out of the 23,000 acre Honolua Ranch.

The complimentary **Kapalua Shuttle** runs throughout the resort for resort guests. While there is no regular schedule, it does make a continuous round of stops at the hotels and villas, tennis courts, golf courses, and the Kapalua-West Maui Airport.

BEACHES AND BAYS

Kapalua Beach

Just past Napili Bay is the equally as nice Kapalua Bay with its fine crescent beach that's popular though usually not overcrowded. Look for access just past the Napili Kai Beach Club. Park in the public lot and follow the path through the tunnel below the Bay Club restaurant to the beach. The well-formed reef has plenty of fish for snorkeling. Also here are restrooms, showers, and a hotel beach concession.

Oneloa Beach

Located around the point from Kapalua Beach, Oneloa is a small sandy beach down a steep path, where swimming is good and locals come to surf. Seldom visited and private; parking available.

D.T. Fleming Beach Park

One of Maui's best—a long wide beach backed by wonderful shade trees. This beach park is on Honoapiilani Highway just past the Ritz-Carlton where the road dips back down to the coast. Here you'll find parking, showers, barbecue grills, and excellent swimming except in winter, when there's a pounding surf. There's fair snorkeling

here and good surfing and body boarding. This has become the beach for the Ritz-Carlton so the south end of the beach closest to the hotel has become a bit exclusive while the rest maintains its very local flavor.

Mokuleia Bay

Also known as "Slaughterhouse," Mokuleia Bay is about 200-300 yards after mile marker 32; walk down to the water through a stand of trees. This beach has great bodysurfing, but terribly dangerous currents in the winter when the surf is rough. Be careful. Follow the trail to the left for the beach. The path straight ahead takes you to a rocky lava flow. This entire area, plus all of adjacent Honolua Bay, is a Marine Life Conservation District and the underwater life is fabulous. Some of the best snorkeling in the area.

Honolua Bay

Just past Mokuleia Bay heading north, look for a dirt road, then park. The bay is good for swimming, snorkeling, and especially surfing. Many people stay the night without much problem. For good views of the surfers, drive a little farther along the road and park along the cliff just as the road reaches the top, or drive down the dirt road at the edge of the pineapple field for a spot—there will be lots of cars on a good wave day.

ACCOMMODATIONS

Kapalua Bay Villas

Several groups of vacation rentals dot this spacious resort. They range from one-bedroom villas to five-bedroom luxury homes. Each is individually owned so all are decorated differently, but all are equipped with full kitchens, a/c and fans, washers and dryers, telephone, and TV, and each has twice-weekly maid service. All groups of villas also have swimming pools, barbecue grills, and maintained gardens. One-bedroom villas with a fairway view start at $185 and climb rapidly to the two-bedroom oceanfront villas for $400. Daily rates for the luxury homes run $995 for three-bedroom to $4,000-5,000 for five-bedroom ones. Some golf packages and car/condo deals are also offered. The Kapalua Villa Reception Center is located at 550 Office Rd., Kapalua, HI 96761. Write or call for information and reservations, tel. (808) 669-8088 or (800) 545-0018, fax (808) 669-5234, website: www.kapaluavillas.com. Luxury.

Ritz-Carlton Kapalua

The green sweep of tended lawns fading into the distant sea foaming azure heralds your entrance into an enchanted realm as you wind your way down the serpentine roadway leading to the Ritz-Carlton Kapalua, One Ritz-Carlton Dr., Kapalua, HI 96761, tel. (808) 669-6200, (800) 262-8440, or (800) 241-3333, fax (808) 665-0026, e-mail: mauiritz@maui.net, website: ritz-carlton.com. At the porte cochere a waiting bellman will park your car. Enter the main hall and relax in the formal parlor of overstuffed chairs, marble-topped tables, and enormous flower arrangements. Evenings in the hall bring mellow entertainment softly illuminated by emerald-green chandeliers. Register, then peer through a huge set of double doors that look straight out into the central courtyard. Walk ahead to the terrace built from Chinese slate and peer into the floral heart of the hotel grounds. Below are seashell-shaped swimming pools and fluttering palms. The roof line of the great hotel, borrowed from the Orient, covers the two wings that descend the hill toward the sea, creating an enormous central area between. Stroll the halls hung with the fine works by prominent island artists and last-century reproductions. Sit in a tiny alcove and let the music of sea and wind lull you into deep relaxation and contemplation. All this, coupled with the dark and rich woodwork, thick patterned carpets, floral drapery, and pineapple-pattern wallpaper, define the Ritz as the epitome of elegance and luxury.

On the beach, a sweeping crescent of white sand is embraced by two sinewy arms of jet-black lava. It becomes immediately obvious why the diminutive promontory was called Kapalua, "Arms Embracing the Sea," by the ancient Hawaiians who lived here. Notice on the rise above the sea a rounded shoulder of banked earth separated from the main hotel grounds by a low hedge: the spirits of the ancient *ali'i* linger here in this an-

cient burial ground. The original construction plans were altered and the hotel was moved away from the area in an attempt to protect it. A *kahuna* was asked to perform the ancient *mele* to appease the spirits, and to reconsecrate the land, passing the *kahu* (caretaking) of it to the Ritz. Although the small parcel was deeded to the state, the hotel management and staff alike take their responsibility very seriously.

The hotel's Village Tennis Center, combined with the Kapalua Tennis Garden a few minutes away, represent the largest private tennis facility in the state. The Village Tennis Center has 10 courts, five lighted for evening play, and a full-service pro shop. A few minutes away by shuttle, in different directions, are three championship golf courses: the Plantation Course, the Village Course, and the Bay Course. Both golf and tennis packages are available. The hotel also has a fitness center complete with stairmasters, massage therapists, beauty salon, sauna, and steam rooms. Other hotel offerings include the Ritz Kids children's program, the Aloha Fridays program of activities, a croquet lawn, putting green, business center, the Art School at Kapalua, and ecotours.

Located in two wings off the main reception hall, the luxury rooms, all with their own private lanai and sensational view, are a mixture of kings, doubles, and suites. Done in muted neutral tones, the rooms feature handcrafted quilts, twice-daily room attendance, turndown service complete with complimentary orchid and rich chocolates, remote control color TV, 24-hour room service, fully stocked honor bar, and an in-room safe. Wardrobes, hung with plush terry robes and plump satin hangers, feature automatic lights, steam irons, and ironing boards. The spacious bathrooms, regal with calcatta fabricatta Italian marble, offer wide, deep tubs, separate commodes, and shower stalls along with dressing and vanity mirrors, double sinks, hair dryers, and name-brand grooming products. Rates begin at $260 for a garden view to $375 for a deluxe oceanfront view. The Ritz-Carlton Club, an exclusive floor with its own concierge, and featuring continental breakfast, light lunch, cocktails, cordials, and a full spread of evening hors d'oeuvres, is $450. Suites from an executive one-bedroom to the magnificent Ritz-Carlton

Suite run $495-2,700. Many special packages are offered. Luxury.

Kapalua Bay Hotel

This, like other grand hotels, is more than a place to stay; it's an experience. The hotel steps down the hillside from its 6th-level entrance. The main lobby is partially open and accented with an enormous skylight. Plants trail from the tall ceiling, and the walls are hung with paintings by Peggy Hopper. All colors are soothing and subdued. A tiny brook splits the Gardenia Court restaurant and Lehua Lounge on the lower level of the lobby, and the view over the garden lawns and out to sea is spectacular. The clean lines of the hotel, its sparse decoration, and contemporary elegance let the view speak for itself without distraction. The ocean view vies for your attention here, while the pool pulls you down to the garden, and the beach lures you to the water. Not overly ornamented, guest rooms are done in muted colors—off whites, tans, and tropical greens. Each spacious room is neatly laid out with an entertainment center, three telephones, electronic safe, a soft couch and easy chairs, and louvered doors to the lanai. The well-lit bathrooms have his and her sinks at each end of the room, separate dressing closets, and individual areas for the tub, shower, and commode. Marble, tile, and chrome are used throughout. Concierge service and twice-daily maid service are additional amenities for guests. There are three restaurants and a lounge in the complex, a fitness room, a small arcade with plenty of shops, a multitude of daily activities including Kamp Kapalua for kids, magnificent golf and tennis nearby, and a resort shuttle to get you to whereever you need to go in the resort. The least expensive room in the hotel is one with a garden view at $275. An ocean view runs $375, oceanfront prime $525, and the suites are $800-1,600; $50 each additional person 18 and older. Available for a reasonable sum, the American plan consists of breakfast and dinner with your room. The Kapalua Bay Hotel is associated with the Halekulani and Waikiki Parc hotels in Honolulu. Contact the Kapalua Bay Hotel at One Bay Dr., Kapalua, HI 9761, tel. (808) 669-5656 or (800) 367-8000, fax (808) 669-4690, website: www.kapaluabay-hotel.com. Luxury.

FOOD

Jameson's Grill and Bar

Don't underestimate this excellent restaurant just because it's located at a golf course. The Kapalua Bay Golf Course provides the backdrop and the restaurant provides the filling delicious food. The main room with its flagstone floor and open beam ceiling is richly appointed with koa wood, and large windows frame a sweeping view of the super-green fairways of the golf course. Sit inside or out on the patio. From the lunch menu select a calamari strip appetizer for $7.95 or a sandwich and salad for under $15. Lunch is served 11 a.m.-3 p.m., dinner 5-10 p.m. The dinner menu is more substantial. Start with an appetizer like Thai summer rolls for $8.95 or seared sashimi for $12.95, and move on to a soup or one of the many fine salads. Entrees include fish of the day for $17.95-23.95, herbed half chicken for $17.95, and rack of lamb at $24.95. To relax and soak up the scenery you can order dessert or sip wine selected from an extensive list. All items can be ordered takeout. An excellent restaurant with a lovely setting at 200 Kapalua Drive. Call (808) 669-5653 for reservations.

Ritz-Carlton Restaurants

Dining at the Ritz-Carlton is a wonderful gastronomic experience with three main restaurants from which to choose, plus a lobby and sunset lounge and a beachside cafe, all under the skillful management of executive chef, Patrick Callarec. **The Terrace Restaurant,** open daily for breakfast 6:30-11:30 a.m. (buffet to 10:30) and for dinner 5:30-10 p.m., informal and relaxed, overlooks the central courtyard with the dramatic sea vista beyond. Tastefully appointed in green and burgundy, the restaurant features Pacific Rim and Asian food, with an emphasis on Japanese cuisine. Although there is an extensive à la carte breakfast menu, the house specialty is a breakfast buffet for $16.50 or $12 for a lighter selection. Apple blintzes, eggs royal and Benedict, Molokai French toast, plump sausages, grilled potatoes, and sizzling strips of bacon are surrounded by fruits, fresh juices, and jams. For dinner, Chef Steve Falsetti starts you with chilled oysters in chili-pepper water mignonette for $12.50, fried tofu and shiitake mushrooms in ginger broth for $8.50, or island clam chowder at $7.50. Main courses include lamb osso bucco for $21; grilled chow mein noodles with clams, shrimp, and scallops in a ginger sauce for $19; or seared salmon with asparagus and fennel $27. Monday evening brings an Asian buffet, Wednesday it's Italian, Friday the buffet is seafood, and Saturday it's a *paniolo* buffet inspired by the cowboys of Hawaii.

The **Anuenue Room,** serving dinner Tues.-Sat. 6-9:30 p.m. and Sunday Champagne brunch 10:30 a.m.-2:30 p.m. ($29 including champagne), is the hotel's most elegant restaurant. Reservations are recommended and resort attire is required. Formal yet intimate, the restaurant offers Hawaiian provincial cuisine prepared by master chef Craig Connole. Appetizers, salads, and soups fit for the *ali'i* include seared duck foie gras and potato risotto for $18, roasted eggplant and Kula tomato soup $12, and grilled quail with lettuce salad with red onion marmalade and balsamic vinegar $14. The finest entrees include herb-crusted onaga for $38, a wonderful sesame-seed rack of lamb with poha berries and pineapple chutney for $39, and grilled marinated chicken breast with basil garlic just $27. Desserts are mango tarte, banana crème brûlée, or a fluffy souffle of the day prepared just for you. The food is wonderful but the view over the lawns, sea, and Molokai in the distance is an added pleasure.

The **Banyan Tree,** an informal poolside restaurant open for lunch and appetizers 11:30 a.m.-4 p.m., is a good stop on your way to or from the beach. Fashioned like a Mediterranean court with stone floor and copper-and-green tiled bar, the restaurant offers seating in high-backed chairs at teakwood tables, with mood lighting reminiscent of old oil lamps. Dine alfresco on the redwood deck and watch cavorting whales just offshore. Selections start with beefsteak tomatoes salad with Upcountry greens and buffalo mozzarella for $15; mahimahi sandwich for $14; or penne pasta smothered in a sauce of roma tomatoes, fried capers, roasted peppers, and garlic for $12.50. Families will enjoy a selection of gourmet pizzas and calzones for $12-16.50, all from a wood-burning oven.

At the **lobby lounge** you'll find appetizers, salads, sandwiches, fruit, and coffee to have while you sit and gaze out over the courtyard from the patio. Down by the beach, on a patio surrounded by a manicured coconut grove, is the **Beachhouse,** serving tropical libations, healthy fruit smoothies, burgers, and sandwiches for under $12.

Kapalua Bay Resort Restaurants

The resort has three dining spots. The elegant **Bay Club,** tel. (808) 669-8008, offers fine dining for lunch 11 a.m.-1:30 p.m. and dinner 6-9:30 p.m. on a promontory overlooking the beach and Molokai in the distance. Traditionally elegant, there is a dress code; expect to spend at least $25 for a superbly prepared Mediterranean entree with overtones of flavors from the Pacific and Asia. Piano music nightly. The open-air and contemporary **Gardenia Court** restaurant on the lower lobby level of the main building serves breakfast and dinner. Best known for its Friday evening seafood buffet and Sunday brunch, Gardenia Court always offers Hawaiian music in the evening. Resortwear required. The casual **Plumeria Terrace** restaurant is located at poolside in the garden below the main building. Stop here for burgers, sandwiches, and light meals, or for a refreshing beer or tropical drink 11 a.m.-5 p.m. Aside from these fine restaurants, the **Lehua Lounge** in the entrance lobby serves *pu pu* and drinks in the evening, always with relaxing music to help let the cares of the day slip away.

Located in the Kapalua Bay Shops is **Sansei** seafood restaurant and sushi bar, which serves more than just Japanese sushi—a whole variety of Pacific Rim food and drinks from the bar. An early bird special is offered 5:30-6 p.m. Open 5:30-11 p.m. Sun.-Wed., until 1 a.m. Thursday and Friday when there is laser karaoke.

The Plantation House

Above Kapalua on the road leading to the Plantation Golf Course Club House, you'll find the lovely Plantation House Restaurant, open daily 8-11 a.m. for breakfast, 11 a.m.-3 p.m. for lunch, and 5:30-9 p.m. for dinner, tel. (808) 669-6299. Inside, the split-level floor, gabled roof, natural wood, and carpeted and marbled floor add elegance, but the real beauty is the natural still life that pours through the floor-to-ceiling French doors. Kapalua lies at your feet, Molokai floats upon the still blue sea, and the West Maui Mountains rise behind in a paisley of emerald green, indigo, and cloud-dappled grays. For breakfast, the extensive menu offers light fare like home-baked muffins for $2; a hearty rancher's break-fast of two eggs, toast, two scoops of rice or breakfast potatoes, grilled ham, bacon, or Por-tuguese sausage all for $8; or smoked salmon Benedict to $10. For lunch, start with pan-fried crab cakes served with roasted pepper aioli for $7, an oriental chicken salad for $8, or black-ened chicken Caesar for $8. A half-pound dou-ble-fisted Plantation House burger is available for $6.50 and a grilled chicken breast sandwich for $8.50. The dinner menu tempts your palate with scallop skewers wrapped in apple-smoked bacon for $8, hot and spicy seared sashimi at a daily quote, and warm goat cheese on a bed of fresh, mixed local greens with passion fruit vinaigrette for $7. The chef prepares *pasta al giorno* for $16, or tops it with scallops or shrimp for $21. Sautéed jumbo prawns with garlic mashed pota-toes costs $21, and broiled double-cut lamb chops, shallots, and rosemary au jus runs $22. To complement your Mediterranean-style din-ner, the mostly Californian wine list also offers a smattering of French and Italian wines, and the full bar can prepare any drink that you may de-sire.

Honolua Store

Just on the right before the Ritz-Carlton, this small general store also serves reasonably priced light meals and sandwiches during the week. The breakfast menu, served 6-10 a.m. offers "The Hobo"—eggs, sausage, and rice for $3.50 —or two pancakes for $2.75. Plate lunches, sandwiches, grilled items, and salads all run under $7 and are served 10 a.m.-3 p.m. Sit at a table on the front porch and overlook the broad lawns and tall pine trees of the exclusive planned community of Kapalua. This is by far the cheap-est place to eat in the area.

Village Cafe

This cafe at the Kapalua Village Golf Course clubhouse serves light meals, better than you would expect from a small snack shop with out-door seating. Burgers, sandwiches, salads, and sides are all available, but the cafe is especially famous for its hot dogs, a steamed Vienna all-beef quarter pounder with all the trimmings on a French roll, and supposedly the best on the is-land. All are reasonably priced.

SHOPPING

Kapalua Shops

A cluster of exclusive shops service the resort, in-cluding **McInerny** with fine women's apparel; **Kapalua Kids** for the younger set; and **Kapalua Logo Shop** if you want to show off that you've at least been to the Kapalua Resort, since all items of clothing sport the butterfly logo. **Mandalay Imports** has a potpourri of silks and cottons from the East, especially Thailand. Visit **La Perle** for pearls, diamonds, and other jewels, and **South Seas** for antiques, art, and jewelry. **La-haina Gallery** has a wonderful collection of is-land artists on display. When you get hungry from all the shopping, stop into the **Sansei** sushi shop and bar for a taste of Japan.

If you're here on Thursday, be sure to stop and see the free ancient hula show 10-11 a.m. On Tuesday 10 a.m.-noon come and listen to slack-key guitar and stories. These shops are connected to those in Kaanapali and Lahaina by the West Maui Shopping Express shuttle.

Honolua Store

This well-stocked, reasonably priced store, open daily 6 a.m.-8 p.m., is a rare find in this expensive neck of the woods. The shelves hold beer, wine, and liquors, basic food items from bananas to sweets, books, and gifts, and even a smattering of sunglasses, shorts, hats, and aloha shirts.

M.G.L. DOMENY DE RIENZI

SOUTH MAUI
MAALAEA

Maalaea is a small community located in the southwestern corner of the Maui isthmus that is home to a handful of houses, a row of condos, two fine restaurants, a small harbor, and the new Maui Ocean Center.

Maalaea Harbor is a bite-size working harbor, one of two on the island where tourist boats dock (the other being Lahaina Harbor). With the comings and goings of all types of craft, the harbor is colorful, picturesque, and always busy. Until the advent of plane travel to and between the islands, Maalaea was a busy port for interisland steamer traffic, principally serving the Maalaea and Kihei area. Maalaea Harbor has the dubious distinction of being the second windiest harbor in the world, with sustained winds averaging 25 knots. Upon entering the village, you are greeted by a small U.S. Coast Guard installation at the east end, and Buzz's Wharf, a well-known restaurant, at the other. Between, you will find restrooms, the Maalaea Activity Center booth at harborside, and the Shinto fishing shrine Ebisuku Kotohira Jinsha, which was constructed

in 1914. The condominiums line Hauoli Street, which culminates in Haycraft Park, the western end of Maalaea Beach.

SIGHTS

Maalaea Beach
Consisting of three miles of windswept sand partially backed by Kealia Pond National Wildlife Refuge, Maalaea Beach has many points of access between Maalaea and Kihei along Rt. 31. The strong winds make the beach undesirable for sunning and bathing, but it's a windsurfer's dream. The hard-packed sand is a natural track for joggers, profuse in the morning and afternoon. The beachcombing and strolling are quiet and productive. From the Maalaea end, you can access the beach from Haycraft Park. If you're up by 6 a.m. you can see the Kihei canoe club practice at the Kihei end; they put their canoes in the water near the Kihei wharf just across the road from Suda's Store.

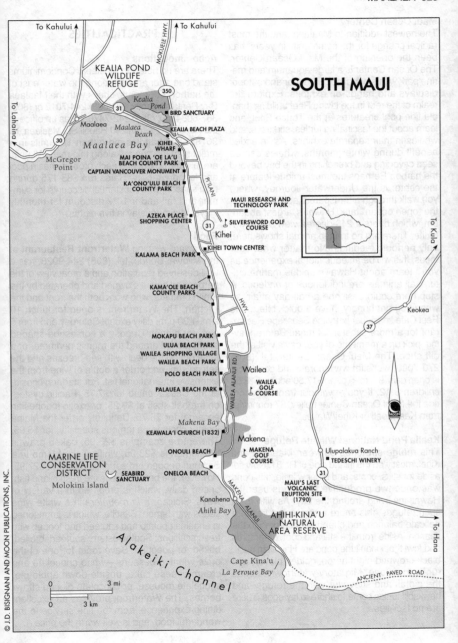

SOUTH MAUI

To Kahului ↑   ↑ To Kahului

MOKUELE HWY

KEALIA POND WILDLIFE REFUGE

350

Kealia Pond

To Lahaina

31

Maalaea

BIRD SANCTUARY

KEALIA BEACH PLAZA

Maalaea Beach

KIHEI WHARF

30

Maalaea Bay

MAI POINA 'OE LA'U BEACH COUNTY PARK

McGregor Point

CAPTAIN VANCOUVER MONUMENT

KA'ONO'ULU BEACH COUNTY PARK

PI'ILANI

MAUI RESEARCH AND TECHNOLOGY PARK

AZEKA PLACE SHOPPING CENTER

31

SILVERSWORD GOLF COURSE

To Kula

Kihei

KIHEI TOWN CENTER

KALAMA BEACH PARK

31 HWY

KAMA'OLE BEACH COUNTY PARKS

Keokea

37

MOKAPU BEACH PARK

ULUA BEACH PARK

WAILEA SHOPPING VILLAGE

WAILEA BEACH PARK

WAILEA ALANUI RD.

Wailea

POLO BEACH PARK

WAILEA GOLF COURSE

PALAUEA BEACH PARK

MOON

Makena Bay

KEAWALA'I CHURCH (1832)

MARINE LIFE CONSERVATION DISTRICT

Molokini Island

SEABIRD SANCTUARY

ONOULI BEACH

ONELOA BEACH

Makena

MAKENA GOLF COURSE

Ulupalakua Ranch

TEDESCHI WINERY

MAKENA ALANUI

37

MAUI'S LAST VOLCANIC ERUPTION SITE (1790)

To Hana

31

Kanahena

Ahihi Bay

AHIHI-KINA'U NATURAL AREA RESERVE

Alakeiki Channel

Cape Kina'u

La Perouse Bay

ANCIENT PAVED ROAD

0   3 mi
0   3 km

Maui Ocean Center

The newest addition to Maalaea, and the most radical change for the community in years, has been the opening of the Maui Ocean Center. The Ocean Center is a large aquarium and marine park with several dozen indoor and outdoor displays and hands-on exhibits. Explore the realm of the reef in the Living Reef building, handle tide pool creatures at the Touch Pool, and learn about the fascinating turtles, stingrays, and whales in their separate exhibits. As an added benefit during winter months, whales can be seen cavorting and breaching in the bay beyond the harbor. Perhaps the most unique feature at the center is the Underwater Journey, where you walk through a transparent acrylic tunnel in the "open ocean" tank, Hawaii's largest aquarium, which offers a 240-degree view of the waterlife. There are no trained animal shows here, only periodic feedings. No matter what your focus, this will be an educational experience as you'll learn about Hawaii's unique marine culture; all animals are indigenous or endemic. A stop here could easily be a half-day affair, so when you get hungry, have a quick bite at the Reef Cafe snack bar or try the Seascape Restaurant for a more substantial meal. Before leaving, pick up a memento of your day's visit at the gift shop. The Maui Ocean Center, tel. (808) 270-7000, website: www.coralworld.com/moc, is open daily 9 a.m.-5 p.m.; $17.50 adults, $12.50 children 3-12. If you're without transportation, ride the Maui Ocean Center trolley, $7 roundtrip, from Kaanapali or Kihei/Wailea.

Kealia Pond National Wildlife Refuge

This refuge stretches between Maalaea and Kihei, mostly on the inland side of Rt. 31. Now set aside for stilts, coots, and other wildlife, this pond was once two productive fishponds used by Hawaiians living around the bay. As with most such refuges, this shore environment lies in a delicate balance and changes according to the season. Aside from the stilt and coot, other birds and fowl that inhabit the pond are Hawaiian duck, black-crowned night heron, golden plover, and ruddy turnstone. Migratory waterfowl such as the pintail and shoveller visit the refuge, and hawksbill turtles come to shore to lay eggs. There are no facilities.

PRACTICALITIES

Accommodations

There are no hotels in Maalaea. Condominiums stand one after another along the water east of the harbor. For rooms, check with the Maalaea Bay Rentals agency, tel. (808) 244-7012 or (800) 367-6084, fax (808) 242-7476. It has an office at the Hono Kai Resort, 280 Hauoli St., Maalaea, HI 96793, and handles more than 100 units in a majority of the condos along this road. All units are fully furnished, and each property has a pool and laundry facility. Rates run $85-175 during high season, with substantial discounts for summer and fall and a 10% discount for monthly stays. Minimum stay is five nights.

Food

The award-winning **Waterfront Restaurant** at the Milowai Condo, tel. (808) 244-9028, has a well-deserved reputation and a great view of the harbor and bay. It's owned and operated by the Smith brothers, who work both the front and the kitchen. The Waterfront is open for lunch 10 a.m.-1:30 p.m. daily except Saturday and from 5 p.m. for dinner. Choose a horseshoe-shaped booth tucked around the room's perimeter or a table out on the deck with sea breezes and the setting sun, and order a bottle of wine from the extensive international list. For starters, consider the Caesar salad for $7.75, Pacific oysters on the half shell at $9.25, or exotic Indonesian escargot for $6.75. Definitely order the Maine lobster chowder, a famous specialty, for $6.95. The entree scampi is $23.95, baked prawns Wellington is $23.95, while rack of lamb in a Sichuan peppercorn sauce is priced at $27.95. However, the best choice is the fresh island fish, priced daily, which is prepared in a variety of ways: Sicilian; à la meuniere in a white wine sauce with lemon; Bastille, which is imprisoned in angelhair potato and sautéed and topped with fresh scallions; Southwestern; sautéed; broiled; baked; or poached. Save room for one of the prize-winning desserts—white chocolate and cream cheese cake, upside-down apple pie, chocolate mousse, or chocolate-dipped strawberries. The Waterfront provides an excellent dining experience, from the fine service to the wonderful food, and is well worth the price.

Buzz's Wharf restaurant, tel. (808) 244-5426, open daily 11 a.m.-11 p.m., specializes in seafood. The waterfront atmosphere and second-story views are unbeatable. It's a favorite spot and often busy. *Pu pu* selections include steamed clams for $12.95, escargot on the shell for $7.95, Buzz's salmon for $6.95, and fresh Pacific oysters on the half shell for $11.95. The lunch menu offers a tossed salad with shrimp for $11.95, an assortment of burgers and fries for under $10, and a Cajun open-faced chicken sandwich for $9.95. For dinner, try prawns Tahitian, the captain's seafood platter, or a mouth-watering cut of prime rib au jus, for $15-30. Enjoy

a liter of house wine for $12 or cocktail for $6. End your meal with dessert followed by a stroll around the moonlit harbor.

The **Tradewinds Deli and Mart,** located at the Maalaea Mermaid, carries groceries, drinks, and alcohol, creates deli sandwiches, and also rents snorkel equipment and boogie boards.

At Maalaea Harbor look for the **Maalaea General Store,** open daily except Monday 8 a.m.-5 p.m., where you have a much better chance of buying fishing tackle than you do a loaf of bread. It does have some very limited groceries and sundries.

KIHEI

Kihei (Shoulder Cloak) takes it on the chin whenever anti-development groups need an example at which to wag their fingers. For the last two decades, construction along both sides of Kihei Road, which runs the length of town, has continued unabated. Since there was no central planning for the development, mostly high-rise condos and a few hotels were built wherever they could be squeezed in: some are lovely, some are crass. There's hardly a spot left where you can get an unobstructed view of the beach as you drive along. That's the "slam" in a nutshell. The good news is that Kihei has so much to recommend it that if you refrain from fixating on this one regrettable feature, you'll thoroughly enjoy yourself, and save money, too.

The developers went "hyper" here because it's perfect as a tourist area. The weather can be counted on to be the best on all of Maui. Haleakala, looming just behind the town, catches rainclouds before they drench Kihei. Days of blue skies and sunshine are taken for granted. On the other side of the condos and hotels are gorgeous beaches, every one open to the public. Once on the beachside, the condos don't matter anymore. The views out to sea are unobstructed vistas of Lanai, Kahoolawe, Molokini, and West Maui, which gives the illusion of being a separate island. The buildings are even a buffer to the traffic noise! Many islanders make Kihei their home, so there is a feeling of real community here. It's quieter than Lahaina, with fewer restaurants and not as much action; but for sun and surf activities, this place has it all.

The six-mile stretch bordered by beach and mountain that makes up Kihei has always been an important landing spot on Maui. Hawaiian war canoes moored here many times during countless skirmishes over the years; later, Western navigators such as Capt. George Vancouver found this stretch of beach a congenial anchorage. A totem pole across from the Maui Lu Hotel marks the spot where Vancouver landed. During WW II, when a Japanese invasion was feared, Kihei was considered a likely spot for an amphibious attack. Overgrown pillboxes and rusting tank traps are still found along the beaches. Many look like cement porcupines with iron quills. Kihei is a natural site with mountain and ocean vistas. It's also great for beachcombing up toward Maalaea, but try to get there by morning because the afternoon wind is notorious for creating minor sandstorms.

Kihei's commercial sections are separated by residential areas. There is no one town center as such, although the highest concentration and greatest number of businesses are near the post office and the Azeka Place shopping centers. From the north, the first commercial area is that around Suda's Store and the Gateway Mall. Following that down the way are business centers around the post office, across from Kalama Beach Park, and fronting the Kamaole beaches.

The new Maui Research and Technology Park has been established above the Silversword Golf Course in Kihei, sprucing up the image of the area a little and bringing in some high-tech white collar jobs at the same time. While only a handful of shiny new office buildings have been built so far, land has been set aside for many more.

BEACHES

Mai Poina Oe Lau Beach Park
On Kihei's northern fringe, fronting Maui Lu Hotel, this beach offers only limited paved parking, otherwise just along the road. Showers, tables, and restrooms front the long and narrow white-sand beach, which has good safe swimming but is still plagued by strong winds by early afternoon. A windsurfer's delight, here you can see upwards of 100 sporting enthusiasts out trying the wind when conditions are optimal.

Kalepolepo Beach Park
Next to the Whale Sanctuary office, this beach is small and good for kiddies. Centuries ago, the thriving community of Kalepolepo occupied this area of Kihei and farmed the six-acre **Koieie Fishpond** here. Remnants of its rock wall can still be seen arcing through the water. Now much reduced in size, the walls once stood higher than high tide. It's estimated that more than 2,000 pounds of fish a year were harvested from these waters when it was a functioning fishpond in the late 1500s.

Kalama Park
This park, located in the middle of town, is more suited to family outings and enjoying the vista than it is for beach activities. Kalama has a large lawn ending in a breakwater, a small beach in summer, and none in winter. However, there are 36 acres of pavilions; tables; barbecue pits; volleyball, basketball, and tennis courts; a baseball diamond; a soccer field; and plenty of expanse to throw a frisbee. With its great views of Molokini and Haleakala, it is considered the best family park in the area. At its extreme southern end, just across the highway bridge, is an area called Cove Park, where locals put small boats in the water.

Kamaole I, II, and III
These beach parks, often referred to as Kam 1, 2, and 3, are at the south end of town near Kihei Town Center. All three have beautiful white sand, picnic tables, lifeguards, and all the amenities.

The swimming and bodysurfing are good. Snorkeling is good for beginners on the reef between II and III, where much coral and many colorful reef fish abound. Kamaole III has a kids' playground. Shopping and dining are nearby.

Kihei Boat Ramp
Just south of Kamaole III Beach is the Kihei Boat Ramp, used by many ocean activity companies in the area to launch boats and rafts.

ACCOMMODATIONS

The emphasis in Kihei is on condos. With keen competition among them, you can save some money while having a more homey vacation. Close to 100 condos, plus a smattering of vacation apartments, cottages, and even a few hotel resorts, are all strung along Kihei Road. As always, you pay more for ocean views. Don't shy away from accommodations on the *mauka* side of Kihei Road. You have total access to the beach, some superior views of Haleakala, and you usually pay less money. The accommodations below are listed north to south.

Hotels
The Kihei area offers three small hotels that are reasonably priced and well appointed. **Maui Lu Resort,** 575 S. Kihei Rd., Kihei, HI 96753, tel. (808) 879-5881, (800) 922-7866, or (800) 321-2558 in Hawaii, attempts to preserve the feeling of old Hawaii with its emphasis on *ohana.* Amenities here include an activities desk, tennis, a Maui-shaped pool, and tiny private beaches strung along its 28 acres. Rooms, located mostly in the new wing that is mountainside and quieter, are priced $99-185, $18 per extra person, and include refrigerators and air-conditioning. This full-service hotel pampers you in the old Hawaiian style. This is an Aston property. Expensive.

The Maui Coast Hotel, 2259 S. Kihei Rd., Kihei, HI 96753, tel. (808) 874-6284 or (800) 895-6284, fax (808) 875-4731, e-mail: mch@maui .net, website: www.maui.net/~mch, is Kihei's newest hotel, completed in 1993. The rooms and suites are bright and cheerful, blending Southwestern pastels and Hawaiian-style furniture. Adding to your comfort are standard amenities like remote-control color TV, a/c and ceiling fans, complimentary in-wall safes, coffee makers, refrigerators, slippers to pad around in, full bathrooms that include a jacuzzi bathtub and a "who asked for one" bathroom scale. A wet bar is in all the larger suites. Guests are also treated to morning coffee, and washers and dryers are on every other floor. This seven-story hotel offers two spas with whirlpools, a swimming pool, lighted guests-only tennis courts, a restaurant, poolside bar with nightly entertainment, sundries shop, and free parking. Rates are $129-139 for a standard room, $149-300 for a suite, $10 each additional person, with discounted off-season and weekly rates. Rental car packages are also available. The Maui Coast Hotel, set back from busy Kihei Road, offers a small oasis of peace and tranquillity with excellent rates for the standard of rooms and amenities offered. Premium.

Maui Oceanfront Inn is at 2980 S. Kihei Rd., Kihei, HI 96753, tel. (808) 879-7744, 874-0145, or (800) 367-5004. This is a very affordable and well-maintained hotel recently given a complete makeover including buildings, furnishings, and grounds. The hotel is fronting a long sandy beach, located just before you get to Wailea at the south end of town. Rates are $95 standard, $100 superior, $110 deluxe, and a one-bedroom family unit is $170; $15 extra person, off-season $10-20 lower. The hotel amenities include air-conditioning, room refrigerators, free morning coffee and donuts, and a garden. You can't go wrong at this terrific little hotel! Expensive.

Condos and Cottages

One of the several condos at the far north end of Kihei at the eastern end of Maalaea Beach is **Sugar Beach Resort,** 145 N. Kihei Rd., tel. (808) 879-7765. All one- and two-bedroom units have full kitchens, ceiling fans and a/c, TV, and lanai, with guest-only tennis courts, swimming pool, spa, sauna, barbecue grills, sundries shop, sandwich shop, and activities desk on property. All are individually owned and decorated. Rates run about $100-150 for one-bedroom and $175-225 for two-bedroom suites. Most rooms here are rented by rental agencies. Contact the following for rooms here and at other condos at this extreme northern end of Kihei: Condominium Rentals Hawaii, tel. (800) 367-5242 or (800)

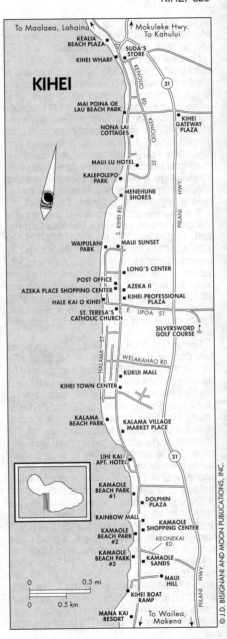

© J.D. BISIGNANI AND MOON PUBLICATIONS, INC.

663-2101 in Canada; Rainbow Rentals, tel. (800) 451-5366; Maui Condominium and Home Realty, tel. (800) 822-4409. Expensive.

Nani Kai Hale, 73 N. Kihei Rd., tel. (808) 875-0630 or (800) 367-6032, is very affordable at $99 for one-bedroom standard for seven days or longer, $105 for fewer than seven days. One-bedroom ocean views run $115/$125, ocean-fronts $135/$145; two-bedroom standards are $135/$145. The two-bedroom oceanfront units go for a $185 nightly rate only. Substantial savings offered during off-season, four-day minimum stay required, monthly rates available. There's a good beach plus sheltered parking, pool, laundry facilities, private lanai, and barbecues on premises. Good views. Expensive.

The Polynesian-style roofs and dark wooden siding might draw you to the **Maalaea Surf Resort,** 12 S. Kihei Rd., tel. (808) 879-1267 or (800) 423-7953, fax (808) 874-2884, but the fully furnished bright interiors, well-tended lawns, tennis courts, swimming pools, and white-sand beach will captivate you. Each unit has a/c and daily maid service. One-bedroom suites run $186 during high season and $165 for low season. Two-bedroom units are $252 and $217, respectively. Luxury.

The first place south of Suda's Store is **Nona Lani Cottages,** 455 S. Kihei Rd., tel. (808) 879-2497 or (800) 733-2688, owned and operated by Dave and Nona Kong. These clean and neat units on the *mauka* side of the road have full kitchens and baths, queen beds, and daybeds. Laundry facilities, public phones, hammocks, chaise lounges, and barbecues are on the premises, and each unit has a raised lanai with tables. Rates are $68 a night or $455 a week during low season, four-night minimum, $7 additional person. There is a seven-night minimum and slightly higher rates in high season, but call to find out if anything's available on a shorter basis or for off-season weekly rates. These individual plantation-style units are about as down-home Hawaiian as you can get, a good place to come if you're looking for relaxation. Moderate.

Menehune Shores, 760 S. Kihei Rd., mailing address P.O. Box 1327, Kihei, HI 96753, tel. (808) 879-3428 or (800) 558-9117, fax (808) 897-5218, is a huge, family-oriented and moderately priced high-rise condo on the beach overlooking an ancient fishpond. The building is high-

lighted with replicas of Hawaiian petroglyphs. On the first floor is Hamilton's Beach Cafe, outside of which is a new swimming pool. The Menehune is used mostly by seniors, except during Christmas when families come. All units have an ocean view and rates are $100-175 for one- to three-bedroom condos in high season, three-day minimum. Low-season rates are a little less, discounts are given for month stays, and special car/room packages can be arranged. Full kitchens with dishwasher, washer and dryer, and disposals are in each unit, which are individually owned, so furnishings vary. Expensive.

Kauhale Makai, 938 S. Kihei Rd., write Maui Condominium and Home Realty, P.O. Box 1840 Kihei, HI 96753, or call (808) 879-5445 or (800) 822-4409. Rates from $70 studio, $80 one-bedroom, $100 two-bedroom, four-night minimum; weekly and monthly discounts given. Fully furnished, individually decorated rooms are a mixture of garden, mountain, and ocean view. A swimming pool, kiddie pool, barbecues, putting green, and sauna are available. Expensive.

The boxy **Leinaala** condos, 998 S. Kihei Rd., tel. (808) 879-2235 or (800) 334-3305, may not attract everyone, but don't let the appearance fool you. Each of the 24 fully appointed units faces the beach. Splash in the condo pool or stroll across the huge lawn to the shore. This lawn and the tennis courts here are part of a county park. Winter rates are $95 and $115 for one- and two-bedroom units during high season. The best time for space is during the summer when rates are $15-20 less; four nights minimum. Reduced rates for AARP and AAA. Expensive.

Just down the back street at 1310 Uluniu Rd., Kihei, HI 96753, tel. (808) 879-2757 or (800) 457-7014, fax (808) 875-8242, is **Hale Kai O Kihei.** This apartment-like cinder block affair, simple and utilitarian, is clean, well-kept, and cute for what it is. Each furnished unit has a direct ocean view with a lanai that looks over the pool, garden, and beach. There is also parking, shuffleboard, barbecue grills, and coin laundry, with maid service on request. Reasonable rates are $110 for a one-bedroom unit ($75 for low season) and $135 for two bedrooms ($100 low season); three nights minimum—15% discount for stays of one month or greater. Cash only, no credit cards. Expensive.

Just south of Kalama Park is **Lihi Kai Cottages,** 2121 Ili'ili Rd., Kihei, HI 96753, tel. (808) 879-2335 or (800) 544-4524. These nine cottages are such a bargain they're often booked by returning guests, particularly during winter months. They're not plush, there's no pool, but they're homey and clean, with little touches like banana trees growing on the property. Rates are $69 daily for three to seven nights, $64 for seven or more nights; three nights minimum. Monthly rates are available on request, no credit cards accepted. For reservations, call or write well in advance c/o Manager, at the above address. Moderate.

Maui Vista, 2191 S. Kihei Rd., tel. (808) 879-7966 or (800) 535-0085, fax (808) 874-5612, is a pleasing 10-acre condo complex that has 38 units managed by Marc Resorts. Three pools, six tennis courts, barbecue grills, and an activities desk are available to all guests. All studios and suites have kitchens, are modern in their appointments, spacious in layout, and have maid service. Studios run $139, one-bedroom suites $149-169, and two-bedroom suites $189-199, $20 less during "value" periods, $15 each extra person. Premium.

At **Kamaole Sands,** 2695 S. Kihei Rd., tel. (808) 874-8700 or (800) 367-5004, all apartments come completely furnished with a full bath and kitchen, roomy living area, and lanai. Prices are: $130 studio, $160-190 one-bedroom, $215-265 two-bedroom, $320-340 three-bedroom, fifth night free; off-season discounts and rental car packages available. Stepping down the hillside, the Kamaole Sands is a full-service, family-oriented condo geared toward making the entire family comfortable. The Sandpiper Grill, situated poolside and for guests only, serves inexpensive breakfasts, lunches, and dinners featuring fresh island fish and pasta. One of the main features of the Kamaole Sands is its wonderful tennis courts, free to guests, with a tennis instructor to help you work on the fine points of your game. The Kamaole Sands is bright, cheerful, and gives you a lot for your money. Premium.

Maui Hill is located at 2881 S. Kihei Rd., tel. (808) 879-6321, (800) 922-7866, or (800) 321-2558 Hawaii. If you want to rise above it all in Kihei come to this upbeat condo with a Spanish motif. This condo resort sits high on a hill and commands a sweeping view of the entire area. The one-, two-, or three-bedroom suites are spacious, bright, and airy; all have ceiling fans and a/c, cable TV, daily maid service, and gourmet kitchens. A concierge service helps with your every need, and all sun and surf activities can be arranged at the ocean activity desk. The grounds are secluded, beautifully maintained, and offer a pool with whale mosaic on the bottom, tennis courts, and spa. Rates are: one-bedroom from $175 (up to four people), two-bedroom from $205 (up to six people), three-bedroom from $260 (up to seven people); $35 less during off-season times. A weekly complimentary mai tai party complete with games, singing, and door prizes is held for guests, along with a continental breakfast at 8 a.m. that offers an orientation on island activities. Guests can also enjoy a weekly afternoon lei-making class and a poolside scuba orientation several days per week. Luxury.

At the south end of Kihei is **Mana Kai Maui** oceanfront resort, 2960 S. Kihei Rd., tel. (808) 879-1561, (800) 367-5242 Mainland, or (800) 663-2101. Hotel features include front desk check-in, an activities desk, daily maid service, a sundries store, swimming pool, and a fine restaurant and bar on premises. Condo units have full kitchens, TV, private lanai, and ceiling fans. All hotel rooms, with outdoor access, air-conditioning, and refrigerators, are on the garden level. Winter rates run $100 for the hotel rooms, $180-210 for a one-bedroom and $190-220 for a two-bedroom suite. Summer rates are about 20% cheaper, and there is a 10% discount for stays of one month or more. Premium.

Aside from the above-listed properties, there are many rental agencies that handle condo units and rental homes. Several of these agencies are: **Condominium Rentals Hawaii,** 362 Huku Li'i Place, #204, Kihei, HI 96753, tel. (800) 367-5242 U.S. or (800) 663-2101 Canada, e-mail: crh@maui.net, website: www.crhmaui.com; **Kihei Maui Vacations,** P.O. Box 1055, Kihei, HI 96753, tel. (808) 879-7581 or (800) 541-6284, website: www.kmvmaui.com/home.html; **Maui Condominium and Home Realty,** P.O. Box 1840, Kihei, HI 96753, tel. (808) 879-5445 or (800) 822-4409, website: www.mauicondo.com; and **Unique Island Homes,** tel. (808) 875-8808 or (800) 961-9196.

Bed and Breakfasts

Owned and operated by Cheryl and Dan Olson, **By The Sea B&B** is tucked under tall palm trees down a side street near Ohukai windsurfing beach at the north end of Kihei. This private home has three units all with separate entrances that look over the back garden and pond. Rooms include a small kitchenette, large bathroom, ceiling fan, TV, and phone, plus daily breakfast; the second floor unit has a deck. Rates run $75-95 a night single, $85-110 double, three nights minimum—no charge for the friendly advice on island activities and places to eat, or for the time you spend lounging in the hammock out back! Weekly discounts are offered and rental cars can be arranged. By The Sea B&B is located at 20 Wailana Place, Kihei, HI 96753, tel. (808) 891-0348 or (888) 879-2700, fax (808) 879-5540, e-mail: bythesea@maui.net, website: www.bythesea.net. Expensive.

Babson's Vacation Rentals, 3371 Keha Dr., Kihei, HI 96753, tel. (808) 874-1166 or (800) 824-6409, fax (808) 879-7906, offers a combination of B&B rooms, separate studio apartment, and private cottage in the quiet residential area of Maui Meadows perched on the hillside between Kihei and Wailea. From this vantage point, you can watch the sun set over the Lahaina Roads with Kahoolawe, Molikini, Lanai, and even Molokai floating on the horizon, or pay closer attention to the finely landscaped gardens that surround the house. All rentals include cable TV, telephone, and laundry facilities. Ann and Bob are happy to recommend their favorite scenic spots, activities, and restaurants, and will provide you with towels and a cooler for a day at the beach. Rates on the main home's B&B rooms, the Bougainvillea and Molokini suite, are $70-85 and include all-you-can-eat continental breakfast. The Hibiscus Hideaway, a first-floor studio priced at $85, has its own bath, kitchen, separate bedroom, and garden. The two-bedroom Sunset Cottage, which can sleep six comfortably, offers a sweeping ocean view, cathedral ceilings, two private baths, and full kitchen, rents for $105. All prices are for double occupancy; $10 for each extra person. Ann and Bob go out of their way to make your stay enjoyable, having mastered the art of allowing you to enjoy it yourself. Moderate.

FOOD

Inexpensive

Azeka's Snacks, Azeka Place, is open daily except Sunday 7:30 a.m.-5 p.m. Basically takeout, the menu features $1.50-1.90 hamburgers and a variety of plate lunches, saimin, and sushi for under $5. Azeka's is popular with locals and terrific for picnics.

International House of Pancakes is toward the rear of Azeka Place. Open daily 6 a.m.-midnight, Friday and Saturday until 2 a.m. Same American standards as on the Mainland with most sandwiches and plate lunches under $8, dinners under $12, and breakfasts anytime around $6. Not exotic, but basic and filling with a good reputation in the area for inexpensive but passable fresh fish and daily specials.

Let the rich aroma of 40 different types of roasting coffee lure you to **The Coffee Store,** Azeka Place II, tel. (808) 875-4244, open Sun.-Thurs. 6 a.m.-9 p.m., Friday and Saturday until 11 p.m. Breakfast fare, served all day, features quiche for $3.75 or a breakfast quesadilla for $5.95. Lunch selections, always served with crusty homemade bread, include a Caesar salad at $4.95—or $6.95 for the large size that can easily feed two—and sandwiches like tuna or turkey for $5.50. The vegetarian sandwiches cost $6.50. Pizza, on a six-inch Boboli crust, ranges $6.50-10. Daily homemade soup for $3.95 including bread and coffee, and stuffed quesadillas of all sorts for $4-6, complete the menu. Enjoy coffee drinks that range in price $1-2.50, along with hot and iced herbal teas, hot chocolate, and Italian cream sodas. A deli case is filled with luscious desserts sure to satisfy any sweet tooth. You can purchase bulk coffee, espresso machines, distinctive aprons, kitchen gadgets, and T-shirts as well. You can dine inside, or sit outside, especially in the evening to hob-nob with local residents who come here to chat and enjoy a rich cup of coffee and snack.

The fountain bar, jukebox, Formica tabletops, leatherette booths, distinctive color scheme, and period decorations and music peg **Peggy Sue** as a classic, theme hamburger joint—with a modern twist. You can order your Big Bopper burger for $7.25 or the Earth Angel garden burger for $6.25, or sample one of the salads, sandwiches, or plate lunches, most for under $9. No '50s joint worth its name would be without that cool summer favorite, so Peggy Sue serves up ice cream, shakes, and fountain drinks. Stop in for the nostalgia rush. At Azeka Place II.

Tie-dyed Deadheads or heat-flushed tourists hoping to chill out should head for **Stella Blue's Cafe and Deli,** located at Longs Shopping Center, tel. (808) 874-3779, open daily 8 a.m.-9 p.m. Inside, the full coffee bar serves up the standards from a cup of house blend to a mocha, along with fresh hot bagels for $2.50, a tuna salad plate for $7.25, or a tossed green salad for $2.25. Sandwiches, everything from roast beef to veggie, average about $7.50. From the grill you can have a tuna melt, veggie burger, or pastrami melt for under $7.75. Breakfast, served 8-11 a.m., features a continental breakfast for $4.85 to homestyle waffles for $6.25. Dinner includes spinach lasagna for $12.95 and chicken parmesan at $13.95. Also, Stella pours frothy mugs of ice-cold beer, perfect to help cool you down before returning to the beach. A few racks hold a small selection of pareus, alohawear, and psychedelic T-shirts, tie-dyed fashions, and stickers.

Kalbi House, in a corner of Longs Shopping Center, open daily except Sunday 9 a.m.-9:30 p.m., offers a full range of Korean standards like barbecued short ribs, fried squid, chicken teriyaki, noodles, stews, and small intestine soup, as well as plate lunches and combination plates. Most everything is under $10; takeout available. The restaurant is basic but clean.

If you've been having too much fun and need a reviving cup of espresso, stop in at the **Kihei Caffe,** at Kalama Village Marketplace, tel. (808) 878-2230, open daily at 5 a.m., Sunday at 6 a.m., and enjoy your coffee along with an excellent assortment of sandwiches and baked goods. This full coffee bar serves up coffee drinks costing $1-2.50. Order a complete breakfast of eggs, bacon, home fries, and biscuits with gravy for $5.50, or a giant raisin muffin for $2.50. Sandwiches, all under $6.25, are served on your choice of homemade bread. Lighter fare includes couscous salad for $6.25, or honey cashew chicken salad for $6.25. Only cold sandwiches after 2 p.m. The cafe provides a few tables and stools inside, and more outside where you can

watch the action on Kihei Road, or across the road through Kamaole Beach Park to the ocean.

A few steps away is **Alexander's Fish and Fowl,** tel. (808) 874-0788, open 11 a.m.-9 p.m. This local long-term establishment is definitely a cut above most fast-food restaurants, and has taken a few steps along the upscale, yuppie, health-conscious road. The menu offers fresh fish, shrimp, and chicken sandwiches for $6.25-7.50. Plate lunches, sides, salads, and drinks, as well as larger baskets for $15.75-19.95, are also on the menu. Full meals are served with cole slaw and french fries or rice. All deep frying is done in canola oil but you can request broiling instead. There's not much decor or atmosphere, but the food is delicious and makes a perfect takeout meal that can be enjoyed at the beach.

Sports Page Bar and Grill, at the Kamaole Beach Center, tel. (808) 879-0602, open 11 a.m.-midnight for cocktails and 11:30 a.m.-10 p.m. for food service, scores big with a full bar and a large-screen TV. Order a mug of beer and a light snack like oyster shooters for $1 or teriyaki chicken breast strips for $6.95. The burger and sandwich menu goes all the way with a San Francisco '49er burger topped with bacon and cheese, a Chicago Cubs hot dog, or a Boston Celtics turkey sandwich, all for under $8.50. There's music on Wednesday evenings 8-10:30 p.m. and comedy 8-10 p.m. on Saturday nights when a $10 cover is charged. Families and even the athletically challenged will be comfortable here and more than welcome. Also in Kamaole Beach Center is **Hawaiian Moon's Deli and Natural Foods,** open Mon.-Sat. 8 a.m.-9 p.m., Sunday until 6 p.m. Stop for a healthy deli sandwich and drink, or shop for groceries, vitamins, and bulk foods.

Denny's at the Kamaole Shopping Center is more than a usual Mainland Denny's. Along with the large and varied selection of food, you have pool tables, games, and the Good Times bar.

For plate lunches from $4.25-6.25, salads, sandwiches, noodles and burgers, try **Sub Tropix** at the Rainbow Shopping Mall. Open 10 a.m.-9 p.m.

Kay's Cafe and Deli at Kai Nani Village Plaza serves smoothies, juices, coffees, and a variety of quick snack deli items.

Moderate

Margarita's Beach Cantina, at 101 N. Kihei Rd in the Kealia Beach Plaza, tel. (808) 879-5275, open daily 11:30 a.m.-midnight, has a well-deserved reputation for good food at fair prices. Formerly vegetarian, it now serves a variety of meat and chicken dishes but still uses the finest ingredients, cold-pressed oils, and no lard or bacon in the bean dishes. The decor is classical Mexican with white stucco walls and tiled floors. There's an outdoor deck affording a great sunset view and sea breezes, or stop by for live music and dancing Friday 5-7 p.m. and Sunday 2:30-5 p.m. The *carta* offers taco salads for $7.95, combination plates for $8.95-12.95, and money-saving daily lunch specials like *carnitas burrito* for under $7. Most entrees are in the $10-12 range, with nothing more than $17. Well drinks are $3, imported beers $3.50; during happy hour 2:30-5:30 p.m., margaritas are only 96 cents or $3 by the pitcher.

Restaurant Isana, located at 515 S. Kihei Rd., tel. (808) 874-5700, is open daily for the best Korean food in the area, and also has Japanese sushi at night. You can either sit at the sushi bar or have dinner cooked at your table. Upstairs is the bar, which has a karaoke sing-along after 10 p.m. Most dinners are in the $15-20 range.

Although you can get appetizers, salads, burgers, shrimp, and chicken at **Tony Roma's,** tel. (808) 875-1104, at the Kukui Mall, Tony's is a place for ribs, ribs, and more ribs. Prepared in several different ways, rib entrees run about $14, with most other entrees less. For a very hungry couple, or a family perhaps, try one of the jumbo orders like honey ribs (40 pieces) for $40.50, or shrimp and ribs for $49.95.

Chuck's Steak House at the Kihei Town Center, tel. (808) 879-4489, open Mon.-Sat. for lunch 11:30 a.m.-2:30 p.m., dinner nightly 5:30-10 p.m., is a family restaurant featuring American standards with an island twist. With a gray-on-gray interior, the restaurant provides a pleasant atmosphere, and although they do not take reservations, they will tell you how busy they are if you call ahead. The lunch menu is affordable with selections like a Reuben sandwich for $5.95 and plate lunches for under $6. The early bird special, priced at a reasonable $10.95, is normally fresh fish or barbecued chicken, and includes the salad bar, homemade bread, and a

choice of white rice or french fries. The dinner menu includes teriyaki steaks for $13.95 and a petite top sirloin priced at $12.95. Chuck's seafood selections include fresh fish or lobster tail for $19.95, and prime rib and lobster tail for $29.95.

In the Rainbow Plaza, **The Thai Chef Restaurant,** tel. (808) 874-5605, offers you a full menu of tasty Thai food at reasonable prices. Like its sister restaurant in Lahaina, you can get appetizers like spring rolls for $7.50 or green papaya salad at $6.50, and various soups for around $10. Entrees include red, green, or yellow curries from $9-11, with noodle, rice, and seafood dishes up to $14. There's a hefty selection for vegetarians, and desserts run $2-3. Well maintained, the decor is casual.

KKO Kai Ku Ono, tel. (808) 875-1007, a semi-sports bar casual dining place, below the more upscale Kihei Prime Rib and Seafood House at Kai Nani Village Plaza, is open 7:30 a.m.-midnight. Grab a pizza and beer and cool off after a day at the beach with a game of pool or darts. Pizzas from their wood-fired oven range $13.95-21.95, and they're also sold by the slice. A variety of sandwiches, ribs, and side dishes are also available, with most items under $15.95. The full bar will set you up drinks, happy hour 3-7 p.m., while you kick back and catch your favorite sporting event on one of the six TVs. For special events, the big screen is turned on.

Tucked into the rear of Kai Nani Village Plaza is the **Greek Bistro,** tel. (808) 879-9330, a wonderful addition to the restaurant scene, where the flavors and textures of the Mediterranean dishes served by the Arabatzi family will excite your palate. Dinner is served 5-10 p.m. and includes souvlakia, spanakopita, moussaka, and lamb kabob, all ranging $14.95-21.95. Other items are stuffed grape leaves for $6.95, Grecian village salad at $7.95, and several family-style platters for around $25. If you're in doubt as to what would be tasty, try the Greek Gods Platter, a sampling of several homemade entrees on the menu. Sit inside or out.

Expensive

The large open pavilion at the Maui Lu Hotel now houses **Ukulele** restaurant, tel. (808) 875-1188. Open for breakfast and dinner, there is Hawaiian entertainment nightly to accompany your evening meal. Available are pancakes, Belgian waffles, eggs Benedict, and such unusual items as a breakfast pizza for under $10. Dinner brings finer but casual dining with a full range of soups, salads, and entrees for $18-25. Prime rib is the specialty, but Ukulele is also known for fish and seafood dishes. Catering to the local populace as well as the tourist, it's a fine place for families.

Expanding from a very successful operation on Kauai, Chef Jean-Marie Josselin has opened **A Pacific Cafe,** tel. (808) 879-0069, at Azeka Place II. Open for dinner nightly 5:30-9:30, this restaurant presents the same kind of fine Hawaiian regional cuisine as at the original. Open, large, and masculine, the simply elegant decor of the dining areas, set off by modernistic touches, surround the exhibition kitchen with its wood-fired pizza oven. Start with a tiger eye *ahi* sushi tempura with tomato and Chinese mustard sauce for $12 or a Caesar salad for $8.95. Soups might be a red Thai curry and coconut with fresh island fish and calamari for $6.75. Entrees average about $25, including grilled Pacific snapper with Indonesian sticky rice roll, Chinese style roasted duck with garlic mashed potatoes, or penne pasta with shrimp, scallop, wild mushrooms, mussels, and purple asparagus. No matter what your choice, the ingredients will be the freshest, the service prompt, and the result memorable.

Upstairs at the Kai Nani Village Plaza at 2511 S. Kihei Rd. is **Kihei Prime Rib and Seafood House,** open from 5 p.m., tel. (808) 879-1954, offering most entrees for $20-32, including a well-stocked salad bar. Sashimi, lobster, and stuffed mushroom appetizers are under $10, and the early bird specials, 5-6 p.m. are $12.95, salad bar included. One of the best choices is rack of lamb for $23.95. An island ambience is created with carvings by Bruce Turnbull and paintings by Sigrid, both well-known local artists.

Overlooking the beach, the casual **Five Palms** restaurant, tel. (808) 879-2607, located at the Mana Kai Maui Resort at the south end of Kihei, is open for breakfast Mon.-Fri. 9-11:30 a.m. and a weekend champagne brunch 8 a.m.-2 p.m. Breakfast includes the usuals like eggs, sausages, pancakes, and the like, while the brunch also gives you the wider options of burgers, soups, salads, sandwiches, and some pastas. For lunch, try sandwiches, soup, pizza, or other entrees for $9-15. Dinner is served 5-9 p.m. (until 10 on Friday and Saturday), with *ahi*

sashimi for $11.95, Kula green salad at $7, roasted rack of lamb for $23.95, broiled lobster for $29.95, and many other delectable items on the menu, but the specialty is fish. Set so close to the water, the location and scenery are an integral part of the dining experience here.

Only steps from Wailea is the fine dining Italian restaurant called **Carrelli's On the Beach,** tel. (808) 875-0001. Open for dinner only 6-10 p.m., bar until 11 p.m., all parking is complimentary valet only because of limited space. If you don't want to deal with parking, take a limo, $15 each way, from along this coast. The excellent reputation and proximity draw many guests from the resorts and condos of Wailea. The seating couldn't be better, with the restaurant set right on the beach, and it's the water and sparkling light off the waves rather than the interior decoration that draws your attention most. Start with an antipasti or calamari friette for $12 and move on to a green salad, Caesar, or soup for $8-18. Pastas include ravioli for $22 and risotto con pettini prosciutto for $28. A bit pricier are the scampi and veal dishes for up to $36. For a bit more casual treat, try a homemade pizza from the wood-fired oven. Although rich and expensive, one of the fine desserts, like tiramisu or tartufo (a gelato ball rolled in chocolate and served with mango puree), might make a fine finish to your meal.

Former Kea Lani chef, Steve Amaral, has opened the new **Cucina Pacifica** restaurant, tel. (808) 875-7831, in the Rainbow Mall. Head upstairs. Food here, tasty, plentiful, and well-presented, is done with a Pacific Rim emphasis; lots of fish and seafood, with an Italian twist. Expect entrees in the $14-27 range. The restaurant has a round bar in the center of the room, a good place for conversation. Entertainment on the weekends. Open for dinner only.

ENTERTAINMENT

Kihei isn't exactly a hot spot when it comes to evening entertainment. Hawaiian music is offered on Friday and Saturday at the Ukulele Restaurant at the Maui Lu Hotel, and you can dance at **Margarita's Beach Cantina** now and again. Try the Maui Coast Hotel **Oasis** poolside bar for nightly music in a relaxed setting. **Kahale Beach Club,** a local bar for people who work in the area, is a place that offers music and dancing on an occasional basis. To its front is the fun little bar **Life's a Beach,** which serves up evening entertainment along with burgers, sandwiches, salads, and *pu pu.* **Hapas,** at 41 E. Lipoa St., is gaining a great reputation with its locally brewed beer, games, entertainment, and dancing nightly. Many of the restaurants offer entertainment on a hit-and-miss basis, usually one artist with a guitar, a small dinner combo, or some Hawaiian music. These are usually listed in the free tourist brochures.

For a different type of entertainment, stop for a movie at the **Kukui Mall Theater** in the Kihei Town Center, which has shows starting at about noon. It's a four-screen theater and admission is $6.50 for adults and $3.75 for seniors.

SHOPPING

While driving the length of Kihei, you will find shopping centers, both large and small, strung along the entire coastal area like shells on a dime store lei. At many you can buy food, clothing, sporting goods, camping and picnic supplies, sundries, photo equipment, cosmetics, resortwear, ice cream, pizza, dinner, and liquor. You can also book activities, order a custom bikini, or just relax with an ice-cold beer while your partner satisfies his or her shopping addiction. In Kihei, you have more than ample opportunity to spend your hard-earned vacation money that would be a sin to take back home. Aloha!

North End Shopping
At the very north end of Kihei as you approach from Kahului or Lahaina is the **Sugar Beach General Store,** with a small clutch of shops selling resortwear, snacks, gifts, and jewelry. The activities company here can set you up for a fun afternoon or rent you a bicycle. Nearby at **Kealia Beach Plaza** is the **Kealia General Store,** and upstairs are the **Pacific Whale Foundation** office and shop, open 9 a.m.-5 p.m. daily, and **Margarita's Beach Cantina.**

Suda's Store is a basic little market with limited food items, but with cold beer, fresh fish, and deli items. Open Mon.-Sat. 7:30 a.m.-5 p.m. and 8 a.m.-3 p.m. on Sunday, it sits along the *mauka* side at 61 S. Kihei Road. A few minutes

down the road from Suda's heading for Kihei, look for the **Nona Lana Cottages** where you can pick up a fresh flower lei for a reasonable price.

One of Kihei's newest shopping center, **Kihei Gateway Plaza,** has opened along Piilani Highway (Rt. 31), the main thoroughfare above Kihei that parallels Kihei Road. The entrance to this small group of shops is marked by a gas station and minimart.

Azeka Place
At the Azeka Place Shopping Center, along S. Kihei Road in what might be considered the center of town, you'll find numerous small shops and fast-food eating establishments. There's also a great community bulletin board listing apartments, yard sales, and odds and ends. Most shops are open daily 9 a.m.-9 p.m. with shorter Sunday hours. **Rainbow Connection** features personalized and Polynesian gifts. **Island Memories** is stocked with carved koa boxes, shells, earrings, woven basketry, a good selection of pottery, and hula instruments, all made in Hawaii. **Tropical Tantrum** specializes in hand-painted clothing by local artists, mostly for women but with a few selections for men as well. In case you need a toggle bolt, try **Kihei Ace Hardware.**

Here as well is the Kihei post office at 1254 S. Kihei Rd., a gas station, and a county Department of Motor Vehicles office. Just down the street is a **Star Market** for all your grocery needs.

Azeka Place II
Located just across the street from the original Azeka's, this new and larger shopping center features a **Maui Dive Shop,** a full-service dive shop and activity center; **The Coffee Store,** a great place for a cup of coffee (40 kinds), a light lunch, or even a late-night snack; **In's Eelskin** for bags, belts, and accouterments made from eel; **Liberty House,** a department store with tasteful island fashions; **Bank of Hawaii,** a full-service bank with ATM machines; **Roland's Shoes** for everything from slippers to hiking boots; **Elephant Walk** filled with gifts and boutique items; and **Postal Connection of Kihei,** open Mon.-Fri. 8:30 a.m.-6 p.m. and Saturday 9 a.m.-5 p.m., for all your boxing, shipping, and copying needs. Also in this center is **General Nutrition Center**

for vitamins, minerals, and supplements; and **Kaiser Permanente Kihei Clinic** for your health concerns.

Longs Shopping Center
Located at 1215 S. Kihei Rd., just up from Azeka Place II, this shopping center is dominated by a huge **Longs Drugs**, stocked with electronics, photo equipment, sundries, cosmetics, stationery, and even sporting goods. Around the center you will find the **T-Shirt Factory** featuring all kinds of discounted wearable take-home gifts; **Mavrik Motorcycles**, which rents the big hogs; and you can do everything from faxing to packing and shipping at **Mail Boxes Etc.** Sports enthusiasts should try **Maui Sporting Goods**, which carries everything from inline skates to spear fishing equipment, or **Maui Sports and Cycle**, for rental and sale of sports equipment. **American Savings Bank** is conveniently located here for all the shopping that you may be doing in this center and along the Kihei strip.

Kukui Mall
At the Kukui Mall, 1819 S. Kihei Rd., are **Waldenbooks, Kihei Kukui Laundromat, J.R.'s Music Store, Whalers General Store** for sundries, and several apparel stores including **Local Motion.** Tired of the beach, or just need to beat the heat? Stop at the multiscreen **Kukui Mall Theater,** the only cinema on this side of the island.

Kihei Town Center
This small shopping center just south of the Kukui Mall offers a 24-hour **Foodland, Hawaii Products Too** for gifts, **Rainbow Attic** consignment shop, and several eateries. Across the street at the corner is the **Aloha Marketplace** covered by awnings and trees, where you can shop for jewelry, clothing, carvings, and other touristy gifts.

Kihei Kalama Village Market Place
Look for this bargain-filled, semi-open-air collection of stalls at 1945 S. Kihei Rd., offering everything from tourist trinkets to fine art; clothes, crafts, and jewelry predominate. Around the periphery are other shops. Among them you will find **Serendipity**, a small, well-appointed boutique that displays imported items mainly from Malaysia and Brazil; **Gallery and Gifts** with

Hawaiian-made items; and the **Treasure Cove** next door with its arts, crafts, crystals, gifts, jewelry, and sculpture. Out front at the corner, **Maui Discount Activity World** will set you with your day's activity, and around back is **Snorkel Bob's** for snorkel and boogie board rentals.

Dolphin Shopping Plaza
This small, two-story plaza at 2395 S. Kihei Rd. includes **Pro Photo Lab**, featuring 40-minute processing, and **Tropical Disk** music store. If you have a craving for pizza try **Pizza Hut.** In a condo and want to cook your own pizza? Try **Pizza Fresh:** "we make it, you bake it." If you need to work off some of those pizza pounds, stop at **Barefoot's Cashback Tours,** where he can set you up with virtually any kind of activity on the island at a 10% discount to you. Or see about some equipment at **Maui Sports and Cycles.** Upstairs, you'll find **Kihei Medical Services** and **Kihei Chiropractic.**

Kamaole Beach Center
A small group of shops between Dolphin and Rainbow plazas, offering several places to eat, **Hawaiian Moon's Deli and Natural Food Store,** and the **Honolulu Surf Company** clothing store.

Rainbow Mall
Yet another small mall just up the road at 2439 S. Kihei Rd. features **South Pacific Kayaks and Outfitters** and **Auntie Snorkel** for the sales and rental of snorkel gear, boogie boards, kayaks, and camping and hiking gear for very reasonable prices. Other shops in the mall are the **Awesome Tees; Maui Custom Beach Wear,** where you can buy off the rack or have a bikini made especially for you; **Premiere Video,** for evening entertainment if you're staying in a condo; **Topaz,** a fine jewelry and watch store; and the **Topaz Gallery** upstairs. **Rainbow Discount Liquor** is located at the back of the mall.

Kamaole Shopping Center
Last in this quick succession of small malls is the slightly larger Kamaole Shopping Center at 2463 S. Kihei Rd. This mall has several inexpensive eateries and various clothing, souvenir, and sundries stores. From its two floors of shops you can buy baubles, beads, some nicer pieces

at **Unique Jewels;** and groceries, liquor, and souvenirs at **Whalers General Store. Lappert's Ice Cream** sells island-made delights and fat-free yogurt. Also in the center is a **Maui Dive Shop,** a complete diving and water sports store offering rentals, swimwear, snorkels, cruises, and windsurfing lessons, and an **Ocean Activities Center** booth for booking water sports.

Kai Nani Village Plaza
This small cluster of shops sits at the south end of Kihei. Aside from the Greek Bistro, Kihei Prime Rib and Seafood House, KKO, and Annie's Deli eateries, you'll find the **International Gift Shop,** and **Sunshine Mart** for sundries and food items.

Swap Meet and Farmers' Market
If you're looking for a bargain on clothes, gifts, craft items, and odds and ends, try the **Kihei swap meet** every Saturday 7 a.m.-4 p.m. across the road from Kalama Beach Park.

A small **farmers' market** is held in the parking lot in front of Suda's Store at 61 S. Kihei Rd., every Tuesday and Friday 1-5:30 p.m. Besides fresh produce, stalls sell shells, T-shirts, and knickknacks of all kinds. There is also a farmers' market in the Longs Shopping Center every Saturday 8 a.m.-noon.

Food/Liquor Stores
Foodland, at Kihei Town Center (open 24 hours), and **Star Market,** at 1310 S. Kihei Rd., are full-service supermarkets with a complete liquor, wine, and beer section. **Rainbow Discount Liquor** has a good selection of liquor, imported beers, and wine at the Rainbow Mall. At the very south end of Kihei at Mana Kai Maui Resort, try **Keawakapu General Store** for groceries, sundries, snacks, and spirits. Open daily 7 a.m.-9 p.m.

Aloha Moon's Natural Foods at the Kamaole Beach Center is a small but full service natural health food store. Stop in for bulk foods, groceries, herbs, organic fruits and vegetables, vitamins, minerals and supplements, juices, bottled water, soy drinks, and beer. There's even a freezer case for ice cream and a deli case for takeout sandwiches.

Kihei Wine and Spirits, located at 300 Ohukai Rd., open daily 10 a.m.-6 p.m., Saturday until 5 p.m., has a fantastic selection of wine and beer and a great little gourmet food section.

Along with your liquor, pick up some imported pasta, sun-dried zucchini or tomatoes, olives, and fancy cheese. Even the most discriminating yuppie will find all necessary items for a first-class picnic at Kihei Wine and Spirits.

The **Pikake Bakery,** open daily 7:30 a.m.-6 p.m. except Sunday, also at 300 Ohukai Rd., bakes some of the best breads and pastries in Kihei. Choose a bread flavored with red onions and olives or red potatoes and rosemary. Order a cup of cappuccino and choose a cinnamon roll with macadamia nuts; a walnut muffin; cheese, custard, or chocolate bear claw; or a passion fruit poppyseed muffin. All breads and pastries are made fresh with the finest ingredients.

The **Kalama Village Bakery,** 1913 S. Kihei Rd. behind Alexander's, also offers the community the best in baked goods. Stop in for a freshly baked loaf of homestyle bread to take home or sit out back on the patio deck and eat your pastry there. With so many selections, your only problem might be what to choose. Whole cakes and tortes are available, and birthday and wedding cakes can be ordered.

DIVE SHOPS AND MARINE RENTALS

The **Maui Dive Shop** has a main store and office at 1455 S. Kihei Rd. near the Star Market in Kihei, and offers a full range of equipment, lessons, and rentals. Open daily 7:30 a.m.-9 p.m., it is one of the oldest and most respected companies in the business. Other locations along this coast are those at the Kamaole Shopping Center, tel. (808) 879-1533, and at the Wailea Shopping Village, tel. (808) 879-3166, with several others around the island.

The **Dive and Sea Center,** 1975 S. Kihei Rd., tel. (808) 874-1952, open Mon.-Sat. 7 a.m.-5 p.m., is a full-service dive shop offering scuba dives, four-day certification classes for $250, air refills, equipment rentals (scuba gear $19.95 per day, snorkel gear $5 per day), and dive/snorkel trips to Molokini Crater (snorkelers pay $65; a one-tank beginner dive costs $85) on a six-passenger Farallon boat so that you are given individual attention and full value for the money.

Snorkel Bob's, tel. (808) 879-8225, is easy to spot at 1913 S. Kihei Road. The weekly prices can't be beat at $15 for snorkel gear or boogie boards (day rentals available too). You also get snorkel tips, a fish I.D. card, and the semi-soggy underwater humor of Snorkel Bob.

Auntie Snorkel, tel. (808) 879-6263, located at the Rainbow Mall and operated by Melissa and Mike McCoy, rents snorkel gear, along with boogie boards, beach chairs, and even ice chests. These are among the lowest prices in the area.

Also at the Rainbow Mall, **South Pacific Kayaks and Outfitters,** tel. (808) 875-4848, open daily 8 a.m.-5 p.m., offers a half-day introductory kayak trip for $65, or an advanced explorer trip along the remote coastline of East Maui for $89. Both tours include lunch along with plenty of snorkeling opportunities as you glide in and out of tiny bays fashioned from jutting lava rock fingers. South Pacific Kayaks offers rentals of single kayaks at $30 and double kayaks at $50, per day.

SeaEscape U-Drive Boat Rental, 1979 S. Kihei Rd., tel. (808) 879-3721, offers seagoing motorized rafts and Boston Whalers that you can pilot yourself to all the snorkel, dive, and picturesque spots of the Lahaina Roads. Rates run $75-95 per hour, two-hour minimum.

Ocean Activities Center, tel. (808) 879-4485, is at the Kamaole Shopping Center. You can book every fun activity on Maui and purchase anything you'll need for sun and surf at this excellent one-stop store.

SERVICES AND INFORMATION

Medical

For medical emergencies try: Kihei Physicians, tel. (808) 879-7781, at 1325 S. Kihei Rd., Suite 103, open 8 a.m.-10 p.m. daily; Kihei-Wailea Medical Center, tel. (808) 874-8100, 41 E. Lipoa St., with physicians, a pharmacy, physical therapy, and a clinical laboratory, open Mon.-Fri. 8 a.m.-8 p.m., Saturday and Sunday until 5 p.m.; Kihei Clinic and Wailea Medical Service, 2349 S. Kihei Rd., tel. (808) 879-1440, open Mon.-Fri. 8 a.m.-7 p.m., Saturday until 6 p.m., and Sunday and holidays 9 a.m.-2 p.m.; or the walk-in Kaiser Permanente Kihei Clinic, tel. (808) 891-3000, in Azeka Place II, open Mon.-Fri. 8 a.m.-5 p.m., closed noon-1 p.m., weekends, and holidays.

Chiropractic services are available at the Chiropractic Clinic of Kihei, tel. (808) 879-7246, 1847 S. Kihei Rd., which specializes in non-force techniques, and Kihei Chiropractic Center, tel. (808) 879-0638, at the Dolphin Plaza. There's also Kihei Acupuncture Clinic, tel. (808) 874-0544, run by Dr. Nancy Macauley, specializing in gentle needling techniques and offering a full selection of Chinese herbs.

Postal

The main post office in Kihei is located at Azeka Place, 1254 S. Kihei Rd., tel. (808) 879-2403. Mail Boxes Etc. at Longs Shopping Center, open weekdays 8 a.m.-6 p.m., Saturday 9 a.m.-5 p.m., Sunday 10 a.m.-3 p.m., offers fax services, copies, notary, and packing and shipping. With basically the same services, you'll find Postal Connection of Kihei at Azeka Place II, open Mon.-Fri. 8:30 a.m.-6 p.m. and Saturday 9 a.m.-5 p.m.

Information

The member organization Kihei Destination Association has a great deal of information about South Maui: hotels, B&Bs, restaurants, activities, shopping, services, real estate, and more. Contact the association at: 101 N. Kihei Rd., #4, Kihei, HI 96753, tel. (808) 874-9400 or 891-0770, fax 879-1283, website: www.maui.net/~kda.

Laundry

At the Kukui Mall is the Kukui Laundromat, tel. (808) 879-7211, open daily 7:30 a.m.-8 p.m., featuring self- or full-service washing. Lipoa Laundry Center, 41 E. Lipoa, tel. (808) 875-9266, is also a full-service laundry and dry cleaning establishment. Open 8 a.m.-8 p.m. with shorter hours on Sunday.

Reading

The Kihei Public library, tel. (808) 875-6833, is across the street from the Kihei Town Center. It has variable daily hours.

For a full-service bookstore browse at Waldenbooks at the Kukui Mall, tel. (808) 874-3688, open Mon.-Sat. 9 a.m.-9 p.m., Sunday 10 a.m.-5:30 p.m. You will find shelves stocked with all kinds of books and titles from fiction to travel guidebooks.

Transportation

From Kihei, shuttles run to various places on the island. **SpeediShuttle** makes numerous daily trips to the airport in Kahului. The old-style trolley-like bus, **"Da Mall" Trolley**, connects Wailea and Kihei to Kaahumanu Center, the Maui Mall, and Maui Marketplace in Kahului for your shopping pleasure. If the malls in Kahului aren't enough to satisfy you shopping needs, the Whalers Village shuttle **Maui Shopping Express** runs from South Maui to the Whalers Village mall in Kaanapali. To reach Maalaea, take the **Maui Ocean Center Shuttle.** For details, see Maui's introduction.

WAILEA

Wailea (Waters of Lea or Joyful Waters) isn't for the hoi polloi. It's a deluxe resort area custom-tailored to fit the egos of the upper class like a pair of silk pajamas. This section of southeastern Maui was barren and bleak until Alexander and Baldwin Co. decided to landscape it into an emerald 1,450-acre oasis of world-class golf courses and destination resorts. Every street light, palm tree, and potted plant is a deliberate accessory to the decor so that the overall feeling is soothing, pleasant, and in good taste. To dispel any notions of snootiness, the five sparkling beaches that front the resorts were left open to the public and even improved with better access, parking areas, showers, and picnic tables—a gracious gesture even if state law does require open access! You'll know when you leave Kihei and enter Wailea. The green, quiet, and wide tree-lined avenues give the impression of an upper-class residential area. Wailea is where you come when quality is the most important aspect of your vacation. The brilliant five-star resorts are first-rate architecturally, and the grounds are exquisite botanical jewel boxes.

Aside from the beaches, the two main attractions in Wailea are the fantastic golf and tennis opportunities. Three magnificent golf courses have been laid out on Haleakala's lower slopes, all open to the public. Tennis is great at the Wailea Tennis Center and many of the hotels and condos have their own championship courts.

Running along the water from one end of Wailea to the other is a 1.5-mile long beach walk. This walkway cuts across all properties in the area from the Renaissance Wailea Beach Resort to the Kai Lani Hotel, and like the beaches is open to the public. Used often in the early morning or late afternoon for exercise by walkers and joggers, it's a convenient way to get to the next beach or to the next resort for lunch or dinner. Even if you're not staying in the area, take a stroll down the path and have a look at the wonderfully landscaped gardens and resort properties here.

You can get to Wailea by coming straight down South Kihei Road through the strip of condos and shopping centers. To miss this area and make better time, take Piilani Highway, Rt. 31. This route takes you up on the hillside, where you have some nice views out over the water and can watch Kihei slip by in a blur below.

Onward and Backward

If you turn your back to the sea and look toward Haleakala, you'll see its cool, green forests and peak wreathed in mysterious clouds. You'll want to run right over, but you can't get there from here! Outrageous as it may sound, you have to double back 18 miles to Kahului and then head down Rt. 37 for another 20 miles just to get to the exact same spot on Rt. 37 that you can easily see. On the map there's a neat little private road that connects the Wailea/Makena area with Upcountry in a mere three-mile stretch, but it's always closed as it traverses ranchland! An ongoing fight over who's responsible for its maintenance keeps it that way. If this appalling situation is ever rectified, you'll be able to travel easily to the Tedeschi Winery and continue on the "wrong way" to Hana, or go left to Kula and Upcountry. For now, however, happy motoring!

BEACHES

If you're not fortunate enough to be staying in Wailea, the best reason for coming here is its beaches. These little beauties are crescent moons of white sand that usually end in lava outcroppings on both ends. This makes for shel-

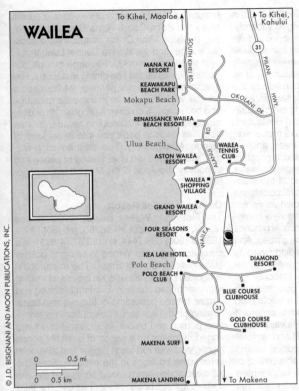

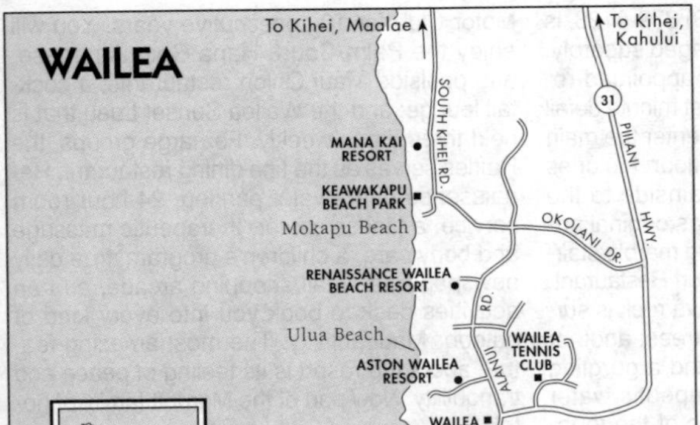
WAILEA
To Kihei, Maalae
To Kihei, Kahului
SOUTH KIHEI RD.
31
PIILANI HWY
MANA KAI RESORT
KEAWAKAPU BEACH PARK
Mokapu Beach
OKOLANI DR.
RENAISSANCE WAILEA BEACH RESORT
Ulua Beach
WAILEA TENNIS CLUB
ASTON WAILEA RESORT
ALANUI RD.
WAILEA SHOPPING VILLAGE
GRAND WAILEA RESORT
FOUR SEASONS RESORT
WAILEA
KEA LANI HOTEL
Polo Beach
POLO BEACH CLUB
DIAMOND RESORT
BLUE COURSE CLUBHOUSE
31
GOLD COURSE CLUBHOUSE
MAKENA SURF
0 0.5 mi
0 0.5 km
MAKENA LANDING
To Makena

© J.D. BISIGNANI AND MOON PUBLICATIONS, INC.

tered swimmable waters and good snorkeling and scuba. Many of the hotel guests in Wailea seem to hang around the hotel pools, maybe peacocking or just trying to get their money's worth, so the beaches are surprisingly uncrowded. The following beaches are listed from north to south, toward Makena.

Keawakapu

The first Wailea beach, almost a buffer between Kihei and Wailea, is just past the Mana Kai Resort. Turn left onto Kamala Place, or proceed straight on S. Kihei Road until it dead-ends. Plenty of parking at both accesses, but no amenities. Keawakapu is a lovely white-sand beach with a sandy bottom. Good swimming and fair snorkeling. There's also a beginner's dive spot offshore where an underwater junkyard of a few hundred cars forms an artificial reef.

Mokapu and Ulua

These two beaches are shoulder to shoulder, separated only by a rock outcropping. Turn right off Wailea Alanui at the first turn past the Outrigger Wailea Resort. The beach is clearly marked, and there's a parking area, showers, and restrooms. Being resort beaches, they're both particularly well-kept. Beautiful white sand and protected waters are perfect for swimming. There's good snorkeling at the outcropping separating the beaches, or swim out to the first reef just in front of the rocks for excellent snorkeling.

Wailea Beach

The Outrigger, Grand Wailea, and Four Seasons resorts front this beach. One-half mile past the Wailea town center, turn right onto a clearly marked access road; at the beach there's good parking, as well as showers and toilets. A short but wide beach of white sand, Wailea offers good swimming and bodysurfing, but the snorkeling is only fair.

Polo Beach

Follow Wailea Alanui toward Makena. Turn right on Kaukahi Street just past the Kea Lani Resort and right again at the clearly marked sign near Polo Beach condo. Here also are paved parking, showers, and toilets. Polo Beach is good for swimming and sunbathing, with few tourists. There's excellent snorkeling in front of the rocks separating Polo from Wailea Beach—tremendous amounts of fish, and one of the easiest spots to get to.

LUXURY ACCOMMODATIONS

Renaissance Wailea Beach Resort

Always a beauty, the Renaissance Wailea, 3550 Wailea Alanui, Wailea, HI 96753, tel. (808) 879-

4900 or (800) 992-4532, fax (808) 879-6128, is like a rich red cabernet that has aged superbly. The Renaissance is a superbly appointed resort with attention given to the most minute detail of comfort and luxury. When you enter the main lobby, you're actually on the fifth floor; the ones below terrace down the mountainside to the golden-sand beach. The lobby has original artworks on the walls and a sweeping marble staircase leading down to the Palm Court Restaurant. A bubbling spa fashioned from lava rock is surrounded by vines and flowering trees; another spa contains three little pools and a gurgling fountain, so that while the therapeutic water soothes your muscles, the music of the fountain soothes your nerves. The hotel boasts the best beach in the area, long known as an excellent vantage point from which to view humpback whales in season. The impeccable grounds have grown into an actual botanical garden. And everywhere there is water, cascading over tiny waterfalls, tumbling in brooks, and reflecting the amazing green canopy in tranquil lagoons.

The white-on-tan rooms are appointed with koa and rattan furniture. Beds are brightened with quilted pillows, and each room is accented with standing lamps, paintings of Hawaiian flora, an entertainment center with VCR and remote-control TV, wall safe, a glass-topped writing desk, even matching *yukata* for an evening of lounging. Sliding doors lead to a lanai where you can relax or enjoy a quiet in-room meal. The bathrooms are small but adequate, with double marble-topped sinks, a queen-size tub, pulsing shower head, vanity mirror, hair dryer, and quality lotions, soaps, and creams.

The hotel features the very private **Mokapu Beach Club,** a detached low-rise wing complete with its own pool and daily continental breakfast, where the hotel's impeccable service rises yet higher with valet service and 24-hour concierge. Room rates are $320 for a standard, $350 for a garden view, $380-435 for an ocean view, $550 for a room in the Makapu Beach Club, and $650 for a one-bedroom suite; $25 additional person. Varying rates include a family plan, where children under 18 stay free if they're in their parents' room, and also a variety of golf and tennis packages.

Renaissance Wailea Beach Resort has been acclaimed as a five-diamond resort by the AAA Motor Club for 10 consecutive years. You will enjoy the Palm Court, Hana Goin Japanese, and poolside Maui Onion restaurants; a cocktail lounge; and the Wailea Sunset Luau that is held three times weekly. For large groups, the Raffles serves as the fine dining restaurant. Renaissance offers valet parking, 24-hour room service, a fitness center, therapeutic massage and body care, a children's program, free daily newspaper, a small shopping arcade, and an activities desk to book you into every kind of outdoor Maui activity. The most amazing feature about the resort is its feeling of peace and tranquillity. Now part of the Marriott family of hotels.

Outrigger Wailea Resort

The Outrigger Wailea Resort, 3700 Wailea Alanui, Wailea, Maui, HI 96753, tel. (808) 879-1922 or (800) 688-7444, fax (808) 874-8331, is a class act. Even the Wrong Way signs politely state *Please,* Do Not Enter. The main lobby, supported by gigantic wooden beams, is inviting with overstuffed chairs in an informal setting and frames a wide panorama of the sea and Lanai floating on the horizon. Walk out onto a stone-tiled portico and below, in a central courtyard ringed by palms, is a series of quiet lily ponds highlighted with red torch ginger and alive with serenading bullfrogs in the evening. Stroll the 22 meticulously landscaped acres and dip into one of the three pools: two for relaxing, the third a lap pool designed to give the illusion that the pool stretches to the sea.

The Outrigger Wailea Resort was the first large hotel property in Wailea. It has roots here. Not only that, but it makes the claim of being the "most Hawaiian hotel in Wailea." From the little touches to the large efforts, many would say that it is so. The hotel has established a position of Director of Hawaiian Activities and runs a Hawaiian cultural program called Ho'olokahi that not only educates the staff about its own Hawaiian heritage but also shares the Hawaiian culture with guests and brings the community to the hotel for cultural exchanges. The Hawaiian cultural program has a varied schedule of activities and workshops presented by knowledgeable Hawaiian elders and teachers. All you need to do to attend is sign up. Some activities are hula demonstrations and contests, a lei festival, an evening torchlight ceremony, and a Friday art and craft display and sale in the hotel lobby. The resort also hosts a Hawaiian sailing canoe regatta, which is accompanied by numerous cultural activities and events. In addition, the restaurant Hula Moons is dedicated to Don Blanding, an early enthusiast of Hawaii and Hawaiian culture from the early 20th century, and it proudly displays some of Blanding's personal belongings and mementos of the times.

At least 70% of the resort's rooms have ocean views, which in most cases are actually oceanfront. Rooms are coordinated with light pastel tones of green-on-tan and beige, appointed with marble-topped writing desks and incidental tables. All have a large entertainment center with remote-control TV, a small refrigerator, coffeemaker, and a double closet with full-length mirror. Marble bathrooms are well-proportioned with a full bath and shower, double sinks, and separate dressing area. Doors open to a terracotta floored lanai, flushed with sunshine and sea breezes, from where you have a private view of the Lahaina Roads. More amenities include room service, a self-service laundry, complimentary valet parking, a beauty salon, and fitness center. For the kids, Keiki Club Gecko fills the day with supervised activities for a nominal fee. Hotel restaurants are Lea's, Hula Moons, and the Lanai Terrace, and they'll certainly please, or pop into the Pa'ani game bar for a friendly little game of foosball and a beer. While you're here, you won't want to miss the award-winning luau and Polynesian show, "Wailea's Finest Luau." Room rates run $219 for a standard garden room to $399 for a deluxe oceanfront room; suites are available for $499-899, $30 per extra person. Special family plans, room and car, honeymoon, and golf packages are available.

Grand Wailea Resort and Spa

A sublime interplay of cascading water, light diffused and brilliant, and the music of natural sound have been entwined with fine art, sculpted landscaping, and brilliant architecture to create the intangible quality of grandeur so apparent at the astounding Grand Wailea Resort and Spa, 3850 Wailea Alanui, Wailea, HI 96753, tel. (808) 875-1234, fax 874-2442, website: grandwailea.com. On arrival the spume of a thunderous waterfall, misting a heroic sculpture of the warrior king, Kamehameha, is the tangible spirit of the grand hotel. Inside the towering reception atrium, alive with the essence of more than 10,000 plants, flowers, and ferns, the water and sculpture interplay continues. Hula dancers both male and female, some with arms outstretched to the sun, others in repose or in a stance of power, are the visual *mele* singing of the ancient times. A mermaid, bronzed, bare-breasted, offers a triton shell of sweet water, and behind, sleek canoes float on a pond of blue. Alcoves and arches frame dramatic scenes in every direction. Ahead the glimmering sea, foaming surf, and wind-tossed palms dance to their immortal tune. Left and right, Fernando Botero's sculpted women —enormous, buxom, and pleasant—lie in alluring repose. Bellmen, in starched white livery, lead you to your room over marble floors embossed with mosaic tiles and laid over with rich carpets.

Rooms, the least of which has an ocean view, feature private lanai that look out over the water and flower gardens below, while inside they are sanctuaries of pure luxury. All are appointed in soothing earth tones with comfortable puff-pillowed chairs, a complete entertainment center with remote color TV, VCR, mini-fridge and bar, in-room safes, multiple phones, twice daily maid service, and turndown service. Rates are $380-445 for standard rooms, and $1,100-2,000 for suites. Guests of the Napua Tower have concierge service and many special amenities. Rooms here run $580, suites $1,400-3,000.

If Nero had the health and relaxation resources found at the hotel's Spa Grande, his fiddle playing would have vastly improved and Rome never would have burned. You enter the facility and the magic begins as soon as you shed your clothing and don a fluffy terry cloth robe. Walk the marble floors and choose a loofah scrub or dip first into a Japanese *ofuro* that unjangles nerves and soothes muscles. From there, a cold dip to revitalize and then into the Terme Circuit, a series of baths, one more intriguing than the other. Choose from a jello green papaya bath, a dark green *limu* bath, a mud bath, or the crystal waters of an aroma bath. Special to the facility are the Hawaiian rejuvenating bath, made from Hawaiian alae salt and a number of spices, and the tropical enzyme bath, especially good for the skin. From there a cascading waterfall massages you with watery fingers, or a jet bath sends 50 penetrating streams of water in varying temperatures that let you know that you are indeed alive. Awaiting you are private massage rooms where you can choose seven different types of massage and five different types of facials. Each room opens to the sea whose eternal rhythm helps to create complete relaxation.

The pool area surrounds a "volcano" and fronts Wailea beach. Here, a formal fountain, surrounded by royal palms, is reflected in a rectangular pool inlaid with white and gold tile forming a giant hibiscus. A canyon river, complete with gentle current, glides you through a series of pools and past small grottoes where you can stop to enjoy a jacuzzi, swing like Tom Sawyer on a suspended rope, swim up to a bar for your favorite drink, or just slip along until you are deposited in the main pool. Waiting is the world's only water elevator, to lift you to the top again and again.

To make a family visit perfect, there is **Camp Wailea**, $40 half day or $65 per day, for children ages 4-12. The day camp, run by professionals, features movies, a preschool playroom, arts and crafts, a computer learning center, video game room, and a kids' restaurant with their own dance floor and soda fountain. Scuba diving lessons, a catamaran sail, and other water activities and rentals are arranged by an outside concession on hotel property near the beach. Periodic tours of the grounds and hotel art are offered. The grounds tour is free and given Thursday at 10 a.m.; the art tour is Tuesday and Friday at 10 a.m., and is free to hotel guests but $6.25 for nonguests. And finally, there is a nondenominational **chapel,** a miniature cathedral with floor-to-ceiling stained-glass windows by renowned Indonesian artist Yvonne Cheng, as well as a number of exclusive shops and boutiques for your shopping pleasure.

Four Seasons Resort Wailea

AAA five-diamond award winner the Four Seasons, 3900 Wailea Alanui, Wailea, Maui, HI 96753, tel. (808) 874-8000 or (800) 334-6284, fax (808) 874-6449, situated on 15 acres at the south end of Wailea Beach, is oriented to the setting sun and opens itself up to the sweet sea breezes. Casually elegant, the open-air lobby is full of cushy chairs and couches, fountains, flowers, fans, and a grand staircase that glides down to the huge pool at beach level. On the way down, say "hello" to Ricky and Lucy, the hotel parakeets who make their home below the staircase. The pool and the colonnade of lobby pillars above it hint at a Romanesque architectural influence, yet the ambience and colors of the hotel say island natural. Original artwork and reproductions hang throughout the lobby and hallways, while huge fossilized sea anemones are displayed on lobby tables, and birds and plants bring the outdoors inside. Countless little details make this resort pleasant and special.

The Four Seasons is a study of cream-on-cream, and this color scheme runs throughout the resort, offset by coral, almond, muted greens, and other pastels. Each large room has a bedroom and sitting area, an exceptionally large bath with separate shower and deep tub, a well-stocked wet bar, TV, room safe, and private lanai; 85% of the rooms have an ocean view and all have twice-daily room service. While air-conditioning is standard, rooms also have sliding screen doors or louvered French doors and overhead fans. Double rooms and suites are even more spacious, with the addition of a second bathroom and/or a dining area. Rates for the standard rooms run $295 for a mountain view to $550 for a prime ocean view, $80 extra person. Depending upon the number of bedrooms and location, suites run $545-5,200. Rates on the Club Floor, which includes on-floor check-in, complimentary continental breakfast, afternoon tea, sunset cocktails and hors d'oeuvres, and a personal concierge, run $625-5,700 a day, $140 extra person. The club lounge on this floor also provides books, newspapers, magazines, and board games; golf, family, room and car, and romance packages are also available.

Other amenities include three top-notch restaurants, a lobby lounge, a game room with a fine collection of surfing memorabilia, meeting rooms for conventions, complimentary valet parking, 24-hour room service, and an early arrival-late departure lounge where you can relax and enjoy the hotel services, store a small bag, or shower off the grit of travel. In addition, the supervised "Kids for all Seasons" program can keep your little ones ages 5-12 busy for all or part of the day, 9 a.m.-5 p.m., with games and

garden of the luxurious Four Seasons Resort

activities. On site are two tennis courts and lawn croquet (for guests only); an expanded health club with exercise machines and a steam room that offers massage and personal training; and organized beach activities. Five shops are also here, among them Viewpoint, for alohawear; Hildgund Jewelers; and Lamonts, a gift and sundries shop. Down by the beach, all beach chairs, cabanas, snorkel equipment (free rental for one hour), boogie boards, and the like are complimentary—added value for guests. These and most hotel amenities are included in the room charge. Although not cheap, you get a lot for your money and great service.

Kea Lani Hotel

While Aladdin napped and dreamed of high adventure, his genie was at work building a pleasure dome more splendid than the great Khan's Xanadu. The Kea Lani Hotel, 4100 Wailea Alanui, Wailea, HI 96753, tel. (808) 875-4100 or (800) 882-4100, fax (808) 875-1200, website: www.kealani.com, is an alabaster fantasy bazaar where turrets and cupolas cover vaulted and coved ceilings suspended above towering pillars. Enter the central lobby, an open-air court with a bubbling fountain, completely sculpted and gilded; sultan's slippers would be appropriate here to pad around on the mosaic floors. A staircase leads to a tranquil pool area fronting a wide sweep of grass and perpetual blue sea. On the second level is a parlor, formal but comfortable, with giant shoji-like mirrors and sculpted harps and lyres embedded in the walls.

Lodging at the Kea Lani is in one-bedroom luxury suites priced $295-525, or in opulent one-, two- and three-bedroom villas priced $900-1,400 that include a car and private pool. Several room/car and room/meal packages are available. Enter the suites, very roomy at just under 900 square feet, to find the rich embossed weave of a Berber carpet contrasting with white-on-white walls. Double doors open to the master bedroom with its own entertainment center, minibar, large dresser/vanity, and brass valet. The parlor, formal but comfy, is appointed with puff-pillowed chairs, a queen-size sleeper sofa, entertainment center, marble-topped tables, and a full bar with microwave and coffeemaker. All rooms are air-conditioned, but there are also ceiling fans. The bathroom, marble from floor to ceiling, features an oversize tub, two pedestal sinks, a huge stall shower, bath products, full-length mirror, a hair dryer, a vanity mirror, and cotton *yukata* for a day of lounging. A steam iron and board are available for last minute touch-ups.

The villas are magnificent. Outside is a private courtyard complete with table, cotton-clad chaise lounges, and a plunge pool, slightly heated and perfect for two. Inside, the bilevel villa includes a completely tiled living room, furnished with an Oriental rug, glass-topped tables, couches and chairs, and a complete entertainment center. The kitchen includes a fridge, stove, microwave, trash compactor, dishwasher, and laundry room. Two downstairs bedrooms, each with full baths, pamper you with queen-size beds. Upstairs, an alcove leads to the master bedroom self-contained with entertainment center; minibar; two pedestal sinks; a deep, almost two-person tub; and a huge shower area. The walk-in closet, as large as many hotel rooms, features a wall safe.

The hotel's pool area is grand, just right for frolicking or for savoring an afternoon siesta. A free-form upper pool, boasting a swim-to bar, and serviced by the Polo Beach Grill, is connected to the lower pool by a 140-foot water slide. The lower area is family oriented with a football-shaped children's pool, but escape is at hand at the casbah pool, inlaid with multi-hued tiles forming an entwined moon and sun around it; adults can shelter in Camelot-like tents providing shade and privacy.

Other amenities include an activities desk, in-house doctor's office, video library, complimentary fitness center, spa, a clutch of swank boutiques, jewelry store, and a hair salon. The children have their own Keiki Lani children's program, open daily 9 a.m.-3 p.m., where children ages 5-12 are entertained with a mixture of fun and educational activities, and even given lunch.

Destination Resorts Hawaii

Located at 3750 Wailea Alanui, Wailea, HI 96753, tel. (808) 879-1595 or (800) 367-5246, fax (808) 874-3554, website: www.destinationresortshi.com, this complex is made up of six separate villages that are scattered along the coast or up around the golf course. Located near the Blue Course, **Ekolu** has one- and two-bedroom condo units for $140-230. Also on the golf links and next to Wailea Tennis Club is **Grand Champions,** with one- and two-bedroom units for $150-240. **Ekahi,** located at the entrance to Wailea and the least expensive of the oceanfront properties, has studio, one- and two-bedroom condos for $149-349. Tucked between two ritzy hotels, **Elua** fronts Ulua Beach and has condominiums ranging $240-600. Right on Polo Beach is **Polo Beach Club,** the only high-rise condo building in the bunch. Rates here are $275-425 for one- or two-bedroom units. The newest and perhaps the most exclusive is **Makena Surf,** on a private section of coast a short way down the road toward Makena. Here one-, two-, and three-bedroom units run $305-600.

Special golf, tennis, car, and romance packages are available. There is a three- to five-night minimum stay, 10-14 nights during the Christmas-New Year's season; $20 extra person. The fifth or seventh night is free depending upon the village. All units are plush and fully furnished, with daily housekeeping service, concierge service, a swimming pool or pools, barbecue grills, and some with tennis courts on the premises. The beach, two golf courses, and additional tennis courts are nearby.

Diamond Resort

Formerly a member-only resort, this condo property is now open to all but gets mostly Japanese visitors. The Diamond Resort, 555 Kaukahi St., Wailea, HI 96753, tel. (808) 874-0500 or (800) 800-0720, fax (808) 874-8778, sits high above the Wailea Blue Golf Course and has a wonderful view over the ocean. The slate roof and stone exterior on the round portion of the main building make a wonderful first impression, and the pools and stream that cascade down between the buildings create a restful feeling. Let the resort's two restaurants fill your belly and the spa soothe your muscles. The spa features Japanese *ofuro,* Scandinavian saunas, and jacuzzis. The 72 large air-conditioned guest suites have ocean or partial-ocean views and come with kitchenettes, TV and VCRs, and lanai. Rates run $170-240 a night.

FOOD

At the Renaissance

The **Palm Court** is the main dining room at the Renaissance. Walk though the lobby and look over the rail to the partially open-air restaurant below, open for breakfast 6-11 a.m. and for dinner nightly from 6 p.m. The menu offers a different buffet every night featuring cuisines ranging from Italian to the Southwestern. The Palm Court is a first-rate restaurant with very reasonable prices, a good choice.

The **Sunset Terrace** just off the lobby is a delightful perch on which to have a drink and survey the grounds and beach below. Every evening brings a dramatic torch-lighting ceremony. The drums reverberate and the liquid melancholy of the conch trumpet sends a call for meditation at day's end. Drinks include the full complement of island specialties, and you can order wonderful gourmet-quality *pu pu*.

The **Maui Onion** is a convenient snack-type restaurant at poolside. Burgers, sandwiches, salads, smoothies, and Maui onion rings, the specialty, are on the limited menu. Prices are reasonable, especially if you don't want to budge from your lounge chair. On Wednesday and Friday evenings 5:30-8:30 p.m., relax here and dine under the stars on a limited choice of entrees.

Outrigger Restaurants

Lea's, the new fine dining restaurant at Outrigger Wailea, is sure to please. Sit inside in the sumptuous booths or out on the balcony overlooking the pool and garden. A breakfast buffet is served for $17, along with a full à la carte menu. In the evening you can hear the poolside music at Hula Moons waft up from downstairs. While there is much more on the menu, Lea's specializes in fresh fish and seafood. Start with a tiger shrimp lumpia for $8.95 and baked Maui onion soup at $4.95. Move on to seafood "Black Thai" risotto, a sautéed combination of lobster, shrimp, and scallops braised with black Thai rice in a spicy Sichuan broth, for $24.95, or stick with a market price fresh catch of the day, charbroiled, steamed, seared, or sautéed. One of the wonderfully rich desserts is certainly an appropriate way to round off your meal. Great care is taken at Lea's to use only the best ingredients; portions are filling, the presentation is pleasing, and there is something on the wine list to accompany any meal. Outrigger's fine dining establishment, Lea's is a class act.

Hula Moons, open daily for lunch and dinner, is a casual indoor/outdoor restaurant draped with awnings for shade and privacy. The name Hula Moons derives from the writings of Don Blanding, Hawaii's poet laureate, who arrived by steamship in 1924, dead broke, and remained for more than 40 years, all the while singing the island's praises. At the restaurant's entrance are opened drawers from Don Blanding's desk filled with memories—Lucky Strike cigarettes, round sunglasses, a box camera, matchboxes, and playing cards—all whispering of the time when Hawaii was a distant land where only the rich and famous came to escape. Nice nostalgic touch. Choose a table or horseshoe booth and for lunch dine on everything from a juicy footlong hot dog for $7 to mahimahi tempura for

$10.50. The poolside menu also offers sandwiches, salads, and appetizers. For dinner, the menu begins with kalua pork spring rolls for $7 and crisp lobster and crab fritters for $9. Entrees include *lilikoi* roast duckling for $21, a whole Maine lobster at $37, medallions of beef tenderloin at $24, and stir-fried Maui vegetables for $14. New to the restaurant, and for the chocoholics in all of us, is the "all-you-care-to-eat" chocolate dessert bar, featuring more than a dozen chocolate concoctions nightly. Hula Moons has an extensive wine list, with selections from France to Australia, and a full bar serving exotic drinks. There's entertainment nightly, with—what else—a hula show for part of the evening.

A special Sunday Champagne Brunch is offered in the Makani Room 10 a.m.-1 p.m. for $28. Let the piano accompaniment soothe your soul as you satiate your body with made-to-order omelettes, fresh fruits and pastries, or mouthwatering entrees of fish, poultry, and meat.

Grand Wailea

The resort has an eclectic mix of restaurants, all landscaped around the central theme of water, art, and flowers, offering a variety of cuisines catering to all tastes and appetites. **The Grand Dining Room Maui** is French with an Oriental twist. Start with wonderful appetizers like lobster noodle soufflé, a Maui Onion broth with Gruère, or a Mandarin chicken salad for $8-12. Entrees beginning at about $27 range from grilled *ahi* niçoise, to hoisin encrusted lamb loin. A fun and informal restaurant more reasonably priced is **Bistro Molokini.** Come for antipasti, pasta smothered in everything from shrimp to pancetta, pizza with fresh tomato, cheeses, and Italian meats, and main dishes like piccata Milanese, veal dipped in Parmesan and served with risotto.

Humuhumu is a thatched-roof Polynesian restaurant afloat on its own lagoon complete with 2,000 varieties of tropical fish in a huge aquarium. The specialties prepared at the Humuhumu come from throughout the Pacific. *Pu pu* like fried coconut shrimp or a dim sum basket are great to nibble on while enjoying a special exotic drink like a Humu Heaven. Entrees are delightful with offerings like wok-seared scallops Sichuan or an enormous porterhouse steak. Delectable but not cheap.

The **Cafe Kula** specializes in "Spa Cuisine," dishes especially prepared with dynamic health in mind. Here the freshest fruits, organic vegetables, and whole grains provide the foundation for most dishes. For breakfast enjoy fresh carrot juice for $5, homemade granola at $7, or apple-stuffed crepes with fresh brandied currants for $10. Healthful entree choices are Basmati rice torte or grilled salmon.

Perhaps the most elegant restaurant is **Kincha,** serving superb Japanese cuisine. Enter over stepping stones past a replica of a golden tea kettle used by Toyotomi Hideyoshi, revered as both a great warrior and a master of the *chanoyu,* the tea ceremony. Follow the stones past stone lanterns that light your way over a humpbacked bridge, a symbol of life, that crosses a tiny stream brimming with orange and white *koi.* Inside a raised *tatami* area awaits with sushi chefs ready to perform their magic. Private rooms, comfortable with *zabuton* backrests, are perfect for a very refined full meal. For a treat order the sashimi moriawase, a sampler of the best sashimi, or start with a hot appetizer like *kani shumai,* deep-fried croquette of crab. Soups and salads are *wafu* salad, *miso wan,* or *cha soba,* tea-flavored buckwheat noodles. Entrees are Japanese favorites like hamachi teriyaki, broiled yellowtail tuna, or tempura, regular or deluxe, with prices from $35 on up.

Four Seasons

Located at the Four Seasons Resort, the elegant **Seasons** restaurant is an experience in fine dining. With table linen, crystal, classical music, and jackets required for men, the Seasons is elegant, but not stuffy. The decor is teal and weathered bamboo, the windows open to let in sea breezes and moonlight, and the island cuisine is offered in a "homelike" presentation. It is here that the freshest of Hawaiian ingredients with a French technique, give this regional cuisine a French soul. Emphasis is on fresh island seafood. Open for dinner only Tues.-Sat. 6-9:30 p.m.; live music and dancing until 10:30. Reservations are recommended, and proper dress required.

The casual **Pacific Grill** restaurant combines a large selection of foods from the Orient and the West. The breakfast buffet is a long-established special, but an à la carte menu is also available. For dinner, entrees are from Asia and the Pacific, some cooked in view of the guests. Pacific edge entree specialties include steamed ehu Oriental style at $28.50 and charred duck breast with a citrus glaze for $27.50; some home-style cooking entrees are roasted half chicken for $21.50 and grilled and herb marinated porterhouse at $32.50. At the Pacific Grill, alohawear and activewear are the norm.

Ferraro's at Seaside serves as two distinct restaurants. For lunch, 11:30 a.m.-3 p.m., dine on healthy light fare, mostly seafood and grilled items. *Pu pu* and drinks are served 3-5 p.m. As Italian as Italian can be, Ferraro's opens at 6 p.m. and serves up with Hawaiian entertainment. Start with an antipasti like deep-fried mozzarella and olives in tomato sauce for $9, and move on to pepper-crusted seared *ahi* at $27, chicken breast wrapped with prosciutto for $22.50, or pasta with tomato, eggplant, and caper sauce for $21.50. Set almost on the water, Ferraro's is a great place to watch the sunset.

Kea Lani

For casual dining any time of the day visit **Cafe Ciao,** rich with the smell of espresso, where the shelves hold homemade jellies, jams, chutney, peppercorn ketchup, and Italian olives. Choose fresh-baked bread, pastries, a spicy focaccia, pesto salad, even ready-to microwave Italian rigatoni and chicken Parmesan. For lunch and dinner try the poolside **Polo Beach Grill and Bar** for a light salad, sandwich, or kiawe-grilled burger.

Towering glass and wooden doors open into **Kea Lani** restaurant, where elegant dining is assured in this sanctuary hung with huge chandeliers and capped with a molded ceiling. Ocean breezes flow freely through louvered windows into the white-on-gray great hall furnished with marble-topped tables. For a romantic evening, choose a table in a more intimate area, where a lowered ceiling and massive sideboard filled with wine and set with pottery create a warmer, candle-lit atmosphere. At the entrance to the restaurant is a lounge area with a hand-rubbed wooden bar that offers evening entertainment, usually a jazz or Hawaiian ensemble. Dinners are a combination of Pacific Rim and European in flavor, with fish as a specialty. Expect entrees from $25, and quality to match.

Diamond Resort

The two restaurants here are the **Taiko** and the **Le Gunji.** Taiko serves breakfast, lunch, and dinner and is open 7 a.m.-9 p.m. The day starts with a Japanese- or Western-style breakfast for

$13; lunch includes sandwiches and burgers, or Japanese *soba, udon,* or other traditional dishes. Dinner entrees, like teriyaki chicken and lobster daiyaki, run $18-27; a whole range of sushi is also available. Le Gunji has limited seating at 6 p.m. and 7:30 p.m. only; reservations are a necessity and a dress code is enforced. Choose from five set menus, ranging $45-75. Here, French food is prepared, unusually, on a *teppan yaki* grill.

Sandcastle Restaurant

Located at Wailea Shopping Village, tel. (808) 879-0606, this moderate restaurant is far enough out of the way that you can count on getting a table, but reservations are recommended anyway. The restaurant, overlooking a small courtyard, has wraparound glass and mirrors, vaulted ceilings, and latticework partitions allowing for some privacy. Lunch served daily 11:30 a.m.-3 p.m. offers a full range of sandwiches from $6.95 to $12.95. Lighter appetites will enjoy a full salad selection for $3.95-8.95, which you can combine with a pizza for a full yet inexpensive meal. Dinner runs 5-9 p.m. Early bird specials, offered 5-6 p.m., are complete dinners for $9.95-14.95, otherwise the dinner menu offers entrees like roasted rack of lamb for $21.95, filet mignon for $19.95, fresh catch at the daily quote, and prime rib of beef au jus for $17.95. The Sandcastle also has a full bar with an excellent wine list. This restaurant is slated to be torn down when the Wailea Shopping Village is demolished for rebuilding.

Golf Ball Soup

The following restaurants are located at the golf links in the area. **The Chart House,** on the 14th fairway of Wailea Blue Course up from the Wailea Shopping Center, 100 Wailea Ike Dr., tel. (808) 879-2875, open daily for dinner from 5:30 p.m., is part of a small chain that deserves its reputation for consistently well-prepared and reasonably priced food. The menu has starters like artichoke salad for $5.25 or a Caesar salad for $8.95. Entrees include the specialty, prime rib, for $22.95 or $26.95 depending on cut, steaks costing $19.95-25.95, grilled teriyaki chicken breast for $16.50, or shrimp Santa Fe at $19.95. There's a children's menu with most dinners priced under $6.95. Aside from the regular menu, there's a daily menu with other tasty choices.

Don't forget about the enticing desserts, like chocolate mousse pie for $4.95 to key lime pie at $4.75 or mud pie for $6.25. The dining area is done in stout sturdy chairs and tables, and the green of the ferns and bamboo inside reflect the fairway green captured in the full glass wall. Also on the premises is the **Sunset Lounge,** an open-air bar, open from 5 p.m. until closing, where you can enjoy an evening cocktail.

The **Lobster Cove Restaurant,** tel. (808) 879-6677, across from the Chart House and open daily 5:30-10 p.m., is a seafood restaurant that shares space with **Harry's Sushi Bar** (as a second Harry's shares space with the Orient Express in Napili). Appetizers include garlic clams for $9.50, sweet and sour crispy shrimp at $11, and lobster cakes for $11.50. These would go well with the rock shrimp Caesar salad at $7.50. Entrees, limited but wonderful, might be seafood ravioli and spiny lobster and shrimp for $22, fresh island fish at market price, or a filet mignon at $24. Choose from an adequate wine list for a bottle to accompany your meal. You can order *pu pu* or make a meal from the offerings at Harry's. The choices of sushi are numerous and run $3.50-6 apiece, and are double that for a plate of sashimi. Also consider such items as California rolls for $5.25 or deep-fried soft-shell crabs at $7.

A little up the hill and across the road at the Wailea Tennis Club is **Joe's Bar and Grill,** tel. (808) 875-7767. Open for lunch 11 a.m.-2 p.m. and again for dinner 5:30-10 p.m., Joe's serves large and tasty portions of honest American, home-style comfort food in a relaxing atmosphere. Joe's is set directly above the tennis courts in a wood-floored open-beamed room, and cool breezes waft through the sliding glass partitions. Owner, operator, and chief schmoozer Joe Gannon is the other half to Haliimaile General Store restaurant's chef Beverly Gannon. Lunch is basically soup, salad, and sandwiches, while dinner offers heartier fare. Entrees range from Joe's famous meatloaf at $17 to filet mignon and grilled prawns for $30. The full bar has a full range of beers and can make any mixed drink that you desire.

At the Wailea Blue Golf Course clubhouse is the **Fairway Restaurant,** tel. (808) 879-4060. Open from 7:30 a.m. for breakfast, Fairway offers everything from eggs Benedict for $5.95 to a simple omelette for $4.75 or buttermilk pancakes, all you can eat, for $3.50. Lunch includes burgers and sandwiches costing $5-7. Dinner selections for $15-20 include filet mignon, New York pepper steak, veal parmigiana, or the salad bar for $11.95. Although the dining room isn't ultra fancy, there's a terrace, and the ambience is peaceful and unhurried. A good place to eat in an area not known for budget restaurants.

More recently, the **SeaWatch** restaurant, tel. (808) 875-8080, has opened at the Emerald Golf Course clubhouse, serving Hawaiian regional cuisine breakfast and lunch both 8 a.m.-3 p.m. Start with fruit for breakfast, or an egg or omelette concoction for $7-12. Salads, sandwiches, and noodle dishes run mostly $6.50-8, while main courses, like linguine, New York steak, and porcini-crusted veal chop range $18-28.

ENTERTAINMENT, SHOPPING, AND SERVICES

Entertainment
If you haven't had enough fun on the Wailea beaches during the day, you can show off your best dance steps at the **Tsunami** nightclub at the Grand Wailea. Easy listening music is performed every evening at the Sunset Terrace lounge on the lobby level of the Renaissance Resort overlooking the gardens, and for hula and local music try **Hula Moons** at the Outrigger Wailea.

Wailea Shopping Village
The only shopping in this area is at **Wailea Shopping Village,** open daily 9 a.m.-7 p.m., Sunday 10 a.m.-6 p.m., just east past the Outrigger Wailea Resort off Wailea Alanui. It has the usual collection of boutiques and shops. **Superwhale** offers alohawear for children. **Weber Goldsmith Galleries** sells fine jewelry, while

Miki's has racks of alohawear at very competitive prices. More exclusive shops are: **Maui's Best** with a range of gifts from the islands; **Isle Style,** a fine-arts gallery with works by local artists; the **Elephant Walk,** a shopping gallery of fine crafts; and **For Your Eyes Only,** which sells sunglasses for every eye and lifestyle. Money needs are handled by the **First Hawaiian Bank; Island Camera** offers accessories and processing; **Whalers General Store** sells food and liquor; **Fox 1-Hour Lab** takes care of your photo needs; and **Sub-Tropix** sells fast food, sandwiches, ice cream, beverages, and gift-food items. The **Maui Dive Shop** is a full-service dive shop with snorkel and scuba rentals, sales, and diving excursions.

The major hotels have an arcade of shops for quick and easy purchases. One of note is the **Coast Gallery, Maui** at the Outrigger Wailea Resort, which displays a wide range of mostly island art, including some unique wood and pottery pieces not usually on display at art galleries.

Medical
For immediate care of a nonemergency nature see Kihei Medical Services, tel. (808) 879-8828, at the Kea Lani Hotel, or contact the concierge at your hotel.

Transportation
The **Wailea Shuttle** is a complimentary jitney that stops at all major hotels and condos, the Wailea Shopping Village, and golf and tennis courts in Wailea about every 20-30 minutes. It operates 6:30 a.m.-8:30 p.m. Be sure to check with the driver about the last pickup times if you are out in the evening. With a little walking, this is a great way to hop from one beach to the next. For information on the schedule and stops, call (808) 879-2828.

MAKENA

Just a skip south down the road is Makena Beach, but it's a world away from Wailea. This was a hippie enclave during the '60s and early '70s, and the freewheeling spirit of the times is still partially evident in the area even though Makena is becoming more refined, sophisticated, and available to visitors. For one thing, "Little Makena" is a famous clothing-optional (unofficial) beach, but so what? You can skinny-dip in Connecticut. What's really important is that Makena is *the last* pristine coastal stretch in this part of Maui that hasn't succumbed to undue development . . . yet. Wailea Point, a promontory of land between Wailea and Makena, is the site of one new development, and others will be following in coming years on both sides of the road.

Aside from the sundries shop at the Maui Prince Hotel, there's nothing in the way of amenities past Wailea, so make sure to stock up on all supplies. In fact, there's nowhere to get *anything* past the hotel except for the lunch wagon

that's usually parked across from the state park entrance. The police come in and sweep the area now and again, but mostly it's mellow. They do arrest the nudists on Little Makena to make the point that Makena "ain't free no more." Rip-offs can be a problem, so lock your car, hide your camera, and don't leave anything of value. Be careful of the *kiawe* thorns when you park; they'll puncture a tire like a nail. The road south of the Maui Prince Hotel to La Perouse Bay is by and large fairly good with a decent surface. It does, however, narrow down to almost a single lane in spots, particularly where it slides past small coves. Drive carefully and defensively.

Makena is magnificent for bodysurfing and swimming. Whales frequent the area and come quite close to shore during the season. Turtles waddled on to Makena to lay their eggs in the warm sand until early in this century, but too many people gathered the eggs and the turtles scrambled away forever. The sunsets from **Red**

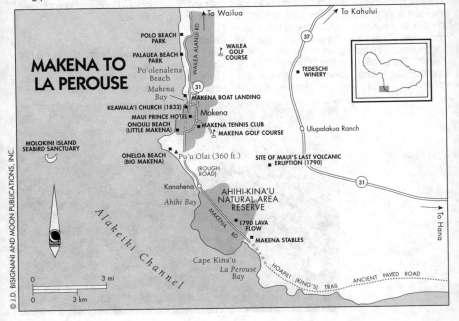

MAKENA TO LA PEROUSE

To Wailua
To Kahului

POLO BEACH PARK
PALAUEA BEACH PARK
Po'olenalena Beach
Makena Bay
MAKENA BOAT LANDING
KEAWALA'I CHURCH (1832)
Makena
MAUI PRINCE HOTEL
ONOULI BEACH (LITTLE MAKENA)
MAKENA TENNIS CLUB
MAKENA GOLF COURSE
WAILEA GOLF COURSE
WAILEA ALANUI RD.
37
TEDESCHI WINERY
31
Ulupalakua Ranch

MOLOKINI ISLAND SEABIRD SANCTUARY

ONELOA BEACH (BIG MAKENA)
Pu'u Olai (360 ft.)
(ROUGH ROAD)
SITE OF MAUI'S LAST VOLCANIC ERUPTION (1790)
31
To Hana

Kanahena
Ahihi Bay
AHIHI-KINA'U NATURAL AREA RESERVE
MAKENA RD.
1790 LAVA FLOW
MAKENA STABLES

Alakeiki Channel

Cape Kina'u
La Perouse Bay
HOAPILI (KING'S) TRAIL
ANCIENT PAVED ROAD

0   3 mi
0   3 km

© J.D. BISIGNANI AND MOON PUBLICATIONS, INC.

Hill (Puu Olai), the cinder cone separating Makena from Little Makena, are among the best on Maui; you can watch the sun sink down between Lanai, Kahoolawe, and West Maui. The silhouettes of pastel and gleaming colors are awe-inspiring. Oranges, russets, and every shade of purple reflect off the clouds that are caught here. Makena attracts all kinds: gawkers, burn-outs, adventurers, tourists, free spirits, and a lot of locals. It won't last long, so go and have a look now!

The Naked Truth

Some years ago in an extremely controversial episode, the Maui police came down hard on the nudists. They arrested nine top-free women from various parts of the U.S. and from foreign countries. The police acted in defiance of a then-recent Hawaii Supreme Court ruling that a woman's breasts when uncovered in appropriate circumstances (i.e., isolated beaches) do not violate the state's "open lewdness" statute. The women, defended by attorney Anthony Ranken, sought compensation for malicious prosecution. Some point directly at former mayor Hannibal Tavares for running a personal crusade against the au naturel sun-worshippers. To show the extent of the conflict, one harebrained scheme actually proposed was to pave a walkway to Red Hill so that Little Makena would no longer be an "isolated beach." The justification was to provide "wheelchair access" to Little Makena although a wheelchair would have to negotiate hundreds of yards of deep sand to get there. Imagine the consternation if the first wheelchair-using sunbather just happened to be a nudist!

Recreation

As the Maui Prince Hotel is a destination resort, on-site recreation possibilities include the beach and the swimming pool. Golf at **Makena Golf Course** and tennis at **Makena Tennis Club** are just across the road and offer world-class courts and links. **Makena Stables** offers trail rides at its location at the end of the road at La Perouse Bay. They also have kayaks and run tours along the coast here.

Keawalai Church

In Makena, you'll pass this Congregational Church, established in 1832. It was restored in 1952, and services are held every Sunday at 9:30 a.m. Many of the hymns and part of the sermon are still delivered in Hawaiian. Notice the three-foot thick walls and the gravestones, many with a ceramic picture of the deceased. A parking lot, restrooms, and showers are across the road for the beach access, which is just down the road. Take Honoiki Road, passing Makena Boat Landing on the way.

Small Beaches

You'll pass by these local beaches, via the Old Makena Road, as you head toward Makena. There are usually few people and no amenities. **Palauea** and **Poolenalena** are about three-quar-

Keawalai Church

ROBERT NILSEN

ters of a mile past Polo Beach. Good swimming and white sloping sands. **Nahuna (Five Graves) Point** is just more than a mile past Polo. An old graveyard marks the entrance. Not good for swimming but great for scuba because of deep underwater caves. Snorkelers can enjoy this area, too. A short distance farther on is the **Makena Boat Landing** (water, restrooms, showers), a launch site for boaters and scuba divers. **Papipi** is along the road 1.5 miles past Polo, but its small sand beach is too close to the road. **Oneuli** (Black Sand Beach) on the north side of Red Crater actually has a salt-and-pepper beach. Turn down a rutted dirt road for a third of a mile. Not good for swimming, but good diving, unofficial camping, and shore fishing. No amenities.

Makena Beach State Park

A few minutes past the Maui Prince Hotel, look for a *kaukau* wagon on the left where you might pick up a snack before turning right onto the access road. Negotiate the excessive speed bumps for a few hundred yards to the parking lot and a few portable toilets; a second beach access is a few hundred yards farther on. This is **Oneloa Beach,** generally called **Makena Big Beach,** a nice long golden strand of sand. Right leads you to **Puu Olai** (Red Hill), a 360-foot cinder cone. When you cross over the point from Big Makena Beach you'll be on **Little Makena,** a favorite clothing-optional beach for locals and tourists alike. You'll know that you're on the right beach by the bare bums and the peace sign outlined in white-painted rocks on the lava outcrop that you just climbed over to get to where you are. Both beaches are excellent for swimming (beware of currents in winter), bodysurfing, and superb snorkeling in front of Red Hill. With families and clothed sunbathers moving in (especially on weekends), Little Makena is no longer so "remote" or isolated. The beginning of the end may be in sight, although there is a movement loosely organized to retain this small sanctuary as a place for those who still wish to swim in the buff.

Ahihi-Kinau Natural Reserve

Look for the sign four miles past Polo Beach. Even this far down toward the end of the road—or perhaps because of it—this stretch of the coast is becoming a bit more populated and fancy homes are popping up here and there.

The jutting thumb of lava is **Cape Kinau,** part of Maui's last lava flow, which occurred in 1790. Here you'll find a narrow beach, the small community of Kanahena, and a desolate, tortured lava flow. Within the reserve, several walking trails start at pullouts along the road and lead to the water. Please stay on established paths and wear sturdy hiking shoes or boots. Dolphins often play off this point and whales can be seen near shore during winter months. Aside from the lava fields, Ahihi-Kinau is also an underwater reserve, so the scuba and snorkeling are first-rate. The best way to proceed is along the reef toward the left, or along the reef to the right if you enter at La Perouse Bay. Beware not to step on the many spiny urchins in the shallow water. If you do, vinegar or urine will help with the stinging.

La Perouse Bay

On the far side of Cape Kinau is La Perouse Bay, named after the French navigator Jean de François La Pérouse, first Westerner to land on Maui in May 1786. The bay is good for snorkelers and divers, but beware of the urchins on entry. If you walk farther around to the south you'll come across a string of pocket-size beaches. The currents can be tricky along here. Past the bay are remnants of the **Hoapili (King's) Trail,** still hikable along some of its distance. The public road ends at the entrance to La Perouse Bay, but with a 4WD you can get a fair distance down the rough track from here for good shore fishing and unofficial camping. Right before the pavement ends you'll find Makena Stables, where you can arrange trail rides in this dry, remote region.

LUXURY ACCOMMODATION

A gleaming wing-shaped building, understated and almost stark on the outside, the **Maui Prince Hotel,** 5400 Makena Alanui, Makena, HI 96753, tel. (808) 874-1111 or (800) 321-6284, fax (808) 879-8763, website: www.sheraton.com, is a fabulous destination resort that opens into an enormous central courtyard, one of the most beautiful in Hawaii. Japanese in its architecture and its sense of beauty, the courtyard is a protected haven of cascading waters, black lava rock, stone lanterns, breeze-tossed palms, and raked

Zen-like gardens. Lean over the hardwood rails of the balconies on each floor and soak in the visual pleasure of the landscape below, where from these balconies cascade flowers and ferns in sympathetic mimicry of Maui's waterfalls.

All rooms have an alcove door so that you can open your front door yet still have privacy and allow the breeze to pass through. Oceanview and oceanfront rooms ranging $260-410 are beautifully accentuated in earth tones and light pastels. The bathrooms have a separate commode and a separate shower and tub. One-bedroom suites, priced $500-1,000, feature a giant living room, three lanai, a large-screen TV and VCR, and white terry cloth robes for lounging. The master bedroom has its own TV, listening center, and king-size bed. A nonsmoking wing is also available. The Prince also offers the very reasonable Prince Special that includes an ocean-view room, midsize rental car, and buffet breakfast for two priced only $235 per night per couple; other honeymoon, golf, tennis, and car packages are also available.

The Maui Prince faces fantastic, secluded Maluaka Beach, almost like a little bay, with two points of lava marking it as a safe spot for swimming and snorkeling. Seven sea turtles live on the south point and come up on the beach to nest and lay their eggs. To the left you can see Puu Olai, a red cinder cone that marks Makena. The boat Kai Kanani arrives each morning and will take you snorkeling to Molokini or arrange other activities throughout the island. The pool area is made up of two circular pools, one for adults, the other a wading pool for kids; two whirlpools; blue cabanas; and a poolside snack bar. There's volleyball, croquet, six plexi-pave tennis courts with a pro on the staff, and the 36 holes of the Makena Golf Course, designed by Robert Trent Jones Jr., the main attraction of the Maui Prince. The concierge desk offers a variety of complimentary activities including a snorkel and scuba introduction. Sign up here for Makena Adventures, an interpretive tour through the entire Makena area via a hotel minivan, or for the Legend of Makena Luau. For the little ones, the Prince Kid's Club children's program can be arranged for $20 for a half day or $40 for a full day of healthy supervised activities. For the big people, see what the complimentary fitness center can do for you.

FOOD

The Prince has three restaurants, and head chef Gregory Gaspar is building an island-wide reputation for exquisite dining. The fanciest restaurant is the **Prince Court,** featuring fine dining for dinner only, except for the truly exceptional Sunday champagne brunch. The evening fare is Hawaiian regional cuisine and then some. Start with appetizers like orange-cured smoked salmon with warm Maui onions for $11.50, or soups and salads that include saffron parsley mussels soup for $9. From the grill, entrees include roasted ginger Kona lobster with poi risotto and shiitake mushrooms for $34, Tahitian peppered *ahi* steak at $29, and grilled tenderloin of beef in a mushroom herb sauce for $30. The room is subdued and elegant, and highlighted with snow-white tablecloths and sparkling crystal. The view is serene facing the courtyard, or dramatic looking out to sea.

When chefs from the best restaurants on Maui want to impress visiting friends with a **brunch,** they come to the Maui Prince on Sunday. For only $34 you can surpass most of your dining fantasies. You start with a table laden with exotic fruits and fresh-squeezed juices. Nearby are plump and steaming rolls, croissants, and pastries rich in chocolates and creams. Then comes an omelette gauntlet, where you pick and choose your ingredients and an attendant chef creates it before your eyes. Hot entrees for the gastronomically timid are offered, from roast beef to fresh fish. But the real delights are the cornucopia of smoked seafood and shellfish. To the left pâté, to the right sushi, and sashimi straight ahead, or choose cracked crab to nibble while you decide. Fat yellow rounds of imported cheeses squat on huge tables. Waiters and waitresses attend with fresh plates, champagne by the glass, and pots of coffee. You couldn't possibly eat like this every day, but *sacrifice* yourself at least once like this while on Maui.

Hakone is a Japanese restaurant and sushi bar with all chefs from Japan. It serves complete dinners like sukiyaki, tempura, and shabu shabu for under $35, and it also serves sushi and sashimi, plus traditional seven- to nine-course *kaiseki* dinners. A special Monday night dinner buffet is offered at $38 where you have your choice from 25 delightful dishes. In keeping with the tradition of Japan, the room is subdued and simple, with white shoji screens counterpointed by dark open beams. The floor is black slate atop packed sand, a style from old Japan.

The main dining room is the more casual **Cafe Kiowai,** open for breakfast, lunch, and dinner, located on the ground level, opening to the courtyard and fishponds. For now, food and accommodations in Makena mean the Maui Prince. The only exceptions are the **Makena Club House Restaurant,** which serves only soups, salads, sandwiches, and grilled items for lunch for under $15.

For nightly entertainment in Makena, the only option is the **Molokini Lounge** at the Maui Prince.

JOHN COSTELLO

HAWAII STATE ARCHIVES

UPCOUNTRY

Upcountry is much more than a geographical area to the people who live there: it's a way of life, a frame of mind. You can see Upcountry from anywhere on Maui by lifting your gaze to the slopes of Haleakala. There are no actual boundaries, but this area is usually considered as running from Makawao in the north all the way around to Kahikinui Ranch in the south, and from below the cloud cover down to about the 1,500-foot level. It swathes the western slope of Haleakala like a large green floral bib patterned by pasturelands and festooned with wild and cultivated flowers. In this rich soil and cool-to-moderate temperatures, cattle ranching and truck farming thrive. Up here, *paniolo* ride herd on the range of the enormous 35,000-acre Haleakala Ranch, spread mostly around Makawao, and the smaller but still sizable 23,000 acres of the Ulupalakua Ranch, which *is* the hills above Wailea. Pukalani, the largest town and expanding residential area, is a way station for gas and supplies, and is pineapple country. While Makawao retains some of its real cowboy town image with saddleries, rodeos, and hitching posts, it has become more sophisticated, with some exclusive shops, fine dining restaurants, art galleries, and alternative healing practitioners.

Kula is Maui's flower basket. This area is one enormous garden producing brilliant blooms and hearty vegetables. Polipoli Spring State Recreation Area is a forgotten wonderland of tall forests, a homogenized stand of trees from around the world. Tedeschi Winery in the south adds a classy touch to Upcountry; a place where you can taste wine and view the winemaking process. There are plenty of commercial greenhouses and flower farms to visit all over Upcountry, but the best activity is a free Sunday drive along the mountain roads and farm lanes, just soaking in the scenery. The purple mists of mountain jacaranda and the heady fragrance of eucalyptus encircling a mountain pasture manicured by herds of cattle portray the soul of Upcountry.

PUKALANI

This way-station town, at the intersection of routes 37 and 365, is a good place to get gas and supplies for a walking or driving trek through Kula. It's a rapidly growing community with many new housing developments around its periphery. There are no outstanding cultural or historical sights in Pukalani, but a fine golf course graces its southern edge.

There's a shopping mall and several minimalls where you can pick up just about anything. **Bullock's** restaurant, just past the T intersection with Makawao Ave., serves a wide assortment of good-value sandwiches. The Moonburger is a tradition, but a full breakfast here for under $6 will give you all the energy you'll need for the day ahead. Bullock's also has plate lunches and some tropical fruit-flavored shakes.

Also at this intersection is the **Pukalani Superette,** a well-stocked grocery store, especially for this neck of the woods, and next door is a tiny **post office** that can take care of basic mailing needs. Here, too, you'll find two **gas stations** and the famous golden arches heralding a **McDonald's.**

The **Upcountry Cafe,** in the pink and gray building on Aewa Place, tel. (808) 572-2395, open daily except Tuesday 6:30 a.m.-3 p.m., Sunday until 1 p.m., and again for dinner Wednesday and Thursday 5:30-8:30 p.m., Friday and Saturday until 9 p.m., has brought upscale yet unpretentious dining to Upcountry. Inside, wooden tables, bent-back chairs, a tiled counter, and a black-on-white Holstein motif set the ambience in this American/island standard restaurant. The breakfast menu has a cholesterol bomb for $5.95, a Belgian waffle for $4.50, or a vegetarian frittata for $4.75. Lunch brings a traditional Reuben for $4.95, or a Crab Supreme on Boboli bread for $7.50. You can also order entrees like sautéed mahimahi for $5.95, or vegetarian lasagna for $6.25. The Upcountry Cafe

is a perfect breakfast or lunch stop while touring Kula. Behind the cafe is **Frenchy's Bakery,** tel. (808) 572-9778, open Mon.-Sat. 6:30 a.m.-6 p.m., where everything is baked fresh daily. Here you can choose from mouthwatering breads and a variety of pastries and cakes, plus soups, salads, and sandwiches.

In the Pukalani Terrace Center are an **Ace Hardware, Upcountry Laundry and Dry Cleaning, Foodland** grocery store, and both a **Bank of Hawaii** and **American Savings Bank,** both of which have teller machines. There is a wide variety of economical eateries here, including a **Subway** sandwich shop, **Royal King's Garden** Chinese restaurant (no MSG), **Mama Son's Barbecue** Korean restaurant, and **Ono Loco Food** mixed-plate shop. Across the street from this shopping center is a large community park with ball fields, basketball courts, and a great swimming center.

One of the best restaurants in the area is the **Pukalani Country Club Restaurant,** open daily 7:30 a.m.-2 p.m. and 5-9 p.m., tel. (808) 572-1325, at the Pukalani Country Club. It has a salad bar and sandwiches, but specializes in "local" and Hawaiian foods such as *kalua* pig and *lau lau* at reasonable prices. Most patrons are local people, so you know that they're doing something right. The only Upcountry golf course on Maui, **Pukalani Country Club,** offers 18 holes of inexpensive golf. In the bargain come spectacular views over the isthmus and up toward Haleakala. Turn south at the Pukalani Terrace Center and follow the road for four or five blocks to reach the golf course.

On Makawao Avenue, going toward Makawao, is a second smaller shopping center, **Pukalani Square.** Here you'll find several medical offices, plus a pharmacy, **The Grill** eatery, and **Upcountry Cycles** for two-wheel transportation.

UPCOUNTRY

To Kahului

36

Paia

HANA HWY.

Haiku

HANA HWY.

360

390

UNION CHURCH

Ulumalu

HOLY ROSARY
CHURCH

RAINBOW COUNTY
PARK

398

365

37

Pu'unene

HALEAKALA RD.

Hali'imaile

BALDWIN AVE.

To Hana Hwy.

Kokomo

To Kahului

KEAHUA RD.

HUI NO'EAU

Makawao

365

POLO
FIELD

RODEO

OLINDA RD.

Pukalani

PUKALANI
COUNTRY CLUB

37

OMAOPIO RD.

LOWER
KULA RD.

PULEHU RD.

377

KIMO RD.

Pulehu

KULA
LODGE

UPCOUNTRY
PROTEA FARM

SUNRISE PROTEA FARM

HOSMER GROVE
CAMPGROUND

HOLY GHOST
CHURCH

HALEAKALA HWY.

HALEAKALA
CRATER RD.

378

Kihei

Waiakoa

UNIV. OF HA. AGR. STA.

KEKAULIKE
AVE.

NATIONAL PARK
HEADQUARTERS

LELEWILI
OVERLOOK

Ka'akaulua Gulch

RICE
PARK

Kula

KULA BOTANICAL
GARDENS

WAIPOU RD.

HALEAKALA
CRATER

Waiohuli Gulch

Kaipoioi Gulch

WAIAKOA
LOOP TRAIL

VISITOR CENTER

Waiohuli

UPPER WAIAKOA TRAIL

Pu'u Ula'Ula (Red Hill)
(10,023 ft.)

MOON

Keokea

KULA HWY.

THOMPSON RD.

SKYLINE TRAIL

0   2 mi

0   2 km

Waimea

31

POLIPOLI
SPRINGS STATE
RECREATION
AREA

KAHUA RD.

Pu'u Keokea

Polipoli
(6,472 ft.)

Makena

31

Pu'u Makua
(5,276 ft.)

MAKEE SUGAR
MILL (1878)

Ulupalakua Ranch

TEDESCHI WINERY

Pu'u Mahoe
(2,660 ft.)

PIILANI

Kahikinui Ranch

Manawainui

To Hana

HWY.

31

© J.D. BISIGNANI AND MOON PUBLICATIONS, INC.

MAKAWAO

Makawao is proud of itself; it's not *like* a cowboy town, it *is* a cowboy town. Depending on the translation that you consult, Makawao means "Eye of the Dawn" or "Forest Beginning." Both are appropriate. Surrounding lowland fields of cane and pineapples give way to upland pastures rimmed with tall forests, as Haleakala's morning sun shoots lasers of light through the town. Makawao was settled late last century by Portuguese immigrants who started raising cattle on the upland slopes. It loped along as a *paniolo* town until WW II, when it received an infusion of life from a nearby military base in Kokomo. After the war it settled back down and became a sleepy village again, where as many horses were tethered on the main street as cars were parked. The majority of its false-front, one-story buildings are a half-century old, but their prototype is strictly "Dodge City, 1850." During the 1950s and '60s, Makawao started to decline into a bunch of worn-out old buildings. It earned a reputation for drinking, fighting, and cavorting cowboys, and for a period was derisively called "Macho-wao."

In the 1970s it began to revive. It had plenty to be proud of and a good history to fall back on. Makawao is *the* last real *paniolo* town on Maui and, with Kamuela on the Big Island, is one of the last two in the entire state. At the Oskie Rice Arena, it hosts the largest and most successful rodeo in Hawaii. Its Fourth of July parade is a marvel of homespun humor, *aloha,* and an old-fashioned good time. Many people ride their horses to town, leaving them to graze in a public corral. They do business at stores operated by the same families for 50 years. Though much of the dry goods are country-oriented, a new breed of merchant has come to town. You can buy a sack of feed, a rifle, designer jeans, and an imported silk blouse all on one street. At its eateries you can have lobster, vegetarian or Mexican food, or a steamy bowl of saimin, reputed to be the best on Maui. Artists of all mediums have found Makawao and the surrounding area fertile ground for their work, and the town has become a hotbed of alternative healing practitioners. Look on any bulletin board in town and you'll see a dozen fliers advertising formulas for better life, better health, reawakening of the spirit, Oriental health therapies, and new-age, new-health concepts.

Everyone, old-timers and newcomers alike, agrees that Makawao must be preserved, and they work together. They know that tourism is a financial lifeline, but shudder at the thought of Makawao becoming an Upcountry Lahaina. It shouldn't. It's far enough off the track to keep the average tourist away, but easy enough to reach and definitely interesting enough to make the side trip absolutely worthwhile.

The main artery to Makawao is through Paia as you travel Rt. 36 (Hana Highway). In Paia turn right onto Baldwin Avenue. From there it's about six miles to Makawao. You can also branch off Rt. 37 (Haleakala Highway) in Pukalani, onto Rt. 365 (some maps show it as Rt. 40), which will lead you to the town.

SIGHTS

En route on Baldwin Avenue (Rt. 390) you pass the Paia **sugar mill,** a real-life Carl Sandburg poem. A smaller sister mill to that at Puunene, it's a green monster trimmed in bare lightbulbs at night, dripping with sounds of turning gears, cranes, and linkbelts, all surrounded by packed, rutted, oil-stained soil. Farther along Baldwin Ave. sits **Holy Rosary Church** and its sculpture of Father Damien. The rendering of Damien is idealized, but the leper, who resembles a Calcutta beggar, has a face that conveys helplessness while at the same time faith and hope. It's worth a few minutes' stop. Coming next is **Makawao Union Church,** and it's a beauty. Like a Tudor mansion made completely of stone with lovely stained-glass windows, the entrance is framed by two tall and stately royal palms. Farther up is **Rainbow County Park,** one of the few noncoastal parks on Maui.

At mile marker 5 along Baldwin Ave., Haliimaile Road turns to the south and leads to the small pineapple town of **Haliimaile.** This tiny community, a combination of old plantation town

ROBERT NILSEN

sculpture of Father Damien at Holy Rosary Church

and new development, offers a wonderful restaurant, the Haliimaile General Store—well worth driving the distance for—and a well-shaded county park that features picnic tables, ball fields, and lighted tennis courts.

Farther up Baldwin Avenue is the **Hui No'eau** (Club of Skills) Visual Arts Center, a local organization that features traditional and modern arts housed at Kaluanui, a mansion built in 1917 by the Baldwin family on their 10-acre estate. The member artisans and craftspeople produce everything from ceramics to *lau hala* weaving. The old house is home to the center office, gift gallery, and periodic shows, while the former stable and carriage house have become studios. Throughout the year classes, lectures, and exhibits are offered, along with an annual Christmas Fair featuring their creations. One of the best features of visiting Hui No'eau is the resplendent mansion itself. Built in a neo-Spanish motif with red-tiled roof and light pink stucco exterior, Kaluanui sits among the manicured grounds that feature a reflection pond just in front of the portico. At 2841 Baldwin Ave., the gift shop and gallery are open Mon.-Sat. 10 a.m.-4 p.m., and you'll often find someone around working in the studios. For information, contact the center at (808) 572-6560, e-mail: hui@maui.net, website: www.maui.net/~hui.

The back way reaches Makawao by branching off Rt. 36 through Ulumalu and Kokomo. Just where Rt. 36 turns into Rt. 360, there's a road to the right. This is Kaupakalua Road, or Rt. 365. Take it through backcountry Maui, where horses graze around neat little houses. Haleakala looms on the horizon; guavas, mangos, and bananas grow wild. At the first Y intersection, bear left to Kaupakalua. Pass a large junkyard and continue to Kokomo. There's a general store here. Notice the mixture of old and new houses—Maui's past and future in microcosm. Here, the neat little banana plantation on the outskirts of the diminutive town says it all. Pass St. Joseph's Church and you've arrived through Makawao's back door. This is an excellent off-track route to take on your way to or from Hana. You can also come up Kokomo Road, Rt. 398, skirting Haiku, or come over Rt. 365 through Pukalani, incorporating Makawao into your Haleakala trip.

Nearby Attractions

Take Olinda Road out of town. All along it custom-designed houses have been built. **Seabury Hall,** a private boarding school for grades 6-12, sits among trees above Makawao. In May, it hosts an arts and crafts fair, with entertainment, food, and games. Look for **Pookela Church,** a coral-block structure built in 1843. In four miles you pass **Rainbow Acres,** tel. (808) 572-8020. Open Friday and Saturday 10 a.m.-4 p.m., it specializes in cactus and succulents. At the top of Olinda turn left onto Piiholo Road, which loops back down. Along it is **Aloha O Ka Aina,** tel. (808) 572-9440, a nursery specializing in ferns. Open Wednesday and Sunday 10 a.m.-4 p.m.

PRACTICALITIES

Accommodations

Built in 1924, the plantation house **Hale Ho'okipa Inn,** 32 Pakani Place, tel. (808) 572-6698, fax 573-2580, e-mail: mauibnb@maui.net, website:

www.maui.net/~mauibnb, has recently been turned into a lovely B&B. Not a modern rendition, this well-loved place has real world, lived-in charm, and is filled with comfortable period-style and antique furniture and furnishings, and artwork by Hawaiian artists. Three rooms have their own private baths, while the two-bedroom suite shares a bath and has use of the big country kitchen. A continental breakfast is served each morning for guests in the rooms. Rates run $60-80 a night for the rooms and $135 for the suite. The inn is within walking distance from town, up above the Eddie Tam Center. Moderate.

Olinda Country Cottages and Inn, tel. (808) 572-1453 or (800) 932-3435, e-mail: olinda@mauibnbcottages.com, website: www.mauibnbcottages.com, is up above Makawao past mile marker 11, at 536 Olinda Road. Located on a protea farm and surrounded by the Haleakala Ranch, this B&B is spacious and comfy. The main house has rooms and there are three separate cottages down below. The two bedrooms in the house have a private entrance and share a sitting room, and each has a private bath. Guests can also use the living room on the first floor, which is filled with antiques and collectibles. Breakfast is provided each morning. The individual cottages are more like small homes, with all the amenities. As each has a kitchen, breakfast is served only the first morning. The County Cottage and Hidden Cottage are older; the Pineapple Sweet Cottage is new. The bedrooms run $95 a night, the cottages $110-140. The rooms have a two-night minimum, the cottages three. Highly recommended for quiet and seclusion yet close enough to get to a fine restaurant in town. Gregarious hosts, good value. The only drawback for some folks might be the windy road leading up to the B&B. Expensive.

Food

All the following establishments are on Makawao or Baldwin Avenue. An excellent place to eat is **Polli's Mexican Restaurant,** tel. (808) 572-7808, open daily 7 a.m.-10 p.m. The sign, Come In and Eat or We'll Both Starve, greets you at the front. The meals are authentic Mexican, using the finest ingredients. Formerly vegetarian—they'll still prepare any menu item in a vegetarian manner—they use no lard or animal fat in their bean dishes. You can have breakfast entrees for $6-8, a full lunch for $8-10, or dinner for $12-16. Margaritas are large and tasty for $4, and the champagne Sunday brunch is particularly good. Monday night is barbecue night, Tuesday is kid's night. Still down home, still wholesome meals, still a happening place.

A surprising and delicious dining experience is found at **Casanova Italian Restaurant and Deli,** tel. (808) 572-0220, located across from Polli's at the main intersection of town. The deli is open daily for breakfast, lunch, and dinner. The interior is utilitarian—a refrigerated case loaded with cold cuts, shelves stocked with Italian delectables and designer chocolates, and a counter for eating. Specials are offered nightly, but the best dishes are the fresh-made lasagna, ravioli, and spaghetti, all smothered in different sauces. Many of the best restaurants on Maui order their pasta from Casanova's. Order at the counter. The best place to sit is on the front porch where you can perch above the street and watch Makawao life go by. Upcountry-yuppie-elegant, Casanova's restaurant occupies the adjoining section of the building, open daily except Sunday, for lunch 11:30 a.m.-2 p.m., and for dinner 5:30-11 p.m., featuring pizza, pasta, and other fine Italian cuisine. Of course, pasta is the staple, but meat, fish, and poultry entrees are also popular. Expect entrees in the $15-25 range. While the food is as good as the deli fare next door, many come for the music and dancing. Having a nightclub atmosphere, and featuring live bands on the weekends, a large dance floor, and a first-class sound system, it draws people not only from Upcountry but also from Central and West Maui. Casual attire is fine, but remember, Upcountry gets cool at night, so long pants would be in order.

Makawao Steak House, tel. (808) 572-8711, is open daily for dinner from 5 p.m., with early bird specials until 6:30, Sunday brunch 9:30 a.m.-2 p.m. Casual, with wooden tables, salad bar, and good fish selections, dinners run upward to around $25. The steak dishes, especially the prime rib, are the best. The lunch menu is more limited. The Makawao Steak House has been around a long time and maintains a good, solid reputation, although it has recently changed hands. The lounge is open from 5 p.m. until closing.

Kitada's, tel. (808) 572-7241, makes the best saimin on Maui, according to all the locals. It's across from the Makawao Steak House; open Mon.-Sat. 6 a.m.-1:30 p.m. Walk in, pour yourself a glass of water, and take a hardboard-topped table. The saimin is delicious and inexpensive. There are plate lunches, too. The walls have paintings of Upcountry by local artists; most show more heart than talent. Bus your own table while the owner, Kitada-*san,* calculates your bill on an abacus. His birthday, May 26, has become a town event.

Komoda's is a corner general store that has been in business for more than 50 years. It sells everything, but the bakery is renowned far and wide. It's open 7 a.m.-5 p.m. except Wednesday and Sunday, and until 2 on Saturday. People line up outside to buy their cream buns and homemade cookies—all gone by 9 a.m.

If you want a break from sightseeing in Makawao, come to **Abbey's Place** in the Courtyard of Makawao, open Mon.-Fri. 7 a.m.-5 p.m., until 3 on Saturday. People come just for the coffee, but you can also get an egg or waffle breakfast, or hot or cold sandwich. Hot meals, including sandwiches and grilled fish and chicken, are available only until 2 p.m.

The **Haliimaile General Store Restaurant,** tel. (808) 572-2666, open Mon.-Fri. 11 a.m.-2:30 p.m., and again 5:30-9:30 p.m., with a Sunday brunch 10 a.m.-2:30 p.m., serves elegant gourmet food to anyone lucky enough to find this Upcountry roadhouse. Located in Haliimaile village along Haliimaile Road between Baldwin Avenue and the Haleakala Highway, the restaurant is housed in what was this pineapple town's general store. Climb the steps to a wide veranda and enter to find the vintage utilitarian wood floored interior transformed into an airy room with tropical fish hung from the ceiling, primitive ceramics and sculptures placed here and there, and paintings of brilliant colors. Choose a table in the casual front room; perch on a canvas chair at the classic wooden bar in front of the open kitchen; or ask for a table in the back room, more formal with dark wood paneling, ceiling fans, track lighting, and floral displays. Master chef Beverly Gannon presents magnificent "Hawaiian regional cuisine with an American and international twist," while her Irish husband, master schmoozer Joe Gannon, presents an equally magnificent Blarney Stone atmosphere! The lunch menu starts with soup of the day for $3.50. Salads are the famous house salad for $5, a Caesar at $7, and a niçoise salad, which is the catch of the day grilled and served with olives, tomatoes, mixed greens, and cucumbers, for $12. Sandwiches, priced under $10, are special and include the grilled catch of the day as well as the Haliimaile BOLT (bacon, Maui onion, lettuce, and tomato), and entrees may be ravioli or baby back ribs, all under $14. Dinner at Haliimaile opens with appetizers like the sashimi Napoleon for $14, or an Asian pear and duck taco for $9. Entrees include *paniolo* ribs for $17, coconut seafood curry for $23, or aged Midwest beef rib eye for $24. The restaurant is also part contemporary boutique and art gallery, with the walls hung with original works and the old grocery shelves filled with distinctive gift items like porcelain plaes, dishes, and teapots. The dining is fine but the setting is casual. Alohawear is okay, but because of the elevation long sleeves and pants might be in order. The Haliimaile General Store has been reborn, and its spirit lives on in this great restaurant.

Food Markets and Liquor
Down to Earth Natural Foods, 1169 Makawao Ave., tel. (808) 572-1488, open daily 8 a.m.-8 p.m., is a first-rate health food store that originated in Wailuku and later opened a branch here in Makawao. Inside you'll find shelves packed with minerals, vitamins, herbs, spices, and mostly organic fruits and vegetables. Bins hold bulk grains, pastas, honey, and nut butters, while a deli case holds sandwiches and drinks. You can even mix up a salad from the salad bar to take out. Down to Earth has a philosophy by which it operates, "to promote the living of a healthy lifestyle by eating a natural vegetarian diet; respect for all forms of life; and concern for the environment."

Nature's Nectar, 3647 Baldwin Ave., tel. (808) 572-9122, open 10 a.m.-4 p.m. daily, is a juice bar that specializes in herbs and natural elixirs. Inside are tinctures, bulk herbs, supplements, and plenty of literature on alternative health. Sterling jewelry, amber, red coral, and crystals are also for sale. From the juice bar order carrot juice, wheatgrass juice, organic salads, or homemade vegetarian soup with whole grain bread. Having expanded, you can now also get simple entrees like vegan lasagna or a nut rice burger for about $6, or choose something from the deli case. Here you can find something for your mind, body, and spirit.

Liquor Shack and Deli, 1143 Makawao Ave., tel. (808) 572-7775, can provide all the fixings for a lunch, or a full range of liquid refreshments.

Rodeo General Store, 3661 Baldwin Ave., is a one-stop shop with a wide selection of natural foods, pastries, produce, fresh fish, wines, spirits, and cigars. Open 6:30 a.m.-10 p.m. daily.

Shopping

Makawao is changing quickly, and nowhere is this more noticeable than in its local shops. The population is now made up of old-guard *paniolo*, yuppies, and alternative people. What a combo! You can buy a bullwhip, a Gucci purse, a cold Bud, or sushi all within 100 feet of each other. Some unique and fascinating shops here can provide you with distinctive purchases.

When Mimi Merrill opened **Miracles Bookery,** at 3682 Baldwin Ave., tel. (808) 572-2317, hours Mon.-Sat. 9 a.m.-9 p.m., Sunday 9 a.m.-8 p.m., she put her heart, soul, and all of her resources into the place, running out of funds before she could finish the floor. Her friends, building off the "miracles do happen" theme of the store, got together and painted it. Every evening for a week they came, and with regular house paint created a mosaic of stones, bricks, and flowers, fashioning what the local people call "the stained-glass floor." Miracles Bookery specializes in books on new-age spiritualism, astrology, Tarot, children's classics, Hawaiiana, general novels and poetry, "pre-loved" books, and even travel guidebooks! A different astrologer, palmist, or Tarot reader is "in residence" every day, and on the third Saturday of every month there's an open house with $5 readings all day long. Miracles also has unique gift items: angels and more angels, petroglyph reproductions, Native American jewelry, bumper stickers with an attitude, T-shirts with a message, posters, and music of all kinds from spiritual to rock.

The Courtyard of Makawao is a consortium of shops at 3620 Baldwin Ave. where you can dine, buy fine art, or watch as glassblowers pursue alchemical art. In the reconstructed Makawao Theater building, **Maui Hands,** tel. (808)

572-5194, is open daily except Sunday 10 a.m.-6 p.m., specializing in Maui-made art and crafts like semiprecious stone necklaces, sterling and gold jewelry, prints, bamboo work, *raku* pottery, primitive basketry, and even some T-shirts. **Viewpoints Gallery,** tel. (808) 572-5979, open daily 10 a.m.-6 p.m., is an artists' cooperative specializing in locally created paintings, sculptures, handicrafts, and jewelry. Some of the art displayed includes: oil paintings by Kathleen MacDonald; impressionistic oils by George Allen; the mixed-media art of Joelle Chichebortiche; and the combination pastel and oils by Diana Dorenzo. Most of the artists live in the area, and with enough notice will come to meet you if time permits. The shop is perfectly suited as a gallery with track lighting and movable partitions, so even the room itself is quite artistic with a feeling of brightness. It is a perfect place to spend an afternoon perusing the contemporary art scene so vibrant in Upcountry. Outside is a pleasant courtyard, around which are several more shops. Here you will find Bill and Sally Worcester making magic at **Hot Island Glass,** open daily 10 a.m.-5 p.m., tel. (808) 572-4527. These very talented glassblowers, assisted by their son Michael, turn molten glass into everything from simple paperweights to gorgeous vases. Just line up at their window and watch the artists work. Between the three of them they have won almost every meaningful art award on Maui and in their former Oregon home. This includes the Art Maui Award that they have brought home every year since 1985. Incidental pieces run as cheap as $10, but the masterpieces go for several thousand. Don't worry about shipping or packing glass; they're also masters at packing so things don't break on the way home.

Upcountry Legends, tel. (808) 572-3523, open daily 10 a.m.-6 p.m., Sunday 11 a.m.-5 p.m., sells handpainted silk shirts, ladies apparel, sterling silver jewelry, huggable teddy bears and other stuffed animals, greeting cards, candles, and baskets.

Collections Boutique, tel. (808) 572-0781, open daily till 6 p.m., Saturday until 4, imports items from throughout Asia: batik from Bali, clothes from India, silk Hawaiian shirts, jewelry, lotions, cosmetics, accessories, sunglasses, and handicrafts from various countries. Operated by Pam Winans.

Hi Hearth and Leisure, tel. (808) 572-4569, has the largest line of wood-burning and gas stoves in Hawaii. That's right, stoves! Nights in the high country can get chilly, and on top of Haleakala downright cold. Also here are fireplaces, chimneys, and accessories, a good selection of cutlery, and a few residuals left over from when it was a great hardware and tack store.

For fine art, check out **David Warren's Studio,** tel. (808) 572-1864, across from the Courtyard. David is one of the featured artists at the prestigious Maui Crafts Guild in Paia, but he chose Upcountry for his studio. His medium is oil, his canvas might be just that or another material like a pottery vase. Farther up Baldwin Ave. is the **S. Reeve Gallery.** Along Makawao Ave. are **Gallery Maui** and **Ola's Makawao,** for contemporary American art, and the newer **Élan Vital's** gallery of contemporary art and sculpture.

Another shop along Baldwin Ave. is **Gecko Trading Co.,** tel. (808) 572-0249, open daily 10 a.m.-5:30 p.m., Sunday 11 a.m.-4 p.m., bright with fashions for men, women, and children; Gecko also sells sterling silver and amber jewelry, handbags, teddy bears, straw hats, old bottles, and imported clothing from Asia and around the world. Listen for tinkling wind chimes to locate **Goodies,** tel. (808) 572-0288, open daily 9:30 a.m.-5:30 p.m., Sunday 10 a.m.-5 p.m., a boutique that looks like a spilled treasure chest. Crystals, silk and cotton casual and elegant clothing, dolls, children's wear, stuffed animals, locally crafted trays, and magic wands fill this shop.

About the only shop in town for men's clothing is **Tropo,** tel. (808) 573-0356, where you can find shorts, polo shirts, aloha shirts, and even hats and ties. Owner Avi Kiriaty helps to design the clothing on sale here. Open Mon.-Sat. 10 a.m.-6 p.m., Sunday 11 a.m.-4 p.m.

Down a narrow alley a few steps from the intersection of Baldwin and Makawao Avenues is **The Dragon's Den Healing Center,** tel. (808) 572-2731, a shop stuffed full of Chinese herbs and medicines, minerals, crystals, teas, gifts, and books on Eastern healing arts. Also in the alley are two new features to the ever-changing face of this Upcountry community: **Healing Hui** health and resource center, tel. (808) 572-6091, for therapeutic massage and colonic therapy, and **Grace Health Clinic,** tel. (808) 572-6091, which specializes in chiropractic, massage, traditional Oriental medicine.

Events

Makawao has a tremendous rodeo season every year. Most meets are sponsored by the Maui Roping Club. They start in the spring and culminate in a massive rodeo on or around July 4, with substantial prize money. These events attract the best cowboys from around the state. Both males and females try their luck in separate groupings. The numerous competitions include barrel racing, breakaway roping, team roping, and calf roping. The organization of the event is headed by long-time resident Brendan Balthazar, who welcomes everyone to participate with only one rule, "Have fun, but maintain safety."

KULA

Kula could easily provide all of the ingredients for a full-course meal fit for a king. Its bounty is staggering: vegetables to make a splendid chef's salad, beef for the entree, flowers to brighten the spirits, and wine to set the mood. Up here, soil, sun, and moisture create a garden symphony. Sweet Maui onions, cabbages, potatoes, grapes, apples, pineapples, lettuce, and artichokes grow with abandon. Herefords and Black Angus graze in knee-deep fields of sweet green grass. Flowers are everywhere: beds of proteas, camellias, carnations, roses, hydrangeas, and blooming peach and tangerine trees dot the countryside like daubs from van Gogh's brush. As you gain the heights along Kula's lanes, you look back on West Maui and a perfect view of the isthmus. You'll also enjoy wide-open spaces and rolling green hills fringed with trees like a lion's mane. Above, the sky changes from brooding gray to blazing blue, then back again. During light rainy afternoons, when the sun streams in from the west, you could easily spot a rainbow form on the hillside, as if sprouting from the rich green pastureland. Kula is a different Maui— quiet and serene.

ROBERT NILSEN

protea

Getting There

The fastest way is the same route to Haleakala Crater. Take Rt. 37 through Pukalani, turn onto Rt. 377, and when you see Kimo Road on your left and right, you're in Kula country. If you have the time, take the following scenic route. Back in Kahului start on Rt. 36 (Hana Highway), but as soon as you cross Dairy Road look for a sign pointing to Pulehu-Omaopio Road on your right. Take it! You'll wade through acres of sugarcane, and in six miles these two roads will split. You can take either, but Omaopio to the left is better because, at the top, it deposits you in the middle of things to see. Once the roads fork, you'll pass some excellent examples of flower and truck farms. You'll also go by the cooperative **Vacuum Cooling Plant** where many farmers store their produce. Then Omaopio Road comes again to Rt. 37 (Kula Highway). Don't take it yet. Cross and continue until Omaopio dead-ends, in a few hundred yards. Turn right onto Lower Kula Road and watch for Kimo (Lower) Drive on your left, and take it straight uphill. This brings you through some absolutely beautiful countryside and in a few miles crosses Rt. 377, where a right will take you to Haleakala Crater Road.

SIGHTS

Curtis Wilson Cost Gallery

In the basement of the Kula Lodge is the Curtis Wilson Cost Gallery, tel. (808) 878-6544 or (800) 508-2278, website: www.costgallery.com. One of Maui's premier artists, Cost captures scenes reflecting the essence of Upcountry Maui; handles color, light, and shadow to perfection; and portrays the true pastoral nature of the area. This is traditional realism with a touch of imagination. Stop in and browse daily 8:30 a.m.-4:30 p.m.

Upcountry Harvest

This little flower shop sits next door to the Kula Lodge and is open daily 8 a.m.-5:30 p.m., tel. (808) 878-2824 or (800) 575-6470. Don't miss seeing the amazing fresh and dried flowers and arrangements. Here you can purchase a wide range of protea and other tropical flowers that can be shipped back home. Live or dried, these flowers are fantastic. Gift boxes starting at $38 are well worth the price. The salespeople are friendly and informative, and it's educational just to visit.

Upper Kimo Road

If you want to be intoxicated by some of the finest examples of Upcountry flower and vegetable farms, come up here. First, head back down Rt. 377 past the Kula Lodge and turn on Upper Kimo Road on your right. One mile up, at the very end, is **Cloud's Rest Protea Farm,** open daily 8 a.m.-4:30 p.m.; for phone orders call (800) 332-8233. The farm has more than 50 varieties of protea and other flowers. You can walk the grounds or visit the gift shop, where they offer gift packs and mail orders. Although harvested year-round since something is always blooming, the ultimate time for viewing and sending protea as gifts is from September through January.

Sunrise Protea Farm

This farm and gift shop is less than half a mile up Haleakala Crater Road. The shop sells gift items, local Maui produce, homemade sweets, sandwiches, and fruit juices. In the flower shop you'll find fresh and dried flowers and arrangements that can be sent anywhere in the country; fresh bouquets from $40, dried arrangements from $30. An easy stop on the way back from Haleakala Crater. Open weekdays 8 a.m.-4 p.m., weekends 7 a.m.-5 p.m., tel. (808) 876-0200 or (800) 222-2797 for phone orders.

Kula Botanical Gardens

Follow Rt. 377 south (it turns into Kekaulike Avenue) and look for the gardens on your left just before the road meets again with Rt. 37. These privately owned gardens, tel. (808) 878-1715, are open daily 9 a.m.-4 p.m.; be sure to start by 3 p.m. to give yourself enough time for a thorough walk-around. Admission is $4, children 6-12 are $1. Here are nearly six acres of identified tropical and semitropical plants on a self-guided tour. There is a stream that runs through the property, a koi pond, and small aviary. Some of the 2,000 different varieties of plants include protea, orchid, fuchsia, native koa, *kukui*, and sandalwood, as well ferns and many introduced species. First opened to the public in 1971, the gardens are educational and will give names to many flowers and plants that you've observed around the island. It makes for a relaxing afternoon, with picnic tables provided. Enter through the gift shop.

Enchanting Floral Gardens

Located across from mile marker 10 on the Kula Highway, this privately owned flower garden is newer and more commercial than Kula Botanical Garden, yet worthy of a look. Its eight acres are neatly laid out, with many of the 1,500 varieties of flowers and plants identified. Stroll down the path and be captivated by the abundance. Plan on about an hour to see the entire lot. Open 9 a.m.-5 p.m., entrance $4; tel. (808) 878-2531.

Polipoli Spring State Recreation Area

If you want quietude and mountain walks, come here, because few others do. Just past the Kula Botanical Gardens look for the park sign on your left leading up Waipoli Road. This 10-mile stretch is only partially paved; the first half zigzags steeply up the hill, and the second half, although fairly flat, is dirt and can be very rutted, rocky, or muddy. Hang gliders use this area, jumping off farther up and landing on the open grassy fields along the lower portion of this road. Hunting is also done in the forests here, and a number of trails lead off this road to prescribed hunting areas. As always, the trip to the end is worth it. Polipoli is an established forest of imported trees from around the world: eucalyptus, redwoods, cypress, ash, cedar, and *sugi* pines. Much of the area was planted in the '20s by the state and in the '30s by the CCC. These trees do well here as the park lies right in that band where moisture laden clouds seem to hang around the mountain. There is a great network of trails in the immediate area, and even one that leads up to the top of the mountain. One of the most popular is the **Redwood Trail,** which you can take to a shelter at the end. These trails are for hiking and mountain biking only—no motorcycles or horses. At 6,200 feet, the camping area can be brisk at night. Camping is free but permits are required and are available from the Division of State Parks, 54 S. High St., Wailuku, HI 96793, tel. (808) 984-8109. Water, picnic tables, and outhouses are provided at the camping spot, which is a small grassy area surrounded by tall eucalyptus trees. The cabin here is a spacious three-bedroom affair with bunks for up to 10 people. It starts at $45 a night for one to four people and goes up $5 per additional person. It's rustic, but all camping and cooking essentials are provided, including a wood-burning stove. If you want to get away from it all, this is your spot.

Others

The University of Hawaii maintains an agriculture experimental station of 20 acres of flowers and other tropical and agricultural plants that change with the seasons. Located on Mauna Place above Rt. 37, open Mon.-Thurs. 7:30 a.m.-3:30 p.m. Check in with the station manager at the office, which is closed during the lunch hour. A self-guided tour map may be available there.

The nursery and flower shop **Proteas of Hawaii,** tel. (808) 878-2533 or (800) 367-7768, website: www.hawaii-exotics.com, is located across the road; hours are 8 a.m.-4:30 p.m. Fresh protea baskets, tropical bouquets, and individual flowers can be purchased and shipped anywhere. Prices start at about $20.

Holy Ghost Church, on Lower Kula Road in Waiakoa, is an octagonal building raised in 1897 by the many Portuguese who worked the farms and ranches of Upcountry. Recently restored, it has many fine statues and an elaborate altar that was sent by the king and queen of Portugal when the church was built.There's a gas station here, as well as **Morihara Store,** spacious but spartan; **Cafe 808,** which serves down-home local food with nothing on the menu more than $8.95; the **Hawaii Institute of Astronomy;** and a post office.

Near the intersection of Highways 37 and 377 is **Rice Park,** a grassy wayside rest area that has a few picnic tables, bathrooms, and a public phone. From here, you get a good view over the lower mountain slope and the coast at Kihei and Wailea.

CONTINUING SOUTH

Keokea

Continue south on Rt. 37 through the town of Keokea, where you'll find gas, Henry Fong's and Ching's general stores, and an excellent park for a picnic. At the far end of the village are two new establishments. **Keokea Gallery** displays works by Maui artists, and next door is **Grandma's Maui Coffee.** Grandma's is open every day, 7:30 a.m.-5 p.m. You can enjoy fresh pastries for breakfast until 10 a.m., and sandwiches, saimin, and pies for lunch. The real treat, however, is the coffee, grown on the slope below and roasted in an old-fashioned coffee machine in the shop. Stop in for a sip or take a package to go. At the end of Thompson Road south of town are Thompson Ranch Riding Stables and Silvercloud guest ranch.

Tedeschi Winery

Past Keokea you'll know you're in ranch country. The road narrows and herds of cattle graze in pastures that seem like manicured gardens highlighting *panini* (prickly pear) cactus. You'll pass Ulupalakua Ranch and then come to the Tedeschi Winery tasting room on the left, tel. (808) 878-6058. Open for tasting daily 9 a.m.-5 p.m., the winery sells bottles of all its wines and cushioned boxes for transporting it. Free, 15-minute tours of the winery are offered as well, every hour on the half hour 9:30 a.m.-2:30 p.m. Here, Emil Tedeschi and his partner Pardee Erdman, who also owns the 23,000-acre Ulupalakua Ranch, offer samples of their wines. This is one of two wineries in Hawaii. When Erdman moved here in 1963 from California and noticed climatic similarities to the Napa Valley, he knew that this country could grow decent wine grapes. Tedeschi comes from California, where his family has a small vineyard near Calistoga. The partners have worked on making their dream of Maui wine a reality since 1974.

It takes time and patience to grow grapes and turn out a vintage wine. While they waited for their carnelian grapes (a cabernet hybrid) to mature and be made into a sparkling wine, they fermented pineapple juice, which they call Maui Blanc. If you're expecting this to be a sickeningly sweet syrup, forget it. Maui Blanc is surprisingly dry and palatable. In 1984 the first scheduled release of the winery's carnelian champagne, Maui Brut, celebrated the patience and craftsmanship of the vintners. Maui Blush, a zinfandel-like light dinner wine, and Maui Nouveau, a young red wine, were then added to the list. Most recently, Plantation Red, a very dry, oaky, red wine; Maui Splash, a sweet dessert wine which is a combination of pineapple and passion fruit; the fruity Pineapple Sparkling Wine; the mellow Ulupalakua Red table wine; and the dry salmon-colored Rose Ranch Cuvee Champagne have made their debut. You can taste these wines at the white ranch house set among the tall proud trees just off the highway, once visited by King Kalakaua in 1874. From here, the tour takes you to the working winery buildings just a few steps away. Hugging the ground closer to the road is a 100-year-old plaster and coral building that used to be the winery's tasting room. Formerly, it served as the jailhouse of the old Rose Ranch owned by James Makee, a Maui pioneer sugarcane planter. Look for the 22-acre vineyard one mile before the tasting room on the ocean side of the highway. Tedeschi wines are available in restaurants and stores around the island.

Across the street are remains of the old **Makee Sugar Mill** and down the road, the Ulupalakua

Ranch office and the ranch store and deli. Hanging around the store like old plantation workers after a hard day's work are several carved and painted lifelike figures, representing various groups of people who've contributed to Maui's past. Sit down and have a chat.

ACCOMMODATIONS AND FOOD

Kula Lodge

The Kula Lodge, RR 1, Box 475, Kula, HI 96790, tel. (808) 878-1535 or (800) 233-1535, fax (808) 878-2518, is on Rt. 377 just past Kimo Road and just before Haleakala Crater Road. Lodging here is in five detached chalets ranging $100-165; check-in is at the restaurant. Two have fireplaces with wood provided, four have lofts for extra guests, and all have lanai and excellent views of lower Maui. With their dark wood, carpets, and cathedral ceilings, they are almost contemporary in appearance. The Kula Lodge is a fine establishment with a wonderful location. Elevation 3,200 feet. Expensive.

The lobby and dining area of the **Kula Lodge Restaurant,** tel. (808) 878-1535, are impressively rustic, with open beamwork and framing, dark wood, and stone. This building started as a private residence some 50 years ago. The walls are covered with high-quality photos of Maui: windsurfers, silverswords, sunsets, cowboys, and horses. The large main dining room has a giant bay window with a superlative view. Breakfast is served daily 6:30-11:45 a.m., lunch 11:45 a.m.-4:45 p.m., dinner 4:45-9 p.m. The menus are surprisingly large. Try Hawaiian buttermilk griddle cakes or vegetarian Benedict for breakfast, or a sandwich or grilled chicken breast for lunch. Start dinner with wild mushroom risotto or Maui greens salad, and move on to a salmon filet, pepper steak, or pasta. The assortment of gourmet desserts includes a tasty mango pie, and one of these should round out your meal. There may be entertainment in the evenings. Before or after dinner, sit at the bar for a drink or warm yourself on the couches that front the stone fireplace. Perhaps the only drawback is the clamor created when riders on the Haleakala downhill bike trips arrive in a large group for breakfast. Be up early so as not to be disturbed.

The **Terrace Garden Restaurant** below at the garden level is only open for lunch, and everything is cooked in a wood-fired stove near the gazebos. While you wait for your meal, have a short stroll through the very lovely but diminutive flower gardens there.

Kula Sandalwoods Restaurant

This restaurant is just up the road from the Kula Lodge, set on the uphill side of the road, tel. (808) 878-3523. Breakfast, lunch, and a Sunday brunch are served. Here you can get breakfast for under $9 and lunch for about $12. Some bike groups stop here on their way down the mountain so you may have competition for service at certain times of the morning. The scenery from here isn't bad if you can ignore the power lines that drape across the view.

Kula Hula Inn

Located at 112 Ho'opalua Dr. in the lower Kula area not far out of Pukalani, this B&B has a room in the main house and two separate cottages. The room has its own bath, entrance, and lanai. It rents for $85. For $100 you can get the three-room Suite Plumeria. The larger and more private two-bedroom Hula Moon Cottage with full bath and kitchen goes for $115. Breakfast is included for all except the cottage, where it's optional for an additional charge. A large lawn surrounds this property. For information, contact the inn at (808) 572-9351 or (888) 485-2466, e-mail: kulahula@maui.net, website: www.maui.net /~kulahula. Moderate.

Silvercloud Upcountry Guest Ranch

A good place for groups, the Silvercloud, RR 2, Box 201, Kula, HI 96790, tel. (808) 878-6101 or (800) 532-1111, fax (808) 878-2132, e-mail: slvr-cld@maui.net, website: www.maui.net/~slvrcld, has six rooms and five studios in two separate buildings and a cottage up behind. All are surrounded by pastureland and have unobstructed views down on the green lower slopes of the mountain. Rooms in the large well-appointed main house run $85-125. Everyone has access to the kitchen, living room, and dining room, and each bedroom has a private bath. The studios run $105 and $145, and come with a bath, kitchen, and private lanai. The cottage is the most private and is a fully furnished unit, $150. The guest ranch is located at the end of Thompson Road, just out of Keokea. Moderate.

HALEAKALA NATIONAL PARK

Haleakala (House of the Sun) is spellbinding. Like seeing Niagara Falls or the Grand Canyon for the first time, it makes no difference how many people have come before you; it's still an undiminished, powerful, personal experience. The mountain is a power spot, a natural conductor of cosmic energy. *Kahuna* brought their novitiates here to perform final rites of initiation. During their heyday, intense power struggles took place atop the mountain between the healing practitioners, the *kahuna lapa'au,* and their rivals the *kahuna ana'ana,* the "black magic" sorcerers of old Hawaii. **Kawilinau,** the "Bottomless Pit," a natural feature on the crater floor, was the site of an ancient battle between Pele and one of her siblings, and thus held tremendous significance for both schools of *kahuna.* Average Hawaiians did not live on Haleakala, but came now and again to quarry tool-stones. Only *kahuna* and their apprentices lived here for any length of time, as a sort of spiritual preparation and testing ground. Today, students of higher consciousness from around the world are attracted to this natural cosmic empire because of the rarefied energy. They claim that it accelerates personal growth, and compare it to remote mountain and desert areas in the Holy Lands. Even the U.S. Air Force has a facility here, and their research indicates Haleakala is *the* strongest natural power point in America. Not only is there an energy configuration coming from the earth itself, but there is also a high focus of radiation coming from outside the atmosphere. No one is guaranteed a spiritual experience on Haleakala, but if you're at all sensitive, this is fertile ground.

Natural Features
Haleakala is the world's largest dormant volcano, composed of amazingly dense volcanic rock, almost like poured cement. Counting the 20,000 feet or so of it lying under the sea makes it one of the tallest mountains on earth. Perhaps this mass accounts for the strange power of Haleakala as it sits like a mighty magnetic pyramid in the center of the North Pacific. The park's boundaries encompass 28,655 variable acres, which stretch from Hosmer Grove to Kipahulu

and include dry forests, rainforests, desert, and subtropical beaches. The most impressive feature is the crater itself. It's 3,000 feet deep, 7.5 miles east to west, and 2.5 miles north to south, accounting for 19 square miles, with a circumference of 21 miles. A mini-mountain range of nine cinder cones marches across the crater floor. They look deceptively tiny from the observation area, but the smallest is 600 feet, and the tallest, Puu O Maui, is 1,000 feet high. Haleakala was designated as a national park in 1961. Before that it was part of the Big Island's Volcanoes National Park. The entire park is a nature preserve dedicated to Hawaii's quickly vanishing indigenous plants and animals, and it was recognized as an International Biosphere Reserve by the United Nations in 1980. Only Volcanoes and Haleakala are home to the *nene,* the Hawaiian wild goose, and the **silversword,** a fantastically adapted plant.

Weather
As high as it is, Haleakala helps to create its own weather. Sunshine warms air that rises up the mountainside. When this moisture-laden air pushes into a cooler strata, it creates a band of clouds that moisten the forest and create what is known as the cloud forest. Often, these clouds will push up into the crater itself, gushing up through the Koolau and Kaupo gaps, sometimes obscuring the crater from view. In the cool of the evening, these clouds retreat back down the mountainside, leaving the crater clear once again. As air temperature drops about three degrees for every 1,000 feet, the top may be more than 30° cooler than the sunny beaches along the Kihei coast below. Haleakala also traps moisture from the trade winds, so the high mountain slopes above Hana get about 400 inches of rain a year, creating thick forest cover, while the slopes above Kihei, mostly dry and scrubby, get only a dozen inches yearly.

The Experience
If you're after *the* experience, you must see the sunrise or sunset. Both are magnificent, but both perform their stupendous light show with astonishing speed. Also, the weather must be coop-

HALEAKALA NATIONAL PARK

To Hana

To Kahului

To Kaupo

Waimoku Falls

KAPAHULU AREA

RANGER STATION

KIPAHULU CAMPGROUND

Ohea Gulch

Palikea Stream

Palikea (2,224 ft.)

Koukoui

Palikea Gulch

Kipahulu Valley

SCIENTIFIC RESEARCH AREA (CLOSED)

Kalapawili Ridge

▲ (8,907 ft.)

Ko'olau Gap

▲ (8,105 ft.)

PALIKU CABIN ▲

Kaluaiki

KAUPO TRAIL

▲ (4,772 ft.)

To Kaupo and Hwy. 31 (4 miles)

Kaupo Gap

▲ (8,201 ft.)

(6,300 ft.)

Oili Puu

Namana O Ke Akua

Mauna Hina

Honokahua

Puu Kumu

Puu Naue

Puu Maile

Ka Moa O Pele

SANDS

KAPALAOA CABIN ▲

SLIDING

HALEAKALA WILDERNESS

HALEMAUU TRAIL

SILVERSWORD LOOP

HOLUA CABIN ▲

Leleiwi Overlook

Kalahaku Overlook

▲ (9,324 ft.)

Bottomless Pit (Kawilinau)

Halalii

Puu O Maui

Puu O Pele

Kalua O Ka Oo

Kamoali

Haupaakea Peak (9,157 ft.)

PARK HEADQUARTERS

HALEAKALA CRATER RD.

▲ (6,849 ft.)

HOSMER GROVE ▲

VISITOR CENTER

Puu Ulaula Overlook (10,023 ft.)

▲ (9,357 ft.)

KALEAKALA OBSERVATORY

(31)

NOTE: BE AWARE OF FREE RANGE CATTLE ALONG THE HIGHWAY, ESPECIALLY AT NIGHT

0   1 mi
0   1 km

© J.D. BISIGNANI AND MOON PUBLICATIONS, INC.

erative. Misty, damp clouds can surround the crater, blocking out the sun, or pour into the basin, obscuring even it from view. The *Maui News* prints the hours of sunrise and sunset (on a daily basis) as they vary with the season, so make sure to check. The National Weather Service provides a daily weather recording at (808) 871-5054. For more specific information, you can call the ranger station at (808) 572-7749 for a recorded message, or call (808) 572-9306 for a ranger. Plan on taking a minimum of 90 minutes to arrive from Kahului, and to be safe, arrive at least 30 minutes before dawn or dusk, because even one minute is critical. The sun, as it rises or sets, infuses the clouds with streaks, puffs, and bursts of dazzling pastels, at the same time backlighting and edging the crater in glorious golds and reds. Prepare for an emotional crescendo that will brim your eyes with tears at the majesty of it all. Engulfed by this magnificence, no one can remain unmoved.

Note: If you want to avoid downhill bikers and tourists you can also get a great view from the Kalahaku Overlook. When you drive back down the mountain, shift into a low gear to control your speed to prevent riding the brakes.

Crater Facts

Haleakala was formed primarily from pa'hoehoe lava. This lava is the hottest natural substance on earth, and it flows like swift fiery rivers. Because of its high viscosity, it forms classic shield volcanoes. Plenty of a'a is also found in the mountain's composition. This rock comes out partially solidified and filled with gases, then breaks apart and forms clinkers. You'll be hiking over both, but be especially careful on a'a, because its jagged edges will cut you as quickly as coral. The crater is primarily formed from erosion, not from caving in on itself. The erosion on Hawaii is quite accelerated due to carbonic acid build-up, a by-product of the quick decomposition of abundant plant life. The rocks break down into smaller particles of soil which are then washed off the mountain by rain, or blown off by wind. Natural drainage patterns form, and canyons begin to develop and slowly eat their way to the center. The two largest are **Keanae Valley** in the north and **Kaupo Gap** in the south. These canyons, over time, moved their heads past each other to the center of the mountain,

where they took several thousand feet off the summit and formed a huge amphitheater-like crater.

Some stones that you encounter while hiking will be very light in weight. They once held water and gases that evaporated. If you knock two together, they'll sound like crystal. Also, be observant for **Maui diamonds.** They are garnet stones, a type of pyroxene or crystal.

The cinder cones in the crater are fascinating. They're volcanic vents with a high iron content and may form electromagnetic lines from the earth's center. On top, they are like funnels, transmitters and receivers of energy, natural pyramids. Climbing them violates park rules made to protect endangered plants and threatened insects that pollinate them. Notice the color of the compacted earth on the trails. It's obvious why you should remain on them. All the plants (silverswords, too) are shallow-rooted and live by condensing moisture on their leaves. Don't walk too close to them because you'll compact the earth around them and damage the roots. The ecosystem on Haleakala is very delicate, so please keep this in mind to better preserve its beauty for future generations.

SIGHTS

You'll start enjoying Haleakala long before you reach the top. Don't make the mistake of simply bolting up the mountain without taking time to enjoy what you're passing. Route 37 from Kahului takes you through Pukalani, the last big place to buy supplies. There it branches to clearly marked Rt. 377; in six miles it becomes the zigzag of Rt. 378 or **Haleakala Crater Road.** Along the way are forests of indigenous and introduced trees, including eucalyptus, beautifully flowering jacaranda, and stands of cactus. The vistas change rapidly from one vantage point to the next. Sometimes it's the green rolling hills of Ireland, and then instantly it's the tall, yellow grass of the plains. This is also cattle country, so don't be surprised to see all breeds, from Holsteins to Brahmans.

Headquarters

After paying your entrance fee, the first stopping point in the park is **Hosmer Grove Camp-**

ground (see below) a short way down a secondary park road on your left. Proceed past here a few minutes and you'll arrive at **park headquarters,** elev. 7,000 feet, open daily 7:30 a.m.-4 p.m. Campers can get their permits here and others will be happy to stop for all manner of brochures and information concerning the park, for water, or to use the toilet or pay phone. There are some silverswords outside, and a few *nene* can occasionally be seen wandering the area. After you pass the park headquarters, zig and zag a couple more times, there's parking for Halemauu Trail on your left (see below). Following are two overlooks, **Leleiwi** and **Kalahaku.** Both offer tremendous views and different perspectives on the crater. They shouldn't be missed—especially Kalahaku, where there are silverswords and the remnants of a travelers' lodge from the days when an expedition to Haleakala took two days.

Visitors Center

Near road's end is the visitors center, elev. 9,740 feet, approximately 10 miles up the mountain from headquarters, and a half-hour drive. You get one of the best views into the crater from here. It's open from sunrise to 3 p.m. and contains a clear and concise display featuring the geology of Haleakala. Maps and books are available, and periodic ranger talks are particularly informative, delving into geology and the legends surrounding the great mountain. Various ranger-led hikes are also given, including the hike down Sliding Sands Trail, daily interpretive talks at the summit, and the Hosmer Grove forest walk. Additional interpretive talks and ranger-led hikes are conducted at the Kipahulu ranger station. Check with the park headquarters or the visitors center for times and days of programs. All mule and horse rides into the crater and bike trips down the mountainside through the park start from the parking lot to the front of the visitors center. By 10 a.m., there will be lots of people at the top, so enjoy the time between when the bikers leave and the buses arrive.

Bikes going down the mountain travel about 20-25 miles an hour, sometimes faster. If you're caught behind a string of bikes on your way down, just slow down and wait for them to pull over and let you pass.

HIKING AND CAMPING

Walks

One of the outside paths leads to **Pakaoao** (White Hill). An easy quarter-mile hike will take you to the summit, and along the way you'll pass stone shelters and sleeping platforms from the days when Hawaiians came here to quarry the special tool-stone. It's a type of whitish slate that easily flakes but is so hard that when you strike two pieces together it rings almost like iron. Next comes **Puu'ulaula** (Red Hill), the highest point on Maui, at 10,023 feet. Atop is a glass-encased observation area (open 24 hours). This is where many people come to view the sunrise and sunset. From here, if the day is crystal clear, you can see all of the main Hawaiian Islands except Kauai. To add some perspective to size and distance, it's 100 miles from the top of Haleakala to the volcanic peak Mauna Kea on the Big Island to the southeast. Behind you on the slope below is **Maui Space Surveillance Complex,** tel. (808) 243-1313, a research facility with eight telescopes that's manned by the University of Hawaii and the Department of Defense. Open to the public one day a month; tours are booked months in advance.

The easy **Hosmer Grove Nature Trail** leads you through a stand of introduced temperate zone trees that was planted in 1910 to see if any would be good for commercial lumber use. There are perhaps a dozen different species of trees here, and the walk should take a half hour or so over mostly level ground. Originally planted in separate areas, these trees and others have intermingled now. Here you will see Jeffrey pine, ponderosa pine, lodgepole pine, incense cedar, eucalyptus, Norway spruce, eastern red cedar, Douglas fir, and Japanese *sugi*. Several signs are posted along the trail to explain what the trees are and how the forest developed.

Various **ranger-led walks** are given during the week, leaving either from the visitors center or from Hosmer Grove campground. On Monday and Thursday at 9 a.m. and noon, a naturalist leads a hike down into the Waikamoi cloud forest from Hosmer Grove, and on this hike you'll learn about trees, birds, and natural features of the area. Three hours, three miles, moderately strenuous. A ranger-led hike also goes down the Sliding Sands trail on a Cinder Desert Hike on Tuesday and Friday at 10 a.m. and noon from the trailhead at the visitors center parking lot. Two hours, two miles, moderately strenuous.

Hikes

There are three trails in Haleakala Wilderness Area: Halemauu, Sliding Sands, and Kaupo. **Halemauu Trail** starts at the 8,000-foot level along the road about three miles past the park headquarters. It descends quickly to the 6,600-foot level on the crater floor. En route you'll pass Holua Cabin, Silversword Loop, the Bottomless Pit (a mere 65 feet deep), then a portion of Sliding Sands Trail and back to the visitors center. You shouldn't have any trouble hitching back to your car from here.

Sliding Sands begins at the summit of Haleakala near the visitors center. This is the main crater trail and gives you the best overall hike. It joins the Kaupo Trail at Paliku Cabin; alternatively, at Kapaloa Cabin you can turn left to the Bottomless Pit and exit via Halemauu Trail. This last choice is one of the best, but you'll have to hitch back to your car at the visitors center, which shouldn't be left for the dwindling late-evening traffic going up the mountain.

The **Kaupo Trail** is long and tough. It follows the Kaupo Gap to the park boundary at 3,880 feet. It then crosses private land, which is no problem, and after a steep and rocky downhill grade deposits you in the semi-ghost town of Kaupo. This is the rugged part of the Hana loop. You'll have to hitch west just to get to the scant traffic of Rt. 31, or head nine miles east to Kipahulu and its campground, and from there back along the Hana Road.

For those inclined, there are also horse and mule tours of the crater. Hikers should also consider a day with the professional guide service **Hike Maui**. The guide's in-depth knowledge and commentary will make your trip not only more fulfilling, but enjoyably informative as well. (See **Sports and Recreation** in Maui's introduction.)

Trekkers

Serious hikers or campers must have sturdy shoes, good warm clothes, rain gear, canteens, down bags, and a serviceable tent. Hats and sunglasses are needed. Compasses are useless because of the high magnetism in the rock,

but binoculars are particularly rewarding. No cook-fires are allowed in the crater, so you'll need a stove. Don't burn any dead wood—the soil needs all the decomposing nutrients it can get. Drinking water is available at all of the cabins within the crater, but the supply is limited so bring what you will need. This environment is particularly delicate. Stay on the established trails so that you don't cause undue erosion. Leave rocks and especially plants alone. Don't walk too close to silverswords or any other plants because you'll compact the soil. Leave your pets at home; ground-nesting birds here are easily disturbed. If nature "calls," dig a very shallow hole, off the trail, and pack out your used toilet paper since the very dry conditions are not conducive to it biodegrading.

Camping

Admission to the park is $10 per car, $5 for bikers, hikers, and motorcycles, and is good for seven days (national park discount passes are honored), but camping is free with a necessary camping permit from park headquarters. The Hosmer Grove campground is at the 6,800-foot level, just before park headquarters; the free camping here is limited to three nights and to 25 people, but there's generally room for all. There's water, pit toilets, picnic tables, grills, and a pavilion. It was named after Ralph Hosmer. While here take a stroll along the half-mile forest loop that threads its way through the grove of trees that Hosmer planted.

Kipahulu Campground is a primitive camping area over near Oheo Stream. It's part of the park, but unless you're an intrepid hiker and descend all the way down the Kaupo Trail, you'll come to it via Hana.

There are campsites in the crater at **Holua, Paliku,** and **Kapalaoa.** All three offer cabins, and tent camping is allowed at the first two. Camping at any of these is extremely popular, and reservations for the cabins must be made at least 90 days in advance by mail using only a special cabin reservation request form. Each cabin is reserved for one group of up to 12 people only. A lottery of the applicants chosen for sites keeps it fair for all. Environmental impact studies limit the number of campers to 25 per area per day. Camping is limited to a total of three days per month, with no more than two consecutive days at each spot. Rates for cabin use are $40 for up to six persons and $80 to a maximum of 12 people. For complete details and reservation form contact: Haleakala National Park, P.O. Box 369, Makawao, HI 96768, tel. (808) 572-9306, website: www.nps.gov/hale.

Making Do

If you've come to Hawaii for sun and surf and you aren't prepared for alpine temperatures, you can still enjoy Haleakala. For a day-trip, wear your jogging suit or a sweater, if you've brought one. Make sure to wear socks, and even bring an extra pair as makeshift mittens. Use your dry beach towel to wrap around inside your sweater as extra insulation, and even consider taking your hotel blanket, which you can use Indian fashion. Make rain gear from a large plastic garbage bag with holes cut for head and arms; this is also a good windbreaker. Take your beach hat, too. Don't worry about looking ridiculous in this get-up—you will! But you'll also keep warm! Remember that for every thousand feet you climb, the temperature drops three degrees Fahrenheit, so the summit is about 32° cooler than at sea level. As the sun reaches its zenith, if there are no rain clouds, the crater floor will go from about 50 to 80 degrees. It can flip-flop from blazing hot to dismal and rainy a number of times in the same day. The nights may drop below freezing, with the coldest recorded temperature a bone-chilling 14°. Dawn and dusk are notorious for being bitter. Because of the altitude, be aware that the oxygen level will drop, and those with any impairing conditions should take precautions. The sun is ultrastrong atop the mountain, and even those with deep tans are subject to burning. Noses are particularly susceptible.

M.G.L. DOMENY DE RIENZI

EAST MAUI
THE HANA ROAD

On the long and winding road to Hana's door, most people's daydreams of "paradise" come true. A trip to Maui without a visit to Hana is like ordering a sundae without a cherry on top. The 50 miles that it takes to get there from Kahului are some of the most remarkable in the world. The Hana Highway (Rt. 36) starts out innocently enough, passing Paia. The inspiration for Paia's gaily painted storefronts looks like it came from a jar of jelly beans. Next come some north-shore surfing beaches where windsurfers fly, doing amazing aquabatics. Soon there is a string of "rooster towns," so named because that's about all that seems to be stirring. Then Rt. 36 becomes Rt. 360 and at mile marker 3 the *real* Hana Road begins.

The semi-official count tallies more than 600 rollicking turns and 57 one-lane bridges, inducing everyone to slow down and soak up the sights of this glorious road. It's like passing through a tunnel cut from trees. The ocean winks with azure blue through sudden openings on your left. To the right, streams, waterfalls, and pools sit wreathed with jungle and wildflowers. Coconuts, guavas, mangos, and bananas grow everywhere on the mountainside. Fruit stands pop up regularly as you creep along. Then comes Keanae with its arboretum and taro farms indicating that many ethnic Hawaiians still live along the road. There are places to camp, picnic, and swim, both in the ocean and in freshwater streams.

Along with you, every other car traveling the Hana Highway is on the road to take in the beauty that this coast has to offer. Nearly all pass through, some stay a day or a week, while others take up residence. Islanders, mainlanders, and foreigners alike are enticed by the land, and under its spell they put down roots. Along with George Harrison, who has a house a few miles down the coast in Nahiku, a few well-known individuals who maintain homes here are Jim Nabors, Kris Kristofferson, and Carol Burnett.

Then you reach Hana itself, a remarkable town. The great Queen Kaahumanu was born here, and many celebrities live in the surrounding hills seeking peace and solitude. Past Hana, the road becomes even more rugged and besieged by jungle. It opens up again around Oheo Gulch. Here waterfalls cascade over stupendous cataracts, forming a series of pools until they reach the sea. Beyond is a rental car's no-man's land, where the passable road toughens and Haleakala shows its barren volcanic face scarred by lava flows.

PAIA

Paia (Noisy) was a bustling sugar town that took a nap. When it awoke, it had a set of whiskers and its vitality had flown away. At the beginning of the 19th century, many groups of ethnic field workers lived here, segregated in housing clusters called "camps" that stretched up Baldwin Avenue. Paia was the main gateway for sugar on East Maui, and even a railroad functioned here until about 30 years ago. During the 1930s, its population, at more than 10,000, was the largest on the island. Then fortunes shifted toward Kahului, and Paia lost its dynamism, until recently. Paia was resuscitated in the 1970s by an influx of paradise-seeking hippies, and then again in the '80s came another shot in the arm from windsurfers. These two groups have metamorphosed into townsfolk and have pumped new life into Paia's old muscles. The practical shops catering to the pragmatic needs of a "plantation town" were replaced. The storefronts were painted and spruced up. A new breed of merchants with their

eye on passing tourists has taken over. Now Paia focuses on boutiques, crafts, artwork, and food. Since you've got to pass through on your way to Hana, it serves as a great place not only to top off your gas tank, but also to stop for a bite and a browse. The prices are good for just about everything, and it boasts one of the island's best fish restaurants and art shops. Paia, under its heavy makeup, is still a vintage example of what it always was—a homey, serviceable, working town.

Sights
A mile or so before you enter Paia on the left is **Rinzai Buddhist Temple** located on Alawai Road—reached by going through H.P. Baldwin Park. The grounds are pleasant and worth a look. **Mantokuji Buddhist Temple** on the eastern outskirts of Paia heralds the sun's rising and setting by ringing its huge gong 18 times at dawn and dusk.

H.P. Baldwin Beach County Park is on your left about seven miles past Kahului on Rt. 36, just past Maui Country Club and the well-to-do community of Spreckelsville; this spacious park is good for swimming, shell-collecting, and decent winter surfing. It has full amenities. Unfortunately, Baldwin has a bad reputation. It's one of those places that locals have staked out with the attitude of "us against them." Hassles and robberies have been known to occur. Be nice, calm, and respectful. For the timid, to be on the safe side, be gone.

Mantokuji Buddhist Temple

ROBERT NILSEN

Hookipa Beach Park is about 10 minutes past Paia. There's a high grassy sand dune along the road and the park is down below, where you'll enjoy full amenities—unofficial camping occurs. Swimming is advisable only on calm days, as there are wicked currents. Primarily a surfing beach that is now regarded as one of the best sailboarding areas in Hawaii, this is home to the Aloha Classic, held yearly in October or November. The world's best sailboarders come here, trying to win the $5,000-10,000 prize. Bring binoculars.

Accommodations

One of the few place to lodge in Paia is at the **Nalu Kai Lodge,** located just behind the Wine Corner where Baldwin Avenue meets the Hana Highway, tel. (808) 579-8009; ask for Myrna. This plain and simple two-story cement building offers clean, quiet, adequate rooms. Don't expect anything fancy, just the necessities. Rates vary—Myrna bargains—but expect to spend about $40 for one night, or $350 for a month. There are seven units, one double and six singles. Most people stay long-term. Inexpensive.

About a mile away in Ku'au next to Mama's Fish House is the **Kuau Plaza Condo,** tel. (808) 579-8080, fax 579-8533. Rooms have private baths and color televisions. Laundry facilities are located on premises. Rooms run $30 a night on a weekly rate and $20 a night on a monthly rate; suites are $55 and $40 a night, respectively. Budget.

Food

Picnic's, 30 Baldwin Ave., tel. (808) 579-8021, is open daily 7 a.m.-7 p.m. Breakfast and lunch offer everything from roast beef to vegetarian sandwiches like a scrumptious spinach nut burger or tofu burger, all under $5. The best options are boxed picnic lunches that add a special touch if you're heading to Hana. They start from the basic Upcountry Picnic, which includes sandwiches and sides at $7.95 per person, to the Executive with sandwiches, *kiawe*-broiled chicken, sides, nut bread, condiments, cheeses, and even a tablecloth all in a Styrofoam ice chest for $42.50. (Supposedly feeds two, but with extra buns will feed four!) Numerous others are available. Picnic's is one of the best stops along the Hana Road even for a quick espresso, cappuccino, or frozen yogurt. Or treat yourself with the fresh-baked pastries like macadamia nut sticky buns and the apple and papaya turnovers: worth the guilt!

Another place for boxed picnic lunches is **Peach's Bakery and Delicatessen,** 2 Baldwin Ave., tel. (808) 579-8612, open 6:30 a.m.-6 p.m., Thursday and Friday to 7:30 p.m., where you can enjoy a scone, the famous peach crumble and Hawaiian coconut cake, and a cup of cappuccino. For a boxed lunch try the Hana Bay box at $6.95. Peach's also serves sandwiches made from homemade breads, great spinach lasagna, and fresh pastries of all sorts.

At the corner is **Paia Fish Market Restaurant,** tel. (808) 579-8030, a casual sit-down restaurant with picnic tables inside. Specializing in charbroiled fish, the menu also includes more than a dozen types of fish, all at market price, that can be prepared in one of four different manners. You can also have charbroiled chicken, blackened sashimi, seafood salad, or fresh fish to take home and prepare yourself. The lunch and dinner menus include burgers, pasta, and fajitas. Across the street on the corner, a great place to people-watch or be watched is **Milagros Bar and Restaurant,** tel. (808) 579-8755, for burgers, sandwiches, and fish; eat inside or outside.

Jacques Bistro and bar, 89 Hana Hwy., is a relative newcomer. Seating is inside at tables with white linen or on the patio out back under shade trees. The lunch menu includes mostly sandwiches, salads, and fish, and might be a mahi sandwich for $6.95 or tomato mozzarella salad for $7.95. For dinner, try grilled chicken, *paniolo* cut steak, or seafood linguine. All entrees are under $19.95, except for the seafood bowl at $24.50.

Kihata Restaurant, tel. (808) 579-9035, open Tues.-Sat. 11 a.m.-1:30 p.m. for lunch, and 5-9 p.m. for dinner, is a small Japanese restaurant and sushi bar that you can easily pass by. Don't! It's just where Baldwin Ave. meets Rt. 36 along the main road. The traditional Japanese menu offers *bento* and sushi, with all entrees under $10, mostly $6-8, like *don buri, soba,* and *udon.* The sushi bar opens about 5:30 p.m.

Visit **Raw Experience,** 42 Baldwin Ave., for uncooked, organic, vegan foods. Here you'll find many items, albeit in a different form, that you'd find elsewhere, but with a big twist—no heat is used in preparation. Try a sprouted hummus

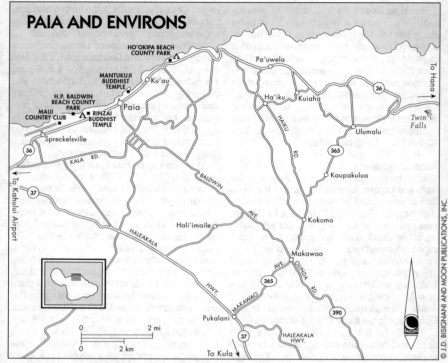

PAIA AND ENVIRONS

HO'OKIPA BEACH
COUNTY PARK

Pa'uwela

MANTUKUJI
BUDDHIST
TEMPLE

Ku'au

H.P. BALDWIN
BEACH COUNTY
PARK

Ha'iku   Kuiaha

MAUI
COUNTY CLUB

RINZAI
BUDDHIST
TEMPLE

Paia

36

To Hana

Spreckelsville

HAIKU RD.

Twin
Falls

Ulumalu

36

KALA RD.

BALDWIN

365

Kaupakulua

To Kahului Airport

37

HALEAKALA

AVE.

Hali'imaile

Kokomo

To Kula

Makawao

AVE.

OLINDA RD.

365

HWY.

MAKAWAO

Pukalani

390

37

HALEAKALA
HWY.

To Kula

0   2 mi
0   2 km

MOON

© J.D. BISIGNANI AND MOON PUBLICATIONS, INC.

appetizer, or angel hair pasta that's made from threads spun from carrots and beets with a sun-dried tomato marinara and vegetables. How about a pizza in the raw, regular or marinated salad, desserts, smoothies, juices, and other drinks. It may sound strange, but it's healthy, wholesome, well-presented food. Friendly, smoke-free environment. Open Mon.-Sat. 10:08 a.m.-8:01 p.m., Sunday 11:30 a.m.-3:30 p.m.

The **Bangkok** Thai cuisine restaurant, tel. (808) 579-8979, an indoor/outdoor cafe with a courtyard area surrounded by palm trees, is open for lunch 11 a.m.-3 p.m. and then again for dinner 5-9:30 p.m. Appetizers ranging $5.50-7.95 include Thai crispy noodles and sateh chicken. Try a green papaya salad or a spicy seafood coconut soup before your entree, which might be the Evil Prince shrimp or fish for $9.95, or seafood combo with broccoli at $11.95. In addition, there are many curry, noodle, fish, and vegetarian dishes. Desserts include tapioca and

warm coconut milk at $2.95. Food here is good value, decently presented, and authentic. Soft drinks and bar drinks available.

For a quick bite you have **Charley's,** tel. (808) 579-9453, a saloon with pool tables and restaurant specializing in pizza, pasta, and sandwiches, open 7 a.m. for breakfast, from 11:30 for lunch, and 5 p.m. for dinner. Charley's is also known for its breakfasts. Breakfast choices include Charley's Eggs Benedict, $8, and huevos rancheros, $7.25; for lunch select a fish sandwich, $9.50, or pasta for around $9. Some specials, like shrimp scampi or chicken marsala at about $15, are more pricey. Soups, salads, and appetizers are priced equally well. This is a big rambling amiable place where tourists and locals alike come for a pleasant time.

The **Vegan Restaurant,** located at 115 Baldwin Ave., tel. (808) 579-9144, open daily 11 a.m.-8:30 p.m. except Monday, is an extraordinary health-conscious restaurant, a "hippie" hangout that others into healthy food frequent. People don't come for the decor—brightly colored wall hangings on no-nonsense walls—they come for the large portions of incredibly delicious food. The Vegan serves only vegetarian food made with organic products and uses no dairy, honey, or animal products of any kind; the food is mostly cholesterol-free. Standard menu items include hummus salad at $4.95, the Vegan burger for $4.75, and veggie lasagna for $8.95; specials nightly. Luscious smoothies are priced at $2.95. There's a great bulletin board, a few tables at which you can eat, or you can call ahead for orders to go.

A short way up Baldwin Avenue, the **Paia Coffee Company,** tel. (808) 579-9296, offers more than coffee. Of course, you can get your morning jolt of espresso, caffe latte, or straight black cup of joe, but you might also like to try a crepe. On Friday nights, it's an all-you-can-eat pasta night for $5. You can't beat it.

Perhaps the most upscale restaurant in Paia itself is **Impromptu,** 71 Baldwin Ave., tel. (808) 579-8477. Open for breakfast, lunch, and dinner, evening entrees are in the $17.95-22.95 range.

Mama's Fish House, reservations highly recommended, tel. (808) 579-8488, is just past Paia on the left heading toward Hana. Look for the turnoffs near the blinking yellow light; you'll see a vintage car with a sign for Mama's, a ship's flagpole, and a fishing boat marking the entranceway. There's plenty of off-road complimentary valet parking. Mama's, serving lunch 11 a.m.-2:30 p.m., cocktails and *pu pu* until dinner at 5 p.m., has earned the best reputation possible—it gets thumbs up from local people even though it is expensive. It's perhaps the best upscale beach shack on the island, set right on the beach surrounded by coconut trees and tiki torches with outrigger canoes drawn on the lawn out front. The fish is fresh daily, with some broiled over *kiawe,* while the vegetables come from local gardens and the herbs are Mama's own. Fish entrees run $30-35, others $25-45. Special Hawaiian touches, wonderful food, friendly professional service, and a great view of Maui's north shore, add to the enjoyment of every meal. A terrific idea is to make reservations here for the evening's return trip from Hana.

Mana Natural Foods, 49 Baldwin Ave., tel. (808) 579-8078, open daily 8 a.m.-8 p.m., is a well-stocked health-food store, maybe the best on Maui. Inside the old building you'll find local organic produce, vitamins, grains, juices, bulk foods, and more. For takeout, try the salad bar or look for picnic items in the cooler. Outside, check out the great community bulletin board for what's selling and happening around Paia.

For boxed and canned goods, picnic items, meats, vegetables, and fresh-cut flowers, try the old-time shop **Horiuchi Market.** Just before Baldwin Ave. along the Hana Highway is **Nagata Store,** a general grocery store, open Mon.-Fri. 6 a.m.-7 p.m., Saturday 6 a.m.-6 p.m., Sunday 6 a.m.-1 p.m.

The **Wine Corner,** appropriately located at the corner of Baldwin Ave. and the Hana Hwy., is a well-stocked bottle shop with wines, liquor, and ice-cold beer. Microbreweries are well represented. Open Monday noon-10 p.m., Tues.-Sun. 9 a.m.-10:30 p.m.

Shopping

Maui Crafts Guild is on the left just as you enter Paia, at 43 Hana Hwy., P.O. Box 609, Paia, HI 96779, tel. (808) 579-9697. Open daily 9 a.m.-6 p.m., the Crafts Guild is one of the best art outlets in Hawaii. It's owned and operated by the artists themselves, now numbering more than two dozen, all of whom must pass a thorough jurying by present members. All artists must be islanders, and they must use natural materials found in Hawaii to create their work except for some specialized clay, fabrics, and printmaking paper. Items are tastefully displayed and you'll find a wide variety of artwork and crafts including pottery, prints, woodwork, bamboowork, stained glass, batik, and jewelry. Different artists staff the shop on different days, but business cards and phone numbers are available if you want to see more of something you like. Prices are reasonable and this is an excellent place to make that one "big" purchase. Upstairs is the gallery of wood sculptor Arthur Dennis Williams.

In town is **Paia Trading Co.,** a discovery shop open Mon.-Fri. 9 a.m.-5 p.m. with collectibles like glass, telephones, aloha shirts, lanterns, jewelry, license plates, oil lamps, flotation balls, old bottles, and a smattering of pottery and antique furniture. Next door is **Boutique II,** open daily 10 a.m.-6 p.m., Sunday to 4 p.m., filled with ladies' apparel and alohawear. **Nuage Bleu,** a boutique open daily 10 a.m.-5 p.m., features distinctive fashions and gift items, mostly for women. **Jaggers,** open daily 9 a.m.-5 p.m., carries alohawear, fancy dresses, replicas of vintage aloha shirts for men, and some umbrellas. Across the street is the **Maui Gecko Factory** for T-shirts; a shaved ice shop; **Sand and Sea,** primarily a sculpture gallery featuring dolphins; and **Paia Bay Gallery** for unique island art.

Walk along Baldwin Avenue for a half block and you'll find a drawerful of boutiques and fashion shops, including **Moon Bow Tropics** carrying women's sun dresses, men's aloha shirts, short, T-shirts, and jewelry; fine batik dresses and shirts made in Indonesia at **Batonga;** and **Alpha and Omega** for ladies' clothing, artwork, glass, and crystal.

Also along Baldwin Avenue are the **Bank of Hawaii,** the **post office,** and a washerette.

For the windsurfer, look for boards and gear at **Hi-Tech Surf Sports,** or **Sailboards Maui.** At these and other places in town, you can dress yourself for the beach and get a board to ride over those waves.

Paia has two gas stations: **Unocal,** which has made-to-order sandwiches at its minimart, and **Chevron,** open 24 hours. These gas stations are the last places to fill your tank before reaching Hana. Next door is **Paia General Store** for groceries, supplies, and sundries, with a takeout snack window called the **Paia Drive Inn** where most items are under $7. Next to that, in what was at one time the Lower Paia Theater, are a gift shop, antique shop, and combination clothing and sailboard shop. Across the street is the Paia Mercantile Shopping Complex, a collection of shops ranging from surfing equipment to **Mandala** for clothing, craft items, and gifts from Asia.

Heading down the road to Hana you'll see the **Maui Community Center** on your right, the Mantokuji Buddhist temple on your left, and a little farther on the **Ku'au Market,** a convenience store to get snacks for the road. Just around the bend is **Mama's Fish House,** and shortly after Hookipa Beach. Near mile marker 14 on the mountain side of the highway you'll come across **Maui Grown Market and Deli.** Housed in a vintage corrugated roof plantation-style building with a porch out front, it carries mostly sandwiches, salads, smoothies and packaged food items, with a limited supply of fresh produce. Lunch boxes are

a specialty. This is the last place before you really start to wind your way down the Hana Highway. A public phone is out front. Open daily 6:30 a.m.-7 p.m. (until 6 p.m. on Sunday). Aside from side trips to Haiku, Pauwela, and Ulumalu, you'll have clear sailing down the road to Hana.

HAIKU

Around mile marker 11, Haiku Road heads up the hill to the little community of Haiku. From Upcountry, follow Kauhikoa Road down the hill after turning off of Rt. 365 below Kokomo and Makawao. Haiku is an old cannery town, canning, boxing, and sending millions of pineapples and guavas to the world over the decades. After the cannery companies stopped production, their industrial buildings were renovated and turned into shops and studios, and have become, along with the Pauwela Cannery down the road, a center for artists and craftsmen. In the largest of the old cannery buildings, the pineapple cannery, you'll find among the many shops here a **True Value Hardware** store, the **Haleakala Bike Company** shop, **Haiku Video, Haiku Pizza and Subs.** To the side of the huge parking lot in a separate building is **Trattoria Haiku,** a wonderful Italian place to eat. Open daily except Monday for dinner only, this restaurant serves honest family food and is especially full on Tuesday when it offers a two-for-one special.

At the main intersection in this little community is **Haiku Grocery,** open seven days a week and a good place to pick up supplies. Across the street are the **post office** and the **Haiku Mart Liquor and Deli.** There's a community bulletin board in front of the grocery store and a few more around town, so you can stop and check out what's happening in the community.

Tucked behind Haiku Mart is **Haiku Town Center,** the second of the big remodeled cannery buildings that's slowly been turned into space for other use. This was the guava cannery. Among other shops that will fill the space you'll find **Sativa,** a store dealing almost entirely with the numerous and various products made from the hemp plant.

Haiku Road runs east, wending its way along the mountain, in and out of gulches, over bridges, and through thickly vegetated forests to Kuiaha. It's a great way to see the back roads of lower mountain Maui. There are lots of roads in this area, and many people have settled here, carving out their little bit of paradise. An alternate road to Kuiaha from the Hana Highway starts just past mile marker 12. Look for W. Kuiaha Road and make a right heading for the old **Pauwela Cannery,** which is less than five minutes up the road. This huge tin can of a building has been divided into a honeycomb of studios and workshops housing fine artists, woodworkers, potters, and sailboard makers. These artists and craftspeople come and go, so you're never sure just who will be occupying the studios. However, all welcome guests to come and browse, and buy. While here, be sure to stop at the **Pauwela Cafe** for a cold drink, hot coffee, salad, sandwich, or pastry. Sit inside or out. Open Mon.-Sat. 7 a.m.-3 p.m., Sunday 8 a.m.-2 p.m. Have a peek at the art and crafts displayed next door at **Makani Hau.** For other needs, try **Okashiro General Store** across the street.

THE ROAD BEGINS

The road to Hana holds many spectacles and surprises, but one of the best is the road itself . . . it's a marvel! The road was hacked out from the coastline and completed in 1927, every inch by hand using pick and shovel. Crushed volcanic rock was the first surface material. Rebuilt and partially paved in 1962, only in 1982 was the road fully paved. Mother nature and man's machines have taken their toll on the road, and in the early '90s, the Hana Highway was widened and again resurfaced. Today it's smooth sailing. An ancient Hawaiian trail followed the same route for part of the way, but mostly people moved up and down this coastline by boat. What makes the scenery so special is that the road snakes along Maui's windward side. There's abundant vegetation and countless streams flowing from Haleakala, carving gorgeous valleys. There are a few scattered villages with a house or two that you hardly notice, and the beaches, although few, are empty. Mostly, however, it's the "feeling" that you get along this road. Nature is close and accessible, and it's so incredibly "South Sea island" that it almost seems artificial. But it isn't.

Hana Road Tips

You've got 30 miles of turns ahead when Rt. 36 (mile marker 22) becomes Rt. 360 (mile marker 0) and the fun begins. The Hana Road has the reputation of being a "bad road," but this isn't true. It's narrow, with plenty of hairpin turns, but it's well banked, has clearly marked bridges, and there's always maintenance going on (which can slow you up). Years back, it was a harrowing experience. When mudslides blocked the road, drivers were known to swap their cars with those on the opposite side and carry on to where they were going. The road's reputation sets people up to expect an ordeal, so they make it one, and unfortunately, drive accordingly. Sometimes it seems as though tourists demand the road to be rugged, so that they can tell the folks back home that they, too, "survived the road to Hana." This popular slogan appears on T-shirts, copyrighted and sold by Hasegawa's famous store in Hana, and perpetuates this belief. You'll have no problem, and you'll see much more if you just take it easy.

Your speed will often drop below 10 miles per hour and will rarely exceed 25. Standard-shift cars are better for the turns. Cloudbursts occur at any time so be ready for slick roads. A heavy fall of fruit from roadside mango trees can also coat the road with slippery slime. Look as far up the road as possible and don't allow yourself to be mesmerized by the 10 feet in front of your hood. If your tire dips off a rough shoulder, don't risk losing control by jerking the wheels back on immediately. Ride it for a while and either stop or wait for an even shoulder to come back on. Local people trying to make time will often ride your rear bumper, but generally they won't honk. Pull over and let them by when possible. Pull-offs on this road are not overabundant, so be sure to choose your spot carefully. As a safety measure and courtesy to others, yield to all oncoming traffic at each bridge.

Driving from Kahului to Hana will take three hours, not counting some recommended stops. The greatest traffic flow is 10 a.m.-noon; returning "car trains" start by 3 p.m. and are heaviest around 5 p.m. Many white-knuckled drivers head for Hana as if it were a prized goal, without stopping along the way. This is ridiculous. The best sights are before and after Hana; the town itself is hardly worth the effort. Expect to spend a long

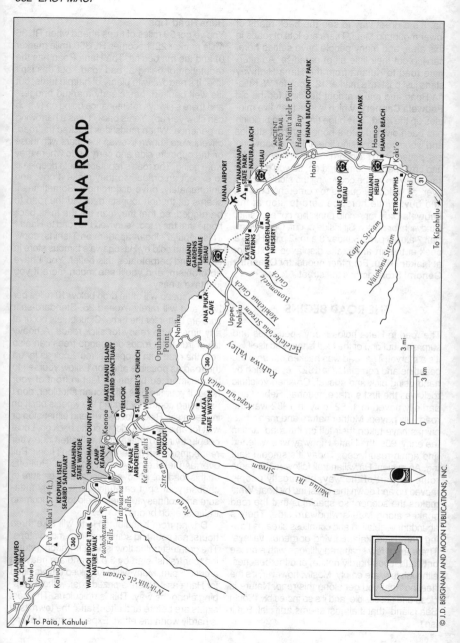

HANA ROAD

KAULANAPUEO CHURCH
Huelo

Pu'u Kuka'i (574 ft.)
Kailua

To Paia, Kahului

WAIKAMOI RIDGE TRAIL NATURE WALK

KEOPUKA ISLET SEABIRD SANCTUARY

KAUMAHINA STATE WAYSIDE

HONOMANU COUNTY PARK

MAKU MANU ISLAND SEABIRD SANCTUARY

CAMP KEANAE

OVERLOOK

ST. GABRIEL'S CHURCH

Keanae

Wailua

KE'ANAE ARBORETUM

Ke'anae Falls

WAILUA LOOKOUT

Haipuaena Falls

Paohokamua Falls

N'āhiku'ele Stream

Ka'no

Wailua Iki Stream

Wailua Stream

PUAAKA STATE WAYSIDE

Kapa'ula Gulch

Kuhiwa Valley

360

Opuhanao Point

Nahiku

ANA PUKA CAVE

Upper Nahiku

Helelike'oha Stream

Mokuhiwa Gulch

Honomaele Gulch

KEHANU GARDENS PI'ILANIHALE HEIAU

KA'ELEKU CAVERNS

HANA GARDENLAND NURSERY

HANA AIRPORT

WAI'ANAPANAPA STATE PARK

HEIAU

Nanu'alele Point

ANCIENT PAVED TRAIL

Hana Bay

HANA BEACH COUNTY PARK

KOKI BEACH PARK

Hamoa

HAMOA BEACH

Hana

HALE O LONO HEIAU

KAULANUI HEIAU

PETROGLYPHS

Kaki'o

Puuiki

Kapi'a Stream

Waiohonu Stream

31

To Kipahulu

MOON

0   3 mi

0   3 km

© J.D. BISIGNANI AND MOON PUBLICATIONS, INC.

day exploring the Hana Road. To go all the way to Oheo Stream and take in some sights, you'll have to leave your hotel at sunup and won't get back until sundown. If your budget can afford it, plan on staying the night in Hana (reservations definitely) and return the next day. This is a particularly good plan if you have an afternoon departing flight from Kahului Airport. Also, most tourists seem terrified of driving the road at night. Actually it's easier. There is far less traffic, road reflectors mark the center and sides like a runway, and you're warned of oncoming cars by their headlights. Those in the know make much better time after dark! In case of **emergency,** a roadside telephone is located *makai* between mile markers 5 and 6. Only 3,000 people live along the entire north coast of East Maui leading to and including Hana.

SIGHTS

Twin Falls

A favorite of locals, the trail to Twin Falls should take about an hour. It's one of the first places to stop and enjoy along the road. Park near mile marker 2 just before the Hoolawa Bridge. A new metal gate marks the jeep trail. This is private property, but everyone seems to use it as if it were open to all. Walk the trail up to the irrigation ditch. On the way, a couple of side trails go off to the left and down to the steam. Guavas grow in this area and you might find ripe fruit at the right time of the year—there used to be a guava cannery in Haiku not far away. Follow the irrigation ditch until you reach the first falls. Alternately, follow the stream. The first pool is feed by two falls that give the area its name. A trail to the right goes up to the top of the falls and on to a second falls a short distance above. There you'll have more privacy. Some people come here to skinny-dip.

Huelo

A few miles past the new bridge and pulloff for Twin Falls is Huelo. Huelo means "Famous Owl," a name given for the birds that used to inhabit trees in the area. In the 1840s, Huelo was bustling sugar town surrounded by cane fields and even sustained a mill. Later, the area grew pineapple, but it's now just a quiet "rooster town"

famous for **Kaulanapueo Church,** built in 1853. The structure is made from coral that was hauled up block by block from Waipio Bay below and is reminiscent of New England architecture. It's still used on the second and fourth Sundays of each month at 10 a.m., and a peek through the door will reveal a stark interior with straight-backed benches and a platform. The pit on the ocean side of the church building was used to make the lime and mortar mix. Few bother to stop, so it's quiet and offers good panoramas of the village and sea below. At the broad turnoff to Huelo between mile markers 3 and 4 there's a public telephone, in case of emergency, and a row of mailboxes.

Kailua

The next tiny town is Kailua. Plenty of mountain apple trees flourish along this stretch. The multicolored trees are rainbow eucalyptus, introduced late last century from Australia and some of the most beautiful trees in Hawaii. Close by is a cousin, *Eucalyptus robusta,* which produces great timber, especially flooring, from its reddish-brown heartwood. This tree, due to its resins, gets extremely hard once it dries, so it must be milled immediately or you can do nothing with it. A few minutes beyond Kailua, notice a sudden difference in the humidity and in the phenomenal jungle growth that becomes even more pronounced.

Waikamoi Ridge

This nature walk (mosquitoes!) is a good place to stretch your legs and learn about native and introduced trees and vegetation. The turnout, good for about half a dozen vehicles, is not clearly marked along the highway past mile marker 9, but look for a metal gate at roadside and picnic tables in a clearing above the road. The well-defined, gradual trail leads through tall stands of trees. It's about one mile long and takes less than an hour. On the way, you will get glimpses of the highway and stream below. For those never before exposed to a bamboo forest, it's most interesting when the wind rustles the trees so that they knock together like natural percussion instruments. Picnic tables are available at the start and end of the trail. Tall mango trees tower over the upper picnic area. Return via the same trail or walk down the jeep path. Back on the road, and at the next bridge, is excellent drinking water. There's a stone barrel with a pipe coming out, and local people come to fill jugs with what they call "living water." It doesn't always run in summer but most times can be counted upon.

Garden of Eden

A new stop along this road is the landscaped Garden of Eden, a private arboretum and botanical garden. Entrance $3; open daily 9 a.m.-2 p.m. Have a stroll here among the tropical trees and flowering bushes, some of which are labeled for easy identification, or walk out to the Puohokamoa Falls overlook where you have a fine view down onto this graceful waterfall.

Puohokamoa Falls

Following is Puohokamoa Falls, where you'll find a nice pool and picnic table. A short trail will take you to the pool and its 30-foot cliff, from which local kids jump off. You'll also find a trail near the falls, and if you go upstream about 100 yards you'll discover another invigorating pool with yet another waterfall. Swimming is great here, and the small crowd is gone. If you hike downstream about one-half mile *through* the stream (no trail), you come to the top of a 200-foot falls from where you can peer over the edge. Be very conscious of water conditions and the dangers of being near the cliff edge.

Wayside Rest and Park

Less than two miles past Waikamoi Ridge are **Kaumahina State Wayside,** along the road, and **Honomanu County Park,** down at Honomanu Bay. Permits are required for camping at the county park. Camping here is in a rainforest with splendid views out to sea overlooking the rugged coastline and the black-sand beach of Honomanu Bay. Honomanu is not good for swimming because of strong currents, but is good for surfing. There are no amenities at Honomanu, but Kaumahina has picnic tables and restrooms. From Kaumahina, you're rewarded with splendid views down the coast to the Keanae Peninsula. Puohokamoa Falls is just a short walk back down the road.

At Nua'ailua Bay, one bay farther on, two roads lead down to the water on either side of the stream. This spot is one where locals come to fish or surf and to spend a leisurely day by the ocean.

Keanae

Going back about five miles toward the center of the mountain, Keanae Valley is the largest valley on the north side of Haleakala. Most of the big valleys that once existed, especially on East Maui, were filled in by lava flows, greatly reducing their original size. Also going deep into the heart of the mountain is Hoomanu Valley, located just before Keanae Valley. Hoomanu Valley has 3,000-foot cliffs and 1,000-foot waterfalls. Unfortunately, the trails here are quite difficult both to find and to negotiate.

Clearly marked on the right side of the highway will be the six-acre **Keanae Arboretum,** established in 1971. A hike through this facility will exemplify Hawaiian plant life in microcosm. There are two sections, one of ornamental tropical plants (identified) and the other of Hawaiian domestic plants. Toward the upper end of the arboretum are taro fields, and the hillsides above are covered with the natural rainforest vegetation. You can picnic along Piinaau Stream. Although the trail is hard to pick out, hardier hikers can continue for another mile or so through the rainforest; at the end of the trail is a pool and waterfall. As there is a gate across the entrance to the arboretum (located at a sharp curve in the road), pull well off the road to park your car and walk in.

Camp Keanae YMCA is just before the arboretum. It looks exactly as its name implies, set in a gorgeous natural pasture. There are three bunkhouses (you must provide your own bedding), two bathrooms with showers, a gymnasium, and a dining room and kitchen for large group events. Camping is allowed on the lawn. Cooking grills are available from the camp caretaker. Arrival time is between 3 and 6 p.m., three-day maximum stay, $10 per person. All accommodations are by reservation only. For more information call the camp at (808) 248-8355; for reservations contact the Maui Family YMCA office in Kahului at (808) 242-9007.

Keanae Peninsula is a thumb-like appendage of land formed by a lava flow that came down the hollowed-out valley from Haleakala Crater. A fantastic lookout is here—look for a telephone pole with a tsunami loudspeaker atop at mile marker 17, and pull off just there. Below you'll see neat little farms, mostly raising taro. Shortly before this lookout, and about 200 yards past the arboretum, a public road heads down into the peninsula to a turnaround by the church. If you walk, park well off the roadway just as you get down the hill. The road makes an arc around to the parking lot by the church, and a trail continues on to the stream. About a mile, this stroll should take less than half an hour, but you may want to stop to chat. Most people living here are native Hawaiians. They still make poi the old-fashioned way: listen for the distinctive thud of poi-pounding in the background. Though *kapu* signs abound, the majority of people are friendly. If you visit, be aware that this is one of the last patches of ground owned by Hawaiians and tended in the old way. Be respectful, please. Notice the lava-rock missionary church. Built in 1860, **Lanikili Ihi Ihi O Lehowa O na Kaua Church** was rebuilt in 1969. Neat and clean, it has straight-back, hardwood pews and a pleasant altar inside. Services are held twice a month. The cemetery to the side is groomed with tropical flowers while the grounds are rimmed by tall coconut trees.

Fruit Stands

Past Keanae between mile markers 17 and 18 is the **Halfway to Hana** roadside refreshment stand, where you can buy hot dogs, shave ice, ice cream, sandwiches, and some fruit. Notice the picture-perfect, idyllic watercress farm on your left.

Do yourself a favor and look for **Uncle Harry's Fruit Stand,** clearly marked on the left past the Keanae Peninsula just beyond the Keanae school. Unfortunately, this *kahuna,* who knew a great deal of the natural pharmacology of old Hawaii and was a living encyclopedia on herbs and all their healing properties, has passed away, but his spirit lives on. Past mile marker 18 on the right is a fruit stand operated by a fellow named Joseph. He not only has coconuts, pineapples, and papayas, but also little-tasted exotic fruits like mountain apples, star fruit, strawberry guavas, and Tahitian lemons. An authentic fruit stand worth a stop. Another one, operated by a Hawaiian woman, is only 50 yards farther on the left. If you have a hankering for fruit, this is the spot. Other fruit stands pop up now and again on this road. It's just a down-home cottage industry. No definite times necessarily, just open when they are. Look for them as you pass, stop to refresh yourself, and leave a little for the local economy.

Wailua

At mile marker 18, you come to Wailua. Similar to Keanae, it too is covered in taro but not to as great an extent, and is a picturesque spot. Turn left here on Wailua Road, following signs for **Coral Miracle Church.** You'll find the **Miracle of Fatima Shrine** here as well, so named because a freak storm in the 1860s washed up enough coral onto Wailua Beach that the church could be constructed by the Hawaiian congregation. Here also are St. Gabriel's Church and St. Augustine's Shrine. There is a lovely and relatively easy-access waterfall nearby. Pass the church, turn right, and park by the large field. Look for a worn path (may be private, but no signs or hassle) that leads down to the falls. Look inland up the valley and you'll see a long sliver of a falls just below the roadway that clings to the *pali.* You can look down on this village and valley from several pulloffs along the highway and from the Wailua Wayside Park, all past the Wailua Road turnoff.

Wailua Wayside Park

Cut into the ridge directly along the roadway is the small parking lot of this tiny wayside park. Drive slowly and keep your eyes peeled as the sign comes up quickly and you have little time to signal your turn to get off the road. A short series of steps leads up under a canopy of overhanging *hao* tree branches to a flat grassy area about 20 feet above the road. From here you have an expansive view down onto Wailua and up along the face of the *pali.* From the rear of the parking area, you can peer into the adjoining *mauka* valley. No facilities.

Puaa Kaa State Wayside

This lovely spot is about 14 miles before Hana. There's no camping, but there are picnic tables, grills, and restrooms. Nearby are Kopiliula and Waikani Falls. A stream provides some smaller falls and pools suitable for swimming.

Nahiku

The village, named after the Hawaiian version of the Pleiades, is reached by a steep but now paved three-mile road and has the dubious distinction of being one of the wettest spots along the coast. The well-preserved and tiny village church near the bottom of the road was constructed in 1867 (renovated in 1993) and is just big enough for a handful of pews. You may see school kids playing ball in the yard next to the church, the only place in the community open and large enough. The turnaround at oceanside is where many locals come to shore-fish. Every evening during the summer months, beginning around 3 p.m., an extended family pod of dolphins enters Nahiku Bay to put on an impromptu performance of water acrobatics just for the joy of it. At one time Nahiku was a thriving Hawaiian village with thousands of inhabitants. Today it's home to only about 70 people, the best-known being former Beatle George Harrison. A few inhabitants are Hawaiian families, but mostly the people are wealthy Mainlanders seeking isolation. After a few large and attractive homes went up, the real estate agents changed the description from "desolate" to "secluded." What's the difference? About $500,000 per house! At the turn of the century it was the site of the Nahiku Rubber Co., the only commercial rubber plantation in the United States. Many rubber trees still line the road, although the venture collapsed in 1912 because the rubber was poor due to the overabundance of rainfall. Some people have augmented their incomes by growing *pakalolo* in the rainforest of this area. However, the alternative-lifestyle people who first came here and have settled in have discovered that there is just as much money to be made raising ornamental tropical flowers ($5,000-10,000 per acre), and have become real "flower children." Many have roadside stands along the Hana Highway where payment for the flowers displayed is on the honor system. Leave what is requested—prices will be marked.

Near mile marker 29 in Upper Nahiku, you'll come upon Nahiku Hawaiian Ti Gallery for gifts and crafts, a pastry and refreshment shop, and a little stand selling baked breadfruit bread.

ACCOMMODATIONS

A number of bed and breakfast establishments and similar accommodations lie along the road to Hana, many in or near Huelo. Only a few are listed below.

Near the end of the road is **Half Way to Hana House.** Surrounded by trees, bamboo, and wild flowers, this B&B has one studio apartment on the lower level of the house. Its private entrance leads into a comfortable room with double bed and mini kitchen. In a separate room is another bed and bath. Breakfast of pastries and fruit from the property is waiting every morning. Room rates are $55 single and $60 double; add $5 per person for a simple continental breakfast. Three nights minimum, 10% discount for a week or more. A kayak and scuba enthusiast, the owner can tell you about good ocean spots to visit. Contact: P.O. Box 675, Haiku, HI 96708, tel. (808) 572-1176, fax 572-3609, e-mail: gailp@mauilnet, website: www.maui.net/~gailp. Moderate.

Not situated along the coast but in the rangeland above Ulumalu is **Lanikai Farm,** P.O. Box 797, Haiku, HI 06708, tel. (808) 572-1111, or fax (808) 572-3498, e-mail: lanibb@maui.net, website: www.maui.net/~lanibb.This "Victorian-European style" newer home lies next to the Koolau forest preserve and is surrounded by tropical fruit trees. The guest rooms have private entrances, TV, small refrigerators, and lanai, and there is use of the washer/dryer and barbecue grill. A scrumptious breakfast of European-style breads and fresh fruit is served every morning. Rates are $65 single, $70 double, or $100 for two rooms; two nights minimum. A studio rental without breakfast runs $80, two rooms is $105. The athletically inclined might want to have a turn on the squash court on property. Moderate.

Hono Huako Tropical Plantation B&B, down behind Kaulanapueo Church on a 300-foot cliff above Waipio Bay, is a peaceful 38-acre retreat and alternative working plantation farm that retains a connection to the past in the guise of a *heiau* while it looks toward the peace and tranquillity of the future. The property is dotted with tropical permaculture orchards and gardens, and the stream was blocked to form a natural heart-shaped pond. Set amidst bamboo, a globe-like kiva meditation hall sits about the main house and office, below which is a heated swimming pool and spa. The two suites on the garden level of the house rent for $80 and $85 a night, or together for $135. The gazebo suite at poolside below the nine-sided office is often used by newlyweds; it runs $125. Overlooking much of the farm and surrounding forested hillsides, the bamboo hexa-hale goes for $100, while the smaller bamboo house set near the heart pond in the orchard is $65. The cliff house, set on the precipice of the 300 foot *pali* next to a waterfall, with a commanding view of the bay, is yours for $250 with a three-night minimum. Breakfast of organic fruits from the property, home-baked muffins and croissants, juice, and tea arrives every morning at your doorstep and is included in the price of the room, even though each unit is equipped with a kitchenette. Come, relax, refresh, and reinvigorate. Write or call for additional information and reservations: P.O. Box 600, Haiku, 96708, tel. (808) 573-1391, fax 573-0141, website: www.maui.net/~bnb/BB.html. Moderate.

Also in the community of Huelo, with a spectacular view up the coast toward Hana, is **Huelo Point Lookout B&B.** Here, the main house and three cottages are scattered around the acreage, which is finely landscaped with tropical trees and bushes. The rock-wall swimming pool is inviting and a soak in the hot tub under a cloudless night sky befits a day on the island. Wake up to the sound of birds singing in the trees, have your breakfast on the lanai, and spend your day leisurely hanging out here or venture out to see the island sights. Once a fisherman's cottage, surrounded by banana trees and heliconia, the remodeled Star Cottage has an indoor/outdoor bathroom, a solarium, and a queen bed and double futon, $125-160. Although smaller, Haleakala Cottage studio has a full kitchen and king bed in one room, $95-125. Outside is an enclosed shower and a covered lanai. The Rainbow Cottage is a newer building, renting for $200-275. Downstairs are the living room and kitchen; a 22-foot tall wall of glass offers the best views of the coast from either floor. Make your way up the handmade wooden spiral staircase to the upstairs bedroom where a king bed lies under a large skylight. Outside is your own private hot tub. The main house also can be rented for families or groups of four for $1,850-2,150 a week.

For additional information: P.O. Box 117, Paia, HI 96779, tel. (808) 573-0914 or (800) 871-8645, fax (808) 573-0227, e-mail: dreamers@maui.net, website: www.maui.net/~dreamers. Expensive.

About one mile down a dirt road near Twin Falls is **Maluhia Hale B&B,** tel. (808) 572-2959, P.O. Box 687 Haiku, HI 96708, e-mail: djg@maui.net, website: www.maui.net/~djg/index.html. Off the main route, this 2.5-acre quiet and relaxing spot is enveloped by greenery yet has the wide ocean vista spreading at your feet. A detached open-beam plantation-style cottage with screened porch and a sitting room has a king bed, a nearly full kitchen, and a detached bathing room that has a clawfoot tub and shower; very commodious. A bit more refined, the suite in the house is decorated with Chinese antiques in a style that says blue and white porcelain. The suite sleeps two, the cottage can accommodate three. Light, open, and airy, both rent for $95 a night with breakfast, two nights minimum. Expensive.

Down at the end of the road is the **Tea House Cottage.** This B&B is "off the grid," generating its own power by photovoltaic cells and collecting its own water. Quiet, with no distractions, from here you have broad views of the ocean. The one cottage has a Japanese "feel," with a living room, kitchen, bedroom, and screened lanai; a few steps away is the redwood bathhouse. Art on the walls is by the owner/artist, and it complements the rattan furniture and oriental rugs. The room rate is $95 a night, two nights minimum; a daily breakfast is provided. A tunnel through the trees leads you to the house, and walkways run throughout the property, one to a small stupa built some 20 years ago by a Tibetan monk. For more information: P.O. Box 335, Haiku, HI 96708, tel. (808) 572-5610, e-mail: teahouse@maui.net, website: www.maui.net/~teahouse. Expensive.

HANA

Hana is about as pretty a town as you'll find anywhere in Hawaii, but if you're expecting anything stupendous you'll be sadly disappointed. For most it will only be a quick stopover at a store or beach en route to Oheo Stream: the townsfolk refer to these people as "rent-a-car tourists." The lucky who stay in Hana, or those not worried about time, will find plenty to explore throughout the area. The town is built on rolling hills that descend to Hana Bay; much of the surrounding lands are given over to pasture, while trim cottages wearing flower corsages line the town's little lanes. Before the white man arrived, Hana was a stronghold that was conquered and reconquered by the kings of Maui and those of the north coast of the Big Island. The most strategic and historically laden spot is Kauiki Hill, the remnant of a cinder cone that dominates Hana Bay. This area is steeped in Hawaiian legend, and old stories relate that it was the demigod Maui's favorite spot. It's said that he transformed his daughter's lover into Kauiki Hill and turned her into the gentle rains that bathe it to this day.

Changing History

Hana was already a plantation town in the mid-1800s when a hard-boiled sea captain named George Wilfong started producing sugar on his 60 acres there. Over the years the laborers came from the standard mixture of Hawaiian, Japanese, Chinese, Portuguese, Filipino, and even Puerto Rican stock. The *luna* were Scottish, German, or American. All have combined to become the people of Hana. Sugar production faded out by the 1940s and Hana began to die, its population dipping below 500. Just then, San Francisco industrialist Paul Fagan purchased 14,000 acres of what was to become the **Hana Ranch.** Realizing that sugar was *pau,* he replanted his lands in *pangola* range grass and imported 300 Hereford cattle from another holding on Molokai. Their white faces staring back at you as you drive past are now a standard part of Hana's scenery. Today, Hana Ranch has about 3,000 acres and raises more than 2,000 head of cattle. Hana's population, at 1,900, is about 48% Hawaiian.

Fagan loved Hana and felt an obligation to and affection for its people. He also decided to retire here, and with enough money to materialize just about anything, he decided that Hana could best survive through limited tourism. He built the Hotel Hana-Maui, which catered to millionaires, mostly his friends, and began operation in 1946. Fagan owned a baseball team, the San Francisco Seals, and brought them to Hana in 1946 for spring training. The community baseball field behind the hotel was made for them. This was a brilliant publicity move because sportswriters came along; becoming enchanted with Hana, they gave it a great deal of copy and were probably the first to publicize the phrase "Heavenly Hana." It wasn't long before tourists began arriving.

Unfortunately, the greatest heartbreak in modern Hana history occurred at just about the same time, on April 1, 1946. An earthquake in Alaska's Aleutian Islands sent huge tsunamis that raked the Hana coast. These destroyed hundreds of homes, wiping out entire villages and tragically sweeping away many people. Hana recovered, but never forgot. Life went on, and the menfolk began working as *paniolo* on Fagan's spread and during round-up would drive the cattle through town and down to Hana Bay where they were forced to swim to waiting barges. Other entire families went to work at the resort, and so Hana lived again. It's this legacy of quietude and old-fashioned *aloha* that attracted people to Hana over the years. Everyone knows that Hana's future lies in its uniqueness and remoteness, and no one wants it to change. The people as well as the tourists know what they have here. What really makes Hana "heavenly" is similar to what's preached in Sunday school: everyone wants to go there, but not everyone makes it.

Hana Festivals

As is the case in most Hawaiian towns, Hana has many local festivals and events. First in the year is the fireworks on New Year's Eve over Fagan's cross. In late March, the weekend **Taro Festival,** website: hookele.com/tarofest, with its traditional ceremonies, games, music, authentic foods and a food market, arts and crafts exhibitions, and hula demonstrations thrills everyone. People come from all over the state to watch and participate; make plans well in advance. Later in June or early July, the children of town get treated to the Makeke, a children's festival, when all sorts of games and celebrations are held. For decades, Hana has had a tie with the great American sport. To honor this connection, a softball tournament is held over the Labor Day weekend, pitting families and friends against one another in friendly but serious competition. As with all of the state, the Aloha Festival is celebrated with gusto. Parades, luau, a fishing tournament, and many other activities are organized.

SIGHTS

Hana Bay
Dominating the bay is the red-faced **Kauiki Hill.** Fierce battles raged here, especially between Maui chief Kahekili and Kalaniopuu of Hawaii, just before the islands were united under Kamehameha. Kalaniopuu held the natural fortress until Kahekili forced a capitulation by cutting off the water supply. It's believed that Kamehameha himself boarded Capt. James Cook's ship after a lookout spotted it from this hill. More importantly, Queen Kaahumanu, Kamehameha's favorite and the Hawaiian *ali'i* most responsible for ending the old *kapu* system and leading Hawaii into the "new age," was born in a cave here in 1768. Until very recent times fish-spotters sat atop the hill looking for telltale signs of large schools of fish.

To get there, simply follow Uakea Road when it splits from the Hana Road at the police station, and follow the signs to the bay. Take it right down to the pier and **Hana Beach County Park,** open 6 a.m.-10 p.m. Hana Beach has full amenities and the swimming is good. It's been a surfing spot for centuries, although the best breakers occur in the middle of the bay. Until the '40s, cane trains rode tracks from the fields above town out onto the pier, where the cut stalks were loaded onto boats to be taken to the mill for processing. To explore Kauiki look for a pathway on your right and follow it. Hana disappears immediately; few tourists come out this way. Walk for a few minutes until the lighthouse comes

clearly into view. The footing is slightly difficult but there are plenty of ironwoods to hang onto as the path hugs the mountainside. A few pockets of red-sand beach eroded from the cinder cone are below. A copper plaque erected in 1928 commemorates the spot of Kaahumanu's birth. This entire area is a great spot for a secluded picnic only minutes from town. Proceed straight ahead to the lighthouse sitting on a small island. To cross, you'll have to leap from one jagged rock to another. If this doesn't suit you, take your bathing suit and wade across a narrow sandy-bottomed channel. Stop for a few moments and check the wave action to avoid being hurled against the rocks. When you've got it timed, go for it! The view from up top is great.

Fagan Memorial
Across from the Hotel Hana-Maui, atop Lyon's hill, is a lava-stone cross erected to the memory of Paul I. Fagan, who died in 1960. The land is privately owned, but it's okay to walk or drive up there if there are no cattle in the pasture. If you drive, you must exchange your license for a gate key to get entry. Whether you walk or drive, always inquire at the hotel if it's all right to go up. The road to the top starts at the hotel guest parking lot. From atop the hill you get the most panoramic view of the entire Hana area. After a rain, magic mushrooms have been known to pop up in the "cow pies" in the pasture surrounding the cross.

Wananalua Church
Near the hotel is the Wananalua Congregational Church, built from coral blocks in 1838 and placed on the National Register of Historic Places in 1988. Sunday service is at 10 a.m. The missionaries deliberately and symbolically built it on top of an old *heiau,* where the pagan gods had been worshipped for centuries. It was the custom of chiefs to build *heiau* before entering battle. Since Hana was always contested ground, dozens of minor *heiau* can be found throughout the region.

Across the street is the newer and lovely St. Mary's Catholic Church. Its wood construction and decorative detail contrast vividly with the plain, sturdy, rather unornamented Wananalua Church. Mass is celebrated Sunday 9 a.m., weekdays 7 a.m., and Friday 5 p.m. Visitors welcome.

Wananalua Church

Hana Cultural Center

Located along Uakea Road on the right, kitty-corner from the Hana Bay entrance road, this center is open daily 10 a.m.-4 p.m.; donations gladly accepted. Founded in 1971 by Babes Hanchett, the Hana Cultural Center, tel. (808) 248-8622, e-mail: hccm@aloha.net, website: www.planet-hawaii.com/hana, occupies an unpretentious building (notice the beautifully carved koa doors, however) on the grounds of the old courthouse and jail. The center houses fine examples of quiltwork: one, entitled "Aloha Kuuhae," was done by Rosaline Kelinoi, a Hana resident and the first woman voted into the State Legislature. There are precontact stone implements, tapa cloth, and an extensive shell collection. Your donation entitles you to visit the courthouse and jail next door. Simple but functional, with bench and witness stand, it makes *Andy of Mayberry* look like big-time. This tiny courthouse was used regularly 1871-1978, and is still used monthly for the same purpose. The jail, "Hana Lockup," was also built in 1871 and finally renovated in 1997. The townsfolk knew whenever it held an inmate because he became the groundskeeper and the grass would suddenly be mowed.

In the ancient Hawaiian style, using traditional materials, a sleeping house, cook house, meeting house, and canoe shed have been constructed to the side and below the center to give you an idea of what types of buildings were used in Hawaii in the past. On the terrace below these structures is a small **ethnobotanical garden** of medicinal and agricultural native plants. Pick up a brochure about the plants inside the museum. Be sure to stop at the cultural center while in Hana to learn a bit about local history and culture.

Hana Gardenland Nursery

On the Hana Highway, you pass several sights east of Nahiku before you actually reach town. The first is Hana Gardenland Nursery, open daily 8:30 a.m.-5 p.m., where you're free to browse. The nursery sells fresh-cut flowers, and the prices are some of the best on Maui. This certified nursery, which can ship plants or cut flowers to the Mainland, sits on more than five acres, over which you can wander at your leisure, and acquaint yourself with the spectacular plantlife that you will encounter throughout the Hana area. Many of the plants are labeled, so it's a bit like a botanical garden, and there are more than 200 varieties of rare palms—a specialty. On the premises is the Jungle Cafe, a "semigourmet window restaurant." Inside the main building is a gift gallery featuring crafts mostly by local artisans.

Ka'eleku Caverns

The newest adventure in Hana is spelunking. There are 50 known caves on Maui and 150 on the Big Island. Only a short section of the Thurston Lava Tube and the Kula Kai Caverns near Ocean View on the Big Island can be entered. Some 30,000 years old, Ka'eleku (Stand-

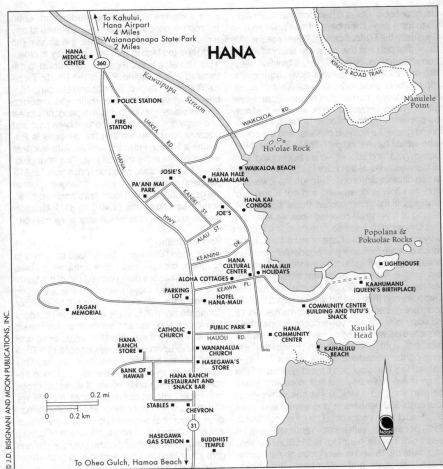

ing in the Dark) Cave near Kahanu Gardens in Hana is the only cave on Maui that's open to the public, and it's a beauty. There is no evidence that Ka'eleku Caverns was ever used for burials like so many on the islands. This cave, like all others in Hawaii, is actually a lava tube 30-40 feet below the surface, so the cave follows the lay of the land up the mountainside. No matter what the temperature is outside, it's always a moderate 64-67° inside. You enter through a skylight and make your way down the steps to the floor of the cave, which once flowed with

molten lava. Here you must let your eyes adjust to the darkness before proceeding. As liquid lava surged through this tube it scored the walls, leaving striations. Here and there, you will also see benches and ledges along the sides where lava cooled faster on the periphery than the middle. Some rubble has fallen from the ceiling or off the walls creating mounds that you'll have to climb around or over. Although you can walk upright most of the way, there are a few sections where you must kneel or even get down on all fours to squeeze through. This is not for the claustrophobic. Still at other spots the tube opens up to form large chambers, at one point with an unusually tall 50-foot ceiling. Other natural features that occur in this cave are lava stalactites and stalagmites, drip columns, a bowling alley-like channeling with gutters down both sides, ropy pahoehoe lava levees, clinkers of rough a'a, side loops, convergent channels, and over tubes. A very unusual feature and one that may be peculiar only to this cave is the delicate, filigreed grape-like botryoid clusters. And the colors, who would have thought? There is gray, blue, brown, gold, and copper—quite astounding. One of the mysteries of this cave is that the air flows in two dfferent directions. Through the lower portion, the flow is downward and out a series of skylights; in the upper section, the air flows uphill, exiting at a yet undiscovered spot. As this cave has only recently been open to visitors, it is still in very pristine condition. Care must be taken not to touch delicate formations or accidentally crush or break anything fragile. "Cave softly and carry a big light" is the owner's motto. Maui Cave Adventures is run by Chuck Thorne and his wife Deborah, and they can set you up with a tour. All tours are guided and are very informative. Chuck is happy to share with you what he knows about this cave as well as other caves in the state. A hard hat, light, and drinks are provided. Wear long pants, closed-toe shoes, and a T-shirt—something that you don't mind getting a little dirty. If you have any interest in caving, you'll be glad you had a look at this one. A two-hour tour costs $50 per person, and adventurers must be at least nine years old. The four-hour tour is $100 per person, with an age requirement of 18 years old. The six-hour tour is $150 per person; you must be 18 and in very good physical condition, and jeans and hiking boots are necessary. Two-person minimum for tours to run. For information and advanced reservations, call or write: Maui Cave Adventures, P.O. Box 40, Hana, HI 96713, tel. (808) 248-7308 (8 a.m.-8 p.m. daily), fax 248-7074, e-mail: hanacave@ maui.net, website: www.maui.net/~hanacave.

Kahanu Gardens

Turn off Hana Highway onto Ulaino Road and proceed toward the ocean. Here, the pavement soon gives way to a dirt track and leads about a mile and a half to Kahanu Gardens, located just past a shallow stream. The gardens are open by appointment only, and may be closed at any time if, because of heavy rains, the stream (no bridge) is too high or moving too swiftly to cross. This 120-acre tropical garden runs down to the tortured lava coastline. Part of the Pacific Tropical Botanical Garden, the Kahanu Gardens contain a huge variety of domestic and imported tropical plants, including a native pandanus forest and large and varied collections of breadfruit and coconut trees. Also within the gardens is **Pii-lanihale Heiau,** Hawaii's largest, with massive walls that rise more than 50 feet. Two-hour guided walking tours are given daily at 1 p.m. for $10 per person (schedule open to change); meet at the gate. Half-hour van tours are also given for $5 at the same time. Call (808) 248-8912 for information and reservations; website: www.ntbg.org.

Pool at Ulaino

Past Kahanu Gardens, Ulaino Road continues to roughen, crosses two more streams, passes several homesites being carved out of the bush, and ends after more than a mile at a parking area near the ocean. This may not be drivable during heavy rains. Walk across the boulders that form the beach at the mouth of the stream and stay along the *pali* for 100 yards or so until you come upon what some people call Blue Pond tucked behind some larger rocks. This hideaway is an old local favorite, a clothing-optional swimming spot where a waterfall drops fresh water into an oceanside pool. Not always blue, it's sometimes murky when water brings large amounts of sediment down from the hillside above. As always at pools, be aware of stones and branches that might come over the top and give you a knot on your noggin as a souvenir of your time in paradise.

Hana Airport

Less than a mile in toward town from Ulaino Road, on Alalele Road, a sign points left to Hana Airport, where **Island Air,** tel. (800) 323-3345, or (808) 248-8328 in Hana, operates two daily flights to Kahului, and **Pacific Wings,** tel. (808) 873-0877, schedules some charter flights. All flights to Hana go through Kahului, from where you can get connecting flights to other Hawaiian cities and the Mainland. Hotel Hana-Maui operates a shuttle between the airport and the hotel for its guests, and can make rental car arrangements for its guests. There is no public transportation in Hana, and only **Dollar Rent A Car,** tel. (808) 248-8237, can provide wheels for you—make reservations *before* arriving in Hana. Aside from the airline counters, there is only a public telephone and restrooms here at this tiny terminal.

Blue Hawaiian helicopters makes one run up the Hana coast that stops at the Hana Airport. Here, it connects with ground transportation by **Temptation Tours,** so you can go one way by air and the other by land, a fly-drive offering. Neither company has an office at the Hana Airport.

Wainapanapa State Park

Only three miles outside Hana, and down a road that's clearly marked along the highway near mile marker 32, this state park offers not only tent camping but houskeeping cabins sleeping up to six. Set some distance from the beach and tenting area, the cabins offer hot water, electricity, a full kitchen, bathroom, bedrooms, and bedding, and rent for $45 a night for up to four people and $5 for each additional person. A deposit is required. They're very popular so book far in advance by writing Division of State Parks or visiting its office at 54 S. High St., Wailuku, HI 96793, tel. (808) 984-8109. The grassy camping area has picnic tables, water, showers, and restrooms. Even for those not camping, Wainapanapa is a "must stop." Pass the office to get to the beach park and its black-sand beach. The swimming is dangerous during heavy surf because the bottom drops off quickly, but on calm days it's mellow. The snorkeling is excellent, and it should be, as Wainapanapa means "Glistening Waters." Just offshore is a clearly visible natural stone bridge.

A short, well-marked trail leads to **Wainapanapa Caves.** The tunnel-like trail passes through a thicket of vines and *hao,* a bush used by the Hawaiians to mark an area as *kapu.* The two small caves are formed from lava. The water trapped inside is clear. These caves mark the site of a Hawaiian legend, in which a lovely princess named Popoalaea fled from her cruel husband Kakae. He found her hiding here and killed her. During certain times of the year millions of tiny red shrimp invade the caves, turning the waters red, which the Hawaiians say is a reminder of the poor slain princess.

Along the coastline here are remnants of the ancient Hawaiian **paved trail** that you can follow for a short distance. To get to the section running north toward the airport, cross the black sand beach and head up the trail on the far side. Most of the way, the trail stays on or near the cliffs; this walk takes about two hours. A section of the trail also runs south along the coast toward Hana. This trail should take about three hours, and along the way you'll pass lava cliffs, blow holes, an old *heiau,* and graves.

BEACHES

Red Sand Beach

Named Kaihalulu (Roaring Waters), this is a fascinating and secluded beach area, but unfortunately the steep walk down is treacherous. The path, after a while, skirts the side of a cliff, and the footing is made tough because of unstable and crumbly cinders. Grave accidents have occurred, and even locals won't make the trip. Follow Uakea Road past the turnoff to Hana Bay. Proceed ahead until you pass the public tennis courts on your right and the community center on your left. The road dead-ends a short way later. Head through the open lot between the community center and hotel property, where you pick up a worn path. Ahead is a Japanese cemetery with its distinctive headstones, some now being lost to wave erosion and a degrading shoreline. Below are pockets of red sand amidst fingers of black lava washed by sky-blue water. There are many tide pools here. Keep walking around Kauiki Head until you are obviously in the hollowed-out amphitheater of the red cinder cone. Pat the walls to feel how crumbly they are—the red "sand" is eroded cinder. The water in the cove is fantastically blue against the redness.

Across the mouth of the bay are little pillars of stone, like castle parapets from a fairy kingdom, that keep the water safe for swimming. This is a favorite fishing spot for local people and the snorkeling is good, too. The beach is best in the morning before 11 a.m.; afterward it can get hot if there's no wind and rough if the wind is from the north—remember the beach's name. The coarse red sand massages your feet, and there's a natural jacuzzi area in foamy pools of water along the shore.

Koki Beach

The beach is a mile or so out of town heading toward Oheo. Look for Haneoo Road on your left with a sign directing you to Koki and Hamoa Beaches. Koki is only a few hundred yards on the left, at the first set of pullouts by the water. The riptides are fierce in here so don't swim unless it's absolutely calm. The winds can whip along here, too, even though at Hamoa Beach, less than a mile away, it can be dead calm. Koki is excellent for beachcombing and for a one-night unofficial bivouac.

A very special person named Smitty lived in a cave on the north side of the beach. A distinguished older man, he "dropped out" a few years back and came here to live a simple monk's existence. He kept the beach clean and saved a number of people from the riptide. He was a long-distance runner who would tack up a "thought for the day" on Hana's public bulletin board. People loved him and he loved them in return. In 1984 the roof of his cave collapsed and he was killed. When his body was recovered, he was in a kneeling position. At his funeral, all felt a loss, but there was no sadness because all were sure that Smitty had gone home.

Hamoa Beach

Follow Hamoa Road a few minutes past Koki Beach to the other side of this small thumb of a peninsula to Hamoa Beach. Between Hamoa and Koki are the remnants of an extensive Hawaiian fishpond, part of which is still discernible. This entire area is an eroding cinder cone known as **Kaiwi O Pele** (The Bones of Pele). This is the spot where the swinish pig god, Kama pua'a, ravished her. Pele also fought a bitter battle with her sister here, who dashed Pele on the rocks, giving them their anatomical name. Out to sea is the diminutive Alau Island, a remnant left over by Maui after he finished up the Hawaiian Islands.

You can tell that Hamoa is no ordinary beach the minute you start walking down the paved, torch-lined walkway. This is the semiprivate beach of the Hotel Hana-Maui. But don't be intimidated, because no one can own the beach in Hawaii. Hamoa is terrific for swimming and snorkeling on calm days or bodysurfing or surfing on days when the wind is up a little. The hotel guests are shuttled here by buses throughout

the day that leave from the hotel on the hour, so if you want this lovely beach to yourself arrive before midmorning and stay after late afternoon. There is a pavilion that the hotel uses for its Tuesday night luau and its lunch buffets, as well as restrooms and showers.

ACCOMMODATIONS

Joe's Place

Down the road from Hana Kai Maui Resort is Joe's Place, tel. (808) 248-7033. A very modest but clean self-serve guesthouse, this is a home that's been split into eight guest rooms. A Maui-style sign reads, "If our office is closed, check key rack at left, and you may use a room and either pay in the morning or lock payment and key in the room before leaving, two persons to a room." Rooms for singles or doubles cost $45, $55 with a private bath. Also available is a cottage for $100 that can sleep three. Cash or traveler's checks only. Checkout time is at 10 a.m. and check-in is at 3 p.m. "or as soon as room is available." Reservations are held until 6 p.m. There's kitchen access, a communal TV room, daily towel change, and maid service on request at an extra charge. Inexpensive.

Hana Maui Vacation Rental

Across from the Heavenly Hana Inn, this is a small place with three new units. Neat and tidy, one has a kitchen while the other two have only microwaves. All have bedrooms separate from the cooking area, bathrooms with showers, and separate entrances. While not large, it's certainly adequate, and the price is right. The room with a kitchen runs $65 a night, with the microwave $55; maximum three per room. Monthly and kama'aina rates available. Call or write for reservations: P.O. Box 455, Hana HI, 96713, tel./fax (808) 248-8087. Inexpensive.

Aloha Cottages

Adjacent to the Hana Cultural Center, these units are owned and operated by Zenzo and Fusae Nakamura and are the best bargain in town. The cottages are meticulously clean, well built, and well appointed. For $60-90 d, $10-20 per additional guest, you get two bedrooms, a full kitchen, living room, deck, and outdoor grills. Mrs. Naka-

a B&B in Hana

mura is very friendly and provides daily maid service. In season, fruit trees on the property provide free fruit to guests. For reservations, contact: P.O. Box 205, Hana, HI 96713, tel. (808) 248-8420. Moderate.

Josie's Hana Hideaway
Josie offers two spartan rooms in the rear of her house and one up at the front. Each large and comfy unit (the front unit is smaller than the ones behind) has a bedroom/sitting room with a kitchenette in the corner, color TV by the queen bed, a full bathroom, and a separate entrance. If you want, you can prepare your meal in the kitchenette on the upper lanai. Daily room rates are $55 s, $65 d, and up to two kids $10 each; five-day, seven-day, and monthly rates also available. Josie also rents the three-bedroom, two-bath house next door for $85 a night, and a cabin behind it for $75 a night. To find Josie's turn off the Hana Highway onto Kauiki Street, near Pa'ani Mai Park, and go down to the bend in the road, where you will find Josie's Hana Hideaway. For information, call Josie Diego at (808) 248-8418, or write P.O. Box 265, Hana HI, 96713. Moderate.

Hana Plantation Houses
Hana Plantation Houses offers a unique service whereby you can rent a private house on the lush, tropical Hana coast. You have 11 homes to choose from ranging from a deluxe cedar one-bedroom, sleeping four and complete with lanai, full kitchen, barbecue, and your own private mini-

garden for $150, to the Lanai Makaalae Studio, a Japanese-style studio for two at $70. Several other newly remodeled homes are available around town, like the two-story Hale Kipa plantation house ($100 downstairs and $135 upstairs), which has full amenities as well as an outdoor jacuzzi, and the two-story two-bedroom The Palms, which can accommodate up to six people for $150 per night. Contact Blair's Original Hana Plantation Houses at P.O. Box 249, Hana, HI 96713, tel. (808) 248-7868, fax 248-8240, or (800) 228-4262 for reservations, e-mail: hana@kestrok.com, website: www.kestrok.com/~hana. Check-in is at Hana Gardenland, open daily 9 a.m.-5 p.m., just past mile marker 30, *mauka* side before entering Hana. Late check-ins should call for instructions. Moderate.

Hana Ali'i Holidays
A second agency in Hana renting everything from a seaside cottage to large plantation homes scattered throughout the Hana area, Hana Ali'i Holidays offers more than a dozen homes to choose from. Rates vary, $75-200 a night; weekly and monthly rentals are also available. Contact Duke; he will set you up: P.O. Box 536, Hana, HI 96713, tel. (808) 248-7742 or (800) 548-0478, fax (808) 248-8595, e-mail: info@hanaalii.com, website: www.hanaalii.com. Moderate.

Flower Farm Rentals
Two tropical flower farms on the outskirts of town that rent rooms or bungalows on their property

are Heavenly Flora and Tradewinds Cottages. **Heavenly Flora** rents two rooms in the main house. Both are tastefully decorated, one with a king bed, the other with a queen bed. Guests have use of the full kitchen, laundry facilities, and swimming pool. The king room is $100 and the queen room runs $80 a night. For information and reservations write or call: P.O. Box 748, Hana, HI 96713, tel. (808) 248-8680. Moderate.

Tradewinds Cottages has two detached houses set in the garden that have full kitchens and bathrooms, queen beds and sleeper sofas, color TV, and ceiling fans. The Tradewinds Cottage runs $115 a night, maximum of six, while the Hana Cabana is $95 a night, maximum of four; $10 each additional person after the first couple. Information: Tradewinds Tropicals Vacation Rentals, P.O. Box 385, Hana, HI 96713, tel. (808) 248-8980 or (800) 327-8097, e-mail: twt@maui .net, website: www.maui.net/~twt/cottage .html. Expensive.

Hana Hale Malamalama

A magnificent place on the lower road into town, Hale Malamalama sits on a steep hillside overlooking an ancient fishpond that's been rebuilt. This is a culturally significant site and numerous artifacts have been found here. Great care has been taken to aesthetically landscape the property so that the buildings seem to fit in as if they have been here for years. Three units make up the compound: set next to the pond, the Royal Suite occupies a two-floor, 1,800-square-foot house made in the Philippines, transported here, and reconstructed; the Garden Suite in set in a rock garden on the hillside; and the Tree House Cottage sits up top over a carport. The Royal suite runs $175, the Garden suite $110, and the Tree House Cottage is $150. This is a perfect place for a honeymoon or for a couple who just wants a little luxury and class without spending an arm and a leg. Call John Romain for reservations, tel. (808) 248-7718, fax 248-7429, or write: Hana Hale Malamalama, P.O. Box 374, Hana, HI 96713, e-mail: hanahale@maui.net. Expensive.

Hana Kai Maui Resort

These resort condos, the only condo rentals in town at 1533 Uakea Rd., are all well maintained and offer a lot for the money. Rates are: studios $125-145, deluxe one-bedrooms $145-195; fifth night free, and weekly and monthly rates available. All have private lanai with exemplary views of the bay, maid service, laundry facilities, and barbecues. The views couldn't be better as the grounds, laid out in a lovely garden highlighting the interplay of black lava rock and multihued blooms, step down the mountainside to Popolana Beach on Hana Bay. For additional information, contact: P.O. Box 38, Hana, HI 96713, tel. (808) 248-8426 or (800) 346-2772, fax (808) 248-7482, website: www.hanakai.com. Premium.

Ekena

Set high above the west end of town is a luxurious vacation rental owned and operated by Robin and Gaylord Gaffney. The upper and lower floors are separate, but only one level is rented at a time—unless the entire building is desired—so you won't be disturbed by anyone. So spacious are these that each floor could be rented by two couples, one on each end, who want to share the cost and enjoy each others' company. Both floors have large living rooms, fully equipped kitchens, two master bedrooms and spacious bathrooms. Ekena is a wonderful pole building with a huge deck and spectacular views both down to the coast and up the mountainside. As it sits high up the hill, it almost always is graced with trade winds, so even if it's dead calm in town it may be breezy up there. At the upper end of the vacation rental bracket, it's not cheap but it's good value for the money. The Jasmine level with one bedroom goes for $150 a night, two bedrooms $190. The Sea Breeze level is $275. Both together run $450 a night. Three nights minimum, no kids younger than 14. For information and reservations, contact: T. Isetorp, P.O. Box 728, Hana HI 96713, tel. (808) 248-7047, e-mail:ekena@maui .net, website: www.maui.net/~ekena. Luxury.

Hamoa Bay Bungalow

Run by Jody Baldwin, this captivating rental sits in a copse of trees and bamboo just off the Hana Highway above Hamoa Beach. Inspired by the architecture of Bali, two stone lions holding umbrellas greet you at the driveway. There is only one second-story unit here but it has all the amenities: living room/bedroom with king-size bed, full kitchen, bath, jacuzzi/shower on the screened porch, and ceiling fans. Cute little place, a fine romantic getaway. Laundry facilities are available. Rates are on a sliding scale: $175 for one night, $165 for each of two nights, $145 for three to six nights, and $135 for seven through 13 nights; monthly rates can be arranged. A continental breakfast is served on the first morning only. Call, fax, or write: P.O. Box 773, Hana, HI 96713, tel. (808) 248-7884, fax 248-8642. Luxury.

Hotel Hana-Maui

The legacy of Paul Fagan, who built it in the late '40s, this is as close to a family-run hotel as you can get; HI 96713, tel. (800) 321-4262 or (808) 248-8211 on Maui. Most personnel have either been there from the beginning, or their jobs have passed to their family members. Guests love it that way, proven by an astonishing 80% in repeat visitors, most of whom feel like they're staying with old friends. The hotel has had only eight managers in the last 50 years. The public areas in the hotel are done in muted tans and browns. It's open and airy with flagstone floors and easy furniture of hardwood and bamboo. All guest rooms have been extensively renovated and the hotel can now proudly take its place among the truly luxury hotels of Hawaii. Rooms, all with their own lanai, surround the beautifully appointed grounds where flowers add a splash of color to the green-on-green blanket of ferns and gently sloping lawn. Inside the colors are subdued shades of white and tan. Morning light, with the sun filtering through the louvered windows, is especially tranquil. All suites have a wet bar and large comfortable lounge area with rattan furniture covered in billowy white pillows. A glass-topped table is resplendent with a floral display, and homemade banana bread greets all guests. There's even fresh Kona coffee that you grind and brew yourself. The floors are a deep rich natural wood counterpointed by a light reed mat in the central area. The beds, all king-size or two twins, are covered with handmade Hawaiian quilts, while Casablanca fans provide all the cooling necessary. The guest-cottage rooms have large free-standing pine armoires; all rooms have two walk-ins. The bathrooms, as large as most sitting rooms, are tiled with earthtone ceramic. You climb a step to immerse yourself in the huge tub, then open eye-level windows that frame a private mini-garden like an expressionist's still life.

The hotel staff adds an intangible quality of friendliness and *aloha* that sets the hotel apart from all others. Upon arrival, you are greeted with a shell lei and a chilled glass of juice. Housekeepers visit twice a day, leaving beige terrycloth robes, and, if you have turndown service, fresh flowers on every pillow. There is a library for use by guests, and a few shops for clothes, necessities, and gifts. The hotel restaurant is open for breakfast, lunch, and dinner, and the Paniolo Bar serves drinks from the late morning until 10:30 p.m. Other facilities and activities include a wellness center, two heated swimming pools, tennis courts, superb horseback riding, a three-hole practice golf course, free bicycle use by guests, hikes to archaeological sites, and a famous luau held every Tuesday, 6 p.m., at the hotel's facilities on Hamoa Beach. Also held at Hamoa Beach, 11:30 a.m.-1:30 p.m. Tuesday, Thursday, Saturday, and Sunday, is a barbecue lunch cookout. All activities are easily arranged by visiting the activities desk that can be counted on to keep family and children happy with Hawaiian language lessons, lei-making, or swaying hula lessons. Free shuttle service is provided by the hotel throughout the area in its vintage vehicles.

Rates start at $395 for a garden-view room and progress up to $795 for the sea ranch cottage suites. An option, for an additional $95, includes three meals under the full American plan, or $75 for breakfast and dinner. Otherwise you can pay as you eat. The entire scene isn't stiff or fancy, but it is a memorable first-class experience! Luxury.

Heavenly Hana Inn

The second most famous Hana accommodation, the Heavenly Hana Inn, resembles a Japanese *ryokan*. Walk through the formal garden and remove your shoes on entering the open-beamed main dining hall. The inn is homey and delightful. Skylights brighten this central area, set around a central hearth. Having undergone renovations, the inn is more beautiful than ever in its simplicity. A variety of woods give warmth to the living areas, shoji screens hide what need not always be present, and the decoration is perfectly authentic. The three suites seem like little apartments broken up into sections by shoji screens. Each has a sleeping room, bathroom with soaking tub, and a sitting room with television. There are no telephones, and no smoking is allowed. Guests stay just three nights only—no exceptions—a Monday arrival with departure on Thursday. Rates are $2,000 for a single or couple, $1,000 for an additional person; most (gourmet) meals are included. An application for reservation, which includes references from people who have stayed at the inn previously, must be filled out by each guest. Write P.O. Box 790, Hana, HI 96713, tel. (808) 248-8442, or e-mail: hanainn@maui.net. Luxury.

FOOD

Hotel Hana-Maui

As far as dining out goes, there's little to choose from in Hana. The Hotel Hana-Maui main dining room offers breakfast, lunch, and dinner. Prices vary according to your choice of options, but expect to spend up to $14 for breakfast, $25 for lunch, and $50 for dinner. Reservations recommended. Hotel guests have first preference, but the hotel will try its hardest to seat. Afternoon snacks are also served at the Paniolo Bar 2:30-5 p.m.

Meals become a long-remembered sumptuous event. Follow the hostesses to your table in the dining room. Here, breakfasts, served 7:30-10 a.m., are all manner of fresh exotic fruits and juices, hot pastries, banana macadamia-nut waffles, eggs poached or herbed into omelettes accompanied by petite steaks, fresh fish, or Hana Ranch sausages. Lunches, 11:30 a.m.-2 p.m., which upon request are prepared as very civilized picnics in wicker baskets, include chilled seafood chowder, Oriental sesame chicken salad, smoked turkey and bacon sandwich, kiawe-grilled chicken breast, and a potpourri of vegetables. Special dinner menus are prepared daily, but you can begin with a sashimi plate, sautéed chicken with peanut sauce, and then move on to an assortment of grilled and roasted fowl, seafood, wild boar, or locally grown beef and lamb, all basted in a variety of gourmet sauces. Vietnamese whole fish for two is especially tantalizing. Desserts are too tempting to resist, and if you can somehow save the room try lime or macadamia nut pie, banana cream cake, coconut mousse, or a rainbow of rich and creamy ice creams and sherbets. Dinner is served 6-9 p.m.

The hotel luau, held every Tuesday at 6 p.m. at Hamoa Beach, and a barbecue lunch cookout at the same site, offered 11:30 a.m.-1:30 p.m. Tuesday, Thursday, Saturday, and Sunday, are other alternatives. Make reservations at the activities desk in the hotel lobby.

Entertainment at the hotel—and that, quite frankly, is it for the whole town—is two informal hula and Hawaiian music shows put on by local families on during the Sunday evening buffet. Aside from that, nightly music is performed at the bar, usually by one or two local musicians on ukulele and/or guitar, who fill the entire building with good cheer and melodious song. The Paniolo Bar is open daily 11:30 a.m.-10:30 p.m. For alternate entertainment, try the frequent evening baseball games at the ballpark behind the hotel.

Hana Ranch Restaurant

The Hana Ranch Restaurant, tel. (808) 248-8255, serves very tasty family-style meals, but it can be stampeded by ravenous tourists heading up or down the Hana Road. Reservations recommended. It's a sturdy place with wood floors, rattan furniture, and heavy slabs of wood as tables. Seating is inside or outside under a timber framework. Breakfast, daily 6:30-10 a.m., is served from an adjoining service window only, but a shaded area with picnic tables is provided. Lunch, also served from the service window daily 11 a.m.-2:30 p.m., is an assortment of sandwiches, saimin, or plate lunches. An inside lunch buffet, served daily 11 a.m.-3 p.m. for adults $12.95, children $6.50, salad only $7.95, includes barbecue beef ribs, teriyaki chicken, baked beans, assorted vegetables, and baked potato. Dinner is served inside Friday and Saturday evenings 6-8 p.m., and Wednesday is pizza night. The dinner menu includes appetizers like fried calamari for $5.50 and crispy onion rings for $3.50, various pizzas range $12.50-18.50, salad, and pasta entrees for around $10. A short wine list is available, or you can choose some other drink from the bar. Not gourmet by any means, it is tasty, filling, and decently priced. The outside window is open daily 4-7 p.m. for plate lunches, burgers, and sandwiches. Besides the Hotel Hana-Maui, this is the only place to have an evening meal in Hana.

Jungle Cafe

Sit surrounded by the blooms and ferns of the Hana Gardenland Nursery and enjoy the delicious food prepared by the Jungle Cafe, tel. (808) 248-8975, a bamboo- and rattan-fronted "window restaurant" open daily 8:30 a.m.-5 p.m. Start your day with the Hana sunrise wrap for $5.50, *ono* steamed eggs and salsa for $5, homemade banana bread for $2.95, waffles at $5.75, or a bowl of health-conscious granola for $3.75. Lunchtime brings mostly sandwiches, soups, and wraps that you can choose your own filling for. Try the smoked turkey sandwich for $6.95, garden island salad for $6.95, wraps at about $6, or lasagna for $8.95. Soups change daily. Refreshing beverages include espresso, cappuccino, fresh-squeezed orange or carrot juice, fruit smoothies, and tropical fruit iced tea for $1.50-3.50. Organic foods and local produce are used as much as possible. The cafe will be happy to prepare your food to go.

Tu Tu's

Tu Tu's Snack Shop, open daily 8 a.m.-4 p.m., is at the community center building at Hana Bay, offering window service with tables available. Eggs, loco moko, French toast, and other breakfast items all under $4.50, sandwiches to $3.75, and plate lunches under $6. Other items include salads, saimin, hamburgers, drinks, and ice cream. This building was donated by Mrs. Fagan, the wife of Paul Fagan, the original owner of the Hotel Hana-Maui, to the community.

SHOPPING

Hasegawa's General Store

In the ranks of general stores, Hasegawa's would be commander-in-chief. This institution, run by Harry Hasegawa, had been in the family for 75 years before it burned to the ground in the fall of 1990. While your gas tank was being filled, you could buy anything from a cane knife to a computer disk. There were rows of food items, dry goods, and a hardware and parts store out back. Cold beer, film, blue jeans, and picnic supplies—somehow it was all crammed in there. Everybody went to Hasegawa's, and it was a treat just to browse and people-watch.

Now housed in the old movie theater in downtown Hana, this store still serves the community and visitors that for so long sustained it. It's just as packed as ever, and it now also has a Bankoh bank machine. The only one-day film processing in town is handled by Hasegawa Gas Station just down the road. Open Mon.-Sat. 8 a.m.-5:30 p.m., Sunday 9 a.m.-4:30 p.m.; tel. (808) 248-8231.

Hana Store

From the Hana Road, make the first right past St. Mary's Catholic Church and go up to the top of the hill to find the Hana Store, open daily 7 a.m.-7 p.m., tel. (808) 248-8261, a general store with an emphasis on foodstuffs. It carries a supply of imported beers, a wide selection of food items, film, videos, and some gifts. The bulletin board here gives you a good idea of what's currently happening in town.

Hana Treasures

In the small complex across from the Hana Ranch Restaurant, look for Hana Treasures, open Mon.-Fri. 10 a.m.-4 p.m., Saturday until 3 p.m., and Sunday 10:30 a.m.-2:30 p.m., operated by Cheryl, a Hana resident who is friendly and willing to offer local information. The small shop features airbrushed T-shirts by Hana artists, an assortment of Hawaiian gifts, particularly those made in the Hana area, and two display cases of silver necklaces, bracelets, and rings.

Hana Coast Gallery

Located at Hotel Hana-Maui, this gallery displays many fine works of art by Hawaiian residents. The gallery, tel. (808) 248-8636, is open daily 9 a.m.-5 p.m.

Hana Gardenland Gift Shop

Inside the main building at the Hana Gardenland Nursery is a gift gallery featuring crafts, mostly by local artisans. The shelves hold a smattering of books on Hawaii, postcards, handmade jewelry, baskets and other woven items, koa wood boxes, some prints, photos, and posters, and T-shirts, of course. Its a nice little collection with quality items to choose from. While here, enjoy a walk through the gardens or stop and have a bite to eat at the Jungle Cafe window.

ACTIVITIES

Hana Bay Kayak

Arranged through the Hotel Hana-Maui activities desk, tel. (808) 248-8811, this adventure heads to Hana Bay for a two-hour session and can take as many as eight people. Kayak and snorkel tours are given at 9:30 a.m. and 2 p.m.; $59 per person, half price under age 12. They'll even videotape underwater for you as you snorkel.

Horseback Riding

Horseback rides are given at the Hana Ranch Stables. The one-hour trail rides, either along the coast or in the upper pastures, leave at 8:30 and 10 a.m. and again at 1:30 p.m. Rides cost $35 per person, and riders must be seven years old. Private rides can be arranged 3-5 p.m. for $70 per person.

Jogging Trail

A walking/jogging trail is maintained on Hana Ranch property, on what was the narrow-gauge sugarcane railbed. The trail runs for a bit more than two miles and starts near the Fagan Memorial. Walk south.

SERVICES

Hana Medical Center

Along the Hana Road at the Y intersection, clearly marked on the right just as you enter town, is Hana Medical Center, tel. (808) 248-8294. Open weekdays 8 a.m.-6 p.m. (until 8 p.m. on Tuesday and Thursday) and Saturday 8 a.m.-noon; closed Sunday. Walk-in, nonemergency treatment. For emergencies, use the phone at the hospital entrance.

Police Station

The police station is at the Y intersection between Hana and Uakea Roads, just as you enter town. For emergencies call 911; otherwise, tel. (808) 248-8311.

Money, Mail, and Books

The Bank of Hawaii, tel. (808) 248-8015, is open Mon.-Thurs. 3-4:30 p.m., Friday 3-6 p.m.; cash advances on Visa and Mastercard can be made there. For an ATM bank machine go to Hasegawa's store. The post office is open weekdays 8 a.m.-4:30 p.m. Both are next door to the Hana Ranch restaurant. The excellent Hana school/public library, tel. (808) 248-7714, is located at the new Hana School on the western edge of town; open weekdays 8 a.m.-5 p.m. (until 8 p.m. on Monday and from 9 a.m. on Tuesday).

Gas

There are two gas stations in town. The Chevron station next to the horse stables is open daily 7:30 a.m.-6 p.m. Hasagawa's gas station and visitor information center is about a hundred yards farther along the highway. Gas in Hana is expensive, about 30-35 cents per gallon higher than elsewhere on the island. Be sure to fill up before leaving town as the nearest gas station west is in Paia; going south around the bottom, the closest is in Keokea.

Rental Cars

Dollar Rent A Car, tel. (808) 248-8237, is the only show in town. It's best to call in advance to ensure a reservation. Cars may be available on short notice during low season, but don't count on it.

BEYOND HANA

About a half mile south of Hana is mile marker 51. From there, the mile markers decrease in number as you continue around the south coast back to Kahului. Now you're getting into adventure. The first sign is that the road becomes narrower, then the twists and turns begin again. After Oheo Gulch, there are a few miles that are still unpaved, and this is followed by a long stretch that's nothing more than a patchwork quilt of potholes. You know you're in a rural area with not much traffic when you come across the sign Caution: Baby Pig Crossing. There are no phones, no gas, only a fruit or flower stand or two, one kaukau wagon, and one store until you reach Ulupalakua Ranch. Although the road is good for most of the year, during heavy rains sections do still wash out and become impassable. The fainthearted should turn back, but those with gumption are in for a treat. There are roadside waterfalls, thick luscious forests, cascading streams filling a series of pools, a hero's grave, tiny plantation communities, some forgotten towns, isolated homesteads, and desolate scrubby ranchland. If you persevere all the way, you pop out at the Tedeschi Winery, where you can reward yourself with a glass of bubbly before returning to civilization.

Waioka Pool

Also referred to by some as Venus Pool, a myth-legend says Waioka Pool was once used exclusively by Hawaiian royalty. At the Waiohonu bridge just past mile marker 48, cross over the fence and hike (public access trail) through the fields above the river to its mouth. There you'll find a spring-fed, freshwater pool scoured out of the solid rock walls of this water course. Used by Hawaiian royalty during centuries past, it's now a refreshing, usually solitary, place for a swim or to sunbathe on the smooth rocks. Be safe and stay out of the ocean—the surf, which is just over the narrow sandbar, is strong. At certain times of the year you may see giant turtles just off the rocks a short way farther down the coast. They are best seen from the road a quarter mile past the river at a sharp turn in the highway. In the fields above and to the north of Waioka Pool are the remains of an old sugar mill and part of the King's Highway, a paved pathway that once ran along the coast.

Wailua Falls

About seven miles after leaving Hana, Wailua and Kanahualui Falls tumble over steep lava *pali*, filling the air with a watery mist and filling their pools below. They're just outside your car door, and a minute's effort will take you to the mossy grotto at the base. There's room to park. If not for Oheo up ahead, this would be a great picnic spot, but wait! Sometimes roadside artists park here, and basket makers plying their trade. Check out the taro fields that have been created on the ocean side of the road. In a few minutes you pass a little shrine cut into the mountain. This is the **Virgin by the Roadside**. It's usually draped with a fresh lei.

KIPAHULU: THE COASTAL BOUNDARY OF HALEAKALA NATIONAL PARK

This is where the enormous **Kipahulu Valley** meets the sea. The majority of this valley, more than a third of the national park area, is off limits to the public, set aside as a scientific research preserve. Palikea Stream starts way up on Haleakala and steps its way through the valley, leaving footprints of waterfalls and pools until it spends itself in the sea. The area was named the Seven Sacred Pools by a publicity person in the late '40s. The area should have been held sacred, but it wasn't. Everything was right here. You can feel the tremendous power of nature: bubbling waters, Haleakala red and regal in the background, and the sea pounding away. Hawaiians lived here but the *heiau* that you would surely expect are missing. Besides that there aren't seven pools; there are more like 24! The name "Seven Sacred Pools" is falling into disfavor because it is inaccurate, with local people and the National Park Service preferring the proper name Kipahulu, or Oheo Gulch, instead. It's about 10 miles out of Hana.

Visitors Center

As you progress along the road, you'll come to a large cement arched bridge (excellent view) and then a parking area to your left with a ranger's station/visitors center, restrooms, and public telephone. The visitors center is relatively new. Information on the Kipahulu district of the national park, area trails and their conditions, the native Hawaiian people who lived in the area and their lifestyle, and the natural resource of the district are all well explained. Check out the koa canoe. It was cracked when the tsunami struck the area in the 1940s. The center also stocks a selection of books about the area. A small bulletin board outside displays other information. The center is open 9 a.m.-5 p.m. daily. The rangers are friendly and informative, so before doing any exploring stop in and ask about trail conditions. They know a tremendous amount of natural history concerning the area and can inform you about the few dangers in the area, such as the flash flooding that occurs in the pools. Interpretive talks are given at the ranger station daily at 12:30, 1:30,

2:30, and 3:30 every afternoon, and occasional cultural programs are offered. Call the ranger station, tel. (808) 248-7375, for information. You can hike the trail by yourself but ranger-led hikes are also given. A short one-mile hike goes to the Bamboo Forest daily at 9 a.m. On Saturday at 9:30 a.m., they lead a group all the way to Waikamoi Falls, four miles there and back. Those intending to hike or camp should bring their own water. The vast majority of the people go to the easily accessible lower pools, but a stiff hike up the mountain takes you to the upper pools, a bamboo forest, and a fantastic waterfall; 99% of park visitors are gone by sundown. From the parking lot, a short dirt trail leads down to the large grassy camping area.

The Lower Pools
Head along the clearly marked path from the parking area to the flat, grass-covered peninsula. The winds are heavy here as they enter the mouth of the valley from the sea. A series of pools to choose from is off to your left. It's delightful to lie in the last one and look out to the sea crunching the shore just a few yards away. Move upstream for the best swimming in the largest of the lower pools. Be careful, because you'll have to do some fairly difficult rock climbing. The best route is along the right-hand side as you face up the valley. Once you're satiated, head

back up to the road along the path on the left-hand side. This will take you up to the bridge that you crossed when arriving, one of the best vantage points from which to look up and down this amazing valley.

In the late '90s, 52 acres were added to the park near the pools, including additional shoreline and the Kanekauila Heiau.

The Upper Pools
Few people head for the upper pools. However, those who do will be delighted. The trail is called **Waimoku Falls Trail,** and it begins at the ranger station. The falls at Makahiku are a half mile uphill and Waimoku Falls is two miles distant. The toughest part is at the beginning as you huff-puff your way straight uphill. About a quarter mile of boardwalk has been constructed through the wettest portions of the trail. The trail leads to a fenced overlook from where you can see the lace-like falls at Makahiku as they plummet 181 feet to the rugged valley floor below. Behind you a few paces and to the left will be a waterworn, trench-like path. Follow it to the very lip of the falls and a gorgeous little pool. You can swim safely to the very edge of the falls. The current is gentle here, and if you stay to the right you can peer over the edge and remain safe behind encircling boulders. Be extremely conscious of the water rising, and get out immediately if it does!

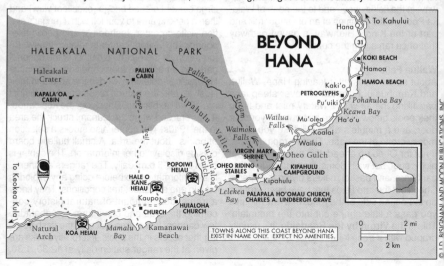

After refreshing yourself, continue on the path through a grassy area. Here you'll cross the creek where there's a wading pool, and then zigzag up the opposite bank. After some enormous mango trees, you start going through a high jungle area. Suddenly you're in an extremely dense bamboo forest—an incredible experience in itself. The trail is well cut as you pass through the green darkness of this stand. If the wind is blowing, the bamboo will sing a mournful song for you. Emerge into more mangos and thimbleberries and there's the creek again. Turn left and follow the creek, without crossing yet, and the trail will become distinct again. There's a wooden walkway, and then, eureka! . . . Waimoku Falls. It cascades over the *pali* and is so high that you have to strain your neck as far as it will go. It's more than a waterfall; it's silver filigree. You can stand in the shallow pool below surrounded by a sheer rock amphitheater. The sunlight dances in this area and tiny rainbows appear and disappear.

One word of warning. As at all such waterfalls on the islands, where the pool beckons to slack the heat and the surrounding scenery is so captivating, rocks and boulders periodically dislodge from the *pali* above and tumble into the pool below. How else have the boulders in the pool gotten to where they are? Usually, although not always, these falling rocks are accompanied by sounds of rock striking rock. Always keep an ear out for danger and an eye upward. At popular and oft-visited waterfalls, warning signs are posted to warn you of such dangers and to keep you out of harm's way. Know the dangers and heed the warnings.

Camping

Kipahulu is part of Haleakala National Park, and camping is free (obtain permit at the visitors center) in designated sites only for a three-day limit. No backcountry camping or camping along the streams. Groups of more than 12 should obtain permits from the park superintendent at: Park Headquarters, P.O. Box 369, Makawao, HI 96768, tel. (808) 572-9306. The campgrounds are primitive and mostly empty, except for holiday weekends when they can be packed. From the parking lot follow the camping sign and continue down the hill on the rutted dirt track. Bear right to a large grassy area overlooking the sea, where signs warn not to disturb an archaeological area. Notice how spongy the grass is here. Move to the trees to escape the wind. Here are clean outhouses, picnic tables, and barbecue grills, but no potable water, so make sure to bring your own.

BEYOND OHEO GULCH

Some of Rt. 31 beyond Oheo is genuinely rugged and makes the car companies cry. But it can be driven, and even the tourist vans make it part of their regular route. Be aware, however, that rough weather can bring landslides; the road may be closed by a locked gate with access available only for official business and local residents. Check the bulletin board at the ranger station for road conditions or ask one of the rangers! In 1.5 miles you come to the well-kept clapboard **St. Paul's Church,** which sits right next to the highway. Services are conducted here twice a month. A little farther along and down a side road is **Palapala Hoomau Church** (founded 1864) and its tiny cemetery, where Charles Lindbergh is buried. People, especially those who are old enough to remember the "Lone Eagle's" historic flight, are drawn here like pilgrims. The public is not really encouraged to visit, but the human tide cannot be stopped. If you go, please follow all of the directions posted. Right next to the church cemetery is the tiny **Kipahulu Lighthouse Point County Park,** which sits on the edge of the cliff overlooking the frothy ocean below. Several trees and picnic tables provide a quiet and shaded place for a bite to eat and a rest. Up the road is Samuel F. Pryor's Kipahulu Ranch. Mr. Pryor was a vice president of Pan Am and a close chum of Lindbergh's. It was he who encouraged Lindbergh to spend his last years in Hana.

Kipahulu Ranch has seen other amazing men. Last century a Japanese samurai named Sentaro Ishii lived here. He was enormous, especially for a Japanese of that day, more than six feet tall. He came in search of work, and at the age of 61 married Kehele, a local girl. He lived in Kipahulu until he died at the age of 102.

Past Sam Pryor's place is **Oheo Riding Stables.** From here two rides a day are taken through the lush vegetation to spots overlooking Makahiku and Waimoku Falls, both in the national park. About three hours are spent in the saddle. Past here the road really begins to get rugged and narrow, but only about four miles remains unpaved.

Kaupo

Once you get to the Kaupo Gap, the tropical vegetation suddenly stops and the landscape is barren and dry. Here Haleakala's rain shadow creates an environment of yellow grassland dotted with volcanic rock. Everywhere are *ahu,* usually three stacked stones, that people have left as personal prayers and wishes to the gods. Just after Kaupo, the dirt road becomes a beat-up pothole patchwork that wheels along with the ocean far below. Around mile markers 28 and 29, notice an ancient lava flow that spilled into the sea and created a huge arch. Beyond that, you can look down on Maui's last lava flow and La Perouse Bay. Also, be aware of free-range cattle, which can be in the middle of the road around any turn. Enjoy the road, because in a few minutes the pavement will improve and you'll be back in the civilized world.

Kaupo Store

The vistas open up at the beginning of the Kaupo Gap just when you pass **Hui Aloha Church.** Built in 1859, this church sits on a level grassy spot below the road near the sea; the road down may be very rough and impassable except with a 4WD vehicle. The village of Kaupo and the Kaupo Store follow Hui Aloha Church. After so many years of erratic hours and unpredictable closures, Kaupo Store now has regular hours, Mon.-Sat. 10:30 a.m.-5:30 p.m. A real anachronism, the store serves double duty as unofficial dusty museum and convenience store. Along with the antiques hanging on the walls and filling the shelves (not for sale), the store stocks cold juices and beer, ice cream and chips—mostly snacks and traveling food.

Only a few families live in Kaupo, old ones and new ones trying to live independently. During decades past, Kaupo Store was the center of this community. If only the walls could talk, what stories they would tell. Kaupo is the last of a chain of stores that once stretched all the way from Keanae and were owned by the Soon Family. Nick Soon was kind of a modern-day wizard. He lived in Kaupo, and among his exploits he assembled a car and truck brought piecemeal on a barge, built the first electric generator in the area, and even made from scratch a model airplane that flew. He was the son of an indentured Chinese laborer.

A short distance past Kaupo is **St. Joseph's Church.** Built in 1862, it has recently been remodeled, and services are held here periodically.

Auntie Jane's

Wonders never cease! About 100 yards east of the Kaupo Store is a *kaukau* wagon, owned and operated by Auntie Jane Aki, who, along with her *paniolo* husband Charles, owns and operates a small cattle ranch. Their organic beef is made into the large juicy burgers offered on the limited menu. Definitely stop by if only just to "talk story" with Auntie Jane, a lifelong Hawaii resident, who came to the Kaupo area 35 years ago. Open from "about 11 a.m. to about when the sun goes down, everyday except Thursday" (when she goes for supplies), Auntie Jane offers big juicy regular burgers for $5, along with local ice cream, $5 large and $3 small, and $1 sodas. These huge burgers are loaded with all the trimmings and a meal in themselves. Auntie Jane says, "Everything is made my way, not McDonald's way." When she first opened, Auntie Jane had no sign to advertise her business. To remedy that, the island artist Piero Resta created one for her. What a blessing. Have a look. Also along with her husband, Jane owns and operates **Charley's Trailrides,** which offers guided overnighters from Kaupo to Haleakala Crater. Auntie Jane has "plenty aloha," which is as nourishing to the soul as her burgers are to the belly. Fill up!

M.G.L. DOMENY DE RIENZI

KAHOOLAWE

OVERVIEW

The island of Kahoolawe (The Taking Away) is clearly visible from many points along Maui's south shore. From Lahaina and Maalaea, the outline of Kahoolawe on the horizon resembles the back and dorsal fin of a whale half out of the water, ready to dive. In fact, many whales and dolphins do congregate around the island in summer to calve their young and mate for the coming year. Until recently Kahoolawe was a target island, uninhabited except for a band of wild goats that refused to be killed off.

Kahoolawe was a sacred island born to Wakea and Papa, the two great mythical progenitors of Hawaii. The birth went badly and almost killed Papa, and it hasn't been any easier for her ill-omened child ever since. Kahoolawe became synonymous with Kanaloa, the man-god. Kanaloa was especially revered by the *kahuna ana'ana*, the "black sorcerers" of old Hawaii. Kanaloa, much like Lucifer, was driven from heaven by Kane, the god of light. Kanaloa held dominion over all poisonous things and

ruled in the land of the dead from his power spot here on Kahoolawe. Kanaloa was also revered as the god of voyaging by early Polynesians and as such held an important place in their cast of deities.

For years, a long, bitter feud raged between the U.S. Navy, which wanted to keep the island as a bombing range, and Protect Kahoolawe Ohana, a Hawaiian native-rights organization, which wants the sacred island returned to the people. The Navy has finally agreed to stop bombing and return the island to the state of Hawaii, bringing the Ohana one step closer to its goal.

The Land

Kahoolawe is 11 miles long and six miles wide, with 29 miles of coastline. Its 45 square miles make it the seventh largest of the main Hawaiian islands, larger only than Niihau, and its mean elevation of about 600 feet is lower than all the other islands except for that small private enclave. The tallest hill, Moaulanui, is in the eastern section at 1,477 feet. Across the shallow Lua-makika Crater is the nearly-as-tall hill Moaulaniki, at 1,444 feet. There are no natural lakes or ponds on the island, and all streams except for one or two are seasonal. As Kahoolawe lies in Maui's rain shadow (it's six miles across to South Maui), it receives only about 25 inches of rain a year.

The land is covered by sparse vegetation and is cut by ravines and gulches. Much of the island, particularly the south and east coasts, is ringed by steep *pali,* but the land slides off more gradually to the north and west. There are few beaches on the island, but the best are at the west end between Honokoa Bay and Honukanaenae Bay. Also known as Smuggler Cove, Honukanaenae Bay is said to be the site of a treasure buried on the beach in 1880 and as yet unclaimed. Kealaikahiki Point is the island's western tip, and this rock was used as a beacon during centuries past for canoe travelers to and from the island to the south.

HISTORY

It's perfectly clear that small families of Hawaiians lived on Kahoolawe for countless generations and that religious rites were carried out by many visiting *kahuna* over the centuries, but mostly Kahoolawe was left alone. There are scores of archaeological sites and remnants of *heiau* all over the bomb-cratered face of Kahoolawe, perhaps from as early as A.D. 1150. Most of these sites are close to water near the area known as Hakioawa in the northeast corner of the island, but a few others have been discovered inland. One site of archaeological interest is an adze quarry, located up top and said to be the second largest in the state.

In the early 1800s, Kahoolawe was used as a place of banishment for criminals. It was a harsh sentence, as the island had little food and less water. Yet, many survived and some managed to raid the nearby islands of Maui and Lanai for food and women! The first attempt at sheep ranching was started in 1858 but was not successful. This was followed by a second venture, which also proved largely unproductive because of the great numbers of wild goats that had by that time established themselves on the island. By the turn of the century, Kahoolawe was already overgrazed and a great deal of its bare topsoil blown away into the sea.

In 1917 Angus MacPhee, a cattleman, leased Kahoolawe from the territorial government for $200 per year. The lease would run until 1954 with a renewal option, if by 1921 MacPhee could show reasonable progress in taming the island. Harry Baldwin bought into the **Kahoolawe Ranch** in 1922, and with his money and MacPhee's know-how, Kahoolawe turned a neat profit. Within a few years Kahoolawe Ranch cattle were being shipped regularly to markets on Maui. MacPhee did more than anyone to reclaim the land. He got rid of many of the goats and introduced horses and game birds. While the island supported indigenous vegetation such as ohia, mountain apples, and even Hawaiian cotton and tobacco, MacPhee planted eucalyptus and range grass from Australia, which caught on well and stopped much of the erosion. Gardens were planted around the homestead and the soil proved to be clean and fertile.

The Navy Arrives
In 1939, with the threat of war on the horizon, MacPhee and Baldwin, stimulated by patriotism, offered a small tip of Kahoolawe's southern shore to the U.S. Army as an artillery range. One day after the attack on Pearl Harbor, the U.S. Navy seized all of Kahoolawe to further the "war effort" and evicted MacPhee, immediately disenfranchising the Kahoolawe Ranch. The island was supposed to be returned after the war, but when the lease ran out in 1954 the island was appropriated by Presidential decree for use solely by the military. No compensation was ever given to MacPhee or his family. Kahoolawe has since become the most bombarded piece of real estate on the face of the earth. During WW II the Navy praised Kahoolawe as being *the* most important factor in winning the Pacific War, and it held Kahoolawe until the fall of 1990.

The Protect Kahoolawe Ohana
Founded in 1976, the Protect Kahoolawe Ohana (PKO) is an extended group favoring traditional values based on *aloha aina* (love of the land), which is the primary binding force for all Hawaiians. They would like the island to return to Hawaiian Lands inventory with the *kahu* (stewardship) in the hands of native Hawaiians. The point driven home by the Ohana is that the military has totally ignored and belittled native

KAHOOLAWE

© J.D. BISIGNANI AND MOON PUBLICATIONS, INC.

Hawaiian values, which are now beginning to be asserted. They maintain that Kahoolawe is not a barren wasteland, but a vibrant part of their history and religion. Indeed, Kahoolawe was placed on the National Register of Historic Sites in 1981.

In a formal agreement with the PKO and the state of Hawaii in 1980, the U.S. Navy granted legal access to the island for four days per month. The PKO has built a *halau* (longhouse), and members use the time on Kahoolawe to dedicate themselves to religious, cultural, and social pursuits. The Ohana look to Kahoolawe as

their *pu'uhonua* (refuge), where they gain strength and knowledge from each other and the *aina*. Hopefully Kahoolawe's future as a sacred island is now secure.

Changing Hands

In 1990, then-president George Bush issued an order to immediately halt the bombing of Kahoolawe, and at the same time established a congressional commission to create the terms and conditions for returning the island to the state. At that time, Ka Lahui Hawaii, the Native Nation of Hawaii, founded in Hilo in 1987, demanded that the island, as "totally ceded lands," be given to them as part of their sovereign nation. The Protect Kahoolawe Ohana, in a more moderate stance, suggested "land banking" the island under the control of the state or federal government until the United States recognizes the sovereignty of the Ka Lahui Hawaii. In the meantime, the PKO continues to lobby for exclusive rights to the stewardship of Kahoolawe. Finally, on May 7, 1994, Kahoolawe was returned to the state of Hawaii.

Transition

With the transfer of the island back to state protection, Kahoolawe has become an "island reserve." Congress has dedicated $400 million over a 10-year period (the Navy will be gone in 2003) toward cleaning the island of scrap and unexploded ordnance, and for the rejuvenation of the environment. What appears to be a huge amount of money is already being used at a rapid pace and appears to be only enough to start the process of making the island safe and healthy. The Kahoolawe Island Reserve Commission (KIRC) was established by state law to oversee and manage this effort until the Navy leaves. The reserve includes the island of Kahoolawe plus the waters surrounding the it to a distance of two miles. This total area is one of restricted access.

Now that the goats are gone and some of the ordnance cleaned up, the greatest problem seems to be erosion. While vegetation has a hold in some valleys and clings to spots where goats could not feed, much of the soil covering the island's plateau and gentle slopes has been blown off, exposing red, hardpan earth. Much work has been done; various approaches tried to establish grasses and other plants, and dams of grasses have been placed to prevent dirt from washing down gullies to the sea. Still, much more needs to be done. Introduced species are overtaking the dwindling native plants, and field mice are swiftly eating native seeds. Two other serious problems that must be overcome are the remaining unexploded ordnance, which is both expensive and risky to dispose of, and the perpetual lack of water. While the ordnance clean-up effort continues by the military, Mother Nature must be coaxed to help out with water.

With similar natural conditions to South Maui, the island gets only minimal rain each year. Freshwater comes from rain catchment, and few streams ever run.

The only habitation sites on Kahoolawe are the traditional structures put up by the PKO near Hakioawa and the military installation on the west end of the island. There is currently virtually no infrastructure on the island except for a few rutted dirt roads. Over the years, about 5,000 people have visited the island, mostly to help with the cleanup efforts or to participate in religious and cultural activities. Kahoolawe might be a great cultural resource, a place where Hawaiians could go to practice age-old traditions in a sympathetic environment. But it probably will never be a place for any large-scale habitation, at least not in the foreseeable future.

While the exact plans for the future are still up in the air, it seems most likely that the island will be kept out of the hands of developers and open to visitors if the risk factor finally drops low enough. How the island will be managed and what status it will eventually attain is still undecided.

The Book on Kahoolawe

Inez MacPhee Ashdown lived on the island with her father and was a driving force in establishing the homestead. She has written a book, *Recollections of Kahoolawe,* that chronicles the events from 1917 until the military takeover and is rife with myths, legends, and historical facts about Kahoolawe.

Information

Unless you are one of the lucky few, you must be content to view Kahoolawe from across the water. For information about current happenings relating to this tortured island, log on to the PKO's website: www.kahoolawe.org. Alternately, try that of the KIRC at www.state.hi.us/kirc, or a Navy information site at www.efdpac.navfac.navy.mil/news/kaho/hp1.htm. To contact the PKO, write: P.O. Box 152, Honolulu, HI 96810. For the KIRC: 33 S. King St., Room 501, Honolulu, HI 96813, tel. (808) 586-0761 or (800) 468-4644 from the Neighbor Islands, e-mail: kirc @lava.net.

HAWAII STATE ARCHIVES

LANAI
INTRODUCTION

Lanai, in the long dark past of Hawaiian legend-history, was a sad and desolate place inhabited by man-eating spirits and fiendish bloodcurdling ghouls. It was redeemed by spoiled but tough Prince Kaululaau, exiled there by his kingly father, Kakaalaneo of Maui. Kaululaau proved to be not only brave, but wily too; he cleared Lanai of its spirits through trickery and opened the way for human habitation. Lanai was for many generations a burial ground for the *ali'i* and therefore filled with sacred mana and *kapu* to commoners. Later, reports of its inhospitable shores filled the logs of old sailing vessels. In foul weather, captains navigated desperately to avoid its infamously treacherous waters, whose melancholy whitecaps still outline Shipwreck Beach and give credence to its name.

The vast majority of people visiting the Hawaiian Islands view Lanai from Lahaina on West Maui but never actually set foot upon this lovely quiet island. For two centuries, first hunters and then lovers of the humpback whale have come to peer across the waters of the Auau Channel, better known as the "Lahaina Roads," in search of

these magnificent giants. Lanai in Hawaiian means "Hump," and it's as if nature built its own island-shrine to the whale in the exact spot where they are most plentiful. Lanai is a victim of its own reputation. Most visitors were informed by even longtime residents that Lanai, nicknamed "The Pineapple Island," was a dull place covered in one large pineapple plantation: endless rows of the porcupine plants, sliced and organized by a labyrinth of roads, contoured and planted by improbable-looking machines, and tended by mostly Filipino workers in wide-brimmed hats and goggles. Although changing somewhat, this image still persists. It's true that Lanai had the largest pineapple plantation in the world, 15,000 cultivated acres, which accounted for about 90% of U.S. production. The remnants of these fields are still obvious in the swirls of green grasses as you approach the island by air. Now only about 100 acres remain in cultivation out by the airport—as a testimony to a bygone era—and these fruits are raised for local consumption only. All other pineapples on the island are raised by local gardeners. But the island has 74,000 acres that remain untouched and perfect for exceptional outdoor experiences, ranging from golf to mountain biking to snorkeling.

Because of its past reputation as a place where almost no one went and recent shift from pineapple production to tourism that caters to the well-to-do who want their peace and quiet, Lanai is once again becoming known as the "Secluded Island."

AN OVERVIEW

The people of Lanai live in one of the most fortuitously chosen spots for a working village in the world: Lanai City. All but about two dozen of the island's 2,800 permanent residents make their homes here. Nestled near the ridge of mountains in the northeast corner of the Palawai Basin, **Lanai City** (elevation 1,600 feet) is shel-

tered, cooled, and characterized by a mature and extensive grove of Cook pines planted in the early 1900s by the practical New Zealand naturalist George Munro. This evergreen canopy creates a parklike atmosphere about town while reaching tall green fingers to the clouds. A mountainous spine tickles drizzle from the water-bloated bellies of passing clouds for the thirsty, red, sunburned plains of Lanai below. The trees, like the bristled hair of an annoyed cat, line the **Munro Trail** as it climbs Lanaihale, the highest spot on the island (3,370 feet). The Munro Trail's magnificent panoramas encompass sweeping views of no less than five of the eight major islands as it snakes along the mountain ridge, narrowing at times to less than 30 yards across.

Maunalei Gulch, a vast precipitous valley, visible from "The Trail," was the site of a last-ditch effort of Lanai warriors to repel an invasion by the warrior king of the Big Island at the

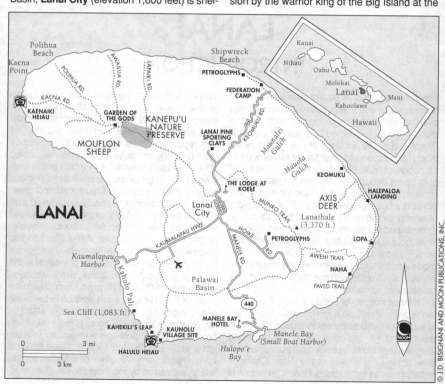

the south coast of Lanai

turn of the 18th century. Now its craggy arms provide refuge to mouflon sheep as they execute death-defying leaps from one rocky ripple to the next. On the valley floors roam axis deer, and, until recently, on the northwest grasslands were the remnants of an experimental herd of pronghorn antelope brought from Montana in 1959. After saturating yourself with the glories of Lanai from the heights, descend and follow a well-paved road from Lanai City to the southern tip of the island. Here, **Manele** and **Hulopoe** bays sit side by side. Manele is a favorite spot of small sailing craft that have braved the channel from Lahaina. Hulopoe Bay, just next door, is as salubrious a spot as you can hope to find. It offers camping and all that's expected of a warm, sandy, palm-lined beach. With its virtually untouched underwater marine park, Hulopoe is regarded as one of the premier snorkeling spots in the entire island chain.

You can hike or 4WD to **Kaunolu Bay,** one of the best-preserved ancient Hawaiian village sites. Kamehameha the Great came to this ruggedly masculine shore to fish and frolic his summers away with his favorite cronies. Here, Kahekili leaped from a sea cliff to the ice-blue waters below, and challenged all other warriors to prove their loyalty to Kamehameha by following his example and hurtling themselves off what today is known as **Kahekili's Leap.**

You can quickly span a century by heading for the southeast corner of Lanai and its three abandoned villages of **Lopa, Naha,** and **Keomuku.**

Here legends abound. *Kahuna* curses still guard a grove of coconut trees, which are purported to refuse to let you down if you climb for their nuts without offering the proper prayers. Here also are the remnants of a sugar train believed to have caused its cane enterprise to fail because the rocks of a nearby *heiau* were disturbed and used in its track bed. A decaying abandoned Hawaiian church in Keomuku insists on being photographed.

You can head north along the east shore to **Shipwreck Beach,** where the rusting hulk of a liberty ship, along with timbers and planks from the great wooden square-riggers of days gone by, lie along the beach, attesting to the authenticity of its name. Shipwreck Beach is a shore stroller's paradise, a real beachcomber's boutique. Also along here are some thought-provoking petroglyphs. Other petroglyphs are found on a hillside overlooking the former "pine" fields of the Palawai Basin.

If you hunger for a totally private beach, head north for the Polihua Trail. En route, you'll pass through a fantastic area of ancient cataclysm aptly called **The Garden of The Gods.** This raw, baked area of monolithic rocks and tortured earth turns incredible shades of purple, red, magenta, and yellow as the sun plays upon it from different angles. You have a junction of trails here. You can bear left to lonely **Kaena Point,** where you'll find Lanai's largest *heiau,* a brooding setting full of weird power vibrations. If you're hot and dusty and aching for a dip, continue due north to trail's end where the desolation of the garden suddenly gives way to the gleaming brightness of virtually unvisited **Polihua Beach.**

After these daily excursions, return to the green serenity of Lanai City. Even if you're only spending a few days, you'll be made to feel like you're staying with old friends. You won't have to worry about bringing your dancing shoes, but if you've had enough hustle and bustle and yearn to stroll in quietude, sit by a crackling fire, and look up at a crystal-clear sky, head for Lanai. Your jangled nerves and ruffled spirit will be glad you did.

THE LAND

The sunburned face of Lanai seems parched but relaxed as it rises in a gentle, steady arc from sea level. When viewed from the air it looks like an irregularly shaped kidney bean. The sixth largest of the eight main islands, Lanai is roughly 140 square miles, measuring 18 miles north to south and 13 miles east to west at its longest points, with 47 miles of coastline. A classic single-shield volcano, at one time Lanai was probably connected to Maui, Molokai, and Kahoolawe as a single huge island. Marine fossils found at the 1,000-foot mark and even higher in the mountains indicate its slow rise from the sea. Its rounded features appear more benign than the violent creases of its closest island neighbors; this characteristic earned it the unflattering Hawaiian name of "Hump." More lyrical scholars, however, have refuted this translation and claim the real meaning has been lost to the ages, but Lanai does look like a hump when viewed from a distance at sea.

Its topography is simple. A rugged mountain ridge runs northwest to southeast through the eastern half of the island, and its entire length is traversed by the Munro Trail. The highest peak is Lanaihale (3,370 feet). This area is creased by precipitous gulches: the two deepest are Maunalei and Hauola at more than 2,000 feet. The topography tapers off steadily as it reaches the sea to the east. Beaches stretch from the white sands of Polihua in the north, along the salt-and-pepper sands of Naha on the east, and end with the beautiful rainbow arches of Manele and Hulopoe in the south. Until 1993, Palawai, Lanai's central basin, was completely cultivated in manicured, whorled fields of pineapple. Early this century, Palawai was covered in cactus; now cattle graze across sections of the plain and some wheat is grown. The southwest and west coasts have phenomenal sea cliffs accessible only by boat. Some of the most majestic are the **Kaholo Pali,** which run south from Kaumalapau Harbor, reaching their most amazing ruggedness at Kaunolu Bay. At many spots along this stretch the sea lies more than 1,500 feet below. Starting at Lanai City in the center, a half hour of driving in any direction presents a choice of this varied and fascinating geography.

Climate
The daily temperatures are quite balmy, especially at sea level, but it can get blisteringly hot in the basin and on the leeward side, so be sure to carry plenty of water when hiking or four-wheel driving. Lanai City gets refreshingly cool in the evenings and early mornings, but a light jacket or sweater is adequate, although thin-blooded residents bundle up.

Water
Lying in the rain shadow of the West Maui Mountains, even Lanai's windward side receives only 40 inches of rainfall a year. The central basins and leeward shores taper off to a scant 12 inch-

LANAI TEMPERATURE AND RAINFALL

	JAN.	MARCH	MAY	JUNE	SEPT.	NOV.
High	70	71	75	80	80	72
Low	60	60	62	65	65	62
Rainfall	3	3	2	0	2	4

Note: Temperature is expressed in degrees Fahrenheit; rainfall in inches.

es, not bad for pineapples and sun worshippers. Lanai has always been short of water, but wells now help satisfy the needs of the residents. Its scruffy vegetation and red-baked earth are responsible for its inhospitable reputation. There are no real rivers, and the few streams, found mostly in the gulches of the windward mountains, carry water only when the rains come and are otherwise dry. Most ventures at colonizing Lanai, both in ancient and modern times, were kept to a minimum because of this water shortage. The famous Cook pines of Lanai City, along with other introduced greenery, greatly helped the barrenness of the landscape and provided a watershed. They tickle the underside of and drink water from the clouds that graze the highland ridge. But the rust-red earth remains unchanged, and if you get it onto your clothes, it'll remain there as a permanent souvenir.

FLORA AND FAUNA

Most of Lanai's flora and fauna have been introduced. In fact, the Cook pine and the regal mouflon sheep were a manmade attempt to improve the natural, often barren habitat. These species have adapted so well that they now symbolize Lanai, as the ubiquitous pineapple once did. Besides the mouflon, Lanai boasts axis deer and a few feral goats. A wide variety of introduced game birds include the Rio Grande turkey, ring-necked pheasant, and an assortment of quail, francolins, and doves. Like the other Hawaiian islands, Lanai, unfortunately, is home to native birds that are headed for extinction. Along the Munro Trail and on the windward coast you pass through forests of Cook pines, tall eucalyptus stands, shaggy ironwoods, native koa, and silver oaks. Everywhere, dazzling colors and fragrances are provided by Lanai's flowers.

Flowers
Although Lanai's official flower is the *kaunaoa,* it's not really a flower, but an airplant that grows wild. It's easily found along the beach at Keomuku. It grows in conjunction with *pohuehue,* a pinkish-red, perennial seashore morning glory. Native to Hawaii, the *pohuehue* grows in large numbers along Lanai's seashore. It's easy to spot, and when you see a yellow-orange vinelike

airplant growing with it, you've found Lanai's *kaunaoa,* which is traditionally fashioned into lei. The medicinal *ilima,* used to help asthma sufferers, is found in large numbers in Lanai's open fields. Its flat, open yellow flower is about one inch in diameter and grows on a waist-high shrub. Two other flowers considered by some to be pests are the purple *koali* morning glory and the miniature red and yellow flowering lantana, known for its unpleasant odor. Both are abundant on the trail to the Garden of the Gods.

Cook Pines
These pines were discovered by Captain Cook. Imported in great numbers by George Munro, they adapted well to Lanai and helped considerably to attract moisture and provide a firm watershed. Exquisitely ornamental, they can also be grown in containers. Their perfect cone shape makes them a natural Christmas tree, used as such in Hawaii; some are even shipped to the Mainland for this purpose.

Endemic Birds
The list of native birds still found on Lanai gets smaller every year, and those still on the list are rarely seen. The *amakihi* is about five inches long with yellowish-green plumage. The males deliver a high-sounding tweet and a trilling call. Vegetarians, these birds live mostly on grasses and lichen, building their nests in the uppermost branches of tall trees. Some people believe that the *amakihi* is already extinct on Lanai.

The *ua'u* or Hawaiian petrel is a large bird with a 36-inch wingspan. Its head and back are shades of black with a white underbelly. This "fisherbird" lives on squid and crustaceans that it regurgitates to its chicks. Unfortunately, the Hawaiian petrel nests on the ground, sometimes laying its eggs under rocks or in burrows, which makes it an easy prey for predators. Its call is reported to sound like a small yapping dog.

The *apapane* is abundant on the other main islands, but dwindling rapidly on Lanai. It's a chubby red-bodied bird about five inches long with a black bill, legs, wingtips, and tail feathers. It's quick, flitty, and has a wide variety of calls and songs from beautiful warbles to mechanical buzzes. Its feathers were sought by Hawaiians to produce distinctive ornate featherwork.

Axis Deer

This shy and beautiful creature came to Lanai via Molokai, where the first specimens arrived in 1868 as a gift from the Hawaiian consul in Hong Kong. Its native home is the parkland forests of India and Sri Lanka. The coats of most axis deer are golden tan with rows of round lifetime spots, along with a black stripe down the back and a white belly. They stand three to four feet at the shoulder, with bucks weighing an average of 160 pounds and does about 110. The bucks have an exquisite set of symmetrical antlers that always form a perfect three points. The antlers can stand 30 inches high and more than 20 inches across, making them coveted trophies. Does are antlerless and give birth to one fawn, usually between November and February, but Hawaii's congenial weather makes for good fawn survival anytime of year. Axis deer on Lanai can be spotted anywhere from the lowland *kiawe* forests to the higher rainforests along the Munro Trail. Careful and proper hunting management should keep the population stable for many generations. The meat from axis deer is reported to have a unique flavor, different from Mainland venison—one of the finest tasting of all wild game.

Mouflon Sheep

Another name for these wild mountain sheep is Mediterranean or European bighorn. One of only six species of wild sheep in the world, mouflon are native to the islands of Sardinia and Corsica, whose climates are quite similar to Hawaii's. They have been introduced throughout Europe, Africa, and North America. Although genetically similar to domestic sheep, they are much more shy, lack a woolly coat, and only infrequently give birth to twins. Both rams and ewes are a similar tannish brown, with a snow-white rump, which is all that most people get to see of these always-alert creatures as they quickly and expertly head for cover. Rams weigh about 125 pounds (ewes a bit less) and produce a spectacular set of recurved horns. They need little water to survive, going for long periods on only the moisture in green plants. On Lanai they are found along the northwest coast in the grasslands and in the dry *kiawe* forests.

HISTORY

Kakaalaneo peered across the mist-shrouded channel between West Maui and Lanai and couldn't believe his eyes. Night after night, the campfire of his son Kaululaau burned, sending its faint but miraculous signal. Could it be that the boy was still alive? Kaululaau had been given every advantage of his noble birth, but still the prince had proved to be unmanageable. King Kakaalaneo had even ordered all children born on the same day as his son to be sent to Lahaina, where they would grow up as his son's friends and playmates. Spoiled rotten, young Kaululaau had terrorized Lahaina with his pranks and one day went too far: he destroyed a new planting of breadfruit. Even the chief's son could not trample the social order and endanger the livelihood of the people. So finally the old *kahuna* had to step in. Justice was hard and swift: Kaululaau must be banished to the terrible island of Lanai, where the man-eating spirits dwelled. There he would meet his fate, and no one expected him to live. But weeks had passed and Kaululaau's nightly fires still burned. Could it be some ghoulish trick? Kakaalaneo sent a canoe of men to investigate. They returned with incredible news. The boy was fine! All the spirits were banished! Kaululaau had cleansed the island of its evil fiends and opened it up for the people to come and settle.

Oral History

In fact, it's recorded in the Hawaiian oral genealogical tradition that a young Kaululaau did open Lanai to significant numbers of inhabitants in approximately A.D. 1400. Lanai passed through the next few hundred years as a satellite of Maui, accepting the larger island's social, religious, and political dictates. During this period, Lanai supported about 3,000 people who lived by growing taro and fishing. Most inhabited the eastern shore facing Maui, but old home sites show that the population became established well enough to homestead the entire island. Lanai was caught up in the Hawaiian wars that raged in the last two decades of the 1700s, and was ravaged and pillaged in 1778 by the warriors of Kalaniopuu, aging king of the Big Island. These hard times marked a decline in Lanai's population; accounts by Western sea captains who passed even a few years later noted that the island looked desolate, with no large villages evident. Lanai began to recover and saw a small boost in population when Kamehameha the Great established his summer residence at Kaunolu on the southern shore. This kept Lanai vibrant for a few years at the beginning of the 19th century but it began to fade soon thereafter. The decline continued until only a handful of Hawaiians remained by the 20th century. The old order ended completely when one of the last traditional *kanaka,* a man named Ohua, hid the traditional fish god, Hunihi, and died shortly thereafter in his grass hut in the year 1900.

Early Foreign Influences

No one knows his name, but all historians agree that a Chinese man tried his luck at raising sugarcane on Lanai in 1802. He brought boiling pots and rollers to Naha on the east coast, but after a few years of hard luck gave up and moved on. About 100 years later a large commercial sugar enterprise was attempted in the same area. This time the sugar company even built a narrow-gauge railroad to carry the cane. A story goes that after disrupting a local *heiau* to make ballast for the rail line, the water in the area, never in great abundance to begin with, went brackish. Again sugar was foiled.

In 1854 a small band of Mormon elders tried to colonize Lanai by starting a "City of Joseph" at Palawai Basin. This began the career of one of Hawaii's strangest, most unfathomable yet charismatic early leaders. Walter Murray Gibson came to Palawai to start an idyllic settlement for the Latter-day Saints. He energetically set to work improving the land with funds from Utah and hard work of the other Mormon settlers. The only fly in Gibson's grand ointment occurred when the Mormon Church discovered that the acres of Palawai were not registered to the church at all but to Walter Murray Gibson himself! He was excommunicated and the bilked settlers relocated. Gibson went on to have one of the strangest political careers in Hawaiian history, including championing native rights and enjoying unbelievable influence at the royal Hawaiian court. His land at Palawai passed on to his daughter who became possessed by the one evil spirit Kaululaau failed to eradicate: she

tried to raise sugarcane, but was fated, like the rest, to fail.

A few other attempts proved uneconomical, and Lanai languished. The last big attempt at cattle raising produced The Ranch, part of whose lands make up the Cavendish Golf Course in Lanai City. This enterprise did have one bright note. A New Zealander named George Munro was hired as the manager. He imported all manner of seeds and cuttings in his attempt to foliate the island and create a watershed. The Ranch failed, but Munro's legacy of Cook pines stands as a proud testament to this amateur horticulturist.

The Coming of Pineapples

The purchase of Lanai in 1922 was one of the niftiest real estate deals in modern history. James D. Dole, the most enterprising of the pineapple pioneers, bought the island—lock, stock, and barrel—from the Baldwins, an old missionary family, for $1.1 million. That comes to only $12 per acre, though many of those acres were fairly scruffy, not to mention Lanai's bad economical track record. Dole had come from Boston at the turn of the century to figure out how to can pineapple profitably. Dole did such a remarkable job of marketing the "golden fruit" on the Mainland that in a few short years, Midwestern Americans who'd never even heard of pineapples before were buying cans of it regularly from the shelves of country grocery stores. In 1922, Jim Dole needed more land for his expanding pineapple fields, and the arid basin of Palawai seemed perfect.

Lanai Plantation was an oligarchy during the early years, with the plantation manager as king. One of the most famous of these characters was H. Broomfield Brown, who ran Lanai Plantation in the '30s. He kept watch over the fields from his house through a telescope. If anyone loafed, he'd ride out into the fields to confront the offender. Mr. Brown personally "eyeballed" every new visitor to Lanai: all prostitutes, gamblers, and deadbeats were turned back at the pier. An anti-litter fanatic, he'd even reprimand anyone who trashed the streets of Lanai City. During the labor strikes of the 1960s, workers' grievances were voiced and Lanai began to function as a more fair enterprise. With pineapple well established on the world market, Lanai finally had a firm economic base. From a few thousand fruits in the early days, the flow at its peak reached a million fruits per day during the height of the season. They were shipped from the man-made port at Kaumalapau, which was specially built to accommodate Lanai's "pines."

Crushed Pineapples

At its height, Lanai had 18,000 acres of pineapples under production (15,000 acres for most of its heyday). These acres made up the largest single pineapple plantation in the world. Virtually the entire island was operated by The Dole Co., whose name had become synonymous with pineapples. In one way or another, everyone on Lanai owed their livelihood to pineapples, from the worker who twisted his ankle in a pine field to the technician at the community hospital who X-rayed it. Now, all has changed and only a few plots remain, mostly for use by the hotels.

Foreign production, especially in the Philippines, has greatly increased, and the Lanai pineapple industry has virtually folded. As acreage was taken out of pineapple production, and as the population of the island and number of visitors have increased, the company has experimented with raising various organic vegetables, grains, and cattle to diversify the island's economy. This seems to be a pet project of David Murdoch, and the hope is to make the economy of Lanai more locally sustainable and less dependent on imports from the other islands and the Mainland.

Changing Lanai

Most are amazed that George Munro's pines still shelter a tight-knit community that has remained untouched for so long. But all that's changing, and changing quickly. Two new hideaway luxury hotels have risen, and they're beauties. The coming of these resorts has brought the most profound changes to Lanai since James Dole arrived at the turn of the century. Castle and Cooke, practically speaking, owns the island (98%). David Murdoch is the CEO of Castle and Cooke, and the hotels are his babies. He developed them and the two golf courses, and continues to develop residential lots (up to 700 in the next 10 years) through a permutation of companies that is now called the Lanai Company. This company employs a staff of about 1,200

or so, more than all the workers needed to tend the pineapple fields, which was just over 500 people. The hotels have brought an alternative job market, new life to the downtown area, and a housing spurt. One fact was undeniable concerning Lanai: if you wanted to make a living you either had to work the pineapple fields or leave. Now that has changed. To stop the disenfranchisement of the local people, which was generally the case with rapid development, the Lanai Company has built several new housing projects, which have come with a promise. Local people, according to seniority with the company and length of residence on Lanai, have first choice. One group of houses is multiple-family, geared to the entry-level buyer, and the second is single-family homes. Million-dollar homes are also starting to pop up above town and now begin to line the fairways of the new golf courses. This isn't all *heart* on the part of the Lanai Company. It wants to ensure that the hotels will have a steady and contented workforce to keep them running without a hitch and to make the whole venture economically viable.

Downtown Lanai is inadequate. It couldn't possibly handle the hotel guests and all the new workers and their families who have moved to the island. Old buildings have been refurbished, some torn down and replaced, with more upscale businesses taking their place. The tired little shops in town are on Lanai Company property, most with month-to-month leases. The Lanai Company again promises to be fair, but like the rest of Lanai, they'll have a choice: progress or perish. Most islanders are optimistic, keeping an open mind and adopting a "wait and see" attitude concerning the inevitable changes and the promises that have been made for a better life.

THE PEOPLE

Lanai is characterized by the incredible mix of racial strains so common in Hawaii—Filipino, Japanese, Hawaiian, Chinese, and Caucasian. It is unique, however, in that 60% of its people are Filipino. The Filipinos, many recent immigrants, were solicited by Castle and Cooke to work as laborers on the pineapple plantation. Mostly young men, the majority speak Ilocano and may have come to join relatives already on

Lanai. Most arrive on their own; they learn English and from Lanai they spread out. As workers they were perfect: industrious and quiet. At night you wonder where they all are. Due to the tremendous shortage of eligible women, most workers stay home or fish or have a beer in the back yard with buddies. And on Sundays, there is the illegal (officially nonexistent) cockfight. For high living, everyone heads for Maui or Oahu.

The next largest racial groups are Japanese (14%), Hawaiian (12%), and whites (11%). The Japanese started as the field workers before the Filipinos but now, along with the whites, are Lanai's professionals and middle management. The races coexist, but there are still unseen social strata. There's even a small Chinese population (1%), who continue their traditional role as shopkeepers. Finally, about 2% fall into the "mixed" category, with many of these Filipino-Hawaiian.

Community

Lanai has a strong sense of community and uniqueness that keeps the people close. For example, during a bitter three-month strike in 1964, the entire community rallied and all suffered equally: laborers, shopkeepers, and management. All who remember say that it brought out the best in the island tradition of *aloha*. If you

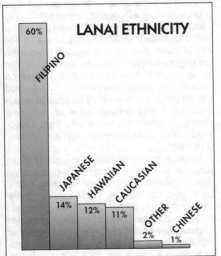

really want to meet Lanaians, just sit in the park in the center of Lanai City for an hour or two. You'll notice a lot of old-timers, who seem to be very healthy. You could easily strike up a conversation with some of them.

Other Faces

It once might have struck you that most of the people you saw around Lanai were men. That in itself was a social comment about Lanai, where men worked the fields and women stayed at home in their traditional roles, nurturing and trying to add the pleasantries of life. Now you will see more and more women about, many who work at the hotels. You might notice that there are no famous crafts of Lanai and few artists working commercially. This is not to say there is no art on Lanai, but the visitor rarely sees it. One reason that Lanai produces so little commercial art is that it's a workers' island with virtually no unemployment, so everyone is busy making a living. Old-timers are known to make superb fishing poles, nets, and even their own horseshoes. The island ladies are excellent seamstresses and, with the rising interest in hula, make lovely lei from the beautiful *kaunaoa,* Lanai's flower. If you turn your attention to the young people of Lanai, you'll see the statewide problem of babies having babies. Although the situation is getting better, teenage parents are still not uncommon. Young guys customize their 4WDs although there's no place to go. If as a young person you wish to remain on Lanai, then in almost every case your future will be tied to the Lanai Company. If you have other aspirations, it's "goodbai to Lanai." These islanders are some of the most easygoing and relaxed people you'll encounter in Hawaii, but with the electronic age extending its long arms of communication, even here they're not nearly as "backwater" as you might think.

ACCOMMODATIONS

Hotel Lanai

Being the only hotel on the island until 1990, you'd think the lack of competition would have made Hotel Lanai, P.O. Box 520, Lanai City, HI 96763, tel. (808) 565-7211 or (800) 795-7211 (7 a.m.-7 p.m. local time), arrogant, indifferent, and expensive. On the contrary: It is delightful. The hotel has gone through a few cosmetic changes since it was built in 1923 as a guest lodge, then called "The Clubhouse," primarily for visiting executives of Dole Pineapple Co., the progeny of which still owns it. Its architecture is simple plantation-style Hawaiiana, and its setting among the tall Cook pines fronted by a large lawn is refreshingly rustic. With a corrugated iron roof, board and batten walls inside and out, wooden floors, and two wings connected by a long enclosed veranda, it looks like the main building at a Boy Scout camp. But don't be fooled. The 10 remodeled rooms may not be plush, but they are cozy as can be. All have been painted in lively colors, and are immaculate with refurbished private baths. All have pine dressers and tables, floor lamps, area rugs, and ceiling fans, and patchwork quilts like grandma used to make cover each comfortable bed. A newly renovated cottage behind the main building, at one time the manager's house, has its own private yard and bath. Room rates are $95-135; checkout is 11 a.m.

The hotel has the only in-town bar, where guests and at times a few islanders have a quiet beer and twilight chat. The dining room, which occupies the center of the hotel, is paneled in knotty pine boards and lined with hunting trophies. So if you're lured by the quiet simplicity of Lanai and wish to avail yourself of one of the last family-style inns of Hawaii, stay at the lovely little Hotel Lanai. Expensive.

The Manele Bay Hotel

Glass doors curved in a traditional Roman arch sympathize with the surging Pacific as you enter the seaside 250-room Manele Bay Hotel, P.O. Box 310, Lanai City, HI 96763, tel. (808) 565-3800 or 565-7700, (800) 321-4666, website: www.sheraton.com, Lanai's newest luxury resort fashioned in a fusion of Mediterranean, Oriental, and Hawaiian architecture. The open reception area, all marble and glass, holds two massive murals of Lanai and the wide Pacific dotted with islands. Heroic paintings depict pioneering Polynesians in a double-hulled canoe sighting the Hawaiian Islands and the rascal Prince Kaululaau, redeemer of Lanai, standing triumphantly on a windswept beach after banishing the vexatious specters of Lanai. Underfoot,

a fern and pineapple motif is woven into the rich carpet, and chandeliers hang overhead from coved and molded ceilings. The lower lobby in contrast has a decidedly Oriental feel, with hints of Hawaii and the Southwest. High on the upper walls are painted huge murals depicting Chinese scenes. Below, salubrious chairs and cushions invite you to relax, Asian-style adornments please the eye, and a huge Hawaiian-theme chandelier provides light. Throughout the hotel are sitting areas and niches where you will find velvet-covered chairs and marble-topped or lacquer tables. Mythical dragons fashioned from mirrors and gold filigree, lamps of Chinese flute players, carved elephant tusks, and billowy curtains add a touch of style. For an elegant evening, order a drink and have it in the hotel library, a salubrious room filled with leather-bound tomes, globes, and models of sailing ships. Overhead, the recessed wooden ceiling has been painted with various emblems of Hawaii; the floor is the intricate paisley of tasseled Persian carpets. Sit in a highbacked chair just near the Library's balcony and enjoy the vantage point overlooking Hulopo'e Court below.

From the main reception area, descend a grand staircase and pass a formidable lava rock wall draped with the purples and pinks of living bougainvillea. Here is the grand cloverleaf pool encircled by a marble apron where you can relax upon white chaise lounges softened with billowy pillows and shaded by white canvas umbrellas. Near the pool is the hotel spa and fitness center, complete with steam rooms, saunas, fitness machines, free weights, and professional staff. The formal gardens, two on the east and three on the west, are tranquil oases where rivulets drop into koi ponds surrounded by patches of broadleafed taro and swaying stands of bamboo. It's a marvelous setting, but perhaps the best outdoor feature of all is the unobstructed natural beauty of Hulopoe Bay

The hotel rooms and suites are mainly in two wings, east and west. East rooms bear marine names derived from the sea; the west rooms are named after flowers. These oversize guest rooms ranging in price $275-525, designed with Mediterranean and Oriental themes, offer woolen carpets, four-poster mahogany beds covered with thick quilts, double-wide louvered closets, wicker lounge chairs, wet bars, and user-friendly entertainment centers. The tiled bathroom, a study in relaxation with thick white carpets on marble floors, features extra-deep soaking tubs, double sinks and vanity, separate commodes, glass-enclosed shower stalls big enough for two, name-brand bath products, hair dryers, and slippers and robes for lounging. Each room has its own private lanai that either overlooks one of the gorgeous gardens or offers an ocean panorama. The hotel also offers 12 suites that range in price $525-2,000. A typical midrange suite offers a formal parlor and separate master bedroom with a dressing room attached. Butlers will pack and unpack clothing, make dinner reservations, and act as your personal liaison at the hotel. They will draw hot baths, pour cold champagne, and tuck you and your teddy bear in for the night.

The hotel also offers valet parking, tennis courts, a children's program, three restaurants, and a cocktail lounge. At the Manele Bay Hotel Gift Shop you can get a windbreaker, polo shirt, sweatshirt, children's alohawear, stuffed animals, incidental bags, jewelry, or light reading material. Saturdays and Sundays are special with *keiki* hula dancers who come to perform their special magic in the Hulopo'e Court. Complimentary afternoon tea is also served here daily as well. Another treat is to walk a few minutes to the hotel's **Lanai Conference Center,** where the antechamber holds museum-quality artifacts. In glass cases, you will find stone im-

plements ranging from *ulu maika,* Hawaiian bowling stones similar to Italian boccie, to *poho kukui* (*kukui* nut oil lamps). Most of these implements, including a petroglyph stone, have been gathered from Lanai. There is also a very impressive replica of a Hawaiian double-hulled canoe. If you care to explore a bit farther, try a section of the old king's trail that runs from the beach and up along the coast by the golf course. Luxury.

The Lodge at Koele

A stately row of Cook pines bids welcome as they line the red brick driveway leading to this grand manor house perched in genteel quietude just a 10-minute walk from downtown Lanai City. An upland country hotel befitting this area of trees and cool summers, it's gracefully done in neo-Victorian style. Here, a huge pineapple mural painted above the front entrance greets everyone upon arrival. "Koele" is variously interpreted as black sugarcane, the banging together of hula sticks, or the summoning of a commoner to do tithe work for an *ali'i*. The Lodge at Koele, P.O. Box 310, Lanai City, HI 96763, tel. (808) 565-3800 or 565-7300, (800) 321-4666, with its encircling veranda and sweep of broad lawn, exudes gracious relaxation. You enter into the Great Hall where the back ceiling is a translucent skylight through which the sun casts diffused beams onto the formal Victorian parlors below. Encircled by a rich koa balcony, the Great Hall holds two immense fireplaces, the largest in

The Lodge at Koele

ROBERT NILSEN

Hawaii. Parlor settings of green velvet chairs, lace doilies, pink couches, with wicker lounges, credenzas covered in flowers and ferns, and lustrous end tables are perfect for a lazy afternoon of perusing the newspapers and magazines of the world. At each corner of the spacious Great Hall is a hexagonal room of beveled windows: one for dining; one for music; one a library; and the last a game room with backgammon, chess, and dominoes.

An unexpected favorite for many guests is the hotel's Visiting Artist Program. Started in 1992, this ongoing cultural event brings writers, musicians, chefs, poets, filmmakers, and a whole host of other creative people to the hotel for informal gatherings and presentations.

Out front is a croquet lawn, to the side a bowling green. Out back through glass French doors are the swimming pool and spa, gazebo and reservoir, Japanese strolling garden, orchid house, palm and fruit gardens, and an executive putting green—a professionally designed "miniature" but real golf course. Here, with putter and a glass of chilled champagne and chocolate-dipped strawberries, you can test your skill against tiny sand traps, puddle-size water traps, and challenging Chihuahua-inspired doglegs both left and right.

Walk along the wide covered veranda past a row of rocking chairs to the two wings off the Great Hall, where you will find the 102 guest rooms, which range in price from $325 for a garden view to $1,500 for the best suite. Once inside, you can take the brass-doored elevator but climb instead the sweeping wooden staircases bearing carved pineapples, the symbol of hospitality, and walk the broad hardwood hall hung with the works of island artists (ask the concierge for an art list for the hotel), letting period wall lamps light your way. Rooms are furnished in a combination of wicker and heavy knotty pine, with a four-poster bed—each topped with a carved pineapple—covered by a downy quilt, while billowy printed curtains flutter past a window seat. Along with this turn-of-the-century charm comes a full entertainment center with remote-control color TV, video viewer, in-room safe, and wet bar. Each room has its own lanai with tile floor and wooden furniture. The bathroom, perhaps blue- or black-on-white marble, features a pedestal sink and deep soaking tub with old-fashioned brass knobs,

a full assortment of name-brand bath care products, huge towels, and separate commode. Each room also has multiple phones, ceiling fans, even walking sticks for an afternoon foray into the surrounding hills.

Two in-house restaurants are here to serve the guests. You can find sundries at the hotel shop, open 8 a.m.-9 p.m., and all hotel and island activities, including croquet, tennis, golf, hunting, horseback riding, jeep tours, sporting clays, and beach and boating activities, can be arranged by the concierge. There is free shuttle service to meet all arriving and departing planes, to and from Lanai City, and to Manele and Hulopoe Bays.

Both the Lodge at Koele and the Manele Bay Hotel have become part of The Luxury Collection of Starwood Hotels and Resorts Worldwide, Inc., which means that information and reservations for these hotels on Lanai can be made through the Starwood organization. Contact The Luxury Collection at (800) 325-3589 in the United States and Canada or check the internet at www.luxurycollection.com. Luxury.

B&Bs and Vacation Rentals

For a more homey stay on the Pineapple Island, try one of the few bed and breakfast inns or vacation rentals on Lanai, all of which are in Lanai City. These places offer a substantially cheaper alternative to staying on Lanai than the resorts and they get you into the community.

Dreams Come True, tel. (808) 565-6961, fax 565-7056, or (800) 566-6961, website: www.gonative.com/inns/0117.html, a true B&B in the oldest part of town at 12th and Olapa St., is surrounded by lots of trees and flowers. Three rooms in this plantation house are rented to guests, each with its own bathroom and use of the common room. Not large or luxurious by any means, but decent size for the island, one room has a queen bed and a single while the others have queen beds. A continental breakfast is served each morning. Rates are $67.50 s, $82.50 d; $10 extra for a child in the same room as parents. The owners, Michael and Susan Hunter, also have two vacation rental houses, website: www.10kvacationrentals.com/dreamscometrue/index.pht, one original plantation house and one new, a two-bedroom, two-bath unit and a three-bedroom, two-bath unit. Moderate.

Hale Moe, tel. (808) 565-9520, on the south side of town at 502 Akolu St., P.O. Box 196, Lanai City, HI 96763, rents three rooms, each with a bathroom. Usually no breakfast is served, but guests can make use of the kitchen. Two rooms go for $60, and the third, at $70, has a deck off the room. Moderate.

Hale O Lanai, tel. (808) 247-3637, fax 235-2644, e-mail: hibeach@lava.net, website: www.hotspots.hawaii.com/beachrent1.html, is a newer two-bedroom, two-bath house on 4th and Lanai Ave. that has all the amenities for a fine vacation stay. It rents for $95 a night, two nights minimum; weekly rates available. Expensive.

Aside from these, try Dolores Fabrao, tel. (808) 565-6134, who rents rooms in the family house for $45 s, $55 d and also has a larger room that's often used by hunting groups. Inexpensive.

For additional information, contact any of the bed and breakfast associations listed in Maui's introduction.

Okamoto Realty
This is Lanai's first house rental agency. Although the number of houses in its listing varies, there are always a handful available from two-bedroom affairs at $150 a night to a four-bedroom, three-bath cedar house for $395 a night. All houses are completely furnished including linens and kitchen utensils, and most have washer/dryer and TV. Houses are rented by the day, week, or month. Write Okamoto Realty, 730 Lanai Ave., P.O. Box 552, Lanai City, HI 96763, tel. (808) 565-7519, fax 565-6106, for current information.

Camping
The only official camping permitted to nonresidents is located at Hulopoe Bay, administered by the Lanai Company. Reservations for one of the six official campsites on the grass here are a must, although unbelievably there's usually a good chance of getting a space. Lanai Company officials state that they try to accommodate any "overflow" unreserved visitors, but don't count on it. Since Lanai is by and large privately owned by Castle and Cooke Inc., the parent company of the Lanai Company, you really have no recourse but to play by their rules. It seems they want to hold visitors to a minimum and keep strict tabs on the ones that do arrive.

Nonetheless, the campsites at Hulopoe Bay are great. Lining the idyllic beach, they're far enough apart to afford some privacy. The showers are designed so that the pipes, just below the surface, are solar heated. This means a good hot shower during daylight and early evening. Campsite use is limited to seven nights. The fee includes a one-time $5 group registration and is $5 per person per night. For reservations write to the Lanai Land Co., P.O. Box 310, Lanai City, Lanai, HI 96763, or call (808) 565-3978. Permits, if not mailed in advance, are picked up at the Lanai Company office. If visiting on the spur of the moment from a neighboring island, it's advisable to call ahead.

Note: While hiking or four-wheel driving the back roads of Lanai, especially along Naha, Shipwreck, and Polihua beaches, a multitude of picture-perfect camping spots will present themselves, but they can be used only by Lanai residents, although there's little supervision. A one-night bivouac would probably go undetected. No other island allows unofficial camping, and unless it can be statistically shown that potential visitors are being turned away, it seems unlikely that the Lanai Company will change its policies. If you're one of the unlucky ones who have been turned down, write your letter of protest to parent company Castle and Cooke, 650 Iwilei Rd., Honolulu, HI 96817, tel. (808) 548-4811.

RESTAURANTS

Aside from the new hotels, Lanai City is the only place on the island where you can dine, shop, and take care of business. Until recently, the food situation on Lanai was discouraging. Most everything had to be brought in by barge, and the fresh produce, fish, and meat was at a premium. People surely ate differently at home, but in the two tiny restaurants open to the traveler, the fare was restricted to the "two-scoop rice and teri beef" variety, with fried noodles and Spam as the pièce de résistance. But, "the times they are a-changin'!" Now, there are more options from which to choose, and more culinary variety.

By far the best restaurant in town is **Henry Clay's Rotisserie** at the Hotel Lanai, tel. (808) 565-7211; open for dinner. Henry Clay has worked under Gerard Reversade of Gerard's in Lahaina, so he's had good training. Evening appetizers run the gamut from oyster shooters at $1.35 apiece to Cajun shrimp for $10.95. A soup or salad prepares the way for an entree, be it eggplant creole and angel hair pasta at $16.95, baby back ribs at $16.95, or hunter-style rabbit at $24.95. Gourmet pizzas are also served and don't forget dessert. Order a variety of beers from around the world or a glass of wine with your meal or simply stop by the bar for a drink.

The banging screen doors announce your presence as you enter the plantation-era wainscoted **Blue Ginger Cafe,** tel. (808) 565-6363, open daily 6 a.m.-2 p.m. and 3-9 p.m., which could actually be called chic for Lanai. Upon entering, baked goods in a case let you know that not long ago it was Dahang's Bakery, a Lanai institution whose motto, "Mo betta grind ova hea" has also survived. It offers a full breakfast menu with choices like two eggs with sausage for $4.75, along with plenty of side orders, and fresh pastries. Plate lunches are $6 or so, while a bowl of saimin goes for $2.95. Burgers, sandwiches, pizza, and Dave's Ice Cream are also on the menu at comparable prices. Varying nightly, dinner specials, served with rice "toss" salad or macaroni salad, run $8-16. Eat inside or on the veranda, where you can see everything there is to see in Lanai City.

An authentic workers' restaurant and sundries store, **Tanigawa's** (formerly S.T. Property), open daily except Wednesday for breakfast and lunch 6:30 a.m.-1 p.m., is one of those places that you must visit at least for morning coffee. Totally down-home, but a pure cultural experience. Arrive before 7 a.m. when many of the older people come to "talk story." Just one look around at the crinkled faces will reveal the tough but sweet spirit of Lanai.

For a healthy, quick, light meal, try **Pele's Other Garden,** tel. (808) 565-9628. This juice bar, pizzeria, and deli is open daily 11 a.m.-7 p.m. (until 9 p.m. on Friday and Saturday). Eat in or take out. Try a turkey, veggie, or other sandwich for $4.45-4.99, or a hot entree for less than $6. Pizzas run $13-26, or choose something else from the deli case. A picnic basket might be a good choice if you're going to be away from town all day. Be sure to check the special board, as you never know what scrumptious delicacy will be offered each day.

Hotel Restaurants

The master chef, aided by a hand-picked staff at the Manele Bay Hotel's formal **Ihilani Dining Room** (jackets required) offers two fixed menus nightly, along with a complete menu of à la carte suggestions. Expect entrees in the $35-45 range. Begin with ravioli of Hawaiian goat cheese in a sauce of parsley and sun-dried tomatoes, or Maine lobster with Hayden mango and arugula salad. Second courses can be a delicately roasted squab breast in a marmalade of onions and a Molokai sweet potato puree. Entrees are roasted Chinese duck with Hawaiian seasoning, Oriental rice, and pickled ginger plum sauce, or an array of curries from Thai shrimp red curry and pan-fried *onaga* in a North Indian style. Grill selections include catch of the day, or Colorado lamb chops with polenta topped by a roasted garlic sauce. All of this, with a superb view of the bay and beach—magnifique!

The less formal but still extremely elegant **Hulopo'e Court** offers breakfast and dinner of contemporary Hawaiian regional cuisine, with prices similar to the Ihilani. This is perhaps the best breakfast spot on the island. Begin the day with a continental breakfast of assorted pastries, sliced fruits, a selection of cereals, chilled juices, and rich Kona coffee, or choose all manner of traditional favorites from the breakfast buffet (à la carte selections available as well). Lunch and dinner begin with appetizers like Chinese spring rolls, seared *ahi* in a spicy crust, or a fresh dim sum basket. Soups and salads include Maui onion soup, Caesar salad with croutons, and Lanai field greens in a *lilikoi* vinaigrette. Entrees are fresh pasta, Chinese noodles with duck covered in a chili oyster sauce, or penne pasta primavera. You can also have a gourmet pizza of Tandoori chicken or Peking duck. An excellent selection of domestic and imported beer and wine completes the meal.

The least formal dining setting is poolside at **The Pool Grill,** an alfresco restaurant serving appetizers like chicken quesadilla or cocktail of Pacific shrimp. Lighter appetites will enjoy main course salads including marinated grilled vegetables, Cobb salad, or seafood salad. The sandwich board features a good old-fashioned club, a grilled beef burger, or hot dog. Special offerings are Hawaiian favorites like grilled fresh catch, or a steamy bowl of savory saimin.

One must not forget the **Clubhouse Restaurant** at the Challenge at Manele golf course, which has superb underwater scene murals painted on its walls by John Wulbrandt. The view from here is perhaps the best on the property, overlooking both the hotel and bay, with Haleakala in the background, particularly on a night when the full moon is rising early. Food is served all day, dinner nightly except Sunday. Small plates are the theme here. Some selections are shrimp satay, spiced lamb, and grilled *ahi* with white bean cassoulet, all for under $15 a plate.

In harmony with the rest of the Lodge at Koele, the dining rooms are impeccably furnished. **The Terrace,** set in a section off the Great Hall and the more casual of the two restaurants, looks out over the exotic gardens, while the separate dinner-only **Formal Dining Room** lends itself to evening attire—jackets required. Breakfast selections include continental breakfast, eggs Benedict, and sweet rice waffles with *lilikoi*-coconut chutney. At midday satisfy your hunger with jumbo shrimp with papaya relish, pan-fried Kona crab cakes with a spicy remoulade, grilled pastrami of striped marlin on a tomato fennel salad, spinach pasta with grilled scallops, or smoked salmon and herbed goat cheese on a salad of field greens and vegetables with cilantro dressing. Simple tastes might also enjoy a barbecued pork sandwich on a sesame bun with cabbage slaw, or ask for a picnic basket for two and find a shady tree where you can enjoy an alfresco lunch. Dinner, like the other daily fare, is made from the freshest island ingredients. Choose standards like rack of lamb, prime rib, a superbly prepared catch of the day, or, for a special treat, the Lanai mixed pheasant, quail, and axis deer sausage with Pinot Noir sauce.

In the Formal Dining Room you'll have a grand dining experience. It always gets rave reviews form diners who are into serious eating. Once again, the freshest island ingredients are used to prepare each meal that leaves the kitchen. Not only are they sumptuous but they are presented in a pleasing manner. All this elegance doesn't come cheap, however. Expect prices in the $40-50 range for an entree.

The **Clubhouse** at the **Experience at Koele** golf course sells excellent soups, sandwiches, and salads at very reasonable prices. Everyone is welcome, and the standing room only lets you know that the food is very good. Try a roasted eggplant sandwich with mozzarella cheese, Caesar salad, or one of the many pasta dishes for $6-21. Dinner is now served as well on Friday and Saturday 5:30-8:30 p.m. Indoor or outdoor seating, with a great view of the 18th green.

SHOPPING

Except for the clutch of shops at the Lodge at Koele and Manele Bay Hotel, and the gift shop at the airport, shopping on Lanai means shopping in Lanai City. Be aware that all but a few are closed on Sunday, and remember that some shops in town may close their doors for an hour or longer at midday for a siesta.

The two grocery stores in town are fairly well stocked with basics. The markets are almost next door to each other. **Pine Isle Market,** tel. (808) 565-6488, run by Kerry Honda and open 8 a.m.-7 p.m. every day except Sunday, is Lanai's closest equivalent to a supermarket. **Richards Shopping Center,** tel. (808) 565-6047, is open Mon.-Sat. 8:30 a.m.-6:30 p.m. A small grocery and sundries store, it supplies all your basic camping, fishing, and general merchandise needs, including clothing and medicines, some groceries, liquor, and odds and ends.

Lying between these two is **Akamai Trading Company,** tel. (808) 565-6587, which sells furniture and gifts, hardware and books, T-shirts and party supplies, espresso and other types of coffee, and also does film processing. Open daily 9 a.m.-5:30 p.m. (until 5 p.m. on Sunday). Around the corner is **International Food and Clothing Center,** tel. (808) 565-6433, where you can pick up not only things to eat and wear, but also hardware and hunting supplies. This is an old-fashioned general store, definitely a local place; open weekdays 8 a.m.-6 p.m., until 1:30 on Sunday, closed Saturday. Across the park is the **Lanai Family Store,** tel. (808) 565-6485, for video rentals and furniture. Next door at **Maria M's Boutique,** tel. (808) 565-9577, you can find clothing items.

Wonders never cease. A health food store has come to Lanai. Opened in 1995, this was the first new store in town in years. **Pele's Garden,** tel. (808) 565-9629, stocks a limited but generous range of packaged items, herbs, juices, vitamins and minerals, and even a few books. It's a full-service health food store in miniature. She'll have most of what you might desire, and you may get a whole nutrition lesson at no extra cost. Owned by Ms. Beverly Zigmond, this fine store is open Mon.-Sat. 9:30 a.m.-6:30 p.m. Out front and connected to her store is **Pele's Other Garden,** opened in 1997, a deli and juice bar that offers cool refreshment and healthy quick food, run by her brother and his wife.

Between these two is **Gifts With Aloha,** tel. (808) 565-6589, a small shop that carries art and craft items from local and other Hawaii residents. Some items include cloth and clothing, jewelry, quilts, and candles. You should be able to find something for that special occasion here.

Heart of Lanai Art Gallery, tel. (808) 565-6678, housed in a vintage plantation-era building in downtown Lanai, open Mon.-Sat. 10 a.m.-5 p.m., is bright with the paintings, sculptures, and handicrafts of its contributing artists, all island and many Lanai residents. The artwork displayed is constantly changing, but some of the regulars include: Margaret Leach, whose watercolors capture the simple spirit of Lanai life; Steve Lance, a longtime resident who moved away but whose surrealistic paintings are filled with the vibrant colors of the islands (Steve is also a very talented wood sculptor and some of his pieces are displayed as well); Sandy Phillips, who creates primitive basketry and paintbrushes made from Lanai bamboo and axis deer hair; Sherry Menze, current Lanai harbormaster and former fisherwoman and boat captain, who has captured her love of the sea in the Japanese technique of *gyotaku,* or fish printing; Ruth Puchek, who arrived on Lanai in 1972 and has captured the mysterious moods of the islands in her paintings. She also sells postcards of her original works. Also exhibited are the works of Rony Doty, a watercolorist who paints the flowers and fauna of Lanai.

Two doors down is the **Lanai Art Program,** tel. (808) 565-7503, open weekdays 9 a.m.-4 p.m. (closed for lunch) and a few irregular hours on the weekend, which has taken the spirit of the Zimbabwe saying "If you can walk, you can dance," and changed it into "If you've got life, you've got art." This co-op of local Lanai citizens has created a nonprofit organization dedicated to developing the artistic talents of its members. Classes, chaired by guest artists, are periodically offered in photography, woodworking, Japanese doll-making, fabric-making, drama, and pen and ink drawing. The showroom offers purchases like hand-dyed silk scarves, stenciled T-shirts, naturally dyed incidental bags, notecards, lovely pareus for women, and even homemade jams and jellies. Pottery and silk painting seem to predominate. The work is always changing, but you are sure to find a distinctive island memento that couldn't be more genuine. All are welcomed, resident or not, so you can drop in on a workshop, pay for your supplies, and create your own art.

For snacks and sundries, you can also try the shop at Lanai City Service. For last-minute souvenirs, have a look at the **airport gift shop** in the terminal building.

SPORTS AND RECREATION

No question that Lanai's forte is its natural unspoiled setting and great outdoors. Traffic jams, neon lights, blaring discos, shopping boutiques, and all that jazz just don't exist here. The action is swimming, hiking, snorkeling, fishing, horseback riding, and some hunting. Tennis and golf round off the activities. Lanai is the place to revitalize your spirits—you want to get up with the birds, greet the sun, stretch, and soak up the good life.

Snorkeling and Scuba

Lanai, especially around Manele/Hulopoe Bay, has some of the best snorkeling and scuba in Hawaii. If you don't have your own equipment, and you're not a guest at one of the hotels, your only choice is to buy it from Pine Isle or Richards stores, but their prices are quite high. If you're the adventurous sort, you can dive for spiny lobsters off Shipwreck or Polihua, but make absolutely sure to check the surf conditions as it can be super treacherous. It would be best to go with a local person.

Trilogy Ocean Sports, tel. (808) 565-2387 or (888) 628-4800, website: www.sailtrilogy.com, operates the new *Trilogy III* catamaran and a rigid-bottom inflatable raft from Manele Boat Harbor for a number of sailing options. The four-hour snorkel/sail ($95) leaves daily at 8:45 a.m. Two scuba adventures, both for around $140, leave around the same time, but not every day. A circle-island rafting tour is also offered ($130), as are an afternoon marine mammal tour ($75) and a two-hour Saturday only champagne sunset sail ($65). Book directly or through the concierge desk at the Manele Bay Hotel or at the Lodge at Koele. Trilogy, in the business for years, has worked out all the kinks, and their boat, crew, and services are truly state-of-the-art. No matter how many times they make the trip, they never seem to forget that it's a new and exciting adventure for you, and they go out of their way to be helpful, upbeat, and caring without being intrusive. *Trilogy III's* aft is set up for easy entry and exit, with steps going down to the water level. Just make like a seal and slither in and out! If the winds are up, the captain will be happy to set sail as they head toward Kahekili's Leap and other famous Lanai landmarks. The experience is not just underwater, but also in the magnificent views of this pristine island that hasn't changed since the days of the Polynesian explorers. On morning sails, you return in the early afternoon with plenty of time left for more sightseeing or just relaxing.

Spinning Dolphin Charters, owned and operated by Capt. Jeff Menze, a long-time Lanai resident, P.O. Box 491, Lanai City, 96763, tel. (808) 565-6613, will take you fishing (children welcome), snorkeling, and whalewatching in season. Captain Jeff is a commercial fisherman and master diver who knows all of the best spots in Lanai's waters. Offered are whole-day and half-day adventures, special off-the-beaten-path dives, and private boat charters.

Swimming
Lanai City has a new swimming pool. Located in town near the high school, it's open to the public daily during summer, and on a limited schedule during other seasons. Each of the two resorts has its own swimming pool and spa. By far the best swimming beach on Lanai is at Hulopoe Bay, but a few other spots for a dip can be found along the coast from Shipwreck Beach to Naha.

Hiking, Biking, and Kayaking
An independent company that caters largely to hotel guests, **Lanai EcoAdventure Centre** can take you along the sheer sea cliffs of west Lanai on a kayak, walking into the Kaiholena Valley, biking down to Shipwreck Beach, or on several other outings on the island. Guided tours and introduction are provided, and rentals can be accommodated. Half-day outings cost $69 per person. Private tours can be arranged. See your hotel concierge or arrange directly: P.O. Box 1394, Lanai City, HI 96763, tel. (808) 565-7737, e-mail: trekmaui@maui.net, website: www.kayak-hawaii.com.

Tennis and Golf
You can play tennis at two lighted courts at the Lanai School. They have rubberized surfaces called royal duck and are fairly well maintained—definitely okay for a fun game. The Lodge at

LANAI GOLF AND TENNIS

GOLF COURSE	PAR	YARDS	FEES	CART	CLUB RENTAL
Cavendish Golf Course tel. (808) 565-9993	36	3,071	Free (Donation)	None	None
Challenge at Manele tel. (808) 565-2222	72	7,039	$175 nonguest $125 hotel guest	Incl.	$35
Experience at Koele tel. (808) 565-4653	72	7,014	$140 nonguest $125 hotel guest	Incl.	$35

TENNIS COURTS	TOWN	LOCATION	NO. OF COURTS	LIGHTED
	Lanai City	The Lodge at Koele	3	Yes
		Near Lanai School	2	Yes
	Manele Bay	Manele Bay Hotel	6	No

Koele and the Manele Bay Hotel have plexi-pave courts that are free to hotel guests and $9 per hour to nonguests. The courts at Manele Bay are newer and in better condition. Equipment rental (rackets and ball machines) and court times are arranged by the concierge. Private lessons and clinics are available.

Golfers will be delighted to follow their balls around Cavendish Golf Course on the outskirts of Lanai City. This nine-hole, 3,071-yard, par-36 course is set among Cook pines. It's free to all, but visitors are requested to leave a donation for maintenance. Unless you're familiar with the course, it's hard to find the first tee. The course is located at the end of Nani Street.

The **Experience at Koele,** a Greg Norman-designed course, won the *Fortune Magazine* Best New Golf Course of 1991 award. This magnificent course, set in the mountains above the Lodge, not only offers challenging links, but a fantastic series of views of Molokai and Maui on a shimmering canvas of sea. With four sets of tees ranging from forward to tournament, the course yardage varies accordingly from 5,425 yards to 7,014 yards. The course also boasts the only bent-grass greens in the state. Two of the finest holes are the number 8, 444-yard par-four, which cascades 250 feet from mountaintop to glen below, and the short but maximum water-challenged number 9, a 180-yard par-three. For information and tee times, call (808) 565-4653.

The **Challenge at Manele,** designed by the legendary Jack Nicklaus, officially opened on Christmas Day, 1993. Employing the five-tee concept, the par-72 course ranges in length 5,024-7,039 yards. Three of the main holes, including the signature number 12 par-three hole, demand a tee shot over the greatest water hazard in the world, the wide Pacific. Call (808) 565-2222 for tee times.

Horseback Riding

The Stables at Koele, tel. (808) 565-4424, open daily, just a few minutes from the Lodge at Koele (contact the concierge at either hotel), offers a variety of mounted excursions. The beginners' Plantation Trail Ride lasts one hour and costs $25, while the Paniolo Lunch Ride lasts three hours, includes lunch, and costs $90. Other rides are available, including a children's pony ride and carriage rides. Lanai enjoys a ranching heritage that goes back to the 1870s. Many of the

trails that you'll be following date from those early days. Riders must be in good health, weigh less than 250 pounds, and wear long pants and shoes. Safety helmets will be provided for all riders.

Hiking and Jogging

All the paved roads and many of the gravel roads on the plateau and in the basin are decent for walking and jogging. Although the traffic is not heavy, be careful if you're on the roadway.

One trail on the island has been marked, the trail to Koloiki Ridge. Start at the rear of the Lodge at Koele and head up through the golf course into a tall stand of pine trees. Cross under the power lines and into Hulopoe Valley, where an abandoned road heads down to the Munro Trail. Once there, turn right and head south, walking into and out of Kukui Gulch, until you round a very eroded "moonscape" on your right. A short way farther, turn left and head through a tunnel in the bushes on the trail to the Koloiki lookout.

Shorter and easier is Fisherman's Trail, a 1.5 mile shoreline trail that runs from Hoopole Bay to the west, below the Manele Bay Hotel. A project of the State Na Ala Hele trail system, this was once part of an ancient trail that circled the island.

Hunting

The first cliché you hear about Lanai is that it's one big pineapple plantation. The second is that it's a hunter's paradise. The first was true, the second still is. Both private and public hunting are allowed. As virtually all of Lanai is privately owned, about two-thirds of the island is set aside as a private reserve, and one-third is leased to the state for public hunting and is cooperatively managed.

The big game action for public hunting is provided by mouflon sheep and axis deer. Various days are open for the hunting of game birds, which include ring-necked and green pheasant; Gambel's, Japanese, and California quail; wild turkey; and a variety of doves, francolins, and partridges. The public hunting area is restricted to the northwest corner of the island. Brochures detailing all necessary information can be obtained free of charge by writing to Dept. of Land and Natural Resources, 1151 Punchbowl St., Honolulu, HI 96813. Contact Derwin Kwon at the Lanai regional office, P.O. Box 732, 911 Fraser Ave., Lanai City, HI 96763, tel. (808) 565-6688. Licenses are required ($15 resident, $100 nonresident) and can be purchased by mail from Dept. of Land and Natural Resources or picked up in person at the office on Lanai.

Public archery hunting of mouflon sheep is restricted to the last Saturday in July and first Saturday in August. The muzzleloader rifle season occurs on the second and third Saturday in August, and for rifles, shotguns, and bows and arrows for the nine following Saturdays. Tags are required and hunters are restricted by public drawing. Axis deer regular season (rifle, shotgun, and bows) opens on the nine consecutive Saturdays starting from the last Saturday in March; it's also restricted by public drawing. Muzzleloader season is the two Saturdays before that, and archery season for axis deer is the two Saturdays preceding the muzzleloader season. Bag limits are one mouflon ram and one buck.

On the private land, only axis deer are hunted. Hunting is done year-round, although the best trophy season is May-November. Hunting dates must be mutually agreed upon by the hunter and the rangers, as there are a limited number of rangers and this is a three-day process, although the hunt itself is only one long day affair. Write three to six months in advance for best results. The rate is $275 per day for a regular hunting permit, or $50 for an archery hunting permit that is good until the Hawaiian hunting license expires. Guide service is not officially mandatory, but you must prove that you have hunted Lanai before and are intimately knowledgeable about its terrain, hunting areas, and procedures. If not, you *must* acquire the services of a guide. Guide service is $750 a day, and this includes a permit and all necessities, except lodging and meals, from airport pickup to shipping the trophy. For all hunters, a Hawaii state hunting license and a hunter safety card are required. For full details write to Gary Onuma, Chief Ranger, The Lanai Co., Game Management, P.O. Box 310, Lanai City, HI 96763, tel. (808) 565-3981, fax 565-3984.

Sporting Clays

An outgrowth of hunting, sporting clays is a sport that helps develop and maintain your hand-eye coordination. Shooting is done from different stations around a course, and the object is to hit a small round clay disk. Different than trap or skeet shooting, sporting clays relies upon moving targets that mimic different animals and birds, hopping along the ground as a rabbit, springing off the ground like a quail, or flying high like a pheasant. Here you can have all the enjoyment of hitting a target without the guilt of killing a living animal. **Lanai Pine Sporting Clays,** tel. (808) 565-3800 or (800) 321-4666, fax (808) 565-3868, is a high-tech operation that services both beginners and the advanced shooter. To satisfy everyone's needs, there are skeet and trap ranges here as well.

Register at the pro shop and pick up your needed supplies and accessories there. A paved path connects each of the 14 stations; take a golf cart or walk the course. The basic package, including 100 targets, gun rental, cartridges, eye and ear protection, and safety vest runs $125 per person; $65 for 50 targets. For experienced shooters, guns, cartridges, targets, and carts can be rented separately, and you may use your own gun. Instruction is also given for beginners at $55; private lessons are available. Pull!

Fishing

Only the Spinning Dolphin Charters fishing boat operates out of Lanai, but that's not to say there are no fish. On the contrary, one of the island's greatest pastimes is this relaxing sport. Any day in Lanai City Park, you'll find plenty of old-timers to ask where the fish are biting. If you have the right approach and use the right smile, they just might tell you. Generally, the best fishing and easiest access on the island is at Shipwreck Beach running west toward Polihua. Near the lighthouse ruins is good for *papio* and *ulua,* the latter running to 50 pounds. Many of the local fishermen use throw-nets to catch the smaller fish such as *manini,* preferred especially by Lanai's elders. Throw-netting takes skill usually learned from childhood, but don't be afraid to try even if you throw what the locals call a "banana" or one that looks like Maui (a little head and a big body). They might snicker, but if you laugh too, you'll make a friend.

Mostly you'll fish with rod and reel using frozen squid or crab, available at Lanai's general stores. Bring a net bag or suitable container. This is the best beachcombing on the island and it's also excellent diving for spiny lobster. There is good shore fishing (especially for *awa*) and easy accessibility at Kaumalapau Harbor, from where the pineapples used to be shipped and where the supplies for the island now come. There is also superb offshore fishing at Kaunolu, Kamehameha's favorite angling spot on the south shore. You can catch *aku* and *kawakawa,* but to be really successful you'll need a boat. Finally, Manele Hulopoe Marine Life Conservation Park has limited fishing, but as the name implies, it's a conservation district so be sure to follow the rules prominently posted at Manele Bay.

SERVICES AND INFORMATION

Money
Try full-service First Hawaiian Bank, tel. (808) 565-6969, in Lanai City for your banking needs. It has the only ATM machine on the island. First Federal Savings, tel. (808) 565-6426, also has a branch here. All major businesses accept traveler's checks. Banks are open Mon.-Thurs., 8:30 a.m.-3 p.m. (First Federal to 4:30 p.m.), until 6 p.m. on Friday.

Post Office
The Lanai post office, tel. (808) 565-6517, on the edge of Dole Park, is across the street from the Lanai Company offices on Lanai Avenue. Open daily 8 a.m.-4:30 p.m., it's full service, but it does not sell boxes or padded mailers in which to send home beachcombing treasures; you can get those at the two general stores in town.

Lanai Playhouse
On the corner of Lanai Ave. and 7th, Lanai Playhouse, tel. (808) 565-7500 is the only theater on the island; it runs current movies.

Laundromat
The laundromat, located next to the art gallery, is open every day from "morning until nighttime": 6 a.m.-9 p.m. Bring coins.

Useful Phone Numbers
Lanai City Service gas station, tel. (808) 565-7227; Dept. of Land and Natural Resources, tel. (808) 565-6688; Lanai Airport, tel. (808) 565-6757; Lanai Community Library (open weekdays), tel. (808) 565-6996; police, tel. (808) 565-6428; weather and surf conditions, tel. (808) 565-6033; Lanai Community Hospital, tel. (808) 565-6411; Lanai Family Health Center, tel. (808) 565-6423; Dr. Nick's Family Dentistry, tel. (808) 565-7801.

Information
For general information about Lanai, and activities and services on the island, contact Destination Lana'i, P.O. Box 700, Lanai City, HI 96763, tel. (808) 565-7600 or (800) 947-4774, fax (808) 565-9316, e-mail: dlanai@aloha.net. Additionally, maps, brochures, and pamphlets on all aspects of staying on Lanai are available free from The Lanai Company, P.O. Box 310, Lanai City, HI 96763, tel. (808) 565-3000.

For an upclose look at local news and what's happening in the community, have a look at the monthly *Lanai Times.*

GETTING THERE

By Air
Hawaiian Airlines, tel. (800) 367-5320 Mainland and Canada, on Lanai (800) 565-7281, flies to Lanai. It currently has morning flights from Honolulu that run Friday, Saturday, and Sunday, and return via Molokai; daily afternoon flights through Molokai return directly to Honolulu. Morning and afternoon flights to Kahului go via Molokai or Honolulu.

Daily flights are available to and from Lanai by **Island Air,** tel. (808) 565-6744, (800) 652-6541 Neighbor Islands, or (800) 323-3345 Mainland. Using some jets and some turbo-props, Island Air flies to and from Honolulu 11 times daily, with three flights daily to/from Kahului, and once daily to Kona on the Big Island.

Lanai Airport is a practical little strip about four miles southwest of Lanai City, out near the remaining pineapple fields. The pleasing new terminal offers a departure lounge, gift shop, bathrooms, and public phones. If you are staying at any of the three hotels, a free shuttle will transport you into town and drop you at the appropriate place. Complimentary airport pickup can also be arranged with either of the two vehicle rental companies if you rent from them. Otherwise **Lanai City Service,** tel. (808) 565-7227, can taxi you into town for $5 per person.

By Boat

Expeditions, a passenger ferry, now plies daily between Lahaina and Manele Bay. No luxury transportation, this shuttle offers speedy and convenient alternative transportation to the island. The crossing takes less than one hour and the ferry leaves Manele Bay at 8 a.m., 10:30 a.m., 2 p.m., 4:30 p.m., and 6:45 p.m. From Lahaina's public loading pier, ferries leave at 6:45 a.m., 9:15 a.m., 12:45 p.m., 3:15 p.m., and 5:45 p.m. The adult fare is $25 one-way while children under 2-11 pay $20; *kama'aina* rates available. Luggage is taken free of charge, except for a $10 fee for bicycles. It's best to reserve a place. For information and reservations call (808) 661-3756 or (800) 695-2624, or write P.O. Box 10, Lahaina, HI 96767.

One other possibility for getting to Lanai is going by pleasure boat from Maui. These are basically tour boats specializing in snorkeling, dinner cruising, whalewatching, and the like, but they may be willing to drop you off and pick you up at a later date. It's an enjoyable way of going. As there are no fixed rates for this service, you'll have to make your own arrangements with the boat captains, most berthed at Lahaina Harbor. Remember that, in effect, you're going standby with these companies, but there is generally room for one more. This alternative is particularly attractive to campers, as they anchor on Lanai at Manele Bay, just a five-minute walk from the campsites at Hulopoe. One company to try is Trilogy, tel. (808) 661-4743 or 565-2387 on Lanai. Another outfit is Club Lanai, tel. (808) 871-1144, but it anchors at its own private beach on very remote east Lanai, with no way of getting anywhere except by a long and dusty hike.

GETTING AROUND

Taxi and Shuttle Transportation

No public bus transportation operates on Lanai, but **Lanai City Service,** tel. (808) 565-7227, or 565-9553 after hours, operates a free airport limousine service if you're renting a car/jeep from them. Otherwise the service to/from the airport to anywhere in Lanai City is $5 per person, and to Manele Bay, $12.50. The company also runs throughout the day from Lanai City to Manele Bay for $10, and from the bay to the

Manele Bay Hotel for $2.50. You can also call 7 a.m.-7 p.m. for service anywhere on Lanai.

Lanai Resort Shuttle

A free shuttle service is offered for guests of the two big resorts and Hotel Lanai. This bus runs daily 7 a.m.-11 p.m. every 30 minutes on the hour and half hour, and picks up passengers at the front of each hotel.

Car, 4WD, and Moped Rental

For a car, or better yet, a jeep, try **Lanai City Service, Dollar Rent A Car,** Lanai City, HI 96763, tel. (808) 565-7227 or (800) 533-7808. You'll be outfitted with wheels and given a drive guide with information about road conditions and where to go. Pay heed! Make sure to tell them your plans, especially if you're heading for a remote area. That way, if you have problems and don't return, they'll know where to send the rescue party! Lanai City Service is a subsidiary of Trilogy Excursions and has a franchise with Dollar Rent A Car. It rents compacts for $59 per day, midsize cars for $79, 4WDs (mostly Jeep Wranglers) for $119 per day, eight-passenger minivans for $129, and 15-passenger maxivans for $175 per day. They also may have a 2WD "hunter's truck" pickup for $145, but check before arrival on the island. Ask about the weekly, monthly, and *kama'aina* rates. No insurance is available for vehicles rented on Lanai. In case of trouble, cellular phones can be rented for $5 a day and the use charge is $1.50 a minute; arrange one at the counter when renting your vehicle. Lanai City Service offers free shuttle service to and from the airport if you rent with them.

For those who just need to zip around town for the day or a set of wheels to get to Hulopoe Beach, mopeds are also available from Lanai City Service at $30 a day, including a helmet.

Red Rover rents four different types of Defender 90 Land Rovers for your off-road pleasure, from four-seater open cabs to a nine-passenger safari van. Rates run $119-159 per vehicle per day. Most have manual transmission, some have hard tops, luggage racks, and/or air conditioning. Each also comes with a tool kit, a winch, and a two-way radio and cell phone (rates apply) that you can use to contact others in your party or call for help if you really get stuck. They'll send out a rescue party. Music tapes, snorkel gear, body boards, and surfboards are also offered free for the use, as is the advice about where to go to use them. The company will pick you up and drop you off at the airport or harbor, or deliver the vehicle to anywhere on the island. For more information, contact Red Rover, Inc., P.O. Box 464, Lanai City, HI 96763, tel. (808) 565-7722, fax 565-7377, or cell phone 565-1155.

Using a 4WD Rental

With only 30 miles of paved road on Lanai and rental cars firmly restricted to these, there is no real reason to rent one. The *real* adventure spots of Lanai require a 4WD vehicle, which on Lanai is actually useful and not just a yuppie showpiece, since mind-boggling spots on Lanai are reachable only on foot or by 4WD. Unfortunately, even the inveterate hiker will have a tough time because the best trailheads are quite a distance from town, and you'll spend as much time getting to them as hiking the actual trails.

Many people who have little or no experience driving 4WDs are under the slap-happy belief that they are unstoppable. Oh, that it were true! They do indeed get stuck, and it's usually miserable getting them unstuck. The rental agencies will give you up-to-the-minute info on the road conditions and a fairly accurate map for navigation. They tend to be a bit conservative on where they advise you to take "their" vehicles, but they also live on the island and are accustomed to driving off-road, which balances out their conservative estimates. Also, remember that road conditions change rapidly: a hard rain on the Munro Trail can change it from a flower-lined path to a nasty quagmire, or wind might lay a tree across a beach road. Keep your eye on the weather, and if in doubt don't push your luck. If you get stuck, you'll not only ruin your outing

and have to hike back to town, but you'll also be charged for a service call, which can be astronomical, especially if it's deemed to be due to your negligence. Most of your off-road driving will be in *compound* 4WD: first gear, low range.

Sightseeing Tours

Personalized escorted van tours to various spots on the island can be arranged by Lanai City Service, tel. (808) 565-7227. Since the tours are changeable, it's best to call in advance to get the rates and times. One of the best is the **4X4 Van Tour.** Departing weekdays around 7:45 a.m., it returns at 1:30 p.m. and shows you around town and many of the sights of the island including the Munro Trail, Shipwreck Beach, and Garden of the Gods. The rate is $79 per person, including a continental breakfast, lunch, and snacks as you go. If you are unsure about driving off-road or may not want to rent a jeep for the out-of-the-way places, leave the driving to the professionals. It can be a good deal.

Uncle Sam Shin also does a personalized tour, arranged through Lanai City Service, which can be adjusted to your liking. These usually last about four hours and run $80 per person.

Hitchhiking

Like everywhere else in Hawaii, hitching is technically illegal, but the islanders are friendly and quite good about giving you a lift. Lanai, however, is a workers' island, and the traffic is really skimpy during the day. You can only reasonably expect to get a ride from Lanai City to the airport or to Manele Bay since both are on paved roads and frequented by normal island traffic, or to Shipwreck Beach on the weekends. There is only a very slim chance of picking up a ride farther afield, toward the Garden of the Gods or Kaunolu, for example, so definitely don't count on it.

EXPLORING LANAI

LANAI CITY

Lanai City (pop. 2,800) would be more aptly described and sound more appealing if it were called Lanai Village. A utilitarian town, it was built in the 1920s by Dole Pineapple Company. The architecture, field-worker plain, has definitely gained "character" in the last 70 years. It's an excellent spot for a town, sitting at 1,600 feet in the shadow of Lanaihale, the island's tallest peak. George Munro's Cook pines have matured and now give the entire town a green, shaded, park-like atmosphere. It's cool and breezy—a great place to launch from in the morning and a welcome spot to return to at night. Most visitors head out of town to the more spectacular sights and never take the chance to explore the back streets.

Houses

As you'd expect, most houses are square boxes with corrugated roofs, but each has its own personality. Painted every color of the rainbow, they'd be garish in any other place, but here they break the monotony and seem to work. The people of Lanai used to make their living from the land and can still work wonders with it. Around many homes are colorful flowerbeds, green gardens bursting with vegetables, fruit trees, and flowering shrubs. When you look down the half-dirt, broken-pavement roads at a line of these houses, you can't help feeling that a certain nobility exists here. The houses are mud-spattered where the rain splashes red earth against them, but inside you know they're sparkling clean. Some modern suburban homes sprawl on the south end of town. Most of these belong to Lanai's miniature middle class and would fit unnoticed in any up-and-coming neighborhood on another island. On the north edge of town are few new apartments and multi-family buildings, and on the slope above town are the townhouses and luxury homes that will over the years become more predominant if development goes as planned.

Around Town

Lanai City streets running east-west are numerical starting with 3rd Street and running to 13th Street; the streets running north-south have alphabetical first letters and include Fraser, Gay, Houston, Ilima, Jackaranda, Koele, and Lanai Avenues, with a few more streets beyond this central grid, mostly new residential areas. If you manage to get lost in Lanai City you should seriously consider never leaving home.

Downtown

If you sit on the steps of Hotel Lanai and peer across its huge front yard, you can scrutinize the heart of downtown Lanai City. Off to your right are the offices of the Lanai Company sitting squat and solid. In front of them, forming a type of town square, is Dole Park where old-timers come to sit and young mothers bring their kids for some fresh air. No one in Lanai City rushes to do anything. Look around and you'll discover a real fountain of youth: the many octogenarians walk with a spring in their step. Years of hard work without being hyper or anxious is why they say they're still around. The park is surrounded by commercial Lanai. There's nowhere to *go* except over to the schoolyard to play some tennis or to Cavendish Golf Course for a round of nine holes. Lanai City has a movie theater, and its now showing pictures once again. You can plop yourself at the Blue Ginger Cafe or Tanigawa's for coffee, or stay in the park if you're in the mood to strike up a conversation—it won't take long.

Meander down Lanai Avenue past a complex of former agricultural buildings and shops. Once full of heavy equipment, this is where Lanai showed its raw plantation muscle. It has now been tamed and is the site of a new senior citizen's housing complex. Beyond the commercial buildings on both sides of the downtown park are the rows of plantation houses, now with newer subdivisions farther to each end. Do yourself a favor—get out of your rental car and walk around town for at least 30 minutes. You'll experience one of the most unique villages in America.

MUNRO TRAIL

The highlight of visiting Lanai is climbing the Munro Trail to its highest point, Lanaihale (3,370 feet), locally called **The Hale.** As soon as you set foot on Lanai the silhouette of this razorback ridge with its bristling coat of Cook pines demands your attention. Set off for The Hale and you're soon engulfed in its cool stands of pines, eucalyptus, and ironwoods, all colored with ferns and wildflowers. George Munro, a New Zealander hired as the manager of the Lanai Ranch a short time before Jim Dole's arrival, is responsible. With a pouch full of seeds and clippings from his native New Zealand, he trudged all over Lanai planting, in an attempt to foliate the island and create a permanent watershed. Driven by that basic and primordial human desire to see things grow, he climbed The Hale time and again to renew and nurture his leafy progeny. Now, all benefit from his labors.

Getting There

There are two basic ways to go to The Hale, by foot or 4WD. Some local people go on horseback. Head out of town on Rt. 440 toward Shipwreck Beach. Make sure to start before 8 a.m.; cloud cover is common by early afternoon. After less than two miles, still on the Lanai City side of the mountains, take the first major gravel road to the right. In about one-quarter mile the road comes to a Y intersection—go left. You immediately start climbing and pass through a forested area past a series of gulches. Continue and the road forks; again bear left. Always stay on the more obviously traveled road. The side roads look muddy and overgrown and it's obvious which is the main one. Robert Frost would be disappointed.

The Trail

As you climb, you pass a profusion of gulches, great red wounds cut into Lanai's windward side. First comes deep and brooding **Maunalei (Mountain Lei) Gulch,** from where Lanai draws its water through a series of tunnels bored through the mountains. It's flanked by **Kuolanai Trail,** a rugged and dangerous footpath leading all the way to the coast. Next is **Hookio Gulch,** a battleground where Lanai's warriors were vanquished in 1778 by Kalaniopuu and his ferocious fighters from the Big Island. All that remains are a few room-size notches cut into the walls where the warriors slept and piled stones to be hurled at the invaders. After Hookio Gulch, a trail bears left, bringing you to the gaping mouth of **Hauola Gulch,** more than 2,000 feet deep. Keep your eyes peeled for axis deer, which seem to defy gravity and manage to cling and forage along the most unlikely and precipitous cliffs. Be very careful of your footing—even skilled Lanai hunters have fallen to their deaths in this area.

The jeep trail narrows on the ridge to little more than 100 feet across. On one side are the wild gulches, on the other the bucolic green, whorling fingerprints of the former pineapple fields. Along the trail you can munch strawberries, common guavas, and as many thimbleberries as you can handle. At the crest of The Hale, let your eyes pan the horizon to see all the main islands of Hawaii (except for Kauai). Rising from the height-caused mirage of a still sea is the hazy specter of Oahu to the north, with Molokai and Maui clearly visible just 10 miles distant. Haleakala, Maui's magical mountain, has a dominant presence viewed from The Hale. Sweep right to see Kahoolawe, bleak and barren, its body shattered by the bombs of the U.S. Navy, a victim of controversial war games. Eighty miles south of Kahoolawe is the Big Island, its mammoth peaks, Mauna Loa and Mauna Kea, looming like ethereal islands floating in the clouds.

Just past the final lookout is a sign for **Awehi Trail,** which leads left to Naha on the beach. It's extremely rough and you'll definitely need a 4WD in compound-low to get down. Follow the main road down past several more lookouts. Take either Hoike Road, which flattens out and joins with Rt. 44 just south of Lanai City, or head straight ahead and join the highway near where it heads down the hill to Manele Bay. If you have time for only one outing on Lanai or funds budgeted for only one day of 4WD rental, make sure to treat yourself to the unforgettable Munro Trail.

HEADING SOUTH

Joseph Kaliihananui was the last of the free Hawaiian farmers to work the land of Lanai. His great-grandson, Lloyd Cockett, still lives in Lanai City. Joseph made his home in the arid but fertile Palawai Basin, which was later bought by Jim Dole and turned into the heart of the pineapple plantation. Just south of Lanai City on Rt. 440 (Manele Road), the Palawai Basin is the crater of the extinct single volcano of which Lanai is formed. Joseph farmed sweet potatoes, which he traded for fish. He gathered his water in barrels from the dew that formed on his roof and from a trickling spring. His lands supported a few cattle among its now-extinct heavy stands of cactus. Here, too, Walter Murray Gibson attempted to begin a Mormon colony, which he later aborted, supposedly because of his outrage over the idea of polygamy. Nothing noteworthy remains of this colony, but high on a hillside overlooking Palawai are the Luahiwa Petroglyphs, considered to be some of the best-preserved rock hieroglyphics in Hawaii.

Luahiwa Petroglyphs

The route through the fields that leads to the petroglyphs is tough to follow, but the best recipe for success is being pointed in the right direction and adding a large dollop of perseverance. Heading south on Manele Road, look to your left for the back side of a triangular yield sign at Hoike Road. Hoike Road was once paved but has now disintegrated into gravel. After turning left onto Hoike, head straight toward a large water tank on the hill. You pass two round-bottomed irrigation ditches, easily spotted as they're always green with grass due to the water they carry. At the second ditch turn left and follow the road, keeping the ditch on your right. Proceed until you come to a silver water pipe about 12 inches in diameter. Follow this pipe as it runs along a hedgerow until you reach the third power pole. At the No Trespassing sign, bear left.

Follow this overgrown trail up the hill to the boulders on which appear the petroglyphs. The boulders are brownish-black and covered in lichen. Their natural arrangement resembles an oversize Japanese rock garden. Dotted on the hillside are sisal plants that look like bouquets of giant green swords. As you climb to the rocks be very careful of your footing—the ground is crumbly and the vegetation slippery. The boulders cover a three-acre area; most of the petroglyphs are found on the south faces of the rocks.

Some are hieroglyphics of symbolic circles, others are picture stories complete with canoes gliding under unfurled sails. Dogs snarl with their jaws agape, while enigmatic triangular stickmen try to tell their stories from the past. Equestrians gallop, showing that these stone picture-books were done even after the coming of the white man. The Luahiwa Petroglyphs are a very special spot where the ancient Hawaiians still sing their tales across the gulf of time.

Hulopoe and Manele Bays

Proceed south on Rt. 440 to Lanai's most salubrious spots, the twin bays of Manele and Hulopoe. At the crest of the hill, just past the milepost, you can look down on the white, inviting sands of Hulopoe to the right, and the rockier small boat harbor of Manele on the left. The island straight ahead is Kahoolawe, and on very clear days you might be able to glimpse the peaks of Hawaii's Mauna Loa and Mauna Kea. Manele Bay is a picture-perfect anchorage where a dozen or so small boats and yachts are tied up on any given day. Ferries from Maui drop off passengers here, and tour boats also tie up here. In the trees overlooking the harbor are a few picnic tables and a public bathroom. Manele and Hulopoe are a Marine Life Conservation District with the rules for fishing and diving prominently displayed on a large bulletin board at the entrance to Manele. Because of this, the area is superb for snorkeling, and you can often see a pod of spinner dolphins playing in the water. No boats are allowed within Hulopoe Bay except for Hawaiian outrigger canoes.

Hulopoe Bay offers very gentle waves and soothing, crystal-clear water. The beach is a beautiful expanse of white sand fringed by palms with a mingling of large boulders that really set it off. This is Lanai's official camping area, and six sites are available. All are well spaced, each with a picnic table and fire pit. A series of shower stalls made of brown plywood provides solar-heated water and just enough privacy, allowing your head and legs to protrude. After refreshing yourself you can fish from the rock promontories on both sides of the bay, or explore the tide pools on the left side of the bay out near the point. It's difficult to find a more wholesome and gentle spot anywhere in Hawaii.

Kaumalapau Harbor

A side trip to Kaumalapau Harbor might be in order. This manmade facility, which used to ship more than a million pineapples a day during peak harvest, was the only one of its kind in the world. Activity is now way down, with only one ferry a week on Thursday to deliver supplies. As you've probably already rented a vehicle, you might as well cover these few paved miles from Lanai City on Rt. 440 just to have a quick look. En route you pass Lanai's odoriferous garbage dump, which is a real eyesore. Hold your nose and try not to notice. The harbor facility itself is no-nonsense commercial, but the coastline is reasonably spectacular, with a glimpse of the island's dramatic sea cliffs. Also, this area has super-easy access to some decent fishing, right off the pier. An added bonus for making the trek to this lonely area is that it is one of the best places on Lanai from which to view the sunset, and you usually have it all to yourself.

KAUNOLU: KAMEHAMEHA'S GETAWAY

At the southwestern tip of Lanai is Kaunolu Bay. At one time, this vibrant fishing village surrounded Halulu Heiau, a sacred refuge where the downtrodden were protected by the temple priests who could intercede with the benevolent gods. Kamehameha the Great would escape Lahaina's blistering summers and come to these very fertile fishing waters with his loyal warriors. Some proved their valor to their great chief by diving from Kahekili's Leap, a manmade opening in the rocks 60 feet above the sea. The remains of more than 80 house sites and a smattering of petroglyphs dot the area. The last inhabitant was Ohua, elder brother of Joseph Kaliihananui, who lived in a grass hut just east of Kaunolu in Mamaki Bay. Ohua was entrusted by Kamehameha V to hide the *heiau* fish-god, Kuniki; old accounts by the area's natives say that he died because of mishandling this stone god. The natural power still emanating from Kaunolu is obvious, and you can't help feeling the energy that drew the Hawaiians to this sacred spot.

Getting There

Proceed south on Manele Road from Lanai City through Palawai Basin until it makes a hard bend to the left. Here, a sign points you to Manele Bay. Do not go left to Manele, but proceed straight and stay on the once-paved pineapple road. At a dip by a huge silver water pipe, go straight through the pineapple fields until another obvious dip at two orange pipes (like fire hydrants) on the left and right. Turn left here onto a rather small road. Follow the road left to a weatherworn sign that actually says "Kaunolu Road." This dirt track starts off innocently enough as it begins its plunge toward the sea. Only two miles long, the local folks consider it the roughest road on the island. It *is* a bone-cruncher, so take it super slow. Plot your progress against the lighthouse on the coast. This road is not maintained. Because of natural erosion, it may be too rugged for any vehicle to pass. Ask in town about its condition before attempting to proceed down. This area is excellent for spotting axis deer. The deer are nourished by *haole koa,* a green bush with a brown seed pod that you see growing along the road. This natural feed also supports cattle, but is not good for horses, causing the hair on their tails to fall out.

Kaunolu

The village site lies at the end of a long dry gulch that terminates at a rocky beach, suitable in times past as a canoe anchorage. This entire area is a mecca for archaeologists and anthropologists. The most famous was the eminent Dr. Kenneth Emory of the Bishop Museum; he filed an extensive research report on the area. At its terminus, the road splits left and right. Go right to reach a large *kiawe* tree with a rudimentary picnic table under it. Just in front of you is a large pile of nondescript rocks purported to be the ruined foundation of Kamehameha's house. Unbelievably, this sacred area has been trashed out by disrespectful and ignorant picnickers. Hurricane Iwa also had a hand in changing the face of Kaunolu, as its tremendous force hit this area head on and even drove large boulders from the sea onto the land. As you look around, the ones that have a whitish appearance were washed up on the shore by the fury of Iwa.

The villagers of Kaunolu lived mostly on the east bank and had to keep an ever-watchful eye on nature because the bone-dry gulch could suddenly be engulfed by flash floods. In the cen-

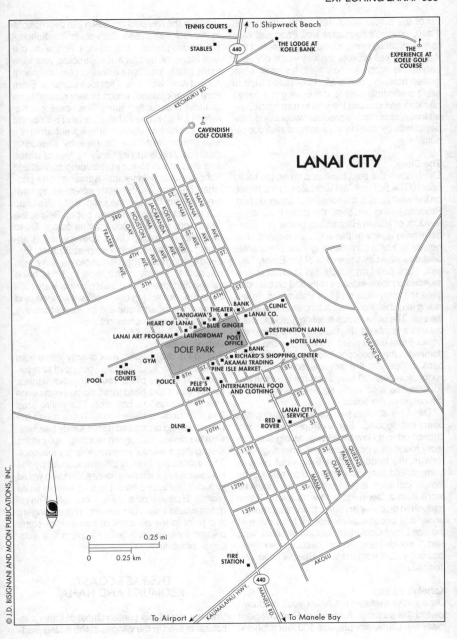

LANAI CITY

TENNIS COURTS
To Shipwreck Beach
STABLES
440
THE LODGE AT KOELE
Bank
THE EXPERIENCE AT KOELE GOLF COURSE
KEOMUKU RD.
CAVENDISH GOLF COURSE

3RD AVE.
FRASER AVE.
GAY AVE.
HOUSTON AVE.
JACARANDA AVE.
KOELE AVE.
IIIMA AVE.
MAHANA AVE.
NANI AVE.
LANAI AVE.
4TH AVE.
5TH AVE.
6TH ST.
ST.
ST.
ST.
ST.

THEATER
BANK
CLINIC
TANIGAWA'S
LANAI CO.
HEART OF LANAI
BLUE GINGER
DESTINATION LANAI
LANAI ART PROGRAM
LAUNDROMAT
POST OFFICE
HOTEL LANAI
PULANI DR.
DOLE PARK
BANK
GYM
RICHARD'S SHOPPING CENTER
AKAMAI TRADING
POOL
TENNIS COURTS
PINE ISLE MARKET
POLICE
8TH ST.
PELE'S GARDEN
INTERNATIONAL FOOD AND CLOTHING
9TH ST.
DLNR
10TH ST.
LANAI CITY SERVICE
RED ROVER
11TH ST.
QUEENS ST.
PALAWAI ST.
12TH ST.
OLAPA ST.
AHA ST.
MANA ST.
13TH ST.

0   0.25 mi
0   0.25 km
MOON

FIRE STATION
440
AKOLU ST.
To Airport
KAUMALAPAU HWY.
MANELE RD.
To Manele Bay

© J.D. BISIGNANI AND MOON PUBLICATIONS, INC.

ter of the gulch, about 100 yards inland, was **Paao,** the area's freshwater well. Paao was *kapu* to menstruating women, and it was believed that if the *kapu* was broken, the well would dry up. It served the village for centuries. It's totally obliterated now; in 1895 a Mr. Hayselden tried to erect a windmill over it, destroying the native caulking and causing the well to turn brackish—an example of Lanai's precious water being tampered with by outsiders, causing disastrous results.

The Sites

Climb down the east bank and cross the rocky beach. The first well-laid wall close to the beach on the west bank is the remains of a canoe shed. Proceed inland and climb the rocky bank to the remains of Halulu Heiau. Just below in the undergrowth is where the well was located. The *heiau* site has a commanding view of the area, best described by the words of Dr. Emory himself: "The point on which it is located is surrounded on three sides by cliffs and on the north rises the magnificent cliff of Palikaholo, terminating in Kahilikalani crag, a thousand feet above the sea. The ocean swell entering Kolokolo Cave causes a rumbling like thunder, as if under the *heiau.* From every point in the village the *heiau* dominates the landscape." As you climb the west bank, notice that the mortarless walls are laid up for more than 30 feet. If you have a keen eye you'll notice a perfectly square fire pit right in the center of the *heiau.*

This area still has treasures that have never been catalogued. For example, you might chance upon a Hawaiian lamp, as big and perfectly round as a basketball, with an orange-size hole in the middle where *kukui* nut oil was burned. Old records indicate that Kuniki, the temple idol itself, is still lying here face down no more than a few hundred yards away. If you happen to discover an artifact, do not remove it under any circumstance. Follow the advice of the late Lloyd Cockett, a *kapuna* of Lanai, who said, "I wouldn't take the rock because we Hawaiians don't steal from the land. Special rocks you don't touch."

Kahekili's Leap

Once you've explored the *heiau,* you'll be drawn toward the sea cliff. **Kaneapua Rock,** a giant tower-like chunk, sits perhaps 100 feet offshore.

Below in the tide pool are basin-like depressions in the rock-salt evaporation pools, the bottoms still showing some white residue. Follow the cliff face along the natural wall obstructing your view to the south. You'll see a break in the wall about 15 feet wide with a very flat rock platform. From here, **Shark Island,** which closely resembles a sharkfin, is perfectly framed. This opening is Kahekili's Leap, named after a Lanai chief, not the famous chief of Maui. Here, Kamehameha's warriors proved their courage by executing death-defying leaps into only 12 feet of water, and clearing a 15-foot protruding rock shelf. Scholars also believe that Kamehameha punished his warriors for petty offenses by sentencing them to make the jump. Kahekili's Leap is a perfect background for a photo. Below, the sea surges in unreal aquamarine colors. Off to the right is Kolokolo Cave, above which is another, even more daring leap at 90 feet. Evidence suggests that Kolokolo is linked to Kaunolu Gulch by a lava tube that has been sealed and lost. On the beach below Kahekili's Leap the vacationing chiefs played *konane,* and many stone boards can still be found from this game of Hawaiian checkers.

Petroglyphs

To find the petroglyphs, walk directly inland from Kaneapua Rock, using it as your point of reference. On a large pile of rocks are stick figures, mostly with a bird-head motif. Some heads even look like a mason's hammer. This entire area has a masculine feeling to it. There aren't the usual swaying palms and gentle sandy beaches. With the stones and rugged sea cliffs, you get the feeling that a warrior king would enjoy this spot. Throughout the area is *pili* grass, used by the Hawaiians to thatch their homes. Children would pick one blade and hold it in their fingers while reciting *"E pili e, e pili e, au hea kuu hale."* The *pili* grass would then spin around in their fingers and point in the direction of home. Pick some *pili* and try it yourself before leaving this wondrous, powerful area.

THE EAST COAST: KEOMUKU AND NAHA

Until the turn of this century, most of Lanai's inhabitants lived in the villages of the now-deserted east coast. Before the coming of Westerners, 2,000 or so Hawaiians lived along these shores, fishing and raising taro. It was as if they wanted to keep Maui in sight so that they didn't feel so isolated. Numerous *heiau* from this period still mark the ancient sites. The first white men also tried to make a go of Lanai along this stretch. The Maunalei Sugar Co. tried to raise sugarcane on the flat plains of Naha but failed and pulled up stakes in 1901—the last time that this entire coastline was populated to any extent. Today, the ancient *heiau* and a decaying church in Keomuku are the last vestiges of habitation, holding out against the ever-encroaching jungle. You can follow a jeep trail along this coast and get a fleeting glimpse of times past.

The shallow coastline that wraps around the north and east coast of Lanai opposes the shallow south coast of Molokai. Although many fewer than on that coast of Molokai, the majority of ancient fishponds of Lanai were located here and their remnants can still be seen. Because of the shallow nature of the water and its rocky bottom, swimming is not particularly good along most of this coast except for a few isolated sandy spots. In fact, the water cannot be seen well from the road most of the way to Naha because of the growth of trees and bushes along the beach. Numerous pullouts and shore access roads have been created, however, so you can get to the water. Unfortunately, inconsiderate visitors have left these pullouts a bit trashy with junk tossed to the ground rather than taken out.

Getting There

Approach Keomuku and Naha from one of two directions. The most straightforward is from north to south. Follow Rt. 440 (Keomuku Road) from Lanai City until it turns to dirt and branches right (south) at the coast, about a half hour. This road meanders for about 12 miles all the way to Naha, another one-half to one hour. Though the road is partial gravel and packed sand and not that rugged, you will need a 4WD in spots. Watch for washouts and fallen trees. It's paralleled by a much smoother route that runs along the beach part way down the coast, but it can only be used at low tide. Many small roads connect the two, so you can hop back and forth between them every 200-300 yards. Consider three tips: First, if you take the beach road, you can make good time and have a smooth ride, but could sail past most of the sights since you won't know when to hop back on the inland road; second, dry sand can easily bog down even a 4WD vehicle, making an expensive rescue mission for a tow truck, so be wise and only drive where sand is hard-packed; third, be careful of the *kiawe* trees—the tough, inch-long thorns can puncture tires as easily as nails.

The other alternative is to take Awehi Trail, a rugged jeep track, about halfway between Lopa and Naha. This trail leads up the mountain to the Munro Trail, but because of its ruggedness it's best to take it down from The Hale instead of up. A good long day of rattling in a jeep would take you along the Munro Trail, down Awehi Trail, then north along the coast back to Rt. 440. If you came south along the coast from Rt. 440, it would be better to retrace your steps instead of heading up Awehi. When you think you've suffered enough and have been bounced into submission by your jeep, remember that many of these trails were carved out by Juan Torqueza. He trailblazed alone on his bulldozer, unsupervised, and without benefit of survey. Now well into his 70s, he can be found in Dole Park in Lanai City, except when he's out here fishing.

Keomuku Village

There isn't much to see in Keomuku (Stretch of White) Village other than an abandoned Hawaiian church. This was the site of the Maunalei Sugar Co. The town was pretty much abandoned after 1901 when the sugar company ceased operations, and most all the decaying buildings were razed in the early 1970s. A few hundred yards north and south of the town site are examples of some original fishponds. They're tough to see (overgrown with mangrove), but a close observation gives you an idea of how extensive they once were. The **Hawaiian church** is worth a stop—it almost pleads to be photographed. From outside, you can see how frail it is, so if you go in, tread lightly. The altar area, a podium with a little bench, remains. A banner on the fading blue-green walls reads *"Ualanaano Jehova Kalanakila Malamalama,* October 4, 1903." Only the soft wind sounds where once strong voices sang vibrant hymns of praise.

A few hundred yards south of the church is a walking trail. Follow it inland to **Kahea Heiau** and a smattering of petroglyphs. This is the *heiau* disturbed by the sugarcane train; its desecration was believed to have caused the sweet water of Keomuku to turn brackish. The people of Keomuku learned to survive on the brackish water and kept a special jug of fresh water for visitors.

Heading South

Farther south a Japanese cemetery and monument were erected for the deceased workers who built **Halepaloa Landing,** from where the cane was shipped. Today, only rotting timbers and stonework remain, but the pier offers an excellent vantage point for viewing Maui, and it's a good spot to fish.

An island venture based on Maui called **Club Lanai,** tel. (808) 871-1144 or (800) 531-5262, has opened the remote east coast of Lanai to visitors. Its six acres of manicured beachfront property sit on one of the nicest stretches of sand, about halfway down the coast. Basically Club Lanai transports tourists from Maui aboard its boats to their its facility for a day of fun, games, and feasting.

The road continues past **Lopa,** ending at **Naha.** On the way, you'll pass several roads heading inland that lead to hunting areas. You also pass a few coconut groves. Legend says that one of these was cursed by a *kahuna*—if you climb a tree to get a coconut you will not be able to come down. Luckily, most tourists have already been cursed by "midriff bulge" and can't climb the tree in the first place. When you get to Naha check out the remnants of the paved Hawaiian walking trail before slowly heading back from this decaying historical area.

SHIPWRECK BEACH

Heading over the mountains from Lanai City to Shipwreck Beach offers you a rewarding scenario: an intriguing destination point with fantastic scenery and splendid panoramas on the way. Head north from Lanai City on Rt. 440 (Keomuku Road). In less than 10 minutes you crest the mountains, and if you're lucky the sky will be clear and you'll be able to see the phenomenon that guided ancient navigators to land: the halo of dark brooding clouds over Maui and Molokai, a sure sign of landfall. Shorten your gaze and look at the terrain in the immediate

vicinity. Here are the famous precipitous gulches of Lanai. The wounded earth bleeds red while offering patches of swaying grass and wildflowers. It looks like the canyons of Arizona have been dragged to the rim of the sea. As you wiggle your way down Keomuku Road, look left to see the rusting hull of a WW II Liberty Ship sitting on the shallow reef almost completely out of the water. For most, this derelict is the destination point on Shipwreck Beach.

The Beach

As you continue down the road, little piles of stones, usually three, sit atop a boulder. Although most are from modern times, these are called *ahu*, a traditional Hawaiian offering to ensure good fortune while traveling. Under no circumstances disturb them. Farther down, the lush grasses of the mountain slope disappear, and the scrub bush takes over. The pavement ends and the dirt road forks left (west) to Shipwreck Beach, or straight ahead (south) toward the abandoned town of Naha. If you turn left you'll be on an adequate sandy road, flanked on both sides by thorny, tire-puncturing *kiawe* trees. In less than a mile is a large open area to your right. If you're into unofficial camping, this isn't a bad spot for a one-night bivouac—the trees here provide privacy and an excellent windbreak against the constant strong ocean breezes. About two miles down the road is Federation Camp, actually a tiny village of unpretentious beach shacks built by Lanai's workers as "getaways" and fishing cabins. Charming in their humbleness and simplicity, they're made mostly from recycled timbers and boards that have washed ashore. Some have been worked on quite diligently and skillfully and are actual little homes, but somehow the rougher ones are more attractive. You can drive past the cabins for a few hundred yards, but to be on the safe side, park just past them and begin your walk.

Petroglyphs

At the very end of the road is a cabin that a local comedian has named the "Lanai Hilton." Just off to your left *(mauka)* are the ruins of a lighthouse. Look for a cement slab where two graffiti artists of bygone days carved their names: John Kupau and Kam Chee, Nov. 28, 1929. Behind the lighthouse ruins an arrow points you to

"The Bird Man of Lanai Petroglyphs." Of all the petroglyphs on Lanai these are the easiest to find; trail-marking rocks have been painted white by Lanai's Boy Scouts. Follow them to a large rock bearing the admonition Do Not Deface. Climb down the path with a keen eye—the rock carvings are small, most only about 10 inches tall. Little childlike stick figures, they have intriguing bird heads whose symbolic meaning has been lost.

Hiking Trail

The trail along the beach goes for eight long hot miles to Polihua Beach. That trip should be done separately, but at least walk as far as the Liberty Ship, about a mile from the cabins. The area has some of the best beachcombing in Hawaii; no telling what you might find. The most sought-after treasures are glass floats that have bobbed for thousands of miles across the Pacific, strays from Japanese fishnets. You might even see a modern ship washed onto the reef, like the Canadian yacht that went aground in the spring of 1984. Navigational equipment has improved, but Shipwreck Beach can *still* be a nightmare to any captain caught in its turbulent whitecaps and long ragged coral fingers. This area is particularly good for lobsters and shore fishing. And you can swim in shallow sandy-bottom pools to refresh yourself as you hike.

Try to time your return car trip over the mountain for sundown. The tortuous terrain, stark in black and white shadows, is awe-inspiring. The larger rocks are giant sentinels: it's easy to feel the power and attraction they held for the ancient Hawaiians. As you climb the road on the windward side with its barren and beaten terrain, the feelings of mystery and mystique attributed to spiritual Lanai are obvious. You come over the top and suddenly see the valley—manicured, rolling, soft, and verdant with pineapples and the few lights of Lanai City beckoning.

THE GARDEN OF THE GODS AND POLIHUA

The most ruggedly beautiful, barren, and inhospitable section of Lanai is out at the north end. After passing through a broad stretch of former pineapple fields, you come to Kanepu'u Preserve, the island's only nature reserve and best example of dryland forest. Just as you pop out the far side of the preserve, you reach the appropriately named Garden of the Gods. Waiting is a fantasia of otherworldly landscapes—barren red earth, convulsed ancient lava flows, tortured pinnacles of stone, and psychedelic striations of vibrating colors, especially moving at sunrise and sunset. Little-traveled trails lead to Kaena Point, a wasteland dominated by sea cliffs where adulterous Hawaiian wives were sent into exile for a short time in 1837. Close by is Lanai's largest *heiau,* dubbed Kaenaiki, so isolated and forgotten that its real name and function were lost even to Hawaiian natives by the middle of the 19th century. After a blistering, sun-baked, 4WD drubbing, you emerge at the coast on Polihua, a totally secluded, pure-white beach where sea turtles once came to bury their eggs in the natural incubator of its soft warm sands.

ROBERT NILSEN

Garden of the Gods

Getting There

Lanai doesn't hand over its treasures easily, but they're worth pursuing. To get to the Garden of the Gods you have to traverse the former pineapple field roads. Head for the Lodge at Koele, and turn right onto the road that runs between the tennis courts and the riding stable. After about one minute, the road turns right. Follow it, keeping the prominent ridge on your right. Proceed for about a half hour until you pass through the Kanepu'u dryland forest preserve. Along the way, you'll come to a sign pointing to Kaena Point; in a minute or so, a sign points to Kuamo'o. Shortly, a marker points you off to the right on Lapaiki Road. Proceed straight ahead to another marker pointing you down Awalua Trail to the right and Polihua straight ahead. Once out the back side of the preserve, you soon begin to see large boulders sitting atop packed red earth, the signal that you're entering the Garden of the Gods. It's about another half hour down to Polihua Beach, and on the way you'll find another marker for Kaena Road, which leads to magnificent sea cliffs and Kaenaiki Heiau.

Note: These roads are very confusing, and oftentimes the signs, due to heavy weather and vandalism, are missing. Check at the jeep rental office for up-to-the-minute road conditions and instructions. Definitely do not attempt the lower reaches of this road without 4WD.

Hiking

Anyone wishing to hike this area should drive to the end of the former pineapple fields. It's close to half the distance and the scenery is quite ordinary. Make sure to bring plenty of water and a windbreaker because the heavy winds blow almost continuously. Sturdy shoes and a sun hat are also needed. There is no official camping at Polihua Beach, but again, anyone doing so overnight probably wouldn't meet with any hassles.

Kanepu'u Preserve

Straddling the road leading to the Garden of the Gods, this 590-acre preserve is the best remaining example of dryland forest on Lanai and a sampling of what covered much of the lower leeward slopes of the Hawaiian Islands before the coming of man. In this forest you'll find *olopua,* a native olive tree, *lama,* a native ebony, *na'u,* Hawaiian gardenia, the *iliahi* sandalwood tree, and numerous other plant varieties, 49 species of which are found only in Hawaii, as well as many species of birds. Over the centuries, these dryland forests were reduced in size by fire, introduced animals, and the spread of nonnative weeds and trees. Erosion control measures, such as the planting of native shrubs and seeds, have been implemented to cover bare spots and fill contour scars. Under the care of the Nature Conservancy and local conservation groups, this forest and others like it are being protected.

As you pass through this preserve, stop at the self-guided loop trail to get a close-up look at some of the trees in the forest. It's about a 15-minute walk over level ground, if you stop and read the posted signs. Overlooking this trail and set on a nearby rise is Kanepu'u (Kane in Hill Form) Heiau.

Every month, guided hikes are offered through the preserve. Call (808) 565-7430 for more information about these hikes or general information about the preserve.

The Garden of the Gods

There, a shocking assault on your senses, is the bleak, red, burnt earth, devoid of vegetation, heralding the beginning of the garden—a Hawaiian Badlands. The flowers here are made of rock, the shrubs are the twisted crusts of lava, and trees are baked minarets of stone, all subtle shades of orange, purple, and sulfurous yellow. While most is obviously created by natural erosion, some piles of stone are just as obviously erected by man. The jeep trail has been sucked down by erosion and the garden surrounds you. While the beginning seems most dramatic, much more spreads out before you as you proceed down the hill. Stop many times to climb a likely outcropping and get a sweeping view. While you can't see Lanai's coastline from here, you do have a nice view of Molokai across the channel. The wind rakes these badlands and the silence penetrates to your soul. Although eons have passed, you can feel the cataclysmic violence that created this haunting and delicate beauty. The Garden of the Gods is perhaps best in the late afternoon when slanting sunlight enriches colors and casts shadows that create depth and mood.

Polihua Beach

Abruptly the road becomes smooth and flat. Straight ahead, like a mirage too bright for your eyes, an arch is cut into the green jungle, framing white sand and moving blue ocean. As you face the beach, to the right it's flat, expansive, and the sands are white, but the winds are heavy; if you hiked eight miles, you'd reach Shipwreck Beach. More interesting is the view to the left, which has a series of lonely little coves. The sand is brown and coarse and large black lava boulders are marbled with purplish-gray rock embedded in long, faulted seams. Polihua is not just a destination point where you come for a quick look. It takes so much effort coming and going that you should plan on having a picnic and a relaxing afternoon before heading back through the Garden of the Gods and its perfectly scheduled sunset light show.

HAWAII STATE ARCHIVES

MOLOKAI
INTRODUCTION

Molokai is a sanctuary, a human time capsule where the pendulum swings inexorably forward, but more slowly than in the rest of Hawaii. It has always been so. In ancient times, Molokai was known as Pule-oo, "Powerful Prayer," where its supreme chiefs protected their small underpopulated refuge, not through legions of warriors but through the chants of their *kahuna*. This powerful, ancient mysticism, handed down directly from the goddess Pahulu, was known and respected throughout the archipelago. Its mana was the oldest and strongest in Hawaii, and its practitioners were venerated by nobility and commoners alike—they had the ability to "pray you to death." The entire island was a haven, a refuge for the vanquished and *kapu*-breakers of all the islands. It's still so today, beckoning to determined escapees from the rat race!

The blazing lights of supermodern Honolulu can easily be seen from western Molokai, while Molokai as viewed from Oahu is fleeting and ephemeral, appearing and disappearing on the horizon. The island is home to the largest number of Hawaiians. In effect it is a tribal homeland: more than 3,000 of the island's 6,700 inhabitants have more than 50% Hawaiian blood and, except for Niihau, it's the only island where they are the majority. The 1920s Hawaiian Homes Act allowed *kuleana* of 40 acres to anyone with more than 50% Hawaiian ancestry. *Kuleana* owners form the grassroots organizations that fight for Hawaiian rights and battle the colossal forces of rabid developers who have threatened Molokai for decades.

AN OVERVIEW

Kaunakakai and West
Kaunakakai, the island's main town, once looked like a Hollywood sound stage where Jesse James or Wyatt Earp would feel right at home. The town is flat, with few trees, and three blocks long. Ala Malama, its main shopping street, is lined with false-front stores; pickup trucks are parked in front where horses and buggies ought

to be. To the west are the prairie-like plains of Molokai, some sections irrigated and now planted in profitable crops. The northern section of the island contains **Palaau State Park,** where a campsite is always easily found, and **Phallic Rock,** a natural shrine where island women came to pray for fertility. Most of the west end is owned by the mammoth 54,000-acre **Molokai Ranch.** Part of its lands supports several thousand head of cattle and herds of axis deer imported from India in 1867.

The 40-acre *kuleana* are here, as well as abandoned Dole and Del Monte pineapple fields. The once-thriving pineapple company towns of **Maunaloa** and **Kualapuu** are now semi-ghost towns since the pineapple companies pulled up stakes in 1975. Undergoing a massive face-lift, Maunaloa is holding on as the ranch is expanding its operations to include more tourism-related activities. The Kualapuu area now produces coffee and attracts its scattered Filipino workers mostly on weekends, when they come to unofficially test their best cocks in the pit. Look for the small A-frame shelters in yards here that house these creatures.

On the western shore is the Kaluakoi Resort and a handful of condos perched above the island's best beaches. Here, 6,700 acres sold by the Molokai Ranch to the Louisiana Land and Exploration Company and later sold to another concern are slowly being developed as homesites. Already there are houses scattered here and there. This area, rich with the finest archaeological sites on the island, is a hotbed of contention between developers and preservationists. The Kaluakoi Resort with its hotel, condominiums, and golf course, however, is often pointed to as a well-planned development, a kind of model compromise between the factions. Its low Polynesian-style architecture blends well with the surroundings and is not a high-rise blight on the horizon.

The East Coastal Road
Highway 450 is a magnificent coastal road running east from Kaunakakai to Halawa Valley. A slow drive along this writhing country thoroughfare rewards you with easily accessible beach parks, glimpses of fishponds, *heiau,* wildlife sanctuaries, and small one-room churches strung along the road like rosary beads. Almost every mile has a historical site, like the **Smith and Bronte Landing Site** where two pioneers of trans-Pacific flight ignominiously alighted in a mangrove swamp, and **Paikalani Taro Patch,** the only one from which Kamehameha V would eat poi.

On Molokai's eastern tip is **Halawa Valley,** a real gem accessible by car. This pristine gorge has a series of waterfalls and their pools, and a beach park where the valley meets the sea. The majority of the population of Halawa moved out in 1946 when a 30-foot tsunami washed their homes away and mangled their taro fields, leaving a thick salty residue. Today only a handful of mostly alternative lifestylers live in the valley among the overgrown stone walls that once marked the boundaries of manicured and prosperous family gardens. Just south on the grounds of Puu O Hoku Ranch is **Kalanikaula,** the sacred *kukui* grove of Lanikaula, Molokai's most powerful *kahuna* of the classic period. This grove was planted at his death and became the most sacred spot on Molokai. Today the trees are dying.

The Windward Coast
Kalaupapa (Flat Leaf) is a lonely peninsula formed by lava flow from the 400-foot-high Kauhako Crater, the highest spot on this relatively flat nub of land. Kalaupapa leper colony, completely separated from the world by a hostile pounding surf and a precipitous 1,600-foot *pali,* is a modern story of human dignity. Kalaupapa was a howling charnel house where the unfortunate victims of leprosy were banished to die. Here humanity reached its lowest ebb of hopelessness, violence, and depravity, until one tiny flicker of light arrived in 1873—Joseph de Veuster, a Belgian priest known throughout Hawaii as Father Damien. In the greatest example of pure *aloha* yet established on Hawaii, he became his brothers' keeper. Tours of Kalaupapa operated by well-informed former patients are enlightening and educational.

East of Kalaupapa along the windward (northeast) coast is a series of amazingly steep and isolated valleys. The inhabitants moved out at the beginning of this century except for one pioneering family that returned a few years ago to carve out a home. Well beyond the farthest reaches of the last road, this emerald-green

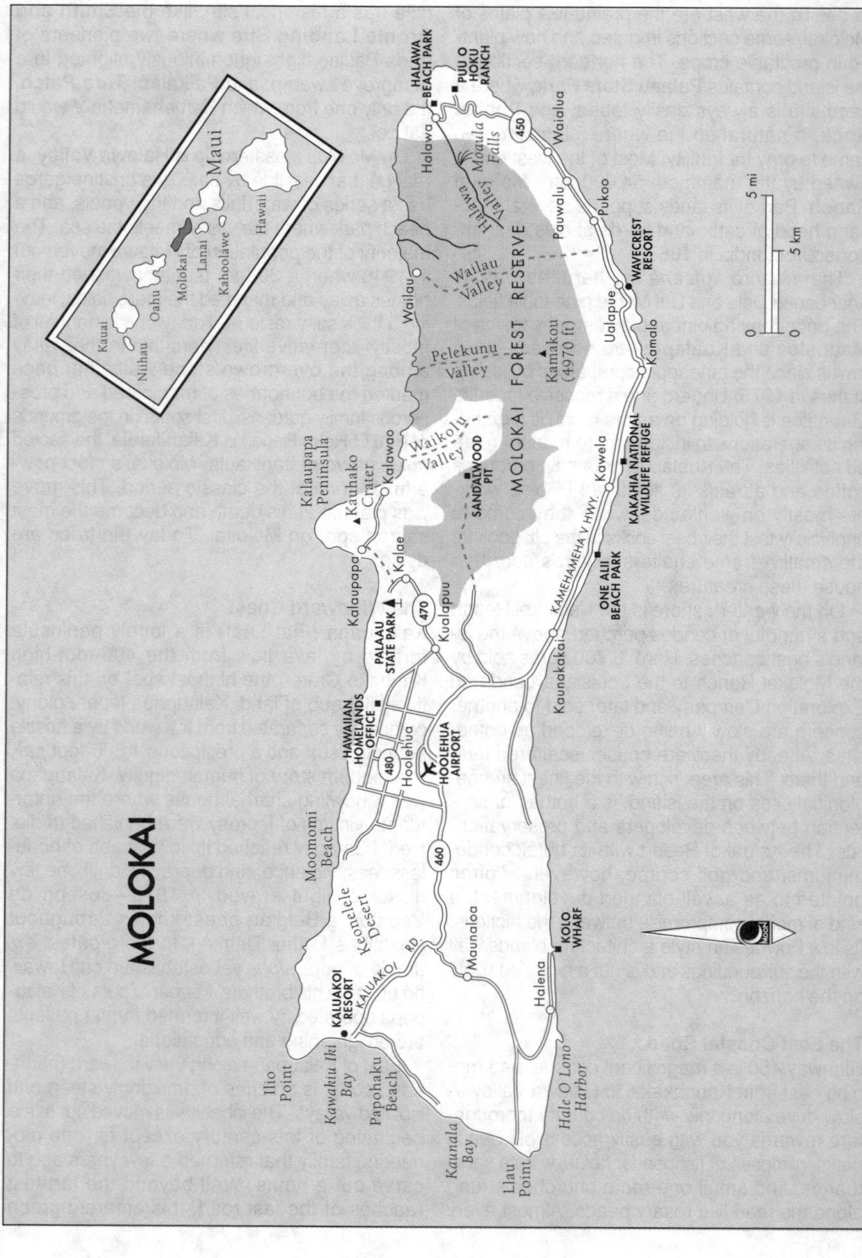

MOLOKAI

Maui
Kauai
Niihau
Oahu
Molokai
Lanai
Kahoolawe
Hawaii

Ilio Point
Kawakiu Iki Bay
Papohaku Beach
KALUAKOI RESORT
Kaunala Bay
Llau Point
Hale O Lono Harbor
Halena
KOLO WHARF
Maunaloa
KALUAKOI RD
Keonelele Desert
Moomomi Beach
HAWAIIAN HOMELANDS OFFICE
Hoolehua
HOOLEHUA AIRPORT
480
460
470
Kualapuu
PALAAU STATE PARK
Kalaupapa
Kalaupapa Peninsula
Kalae
Kauhako Crater
Kalawao

Waikolu Valley
SANDALWOOD PIT
MOLOKAI FOREST RESERVE
Pelekunu Valley
Wailau Valley
Kamakou (4970 ft)
Wailau
KAMEHAMEHA V HWY
Kaunakakai
ONE ALII BEACH PARK
Kawela
KAKAHIA NATIONAL WILDLIFE REFUGE
Kamalo
Ualapue
WAVECREST RESORT
Pukoo
Pauwalu
Waialua
450
Moaula Falls
Halawa Valley
Halawa
HALAWA BEACH PARK
PUU O HOKU RANCH

5 mi
5 km
0

primeval world awaits. The *pali* here mark the tallest sea cliffs in the world (although some dispute this designation), with an "average incline of more than 55 degrees." Many spots are far steeper. About halfway down the coast near Umilehi Point, the cliffs are at their highest at 3,300 feet. Farther to the east and diving headfirst out of a hanging valley is **Kahiwa (Sacred One) Falls,** the highest in Hawaii at 1,750 feet. You get here only by helicopter excursion, by boat in the calmer summer months, or by foot over dangerous and unkempt mountain trails. For now, Molokai remains a sanctuary, reminiscent of the Hawaii of simpler times. Around it the storm of modernity rages, but still the "Friendly Island" awaits those willing to venture off the beaten track.

THE LAND

With 260 square miles, Molokai is the fifth largest Hawaiian island. Its western tip, at Ilio Point, is a mere 22 miles from Oahu's eastern tip, Makapuu Point. Resembling a jogging shoe, Molokai is about 38 miles from heel to toe and 10 miles from laces to sole, totaling 166,425 acres, with just over 88 miles of coastline. Most of the arable land on the island is owned by the 54,000-acre Molokai Ranch, primarily on the western end, and the 14,000-acre Puu O Hoku Ranch on the eastern end. Molokai was formed by three distinct shield volcanoes. Two linked together to form Molokai proper, and a later eruption formed the flat Kalaupapa Peninsula.

Physical Features

Although Molokai is rather small, it has a great deal of geographical diversity. Western Molokai is dry with rolling hills, natural pastures, and a maximum elevation of only 1,381 feet. The eastern sector of the island has heavy rainfall, the tallest sea cliffs in the world, and craggy narrow valleys perpetually covered in a velvet cloak of green mosses. Viewed from the sea it looks like a 2,000-foot vertical wall from surf to clouds, with tortuously deep chasms along the coastline. Mount Kamakou is the highest peak on Molokai, at 4,961 feet. The south-central area is relatively swampy, while the west and especially northwest coasts around Moomomi have rolling sand dunes. Papohaku Beach, just below the Kaluakoi Resort on western Molokai, is one of the most massive white-sand beaches in Hawaii. A controversy was raised when it was discovered that huge amounts of sand were dredged from this area and hauled to Oahu; the Molokai Ranch was pressured and the dredging ceased. A hefty section of land in the north-central area is a state forest where new species of trees are planted on an experimental basis. The 240-acre Palaau State Park is in this cool upland forested area.

East Molokai Mountains

ROBERT NILSEN

MOLOKAI TEMPERATURE AND RAINFALL

	JAN.	MARCH	MAY	JUNE	SEPT.	NOV.
High	79	79	81	82	82	80
Low	61	63	68	70	68	63
Rain	4	3	0	0	0	2

Note: Temperature is expressed in degrees Fahrenheit; rainfall in inches.

Manmade Marvels

Two manmade features on Molokai are engineering marvels. One is the series of ancient fishponds strung along the south shore like pearls on a string—best seen from the air as you approach the island by plane. Dozens still exist, but the most amazing is the enormous **Keawanui Pond,** covering 54 acres and surrounded by a three-foot-tall, 2,000-foot-long wall. The other is the modern **Kualapuu Reservoir** completed in 1969. The world's largest rubber-lined reservoir, it can hold 1.4 billion gallons of water. Part of its engineering dramatics is the Molokai Tunnel, which feeds it with water from the eastern valleys. The tunnel is eight feet tall, eight feet wide, and almost 27,000 feet (five miles) long.

Climate

The average island temperature is 75-85° F (24° C). The yearly average rainfall is 30 inches; the east receives a much greater percentage than the west.

FLORA AND FAUNA

Land animals on Molokai were brought by man: pigs, goats, axis deer, and cattle. The earliest arrival still extant in the wild is the *pua'a* (pig). Molokai's pigs live in the upper wetland forests of the northeast, but they can actually thrive anywhere. Hunters say the meat from pigs that have lived in the lower dry forest is superior to those that acquire the muddy taste of ferns from the wetter upland areas. Pigs on Molokai are hunted mostly with the use of dogs who pin them by the ears and snout while the hunter approaches on foot and skewers them with a long knife.

Offspring from a pair of **goats** left by Captain Cook on the island of Niihau spread to all the islands; they were very well adapted to life on Molokai. Originally from the arid Mediterranean, goats could live well without any surface water, a condition quite prevalent over most of Molokai. They're found primarily in the mountainous area of the northeast.

The last free-roaming arrivals to Molokai were **axis deer.** Molokai's deer came from the upper reaches of the Ganges River, sent to Kamehameha V by Dr. William Hillebrand while on a botanical trip to India in 1867. Kamehameha V sent some of the first specimens to Molokai, where they prospered. Today they are found mostly on western Molokai, though some travel the south coast to the east.

The island is unique in that it harbors a wildlife park on the grounds of the Molokai Ranch. This park has several hundred animals mostly imported from the savannas of Africa. Who knows? Perhaps in a few thousand years after some specimens have escaped there might be such a thing as a "Molokai giraffe" that will look like any other giraffe except that its markings resemble flowers. This sanctuary is now closed to the public, but the ranch still takes seriously its responsibility for the health and well-being of these animals.

Birdlife

A few of Hawaii's endemic birds can be spotted by a determined observer at various locales around Molokai. They include: the Hawaiian petrel (*ua'u*); Hawaiian coot (*alae ke'oke'o*), prominent in Hawaiian mythology; Hawaiian stilt (*ae'o*), a wading bird with ridiculous stick legs that protects its young by feigning wing injury and luring predators away from the nest; and the Hawaiian owl *(pueo),* a bird that helps in its own demise by being easily approached. Molokai has a substantial number of introduced game birds that attract hunters throughout the year.

The nonprofit organization **Nene O Molokai** operates a facility that breeds, releases, and monitors the state bird, the *nene.* Located about four miles east of Kaunakakai, they offer free tours but you must make an appointment to visit. To learn more about these friendly geese, call (808) 553-5992 or visit their website at www .aloha.net/~nene.

Flora

The *kukui* or candlenut tree is common to all the Hawaiian Islands; along with being the official state tree, its tiny white blossom is Molokai's flower. The *kukui,* introduced centuries ago by the early Polynesians, grows on lower mountain slopes and can easily be distinguished by its pale green leaves.

Conservation Controversy

It has long been established and regretted that introduced animals and plants have destroyed Hawaii's delicate natural balance leading to the extinction of many of its rare native species. A number of well-meaning groups and organizations are doing their best to preserve Hawaii habitat, but they don't always agree on the methods employed. Feral pigs, indiscriminate in their relentless hunt for food, are ecological nightmares that virtually bulldoze the rainforest floor into fetid pools and gouged earth where mosquitoes and other introduced species thrive while driving out the natives. Molokai's magnificent Kamakou Preserve, Upper Pelekunu, and Central Molokai Ridges are the last remaining pockets of natural habitat on the island. The Kamakou Preserve, 2,774 pristine acres, is covered, like the others, in ohia forest, prime habitat for the almost-extinct *oloma'o* (Molokai thrush), *kakawahie* (creeper), and the hearty but beleaguered *apapane* and *amakihi.* No one disagrees that the wild boar must be managed to protect these areas, but they do not agree on *how* they should be managed. The Nature Conservancy in its dedication to preserving the rainforest backed a policy to snare the wild boar, maintaining that this was the best possible way of eliminating these pests while placing the forest under the

least amount of stress. In opposition to the practice of snaring is Pono, a local organization of native Molokai hunters that maintains snaring pigs is inhumane, causing the animals to starve to death or to die slowly from strangulation. Pono also abhors the wasting of the meat, and the indiscriminate killing of sows, the future of pigs on Molokai.

Aside from the **Kamakou Preserve,** the Nature Conservancy also maintains 5,714 acres of the Pelekunu Valley on the remote north coast of the island, where there is no public access. There is periodic access, however, to the **Moomomi Preserve,** a 921-acre area of sand dunes west of Moomomi Beach that is safe harbor for several species of endangered plants, seabirds, and green sea turtles.

Another grassroots group, **Na Ala Hele,** with branches on all islands, is dedicated to opening the ancient and extensive Hawaiian trail and access system. As part of its lobbying to open these trails, many of which now cross private property, it is trying to free landowners from any liability for those walking over the trails. So far the progress has been very slow.

HISTORY

The oral chant *"Molokai nui a Hina . . ."* ("Great Molokai, child of Hina") refers to Molokai as the island-child of the goddess Hina and the god Wakea, male progenitor of all the islands; Papa, Wakea's first wife, left him in anger as a result of this unfaithfulness. Hina's cave, just above Kaluaaha on the southeast coast, can still be visited and has been revered as a sacred spot for countless centuries. Another ancient spot, Halawa Valley, on the eastern tip of Molokai, is considered one of the oldest settlements in Hawaii. As research continues, settlement dates are pushed farther back, but for now scholars agree that early wayfarers from the Marquesas Islands settled Halawa in the mid-seventh century.

Molokai, from earliest times, was revered and feared as a center for mysticism and sorcery. **Ili'ili'opae Heiau** was renowned for its powerful priests whose incantations were mingled with the screams of human sacrifice. Commoners avoided Ili'ili'opae, and even powerful *kahuna* could not escape its terrible power. One, Kamalo, lost his sons as sacrifices at the *heiau* for their desecration of the temple drum. Kamalo sought revenge by invoking the help of his personal god, the terrible shark deity Kauhuhu. After the proper prayers and offerings, Kauhuhu sent a flash flood to wipe out Mapulehu Valley where Ili'ili'opae was located. All perished except for Kamalo and his family, who were protected by a sacred fence around their home.

This tradition of mysticism reached its apex with the famous Lanikaula, "Prophet of Molokai." During the 16th century, Lanikaula lived near Halawa Valley and practiced his arts, handed down by the goddess Pahulu, who predated even Pele. Pahulu was the goddess responsible for the "old ocean highway," which passed between Molokai and Lanai and led to Kahiki, lost homeland of all the islanders. Lanikaula practiced his sorcery in the utmost secrecy and even buried his excrement on an offshore island so that a rival *kahuna* could not find and burn it, which would surely cause his death. Hawaiian oral history does not say why Kawelo, a sorcerer from Lanai and a friend of Lanikaula, came to spy on Lanikaula and observed him hiding his excrement. Kawelo burned it in the sacred fires, and Lanikaula knew that his end was near. Lanikaula ordered his sons to bury him in a hidden grave so that his enemies could not find his bones and use their mana to control his spirit. To further hide his remains, he had a *kukui* grove planted over his body. **Kalanikaula** (Sacred Grove of Lanikaula) is still visible today, though most of the trees appear to be dying.

Western Contacts

Captain James Cook first spotted Molokai on November 26, 1778, but because it looked bleak and uninhabited he decided to bypass it. It wasn't until eight years later that Capt. George Dixon sighted the island and decided to land. Very little was recorded in his ship's log about this first encounter, and Molokai slipped from the attention of the Western world until Protestant missionaries arrived at Kaluaaha in 1832 and reported the native population at approximately 6,000.

In 1790 Kamehameha the Great came from the Big Island as a suitor seeking the hand of Keopuolani, a chieftess of Molokai. Within five years he returned again, but this time there was no merrymaking: he came as a conquering em-

peror on his thrust westward to Oahu. His war canoes landed at Pakuhiwa Battleground, a bay just a few miles east of Kaunakakai; it's said that warriors lined the shores for more than four miles. The grossly outnumbered warriors of Molokai fought desperately, but even the incantations of their *kahuna* were no match for Kamehameha and his warriors. Inflamed with recent victory and infused with the power of their horrible war-god Ku ("of the Maggot-dripping Mouth"), they slaughtered the Molokai warriors and threw their broken bodies into a sea so filled with sharks that their feeding frenzy made the waters appear to boil. Thus subdued, Molokai slipped into obscurity once again as its people turned to a quiet life of farming and fishing.

Molokai Ranch

Molokai remained almost unchanged until the 1850s. The Great Mahele of 1848 provided for private ownership of land, and giant tracts were formed into the Molokai Ranch. About 1850, German immigrant Rudolph Meyer came to Molokai and married a high chieftess named Dorcas Kalama Waha. Together they had 11 children, with whose aid he turned the vast lands of the Molokai Ranch into productive pastureland. A man of indomitable spirit, Meyer held public office on Molokai and became the island's unofficial patriarch. He managed Molokai Ranch for the original owner, Kamehameha V, and remained manager until his death in 1897, by which time the ranch was owned by the Bishop Estate. In 1875, Charles Bishop had bought half of the 70,000 acres of Molokai Ranch, and his wife, Bernice, a Kamehameha descendant, inherited the remainder. In 1898, the Molokai Ranch was sold to businessmen in Honolulu for $251,000. This consortium formed the American Sugar Co., but after a few plantings the available water on Molokai turned brackish and once again Molokai Ranch was sold. Charles Cooke bought controlling interest from the other businessmen in 1908 and remained in control of the ranch until 1988 when it was sold to Brierly Investments, a business concern from New Zealand.

Changing Times

Very little happened for a decade after Charles Cooke bought the Molokai Ranch from his partners. Molokai did become famous for its honey production, supplying a huge amount to the world up until WW I. During the 1920s, political and economic forces greatly changed Molokai. In 1921, Congress passed the **Hawaiian Homes Act,** which set aside 43,000 acres on the island for people who had at least 50% Hawaiian blood. By this time, however, all agriculturally productive land in Hawaii had already been claimed. The land given to the Hawaiians was very poor and lacked adequate water. Many Hawaiians had long since left the land and were raised in towns and cities. Now out of touch with the simple life of the taro patch, they found it very difficult to readjust. To prevent the Hawaiians from selling their claims and losing the land forever, the Hawaiian Homes Act provided that the land be leased to them for 99 years. Making a go of these 40-acre parcels *(kuleana)* was so difficult that successful homesteaders were called "Molokai Miracles."

In 1923 Libby Corporation leased land from Molokai Ranch at Kaluakoi and went into pineapple production; Del Monte followed suit in 1927 at Kualapuu. Both built company towns and imported Japanese and Filipino field laborers, swelling Molokai's population and stabilizing the economy. Many of the native Hawaiians subleased their tracts to the pineapple growers, and the Hawaiian Homes Act seemed to backfire. Instead of the homesteaders working their own farms, they were given monthly checks and lured into a life of complacency. Those who grew little more than family plots became, in effect, permanent tenants on their own property. Much more importantly, they lost the psychological advantage of controlling their own future and regaining their pride as envisioned in the Hawaiian Homes Act.

Modern Times

For the next 50 years life was quiet. The pineapples grew, providing security. Another large ranch, **Puu O Hoku** (Hill of Stars) was formed on the eastern tip of the island. It was originally owned by Paul Fagan, the amazing San Francisco entrepreneur who also developed Hana on Maui. In 1955, Fagan sold Puu O Hoku to George Murphy, a Canadian industrialist, for a meager $300,000. The ranch, under Murphy,

became famous for beautiful white Charolais cattle, a breed originating in France.

In the late 1960s "things" started quietly happening on Molokai. The Molokai Ranch sold 6,700 acres to the Kaluakoi Corp., which they controlled along with the Louisiana Land and Exploration Company. In 1969 the long-awaited Molokai reservoir was completed at Kualapuu; finally west Molokai had plenty of water. Shortly after Molokai's water problem appeared to be finally under control, Dole Corp. bought out Libby in 1972, lost millions in the next few years, and shut down its pineapple production at Maunaloa in 1975. By 1977 the acreage sold to the Kaluakoi Corp. started to be developed, and the Molokai Sheraton (now the Kaluakoi Hotel) opened along with low-rise condominiums and 270 fee-simple home sites ranging 5-43 acres selling for a minimum of $150,000 ($350,000 for oceanfront sites). Future plans for this area include two more resorts, additional condominiums, shopping facilities, bridle paths, and an airstrip (it's only 20 minutes to Honolulu). Lo and behold, sleepy old Molokai with the tiny Hawaiian Homes farms was now prime real estate and worth a fortune.

To complicate the picture even further, Del Monte shut down its operations in 1982, throwing more people out of work. In 1986 it did resume planting 250-acre tracts, but now all the pineapple is gone. Recently, coffee has been put into production near the old pineapple town of Kualapuu, some experimental plots of fruits and vegetables have been planted, and the Molokai Ranch has brought in sheep and cattle. After Brierly Investments bought the Molokai Ranch, bigger changes have started to take place, including a total face-lift for the town of Maunaloa and greater emphasis on tourism for a slice of the ranch's income. These new avenues of diversification are still in their infant stages but might possibly lead to greater economic strength and stability. Today Molokai is in a period of flux in other ways. There is great tension between developers, who are viewed as "carpetbaggers" interested only in a fast buck, and those who consider themselves the last remnants of a lost race holding on desperately to what little they have left.

ECONOMY

If it weren't for a pitifully bad economy, Molokai would have no economy at all. At one time the workers on the pineapple plantations had good steady incomes and the high hopes of the working class. With all the pineapple jobs gone, Molokai was transformed from an island with virtually no unemployment to a hard-luck community with a high rate of the people on welfare. With the start of the coffee plantation and the slowly growing tourism industry, this bleak economic situation has lessened somewhat. Inexplicably, Molokai also has the highest utility rates in Hawaii. Some say this is due to the fact that the utility company built a modern biomass plant and didn't have enough biomass to keep it operating—the people were stuck with the fuel tab. The present situation is even more ludicrous when you consider that politically Molokai is part of Maui County. It is lumped together with Kaanapali on Maui's western coast, one of Hawaii's poshest and wealthiest areas, where the vast majority of people are recent arrivals from the Mainland. This amounts to almost no political/economic voice for grassroots Molokai.

Agriculture

The word that is now bandied about is "diversified" agriculture. What this means is not pinning all hope to one crop like the ill-fated pineapple, but planting a potpourri of crops. Attempts at diversification are evident as you travel around Molokai. Fields of corn, wheat, fruits, nuts, and coffee are just west of Kaunakakai; many small farmers are trying truck farming by raising a variety of garden vegetables that they hope to sell to the massive hotel food industry in Honolulu. Watermelon, bell pepper, onions, and herbs are perhaps the most well known. The problem is not in production, but transportation. Molokai raises excellent crops, but little established transport exists for the perishable vegetables. A barge service, running on a loose twice-weekly schedule, is the only link to the market. The lack of storage facilities on Molokai makes it tough to compete in the hotel food business, which requires the freshest produce. Unfortunately, vegetables don't wait well for late barges.

Development

A debate rages between those in favor of tourist development, which they say will save Molokai, and grassroots organizations championed by OHA (Office of Hawaiian Affairs), which insist unchecked tourism development will despoil Molokai and give no real benefit to the people. A main character in the debate is the Kaluakoi Corp., which wants to build condos and sell more home lots. It claims that this, coupled with a few more resorts, will bring in jobs. The people know that they will be relegated to service jobs (maids and waiters), while all the management jobs go to outsiders. Most islanders feel that only rich people from the Mainland can afford million-dollar condos, and that eventually they will become disenfranchised on their own island. Claims are that outsiders have no feeling for the *aina* (land) and will destroy important cultural sites whenever growth dictates.

A few years back the Kaluakoi Corp. hired an "independent" research team to investigate Kawakiu Iki Bay, known to be an ancient adze quarry. After weeks of study, this Maui-based research team reported that Kawakiu was of "minor importance." Hawaii's academic sector went wild. The Society of Hawaiian Archaeology dispatched its own team under Dr. Patrick Kirch, who stated that Kawakiu was one of the richest archaeological areas in Hawaii. In one day they discovered six sites missed by the "independent" research team, and stated that a rank amateur could find artifacts by merely scraping away some of the surface. Reasonable voices call for moderation. Both sides agree Molokai must grow, but the growth must be controlled, and the people of Molokai must be represented and included as beneficiaries.

THE PEOPLE

Aside from the tiny island of Niihau, Molokai has the largest percentage of Hawaiian population, and this is perhaps due in part to relatively small commercial development on the island throughout its history, which did not bring in large numbers of ethnic workers. While sugar was tried early on with some success, it never grew to vast size, and the pineapple production on the island was also limited. Only ranching has really persevered and this doesn't require any large number of laborers. More recently, with the slow development of tourism, white collar workers have filtered into the workforce and there has been some increase in tourism-related jobs, but mostly local Hawaiians make up 48% of Molokai's population; 21% are Filipino, 18% Caucasian, 9% Japanese, 1% Chinese, and 3% various other groups.

Molokai is obviously experiencing a class struggle. The social problems hinge on the economy—the collapse of pineapple cultivation and the move toward tourism. The average income on Molokai is quite low and the people are not consumer-oriented. Tourism, especially "getaway condos," brings in the affluent. This creates friction; the "have-nots" don't know their situation until the "haves" come in and remind them. Today, most people hunt a little, fish, and have small gardens. Some are small-time *pakalolo* growers who get over the hard spots by making a few dollars from some backyard plants. There is no organized crime on Molokai. The worst you might run into is a group of local kids drinking on a weekend in one of their favorite spots. It's a territorial thing. If you come into their vicinity they might feel their turf is being invaded, and you could be in for some hassles. All this could add up to a bitter situation except that the true nature of most of the people is to be helpful and friendly. Just be sensitive to smiles and frowns and give people their space.

Ethnic Identity

An underground link exists between Molokai and other Hawaiian communities such as Waianae on Oahu. Molokai is unusual in that it is still Hawaiian in population and influence, with continuing culturally based outlooks that remain unacceptable to Western views. Ethnic Hawaiians are again becoming proud of their culture and heritage, as well as politically aware and sophisticated, and are just now entering the political arena. Few are lawyers, doctors, politicians, or executives; with ethnic identity returning, there is beginning to be a majority backlash against these professions. Among non-Hawaiian residents, it's put down or unacknowledged as a real occurrence.

Social problems on Molokai relate directly to teenage boredom and hostility in the schools, fueled by a heavy drinking scene. A disproportionate rate of teen pregnancy is a direct by-product. Teachers unofficially admit that they prefer a student who has smoked *pakalolo* to one who's been drinking. It mellows them out. The traditional educational approach is failing.

Ho'opono'opono is a fascinating family problem-solving technique still very much employed on Molokai. The process is like "peeling the onion," where a mediator, usually a respected *kapuna,* tries to get to the heart of a problem. Similar to group therapy, it's a closed family ordeal, never open to outsiders, and lasts until all emotions are out in the open and all concerned feel "clean."

BEACHES

Eastern Beaches

The beaches of Molokai have their own temperament, ranging from moody and rebellious to sweet and docile. Heading east from Kaunakakai along Rt. 450 takes you past a string of beaches that vary from poor to excellent. Much of this underbelly of Molokai is fringed by a protective coral reef that keeps the water flat, shallow, and at some spots murky. This area was ideal for fishponds but leaves a lot to be desired as far as beaches are concerned. The farther east you go, the better the beaches become. The first one you come to is at **One Ali'i Park,** about four miles east of Kaunakakai. Here you'll find a picnic area, campsites, good fish-

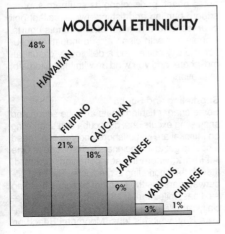

MOLOKAI ETHNICITY

ing, and family-class swimming where the kids can frolic with no danger from the sea. Next you pass **Kakahai'a Beach Park** and **Kumimi Beach,** one of a series of lovely sandy crescents where the swimming is fine. Just before you reach Pukoo, a small dirt road on your right goes to a hidden beach perfect for a secluded swim.

Halawa Bay, on Molokai's far east end, is the best all-around beach on the island. It's swimmable year-round, but be extra careful during the winter months. The bay protects the beach for a good distance; beyond its reach the breakers are excellent for surfing. The snorkeling and fishing are good to very good.

West End Beaches

The people of Molokai favor the beaches on the northwest section of the island. **Moomomi Beach** is one of the best and features good swimming, fair surfing, and pleasurable snorkeling along its sandy, rocky bottom. You have to drive over a very rutted dirt road to get there. Although car rental agencies are against it, you can make it, but only in dry weather. From Moomomi you can walk west along the beach and find your own secluded spot.

Very few visitors go south from Maunaloa town, but it is possible and rewarding for those seeking a secluded area. As you enter Maunaloa town a dirt track goes off to your right. Follow it through the Molokai Ranch and down the hill to **Hale O Lono Harbor,** start of an Outrigger Canoe Race. The swimming is only fair but the fantasy-feeling of a deserted island is pervasive.

Papohaku and **Kepuhi Beaches** just below the Kaluakoi Resort are excellent, renowned for their vast expanses of sand. Unfortunately, they're treacherous in the winter with giant swells and heavy rips, which make them a favorite for surfers. Anyone not accustomed to strong sea conditions should limit themselves to sunning and wading only to the ankles. During the rest of the year this area is great for swimming, becoming like a lake in the summer months. North of Kepuhi Bay is an ideal beach named **Kawakiu.** Although it's less than a mile up the coast, it's more than 15 miles away by road. You have to branch off Rt. 460 and follow the seven-mile dirt track north well before it forks toward the Kaluakoi. This area is well established as an archaeological site, and access to the beach was

a hard-fought controversy between the people of Molokai and the Molokai Ranch. Good swimming, depending upon tide conditions, and free camping on weekends.

SPORTS AND RECREATION

Since Molokai is a great place to get away from it all, you would expect an outdoor extravaganza. In fact, Molokai is a "good news, bad news" island when it comes to recreation, especially in the water. Molokai has few excellent beaches with the two best, Halawa and Papohaku, on opposite ends of the island; **Papohaku Beach** on the west end is treacherous during the winter months. Surfers and windsurfers will be disappointed with Molokai except at a few locales at the right time of year, while bathers, sun worshippers, and families will love the small secluded beaches with gentle waves located around the island.

Molokai has a small population and plenty of undeveloped "outback" land. This *should* add up to great trekking and camping, but the land is mostly privately owned and the tough trails are poorly maintained. However, permission is usually granted to trek across private land, and those bold enough to venture into the outback will virtually have it to themselves. Day-hiking trails and lightly used camping areas with good facilities are no problem. Molokai has tame, family-oriented beach parks along its southern shores, superb hunting and fishing, two excellent golf courses, and a handful of fine tennis courts. Couple this with clean air, no industrial pollution, no city noise, and a deliciously casual atmosphere, and you wind up with the epitome of relaxation.

Snorkeling and Scuba

Some charter fishing boats arrange scuba and snorkeling excursions, but scuba and snorkeling on Molokai are just offshore and you don't need a boat to get to it. Beginners will feel safe at **One Ali'i Park,** where the sea conditions are mild, though the snorkeling is mediocre. The best underwater area is the string of beaches heading east past mile marker 18 on Rt. 450, and especially at mile marker 20. You'll wind up at Halawa Bay, which is tops. Moomomi Beach on the northwest shore is very good, and Kawakiu Beach out on the west end is good around the rocks, but stay away during winter. For those staying at Molokai Ranch, Halena and Kolo Beaches along the south coast also offer descent snorkeling.

Molokai Fish and Dive in Kaunakakai, tel. (808) 553-5926, is a full-service snorkel shop. It has very good rental rates ($9 a set), can give you directions to the best spots, and arranges excursions.

Bill Kapuni's Snorkel and Dive Adventure, tel. (808) 553-9867, P.O. Box 1962, Kaunakakai, HI 96748, is an excellent way to enjoy Molokai's underwater spectacle, with Bill Kapuni, a native Hawaiian, who is intimately familiar with both the marine life that you will encounter and the Hawaiian myths and legends of his heritage. Bill's trips, 7:30 a.m., 10:30 a.m., and 1 p.m., including complimentary snacks, are $45 for snorkeling and $85 for a one-tank dive. Bill offers professional PADI instruction and has a compressor to fill tanks for certified divers.

Ma'a Hawaii, Molokai Action Adventures

Walter Naki knows Molokai—its mountains, seas, shores, trails, flowers, trees, and birds. His one-man action-adventure company, Ma'a Hawaii, P.O. Box 1269, Kaunakakai, HI 96748, tel. (808) 558-8184, loosely translates as "used to, accustomed to, familiar with Hawaii." As a native Hawaiian raised on the island and versed in its myths and mysteries, his spirit is strengthened and revitalized by the *aina* to which he is so closely attached. Walter has won the Hawaiian decathlon five times—a 10-event competition that includes sprinting, spear throwing, heaving a 28-pound stone, and swimming. He has also proven to be one of Hawaii's most renowned athletes in statewide spearfishing and free diving contests, training himself to stay underwater for more than two minutes while descending to depths of 85 feet. Walter's modest but lovingly tended home, which he shares with his two children, is lined with his trophies. Outside a pet deer, Pua (Flower), which he has raised since she was a tiny fawn, comes when he calls, loves sweets, and follows his truck like a puppy whenever he leaves. If it has to do with the outdoors Walter does it. Hunting for axis deer, wild boar, or goats on private land costs $200 per day for

bow hunters and $300 per day for rifle hunts (two hunters per day only). Hiking and "camera safaris" over many of the same hunting trails cost $50 for a half day (up to six people only), while snorkeling, skin-diving, spear fishing, and reef fishing are $50 per half day; kayak trips are available on request. Walter is extremely ecologically minded, employing practical knowledge that he has learned from years of living *with* the land and sea. The wild game that he hunts is used for food, not just trophies, and by taking pig, goats, and deer, he helps to manage the forest, balancing the destruction caused by these introduced animals so that native species can survive.

Walter is a great guide, but he is definitely "fo real," absolutely genuine with no glitz or glamour. He transports his gear, much of which is homemade and which he pulls from a shed in his back yard, in a used but not abused old truck, and he takes you to sea in a very seaworthy 21-foot Boston Whaler with twin 90s on the back, capable of going around to the north coast. Walter will do everything that he can to make your day safe and enjoyable, even stopping at his friend's taro patch to give you a glimpse of preserved island life. Remember, however, that it is up to you to be completely honest about your physical abilities, especially underwater, because with Walter's great skills and enthusiasm, it is easy for him to push you to your limit while he is just taking a stroll in the park. Whether it's snorkeling, diving, reef fishing, hiking, or camping in an north coast valley, Walter can do it all. If you seek a unique experience where you can touch the spirit of Molokai, travel for a day with Walter Naki. It will make all the difference.

Kayaking

Whether its to the calm south shore with its reef and many fishponds, or the rugged north shore and its isolated valleys, **Lani's Kayak Tours and Rentals,** tel. (808) 558-8563, can get you there. Destinations may depend upon the season and water conditions. South shore trips are $45 and north shore trips $65, $10 extra for snorkeling gear.

Sailing

Molokai is nearly devoid of charter sailboats. However, for those who like to feel the salty sea breeze in their hair, hear the snap of a full-furled sail, or enjoy the sunset from the deck of a sailing ship, try an excursion with **Molokai Charters,** tel. (808) 553-5852, P.O. Box 1207, Kaunakakai, HI 96748. The only charter sailing ship on the island is its 42-foot sloop *Satan's Doll,* berthed at the Kaunakakai wharf. Tours offered are a two-hour sunset sail for $40 and a full day sail to Lanai for swimming and snorkeling for $90. In season, whalewatching tours are also run for $50. Four-person minimum.

Surfing
The best surfing is out on the east end past mile marker 20. Pohakuloa Point has excellent breaks, which continue eastward to Halawa Bay. Moomomi Beach has decent breaks as does Kepuhi Beach in front of Kaluakoi Resort; Kawakiu's huge waves during the winter months are suitable only for experts.

Horseback Riding
For riding options on Molokai, there's slim pickin's. The **Molokai Ranch,** tel. (808) 552-2767, which offers a variety of rides over its ranch lands as part of the all-inclusive accommodation/activity packages, will also take nonguests. The **Molokai Horse and Wagon Ride,** tel. (808) 558-8380 or 588-8132, near Pukoo also does rides along with the wagon ride through the Mapulehu mango grove and up to the Ili'ili'opae Heiau, largest on the island.

Molokai Ranch
While daily activities are included in the cost of staying at the Molokai Ranch, other guests may also sign up for these outings. Activities include horseback riding, mountain biking, and hiking. Sign up at the Molokai Ranch Outfitters Center in Maunaloa, or call (808) 552-2791.

Golf
Molokai's two golf courses are as different as custom-made and rental clubs. The **Kaluakoi Golf Course,** tel. (808) 552-2739, is a picture-perfect beauty that would challenge any top pro. Laid out by master links designer Ted Robinson, it's located out at the Kaluakoi Resort. The 6,564-yard, par-72 course winds through an absolutely beautiful setting including five holes strung right along the beach. There's a complete pro shop, driving range, and practice greens. Golf lessons by the hour are also available. Greens fees for 18 holes are $45 for resort guests and $65 for nonguests; twilight specials available.

Molokai's other golf course is the homey **Ironwood Hills Golf Club,** tel. (808) 567-6000. Open 7 a.m.-5 p.m. daily, this rarely used but well-maintained mountain course is nine holes, par 34, and 3,086 yards long. Pay the affordable greens fee, $10 for nine holes and $14 if you want to loop the course twice, to the office manager or to a groundskeeper who will come around as you play. Twilight rates, club rental, riding cart, and hand cart are also available. The course is located up in the hills in Kalae at 1,200 in elevation, just before the Meyer Sugar Mill—look for the sign. Ironwood Hills is turning from a frog to a prince. Recent work has concentrated on improving the grounds. Even today there is no pro shop or snack shop available—all these will

MOLOKAI GOLF AND TENNIS

GOLF COURSE	PAR	YARDS	FEES	CART	CLUB RENTAL
Ironwood Hills Golf Club tel. (808) 567-6000	34	3,086	$10/9 holes $14/18 holes	$7	$7
Kaluakoi Golf Course tel. (808) 552-2739	72	6,564	$45 guest $75 nonguest	$15 $15	$22

TENNIS COURTS	TOWN	LOCATION	NO. OF COURTS	LIGHTED
	Kaunakakai	Community Center	2	Yes
	Hoolehua	Molokai High	2	Yes

come in time—and only a small mobile building as an office.

Tennis
Two courts are available at the **Ke Nani Kai Condos**, near the Kaluakoi Resort, which are free to guests. Two courts at the **Wavecrest Condo** east of Kaunakakai on Rt. 450 are also free to guests. Public courts are available at Molokai High School in Hoolehua and at the Community Center in Kaunakakai, but you may have to reserve a spot with the office in the Mitchell Pauole Center next door for the courts in town.

Fishing
The Penguin Banks of Molokai are some of the most fertile waters in Hawaii. Private boats as well as the commercial fishing fleets out of Oahu come here to try their luck. Trolling produces excellent game fish such as marlin, mahimahi, *ahi* (a favorite with sashimi lovers), and *ono,* with its reputation of being the best-tasting fish in Hawaii. Bottom fishing, usually with live bait, yields *onaga* and *uku,* a gray snapper favored by local people. Molokai's shoreline, especially along the south and west, offers great bait-casting for *ulua* and *ama ama. Ulua* is an excellent eating fish, and with a variance in weight from 15 to 110 pounds, can be a real whopper to catch from shore. Squidding, *limu* gathering, and torch-fishing are all quite popular and productive along the south shore, especially around the old fishpond sites. These remnants of Hawaii's one-time vibrant aquaculture still produce mullet, the *ali'i*'s favorite; an occasional Samoan crab; the less desirable, introduced tilapia; and the better-left-alone barracuda.

The *Alyce C.,* tel. (808) 558-8377, is a 31-foot, fully equipped diesel-powered fishing boat, owned and operated by Capt. Joe Reich, who can take you for full- or half-day charters and offers whalewatching tours in season.

The **Molokai Fish and Dive Co.,** tel. (808) 553-5926, also arranges deep-sea charters as well as excursions and shoreline sailing.

Hunting
Some of the best hunting on Molokai is on the private lands of the 54,000-acre **Molokai Ranch,** tel. (808) 552-2741, open to hunting year-round.

However, the enormous fees charged by the Ranch have effectively stopped hunting on their lands to all but the very determined or very wealthy. Ecological conditions may also affect hunting at certain times of the year. A permit to hunt game animals including black buck, aoudad sheep, eland antelope, and axis deer costs $400 per day for a guided hunt with an additional fee of $250 per person (up to three). Game fees are $1000 for each of the animals, except that the trophy fee (certain animals of a certain size) is $1,500! Game bird hunting is also offered during regular state hunting season, following state rules and regulations, at $150 per day.

Public hunting lands on Molokai are open to anyone with a valid state hunting license. Wild goats and pigs can be hunted in various hunting units year-round on weekends and state holidays except when bird hunting is in effect. Bag limits are two animals per day. Hunting game birds (ring-necked pheasants, various quails and doves, wild turkeys, partridges, and francolins) is open on public lands from the first Saturday in November to the third Sunday in January. A special dove season runs late January through March. For full information, license, and fees (as well as State Park and Forest Service camping permits) contact the Division of Forestry and Wildlife, P.O. Box 347, Kaunakakai, HI 96748, tel. (808) 533-5019.

Camping
The best camping on Molokai is at **Pala'au State Park** at the end of Rt. 470, in the cool mountains overlooking Kalaupapa Peninsula. It's also the site of Molokai's famous Phallic Rock. Here you'll find pavilions, grills, picnic tables, and freshwater. What you won't find are crowds; in fact, most likely you'll have the entire area to yourself. The camping here is free, but you need a permit, good for seven days, from the camp headquarters office in Kalae or from the Division of State Parks in Wailuku on Maui. Camping is permitted for up to a week at **Waikolu Lookout** in the Molokai Forest Reserve, but you'll have to follow a tough dirt road (Main Forest Road) for 10 miles to get to it. A free permit must be obtained from the Division of Forestry and Wildlife, Olo Ave., about one mile west of Kaunakakai. tel. (808) 553-5019.

tentalow,
Molokai Ranch

ROBERT NILSEN

Seaside camping is allowed at **One Ali'i Park,** just east of Kaunakakai, and at **Papohaku Beach Park,** west of Kaunakakai. These parks have full facilities but due to their beach location and easy access just off the highway they are often crowded, noisy, and bustling. Also, you are a target here for any rip-off artists. A county permit ($3 per day) is required and available from County Parks and Recreation at the Mitchell Pauole Center in Kaunakakai, tel. (808) 553-3204.

Hawaiian Homelands, P.O. Box 198, Hoolehua, HI 96729, tel. (808) 567-6104 or 567-6296, fax 567-6665, offers camping at **Kioea Park,** one mile west of Kaunakakai. The permit to this historical coconut grove costs $5 a day. Be sure to reserve well ahead of time; graduation, summer, and December are usually booked. One of the most amazing royal coconut groves in Hawaii, it's a treat to visit, but camping here, though quiet, can be hazardous. Make sure to pitch your tent away from any coconut-laden trees if possible, and vacate if the winds come up.

You may be able to camp free (unofficially) at Moomomi Beach on the island's northwest shore on a grassy plot near the pavilion, or at isolated Kawakiu Iki Bay farther to the west. You can't officially camp at Halawa Bay Beach Park either, but if you continue along the north side of the bay you'll come to a well-used but unofficial campground fringed by ironwoods and recognizable by old fire pits. This area does attract down-and-outers so don't leave your gear unattended.

Hiking

Molokai should be a hiker's paradise and there are exciting, well-maintained, easily accessible trails, but others cross private land, skirt guarded *pakalolo* patches, are poorly maintained, and tough to follow. This section provides a general overview of the trekking possibilities available on Molokai. Full info is given in the respective sections.

One of the most exciting hassle-free trails descends the *pali* to the **Kalaupapa Peninsula.** You follow the well-maintained mule trail down, and except for some "road apples" left by the mules, it's a totally enjoyable experience suitable for an in-shape family. You *must* have a reservation with the guide company to tour the former leper colony, however (see **Kalaupapa**).

Another excellent trail is at **Halawa Valley,** following Halawa Stream to cascading Moaula Falls, where you can take a refreshing dip if the famous *moo,* a mythical lizard said to live in the pool, is in the right mood. This trail is strenuous enough to be worthwhile and thrilling enough to be memorable. In years past anyone could walk up into Halawa Valley; however, due to abuse, disrespect, and degradation of the land, it was closed to the public for two years. It has been opened again, but entrance is restricted to those who go in with **Pilipo's Halawa Valley Hike.** Tour leader Pilipo Solitorio was born and bred in the valley, so a walk with him is like having a private historical and cultural lesson. For reservations, call (808) 553-4355 in the early evening.

Molokai Forest Reserve, which you can reach by driving about 10 miles over the rugged Main Forest Road (passable by 4WD only in the dry season), has fine hiking. At road's end you'll find the Sandalwood Measuring Pit. The hale and hearty who push on will find themselves overlooking Waikolu and Pelekunu, two fabulous and enchanted valleys of the north coast.

The most formidable trail on Molokai is the one that completely crosses the island from south to north and leads into **Wailau Valley.** It starts innocently enough at Iliʻiliʻopae Heiau about 15 miles east of Kaunakakai, but as you gain elevation it gets increasingly tougher to follow. After you've trekked all day, the trail comes to an abrupt halt over Wailau. From here you have to pick your way down an unmarked, slippery, and treacherous 3,000-foot *pali*. Don't attempt this trail alone. It's best to go with the Sierra Club, which organizes periodic hikes, or with a local person who knows the terrain. Wailau Valley is one of the last untouched valleys of bygone days. Here are bananas, papayas, and guavas left over from the last major inhabitants, who left early in this century. The local people who summer here, and the one family who lives here year-round, are generous and friendly, but also very aware and rightfully protective of the last of old Hawaii in which they live. If you hike into Wailau Valley remember that in effect you are a guest. Be courteous and respectful and you'll come away with a unique and meaningful island experience.

SHOPPING

Coming to Molokai in order to shop is like going to Waikiki and hoping to find a grass shack on a deserted beach. Molokai has only a handful of shops where you can buy locally produced crafts and Hawaiiana. Far and away, most of Molokai's shopping is centered along Ala Malama Street in downtown Kaunakakai. All three blocks of it! Here you'll find the island's only health food store, three very good food markets, a drugstore that sells just about everything, and a clutch of souvenir shops. Away from Kaunakakai the pickin's get mighty slim. Heading west you'll find the

Kualapuu General Store off Rt. 470 on the way to Kalaupapa, and a sundries store along with a Liberty House at the Kaluakoi Resort on the far west end. The Maunaloa Road (Rt. 460) basically ends in Maunaloa town. Go there! The best and most interesting shop, **The Big Wind Kite Factory,** is in town and is worth a visit in its own right. Also, in Maunaloa you'll find a market and a restaurant. Heading east from Kaunakakai is another shoppers' wasteland with only the sundries store at the Molokai Shores condo and the store and lunch window at Pukoo Neighborhood Store for anything to buy.

GETTING THERE

Hawaiian Airlines, tel. (800) 367-5320 or (808) 533-3644 on Molokai, has two regularly scheduled flights each way connecting Molokai and Honolulu. The morning flight from Honolulu and the afternoon flight to Honolulu go through Lanai. The second morning flight to Honolulu continues on to Kahului.

Island Air, tel. (808) 567-6115 or (800) 323-3345 Mainland, offers flights connecting Molokai with Oahu and Maui. There are 11 daily flights to Honolulu 6:35 a.m.-6:25 p.m. The two daily flights from Hana go through Kahului, from where there are an additional three daily flights.

Molokai Air Shuttle, tel. (808) 567-6847 Molokai or (808) 545-4988 Oahu, flies a Piper Aztec to/from Honolulu and Molokai for $50 roundtrip. This is not a scheduled route: you call and let them know when you want to fly and they will tell you what's available that day. Aside from this flight, Molokai Air Shuttle runs roundtrip charter service from Honolulu and Molokai to Lanai for $275 from Molokai. A 20-minute air tour of the north coast of Molokai is offered for $52, and they can fly you down to Kalaupapa, connect you with a tour of the settlement there, and fly you back for around $80. Always call to ask what's available on the day you want to go.

Paragon Air, tel. (808) 244-3356 or (800) 428-1231, does island-wide air charters in small aircraft, including from Molokai to Honolulu.

Pacific Wings, tel. (888) 575-4546, flies out of Kahului for Molokai (four a day), Hana (three a day), and Kamuela on the Big Island (one a day), as well as from Honolulu to those three destinations, no more than twice daily, using eight-seat, twin engine Cessna 402C aircraft.

Molokai Airport

The **Hoolehua Airport** has a small terminal with an open-air baggage claim area to the far right, check-in counters next to that, and the waiting lounge on the left side. In the baggage claim area, Dollar and Budget have rental car booths, and each has a base yard a few steps away across the free public parking lot out front. Ground transportation waits at the front but doesn't hang around long after a plane arrival. Also at the airport you'll find a lounge and lunch counter with not-too-bad prices, toilets, and public telephones. Pick up a loaf of excellent Molokai bread, the best souvenir available, or a lei from the small gift shop. Tourist brochures are available from a rack in the arrival area.

By Sea

Currently there is no scheduled sea connection to Molokai. The *Maui Princess* used to sail daily from Kaunakakai wharf to Lahaina, but for economic reasons the service was stopped in 1997, affecting many businesses on Molokai. Hopefully, it will be restarted at some point in the future, as it provides a fun and economical way to reach the island. The *Maui Princess* does, however, offer several day and overnight tour packages to Molokai. For information and reservations call (808) 661-8397 or (800) 833-5800.

GETTING AROUND

Public Transportation

No public bus transportation services Molokai. The following are taxi and limousine services that also provide some limited tours. **Kukui Tours and Limousines,** tel. (808) 553-5133, is a 24-hour taxi service, taking reservations 8 a.m.-5 p.m. **Molokai Off-road Tours and Taxi,** tel. (808) 553-3369, is another option. **Friendly Isle Tours and Transportation,** tel. (808) 553-9046, does transfers from the airport 8 a.m.-6 p.m. for $7 per person ($8 after hours), minimum of three.

Rental Cars

Molokai offers a limited choice of car rental agencies—make reservations to avoid being disappointed. Rental car booths close after the last flight of the day has arrived. Rental car companies on Molokai dislike their cars being used on dirt roads (there are plenty) and strongly warn against it. No jeeps are available on Molokai at this time, but it's always in the air that one of the car companies will make them available sometime in the future. **Dollar Rent A Car,** tel. (808) 567-6156, provides professional and friendly service, also offering some of the best rates on the island; **Budget Rent A Car,** tel. (808) 567-6877, is another option. These companies have booths and base yards at the airport. Pick up a copy of the *Molokai Drive Guide* magazine for maps and useful information on sights and activities.

The new guy in the market is a local company called **Island Kine Auto Rental.** Its slant is to rent the kind of vehicle that the big companies don't. It has a handful of cars, pickups, and vans, all used but well-maintained, that start at $30 a day. For further information and reservations, contact the company at: 51 Ilio Rd., P.O. Box 1018, Kaunakakai, HI 96748, tel. (808) 553-5242, fax 553-3880, e-mail: cars@molokai-aloha, website: www.molokai-aloha.com/cars.

A few unofficial rental car dealers exist on the island that "lend" vehicles and accept only "donations." Their vehicles are usually used and "local." Unless you personally know someone who runs this sort of business, be cautious.

Hitchhiking

The old thumb gives fair to good results on Molokai. Most islanders say they prefer to pick up hitchers who are making an effort by walking along, instead of lounging by the side of the road. It shows that you don't have a car but do have some pride. Getting a ride to or from Kaunakakai and the airport is usually easy.

GUIDED TOURS

Only a few limited tours are offered on Molokai. Mostly, it's you and your rental car. **Friendly Isle Tours and Transportation,** tel. (808) 553-9046, runs a four-hour van tour for $49 from the Kaluakoi Resort or the airport that hits many of the highlights of the island. Also offered is a two-hour tour of the upcountry area around Kalae for $36.

For a similar tour of the highlights of the island contact **Kukui Tours and Limousines,** tel. (808) 553-5133.

Molokai Off-road Tours and Taxi, tel. (808) 553-3369, offers half- and full-day narrated tours by van or 4WD Mon.-Sat., reservations required. The "Rainforest Adventure" for $53 takes you up into the forest preserve (minimum four people). Bring lunch.

One of the most fun-filled cultural experiences that you can have is to spend an afternoon on the **Molokai Horse and Wagon Ride,** tel. (808) 558-8380, 588-8132, or (800) 670-6965, e-mail: wgnride@aloha.net, website: www.visitmolokai .com/wgnride. Rides are given Mon.-Sat. 10:30 a.m. until finished. Call at least a day in advance. Rates are $35 for the wagon ride ($17.50 for kids under 12), $40 if you would like to go along on horseback, and lunch is provided. The experience starts and ends from a hidden beach just past mile marker 15 on the east end of the island along Rt. 450. As you drive, look to the right for a sign to Mapulehu Mango Grove; you'll follow the road to a small white house and a picnic area prepared on the beach. The wonderful aspect of this venture is that it is a totally local operation completely devoid of glitz, glamour, and hype. It's run by Junior Rawlins, wagonmaster, and his wife, Nani.

After loading, the wagon leaves the beach and rolls through the **Mapulehu Mango Grove,** one of the largest in the world, with more than 2,000 trees and 32 varieties. Planted by the Hawaiian Sugar Co. in the 1930s in an attempt to diversify, trees came from all over the world, including Brazil, India, and Formosa. Unfortunately, most of the U.S. was not educated about eating exotic fruits, so the mangos rotted on the tree unpicked, and the grove became overgrown. The ride proceeds down a tree-shrouded lane with music, singing, and anecdotes along the way. In about 20 minutes you arrive at **Ili'ili'opae Heiau,** among the largest Hawaiian places of worship in the islands. You are told about the history of the *heiau,* pointed out exotic fruits and plants in the area, and led atop the *heiau* for a photo session. You then return to the beach for a barbecue lunch and a demonstration of coconut husking, throw-netting (one of the oldest and most fascinating ways of catching fish), and maybe even a hula lesson. You can also count on the Hawaiian tradition of hospitality. These guys know how to treat you well, but remember that this is a *real* experience, so don't expect anything fancy or pretentious.

Coupled with a tour of the Kalaupapa settlement, the **Molokai Mule Ride** runs tours from topside down to the peninsula. The well-trained mules will transport you roundtrip down and up the 1,600-foot *pali* face, expertly negotiating 26 hairpin switchbacks on the trail. The ride each way is about 90 minutes. Conducted 8 a.m.-3:30 p.m. daily except Sunday, this tour is $120 and includes the ground tour of the settlement and lunch. No riders over 240 pounds please; all must be at least 16 years old and in good physical shape. Molokai Mule Ride can also arrange the ground tour for you ($38) if you desire to hike down the hill, or a fly-in from Hoolehua Airport and ground tour for $88. An accommodation and tour package, as well as air transportation from Honolulu and tour, are also available. For information and reservations, call (808) 567-6088 or (800) 567-7550, e-mail: muleman@aloha.net, website: www.muleride.com.

The **Meyer Ranch** in Kalae has opened part of its 1,800 acres to guided mountain bike and 4WD tours. All tours leave from the Molokai Museum and Cultural Center, which is included as part of the tour. Call (808) 567-6624 or (800) 962-9989 for complete information and details.

Helicopter and Airplane Flights

An amazing way to see Molokai—particularly its north coast—is by helicopter. This method is admittedly expensive, but dollar for dollar it is *the* most exciting way of touring and can get you places that no other means can. A handful of companies operate mostly from Maui and include overflights of Molokai. Though helicopter trip will put a big hole in your budget, most agree they are among the most memorable experiences of their trip. Try **Sunshine Helicopters,** tel. (808) 871-0722 or (800) 544-2520; **Hawaii Helicopters,** tel. (808) 877-3900 or (800) 994-9099; **Air Maui,** tel. (808) 877-7005; and **Blue Hawaiian Helicopters,** tel. (808) 871-8844 or (800) 786-2583.

Molokai Air Shuttle, tel. (808) 567-6847 on Molokai, (808) 545-4988 on Oahu, does scenic flights around Molokai and down to Kalaupapa. If you are lucky, your regularly scheduled flight from Kahului to Hoolehua will also fly along the north coast and give you a glimpse, although not real close, of this spectacular line of *pali* and valley.

INFORMATION AND SERVICES

Telephone numbers for service agencies that you might find useful: emergency, 911; police, tel. (808) 553-5355; County Parks and Recreation, tel. (808) 553-3204; Division of Forestry, tel. (808) 553-5019; Hawaiian Homelands, tel. (808) 567-6104 or 567-6296; Molokai Public Library (1937), tel. (808) 553-5483; Office of Hawaiian Affairs (OHA), tel. (808) 553-3611; Kaunakakai post office, tel. (808) 553-5845; Bank of Hawaii, tel. (808) 553-3273; American Savings Bank, tel. (808) 553-3263.

Molokai Visitors Association
The MVA, tel. (808) 553-3876, (800) 553-0404 statewide, or (800) 800-6367 Mainland, e-mail: mva@molokai.com, website: www.molokai.com /mva, is an excellent organization that can help with every aspect of your trip to Molokai. Lawrence Aki and his friendly staff dispense up-to-the-minute information on hotels, car rentals, activities, and services. Molokai Visitors Association should be your first contact if you are contemplating a visit to Molokai. Open Mon.-Fri. regular business hours.

For general information about the island, try the websites www.molokai-aloha.com and molokai-hawaii.com.

Newspapers
For a local look at what's happening on the island of Molokai, check out either of the island's two newspapers. The larger and more mainstream is *The Dispatch,* published in Maunaloa, while the more humble *Molokai Advertiser-News* is published in Kaunakakai by solar power.

Medical
Molokai is a small place with a small population so there is not as much available here in the way of medical treatment as on Maui or the other larger islands. Yet Molokai has Molokai General Hospital, tel. (808) 553-5331, which is located at the end of Home Olu Street just above Ala Malama Ave. in Kaunakakai. There are half a dozen doctors on the island and half as many dentists. For alternative care, try the Healing Touch Center, tel. (808) 553-3595, for massage, acupuncture, and chiropractic. Try Molikai Pharmacy, tel. (808) 553-5790, in the new Kamo'i Professional Center, one block off the main drag, for prescription drugs, first aid items, potions, lotions, and sundries. It's open Mon.-Sat. 8:45 a.m.-5:45 p.m.

Laundry
Molokai Dry Cleaning, located next to the Pizza Cafe, is open Mon.-Fri. 9 a.m.-5 p.m., Saturday 9 a.m.-1 p.m., closed Sunday. There is also a laundromat behind Outpost Natural Foods.

KAUNAKAKAI

No matter where you're headed on the island you have to pass through Kaunakakai (Beach Landing), the tiny port town and economic and government center that is Molokai's hub. An hour spent walking the three blocks of Ala Malama Street, the main drag, gives you a good feeling for what's happening. As you walk along you might hear a mechanical whir and bump in the background—Molokai's generating plant almost in the middle of town! If you need to do any banking, mailing, or shopping for staples, Kaunakakai's the place. Hikers, campers, and even day-trippers should get all they need here since shops, both east and west, are few and far between, and mostly understocked. Evenings are quiet here, with no bars or nightspots, neon or glamour.

SIGHTS

Head toward the lagoon and you'll see Kaunakakai's wharf stretching out into the shallow harbor for over a half mile. Townsfolk like to drive their cars onto it, but it's much better to walk out. The fishing from the wharf isn't great but it's handy and you never can tell. If you decide to stroll out here, look for the remains of Lot Kamehameha's summer house (circa 1864), a raised platform surrounded by stone, near the canoe shed along the shore west of the road.

Kapuaiwa Coconut Grove

A three-minute drive or a 10-minute walk west brings you to this 11-acre royal coconut grove planted in the 1860s for Kamehameha V (Lot Kamehameha), or Kapuaiwa to his friends. Kapuaiwa Coconut Grove was originally built because there were seven pools here in which the *ali'i* would bathe, and the grove was planted to provide shade and seclusion. The grove also symbolically provided the king with food for the duration of his life. The grove has diminished from the 1,000 trees originally planted, but more than enough remain to give a sense of grandeur

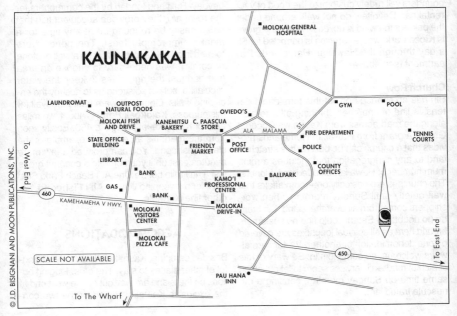

small Molokai church

to the spot. Royal coconut palms are some of the tallest of the species, and besides providing nuts, they served as natural beacons pinpointing the spot inhabited by royalty. These here are more than 80 feet tall. Now the grove has a park-like atmosphere and mostly you'll have it to yourself. Pay heed to the signs warning of falling coconuts. An aerial bombardment of hefty five pounders will rudely customize the hood of your rental car. Definitely do not walk around under the palms if the wind is up. Just next to the grove is **Kioea Park,** where camping is permitted for $5 a day through the Hawaiian Homelands Department (see above).

Church Row

Sin has no chance against this formidable defensive line of churches standing altar-to-altar along the road across from Kapuaiwa Coconut Grove. A grant from Hawaiian Homelands provides that a church can be built on this stretch of land to any congregation that includes a minimum number of Hawaiian-blooded parishioners. The churches are basically one-room affairs that wait quietly until Sunday morning when worshippers come from all over the island. Let there be no doubt: old Satan would find no customers around here as all spiritual loopholes are covered by one denomination or another. Visitors are always welcome, so come join in. Be wary of this stretch of road—all services seem to let out at the same time on Sunday morning, causing a minuscule traffic jam.

Classic Fishponds

Molokai is known for its fishponds, which were a unique and highly advanced form of aquaculture prevalent from at least the early 13th century. Molokai, because of an abundance of shallow, flat waters along its southeastern shore, was able to support a network of these ponds numbering more than five dozen during their heyday. Built and tended by the commoners for the royal *ali'i,* they provided succulent fish that could easily be rounded up at any time for a meal or impromptu feast. The ponds were formed in a likely spot by erecting a wall of stone or coral. It was necessary to choose an area that had just the right tides to keep the water circulating, but not so strong as to destroy the encircling walls. Openings were left in the wall for this purpose. **Kalokoeli Pond** is about two miles east of Kaunakakai along Rt. 450. Easily seen from the road, it's an excellent example of the classic fishpond. You can proceed a few more minutes east until you come to a coconut grove just a half mile before One Ali'i Beach Park. Stop here for a sweeping view of **Ali'i Fishpond,** another fine example.

ACCOMMODATIONS

Besides camping, Kaunakakai has only a handful of other places to stay. The other lodging options on the island are way out on the west end at the exclusive Kaluakoi Resort or the two condos that surround it, and at the Wavecrest Condo east of Kaunakakai along the south coast. A few bed and breakfasts are also available, many along the road to the east. Head for Kaunakakai and its limited but adequate accommodations if you want to save money.

Pau Hana Inn

For years the Pau Hana (Work's Done) Inn had the reputation for being *the* budget place to stay on Molokai. Now all that's left is the reputation, although it's still not too expensive. It still has a strong "local" feel, just right for laid-back Molokai. The owner is Molokai Beach, Ltd., and many changes have been made in the last few years; rooms are refurbished, and the whole place is spiffed up. Special touches still remain, though, like leaving the windows of the dining room open so that birds can fly in to peck crumbs off the floor. A fireplace is lit in the morning to take the chill off the place; hanging over it is a noble stag with wide, perfect antlers and tearful eyes. Breakfast and lunch are served daily, with dinner only on Friday and Saturday evenings. Outside, in the courtyard bar, a magnificent Bengalese banyan provides the perfect setting in which to sit back and relax. The waitresses are friendly and go out of their way to make you feel welcome and comfortable. The Pau Hana Bar is a favorite with local people. Friday and Saturday nights feature live music and dancing under the banyan tree. Room rates are: Long House, a barracks-type building, clean with carpeted floors $47.50; cottages $55, studio with kitchenette $97.50, poolside unit $78.50, oceanfront $97.50, suite $125; extra person $10. For reservations contact Pau Hana Inn, P.O. Box 860, Kaunakakai, HI 96748, tel. (808) 553-5342. Inexpensive.

Molokai Shores Suites

This is a relatively new condo a few minutes east of the Pau Hana with full kitchens, large living rooms, and separate bedrooms. The white walls contrasting with the dark brown floors are hung with tasteful prints. Plenty of lounge furniture is provided along with a table for outside dining and barbecues. The upper floor of the three-story building offers an open-beam ceiling including a full loft. Some units have an extra bedroom built into the loft. The grounds are very well kept, quiet, and restful. The swimming pool

fronts the gentle but unswimmable beach, and nearby is a classic fishpond. The only drawback is the architecture: it's pragmatic and neat, but not beautiful. Rates are $144 one-bedroom oceanfront, $189 two-bedroom oceanfront; $15 for each additional person. For information, call (808) 553-5954 direct or call central reservations, tel. (800) 535-0085, fax (800) 633-5085. A Marc Resorts Hawaii property. Premium.

Hotel Molokai

This 45-room hotel was built in 1966 by an architect (Mr. Roberts) enamored with the South Seas, who wanted to give his hotel a Polynesian village atmosphere. He succeeded. The buildings are two-story, semi-A-frames with sway-backed roofs covered with split wood shingles. Outside staircases lead to the large, airy studios that feature a lanai with swing. This hotel had its heyday before the big resort and the big money came to the island. After a change of ownership in 1998, Hotel Molokai was closed for extensive renovation. By the beginning of 1999, the hotel was once again entertaining guests. The Molokai hotel was always known for good dining, weekend entertainment, a well-appointed gift shop, a swimming pool, and a poolside lounge. With luck, all will again be better than ever. The restaurant and lounge are open daily and rooms run $75-130. For current information on dining and room availability, contact Hotel Molokai directly at tel. (808) 553-5347 or (800) 423-6656, or Castle Resorts, tel. (800) 367-5004 from the Mainland and Canada or (800) 272-5275 in Hawaii.

FOOD

Like the hotel scene, Molokai has only a handful of places to eat, but among these are veritable institutions that if missed make your trip to Molokai incomplete. The following are all located on Kaunakakai's main street, or just a minute away. Just ask anyone where they are.

The 50-year-old **Mid-Nite Inn** in "downtown" Kaunakakai was started as a saimin stand by Mrs. Kikukawa, the present owner's mother. People would come here to slurp noodles while waiting for the midnight interisland steamer to take them to Honolulu. The Mid-Nite was well known for its large, tasty, island-inspired meals, and very friendly service. The steamers are gone but the restaurant remains, sort of. The Mid-Nite Inn was gutted by fire some years ago, and while townsfolk hope that someone will reopen a restaurant on the same spot, nothing has yet taken place.

The **Kanemitsu Bakery,** tel. (808) 553-5855, has been in business for more than 70 years and is still run by the same family. The bakery is renowned for its Molokai breads, boasting cheese and onion among the best of its 19 varieties. Mrs. Kanemitsu's cookies are scrumptious, and anyone contemplating a picnic or a day hike should load up. The bakery is open 5:30 a.m.-6:30 p.m., closed Tuesday. There's a lunch counter in the back where you can get eggs, pancakes, and omelettes for breakfast, and local Hawaiian foods for lunch, open 5:30 a.m.-1 p.m.

Oviedo's Filipino Restaurant is the last building on the left along Ala Malama, where every item on the menu is about $5. Choose from ethnic selections like pork *adobo,* chicken papaya, tripe stew, sweet and sour ribs, pig's feet, mongo beans, and a good selection of ice cream for dessert. Oviedo's is small, run-down, but clean. The decor is worn linoleum floors and Formica tables, and the cooling is provided by breezes that readily pass through large cracks in the walls.

Kamo'i Snack-N-Go is in the new Kamo'i Professional Center. Stop here for Dave's ice cream, candies, cold drinks, and other snacks. Open daily until 9 p.m.

The **Molokai Drive-In,** open daily 6 a.m.-10 p.m., is along Kamehameha Hwy. in a bluish-gray, flat-roofed building that has the look of the '60s. You order from the window and then take your meal to eat under an awning, or step into the air-conditioned inside to find a few tables. Breakfast offers omelettes, eggs, spam, bacon, or ham along with sides of rice, hash browns, or toast for under $5. Lunch is chili dogs, nachos, subs, fish, shrimp, and chicken burgers, with a special featured every day. The drive-in is actually tasteful, bright, and clean. It's a local place with decent food and very affordable prices. It would make a great stop for a picnic lunch to go, especially if you're heading to Halawa and points east.

Don't let the name **Molokai Pizza Cafe,** tel. (808) 553-3288, fool you! Although this bright and cheery restaurant makes designer pizza, the emphasis is on *cafe*. Owned by Julie and Sean Connolly, and located wharfside of the junction of Routes 450 and 460, this eatery is open daily 11 a.m.-10 p.m. (until 11 p.m. on Friday and Saturday). Molokai's answer to upscale dining, the cafe is fast food with a flare. Pizzas come in three sizes and range in price from a Molokai small for $7.80 up to their giant Big Island with everything including green peppers, onions, sausage, beef, and bacon for $21.95. Sandwiches can be an Italian sub laden with turkey, ham, and roast beef, or a plump fresh-baked pocket sandwich. Hearty appetites will enjoy meals like pasta in marinara sauce, barbecued spareribs (great!), or the fresh catch. Order it! Caught in these waters, the fish comes in the back door, is filleted, cooked, and served to you as fresh as it can be. For dessert, you can be repentant and go for a low-fat frozen yogurt, be brazen and order the strawberry shortcake, or let the devil take the hindmost and order the Chocolate Suicide. The Molokai Pizza Cafe delivers, perfect for anyone staying in a condo. Takeout available.

Outpost Natural Foods, tel. (808) 553-3377, serves wholesome, healthy, nutritious quick foods from its inside window, Sun.-Fri. 10 a.m.-3 p.m. Here you can find various sandwiches for less than $5, burritos for up to $4.25, salads, veggie and tempeh burger around $5, and the daily lunch specials for under $6. In addition, there is an assortment of fresh juices and smoothies. While there, pick up any groceries that you'll need for your time on the island.

The restaurant at the **Pau Hana Inn** serves breakfast and lunch daily and dinner on Friday and Saturday evenings; American and Hawaiian fare. The Pau Hana Bar has a daily happy hour with *pu pu* 4-6 p.m. Here you can relax under the famous banyan tree for an early evening cocktail. On Friday and Saturday evenings there is live music and dancing, but there may be an annoying cover charge, even for hotel guests who only want a quiet drink.

SHOPPING

Molokai Fish and Dive in downtown Kaunakakai, tel. (808) 553 5926, sounds very practical, and it is, but it has a good selection of souvenirs, T-shirts and fashions, books (including a couple written by shop owner James Brocker), maps of Molokai, island music, jewelry, and a good assortment of film along with its fishing equipment. They can give you detailed information about fishing and water sports on Molokai, and they rent some water gear like snorkel sets, boogie boards, or a rod and reel for $9 a day.

Molokai Island Creations, connected to Molokai Fish and Dive and also open daily 9:30 a.m.-4:30 p.m., features authentic Molokai designs on ladies' blouses, tank tops, and men's T-shirts. It also has original Molokai glassware, china, and porcelain, along with Hawaiian cards and notebooks. Fashions also include pareus, children's alohawear, shorts, hats, aloha shirts, muumuu, swimwear, a good selection of jewelry, and a rack of cosmetics and perfumes in island scents.

Imamura's, open daily except Sunday 8:45 a.m.-5:45 p.m., is a very friendly down-home shop that sells everything from flip-flops to fishnets. It also specializes in lei-making needles and has a great selection of inexpensive luggage. The shelves hold beach mats and hats, T-shirts, pots and pans, and kitchen utensils. The sales staff are all friendly and slow-paced; when you return, they'll smile a welcome.

Lourdes Shoes Clothing and Jewelry is a basic local shop offering a smattering of alohawear, handbags, jogging shoes, baby clothes, towels, and women's clothing. **Mango Video,** tel. (808) 553-3600, is a place to find entertainment for the evening. It rents camcorders and even sells a smattering of snorkel gear. There is no theater in Kaunakakai, but since 1998 there has been one in Maunaloa. People who want to watch a big screen show must now travel to the west end for it—and they do.

Molokai Surf, open daily except Sunday 9 a.m.-6 p.m., has bathing suits, sandals, T-shirts, shorts, and alohawear.

Dudoit Imports, which used to be on the main drag but has moved to the little row of shops by Molokai Pizza Cafe, features wicker baskets, rattan furniture, handcrafted items made on Molokai, arts and collectibles, and, what else, lots of imports.

For those into wholesome health food, **Outpost Natural Foods,** tel. (808) 553-3377, is at 70 Makaena Place across from the government buildings and near Kalama's Gas Station. It's the only store of its kind on Molokai, but it's excellent. It's open Sun.-Thurs. 9 a.m.-6 p.m., Friday 9 a.m.-3 p.m., closed Saturday. The fruits and vegetables are locally and organically grown as much as possible. Along with the usual assortment of health foods you'll find bulk grains, granola, nuts, and dried fruits. The jam-packed shelves also hold rennetless cheese, fresh yogurt, nondairy ice cream, vitamins, minerals, supplements, and a good selection of herbs, oils, and spices. If you can't find what you need, ask Dennis, the owner, or the general manager on duty. The juice bar, open Sun.-Fri. 10 a.m.-3 p.m., is a great place for a healthy lunch and cold drink. Shaded picnic tables are provided out back.

For general shopping along Ala Malama Street, the **Friendly Market,** open Mon.-Fri. 8:30 a.m.-8:30 p.m., Saturday to 6:30 p.m., is by far the best-stocked grocery store on Molokai. There's a community bulletin board outside. It might list cars for sale, Hawaiian genealogies, or fund-raising sushi sales. Have a look!

Just down the street **Takes Variety Store** and **Misaki's Groceries and Dry Goods** a few steps farther along sell just about everything in food and general merchandise that you'll require. Across from the Mid-Nite Inn is the minimart **C. Paascua Store** for snack items and drinks.

The **Kaunakakai Market,** along the main drag, open 7 a.m.-10:30 p.m., is fairly well-stocked, with a selection of canned goods and some fresh veggies.

For that special evening, try **Molokai Wines and Spirits,** open Sun.-Thurs. 9 a.m.-10 p.m., until 10:30 p.m. Friday and Saturday, which has a small but good selection of vintage wines as well as beer and gourmet treats.

Molokai Drugstore, tel. (808) 553-5313, open daily 8:45 a.m.-5:45 p.m., closed Sunday, is the only full-service pharmacy and drugstore on the island. Don't let the name fool you because it sells much more than potions and drugs. You can buy anything from sunglasses to film, watches, toys, baby food, small appliances, and garden supplies. It has the best selection of film on Molokai, with a very good selection of books, especially on Hawaiiana. Film processing, including slides, takes 48 hours. It too has moved from its spot on the main street to the town's newest mall, the small Kamo'i Professional Center, one street back. Also in this center is **Kamo'i Snack-N-Go** for ice cream, candies, snacks, and cold drinks; open daily until 9 p.m.

EAST TO HALAWA VALLEY

The east end of Molokai, from Kaunakakai to Halawa Valley, was at one time the most densely populated area of the island. At almost every milepost is a historical site or point of interest, many dating from precontact times. A string of tiny churches attests to the coming of the missionaries in the mid-1800s, and a crash-landing site was an inauspicious harbinger of the deluge of Mainlanders bound for Hawaii in this century. This entire stretch of Rt. 450 is almost entirely undeveloped, and the classical sites such as *heiau*, listening stones, and old battlegrounds are difficult to find, although just a stone's throw from the road. The local people like it this way, as most would rather see the south shore of Molokai remain unchanged. A determined traveler might locate the sites, but unless you have local help, it will mean hours tramping around in marshes or on hillsides with no guarantee of satisfaction. Some sites such as **Ili'ili'opae Heiau** are on private land and require permission to visit. It's as if the spirits of the ancient *kahuna* protect this area.

SIGHTS

It's a toss-up whether the best part about heading out to the east end is the road itself or the reward of Halawa Valley at the end. Only 30 miles long, it takes 90 minutes to drive. The road slips and slides around corners, bends around huge boulders, and dips down here and there into coves and inlets. The cliff face and protruding stones have been painted white so that you can avoid an accident, especially at night. Sometimes the ocean and road are so close that spray splatters your windshield. Suddenly you'll round a bend to see an idyllic house surrounded by palm trees with a gaily painted boat gently rocking in a protected miniature cove. Behind is a valley of verdant hills with colors so vibrant they shimmer. You negotiate a hairpin curve and there are Lanai and Maui, black on the horizon, contrasted against the waves as they come crashing in foamy white and blue. Down the road chugs a pickup truck full of local people. They wave you a "hang loose" as their sincere smiles light up your already glorious day. Out in one of the innumerable bays are snorkelers, while beyond the reef, surfers glide in exhilarating solitude.

The local people think of the road as "their road." Why not? They use it as a sidewalk, playground, and extension of their back yards. Dogs snooze on it, while the rumps of grazing stock are only inches away from your fender. The speed limit is 35, but go slower and enjoy it more. The mile markers stop at mile 17, then four miles farther you come to the best part. Here, the well-tended two-lane highway with the yellow stripe plays out. The road gets old and bumpy, but the scenery gets much more spectacular. It's about nine miles from where the bumpy part begins until you reach the overlook at Halawa Valley. Come with a full tank of gas, plenty of drinking water, a picnic lunch, and your sense of wonder.

One Ali'i Beach Park

A few minutes east of Kaunakakai the road brings you to a stand of perhaps 80 coconut palms. Here is a little-used, unnamed beach park with an excellent view of one of the string of fishponds that are famous in this area. One Ali'i Beach Park, only a few minutes farther along, is open for camping. It's too close to the road, not well shaded, and a bit too overused to be comfortable. The swimming here is only fair for those who like a challenging surf, but excellent for families with little children who want calm waters. Clean restrooms and showers are available and the grounds are generally in good shape. Those not camping here would find it pleasant enough for a day excursion, but it's nothing compared with what's farther east along the road.

picturesque coconut grove and fishpond typical of east Molokai

About two minutes past One Ali'i, Makanui Road leads up the hillside on the *mauka* side of the road. A two-minute ride up this road exposes the beginnings of a condo development. As you gain height (one of the only roads that allows you to do so) you'll have an excellent view of the coastline with a panorama of the fishponds below and Lanai and Maui out to sea. Beyond this road is another just like it, leading into a future subdivision with much the same overview.

Kawela

The Kawela area was a scene of tragedy and triumph in Molokai's history. Here was Pakuhiwa, the battleground where Kamehameha I totally vanquished the warriors of Molokai on his way to conquering Oahu. In nearby Kawela Gulch was Pu'u Kaua, the fortress that Kamehameha overran. The fortress oddly doubled as a *pu'uhonua,* a temple of refuge, where the defeated could find sanctuary. Once the battle had been joined, and the outcome inevitable, the vanquished could find peace and solace in the very area that they had so recently defended.

Today the area offers refuge as **Kakahai'a County Beach Park and National Wildlife Refuge.** The beach park is not used heavily: it, too, is close to the road. The fishpond here is still used though, and it's not uncommon to see people in it gathering *limu.* This is also an excellent area for coconut trees, with many nuts lying on the ground for the taking. The refuge is an area where birdwatchers can still be captivated by the sight of rare endemic birds.

Kamalo to Pukoo

This six-mile stretch is loaded with historical sites. Kamalo is one of Molokai's natural harbors and was used for centuries before most of the island commerce moved to Kaunakakai. In the late 1800s, **Kamalo Wharf** (turn right down the dirt road at mile marker 10) was the island's principal landing site. Tracks once ran out on the wood and stone "mall" to help unload ships.

Saint Joseph Church, next in line, was built in 1876 by Father Damien. It's small, no more than 16 by 30 feet, and very basic. Inside is a small wooden altar adorned with flowers in a canning jar. A picture of Father Damien and one of St. Joseph adorn the walls. Outside is a black metal sculpture of Damien.

One mile or so past St. Joseph's is the **Smith and Bronte Landing Site.** These two aviators safely crash-landed their plane here on July 14, 1927, completing the first trans-Pacific civilian flight in just over 25 hours. All you can see is a mangrove swamp, but it's not hard to imagine the relief of the men as they set foot even on soggy land after crossing the Pacific. They started a trend that would bring more than six million people a year to the islands. The Wavecrest Resort Condominium is nearby at mile marker 13.

Before Pukoo are two noteworthy sites. **Kalua'aha Church** looks like a fortress with its tiny slit windows and three-foot-thick plastered walls and buttresses. It was the first Christian church on Molokai, built in 1844 by the Protestant missionaries Rev. and Mrs. Hitchcock, and is considered by some to be the most significant building on the island. Used for worship until the 1940s, it has since fallen into disuse. In 1967, the bell and steeple came down, the roof is caving in, and the rest is mostly in ruins. While parishioners had repair plans, it is doubtful that the structure can be saved without major rehabilitation.

Then comes **Ili'ili'opae Heiau,** one of Hawaii's most famous human-sacrifice temples, and a university of sorcery, as it were, where *kahuna* from other islands were tutored. (For a unique tour of this area, along with nearby Mapulehu Mango Grove, see the description of the Molokai Horse and Wagon Ride, under **Guided Tours.**) All of the wooden structures on the 267-foot stone platform have long since disappeared. Legend holds that all of the stone was carried across the island from Wailau Valley and perfectly fitted in one night of amazing work. Legend also holds that the sorcerers of Ili'ili'opae once sacrificed nine sons of a local *kahuna*. Outraged, he appealed to a powerful shark-god for justice. The god sent a flash flood to wipe out the evil sorcerers, washing them into the sea where the shark-god waited to devour them. The trailhead for Wailau Valley begins at Ili'ili'opae, but since

the temple is now on private land it is necessary to receive permission to visit it. This *heiau* is now on the National Register of Historic Places.

Our Lady of Sorrows Church, another built by Father Damien in 1874 and rebuilt by the parishioners in 1966, is next. Inside are beautiful pen-and-ink drawings of the Stations of the Cross imported from Holland. Just past Our Lady of Sorrows are the **bell stones,** but they're almost impossible to locate.

Before Pukoo, near mile marker 16, is the **Manee Canoe Club** with its well-tended lawns and tiny inlets. There has recently been a controversy about public access to the beach on the bay across from the canoe club, which has been the norm for generations. The situation culminated in public protests and walks to the beach. There is, however, public access to the old wharf area directly west of the canoe club, but it's not good for swimming.

Just past Pukoo is the **octopus stone,** a large stone painted white next to the road. It is believed that this is the remainder of a cave inhabited by a mythical octopus, and that the stone still has magical powers.

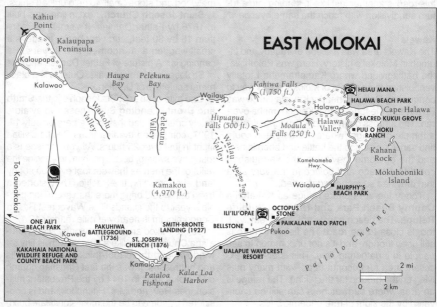

EAST MOLOKAI

More East End Beaches

Waialua Beach, almost at mile marker 19, is one of the best beaches on the island for swimming, snorkeling, and beginner surfing. A freshwater stream entering the ocean is very convenient for rinsing off.

Two minutes past mile marker 19 is a sand and coral beach where you can walk knee-deep out to the reef. At high tide, it's chest high.

Mile Marker 20 Beach, with its huge strand of white sand and protected lagoon, is the main beach on the east end. Pull off at a handy spot and enjoy the great snorkeling, although the swimming is only mediocre. It's very safe and perfect for a family outing.

Note: All of these beaches have sharp coral. Wear a pair of reef walkers or good old sneakers. You do not want to go out there barefoot!

On to Halawa Valley

Past Pukoo, the road gets very spectacular. Many blow-your-horn turns pop up as you wend around the cliff face following the natural roll of the coastline. Coming in rapid succession are incredibly beautiful bays and tiny one-blanket beaches, where solitude and sunbathing are perfect. Be careful of surf conditions! Some of the fruitful valleys behind them are still cultivated in taro, and traditional community life beckons young people from throughout the islands to come and learn the old ways. Offshore is the crescent of **Moku Ho'oniki Island,** and Kanaha Rock in front. The road swerves inland, climbing the hills to the 14,000 acres of **Puu O Hoku (Hill of Stars) Ranch.** People often mistake one of the ranch buildings along the road for a store. It's the ranch office, but the people inside can direct you to an overlook where you can see the famous and sacred *kukui* grove where Lanikaula, one of the most powerful sorcerers of Molokai, is buried. The different-looking cattle grazing these hilly pastures are French Charolais, imported by Puu O Hoku Ranch and now flourishing on these choice pasturelands. The road comes to a hairpin turn where it feels like you'll be airborne. Before you is the magnificent chasm of Halawa Valley with its famous waterfalls sparkling against the green of the valley's jungle walls. Hundreds of feet below, frothy aquamarine breakers roll into the bay.

Halawa Valley and Bay

This choice valley, rich in soil and watered by Halawa Stream, is believed to be the first permanent settlement on Molokai, dating from the early seventh century. Your first glimpse is from the road's overlook from which you get a spectacular panorama across the half-mile valley to Lamaloa Head forming its north wall, and eastward, deep into its four-mile cleft, where lies Moaula Falls. Many people are so overwhelmed when they gaze from the overlook into Halawa that they don't really look around. Turn to your right and walk only 15 yards directly away from Halawa. This view gives a totally different perspective of a deep-V valley and the pounding surf of its rugged beach—so different from the gently arcing haven of Halawa Bay. For centuries, Halawa's farmers carved geometric terraces for taro fields until a tsunami of gigantic proportions inundated the valley in 1946 and left a plant-killing deposit of salt. Most people pulled out and left their homes and gardens to be reclaimed by the jungle.

Follow the paved road into the valley until you see a house that was obviously a church at one time. Cross Halawa Stream and follow the road as far as you can. Here you have a choice of bathing in the cool freshwater stream or in the surf of the protected bay. Don't go out past the mouth of the bay because the currents can be treacherous. This area is great for snorkeling and fishing, and is one of the only good surfing beaches on Molokai.

Halawa Bay is a beach park, but it's not well maintained. There are toilet facilities and a few dilapidated picnic tables, but no official overnight camping, and the water is not potable. You can bivouac for a night on Puu O Hoku Ranch land at the far north end of Halawa Bay under a canopy of ironwood trees, but be aware that this area attracts rip-offs and it's not safe to leave your gear unattended.

Moaula Falls

One of *the* best walks on Molokai, mosquitoes notwithstanding, is to the famous 250-foot Moaula (Red Chicken) Falls. Halawa Stream can be a trickle or torrent, depending upon recent rains. If Moaula Falls is gushing, the stream too will be roaring. The entire area up toward the falls harbors the remains of countless taro patches and home sites. Groves of *kemani* trees mark the sites where *ali'i* were buried; their tall trunks at one time were used by Hawaiian fishermen and later by sailors as a landmark. Legend recalls that a female lizard, a *moo*, lives in the gorgeous pool at the bottom of the falls. Sometimes she craves a body and will drag a swimmer down to her watery lair. The only way to determine her mood is to place a ti leaf (abundant in the area) in the pool. If it floats you're safe, but if it sinks the lady lizard wants company—permanently! Minor gods who live in the rocks above Moaula Falls pool want to get into the act too. They'll drop tiny rocks on your head unless you make an offering (a penny under a ti leaf will do). Above Moaula Falls you can see **Upper Moaula Falls**, and beyond that the cascading brilliance of 500-foot **Hipuapua Falls**. For some years the trail to this waterfalls was closed; it goes across private property. You can once again gain access but only through a guided tour led by a man who was born and raised in the valley. (See **Hiking** for details.)

ACCOMMODATIONS AND FOOD

First down the line is **Ka Hale Mala,** just less than five miles east of Kaunakakai on Kamakana Place. This vacation rental is the ground floor of a family house, set amidst a tropical garden. Here you have a large living room, full kitchen and bath, and a laundry room, plus use of a bicycle or snorkel gear. Rates are $60 without breakfast or $70 with. For more information, contact Cheryl Corbiell, P.O. Box 1582, Kaunakakai, HI 96748, tel./fax (808) 553-9009, e-mail: 73124.1477@compuserve.com, website: www.molokai.com/kahalemala. Moderate.

Depending on your point of view the **Wavecrest Resort** is either a secluded hideaway, or stuck out in the sticks away from all the action. It's east of Kaunakakai on Rt. 450 just at mile marker 13. You'll find *no* hustle, bustle, anxiety, nightlife, restaurants, or shopping. This condominium sits on five well-tended acres fronting a lovely-to-look-at lagoon that isn't good for swimming. It catches the morning sun and looks directly across the Pailolo Channel to Kaanapali on Maui. Enjoy a putting green, shuffleboard court, newly refurbished swimming pool, and two lighted tennis courts free to guests. Be aware that there are no phones in any of the units. For those who need to call, there are two pay phones at the front office. In each unit is a fully furnished kitchen, spacious living room, ceiling fan, television, and lanai. A laundry room is located on each floor for guest use. Even if you feel that you're too far from town, remember nothing is going on there anyway. Another attraction is that local fishermen may put in just next to the Wavecrest and sell their fish for unbeatable prices. Guests can barbecue on gas grills provided. Rates: one-bedroom ocean or garden view $119, one-bedroom oceanfront $149; two-bedroom oceanfront $189; $15 extra person. Car/condo packages are also available. Attractive monthly and low-season discounts available. Call the Wavecrest direct, tel. (808) 558-8103, or central reservations, tel. (800) 535-0085 or fax (800) 535-0085. A Marc Resorts Hawaii property. Premium.

Kamalo Plantation, HC 01, Box 300, Kaunakakai, HI 96748, tel./fax (808) 558-8236, e-mail: kamaloplantation@aloha.net, is a five-acre tropical fruit orchard, where Glenn and Akiko Foster welcome guests. About 10 miles east of Kaunakakai, and across from Father Damien's St. Joseph Church, Kamalo Plantation is surrounded by well-vegetated grounds and even has a *heiau* on the property. The Fosters can accommodate you in a fully contained private studio cottage with full kitchen, indoor and outdoor showers, and deck for $75, or as a B&B guest in a guest suite with private bath and private entry in the main house for $65. This large suite is secluded at one end of the house and has a sitting area, some cooking appliances, and an outside deck. A breakfast of fruit and baked breads and a tour of the grounds are part of the price. A fine place. Moderate.

A short distance down the road is **Kumu'eli Farms B&B,** P.O. Box 1829, Kaunakakai, HI 96748, tel./fax (808) 558-8284, or 558-8281, e-mail: dcurtis@aloha.net, website: www.visit-molokai.com/kumueli. This lovely, contemporary-style wooden house has only one rental suite, which is set to the side of the main house. It has a private entrance off the connecting deck, and there is a lap pool off the back deck. The suite has a queen bed, ceiling fan, TV, and refrigerator, and runs $75 a night, two nights minimum. A homemade breakfast is served each morning. For more information, contact Dorothea or David Curtis, longtime Molokai residents. Moderate.

At the far eastern end of the island, overlooking the lands of Puu O Hoku Ranch is **Puu O Hoku Country Cottage,** a vacation rental that was once a guest cottage at the ranch manager's residence. Check in at the ranch office along the highway near mile marker 25. If you're looking for a place to really be away, this is it. This cottage is a large two-bedroom house that has been renovated but is still charming in its simplicity. It has a living room with a wall of glass, dining room, and full kitchen. Each of the two bedrooms has a private bath. No television, radio, or telephone unless requested. Feel free to use the swimming pool up at the main house. The rental rate is $85 a night or $510 a week with the seventh night free. Contact: Puu O Hoku Ranch, HC 01 Box 900, Kaunakakai, HI 96748, tel. (808) 558-8109, fax 558-8100, e-mail: hoku @aloha.net. Moderate.

The only place to find food on this end of the island is the **Neighborhood Store** in Pukoo. This convenience store carries basic necessities. Connected is a lunch window that serves breakfasts and lunches. Open 8 a.m.-6 p.m. daily.

MIDDLE MOLOKAI AND KALAUPAPA

As you head west from Kaunakakai on Rt. 460 toward Hoolehua Airport you pass fields planted in various crops. These are Molokai's attempt at diversified agriculture since the demise of pineapple a few years ago. Iowa-like cornfields make it obvious that the experiment is working well and has a chance, if the large corporations and the state government get behind it. The cultivated fields give way to hundreds of acres filled with skeletons of dead trees. It's as if some eerie specter stalked the land and devoured their spirits. Farther along and just before a bridge, the **Main Forest Road** intersects, posted for 4WD vehicles but navigable in a standard car during dry weather. This track leads to the Sandalwood Measuring Pit, a depression in the ground that is a permanent reminder of the furious and foolhardy trading of last century. Here too along little-used trails are spectacular views of the lost valleys of Molokai's inaccessible northeast shore.

West on Rt. 460 another branch road, Rt. 470, heads due north through Kualapuu, Del Monte's diminished pineapple town, to road's end at Palaau State Park, Molokai's best camping area and home to the famous Phallic Rock. Near the state park entrance is the lookout for Kalaupapa Peninsula and the beginning of the mule trail, which switchbacks down more than 1,600 feet to the humbling and uplifting experience of Kalaupapa.

MAIN FOREST ROAD

Head west on Rt. 460 from Kaunakakai, and just before mile marker 4 turn right over a bridge (just past the Seventh-day Adventist Church). After a few hundred yards is a red dirt road called Main Forest or Maunahui Road, which heads into the mountains. Your car rental agency will tell you that this road is impassable except in a 4WD, and they're right—if it's raining! But, even if it isn't, this road is rough. Follow the rutted road up into the hills and you'll soon be in a deep forest of ohia, pine, eucalyptus, and giant ferns thriving since their planting early this century. The cool, pleasant air mixes with rich earthy smells of the forest. In just under six miles is a main intersection where you turn right. Proceed a few hundred yards and look for a sign pointing out a Boy Scout/Nature Conservancy Camp. Ignore many small roads branching off.

After 10 miles, look for the road sign, "Kamiloloa"; park 100 yards past in a turnout and walk five minutes to the **Sandalwood Measuring Pit** (Lua Na Moku Iliahi). It's not very spectacular, and this is a long way to go to see a shallow hole in the ground, but the Sandalwood Pit is a permanent reminder of the days of mindless exploitation in Hawaii when money and possessions were more important than the land or the people. Hawaiian chiefs had the pit dug to measure the amount of sandalwood necessary to fill the hold of a ship. They traded the aromatic wood to Yankee captains for baubles, whiskey, guns, manufactured goods, and tools. The traders carried the wood to China where they made huge profits. The trading was so lucrative that the men of entire villages were forced into the hills to collect it, even to the point where the taro fields were neglected and famine gnawed at the door. It only took a few years to denude the mountains of their copious stands of sandalwood, even more incredible when you consider that all the work was done by hand and all the wood was carried to the waiting ships on the coast using the *maka'ainana* as beasts of burden.

Travel past the Sandalwood Pit (beware the mud) for about one mile and you'll come to **Waikolu (Three Waters) Overlook.** From here you can peer down into the pristine valley 3,700 feet below. If rains have been recent, hundreds of waterfalls spread their lace as they fall to the green jungle. The water here seeps into the ground, which soaks it up like a huge dripping sponge. A water tunnel, bored into the valley, collects the water and conducts it for more than five miles until it reaches the 1.4 billion gallon Kualapuu Reservoir. Drive to this area only on a clear day, because the rain will not only get you stuck in mud, but also obscure your view with heavy cloud cover.

Hiking trails through this area are poorly marked, poorly maintained, and strenuous—great qualifications for those who crave solitude and adventure. Up-to-the-minute information and maps are available from the Division of Forestry and Wildlife, Olo Ave., about one mile west of Kaunakakai, tel. (808) 553-5019. **Hanalilolilo Trail** begins not far from Waikolu Lookout and winds through high mountain forests of ohia until it comes to a breathtaking view of **Pelekunu (Foul Smelling, No Sunshine) Valley.** Don't let the name fool you. Hawaiians lived happily and well in this remote, north shore valley for centuries. Time, aided by wind and rain, has turned the 3,300-foot sea cliffs of Pelekunu into some of the tallest in the world. Today, Pelekunu is more remote and isolated than ever. There are no permanent residents, although islanders come sporadically to camp in the summer, when the waters are calm enough to land.

The Hanalilolilo Trail is in the 2,774-acre **Kamakou Preserve,** established by the Nature Conservancy of Hawaii in 1982. It seeks to preserve this unique forest area, home to five species of endangered Hawaiian birds, two of which are endemic only to Molokai. There are 250 species of Hawaiian plants and ferns, 219 of which grow nowhere else in the world. Even a few clusters of sandalwoods tenaciously try to make a comeback. The land was donated by the Molokai Ranch, which kept control of the water rights. Two officials of the ranch are on the conservancy board, which causes some people to look suspiciously at their motives. Most trails have been mapped, and hunting is encouraged throughout most of the area. If interested in obtaining a map, ask the preserve manager: P.O. Box 220, Kualapuu, HI 96757, tel. (808) 553-5236.

KUALAPUU AND KALAE

Kualapuu was a vibrant town when pineapple was king and Del Monte was headquartered here. Now, coffee is king and some of the town's former vibrancy has resurfaced. It is the only

CENTRAL MOLOKAI

KALAUPAPA AIRFIELD · Kahiu Point
Kalaupapa Peninsula
Iliopii Beach · KALAUPAPA NATIONAL HISTORICAL PARK
Kauhako Crater
Kalaupapa
Puu Uao (405 ft.) · FATHER DAMIEN MONUMENT
PALAAU STATE PARK · MULE TRAIL
IRONWOOD HILLS GOLF COURSE
480 · KALAE HWY.
470 · Kalae
Kualapuu
MAUNAHUI RD. · (MAIN FOREST RD.) · SANDALWOOD MEASURING PIT
WAIKOLU OVERLOOK
MAUNALOA HWY.
460
To Maunaloa
Kaunakakai · PAU HANA INN
Kaunakakai Harbor
KAMEHAMEHA HWY. · To Halawa
ONE ALII BEACH PARK
0   2 mi
0   2 km

© J.D. BISIGNANI AND MOON PUBLICATIONS, INC.

town where you can find basic services on the way to Kalaupapa.

Right at the turnoff onto Farrington Avenue is the restored Plantation Store and lunch counter. Displayed in the store are many attractive island gifts, and the lunch counter has pastries, sandwiches, and various coffee and juice drinks. This is now coffee country, so pick up a bag of Mululani Estate or Muleskinner coffee at the store or try a cup at the lunch counter. Both are open daily 10 a.m.-3 p.m.

Weekday tours are given at the 500-acre **Coffees of Hawaii** coffee plantation. Pulled by Sherman and Goliath, the mule wagon takes you through the fields for an up-close look at the coffee plants, then heads to the mill and roasting room to see what happens to the beans once they are picked. The hour-long tours run at 10 a.m. and again at 1 p.m. Mon.-Fri., 10 a.m. only on Saturday, and cost $14 adult or $7 child; advance reservations required. For more information, call (808) 567-9270 or (800) 709-BEAN, website: www.planet-hawaii.com/coffeeshawaii.

A minute down Farrington Avenue you'll come to the **Kualapuu Market,** open daily 8:30 a.m.-6 p.m. except Sunday. Here you'll find a selection of foodstuffs, fresh produce and beef, and general merchandise as well as the only gas pump in the area. The pumps are across the road.

Open 7:30-11:30 a.m. and 12:30-4:30 p.m., the Kualapuu post office is located to the side of the market.

Across the street is the **Kualapuu Cookhouse,** tel. (808) 567-6185, open daily except Sunday 7 a.m.-9 p.m., serving country-cooked foods of a local variety. Hearty breakfasts run $5-8, while the lunch menu has burgers, sandwiches, soups, and plate lunches for $7-9. The dinner menu is a notch or two fancier with items $8-18. It boasts about its homemade pies and cakes. The Kualapuu Cookhouse, headquarters of "The Slow Food Chain," is very friendly, meticulously clean, reasonably priced, and, well . . . slow! Takeouts available.

Notice also the world's largest rubber-lined reservoir across the highway from town. Holding 1.4 billion gallons, its water comes via a five-mile-long, eight-foot-round tunnel from the water-filled valleys to the east.

Purdy's Macadamia Nut Farm

A few miles west of Kualapuu, on Lihi Pali Ave, is **Purdy's Na Hua 'O Ka Aina Farm.** A former airline employee, Mr. Purdy grew up just down the road. When the airline pulled out of Molokai, he decided to stay home, become a farmer, and teach people about the exquisite macadamia nut. His farm has 50 trees that are about 70 years old. These trees still produce nuts prodigiously and continuously for 10 months of the year—Sept.-June—with nuts at all different stages of maturity on the tree at one time. When mature, nuts fall to the ground. Harvested from the ground, they are taken to be cracked and either kept raw or roasted and lightly salted. This one-acre grove of trees is farmed naturally, but Mr. Purdy has put in about 250 trees at another location on the island that are fertilized and treated with pesticides. Purdy's is the only mac nut farm on Molokai, and his yield is about 250-300 pounds of unshelled nuts per tree, as opposed to the 150-200 pounds on the thousand-acre farms of the Big Island. Visit the shop at the farm where Mr. Purdy tells everyone about the trees. Have a go at cracking one of the nuts, and have a taste of its rich fruit. Bags of nuts are sold here—a little treat to yourself for the road—and can be mailed anywhere in the country for you.

Molokai Museum and Cultural Center

Along Rt. 470, two miles past Kualapuu in the village of Kalae, you'll discover the old R.W. Meyer Sugar Mill, now part of the Molokai Museum and Cultural Center, tel. (808) 567-6436. Open Mon.-Sat. 10 a.m.-2 p.m., the mill tour is $2.50 adults, $1 students 5-18; entrance to the cultural center building with its few displays, gift and book shop, and historical video is free. Proceeds go into a fund to construct a new museum building. Built in 1878, the restored mill (1988) is on the National Register of Historic Places. It is in functioning order and clearly shows the stages of creating sugar from cane. As the smallest commercial mill in the state, it was used only until 1889, and it ground cane from 30 nearby upland acres. The museum and cultural center focus on preserving and demonstrating Hawaiian arts and handicrafts like quilting, *lau hala* weaving, woodcarving, plus demonstrations of lei-making and hula. The idea is to share and revive the arts of Hawaii, especially those of Molokai, in this interpretive center. As an outgrowth, the center is used as the Elderhostel campus for Molokai. In August, the annual Molokai music and dance festival takes place at the center. Hula is performed, local musicians play, and the whole community turns out.

Just beyond the center is the Meyer cemetery. You can enter, but be respectful. It is here that Rudolph Meyer, his wife, and children are buried. Up in among the trees above the mill is the Meyer home—not open to the public. Partially restored in 1973, it's now in disrepair. Perhaps one day it to will be restored again and preserved as another tangible link to the family that helped shape the history and economy of the island. The three acres that the cultural center sits on were graciously donated by the Meyer family. Aside from sugarcane, coffee, vegetables, fruits, and dairy cattle were raised on Meyer land, and the present Meyer Ranch still occupies a large tract of the surrounding upland area.

Kalae Cocks

A minute or two past the sugar mill is a surrealistic scene amidst the bucolic highland fields of knee-deep grass. Keep your eyes peeled for a tall cyclone fence topped with nasty looking barbed wire. Inside are row after row of tiny green A-frames, like the pup tents of a brigade of GIs on bivouac. Restrained by leashes just long enough to prevent mortal combat are hundreds of plumed, crowing roosters. Molokai's Filipino population has long been known for cockfighting, an illegal activity, but no law prevents the raising of the fighting birds. These glorious cocks, displaying their feathers while clawing the earth, challenge each other with quite a show of devil-may-care bravado. The spectacle is easily seen from the road.

Palaau State Park

A few minutes past Kalae are the stables for Molokai Mule Rides, which take you down to Kalaupapa. Even if you're not planning a mule ride, make sure to stop and check out the beauty of the countryside surrounding the mule stables. Follow the road until it ends at the parking lot for Palaau State Park.

In the lot, two signs direct you to the Phallic Rock and to the Kalaupapa Overlook (which is not the beginning of the trail down to the penin-

sula). Palaau State Park offers the best camping on Molokai although it's quite a distance from the beach. Follow the signs from the parking lot for about 200 yards to **Phallic Rock** (Kauleomamahoa). Nanahoa, the male fertility god inhabiting the anatomical rock, has been performing like a champ and hasn't had a "headache" in centuries! Legend says that Nanahoa lived nearby and one day sat to admire a beautiful young girl who was looking at her reflection in a pool. Kawahuna, Nanahoa's wife, became so jealous when she saw her husband leering that she attacked the young girl by yanking on her hair. Nanahoa became outraged in turn and struck his wife, who rolled over a nearby cliff and turned to stone. Nanahoa also turned to stone in the shape of an erect penis, and there he sits pointing skyward to this day. Barren women have come here to spend the night and pray for fertility. At the base of the rock is a tiny pool the size of a small bowl that collects rainwater. The women would sit here hoping to absorb the child-giving mana of the rock. You can still see offerings and of course graffiti. One says "Zap"—parents thankful for twins maybe.

Return to the parking lot and follow the signs to **Kalaupapa Overlook.** Jutting 1,600 feet below, almost like an afterthought, is the peninsula of Kalaupapa, which was the home of the lost lepers of Hawaii, picked for its remoteness and inaccessibility. The almost-vertical *pali* served as a natural barrier to the outside world. If you look to your right you'll see the mule trail switchbacking down the cliff. Look to the southeast sector of the peninsula to see the almost perfectly round **Kauhako Crater,** the remnant of the separate volcano that formed Kalaupapa.

THE KALAUPAPA EXPERIENCE

No one knew how the dreaded disease came to the Hawaiian Islands, but they did know that if you were contaminated by it your life would be misery. Leprosy has caused fear in the hearts of man since biblical times, and last century King Kamehameha V and his advisors were no exception. All they knew was that lepers had to be isolated. Kalawao Cove, on the southeast shore of Kalaupapa Peninsula, was regarded as the most isolated spot in the entire kingdom. So, starting in 1864, it was to Kalawao that the lepers of Hawaii were sent to die. Through crude diagnostic testing, anyone who had a suspicious skin discoloration, ulcer, or even bad sunburn was rounded up and sent to Kalawao. The islanders soon learned that once sent, there was no return. So the afflicted hid. Bounty hunters roamed the countryside. Babies, toddlers, teenagers, wives, grandfathers—none were immune to the bounty hunters. They hounded, captured, and sometimes killed anyone who had any sort of skin ailment. The captives were ripped from their villages and loaded on a ship. No one would come near the suspected lepers on board and they sat open to the elements in a cage. They were allowed only one small tin box of possessions. As the ship anchored in the always choppy bay at Kalawao, the cage was opened and the victims were tossed overboard. The contaminated cage was followed by a few sealed barrels of food and clothing that had been collected by merciful Christians. Those too weak or sick or young drowned; the unlucky made it to shore. The crew waited nervously with loaded muskets in case any of the howling, walking nightmares on shore attempted in their delirium to board the ship.

Hell on Earth

Waiting for the newcomers were the forsaken. Abandoned by king, country, family, friends, and apparently the Lord himself, they became animals—beasts of prey. Young girls with hardly a blemish were raped by reeking deformed men in rags. Old men were bludgeoned, their tin boxes ripped from their hands. Children and babies cried and begged for food, turning instinctively to the demented women who had lost all motherly feelings. Finally too weak even to whimper, they died of starvation. Those victims who could make rude dwellings of sticks and stones,

while others lived in caves or on the beach open to the elements. Finally, the conscience of the kingdom was stirred in 1866: the old dumping ground of Kalawao was abandoned and the lepers were exiled to the more hospitable Kalaupapa side of the peninsula, just a few hundred yards to the west.

The Move to Kalaupapa

The people of the sleepy village of Kalaupapa couldn't believe their eyes when they saw the ravaged ones. But these lepers now sent to Kalaupapa were treated more mercifully. Missionary groups and *kokua* (helpers) provided food and rudimentary clothing. An end was put to the lawlessness and depravity. Still, the lepers were kept separate. For the most part they lived outdoors or in very rude huts. They never could come in direct contact with the *kokua*. If they met a healthy person walking along a path, they had to grovel at the side. Most fell to the ground, hiding their faces and attempting to crawl like beaten dogs under a bush. Many *kokua*, horrified by Kalaupapa, left on the next available boat. With no medical attention, death was still the only release from Kalaupapa.

Light in Hell

It was by accident or miracle that **Joseph de Veuster, Father Damien**, a Catholic priest, came from Belgium to Hawaii. His brother, also a priest, was supposed to come, but he became ill and Father Damien came in his place. Damien spent a few years in Hawaii, building churches and learning the language and ways of the people, before he came to Kalaupapa in 1873. What he saw touched his heart. He was different from the rest, having come with a sense of mission to help the lepers and bring them hope and dignity. The other missionaries saw Kalaupapa not as a place to live, but to die. Damien saw the

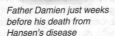

Father Damien just weeks before his death from Hansen's disease

lepers as children of God who had the right to live and be comforted. When they hid under a bush at his approach, he picked them up and stood them on their feet. He carried water all day long to the sick and dying. He bathed their wounds and built them shelters with his own two hands. When clothes or food or materials ran short, he walked topside and begged for more. Other church groups were against him and the government gave him little aid, but he persevered. Damien scraped together some lumber and fashioned a flume pipe to carry water to his people, who were still dying mainly from pneumonia and tuberculosis brought on by neglect. Damien worked long days alone, until he dropped exhausted at night.

Father Damien modified **St. Philomena Church,** a structure that was originally built in Honolulu by Brother Bertrant in 1872, and shipped it to Molokai in segments. Father Damien invited his flock inside, but those grossly afflicted could not control their mouths, so spittle would drip to the floor. They were ashamed to soil the church, so Damien cut squares in the floor through which they could spit onto the ground. Slowly a light began to shine in the hearts of the lepers and the authorities began to take notice. Conditions began to improve, but there were those who resented Damien. Robert Louis Stevenson visited the settlement, and after meeting Damien wrote an open letter that ended ". . . he is my father." Damien contracted leprosy, but by the time he died in 1889 at age 49, he knew his people would be cared for. In 1936, Damien's native Belgium asked that his remains be returned. He was exhumed and his remains sent home, but a memorial still stands where he was interred at Kalaupapa. After lengthy squabbles with the Belgian government, Father Damien's right hand was returned to Kalaupapa in 1995 and has been reinterred as a religious relic. He has since been beatified by the Pope.

The Light Grows Brighter

Brother Dutton, who arrived in 1886, and Mother Marianne Cope, a Franciscan nun from Syracuse, New York, who came in 1888 with two other Sisters of Saint Francis, carried on Damien's work. In addition, many missionary groups sent volunteers to help at the colony. Thereafter the people of Kalaupapa were treated with dignity

and given a sense of hope. In 1873, the same year that Damien arrived at Kalaupapa, Norwegian physician Gerhard Hansen isolated the bacteria that causes leprosy, and shortly thereafter the official name of the malady became Hansen's disease. By the turn of this century, adequate medical care and good living conditions were provided to the patients at Kalaupapa. Still, many died, mostly from complications such as TB or pneumonia. Families could not visit members confined to Kalaupapa unless they were near death, and any children born to the patients—who were now starting to marry—were whisked away at birth and adopted, or given to family members on the outside. Even until the 1940s people were still sent to Kalaupapa because of skin ailments that were never really diagnosed as leprosy. Many of these indeed did show signs of the disease, but there is always the haunting thought that they may have contracted it after arrival at the colony. Jimmy, one of the guides for Damien Tours, was one of these. He had some white spots as a child that his Hawaiian grandmother would treat with herbs. As soon as she stopped applying the herbs, the spots would return. A public health nurse at school saw the spots, and Jimmy was sent to Kalaupapa. At the time he was given only 10 years to live.

In the mid-1940s sulfa drugs were found to arrest most cases of Hansen's disease, and the prognosis for a normal life improved. By the 1960s further breakthroughs made Hansen's disease noncontagious, and in 1969 the quarantine on patients was eliminated. Patients at Kalaupapa were then free to leave and return to their homes. No new patients were admitted, but most, already living in the only home they'd ever known, opted to stay. In total over the years, there have been about 8,000 unfortunate individuals who have been exiled to this forgotten spit of land. Almost as if it were an accident of fate designed to expunge evidence of the damning past, the community hospital along with all its records burned to the ground in the early '90s. No help was afforded by the local fire truck, which was unable to be started. Nonetheless, medical treatment continues and all needed care is still provided. The community of resident patients numbers less than 60 today—the average age is about 70—and state caretakers and federal employees in the community now outnumber patients. In all of Hawaii today, there are about 450 people registered with Hansen's disease; all but those at Kalaupapa live at home with their families. Each year on average, about 18 new cases are diagnosed in the state. Still the number of patients continues to drop as the old-timers die. Kalaupapa has been turned into a national historical park, jointly administered by the state Department of Health, but the residents are assured a lifetime occupancy and free care.

Getting There

It shouldn't be a matter of *if* you go to Kalaupapa, but *how* you go. You have choices. You can fly, walk, or ride a mule. No matter how you go, you *cannot* walk around Kalaupapa unescorted. You *must* take an official tour, and children under 16 are not allowed. If you're going by mule, arrangements are made for you by the company, but if you're walking down or flying in you have to call ahead to Richard Marks at **Damien Tours,** tel. (808) 567-6171, the only tour company now operating, and he will give you an exact place and time to meet once down on the peninsula. Damien Tours charges $32 for a fascinating, four-hour tour conducted by one of the residents. Definitely worth the money; the insight you get from the resident tour guide is priceless and unique. No food or beverages, except water, are available to visitors, so make sure to bring your own.

"I'd rather be riding a mule on Molokai" is an eye-catching bumper sticker sported by those lucky enough to have made the decent to Kalaupapa aboard sure-footed mules. After several years of closure for trail repair, the **Molokai Mule**

Ride is now back in business. The well-trained mules will transport you down the 1,600-foot *pali* expertly negotiating 26 hairpin switchbacks on the trail to the bottom. After your tour of the settlement, these gutsy animals carry you right back up so you too can claim your bumper sticker and ride-completion certificate. You are on the mule about 90 minutes each way. This tour runs $120 and includes the ground tour of the settlement and lunch. No riders over 240 pounds please; you must be at least 16 years old and in good physical shape. For reservations, call (808) 567-6088 or (800) 567-7550.

If you're walking to Kalaupapa, follow the mule trail, cut by Manuel Farinha in 1886. Go about 200 yards past the stables and look for a road to the right. Follow this track down past pastureland to the trailhead, where there is a small metal building with an odd sign that reads "Advance Technology Center Hawaii USA" just near an overgrown observation point for the peninsula. The three-mile, 90-minute trail going down the steep north face of the *pali* is well maintained and only mildly strenuous. It will be rutted and muddy in spots, and you'll have to step around the road apples, so wear hiking boots if possible.

You can fly in and out, or out only, which is a good alternative and relatively cheap. **Molokai Air Shuttle** from Hoolehua offers roundtrip flights for $50. Flights are limited so call for schedules. When you fly in you must still arrange for the ground tour through Damien Tours before you will be sold a ticket. If you decide to fly, notice the breakers at the end of the runway sending spray 90 feet into the air. The pilots time their takeoff to miss the spray!

MOLOKAI'S WEST END

Long before contact with the Europeans, the west end of Molokai was famous throughout the Hawaiian Islands. The culture centered on Maunaloa, the ancient volcanic mountain that formed the land. On its slopes the goddess Laka learned the hula from her sister and spread its joyous undulations to all the other islands. Not far from the birthplace of the hula is Kaluakoi, one of the two most important adze quarries in old Hawaii. Without these stone tools, no canoes, bowls, or everyday items could have been fashioned. Voyagers came from every major island to trade for this perfect stone of Kaluakoi. With all this coming and going, the always-small population of Molokai needed godly protection. Not far away at Kalaipahoa, the "poison wood" sorcery gods of Molokai lived in a grove that supposedly sprouted to maturity in one night. With talismans made from this magical grove, Molokai kept invading warriors at bay for centuries.

Most of the island's arable land is out here. The thrust west began with the founding of the Molokai Ranch, whose 54,000 acres make up about 50% of the good farmland on the island, or about one-third of the island. The ranch was owned last century by Kamehameha V, and after his death it was sold to private interests who began the successful raising of Santa Gertrudis cattle imported from the famous Texas King Ranch. The ranch still employs *paniolo*, with the life of riding the range and rodeo still strong. Today, anywhere between 6,000-10,000 head of Brahman and Brangus cattle roam ranch land with about 80 horses to do the work.

THE NORTHWEST

The northwest section of Molokai, centered at **Hoolehua,** is where the Hawaiian Homes parcels are located. The entire area has a feeling of heartland America, and if you ignore the coastline in the background you could easily imagine yourself in the rolling hills of Missouri. Don't expect a town at Hoolehua. All that's there is a little post office and a government office.

Moomomi Beach

The real destination is Moomomi (Jeweled Reptile) Beach. Follow Rt. 460 until it branches north at Rt. 480 a mile east of the airport. Follow Rt. 480 until it turns left onto Farrington Avenue in Hoolehua, and continue for about four miles until it turns into a red dirt road. This road can be extremely rutted, even tipping your car at a very precarious angle. Be advised! Continue for about 10 minutes until you come to a pavilion. Below you is Moomomi. This area is a favorite with local people who come here to swim, fish, and surf. The swells are good only in winter, but the beach becomes rocky at that time of year. The tides bring the sand in by April and the swimming until November is good. Unofficial camping is probably okay on this grassy area, and a toilet and water are available at the pavilion.

Moomomi Beach goes back in Hawaiian legend. Besides the mythical lizards that inhabited this area, a great shark-god was born here. The mother was a woman who became impregnated by the gods. Her husband was angry that her child would be from the spirit world, so he directed her to come and sit on a large rock down by the beach. She went into labor and began to cry. A tear, holding a tiny fish, rolled down her cheek and fell into the sea and became the powerful shark-god. The rock upon which his mother sat is the large black one just to the right of the beach.

If you feel adventurous you can head west along the beach. Every 10 minutes or so you come to a tiny beach that you have entirely to yourself. Since this area is so isolated, be extremely careful of surf conditions. About two miles west of Moomomi is **Keonelele,** a miniature desert of sand dunes. The wind whips through this region and carries the sand to the southwest shore. Geologists haunt this area trying to piece together Molokai's geological history. The Hawaiians used Keonelele as a burial site, and strange footprints found in the soft sandstone supposedly foretold the coming of white men. Today, Keonelele is totally deserted; although small, it gives the impression of a vast wasteland.

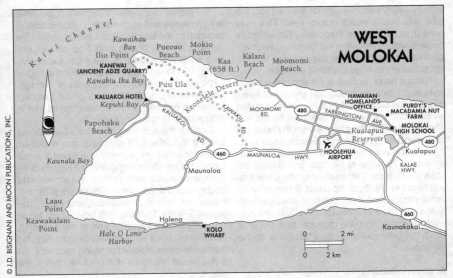

© J.D. BISIGNANI AND MOON PUBLICATIONS, INC.

Kawakiu Beach

This secluded and pristine beach on the far northwestern corner of Molokai was an item of controversy between the developers of the Kaluakoi Corp. and the grassroots activists of Molokai. For years access to the beach was restricted, and the Kaluakoi Corp. planned to develop the area. It was known that the area was very important during precontact times and rich in unexplored archaeological sites. The Kaluakoi Corp. hired a supposed team of "experts" who studied the site for months and finally claimed that the area had no significant archaeological importance. Their findings were hooted at by local people and by scholars from various institutions who knew better. This controversy resulted in Kawakiu Beach being opened to the public with plans of turning it into a beach park; the archaeological sites will be preserved.

The swimming at Kawakiu is excellent with the sandy bottom tapering off slowly. To get there go to the Paniolo Hale Condo at Kaluakoi Resort (see following) and park at the end of the dirt road that heads toward the sea, past the last paved parking lot of the condo. Walk across the golf course fairway of the 10th hole to the beach. Follow it north for three-quarters of a mile, dodging the tide until you come to Kawa-

kiu—definitely not recommended during periods of high surf, when swimming would be too dangerous anyway. If you have lots of time and energy, walk on farther to the ancient adze quarry and abandoned Coast Guard station on Lio Point. You can also drive there by following the dirt road past the condos until it branches inland. It eventually swings back and takes you to Kawakiu. The road is rough, and the hike mildly strenuous, but Kawakiu is definitely worth it.

Papohaku Beach

The best attraction in the area doesn't have a price tag. Papohaku Beach is the giant expanse of white sand running south from the Kaluakoi Resort. The sands here are so expansive that they were dredged and taken to Oahu in the 1950s. During the winter months a great deal of sand is stripped away and large lava boulders and outcroppings are exposed. Every spring and summer the tides carry the sand back and deposit it on the enormous beach. Camping is permitted at the **Papohaku County Beach Park** just past the resort. Pick up your permit at the Mitchell Pauole Center in Kaunakakai, tel. (808) 553-3204, before you come all the way out here. Here you'll find a large grassy play area, toilets, showers, picnic tables, grills for cooking, and a virtually empty beach. A sign on the road past the park tells you to watch out for deer. This road runs through a huge Papohaku Ranchlands home development area, with several beach access roads and parking areas that lead to other spots along this huge expanse of beach.

The last beach access at the end of the paved road leads to a secluded and protected small bay and fine sand beach that is even safe during winter months when other beach areas are not. The Kaupoa Trail starts from the south end of this beach and runs into Molokai Ranch lands.

One of the attractions of Molokai is its remoteness. Here the sky is clear and at night the stars are brilliant. Yet, even here you know that you're not too far from the crush of humanity for directly across the Kaiwi Channel you can clearly see the glow of Honolulu, Wailua, and Kaneohe shimmering in the distance, and, closer at hand, the more muted lights of Maunaloa on the hill above.

Accommodations

Much of the west end of Molokai is the Kaluakoi Resort. The complex includes the Kaluakoi Hotel, two resort condominiums, world-famous Kaluakoi Golf Course, private home sites, and Papohaku, Hawaii's largest white-sand beach.

The **Kaluakoi Hotel and Golf Club,** P.O. Box 1977, Maunaloa, HI 96770, tel. (808) 552-2555, (800) 435-7208 statewide, or (800) 552-2550 Mainland, fax (808) 552-2821, e-mail: Kaluakoi @juno.com, website: www.kaluakoi.com, is the destination point for most of the people coming to Molokai. The low-rise buildings, made primarily of wood, blend with the surrounding countryside. The well-kept grounds are covered in manicured trees and shrubbery. All rooms have color TV, VCRs (video rental is at the front desk), and small refrigerators, and those on the second floor have open-beam construction. Some of the rooms have stovetops, while the cottages have kitchens. Many rooms sit along the fairways of the golf course and most have at least a partial ocean view. Because of the constant cool breezes, no air-conditioning is necessary, but there are ceiling fans. A guest laundry is located on premises. At more than 20 years old, this resort is beginning to show its age; it's becoming a little frayed around the edges. While not luxury, it is, nonetheless, quite adequate.

The rooms, many newly refurbished, are done in light pastels and earth colors. Dynamic color is provided by the large windows that open onto the fairways and the sea beyond. The least expensive hotel room is $105, the most expensive $275. Condo units go from $155 for a studio to $220 for a one-bedroom oceanfront cottage. Third person is $15. All guests of the Kaluakoi Hotel can golf free ($15 cart fee only) as part of their room charge. Expensive.

Consult the activities desk for what's doing around the island. It can help you make all arrangements. On property you'll find a small Liberty House shop, along with the Kepuhi Sundries store, which sells snacks, magazines, and liquor, and the Laughing Gecko shop for antiques, art, jewelry, Hawaiiana, and locally designed T-shirts. Past the 10th hole, which would basically be the far north end of the property, you'll overlook a very private beach. Beyond that is one more. No rules or prying eyes here, so if you would like to swim au naturel, this is the place.

Some of the units at the resort complex, collectively called the **Kaluakoi Villas,** 1131 Kaluakoi Rd., Maunaloa, HI 96770, tel. (808) 552-2721 or (800) 367-5004 U.S. and Canada, (800) 272-5275 statewide, are managed by the Castle Group. Each studio, suite, and cottage has been tastefully decorated and includes a color TV, lanai, and refrigerator, and guests can use the resort's restaurants and all its recreational facilities. Rates range $125-150 for a studio, $150-180 for a suite, and $200 for the cottage; fourth night free. Premium.

Built in 1981, the **Ke Nani Kai Condos** are *mauka* of the road leading to the Kaluakoi Resort, and they cost $149-159 for one of the fully furnished one-bedroom apartments; two bedrooms rent at $179-199. All apartments are large and in excellent condition. Contact Ke Nani Kai, P.O. Box 289, Maunaloa, HI 96770, tel. (808) 552-2761 or (800) 535-0085, fax (808) 633-5085. A Marc Resort Hawaii property. Luxury.

Newer yet, **Paniolo Hale** is another condo complex set in the trees surrounded by fairways. These buildings have more style than others on the area, and the whole complex a little more classy. The swimming pool, paddle tennis, and barbecue grill are for the use of all guests. Maid service is provided for stays of one week or longer, and each unit has a washer and dryer. Garden and ocean studios run $95 and $135, $115 and $160 for one bedroom, $145 and $195 for two bedrooms; $20 more in high season. Three nights minimum. Two-bedroom units have a hot tub and enclosed lanai. Contact Paniolo Hale, P.O. Box 190, Maunaloa, HI 96770, tel. (808) 552-2731 or (800) 367-2984, fax (808) 552-2288, e-mail: paniolo@lava.net, website: www .lava.net/paniolo. Expensive.

Food

The Kaluakoi Resort's **Ohia Lodge**, tel. (808) 552-2555, is an uninspired restaurant serving breakfast and dinner daily. It is the only restaurant at the resort and, aside from the Village Grill in Maunaloa, the only one on the west end of the island. Nice sunset views; reservations suggested. The garden-side snack bar is open daily 11 a.m.-4 p.m., selling sandwiches, burgers, and plate lunches, with most everything under $6. The **Ohia Lounge** is open all day and provides live local entertainment on Friday and Saturday.

MAUNALOA AND THE SOUTHWEST COAST

According to legend, the hilltop area of Maunaloa was the first place in the islands that the Hawaiians received hula instruction. Today, there are many *hula halau* on Molokai, and the yearly Molokai Hula Ka Piko festival is held down the hill at Papohaku State Park to honor this ancient music and dance form.

Most people heading east-west between Kaunakakai and the Kaluakoi Resort never make it into Maunaloa town. That's because Rt. 460 splits just east of Maunaloa, and Kaluakoi Road heads north toward the Kaluakoi Resort and away from the town. Until recently, with the pineapple gone and few visitors, the town barely hung on. Maunaloa was a wonderful example of a plantation town. It was a little patch of humble workers' houses carved into a field. In front you were likely to see a tethered horse, a boat, or glass fishing floats hanging from the lanai. Overhead you could see a kite flying—a sign that you had arrived in Maunaloa. The townsfolk were friendly and if you were looking for conversation or a taste of Hawaiian history, the old-

timers hanging around under the shaded lean-to near the post office were just the ticket.

But the winds of change have started to blow in Maunaloa and the force increases. The Molokai Ranch, which owns the town, has begun to institute a new grand development scheme to completely "rejuvenate" the town. Most of the old homes, many falling apart and maybe uninsurable, have been torn down and have been replaced by new, similar-style homes. Bunched together away from the downtown area, these homes are set closer together than the old houses were. Starting at about $139,000, they are pricy yet affordable for many. Local people have been given first choice, and many have taken the deal. Additionally, streets have been paved and new ones laid out. A new sewer system and water reservoir have been installed. While several of the old standby commercial establishments have remained, others are being built. Already a movie theater, KFC, and ranch activities center are up and running. Future plans include a lodge, an old-town museum and cultural center, a city park, and new housing areas for custom homes. With all these changes there is certain to be some disagreement about their effect. While many take a wait-and-see attitude, others who live and/or work in town seem to think that the changes are for the better.

The only public access beach on this part of the island is **Hale O Lono**—follow the only road south of town and keep to the major track of crushed coral. A fine white-sand beach, Hale O Lono is the launch point for the annual Bankoh Molokai Outrigger Canoe Championship race to Waikiki. This is an old harbor that services the ranch, a few commercial boats related to the ranch, and the occasional passing ship. From here, the sand of Papohaku Beach was shipped to Oahu in the 1950s.

If you are staying at the Molokai Ranch, other spots along the coast might be of interest. About a mile east of Hale O Lono is **Halena Beach**, where there is an old Boy Scout camp and pavilion. East of there down the coastal dirt track is **Kolo Beach**, a fine long strand that sports the dilapidated **Kolo Wharf** at its far end. Kolo Wharf was where Molokai once shipped its pineapples. Now only naked pilings stand to mark the spot. On the far western end of the island is **Kaupoa Beach**, an old-time favorite of island residents.

Molokai Ranch

The only place to stay in Maunaloa in at the Molokai Ranch, but you don't just sleep there; activities are included. Accommodations are in three camps, placed in isolated yet picturesque spots. Paniolo Camp is set up near the rodeo arena, Kolo Camp overlooks the water near the old Kolo Wharf on the south shore, and Kaupoa Camp sits on a perfect white-sand crescent beach at the extreme west end. Paniolo and Kaupoa Camps have "tentalows," and Kolo has yurts. Wood-frame structures covered with heavy canvas, all are set up on wooden platforms that hold umbrella-covered patio tables, chairs, and benches. Inside are comfortable queen beds, a chest of drawers, and a chair. Set off to the side of the lanai is a composting toilet and no-roof shower that uses solar energy to heat the water. Electricity in each camp is powered by solar batteries. All this is done to impact the environment as little as possible. This is rustic simplicity—but luxurious for camping. Rates are on a sliding scale from $185-245 a night; children 4-12 are $75. These prices include morning and afternoon activities, three home-cooked meals a day, evening entertainment, and transportation to and from the airport and around the ranch property. For activities, you might choose horseback trail riding, *paniolo* roundup in the corral, a ropes course, mountain biking, hiking, kayaking, outrigger canoeing, sailing or whalewatching in season, or beach games; all equipment is provided. Multiday packages are available, and other island activities can be arranged at additional cost. For information and reservations contact Molokai Ranch, P.O. Box 259, Maunaloa, HI 96770, tel. (808) 552-2734 or (800) 254-8871, e-mail: info@molokai-ranch.com, website: www.molokai-ranch.com. Luxury.

Other Practicalities

A good reason to make the trek to Maunaloa is to visit the **Big Wind Kite Factory,** P.O. Box 10, Maunaloa, HI 96770, tel. (808) 552-2364, e-mail: bigwind@aloha.net, website: www.molokai.com/kites, open Mon.-Sat. 8:30 a.m.-5 p.m., Sunday 10 a.m.-2 p.m., owned and operated by Jonathan Sosher and his wife Daphane. The handcrafted kites and windsocks from this down-home cottage industry are the same ones that sell at Honolulu's slick Ala Moana Mall, and at Kyle's Kites at The Plantation on Kauai. All are made on the premises by Jonathan, Daphane, son Zachary, and a few workers, who come up with designs like panda bears, rainbow stegosauruses, geckos with sunglasses, and hula girls in ti-leaf skirts—ask for a free factory tour. Jonathan will give you a lesson in the park next door on any of the kites, including the two-string-controllable ones. Prices range $10-200 for a rip-stop nylon kite; they make beautiful, easily transportable gifts that'll last for years.

The shop itself is ablaze with beautiful colors, as if you've walked into the heart of a flower. This is a happy store. Part of it, **The Plantation Gallery,** sells a variety of crafts by local artists—Hawaiian quilt pillowcases, Pacific isle shell jewelry, scrimshaw (on deerhorn), earrings, bracelets, boxes, bamboo xylophones, and other wood objects. Island cypress, Japanese *sugi* from a local tree, and *milo* have been carved by a local artist named Robin. Part of the boutique has batiks, Balinese masks, woodcarvings, quilts, and sarongs; especially nice are carved mirror frames of storks, birds, and flowers. And if you just can't live without a blowgun from Irian Jaya, this is the place. Here too you'll find perhaps the island's best selections of books on Hawaii. After you've run through a million tourist shops and are sick of the shell lei, come here to find something truly unique. The Big Wind Kite Factory is *the* most interesting shop on Molokai.

Maunaloa General Store, tel. (808) 552-2868, is open Mon.-Sat. 9 a.m.-7 p.m., Sunday 10 a.m.-7 p.m. It's a well-stocked store where you can pick up anything that you'll need if you'll be staying in one of the condos at Kaluakoi. You can buy liquor, wine, beer, canned goods, meats, and vegetables.

The old Jojo's Cafe has been totally renovated and now operates with a new menu as **The Village Grill,** tel. (808) 552-0012. However, the bar that once did duty at the Pearl City Tavern in Oahu still occupies a spot in this new restaurant but has been retopped in bronze with cowboy designs added. Open 11 a.m.-2 p.m. for lunch, serving sandwiches, burgers, stir-fry, pasta, ribs, and pizza. For dinner, 6-9 p.m., the restaurant is more like a steakhouse with many meat and fish dishes, some pasta, and salads and dessert; entrees are in the $9-18 range.

To some people's delight and others' chagrin, there is now a KFC in town in the theater building. Usual fare, but limited; usual prices.

There was a theater is Maunaloa until the mid-1970s, after which the only one on the island was in Kaunakakai. When that closed, the island was without until the **Maunaloa Theater** was newly built in 1997. This triplex theater shows first movies and not only draws people from Maunaloa, but also from Kaluakoi and Kaunakakai as well.

While in Mauna Loa, stop at the Molokai Ranch Outfitters Center and have a peek at the mini-museum displaying photos and artifacts of Molokai culture and history. Open daily 7 a.m.-7 p.m. for self-guided tours; tel. (808) 552-2791.

DIANA LASICH HARPER

OAHU

. . . but a diversion, the most common is upon the water . . . the men lay themselves flat upon an oval piece of plank . . . they wait the time for the greatest swell that sets on shore, and altogether push forward with their arms to keep on its top, it sends them in with a most astonishing velocity . . .

~James King, c. 1779

M.G.L. DOMENY DE RIENZI

INTRODUCTION

It is the destiny of certain places on earth to be imbued with an inexplicable magnetism, a power that draws people whose visions and desires combine at just the right moment to create a dynamism so strong that it becomes history. The result for these "certain places" is greatness . . . and Oahu is one of these.

It is difficult to separate Oahu from its vibrant metropolis, Honolulu, whose massive political, economic, and social muscle dominate both the entire state and its home island. But to look at Honolulu *as* Oahu is to look upon only the face of a great sculpture, ignoring the beauty and subtleties of the whole. The words "Honolulu," "Waikiki," and "Pearl Harbor" conjure up visions common to people the world over. Immediately imaginations flush with palm trees swaying, a healthy tan, bombs dropping with infamy, and golden moons rising romantically over lovers on white-sand beaches.

Oahu is called the "Gathering Place," and to itself it has indeed gathered the noble memories of old Hawaii, the vibrancy of a bright-eyed fledgling state, and the brawny power so necessary for the future. On this amazing piece of land adrift in the great ocean, 885,000 people live; nearly seven times that number visit yearly, and as time passes Oahu remains strong as one of those "certain places."

OVERVIEW

Oahu is partly a tropical garden, bathed by soft showers and sunshine, and swaying with a gentle but firm rhythm. You can experience this feeling all over the island, even in pockets of downtown Honolulu and Waikiki. However, its other side is brash—dominated by the confidence of a major American city perched upon the Pacific Basin whose music is a pounding staccato jackhammer, droning bulldozer, and mechanical screeching of the ever-present building-crane. The vast majority of first-time and return visitors land at Honolulu International and spend at least a few days on Oahu, usually in Waikiki.

People are amazed at the diversity of experiences the island has to offer. Besides the obvious (and endless) beach activities, it offers museums, botanical gardens, a fantastic zoo and aquarium, nightclubs, extravagant shows, free entertainment, cultural classes, theaters, sporting events, a major university, historical sights galore, an exotic cosmopolitan atmosphere, backcountry trekking, and an abundance of camping—all easily accessible via terrific public transportation. Finally, to sweeten the pot, Oahu can easily be the least expensive of the Hawaiian Islands to visit.

Waikiki

Loosely, this world-famous beach is a hunk of land bordered by the **Ala Wai Canal** and running eastward to **Diamond Head.** Early last century these two golden miles were little more than a string of dirty beaches backed by a mosquito-infested swamp. Until 1901, when the Moana Hotel was built, only Hawaii's few remaining *ali'i* and a handful of wealthy *kama'aina* families had homes here. Now, more than 120 hotels, condos, and other lodgings provide more than 31,000 rooms, and if you placed a $20 bill on the ground, it would barely cover the cost of the land beneath it!

This hyperactive area will delight and disgust you, excite and overwhelm you, but never bore you. Waikiki gives you the feeling that you've arrived *someplace*. Besides lolling on the beach and walking the gauntlet of restaurants, hotels, malls, and street merchants, you can visit the **Waikiki Aquarium** or **Honolulu Zoo.** Then, ever-present Diamond Head, that monolith of frozen lava so symbolic of Hawaii, is easily reached by a few minutes' drive and a leisurely stroll to its summit.

Downtown Honolulu

Head for downtown and give yourself a full day to catch all the sights. It's as if a huge grappling hook attached to the heart of a Mainland city and hauled it across the sea. But don't get the idea that Honolulu is not unique, because it is! You'll find a delightful mixture of quaintly historic and future-shock new; exotic and ordinary. The center is **Iolani Palace,** the only royal palace in America, heralded by the gilded statue of Kamehameha I. In an easy walking radius are the **State Capitol** and attendant government buildings. Chrome and glass skyscrapers holding the offices of Hawaii's economically mighty shade small stone and wooden structures from the last century: **Mission Houses Museum, Kawaiahao Church,** and **St. Andrew's Cathedral.**

Down at the harbor **Aloha Tower** greets the few passenger ships that still make port; nearby is the floating museum ship, *Falls of Clyde,* a nostalgic reminder of simpler times. Hotel Street takes you to old but not always venerable **Chinatown,** filled with alleyways housing tiny temples, herbalists, aromatic markets, inexpensive eateries, rough nightspots, dives, and the strong, distinctive flavor of transplanted Asia.

If the hustle and bustle gets to be too much, head for **Foster Botanical Gardens.** Or hop a bus for the serenity of the **Bishop Museum and Planetarium,** undoubtedly *the* best Polynesian cultural and anthropological museum in the world.

Pearl Harbor

Hawaii's only interstate, H-1, runs west of the city center to Pearl Harbor. You can't help noticing the huge military presence throughout the area, and it becomes clear why Hawaii is considered the most militarized state in the country. The attraction here, which shouldn't be missed, is the **USS *Arizona* Memorial.** The museum, visitors center, and tours, operated jointly by the U.S. Navy and the National Park Service, are both excellent and free. Nearby is the **USS *Bowfin* Submarine Museum and Park,** another worthy stop.

Heading for the Hills

Behind the city is the **Koolau Range.** As you head for these beckoning hills, you can take a side trip over to the **University of Hawaii** and the **East-West Center** while passing through Manoa Valley, epitome of the "good life" in Hawaii. Route 61 takes you up and over Nuuanu Pali to Oahu's windward side. En route you'll pass **Punchbowl,** an old crater holding some of the dead from WW II and the Korean and Vietnam wars in the **National Cemetery of the Pacific.**

As you climb, the road passes the **Royal Mausoleum,** final resting place for some of Hawaii's last kings, queens, and nobility. Then comes **Queen Emma Summer Palace,** a Victorian home of gentility and lace. Next is **Nuuanu Pali,** where Kamehameha drove 16,000 Oahu warriors over the cliff, sealing his dominance of the island kingdom with their blood. The view is hauntingly beautiful, as the mountains drop suddenly to the coast of windward Oahu.

Central Oahu

Pearl Harbor is ringed by rather ordinary communities, suburbs of Honolulu, but farther up the plateau the land has been put to other uses. Early in the 19th century, huge pineapple plantations were started on the rich soil, and today vast tracts are still planted in this fruit. The **Pineapple Variety Garden** is a good place to stop for an introduction to the history of pineapple production on the island. Also dominating huge areas of this central plain are the broad and beautiful **Schofield Barracks** Army base and **Wheeler Air Force Base,** two of the island's important military installations and significant players in America's armed conflicts in the Pacific and Asia.

Southeast Oahu

Head eastward around the bulge of Diamond Head and passing exclusive residential areas, and you soon find a string of secluded beaches. Around this tip you pass **Koko Head Crater,** a trekker's haven; **Hanauma Bay,** an underwater conservation park renowned for magnificent family-class snorkeling; **Sea Life Park,** an extravaganza of the deep; and the sleepy village of **Waimanalo Beach.** Nearby at **Bellow's Field Beach Park** is camping, where it's hard to believe the city's just 10 miles back.

Windward Oahu

On the windward side, **Kailua** and **Kaneohe** have become suburban bedroom communities for Honolulu; this entire coast has few tourist accommodations, so it remains relatively uncrowded. The beaches are excellent, with beach parks and camping spots one after another, and the winds make this side of the island perfect for windsurfing. North of Kaneohe is **Valley of the Temples,** where a Christian cross sits high on a hill, and Buddha rests calmly in the **Byodo-In Temple.**

Just up Rt. 83, the coastal highway, comes **Waiahole,** Oahu's outback, where tiny farms and taro patches dot the valleys and local folks move with the slow beat of bygone days. A quick succession of beaches follows, many rarely visited by more than passing fishermen. **Punaluu** comes next, offering some of the only accommodations along this coast and a lovely walk to **Kaliuwaa,** the Sacred Falls. In **Laie** is the **Polynesian Cultural Center,** operated by the Mormon Church. **Brigham Young University** is here too, along with a solid Mormon temple open to visitors.

North Shore

The North Shore is famous for magnificent surf. From **Sunset Beach** to **Haleiwa,** world-class surfers come to be challenged by the liquid thunder of the **Banzai Pipeline** and **Waimea Bay.** Art shops, boutiques, tiny restaurants, and secluded hideaways line these sun-drenched miles. At the far western end is **Dillingham Airfield** where you can take a glider ride or air tour of the island. The road ends with a very rugged jeep trail leading to **Kaena Point,** renowned for the most monstrous surf on the North Shore.

Leeward Coast

The western end of the island is the **Waianae Coast.** The towns of **Maili, Waianae,** and **Makaha** are considered the last domain of the locals of Oahu. This coastal area has escaped development so far, and it's one of the few places on the island where ordinary people can afford to live near the beach. Sometimes an attitude of resentment spills over against tourists; mostly, though, lovely people with good hearts live here, who will treat you as nicely as you're willing to treat them.

World-class surfing beaches along this coast are preferred by many of the best-known surfers from Hawaii. Many work as lifeguards in the beach parks, and they all congregate for the annual surfing championships held in Makaha. Here is a perfect chance to mingle with the people and soak up some of the last real *aloha* left on Oahu.

THE LAND

When Papa, the Hawaiian earth mother, returned from vacationing in Tahiti, she was less than pleased. She had learned through a gossiping messenger that her husband, Wakea, had been playing around. Besides simply philandering, he'd been foolish enough to impregnate Hina, a lovely young goddess who bore him island children. Papa, scorned and furious, showed Wakea that two could play the same game by taking a handsome young lover, Lua. Their brief interlude yielded the man-child Oahu, sixth of the great island children. Geologically, Oahu is the second oldest main island after Kauai. It emerged from beneath the waves as hissing lava a few million years after Kauai and cooled a little quicker than Papa's temper to form Hawaii's third largest island.

Land Facts

Oahu has a total land area of 597 square miles, and measured from its farthest points it is 44 miles long by 30 miles wide. The 112-mile coastline holds the two largest harbors in the state, **Honolulu** and **Pearl.** The **Koolau Range** run north-south for almost the entire length of the island, dramatically creating windward and leeward Oahu. The **Waianae Range** is smaller, confined to the western section of the island. It too runs north-south, dividing the **Waianae Coast** from the massive **Leilehua Plateau** of the interior. **Mount Ka'ala,** at 4,020 feet, in the northern portion of the Waianae Range, is Oahu's highest peak. Even with these two mountain ranges, 45% of Oahu is less than 500 feet in elevation, the lowest of the six major islands. The huge Leilehua Plateau is still covered in pineapple and sugarcane. Lying between the two mountain ranges, it runs all the way from Waialua on the north shore to Ewa, just west of Pearl Harbor. At its widest point, around Schofield Barracks, it's more than six miles across.

Oahu's most impressive natural features were formed after the heavy volcanic activity ceased and erosion began to sculpt the island. The most obvious is the wall-like cliffs of the **Pali**— mountain heads eroded by winds from the east,

valleys cut by streams from the west. Perfect examples of these eroded valleys are **Nuuanu** and **Kalihi.** Other impressive examples are **Diamond Head, Koko Head,** and **Punchbowl,** three "tuff-cone" volcanoes created after the heavy volcanic activity of early Oahu. A tuff cone is volcanic ash cemented together to form solid rock. Diamond Head is the most dramatic,

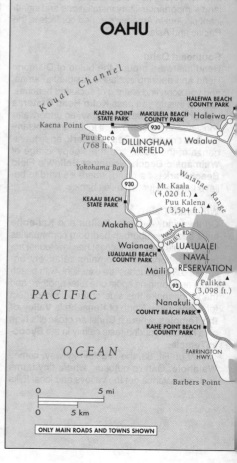

OAHU

formed after a minor eruption about 100,000 years ago and rising 760 feet from its base.

Oahu has the state's longest stream, **Kaukonahua,** which begins atop Puu Kaaumakua at 2,681 feet in the central Koolau Range and runs westward 33 miles through the Leilehua Plateau. En route, it passes the **Wahiawa Reservoir** which, at 302 acres, forms the second largest body of fresh water in Hawaii. Oahu's tallest waterfalls are 80-foot **Kaliuwaa** (Sacred Falls) just west of Punaluu; and **Waihee Falls** in famous Waimea Park on the North Shore, which have a

sheer drop of more than 40 feet. Oahu's main water concern is usage that outstrips supply, and major municipal water shortages are expected by the year 2000 unless conservation measures and new technology are employed.

Rivers and Lakes

Oahu has no navigable rivers, but there are hundreds of streams. The two largest are Kaukonahua Stream, which runs through central Oahu, and Waikele Stream, which drains the area around Schofield Barracks. A few reservoirs dot

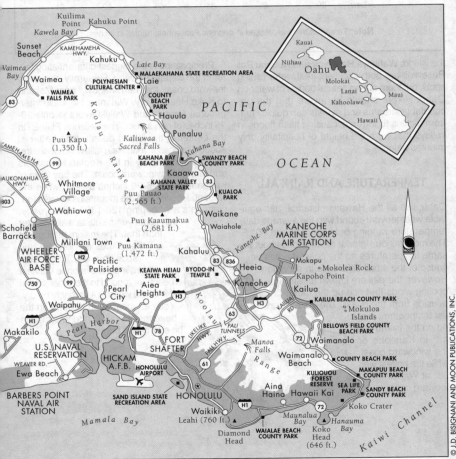

© J.D. BISIGNANI AND MOON PUBLICATIONS, INC.

OAHU TEMPERATURE AND RAINFALL

TOWN		JAN.	MARCH	MAY	JUNE	SEPT.	NOV.
Honolulu	High	80	82	84	85	82	81
	Low	60	52	68	70	71	68
	Rain	4	2	0	0	0	4
Kaneohe	High	80	80	80	82	82	80
	Low	67	62	68	70	70	68
	Rain	5	5	2	0	2	5
Waialua	High	79	79	81	82	82	80
	Low	60	60	61	63	62	61
	Rain	2	1	0	0	1	3

Note: Temperature is expressed in degrees Fahrenheit; rainfall in inches.

the island; Wahiawa Reservoir and Nuuanu Pali Reservoir are both excellent freshwater fishing spots, but there are no natural bodies of water on Oahu. Hikers should be aware that the uncountable streams and rivulets can quickly turn from trickles to torrents, causing flash floods in valleys that were the height of hospitality only minutes before.

TEMPERATURE AND RAINFALL

Oahu, like all the Hawaiian Islands, has equitable weather year-round with the average daily temperature ranging between 71° and 80° F. The mountainous interior experiences about the same temperatures as the coastal areas because of the small difference in elevation. However, the *pali* are known for strong, cooling winds that rise up the mountainside from the coast. The coldest temperature recorded on the island was 43° in Kaneohe on the windward coast, while the hottest was 96° at Waianae on the leeward coast.

Precipitation is the biggest differentiating factor in the climate of Oahu. Generally, the entire leeward coast, the "rain shadow," from Makaha to Koko Head, is dry. Waianae, Honolulu International Airport, and Waikiki average only 20-25 inches of rain a year. The Leilehua Plateau in the center of the island does a little better at about 40 inches a year. Rain falls much more frequently and heavily in the Koolau Mountains and along the windward coast. The bay town of Kaneohe sees 75-90 inches a year, while the Nuuanu Reservoir in the mountains above Honolulu gets a whopping 120-130 inches yearly, with some years substantially greater than that. The maxim throughout the islands is "don't let rain spoil your day." If it's raining, simply move on to the next beach, or around to the other side of the island where it'll probably be dry. You can most often depend on the beaches of Waikiki and Waianae to be sunny and bright.

LOUISE FOOTE

apapane

FLORA AND FAUNA

You would think that with Oahu's dense human population, little room would be left for animals. In fact, they are environmentally stressed, but they do survive. The interior mountain slopes are home to **wild pigs,** and a small population of **feral goats** survives in the Waianae Range. Migrating **whales** pass by, especially along the leeward coast where they can be observed from lookouts ranging from Waikiki to Koko Head. Half a dozen introduced game birds are found around the island, but Oahu's real animal wealth is its indigenous birdlife.

Birds

The shores around Oahu, including those off Koko Head and Sand Island, but especially on the tiny islets of Moku Manu and Manana on the windward side, are home to thriving colonies of marine birds. On these diminutive islands it's quite easy to spot a number of birds from the **tern** family, including the white, gray, and sooty tern. All have a distinctive screeching voice and approximate wingspan of 30 inches. Part of their problem is that they have little fear of humans. Along with the terns are **shearwaters.** These birds have a normal wingspan of about 36 inches, and make a series of moans and wails, oftentimes while in flight. For some reason shearwaters are drawn to the bright lights of the city, where they fall prey to house cats and automobiles. Sometimes Moku Manu even attracts the enormous **Laysan albatross** with its seven-foot wingspan. **Tropic birds** with lovely, streamerlike tails, are quite often seen along the windward coast.

OAHU BOTANICAL GARDENS

Honolulu Botanical Gardens are five separate gardens supported and maintained by the county. All are open daily 9 a.m.-4 p.m. No admission fee, except for the Foster Botanical Garden.

1) **Foster Botanical Garden,** 50 N. Vineyard Blvd., tel. (808) 522-7065. Fifteen-acre oasis of exotic trees and rare plants. Guided tours Mon.-Fri. at 1 p.m.

2) **Ho'omaluhia Botanical Garden,** 45-680 Luluku Rd., Kaneohe, tel. (808) 233-7323. Some guided hiking tours are offered

3) **Koko Crater Botanical Garden,** in Koko Head Regional Park, tel. (808) 522-7060.

4) **Lili'uokalani Botanical Garden,** between Kuakini and School Streets, Honolulu, tel. (808) 522-7066.

5) **Wahiawa Botanical Garden,** 1396 California Ave., Wahiawa, tel. (808) 621-7321. Twenty-seven acres of cultivated trees, flowers, and ferns from around the world.

Ha'iku Gardens, 46-336 Haiku Rd., Kaneohe. Many acres of flowers, ornamental trees, and ponds. Chart House Restaurant on site.

Lyon Arboretum, 3860 Manoa Rd., Honolulu, tel. (808) 988-3177 or (808) 988-7378. Dr. Lyon planted 194 acres of trees and flowers in the late 1800s. Research facility of the University of Hawaii. Open Mon.-Sat. 9 a.m.-3 p.m. Some guided tours offered.

Moanalua Gardens, 1352 Pineapple Pl., tel. (808) 833-1944. Former Damon Estate property. Open to public for self-guided walks by reservation only. Guided tours given weekends at 9 a.m.; call (808) 839-5334.

Senator Fong's Plantation and Gardens, 47-285 Pulama Rd., Kaneohe, tel. (808) 239-6775. Open daily 10 a.m.-4 p.m., except Christmas and New Year's Day. Offers 725 acres of natural and cultivated flower, tree, palm, and fern gardens. Admission.

Waimea Arboretum and Botanical Garden, at Waimea Falls Park, tel. (808) 638-8511. Collects, grows, and preserves rare Hawaiian flora. Flowers and plants labeled.

To catch a glimpse of exotic birds on Oahu you don't have to head for the sea or the hills. The city streets and beach parks are constantly aflutter with wings. Black **mynah birds** with their sassy yellow eyes are common mimics around town. **Sparrows,** introduced to Hawaii through Oahu in the 1870s, are everywhere, while **munia,** first introduced as cage birds from Southeast Asia, have escaped and can be found almost anywhere around the island. Another escaped cage bird from Asia is the **bulbul,** a natural clown that perches on any likely city roost and draws attention to itself with loud calls and generally ridiculous behavior.

If you're lucky, you can also catch a glimpse of the *pueo* (Hawaiian owl) in the mountainous areas of Waianae and the Koolau Range. Also, along trails and deep in the forest from Tantalus to the Waianae Range you can sometimes see elusive native birds like the *elepaio, amakihi,* and fiery red *'i'iwi.*

Oahu also is home to a number of game birds found mostly in the dry upland forests. These include two varieties of **dove,** the **Japanese quail,** both the **green** and **ring-necked pheasant,** and **Erkel's francolin.** Hunting of these birds occurs during different periods year-round and information can be had by contacting the Oahu branch of the Division of Forestry and Wildlife.

Oahu Wildlife Refuges and Preserves

Two areas at opposite ends of the island have been set aside as national wildlife refuges (NWR): **James Campbell NWR,** above the town of Kahuku on the extreme northern tip; and **Pearl Harbor NWR,** at the West Loch of the harbor. Both were established in the mid-'70s and are managed by the U.S. Fish and Wildlife Service. They serve mainly as wetland habitats for the endangered Hawaiian gallinule *(alae'ula),* stilt *(ae'o),* and coot *(alae ke'oke'o).* Clinging to existence, these birds should have a future as long as their nesting grounds remain undisturbed. These refuges also attract a wide variety of other birds, mostly introduced species such as **cattle egrets, herons,** a few species of **doves, munia, cardinals,** and **common finch.**

Much of the area within the refuges is natural marshland, but ponds, complete with water-regulating pumps and dikes, have been built. The general public is not admitted to these areas without permission from the refuge managers. For more information, and to arrange a visit, contact Refuge Manager, Hawaiian and Pacific Islands NWR, U.S. Fish and Wildlife Service, Federal Bldg., Room 5231, Box 50167, Honolulu, HI 96850; tel. (808) 541-1201.

The Nature Conservancy of Hawaii maintains two nature preserves in coordination with one public and one private owner. **Honouliuli,** a 3,692-acre tract located on the southeast slope of the Waianae Mountains above Makakilo and Schofield Barracks, is home to more than 60 rare and endangered plants and animals, including a handful found nowhere else on earth. Two guided hikes into the preserve are offered once a month on Saturday or Sunday. Much smaller in size is the 30-acre **Ihi'ihilauakea** preserve. In this shallow crater above Hanauma Bay at the southeastern tip of the island is a totally unique vernal pool and a very rare *Marsilea villosa* fern. Because of the nature of this extremely fragile ecosystem, visitation is limited. For more information on hikes or volunteer activities, contact the Nature Conservancy at (808) 537-4508.

Flora

Oahu, a huge tropical garden, has been long planted with every type of flower, tree, fern, and fruit found in the islands. For a description of Hawaii's indigenous flora and other fauna not touched on here, please see **Flora and Fauna** in the general introduction.

GOVERNMENT

Oahu has been the center of government for about 150 years, since King Kamehameha III permanently established the royal court here in the 1840s. In 1873-74, King David Kalakaua built Iolani Palace as the central showpiece of the island kingdom. Liliuokalani, the last Hawaiian monarch, lived after her dethronement in the nearby residence, Washington Place. While Hawaii was a territory, and for a few years after it became a state, the palace was used as the capitol building, the governor residing in Washington Place. Modern Oahu, besides being the

HOUSE DISTRICTS

Oahu

45

46-47

43-44

32-40

41-42

48-51

17-31

15-16

Honolulu

SENATORIAL DISTRICTS

Oahu

22

23

21

15, 17-18

19-20

24-25

16

9-14

8

Honolulu

center of state government, governs itself as the **City and County of Honolulu.** The county covers the entire island of Oahu as well as the far-flung Northwestern Islands, except for Midway, which is under federal jurisdiction.

City and County of Honolulu

The island of Oahu has three times as many people as the other islands combined. Nowhere is this more evident than in the representation of Oahu in the state House and Senate. Oahu claims 18 of the 25 state senators and 37 of the 51 state representatives. These lopsided figures make it obvious that Oahu has plenty of clout, especially Honolulu urban districts, which elect more than 50% of Oahu's representatives. Frequent political battles ensue, since what's good for the city and county of Honolulu isn't always good for the rest of the state. More often than not, the political moguls of Oahu, backed by huge business interests, prevail.

Like the rest of the state, the voters on the island of Oahu are principally Democratic in orientation, but not in as great a percentage as on the other islands. The current mayor is Jeremy Harris, Democrat. He is assisted by an elected county council consisting of nine members, one

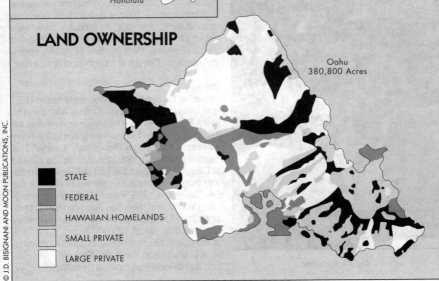

LAND OWNERSHIP

Oahu
380,800 Acres

STATE

FEDERAL

HAWAIIAN HOMELANDS

SMALL PRIVATE

LARGE PRIVATE

from each council district around the island. The Oahu state senators are overwhelmingly Democratic, except for two Republicans from the Koko Head and Kailua districts. Democratic state representatives also outnumber Republicans, but not by quite as huge a margin. Most of the 10 Republican districts are in urban Honolulu and the suburban communities of Kailua and Kaneohe.

ECONOMY

Economically, Oahu dwarfs the rest of the islands combined. It generates income from government spending, tourism, and agriculture. A huge military presence, an international airport that receives the lion's share of visitors, and, unbelievably, half of the state's best arable lands, keep Oahu in the economic catbird seat. The famous "Big Five" maintain their corporate offices in downtown Honolulu, from where they oversee vast holdings throughout Hawaii and the Mainland. These offices are located in about the same spots they were when their founders helped overthrow the monarchy. For the Big Five, things are about the same as then, except that they're going strong, while the old royalty of Hawaii has vanished.

Tourism

The flow of visitors to Oahu has remained unabated ever since tourism outstripped sugar and pineapples in the early 1960s, becoming Hawaii's top moneymaker. Of the more than six million people who visit the state yearly, more than one half stay on Oahu. This means that on any given day, Oahu plays host to about 80,000 visitors. Waikiki is still many people's idea of paradise. Most all the rest, en route to the Neighbor Islands, at least pass through. Hotels directly employ more than 18,000 workers, half the state's total, not including all the shop assistants, waiters and waitresses, taxi drivers, and everyone else needed to ensure carefree vacation. Of Hawaii's 70,000 accommodation units, Oahu claims 36,000; of those, more than 31,000 are in Waikiki. The Oahu hotels consistently have the highest occupancy rates in the state, hovering around 80%. The tourism industry generates about $11 billion of yearly revenue from direct visitor spending. With the flow of visitors seemingly endless, Oahu has a bright economic future.

Military

Hawaii is the most militarized state in the U.S., and Oahu is the most militarized island in the state. The U.S. military has been in Hawaii since 1887, when Pearl Harbor was given to the Navy as part of the "Sugar Reciprocity Treaty." The Spanish-American War saw U.S. troops billeted at Camp McKinley at the foot of Diamond Head, and Schofield Barracks opened to receive the 5th Cavalry in 1909. Pearl Harbor's flames igniting WW II, and there has been no looking back since then. On Oahu today, the combined military services hold about 100,000 acres, a full 26% of the island. Much of this land, used for maneuvers, is off-limits to the public. Besides Pearl Harbor, so obviously dominated by battleship gray,

Mainland visitors

the largest military lands are around Schofield Barracks and the Kahuku-Kawailoa Training Area. About 44,000 military personnel are stationed on Oahu (99% of those in the state), with a slightly higher number of dependents.

Agriculture

You'd think that with all the people living on Oahu, coupled with the constant land development, there'd be hardly any room left for things to grow. But that's not the case. The land is productive, though definitely stressed. It is startling to realize that in downtown Honolulu and Waikiki, so many trees have been removed to build parking lots the asphalt becomes overheated from the lack of shade, raising temperatures once moderated by trade winds.

Changing times and attitudes led to a "poi famine" that hit Oahu in 1967 because very few people were interested in the hard work of farm-ing this staple. While Oahu has, by far, the smallest acreage in farms and the smallest average size of farm in the state, it still manages to produce a considerable amount of sugarcane, pineapples, and the many products of diversified agriculture. Sugar lands account for 22,000 acres, most owned by the James Campbell Estate, located around Ewa, north and west of Pearl Harbor, with some acreage around Waimea and Waialua on the North Shore. Pineapples cover 11,500 acres, with the biggest holdings on the Leilehua Plateau belonging to Dole, a subsidiary of Castle and Cooke. In the hills, entrepreneurs raise *pakalolo,* which has become the state's most productive cash crop. Oahu is also a huge agricultural consumer, demanding more than four times as much vegetables, fruits, meats, and poultry to feed its citizens and visitors than the remainder of the state combined.

PEOPLE

For most visitors, regardless of where they've come from, Oahu (especially Honolulu) will be the first place they've ever encountered such an integrated multiracial society. Various countries may be cosmopolitan, but nowhere will you meet so many individuals from such a diversity of ethnic groups, and mixes of these groups. You could be driven to your hotel by a Chinese-Portuguese cab driver, checked in by a Japanese-Hawaiian clerk, served lunch by a Korean waiter, and serenaded by a Hawaiian-Italian-German musician, while an Irish-English-Filipino-French chambermaid tidies your room. This racial symphony is evident throughout Hawaii, but it's more apparent on Oahu, where the large population creates more opportunity for a racial hodge-podge. The warm feeling you get almost immediately upon arrival is that everyone belongs.

Population Figures

Oahu's 877,000 or so residents account for 74% of the state's population. All these people are on an island comprising only nine percent of the state's land total. Sections of Waikiki can have a combined population of permanent residents and visitors as high as 90,000 per square mile, making cities like Tokyo, Hong Kong, and New York seem quite roomy by comparison. The good news is that Oahu *expects* all these people and knows how to accommodate them comfortably.

About 400,000 people live in greater Honolulu, the built-up area from Aiea to Koko Head. The next most populous urban centers after Honolulu are the Kailua-Kaneohe area with about 100,000 residents, followed by Pearl City and

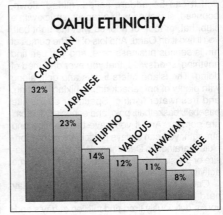

OAHU ETHNICITY

CAUCASIAN 32%
JAPANESE 23%
FILIPINO 14%
VARIOUS 12%
HAWAIIAN 11%
CHINESE 8%

Waipahu with a combined total of about 70,000. On the Leilehua Plateau, 47,000 live in Mililani Town and Wahiawa. The strip of towns on the leeward coast, including Waianae, totals about 33,400 inhabitants. In the last decade, the areas that have had the greatest increase in population are Wahiawa and Ewa. On Oahu, 96% of the population are urban dwellers while only four percent live rurally.

With all of these people, and such a finite land resource, real estate on the island is sky-high. A average single-family home on Oahu sells for $375,000 ($50,000 higher than the state average), while a condo averages about $180,000. And for plenty of prime real estate, these figures would barely cover the down payment!

So where is everybody? Of the major ethnic groups, you'll find the Hawaiians clustered around Waianae and on the windward coast near Waiahole; the whites tend to be in Wa-hiawa, around Koko Head, in Waikiki, and in Kailua-Kaneohe; those of Japanese ancestry prefer the valleys heading toward the *pali*, including Kalihi, Nuuanu, and Tantalus; Filipinos live just east of the airport, in downtown Honolulu, around Barbers Point, and in Wahiawa; the Chinese are in Chinatown and around the Diamond Head area. Of the minor ethnic groups, the highest concentration of blacks is in the Army towns around Schofield Barracks; Samoans live along with the Hawaiians in Waianae and the windward coastal towns, though they are most concentrated in downtown Honolulu not far from Aloha Tower; Koreans and Vietnamese are scattered here and there, but mostly in Honolulu. The ethnic breakdown of Oahu's 877,000 residents is as follows: 32% White, 23% Japanese, 14% Filipino, 11% Hawaiian, 8% Chinese, and 12% other.

SPORTS AND RECREATION

Oahu is a playground for young and old with sports, games, and activities galore. Everyone can find something to enjoy, and most activities are free, relatively cheap, or once-in-a-lifetime thrills that are worth the money. The sea is the ideal playground. You can swim, snorkel, scuba, surf, fish, sail, canoe, kayak, windsurf, bodysurf, parasail, cruise, or merely stroll along the shore picking up shells or exploring tidepools.

If it can be ridden, sailed, glided, flown, bounced, smashed with a racket, struck with a club, bat, or foot, or hooked with the right bait, you'll find it on Oahu. And lots of it! The pursuit of fun is serious business here, and you can find anything, sportswise, that you ever dreamed of doing. The island offers tennis and golf, along with plenty of horseback riding, hiking, hunting, and freshwater fishing. Spectator sports like baseball, basketball, polo, and especially football are popular. And if you have the stamina and strength, you can always participate in the Honolulu Marathon in December. Whatever your desire or physical abilities may be, there'll be some activity that strikes your fancy.

One of the best tonics for relaxation is to play hard at something you thoroughly enjoy, so you're deliciously tired and fulfilled at day's end. For you this might be hooking onto an 800-pound marlin that'll test you to the limit, or perhaps just giving yourself to the sea and floating on gentle waves. Hawaii is guaranteed to thrill the young and invigorate the once-young. It'll put a twinkle in your eye and a bounce in your step.

CAMPING

Few people equate visiting Oahu with camping. The two seem mutually exclusive, especially when you focus on the mystique of Waikiki, and the dominance of a major city like Honolulu. But among state, county, and private campgrounds, you have about 20 spots to choose from all over the island. Camping on Oahu, however, is a little different from camping on the Neighbor Islands, which are simply more amenable to camping. In an island state, they're considered "the woods, the sticks, the backcountry," and camping seems more acceptable there.

Although totally legal to camp, and done by both visitors and residents, Oahu's camping problems are widely divergent, with social and financial implications. When the politically powerful tourist industry thinks of visitors, it imagines people sitting

OAHU CAMPING

NOTE: PARKS ARE OPEN FOR CAMPING ON A ROTATING BASIS. CHECK FIRST

© J.D. BISIGNANI AND MOON PUBLICATIONS, INC.

by a hotel pool, drinking mai tais, and dutifully spending money. Campers just won't cooperate in parting with their quota of dollars, so there's not much impetus to cater to their wants and needs. Moreover, Honolulu is an international city that attracts both the best and worst kinds of people. The tourist industry, supported by the civil authorities, has a mortal dread that low-lifers, loafers, and bums will ensconce themselves on Oahu's beaches. This would be disastrous for Oahu's image! Mainland cities, not so dependent upon tourism, can obviously be more tolerant of their citizens who have fallen through the social net. So in Oahu they keep a close eye on the campgrounds, enforcing the rules, controlling the situation. The campgrounds are patrolled, adding a measure of strictness along with a measure of security. Even decent people can't bend the rules and slide by a little, where they normally might on the Neighbor Islands.

An odd, inherent social situation adds to the problem. Not too long ago, the local people either lived on the beach or used them extensively, oftentimes for their livelihoods. Many, especially fishermen and their families, would set up semipermanent camps for a good part of the year. You can see the remnants of this practice at some of the more remote and ethnically claimed campgrounds. As Oahu, much more than the Neighbor Islands, felt the pressures of growing tourism, beachfront property became astronomically expensive. Local people had to relinquish what they thought of as their beaches. The state and county, in an effort to keep some beaches public and therefore undeveloped, created **beach parks.** This ensured all could use the beaches forever, but it also meant their access would be governed and regulated.

Local people, like visitors, must follow the rules and apply for camping permits limited by the number of days that you can spend in any one spot. Out went the semipermanent camp and with it, for the local people, the idea of *our* beach. Now, you have the same right to camp in a spot that may have been used, or even owned, in past generations, by the family of dark-skinned people next to you. They feel dispossessed, infringed upon, and bitter. And you, especially if you have white skin, can be the focus of this bitterness. This situation, although psychologically understandable, can be a monumental drag. Of course, not all island people have this attitude, and chances are very good nothing negative will happen. But you must be aware of underlying motivations so that you can read the vibes of the people around your camp spot.

If all of these "problems" haven't made you want to pull up your tent stakes and head into a more congenial sunset, you can have a great and inexpensive time camping on Oahu. All of this is just the social climate that you *may* have to face, but most likely, nothing unpleasant will happen, and you'll come home tanned, relaxed, and singing the praises of the great outdoors on Hawaii's capital island.

State Parks

Oahu boasts 22 state parks, recreation areas, waysides, and monuments. A majority offer a beach for day use, walking paths, picnic areas, toilets, showers, and/or pavilions. Included in these state properties are three *heiau,* **Iolani Palace,** the **Royal Mausoleum,** and **Diamond Head.** Of the 22, three are registered National Historical Landmarks and one is a National Natural Landmark.

Oahu state parks close their gates and parking lots at night. Those *not* offering camping are open 7 a.m.-7:45 p.m. from April 1 to Labor Day, closing during the remainder of the year at 6:45 p.m.

Four state parks currently offer tent camping: **Sand Island State Recreation Area,** just a few minutes from downtown Honolulu; **Keaiwa Heiau State Recreation Area,** in the interior on the heights above Aiea; **Malaekahana Bay State Recreation Area,** a mile north of Laie on the windward coast; and **Kahana Valley State Park** between Punaluu and Ka'a'awa on the windward coast.

To camp at Sand Island, Keaiwa Heiau, and Kahana Valley parks, you must acquire a permit

(free) from the Dept. of Land and Natural Resources, Division of State Parks, P.O. Box 621 (1151 Punchbowl St.), Honolulu, HI 96809, tel. (808) 587-0300, open weekdays 8 a.m.-3:30 p.m. Oahu campsite **permit reservations** can be made only 30 days prior to the first day of camping, but *must* be made at least one week in advance. Write for a permit application form. Information needed includes your name, address, phone number, names and identification numbers of all persons over 18 years of age in your party, type of permit requested, duration of your stay, and specific dates requested. The permits can be picked up on arrival with proof of identification.

On Oahu campsites are at a premium and people line up at 8 a.m. on the first-floor breezeway on the Beretania Street side of the issuing office, just outside the double glass doors, where you are given a number on a first-come, first-served basis (usually no hassle except on three-day holiday weekends). After this, go to the third floor where the office is located.

Note: Camping is allowed *only* from Friday 8 a.m. to Wednesday 8 a.m. (closed all day Wednesday and Thursday for camping—other activities okay) with the shutdown, supposedly, for regrowth. Camping on Sand Island SRA only is Friday through Monday. Camping is allowed for only five consecutive days in any one month, and don't forget a parking permit for your vehicle, which must remain within the locked park gates at night. *Aloooohaaa!*

Camping at Malaekahana State Recreation Area is handled by the Friends of Malaekahana, P.O. Box 305, Laie, HI, 96762, tel. (808) 293-1736 or fax 293-2066. Reservations are taken up to 12 months in advance and at least 14 days before planned arrival; two nights minimum stay. Check-in is handled 3-5 p.m.; check out time is noon. The office is open Mon.-Fri. 10 a.m.-3 p.m. Write or call for information and reservation applications. Firearms, fireworks, pets, and drinking of alcoholic beverages are prohibited in the park, and a quiet time is enforced 10:30 p.m.-8 a.m. Sleeping up to 10, half a dozen beach houses run $66 a night during the week and $80 on weekends. Tent campers pay $5 a night. There also are a few yurts on the property that can be rented when not occupied by students during the school year. The yurts do not have bath or cooking facilities, but they have floors and electricity. Outside hot showers and bathroom facilities are shared. Bring mosquito repellent. The pavilion can be rented for day events or for the day and night ($250)—it sleeps 15. Parking is limited. Make sure to call and make arrangements with the staff if you will be arriving later than office hours. The park gate is locked—for your security—7 a.m.-7 p.m.

The park service offers special culture and arts programs at Kahana Valley State Park and talks and guided tours weekdays at the Royal Mausoleum. Tours and other services at Iolani Palace are provided by the nonprofit Friends of Iolani Palace.

County Parks

There are nearly 300 county parks on the island of Oahu. The city and county of Honolulu has opened 13 (these change periodically) of its 62 beach parks around the island to tent camping, and most allow trailers and RVs. Unfortunately, these are the very parks at which you're more likely to encounter hassles. A free permit is required, and camping is allowed only from Friday at 8 a.m. until the following Wednesday at 8 a.m., at which time your campsite must be vacated (no camping Wednesday and Thursday evenings). A few of these parks have camping only on the weekends and one allows it only during summer months, so be sure to ask for particulars. These campsites are also at a premium, but you can write for reservations and pick up your permits on arrival with proper identification. For information and reservations write or visit City and County of Honolulu, Dept. of Parks and Recreation, Permit Section, 650 S. King St., Honolulu, HI 96813, tel. (808) 523-4525. Permits are also available from the satellite city halls around the island.

Note: All of the beach parks are closed during designated months (they differ from park to park) throughout the year. This is supposedly for cleaning, but really it's to reduce the possibility of squatters moving in. Make sure, if you're reserving far in advance, that the park will be open when you arrive! Don't count on the Parks and Recreation Department to inform you!

Note: For private group camps, mostly church-affiliated, see "Camps" in the *Yellow Pages*.

HIKING

The best way to leave the crowds of tourists behind and become intimate with the beauty of Oahu is to hike it. Although the Neighbor Islands receive fewer visitors, a higher percentage of people hike them. Don't get the impression that you'll have the island to yourself, but you will be amazed at how open and lovely this crowded island can be. Some cultural and social hikes can be taken without leaving the city, like a stroll through Waikiki and a historical walking tour of downtown Honolulu and Chinatown. But others —some mere jaunts, others quite strenuous— are well worth the time and effort.

Remember that much of Oahu is privately owned, and you must have permission to cross this land, or you may be open to prosecution. Usually private property is marked by signs. Another source that might stomp your hiking plans with their jungle boots is the military. A full 25% of Oahu belongs to Uncle Sam, and he isn't always thrilled when you decide to play in his back yard. Some of the finest walks (like to the summit of Mt. Ka'ala) require crossing military lands, much of which has been altered by very unfriendly looking installations. Always check and obey any posted signs to avert trouble. The following listings are by no means all-inclusive, but should help you choose a trail that seems interesting and is within your ability level.

Diamond Head

The most recognized symbol of Hawaii, this is the first place you should head to for a strikingly beautiful panorama of Waikiki and greater Honolulu. Called Leahi (Casting Point) by the Hawaiians, it was named Diamond Head after a group of wild-eyed English sailors espied what they thought to be diamonds glistening in the rocks. Hawaii had fulfilled so many other dreams, why not a mountain of diamonds? Unfortunately, the glimmer was caused by worthless calcite crystals. No fortune was made, but the name stuck.

To get here, follow Kalakaua Avenuw south from Waikiki until it leads onto Diamond Head Road; right away a sign points you to Diamond Head Crater. Pass through a tunnel and into the heavily militarized section in the center of the crater; the trail starts here. Although the hike is moderate, you should bring along water, flashlight (a must), and binoculars if you have them. Run by the Division of State Parks, the park is open daily 6 a.m.-6 p.m. Entrance is $5 per car and $1 to walk the trail. A sign at the beginning describes the rigors you'll encounter, and informs that the trail is seven-tenths of a mile long and was built to the 760-foot summit of Leahi Point in 1908 to serve as a U.S. Coast Artillery Observation Station. It was heavily fortified during WW II, and part of the fun is exploring the old gun emplacements and tunnels built to link and service them.

Though only 10 minutes from Waikiki, wildflowers and chirping birds create a peaceful setting. When you come to a series of cement and stone steps, walk to a flat area to the left to find an old winch that hauled the heavy building materials to the top. Here's a wide panorama of the sea and Koko Head, and notice too that atop every little hillock is an old gun emplacement. Next comes a short but dark tunnel (bring a flashlight) and immediately series of 99 steps. You can avoid the steps by taking the trail to the left, but the footing is slippery and there are no guard rails. Following the steps is a spiral staircase that leads down into a large gun emplacement, through which you walk and come to another tunnel. If you haven't brought a flashlight, give your eyes a few minutes to adjust; there's enough light to make it. Once on top, another stairway and ladder take you to the very summit.

Judd Trail

This is an excellent trail to take to experience Oahu's "jungle" while visiting the historic and picturesque **Nuuanu Pali**. From Honolulu take H-1 and turn onto Rt. 61, the Pali Highway. Turn right onto Nuuanu Pali Drive. Follow it for just under a mile to a reservoir spillway. The trail begins to the right of the water company building near the spillway and leads through fragrant eucalyptus and a dense stand of picture-perfect Norfolk pines. It continues through the forest reserve and makes a loop back to the starting point. En route you pass **Jackass Ginger Pool**. In the immediate area are "mud slides," where you can take a ride on a makeshift toboggan of *pili* grass or ti leaves, or on a piece of plastic if you've brought one. This activity is rough on

your clothes, and even rougher on your body. The wet conditions after a rain are perfect. Afterward, a dip in Jackass Pool cleans away mud and refreshes at the same time. Continue down the trail to observe wild ginger, guava, and *kukui*, but don't take any confusing side trails. If you get lost, head back to the stream and follow it until it intersects the main trail.

Tantalus and Makiki Valley Trails

Great sightseeing and hiking can be combined when you climb the road atop Tantalus. A range of trails in this area offers magnificent views. A few roads lead up Tantalus, but a good one heads past Punchbowl along Puowaina Drive; just keep going until it turns into Tantalus Drive. The road switchbacks past some incredible homes and views until it reaches the 2,013-foot summit, where it changes its name to Round Top Drive, then heads down the other side.

The best place to start is at the top of Tantalus at the **Manoa Cliff Trailhead,** where a number of intersecting trails give you a selection of adventures. Once on Round Top Drive, pass a brick wall with the name Kalaiopua Road imbedded in the stonework, and continue until you pass Forest Ridge Way, right after which is a large turnout on both sides of the road near telephone pole no. 56. To the right is the beginning of half-mile-long **Moleka Trail,** which offers some excellent views and an opportunity to experience the trails in this area without an all-day commitment. The trails are excellently maintained by the State Division of Forestry and Wildlife. Your greatest hazard here is mud, but in a moment you're in a handsome stand of bamboo, and in 10 minutes the foliage parts onto a lovely panorama of Makiki Valley, with Honolulu in the background. These views are captivating, but remember to have "small eyes"—check out the varied-colored mosses and fungi, and don't forget the flowers and fruit growing around you.

A branch trail to the left leads to Round Top Drive, and if you continue, the trail splits into three: to the right is the **Makiki Valley Trail,** which cuts across the valley starting at a Boy Scout camp on Round Top Drive and ending atop Tantalus; **Ualakaa Trail** branches left and goes for another half mile, connecting the Makiki Valley Trail with Puu Ualakaa State Park; straight ahead is the **Makiki Branch A Trail,** which descends for one-half mile, ending at the Division of Forestry Baseyard at the bottom of the valley.

On the mountainside of the Manoa Cliffs Trailhead is the **Connector Trail**. This pragmatic-sounding trail does indeed connect the lower trails with **Manoa Cliffs Trail**, skirting around the backside of Tantalus and intersecting the **Puu Ohia Trail**, which leads to the highest point on Tantalus and the expected magnificent view.

Maunawili Falls Trail

Maunawili Falls is on the other side of Nuuanu Pali, near Maunawili town. This trail offers adventure into Oahu's jungle, with a rewarding pool and falls at the end. At the third red light as you head down the windward side of the Pali Highway, make a right onto Auloa Road. In a few hundred yards, take the left fork onto Maunawili Road and follow it toward the mountains through a residential area. Turn right onto Aloha Oe Drive, follow it to the end, and make a right on Maleko Road, which ends in a cul-de-sac. **Warning:** Do not trespass on any private land. There is no public right-of-way! Just before you get to the end of the cul-de-sac look for an open space on the right with a short trail leading down to a culvert. Follow the culvert for about 100 yards, and turn left onto a heavily used jeep trail that soon becomes a walking path. In 400 yards, at three telephone poles, the trail splits into three branches; take the center branch and go straight ahead downhill until you intersect a trail that leads right along the creek. This trail is very muddy, but worth it. Follow it for about 15 minutes until you come to Maunawili Falls—deep enough to dive in. You can also see an upper falls. Above them is an open field perfect for an overnight camp. To the left a path leads past a small banana plantation, along an irrigation ditch cut into the mountainside and paralleled by a wooden walkway. Very few people venture into this safe but fascinating area.

Maunawili Demonstration Trail

This is one of Oahu's most accessible and newest trails. Soon after passing the Pali Lookout, which is clearly marked along the Pali Highway, you will go through a tunnel. Almost immediately, a sign points to a scenic overlook. Pull off into the parking area and walk back up the highway for about 100 yards where you'll see a break in the guardrail and a sign for *"Na'ala Hele,"* the Hawaiian Trail and Access System. The beauty of this trail is that it is reasonably flat with little elevation gain or loss as it winds its way along the windward side of the Koolau Range. The whine of the Pali Highway abates almost immediately and you are suddenly in a brilliant highland tropical forest. You can continue to the end (about three hours one-way) for a full day's hike, or just find a secluded spot after a mile or so for a picnic. The views are spectacular and there are vantage points where you can see the coast all the way from Rabbit Island to Chinaman's Hat. Remember, however, that like all Hawaiian trails, recent rainfall makes for treacherous footing.

Hauula Loop Trails

Built by the Workers Civilian Conservation Corps (WCCC) during the Depression, these manicured trails run up and down two ridges and deep into an interior valley, gaining and losing height as they switchback through the extraordinary jungle canopy. The **Gulch and Papali trails,** branches of the Hauula Loop Trail, start from the same place. The Hauula Trail is wide with good footing. There're a few stream crossings, but it's not muddy even after a heavy rain, which can shut down the Sacred Falls Trail just a few miles north. The hard-packed trail, covered in a soft carpet of ironwood needles, offers magnificent coastal views once you reach the heights, or you can look inland into verdant gulches and gullies (valleys).

You'll be passing through miniature ecosystems very reminiscent of the fern forests on the Big Island, but on a much smaller scale. The area flora is made up of ironwoods, passion fruit, thimbleberries, ohia, wild orchids, and fiddlehead ferns. To get there, head for Hauula on coastal Rt. 83 (Kamehameha Hwy.). Between mile markers 21 and 22, look inland for Hauula Homestead Road. Take it for a minute, and continue on Maakua Road until you see the well-marked sign leading to the trails.

Sacred Falls

On coastal Rt. 83, between Hauula and Punaluu (mile markers 22 and 23), an HVB Warrior points you to Sacred Falls. Note that you *cannot* drive to the falls. An old commercial venture put out this misinformation, which persists to this day. The walk is a hardy stroll, so you'll need jogging shoes, not thongs. The area becomes a narrow canyon, and the sun sets early; don't start out past 3 p.m., especially if you want a dip in the stream. The trail was roughed up by Hurricane Ewa, and a sign along it says "Danger. Do not go past this point." Many people ignore this sign; the path is a little more treacherous but is passable.

The area's Hawaiian name was Kaliuwaa (Canoe Leak), and although the original name isn't as romantic as the anglicized version, the entire area was indeed considered sacred. En route, you pass into a very narrow valley where the gods might show disfavor by dropping rocks onto your head. Notice many stones, each wrapped with a ti leaf. This is an appeasement to the gods, so they're not tempted to brain you. Go ahead, wrap a rock; no one will see you! You can hear the falls dropping to the valley floor. Above you the walls are 1,600 feet high, but the falls drop only 90 feet or so. The pool below is ample for a swim, but the water is chilly and often murky. A number of beautiful picnic spots are on the large flat rocks.

North Oahu Treks

Some of the hiking in and around northwest Oahu is quite difficult. However, you should take a hike out to **Kaena Point**, where there is huge surf, sometimes 30 feet high. You have two choices: you can park your car at the end of the road past Dillingham Airfield on the north coast and hike in, or you can park your car at the end of the road past Makua on the Waianae coast and hike in. Both are hardy but not difficult. The trail is only two miles from each end, and few people come here except some local fishermen.

Peacock Flat is a good family-style trail that offers primitive camping. Follow Rt. 93 toward Dillingham Airfield and just before getting there turn left onto a dirt road leading toward the Kawaihapi Reservoir. If you want to camp, you need permits from the Division of Forestry and a waiver from the Mokuleia Ranch, tel. (808) 637-4241, which you can get at their office, located at the end of a dirt road just before the one leading to Kawaihapi Reservoir. They will also provide instructions and a key to get through two locked

gates before reaching the trailhead, if you decide to go in from that end. Heading through the Mokuleia Forest Reserve, you can camp anywhere along the trail, or at an established but primitive campground in Peacock Flat. This area is heavily used by hunters, who are mostly after wild pigs.

Dupont Trail takes you to the summit of Mt. Ka'ala, highest point and by far the most difficult hike on the island. The last mile is downright dangerous, and has you hanging on cliff edges, with the bottom 2,000 feet below! This is not for the average hiker. Follow Rt. 930 to Waialua, make a left at Waialua High School onto a cane road, and follow it to the second gate, about 1.5 miles. Park there. You need a hiking permit from the Division of Forestry and a waiver from the Waialua Sugar Company, tel. (808) 637-3521. Atop Ka'ala, although the views are magnificent, you'll also find a mushroom field of FAA satellite stations.

CAMPING AND HIKING RESOURCES

Hiking Groups and Information

The following organizations can provide information on organized hiking trips. **Hawaiian Trail and Mountain Club,** P.O. Box 2238, Honolulu, HI 96804, tel. (808) 262-2845 or 488-1161, meets behind Iolani Palace on Saturday at 9 a.m., and Sunday at 8 a.m.; free for members and $2 for nonmembers. Their hikes are announced in the *Honolulu Star Bulletin*'s "Pulse of Paradise" column. For their Hiker's Guide, send $1.50 and a SASE to the above address or check their website: www.geocities.com/yosemite/trails/3660. **Sierra Club, Hawaii Chapter** P.O. Box 2577, Honolulu, HI 96803, tel. (808) 538-6616, organizes weekly hikes, $1 for members and $3 for nonmembers. Information about the organization and their hikes is listed in their newsletter and on their website: www.hi.sierraclub.org. Additional information about hiking in Hawaii can be found on the website: www2.edu /~turner/htmc/hi-hike.htm, and about camping at: www.visit.hawaii.org/hokeo/activity/camping.html. **Hawaii Audubon Society** can be reached at P.O. Box 22832, Honolulu, HI 96822 for information about their birdwatching hikes, or call the **Hawaii Nature Center,** at (808) 955-0100 for information about hikes they sponsor. Since 1997, the eco-tour operator **Oahu Nature Tours,** P.O. Box 8059, Honolulu, HI 96830, tel. (808) 924-2473 or (800) 861-6018, website: www.OahuNatureTours.com; e-mail: nature-guide@OahuNatureTours.com, has offered two daily hiking tours that focus on native birds and plants. The morning tour to the southeast corner of the island runs 7:30-11:30 a.m. and the afternoon tour into the Koolau Mountains 1:30-5:30 p.m.; both run $37.50 apiece. Conducted by owner Michael Walther and with a limit of six participants, each tour is a environmental education experience as well as a fun outing. For half- or full-day hikes, try **Hike Hawaii,** 91-261 Hanapouli Circle, #W, Ewa Beach, HI 96706, tel. (808) 683-3967. Hiking destinations vary from the coast to mountain and rainforest, but here is always information about the flora, fauna, environment, and history of the island. Maximum of six; good for novice hikers to the experienced. Transportation, lunch or snacks, and rain gear are included; $50 half day, $65 for the full day.

Camping Gear and Rentals
If you've come without camping gear and wish to rent some try **The Bike Shop,** 1149 S. King St., Honolulu, tel. (808) 596-0588, renting two-person tents and backpacks at $35 for a weekend or $70 for the week, for either. They require a $200 deposit that's returned when you return their equipment. **Omar the Tentman,** 94-158, Leoole St., Waipahu, tel. (808) 677-8785 rents a wider variety of equipment, with prices for 1-3 day or 4-7 day periods. Their dome tent runs $25/$30, a six-person tent $52/$57, sleeping bags $15/$20, backpacks $15/$20, stoves $14/18, and lanterns (you supply to fuel) $14/$18. They have no backpacking tents.

Topographical Maps
On Oahu, a wide range of topographical maps can be purchased at the **Pacific Map Center,** 560 N. Nimitz Hwy., 206A, Honolulu, HI 96817, tel. (808) 545-3600, or at **Hawaii Geographic Maps and Books,** 49 S. Hotel St., Honolulu, tel. (808) 538-3952.

GOLF

With 37 private, public, and military golf courses scattered around such a relatively small island, *(continues on page 709)*

OAHU GOLF COURSES

COURSE	STATUS	PAR	YARDS	FEES	CART	CLUBS
Ala Wai Golf Course 404 Kapahulu Ave. Honolulu, HI 96851 tel. (808) 733-7387	Municipal	70	5,817	$40	$14	$25
Barbers Point Golf Course NAS, Barbers Point, HI 96862 tel. (808) 682-1911	Military	72	6,394	$28	$10	$5
BayView Golf Links 45-285 Kaneohe Bay Dr. Kaneohe, HI 96744 tel. (808) 247-0451	Public	60	3,430	$73	Incl.	$21
Ewa Beach International Golf Club 91-050 Fort Weaver Rd. Ewa Beach, HI 96706 tel. (808) 689-8351	Semiprivate	72	5,998	$135	Incl.	$35

(continues)

OAHU GOLF COURSES

(continued)

COURSE	STATUS	PAR	YARDS	FEES	CART	CLUBS
Ewa Village Golf Course Mango Tree Road Ewa, HI 96706 tel. (808) 681-0220	Municipal	72	7,100	$40	$14	No
Fort Shaffer Golf Course USAG-HI Golf Bldg. 2104, Schofield Barracks, HI 96857 tel. (808) 438-9587	Military	68	5,800	$21	$8	$6
Hawaii Country Club 94-1211 Kunia Rd. Wahiawa, HI 96786 tel. (808) 621-5654	Public	72	5,916	$40	Incl.	$20
Hawaii Kai Championship **Golf Course** 8902 Kalanianaole Hwy. Honolulu, HI 96825 tel. (808) 395-2358	Public	72	6,222	$120	Incl.	$30
Hawaii Kai Executive Golf Course 8902 Kalanianaole Hwy. Honolulu, HI 96825 tel. (808) 395-2358	Public	55	2,386	$42	Incl.	$15
Hawaii Prince Golf Club 91-1200 Fort Weaver Rd. Ewa Beach, HI 96706 tel. (808) 689-8361	Resort	36**	6,214	$135	Incl.	$35
Hickam Mamala Bay Golf Course 625 Worchester Ave. Hickam AFB, HI 96853 tel. (808) 449-6490	Military	72	6,412	$32	$8.50	$10
Hickam Par Three Golf Course 625 Worchester Ave. Hickam AFB, HI 96853 tel. (808) 449-2093	Military	27*	1,400	$7	$3 (pull)	$3.50
Honolulu Country Club 1690 Ala Puunalu St. Honolulu, HI 96818 tel. (808) 833-4541	Private	71	5,987	$46	Incl.	$25
Kahuku Golf Course P.O. Box 417 Kahuku, HI 96731 tel. (808) 293-5842	Municipal	35*	2,699	$20	$2 (pull)	$10
Kalakaua Golf Course USAG-HI Golf Bldg. 2104, Schofield Barracks HI 96857 tel. (808) 655-9833	Military	72	6,186	$25	$8	$6

* 9-hole course   ** 27-hole course (par 36 per 9)

COURSE	STATUS	PAR	YARDS	FEES[†]	CART	CLUBS
Kaneohe Klipper Golf Course MCBH Bldg. 3088 Kaneohe, HI 96863 tel. (808) 254-1745	Military	72	6,216	$35	$8	$10
Kapolei Golf Course 91-701 Farrington Hwy. Kapolei, HI 96707 tel. (808) 674-2227	Semiprivate	72	6,136	$90	Incl.	$30
Ko Olina Golf Club 92-1220 Alii Nui Dr. Kapolei, HI 96707 tel. (808) 676-5300	Resort	72	6,480	$145	Incl.	$40
Koolau Golf Course 45-550 Kionaole Rd. Kaneohe, HI 96744 tel. (808) 236-4653	Private	72	6,857	$90	Incl.	$30
Leilehua Golf Course USAG-HI Golf Bldg. 2104 Schofield Barracks HI 96857 tel. (808) 655-4653	Military	72	6,521	$31	$8	$6
Luana Hills Country Club 770 Auloa Rd. Kailua, HI 96734 tel. (808) 262-2139	Semiprivate	72	5,308	$80	Incl.	$30
Makaha Valley Country Club 84-627 Makaha Valley Rd. Waianae, HI 96792 tel. (808) 695-9578	Private	71	6,091	$65	Incl.	$30
					(continues on next page)	
Mid-Pacific Country Club 266 Kaelepulu Dr. Kailua, HI 96734 tel. (808) 261-9765	Private	72	6,509	$125	Incl.	$25
Mililani Golf Club 95-176 Kualelani Ave. Mililani, HI 96789 tel. (808) 623-2222	Semiprivate	72	6,239	$95	Incl.	$25
Moanalua Golf Club 1250 Ala Aolani St. Honolulu, HI 96819 tel. (808) 839-2411	Semiprivate	36*	2,972	$25	$14	No
Navy-Marine Golf Course 943 Valkenburgh St. Honolulu, HI 96818 tel. (808) 471-0142	Military	72	6,566	$40	$10	$5
Oahu Country Club 150 Country Club Rd. Honolulu, HI 96817 tel. (808) 595-3256	Private	71	5,820	$40	Incl.	$25

* 9-hole course   ** 27-hole course (par 36 per 9)

(continues)

OAHU GOLF COURSES
(continued)

COURSE	STATUS	PAR	YARDS	FEES	CART	CLUBS
Olomana Golf Links 41-1801 Kalanianaole Hwy. Waimanalo, HI 96795 tel. (808) 259-7926	Private	72	5,887	$90	Incl.	$25
Pali Golf Course 45-050 Kamehameha Hwy. Kaneohe, HI 96744 tel. (808) 266-7612	Municipal	72	6,494	$40	$14	$30
Pearl Country Club 98-535 Kaonohi St. Aiea, HI 96701 tel. (808) 487-3802	Semiprivate	72	6,232	$80	Incl.	$20
Sheraton Makaha Golf Club 84-626 Makaha Valley Rd. Makaha, HI 96792 tel. (808) 695-9544	Resort	72	6,414	$120	Incl.	$30
Ted Makalena Golf Course 93-059 Waipio Point Access Rd., Waipahu, HI 96797 tel. (808) 675-6052	Municipal	71	5,946	$40	$14	$No
The Links at Kuilima 57-091 Kamehameha Hwy. Kahuku, HI 96731 tel. (808) 293-8574	Resort	72	6,225	$125	Incl.	$30
Turtle Bay Country Club 57-091 Kamehameha Hwy. Kahaku, HI 96731 tel. (808) 293-8574	Resort	36*	3,204	$25	Incl.	$25
Waialae Country Club 4997 Kahala Ave. Honolulu, HI 96816 tel. (808) 732-1457	Private	72	7,012	$150	Incl.	$25
Waikele Golf Club 94-200 Paioa Place Waipahu, HI 96797 tel. (808) 676-9000	Semiprivate	72	6,261	$110	Incl.	$30
West Loch Golf Course 91-1126 Okupe St. Ewa Beach, HI 96706 tel. (808) 675-6076	Municipal	72	5,849	$47	Incl.	$15

* 9-hole course ** 27-hole course (par 36 per 9)

it's a wonder that it doesn't rain golf balls. These courses range from modest nine-holers to world-class courses whose tournaments attract the biggest names in golf today. Prices range from $20 a round up to $150. An added attraction of playing Oahu's courses is that you get to walk around on some of the most spectacular and manicured pieces of real estate on the island. Some afford sweeping views of the coast, such as the **Ko Olina Golf Club,** while others, like the **Pali Golf Course,** have a lovely mountain backdrop, or, like Waikiki's **Ala Wai Golf Course,** are set virtually in the center of all the downtown action. The Ala Wai Golf Course also must be one of the busiest courses in the country as some 500 rounds of golf are played there daily! In 1994, the PGA rated the **Koolau Golf Course** the toughest course in the United States. Tough or easy, flat or full of definition, Oahu provides ample opportunity and variety for any golfer.

The **Hawaiian Open Golf Tournament** held in late January or February at the Waialae Country Club brings the world's best golfers. Prize money is close to $1 million, and all three major TV networks cover the event. This is usually the only opportunity the average person gets to set foot on this course.

For ease of use for municipal golf courses, the City and County of Honolulu has set up an automated tee time reservation and information system. Call (808) 296-2000 to make or check your reservation or to have your inquiry answered.

TENNIS

Grease up the old elbow, because Oahu boasts 181 county-maintained tennis courts, 124 of which are lighted. Most courts also have backboards. Get a complete list of them by writing a letter of inquiry and enclosing a SASE to the Dept. of Parks and Recreation, Tennis Division, 3908 Paki Ave., Honolulu, HI 96815, or by calling (808) 971-7150. Alternately, you can stop by the Diamond Head Tennis Center at the above address and pick up a copy yourself. The chart on the following page is a partial listing of what's available.

SCUBA, SNORKELING, AND SNUBA

Oahu has particularly generous underwater vistas open to anyone donning a mask and fins. Some well-known favorites are Hanauma Bay, Black Point off Diamond Head, the waters around Rabbit Island, Sharks Cove on the North Shore, Maunalua Bay between Koko and Diamond Heads (good for green sea turtles), Magic Island near Ala Moana Beach Park, and some sunken ships and planes just off the Waianae coast.

Dive Shops and Rentals

In the Honolulu area, try the following. **Waikiki Diving,** at 1734 Kalakaua, tel. (808) 955-5151, closed Sunday, does PADI certification. No snorkeling tours, but they rent snorkeling equipment at $8 for 24 hours. A three-day certification course costs $300 plus tax; books are extra and run $35. Open-water, two-tank, two-location boat dives run $75. **South Seas Aquatics,** 2155 Kalakaua Ave., Suite 112, tel. (808) 922-0852, is a full service dive shop with competitive pricing for certification, tours, and rentals. **Dan's Dive Shop,** 660 Ala Moana Blvd., tel. (808) 536-6181, is open daily and offers several different dive tours. A beginner's tour is $70 for instruction and a one tank dive, while nonbeginners have two locations and two tanks for $80. Scuba equipment rental is $40 and snorkel equipment $10.

Surf and Sea, 62-595 Kamehameha Hwy., tel. (808) 637-9887, is a complete dive shop on the North Shore in Haleiwa offering certification, rentals, charters, and tours. **Aaron's Dive Shop,** at 602 Kailua Rd., Kailua, tel. (808) 262-2333, or in Pearl City at (808) 487-5533, is a full-service dive shop. A snorkel outfit runs $7 for 24 hours. They have a four-day scuba certification course for $390 and two-week course for $170. Two tank boat dives run $80-90 and a one tank dive off the beach is $90. In Kailua, try **Windward Dive Center,** 789 Kailua Rd., tel. (808) 263-2311, website: www.divehawaii.com, offering various PADI instruction courses. A two-week, open-water dive class is about $120, while a tailor-made short course runs about $300. More advanced courses are also taught here. **Aloha Dive Shop,** at Koko Marina (on the way to

OAHU TENNIS COURTS

COUNTY COURTS

Under the jurisdiction of the Department of Parks and Recreation Tennis Division, 3908 Paki Ave., Honolulu, HI 96815, tel. (808) 971-7150. Courts listed are in Honolulu, Waikiki, and main towns only.

TOWN	LOCATION		NO. OF COURTS	LIGHTED
Aiea	Aiea District Park	99-350 Aiea Heights Dr.	2	Yes
Ewa	Ewa Beach Community Park	91-955 North Rd.	4	Yes
Kahala	Kahala Community Park	4495 Pahoa Ave.	2	No
Kailua	Kailua District Park	21 S. Kainalu Dr.	8	Yes
Kaimuki	Kaimuki Community Park	3521 Waialea Ave.	2	Yes
Kaneohe	Kaneohe District Park	44-660 Keaahala Rd.	6	No
Keehi	Keehi Lagoon Courts	405 Lagoon Dr.	12	Yes
Koko Head	Koko Head District Park	423 Kaumakani St.	6	Yes
Manoa	Manoa Valley District Park	2721 Kaaipu St.	4	Yes
Maunawili	Maunawili Valley Park	962 Maunawili Rd.	2	Yes
Mililani	Mililani District Park	94-1150 Lanikuhana	4	No
Pearl City	Pearl City District Park	785 Hoomaemae St.	2	Yes
Sunset Beach	Sunset Beach Neighborhood Park	59-360 Kam. Hwy.	2	Yes
Wahiawa	Wahiawa District Park	1139-A Kilani Ave.	4	Yes
Waialua	Waialua District Park	67-180 Goodale Rd.	4	Yes
Waianae	Waianae District Park	85-601 Farrington Hwy.	8	Yes
Waikiki	Ala Moana Park	1201 Ala Moana Blvd.	10	Yes
	Diamond Head Tennis Center	3908 Paki Ave.	10	No
	Kapiolani Tennis Courts	2740 Kalakaua Ave.	4	Yes
Waimanalo	Waimanalo District Park	41-415 Hihimanu St.	4	No
Waipahu	Waipahu District Park	92-230 Paiwa St.	4	Yes

HOTEL AND PRIVATE COURTS THAT ARE OPEN TO THE PUBLIC

TOWN	LOCATION	TEL. (808)	COST
Ainahaina	Honolulu Tennis Academy	373-1282	$20/hr.
Ewa Beach	Hawaii Prince Golf Club	944-4567	$8/hr.
Kahuku	Turtle Bay Resort	293-8811	$20/hr.
Kopolei	Ihilani Resort	679-0079	$24/hr.

Hanauma Bay), tel. (808) 395-5922, does it all from snorkeling to boat dives. Excellent rates, good service. This shop is owned and run by Jackie James, the "First Lady of Diving" in Hawaii, with nearly 30 years of experience.

Snorkel Rentals
Snorkel Bob's, tel. (808) 735-7944, at the corner of Kapahulu and Mooheau Avenues, has very inexpensive deals on snorkeling. Prices start at $3.50 a day or only $9 per week for full snorkel gear, which you can take to Maui, Kauai, and Big Island locations and return there ($3 extra). The better equipment (still a deal) gets progressively more expensive. Snorkel Bob's also has underwater cameras, boogie boards for $6.50

exploring the reefs of Oahu

a day or $26 a week, and wet suits at $15 a week. It's best to stop in an peruse their selection for just what you need. **Haunama Bay Snorkeling,** tel. (808) 373-5060, rents full equipment for $6.25 a day and underwater cameras for $17. They offer tours to Hanauma Bay from Waikiki for $18.75, which includes transportation, equipment, instruction, a fish I.D. chart, and a map of the reef. Also try **Paradise Snorkel Adventures,** tel. (808) 923-7766. They rent top-of-the-line equipment for $6.95 a day, and run a shuttle to Hanauma Bay for $9.95 with equipment. Disposable underwater camera go for $19.95, and the better ones are $20-25, for 24 or 36 exposures, respectively.

Snuba
Snuba Tours of Oahu, tel. (808) 396-6163, offers a hybrid sport that is half snorkeling and half scuba diving. Snuba tours include instruction and transportation, and free swim time runs about 30 minutes. Four times a day, Mon.-Fri., tours are offered to Waikiki beach for about $70 and to Hanauma Bay for $90. For $80, Mon.-Sat., you can snuba the waters of Maunalua Bay on any of three tours.

SURFING AND WINDSURFING

All the Hawaiian Islands have incredibly good surfing conditions, but Oahu has the best. If there is such a thing as "the perfect wave," Oahu's wa-ters are a good place to look for it. Conditions here are perfect for both rank beginners and the most acclaimed surfers in the world. Waikiki's surf is predictable, and just right to start on, while the **Banzai Pipeline** and **Waimea Bay** on the North Shore have some of the most formidable surfing conditions on earth. **Makaha Beach** in Waianae is perhaps the best all-around surfing beach, frequented by the living legends of this most graceful sport. Summertime brings rather flat action around the island, but the winter months are a totally different story, with monster waves on the North Shore, and heavy surf, at times even in the relative calm of Waikiki.

Note: For surfing conditions, call (808) 973-4383 or 296-1818, ext. 9800. Heed all warnings!

Surfing Lessons
A number of enterprises in Waikiki offer beach services. Often these concessions are affiliated with hotels, and almost all hotel activities desks can arrange surfing lessons for you. An instructor and board go for about $25 per hour—most guarantee that they will get you standing. A board alone is half the price, but as in skiing, a few good lessons to start you off are well worth the time and money. Some reputable surfing lessons along Waikiki are provided by: Outrigger Hotel, 2335 Kalakaua Ave., tel. (808) 923-0711; and Hilton Hawaiian Village, 2005 Kalia Rd., tel. (808) 949-4321. Also check near the huge rack of surfboards along Kalakaua Avenue, just near Kuhio Beach at the Waikiki Beach Center, where you'll

find a number of beachboy enterprises at competitive rates. Also in Honolulu, try **Hans Hedemann Surf,** tel. (808) 591-7778, and **Hawaiian Water Sports,** tel. (808) 255-4352, for instructions and lessons, and in Haleiwa on the North Shore, try **Surf and Sea,** tel. (808) 637-9887.

For rentals, try those place that give lessons or contact **Blue Water Rentals,** tel. (808) 926-1477, or **Local Motion,** tel. (808) 955-7873.

Windsurfing

Far and away the most famous windsurfing beach on Oahu is Kailua Beach Park on the windward coast. Daily, a flotilla of windsurfers glide over its smooth waters, propelled by the always blowing breezes. Along the shore and in town a number of enterprises build, rent, and sell sailboards. There is also windsurfing along the North Shore. Commercial ventures are allowed to operate along Kailua Beach only on weekdays and weekend mornings, but weekend afternoons and holidays are *kapu!* Here are some of the best.

Windsurfing Lessons and Rentals

Kailua Sailboard Company, with a perfect location only a minute from the beach in Kailua at 130 Kailua Rd., tel. (808) 262-2555, open 9 a.m.-5 p.m. daily, is a full-service sailboard and kayak store. Sailboard rentals are $30 per day (24 hours), half day $25, double day and weekly rates are also available. Beginning group lessons are $39 for a three-hour session. During the week they have equipment right at the beach so you don't have to have a car to transport it. Weekends they provide a push cart or a roof rack at no additional charge. They also have boogie boards for $7.50 per day. Ocean kayaks run $22 a half day, $28 full day, and $120 a week. Double kayak rentals are $29, $39, and $165, respectively. If you're in Waikiki, transportation to and from is included in the rental price—a good deal. If you drive here, owner Aidin Schmer and his Doberman pinschers will watch your car.

Naish Hawaii, 155 A Hamakua Dr., tel. (808) 262-6068 or (800) 767-6068, open 9-5:30 daily, are very famous makers of custom boards, production boards, sails, hardware, accessories, and repairs. They also have T-shirts, bathing suits, beach accessories, hats, and slippers primarily for men, but plenty of their fashions would be attractive on women as well. Naish is the largest and oldest windsurfing company in Hawaii. The famous Naish Windsurfing School, located at Kailua Beach, gives 90 minutes of personal instruction and an additional hour of board use for $55 including all equipment; $75 for two people.

On the North Shore in Haleiwa, try **Surf and Sea,** tel. (808) 637-9887, and **Hawaiian Water Sports,** tel. (808) 255-4352, in Honolulu.

Boogie Boarding

The most highly acclaimed boogie-boarding beach on Oahu is Sandy Beach. It also has the dubious distinction of being the most dangerous beach in Hawaii, with more drownings, broken backs, and broken necks than anywhere in the state. Waikiki is tame and excellent for boogie boarding, while Waimanalo Beach, on the southeast side, is more for the intermediate boogie-boarder.

OTHER WATER ACTIVITIES

Kayaks, Jet Skis, Water Skis

Go Bananas Hawaii, 732 Kapapulu, tel. (808) 737-9514, and at 98-406 Kamehameha Hwy., Pearl City, tel. (808) 484-0606, are into kayaks, wave skis, and water toys. Single-person kayaks are $25 per day, $40 for two-person kayaks; $10 extra for 24 hours. Guided tours are offered at $50 for the first person, $40 for the second, and $30 for each additional member. Aside from wave skis, the store sells inflatable kayaks, aqua socks for walking on the reef, books, soaps, sunglasses, and T-shirts.

Located near the beach in Kailua, **Kailua Sailboard Company** also rents kayaks. They're a good company with a great location and competitive prices. They even provide shuttle service from Waikiki. **Twogood Kayaks Hawaii,** just down the block from Naish Hawaii (see above) at 345 Hahani St., tel. (808) 262-5656, offers kayak rentals, sales, and lessons. Good service, good prices. Full day rental $32, tandem $42, and they'll drop the kayak off for free at the Kailua Beach Park ($10 delivery fee for other locations in Kailua). Open Mon.-Fri. 9 a.m.-5 p.m. and Sat.-Sun. 8 a.m.-5 p.m.

Waikiki Beach Services, tel. (808) 924-4941, rents jet skis along Waikiki. At the Koko Marina Shopping Center, check with both **Fun Island Water Sports**, tel. (808) 395-4386, and **Sea Breeze Water Sports Ltd.**, tel. (808) 396-0100. In Haleiwa, try **Jet Ski Plus**, tel. (808) 637-8006, for jet skis and other water crafts. Expect to pay about $50 for a half hour.

If you like water-skiing, **Suyderhoud Water Ski Center**, tel. (808) 395-3773, at the Koko Marina Shopping center, can provide all your equipment, rentals, and lessons. Rates are $49 each for two people, skis included, for a half-hour session, $98 for an hour. Suyderhoud's is a full pro shop, so you can find all the best equipment and accessories here.

Parasailing

For a once-in-a-lifetime treat try **Aloha Parasail**, tel. (808) 521-2446. Strapped into a harness complete with lifejacket, you're towed aloft to glide effortlessly over the waters off Waikiki. Aloha Parasail has free hotel pickup. Others are: **Big Sky Parasail**, tel. (808) 396-0564, and **Sea Breeze Water Sports**. at the Koko Marina Shopping Center, tel. (808) 396-0100; and **Hawaii Kai Parasail**, at the Hawaii Kai Shopping Center, tel. (808) 396-9224. At Waikiki, check out **Waikiki Beach Services**, tel. (808) 924-4941. Rides go for $40-50 and last about 10 minutes. Boats usually have up to six riders so you might be on the water for about an hour.

Power Rafts

New to the Honolulu water scene is **Banana Boat Riders of Hawaii**, P.O. Box 8984, Honolulu, HI 96830, tel. (808) 922-5588 or (888) 922-5588, fax (808) 739-2962. The banana boat is a 32-foot inflatable yellow raft powered by twin 225 hp engines. It seats up to 21 and skims and bounces over the waves along the south coast. Riders straddle three inflatable tubes in the center of the craft and hang on to ropes for the safe but wild ride. The one-hour rides leave throughout the day starting at 9 a.m. and cost $39 for adults and $34 for children 3-11. Pregnant women and those with back problems should not consider riding. This thrill of a ride is sure to please—and get you wet. Wear a swimsuit or clothes that don't need to stay dry, and bring a

towel. From Jan.-April, tamer whalewatching rides are also offered for the same cost. Call (808) 922-5588 for information and reservations.

Royal Hawaiian Cruises, tel. (808) 848-6360 or (800) 852-4183, also offers hosted whalewatching tours on cushy, canopied, 49-passenger rafts during the winter months. All run $29 ($21.95 for kids 5-11) and leave early morning, late morning, and early afternoon from Honolulu's Kewalo Basin.

BICYCLING

Pedaling around Oahu can be both fascinating and frustrating. The roads are well paved, but the shoulders are often torn up. Traffic in and around Honolulu is horrifying, and the only way to avoid it is by leaving very early in the morning. Many, but not yet all, of the city buses have been installed with bike racks, so it's easier than before to get your bike from one part of the city to another or out of town. Once you leave the city, traffic, especially on the secondary interior roads, isn't too bad. Unfortunately, all of the coastal roads are heavily trafficked. Peddling around Waikiki, although congested, is usually safe, and a fun way of seeing the sights. Always use a helmet, always lock your bike, and always take your bike bag.

Bike Rental and Bike Shops

For bicycle rentals try: **Big Mountain Rentals**, 2426 Kuhio Ave., tel. (808) 926-1644; **Island Triathlon and Bike**, 569 Kapahulu Ave., tel. (808) 732-7227 (also in Wahiawa and at Hickam AFB); or **Paradise Isle Rentals**, 151 Uluniu Ave., tel. (808) 922-2224. Most rental bikes are mountain bikes or hybrids. Expect to pay about $15-20 a day or $50-70 a week, depending upon the type.

For sales and repairs try: **The Bike Shop**, at 1149 S. King St., tel. (808) 596-0588 (locations also in Aiea and Kaneohe); **Eki Cyclery**, 1603 Dillingham Blvd., tel. (808) 847-2005; **Island Triathlon and Bike**, 569 Kapahulu Ave., tel. (808) 732-7227; **McCully Bicycle**, 2124 S. King St., tel. (808) 955-6329; and **Barnfields Raging Isle Surf and Cycle**, 66-250 Kamehameha Hwy. in Haleiwa, tel. (808) 637-7707.

FISHING

Deep-Sea Fishing

Oahu's offshore waters are alive with game fish. Among these underwater fighters are marlin, *ahi, ono,* mahimahi, and an occasional deep-water snapper. The deep-sea boats generally troll the Penguin Banks and the generally calm waters along the Waianae Coast, from Barbers Point to Kaena Point.

The vast majority of Oahu's fleet moors in **Kewalo Basin,** in Honolulu Harbor along Ala Moana Boulevard next to Fisherman's Wharf. The boat harbor is a sight in itself, and if you're contemplating a fishing trip, it's best to head down there the day before and yarn with the captains and returning fishermen. This way you can get a feel for a charter to suit you best.

For a charter organization try **Island Charters,** tel. (808) 596-2086. Many private boats operating out of Kewalo Basin include: *Sea Verse,* tel. (808) 591-8840; **E.L.O. Sport Fishing,** tel. (808) 947-5208; *Maggie Joe* and *Sea Hawk,* tel. (808) 591-8888; and **The Wild Bunch,** tel. (808) 596-4709.

A few boats operate out of **Pokai Bay,** in Waianae on the northern leeward coast, and there are even a few berthed in Haleiwa on the North Shore.

Freshwater Fishing

The state maintains two public freshwater fishing areas on Oahu. The **Wahiawa Public Fishing Area** is 300 acres of fishable waters in and around the town of Wahiawa. It's basically an irrigation reservoir used to hold water for cane fields. Species regularly caught here are large and smallmouth bass, sunfish, channel catfish, *tucunare,* oscar, carp, snakehead, and Chinese catfish. The other area is the **Nuuanu Reservoir no. 4,** a 25-acre restricted watershed above Honolulu in the Koolau Mountains. It's open for fishing only three times per year in May, August, and November. Fish caught here are tilapia and Chinese catfish.

OTHER SPORTS

Horseback Riding

A different and delightful way to see Oahu is from the back of a horse. The following are a few outfits operating trail rides on different parts of the island. **Kualoa Ranch,** in Kualoa on north windward Oahu, tel. (808) 237-8515, by reservation only, offers picnic rides into Ka'a'awa Valley as part of their all-day adventures. Hotel pickup available. The stable at **Turtle Bay Hilton,** tel. (808) 293-8811, on the North Shore, welcomes nonguests. Guided trail rides through the forest and along the beach are given several times daily; adults $35, children $22 for a 45-minute ride. Ride every day except Monday in the hills above Waimanalo with **Correa Trails Hawaii,** tel. (808) 259-9005, or daily on the north shore with **Happy Trails Hawaii,** tel. (808) 638-7433.

Hang Gliding

North Shore Hang Gliding, tel. (808) 637-3178, sells hang gliders and can hook you up with a tandem instructor for lessons toward certification. They can also give you tips on where to fly on Oahu, if you're already certified.

Spectator Sports

Oahu is home to a number of major sporting events throughout the year. Many are "invitationals" that bring the cream of the crop from both collegiate and professional levels. Here are the major sports happenings on the island.

Football is big in Hawaii. The University of Hawaii's Rainbows play during the normal collegiate season at Aloha Stadium near Pearl Harbor. The December **Aloha Bowl** is a post-season collegiate game. In early January, the **Hula Bowl** brings together two all-star teams from the nation's collegiate ranks. You can hear the pads crack in February, when the NFL sends its best players to the **Pro Bowl.**

Basketball is also big on Oahu. The University of Hawaii's Rainbow Warriors play at the Neal S. Blaisdell Center in Honolulu at 777 Ward Street. The **Outrigger Hotels Rainbow Classic** tournament gathers eight heavy-hitting college teams from around the country for holiday sports entertainment. Mid-April sees some of the nation's best collegiate hoopballers make up four teams to compete in the **Aloha Basketball Classic.**

You can watch the Islanders of the Pacific Coast League play **baseball** during the regular season at Aloha Stadium. Baseball goes back well over 100 years in Hawaii, and the Islanders receive extraordinary fan support.

Watersport festivals include surfing events, usually Nov.-February. The best-known are: the **Triple Crown of Surfing, Hawaiian Pro Surfing Championships, Duke Kahanamoku Classic, Buffalo's Big Board Classic,** and the **Haleiwa**

Sea Spree, featuring many ancient Hawaiian sports. You can watch some of the Pacific's most magnificent yachts sail into the **Ala Wai Yacht Basin** in mid-July, completing their run from Los Angeles in the annual **Trans Pacific Yacht Race.**

FESTIVALS, HOLIDAYS, AND EVENTS

The following events and celebrations are either particular to Oahu, or they're celebrated here in a special or different way. This central island has more festivities and events than all the others, and these times provide great social opportunities for meeting people. Everyone is welcome to join in the fun, and most times the events are either free or nominally priced. There's no better way to enjoy yourself while vacationing than by joining in with a local party or happening.

JANUARY

January 1: **Hauoli Makahiki Hou.** Start the New Year off right by climbing to the top of Koko Crater on Oahu. A great way to focus on the limitless horizons of the coming year and a great hangover remedy. See the HVB for details. Or continue the party with the **Sunshine Music Festival** rock concert at Diamond Head Crater.

January 2: **Queen Emma Museum Open House.** This is Queen Emma's birthday, and the public is invited to visit her summer home and view a well-preserved collection of her personal belongings; tel. (808) 595-3167.

First Saturday: Watch the old pigskin get booted around in the **Hula Bowl Game,** Aloha Stadium, Honolulu. Annual college all-star football classic. Call (808) 947-4141 for specifics.

Mid-January to early February: **The Narcissus Festival** in Honolulu's Chinatown starts with the parade and festivities of Chinese New Year, with lion dances in the street, fireworks, a beauty pageant, and a coronation ball; call (808) 533-3181 for locations.

Late January: **Robert Burns Night** at the Ilikai Hotel, Honolulu. Scots from Canada and Mainland U.S. celebrate the birthday of Scotland's poet Robert Burns.

The **Cherry Blossom Festival** in Honolulu can begin in late January and last through March. Events include a Japanese cultural and trade show, tea ceremony, flower arranging, queen pageant, and coronation ball. Check newspapers and free tourist magazines for dates and times of various Japanese cultural events; tel. (808) 949-2255

FEBRUARY

Early February: **NFL Pro Bowl,** Aloha Stadium, Honolulu. Annual all-star football game offering the best from both conferences; tel. (808) 486-9300.

Punahou School Carnival, Honolulu. Arts, crafts, and a huge rummage sale at one of Hawaii's oldest and most prestigious high schools. Great ethnic foods. You'd be surprised at what Hawaii's oldest and most established families donate to the rummage sale. Call (808) 944-5711 for details.

The Hawaiian Open Golf Tournament, in Honolulu at Waialae Country Club. Huge prize money lures the best PGA golfers to this tournament, which is beginning its second decade.

Mid-February: **Haleiwa Sea Spree** on Oahu's North Shore. Surfing championships, outrigger canoe races, and ancient Hawaiian sports, topped off by an around-the-island bicycle race. Competitions last four days.

Late February-early March: **Buffalo's Annual Big Board Surfing Classic** at Makaha Beach, Oahu. Features the best of the classic board riders. A real cultural event complete with entertainment, crafts, and food. A two-day event held the last weekend in February and again on the first weekend in March.

MARCH

Hawaiian Song Festival and Song Composing Contest, Kapiolani Park Bandstand in Waikiki. Determines the year's best Hawaiian song. Presented by top-name entertainers.

Emerald Ball. An elegant affair sponsored by the Society of the Friendly Sons of St. Patrick that features dinner as well as dancing to a big-name band. Also, the **Saint Patrick's Day Parade,** Kalakaua Avenue, Waikiki.

Kamehameha School Annual Song Contest, Blaisdell Center Arena, Honolulu. Competition among secondary-grade students of Hawaiian ancestry. Kamehameha Schools, tel. (808) 842-8211 or 842-8495.

Late March: **Hawaiian Highland Gathering,** Honolulu. A gathering of the clans for Scottish games, competition, Scottish foods, highland dancing, and pipe bands. Great Scotsmen with kilts and lei too. Richardson's Field, Pearl Harbor, tel. (808) 523-5050.

Hawaii Challenge International Sport Kite Championship and **Oahu Kite Festival,** both at Kapiolani Park. Call (808) 735-9059 for times and information.

APRIL

Early April: **Easter Sunday,** Sunrise Service at the National Memorial Cemetery of the Pacific, Punchbowl Crater, Honolulu.

Annual Hawaiian Festival of Music, Waikiki Shell, Honolulu. A grand and lively music competition of groups from all over the islands and the Mainland. A music lover's smorgasbord offering everything from symphony to swing and all in between.

April 8: **Wesak or Buddha Day** on the closest Sunday to April 8. Celebrates the birthday of Gautama Buddha. Ornate offerings of tropical flowers at temples throughout Hawaii. Great sunrise ceremonies at Kapiolani Park, Honolulu. Mainly Japanese in their best *kimono.* Flower festival pageant and dance programs in all island temples.

International Bed Race Festival (formerly Carole Kai Bed Race) down Kalakaua Avenue in Waikiki and a free concert at the Waikiki Shell the

night before. There's a race and appearances by Hawaii's name entertainers in this fun-filled charity fund-raiser.

Mid-April: **Aloha Basketball Classic,** Blaisdell Center Arena, Honolulu. Top college seniors are invited to Hawaii to participate in charity games made up of four teams. Blaisdell Center, tel. (808) 527-5400.

Late April or early May: **Pacific Handcrafters Guild Spring Fair,** at Thomas Square Park, Honolulu. An opportunity to see the "state of the arts" in Hawaii. Some of the islands' finest craftsmen in one spot selling their creations; tel. (808) 254-7688.

MAY

May 1: **Lei Day.** May Day to the rest of the world, but in Hawaii red is only one of the colors when everyone wears a lei. Festivities throughout Hawaii with special goings-on at Kapiolani Park, Waikiki.

Late May: **Memorial Day.** Special military services held at Honolulu, National Memorial Cemetery of the Pacific, on the last Monday in May. Call (808) 566-1430.

50th State Fair, at Aloha Stadium, Honolulu. Agricultural exhibits, down-home cooking, entertainment, and produce. Lasts four weekends. Call (808) 488-3389 or 923-1811 for information.

JUNE

Early June: **Mission Houses Museum Fancy Fair** and **Festival of Hawaiian Quilts,** Honolulu. A top-notch collection of Hawaii's best artists and craftsmen for the fair, and Hawaii's best stichery for the quilt show. A great chance to browse and buy. Also, foods and entertainment; tel. (808) 531-0481.

June 11: **King Kamehameha Day** is a Hawaiian state holiday honoring Kamehameha the Great, Hawaii's first and greatest universal king. Lei-draping ceremony at King Kamehameha statue and parades complete with floats and pageantry featuring a *ho'olaule'a* (street party) in Waikiki. Civic Center, downtown Honolulu.

Mid-June: **Annual King Kamehameha Traditional Hula and Chant Competition.** Blaisdell Center; tel. (808) 536-6540.

Annual Hawaiian Festival of Music, Waikiki Shell, Honolulu. A repeat of the April festivities, but no less a music lover's delight as local and Mainland bands compete in genres from symphony to swing.

Late June: **Annual Pan-Pacific Festival—Matsuri.** Dances and festivities, parades and performances, music, and arts and crafts in Honolulu at Kapiolani Park and other locations. It's a show of Japanese culture in Hawaii. Also, *bon odori*, the Japanese festival of departed souls, which features dances and candle-lighting ceremonies at numerous Buddhist temples throughout the islands. These festivities change yearly and can be held anytime from late June to early August. Call (808) 923-0492 for information.

The annual **Wai'anae Coast Community Cultural Festival** takes place at various spots along the Leeward Coast from mid-June to early August. Events include music and dance, arts and crafts, story telling, foods, and a fishing competition.

JULY

Early July: **Tin Man Triathlon,** Honolulu. More than 1,000 triathletes gather to swim 800 meters, bike 25 miles, and finish with a 10,000-meter (6.2 miles) run around Diamond Head and back to Kapiolani Park in Waikiki.

Trans Pacific Yacht Race, from Los Angeles to Honolulu during odd-numbered years. Yachties arrive throughout the month and converge on the Ala Wai Yacht Basin, where "party" is the password. They head off for Hanalei Bay, Kauai, to begin the year's yachting season.

July 4: **Hawaiian Islands Tall Ships Parade.** Tall-masted ships from throughout the islands parade from Koko Head to Sand Island and back to Diamond Head. A rare treat and taste of days gone by.

Mid-July: **Prince Lot Hula Festival,** Honolulu. A great chance for visitors to see authentic hula from some of the finest *hula halau* in the islands. Moanalua Gardens, tel. (808) 839-5334.

Annual Ukulele Festival, held on the last Sunday of the month 11 a.m.-1:30 p.m. at Kapiolani Park Bandstand, Waikiki. Hundreds of ukulele players from throughout the islands put on a very entertaining show. For information, call (808) 971-2525.

Pacific Handcrafters Guild Summer Fair, Thomas Square Park, Honolulu. A chance to see the "state of the arts" all in one locality. Browse, buy, and eat ethnic foods at various stalls; tel. (808) 254-6788.

Late July: **International Sailboard Championship Invitational** held at Diamond Head. Watch the amazing "aquabatics" as windsurfers run before the wind on their amazing one-person crafts.

AUGUST

Early August: **Honolulu Zoo Day,** Waikiki. A day of family fun where kids of all ages get a close-up look at the animals and a day of entertainment.

Hula Festival, Kapiolani Park, Waikiki. Recent hula graduates from Honolulu's Summer Fun classes perform hula they have learned. Some amazing bodily gyrations.

Late August: **Hawaiian Open State Tennis Championships,** Honolulu. Held at various courts around town offering substantial prizes. For info call Don Andrews, tel. (808) 971-7150.

Queen Liliuokalani Keiki Hula Competition, Kamehameha Schools, Honolulu. Children ages 5-12 compete in a hula contest. Caution: "Terminal Cuteness."

SEPTEMBER

Early September: **Waikiki Rough Water Swim,** Honolulu. A two-mile open-ocean swim from Sans Souci Beach to Duke Kahanamoku Beach. Open to all ages and abilities.

Late September: **Aloha Festivals** celebrates Hawaii's own "intangible quality," *aloha*. There are parades, luau, historical pageants, balls, and various other entertainment on all islands. The spirit of *aloha* is infectious and all are welcomed to join in. Check local papers and tourist literature for happenings near you. Downtown parades attract thousands, and even parking lots do their bit by charging a $1 flat fee during these festival times. The savory smells of ethnic foods fill the air from a multitude of stands, and the Honolulu Symphony performs at the Blaisdell Center, while free concerts are given at the Waikiki Shell. Various locations on all islands; tel. (800) 852-7690.

Molokai to Oahu Canoe Race. Women (men in October) in Hawaiian-style canoes race from a remote beach on Molokai to Fort DeRussy in Honolulu. In transit they must navigate the rough Kaiwi Channel.

Pacific Handcrafters Guild Fall Fair, Thomas Square Park. A fall show of the best works of Handcrafters Guild members. Perfect for early-bird and unique Christmas shopping; tel. (808) 254-6788.

OCTOBER

Makahiki Festival, Waimea Falls Park, Oahu. Features Hawaiian games, crafts, and dances, reminiscent of the great Makahiki celebrations of ancient Hawaii. On an 800-acre tropical preserve.

Molokai to Oahu Canoe Race. Men (women in September) navigate Hawaiian-style canoes across the rough Kaiwi Channel from a remote beach on Molokai to Fort DeRussy, Honolulu.

Oktoberfest. Where else would you expect to find German oom-pah bands, succulent Wiener schnitzel, *und* beer, than in Honolulu. At the Budweiser Warehouse, 99-877 Iwaena St., Aiea, from noon until 10 p.m.

Annual Orchid Plant and Flower Show. Hawaii's copious and glorious flowers are displayed. Blaisdell Center Exhibition Hall, Honolulu. Blaisdell Center, tel. (808) 527-5400.

Late October: **Bishop Museum Festival.** A superb time to visit the world's best museum on Polynesia and Hawaii. Arts, crafts, plants, and tours of the museum and planetarium. A full day for the family, with special "back room" exhibits open to the public that are usually not seen. Bishop Museum, Honolulu, tel. (808) 847-3511.

NOVEMBER

Early November: **Ho'olaule'a in Waianae.** The military lets down its hair and puts on a display accompanied by top entertainers, food, and music in this very ethnic area. All-day event.

November 11: **Veterans Day Parade.** National holiday. A parade from Fort DeRussy to Queen Kapiolani Park, Waikiki. American Legion, tel. (808) 949-1140.

Christmas in November: **Mission Houses Museum Annual Christmas Fair.** Quality items offered by Hawaii's top craftsmen in an open-air bazaar; tel. (808) 531-0481.

Late Nov.-Dec.: **Triple Crown of Surfing:** Hawaiian Pro, World Cup of Surfing, Pipeline Masters. The best surfers in the world come to the best surfing beaches on Oahu. Wave action determines sites except for the Masters. Big money and national TV coverage. Call (808) 377-5850 or 325-7400 for dates and locations.

Artists of Hawaii Annual Exhibition. The best works of Hawaii's contemporary fine artists. The Honolulu Academy of Arts, tel. (808) 532-8701.

Hawaii International Film Festival. The best films from the East, West, and Oceania. Various locations on all islands. For information, call (808) 528-3456 or (800) 752-8193, website: www.hiff.org.

DECEMBER

Christmas celebrations: **Kamehameha Schools Christmas Concert,** Blaisdell Center Concert Hall, Honolulu.

Pacific Handcrafters Guild Winter Fair, Thomas Square, Honolulu. The best by the best, just in time for Christmas. Open air. Pacific Handcrafters, tel. (808) 254-6788.

Annual **Honolulu Marathon.** An institution in marathon races. One of the best-attended and very prestigious races in the country, where top athletes from around the world turn out to compete. Call (808) 734-7200 or 422-0561.

Annual Rainbow Classic. Invitational tournament of collegiate basketball teams. Blaisdell Center Arena, Honolulu.

Aloha Bowl Game. Collegiate football. Aloha Stadium, Honolulu. Call (808) 947-4141.

On **New Year's Eve** hold onto your hat, because they do it up big in Hawaii. The merriment and alcohol flow all over the island. Firecrackers are illegal, but they go off everywhere. Beware of hangovers and "amateur" drunken drivers. For a no-alcohol event, head downtown for the **First Night** festival of entertainment and the arts.

SHOPPING

You can't come to Oahu and *not* shop. Even if the idea of it doesn't thrill you, the lure of almost endless shops offering every imaginable kind of merchandise will sooner or later tempt even the most "big-waste-of-time" mumbler through their doors. So why fight it? And if you're the other type, who feels as though a day without shopping is like being marooned on a deserted island, have no fear of rescue, because everywhere on the horizon is "a sale, a sale!"

You can use "much much more" as either an aspersion or a tribute when describing Oahu, and nowhere does this qualifier fit better than when describing its shopping. More than a dozen major and minor shopping centers and malls are in Honolulu and Waikiki alone! Population centers around the island, including those in the interior, the south shore, windward shore, and north shore, all have shopping centers in varying degrees—at the very least, a parking lot rimmed with a half-dozen shops that can provide immediate necessities.

On the Neighbor Islands, a major shopping mall is usually found only in the island's main city, with mom 'n' pop stores and small superettes taking up the slack. On Oahu, you've got these too, but you're never very far from some serious shopping centers. The tourist trade fosters the sale of art and artifacts, jewelry and fashions, and numerous boutiques selling these are strung around the island like a shell necklace. Food costs in supermarkets tend to be reasonable because Oahu is the main distribution center, and with all the competition, prices in general seem to be lower than on the other islands. If your trip to Hawaii includes a stop on Oahu, do most of your shopping here, because of the cut-rate prices and much greater availability of goods. When most Hawaiians go on a shopping spree, they head for Oahu. Don't underestimate a simple trip to the grocery store. Often, but not always, you can find uniquely Hawaiian gifts like coffee, macadamia nut liqueur, coconut syrup, and even an assortment of juices much cheaper than in the gift shops. Remember, even thrift and consignment shops may hold some treasures, like older T-shirts, many with distinctive local flavor.

Note: The following are merely general listings; refer to **Shopping** in the travel sections for listings of specific shops, stores, and markets.

SHOPPING CENTERS

Honolulu Shopping Centers

Since it serves as the main terminal for TheBus, you could make a strong case that **Ala Moana** Shopping Center is the heart of shopping on Oahu. At one time billed as the largest shopping center in the country, today it settles for being the largest in the state, with its hundreds of stores covering 50 acres. It's on Ala Moana Blvd., just across from the Ala Moana Beach Park. **The Ward Warehouse** is just a few blocks west of the Ala Moana Center, at 1050 Ala Moana Boulevard. The **Ward Centre** on Ala Moana across from Ward Warehouse, is a relatively new shopping center that's gaining a reputation for some exclusive shops.

Waikiki Shopping

Shopping in Waikiki is as easy as falling off a surfboard. In two or three blocks of Kuhio and Kalakaua Avenues are no less than seven shopping centers. If that's not enough, there are hundreds of independent shops, plus plenty of street vendors. Main shopping centers include the **Royal Hawaiian Shopping Center,** the **Waikiki Shopping Plaza,** and the **International Market Place,** an open-air shopping bazaar across from the Moana Hotel at 2330 Kalakaua Ave., open daily from 9 a.m. until the vendors get tired at night.

The **Hyatt Regency Shopping Center** is located on the first three floors of the Hyatt Regency Hotel, at 2424 Kalakaua Avenue. The **King's Village** is at 131 Kaiulani Ave., the **Waikiki Trade Center** is on the corner of Seaside and Kuhio Avenues, and the **Rainbow Bazaar** is a unique mall located at the Hilton Hawaiian Hotel, at 2005 Kalia Road.

Around the Island

Heading east from Waikiki on Rt. 72, the first shopping opportunity is the **Niu Shopping Center** on your left, about four miles before Hanauma Bay. The Time Supermarket is known for good prices. Also on the left is the **Koko Marina Shopping Center,** just before Hanauma Bay, with several banks, a few art galleries, sports shops, and Foodland Supermarket. Nearby is the **Hawaii Kai Shopping Center.** Kailua and Kaneohe bedroom communities have shopping malls. Try the **Kaneohe Bay Shopping Center, Windward City Shopping Center,** and **Windward Mall. Kahaluu Sportswear,** along the Kahekili Hwy., about five minutes north of Byodo-In Temple, is a garment factory outlet store with decent prices and the ugliest collection of mannequins in the Pacific. Numerous shops are found along the North Shore from Haleiwa to Waimea, including surf shops, art galleries, boutiques, and plenty of fast food and restaurants. The **Pearlridge Shopping Center,** in Pearl City at the corner of the Kamehameha Hwy. and Waimano Home Rd., is a full shopping complex with more than 150 stores. The **Waianae Mall,** 86-120 Farrington Hwy., serves the Waianae coast with a supermarket, drugstore, fast foods, and sporting goods, and the **Waipahu Town Center** in Waipahu is a good place to start when up in the center of the island.

SUPERMARKETS AND OTHER MARKETS

Around the island plenty of mom 'n' pop grocery stores provide fertile ground for a cultural exchange, but they're expensive. Oahu's large su-

---

OAHU MUSEUMS AND GALLERIES

Bishop Museum, 1525 Bernice St., Honolulu, HI 96817, tel. (808) 847-3511, website: www.bishop.hawaii.org.Open daily 9 a.m.-5 p.m.The best collection in the world on Polynesia in general and Hawaii specifically. A true cultural treat. Should not be missed.

The Contemporary Museum, 2411 Makiki Heights Dr., Honolulu, HI 96822, tel. (808) 526-1322, open Tues.-Sat. 10 a.m.-4 p.m., Sunday noon-4 p.m., closed Monday. The focus is on exhibitions, not collections, although works by David Hockney are on permanent display. Changing exhibits reflect different themes in contemporary art.

Damien Museum, located at Saint Augustine Catholic Church, 130 Ohua Ave. in Waikiki, tel. (808) 923-2690. Displays photographs, papers, artifacts, and mementos of the legendary Father Damien. Open weekdays only 9 a.m.-3 p.m. Donations gratefully accepted.

Hawaii Maritime Center, at Pier 7, Honolulu Harbor, HI 96813, tel. (808) 536-6373. Open daily 8:30 a.m.-5 p.m. A museum chronicling the exploration and exploitation of Hawaii by the seafarers who have come to its shores. Visit the famous double-hulled canoe *Hokule'a* and the tall-masted *Falls of Clyde.*

Hawaii's Plantation Village, 94-695 Waipahu St., Waipahu, HI 96797, tel. (808) 677-0110. An open-air museum portraying sugar plantation life and the ethnic mix of plantation workers. Restored buildings and memorabilia. Open for guided tours only Mon.-Fri. 9 a.m.-3 p.m. and Saturday 10 a.m.-3 p.m.

Honolulu Academy of Arts, 900 S. Beretania St., Honolulu, HI 96814, tel. (808) 532-8700, website: www.honoluluacademy.org. Open Tues.-Sat. 10 a.m.-4:30 p.m., Sunday 1-5 p.m. Collects, preserves, and exhibits works of art, classic and modern, with a strong emphasis on Asian art. Permanent and special exhibitions, with tours, classes, lectures, and films.

Honolulu Art Center, across from the Academy of Arts, displays student artwork. Contemporary Hawaiian works.

Iolani Palace, on the Iolani Palace Grounds, P.O. Box 2259, Honolulu, HI 96804, tel. (808) 522-0832. The only royal palace in the United States. Vintage artwork and antiques. Guided tours. Open Tues.Sat. 9 a.m.-2:15 p.m.

Mission Houses Museum, 553 S. King St., Honolulu, HI 96813, tel. (808) 531-0481. Open Tues.-Sat. 9 a.m.-4 p.m. Two homes, a printing house, and a library; an early mission compound. Guided tours. Excellent.

permarkets include **Times, Safeway, Foodland, and Star Markets.** Preference is highly individual, but Times has a good reputation for fresh vegetables and good prices. Japanese **Holiday Mart** has stores around the island. They've got some bargains in their general merchandise departments, but because they try to be everything, their food section suffers, especially the fruits and vegetables.

Chinatown offers an open market at the Cultural Plaza, located at the corner of Mauna Kea and Beretania Streets. Besides produce, you'll find fresh fish, meats, and poultry; the **Oahu Fish Market** is in the heart of Chinatown along King Street. The shops are run-down but clean, and sell everything from octopus to kimchi.

People's Open Market

A highly organized venture overseen by the county, the People's Open Market has been going strong since 1973. This rotating farmer's market offers the best and freshest products from farm and sea at prices lower than at any store. A wonderful practice in and of itself, it also helps to vitalize the local economy while offering a place for people to gather in an age-old tradition. The market is held at 22 different locations and times throughout the week—every day except Sunday. On Monday, Wednesday, Friday, and Saturday, the market is in the greater Honolulu area. On Tuesday, it moves up to Waipahu and over to the leeward coast, while Thursday finds it on the windward coast. Three market sites that will be easy to locate are the City Hall parking lot deck, 11:45 a.m.-12:30 p.m. on Monday; Queen Kapiolani Park, 10-11 a.m. on Wednesday; and Waimanalo Beach Park, 7:15-8:15 a.m. on Thursday. Call (808) 522-7088 for full in-

---

Pacific Aerospace Museum, tel. (808) 839-0777, at the Honolulu International Airport, is open daily 9 a.m.-6 p.m. The focus is on aerospace travel and the aviation history of Hawaii, with interactive displays and an interpretive film.

Queen Emma's Summer Palace, 2913 Pali Hwy., Honolulu, HI 96817, tel. (808) 595-3167. Open daily 9 a.m.-4 p.m., except major holidays. Restored historic home, built about 1848. Furniture and mementos of Queen Emma and her family. Some items belong to other members of royal family.

Queen's Medical Center Historical Room, 1301 Punchbowl St., Honolulu, HI 96813, tel. (808) 547-4397. Exhibits display the history of the Queen's Medical Center (founded 1859) and the history of medicine in Hawaii. Open weekdays 8:30 a.m.-3:30 p.m.; no charge.

Tennent Art Foundation Gallery, 201-203 Prospect St., Honolulu HI, 96813 tel. (808) 531-1987. Shows work of Madge Tennent and other, mostly contemporary, works of art.

Tropic Lightning Museum, located directly up from Macomb Gate on Schofield Barracks. Military museum on the history of Schofield Barracks Army Base and the 25th Infantry Division. Open 10 a.m.-4 p.m. Tues.-Sat., tel. (808) 655-0438.

University of Hawaii Art Gallery, 2535 The Mall, Honolulu, HI 96822, tel. (808) 956-6888. On the third floor of the student center. Showcases faculty, student, and traveling exhibitions. Open Mon.-Fri.10 a.m.-4 p.m. and Sunday noon-4 p.m. Gallery closed between exhibitions.

U.S. Army Museum of Hawaii, Fort DeRussy, Waikiki, tel. (808) 438-2821. Open Tues.-Sun. 10 a.m.-4:30 p.m. Military history of Hawaii from the time of Kamehameha I to the activities of the U.S. Army in east Asia and the Pacific islands.

USS *Arizona* Memorial, Arizona Memorial Dr., Pearl Harbor, HI 96818, tel. (808) 422-2771 or 422-0561. A free tour of the sleek 184-foot white concrete structure that spans the sunken USS *Arizona*. Free Navy launches take you on the tour of "Battleship Row." Open daily 7:30 a.m.-5 p.m. No reservations-first-come, first-served. Launches every 15 minutes. Visitor center offers graphic materials and film, reflecting events of the Pearl Harbor attack.

USS *Bowfin* Submarine Museum, 11 Arizona Memorial Dr., Honolulu, HI 96818, tel. (808) 432-1341, fax 422-5201, website: www.aloha.net/~bowfin, e-mail: bowfin@aloha.net. Open daily 8 a.m.-5 p.m. Fully restored WW II submarine. Insight into the underwater war. Guided tours. Fascinating. Next door to *Arizona* Memorial.

formation on locations and times. Come indulge in the sights and smells.

Health Food Stores

Brown rice and tofu eaters can keep that special sparkle in their eyes with no problem on Oahu—there are some excellent health food stores. Most have a snack bar where you can get a delicious and nutritious meal for bargain prices. **Down to Earth**, 2525 S. King St., tel. (808) 947-7678, is an old standby where you can't go wrong; great stuff at great prices. **Kokua Market Natural Foods Co-op**, 2643 S. King St., tel. (808) 941-1922, is a full-service store with organic and fresh produce, cheese, milk, juices, bulk foods, and breads. **Vim and Vigor Foods** has four stores on Oahu, including at the Ala Moana Center, tel. (808) 955-3600. **Celestial Natural Foods,** at the Haleiwa Shopping Plaza on the North Shore, tel. (808) 637-6729, is also top-notch, and **The Source Natural Foods,** 32 Kaneohe in Kailua on the windward side, tel. (808) 262-5604, is open daily.

BOOKSTORES

Oahu has plenty of excellent bookstores. In Honolulu, try the **Honolulu Book Shops**, with four locations at the Ala Moana Center, tel. (808) 941-2274; in downtown Honolulu at 1001 Bishop St., tel. (808) 537-6224; at the Pearlridge Center, tel. (808) 487-1548; and at the Kailua Shopping Center, tel. (808) 261-1996. **Waldenbooks** has several locations in the city, including at the Pearlridge Center, tel. (808) 488-9488; at Kahala Mall, tel. (808) 737-9550; and Waikiki Shopping Plaza, tel. (808) 922-4154. **Borders Books and Music** also has two full-selection stores in Honolulu, one in the Waikele Center, tel. (808) 676-6699, and the other at the Ward Centre, tel. (808) 591-8995. For a fine selection of Hawaiiana try the **Bishop Museum and Planetarium Bookshop** at the Bishop Museum, 1525 Bernice St., tel. (808) 848-4158, and at the **Mission Houses Museum** in downtown Honolulu at 553 S. King St., tel. (808) 531-0481. You can

OAHU LIBRARIES AND ARCHIVES

Bishop Museum Library and Archives, 1525 Bernice St., Honolulu, HI 96817, tel. (808) 848-4148. The archives are open Tues.-Fri. 10 a.m.-3 p.m., Saturday 9 a.m.-noon, while the library is open Tues.-Fri. 1-4 p.m. and Saturday 9 a.m.-noon. Extensive historical and cultural collection.

Episcopal Church of Hawaii, 229 Queen Emma Square, Honolulu, HI 96813, tel. (808) 536-7776. Records and photos of church history in Hawaii from 1862.

Hawaii Chinese Historical Center, 111 N. King St. Room 410, Honolulu, HI 96813, tel. (808) 521-5948. Open 12 hours per week; call. Rare books, oral histories, and photos concerning the history of Chinese in Hawaii.

Hawaiian Historical Society, 560 Kawaiahao St., Honolulu, HI 96813, tel. (808) 537-6271. Open Mon.-Fri. 10 a.m.-4 p.m. Extensive collection of 19th-century materials on Hawaiian Islands, including 3,000 photos, 10,000 books, maps, microfilm. Adjacent to Hawaiian Mission Children's Society. Should be seen together. Should not be missed.

Hawaiian State Archives, Iolani Palace Grounds, Honolulu, HI 96813, tel. (808) 586-0329. Open Mon.-Fri. 7:45 a.m.-4:30 p.m. Archives of the government of Hawaii. Private papers of Hawaiian royalty and government officials, photos, illustrations, etchings recording Hawaiian history. For anyone seriously interested in Hawaii. Shouldn't be missed.

Hawaii State Library, Iolani Palace Grounds, Honolulu, tel. (808) 586-3500. Main branch of statewide library system.

Mission Houses Library, 553 S. King St., Honolulu 96813, tel. (808) 531-0481. Open Tues.-Sat. 9 a.m.-4 p.m. Records, personal journals, letters and photos of early 19th-century Congregational missionaries to the Hawaiian Islands; archive of the Congregational Church in the Pacific. Shouldn't be missed.

University of Hawaii Library, 2425 Campus Rd., Honolulu 96822, tel. (808) 956-7204. Manoa campus. The Hamilton Library 4th floor holds the Hawaiian/Pacific Collection.

find a good selection of books on Hawaiian outdoors, hiking, camping, and recreation, as well as fine maps at the **Hawaii Geographic Maps and Books** shop, 49 S. Hotel St. in Honolulu, tel. (808) 538-3952. The **East-West Center bookstore** also carries a substantial collection of Hawaiiana as well as books on Asia, many of them published by the center.

SUNDRIES AND PHOTOGRAPHY

ABC has more than a dozen mini-marts in and around Waikiki. Their prices are generally high, but they do have some good bargains on suntan lotions, sunglasses, and beach mats. The cheapest place to buy **film** is at **Sears** and **Longs Drugs**. All have good selections, cheap prices, and stores all over the island. Open seven days a week, **Francis Camera Shop** in the Ala Moana Center, is extremely well stocked with accessories. For a large selection of military surplus and camping goods try the **Camouflage Shop Inc.** at 38 Wilikina Dr., in Wahiawa.

If gadgetry fascinates you, head for **Shirokiya Department Store** at the Ala Moana and Pearlridge centers. Besides everything else, they have a wonderful selection of all the gimcracks and doohickeys that Nippon has to offer. The atmosphere is somewhat like a trade fair. Those who can't imagine a tour with anything on their feet but Birkenstock can have their tootsies accommodated, but they won't be entirely happy. If you get a sole blowout, **Birkenstock Footprints** at Ward Center, will resole them for $14, but they want a full week to do it. For one-day service, they'll refer you to a shoemaker, **Joe Pacific** at 1680 Kapiolani Blvd., but he wants a toe-twisting $25 for the service!

FLEA MARKETS AND SWAP MEETS

Amidst the junk, these are the cheapest places to find treasures. Two operate successfully on Oahu and have a regular following. **Aloha Flea Market,** weekends tel. (808) 486-1529, weekdays tel. (808) 732-9611, is at Aloha Stadium every Wednesday, Saturday, and Sunday and most holidays 6 a.m.-3 p.m. It's the biggest flea market on Oahu, selling everything from bric-a-brac to real heirlooms and treasures.

Kam Swap Meet, tel. (808) 483-5933, inside the Kam Drive-In Theater (look for the two big screens), 98-850 Moanalua Rd., Pearl City, is open Wednesday, Saturday, and Sunday, 5:30 a.m.-1 p.m. Vendors from regular stall holders to housewives cleaning out the garage offer great fun and bargains.

ARTS AND CRAFTS

The following are a few of Oahu's many art shops and boutiques, just to get you started. An excellent place to find original arts and crafts at reasonable prices is along **The Fence** surrounding the Honolulu Zoo fronting Kapiolani Park. Island artists come here every weekend 10 a.m.-4 p.m. to display and sell their artwork. The **Honolulu Academy of Arts** is not only great to visit, but has a fine gift shop that specializes in Asian art. The same high-quality and authentic handicrafts are available in both the **Hawaiian Mission Houses Museum** and **Bishop Museum** gift shops. **Ka'ala Art,** in Haleiwa, is a great one-stop shop for fine arts, pop art, and handicrafts, all by aspiring island artists. The **Punaluu Gallery,** is the oldest gallery on the windward coast. It's been there more than 30 years and is now operated by candle maker extraordinaire Scott Bechtol.

ACCOMMODATIONS AND FOOD

The innkeepers of Oahu would be personally embarrassed if you couldn't find adequate lodging on the island. So long as Oahu has to suffer the "slings and arrows" of development gone wild, at least you can find all kinds, qualities, and prices of places in which to spend your vacation. Of the nearly 70,000 rooms available in Hawaii, 36,000 are on Oahu, with 31,000 of them in Waikiki alone! Some accommodations are living landmarks, historical mementos of the days when only millionaires came by ship to Oahu, dallying as if it were their own private hideaway. When the jumbo jets began arriving in the early '60s, Oahu, especially Waikiki, began to build frantically. The result was hotel skyscrapers that grew faster than bamboo in a rainforest. These monoliths, which offered the "average family" a place to stay, marked a tremendous change in social status of visitors to Oahu. The runaway building continued unabated for two decades, until the city politicians, supported by the hotel keepers themselves, cried "Enough!" and the activity finally slowed down.

Now a great deal of money is put into refurbishing and remodeling what is already built. Visitors can find breathtakingly beautiful hotels that are the best in the land next door to more humble inns that can satisfy most anyone's taste and pocketbook. On Oahu, you may not get your own private beach with swaying palms and hula girls, but it's easy and affordable to visit one of the world's most exotic and premier vacation resorts. The following is an overview of the accommodations available on Oahu.

For listings of specific accommodations, refer to the **Accommodations** sections in the specific travel chapters below.

The Range

At almost any time of year, bargains, plenty of them, may be found including fly/drive/stay deals, or any combination thereof, designed to attract visitors while keeping prices down. You don't even have to look hard to find roundtrip airfare, room, and rental car for under $500 a week from the West Coast, based on double occupancy. Rooms on Oahu may be found in all sorts of hotels, condos, and private homes. Some venerable old inns along **Waikiki Beach** were the jewels of the city when only a few palms obscured the views of Diamond Head. However, most of Waikiki's hotels are now relatively new highrises. In Waikiki's five-star hotels, prices for deluxe accommodations, with all the trimmings, can run $250 per night. But a huge inventory of rooms go for half that amount and less. If you don't mind being one block from the beach, you can easily find nice hotels for $60-90. You can even find these prices in hotels on the beach, though most tend to be a bit older and heavily booked by tour agencies. You, too, can get a room in these, but expect the staffs to be perfunctorily friendly, and the hotels to be a bit worn around the edges. Waikiki's side streets also hold many apartment-hotels that are, in effect, condos. In these you get the benefit of a full kitchen for under $100. Stays of a week or more bring further discounts.

Central Honolulu has few acceptable places to stay except for some no-frills hotels in and around Chinatown. Bad sections of Hotel Street have dives frequented by winos and prostitutes, not worth the hassle for the few dollars saved. Some upscale hotels around Ala Moana put you near the beach, but away from the heavy activity of Waikiki. For those just passing through, a few overnight-style hotels are near the airport.

The remainder of the island, outside Waikiki, was mostly ignored as far as resort development was concerned. In the interior towns, and along the south and most of the windward coasts, you'll be hard pressed to find a room because there simply aren't any. Even today, only a handful of hotels are found on the **leeward coast,** mostly around Makaha, with the exception of the new and luxurious Ihilani Resort and Spa. The area has experienced some recent development with a few condos and full resorts going up, but it remains mostly undeveloped. **Windward Oahu** does have a few established resorts at Turtle Bay and Punaluu, but most of the lodging there is in beachhouse rentals and tiny, basic inns.

To round things off, there is a network of bed and breakfasts, YM/WCAs, youth hostels, elderhostels, and summer sessions complete with

Hilton Hawaiian Village

room and board at the University of Hawaii. Oahu also offers plenty of spots to pitch a tent at both state and county campgrounds.

Hotel/Condo Booking and Reservations

The following is a partial list of booking agents handling a number of properties on Oahu.

Aston Hotels and Resorts, 2250 Kuhio Ave., Honolulu, HI 96815, tel. (808) 931-1400 or (800) 922-7886 Mainland, (800) 445-6633 Canada, or (800) 321-2558 in Hawaii.

Go Condo Hawaii, tel. (800) 452-3463, website: www.gocondohawaii.com.

Hawaii Resort Management, 75-5776 Kuakini Hwy., Suite 105C, Kailua-Kona, HI 96740, tel. (808) 329-9393, fax 326-4136.

Homes and Villas in Paradise, 116 Hekili St., Suite 201, Kailua, HI 96734, tel. (808) 262-4663 or (800) 282-2736, website: planet-hawaii .com/homes-villas.

Marc Resorts Hawaii, 2155 Kalakaua Ave., Honolulu, HI 96815, tel. (808) 926-5900 or (800) 535-0085.

FOOD

Luau

The following is a listing of the luau available on Oahu at the present time. The **Royal Hawaiian Luau** on the Ocean Lawn of the Royal Hawaiian Hotel, every Monday only 6-8:30 p.m., tel. (808) 931-7194, *is* the classic Hawaiian feast, complete with authentic foods, entertainment, and richly spiced with *aloha.* Authenticity is added by lawn seating on traditional *lau hala* mats (table seating too) while the sun sets on Waikiki Beach and the stars dance over Diamond Head. Entertainment is an hour-long Polynesian extravaganza featuring Tahitian and traditional hula, a Samoan fire dance, bold rhythmic drumming, all done by Tihati. The buffet is a lavish feast of *kalua* pig, salmon, mahimahi, steak, and sides of poi, *haupia,* and a sinful but scrumptious table of desserts like coconut cake, *lilikoi* chiffon pie, banana bread, and guava chiffon pie. You are presented with a fresh-flower lei and welcomed at the open bar for mai tais and other tropical drinks. Cost is $78 adults, $48 for children 5-12.

Germaine's Luau, tel. (808) 941-3338, often claimed by local people to be *the* best, is held at a private west shore beach, Tues.-Sun. 6-9 p.m. The cost for dinner, cocktails, and the Polynesian show runs $46 for adults and $25 for kids 6-12. A free shuttle (reservations required) from Waikiki area hotels can be booked when calling for tickets.

Paradise Cove Luau at the Ko Olina Resort boasts a wonderful dinner with arts and crafts displays on a private beach along the leeward coast. It's held 5-8:30 p.m., and tickets run $49.50 for adults and $29.50 for kids 6-12. The Royal Ali'i package, at $59.50 adult and $39.50 kids, gives you the standard luau and transportation plus several special extras. Transportation by shuttle bus from Waikiki is included in the price of admission. The shuttle bus departs from various hotels starting at 3:45 p.m. and returns by about 9:30 p.m. Call (808) 973-5828 or (800) 775-2683 for reservations.

In Laie on the windward coast, try the **Ali'l Luau** at the Polynesian Cultural Center. The dinner and show run 5:30-9:30 p.m. and cost $49 adult and $30 children.

GETTING THERE

The old adage of "all roads leading to Rome" applies almost perfectly to Oahu, though instead of being cobblestones, they're sea lanes and air routes. Except for a handful of passenger ships still docking at Honolulu Harbor, and some limited nonstop flights to Maui and the Big Island, all other passengers to and from Hawaii are routed through **Honolulu International Airport.** These flights include direct flights to the Neighbor Islands, which means stopping over at Honolulu International and continuing on the same plane, or more likely changing to an interisland carrier whose fare is included in the original price of the flight.

Honolulu International Airport

This international airport is one of the busiest in the country, with hundreds of flights to and from cities around the world arriving and departing daily. In a routine year, more than 15 million passengers utilize this facility. The two terminals (directions given as you face the main entranceway) are: the main terminal, accommodating international and Mainland flights, with a small wing at the far left end of the ground floor for a few commuter airlines; and the interisland terminal in a separate building at the far right end of the main terminal.

The ground floor of the **main terminal** is mostly for arriving passengers and contains the baggage claim area, baggage lockers, car rental agencies, and international and domestic arrival doors, which are kept separate. The second floor is for departing passengers, with most activity centered here, including ticket counters, shops, lounges, baggage handlers, the Pacific Aerospace Museum, a business center, and the entrance to most of the gates. From both levels you can board taxis and TheBus to downtown Honolulu and Waikiki.

The **interisland terminal** services flights aboard Hawaii's own interisland carriers. It has its own snack bars, car rental booths, transportation to and from the city, lounges, information windows, and restrooms. It is only a leisurely five minute stroll between the two terminals, which is fine if you don't have much baggage; if you do, there are plenty of shuttles every few minutes . . . supposedly!

Services, Information, Tips

For general airport information and arrival and departure information, call (808) 836-6431.

The main **information booth,** tel. (808) 836-6413, is located on the ground level just near the central escalators. Besides general infor-

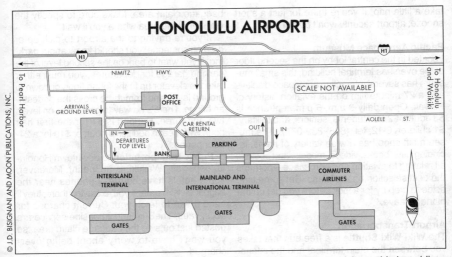

HONOLULU AIRPORT

SCALE NOT AVAILABLE

© J.D. BISIGNANI AND MOON PUBLICATIONS, INC.

mation, they have good maps of the airport, Oahu, Honolulu, and Waikiki. Also, inquiry booths lined up along the ground level and at the interisland terminal are friendly and helpful, but not always stocked with as many maps as the main information booth.

The **lost and found** is located on the ground level of the main terminal, and also at the interisland terminal, call (808) 836-6547. The **post office** is across the street from the main entranceway toward the interisland terminal.

Storage lockers are located on both levels of the main terminal and at the interisland terminal. Locker rental is for a 24-hour period, with a refundable key deposit. Baggage lockers and a long-term baggage storage facility are located in the parking structure. Prices depend on the size of baggage and length of storage. You *must* have your claim ticket to retrieve your belongings. The service is well run and efficient.

Money can be a hassle at the airport, especially getting change, which is a downright rip-off, and very bad public relations for visitors. Unfortunately, no one will give you change, putting you at the mercy of $1 bill-change machines located throughout the airport. These machines happily dispense 85 cents for every $1 you put in, so if you want to make a phone call or the like, you're out of luck. The snack bars will only change money for you with a purchase. For a state that prides itself on the *aloha* spirit and depends on

good relations with its visitors, this is a ridiculously poor way of greeting people or of giving them a last impression before they return home. The **foreign currency exchange** is on the second floor of the main terminal along the concourse behind the United Airlines ticket window. Here, and at a few smaller exchanges on the ground floor, the charge is one percent per transaction on foreign currency, and the same on traveler's checks no matter where they're from, with a minimum charge of $1.50.

To refresh and relax, you might visit the **Airport Mini-Hotel**, tel. (808) 836-3044, on the second level central area of the terminal, with 19 private, single-bed rooms. You can have a shower for $8.25, which includes soap, towel, shampoo, deodorant, and hair dryers. An eight-hour sleep and a shower runs $33, four hours is $30.25, three hours runs $24.75, and two hours goes for $19.75. You should make reservations if you want a room after 9 p.m. as it probably will be full. Also, **The Shower Tree**, 3085 N. Nimitz Hwy., tel. (808) 833-1411, is only five minutes from the airport with transportation available and luggage storage. This place is a bit like a hostel, with double-bed rooms for $27.25-32.70, and bunk rooms at $39.24 (for two). The bathroom and TV lounge are down the hall. If these seem a bit pricey, use the airport's public bathrooms for a quick wash, then choose any one of three small gardens near the central concourse to take a little nap. If you're there for just a short snooze, airport security won't bother you.

Pacific Aerospace Museum

Located in the central lobby on the second floor of the overseas terminal building, this small museum has several interactive aerospace displays and a 27-minute film on the aviation history of Hawaii. Open daily 9 a.m.-6 p.m., entrance is $3 adults, $2.50 students, seniors, and military, $1 children 6-12; tel. (808) 839-0777. The museum gift shop has a wide variety of items, including hats, books, videos, models, and posters, all relating to aviation and aerospace—perhaps the best selection on the island. Set some time aside to drop by for a look before you get on the plane to leave.

Airport Transportation

The **Wiki Wiki Shuttle** is a free bus that takes you between the main terminal and the interisland terminal. Staffed by courteous drivers, it is efficient—most of the time. When it's not, a nickname could be the "Tricky Tricky Shuttle." Transfer time between the two terminals is only about 10 minutes, which does not include baggage transfer. If you'll be going on to a Neighbor Island, make sure the carrier you are using has an interline agreement with the Hawaiian domestic carrier. If not, you must fetch your own bags, place them on the shuttle, and bring them with you to the interisland terminal. Also, if a flight is delayed, it is up to the carrier to notify the Wiki Wiki Shuttle so that adjustments can be made and they are waiting for you. If your carrier does not contact them, the shuttle bus will follow the normal schedule and may not arrive in time to get you to the interisland terminal. Usually, this is a routine procedure with few problems, but if your connecting schedule is tight, and especially if your carrier has no interline agreement (the airline or your travel agent can tell you) be aware and leave extra time!

Car rental agencies are lined up at booths on the ground floors of both terminals. Many courtesy phones for car rental agencies not at the airport are located in and around the baggage claim area; call for a free van to pick you up and take you to their nearby facility. This procedure even saves the hassle of maneuvering through heavy airport traffic—you usually wait at the island in the middle of the road just outside the baggage claim area. Make sure to specify the number of the area where you'll wait.

If you're driving to the airport to pick up or drop off someone, you should know about **parking.** If you want to park on the second level of the parking garage for departures, you must either take the elevator up to the fourth floor, or down to ground level, and from there cross the pedestrian bridge. There's no way to get across on levels two and three. Parking is $1 for the first half hour, $1 for each additional hour, or $10 for a 24-hour period.

Public transportation to downtown Honolulu, especially Waikiki, is abundant. Moreover, some hotels have courtesy phones near the baggage claim area; if you're staying there, they'll send a van to fetch you. Current charges for taxis, vans, TheBus, and limousine service are posted just outside the baggage claim area, so you won't have to worry about being overcharged.

Only **Taxis** that contract with the airport can pick up at the terminal. All others can drop off there, but are allowed to pick up only outside the terminal, at a car rental office, for example. From the terminal to Waikiki costs about $21-26, not counting bags. Splitting the fare with other willing passengers can save money. Some companies charge a flat fee of $15 from outside the terminal to Waikiki. A number of vans and motorcoaches leave from the central island in the roadway just outside the baggage claim. They charge about $8, but a wait of up to 45 minutes for one is not out of the ordinary. Moreover, they drop passengers at hotels all over Waikiki, so if you're not one of the first stops by chance, it could be an hour or so after reaching Waikiki before you're finally deposited at your hotel.

Airport Express, tel. (808) 866-7250, charges $8 per person ($4 for children) between the airport and Waikiki, and $13 roundtrip. When going to the airport, you must reserve two days in advance.

You can take **TheBus** (no. 19 or no. 20) to Waikiki via the Ala Moana Terminal, from which you can get buses all over the island. If you're heading north, pick up bus no. 20, 51, or 52 just outside the airport. TheBus only costs $1, but you are allowed only one carry-on bag, which must be small enough to hold on your lap. Drivers are sticklers on this point.

GETTING AROUND

Touring Oahu is especially easy, since almost every normal (and not so normal) mode of conveyance is readily available. You can rent anything from a moped to a pedicab, and the competition is very stiff, which helps keep prices down. A few differences separate Oahu from the other islands. To begin with, Oahu has a model public transportation system called The-Bus—not only efficient, but very inexpensive. Also, Oahu is the only island that has a true expressway system, though along with it came rush hour and traffic jams. A large part of Oahu's business is processing people, even if it's only to send them on to another island. The agencies operating these businesses on the island are masters at moving people down the road. With the huge volume of tourists who visit every year, it's amazing how smoothly it works. The following is a cross section of what's available and should help you decide how to get around. Have fun!

CAR RENTALS

Every reputable nation-, state-, and island-wide car rental agency is here, along with some car rental hucksters that'll hook you and land you like mahimahi if you're not careful. Most of the latter are located along the main tourist drags of Waikiki. The rule of thumb is, if their deal sounds too good to be true, it is. The competition is so fierce among the reputable agencies, however, that their deals are all equally good. Always check with your travel agency for big savings on fly/drive or stay/drive packages. Make sure your car comes with a flat daily rate and unlimited mileage. If you're lured into renting a "bargain" car, don't be whacked with a mileage charge. Extra benefits from many firms include a free *Drive Guide* that has good maps and lists the island's main attractions; oftentimes you receive a booklet of coupons that entitle you to free or reduced prices on services, admissions, dining, and entertainment. Seven pages of car rental agencies grace the Honolulu *Yellow Pages,* from firms that rent Mercedes convertibles down to low-budget operations with a few dented and dated Datsuns. Don't get the impression that all the backyard firms are rip-offs. You can get some great deals, but you have to choose wisely and be willing to settle for a less-than-prestigious car.

Reserving a car on Oahu is doubly important because of the huge turnover that can occur at any time. Be aware of **drop-off charges;** for example, if you rent in Waikiki and leave the car at the airport, you'll be charged. It's convenient to rent a car at the airport. But it's also convenient to take an inexpensive shuttle to and from Waikiki and rent there. Many firms have offices in Waikiki, and you can even rent a car from your hotel desk and have it delivered to you. This saves you the hassle of dealing with traffic and unfamiliar roads during arrival and departure, and avoids drop-off fees—but you don't always get the cheapest rates.

National Agencies

All of the following national companies have locations in Waikiki. The local phone numbers given are for the main location at Honolulu International Airport and/or other reservations numbers. Call for more details.

Dollar Rent A Car, tel. (808) 831-2330, 944-1544, (800) 342-7398 statewide, or (800) 800-4000 worldwide, website: www.dollarcar.com.

Alamo, tel. (808) 833-4585, or (800) 327-9633, website: www.goalamo.com.

National Car Rental, tel. (808) 831-3800, or (800) 227-7368 worldwide, website: www.nationalcar.com.

Avis, tel. (808) 834-5536, 841-5295, or (800) 321-3712 nationwide, website: www.avis.com.

Budget, tel. (808) 537-3600, or (800) 527-0700 worldwide, website: www.drivebudget.com.

Hertz, tel. (808) 831-3500, or (800) 654-3011 worldwide, website: www.hertz.com.

Thrifty, tel. (808) 833-0046, or (800) 367-2277 worldwide, website: www.thrifty.com.

Enterprise, tel. (800) 736-8222 in Honolulu, or (800) 325-8007 out of town, website: www.pick-enterprise.com.

Sears, tel. (808) 599-2205, or (800) 527-0770 elsewhere, www.sears.com.

Local Agencies

These firms offer bargain rates and older cars. Many of these rent without a major credit card, but they require a stiff deposit. Sometimes they even rent to those under 21, but you'll have to show reservations at a major hotel. Some where you usually make out all right are: **VIP** (Very Inexpensive Prices), tel. (808) 488-6187 or 924-6500; **JN,** 831-2724, which also has trucks and vans; and **Paradise Isle Rentals,** tel. (808) 922-2224, which carries Jeeps, sports cars and convertibles, motorcycles, and mopeds.

Fantasy and Vanity Rentals

The most distinctive and fun-filled cars on Oahu are the sports cars and luxury imports available from **Ferrari Rentals,** in Waikiki at 1879 Kalakaua Ave., tel. (808) 942-8725. These guys have a fleet of American and European classic cars, like Viper, Corvette, Ferrari, Porsche, Jaguar, Mercedes, and BMW. Their magnificent Lamborghini Diablo goes for the equally magnificent price of $1,300 per day, while they let the lowly Corvette out for the mere pittance of only $260 per day.

Motorcycles and Mopeds

For rentals, try **Paradise Isle Rentals,** 151 Uluniu in Waikiki, tel. (808) 922-2224, where you can ride away with the wind in your face on a Nighthawk, Ninja, or Harley-Davidson for $79-99 a day, or scoot away on a 50cc moped for a daily rate of $20. Also look for mopeds in Waikiki at **Adventure Moped Rentals,** 1705 Kalakaua Ave., tel., 941-2222; **Adventure Rentals,** 1946 Ala Moana Blvd., tel. (808) 944-3131; **Big Mountain Rentals,** 2426 Kuhio Ave., tel. (808) 926-1644; and **Big Sky Rentals,** 1920 Ala Moana Ave., tel. (808) 947-0101.

ALTERNATE TRANSPORTATION

TheBus

If Dorothy and her mates had TheBus to get them down the Yellow Brick Road, she might have chosen to stay in Oz and forget about Kansas. TheBus, TheBus, ThewonderfulBus is the always-coming, slow-moving, go-everywhere friend of the budget traveler. Operated by Oahu Transit Services, Inc. (OTS), it could serve as a model of efficiency and economy in any city of the world. What makes it more amazing is that it all came together by chance, beginning as an emergency service in 1971. These brown, yellow, and orange coaches go up and down both the windward and leeward coasts, through the interior, while passing through all of the major and most of the minor towns in between, and most often stopping near the best sights.

Route signs are located on the front of the bus and near the bus doors. The direction in which TheBus travels is posted after the number and the name of the town. They are designated as EB (eastbound toward Diamond Head) and WB (westbound toward the airport). The fare is only $1 adult, 50 cents for students between

Waikiki Trolley

ages 6-19, while kids under six who can sit on their parent's lap aren't charged at all. The fare is paid in *exact change* upon entering. Even putting excess money into the box and not expecting change is unacceptable. Adult **monthly bus passes,** good at any time and on all routes, are $25, but be aware that they are good only from the first to the last day of every month. If you buy a pass in midmonth, or even later, it's still full price! A student monthly pass is $12.50. Passes for senior citizens and disabled passengers are $20 and good for two years, or $6 for a half-fare discount card that's good for four years but which you need only pay 50 cents for each ride. Seniors (65 or older) must furnish proof of age, and will be given the pass within a few minutes of having an ID photo taken. Monthly passes are available at **TheBus Pass Office,** open Mon.-Fri. 7:30 a.m.-3:30 p.m., at 811 Middle St., tel. (808) 848-4500. Route 1, Kalihi Bus stops within a few feet of TheBus Pass Office.

Transfers are free and are issued upon request when entering TheBus, but you can only use them for ongoing travel in the same direction, and on a different line (numbered bus). They are also timed and dated, good for approximately one half-hour to one hour.

Only baggage that can be placed under the seat or on one's lap is permitted; baby strollers that fold up are allowed. Seeing-eye dogs and other similar service animals can accompany a passenger, but all other animals must be in a carrier that fits under the seat or on the lap. No smoking is allowed, and eating and drinking is not permitted. Please use radios or similar devices with headphones only.

Many, but not all, buses are now equipped with bike racks, which makes it easier to get around town or out of town, without having to jostle with all the traffic. Bike racks carry two bikes only. First, let the bus driver know that you wish to load your bike. Then pull down to unfold the rack, if it isn't down already, and securely set the bike wheels into the slots. Pull up on the securing arm to lock your bike in, then board. When leaving the bus, be sure to let the driver know that you want to unload your bike, or the bus may go on to the next stop with your bike. For additional instructions, consult the *How to Use the New Bike Rack for Buses* booklet, available from TheBus office.

There are about 75 routes in the system. Get full **route and schedule information** by calling TheBus at (808) 848-5555, 5:30 a.m.-10 p.m., or by visiting the information booth at the Ala Moana Terminal, where you can pick up fliers and maps. For other general information and attractions along the routes call (808) 296-1818 with access code 8287. An excellent, inexpensive little guide is *Hawaii Bus and Travel Guide* by Milly Singletary, available in most bookstores. Recorded information on routes and attractions is available 24 hours a day at (808) 296-1818. TheBus Lost and Found office can be contacted at (808) 848-4444.

The following are some popular destinations and their bus numbers, all originating from the Ala Moana Terminal: **Aloha Tower,** no. 19, 20, 47; **Airport,** no. 19 or 20; *Arizona* **Memorial, Pearl Harbor,** no. 20, 47, 50, or 52 Wahiawa (not no. 52 Kaneohe); **Bishop Museum,** no. 2 School; **Chinatown,** no. 1, 2, 4, 19, 20, 47, 51, or 52 Wahiawa; **Fisherman's Wharf,** no. 19, 20, or 52 Kaneohe; Hanauma Bay, no. 1, 22, or 58, beach bus weekends; **Honolulu (downtown),** no. 1, 2, 3, 4, 9, 11, or 12; **Punchbowl,** no. 15; **Polynesian Culture Center,** 52 Wahiawa/circle island, 55 Kaneohe/circle island; **Queen Emma's Summer Palace,** no. 4; **Sea Life Park,** no. 22, 57, 58; **Waikiki Beach,** no. 2, 4, 8, 14, or 20.

The **Beach Bus,** no. 22, starts on Kuhio Ave. near Kalakaua Ave. and services all of the beach areas, including Hanauma Bay and Sandy Point; Sea Life Park is its terminus. Once a seasonal service, the Beach Bus now operates year-round.

Circling the island by bus is a terrific way to see the sights and meet people along the way. The circle route takes about four hours if you ride the entire loop, but you can use the transfer system to give yourself a reasonable tour of only the sights that strike your fancy. The **circle-island** bus is no. 52, but remember that there are two no. 52 buses, going in different directions. The buses are labeled: **no. 52 Wahiawa Kaneohe** goes inland to Wahiawa, north to Haleiwa, along the north shore, down the windward coast to Kaneohe and back over the *pali* to Honolulu; **no. 52 Kaneohe Wahiawa** follows the same route but in the opposite direction. If you'll be taking this bus to Pearl Harbor, be absolutely sure to take no. 52 Wahiawa Kaneohe, because if you took the other, you'd have to circle the entire island before arriving at Pearl!

Trolley and Shuttles.
The **Waikiki Trolley,** tel. (808) 596-2199, an open-air trolley-like bus, will take you on a tour of Waikiki and Honolulu for $18, or $8 children. This all-day pass lets you board, exit, and re-board at 20 different stops. Multiday passes for five consecutive days are available for $30 and $10. Starting from the Royal Hawaiian Shopping Center in Waikiki, the trolley runs two routes, a shopping route and sightseeing route, with several overlapping stops. The red line (sightseeing route) operates 8:30 a.m.-6:30 p.m., leaving its last starting point at 4:30 p.m. The yellow line (shopping route) runs from 9 a.m. to about 10 p.m. Pick up a map/brochure from any activity desks or call the number above.

In addition to this trolley, there are several shuttles that run only to specified sites. All leave from various hotels in Waikiki. The **Arizona Memorial Shuttle Bus** runs every 90 minutes 7 a.m.-1 p.m. Call (808) 539-0911 for reservations (a must); $3 per person, one way. The **Hilo Hattie/Dole Cannery Bus** runs daily to those two shopping sites, leaving every 30 minutes 8:30 a.m.-3:30 p.m. No charge. Going to see the marine exhibits? Take the free, daily **Sea Life Park Hawaii Shuttle.** Call (808) 955-3474 for times and pickup points. The **Waimea Valley Shuttle** runs daily at no cost to the north shore's best known tourist attraction. For a schedule and boarding locations, call (808) 955-8276.

Taxis
The law says that taxis are not allowed to cruise around looking for fares, so you can't hail them. But they do and you can, and most policemen have more important things to do than monitor cabs. Best is to summon one from your hotel or a restaurant. All are radio-dispatched, and they're usually there in a flash. The fares, posted on the taxi doors, are set by law and are fair, but still expensive for the budget traveler. The rates do change, but expect about $2 for the flag fall, and then 25 cents for each additional one-eight mile. The airport to Waikiki is about $25, though luggage costs extra. Most cab drivers are quite good, but you may pause and consider if your cab sports the bumper sticker "Caution! I drive like you do!"

Of the many taxi companies, some with good reputations are: **SIDA,** a cooperative of owner-drivers, at (808) 836-0011; **Aloha State Taxi,** tel. (808) 847-3566; **Charley's,** tel. (808) 531-1331; **TheCab,** tel. (808) 422-2222, and **City Taxi,** tel. (808) 524-2121. If you need some special attention like a Rolls-Royce limo, try: **Cloud 9 Limousines,** tel. (808) 524-7999. They are one of at least four dozen limo services on the island.

If you need wheelchair or other special-needs transport, call **Handicabs of the Pacific,** tel. (808) 524-3866.

Hitchhiking
Hitchhiking varies from island to island, both in legality and method. On Oahu, hitchhiking is legal, and you use the tried-and-true style of facing traffic and waving your thumb. But, city ordinance specifies that you can only hitchhike from a bus stop! Not many people try so the pickings are reasonably easy. TheBus, however, is only $1 for anywhere you want to go, and the paltry sum that you save in money is lost in "seeing time."

Two things against you: many of the people are tourists and don't want to bother with hitchhikers, and many locals don't want to bother with nonlocal hitchhikers. When you do get a ride, most of the time it will be from a *haole* who is either a tourist on his own or a recent island resident. If you are just hitchhiking along a well-known beach area, perhaps in your bathing suit and obviously not going far, you can get a ride more easily. Women should exercise caution like everywhere else in the U.S., and avoid hitchhiking alone.

SIGHTSEEING TOURS

Guided land tours are much more of a luxury than a necessity on Oahu. Because of the excellent bus system and relatively cheap rental cars, you spend a lot of money for a narration and to be spared the hassle of driving. If you've come in a group and don't intend on renting a car, they may then be worth it. Sea cruises and air tours are equally luxurious, but provide glimpses of this beautiful island you'd normally miss. The following partial list of tour companies should get you started.

Note: For ocean, bicycling, and hiking tours, refer to **Sports and Recreation.**

Land Tours

If you're going to take a land tour, you must have the right attitude, or it'll be a disaster. Your tour leader, usually driving the van or bus, is part instructor, comedian, and cheerleader. There's enough "corn" in the jokes to impress an Iowa hog. On the tour, you're expected to become part of one big happy family, and most importantly, to be a good sport. Most guides are quite knowledgeable about Oahu and its history, and they honestly try to do a good job. But they've done it a million times before, and their performance can be as stale as week-old bread. The larger the tour vehicle and the shorter the miles covered, the worse it is likely to be. If you still want a tour, take a full-day jaunt in a small van: you get to know the other people and the guide, who'll tend to give you a more in-depth presentation. Tips are cheerfully accepted. Also, be aware that some tours get kickbacks from stores and restaurants they take you to, where you don't always get the best bargains. Most companies offer free hotel pickup and delivery. Lunch or dinner is not included unless specified, but if the tour includes a major tourist spot like Waimea Falls Park or the Polynesian Culture Center, admission is usually included.

About half a dozen different tours offered by most companies are variations on the same theme, and the cost is fairly uniform. One of the more popular is a **circle-island tour,** including numerous stops around Waikiki, the windward coast, north shores, and center of the island. These usually run about $50, and half for children. An afternoon and evening **Polynesian Culture Center Tour,** including admission and dinner show, costs close to $60. Tours to **Pearl Harbor and the** *Arizona* **Memorial** and to **Diamond Head** both run around $25.

Some reputable companies include: **Polynesian Adventure Tours,** tel. (808) 833-3000; **Robert's Hawaii Tours,** tel. (808) 539-9400; and **E Noa Tours,** tel. (808) 591-2561. Hotel activities desks and activity centers around Waikiki can also arrange tours for you or point you in the right direction.

Special Walking Tours

The following are special tours that you should seriously consider.

"Walking Tour of Chinatown," tel. (808) 533-3181, by the **Chinese Chamber of Commerce,** leaves every Tuesday at 9:30 a.m. from in front of their offices at 42 N. King Street. The cost is $5 for the 2.5-hour tour. The **Hawaiian Heritage Center** offers a similar historical and cultural two-hour tour of Chinatown, leaving from the Ramsey Galleries at 1128 Smith St. every Friday at 9:30 a.m. The cost is $5 per person. Call (808) 521-2749 for reservations.

"Walking Tour of Honolulu," is a three-hour tour led by a very knowledgeable volunteer from the **Mission Houses Museum,** who is probably a member of the Cousin's Society and a descendant of one of the original Congregationalist missionaries to Hawaii. Starting with a walk through the houses of the museum, you're led on a wonderfully anecdoted walk through the historical buildings of central Honolulu for only $8 (reduced fees for seniors, *kama'aina,* military, and students). Tours are given on Thursday only and start at 9:30 a.m. from the Mission Houses Museum. Reservations are required; call (808) 531-0481.

Honolulu Time Walks, 2634 S. King St., Suite 3, Honolulu, HI 96826, tel. (808) 943-0731, offers fascinating interpretive walking tours focusing on the city's colorful past. The tours, ranging in price $5-40 (most about $10), sometimes including dinner, are thematic and change regularly. Expect topics like "A Journey to Old Waikiki," "Mysteries of Moilili," "Scandalous Days of Old Honolulu," and the very popular "Ghosts of Honolulu." Master storyteller Glen Grant, in costume, hosts many of the tours. Thematic bus and trolley tours are also offered, and several historical shows are performed at the Waikiki Heritage Theater in the International Marketplace. Extremely authentic and painstakingly researched, these tours and shows are immensely educational and entertaining. You can't find better. Reserve!

The **Hawaii Nature Center,** 2131 Makiki Heights Dr., Honolulu, HI, tel. (808) 955-0100, is a nonprofit organization dedicated to environmental education through a "hands on" approach. Primarily geared toward school-age children, but welcoming the young at heart, the Hawaii Nature Center offers weekend community programs for families and the public to share in the wealth of Hawaii's magnificent natural environment through interpretive hikes, earth care projects, and nature crafts. This is a wonderful opportunity for visitors to explore Hawaii through direct interaction with the environment.

The volunteer organization, **Clean Air Team,** 720 South St., #184, Honolulu, HI 96813, tel. (808) 948-3299, hosts a hike up Diamond Head every Saturday 9 a.m.-noon, regardless of weather, leaving from the front entrance of the Honolulu Zoo. There is no cost for this hike, but donations are accepted to further programs of this nonsmoker's rights advocacy group.

Kapi'olani Community College offers a no-credit program of walking and bus tours for senior citizens. Both state residents and visitors may participate. Offered at various times throughout the year, these tours focus on sites of local historic and natural interest. Tours are run 8 a.m.-1 p.m. and cost $12. For information on registration, contact the Office of Continuing Education and Training, Kapi'olani Community College, 4303 Diamond Head Rd., Honolulu, HI 96816; tel. (808) 734-9234.

If you don't want to follow the leader, but still desire to get out and stretch your legs while soaking up a bit of the local color, try a **city walking tour.** In order to promote good health and exercise, the Hawaii Department of Health has put together a fun brochure/map briefly outlining 15 different walks in the downtown Honolulu, Waikiki, and Diamond Head areas. To get a copy so you too can go on your own, write to the Physical Activity Promotion Project, Hawaii Department of Health, Room 217, 1250 Punchbowl St., Honolulu, HI 96813, and ask for the *Honolulu Walking Map.* Be sure to include a business-size SASE.

Oahu by Air

When you soar above Oahu, you realize just how beautiful this island actually is, and considering that the better part of a million people live in this relatively small space, it's amazing just how much undeveloped land still exists in the interior and even along the coast. The following are some air tours worth considering. Remember that small one- or two-plane operations come and go as quickly as cloudbursts. They're all licensed and regulated for safety, but if business is bad, the propellers stop spinning.

Novel air tours are offered from Dillingham Airfield, located in the northwest section of Oahu, a few miles down the Farrington Hwy. from Waialua. Once in the air, you can soar silently above the coast with **Glider Rides,** tel. (808) 677-3404,

an outfit offering one- or two-passenger piloted rides infinitely more exciting than the company's name. A plane tows you aloft and you circle in a five-mile radius with a view that can encompass 80 miles on a clear day. The rides are available daily, 10:30 a.m.-5 p.m., on a first-come, first-served basis. Cost is $60 each if there are two passengers and $100 for a single person; rides last about 20 minutes. Check in with "Mr. Bill."

Also located at the Dillingham Airfield is **Soar Hawaii Sailplanes,** tel. (808) 637-3147. This company offers 20-, 30-, 40-, and 50-minute rides for $120, $140, $150, and $160, respectively, for two persons; and aerobatic rides for a pilot and one passenger (with parachute!) that are the same length as the standard rides but $10 less per ride. Open 10 a.m.-6 p.m.; reservations are recommended.

Islands in the Sky is a one-day flying extravaganza, offered by the most reputable island-based airline, **Hawaiian Airlines,** Using regularly scheduled flights, this daily tour goes from Honolulu to Kona on the Big Island, on to Maui, and then back to Oahu for $315 adults or $295 for kids age 2-11. Stops in Kona and on Maui include dinner and transportation; transport to and from your hotel in Honolulu is also included. Call (808) 838-1555 for reservations.

Eco Air Tours Hawaii, tel. (808) 839-1499, flies out of Honolulu in a nine-passenger Piper Chieftain. Minimum six passengers to fly. Six-island, full- and half-day scheduled excursions are offered, starting from $150 per person. A two-hour flight over Oahu, Kauai, and Niihau is also available. All flights include a narration on ecology, culture, and history of the islands. Ground tours are an added option with the six-island flight, and private charters can be scheduled at $400 an hour for the plane. Reservations are necessary at least 24 hours in advance.

Panorama Air Tours, tel. (808) 244-3356 or (800) 428-1231, has tailor-made tours leaving mostly from Maui, although a nine-seater does operate out of Oahu. Most flights will be in the $120-600 range, depending upon the itinerary. Call for options available.

Ever dreamed of taking off from and landing in Hawaiian waters, like the early air travelers to Hawaii did? **Island Seaplane Service, Inc.,** 85 Lagoon Dr., tel. (808) 836-6273, provides a way to fulfill your dream by offering a 30-minute flight along the south coast of Oahu for $79 and a one-hour flight circling the eastern half of the island for $129. The company's two seaplanes (a four-passenger Cessna 206 and a six-passenger DeHavilland Beaver) use Keeki Lagoon as their runway. Shuttle service from Waikiki is provided for those without transportation.

Helicopter companies rev up their choppers to flightsee you around the island, starting at about $70 per person for a short trip over Honolulu/Waikiki. Prices rise up from there to about $170 for a full island tour. Usually, transport to and from the heliport is included in the cost. Chopper companies include: **Hawaii Helicopters,** tel. (800) 994-9099, website: www.hawaiiheli .com; **Hawaiian Breeze Helicopters,** tel. (808) 223-2404; and **Rainbow Pacific Helicopters,** tel. (808) 834-1111.

Sail and Dinner Cruises

If you're taking a tour at all, your best bet is a sail or dinner cruise. They're touristy, but a lot of fun, and actually good value. Many times money-saving coupons for them are found in the free tourist magazines, and plenty of street buskers in Waikiki give special deals. The latter are mostly on the up and up, but make sure you know exactly what you're getting. Most of these cruises depart around 5:30 p.m. from the Kewalo Basin Marina, near Fisherman's Wharf, or from one of the piers near the Aloha Tower, and cruise Waikiki toward Diamond Head before returning about two hours later. On board are a buffet, an open bar, live entertainment, and dancing. Costs vary but run from $50 on up, per person.

Some of the better dinner sails and cruises follow. **Windjammer Cruises,** tel. (808) 537-1122 or (800) 367-5000, sets sail from pier 7A near the Aloha Tower on a sunset dinner cruise, where all food is cooked onboard. There are four options: luau at sea for $39, the standard buffet dinner for $49 per person, a sit-down dinner for $69, and the sit-down steak and lobster dinner for $99; reduced fares for children. All include a couple of complimentary drinks, the hula show, and dancing. As fine as the food and entertainment are, don't think that this is a getaway. Their sailing ship *Kulamanu* can carry 1,000 passengers.

High-tech hits the high seas on the *Navatek I,* tel. (808) 848-6360 or (800) 852-4183, a unique bi-hulled ship that guarantees the "most stable ride in the islands." Sailing from Pier 6, you have a choice of an early morning Pearl Harbor cruise ($45, $26.50 for children 2-11), midday luncheon cruise ($47, $28.50), the ultimate sunset/dinner cruise ($140, $110) featuring gourmet food and some of the best island entertainers, and the late evening skyline dinner cruise ($75 for main deck, $125 for in the upper salon). *Kama'aina* rates available. During the winter, these become whalewatching cruises with naturalists onboard. The parent Company, Royal Hawaiian Cruises, continues its policy of donating a percentage of its ticket proceeds to marine mammal research and preservation.

Dream Cruises, tel. (808) 592-5200 or (800) 400-7300, offers a seasonal (April-Dec.) dolphin watching tour along the leeward coast onboard the *Rainbow I* catamaran. Early and late morning 2.5-hour sails leave form Waianae small boat harbor and includes a small breakfast; $45.95 adults, $24.95 for children 17 and under, transportation from Honolulu included. December to April, several daily whalewatching tours leave from Honolulu's Kewalo Basin and cruise off Waikiki and Diamond Head; $19.95 adults and $12.95 for children. Their *Lin Wa II,* a craft that resembles a Chinese junk, runs a tame bottom fishing tour in Honolulu harbor once in the afternoon ($45.95) and later a sunset fishing and dinner cruise ($59.95). The crew will cook what you catch on both of these tours. Nonfishermen and children have reduced fares. Other offerings include the twice an evening dinner/dance cruise off Waikiki ($45.95/$24.95) and a morning Pearl Harbor Coastal Cruise ($19.95/$12.95). The newer mid-day Pacific Splash tour ($59.95/ $29.95) takes you to a mooring spot where you can play with the water toys, swim, and use the two-story waterslide and trampoline. The use of snuba equipment and jet skis, for an additional $40 and $30 pre-paid, respectively, are options for this leisurely fun-filled splash cruise.

Paradise Cruises, tel. (808) 983-7827, also does dinner cruise and show combinations on their *Star of Honolulu, Starlet I,* and *Starlet II* ships. They leave out of the Kewalo Basin at 5:15-5:30 for 2-3.5 hour cruises. Prices range from $31 adult for the Sunset Grill to the $199 five-star, seven-course French dinner cruise with all the extras.

The **Ali'i Kai Catamaran** packs them in for their sunset dinner cruise and live band dance. At $49 adult and $29 for kids 2-11, the ride includes dinner, a Polynesian show, three free cocktails, and dancing. Call (808) 539-9400 for reservations.

Captain Bob's Picnic Sail, tel. (808) 942-5077 or (800) 262-8798, tours Kaneohe Bay daily (except Sunday), and features lunch and all the water activities that you can handle on its four-hour sail 10:30 a.m.-2:30 p.m. Prices run $69 adults, $55 for ages 13-17, and $49 for kids 3-12. You can work off lunch snorkeling or playing volleyball on the beach. The food is passable, but the setting offshore with the *pali* in the background is world-class. Transportation from Waikiki is included.

Outrigger Canoe Tour

Perhaps the most culturally sensitive, if not the most unusual tour that you might try while on Oahu is a day-long outrigger sailing canoe trip with **Hawaiian Experience.** Although the trade winds always blow on this side and help push the canoe along, you will paddle too. You start the day at Kailua Bay and head south to Mokapu Point. From there you return north to Kaneohe Bay for leisurely water activities on the sandbar. A stop at Kualoa Beach is included before the return to Kailua Bay. Your guides will teach you about the water and marine life, the flora, fauna, and geology of the coast, and of Hawaiian culture. This tour runs $150 per person. For all details, contact Hawaiian Experience, 327-111A Hekili St., Kailua, HI 96734, tel. (808) 261-5751 or fax 261-6634. Three- and four-day trips on Oahu and the Big Island are also offered.

Underwater Cruises

A beautiful as Oahu is topside, it can be more exquisite below the waves. **Atlantis Submarines,** tel. (808) 973-9800 or (800) 548-6262, website: goatlantis.com, costs $89 adult, $39 children 12 and under, and departs daily every hour on the hour 7 a.m.-4 p.m., from the Hilton Hawaiian Village, where you board the Hilton Rainbow Catamaran, which ferries you to the waiting sub. Once aboard, you're given a few instructions and then it's "run silent, run deep, run excited" for about one hour. The sub is amazingly comfortable. Seats are arranged so that everyone gets a prime view through the large windows, and

the air is amazingly fresh. In early 1994 a futuristic sub was launched that measures 96 feet and carries 64 passengers (the original sub seats 48). Outfitted with videocams, it allows the passengers to view the undersea world in every direction, while listening to explanations of the varied sea life through a multilanguage audio system. A thrill of a lifetime.

A similar tour is offered by **Voyager Submarine,** tel. (808) 592-7850. Although you can't live in their yellow submarine, they'll escort you to the sea of green. From the comfort of their new sub, you can view the wonders of life below the waves. Captain, captain, full speed ahead.

If you get seasick out on the water, try Dramamine or Bonine tablets, although these may make you sleepy or give you a dry mouth. Benadryl also works, but again can cause sleepiness. Some people swear by ginger tablets, and others try an accupressure wristband like Seabands.

SPECIAL NEEDS

Oahu Services

At Honolulu International Airport, parking spaces are on the fourth floor of the parking garage near each pedestrian bridge, and on each level near the elevators at the interisland terminal. Be aware that the Wiki Wiki Bus, all other buses and vans, and taxis to town have steps.

For getting around, the City of Honolulu offers a curb-to-curb service for people with disablities, $1.50 each way; call **Handi-Van,** tel. (808) 456-5555. You must make arrangements at least a day in advance or up to two weeks in advance. A private special taxi company operating all over the island is **Handi-Cabs of the Pacific,** tel. (808) 524-3866 in Honolulu. They take people who use wheelchairs. Most of the large **rental car companies** can put hand controls (right or left) on their cars, but some restrict these controls to certain size or type vehicles. They generally require prior arrangements, one or two days at least, preferably when making your advance reservation. Rates are comparable with or the same as for standard rental cars. **Accessible Vans of Hawaii,** tel. (808) 879-5521, fax 879-0649, or (800) 303-3750, rents wheelchair-lift equipped vans on Oahu, Maui, and the Big Island for $109 a day or $560 a week. This is a full service travel agency and a good source of information on traveling with disabilities. Valid, out-of-state, **handicapped parking placards** may be used throughout the state of Hawaii. To apply for a Hawaii parking permit, contact the Department of Transportation Services, tel. (808) 523-4245, for an application form and all requirements. Passes for disabled but ambulatory persons using **TheBus** cost $20 and are good for two years. Check at TheBus Pass Office at 811 Middle St., tel. (808) 848-4500; open Mon.-Fri. 7:30 a.m.-3:30 p.m.

For **medical equipment rental** see the following establishments for all kinds of apparatus: Honolulu Orthopedic Supply, tel. (808) 847-0099; American Home Care System, tel. (808) 486-4954; C. R. Newton Co., tel. (808) 949-8389; Ali'i Medical Supply, tel. (808) 524-2279; and Center Pharmacy, tel. (808) 622-2773. If you are staying for any length of time on the island, medical help, nurses, and companions might be arranged through Hawaii Centers for Independent Living, tel. (808) 537-1941.

Medical services are available 24 hours a day from **Doctors on Call Waikiki**, tel. (808) 971-6000. For hospitals and medical care, see **Health Care.**

INFORMATION AND SERVICES

For police, fire, and ambulance anywhere on Oahu, dial 911.

Civil Defense: In case of natural disaster such as hurricanes or tsunamis on Oahu, call (808) 523-4121 or 527-5373.

Coast Guard Search and Rescue: tel. (808) 541-2450 or (800) 552-6458.

Life Guard Service: tel. (808) 922-3888.

Sex Abuse Treatment Center Hotline: call (808) 524-7273 for cases involving sexual assault or rape crisis.

Time of day: tel. (808) 983-3211

Honolulu Harbor, daily ship arrival and departure recording, tel. (808) 537-9260;

The Aloha Pages, at the front of the *Yellow Pages* phone directory is a font of at-your-fingertip information for visitors to the island. The Audio Pages section, tel. (808) 296-1818, is a free 24-hour "talking telephone" information service on a variety of topics including weather, news, sports, community service, and entertainment. For specific information, dial the above number, followed by a four-digit code number as directed, or check your local Hawaiian phone book for a complete listing of available topics.

Weather, Marine, and Surf Reports

For recorded information on local island weather, call (808) 973-4381; for marine conditions, call (808) 973-4382, and for the surf report, call (808) 973-4383.

Consumer Protection and Tourist Complaints

If you encounter problems with accommodations, bad service, or down-right rip-offs, try the following: The Chamber of Commerce of Hawaii, tel. (808) 545-4300; Hawaii Hotel Association, tel. (808) 923-0407; Office of Consumer Protection, tel. (808) 587-3222; or the Better Business Bureau, tel. (808) 941-5222. For general information, or if you have a hassle, try the City Hall's Office of Information, tel. (808) 523-4385, or the Office of Complaint, 523-4381.

Tourism Information

The Hawaiian Visitors Bureau Administrative Office is at the Waikiki Business Plaza, 2270 Kalakaua Ave., Suite 801, Honolulu, HI 96815, tel. (808) 923-1811 or (800) 464-2944. Oahu Visitors Bureau, 733 Bishop St., Suite 1872, Honolulu, HI 96813, tel. (808) 824-0722 or (877) 525-6248, website: www.visit-oahu.com, has information about the island of Oahu. For general information about Oahu and specific accommodation and activities listings, ask for their official vacation planner, or check it on the web at www.hshawaii.com/ovp.

Other Tourism-related Information Source

The Airport Visitor Information center, tel. (808) 836-6413, is a good sources of information available on arrival.

The Japanese Chamber of Commerce has special information on things Japanese, tel. (808) 949-5531; the Chinese Chamber of Commerce offers information and tours on Chinatown, tel. (808) 533-3181. State Foundation on Culture and Arts, 44 Merchant St., Honolulu, HI 96813, tel. (808) 586-0300, dispenses information on what's happening culturally on Oahu. For general information, or if you're trying to solve a hassle, try the Mayor's Complaint Office, tel. (808) 523-4381.

Health Care
Full-service hospitals include: The Queen's Medical Center, 1301 Punchbowl St., Honolulu, tel. (808) 538-9011; Kaiser Permanente, 3288 Moanalua Rd., Honolulu, tel. (808) 834-5333; Castle Medical Center, 640 Ulukahiki St., Kailua, tel. (808) 263-5500; St. Francis Medical Center, 2230 Liliha, Honolulu, tel. (808) 547-6011; Straub Clinic and Hospital, 888 S. King St., Honolulu, tel. (808) 522-4000; and Kuakini Medical Center, 347 N. Kuakini St., Honolulu, tel. (808) 536-2236.

Medical services and clinics include: Doctors On Call, tel. (808) 971-6000 (for Japanese speaking doctors call 808-923-9966), for emergencies and "house calls" to your hotel, 24 hours a day; Kuhio Walk-in Medical Clinic, tel. (808) 924-6699, at 2310 Kuhio Ave, Suite 223, in Waikiki; and Waikiki Health Center, 277 Ohua Ave., tel. (808) 922-4787, for low-cost care including pregnancy and confidential VD testing, open 9 a.m.-8 p.m. Mon.-Thurs., until 4:30 p.m. Friday, until 2 p.m. Saturday. You can get a free blood pressure check at the fire station in Waikiki, corner of Paki and Kapahulu Streets, daily 9 a.m.-5 p.m.

For a referral to a doctor, try the Queens Referral Line, tel. (808) 537-7117 or Physicians Exchange of Honolulu, tel. (808) 524-2575. For dental referrals call the Hawaii Dental Association information hotline at tel. (808) 536-2135, 24-hour service.

There are dozens of pharmacies around the island, including: Kuhio Pharmacy, at the corner of Kuhio and Nahua, tel. (808) 923-4466; Center Pharmacy, 302 California Ave., tel. (808) 622-2773; Longs Drugs, in Honolulu at the Ala Moana Shopping Center, tel. (808) 941-4433, at the Kaneohe Bay Shopping Center, tel. (808) 235-4511, and at more than 20 other locations around the island; Waianae Drugs at 85-910 Farrington Hwy., Waianae, tel. (808) 696-6348; and Waipahu Drug, 94-748A Hikimoe, tel. (808) 677-0794.

For alternative health care try: Acupuncture Clinic, 111 N. King St., tel. (808) 545-8080; Honolulu School of Massage, 1123 11th Ave., Suite

301, tel. (808) 733-0000; Ed Hoopai is an excellent masseur whose motto is "You're in good hands," tel. (808) 926-9045, at 250 Lewers St., second floor of the Outrigger Village Hotel, Suite 1. He deals basically in headaches, neck and shoulders, and lower backs. Chiropractic Referral Service, tel. (808) 478-4022, offers free information and referral to qualified chiropractors. For other chiropractors, acupuncturists, and alternative health care providers, please refer to the *Yellow Pages.*

Post Offices
There are more than a dozen post offices in Honolulu, and one in each of the major towns on the island. Window service is offered Mon.-Fri. 8:30 a.m.-4 p.m.; some offices are open Saturday 10 a.m.-noon. For all postal information on Oahu, call (800) 275-8777. The main post office in downtown Honolulu is at 3600 Aolele Street. In Waikiki, it is at 330 Saratoga Road.; in Kailua, at 335 Hahani; in Waianae, at 86-014 Farrington Hwy.; in Haleiwa, at 66-437 Kamehameha Hwy.; and in Wahiawa, at 115 Lehua.

Reading Material
Besides a number of special-interest Chinese, Japanese, Korean, Filipino, and military newspapers, two major dailies are published on Oahu. The *Honolulu Advertiser,* tel. (808) 525-8000, is the morning paper, and the *Honolulu Star Bulletin,* tel. (808) 525-8000, is the evening paper. They combine to make a Sunday paper. The alternative press *Honolulu Weekly,* tel. (808) 528-1475, adds a different perspective to the mix. Aside from feature articles on pertinent local issues, it does a calendar of local arts and events. This free weekly is available throughout Oahu at more than 600 locations. A money-saving paper is the *Pennysaver,* tel. (808) 841-4444, featuring classified ads on just about anything. Call for distribution points.

Don't miss out on the free tourist literature available at all major hotels, shopping malls, the airport, and stands along Waikiki's streets. They all contain up-to-the-minute information on what's happening, and a treasure trove of free or reduced-price coupons for various attractions and services. Always featured are events, shopping tips, dining and entertainment, and sightseeing. The main ones are: *This Week Oahu,* the best and most complete; *The Best of Oahu;* and *Spotlight Hawaii,* with good sections on dining and sightseeing. Two free tabloids, *Waikiki Beach Press* and *Island News,* offer entertainment calendars and feature stories of general interest to visitors. *Oahu Drive Guide,* handed out by all the major car rental agencies, has some excellent tips and orientation maps. Especially useful to get you started from the airport.

There are 22 public libraries on Oahu, and these include: Hawaii State Library, in Honolulu at 478 S. King St., tel. (808) 586-3500; Kailua Library, 239 Kuulei Rd., tel. (808) 266-9911; Library for the Blind and Physically Handicapped, 402 Kapahulu Ave., tel. (808) 733-8444; Waikiki branch next door, at 400 Kapahulu, tel. (808) 733-8488.

Island Radio

Several dozen radio stations of all stripes broadcast on Oahu. You will find one that you like when you spin the dial. Among those that are popular are: KCCB FM 100 playing Hawaiian and reggae 24-hours a day; KKLV 98.5 FM for classical rock and roll; The Edge 97.5 FM for alternative rock; KIKI FM 94, which gives you rap, dance, and modern R&B; and KIPO FM 89.3, Hawaii Public Radio.

Island Facts

Oahu's nickname is "The Gathering Place." Its color is yellow, the island flower is the *ilima,* and the island lei is strung from its bold blossoms. At 597 square miles, Oahu follows Hawaii and Maui in size and has nearly the same area as Kauai.

HAWAII STATE ARCHIVES

HONOLULU

Honolulu is the most exotic city in the world. It's not any one attribute that makes this so; it's a combination of things. Honolulu's like an ancient Hawaiian goddess who can change her form at will. At one moment you see a black-eyed beauty, swaying provocatively to a deep and basic rhythm, and in the next a high-tech scion of the computer age sitting straight-backed behind a polished desk. The city is the terminus of "manifest destiny," the end of America's relentless westward drive, until no more horizons were left. Other Mainland cities are undoubtedly more historic, cultural, and perhaps, to some, more beautiful than Honolulu, but none come close to having all of these features in the same overwhelming combination. The city's face, though blemished by high-rises and pocked by heavy industry, is eternally lovely. The Koolau Mountains form the background tapestry from which the city emerges; the surf gently foams along Waikiki; the sun hisses fire-red as it drops into the sea, and Diamond Head beckons with a promise of tropical romance.

In the center of the city, skyscrapers rise as silent, unshakable witnesses to Honolulu's economic strength. In glass and steel offices, businesspeople wearing conservative three-piece uniforms are clones of any found on Wall Street. Below, a fantasia of people live and work. In nooks and crannies are an amazing array of arts, shops, and cuisines. In a flash of festival the streets become China, Japan, Portugal, New England, old Hawaii, or the Philippines.

New England churches, a royal palace, bandstands, tall-masted ships, and coronation platforms illustrate Honolulu's history. And what a history! You can visit places where in a mere twinkle of time past, red-plumed warriors were driven to their deaths over an impossibly steep *pali,* or where the skies were alive with screaming Zeros strafing and bombing the only American city threatened by a foreign power since the War of 1812. In hallowed grounds throughout the city lie the bodies of fallen warriors. Some are entombed in a mangled steel sepulchre below the waves, others from three wars rest in a natural bowl of bereavement and silence. And a nearby royal mausoleum holds the remains of those who were "old Hawaii."

Honolulu is the pumping heart of Hawaii. The state government and university are here. So are botanical parks, a fine aquarium and zoo, a floating maritime museum, and the world's foremost museum on Polynesia. Art flourishes like flowers, as do professional and amateur entertainment, extravaganzas, and local and world-class sporting events. But the city isn't all good clean fun. The seedier side includes "girlie" shows, raucous GI bars, street drugs, and street people. But somehow this blending and collision of East and West, this hodgepodge of emotionally charged history, this American city superimposed on a unique Pacific setting works well as Honolulu, the "Sheltered Harbor" of man and his dreams.

SIGHTS

The best way to see Honolulu is to start from the middle and fan out on foot to visit the inner city. You can *do* downtown in one day, but the sights of greater Honolulu require a few days to see. It's a matter of opinion where the center of downtown Honolulu actually is, but the King Kamehameha statue in front of Aliiolani Hale is about as central as you can get, and a perfect landmark from which to start. If you're staying in Waikiki, leave your rental car in the hotel garage and take TheBus (no. 2) for downtown sightseeing.

Parking and Transportation, Downtown Honolulu

If you can't bear to leave your car behind, head for Aloha Tower. When you get to where you can see the Aloha Tower off the S. Nimitz Hwy., look for a sign pointing you left to "Piers 4 and 11, Aloha Tower." Enter to find plenty of parking. The traffic is not as congested here and the large lot is open 24 hours, at $1 per hour, with a four-hour maximum on the meter. Bring change, as none is available. You might have to come back and feed the meter again if you want to go as far as Chinatown, but this will be plenty of time for the local attractions that are well within walking distance.

For various sights outside the downtown area, your rental car is fine. Some shuttles running out to the *Arizona* Memorial are more expensive than TheBus, but so convenient that they're worth the extra few coins. The **Waikiki Trolley,** tel. (808) 596-2199, conducts tours throughout the downtown area. It looks like a trolley but it's a bus that's been ingeniously converted. For $18 adults, $8 children, you can ride it all day long. Multiday passes are available for $30 and $10, respectively. The trolley departs daily at 15-minute intervals 8:30 a.m.-6:30 p.m. from the Royal Hawaiian Shopping Center. You can get off and on at any of the 20 stops along the way or ride along for the entire two-hour trip.

IOLANI PALACE AREA

The **Statue of King Kamehameha** is at the junction of King and Mililani Streets. Running off at an angle is **Merchant Street,** the oldest thoroughfare in Honolulu, and you might say it's "the beginning of the road to modernity." The statue is much more symbolic of Kamehameha's strength as a ruler and unifier of the Hawaiian Islands than as a replica of the man himself. Of the few drawings of Kamehameha that have been preserved, none is necessarily a good likeness. Kamehameha was a magnificent leader and statesman, but by all accounts not very good-looking. This statue is one of three. The original, lost at sea near the Falkland Islands en route from Paris where it was bronzed, was later recovered, but not before insurance money was used to cast this second one. The original is in the town of Kapaau, in the Kohala District of the Big Island, not far from where Kamehameha was born, but although they supposedly came from the same mold, they somehow seem quite different. The third stands in Washington, D.C., dedicated when Hawaii became a state. The Honolulu statue was dedicated in 1883, as part of King David Kalakaua's coronation ceremony. Its black and gold colors are striking, but it is most magnificent on June 11, King Kamehameha Day, when 18-foot lei are draped around the neck and the outstretched arms.

Behind Kamehameha stands **Aliiolani Hale,** now the State Judiciary Building. This handsome structure, designed by an Australian architect and begun in 1872, was originally commissioned

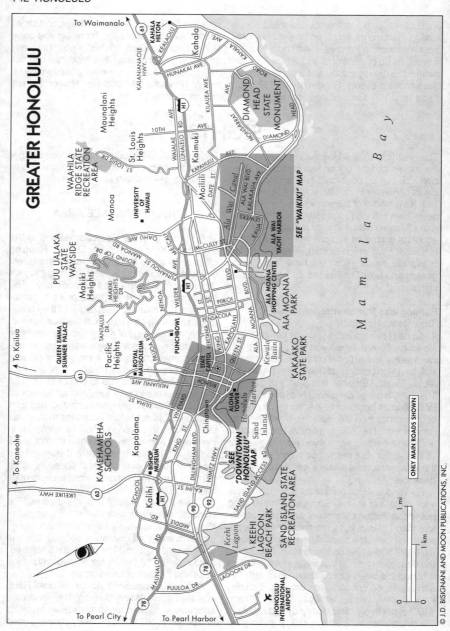

GREATER HONOLULU

To Waimanalo

To Kailua

To Kaneohe

To Pearl City

To Pearl Harbor

Mamala Bay

ONLY MAIN ROADS SHOWN

© J.D. BISIGNANI AND MOON PUBLICATIONS, INC.

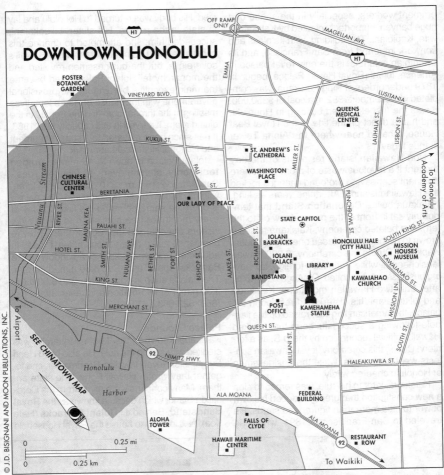

DOWNTOWN HONOLULU

© J.D. BISIGNANI AND MOON PUBLICATIONS, INC.

SEE CHINATOWN MAP

To Airport

Honolulu Harbor

0   0.25 mi

0   0.25 km

Foster Botanical Garden

Chinese Cultural Center

Our Lady of Peace

St. Andrew's Cathedral

Washington Place

State Capitol

Iolani Barracks

Iolani Palace

Bandstand

Honolulu Hale (City Hall)

Library

Kamehameha Statue

Post Office

Kawaiahao Church

Mission Houses Museum

Queens Medical Center

To Honolulu Academy of Arts

Aloha Tower

Falls of Clyde

Hawaii Maritime Center

Federal Building

Restaurant Row

To Waikiki

Vineyard Blvd.

Kukui St.

Beretania

Pauahi St.

Hotel St.

King St.

Merchant St.

Queen St.

Nimitz Hwy.

Ala Moana

Haleakuwila St.

Ala Moana

Magellan Ave.

Emma

Lusitania

Nuuanu Stream

River St.

Mauna Kea

Smith St.

Nuuanu Ave.

Bethel St.

Fort St.

Bishop St.

Alakea St.

Richards St.

Miller St.

Punchbowl St.

South King St.

Kawaiahao St.

Mission Ln.

South St.

Lauhala St.

Lisbon St.

Pali

---

by Kamehameha V as a palace, but was redesigned as a general court building. It looks much more grand than Iolani Palace across the way. Kamehameha V died before it was finished, and it was officially dedicated by King Kalakaua in 1874. Less than 20 years later, on January 17, 1893, at this "hall of justice," the first proclamation by the Members of the Committee of Safety was read, stating that the sovereign nation of Hawaii was no more, and that the islands would be ruled by a provisional government.

On the ground floor of this building, the **Judiciary History Center,** tel. (808) 539-4999, offers free exhibits Tues.-Thurs. 10 a.m.-3 p.m.

Next door is the **Old Federal Building,** which is home to several state department offices and the downtown post office station.

Iolani Palace

As you enter the 11-acre parklike palace grounds, notice the emblem of Hawaii in the center of the large iron gates. They're often draped with simple lei of fragrant *maile*. The quiet grounds are a favorite strolling and relaxing place for many government workers, especially in the shade of a huge banyan, purportedly planted by Kalakaua's wife, Kapiolani. The building, with its glass and ironwork imported from San Francisco, and its Corinthian columns, is the only royal palace in America. Iolani (Royal Hawk) Palace, begun in 1879 under orders of King Kalakaua, was completed in December 1882 at a cost of $350,000. It was the first electrified building in Honolulu, and had a direct phone line to the Royal Boat House, located near where the Aloha Tower stands today.

Non-Hawaiian island residents of the day thought it a frivolous waste of money, but here poignant scenes and profound changes rocked the Hawaiian islands. After nine years as king, Kalakaua built a **Coronation Stand** that temporarily sat in front of the palace (now off to the left). In a belated ceremony, Kalakaua raised a crown to his head and placed one on his queen, Kapiolani. During the ceremony, 8,000 Hawaiians cheered, while Honolulu's foreign, tax-paying businessmen boycotted. On August 12, 1898, after only two Hawaiian monarchs, Kalakaua and Liliuokalani (his sister), had resided in the palace, the American flag was raised up the flagpole following a successful coup that marked Hawaii's official recognition by the U.S. as a territory. During this ceremony, loyal Hawaiian subjects wept bitter tears, while the businessmen of Honolulu cheered wildly.

Kalakaua, later in his rule, was forced to sign a new constitution that greatly reduced his own power to little more than figurehead status. He traveled to San Francisco in 1891, where he died. His body was returned to Honolulu and lay in state in the palace. His sister, Liliuokalani, succeeded him; she attempted to change this constitution and gain the old power of Hawaii's sovereigns, but the businessmen revolted and the monarchy fell. Iolani Palace then became the main executive building for the provisional government, with the House of Representatives meeting in the throne room and the Senate in the dining room. It served in this capacity until 1968. It has since been elevated to a state monument and National Historical Landmark.

Iolani Palace is open to 45-minute **guided tours only,** starting every 15 minutes Tues.-Sat. 9 a.m.-2:15 p.m.; $10 adults, $3 children, with no children under five admitted. The palace is open the same hours on the first Sunday of every month for free admission to *kama'aina;* visitors are charged the regular fees. They're popular so make reservations at least a day in advance. Tickets are sold at a window at the Barracks, open Tues.-Sat. 8:30 a.m.-3:30 p.m. The Palace shop is open Tues.-Sat. 8:30 a.m.-3:30 p.m. For information and reservations call (808) 522-0832.

Palace Grounds

Kalakaua, known as the "Merrie Monarch," was credited with saving the hula. He also hired Henri Burger, first Royal Hawaiian Bandmaster, and together they wrote "Hawaii Pono," the state anthem. Many concerts were given from the Coronation Stand, which became known as the **Royal Bandstand.** Behind it is **Iolani Barracks** (Hale Koa), built in 1870 to house the Royal Household

Iolani Palace, the only royal residence in the United States

Guards. When the monarchy of Hawaii fell to provisional government forces in 1893, only one of these soldiers was wounded in the nearly bloodless confrontation. The barracks were moved to the present site from nearby land on which the State Capitol was erected.

To the right behind the palace are the **State Archives,** tel. (808) 586-0329. This modern building, dating from 1953, holds records, documents, and vintage photos. A treasure trove to scholars and those tracing their genealogy, it is worth a visit by the general public to view the old photos on display. Open Mon.-Fri. 7:45 a.m.-4:30 p.m.; free. Next door is the **Hawaii State Library,** housing the main branch of this statewide system. As in all Hawaii state libraries, you are entitled to a card on your first visit and are then eligible to take out books. Library cards are available free for Hawaii state residents and military personnel stationed in Hawaii, $25 for nonresidents, and $10 for up to three months for visitors. The central courtyard is a favorite lunch spot for many of the government workers. Some of the original money to build the library was put up by Andrew Carnegie. For information call (808) 586-3500.

Government Buildings

Liliuokalani was deposed and placed under house arrest in the palace for nine months. Later, after much intrigue that included a visit to Washington, D.C., to plead her case and an aborted counterrevolution, she sadly accepted her fate and moved to nearby **Washington Place.** This solid-looking structure fronts Beretania Street and was originally the home of sea captain John Dominis. It was inherited by his son John Owen Dominis, who married a lovely young Hawaiian aristocrat, Lydia Kapaakea, who became Queen Liliuokalani. She lived in her husband's home, proud but powerless, until her death in 1917. Washington Place is now the official residence of the governor of Hawaii. To the right of Washington Place is the **War Memorial.** Erected in 1974, this memorial replaced an older one and is dedicated to the people who perished in WW II. A courtyard and benches are provided for quiet meditation.

Directly in front of you is the magnificent **Hawaii State Capitol,** built in 1969 for $25 million. The building itself is a metaphor for Hawaii: the pillars surrounding it are palms, the reflecting pool is the sea, and the cone-shaped rooms of the Legislature represent the volcanoes of Hawaii. It's lined with rich koa wood from the Big Island, and is further graced with woven hangings and murals, with two gigantic, four-ton replicas of the State Seal hanging at both entrances. The inner courtyard has a 600,000-tile mosaic, *Aquarius,* rendered by island artist Tadashi Sato, and on one side is a poignant sculpture of *Father Damien of the Lepers.* The State Legislature is in session January to March, and opens with dancing, music, and festivities at 10 a.m. on the third Wednesday in January, public invited. Peek inside, then take the elevator to the fifth floor for outstanding views of the city.

A few steps away, on the corner of Punchbowl and King Streets, stands **Honolulu Hale,** Honolulu City Hall. Built in 1928, with additions in 1951, this office building is open 7:45 a.m.-4:30 p.m. weekdays and houses the office of the mayor, the city council, and a few city departments. It too has a courtyard where music, art, and other public events are held.

St. Andrew's Cathedral

To the left of Washington Place, the governor's residence, is St. Andrew's Cathedral. Construction started in 1867 as an Anglican church, but wasn't really finished until the late 1950s. Many of its stones and ornaments were shipped from England, and its stained glass windows and bell tower are of particular interest. Hawaii's monarchs worshipped here, and the church is still very much in use. Open 8 a.m.-4 p.m. Mon.-Fri.; call (808) 524-2822 for information concerning tours.

MISSION HOUSES MUSEUM

The days when tall ships with tattered sails crewed by rough seamen bore God-fearing missionary families dedicated to Christianizing the savage islands are alive in the halls and buildings of the Mission Houses Museum, 553 S. King St., Honolulu, HI 96813, now a Registered National Historical Landmark. Across from Kawaiahao Church (oldest in Honolulu), the complex includes two main houses, a printing house annex, a library and a fine, inexpensive gift shop, and is operated by the **Hawaiian Mission Children's Society** (or Cousins' Society), whose members serve as guides and hosts. Many are direct descendants, or spouses of descendants, of the Congregationalist missionaries who built these structures. One-hour tours are conducted at various times throughout the day, Tues.-Sat. 9 a.m.-4 p.m.; closed Sunday and Monday. Guided tours of the Frame House, oldest wooden structure in Hawaii are offered 9:30 a.m.-3 p.m. Admission is $6 adults; $5 kama'aina, seniors, and military; $3 college students and $2 children ages 4-12. Call (808) 531-0481 for information; e-mail: mhm@lava.net, website: www.lava.net/~mhm/main.htm (see **Special Programs**).

Construction

If you think that precut modular housing is a new concept, think again. The first structure that you enter is the **Frame House,** the oldest wooden structure in Hawaii. Precut in Boston, it came along with the first missionary packet in 1819. Since the interior frame was left behind and didn't arrive until Christmas Day, 1820, the missionary families lived in thatched huts until it was erected. Finally the Chamberlain family occupied it in 1821. Many missionary families used it over the years, with as many as four households occupying this small structure at the same time. This is where the Christianizing of Hawaii truly began.

The missionaries, being New Englanders, first dug a cellar. The Hawaiians were very suspicious of the strange hole, convinced that the missionaries planned to store guns and arms in this "fort." Though assured to the contrary, King Liholiho, anxious to save face and prove his omnipotence, had a cellar dug near his home twice as deep and large. This satisfied everyone.

Notice the different styles, sizes, and colors of bricks used in the structures. Most of the ships of the day carried bricks as ballast. After unloading cargo, the captains either donated or sold the bricks to the missionaries, who incorporated them into the structures. A common local material was coral stone: pulverized coral was burned with lime to make a rudimentary cement, which was then used to bind cut-coral blocks. The pit that was used for this purpose is still discernible on the grounds.

Kitchen

The natives were intrigued with the missionaries, whom they called "long necks" because of their high collars. The missionaries, on the other hand, were a little more wary of their "charges." The low fence around the complex was symbolic as well as utilitarian. The missionaries were obsessed with keeping their children away from Hawaiian children, who at first ran around naked and played many games with overt sexual overtones. Almost every evening a small cadre of Hawaiians would assemble to peer into the kitchen to watch the women cook, which they found exceedingly strange because their kapu said that men did the cooking. In the kitchen, actually an attached cookhouse, the woodburning stove kept breaking down. More often than not, the women used the fireplace with its built-in oven. About once a week, they fired up the oven to make traditional New England staples like bread, pies, cakes, and puddings. The missionaries were dependent on the Hawaiians to bring them fresh water. Notice a large porous stone through which they would filter the water to remove dirt, mud, and sometimes brackishness.

The Hawaiians were even more amazed when the entire family sat down to dinner, a tremendous deviation from their beliefs that separated men and women when eating. When the missionaries assembled to dine or meet at the "long table," the Hawaiians silently stood at the open door to watch the evening soap opera. The unnerved missionaries eventually closed the door and cut two windows into the wall, which they could leave opened but draped. The long table took on further significance. The one you see is a replica. When different missionaries left the islands, they, like people today, wanted a souvenir. For some odd reason, they elected to saw a bit off the long table. As years went by, the table got shorter and shorter until it was useless.

Residents

The house was actually a duplex. Although many families lived in it, two of the best known were the Binghams and the Judds. Much of the furniture here was theirs. Judd, a member of the third missionary company, assumed the duties of physician to all the missionaries and islanders. He often prescribed alcohol of different sorts to the missionary families for a wide variety of ailments; many records remain of these prescriptions, but not one record of complaints from his patients. The Binghams and Judds got along very well, and entertained each other and visitors, most often in the Judds' parlor because they were a little better off. The women would often congregate here to do their sewing, which was in great demand, especially by members of the royal household. Until the missionary women taught island girls to sew, providing clothing for Hawaii's royalty was a tiresome and time-consuming obligation.

The missionaries were self-sufficient, and had the unbounded energy of youth, as the average age was only 25. The husbands often built furniture for their families. Reverend Bingham, a good craftsman, was pressed by Queen Kaahumanu to build her a rocking chair after she became enamored of one made for Mrs. Bingham. The queen weighed almost 400 pounds, so building her a suitable chair was no slim feat! Still, the queen could only use it in her later years when she'd lost a considerable amount of weight. After she died, the Binghams asked for it to be returned, and it sits in their section of the house. Compare Bingham's chair to another in the Judds' bedroom, jury-rigged by a young missionary husband from a captain's chair. An understatement, found later in his diary, confirmed that the young man was not a carpenter.

When you enter the Judds' bedroom, note how small it is, and consider that two adults and five children slept here. As soon as the children were old enough, they were sent back to the Mainland for schooling, no doubt to relieve some of the congestion. Also notice that the windows were fixed, in the New England style, and imagine how close it must have been in these rooms.

The Binghams' bedroom is also small, and not as well furnished. Bingham's shaving kit remains, and is inscribed with "The Sandwich Isles." In the bedroom of Mary Ward, a missionary woman who never married, the roof was raised to accommodate her canopy bed.

Another famous family that lived in the complex were the Cookes. When the missionary board withdrew its support, the Cookes petitioned them to buy the duplex, which was granted. Shortly thereafter, Mr. Cooke, who had been a teacher, formed a partnership with one Mr. Castle, and from that time forward Castle and Cooke grew to become one of Hawaii's oldest and most powerful corporations.

The largest building in the compound is the **Chamberlain House.** This barnlike structure was completed in 1831 and used as a warehouse and living quarters for Levi Chamberlain's family. Goods were stored in most of the structure, while the family occupied three modest rooms.

Printing House
The missionaries decided almost immediately that the best way to convert the natives was to speak to them in their own language, and to create a written Hawaiian language that they would teach in school. To this end, they created the **Hawaiian alphabet,** consisting of 12 letters, including the five vowels and seven consonants. In addition, to disseminate the doctrines of Christianity, they needed books, and therefore a printing press. On the grounds still stands the Printing House, built in 1841 but first used as annex bedrooms by the Hall family. The original printing house, built in 1823, no longer exists. In the Printing House is a replica of the Ramage press brought from New England, first operated by Elijah Loomis. He returned to the Mainland when he was 28 and soon died of tuberculosis, but not before he had earned the distinction of being the first printer west of the Rockies. Here were printed biblical tracts, textbooks, or anything that the king or passing captains were willing to pay to have printed. Although it took eight hours of hard work to set up one page to be printed, it is estimated that in the 20 years the press operated under the missionaries, more than seven million pages were produced.

Gift Shop
While on the grounds make sure to visit the bookstore and gift shop. It's small but has an excellent collection of Hawaiiana, and some very inexpensive but quality items, such as tapa bookmarks for only 25 cents, and an outstanding collection of Niihau shellwork, considered the finest in Hawaii. The shelves hold tasteful items like woodcarvings, bread boards, hats, weavings, chimes, flags of old Hawaii, and stuffed pillows with classic Hawaiian quilt motifs, as well as a good collection of Hawaiian dolls, for kids and adults. Between the bookstore and the research library are restrooms.

Special Programs

Along with other programs, the museum hosts Hawaii's only **living history program**, with actors who dress in fashions of the period and assume the roles of missionaries in 1830 Honolulu. Feel free to interact and ask questions, but remember that they stay in character, so the answers may surprise you. The living history program is usually offered every Wednesday and on the second Saturday of the month, 9 a.m.-4 p.m., regular admission. Other special programs are also offered like tea with the 19th-century Reverend Hiram and Mrs. Sybil Bingham in their parlor; call (808) 924-1911 for details. Also, consider the historic walking tour offered by the museum 9:30 a.m.-12:30 p.m. that guides you through the houses of the museum and then on to downtown Honolulu, hitting all the historic sights with an extremely knowledgeable narration by one of the museum's guides. The walking tour is conducted on Thursday only; reserve two days in advance. The cost is $8 for adults; $7 for seniors, military, and *kama'aina*; $5 for college students and other students ages 13-18; $4 for children ages 4-12; and free for children under four.

KAWAIAHAO CHURCH

This church, so instrumental in Hawaii's history, is the most enduring symbol of the original missionary work in the islands. A sign welcomes you and bids the blessing, "Grace and peace to you from God our Father." Hawaiian-language services are given here every Sunday, along with English-language services. The church was constructed 1836-1842 according to plans drawn up by Hiram Bingham, its minister. Before this, at least four grass shacks of increasing size stood here. One was destroyed by a sailor who was reprimanded by Reverend Bingham for attending services while drunk; the old sea dog returned the next day and burned the church to the ground. Kawaiahao (Water of Hao) Church is constructed from more than 14,000 coral blocks quarried from offshore reefs. In 1843, following Restoration Day, when the British returned the Hawaiian Islands to sovereignty after a brief period of imperialism by a renegade captain, King Kamehameha III uttered here the profound words in a thanksgiving ceremony that were destined to

become Hawaii's motto, *"Ua mau ke ea o ka aina i ka pono"* ("The life of the land is preserved in righteousness").

Other noteworthy ceremonies held at the church were the marriage of King Liholiho and his wife Queen Emma, who bore the last child born to a Hawaiian monarch. Unfortunately, little Prince Albert died at the age of four. On June 19, 1856, Lunalilo, the first king elected to the throne, took his oath of office in the church. A bachelor who died childless, he always felt scorned by living members of the Kamehameha clan, and refused to be buried with them at the Royal Mausoleum in Nuuanu Valley; he is buried in a tomb in the church's cemetery. Buried along with him is his father, Charles Kanaina, and nearby lies the grave of his mother, Miriam Kekauluohi. In the graveyard lies Henri Burger, and many members of the Parker, Green, Brown and Cooke families, early missionaries to the islands. Liliuokalani's body lay in state in the church before it was taken to the Royal Mausoleum. A jubilation service was held in the church when Hawaii became a state in 1959. Kawaiahao holds beautiful Christmas services with a strong Polynesian and Hawaiian flavor. Hidden away in a corner of the grounds is an unobtrusive adobe building, remains of a schoolhouse built in 1835 to educate Hawaiian children.

HONOLULU HARBOR AREA

Maritime Center

The development of this center is a wonderful concept whose time has finally come. It's amazing that a state and former nation, whose discovery and very birth are so intimately tied to the exploration, navigation, and exploitation of the sea, has never had a center dedicated exclusively to these profoundly important aspects of its heritage. Now the Hawaii Maritime Center, at Pier 7, Honolulu Harbor, Honolulu, HI 96813, tel. (808) 536-6373, is exactly that . . . and it needs your support as a visitor. Open since 1989, the center consists of three attractions: the Maritime Center building with displays of Hawaii's past; the classic, and last remaining, fully rigged, four-masted *Falls of Clyde* floating museum; and the reproduction of a Hawaiian sailing canoe, the *Hokule'a,* which recently sailed back in time using ancient navigational methods to retrace the steps of Hawaii's Polynesian explorers. Take bus no. 8 or 20 from Waikiki and you're deposited right in front. Admission for all attractions is $7.50 adults, $4.50 for children 6-17, and free for the younger kids; open 8:30 a.m.-5 p.m. every day except Christmas.

The main building of the center is the two-story museum. Behind is Pier Seven Restaurant, a seafood restaurant, and an area called Kalakaua Park, a garden and observation area perfect for lunch. Eighty-one steps lead to the "crow's nest" and "widow's walk," with great views of the harbor and city.

Upon entering you find a glass case filled with trophies and memorabilia from the days of King Kalakaua. His words have a sadly prophetic ring. "Remember who you are. Be gracious, but never forget from whence you came for this is where your heart is. This is the cradle of your life." Notice the phones installed throughout the capital in 1887, a few years before California had electricity. Kalakaua had previously installed telephones between his boathouse and the palace in 1878, just two years after Bell's invention. The bottom floor of the center recalls ancient fishing methods and the traditional division of land and sea resources among the people.

Another fascinating display traces the development of surfing through the ages, from original boards, more like seagoing canoes at 18 feet long, until the modern debut of the fiberglass board. You can spot a vintage album of *Surfin Safari* by The Beach Boys. Here, too, is a land-surfing sled used for games during the Makahiki Festival. It measures six inches wide and 10-14 feet long. Trails to accommodate it were up to a mile long. Built on steep hills, they were paved in stone, layered with earth and topped with slippery grass. Once launched there was no stopping until the bottom. Yippee!

One corner of the museum is dedicated to tattooing, Polynesian and Western. It shows traditional tattoos worn by both men and women, and then how the Western style became more popular, as Hawaii was a main berth for sailors, who sported these living souvenirs from around the world. **Mail buoys** sounds uninteresting, but these tidbits of old Hawaiiana, still alive today, are fascinating. Fashioned from gaily painted metal cans, passing ships, mainly from Peru and Equador, still radio Honolulu Harbor that they are dropping one. Someone, anyone, who heard the message, would fetch them. Inside are little gifts for the finder, who takes the enclosed mail and sends it on its way.

The second floor is dedicated to the discovery of Hawaii, both by the Polynesians and Westerners. Through ledgers, histories, and artifacts, it traces original discovery, Western discovery, the death of Captain Cook, and the role of the sea otter pelt, which brought the first whalers and traders after sandalwood. The whaling section is dripping with blood and human drama. Look at the old harpoons and vintage film footage. Yes, film footage, and photos. A remarkable display is of scrimshaw from the whaling days. Sailors would be at sea for five to seven years, and would have untold hours to create beauty in what were dismal conditions. Suspended from the ceiling are replicas of double-hulled sailing canoes, and one of only two fully restored skeletons of the humpback whale (this one is in diving position). One corner is a replica of H. Hackfeld and Co., a whaling supply store of the era. The rear of the second floor shows steamships that cruised between Hawaii, Japan, and the East Coast; a nature exhibit of weather, marine life, and volcanoes; and an auditorium with a video on the *Hokule'a*.

An free audio tape tour of the center, the kind that plays on a personal cassette player that you listen to with earphones, is available for all who desire a narrated tour. Don't just walk past or save this for the last, as it explains the exhibits and gives insight into what you're seeing. Also, stop in at the gift shop for a collectible of Hawaii's vintage past.

Mac Simpson is the historian/exhibit designer for the Maritime Center. A burly guy with a white beard, he looks the part of an old sea dog. If you have questions about the exhibits, ask him.

Falls of Clyde

This is the last fully rigged, four-masted ship afloat on any of the world's oceans and has recently been designated as a National Historic Landmark. She was saved from being scrapped in 1963 by a Seattle bank that was attempting to recoup some money on a bad debt. The people of Hawaii learned of her fate and spontaneously raised money to have the ship towed back to Honolulu Harbor. The *Falls of Clyde* was always a worker, never a pleasure craft. It served the Matson Navigation Company as a cargo and passenger liner 1898-1920. Built in Glasgow, Scotland, in 1878, she was converted in 1906 to a sail-driven tanker; a motor aboard was used mainly to move the rigging around. After 1920, she was dismantled, towed to Alaska and became little more than a floating oil depot for fishing boats. Since 1968, the *Falls of Clyde* has been a floating museum, sailing the imaginations of children and grownups to times past, and in this capacity has perhaps performed her greatest duty.

Hokule'a

The newest and perhaps most dynamic feature of the center is the *Hokule'a*. This authentic recreation of a traditional double-hulled sailing canoe captured the attention of the world when in 1976 it made a 6,000-mile roundtrip voyage to Tahiti. It was piloted by Mau Piailug, a Caroline Islander, who used only ancient navigational techniques to guide it successfully on its voyage. This attempt to relive these ancient voyages as closely as possible included eating traditional provisions only—poi, coconuts, dried fish, and bananas. Toward the end of the voyage some canned food had to be broken out!

Modern materials such as plywood and fiberglass were used, but by consulting many petroglyphs and old drawings of these original craft, the design and lines were kept as authentic as possible. The sails, made from a heavy cotton, were the distinctive crab-claw type. In trial runs to work out the kinks and choose the crew, she almost sank in the treacherous channel between Oahu and Kauai and had to be towed in by the Coast Guard. But the *Hokule'a* performed admirably during the actual voyage. The experiment was a resounding technical success, but it was marred by bad feelings between members of the crew. Both landlubber and sea dog found it impossible to work as a team on the first voyage, thereby mocking the canoe's name, "Star of Gladness." The tension was compounded by the close quarters of more than a dozen men living on an open deck only nine feet wide by 40 feet long. The remarkable navigator Piailug refused to return to Hawaii with the craft and instead sailed back to his native island. Since then,

the *Hokule'a* has made five more voyages, logging more than 60,000 miles, with many ethnically mixed crews who have gotten along admirably.

The *Hokule'a*, owned by the Hawaii Maritime Center but sailed by the Polynesian Voyaging Society, makes Pier 7 its home berth when not at sea. This double-hulled canoe, a replica and much older brother of the significantly larger ones that Captain Cook found so remarkable, will fascinate you too.

Aloha Tower

Next door to the Hawaiian Maritime Center, on Pier 9, is the Aloha Tower, a beacon of hospitality welcoming people to Hawaii for six decades. When this endearing and enduring tourist cliche was built in 1926 for $160,000, the 184-foot, 10-story tower was the tallest structure on Oahu. As such, this landmark, with clocks embedded in all four walls, and emblazoned with the greeting and departing word, "Aloha," became the symbol of Hawaii. Before the days of air transport, ocean liners would pull up to the pier to disembark passengers, and on these "Boat Days," festive well-wishers from throughout the city would gather to greet and lei the arriving passengers. The Royal Hawaiian Band would even turn out to welcome the guests ashore.

When you enter the ground floor, you enter what were the huge U.S. Customs rooms that at one time processed droves of passengers coming to find a new life. Today, the crowds come to find a bargain. Only a few harbormasters on the top floor oversee the comings and goings of cargo ships. When you enter the tower a sign claims that you can only get to the observation area on the top floor by elevator. You can walk up to the ninth floor if you want, but to get to the very top does necessitate taking the elevator, which has the dubious distinction of being one of the first elevators in Hawaii. The elevator is a bit like a wheezy old man, huffing and puffing, but it still gets you to the top. Once atop the tower, you get the most remarkable view of the harbor and the city. A high-rise project planned for next door would surely have ruined the view, but due to good sense and citizens with clout, this ill-considered idea has thankfully met a timely end. A remarkable feature of the vista is the reflections of the city and the harbor in many of the neighboring steel and reflective glass high-rises. It's as if a huge mural were painted on them. The tower is open free of charge Mon.-Fri. 9 a.m.-4 p.m., Saturday 9 a.m.-10 p.m., and Sunday 9 a.m.-6 p.m.

PALI HIGHWAY

Cutting across Oahu from Honolulu to Kailua on the windward coast is Rt. 61, better known as the Pali Highway. Before getting to the famous Nuuanu Pali Lookout at the very crest of the Koolau Mountains, you can spend a full and enjoyable day sightseeing. Stop en route at Punchbowl's National Memorial Cemetery, followed by an optional side trip to the summit of Tantalus for a breathtaking view of the city. You can also visit the **Royal Mausoleum State Monument** in the vicinity. Take the H-1 freeway to Vineyard Boulevard (exit 22), cross the Pali Highway to Nuuanu Avenue and follow it to the mausoleum. In a minute or two, if you continue up Nuuanu Avenue, it intersects the Pali Highway, but you'll have passed the Punchbowl turnoff (see following). This small chapel, built in 1865 by Kamehameha IV, holds the bodies of most of the royal family who died after 1825. Their bodies were originally interred elsewhere but were later moved here. The mausoleum at one time held 18 royal bodies but became overcrowded, so they were moved again to little crypts scattered around the three-acre grounds. Of the eight Hawaiian monarchs, only King Kamehameha I and King William Lunalilo are buried elsewhere— King Kamehameha I somewhere on the Big Island and Lunalilo at Kawaiahao Church. Few tourists visit this serene place open weekdays 8 a.m.-4 p.m., tel. (808) 536-7602.

Next comes Queen Emma Summer Palace and the Dai Jingu Temple, a Baptist college, and a Catholic church. It almost seems as though these sects were vying to get farther up the hill to be just a little closer to heaven.

A sign, past Queen Emma Summer Palace, points you off to **Nuuanu Pali Drive.** Take it! This few-minutes' jog off the Pali Highway (which it rejoins) takes you through some wonderful scenery. Make sure to bear right as soon as you pull off and not up the Old Pali Highway, which has no outlet. Immediately the road is canopied with trees, and in less than half a mile there's a bubbling little waterfall and a pool. The homes in here are grand, and the entire area has a parklike effect. One of the nicest little roads that you can take while looking around, this side trip wastes no time at all.

Queen Emma Summer Palace

This summer home is more the simple hideaway of a well-to-do family than a grand palace. The 3,000-square-foot interior has only two bedrooms and no facilities for guests. The first person to put a house on the property was John George Lewis. He purchased the land for $800 from a previous owner by the name of Henry Pierce, and then resold it to John Young II. The exterior has a strong New England flavor, and indeed the house was prefabricated in Boston. The simple square home, surrounded by a lanai, was built 1843-1847 by John Young II, Queen Emma's uncle. When he died, she inherited the property and spent many relaxing days here, away from the heat of Honolulu, with her husband King Kamehameha IV. Emma used the home little after 1872, and following her death in 1885 it fell into disrepair.

Rescued from demolition by the Daughters of Hawaii in 1913, it was refurbished and has operated as a museum since 1915. In the '70s, the Summer Palace was added to the National Register of Historic Sites. The palace, at 2913 Pali Hwy., tel. (808) 595-3167, is open daily 9 a.m.-4 p.m., except for major holidays; admission $5, seniors $4, children 16 and under $1. Although it's just off the Pali Highway, the one and only sign comes up quickly, and many visitors pass it by. If you pass the entranceway to the Oahu Country Club just across the road, you've gone too far.

As you enter, notice the tall *kahili,* symbols of noble rank in the entranceway, along with *lau hala* mats on the floor, which at one time were an unsurpassed specialty of Hawaii. Today they must be imported from Fiji or Samoa. The walls are hung with paintings of many of Hawaii's kings and queens, and in every room are distinctive Hawaiian artifacts, such as magnificent feather capes, fans, and tapa hangings.

The furnishings have a very strong British influence. The Hawaiian nobility of the time were enamored with the British. King Kamehameha IV traveled to England when he was 15 years old;

he met Queen Victoria, and the two become good friends. Emma and Kamehameha IV had the last child born to a Hawaiian king and queen on May 20, 1858. Named Prince Albert after Queen Victoria's consort, he was much loved but died when he was only four years old on August 27, 1862. His father followed him to the grave in little more than a year. The king's brother, Lot Kamehameha, a bachelor, took the throne but died very shortly thereafter, marking the end of the Kamehameha line; after that, Hawaii elected her kings. Prince Albert's canoe-shaped cradle is here, made in Germany by Wilhelm Fisher from four different kinds of Hawaiian wood. His tiny shirts, pants, and boots are still laid out, and there's a lock of his hair, and one from Queen Emma. In every room there is royal memorabilia. The royal bedroom displays a queen-size bed, covered with an exquisite bedspread or quilt that changes periodically. There's vintage Victorian furniture, and even a piano built in London by Collard and Collard. A royal cabinet made in Berlin holds porcelains, plates, and cups. After Queen Emma died, it stood in Charles R. Bishop's drawing room but was later returned. The grounds are beautifully manicured, and the house is surrounded by shrubbery and trees, many of which date from when the royal couple lived here. Restrooms are around back.

The Daughters of Hawaii have added a gift shop around back, which is open the same hours as the palace. It's small but packed with excellent items like greeting cards, lei, travel guidebooks, beverage trays (reproductions of the early Matson Line menus), little Hawaiian quilt pillows, needlepoint, wraparounds from Tahiti, T-shirts with Queen Emma Summer Palace logo, and Niihau shellwork, the finest in Hawaii.

Walk around back past the basketball court and keep to the right. Soon you'll see a modest little white building. Look for a rather thick and distinctive rope hanging across the entranceway. This is the Shinto temple **Dai Jingu**. It's not nearly as spectacular as the giant trees in this area, but it is authentic and worth a quick look. Shake the bell rope and clap your hands three times as you walk up to the entranceway. For fun, place 25 cents into the *oni kuji* wooden box and out comes a good luck fortune on the back of a small piece of paper. So, for a quarter, find out about love, marriage, business, health, and that sort of thing, and help out the temple at the same time.

Nuuanu Pali Lookout

This is one of those extra-benefit places where you get a magnificent view without any effort at all. Merely drive up the Pali Highway to the well-marked turnout and park. Rip-offs happen, so take all valuables. Before you, if the weather is accommodating, an unimpeded view of windward Oahu lies at your feet. Nuuanu Pali (Cool Heights) lives up to its name; the winds here are chilly and extremely strong, and they funnel right through the lookout. You definitely need a jacket or windbreaker. On a particularly windy day just after a good rainfall, various waterfalls tumbling off the *pali* will actually be blown uphill! A number of roads, punched over and through the *pali* over the years, are engineering marvels. The famous "carriage road" built in 1898 by John Wilson, a Honolulu boy, for only $37,500, using 200 laborers and plenty of dynamite, was truly amazing. Droves of people come here, many in huge buses, and they all go to the railing to have a peek. Even so, by walking down the old road built in 1932 that goes off to the right, you actually get private and better views. You'll find the tallest point in the area, a huge needlelike rock. The wind is quieter here.

Nuuanu Pali figures prominently in Hawaii's legend history. It's said, not without academic skepticism, that Kamehameha the Great pursued the last remaining defenders of Oahu to these cliffs in one of the final battles fought to consolidate his power over all of the islands in 1795. If you use your imagination, you can easily feel the utter despair and courage of these vanquished warriors as they were driven ever closer to the edge. Mercy was not shown nor expected. Some jumped to their deaths rather than surrender, while others fought until they were pushed over. The estimated number of casualties varies considerably, from a few hundred to a few thousand, while some believe that the battle never happened at all. Compounding the controversy are stories of the warriors' families, who searched the cliffs below for years, and supposedly found bones of their kinsmen, which they buried. The Pali Lookout is romantic at night, with the lights of Kailua and Kaneohe in the distance, but the best nighttime view is from Tantalus Drive, where all of Honolulu lies at your feet.

PUNCHBOWL, NATIONAL CEMETERY OF THE PACIFIC

One sure sign that you have entered a place of honor is the hushed and quiet nature that everyone adopts without having to be told. This is the way it is the moment that you enter this shrine. The Hawaiian name, Puowaina (Hill of Sacrifice), couldn't have been more prophetic. Punchbowl is the almost perfectly round crater of an extinct volcano that holds the bodies of more than 33,000 men and women who fell fighting for the United States, from World War II to Vietnam, and a few notable individuals who have served the country in other ways. At one time, Punchbowl was a bastion of heavy cannon and artillery trained on Honolulu Harbor to defend it from hostile naval forces. In 1943 Hawaii bequeathed it to the federal government as a memorial; it was dedicated in 1949, when the remains of an unknown serviceman killed during the attack on Pearl Harbor were the first interred. One of the more recent to be buried here was astronaut Ellison Onizuka, who died in 1986 aboard the *Challenger* space shuttle. To attest to its sacredness and the importance of those who lie buried here, more than five million visitors stop here yearly to pay their respects, making this the most visited site in the state. In addition, the annual Easter sunrise service held here draws thousands.

As you enter the main gate, a flagpole with the Stars and Stripes unfurled is framed in the center of a long sweeping lawn. A roadway lined with monkeypod trees adds three-dimensional depth to the impressionistic scene, as it leads to the steps of a marble, altarlike monument in the distance. The eye has a continuous sweep of the field, as there are no elevated tombstones, just simple marble slabs lying flat on the ground. The field is dotted with trees, including eight banyans, a special tree and symbolic number for the many Buddhists buried here. Brightening the scene are plumeria and rainbow shower trees, often planted in Hawaiian graveyards because they produce flowers year-round as perennial offerings from the living to the dead when they can't personally attend the grave. All are equal here: the famous, like Ernie Pyle, the stalwart who earned the Congressional Medal of Honor, and the unknown who died alone and unheralded on muddy battlefields in godforsaken jungles. To the right just after you enter is the office, tel. (808) 566-1430, with brochures and restrooms. The cemetery is open free of charge 8 a.m.-5:30 p.m. Sept. 30-March 1 and until 6:30 p.m. March 2-Sept. 29, except for Memorial Day when the grounds are open 7 a.m.-7 p.m. Guided walking tours are conducted by the American Legion Mon.-Fri. at 11 a.m. These two-hour tours cost $15 per person and reservations must be made by calling (808) 946-6383. Tour buses, taxis, and limousines line up at the front. Don't leave valuables in your car.

To get to Punchbowl take the H-1 freeway to Rt. 61, the Pali Highway, and exit at 21B. Immediately get to the right, where a sign points you to Punchbowl. You'll make some fancy zigzags through a residential area, but it's well marked and you'll come to Puowaina Street, which leads you to the main gate. Make sure to notice landmarks going in, because as odd as it sounds, no signs lead you back out and it's easy to get lost.

The Monument

Like a pilgrim, you climb the steps to the monument, where on both sides marble slabs seem to whisper the names of 28,778 servicemen, all MIAs whose bodies were never found or those who were buried at sea, but whose spirits are honored here. The first slabs on the right are for the victims of Vietnam, on the left are those from WW II, and you can see that time is already weathering the marble. Their names stand together, as they fought and died . . . men, boys, lieutenants, captains, private soldiers, infantrymen, sailors . . . from everywhere in America. "In proud memory . . . this memorial has been erected by the United States of America."

At the monument itself, built in 1966, is a chapel, and in the middle is a statue of a woman, a woman of peace, a heroic woman of liberty. Around her on the walls are etched maps and battles of the Pacific War whose names still evoke passion: Pearl Harbor, Wake, Coral Sea, Midway, Iwo Jima, the Gilbert Islands, Okinawa. Many of the visitors are Japanese. Many of Hawaii's war dead are also Japanese. Four decades ago we battled each other with hatred and malice. Today, on bright afternoons we come together with saddened hearts to pay reverence to the dead.

UNIVERSITY OF HAWAII

You don't have to be a student to head for the University of Hawaii, Manoa Campus. For one, it houses the **East-West Center,** which was incorporated in 1975 and officially separated from the university; here nations from Asia and the Pacific present fascinating displays of their homelands. Also, Manoa Valley itself is one of the loveliest residential areas on Oahu. To get to the main campus follow the H-1 freeway to exit 24B (University Avenue). Don't make the mistake of exiting at the University's Makai Campus. Follow University Avenue to the second red light, Dole Avenue, and make a right onto campus. Stop immediately at one of the parking lots and get a parking map! Parking restrictions are strictly enforced, and this map not only helps to get you around, but saves you from fines or having your car towed away. Parking is 50 cents an hour, even for visitors, so think about taking The-Bus, which services this area quite well.

Two six-week summer sessions beginning late May and in early July are offered to bona fide students of accredited universities at the University of Hawaii at Manoa. Reasonable rates are available in residence halls (mandatory meals) and in apartments on campus; special courses have an emphasis on Polynesian and Asian culture and languages, including China and Japan. Unbeatably priced tours and outings to points throughout the islands for students and the general public can be arranged at the Summer Session Activities Office. For information, catalog, and enrollment, write Summer Session Office, University of Hawaii, 2500 Dole St., Krauss Hall 101, Honolulu, HI 96822, tel. (808) 956-6894.

Student Center

Make this your first stop. As you mount the steps, notice the idealized mural of old Hawaii: smiling faces of contented natives all doing interesting things. Inside is the **Information Center,** which dispenses info not only about the campus, but also about what's happening socially and culturally around town. Stop here for a campus map and self-guided tour brochure. It even has lists of cheap restaurants, discos, and student hangouts. The food in the cafeteria is institutional but cheap, and has a Hawaiian twist. The best place

to eat is **Manoa Gardens** in the Hemenway Center, where you can get a tasty stir-fry or good vegetarian dishes for $3.50 and up.

The **University Bookstore** is excellent, open Mon.-Fri. 8:15 a.m.-4:15 p.m., Saturday 8:15-11:45 a.m. The bookstore is worth coming to for its excellent range of specialty items, like language tapes, and its extensive assortment of travel guidebooks. The **University Art Gallery** is on the third floor, and is worth a look. Free! The exhibits change regularly. Next to the gallery is a lounge filled with overstuffed chairs and big pillows, where you can kick back and even take a quick snooze. This is not a very social campus. By 4:30 or 5 p.m. the place is shut up and no one is around. Don't expect students gathered in a common reading room, or the activity of social and cultural events. When school lets out at the end of the day, people simply go home.

East-West Center

Follow Dole Avenue to East-West Road and make a left. Free tours, Wednesdays only at 1:30 p.m., originate from Imin Center-Jefferson Hall opposite Kennedy Theater. For more info contact the Friends of the East-West Center, 1777 East-West Rd., Honolulu, HI 96848, tel. (808) 944-7691. The center's 21 acres were dedicated in 1960 by the U.S. Congress to promote better relations between the countries of Asia and the Pacific with the United States. Many nations, as well as private companies and individuals, fund this institution of cooperative study and research. The center's staff, with help from University of Hawaii students and scholars and professionals from throughout the region, focus on four broad but interconnected issues: regional security, social and cultural changes, the changing domestic political scene in nations of the region, and regional economic growth and its resultant consequences. John Burns Hall's main lobby dispenses information on what's happening, along with self-guiding maps. Imin Center-Jefferson Hall, fronted by Chinese lions, has a serene and relaxing Japanese garden behind, complete with a little rivulet and a teahouse named Jakuan, "Cottage of Tranquility." The murals inside are excellent, and it also contains a large reading room with relaxing couches. While here, check out the bookstore, which carries an impressive selection of Hawaiiana and books on Asia.

The impressive Thai Pavilion was a gift from the king of Thailand, where it was built and sent to Hawaii to be reconstructed. This 23-ton, solid teak sala is a common sight in Thailand. The Center for Korean Studies (not part of the East-West Center) is also outstanding. A joint venture of Korean and Hawaiian architects, its inspiration was taken from the classic lines of Kyongbok Palace in Seoul. Most of the buildings are adorned with fine artworks: tapa hangings, murals, calligraphy, paintings, and sculpture. The entire valley is tranquil, and along with the John F. Kennedy Theater of Performing Arts just across the road, is indeed fulfilling its dedication as a place of sharing and learning, culture and art.

MANOA VALLEY

Manoa Valley, a tropical palette of green ablaze with daubs of iridescent color, has a unique designation most aptly described as "urban rainforest." Although not technically true, the valley receiving more than 100 inches of rainfall per year is exceptionally verdant even by Hawaiian standards. However, it wasn't always so. In the late 1800s, the overpopulated valley was almost denuded of trees, only to be reforested by Dr. Lyon, the founder of Lyon Arboretum, who planted trees gathered from around the world. A literal backwater, the runoff from Manoa would flood the relatively dry Waikiki until the Ala Wai Canal was built in the 1920s as a catchment for its torrential flash floods. Only a short drive from arid Waikiki, Manoa was the first place in Hawaii where coffee was grown and where pineapple was cultivated. The great Queen Kaahumanu, who died here in 1832, favored the cool hills of the valley as a vacation spot to escape the summer heat. Manoa, favored by royalty ever since, has maintained itself as one of the most fashionable residential areas in Hawaii, even boasting its own country club at the turn of the century, which is yet memorialized by the Manoa Cup held yearly at the Oahu Country Club. In 1893, just before annexation, a bewildered and beaten group of royalists came to Manoa to hide out. They were subsequently captured by a contingency of pursuing U.S. Marines and imprisoned in an area called The Pen, located on the grounds of the now defunct Paradise Park.

THE LEGENDS OF MANOA VALLEY

Kahala-o-puna, known for her exceptional beauty, was betrothed to Kauhi, a young chief who was driven mad by unfounded jealousy. He falsely accused his lovely wife of faithlessness and killed her five times, only to have her resurrected each time by her sympathetic guardian *aumakua*. Finally, left for dead, Kahala-o-puna was found by a young prince who fell in love with her. Beseeching his animal spirits, he brought her to life one last time, and through them turned the jealous Kauhi into a shark. Kahala-o-puna, warned never to go into the ocean, disobeyed, and was seized in the massive jaws of Kauhi, who finally crushed the life from her, never to be rekindled. The warm misty rains of Manoa are the tears of the mother of Kahala-o-puna, and the gentle winds are the soft sobs of her bereaved father, who together forever lament the loss of their beloved daughter.

Another legend sings of the spring, Wai-a-ke-akua, created spontaneously by the great gods Kane and Kaneloa, who came to visit this valley. While overindulging in *awa* they became intoxicated, and decided that they would dawdle in the lovely valley. Lying down, the gods could hear water running underground, so Kane took his great staff and struck the earth, causing Wai-a-ke-akua to appear. Because of the spring's divine origin, it became known as "water of the gods," making it *kapu* to all but the highest *ali'i*. When Kamehameha conquered Oahu, only he could drink from the spring, which flows with cool sweet water to this day.

Taking Manoa Road past the University of Hawaii you pass **Punahou School,** one of the oldest and most prestigious high schools in Hawaii. Built in 1841 from lava rock, children of the missionary families of wealthy San Franciscans attended, getting the best possible education west of the Rockies.

Manoa Road eventually crosses Oahu Avenue. Follow it to **Waioli Tea Room,** 3016 Oahu Ave., owned and operated by the Salvation Army. It's a small park with a snack bar that features fresh-baked pastries and serves lunch daily. Also featured here is the **Little Grass Shack** supposedly lived in by Robert Louis

Stevenson when he was a resident of Waikiki. Visit the chapel with its distinctive stained-glass windows. Waioli Tea Room is open daily except Monday, 8 a.m.-3:30 p.m.

Paradise Park, 3737 Manoa Rd. (at the very end), closed in late 1993, is 13 acres of lush tropical plants founded by James Wong about 25 years ago. Magnificent blooms compete with the wild plumage of 50 species of exotic birds. However, the Treetop (literally) Restaurant, located here and offering very good food and superlative views, is still operating.

The **Lyon Arboretum,** tel. (808) 988-3177 or 988-7378, is situated on 194 acres at the upper end of Manoa Road. Open to the public, it's principally a research facility and academic institution of the University of Hawaii. You can visit on your own Mon.-Sat. 9 a.m.-3 p.m., but guided tours are also offered on the first Friday and third Wednesday of the month at 1 p.m. and on the third Saturday at 10 a.m. Walking tour maps are available.

BISHOP MUSEUM

Otherwise known as the Museum of Natural and Cultural History, this group of stalwart stone buildings holds the greatest collection of historical relics and scholarly works on Hawaii and the Pacific in the world. Referring to itself as a "museum to instruct and delight," in one afternoon walking through its halls you can educate yourself about Hawaii's history and people and enrich your trip to the islands tenfold.

Officially named Bernice Pauahi Bishop Museum, its founding was directly connected to the last three royal women of the Kamehameha dynasty. Princess Bernice married Charles Reed Bishop, a New Englander who became a citizen of the then-independent monarchy in the 1840s. The princess was a wealthy woman in her own right, with lands and an extensive collection of "things Hawaiian." Her cousin, Princess

Ruta Keeikolani, died in 1883 and bequeathed Princess Bernice all of her lands and Hawaiian artifacts. Together, this meant that Princess Bernice owned about 12% of all Hawaii! Princess Bernice died less than two years later, and left all of her landholdings to the **Bernice Pauahi Bishop Estate,** which founded and supported the Kamehameha School, dedicated to the education of Hawaiian children. (Though this organization is often confused with the Bishop Museum, they are totally separate. The school shared the same grounds with the museum, but none of the funds from this organization were, or are, used for the museum.) Bernice left her personal property, with all of its priceless Hawaiian artifacts, to her husband, Charles. Then, when Queen Emma, her other cousin, died the following year, she too desired Charles Bishop to combine her Hawaiian artifacts with the already formidable collection and establish a Hawaiian museum.

True to the wishes of these women, he began construction of the museum's main building on December 18, 1889, and within a few years the museum was opened. In 1894, after 50 years in Hawaii, Bishop moved to San Francisco, where he died in 1915. He is still regarded as one of Hawaii's most generous philanthropists. In 1961, a science wing and planetarium were added, and two dormitory buildings are still used from when the Kamehameha School for Boys occupied the same site.

Getting There

To get there, take exit 20A off the H-1 freeway, which puts you on Rt. 63, the Likelike Highway. Immediately get into the far right lane. In only a few hundred yards, turn onto Bernice Street, where you'll find the entrance. Or, exit H-1 onto Hofftailing Street, Rt. 61, exit 20B. Keep your eyes peeled for a clearly marked but small sign directing you to the museum. TheBus no. 2 (School-Middle Street) runs from Waikiki to Kapalama Street, from which you walk two blocks.

Princess Bernice

HAWAII STATE ARCHIVES

Admission and Information

The museum is located at 1525 Bernice St., Honolulu, HI 96817, tel. (808) 847-3511, website: www.bishop.hawaii.org, and is open seven days a week 9 a.m.-5 p.m. Admission is $14.95 adults, $11.95 for those ages 6-17 and for seniors; kids five and younger and museum members are free, but some exhibits and the planetarium are closed to children under six. *Kama'aina,* military, and other discounts are available but you must ask. It's sometimes best to visit on weekends because many weekdays bring teachers and young students who have more enthusiasm for running around than checking out the exhibits. Food, beverages, smoking, and flash photography are all strictly prohibited in the museum. The natural light in the museum is dim, so if you're into photography you'll need super-fast film (400 ASA performs only marginally). Daily tours of the Hawaiian Hall are given at 10 a.m. and noon. Throughout the week, the hall offers demonstrations in various Hawaiian crafts like lei-making, featherwork, and quilting 9 a.m.-2

Bishop Museum

ROBERT NILSEN

p.m. Before leaving the grounds make sure to visit **Hawaiian Halau,** where a hula is performed Mon.-Fri. at 11 a.m. and 2 p.m. The **planetarium** opens up its skies daily at 11:30 a.m., 1:30 p.m., and 3:30 p.m., and Fri.-Sat. evenings at 7 p.m. by reservation; call (808) 848-4136. Both the library and archives are open to the public, the library on Tues.-Fri. 1-4 p.m. and the archives Tues.-Fri. 10 a.m.-3 p.m., while both open Saturday 9 a.m.-noon. For library reference services, call (808) 848-4148. The snack shop has reasonable prices, and **Shop Pacifica,** the museum bookstore and boutique, has a fine selection of materials on Hawaii and the Pacific, and some authentic and inexpensive souvenirs. Although it has a limited menu, try the **museum cafe** for a snack.

Exhibits

It's easy to become overwhelmed at the museum, so just take it slowly. The number of exhibits is staggering: more than 180,000 artifacts; about 20 million(!) specimens of insects, shells, fish, birds, and mammals; an extensive research library; a photograph collection; and a fine series of maps. The main gallery is highlighted by the rich tones of koa, the showpiece being a magnificent staircase. Get a map at the front desk that lists all of the halls, along with a description of what theme is found in each, and a suggested route to follow. Guided tours are given Mon.-Fri. at 10 a.m. and noon. The following is just a small potpourri of the highlights that you'll discover.

To the right of the main entranceway is a fascinating exhibit of the old Hawaiian gods. Most are just called "wooden image" and date from the early 19th century. Among them are: Kamehameha's war-god, Ku; the tallest Hawaiian sculpture ever found, from Kauai; an image of a god from a temple of human sacrifice; and lesser gods, personal *aumakua* that controlled the lives of Hawaiians from birth until death. You wouldn't want to meet any of them in a dark alley! Outside, in what's called the **Hawaiian Courtyard,** are implements used by the Hawaiians in everyday life, as well as a collection of plants that are all identified. The first floor of the main hall is perhaps the most interesting because it deals with old Hawaii. Here are magnificent examples of *kahili,* feathered capes, plumed helmets . . . all the insignia and regalia of the *ali'i.* A commoner sits in a grass shack, a replica of what Captain Cook might have seen.

Don't look up! Over your head is a 55-foot sperm whale hanging from the ceiling. It weighed more than 44,000 pounds alive. You'll learn about the ukulele, and how vaudevillians spread its music around the world. Hula-skirted damsels from the 1870s peer provocatively from old photos, bare-breasted and with plenty of "cheesecake." Tourists bought these photos even then, although the grass skirts they're wearing were never a part of old Hawaii but were brought by Gilbert Islanders. See authentic hula instruments like a "lover's whistle," a flute played through the nose, and a musical bow, the only stringed pre-European Hawaiian instrument.

Don't miss the koa wood collection. This accomplished artform produced medicine bowls, handsome calabashes, some simple home bowls, and others reputed to be the earthly home of the wind goddess, which had to be refitted for display in Christianized Iolani Palace. A model *heiau* tells of the old religion, and the many strange *kapu* that governed every aspect of life. Clubs used to bash in the brains of *kapu*-breakers are next to benevolent little stone gods, the size and shape of footballs, that protected humble fishermen from the sea. As you ascend to the upper floors, the time period represented becomes increasingly closer to the present. The missionaries, whalers, merchants, laborers, and Westernized monarchs have arrived. Yankee whalers from New Bedford, New London, Nantucket, and Sag Harbor appear determined and grim-faced as they scour the seas, harpoons at the ready. Great blubber pots, harpoons, and figureheads are preserved from this perilous and unglamorous life. Bibles, thrones, the regalia of power and of the new god are all here.

OTHER MUSEUMS AND GALLERIES

Honolulu Academy of Arts

Enjoy the magnificent grounds of this perfectly designed building, a combination of East and West with a Hawaiian roof and thick white stucco walls reminiscent of the American Southwest, created by architect Bertram Goodhue and benefactor Mrs. Charles Montague-Cooke expressly as a museum. The museum, at 900 S. Beretania St. (TheBus no. 2) opposite Thomas Square, tel. (808) 532-8700, website: www.honolulu-academy.org, is open Tues.-Sat. 10 a.m.-4:30 p.m., Sunday 1-5 p.m., closed Monday. Admission fees are $5 general and $3 for seniors, students, and military personnel. Members and children under 12 are free, as is everyone on the first Wednesday of the month. Guided docent tours are conducted daily at 11 a.m. The academy houses a brilliant collection of classic and modern art, strongly emphasizing Asian artwork.

James Michener's outstanding collection of Japanese *ukiyo-e* is here. The story goes that an unfriendly New York cop hassled him on his way to donate it to a New York City museum, while a Honolulu officer was the epitome of *aloha* when Michener was passing through, so he decided that his collection should reside here. This collection is rotated frequently and displayed in a specially designed gallery to highlight and protect the prints. Magnificent Korean ceramics, Chinese furniture, and Japanese prints, along with Western masterworks from the Greeks to Picasso, make the academy one of the most well-rounded art museums in America. Some collections are permanent while others change, so the museum remains dynamic no matter how many times you visit.

Enter through the foyer and pass to the courtyard that gets you away from the hustle and bustle of downtown. Great for a little respite from noise. Pass through double French doors to the thick white-walled galleries that create a perfect atmosphere for displaying fine works of art. Discover delights like Paul Gauguin's *Two Nudes on a Tahitian Beach,* James Whistler's *Arrangement in Black No. 5,* John Singer Sargent's *Portrait of Mrs. Thomas Lincoln Hansen Jr.* An entire wing is dedicated to religious art, while another holds furniture from medieval Europe. The courtyards are resplendent with statuary from the 6th century A.D. and a standing figure from Egypt, circa 2500 B.C. The Hawaiian climate is perfect for preserving artwork. In addition to the art exhibitions, educational programs, films, and concerts are supported by the museum.

Stop at the **Academy Shop,** specializing in art books, museum repros, Hawaii out-of-prints, jewelry, notebooks, and postcards. The **Garden Cafe** is open Tues.-Sat. 11 a.m.-2:30 p.m. It has a light but terrific menu, and besides, a trip to the academy demands a luncheon in the cafe.

Honolulu Art Center

Catty-corner from the Academy of Arts, and affiliated with it, is the Honolulu Art Center. Built in 1908 as McKinley High School, and later used as Lincoln (Line Kona) Elementary School, it is now on both the national and state registers of historic places. The building was renovated and reopened in 1990 as a place where art students can do and display their artwork. As the displays change periodically, what you'll get is potluck, but prints and quilts seem to be prominent. As it's a functioning art center, it's a good place to see what kind of artwork young, contemporary Hawaiian artists are doing. Works are displayed in a large, wooden-floored room with a high vaulted ceiling, perhaps the old school gymnasium, where banks of windows provide plenty of natural light.

The Contemporary Museum

Under the direction of Georgiana Lagoria, at 2411 Makiki Heights Dr., tel. (808) 526-1322, the museum welcomes you with two copper-green gates that are sculptures themselves. This open and elegant structure, the former Spalding House, has yielded seven galleries, a shop, and an excellent gourmet restaurant, the Contemporary Cafe. Acquired through the generosity of the *Honolulu Advertiser*'s stockholders, the building was donated to the museum as a permanent home in 1988. The focus is on exhibitions, not collections, although works by David Hockney are on permanent display. Always-changing exhibits reflect different themes in contemporary art. Open Tues.-Sat. 10 a.m.-4 p.m., Sunday noon-4 p.m., closed Monday and major holidays; admission $5 general, $3 students and seniors, except on the third Thursday of the month when admission is free. The museum also has a ritzy little restaurant, so you don't have to step out for a bite to eat.

Surrounding the building are three magnificent acres sculpted into gardens perfect for strolling and gazing at the sprawl of Honolulu far below. Led by museum volunteers, a 45-minute tour of the gardens is offered by appointment only. Call the museum for details at least a week in advance.

Aside from the main galleries, works are displayed at the museum cafe; at the museum galleries at the *Honolulu Advertiser,* 605 Kapiolani Blvd.; and at the First Hawaiian Center, 999 Bishop Street. The cafe hours are Tues.-Sat. 10 a.m.-3 p.m. and Sunday noon-3 p.m. The museum gallery hours at the *Honolulu Advertiser* are Mon.-Fri. 8:30 a.m.-5 p.m. For the First Hawaiian Center gallery, the gallery is open Mon.-Thurs. 8:30 a.m.-3 p.m. and Friday until 6 p.m. Admission is free at both the *Honolulu Advertiser* and First Hawaiian Center galleries.

Tennent Art Foundation Gallery

At 201-203 Prospect St., on the *ewa* slope of Punchbowl, the foundation is open Tues.-Sat. 10 a.m.-noon, Sunday 2-4 p.m., tel. (808) 531-1987. Free. There is a library and the walls hold the paintings of Madge Tennent, one of Hawaii's foremost artists, as well as many other contemporary works. It's beautiful, quiet, and worth a visit. Head up Ward Avenue until it meets Prospect Street. Turn left and proceed until Prospect Street veers off to the right. From there it's not far. Look for the salmon-colored wall and gate. The gallery now sits behind a condo.

GARDENS, GUIDED TOURS, ETC.

Foster Botanical Garden

Many of these 13.5 acres of exotic trees have been growing in this manicured garden for more than 100 years. It was at one time the private estate of Dr. Hillebrand, physician to the royal court; he brought many of the seedlings from Asia. Two dozen of these trees enjoy lifetime protection by the state. Located at 50 N. Vineyard Blvd., tel. (808) 522-7065, open daily except Christmas and New Year's Day 9 a.m.-4 p.m. Admission is $5 for nonresidents, $3 for residents, $1 for children 6-12, and free for those under age six; a self-guiding brochure sells for $1. Guided tours are given Mon.-Fri. at 1 p.m.; call (808) 522-7066 for reservations. Bring insect repellent. Many nature hikes on Oahu are sponsored by the gardens. Along with four others on the island, these gardens are administered by the Honolulu Botanical Gardens. Before leaving, stop in for a look at the Foster Garden Gallery and Bookstore for books, postcards, tapa cloth, T-shirts, and other such gift items. The closest stops on TheBus are no. 4 from Waikiki, no. 2 and no.13 to Chinatown.

A stone's throw to the north and set along the Nuuanu Stream on the opposite side of the freeway are the 7.5 acres of the **Lili'uokalani Botanical Garden.** Once the private garden of the last Hawaiian monarch, it's now part of the Honolulu Botanical Garden system. Unlike the imported magnificence of the Foster Botanical Garden, this garden features native Hawaiian plants.

Moanalua Gardens

The private gardens of the Damon Estate, at 1352 Pineapple Pl., tel. (808) 833-1944, were given to the original owner by Princess Bernice Bishop in 1884. Just off the Moanalua Freeway, and open to the public, these gardens are not heavily touristed, a welcome respite from the hustle and bustle of the city. Some magnificent old trees include a Buddha tree from Ceylon and a monkeypod called "the most beautifully shaped tree" in the world by *Ripley's Believe It or Not.* The Moanalua Foundation also sponsors walks deep into Moanalua Valley for viewing the foliage of "natural Hawaii." You can walk on your own through the garden, but only after making arrangements at the number above. Free guided walks begin at 9 a.m. usually on weekends; make arrangements, preferably a week in advance, by calling (808) 839-5334.

HONOLULU BEACHES AND PARKS

The beaches and parks listed here are found in and around Honolulu's city limits. World-famous Waikiki has its own section (see **Waikiki**). The good thing about having Waikiki so close is that it lures most bathers away from other city beaches, which makes them less congested. The following list contains most of Honolulu's beaches, ending at Fort DeRussy Beach Park, just a few hundred yards from where the string of Waikiki's beaches begins.

Sand Island State Recreation Area

You enter this park by way of the Sand Island Access Road, clearly marked off the Nimitz Highway. On the way, you pass through some ugly real estate-scrapyards, petrochemical tanks, and other such beauties. Don't get discouraged, keep going! Once you cross the metal bridge, a favorite fishing spot for local people, and then pass the entrance to the U.S. Coast Guard base, you enter the actual park, 14 acres landscaped with picnic and playground facilities. Follow the road into the park; you pass two observation towers that have been built in the middle of a grassy field, from where you can get an impressive view of Honolulu, with Diamond Head making a remarkable counterpoint. The park is excellently maintained, with pavilions, cold-water showers, walkways, and restrooms, all for day use only; the park closes at 6:30 p.m. However, the camping area is usually empty (state permit required). The sites are out in the open, but a few trees provide some shade.

Unfortunately, you're under one of the main glide paths for Honolulu International Airport. Many local people come to fish, and the surfing is good, but the beaches for snorkeling and swimming are fair at best. Some of the beach area is horrible, piled with broken stone, rubble, and pieces of coral. However, follow the road past the tower and park in the next lot; turn right and follow the shore up to a sandy beach. The currents and wave action aren't dangerous, but remember that this part of the harbor receives more than its share of pollutants. For delicious and inexpensive plate lunches, make sure to stop at Penny's Lunch Wagon, next door to Dancers strip joint, on your way down the access road.

La Mariana Yacht Sailing Club

This small marina at 50 Sand Island Access Rd. is a love song in the middle of an industrialized area. The marina is Annette La Mariana Nahinua's labor of love that has remained true since 1955. You can read her fantastic story on the menu of the marina's Hideaway Restaurant, the only real restaurant on Sand Island. In 1955 this area was forgotten, forsaken, and unkempt. Ms. Nahinua, against the forces of nature, and the even more unpredictable and devastating forces of bureaucracy, took this land and turned it into a yacht harbor. The main tools were indefatigable determination, God listening to her prayers, and a shovel and rake. It's one of the last enclaves of old Hawaii, a place to come for dinner, a drink, or just to look at the boats. The nighttime bartender, Mr. Lee, is friendly but stoic after decades of seeing and hearing it all. Annette, the founder, is now a little gray-haired woman, a motherly type in Birkenstocks, who lives right here above the Hideaway. In the daytime she wanders around spreading her magic while talking to old salts or new arrivals.

The marina is adjacent to an open waterway, which means that you don't have to pay for anchorage. It comes under the old "rights of sailors" to find a free port in which to berth. This unique setup has created an atmosphere in which a subculture of people have built subsistence shacks on the little islands that dot the bay. Some also live on old scows, shipshape yachts, or on very imaginative homemade crafts, afloat and semi-afloat on this tranquil bay. Many are disillusioned and disenfranchised Vietnam vets who have become misanthropes. You'll see the Stars and Stripes flying from their island hooches. Others are yachties who disdain being landlubbers, while others are poor souls who have fallen through the social net. La Mariana is a unique statement of personal freedom in a city where unique statements are generally not tolerated.

Keehi Lagoon Beach Park
Located at the eastern end of Honolulu International Airport, at the northern tip of Keehi Lagoon, this park is just past the **Pacific War Memorial** on Rt. 92 (the Nimitz Hwy.). Here are restrooms, picnic facilities, and a pay phone. This park is polluted, but some people do swim here. Mostly, local people use the area for pole fishing and crabbing.

Kakaako (Point Panic) Waterfront Park
This small facility was carved out of a piece of land donated by the University of Hawaii's Biomedical Research Center. Next to Kewalo Basin Harbor, follow Ahui Street, off Ala Moana Boulevard. You'll come to some landscaped grounds with a cold-water shower and a path leading to the bathing area. Kewalo Basin, developed in the '20s to hold Honolulu's tuna fleet, is home to many charter boats. If you're lucky, you may even spot a manta ray, which are known to frequent these waters. This area is poor for swimming, known for sharks, but great for fishing and bodysurfing. Unfortunately, novices will quickly find out why it's called Point Panic. A long seawall with a sharp dropoff runs the entire length of the area. The wave action is perfect for riding, but all wash against the wall. Beginners stay out! The best reason to come here is for the magnificent and unobstructed view of the Waikiki skyline and Diamond Head.

Ala Moana Beach Park
Ala Moana (Path to the Sea) Beach County Park is by far Honolulu's best. Most visitors congregate just around the bend at Waikiki, but residents head for Ala Moana, the place to soak up the local color. During the week, this beautifully curving white-sand beach has plenty of elbow room. Weekends bring families that come for every water sport Oahu offers. The swimming is great, with manageable wave action, plenty of lifeguards, and even good snorkeling along the reef. Board riders have their favorite spots, and bodysurfing is excellent. The huge area has a number of restrooms, food concessions, tennis courts, softball fields, a bowling green, and parking for 500 cars. Many Oahu outrigger canoe clubs practice in this area, especially in the evening; it's great to come and watch them glide along. A huge banyan grove provides shade and strolling if you don't fancy the beach, or you can bring a kite to fly aloft with the trade winds. Ala Moana Park stretches along Ala Moana Blvd., between the Ala Wai and Kewalo Basin boat harbors. It's across from the Ala Moana Shopping Center, so you can rush right over if your credit cards start melting from the sun.

Aina Moana (Land from the Sea) State Recreation Area used to be called Magic Island because it was reclaimed land. It is actually the point of land stretching out from the eastern edge of Ala Moana, and is contiguous with it. All the beach activities are great here, too. Jutting out from the western end of Ala Moana, making one arm of land that creates Kewalo Basin Marina, is the much smaller **Kewalo Basin State Park.**

If you're here in the early morning hours, check out the Honolulu Fish Auction at Kewalo Basin. Your dinner might be coming off one of these boats.

ACCOMMODATIONS

The vast majority of Oahu's hotels are strung along the boulevards of Waikiki. Most are neatly clustered, bound by the Ala Wai Canal, and run eastward to Diamond Head. These hotels will be discussed in the Waikiki section. The remainder of greater Honolulu has few hotels, but those that do exist are some of Oahu's cheapest. Most are clean, no-frills establishments, with a few others at the airport, or just off the beaten track.

BUDGET ROOMS

Oahu has a number of YM/WCAs from which to choose, and the only official youth hostel in the state. The Ys vary as far as private rooms and baths are concerned, facilities offered, and prices. Expect to pay $25-30 single with a shared bath, and more for a double with a private bath.

The **YMCA Central Branch** (men only) at 401 Atkinson Dr., Honolulu, HI 96814, tel. (808) 941-3344, is the most centrally located and closest to Waikiki. You can call ahead, but there are no reservations, no curfew, no visitors after 10 p.m.; it has an outside pool, singles, doubles, and private baths. Rates are $29 a night with a $10 key deposit. This Y is located just across from the eastern end of Ala Moana Park, only a 10-minute walk to Waikiki.

YMCA Nuuanu (men only), 1441 Pali Hwy., Honolulu, HI 96813, tel. (808) 536-3556, just near the intersection of S. Vineyard Blvd., is a few minutes' walk from downtown Honolulu. You'll find a modern, sterile facility with a pool, shared and single rooms, and communal bathroom; $25 a night, $143 a week, with a $5 key deposit.

YMCA Atherton Branch, 1810 University Ave., Honolulu, tel. (808) 946-0253, is near the University of Hawaii. Men and women students are given long-term residence here during the school year. It's dormitory style, with no recreational facilities. Only during the summertime can you rent a room here. It's the cheapest in town, but there's a three-night minimum and a one-time membership fee of $5.

YWCA Fernhurst (women only), 1566 Wilder Ave., Honolulu, HI 96822, tel. (808) 941-2231, fax 949-0266, e-mail: fernywca@gte.net, just off Manoa Rd., across from the historical Punahou School, offers singles and doubles with shared bath. Daily rates are $30 single or $25 shared. Breakfast and dinner included Mon.-Friday. Long-term stays are paid weekly. Security is 24 hours. Women can stay for up to one year, and many women from around the world add an international flavor. Reserve by phone, fax, or e-mail.

The **Honolulu International Youth Hostel,** 2323 A Seaview Ave., Honolulu, HI 96822, tel. (808) 946-0591, is located near the University of Hawaii. As an official American Youth Hostel, AYH members with identity cards are given priority, but nonmembers are accepted on a space-available day-by-day basis. A bed in a bunk room runs $12.50 a night for members and $15.50 for nonmembers. There are no couples' rooms. The office is open 8 a.m.-noon and again 4 p.m.-midnight. This YH is always busy, but will take reservations by phone with a credit card. For information and noncredit card reservations write to the manager, and include an SASE. For information about AYH and membership cards write American Youth Hostels, 1332 I St. NW, Suite 895, Washington, D.C. 20005.

HOTELS

The **Town Inn** (formerly Kobayashi Hotel) at 250 N. Beretania St., Honolulu, HI 96817, tel. (808) 536-2377, is in Chinatown, and it's an old standby as an inexpensive but clean hotel. It's away from all the Waikiki action, and the spartan, linoleumed rooms rent for under $41.80 or $46.20 for air-conditioning single or double. Plenty of travelers pass through here, and the hotel's restaurant serves authentic Japanese food at moderate prices. Inexpensive.

The **Nakamura Hotel** is a little bit more "uptown" both price- and location-wise. It's at 1140 S. King St., Honolulu, HI 96814, tel. (808) 593-9951. The rooms are well-appointed, carpeted, and have large bathrooms. Some a/c rooms face busy King Street; the *mauka* side rooms

ROBERT NILSEN

Manoa Valley Inn

are quieter, with plenty of breezes to keep you cool. Often you can find a room at this meticulously clean hotel when others are booked up, only because it's out of the mainstream. Rates are $43 s and $48 d. Inexpensive.

The **Pagoda Hotel,** 1525 Rycroft St., Honolulu, HI 96814, tel. (808) 941-6611 or (800) 367-6060, is behind Ala Moana Park between Kapiolani Blvd. and S. King Street. Because this hotel is away from the "action," you get very good value for your money. Rooms with kitchenettes start at about $85, with two-bedroom suites at around $120. Substantial discounts are given to residents. All rooms have TV, a/c, and parking, and there's a swimming pool as well as access to the well-known Pagoda Restaurant. Moderate.

Another in the same category is the **Holiday Inn Waikiki,** at 1830 Ala Moana Blvd., tel. (808) 955-1111. Rooms here are clean, decent, away from the action, and reasonably priced at $93-130. Expensive.

The **Ala Moana Hotel,** 410 Atkinson Dr., Honolulu, HI 96814, tel. (800) 228-3278, on Oahu (808) 955-4811, is another hotel where you're just off the Waikiki strip. It's located just behind Ala Moana Park between Ala Moana and Kapiolani Boulevards, with a walking ramp connecting it directly with the Ala Moana Shopping Center. Rooms start at $120 and go up to around $345 for a two-bedroom suite (six people). There's a/c, TV, swimming pools, an all-night coffee shop, nightclub, and the **Summit Supper Club**

on the top of this 36-story, 1,200-room hotel. Premium.

BED AND BREAKFAST

The **Manoa Valley Inn,** at 2001 Vancouver Dr., Honolulu, HI 96822, tel. (808) 947-6019 or (800) 634-5115, fax (808) 946-6168, offers a magnificent opportunity to lodge in early-century elegance. Formerly the John Guild Inn, this "country inn" is listed on the national and state registers of historic places. Built in 1915 by Milton Moore, an Iowa lumberman, the original structure was a very modest, two-story, boxlike home. It was situated on seven acres, but the demand for land by growing Honolulu has whittled it down to the present half acre or so. Moore sold the house to John Guild in 1919. Guild, a secretary to Alexander and Baldwin, added the third floor and back porch, basically creating the structure that you see today. The home went through several owners and even did a stint as a fraternity house. It ended up as low-priced apartment units until it was rescued and renovated in 1982 by Rick Ralston, the owner of Crazy Shirts and one of Hawaii's successful self-made men, a patron of arts and antiques. He outfitted the house from his warehouse of antiques with furnishings not original to the house, but true to the period. It was sold again in 1990, at which time it went through another refurbishing and landscaping.

Rooms with double beds and a shared bath run a reasonable $99-120, while the larger rooms with private baths and queen- or king-size beds are $140. One suite with a king bed goes for $190, and the detached cottage with its double bed runs $165. A continental breakfast, evening wine and cheese service, and local phone calls are all included in the room charge. Free off-street parking is provided. Check-in is at 3 p.m. and checkout at 11 a.m.

The exemplary continental breakfasts are prepared on the premises. In the morning, the aroma of fresh-brewed coffee wafts up the stairs. The breakfast selections are bran muffins, croissants, little sticky buns, fresh fruit of the season, and hand-squeezed juices. The daily and Sunday newspapers are available. Pick one and sink into the billowy cushions of a wicker chair on the lava-rock-colonnaded back porch. Both inside and out, you'll find coffee tables surrounded by overstuffed chairs and, nearby, decanters of port and sherry and dishes filled with chocolates. Every evening, wine and gourmet cheese, along with crackers and fresh fruits, are presented. Expensive.

FOOD

The restaurants mentioned below are outside of the Waikiki area, although many are close, even within walking distance. Others are located near Ala Moana, Chinatown, downtown, and the less touristed areas of greater Honolulu. Some are first-class restaurants; others, among the best, are just roadside stands where you can get a satisfying plate lunch. The restaurants are listed according to price range and location, with differing cuisines mixed in each range. Besides the sun and surf, it's the amazing array of food found on Oahu that makes the island extraordinary.

SHOPPING CENTER DINING

Ala Moana Shopping Center
The following are all located at the Ala Moana Shopping Center along Ala Moana Boulevard. Most are located in the **Makai Food Court,** a huge central area where you can inexpensively dine on dishes from San Francisco to Tokyo—most for under $10. Counter-style restaurants serve island favorites, reflecting the multiethnic culinary traditions from around the Pacific. You take your dish to a nearby communal dining area, which is great for people-watching. The **China House,** tel. (808) 949-6622, is open daily for lunch and dinner. This enormous dining hall offers the usual selection of Chinese dishes, but is famous for its dim sum (served 11 a.m.-2 p.m.); you pick and choose bite-sized morsels from carts.
Patti's Chinese Kitchen, tel. (808) 946-5002, first floor facing the sea, has all the ambience

you'd expect from a cafeteria-style Chinese fast-food joint, plus lines about a block long. But don't let either discourage you. The lines move incredibly quickly, and you won't get gourmet food, but it's tasty, plentiful, and cheap. The Princess-Queen Special is steamed rice, fried rice or noodles, a chow mein, plus two entrees like sweet and sour pork or a chicken dish—for around $3. The Queen is the same, but add an entree—under $4. You can even have four entrees, which fills two large paper plates. The princesses who eat this much food aren't tiny-waisted damsels waiting for a rescuing prince—they can flatten anyone who hassles them on their own.

Plate lunches, noodle soups, pizza, and a variety of munchies can be ordered from the **Ala Moana Poi Bowl.** The **Aloha Grill** has hot dogs, chili dogs, etc.

Ward Warehouse
This shopping center, located at 1050 Ala Moana Blvd., has a range of restaurants, from practical to semi-chic, all reasonably priced. **Benkei,** tel. (808) 591-8713, is a Japanese restaurant that's beautifully appointed with a rock garden at the entranceway that continues to the inside. It's bright and airy, neo-Japanese traditional. Prices are reasonable, with set menu dishes like *unagi kabayaki* for $12.95, miso-fried fish at $9.25, combination dinners for around $14, and plate lunches for about $6. It has a wide selection of *don buri,* yakitori, and tempura for around $6. Open Mon.-Sat. 11 a.m.-2 p.m. for lunch, and for dinner from 5 p.m. Nearby is the opposite side of

the coin. A small lunch stand sells saimin and yakitori for under $4. Mostly you stand and eat, but there are a few tables in the common mall area. Also, you'll find **Korean Barbecue Express** and **L&L Drive-In** for a quick bite to eat.

The Old Spaghetti Factory, tel. (808) 591-2513, is a huge place that feels a bit like you might imagine a San Francisco eatery at the turn of the century—almost Victorian. It serves a wide variety of pasta not quite like Mama makes, but passable, and at a reasonable price. Try chicken parmigiana for $7.95, spinach and cheese ravioli for $6.50, or meatballs, Italian sausage, and spaghetti with meat sauce for $7.45. Following your meal, linger over an Italian soda, coffee, tea, draft beer, or house wine. Open Mon.-Fri. for lunch, daily for dinner.

More modern, upscale, and expensive is **Kincaid's Fish Chop & Steak House,** tel. (808) 591-2005, with such items on the dinner menu as sirloin steak for $16.95, pasta and roast chicken Dijon for $11.95, and grilled mixed seafood at $18.95. The lunch menu includes many sandwiches in the $7.95-9.95 range, Korean *kalbi* ribs for $9.95, Sonora pork chops with garlic plum sauce for $10.95, and grilled northern Pacific salmon for $13.95. Soups and salads are à la carte, and a few desserts round out the list.

For those into health foods **Aloha Health Food,** primarily a vitamin and mineral store, has some prepared food and drinks in a cooler. Right across is **Coffee Works,** specializing in gourmet coffee and tea. It has a bakery and sandwiches for under $5, croissants $1.50. So take your vitamins on one side and get jazzed on the other. For any number of fresh fruit juices and smoothies try the **Juice Stop.**

Orson's Restaurant, tel. (808) 591-8681, is a seafood house on the second floor. It's actually quite elegant considering the location, with a prize-winning sunset view of the small boat harbor at Kewalo Basin across the way. The inside, too, is richly appointed in wood and glass. Prices are $12-15 for fresh catch of the day complemented by an extensive wine list.

The **Chowder House,** tel. (808) 596-7944, on the ground floor has fresh-grilled *ahi,* snow crab salad, Manhattan clam chowder, bay shrimp cocktail, deep-fried shrimp, daily specials, and an all-you-can-eat crab night on Thursday.

Ward Centre

This upscale shopping center is directly across the street from Ala Moana Park and next door to the Ward Warehouse. The following are some of its restaurants and eateries, where you can enjoy not only class, but quality as well.

R. Field Wine Co. is not really a restaurant, but a purveyor of exquisite food, fine wines, crackers, cookies, cheeses, imported pastas, and caviar. Most of the wines are top shelf Californian like Kiestler, Dominus, Opus I, and Robert Mondavi, with a nice variety of their reserve wines going back to 1968. Older French wines, as well as German wines, are also available, and while you're there peruse the humidor for a fine cigar. Most recent has been the addition of local organic produce and other Hawaiian food products. Look here for something for that special evening.

Chocoholics would rather visit the **Honolulu Chocolate Company** than go to heaven. Mousse truffles, Grand Marnier truffles, chocolate eggs with pistachio or English walnut all will send you into eye-rolling rapture. If you enter, forget any resolve about watching your weight. You're a goner!

For a quick lunch try **Mocha Java Cafe,** a yuppie, upscale, counter-service-type place with a few tables. It has a selection of sandwiches with an emphasis on vegetarian. If you want a designer lunch, that's the place to go.

The premier, or at least best-known, restaurant in the complex is **Keo's Thai Cuisine,** tel. (808) 596-0020, known for its mouthwatering Thai dishes and for its beautiful decor. The menu is extensive, with plenty of dishes for non-meat-eaters. Prices can be quite reasonable for Thai noodles, chicken, shrimp, or vegetarian ($6.95-8.95), house salad ($4.95), green papaya salad ($4.95), spring rolls (four for $4.95), and tofu, shrimp, or chicken satay for under $9. Try the delicious soups like spicy lemongrass or Thai ginger for $3.75 per serving. Entrees like the Evil Jungle Prince have quite a spicy reputation, or tame down with Asian watercress stir-fried with garlic, yellow bean sauce, and beef, shrimp, or veggies ($6.95-8.95). Keo's has another location, 625 Kapahulu, tel. (808) 737-8240, and operates the **Mekong I and II,** simpler and less expensive restaurants, located at 1295 S. Beretania and 1726 S. King St., respectively. Keo's is known for its beautiful flower displays of torch ginger, orchids, or plumeria on every table, and you may eat inside or outside.

The **Yum Yum Tree,** tel. (808) 592-3580, is an affordable American standard restaurant that features pies and cakes from its bakery, along with homestyle fresh pasta. It has an extensive dining area, quite cheerful with dark wood floors, ferns, hanging greenery, and an open-beam ceiling. Breakfast is 7 a.m.-noon, lunch 11 a.m.-5 p.m., dinner 5 p.m. to midnight, cocktails 7 a.m.-closing.

Compadres Mexican Bar and Grill, tel. (808) 591-8307, open Mon.-Fri. 11 a.m.-1 a.m., Sat.-Sun. noon-1 a.m., serves from a smaller, late menu 10 p.m.-1 a.m. Although part of a small chain with restaurants in Maui, Palo Alto, and Napa Valley, Compadres offers made-to-order health-conscious Mexican cuisine that was voted as the Best on Oahu by the small but discerning local Mexican population. The open-beamed dining room overlooking Ala Moana park is a mixture of South Seas and south of the border with plenty of ferns and foliage, round-topped wooden tables, bent-backed chairs upholstered in primary reds and greens, with Mexican masks, bronze parrots and ceramic macaws hanging from the walls and ceilings. The huge menu, featuring handmade tortillas made either from white flour, whole wheat, blue corn, or regular old yellow corn, along with homemade chips and salsa, uses no lard in any of the dishes except carnitas, which are pork anyway. The most unique offerings are the **Quesadillas Internacionales,** priced $7.95-9.95. Flavors vary but include Baja with shrimp, spinach, and Monterey jack cheese; and Texas with chicken or steak and fiery sauce. Joining the international festival are the big, double-handed burritos for $5.95, which include Thai with spicy chicken breast, sprouts, carrots, green onions, cilantro, chili peanut paste, rice, and black beans; Baja with barbecued shrimp, whole beans, fiesta rice, jack cheese, and salsa fresca; and Hawaiian with teriyaki chicken thighs, whole beans, fiesta rice, and pineapple salsa. Besides quesadillas, there are standard burritos, tacos, and plenty of vegetarian selections like the Joy Enchilada, which will make you giggle all the way to Tijuana, or Compadres Tostada filled with beans, avocado, fresh salsa, and chopped olives. No dish is more than $16.50. The bar complements the meal with a full selection of domestic and imported beer, a selection of microbrewery beers like Samuel Adams and Sierra Nevada, 10 different kinds of tequila, margaritas by the glass or pitcher, and island exotic drinks for under $5. Compadres is an excellent choice for a "budget gourmet" meal in a hospitable atmosphere where the prices are right and the service excellent. There's even live music offered now and again. You can't go wrong!

Ryan's Grill, tel. (808) 591-9132, open daily 11:15 a.m.-1:45 a.m., is an ultramodern yet comfortable establishment appointed with black leather chairs, chrome railings, marble-topped tables, and a hardwood floor, which are all dominated by a huge bar and open kitchen. The menu offers standards along with nouveau cuisine and includes onion soup ($4.95), sesame chicken salad ($8.95), and tossed fettuccine with sliced breast of chicken and Cajun sauce ($11.95). Sandwiches are everything from hot Dungeness crab to a grilled chicken club, all for about $10. More substantial meals from the grill include Cajun seafood jambalaya ($11.95). The bar prepares all of the usual exotic drinks and has plenty of draft beer selections from which to choose. Most menu items along with plenty of munchies and *pu pu* are served until 1 a.m., so Ryan's Grill makes a perfect late night stop!

Offering pizza, pasta, and (as they say) pizzazz, **Scoozees a Go Go Bakery and Deli,** tel. (808) 597-1777, is a modern and tasteful restaurant and deli. Imported pastas, prosciutto, cheese, stromboli, and fresh baked goods are available from the counter. Menu items include Italian sausage and pepper sandwich or marinated chicken breast grilled with orange macadamia nut pesto for $8.50, and a multitude of pastas and pizzas for around $8-10. Italian desserts, soft drink, coffees, and smoothies round out what's available. Hours are Sun.-Thurs. 11 a.m.-10 p.m., Fri.-Sat. 11 a.m.-11 p.m.

Sushi Masa, tel. (808) 593-2007, serves reasonable Japanese food like tempura, shrimp, and vegetables for $9.50, chicken teriyaki for $7.75, and tanuki udon for $6.50. You can get a sashimi combination plate for $22 or a sushi special for $16.50-18.50.

Aloha Tower Marketplace

A few years ago, a law was passed in Hawaii allowing beer to be sold at the place at which it was made. This allowed breweries to open pubs on premises. **Gordon-Biersch Brewery & Restaurant,** tel. (808) 599-4877, open Sun.-Wed. 11 a.m.-10 p.m., Thurs.-Sat. until 11 p.m., has taken advantage of this opportunity and opened a fine establishment at the Aloha Tower Marketplace. Three beers are brewed here: GB Export, a smooth, medium hop, full-bodied beer similar to a pilsner but less bitter; GB Marzen, an Oktoberfest beer with a little extra oomph from a combination of malts; and GB Dunkles, a dark beer, the house specialty, served unfiltered in the old Bavarian tradition. Aside from these beers, there is a selection of wines, coffees, soft drinks, milk, and juices, but no tropical mixed drinks. A short brewery tour is given free every Saturday at noon. Plan to stay for lunch. The lunch and dinner menus are similar, aside from the sandwiches offered at lunch, but lunch prices are about 25% less. Appetizers include garlic fries for $3.95 and sashimi for $12.95, and the small pizzas run $8.95-9.95. These and the various salads are just preparation for the main courses. Try the risotto with grilled vegetables, Italian sausage, Japanese eggplant, and rosemary and black olive bruchetta for $14.95; the guava-glazed roast duck with scallions, noodle cake, and braised greens for $16.95; or the pan-seared *ahi* tuna on a bed of linguini tossed with anchovies, capers, oregano, and arugula for $18.95. An assortment of wonderful desserts tops off the meal. Dine inside or out. Inside, with its leather booths, is more elegant and quieter for conversation. In the more casual alfresco portico, sit at stout wooden tables under canvas umbrellas and watch the tugboats shuttle ships through the harbor as the lights of the city sparkle across the water. The inside bar is good for a quiet drink, while you can boogie at the outside bar, where different bands come to play every night—never a cover.

Restaurant Row

This new-age complex at 500 Ala Moana Blvd. (across from the Federal Building) points the way to "people-friendly" development in Honolulu's future. It houses shops and businesses, but mostly restaurants, all grouped together around a central courtyard and strolling area. Some restaurants are elegant and excellent, while others are passable and plain. But they are all in a congenial setting, and you can pick your palate and style preference as easily as you'd pick offerings at a buffet. Start at the central fountain area with its multicolored modernistic Lego-inspired tower. Every Saturday at 8 p.m. jazz is offered here overlooking the waterfront.

The **Sunset Grill,** tel. (808) 521-4409, is on the corner. With wraparound windows, a long and open bar, and comfortable maple chairs, it lives up to its name. This is the place to come for a quiet evening drink in the downtown area. The food is prepared in full view on a *kiawe*-fired grill, wood-roasting oven, and Italian rotisserie. Choices include a variety of pasta, gourmet salads, calamari, fresh fish, oysters, chicken, veal, and lamb. Lunch is a wide variety of plump juicy sandwiches of turkey, sausage, beef, fish, or chicken. The chefs at the Sunset aren't afraid to blend East with West in a wide variety of creations. Open daily 11 a.m.-11 p.m., Fri.-Sat. 11 a.m.-midnight, and Sunday 9:30 a.m.-10 p.m.

In the middle of the complex is **The Row,** an outdoor bar with finger food. The **Honolulu Chocolate Co.** is next. Like a smug little devil, it tempts with chocolate truffles, mocha clusters, and fancy nut rolls. So sin! You're on vacation. The **Paradise Bakery Cafe** is a simple counter restaurant with pie, coffee, and donuts.

Prima Trattoria offers very special Italian dishes from the Abruzzi, a coastal and mountainous region along the Adriatic known for its hearty cooking. Choose an antipasto from Italian cold cuts to clams in red wine sauce for $7 and under. Assorted soups and salads range from $3 to $6 for *insalata calamari.* Select your favorite pasta, and then cover it with one of 201 delectable sauces, most under $10. Chicken, veal, and steak are grilled, simmered in wine sauce, or made into parmigiana, or choose a traditional lasagna, *gnocchi,* or a good old pizza. The interior is sharp with neon strips and black marble tables and chairs.

A few others in the Row include **Jamaican Cuisine Bar and Grill, Kin Chan Sushi,** and the **Payao Thai Restaurant.**

INEXPENSIVE DINING
AROUND TOWN

The following restaurants are located in and around the greater Honolulu area.

In central Honolulu, mostly along Bishop Street's financial district, you'll find excellent and inexpensive restaurants that cater to the district's lunch crowd.

At the corner of Pali Hwy. and Vineyard is **People's Cafe,** tel. (808) 536-5789. Run by Newton and Adelle Oshiro, two going on three generations of the same Japanese family have been serving the full range of excellent and inexpensive Hawaiian food at this down-home restaurant. Plate lunches and other lunches run about $5.50. Combination lunches like the Laulau plate, which is lomi salmon, pipikaula, chicken luau or chicken long rice, poi or rice, are $9-9.50 and served on sectioned trays. While there's no decor to speak of, the place is clean and the people are very friendly. If you want a real Hawaiian meal at a reasonable price, this is the place to come. It's not fancy, but the food is good and the surroundings clean. The People's Cafe is open Mon-Sat. 10:30 a.m.-7:30 p.m.

Down to Earth Natural Foods and Deli, tel. (808) 947-7678, open Mon.-Sat. 10 a.m.-8:30 p.m., Sunday 10 a.m.-6 p.m., at 2525 S. King St., is a kind of "museum of health food stores" serving filling, nutritious health food dishes for very reasonable prices. Sandwiches, like a whopping avocado, tofu, and cheese, are under $5. Daily full-meal specials, like veggie stroganoff, eggplant parmigiana, and lasagna are around $4, including salad. There are plenty of items on the menu that will fill you up for under $3. Healthwise, you can't go wrong!

Kokua Market, tel. (808) 941-1922, at the corner of S. Beretania and Isenberg, is open to the public Mon.-Sat. 9 a.m.-8:30 p.m. It's a full-service store with organic and fresh produce, cheese, milk, juices, bulk foods, breads, and a deli case full of sandwiches and other prepared foods.

Suehiro's at 1824 S. King, tel. (808) 949-4584, open daily for lunch and dinner, with take-out service, gets the nod from local Japanese people. The menu here is authentic, the decor strictly Americana, and the food well prepared and moderately priced.

Another of the same is the **Hungry Lion Coffee Shop,** tel. (808) 536-1188, at 1613 Nuuanu Avenue. Open 24 hours, it serves everything from Asian food to steaks. Many local people come here after a night out. Nothing special, but decent wholesome food on formica tables.

At the Hawaii Maritime Center you'll find the seafood establishment **Pier Seven Restaurant** tucked away in the rear overlooking Honolulu Harbor. More interesting and definitely more local is **Pier Eight Restaurant** sandwiched under the huge elevated pier area just nearby the Maritime Center. Basic, Chinese, fast food to go, open daily 10 a.m.-5 p.m.

The **University of Hawaii,** Manoa Campus, hosts a number of restaurants, ranging from an inexpensive cafeteria to international cuisine at the East-West Center. Inexpensive to moderate restaurants include: **Manoa Gardens,** salad and snacks; **Campus Center Dining Room,** for full meals; and the **International Garden,** at Jefferson Hall in the East-West Center.

Sekiya's Restaurant and Deli at 2746 Kaimuki Ave. tel. (808) 732-1656, looks like a set from a 1940s tough-guy movie. The food is well prepared and the strictly local clientele will be amazed that you even know about the place. Closed Monday.

Hale Vietnam, 1140 12th Ave. in Kaimuki, tel. (808) 735-7581, is building an excellent reputation for authentic and savory dishes at very moderate prices. It gets the highest praise from local people, who choose it again and again for an inexpensive evening of delicious dining. Hours are daily 11 a.m.-9:45 p.m.

Penny's Lunch Wagon, on the Sand Island Access Rd., tel. (808) 845-6503, is one of the least expensive and most authentic Hawaiian plate-lunch stands you can find. The most expensive lunch is *lau lau,* pork and butterfish wrapped in a ti leaf, at around $4. You can also try baseball-sized *manapua* for around 60 cents. Penny's is out of the way, but definitely worth a stop.

You can't get much cheaper than free, and that's what the **International Society for Krishna Consciousness** offers every Sunday at 5:30 p.m. for its vegetarian smorgasbord. Their two-acre compound is just off the Pali Hwy. at 51 Coelho Way, tel. (808) 595-5339. Of course there're a few chants for dessert. *Hare Krishna!*

lunch wagon

For **shave ice** try the **Waiola Store,** on the corner of Paani and Waiola. You can get it in Waikiki, but for the real stuff in all its syrupy glory come here.

Art and the Sandwich

In Honolulu there are a few opportunities to feed your mind and soul along with satiating your appetite.

The **Garden Cafe,** at the Honolulu Academy of Arts, 900 S. Beretania, tel. (808) 532-8734, is a classy place for lunch. Open Tues.-Sat. 11 a.m.-2:30 p.m. The cafe has grown from a volunteer operation to serving a full luncheon under professional management. Dine inside or out; it's a fine place to get away from the hustle and bustle of the city. Menu items include a chilled tomato and avocado soup with coriander garnish for $3.75, soup or salad and half sandwich for $7.35, and a turkey sandwich for $8.25. An assortment of desserts, beverages, and drinks can also be ordered. The food is delicious, but be aware that the portions are not for the hungry, being designed primarily for patrons of the arts who seem to be wealthy matrons from the fashionable sections of Honolulu who are all watching their waistlines.

Don't let the Porsches, Mercedeses, and BMWs parked vanity plate to vanity plate in the parking lot discourage you from enjoying the **Contemporary Cafe,** tel. (808) 523-3362 (reservations recommended), at the Contemporary Museum, 2411 Makiki Heights Drive. The small but superb menu is as inspired as the art in the museum, and the prices are astonishingly inexpensive. Dine inside or out, or perch on the porch. Appetizers are sautéed mushrooms, fruit, or smoked salmon for under $10. Salads include home-smoked mahimahi and papaya vinaigrette salad, Malaysian shrimp salad, Greek salad, or chicken salad for under $11. Sandwiches are a fine selection including smoked breast of turkey or *ahi* Caesar for under $10. Desserts run from cheesecake to flourless chocolate roulade, and beverages include homemade lemonade and cappuccino. For a wonderful cultural outing combined with a memorable lunch, come to the Contemporary Cafe. Open Tues.-Sat 11 a.m.-2 p.m. for the main menu, and 2-3 p.m. for drinks and desserts only. Sunday hours are noon-3 p.m. It's just so . . . contemporary! When in downtown Honolulu, check out the branch Contemporary Cafe at the First Hawaiian Center near Bishop and Market Streets.

HAWAIIAN REGIONAL CUISINE

As large a city as Honolulu is, it's able to support many innovative restaurants where locally grown foods are combined with preparation techniques from around the world to produce new and intriguing flavors. The following are restaurants where something new is always on the menu and the combination of ingredients, textures, and tastes is sure to please. Reservations are recommended.

Located in the semi-industrial area of Iwilei, **Sam Choy's Breakfast, Lunch, and Crab,** tel. (808) 732-8645, is as popular as every other Sam Choy restaurant in the islands. The Kona poke and beef stew omelettes are much-requested breakfast items, while various crab entrees appear for dinner depending on the season. Always generous portions at reasonable prices.

Indigo, 1121 Nuuanu Ave. in Chinatown, tel. (808) 521-2900, serves what some classify as Eurasian cuisine. Chef Glenn Chu offers such savory items as Chinese steamed buns filled with eggplant and sun-dried tomatoes, crispy goat cheese wonton filled with fruit sauce, fresh corn polenta, or grilled Atlantic salmon with tomato salsa and shiitake mushroom pepper relish. Some vegan items available.

Located at the Ward Center is **A Pacific Cafe,** tel. (808) 593-0035, where Chef Jean Marie Josselin creates tasty treats like spinach and wild mushroom cannelloni, Australian salmon with Moroccan spice and lentils, and *opakapaka* crusted with porcini and fresh herbs with fennel and sun-dried tomato Israeli couscous.

For two years running, **Alan Wong's** has been awarded Best Restaurant of the Year by the *Honolulu Magazine*. Here you can try such delicacies as shredded *kalua* pig wrapped in taro pancake on poi vinaigrette with lomi tomato relish, grilled lamb chops with coconut macadamia nut crust, or a vegetarian entree consisting of mashed potatoes, black bean salsa, grilled asparagus, and roasted shiitake mushrooms. Yum! Alan Wong's is located just north of Waikiki at 1857 S. King St., tel. (808) 949-2526.

At 3660 Waialea Ave. near where the road crests the hill in Kaimuki is **3660 On The Rise,** tel. (808) 737-1177, a casually elegant place where you can watch the cooks create behind the glass wall of the kitchen. While the menu changes somewhat every night, Chef Russel Siu's "first flavors" include frizzled shrimp wrapped in shredded phyllo pastry or potato crusted crab cakes, while "second flavors" are soups and salads. "Feature presentations" might be shichimi seared breast of chicken with shiitake mushrooms and soy citrus butter sauce or Chinese steamed fillet of *opakapaka* lightly seared and simmered in a Chinese black bean broth. Round out your meal with one of the "sweet endings": harlequin crème brûlée or mile-high Wailea pie,

perhaps, or indulge in a cup of coffee or glass of cognac or port. Delightful presentation and attentive service. Open Sunday and Tues.-Thurs. 5:30-9:30 p.m., Friday and Saturday until 10 p.m., closed Monday.

The newest fine restaurant to enter the market is **Chef Mavro Restaurant,** 1969 S. King St., tel. (808) 944-4714. Formerly the executive chef of the Four Seasons Resort on Maui and prior to that the executive chef at the Halekulani in Waikiki, chef Mavro offers a mix of à la carte and prix fixe menu options. No matter what you choose, the freshest of Hawaiian produce and seafood are always infused with subtle yet intense flavors and prepared with a French flare, resulting in a tropical cuisine with a French soul.

MODERATE DINING AROUND TOWN

The following listings are for restaurants where two can dine for around $40, not including drinks.

Fisherman's Wharf, tel. (808) 538-3808, at 1009 Ala Moana Blvd. on the Kewalo Basin, is a Honolulu institution. This restaurant has been here since 1952, when it took over from Felix's Italian Garden Restaurant, which had been on this spot since the '40s. The restaurant's design gives you the feel of being aboard ship. Its theme is nautical, displaying a collection of ship's accessories, riggings, and figurines, and trophy catches from the sea. Even a few unique museum-quality items adorn the walls. The place exudes the feel of a Honolulu of days past, and you can sit and watch through the windows as fishing boats and cruise ships arrive and depart as they have done for decades, or look out past Waikiki to Diamond Head. Upon entering the first floor Seafood Grotto, you pass a live lobster tank. For lunch, start with shrimp cocktail or oysters on the half shell for under $9. Follow this with Boston-style clam chowder at $3.50 a bowl and a Caesar salad for $4.95. Sandwiches range $5.95-11.95, or choose fresh fish done in a variety of ways at market price, mahimahi strips for $7.95, batter-fried mahi, shrimp, scallops, and clam strips for $11.95, or one of the special entrees from chicken stir-fry to seafood medley $13.95-29.75. The dinner menu is similar, but without the sandwiches and with the addition of pastas and other special entrees. Some additional dinner dishes are seafood parmesan, shrimp curry, combination filet mignon with king crab or shrimp, seafood medley, and lobster for $15.25-27.95. Upstairs, the Captain's Bridge is like a cabaret club that serves light meals, soups, and salads, with a full range of drinks. Friday and Saturday nights there's karaoke, so come up and dance.

The Hideaway Restaurant, at La Mariana Yacht Sailing Club, 50 Sand Island Access Rd., is the only real restaurant on Sand Island. Henry, for many years a ship's cook, can cook everything well—maybe not great, but well. If a Chinese person came here and wanted chop suey Henry could do it. If a guy wanted steak and potatoes, you got it! Pasta? Here it is! The Hideaway serves appetizers like sashimi, lumpia, and sautéed mushroom buttons. From the broiler come steaks, pork chops, and burgers with all the fixings; the most expensive is $14.95. From the sea, seafood brochette, shrimp scampi served over linguini, or *ahi* Cajun style fill your plate. Chicken, lobster, and nightly specials fill out the menu. The lunch menu is simpler, with soups, salads, hot and cold sandwiches, and a handful of fish and stir-fry selections. Henry is also known for his onion rings. They're not on the menu; you have to know about them. Now you know.

While the decor has recently been upgraded, it's still very Polynesian and nautical in essence. Inside hang Japanese glass floats that at night are diffused with different colors, providing mood lighting for the cozy black booths and wooden tables with wicker chairs, tiki posts, and decorations scavenged from defunct former restaurants in town. The Hideaway is an out-of-the-way place, local, and real Hawaiiana. Located at a working marina, this is where all the yachties come. Half hidden behind a stand of trees, there is only one small sign at the entrance to point the way. The restaurant serves food Mon.-Fri. 11:30 a.m.-2 p.m. and 5-9 p.m. and Sat.-Sun. noon-5 p.m. On Friday and Saturday 9 p.m.-midnight, Ron Miyashiro and Singers croon the night away to piano music so stop by for a drink at the bar and enjoy.

Shiruhachi, at 1901 Kapiolani Blvd., tel. (808) 947-4680, is a completely authentic Japanese sushi bar operated by Hiroshi Suzuki. As a matter of fact, until recently 90% of the clientele was

Japanese, either visiting businessmen or locals in the know, and the menu was only in Japanese. However, everyone is more than welcome. With a beer, you get free *otsumami* (nibbles), with a wide selection of sushi and other finger foods like yakitori at about $2 for two skewers. A separate section of the restaurant turns into a cocktail lounge, somewhat like an *akachochin,* a neighborhood Japanese bar where people go to relax. There's taped music and a dance floor. If you're into authentic Japanese, this is a great one.

Auntie Pasto's, at 1099 S. Beretania and the corner of Pensacola, tel. (808) 523-8855, is open Mon.-Thurs. 11 a.m.-2:30 p.m., Friday 11 a.m.-11 p.m., Saturday 4-11 p.m., and Sunday and holidays 4-10:30 p.m. The vibe is upbeat pizza parlor, where you can even bring your own wine. Most of the Italian menu entrees are $8.50-12, and these include eggplant parmesan for $8.50, calamari steak for $9.25, and veal marsala for $11.95. Soups come by the cup, $1.95, or bowl, $2.50; the large salads range from a $2.95 garden salad to a chicken Caesar for $6.95. Antipasto plates, sides, and desserts run $3-6. No reservations necessary, quiet, comfortable.

Wo Fat's, at 115 N. Hotel St., tel. (808) 533-6393, has had a little experience satisfying customers—the oldest eatery in Chinatown, it's been at the same location for more than 80 years, and open for business for 100! Besides serving delicious food from a menu with hundreds of Cantonese dishes, the building itself is monumentally ornate. You're entertained just checking out the decor of lanterns, dragons, gilt work, and screens. Most dishes are reasonably priced and start at around $5. This restaurant is highly respected by the people of Chinatown and is part of the Chinatown tour offered by the chamber of commerce.

EXPENSIVE DINING AROUND TOWN

Sometimes only the best will do, and Honolulu can match any city for its fine restaurants. For more fine dining see the Waikiki chapter.

Won Kee Seafood Restaurant, 100 N. Beretania, tel. (808) 524-6877, is a splurge joint where you get delicious seafood. Free parking on Maunakea Street. This is the place for Honolulu's in-the-know crowd. Tasteful and elegant surroundings.

Right next door to the Won Kee is the **Forum Restaurant,** tel. (808) 599-5022. Open daily 11 a.m.-2:30 p.m. and 5-11 p.m., this too is a classy joint with everything from the usual rice dishes to braised imperial shark fin soup for $38 per person.

The **Legend Seafood Restaurant,** tel. (808) 532-1868, two doors down from the Won Kee, emphasizes fish and seafood, but also serves Hong Kong-style dim sum for $1.50, $2.40, $3.25, and $4.25 for small, medium, large, and super size plates, respectively.

The Chart House, at 1765 Ala Moana Blvd. near Ala Wai Yacht Harbor, tel. (808) 941-6660, is open daily 4 p.m. (Sunday 5 p.m.) till 2 a.m. It offers a happy hour until 7 p.m., pu pu until midnight, and nightly entertainment. Shellfish specialties start at $15, with chicken and beef dishes a few dollars cheaper.

India House, 2632 S. King St., is open daily for lunch and dinner, tel. (808) 955-7552. Extraordinary Indian dishes are prepared by chef Ram Arora. A wide selection of curries, vegetarian dishes, special naan bread, kabobs, and fish tikka. Specialty desserts include homemade ice cream and toppings.

Keo's Thai Cuisine, 625 Kapahulu, tel. (808) 737-8240, open nightly 5:30-11 p.m., has become an institution. It serves great Thai food at expensive prices. They pride themselves on the freshest ingredients and spices tuned up or down to suit the customer, and Keo's recipes are taught to each chef personally. There's always a line, with a few benches in the parking lot for waiting customers, but no reservations are taken. The eight-page menu offers most of Thailand's delectables, and vegetarians are also catered to. You can save money and still have the same quality food at **Mekong I and II.** Also owned by Keo's, they're not as fancy.

ENTERTAINMENT

Dancing, Disco, and Lounge Acts
Anna Bannana's, at 2440 S. Beretania, tel. (808) 946-5190, is the "top banana" for letting your hair down and boogying the night away. It's out by the university just across from Star Market. This dance joint has a laid-back atmosphere, reasonable beer prices, a small cover which goes to the band, no dress code, and a friendly student crowd. Dancing is upstairs, light dining downstairs, and a backyard to cool off between sets. Great place, great fun!

The **Club Jubilation,** at 1007 Dillingham Blvd., tel. (808) 845-1568, sways with Hawaiian music every night but Monday. Listen to hula tunes on traditional and quickly fading slack-key guitar. People from the audience, when moved by the music, will take to the dance floor or the stage for an impromptu performance. What they lack in polish they make up for in sincerity. Everybody's welcome. Beer around $3, with plenty of pu pu, like watercress with mayonnaise and soy sauce, along with regular island munchies.

Ocean Club (formerly Studebaker's) at Restaurant Row, 500 Ala Moana, tel. (808) 526-9888, is Honolulu's newest hot spot. Open from late afternoon to early morning, except Sunday and Monday.

Rumours Nightclub, in the Ala Moana Hotel, 410 Atkinson St., tel. (808) 955-4811, is an established disco that cranks up around 9 p.m. and features the newest in dance and rock videos.

Also along Restaurant Row is **Blue Zebra,** a popular disco nightclub with a good dance floor, a fine selection of music, and a reasonable dress code. Blue Zebra is open seven nights a week until the wee hours of the morning.

Nearby, find the **World Cafe** nightclub. The dance floor and pool tables draw a blend of locals and tourists.

The **Fast Zone** at the Fort Street Mall generally draws a younger crowd, many of them students from Hawaii Pacific University. There's no dancing, but it's a place to have a beer and conversation and listen to the strains of hard core alternative music.

TGI Fridays, 950 Ward Ave., tel. (808) 523-5841, is a lively night spot. Good food, large portions, reasonable prices, and music.

Pecos River Cafe, at 99-016 Kamehameha Hwy., tel. (808) 487-7980, has country music by local country bands. On Wednesday evening instructors teach country line dancing and square dancing. Have a few lessons so you can dance to the live band with confidence.

The **Pier Bar** at the Aloha Tower Marketplace has an elevated stage with live acts throughout the week, ranging from Hawaiian to contemporary rock to R&B. The music is potluck, but you're right on the harbor, so you can watch the sunset and always have a great time.

Note: Also see the Waikiki chapter.

Girlie Bars and Strip Joints

You'll have no excuse if your maiden Aunt Matilda or local chapter of Fed Up Feminists Inc. ever catches you going into one of these joints, sonny boy! There's not even a hint of a redeeming social value here, and the only reason they're listed is to let you know where *not to go.* Many of these "lounges," as they're called, are strung along the 1600 and 1700 blocks of Kapiolani Blvd., and in the little alleys running off it. Mostly, tough-looking Asian men own or operate them, and they open and shut quicker than a streetwalker's heart. Inside are two types of women: the dancers and the lap sitters, and there's definitely a pecking order in these henhouses. Most patrons are local men or GI types, with only a smattering of tourists. Personal safety is usually not a problem, but a fool and his money are soon parted in these bars.

Chinatown's **Hotel Street** has hookers, both male and female, walking the heels off their shoes. They cruise during the day, but the area really comes alive at night. Mostly, these people are down-and-outers who can't make it against the stiff competition along the main areas of Waikiki. The clientele is usually servicemen and hard-core locals. A few clubs in this area offer strippers. Always be prepared for fights and bad vibes in any of these joints.

Freebies

At **Centerstage,** Ala Moana Center, various shows are presented-mostly music (rock, gospel, jazz, Hawaiian) and hula. Performances usually start at noon. The **Young People's Hula Show,** every Sunday at 9:30 a.m., is fast becoming an institution. Here, hula is being kept alive, with many first-time performers interpreting the ancient movements that they study in their *halau.*

The **Royal Hawaiian Band,** founded more than 150 years ago, performs Friday at noon on the Iolani Palace Bandstand, and on Sunday at 12:45 p.m. and 2 p.m. at the Kapiolani Bandstand. Call (808) 527-5666 for other band performance locations.

Everyone is invited to enjoy the **Friday noon-time music** at Tamarind Park, on the corner of King and Bishop Streets, where anything from pop to traditional may be performed.

Honolulu Hale (City Hall) presents periodic free musical concerts in the central courtyard and art exhibitions in the central courtyard, Lane Gallery, or Third Floor Gallery. All are welcome.

Various hula and other cultural programs are performed around dusk on Saturday and Sunday at the Kuhio Beach Banyan Tree Park.

Sometimes the University has free noontime shows at the student center and evening musical concerts at the Manoa Gardens restaurant. Call the information center, tel. (808) 956-7235, for current happenings.

Hilo Hattie, 700 Nimitz Hwy., the largest manufacturer of alohawear in the state, conducts free tours of the factory, complete with complimentary shuttle ride from Waikiki (the shuttle also passes Dole Cannery Square). Up to 40,000 garments are on display in the showroom, plus countless gifts and souvenirs. It's hard to resist spending: prices and craftsmanship are good, and designs are the most contemporary. Open daily 7 a.m.-6 p.m., tel. (808) 537-2926 or (800) 272-5282.

SHOPPING

If you don't watch the time, you'll spend half your vacation moving from one fascinating store to the next. Luckily, in greater Honolulu the majority of shopping is clustered in malls, with specialty shops scattered around the city, especially in the nooks and crannies of Chinatown. For a general overview of what the island has for sale, along with listings for bookstores, food outlets, flea markets, sundries, and art shops, see **Shopping** in the Honolulu introduction.

Ala Moana Shopping Center

This is the largest shopping center in the state, and if you want to get all of your souvenir hunting and special shopping done in one shot, this is the place. It's on Ala Moana Blvd. just across from the Ala Moana Beach Park, open weekdays 9:30 a.m.-9 p.m., Saturday 9:30 a.m.-5:30 p.m., Sunday 10 a.m.-5 p.m., tel. (808) 946-2811. Recently, the Ala Moana Shopping Center has taken off its comfortable Hawaiian shirt and shorts and donned designer fashions by Christian Dior and Charles Jordan. Local people are irritated, and they have a point, to a point. The center has plenty of down-home shopping left, but it now caters as much to the penthouse as it does to the one-room efficiency. It used to be where the *people* shopped, but now portions are being aimed at the affluent tourist, especially the affluent Japanese tourists who flaunt designer labels like politicians flaunt pretty secretaries. If anything, the shopping has gotten better, but you'll have to look around a bit more for bargains.

Plenty of competition keeps prices down, with more than enough of an array to suit any taste and budget. There are about 200 stores including all of Hawaii's major department stores like **Sears, JCPenney,** and **Liberty House.** Utilitarian shops like shoe makers, eateries, banks, and boutiques feature everything from flowers to swim fins. It's also a great place to see a cross-section of Hawaiian society. Another pleasantry is a free hula show every Sunday at 9:30 a.m. on the Centerstage. The **Hawaii Visitors Bureau** maintains an information kiosk just near Centerstage. The following is a mere sampling of what you'll find.

The restaurants in the **Makai Food Court** are exceptional, if not for taste, at least for price, and are unbelievable for the variety of cuisines represented. In a huge open area you'll find dishes from Bangkok to Acapulco, from Tokyo to San Francisco. Most of these restaurants have only counters for ordering, with tables in a common dining area. Great for people-watching, too!

House of Music, tel. (808) 949-1051, sells records and tapes. On the ground floor, this is a good store to shop for those island sounds that'll immediately conjure up images of Hawaii whenever they're played.

The Honolulu Book Shop, tel. (808) 941-2274, has the one of the largest selection of books in the state, especially in the Hawaiiana section. Books make inexpensive, easy-to-transport, and long-lasting mementos of your trip to Hawaii. Ground level near Centerstage.

Francis Camera Shop, tel. (808) 973-4480, is a well-stocked camera store with a fine selection of merchandise sure to please the most avid camera buff. If you need something out of the ordinary for your camera bag, this is a good place to come. The staff is friendly and will spend time giving you advice. However, the best place to buy film is at **Sears** (no credit cards). **Longs Drugs** also has good prices, but for cheap and fast developing try **Fromex One Hour Photo,** tel. (808) 955-4797, street level, ocean side.

The Crack Seed Center, tel. (808) 949-7200, offers the best array of crackseed (spiced nuts, seeds, and fruits) that have been treats for island children for years. There're also dried and spiced scallops at $68 per pound and cuttlefish at $2.50 per pound—such a deal! Prices are inflated here, but the selection can't be beat, and you can educate yourself about these same products in smaller stores around the island. Crackseed is not to everyone's liking, but it does make a unique souvenir. Spirolina hunters can get their organic fix at **Vim and Vigor,** featuring vitamins, supplements, and minerals.

Shirokiya is a Japanese-owned department store between JCPenney and Liberty House on the mountain side of the complex. It has a fascinating assortment of gadgetry, knickknacks, handy items, and nifty stuff that Nippon is so famous for. It's fun just to look around, and the prices are reasonable. Japanese products are also available at **S.M. Iida Limited,** tel. (808) 973-0320, a local store dating back to the turn of the century, featuring garden ornaments and flower-arrangement sets.

Specialty shops in the center include **Hawaii Too** and **Irene's Hawaiian Gifts,** selling a wide assortment of island-made goods and souvenirs, from cheap to exquisite; **Tahiti Imports,** with bikinis, muumuu, and a wide selection of handicrafts from throughout Polynesia; and **Jeans Warehouse** for you aloha buckaroos.

Ward Warehouse

Located just a few blocks west of Ala Moana Center, at 1050 Ala Moana Blvd., open weekdays 10 a.m.-9 p.m., Saturday 10 a.m.-5 p.m., Sunday 11 a.m.-4 p.m., tel. (808) 591-8411, this modern two-story complex lives up to its name as a warehouse, with a motif from bygone days when stout wooden beams were used instead of steel. The wide array of more than 75 shops here includes a number of inexpensive restaurants, but the emphasis is on arts and crafts.

Give the tots their first lesson in impulse buying at **Hello Kiddie's,** a toy store, or show them how a pro does it by wandering into **Blue Ginger** for men's and women's fashionable alohawear.

Repent past gluttonies at **Aloha Health Food,** primarily a vitamin and mineral store. Or dress your feet at **Thongs 'n Things,** with everything in thongs from spiked golfing thongs to Teva sandals, the best all-around footwear for the island.

Other shops include **Runners Route,** selling jogging shoes, shorts, and some backpacks; **Island Sunspot** and **Villa Roma** for ladies' fashions; and **Beyond the Beach,** which stocks men's and women's alohawear, casual clothing, and sunglasses.

Perhaps the premier shop in the Warehouse is **Nohea Gallery** (*nohea* means beautiful or handsome in Hawaiian), tel. (808) 596-0074, owned and operated by Gail and Lorie Baron, who personally choose for display works by more than 500 local artists and craftspeople. Some of the finest works are created by more than 100 island woodworkers who make everything from rocking chairs and rolltop desks to traditional canoe paddles using rich grained woods like koa, mango, and rosewood. One of the most ac-

claimed woodworkers on display is **Kelly Dunn,** who, from his shop in Hawi on the Big Island, turns out bowls from Norfolk Island pine that are so thin you can actually see through them. Other artists displaying their talents include: Kurt McVay, who creates masterpieces in glass primarily in cobalt blues and emerald greens highlighted with daubs of oranges and yellows; Diana Lehr, who uses oils and pastels to capture the dramatic skyscapes and colors of Hawaii's sunsets and sunrises; Fabienne Blanc, who works in ultravibrant watercolors creating surrealistic close-up images of plants and foliage; Russell Lowrey, Fabienne's husband, who watercolors and pastels, creating soft, feminine images of the islands; a very talented local couple, under the name of Ulana O Kukui, make beautiful jewelry such as rings of gold and silver that they fashion like traditional *lau hala* weaving along with fused and blown glass, and woven baskets of all natural materials; and Rick Mills, a University of Hawaii professor, another glass artist who favors cobalt blue. Distinctive and affordable treasures include backgammon games, jewelry boxes, bowls, all kinds of jewelry, prints, and even distinctive postcards. Nohea Gallery is where you can see the "heart of Hawaii" through the eyes of its artists. Have a look!

The **Ward Farmer's Market** is just across the street, at 1020 Auahi, where you can pick up fresh produce and flowers. Down the street at 1116 Auahi St. is **Ward Village Shops,** and more shops are located nearby in **Ward Gateway Center** at 333 Ward Avenue.

Ward Centre

Across the street from the Ward Warehouse, this relatively new shopping center is gaining a reputation for some exclusive shops. The Ward Centre, tel. (808) 531-6411, open weekdays 10 a.m.-9 p.m., Saturday 10 a.m.-5 p.m., Sunday 11 a.m.-4 p.m., is appointed in light wood and accentuated by brick floors that give the feeling of an intimate inside mall, although much is outside.

The Colonnade is a cluster of shops inside the Ward Centre. It includes **Willowdale Galleries,** twinkling with elegant antiques, crystal place settings, chandeliers, and even candelabra for those closet Liberace wannabes. It's like looking into a giant china closet filled with the best place settings and crystal.

Art A La Carte is a 12-member co-op featuring the works of well known island artists including Gail Bakutis, Cindy Conklin, Helen Iaea, and Masao Yamanoha. Hanging on the walls are landscapes, seascapes, and a variety of portraits done in oils, paper, and watercolors, while cases hold the distinctive *raku*-style ceramics of Carl Fieber.

You can find that just-right gift at **Gems of the Pacific,** which mainly deals in coral and black onyx jewelry. **Size Me Petite** is for the smaller women and young girls, and **Allure** offers designer bikinis and bathing suits.

Vibrating from a remote corner of the mall, where mystics feel more at home, is **Sedona,** tel. (808) 591-8010, a metaphysical new-age store. Inside, its shelves and cases are stocked with aromatherapy and massage oils, natural crystals, agates, books, jewelry, figurines, carvings, posters, postcards, and consciousness-lifting tapes. Recharge your spiritual batteries with a personal psychic reading done by various practitioners in a private upstairs area.

Borders Books and Music has a full-selection outlet here, with books, music, newspapers and magazines from around the world, and a gallery and coffee shop upstairs. It has a good Hawaiiana section. Open Mon.-Thurs. 9 a.m.-11 p.m., Fri.-Sat. to midnight, and Sunday 9 a.m.-9 p.m. Call (808) 591-8995 for book information, (808) 591-8996 for music, or (800) 591-8995 from the Neighbor Islands.

Aloha Tower Marketplace

Constructed in 1994, the Aloha Tower Marketplace is one of the newest mall/shopping plazas in Honolulu, one frequented not only by tourists but by locals. Surrounding the Aloha Tower and fronting the working harbor of Honolulu where ships from all over the world load and unload their goods, this marketplace is an old warehouse that's been tastefully converted into an upscale group of more than 100 shops offering food and beverages, apparel, art, gifts, jewelry, and specialty items. An indoor-outdoor affair, where the sea breezes blow right through, the center atrium area looks out over the tower. This central courtyard atrium is also the spot for musical entertainment performed free throughout the day. The outside area is called the Boat Days Bazaar, and it's filled with cabana-type booths selling mostly apparel, gifts, and souvenirs. Inside, find fashions at **Daniella** and **Beyond the Beach,** among others. **Magnet Five-Oh** has all sorts of magnets from floor to ceiling. If you can't find one here, you haven't looked hard enough. The **World of Time** carries everything from Swatch watches to pocket watches, and **Powder Edge** has outdoor gear. Then there is **Perfumania,** and its name says it all. Browse through **Hula Prints** and **Wyland Galleries. Martin & MacArthur** carries mostly koa wood furniture and furnishings. Also check out the **Endangered Species Store,** which stocks nature-inspired gift items. Part of the profits go to protect endangered species of the world. Most of the shops in this complex are locally owned and nonchain outfits. Have a walk through and support the local economy.

After having a look at the shops, sit down for a snack at one of the many food vendors in the building. Try **Gordon-Biersch Brewery & Restaurant** for lunch and a chilled local brew, or the **Rodeo Cantina** for other drinks; **Villa Pizza** for a quick bite; or **Belinda's Aloha Kitchen** or **Big Island Steakhouse** for a more substantial meal. If you're at the marketplace for dinner, you can also enjoy the free concert at the main stage.

A vintage-looking, open-air trolley runs between here and Waikiki, charging $2 each direction for adults and $1 for children 3-11. The trolley starts around 9:15 a.m. and runs ever 20 minutes until 10:45 p.m. Pickups are at 10 hotels and landmarks in Waikiki, and it drops you off right in front of the marketplace.

Downtown Shopping

If you're touring the historical sights of downtown Honolulu, take a short stroll over to the corner of Bishop and King Streets, as good a place as any to call the center of the financial district. The names atop the buildings, both vintage and new, trace "big business" in Hawaii. There's good food to be enjoyed in the restaurants in this area along with some shops stuck away in the corners of the big buildings. **Longs Drugs** is at 1088 Bishop for any sundries and necessities.

The full-service **Honolulu Bookshop** is on the corner of Bishop and Hotel, tel. (808) 537-6224. The selections are excellent. **Hawaiian Islands Stamp and Coin,** tel. (808) 531-6251, at

1111 Bishop St., street level in the International Savings Building, displays rare coins, stamps, and paper money of Hawaii, the U.S., and worldwide. **Discount Mutual,** 1020 Auahi, tel. (808) 591-9441, sells TVs, VCRs, radios, electronic gear, and more. The **Lion Coffee Co.,** at 894 Queen St., tel. (808) 591-1199, offers a great little tour of its roasting facilities and will mail out a colorful little newsletter on request. For classic Hawaiian shirts head for **Bailey's Antique and Aloha Shirts,** 517 Kapahulu, tel. (808) 734-7628, where you will find thousands of the vintage "collectible garments" on display. The best are made from rayon that was manufactured before 1950. Prices can range from $100 to $2,000.

Dole Cannery Square

Look for the giant pineapple rising 200 feet into the air. A landmark of Honolulu, it was built in Chicago and erected here in 1928. It is still used as a reservoir and holds 100,000 gallons of water that's piped throughout the Dole Cannery, whose outer buildings were transformed in 1988 to a minimall located at 650 Iwilei Road. Upon entering the atrium area, look high on the walls to see reproductions of Dole Pineapple can labels. They're pop art, and convey a feeling of simpler times past. Downstairs you can watch a video about Dole and the cannery. Here also is the **Food Court,** providing snacks, salads, sandwiches, and soups for a quick lunch.

On the two levels you'll find a cluster of some 60 shops laid out as traditional storefronts and featuring items made in Hawaii. **Jungle Jerky Shop** has jerky of all sorts and sells stuffed animals, all life-size, as well as cotton cloth flowers. New shops like **Island Princess** have an added elegance with their fashions, or you can take care of your sweet tooth at **Sharyn's Hawaiian Island Cookies.** One of the nicest shops is the **Village Beach Shop.** It's a complete resortwear store with plenty of muumuu, sandals, and even boogie boards to choose from. It has a fine selection of T-shirts with gold designs by Ericka Paeis, a very creative and distinctive designer in the crowded field of Hawaiian T-shirts.

In the factory itself, workers stay busy processing the fruit. Used is the newest generation of the marvelous Ginaca machine, first built in 1913 by Henry Ginaca, a draftsman hired by James Dole to modernize the industry. This whirring wonder can peel, core, cut, slice, and dice 100 fruits per minute. Within 20 minutes of reaching the machine, the canned fruit's ready for the grocer's shelf. Millions of Hawaii's fruits are canned, juiced, and sliced here for shipment around the world. In the summertime, at the height of the harvest, this factory can process more than three million cans of fruit per day!

Kahala Mall

A smaller version of the city center malls, although large enough in its own right, is the Kahala Mall. **Liberty House, Longs Drug, Star Market,** and the eight-plex **Kahala Theaters** anchor this mall, surrounded by dozens of apparel outlets, gift shops, and novelty stores. Both **Barnes and Noble** and **Waldenbooks** have shops here. On the east end of the city this is the shopping center of choice.

Bargains and Discounts

For discounts and bargains, try the following. **Crazy Shirts Factory Outlet,** at 99-969 Iwaena St., Aiea, tel. (808) 487-9919, sells seconds and discontinued styles, with a minimum savings of 50%. **Swim Suit Warehouse,** in the Royal Hawaiian Shopping Center, has women's swimsuits under $20, plus shorts and tops. **The Muumuu Factory,** 1423 Kapiolani Blvd., offers great sales—get there early and bring your helmet and shoulder pads to fight off the crowds. **Goodwill Thrift Shop,** at 780 S. Beretania St., displays the same bargains as on the Mainland, but with a wide assortment of alohawear. **Pzazz** at 1419 Kalakaua Ave. has won accolades for being the best designer resale shop in town for moderately priced quality women's clothing.

Miscellaneous

Everyone, sooner or later, needs a good hardware store. You can't beat the selection at **Kilgo's,** 180 Sand Island Rd., tel. (808) 832-2200.

CHINATOWN

Chinatown has seen ups and downs in the last 130 years, ever since Chinese laborers were lured from Guangdong Province to work as contract laborers on the pineapple and sugar plantations. They didn't need a fortune cookie to tell them that there was no future in plantation work, so within a decade of their arrival they had established themselves as merchants, mostly in small retail businesses and restaurants. Chinatown is roughly a triangle of downtown Honolulu bordered by Nuuanu Street on the southeast, N. Beretania Street on the northeast, and S. King Street forming the hypotenuse. Twice this area has been flattened by fire, once in 1886 and again in 1900. The 1900 fire was deliberately set to burn out rats that had brought bubonic plague to the city. The fire got out of control and burned down virtually the whole district. Some contended that the fire was allowed to engulf the district in order to decimate the growing economic strength of the Chinese. Chinatown reached its heyday in the 1930s when it thrived with tourists coming and going from the main port at the foot of Nuuanu Street.

Today, Chinatown is a mixed bag of upbeat modernization and run-down sleazy storefronts. Although still strongly Chinese, there are Japanese, Laotians, Vietnamese, and even an Irish pub, O'Toole's, on Nuuanu Avenue. This is Asia come to life: meat markets with hanging ducks, and Chinese, Korean, Japanese, and Vietnamese food with their strange aromatic spices all in a few blocks. The entire district takes only 10 minutes to walk and is a world apart from "tourist" Oahu. Crates, live chickens, incredible shops, down-and-outers, tattoo parlors, and temples all can be found in this quarter. When Hotel Street meets River Street, with the harbor in the background, it all abruptly ends. This is a different Honolulu, a Pacific port, crusty and exciting.

SIGHTS

Look for the pagoda roof of **Wo Fat's** on the corner of Hotel and Maunakea Streets. This is the oldest chop suey house in Honolulu, started in 1886 by Mr. Wo Fat, a baker. It's a good landmark for starting your tour. The Chinatown landmark (circa 1922), **Hawaii Theater,** has been renovated and once again is open to the public. One-hour tours of this historic building are given on the first Monday of every month at 10 a.m. and 2 p.m., $5 admission. Call (808) 528-0506 for additional information. You can easily do Chinatown on your own, but for another view and some extremely knowledgeable guides try the **Chinese Chamber of Commerce** tour, tel. (808) 533-3181, which has been operating as a community service for almost 30 years. A guide will show you around Chinatown for only $5. This tour is offered Tuesday mornings at 9:30 a.m. only and starts from the chamber office at 42 N. King Street. Or try the **Hawaiian Heritage Center** Chinatown Historical and Cultural Walking Tour, which starts from the Ramsay Galleries at 1128 Smith St., every Friday at 9:30 a.m. The two-hour tours are $5 per person, minimum of three for tours to go; call (808) 521-2749 for reservations, or write to P.O. Box 37520, Honolulu, HI 96837. An excellent source of general information is the **Hawaii Chinese Historical Center,** 111 N. King St., Honolulu, HI 96817.

If you want to clear your head from the hustle and bustle, visit the **Kuan Yin Temple,** where Buddha is always praised with some sweet-smelling incense, or peek into the **Taoist Temple.** If that's not enough to awaken your spiritual inner self, visit the **Izumo Taisha Jinja,** a Japanese Shinto shrine. All the accoutrements of a shrine are here—roof, thick coiled rope, bell, and prayer box. This one houses a male deity. You can tell by the cross on the top. There's a ferroconcrete example of a torii gate. If you've never visited a Japanese Shinto shrine, have a look here but be respectful and follow the rules. **Lum Sai Ho Tong,** across the street from the Shinto shrine on River St., is a basic Chinese Buddhist temple, very small and usually closed after 2 p.m.

For peace and quiet, or to check out some old-timers playing checkers or dominoes, cross the river and enter **Aala Triangle Park,** or treat yourself by walking a few minutes north to **Fos-**

ter **Botanical Garden** at 180 N. Vineyard for a glimpse of rare and exotic flora from around the world.

SHOPPING

For shopping head to the **Cultural Plaza,** on the corner of Maunakea and Beretania Streets, but note that it has been struggling lately and shops come and go with regularity. It's more fun to look at than to shop. You'll find Dragongate Bookstore, Tak Wah Tong Chinese Herbalist, Excellent Gem and Diamonds, Peninsula Jewelry. The Cultural Plaza Moongate Stage is the centerpiece. Here they perform Chinese dances and plays, and herald in the Chinese New Year. If there is a presentation happening, attend. Out back, in a little parklike area, you'll find local men spending the afternoon chatting or playing dominoes, Go, or other board games.

Nearby and close to the river is an open market, a cooperative of open-air stalls selling just about everything that Chinatown has to offer at competitive prices. Follow your nose to the pungent odors of fresh fish at **Oahu Market** on King St., where ocean delectables can be had for reasonable prices.

The **Wingon Co.,** at 131 Hotel, has porcelain ware, but the feature is the big crocks of crackseed. If you want it the way it *was* made, this is it.

Pegge Hopper Gallery, tel. (808) 524-1160, is at 1164 Nuuana St., open Mon.-Fri. 11 a.m.-5 p.m. and Saturday 11 a.m.-3 p.m. Ms. Hopper is one of the three most famous working artists in all of Hawaii. Her original works grace the walls of the most elegant hotels and homes in the islands. If you would like to purchase one of her bold and amazing serigraphs, this shop has the best and widest selection.

Cindy's Flower Shop is just next to Wo Fat's, and it has fresh lei at cheap prices. Located right where S. Beretania turns into N. Beretania, at Smith St. across from the Honolulu Towers, is a garland of flower shops like Lita's Lei and Mauna Kea Lei, famous for good products and prices. Also, at the corner of Pauahi and Maunakea look for **Aloha Lei and Flowers,** which is locally famous for its lei, which it can ship to the Mainland. Several other flower shops in the vicinity of Beretania and Maunakea Streets, selling authentic lei and other flowers, are Maunakea Florist, which is right on the corner, Sweetheart's Lei Shop, just down the street, and Lauli'ilani's Lei and Flowers.

Chinese Acupuncturists and Herbalists, Etc.
Ted J. Kaptchuk, O.M.D., in his excellent book *The Web That Has No Weaver* says, "Actually, Chinese medicine is a coherent and independent system of thought that has been developed over two millennia." Chinese practitioners, unlike most of their Western counterparts, look at the entire individual, not just the acute symptom, and try to pinpoint what they refer to as "internal disharmony." Their diagnosis might be "dampness in the liver" or "fire in the kidney," for which they may prescribe a combination of acupuncture, herbs, dietary supplements and even exercise. The practitioners listed below are all licensed to practice Chinese medicine. A visit, where they will check your overall appearance and a number of "pulses," costs about $10. The herbs that they prescribe, usually dispensed from a wall of drawers labled with Chinese characters, will probably cost under $10 depending upon the malady.

Yuan Chai Tong Ltd. Oriental Herbs and **Dr. W.S. Lam,** licensed acupuncturist, occupy a storefront on the corner of River and N. King. Nearby on King St. is **Fook Sau Tong's,** another Chinese herb specialist. Look in the window to see coiled snake skin, a few dried-out snakes, some flat-looking lizards, and who-knows-what. If you need the bounce put back in your step, maybe some tonics or a few needles in the ear are just what the doctor will order. **Kam Sang Chun,** 1121 Nuuanu Ave., open daily 9 a.m.-noon and again 2-5:30 p.m., Sunday 9 a.m.-noon, is another long established acupuncturist and herbalist.

Down Smith St. is **Kam Mau Co.,** whose shelves are stacked with every conceivable (and inconceivable) Asian food. This is a great place to sample authentic crackseed. If your tummy revolts or if you need a quick tonic head next door to **Lai An Tong's** herb shop where some mashed antelope antler or powdered monkey brain will set you straight again.

FOOD

You can eat delicious ethnic food throughout Chinatown. If not Honolulu's best, the entire district, food-wise, is definitely Honolulu's cheapest. On almost every corner you've got places like **Mini Garden Noodle House** and **Cafe Paradise** for breakfast, lunch, and dinner. They're basic and cheap eateries whose ambience is a mixture of formica-topped tables and linoleum floors. In almost all, the food is authentic, with most featuring Asian food. You can easily get meals here for $3-5. Some eateries appear greasier than the Alaska Pipeline, so you'll have to feel them out. The local people eat in them regularly, and most are clean enough.

Right at the corner of N. Hotel and Maunakea, you'll see **Wo Fat's Restaurant,** tel. (808) 524-1628, the oldest chop suey house in Hawaii, where you're guaranteed an authentic meal at reasonable prices. A visit to Chinatown is incomplete without lunch at Wo Fat's, or at least a tour of this extremely ornate restaurant. The three floors are covered with paintings of dragons, birds, flowers, and a variety of land- and seascapes. Murals, carvings, and hanging lanterns create the mood of "rococo Chinese." The menu is like a small phone book, with literally hundreds of choices of fish, fowl, beef, and vegetarian dishes. It's hard to spend more than $10 per person, with many dishes considerably less.

Rosarina Pizza, at 1111 Maunakea St., tel. (808) 533-6634, is an alternative to the Asian cuisine. They will sell you a slice of pizza for only $1.40, or a whole pie ranging from a small cheese for $8 to a large combo at $15.25. You can also order a 12-inch sublike pastrami and provolone for $4.75, or an à la carte dinner like spaghetti with meat sauce or sausage, cannelloni, or manicotti, all for under $7.

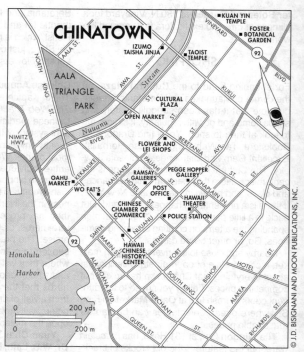

One place that you shouldn't miss is **Shung Chong Yuein,** a Chinese cake shop at 1027 Maunakea. Look in to see yellow sugar cakes, black sugar cakes, shredded coconut with eggs, salted mincemeat, Chinese ham with egg, lotus seeds, and steamed buns.

Chinatown Joe's, at the corner of Hotel and Nuuanu Streets, is a classic tavern complete with dartboard and mugs of draft beer. Laid-back, local, and friendly, it's a good place to stop in for a breather, or to have a classic pastrami or tuna, ham, and Swiss sandwich.

At the Chinatown Cultural Plaza
As with the shops in the plaza, the restaurants also come and go. One to check is **Buddhist Vegetarian Restaurant,** tel. (808) 532-8218. The Buddhist Vegetarian Restaurant is basic and about as antiseptic as a monk's cell, but the food is healthy. The varied menu includes inexpensive dim sum dishes, stir-fry vegetables for $9.50, spicy hot and sour soup for $6.50, and

many braised or fried vegetable or tofu dishes for about $7.50. Most are in the under-$10 category, but the Buddhist supreme vegetarian plate goes for $23.95. Lunch is served 10:30 a.m.-2 p.m., dinner 5:30-9 p.m.

Doong Kong Lau Seafood Restaurant offers Hakka cuisine and sizzlers. It's on the river side of the Cultural Plaza, tel. (808) 531-8833. Inside it's utilitarian with leatherette seats and formica tables. You come here for the food. Savories include stir-fried squid with broccoli for $5.95, stir-fried scallops with garlic sauce for $7.95, stir-fried oysters with black beans for $6.95, sizzle plates like seafood combo at $7.95, or shark fin with shredded chicken, $16.50. The menu reads, "The chief recommends deep fried shrimp with toast." Who's to argue with the chief! **Won Kee Sea Food Restaurant** is another restaurant in the Cultural Plaza. Locals swear by it, especially the lunch specials for $4.95. At another stall in this complex is the **Royal Kitchen,** tel. (808) 524-4461, a very popular place with local families and businesspeople. It's especially known for its takeout baked *manapua,* soft dough buns stuffed with pork, charsiu, or vegetables, and for its Chinese sausage, *lupcheung.* Open very early in the morning. Stuck in the corner is the reasonably priced **Cheuk's Chinese Restaurant.** Open Monday 10:30 a.m.-2:30 p.m., Tues.-Sun. 10:30 a.m.-8:30 p.m., this is a simple, down-home place, with items like soups and pot stickers for $4.50, beef and pork dishes for about $6, and seafood dishes for around $8.

Chinatown's Vietnamese Restaurants

A recent phenomenon is a number of excellent Vietnamese restaurants that have sprung up like bamboo sprouts along Chinatown's streets. The majority are meticulously clean, and the moderately priced food is "family-pride-gourmet." The decor ranges from oilcloth tablecloths topped by a "bouquet" of plastic flowers and a lazy Susan filled with exotic spices and condiments, to "down-to-earth chic" with some mood lighting, candles, and even linen place settings. As a group, they represent the best culinary deals on Oahu today. Many selections, like the grilled seasoned meatballs or marinated pork (under $8), come with noodles, fresh lettuce, mint, cucumber, bean sprouts, and ground peanut sauce

that you wrap in layers of rice paper to make your own version of what can best be described as an "oriental taco." Simply moisten a few sheets of the rice paper in the bowl of water provided and wrap away. Great fun, and they'll show you how! There are plenty of savory vegetarian menu choices as well.

Maxime's Vietnamese Restaurant, 1134 Maunakea St., tel. (808) 545-4188, open Tues.-Fri. 9 a.m.-9 p.m., Sat.-Sun. until 10 p.m., Monday till 5 p.m., is as authentic as its name is contrived. To get an idea, ask to use the bathroom. You'll pass through the cramped but meticulously clean kitchen filled with boiling pots that are tended by about three generations of the family. In the dining room, it's just formica tables and red Naugahyde chairs, but the people couldn't be more friendly. Try Maxime's special noodles with pork, shrimp, crab, bean sprouts, lettuce, and pork soup on the side for only $6.50, or an order of shrimp rolls—light aromatic rolls with shrimp, pork, and garden vegetables and rice noodles rolled up in rice paper served with sauce for $4, or only $1.50 as an appetizer. The selections of *pho* soup, which can be beef or chicken (*pho ga*) come with rice noodles, onions, Chinese parsley, basil, bean sprouts, and wine. You can either have the meat in the soup or on the side, for only $4.50 or $5 for the jumbo size. Beverages are lemonade, iced coffee with condensed milk, jasmine tea, fresh coconut juice, sweet and sour lemon juice, and soybean milk. Top off your meal with desserts like caramel custard or sweet beans with coconut milk for under $2.

A Little Bit of Saigon, 1160 Maunakea, tel. (808) 528-3663, open daily 10 a.m.-10 p.m., is the fanciest of the lot, although it is still quite basic. Specialties are "roll ups" that include savory beef, pork or chicken, served with lettuce, fresh herbs, vegetables, sweet and sour fish sauce, and peanut or pineapple and anchovy sauce along with thin rice paper that you use to roll-your-own for $5.95-8.95. Good yet inexpensive selections are stir-fried vegetables that you can have either by themselves or with fresh fish, prawns, chicken, beef, tofu, or scallops, all for under $7.95. For the hearty appetite try the seven-course dinner for two at $29.95 that gives a good sample of the menu. Finish with agar served with tapioca and coconut milk for $1.75.

To Chau Vietnamese Restaurant, at 1007 River, tel. (808) 533-4549, and **Ha Bien,** at 198 N. King St., serve basic Vietnamese fare for under $7 for most dishes. They're around the corner from the action of Hotel St., and are family-oriented. Ha Bien is open strange hours, Monday 8 a.m.-4 p.m., open the remainder of the week until 6 p.m.

CHINATOWN NIGHTS

Chinatown is relatively safe, especially during the daytime, but at night, particularly along infamous Hotel Street, you have to be careful. When the sun sinks, the neon lights and the area fires up. Transvestites and hookers slide down the street, shaking their wares and letting you know that they're open for business. Purchasing might leave you with a few souvenirs that you'd never care to *share* with the folks back home.

Not many tourists come this way. But walking down Hotel Street is really an adventure in and of itself. If you stay on the main drag, right down the middle, you'll be okay. At Hotel and Nuuanu

Streets you'll find the Honolulu Police Department downtown substation.

There are a lot of nondescript places that open to the street like a wound oozing the odor of stale beer and urine. The **Hubba Hubba Club,** with its live nude shows, no cover, and not-too-inflated drinks, is the best of Hotel Street. This is not a place for candy-asses, wimps, or missionaries. Simply put, there are naked women in there doing exotic and bizarre acts. The Hubba Hubba is basically a clip joint on the up and up. Inside are flashing lights, a runway, and $3 beers, with only mild pressure as you sit and watch the act. As you walk down Hotel Street toward the river it gets sleazier. **Elsie's Bar,** at 145 N. Hotel St., open 6 a.m.-2 a.m., looks meaner than a tattooed snake, but it's a safe place. So if you want to have a night of fun and relaxation come in here. It offers Hawaiian music along with fairly decent Hawaiian food. A few doors down are steps leading upstairs to the **Original Bath Palace.** The *original* place where drunken fools were taken to the cleaners.

HAWAII STATE ARCHIVES

WAIKIKI

Waikiki (Spouting Water) is like a fresh young starlet from the sticks who went to Hollywood to make it big, and did, though maybe too fast for her own good. Everyone always knew that she had a double-dip of talent and heart, but the fast lane has its heartaches, and she's been banged around a little by life. Even though her figure's fuller, her makeup's a little askew, and her high heels are worn down, she has plenty of chutzpah left, and when the curtain parts and the lights come up, she'll play her heart out for her audience.

Waikiki is a classic study of contradictions. Above all, it is an example of basic American entrepreneurialism taken to the nth degree. Along the main strip, high-powered businesspeople cut multimillion-dollar deals, but on the sidewalks it's a carnival midway with hucksters, handbillers, and street people selling everything decent and indecent under the tropical sun. To get a true feeling for Waikiki, you must put this amazing strip of land into perspective. The area covers only seven-tenths of a square mile, which at a good pace, you can walk in 15 minutes. On any given day, about 110,000 people crowd its beaches and boulevards, making it one of the most densely populated areas on earth. Sixty thousand of these people are tourists; 30,000 are workers who commute from various towns of Oahu and cater to the tourists, and the remaining 20,000 actually call Waikiki home. The turnover is about 80,000 new tourists per week, and the pace never slackens.

To the head shakers, these facts condemn Waikiki as a mega-growth area gone wild. To others, these same figures make Waikiki an energized, fun-filled place to be, where "if you don't have a good time, it's your own fault."

It is the meeting place of East and West. The very new rubs shoulders with the immeasurably old. And if you have not found the romance you expected you have come upon something singularly intriguing.

~W. Somerset Maugham

For the naive or the out-of-touch looking for "grass-shack paradise," the closest they'll come to it in Waikiki is painted on a souvenir ashtray. Those drawn to a smorgasbord of activities, who are adept at choosing the best and ignoring the rest, can't go wrong! People and the action are as constant in Waikiki as the ever-rolling surf.

History

The written record of this swampy area began in the late 1790s. The white man, along with his historians, cartographers, artists, and gunpowder, were already an undeniable presence in the islands. Kalanikupule, ranking chief of Oahu, hijacked the *Jackall*, a small ship commanded by Captain Brown, with which he intended to spearhead an attack against Kamehameha I. The chief held the *Jackall* for a while, but the sailors regained control just off Diamond Head and sent the Hawaiians swimming for land. The ship then hastened to Kamehameha to report the treachery, and returned with his armada of double-hulled canoes, which beached along Waikiki. The great king then defeated Kalanikupule at the famous battle of Nuuanu Pali and secured control of the island. Therafter Waikiki, pinpointed by Diamond Head, became a well-known landmark.

Waikiki's interior was low-lying swampland, long known to be good for fishponds, taro, rice, and bananas, but hardly for living. The beach, however, was always blessed with sunshine and perfect waves, especially for surfing, a sport heartily loved by the Hawaiians. The royalty of Hawaii, following Kamehameha, made Honolulu their capital and kept beach houses at Waikiki. They invited many visiting luminaries to visit them at their private beach. All were impressed. In the 1880s, King Kalakaua was famous for his beach house hospitality. One of his favorite guests was Robert Louis Stevenson, who spent many months here writing one of his novels. By the turn of the 20th century Waikiki had become a highly exclusive vacation spot.

In 1901 the Moana Hotel was built, but immediately a protest was heard because it interfered with the view of Diamond Head. In 1906, Lucius Pinkham, then director of Hawaii's Board of Health, called the mosquito-infested area "dangerous and unsanitary," and proposed to drain the swamp with a canal so that "the whole place can be transformed into a place of unique beauty." By the early 1920s, the Ala Wai Canal was built, its dredgings used to reclaim land, and Waikiki was demarcated. By the end of the 1920s, the Royal Hawaiian Hotel, built on the site previously occupied by the royal beach house, was receiving very wealthy guests who arrived by ocean liner, loaded down with steamer trunks. They ensconced themselves at Waikiki, often staying for the duration of the season.

For about 40 years, Waikiki remained the enchanted domain of Hollywood stars, dignitaries, and millionaires. But for the brief and extraordinary days of WW II, which saw Waikiki barricaded and barbed-wired, GIs—regular guys from the Mainland—were given a taste of this "reserved paradise" while on R&R. They brought home tantalizing tales of wonderful Waikiki, whetting the appetite of middle America.

Beginning just before statehood and continuing through the '60s to the mid-'70s, hotels and condos popped up like fertilized weeds, and tourism exploded with the advent of the jumbo jet. Discounted package tours began to haul in droves of economy-class tourists. Businesses catering to the tastes of penny-pinchers and first-timers elbowed their way into every nook and cranny. For the first time Waikiki began to be described as tacky and vulgar. For the old-timers, Waikiki was in decline. The upscale and repeat visitors started to snub Waikiki, heading for hidden resorts on the Neighbor Islands. But Waikiki had spirit and soul, and never gave in. In the last few years, its declining hotels started a campaign to regain their illustrious images. Millions upon millions of dollars have been poured into renovations and remodeling. Luxury hotels renting exclusive and expensive rooms have reappeared and are doing a booming business.

Waikiki Today

The Neighbor Islands are pulling more and more tourists away, and depending on your point of view, this is either a boon or a bust for Waikiki. Direct flights to Maui and the Big Island allow more tourists than ever to bypass Oahu, but still a whopping 80% of the people visiting the islands spend at least one night in Waikiki hotels, which offer the lowest room rates in Hawaii. The sublime and the gaudy are neighbors in Waikiki. Exclusive shops are often flanked by buskers

WAIKIKI

© J.D. BISIGNANI AND MOON PUBLICATIONS, INC.

DETAIL

- KEALOHILANI AVE
- EDWARD ST
- WAIKIKI HANA
- IIUOKALANI AVE
- PRINCE
- KING'S VILLAGE
- KOA
- HYATT REGENCY
- KALAKAUA
- KAIULANI AVE
- SHERATON MOANA SURFRIDER
- PACIFIC BEACH HOTEL
- PRINCE KUHIO BEACH PARK

- KALAKAUA AVE
- PAKI AVE
- KAPAHULU AVE
- MONSARRAT AVE
- HONOLULU ZOO
- WAIKIKI SHELL
- KAPIOLANI PARK BANDSTAND
- KAPIOLANI PARK
- QUEEN KAPIOLANI
- THE FENCE (ART)
- WAIKIKI BEACHSIDE
- EWA
- HAWAIIAN REGENT
- WAIKIKI AQUARIUM
- To Diamond Head
- KUHIO AVE
- PAOAKALANI AVE
- OHUA AVE
- Kuhio Beach
- ST. AUGUSTINE CATHOLIC CHURCH
- LILIUOKALANI AVE
- KOA
- PACIFIC BEACH
- SEE DETAIL
- Waikiki Beach

- Ala Wai Canal
- Ala Wai Blvd
- Manoa-Palolo Drainage Canal
- ILIMA HOTEL
- WALINA
- NAHUA
- NOHONANI
- MIRAMAR AT WAIKIKI
- HONOLULU PRINCE
- BEACHCOMBER
- PACIFIC MONARCH
- INTERNATIONAL MARKET PLACE
- WAIKIKI TOWN CENTER
- SEASIDE
- WAIKIKI BUSINESS PLAZA
- OUTRIGGER REEF
- ALOHA DR
- MANIKAI
- WAIKIKI TRADE CENTER
- WAIKIKI SHOPPING PLAZA
- ROYAL HAWAIIAN SHOPPING CENTER
- SURFRIDER
- OUTRIGGER CORAL SEAS
- LEWERS ST
- KAIULANI
- OUTRIGGER EDGEWATER
- ROYAL HAWAIIAN
- SHERATON WAIKIKI
- HELUMOA
- HALEKULANI
- Gray's Beach

- B a y
- M a m a l a
- M a m a l a   B a y

- McCULLY ST
- HAWAII CONVENTION CENTER
- HAWAIIAN MONARCH
- KEONIANA ST
- POST OFFICE
- BREAKERS
- FORT DERUSSY MILITARY RESERVATION
- U.S. ARMY MUSEUM OF HAWAII
- BEACH WALK
- SARATOGA RD
- Fort Derussy Beach
- DOUBLETREE ALANA HOTEL
- ENA RD
- KALIA RD
- MALUHIA RD
- PAOA PL
- RAINBOW BAZAAR
- HILTON HAWAIIAN VILLAGE
- WESTON ILIKAI
- Hilton Lagoon
- DUKE KAHANAMOKU BEACH
- ALA WAI YACHT HARBOR
- HOLOMANA ST
- HOBRON LN
- ALA MOANA BLVD
- KALAKAUA AVE
- To Ala Moana Shopping Center
- 92

- NOT ALL HOTELS ARE SHOWN
- 0.25 mi
- 0.25 km
- 0

selling plastic hula dolls. Burgers and beer mingle their pedestrian odors with those of Parisian cuisine. Though Waikiki in many ways is unique, it can also come off as "Anytown, U.S.A." But most importantly it somehow works, and works well. You may not find "paradise" on Waikiki's streets, but you will find a willing "dancing partner," and if you pay the fiddler, she'll keep the beat.

Non-Americans, especially Japanese, still flock for dream vacations, mostly staying at Waikiki hotels, 25% of which are owned by Japanese firms. Mainlanders and locals alike are disgruntled when they see the extent to which Waikiki has become a Japanese town. It's one of the only cities in America where you can have trouble ordering a meal or making a purchase if you don't speak Japanese! The visiting Japanese have been soundly warned by the tour operators before they arrive to never talk to strangers, especially someone on the street. Unfortunately for them, this means a vacation in which they never really leave Japan. They're herded into Japanese-owned shops and restaurants where prices are grossly inflated, and from which the tour operators get kickbacks. Local shopkeepers, not on the list, are aggravated. They say that the once-timid Japanese visitor will now show irritation if the shopkeeper doesn't speak Japanese, and will indignantly head for the door if there is no one provided to deal with them in their native tongue. Also, these visitors have been taught to bargain with American shopkeepers, who they are told inflate prices. This makes for some rugged interaction when the price is already fair, but the Japanese visitor won't believe it. While on average the Japanese tourist spends $340 per day, as opposed to a Mainlander who spends $130 per day, the Japanese really don't spread their money around as much as you would think. The money spent in Japanese shops primarily goes back to Japan. It's an incestuous system that operates in Waikiki.

Getting Around

By far and away the best way to get around Waikiki is on foot. For one, it's easily walked from one end to the other in less than 20 minutes, and walking will save you hassling with parking and traffic jams. Also, TheBus and taxis are abundant. Those who have opted for a rental car should note that many of the agencies operate Waikiki terminals, which for some can be more convenient than dropping your car at the airport on the day of departure. Check to see if it suits you. The following information is specific to Waikiki, and offers some limited alternatives.

In mid-1987, **pedicabs,** for all intents and purposes, were outlawed in Waikiki. There used to be 150-160 pedicabs that offered short taxi rides. They took people shopping, sightseeing, and between hotels, but basically they were a joyride. Mainstream businesspeople considered them a nuisance, and there were rumors that some drivers dealt drugs, so they were finally outlawed. Now only 10-12 legal pedicabs operate in and around Waikiki. They're not allowed to go along Kalakaua Avenue, pick up or drop off at hotels, or use any of the main drags. They stay on the back streets or in the park, where they are constantly watched by the police. Charges are a hefty $3 per minute. The main customers are Japanese tourists who marvel at being peddled around town by a muscular *gaijin* in a rickshaw-type conveyance never seen in their own homeland any longer.

The **Waikiki Trolley,** tel. (808) 596-2199, offers tours throughout Waikiki and downtown Honolulu on two different routes, both starting at the Royal Hawaiian Shopping Center. A day pass costs $18 adults, $8 children, and you can get on and off as much as you like. The trolley is really an open-air bus, but it's well done and plenty of fun. Pick up a route map at an activity desk, or call the number above for times and stops.

Waikiki does an excellent job of conveying traffic, both auto and pedestrian, along Kalakaua Avenue, the main drag fronting Waikiki. The city has installed very clear yet unattractive combinations of stoplights and street names. These are metal L-shaped beams, painted a dull brown, that straddle the roadways, clearly pinpointing your location. Unfortunately, they match the area about as well as work boots match a hula dancer. To give the feeling of an outdoor strolling mall, sidewalks along Kalakaua have been widened and surfaced with red brick.

The **Kapiolani Park Kiosk** is on the corner of Kapahulu and Kalakaua Avenues. The kiosk uses vintage photos to give a concise history of Kapiolani Park. An overview map shows all the features of the park. Information is available here concerning events at the Aquarium, Zoo, Waikiki Shell, the Kodak Hula Show, the Art Mart (a collection of island artists selling their creations along the Zoo), and the Kapiolani Bandstand, where you're treated to free concerts by top-name bands and orchestras.

Public parking in Waikiki can be a hassle, although there are plenty of parking garages. A good place to park not far from the beach is the strip running parallel to Kapiolani Park at one end and along Saratoga Street at the other. There are plenty of two-hour parking meters available, especially if you arrive before 9 a.m. Also, inexpensive (for Waikiki) parking is available at the ramp adjacent to the Waikiki 3 Theaters along Seaside Road, but only after 5:30 p.m.

SIGHTS

To see Waikiki's attractions, you have to do little more than perch on a bench or loll on a beach towel. Its boulevards and beaches are world-class for people-watching. Some of its strollers and sunbathers are *visions,* while others are real *sights.* And if you keep your ears open, it's not hard to hear every American accent and a dozen foreign languages. Some actual sights are intermingled with the hotels, boutiques, bars, and restaurants. Sometimes, too, these very buildings are the sights. Unbelievably, you can even find plenty of quiet spots—in the gardens of Kapiolani Park, and at churches, temples, tea-rooms, and ancient Hawaiian special places sitting unnoticed amidst the grandiose structures of the 20th century. Also, both the Honolulu Zoo and Waikiki Aquarium are well worth a visit.

DIAMOND HEAD

If you're not sandwiched in a manmade canyon of skyscrapers, you can look eastward from anywhere in Waikiki and see Diamond Head. Diamond Head *says* Waikiki. Western sailors have used it as a landmark since the earliest days of contact, and the Hawaiians undoubtedly before that. Ships' artists etched and sketched its motif long before the names of the newfound lands of Hawaii, Waikiki, and Oahu were standardized and appeared on charts as Owyhee, Whytete, and Woohoo. The Hawaiian name was Leahi (Brow of the Ahi); legend says it was named by Hi'iaka, Madame Pele's younger sister, because she saw a resemblance in its silhouette to the yellowfin tuna. The name "Diamond Head" comes from a band of sailors who found calcite crystals on its slopes and thought they'd dis-

covered diamonds. Kamehameha I immediately made the mountain *kapu* until his adviser John Young informed him that what the seamen had found, later known as "Pele's tears," were, except as souvenirs, worthless. Diamond Head was considered a power spot by the Hawaiians. Previously, Kamehameha had worshipped at a *heiau* located on the western slopes, offering human sacrifice to his bloodthirsty war-god, Ku.

Geologically, the 760-foot monolith is about 350,000 years old, formed in one enormous explosion when seawater came into contact with lava bubbling out of a fissure. No new volcanic activity has been suspected in the last 200,000 years. The huge rock is now Hawaii's state monument and a national natural landmark. Its crater serves as a Hawaii National Guard depot; various hiking trails to the summit bypass installations left over from WW II. Getting there takes only 15 minutes from Waikiki, either by TheBus no. 57 or by car along Diamond Head Road. The southeast *(makai)* face has some of the most exclusive and expensive real estate in the islands. The Kahala Mandarin is regarded by many to be one of the premier hotels in the world, and nearby is the super-snobbish Waialae Country Club. Many private estates—homes of multimillionaires, Hollywood stars, and high-powered multinational executives—cling to the cliffside, fronting ribbons of beach open to the public by narrow rights-of-way that oftentimes are hemmed in by the walls of the estates.

HONOLULU ZOO

The trumpeting of elephants and chatter of monkeys emanates from the jungle at the Honolulu

Diamond Head from Halekulani

Zoo, 151 Kapahulu Ave., tel. (808) 971-7171, open daily 9 a.m.-4:30 p.m., with special evening concerts featuring local artists every Wednesday 6-7 p.m. June-August. For the free evening show, the gates reopen at 4:35 p.m. and there is no admission. General admission is $6 for 13 years and older, $4 for locals, children 6-12 with an adult $1, and children under five free; the Honolulu Zoo family pass is $25. As you walk along, you find the expected animals from around the world: monkeys, giraffes, lions, big cats, a hippo, even a sun bear (what else in Hawaii!). The Honolulu Zoo has the only large snake in Hawaii—a male Burmese python named Monty —housed in the Reptile House. (Only the zoo can legally import snakes, geckos, iguanas, and similar reptiles.) Many islanders love this exhibit, because snakes in Hawaii are so exotic! But the zoo is much more than just a collection of animals. It is an up-close escapade through the jungle of Hawaii, with plants, trees, flowers, and vines all named and described. Moreover, the zoo houses Hawaii's indigenous birdlife, which is fast disappearing from the wild: Hawaiian gallinules, coots, hawks, owls, and the *nene,* the state bird, which is doing well in captivity, with breeding pairs being sent to other zoos around the world. The zoo is also famous for its Manchurian cranes, extremely rare birds from East Asia, and for successfully mating the Galapagos turtle. A **petting zoo** of barnyard animals is great for kids. A concession stand serves typical junk food and soft drinks. Before leaving,

have a look at the Zootique shop where you can pick up T-shirts, postcards, posters, stuffed animals, books, and other gift items.

WAIKIKI AQUARIUM

The first Waikiki Aquarium was built in 1904, its entranceway framed by a torii gate. Rebuilt and restocked in 1954, it has just undergone another face-lift with a new entranceway, "touch tanks," and an opening directly to the sea. The aquarium, located at 2777 Kalakaua Ave., tel. (808) 923-9741, website: www.aquarium.mic/hawaii .edu, is open daily 9 a.m.-5 p.m. (entrance until 4:30 p.m.), admission $6 adults, $4 seniors, $2.50 youths 13-17, and free to children under 12. An audio tour ("magic wand" device) in English and Japanese is available for a small fee. Walk or take TheBus no. 2.

Although more than 300 species of Hawaiian and South Pacific fish, flora, and mammals live in its sparkling waters, the aquarium is much more than just a big fish tank. The floor plan contains four galleries of differing themes, and a seal tank. The **South Seas Marine Life** exhibit shows fish found in waters from Polynesia to Australia. The tanks hold sharks, turtles, eels, rays, clams, a seahorse, and colorful coral displays. Another exhibit, **Micronesia Reef Builders,** is perhaps the most amazing of all. It contains live coral that seem more like extraterrestrial flowers than specimens from our own seas. Some are long strands of spaghetti with bulbous ends like lima beans, others are mutated roses, or tortured camellias, all moving, floating, and waving their iridescent purples, golds, and greens in a watery bouquet.

Watch the antics of the monk seals, shameless hams, from the side of their 85,000 gallon tank, which now has a "variegated coastline" of natural nooks and crannies patterned after sections of Oahu's Pupukea and Kahe Point. Hawaiian monk seals are one of only two species of tropical seals on earth. Endangered, there are only about 1,500 individuals still surviving, and the "performances" are more of a detailed description of the seals day-to-day life in their dwindling environment. The three seals inhabiting the tank are all males, since placing a breeding couple would almost certainly result in the birth of a pup. Marine biologists anguished over the decision. It was felt that seals raised in captivity and then released back into the natural environment might introduce a devastating disease to the native population. This was considered too great a danger to risk.

The aquarium contains a bookshop with a tremendous assortment of titles on the flora and fauna of Hawaii. Restrooms are behind the bookshop area as you face the main gate. The University of Hawaii offers seminars and field trips through the aquarium, everything from guided reef walks to mini-courses in marine biology; information is available at the aquarium.

The Waikiki Aquarium is a very special opportunity for fun and education that will be enjoyed by the entire family. Don't miss it!

Just near the aquarium is the **Natatorium,** a saltwater swimming pool built in 1927 as a WW I memorial, which was allowed to decay over the years until it was closed in 1980. Plans are constantly afoot in the House of Representatives calling for either a restoration or its demolition, but no decision has yet been reached about its fate.

U.S. ARMY MUSEUM OF HAWAII

This museum, with the hulks of tanks standing guard, is one long corridor where you feel the strength of the super-thick reinforced walls of this once-active gun emplacement. Located at Battery Randolf in Fort DeRussy, on the corner of Kalia and Saratoga Roads, the U.S. Army Museum of Hawaii, tel. (808) 438-2821, is open Tues.-Sun. 10 a.m.-4:30 p.m., except Christmas and New Year's Day, for self-guiding tours. An optional hour-long audiocassette can be rented for $3.50 that will guide you through the museum. Guided tours can be arranged for large groups by calling several weeks in advance. Battery Randolph once housed two 14-inch coast artillery rifles meant to defend Honolulu and Pearl Harbors. The architecture is typical of the Taft Period forts constructed between 1907 and 1920. The battery is listed in the National Register of Historic Places. As you enter there is a shop dedicated to "things military," flying jackets to wall posters. Walk the halls to learn the military history of Hawaii traced as far back as Kamehameha I. Here are rifles, swords, and vintage photos of Camp McKinley, a turn-of-the-century military station in the shadow of Diamond Head.

A side room holds models of artillery used to defend Waikiki from times when Battery Randolph was an active installation. One room shows how the guns worked in a method called "disappearing guns." The gun would raise up and fire and then disappear. The recoil of the gun would lock it back in position, and after it was reloaded a 50-ton counterweight would pop it up ready to fire. The explosive sound would rattle the entire neighborhood so they were seldom test-fired.

Exhibits show the fledgling days of Army aviation in Hawaii, when on July 13, 1913, 14 officers began a military flying school. There are beautiful models of military equipment, especially one of an old truck unit. Then comes the ominous exhibit of "Rising Japan" with its headlong thrust into WW II. Hawaii, grossly overconfident, felt immune to attack because of the strong military presence. Photos from the '30s and '40s depict the carefree lifestyle of visiting celebrities like Babe Ruth and Shirley Temple, which ended abruptly on December 7, 1941, in the bombing of Pearl Harbor.

An entire room is dedicated to the Pearl Harbor attack and is filled with models of Japanese planes, aircraft carriers, and real helmets and goggles worn by the Zero pilots. Most interesting are the slice-of-life photos of Hawaii mobilized for war: defense workers, both men and women, sailors, soldiers, entertainers, and street scenes. Pamphlets from the time read, "Know Your Enemies," and there's a macabre photo of people gathered at a stadium to see a demonstration of the devasting effect of flame throwers that would be employed upon the Japanese enemy. Bob Hope is here entertaining the troops, while a 442nd Regimental Battle Flag bears testament to the most decorated unit in American history, comprised mostly of *nisei* Japanese from Hawaii. Then come photos and exhibits from the soul-wrenching conflicts in Korea and Vietnam. Finally a room, like a whispering tomb, tells of the heroics of Hawaiian soldiers who have been awarded the Congressional Medal of Honor, almost all posthumously.

Make sure to go outside to the upper level exhibit where you'll see one of the old guns still pointing out to sea, which seems incongruous with sunbathers just below on the quiet and beautiful stretch of beach. On the upper deck are depth charges, torpedoes, and shells, along with a multimedia slide show. Your eyes will take a few minutes to refocus to the glorious sunshine of Waikiki after the cold gloom of the bunker. Perhaps our hearts and souls could refocus as well.

FREE SIGHTS AND CURIOSITIES

On the beach near the Sheraton Moana Surfrider Hotel are the **kahuna stones,** a lasting remnant of old Hawaii. The Hawaiians believed these stones were imbued with mana by four hermaphroditic priests from Tahiti: Kinohimahu, Kahaloamahu, Kapunimahu, and Kapaemahu (*mahu* in Hawaiian signifies homosexuality). They came to visit this Polynesian outpost in ancient times and left these stones for the people, who have held them in reverence for more than 600 years. About 40 years ago, a group of local historians went looking for the stones but couldn't find them. Around that time, there was a bowling alley along the beach, and when it was finally torn down, it was discovered that the stones had been incorporated into the foundation. Today, the vast majority of visitors and islanders alike no longer revere the stones, often using them as a handy spot to scrape sand off their feet. *Kapuna* versed in the old ways say

that the mana, once put in and strengthened by reverence, is now dissipating.

Delineating Waikiki from the rest of the city is the nearly two-mile-long **Ala Wai Canal.** Created in the '20s to drain the swamps that filled this flat oceanfront land, it now channels runoff from the mountains to the sea. The banks of the canal are used extensively by walkers, joggers, and runners, particularly shortly after sunrise and again before sunset; many come here to sit, relax, and watch the parade of paddlers practice for outrigger canoe races. It's cheap entertainment for one of Hawaii's favorite sports. Fishermen also make use of the canal, trying their luck near its mouth near the Ala Moana bridge.

Just across the canal from Waikiki proper is the new and impressive **Hawaii Convention Center.** Built to attract more convention business to the state, it's a combination of large and small meeting halls, exhibition rooms, and banquet facilities, with high-tech sound and light capabilities and instantaneous translation services. Appealing to the aesthetic side of anyone who takes the time to look inside are several waterfalls and pools, tall palm trees, numerous artworks, and a glass ceiling that seems to bring the outside in.

Even if you're not a guest at the following hotels, you should at least drop by their lobbies for a quick look. Dramatically different, they serve almost as a visual record of Waikiki's changing history. Those who have a fondness for the elegance of days gone by should take a tour of the **Sheraton Moana Surfrider Hotel** and steep in the history of the hotel, admiring its turn-of-the-century artifacts and memorabilia. The Moana, Waikiki's oldest hotel, dating from 1901, is a permanent reminder of simpler times when its illustrious clientele would dance the night away at an open-air nightclub suspended over the sea. The Moana houses the Banyan Court, named for the enormous banyan tree just outside. From here, *Hawaii Calls* beamed Hawaiian music to the Mainland by shortwave for 40 years beginning in 1935. In its heyday, the show was carried by more than 700 stations. The hotel's architecture is a classic example of the now quaint "colonial style." Daily tours start at 11 a.m. from the concierge desk.

Across the street are the giant, modernistic, twin towers of the **Hyatt Regency.** The lobby, like those of most Hyatts, is wonderful, with a huge waterfall and a jungle of plants, all stepped down the series of floors, making an effect like the Hanging Gardens of Babylon. Even if you're not a guest here, have a look at the Hawaiian craft items displayed at the hotel museum. It's open 9 a.m.-5 p.m. Mon.-Fri., and it's free. The **Pacific Beach Hotel,** at 2490 Kalakaua Ave., is a first-rate hotel and a great place to stay in its own right. But if you don't, definitely visit the lobby, where the Oceanarium Restaurant has an immense three-floor-high aquarium dedicated to holding 280,000 gallons of sea water. The old mafia dons used to send their rivals to "sleep with the fishes"; here, you have an opportunity to dine with the fishes. Usually you go snorkeling to watch the fish eat, but in this particular instance the fish watch you eat.

The **Royal Hawaiian Hotel,** built in 1927 on the site of the old royal beach house, once had fresh pineapple juice running in its fountains. Now surrounded by towering hotels, it's like a guppy in a sea of whales. However, it does stand out with its Spanish-Moorish style, painted in distinctive pink. In the old days, only celebrities and luminaries came to stay—who else could afford $3 per day? Although it's younger than the Moana, many consider it the grande dame of Hawaiian hotels. The entranceway is elegantly old-fashioned, with rounded archways, over-stuffed couches, and lowboys. You pass through the lobby on a shocking cerise and green rug. All the rooms are appointed in the trademark pink, with matching towels, sheets, and pillowcases. When you visit the Royal Hawaiian, the most elegant lobby is not where you check in. Rather, turn right from there and follow the long hallway toward the sea. This becomes an open breeze-way, with arches and columns in grand style. You'll come to a small circular area in the hotel. Here is the heart, with Diamond Head framed in the distance.

The **Urusenke Teahouse,** tel. (808) 923-3059, is an authentic teahouse donated to Hawaii by the Urusenke Foundation of Kyoto. It is located at 245 Saratoga Rd., which lies along the Waikiki side of Fort DeRussy. Every Wednesday and Friday 10 a.m.-noon, tea master Takashi Machita performs the ancient and aesthetic art of *chanoyu* (tea ceremony). The public is invited to watch the ceremony for free, but a donation of $2 is asked of those who want to partake of the frothy *matcha,* a grass-green tea made from the delicate tips of 400-year-old bushes, and the accompanying sweets. To find delight and sanctuary in this centuries-old ritual among the clatter and noise of Waikiki offers a tiny glimpse into the often puzzling duality of the Japanese soul.

As you walk along Kalakaua Avenue, directly across from Waikiki Beach proper is **St. Augustine Catholic Church.** This modernistic building squashed between high-rises is worth a quick look. The interior, serene with the diffused light of stained glass, looks like a series of A-frames. The **Damien Museum** is housed here, displaying photos and other artifacts of Father Damien, the Belgian priest who humanely cared for the lepers of Kalaupapa, Molokai, until his own death from complications of leprosy. The museum is open daily 9 a.m.-3 p.m. and is free, although donations are gratefully accepted as they are the museum's only source of revenue.

Believe it or not, you should pass through the McDonald's at the Royal Hawaiian Shopping Center to see a permanent collection of Hawaiian art on display. Among the exhibits are carvings, paintings, macramé, and featherwork. Many of the works are by Rocky Kaiouliokahihikoloehu Jensen, a famous island artist.

WAIKIKI BEACHES AND PARKS

In the six miles of shoreline from Kahanamoku Beach fronting the Hilton Hawaiian Village at the west end of Waikiki to Wailupe Beach Park in Maunalua Bay just east of the Kahala Mandarin, there are at least 17 choice spots for enjoying surf activities. Most of the central Waikiki beaches are so close to each other you can hardly tell where one ends and another begins. All of these are generally gentle, but as you head east the beaches get farther apart and have their own personalities. Sometimes they're rough customers. As always, never take *moana* for granted, especially during periods of high surf. To get information on the presence of lifeguards, call Ocean Safety at (808) 922-3888; people with disabilities can get information on beach and facility accessibility by calling (808) 586-8121. Now that you've finally arrived at a Waikiki beach, the one thing left to do is kick back and R-E-L-A-X.

Waikiki Beach stretches for two miles, broken into separate areas. A multitude of concession stands offer everything from shave ice to canoe rides. It's not news that this beach is crowded. Sometimes when looking at the rows of glistening bodies, it appears that if one person wants to tan his other side, everybody else has to roll over with him. Anyone looking for seclusion here is just being silly. Take heart—a big part of the fun is the other people.

Umbrella stands set up along Waikiki Beach fronting Kalakaua Avenue rent boogie boards, surfboards, paddle boats, and snorkel gear. They're convenient, but their prices are much more than many shops offering the same. The guys by the big banyan tree are slightly cheaper than those set up by the breakwater just before Kapiolani Park. However, all offer decent prices for surfing lessons and rides in outrigger canoes, which gets you three waves and about 20 minutes of fun. Bargaining is acceptable. Find other outrigger canoe rides—you help paddle—in front of the big hotels (try the Outrigger Waikiki). They're great fun and a bargain at $5 per person.

Kahanamoku Beach

This stretch of sand in front of the Hilton Hawaiian Village is named after Hawaii's most famous waterman, Duke Kahanamoku. The manmade beach and lagoon were completed in 1956. A system of pumps pushes water into the lagoon to keep it fresh. The swimming is great, and plenty of concessions offer surfboards, beach equipment, and catamaran cruises.

Fort DeRussy Beach

You pass through the right-of-way of Fort DeRussy military area, where you'll find restrooms, picnic facilities, volleyball courts, and food and beverage concessions. Lifeguard service is provided by military personnel—no duty is too rough for our fighting men and women! A controversy has raged for years between the military and developers who covet this valuable piece of land. The government has owned it since the turn of the century, and has developed what once was wasteland into the last stretch of non-cement, non-high-rise piece of real estate left along Waikiki. Since the public has access to the beach, and since Congress voted a few years back that the lands cannot be sold, it'll remain under the jurisdiction of the military.

Gray's Beach

This section's name comes from Gray's-by-the-Sea, a small inn once located here. The narrow white-sand beach lies in front of the Halekulani Hotel, which replaced Gray's. Take Lewers Street off Kalakaua Avenue and park along Kalia Road; a right-of-way is between the Reef and Halekulani hotels. The sea is generally mild here and the swimming is always good, with shallow waters and a sandy bottom. Offshore is a good break called **No. 3's,** a favorite with surfers.

Next door is **Royal Moana Beach,** lying between Waikiki's oldest manmade landmarks, the Moana and Royal Hawaiian hotels. Access is unlimited off Kalakaua Avenue. The inshore waters here are gentle and the bottom is sandy and generally free from coral. Offshore are three popular surfing areas, **Popular's, Queen's,** and **Canoes.** Many novices have learned to surf here because of the predictability of the waves, but with so many rookies in the water, and beach activities going on all around, you have to remain alert for runaway boards and speeding canoes.

Waikiki Beach Center and Prince Kuhio Beach Center

When people say "Waikiki Beach," this is the section to which they're referring. Both beaches front Kalakaua Avenue, and a long sand retaining wall called Slippery Wall fronts both beaches, creating a semi-enclosed saltwater pool. Here, you'll find surfing, canoeing, snorkeling, and safe year-round swimming along the gently sloping, sandy-bottomed shoreline. There are comfort stations, concession stands, and lifeguards. Be careful of the rough coral bottom at the Diamond Head end of Kuhio Beach. Covered with a coating of slick seaweed, Slippery Wall definitely lives up to its name. Though local youngsters play on the wall, the footing is poor and many knees have been scraped and heads cracked after spills from this ill-advised play. The surf on the seaward side of the wall churns up the bottom and creates deep holes that come up unexpectedly, along with an occasional rip current.

Kapiolani Regional Park

In the shadow of Diamond Head is Kapiolani Park, a quiet 140-acre oasis of greenery, just a coconut's roll away from the gray cement and flashing lights of Waikiki. It has proved to be one of the best gifts ever received by the people of

Honolulu, ever since King Kalakaua donated this section of crown lands to them in 1877, requesting that it be named after his wife, Queen Kapiolani. In times past, it was the site of horse and car races, polo matches, and Hawaii's unique *pa'u* riders, fashionable ladies in long flowing skirts riding horses decked out with lei. The park was even the site of Camp McKinley, the U.S. Army headquarters in the islands 1898-1907.

It remains a wonderful place for people to relax and exercise away from the hustle of Waikiki. The park is a mecca for jogging and aerobics, with many groups and classes meeting here throughout the day. It also serves as the starting point for the yearly **Honolulu Marathon,** one of the most prestigious races in the world.

Its **Waikiki Shell,** an open-air amphitheater, hosts many visiting musical groups, especially during Aloha Week. The Honolulu Symphony is a regular here, providing free concerts, especially on summer evenings. Nearby, the **Kapiolani Bandstand** hosts the Royal Hawaiian Band on Sunday afternoons. Also, under the shade of the trees toward Waikiki Beach, plenty of street entertainers, including clowns, acrobats, and jugglers, congregate daily to work out their routines to the beat of conga drums and other improvised music supplied by wandering musicians. Families and large groups come here to picnic, barbecue, and play softball. The park grounds are also home to the free **Kodak Hula Show,** Elks Club, prestigious Outrigger Canoe Club founded at the turn of the century, Waikiki Aquarium, and 45-acre Honolulu Zoo.

Just in front of the zoo, by the big banyan, are hundreds and hundreds of pigeons, the "white phantoms of Waikiki." In the morning they are especially beautiful darting through the sunshine like white spirits. Go to the Stop N Go or the ABC Store at the corner of Kapahulu and Kapiolani and buy birdseed. Take a few handfuls and stand among the pigeons. They will perch on your arms, shoulders, and head and peck away. If you're not wearing toe-covering shoes be advised that if you drop seed between your toes, you'll get an instant and free pedicure by the hungry birds. This is great fun and free!

The Kapiolani Beach Park section is the only spot along Waikiki with facilities for barbecueing and picnicking. Although it's only a short stroll down the beach from Waikiki central, it gets much less use. This is where local families and those in the know come to get away from the crowds, just a few beach-blanket lengths away. In the park and along the beach are restrooms, volleyball courts, picnic tables, lifeguard towers, a bath house, and a concession stand. Activities include surfing, fishing, snorkeling, and year-round safe swimming. Just be careful of the rocky bottom that pops up unexpectedly here and there. **Kapiolani Park Center** is the beach closest to Waikiki. The swimming is good here, with the best part at the Waikiki end. The beach is at its widest, and the bottom is gently sloping sand. The area called **The Wall** has been des-

Kapiolani
Regional Park

ignated as a special bodysurfing area. Supposedly, board riders are restricted from this area, but if the surf is good they're guaranteed to break the rules. Experts can handle it, but novices, especially with runaway boards, are a hazard. Kapiolani Park incorporates **Sans Souci Beach** at the eastern end. Many families with small children come to Sans Souci because it is so gentle. This beach, in front of the Colony Surf and New Otani Kaimana hotels, has unlimited access. Changing facilities are found at the deteriorating Natatorium, a saltwater pool built in the '20s. Unless something has been done to the Natatorium by the time you arrive, avoid its murky waters and be careful of the rocky areas to the front of its stone enclosure.

Around Diamond Head

Kaluahole Beach is located at the Waikiki side of Diamond Head. The water conditions are safe all year-round, but the beach is small and lies along a seawall. Once a large beach, it was paved over for building purposes. It has one public right-of-way, poorly marked and sandwiched between private homes. It's almost at the end at 3837 Kalakaua Avenue. The surfing in this area is generally good, and the breaks are known as "Tongg's," named after a local family that lived along this shore.

Diamond Head Beach Park is an unlimited access area along Beach Road (marked). It covers almost two acres of undeveloped shoreline. Unfortunately, the beach is very narrow and surrounded by unfriendly rock and coral. The waters, however, are quite protected and generally safe, except in periods of high surf. This area is good for fishing and finding quiet moments.

Kuilei Cliffs Beach Park lies below Diamond Head Road, with access available from three lookout areas along the road. You must walk down the cliff trails to the beaches below. Here are plenty of secluded pockets of sand for sunbathing, but poor swimming. The surf is generally rough, and the area is always frequented by

surfers. When the winds are right, windsurfers also come. Offshore is hazardous with submerged rocks, but this makes it excellent for diving and snorkeling—for experts only! Currents can be fierce, and you can be dashed against the rocks. Whales can sometimes be spotted passing this point, and to add to the mystique, the area is considered a breeding ground for sharks. Most visitors just peer down at the surfers from Diamond Head Road, or choose a spot of beach for peace and quiet.

Farther east is **Kaalawai Beach.** The swimming is good here and generally safe because of a protecting reef. Many locals come to this area to fish, and it is good for bodysurfing and snorkeling. The waters outside the reef are excellent for surfing, and produce some of the biggest waves on this side of the island. Access is by public right-of-way, marked off Kulumanu Place, or a small side road running off Kahala Avenue, or by walking along the shoreline from Kuilei Beach.

Kahala Beach, lying along Kahala Avenue, can be reached by a number of marked rights-of-way located between the high fences of estates in the area. The swimming is not particularly good, but there are plenty of pockets of sand and protected areas where you can swim and snorkel. Local people come to fish, and the surfing is good beyond the reef. The Hilton is located along this beach at the eastern end. The public can use "their" beach by walking from Kahala Beach. The swimming here is always safe and good because the hotel has dredged the area to make it deeper. Concession stands and lifeguards are provided by the hotel.

Wailupe Beach Park lies on the Waikiki side of Wailupe Peninsula in Maunalua Bay, and is the last beach covered by this chapter. This beach park, clearly marked off the Kalaniana'ole Highway, provides restrooms and picnic facilities. Swimming is officially not recommended. Be careful of the boat channel surrounding the area because the deep dropoff is very abrupt.

ACCOMMODATIONS

Waikiki is loaded with places to stay: 120 properties holding 31,000 rooms jammed into one square mile. And they come in all categories of hotels and condos, from deluxe to dingy. Your problem won't be finding a place to stay, but choosing from the enormous selection. During peak season (Christmas to Easter and again in summer) you'd better have reservations, or you could easily be left out in the *warm*. The good news is that, room for room, Waikiki is the cheapest place to stay in the state. Hotels along the beach tend to be slightly more expensive than their counterparts on a side street or back lane. The beachfront hotels have the surf at the doorstep, but those a block away have a little more peace and quiet. The following listings are not exhaustive. They couldn't be! Here are just some from all categories which you can use as a barometer to measure what's available.

MILITARY PERSONNEL ONLY

Hale Koa, tel. (808) 955-0555, website: www .halekoa.com, is located on the beach in Fort DeRussy; it is maintained especially for active-duty U.S. military personnel, Department of Defense civilians, and a few other categories of former military and defense-related personnel. This well-run and well-maintained hotel has all the dining facilities, entertainment options, and other amenities of other large hotels in Waikiki. Depending upon military rank or government status, there is a bewildering array of rates for the eight categories of rooms. Call for specifics.

BUDGET

Hale Aloha Youth Hostel, a member of the American Youth Hostel Association, is located in Waikiki at 2417 Prince Edward St., Honolulu, HI 96815, tel. (808) 926-8313. Walk down Kalakaua until you see the Hyatt Regency. Two streets directly behind is Prince Edward. Directions are also available at the airport information counter. A dorm room bunk is $16 for YH members and

$19 for those who are not International Youth Hostel Association members. Dorm rooms are not sexually integrated, and you must be at least age 18 to stay unaccompanied by an adult. Couples can rent a studio for $40 members and $46 nonmembers. It's recommended that reservations be made at least two weeks in advance, particularly during peak season. Credit cards can be used for reservations; the business office is open 24 hours a day. The hostel closes at 11 p.m. and all must leave daily 11 a.m.-5 p.m. The maximum three-day stay, especially during peak seasons, can sometimes be extended at the discretion of the manager. Requests must be made before 10 p.m. the previous day. Baggage may be left for the day for $2. Key deposits will not be returned if keys are not returned by 11 a.m., checkout time. Visitors are not allowed at any time, and neither alcohol nor smoking is permitted. Chores are required. Lockers—small, gym locker-types not big enough for a backpack but adequate for valuables—are available, but you must provide your own lock. The hostel gets visitors from around the world. It's clean and safe. The common area, kitchen, and bathrooms are shared by all.

Inter-Club Hostel Waikiki, at 2413 Kuhio Ave., Honolulu, HI 96815, tel. (808) 924-2636, has self-service laundry facilities, a relaxed island-style TV lounge, and a game room with ping pong and pool tables. Unlike some hostels, it's all right to drink beer on premises. You must be an international traveler or an American with an onward-going ticket to bunk here. Most rooms are dorm style (five to seven beds in each), $16.35 per night, but couples rooms run $32.70 and private rooms $49 for two, with $10 for an extra person; $10 key deposit. Rooms are usually segregated according to gender, but may not be if they are full. Reservations are accepted and are most often necessary; a credit card helps with reservations but is not necessary. The kitchen is used by the staff only. A continental breakfast is served 8-11 a.m. daily; dinner is served only on Monday, Wednesday, Friday, and Saturday for $3.50-4. Large lockers, big enough for a backpack, are $1; small lockers are 50 cents. Safe deposit boxes are also available for your most valuable possessions. Phone cards are sold here, and boogie boards, snorkels, and other water equipment are free for the use with a deposit.

Hawaiian Seaside Hostel, 419 Seaside and Kuhio, Honolulu, HI 96815, tel. (808) 924-3306, is a private hostel for international travelers, who must show a passport and an onward-going ticket. United States citizens are welcomed if they are travelers bound for a foreign destination (onward-going ticket necessary). Rates are $9.75 for the first night, plus a $10 deposit which is returnable upon checkout. After the first night, the rate goes up to $14.30 per night. Reservations are not required but can be accepted with a credit card. Accommodations are in nine mixed dorms, each with bunks and double beds. Bedding is provided. Each dorm has a refrigerator, a bathroom, air-conditioning, and a locker for each bed. Other helpful amenities include free safe deposits, free long-term storage, laundry facilities, a lounge with a wide-screen TV, free videos, and a lanai. The hostel has a common communal kitchen. Semiprivate rooms for two go for $16.50. Weekly rates give you seven nights for the price of six. One private room goes for $40 a night. The hostel, located on a cul-de-sac across from the Honolulu Zoo, is quiet for being so close to the action. It's the closest hostel to the beach. Most of the international travelers that you will find there are Australians, Brits, Germans, and Swedes. Beach mats, boogie boards, surfboards, and snorkeling equipment can be borrowed for your enjoyment on the beach. A hostel van makes a run to various spots of the North Shore three times a week—Monday, Wednesday, and Saturday; $5 for the roundtrip ride. Also, on Wednesday and Saturday, parties are thrown to facilitate socializing, so you can party hearty with new friends. A weekly barbecue at 3 p.m. on Sunday goes for $5.

The management also runs the nearby **Waikiki Beachside Hostel** at 2556 Lemon Rd., tel. (808) 923-9566. Rates start at $15 per person for a bunk bed and increase to $35 for a semiprivate room in a unit. A full unit with kitchen goes for $66 a night.

Just down the road at 2584 Lemon Rd., tel. (808) 922-1340, fax 955-4470, is the **Polynesian Hostel Beach Club.** Dorm rooms run $12-

15, single/double rooms with a shared bath are $30-40, and a studio with bath and kitchen is $45. The hostel has a common room for reading and TV watching, a communal kitchen, storage lockers for valuables, free use of some water equipment, frequent in-hostel activities, and inexpensive excursions. It is only one block from the beach. The management here also runs the Northshore Inn in Wailiku on Maui.

On the other end of Waikiki at 1946 Ala Moana Blvd., located inside the Hawaiian Colony Building across from Fort DeRussy, is **Island Hostel,** tel. (808) 942-8748. Each hostel room has a bathroom, small refrigerator, and a/c. Bunks run $16.50 per person, and private rooms cost $45 a night. A communal kitchen is located in the office, the lounge is open for community activities, and laundry facilities, lockers, and telephones are available.

When the YHs are full try the **Waikiki Prince** just next door to Hale Aloha YH, at 2431 Prince Edward St., tel. (808) 922-1544. Listed as a hotel, it is about the cheapest in Waikiki at $25-35 per night during low season.

Honolulu's YM/WCAs and AYH hostel near the university are near, but not technically in Waikiki. Find a complete list in the Honolulu chapter.

INEXPENSIVE

The **Royal Grove Hotel,** at 151 Uluniu Ave., Honolulu, HI 96815, tel. (808) 923-7691, built in 1951 and run by the Fong family since 1970, gives you a lot for your money. You can't miss its "paint-sale pink" exterior, but inside it's much more tasteful. Rooms in the older and cheaper wing run $42.50-75 for two, $10 for an extra person; the newer upgraded wing with a/c is $57-75. Most are studios and one-bedroom apartments with full facilities. A tiny pool in the central courtyard offers some peace and quiet away from the street. The Royal Grove passes the basic tests of friendliness and cleanliness. It's used but not abused. During low season it offers reduced weekly and monthly rates.

Hale Pua Nui, at 228 Beachwalk, Honolulu, HI 96815, tel. (808) 923-9693 or 921-4398, offers very reasonable accommodations only a few minutes' walk from Waikiki Beach. A studio apartment with a kitchenette is only $45 off season and $55 during peak season, $269 a week, and $880 a month. The on-site parking is $5 a night. Hale Pua Nui, clean and adequate, is a touch above spartan, with ceiling fans but no a/c, cable TV, phone, and fully equipped kitchen. Unfortunately, the "House of the Big Flower" is a bit wilted. The hotel is geared to repeat clientele, mostly from Canada, who book a year in advance, and not really open to new clientele, especially those who just drop in. If you want a room, call well in advance, and it will send you a form with the house rules (plenty). Remember, too, that there is no elevator, so you must carry your bags to the upper floors.

A two-minute walk puts you on Waikiki Beach when you stay at the **Waikiki Malihini Hotel,** 217 Saratoga Rd., Honolulu, HI 96815, tel. (808) 923-9644 or 923-3095, which bills itself as a "small, plain hotel with no extra frills. Just a place to stay in an excellent location." And, that's just what it is! In a semi-quiet area just across from Fort DeRussy, the hotel's 30 units have kitchenettes, daily maid service, fans (no a/c in most units), rental TV, and convenient but not complimentary parking next door. The management, not unfriendly but not overly congenial either, "strongly requests" that you contact them and fill out a card that will inform them of your dates of stay, number in party, etc., *before* they will make reservations. A well-laid lava rock wall in front provides some privacy for a small picnic area complete with tables and charcoal grills. Rates are studios $40-50, family suites $70-80 (some have a/c). There's a three-day minimum stay during peak season, and payment is by cash only!

MODERATE

The **Waikiki Beachside Apartment Hotel,** at 2556 Lemon Rd., Honolulu, HI 96815, tel. (808) 923-9566, is owned and operated by Mr. and Mrs. Wong, who keep a close eye on who they admit, as they run a very "decent" clean hotel. They rent weekly, charging from $385; off season may be cheaper. Per diem rooms are available during the winter rush at $66 a room, $35 for a semiprivate room, or $16.50 for a dorm bed. Furnished units have full kitchens and baths with twin beds and a convertible sofa and accommodate up to three people at no extra charge.

There are laundry facilities, but no maid service is available. Reservations are reluctantly accepted (they like to see you first), and parking is extra. Mrs. Wong says that they are going to renovate the hotel because it has become rundown. There are no firm plans for completion, but when and if they are carried out, the rates will go up. Be advised!

The **Outrigger Coral Seas Hotel,** at 250 Lewers St., Honolulu, HI 96815, tel. (808) 923-3881 or (800) 367-5170, is an old standby for budget travelers. This is the epitome of the economy tourist hotel and houses **Perry's Smorgasbord.** It's one of the Outrigger Hotels, and seems to get all the hand-me-downs from the others in the chain. There's a restaurant, cocktail lounge, TV, pool, and parking. Rates are an economical $75-85, extra person $15, and $130 for a kitchenette. Not to everyone's taste, but with plenty of action and the beach only a few steps away.

The **Waikiki Hana Hotel** at 2424 Koa Ave., Honolulu HI 96815, tel. (808) 926-8841 or (800) 367-5004, sits just behind the massive Hyatt Regency on a quiet side street. The hotel has just 73 rooms, so you won't get lost in the shuffle, and the friendly staff go out of their way to make you feel welcome. The Waikiki Hana is surrounded by high-rise hotels, so there's no view, but the peace and quiet just one block from the heavy action more than makes up for it. Rooms start at a very reasonable $79 and go to $119 for a superior with kitchenette. All rooms have telephones, a/c, color TV, in-room safes, and are gaily appointed with bright bedspreads and drapes. The **Super Chef Restaurant,** on the ground floor of the hotel, is one of the best in Waikiki for atmosphere, food, and very reasonable prices. On-site parking is another good feature in crowded Waikiki, but the charge is $10 a day. For a quiet, decent, but basic hotel in the heart of Waikiki, the Waikiki Hana can't be beat!

EXPENSIVE

The **Outrigger Hotels** chain has 20 locations in and around Waikiki offering thousands of rooms. Many of the hotels are on quiet side streets, others are on the main drags, while still more perch on Waikiki Beach. Although most are not luxurious, they do offer good accommodations and all have pools, restaurants, a/c, TV, and parking. Several have recently been renovated. Rates vary from hotel to hotel; their cheapest rates are $85 and from there run up to $660 for a two-bedroom ocean suite at the Prince Kuhio; $15 additional person. Special discounts of 20% are offered to travelers over 50 years old. For information and reservations call (800) 668-7444 or check the Outrigger website: at www.outrigger.com. Three of the chain's best hotels in Waikiki are the **Outrigger Reef, Outrigger Waikiki** (both on the beach), and the **Outrigger Prince Kuhio.** Others include the **Outrigger Waikiki Tower, Outrigger Royal Islander, Outrigger Edgewater,** and the **Outrigger Coral Seas.**

The **Outrigger Edgewater Hotel,** at 2168 Kalia Rd., Honolulu, HI 96815, tel. (808) 922-6424, is an old standby in the palpitating heart of Waikiki. Rates begin at a reasonable $90, rising to $145 for a kitchenette suite, $15 extra person. Kitchenettes run $100. Facilities include a swimming pool, a good Italian restaurant (open for dinner only), limited parking ($8 for 24 hours), TV, and maid service.

You can capitalize on the off-beach location of the **Aston Honolulu Prince,** at 415 Nahua St., Honolulu, HI 96815, tel. (808) 922-1616 or (800) 922-7866, where you'll find a hotel/condo offering remarkably good value for your money. The hotel/condo invites you into its fully furnished one- and two-bedroom suites. All offer a/c, color cable TV, fully equipped kitchens, and daily maid service. Prices begin at $90 for a standard room and $105 for superior, $135 one bedroom, and $155 two bedroom, with substantial discounts during low season. The apartments are oversize, with a huge sitting area that includes a sofa bed for extra guests. The Honolulu Prince is not fancy, but it is clean, decent, and family-oriented. A fine choice for a memorable vacation at affordable prices.

The **Breakers Hotel,** 250 Beach Walk, Honolulu, HI 96815, tel. (808) 923-3181 or (800) 426-0494, is a very friendly family-style hotel, where if you're a repeat visitor, the staff remembers your name. Only minutes from the beach, this little gem of a hotel somehow keeps the hustle and bustle far away. Every room has a kitchenette and overlooks the shaded courtyard of coconut and banana trees. The rates for studios are $88-95 s, $91-97 d, additional person

$8. The garden suites, which are equipped for up to four people, are $120-146. All units have a full kitchenette, a/c, color TV, a safe, and limited parking. There is also a swimming pool, and the **Hotel Cafe Terrace** where you can have a snack or light meal.

Varying shades of Italian Trabertine marble covered with pink floral carpets, filigreed mirrors, tables of black lacquer bearing Chinese porcelains, and ornate Louis XV chests under cut crystal chandeliers are the signature touches of the chinoiserie decor (combination of Chinese and European) at the **Aston Waikiki Beachside Hotel,** 2452 Kalakaua Ave., Honolulu, HI 96815, tel. (808) 931-2100, (800) 922-7866 Mainland, (800) 445-6633 Canada, or (800) 321-2558 Hawaii, another of Aston's boutique hotels. A Chinese lord and his concubine sit under an umbrella in a hand-painted silk portrait, while two bronze lions guard the marble staircase leading to a formal parlor on the second floor. Here, white silk couches with puffy pillows, a magnificent Chinese folding screen depicting courtly life, and an 18th-century Chinese secretary in red and black lacquer especially made for the "British market" are the decor. Outside, a tiny courtyard serenaded by a bubbling Italian fountain is set with wooden tables protected by canvas umbrellas. Mornings are perfect here with complimentary coffee and croissants. In the 12 floors above, only 77 luxurious rooms await, ranging in price from $105 for a superior to $290 for a VIP oceanfront (ask for discounted specials). Small, but space-consciously designed, the rooms are vibrant with melba peach carpet and wallpaper with a counterpoint of black. Amenities include air-conditioning, or functional windows to catch the Waikiki breeze, an entertainment center with remote-control color TV and VCR, a mini-fridge stocked with a selection of complimentary soft drinks, and a voice mail message system. Your stay is made even more relaxing with twice daily maid service and turndown service with a special treat left on your pillow, a free morning newspaper, and concierge service for all activities and travel plans. Tastefully decorated, the rooms are appointed with Chinese vases, folding screens painted with birds and flowers, jewelry boxes, and goosedown pillows imported from London. The bathrooms are done in Italian marble and feature glass shower stalls (no baths), floor-to-ceiling mirrors, pedestal sinks with black fixtures from Germany, his-and-her *yukata* (robes), a makeup mirror, a hair dryer, and bath products including shampoo, moisturizer, and French-milled soaps. Ocean view rooms have their own lanai, but be aware that some inside rooms are windowless.

The **Queen Kapiolani Hotel** is at 150 Kapahulu Ave., Honolulu, HI 96815, tel. (808) 922-1941 or (800) 367-5004. With its off-the-strip location and magnificent views of Diamond Head, this is perhaps the best, and definitely the quietest, hotel for the money in Waikiki. You're only seconds from the beach, and the hotel provides a spacious lobby, parking, a restaurant, TV, a/c, shops, and a swimming pool. Rates begin at $107 standard to $127 for a superior and go up to $165 with kitchenettes. Suites with kitchenettes run $250-380 a night. The main lobby has been rejuvenated with a $2 million face-lift. The stately marble columns have been redone, new wallpaper has been applied, and the shopping area has been upgraded. The overall effect is open and airy with the living mural of Diamond Head in the background. Select rooms have been made first-class with new carpeting, draperies, furnishing, and amenities. Most boast a spectacular view of Diamond Head. An excellent choice for the money. Also featured, in the **Peacock Dining Room,** is one of the best buffets in Waikiki.

The **Ilima Hotel,** 445 Nohonani St., Honolulu, HI 96815, tel. (808) 923-1877 or (800) 367-5172, is two streets back from the Ala Wai Canal and overlooks the Ala Wai Golf Course. This condo-style hotel is a few blocks from the beach—quiet atmosphere and budget rates. Studio units begin at a reasonable $109, $10 extra persons, one bedroom $144, two bedroom $187. All units have full kitchens, a/c, and TV, along with a pool, parking, and maid service. Discounts are given for those over age 55. **Sergio's Italian Restaurant,** on premises, is open for dinner. Good value.

A reasonably priced accommodation is the **Coconut Plaza Hotel,** at 450 Lewers St., tel. (808) 923-8828. Rates are $110-125 d during peak season. Off season is cheaper, with special day rates for bona fide business travelers on a space-available basis. A complimentary continental breakfast is offered daily in the lobby. All rooms are fully air-conditioned, and there is a hotel pool.

PREMIUM

Miramar at Waikiki, 2345 Kuhio Ave., Honolulu, HI 96815, tel. (808) 922-2077 or (800) 367-2303, is in the heart of Waikiki. The hotel offers generous-size rooms, with lanai, a pool, a restaurant, a/c, TV, and parking ($7 for 24 hours). Rates range $120-140, $20 extra per person.

You can't beat the value at the **Pacific Monarch Hotel/Condo** located directly behind the Hyatt Regency at 142 Uluniu Ave., Honolulu, HI 96815, tel. (808) 923-9805. It offers some great features for a moderately priced hotel. Fully furnished studios begin at $125 and go up to $145; one-bedroom condo apartments cost $160-190, all a/c, with on-site parking ($9 a night). The rooms are bright and cheery with full baths, living/dining areas, and cable TV. End units of each floor are larger, so request one for a large or shared party. The swimming pool, with a relaxing jacuzzi, perches high over Waikiki on the 34th floor of the hotel, offering one of the best cityscapes in Honolulu. The lobby is sufficient but small. It's accented with a lava fountain and two giant brass doors. A security key allows guests through the main door to the elevators. Save money and have a great family experience by setting up temporary housekeeping at the Pacific Monarch.

Sometimes you just hit it lucky and find yourself in a situation where you get more for your money than you expected, and delightfully so. The **Waikiki Beachcomber Hotel,** 2300 Kalakaua Ave., Honolulu, HI 96815, tel. (808) 922-4646, (800) 622-4646 Mainland, or (800) 338-6233 Canada, website: www.waikikibeachcomber.com, is definitely one of those *sometimes* things. The Beachcomber, living up to its name, is just a minute from the beach, and with a professional and amiable staff, knows exactly what you want and how to deliver it. Newly renovated to the tune of $5 million, the 500 guest rooms, outfitted in new furniture and carpet, and painted in soothing tropical tones, all feature a private lanai, a/c, TV, phone, room safe, and convenient refrigerator. On the property is a pool, the **Hibiscus Cafe,** boutique shops, parking, and laundry facilities. Offered through the summer months, the Beachcomber Kids program can entertain and feed children while their parents are off doing other activities. Every evening at 7 p.m., except Friday and Saturday, enjoy the voice and humor of one of Hawaii's consummate entertainers, Don Ho, as he presents his musical extravaganza as he has done in Waikiki for years. To add to its image as an entertainment center, the Beachcomber also presents the Magic of Polynesia Show. The rates for guest rooms range from $170 to $295 for a suite with $22 for an additional person, children under 17 free in their parents' room. A bargain special at only $140 puts you in a city view room with a rental car included or a breakfast buffet for two. To stay within budget, while having a quality experience, the Beachcomber is a sure bet!

LUXURY

Doubletree Alana Waikiki Hotel

At 1956 Ala Moana Blvd., tel. (808) 941-7275 or (800) 367-6070, fax (808) 951-3114, this "intimate boutique hotel" provides all needed amenities in a casual and relaxed atmosphere. All rooms are comfortably outfitted and have a/c, TV, computer hookups, lanai, and Italian marble entryways and baths. Rooms run $160-200, suites $240-550, and the Royal Amethyst Suite (a combined three-suite unit with boardroom) goes for $2,000. Artworks adorn the walls and works by local artists hang in the hotel's gallery. A full-service business center is available for those on working assignments, and everyone can enjoy the fitness center and swimming pool. The fine-dining **Harlequin** restaurant serves breakfast and "Pacific Northwest Rim cuisine" for dinner, while the more casual **Cafe Picasso** is a little easier going and combines dinner with entertainment. In the Doubletree tradition, every guest is welcomed to the hotel with freshly baked chocolate chip cookies.

Hawaiian Regent Hotel

The Hawaiian Regent, at 2552 Kalakaua Ave., Honolulu, HI 96815, tel. (808) 922-6611 or (800) 367-5370, has a long history of treating guests like royalty. The hotel now stands on what was the original site of Queen Liliuokalani's summer cottage. The Regent was the first major Hawaiian project of master designer Chris Hemmeter, famed for his magnificent Westin Kauai and

Hyatt Regency Waikaloa hotels. The grand tradition of the hotel is reflected in the open sweeping style that marks a Hemmeter project. After two decades, the Regent appears extremely modern because its design was so visionary when it was built. With almost 1,400 units, the hotel ranks as the third-largest hotel in Hawaii after the Hilton Hawaiian Village and the Sheraton Waikiki. Rates are $165-270 for a standard room up to $1,000 for a deluxe suite. Children are especially taken care of with the "Kid Quest," a summer program, and honeymooners can choose a junior suite with special amenities for a reduced price. All rooms are oversize and include cable TV, a/c, nightly turndown service, and in-room safes. You can step across the street to mingle with the fun-seekers on Waikiki Beach, or relax at one of the hotel's two pools. A championship Laykold tennis court is open from sunrise to sunset, with lessons and rackets available. The hotel offers a variety of exclusive shops in an off-lobby mall area like Shirokiya and Sandcastles for alohawear and evening wear. An onsite beauty shop and Japanese acupressure/massage service are there to revitalize you after a hard day of having fun in the sun. The Regent is renowned for its fine dining, entertainment, and late-night disco. The **Lobby Bar** is a perfect spot to perch while listening to relaxing Hawaiian music. The **Cafe Regent,** an open-air restaurant just off the main lobby, is open for breakfast, buffet, and lunch selections 6 a.m.-2:30 p.m. The **Tiffany Restaurant,** dinner only, has casual dining in an elegant atmosphere, with a stained-glass ceiling and shuttered windows. The **Ocean Terrace,** designed for kicking back and watching life go by, is a poolside bar serving sandwiches and hamburgers at very good prices. The premier restaurant of the hotel, and one of Waikiki's consistently best, is the award-winning **The Secret,** previously known as the Third Floor, where you can not only dine in Polynesian splendor, but be treated to a magnificent selection of wines collected by Richard Dean, one of only two sommeliers in all of Hawaii.

Enjoy a daily international buffet or spectacular Sunday brunch at **The Summery,** or a traditional Japanese meal at the **Regent Marushin.** You won't be told to hush while you dance or relax to the sounds of live music in **The Library.** And, if you have "dancing feet" take them to **The**

Point After, one of Waikiki's swingingest high-tech discos, which will rock you until the wee hours. If you're after peace and quiet, head for the **Garden Courtyard,** a multipurpose area in the center of the hotel. Sit among flowers and full-grown coconut and bamboo trees. Every Monday, Wednesday, and Friday 10 a.m.-noon learn lei-making, hula, or even Hawaiian checkers from *kapuna* who come just to share their *aloha.* The Hawaiian Regent is a first-class hotel that really knows how to make you feel like a visiting monarch. Rule with joy! (E-mail: hwnrgnt@aloha.net, website: hawaiianregent.com.)

Waikiki Parc Hotel

Just off Lewers St. at 2233 Helumoa Rd. is the modern but casual Waikiki Parc Hotel, tel. (808) 921-7272. The beach is just a stroll away. The entranceway is done in marble, carpet, and subdued lighting, and coolness seems to permeate the entire property. Rooms are not spacious, but efficient, some with lanai and others with balconies. On the ocean-view side, you look down on the distinctive orchid pool at the Halekulani Hotel. Depending upon location in the building, rooms run $170-255 a night. Open for breakfast, lunch, and dinner are the **Parc Cafe,** the hotel's main dining room, and the Japanese restaurant **Kacho.** The Parc Cafe features buffets at all meals, but the specialty is the weekend evening seafood buffet. The hotel pool is on the eighth floor, and there too you can get light meals and refreshments.

Aston Waikiki Joy Hotel

Upon arrival, step onto a path of white tile leading through a tiny but robust garden to a translucent dome sheltering the outdoor reception area of the Aston Waikiki Joy Hotel, a lotus flower that blooms in the heart of Waikiki, at 320 Lewers St., Honolulu, HI 96815, tel. (808) 923-2300, (800) 922-7866 Mainland, or (800) 321-2558 Hawaii. Blocks of glass, veined marbles in pinks, whites, and grays, and polished chrome are part of its petals. Immediately, marble steps rise to a veranda, where every morning a complimentary continental breakfast is served accompanied by the soft background chanting of a tiny fountain. The hotel, with only 94 rooms, is divided into two towers, the Hibiscus and the Gardenia. It's intimate enough to make everyone feel like an hon-

ored guest. Typical rooms, $170-195, are amazingly spacious. You enter through a vestibule to find an ultramodern room of slate blue and pastel pink contrasted with the embossed effect of a tan Berber carpet. Two accommodating wicker chairs wait to hug you with their overstuffed pillow arms. At the foot of each bed is an ottoman, great for perching on while dressing, and a dresser built in as part of the wall. The hotel rooms each feature a refrigerator and writing desk, which has a believable rendition of Miss Muffet's tuffet as its chair. A king-size bed with a slanted headboard perfectly designed for propping pillows is the "nerve center" of the room. Here, in easy reach, is a dimmer switch for all lighting, a temperature control, and a phone featuring a personalized voice message system. In front of the bed is an entertainment center with remote-control color TV and a stereo system with tape deck. The bathroom, done in pastel barber stripes, is a sanctuary of relaxation where you can slide every evening into a large and bubbling jacuzzi tub. The suites in the Gardenia Tower feature a bedroom and attendant sitting area complete with couch, and a large private lanai. Suite kitchens have a standard-size refrigerator, two-burner stove, double sink, microwave, toaster, and coffee maker. Here too, the bathrooms feature the wonderful jacuzzi tub. The Waikiki Joy is also very special with a 15-room karaoke studio, the largest and most modern in Waikiki (reservations recommended). The karaoke studio also features a lounge at the entrance, open weekdays 5 p.m.-2 a.m., weekends until 4 a.m., where you can order exotic drinks, standard cocktails, assorted iced teas, and island inspired *pu pu* from tofu to breaded calamari sticks. The hotel restaurant is **Cappuccino's,** a European-style bistro featuring live entertainment on the weekends. The Waikiki Joy, aptly named, is the epitome of the adage that "wonderful things come in small packages," but in this case, the wonderful thing *is* the package!

Aston Waikiki Shores Condominium

All you have to do is literally roll out of bed, walk out your door, and pick a spot on Waikiki Beach when you stay at the Aston Waikiki Shores Condominium, 2161 Kalia Rd., Honolulu, HI 96815, tel. (808) 926-4733 or (800) 367-2353. Individually owned, the decor in each unit differs, but most are tasteful with island-style furnishings, and all are immense. Typical is a one-bedroom laid out with a sitting area, living room, dining area, two baths with dressing rooms, and a kitchen complete with microwave, dishwasher, coffee maker, and garbage disposal. To make your stay more pleasant, there's daily maid service, private lanai, cable TV, in-room washers and dryers, beach towels, and limited parking, and children stay free with their parents. Rates, especially for what you get, are very reasonable, and start at $180 for a studio with deluxe ocean view, $260 for a one-bedroom unit, and up to $495 for a two-bedroom deluxe ocean front (10% off-season discount—ask!).

Sheraton Waikiki

Dominating the center of Waikiki are the 30 floors and 1,852 rooms of the Sheraton Waikiki Hotel, 2255 Kalakaua Ave., Honolulu, HI 96815, tel. (808) 922-4422, fax 923-8785, website: www.sheraton.com. Built in 1971 as one of the area's first convention centers, it has a perfect location on the beach. Think of it as a miniature global village where 7,000-8,000 people come and go every day. Over the next few years, the Sheraton company will put several million dollars into refurbishing this complex, bringing the spirit of the sea into the hotel. In conjunction, the *honu* (green sea turtle), which has come back from the brink of extinction and feeds in the evening in the waters of Waikiki, has been incorporated into the hotel logo. Rooms are either ocean view or city view, and all have full amenities, including air-conditioning, TV and movies, mini-refrigerators, and in-room safes. Ocean view rooms run $315-430, city and mountain view rooms $195-300, suites from $600. The hotel has a clutch of shops for apparel, jewelry, gifts, camera needs, and sundries; two freshwater pools; its own nightclub; three cocktail lounges; and three restaurants, including the **Hanohano Room** (its signature restaurant on the 30th floor) the **Ciao!** Italian restaurant, and the more casual **Ocean Terrace Restaurant.** Free to guests are fun runs Mon.-Sat. at 7 a.m. with marathoner Max Telford, aerobic fitness training Mon.-Fri. at 5 p.m., tai chi on Tuesday and Thursday at 4 p.m., and a leisurely guided historical tour along the beach at 9 a.m. every Wednesday. The Keiki Aloha Club can keep your kids (ages 5-12) busy with age-appropriate, supervised activities 9 a.m.-9 p.m. from mid-June through mid-August and 9 a.m.-5 p.m. the rest of the year. Baby-sitting services are also available. Golfers can easily schedule tee times at the Sheraton Makaha Golf Club through the dining and activities desk, while guests who have early arrivals or late-night departures can make use of the lockers, showers, restrooms, and lounge in the Hospitality Center 6:30 a.m.-9:30 p.m.

Hilton Hawaiian Village

This glorious first-rate hotel, an oasis of tranquility, sits in its own quiet corner of Waikiki. The Hilton, at 2005 Kalia Rd., Honolulu, HI 96815, tel. (808) 949-4321 or (800) 445-8667, website: www.hawaiianvillage.hilton.com, is at the far western end of Waikiki, just below Fort DeRussy. Enter along 200 yards of the private hotel driveway, passing the village, a small mall with exclusive shopping and dining. Facing you are the Hilton's "towers," the Tapa, the Diamond Head, the Rainbow, and the prestigious Alii Tower. Rainbow Tower, so called because of the huge multistoried rainbow on the entire side of this building, is, according to the *Guinness Book of World Records,* the tallest ceramic-tile mosaic in the world. All the rooms are deluxe with magnificent views. Amenities include color TV, a/c, self-service bar, refrigerator, 24-hour room service, voice mail, and a safe for personal belongings. Children will also be delighted with the **Rainbow Express,** a year-round program that entertains and educates with everything from hula lessons to a trip to the Honolulu Zoo ($17 half day, $32 full lunch included).

The Alii Tower pampers you even more with a private pool with nightly gourmet *pu pu,* turndown service, fresh flowers, fruit baskets, concierge service, flowers, a fitness center, a sauna, and bath accessories. Rates are $240-310 throughout the Village and $229-340 in the Alii Tower.

The towers form a semicircle fronting the beach, not a private beach because none can be private, but about as private a public beach as you can get. Few come here unless they're staying at the Hilton. It's dotted with palms—tall royal palms for elegance, shorter palms for shade. The property has three pools. The main pool, surrounded by luxuriant tropical growth, is the largest in Waikiki. The lagoon area creates the music of water in bubbling rivulets, tiny waterfalls, and reflecting pools. Torches of fire, and ginger, banana trees, palms, ferns, and rock gardens are the grounds. The concierge can arrange a guided tour of the grounds (free) by a grounds-keeper, who will explain the habitat, life cycle, and characteristics of each plant.

The *action* of Waikiki is out there, of course, just down the driveway, but you don't feel it unless you want to. Relax and enjoy the sunset accompanied by music at any one of 10 lounges like the **Shell Bar,** or in the main foyer where another small casual bar swings to the tunes of a piano stylist. Exotic and gourmet dining from throughout the Pacific rim is available at the Village's 10 restaurants, especially the hotel's signature **Bali by the Sea** and **Golden Dragon** restaurants.

As you pull into the driveway there's a geodesic dome, like a giant stereo speaker, entertainment shows are performed. A miniature golf course has been added to the grounds and an entertainment center, with karaoke and video games, is now located in Joy Square. The hotel has everything to keep its "villagers" contented and happy. As a complete destination resort where you can play, relax, shop, dine, dance, and retreat, the Hilton Hawaiian Village knows what it's about and has found its center.

Aston Waikiki Sunset Hotel

Twinkling lights descending the residential valleys of the Koolau Range with Diamond Head framed in perfect symmetry are an integral part of the natural room decor of the Aston Waikiki Sunset Hotel, 229 Paoakalani St., Honolulu, HI 96815, tel. (808) 922-0511, (800) 922-7866 Mainland, or (800) 321-2558 Hawaii, one of Waikiki's newest suite-hotels. Charmingly refurbished from head to toe in 1991, the Waikiki Sunset, although *feeling* like a condominium, offers all of the comfort and convenience of a hotel including 24-hour front desk service, daily maid service, and amenities like a swimming pool, sauna, tennis court, travel desk, minimart, and even a restaurant. The entrance, cooled by Casablanca fans whirring over marble floors, sets the mood for this charming hotel tucked away only one block from the Waikiki strip. Units range $245-280. All feature full kitchens outfitted with a large refrigerator, coffee maker, electric stove and oven, disposal, and complete utensils for in-room cooking and dining. All suites feature a private lanai and entertainment center with remote-control color TV, and a tiled bath with a Japanese-style *ofuro,* a soaking tub perfect for the start of a cozy evening. The larger suites have a sitting room, modern and chic with rattan furniture, a bar/breakfast nook, and separate master bedroom. The **Manbow Inn,** on the sixth floor, open 7:30 a.m.-9 p.m., serves breakfast, lunch, and dinner at reasonable prices. The minimart, open 7 a.m.-11 p.m., provides everything from suntan lotion to takeout pizza. Here, too, you can rent sporting equipment like snorkel sets and boogie boards, with a 10% discount offered to hotel guests.

Hawaii Prince Hotel

The dynamic seascape of the tall masted ships anchored in the Ala Wai Yacht Harbor reflects in the shimmering pink-tinted glass towers of the Hawaii Prince Hotel, at 100 Holomoana St., Honolulu, HI 96815, tel. (808) 956-1111 or (800) 321-6248, www.sheraton.com, the city's newest luxury hotel. This hotel is also represented by Westin Resorts, tel. (800) 228-3000. The twin towers, Diamond Head and Ala Moana, are scaled by a glass elevator affording wide-angled vistas of the Honolulu skyline. Decorated in green and tan with light burnished maple, the rooms, all ocean view, feature a marble-topped desk with full mirror, a/c, functional windows, and a full entertainment center with remote-control color TV and VCR. Each room has its own refrigerator, walk-in closet with complimentary safe and terry cloth robes, and a king-size bed with fluffy down pillows. The marble bathrooms have separate shower stalls, tubs, and commodes with a full set of toiletries, lighted makeup mirrors, and hair dryers. Room rates are from $250 for an Oceanfront Marina to $410 for an Oceanfront Top (floors 30-33), while suites range up to $2,500; $45 per extra person. Special business rates are offered (ask when booking), and a special golf package is available for $275. Ride the elevator to the fifth floor, where you will find a keyhole-shaped pool and canvas shade umbrellas overlooking the harbor below. Here as well is the **Promenade Deck Snack Shop** serving coffee, jumbo hamburgers, and other munchies beginning at 11 a.m. The business center on the 29th floor gives you access to a secretary, computers, fax machines, modems for e-mail, and a conference room. Fees vary according to services rendered. Other amenities include three excellent restaurants, the **Takanawa, Prince Court,** and **Hakone;** a lobby lounge; a full fitness center; turndown service upon request; valet parking; and a Waikiki/Ala Moana Shuttle. The Hawaii Prince boasts its own golf course, the **Hawaii Prince Golf Club,** the only one of its kind belonging to a Waikiki hotel. Located at Ewa Beach, 35 minutes away by complimentary shuttle, the Arnold Palmer-designed 27-hole championship course includes a fully equipped golf shop, practice range, putting greens, chipping greens, locker and shower facilities, clubhouse dining, and tennis courts. The Hawaii Prince, located at the "gateway to Waikiki" is away from the action of the frenetic Waikiki strip, but close enough to make it easily accessible.

Sheraton Moana Surfrider

The Moana, 2365 Kalakaua Ave., Honolulu, HI 96815, tel. (808) 922-3111 or (800) 325-3535, fax (808) 923-0308, website: www.sheraton.com, is the oldest and most venerable hotel in Waikiki. More than just recapturing turn-of-the-century grandeur, the Moana has surpassed itself by integrating all of the modern conveniences. The original Italian Renaissance style is the main architectural theme, but like a fine opera, it joins a ariety of architectural themes that blend into a soul-satisfying finale. The restoration has connected the three main buildings, the Moana, Ocean Lanai, and Surfrider, to form an elegant complex of luxury accommodations, gourmet dining, and distinctive shopping. The renovated Moana, filled with memories of times past, is magical. It's as if you stood spellbound before the portrait of a beautiful princess of long ago, when suddenly her radiant granddaughter, an exact image, dazzling in jewels and grace, walked into the room.

You arrive under the grand columns of a porte cochere, where you are greeted by doormen in crisp white uniforms and hostesses bearing lei and chilled pineapple juice. The lobby is a series of genteel parlor arrangements conducive to very civilized relaxation. Art, urns, chandeliers, sofas, koa tables, flowers, vases, and pedestaled glass-topped tables wait in attendance. An elevator takes you to the second floor, where a room filled with 80 years of memorabilia whispers names and dates of the Moana's grand past. After a fresh chilled glass of pineapple juice, you are escorted to check-in.

Upstairs, the rooms are simple elegance. Queen-size beds in the Banyan Wing, rattan chairs, and fat fluffy pillows and bedspreads extend their waiting arms. All rooms have a/c, and the Banyan Wing features a remote-control master keyboard for TV, lights, and music. But this is the Moana! Sachet-scented closets hold *yukata* (robes), terry slippers, and satin hangers. Bathrooms are tile and marble appointed with huge towels and stocked with fine soaps, shampoos, creams, makeup mirrors, and a bathroom scale, which you can hide under the bed.

Being the first hotel built in Waikiki, it sits right on the beach with one of the best views of Diamond Head along the strip. A swimming pool with sundeck is staffed with attentive personnel, and the activities center can book you on a host of activities, including a classic outrigger canoe ride or a sunset sail on a catamaran. Four restaurants, a grand ballroom, a snack bar, and three lounges take care of all your dining needs. Rooms in the Moana wing overlook Banyan Court, scene of a nightly entertainment that can be chamber music provided by a pianist or harpist. Open the windows, allowing the breezes to billow the curtains while the waves of Waikiki join with the music below in a heavenly serenade. Rooms are $250-485, with suites priced from $900. The Sheraton Moana Surfrider is a superb hotel offering exemplary old-fashioned service. Whether you're a guest here or not, feel free to join one of the guided tours of the hotel's restored and refurnished original section, offered twice daily at 11 a.m. and 5 p.m.

Royal Hawaiian Hotel

The Royal Hawaiian, second oldest hotel built along Waikiki, at 2259 Kalakaua Ave., Honolulu, HI 96815, tel. (808) 923-7311 or (800) 325-3535, fax (808) 924-7098, website: www.sheraton.com, provides an ongoing contemporary experience in turn-of-the-century charm. The Royal Hawaiian has also recently completed a $25 million restoration, which has recaptured the grand

Royal Hawaiian Hotel

them. Rooms might have four-poster beds, canopies, twins, or kings, depending upon your preference. All rooms have remote-control TV, refrigerators, electronic safes, and computer hookups on telephones for lap-top computers. Furniture is French provincial, with bathrooms fully tiled. Completely renovated rooms in the original section have kept the famous pink motif, but are slightly more pastel. They have a marble tile bathroom, a brass butler, louvered drawers, and a huge bed. The tall ceilings are even more elegant with molded plaster cornices. Guests are treated to banana bread on arrival, a daily newspaper, and turndown service with a complimentary late-night sweet treat. Preferential tee-off times at the Makaha Resort are also offered. Each floor of the original Royal has a pool elevator, so guests in beachwear don't clash with the early evening black-tie set. A Hospitality Suite is provided for early morning check-ins or late checkouts and offers complimentary shower facilities, maid service six times during the day, coffee-making facilities, and a sitting and lounging area.

Some of the prestige suites are truly luxurious and feature huge balconies with tiled floors, where a party of 25 could easily be entertained. The tastefully carpeted bedrooms boast a quilt-covered bed heaped with a half dozen pillows. The huge bathrooms overlook the beach and have a small built-in jacuzzi. In the massive Governor's Suite is a formal dining room, two huge bedrooms, two magnificent sitting areas—one a formal parlor, the other an "informal" rec room. The Royal Towers, an addition dating from 1969, are preferred by many guests because every room has an ocean view. From the balcony of most, you look down onto the swimming pool, the beach, palm trees, and Diamond Head in the distance. Not as large as its neighbors, the Royal Hawaiian has 527 rooms, 49 of which are suites. A basic guest room is $290-540, with suites ranging from $475 to more than $1,600.

If you stay at the Royal Hawaiian, you can dine and sign at the Moana Surfrider, Sheraton Waikiki, or Princess Kaiulani, all operated by Sheraton Hotels. One of the best features of the Royal, open to guest and nonguest, is the remarkable luau every Monday night and the extraordinary food and entertainment provided Tues.-Sat. by the Brothers Cazimero in the

elegance of days past. Doors first opened in 1927, at a cost of $4 million, an unprecedented amount of money in those days for a hotel. The Depression brought a crushing reduction to Hawaiian tourism, bringing the yearly total down from a whopping 22,000 to under 10,000 (today more visitors arrive in one day), and the Royal became a financial loss. During WW II, with Waikiki barbed-wired, the Royal was leased to the Navy as an R&R hotel for sailors from the Pacific Fleet. After the war, the hotel reverted to Matson Lines, the original owner, and reopened in 1947 after a $2 million renovation. Sheraton Hotels purchased the Royal in 1959, built the Royal Tower Wing in 1969, sold the hotel in 1975, but continued to remain as operating manager.

Original double doors featured one solid door backed by a louvered door so you could catch the ocean breezes and still have privacy. Today, the hotel is fully air-conditioned, so the old doors have been removed and new solid rosewood doors carved in the Philippines have replaced hotel's famous and elegant **Monarch Dining Room.** The Royal Hawaiian, a Waikiki classic, is worth a visit even if you don't stay there.

Halekulani

The Halekulani Hotel, in mid-Waikiki at 2199 Kalia Rd., Honolulu, HI 96815, tel. (808) 923-2311 or (800) 367-2343, website: www.halekulani.com, was an experiment of impeccable taste that paid off. Some years ago the hotel was completely rebuilt and refurnished with the belief that Waikiki could attract the luxury-class visitor, and that belief has proven accurate. Since opening, the hotel has gained international recognition and has been named as a member of the prestigious Leading Hotels of the World, and Preferred Hotels and Resorts Worldwide. It is one of four AAA five-diamond hotels in Hawaii and the only one on Oahu. In addition, its signature restaurant, La Mer, has also been given a five-diamond rating, making the Halekulani one of the best.

The soothing serenade of the Halekulani begins from the moment you enter the porte cochere where an impressive floral display of protea, anthuriums, orchids, and ferns arranged in the *sogetsu* style of *ikebana* by Kanemoto-san awaits to welcome you. The property was first developed in 1907 by Robert Lewers as a residential grouping of bungalows, none of which survive. However, still preserved is the **Main Building,** dating from the 1930s when the hotel became a fashionable resort owned by Juliet and Clifford Kimball. The Main Building, a plantation-style mansion, houses the hotel's award-winning **La Mer Restaurant,** along with the **Orchids Dining Room,** serving breakfast, lunch, and dinner; **Lewer's Lounge** for an intimate cocktail and nightly entertainment; the very genteel **Living Room,** where you can enjoy refreshments and watercress sandwiches; and the veranda where the afternoon tea is held. Notice the Main Building's distinctive "Dickey Roof," patterned after a Polynesian longhouse, perfectly sloped in such as way as to catch island breezes while repelling a sudden rain squall.

Wander the grounds to be pleasantly surprised that a full 50% is given to open space accented with trimmed lawn, reflecting pools, and bubbling fountains. The heated **Orchid Pool,** with its signature mosaic orchid, is always inviting and within earshot of the foaming surf. Close by is **House Without a Key,** an indoor/outdoor buffet restaurant also serving light snacks and perhaps the best locale in all of Waikiki for a sunset cocktail. Upon arrival, you are escorted directly to the privacy of your own guest room where you register. Awaiting is a platter of fine china bearing a display of fresh fruit and complimentary "Bakeshop" chocolates. Each evening, with turndown service, a dainty orchid and delicate shell are left upon your pillow, along with a once-per-week recipe card from one of the fine hotel restaurants. Enter the guest room through a solid teak door into an antechamber that opens into a room, done in seven shades of white. The floors are covered in rich Berber carpet while the king-size beds are dressed with soft white quilts. For ultimate relaxation and added convenience, all of the rooms feature a writing desk, small couch, reclining chair, and marble-topped accessory tables softly lit by Oriental-style lamps. A remote-controlled entertainment center, mini-fridge, three telephones, an in-room safe, and a collection of wooden and satin covered hangers complete the amenities. Sliding louvered doors lead to a tiled lanai, private and perfect for in-room dining. The bathroom, with floor to ceiling tile, features a deep soaking tub, a shower stall, two sinks, a separate commode, and a hairdryer. The louvered and glass doors can be opened so that you have a view from your tub directly past the lanai to Diamond Head in the distance. Prices are $310-520 for guest rooms, $700-1,700 for suites, with the President Suite at $4,000 and Royal Suite at $4,500 a night. A third-person charge for over 18 years of age is $125 or $40 for a child if a roll-away bed is needed. Additional amenities include swimming pool, beach service, daily newspapers, free local telephone calls, and a full-service fitness center where you can sign up to go on a fun run with world-class marathon runner Max Telford on Monday, Wednesday, or Friday, or attend an aerobics class on Tuesday, Thursday, and Saturday. The Halekulani awaits to show you its version of classic island charm. You won't be disappointed.

Kahala Mandarin Oriental

Cast-up treasures of sand-tumbled glass is the theme captured in the distinctive multihued chandeliers that hang from the 30-foot vaulted ceilings of the grand hallway, the entrance to the Kahala Mandarin. Long considered a standard-setter for Hawaiian deluxe hotels, the Kahala Mandarin, 5000 Kahala Ave., Honolulu, HI 96816, tel. (808) 739-8888, fax 739-8800, or (800) 367-2525, is not technically in Waikiki, but in Kahala, an exclusive residential area just east of Diamond Head. The hotel, built 30 years ago and refurbished in '96-97 to the tune of $80 million, is proud that most of its key employees have been there from the first days and that they have formed lasting friendships with guests who happily return year after year. Surrounded by the exclusive Waialae Country Club (not even hotel guests are welcome unless they are members), the hotel gives a true sense of peace and seclusion and rightly boasts a "Neighbor Island Experience" only minutes from bustling Waikiki. A grand staircase fashioned from lava rock wears a living lei of green ferns and purple orchids, as it descends to **Hoku,** the hotel's formal restaurant, open for lunch and dinner and specializing in Pacific Rim cuisine with a Hawaiian twist. The hotel's informal **Plumeria Beach Cafe,** open 6:30 a.m.-11 p.m., is famous for its impossible-to-resist pastries. Entertainment at the hotel is offered in the evening at the **Plumeria Bar** at beachside and at the lobby lounge. A beach shack offers all kinds of pool-side snacks and boasts the best hamburgers on Oahu.

The hotel, fronting the sheltered Mauna Lua Bay, features a perfect crescent beach, swimming pool, and beach cabana with all watersports gear available including kayaks, rafts, boogie boards, and snorkel gear. Behind, a waterfall cascading from a free-form stone wall forms a rivulet that leads to a dolphin lagoon (feeding daily at noon, 2 p.m., and 4 p.m.) and a series of saltwater ponds teeming with reef fish. A daily 30-45-minute dolphin experience is offered by lottery and runs $90 per adult and $50 for kids 7-12 years old. Other offerings are its arcade shops, scheduled shuttle service to Waikiki and major shopping malls, its new fitness and executive business centers, and its Hawaiian cultural program.

Average rooms are extra large and have in-room safes and small refrigerators. Rates are $295 for a garden view room, $340 for a mountain view room, and up to $440 for an ocean view room; the 29 suites are more yet. The Kahala Mandarin isn't for everyone, but there's no doubt that you get all that you pay for.

Aston Waikiki Beach Tower Hotel

A tunnel of white thumbergia tumbling from a welcoming arbor leads to the entrance of the Aston Waikiki Beach Tower Hotel, 2470 Kalakaua Ave. Honolulu, HI 96815, tel. (808) 926-6400, (800) 922-7866 Mainland, or (800) 321-2558 Hawaii, one of Waikiki's newest mini-luxury condo hotels. A lustrous patina shines from brown on tan marble floors while glass-topped tables of black and gold lacquer hold magnificent displays of exotic blooms, and fancy French mirrors and cut glass chandeliers brighten the small but intimate reception area. Enter your suite through a vestibule of brown marble and glass onto a white carpet leading to a combination dining/living room. This common area, accented with contemporary paintings and highlighted by koa trim, offers a full wet bar, drum and glass tables, high-backed chairs, a pastel rainbow couch, and an entertainment center with remote-control TV. The ultramodern kitchen is complete with standard-size refrigerator with ice maker, a rice cooker, a blender, a coffee maker, a microwave, a four-burner stove and oven, a dishwasher, a double sink, and koa cabinets. The master bedroom has its own entertainment center and private lanai from which you can overlook Waikiki. The bathroom has a double sink, commode, and shower, and a huge walk-in closet holding a complimentary safe, steam iron and board, and a washer and dryer. Rates range $450-680. Special amenities include twice daily maid service, turndown service, concierge desk, valet parking, a paddle tennis court, a swimming pool, spa and sauna, and also meeting rooms and a family plan.

FOOD

The streets of Waikiki are an international banquet, with more than a dozen cuisines spreading their tables for your enjoyment. Because of the culinary competition, you can choose restaurants in the same way that you peruse a smorgasbord, for both quantity and quality. Within a few hundred yards are all-you-can-gorge buffets, luau, dinner shows, fast foods, ice cream, and jacket-and-tie restaurants. The free tourist literature runs coupons, and placards advertise specials for breakfast, lunch, and dinner. Bars and lounges often give free *pu pu* and finger foods that can easily make a light supper. As with everything in Waikiki, its restaurants are a close-quartered combination of the best and the worst, but with only a little effort it's easy to find great food, great atmosphere, and mouthwatering satisfaction.

Note: At many of the moderately priced restaurants listed below and at all of the expensive restaurants *reservations are highly recommended.* It's much easier to make a two-minute phone call than it is to have your evening spoiled, so please call ahead. Also, many of the restaurants along the congested Waikiki strip provide valet parking (usually at no charge), or will offer validated parking at a nearby lot. So check when you call to reserve. Attire at most Hawaiian restaurants is casual, but at the better restaurants it is dressy casual, which means closed-toe shoes, trousers, and a collared shirt for men, and a simple but stylish dress for women. At some of the very best restaurants you won't feel out of place with a jacket, but ties are not usually worn.

INEXPENSIVE

Eggs And Things, at 1911 Kalakaua Ave., just where it meets McCully, tel. (808) 949-0820, is a late-night institution open 11 p.m.-2 p.m. the following afternoon. A number of discos are just around the corner, so the clientele in the wee hours is a mix of revelers, hotel workers, boat captains, and even a hooker or two. The decor is wooden floors and formica tables, but the waitresses are top-notch and friendly. The food is absolutely excellent and it's hard to spend more than $10. Daily specials are offered 1-2 a.m., while the morning special 5-8 a.m. gets you three pancakes and two fresh eggs cooked as you like for just a few dollars. Waffles and pancakes are scrumptious with fresh fruit or homemade coconut syrup. Besides the eggs and omelettes the most popular item is fresh fish, which is usually caught by the owner himself, Mr. Jerry Fukunaga, who goes out almost every day on his own boat. It's prepared Cajun-style, or sautéed in garlic and butter, with two fresh eggs and a choice of pancakes, rice, or home-fried potatoes. Prices vary according to market price. Casual attire is acceptable, and BYO wine or beer is okay.

Around the corner is **The Dynasty Restaurant,** tel. (808) 947-3771, at 1778 Ala Moana Blvd., in Discovery Bay across from the Ilikai Hotel. It has an enormous menu of various Chinese cuisines that is acceptable but not memorable. The servers are friendly and courteous, and it's open daily 10 a.m.-6 a.m. For a very late night repast after "doing the town," the food definitely hits the spot!

Almost across the street and tucked into a nook close to the Hilton Hawaiian Village is the **Saigon Cafe,** at 1831 Ala Moana Blvd., tel. (808) 955-4009, open daily 6:30 a.m.-10 p.m. The Saigon Cafe is a friendly, meticulously clean, unpretentious, family-run affair that definitely offers "budget gourmet" food. Order tureens of soup for two, spiced with lemongrass, hot garlic sauce, and floating with dollops of seafood, chicken, beef, tofu, or pork for under $7. Roll your own spring rolls, which come with slices of meat, fresh vegetables, mint, dipping sauces, and transparently thin rice paper that you dip in water to soften before rolling away. Noodle dishes are large and hearty, while breakfast brings an assortment of eggs, pancakes, and waffles. It's hard to spend more than $10 on a meal that is not only delicious, but fresh, made to order, and healthy as well. Great choice!

Right across from the Hilton Hawaiian Village, downstairs below the California Pizza kitchen is the tastefully arranged **Singha Thai Cuisine.** Lunch is served Mon.-Fri. 11 a.m.-4 p.m., and dinner is served nightly 4-11 p.m. Thai dancers perform every night 6:45-9 p.m. Vegetarian spring rolls for $5.95 and chicken or shrimp sauté for $7.95 are two of the appetizers on the menu; soups run about $6.95. Entrees include a Thai-style spicy eggplant dish for $7.95 lunch or $11.95 dinner, barbecued chicken for $8.95 lunch or $11.95 dinner, grilled jumbo black tiger prawn curry for $17.95, seafood noodles for $14.95, and vegetarian fried rice for $8.95. Ranging $15-25 are the most expensive entrees like fresh local fish, grilled rack of lamb, and lobster with pineapple and yellow curry. This is an upscale place, but authentic Thai.

Right next to the reasonable Royal Grove Hotel, at 151 Uluniu St., tel. (808) 926-9717, is **Na's Barbecue,** serving Korean food. Open 7 a.m.-10 p.m. daily, it's a tiny place, with plastic chairs and one formica table inside and a small courtyard outside, but the people are friendly, the food well-prepared, and the prices are good. Try a plate of *kalbi,* which is marinated and grilled beef short ribs, for $6.99, charbroiled chicken for $6, *mandu,* or fried stuffed dumplings, for $5.99, or various soups for $8-9. Hawaiianized Korean dishes are also on the menu.

Da Smokehouse, 470 Ena Rd., tel. (808) 946-0233, open daily 11:30 a.m.-midnight, is one of those places where the food is excellent, but you wouldn't want to eat there. Why? Because it is primarily a takeout restaurant with only a few booths stuck in the back where *da* smoke and *da* grease from *da* wood-fired smoker is *da* decor. Actually, owner Shirley Jones has recently moved *da* wood-fired smoker out back and added a few new tables. *Da* decor is now compromised. Next will come color-coordinated tableware. God forbid! Your choices are smoked beef, pork, chicken, and ham all served picnic style, with two choices of sides including homemade potato salad, baked beans, rice, coleslaw, or french fries. Price ranges are $5.95 for a quarter barbecued chicken, $8.95 for a half barbecued chicken, $9.95 for barbecued ham, $11.95 for barbecued pork or beef ribs. The combo plate of all of the above, which can easily feed two, is only $20.95. Desserts for $2.50 include *lilikoi* pie, cheesecake, mud pie, and sorbet. No liquor, so BYO A small delivery charge of $1.35 makes Da Smokehouse a perfect alternative to inflated room service prices at sur-rounding hotels, or for a home-cooked dinner in your condo. You'll love it!

LNT Spaghetti Hale, tel. (808) 949-3216, at 474-A Ena Rd., is a tiny family-run place with only a handful of tables—takeout available. The food is Italian, the cooks, Asian; a good mix with wonderful results, yet nothing fancy. Some available items are seafood and vegetables for $9.49, and spaghetti with various sauces from $4.99 to $7.

Ena Restaurant, 432 Ena Rd., tel. (808) 951-0818, open daily 10 a.m.-11:30 p.m., is a small Chinese restaurant with little atmosphere, but with good food at good prices. Appetizers and soups include crispy wonton $2.95, chicken salad $5.95, and scallop soup for $2.95. Lunch specials like lemon chicken or beef with vegetables are $4.75, while entrees like mixed seafood and vegetables, fillet of fish in hot red sauce, roast duck, twice-cooked Sichuan-style pork, or Hunan-style tofu are $5.95-8.95. The Ena Restaurant, away from the hustle and bustle, is a good choice for a basic meal with no frills.

Ruffage Natural Foods, at 2442 Kuhio, tel. (808) 922-2042, is one of a very few natural food restaurants in Waikiki. It serves a wide assortment of tofu sandwiches, burritos, natural salads, tofu burgers, fresh island fruits, and smoothies for lunch and dinner. Everything is homemade, and the restaurant tries to avoid, as much as possible, processed foods. Just about everything on the menu is less than $6. Aside from the menu items, food supplements, minerals, vitamins, and things of that nature are also available. It's a small hole-in-the-wall type eatery that's easy to miss. A few wooden tables outside under a portico are the ambience.

Ezogiku is a chain of Japanese restaurants. Open till the wee hours, these no-atmosphere restaurants serve inexpensive hearty bowls of Sapporo *ramen* (renowned as the best), curry rice, and *gyoza.* It has multiple locations in and around Waikiki at 2083 Kuhio Ave., 2420 Koa Ave., 2546 Lemon Rd., and 2141 Kalakaua Avenue. Ezogiku is a no-frills kind of place. Small, smoky, counter seating, and totally authentic. It's so authentic that on the dishes they spell *ramen* as *larmen.* You not only eat inexpensively, but you get a very authentic example of what it's like to eat in Japan . . . cheaply. Eat heartily for around $6.

The Jolly Roger, 150 Kaiulani, is an American standard restaurant with a Hawaiian flair. If you're after good old-fashioned tuna salad sandwiches, hot roast beef, a tostada even, or just plain soup and salad, this would be your best bet in Waikiki. The Jolly Roger borders on tasteful with a dark green decor accented with bronze, pleasant booth seating, and a profusion of ferns and hanging plants. Open 6:30 a.m.-1 a.m.; breakfast fare includes waffles, pancakes, omelettes, and meats, but try the orange bread as standard or French toast. A lunch special is hamburger steak, $4.95, with dinners well under $10. Happy hour is 6 a.m.-6 p.m., when exotics are poured for $1.75, draft beer $1.50. Free *pu pu* is available 4-6 p.m.

Man Lee's Chinese Restaurant, 124 Kapahulu, tel. (808) 922-6005, is a basic Chinese restaurant that offers daily lunch and dinner specials, for $4.25 and $6, respectively. The atmosphere is quiet since it's around the corner from most of the action, and the food is acceptable but not memorable. A belly-filler only, it's open 11 a.m.-2 p.m. and then again 5-9 p.m.

Wong and Wong, at 1023 Maunakea, tel. (808) 521-4492, is a simple and basic Chinese restaurant where you can have a good and filling meal at a reasonable price. Many people who live and work in and around Waikiki choose to go here for Chinese food.

Perry's Smorgy, at 2380 Kuhio Ave., tel. (808) 926-0184, and at the Coral Seas Hotel, 250 Lewers St., tel. (808) 922-8814, is the epitome of the budget travelers' "line 'em up, fill 'em up, and head 'em out" kind of restaurant. There is no question that you'll waddle away stuffed, but forget about any kind of memorable dining experience. When you arrive, don't be put off by the long lines. They move! First, you run a gauntlet of salads, breads, and potatoes, in the hopes that you'll fill your plate. Try to restrain yourself. Next comes the meat, fish, and chicken. The guys serving up the roast beef are masters of a whole lot of movement and very little action. The carving knife whips around in the air, but does very little damage to the joint of beef. A paper-thin slice is finally cut off and put on your plate with aplomb. The carver then looks at you as if you were Oliver Twist asking for more. Added pressure comes from the long line of tourists behind, who act as if they have just escaped from a Nazi labor camp. The breakfast buffet is actually very good, with all the standard eggs, meats, juices, and rolls, and the food in general, considering the price, is more than acceptable. You can't complain. The all-you-can-eat dinner is $8.99.

The Shorebird, open for breakfast, lunch, and dinner (from 5 p.m.), is on the beach behind the Outrigger Reef Hotel at 2169 Kalia Rd., tel. (808) 922-2887, giving this budget restaurant the best gourmet location in all of Waikiki. Here you'll find a limited but adequate menu of cook-your-own selections for under $15 (discount tickets save you more). Walk through the lobby to the beach for a remarkable sunset while dining. Included is a good, fresh salad bar of vegetables and fruits. Beverages are included, the setting is wonderful, and the value excellent, but you do pay extra for bread. Karaoke is offered nightly for all those Don Ho "wannabes."

The Islander Coffee House, on Lewers St., tel. (808) 923-3233, in the Reef Towers Hotel, open daily 6 a.m.-midnight, has inexpensive breakfasts of two pancakes, eggs, and bacon for $2.69. It also offers steak and eggs Benedict for $4.29, chef salad for $6, hamburgers under $5, and specials every day for inexpensive prices. No dining experience whatsoever, but down-home prices in the heart of Waikiki.

The **Beach Street Cafe,** in the Outrigger Reef Hotel, 2169 Kalia Rd., open daily 7 a.m.-9 p.m., is literally on the beach. Breakfast, 7-11 a.m., starts at $2.99 for a scrambled-egg platter, and just $1.95 for cereal and yogurt. Other munchies like burgers and plate lunches are under $4. Cafeteria-style, the cafe has no decor except for a huge open window that frames the living sculpture of Waikiki.

Kapahulu Avenue

Once Kapahulu Avenue crosses Ala Wai Boulevard, it passes excellent inexpensive to moderately priced restaurants, strung one after the other. Kapahulu was the area in which the displaced Chinese community resettled after the great Chinatown fire at the turn of the century. Kapahulu basically means "poor soil," and unlike most areas of Hawaii could barely support vegetables and plants. Undaunted, the Chinese brought in soil with wagons and wheelbarrows, turning the area productive and verdant.

The first eatery is **Rainbow Drive-In**, at the corner of Kanaaina Avenue. It's strictly local, with a kids' hangout feel, but the plate lunches are hearty and well-done for under $4. Another of the same, **K C Drive-In**, just up the road a few blocks at 1029 Kapahulu, specializes in waffle dogs and shakes and even has carhops. Both are excellent stops to pick up plate lunches on your way out of Waikiki heading for the H-1 freeway.

The first sit-down restaurant on the strip is **Irifune Japanese Restaurant**, at 563 Kapahulu, tel. (808) 737-1141, open for lunch Tues.-Fri. 11:30 a.m.-1:30 p.m., for dinner Tues.-Sun. 5-9 p.m., directly across from **Zippy's**, a fast-food joint. Irifune serves authentic, well-prepared Japanese standards in its small dining room. Most meals begin at $8, with a nightly special for around $10. One item that Irifune has become especially known for is its garlic *ahi*, which goes for $11. You're also given a card that is punched every time you eat there; after 20 meals, you get one free. Irifune is a great deal for Japanese food, and is much cheaper and easily as good as most other Japanese restaurants on the Waikiki strip. Known more for its food than its decor, it's a winner! Get there early; it's a popular place.

The next restaurant in line is **Ono Hawaiian Foods**, 726 Kapahulu, tel. (808) 737-2275, open Mon.-Sat. 11 a.m.-7:30 p.m., an institution in down-home Hawaiian cooking. This is the kind of place that a taxi driver takes you when you ask for "the real thing." It's clean and basic, with the decor being photos of local performers—all satisfied customers—hung on the wall. If you want to try *lomi lomi* salmon, poi, or *kalua* pig, this is *da kine place, brah!* Prices are cheap; the most expensive item, a combination plate, is only $9.50. And, if you have a sweet tooth, try **Leonard's Bakery,** which specializes in *malasadas* and *pao dolce.*

The **Rama Thai Restaurant,** on the corner of Kapahulu and Winam Streets, open daily for dinner 5-10 p.m., tel. (808) 735-2789, is *uptown* with some track lighting and linen tablecloths, but the prices and food are still *downtown* Bangkok. A wonderful choice is Thai crisp noodles for $5.50, Rama chicken wings at $8.75, chicken and ginger soup in a coconut-milk spicy broth at $7.50, or Thai curried beef, chicken, or shrimp for $7.95. Almost half of the menu is vegetarian; each of the veggie items is $5.95. All items are à la carte, so it's not that cheap; a complete meal costs around $15. The fish-ball soup is out of this world, with plenty for two. The tofu in coconut milk is also a great choice. Try the Wednesday evening buffet for $13.95 to get a sampling of food so you can come back and know what to order.

New to this row is **Sam Choy's Diamondhead Restaurant,** 449 Kapahulu Ave., tel. (808) 732-8645. Open Mon.-Thurs. for dinner 5:30-9:30 p.m. and Fri.-Sun. 5-10 p.m. Reservations are accepted, and there is complimentary validated parking. Island chef Sam Choy prepares food using mostly local produce and meat and fish from Hawaiian waters, mixing and embellishing the varied ethnic cuisine traditions of the islands. There are set and daily special menus. Soups run $6.95-9.95 while entrees range $18.95-29.95. Various soups and salads are also on the menu. The restaurant also has a full bar and wine selection. The decorations are as soothing as the food is delicious.

Also relatively new is the **Internet Cafe,** 559 Kapahulu Ave., tel. (808) 735-5282, website: www.aloha-cafe.com. Food, drinks, and Internet connections are available 24 hours a day, seven days a week. Try a focaccia sandwich for $2.95, a personal pizza à la Wolfgang Puck for $6.75, or cheesecake for $3.95 to go along with your coffee, tea, or Italian soda. Power Macs with printers and full Internet access are also served up for $1.50 for 15 minutes or $6 an hour if you didn't bring your computer with you. Internet or chat classes are held here Monday and Wednesday evenings 6-8 p.m. and Saturday morning 11 a.m.-1 p.m. Your basic cinderblock affair, it's clean and friendly.

The Pyramids, 758-B Kapahulu Ave., tel. (808) 737-2900, is the place to head for Greek and Mediterranean cuisine. Open Mon.-Fri. 11 a.m.-2 p.m. for lunch and daily 5:30-10 p.m. for dinner. Being here, you might imagine yourself to be inside King Tut's tomb with hieroglyphics and painted stone blocks on the walls. Live music and belly dancing accompany the meal every evening at 7:15 p.m. and again at 8:30 p.m. Lunch appetizers include tabouli at $4.95, hummus for $4.25, and spanakopita for $3.95. Try a chicken salad for $6.95 to accompany a sandwich of ground beef and lamb, parsley, and onions, charbroiled and topped with tahini sauce at $5.85. Select from entrees like shish kabob at $12.25 or moussaka for $10.95. Dinner appetizers and entrees are roughly the same items but run about $1 more.

Fast Foods and Snacks

There are enough formica-tabled, orange-colored, golden-arched, belly-up-to-the-window places selling perfected, injected, and inspected ground cow, chicken, and fish to feed an army . . . and a navy, and marine corps too. Those needing a pre-fab meal can choose from the royal **Burger King** and **Dairy Queen, Jack-in-his-Box, Ronnie McDonald, Pizza Hut-2-3-4, Wendy's,** and dippy **Zippy's Drive-In.** Zippy's is a local chain and has much more than the usual hamburger and fries. Fast food addicts easily find pushers throughout Waikiki!

You can't miss the pink, white, and magenta of **J.R.'s Fast Food Plate Lunch Restaurant,** at the corner of Lewers and Helumoa, where $6 or less will get you a hefty plate of rice, macaroni salad, and a slice of teriyaki beef, roast pork, or mahimahi. The food is fair, the portions hefty, and with a touch of local color is far superior to the nondescript national fast food chain restaurants in the area. Upstairs is a dining veranda where you can perch above the endless crowd.

Fatty's Chinese Fast Food, 2345 Kuhio, tel. (808) 922-9600, is very inexpensive. For about $3.50 you get a giant plate of Chinese fast food. A belly-filler only, but not bad.

MODERATE

Roberto and Laura Magni, a couple from Milano, one day discussed moving to Hawaii. With Italian spontaneity and gusto, they looked at each other and simultaneously said "perche no!" **Caffelatte,** at 339 Saratoga Rd. (across from the post office), tel. (808) 924-1414, open daily 5:30 p.m.-1 a.m., on the second floor of a clapboard "New England-Hawaiian style" house encircled by a veranda, is the result of their impetuousness. The cosmopolitan interior, simple and basic, is white on green with wrought-iron tables set with starched white linens. Hardwood floors, framed paintings both traditional and modern, a horseshoe bar, and subdued globed lighting complete the casual but stylish effect. The Mediterranean-inspired service is slow, but very friendly, and very professional. Each waitperson is intimately familiar with the menu and will be happy to recommend and describe each dish. The menu features homemade pasta ranging in price $11.50-20 with offerings like Spaghetti Paradiso with tomato sauce, or *daglia talle,* a flat thin pasta with Italian sausage for $12.50. Traditional favorites are sure to please with lasagna Leonardo da Vinci at $15, various polenta smothered in everything from a simple calamari to brosola, a rolled and herb-stuffed steak, gnocchi for $14.50, and ricotta and spinach ravioli at $17. Top off dinner with Italian desserts like peaches and strawberries in wine, or oranges and bananas in Russian vodka. The bar serves Italian wine by the bottle or glass, along with bubbling spumante and various champagnes. Italy in Hawaii? . . . *Perche no?*

The **Super Chef Restaurant,** at the Waikiki Hana Hotel, 2424 Koa Ave., tel. (808) 926-7199, is a sleeper. It is definitely one of *the* best moderately inexpensive restaurants in Waikiki, where you can get an *almost* gourmet meal for a terrific price. Being in a small hotel on a side street keeps the crowds away, so the quality of the food and service never suffers. The restaurant decor is not spectacular, but it is classy with small linen-covered tables and drum-seat chairs in a open and cheery room. The staff is very friendly, and the chefs prepare each meal individually behind a tile counter. Breakfast is served 6:30-10:30 a.m., when they feature buttermilk pancakes, bacon and ham, or Portuguese sausage with a large juice for just $2.25; or choose a *wiki wiki* breakfast of pastry, juice, and Kona coffee for only $1.75. No lunch menu, but dinner is served 5-10 p.m. One special is a complete dinner of steak with two lobster tails for only $11.95, or rack of lamb for $8.95. The portions are moderate but definitely not minuscule, and on top of it the cooking is just a half step below excellent. Definitely worth a try.

The **Peacock Dining Room,** at the Queen Kapiolani Hotel, 150 Kapahulu, tel. (808) 922-1941, open 5:30-9 p.m., offers one of the most outstanding buffets in Waikiki for both price and quality. Different nights feature different cuisines. All are special but the Japanese buffet on Wednesday and Thursday and the seafood buffet on Friday are extraordinary. All range $12.95-15.95. The room itself is tasteful with white tablecloths and full service. Every time you return to the buffet just leave your empty plate and it will be taken away for you. Help yourself from an amazing array of entrees that are expertly prepared. The salad bar is extremely varied, and the desserts will make you wish that you saved room. Excellent value.

Carlos Castaneda wouldn't even notice as he walked past two psychedelic green cactuses into **Pepper's**, at 150 Kaiulani Ave., tel. (808) 926-4374, open daily for lunch 11:30 a.m.-4 p.m., dinner 4 p.m.-1:30 a.m. The interior is Yuppie-Mex with a wraparound rectangular bar with a fat wooden rail, and low ceilings done in a Mexican-style stucco. The specialties of the house are prepared in a wood-fired oven for that hearty outdoor flavor in the heart of "Rancho Waikiki." Light meals are chicken taco salad for $9.95, the Pepper club ($6.95), and tuna melt ($5.95), with a good selection of salads. But you can get these anywhere so go "south of the border" for burrito madness ($8.50), complete flautas dinner ($9.95), or selections from the lavarock grill like marinated chicken breast ($12.95), or baby-back ribs (full slab, $15.95). You can also pick Mexican favorites like tacos, enchiladas, and fajitas, all served with rice, beans, and Mexican salad. Nothing on the Mexican side is more than $12.95, with most around $9. Eat, *hombre!*

Eating at **Caffe Guccinni**, at 2139 Kuhio Ave., tel. (808) 922-5287, open daily 5-10:30 p.m., is like following a Venetian gondolier to his favorite restaurant. It's not fancy but the food is good and plentiful, and the pasta is made fresh daily. The staff is usually a cook and a waiter who seats you at one of a dozen tables, most outdoors. It's easy to miss because it's stuck back off the street, which means a nice, quiet area. For a light meal choose garlic bread and Caesar salad, or for a full meal try one of the house specialties (with soup or salad), like eggplant parmigiana, pasta contesto, spaghetti and meatballs, or manicotti; most are under $14. The cappuccino and espresso are freshly brewed and extraordinarily good. For dessert have *cannoli,* a flaky pastry stuffed with ricotta and smothered with slivers of almond and chocolate—excellent! Other desserts include carrot cake, chocolate

torte, New York cheesecake, amaretto cheesecake, and crème brûlée; all are $3.50. The owner, Jocelyn Batista, started with a pastry shop and was rightfully proud of her desserts, so give one a try.

Hernando's Hideaway, at 2139 Kuhio, tel. (808) 922-7758, open daily 10:30 a.m.-2 a.m., sits well off the street and is a very casual Mexican restaurant where the emphasis is on plenty of good food and having a good time. Tables are mostly outside under an awning, and every day a special drink is featured. Some of the best offerings are chicken enchilada dinner for $6.75, or an overstuffed calzone for $5.75. Every night, 6-7 p.m. is "power hour," when all well drinks are $1, followed by "pizza hour" 7-8 p.m., when pizza is only $1 per slice. All this activity attracts a younger crowd of both resort workers and vacationers. You can eat until you're as stuffed as a burrito for under $10.

La Provence, 2139 Kuhio, tel. (808) 924-6696, is open Tues.-Sun. 5ish-10:30 p.m., with a full fancy French menu at reasonable prices. Start with an hors d'oeuvre like escargot for $6 or tabouli à la menthe fraiche for $5.50. Move on to a ratatouille at $9.50, giant prawns sautéed with thyme and served with saffron and rice for $15, or a traditional beef stew smoldered in orange zest and herbed red wine sauce served with new potatoes at $12.50. A few more expensive specialty dishes must be ordered 24 hours in advance. The motif is blue on blue, and if you're in a blue mood, eating here will surely raise your spirits.

Pieces of Eight is in the Coral Seas Hotel, tel. (808) 923-6646, open daily 5-11 p.m., happy hour 4-6 p.m., piano bar nightly. This steak and seafood house has managed to create a comfortable and relaxed atmosphere where it serves up excellent steaks and very good fish dishes at a moderate price. The decor is dark wood and burnished brass in a romantically lit main room. A piano stylist tickles the ivories in the background. It's the perfect combination of restaurant that will match itself to your mood. Come for that special night out or just a casual evening meal. "Early birders" 5-7 p.m. can pick selections like garlic chicken or fish and chips with salad bar for $6.95. Entrees are 10-ounce top sirloin ($13.95), ground beef sirloin ($8.95), filet mignon ($15.95), and mahimahi amandine

($11.95). All dinners include choice of potato, rice, or bread, and salad bar is $3.50 extra. A great choice for good food and a pleasant setting at affordable prices. The **Cellar Bar** open from noon to the wee hours serves exotic drinks and light meals like a simple pizza, hamburger, or fish bake combination. If you are out on the town, it is a good choice to munch while enjoying a video game or a game of pool.

The House of Hong, 260 Lewers St., tel. (808) 923-0202, open daily 11 a.m.-10:30 p.m., Sunday from 4 p.m., is a standard, no surprises Chinese restaurant with a flair. The decor borders on tasteful with some tables outfitted in starchy white tablecloths accented by inlaid wall murals and painted ceilings of China scenes. The Cantonese lunch special is weekdays 11 a.m.-3 p.m. for $5.95, with "early bird specials" 4-6 p.m.— dishes like egg flower soup, chicken chow mein, sweet and sour pork, crispy wonton, fried rice, fortune cookie, and Chinese tea for $9.95. Not great, but no complaints either.

The **Oceanarium** at the Pacific Beach Hotel, 2490 Kalakaua Ave., tel. (808) 922-1233, offers a full breakfast, lunch, and dinner menu. For lunch, try the tropical fruit plate at $7.50, or an entree such as Cajun five-spice chicken for $7.50. Dinner appetizers such as Cajun calamari begin at $4.95, while entrees such as New York peppercorn steak are $19.95, and specials such as live Maine lobster are $21.95. Also featured are fresh island catches at market prices. The Oceanarium is done in elegant muted colors as if you were under water.

Trattoria, in the Edgewater Hotel, 2168 Kalia Rd., tel. (808) 923-8415, serves savory dishes from northern Italy. Particularly good are the veal plates with an appropriate bottle of Italian wine. The interior is upscale with bent-wood chairs and white linen tablecloths set with crystal. Antipasti selections include escargot ($8.25) and spinach salad ($7.75). Combine these with pasta dishes like spaghetti puttanesca, a savory dish of fillet of anchovy and melted butter cooked in a hot sauce with tomatoes and black olives ($10.75). Complete dinners, ranging in price $17.95-24.95, include choice of minestrone soup or dinner salad, and lasagna, eggplant or tortellini. Trattoria is a good choice for a moderate restaurant with a pleasant atmosphere and better-than-average cooking. Dinner only.

Benihana, at the Hilton Rainbow Bazaar, 2005 Kalia Rd., open daily for lunch 11:30 a.m.-2 p.m., and for dinner 5:30-10:30 p.m., tel. (808) 955-5955, is a medium-priced Japanese restaurant for those who are jittery about the food and prices. Meals are designed to fit *gaijin* taste, and cooks flash their knives and spatulas at your table—as much a floor show as a dining experience. Good, basic Japanese food, *teppan*-style.

Mandarin Palace, at the Miramar Hotel, 2345 Kuhio Ave., tel. (808) 926-1110, is open for lunch and dinner. Highly rated for its Asian cuisine in a full-blown Chinese atmosphere.

White and pink canvas umbrellas shade the outdoor tables of the **Cafe Princess Garden,** just next to its sister restaurant the **Cafe Princess** (indoor restaurant with full table service), both set in a carved garden grotto surrounded by the Royal Hawaiian and Sheraton Hotels. Here, in the heart of Waikiki, but buffered from the crowds, you can enjoy a reasonably priced breakfast special of two scrambled eggs, link

Beat the crowds inside the Cafe Princess

sausage, and a croissant for $3.50, or lunch specials, served 11:30 a.m.-5 p.m., like soup and a sandwich for $6.50 or a plate lunch for $5.75. Dinner specials served 5-10 p.m. in the Princess Garden feature steak and lobster for $18.95, while those opting for the inside Cafe Princess can choose jumbo prawns or char-broiled steak for $16.95, or roast prime rib for $11.95. The outdoor Cafe Princess Garden is an excellent people-watching perch from which to enjoy happy hour drinks, 11:30 a.m.-6 p.m., and 10 p.m. until closing, when mai tais are $2.25, pitchers of Bud are $5.50, and frothy chi-chis are only $3.

Duke's Canoe Club, tel. (808) 922-2268, at the Outrigger Waikiki Hotel, has an unbeatable location fronting Waikiki beach. Basically a steak and seafood restaurant, it's a happening place, with plenty of Duke Kahanamoku and surfing memorabilia on the wall, and cocktails and music in the evening.

CASUAL GOURMET

The following restaurant is unique in that it serves inspired gourmet food in a lovely setting for very reasonable prices. Though technically not in Waikiki, but located in Hawaii Kai about 20 minutes away, it is definitely worth the trip.

The word "genius" is oftentimes overused and misapplied, causing it to loose its oomph, but when it comes to creativity with food, Roy Yamaguchi is a genius, par excellence! **Roy's Restaurant,** 6600 Kalanianaole Hwy. and Keahole Dr., tel. (808) 396-7697, in Hawaii Kai Corporate Plaza, open Sun.-Thurs. 5:30-9:30 p.m., until 10:30 p.m. Fri.-Sat., from 5 p.m. Saturday and Sunday, presents Euro-Asian cuisine (Pacific Rim) at its very best. The young master chef, through experimentation and an unfailing sense of taste, has created dishes using the diverse and distinctive flavors of French, Italian, Chinese, Japanese, Thai, and Hawaiian cuisine and blended them into a heady array of culinary delights that destroy the adage that "East is East and West is West." The twain have definitely met, and with a resounding success. Roy's dining room is "elegant casual" much like the food, featuring an open kitchen, and although pleasant enough with a superb view, it is not designed

for a lengthy romantic evening. Roy's dining philosophy seems to be the serving of truly superb dishes posthaste with the focus on the "food as the dining experience," not the surroundings. The presentation of every dish, under the direction of executive chef Gordon Hopkins, who has been with Roy's since its inception, is flawless, and as pleasing to the eye as it is titillating to the palate. The mastery is in "the blend," which can take you to heights of satiation rarely experienced before. Start with the charred *ahi* and *opakapaka* pot stickers, hibachi-style salmon with Maui onions, grilled shrimp risotto with fresh mushrooms, herbs, and lobster essence, or even an individual *imu*-oven pizza smothered with grilled chicken, feta cheese, olives, and pesto, most for under $8. Salads feature island-grown greens and vegetables and include such wonderful concoctions as crispy calamari with baby romaine at $7.95, and Chinese chicken with candied pecans and soy ginger dressing at $7.95. Entrees are wonders like grilled loin of lamb with rosemary, crabmeat, and risotto sauce at $17.95, Thai stuffed chicken for $14.95, or a nightly special such as lemongrass encrusted mahimahi with crispy duck cakes in *lilikoi* mustard sauce. Part of the menu changes every night, but there is always fish, which might be garlic-seared red tombo *ahi* with crispy bacon parmesan aioli for $22.95. Desserts by pastry chef Rick Chang are also superb, and include individually prepared (order at beginning of dinner) fresh fruit cobbler in sauce anglaise, or a richer than rich chocolate souffle. Although Roy's has only been open since 1988, it is *the* trendsetter in new and inspired cuisine, receiving the praise and adulation of other fine chefs throughout the islands who try to mimic and match Roy's flair and style.

CLASSY DINING

Halekulani Dining

Softly the soprano sea sings, while the baritone breeze whispers in melodious melancholy, as you float ephemerally above the waves at **La Mer,** the open-air signature dinner restaurant at the Halekulani Hotel. Splendid in its appointment, the walls, filigreed panels of teak covered in Chinese silkscreen, are predominantly browns and whites, the traditional colors of Hawaiian tapa. Seating is in high-backed upholstered chairs with armrests, and every table is either illuminated by flickering candles or by recessed ceiling lamps that seem to drip the soft gold light of the melting sun upon the table. The superb Continental French menu, with its numerous selections of seafood, is bolstered by a huge wine list and a platter of select cheeses to end the meal. La Mer sets the standard, and if you were to choose one restaurant for a night of culinary bliss, this is a perfect choice.

The House Without a Key, open for breakfast 7-10 a.m. buffet, lunch 11 a.m.-5 p.m., and dinner 5-9 p.m., is a casual outdoor-indoor restaurant in a magnificent oceanside setting. Named after the first novel written about Charlie Chan, Honolulu's famous fictional detective, the restaurant offers unsurpassed views in every direction, and is perhaps the best spot on the island to enjoy a sunset cocktail. Although casual, the seating is very comfortable with padded chairs at simple wood-trimmed tables. The breakfast buffet, including fresh omelettes, is $18.50. Lunch offers main course salads like Oriental chicken salad, grilled beef fajita salad, or a pasta dish like seafood penne or spaghetti bolognese all for under $15. Sandwiches range from a classic triple-decker club sandwich at $12, to grilled mahimahi on nori bread for $15, while entrees are New York steak at $21 or grilled salmon at $19. Dinner starts with cocktail *pu pu,* including chilled jumbo shrimp at $13.50 or scallops wrapped in bacon for $10.50, with the sandwiches, salads, and entrees about the same as the lunch menu. Desserts, designed to soothe your palate as the setting sun soothes your soul, include chocolate macadamia-nut creme pie, Toblerone chocolate mousse, or *lilikoi* cheesecake all priced at $6. Entertainment, nightly 5-8 p.m., performed by **The Islanders** or the **Hiram Olsen Trio,** is great for dancing under the stars. In addition, Mon.-Sat. evenings be entranced by the graceful beauty of the hula dances done by former Miss Hawaii, Konoe Miller; on Sunday, Debbie Nakanelua, another former Miss Hawaii, does the honor of performing the hula. Remember, the door is never locked at House Without a Key.

White, purple, and yellow orchids tumble from trellises, cascade from clay planters, and always grace your table at **Orchids Dining Room,** also at the Halekulani, open daily 7:30-11 a.m. breakfast, 11:30 a.m.-2 p.m. lunch, and 6-10 p.m. dinner, and is another seaside, indoor-outdoor restaurant. Specializing in contemporary American cuisine, Orchids is also famous for its fabulous Sunday brunch at $29.50 adults, $18.50 children. Chefs Keith Hirata and Shawn Smith make freshness a priority, buying ingredients as locally as possible—vegetables, beef, prawns, and especially fish. Beautifully appointed with teak wood and Hawaiian eucalyptus flooring, the setting is casual-elegant with white starched linen tablecloths, captain-style chairs with blue and white pillows, and of course heavy silver and crystal. Arranged with a tri-level central dining area that spreads out to a covered veranda, all tables enjoy a panoramic view of the sea with Diamond Head in the distance. Start the day with a continental breakfast including fresh fruit juice, pastry basket, and beverage at $12.50, or an American breakfast with all of the above plus eggs and a breakfast meat at $16.50, or try Japanese style with grilled fish, steamed rice, pickles, miso soup, seaweed, and green tea, at $19.50. There are also whole wheat pancakes with macadamia nuts and coconut syrup at $9, or just a basket of pastries and coffee for $6.75. The daily brunch is served 8:30-10 a.m., at $20.75. Start your engine with a mimosa, Bloody Mary, screwdriver, or tropical fruit, along with eggs Benedict, frittata, smoked salmon and cream cheese, and various pastries. Lunch begins with an assortment of delicious appetizers like seared *ahi* with mustard shoyu for $15, or a simple salad of mixed greens with various dressings for $6. Soups, all priced at $5, include Portuguese bean and chilled tropical fruit soup. Special dishes are an assortment of pasta under $15, curry including lamb, Thai chicken for around $18, and broiled Hawaiian fish wth herbs at $18. A full-course table d'hôte is $25, and all desserts are $6.50. Dinner entrees are luscious seafood platters of charbroiled *a'u* with kula tomato and herbed pasta at $27, pepper crusted *opakapaka* at $29.50 or rack of lamb Provençale at $33. A taster's menu at $54 is a full five-course meal.

Hilton Hawaiian Village Dining

The Hilton Hawaiian Village, at 2005 Kalia Rd., is one of the finest destination resorts in Hawaii. Its two signature restaurants, both *Travel Holiday* award winners, complement the resort perfectly. **Bali by the Sea,** tel. (808) 941-2254, open daily for dinner 6-10 p.m., may sound like Indonesian cuisine, but it's more continental than anything else. The setting couldn't be more brilliant. Sit by the open windows so that the sea breezes fan you as you overlook the gorgeous Hilton beach with Diamond Head off to your left. The room is outfitted in a tropical green paisley carpet, high-backed, armrest-type chairs, white tablecloths, and classical place settings with silver service. Upon ordering, you are presented with a complimentary platter of hors d'oeuvres. Choose appetizers like Hawaiian pot stickers with lemongrass and Thai peanut sauce, or fresh lobster tartare flavored with coriander and cucumber. Soups include the Kona crab chowder flavored with sweet mixed peppers and laced with brandy, or Maui onion soup glazed with Gruyère cheese. Entrees are a magnificent selection of fish from Hawaiian waters baked, sautéed, or broiled and then covered in a variety of sauces. Meat entrees are breast of chicken and lobster, or medallions of veal with honey. The meal ends with a fine presentation of desserts, or a complimentary "steaming chocolate Diamond Head." Bali by the Sea is a superb choice for an elegant evening of fine dining.

The **Golden Dragon,** tel. (808) 946-5336, open nightly for dinner 6-10 p.m., would tempt any knight errant to drop his sword and pick up chopsticks. This too is a fine restaurant where the walls are decorated with portraits of emperors, and the plates carry the Golden Dragon motif. The interior color scheme is a striking vermilion and black, with the chairs and tables shining with a lacquerware type of patina. The floor is dark koa. Outside, the terrace has pagoda-style canopies under which you may dine. Obviously the Golden Dragon isn't your average chop suey house, but the menu has all of the standard Chinese fare from lemon chicken to . . . well, chop suey, but it doesn't end there. The food is expertly prepared, and two fine choices are the exotic Imperial Beggar's Chicken, feeding two for $39.50, which is a chicken wrapped in lotus leaves, encased in clay, and baked (requires 24 hours notice to prepare); and Chef Chang's Signature Selection (for two), which includes seafood and vegetable egg rolls, crispy won-

tons, island pork charsiu, hot and sour soup, stir-fry chicken, wok-seared scallops, beef with vegetables, lobster and shrimp, and pepper and duck fried rice, with litchi ice cream for $31 per person. For a first-class restaurant with impeccable food and service, the prices at the Golden Dragon are very, very reasonable.

Sheraton Waikiki Dining

The signature restaurant at the Sheraton Waikiki is the **Hanohano Room,** located atop the building on its 30th floor. From here, the vista before you sweeps from Pearl Harbor to Diamond Head, and behind you, the city of Honolulu runs up into the hills. While noteworthy during the day, the view at night is stunning with the twinkle of city lights below. Aside from the usual breakfast fare, the Hanohano room serves a breakfast buffet that seems to have endless options. Along with breakfast Saturday morning, the room hosts the ever-popular Parry and Price live radio show on KSSK. The 10 a.m.-1 p.m. Sunday champagne brunch buffet is an outstanding feed, but pricey. In the evening, the restaurant features Pacific Island cuisine. Start with an hors d'oeuvre like Scottish smoked salmon for $9.95 or fresh island *ahi* sashimi with shredded radish and wasabi for $12.95. Move on to essence of shiitake mushroom soup at $7.95 and chilled asparagus and prawns salad for $7.95. Make your selection of entrees from such items as chicken stuffed with lobster meat to filet mignon and lobster tail, ranging $26.95-48.95. If all the choices are too difficult, try one of the four select menu combinations, $53-75. A wonderful meal may be even more romantic here when a local trio called Stardust plays contemporary jazz and top 40 tunes; the dance floor is always open.

On the first floor, near the hotel entrance, is the **Ciao!** Italian restaurant. More moderate in price, Ciao! offers a pasta buffet every night along with its menu selections. Items from the menu include appetizers for under $9, pizza for $11.50-16, pasta marinara for $11.50, and open face lasagna with shrimp and scallops for $17.95. Filet mignon, rib-eye, and New York steaks come from the broiler for $21-37.50, a grilled and marinated boneless chicken breast with mixed greens and roasted potatoes is $15.50, and the live Maine lobster, steamed or broiled, runs $32.50. Of course, there is a good selection of

Italian and California wines to accompany any meal.

The **Ocean Terrace Restaurant** is more casual. Although you can order off the menu for such items as bacon and cheese over hash browns with coffee or tea at $8.95 for breakfast, mahimahi burger with tartar sauce and curly fries at $10.95 for lunch, or stir-fry tender beef and vegetables with firecracker fried rice at $15.75 for supper, the Ocean Terrace is known for its buffets. The ordinary breakfast buffet is $18.85, while the continental breakfast buffet runs $13.85. Buffet lunch goes for $19.25 and the dinner buffet is $28.75. Dinner buffets vary nightly among international cuisines. Enjoy any meal here with the Great Moana herself as the backdrop, while every night brings different local entertainers to the restaurant stage.

If you don't want to leave your place on the beach or loose your spot at the shell-shaped pool, and still require a midafternoon snack, try the **Kau Kau Express.** Here you can order a Japanese *bento* box lunch, fresh fruit, health-conscious sandwich, or pizza, and a full range of drinks. The **Sand Bar** serves up poolside drinks.

Hawaii Prince Hotel Dining

The Hawaii Prince Hotel at 100 Holomoana St., tel. (808) 956-1111, features three distinctive restaurants. **Takanawa,** with posts of *sugi* pine, floor-to-ceiling windows, and a koi pond in the center of a Japanese garden, is the hotel's sushi bar. In addition, a buffet of Japanese food is served here for $16.50 every evening.

The Prince Court, the main dining room, offers breakfast, lunch, and dinner. Breakfast, served 5:30-10:30 a.m., starts with juices and fruits ($4-7), seasonal berries and cream ($6), continental breakfast ($10.50), and a buffet breakfast ($15). On Sunday, there's an additional full American breakfast for $30. Lunches start with appetizers like grilled fresh mozzarella ($6.50), barbecued Pacific oysters and fried onions ($9.50), and Cobb salad with Dungeness crab ($9.50). Sandwiches like sliced avocado, tomato, sprouts, and cucumber in pocket bread start at $6.50, while pasta selections are $9-13.50. Dinner offers entrees like the fresh fish of the day, cooked five possible ways including being baked in a cornbread crust or sautéed with angel hair pasta for a reasonable $17.50, or

a mixed grill of local slipper lobster, *kahuku* shrimp, and sea scallops for $24.

Hakone, the hotel's fine Japanese restaurant, is appointed with shoji screens and wooden tables with high-backed chairs in front of a glass wall that frames the still life of the Ala Wai Yacht Harbor. Dishes are typical, with set menus *(teishoku)* of chicken teriyaki ($23), katsura steak ($29.50), and the Kaiseki Hakone, a full seven course meal for $60. A Japanese lunch buffet is also served.

Around Waikiki

One of the most laudable achievements in the restaurant business is to create an excellent reputation and then to keep it. **Nick's Fishmarket** at the Waikiki Gateway Hotel, 2070 Kalakaua, tel. (808) 955-6333, open nightly for dinner 6-11:30 p.m., has done just that . . . and keeps doing it. Many gourmets consider Nick's *the* best dining in Waikiki, and it's great fun to find out if they know what they're talking about. Owner Randy Schoch pays personal attention to every detail at Nick's, while executive chef Mariano Lalica creates the culinary magic. Lalica placed first in the "Seafood Olympics" recently held in Hawaii, and is a marvel at preparing fresh fish, which he accents with Thai peanut sauce and balsamic vinegar, rock shrimp sauce with stone ground mustard and macadamia nuts, or roasted garlic and sun-dried tomato vinaigrette. Adventurous and highly skilled, Chef Lalica, like the master of an old sailing ship, will take you to culinary ports of call rarely, if ever, visited. Highly professional waiters, knowledgeable about every dish, are friendly and efficient, and always at hand to suggest just the right wine from the extensive list to perfectly complement your choice of dish. Start with fresh-baked clams casino ($9.95), smoked salmon ($10.50), or, if you're in the mood, how about beluga caviar (don't ask). For soup order the Fish Market Chowder, while the Caesar salad prepared at your table has long won honors as the best available west of California! Although Nick's is primarily renowned for its fish, don't overlook the veal, steaks, and chicken with sides of pasta. An excellent choice is one of Nick's complete dinners featuring entree, soup or salad, vegetables, and hot drink. Other great choices are veal picatta, succulent rack of lamb with a Hawaiian mango chutney, and perfectly prepared abalone imported from the cold waters of the California coast. The sinless along with those expecting salvation "tomorrow" will enjoy the dessert menu, which features Nick's vanbanna pie, a tempting concoction of banana mousse and almond vanilla ice cream dripping with a caramel sauce, New York inspired cheesecake, or a lighter tropical sorbet. A Cafe Menu has recently been added from which you can order until the wee hours while listening to live entertainment in the lounge area. Lobster fried rice, crispy calamari, pasta à la Hawaii, or plump tacos can all be enjoyed, and are all very reasonably priced under $10. Dancing to live music is featured nightly along with special events such as wine-tasting evenings scheduled throughout the year. The bar prepares a host of exotic island drinks along with a fine cup of cappuccino, and is known for its extensive microbrewery beer selections. If you had only one evening in Waikiki and you wanted to make it memorable, you'd have a hard time doing better than Nick's Fishmarket.

Sergio's, at the Ilima Hotel, 445 Nohonani, open daily for dinner 5:30-11:30 p.m., tel. (808) 926-3388, is one of the finest Italian restaurants in Honolulu. The interior is romantic, subtle, and simple with a combination of booths and tables. Sergio prepares foods from all regions of Italy, blending and matching hearty peasant soups, fresh salads, and antipasti garnished with aromatic cheeses and spicy prepared meats, pasta dishes, entrees, and desserts. The more than a dozen choices of pasta come with sauces of savory meat, or delicate vegetables, and seafood. Entrees of chicken, beef, and fresh fish make your taste buds rise and shout "Bravo! Sergio! Bravo!"

Michel's, at the Colony Surf Hotel, 2895 Kalakaua Ave., tel. (808) 923-6552, open daily for dinner only, is literally on the beach, so your appetite is piqued not only by sumptuous morsels, but by magnificent views of the Waikiki skyline boldly facing the Pacific. The interior is "neo-French elegant," with the dining rooms appointed in soft pastels, velour chairs with armrests, white tablecloths, crystal chandeliers, heavy silver service, and tasteful paintings. The bar is serpentine and of polished koa. Food is French Continental and dinner is *magnifique* with such entrees as fresh Maine lobster on ice, delicate baby coho salmon garnished with shrimp served in its own sauce, or tournedos rossini, a center cut of tenderloin with goose liver and truffles. The dining experience at Michel's is completely satisfying with outstanding food and outstanding service, all in an outstanding setting.

Also located at the Colony Surf is **David Paul's Diamond Head Grill.** Following the success of his award-winning restaurant in Lahaina, Maui, Chef David Paul Johnson hopes to create as big a splash here in the big city. He is one of a new breed of young chefs serving innovative local foods created with Hawaiian, Asian, American and/or European preparation techniques. *Kalua* duck and tequila shrimp with firecracker rice are only two of the entrees that are certain to please.

Matteo's, in the Marine Surf Hotel, 364 Seaside, tel. (808) 922-5551, open 6 p.m.-2 a.m., is a wonderfully romantic Italian restaurant that sets the mood even outside by welcoming you with a red canopy and brass rail that leads to a carved door of koa and crystal. Inside is dark and stylish, with high-backed booths, white tablecloths, and marble-top tables. On each is a rose, Matteo's signature. Dinners begin with hot antipasti priced $7-14, such as stuffed mushrooms à la Matteo, seafood combo or cold antipasto for two. Light fare of *ensalada e zuppa* (salad and soup), hearts of romaine lettuce, or clam soup matched with garlic bread or pizza bread make an inexpensive but tasty meal. Entree suggestions are chicken *rollatini,* veal *rollatini* (rolled veal stuffed with bell peppers, mushrooms, onions, spinach, and mozzarella), or *bragiola* (rolled beef with mozzarella cheese, garlic, fresh basil, and baked with marinara sauce), all under $20. Complete dinners come with Matteo's special salad, pasta, vegetables, and coffee or tea and include mahimahi Veronica (sautéed fish in lemon sauce and seedless grapes) or veal parmigiana and are priced under $28. Pastas are very reasonable and besides the usual linguine dishes include gnocchi and manicotti à la Matteo. An extensive wine list complements the food. If you are out for a special evening of fine dining and romance, Matteo's will set the mood, and the rest is up to you.

The **Surf Room** is in the Royal Hawaiian Hotel, 2259 Kalakaua Ave., tel. (808) 931-7194. The menu is solid but uninspired. However, the setting couldn't be lovelier, and the buffet is staggeringly huge.

Hy's Steak House, 2440 Kuhio Ave., tel. (808) 922-5555, is one of those rare restaurants that is not only absolutely beautiful, but serves great food as well. Decorated like a Victorian sitting room, its menu offers things other than steaks and chops, but these are the specialties and worth the stiff-upper-lipped price.

Restaurant Suntory, Royal Hawaiian Shopping Center, tel. (808) 922-5511, is a very handsome restaurant with different rooms specializing in particular styles like *shabu shabu, teppanyaki,* and sushi. The prices used to be worse, but they're still expensive. However, the food preparation and presentation are excellent, and the staff is very attentive. Open for lunch and dinner.

Furusato Sushi, right next to the Hyatt Regency at 2424 Kalakaua Ave., tel. (808) 922-4991, and **Furusato Tokyo Steak,** downstairs, are both expensive but top-notch Japanese restaurants. The food and service are authentic, but they are geared toward the Japanese tourist who expects, and almost demands, to pay high prices. In the steakhouse, expect steak since very little else is on the menu. Upstairs is sushi. Free valet parking is great for this congested part of Waikiki.

Three other exceptional restaurants worth visiting for authentic Japanese food are **Miyako** at the New Otani Beach Hotel, tel. (808) 921-7077; **Kacho** at the Waikiki Parc Hotel, tel. (808) 924-3535; and the **Kyo-ya** at 2057 Kalakaua Ave., tel. (808) 947-3911.

For a variety of Mediterranean cuisine with a Hawaiian twist visit **Cascada** restaurant at the Royal Garden Hotel, tel. (808) 945-0270. Open for breakfast, lunch, and dinner.

ENTERTAINMENT

Waikiki swings, beats, bumps, grinds, sways, laughs, and gets down. If Waikiki has to bear being called a carnival town, it might as well strut its stuff. Dancing (disco and ballroom), happy hours, cocktail shows, cruises, lounge acts, Polynesian extravaganzas, and the street scene provide an endless choice of entertainment. Small-name Hawaiian trios, soloists, pianists, and sultry singers featured in innumerable bars and restaurants woo you in and keep you coming back. Big-name island entertainers and visiting international stars play the big rooms. Free entertainment includes hula shows, ukulele music, street musicians, jugglers, artists, and street-walkers. For a good time, nowhere in Hawaii matches Waikiki. Also see the Honolulu chapter for other listings.

Bars and Lounge Acts
Brother Noland is a local talent who appears here and there around town. He's the cutting edge for ethnic Hawaiian groups playing hot reggae, originals, and plenty of Stevie Wonder, solo or with a group, and shouldn't be missed.

Theresa Bright is an excellent Hawaiian musician. Her sound is a melodious mixture of traditional and contemporary. An accomplished musician with a beautiful voice, she often appears at various venues around town.

In the Park Shore Hotel, 2586 Kalakaua Ave., **The Bar** is a quiet, relaxing place to have a drink. Sometimes, a guest pianist plays.

The **Irish Rose Saloon,** at 227 Lewers, presents live entertainment nightly with dancing till 4 a.m. and features sporting events on its big-screen TV. Happy hour is 3-8 p.m. It's right across the street from the Outrigger Coral Seas Hotel, just at the entrance of the Al Herrington Show.

A great little bar, the **Brass Rail,** serves up cold draft beer and deli sandwiches (until 4 p.m.). It's into sports and especially Monday Night Football, which usually begins in Hawaii at 7:30 p.m. Located on the ground floor of the Outrigger Waikiki Hotel, at 2335 Kalakaua.

The **Rose and Crown Pub** in King's Village has a pianist playing sing-along favorites in what is a very close rendition of an English-style pub. It has daily specials; for example, on Saturday if you wear your Rose and Crown hat you have happy hour prices all night long. So drink hearty, and hold on to your hat! The crowd is intent on swilling beer and partying. Noisy, raucous, and fun.

Jolly Roger Restaurant, at 150 Kaiulani, presents a changing mixture of live music nightly in its lounge, open until 2 a.m. A good spot for listening to music and enjoying conversation around the bar.

In the International Market Place, **Coconut Willy's** offers free entertainment, with no minimum or cover.

Baron's Studio, Waikiki Plaza Hotel, tel. (808) 946-0277, is open nightly. Quiet drinks, fine background tunes.

The **Paradise Lounge** at the Hilton Hawaiian Village, tel. (808) 949-4321, has entertainment Wednesday, Friday, and Saturday evenings; no cover.

A tradition at the **Lobby Bar** at the Hawaiian Regent is its no-cover entertainment by well-respected Waikiki's musicians.

Visit the **Hanohano** room on the 30th floor of the Sheraton Waikiki Hotel for jazz and contemporary music of Stardust.

The five-diamond Halekulani hotel offers superb nightly entertainment. There is no lovelier location for a sunset cocktail than **House Without a Key,** where The Islanders or The Hiram Olsen Trio perform contemporary tunes nightly 5-8:30 p.m. Gracing the stage are two former Miss Hawaiis, Konoe Miller and Debbie Nakanelua, who perform their inspired hula (Debbie on Sunday, Kanoe the rest of the week). Sunday brunch at the hotel's **Orchids Dining Room** is made even more genteel with the musical strains of harpist Susanne Hussong, accompanied by flutist Susan Gillespie, who perform the hit songs of Broadway musicals. Nightly 8:30-10 in the Orchids Dining Room and 10:15-midnight from the wood-paneled **Lewers Lounge** flows contemporary jazz selections with either Noly Paa on piano or the duo of Jim Howard on keyboard and Bruce Hamada on bass and vocals.

Enjoy a free steel guitar and hula show at the **Banyan Court** at the Sheraton Moana Surfrider Hotel.

Discos, Dancing, and Nightclubs

Ballroom dancers will enjoy **Tea Dancing at the Royal** in the Monarch Room of the Royal Hawaiian Hotel, featuring the 14-piece Del Courtney Orchestra, Monday 5:30-8:30 p.m.

Nick's Fishmarket at the Gateway Hotel, 2070 Kalakaua Ave., swings with contemporary dance music until 1:30 a.m. Expect a mixed but mostly mature crowd who have stayed on to dance after a magnificent meal, which Nick's is known for. Music is provided by No Excuse, headliners who make Nick's their home when not on tour.

The **Paradise Lounge** in the Rainbow Tower of the Hilton Hawaiian Village is a jazz nightclub, perfect for a night of relaxing entertainment. It has a pianist nightly and a polished wooden dance floor. Weekends bring a variety of jazz ensembles for your listening and dancing pleasure. Perfect for a romantic evening.

The Wave, 1877 Kalakaua Ave., tel. (808) 941-0424, is a rock and roll and new wave hotspot with live music nightly. Every Tuesday, hear Willie Kay, a popular Hawaiian performer, jam with other hot island musicians. They let it rip. The Wave has become an institution of late-night fun and dancing. The crowd is mixed, and you can either choose to dance, perch upstairs in the balcony behind glass where you can check out the dancers below, or have a few drinks and some conversation. The Wave is a sure bet for a night of fun.

The **Waikiki Hard Rock Café,** the fast food joint of nightspots, has jazzed up its act by putting on live music Friday and Saturday evenings. It's located at Kalakaua Ave. and Kapiolani Boulevard.

The following are disco nightclubs in and around Waikiki. Most have videos, a theme, a dress code of alohawear and shoes, no sandals, and start hopping around 9 p.m. with the energy cutoff around 4 a.m.

The **Cellar,** 205 Lewers St., tel. (808) 923-9952, features mostly rock and roll spun by the DJ. The place jumps till 4 a.m. and has plenty of special nights like Thirsty Tuesdays and Ladies' Night. Put on your dancin' shoes and casual attire.

Lewers Street Annex, at 270 Lewers, is a basic disco dance spot featuring top 40 tunes. The clientele is mostly young visitors and some local workers who stop in for a late-night drink. A special feature is the 12 O'clock High, basically happy hour prices noon-midnight. Standard drinks $1.50, domestic beers $1.50, margaritas and mai tais $1.50. Good for casual drinking, dancing, and meeting people.

Everyone trumpets the mating call at **Moose McGillycuddy's Pub and Cafe,** 310 Lewers in Waikiki, tel. (808) 923-0751, especially every Thursday, which is Ladies' Night. Standard but good food and plenty of dancing. Try here to answer the call of the wild.

Across the street from Moose McGillycuddy's is **The Jungle,** so after trumpeting your moose calls, all you apes and apesses can lope across the street and swing until the late hour. You never know if the music will be from the '60s, '70s, '80s, or year 2010—it's a jungle in there.

The Esprit, at the Sheraton Waikiki, presents dance music from the '40s to the present Tues.-Sat. from 8:30 p.m. by a local band. Come casual or dressed to the hilt. Good dance floor, no cover, and it's the only nightclub right on the beach.

Eurasia, 2552 Kalakaua Ave., is a disco that's attracting dancers who once filled other discos in the area that have since closed their doors. Also try **Scruples Beach Club** on Kuhio Ave. for international DJ disco music.

Red Lion Dance Palace, 240 Lewers St., tel. (808) 922-1027, offers live rock and roll Wed.-Sat. and high-tech video and disco the remaining nights. Nice dance floor. Beachwear is okay. Open 2 p.m.-4 a.m.

Exotic live dancers, like exotic live plants, need a unique atmosphere in which to bloom. Both seem to crave light, one sunlight, the other a spotlight. Most of the flashy fleshy nightspots of Waikiki used to be a few blocks away along Kapiolani Blvd., but they have been moving ever closer to the heart of Waikiki. Now they are strung along Kuhio Avenue, where they're easily recognizable by their garish neon lights advertising their wares. The Kuhio Avenue exotic dance spots are supposedly a step up in class from their Kapiolani Boulevard counterparts, but when their dancers strip to the buff, the difference is hardly noticeable . . . or very noticeable, depending upon point of view. The names of the strip joints really don't matter, just look for the signs of "exotic dancers." Usually a $10 cover and $5 for a drink.

Dinner Shows and Polynesian Extravaganzas

The **Don Ho Show,** an institution that played at the Hilton Hawaiian Village for years, is no longer. Mr. Ho has moved to the Waikiki Beachcomber at 2300 Kalakaua Ave., tel. (808) 922-4646, where he plays two shows nightly, Thurs.-Sunday. The 7 p.m. dinner show costs $46, and the 9 p.m. cocktail show is $28. Either show is recommended. Gone is the glitz and glamour, just Ho and his organ much in the same way as he performed at Duke Kahanamoku's Club in the 1960s. Don Ho is still a great performer, and "the godfather of modern Hawaiian music." Pro-

fessional funster **Frank De Lima** hosts Tropical Madness in the Polynesian Palace nightly except Monday, at 9 p.m. De Lima, supported by a cast of various loonies, is guaranteed to tickle your funny bone, "island style."

The new multi-million dollar showroom at the Waikiki Beachcomber Hotel fills with magical vibrations when headliner John Hirokawa suddenly appears out of nowhere. The **Magic of Polynesia** is a journey into the realm of enchantment and beauty that the entire family can enjoy. Sleight of hand, disappearing maidens, swaying hula dancers, fantastic costumes, and audience participation are all part of the magical extravaganza. Two shows nightly: dinner seating at is at 5 p.m. for the 6:30 p.m. show, adults $64, children $44; cocktail show at 8:45 p.m., adults $35, children $25. The deluxe package for $129 gives you preferred seating and a fancier menu.

Society of Seven, a well-established local ensemble, appears nightly at the Outrigger Main Showroom performing a variety of musical tunes from the last 50 years. In various permutations, this band has been performing locally since the late '60s.

Performing two shows nightly in the Outrigger Polynesian Palace is the **Yes! International Revue,** an absorbing collaboration of magic, dance, illusion, and mime.

If you missed them the first time, here's your chance to see the world's greatest entertainers when unbelievably realistic impersonators perform **Legends in Concert,** a Las Vegas-style spectacular presented nightly at the Aloha Showroom of the Royal Hawaiian Shopping Center.

The Ainahau Showroom at the Sheraton Princess Kaiulani Hotel presents the **Sheraton Spectacular Polynesian Revue** nightly for dinner and cocktail shows at 5:30 and 8 p.m.

Free or Small Fee Entertainment

Check the newspapers and free tourist literature for times to the following events.

The **Royal Hawaiian Band** plays free concerts on Sunday afternoons at 12:45 p.m. and 2 p.m. at the bandstand in Kapiolani Park, oftentimes with singers and hula dancers, and again on Friday at 12:15 p.m. at the Iolani Palace. Formed in 1836, the band plays mostly classical music and Hawaiian traditional tunes. Also in the park, free concerts are periodically given by a variety of local and visiting musicians at the Waikiki Shell.

Every evening at King's Village across the street from the Hyatt Regency, a changing of the guard show is performed by the King's Guards in uniforms from the period of the monarchy to give you a peek into one of the rituals of royal ceremony.

The **Kodak Hula Show** is very popular. The show is held on Tues.-Thurs. at 10 a.m. at the Waikiki Shell in Kapiolani Park, but people start lining up at 8 a.m.; be there by 9 if you want a seat. You sit on bleachers with 3,000 people, while Hawaiian *tutu* bedecked in muumuu, lei, and smiles play ukuleles and sing for the ti-leaf-skirted dancers. You can buy film and even rent a camera, as befits the show's sponsor, the East-man Kodak Company—snap away with abandon. The performance dates back to 1937, and some of the original dancers, now in their eighties, still participate. At the finale, the dancers line up on stage with red-lettered placards that spell out H-A-W-A-I-I, so you can take your own photo of the most famous Hawaiian postcard. Then the audience is invited down for a free hula lesson. People who are too hip hate it, *kama'aina* shy away from it, but if you're a good sport, you'll walk away like everyone else with a big smile on your face.

A potpourri of contemporary entertainment is also found in Kapiolani Park on weekends. Just across from the zoo, musicians, jugglers, clowns, unicyclists, and acrobats put on a free, im-promptu circus. Some of the best are B.J. Patch-es, Twinkles, and Jingles from a local troupe called Clown Alley.

The **Ukulele Tree Hawaiian Music Show** is held in the Outrigger East Hotel Saturday, Sunday, and Monday 5-7 p.m., for free; local musicians and sometimes well-known guests come to play and be heard. For information call (808) 922-5353.

The **Royal Hawaiian Shopping Center** provides free crafts demonstrations and lessons at various times throughout the week: quilting, *lau hala* weaving, coconut weaving, hula, lei-making, ukulele instruction, and *haku* (floral wristband) weaving. The Polynesian Cultural Center puts on a torchlighting ceremony with song and dance every Monday, Wednesday, and Friday 6-6:45

p.m., and Tuesday and Thursday 10-11:30 a.m. they perform songs and dances. Tuesday, Thursday, Saturday, and Sunday 6-6:15 p.m. is a mini-torchlighting ceremony. Free musical entertainment is also scheduled daily and throughout the day at the fountain court. For specific times for the crafts, call (808) 922-0588.

A free hula show and fireworks are performed every Friday 6:30-7:30 p.m. at the super pool next to the main lobby at the Hilton Hawaiian Village. Anyone can come and stand for the show, but if you occupy one of the seats you must purchase at least one drink.

Molehu I Waikiki, a torchlighting ceremony complete with authentic hula performed by various *halau,* is offered to the public free of charge at Kuhio Beach Park every Saturday and Sunday at 6:45 p.m.

Every Friday evening 8-10 p.m., Kalakaua Avenue comes alive with the music and dance of hula as the **Strolling Hula on Kalakaua** makes seven stops between Beach Walk Street and the Waikiki Shopping Center.

Sometimes, "free" tickets to some of Waikiki's most popular Polynesian Extravaganzas are handed out by condo time-share outfits stationed in booths along the main drags. For attending their sales presentations, usually 90 minutes, you can get tickets, but they might be the toughest freebies you've ever earned. The presentation is a pressure cooker where hardened sales pros try every imaginable technique to get you to sign . . . "right now, because this is the only time that this deal can be offered." If you're really interested in time-sharing, the deals aren't too bad, but if you're there only for the tickets, what a waste of time!

The **Hawaii IMAX Theater,** 325 Seaside Ave. in Waikiki, screens several shows everyday 11 a.m.-9 p.m. These exciting documentary films on Hawaiian subjects start every hour on the hour, run about 40 minutes in length, and are scheduled on a rotating basis. Adults $7.50, children 3-11 $5. You can see two or more of the different shows on any one day for a reduced fee. Call for current showings and ticket prices; tel. (808) 923-4629.

Just for the thrill of it (and for the spectacular scenery), ride the outside glass elevators of either the Sheraton Waikiki or Ilikai Hotel.

SHOPPING

The biggest problem concerning shopping in Waikiki is to keep yourself from burning out over the endless array of shops and boutiques. Everywhere you look someone has something for sale, and with the preponderance of street stalls lining the boulevards, much of the merchandise comes out to greet you. The same rule applies to shopping as it does to everything in Waikiki—class next door to junk. Those traveling to the Neighbor Islands should seriously consider a shopping spree in Waikiki, which has the largest selection and most competitive prices in the islands. A great feature about shopping in Waikiki is that most shops are only a minute or two from the beach. This enables your sale-hound companion to hunt while you relax. There's no telling how much money your partner can save you! "Ingrate! This bathing suit could have cost $50, but I got it for $25. See, you saved $25 while you were lying here like a beached whale." Everyone concerned should easily be mollified. Charge!

The Fence

The best place to find an authentic island-made souvenir at a reasonable price is at The Fence, located along the fence of the Honolulu Zoo fronting Kapiolani Park. Also referred to as Artists of Oahu/Sunday Exhibit and Art Mart, some of the island's best artists congregate here to display and sell their works on Tuesdays and weekends 10 a.m.-4 p.m. Individual artists are only allowed to display one day a week. The Fence was the good idea of Honolulu's former mayor, Frank Fasi, who decided that Oahu's rich resource of artists shouldn't go untapped. There are plenty of excellent artists whose works are sure to catch your fancy. Also, about once a month on a Saturday or Sunday, booths are set up on the grassy area closer to the zoo, and an arts and crafts fair is held.

Gifts and Souvenirs

ABC Stores scattered throughout Waikiki were founded by a local man, Sid Kosasa, who learned the retail business from his father. This "everything store" sells groceries, sundries, and souvenirs. Prices are good, especially on specials like lotions and beach mats. Very convenient.

Those who just couldn't return home without a deep Hawaiian tan can be helped by visiting **Waikiki Aloe,** 2168 Kalakaua Ave. It specializes in skin-care products, lotions, and tanning supplies.

The **Waikiki Business Plaza,** 2270 Kalakaua Ave., houses a number of jewelry stores. In one stop you can get a pretty good idea of prices and availability. Look for jewelry boxes laden with jade, gold, turquoise, pearls, coral, and *puka* shells, and eel, snake, and leather goods.

Military Shop of Hawaii, 833 Kalakaua Ave., has an entire wall dedicated to military patches, along with clothes, memorabilia, and collectibles.

Those with good taste but a limited budget should check out **Hawaiian Wear Unlimited,** 205 Lewers St., liquidators of alohawear from most of Hawaii's big manufacturers. Also, **Pzazz** "consignment boutique" sells used designer clothing at 1419 Kalakaua Avenue.

Up Kapahulu Avenue, along Restaurant Row, is **Bailey's Antiques,** tel. (808) 734-7628, which specializes in vintage Hawaiian shirts. Reproductions of these old wearable artworks are also available, as are clothing, jewelry, lamps, figurines, and the like. Nearby is **Peggy's Picks,** with new and used gifts, treasures, and collectibles from around the world.

For a full range of **photo supplies** at bargain prices try: **Woolworth's,** 2224 Kalakaua Ave.; **Fox Photo** in the Waikiki Town Center and Royal Hawaiian Shopping Center, and at the Hilton Hawaiian Village and Sheraton Moana Surfrider; and **Island Camera and Gift Shops** at Princess Kaiulani, Sheraton Waikiki, Royal Hawaiian, and Sheraton Moana Surfrider Hotels. Handbillers often give money-saving coupons to a variety of photo stores. Also for camera and photo supplies, **Central Camera,** 159 Kaiulani Ave., Suite 109, is a fine store where the salespeople are very helpful. Other photo stores are located here and there along Kalakaua, Kuhio, Kalia, and Lewers Streets.

Duty-free goods are always of interest to international visitors. You can find a duty-free store at the Hilton Hawaiian Village. Also, if you want to see a swarm of Japanese jostling for position in a tiny little store trying to feed a buying frenzy, that's the spot.

Waikiki Shopping Centers

The largest credit card oasis is the **Royal Hawaiian Shopping Center.** This massive complex is three stories of nonstop shopping, running for three blocks in front of the Sheraton and Royal Hawaiian hotels. It's open daily 9 a.m.-10 p.m., till 9 p.m. on Sunday, tel. (808) 922-0588. This complex provides an excellent mixture of small intimate shops and larger department stores. There's a post office on the second-floor "B" building. The second and third floors of this shopping center are pretty quiet. It's off the street so not as many tourists find their way here. It's a good place to do some comparative browsing before making your purchases. If jewelry is an interest of yours, head up to the third floor and have a look at the Hawaiian Heirloom Jewelry Factory and the intriguing heirloom jewelry museum next door.

Where the Royal Hawaiian Shopping Plaza ends the **Waikiki Shopping Plaza** begins, but on the other side of the street. Here, you'll find multilevel shopping. The mall's centerpiece is a five-story waterfall, an impressive sculpture of water and plexiglass, while other fountains grace the lower level. Another feature of this mall is Waikiki Calls, a free hula show. Many inexpensive eateries are located on the bottom floor, while fancier Chinese and Japanese restaurants are on the fourth and fifth floors. Clothing and accessory shops seem to predominate. The plaza is open daily 9 a.m.-11 p.m., tel. (808) 923-1191. While here, take a ride to the top floor of the Waikiki Business Plaza next door to the Shopping Plaza, where you'll get a fine overview of the Honolulu-Waikiki area. Out behind the plaza is an open-air bazaar called **The Royal Market,** where you can find a few treasures among the lesser quality goods.

The **International Market Place** is an open-air shopping bazaar that feels like Asia. Its natural canopy is a huge banyan, and the entire complex is across from the Moana Hotel at 2330 Kalakaua Ave., open daily from 9 a.m. until the vendors get tired at night, tel. (808) 923-9871. Among some fine merchandise and a treasure or two is great junk! If you're after souvenirs like bamboo products, shellwork, hats, mats, lotions, alohawear, and carvings, you can't do better than the International Market Place. The worst thing is that everything starts to look the same; the best is that the vendors will bargain. Make offers and try hard to work your way through the gauntlet of shops without getting scalped. Check out the Elvis Store and Museum, which must be seen to be believed.

Waikiki Bazaar

Directly behind the marketplace is the **Waikiki Town Center,** 2301 Kuhio Avenue. Basically the same theme with open-air shops: gifts, fashions, food, and handmade artifacts. Enjoy the free Polynesian Show nightly at 7 and 8 p.m. This is a little older, funkier mall, one grade up from what you would find in the International Market Place and Duke's Alley. If you want a low-key place to discover "treaure junk" this mall is good. It's even better than the International Market Place because it's more low-key. There aren't nearly as many people here and the salespeople are not as pushy.

For those who can't stand to waste an opportunity to shop, they can do so while passing through **Duke's Alley,** a shortcut between Kuhio and Kalakaua Avenues. Here you'll find a row of stalls selling basically the same merchandise as in the International Market Place.

The **Hyatt Regency Shopping Center,** also called the **Atrium Shops,** is located on the first three floors of the Hyatt Regency Hotel, 2424 Kalakaua Ave., tel. (808) 922-5522, open daily 9 a.m.-11 p.m. The 70 or so shops are mighty classy: if you're after exclusive fashions or a quality memento, this is the place. There's a continental-style sidewalk cafe, backed by a cascading indoor waterfall. Often free entertainment and fashion shows are put on by the various shops.

Smaller Malls
King's Village, at 131 Kaiulani Ave., just next to the Hyatt Regency, takes its theme from last century, where boardwalks pass 19th-century look-alike shops, complete with a changing-of-the-guard ceremony nightly at 6:15 p.m. This attractive complex offers free entertainment and attracts some of the best local street artists, who usually set up their stands at night. The **Waikiki Trade Center** is on the corner of Seaside and Kuhio Avenues with some of Waikiki's most elegant shops, featuring sophisticated fashions, exquisite artwork, and fine dining. The **Rainbow Bazaar** is a unique mall located at the Hilton Hawaiian Village, 2005 Kalia Road. Fun just to walk around, shops feature three main themes: Imperial Japan, Hong Kong Alley, and South Pacific Court.

The newest shopping complex to grace the streets of this already shop-filled town is the **King Kalakaua Plaza** located toward the western end of the strip. Nike Town fills a good portion of this building, as does a Banana Republic store.

Street Artists and Vendors
You don't have to try to find something to buy in Waikiki—in fact, if you're not careful, the merchandise will come after you! This takes place in the form of street vendors, who have been gaining a lot of attention lately. Some view them as a colorful addition to the beach scene, others as a nuisance. These carnival-type salespeople set up their mobile booths mainly along Kalakaua Avenue, with some on Kuhio Avenue and the side streets in between. In dealing with them you can have a positive experience if you remember two things: they have some pretty nifty junk, and you get what you pay for.

Also, street artists set up their easels along busy thoroughfares, and especially at the entrances to small shopping malls. Most draw caricatures of patrons in a few minutes for a few dollars—fun souvenirs.

Right here under the Waikiki banyan is a gentleman named Coco who makes coconut-frond hats, basically a dying art. Just near the canoe rides, you'll see his hats and baskets. Depending on the hat, you can get one for $15 or so. The baskets, good for holding fruit, incidentals, or whatever, are a real souvenir of Hawaii. With Coco making them right before your very eyes, you can't get more authentic than that. Coco says you can still learn how to weave in the Hawaiian tradition. His dad, Uncle Harry Kuikai, weaves at the Royal Hawaiian Shopping Center every Tuesday and Thursday 9:30-11:30 a.m. He'll teach you the basics of weaving and you can make your own souvenir (free). For longer-term tourists, there's an eight-week weaving class sponsored by the Kamehameha School. Just call the high school and inquire as to time and fees.

As you walk around Waikiki you'll see plenty of street-side booths offering unbelievable prices like "rent a car for $5, a jeep for $15, Pearl Harbor Cruise $5, Don Ho Show $20." Why so cheap? It's basically an advertising firm that signs you up to listen to a 90-minute spiel on a time-share condo. What happens during and after the 90-minute hard pitch is up to you, but you do get the payoff at the end.

Activities and Rentals

Not all activities and sports rentals in Waikiki are done at the umbrella stands set up along Waikiki Beach. For a reputable shop, try **Blue Sky Rentals,** 1920 Ala Moana Blvd., tel. (808) 947-0101. Owner Luis Merino can arrange activities and rent equipment for most of your ground, air, and sea needs. Bicycles and mopeds rent for $15 per half day or $20 a full day. Snorkeling gear is $10 a day, boogie boards $10. Introductory scuba dives start from $75, a full-day deep-sea fishing tour from around $100, a tandem ski diving jump at $225, and a glider ride for $60. You'll find these and many more options at Blue Sky Rentals.

Of the beachside sport rental shops, **Prime Time Sports,** tel. (808) 949-8952, is a good bet. Located at Fort DeRussy Beach in front of the Hale Koa Hotel, it rents all sorts of water equipment and gives scuba, surf, and windsurfing lessons, all at reasonable prices.

M.G.L. DOMENY DE RIENZI

CENTRAL OAHU

For most uninformed visitors, central Oahu is a colorful blur as they speed past in their rental cars en route to the North Shore. Slow down, there are things to see! For island residents, the suburban towns of Aiea, Pearl City, Waipahu, Mililani, and Wahiawa are home. Both routes heading north from Honolulu meet in **Wahiawa,** the island's most central town. The roads cross just near the entrance to **Schofield Barracks,** a warm-up target for Japanese Zeros as they flew on their devastating bombing run over Pearl Harbor.

AIEA, PEARL CITY, AND VICINITY

The twin cities of Aiea and Pearl City, except for the USS *Arizona* Memorial, USS *Bowfin* Submarine Museum, and perhaps a football game at Aloha Stadium, have little to attract the average tourist. Mainly they are residential areas for greater Honolulu, and for the large numbers of military families throughout this area. Likewise, Waipahu doesn't hold much attraction to the tourist because of its largely agricultural base, but **Hawaii's Plantation Village** is an attempt to interpret the importance of plantation culture for visitors.

PEARL HARBOR:
USS *ARIZONA* MEMORIAL

Even as you approach the pier from which you board a launch to take you to the USS *Arizona,* you know that you're at a shrine. Very few spots in America carry such undeniable emotion so easily passed from one generation to another: here, Valley Forge, Gettysburg, not many more. On that beautiful, cloudless morning of December 7, 1941, at one minute before 8 o'clock, the

United States not only entered the war, but lost its innocence forevermore.

The first battle of WW II for the U.S. actually took place about 90 minutes before Pearl Harbor's bombing, when the USS *Ward* sank an unidentified submarine sliding into Honolulu. In Pearl Harbor, dredged about 40 years earlier to allow superships to enter, the heavyweight champions of America's Pacific Fleet were lined up flanking the near side of Ford's Island. The naive deployment of this "Battleship Row" prompted a Japanese admiral to remark that never, even in times of maximum world peace, could he dream that the military might of a nation would have its unprotected chin stuck so far out, just begging for a right cross to the jaw. When it came, it was a roundhouse right, whistling through the air, and what a doozy!

Well before the smoke could clear and the last explosion stopped rumbling through the mountains, 3,581 Americans were dead or wounded, six mighty ships had sunk into the ooze of Pearl, 12 others stumbled around battered and punch-drunk, and 347 warplanes were useless heaps of scrap. The Japanese fighters had hardly broken a sweat, and when their fleet, located 200 miles north of Oahu, steamed away, the "east wind" had indeed "rained." But it was only the first squall of the American hurricane that would follow.

Getting There

There are a few options on how to visit Pearl Harbor and the USS *Arizona* Memorial. If you're driving, the entrance is along Rt. 99, the Kamehameha Highway, about a mile south of Aloha Stadium; well-marked signs direct you to the parking area. If you're on H-1 west, take exit 15A and follow the signs. You can also take TheBus, no. 50, or 52 from Ala Moana Center, or no. 20 Airport from Waikiki, and be dropped off within a minute's walk of the entrance. Depending upon stops and traffic, this can take well over an hour.

Arizona Memorial Shuttle Bus, tel. (808) 839-0911, a private operation from Waikiki, takes about 20 minutes and will pick you up at most Waikiki hotels. It charges $3 one-way; reservations are necessary. Returning, no reservations are necessary; just buy a ticket from the lady selling them under the green umbrella in the parking lot.

The **Arizona Memorial Visitor Center** is a joint venture of the U.S. Park Service and the Navy, and is free! The Park Service runs the theater and museum, and the Navy operates the shuttle boats that take you out to the memorial shrine. The complex is open daily 7:30 a.m.-5 p.m., with daily programs 8 a.m.-3 p.m. (closed Thanksgiving, Christmas, New Year's Day), when you can visit the museum and the theater, and take the shuttle boats out to the memorial. If the weather is stormy, or waves rough, they won't sail. For recorded information call (808) 422-0561 or 422-2771. As many as 3,000 people visit per day, and your best time to avoid delays is before 9:30 a.m.

Also, a number of boats operate out of Kewalo Basin doing **Pearl Harbor Cruises.** Costing about $25 for an extensive tour of Pearl Harbor, they are not allowed to drop passengers off at the memorial itself.

Bookstore and Theater

As you enter, you're handed a numbered ticket. Until it's called, you can visit the bookstore/gift shop and museum or, if the wait is long, the USS *Bowfin* moored within walking distance (see following). The bookstore specializes in volumes on WW II and Hawaiiana. The museum is primarily a pictorial history, with a strong emphasis on the involvement of Hawaii's Japanese citizens during the war. There are instructions of behavior to "all persons of Japanese ancestry," from when bigotry and fear prevailed early in the war, as well as documentation of the 442nd Battalion, made up of Japanese soldiers, and their heroic exploits in Europe, especially their rescue of Texas's "lost battalion." Preserved newspapers of the day proclaim the "Day of Infamy" in bold headlines.

When your number is called you proceed to the comfortable theater where a 20-minute film includes actual footage of the attack. The film is historically factual, devoid of an overabundance of flag waving and mom's apple pie. After the film you board the launch: no bare feet, no bikinis or bathing suits, but shorts and shirts are fine. Twenty years ago visitors wore suits and dresses as if going to church!

The Memorial

The launch, a large mostly open-air vessel handled and piloted with professional deft, usually by female Naval personnel, heads for the 184-foot-long alabaster memorial straddling the ship that still lies on the bottom. Some view the memorial as a tombstone; others see it as a symbolic ship, bent by struggle in the middle, but raised at the ends pointing to glory. The USS *Arizona* became the focus of the memorial because her casualties were so severe. When she exploded, the blast was so violent that it lifted entire ships moored nearby clear out of the water. Less than nine minutes later, with infernos raging and huge hunks of steel whizzing through the air, the *Arizona* was gone. Her crew went with her; nearly 1,100 men were sucked down to the bottom, and only 289 somehow managed to struggle to the surface. To the left and right are a series of black and white moorings bearing the names of the ships that were tied to them on the day of the attack.

The deck of the memorial can hold about 200 people; a small museum holds the ship's bell, and a chapel-like area displays a marble tablet with the names of the dead. Into a hole in the center of the memorial, flowers and wreaths are dropped on special occasions. Part of the superstructure of the ship still rises above the waves, but it is slowly being corroded away by wind and sea water. The flag, waving overhead, is attached to a pole anchored to the deck of the sunken ship. Sometimes, on weekends, survivors from the attack are aboard to give firsthand descriptions of what happened that day. Many visitors are Japanese nationals, who often stop and offer their apologies to these Pearl Harbor survivors, distinguished by special military-style hats. The Navy ordered that any survivor wishing to be buried with his crew members had that right. In 1982 a diver took a stainless-steel container of the ashes of one of the survivors to be laid to rest with his buddies.

USS *Bowfin* Submarine Museum and Park

The **USS *Bowfin,*** a WW II submarine moored within walking distance of the *Arizona* Memorial Center, has been turned into a museum. It's open daily 8 a.m.-5 p.m. except Thanksgiving, Christmas, and New Year's Day; admission is $8 adults or $4 for the museum tour only, $3 children ages 4-12 or $2 for the museum tour only. Children three and under are free for the museum tour but not admitted into the submarine. The rate for *kama'aina,* senior citizens, and active military personnel is $6. Topside are a gift shop, snack bar, and the museum building containing many items once on display at the Pacific Sub-

Under attack: the Japanese attack on Pearl Harbor set off a chain of events that would make the U.S. the domineering power of the Pacific.

NATIONAL ARCHIVES

marine Museum. Here and there across the extensive four-acre grounds lie artillery pieces, torpedoes, missiles, and the conning tower and periscope of the **USS Parche**. Guided tours lead you into the sub; the last tour starts at 4:30 p.m. The private, nonprofit organization Pacific Fleet Submarine Memorial Association maintains the park and museum as a memorial and educational exhibit.

Launched one year to the day after the Pearl Harbor attack, the USS *Bowfin* (SS-287) completed nine patrol tours during WW II. Retired in 1979, restored and opened to the public in 1981, it was put on the National Historical Landmark list in 1986. It's a 312-foot-long sausage of steel with a living area only 16 feet in diameter. As you enter the sub, you're handed a telephonelike receiver; a recorded transmitted message explains about different areas on the sub. The deck is made from teak wood, and the deck guns could go fore or aft depending on the skipper's preference. You'll also notice two anchors. As you descend, you feel as if you are integrated with a machine, a part of its gears and workings. In these cramped quarters of brass and stainless steel lived 90 to 100 men, all volunteers. Fresh water was in short supply, and the only man allowed to shower was the cook. Officers were given a dipper of water to shave with, but all the other men grew beards. With absolutely no place to be alone, the men slept on tiny stacked shelves, and only the officers could control the light switches. The only man to have a minuscule private room was the captain.

Topside, twin 16-cylinder diesels created unbelievable noise and heat. A vent in the passageway to the engine room sucked air with such strength that if you passed under it, you'd be flattened to your knees. When the sub ran on batteries under water, the quiet became maddening. The main bunk room, not much bigger than an average bedroom, slept 36 men. Another 30 or so ran the ship, while another 30 lounged. There was no night and day, just shifts. Coffee was constantly available, as well as fresh fruit, and the best mess in all the services. Subs of the day had the best radar and electronics available. Aboard were 24 high-powered torpedoes, and ammo for the topside gun. Submariners, chosen for their intelligence and psychological ability to take it, knew that a hit from the enemy meant certain death. The USS *Bowfin* is fascinating and definitely worth a visit.

In the museum building, you're presented with a short pictorial history of man's progress in undersea travel and warfare, from Revolutionary times to the present. Battle flags, recruiting posters, photographs, uniforms, military medals, and a variety of weapons and hardware are displayed, while a cutaway model of the *Bowfin* shows life aboard ship. New to the museum, and the only one displayed for public viewing, is a daunting Poseidon C-3 submarine missile. An ongoing film in the mini-theater describes life below the surface for the modern submarine force. For the real aficionado, the museum archives and library of submarine-related literature is open by appointment only.

The museum and park is located at 11 Arizona Memorial Dr., Honolulu, HI 96818, tel. (808) 423-1341, fax 422-5201, website: www.aloha.net/~bowfin, e-mail: bowfin@aloha.net. If you are coming by bus, use no. 20 or 47 from Waikiki, or no. 20, 47, 52, or 62 from the Ala Moana Shopping Center.

USS *Missouri*

On June 22, 1998, the USS *Missouri* came home. Whereas the destruction of the USS *Arizona* and other ships in the harbor and the incredible loss of life and innocence brought the United States into war with Japan, it was on the deck of the USS *Missouri* that Japan, bruised and bloodied, surrendered to the U.S., ending this most costly of world conflicts. Temporarily docked on Ford Island just a stone's throw from the USS *Arizona,* it will be moved down "battleship row" in a few years to new and permanent moorings. Money collected by the private, nonprofit USS *Missouri* Memorial Association is going into refurbishing and maintaining the "Mighty Mo," which saw battle during WW II, the Korean War, and the Persian Gulf War. From January 1999, visitors have been allowed onto the deck, where the signing of the surrender took place, and to view the bridge, some dining and sleeping rooms, and the huge 16-inch guns that the ship was well known and feared for. In future years, other areas of the ship may also be opened to tourists. Tours run about $12. Launches to the battleship leave from the USS *Missouri* Visitors Center, set next to the USS *Arizona* Visitors Center. For more information contact the USS Missouri Memorial Association, P.O. Box 6339, Honolulu, HI 96818, tel. 545-2263 or (888) 877-6477, e-mail: bigmo@pixi.net, website: www .ussmissouri.com.

Visit Ships Program

The Navy holds an **open house** on one of its ships berthed at Pearl Harbor on the first Saturday of each month noon-4 p.m. For information call (808) 471-0281. You must enter through the main Nimitz Gate, and then follow the signs to the ship, which is usually at the Bravo or Mike piers. On your way to the docking area you stop at the Family Services area where you can pick up some snacks or ice cream at the concession. The sailors conducting the tour are polite and knowledgeable, and the tour is free. Those never in the service can always spot the officers—the guys with the white shoes.

BEACHES AND SIGHTS

Keaiwa Heiau State Recreation Area

As you travel up Aiea Heights Rd., an exit off H-1, you get a world-class view of Pearl Harbor below. It's not glorious because it is industrialized, but you do ride through suburban sprawl Hawaiian style until you come to the end of the road at Keaiwa Heiau State Recreation Area. In the cool heights above Aiea, these ancient grounds have a soothing effect the minute you enter. Overnight tent camping is allowed here (free permit required), with exceptionally large sites; for the few other visitors, the gates open at 7 a.m. and close at 6:45 p.m. As you enter the well-maintained park (a caretaker lives on the premises), tall pines to the left give a feeling of alpine coolness. Below, Pearl Harbor lies open, like the shell of a great oyster.

Keaiwa Heiau was a healing temple, surrounded by gardens of medicinal herbs tended by Hawaii's excellent healers, the *kahuna lapa'au.* From the gardens, roots, twigs, leaves, and barks were ground into potions and mixed liberally with prayers and love. These potions were amazingly successful in healing Hawaiians before the white man brought his diseases. Walking onto the stone floor of the *heiau,* it's somehow warmer and the winds seem quieter. Toward the center are numerous offerings, sim-

ple stones wrapped with a ti leaf. Some are old, while others are quite fresh. Follow the park road to the **Aiea Loop Trail,** which heads back 4.8 miles roundtrip onto one of the ridges descending from the Koolau Mountains. Pass through a forest of tall eucalyptus trees, viewing canyons to the left and right. Notice, too, the softness of the "spongy bark" trees growing where the path begins. Allow three hours for the loop.

Blaisdell County Park

The park's waters, which can be considered part of Pearl Harbor, are too polluted for swimming. It's sad to think that at the turn of the century it was clear and clean enough to support oysters. Pearl Harbor took its name from Waimomi, "Water of Pearls," which were indeed harvested from the oysters and a certain species of clam growing here. Today, sewage and uncountable oil spills have done their devastation. Recently, oysters from the Mainland's East Coast have been introduced and are being harvested from the mudflats. Supposedly, they're fit to eat. Facilities include a pay phone, tables, and restrooms. Access is off Rt. 99 just past Aloha Stadium and before you enter Pearl City.

Hawaii's Plantation Village

Hawaii's Plantation Village in Waipahu Cultural Park, 94-695 Waipahu St., Waipahu, HI 96797, tel. (808) 677-0110, offers a stroll down memory lane into a once-working plantation village, now an open-air museum. This group of 30 homes, some original and others replicas, and the photos, artifacts, and memorabilia that they contain are a testament to the hard work performed by Hawaii's sugar plantation communities and an insight into the eight ethnic groups represented. Open for guided tours only Mon.-Fri. 9 a.m.-3 p.m. and Saturday 10 a.m.-3 p.m. Tours run about 90 minutes and start every hour. Admission is $5 for adults, $4 for seniors, and $3 for students 5-18.

Hawaiian Railway Line

While there are no commercial passenger train lines operating on the islands, two trains do run for tourists: the Sugar Cane Train on Maui and the Hawaiian Railway train on Oahu. Located in Ewa at 91-1001 Renton Rd., tel. (808) 681-5461, the Hawaiian Railway Society gives rides, restores and exhibits engines and train cars,

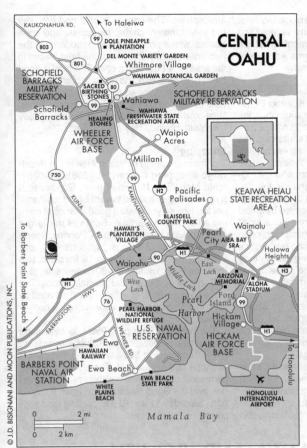

leeward coast, just past the Ko Olina Resort. Don't expect a rail burner—this baby moves at a mild 15 miles an hour. All aboard!

At one time, the Oahu Railway and Land Co. (OR&L) railroad totaled 72 miles of track that ran from Honolulu around Pearl Harbor, up the leeward coast, and across the north coast all the way to Kahuku, with another line up from Honolulu to the central island town of Wahiawa. It was a workhorse of a system, hauling people and goods (mostly sugar and molasses), servicing farms and commercial establishments, and, later, transferring troops and bulk items during WW II. After the war, the railroad couldn't compete with the burgeoning bus and trucking firms and the growing importance of the private automobile, so the line was shut down at the end of 1947, after 58 years of service, and most of the track taken up. After much labor was expended restoring a section of the remaining track and some rolling stock, the Hawaiian Railway Society began to offer rides to the public in 1989.

and maintains an open-air train exhibit and gift shop. This organization does more than give tourist rides, however; it provides an educational adventure. The 90-minute roundtrip, fully narrated rides start at 12:30 p.m. and 2:30 p.m. on Sunday only; $8 adults and $5 for seniors and children under 12. On the second Sunday of every month, the Dillingham parlor car is added to the train on both runs. Fares for a seat in the parlor car are $15, with no children under age 13 allowed. Group charter rides can be arranged Mon.-Fri. mornings. The train runs about six miles along narrow-gauge track from the Ewa station at the end of Renton Road west to the

PRACTICALITIES

Accommodations

Except for long-term apartment hotels and bed and breakfasts, accommodations are virtually nonexistent in this area.

The **Pepper Tree Apartment Hotel,** at 98-150 Lipoha Place, Aiea, HI 96701, tel. (808) 488-1993 or (800) 779-8058, offers furnished studios and apartments, all with complete kitchens and baths, TV, and phones. Rooms start at $65 s or $94 d, with a weekly rate of $385, cash only. A laundromat and swimming pool are also available. Many military personnel use this facility as temporary housing. Just down the block, two other places have approximately the same services and rates: **Hawaiian Horizon Apartment Hotel,** tel. (808) 488-4900, and **Harbor Arms Apartment Hotel,** tel. (808) 488-5556. Expensive.

Food
Buzz's Steak House, 98-751 Kuahao Pl. (at the corner of Moana Loa and Kaahumanu), tel. (808) 487-6465, is open for lunch 11 a.m.-2 p.m. and again for dinner 5-10 p.m. It's futuristic, like something a kid would build with an erector set. It'd be perfect if it were down by the sea, where you could see something, but from where it's located you can peer at Pearl Harbor in the distance or have a world-class view of the freeway. The steakhouse is owned and operated by an old island family whose business grew into a small chain of restaurants from the original location in Kailua. This is one of the remaining two. Buzz's is an institution where islanders go when they want a sure-fire good meal. There's a salad bar and you prepare your own charbroiled steaks and fish. The prices are reasonable.

In the Waimalu Shopping Plaza, try **Stuart Anderson's Cattle Co. Restaurant,** tel. (808) 487-0054, open daily for lunch and dinner. The lounge is open until 2 a.m. weekends, serving huge steaks and all the trimmings.

Across the road is the **Elephant and Castle Restaurant,** at 98-1247 Kaahumanu, tel. (808) 487-5591, open daily for lunch and dinner, breakfast on weekends only. This restaurant has done an excellent job of creating an English-style pub atmosphere. The interior is cool and rich with red velvet, heavy chairs, tapestries, and open beams, with a pool table and dartboards in the pub area. Nightly, it's one of the best places in the area for a beer and a chat. The food is good too. Try English fish and chips, a burger platter, hot sandwiches, or soup and sandwich. Specials on weekends are English prime rib dinner, New York steak, and seafood scampi. Enjoy merry old England Hawaiian style.

Shopping
The main shopping center in Aiea is the **Pearlridge Shopping Center,** tel. (808) 488-0981, open Mon.-Sat. 10 a.m.-9 p.m., Sunday to 5 p.m., with prices geared toward island residents, not tourists, so you have a good chance of coming away with a bargain. Some of the larger stores include Liberty House, JCPenney, Sears, Star Supermarket, Longs, Waldenbooks, and Woolworth's. There are also 16 theaters, two food courts with more than 30 restaurants, plus 150 smaller boutiques and specialty shops. The entire complex is air-conditioned and serviced by an in-house monorail for your shopping convenience.

The **Waimalu Shopping Plaza,** located along Kaahumanu St. between the Kamehameha Hwy. (Rt. 99) and the H-1 freeway, has a small cluster of shops and restaurants. There's a Times Supermarket, open 24 hours with its pharmacy and deli, and the Good Health Store, open 9 a.m.-7 p.m., Saturday 11 a.m.-6 p.m., selling food supplements and minerals.

WAHIAWA AND VICINITY

Wahiawa is like a military jeep: basic, ugly, but indispensable. This is a soldiers' town, with servicemen from Schofield Barracks or nearby Wheeler A.F.B. shuffling along the streets. Most are young, short-haired, short-tempered, and dressed in fatigues. Everywhere you look are cheap bars, burger joints, run-down discos perfumed with sweat and spilled beer, and used-furniture stores. Route 99 turns into Rt. 80 which goes through Wahiawa, crossing California Avenue, the main drag, then rejoins Rt. 99 near the Del Monte Pineapple Variety Garden. Wahiawa has seemingly little to recommend it, and maybe because of its ugliness, when you do find beauty it shines even brighter.

Wahiawa was of extreme cultural and spiritual importance to the early Hawaiians. In town are **healing stones,** whose mystic vibrations were said to cure the maladies of sufferers. In a field not far from town are the **Kukaniloko,** the royal birthing stones, where the ruling *ali'i* labored to give birth to the future nobles of the islands. While in town you can familiarize yourself with Oahu's flora by visiting the **Wahiawa Botanical Garden,** or take a quick look at a serene Japanese temple.

As you gain the heights of the **Leilehua Plateau,** sandwiched between the Waianae and Koolau Ranges, a wide expanse of green is planted in cane and pineapple. Just like on supermarket shelves, Del Monte's **Pineapple Variety Garden** competes with Dole's **Pineapple Pavilion,** a minute up the road. As a traveler's way station, central Oahu blends services, amenities, and just enough historical sites to warrant stretching your legs, but not enough to bog you down for the day.

SIGHTS

The Healing Stones

Belief in the healing powers of these stones has been attracting visitors since ancient times. When traveling down Oahi Street (Rt. 80) take a left on California Avenue, and follow it to Kaalalo Place. To glimpse the religion of Hawaii in microcosm, in a few blocks you pass the Riusenji Soto Buddhist Mission, followed by the healing stones, next door to Olive United Methodist Church. If you've never experienced a Buddhist temple, make sure to visit the grounds of **Riusenji Soto Mission.** Usually no one is around, and even if the front doors are locked you can peer in at an extremely ornate altar graced by Buddha, highlighted in black lacquer and gold. On the grounds look for a stone *jizo,* patron of travelers and children. In Japan he often wears a red woven hat and bib, but here he has on a straw hat and muumuu.

An HVB Warrior marks the stones, just past the Kaalala Elementary School, across the street from a beautiful eucalyptus grove. A humble cinder-block building built in 1947 houses the stones. When you swing open the iron gate it strikes a deep mournful note, as if it were an instrument designed to announce your presence and departure. Inside the building, three stones sit atop rudimentary pedestals. Little scratches mark the stones, and an offertory box is filled with items like oranges, bread, a gin bottle, coins, and candy kisses. A few votive candles flicker before a statue of the Blessed Virgin.

Kukaniloko, the Birthing Stones

Follow Rt. 80 through town for about a mile. At the corner of Whitmore Avenue is a red light:

right takes you to Whitmore Village and left puts you on a dirt track that leads to another eucalyptus grove marking the birthing stones. About 40 large boulders are in the middle of a field with a mountain backdrop. One stone looks like the next, but on closer inspection you see that each has a personality. The royal wives would come here, assisted by both men and women of the ruling *ali'i,* to give birth to their exalted offspring. The baby's umbilical cord, a sacred talisman, would be hidden in the cracks and crevices of the stones. Near the largest palm tree is a special stone that appears to be fluted all the way around, with a dip in the middle. It, along with other stones nearby, seem perfectly fitted to accept the torso of a woman in a reclining position. Notice that small fires have been lit in the hollows of these stones, and that they are discolored with soot and ashes.

Wahiawa Botanical Garden

In the midst of town is an oasis of beauty, 27 acres of developed woodlands featuring exotic trees, ferns, and flowers gathered from around the world. Located at 1396 California Ave., tel. (808) 621-7321, it's open daily except Christmas and New Year's, 9 a.m.-4 p.m., admission free. The parking lot is marked by an HVB Warrior; walk through the main entranceway and take a pamphlet from the box for a self-guiding tour. When it rains, the cement walkways are treacherously slippery, especially if you're wearing thongs. The nicer paths have been left natural, but they can be muddy. Inside the grounds are trees from the Philippines, Australia, Africa, and a magnificent multihued Mindanao gum from New Guinea. Your senses will be bombarded with fragrant camphor trees from China and Japan, and the rich aroma of cinnamon. Everywhere are natural bouquets of flowering trees, entangled by vines and highlighted by rich green ferns. Most specimens have been growing for a minimum of 40 years, so they're well established.

Schofield Barracks

Stay on Rt. 99, skirt Wahiawa to the west, and go past the entrance to Schofield Barracks. Schofield Barracks dates from the turn of the century, named after Gen. John Schofield, an early proponent of the strategic importance of

Pearl Harbor. A sign tells you that it is still the "Home of the Infantry, Tropic Lightning." Open to the public, the base remains one of the prettiest military installations in the world. With permission, you can proceed to the Kolekole Pass, from where you get a sweeping view of inland and coastal Oahu. While heading north on 99 as you pass Schofield Barracks, notice a few run-down shops about 50 yards past the entrance. Stop here and look behind the shops at a wonderful still life created by the Wahiawa Reservoir.

On base, you can visit the small **Tropic Lightning Museum** with memorabilia going back to the War of 1812. There are planes from WW II, Chinese rifles from Korea, and deadly *pungi* traps from Vietnam. The museum has lost many of its exhibits in recent years to the U.S. Army Museum at Fort DeRussy in Waikiki, so it remains mostly a portrayal of the history of Schofield Barracks and the 25th Infantry "Tropic Lightning" Division. There is no charge for the museum, which is open Tues.-Sat. 10 a.m.-4 p.m., except federal holidays; tel. (808) 655-0438. Entrance is via the main gate on Kunia Road, and from there you must follow the signs.

Pineapples

A few minutes past the entrance to Schofield Barracks, Rt. 803 bears left to Waialua, while Rt. 99 goes straight ahead and begins passing rows of pineapple. At the intersection of Rt. 80 is the **Del Monte Variety Garden.** You're free to wander about and read the descriptions of the history of pineapple production in Hawaii, and of the genetic progress of the fruit made famous by the islands. This exhibit is much more educational and honest than the **Dole Pineapple Pavilion** just up the road, the one with all the tour buses lined up outside.

While at the Dole Plantation, visit the "World's Largest Maze." Certified by the Guiness Book of World Records, this maze is nearly two acres in area and formed by more than 11,000 native Hawaiian bushes and flowering plants. Open 9 a.m.-6 p.m., admission $4.50 adults and $2.50 children.

PRACTICALITIES

Dot's Restaurant, off California Avenue at 130 Mango St., tel. (808) 622-4115, is a homey restaurant specializing in American-Japanese food that gives a good square meal for your money. The interior is a mixture of Hawaiian/Asian in dark brown tones. Lunch specials include butterfish, teriyaki chicken, pork, or beef plates all for around $4.50. Miso soup is $2, and simple Japanese dishes go for about $3.50. The most expensive item on the menu is steak and lobster for $15. Dot's is nothing to write home about, but you definitely won't go hungry. Open 6 a.m.-9 p.m.

The streets of Wahiawa are lined with stores that cater to residents, not tourists. This means that the prices are right, and if you need supplies or necessities, this would be a good place to stock up. On the corner of California and Oahi Streets is a **Cornet Store,** an old-fashioned five and dime, where you can buy anything from suntan lotion to a crock pot. The **Big Way Supermarket** is at the corner of California and Kilani Avenues.

Schofield Barracks

HAWAII STATE ARCHIVES

SOUTHEAST OAHU
KOKO HEAD TO WAIMANALO

It's amazing how quickly you can leave the frenzy of Waikiki behind. Once you round the bend past Diamond Head and continue traveling east toward Koko Head, the pace slackens measurably . . . almost by the yard. A minute ago you were in traffic, now you're cruising. It's not that this area is undeveloped; other parts of the island are much more laid-back, but none so close to the action of the city. In the 12 miles you travel from Honolulu to Waimanalo, you pass the natural phenomenon of Koko Crater, a reliable blowhole, the most aquatically active underwater park in the islands, and a string of beaches, each with a different personality.

Man has made his presence felt here, too. The area has some of the most exclusive homes on the island, as well as Hawaii Kai, a less exclusive project developed by the visionary businessman Henry Kaiser, who 20 years ago created this harbinger of things to come. There's Sea Life Park, offering a day's outing of fun for the family, plus shopping centers, the mostly Hawaiian town of Waimanalo, and Bellows Air Force Base, unused by the military and now one of the finest camping beaches on the island. Besides camping, few accommodations are found out here, and few restaurants. This lack of development preserves the area as scenic and recreational, prized attributes that should be taken advantage of before this sunny sandbox gets paved over.

SIGHTS, BEACHES, AND PARKS

The drive out this way accounts for half of the 360 degrees of what is called **The Circle Route.** Start by heading over the Pali Highway down to Kailua, hitting the sights on the way, or come this way first along Diamond Head Rd. to Rt. 72 as you make the loop back to the city. The only consideration is what part of the day you'd rather stop at the southeast beaches for a dip. For the most part, the beaches of this area *are* the sights. The road abounds with scenic points and overlooks. This is the part of Oahu that's absolutely beautiful in its undevelopment. It's hard to find a road on any of the Hawaiian islands that's going to be more scenic than this. At first the countryside is dry because this is the leeward side. But as you approach Waimanalo it gets much more tropical. The road is a serpentine ribbon with one coastal vista after another, a great choice for a joyride just to soak in the sights. The following listings assume that you follow Rt. 72 east from Waikiki to Waimanalo.

Maunalua Bay

Maunalua (Two Mountain) Bay is a four-mile stretch of sun and surf between Diamond Head and Koko Head, with a beach park about every half mile. The first is **Waialae Beach County Park** in Kahala. Go straight ahead on Kahala Avenue for one minute instead of going left on Rt. 72 to join H-1 on to Hanauma Bay. This section is the Beverly Hills of Honolulu, as many celebrities like Tom Selleck and Carol Burnett have homes here. The least expensive home in this section easily pushes $1 million asking price. Waialae is a popular windsurfing spot, crowded on weekends. It's a small beach park with basic amenities in a beautiful location where Makapuu Head wraps around and gives the impression that there are two islands off in the distance, but it's just the way Oahu bends at this point.

Next comes **Kawaikui Beach Park.** No lifeguard, but the conditions are safe year-round, and the bottom is shallow, muddy, and overgrown with seaweed. In times past, islanders came to the confluence of a nearby spring to harvest special *limu* that grow only where fresh water meets the ocean. You'll find unlimited access, parking stalls, picnic facilities, and restrooms. Few people use the park, and it's ideal for sunning, but for frolicking in the water, give it a miss.

In quick succession come **Niu and Paiko Beaches,** lying along residential areas. Although there is public access, few people take advantage of them because the swimming, with a coral and mud bottom, is less than ideal. Some residents have built a pier at Niu Beach past the mudflats, but it's restricted to their private use. Paiko Lagoon is a state bird sanctuary; binoculars will help with sightings of a variety of coastal birds.

The residential area in the hills behind **Maunalua Bay Beach Park** is Hawaii Kai, built by Henry Kaiser, the aluminum magnate. The controversial development was often denigrated as "suburban blight." Many felt it was the beginning of Oahu's ruination. The park fronts Kuapa Pond, at one time a huge fishpond, later dredged by Kaiser, who used the dredged material to build the park, which he donated to the city in 1960. Now, most of the land has been reclaimed except for Koko Marina, whose boat launch constitutes the primary attraction of the park.

Except for the boat launch (the only one on this side of the island), the area is of little recreational use because of the mud or coral bottom. However, swimming is possible and safe, but be careful of the sudden drops created by the dredged boat channels. Two undeveloped parks are located at the end of Poipu Drive, **Kokee and Koko Kai Parks.** The currents and beach conditions make both unsuitable for swimming, but they're popular with surfers. Few others come here, but the views of the bay are lovely with glimpses of Molokai floating on the horizon to the south.

Hanauma Bay State Underwater Park

One of the premier beach parks in Hawaii is located in the sea-eroded crater of an extinct volcano just below Koko Head. People flock here to snorkel, scuba, picnic, and swim. During the day, the parking lot at the top of the hill overlooking the crescent bay below looks like a used car lot, jammed with Japanese imports, vans, and tour buses. A shuttle bus runs up and down the hill, and you can rent snorkeling equipment at the concession stand. If you want to avoid the crowds come in the early morning or after 4 p.m. when the sun dips behind the crater and most tourists leave on cue. There's still plenty of daylight, so plan your trip accordingly.

The reef protects the bay and sends a maze of coral fingers right up to the shoreline. A large sandy break in the reef, **Keyhole,** is a choice spot for entering the water and for swimming. The entire bay is alive with tropical fish. Many have become so accustomed to snorkelers that they've lost their fear entirely, and willingly accept food from your fingers—some so rudely you had better be careful of getting your fingers nibbled. The county provides lifeguards, restrooms, showers, picnic facilities, a pavilion, and food concession.

Before you enter the water, do yourself a favor and read the large bulletin board near the pavilion that describes conditions. It divides the bay into three areas ranging from beginner to expert, and warns of sections to avoid. Be especially careful of **Witches Brew,** a turbulent area on the right at the mouth of the bay that can wash you into the Molokai Express, a notoriously dangerous rip current. Follow a path along the lefthand seacliff to **Toilet Bowl,** a natural pool that rises and falls with the tides. If the conditions are right, you can sit in it to float up and down in a phenomenon very similar to a flushing toilet.

Note: Environmental Alert. Because severe overuse was threatening the fragile ecosystem of the bay, tour companies are now banned from dropping people in the park expressly for snorkeling. Tour buses can now only stop at the top of the hill for a 15-minute overview, and then must leave. People wishing to explore the bay may come by rental car, moped, bicycle, or city bus, which has a stop within the park. However, once the parking lot is filled, it is closed! And, the park is closed to all visitors on Tuesday when sorely needed maintenance is performed. Also, please do not feed the fish anything but approved fish food. Peas and bread are only appetizing to large-mouthed fish and severely cut down on the variety of fish that would normally live within the reef. Most importantly, the very reef is being destroyed by people walking upon it. Please do everything you can to avoid this. A few tour companies have tried to continue bringing people into the park and have found ways to violate the *spirit,* if not the *letter* of the restrictions. Please do not patronize them. With care, Hanauma Bay will remain beautiful for all future generations.

One group that you *should* patronize is the volunteers of the **Hanauma Bay Educational Program** (HBEP), a Sea Grant Program out of the University of Hawaii. The HBEP works toward the conservation and preservation of the bay, and the volunteers run a daily (except Tuesday when the bay is closed) educational tour, starting between 8 and 9 a.m. Come join the tour and learn about this important environmental work.

Koko Head Hike

For a sweeping view, hike to the summit of **Koko Head,** not to be confused with Koko Crater, another good hike but farther east on Rt. 72. To start your trek, look for a paved road closed off to vehicles by a white metal fence, on the right before the road to the parking lot. A 15-minute hike takes you to the 646-foot summit of Koko (Blood) Head. This was the last place that young, wandering Madame Pele attempted to dig herself a fiery nest on Oahu; as usual, she was flooded out by her jealous sister. From the summit you get an unobstructed view of Molokai 20 miles across the Kaiwi Channel, the bowl of Hanauma Bay at your feet, and a sweeping panorama of Diamond Head and the Koolau Mountains. Below are two small extinct craters, Nono'ula and Ihi'i-hilauakea.

Koko Crater

Koko Crater's Hawaiian name is Kohelepelepe (Fringed Vagina). Legend says that Pele's sister, Kapo, had a magical "flying vagina" that could fly and that she could send anywhere. Kamapua'a, the pig-god, was intent on raping Pele when Kapo came to her aid. She dispatched her vagina to entice Kamapua'a, and he followed it to Koko Head, where it made the crater and then flew away. Kamapua'a was unsuccessful when taking a flying leap at this elusive vagina.

You can either hike or drive to the crater. To begin the hike, look for the road to the Hawaii Job Corps Training Center just across from Hanauma Bay. Follow the road down past a rifle range and park at the job training building. Behind is an overgrown tramway track. The remaining ties provide a rough but adequate stairway to the top. At the 1,208-foot summit is an abandoned powerhouse and tramway station. The wood is rotted and the floors are weak! The crater itself lies 1,000 feet below. An easier but less exciting route is to follow Rt. 72 for two miles to Wawamalu Beach near the Hawaii Kai Golf Course and then take a left on Kealahou Street. Nearby is a walking path that leads into the crater.

On the floor of Koko Crater is a 60-acre botanical garden that, due to the unique conditions, specializes in succulents, cacti, and other dry land plants. Little developed yet except for one trail through the garden, the garden has no amenities. Free admission.

Halona Cove

As you round a bend on Rt. 72 you come to the natural lookout of Halona Cove, which means "The Peering Place," an excellent vantage point from which to see whales in season. Just before Halona, a sign will point you to the **Honolulu Japanese Casting Club,** with a stone wall and a monument. The monument at one time was of O Jisan, the Japanese god of protection, destroyed by overzealous patriots during WW II. The current monument was erected after the war, and O Jisan was carved into it. Below is a secluded little beach that's perfect for sunbathing. The only way to it is to scramble down the cliff. Swim only on calm days, or the waves can pull you out to sea and then suck you into the chamber of the famous **Halona Blowhole** just around the bend. There's a turnout at the blowhole for parking. The blowhole is a lava tube at the perfect height for the waves to be driven into it. The water compresses, and the pressure sends a spume into the air. Be extremely cautious around the blowhole. Those unfortunate enough to fall in face almost certain death.

Sandy Beach Park

Sandy Beach is one of the best bodysurfing beaches on Oahu, and the most rugged of them all. More necks and backs are broken on this beach than on all the other Oahu beaches combined. But because of the east-breaking waves, and bottom, the swells are absolutely perfect for bodysurfing. The lifeguards use a flag system to inform you about conditions. The **red flag** means "stay out." When checking out Sandy Beach, don't be fooled by bodysurfers who make it appear easy. These are experts, intimately familiar with the area, and even they are injured at times. Local people refer to the beach as "Scene Beach" because this is where young people come to strut their stuff. This is where the boys are because this is where the girls are. There are restrooms, a large parking area, and two lifeguard towers. Rip-offs have happened, so don't leave valuables in your car. *Kaukau* wagons park in the area, selling a variety of refreshments.

As the road skirts the coastline, it passes a string of beaches that look inviting but are extremely dangerous because there is no protecting reef. The best known is **Wawamalu,** where people come to sunbathe only. Across the road is **Hawaii Kai Golf Course,** an excellent public course.

Makapuu Beach Park

This beach park is below Makapuu (Bulging Eye) Point, a projection of land marking Oahu's easternmost point, and a favorite launching pad for hang gliding. Makapuu is *the* most famous bodysurfing beach in the entire state, but it can be extremely rugged; more people are rescued here than at any other beach on Oahu—except Sandy Beach. In winter the conditions are hazardous, with much of the beach eroded away, leaving exposed rocks. With no interfering reef, the surf can reach 12 feet—perfect for bodysurfing, if you're an expert. Board riding is prohibited. In summer, the sandy beach reappears, and the wave action is much gentler, allowing recreational swimming. There are restrooms, lifeguard towers with a flag warning system, and picnic facilities.

Overlooking Makapuu Beach Park is the lighthouse on Makapuu Point. A moderate hike leads to the top. This lighthouse uses prism glass in its

The lifeguards do a great job at Sandy Beach.

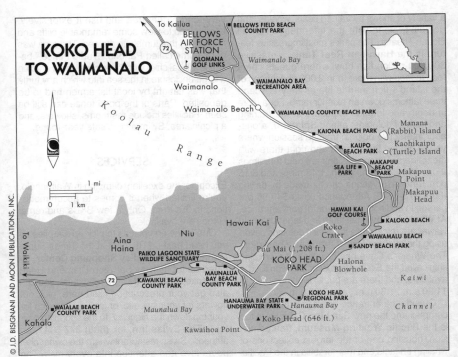

KOKO HEAD TO WAIMANALO

To Kailua
BELLOWS FIELD BEACH COUNTY PARK
BELLOWS AIR FORCE STATION
OLOMANA GOLF LINKS
Waimanalo Bay
Waimanalo
WAIMANALO BAY RECREATION AREA
Waimanalo Beach
WAIMANALO COUNTY BEACH PARK
Koolau Range
KAIONA BEACH PARK
Manana (Rabbit) Island
KAUPO BEACH PARK
Kaohikaipu (Turtle) Island
SEA LIFE PARK
MAKAPUU BEACH PARK
Makapuu Point
Makapuu Head
0   1 mi
0   1 km
HAWAII KAI GOLF COURSE
KALOKO BEACH
Niu
Koko Crater
WAWAMALU BEACH
Aina Haina
Puu Mai (1,208 ft.)
SANDY BEACH PARK
Hawaii Kai
KOKO HEAD PARK
Halona Blowhole
Kaiwi
PAIKO LAGOON STATE WILDLIFE SANCTUARY
KAWAIKUI BEACH COUNTY PARK
MAUNALUA BAY BEACH COUNTY PARK
KOKO HEAD REGIONAL PARK
Channel
WAIALAE BEACH COUNTY PARK
HANAUMA BAY STATE UNDERWATER PARK
Hanauma Bay
Kahala
Maunalua Bay
Koko Head (646 ft.)
Kawaihoa Point
To Waikiki

© J.D. BISIGNANI AND MOON PUBLICATIONS, INC.

lamp and has been functioning for more than 100 years. Bunkers near the top were constructed during WW II and referred to by James Jones in his novel *From Here to Eternity.* They were manned during the war to protect the deepwater Makapuu Bay from possible Japanese attack.

Offshore is **Manana (Rabbit) Island.** Curiously, it does resemble a rabbit, but it's so named because rabbits actually live on it. They were released there in the 1880s by a local rancher who wanted to raise them but who was aware that if they ever got loose on Oahu they could ruin much of the crop lands. During the impotent counterrevolution of 1894, designed to reinstate the Hawaiian monarchy, Manana Island was a cache for arms and ammunition buried on its windward side. Nearby, and closer into shore, is tiny Kaohikaipu (Turtle) Island, which, along with Manana and several other islands along this coast, is reserved as a seabird sanctuary. Efforts are being made by the National

Audubon Society to attract albatross to this island from nearby Kainuio Marine Corps Air Base. Establishing a colony here would keep these ground-nesting animals away from natural predators like mongooses, cats, and dogs.

Sea Life Park Hawaii

Nestled below the lush Koolau Mountains west of Makapuu Point is Sea Life Park Hawaii, tel. (808) 259-7333 or (800) 767-8046, a cluster of tanks holding an amazing display of marine animals that live freely in the ocean just a few hundred yards away. Admission for adults is $19.95, $15.95 for seniors, juniors 4-12 $9.95, under four free. Open daily 9:30 a.m.-5 p.m. On Friday, the park is open until 10 p.m., so there's plenty of time to see the sights and take in the free Hawaiian concert put on at 8:30 p.m. A free shuttle bus runs from major Waikiki hotels (call 808-955-3474 for details), or take TheBus no. 57 from Ala Moana Center, or no. 58, which comes straight up Kuhio Avenue. The park hosts a variety of shows by trained seals, whales, and dolphins, along with the informative Hawaii Ocean Theater. The park's most impressive feature is the **Hawaiian Reef Tank,** a massive 300,000-gallon fish bowl where guests come face to face with more than 2,000 specimens of the island's rich marine life as they descend three fathoms down an exterior ramp. For a more in-depth and intense exposure to the training and care of dolphins, attend **Splash U,** a one-hour interactive dolphin training session where you're behind the scenes and right there with the trainers. These sessions are held four times a day at 10:45 a.m., noon, 1:45 p.m., and 3:15 p.m., and reservations can be made by calling (808) 973-9825. Attendance costs $49.95 per person in addition to the general park entrance. At **Whaler's Cove,** tall tales and legends of old Hawaii are retold while the park's dolphins cavort using the offshore Rabbit Island as a backdrop. The Whaler's Cove has a replica of a whaling ship called the *Essex Nantucket.* Sea lion food is available, and there are public feedings daily at 11:30 a.m., 1:30 p.m., and 3:30 p.m.

Outside the entrance turnstile is a shopping complex and the new **Sea Lion Cafe.** Here too is the **Pacific Whaling Museum,** free admission, housing one of the largest collections of whaling artifacts and memorabilia in the Pacific. Sea Life Park Hawaii is a great learning and entertaining experience for the entire family, or for anyone interested in exploring Hawaii's fascinating marine life.

Kaupo Beach Park

This is the first park that you come to along the southeast coast that is safe for swimming. It is between Sea Life Park and Waimanalo. The park is undeveloped and has no lifeguards, so you are advised to exercise caution. The shore is lined with a protective reef or rocks, and the swimming is best beyond the reef. Close to shore, the jutting rocks discourage most swimmers. Surfers frequent Kaupo, especially beginners, lured by the ideal yet gentle waves.

Kaiona Beach Park

Just before you enter the ethnically Hawaiian town of Waimanalo, you pass Kaiona Beach Park, which you can spot because of the semipermanent tents pitched there. Local people are

very fond of the area and use it extensively. Look inland to view some remarkable cliffs and mountains that tumble to the sea. The area was at one time called Pahonu, "Turtle Fence," because a local chief who loved turtle meat erected a large enclosure in the sea into which any turtle that was caught by local fishermen had to be deposited. Parts of the pond fence can still be seen. Facilities include restrooms, showers, and a picnic area. Swimming is safe year-round.

SERVICES

Except for the excellent camping in Waimanolo, you're limited when it comes to accommodations in this area. Only a few B&Bs and rental homes are available.

One of the first places to pick up supplies as you head east on Rt. 72 is at the Times Super Market in the **Niu Valley Shopping Center,** located about halfway between Diamond Head and Koko Head. Aside from foodstuffs, you can also get your prescription filled here, pick up flowers for your sweetie, or grab a sandwich for your trip down the highway. In the shopping center is **The Swiss Inn,** tel. (808) 377-5447, an authentic Swiss restaurant where the owner/chef pours love and attention into every dish. The food is superb, well prepared, and reasonably priced for the quality; closed Monday and Tuesday. After your meal, have dessert at **Dave's Ice Cream,** also in the center.

A little less ideal for location and a bit closer to Diamond Head, the **Aina Haina Shopping Center** still has many restaurants, a Foodland Supermarket, two banks, a branch post office, and a gas station. Go in on Hind Drive.

Koko Marina Shopping Center

Located along the highway in Hawaii Kai, this center is the largest and easiest access shopping center that you'll find on the way to Hanauma Bay. For photo supplies and sundries, try Thrifty Drugs, Ben Franklin's, Clic Photo, and Surfside Camera. There are two banks, a Waldenbooks, The Bike Shop, and a satellite city hall for camping permits. Foodland provides most supplies for picnics and camping, and you can dine at Chuck's Steak House, McDonald's, Magoo's Pizza, Baskin-Robbins Ice Cream, Sizzler, Kentucky Fried Chicken, Zippy's, Marina Grill, or Kozo Sushi.

Note: For Hawaii Kai's outstanding gourmet option, Roy's Restaurant, see the Waikiki chapter.

The Aloha Dive Shop at the Koko Marina is a full-service dive shop. You can rent or buy snorkeling and scuba gear. So, if you haven't picked up rentals from Waikiki and you're heading out to Hanauma Bay, come here. Dives start at $75 for beginners, featuring all-boat diving at Maunalua Bay, Koko Head, and Diamond Head. Open-water, advanced, and search and rescue certification courses are given for $375. This is the shop of Jackie James, first lady of Hawaiian diving. She's been diving here for more than 25 years.

The Japanese own the Koko Marina Center. In the center are thrill-ride (jet skis, parasails, etc.) booking agencies that will take non-Japanese tourists, but are more for the Japanese tourists who come here by the busload and immediately head out on one of these thrill rides. They've already booked from Japan, so it's all set up and off they go.

Big Sky Parasail, tel. (808) 395-2760, can pull you aloft on a wing (and a prayer) for that parasail ride that you've always dreamed about. Upstairs in the center is **Fun Island Water**

Sports, tel. (808) 395-4386, which does parasailing, water trampolines, water slides, jet boats, boogie boards, and kayaks, as well as renting snorkeling gear. Fun Island is a floating barge that's towed out into the water where you can splash away to your heart's content. The price is $39 for the basic activities, or $59 including jet boating and $98 with jet boating and parasailing; parasailing alone is $39. Also on the second floor of the center is **Sea Breeze Water Sports Ltd.,** tel. (808) 396-0100. It offers jet skiing at $49 for 30 minutes, speedboat rides for the same price and time, and a two-tank scuba dive for $49. Sea Breeze advertises that if you can find a better price anywhere, it will match it.

If you prefer to be pulled across the water behind a boat, try **Suyderhoud Water Ski Center,** tel. (808) 395-3773. They'll take out two people for $49 a half hour or $98 an hour, including skis and a short lesson.

Hawaii Kai Corporate Plaza

For those of you who haven't yet had enough shopping, try Marshall's Store, Payless Shoes, General Nutrition Center, or Costco in this shopping plaza. To fill your stomach, stop at Andre's or Dave's Ice Cream.

WAIMANALO

This small rural town was at one time the center of a thriving sugar plantation owned by the *hapa* Hawaiian nobleman, John Cummins, who was responsible for introducing rabbits to Manana Island. It has fallen on hard times ever since the plantation closed in the late 1940s, and now it produces much of Honolulu's bananas, papayas, and anthuriums from small plots and farms. The town sits in the center of Waimanalo Bay, which is the longest (three miles) stretch of sand beach on Oahu. To many people, especially those from Oahu, it is also the best. Few but adequate travelers' services are in town.

The **Olomana Golf Links,** a relatively easy public course, is close to town. It's also a good place to go for breakfast. You think you're in Waimanalo when you pass a 7-Eleven Store and McDonald's in a built-up area, but that isn't it. You keep going about a mile or two and then you'll come to the older section of town which is Waimanalo proper.

BEACHES AND PARKS

Waimanalo County Beach Park

This park provides camping with a county permit. The beach is well protected and the swimming is safe year-round. Snorkeling is good, and there are picnic tables, restrooms, and recreational facilities, including a ball park and basketball courts. The park is right in the built-up beach area, and not secluded from the road. Although the facilities are good, the setting could be better.

Waimanalo Bay State Recreation Area

Just up the road is Waimanalo Bay State Recreation Area, which remains largely undeveloped, and is much better situated. The access road is hard to spot, but just after McDonald's look for a tall wire fence with the poorly marked entrance in the center. It is good for picnicking and swimming, which can sometimes be rough.

The area, surrounded by a dense ironwood grove, is called "Sherwood Forest," due to many rip-offs by thieves who fancy themselves as Robin Hood, plundering the rich and keeping the loot for themselves. Guess who the rich guys are? Fortunately, this problem of breaking into cars is diminishing, but take necessary precautions. This is the best beach on this section of the island.

For those who enjoy the sport of kings, polo matches are held at 2 p.m. on some Sundays of the year at the polo field in Waimanalo across from Waimanalo Bay State Recreation Area.

Bellows Field Beach County Park

Part of this one-time active Air Force base is now one of Oahu's finest beach parks, and there's camping too! As you enter a sign warns that "This military installation is open to the public only on the following days: weekends—noon Friday to 6 a.m. Monday; federal and state holidays—6 a.m. to 6 a.m. the following day. Camping is authorized in this park by permit from the City and County of Honolulu, Parks and Recreation Board, only." They mean it! The water is safe for swimming year-round, but lifeguards are on duty only during the above-stated hours. Bodysurfing and board surfing are also excellent in the park, but snorkeling is mediocre. Surfboards are not allowed in the area between the two lifeguard towers. After entering the main gates, follow the road for about two miles to the beach area. You'll find picnic tables, restrooms, and cold-water showers. The combination of shade trees and adjacent beach make a perfect camping area. The park is marked by two freshwater streams, Waimanalo and Puha, at either end.

FOOD AND SHOPPING

As you enter Waimanalo, look on the right for a sandwich-board sign painted with a bright red chili pepper that marks the **Bueno Nalo Cafe** at 41865 Kalanianaole Hwy. (next door to Bobby's Market), tel. (808) 259-7186, open daily 11:30 a.m.-9 p.m., which offers a very tasty and inexpensive selection of Mexican food à la Hawaiiana. Hearty *menudo* soup covered in melted cheese is only $4.50 while à la carte tacos, tostadas, tamales, and burritos range $2.75-8.25, and combination dinners are priced at $9.25-10.25. The desserts are real pleasers as well. No drinks are served but you can bring your own. The service is friendly, the atmosphere relaxed, and the food is *muy bueno.*

A short "mile" past Bueno Nalo is **Mel's Market,** where you can pick up almost all camping supplies. Keep going along the Kalanianaole Highway for a mile or so to find **Waimanalo Shopping Center** in the middle of town. Here you can do all your business, pick up lunch and supplies, and head on down the road or go to the beach. In the shopping center is also a **visitor information booth, Woolworth's,** and **Waimanalo Fish Market,** where you can also get plate lunches for about $7.50.

Frankie's Drive-In, at the bottom of the hill, is a local favorite plate lunch drive-in, where you can fill up on teriyaki beef or chicken, fried mahi-mahi, or hamburger steak along with two big scoops of rice and a whack of mac-salad for under $5. Frankie's is great for takeout that can be enjoyed at one of the nearby beaches. Its specialty is a *lilikoi* milkshake, a true island delight!

Pine Grove Village is an open-air bazaar where local people come to sell handmade products and produce. The majority of items are authentic and priced well below similar products found in Honolulu. Participants and times vary, but a group is usually selling daily until 6 p.m. Some excellent buys include local fruits and vegetables, lei, shellwork, hand-dipped candles, bikinis, jewelry, and leather goods. Price haggling is the norm; when the seller stops smiling, that's about the right price.

M.G.L. DOMENY DE RIENZI

WINDWARD OAHU

Oahu's windward coast never has to turn a shoulder into a harsh and biting wind. The trades do blow, mightily at times, but always tropical warm, perfumed with flowers, balmy and bright. Honolulu is just 12 miles over the hump of the *pali,* but a world apart. When *kama'aina* families talk of going to "the cottage in the country," they're most likely referring to the windward coast. In the southern parts, the suburban towns of **Kailua** and **Kaneohe** are modern in every way, with the lion's share of the services on this side. Kailua has Oahu's best windsurfing beach and a nearby *heiau,* preserved and unvisited, while Kaneohe sits on a huge bay dotted with islands and reef. The coastal **Kamehameha Highway** (Rt. 83) turns inland to the base of the *pali,* passing the **Valley of the Temples,** resplendent with universal houses of worship. At **Kahaluu** starts a string of beaches running north, offering the full range of Oahu's coastal outdoor experience. You can meander side roads into the mountains near the Hawaiian villages of **Waiahole** and **Waikane,** where the normal way of life is ramshackle cottages on small subsistence farms.

The coast bulges at **Ka'a'awa,** where the **Crouching Lion,** a natural stone formation, seems ready to pounce on the ever-present tour buses that disturb its repose. North is **Sacred Falls State Park,** a short hike to a peak at Oahu's beautiful and natural heart (if it isn't muddy). Suddenly, you're in manicured **Laie** where Hawaii's Mormon community has built a university, a temple perfect in its symmetry, and the **Polynesian Cultural Center,** a sanitized replica of life in the South Seas, Disney style. The northern tip at **Kahuku** is the site of one of Oahu's oldest sugar mills. Just outside of town is the **James Campbell National Wildlife Refuge,** and beyond that **Kahuku Point,** where the North Shore begins.

It makes little difference in which direction you travel the windward coast, but the following will be listed from south to north from Kailua to Kahuku. The slight advantage in traveling this direction is that your car is in the right-hand lane, which is better for coastal views. But, as odd as it may seem, this dynamic stretch totally changes its vistas depending upon the direction that you travel. You can come one way and then retrace your steps, easily convincing yourself that you've never seen it before. The road is clearly marked with mile markers. They decrease as you head north from Kaneohe on Rt. 83, the Kamehameha Highway.

Beaches and Parks

More than a dozen beaches line the 24 miles of the windward coast from Kailua to Kahuku. The majority offer a wide range of water sports and camping. A few offshore islands, refuges for Hawaiian water birds, can be visited and explored. You can walk to these islands during low tide, and even camp there.

KAILUA AND VICINITY

The easiest way into Kailua (Two Seas) is over the Koolau Range on Rt. 61, the Pali Highway. As soon as you pass through a long tunnel just after the Nuuanu Pali Lookout and your eyes adjust to the shocking brilliance of sunshine, look to your right to see Mt. Olomana. Its 1,643-foot peak is believed to be the volcanic origin of Oahu, the first land to emerge from the seas. Below lies Kailua and the Kawainui swamp, perhaps the oldest inhabited area on this side of the island. Kamehameha I, after conquering Oahu in 1795, gave all this land to his chiefs who had fought for it. The area became a favorite of the ruling *ali'i* until the fall of the monarchy at the turn of this century. The Kawainui Canal drains the marsh and runs through Kailua. A good vantage point from which to observe it is along Kalaheo Avenue, the main road running along the coast in Kailua. Kailua is developed with shopping centers, a hospital, and the *best* windsurfing beach in the state. Six golf courses surround the town, and a satellite city hall dispenses camping permits.

SIGHTS

A good touring loop is to continue straight on Rt. 61 until it comes to the coast. Turn right onto Kalaheo Road, which takes you along the coast to Kailua Beach Park. In the waters offshore will be a spectacle of windsurfers, with their sails puffed out like the proud chests of multicolored birds. To the left of the beach is **Mokapu (Sacred Area) Peninsula,** home of the Kaneohe Marine Corps Base, closed to civilians except 1-5 p.m. on Sunday when only certain areas are open. Notice that the rock that separates the peninsula creates a large natural archway navigable by sizable boats. Most of the little islands in the bay

are bird sanctuaries. The farthest, **Moku Manu,** is home to terns and man-o'-wars, birds famous for leading fishermen to schools of fish. Up on the coastal bluffs is a gray house with a flat roof, the residence of a local woman called the "Bird-lady of Kailua." The woman has a reputation for taking care of any sick or injured birds that people bring to her. Her entire home is carved from rock, including the chairs and table. Every once in a while tours are offered to the house for a few dollars. They're irregular, so check the local papers, and you may be lucky enough to be there at just the right time.

A'alapapa Drive gains the heights from the beach and takes you through an area of beautiful homes until you come to **Lanikai Beach.** At one time trees came down to the shoreline, but it has steadily eroded away. The Navy attempted to start a retaining reef by dumping barge loads of white bath tile just offshore. Their efforts were not successful, but many homes in town now have sparkling, new, white-tiled bathrooms! As A'alapapa Drive loops back to town, it changes names to Mokulua; a pulloff here affords an expansive panorama of the bay below. By daytime it's enjoyable, but in the evening local kids come here to hang out and drink beer.

Ulupo Heiau State Monument

Ulupo is dedicated to the Ulu line of *ali'i,* who were responsible for setting up *heiau* involving the sacred births of chiefs. Oftentimes the umbilical cord was cut just as a drum was sounded, then the cord *(piko)* was placed in a shallow rock depression at a *heiau.* This temple, supposedly built by the legendary *menehune,* shows remarkable stone craftsmanship, measuring 140 feet wide and 30 feet high. Atop the temple is a pathway that you can follow. Notice small stones wrapped in ti leaves placed as offerings. The *heiau* overlooks Kawainui marsh. To get there, as you approach Kailua on Rt. 61 look for a red light and a 7-Eleven store. Turn left onto Uluoa Street, following it to Manu Aloha Street, where you turn right. Follow it to the end and park in the YMCA lot.

BEACHES

Along the shoreline of an exclusive residential area, just south of Kailua, sits **Lanikai Beach.** Three clearly marked rights-of-way run off Mokulua Drive, the main thoroughfare. No facilities, but good snorkeling and swimming year-round, with generally mild surf and a long, gently sloping, sandy beach. The beach runs south for almost a mile, broken by a series of seawalls designed to hold back erosion. Many small craft use the sandy-bottomed shore to launch and land. Popular with local people, but not visited much by tourists.

Kailua Beach Park is the main beach in the area. In the last few years, it has become the windsurfing capital of Hawaii. Local people complain that at one time the beach was great for family outings, with safe conditions and fine facilities. Now the wind has attracted a daily flotilla of windsurfers, kayak racers, and jet skiers. The congested and contested waters can be dangerous for the average swimmer. Many windsurfers are beginners, so if you're a swimmer, be careful of being run over. The conditions are similar to out-of-control skiers found on the slopes of many mountains. The windsurfing area is clearly marked with buoys, which recently were moved 100 yards northeastward, making the area larger.

The park boasts a pavilion, picnic facilities, restrooms, showers, lifeguards, a boat ramp, and sometimes a food concession (they come and go). The surf is gentle year-round, and the swimming safe. Children should be careful of the sudden drop-offs in the channels formed by the Kaelepulu Canal as it enters the sea in the middle of the beach park. Good surfing and diving are found around Popoi'a Island just offshore. Follow Rt. 61 through Kailua until it meets the coast, and then turn right on S. Kalaheo Street following it to the beach park.

Kalama Beach is reached by making a left onto N. Kalaheo. This beach has no facilities and is inferior to Kailua Beach Park, but the swimming is good, and sections of the beach have been made off-limits to any surf-riding vehicles.

ACCOMMODATIONS

Most options here are cottages, rental homes, and bed and breakfasts.

One of the finest guest homes in Kailua is **Sharon's Serenity,** tel. (808) 262-5621 or (800) 914-2271. This beautiful property sits on a quiet side street fronting the picturesque Kawainui

Kailua Beach, the windsurfing capital of Oahu

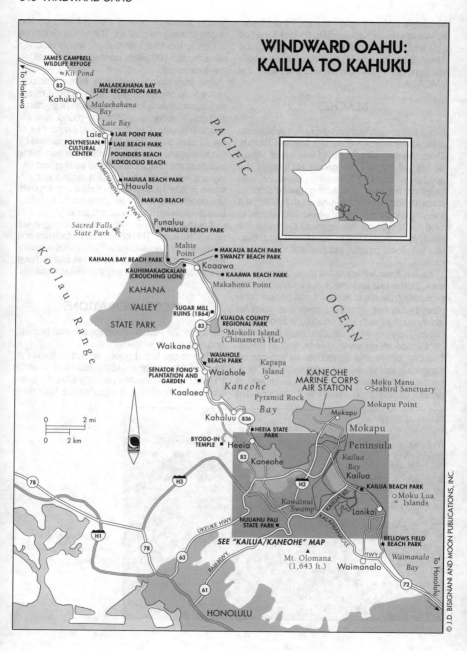

WINDWARD OAHU:
KAILUA TO KAHUKU

JAMES CAMPBELL WILDLIFE REFUGE

Kii Pond

MALAEKAHANA BAY STATE RECREATION AREA

Kahuku

Malaekahana Bay

Laie Bay

Laie

LAIE POINT PARK

POLYNESIAN CULTURAL CENTER

LAIE BEACH PARK

POUNDERS BEACH

KOKOLOLIO BEACH

HAUULA BEACH PARK

Hauula

MAKAO BEACH

Punaluu

Sacred Falls State Park

PUNALUU BEACH PARK

Mahie Point

MAKAUA BEACH PARK

SWANZY BEACH PARK

KAHANA BAY BEACH PARK

Kaaawa

KAUHIIMAKAOKALANI (CROUCHING LION)

KAAAWA BEACH PARK

Makahonu Point

KAHANA VALLEY STATE PARK

Koolau Range

SUGAR MILL RUINS (1864)

KUALOA COUNTY REGIONAL PARK

Mokolii Island (Chinamen's Hat)

Waikane

WAIAHOLE BEACH PARK

Kapapa Island

KANEOHE MARINE CORPS AIR STATION

Moku Manu Seabird Sanctuary

SENATOR FONG'S PLANTATION AND GARDEN

Waiahole

Kaneohe Bay

Pyramid Rock

Mokapu Point

Kaalaea

Kahaluu

BYODO-IN TEMPLE

Heeia

HEEIA STATE PARK

Mokapu

Mokapu Peninsula

Kaneohe

Kailua Bay

Kailua

KAILUA BEACH PARK

Moku Lua Islands

Kawainui Swamp

Lanikai

NUUANU PALI STATE PARK

SEE "KAILUA/KANEOHE" MAP

BELLOWS FIELD BEACH PARK

Mt. Olomana (1,643 ft.)

Waimanalo Bay

Waimanalo

To Honolulu

To Haleiwa

HONOLULU

PACIFIC

OCEAN

0   2 mi

0   2 km

MOON

© J.D. BISIGNANI AND MOON PUBLICATIONS, INC.

Canal. Sharon goes out of her way to make you feel comfortable and welcome. The coffee is always fresh-perked. Sharon also takes the time to sit with you, giving advice on where to dine, what to see, and a candid description of activities that are worthwhile. She also goes weekly to the People's Market (she'll take you along early Thursday morning) for lovely island blooms including anthuriums, ginger, and heliconia, which she arranges and places throughout the home to add a touch of beauty. The meticulously clean, beautifully appointed home features guest rooms with color TV, Mexican tile throughout, a spacious family room, swimming pool, lanai, and views of the stream, golf course, and mountains beyond. The main guest room has its own attached private bath done in tile and oak cabinetry. In here, the bed is queen-size, and next to it is a comfortable leather recliner with green-shaded reading lamp close at hand. Another bedroom could easily accommodate a family, with a queen-size bed and a twin bed set up like a daybed. It features in-room sliding doors for privacy and its own bath just across the hall. Rates are $55 s, $60-65 d. The price includes a continental breakfast, which Sharon will have waiting in the morning. Sharon's Serenity is an excellent choice for the windward coast, and perfect for getting away from it all. Moderate.

Kailua Beachside Cottages, tel. (808) 262-4128, fax 261-0893, has 33 separate units in Kailua, ranging in price $60-450 a night. All are fully furnished, and most are close to the water. If you can't find something from this group that meets your needs, you aren't trying. Moderate.

Pacific Hawaii Bed and Breakfast, tel./fax (808) 486-8838 or (800) 999-6026, or **Affordable Paradise,** tel. (808) 261-1693 or (800) 925-9065, both with offices in Kailua, list private homes in and around town, as well as throughout the state. Rates and homes differ dramatically, but all are guaranteed to be comfortable and accommodating.

FOOD

The **Kailua Shopping Center,** 540 Kailua Rd., has a few inexpensive restaurants. One is **Okazu-ya,** just a takeout lunch window, Japanese and Korean style. In the same small com-

plex is **Chef's Grill,** for sandwiches and plate lunches; **Yoshi's,** for Japanese food; and a **Baskin-Robbins** for your sweet tooth.

The **Holiday Food Mart Food Court,** at 345 Hahani St., has three eateries where you order at a counter and eat outside. **Good Friend Chinese Chicken** serves plate lunches along with the usual assortment of Chinese dishes. For something a bit heartier, try **Yummy's Korean Barbecue** where you can fill yourself with barbecued short ribs, barbecued chicken, noodle soups, or a combination plate. A good place for a breakfast croissant and a coffee pick-me-up is **Baile,** a French sandwich shop.

Hekili Street Eateries

The 100 block of Hekili Street could be Kailua's mini-version of Honolulu's Restaurant Row. Along this street is **Princess Chop Suey,** tel. (808) 839-0575, your basic chop suey joint. Open Mon.-Sat. 10:30 a.m.-9 p.m., Sunday noon-9 p.m. Naugahyde booths and Formica tables. Everything under $7.95.

Next door is **Sisco's Cantina,** tel. (808) 262-7337, featuring complete Mexican cuisine, open Sun.-Thurs. 11 a.m.-10 p.m., Friday and Saturday 11 a.m.-11 p.m. Tostadas, tacos, burritos, enchiladas, and chiles rellenos are all under $10. More expensive dishes are shrimp Veracruz ($14) and fajitas ($16.25, for two $20.95). All come with Mexican corn, sautéed Tex-Mex mushrooms, and salad. Inside, the south-of-the-border atmosphere is created with hanging piñatas, stucco walls, and blue-tile tables.

A minute down the street is **Detroit Italian Deli,** featuring subs and ice cream.

Around Town

Let the pungent aroma of garlic frying in olive oil lead you to **Assaggio's Ristorante Italiano,** 354 Uluniu St., tel. (808) 261-2772, open Mon.-Fri. for lunch, 11:30 a.m.-2:30 p.m., dinner nightly 5-10 p.m. You are welcomed into a bright and open room done in the striking colors of black, red, teal, and magenta. A wall running down the center of the restaurant separates the bar from the dining room, where tables covered in white linen and black upholstered chairs line the long window area. The typical Italian menu, served with crusty Italian bread, begins with antipasti priced $5.90-9.90, fresh clam scampi at $6.90, and the light and classic prosciutto and melon at $6.90. Soups are pasta fagioli (macaroni and beans, the favorite of Italian contadina), minestrone, tortellini imbrodo (tortellini with ricotta in broth), or vichysoisse served as a cup or bowl, for $1.90 or $2.90. Pasta ranging in price $8-12 includes linguine, fettuccine, and ziti. Dishes come in two sizes, small (about $2 less) and regular, and are covered in marinara, clam, carbonata, or pesto sauce. Entrees are chicken cacciatore or chicken rolatini, stuffed with ricotta cheese, both at $12.90; baked ziti with eggplant and mozzarella for $9.90; or lasagna for $11.90. Meat dishes are New York steaks, pork chops, or *osso bucco* (veal shanks with onions), all for around $14.90. From the sea comes fresh fish sautéed in garlic oil for $15.90, scallops and shrimp in wine, garlic butter, and snow peas for $17.90, or calamari alla parmigiana at $12.90. Desserts are homemade cheesecake, cannelloni, spumoni, and chocolate mousse all around $4. The full bar serves imported and domestic beers, liquors, coffees, espressos, and plenty of wine varietals.

On a side street near Assaggio's, Solana features Mediterranean regional cuisines. Open Mon.-Fri. 5:30-9:30 p.m., until 10:30 Saturday and Sunday; call (808) 263-1227 for reservations. Look for the tiki torches at 30 Aulike Street. Inside are wooden tables, tile floors, and a solarium-like room. To create a feeling of intimacy, you can watch the cook prepare your food in the open kitchen. Try the North African-style seared *ahi* with white bean and baby artichoke salad and twin pestos as an appetizer for $9.95, or save room for the Moroccan-style *osso bucco* served on a bed of vegetables, with couscous in a tomato and veal sauce with blonde raisins and kalamata olives for $17.50. That's Mediterranean! The grilled, marinated lamb at $24.50 is the most expensive item on the menu, but most entrees are under $18. As wonderful as the main dishes are the appetizers and soups. It's casual gourmet and the service is excellent. Give it a try.

El Charro Avitia, 14 Oneawa St., tel. (808) 263-3943, open daily for lunch and dinner, is a better than average Mexican restaurant. Simple yet tasteful, the south-of-the-border inspired decor is achieved with adobe-like arches, wooden tables, Mexican ceramics placed here and there, and plenty of cacti and hanging plants. The menu features combination dinners of bur-

ritos, chili verde, enchiladas, or tacos, all priced under $12. The specialty of the house is the flame-broiled catch of the day at $14.50. Other entrees include fish Veracruzana, as good as you'll find anywhere, carne asada, or *camarones al mojo de ajo* (jumbo shrimp sautéed in butter, garlic, and white wine), all for under $15, and all served with rice, black beans, fresh vegetables, and a fresh fruit garnish. Less expensive dishes are chimichangas, burritos, taco salad, and Mexican pizza, which is two deep-fried tortillas topped with cheddar cheese, jack cheese, beans, tomatoes, olives, and lettuce, all around $9. Huevos Mexicana, rancheros, and revueltos, served throughout the day, are $8.50. The bar mixes mean margaritas, which come in normal sizes up to a fiesta 40-ounce that will definitely have you yelling ¡olé! El Charro Avitia is definitely worth the money!

Just up Oneawa Street is **Ching Lee Chop Suey,** a down-home, inexpensive Chinese restaurant where you can have a complete meal for under $5.

Buzz's Original Steakhouse, at 413 Kawailoa Rd., tel. (808) 261-4661, is really *the* original steakhouse of this small island chain owned by the Schneider family. Buzz's is just across the road from Kailua Beach Park, situated along the canal. This restaurant is an institution with local families. It's the kind of place that "if you can't think of where to go, you head for Buzz's." The food is always good, if not extraordinary. It has top sirloin ($14.95), pork chops ($13.95), chicken teri ($11.75), fresh fish (usually about $18), and mahimahi ($12.95). Salad bar is included with all entrees, and separately for $7.95. Everything is charbroiled. Remember, no credit cards.

Saeng's Thai Cuisine, at 315 Hahani, tel. (808) 263-9727, open Sat.-Sun. 5-9:30 p.m., Mon.-Fri. 11 a.m.-2:30 p.m. and again 5-9:30 p.m., offers spicy Thai food with an emphasis on vegetarian meals. Appetizers and starters are Thai crisp noodles ($5.25), sautéed shrimp ($9.95), salads like green papaya salad ($5.25), *yum koong* (shrimp salad, $7.95), and chicken coconut soup ($6.95). Specialties include spicy stuffed calamari ($9.95), Thai red curry ($7.95), and à la carte beef, pork, and chicken dishes, all under $8. Vegetarians can pick from mixed veggies with yellow bean paste ($5.95), mixed veggies with oyster sauce ($5.95), or zucchini tofu ($5.95). Saeng Thai is a good change of pace at a decent price.

Harry's Cafe and Deli, 629 Kailua Rd., tel. (808) 261-2120, is open Mon.-Sat. 11 a.m.-3 p.m. and 5:30-9 p.m. Owned and operated by Tim Owens, son of songwriter and radio personality Harry Owens, this casual place is decorated with a strong Hawaiian flavor, including some sheet music covers from the '30s, when Harry penned the famous song "Sweet Leilani." It was Harry, along with Webley Edwards, who inaugurated the radio broadcast *Hawaii Calls* in 1935, introducing millions of Americans to the sweet sounds of island music during the bleak days of the Depression. The lunch menu strongly favors sandwiches like the club sandwich at $5.50, Reuben at $6.50, and the veggie avocado at $4.50. Also try the soups and salads or the daily special, like the pita pocket filled with curried turkey salad, cucumber slices, sprouts, and onions for $7.50. The dinner menu is a bit more substantial yet very reasonably priced. Choose between such items as fettuccine and sautéed chicken with basil, pesto, and cream for $9.95, or black tiger shrimp for $11.95.

Family-run **Brent's Restaurant and Delicatessen,** next to Harry's, tel. (808) 262-8588, is a slice of New York in paradise. Choose sausage, corned beef, lox, or cheese from the deli case or order a lunch sandwich off the menu. Hearty breakfasts are also served as are à la carte dinners. All items are reasonably priced. Brent's is open daily except Monday 7 a.m.-9 p.m., until 8 p.m. on Sunday.

At the Enchanted Lake Shopping Center is **Yen Yen Chinese Restaurant,** tel. (808) 262-2218, a friendly and inexpensive place to stop for the food, not necessarily for the decor. One of the favorite dishes is prawns with walnuts at $7.50. Vegetarian dishes run $5-6, rice and noodle dishes around $7, and most other main dishes under $10. Appetizers and soups fill out the rest of the menu.

Uluniu Street: Inexpensive Dining

Uluniu Street has inexpensive places to eat, one after the other. After making a left from Kuulei Road (Rt. 61) onto Oneawa, a main thoroughfare, turn right onto Uluniu just at the large Kailua Furniture. First is an authentic but very basic

hole-in-the-wall Japanese restaurant, **Kailua Okazuya.** It specializes in *donburi,* a bowl of rice smothered with various savories. Try the *o yakodon buri,* chicken and egg with vegetables over rice for under $4. It serves plate lunches and a sushi special that can't be beat, which includes fresh fish, shrimp, abalone, and octopus for only $5! Next door is **Kolohe Hawaiian Restaurant,** and up the street is the **New Chinese Garden,** a basic Chinese restaurant with decent prices. None of these restaurants is remarkable, but all will fill you up with good enough food for a very reasonable price.

Health Foods

A well-established health food store in Kailua is **The Source,** tel. (808) 262-5604, at 32 Kainehe Street. This place has vitamins and minerals, bulk foods, some organic fresh produce, cosmetics and hygiene products, as well as lots of essences, oils, and natural healing products to help with whatever ails you and to keep you on the straight and narrow. Fresh juices are available from the juice bar, and from the food bar you can order organic burgers, salads, homemade soups, sushi, smoothies, and the like at very reasonable prices. The food bar is open Mon.-Fri. 10 a.m.-8 p.m., Saturday and Sunday 10 a.m.-4 p.m.

For a little pick-me-up, try **Agnes Bake Shop** across the street for Portuguese-based *malasadas* and *pao dolce,* or soup, salad, cappuccino, or espresso.

SHOPPING

The two towns of Kailua and Kaneohe have the lion's share of shopping on the windward coast. You can pick up basics in the small towns as you head up the coast, but for any unique or hard-to-find items, Kailua/Kaneohe is your only bet. The area offers a few shopping centers. The **Windward Mall,** at 46-056 Kamehameha Hwy., Kaneohe, tel. (808) 235-1143, open weekdays 9:30 a.m.-9 p.m., Saturday to 5:30 p.m., Sunday 10 a.m.-5 p.m., is the premier, full-service mall on the windward coast. Besides department stores like Liberty House and Sears, there are shops selling everything from shoes to health foods.

The **Kaneohe Bay Mall** across from the Windward Mall is a little more down-home, and features a Longs Drugs, especially good for photo supplies. The **Aikahi Park Shopping Center** along Kaneohe Bay Dr., at the corner of Mokapu Blvd., is a limited shopping center whose main shops are a Safeway and a Sizzler Restaurant. The **Kailua Shopping Center,** at 540 Kailua Rd., also has limited shopping that includes a **Time's Supermarket,** open till 10 p.m., and a well-stocked **Honolulu Bookshop,** tel. (808) 261-1996, open Mon.-Fri. 9:30-9, Saturday 9:30-5:30, Sunday till 5 p.m., for a full range of reading material. There's also a **Cornet Store** along Kailua Ave. for sundries, lotions, and notions, and a **Longs Drugs.** You never know what kind of treasure lurks at a thrift shop, so have a look at the **Salvation Army Thrift Store** on Uluniu St. to see what kind of bargain you can find.

You'll find just about anything at **Holiday Mart** on Hahani Rd., or picnic supplies, beach accessories, or cappuccino at the upgraded landmark **Kalapawai Market,** at the corner of Kailua and Kalaheo roads, which marks the best entrance to Kailua's windsurfing beaches.

Thursday mornings bring a **farmers' market** into town for only one hour, 8:50-9:50 a.m. Those in the know arrive early to get a number at their favorite stalls, which can sell out within minutes of opening. Great for fresh flowers and fruits.

You might pick up an heirloom at **Heritage Antiques,** at the corner of Kailua Rd. and Amakua St., tel. (808) 261-8700, open daily 10 a.m.-5:30 p.m., which is overflowing with Asian, Hawaiian, and Americana antiques. Here too are **jewelers,** H.W. Roberts and J.K. Phillips, who also specialize as gemologists. **The Hunter Antiques,** across the street from Heritage Antiques, specializes in Depression glass.

Island Treasures, 629 Kailua Rd., tel. (808) 261-8131, is a relatively new art gallery in Kailua. Owned and operated by Debbie Costello, who comes from a family of artists, the shop is open daily 10 a.m.-6:30 p.m. Debbie, an artist in her own right, does the beautiful stained glass pieces in the shop. Other artists she represents are John Costello, who does fantasy scenes in acrylics and pastels; Tom Cohen, a master with jewelry, precious stones, and crystals; potters Jerry Meek and Stephen Hatland; Bud Morrison, who works bamboo into objects emanating a Japanese feel; bronze artist Holly Young; Teri Inouye, who renders the flora of Hawaii in colored pencils; and photographer Randy Braun.

SERVICES

Campers can reach the satellite city hall, 1090 Keolu Dr., for information and permits by calling (808) 261-8575. A post office is at the corner of Kailua and Hahani, just across from the Hawaiian National Bank. Medical aid is available from Castle Medical Center, tel. (808) 263-5500.

KANEOHE AND VICINITY

The bedroom community of Kaneohe (Kane's Bamboo) lies along Kaneohe Bay, protected by a huge barrier reef. Around the edge of the bay lie six of the original 30 fishponds that once graced this fine shore. A lush, fertile land of bountiful farms, Kaneohe was the second most populous area on the island. Through the years, the major crops of this coastal town have shifted from taro to rice, sugarcane, pineapples, and bananas, and today a variety is still grown.

Where Rt. 83 intersects the Likelike Highway on the southern outskirts of Kaneohe, it branches north and changes its name from the Kamehameha Highway to the Kahekili Highway until it hits the coast at Kahaluu. This four-mile traverse passes two exceptionally beautiful valleys: Ha'iku Valley and the Valley of the Temples. Neither should be missed.

Within the town is **Ho'omaluhia Botanical Garden,** 45-680 Luluku Rd., Kaneohe, tel. (808) 233-7323, so large that guided hikes are offered on a daily basis. This garden is one component of the Hawaiian Botanical Garden system. A 400-acre tract, it includes a 32-acre lake, a dammed reservoir that's part of the flood control for Kaneohe. Day-use and overnight facilities are available, horseback riding is permitted, and walking, jogging, and bicycling are encouraged. Guided nature walks are given 10 a.m. on Saturday, 1 p.m. on Sunday, and Hawaiian plant use walks are run daily 10 a.m.-noon.

KAILUA / KANEOHE

© J.D. BISIGNANI AND MOON PUBLICATIONS, INC.

Offshore is Moku o' Loe, commonly called **Coconut Island.** It became famous as the opening shot in the TV show *Gilligan's Island,* although the series itself was shot in California. In ancient times, it was *kapu* and during WW II served as an R&R camp for B-29 crews. Many of the crews felt the island had bad vibes, and reported having a streak of bad luck. In recent times, Frank Fasi, Honolulu's former mayor, suggested that Hawaii's gate-crashing guests, Ferdinand and Imelda Marcos, should lease Coconut Island. It never happened.

A sandbar has been building in the center of Kaneohe Bay that has made a perfect anchorage for yachts and powerboats. These boat people drop anchor, jump off, and wade to the bar through waist-deep, clear waters. It has become an unofficial playground where you can fling a Frisbee, drink beer, fly a kite, or just float around. Part of the sandbar rises above the water and some barbecue chefs even bring their hibachis and have a bite to eat. Surrounding you is Kaneohe Bay with Chinaman's Hat floating off to your right, and a perfect view of the *pali* straight ahead. The epitome of la dolce vita, Hawaiian style. Fortunately, in recent years, the once crystal-clear bay, which was becoming murky with silt because of development, is clearing again due to conservation efforts.

For a fun-filled day on the water, far from the crowds of Waikiki, try **North Bay Aquatics** located on the grounds of Schrader's Windward Marine Resort, 47-039 Lihikai Dr., Kaneohe, tel. (808) 239-5711. A boat ($10) runs from the resort property to the sandbar on Tuesday and Saturday, where you can swim, snorkel, kayak, or hydrobike to your heart's content. Departure times depend on the tides, so call a day in advance.

Ha'iku Gardens

Ha'iku (Abrupt Break) Gardens is a lovely section of a commercial area that includes a restaurant and some quiet condominiums. After you pass a community college, Ha'iku Road is past two red lights. Turn left and proceed for about one-half mile until you see the entrance. The gardens date from the mid-1800s, when Hawaiian *ali'i* deeded 16 acres to an English engineer named Baskerville. He developed the area, creating a series of spring-fed lily ponds, a number of estate homes, and planting flowers, fruits, and ornamental trees. Later a restaurant was built, and the grounds became famous for their beauty, often used for outdoor weddings and special gatherings.

You're welcome to walk through the gardens. Proceed from the restaurant down a grassy area to a pond, where perhaps you'll attract an impromptu entourage of ducks, chickens, and guinea fowl that squawk along looking for handouts. Amidst the lush foliage is a grass shack used for weddings. A path leads around a larger pond whose benches and small pavilions are perfect for contemplation. The path leads under a huge banyan, while a nearby bamboo grove serenades with sonorous music if the wind is blowing.

Valley of the Temples

The concept of this universal faith cemetery is as beautiful as the sculpted *pali* that serves as its backdrop. A rainy day makes it better. The *pali* explodes with rainbowed waterfalls, and the greens turn a richer emerald, sparkling with dewdrops. Don't miss the Valley of the Temples Memorial Park, 47-200 Kahekili Hwy., tel. (808) 239-8811. Open daily 8 a.m.-4:30 p.m.; admission is $2 per person, $1 for seniors and children under 12, or *kama'aina* rates of $5 per carload, but you have to prove you're from Hawaii. Admission is charged only until 4:30 p.m. After that, you can walk in to see the grounds, but the buildings will not be open. High on a hill sits a Christian chapel, an A-frame topped by a cross.

The views can be lovely from up here, but unfortunately the large windows of the chapel perfectly frame some nondescript tract housing and a supermarket below. Great planning!

The crown jewel of the valley is **Byodo-In Temple** (Temple of Equality), a superbly appointed replica of the 900-year-old Byodo-In of Uji, Japan (depicted on the 10-yen coin). This temple dates from June 7, 1968, 100 years to the day when Japanese immigrants first arrived in Hawaii. It was erected through the combined efforts of an American engineering firm headed by Ronald Kawahara in accordance with a plan designed by Kiichi Sano, a famed Kyoto landscape artist. Remove your shoes before entering the temple. A three-ton brass bell, which you're invited to strike after making an offering, creates the right vibrations for meditation, and symbolically spreads the word of Amida Buddha.

The walls hold distinctive emblems of different Buddhist sects. Upstairs wings are roped off, with no entry permitted. Stand on the gravel path opposite the main temple. You'll see a grating with a circle cut in the middle. Stick your face in to see the perfectly framed contemplative visage of Buddha. Cross a half-moon bridge to the left of the temple and follow the path to a small gazebo. Here a rock, perfectly and artistically placed, separates a stream in two, sending the water to the left and right. The pagoda at the top of the path is called the Meditation House. Go to this superbly manicured area to get a sweep-

Byodo-In Temple

ing view of the grounds. In front of the Meditation House is a curious tree; pick up one of the fallen leaves, and feel the natural velvet on the backside.

The grounds are alive with sparrows and peacocks, and from time to time you'll hear a curious-sounding "yip, yip, yip" and clapping hands. Follow it to discover Mr. Henry Oda, who, with crumbs in his fingers, feeds a boiling cauldron of koi in the waters below with mouths agape demanding to be fed. He mostly feeds the fish while Mr. Hisayoshi Hirada, the original "Birdman of Byodo-In," feeds the birds. Mr. Hirada translates his first name into "long live a good man," and he, in his 80s, is living proof. Mr. Hirada began training the birds and carp of Byodo-In after his *first* retirement. He would come daily to feed the fish, clapping his hands while he did so. Soon the Pavlovian response took over. Simultaneously, a small and courageous bird, which Hirada-san calls Charlie, began taking crumbs from his fingers. After that, all the birds wanted some. Mr. Oda does a great job of showing visitors around. Mr. Hirada is also there most days, and if you happen to meet him while you're visiting, you have been blessed by the great Buddha of Byodo-In.

A small gift shop selling souvenirs, cards, film, and some refreshments is to the right of the temple. If you wish to photograph the complex, it's best to come before noon, when the sun is at your back as you frame the red and white temple against the deep green of the *pali*.

BEACHES

Kaneohe Bay offers Kaneohe Beach Park, Heeia State Park, and Laenani Beach Park, all accessible off Rt. 836 as it heads northward along the coast. All are better for the views of Kaneohe Bay than for beach activities. They have restrooms and a few picnic tables. The water is safe year-round, but it's murky and lined with mudflats and coral heads. The same conditions hold true for **Waiahole Beach Park** about four miles north, but this area is much less developed, quieter, and good for beachcombing.

Heeia State Park lies along Rt. 836 between Kaneohe and Kahaluu and is designated as an "interpretive park." It sits high on Kealohi Point overlooking Heeia Fishpond below. Kealohi translates as "The Shining," because it was a visible landmark to passing voyagers, but there is a much deeper interpretation. To the Hawaiians this area was a "jumping-off point into the spirit world." It was believed that the souls of the recently departed came to this point and leapt into eternity. The right side, Heeia-kei, was the side of light, while the left side, Heeia-uli, was the domain of darkness. The wise *kahuna* taught that you could actually see the face of God in the brilliant sun as it rises over the point.

On the grounds are a main hall, pavilion, restrooms, and various short walks around the entire area with magnificent views of Kaneohe Bay. The park contains numerous indigenous plants and mature trees, the perfect laboratory for the educational goals set by The Friends of Heeia State Park. As an interpretive park, programs are offered for the community and visitors alike. Bernadette Lono, the Director of Hawaiian Studies, gives personal tours of the area. Her family has been part of this *ahuapua* (ancient land division) for countless generations. Bernadette first acquaints you with the area by asking you to sit Hawaiian style on the grass. The earth or *aina* is fundamental to the Hawaiian belief system, and you should start connected to it. She goes on to explain the symbiotic relationship between inland farmers whose fields stretched to Eolaka, the top of the *pali*, and the fishermen who plied the waters of Mokapu on the other side of the peninsula.

Below, Heeia Fishpond is now privately owned by a Mr. Brooks, who has taken over the management of the pond from the Bishop Estates on a 20-year lease. He will raise mullet *(ama)*, the traditional fish raised by the ancient Hawaiians and *kapu* to all except the *ali'i*.

ACCOMMODATIONS AND FOOD

Camp Kokokahi, located at the pier, at 47-035 Kaneohe Bay Dr., tel. (808) 247-2124, e-mail: kokokahi@gte.net, has private and semiprivate cottages and camping. Rates are $20 single, $15 double or a bunk, and $8 tent. Amenities include barbecue and laundry facilities. Budget

The **Schrader's Windward Marine Resort** in Kaneohe has been operating for years. It's a hodgepodge of a place, a "cottage hotel," with some fully furnished units and others with kitchenettes. There are some separate units along the bay, while others are quite nondescript. A swimming pool, laundry, and barbecue pit are on the premises, and maid service is offered every third day. Rates run about $50-190, but a room/car/activity package is also an option. For information contact Schrader's Windward Marine Resort, 47-039 Lihikai Dr., Kaneohe, HI 96744, tel. (808) 239-5711 or (800) 735-5711. Inexpensive.

Fortunately, or unfortunately, Kaneohe is a bit of a wasteland as far as tourist services, nightlife, and eating out are concerned. Most people who live here head for the action in Honolulu. There are a few limited choices. **Fuji's Delicatessen,** at 45-270 Wm. Henry Rd., tel. (808) 235-3690, is a local favorite known for its down-home Japanese, Korean, and Hawaiian cooking served family style on long communal tables.

The best cheap deal in town is at **Kim Chee One,** at 46-010 Kamehameha Hwy., tel. (808) 235-5560, which has a few sister restaurants scattered around Oahu. The setting is plain, but

you'll have trouble finishing the excellent Korean mixed barbecued plate for $6.95, easily enough for two.

The **Chart House at Ha'iku Gardens,** true to its name, sits surrounded by a fragrant garden in a lovely, secluded valley. It's considered one of the most beautiful places on Oahu, and people still come here to be married. The restaurant is part of a small island chain with an excellent reputation for good food. Most entrees are in the $19-25 range, so it's not inexpensive. A variety of appetizers, soups, and salads start the meal, after which you can choose entrees including teriyaki chicken breast for $16.50 and salmon or a combination top sirloin and shrimp for $22.95. The house specialty is a thick cut of prime rib that goes for $21.95. Sit back and relax over a pie, drinks, coffee, or tea while enjoying the lighted evening garden before leaving. On Sunday evening, the local classical and slack key guitar player Ellsworth Simeona provides the entertainment. Open Mon.-Thurs. 5:30-9 p.m., Fri.-Sat. 5-10 p.m., and Sunday 5-9 p.m.; call (808) 247-6671 for reservations.

NORTH KANEOHE BAY

KAHALUU

This town is at the convergence of the Kahekili Hwy. and the Kamehameha Hwy. (Rt. 83) heading north. Also, Rt. 836, an extension of the Kamehameha Highway, hugs the coastline heading down to Kailua/Kaneohe. It offers some of the most spectacular views of a decidedly spectacular coast, with very few tourists venturing down this side road. Kahaluu Town is a gas station and a little tourist trap selling junk just in case you didn't get enough in Waikiki. The Hygienic Store sells liquor, groceries, soda, and ice, all you'll need for an afternoon lunch. The Waihee Stream, meandering from the *pali,* empties into the bay and deposits fresh water into the ancient **Kahaluu Fish Pond,** a picture-perfect tropical setting. So picture-perfect is the place that it has provided the background scenery to TV and Hollywood productions such as an episode from *Jake and the Fat Man,* a setting for *Parent Trap II,* and the famous airport and village scene from

The Karate Kid II. All of the movie sets have been torn down, but you can still overlook the fishpond by taking a short walk just behind the bank in town.

Senator Fong's Plantation and Gardens

Senator Fong's Plantation and Gardens, 47-285 Pulama Rd., Kaneohe, HI 96744 (in Kahaluu), tel. (808) 239-6775, is open daily 10 a.m.-4 p.m., except Christmas and New Year's Day. Admission is $10 adults, $8 seniors, and $6 children 5-12. Guided tram tours run at 10:30 a.m., 11:30 a.m., 1 p.m., 2 p.m., and 3 p.m. One of Hawaii's newest attractions, the plantation is a labor of love created by Senator Hiram Fong, who served as state senator 1959-77. Upon retirement he returned to his home and ever since has been beautifying the gardens he started more than 40 years ago. The result is 725 acres of natural beauty rising from 80 feet in elevation to 2,600 feet at the ridge of the Koolau Range above. The gardens preserve the native flora and fauna of the land, along with planted flower and fruit gardens, and groves of trees, palms, bushes, and ferns. When you first arrive, there is a large open-air pavilion housing a snack window serving sandwiches, plate lunches, and saimin. Inside is also a small but well-appointed souvenir shop where you can get everything from aloha shirts to postcards. Notice a table set with baskets of flowers where you can make your own keepsake lei for $6.50. **Horseback rides** are also given at $34 an hour; make reservations by calling Aloma Trail Rides at (808) 293-7857.

WAIAHOLE AND WAIKANE

If you want to fall in love with rural, old-time Oahu, go to the northern reaches of Kaneohe Bay around Waiahole and Waikane, a Hawaiian grassroots area that has so far eluded development. Alongside the road are many more fruit stands than in other parts of Oahu. For a glimpse of what's happening look for the Waiahole Elementary School, and turn left up Waiahole Valley Road. The road twists its way into the valley, becoming narrower until it turns into a dirt track. Left and right in homey, ramshackle houses lives down-home Hawaii, complete with taro patches in the back yards. Another road of the same type is about one-half mile up Rt. 83 just before you enter Waikane. If you're staying in Waikiki, compare this area with Kuhio Avenue only 45 minutes away!

Route 83 passes a string of beaches, most with camping. Offshore from Kualoa County Park is Mokolii (Small Reptile) Island, commonly called **Chinaman's Hat** (between mile marker 30 and 31) due to its obvious resemblance to an Asian chapeau. Kualoa Park has undergone extensive renovations. There is an expansive parking area, plenty of picnic tables, and a huge grassy area fronting the beach. The road passes through what was once sugarcane country. Most of the businesses failed last century, but you will see the ruins of the Judd Sugar Works a mile or so before reaching Ka'a'awa. The dilapidated mill stands although it was closed more than a century ago. Entering is not advised!

Kualoa County Regional Park
With the *pali* in the background, Chinaman's Hat Island offshore, and a glistening white strand shaded by swaying palms, Kualoa is one of the finest beach parks on windward Oahu. One of the most sacred areas on Oahu, the *ali'i* brought their children here to be reared and educated, and the area is designated in the National Register of Historic Places. It has a full range of facilities and services, including lifeguards, restrooms, and picnic tables. The park is open daily 7 a.m.-7 p.m., with overnight camping allowed with a county permit (mandatory). The swimming is safe year-round along a shoreline dotted with pockets of sand and coral. The snorkeling and fishing are good, but the real treat is walking the 500 yards to Chinaman's Hat at low tide. You need appropriate footgear (old sneakers are fine) because of the sharp coral heads. The island is one of the few around offshore Oahu that is not an official bird sanctuary, although many shorebirds do use the island and should not be molested.

Because of its exposure to winds, Kualoa is sometimes chilly. Although the park is popular, it is not well marked. It lies along Rt. 83, and if you're heading north, look for a red sign to the Kualoa Ranch. Just past it is an HVB Warrior pointing to the park and Chinaman's Hat. Heading south the entrance is just past the HVB Warrior pointing to the Kualoa Sugar Mill ruins.

Kualoa Ranch and Activity Club
The Kualoa Ranch, P.O. Box 650, Ka'a'awa, HI 96730, tel. (808) 237-7321 or (800) 231-7321, offers three organized, pre-packaged, outdoor activity tours. Your choice of activities includes horseback riding, jet-ski rides, ATV dune cycle rides, gun range firing, tennis, snorkeling, a helicopter ride, and a trolley ride. Other games, a petting zoo, and Hawaiian exhibits are also available. The Activity Adventure Tour runs $99 for adults, $65 for children 2-11 and includes a full-day pass for up to four activities except the helicopter ride. With the Secret Island and Activity Tour, you get a half day and two activities at the ranch and a half day at the island for water sports. Rates run $79 for adults and $52 for children 2-11. With both these tours, a helicopter ride may be purchased separately for $39 per person. For $69 adult and $45 for children 2-11, the Secret Island and Snorkel Tour gets you a full-day pass at the ranch island for snorkeling and other water activities. For some activities,

there are stipulations for the age of participant and adult accompaniment. A balanced, filling buffet lunch and free transportation from various Waikiki hotels are provided with all tours. First pickup is at 7:30 a.m. and tours last eight hours. Kualoa Ranch is open Mon.-Fri. for the ranch activities tours and Mon.-Sat. for the Secret Island and Snorkel tour; closed on national holidays. Call for reservations. (Website: www.pixi.com/~kualoa.)

Food and Shopping
Kahaluu Sportswear, at 47-102-A1 Wailehua Rd., is a garment factory outlet store that sells inexpensive alohawear. Some is made from unbearable and unwearable polyester, but a great deal are made from cotton or rayon. Prices are about 10-20% cheaper than what you'll find in the malls, or city area.

The **Hygienic Store** along Rt. 83 just past the Valley of the Temples sells groceries and supplies. It's flanked by stalls selling fruits and shellwork at competitive prices. Although they may not always be around, look for little trucks parked along the road near the Hygienic Store selling hot *ono laulau,* which are snacks that come out of the *imu* oven.

Follow the Kahekili Highway to Rt. 83 past Waiahole and Waikane, where you'll find some of the best roadside fruit stands on Oahu. One is located just near the Waiahole Elementary School (mile marker 34.5), and another just a few minutes north along Rt. 83 has cold drinking coconuts. Do yourself a favor and have one. Sip the juice, and when it's gone, eat the custardlike contents. A real island treat, nutritious and delicious.

KA'A'AWA TOWN AND VICINITY

SIGHTS AND BEACHES

When you first zip along the highway through town you get the impression that there isn't much, but there's more than you think. The town stretches back toward the *pali* for a couple of streets. On the ocean side is **Ka'a'awa Beach Park,** a primarily local hangout. Across the road is the post office, and the **Ka'a'awa Country Kitchen,** which serves breakfast and plate lunches, where you can easily eat for $5. It has a few tables, but the best bet is to get your plate lunch and take it across the street to the beach park. Next door is a 7-Eleven with gas and incidentals. Behind the post office is **Pyramid Rock,** obviously named because of its shape.

Oahu's *pali* is unsurpassed anywhere in the islands, and it's particularly beautiful here. Take a walk around. Stroll the dirt roads through the residential areas and keep your eyes peeled for a small white cross on the *pali* just near Pyramid Rock. It marks the spot where a serviceman was killed during the Pearl Harbor invasion. His spirit is still honored by the perpetually maintained bright white cross. While walking you'll be treated to Ka'a'awa's natural choir—wild roosters crowing any time they feel like it, and the din of

cheeky parrots high in the trees. A pair of parrots escaped from a nearby home about 10 years ago, and their progeny continue to relish life in the balmy tropics.

As you come around the bend of Mahie Point, staring down at you is a very popular stone formation, the **Crouching Lion.** Undoubtedly a tour bus or two will be sitting in the lot of the Crouching Lion Inn. As with all anatomical rock formations, it helps to have an imagination. Anyway, the inn is much more interesting than the lion. Built by George Larsen in 1928 from rough-hewn lumber from the Pacific Northwest, the huge stones were excavated from the site itself. The inn went public in 1951 and has been serving tourists ever since.

Three beach parks in as many miles lie between Ka'a'awa Point and Kahana Bay. The first heading north is **Ka'a'awa Beach County Park,** a popular beach with restrooms, lifeguards, and picnic facilities. An offshore reef running the entire length of the park makes swimming safe year-round. There's a dangerous rip at the south end of the park at the break in the reef.

Swanzy Beach County Park, two minutes north, has camping with a county permit—weekends only. The sand and rubble beach lies below a long retaining wall, often underwater during high tide. The swimming is safe year-round, but is not favorable because of the poor quality of the beach. Swanzy is one of the best squidding and snorkeling beaches on the windward coast. A break in the offshore reef creates a dangerous rip and should be avoided.

Kahana Bay Beach Park is a full-service park with lifeguards, picnic facilities, restrooms, and the area's only boat launch. Camping is allowed with state permit at the beach. Swimming is good year-round, although the waters can be cloudy at times. A gentle shorebreak makes the area ideal for bodysurfing and beginner board riders. This entire beach area is traditionally excellent for *akule* fishing, with large schools visiting the offshore waters at certain times of year. It once supported a large Hawaiian fishing village; remnants of fishponds can still be seen.

Running the valley from Kahana Beach is **Kahana Valley State Park.** Few visit here, and it's perfectly situated for a quiet picnic under the coconut trees. Or to stretch your legs, you can follow the trail about five miles along the stream up the valley.

Huilua Fish Pond lies outside the park boundary. Look to the mountainside for Trout Farm Road and immediately to your right, on the ocean side, is the fishpond. Spot a small bridge and a great launching area for a canoe, kayak, or flotation device. Once in, go left under the traffic bridge. Follow Kahana Stream as it gets narrower and narrower (but passable) as it heads inland. You can even use the overhanging ferns to pull yourself along. It's deep so be aware. If you go to the right, you'll reach the bay. It's fairly safe until you come to open ocean. TheBus stop is directly across from the launching area so you can get off here, enjoy the sights, and then continue on.

PRACTICALITIES

Crouching Lion Inn

There was a time when *everyone* passing through Ka'a'awa stopped at the Crouching Lion Inn. Built in 1926, it was the only place *to* stop for many, many years. The inn has seen its ups and downs, and now, fortunately, it is under new management and on the upswing again. The inn, along Rt. 83 in Ka'a'awa, tel. (808) 237- 8511, open daily for lunch 11 a.m.-3:30 p.m., and for dinner 5-9 p.m., is beautiful enough to stop at just to have a look, but if you want a reasonably quiet meal, avoid lunchtime and come in the evening when all of the tour buses have long since departed. Sitting high on a verdant green hill, the inn's architectural style is a mixture of English Tudor and country Hawaiian. Inside it is cozy with a few fireplaces as well as open-beamed ceilings, while the view from the veranda is especially grand. Lunch can be a simple order of Portuguese bean soup that comes with a delicious flavored bun at only $3.75 per bowl, or appetizers ($7.25-10.95) like royal shrimp cocktail, sashimi, or honey garlic shrimp. Salad entrees ($9.50-10.25) include Oriental chicken, shrimp parmesan, and fruit of king's salads. The complete salad bar runs $9.95. Regular entrees are chopped steak, chicken macadamia, or *kalua* pork plate all priced under $12. Sandwiches like teriyaki steak and *kalua* pork are $8.25, while various burgers cost $7.50-8.50. Dinner entrees, with fresh-baked rolls, soup or salad, vegetables, and choice of rice, potatoes, or garlic pasta, include Slavonic steak, teriyaki steak, filet mignon, or prime rib for $19.50-24.95. Chicken macadamia and coconut island chicken are $15.75, and *kalua* pork is $14.95, while seafood selections and vegetarian pleasing stir-fry tempura complete the menu. The inn's famous mile-high coconut pie, macadamia nut cream pie, or double-crusted banana pie, for under $4, are absolutely delicious. To complement your menu selection there is also a full bar serving cocktails, beer, wine, and liquors.

On the premises is the **Livingston Galleries,** open daily 10:30 a.m.-7:30 p.m., tel. (808) 237-7165, which displays original prints, sculptures, and edition prints of both internationally acclaimed and local island artists. The artists displayed include: Jiang, He Neng, and Hede Guang, all of the Yunnan School of Art that emerged in China after long years of repression under the Mao regime. Using various media including pastels, watercolors, and chalk the Yunnan artists have created works reminiscent of stained-glass windows that seemingly pre-existed inside their souls waiting for the light to illuminate their beauty. Other artists include Tony Bennett, the famous crooner, whose works burst with intense emotion; the fantastic underwater-earth-cosmic paintings of John Pitre or Dana Queen, his wife and colleague; the foggy coasts and misty *pali* captured by Sumner; bronze sculptures by Bruce Stanford; and the terminally cute children rendered by Mary Koski. Also displayed is Beverly Fettig, an Oahu artist long renowned for her land- and seascapes; Dennis Morton, who does landscapes and seascapes in oils; wildlife artist Daniel Van Zyle; and one-of-a-kind blown glass by Tracy and Denise from North Shore Glass and Diane Kelley and Bruce Clark. Some jewelry, kaleidoscopes, and natural flower oil and botanical perfumes are also sold.

PUNALUU AND HAUULA

PUNALUU

Punaluu (Coral Diving) is a long and narrow ribbon of land between the sea and the *pali,* a favorite place to come for a drive in the "country." Its built-up area is about a mile or so long, but only a hundred yards wide. It has gas, supplies, camping, and some of the cheapest accommodations anywhere on Oahu, along with the **Punaluu Art Gallery,** operated by Scott Bechtol, famous candle artist. On the northern outskirts of town, a sign points to **Sacred Falls,** an excellent hike, weather permitting.

In town is **St. Joachim Church.** There's nothing outstanding about it, merely a one-room church meekly sitting on a plot of ground overlooking the sea. But it's real home-grown, where the people of this district come to worship. Just look and you might understand the simple and basic lifestyle that still persists in this area.

HAUULA

This speck of a town is just past Punaluu between mile markers 21 and 22. The old town center is two soda machines, two gas pumps, and two limited supply stores, Masa's and Ching Jong Leong's. Another store, Segame's, sells cold beer and liquor. At the estuary of a stream is **Aukai Beach Park,** a flat little beach right in the middle of town. A 7-Eleven and a little church up on the hill with the *pali* as a backdrop add the seemingly mandatory finishing touches. Just near the bus stop on the south end, look for a local man who is usually there selling lei. The flowers and vines are fresh-picked from the immediate area, and the prices and authenticity are hard to beat.

Outdoor enthusiasts will love the little-used **Hauula Loop Trails.** These ridge trails head up the valleys gaining height along the way. They offer just about everything that you can expect from a Hawaiian trail: the mountains, the valleys, and vistas of the sea. Built by the Civilian Conservation Corps during the Depression, the trails are wide, and the footing is great even in rainy periods that can shut down the nearby **Sacred Falls Trail.**

BEACHES

Right along the highway is **Punaluu Beach County Park.** Punaluu provides shopping, and the beach park has restrooms, cooking facilities, but no lifeguards. The swimming is safe year-round inside the protected reef. Local fishermen, usually older Filipino men who are surf-casting, use this area frequently. They're friendly and a great source of information for anyone trying to land a fish or two. They know the best baits and spots to dunk a line.

Hauula Beach County Park is an improved beach park with picnic facilities, restrooms, pavilion, volleyball court, and camping (permit). There's safe swimming year-round inside the coral reef, with good snorkeling; surfing is usually best in the winter months. Rip currents are present at both ends of the beach at breaks in the reef, and deep holes in the floor of a brackish pond are formed where Maakua Stream enters the sea. Across the road are the ruins of the historic **Lanakila Church** (1853), partially dismantled at the turn of the century to build a smaller church near Punaluu.

PRACTICALITIES

Accommodations

Countryside Cabins is a wonderful and inexpensive place to stay. Owned and operated by Margaret Naai, until she passed away in her late '90s, it is now run by other members of her family who have updated the accommodations. The cabins' entrance is hard to spot, but it's located *mauka*. Look for the small white sign that says Cabins. It's only a few minute's walk from the beach. Completely furnished studios are $45 daily or $598 monthly. For information and reservations, write Countryside Cabins, 53-224 Kamehameha Hwy., Hauula HI 96717, tel. (808) 237-8937. Inexpensive.

Food

An institution along the windward coast, **Pat's at Punaluu**, tel. (808) 293-2624, open daily except Monday 11 a.m.-9 p.m., and breakfast on the weekends only, has an extraordinary view of the coast. The interior is quite tasteful with open beams, ceiling fans, high-backed wicker chairs, and a long, polished koa bar. The feeling is warm, peaceful, and very tropical. There's a little bandstand, some fish tanks, and a large lava rock wall that counterpoints the white stucco. Breakfast (weekends only) features three-egg omelettes, bacon or sausage and eggs, or a local artery-clogging loco moco for under $6. Lunch includes a variety of appetizers like beer-battered mahimahi, salads, and sandwiches. Full meals are served with salad, potato or rice, rolls, and vegetables, and include a captain's platter of seasonal fish and seafood in a crispy beer-batter tempura at market price, a Hawaiian plate of *kalua* pork, grilled fish, *lomi* salmon and steamed rice, and an order of baby-back ribs. No trip to Pat's is complete without sampling the fresh tarts famous since 1945—your choice of banana, pineapple, or coconut ladled into an oven-fresh tart shell and mounded with whipped cream. Pat's is also famous for mai tais, made fresh, and so laced with booze that if you intend on driving, it would be good to have a designated driver. Pat's, long renowned as a good, old-fashioned, Hawaiian-style restaurant, has been going through a transition in the last few years. Luckily, it is definitely back on the right track.

The previous owners tried to make it a tourist trap complete with mediocre cafeteria to cater to the tour-bus crowd. The new owners have reclaimed Pat's and saved it from a fate worse than deep-fried mahimahi. They're restoring Pat's to its old island-style tradition, and doing an admirable job. Pat's is back, and is definitely worth a stop.

Don Ho's **Punaluu Cafe**, tel. (808) 237-8020, is basically a easy-going country bar and restaurant; open Mon.-Thurs. 11 a.m.-11 p.m. and Fri.-Sun. 11 a.m.-2 a.m. Lunch is served 11 a.m.-3 p.m., dinner 5-9 p.m. A live band plays Sunday 2-6 p.m., and on other nights they do karaoke, so you can croon for your friends. Lunches include salads, sandwiches, and plate lunches, plus such hearty items as beef stew and baby-back ribs. The dinner menu is similar, with the addition of daily specials. Most entrees are under $13.

Shopping

The **Punaluu Art Gallery,** in Punaluu around mile marker 24, tel. (808) 237-8221, is the oldest art gallery on windward Oahu. Open Thurs.-Mon. 10:30 a.m.-6:30 p.m.; closed Tuesday and Wednesday. Owner and candle artist Scott Bechtol is dedicated to showcasing the works of an assortment of the finest artists that the North Shore has to offer. Scott is well known for his wonderful sculpted candles, all made from the finest beeswax. Some are lanterns shaped like a huge pita bread with the top third cut off. The remainder is sculpted with a scene that glows when the candle is lit. Others are huge tikis, dolphins, or flowers, all inspired by the islands. There's even a 10-foot whale! Some of the larger candles are $70, the man-size tiki is about $800, and Scott's unique "crying tiki" sells for only $20; small tapers go for $5. Scott creates all of this beautiful glowing art with just one precision carving tool . . . a Buck knife! Another artist shown is Bill Cupit, who creates "bananascapes." Bill removes the outer bark from the banana tree, then he tears and cuts it to make a scene of boats or mountains. The result is a three-dimensional piece. Bill's wife is an artist who specializes in seascapes made with seaweed, while Janet Stewart does watercolors and prints. Other beauty is added by Janet Holiday's silkscreen prints, Peter Hayward's landscapes and seascapes in oil, and the dramatic tropical beauty of the North Shore captured by long-time resident, Edgardo Garcia. The Punaluu Art Gallery is a jewel case of manmade beauty surrounded by natural beauty. They harmonize perfectly.

The **Sacred Falls Bazaar,** seaside on the north end of Punaluu, open daily 9:30 a.m.-6:30 p.m., sells an assortment of neat touristy junk including aloha shirts, shell lei, tie-dyed T-shirts, and fresh island fruit. A minute farther north is the **Jhing Leong Store,** painted shocking pink,

where you can pick up a smattering of supplies.

In Hauula look for the **Hauula Kai Center,** a small shopping center with a post office and stores for groceries, food, and supplies. Also in Hauula is the **Rainbow Shopping Plaza,** an unabashed tourist trap, classic in its obvious tastelessness. Here you'll find beads and baubles, the **Rainbow Barbecue** for something to eat and the **Rainbow Lounge** where you can have a drink.

LAIE TO KAHUKU

LAIE

The "Saints" came marching into Laie (Leaf of the Ie Vine) and set about making a perfect Mormon village in paradise. What's more, they succeeded! The town itself is squeaky clean, with well-kept homes and manicured lawns that hint of suburban Midwest America. Dedicated to ed-

Polynesian Cultural Center

ucation, they built a branch of **Brigham Young University** (BYU) that attracts students from all over Polynesia, many of whom work in the nearby Polynesian Cultural Center. The students vow to live a clean life, free of drugs and alcohol, and not to grow beards. In the foyer of the main entrance look for a huge mural depicting Laie's flag-raising ceremony in 1921, which symbolically established the colony. The road leading to and from the university campus is mazelike but easily negotiable.

The first view of the **Mormon Temple,** 55-600 Naniloa Loop, Laie, tel. (808) 293-9297, built in 1919, is very impressive. Square, with simple architectural lines, this house of worship sits pure white against the *pali* and is further dramatized by a reflecting pool and fountains spewing fine mists. The visitor's center of this tranquil, shrinelike church is open daily 9 a.m.-8 p.m., when a slide show telling the history of the Laie colony is presented, along with a guided tour of the grounds. "Smoking is prohibited, and shirts (no halter tops) must be worn to enter." The temple attracts more visitors than any other Mormon site outside of the main temple in Salt Lake City.

Polynesian Cultural Center
The real showcase is the Polynesian Cultural Center. PCC, as it's called by islanders, began as an experiment in 1963. Smart businessmen said it would never thrive way out in Laie, and tourists didn't come to Hawaii for *culture* anyway. Well, they were wrong, and the PCC now rates as one of Oahu's top tourist attractions, luring about one million visitors annually. Miracles do happen! PCC is a nonprofit organization, with pro-

ceeds going to the Laie BYU, and to maintaining the center itself.

Covering 42 acres, the primary attractions are seven model villages including examples from Hawaii, Samoa, the Marquesas, Fiji, New Zealand, Tonga, and Tahiti. Guides lead you through the villages either on a walking tour, or by canoe over artesian-fed waterways. A shuttle tram runs outside the center, and will take you on a guided tour to the BYU campus, the temple, and a short tour of the community (it would be okay except for the missionary hard sell). The villages are primarily staffed with people from the representative island homelands. Remember that most are Mormons, whose dogma colors the attitudes and selected presentations of the staffers. Still, all are genuinely interested in dispensing cultural knowledge about their traditional island ways and beliefs, and almost all are characters who engage in lighthearted bantering with their willing audience. The undeniable family spirit and pride at PCC makes you feel welcome, while providing a clean and wholesome experience, with plenty of attention to detail.

The morning begins with the **Fiafia Festival,** a lei greeting that orients you to the center. Next comes **Music Polynesia,** a historical evolution of island music presented by singers, musicians, and dancers. A brass band plays from 5:30 p.m., touring the different villages, and the **Pageant of Canoes** sails at 2 and 3 p.m. All day, the Keiki Activities program offers children the opportunity to tune into these cultures with kid-oriented experiences. The largest extravaganza occurs during an evening dinner show called **Horizons.** Beginning at 7:30 p.m., the center's amphitheater hosts about 3,000 spectators for this show of music, dance, and historical drama. The costumes and lighting are dramatic and inspired; it's hard to believe that the performers are not professionals. In addition, the **Imax** theater gives you a real sense of what it's like to take a canoe around the shores of Fiji, or to tramp the mountains of New Zealand.

Food is available from a number of snack bars, or you can dine at the **Gateway Buffet Restaurant,** which serves you a buffet dinner as part of a package including the Polynesian extravaganza.

PCC is open daily except Sunday 12:30-6 p.m. for general admission, $27 adult, $16 children, under five free. A variety of packages are also available including an all-day pass, with dinner and evening show, which lasts until about 9 p.m. The **Ali'i Luau** and dinner show run $49 adults, $30 children. For more information contact PCC at (808) 293-3333 or (800) 367-7060. TheBus no. 52 leaves from Ala Moana to the center and takes about two hours. Most island hotels and tour companies can arrange a package tour to PCC.

Malaekahana Bay State Recreation Area

This state recreation area is the premier camping beach and park along the north section of the windward coast. Separated from the highway by a large stand of shade trees, this 37-acre park offers showers, restrooms, picnic facilities, pavilion, and camping. For camping permits, contact Friends of Malaekahana at P.O. Box 305, Laie, HI 96762, tel. (808) 293-1736; office hours are Mon.-Fri. 10 a.m.-3 p.m.

Malaekahana was Pu'uhonua of Laie, a place of refuge, and, according to legend, the only spot on Oahu not conquered by King Kamehameha. The recent restructuring of the recreation area was intended to bring back its traditional role as a healing and gathering place. An alternative learning center erected here is connected to Kahuku High School, where students come to reconnect culturally and spiritually.

Offshore is Moku'auia, better known as **Goat Island.** The island is only a stone's throw from shore. Reef walkers or tennis shoes are advised. You can reach this seabird sanctuary by wading across the reef during low tide. You'll find a beautiful crescent white-sand beach and absolute peace and quiet. Relax and look for seabirds, or try to spot hawksbill or green sea turtles. The swimming inside the reef is good, and it's amazing how little used this area is for such a beautiful spot. Further offshore, about 200-300 yards, is a small island. *You cannot wade to this island. It is too far, and the currents are strong.* Be aware that there are two entrances to the park. The north entrance, closest to Kahuku, puts you in the day-use area of the park, where there are restrooms and showers. The entrance to the camping section is south a minute or two (around mile marker 17) and is marked by a steel gate painted brown and a sign welcoming you to Malaekahana Bay State Recreation Area. Be aware that the gates open at 7 a.m. and close at 7 p.m.

BEACHES

At the southern end of Laie is **Pounder's Beach,** so named by students of BYU because of the pounding surf. The park area is privately owned, open to the public, and has few facilities. This beach experiences heavy surf and dangerous conditions in the winter months, but its excellent shoreline break is perfect for bodysurfing. The remains of an old pier at which interisland steamers once stopped is still in evidence.

Laie Beach County Park is an unimproved beach park with no facilities, but a one-mile stretch of beach. The shoreline waters are safe for swimming inside the reef, but wintertime produces heavy and potentially dangerous surf. Good snorkeling, fishing, and throw-netting by local fishermen; get there by following the stream from the bridge near the Laie Shopping Mall.

PRACTICALITIES

Accommodations

Lora Dunn's House is at 55-161 Kamehameha Hwy., Laie, HI 96762, tel. (808) 293-1000 (between mile markers 19 and 20, ocean side). Lora admits people on a first-come, first-served basis, but will happily take phone reservations for which she requires a deposit. Chances of turning up and finding a vacancy are poor, so at least call from the airport to check availability. A separate studio for two people is $50 a day, while the downstairs self-contained, two-bedroom, full-kitchen unit of her home, which is larger and can accommodate four people, runs $66 per day. There is a two-day minimum. Good value in a quiet, if not spectacular, setting. Inexpensive.

The **Rodeway Inn Hukilau Resort,** 55-109 Laniloa St., Laie, HI 96762, tel. (808) 293-9282 or (800) 526-4562, is just outside the Polynesian Cultural Center. Rooms are $84 queen, $89 double, $94 king, with a $5 reduction during off season. The fee includes continental breakfast, free local calls, parking, and 10% off tickets to the Polynesian Cultural Center. All rooms have a/c,

TV, refrigerators, and microwaves. It's a cinderblock building, as neat as a pin but basic. Expensive.

Food and Shopping

When you enter Laie you will be greeted by the Stars and Stripes flying over the entrance of the Polynesian Cultural Center. Next door is a whopper of a **McDonald's,** and in keeping with the spirit of Polynesian culture, it looks like a Polynesian longhouse.

On the ocean side of the road is **Masa's Market,** which couldn't be more local with counters stocked with everything from lotus root to lamb. A few minutes south is the **Haaula Kai Shopping Center,** which provides a small variety of dining spots and shopping.

Between Kahuku and Laie is a new **Laie Village Shopping Center,** where you'll find a large and modern Foodland, along with a Bank of America, a small convenience store, Lindy's Food, The Gallery Restaurant, Laie Chop Suey, Laie Cinemas, and a post office.

KAHUKU

This village, and it is a village, is where the *workers* of the North Shore live. Kahuku is "fo' real," and a lingering slice of what *was* not so long ago. Do yourself a favor, and turn off the highway for a two-minute tour of the dirt roads lined by proudly maintained homes that somehow exude the feeling of Asia.

Practicalities

You can pick up supplies at the **Kahuku Superette,** clearly marked along Rt. 83, or better yet look for a little white *kaukau* wagon that sits across the roadway from the school—most days. It sells great food that they bring from Honolulu's Chinatown fresh every day. Unfortunately, it's here only during school hours, when you can pick up a tasty and inexpensive lunch.

Keep a sharp eye out for a truck and a sign featuring shrimp just along the road. Follow it to **Ahi's Kahuku Restaurant,** operated by Roland Ahi and son, open daily 11 a.m.-9 p.m. The shrimp couldn't be fresher as it comes from local fishermen. The longest that these plump babies have been out of the water is 48 hours, so you are definitely getting *the* best. In this no-frills but super-friendly restaurant, you can have your shrimp cooked to order as scampi, deep-fried, tempura, sautéed, or in a cocktail for $8.25, or $9.50 for a sampler plate. You get about eight shrimp, depending on the size. The shrimp is the pièce de résistance, but basic sandwiches and burgers for under $5.50 are also on the menu, as well as entrees like spaghetti with meat sauce for $6.50 and steak and mahimahi combo for $11.95. Complete meals come with green salad, fresh vegetables, bread, rice or potatoes, and tea. There are plenty of appetizers and side dishes on the menu and a good selection of beer and wine. On Friday and Saturday nights, various local musicians perform until closing. Ahi's serves all of its great food with authentic *aloha.* Stop in! You'll be glad you did!

On the north end of town is the **Mill Shopping Center,** which is really the town's old sugar mill that has been recycled. The interior is dominated by huge gears and machinery, power panels, and crushers that are the backdrop for a string of shops, a restaurant, and the Kahuku Theater. The 10-foot gears and conveyor belts have all been painted with bright colors, and seem like a display of modern art pieces. Outside under a covered area is a little bazaar of shops selling everything from pottery to herbal medicine and fruits and vegetables to aloha shirts. This is the Kahuku Village Association, open daily except Sunday 9 a.m.-5 p.m. Also at the shopping center are a **Circle K** food store and gas station, **Lee's Gifts and Jewelry, Island Snow** for shave ice, and a post office. Located under the veranda behind the gas station at the Mill Shopping Center is the **Country Kitchen,** tel. (808) 293-2110, serving mostly Korean, American standard, and Filipino foods. An indoor-outdoor restaurant with a walk-up window, it is open daily 8 a.m.-6 p.m. for breakfast and lunch. Most dishes are in the under-$10 range.

Just past is the **Tanaka Plantation Store,** at 56-901 Kamehameha Hwy., Kahuku, a refurbished turn-of-the-century company store that now houses a clutch of boutiques and shops. Make sure to visit **The Only Show In Town,** open daily 10:30 a.m.-5:30 p.m., tel. (808) 293-1295. Blown to Oahu's North Shore from Kauai by

Hurricane Iniki, Paul Wroblewski has reopened his antiques and collectibles shop and once again jammed it with Hawaiian artifacts, old bottles, costume jewelry, license plates, Japanese glass fishing floats, netsuke, scrimshaw, a collection of Marilyn Monroe memorabilia, and a full line of antique jewelry. Paul's an amiable fellow and is open to any reasonable offer. Remember, he may price according to your attitude. Also, if you have a collectible that you want to sell or get an estimate of value on, ask Paul to take a look.

Next door is **Imua Shop Polynesia,** open daily 10 a.m.-6 p.m., tel. (808) 293-5055, with craft items, carvings, tapa, tiki, aloha shirts, shells, jewelry, Hawaiian quilts, and postcards. If you have any questions on the origin or authenticity of these items, talk to the owner Doris.

Perhaps the most interesting shop in the complex is the **Amazonian Forest Store,** owned and operated by Brazilian world travelers Cesar Olivera and Katia Ferz. Open daily 11 a.m.-6 p.m.; tel. (808) 293-5053. It specializes in authentic artifacts gathered from the Amazon and other rainforest regions around the world, including Hawaii and Indonesia. Some of the most amazing artifacts are headdresses and paintings by Brazil's Xindu Indians, along with basketry, parasols, coconut purses, string and cotton hammocks, and semiprecious gemstones gathered from throughout South America. If these aren't enough to make you "bug eyed" perhaps a Brazilian string bikini will. They've added a boutique with ladies dresses, sundresses, and beach apparel, and men's casual beachwear.

GEOGRAPHICAL NOTE

The following chapter, The North Shore, begins at the west end in Waialua/Haleiwa and works eastward toward Kahuku. That's because most people visiting the North Shore proceed in this direction, while those heading for Windward Oahu start in Kailua/Kaneohe and proceed up the coast. So, the end of this chapter follows geographically with the end of The North Shore chapter. Don't let it throw you.

HAWAII STATE ARCHIVES

THE NORTH SHORE

This shallow bowl of coastline stretches from Kaena Point in the west to Turtle Bay in the east. **Mount Ka'ala,** verdant backdrop to the area, rises 4,020 feet from the Waianae Range, making it the highest peak on Oahu. The entire stretch is a day-tripper's paradise with plenty of sights to keep you entertained. But the North Shore is synonymous with one word: surfing.

Thunderous winter waves, often measuring 25 feet (from the rear!), rumble along the North Shore's world-famous surfing beaches lined up one after the other—**Waimea Bay, Ehukai, Banzai Pipeline, Sunset.** They attract highly accomplished athletes who come to compete in prestigious international surfing competitions. Be aware that *all* North Shore beaches experience very heavy surf conditions with dangerous currents from October through April. The waters, at this time of year, are not for the average swimmer. Please heed all warnings. In summertime *moana* loses her ferocity and lies down, becoming gentle and safe for anyone—leap in!.

The main attractions of the North Shore are its beaches, but interspersed among them are a few sights definitely worth your time and effort.

The listings below run from west to east. The most-traveled route to the North Shore is from Honolulu along the H-2 freeway to Wahiawa, and then directly to the coast from there along Rt. 99 or Rt. 803. At Weed Circle or Thompson Corner, where these routes reach the coast, turn left along the Farrington Highway, following it to road's end just before Kaena Point, or turn right along the Kamehameha Hwy. (Rt. 83), which heads around the coast all the way to Kailua.

Haleiwa is fast becoming the central town along the North Shore. The main street is lined with restaurants, boutiques, art galleries, small shopping malls, and sports equipment stores. **Waialua,** just west, is a "sugar town" with a few quiet condos for relaxation. Farther west is **Dillingham A.F.B.** (inactive), where you can arrange to fly above it all in a small plane or soar silently in a glider. The road ends for vehicles not far from here, and then your feet have to take you to Kaena Point, where *the* largest waves pound the coast. Heading east, you'll pass a famous *heiau* where human flesh mollified the gods, a monument to a real local hero, and **Waimea Falls Park,** the premier tourist attraction of the North Shore. Then come the great surfing beaches and their incredible waves. Here and there are tidepools rich with discovery.

Places to stay are quite limited along the North Shore. The best deals are beach homes or rooms rented directly from the owners, but this is a hit-and-miss proposition, with few agencies handling the details. You have to check the local papers. The homes vary greatly in amenities. Some are palaces, others basic rooms or shacks, perfect for surfers or those who consider lodging secondary. Check the bulletin boards outside the Surf and Sea Dive Shop in Haleiwa and Foodland supermarket.

ALONG THE FARRINGTON HIGHWAY

WAIALUA

The first town is Waialua (Two Waters). At the turn of the century, Waialua, a stop along the sugar-train railway, was a fashionable beach community complete with hotels and vacation homes. Today, it's hardly ever visited, and it's not uncommon to see as many horses tied up along the main street as it is to see parked cars in this real one-horse town. Sundays can also attract a rumble of bikers who kick up the dust on their two-wheeled steeds.

The sugar mill, an outrageously ugly mechanical monster, is still operating and is central to the town. Quiet Waialua, with its main street divided by trees running down the middle, *is* rural Oahu. There's a general store for supplies, a post office, and snacks at the **Sugar Bar,** a restaurant in the old Bank of Hawaii building that features an international menu—hot dogs from America to bratwurst from Germany. *Magnifique!*

If you're heading to Haleiwa take Haleiwa Road, a back way through residential areas. Look for Paalaa Road on the right and take it past a small Buddhist temple that holds an *o bon* festival honoring the dead, traditionally observed in July.

If polo is your game or if you're just curious, head west of town to the Mokuleia Polo Field and catch a Hawaii Polo Club match, Sunday at 2 p.m.

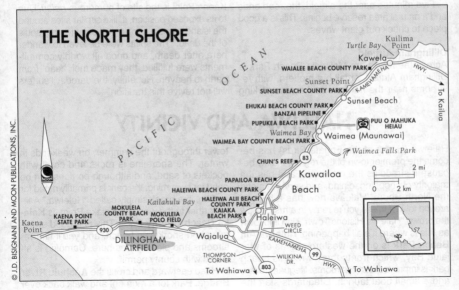

THE NORTH SHORE

Beach Areas

Mokuleia Beach County Park is the main public access park along the highway. It provides picnic facilities, restrooms, lifeguards, a playground area, and camping (county permit). In summertime, swimming is possible along a few sandy stretches protected by a broken offshore reef. Mokuleia Army Beach is a wider strand of sand. It's very private, and the only noise interrupting your afternoon slumber might be planes taking off from the airfield. Local people have erected semipermanent tents in this area and guard it as if it were their own. A minute farther toward Kaena is an unofficial area with a wide sand beach. During the week you can expect no more than a half dozen people on this 300-yard beach. Remember that this is the North Shore and the water can be treacherous. Careful!

Camp Harold Erdman is next, one of the best-known camps on Oahu. This YMCA facility is named after a famous Hawaiian polo player killed in the '30s. The facility is used as a summer camp for children, throughout the year for special functions, and as a general retreat area by various organizations. Access is limited to official use.

Five minutes past the airfield, the road ends and a natural area reserve begins. This is a good place to check out giant waves.

Dillingham Airfield

Across the road from Mokuleia Beach Park is Dillingham Airfield, small but modern, with restrooms near the hangars and a new parking area. A public phone is available in hangar G-1. Most days, especially weekends, a few local people sell refreshments from their cars or trucks. The main reason for stopping is to take a small plane or glider ride. **Glider Rides,** tel. (808) 677-3404, takes you on a 20-minute flight. Talk to owner Bill Star, who has been flying from here since 1970. A second company, **Soar Hawaii Sailplanes,** tel. (808) 637-3147, does a variety of rides.

Kaena Point State Park

Kaena Point lies about 2.5 miles down the dirt track after the pavement gives out. Count on three hours for a return hike and remember to bring water. The point can also be reached from road's end above Mahuka on the Waianae (leeward) side of the island. Kaena has *the* largest waves in Hawaii on any given day. In wintertime, these giants can reach above 40 feet, and their power, even when viewed safely from the high ground, is truly amazing. Surfers have actually plotted ways of riding these waves, which include being dropped by helicopter with scuba tanks. Reportedly, one surfer named Ace Cool has already done it. For the rest of us mortals . . . "who wants to have that much fun anyway!" Kaena Point is the site of numerous *heiau.* Due to its exposed position, it, like similar sites around the islands, was a jumping-off point for the "souls of the dead." The spirits were believed to wander here after death, and once all worldly commitments were fulfilled, they made their "leap" from earth to heaven. Hopefully, the daredevil surfers will not revive this tradition!

HALEIWA AND VICINITY

Haleiwa (Home of the Frigate Birds) has become the premier town of the region, mainly because it straddles the main road and has the majority of shopping, dining, and services along the North Shore. Haleiwa now has a bypass around town. Unless you're really in a rush, follow the brown "Haleiwa Historic Town" sign into town as this is where it's all happening. **Haleiwa Alii Beach Park** is on the western shores of Waialua Bay, which fronts the town. This beach park is improved with restrooms, lifeguard tower, and a small boat launch. Lifeguards staff the tower throughout the summer, on weekends in winter. The shoreline is rocks and coral with pockets of sand, and although portions can be good for swimming, the park is primarily noted for surfing, in a break simply called "Haleiwa." A little farther to the west, on Kaiaka Point, is **Kaiaka Beach County Park.** This is a good swimming and snorkeling beach, and you'll find restrooms and picnic areas here. Camping is allowed with county permit.

Head eastward and cross the **Anahulu River Bridge.** Park for a moment and walk back over

typical rural Buddhist temple, on the outskirts of Haleiwa

the bridge. Look upstream to see homes with tropical character perched on the bank with a bevy of boats tied below. The scene is reminiscent of times gone by.

A much better park is **Haleiwa Beach Park,** clearly marked off the highway on the eastern side of Waialua Bay. Here you'll find pavilions, picnic facilities, lifeguards, restrooms, showers, and food concessions, but no camping. The area is good for fishing, surfing, and most importantly, for swimming year-round! It's about the only safe place for the average person to swim along the entire North Shore during winter.

Kawailoa Beach is the general name given to the area stretching all the way from Haleiwa Beach County Park to Waimea Bay. A string of beaches **(Papailoa, Laniakea,** and **Chun's Reef)** is just off the road. Cars park where the access is good. None of these beaches is suitable for the recreational swimmer. All are surfing beaches, with the most popular being Chun's Reef. One area, about in the center of this line of beaches, is being developed as **Kawailoa Beach Park.**

ACCOMMODATIONS

Located on the back side of Lokoea Pond in town is the **Surfhouse,** 62-202 Lokoea Pl., Haleiwa, HI 96712, tel. (808) 637-7146. A budget accommodation, this new white house offers shared and private rooms. The dorm rooms each have six beds and run $15 a night or $95 a week; private rooms are $45 a night or $280 a week. Campers can find a space on the lawn for $9 a night or $56 a week. Laundry service is available and the kitchen can be used for preparing your own meal. Bicycles and water equipment can be rented at inexpensive rates. Make your arrangements with Sofie or Lee. Budget.

FOOD

Inexpensive Food

Near Pizza Hut, but a culinary world apart, is **Celestial Natural Foods,** tel. (808) 637-6729, open weekdays 9 a.m.-6:30 p.m., Sunday 10 a.m.-6 p.m. Up front is a complete natural and health food store. In back, and called **Paradise Found,** is a lunch counter that serves vegetarian meals. Some items are nachos for $2.95, couscous at $3.95, pita pockets and chapati wraps for $5.25, and veggie sandwiches at $3.95. Smoothies, fresh juice drinks, teas, sodas, and sweets are also available. The food is healthful and nutritious, but portions are definitely not for the hungry.

Cafe Haleiwa, a hole-in-the-wall eatery on your left just as you enter town, serves one of the best breakfasts on Oahu. Lunch is served too; hours are Mon.-Fri. 6 a.m.-3 p.m., Saturday 7 a.m.-3 p.m., and Sunday 7 a.m.-2 p.m. The "dawn patrol" 6-7 a.m. includes eggs and whole-wheat pancakes for $2.50. Specials of the house are whole-wheat banana pancakes, French toast, spinach and mushroom quiche, and steaming-hot Kona coffee. One of the partners, Jim Sears, is called "the wizard of eggs" and has built up a local following. The cafe attracts many surfers, so it's a great place to find out about conditions.

Another tiny place with great treats is **Kua Aina,** for sandwiches and—some claim—the best burgers on the island.

If you're tired or just need a pick-me-up head for the North Shore Marketplace (after McDonald's, mountain side), where you'll find the **Coffee Gallery,** tel. (808) 637-5571, open daily 6 a.m.-9 p.m., which has the largest selection of fresh roasted gourmet coffees in Hawaii, including Kona coffees and international selections of organically grown coffee from Sumatra and elsewhere in Indonesia, Guatemala, and South America. You can enjoy a steaming cup from its full service espresso bar along with fresh carrot juice, and vegan pastry made without dairy products or eggs. Other more bliss-inducing pastries are blackberry apple crumble pie, super chocolaty brownies, fresh fruit bars, and racks of various cookies and muffins. Every day there is a homemade soup, fresh salad, and a fine selection of deli sandwiches that range from a vegetarian garden burger on a whole wheat bun with lettuce and tomatoes, Maui onion, guacamole, and a side of tortilla chips to pita bread filled with eggplant, pesto, and veggies all priced around $6. It's all vegetarian. Sit outside in the shaded and screened dining area and watch the character-laden "characters" of the North Shore come and go. Coffee Gallery has expanded, with shops now in Honolulu, Wahiawa, and Hawaii Kai.

The **China Chop Suey** restaurant, tel. (808) 637-5281, serves basic Chinese food in a basic place at moderate prices. Most dishes are under $8, but the special dinner for two runs $22. Here also is the **Haleiwa Chinese Restaurant,** tel. (808) 637-3533, open daily 10 a.m.-9 p.m. The interior is nothing special, but the food is very good. The steamed sea bass and kung pao chicken are both excellent. A gigantic bowl of tofu soup is $5, while most main courses are under $6. One of the best inexpensive eateries on the North Shore.

For south-of-the-border food, try **Cholo's Homestyle Mexican Restaurant,** tel. (808) 637-3059. Plate items, which include rice and beans, run $4-7.50; dinners include rice, beans, salad, chips, salsa, and a choice of meat and go for $6.25-9.50. Many combinations are also available. The walls are festooned with masks, paintings, prints, and other works of art and crafts.

You can tell by the tour buses parked outside that **Matsumoto's** is a very famous store on the North Shore. What are all those people after? Shave ice. This is one of the best places on Oahu to try this island treat. Not only do the tourists come here, but local families often take a "Sunday drive" just to get Matsumoto's shave ice. Try the Hawaiian Delight, a mound of ice smothered with banana, pineapple, and mango syrup. If lines are too long here or if you want to frequent the competition, try **Aoki's** shave ice up the way.

Moderate/Expensive Food

Rosie's Cantina, in the Haleiwa Shopping Plaza, open Sun.-Thurs. 7 a.m.-10 p.m., Fri.-Sat. 7 a.m.-11 p.m., prepares hearty Mexican dishes for a good price. The inside is "yuppie Mex" with brass rails, painted overhead steam pipes, and elevated booths. Expect to pay $5 for enchiladas and burritos, while meat dishes are $9-10. Order the enchilada stuffed with crab; add a salad and two could easily make this a lunch. **Pizza Bob's,** also in the plaza, has an excellent local reputation, and its little pub serves up not only delicious pizza, but a variety of salads, lasagna, and sandwiches. People are friendly, there's plenty of food, and the price is right.

Situated in the North Shore Marketplace is **Portofino,** tel. (808) 637-7678, an Italian restaurant that also does a delivery service under the name North Shore Pizza Company; the delivery number is (808) 637-2782. Here they use a wood-fired pizza oven so you know that it's the real McCoy. Aside from pizza, soups, salads, pastas, and fish dishes are also served. Give it a try. It's a friendly place with wholesome food.

Jameson's by the Sea, 62-540 Kamehameha Hwy., tel. (808) 637-4336, is open daily for lunch, dinner, and cocktails. Located at the north end of Haleiwa overlooking the sea, its outdoor deck is perfect for a romantic sunset dinner, while inside the romantic mood is continued with track lighting, shoji screens, cane chairs with stuffed pillows, candles with shades, and tables resplendent with fine linen. Appetizers include a salmon pâté for $7.50, stuffed mushrooms with escargot for $7.50, fresh oysters for $8.95, and a bowl of creamy clam chowder for $4.50. Soups are priced under $5. Try the Yokohama soup, as well as salad with any of the homemade dressings. Main dishes like mahimahi, stuffed shrimp, shrimp curry with mango chutney, and sesame chicken range $18.50-25. For dessert have the lemon macadamia nut chiffon pie for $4.50. The pub downstairs serves lunch from a slightly different menu. It's quiet at night and serves a variety of imported beers; try South Pacific, imported from New Guinea. Breakfast is served Saturday and Sunday 9 a.m.-noon. Reservations highly recommended. Request a window seat for the sunset.

The **Chart House,** at 66-011 Kamehameha Hwy., Haleiwa, tel. (808) 638-8005, open daily for dinner 5-10 p.m., for lunch Thurs.-Sun. 11 a.m.-3 p.m., is part of a small chain known for good food, located in a green cinder-block building on the left before you cross the Anahulu River bridge. Although purely utilitarian on the outside, the inside is modern and tasteful with plenty of tile work, track lighting, bent-back chairs, and ceiling fans. Most appetizers, ranging from artichokes to chowder, are under $8, while the salad bar (included with an entree) is a bit more. Steaks, the specialty of the house, and most entrees are in the $19-25 range. Specials are offered daily, and there's a "wine of the month" chosen to enhance your meal. For dessert try the mud pie or the key lime pie. Although the Chart House is not quite gourmet, the food is good and wholesome, with the price right for what you get.

SHOPPING AND SERVICES

Art Galleries and Shops

Ka'ala Art, open 9 a.m.-6 p.m. daily, tel. (808) 637-7065, as you enter Haleiwa (across from McDonald's), is a perfect place to stop, with some of the best shopping on the North Shore. The brothers Costello, John and Jim, who own and operate the shop, are knowledgeable, longtime residents of the North Shore who don't mind dispensing directions and information. The premier items are John's original artwork, wonderful paintings that are impressionistic and magical, with many of these unique designs silk-screened onto 100% cotton T-shirts or made into inspiring posters. John has also turned his hand to carvings of dolphins and other Hawaiian themes. Also featured are fine carvings from Tonga, Tahiti, and Bali that John has hand-selected on his travels, along with excellent examples of local Hawaiian woodcarvings. Small but wonderful items are tapa cloth made by Sella, a Tongan woman who lives nearby, batiks from Thailand, and jewelry made locally and from Asia. The Costello brothers travel to buy, and they have a keen eye for what's happening and distinctive. Brother Kevin offers a fine selection of imported clothing from Thailand, which is available through the gallery by appointment. A rainbow has spilled in a corner of the shop, where 100% cotton pareu ($18-35) from Hawaii, Tahiti, and Indonesia vibrate in living color. More "art-clothing" includes a rack of beach cover-ups designed by John, tie-dyed and silk-screened using ecologically minded nontoxic colors. There's also a fine postcard selection just to remind the folks back home that you are in Hawaii.

Iwa Gallery, open daily except Tuesday and Wednesday 10:30 a.m.-6:30 p.m., is across the street from the Protestant church, founded in 1892, and next door to Aoki's Shave Ice. This co-op shows the efforts of local artists who have been juried in order to place their artwork on consignment. Featured are the fine candle sculptures of Scott Bechtol. Other artists displayed at the gallery include: Angela Kanas, a watercolor artist who does fanciful renditions of Hawaiian gods, goddesses, and traditional folk; Janet Stewart, who depicts island themes like Madame Pele lying with the blood of her hot lava flowing from her body, or a *keiki* hula dancer with a look of concentration on her face, or a kindly *tutu* in a red muumuu; Bill Cupit uses the bark of banana trees to create entire island scenes like ships departing a sheltered harbor. The oil paintings of Peter Hayward, who died at age 87, survive him. Many show translucent waves crashing on lonely shores. Serigraphs and cards by Janet Holiday are often depictions of flowers in bold primary colors; Peggy Pai, born and raised in China, creates silk batik with ephemeral, beautiful, cloudy landscapes; James Rack uses his palette and brush to catch scenes of idyllic Hawaii; and Norman Kelly catches children at play or surfers on towering waves in his fluid watercolors.

Wyland Gallery, across the street from the Haleiwa Shopping Center, is open daily 9 a.m.-6 p.m., tel. (808) 637-7498. Wyland is a famous environmental artist known for his huge whale and marine life murals, in addition to watercolors and fine oil paintings. The gallery is large, spacious, and well lit. Everything has a Hawaiian or sea theme, and there's even a huge fish tank filled with tropical fish. There're watercolors of Hawaiian maidens by Janet Stewart, lithographs by Roy Tabora of palm trees and cliffs with Michelangelo skies, waterfall paintings by James Coleman, strong and dramatic oils of young Walfrido, and bronze sculptures of the sea by Scott Hanson. You can walk away with a limited-edition lithograph by Wyland with original watercolor mark framed in koa for $1,550. If the original artwork is too expensive, there are posters, miniprints, and postcards. Wyland's gold jewelry sculpture is also beautiful, distinctive, and affordable.

On the ground floor of Jameson's By the Sea is **Galerie,** tel. (808) 637-8866. Owner-operator Christian Reese Lassen works in oil, acrylic, and watercolor, but in all he displays fantastic seascapes in vibrant brilliant color. Also featured are oil painter William Dechasazo and sculptors Joseph Quillan and Douglas Wylie.

North Shore Marketplace

The North Shore Marketplace, along the Kamehameha Hwy. between McDonald's and the Haleiwa Shopping Center, is a small complex with some inexpensive and unique shops. The most interesting shop is **Jungle Gem's,** tel. (808) 637-6609, open 10 a.m.-6 p.m., with a metaphysical assortment of crystals, crystal balls, African trading beads, and gems. The shop specializes in locally made jewelry that is reasonably priced and of excellent quality. The owners, Brent Landberg and Kimberely Moore, are knowledgeable gemologists and fine jewelers who do much of the work on display.

Another good shop is **More or Less Beach Wear,** tel. (808) 637-6859, open 9 a.m.-6 p.m. daily, where they make custom bathing suits for women and men and sell hand-painted T-shirts by local artists. The owner and chief designer, Lucinda Vaughen, will take a personal hand in fit-

ting and designing just the right suit for you. Other clothing stores are **Pomegranates In The Sun** and **Patagonia.**

Strong Current North Shore Hawaii, tel. (808) 637-3406, is open daily 9:30 a.m.-6:30 p.m. This is a surf shop that also has beachwear, but it's more than that. It's almost like a museum of surfing with all the collectibles on display. Stop in and reminisce about the '50s and '60s classic era of surfing.

To the left as you drive into the parking lot is **Barnfield's Raging Isle Sports,** tel. (808) 637-7707, a full-service mountain bike and surf shop open daily 10 a.m.-6:30 p.m. Aside from selling and repairing bikes, they rent mountain bikes for $35 a day and lead bike tours. The shop also manufactures surfboards here, the only place on the North Shore legally doing so. Board repairs are also made. Casual clothing and surf wear are stocked, as well as snowboards, bindings, and snow clothing.

Island Inspired is run by the husband and wife team of Michael and Ilona Hemperly. Have a look at the prints done on rice paper, pen and ink drawings, and acrylic washes.

Twelve Tribes International Imports, tel. (808) 637-7634, is a multicultural emporium with items from the global village.

Around back is **North Shore Glass,** tel. (808) 637-4853, where Traci and Dennis produce hand-blown art glass in their open-air studio. Most of what they make goes to the hotels, but they do have a small rack of retail items that they sell in the studio. Check them out to see how the work is done.

Along the Kamehameha Highway

As you move down the Kamehameha Hwy. you'll pass in rapid succession the **Haleiwa Flower Shop** on the left selling lei and fresh-cut flowers. Next comes **Oogenesis Boutique,** with original fashions for women, and almost next door is **Haleiwa Acupuncture Clinic,** tel. (808) 637-4449, with Richard Himmelmann, in cooperation with Healing Touching Massage by Brenda McKinnon, and chiropractic care by Dr. Edward Bowles, who will make house calls. Nearby is **Haleiwa Family Health Center,** a walk-in clinic, tel. (808) 637-5087, open 8 a.m.-5 p.m. daily, closed Sunday.

Also along the highway is **Haleiwa Shopping Center,** which provides all the necessities in one-stop shopping: boutiques, pharmacy, photo store, and general food and merchandise. For food and picnic supplies try the **Haleiwa IGA.**

Services
The best sources of general information for the North Shore are the bulletin boards outside of Surf and Sea and the Foodland supermarket.

As you enter Haleiwa from the west, you'll pass a Shell gas station and a full-service post office.

Sporting Goods and Rentals
The following shops are all located along the Kamehameha Highway, the main drag through Haleiwa.

Barnfield's Raging Isle Sports, in the North Shore Marketplace, tel. (808) 637-7707, open 10 a.m.-6:30 p.m. daily, is primarily a surf shop and manufacturer of Barnfield's Raging Isle Boards, but it also sells, rents, and repairs bikes.

For surfboards, sailboards, boogie boards, snorkeling equipment, sales and rentals, try **Hawaii Surf and Sail,** 66-214 Kamehameha Hwy., tel. (808) 637-5373; **Hawaiian Surf,** 66-250 Kamehameha Hwy., tel. (808) 637-8316; or **Surf and Sea,** 62-595 Kamehameha Hwy., tel. (808) 637-9887.

WAIMEA BAY AND VICINITY

The two-lane highway along the North Shore is pounded by traffic; be especially careful around Waimea Bay. The highway sweeps around till you see the steeple of **St. Peter and Paul Mission** with the bay below. The steeple is actually the remnants of an old rock-crushing plant on the site. **Waimea Bay Beach County Park** has the largest rideable waves in the world. This is the heart of surfers' paradise. The park is improved with a lifeguard tower, restrooms, and a picnic area.

During a big winter swell, the bay is lined with spectators watching the surfers ride the monumental waves. In summertime, the bay is calm as a lake. People inexperienced with the sea should not even walk along the shorebreak in winter. Unexpected waves come up farther than you'd think, and a murderous rip lurks only a few feet from shore. The area is rife with tales of heroic rescue attempts, many ending in fatalities. A plaque commemorates Eddie Aikau, a local lifeguard credited with making thousands of rescues. In 1978, the *Hokule'a,* the Polynesian Sailing Society's double-hulled canoe, capsized in rough seas about 20 miles offshore. Eddie was aboard and launched his surfboard to swim for help. He never made it, but his selfless courage lives on.

Waimea Valley, Home of Waimea Falls Park
Look for the well-marked entrance to Waimea Falls Park, mountain side from the bay, and then drive for quite a ways into the lush valley before coming to the actual park entrance. Along with the Bishop Museum, the park is the most culturally significant travel destination on Oahu. Although open to the public and more than happy to welcome visitors, Waimea Falls Park has not lost sight of its ancient *aloha* soul, which it honors while providing a wonderful day of excitement and education. Primarily a botanical garden, with a fascinating display of flowers and plants all labeled for your edification, the Waimea Arboretum collects, grows and preserves extremely rare specimens of Hawaii's endangered flora. If you choose not to walk, an open-air tour bus will take you through, narrating all the way. A thrilling event is the professional diving from the 55-foot rock walls into the pool below Waimea Falls. Culturally enlightening are displays of ancient hula *(kahiko)* performed by very accomplished dancers, a display of Hawaiian games, carving demonstrations, and walks along forest paths that end at fascinating historical sites. On the property is Hale o Lono, one of the island's largest and most ancient *heiau* dedicated to the god Lono.

Admission is $19.95 adults and $9.95 for juniors age 6-12, open daily 10 a.m.-5:30 p.m.; tel. (808) 638-8511 or (800) 767-8046. Four-wheel drive ATV vehicle and horseback tours are available ($20-75), mountain bikes can be rented (about $50) for use on the park's course, and kayak tours ($20-50) are guided down the river to the sea. The **Proud Peacock** serves dinner until 9 p.m. A free guided moon-viewing tour on the Friday night closest to the full moon used to be offered on a regular basis. This ceased

hula dancers at
Waimea Falls Park

for about a year but there are plans to revive it on an intermittent basis. If you're interested, call the park to see if it's happening.

For those coming from Waikiki intending to visit only the park, consider taking the free park shuttle bus. Call (808) 955-8276 for pickup times and locations.

Pupukea Beach Park

A perfect place to experience marine life is the large tidepool next to Pupukea Beach Park, the first one north of Waimea Bay, across the street from the Shell gas station. A long retaining wall out to sea forms a large and protected pool at low tide. Wear footgear and check out the pools with a mask. Don't be surprised to find large sea bass. A sign warns against spearing fish, but the local people do it all the time. Be careful not to step on sea urchins, and stay away from the pool during rough winter swells, when it can be treacherous. The beach park has restrooms, picnic facilities, and fair swimming in sandy pockets between coral and rock, but only in summertime.

The middle section of the park is called **Shark's Cove,** though no more sharks are here than anywhere else. The area is terrific for snorkeling and scuba in season. Look to the mountains to see **The Mansion** (see following), and next to it the white sculpture of the **World Unity Monument.** If you had to pick a spot from which to view the North Shore sunset, Pupukea Beach Park is hard to beat!

Farther down the road, as you pass mile marker 9 you can't help noticing a mammoth redwood log that has been carved into a giant statue representing an ancient Hawaiian. Peter Wolfe, the sculptor, has done a symbolic sculpture for every state in the union, this being his 50th. This statue is extremely controversial. Some feel that it looks much more like an American Indian than a Hawaiian, and that the log used should have been a native koa instead of an imported redwood from the Pacific Northwest. Others say that its *intention* was to honor the living and the ancient Hawaiians, and that is what's important.

Puu O Mahuka Heiau

Do yourself a favor and drive up the mountain road leading to the *heiau* even if you don't want to visit it. The vast and sweeping views of the coast below are incredible. About one mile past Waimea Bay the highway passes a Foodland on the right. Turn here up Pupukea Road and follow the signs. There is a warning at the beginning of the access road, but the road is well maintained and many people ignore the sign.

Puu O Mahuka Heiau, the largest on Oahu, covers a little more than five acres. Designated as a national historical landmark, its floorplan is huge steps, with one area leading to another just below. The *heiau* was the site of human sacrifice. People still come to pray as is evidenced by many stones wrapped in ti leaves placed on small stone piles lying about the grounds. In the upper section is a raised mound surrounded by stone in what appears to be a central altar area. The *heiau*'s stonework shows a high degree of craftsmanship throughout, but especially in the pathways. The lower section of the *heiau* appears to be much older, and is not as well maintained.

Drive past the access road leading to the *heiau* and in a minute or so make a left onto Alapio Road. This takes you through an expensive residential area called Sunset Hills and past a home locally called **The Mansion**—look for the English-style boxwood hedge surrounding it. The home was purported to be Elvis Presley's island hideaway. Almost next door are the grounds of the **Nichiren Buddhist Temple**, resplendent with manicured lawns and gardens. This area is a tremendous vantage point from which to view Fourth of July fireworks lighting up Waimea Bay far below.

The Great Surfing Beaches

Sunset Beach runs for two miles, one of the longest white-sand beach on Oahu. This beach is the site of yearly international surfing competitions. Winter surf erodes the beach, with coral and lava fingers exposed at the shoreline, but in summertime you can expect an uninterrupted beach usually 200-300 feet wide. The entire stretch is technically Sunset Beach, but each world-famous surfing spot warrants its own name though they're not clearly marked and are tough to find . . . exactly. Mainly, look for cars with surfboard racks parked along the road. The beaches are not well maintained either. They're often trashed, and the restrooms, even at Waimea Bay, are atrocious. The reason is politics and money. Efforts all go into Waikiki, where the tourists are. Who cares about a bunch of crazy surfers on the North Shore? They're just a free curiosity for the tourists' enjoyment!

The **Banzai Pipeline** is probably the best-known surfing beach in the world. Its notoriety dates from *Surf Safari*, an early surfer film made in the 1950s, when it was dubbed "Banzai" by Bruce Brown, maker of the film. The famous tubelike effect of the breaking waves comes from a shallow reef just offshore, which forces the waves to rise dramatically and quickly. This forces the crest forward to create "the Pipeline." A lifeguard tower near the south end of the beach is all that you'll find in the way of improvements. Parking is along the roadway. Look for Sunset Beach Elementary School on the left, and the Pipeline is across the road. You can park in the school's lot on non-school days.

Ehukai Beach County Park is the next area north. It has a lifeguard tower and restroom, and provides one of the best vantage points from which to watch the surfing action on the Pipeline and Pupukea, the area to the right.

Don't expect much when you come to **Sunset Beach County Park** itself. Except for a lifeguard tower, there is nothing. Almost as famous as the surfing break is the **Sunset Rip**, a notorious current offshore that grabs people every year. Summertime is generally safe, but never take *moana* for granted.

NORTH SHORE SURF BEACHES

SUNSET BEACH

BANZAI PIPELINE

83

SHARK'S COVE

FOODLAND

PUPUKEA RD.

RUBBER DUCKIES

BEACH PARK

"THREE TABLES"

CATHOLIC CHURCH

PINBALLS

MARIJUANA'S

WAIMEA BAY

TO HALEIWA

NOT TO SCALE

© J.D. BISIGNANI AND MOON PUBLICATIONS, INC.

ACCOMMODATIONS

Budget Surfer Rentals

The North Shore of Oahu has long been famous for its world-class surfing. The area attracts enthusiasts from around the world who are much more concerned with the daily surfing report than they are with deluxe accommodations. The Kamehameha Highway is dotted with surfer rentals from Haleiwa to Turtle Bay. Just outside their doors are the famous surfing breaks of Marijuana's, Rubber Duckies, and Pinballs, all famous and known to world-class surfers. Some of these accommodations are terrific, while others are barely livable. Here's a sample of what's offered.

Backpacker's Vacation Inn and Hostel, 59-788 Kamehameha Hwy., Haleiwa, HI 96712, tel. (808) 638-7838 (courtesy phone at airport, no charge), specializes in budget accommodations for surfers, backpackers, and families. Owned and operated by the Foo Family, the main building in this small cluster of buildings is at mile marker 6, the fourth driveway past the church tower coming from Waimea Bay. There are a number of facilities and room styles that could put you on the beach or mountainside, depending on availability and your preference. Basic rates are $14-16 (a little more during high season) for a bunk in the hostel-style rooms, which includes cooking and laundry facilities, and TV in the communal room. Each room has four bunks, microwaves, a shower, and a bath. The feeling is definitely not deluxe, but it is adequate. A complex on the beach, $70 daily, $420 weekly, sleeps four, has a complete kitchen, two double beds, a roll-out couch, a ceiling fan, and a world-class view of the beach from your lanai. The back house, on the mountainside, is farther away from traffic and is among the trees. It's on stilts, and has an open ceiling and rustic common area. Rates are $40 for the main rooms (two people), $25 for a private loft (it gets hot up there), or $14 for a shared bunk. The Vacation Inn has only two rules: use common sense, and clean up after yourself. It provides free boogie boards and snorkeling gear and can arrange whalewatching or sunset sails and scuba and kayak rental. Airport transportation (directly opposite the baggage claim) is free *to* the inn and

$5 for the return trip. Everyone's friendly and laid-back. Book ahead. A good choice.

The **Plantation Village** at 59-754 Kamehameha Hwy., tel. (808) 638-7838, operated by Backpacker's, lies across from Three Tables Beach by Shark's Cove, between mile markers 6 and 7. It's on TheBus line and only a five-minute walk from a Foodland store for supplies. The Plantation Village, once a real Filipino working village, has cottages by the sea, secure behind a locked gate and furnished with cable, stereo, linens, a full kitchen, dishes, washers and dryers, ice machines, and cleaning service. Many of the fruit trees on the grounds provide the guests with complimentary bananas, papayas, breadfruit, or whatever is ripe. Prices are $16 for a shared room and bath with two or three others. The small (300 square feet) private cottages, once the homes of real plantation workers, sleep two and are $40 per night, or $245 per week. A $100 per night deluxe cottage sleeps four, and you get a large front lanai, two couches, wicker furniture in a sitting room, cable TV, a/c, fan, full bath with vanity, and a kitchen fully furnished with microwave, stove, and fridge. The Backpacker's van also services the Plantation Village. During surfing season the place is booked up. Reserve one month in advance, full deposit during high season (Dec.-Feb.), one-half deposit other months. No refund policy in high season.

Located at a quintessential surfing spot along the North Shore is **Breck's Hostel,** 59-043 Huelo St., Sunset Beach, HI 96712, tel. (808) 638-7873, but you don't have to be a surfer to enjoy the ambience. The beach is just across the highway, and nearby are shops, eateries, and the bus. Guests here have free use of the hostel's bodyboards, surfboards, snorkeling equipment, and bicycles, and rides to and from the airport can be arranged. Rates are charged by the day or the week: $12.50 for a basic dorm bed, $15.40 for the deluxe dorm, $35-45 for a private room or studio, and $16.50 per person in the ocean-view apartment (sleeps eight).

Condo

Ke Iki Hale is a small condo complex operated by Alice Tracy, 59-579 Ke Iki Rd., Waimea, HI 96712, tel. (808) 638-8229. Pass the Foodland supermarket heading north and look for a school sign. Turn left to the beach to find the condo. The property has 200 feet of private beach with a sandy bottom that goes out about 300 feet (half that in winter). The condo is quiet with a home-away-from-home atmosphere. Rates are: one-bedroom beachfront, $135 per day or $875 per week; two-bedroom beachfront, $185 per day or $1,155 per week; and a two-bedroom compact, $165 per day or $1,106 per week In addition, there is a cottage at $160 a day or $1,050 per week. Streetside units are about 30% less. A one-time cleaning fee is charged, and this ranges $35-65, depending upon the length of stay. Premium.

Luxury Resort

The **Hilton Turtle Bay Golf and Tennis Resort** is a first-class resort on Turtle Bay, the northern extremity of the North Shore, P.O. Box 187, 57-091 Kamehameha Hwy., Kahuku, HI 96731, tel. (808) 293-8811 or (800) HILTONS, website: www.turtlebayresort.hilton.com. Once a Hyatt hotel, it was built as a self-contained destination resort and is surrounded by sea and surf on Kuilima Point, which offers protected swimming year-round. The entrance road to the hotel is lined by blooming hibiscus that outline a formal manicured lawn. In 1993, *Golf Magazine* rated the 27-hole, Arnold Palmer-inspired Links at Kuilima one of the "top 10 best new courses in the U.S., while *Tennis Magazine* rated the hotel's tennis facilities among the top 50 tennis resorts in the entire world! The resort also offers a pool, full water activities including windsurfing and scuba lessons, horseback riding, shopping, and the fanciest dining on the North Shore. Since the hotel is an oasis unto itself, you should *always* call ahead to book any of these activities, even as a guest staying at the hotel, to avoid disappointment. There's very little shopping in this area, so if you're after film, or basic picnic supplies, stop at the hotel's minimall. The resort's newest feature is a seaside **Wedding Chapel,** splendid with open-beamed ceiling, stained glass, and eight-foot beveled windows that can be thrown open to allow the ocean breezes to waft through. All guest rooms are ocean view, but not all are oceanfront. Oceanfront is slightly more expensive, but is worth the price, especially Dec.-April when humpback whales cavort in the waters off the point. Rooms are furnished with full baths, a mini-fridge, a

dressing room, a large vanity, ample closets, a/c, and remote control cable TV. Junior suites come complete with a library, a large bathroom and changing room, two couches, a sitting area, a queen-size bed, and a large enclosed lanai. The Hilton has upgraded and refurbished with new carpets, drapes, bedspreads, wallpaper, and upholstered furniture. Rates are $160-200 for a standard with an ocean, mountain, or bay view; cabanas go for $285; and suites cost $400-1,500; $30 extra person. The Hilton family plan allows children free when they stay in a room with their parents. The Hilton is a first-class destination resort, but because of its fabulous, yet out-of-the-mainstream location, you get much more than what you pay for. The Hilton Turtle Bay is an excellent choice for a vacation with the feel of being on a Neighbor Island.

FOOD

Inexpensive/Moderate

East from town, across from Shark's Cove, is **Shark's Shack,** a *usually* open lunch wagon that'll fix you a sandwich or rent you snorkeling gear. Next door is **Pupukea Shave Ice** for an island treat. Farther toward Sunset Beach (around mile marker 9) look for **D'amico's Pizza,** open for breakfast, lunch, and dinner (slow but friendly service). The Sunset Beach store has basic items but is the home of **Ted's Bakery,** where you can get a fine assortment of loaves and pastries. For food supplies, shop **Foodland,** along the highway past Waimea Bay.

The **Proud Peacock,** Waimea Falls Park, tel. (808) 638-8531, is open daily for a lunch buffet and dinner 5-9 p.m. It's fun to dine here even if you don't enter the park. From the dining room, you can look into some of the nicest gardens while feeding crumbs to the peacocks. The beautiful mahogany bar was made in Scotland almost 200 years ago. You can have a light soup and salad, but their seafood *pu pu* platter is hard to beat. Roast pork and roast beef are well-prepared favorites here.

Classy Dining

If you're looking for gourmet dining in an incredibly beautiful setting head for the Hilton Turtle Bay Golf and Tennis Resort. The **Cove Res-**

taurant, open 6-9:30 p.m. (reservations advised), is the signature restaurant at the resort and welcomes you for an evening of fine dining. Slowly stroll a wooden walkway leading past tiny waterfalls and a profusion of plants to the main room that overlooks the manicured grounds and pool. Start with lobster bisque in a puff pastry shell or a variety of fresh island salads for $6. Move on to filet mignon, veal chops, fresh tiger prawns, and lobster that you choose fresh from the tank. The fresh catch, always an excellent choice, is a very reasonable $19.95. If you really want to treat yourself, order the North Shore potpourri, a silver bowl mounded with ice that cradles opihi, shrimp, sashimi, oysters, and fresh fish that come with savory dipping sauces from a basic shoyu and hot mustard to a papaya salsa. Enjoy dessert while gazing through floor-to-ceiling windows that frame the living mosaic of Turtle Bay turned brilliant by a legendary North Shore sunset.

The **Sea Tide Room** is synonymous with Sunday brunch. It enjoys a wonderful reputation, and if friends or family come visiting, islanders take them here to impress. Brunch is buffet style 9 a.m.-2 p.m. and features mounds of fresh fruits and pastries, fresh-squeezed fruit juices, imported cheeses, eggs Florentine and Benedict, fresh fish, seafood, sashimi, shrimp, crab claws, and flowing champagne. Reservations are not taken, $25 adults. Expect a wait, which goes quickly as you enjoy the magnificent scenery.

The **Palm Terrace** is the most "ordinary" of the hotel's restaurants, but ordinary par excellence! Open 6:30 a.m.-10 p.m., the restaurant serves hearty American favorites from all 50 states,

supplemented by dishes from around the world. You can dine on smoked Pacific fish, saimin with crispy bread, curried chicken papaya, or a seafood tostada. You will enjoy lunch sandwiches like Portuguese sausage on rye or a clubhouse special. There are hamburgers, of course—the basic burger, right down to a North Shore burger with grilled onions and peppers. For dessert order a cinnamon tulip: macadamia nut ice cream, split bananas, chocolate, and Kahuku watermelon all in a cinnamon tostada pastry shell. The views overlooking Turtle Bay combined with excellent value for the money make the Palm Terrace the best ordinary restaurant on the North Shore.

The **Bay View Lounge** is a casual restaurant/nightclub offering a deli-luncheon buffet. It's open 11:30 a.m.-1 a.m. and serves complimentary pu pu around sunset, which is a perfect time to drop in. On weekends the Bay View Lounge is the hotspot disco, ID required after 9 p.m.; dress code is collared shirts and closed-toe shoes.

GEOGRAPHICAL NOTE

The previous chapter, Windward Oahu, begins in Kailua/Kaneohe and works its way up the coast simply because most people visiting that coast approach it from the south. Those heading for the North Shore usually come from Haleiwa in the west and proceed northeast toward Kahuku. So, the end of this chapter follows geographically with the end of the Windward Oahu chapter. Don't let it throw you.

M.G.L. DOMENY DE RIENZI

THE LEEWARD COAST

The Waianae (Mullet Waters) coast, the leeward face of Oahu, is separated physically from the rest of the island by the Waianae Range. Spiritually, culturally, and economically, the separation is even more profound. This area is Oahu's last stand for ethnic Hawaiians, and for that phenomenal cultural blending of people called *locals*. The idea of "us against them" permeates the consciousness of the area. Guidebooks, government pamphlets, and word of mouth warn tourists against going to Waianae because "the natives are restless." If you follow this poor advice, you not only miss the last of undeveloped coastal Oahu, but the absolute pleasure of meeting people who will treat you with genuine *aloha*. Along the coast are magnificent beaches long known for their surf, new condos and developments nestled in secure valleys, and prime golfing. Inland, roads will take you to the roof of Oahu. Waianae is the home of small farms, rundown shacks, and families that hold luau on festive occasions, where the food and entertainment are the real article. Anyone lucky enough to be invited into this quickly disappearing world will be blessed with one of the last remaining authentic cultural experiences in Hawaii.

The possibility of hassles shouldn't be minimized because they do happen, but every aggressor needs a victim. The biggest problem is thievery, of the sneak-thief variety. You're marked as a tourist because of your new rental car. If you leave valuables in it, or lying unattended on the beach, they have a good chance of disappearing. But who does silly things like this *anywhere* in the U.S.? You won't be accosted, or held up at gunpoint, but if you bother a bunch of local guys drinking beer, you're asking for trouble. Moreover, the toughness of Waianae is self-perpetuating, and frankly the locals *like* the hard reputation. A few years back a feature writer reported that when he visited Waianae some toughs threw rocks at him. No one had ever reported this before, but after a big stink was made about it, more and more people had rocks thrown at them when they visited here. In recent years *pakalolo* has had a tremendous effect on the area. Local guys began growing and smoking it. This brought some money back into the depressed region, and it changed the outlook of some of the residents. They felt a camaraderie with other counterculture people, many of whom happened to be *haole*. They could relax and not feel so threatened with pursuing an often elusive materialistic path. Many became more content with their laid-back lifestyle, and genuinely less interested with the materialistic trip all the way around.

In truth, *we* shouldn't be warned about *them,* but vice versa. The people of Waianae are the ones being infringed upon, and it is they who, in the final analysis, will be hassled, ripped off, and ultimately dispossessed. Recent articles by Oahu's Development Conference strongly state that future development will center on the island's northwestern shore . . . the Waianae coast! A few rocks are poor weapons against developmental progress, which is defined by the big

boys with the big dreams and the big bucks to back them up.

When you go through Maili, you'll see what's been happening here since development has come to Waianae. As you drive through town notice a giant outcropping, Maili Point, which meets the sea like a giant fist. It has the same dominant presence as Diamond Head. Pull off at Maili Beach County Park, and to your right are the modest homes of local people. Look up the coast to where the mountains come down to the sea. Out on that headland you can see a giant resort, and on the bending backbone leading up to it, modest homes of the local people.

BEACHES AND SIGHTS

The Waianae coast is very accessible. One road takes you there. Simply follow the H-1 freeway from Honolulu until it joins the Farrington Highway (Rt. 93). It runs north, opening up the entire coast. A handful of side roads lead into the interior, and that's about it! A strange recommendation, but sensible on this heavily trafficked road, is to drive north to the end of the line and then stop at the scenic sights on your way back south. This puts you on the ocean side of the highway where you won't have to worry about cutting across two lines of traffic, which can be a steady stream making it tough to navigate. The Bus no. 51 runs the entire Waianae coast and stops at all of the following beaches.

Note: Four of the beach parks along this coast offer **camping,** but their status periodically changes to no camping without notice. Many of the other campers are local people in semipermanent structures; the reason that the status changes quickly is to prevent these people from squatting. Also, remember that this is the leeward coast, which gets plenty of sunshine. Many of the beach parks do not have shade trees, so be prepared. June is the prettiest month because all the flowers are in bloom, but it's one of the worst times for sunburn. The entire coast is great for snorkeling, with plenty of reef fish. However, keep your eyes on the swells, and always stay out during rough seas, when waves can batter you against the rocks. The parks listed below run from south to north.

Barbers Point Beach County Park
The first beach is Barbers Point Beach County Park, at the end of Kalaeloa Boulevard. Turn down it where H-1 and the Farrington Highway join. The point was named after Capt. Henry Barber, who was shipwrecked here in 1795. Few people, even island residents, visit this beach park. It's in an industrial area and the shoreline is rocky. One pocket of white-sand beach is open to the public, though it fronts a private residence. The swimming is safe only in summer; snorkeling is better, and you'll find picnic facilities and restrooms.

Kahe Point and Tracks Beach County Parks
Kahe Point and Tracks Beach County Parks are just where the Farrington Highway curves north along the coast. They're the first two *real* Waianae beaches, and they're symbolic. You come around the bend to be treated to an absolutely pristine view of the coast with the rolling sea, a white-sand beach, a cove, and the most hideous power plant you've ever seen. Facilities at Kahe Point Beach County Park are restrooms and a phone. The beach is poor except for a section just east of the improved park. Swimming is dangerous except on calm summer days, when a lifeguard is present. More often, you'll find people surfing and bodysurfing here. Camping is allowed with a county permit, although periodically this camping area closes temporarily.

The Hawaiian Electric Beach Park, across

typical camping beach, leeward coast

from the power plant, is known as "Tracks" to island surfers because of the railroad tracks that run along the shore here. Facilities include picnic tables, a pavilion, restrooms, showers, and parking along the highway. The white-sand beach is wide, and the swimming generally safe. The mild waves are perfect for learning how to surf. If you keep your eyes trained out to sea, the area is beautiful. Don't look inland!

Nanakuli Beach County Park

Nanakuli Beach County Park is on the southern outskirts of Nanakuli (Pretend to be Deaf) town, which is the first real town of the Waianae coast. If you get to the red light you've gone a little too far. The beach park is community-oriented, with recreational buildings, basketball courts, a baseball diamond, and kiddies' play area. Camping is permitted with a county permit. Lifeguards work on a daily basis, and the swimming is generally safe except during periods of high winter surf. The northern end of the beach, called Kalanianaole, is generally calmer than the southern end. They're divided by a housing project, but connected by a walkway. The southern section is fronted by a cliff with a small cove below. During periods of calm surf, the waters are crystal clear and perfect for snorkeling.

Ulehawa Beach County Park

Ulehawa Beach County Park, just north of Nanakuli, offers restrooms, picnic facilities, lifeguards, and sometimes camping. The best swim-

ming is in a sandy pocket near the lifeguard tower. Surf conditions make for good bodysurfing. Most of the park, along a rocky cliff, is undeveloped. Here you'll find useful fishing spots. A shallow lagoon is generally safe for swimming year-round. As always, it's best to check with the local people on the beach.

Maili Beach County Park

Maili Beach County Park is at the southern end of Maili (Many Small Stones) town. It lies between two streams coming down from the mountains. Amenities include restrooms, picnic facilities, and a lifeguard tower. The best swimming is in front of the lifeguard tower. The beach is broken into three parts by a housing development. In wintertime the beach disappears, but it returns wide and sandy for the summer. Most of the park is undeveloped. Plenty of coral pockets offer good snorkeling. Don't just jump in. Ask the locals or swing by the lifeguard tower to make sure that it's safe.

Lualualei Beach County Park

Lualualei Beach County Park has restrooms, picnic facilities, and camping during summer months. The entire park is largely undeveloped and lies along low cliffs and raised coral reef. Swimming is almost impossible. It's primarily good for fishing and looking.

Pokai Beach County Park

Pokai Beach County Park is one of the nicest

along the Waianae coast, located just south of Waianae town. It provides restrooms, picnic facilities, lifeguards, and a boat ramp, which brings plenty of small craft into the area. Don't be surprised to see a replica of a double-hulled canoe, often used for publicity purposes. It has appeared in a beer commercial. The park is clean, well maintained, reasonably secure, and family-oriented. There's surfing, snorkeling, and safe swimming year-round. If you're heading for one beach along Waianae, this is a top choice.

Waianae Harbor

To get a look at a small working harbor or to hire a fishing boat, visit Waianae Boat Harbor as you head north from town. Huge installed stones form an impressive manmade harbor, with everything from luxury yachts to aluminum fishing boats. Some cruises and whale-watching tours start from here.

Waianae Valley Road

To head inland take Waianae Valley Road. You quickly gain the heights of the Waianae Range, and eventually come to a sentry box with a soldier inside. From here Kolekole Road is closed to the public, but if you stop and identify yourself, you might be given permission to go to **Kolekole Pass**. The awesome view is well worth the trip.

Makaha Beach County Park

Makaha Beach County Park is famous for surfing, and as you approach, you can't help spotting a dominant headland called **Lahi Lahi**, which was a one-time island. Called "Black Rock" by the local fishermen, and

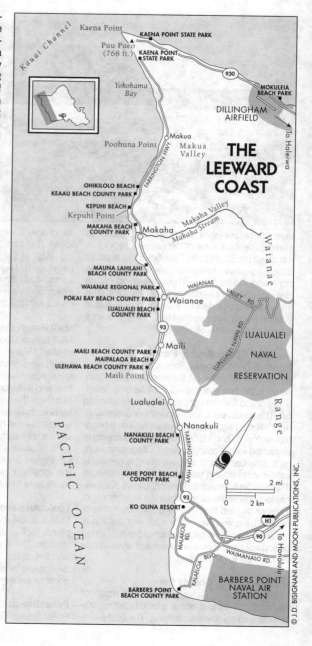

used as a landmark, it still marks Makaha. Surfing competitions have been held here since the Makaha International Surfing Competition began in 1952. In recent years, a local lifeguard named Richard "Buffalo" Keaulana, known to all who've come here, has begun the Annual Buffalo Big Board Riding Championship. Paul Strauch Jr., inventor of the "hang five," comes to Makaha whenever he has a chance, along with Buffalo's sons and other pro surfers, many of whom live in the area. In 1995, Buffalo retired after 36 years as a lifeguard. He has passed the torch on to his son Brian, who now becomes captain of the whole east side. Along with protecting the beach and riding the waves, Brian has a budding acting career as a stunt man for Hollywood. The swimming can be dangerous during high surf, but excellent on calm days. Winter brings some of the biggest surf in Hawaii. Always pay heed to the warnings of the lifeguards.

Makaha

Although Makaha can translate as "water breaking out to sea" because of the area's propensity of damming runoff waters from the mountains behind the beach until enough pressure forces it to "break out," there is another meaning for Makaha that doesn't help its image. The second translation, meaning "Fierce," aptly describes a gang of bandits who long ago lived in the surrounding hills and terrorized the region. They would wait for small bands of people walking the road, then swoop down and relieve them of their earthly goods.

If you follow Makaha Valley Road inland, you pass condos and high-rises clinging to the arid walls of this leeward valley. Surrounded by an artificial oasis of green, this developed resort area provides golfing at the Sheraton Makaha Golf Club and all the amenities of a destination resort. Visit the **Kaneaki Heiau,** a 17th-century temple restored by the resort under the direction of the Bishop Museum. This temple was dedicated to Lono, the benevolent god of harvest and fertility. The grass and thatched huts used as prayer and meditation chambers, along with a spirit tower, have all been replicated.

Once past Makaha, the road gets rugged, with plenty of private places to pull off. This crab claw of land, which ends at Kaena Point, forms a bay. The seascape demands attention but look into the interior. The mountains seem naturally terraced as they form dry, deep valleys. All are micro-habitats, each different from the other. On top of one notice a gigantic golf ball, really a radar tracking station, that lets you know you're coming to the end of the passable road.

Keaau Beach County Park

Keaau Beach County Park has restrooms, picnic facilities, and camping (county permit). The improved part of the park has a sandy beach, but mostly the park is fronted by coral and lava, and is frequented mostly by fishermen and campers. The unimproved section is not good for swimming, but it does attract a few surfers, and is good for snorkeling and scuba but only during calm periods. The improved section is a flat grassy area with picnic tables, shade trees, and pavilions.

Kaena Point State Park

Yokohama Bay is the end of the line; the pavement ends here. If you're headed for Kaena Point or beyond to the north coast you'll have to walk through this windswept coastal park. Yokohama Bay is a long stretch of sandy beach that is mostly unimproved. A lava-rock bathhouse is on the right, just after the entrance. The area was named because of the multitude of Japanese fishermen who came to this lonely site to fish. It's still great for fishing! The swimming can be hazardous because of the strong wave action and rough bottom, but the snorkeling is superb. Lifeguards are on duty during the summer months. Mostly the area is used by surfers and local people, including youngsters who dive off the large lava rocks. This is inadvisable for people unfamiliar with the area. Yokohama is a great place to come if you're after a secluded beach. Weekdays, you'll have it to yourself, with a slightly greater number of people on the weekends. Definitely bring cold drinks, and remember that there are no shade trees, so a hat or beach umbrella is a necessity. Many camp here unofficially.

Kaneana Cave is a few minutes south of Yokohama Bay on your left as you head back down the coast. You probably didn't notice it on your way north because of the peculiar land formation that conceals the mouth in that direction. Legend has it that this cave was the home of

Nanue the shark man. Unfortunately, people have come here with spray cans and trashed the cave. If you can overlook that, it's a phenomenon—a big one. You can spot it by looking for three cement blocks, like road dividers, right in front of the entrance. It's at the foot of a 200-foot outcropping of stone. When you see local people defacing the natural beauty like this, it's hard to believe that the Hawaiians had such a spirit bond with the *aina*.

PRACTICALITIES

ACCOMMODATIONS

Inexpensive Condos

Except for camping, the only inexpensive places to stay along the Waianae coast are condos, which cost about $350 a week and require a minimum stay of seven days. Some local people let rooms for a good rate, but there is no way to find this out in advance. Your best bet is to check out the bulletin boards at various stores along the coast.

The **Maili Cove**, 87-561 Farrington Hwy., Waianae, HI 96792, tel. (808) 696-4447, rents one-bedroom apartments for $350-450 per week. It has a swimming pool, parking, and TV, along with a few hotel units.

The **Makaha Beach Cabanas**, 84-965 Farrington Hwy., tel. (808) 696-2166, are in Makaha along the beach just past the high school. All units have a lanai overlooking the water. They're not fancy, but are spotlessly clean and serviceable. All units are fully furnished with complete kitchens; from $350 per week.

The **Makaha Shores** are privately owned units that overlook a beautiful white-sand beach and provide great viewing of the surfers challenging the waves below. All units are fully furnished. The least expensive accommodations are at the **Makaha Surfside**. The beach is rocky near the condo, but it makes up for this with two pools and a sauna. All units are individually owned and fully furnished. **Makaha Valley Towers** rise dramatically from Makaha Valley, but they don't fit in. They're either a testament to man's achievement or ignorance, depending on your point of view. In keeping with the idea of security, you drive up to a gate manned by two guards. You're stopped, asked your business, and sent unsmilingly on your way. The condo provides fully furnished units, a/c, TV, and pool. If you're staying in this ill-fitting high-rise, at least try to get a top floor where you can take advantage of the remarkable view. Of the three condos, these have the most expensive units. Rates vary according to property, but generally fall into the $250-450 a week range for studios, $350-550 for one-bedroom units, and up to $750 for two bedrooms per week. Monthly rates are also available, and you get substantial savings for longer rentals. For rental information, contact Hatfield's Realty, tel. (808) 696-8415; Sugar Kane Realty, tel. (808) 696-5833; Waianae Coast Realty, tel. (808) 696-6366; or Sun Estates, tel. (808) 487-0000.

Ihilani Resort and Spa

The courtiers anxiously waited for the grand night when the torches would be lighted and the drums beaten to announce the lovely princess as she was presented to the assembled *ali'i*. Those closest to the young beauty were confident that their years of training had refined the grace and nobility that matched her dignified heritage. She had proven to be an enthusiastic and willing student, endearing herself to all because of her gaiety, sweetness, and loving heart. But to assume her rightful place with the most powerful in the land, she would have to gain the self-possessed assurity that only comes from the wisdom of experience. It is much the same with the Ihilani Resort and Spa, at 92-1001 Olani St., Kopolei, HI 96707, tel. (808) 679-0079, (800) 626-4446, website: www.ihilani.com. The hotel, an alabaster specter floating amidst the 640 emerald-green acres of the Ko Olina Resort, rises above a white-sand beach at the southern end of the Waianae coast. It's about 25 minutes west of the Honolulu airport—simply follow the H-1 expressway to the clearly marked Ko Olina exit. You approach the resort by way of a cobblestone drive that winds its way up to a porte cochere where valets and lei-bearing hostesses wait to greet you. The open breezeway leads to a towering glass-domed atrium brightened by cascading trellised flowers, and ringed by living green ferns. Below, rivulets trickle through a series of free-form ponds, some like glass-reflecting sculptures, others alive and tinkling a natural refrain. The guest rooms, huge at almost 700 square feet, are pleasantly appointed in pastels and white and all feature a/c, ceiling fans, louvered doors, remote-control entertainment centers, in-room safes, minibars, and luxurious cushioned teak furniture including a dining table and lounge awaiting you on your private lanai. A futuristic feature is a bedside master control telephone system from where you can regulate the room's lighting, a/c, and voice mail service at the touch of a finger. Bathrooms, an intricate play of marble and tile, feature double sinks, hair dryers, a basket of fine toiletries, separate commode and shower stalls, and deep oversize tubs. Evening brings turndown service when little gifts of mineral bath gels or soothing facial compresses are left on your pillow, compliments of the spa. Terrace view rooms run $295, the golf-mountain view rooms $325, while the ocean-view rooms go for $415 a night. Many spa, golf, and tennis packages are also available, and they save a good deal on room rates. Other amenities are 24-hour room service, concierge service, tennis courts, and a beauty salon. With time and maturity, the Ihilani Resort and Spa, tucked away from the madding crowd, gives every indication of becoming one of Oahu's premier destinations. In fact, for 1998, it received the prestigious AAA Five Diamond Award for excellence in service and accommodations.

Dining at the Ihilani is in the masterful and infinitely creative hands of executive chef, Katsuo Sugiura (Chef Suki), who has created dishes in what he describes as "Tropical Pacific." This fantastic blending of East and West relies heavily on locally grown herbs, vegetables, meats, and most importantly, island seafood. It is a blissful marriage built on Mediterranean, Oriental, and Hawaiian cuisine that can easily be influenced by Scandinavian, Caribbean and Southwestern ingredients. Mostly, Chef Suki is an artist who is constantly experimenting and creating new presentations on a daily basis. Using smoking techniques that he has perfected over the years, Suki not only creates distinctive individual dishes, but he creates them especially for each guest, sealing the recipe and repeating it when you return, if you so desire. The Ihi-

lani's signature restaurant is the dinner-only **Azul,** complemented by a magnificent wine cellar, with breakfast, lunch, and dinner served at the open-air **Naupaka Terrace.** Health-conscious cuisine for breakfast and lunch is offered at the **Spa Cafe,** on the sixth level of the Ihilani Spa. Traditional Japanese fare is offered for dinner only at the **Ushio-tei.** And golfers or those into a more casual setting will enjoy clubhouse dining for lunch at the Ko Olina Golf Course's **Niblick Restaurant.** For snacks during the day, try the **Poolside Grill** or **Hokule'a Bar.**

Located in a separate facility just a short walk across from the main entrance is the **Ihilani Spa,** a magnificently soothing, revitalizing, and uniquely Hawaiian spa experience. This facility is centered around Thalasso water therapy, a computer-controlled water-jet massage utilizing fresh seawater and seaweed. After being immersed in this state-of-the-art tub, you move on to the Vichy Shower, Grand Jet, or Needle Pavilion, where 12 shower heads poke stimulating sprays into every nook and cranny. Next, the superbly trained staff offers hands-on experiences in the form of therapeutic massage including Swedish, *lomi lomi,* or shiatsu. You can also opt for a manicure, pedicure, or skin-rejuvenating facial. To keep trim and supple, head for the fitness facility on the third level where you will find a lap pool, jacuzzi, aerobics room, and strengthening equipment.

The green velvet of the **Ko Olina Championship Golf Course,** designed by Ted Robinson and named as one of the finest courses in America by *Golf Digest,* fronts the hotel. Open since 1990, the course is fully matured and has already hosted a number of prestigious tournaments. If you'd rather play tennis, the resort's six Kramer-covered tennis courts await your pleasure. Luxury

FOOD AND SERVICES

For anyone with an urge to eat a two-scoop plate lunch, no problem. Little drive-in lunch counters are found in almost every Waianae town. Each serves hearty island food such as teriyaki chicken, pork, or mahimahi for under $5. A favorite is the **Makaha Drive-In.**

You also see plenty of fruit sellers parked along the road. Their produce couldn't be fresher, and stopping provides you not only with the perfect complement to a picnic lunch but with a good chance to meet some local people.

For your shopping and dining needs in Nanakuli, try the **Pacific Shopping Mall**, where you'll find Sac and Save Supermarket, the largest in the area. In the complex is **Nanakuli Chop Suey Restaurant,** open 10 a.m.-8:30 p.m., tel. (808) 668-8006, serving standard Chinese fare at local down-home prices. Just behind McDonald's is the **Eden BBQ Lounge,** tel. (808) 668-2722, with sit-down and takeout Korean food at moderate prices; open 10 a.m.-9 p.m. daily.

The **Waianae Mall** is a complete shopping facility. Don't worry about bringing supplies or food if you're on a day excursion. You'll find all that you need at the mall, which includes Red Baron Pizza, Waianae Chop Suey, Subway Sandwiches, Woolworth's, and Longs. Have no fear if you're addicted to fast foods. Some major franchises have decided that your trip to lee-ward Oahu wouldn't be complete without something processed in a Styrofoam box. If you're looking for ethnic flavor try the **Tamura Superette,** which stocks plenty of ingredients used in ethnic foods. An **L&L Drive-In** is here as well for the plate lunch lovers. For banking needs, try the Bank of America branch office. You'll spot a number of gas stations in the middle of town, along with Circle K and 7-Eleven convenience stores. Makaha has Woolworth's and a shopping basket of neighborhood markets.

Arts and Crafts

The **Waianae Hawaiian Heritage Cultural Center** offers workshops in lei-making, *lau hala* weaving, hula, and the Hawaiian language. The center welcomes people either to observe or participate in the programs. For times and schedules contact the State Foundation on Culture and Arts, tel. (808) 586-0300.

KAUAI

O, how my spirit languishes
to step ashore in the Sanguishes . . .
    –Robert Louis Stevenson, circa 1888

INTRODUCTION

Kauai is the oldest of the main Hawaiian Islands, and nature has had ample time to work, sculpting Kauai into a beauty among beauties. Flowers and fruits burst from its fertile soil, but the "Garden Island" is much more than greenery and flora—it's the poetry of land itself. Its mountains have become rounded and smooth, and its streams tumbling to the sea have cut deep and wide, giving Kauai the only navigable river in Hawaii. The interior is a dramatic series of mountains, valleys, and primordial swamp. The great gouge of Waimea Canyon, called the "Grand Canyon of the Pacific," is an enchanting layer of pastels where uncountable rainbows form prismatic necklaces from which waterfalls hang like silvery pendants. The northwest is the seacliffs of Na Pali, mightiest in all of Oceania, looming more than 3,000 feet above the pounding surf.

After only 35 minutes by air from Honolulu (103 miles), you land just about the time you're finishing your in-flight cocktail. Everything seems quieter here, rural but upbeat, with the main town being just that, a town. The pursuit of carefree relaxation is unavoidable at five-star hotels, where you're treated like a visiting *ali'i,* or at campsites deep in interior valleys or along secluded beaches where reality *is* the fantasy of paradise.

Kauai is where Hollywood comes when the script calls for "paradise." The island has a dozen major films to its credit, everything from idyllic scenes in *South Pacific* to the lurking horror of Asian villages in *Uncommon Valor. King Kong* tore up this countryside in search of love, and Tattoo spotted "de plane, boss" in *Fantasy Island.* In *Blue Hawaii,* Elvis's hips mimicked the swaying palms in a famous island grove, while torrid love scenes from *The Thorn Birds* were steamier than the jungle in the background. More recently, parts of *Outbreak* and *Jurrasic Park* were filmed here. Perhaps its greatest compliment is that Kauai is where other islanders come to look at the scenery.

AN OVERVIEW

Kauai is the most regularly shaped of all the major islands—more or less round, like a partially deflated beach ball. The puckered skin around the coast forms bays, beaches, and inlets, while the center is a no man's land of mountains, canyon, and swamp.

Lihue
Almost everyone arrives at the airport in Lihue. The small strip in Princeville, once serviced by

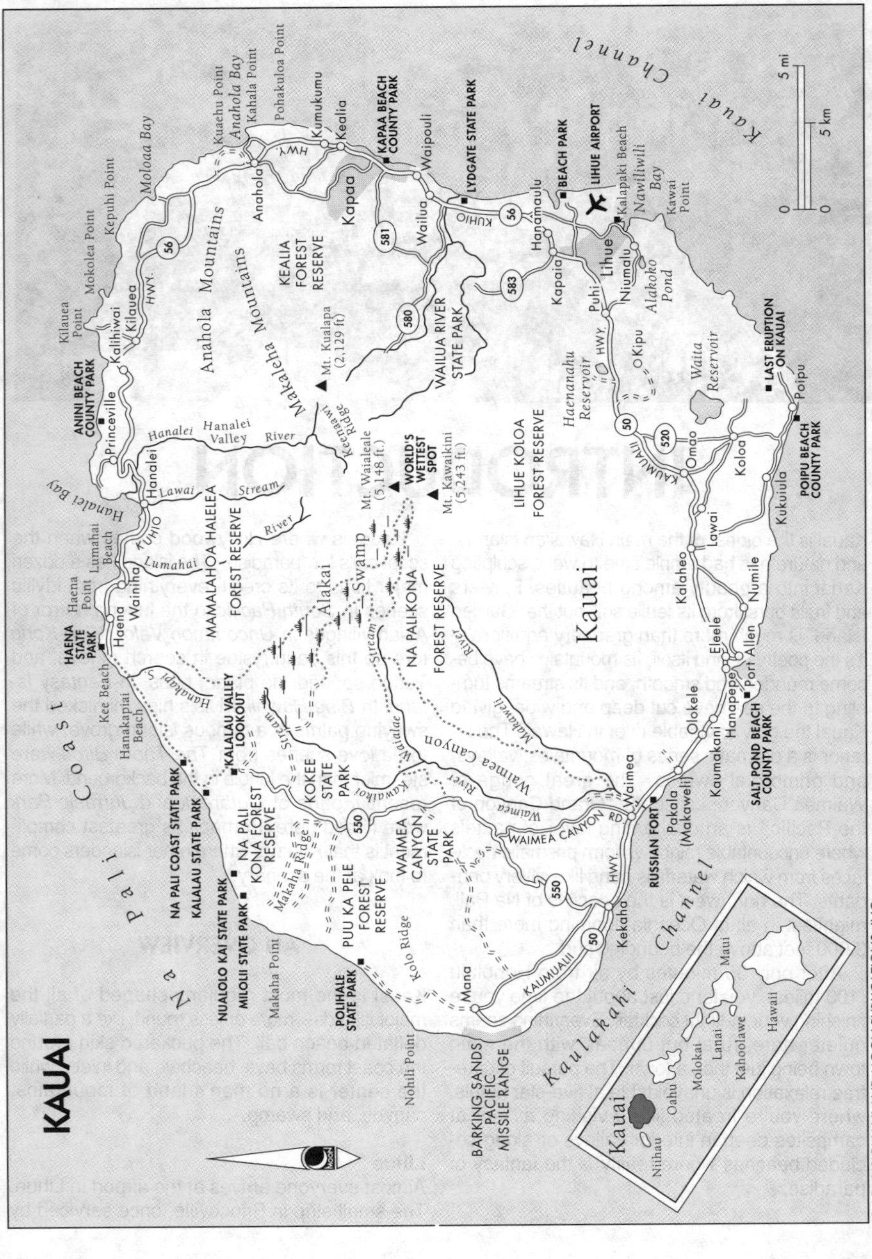
KAUAI
Kauai
Kaulakahi Channel
Kauai Channel
Na Pali Coast
Hanalei Bay
Moloaa Bay
Anahola Bay
Nawiliwili Bay
Kilauea Point
Mokolea Point
Kepuhi Point
Kuaehu Point
Kahala Point
Pohakuloa Point
Haena Point
Kawai Point
Makaha Point
Nohili Point
ANINI BEACH COUNTY PARK
HAENA STATE PARK
NA PALI COAST STATE PARK
KALALAU STATE PARK
NUALOLO KAI STATE PARK
MILOLII STATE PARK
POLIHALE STATE PARK
KALALAU VALLEY LOOKOUT
KOKEE STATE PARK
WAIMEA CANYON STATE PARK
WAILUA RIVER STATE PARK
LYDGATE STATE PARK
KAPAA BEACH COUNTY PARK
BEACH PARK
LIHUE AIRPORT
SALT POND BEACH COUNTY PARK
POIPU BEACH COUNTY PARK
LAST ERUPTION ON KAUAI
RUSSIAN FORT
BARKING SANDS PACIFIC MISSILE RANGE
NA PALI KONA FOREST RESERVE
PUU KA PELE FOREST RESERVE
WAIMEA CANYON
NA PALI-KONA FOREST RESERVE
MAMALAHOA HALELEA FOREST RESERVE
KEALIA FOREST RESERVE
LIHUE KOLOA FOREST RESERVE
WORLD'S WETTEST SPOT
Mt. Waialeale (5,148 ft.)
Mt. Kawaikini (5,243 ft.)
Mt. Kualapa (2,129 ft)
Alakai Swamp
Anahola Mountains
Makaleha Mountains
Hanalei Valley
Hanalei River
Lumahai
Lawai Stream
Waimea River
Makaweli River
Waialae Stream
Kawaikoi Stream
Makaha Ridge
Kolo Ridge
Keenaa Ridge
Hanakapiai Beach
Kee Beach
Lumahai Beach
Kalapaki Beach
Haenanahu Reservoir
Waita Reservoir
Alakoko Pond
Princeville
Kalihiwai
Kilauea
Hanalei
Wainiha
Haena
Anahola
Kumukumu
Kealia
Kapaa
Waipouli
Wailua
Hanamaulu
Kapaia
Lihue
Puhi
Niumalu
Kipu
Omao
Koloa
Poipu
Kukuiula
Lawai
Kalaheo
Numila
Eleele
Port Allen
Hanapepe
Olokele
Kaumakani
Pakala (Makaweli)
Waimea
Kekaha
Mana
KUHIO HWY.
KAUMUALII HWY.
WAIMEA CANYON RD.
56
50
520
550
580
581
583
0 5 mi
0 5 km
Niihau
Oahu
Molokai
Lanai
Maui
Kahoolawe
Hawaii

commuter aircraft, has been closed since the mid-90s. Lihue is the county seat and major town with government agencies, full amenities, and a wide array of restaurants and shopping. Lihue also boasts some of the least expensive accommodations on the island, in small family-operated hotels; however, most visitors head north for Wailua/Kapa'a or Princeville, or west to the fabulous Poipu Beach area. Lihue's Kauai Museum is a must stop, where you'll learn the geological and social history of the island, immensely enriching your visit.

On the outskirts of town is the oldest Lutheran church in the islands and the remarkably preserved Grove Farm Homestead, a classic Hawaiian plantation that is so intact that all that seems to be missing are the workers. At Nawiliwili Bay you can see firsthand the Menehunes' handiwork at the Menehune (Alakoko) Fish Pond, still in use. Just north are the two suburbs of Kapaia and Hanamaulu. Here too you'll find shops and restaurants and the junction of Rt. 583 leading inland through miles of sugarcane fields and terminating at a breathtaking panorama of Wailua Falls.

East Coast

Heading northeast from Lihue along Rt. 56 takes you to **Wailua** and **Kapa'a**. En route, you pass Wailua Municipal Golf Course, beautiful, cheap, and open to the public. Wailua town is built along the Wailua River, the only navigable stream in Hawaii. At the mouth of the river are two enchanting beach parks and a temple of refuge, while upstream are more *heiau,* petroglyphs, royal birth stones, the heavily touristed yet beautiful Fern Grotto, and the Kamokila Hawaiian folk village, all within the Wailua River State Park. Here too are remarkable views of the river below and the cascading Opaekaa Waterfalls.

Along Rt. 56 toward Kapa'a you pass The Market Place, an extensive mall that'll satisfy your every shopping need and then some. In the vicinity, a clutch of first-rate yet affordable hotels and condos line the beach. Kapa'a is a workers' town with more down-home shopping, and good, inexpensive restaurants. Heading north toward Hanalei, you pass Pohakuloa Point, an excellent surfers' beach; Anahola Beach Park, where the water and camping are fine; and Moloa'a Bay, a secluded beach that you can have mostly to yourself.

Hanakapi'ai Stream

North Coast

Before entering **Kilauea**, the first town in the Hanalei District, unmarked side roads can lead you to secret beaches and unofficial camp spots. A small coastal road leads you to Kilauea Lighthouse, a beacon of safety for passing ships and for a remarkable array of birds that come to this wildfowl sanctuary. **Princeville** is next, the largest planned resort in Hawaii. Here an entire modern village is built around superb golf courses and an exclusive deluxe resort.

Down the narrowing lane and over a single-lane steel-strut bridge is **Hanalei**. Inland is a terraced valley planted in taro just like in the old days. Oceanside is Hanalei Bay, a safe anchorage and haven to seagoing yachts, which have made it a port of call ever since Westerners began coming to Hawaii. On the outskirts is Waioli Mission House, a preserved home and museum dating from 1837. Then comes a string of beaches, uncrowded and safe for swimming and snorkeling. You pass through the tiny village of Wainiha, and then Haena, with the island's "last resort." In quick succession come Haena Beach County Park, the wet and dry caves, and the end of the road at Ke'e Beach in Haena State Park. Here are beach houses for those who want to get away from it all, Kaulu Paoa Heiau dedicated to hula, and the location where the beach scenes from *The Thorn Birds* were filmed. From here only your feet and love of adventure take you down the Kalalau Trail to back-to-nature camping. You pass along a narrow foot trail down the **Na Pali Coast,** skirting emerald valleys cut off from the world by impassable 4,000-foot seacliffs. All along here are *heiau,* ancient village sites, caves, lava tubes, and the romantic yet true Valley of the Lost Tribe just beyond trail's end.

South Coast

From Lihue west is a different story. Route 50 takes you past the Kukui Grove Center and then through **Puhi,** home of Kauai Community College. As the coastal Hoary Head Mountains slip past your window, Queen Victoria's Profile squints down at you. Maluhia Road, famous for its tunnel-like line of eucalyptus, branches off toward **Koloa,** a sugar town now rejuvenated with shops, boutiques, and restaurants. At the coast is **Poipu Beach,** the best on Kauai with its bevy of beautiful hotels and resorts.

Westward is a string of sugar towns. First is **Kalaheo,** where an island philanthropist, Walter McBryde, gave the munificent land gift that has become Kukui O Lono Park. Here you'll find a picture-perfect Japanese garden surrounded by an excellent yet little-played golf course. West on Rt. 50 is **Hanapepe,** a good supply stop famous for its art shops and inexpensive restaurants. The road skirts the shore, passing **Olokele,** a perfect caricature of a sugar town with its neatly trimmed cottages, and **Pakala,** an excellent surfing beach. Quickly comes **Waimea,** where Captain Cook first came ashore, and on the outskirts is the Russian Fort, dating from 1817, when all the world powers were present in Hawaii, jockeying to influence this Pacific gem.

In Waimea and farther westward in **Kekaha,** the road branches inland, leading along the rim of **Waimea Canyon.** This is what everyone comes to see, and none are disappointed. The wonderfully winding road serves up lookout after lookout and trail after trail. You end up at Koke'e State Park and the Kalalau Valley Lookout, where you're king of the mountain, and 4,000 feet below is your vast domain of Na Pali. Past Kekaha back on Rt. 50 is a flat stretch of desert vast enough that the military has installed Barking Sands Missile Range. The pavement ends and a good tourist-intimidating "cane road" takes over, leading you to the seclusion of Polihale State Park, where you can swim, camp, and luxuriate in privacy. If Madame Pele had had her choice, she never would have moved.

THE LAND

Kauai, 100 miles northwest of Oahu, is the northernmost of Hawaii's six major islands and fourth largest. It is approximately 33 miles long and 25 miles wide at its farthest points, with an area of 552 square miles and 90 miles of coastline. The island was built by one huge volcano that became extinct about six million years ago. Mount Waialeale in central Kauai is its eastern rim, and speculation holds that Niihau, 20 miles off the west coast, was at one time connected. The volcanic "hot spot" under Kauai was sealed by the weight of the island; as Kauai drifted northward the hot spot burst through again and again, building the string of islands from Oahu to Hawaii.

A simplified but chronologically accurate account of Kauai's emergence is found in a version of the Pele myth retold in *The Kumulipo*. It depicts the fire goddess as a young, beautiful woman who visits Kauai during a hula festival and becomes enraptured with Lohiau, a handsome and mighty chief. She wants him as a husband and determines to dig a fire pit home where they can reside in contented bliss. Unfortunately, her unrelenting and unforgiving sea-goddess sister pursues her, forcing Pele to abandon Kauai and Lohiau. Thus, she wandered and sparked volcanic eruptions on Oahu, Maui, and finally atop Kilauea Crater on Hawaii, where she now resides.

Phenomenal Features of Kauai

Located almost smack-dab in the middle of the island are **Mount Kawaikini** (5,243 feet) and adjacent **Mount Waialeale** (5,148 feet), highest points on Kauai. Mount Waialeale is an unsurpassed "rain magnet," drawing an estimated 480 inches (40 feet) of precipitation during the approximately 350 days it rains per year, and earning itself the dubious distinction of being "the wettest spot on earth." Don't be intimidated—this rain is amazingly localized, with only 20 inches per year falling just 20 miles away. Visitors can now enter this mist-shrouded world aboard helicopters that fly through countless rainbows and hover above a thousand waterfalls.

Draining Waialeale is **Alakai Swamp,** a dripping sponge of earth covering about 30 square miles of trackless bog (construction of an elevated boardwalk is underway). This patch of mire contains flora and fauna found nowhere else on earth. For example, ohia trees, mighty giants of upland forests, grow here as natural bonsai that could pass as potted plants.

Boardering the Alakai Swamp on the west is **Waimea Canyon,** where eons of whipping winds, pelting rain, and the incessant grinding of streams and rivulets have chiseled the red bedrock to depths of 3,600 feet and expanses 10 miles wide. On the western slopes of Waimea Canyon is the **Na Pali Coast,** a scalloped, undulating vastness of valleys and *pali* forming a bulwark 4,000 feet high.

Other mountains and outcroppings around the island have formed curious natural formations. The **Hoary Head Mountains,** a diminutive range barely 2,000 feet tall south of Lihue, form a profile of Queen Victoria. A ridge just behind Wailua gives the impression of a man in repose and has been dubbed The Sleeping Giant. Another small range in the northeast, the **Anahola Mountains,** had until recently an odd series of boulders that formed "Hole in the Mountain," mythologically created when a giant hurled his spear through sheer rock. Erosion has collapsed the formation, but the tale lives on.

Channels, Lakes, and Rivers

Kauai is separated from Oahu by the **Kauai Channel.** Reaching an incredible depth of 10,900 feet and a width of 72 miles, it is by far the state's deepest and widest channel. Inland, man-made **Waita Reservoir** north of Koloa is the largest body of fresh water in Hawaii, covering 424 acres with a three-mile shoreline. The **Waimea River,** running through the floor of the canyon, is the island's longest at just under 20 miles, while the **Hanalei River** moves the greatest amount of water, emptying 150 million gallons per day into Hanalei Bay. But the **Wailua River** has the distinction of being the state's only navigable stream, although passage by boat is restricted to a scant three miles upstream. The flatlands around Kekaha were at one time Hawaii's largest body of inland water. They were brackish and drained last century when the Waimea Ditch was built to irrigate the cane fields.

CLIMATE

Kauai's climate will make you happy. Along the coastline the average temperature is 80° F in spring and summer, and about 75 during the remainder of the year. The warmest areas are along the south coast from Lihue westward, where the mercury can hit the 90s in midsummer. To escape the heat any time of year, head for Koke'e atop Waimea Canyon, where the weather is always moderate.

Precipitation

Although Mt. Waialeale is "the wettest spot on earth," in the areas most interesting to visitors, rain is not a problem. The driest section of Kauai is the southwestern desert, from Polihale to Poipu Beach, which gets from five inches per year up to a mere 20 inches around the resorts. Lihue receives about 30 inches. As you head northeast toward Hanalei, rainfall becomes more frequent but is still a tolerable 45 inches per year. Cloudbursts in winter are frequent but short-lived.

Hurricanes Iwa and Iniki

The Garden Island is much more than just another pretty face—the island and its people have integrity. Thanksgiving was not a very nice time on Kauai back in November 1982. Along with the stuffing and cranberries came an unwelcome guest who showed no *aloha,* **Hurricane Iwa.** What made this rude 80-mph party-crasher

KAUAI TEMPERATURE AND RAINFALL

TOWN		JAN.	MARCH	MAY	JUNE	SEPT.	NOV.
Hanapepe	high	79	80	81	84	82	80
	low	60	60	61	65	62	61
	rain	5	2	0	0	2	3
Lihue	high	79	79	79	82	82	80
	low	60	60	65	70	68	65
	rain	5	3	2	2	5	5
Kilauea	high	79	79	80	82	82	80
	low	62	64	66	68	69	65
	rain	5	5	3	3	1	5

Note: Temperature is expressed in degrees Fahrenheit; rainfall in inches.

so unforgettable was that she was only the fourth such storm to come ashore on Hawaii since records have been kept and the first since the late 1950s. All told, Iwa caused $230 million dollars' worth of damage. A few beaches were washed away, perhaps forever, and great destruction was suffered by beach homes and resorts, especially around Poipu. Thankfully, no lives were lost. The people of Kauai rolled up their sleeves and set about rebuilding. In short order, the island recovered, and most residents thought "that was that."

Unfortunately on Friday, September 11, 1992, **Hurricane Iniki,** with unimaginable ferocity, ripped ashore with top wind speeds of 175 mph, and slapped Kauai around like the moll in a Bog-

art movie. "Iniki" has two meanings in Hawaiian: "piercing winds" or "pangs of love," both devastatingly painful in their own way. The hurricane virtually flattened or tore to shreds everything in its path. No one was immune from the savage typhoon. Renowned director, Steven Spielberg and his cast, including Laura Dern, Jeff Goldblum, Richard Attenborough, and Sam Neill, were on the island filming scenes for the blockbuster *Jurassic Park*. They along with other guests, bellhops, maids, groundskeepers, and cooks, rode out the storm huddled in the ballroom of the Westin Kauai Lagoons. Afterward, Mayor JoAnn Yukimura and her staff worked day and night from her then roofless office in Lihue. Hanalei taro farmers opened their humble

*the destruction wrought
by Hurricane Iniki*

doors to homeless neighbors and strangers alike, while a general manager of a luxury resort on the eve of his wedding pleaded with invited guests to give donations to various charitable organizations in lieu of gifts. There was hardly a structure on the entire island that wasn't damaged in one way or another. Proud yachts were thrown like toy boats into a jangled heap; cars were buried whole in the red earth; a full third of Kauai's 20,000 homes were broken into splinters; and 4,200 hotel rooms became a tangled heap of steel and jagged glass. By the grace of god, and because of a very competent warning system, only eight lives were lost and fewer than 100 people had to be admitted to the hospital due to injury. Psychologically, however, many people who lost everything were scared; special counseling services were set up to offer techniques to deal with the stress and sense of loss. Insurance companies were stressed to the breaking point, with some very slow to pay. Locals checked their policies and prayed desperately that they wouldn't be "HIG-positive"; Hawaii Insurance Group, a popular island-based insurance company that literally went broke trying to pay all of the claims brought against it.

An estimated $1.9 billion worth of damage was caused by Hurricane Iniki. Undaunted and with pride and will that far surpassed the fury of the storm, Kauai's people immediately set about rebuilding homes, while nature took care of the rest. Some philosophical souls hold Kauai wasn't hurt at all, and only a bunch of manmade buildings were destroyed. They contend in its millions of years of existence, Kauai has been through many storms, and Hurricane Iniki was merely a "$1.5 billion pruning . . . for free." Though trees were twisted from the ground and bushes were flattened, Kauai is strong and fertile and the damage was temporary. Now, Iniki is mostly a memory and Kauai has emerged a touch more self-assured and as beautiful as ever.

FLORA AND FAUNA

Kauai exceeds its reputation as the Garden Island. It has had a much longer time for soil building and rooting of a wide variety of plantlife, so it's lusher than the other islands. Lying on a main bird migratory route, lands such as the Hanalei National Wildlife Sanctuary have long since been set aside for their benefit. Impenetrable inland regions surrounding Mt. Waialeale and dominated by the Alakai Swamp have provided a natural sanctuary for Kauai's own bird- and plantlife. Because of this, Kauai is home to the largest number of indigenous birds extant in Hawaii, though even here they are tragically endangered. As on the other Hawaiian Islands, a large number of birds, plants, and mammals has been introduced in the past 200 years. Most have either aggressively competed for, or simply destroyed, the habitat of indigenous species. As the newcomers gain dominance, Kauai's own flora and fauna slide inevitably toward oblivion.

Indigenous Forest Birds
Kauai's upland forests are still home to many Hawaiian birds. You may be lucky enough to spot the **Hawaiian owl** *(pueo),* one of the friendliest *aumakua* (ancestral spirit) in ancient Hawaii; the *elepaio,* an indigenous bird found around Koke'e, and the bright red *'i'iwi.*

Anianiau is a four-inch yellow-green bird found around Koke'e. Its demise is due to a lack of fear of humans. The **nukupu'u,** extinct on the other islands except for a few on Maui, is found in Kauai's upper forests and on the borders of the Alakai Swamp. It's a five-inch bird with a drab green back and a bright yellow chest.

Birds of the Alakai Swamp
The following scarce birds are some of the last indigenous Hawaiian birds, saved only by the inhospitability of the Alakai Swamp. All are endangered species and under no circumstances should they be disturbed. The last survivors include: the **o'u,** a chubby seven-inch bird with a green body, yellow head, and lovely whistle ranging half an octave; the relatively common **Hawaiian creeper,** a hand-size bird with a light green back and white belly, which travels in pairs and searches bark for insects; the **puaiohi,** a dark brown, white-bellied seven-inch bird so rare its nesting habits are unknown.

O'o'a'a', although its name may resemble the sounds you make getting into a steaming

KAUAI BOTANICAL GARDENS

For those interested in the flora of Kauai, beyond what can be seen out of the car window, a visit to the following will be both educational and inspiring.

Koke'e Natural History Museum, tel. (808) 335-9975, just past the Koke'e State Park Headquarters, has exhibits explaining the geology and plant and animal life of the park and the surrounding upper mountain and swamp regions of the island. It is free and open daily 10 a.m.-4 p.m.

National Tropical Botanical Garden, in Poipu, tel. (808) 742-2623, is the only research facility for tropical plants in the country and the premier botanical garden on Kauai. Tours lasting about 2.5 hours are given daily except Sunday. The visitor center/museum/gift shop is open Mon.-Sat. 8:30 a.m.-5:30 p.m. for walk-in visitors. You can take a short self-guided tour of the plants around this building (map provided), but to go into the gardens you need reservations in advance.

Kiahuna Plantation Gardens, tel. (808) 742-6411, are located at the Kiahuna Plantation Resort in Poipu. Over a 27-year period during the mid-1900s, five acres of this former plantation site were cultivated with about 2,500 plants from Africa, the Americas, the Pacific, and India, and include cactus and aloe sections. Open daily during daylight hours, free guided tours of the property are given weekdays at 10 a.m.

Smith's Tropical Paradise, tel. (808) 821-6892, a finely manicured and well-kept botanical and cultural garden with a bountiful, beautiful collection of ordinary and exotic plants (many labeled), is on 30 riverfront acres adjacent to the Wailua marina. Have a look here before heading upcountry. Open 8:30 a.m.-4:30 p.m. for a $5 entrance fee, then open for a luau and show ($43.75).

Limahuli Botanical Garden, tel. (808) 828-1053, on Kauai's extreme North Shore in the last valley before the beginning of the Kalalau Trail, open Tues.-Fri. and again on Sunday 9:30 a.m.-3 p.m., showcases tropical plants both ancient and modern. It's part of the National Tropical Botanical Gardens and there are both a self-guided ($10) and guided ($15) walking tours. As you walk this three-quarter-mile loop trail, you'll pass patches of taro plants introduced to Hawaii by early Polynesians, living specimens of endangered native species, and post-contact tropicals, all while enjoying listening to the legends of the valley.

---

hot tub, is an eight-inch black bird which played a special role in Hawaiian history. Its blazing yellow leg feathers were used to fashion the spectacular capes and helmets of the *ali'i*. Even before white people came, this bird was ruthlessly pursued by specially trained hunters who captured it and plucked its feathers. Finally there is the *akialoa,* a seven-inch greenish-yellow bird with a long, slender, curved bill.

Marine and Water Birds

Among the millions of birds that visit Kauai yearly, some of the most outstanding are its marine and water birds. Many beautiful individuals are seen at **Kilauea Point,** where they often nest in the trees on the cliff or on **Moku'ae'ae Islet.** Among them are the **Laysan albatross** *(moli),* which also nests along Barking Sands, the **wedge-tailed shearwater** *(ua'u kani),* and the **red-footed booby.** Kiting from the same cliffs is the **white-tailed tropic bird,** and one of the most amazing is the **great frigate bird,** which nests off Kilauea Point and are also seen along Kalalau Trail, and even at Poipu Beach.

Many of Kauai's waterbirds are most easily found in the marshes and ponds of Hanalei National Wildlife Refuge, though they have also been spotted at some of the island's reservoirs, especially at Menehune Fish Pond in the Huleia National Wildlife Refuge and its vicinity. Some that are seen are the **Hawaiian stilt** *(ae'o),* the **Hawaiian coot** *(alae ke'oke'o),* the **Hawaiian gallinule** *(alae'ula),* and the **Hawaiian duck** *(koloa maoli).*

Introduced Common Birds

Kauai is rich in all manner of birds, from migratory marine birds to upland forest dwellers. Many live in areas you can visit; others you can see by taking a short stroll and remaining observant. Some, of course, are rare and very difficult to spot. Some of the most easily spotted island birds frequent almost all areas from the Kekaha Salt Ponds to Kalalau and the upland regions of Koke'e, including the blazing red **northern cardinal;** the comedic, brash **common mynah;** the operatic **western meadowlark,** introduced in 1930 and found in Hawaii only on Kauai; the ubiquitous **Japanese white eye;** sudden fluttering flocks of **house finches;** that Arctic traveler the **golden plover,** found along mudflats everywhere; the **cattle egret,** a white, 20-inch-tall heron found anywhere from the backs of cattle to the lids of garbage cans.

Introduced Fauna and Game Animals

One terribly destructive predator of native ground-nesting birds is the **mongoose.** Introduced to Hawaii last century as a cure for a rat infestation, the mongoose has only recently made it to Kauai, where a vigorous monitoring and extermination process is underway. Game mammals found in Kauai's forests include feral goats and pigs, although they too have caused destruction by uprooting seedlings and by overgrazing shrubs and grasses. Game fowl that have successfully acclimatized include francolins, ring-necked pheasants, and an assortment of quail and dove.

One game animal found in Hawaii only on Kauai is the **black-tailed deer.** Kauai's thriving herd of 700 started as a few orphaned fawns from Oregon in 1961. These handsome animals, a species of western mule deer, are at home on the hilly slopes west of Waimea Canyon. Although there is little noticeable change in seasons in Hawaii, bucks and does continue to operate on genetically transmitted biological time clocks. The males shed their antlers during late winter months and the females give birth in spring.

HISTORY

Kauai is the first of the Hawaiian islands in many ways. Besides being the oldest main island geologically, it's believed that Kauai was the first island to be populated by Polynesian explorers. Theoretically, this colony was well established as early as A.D. 200, which predates the populating of the other islands by almost 500 years. Even Madame Pele chose Kauai as her first home and was content here until her sister drove her away. Her fires went out when she moved on, but she, like all visitors, never forgot Kauai.

Written History

The written history of Hawaii began when Capt. James Cook sailed into Waimea Bay on Kauai's south shore on the afternoon of September 20, 1778, and opened Hawaii to the rest of the world. In the years just preceding Cook's discovery, Hawaii was undergoing a unique change. Kamehameha the Great, a chief of the Big Island, was in the process of conquering the islands and uniting them under his rule. King Kaumualii of Kauai was able to remain independent from Kamehameha's rule by his use of diplomacy, guile, and the large distances separating his island from the others. Finally, after all the other islands had been subjugated, Kaumualii joined Kamehameha through negotiations, not warfare; he retained control of Kauai by being made governor of the island by Kamehameha. After Kamehameha died, his successor, Kamehameha II, forced Kaumualii to go to Oahu, where arrangements were made for him to marry the great queen Kaahumanu, the favorite wife of Kamehameha, and the greatest surviving *ali'i* of the land. Kaumualii never returned to his native island.

Hawaii was in a great state of flux at the beginning of the 1800s. The missionaries were coming, along with adventurers and schemers from throughout Europe. One of the latter was George Scheffer, a Prussian in the service of Czar Nicholas of Russia. He convinced Kaumualii to build a Russian fort in Waimea in 1817, which Kaumualii saw as a means of discouraging other Europeans from overrunning his lands. A loose alliance was made between Kaumualii and Scheffer. The adventurer eventually lost the czar's support, and Kaumualii ran him off the island, but the remains of Fort Elizabeth still stand. Around the same time, George Kaumualii, the king's son who had been sent to Boston to be educated, was accompanying the first missionary packet to the islands. He came with Rev. Sam Whitney, whom Kaumualii invited to stay, and who planted the first sugar on the island and taught the natives to dig wells. Waioli Mission House, just north of Hanalei, dates from 1836 and is still standing as a museum. Nearby, Hanalei Bay was a commercial harbor for trading and whaling. From here, produce such as oranges were shipped from Na Pali farms to California. In Koloa, on the opposite end of the island, a stack from the Koloa Sugar plantation, started in 1835, marks the site of the first successful sugar-refining operation in the islands.

Another successful enterprise was Lihue Plantation. Founded by a German firm in 1850, it prospered until WW I, when anti-German sentiment forced the owners to sell out. In Lihue Town, you can still see the Haleko Shops, a cluster of four two-story buildings that show a strong German influence. If you go into the Lihue Lutheran Church you can view an ornate altar very similar to ones found in old German churches.

During the 1870s and '80s, leprosy raged throughout the kingdom and strong measures were taken. Those believed to be afflicted were wrenched from their families and sent to the hideous colony of Kalaupapa on Molokai. One famous Kauaian leper, Koolau, born in 1862 in Kekaha, refused to be brought in and took his family to live in the mountain fortress of Na Pali. He fought the authorities for years and killed all those sent to take him in. He was made popular by Jack London in his short story, "Koolau, the Leper."

When WW II came to Hawaii, Nawiliwili Harbor was shelled on December 31, 1941, but there was little damage. The island remained much the same, quiet and rural until the late 1960s when development began in earnest. The first resort destination on the island was the Coco Palms Hotel in Wailua, followed by development in Poipu, and more in Princeville. Meanwhile, Hollywood had discovered Kauai and featured its haunting beauty as a "silent star" in dozens of major films. Today, development goes on, but the island remains quiet, serene, and beautiful.

GOVERNMENT

Kauai County

Kauai County is composed of the inhabited islands of Kauai and Niihau and the uninhabited islands of Kaula and Lehua. Lihue is the county seat. It's represented by two state senators elected from the 6th District—a split district includ-

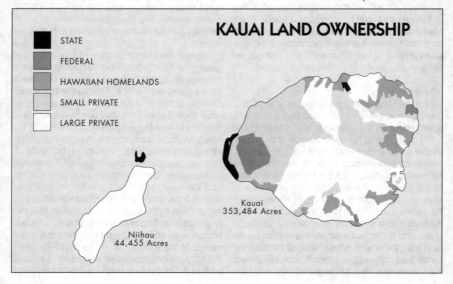

ing north Kauai and portions of the Kihei and Upcountry regions of Maui—and the 7th District, which includes all of southern Kauai and Niihau. Kauai has three state representatives—from the 12th District, which is again a split district with north Kauai and eastern Maui; the 13th District around Lihue; and the 14th District, which includes all of southwestern Kauai and Niihau. The current mayor of Kauai is Maryanne W. Kusaka, a Republican who won a second term of office in 1998.

ECONOMY

The economy of Kauai, like that of the entire state, is based on agriculture, the military, and tourism, the fastest-growing sector.

Tourism

Kauai, in a tight race with the Big Island, is the fourth most visited island. Regaining momentum after Hurricane Iniki, it is once again attracting about one million visitors annually. When completely recovered, approximately 6,800 hotel and condo units will be available, and the current accommodations now averaging a 70% occupancy rate. At one time, Kauai was the most difficult island on which to build a resort because of a strong grassroots antidevelopment faction. This trend has been changing due to the recession that hit everyone after Hurricane Iwa and then Iniki scared off many tourists. Island residents realized how much their livelihood was tied to tourism, and a recent ad campaign depicting tourists as visitors (rather than unwelcome invaders) has helped in their acceptance. Also, the resorts being built on Kauai are first rate, and the developers are savvy enough to create "destination areas" instead of more high-rise boxes of rooms.

Agriculture

Agriculture still accounts for a hefty portion of Kauai's income, although **sugar,** once the backbone of the agricultural economy, has taken a

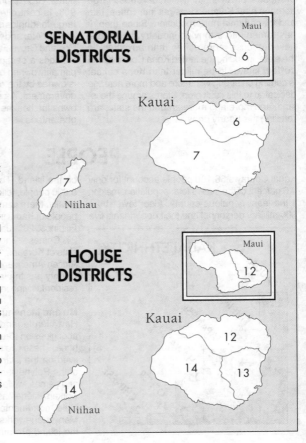

downward trend and as of 1996 is no longer grown commercially on the island. Kauai produces about six percent of the state's diversified agricultural crop, with a strong yield in **papayas.** In 1982, California banned the importation of Kauai's papayas because they were sprayed with EDB, a fumigant used to control fruit flies. The chemical is no longer used, and the papaya market has rebounded. Hanalei Valley and many other smaller areas produce five million pounds of taro, which is quickly turned into poi, and the county produces two million pounds of guavas, as well as pineapples, beef, and pork for its own use. A growing aquaculture industry produces prawns. In the mid-1980s, large acreage near Kalaheo was put into coffee, tea, and macadamia nut production. Since then, it has turned into a thriving industry, and Kauai now produces more coffee than anywhere in the state, including the famed Kona Coast. **Kauai coffee,** known to be milder than Kona coffee, is coming on strong with more and more acreage dedicated to this cash crop. Stores around the island, and more and more around the state, are retailing this hearty brew.

Military

The military influence on Kauai is small but vital. NASA's major tracking facilities in Koke'e Park were turned over to the Navy and Air Force. At **Barking Sands,** the Navy operates BARSTUR, an underwater tactical range for training in anti-submarine warfare. Also along Barking Sands (a fitting name!) is the **Barking Sands Pacific Missile Range,** operated by the Navy but available to the Air Force, Department of Defense, NASA, and the Department of Energy.

Land Ownership

Of Kauai's total usable land area of 353,484 acres, 62% is privately owned. Of this, almost 90% is controlled by only half a dozen or so large landholders, mainly Gay and Robinson, Amfac, Alexander and Baldwin, C. Brewer and Co., and Grove Farm. The remaining 38%, which includes a section of Hawaiian Homelands, is primarily owned by the state, and a small portion is owned by the county of Kauai and the federal government. As everywhere in Hawaii, no one owns the beaches and public access to them is guaranteed.

PEOPLE

Kauai County's 56,100 people account for only 4.6 percent of the state's total population, making it the least populous county. Also, fewer than 300 military personnel and their dependents live

on the island. The largest town is Kapa'a with 8,200 people, followed by Lihue with 5,500. Ethnically, there is no clear majority on Kauai. The people of Kauai include: 35% Caucasians, 25% Filipinos, 20% Japanese, 15% Hawaiians, and 2% Chinese. The remaining three percent consists of Koreans, Samoans, and a smattering of African-Americans and Native Americans. Kauai County has the largest percentage (45%) of its residents living in rural areas.

Mu and Menehune

Hawaiian legends give accounts of dwarflike aborigines on Kauai called the Mu and the Menehune. These two hirsute tribes were said to have lived on the island before and after the arrival of the Polynesians. The Mu were fond of jokes and games, while the Menehune were dedicated workers, stonemasons par excellence, who could build monumental structures in just one night. Many stoneworks that can still be seen around the island are attributed to these hardworking nocturnal people, and a wonderfully educational exhibit concerning them is presented at the Kauai Museum.

Anthropological theory supports the legends that say that some non-Polynesian peoples actually did exist on Kauai. According to oral history, their chief felt that too much interplay and intermarriage was occurring with the Polynesians. He wished his race to remain pure so he ordered them to leave on a "triple-decker floating island," and they haven't been seen since—though if you ask a Kauaian whether he or she believes in the Menehune, the answer is likely to be, "Of course not! But they're there, anyway." Speculation holds that they may have been an entirely different race of people, or perhaps the remaining tribes of the first Polynesians. It's possible that they were cut off from the original culture for so long they developed their own separate culture, and the food supply became so diminished their very stature became reduced in comparison to other Polynesians.

SPORTS AND RECREATION

Kauai is an exciting island for all types of sports enthusiasts, with golf, tennis, hunting, fresh- and saltwater fishing, and all manner of water sports. You can rent horses, camp and hike the hidden reaches of the Na Pali coast, or simply relax on a cruise. The following should start the fun rolling. For ocean and helicopter tours see **Sightseeing Tours.**

Kauai is very hospitable to campers and hikers. More than a dozen state and county parks offer camping, and a network of trails leads into the interior. There are different types of camping to suit everyone: you can drive right up to your spot at a convenient beach park, or hike for a day through incredible country to build your campfire in total seclusion. A profusion of "secret beaches" have unofficial camping, and the State Division of Forestry even maintains free campsites along its many trails. Koke'e State Park provides affordable self-contained cabins. RV camping is permitted only at Koke'e and Polihale state parks, and at Haena, Hanamaulu, and Niumalu county parks.

Hikers can take the Kalalau Trail—perhaps the premier hiking experience in Hawaii—or go topside to Koke'e and follow numerous paths to breathtaking views over the bared-teeth cliffs of Na Pali. Hunting trails follow many of the streams into the interior; or, if you don't mind mud and rain, you can pluck your way across the Alakai Swamp (boardwalk under construction). Wherever you go, enjoy but don't destroy, and leave the land as beautiful as you find it.

Polihale State Park

CAMPING

General Information

All the campgrounds, except for the state parks along Na Pali, provide grills, pavilions (some with electricity), picnic tables, cold-water showers, and drinking water. No one can camp "under the stars" at official campgrounds; all must have a tent. Campsites are unattended, so be careful with your gear—especially radios, stereos, and cameras (your tent and sleeping bag are generally okay). Always be prepared for wind and rain, especially along the north shore.

Note: Recently, the police have been aggressively issuing tickets and fines of $50-300 for illegal camping, especially along North Shore beaches. Multiple offenders can even be sentenced to 30 days in jail. *Sometimes* they will merely issue a warning, but definitely do not count on it!

County Parks

A permit is required for camping at all county-maintained parks. The cost is $3 per person per day, children under 18 free if accompanied by parent or guardian. Permits are good for four nights, with one renewal possible, for a total of seven nights per campground. Camping is limited to 60 days total in any one-year period. The permit-issuing office is the Division of Parks and Recreation, 4444 Rice St., Suite 150, Lihue, HI 96766, tel. (808) 241-6670, open Mon.-Fri. 8 a.m.-5 p.m. At all other times, including weekends and holidays, you can pick up your permit at the Kauai Police Department, Lihue Branch, 3060 Umi St., tel. (808) 245-9711. Write in advance for information and reservations, but do not send money. They'll send you an application. Return it with the appropriate information, and your request will be logged in their reservations book. You'll also receive brochures and maps of the campgrounds. When you arrive, you must pick up

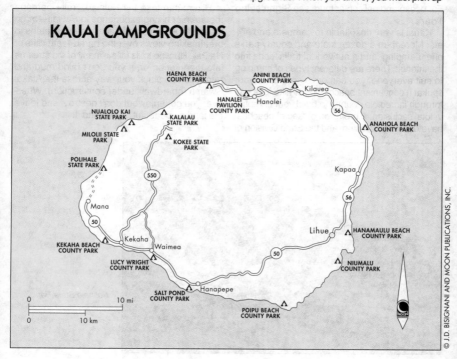

KAUAI CAMPGROUNDS

HAENA BEACH COUNTY PARK
ANINI BEACH COUNTY PARK
Kilauea
HANALEI PAVILION COUNTY PARK
Hanalei
NUALOLO KAI STATE PARK
KALALAU STATE PARK
56
MILOLII STATE PARK
KOKEE STATE PARK
ANAHOLA BEACH COUNTY PARK
POLIHALE STATE PARK
550
Kapaa
Mana
56
50
Lihue
HANAMAULU BEACH COUNTY PARK
KEKAHA BEACH COUNTY PARK
Kekaha
Waimea
NIUMALU COUNTY PARK
LUCY WRIGHT COUNTY PARK
50
SALT POND COUNTY PARK
Hanapepe
0   10 mi
0   10 km
POIPU BEACH COUNTY PARK

and pay for your permit at the Parks and Recreation office or the police station.

State Parks

A camping permit (free) is required at all state parks. Camping is restricted to five nights within a 30-day period per campground, with a two- and three-night maximum at some of the stopovers along the Kalalau Trail. You can pick up the permits at the Dept. of Land and Natural Resources (DLNR), Division of State Parks, 3060 Eiwa St., Room 306, Lihue, HI 96766, tel. (808) 274-3444. Permits can be picked up Mon.-Fri. 8 a.m.-4 p.m. only. *No* permits will be issued without proper identification. You can write well in advance for permits which will be mailed to you, but you must include photocopies of identification for each camper over 18. Children under 18 will not be issued a permit, and they must be accompanied by an adult. Allow at least one month for the entire process, and no reservations are guaranteed without at least a seven-day notice. Include name, dates, number of campers (with ID photocopies!), and numbers of tents.

Camping is allowed at Koke'e State Park, and the **Koke'e Lodge** also provides self-contained housekeeping cabins. They are furnished with stoves, refrigerators, hot showers, cooking and eating utensils, bedding, and linen; wood is available for the fireplaces. The cabins vary from one large room that accommodates three, to two-bedroom units that sleep seven. The cabins are tough to get on holidays, during trout-fishing season (August and September), and during the wild plum harvest in June and July. For reservations write Koke'e Lodge, P.O. Box 819, Waimea, Kauai, HI 96796, tel. (808) 335-6061. Please include a SASE, number of people, and dates requested. One night's deposit is required for confirmation of reservation. Full payment is required within two weeks of making reservations. Write well in advance. Check-in is from 2 p.m. (call if you will arrive after 5 p.m.), checkout is before 11 a.m. The lodge is open Mon.-Thurs. 8:30 a.m.-5:30 p.m., and until 10 p.m. Friday and Saturday. Breakfast and lunch are served daily, while dinner is available Friday and Saturday 6-9 p.m. The lodge has a bar and small shop selling sundries and snacks. The nearest town, Kekaha, is 15 miles down the mountain, on the coast.

HIKING

More than 90% of Kauai is inaccessible by road, making it a backpackers' paradise. Treks range from overnighters requiring superb fitness and preparedness to 10-minute nature loops just outside your car door. Most trails are well marked and maintained, and all reward you with a swimming hole, waterfall, panoramic overlook, or botanical or historical information.

Through its various divisions, the Department of Land and Natural Resources, 3060 Eiwa St., Lihue, Kauai, HI 96766, provides free detailed maps and descriptions of most trails. For state park trails (Kalalau and Koke'e), direct letters to the Department's Division of State Parks; for forest reserve trails, the Division of Forestry; for hunting trails, the Division of Fish and Game.

Tips and Warnings

Many trails are used by hunters after wild boar, deer, or game birds. Oftentimes the forest reserve trails, maintained by the State Division of Forestry, have a check-in station at the trailhead. Trekkers and hunters must sign a logbook, especially if they intend to use the camping areas along the trails. The comments by previous hikers are worth reading for up-to-the-minute information on trail conditions. Many roads leading to the trailheads are marked for 4WD vehicles only. Heed the warning, especially during rainy weather, when roads are very slick and swollen streams can swallow your rental car. Also remember that going in may be fine, but a sudden storm can leave you stranded.

Maps of the trails are usually only available in Lihue from the various agencies, not at trailheads. Water found along the trails is unsafe to drink unless treated, so carry your own or drink only from catchment barrels. Expect wind and rain at any time along the coast or in the interior. Make sure to log in at the check-in stations and leave your itinerary. A few minutes of filling in forms could save your life. Never attempt to climb up or down a *pali* while hiking. For example, you *cannot* go from Koke'e down to the valleys of Na Pali. Every now and again someone attempts it and is killed. The cliffs are impossibly steep and brittle, and your handholds and footholds will break from under you. Don't be foolish.

If you're going into the Alakai Swamp, remember that all the birds and flora you encounter are unique, and most of them are fighting extinction. Also, your clothes will become permanently stained with swamp mud—a wonderful memento of your trip. Before attempting any of the trails, please sign in at park headquarters.

Eastern Kauai Trails
A number of trails can be hiked in the mountains behind Wailua. Most start off Rt. 580, which parallels the Wailua River. These hikes provide fantastic vistas from Nonou Mountain, known as the Sleeping Giant, and are covered in the **Wailua** chapter.

Na Pali Coast Trails
No roads penetrate the Na Pali Coast area, but trailheads are accessible from either end of the road. From the southwest approach, you can access trails that head east from Koke'e State Park to the coast. This area is covered in the **Southwest Kauai** chapter. Approaching the Na Pali Coast from the northeast gives you access to *the* premier hiking experience on Kauai, the **Kalalau Trail.** It not only leads you physically along the Na Pali Coast, but back in time to classic romantic Hawaii. The Kalalau is a destination in and of itself, and those who have walked these phenomenal 11 miles never forget it. This hike is covered at the end of the **North Shore** chapter.

Rental Equipment and Sales
Na Pali Outfitters, a division of Kayak Kauai, P.O. Box 508, Hanalei, HI 96714, tel. (808) 826-9844, and in Kapa'a at tel. (808) 822-9179, open daily 8 a.m.-5 p.m., sells and rents camping equipment. At both locations you can find all sorts of camping gear including metal cups and dishes, insect repellent, backpacks, day packs, ground cloths, camping gas, candles, and tube tents.

Pedal and Paddle, tel. (808) 826-9069, in Hanalei's Ching Young Center, open daily 9 a.m.-5 p.m. in winter, 9 a.m.-6 p.m. in summer, rents and sells backpacking equipment. Rental rates are two-person dome tent $10 a day, $30 a week; backpack $5 and $20; light blanket $3 and $10; and day packs $4 and $12. A rental day begins at the time you rent and ends at 5 p.m. the following day. Bikes, snorkel gear, surfboards, and boogie boards are also available.

The **Wainiha Store,** just a few miles before the beginning of the Kalalau Trail, open daily 9:30 a.m.-6:30 p.m., tel. (808) 826-6251, sells few supplies and sundries. Campers and cyclists heading down the Kalalau Trail can store bags here for $2 per bag per day and bikes for $5 a day. A three-day camping equipment package including tent, lantern, stove, utensils, and backpack is $30 (no sleeping bags). Remember that camping permits must be picked up at the DLNR at the State Building way back in Lihue.

Other camping supply outlets are **Dan's Sports Shop,** in the Kukui Grove Center, tel. (808) 246-0151, and **Jungle Bob's,** in Hanalei, tel. (808) 826-6664. Also try the very local **Mandala Store,** at 3122 Kuhio Hwy. in Lihue, which carries mosquito nets and hammocks.

SWIMMING AND BEACHES

With so many beaches to choose from, the problem on Kauai is picking which one to visit. If you venture farther than the immediate area of your hotel, the following will give you some help in deciding just where you'd like to romp about. This is a simple listing only. For more details see the specific listings in the appropriate travel chapters.

Lihue Area Beaches
Kalapaki Beach in Lihue is one of the best on the island, and convenient to Kauai's principal town center. This beach's gentle wave action is just right for learning how to bodysurf or ride the boogie board; snorkeling is fair. Two small crescent beaches lie just below the lighthouse at the far end of the beach. Water is rougher there, with much exposed rock; snorkeling should be done on calm days only. Also accessible but less frequented is **Hanamaulu Bay,** just up the coast, with a lagoon, picnic spots, and camping (with permit) at **Ahukini Recreation Pier State Park.**

Kapa'a, Wailua, and Vicinity
Like its accommodations, the beaches of Wailua are few but very good. **Lydgate Beach** has two

lava pools, and the beaches below Wailua Municipal Golf Course offer seclusion in sheltered coves where there's fine snorkeling. **Waipouli Beach** and **Kapa'a Beach** flank the well-developed town of Kapa'a, while out along a cane road near Pohakuloa is the little-frequented **Donkey Beach,** known for its good surfing and snorkeling. The undertow is quite strong at Donkey Beach so don't venture out too far if you don't swim well. (A permit issued by the Lihue Sugar Co. is technically necessary—and advised—to use the cane road.)

Anahola Beach, at the south end of Anahola Bay, has safe swimming in a protected cove, freshwater swimming in the stream that empties into the bay, picnicking, and camping (with permit). Snorkel a short distance up the shore to where the reef comes in close—an area where locals come for shore fishing. Still farther north is **Moloa'a Beach,** a little-visited half-moon swath of sand.

North Kauai Beaches

Just south of Kilauea is **Secret Beach,** all that its name implies. At the end of a tiny dirt road, the start of which eludes many people, is a huge stretch of white sand. You're sure to find it nearly empty. Camping is good, and no one is around to bother you. North of town is **Kalihiwai Beach,** great for swimming and bodysurfing during the right conditions. People camp in the ironwood trees that line the beach. There is a park at **Anini Beach,** a great place to snorkel as it has the longest exposed reef in Kauai, and a wonderful place to learn windsurfing because of the shallow water inside the reef.

Hanalei Bay is a prime spot on the north coast. Swim at the mouth of the Hanalei River (but watch out for boats) or on the far side of the bay. Experienced surfers ride the waves below the Sheraton; snorkeling is good closer to the cliffs. West of Hanalei is **Lumahai Beach,** a beautiful curve of white sand backed by cliffs and thick jungle that was the silent star of the movie *South Pacific.* The inviting water here has a fierce riptide, so enter only when the water is calm. **Haena Beach** and nearby **Tunnels** are terrific swimming and snorkeling spots.

At the end of the road is **Ke'e Beach,** a popular place with some amenities and good swimming in summer with adequate snorkeling. Many secluded beaches at the foot of the Na Pali cliffs dot the coast to the west along the Kalalau Trail. **Hanakapi'ai Beach** is reached after one hour on the trail and is fine for sunbathing; the water, especially in winter, can be torturous so stay out. **Kalalau Beach** is a full day's hike down this spectacular coast, while some beaches here can only be reached by boat.

South Kauai Beaches

The **Poipu Beach** area is the most developed on the island—accommodating, tame, and relaxing. You can swim, snorkel, and bodysurf here to your heart's content.

Down the coast are **Salt Pond Beach,** one of the island's best and good for swimming and windsurfing, and **Pakala Beach,** popular with surfers but also good for swimming and snorkeling. The golden strand of **Kekaha Beach** runs for miles with excellent swimming, snorkeling, and surfing, and stretches into Barking Sands Pacific Military Base, where you can go, with permission, for good views of Niihau when no military exercises are in progress.

Polihale Beach is the end of the road. Swimming is not the best as the surf is high and the undertow strong, but walk along the shore for a view of the south end of the great Na Pali cliffs.

SCUBA AND SNORKELING

The best beaches for snorkeling and scuba are along the northeast coast from Anahola to Ke'e. The reefs off Poipu, roughed up by Hurricane Iwa and Iniki, are making a remarkable comeback. Those interested can buy or rent equipment in area dive shops and department stores. Sometimes condos and hotels offer snorkeling equipment free to their guests, but if you have to rent it, don't do it from a hotel or condo; go to a dive shop where it's much cheaper—about $5 per day, $15 per week. Scuba divers can rent gear for $50-60 from most shops. To get just what you need at the right price, be sure to call ahead and ask for particulars about what each company offers.

Scuba/Snorkel Rentals

The following full-service shops rent and sell scuba and snorkel equipment, and most offer scuba certification courses.

Kauai Water Ski and Surf Co., in the Kinipopo Shopping Village, 4-356 Kuhio Hwy., Kapa'a, HI 96746, tel. (808) 822-3574, open daily 9 a.m.-7 p.m., is a complete water-sports shop that offers snorkel gear by the day or week.

Aquatic Adventures, at 4-1380 Kuhio Hwy., Kapa'a, HI 96746, tel. (808) 822-1434, open Mon.-Fri. 7:30 a.m.-7 p.m. and Sat.-Sun. 7:30 a.m.-5 p.m., owned and operated by Janet Moore, is a dive shop offering rentals, excursions, and certification courses.

Also in Kapa'a, **Bubbles Below,** tel. (808) 822-3483, runs the most unusual dives (and perhaps the most expensive); they go to Lehua Island off Niihau—diving there, where the water is clear to depths of more than 100 feet, is tops. Or you might try **Sunrise Diving Adventures,** tel. (808) 822-7333.

The second concentration of dive shops is in Koloa. **Fathom Five Divers,** about 100 yards past the left-hand turn to Poipu, tel. (808) 742-6991 or (800) 972-3078, open daily 9 a.m.-6 p.m., owned and operated by Karen Long-Olsen, is a complete diving center offering lessons, certification, and rentals. Two-tank boat dives for certified divers, including gear, are $95, or $79 if you have your own equipment. Introductory dives, lesson and gear included, are $129; and a one-tank shore dive is $64. Certification courses take five days and average about $359 (group); tank refills are also available. Fathom Five also does half-day snorkeling cruises that include lessons and gear for $64. Snorkel rental is $5 per day, $15 per week.

Sea Sports Divers, at Poipu Plaza, 2827 Poipu Rd., tel. (808) 742-9303 or (800) 685-5889, is a scuba/snorkel/surf shop. Rentals include snorkel masks, fins, and snorkels all for $5 per hour, $15 per day (includes complimentary lesson), $30 for a reef tour; surfboards for $5-10 per hour, $15-20 per day, depending on quality (surfing lessons are $30). A two-tank introductory scuba dive runs $110, a one-tank certified dive $75, and a three-day certification course $395 (dive video available at $39.95). Sea Sports Kauai is also a sports boutique with boogie boards, surfboards, underwater equipment, T-shirts, sandals, and unique bags in the form of sharks and colorful reef fish.

The **Captain's Cargo Company,** 9984 Kaumuali'i Hwy. (Rt. 50), Waimea, tel. (808) 338-

0333, and office of **Liko Kauai Cruises,** is operated by Debra Hookano, wife of Captain Liko. Rental rates are $2 per hour, $5 per day for mask, fins, and snorkel.

Sea Fun, P.O. Box 3002, Lihue, HI 96766, tel. (808) 245-6400 or (800) 452-1113, offers guided snorkeling tours, wetsuits, optical masks, an optional video of your adventure, and juices and snacks.

Good old **Snorkel Bob,** at 4480 Ahukini Rd., in Lihue on the way to the airport, tel. (808) 245-9433, and also in old Koloa Town along Poipu Beach Rd., tel. (808) 742-2206, offers some of the best deals for snorkel rental in Hawaii (and free snorkeling maps and advice). Basic gear is $14 per week; better, silicone gear is $19-29, or $2.50 to $6.50 a day; boogie boards run $4.50-6.50 daily, $15-26 weekly. If you'll be island hopping, Snorkel Bob allows you to take the gear with you and drop it off at a Snorkel Bob location on the next island.

Other shops are **Ocean Odyssey,** tel. (808) 245-8661; and **Hanalei Surf Co.,** tel. (808) 826-9000, in Hanalei.

For additional information about scuba diving and diving clubs in Hawaii, contact **Hawaii Council of Dive Clubs,** P.O. Box 298, Honolulu, HI 96809.

Snuba Tours of Kauai, tel. (808) 823-8912, offers an underwater adventure free of the normal scuba tanks. You are tethered to a sea sled that carries the tanks. Depth is limited, but the fun isn't. Tours conducted off of Poipu's Lawai Beach cost $55

SURFING, SAILBOARDING, AND BOOGIE BOARDING

Surfing has long been the premier water sport in Hawaii. Locals, and now "surfies" from all over the world, know where the best waves are and when they come. While Anahola Beach was a traditional surfing spot for Hawaiians of yesterday, the north shore has the beaches of choice today. The east side of Hanalei Bay provides a good roll in winter for experts, as does Tunnels. Quarry Beach, near Kilauea, and Donkey Beach, north of Kapa'a, are used mostly by locals. On the south coast, the surfers' favorite is the area in front of the Waiohai Resort, or west of there near

Pakala. Listen to local advice as to where and when to ride and why. The sea is unforgiving—and particularly unpredictable in winter.

Surfing lessons are available. Companies offering them include **Mike Smith International Surfing School,** tel. (808) 245-3882; world champion **Margo Oberg**'s school on Poipu Beach, tel. (808) 742-6411 or 742-1750; and **Garden Island Windsurfing,** tel. (808) 826-9005, where Nancy Palmer offers surfing lessons at the Lawai Beach Resort.

Kauai Water Ski and Surf Co., tel. (808) 822-3574, open daily 9 a.m.-7 p.m., in the Kinipopo Shopping Village, 4-356 Kuhio Hwy., Wailua, HI 96746, is a complete water-sports shop that offers surfboard and boogie-board rentals by the day or week.

Sea Sports Kauai, located at the Poipu Plaza, 2827 Poipu Rd., tel. (808) 742-9303 or (800) 685-5889, offers rental boards and surfing lessons.

In Poipu, **Sea Star,** tel. (808) 332-8189, rents windsurfing gear (rack included) but does not offer lessons.

Hanalei Surf Co., tel. (808) 826-9000, just a few minutes from a great beginners' surfing area at Hanalei, offers surfing lessons or board rentals without lessons (boogie boards, too). Hanalei Bay goes completely flat in summer, so call ahead for surfing conditions.

The **Captain's Cargo Company,** 9984 Kaumuali'i Hwy. (Rt. 50), tel. (808) 338-0333, which is also the office of **Liko Kauai Cruises,** rents and sells surfboards and boogie boards. Rental rates are $5 per hour or $15 per day for boogie boards, $5 and $20 for surfboards.

Pedal and Paddle, tel. (808) 826-9069, in Hanalei's Ching Young Center, open daily 9 a.m.-5 p.m. in winter and 9 a.m.-6 p.m. in summer, rents body boards with fins for $8 a day, $25 a week; surfboards for $12 and $36.

Windsurfing

Windsurfing has become very popular on Kauai in the last few years. The best spots for beginners are at Anini Beach on the north coast, and Poipu Beach on the south. For the advanced only, Haena Beach on the north coast is preferred.

For windsurfing rental gear and other beach rentals and sales, contact **Hanalei Sailboards,** tel. (808) 826-9733; they're the best in the business.

Anini Beach Wind Surf Company, P.O. Box 1602, Hanalei, HI 96714, tel. (808) 826-9463, is a one-man operation. Owner Keith Kabe will load his truck with windsurfing gear and come to you. Keith is well known on the North Shore, buys and sells equipment, and will tailor your windsurfing lesson to fit your ability. Call for an appointment and to arrange a time and place for your windsurfing adventure.

Wind Surf Kauai, owned by Celeste Harvel, P.O. Box 323, Hanalei, HI 96714, tel. (808) 828-6838, specializes in beginner lessons. Three-hour group lessons (six people maximum) are $60 with equipment (individual lessons, too).

Also contact **Sand People,** tel. (808) 826-6981, in Hanalei; **Kalapaki Beach Center,** tel. (808) 245-5595, in Nawiliwili; **Ray's Rentals and Activities,** 1345 Kuhio Hwy., downtown Kapa'a, tel. (808) 822-5700; or any of the sports shops on the island.

WATER-SKIING

When you think of recreation on Kauai, water-skiing might not necessarily come to mind. **Kauai Water Ski and Surf Co.** tel. (808) 822-3574, open daily 9 a.m.-7 p.m., in the Kinipopo Shopping Village, 4-356 Kuhio Hwy., Wailua, HI 96746, has established itself as the main water-skiing company. Skimming placid Wailua River, freshwater skiers pass tour boats going to and from the Fern Grotto. Water-skiing fees include boat, driver, gas, skis, and other equipment; instruction at all levels can be arranged. They also sell beach clothes and water sports equipment. Rentals include kayaks, surfboards, boogie boards, and snorkel equipment. Inquire here about the Terheggen International Ski Club.

POWER GLIDING

Birds in Paradise, tel. (808) 639-1067, instructs you how to soar above the emerald green and azure blue of Kauai in a 70 horsepower ultra-light power glider. Instructor Gerry Charleboiss has thrilled more than 2,000 brave and slightly wacky souls in the skies above Kauai. He describes his apparently skyworthy craft as a "motorcycle with wings." Safety features include a backup rocket parachute that will bring the entire craft safely to the ground, and a surprising structural strength certified twice as strong as a Cessna and capable of withstanding six Gs positive load and three Gs negative. This state-of-the-art tandem glider needs only about 100 feet for take off and landing, and Gerry has mounted both a video and a still camera so you can write back home, "Look, Mom. No hands"—and, as she's always said, not much sense either. For those who enjoy pushing the envelope in a contraption soaring at 55 mph, prices are $75 for

KAUAI GOLF COURSES

COURSES	PAR	YARDS	FEES	CART	CLUB RENTAL
Grove Farm Golf Course at Puakea 4315 Kalepa St. Lihue, HI 96766 tel. (808) 245-8756	40 (10 holes)	3,500	$35 (10) $60 (20)	incl.	$15 (10) $25 (20)
Kauai Lagoons Resort 3351 Hoolaulea Way Lihue, HI 96766 tel. (808) 241-6000 or (800) 634-6400					
Kiele Course	72	6,164	$145	incl.	$30
Lagoons Course	72	6,136	$100	incl.	$30
Kiahuna Golf Club 2545 Kiahuna Plantation Dr. Koloa, HI 96756 tel. (808) 742-9595	70	5,631	$65	incl.	$30
Kukui O Lono Golf Course 854 Puu Road Kalaheo, HI 96741 tel. (808) 332-9151	36	2,981	$7	$6	$6
Princeville Golf Club, Makai Courses P.O. Box 3040 Princeville, HI 96722 tel. (808) 826-3580 or (800) 826-4400					
Ocean Course	36	3,157	$115	incl.	$30
Woods Course	36	3,208	$115	incl.	$30
Lake Course	36	3,149	$115	incl.	$30
Princeville Golf Club, Prince Course P.O. Box 3040 Princeville, HI 96722 tel. (808) 826-5000 or (800) 826-4400	72	6,521	$150	incl.	$30
Poipu Bay Resort Golf Course 2250 Ainako St. Koloa, HI 96756 tel. (808) 742-8711 or (800) 856-6300	72	6,499	$140	incl.	$35-55
Wailua Municipal Golf Course P.O. Box 1017 Kapa'a, HI 96746 tel. (808) 241-6666	72	6,585	$20	$14	$15 $30 (weekends)

30 minutes, $150 for one hour, and $250 for a tailor-made flight of more than two hours.

GOLF

Kauai offers varied and exciting golfing around the island. Kukui O Lono Golf Course, a mountaintop course in Kalaheo, is never crowded and is worth visiting just to see the gardens. Wailua Municipal Golf Course is a public course with a reasonable greens fee, considered excellent by visitors and residents. Princeville boasts 46 magnificent holes sculpted around Hanalei Bay. A favorite for years, Kauai Lagoons Golf Club has recently added Kiele Course, designed by Jack Nicklaus. In Poipu, Kiahuna Golf Course and the new Poipu Bay Resort Golf Course, designed by Robert Trent Jones Jr., are fabulous courses.

Oftentimes, if you are a guest of one of the hotels affiliated with a golf course, you are offered guest golfing rates at substantial savings. Also worth checking out is the **Kauai Golf Challenge,** a booklet of coupons that allows you to golf at Princeville's Prince Course, the Lagoons Kiele Course, and the Poipu Bay Resort Golf Course for reduced rates.

TENNIS

The accompanying chart lists private and public tennis courts. Many hotel tennis courts are open to nonguests, usually for a fee. The Mirage Princeville Tennis Club has a few clay courts for those who prefer that surface.

BICYCLING

Riding a bike around Kauai is fairly easy, thanks to the lack of big hills—except for the road up to Koke'e State Park. Traffic is moderate, especially in the cool of early morning, when it's best

KAUAI TENNIS COURTS

COUNTY COURTS

Under jurisdiction of the Department of Parks and Recreation, P.O. Box 111, Lihue, HI 96766, tel. (808) 245-4751. Courts listed are in Lihue and near the Wailua and Poipu areas. There are also additional private locations around the island.

TOWN	LOCATION	NO. OF COURTS	LIGHTED
Hanapepe	next to stadium	2	Yes
Kalahea	Kalawai Park	2	Yes
Kapaa	New Park	2	Yes
Kekaha	next to park	2	Yes
Koloa	next to fire station	2	Yes
Lihue	next to convention hall	2	Yes
Wailua	Wailua Park	4	Yes
Waimea	next to high school	4	Yes

HOTEL AND PRIVATE COURTS THAT ARE OPEN TO THE PUBLIC

TOWN	LOCATION	NO. OF COURTS	LIGHTED
Hanalei	Hanalei Bay Resort	8	Yes
Kapaa	Aston Kauai Beachboy	1	No
Poipu	Hyatt Regency	4	Yes
	Poipu Kai Resort (fee for nonguests)	9	No
Poipu Beach	Kiahuna Tennis Club (fee)	10	Yes
Princeville	Princeville Resort Tennis Club	6	No

for making some distance. Roads are generally good, but shoulders aren't wide and are sometimes nonexistent. Peak season brings a dramatic increase in traffic and road congestion. Take care! Perhaps the best riding is by mountain bike on the cane haul roads that head into the interior.

Outfitters Kauai, an ecology-minded sports shop specializing in kayaking and mountain biking, is owned and operated by Rick and Julie Havilend in the Poipu Plaza, at 2827-A Poipu Rd., P.O. Box 1149, Poipu Beach, HI 96756, tel. (808) 742-9667, open Mon.-Sat. 9 a.m.-5 p.m. and Sunday by arrangement. Their Poipu "interpretive bike course," self-guided with map and narrative information, is $20-33, depending upon the grade of bicycle chosen ($35 tandem). Mountain-bike rentals include helmet and water bottles for $20 a day and up (multiday discounts). Biking and kayaking incidentals are also available for purchase along with Patagonia clothing. Bike/hike and bike/hike/snorkel tours are offered for $78 and $65.

An excellent choice is **Bicycle John's,** a full-service bicycle shop offering sales, repairs, and rentals. Located along Rt. 56 as you enter Lihue, tel. (808) 245-7579, the shop is open Mon.-Fri. 9 a.m.-5 p.m., Saturday 10 a.m.-4 p.m., and Sunday noon-4 p.m. Rental bicycles range from an 18-speed basic cruiser to a custom road bike, and prices range from $25 per day to $65 for four days with a price break for multiday rentals. You're not required to salute John Sargent, the **Bike Doctor,** in Hanalei, tel. (808) 826-7799, open Mon.-Sat. 9 a.m.-5 p.m., who has a shop stocked with everything for both casual and serious cyclists. John sells road bikes, sells and rents Marin mountain bikes, and offers special *wiki wiki* repair service to visiting cyclists whose equipment has broken down. Rental prices are $25 a day, $100 per seven-day week, including helmet, tool box, and water bottle. The Bike Doctor is intimately familiar with roads and trails all over the island and is happy to give advice on touring. Happy pedaling!

Bicycle Kauai, at 1379 Kuhio Hwy., Kapa'a, tel. (808) 822-3315, open Mon.-Fri. 9 a.m.-6 p.m., Saturday 9 a.m.-4 p.m., and Sunday 10 a.m.-3 p.m., is a complete bicycle shop with sales, repairs, helmets, riding clothes, and rentals. Trek mountain bikes are $20 per day or $100 per week, including helmet, lock, and a car rack. The staff is friendly and knowledgeable, offering plenty of advice on bike routes and where and when to ride.

Pedal and Paddle, tel. (808) 826-9069, in the Ching Young Center in Hanalei, open daily 9 a.m.-5 p.m. in winter, 9 a.m.-6 p.m. in summer, rents bicycles as well as camping gear, snorkel gear, and surfboards. Prices are $10 per day, $40 per week for a cruiser bike and $50 and $80 for a mountain bike; prices include lock, helmet, and car rack if desired.

Or try **Dan's Sport Shop,** tel. (808) 246-0151, a full-service sporting goods store located at the Kukui Grove Shopping Center.

Bicycle Tours
Outfitters Kauai, tel. (808) 742-9667, offers mountain bike and hike ecotours to Koke'e on Wednesday 7:30 a.m.-1:30 p.m., or by special arrangement. The 16-mile relaxed-pace ride contains a few vigorous climbs and focuses on the natural history of the area. Cold drinks and a full lunch are included for $78 per person. Rick and Julie are excellent athletes who know the mountains and seas of Kauai intimately. Their tours are educational as well as highly adventuresome; you couldn't find a better outfit to travel with.

HORSEBACK RIDING

One of the most exciting and intimate ways to discover Kauai is from atop a well-trained horse. Most of the guides are extremely knowledgeable about the area's unique flora and fauna and are able to talk story about the ancient tales and legends pertaining to the ride site. For your safety and comfort, make sure to have long riding pants (jeans are the best) and closed-toe shoes (boots if possible). Also, don't forget about the tropical sun—bring a hat and sunblock as well.

You can hire mounts from **CJM Country Stables,** tel. (808) 742-6096, just past the Hyatt in Poipu. CJM offers two rides: a secret beach breakfast ride starting at 8:30 a.m. and lasting three hours for $71; and a hidden beach surprise ride at 10 a.m. and again at 2 p.m., juice provided—lasting two hours for $56.

Princeville Ranch Stables, closed Sunday, tel. (808) 826-6777, along Rt. 56 near Princeville, also offers a variety of rides—lunch, snacks, and drinks are provided on most of them. The deluxe, four-hour ride is $105 and meanders across the verdant interior land of the North Shore, ending at an inland waterfall. Shorter rides take you to overlooks of Hanalei Valley and into the foothills of the surrounding mountains, $55-95.

Silver Falls Ranch, tel. (808) 828-6718, on the North Shore off Rt. 56 along Kalihiwai Ridge, offers rides daily 9 a.m.-4 p.m. (check in 30 minutes before). You can choose the *Hawaiian Discovery Ride,* two hours long with refreshment provided for $70, or the *Silver Falls Ride,* a three-hour ride including a picnic and swim for $95.

Espirit De Corps Riding Academy, in the Kapaa area, tel. (808) 822-4688, appointment only, will take you on a three-hour ride for $79, a four-hour ride with snacks for $99, and a deluxe eight-hour ride with lunch for $179. Closed Sunday.

FISHING

Deep-Sea Fishing Charters

There are excellent fishing grounds off Kauai, especially around Niihau, and a few charter boats for hire. Most are berthed at Nawiliwili Harbor, with some on the north coast.

The following charter boats have good reputations. **Gent-Lee,** tel. (808) 245-7504, captained by Bo Jordan, is a 36-foot full cabin cruiser complete with full galley, berths for six, and a hot shower. The *Gent-Lee* is "disabled-person-friendly"—set up to take people with disabilities (who *are* encouraged to fish). *Gent-Lee* also operates the **Fisherman's Restaurant,** tel. (808) 246-4700, in Puhi, where your catch is prepared for your gustatory enjoyment; **Sea Lure Fishing Charters,** tel. (808) 822-5963, offers a modern 30-foot Radon Sportsfisher departing from Nawiliwili harbor that'll take you out for the big ones; **Ahukini Charters,** tel. (808) 822-3839, operates a 32-foot Radon. Others include **Sport Fishing Kauai,** tel. (808) 742-7013, with a 38-foot Bertram; **Mana Kai Adventures,** tel. (808) 742-9849, offering a 33-foot Fiberform; and **True Blue Charters,** tel. (808) 246-6333, with a 30-foot Force.

Anini Fishing Charters, tel. (808) 828-1285, with skipper Bob Kutowski at the helm of *Sea Breeze IV,* specializes in bottom fishing. He and **Robert McReynolds Charters,** tel. (808) 828-1379, both leave from Anini Beach. McReynolds uses medium tackle and fishes the area off Kilauea Lighthouse. Going with him is perhaps the best introduction to sportfishing in Kauai.

Only real fisherpeople need contact **Joseph "Toby" Bento,** tel. (808) 828-6107 or cellular 639-6594, P.O. Box 3451, Princeville, HI, 96722, for a day's outing; the emphasis here is on catching fish, not playing around in the ocean. His boat is the *Linaka B.* Toby, who was born and raised in Hawaii, has been fishing for 35 years, having learned the trade from his dad, who has the distinction of having been twice elected Commodore of the Honolulu Yacht Club and who has designed lures that are legendary for catching marlin. Toby holds a commercial license to captain any boat up to 100 tons and, unlike many other captains, actually supports his family through fishing. Although he has caught two massive 800-pound marlins, he focuses on "what's biting," and if you are truly after fish and not a suntan, you won't find anyone more authentic than Toby Bento.

Freshwater Fishing

Kauai has trout and bass. Rainbow trout were introduced in 1920 and thrive in 13 miles of fishable streams, ditches, and reservoirs in the Koke'e Public Fishing Area. Large and small bass and the basslike *tucunare* are also popular game fish on Kauai. Introduced in 1908, they're hooked in reservoirs and in the Wailua River and its feeder streams.

For full- and half-day bass fishing excursions, mostly in the reservoirs around Kalaheo and Kapa'a, contact **Cast & Catch,** tel. (808) 332-9707. You'll take their 17-foot bass boat to one of Kauai's lovely freshwater reservoirs. All tackle, bait, and soft drinks are provided along with airport/hotel pickup and delivery. Also try **J.J.'s Big Bass Tours,** tel. (808) 332-9219, with 1993 Big Bass Hawaii State Champion, John Jardin. Tackle, license, refreshments, and hotel pickup are included.

Fishing Licenses and Regulations

No license is needed for recreational saltwater

fishing. A freshwater game fishing license is needed for certain freshwater fish during their seasons (inexpensive temporary visitor's licenses available). Licenses and a digest of fishing laws and rules are available from the State Division of Conservation and Resources Enforcement or from most sporting goods stores. For free booklets and information, write Division of Aquatic Resources, 1151 Punchbowl St., Honolulu, HI 96813. On Kauai, write to Division of Aquatic Resources, Department of Land and Natural Resources, 3060 Eiwa St., tel. (808) 274-3344.

Nearly all game fish may be taken year-round, except trout. Trout, only in the Koke'e Public Fishing Area, may be taken for 16 days commencing on the first Saturday of August. Thereafter, for the remainder of August and September, trout can be taken only on Saturday, Sunday, and state holidays.

HUNTING

All game animals on Kauai have been introduced. Hunters go for feral pigs and goats, both found on all islands except Lanai, and black-tailed deer, found only on Kauai. Black-tailed deer come from Oregon. Forty were released on Kauai in 1961; the herd is now stabilized at around 700 and they're hunted in October by public lottery. Because they thrive on island fruits, their meat is sweeter and less gamey than that of Mainland deer.

A number of game birds are found on Kauai. Bag limits and hunting seasons vary, so check with the Division of Forestry and Wildlife for details. Ring-necked pheasants are one of the best game birds. Also on the list are francolins—gray, black, and Erkel's—chukar, a number of quail, including the Japanese and California varieties, and doves.

FESTIVALS, HOLIDAYS, AND EVENTS

January

The **Kauai Loves You Triathlon** is held at lovely Hanalei Bay. Amateurs and professionals are welcome. Covered by CBS, it can alternatively occur in December.

February

The **Hawaii International Scrimshaw Competition,** held throughout the entire month of February and sponsored by Ye Old Ship Store at the Coconut Marketplace, brings the best scrimshanders from around the world to display their phenomenal artwork. An excellent opportunity to experience this revived sailors' art.

The three-day **Captain Cook Festival,** a.k.a. Waimea Town Celebration, is held at Waimea, the spot where this intrepid Pacific explorer first made contact. Food, entertainment, canoe races, and a partial marathon add to the fun. Sometimes occurs in March.

March

Midmonth features feminine beauty, grace, and athletic ability at the **Miss Kauai Pageant,** at the Kauai War Memorial Convention Hall, Lihue.

The **Prince Kuhio Festival,** at Prince Kuhio Park in Koloa and in Lihue, features festivities from the era of Prince Kuhio along with canoe races, a 10k run, and a royal ball in period dress.

The **Prince Kuhio Rodeo** is held at Po'oku Stables, in Princeville. Call (808) 826-6777 for details.

The **LPGA Women's Kemper Open Golf Tournament** is held at the Princeville Prince Golf Course in late February or early March.

April

Wesak, or **Buddha Day,** is on the closest Sunday to April 8 and celebrates the birthday of the Buddha. Ornate offerings of tropical flowers are placed at temple altars throughout Hawaii. Enjoy the flower festivals, pageants, and dance programs at many island temples.

May

May 1 is May Day to the communist world, but in Hawaii red is only one of the colors when everyone dons a lei for **Lei Day.** Festivities abound throughout Hawaii; check out the activities at the Kauai Museum in Lihue.

Armed Forces Week brings military open houses, concerts, and displays in and around the islands. Hawaii is the most militarized state in the country, and that fact becomes obvious this week. Call Military Relations at (808) 438-9761 for details.

Filipino Fiesta is a monthlong celebration of the islands' Filipino population. Food, various festivities, and a beauty contest are parts of the fiesta.

The **Prince Albert Music Festival** at Princeville presents a mixture of Classical and Hawaiian music, children's hula, and various other cultural events.

June
King Kamehameha Day, June 11, is a state holiday honoring Kamehameha the Great with festivities on all islands. Check local papers for times and particulars. On Kauai, enjoy parades, *ho'olaule'a,* and arts and crafts, concentrated around the Kauai County Building and the Kukui Grove Center.

Koke'e Wilderness Festival is an event that combines a 5k and a 10k footrace and a mountain-bike race. Events start in Poipu in mid-June.

July
The week of the **Fourth of July** offers the all-American sport of rodeo along with parades, carnivals, and contests on every island.

The **Trans Pacific Race** from Los Angeles to Honolulu sails during odd-numbered years. Yachties arrive throughout the month and converge on Ala Wai Yacht Basin, where "party" is the password. They head off for Hanalei Bay to begin the year's yachting season.

The **Na Hula O Kaohikukapulani** features Hawaiian hula and Polynesian dances performed by the children of this well-known hula *halau.* Held in Lihue.

August
The **Annual Hanalei Stampede** is held at the Po'oku Stables, Princeville.

August 17 is **Admissions Day,** a state holiday recognizing the day that Hawaii became a state.

At the **Kauai County Fair,** gardeners, stockmen, and craftspeople of the Garden Island display their wares at the War Memorial Center in Lihue. There are pageantry, great local foods, and terrific bargains to be had.

The **West Kauai Summer Festival** in Waimea features a beach party, luau, hula, arts and crafts booths, games, races, concerts, a beauty pageant, and more.

September
In early September, the **Garden Island Marathon and Half-Marathon** starts in Kapa'a.

Aloha Week, in late September, brings festivities on all of the islands as everyone celebrates Hawaii's own intangible quality, *aloha.* There are parades, luau, historical pageants, balls, and various other entertainments. The spirit of *aloha* is infectious and all are welcome to join in. Check local papers and tourist literature for happenings near you.

The **Mokihana Festival,** held in late September mainly in Lihue and Waimea with festivities at some of the big hotels, is a grassroots festival featuring lei making, hula, and ukulele competitions, along with folk-arts workshops and local entertainment.

October
The **Kauai Taro Festival,** held in Hanalei, honors taro, the staple of ancient Hawaii still actively cultivated along the North Shore. Festivities also include entertainments, arts and crafts, and a farmer's market.

November
November 11, **Veterans Day,** is a national holiday celebrated with a large parade from Fort DeRussy to Queen Kapiolani Park in Waikiki, Oahu. All islands have parades, though; for information about the one on Kauai, contact the Kauai Chamber of Commerce, tel. (808) 245-7363.

December
The **Kauai Junior Miss Presentation,** at the Kauai War Memorial Convention Hall, Lihue, is where young hopefuls get their first taste of the "big time."

The **Festival of Trees** is when the business community pitches in and markets gaily decorated Christmas trees, giving the proceeds to charity. It's held in Wailua, at the Coco Palms Hotel's Queen's Audience Hall.

The **Kauai Museum Holiday Festival** is an annual Christmas event known for attracting the island's best in handcrafted items and home-baked goodies. At the Kauai Museum, Lihue, tel. (808) 245-6931.

Bodhi Day is ushered in with ceremonies at Buddhist temples to commemorate Buddha's day of enlightenment.

The **Christmas Concert** by the Kauai High School Band and Chorus includes a medley of classic, contemporary, and Hawaiian Christmas carols and other tunes. At the Kauai War Memorial Convention Hall, Lihue, tel. (808) 245-6422.

SHOPPING

Kauai has plenty of shops of all varieties: food stores in every town, boutiques, and specialty stores here and there. There are health food stores and farmers' markets, two extensive shopping malls, and even a flea market. The following is merely an overview; specific stores, with their hours and descriptions, are covered in the appropriate travel sections.

SHOPPING CENTERS

In and around Lihue

The **Kukui Grove Shopping Center,** tel. (808) 246-6753, is one of the two largest malls on Kauai. It's a few minutes west of Lihue along the Kaumualii Hwy. (Rt. 50). Clustered around an open courtyard, its more than 50 shops have everything from food to fashions, sports gear to artwork. Across Rt. 58 and toward the city from this complex is a cluster of offices and shops that includes fast-food restaurants, banks, boutiques, shoe store, and a nearby Kmart.

Lihue has four small shopping centers off Rice Street. **Lihue Shopping Center,** tel. (808) 245-3731, is a small clutch of shops, a restaurant or two, a bank, a supermarket, and a discount store. The **Rice Shopping Center,** tel. (808) 245-2033, features variety stores, a natural food and nutrition center, a laundromat, and a karaoke bar. In Nawiliwili is the **Pacific Ocean Plaza,** and, just across the road at 3416 Rice St., is the **Anchor Cove Shopping Center,** bright and new with clothing stores, several good restaurants, a convenience store, and various boutiques. The Wal-Mart is located along Rt. 56 as you're entering Lihue from the airport; the Kmart is adjacent to the Kukui Grove Shopping Center.

In and around Kapa'a

The **Coconut Market Place,** tel. (808) 822-3641, an extensive shopping mall, is along the Kuhio Hwy. (Rt. 56) in Waipouli between Wailua and Kapa'a. The Market Place is even larger than Kukui Grove and offers more than 70 shops in a very attractive open-air setting. Aside from the clothing and gift shops, there are a bookstore, a cinema, a good activity and information center, and more than a dozen eateries. In its courtyard are a huge banyan tree, a lookout tower, and colorful sculptures made of pipes, fittings, and machinery from old sugar mills.

The **Kauai Village,** built on the theme of an 18th-century Main Street and boasting its own museum, is modern, large and diverse. One of Kauai's newest shopping centers, the Kauai Village, at 4-831 Kuhio Hwy. between Wailua and Kapa'a, offers a Safeway Supermarket, open 24 hours; Long's, a complete variety store with photo equipment and a pharmacy; an ABC Store for everything from suntan lotion to beach mats; a well-stocked Waldenbooks; Blockbuster Video, for home/condo entertainment; a cluster of fast-food restaurants, and small inexpensive eateries; Papaya's Market Cafe, the island's best natural health food store; and the Pacific Cafe, a fantastic restaurant featuring Pacific Island cuisine prepared by master chef Jean-Marie Josselin. Other stores are Mango's for Men, featuring gentlemen's alohawear; Sunglass Hut, where you can buy all kinds of sunglasses; Kahn Gallery, resplendent with some of the finest artworks in Hawaii; and the always good Crazy Shirts.

Along the Kuhio Highway, in Wailua, Waipouli, and Kapa'a, are six smaller shopping centers. Starting from the Rt. 580 turnoff, they are the **Kinipopo Shopping Center** just across from Sizzler; **Waipouli Town Center, Waipouli Plaza,** and **Waipouli Complex** on the *mauka* side of the highway in rapid succession. Finally, just before you enter the main part of Kapa'a, you'll see **Kapa'a Shopping Center,** tel. (808) 245-2033, the largest of these complexes with the greatest variety of stores.

In and around Poipu

Across the road from the Kiahuna Plantation Condominiums in Poipu is the **Poipu Shopping Center,** tel. (808) 851-1200, an attractive cluster of shops and restaurants geared toward the tourist. The proletarian **Ele'ele Shopping Center,** tel. (808) 245-2033, at the Rt. 541 turnoff to the Port Allen harbor, is the only one farther to the west along the south shore.

Along the North Shore

The north coast has but two shopping centers. **Princeville Center,** tel. (808) 826-3320, the newest, largest, and open to everyone, provides the main shopping for the residents of this planned community. In Hanalei, you'll find limited shopping at the **Ching Young Shopping Village,** tel. (808) 826-7222.

SPECIALTY SHOPS, ARTS, AND BOUTIQUES

Fine Art Galleries

The longest-lasting part of a journey is its memory of that journey, which can instantly transport you through space and time to recapture the sublime beauty of the moment. One of the best catalysts for recapturing this memory is an inspirational work of art. **Kahn Galleries** specializes in original artworks and limited-edition prints created by some of the finest artists Hawaii has to offer. The Kahn Galleries, open daily 9 a.m.-10 p.m., are located in Hanalei Town right in the old schoolhouse, tel. (808) 826-6677; in Koloa in the main building that faces you as you enter town, tel. (808) 742-2277; at the Kilohana Plantation, just west of Lihue, tel. (808) 246-4454; and in the Kauai Village Shopping Center, tel. (808) 822-4277. Some of the master artists and works displayed by Kahn Galleries include Roy Tabora, who creates dramatic seascapes of wind-whipped palms and crashing surf made magically mysterious by the light of a translucent moon or illuminated by a glorious sunset; H. Leung and his sons, Thomas and Richard, are landscape impressionists who blend the techniques of East and West into paintings of provocative, dazzling beauty; world-famous George Sumner, a much-copied but never equaled environmental impressionist who insists on historical correctness

KAUAI MUSEUMS

Grove Farm Homestead, P.O. Box 1631, Lihue, HI 96766, tel. (808) 245-3202, is open by reservation for two-hour tours Monday, Wednesday, and Thursday 10 a.m. and 1 p.m.; adults $5, children 2-12 $2. Displayed are the records, business, and personal papers of early sugar planter George N. Wilcox. Plantation owner's home, workers' cottages, outbuildings, and garden. Definitely worth a visit. Personalized tours.

Kauai Museum, 4428 Rice, Lihue, HI 96766, tel. (808) 245-6931. Open Mon.-Fri. 9 a.m.-4 p.m. and Saturday 10 a.m.-4 p.m.; adults $5, seniors $4, students 13-17 $3, children 6-12 $1. Two buildings. The story of Kauai told through art and ethnic exhibits. Hawaiiana books, maps, and prints available at museum shop.

Koke'e Natural History Museum, P.O. Box 100, Kekaha, HI, 96752, tel. (808) 335-9975. Open daily 10-4; free. Exhibits interpreting the geology and unique plants and animals of Kauai's mountain wilderness. Great to visit while at Waimea Canyon.

Waioli Mission House, (808) 245-3202, run by the same group that shows the Grove Farm Homestead, is open Tuesday, Thursday, and Saturday 9 a.m.-3 p.m. No reservations are needed. Entrance by donation only.

and who brings us, among other images, the beauty of whales like cosmic ballerinas twisting to the surface to drink deep of life-giving oxygen; the finely detailed sculptures of Randy Puckett; and the extremely talented Makk family—Meriko, Eva, and A.D.—who work in oil on canvas rendering soulful portraits of American presidents and first ladies as well as immense murals in cathedrals around the world. Kahn Galleries also offer unbelievable prints produced by a computer-based method called *giclee*. A picture of the original is made into a transparency that is scanned to match subtle strokes and color variations perfectly, and then airbrushed at four million droplets per second (each one-fourth the diameter of a human har) on to paper or canvas, creating a cyberspace copy of near-perfect similarity to the original.

If the price of original artwork puts too much of a strain on your budget, then **Island Images,** offering fine art prints and posters, might have just what you need at an affordable price. Island Images, is at Kapa'a's Coconut Market Place, tel. (808) 822-3636, open daily 9 a.m.-5 p.m. Posters average $30, with framing and shipping available. Island Images also has *some* original artwork sold at discount prices.

Old Hanapepe Town has a string of fine art shops and studios along the main drag. The first is the **James Hoyle Gallery,** housed in a two-story building just as you enter town, tel. (808) 335-3582, open daily 9 a.m.-6 p.m. and by appointment. James Hoyle has been able to capture the spirit of Hawaii through color and movement. His medium is a mixture of oil, pastel, and polymer that he applies on canvas in a distinctive style of macro-pointillism. Each daub, like a melted jelly bean, is a fantastic shade of deep purple, orange, magenta, yellow, and various shades of green. The sense permeating Hoyle's work is that in Hawaii humankind can not conquer nature, but must learn to live in harmony with the *aina,* which is very much alive. These fine works range in price $800-40,000.

A minute down the road is the **Lele Aka Studio and Gallery,** wild with fantastic demons rising from the sea and goddesses with silvery moonbeams emanating from their foreheads. In stark contrast, there are also portraits depicting the lovely bright faces of Kauai's children.

Another minute's stroll brings you to **Kauai Fine Arts,** 3848 Hanapepe Rd., P.O. Box 1079, Hanapepe, HI, 96716, tel. (808) 335-3778, open Mon.-Fri. 10 a.m.-5 p.m., Saturday and Sunday by appointment. The interior gives the impression that you are inside a handcrafted jewelry box. When you view it yourself, you'll see what I mean. From floor to wall to ceiling, it's all natural wood. The floor is hardwood and the walls and ceiling are pine. Owned and operated by Caribbean islander Mona Nicolaus, Kauai Fine Arts specializes in original engravings, original antique prints mainly of the Pacific Islands, antique maps, and vintage natural science photos from as far afield as Australia and Egypt. The shelves also hold a collection of antique bottles.

A co-op of four goldsmiths displays its craftsmanship at **The Goldsmith's Gallery,** tel. (808) 822-4653, in the Kinipopo Shopping Village, Waipouli.

Nearly three dozen first-rate island artists display their artwork at the **Artisans' Guild of Kauai,** tel. (808) 826-6441, in Hanalei.

Specialty Shops and Boutiques

You can't go wrong in the following shops. The **Kauai Museum Shop** on Rice St. in Lihue, tel. (808) 245-6931, has perhaps the island's best selection of Kauaian arts and crafts at reasonable prices, as well as books on Hawaii. **Kapaia Stitchery,** tel. (808) 245-2281, has beautiful handmade quilts, embroideries, and 100% cotton alohawear. Many shops can be found at **Kilohana,** tel. (808) 245-5608, west of Lihue on the way to Puhi. Most rooms in this 1930 plantation estate of Gaylord Wilcox have been turned into high-end boutiques featuring gifts, artwork, clothing, jewelry, antiques, or plants. **Remember Kauai,** 4-734 Kuhio Hwy. between Wailua and Kapa'a, tel. (808) 822-0161, sells a wide selection of coral and shell necklaces, featuring famous Niihau shellwork, bracelets, earrings, buckles, and chains.

The old standby in Kilauea is **Kong Lung Store,** which prides itself on being an ever-changing consignment store. One section offers such things as jewelry and upscale gift items, while another has been taken over by the Indo Pacific Trading Company.

Kilauea is also home to the **Island Soap Co.,** owned and operated by Stephen and Marlena Connella at P.O. Box 846, Kilauea, HI 96754, tel. (808) 828-1120 or (800) 300-6067. Here, the husband and wife team hand-pours soap and perfumes the raw bars with heady fragrances like coconut, plumeria, and ginger. They also produce self-pampering products like scented coconut oils, lotions, and bath gels capturing the scents of the islands. Island Soap Co. products are available at boutiques throughout Hawaii and can also be purchased by mail order.

Flea Markets

Excellent bargains are found at **Spouting Horn Flea Market** near Poipu Beach, where buskers set up stalls selling cut-rate merchandise.

At the **Roxy Swap Meet,** held every Saturday, tel. (808) 822-7027, is in the middle of Kapa'a with tables set up under numerous tents. People from all over come to barter and sell everything and anything.

Bookstores

The most extensive bookstores on Kauai are the **Waldenbooks** shops at the Kukui Grove Shopping Center in Lihue, tel. (808) 245-7162, the Coconut Market Place in Waipouli, tel. (808) 822-9362, and at the Kauai Village between Wailua and Kapa'a, tel. (808) 822-7749, all generally open Mon.-Sat. 9 a.m.-8 p.m. and Sunday 9 a.m.-5 p.m., featuring racks of books on everything from Hawaiiana to travel, along with maps, postcards, stationery and souvenirs.

Borders Books and Music, tel. (808) 246-0862, in the Kukui Grove Shopping Phase II, near the Kmart, is an excellent full-service bookstore, music center, and coffee bar. Shelves, attended by a very knowledgeable staff, hold bestsellers, Hawaiiana, children's books, travel guides, and a wide variety of special-interest publications. There is a computer center and a fine coffee lounge where you can revitalize with a latte and a sweet while perusing your new purchase.

Perhaps the place with the widest selection of Hawaiiana, Kauaiana, and guidebooks is the **Kauai Museum Shop;** other stores to check for books on these subjects are the **Koke'e Natural History Museum** in Koke'e State Park, the **Hawaiian Art Museum and Bookstore** and **Kong Lung Store** in Kilauea, and **Happy Talk** and **Hanalei Camping and Backpacking** in Hanalei. Books on metaphysics, spirituality, self-help, health, cooking, and natural foods, can be found at **Papaya's Natural Food Cafe** in Kapa'a, and at **Hanalei Health and Natural Foods** in Hanalei.

FOOD STORES

Supermarkets

Groceries and picnic supplies can be purchased in almost every town on the island. Many of the markets in the smaller towns also sell a limited selection of dry goods and gifts. The general rule is the smaller the store, the bigger the price. The largest and cheapest stores with the biggest selections are in Lihue and Kapa'a. **Big Save Value Centers** sell groceries, produce, and liquors in Ele'ele, Hanalei, Kapa'a, Koloa, Lihue, and Waimea. Most stores are open weekdays 8:30 a.m.-9 p.m., weekends until 6 p.m.

Large **Foodland** supermarkets, open 5 a.m.-midnight, operate at the Waipouli Town Center and the Princeville Center. The Princeville store is the largest and best-stocked market on the north shore.

Star Super Market is a well-stocked store in the Kukui Grove Shopping Center, while the smaller but well-stocked **Menehune Food Marts** are found in Kekaha, Kalaheo, and Kilauea.

Safeway, open 24 hours, in the Kauai Village Shopping Center, along the Kuhio Hwy., in Waipouli between Wailua and Kapa'a, is a large well-stocked supermarket.

Smaller individual markets around the island include **Kojima's** and **Pono Market** in Kapa'a, where you can stock up not only on food items and dry goods, but also on local color. North from Kapa'a are **Whalers General Store** in Anahola, the **farmers' market** in Kilauea, and the limited-selection "last chance" **Wainiha Store** in Wainiha.

Note: The following stores in and around the Poipu area are all making a comeback since Hurricane Iniki. Some are up and running, while others are still under repair. Along the south coast look for the **Sueoka Store** in Koloa, the **Kukuiula Store** at the turnoff to Spouting Horn, **Whalers General Store** in the Kiahuna Shopping Village, **Matsuura Store** in Lawai, **Mariko's Mini Mart** in Hanapepe, and the **Ishihara Market** in Waimea.

Health-Food Stores

Papaya's Natural Food Cafe, at the Kauai Village Shopping Center, 4-831 Kuhio Hwy., open daily except Sunday 9 a.m.-8 p.m., tel. (808) 823-0190, is not only the largest but also the best natural-food store on Kauai. Coolers and shelves are stocked with organic fruits and vegetables, beers and wines, whole-grain breads, organic teas and flavored coffees, grains, dried beans, spices, homeopathic medicines, cruelty-free cosmetics, vitamins, minerals, and an assortment of biodegradable cleaning products. The cafe section has a display case filled with cheesecakes and other goodies, salads and entrees by the pound, and freshly made sandwiches, all packed and ready to go. If you are into healthy organic food, there is no place better than Papaya's!

If not the best, at least the most down-to-earth health-food store on Kauai is **Ambrose's Kapuna Natural Foods,** along the Kuhio Hwy. across from the Foodland Supermarket in Kapa'a, tel. (808) 822-7112 or 822-3926. Ambrose is a character worth visiting just for the fun of it. He's well stocked with juices, nuts, grains, island fruits, vitamins and minerals, and plenty of bananas. Ambrose has one of the largest collections of the big old boards on the island (he has new surfboards too). If he's not in the store just give a holler around the back. He's there!

General Nutrition Center, tel. (808) 245-6657, in the Kukui Grove Center, is a full-service health-food store.

Hale O' Health, tel. (808) 245-9053, in the Rice Shopping Center in Lihue, open Mon.-Fri., 8 a.m.-5 p.m. and Sat.-Sun. until 3 p.m., specializes in vitamins and minerals. The shelves are stocked with everything from whole-wheat flour to spices, organic pastas, oils, and a good selection of teas. The back deli case holds a small selection of fresh organic vegetables and prepared deli sandwiches.

On the north shore, try **Hanalei Health and Natural Foods,** in the Ching Young Shopping Village, open daily 8:30 a.m.-8:30 p.m., tel. (808) 826-6990. Although cramped, this little store has a good vibe and a reasonable selection of bulk foods, fresh produce, hand-squeezed juices, vitamins, and books. They also have a good selection of cosmetics, incense, candles, and massage oils.

Farmers' Markets and Fresh Fish

Farmers' markets are also found on Kauai; each must have at least 20 vendors. The **Sunshine Farmers' Market,** featuring backyard produce from people's garden surplus, is held six days a week: Monday at noon at the baseball field in Koloa; Tuesday at 3 p.m. at the Kalaheo Neighborhood Center; Wednesday at 3 p.m. at the beach park in Kapa'a; Thursday at the Kilauea Neighborhood Center and in Old Hanapepe from 4:30 p.m. (get there early; the best pickings are gone in the first hour); Friday at 3 p.m. in Lihue at Vidinha Stadium; and Saturday at 9 a.m. at the Kekaha Neighborhood Center. Local gardeners bring their produce to town; a large selection of island produce can be had at very good prices. The stories and local color are even more delicious than the fruit. Contact the County Information and Complaint Office, tel. (808) 245-3213, for exact times and places.

Every Tuesday 3-5 p.m. pick up some farm-fresh fruit and vegetables from the **Hawaiian Farmers of Hanalei** farmers' market located one-half mile west of Hanalei, in Waipa, on the road to Haena. Look for the sign along the road on the left.

An excellent fish store is the **Pono Fish Market,** in Kapa'a, open Mon.-Sat. 9 a.m.-8:30 p.m. and Sunday till 6 p.m. They have fresh fish daily and often offer specials.

G's Fishco, 4361 Rice St., Lihue, tel. (808) 246-4440, open weekdays 10 a.m.-8 p.m., Saturday until 7 p.m., and Sunday until 5 p.m., offers cold cases filled with whole fish, *poki,* sashimi, and assorted seafood.

Ara's Sakamaya, open Mon.-Sat. 9 a.m.-7 p.m. and Sunday 9 a.m.-5 p.m., tel. (808) 245-1707, in the Hanamaulu Plaza in Hanamaulu (clearly marked along Rt. 56), is a takeout deli-restaurant that offers plate lunches, Japanese *bento,* and fresh fish daily.

Other stores include **The Fish Express** at 3343 Kuhio Hwy. in Lihue, and **Nishimura's Market** in Hanapepe.

ACCOMMODATIONS

Kauai is very lucky when it comes to places to stay. It's blessed by a combination of happenstance and planning. The island was not a major Hawaiian destination until the early '70s. By that time, all concerned had wised up to the fact that what you *didn't do* was build endless miles of high-rise hotels and condos that blotted out the sun and ruined the view of the coast. Besides that, a very strong grassroots movement here insisted on tastefully done low-rise structures that blend into and complement the surrounding natural setting. This concept mandates "destination resorts," the kind of hotels and condos that lure visitors because of their superb architecture, artistic appointments, and luxurious grounds. There is room for growth on Kauai, but the message is clear: Kauai is the most beautiful island of them all, and the preservation of this delicate beauty benefits everyone. The good luck doesn't stop there. Kauai leads the other islands in offering the best quality rooms for the price.

Hotel/Condo Choices

Kauai has approximately 168 properties with a total of 6,800 rooms available, of which 45% are condominium units. Almost all the available rooms on Kauai are split between four major destinations: Poipu Beach, Lihue, Wailua/Kapa'a, and Princeville/Hanalei. Except for Koke'e Lodge overlooking Waimea Canyon and Waimea Plantation Cottages in Waimea, little is available west of Poipu. Specialized and inexpensive accommodations are offered inland from Poipu at Kahili Mountain Park, but these very basic cottages are just a step up from what you'd find at a Boy Scout camp. Long stretches along the coast between the major centers have no lodgings whatsoever. The north shore past Hanalei has one resort, a few condos, and some scattered guest homes, but you won't find any large concentration of rooms. Aside from hotel/condo or cottage rooms, rental homes are peppered throughout the island.

Poipu, the best general-purpose beach and most popular destination on Kauai, has several major hotels and a host of condos. Prices are reasonable to expensive, and most of the condos offer long-term discounts.

For years Lihue had only one luxury hotel, the Kauai Surf, which became the fabulous Westin Kauai. It was heavily hit by Iniki and has arisen as the Kauai Marriott. In and around Lihue are most of Kauai's inexpensive hotels, guest cottages, and one mandatory fleabag. Small hotels, and especially the guest cottages, are family run. They're moderately priced, very clean, and more than adequate. However, they are in town and you have to drive to the beach. Just a

cabin at Kahili
Mountain Park

ROBERT NILSEN

few minutes away is the Outrigger Beach Hotel and its neighbor, the Aston Kauai Beach Villas, two fine properties that are affordable.

Wailua/Kapa'a on the east coast has good beaches and a concentration of accommodations, mostly hotels. Here you'll find the Holiday Inn Sunspree Kauai, formerly the Kauai Resort, which traditionally brought most of the big-name entertainment to Kauai. The Coco Palms in Wailua was a classic. Used many times as a Hollywood movie set, it had a very loyal clientele, the sure sign of a quality hotel. Unfortunately, The Coco Palms was heavily hit by Iniki, and has not been rebuilt. The Coconut Plantation is just east of Coco Palms and includes an extensive shopping center, three large hotels, and a concentration of condos. Almost all sit right on the beach and offer superior rooms at a standard price.

Princeville is a planned "destination resort" that boasts golf courses, a shopping center, 1,000 condo units, and the Princeville Hotel, a showcase resort overlooking Hanalei Bay. From here to Haena are few accommodations until you get to the Hanalei Colony Resort—literally the last resort.

Hotel/Condo Booking and Reservations

Another way to find vacation or long-term rentals is through a rental/real estate agent. This can be handled either on Kauai or through the mail. If handled through the mail, the process may take considerably longer, and you take a chance getting the type of place you want. Throughout the island, everything from simple beach homes to look-alike condominiums and luxurious hideaways are put into the hands of rental agents. The agents have descriptions of the properties and terms of the rental contracts, and many will furnish photographs. When contacting an agency, be as specific as possible about your needs, length of stay, desired location, and how much you're willing to spend. Write several months in advance. Be aware that during high-season, rentals are at a premium; if you're slow to inquire there may be slim pickings.

The following is a partial list of booking agents handling a number of properties on Kauai.

Aloha Rental Management, tel. (808) 826-7288 or (800) 487-9833.

Aston Hotels and Resorts, 2250 Kuhio Ave., Honolulu, HI 96815, tel. (808) 931-1400 or (800) 922-7866 Mainland, (800) 445-6633 Canada, or (800) 321-2558 in Hawaii.

Grantham Resorts, P.O. Box 983, Koloa, HI 96756, tel. (808) 742-7220 or (800) 742-1412.

Kauai 800, P.O. Box 295, Lawai, HI 96765, tel. (800) 443-9180.

Kauai Paradise Vacations, tel. (808) 826-7444 or (800) 826-7782.

Kauai Vacation Rental and Real Estate, 3-3311 Kuhio Hwy., Lihue, HI 96766, tel. (808) 245-8841 or (800) 367-5025.

Marc Resorts Hawaii, 2155 Kalakaua Ave., Honolulu, HI 96815, tel. (808) 926-5900 or (800) 535-0085.

North Shore Properties and Vacation Rentals, Princeville Center, Princeville, HI 96714, tel. (808) 826-9622 or (800) 488-3336.

R&R Realty and Rentals, 2827 Poipu Rd., Koloa, HI 96756, tel. (808) 742-7555 or (800) 367-8022.

Hostels

Kauai offers one hostel, the **Kauai International Hostel,** at 4532 Lehua St., Kapa'a HI 96746, tel. (808) 823-6142, just across from the Kapa'a Library.

GETTING THERE

Kauai's Lihue Airport is connected to all the Hawaiian Islands by direct flight. Most Mainland and international passengers arrive via Honolulu, from which the interisland carriers offer numerous daily flights. Currently, there is only one nonstop connection directly from the Mainland and that is flown daily by United Airlines between Los Angeles and Lihue.

Kauai's Airport

Lihue Airport, less than two miles from downtown Lihue, receives all of Kauai's flights. No public transportation to or from the airport is available, so you must rent a car or hire a taxi. The new terminal, long and low, has a restaurant and cocktail lounge, snack shop, flower shop, gift shop, restrooms, and a handful of suitcase-size coin lockers ($1) in the lobby. The gift shop sells pre-inspected island fruit that's boxed and ready to transport; tel. (808) 245-6273. All major car rental agencies and a good number of local firms maintain booths outside the main entranceway; other agencies send vans to the airport to pick up customers. Baggage pickup is at either end of the building—follow the signs. Check-in counters are along the outside corridor. All non-carry-on baggage must go through an agricultural inspection at the terminal entrance; carry-on luggage is run through X-ray machines.

Airline Carriers

Hawaiian Airlines, tel. (808) 245-1813 on Kauai, (800) 367-5320 nationwide, or (800) 882-8811 in Hawaii, offers the largest number of daily flights. From Honolulu, Oahu, 19 nonstop flights go 5:30 a.m.-8 p.m.; from Kahului, Maui, 14 flights run 6:30 a.m.-5:45 p.m., all running through Honolulu; from Kona, Hawaii, nine flights are available 6:30 a.m.-6:05 p.m. with a stopover in Honolulu; from Hilo, Hawaii, seven flights leave 6:30 a.m.-5:15 p.m. but all stop in Honolulu; and from Lanai, there is one morning and one afternoon flight via Honolulu.

Aloha Airlines, tel. (808) 245-3691, (800) 367-5250 nationwide, or (800) 235-0936 Canada, has a jet fleet of 737s connecting Kauai to Honolulu, Maui, and both Kona and Hilo on Hawaii. Aloha's routes to Lihue are: from Honolulu, 22 flights 5:30 a.m.-8 p.m.; from Maui, 20 flights via Honolulu, 6:12 a.m.-7 p.m.; from Kona, 15 flights via Honolulu and/or Maui, 6:30 a.m.-6:40 p.m.; and from Hilo, nine flights, 7:40 a.m.-6:35 p.m.

Charter Airlines

If you've got the bucks or just need to go when there's no regularly scheduled flight, try **Paragon Air,** tel. (808) 244-3356 or (800) 428-1231; or **Seaplane Safari,** tel. (800) 732-7526.

GETTING AROUND

The most common way to get around Kauai is by rental car. The abundance of agencies keeps prices competitive. As always, reserve during peak season, but in the off-season you may take your chances by shopping around to score a good deal. Kauai also has limited shuttle-bus service; expensive taxis; reasonable bicycle, moped and scooter rentals; and the good old (legal) thumb.

Auto Rental Companies

The following are major firms that maintain either a booth or courtesy pickup vans at Lihue Airport. **Dollar,** tel. (808) 245-3651, (800) 342-7398 statewide, or (800) 800-4000 worldwide, website: www.dollarcar.com, has an excellent reputation and very competitive prices. Dollar rents all kinds of cars as well as jeeps and convertibles. Great weekly rates, and all major credit cards accepted.

Alamo has good weekly rates, tel. (808) 246-0645 or (800) 327-9633, website: www.goalamo.com.

National Car Rental, tel. (808) 245-5636 or (800) 227-7368 nationwide, website: www.nationalcar.com, features GM and Nissan cars and accepts all major credit cards. They sometimes rent without a credit card if you leave a $100/day deposit—less if you take full insurance coverage.

Avis, tel. (808) 245-3512, 826-9773 in Princeville, or (800) 831-8000 nationwide, website: www.avis.com, features late-model GM cars as well as most imports and convertibles.

Budget, tel. (808) 245-1901 or (800) 527-0700, website: www.drivebudget.com, offers competitive rates on a variety of late-model cars.

Hertz, tel. (808) 245-3356 or (800) 654-3131, website: www.hertz.com, is competitively priced with many fly/drive deals. They also maintain desks at the Princeville Airport.

A local company with a reliable reputation is **Westside-U-Drive,** tel. (808) 332-8644.

Scooters and Mopeds

These tiny two-wheelers are available from **South Shore Activities,** tel. (808) 742-6873, at Poipu Beach, and from **Budget** at Kiahuna Plantation in Poipu.

ALTERNATIVE TRANSPORTATION

Bus

One of the benefits to come out of the destruction caused by Hurricane Iniki was the establishment of limited public transportation. The Iniki Express, free at one time, has become the **Kauai Bus,** 4396 Rice St., #104, Lihue, HI 96766, tel. (808) 241-6410 for current routes. Operating times are Mon.-Sat. 6 a.m.-6:30 p.m. (no operation Sunday and holidays); fare is $1, or 50 cents for seniors, students, and people with disabilities (with I.D.); $25 for a monthly pass. Wait at any of the designated bus stops. The bus will not allow large bags or items—including backpacks and boogie boards—nor will it stop or pick up at undesignated spots, so be aware. The bus runs main routes only from the airport to Lihue, as far north as Hanalei, as far west as Kekaha, and as far south as Poipu. Running approximately every 40 minutes during the morning and slowing to once an hour in the afternoon, it is not uncommon for there to be a lapse of two hours between buses. In September 1996, the U.S. Dept. of Transportation passed an appropriations bill allocating $3.2 million for Kauai's public transportation.

Taxis

Taxis are all metered and charge a hefty price for their services; all have the same rates. Airport taxis have a monopoly on pickups at the airport, although others can drop off there. Sample fares are $5.50 from Lihue and $35 from Poipu to the airport, $30 from Lihue to Poipu, $60 from Lihue to Princeville, and $25 from Princeville to Ke'e Beach and the Kalalau trailhead. Reputable taxi companies include **Akiko's,** tel. (808) 822-3613, in Wailua; **A-1,** tel. (808) 742-1390, in Poipu; **North Shore Taxi,** tel. (808) 826-6189, in Hanalei; and **Kauai Cab,** tel. (808) 246-9554, in Lihue.

Hitchhiking

Using your thumb to get around is legal on Kauai, but you must stay off the paved portion of the road. For short hops in and around the towns—like from Koloa to Poipu or from the airport to Lihue—thumbing isn't difficult. But getting out to the Kalalau Trail or to Polihale on the west end when you're toting a backpack and appear to be going a longer distance is tough. As on all the islands, your best chance of being picked up is by a visiting or local *haole*. Sometimes locals in pickup trucks will stop to give you a ride for short distances. Women *should not* hitch alone!

SIGHTSEEING TOURS

Magnificent Kauai is fascinating to explore by land, sea, or air. Looking around on your own is no problem, but some of the most outstanding areas are more expediently seen with a professional guide. Some options are discussed below.

Van and Bus Tours

On Kauai, most tour companies run vans, but some larger companies also use buses. Though cheaper, tours on full-size coaches are generally less personalized. Wherever a bus can go, so can your rental car—but on a tour you can relax and enjoy the scenery without worrying about driving. Also, tour drivers are very experienced with the area and know many stories and legends with which they annotate and enrich your trip. Coach tours vary, but typical trips go to Hanalei and the north coast, to Waimea Canyon and south coast sights, or combine one of these tours with a trip to the Wailua River. Each agency has its own routes and schedules, but all hit the major tourist sites.

Rates sometimes include entrance fees and lunch. Half-day fares run $55-65, while full-day fares run $75-85; children's fares are about 25% less. Fares also vary according to area of pickup and route. Often a tour to the Fern Grotto is considered the highlight—that should say it all! Companies offering these tours include **Trans Hawaiian**, tel. (808) 245-5108, **Robert's Hawaii**, tel. (808) 245-9558, **Kauai Paradise Tours**, tel. (808) 246-3999 (German-speaking guide available), and **Polynesian Adventure Tours**, tel. (808) 246-0122.

One unique tour company is **Aloha Kauai Tours**, P.O. Box 3069, Lihue, HI 96766, tel. (808) 245-7224 or (800) 452-1113, fax (808) 245-4888, e-mail: tours@gte.net. It alone is licensed to operate tours in Koke'e State Park and the Pali-Kona Forest Preserve. Knowledgeable guides take you into the back country over dirt roads by a/c12-passenger 4WD vans, with an informed narrative on the way. They let you see a part of Kauai not reached by anyone who doesn't walk in. Traveling is rough, but the sights are unsurpassed; truly, this is one of the few ways in Kauai to get off the beaten path. The company's guides, all local people, are excellent and have a tremendous amount of knowledge about the island's flora, fauna, and history. Their eight-hour Kaui Mountain Tour costs $88 plus tax ($58 for children under 12) and includes a deli/picnic lunch (vegetarian too!) Tours start about 8 a.m. with free pickup in the Wailua and Poipu areas. A four-hour Kauai Backroads Tour is also offered at $44 adult and $38 children, as is a four-hour Sea Fun Tour for $63 and $50, respectively.

Air Tours

Flying in a chopper is a thrilling experience, like flying in a light plane—with a twist. It can take you into all kinds of otherwise inaccessible little nooks and crannies. Routes cover the entire island, but the highlights are flying through Waimea Canyon, into the Mount Waialeale crater—where it almost never stops raining—and over the Alakai Swamp, where you see thousands of waterfalls and even 360-degree rainbows floating in midair. Then, to top it off, you fly to the Na Pali coast, swooping along its ruffled edge and dipping down for an up-close look at its caves and giant sea-cliffs. Earphones cut the noise of the aircraft and

play soul-stirring music as a background to the pilot's narration. The basic one-hour around-the-island flight runs about $150 per person; other flights are 45-75 minutes long and cost from $100-130. Some companies tailor flights to your interests; a flight might include a swim at a remote pool along with a champagne lunch. But these are, of course, more costly. Niihau Helicopters also flies periodically to points on Niihau. Its flights are more expensive, but it's the only way to get to see this island up close. Discounts of up to 15% from some of the companies are always featured in the ubiquitous free tourist brochures and are also occasionally offered through tourist-activity and information centers.

Outdoor purists disparage this mode of transport, saying, "If you can't hike in you shouldn't be there"—but that's tunnel vision and not always appropriate. To go deep into the mist-shrouded interior, especially through the Alakai Swamp, the average traveler "can't get there from here"—it's just too rugged and dangerous. The only reasonable way to see it is by helicopter and, except for the noise, choppers actually have less of an impact on the ecosystem than hikers do! A compromise—limiting numbers and times of flights—seems to be the best answer.

Everyone has an opinion on which company offers the best ride, the best narration, or the best service. All the helicopter companies on Kauai are safe and reputable, and most fly A-Stars, with a few Bell Jet Rangers still in use. Some helicopters accommodate only four passengers, while others take five; some have two-way microphones so you can ask questions of the pilot. Remember, however, that the seating arrangement in a helicopter is critical to safety. The pre-flight crew is expertly trained to arrange the chopper so that it is balanced, and with different people in various sizes flying every day, their job is very much like a chess game. This means that the seating goes strictly according to weight. If you are not assigned the seat of your choice, for safety's sake, please do not complain. Think instead that you are part of a team whose goal is not only enjoyment but also to come back safe and sound. It's very difficult not to have a fascinating flight—no matter where you sit.

Of the nearly two dozen helicopter companies on Kauai, the majority operate from Lihue

Airport, with a handful flying from Burns Field in Hanapepe. The following have top-notch reputations. **Ohana Helicopter Tours,** at the Anchor Cove Shopping Center, 3416 Rice St., tel. (808) 245-3996 or (800) 222-6989, is an owner-operated company that gives personalized service. Ohana offers complimentary shuttle service (Kapa'a and Poipu areas) to their office, where flight procedures are explained. They want you to have the time of your life—not hard to achieve with this experience. The owner, Bogart Kealoha, has years of commercial and military experience and *knows* this island of his birth. Kealoha's hands-on approach, coupled with a flawless flight record since the day he opened for business more than 10 years ago, has allowed Ohana Helicopters to grow into one of the largest and best-regarded helicopter companies on the island. Ohana now employs five pilots running three modern A-Stars into Kauai's wondrous interior. All pilots are handpicked and trained by Bogart, whose chief task has become the maintenance and safety of the crafts. The pilots use his wealth of knowledge as they point out historical, geological, and mythological areas during your flight. From smooth liftoff to gentle landing, you are in good hands with Ohana.

The granddaddy of them all is **Jack Harter Helicopters,** P.O. Box 306, Lihue, HI 96766, tel. (808) 245-3774 or (888) 245-2001, e-mail: jharter@aloha.net, website: www.helicopters-kauai.com. Jack, along with his wife, Beverly, literally started the helicopter business on Kauai and has been flying the island for more than 20 years. Jack doesn't advertise but he is always booked up. He knows countless stories about Kauai and just about everywhere to go on the island. He gives you a full hour and a half in the air, and his slogan—"Imitated by all, equaled by none"—says it all.

Safari Helicopter, tel. (808) 246-0136 or (800) 326-3356, is owned and operated by pilot Preston Myers, who learned to fly in the '60s and has been flying over Kauai for more than 10 years. Safari prides itself on offering a luxury tour in its state-of-the-art A-Star helicopters, complete with two-way sound system, unobstructed view, a/c compartments, and an all-seeing video camera system that records your trip for future enjoyment. Prices range from a 40 minute mini-tour for $89 to a one hour flight including video of your tour for $148.

Other companies with good reputations and competitive prices flying out of Lihue Airport are: **Island Helicopters,** P.O. Box 3101, Lihue, HI 96766, tel. (808) 245-8588 or (800) 829-5999, owned and piloted by Curt Lofstedt, who also employs Rudy Dela Cruz, a local instructor with the Air National Guard; **South Sea Helicopters,** P.O. Box 1445, Lihue, HI 96766, tel. (808) 245-2222 or (800) 367-2914, is owned and operated by Dennis Esaki, a local pilot with plenty of knowledge and experience; **Will Squyre Helicopters,** tel. (808) 245-8881, a one-man operation with personalized service from an owner who loves his work.

Several reputable companies fly from Burns Field in Hanapepe. **Bali Hai,** tel. (808) 355-3166 or (800) 325-8687, is one; **Niihau Helicopters,** P.O. Box 370, Makaweli, HI 96769, tel. (808) 335-3500, is another. The primary purpose of Niihau Helicopters is to provide medical and emergency treatment for the residents of Niihau. However, to defray costs, occasional non-scheduled tourist charters are offered on its twin-engine Agusta 109A. Two of their flights last 90 and 110 minutes, each with 30-minute stops on secluded beaches on Niihau; fares are $185 and $235, respectively. Two other options are an overflight of Niihau for $135 and a tour of the Na Pali coast with a Niihau overflight for $235. While it cannot compete with helicopter companies that regularly fly only over Kauai, it does offer you the only way to see Niihau up close. Let pilot Tom Mishler show you a bit of this Forbidden Island.

Fly Kauai and **Kumulani Air,** tel. (808) 246-9123, will take you above Kauai's sand and surf in their fixed-wing Cessna aircraft. A variety of tours are offered including flyovers of Niihau.

Special Note

On October 26, 1995, the FAA instituted regulation S472, stipulating that all commercial air-tour operators fly at an elevation of no less than 1,500 feet and maintain a lateral standoff of 1,500 feet from canyon walls. The majority of the helicopter tour operators now have been granted an elevation deviation of 1,000 feet, but the lateral standoff remains. If you have flown on Kauai before and remember descending deep into the canyons and hovering within an arm's length of waterfalls, don't expect a repeat per-

ROBERT NILSEN

tourist boat on the Wailua River cruising to the Fern Grotto

formance. Don't be discouraged, though; despite the new restrictions, the tours are still outstanding and offer the thrill of a lifetime.

Wailua River Cruises

You too can be one of the many cruising up the Wailua River on a large, canopied, motorized barge. The Fern Grotto, where the boat docks, is a natural amphitheater festooned with hanging ferns—one of the most touristed spots in Hawaii. The oldest company is **Smith's Motor Boat Service**, tel. (808) 822-6892, in operation since 1947. The extended Smith family still operates the business, and members serve in every capacity. During the 20-minute ride upriver you're entertained with music and a recounting of legends, and at the Fern Grotto a small but well-done medley of island songs is performed. Daily cruises depart every half hour from Wailua Marina 9 a.m.-2:30 p.m., to 3:30 p.m. Monday, Wednesday, and Friday. Adults cost $10, children $5, discounts for seniors and *kama'aina* available. Evening cruises are only offered to large groups by special request.

Waiaideale Boat Tours, tel. (808) 822-4908, is Smith's only competition. Also at the marina, they're a smaller operation with competitive rates. Daily tours leave approximately every half hour between 9 a.m. and 3:30 p.m. and cost $15 adults, $7.50 children; senior and *kama'aina* rates available.

Zodiacs

The exact opposite experience from the tame Wailua River trip is an adventurous ride down the Na Pali coast in a very tough, motorized rubber raft that looks like a big horseshoe-shaped inner tube that bends and undulates with the waves like a floating waterbed. These seaworthy craft, powered by twin engines, have five separate air chambers for unsinkable safety. Seating 12 or so, they'll take you for a thrilling ride down the coast, pausing along the way to whisk you into caves and caverns. Once at Kalalau Valley, you can swim and snorkel before making the return ride; the roundtrip, including the stop, takes about five hours. You roll with the wind and sea going down the coast and head into it coming back. The wind generally picks up in the afternoon, so for a more comfortable ride, book the morning cruise.

Other Zodiac trips include a hike to an archaeological site at Nualolo Kai Beach, a whale-watching tour, and a trip to Kipu Kai or up little-visited rivers on the south coast. All are popular so make reservations. Rates vary with the season and particular expedition, but the ultimate once-in-a-lifetime ride is around $120. Shorter trips run $60-65. Bring a bathing suit, snorkel gear (rental available), lunch, drinks (cooler provided), camera (in a plastic bag for protection), sneakers for exploring, and a windbreaker for the return ride. Summer weather permits excursions almost every day, but winter's swells are turbulent and these experienced seamen won't go if it's too rough. Take their word for it! Pregnant women and individuals with bad backs are not advised to ride.

Because of changes in the accessibility to the Na Pali coast by sea and the use of certain motorized water craft in the Hanalei Bay, the number of companies offering these tours has been cut drastically. Try **Na Pali Explorer,** tel. (808) 335-9909, which offers a five hour trip.

Another reputable company offering Zodiac tours is **Hanalei Sea Tours,** tel. (808) 826-7254 or (800) 733-7997, P.O. Box 1447, Hanalei, HI 96714, website: www.hshawaii.com/kvp/hanaleisea. Their trips run out of Nawiliwili Harbor near Lihue

Kayaks

Outfitters Kauai, 2827-A Poipu Rd., P.O. Box 1149, Poipu Beach, HI 96756, tel. (808) 742-9667, offers a South Shore Sea Kayaking Tour on Thursday or by arrangement; check in at 1:15 p.m., return by 5 p.m. Single or double kayaks are available, and the adventure includes snacks and cold drinks for $48 per person. Also offered is the River Kayak Adventure, which takes you up Kauai's navigable rivers; $45 for a double kayak, $30 for a single.

Kayak Kauai Outbound, P.O. Box 508, Hanalei, HI 96714, tel. (808) 826-9844 or (800) 437-3507, and in Kapa'a at tel. (808) 822-9179, e-mail: info@kayakkauai.com, website: www.kayakkauai.com, open daily 8 a.m.-5 p.m., has extensive experience—its owners are world-class kayak experts and the staff are sensitive people who provide good service while having a good time. Two-person kayaks rent for $48-60 per day, and one- and three-person kayaks for $35-75. From May to October, the company leads ocean tours up the Na Pali coast for $130. It also rents and sells surf-skis, boogie boards, masks, fins, *tabi* (robber-soled water shoes), tents, and other beach and camping gear. Staff will rig your car to carry the kayak and will provide drop-off and pickup service at Ke'e Beach for $8, or at Polihale State Park for $40—when it's safe to be on the ocean. During the summer, guided tours are taken along the Na Pali coast, and when conditions are too harsh there, trips are run to Kipu Kai along the south coast. Kayak tours on the Wailua River, a botanical hiking tour, and a six-day kayak/hiking tour are also offered. All of the above provide good family-style fun.

Kauai Water Ski and Surf, tel. (808) 822-3574, open daily 9 a.m.-7 p.m., in the Kinipopo Shopping Village, 4-356 Kuhio Hwy., Wailua, HI 96746, is a complete water-sports shop that offers kayak rentals.

Ray's Rentals and Activities, 1345 Kuhio Hwy., downtown Kapa'a, tel. (808) 822-5700, rents kayaks at reasonable prices, and **Kayak Kauai** (see above) has a rental outlet across the road from Ray's, open daily 9 a.m.-4 p.m., tel. (808) 822-9179.

Cabin Cruisers and Sailing Ships

For those who want an adventure but a smooth ride, try a cabin cruiser, Boston whaler, or catamaran. Boston whalers are stable, V-hulled ships—the fastest on the coast—while catamarans ride on two widely spaced hulls. Both provide smooth sailing down the coast and get you back in great comfort. Like the Zodiacs, each ventures into the sea caves (sea conditions permitting), stops for you to snorkel, and provides complimentary snacks after your swim. Tours vary, but typically a half day run runs $65; five hours, with a hike to an ancient fishing village site at Nualolo Kai, costs $90; whalewatching trips on the north or south coast are $45-65; and, during the summer, sunset tours run $80. When calling, be sure to ask about the particulars of each trip and what extras each company provides.

Liko Kauai Cruises, P.O. Box 18, Waimea, HI 96796, tel. (808) 338-0333, e-mail: liko@aloha.net, website: www.extremehawaii.com/activities/liko, is a new cruise company owned and operated by native Hawaiian Captain Liko Hookano. Unlike all the other cruises, Liko Kauai takes you down the Na Pali coast from the *west end* departing from Kikiaola Harbor just two miles from Waimea, offering vistas and sights unseen by any of the other companies. Born and raised on Kauai, Captain Liko worked for 10 years as a supervising lifeguard on the west end, and no one knows these waters better than he. After boarding the 38-foot cabin cruiser and setting sail down the coast, Captain Liko begins telling Hawaiian tales, especially about Niihau, the island of his ancestors. En route you pass Barking Sands Pacific Missile Range, Polihale, the secluded Milolii Beach, and the little-visited Marconi or Treasure Beach, where the snorkeling is superb. The tour offers a lunch of sandwiches, chips, sides, and soft drinks (BYO beer okay). On the way back, since the boat is completely outfitted for fishing charters, some lucky person gets to reel in whatever bites. The boat, built not only for speed, but also for comfort, has a large, comfortable bathroom and freshwater showers for rinsing off. The 4-5 hour tour meets at 8:30 a.m. at the offices of **Captain's Cargo Company,** 9984 Kaumuali'i Hwy. (Rt. 50). It is clearly marked just as you enter Waimea from the east end. Rates are $85 adults, $65 children 4-14, free under age four. Captain Liko's wife, Debra, *capo de captain,* runs this boutique and the office for the tours.

Hanalei Sea Tours, tel. (808) 826-7254 or (800) 733-7997, P.O. Box 1447 Hanalei, HI 96714, e-mail: napali@pixi.com, website: www .napali.com, offers Zodiac and catamaran trips out of Nawiliwili harbor. This reputable company features comfortable boats with limited passengers, knowledgeable skippers, and friendly crews. Definitely one of the best.

Na Pali Adventures, P.O. Box 1017, Hanalei, HI 96714, tel. (808) 826-6804 or (800) 659-6804, provides environmentally responsible interpretive tours in their specially outfitted catamarans on which you can sail, snorkel, or whalewatch in season. Based primarily in Hanalei, they will also sail from Nawiliwili or Port Allen, depending upon ocean conditions. Rates are $55-80 ($60 for children 3-12), depending on which tour you choose, and include a snorkel stop with instructions and equipment, snacks, beverages, and deli sandwiches.

Running under sail is also possible around Kauai. Captain Andy of **Captain Andy's Sailing Adventures,** tel. (808) 822-7833, e-mail: fun@sailing-hawaii.com, website: www.sailing-hawaii.com, lets the wind power his 46-foot catamaran along the south coast in winter and the north coast in summer. A real jolly fellow, he will take you for a half day of sailing, snorkeling, and

beachcombing for $95 or for a two-hour sunset cruise for $45, $75 and $35 for children; lunch and snacks included.

Bluewater Sailing, tel. (808) 822-0525, runs a 42-foot ketch-rigged yacht also on the south coast in winter and the north coast in summer. This is Kauai's only monohull charter sailing vessel. Half-day rates are $75, all day $115, a sunset sail is $45. Hourly, daily, and weekly charters can be arranged.

Blue Dolphin Charters, tel. (808) 246-4482, welcomes you aboard a 49-passenger, 56-foot trimaran named *Tropic Bird,* on which you can sail, snorkel, and watch the sun go down.

SPECIAL NEEDS

Kauai Services
At Lihue Airport, handicapped parking is available in an adjacent lot and across the street in the metered area.

For emergency services, call (808) 245-3773; visitor info is available at (808) 246-1440. For medical services, Kauai Medical Group at Wilcox Hospital will refer, tel. (808) 245-1500. For emergency room, long-term, and acute care contact Wilcox Memorial Hospital, 3420 Kuhio Hwy., Lihue, tel. (808) 245-1100.

To get around, arrangements can be made if the following are contacted well in advance: the county Office of Elderly Affairs, tel. (808) 245-7230, and Akita Enterprises, tel. (808) 245-5344. Avis will install hand controls on cars, but they need a month's notice. There are very few sidewalks and fewer cut curbs on Kauai—and none in Lihue. Special parking permits (legal anywhere, anytime) are available from the police station in Lihue. Medical equipment rentals are available from: American Cancer Society, tel. (808) 245-2942; Pay 'n Save, tel. (808) 245-6776; and Easter Seals, tel. (808) 245-6983. For medical support and help contact Kauai Center for Independent Living, tel. (808) 245-4034.

INFORMATION AND SERVICES

For police, fire, and ambulance anywhere on Kauai, dial 911.

To reach the Coast Guard Search and Rescue on Kauai call (808) 245-4521, (800) 552-6458.

In case of natural disaster such as hurricanes or tsunamis on Kauai call civil defense, tel. (808) 245-4001.

Crisis Intervention Helpline, tel. (808) 245-3411; Rape Crisis Hotline, tel. (808) 245-4144; and Kauai Hotline, tel. (808) 822-4114.

For time, tel. (808) 245-0212.

Ask-2000, Information and Referral Service, tel. (808) 275-2000.

Aloha Pages, tel. (808) 246-4441, is a free 24-hour "talking telephone" information service on a variety of topics including entertainment, sports, health, weather, and community services. For specific information, dial the above number or check your local Hawaiian phone book for a complete listing of available topics.

The area code for all Kauai telephone numbers is 808.

Weather and Marine Conditions

For a recorded message 24 hours a day, call (808) 245-6001. For marine weather call (808) 245-3564.

Consumer Protection

If you encounter accommodations problems, bad service, or downright rip-offs while on Kauai, try the following: Chamber of Commerce, tel. (808) 245-7363; Hawaii Hotel Association, tel. (808) 923-0407; Office of Consumer Protection, tel. (808) 241-3365; and the Better Business Bureau of Hawaii of Oahu, tel. (808) 942-2355.

Tourist Information

The best information on Kauai is dispensed by Kauai HVB, 3016 Umi St., Suite 207, Lihue, HI 96766, tel. (808) 245-3971, website: www.kauai-visitorsbureau.org.

For general information about Kauai and specific accommodation and activities listings, ask for their official vacation planner, or check it on the web at www.hshawaii.com/kvp.

For information by radio, convenient while driving, tune to 98.9 FM for a short-range broadcast about area sites.

Post Offices

Normal business hours are Mon.-Fri. 8 a.m.-4:30 p.m., Saturday 8 a.m.-noon. The central post office on Kauai is at 4441 Rice St., Lihue, tel. (808) 245-4994. Main branches are located at Kapa'a, tel. 822-5421, and Waimea, tel. (808) 338-9973, with 13 others scattered throughout the island. Most larger hotels offer limited postal services.

Hospitals

Wilcox Memorial is at 3420 Kuhio Hwy., Lihue, tel. (808) 245-1100; Kauai Veterans is in Waimea, tel. (808) 338-9431; and Samuel Mahelona Hospital is in Kapa'a, tel. (808) 822-4961.

Medical Clinics and Physicians

Kauai Medical Group is at 3420 B Kuhio Hwy., tel. (808) 245-1500, after hours call (808) 245-1831. Office hours are "urgent care clinic" Mon.-Sat. 9 a.m.-6 p.m., Sunday 10 a.m.-4 p.m.; "regular clinic," weekdays 8 a.m.-5 p.m. and weekends 8 a.m.-noon. Offices are also at Kapa'a, Koloa, Kukui Grove Shopping Center, Kilauea, and Princeville.

Garden Island Medical Group is in Waimea, tel. (808) 338-1645, after hours call (808) 338-9431. Office hours are weekdays 8 a.m.-5 p.m. and weekends 8 a.m.-noon. They also have offices at Eleíele and Koloa. Hawaiian Planned Parenthood can be reached at (808) 245-5678.

Contact Natural Health and Pain Relief Clinic at (808) 245-2277.

A fine pediatrician with four young children of his own is Dr. Terry Carolan, at 4491 Rice St., Lihue, tel. (808) 245-8566.

Pharmacies

Southshore Pharmacy in Koloa, tel. (808) 742-7511, gives senior discounts. Westside Pharmacy is in Hanapepe, tel. (808) 335-5342; Shoreview Pharmacy is in Kapa'a, tel. (808) 822-1447; Longs Drugs is in the Kukui Grove Shopping

Center, tel. (808) 245-7771; and Pay 'n Save is in Lihue, tel. (808) 245-8896. Hospitals and medical groups have their own pharmacies.

Reading Material

The central library is at 4344 Hardy St., Lihue, tel. (808) 245-3617. Branch libraries are located in Hanapepe, Kapa'a, Koloa, and Waimea. Check with the main library for times and services.

Free tourist literature, such as *This Week Kauai, Spotlight Kauai,* and *Kauai Beach Press,* is available at all hotels and most restaurants and shopping centers around the island. They come out every Monday and contain money-saving coupons and up-to-the-minute information on local events. *Kauai Drive Guide* is available from the car rental agencies and contains tips, coupons, and good maps. The AAA Hawaii *Tourbook* is also very useful.

There are two island newspapers, *The Garden Island,* published four times weekly, and the *Kauai Times,* appearing once a week. The *Garden Island* maintains an online edition at www.planet-hawaii.com/gardenisland, which offers not only news, but events, local issues, and links to other Kauai organizations. Hawaii's two main English-language dailies are the *Honolulu Star Bulletin,* and the *Honolulu Advertiser.* The Japanese-English *Hawaii Hochi* and the Chinese *United Chinese Press* are also available. The last four are published on Oahu but are available on Kauai. Magazines to look for that deal with Kauai are *The Sandwich Islands Quarterly, The North Shore Quarterly, Kauai,* and *Kauai Dining.* Others of interest that have ads, stories, and information, about all the islands are *Art to Onions,* a fine art and leisure magazine, and the inflight magazines of Aloha and Hawaiian airlines.

Island Radio

Among the numerous radio stations that broadcast on Kauai, several that are popular are KFMN 97 FM, KONG 570 AM and 93.5 FM, and KUAI 720 AM.

Island Facts

Kauai's nickname is "The Garden Island," and it is the oldest of the main Hawaiian Islands. Its lei is made from the *mokihana,* a small native citrus fruit of purple color.

HAWAII STATE ARCHIVES

LIHUE

The twin stacks of the **Lihue Sugar Company** let you know where you are: in a plantation town on one of the world's most gorgeous islands. Lihue (Open to Chill) began growing cane in the 1840s, and until the last cane harvest in 1996, its fields were among Hawaii's most productive. The town has correspondingly flourished and boasts all the modern conveniences including chrome-and-glass shopping centers, libraries, museums, and a hospital. But the feel is still that of a company town. Lihue, the county seat, has 5,500 residents and two traffic lights. It isn't the geographical center of the island (Mount Waia-leale has that distinction), but it is halfway along the coastal road that encircles the island, making it a perfect jumping-off point for exploring the rest of Kauai. It has the island's largest concentration of restaurants and the most varied shopping, a major resort, and right-priced accommodations. If you're going to find any nightlife at all on Kauai, beyond the lounges at the big resorts, it'll be here (don't expect much). Good beaches are within a five-minute drive, and you can be out of town and exploring long before your shave ice begins to melt.

SIGHTS

KAUAI MUSEUM

If you really want to enrich your Kauai experience, this is the first place to visit. Spending an hour or two here infuses you with a wealth of information regarding Kauai's social and cultural history. The two-building complex is at 4428 Rice St. in downtown Lihue, tel. (808) 245-6931, open Mon.-Fri. 9 a.m.-4 p.m. and Saturday from 10 a.m.; admission is $5, $4 seniors 65 and older, $3 students 13-17, $1 children 6-12, and free under six. The main building was dedicated in 1924 to Albert Spencer Wilcox, son of pioneer missionaries at Hanalei. It has a Greco-Roman facade and was the public library until

1970. Its two floors house the main gallery, devoted to ethnic heritage and island art exhibits that are changed on a regular basis. The **Museum Shop** sells books, Hawaiiana prints, and a fine selection of detailed U.S. Geological Survey maps of the entire island. Some inexpensive but tasteful purchases include baskets, wooden bowls, and selections of tapa. (The tapa is made in Fiji, but native craftspeople are studying Fijian techniques and hope to re-create this lost art.) The main room contains an extensive and fascinating exhibit of calabashes, koa furniture, quilts, and feather lei. One large calabash belonged to Princess Ruth, who gave it to a local child. Its finish, hand rubbed with the original *kukui* nut oil, still shows a fine luster. The rear of the main floor is dedicated to the **Senda Gallery,** with its collection of vintage photos shot by W.J. Senda, a Japanese immigrant from Matsue who arrived in 1906. These black and whites are classics, opening a window onto old Kauai.

Kauai's fascinating natural and cultural history begins to unfold when you walk through the courtyard into the second half of the museum, the **William Hyde Rice Building.** Notice the large black iron pot used to cook sugarcane. The exhibits are self-explanatory, chronicling Kauai's development over the centuries. The windows of the Natural History Tunnel show the zones of cultivation on Kauai, along with its beaches and native forests. Farther on is an extensive collection of Kauai shells, old photos, and displays of classic muumuu. The central first-floor area has a model of a Hawaiian village, an extensive collection of weapons, some fine examples of adzes used to hollow canoes, and a model of HMS *Resolution* at anchor off Waimea. An excerpt from the ship's log records Captain Cook's thoughts on the day that he discovered Hawaii for the rest of the world.

As you ascend the stairs to the second floor, history continues to unfold. Missionaries stare from old photos, their countenances the epitome of piety and zeal. Just looking at them makes you want to repent! Most old photos record the plantation era. Be sure to see the **Spalding Shell Collection,** gathered by Colonel Spalding, an Ohio veteran of the Civil War who came to Kauai and married the daughter of Capt. James Makee, owner of the Makee Sugar Company. Besides shells from around the world are examples of magnificent koa furniture, table settings, children's toys, dolls, and photos of Niihau—about all that the outside world ever sees.

Follow the stairs to the ground floor and notice the resplendent examples of feather capes on the wall. On the main floor, in an alcove by the front door, push the button to begin a 15-minute aerial-view video of Kauai. This pictorial is a treat for the eyes; soothing Hawaiian chanting in the background sets the mood. If you're seeking further enrichment, (bring the children) the museum staff conducts a tour (free with admission) Wednesday at 10:30 a.m. and upon request. Time permitting, they will also take you on private tours if you call in advance. On Friday, there is an orchid sale in the museum yard, where you can delight in the magic of these lovely flowers. Outside in the courtyard is **A Matter of Taste,** an espresso bar where you can refresh yourself with a coffee, cool drink, or light lunch.

GROVE FARM HOMESTEAD

Grove Farm is a plantation started in 1864 by George Wilcox, the son of missionaries who worked for the original owner of the surrounding acreage. The first owner saw no future in the parched land and sold 500 acres to Wilcox for $1,000. Through a system of aqueducts, Wilcox brought water down from the mountains and began one of the most profitable sugar plantations in Hawaii. The homestead was a working plantation until the mid-1930s, when George died and operations were moved elsewhere. The remaining family continued to occupy the dwellings and care for the extensive grounds. In 1971, Mabel Wilcox, a niece of the founder, dedicated the family estate to posterity. Well advanced in years but spirited in mind, she created a nonprofit organization to preserve Grove Farm Homestead as a museum. Reap the benefits of her efforts by visiting this self-sufficient farm Monday, Wednesday, or Thursday. Well-informed guides take you on a two-hour tour of the grounds and various buildings; admission $3 adults, $1 children under 12. Tours are *by reservation only!* Drop-in visitors will be turned away. Telephone (808) 245-3202 at least 24 hours in advance to make arrangements. Mail reservations are accepted up to three months

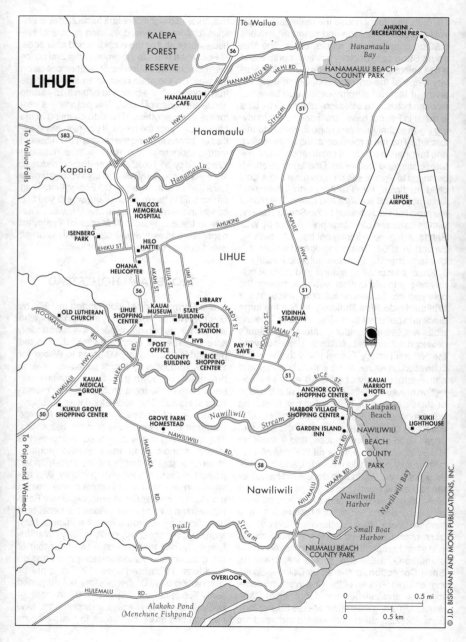

George's desk

in advance; write to Grove Farm Homestead, P.O. Box 1631, Lihue, HI 96766. The homestead is located off Nawiliwili Rd.; precise directions are given when you call. Group size is limited to give full attention to detail and minimize wear and tear on the buildings. Tours begin at 10 a.m. and 1 p.m. Please be prompt!

Living History

The first thing you notice when entering Grove Farm is the rumble of your tires crossing a narrow-gauge railroad track. The tracks meant sugar, and sugar meant prosperity and change for old Hawaii. The minute you set foot upon Grove Farm Homestead you can feel this spirit permeating the place. This is no "glass-case" museum. It's a real place with living history, where people experienced the drama of changing Hawaii.

George Wilcox never married. In love once, he was jilted, and that ended that. In 1870, his brother Sam came to live on the homestead. In 1874,

Sam married Emma, daughter of missionaries from the Big Island. She had been educated in Dearborn, Michigan, and had recently returned to Hawaii. The couple had six children—three boys and three girls. Two of the boys survived to manhood and managed the farm, but later both met with tragic deaths. Of the girls, only Henrietta, the oldest, married. The two other sisters, Miss Elsie and Miss Mabel, were single all their lives. Elsie became very involved in politics, while Mabel went to Johns Hopkins University and earned a degree as a registered nurse. Her parents wouldn't let her leave home until she was 25 years old, when they felt she could cope with the big, bad world. She returned in 1911 and opened a public health office on the grounds.

The Tour

You meet your guide at the plantation office. The buildings, furnishings, orchards, and surrounding lands are part of what was the oldest intact sugar plantation in Hawaii. The office contains a safe dating from 1880, when it was customary to pay for everything in cash. On top sits a cannonball that's been there as long as anyone can remember. Perhaps it was placed there by Mr. Pervis, the original bookkeeper. As time went on the safe's combination—which is in letters, not numbers—was lost. A safecracker was eventually hired to open it, and inside was the combination written in a big, bold hand: "B-A-L-L."

You cross the grounds to a simple dwelling and enter the home of the Moriwakis. Mrs. Moriwaki came to Grove Farm as a "picture bride," though she was born in Hawaii and taken back to Japan as a child. She was the cook at the big house for almost 50 years. After the grounds opened to the public and until her death in 1986, she returned on tour days to explain her role in running the homestead. Her home is meticulously clean and humble, a symbol of Japanese plantation workers' lives on Hawaii. Notice the food safe; most workers in Hawaii had no iceboxes and kept vermin away by placing sardine cans filled with water or kerosene inside, into which the pests fell and were drowned. A small print of Mt. Fuji and a geisha doll in a glass case are simple yet meaningful touches. Together they signify the memory of the past along with the hope of a brighter future which all plantation workers sought for their children.

As you walk around, notice how lush and fruitful the grounds are, with all sorts of trees and plants. At one time the workers were encouraged to have their own gardens. A highlight is a small latticework building half submerged in the ground. This is the **fernery,** at one time a status symbol of the good life in Hawaii. There was great competition among the ladies of Victorian Hawaii, who were proud of their ferns, and you became an instant friend if you presented a new and unique variety while on a social visit. Behind the Wilcox Home is a small schoolhouse built in 1900. It later became Mabel Wilcox's public health office; now a depository for all sorts of artifacts and memorabilia, it's called the **Trunk Room.** A photo of Mabel shows her in a Red Cross uniform. By all accounts, Mabel was a serious but not humorless woman. Her dry and subtle wit was given away only by her sparkling eyes, which are evident in the photo.

Wilcox Home

Remove your shoes before entering this grand mansion. The Wilcoxes were pleasant people given to quiet philanthropy, but their roots as New England missionaries made them frugal. The women always wore homemade cotton dresses and in the words of a tour guide, "nothing was ever thrown away by this family." The home is comfortable and smacks of culture, class, and money—in the old-fashioned way. As you enter, you'll be struck with the feeling of space. The archways were fashioned so they get smaller as you look through the house. This shrinking perspective gives an illusion of great length. The walls and staircase are of rich, brown koa. Much of the furniture was bought secondhand from families returning to the Mainland. This was done not out of a sense of frugality, but simply because it was often the only good furniture available.

The piano here belonged to Emma Wilcox; the profusion of artwork includes many original pieces, often done by visitors to the homestead. One longtime visitor, a sickly girl from the East Coast, did some amazing embroidery. Her finest piece on display took 10 years to complete. Portraits of the family include a good one of George Wilcox. Notice a Japanese chest that Miss Mabel won in a drawing while she was in Japan with her sister Elsie and Uncle George in 1907. Notice,

too, the extensive collection of Hawaiiana that the family accumulated over the decades. In the separate kitchen wing is a stove that is still functional after 100 years of hard use. A porch, obviously homey during rainstorms, looks out onto a tea house. Everything in the home is of fine quality and in good taste. It's a dwelling of peace and tranquillity.

The Cottage

Finally you arrive at the private home of a private man, George Wilcox himself. It is the picture of simplicity. Only an old bachelor would have chosen these spartan surroundings. An inveterate cigar smoker along with his brother Sam, both were forbidden by the ladies to smoke in the main house. Here, he did as he pleased. Maybe the women were right; George died of throat cancer . . . in 1933 at the age of 94!

The first room you enter is his office. George was a small man and a gentleman. Whenever he left the house, he donned a hat. You'll notice a collection of his favorites hanging on pegs in the hallway. One of his few comforts was a redwood tub he'd soak in for hours. This self-made millionaire kept his soap in an old sardine tin, but he did use fine embroidered towels. His bedroom is simple, bright, and airy. The mattress is of extremely comfortable horse hair. Outside his window is a profusion of fruit trees, many of which George planted himself. As the tour ends you get the feeling that these trees are what Grove Farm is all about—a homestead where people lived, and worked, and dreamed.

OTHER SIGHTS

Kilohana Plantation

The manor house at Kilohana Plantation was built in 1935 by the wealthy *kama'aina* planter, Gaylord Wilcox, to please his wife, Ethel. She was enamored with Hollywood and its glamorous Tudor-type mansions, which were the rage of the day. Sparing no expense, Gaylord spent $200,000 building an elaborate 16,000-square-foot home; estimates are that it would cost about $3 million by today's standards. A horse and carriage waits to take visitors on a tour (nominal fee) of the 35 lush acres that surround the home, which was the center of a working farm—a feeling that lingers. Inside, **Gaylord's Restaurant** occupies the actual dining room. Original furniture includes a huge table which seats 22 and a stout sideboard fit for a truly regal manor house. As you pass from room to room—some of which are occupied by fine boutiques, jewelry shops, and art galleries—notice the coved ceiling, lustrous wood molding, and grand staircase. A mirror from the '30s (mirrors in Hawaii have a tough time holding up because of the moisture) still hangs just inside the tiled, atriumlike main entranceway. Walk straight through a set of double doors onto the flagstone veranda (also occupied by Gaylord's for alfresco dining) to view a living tapestry of mountain and cloud, even more ethereal when mist shrouds magical Mt. Waialeale in the distance. To arrive, take Rt. 50 (Kaumuali'i Hwy.) west from Lihue for about two miles toward the tiny village of Puhi, and look on the mountain side for the clearly marked entrance.

Lihue's Churches

When Rt. 56 becomes Rt. 50, just as you pass the Lihue Sugar Mill, look for the HVB Warrior pointing you to the **Old Lutheran Church.** Just before the bridge, follow Hoomana Road to the right through a well-kept residential area. Built in 1883, it has everything a church should have, including a bell tower and spire, but it's all miniature. The church reflects a strong German influence that dominated Lihue and its plantation until WW I. The turn-of-the-century pastor was Hans Isenberg, brother of the plantation founder and husband to Dora Rice from the old *kama'aina* family. Pastor Isenberg was responsible for procuring the Lihue Horse Trough, an ornate marble work imported from Italy in 1909 and now on display at the Haleko Shops' botanical gardens in downtown Lihue (see below). The outside of the church is basic New England, but inside, the ornate altar is reminiscent of baroque Germany. Headstones in the yard to the side indicate just how old this congregation is.

On a nearby hill is **Lihue Union Church,** which was mostly attended by workers and their families. Its cemetery is filled with simple tombstones, and plumeria trees eternally produce blossoms for the departed ones.

Around Town

Across the street from Lihue Shopping Center, a stone's throw from the twin stacks of the sugar mill, are four solid-looking buildings known as the **Haleko Shops.** Once the homes of German plantation managers—before they gave up their holdings during WW I—they're now occupied by restaurants and shops; part of the shopping center across the road. Around them is a botanical garden. Each plant carries a description of its traditional use and which ethnic group brought it to the island. (Look for the Lihue Horse Trough imported by Pastor Isenberg.)

Follow Umi Street off Rice to Hardy Street. At the corner is the **Kauai Library.** In the entrance is a batik wall hanging by Jerome Wallace —the largest painting of its type in the world.

Follow Rice Street toward Nawiliwili Harbor and it turns into Rt. 51, known as Waapa Road. You'll come to the junction with Rt. 58 (Nawiliwili Road). Take Nawiliwili to Niumalu Road and turn left, following it to Hulemalu Road. You pass the predominantly Hawaiian settlement of Niumalu. Along Hulemalu Road is a lookout, below which is **Alakoko (Rippling Blood) Pond,** commonly known as Menehune Fishpond. You have a sweeping view of Huleia Stream, the harbor, and the Hoary Head Mountains in the background. The 900-foot mullet-raising fishpond is said to be the handiwork of the Menehune. Legend says that they built this pond for a royal prince and princess and made only one demand: that no one watch them in their labor. In one night, the indefatigable Menehune passed the stones needed for the project from hand to hand in a double line that stretched for 25 miles. But the royal prince and princess could not contain their curiosity and climbed to a nearby ridge to watch the little people. They were spotted by the Menehune, who stopped building, leaving holes in the wall, and turned the royal pair into the twin pillars of stone still seen on the mountainside overlooking the pond.

Wailua Falls

Heading north, in Kapaia, Rt. 583 branches from Rt. 56 and heads into the interior. The road lifts up and away from the ocean to rolling terrain surrounded by lofty mountain peaks. To the left and right are small homes with the usual patches of tropical fruit trees. Route 583 ends at mile marker 3. Far below, Wailua Falls tumbles 80 feet over a severe *pali* into a large round pool. It's said that the *ali'i* would come here to dive from the cliff into the pool as a show of physical prowess; commoners were not considered to be infused with enough mana to perform this feat.

Many of the trees here are involuntary trellises for rampant morning glory. Pest or not, its blossoms are still beautiful as it climbs the limbs. A trail down to the falls is particularly tough and steep. If you make it down, you'll have the falls to yourself, but you'll be like a goldfish in a bowl with the tourists—perhaps jealously—peering down at you.

BEACHES AND PARKS

Lihue has very convenient beaches. You can sun yourself within 10 minutes of anywhere in town, with a choice of beaches on either Nawiliwili or Hanamaulu Bay. Few tourists head to Hanamaulu Bay, while Nawiliwili Bay is a classic

Wailua Falls

example of "beauty and the beast." There is hardly a more beautiful harbor than Nawiliwili's, with a stream flowing into it and verdant mountains all around. However, it is a working harbor complete with rusting barges, groaning cranes, and petrochemical tanks. Private yachts and catamarans bob at anchor with their bright colors reflecting off dappled waters, and as your eye sweeps the lovely panorama it runs into the dull gray wall of a warehouse where raw sugar was stored before being shipped to the Mainland to be processed. It's one of those places that separates perspectives: some see the "beauty," while others focus on the "beast."

Kalapaki Beach

This most beautiful beach at Nawiliwili fronts the lavish Kauai Marriott (formerly the Westin Kauai). Just follow Rice Street until it becomes Rt. 51; you'll soon see the bay on your right and the entrance to the hotel on your left. The hotel serves as a type of giant folding screen, blocking out most of the industrial area and leaving the lovely views of the bay. Park in the visitors' area at the hotel entrance, or to the rear of the hotel at the north end of Nawiliwili Beach Park, where a footbridge leads across the Nawiliwili Stream to the hotel property and the beach. Access to the beach is open to anyone, but if you want to use the hotel pool and showers, you'll have a lot less hassle if you order a light breakfast or lunch at one of the restaurants. The homemade ice cream at the hotel ice cream shop is delicious!

The wave action at Kalapaki is gentle at most times, with long swells combing the sandy-bottomed beach. Kalapaki is one of the best swimming beaches on the island, fair for snorkeling, and a great place to try bodysurfing or begin with a board. Two secluded beaches in this area are generally frequented by local people. Head through the hotel grounds on the road to the right past the few private homes that overlook this bay. From here you'll see a lighthouse on Ninini Point. Keep the lighthouse to your left as you walk across the golf course to the bay. Below are two small crescent beaches, both good for swimming and sunbathing. The right one has numerous springs that flow up into the sand. You can also head for **Nawiliwili Beach County Park** by following Rt. 51 downhill past the Kauai Marriott until you come to the water; on the

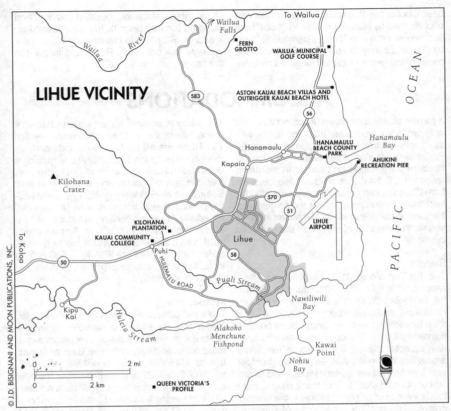

LIHUE VICINITY

To Wailua

Wailua Falls

FERN GROTTO

WAILUA MUNICIPAL GOLF COURSE

Wailua River

583

ASTON KAUAI BEACH VILLAS AND OUTRIGGER KAUAI BEACH HOTEL

56

Hanamaulu

Kapaia

HANAMAULU BEACH COUNTY PARK

Hanamaulu Bay

AHUKINI RECREATION PIER

Kilohana Crater

570

KILOHANA PLANTATION

KAUAI COMMUNITY COLLEGE

Puhi

HULEMALU ROAD

51

58

Lihue

LIHUE AIRPORT

PACIFIC OCEAN

To Kaloa

50

Puali Stream

Nawiliwili Bay

Kipu Kai

Huleia Stream

Alakoko Menehune Fishpond

Kawai Point

Nohiu Bay

0   2 mi

0   2 km

QUEEN VICTORIA'S PROFILE

© J.D. BISIGNANI AND MOON PUBLICATIONS, INC.

left is the beach park. Here are showers, picnic tables, and a pavilion along with some shady palm trees for a picnic. A seawall has been erected here, so for swimming and sunning it's much better to walk up to your left and spend the day at Kalapaki Beach.

Niumalu Beach County Park

This county-maintained beach park lies along the Huleia Stream on the west end of Nawiliwili Harbor. Many small fishing and charter boats are berthed nearby and local men use the wharf area to fish and "talk story." There is no swimming and you are surrounded by the industrial area. However, you are very close to Lihue and there are pavilions, showers, toilets, and camping both for tents and RVs (permit required). To

get there, take Rt. 51 to Nawiliwili Harbor. Continue on Waapa Road along the harbor until you arrive at the beach park.

Ahukini Recreation Pier

As the name implies, this state park is simply a pier from which local people fish. And it's some of the best fishing around. Follow Rt. 57 to Lihue Airport. With the airport to your right, keep going until the road ends at a large circular parking lot and fishing pier. The scenery is only fair, so if you're not into fishing give it a miss.

Hanamaulu Beach County Park

This is a wonderful beach, and although it is very accessible and good for swimming, very few tourists come here. There is not only a beach, but to the right is also a lagoon area with pools formed by Hanamaulu Stream. Local families frequent this park, and it's particularly loved by children as they can play Tom Sawyer on the banks of the heavily forested stream. There are picnic tables, showers, toilets, a pavilion, and camping (county permit). In Hanamaulu, turn *makai* off Rt. 56 onto Hanamaulu Road, take the right fork onto Hehi Road, and follow it to the beach park.

ACCOMMODATIONS

If you like simple choices, you'll appreciate Lihue; only two fancy resorts are here, the rest are either family-run hotel/motels or apartment hotels. Prices here are also better than on the other islands because Lihue isn't considered a prime resort town. But it makes an ideal base, because from Lihue you can get *anywhere* on the island in less than an hour. Although it's the county seat, the town is quiet, especially in the evenings, so you won't have to deal with noise or hustle and bustle.

Budget

The **Tip Top Motel,** 3173 Akahi St. (for reservations, write P.O. Box 1231, Lihue, HI 96766), tel. (808) 245-2333, is a combination lounge, restaurant, and bakery popular with local folks. It's a functional, two-story, cinder-block building painted light gray. The lobby/cafe/bakery is open daily except Monday 6:45 a.m.-9 p.m. The rooms are antiseptic in every way—a plus, as your feet stay cool on the bare linoleum floor—and all are air-conditioned. Just to add that mixed-society touch, instead of a Gideon's Bible in the dresser drawer, you get The Teachings of Buddha, placed by the Sudaka Society of Honolulu. Rates are $50 for four, with a few cheaper rooms available.

The **Hale Lihue,** 2931 Kalena St., Lihue, HI 96766, tel. (808) 245-2751, has made an excellent comeback! Don't expect anything fancy from this pink, two-story, cinder-block hotel, but the manager, Benki M. Somera (cellular tel. 808-639-8896 for emergencies), runs a well-managed, clean hotel with a screened-in lobby. Perfect for no-frills, budget accommodations. Rates are $22 s, $25 d, $30 t; with kitchenettes, $30 s, $40 d, and good weekly rates.

Motel Lani, owned and operated by Janet Naumu, offers clean, inexpensive rooms at 4240 Rice St.; for reservations write Motel Lani, P.O. Box 1836, Lihue, HI 96766; tel. (808) 245-2965.

The lobby is actually an extension of Janet's home, where she and her children often watch TV. There are 10 sunburn-pink units and, although close to the road, they're surprisingly quiet. Each room has a small desk, dresser, bath, fan, and refrigerator and is cross-ventilated. Some have air-conditioning. No TVs. Janet usually doesn't allow children under three years old, especially if they misbehave, but she's reasonable and will make exceptions. A small courtyard with a barbecue is available to guests. Rates for two nights are $32-40 d, $40 and up triple, $14 for an additional person, slightly more for one night. Budget.

Inexpensive

The loved but worse-for-wear Ocean View Motel, built and operated by the irascible but lovable Spike Kanja, several years ago reopened as the refurbished and very attractive **Garden Island Inn,** at 3445 Wilcox Rd., Nawiliwili, HI 96766, tel. (808) 245-7227 or (800) 648-0154. The new owners, Steve and Susan Layne, did a wonderful job of turning the once character-laden hotel into a bright and cheery inn. Head down Rice Street toward Nawiliwili; the inn is at the corner of Wilcox Road, across from Nawiliwili Beach Park, just a stroll from Kalapaki Beach. Each room has a color TV, microwave, refrigerator, and coffeemaker with Lappert's Kona coffee complimentary. The Inn also provides boogie boards, snorkeling gear, beach mats, bicycles (if you're nice), and ice chests for a day's outing. The ground floor rooms, $55 d, are appointed with textured bamboo-motif wallpaper and are cooled by louvered windows and ceiling fans. Second floor rooms, $65 d, are about the same, but each has its own lanai. The best rooms ($75-85) are on the third floor, from where you look down on a fully matured banana grove. Is this the tropics or what! More like mini-suites, third-floor rooms give you two full rooms that can easily accommodate four people comfortably. The front sitting room, doubling as a kitchen, is bright with a wraparound lanai from where you can watch the goings on in Nawiliwili Harbor and have an unobstructed view of the cement works! Fortunately, Kauai always seems to give more than it takes. Walk out to the cement works in the evening and look over the seawall. You're likely to spot green sea turtles as they breaststroke through the darkening sunset waters looking for food and a quiet nook in which to relax. Across the street from the inn is a family-oriented playground great for the kiddies and a new volleyball court kept green by a year-round sprinkler system. For the money, the Garden Island Inn is one of the best deals on Kauai.

Expensive to Premium

The **Aston Kauai Beach Villas,** at 4330 Kauai Beach Dr., Lihue, HI 96766, tel. (808) 245-7711, (800) 922-7866 Mainland and Canada, or (800) 321-2558 Hawaii, are perfectly located midway between the airport and Kapa'a. It is a fine condominium resort that has consistently earned the AAA "Three-Diamond Award." The spacious units, a signature of Aston Resorts, differ slightly, but expect a terra-cotta foyer leading to a living room with comfortable bamboo furniture with puff pillows, a fold-out couch, and remote-control color TV. The dining area has a marble-topped table with highback chairs adjacent to the full kitchen with refrigerator, dishwasher, garbage disposal, coffeemaker, four-burner electric stove, hood fan, microwave oven, toaster, and all the necessary utensils. A washer-dryer combination is tucked into its own utility closet. Master bedrooms have queen-size beds, private baths, plenty of closet space, and complimentary safes. Ceiling fans, air-conditioning, and phones are part of the amenities. Each unit has a lanai with outdoor tables, chairs, and lounges. Rates are $99 for a studio with kitchen, $140 for one-bedroom units, $195 for a two-bedroom with a garden view, and $255 for a two-bedroom, two-bath suite with ocean view. The Aston Kauai Beach Villas are adjacent to the Outrigger Kauai Beach Hotel (a former Hilton), with which it shares all amenities including the free-form pool.

The **Outrigger Kauai Beach Hotel** is one of Kauai's newest hotel/condos. On 25 landscaped acres overlooking Hanamaulu Beach, it offers 350 hotel rooms—all with mini-refrigerators—and 136 villas with full kitchens and laundry facilities. The hotel pool is in three sections connected by tiny waterfalls and cascades. Dining amenities include late-night room service, lobby lounge, pool bar and restaurant, **Gilligan's** for drinks and dancing, and the casual **Jacaranda Terrace,** the hotel's main dining hall. There are four tennis courts, two whirlpools, and watersports equipment. Prior to the nightly luau, a torchlighting ceremony is performed, and a wide range of events is run by the activities desk. Rates are $125-175 hotel, $140-200 one-bedroom villa, $190-250 two-bedroom villa (up to four people). Special honeymoon, tennis, and golf packages are available. For information, write 4331 Kauai Beach Dr., Lihue, HI 96766; tel. (800) 462-6262 or (808) 245-1955.

Luxury

The **Kauai Marriott on Kalapaki Beach,** at Kalapaki Beach, Lihue, Kauai, HI. 96766, tel. (808) 245-5050 or (800) 220-2925, is a testament to man's perseverance coupled with the forgiving personality of Mother Nature. In 1987, the hotel was completely refurbished and rebuilt, emerging as the Westin—at the time, the most luxurious property on Kauai. Hurricane Iniki then furiously blew ashore, raking the island and mangling the hotel. Afterward, the Marriott chain purchased the property and set about restoring it to its former grandeur. The result is, once again, a fabulous hotel that co-operates as a time-share condominium. Upon arrival, you are greeted with valet parking and enter through a grand foyer. Descending the escalator you emerge on a flagstone path, which winds along the perimeter of **Kamalao Kalapaki,** a formal garden that says "Hawaii" unmistakably. Enter the garden and immediately you're embraced by the foliage and the feeling that you're walking the grounds of a grand estate where you can enjoy a quiet moment or a slow meditative stroll enhanced by twittering birds and the soft swish of palms tussled by sea breezes. Suddenly you'll see a delightful burst of flowers amidst the subtle shades of tranquil green that carpets the gardens. You'll be serenaded by a small, lava-rock waterfall that showers the surrounding ferns and foliage with mist. If you continue straight along the colonnaded main walkway, you'll soon descend a flight of marble stairs into the reception area. Displayed here is a lustrous original koa canoe that belonged to royal Prince Kuhio. In the care of a local Hawaiian family over the generations, the canoe was leased to Marriott with the understanding that funds be used in a scholarship that directly benefits a child of Hawaiian ancestry. The central area of the hotel is an extensive free-form pool surrounded by five neoclassical thrust proscenium porticos bubbling with soothing jacuzzis.

Rooms are classified into garden view ($229), pool/ocean view with car and complimentary health club ($269/$285), and deluxe ocean ($375); all prices include breakfast for two. Although the Marriott considers itself "family deluxe," the rooms are pure luxury. A comfy bed with six puffy pillows faces an entertainment center complete with remote-control color TV. The walls are painted a muted sand color reminiscent of the beach and brightened by Hawaiian-themed paintings and prints, while the carpeting is the soft green of new-mown grass. Some rooms have reclining chairs with footrests, others have love seats that convert to double beds. The furniture is generally a blend of bent bamboo and rattan. Each room boasts air-conditioning, a mini-fridge, tiled full bath with separate dressing area, a steam iron and ironing board, coffee maker with compli-

mentary Kona coffee, and mailbox. Full-service amenities include in-room dining and cocktails, an activities desk, concierge service, and complimentary airport shuttle. The hotel's mini-mall (most shops open daily 9 a.m.-9 p.m.) includes Lamonts Gifts and Sundries, for everything from grocery items to glass anthuriums; Aveda Concept Salon, where owner April Lane offers hair styling, facials, manicures, and pedicures; Tropical Tantrum, for ladies' original resort and alohawear; The Sandal Tree, where you can dress your feet in anything from elegant pumps to flip-flops; the Marriott Logo Shop, for an assortment of articles including those fashioned from comfortable, wrinkle-resistant "micro-wear"; Collections, with alohawear, hats, and ladies' and men's bathing suits and bikinis, presented by Liberty House.

The hotel also offers a cocktail lounge, a poolside snack bar, and the **Kukui Buffet,** an indoor/outdoor restaurant for breakfast, lunch, and dinner overlooking the central pool area. Although you're surrounded by luxury at the Marriott, you experience the feeling of a quieter, more casual place. The hotel is very much like the stunning sister who decided to stay close to home instead of heading for the bright lights where her beauty would easily have dazzled everyone.

FOOD

Dining in Lihue is a treat—good to your palate and your budget. The roster of restaurants in and around town is the most extensive on the island. You can have savory snacks at saimin shops or at bargain-priced eateries frequented by local people. You'll find pizza parlors and fast-food chains. Stepping up in class, there are continental, Italian, and Japanese restaurants, while moderately priced establishments serve up hearty dishes of Mexican, Chinese, and good old American fare. Fancier dining is found in some of the big hotels.

Inexpensive in and around Lihue

If you ask anyone in Lihue where you can chow down for cheap, they'll send you to **Ma's Family Inc.,** an institution owned and operated by matriarch Akiyo Honjo, a third-generation Kaua-

ian, who is assisted at times by her great-grandchildren. To arrive make a right off of Rice Street onto Kress Street and follow Kress to the corner, where you'll find Ma's at 4277 Halenani St., tel. (808) 245-3142, open weekdays 5 a.m.-1:30 p.m. and Saturday, Sunday, and holidays 5-10 a.m. (or until customers stop coming). The building is old and a bit run-down, but clean. A few tourists find it, but mostly it's local working people who come here for a hearty and filling meal. Lunches are good, but the super deals are breakfast and the Hawaiian specialties. The coffee, free with breakfast and served with condensed milk, arrives in a large pot about as soon as your seat hits the chair. The menu is posted above the kitchen. You can start the day with The Works, which includes either potatoes or fried noodles, bacon or sausage, and toast for $5. From the

Hawaiian menu, try *kalua* pork with two eggs and rice, poi, and *lomi* salmon, or Kauai sausage—all for under $6. For the famished (or a traveling wrestling team), the menu also offers a pound of *kalua* pork. (If this last item is ordered by one guy who appears grumpy before his gallon of morning coffee, don't bother him!) Ma also serves hamburgers from $1.75 and an assortment of sandwiches including teriyaki beef—the most expensive at $2.50.

Hamura Saimin Stand, at 2956 Kress St., tel. (808) 245-3271, open daily 10-2 a.m. (depending upon business), is just around the corner from Ma's. People flock to the orange countertops of this restaurant all day long, where they perch on short stools to eat giant steaming bowls of saimin. But the real show is around 2 a.m., when all the bars and discos let loose their revelers. There is no decor here (beyond the sign admonishing, Please do not stick gum under counter), just good food. Your first time, try the Saimin Special, which gives you noodles, slivers of meat and fish, vegetables, won ton, and eggs, all floating in a golden broth. Other items on the small menu are variations on the same theme, with nothing more than $5. On the counter will be hot sauce, mustard, and *shoyu*—condiments that you mix yourself in the small bowls that accompany your soup. Enjoy not only the saimin, but also the truly authentic Kauai experience.

Halo Halo Shave Ice occupies a second counter in the same building—use the side entrance. Here you can get some of the best throat coolers on the island.

A replica of a 1920's delivery truck sets the theme at **Ye Old Espresso Court,** open Mon.-Sat. 8 a.m.-5 p.m., directly behind the Exotic Bird Emporium at Paena Court. Here at the bottom of Rice Street, Billie Ann Walker serves up steaming mugs of espresso, cappuccino, and café latte, along with Italian sodas, sun tea, real Ghirardelli cocoa, and spiced *chai*. After you and your taste buds are caffeine-dancing, take care of those early-morning hunger pangs with a fresh pastry baked by the local gourmet Garden Island Bakery. If time permits, Billie will join you at one of the outside tables to "talk story." A great stop for a revitalizing pick-me-up.

A Matter of Taste, located at the Kauai Museum, 4428 Rice St., open during museum hours, (Mon.-Fri. 9:30 a.m.-4 p.m., Saturday until

1 p.m.) is nestled in the quiet museum courtyard. Owner Barbara Watts is a travel enthusiast and will be happy to pour you a house coffee, latte, mocha, cappuccino, or refreshing piña colada or mocha slush. Nibbles include luscious cappuccino and *lilikoi* cheesecake and chocolate-macadamia nut croissants, while light lunches include quiche, minestrone soup, and feisty turkey chili.

Yokozuna's Ramen, a cafeteria-style *ramen* shop with long communal tables and a few potted plants for decor, is located along Rt. 56 as you enter Lihue, just across from McDonald's, tel. (808) 246-1008, and open Mon.-Sat. 10:30 a.m.-2 p.m. and 4:30 p.m.-10 p.m. Try *wakame* (seaweed) *ramen* for $5.60, Yokozuna *ramen,* the house specialty for $6.75, or cold *ramen* for $5.35. Plate lunches and dinners include breaded shrimp for $5.75, beef curry and rice for $5.95, grilled mahimahi for $5.85, or chicken tofu for $6.55. Yokozuna's Ramen is very local, very clean, and known for its good food.

Da Box Lunch, along Rt. 56 as you are entering Lihue from the airport, open for breakfast and lunch Mon.-Sat. 5:30 a.m.-2 p.m., is a small local place appointed in blue with picnic-table seating that has made a pretty good attempt at being "down-home chic." The limited menu presents Belgian waffles or two eggs with a choice of bacon, Portuguese sausage, or buttermilk pancakes, all priced around $5. Box lunches, priced $4-6, might include teriyaki meat, fresh noodles, rice, and the mandatory scoop of mac-salad.

Tip Top Restaurant/Bakery, at 3173 Akahi St. between Rice and Rt. 57, open daily except Monday 6:45 a.m.-9 p.m., tel. (808) 245-2333, doubles as the downstairs lobby of the Tip Top Motel. A local favorite with unpretentious but clean surroundings, the food is wholesome but uninspired—just like the service. Breakfast is the best deal, at around $5, and the macadamia nut pancakes are delish! Plate lunches are under $6 and dinners under $8. You can choose anything from pork chops to teriyaki chicken, and you get soup, salad, rice, and coffee. The *bento* (box lunches), either American-style or Asian, are a good deal. Visit the bakery section and let your eyes tell your stomach what to do. The *malasadas* are fresh daily.

Dani's, 4201 Rice St., toward Nawiliwili near the fire department, tel. (808) 245-4991, open

Mon.-Fri. 5 a.m.-1:30 p.m., Saturday 5 a.m.-1 p.m., closed Sunday, is a favorite with local people. It's been around a while and has a good reputation for giving you a hearty meal for a reasonable price. The food is American-Hawaiian-Japanese. Most full meals range from $4.50 to $8, and you have selections like *lomi* salmon, tripe stew, teri beef and chicken, and fried fish. Unpretentious, the cafeteria-style interior displays formica-topped tables and linoleum floors. Service is friendly, and the food is good.

You won't have to wonder what the future will bring as far as your evening meal if you choose the **Fortune Cookie Restaurant,** 4261 Rice St., tel. (808) 246-0855, open Mon.-Thur. 9:30 a.m.-8 p.m., Friday 9 a.m.-9 p.m., and Saturday 10 a.m.-9 p.m., free delivery in the Lihue area with a $10 minimum purchase. The menu offers a "super *bento*" of deep-fried prawns, *kaugee*, spare ribs, crispy chicken, mixed vegetables, chow mein, and steamed rice for $6.45, deep-fried vegetarian egg rolls $5.25, deep fried wonton soups $7.25, house fried rice $6.50, shrimp Canton $6.50, and a variety of chow meins from $5.95 to $6.45. Fortune Cookie caters to vegetarians with items like braised tofu and Sichuan broccoli (each $5.95). The decor in this one room restaurant is lean and practical.

The **Garden Island Barbecue,** across from the newly renovated Yoneji Bldg. at 4252 Rice St., tel. (808) 245-8868, open Mon.-Sat. 10:30 a.m.-9 p.m., is a simple, clean, and economical eat-in or takeout restaurant. The menu offers varied dishes from the mix of ethnic groups on Kauai including crispy *kaugee* mein at $6.25, pot-roast chicken for $5.95, shrimp and vegetables for $6.25, and oxtail soup for $5.95. Cheaper but equally filling items include loco moco at $5.50, an array of sandwiches and hamburgers priced from only $1.25 to $2.25, and "mini" and regular plate lunches heaped with barbecued short ribs, shrimp curry, or mahi from $3.75 to $5.75, depending on your choices. The food is good, the surroundings adequate, and the service friendly.

Kunja's Korean Restaurant, open Mon.-Sat. 9:30 a.m.-8 p.m. at 4100 Rice St., in the small shopping center next door to Ben Franklin's, tel. (808) 245-8792, is a sit-down or takeout restaurant that serves authentic Korean food. Dishes include short ribs, marinated beef strips, mixed rice and vegetables, and various noodle soups, priced from $3.50 to $6.75. Many are made with the Hawaiian palate in mind, but for a really spicy dish try O-jing-o Po Kum for $5.50 or kimchi soup for $5.50. Clean and tidy, with only a few tables.

Look for an anchor chain marking the two-tone blue **Beach Hut,** open daily except Sunday 7 a.m.-4 p.m. at the bottom of Rice St., just before Nawiliwili Harbor. This upscale window-restaurant offers limited seating in the upstairs "crow's nest," from where you get a great view of the harbor. With a good reputation among local clientele, it serves breakfast and lunches of fish and chips, mahimahi, and charbroiled chicken for under $7.50. The specialty is large, juicy buffalo burgers with all the fixings, but turkey burgers and traditional beef burgers are also offered. Unpretentious, the Beach Hut is an excellent choice for lunch in the Nawiliwili area.

The Nawiliwili Tavern, housed in the old Hotel Kuboyama, at the bottom of Rice St. along Paena Loop Rd., tel. (808) 245-7267, open 11 a.m.-2 a.m., is a friendly neighborhood bar and restaurant where you can mix with local people and tourists alike who are having fun playing pool, shuffleboard, or darts. Enjoy a cold beer in the casual and attractive surroundings, or satisfy your appetite by ordering a teriyaki burger for $6.50, pastrami and Swiss for $6.95, various plate lunches for $8.95, *pu pu* like sashimi at $7.95, or chicken strips for $3.95 (daily lunch special is $5.50).

Don't let the name **Lihue Bakery and Coffee Shop** fool you into thinking of just the familiar styrofoam cup of coffee and powdered donut. Located in the Rice Shopping Center and open Mon.-Sat. 5:30 a.m.-6 p.m. and Sunday 5 a.m.-1 p.m., this storefront restaurant specializes in Filipino foods and pastries. Choose your selection from a hot table laden with ethnic dishes like *pinkabet* and chicken or pork *adobo*. You can have from one to three selections for $4, $4.50, and $5, and top it off with a Filipino pastry.

The **Kukui Grove Shopping Center** has a number of sit-down and sidewalk restaurants. They include the **Deli and Bread Connection,** a kitchenware store with a deli counter offering sandwiches for around $3 and an assortment of soups and salads; **Kauai Cinnamons,** a bake shop specializing in cinnamon rolls; **Si Cisco's,** a Mexican restaurant nicely appointed with a tile floor and a full bar; **Joni Hana,** a walk-up counter with *bento* and plate lunches priced $2-5; and **J.V. Snack Bar,** featuring shave ice and light sandwiches.

One of the mall's best restaurants for Cantonese food at very reasonable prices is **Ho's Garden,** where most dishes are under $7.

Fast Foods

Yes, the smell of the colonel's frying chicken overpowers the flower-scented air, and the golden arches glimmer in the bright Kauai sun. **Pizza Hut, Jack in the Box, McDonald's, Kentucky Fried Chicken, Zack's Frozen Yogurt, Domino's, Baskin-Robbins,** and **Subway Sub Shop** are all located along Rt. 56 as you are entering Lihue. **Burger King** and **Taco Bell** are at the Kukui Grove Shopping Mall, and a **Dairy Queen** brazier can be found on Rice St. across from the Rice Street Shopping Center.

Moderate in and around Lihue

The restaurants in and around Lihue charge as little as $5 for an entree, with the average around $10. Most of these restaurants advertise specials and discounts in the free tourist literature.

Restaurant Kiibo, 2991 Umi St., tel. (808) 245-2650, serves authentic Japanese meals without a big price tag. Many Japanese around town come here to eat. The low stools at the counter are reminiscent of a Japanese *aka-chochin* or *sushiya.* In fact, the sushi bar is a recent addition. The menu listing savory offerings of udon, tempura, teriyaki, and a variety of *teishoku* (specials) includes pictures showing you just what you'll get. The service is quick and friendly; most offerings are under $10. Restaurant Kiibo is *ichiban!* Located just off Rice St., it's open for lunch 11 a.m.-1 p.m. (attracts many office workers) and for dinner 5:30-9 p.m., closed Sunday and holidays. Just around the corner is the **Lihue Cafe** for Japanese and Chinese food. Unpretentious setting, basic food. Open Mon.-Sat. 4:30-9 p.m. (to 10 p.m. on Friday); tel. (808) 245-6471.

The **Barbecue Inn** has been in business for three decades, and if you want a testimonial, just observe the steady stream of local people, from car mechanics to doctors, heading for this restaurant. Word has it that it's better for lunch than dinner. The atmosphere is "leatherette and

formica," but the service is homey, friendly, and prompt. Japanese and American servings are huge. More than 30 entrees include a chicken platter, seafood, even prime rib. The Friday teriyaki platter is a good choice. The scampi is perhaps the best for the price on the island. Most meals come complete with soup or salad, banana bread, vegetables, beverage, and dessert for around $6 and up. Breakfast goes for a reasonable $2, with lunch at bargain prices. The homemade pies are luscious. Cocktails. No credit cards accepted; 2982 Kress St., open Mon.-Sat. 7:30 a.m.-8:45 p.m.; tel. (808) 245-2921.

Tokyo Lobby, in Nawiliwili, at the Pacific Ocean Plaza, 3501 Rice St., Suite 103, tel. (808) 245-8989, open Mon.-Sat. for lunch 11 a.m.-2 p.m., dinner daily 5-9:30 p.m., prides itself on the freshness of the food, especially the seafood. Appointed with shoji screens, a pagoda-style roof over the sushi bar, paper fans, and paper lanterns, the Tokyo Lobby creates an authentic Japanese atmosphere. Most meals are presented in small wooden boats, the signature of the restaurant. For lunch, start with combination *nigiri* sushi or sashimi priced around $9.50, various *don buri* (a bowl of rice with savory bits of meat, egg, and vegetables on top) for $6.50-11.95, or *nabeyaki,* assorted seafood with vegetables, and noodles in a broth for $8.95. The dinner menu starts with appetizers like chicken teriyaki or deep-fried soft-shell crab for $3.75-8.95. Soups and salads include miso for $1.50, or *sunomono,* seafood and cucumber in a light vinegar sauce, for $6.50. Sashimi and sushi platters are served with soup and *tsukemono* (cabbage salad), and range from $8.95 to $19.95 for the deluxe combination. Dinner entrees include calamari steak, curried chicken, and beef teriyaki, all priced under $13.95, or combination dinners like sesame chicken with sashimi for $19.95. The house specialty is the Tokyo Lobby Love Boat (minimum two people), including soup, steamed rice, New York steak, teri chicken, California roll, sashimi, and tempura for $21.50 per person.

The plantation-style **Pacific Bakery and Grill,** 4479 Rice St., tel. (808) 246-0999, will fill your belly without breaking your pocketbook. It's open daily for breakfast and lunch, but dinner is served only Thursday, Friday, and Saturday. Try a fresh pastry or a delicacy from their wood-burning oven.

Kauai Chop Suey, also located in Nawiliwili's Pacific Ocean Plaza, tel. (808) 245-8790, open daily except Monday for lunch 11 a.m.-2 p.m. and for dinner 4:30-9 p.m., is a reasonably priced Chinese restaurant. The restaurant's two dining rooms, separated by a keyhole archway, are alive with plants and brightened by Chinese lanterns hanging from the open-beamed ceiling. The simple but pleasing decor also features tables set with white linen, all dominated by large lazy Susans, perfect for easy sampling of the savory dishes chosen from the menu. Begin with scallop soup or rainbow tofu soup, priced under $7.50. Entrees include sizzling shrimp with lobster sauce for $8.15 (Mama Lau, the owner, says this is the best!), boneless chicken with mushrooms for $7.75, or beef or pork with tomato for under $8. House specials are Kauai Chop Suey for only $7.25, and a variety of noodle dishes, all under $7.50. Kauai Chop Suey also offers plate lunches and dinners to go, and has a steady local clientele, a sure sign of good food at reasonable prices.

Rob's Goodtime Grill is one of Lihue's only "neighborhood bars," where you can watch sports on a big screen TV, hobnob with the locals, sing your heart out when the karaoke fires up, and have a reasonable meal. Located in the Rice Shopping Center, open daily 10-2 a.m., with takeout orders available 10 a.m.-midnight; tel. (808) 246-0311. The menu includes zucchini sticks, shrimp cocktail, chef's salad, or Pacific catch salad (seafood, crabmeat, and jumbo shrimp), all priced $5-6.75. Sandwiches run from pastrami and Swiss for $5.50 down to a veggie for $5.25, while burgers are under $6. Entrees include a mahi platter or stir-fry for $6.75, with a special offered daily. The interior is a mixture of booths, tables, and bar seating, and the service and atmosphere are friendly.

The Beach Club, at the Anchor Cove Shopping Center in Nawiliwili, owned and operated by Charlie Vespoli, is open daily 8-11 a.m. for breakfast, 11 a.m.-5 p.m. for lunch, and 5 a.m.-10 p.m. for dinner with the bar open until closing. However, time permitting, Charlie, the chief cook, will serve you whatever you want at any hour. Breakfast starts with a veggie omelette for $6.95, shrimp omelette for $8.95, or the normal bacon, Portuguese sausage, or green onion and cheddar cheese for $7.95. An espresso bar opens your eyes with cappuccino, espresso Roma, latte, or mocha, all priced $1.95-2.95. There is wine by the glass or the bottle, along with beer and mixed drinks from the full-service bar. Lunch brings cowboy ribs at $6.95, ham-wrapped shrimp for $7.95, special wonton for $5.95, or New England clam chowder for $9.95. Lunch specialties include Caesar salad for $5.95 or sandwiches such as barbecued beef, grilled *ahi,* or a sirloin burger—each $8.95. More hearty dinner dishes inspired by Southern Italian cuisine include Vespoli esposito marinara for $11.95, eggplant parmigiana for $14.95, or scampi at $19.95. Island-style entrees include fresh local fish for $19.95 done with macnut breading, Cajun cream sauce, or garlic champagne. Although the food is good, the Beach Club is still trying to find its niche. The interior, designed originally as a supper club, features a parquet floor, track lighting, and giant windows that open to the beauty of Nawiliwili. But overall, the place has a transitional feeling. The waitpeople are enthusiastic and friendly but still need some training in the finer points of service.

The **Fisherman's Galley,** along Rt. 50 in Puhi (look for the blue marlin and yellowfin tuna on the roof), tel. (808) 246-4700, open daily for lunch and dinner, is the seafood restaurant affiliate of Gent-Lee fishing charters. Here, you can dine on the freshest of fish, creamy chowders, steak and lobster, and, for the landlubber, even burgers (takeout available). The full bar serves bottled and draught beers, wine, and cocktails. Choices include smoked or fresh fish salad for $8.95, fish and chips in various sizes priced $5.95-8.95, and a fresh tuna melt for $6.95. Larger meals include a Hawaiian fish platter for $15.95, a New York Steak at $13.95, or the whopping Captain Bo's Platter, with prawns, steak, and fresh fish, for $25.95.

Hanamaulu Dining

Heading north, in Hanamaulu and clearly marked along Rt. 56, is the **Hanamaulu Restaurant and Tea House and Sushi Bar,** tel. (808) 245-2511, where they must be doing something right-they've lasted in the same location for more than 70 years! Open 9 a.m.-1 p.m. for lunch and 4:30-9 p.m. for dinner. The menu, which includes sushi, *yakiniku,* and a variety of other Japanese and Chinese dishes, is priced right. Ho Tai, the pudgy happy Buddha, greets you as you enter the room, which has shiny parquet flooring and is partitioned by shoji screens and hanging plants. Next door and part of the same restaurant is a sushi bar with tatami-floored rooms that look over a fishpond and a lovely Japanese garden. In the sushi bar section is an elevated tatami made private by sliding screens. The gardens behind and next door to the restaurant are wonderful and well worth a stroll.

The Planter's also sits along Rt. 56 in Hanamaulu, tel. (808) 245-1606. The menu is long and varied, but the specialty is *kiawe*-broiled prime rib and steak. Most meals run in the $12-18 range. Open windows let in the breeze as well as the traffic noise along the highway. The bar is open 3:30-10:30 p.m., happy hour runs until 5:30 p.m., and dinner is served daily except Sunday 5-9:30 p.m. In the large green building next door (built 1908) are the post office, a few shops, and the **Big Wheel Donut Shop** for a quick sugar fix.

The Hanamaulu Plaza in Hanamaulu is also clearly marked along Rt. 56. It is a small but practical shopping center featuring a laundromat and **Ara's Sakamaya,** tel. (808) 245-1707, open Mon.-Sat. 9 a.m.-7 p.m. and Sunday 9 a.m.-5 p.m. It is a takeout deli-restaurant that offers plate lunches, Japanese *bento,* and fresh fish daily.

Across the street is a 7-Eleven and a Shell gas station.

Fine Dining

The rear flagstone veranda and original dining room at Kilohana, the restored 1935 plantation estate of Gaylord Wilcox, have been turned into the breezy **Gaylord's,** at 3-2087 Kaumuali'i Hwy., Lihue, tel. (808) 245-9593, open daily for lunch 11 a.m.-3 p.m., for dinner from 5 p.m., and Sunday for brunch 9:30 a.m.-2:30 p.m.; reservations recommended. Visiting the vintage estate is a must, and if you can't stay for dinner, try lunch, starting with salads and munchies like a Kilohana fruit platter, fresh shrimp cocktail, baked brie in phyllo, or honey-baked brie with macadamia nuts served with fresh fruit and baguette slices for $8.95. The sandwich board offers turkey, beef, and brie, or hot teriyaki or Cajun chicken croissant, at $8.95, along with standards like a grilled cheese or peanut butter sandwich for the children for $3.95. More substantial yet still health-conscious choices include Cajun and regular chicken Caesar salads for $8.95, peppered *ahi* Caesar at $9.95, Gaylord's Papaya Runneth —a papaya stuffed with turkey salad or bay shrimp salad at $7.95—and the very popular Oriental chicken salad at $9.95. The dinner menu begins with appetizers such as blackened prawns and pan-seared sashimi priced around $8.95. Dinner entrees include herb-crusted whole rack of lamb ($24.95), blackened prime rib ($19.95 or $21.95), and chicken *moutard* and free-range Cornish game hen (either $16.95). Fish and game lovers will greatly enjoy the seafood rhapsody, where your taste buds will thrill to Mozart for $26.95; one of three choices of fresh fish (market price) that can be char-broiled, sautéed, or sesame crusted; or Gaylord's famous farm-raised venison marsala—medallions of tender, lean venison (saddle cuts) sautéed and served with artichoke hearts, sun-dried tomato, and basil. Twirl your fork into savory pasta dishes like angel-hair pasta with marinara sauce, Greek-style pasta with grilled chicken, or seafood linguine, all priced $16.95-18.95. For dessert, choose a fabulous Kilohana mud pie, a rich cheesecake, or fantastic banana cream pie, all guaranteed to please. Finish your meal with a cappuccino or coffee mocha prepared on a century-old espresso machine, resplendent in its battered yet burnished glory. Gaylord's also prides itself on having one of the largest wine cellars on Kauai, featuring more than 100 vintages from around the world representing more than two dozen varietals.

Sunday brunch, basically à la carte, features the hearty Plantation Breakfast, cheese blintzes, French toast, Gaylord's eggs Benedict, and Gaylord's waffle topped with real maple syrup or the specially prepared topping of the day. Breakfast meats, served with all types of eggs and omelettes, include ham, bacon, Portuguese sausage, and even spring ham. Prices for a complete brunch are $9.95-14.95 and include a fresh-baked sweet roll, potatoes, and a fresh fruit cup. If you want to move away from the breakfast menu, there is a special Sunday pasta, teriyaki chicken, or even a hamburger. Gaylord's is a wonderful restaurant to visit just to spend a quiet afternoon. The dining facility is indoor/outdoor, utilizing the plantation home's generous veranda, with a more formal dining room inside. Formal tables, surrounded by upholstered chairs, are graced with floral displays set upon fine starched linens. The feeling is one of gentility, as if you were a guest at a very civilized garden party.

J.J.'s Broiler, in the Anchor Cove Shopping Center at 3416 Rice St., tel. (808) 246-4422, open daily 11 a.m.-5 p.m. for lunch, until 10 p.m. for dinner, and until midnight for cocktails and light meals, was known in Kapa'a for more than 30 years as Kauai's original steak house and was famous for its juicy Slavonic steak; it has now moved to Nawiliwili. Richard Jasper, son of the original owner, lolled in his crib to the sizzle of barbecue and the aroma of heady spices, and now owns and operates the restaurant, assisted by executive chef Mark Caeson. The menu offers grain-fed aged beef from the Midwest and four daily choices of fish caught by local captains and delivered fresh. Upon entering, the living landscape of Nawiliwili Bay glistening through the huge windows creates the backdrop for the bi-level interior, done in light wood counterpointed by blue carpeting. The first level is more casual, with a full bar, wooden tables, and bentwood chairs. You can also dine alfresco on the veranda under large yellow umbrellas, but wherever you choose, you are not far from the sea. The tiered upstairs offers horseshoe booths and intimate tables, along with another full bar and wrap-around windows that open to cooling sea breezes. Hanging from the ceiling are replicas of 12-meter racing yachts, exactly like those entered in the America's Cup (not models, these authentic, seaworthy craft are more like one-person go-carts for the ocean). Lunch at J.J.'s starts with potato skins for $7.25, a clam bucket for $6.75, or mozzarella sticks for $6.95. There are also calamari ringers for $6.95, and soups including the specialties—French onion and Hawaiian Ocean Chowder—each for $5.25. You can also have a very reasonable soup and dinghy sandwich (one tuna or one turkey on croissant) for $6.95. Salads include Oriental chicken ($8.50), Italian tortellini ($8.75), and Fisherman's Net—crab, shrimp, and smoked fish on a bed of greens—for $9.95. Sandwiches range from the Kalapaki Yacht Club (turkey, bacon, and avocado for $8.25) to J.J.'s steak sandwich for $9.75. Burgers range from $6.25 to $7.50. Dinner can begin with J.J.'s house es-

cargot or crab cakes (each $8.95). From the broiler, choose New York steak for $19.95, prime rib of beef for $20.25, roasted macadamia or lamb rack for $23.95, or broiled scallops with crisp taro for $18.95. Specialties include a Chinese fajita platter at $19.95, medallions of beef tenderloin for $29.95, and seafood linguine for $22.95. For those wondering about Slavonic steak, it's broiled tenderloin dipped in a special sauce of butter, wine, and garlic and ordered alone or in combination with teriyaki chicken or lobster tail. Daily specials for both lunch and dinner are offered to help save money at this fine steak and seafood restaurant.

The heady aroma of sautéed garlic mixed with the sweet scents of oregano and rosemary floats from the kitchens of **Cafe Portofino.** This authentic Italian restaurant, owned and operated by Giuseppi Avocadi, is located on the second level of the Pacific Ocean Plaza, tel. (808) 245-2121, and is open for lunch Mon.-Fri. 11 a.m.-2 p.m. and daily for dinner 5-10 p.m. Sliding wooden doors open to the distinctive wooden bar—a bold statement of high chic topped with pink-and-black marble and surrounded by marble-topped tables and floral upholstered captain's chairs. The open-beamed wooden ceiling is dotted with fancy fans, track lighting, and a baby spot illuminating a rosewood piano. The main dining room, encased in beveled glass windows, is studded with gray-on-pink tables formally set, and counterpointed by a black-and-white tiled floor. Flowers and ferns add island color, and an outdoor veranda is perfect for a romantic evening. The dinner menu begins with antipasto Portofino for $8, and offers choices like steamed clams, calamari friti, or escargot from $6.50 to $8.75. Salads include the house salad for $4.25 and the ensalate de patate—a warm potato salad with bacon strips—for $5.25, while soups of the day, like minestrone Portofino, are priced at $4.25. Tempting Italian entrees include spaghetti marinara at $13.75, fettuccine Cafe Portofino (noodles sautéed in tomato, mushroom, garlic, butter, oregano, and cheese sauce) for $19, and specialties of the house like scampi with fettuccine for $19, or eggplant parmigiana at $15. Fresh fish, broiled, baked, or sautéed, is served with fresh homemade condiments (daily quote), while an assortment of chicken dishes, from cacciatore to al forno, are all priced around $14.50.

There is a full wine list, and desserts are complemented by a cup of coffee or cappuccino from the full espresso bar. The lunch menu is smaller, both in portion size and price, with most offerings available for under $12. Every night, you are serenaded with live contemporary music, including light jazz, or soloists on saxophone, piano, or harp. Cafe Portofino's newest addition is a formal but comfortable banquet room that can seat up to 100 people. Cafe Portofino is an excellent choice for an evening of romance and fine dining. Buon appetito!

Duke's Canoe Club, on Kalapaki Bay at the Kauai Marriott Resort, tel. (808) 246-9599, open daily 5-10 p.m. for dinner and 4 p.m.-12:30 a.m. for drinks, *pu pu,* and light meals at the Barefoot Bar, with live Hawaiian music nightly, is as much an Hawaiian class act as its namesake, the legendary Duke Kahanamoku. Duke's is one of those places, with an exemplary setting just off the beach, a lustrous wood and thatched interior illuminated by torches and moonlight, that pleasantly overwhelms you with the feeling that you're *really in Hawaii.* At the Barefoot Bar, you feel compelled to quaff a frothy brew and, well . . . kick off your shoes as you listen to the natural melody of wind and waves just a palm tree away. You can order sandwiches, plate lunches, pizza, burgers, and salads, all for well under $10, and you can enjoy a variety of island drinks prepared at the full-service bar. Upstairs, still casual but elegant enough for a romantic evening, the menu offers fresh catch ($17.95-19.95) expertly baked in a glaze of lemon and basil, or ginger, orange, and macadamia, or offered teriyakied, sautéed, or simply broiled. You can also order prime rib for $19.95, shrimp scampi for $17.95, or twist your fork into pasta primavera for a reasonable $9.95. Duke's is Hawaii at its best: relaxed, charming, idyllic, and offering fine cuisine.

Farmers' Market

If you're making your own meals while visiting Kauai, remember that locally grown fresh fruit and vegetables are available from vendors at the farmers' market every Friday at 3 p.m. at Vidinha Stadium in Lihue.

ENTERTAINMENT

Lihue is not the entertainment capital of the world, but if you have the itch to step out at night, there are a few places where you can scratch it.

The **Outrigger Kauai Beach Hotel** has dancing and entertainment at **Gilligan's.** Weekends are popular here with locals from Lihue and Kapa'a who are looking for a night out on the town. The music seems to get louder as the night wears on, and the dance floor is seldom empty. Open Sun.-Thurs. 8 p.m.-2 a.m., Fri.-Sat. 8 p.m.-4 a.m. Dress code.

For a more sophisticated evening, try the Monday evening "A Night of Broadway" dinner show at the Outrigger, where three musical acts are performed between courses of your meal. The evening's entertainment runs $65 for adults and $30 for kids age 6-12. For information and reservations, call (808) 742-6511 or 246-0894.

If you desire slower dancing and quieter music, find your way to the **Lihue Neighborhood Center,** tel. (808) 822-4836, any Friday evening 7:30-9:30 p.m. for down-home square dancing. A $1 donation is requested at the door. Records provide the music, and a caller helps even the novice become proficient by the end of the evening.

Sometimes the **Kukui Grove Shopping Center** presents free entertainment, usually of a Hawaiian nature. The schedule varies, but these shows mainly occur on weekends. Check the free tourist literature to see if anything's going on —these events are worth the effort!

Enjoy a night of shared karaoke fun at **Rob's Goodtime Grill** (formerly Kay's Pub), open Mon.-Sat. 10 a.m.-1 a.m. in the Rice Street Shopping Center. A would-be crooner is given the microphone and sings along with the music— the video and words to which are projected on a screen in the corner. A funky, dark little place with booths and formica tables, it's become a local hangout. Even if your mom used to ask you to stop singing in the shower, here you can join in the fun. Everyone gets applause, and beer and drinks are reasonably priced.

If you're lucky, you can "strike out" at the **Lihue Lanes Bowling Alley,** in the Rice Shopping

Center, 4303 Rice St., tel. (808) 245-5263, open daily 9 a.m.-11 p.m.

Hap's Hideaway Tavern is a friendly neighborhood bar where you can have a quiet beer. The address is 2975 Ewalu St., tel. (808) 245-3473, and although you'll see the sign on Rice Street, you have to go around back to enter.

For 20 years, the **Kauai Community Players** have presented the island with virtually its only theatrical performances. Four times a year—November, February, April, and July—this non-professional community theater group puts on well-known and experimental plays, usually in the Lihue Parish Hall across Nawiliwili Road from the Kukui Grove Shopping Center. Curtain time is 8 p.m., and ticket prices are $7 adults, $5 students and senior citizens (a dollar less with advance purchase). For information on what's currently showing, call (808) 822-7797.

Another possibility for evening entertainment is the nightly luau and torchlighting ceremony at the Outrigger Kauai Beach Hotel.

SHOPPING

Lihue makes you reach for your wallet—with good cause. A stroll through one of the city's four shopping centers is guaranteed to send you home with more in your luggage than you came with. Kauai's best selections and bargains are found here in the city. It helps that Lihue is a *resort* town—second to being a *living* town. Kauaians shop in Lihue, and the reasonable prices that local purchasing generates are passed on to you.

Shopping Centers

The **Rice Shopping Center**, at 4303 Rice St., tel. (808) 245-2033, features a laundromat, a bowling alley, inexpensive eateries, a health-food store, a pet center, and a karaoke bar.

The **Lihue Shopping Center**, in downtown Lihue along Rt. 56, features Gem, a large discount store filled with everything from sporting goods to alohawear, and the Big Save Supermarket, open daily 7 a.m.-11 p.m.

The **Kukui Grove Shopping Center**, tel. (808) 245-7784, along Rt. 50 just a few minutes west of Lihue, is Kauai's largest shopping mall. The center's main stores include Liberty House, for general merchandise and apparel (may be closing); Longs Drugs and Woolworth's for sundries, sporting goods, medicines, and photo needs; Sears; Foot Locker and Kinney Shoes, where you can dress your tootsies appropriately; and Waldenbooks, a first-class complete bookstore. Some distinctive boutiques and shops found at the mall include Alexandra Christian, which has racks of ladies' high fashion including cocktail dresses and evening gowns; Deja Vu, a surf shop with T-shirts, sun hats, glasses, wrap-around dresses, bikinis, boogie boards, surfboards, sandals, and a smattering of dress shirts and shoes; Easy Discount Store, with sundries and souvenirs from sunglasses to beach balls for the kids. Shades of California will protect your eyes with a large assortment of sunglasses, while Zales and Prestige Jewelers offer fine jewelry. To pick up classic, contemporary, or island tunes, head for Tempo Music Shop; for anything electronic that beeps or buzzes, head for Radio Shack. Other shops include Pictures Plus for island prints and custom framing; Rave, another store for the younger set with dresses, bikinis, and alohawear; Kauai Beach Co., a great shop for T-shirts and distinctive men's and women's fashions; Dan's Sports Shop, tel. (808) 246-0151, for golf clubs, tennis racquets, baseball caps, mitts, dartboards, and water gear; General Nutrition Center for the health conscious; Kaybee Toys, for children, with a large selection of stuffed animals and games; the IndoPacific Trading Co., the most intriguing store in the mall; and, finally, the Kauai Product Store, which offers muumuu, dolls, koa boards, carvings, art work, post cards, and a smattring of jewelry, all made on Kauai.

The **Anchor Cove Shopping Center**, at 3416 Rice St., just a minute from Kalapaki Beach and Nawiliwili Harbor, is Lihue's newest shopping and dining mall. Among the semidetached kiosks, you will find an ABC Store, open daily 7 a.m.-10:30 p.m., selling sundries, beachwear, groceries, film, drugs, cosmetics, and also liquor; Aloha Wear, open daily 9 a.m.-5 p.m. and until 6 on Monday and 9 Sunday, selling discounted alohawear for the entire family; Feet First, open daily 9 a.m.-9 p.m., where you can not only dress your tootsies in anything from froufrou golden slippers to tough but tasteful Tevas, but also find aloha shirts, matching cabana sets, discounted bathing suits, beach cover-ups, and shorts; another store is Crazy Shirts, open daily 9 a.m.-9 p.m., with well made and distinctive designed T-shirts; Sunglass Hut International, open daily 9 a.m.-9 p.m., which can protect your eyes and enhance your image with sunglasses from famous makers like Revo, Ray Ban, Oakley, and Maui Jim—with 1,700 stores in their chain, they offer excellent prices, and satisfaction is guaranteed even at a store in your home area; Royal Hawaiian Heritage, open Mon.-Sat. 10 a.m.-9 p.m. and Sunday 10 a.m.-6 p.m., sparkles with Hawaiian-inspired jewelry including personalized pendants and bracelets all in solid 14-karat gold; Sophisticated You, owned and operated by former beauty queen Therese Jasper and open daily 10 a.m.-5 p.m. and Sunday 11 a.m.-3 p.m., features ladies' fine apparel for sale or rent, and rents wedding gowns and tuxedos, just in case the tropical sun goes to your head and you decide to tie the knot. Other establishments in the center include Ohana Helicopter Tours, J.J.'s Broiler, and The Beach Club, a newcomer to the dining scene trying to get established.

Pay 'n Save is on Rice St. with a row of shops including Daylight Donuts. In Nawiliwili is the **Pacific Ocean Plaza,** just across from Anchor Cove, with clothing stores, several restaurants, and an art gallery.

Along Rt. 56 just as you enter Lihue, you'll see a classic building dating from 1923. Once the home of Garden Island Motors Limited, it's now a mini-mall housing Subway Sandwich Shop, a national chain; Photo Spectrum, offering one-hour film processing; and Baskin-Robbins 31 Flavors.

Clothing and Specialty Shops

Don't pass up **Hilo Hattie**, 3252 Kuhio Hwy., at the intersection with Rt. 57, tel. (808) 245-3404, an institution of alohawear, to at least educate yourself on products and prices. Though their designs may not be one-of-a-kind, their clothing is very serviceable and well made. Specials are always offered in the free tourist literature and on clearance racks at the store itself. They also have a selection of gifts and souvenirs. Among the abundance of incentives to get you in is the free hotel pickup from Poipu to Kapa'a, a tour of the factory, free refreshments while you look around, and free on-the-spot alterations. Open every day 8:30 a.m.-5 p.m.

Kapaia Stitchery is where you find handmade and distinctive fashions. This shop is along Rt. 56 in Kapaia, a tiny village between Hanamaulu and Lihue. The owner is Julie Yukimura, who, along with her grandmother and a number of very experienced island seamstresses, creates fashions, quilts, and embroideries that are beautiful, painstakingly made, and priced right. You can choose a garment off the rack or have one tailor-made from the Stitchery's wide selection of cotton fabrics. You can't help being pleased with this fine shop!

Clothing at discount prices is found at **Garment Factory to You** in the Lihue Shopping Center. This store is as practical as its name.

Bamboo Lace, tel. (808) 245-6007, in the Pacific Ocean Plaza at 3501 Rice St., Nawiliwili, open Mon.-Sat. 11 a.m.-7 p.m., offers dresses, blouses, hats, jewelry, and a smattering of alohawear. It's owned and operated by Nadine, who handpicks fashionable clothing from the continent. Shelves also hold bath and skin-care products, gift items, lingerie, fancy shoes, and straw hats. Basically, Bamboo Lace is a women's fine apparel store, which Nadine says resembles her closet, only a lot bigger.

You can find everything you need to try your luck in Kauai's waters at **Lihue Fishing Supply,** 2985 Kalena St., tel. (808) 245-4930, open Mon.-Fri. 8:30 a.m.-5 p.m. and Saturday 8:30 a.m.-4:30 p.m.

Arts, Crafts, and Souvenirs

The longest-lasting part of a journey is the memory of that journey, capable of instantly transporting you through space and time to recapture the sublime beauty of the moment. One of the best catalysts for recapturing this memory is an inspirational work of art.

Kahn Galleries specializes in original artworks and limited-edition prints created by some of the finest artists Hawaii has to offer. The Kahn Galleries, open daily 9 a.m.-10 p.m., are located in Hanalei Town right in the old schoolhouse, tel. (808) 826-6677; in Koloa in the main building that faces you as you enter town, tel. (808) 742-2277; at the **Kilohana Plantation,** just west of Lihue, tel. (808) 246-4454; in the Kauai Village Shopping Center, tel. (808) 822-4277; and at Kapaa Coconut Marketplace, in a slightly different venue called Island Images, where some of the great art is sold at discount prices. Some of the master artworks shown by Kahn Galleries include Tabora's dramatic seascapes of wind-whipped palms and crashing surf, made magically mysterious by the light of translucent moon or illuminated by a glorious sunset; the landscapes of father and sons H., Thomas, and Richard Leung, impressionists who blend the techniques of East and West into paintings of provocative, dazzling beauty; the environmental impressionism of world-famous George Sumner; and the finely detailed sculptures of Randy Puckett. Kahn Galleries also offers unbelievable prints produced by a computer-based operation called *giclee,* where a picture of the original is made into a transparency that is scanned to match subtle strokes and color variations perfectly, and then airbrushed at 4 million droplets per second (each 4 times smaller than a human hair) to paper or canvas, creating a cyberspace copy of amazing exactness.

The Country Store, at the Kilohana Plantation, open daily 9 a.m. to late evening, specializes in Hawaiian-inspired souvenirs, wind chimes, wicker picnic baskets, cutlery, Hawaiian quilted pillows, vintage fabric handbags, hand-blown and hand-etched glass, and lovely silver jewelry. Master crafts from local artists include koa boxes by Robert Brackbill and Roy Tsumoto; koa, camphor, and kamani bowls by Robert Bouman; throws (small blankets) by local artist Anne Oliver, who hand-dyes and -sews her work; and cobalt blue glass, hand-blown and -etched by Jennifer Pontz.

Upstairs and down (the koa banister is a delight to run your hand over) in the vintage Kilohana Plantation Home you will also find **Sea Reflections,** glimmering with glass, jewelry, and carvings; **Grande's,** for that impulse purchase of a gold bracelet or pearl necklace; **Kilohana Gallery,** offering eye-catching *tapa* prints, wooden bowls, and inexpensive souvenir items; and the somehow politically incorrect-sounding **Dolls and Furry Little Critters** (whose name, said in the wrong context, could get your face slapped), selling fuzzy-wuzzies and doll babies.

If you're after just filling a shopping basket with trinkets and gimcracks for family and friends back home, go to **Gem** in Lihue or **Longs Drugs** in the Kukui Grove Shopping Center. Their bargain counters are loaded with terrific junk for a buck or two.

The IndoPacific Trading Co. at the Kukui Grove Shopping Center (also at the Coconut Market Place in Kapa'a and at Kong Lung Complex in Kilauea), tel. (808) 246-2177, is a distinctive boutique selling artifacts, incense, local island perfumes, and cotton and rayon clothing mostly from Indonesia and Thailand, including replicas of classic Hawaiian shirts. Artworks include sculpted ducks, fish, primitive artwork from New Guinea, Borneo, and Australia and a beautiful collection of Balinese masks. Richly embroidered Burmese tapestries, baskets, hammocks, and wind chimes imported from Java, Sumatra, and other parts of Oceania hang on the walls. Amazing pieces of furniture including hand-carved teak chests, a beveled glass mirror intricately etched, a Balinese temple door, prancing horses, and bentwood chairs are also on display.

For better-quality souvenirs, along with custom jewelry, try **Linda's Creation,** at 4254 Rice Street. This shop, owned and operated by Joe and Linda Vito, is well stocked with items ranging from silk wallets for $2 to lovely vases for more than $100.

Kauai Museum Shop, at the Kauai Museum has authentic souvenirs and items Hawaiian with competitive prices.

The Gift Gallery, at the Pacific Ocean Plaza at 3501 Rice St., just near Nawiliwili Harbor, open Tues.-Sat. 10 a.m.-9 p.m., is filled with stuffed animals, koa woodwork, tile whales, and decorative exotic birds, mugs, wind chimes, serving platters, glasswork, and a good collection of postcards.

Longi's Crackseed Center, in the Rice Shopping Center, open Mon.-Fri. 8:30 a.m.-9 p.m., Saturday 8:30 a.m.-4:30 p.m., and Sunday 10 a.m.-4 p.m., is packed with large glass jars filled with crackseed, preserved and spiced fruits, seeds, and nuts.

Listen for the chatter of a cheeky cockatoo leading you into **Exotic Bird Emporium,** at 3470 Paena Loop Rd. at the bottom of Rice St. just before the harbor, tel. (808) 246-6707, open Mon.-

Sat. 9 a.m.-8 p.m. and Sunday 10 a.m.-6 p.m., where owners Bob and Geri Jasper are proud to offer "the world's finest hand-fed baby birds" (read "spoiled rotten"). These magnificently plumed "living feather dusters" include everything from Moluccan cockatoos to hyacinth macaws and range in price from $1,000 to $20,000. All are U.S. bred from incubated eggs, so the Emporium's birds are no threat to the deterioration of the rain forest or the natural populations of their wild relatives. The health of all birds is 100% guaranteed, and they are imprinted from birth to accept human contact. Bob and Geri will ship them anywhere in the continental U.S.

In the humble and poorly marked Kalapaki Shopping Center, just a minute from the Anchor Cove Shopping Center towards Nawiliwili Harbor, is the **Bead Store,** open daily 9 a.m.-5 p.m., tel. (808) 245-8713, sparkling from floor to ceiling with baubles, bangles, and beads. Look for a couple of hanging shell baskets and a makeshift sign reading Beads. Inside, the shimmering faux jewels—some pre-strung, others waiting for nimble fingers—come from all over the world, including the Philippines, Czechoslovakia, and Native American beads from throughout the southwest. Other items include Hawaiian fishhooks, a case full of sterling silver, gaping shark jaws, crystals, and plenty of carvings of horses, fish, and turtles. A grab bag called "findings" offers bits and pieces of the various baubles at a large markdown.

The **Kalapaki Bay Gallery,** at Pacific Ocean Plaza, tel. (808) 245-5125, open daily noon-10 p.m., features a collection of works that attempt to capture the lighted soul of Hawaii. Here are the famed seascapes, waterfalls, and landscapes of Edgardo Garcia and the oils of famed Maui artist James O'Neill. The owner is artist D.J. Khamis, who, in a collaboration with O'Neill, brings to life a cavorting humpback whale rising from the deep along Kauai's dramatic Na Pali Coast, and in a solo piece raises Madame Pele triumphantly from her ancient volcano home on Kauai. Khamis has another gallery just across the courtyard called **Kauai Collections,** filled with the works of aspiring artists capturing scenes from around the entire state. One artist, Mark D'Amato, works in fossilized ivory, creating amazing miniatures of fishhooks, roses, and even feathers. Another is Roman Hubbel, a sculptor/potter who is just as adept at working in free-form as he is in classic form. Some of the paintings are by a recent arrival, Rafal Chlodzinski, an internationally known watercolorist and graduate architect who renders Hawaii in a bright and whimsical style.

The soothing rich aroma of a premium cigar wafts from the **Kapaia Trading Company** into the big dip along Rt. 56, just at the turnoff to Wailua Falls, at 3-601 A Kuhio Hwy., Lihue, HI 96766, tel. (808) 246-6792, open daily 9 a.m. to sunset. Owned and operated by Bill Carl, this one-time gas station is a great place for both men and women to peruse. The swirl of burly koa and other native woods lend natural luster to the handmade humidors and fine furniture that Bill has crafted. If you enjoy a fine cigar, write or call Bill in advance to get a list of the cigars he carries (which includes Mackanudos, Fuente, Partigas, Fonseca, and Griffins, among many others). You can pack your purchases in one of many styles of humidors boasting brass hinges, a built-in sponge and bentonite clay holder to keep the humidity constant, a humidity gauge, drawers perfectly designed to hold different shapes of cigars, and a lifetime guarantee (from the builder). From cigar-box-size to a desktop model, these beauties go for from $250 to $1,650. The hand-built furniture on display includes everything from a dining set to an ice bucket of solid koa and a wine rack with glass holder and built-in fruit and cheese tray. Kapaia Trading Company also hosts a monthly cigar tasting for $45 that includes three excellent cigars, fine port, wine, whiskey or cognac, and gourmet hors d'oeuvres. The Kapaia Trading Company, more than just a shopping stop, is a "real" working man's gallery, where years of carpentry experience has been called upon to create exquisite pieces of fine art.

Photo Needs

For a full-line photo store go to **Don's Camera Center,** 4286 Rice St., tel. (808) 245-6581. You'll find all you'll need from a wide selection of famous brands to camera repair and one-day processing. **Longs Drugs, Woolworth's,** and **Kauai 1-hour Photo** at the Kukui Grove Shopping Center have inexpensive film and processing. **Senda Studio,** at 4450 Hardy St., is a studio and supply shop.

Supermarkets and Health Food Stores
The **Big Save Supermarket,** 4444 Rice St., tel. (808) 245-6571, is open daily 7 a.m.-11 p.m. The well-stocked **Star Super Market** is in the Kukui Grove Shopping Center.

Also in the Kukui Grove Shopping Center is **General Nutrition Center,** a full-service health food store.

Hale O' Health, tel. (808) 245-9053, in the Rice Shopping Center, open Mon.-Fri. 8 a.m.-5 p.m. and Sat.-Sun. until 3 p.m., specializes in vitamins and minerals. The shelves are stocked with everything from whole-wheat flour to spices, organic pastas, and a good selection of teas. The back deli case holds a small selection of fresh organic vegetables and prepared deli sandwiches.

M.G.L. DOMENY DE RIENZI

WAILUA

Wailua (Two Waters) is heralded by the swaying fronds of extra-tall royal palms; whenever you see these, like the *kahili* of old, you know you're entering a special place. The Hawaiian *ali'i* knew a choice piece of real estate when they saw one, and they cultivated this prime area at the mouth of the Wailua River as their own. Through the centuries they built many *heiau* in the area, some where unfortunates were slaughtered to appease the gods, others where the weak and vanquished could find succor and sanctuary. The road leading inland along the Wailua River was called the King's Highway. Commoners were allowed to travel along this road and to approach the royal settlement by invitation only. The most exalted of the island's *ali'i* traced their proud lineage to Puna, a Tahitian priest who, according to the oral tradition, arrived in the earliest migrations and settled here.

Even before the Polynesians came, the area was purportedly settled by the semimythical Mu. This lost tribe may have been composed of early Polynesians who were isolated for such a long time that they developed different physical characteristics from their original ancestral stock. Or perhaps they were a unique people altogether, whom history never recorded. But like another island group, the Menehune, they were said to be dwarfish creatures who shunned outsiders. Unlike the industrious Menehune, who helped the Polynesians, the Mu were fierce and brutal savages whose misanthropic characteristics confined them to solitary caves in the deep interior along the Wailua River, where they led unsuspecting victims to their deaths.

Wailua today has a population of more than 2,000, but you'd never know that driving past it, as most houses are scattered in the hills behind the coast. Though an older resort area, it's not at all overdeveloped. The natural charm is as vibrant as ever. Depending on conditions, the beaches can be excellent, and shops, restaurants, and nightlife are close at hand. With development increasing both to the east and west, perhaps now, as in days of old, the outstanding beauty of Wailua will beckon once again.

SIGHTS

Wailua is famous primarily for two attractions, one natural, the other manmade. People flock to these, but there also exist, in the hills behind the settlement along King's Highway, deserted *heiau*, sacred birthing stones, old cemeteries, and vantages for meditative views of the river below.

Fern Grotto

Nature's attraction is the Wailua River itself, Hawaii's only navigable stream, which meanders inland toward its headwaters atop forbidding Mt. Waialeale. Along this route is the Fern Grotto, a tourist institution of glitz, hype, and beauty rolled into one. Two local companies run sightseeing trips to the grotto on large motorized barges. As you head the two miles upriver, the crew tells legends of the area and serenades visitors with Hawaiian songs. A hula demonstration is given, where you are encouraged to get up and swing along. The grotto itself is a huge rock amphitheater, whose ever-misty walls create the perfect conditions for ferns to grow. And grow they do, wildly and with abandon, filling the cavern with their deep musty smell and penetrating green beauty. Partially denuded of its lush green coat by Hurricane Iniki, the grotto is slowly filling in and becoming again the beauty it once was. Although the grotto is smaller than one might imagine, the resonating acoustics are wonderful from inside. Here in the natural cathedral, musicians break into the Hawaiian Wedding Song; over the years a steady stream of brides and grooms have come to exchange vows. The Fern Grotto trip is an amusement ride, but it's also the only way to get there. It's enjoyable and memorable, but you have to stay in the right frame of mind; otherwise, it's too easy to put down. (For tour information, see **Getting Around**)

Smith's Tropical Paradise

Set along the Wailua River is this 30-acre botanical and cultural garden. A large entranceway welcomes you and proclaims it a "tropical paradise." Inside, most plants are labeled; many are ordinary island foliage, but others are rare and exotic even for the Garden Island. The entire area is sheltered and well watered, and it's easy to imagine how idyllic life was for the original Hawaiians. The array of buildings includes a luau house and a lagoon theater used in the evenings for an international musical show and luau. Peacocks and chickens pecking beneath the trees are natural groundskeepers, preventing insects and weeds from overpowering the gardens. The "villages"—Japanese-, Philippine-, and Polynesian-inspired settlements—are merely plywood facsimiles. However, the grounds themselves are beautifully kept and very impressive. For those who won't be trekking into the Kauai backcountry (especially for those who will), this garden provides an excellent opportunity to familiarize yourself with Kauai's plants, flowers, and trees. You are welcome to walk where you will, but signs guide you along a recommended route. Scheduled mini-trams carry tourists around the grounds for an additional fee. Entrance fees are $5 adults, $2.50 children 2-11; the tram tour is an additional $3 for adults, $2 for children. The entrance fee is good 8:30 a.m.-4:30 p.m., after which the gardens are readied for the evening entertainment. The luau/musical show costs $43.75 for adults and $26 for children ($10.50 and $5.25 for the show only). Reservations are necessary for both. Rated the favorite luau show on the island, this spectacle includes Hawaiian music, a fiery volcanic eruption, and dances from all over the Pacific. For information, call (808) 821-6892 or 821-6893 or pick up tickets at the Smith's booth across from the entrance to the Coco Palms Hotel on the north side of the river mouth. To get to the gardens, follow the road past the Wailua Marina on the south side of the river and park in the large lot.

Kamokila Hawaiian Village

Situated at a bend in the Wailua River on the way to the Fern Grotto is Kauai's only re-created folk village. Kamokila (Stronghold) has been cut from the jungle on the site of an *ali'i* village, the first of seven ancient villages in this valley; the villages farther up were for common laborers. The prominent ridge across the river indicates the boundary past which the ordinary man could not tread for fear of his losing his life.

The old village sat on terraces on the hillside above the river, and fields were cultivated where the village now lies. Kamokila has been resurrected to give visitors a glimpse of what island life was like for the ancient Hawaiians. Created in 1981, it was destroyed almost immediately by Hurricane Iwa in 1982, and badly knocked around again by Hurricane Iniki in 1992. It is continually going through renovation to make it more authentic; there are examples of buildings, agricultural plots, fruit trees and medicinal plants, and demonstrations of ancient crafts and activities of everyday life. Taro is grown and poi made, mats and skirts are woven, and traditional medicines prepared. A *hale noa* (chief's sleeping quarters), *hale koa* (warrior's house), *pahoku hanau* (birthing house), *hale ali'i akoakoa* (assembly hall), *laola pa'au* (herbal medicine office), and *lana nu'u mamao* (oracle tower) have been erected. The *imu* pits for cooking are functional, and there is an athletic ground used for games at festive times of the year. There are also tikis (spirit containers) and *aumakua* (ancestral spirit icons) set up at propitious spots around the village.

A guide escorts you and explains the importance of each site, the methods of creating handicrafts and tools, the use of both the ordinary and medicinal plants, and how the village operated on a daily basis. You may drive down to

the village by following a steep one-lane track that skirts the ridge—the turnoff is just above the Opaeka'a Falls overlook on Rt. 580. A free shuttle bus service is available from hotels in the Wailua and Kapa'a area. Future plans include a ferry ride from the Wailua Marina to the village. The entrance fee is $5 for adults, $2.50 for children under 12; open Mon.-Sat. 9 a.m.-5 p.m. A trip to this inspiring village is well worth the time and effort and will certainly add to your knowledge of the roots of Hawaiian life. For more information, call (808) 822-3350.

Historical Sites and *Heiau*

The King's Highway (Rt. 580), running inland from Wailua, and Rt. 56, the main drag, have a number of roadside attractions and historical sites dating from the precontact period. Most are just a short stroll from your car and well worth the easy effort. The mountains behind Wailua form a natural sculpture of a giant in repose, aptly called the **Sleeping Giant.** You have to stretch your imagination just a little to see him (his outline is clearer from farther up, toward Kapa'a), and although not entirely a bore, like most giants, he's better left asleep. This giant and his green cover are part of the Nounou Forest Reserve.

Along Rt. 56 just before the Coco Palms Hotel, a tall stand of palms on the east side of the Wailua River is part of Lydgate State Park and marks the spot of **Hauola O' Honaunau,** a tem-

From the bell stones you can look over the Wailua River and Coco Palms Resort to the sea.

ROBERT NILSEN

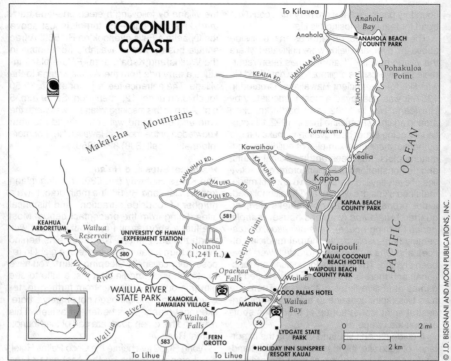

COCONUT COAST

To Kilauea

Anahola Bay

Anahola

ANAHOLA BEACH COUNTY PARK

Pohakuloa Point

KEALIA RD.

HAUAALA RD.

KUHIO HWY

Makaleha Mountains

Kumukumu

Kawaihau

Kealia

Kapaa

KAWAIHAU RD.

HAUIKI RD.

KAAPUNI RD.

WAIPOULI RD.

581

KAPAA BEACH COUNTY PARK

PACIFIC OCEAN

KEAHUA ARBORETUM

Wailua Reservoir

UNIVERSITY OF HAWAII EXPERIMENT STATION

580

Nounou (1,241 ft.)▲

Sleeping Giant

Waipouli

KAUAI COCONUT BEACH HOTEL

WAIPOULI BEACH COUNTY PARK

Opaekaa Falls

Wailua

COCO PALMS HOTEL

Wailua River

WAILUA RIVER STATE PARK

KAMOKILA HAWAIIAN VILLAGE

MARINA

Wailua Bay

Wailua River

Wailua Falls

583

FERN GROTTO

56

LYDGATE STATE PARK

To Lihue

To Lihue

HOLIDAY INN SUNSPREE RESORT KAUAI

0   2 mi

0   2 km

© J.D. BISIGNANI AND MOON PUBLICATIONS, INC.

ple of refuge that welcomed offending *kapu*-breakers of all social classes. Here miscreants could atone for their transgressions and have their spiritual slates wiped clean by the temple priests, enabling them to return to society without paying with their lives. Both the refuge and **Hikina Heiau** are marked by a low encircling wall. The area is extremely picturesque here, where the Wailua River meets the sea. Perhaps it's knowledge about the temple of refuge that creates the atmosphere, but here, as at all of these merciful temple sites, the atmosphere is calm and uplifting, as if some spiritual residue has permeated the centuries. It's a good spot to relax in the cool of the grove, and there are picnic tables available.

As Rt. 580 meanders inland, you pass **Wailua River State Park.** Then immediately look for **Poaiahu Arboretum** and its convenient turnout. The arboretum is merely a stand of trees along the roadside. Across the road is **Holo Holo Ku Heiau,** where the unfortunate ones who didn't make it to the temple of refuge were sacrificed to the never-satisfied gods. This temple is one of Kauai's most ancient; the altar itself is the large slab of rock near the southwest corner. Behind the *heiau,* a silver guardrail leads up the hill to a small, neatly tended Japanese cemetery. The traditional tombstones chronicling the lives and deaths of those buried here have turned green with lichens against the pale blue sky. As if to represent the universality of the life-death cycle, **Pohaku Hoo Hanau,** the "royal birthing stones," are within an infant's cry away. Royal mothers came here to deliver the future kings and queens of the island. The stones somehow look comfortable to lean against, and perhaps their solidity reinforced the courage of the mother.

Back on Rt. 580, you start to wend your way uphill. You can see how eroded and lush Kauai is from this upland perch. On your left is the verdant Wailua Valley, watered by the river, and on your right, separated by a spit of land perhaps only 200 yards wide, is a relatively dry gulch. Notice, too, the dark green freshwater as it becomes engulfed by the royal blue of the ocean in the distance. As you climb, look for an HVB Warrior pointing to **Opaeka'a Falls.** The far side of the road has an overlook; below is the Wailua River and the Kamokila Hawaiian Village. Take a look around to see how undeveloped Kauai is. Across the road and down a bit from the Opaeka'a turnoff is **Poliahu Heiau,** supposedly built by the Menehune. Nothing is left but a square wall enclosure that is overgrown on the inside. Do not walk on the walls as it's believed that the spirits of the ancestors are contained in the rocks. Down the ridge, at the end of a gravel track, are the **bell stones;** pounded when a royal *wahine* gave birth, their peals could be heard for miles. From here, there is a great view over the river and down to the coast.

Beaches, Parks, and Recreation

Wailua has few beaches, but they are excellent. **Wailua Municipal Golf Course** skirts the coast, fronting a secluded beach, and because of its idyllic setting is perhaps the most beautiful public links in Hawaii. Even if you're not an avid golfer, you can take a lovely stroll over the fairways as they stretch out along the coastline. The greens fees are a reasonable $20 weekdays, $30 weekends, with carts and clubs for rent. The driving range is open until 10 p.m. For the convenience of golfers, the clubhouse has a dining room and snack bar open daily. For information or links reservations call (808) 241-6666. Below the links is a secluded beach. You can drive to it by following the paved road at the western end of the course until it becomes dirt and branches toward the sea. The swimming is good in the sheltered coves and the snorkeling is better than average along the reef. Few people ever come here, and plenty of nooks and crannies are good for one night's bivouac.

Lydgate Beach is a gem. It's clearly marked along Rt. 56 on the south side of the Wailua River, behind the Holiday Inn Sunspree Resort complex. Two large lava pools make for great swimming even in high surf. The smaller pool is completely protected and perfect for tots, while the larger is great for swimming and snorkeling. Stay off the slippery volcanic rock barrier. This beach is never overcrowded, and you can find even more seclusion by walking along the coast away from the built-up area. If you head to the river, the brackish water is refreshing, but stay away from the point where it meets the ocean; the collision creates tricky, wicked currents. **Lydgate State Park** also provides sheltered picnic tables under a cool canopy provided by a thick stand of ironwoods, plus grills, restrooms, and showers, but no camping. The beach across the river fronting the Coco Palms is treacherous and should only be entered on calm days when lifeguards are in attendance.

East Kauai Trails

All these trails are in the mountains behind Wailua. Most start off Rt. 580, which parallels the Wailua River. Here are an arboretum and some fantastic vistas from Nonou Mountain, known as the Sleeping Giant.

Nonou Mountain Trail, East Side, begins off Haleilio Road just north of the junction of Routes 56 and 580, at the Kinipopo Shopping Village. Follow Haleilio Road for 1.2 miles to pole no. 38. Park near a water pump. The trailhead is across the drainage ditch and leads to a series of switchbacks that scales the mountain for 1.75 miles. The trail climbs steadily through native and introduced forest, and ends at a picnic table and shelter. From there you can proceed south through a stand of monkeypod trees to a trail that leads to the Giant's face. The going gets tough, and unless you're very sure-footed, stop before the narrow ridge (500-foot drop) that you must cross. The views are extraordinary and you'll have them to yourself.

Nounou Mountain Trail, West Side, is found after turning onto Rt. 580 at the Coco Palms. Follow it a few miles to Rt. 581, turn right for just over a mile and park at pole no. 11. Follow the right of way until it joins the trail. This will lead you through a forest of introduced trees planted in the 1930s. The West Trail joins the East Trail at the 1.5-mile marker and proceeds to the picnic table and shelter. This trail is slightly shorter and not as arduous. For both, bring water as there is none on the way.

Follow Rt. 580 until you come to the University of Hawaii Experimental Station. Keep going until the pavement ends and then follow the dirt road for almost a mile. A developed picnic and freshwater swimming area is at Keahua Stream. On the left is a trailhead for **Keahua Arboretum.** The moderate trail is one-half mile through a forest reserve maintained by the Division of Forestry; marked posts identify the many varieties of plants and trees. The **Kuilau Trail** begins about 200 yards before the entrance to the arboretum, on the right. This trail climbs the ridge for 2.5 miles, en route passing a picnic area and shelter. Here are some magnificent views of the mountains; continue through a gorgeous area complete with waterfalls. After you cross a foot-bridge and climb the ridge, you come to another picnic area. A few minutes down the trail from here you join the **Moalepe Trail,** which starts off Olohena Road, 1.5 miles down Rt. 581 after it branches off Rt. 580. Follow Olohena Road to the end and then take a dirt road for 1.5 miles to the turnaround. The last part can be extremely rutted and slick in rainy weather. This hike is a popular horseback-riding trail. It gains the heights and offers some excellent panoramas before joining the Kuilau Trail.

PRACTICALITIES

ACCOMMODATIONS

The hotels in Wailua are like the beaches—sparse but good. Your only hotel choice is the Holiday Inn Sunspree, with its admirable location fronting Lydgate State Park, as the famous Coco Palms not reopened again. Wailua also has one B&B.

Holiday Inn Sunspree Resort Kauai
A $5 million renovation and property management change has transformed the old Kauai Resort in the 216-room oceanfront Holiday Inn Sunspree Resort Kauai, at 3-5920 Kuhio Hwy., Kapaa, HI 96746, tel. (808) 823-6000 or (888) 823-5111, fax (808) 823-6666, e-mail: info@holidayinn-kauai.com, website: www.holidayinn-kauai.com. This hotel has a lovely setting above Lydgate Park, with the Hauola Temple of Refuge adjacent to the grounds. Incorporated into the architecture are a series of cascading pools and a koi pond that boils with frenzied color at feeding time. The main lobby is a huge affair with swooping beams in longhouse style. The hotel facilities include two swimming pools, jacuzzi, a fitness room, tennis, volleyball, and shuffleboard courts, as well as a restaurant, lounge, snack bar, and market deli. Most rooms have ocean views; rates run $150-175 and suites $190-225. Cabanas with kitchenettes are separate from the main facility and have unobstructed views of the beach. Luxury.

Fern Grotto Inn
A unique lodging alternative is the Fern Grotto Inn, a bed and breakfast surrounded by Wailua River State Park. This plantation home on the Wailua River offers three tastefully furnished bedrooms with private baths, gourmet breakfast especially tailored for the health-conscious traveler, and a private garden perfect for an evening stroll. Rates range $80-100 per night, or the entire home can be rented for $1,250 per week. For information, contact the Fern Grotto Inn at 4561 Kuamoo Rd., Wailua, HI 96746, tel. (808) 822-2560, or on Oahu at (808) 521-5521. Moderate.

Coco Palms Resort
The Coco Palms Resort was a classic Hawaiian hotel, one of the first tourist destinations built on the island, but it took a terrible beating during Hurricane Iniki. There is talk of it reopening or being replaced by another resort, but don't hold your breath. The Polynesian-inspired buildings are interspersed through a monumental coconut grove planted by a German immigrant in the early 1800s. His aspiration was to start a copra plantation, and although it failed, his plantings matured into one of the largest stands of coconut trees in the islands. When Hollywood needed "paradise" it came here. The Coco Palms served as movie backdrop for Elvis in *Blue Hawaii* and for Rita Hayworth in the movie *Sadie Thompson,* bringing the hotel (and the island) notoriety. Nightly, the hostelry's famous torch-lighting ceremony took place under the palm canopy, which encircles a royal lagoon once used to fatten succulent fish for the exclusive use of the *ali'i.* The Coco Palms was a peaceful garden brought to its knees by the hurricane. The greenery will rebound. One only wonders if the hotel will as well.

FOOD

Inexpensive

In the Wailua Shopping Center behind Sizzler is the pick-and-choose, hot-table-style **Manila Fastfood Restaurant,** tel. (808) 823-0521, serving breakfast 7-9:30 a.m., lunch 10 a.m.-3 p.m., and dinner 4-7 p.m. A mixture of Filipino and American dishes are served for around $5.

Wah Kung Chop Suey, in the Kinipopo Shopping Village just across from the Sizzler Steakhouse, tel. (808) 822-0560, open daily 11 a.m.-8:30 p.m., is a clean, no-decor restaurant offering Chinese and local food. Lunch specials 11 a.m.-2 p.m. (all around $5) include items like kung pao with vegetables, rice, or noodles; beef broccoli; fried chicken; lemon chicken; and egg foo yung. Soups made from scallops, abalone, and pork are $4.50-5.50. Standards like chop suey and chow mein are under $6, and at $7.50 shrimp, scallops, and mahimahi are the most expensive dishes on the menu. Wah Kung has a good reputation with local people, so it must be doing something right!

Moderate

The **Wailua Marina Restaurant,** tel. (808) 822-4311, overlooking the Wailua River, offers inexpensive to moderately priced "local-style" food and free hotel pickup in the Wailua area for dinner. If you're going on a Fern Grotto boat trip, consider eating here. Breakfast, 8:30-11 a.m., is under $5; lunches, until 2 p.m., include dishes like a small tenderloin, fries, and a tossed green salad for $7.25; dinner, 5-9 p.m., features entrees like Korean barbecued ribs or breaded veal cutlets in mushroom sauce for under $11. It's convenient, and there's never a wait after the last boat upriver.

Mema's Thai Chinese Restaurant, in Wailua Shopping Plaza behind Sizzler, tel. (808) 823-0899, open Mon.-Fri. 11 a.m.-2 p.m. for lunch and nightly 5-9:30 p.m. for dinner, is a casual family-operated restaurant with a touch of class. The ornate chairs and tables, made of imported wood from Thailand set the theme. Waiters, dressed in green silk shirts, carry their trays past a profusion of potted plants and flowers. The booklike menu starts with crispy noodles at $6.95, fish cakes for $7.95, satay for $7.95-9.95

depending upon choice of fish or meat, fried calamari at $7.95, and exotic Thai soups ($7.95-10.95) like spicy lemongrass or Thai ginger coconut. Most entrees can be prepared vegetarian but might include cashew chicken at $8.25; garlic with mixed vegetable, chicken, pork, shrimp, or beef for $7.95-9.50; spicy sweet and sour chicken, beef, vegetables, seafood, or pork for $7.95-14.95; or savory curries—red, green, or yellow—$8.95-15.95. The assortment also includes rice and noodle dishes to please all palates and pocketbooks. If you are overwhelmed by choices, try the fixed dinners for two to six people ranging in price from $32.95 to $89.95. Mema's offers complete wine, beer, and dessert menus. If you are looking for a restaurant with excellent exotic food where you can enjoy a romantic evening for a reasonable price, Mema's should be at the top of your list.

Some will be happy, others sad, to hear that the aroma of fast food wafts on the breezes of Wailua. Just past the venerable Coco Palms is the **Sizzler Steakhouse,** at 4361 Kuhio Hwy., tel. (808) 822-7404, open Fri.-Sat. 6 a.m.-11 p.m. and Sun.-Thurs. 6 a.m.-10 p.m., serving breakfast and the familiar steaks, burgers, and salad bar, in this better-than-average fast-food environment.

Expensive

The Japanese legend of Kintaro, a pint-size boy born to an old couple from inside a peach pit, is slightly less miraculous than the excellent and authentic Japanese restaurant named for him, owned and operated by a Korean gentleman, Don Kim. From the outside, **Restaurant Kintaro** is nothing special, but inside it transforms into the simple and subtle beauty of Japan. The true spirit of Japanese cooking is presented, with the food as pleasing to the eye as to the palate. The sushi bar alone, taking up an entire wall, is worth stopping in for. The dinners are expertly and authentically prepared, equaling those served in fine restaurants in Japan. If you have never sampled Japanese food before, Restaurant Kintaro is Kauai's best place to start. Those who *are* accustomed to the cuisine can choose from favorites like tempura, sukiyaki, a variety of soba, and the old standby teriyaki. Open daily 5:30-9:30 p.m. for dinner only, along Rt. 56 just past the Coco Palms. Reservations are often necessary; call (808) 822-3341.

SHOPPING

The **Kinipopo Shopping Village,** a diminutive seaside mall, at 4-356 Kuhio Hwy., just across from Sizzler, offers most of Wailua's one-stop shopping. Here you can find the **Goldsmith's Gallery,** tel. (808) 822-4653, open Mon.-Sat. 9:30 a.m.-5:30 p.m. and Friday until 7 p.m., a store shimmering with brilliant jewelry. Five jewelers make the individual pieces, and for their artistry were named the 1992 "Jewel Designers of the Year" for the State of Hawaii. Diamonds, gold, and Australian opals add brilliance (and hefty price tags) to the artwork. Much of the jewelry is commissioned, but there is plenty on display to choose from. One of their distinctive lines, all with island motifs, features pieces shaped like flowers, clam shells, sailfish, petroglyphs, birds, and tropical fish, all fashioned into bracelets, earrings, brooches, and charms.

Kauai Water Ski and Surf Co., tel. (808) 822-3574, open daily 9 a.m.-7 p.m., also in the Kinipopo Shopping Village, is a complete watersports shop. Bathing suits, bikinis, sun visors, men's shorts, surfboards, boogie boards, wetsuits, fins, masks, snorkels, underwater watches, and even a few backpacks and daypacks line the shelves of this small but jam-packed shop. A water-skiing rental package comes complete with boat, professional driver, all equipment, and instruction for beginners to advanced for $85 an hour; kayaks rent for $25 a day single, $50 a day double; snorkel gear is $5 a day, $20 per week; boogie boards are $5 and $20; and surfboards are $10 and $30.

Bachman's, also in the Kinipopo Village, handles clothes, shells, and gift items, while **A Unique Emporium,** open daily except Monday 10 a.m.-5 p.m., tel. (808) 823-0455, is a cutesy-pie shop. Dolls, umbrellas, quilts, pillows, some wicker furniture, and a few display cases filled with jewelry make it as sweet as a double-fudge brownie.

Tony's Minit Mart and the **Shell Station Mini-Mart,** just next door, sell sundries, snacks, beer, and packaged foods.

May and Joy of Hawaii, tel. (808) 823-6276, just across the street, is a surprisingly neat souvenir stand. Inside you will find cut flowers and lei, and a good selection of touristy "junque" including some fine lei fashioned from amethyst and semiprecious stones.

Almost next door, the **Kinipopo General Store** sells groceries, sundries, and liquors.

D.S. Collections, next to Restaurant Kintaro, just past the Kinipopo Shopping Center, is a women's fine apparel store with a smattering of jewelry and some lovely ceramic bowls.

HAWAII STATE ARCHIVES

KAPA'A

Kapa'a means "fixed," as in "fixed course." In the old days, when the canoes set sail to Oahu, they'd always stop first at Kapa'a to get their bearings, then make a beeline directly across the channel to Oahu. Yachts still do the same today. Kapa'a is a town of unusual contrasts. At the south end along the main drag is **Waipouli** (Dark Water), actually a separate municipality (though you'd never know it). Clustered here are newish hotels, condos, a full-service shopping mall, restaurants, nightlife—all in all sort of a live-in resort atmosphere. The heart of Kapa'a itself is a workers' settlement, with modest homes, utilitarian shops, some downhome eateries, and a funky hotel.

Actually, more people live here than do in Lihue, and the vibe is a touch more local. There are no sights per se. You spend your time checking out the shops, scanning the color-mottled mountains of the interior, and combing the beaches, especially those to the north, toward Hanalei. Two minutes upcoast you're in wide-open spaces. Cane roads cut from Rt. 56 and rumble along the coast. Small oceanside communities pop up, their residents split between beachhouse vacationers and settled *kama'aina*.

What distinguishes Kapa'a is its unpretentiousness. This is "everyday paradise," where the visitor is made to feel welcome and stands in line with everyone else at the supermarket. Generally, the weather is cooperative throughout the area, prices on all commodities and services are good, beaches are fair to spectacular, and the pace is unhurried. Kapa'a isn't the choicest vacation spot on the island, but you can have a great time here and save money.

BEACHES AND PARKS

Central Kapa'a's beaches begin at **Waipouli Beach County Park,** fronting the cluster of hotels just north of the Coconut Market Place Shopping Center, and end near the royal coconut grove by the Kauai Coconut Beach Resort. The town interrupts the beach for a while south of the Waikaea Canal, and then the beach picks up again at **Kapa'a Beach County Park,** running north for almost a mile until it ends near a community swimming pool and the Kapa'a Library. A number of small roads lead off to the beach from Rt. 56. Kapa'a Beach County Park has just over 15 acres, with a pavilion, picnic tables, showers, toilets, and grills. The beach is pretty to look at, but this section of town is run-down. The feeling here is that it belongs to the locals, although no undue hassles have been reported.

As soon as you cross the Kapa'a Stream on

the north end of town you're in the one-store village of Kealia. Past mile marker 1, look for Ray's Auto Saloon, and turn off onto the cane road. At the junction is **Kealia Beach**. This wide, white strand curves along the coast for a half-mile. It's not a beach park, so there are no facilities, but during calm weather the swimming is good—particularly at the north end—and few people are ever here except for some local fishermen and surfers.

Continue along Rt. 56 heading north, and just past mile marker 12 you'll find cars parked along the side of the road. Walk to the nearby cane road and continue for 10 minutes until you come to a surfing beach that the locals call **Donkey Beach**. Look for a tall stand of ironwoods, a rutted, makeshift pulloff, and a wide sandy beach below. A footpath leads down to it. This area is very secluded and good for unofficial camping, while others come here to spend time au naturel. Unfortunately, the undertow is severe, especially during rough weather, and only experienced surfers challenge the waves here. You can sunbathe and take dips, but remain in the shallows close to shore.

Note: There is access to the cane roads from Kealia Beach, but these are often chained and locked. Technically, you need (and should get) a permit issued at the Lihue Sugar Co. office in Lihue to travel them. As you skirt the coastline on this road, heading for **Pohakuloa Point** and Donkey Beach, the ride is much more picturesque than Rt. 56. Continue north on the cane road until it intersects Rt. 56 again.

PRACTICALITIES

ACCOMMODATIONS

Budget
Kauai International Hostel, at 4532 Lehua St., Kapa'a, HI 96746, tel. (808) 823-6142, just across from the Kapa'a Library, welcomes international guests with a friendly staff that speaks German, French, and good old English. Rates are $16 for a dorm bunk (no reservations, 40 bunks, private female dorm available), and $40 for a private room with double bed (reservations accepted, 6 rooms). Although open 24 hours, "lights out" (read "no more noise") is at 11 p.m.; checkout is by 10 a.m., with a loss of $10 key deposit if you're late. Occasionally, staff members or guests organize an impromptu barbecue/luau, and the hostel runs van tours ($20)—mostly hikes to waterfalls, canyons, and pristine beaches, along with airport pickup on arrival before 10 a.m. and after 6 p.m. Facilities include a communal kitchen with good appliances, a lounge with comfortable couches and cable TV, and a laundry room. Dorm rooms, each with its own sink and private bath, contain either four or six bunks. The private rooms are small but cheery (shared bath). The hostel is clean and well managed and has a maximum seven-night stay.

Inexpensive
Hotel Coral Reef, at 1516 Kuhio Hwy., Kapa'a, HI 96746, tel. (808) 822-4481 or (800) 843-4659, is relatively inexpensive and definitely has character. Toward the north end of Kapa'a between the main road and the beach, this family-style hotel, one of the first built in the area, has a deluxe view of the bay, is clean, and attracts a decent clientele. Enter the office past a mini-garden, and notice a seascape mural of the bay as you recline on the covered lanai. The rates (based on double occupancy) for the recently refurbished rooms are: mountain or garden view $49, ocean view $59, oceanfront $89, two-room suite $79 ($10 charge for additional guests). The hotel offers "room and car packages" and senior citizen discounts. Rooms, outfitted in tropical decor, feature refrigerators, sliding glass doors, daily maid service, free parking, a pay telephone in the lobby, color television, complimentary coffee, activity bookings and equipment rental, and private beachfront lanai. The Hotel Coral Reef is family run, neat as a pin, and very affordable for a family vacation.

For those island visitors "who value their personal health, and who seek inner growth and the opening of creative potential," the **Keapana Center**, 5620 Keapana Rd., Kapa'a, HI 96746, tel. (808) 822-9768 or (800) 822-7968, may be the place for you. Gabriela, the multitalented owner, has had varied careers from college professor to dance instructor but now calls herself simply an artist. Living on Kauai for more than 20 years and being an avid hiker and outdoor person, Gabriela is accommodating and helpful in giving tips on hikes and nature trails and is also well-versed in the Hawaiian culture, especially the healing arts. In touch with local practitioners, she can make arrangements for instruction or sessions of massage and body work, naturopathic medicine, yoga, tai chi, 12-step programs, and other healing and wellness programs in this restful but stimulating (and nonsmoking) environment. Guest rooms are very island, very Hawaiian. Floors are covered with sisal matting, and most furniture is rattan or wicker. Shoji-screen paper lanterns add soft lighting, and beautiful floral displays brighten every room. Beds are covered with batik bedspreads, while Balinese masks, Chinese peasant hats, and hula skirts hang from the walls. The common area, open to the elements, is serene with its own indoor/outdoor garden. The lanai offers sweeping vistas over the lush hillside, which descends to the beach only five minutes away. A solar jacuzzi waits to knead the muscles of any intrepid hikers. Rooms with shared/private baths are $40/$65 s, $55/$70 d, with weekly rates available. Each morning the continental breakfast includes homemade bread, health-conscious muffins, and unique island fruits like sour sop or star fruits, which grow on the property and are delightfully unfamiliar to most guests. Bowls of papayas and hands of bananas, all organic and all also from the property, are left in the downstairs area for the guests. There is a kitchenette, with refrigerator and microwave available. Gabriela also offers a freestanding 24-foot yurt with its own kitchen and hot outdoor shower. The rate is $60 (maximum four people), with a five-day minimum, (discount thereafter). The yurt can accommodate children, whereas the house is an adult-only atmosphere to ensure the serenity of the environment.

Moderate

The **Royal Drive Cottages,** 147 Royal Dr., Kapa'a, HI 96746, tel. (808) 822-2321, owned and operated by Bob Levine, are nestled in the mountains high above Kapa'a. Very private, the self-contained cottages are complete with kitchenettes; $75 d, with weekly discounts available.

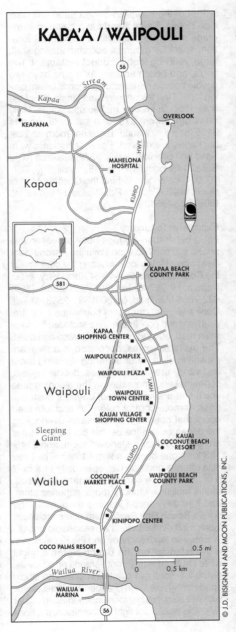

© J.D. BISIGNANI AND MOON PUBLICATIONS, INC.

Part of the Hawaiian-owned Sand and Seaside Hotels, **Kauai Sands** is a better-than-average moderate hotel with a convenient location, spacious grounds, accommodating staff, large, relaxing lobby, budget restaurant, two pools, and beach access. All rooms have two double beds, a refrigerator, air conditioning, ceiling fans, TVs, telephones, and lanais. What the hotel lacks in luster it makes up in price. Daily rates range from $75 for a standard room to $135 for a junior suite. Excellent room and car packages are offered. For reservations, write Sand and Seaside Hotels, 2222 Kalakaua Ave., Suite 714, Honolulu, HI 96815, or call (800) 367-7000. Located just behind the Coconut Market Place, at 420 Papaloa Rd., Wailua, HI 96746, tel. (808) 822-4951.

Expensive to Luxury

For a better-than-average hotel at reasonable prices, you can't go wrong with the **Aston Kauai Beachboy Hotel,** located along the coastline at the Coconut Plantation, 4-484 Kuhio Hwy. #100, Kapa'a, HI 96746, tel. (808) 321-2558, (800) 922-7866 Mainland, or (800) 321-2558 Hawaii. Cool and quiet, the hotel surrounds a central courtyard and pool that is quite secluded from the main road, offering an oasis of peace and quiet. The oversize rooms, decorated in a pleasant Hawaiian style, offer separate dressing room and vanity areas, mini-fridges, double closets, coffeemakers, and safes. In the sleeping area you'll find a king-size bed, daybed, business desk, remote-control color TV, and louvered doors that open to a private lanai overlooking the ocean or into the central pool area. Rates are $98-138 d for a standard room, and $145-185 for a one bedroom with kitchen. The hotel also offers a poolside bar, open daily 11 a.m.-7 p.m., full-service bar, shuffleboard, volleyball, tennis facilities, laundry room, sundries store, and free daily scuba lessons for guests. The hotel's **Beach Boy Restaurant** offers breakfast, lunch, and dinner buffets at reasonable prices.

Between the Beachboy and the Kauai Sands is the **Islander on the Beach Hotel,** a bright white structure with a front veranda on all levels, giving it a Southern plantation look. The studio apartments have been changed into hotel rooms with wet bars, refrigerators, coffeemakers, color TVs, and lanais. Set right on the beach, the hotel has a pool, a beach activities center, and a gift shop. Room rates are $95 for a standard to $185 for an oceanfront suite; add $10 during high season. Write Islander on the Beach, 484 Kuhio Hwy., Kapa'a, HI 96746, or call (808) 822-7417 or (800) 847-7417.

Amidst a huge grove of swaying palms, encircling a central courtyard, sits the sand-colored, low-rise **Kauai Coconut Beach Resort,** at P.O. Box 830, Kapa'a, HI 96746, tel. (808) 822-3455 or (800) 222-5642. The palm grove once belonged to the family of the famous swimmer and actor Buster Crabbe, of *Buck Rogers* fame. He and his twin brother, Bud, were born and raised right here, and Buster learned to swim along this very coast. After entering the main lobby, turn around and look at the grove—a natural buffer offering peace and tranquillity—and notice the diminutive indoor coconut trees placed here and there, creating the illusion that the grove continues inside. The lobby is alive with trees, flowers, and vines trellised from the balconies. Wicker chairs, stained glass depicting a sailing canoe departing at sunset, and a 40-foot waterfall, reminiscent of the real thing at Hanakapi'ai, add comfort and grandeur. A bas relief encircles the reception area, and as your eyes sweep from panel to panel it tells the story of how the Hawaiians became a "people," migrating originally from Indonesia until they found their fabled "homeland in the north." All rooms have remote-control color TVs, air conditioning, mini-fridges, safes, coffeemakers with complimentary Kona coffee, private lanais, and room service available 7 a.m.-9:30 p.m. The pastel green walls are decorated with an original painting in a Hawaiian theme, and the headboards in the upgraded rooms are carved with palm tree motifs repeated in the armoires. Carpets are bluish-green, and bed quilts are bright with printed flowers and ferns. Large pedestal lamps light conversation nooks made comfortable with high-backed armchairs surrounding marble-topped tables. The junior suites (all fronting the ocean) are massive, and feature separate dressing nooks just off the baths, ceiling fans, and Victorian wicker *punees,* perfect to while away the afternoon reclining and sipping a refreshing mint julep. Rates are $95 for a standard room to $250 for a VIP suite, which includes a full buffet breakfast.

For your convenience, the hotel offers two full-service activity desks where you can arrange everything from helicopter rides to horseback riding, with concierge service taking care of all travel details. Wednesday evenings during whalewatching season (late November through early May), a marine slide show comes to the Chart Room, a comfortable, quiet area hung with authentic maps and charts from the days of the tall ships. A lobby table is always reserved for local craftspeople, who offer their authentic handmade creations—anything from carvings to quilts. The hotel's three tennis courts, free to guests, are supervised by Coco, the onsite tennis pro. The hotel's **Voyage Room/Flying Lobster** is an indoor/outdoor restaurant featuring original artwork. Have a drink and listen to nightly entertainment at the Royal Coconut Grove Lounge, or try the hotel luau, one of the best on the island.

Condos

Kapa'a also has several other condos in the moderate-to-expensive price range.

A reasonably priced condominium in the area is the **Kapa'a Sands,** with pool and maid service. The oldest condo on the island—since 1968—Kapa'a Sands is kept clean and up to date and has been completely refurbished since Hurricane Iniki. It is situated on old Japanese grounds that once were the site of a Shinto shrine. The Japanese motif is still reflected in the roofline of the units and the torii design above each door number. Each unit has a full kitchen, ceiling fans in all rooms, and a lanai. Two-bedroom units occupy two levels, and even the garden units have limited views of the ocean. Room rates are $75 for garden studios, $85 for oceanfront studios, $99 for two-bedroom garden units, and $109 for two-bedroom oceanfront units. Monthly rates are available; minimum stay is three days except during winter, when it is seven days. For reservations, write Kapa'a Sands, 380 Papaloa Rd., Kapa'a, HI 96746, or call (808) 822-4901 or (800) 222-4901.

The **Kapa'a Shore Condo** is along the main road just north of the Coconut Plantation, at 40-900 Kuhio Hwy., Kapa'a, HI 96746, tel. (808) 822-3055. These one- and two-condo units offer a swimming pool, jacuzzi, tennis courts, and maid service on request. All units are bright and cheerful, with full kitchens and dishwashers.

One-bedroom garden-view units accommodate up to four for $110, one-bedroom ocean view units run $120, and two-bedroom ocean view units house up to six for $150. For reservations, call Kauai Vacation Rentals, tel. (808) 245-8841 or (800) 367-5025.

The **Pono Kai,** at 1250 Kuhio Hwy., Kapa'a, HI 96746, is a step up in class, offering one-bedroom units at $109-135, and two bedrooms at $135-160. All units have full kitchens, color cable TVs, and lanais. For reservations, call Kauai Vacation Rentals, tel. (808) 243-8427 or (800) 535-0085.

The **Plantation Hale,** at 484 Kuhio Hwy., Kapa'a, HI 96746, tel. (808) 822-4941 or (800) 775-4253, is a condominium that also offers daily rates. It's across the street from Waipouli Beach County Park just beyond the Coconut Market Place. There are only one-bedroom units; however, each is like a small apartment with full kitchen, bath, dining room, and living area. Rates for up to four people are $115-150.

A touch more classy than their Plantation Hale is the **Lae Nani,** offering one- and two-bedroom units on the beach. The rich decor varies by unit, but all have full kitchens, lanais, ceiling fans, and one and a half baths; most have ocean views. There is a laundry room, daily maid service, a swimming pool, tennis courts, and barbecue grills on the lawn. A small *heiau* is on the property beachside. One-bedroom units for up to four people are $150-179, and the two-bedroom units are $185-205, maximum six persons; rates are $20 cheaper during low season. The condo is at 410 Papaloa Rd., Kapa'a, HI 96746. For reservations, call (808) 822-4938 or (800) 367-7052.

Colony Resorts manages one deluxe condo in and around the Coconut Plantation. The **Lanikai,** is next door to the Lae Nani at 390 Papaloa Rd., tel. (808) 822-7456. Here there are only two-bedroom, two-bath units that rent for $200 a day, $20 cheaper during low season. For reservations, contact Colony Resorts, tel. (800) 367-5004.

FOOD

From the Coconut Market Place to the north edge of Kapa'a, there are dozens of places to eat. The vast majority are either inexpensive diners or mid-priced restaurants, but there are also a fine restaurant, several luau and buffets, the ubiquitous fast-food chains, and several bakeries, fruit stands, markets, and grocery stores.

Inexpensive Food in Shopping Malls

Surrounded by hotels and condos, the **Coconut Market Place** is the island's largest shopping center. In this huge complex are more than a dozen eateries.

For a quick, cool snack try **Lappert's** for ice cream, or **Rainbow Frozen Yogurt** for a more healthful snack, and for quick counter food try **The Fish Hut** or **Island Chicken**.

For more substantial food, check out **South of the Border,** a restaurant and cantina serving steak and Mexican food and even live music now and again, especially on weekends; **Tradewinds Bar,** tel. (808) 822-1621, open 10 p.m.-2 a.m., serving drinks and food and offering karaoke nightly; **Taco Dude,** receiving high praise from local people, is open for lunch and dinner and serves beef, chicken, or bean tacos for $1.75, tostadas for $2.25, burritos at $3.75-4.75, and taco salad for $4.75. A counter restaurant, it serves fresh food made to order at reasonable prices. Others include the **Banyan Tree Cafe** and **Aloha Kauai Pizza.** At **Don's Deli and Picnic Basket** you can get a large sandwich for $2.50-4.50, subs, or a picnic basket for your day on the beach or your trip to the north coast. **Auntie Sophie's Grill** serves burgers, hot dogs, and sandwiches, while **Harley's Ribs and Chicken** says it all with its name. For a cup of fine coffee and a selection of baked goods, try the **Cafe Espresso.** For your sweet tooth, step in to see what mouthwatering delicacies the **Rocky Mountain Chocolate Factory** and **Nut Cracker Sweet** shops have to offer, or go healthy with **Zack's Frozen Yogurt.**

A short way up the highway, *mauka* from the road, is the **Waipouli Town Center,** marked by **McDonald's** and **Pizza Hut.** Near the yogurt shop is **Waipouli Restaurant,** a favorite local eatery open daily 7 a.m.-7 p.m. except Monday, when it closes at 3 p.m. The daily breakfast special, served 7 a.m.-11 a.m., brings a pancake, two pieces of bacon, and eggs for $2.99. Or choose a menu item like papaya for $1.39, or omelettes with a choice of bacon, ham, Portuguese sausage, or Spam for $5.49. Sandwiches range from hamburgers to teriyaki beef

and are all priced under $3. For a local treat, try the Kauai Super Saimin at $5.79, or miso saimin at $4.79. The lunch menu, mostly under $7, features shrimp tempura, beef broccoli, or a mixed plate of barbecued steak, fried chicken, and fried noodles. The best deals are the daily specials, priced at only $6.39, offering choices like fresh *ono,* chicken cutlet, and beef stew. The dinner menu ranges $8.49-12.99 for a sirloin steak or shrimp tempura—the most expensive items listed. You can also order a rice bowl topped with anything from the menu for only $2.79. The Waipouli Restaurant is basic, friendly, and clean —and the prices can't be beat!

The Waipouli Town Center has one of the best moderately priced restaurants on the island, **The King and I,** tel. (808) 822-1642, open Sun.-Thurs. 4:30-9:30 p.m. and Friday and Saturday 4:30-10 p.m. This Thai restaurant serves wonderful food that will make your taste buds stand up and be counted. Most dinners are $5-8. Also in the center is the Chinese restaurant the **Dragon Inn,** which has a well-deserved reputation for filling meals at reasonable prices. There is a menu as long as your arm, and most dinners go for $5-7. Stop in for lunch Tues.-Sat. 11 a.m.-2 p.m., for an all-you-can-eat buffet at $6.95, and nightly for dinner 4:30-9:30 p.m.

Recently opened in the center is the **Lizard Lounge and Deli,** tel. (808) 821-2205, open 7 a.m.-1 a.m., and offering everything from a limited breakfast buffet to deli sandwiches and pizza by the slice.

In the Waipouli Complex, another tiny mall along Kuhio, is the **Aloha Diner,** tel. (808) 822-3851. Open daily except Sunday 11:30 a.m.-3 p.m. and 5:30-9 p.m., this diner serves Hawaiian food. It offers à la carte selections like *kalua* pig, chicken luau, *lomi* salmon, rice and poi, *haupia,* and *kulolo.* Dinner specials run $5-6, with full dinners $7.50-9.50. Takeout is available. There is no atmosphere, the service is slow but friendly, and most people eating here are residents. Next door is the Japanese **Restaurant Shiroma,** which also serves Chinese standards. The daily lunch and dinner specials include items like shrimp tempura, pork tofu, teriyaki steak, or seafood combo. A money-saving lunch is a huge bowl of *wonton min* and a side of rice. And you must have a slice of the homemade pineapple or passion fruit chiffon pie for $1. Shiroma is open Fri.-Sun. 7 a.m.-9 p.m., and Monday, Wednesday, and Thursday 7 a.m.-2 p.m.; closed Tuesday.

For inexpensive plate lunches, try the **Barbeque House,** in the Kapa'a Shopping Center, open Mon.-Sat. 10:30 a.m.-8 p.m., where most selections are under $5.

Papaya's, a natural-food cafe and market, at the Kauai Village, 4-831 Kuhio Hwy., tel. (808) 823-0190, open daily except Sunday 9 a.m.-8 p.m., is not only the largest, but also the best natural-food store and cafe on Kauai. From the cafe section (outdoor tables available) come daily specials like vegan baked tofu over brown rice with green salad for $4.95, a tri-plate with your choice of three salads (one pound total) for $8.50, soup du jour $1.95-4.95 depending upon the size, and two-fisted sandwiches like veggie with cheese ($5.50), nutty burger ($6), or a good old-fashioned tempe burger for $5.50. Gourmet coffees, herbed teas, and fresh juices are also a specialty. Papaya's is famous for its hot entrees, including stuffed peppers, vegetarian lasagna, chicken enchiladas, spanakopita—a Greek dish with feta cheese and phyllo dough—and stuffed baked potatoes, all sold by the pound for about $4 and up; all can be packed to go. If you are into healthy organic food, there is no place better than Papaya's!

Inexpensive Eateries in and around Kapa'a
In Kapa'a, just south of the Waipouli Shopping Center, you'll find **Local's Fast Food,** open daily 6 a.m.-midnight, where you can get items like a loco moco—hamburger, two fried eggs, brown gravy, and rice—for $3.49, hamburger steak plate lunch for $2.99, and a variety of topped hot dogs. The food isn't great, but the prices are right and it's not the typical fast-food styrofoam junk.

Almost next door is **Margarita's.** Billed as a "Mexican restaurant and watering hole," it's open daily from 4 p.m. for cocktails and from 5 p.m. for dinner.

Marilyn Monroe, skirt tossed by the Kauai breeze, and the big bow tie and bigger smile of owner and chief soda jerk Chris Erickson welcome you to **Beezers,** a vintage '50s soda fountain, open daily 11 a.m.-10 p.m., tel. (808) 822-4411, along Rt. 56 in downtown Kapa'a. Chris, a bartender for two decades, researched the soda-fountain idea for years before opening Beezers—and actually got his best idea after visiting Disneyland. He scoured Hawaii and then finally the Mainland before finding a real soda fountain. The floor of red, black, and white tiles leads to low stools facing a counter made from glass brick and featuring a light show inside that matches the tunes coming from a real jukebox in the corner. The ice cream served is Hawaii's own Lappert's—some of the best in the world. Besides standard cones, Beezers serves an old-fashioned banana split for $7.95, a Mustang Sally—a rich chocolate brownie with two scoops of creamy vanilla—for $6.25, and an American Bandstand deluxe—a decadent combination of white chocolate, macadamia nuts, Kona coffee, and chocolate ice cream all covered with hot fudge, hot butterscotch, and marshmallow toppings, whipped cream, chopped nuts, and a cherry—for $7.95. Chris also handmakes malts, shakes, and flavored Cokes, and serves brownie wedges, oatmeal molasses cookies, coffee, tea, lemonade, and juices. Beezers is the kind of place where if you're not smiling going in, you're definitely smiling coming out.

Look for yellow and white umbrellas shading a few picnic tables that mark **Bubba's,** at 1384 Kuhio Hwy., tel. (808) 823-0069, open Mon.-Sat. 10:30 a.m.-6 p.m. and sometimes on Sunday, where you can have a Bubba burger for $2.75 or a Big Bubba for $5. Other menu items include a "Slopper," an open-faced burger smothered in Bubba's famous Budweiser beer chili, for $4.50; a Hubba Bubba, a scoop of rice, hamburger, and grilled hot dog smothered in beer chili with diced onion for $5.50; or a simple order of fish and chips, chicken burger, or corn dog, all for under $4.50. Sides include french fries, onion rings, and "frings," a combo of both. On entering, you can try your hand at a coin toss, and if you manage to place your coin in the right slot, you win a soda, lunch, or a free T-shirt. Also, check out the community bulletin board to see what's happening and what's for sale in the Kapa'a area. Bubba's is a throwback to the days when a diner owner was also the short-order cook and all the burgers were handmade. Rock and roll, grease, and Elvis lives, man! Enjoy!

Kapa'a Bagelry and Espresso Bar, near Bubba's at 1384 Kuhio Hwy., tel. (808) 823-6008, open Mon.-Fri. 7 a.m.-3 p.m. and Sat.-Sun. 7:30 a.m.-2:30 p.m., occupies an old bank building and, to keep up with the catch-your-eye local paint jobs, is bright orange. Here too, everything is handmade, but instead of old-fashioned burgers, the offerings are mostly organic and healthful. All sandwiches are served on hand-rolled bagels boiled in the traditional way. Choose one of the many flavors and then have a sandwich like the Napili, with green onion spread, cukes, tomato, and sprouts for $2.75; the Kilohana, a combo of hummus, olives, red onions, and sprouts for $2.95; or the Kalalau, with roast turkey, avocado, red onions, and sprouts for $3.75. Lighter appetites will enjoy a bagel (90 cents plain) covered with roasted red peppers for $1, smoked marlin for $1.25, or *lomi lomi* salmon for $1.25. You can also enjoy homemade soup like spring garlic and potato, and black bean chili over rice with sour cream, both including bread, for $3.75. Drinks from espresso to hot chocolate, priced $1.50-2.95, fresh organic juices priced $1.50-3.95, and even iced *chai* and tropical smoothies ($2.50) are offered. The Kapa'a Bagelry is unpretentious, homey, healthful, and "culinarily correct," a welcome haven for yuppies and born-again-hippies. Peace, brotherhood, Birkenstocks, and Volvos forever!

Hana-Ya Sushi, in downtown Kapa'a, at 1394 Kuhio Hwy., tel. (808) 822-3878, open Mon.-Fri. 11:30 a.m.-2 p.m. for lunch and Mon.-Sat. 5:30-9:30 p.m. for dinner, is an authentic sushi bar owned by sushi chef Matomu Hanaya and serves up tasty tidbits and classic Japanese dishes. For lunch, try *oyaku donburi* or chicken katsu (each $5.95), or a 16-piece tray of assorted sushi for $8.55. Dinner prices are about $1 more for the fixed dishes, and $16.55 for a tray of 19 pieces of assorted sushi. Hanaya *san* has no liquor license, but it's okay to bring your own sake or beer. *Itadakemas!*

The Olympic Cafe, a fixture in Kapa'a for more than half a century but torn up by Hurricane Iniki (then painted purple, perhaps to ward off the wrath of future "big wind goddesses" with the right vibes), is back in business at 1387 Kuhio Hwy., tel. (808) 822-5731, open daily 6 a.m.-2 p.m. for breakfast and lunch and 5-9 p.m. for dinner. This linoleum and formica restaurant fixes American, Japanese, and Hawaiian standards. Breakfasts of eggs, meats, rice, and potatoes are under $6, and lunches of chopped steak or breaded pork cutlets are under $7. Island favorites like saimin and pork soup are about

$4.50, and the mahi plate is under $6.50. The dinner menu, priced $6.95-11.95, includes shrimp tempura, chicken or pork *katsu,* pork or chicken hecca, and the fresh catch of the day. A children's menu offers items priced less than $5. Beer, wine, and cocktails are served. There's no atmosphere, but the service is friendly, the restaurant clean, and the food plentiful and good.

Sideout Bar and Grill, a neighborhood bar and restaurant in downtown Kapa'a, tel. (808) 822-0082, open daily 11 p.m.-1:30 a.m., offers inexpensive sandwiches, burgers, and light meals along with cold drafts, wine, liquor, and imported beer. Sideout patrons are a fun-filled potpourri of sunburned tourists, tattooed locals, and multi-earringed men and women of various sexual persuasions. The restaurant has a dining deck out back where you can enjoy local fare like meatloaf, pork *adobo,* fish cakes, and fresh catch when available. Prices for all are only around $7.

A diner with formica tables and a lunch counter, **T. Higashi Store** also caters mostly to local residents, tel. (808) 822-5982. Serving everyday Japanese food, it's open 6 a.m.-8 p.m.

Moderate

The **Ono Family Restaurant,** downtown Kapa'a, at 4-1292 Kuhio Hwy., open daily 7 a.m.-3 p.m., tel. (808) 822-1710, is cozy and functional, with nice touches like carpeted floors, ceiling fans, and even a chandelier. Creative breakfasts include eggs Canterbury, with turkey, tomatoes, and hollandaise sauce over poached eggs on an English muffin; pancakes; and a variety of omelettes like a Local Boy, which combines Portuguese sausage and kimchi. Lunch salads run about $4.50, and the Island's Best Burger is $5.50. You can't go wrong with a mushroom melt burger for $6.95, and from the broiler or grill try sirloin steak, barbecued ribs, or teri chicken. For those with a taste for the exotic, you can even get a real buffalo burger here, from American bison raised in Hanalei and Kansas. The daily fish special is always terrific and, depending upon the catch, goes for about $13.

If the moon hits your eye like a big pizza pie, go to **Rocco's Italian Restaurant** at the Pacific House Complex in downtown old Kapa'a across from the ABC store, tel. (808) 822-4422, open Mon.-Sat. 11 a.m.-4 p.m. for lunch and daily 5-10 p.m. for dinner. Enter to a valiant attempt at creating a homey Italian atmosphere—red and green curtains, Chianti bottles hanging from an open beamed ceiling, and a recessed bar separated from the downstairs dining area by a glass brick wall. Upstairs, you'll find a more intimate seating area where you can look over a balcony railing festooned with artificial grapes and garlic bunches to the flagstone floor below. Lunch specials are Caesar salads with shrimp, fresh fish, or chicken, priced $7.95-9.95, as well as soups like minestrone or onion for around $3.50 and sandwiches, including Sofia's Garden Sub at $6.50, or Cynthia's Chicken Parmesan Sub, at $7.95. Pizza by the slice goes for $2.50 and up, depending on toppings. Or choose lasagna at $7.95 or ravioli at $6.95. The dinner menu starts with sautéed mushrooms for $5, white pizza for $6, or their raved-about sautéed garlic shrimp at $9.95. Pastas offered include linguine, manicotti, and cannelloni, ranging $8.95-12.95, while entrees of eggplant, chicken, or pork parmigiana go from $11.95 to $12.95, and a specialty of chicken "franchisee" (like marsala) is $12.95. For snacks to go with a beer or a glass of wine from the full-service bar, order garlic bread with ricotta cheese for $7.50, or meatballs with marinara sauce for $3.50. Satisfy your sweet tooth with New York cheesecake or tiramisu, priced $2.25-4. Rocco's food is better than average, and the atmosphere is friendly, with the strong appeal of a cozy neighborhood ristorante.

Look for the blue and white awning on the left as you're leaving Kapa'a heading north. It marks **Charlie's Place**, tel. (808) 822-3955, open for breakfast Tues.-Sun. 7:30-11:30 a.m., for lunch Tues.-Fri. 11:30 a.m.-3 p.m., and for dinner Tues.-Sat. 6-10 p.m. (they plan to have dinner on Sunday nights as well, so check). The bar is open Tues.-Sat until midnight or so, with happy hour 3-6 p.m., during which well drinks are $2 and draft Steinlager is $1.50. Charlie's hops with live music from local bands, and features changing themes like "songwriters round" on Tuesday, female country rock Wednesday, folk rock Thursday, rock and roll on Friday, and Saturday-night potpourri. Charlie's is an indoor/outdoor restaurant/bar right across the street from Kapa'a Beach Park. They have a lanai, where you can catch the breeze, and inside are hanging plants, blue tables, and an old piano in the corner. The breakfast menu at Charlie's Place includes eggs with bacon or ham and sausage for $5.25, eggs Benedict for $7.50, omelettes $4.50-5.95, and waffles $2.95-3.95. Lunch brings a tropical seafood burrito for $8.95, fish and chips for $7.95, barbecued ribs for $7.95, a full range of burgers from $5, a garden vegetarian sandwich at $6.95, and a small children's menu. For dinner choose Cajun-style fresh catch—the house specialty—at $13.95, tropical seafood plate or ginger chicken for $11.95, teriyaki chicken for $10.95, or a vegetarian platter for $10.95. Charlie's is a good-time local bar with a mixed clientele where you can have a toe-tapping evening or a quiet beer and a chat.

When you don't want to fool around deciding where to get a good meal, head for the north end of Kapa'a and the local favorite, **Kountry Kitchen.** Open daily 6 a.m.-9 p.m., the tables are usually packed with regulars during peak dining hours. Breakfasts are full meals of hefty omelettes for $3-4 or the Hungryman Special, for $6. Lunches range $4-6, and full dinners of country ribs, sesame shrimp, or baked ham served with soup, bread, potatoes or rice, and veggies are $7-9. The food is tasty, the service prompt and friendly, and the portions large. The Kountry Kitchen is at 1485 Kuhio Hwy., tel. (808) 822-3511.

Nearby is the **Makai Restaurant,** tel. (808) 822-3955, which serves Hawaiian, Mediterranean, and continental food. Try their fish and chips, gyros, or moussaka (you can get it to go). The open windows let in the breeze and morning sunlight but, as the place is close to the road, they also let in the sounds of passing cars.

Norberto's El Cafe, at the intersection of Kukui St. and Rt. 56 in downtown Kapa'a, tel. (808) 822-3362, open daily 5:50-9 p.m., is a family-run Mexican restaurant. Then what's it doing on a side street on a Pacific Island, you ask? Hey, gringo, don't look a gift burro in the face! They serve nutritious, delicious, wholesome food, and they cater to vegetarians—all dishes are prepared without lard or animal fats. The smell of food wafting out of the front door around dinnertime is its best advertisement. They serve the best Mexican food on the island. Full-course meals of burritos, enchiladas, and tostadas are $11.50-12.95, children's plates are $6.95, and à la carte dishes are $2.95-6.95. The best deals are the chef's specials of burrito el *cafe,* Mexican salad, and chiles rellenos, all for under $7, or fajitas for $13.95. Other entrees are rellenos tampico, chimichangas, tacos, and quesadillas. Dinners are served with soup, beans, and rice; chips and salsa are complimentary. There's beer on tap, or if you really want to head south of the border (by way of sliding under the table), try a pitcher of margaritas. If you have room after stuffing yourself like a chimichanga, try a delicious chocolate-cream pie or homemade rum cake. The cafe is extremely popular with local folks and tables fill as soon as they're empty.

At the Coconut Market Place is **Buzz's Steak and Lobster** restaurant, tel. (808) 922-7491, open for lunch 11 a.m.-3 p.m., *pu pu* and happy hour 3-5 p.m., and dinner 5-10:30 p.m. They offer a $7.95 early-bird special 5-6:30 p.m. with your choice of teriyaki chicken, ground sirloin, or fried island fish. Buzz's started serving steaks and seafood in Waikiki in 1957 and, with its signature restaurant still open on Oahu, continues to do the same. You enter through large koa doors into a subdued interior rich with more koa and highlighted by lava rock. An open kitchen presides over a comfortable dining area with high-backed wicker chairs, while palm fronds and a hanging canoe add a Polynesian flair. Take time to notice the collection of artifacts, paintings, basketry, lei, and antiques gathered from Tahiti and the islands of the South Pacific. Word on the street says the salad bar here is the best. For lunch, Buzz's offers soup of the day at $2.95, tuna and avocado salad at $6.95, a tuna salad sandwich for $4.95, and a mahimahi burger for $6.50. Desserts include New York-style cheesecake and homemade ice-cream pie, both priced at $3.95. Appetizers, served at both lunch and dinner, include calamari at $5.95, deep-fried zucchini and teriyaki beef sticks both priced at $4.50. Dinner entrees are ground sirloin for $8.95, various steaks priced $12.95-17.95, prime rib (Fri.-Sat. only) at $17.95, golden fried chicken for $10.95, and baby-back pork ribs for $14.95. Seafood offered is lobster tail (daily quote), oven-broiled mahi for $11.95, fish and fries for $8.95, and various fresh catch at market price. As an added benefit, you can sit at the bar after dinner and listen to nightly entertainment 9 p.m.-midnight.

The **Jolly Roger Restaurant,** open 6 p.m.-2 a.m., claims to have the longest happy hour on the island-6:30 a.m.-7 p.m. They're not known for exceptional food, but you always get hearty, substantial portions no matter what time of day you come to dine. A breakfast special brings pancakes, eggs, and bacon for $3.99, while a steak and shrimp dinner special is $7.99. Evening entertainment features a lively karaoke bar. You can find Jolly Roger behind the Coconut Market Place Shopping Center, near the Islander on the Beach Hotel, tel. (808) 822-3451.

Al and Don's Restaurant, in the Kauai Sands Hotel, tel. (808) 822-4221, is open daily 7 a.m.-8 p.m. The service and food are good but not memorable. However, the view from the spacious booths overlooking the seacoast is magnificent. Prices are reasonable for their numerous dinner and breakfast selections. Perhaps this is the problem: though you don't get the bum's rush, the place feels like one of those feeding troughs in Waikiki that caters to everyone and pleases no one. However, you can't complain about the large portions; breakfast is $3.85 for all-you-can-eat hotcakes, one egg, grilled ham, and coffee. And you won't be disappointed with their build-your-own omelette. Most breakfasts are under $4, and there are plenty of evening specials, with most dinners under $10. Dinner includes soup and salad bar with adequate entree choices like *ahi,* swordfish, top sirloin, and chicken exotica. The bar serves good drinks for reasonable prices. When you leave Al and Don's, you won't feel like complaining, but you won't rush back either.

The **Bull Shed,** 796 Kuhio Hwy., down the little lane across from McDonald's, tel. (808) 822-3791, is known for prime rib; its chicken and seafood dishes are also praised ($9.95-18.95). The wine list is better than average and includes Domaine Chandon champagne ($22.95). Insiders go for the extensive salad bar for only $6.95—but be forewarned: the pickings get all jumbled together as the night goes on, and the salad bar peaks out by 7:30. The Bull Shed is open for cocktails and dinner daily 5:30-10 p.m.

Diners at **Noe's,** in the Kauai Village Shopping Center, tel. (808) 821-0110, open daily for lunch 11 a.m.-5 p.m., for dinner 5 p.m.-10:30 p.m., and for happy hour 4-6 p.m., get plenty of hands-on attention from owner Linda Chong. Appetizers begin at $4.95 and include mozzarella sticks, quesadilla rolls, breaded dill pickles, and standards like wing dings or onion rings at $6.95. The lunch menu continues with Cobb salad at $8.95, fish and chips for $7.95, steak sandwich for $9.95, burgers made your way from $5.95, or a bacon cheeseburger for $6.50. Well priced dinner specials include stir-fry local-style beef, chicken, or shrimp for $12.95, scampi at $14.95, and mahi magic for $12.95. A house specialty is shri island pie, made with Oreos and Kona coffee ice cream, all covered with fudge for $3.50. Noe's interior is island casual with a touch of Dublin and sports a long bar with green stools, and booths or tables with bamboo captains' chairs. A huge hammerhead shark leers beady-eyed from the wall, somewhat like a "hammered" tourist leering at the bikini babes.

Walk the gangplank to enter the **Kapa'a Fish and Chowder House,** in a two-tone blue building on Kapa'a's north end, tel. (808) 822-7488, offering a happy hour daily 4-6 p.m. and dinner from 5:30 p.m. Tastefully appointed, the interior of this comfortably casual restaurant is nautical, featuring a ship's wheel, hanging nets, and ocean-blue carpet. Start with steamed clams (market price), Pacific shrimp cocktail at $7.95, a pot of clam or fish chowder at $4, or a Caesar salad for $6.95. Seafood selections are coconut shrimp, Alaska snow crab clusters, charbroiled lobster tails, or tiger prawns priced $14.95-18.95. Landlubbers can order New York strip steak at $19.95, ginger chicken for $10.95, or New York pepper steak for $20.95, along with multiple combination plates for around $21.95. A selection of pasta dishes like calamari sauté and shrimp scampi is $14.95-15.95. The full bar serves wine, beer, and exotic drinks and offers a special every night. The Kapa'a Fish and Chowder House is a decent restaurant, with good value for the money.

Fine Dining

Master chef Jean-Marie Josselin knows a good thing when he sees it and, moreover, knows how to prepare it exquisitely. You can enjoy his excellent food at the **Pacific Cafe,** at the Kauai Village, 4-831 Kuhio Hwy., tel. (808) 822-0013, open 5:30-10 p.m. Although it's in a shopping center, the Pacific Cafe creates a casually elegant atmosphere appointed with a cove and molded ceiling, ferns and flowers placed here and there, bamboo chairs, and an open kitchen so that you can witness the food preparation. Appetizers range $7.25-9.75 and include such delicacies as deep-fried tiger-eye sushi with wasabi ($9.75) or *beurre blanc* pan-fried shrimp or salmon with sweet Thai pepper sauce for $8.25. Soups and salads are mouthwatering; a special Thai coconut curry basil soup with fresh island fish and shrimp is $5.75, seared spicy *ahi* salad with Kauai, romaine, and Caesar dressing is $7.45. Order from the woodburning grill—you can't go wrong! Try grilled *ahi* marinated in coriander, fennel seeds, white truffle mashed potatoes, and peppercorn sauce for $22.95, or the grilled rack of lamb—Hunan style—with dried cherry port sauce for $24. Specialties of the Pacific Cafe include wok-charred mahimahi with garlic sesame crust and lime ginger sauce for $24, or herb crust of *opakapaka* with black rice and basil, and coconut chardonnay vinaigrette for $22.50. The Pacific Cafe is an excellent restaurant with the perfect mixture of fine food, fine service, and superb presentation; by far the best that the area has to offer.

Luau and Buffet

The **Voyage Room,** at the Kauai Coconut Beach Resort, offers a sumptuous breakfast buffet including vegetarian and health-conscious fare like fresh fruit, yogurt, and cereal along with the traditional breakfast fixings of sausage, home-fried potatoes, eggs, and a good assortment of croissants and pastries. An excellent way to save money is to choose from the hotel's dining plans: one includes breakfast, another includes both breakfast and dinner.

In the evenings, the Voyage Room transforms into **The Flying Lobster.** The surf-and-turf oriented menu begins with *pu pu* such as jumbo shrimp cocktail for $7.50, sashimi at market price, or deep-fried wonton for $3.75. Seafood lovers will enjoy featured entrees like the spiny lobster dinner—one tail for $19.75, or a 10-ounce dinner for $23.95—or choose a filling combination like lobster and mahi for $22.50, and top sirloin teriyaki steak and lobster for $25.50. From the broiler, you can dine on New York steak at $19.75, or try a Hawaiian Luau sampler—a trio of *imu* baked pork, teriyaki beef, and *mahi* served with *lomi* salmon and poi for $16.25. Other selections include the fresh catch of the day, which can be broiled, sautéed with lemon butter, or stuffed with crab and priced $17.50-20, or try Chinese-style shrimp and scallops—a true delight for $22.50. For lighter appetites and the budget conscious, choose from a selection of pastas that include Italian sausage and fettucini at $11.25 and shrimp and sausage over fettucine for $14.15. Salads and sandwiches include a lobster bisque and salad bar for $9.75 and a seafood salad sandwich for $9.50. Top off your meal with a scrumptious dessert like Coconut Beach sand pie, a trio of coffee, chocolate, and vanilla ice creams for $3.75, or a real island special such as "tutu's" banana treat—bananas flambéed in brown sugar and butter, and topped with a blend of fine liqueurs over vanilla ice cream for $3.75. Follow the example of the locals who come to the Flying Lobster on Friday and Saturday evenings 5:30-9:30 p.m. for the seafood and prime-rib buffet—lobster, crab, shrimp, oysters, prime rib, and fresh fish cooked to order before your very eyes. Prices are extremely reasonable at $19.95 adults, $10.95 children ages 6-10, and free for little ones under five. Sunday evenings bring the prime rib *paniolo* barbecue buffet, a Hawaiian cowboy cookout, also priced at $19.95. Make reservations at tel. (808) 822-3455; they're recommended because both are very popular with local people, who know quality and a fantastic price when they see them.

The real treat is the **Kauai Coconut Beach Resort Luau,** which everyone agrees is one of the best on the island. It's held every night in the special luau *halau* under a canopy of stars and palm trees. The luau master starts the *imu* every morning; stop by and watch. He lays the hot stones and banana stalks so well that the underground oven maintains a perfect 400°. In one glance, the luau master can gauge the weight and fat content of a succulent porker and decide just how long it should be cooked. The water in the leaves covering the pig steams and roasts the meat so that it falls off the fork. Local wisdom has it that "All you can't eat in the *imu* are the hot stones." The dining begins at 7 p.m., with cocktails ongoing until 8 p.m., when the show begins. Tables are laden with pork, chicken, Oriental beef, salmon, fish, exotic fruits, salads, coconut cake, and *haupia*. Afterwards, you lean back and watch authentic Hawaiian hula and entertainment choreographed by Kawaikapookala-

wai (a.k.a. Frank Hewett). The enthusiastic entertainment is a combination of *kahiko* (ancient hula) and *awana* (modern hula), performed by an accomplished troupe of both men and women. Most numbers are *kahiko*—dignified, refined, and low-keyed portrayals of the tales and myths of ancient Hawaii. Intermixed are a few *awana* numbers, startling, colorful, and reminiscent of the days when Elvis was still the gyrating king of *Blue Hawaii.* Prices are $49 adults, half-price for children under 12, discounts available for seniors, and Tuesday and Saturday family nights, on which one child is admitted free; reservations suggested, tel. (808) 822-3455.

On a day that you can eat a lot, want to try a little bit of everything, and don't want to bust your wallet, stop in at the **Beach Boy Restaurant,** at the Aston Kauai Beachboy Hotel, tel. (808) 822-7163, which offers an extremely economical and well presented buffet, open daily for breakfast ($6.95) 6:30-10 a.m., lunch ($7.95) 11 a.m.-1:30 p.m., and dinner ($11.95) 5-9 p.m., with discounts offered for seniors and children. Breakfast is a full array of eggs, meats, coffee, croissants, toast, and fresh fruit, while lunch consists of platters of roasted chicken with Cajun spice, baked mahi, beef stew, and a complete salad bar including cakes, fresh fruits, and various desserts. Dinner changes its theme every day with dishes from Japan, the Philippines, China, Hawaii, and typical American standards including main courses like roast turkey, baked mahi with wasabi glaze, *kalua* pork and cabbage, an assortment of pasta and sauces, and, again, the full salad bar. The room itself is large but not impersonal, with floor-to-ceiling windows open to the courtyard of the hotel. The food is good quality, well presented, and you certainly get your money's worth.

ENTERTAINMENT

The night scene in Kapa'a isn't very extensive, but there is enough to satisfy everyone.

The **Jolly Roger Restaurant** at the Coconut Market Place offers karaoke nightly. You can listen, sing, and even dance nightly 9 p.m.-1:30 a.m. The atmosphere is casual, the talk friendly. A good watering hole, where you can find cool drinks and good conversation, is the **Tradewinds**

Bar, also at the Coconut Market Place. **South of the Border,** a Mexican cantina in the same center, sometimes has live music (especially on weekends). Nearby, **Buzz's** also has nightly entertainment—usually a small band playing contemporary, original, and country-and-western music. You can sit at the bar and enjoy the casual Polynesian setting.

The Coconut Market Place also hosts a free **Polynesian Hula Show** Monday, Wednesday, Friday, and Saturday at 5 p.m. The young local dancers and musicians put as much effort into their routines as if this were the big time. (Be forewarned that local sneak thieves rifle cars in the parking lot, knowing that their owners are occupied watching the show.) The shopping center also has something to offer moviegoers: the **Plantation Cinema 1 and 2.**

The **Kauai Coconut Beach Resort** offers a little of everything. You can enjoy free *pu pu* and entertainment at Royal Coconut Grove Lounge, just off the gardens and pool deck—happy hour is 4-6 p.m. Every evening 8-11 p.m., listen to pop, contemporary, and standard hits by local musicians. The dinner show in the Paddle Room presents a full performance of Hawaiian dance and music. Swing, rock, and Hawaiian music, as well as hula of the Polynesian Show, also accompany the luau.

Margarita's, along the Kuhio Hwy., just near the Waipouli Shopping Center, jams with live entertainment on the weekends.

SHOPPING

Kapa'a teems with shopping opportunities. Lining Kuhio Highway are a major shopping mall—the Coconut Market Place—and several other smaller shopping plazas. All your needs are met by a variety of food stores, health stores, drugstores, a farmers' market, fish vendors, and some extraordinary shops and boutiques tucked away here and there. You can easily find photo supplies, sporting equipment, "treasures," and inexpensive lei to brighten your day. Like dealing with the sun in Hawaii, enjoy yourself but don't overdo it.

The Coconut Market Place

Prices at this cluster of more than 70 shops, restaurants, galleries, and movie theaters are kept down because of the natural competition of so many shops, each of which tries to specialize, which usually means good choices for what strikes your fancy. As you walk around, notice the blown-up photos that give you a glimpse into old Hawaii. **Ye Old Ship Store** displays the best collection of scrimshaw on Kauai and some sea paintings by local artists. Any of the jewelry shops have enough stock on hand to drop even Mr. T to his knees. With so many apparel and footwear shops, the job of finding just the right aloha shirt, muumuu, or sports clothing shouldn't be a problem. **Pottery Tree** overflows with everything from junk to fine pieces. Select from stained-glass chandeliers, I Love Hawaii mugs, and cheap yet nice shell mobiles. **Kauai Gold Limited** sells scrimshaw and Niihau shells, while **Kauai Vision Kites** allows you to fly with the breezes over the island, and the **Ship Store Gallery** sets sail for adventure with nautical artwork of tall-masted ships and contemporary Japanese art in a gallery that's filled with cannons, pistols, and swords.

If the price of original artwork puts too much of a strain on your budget, then **Island Images,** offering fine art prints and posters, might have what you need at an affordable price. Island Images, open daily 9 a.m.-5 p.m., tel. (808) 822-3636, offers posters for around $30, with framing and shipping available, and a smattering of original artwork at discounted prices.

Some other specialty shops include **Pure Hawaiian,** with tapa cloth, drums, koa bowls, straw hats, muumuu, and casual dresses; **Golden Nugget,** for fine jewelry; **Kii Hale,** selling dolls from around the world but specializing in Hawaiian dolls; **Coconut Coast,** for women's and children's casual wear; **Island Surf Shop,** where you can purchase a boogie board, travel bag, a pareu, beach hat, and T-shirts; if yours becomes one of the sunburned bodies, you might be interested in the **Aloe Connection; Russian Treasures** is filled with Russian dolls; and **Collectors Corner** sells shells; mailboxes shaped like mermaids, cats, and cockatoos; aloha shirts, and Hawaiian dolls.

If your heart desires Hawaiian delicacies like Kona coffee, Maui onion mustard, macadamia nuts, island candy, Kauai Kookies, Kukui jams and jellies, or just a souvenir to take home, head for **The Nut Cracker Sweet** and just see if you can pull yourself away. For the ordinary purchase, head for **Whaler's General Store. Fox One-Hour Photo** will develop film, and the **Kauai Visitors Center** can give you information about things to see, places to go, and adventures to explore.

Kauai Village

Built around a theme of an 18th-century Main Street, this very modern, very large, and very diverse shopping center, one of the newest and best that Kauai has to offer, complete with its own museum, is at 4-831 Kuhio Hwy. It contains a **Safeway** supermarket, open 24 hours; **Longs Drugs,** open Mon.-Sat. 8 a.m.-9 p.m. and Sunday until 6 p.m., a complete variety store with photo equipment and a pharmacy; an **ABC** store, for everything from suntan lotion to beach mats; a **Waldenbooks,** tel. (808) 822-7749, open Mon.-Sat. 9 a.m.-8 p.m. and Sunday 9 a.m.-5 p.m., well stocked with everything from Hawaiiana to travel; a cluster of fast-food restaurants and small, inexpensive eateries; also located here are **Papaya's,** the island's best natural health-food store, and the **Pacific Cafe,** a fantastic restaurant featuring Pacific Island cuisine prepared by master chef Jean-Marie Josselin. Other stores are **Mango's for Men,** featuring gentlemen's alohawear; **Sunglass Hut,** where you can buy all kinds of sunglasses; a **Kahn Gallery,** resplendent with some of the finest artworks in Hawaii; and the always good **Crazy Shirts.**

Kapa'a Shopping Center

Marked by a Shell station and a Burger King at 4-1105 Kuhio Hwy., is this bite-size, functional shopping center. Here, you'll find a **Big Save Market,** a well-stocked food store, open daily 7 a.m.-10 p.m.; **Clic Photo,** for inexpensive film and fast developing; **Kapa'a Bakery,** filled with goodies; **Kapa'a Laundry,** for do-it-yourselfers; **Kapa'a Sports Center** with all kinds of sporting goods; and **Kauai Video.** Also in this shopping center are the Kapa'a clinic of the Kauai Medical Group, a full-service post office, an inexpensive restaurant or two, and Mail Boxes Kauai for mailboxes, faxes, and mailings of all sorts.

Small Shopping Malls

Across the highway from another Shell station, in the **Waipouli Complex,** is Popo's Cookies. Closed Mon.-Wed., it is open Thurs.-Fri. 8 a.m.-5 p.m., Saturday until 3 p.m., and Sunday until 2 p.m. Nearby, in the **Waipouli Plaza,** are several clothing shops and a seashell merchant who sells retail and wholesale. Farther down the road, in the **Waipouli Town Center,** you'll find Foodland, open 5 a.m.-midnight; Fun Factory arcade for games; Blockbuster Video, for home/condo entertainment; and JM's jewelry store.

Boutiques and Souvenirs

Right next door to Ambrose's Kapuna Natural Foods and across from Foodland is **Marta's Boat,** open Mon.-Sat. 10:30 a.m.-6 p.m., tel. (808) 822-3926. Primarily a children's boutique, the overflowing shelves also hold handmade quilts by local ladies, T-shirts, shorts, casual wear, elegant evening wear, and beautiful lingerie. A rack of games and educational items will help to keep the little ones happy on a return plane voyage or during an evening in the condo.

Follow the reggae beat and your dancing feet to **Jamaican Style,** in the Waipouli Town Center, open daily noon-9 p.m., tel. (808) 823-6100, owned and operated by Jimmy Dread. Racks hold Jamaican Style's own brand of 100% cotton preshrunk T-shirts and the island's largest selection of junior bikinis. The wall is filled with CDs and tapes of reggae music from Alpha Blonde to Ziggy Marley.

Ye Old Ship Store, located in the Coconut Market Place, and distinguished as the center's oldest retail store, is the premier shop on Kauai for scrimshaw. The shelves are filled with collectors' pieces and museum-quality artwork scrimmed from fossilized walrus, mammoth, and mastodon ivories that have been worked by extremely talented contemporary artists. Every February, Ye Old Ship Store sponsors the **Hawaii International Scrimshaw Competition,** drawing competitors from throughout the U.S. and Canada. Pieces created by these master scrimshanders are like any other original works of art, carrying price tags up to $10,000 and beyond. Some of the top scrimshanders on display are Jerry DuPont who won the top color nautical category; Ray Peters from Hawaii, winner of the black and white category; Kelly Mulford, a fine artist who took top honors in color whale, and Best of Hawaii category; Anna Good, winner of the Niihau Award for most unique in the open category with her rendering of a geisha at a tea ceremony; and the phenomenal Jesus Arick, who captured the drama and pathos of the Greek hero Prometheus. Cases hold other items, not just scrimshaw, in a wide variety of price ranges—Hawaiian fishhooks made from wild pig bone by local hunters ($66); copies of fishhooks from the Philippines ($20); turtles, whale tails, and money clips priced $9.95-75. Another local artist on display is Curt Danette, who specializes in tikis fashioned in the traditional way, from native woods like milo, koa, and even the very scarce sandalwood. Ye Old Ship Store has other interesting items that will delight the entire family. If scrimmed knives, letter openers, and fine jewelry isn't enough, look for the distinctive "Spirit of Aloha Kauai Bottle," made from Kauai's land, sea, and air, and each blessed with a Hawaiian prayer, or for an extremely accurate Hawaiian Islands map T-shirt depicting Hawaii during the times of first contact, made more fancy with a border of ancient Hawaiian tattooing. Ye Old Ship Store is a perfect stop to make a purchase that says "Hawaii," or just to have a close-up look at a very intriguing artform.

Remember Kauai, 4-734 Kuhio Hwy., tel. (808) 822-0161, open daily 9:30 a.m.-5:30 p.m., just past the Kauai Coconut Beach Resort, specializes in unique Hawaiian jewelry, like necklaces made from shells, beads, wood, and gold. The counters shine with belt buckles, pins, and a large collection of gemstones from around the world. Niihau shellwork is available, and fine specimens run up to $12,000. The scrimshaw, worked by Kauai artists on fossilized walrus ivory, adds rich texture to everything from knives to paperweights. Any place like this, with a rainbow painted on its roof, is worth a look.

Cathy and Karlos travel to Indonesia where they purchase the magnificent fabrics they design of 100% cotton or rayon for exclusive clothing to bring back to their shop **Bokumarue,** at 1388 Kuhio Hwy., Kapa'a, HI 96746, tel. (808) 822-1766, open 10 a.m.-6 p.m. They have taken on a new partner, Zayda, who helps with the designs and in the retail shop. Cathy, who has been in the garment design business for more than 20 years, offers affordable yet classy garments that include casual dresses, lace dresses, and island-style shirts. Karlos specializes in pareus and sarongs all of which are either hand-stamped or handpainted, and boasts the largest and best-priced selection on Kauai. Kathy also offers a personal line of lotions, potions, and bath gels called **Body Paradise Kauai.** She blends and bottles more than 25 different essential oils on the premises from which to choose and create your own distinctive scent. Other items include *ikat* blankets (a real deal at $20), temple carvings, and gaily painted masks, angels, and winged creatures priced $30-50. There is even some amazing primitive basketry from Borneo, and handpainted 100% cotton quilts from Indonesia for $175. Bokumarue, although not typically Hawaiian, is a real find!

Earth Beads, owned by Angelika Riskin, just a step from Bokumarue, tel. (808) 822-0766, open daily except Sunday 10 a.m.-6 p.m., specializes in beads and imported items from India, Africa, and South America. Shimmering in the tiny shop are earrings, belts, incidental bags, and sterling silver jewelry from Thailand, as well as locally made designs. A smattering of primitive basketry, incense, perfumed oils, T-shirts, "jungle" umbrellas and very unusual greeting cards complete the stock of this great little shop.

Walk into the **Island Hemp and Cotton Company,** tel. (808) 821-0225, open Mon.-Sat. 10 a.m.-6 p.m., and suddenly you're in Asia. Stride across the reed mat floor while the soulful eyes of a Buddha sitting serenely atop a glass counter follow you in. Across from the ABC store in downtown Kapa'a, the shop is owned and operated by Nancee McTernan, a long distance traveler and "old Asia hand" who has personally chosen every item in the store. Some special items include: tall drums made by Sage Adamson, a local artisan who sold one of his creations to Mickey Hart of Grateful Dead fame; Buddhas from Borneo; baskets from Bali; purses from Southeast Asia; carved bone necklaces from New Zealand; local puka shell jewelry; Niihau shellwork; and antique wood carvings from all parts of Indonesia. The clothing, all made from organic cotton, hemp, and linen, is machine washable and requires no ironing. Items include everything from casual shirts to elegant dresses ranging in price from $34 to $150. If you are after a truly distinctive gift, one-of-a-kind clothing, or an original artifact, you can't do better than visiting Nancee at Island Hemp and Cotton Company.

Far Fetched Designs, in downtown Kapa'a across from the Olympic Cafe, tel. (808) 823-8235, open daily 10 a.m.-6 p.m., sells art, curios, curiosities, and bric-a-brac from around the world. The jam-packed shop offers clocks bearing angels, rabbits, and mythical paintings; carved furniture from Indonesia; babushka dolls from Russia; glassware, kaleidoscopes, and island jewelry. There's a smattering of postcards and a good selection of local art by Kimberlin Blackburn, who works on handmade paper with pastels to create stylized seascapes and landscapes; Terri Scarborough, who employs pigments from local plants, roots, and fibers to dye her paper, which is then laid down in a silkscreen fashion to create Hawaii's flora, fauna, and waterfalls; and Sally French, who works in reverse acrylic on glass.

Kama'aina Clothing and Vintage Prints, located next to Beezers in downtown Kapa'a, open daily 9 a.m.-6 p.m., tel. (808) 822-0916, sells T-shirts with distinctive turn-of-the-century travel poster prints, "red dirt" T-shirts, and actual prints (framed in koa, if you like).

Look for **M. Miura Store,** at the north end of Kapa'a, mountain side, open Mon.-Sat. 9 a.m.-5 p.m. Local people shop at this dry goods store for alohawear, T-shirts, caps, men's and women's shorts, and a good selection of bikinis.

As shiny and glittering as the sunbeams pouring through the windows, **Kela'a Glass Gallery,** in the Hefat Market Place, at 4-1354 Kuhio Hwy., Kapa'a, HI 96746, tel. (808) 822-4527, owned and operated by Larry Barton, is a showcase for more than 60 contemporary artists working in glass. A few of the more famous are Daniel Lotton, Cohn-Stone, Bruce Freund, Bob Eickholt, and Steve Schlanser. The gallery features everything from classic vases to free-form sculptures ranging in price from $10-2,000. Kela's also sells and ships (disassembled but with pieces numbered for easy re-assembly) wooden flowers that are hand-carved and hand-painted in Indonesia. There are 30 different flowers represented including hibiscus, irises, calla lilies, various ginger, and heliconia. Prices range between $8 and $45, with the bulk priced $12 to $25.

If you are an aficionado of old Hawaii, make sure to drop into the **Tin Can Mailman,** at 4-1353 Kuhio Ave., downtown Kapa'a, tel. (808) 822-3009, open daily except Sunday 10 a.m.-5:30 p.m. The Tin Can Mailman has definitely found a heart for out-of-print books on Hawaii and Polynesia, battered travel guides filled with memories, antique maps, vintage menus, early botanical prints, rare Missionary items, and even new books. The shop is small, jam-packed, and bursting with ancient voices still quietly singing their songs.

The **Roxy Swap Meet,** held every Saturday and during the week (days to be announced), tel. (808) 822-7027, is in the middle of Kapa'a with tables set up under numerous tents. People from all over come to barter and sell everything and anything.

Photo Needs

Across from Remember Kauai is **Cameralab,** tel. (808) 822-7338, for all your photofinishing needs. In downtown Kapa'a, **Pono Studio** also develops film, carries photographic equipment, and has a studio for portraits. At the Coconut Market Place, **Fox One-Hour Photo** and **Plantation Camera and Gifts** also do photo developing.

Small Food Shops

Papaya's, a natural-food cafe and market, at the Kauai Village, 4-831 Kuhio Hwy., is open daily except Sunday 9 a.m.-8 p.m., tel. (808) 823-0190. Coolers and shelves hold items like wild tropical guava juice, organic sprouted hotdog buns, and mainstays like organic fruits and vegetables, yogurt, whole-grain bread and bulk foods. The new owners, Eric and Leslie Wing, have added an extensive collection of premium microbrewery beers, along with racks of fine wines, and boast the best selection and prices on Kauai. There is also a good selection of organic teas and flavored coffees. Spices, oils, vinegars, organic salad dressings, homeopathic medicines, cruelty-free cosmetics, vitamins, minerals, and an assortment of biodegradable cleaning products are also well represented. A large display case holds all kinds of goodies like cheesecakes, pumpkin and carrot cake, mango moussecake, and chocolate flan. If you are into healthy organic food, there is no place better than Papaya's.

There are several other markets and groceries in the Waipouli/Kapa'a area where you can pick up food if you're cooking for yourself. **Ambrose's**

Ambrose's Kapuna Natural Foods is perfect for all your whole-grain needs.

Kapuna Natural Foods (in a funky yellow building), tel. (808) 822-7112 or 822-3926, across from Foodland in the Waipouli Town Center, serves the community's produce and bulk- and health-food needs. Ambrose and his friends are real storehouses of information about the island; they have the "scoop" on what's happening and where. While visiting Ambrose, take a peek just next door at the **Kapa'a Missionary Church**, made from beautifully laid lava rock. If you have kids, check **Marta's Boat**.

There's a **farmers' market** every Wednesday at 3 p.m. at the Kapa'a Beach Park, while the local **Pono Market**, open Mon.-Sat. 7 a.m.-9 p.m. and Sunday 8 a.m.-4 p.m., is stuffed to the gills with grocery items, along with takeout sushi, *bento,* and deli sandwiches. As you're coming into Kapa'a heading north look for the **Sunnyside Farmers Market**, open daily 8 a.m.-8 p.m., where you can get fresh fruits and vegetables from around the island. **Kojima's** grocery, for produce, meat, liquor, beer, and picnic supplies, is beyond the Aloha Lumber yard at the north end of town. Currently painted blue, this well-stocked store is on the mountain side of the road.

Sports and Recreation

One of the best bike shops on the island for sales and repair is **Bicycle Kauai**, at 1379 Kuhio Hwy. in Kapa'a, tel. (808) 822-3315, open Mon.-Fri. 9 a.m.-6 p.m., Saturday 9 a.m.-4 p.m., and Sunday 10 a.m.-1 p.m. Stop in and talk to the guys; they can give you great advice on where to ride for your type of bike. Cannondale mountain bikes rent for $20 a day or $85 per seven-day week, including helmet, lock, and a car rack. You can also arrange a mountain-bike tour of 3-6 hours (full-day tours by appointment only) for $50-100, depending on the length and location of the tour (price includes a lunch prepared by Anahola's famous Duane's Ono Charburger).

Aquatic Adventures, at 4-1380 Kuhio Hwy., Kapa'a, HI 96746, tel. (808) 822-1434, open daily 7:30 a.m.-5 p.m., owned and operated by Janet Moore, is a full-service dive shop offering rentals, excursions, and certification courses. PADI courses, lasting 3-5 days for open-water certification, are $450 for the total package ($300 for a refresher course). Beginners can start with an introductory shore dive for $100 or a boat dive for $140. Other possibilities include a two-tank boat dive ($80, $95 with equipment), a one-tank shore dive or a one-tank night dive ($70 and $80); and a three-tank dive to Niihau, Thursday 7 a.m.-5 p.m. ($200 and $215). All dives are on a 30-foot Raddon especially designed for scuba diving and comfort with an onboard hot shower. Janet also sells a full complement of underwater gear including knives, wet suits, masks, fins, spearfishing gear, and carry bags.

Chris The Fun Lady, at 4-746 Kuhio Hwy. across from the Waipouli Shopping Center, tel. (808) 822-7759, open daily 8 a.m.-6 p.m., offers boogie-board rentals at $5-8 a day; kayaks for $25 single, $50 double with coolers, dry bags, life vests, car racks, and waterproof maps included; top-of-the-line snorkel gear (prescription masks, too), golf clubs, fishing equipment, and surfboards at $10 per day. Chris is an expert at arranging all ocean, air, and luau activities, claiming that her years of experience on Kauai don't always get you the cheapest but do always gets you the best.

There's no problem planning a fun-filled day with the help of **Ray's Rentals and Activities,** 1345 Kuhio Hwy., in downtown Kapa'a, tel. (808) 822-5700. Ray's rents boogie boards, snorkel gear, bicycles, surfboards, and kayaks. It also rents Harleys for the macho, Hondas for the minnow, and mopeds for the micro. The big Harleys are $175 per day, small Harleys are $150, Hondas $125, and mopeds $35 (longer-use discounts are available). Ray's functions as a booking agency for activities like helicopter rides, scuba diving, snorkeling, and luau. They claim to beat all prices, so it's worth calling to see what they can do.

Kayak Kauai, across the road from Ray's, open daily 8 a.m.-5 p.m., tel. (808) 822-9179, rents two-person kayaks for $48-60 per day and single kayaks for $25-35. Its owners are world-class kayak experts, and the staff are sensitive people who provide good service while having a good time. From May to October they lead ocean tours up the Na Pali coast for $130. They also rent and sell surf-skis, boogie boards, masks, fins, *tabi,* tents, and other beach and camping gear. They will rig your car to carry the kayak and provide drop-off and pickup service at Kee Beach for $8 or at Polihale State Park for $40—when it's safe to be on the ocean. During the summer, guided tours are taken along the Na Pali coast, and when conditions are too harsh up there, trips are run to Kipu Kai along the south coast. All of the above are good family-style fun. Kayak Kauai has another shop in Hanalei, tel. (808) 826-9844, which provides the same services.

Ambrose of **Ambrose's Kapuna Natural Foods,** in the funky yellow building across from Foodland in the Waipouli Town Center is a surfer's advocate, philosopher, and generally good guy. He has one of the largest collections of big boards and old surfboards on the island, and some new ones, too. If you are a surfer coming on vacation and you let Ambrose know in advance what you want and are qualified to use, he'll have it waiting when you get here. He doesn't rent boards, but he'll buy back the ones he sells at a very equitable rate. On his neighborhood beaches, Ambrose also offers surfing lessons tailor-made to the individual beginner or advanced board rider. Rates are $25 per hour.

INFORMATION AND SERVICES

Aside from the hotel activity desks, there are four places in Waipouli/Kapa'a where you can get tourist information. Very helpful is the Kauai Visitors Center in the Coconut Market Place, tel. (808) 245-3882. They have a complete range of free information on all the island's activities, are able to make reservations, and have an eye for the deals.

K.B.T.C. also has the full range of information and sometimes gets discount deals. Stop in at their main booth at the Pono Kai Condo or at their cubbyhole office below Jimmy's Grill in downtown Kapa'a, or call (808) 822-7447.

Your Kauai Office, tel. (808) 822-5504, open Mon.-Sat. 8 a.m.-6 p.m., can answer all of your shipping and office needs, including fax, photocopies, and UPS.

For a rejuvenating and revitalizing massage contact Aunty Daisy's Polynesian Massage. Aunty Daisy is "the lady with the *aloha* hands" and works in the small Waipouli Complex at 971 D Kuhio Hwy., tel. (808) 822-0305, open Tuesday and Wednesday 8:30 a.m.-5:30 p.m., Thursday and Friday 11 a.m.-10 p.m., and Saturday, 9:30 a.m.-2:30 p.m.

THE NORTH SHORE

The north shore is a soulful song of wonder, a contented chant of dream-reality, where all the notes of the Garden Island harmonize gloriously. The refrain is a tinkling melody, rising, falling, and finally reaching a booming crescendo deep in the emerald green of Na Pali. In so many ways this region is a haven: tiny towns and villages that refused to crumble when sugar pulled out; a patchwork quilt of diminutive *kuleana* of native Hawaiians running deep into luxuriant valleys, where ageless stone walls encircle fields of taro; a winter sanctuary for migrating birds, and gritty native species desperately holding on to life; a refuge for myriad visitors—the adventuring, vacationing, life-tossed, or work-weary who come to its shores seeking a setting conducive to finding peace of body and soul.

The north shore is only 30 miles long, but, oh, what miles! Along its undulating mountains, one-lane roads, and luminescent bays are landlocked caves still umbilically tied to the sea; historical sites, the remnants of peace or domination once so important and now reduced by time; and living movie sets, some occupied by villas of

stars or dignitaries, enough to bore even the worst name-dropper. Enduring, too, is the history of old Hawaii in this fabled homeland of the Menehune, overrun by the Polynesians who set up their elaborate kingdoms built on strict social order. The usurpers' *heiau* remain, and from one came the hula, swaying, stirring, and spreading throughout the island kingdoms.

Starting in **Kilauea,** an old plantation town, you can search out the spiritual by visiting two intriguing churches, browse an "everything" general store, or marvel at the coastline from bold promontories pummeled by the sea. Then there are the north shore beaches—fans of white sand, some easily visited as official parks, others hidden, the domains of simplicity and free spirits. **Princeville** follows, a convenient but incongruous planned community, vibrant with its own shopping mall and flexing condo muscles. Over the rise is **Hanalei,** even more poetic than its lovely name, a tiny town, a yachties' anchorage with good food, spirited, slow, a bay of beauty and enchantment. Movie cameras once rolled at neighboring **Lumahai Beach** and an entire generation shared the dream of paradise when they saw this spot in *South Pacific*. Next in rapid succession are **Wainiha**, and **Haena** with its few amenities, the last available indoor lodging, a restaurant, a bar, and a little of the world's most relaxed lifestyle. The road ends at **Ke'e Beach**, where adventure begins with the start of the **Na Pali Coast Trail.** The north shore remains for most visitors the perfect setting for seeking and maybe actually finding peace, solitude, the dream, yourself.

HEADING NORTH: ANAHOLA AND VICINITY

Route 56 north from Kapa'a is a visual treat. Out your window, the coastline glides along in an ever-changing panorama. Development is virtually nonexistent until you get to Kilauea in the Hanalei District. To your left are the **Anahola Mountains,** jagged, pointed, and intriguing. Until recently, you could crane your neck and see **Hole-in-the-Mountain,** a natural arrangement of boulders that formed a round *puka* (legend says it was formed by an angry giant who hurled his spear with such force that he made the hole), but time and storms have taken their toll and the hole has collapsed.

Villages, Beaches, and Practicalities

The first village that you come to is **Anahola.** Just before mile marker 14 is the **Whaler's General Store,** open daily 6:30 a.m.-9:30 p.m., selling groceries, souvenirs, vegetables, and liquor.

Next door to the general store is a post office and **Duane's Ono Charburger,** open Mon.-Sat. 10 a.m.-8 p.m. and Sunday 11 a.m.-6 p.m., a clean, friendly roadside stand where you can get burgers or fish and chips. Some of the double-fisted burgers include the Ono at $3.90; an Old Fashioned, with cheddar, onions, and sprouts on a Kaiser roll, at $4.95; the Local Boy, made with teriyaki, cheddar cheese, and pineapple for $5.65; and a Local Girl, made with teriyaki and Swiss cheese. The burgers are oversize, and heavy with cheese and trimmings. For an extra treat, try a delicious marionberry shake. Tables are available, but hold your appetite for a few minutes and make it a picnic at the nearby beach.

Across the road from Duane's, look for the Anahola Baptist Church and a small lane leading to **Hawaiian Barbecue Chicken,** tel. (808) 822-7144, owned and operated by Lee and his family, open Tues.-Sun. when the family is there. The Hawaiian Barbecue is a hut in a grove of trees with two green picnic tables out front. Cooking is done on an enormous barbecue Lee fashioned from an old flatbed truck, its grills flipped by a motorized chain. Lee and his family offer plate lunches such as a half chicken with a scoop each of rice and mac salad for only $6.50. Treats include shave ice, smoothies, cold coconut, and, for a touch of beauty, fresh lei. Hawaiian Barbecue is downhome, clean, friendly, inexpensive, delicious, and filled with the aloha spirit. You can't go wrong.

Just a minute up the road, look to your right for Aliomanu (Oil of the Shark) Road and follow it for a few minutes to the mouth of the Anahola River as it spills into the bay. Or take Anahola Road off Rt. 56 just before the Whaler's General Store to a long strand of white sand that forms one of the best beaches on the north shore. The south end of the bay is **Anahola Beach County Park,** with a developed picnic area, shower, grills, restrooms, and camping (county permit). Tall ironwood trees provide a natural canopy. The swimming is safe in the protected cove near the beach park and in the freshwater river, good for a refreshing dip. As you walk north the waves and rips get tougher—Anahola means "easily broken." It's not advisable to enter the water, although some experienced board riders do challenge the waves here, as the Hawaiians did long ago. However, the reef comes close to shore at this end, and wherever you can find a sheltered pocket is good for snorkeling. Local anglers love this spot for near-shore fishing. The entire area is popular with local people, and at times begins to look like a tent city of semipermanent campers and squatters. This is a place to camp for a few days, or just to stop in for a refreshing plunge on the way to or from the north shore.

The turnoff to **Moloa'a (Matted Roots) Bay** is between mile markers 16 and 17. Turn down the rough Koolau Road, follow it to Moloa'a Road, and take this narrow but paved road to the end. Look for the brilliant poinsettias blooming in early winter along Koolau Road—they are the island's clue that Christmas and New Year are near. Moloa'a Bay is a magnificent but rarely visited beach. The road leading down is a luscious little thoroughfare, cutting over domed hillocks in a series of switchbacks. The jungle canopy is thick and then opens into a series of glens and pastures. Off to the sides are vacation homes perched on stilts made from telephone poles. A short drive takes you to road's end and a small cluster of dwellings where there is limited space to put your vehicle. Park here and follow the right-of-way to the beach signs. Here, a stream comes into the bay providing a great place to wash off the ocean water after a dip.

The beach is lovely, bright, and wide, forming a crescent moon. To the north the beach ends in a grassy hillock; south, it's confined by a steep *pali* (this is where the swimming is best). As at all north shore beaches, swimming is advised only during calm weather. Snorkeling is good, but you'll have to swim the channel out to the base of the *pali,* which is unadvisable if the waves are rough. Although a few homes are around, Moloa'a is a place of peaceful solitude. Sunsets are light shows of changing color, and you'll probably be a solitary spectator.

KILAUEA

There's no saying *exactly* where it begins, but Kilauea is generally considered the gateway to the north shore. The village proper was built on sugar, but that foundation melted away almost 20 years ago. Now the town holds on as a way station to some of the most intriguing scenery along this fabulous coast. Notice the bright, cheery, well-kept homes as you pass through this community. The homeowners may be short on cash but are nonetheless long on pride and surround their dwellings with lovingly tended flower gardens. The bungalows—pictures of homey contentment—are ablaze with color.

To get into town, look for mile marker 23 and a Shell gas station on your right, along with the Menehune Food Market, a small store selling sundries and general groceries. This is where you turn onto Kolo Road, following the signs to Kilauea Lighthouse and National Wildlife Refuge. The promontory that it occupies, Kilauea Point, is the northernmost point of the main Hawaiian Islands.

A second way into Kilauea is by turning off the highway just before mile marker 23 at Ho'okui Road, which is marked by Mango Mama's Fruit Stand (a farmers' market is held every Saturday at noon in the Crater Hills schoolyard next door). Go one block and turn left. Pass St. Sylvester's Church and proceed over a bridge, past the Kilauea School, and on into town.

Alternatively, just before you arrive at the turnoff to Kilauea, look left to see a sign pointing to **Kai Guava Plantation,** open daily 9 a.m.-5 p.m., where you can take a (free) self-guided map tour through lush gardens. Proceed along the access road lined with ferns, banana trees, ironwoods, and flowering bushes, and stop in at the gift shop to pick up a map of the grounds. They also sell guava products, T-shirts, and sundries. Follow a well-trodden path through a covered archway where tropical plants grow, and cross a tiny stream to find many of Hawaii's flowers and plants labeled by name. The path winds along for just 10 minutes and leads to a pond surrounded by taro, bird of paradise, hibiscus, torch ginger, ferns, and various palms. Near the pond, you'll find a round, thatched gazebo, and a picnic table for your enjoyment. Finally, cross the stream on two rustic, wooden half-moon bridges while listening to the babbling water and whispering wind, just as the ancient Hawaiians did while tending their water-terraced fields.

SIGHTS

As you head down Kolo Road from the gas station, you pass the post office. Where Kolo intersects Kilauea Road sits **Christ Memorial Episcopal Church** on the right. Hawaii seems to sprout with as many churches as bamboo shoots, but this one is special. The shrubbery and flowers immediately catch your eye, their vibrant colors matched by the stained-glass windows (imported from England). The present church was built in 1941 from cut lava stone. Inside is a hand-hewn altar, and surrounding the church is a cemetery with several tombstones of

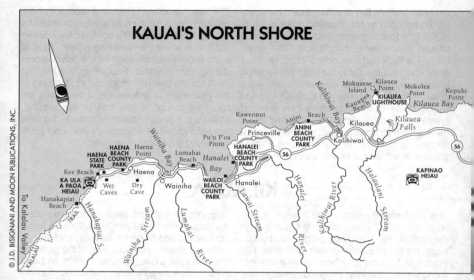

KAUAI'S NORTH SHORE

© J.D. BISIGNANI AND MOON PUBLICATIONS, INC.

long-departed parishioners. Go in, have a look, and perhaps meditate for a moment.

Before turning on Kilauea Road have a look at **St. Sylvester's Catholic Church.** This house of worship is octagonal, with a roof resembling a Chinese hat. Inside are murals painted by Jean Charlot, a famous island artist. The church, built by Friar John Macdonald, was an attempt to reintroduce art as one of the bulwarks of Catholicism.

Head down Kilauea Road past the Kong Lung Store and keep going until Kilauea Road makes a hard swing to the left. Proceeding straight ahead up Mihi Road brings you to a little Japanese cemetery on your right. This road has been blocked—it's now privately owned and closed to the public—but it leads to Mokolea Point's **Crater Hill,** where, 568 feet straight down, is the Pacific, virtually unobstructed until it hits Asia. The seacliff is like a giant stack of pancakes, layered and jagged, with the edges eaten by age, and covered with a green syrup of lichen and mosses. The cliff is undercut and gives the sensation of floating in midair. There is a profusion of purple and yellow flowers all along the edge. The cliffs serve as a giant rookery for seabirds and, along with Mokolea Point to the east, are now part of the **Kilauea National Wildlife Refuge,** which also encompasses Kilauea Point.

For a more civilized experience of the same view with perhaps a touch less drama, head down Kilauea Road to the end and park at **Kilauea Lighthouse,** a designated national historical landmark. This facility, built in 1913, was at one time manned by the Coast Guard but is now under the jurisdiction of the Department of the Interior's Fish and Wildlife Service. Boasting the largest "clamshell lens" in the world, it is capable of sending a beam 90 miles out to sea. The clamshell lens has not been used since the mid-'70s, however, and a small, high-intensity light now shines as an important reference point for mariners.

The area is alive with permanent and migrating birds. Keep your eyes peeled for the great frigate bird kiting on its eight-foot wingspan, and the red-footed booby, a white bird with black wingtips darting here and there, always wearing red dancing shoes. At certain times of the year, Hawaiian monk seals and green turtles can be seen along the shore and around Moku'ae'ae Island just off Kilauea Point. Dolphins and whales are also spotted offshore. Information at the visitors center gives you a fast lesson in birdlife and a pictorial history of the lighthouse—worth reading. Also available are a good selection of books on Hawaiian flora, fauna, history, and hiking, as well as maps of the islands. The center also signs out

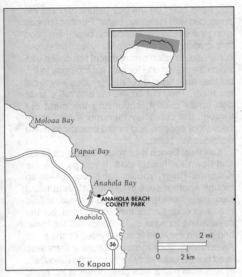

Moloaa Bay

Papaa Bay

Anahola Bay

**ANAHOLA BEACH
COUNTY PARK**

Anahola

0   2 mi

0   2 km

56

To Kapaa

A leisurely walk takes you out onto this amazingly narrow peninsula, where you can learn more about the plant- and birdlife in the area. Don't keep your eyes only in the air, however. Look for the coastal *naupaka* plants, which surround the parking lot and line the walk to the lighthouse. Common along the seashore and able to grow even in arid regions, these plants have bunches of bright green, moisture-retaining, leathery leaves; at their center are white half-flowers the size of a fingernail and small white seeds. The refuge plans to establish a four-mile-long walking trail from Kilauea Point around Crater Hill to Mokolea Point that will be used strictly for tours led by refuge personnel.

This facility is open Mon.-Fri. 10 a.m.-4 p.m., closed weekends and federal holidays. The entrance fee is $2 adults, free for children under 16, $10 for an annual refuge permit; the Golden Eagle Pass, Golden Access Pass, Golden Age Pass, and a Federal Duck Stamp are also honored for free entrance.

binoculars for free to view the birds, and there are usually informative docents in the yard with monoculars trained on particular birds or nesting sites on the nearby cliffs.

The wildlife refuge is attempting to relocate albatross from the Midway Islands, where they nest on runways. The refuge has successfully relocated more than 40, and you can watch them floundering around on nearby Albatross Hill.

BEACHES

The Kilauea area has some fantastic beaches. One is a beach park with full amenities and camping, one is hidden and rarely visited, others are for fishing or just looking.

Kauapea Beach, more commonly called **Secret Beach,** deserves its name. After passing

Kilauea Lighthouse

ROBERT NILSEN

through Kilauea, look for Banana Joe's tropical fruit stand on the left; just past it is Kalihiwai Road. Make a right onto Kalihiwai and then take the very first dirt road on the right. Follow this tiny road for about one mile, until it turns right at an iron gate. Continue down the hill to a parking area and a little homemade sign announcing the beach trail. Follow the signs (if there are signs it can't be too secret, right?). Even some local residents ruefully admit that the secret is out. However, if you venture to this beach, be conscious that there are private homes nearby and that it's a place locals come to enjoy away from the crowds of tourists.

Walk beside the barbed-wire fence and start down the slippery slope to the beach. You pass through some excellent jungle area before emerging at Secret Beach in less than 15 minutes. If you expect Secret Beach to be small, you're in for a shock. This white-sand strand is huge. Off to the right you can see Kilauea Lighthouse, dazzling white in the sun. Along the beach is a fine stand of trees providing shade and perfect for pitching a tent. (Recently the police have been patrolling and issuing tickets for camping without a permit! Sometimes, they issue a warning only, but don't count on it.) A stream coming into the beach when you come down the hill is okay for washing in, but not drinking. For drinking water, head south along the beach and keep your eyes peeled for a freshwater spring coming out of the mountain. What more can you ask for? The camping is terrific and generally free of hassles.

Kilauea Bay offers great fishing, unofficial camping, and beautiful scenery. Proceed through Kilauea along Kilauea Road and pass Kong Lung Store. Take the second dirt road to the right; it angles through cane fields about 100 yards past the Martin Farm produce stand. Follow this rutted road 1.5 miles down to what the local people call **Quarry Beach,** also known as Kahili Beach. At the end of the road is the now-abandoned Kahili Quarry. Although easy to get to, this wide sandy beach is rarely visited. Characteristic of Kauai, Kilauea Stream runs into the bay. From the parking lot, you must wade across the stream to the beach. The swimming is good in the stream and along the beach, but only during calm periods. Some local residents come here to surf or use boogie boards; do this only if you have been on the bay before and are experienced with Hawaiian water. Plenty of places along the streambank or on the beach are good for picnicking and camping. Many local fishermen come here to catch a transparent fish called *o'io,* which they often use for bait. It's too bony to fry, but they have figured out an ingenious way to get the meat. They cut off the tail and roll a soda pop bottle over it, squeezing the meat out through the cut. They then mix it with some water, hot pepper, and bread crumbs to make delicious fish balls.

Kalihiwai Beach is just past Kilauea, off Rt. 56 and down Kalihiwai Road. If you go over the Kalihiwai River, you've gone too far—even though another section of the Kalihiwai Road also leads from there down to the coast. This road was once part of the coastal road, but the devastating tsunami of 1946 took out the lower bridge and the road is now divided by the river. As on many such rivers in Kauai, a ferry was used here to ease early transportation difficulties. In less than half a mile down the first Kalihiwai Road you come to an off-the-track, white sand beach lined with ironwoods. The swimming and bodysurfing are outstanding, given the right conditions. The river behind the ironwoods forms a freshwater pool for rinsing off, but there are no amenities whatsoever. People can camp among the ironwoods without a problem. The second Kalihiwai Road leads you to the beach on the west side of the river where some people come to fish.

Go over the bridge and turn right on the second Kalihiwai Road. Follow this to a Y, take the left fork—Anini Road—and follow it to its end at the remarkable **Anini Beach County Park.** The reef here is the longest exposed reef off Kauai; consequently, the snorkeling is first-rate. Anini was traditionally called *Wanini.* It was known as one of the best fishing grounds and was reserved for the exclusive use of the *ali'i.* But time and sea air weathered a latter-day sign until the "W" rusted off completely. Newcomers to the area mistakenly called it Anini, and the name stuck. It's amazing to snorkel out to the reef in no more than four feet of water and then turn to peer over the edge into waters that seem bottomless. Windsurfers also love this area, and their bright sails can be seen year-round. Those in the know say this is the best spot on Kauai for beginning windsurfers as the winds are generally steady, the water is shallow, and the beach protected. Several shops in Hanalei give lessons here.

Follow the road to the end, where a shallow, brackish lagoon and a large sandbar make the area good for wading. This beach has full amenities—toilets, picnic tables, grills, and a pavilion. There are private homes at both ends of this beach, so be considerate when coming and going.

A polo ground is across the road from the open camping area, and several Sundays each month matches are held here beginning at 3 p.m. and lasting until 5 p.m. Admission is $3 per person or $6 per car, and the exciting matches are both fun and stylish. The local horsemen are excellent players who combine with their trusty mounts to perform amazing athletic maneuvers.

PRACTICALITIES

Accommodations
The **Kai Mana,** P.O. Box 612, Kilauea, tel. (808) 828-1280 or (800) 837-1782, is filled with the healing vibrations of its internationally acclaimed owner, Shakti Gawain, author of Creative Visualization, and of the powerful natural forces so evident on Kauai. Here, the emphasis of your vacation is not only on relaxation, but also on revitalization. Part of your stay can involve private counseling with Shakti when she is in residence, a session with a massage practitioner or meditation instructor, or a simple nature-attunement excursion. Rates are $75 s, $95 d standard room; $95 s, $115 d deluxe corner room; self-contained cottage for $125 per night, $750 per week. All rooms have their own private entrances and private baths; light breakfast food is provided, and a kitchenette is open to guests. Expensive.

Food, Shopping, and Services
In Kilauea across from the Shell station look for **Shared Blessing Thrift Shop,** open Tuesday and Thursday 2-5 p.m. and Wednesday and Saturday 9 a.m.-noon in a vintage plantation building, a good place to pick up secondhand treasures or curios from Kauai here among everything from binoculars to boogie boards.

The **Hawaiian Art Museum,** housed in a plantation building on the left about 50 yards past the sign pointing to Kilauea Lighthouse in downtown Kilauea, tel. (808) 828-1253, open Mon.-Fri. 1-5 p.m. and Sunday 10-11 a.m., offers "talk story" on Sunday morning by Serge King, an internationally known author and lecturer proficient in his knowledge of huna and ancient Hawaiian arts and crafts. The shelves and counters are filled with artifacts like poi pounders and bowls, a remarkable carved statue of a god doing a handstand, a model village alive with dancers and warriors, descriptions of different canoes, makini masks with their distinctive owl-like eyes, ferocious-looking palau war clubs, and Hawaiian musical instruments. The museum is also the home of **Aloha International,** founded by Serge King and dedicated to the practice and philosophy of huna. You can contact the center for a free brochure listing the weeklong summer courses offered and a list of their various products. The curator, Bev Brody, a certified instructor in huna, is also intimately familiar with the fauna and flora in the area, and may lead you on a nature hike if you call in advance to make arrangements and if time permits.

Look for the blue and white kiosk in a banana grove marking **Mango Mama's Fruit Stand** at the south entrance to Kilauea along Rt. 56. Mango Mama's is ripe with papayas, bananas, mac nuts, fresh juices, sugarcane, honey, and health-conscious sandwiches.

An institution in this area is **Kong Lung Store,** located along Kilauea Lighthouse Rd. at the intersection of Keneke St., tel. (808) 828-1822, open Mon.-Fri. 10 a.m.-6 p.m., Saturday 9 a.m.-6 p.m., and Sunday 10 a.m.-5 p.m., which has been serving the needs of the north shore plantation towns for almost a century. But don't expect bulk rice and pipe fittings. The upstairs section of the store is called **Reinventions** and sells consignment clothing for both men and women; downstairs, the items change constantly, but there are always hats, furniture, bath products, and artworks. The **Indo Pacific Trading Co.,** a store featuring arts and artifacts from throughout Asia and Polynesia, also has a section of the old Kong Lung Store.

The **Roadrunner Bakery and Cafe,** at 2430 Oka St. (turn at Garden Isle Missionary Baptist Church just before Kong Lung), tel. (808) 828-

8226, open Mon.-Fri. 7 a.m.-8 p.m., to 8:30 p.m. Saturday, would make even Wile E. Coyote give up Acme Exploding Enchiladas with its excellent and very affordable Mexican food. Shuffle across a sand floor and spin like a piñata to view the interior painted floor and a ceiling with a Mexican motif. Chew your chimichanga while Aztec Indians tend their crops, horses gallop past, buses laden with chickens and baggage cruise along through cactus fields, and *charros* roast a side of beef over a campfire. It's owned and operated by Denis Johnston, who arrives at 3 a.m. to fire up the ovens. You order through a window that looks back into the bakery, then sit at green tables amidst full-size trees and strings of hanging chilies. Breakfast gets you rolling with huevos—rancheros, Mexicana, or Americano— all priced under $6. Lunch brings appetizers like chips and salsa at $4.75, guacamole and chips at $5.25, and entrees like chicken flautas at $4.75. A range of salads priced $5.75-6.75 includes grilled vegetable and mahi selections. Regular Mexican fare includes tostadas smothered with roasted chicken, pork, steak, or fresh catch, all under $7.75; or tortas bulging with pinto beans, rice, lettuce, salsa fresca, and your choice of steak, roast pork, or roast chicken, all at $5.25. Roadrunner also offers tacos, tamales, and enchiladas, all handmade fresh on the premises. Beverages are coffee, iced tea, and fresh-squeezed orange juice. From the bakery you can order Hanalei taro rolls, bagels, sourdough, cracked pepper, honey wheat, and Rhine molasses bread, along with all sorts of goodies. Roadrunner is a hands-on business run with pride, friendliness, and a commitment to fresh and excellent food at reasonable prices.

Windows all around open to a miniature garden and lanai where you can dine alfresco at **Casa di Amici Ristorante.** Located next door to Kong Lung Store, tel. (808) 828-1555, open for dinner 5:30-9 p.m., it is the best Italian restaurant on the north shore. Chef Randall Yates and his professional staff make you feel right at home in this "house of friends." Inside, the ristorante is classic, with green-topped tables trimmed in wood and comfortable chairs with padded armrests. In the center, a diminutive fountain performs a tinkling melody while an ensemble of magnificent Hawaiian flowers dances gently in the breeze. Start with antipasti, a plate laden with greens, pepperoncini, olives, eggs, provolone, salami, prosciutto, and anchovies for $10, or try the gorgonzola mushroom polenta served with Roma tomatoes, or the risotto quatro fromagio with fresh basil and tomatoes, each at $8. Soups and salads include minestrone for $5, the savory *zuppa di casa*—New Zealand mussels with fresh tomatoes, capers, tri-colored bell peppers, and leeks in a rich *femet depoission* for $6, or Caesar salad $6, and mixed salad for $5. Pasta dishes are a choice of linguine, fettuccine, capellini, tortellini, or penne covered in zesty sauces like pesto, marinara, arabiato, or Alfredo; entrees include lasagna, chicken cacciatore, veal marsala, and chicken picatta, all priced $16-22. The ristorante also has a full-service bar serving top-shelf liquors and imported draft beers, along with a fine wine selection prominently displayed for your perusal. There's espresso or cappuccino to complete your meal, and, to add to your dining pleasure, soothing piano music is performed Thurs.-Saturday.

Just behind Casa di Amici is the **Kilauea Bakery and Pau Hana Pizza,** tel. (808) 828-2020, open daily except Sunday 6:30 a.m.-9 p.m. Using all natural ingredients, Kilauea Bakery supplies some of the best restaurants along the north shore. The extensive selection of baked goods is tempting, and occasionally they put out something a bit offbeat like pumpkin coconut muffins (the breadsticks are great). As with the other shops in this little complex, Kilauea Bakery succeeds in offering something special. Their pizzas are made with organically grown California olive oil and whole-milk mozzarella on a whole-wheat or sourdough crust. All are gourmet, topped with sautéed mushrooms, feta cheese, grated Parmesan, homemade pesto, sun-dried tomatoes, or locally grown peppers, priced $7.25 for a small to $16.25 for a 16-inch large, or $2.75 by the slice. Enjoy your treat inside, or sit on the tiny veranda under a shade umbrella. Coffee, made by the cup, is also served.

Next door to Casa di Amici is the Kilauea neighborhood center and theater, and beyond that is **The Farmers' Market,** a deli/grocery store, open 9 a.m.-9 p.m. The deli carries food items and beverages and makes filling homemade soups and sandwiches for those who want something substantial but don't want a full sit-down meal. Much of their produce is organic, when possible, and they have a gourmet section with imported cheeses and fine food items. Behind the center is a small community park.

Kilauea is also home to the **Island Soap Co.**, owned and operated by Stephen and Marlena Connella, at P.O. Box 846, Kilauea, HI 96754, tel. (808) 828-1120 or (800) 300-6067. The husband and wife team hand-pours its soap, perfuming the raw bars with heady fragrances like coconut, plumeria, and ginger. They also produce self-pampering products like scented coconut oils, lotions, and bath gels capturing the scents of the islands. Island Soap Co. products are available at boutiques throughout Hawaii and can also be purchased by mail.

To experience the living beauty of your trip to Kauai, try a bouquet of lovely orchids from **Makai Farms**, tel. (808) 828-1874, open Sat.-Tues. 9 a.m.-4 p.m., or by appointment. Look for the sign to the entrance past mile marker 21, *makai* along a white fence.

Martin Farm Produce Stand is just beyond town. Open Mon.-Sat. 9 a.m.-5 p.m., it operates on the self-service honor system. Select what you want, add up the cost marked on each item, and drop your payment in the box. Nearby, at the corner of Oka St., is the Kilauea clinic of the Kauai Medical Group.

After visiting all these places, you need a rest. The perfect stop is just west of town at **Banana Joe's** fruit stand, *mauka* of the highway, tel. (808) 828-1092. Run by Joe Halasey, his wife, and friends, this little yellow stand offers fresh fruit, smoothies and other drinks, packaged fruit baskets, baked goods with fruit, and other fruit products. They have more kinds of fruit than you've ever heard of—try something new. If you're interested and they have the time, you may be able to visit the farm behind the stand and talk to Banana Joe himself, but you'll have to ask first. Not to be outdone in the related-to-a-tropical-fruit department, just before Banana Joe's is **Mango Mama's Fruit Stand.** What's next? Sister Soursop and Brother Breadfruit?

PRINCEVILLE

Princeville is 9,000 acres of planned luxury overlooking Hanalei Bay. Last century, the surrounding countryside was a huge ranch—Kauai's oldest, established in 1853 by the Scotsman R.C. Wyllie. After an official royal vacation to the ranch by Kamehameha IV and Queen Emma in 1860, the name was changed to Princeville in honor of the royal son, Prince Albert. The young heir unfortunately died within two years, and his heartbroken father soon followed.

Since 1969, Consolidated Gas and Oil of Honolulu has taken these same acres and developed them into a prime vacation community designed to keep the humdrum world far away. Previously owned by the Princeville Development Corporation, a subsidiary of Quitex Australia, and now owned by the Japanese consortium of Suntory, Mitsui, and Nippon Shinpan, the community provides everything: accommodations, shopping, dining, recreational facilities (especially golf and tennis), even a fire and police force and a website: www.princeville.com. First-rate condos are scattered around the property, and a new multitiered Princeville Hotel perches over the bay. The guests expect to stay put, except for an occasional day-trip. Management and clientele are in league to provide and receive satisfaction. And without even trying, it's just about guaranteed.

Note: Mile markers on Hwy. 56 going west are renumbered from one at Princeville. It is 10 miles from here to the end of the road at Ke'e Beach.

RECREATION

Golf, Tennis, and Other Athletic Clubs
Those addicted to striking hard, dimpled white balls or fuzzy soft ones have come to the right spot. In Princeville, golf and tennis are the royal couple. The **Princeville Makai Golf Course** offers 27 holes of magnificent golf designed by Robert Trent Jones Jr. This course, chosen as one of America's top 100, hosted the 26th annual World Cup in 1978 and is where the LPGA Women's Kemper Open is played. Radiating from the central clubhouse are three nine-hole, par-36 courses you can use in any combination. They include the Woods, Lake, and Ocean courses—the names highlighting the special focus of each.

Opened in 1987, the 18-hole **Prince Course,** tel. (808) 826-3580, also welcomes the public. It's located off Hwy. 56 just east of the Woods course and has its own clubhouse. For this course, accuracy and control are much more important than power and distance. Many expert golfers judge the Prince extremely difficult—perhaps the most challenging in Hawaii; there's one par-six hole, another hole with the tee 300 feet above the fairway, and ravines and streams among the obstacles. Nine-hole twilight golf is available on any course weekdays after 3 p.m. for a reduced fee. The clubhouse has an extensive pro shop, a snack shop, and club storage. The driving range is open during daylight hours. Plenty of package deals to the resort include flights, accommodations, rental car, and unlimited golf.

You can charge the net on 22 professional tennis courts day or night at the **Princeville Tennis Club,** tel. (808) 826-3620. There are two pro shops, lessons of all sorts, racket rental, ball machines, and even video playback so you can burn yourself up a second time reviewing your mistakes. Several condos in Princeville, such as The Cliffs and the Hanalei Bay Resort, also have tennis courts, but these are for their guests only.

On the lower level of the Princeville clubhouse is the **Hanalei Athletic Club,** tel. (808) 826-7333, open weekdays 7 a.m.-8 p.m., Saturday 8 a.m.-6 p.m., and Sunday 11 a.m.-5 p.m. This is a sister club of the Kauai Athletic Club in Lihue, so you can use both if you are a member. Available are aerobics classes, Nautilus machines, freeweights, an outdoor pool, jacuzzi, and sauna. It also has designated running courses throughout the Princeville resort area. Daily, weekly, and monthly rates are available, with discounts for couples. For those with small children, a babysitting service is available by appointment 8:30-10 a.m. weekdays. Operating through the health club is **Hanalei Health and Sports Massage.** For an appointment, call (808) 826-1455. Licensed, professional staff give *lomi lomi,* shiatsu, Swedish, Esalen, and sports massages.

Horseback Riding

Princeville Ranch Stables, is located a half-mile east of Princeville Center, tel. (808) 826-6777, open Mon.-Sat. 7:30 a.m.-4 p.m. You can rent a mount here for one of three group rides that take you throughout the area's fascinating countryside. Prices are $30, $50, and $75 for the Hanalei Valley, shoreline, and waterfall picnic rides. The Hanalei Stampede, Kauai's largest rodeo, is held at the stables in early August. Call for details.

Nearby is the **Silver Falls Ranch,** P.O. Box 692 Kilauea, HI 96752, tel. (808) 828-6718, which offers tame guided rides on a daily basis. The 1.5-, 2-, and 3-hour rides run $60, $73, and $98 for adults. The three-hour ride includes a picnic lunch and swim in the cascading Silver Falls.

ACCOMMODATIONS

The condos and hotel rooms in Princeville all fall into the luxury range. The best deals naturally occur off-season (fall), especially if you plan on staying a week or more. Oddly enough, a project like Princeville should make booking one of its many condos an easy matter, but it's sadly lacking on this point. Lack of a centralized organization handling reservations causes the confusion. Each condo building can have half a dozen booking agents, all with different phone numbers and widely differing rates. The units are privately owned and the owners simply choose one agency or another. If you're going through a travel agent at home, be aware of these discrepancies and insist on the least-expensive rates. A situation that reduces the number of units available is that many of the condos are moving to exclusively time-share programs while others still offer rental units along with their time-share units, so check out the possibilities.

The Cliffs at Princeville

Set high on the bluff overlooking the Pacific Ocean and having one of the nicest views in the area is The Cliffs at Princeville, tel. (808) 826-6219 or (800) 367-7052. These one-bedroom condo units have full-size baths and small wet bars. At the far end of the L-shaped living and dining room is the fully equipped kitchen; you can prepare everything from a fresh pot of morning coffee to a five-course meal at your leisure and in the comfort of your own living space. Two large lanai, one at each end of the unit, offer both ocean and mountain views. Carpets run throughout the unit and the furniture is of con-

entrance to The Cliffs
at Princeville

ROBERT NILSEN

temporary style. Fresh flowers, potted plants, Hawaiian prints, and artwork counter the pastel colors and the subdued floral patterns of the bedroom linen. The bedrooms have king-size beds and the cushy living-room couch pulls out to sleep two more. Units have color TVs, video and stereo systems, compact washers and dryers, irons and ironing boards, small safes for valuables, and daily maid service. Some third-floor units have two bedrooms. These are basically the same as the one-bedroom units except that the second bedroom is in a loft and the living-room ceiling slants up to the second floor. One-bedroom units are $120-150; one-bedroom units with lofts run $155-200. The property also has a pool and tennis courts free to guests and a breezy common room off the pool with a large-screen TV, reading material, and a laundry room. Premium.

Princeville Hotel

The Princeville Hotel, 5520 Kahaku Rd., Princeville, HI 96722, tel. (808) 826-9644, (800) 826-4400, or (800) 782-9488, website: www .sheraton.com, is a dramatic architectural opus, built in cascading tiers on an extreme point of rugged peninsula. From its perch, all but 16 of the 252 rooms offer breathtaking views of the frothing azure of Hanalei Bay as it stretches toward the emerald green of Bali Hai Peak down the coast. The other rooms offer panoramic views of Puu'poa Marsh, a wildlife conservation wetlands area that offers sanctuary to exotic birdlife. The main lobby offers elegance on a grand scale. The living natural treasures of Kauai spill intimately into the immense room, which is completely encircled by glass. Gold-capped Corinthian columns seem to support banks of clouds as they wander past colossal skylights. Teardrop chandeliers softly illuminate magical fans of tropical flora surrounding a central reflecting pool, its waters lapping the edges in natural syncopation to the wind that whispers through the entire majestic chamber. Here and there are gold-tinged mirrors, Louis XIV chairs, plush couches, and stout coffee tables, and a floor of swirled black and white marble. One special spot is the Living Room, a dignified area serving as library, cocktail lounge, and music room. Choose a plush chair just before sunset, and sip a cocktail as the sun streaks the sky with lasers of light dancing across the endless blue of the wide Pacific. There is entertainment every night: a pianist comes to play Hawaiian and contemporary music, you can enjoy twice-weekly sonorous Hawaiian chanting, and sometimes you can watch the exotic sway of accomplished hula dancers. Cocktails and beverages are served 4 p.m.-midnight, *pu pu* and hors d'oeuvres 5-9 p.m., and dessert 5-10:30 p.m. The hotel has a small mini-mall with a cluster of shops that include the **Princeville Resort Shop,** the hotel's logo boutique, where you can purchase everything from hats to incidental bags, all emblazoned with the hotel's logo; **Lamont's Gifts and Sundries,** stocked with sundresses, bathing suits, film, suntan lotion, and books and magazines; a beauty salon; and **Collectors Fine Arts,** representing internationally acclaimed artists.

All rooms feature bathrooms with double vanities, gold fixtures, lotions, potions, terry robes, slippers, and deep immersion tubs, some of which are mini-spas. Bathroom doors are of liquid crystal that can be controlled to change from opaque for privacy to clear so that you can enjoy the view while you soak. Rooms also feature mini-bars, refrigerators, remote-controlled color TVs, and 24-hour room service. In addition, there are three restaurants (see following), two lounges, romantic beachside dinners, prepared picnic lunches, and an activities desk. The Princeville also offers full pool service—with poolside food service—and a white sand beach fronting the hotel that is perfect for swimming. The reef below, alive with tropical fish, is excellent for snorkeling. At dusk, descend to the pool area and immerse yourself in one of the jacuzzis to watch the sun melt into the Pacific as you melt into the foaming bubbles. Free shuttle service is provided to and from the golf course, tennis courts, shopping center, and Princeville Airport, and guest can also use the facilities at the recently reopened Sheraton Kauai in Poipu. A standard room ranges $350-495, suites are $575 for an executive to $3,500 for a royal, with a $35 third-person charge. Luxury.

Condos

The best deal in Princeville is offered by **Sandpiper Village** condominiums. By chance, they stumbled onto a good thing. When they first opened, they priced their units low to attract clientele. The response was so good, with so many repeat visitors, that they have decided to keep it that way . . . for the time being. For $80-200, you get a roomy one-bedroom unit (one to two people); a two-bedroom, two-bath unit (one to four people); or a three-bedroom unit. (Minimum stay is often required, so ask. *Kama'aina* and long-term stay discounts are available.) A few unadvertised one-room studios with baths but no kitchens run $45 per night; available on a limited basis; you must specifically ask about these. Most units have garden views, with a few offering ocean views. Each has a full kitchen with dishwasher, laundry facilities, color TV, and private lanai. Maid service (fee) is available on re-

quest, and a cleaning charge ($65-85) is added to your bill at checkout. On the grounds are a pool, jacuzzi, barbecue grills, and recreational building, all surrounding well-tended gardens. For reservations and information, contact booking agents Oceanfront Realty at (800) 222-5541. Moderate.

The **Hanalei Bay Resort,** P.O. Box 220, Hanalei, HI 96714, physically at 5380 Honoiki Rd., tel. (808) 826-6522 or (800) 367-5004 Mainland and Canada, or (800) 272-5275 in Hawaii, is a condo resort with some private units. You enter through a spacious open area paved with flagstone and face the **Bali Hai Bar,** done in longhouse style with a palm-frond roof, magnificent koa long bar, and matching koa canoe. From the bar, you have a spectacular panorama of Bali Hai Peak dappled by passing clouds and Hanalei Bay, a sheet of foam-fringed azure. Evening brings live music, with everything from jazz to a local slack-key combo. Stepping down the hillside from the bar is the resort's free-form pool complete with a 15-foot waterfall—all surrounded by landscaping inspired by the area's natural beauty. The resort buildings are like two outstretched arms ready to embrace the bay, and all units are guaranteed to have stupendous views. Amenities include laundry facilities, full kitchens in the condo units, TV, phone, tennis courts, and air conditioning. The resort condo offers single rooms, studios, and one-, two-, and three-bedroom suites in categories from mountain view to ocean deluxe. Rates start at $160 for a mountain-view room to $650 for a three-bedroom suite. Luxury.

Other condos in the development charge a minimum of $100 per night. They're out to please and don't skimp on the luxuries. The **Pali Ke Kua** condos sit right on the cliffs and, along with the nearby **Pu'u Po'a** and **Hale Moi** condominiums are managed by Marc Resorts Hawaii, tel. (800) 535-0085. The Pali Ke Kua boasts one of the best restaurants on the north coast, the units at the Pu'u Po'a are more luxurious and slightly more expensive, and the Hale Moi overlooks the golf course for about half the price.

The **Hanalei Bay Villa,** located just next to the prestigious Princeville Resort, is the area's newest vacation rental and offers large luxury suites at affordable prices. Rates are $140, $175, and $230 for a one-, two-, or three-bedroom unit (weekly and longer-stay discounts available). For reservations and information, contact Oceanfront Realty at tel. (808) 826-6585 or (800) 222-5541. Luxury.

Other good locations include the **Alii Kai II,** where all units are around $100; the **Paniolo;** and weathered gray Cape Cod-ish **Sealodge.** Reservations can be made by calling Hanalei Aloha Rental Management, P.O. Box 1109, Hanalei, HI 96714, tel. (808) 826-7288 or (800) 487-9833.

FOOD

Hanalei Bay Resort

The **Bali Hai,** at the Hanalei Bay Resort, tel. (808) 826-6522, open daily for breakfast 7-11 a.m., lunch 11:30 a.m.-2 p.m., and dinner 5:30-10 p.m., enjoys an excellent reputation not only for its food but also for its superb atmosphere and prizewinning view of the sunset through the wraparound windows of this bilevel and informal yet elegant restaurant. The Bali Hai chefs grow their own herbs on the premises and insist on fresh local vegetables, meat, and fish prepared in a mixture of continental and Pacific Rim cuisine. Settle comfortably into high-backed wicker chairs in the inviting room, which is reminiscent of a Polynesian longhouse, with a vaulted thatched roof from which hangs a koa outrigger canoe. Drink in the spectacular view of Hanalei Bay while a tinkling waterfall keeps a soothing rhythm in the background. Start your day with a chilled fresh coconut for $4.75, a half island papaya for $3.50, or a continental breakfast that includes fresh fruit juices, bakery items, and Kona coffee for $7.25. Go local with a taro patch breakfast of two fried eggs, Portuguese sausage, poi pancakes, and taro hash browns for $8.25, or try specialties like the Bay Breakfast—eggs, ham, bacon or sausage, hash browns, and white rice for $7.25—or the Bay Benedict for $12.50. Lunchtime brings Kauai onion soup for $4, soup and salad for $7.50, and filling salads like spicy beef salad with smoked tofu for under $10. The sandwich board has a Monte Cristo with ham, turkey, and Swiss cheese—for $9.75 and an assortment of burgers, including the Bali Hai, charbroiled and served with cheese and onions, for $8.25. You can start with appetizers like blackened *ahi* sashimi (market price), sesame-crusted chicken for $8, or a *pu pu* platter for $11. Soup selections include soup de jour at $4, gazpacho at $5, and seafood chowder for $6, or try a garden salad with Kilauea organic greens and a choice of dressing for $5.50, or salad entrees like a crab Caesar for $14 ($16 with snow crab legs). Entree specialties are fresh island fish prepared in a variety of tempting sauces including Thai sesame, papaya salsa, and Drambuie herbed butter. Standard but wonderful offerings are teriyaki chicken at $21, spicy scampi for $23, and petite Australian lamb with fresh mint sauce for $25. Nightly, a luau and Hawaiian revue featuring hula and reenactments of Hawaiian legends is offered. You're greeted with cocktails and music provided by a local duet 6-7 p.m., and the luau buffet opens at 6:45 p.m. Tables are laden with Hawaiian favorites like *lomi* salmon, chicken long rice, fresh island catch, *kalua* pork, *hapia,* coconut cake, and hot bread pudding. A cocktail show begins seating at 7:45 p.m., and the revue begins at 8:45 p.m. Prices for luau and revue are $49.95 adults and $12.95 children ages 5-12, $19.50 and $14 for the cocktail show and revue only.

The **Happy Talk Lounge,** also at the Hanalei Bay Resort, mixes its fantastic views of Hanalei Bay with exotic drinks, wine by the glass, and frothy beers for a night of relaxation and entertainment. A limited menu served 3-10 p.m. offers tortilla chips at $4.50, jalapeño poppers at $7.25, a *pu pu* platter for two at $11, and sesame-crusted chicken for $8. Sandwiches and salads served daily 11:30 a.m.-10 p.m. include a bay burger made with the fresh catch of the day for $10.75, chicken breast marinated in teriyaki sauce for $9, honey dipped chicken at $8.75, and a fruit and cheese plate, enough for two at $9.25.

Pali Ke Kua

The **Beamreach Restaurant,** in a freestanding building on the grounds of the Pali Ke Kua condo complex, tel. (808) 826-6143, open nightly for dinner 5:30-9:30 p.m. (reservations suggested), is a casual fine dining restaurant where chef Catalano Domingo offers a mix of island-style and classic American dishes. The bilevel dining room, subdued in shades of tan and brown, is lightly appointed with hanging baskets, throw nets, frescoes depicting Hawaiian mythology, and a display case holding ancient artifacts. A very good sign is that all soups and salad dressings are made on the premises, and fresh organic greens and vegetables are used as much as possible. Stimulate your palate with *poki,* offered raw or seared, at $6.95; teriyaki meat sticks at $5.95; or a pot of fresh steamed clams for $6.95. Move on to entrees, priced $12.95-21.95, like ground sirloin, filet mignon, macadamia nut chicken with tropical sauce, or fresh fish sautéed, broiled, or blackened. Your sweet tooth will be happy with desserts such as Tahitian Lime Pie at $4.50, tropical fruit sherbet for $2.75, or a rum, caramel, or chocolate sundae for $4.50. The Beamreach also has a full-service bar stocked with fine wine, a good selection of beer, and house specialty tropical drinks.

Princeville Hotel
The Princeville Hotel is home to three restaurants. The **Cafe Hanalei,** tel. (808) 826-9644, open for breakfast 6:30-11 a.m., lunch 11 a.m.-2:30 p.m., dinner 6-9:30 p.m., and Sunday brunch, offers indoor or outdoor seating in a casual setting. Breakfast at the Hanalei is either continental for $14.95 or full for $20.95. The continental breakfast is much more than you might expect—a buffet table set with lox and bagels, cream cheese, fresh island fruits, fresh-squeezed juices, an assortment of cereals, yogurt, pastries, and coffee. The full breakfast buffet is complete with an omelette station, and an array of savory breakfast meats. Lunch may be chilled shrimp with rice noodles for $11.50, Thai chicken and beef satay for $10.95, a Caesar salad with croutons and Parmesan for $7.95, sushi nigiri and California rolls for $14, or any of a number of gourmet sandwiches and burgers. Dinner entrees are roasted rack of lamb for $27.95, grilled moon fish *(opa)* for $24.95, seared spicy pepper *ahi* at $27.95, breast of chicken or steamed Kona lobster at $35.95. Finish with desserts like apple cinnamon cheesecake, mango creme brûlé, or flourless chocolate cake, all delicious and prepared daily.

La Cascata, tel. (808) 826-2761, open daily for dinner 6-9:30 p.m., offers tremendous views of the island's inland waterfalls as you dine in this elegant ristorante. Designed after a famous restaurant in Positano, Italy, it features elegant decor including hand-painted terra-cotta floors, inspir-

ing murals, and formally set tables. The Mediterranean-inspired menu features capellini pasta with rosemary chicken and penne primavera with roasted seasonal vegetables, both priced around $24. Grilled island *ahi* with roasted garlic polenta and mushroom medley, garlic breadcrumb baked island snapper, or crisp, slow-roasted duck with stewed lentils are all around $28. Meals are perfectly finished with desserts like classic tiramisu or a chocolate bourbon pecan tart, or with a cup of espresso or cappuccino, or a glass of fine port. For light meals, try the hotel's casual, pavilion-type **Beach Bar and Restaurant,** where you can order snacks, sandwiches, or complete meals. They offer such entrees as grilled Black Angus sirloin steak, grilled salmon or *opakapaka,* and barbecued pork ribs, all priced $30-35. A children's menu, priced $2 for every year of age between 3 and 12, helps keep prices down. For a sunset drink, try the hotel's **Living Room** or swim up to the pool's water bar for a mid-lap mai tai.

Princeville Center and Beyond
At the Princeville Center you'll find **Chuck's Steak House,** tel. (808) 826-9700, open for lunch Mon.-Fri. 11:30 a.m.-2:30 p.m., nightly for dinner 6-10 p.m. Chuck has a very loyal clientele that comes not only for the juicy steaks but for the fresh fish as well. Chuck's is "casual country," with an open-beamed ceiling, a choice of booth or table inside or on the lanai, and a few saddles and barrels placed here and there for effect. The lunch menu has salads and *pu pu* such as "loaded fries," which are covered with bacon, cheese, and sour cream for $4.25; Caesar salad for $5.25; tuna salad $8.95; shrimp Louis for $10.50; and crab Louis for $12.50. Burgers and sandwiches go from a simple burger for $4 to a barbecue prime rib sandwich for $6.75. Dinner is delicious, with the fresh catch charbroiled or sautéed for $18.50, shrimp Hanalei for $21.50, juicy prime rib $16.95-24.50 depending on the cut, teriyaki chicken breast at $15.75, an assortment of combination dinners priced $19.50-26, and the mouth-watering house specialty—barbecued pork ribs. A senior and children's menu relieves the bottom-line total. Chuck's has a full-service bar separate from the dining area and features a local Hawaiian woman who comes to sing and play her ukulele on week-

ends. Chuck's is a good choice for a family-style restaurant offering hearty portions.

Follow the rich aroma of brewing coffee to **Hale O Java,** an upscale, friendly, indoor/outdoor, casual restaurant behind Chuck's Steak House, tel. (808) 826-7255, open daily 6:30-10:30 a.m. for breakfast, 10:30 a.m.-5:30 p.m. for lunch, and until 9:30 p.m. for dinner; it will even deliver from 5 p.m. until closing. The breakfast menu offers an early-bird special (6:30-8 a.m.—two eggs, bacon, toast, and Americano coffee for $3.95), Belgian waffles $3.95-5.50, and tropical granola for $4.50; steaming coffee, latte, cappuccino, or mocha in large Italian-style cups cost around $2; or try a fruit slush or smoothie just to cool off. A glass case is filled with pastries—from sticky buns to bagels—made fresh on the premises and all priced under $2. Lunch menu is basically *panini,* Italian sandwiches made with an assortment of lunch meats and smothered with mozzarella, sliced tomatoes, and fresh pesto, served on focaccia bread for about $6. Pizza, a specialty of Hale O Java, is priced $8.50-18.50, depending on size and toppings. Dinner brings spaghetti or fettucine with marinara, white wine sauce, or pesto, priced $8.50-10.50, with a daily lasagna priced at $8.75. This place is a step or two off the normal tourist track, but it's quiet and offers well-prepared food and decent prices with a friendly staff to make you feel welcome.

Auntie Sophies, near Hale O Java, open daily 11 a.m.-9 p.m., is a Mexican restaurant with seating indoors or outdoors on the lanai. Lunch-menu items such as chicken, beef, or cheese enchiladas ($6.95), burrito ($7.95), or taco salad ($7.95), are all served with Spanish rice and beans. You can also have a chili rice bowl for $4.50, or a gringo hamburger or hot dog with different fixings for $5.95-7.50. Dinner brings a chile relleno for $11.95, baby back ribs for $14.95, or fried chicken at $11.95. Daily specials such as fajitas round out the menu.

Also at the Princeville Center, **Lappert's Ice Cream** will fill a cone for you. You can order guess-what at the **Pizza Burger.**

Don't forget **Amelia's,** open daily 11:30 a.m.-6:30 p.m. at the old Princeville Airport, convenient on your way into or out of town. This friendly pub serves sandwiches, hot dogs, chili, and nachos and has four TVs for live satellite sports.

ENTERTAINMENT

There is little in the way of evening entertainment in Princeville, so you may have to be creative and make your own. However, the following are definitely worth checking out. The **Bali Hai Restaurant** at the Hanalei Bay Resort swings with nightly entertainment Tues.-Sat. 6:30-9:30 p.m.—everything from contemporary music to Hawaiian ballads performed by slack-key artists. A very special performance that shouldn't be missed is the free jazz combo every Sunday 3-6 p.m. Local musical talent is fantastic, but to make things even better, top-name musicians who happen to be on the island are frequently invited to join in. If you love jazz, you can't find a more stunning venue than the Bali Hai.

Weekends bring live music to the **Princeville Golf Course Clubhouse,** where a good mix of local people and tourists come to dance the night away.

The Living Room, in the main lobby of the Princeville Hotel, is a dignified venue for a variety of island-themed entertainment including Hawaiian music, chanting, and hula.

SHOPPING AND SERVICES

Aside from the few shops in some of the larger resorts, the shopping in Princeville is clustered in the **Princeville Center,** with most shops (although not all) open daily 8 a.m.-8 p.m. Since Princeville is a self-contained community, many of these are practical shops: bank, hardware store, sporting-goods outlet, real-estate offices, Kauai Medical Group clinic, post office, restaurants. **Foodland,** open daily 6 a.m.-11 p.m., is important because it offers the cheapest food prices on the North Shore. Before it was built, the local people would drive to Kapa'a to shop; now they come here.

Some of the shops here include **Lappert's Ice Cream,** for a quick pick-me-up; **J Ms Jewels** for a quick pick-*her*-up; the **Kauai Kite Company,** a bursting crayon box filled with stuffed animals, toys, and, of course, kites for a quick lift-it-up; **Hanalei Photo Company,** a full-service photography store offering developing, cameras, and photo supplies and gadgets for a quick pin-it-up;

and **Sand Dunes,** a clothing boutique for men and women with sandals, sun hats, waterproof watches, perfume, ladies' dresses, jewelry, T-shirts, and beach bags. **Pretty Woman,** open Mon.-Sat. 9:30 a.m.-6 p.m., is in the rear of the center, so you'll have to search them out. They sell name-brand ladies' fashions, jewelry, evening dresses, hats, and accessories. Not-so-pretty men are also welcome—especially if they have rolls of wrinkled-up bills bearing pictures of dead presidents—who were not so pretty either. Restrooms, handicapped friendly, are on the first floor of the shopping center just near the Mail Service Center.

The Princeville Medical Clinic, tel. (808) 826-7228, specializing in preventive medicine, is open Mon.-Fri. 9 a.m.-5 p.m. and alternating Saturdays 9 a.m.-1 p.m. Mornings are best for walk-in patients.

The last gas station on the north shore is Princeville Chevron. If your gauge is low make sure to tank up if you're driving back down the coast. They're open Mon.-Thurs. 7 a.m.-7 p.m., Friday and Saturday until 8 p.m., and Sunday until 6 p.m.

The Princeville Health Club and Spa, located at the Princeville Golf Club, tel. (808) 826-5030, open Mon.-Fri. 7 a.m.-8 p.m., Saturday 8 a.m.-8 p.m., and Sunday 8 a.m.-6 p.m., is open to the general public with a charge of $12 a day, and $40 a week. Besides a complete set of exercise equipment, the spa offers massage, body treatments, facials, and aromatherapy wraps.

HANALEI

If Puff the Magic Dragon had resided in the sunshine of Hanalei instead of the mists of Hanalee, Little Jackie Paper would still be hangin' around. You know you're entering a magic land the minute you drop down from the heights and cross the Hanalei River. The narrow, one-lane bridge is like a gateway to the enchanted coast, forcing you to slow down and take stock of where you are. To add to your amazement, as you look up valley over a sea of green taro, what else would you expect to find but a herd of buffalo? (They've been imported by a local entrepreneur trying to cross-breed them with beef cattle.)

Hanalei (Lei-making Town) compacts a lot into a little space. You're in and out of the town in two blinks, but you'll find a small shopping center, some terrific restaurants, beach and ocean activities, historical sites, and a cultural and art center. You also get two superlatives for the price of one: the epitome of a laid-back north shore village, and a truly magnificent bay. In fact, if one were forced to choose the most beautiful bay in all of Hawaii, Hanalei (and Lumahai, the silent star of the movie *South Pacific,* just west of town), would definitely be among the finalists.

SIGHTS

The sights around Hanalei are exactly that—beautiful sweeping vistas of Hanalei Valley and the sea, especially at sunset. People come just for the light show and are never disappointed. When you proceed past the Princeville turnoff, keep your eyes peeled for the Hanalei Valley scenic overlook. Don't miss it! Drifting into the distance is the pastel living impressionism of Hanalei Valley—most dramatic in late afternoon, when soft shadows from deeply slanting sun-rays create depth in this quilt of fields. Down the center, the liquid silver Hanalei River flows until it meets the sea where the valley broadens into a wide flat fan. Along its banks, impossible shades of green vibrate as the valley steps back for almost nine miles, all cradled in the protective arms of 3,500-foot *pali.* Controlled by rains, waterfalls either tumble over the *pali* like lace curtains billowing in a gentle wind or with the blasting power of a fire hose. Local wisdom says, "When you can count 17 waterfalls, it's time to get out of Hanalei." The valley has always been one of the most accommodating places to live in all of Hawaii, and its abundance was ever-blessed by the old gods. Madame Pele even sent a thunderbolt to split a boulder so that the Hawaiians could run an irrigation ditch through its center to their fields.

In the old days, Hanalei produced taro, and deep in the valley the outlines of the ancient fields can still be discerned. Then the white man came and planted coffee that failed and sugar that petered out, and raised cattle that over-grazed the land. During these times, Hanalei had to *import* poi from Kalalau. Later, when Chinese plantation laborers moved in, the valley was terraced again, but this time the wet fields were given to rice. This crop proved profitable for many years and was still grown as late as the 1930s. Then, amazingly, the valley began to slowly revert back to taro patches.

In 1972, 917 acres of this valley were designated **Hanalei National Wildlife Refuge;** native water birds such as the Hawaiian coot, stilt, duck, and gallinule loved it and reclaimed their ancient nesting grounds. Today, the large, green, heart-shaped leaves of taro carpet the valley, and the abundant crop supplies about half of Hawaii's poi. You can go into Hanalei Valley; however, you're not permitted in the designated wildlife areas except to fish or hike along the river. Never disturb any nesting birds. Look below to where a one-lane bridge crosses the river. Just there, Ohiki Road branches inland. Drive along it slowly to view the simple and quiet homesteads, old rice mill, nesting birds, wildflowers, and terraced fields of this enchanted land.

In addition, and more recently, the Hanalei River itself has been designated an "American Heritage River," one of only 14 in the nation to be so noted and the only one whose total length is placed in this category. Federal monies will be used to help protect its unique character and enhance its preservation.

Overlooking the bay, on a tall bluff, are the remains of an old Russian fort (1816) from the days when Hawaii was lusted after by many European powers. It's too difficult to find, but knowing it's there adds a little spice.

For a real cultural event, the North Shore co-operative, operating the **Waipa Taro Farm,** tel. (808) 826-6192, graciously invites lucky volunteers (maximum 15) to help with the final preparation of their famous taro every Thursday 7 a.m.-noon. You must remember that you are there to help, not to observe. You are there to do a job and should hold your questions until work is done when you are free to take a walk through the taro patch.

Down the block, on the right next to Na Pali Zodiac, an old building (the old Ching Young Store) houses the **Native Hawaiian Trading and Cultural Center.** Don't get *too* excited, though, because this good idea doesn't have its act together yet. Aside from a very small museum (open daily 10 a.m.-5 p.m.), it has some authentic Hawaiian crafts and some awful touristy junk, too. You can buy handmade jewelry, shells, clothes, and sweets, but some of the really worthwhile items are lovely fresh plumeria lei and flowers. Upstairs is the **Artisans Guild of Kauai,** a fine co-op where local artists display and sell their arts and crafts.

Waioli Mission House Museum

As you leave town, look to your left to see **Waioli Hui'ia Church.** If you're in Hanalei on Sunday, do yourself a favor and go to the 10 a.m. service; you will be uplifted by a choir of rich voices singing enchanting hymns in Hawaiian. They do

The spacious guest bedroom at the Waioli Mission House Museum is filled with period furniture.

justice to the meaning of *waioli,* which is "healing or singing waters." The Waioli Mission House is a must-stop whenever you pass through. You know you're in for a treat as soon as you pull into the parking lot, which is completely surrounded by trees, creeping vines, ferns, and even papaya. You walk over stepping-stones through a formal garden with the jagged mountains framing a classical American homestead; the acreage was also a self-sufficient farm where the owners raised chickens and cattle. Most mission homes are New England-style, and this one is, too, inside. But outside, it's Southern, because the missionary architect, Rev. William P. Alexander, was a Kentuckian who arrived with his wife, Mary Ann, in 1834 by double-hulled canoe from Waimea. Although a number of missionary families lived in the home in the first few years after it was built in 1837, in 1846 Abner and Lucy Wilcox arrived, and the home became synonymous with this family. Indeed, it was owned and occupied by the *kama'aina* Wilcox family until very recently. It was George, the son of Abner and Lucy, who founded Grove Homestead over by Lihue. Miss Mabel Wilcox, his niece—who died in 1978—and her sister, Miss Elsie, who was the first woman representative of Hawaii in the '30s, set up the nonprofit educational foundation that operates the home.

Your first treat will be meeting Joan, the lovely tour guide. A fusspot in the best sense of the word, she's like a proper old auntie who gives you the "hairy eyeball" if you muss up the doily on the coffee table. Joan knows an unbelievable amount of history and anecdotes, not only about the mission house, but also about the entire area and Hawaii in general. The home is great, and she makes it better. The first thing she says to Mainlanders, almost apologetically, is "Take off your shoes. It's an old Hawaiian custom and feels good to your feet."

You enter the parlor, where Lucy Wilcox taught native girls who'd never seen a needle and thread to sew. (Within a few years, their nimble fingers were fashioning muumuu to cover their pre-Christian nakedness.) In the background, an old clock ticks. In 1866, a missionary coming to visit from Boston was given $8 to buy a clock; here it is keeping time more than 120 years later. The picture on it is of the St. Louis Courthouse. Paintings of the Wilcoxes line the walls. Lucy looks like a happy, sympathetic woman. Abn-

er's books line the shelves. Notice old copies of *Uncle Tom's Cabin* and *God Against Slavery.* Mr. Wilcox, in addition to being a missionary, was a doctor, teacher, public official, and veterinarian. His preserved letters show that he was a very serious man, not given to humor. He and Lucy didn't want to come to Waioli at first, but they learned to love the place. He worried about his sons and about being poor. He even wrote letters to the king urging that Hawaiian be retained as the first language, with English as a second. He and Lucy returned to New England for a visit in 1869, where both took sick and died.

During the time that this was a mission household, nine children—eight of them boys—were born in the main bedroom. Behind it is a nursery, the only room that has had a major change; Lucy and Mabel had a closet built and an indoor bathroom installed there in 1921. Upstairs is a guest bedroom that the Wilcoxes dubbed the "room of the traveling prophet," because it was invariably occupied by visiting missionaries. It was also used by Abner Wilcox as a study, and the books in the room are the original primers printed on Oahu. The homestead served as a school for selected boys who were trained as teachers.

The house has been added to several times and is surprisingly spacious. Around the home are artifacts, dishes, and knickknacks from the last century; notice candle molds, a food locker, a charcoal iron, and the old butter churn. Lucy Wilcox churned butter, which she shipped to Honolulu in buckets and which brought in some good money. Most of the furniture is donated period pieces; only a few were actually used by the Wilcoxes. From an upstairs window, you can still see the view that has remained unchanged from the last century: Hanalei Bay, beautifully serene and timeless. The Waioli Mission House is open Tuesday, Thursday, and Saturday 9 a.m.-3 p.m., and is free! There is a bucket for donations; please be generous. For information, call (808) 245-3202.

BEACHES

Since the days of the migrating Polynesians, Hanalei Bay has been known as one of the Pacific's most perfect anchorages. Used as one of Kauai's three main ports until very recently, it's still a favorite port of call for world-class yachts.

They start arriving in mid-May, making the most of the easy entrance and sandy bottom, and stay throughout the summer. They leave by October, when even this inviting bay becomes rough, with occasional 30-foot waves. When you drive to the bay, the section under the trees near the river is called **Black Pot**. It received this name from an earlier time, when the people of Hanalei would greet the yachties with island *aloha*, which, of course, included food. A fire was always going with a large black pot hanging over it, into which everyone contributed and then shared in the meal. Across the road and upriver a few hundred yards is **Hanalei Canoe Club**. This small local club has produced a number of winning canoe teams in statewide competitions, oftentimes appearing against much larger clubs.

The sweeping crescent bay is gorgeous. The Hanalei River and three smaller streams empty into it, and all around it's protected by embracing mountains. A long pier is in the center, and two reefs front the bay: Queen to the left and King to the right. The bay provides excellent sailing, surfing, and swimming—mostly in the summer. The swimming is good near the river (but watch out for boats and Zodiac rafts, which are launched from here) and at the west end, but rip currents can appear anywhere, even around the pier area, so be careful. The best surf rolls in at the outside reef below Pu'u Po'a Point on the east side of the bay, but it's definitely recommended only for expert surfers. Beginners should try the middle of the bay during summer, when the surf is smaller and gentler. The state maintains three parks on the bay: Black Pot, at the Hanalei River mouth, Pine Trees, in the middle of the bay, and Waipa, on the west side. Black Pot and Pine Trees have picnic areas, restrooms, and showers. Camping is permitted only at Pine Trees. A small *kaukau* wagon sells plate lunches near the river; local fishermen launch their boats in the bay and are often amenable to selling their catch.

Lumahai Beach is a femme fatale, lovely to look at but treacherous. This hauntingly beautiful beach (whose name translates as "Twist of Fingers") is what dreams are made of: white sand curving perfectly at the bottom of a dark lava cliff with tropical jungle in the background. The riptides here are fierce even with the reef, and the water should never be entered except in very calm conditions during the summer. Look for a vista point between mile markers 4 and 5. Cars invariably park here. It's a sharp curve, so make sure to pull completely off the road or the police may ticket you. An extensive grove of hala trees appears just as you set off down a steep and often muddy footpath leading down to the east end of the beach. The best and easiest place to park is among the ironwood trees at the west end of the beach near the bridge that crosses the Lumahai River; an emergency phone is across the road from this parking area. From here you can walk to the south end if you want seclusion.

ACCOMMODATIONS

Hanalei Inn

The moderately priced Hanalei Inn is on the west side of town across from the school. It's tucked in among flowering bushes and trees; with only four studio apartments, it's a quiet, relaxing place. Each unit has a living/bedroom areas with queen-size bed, an efficiency kitchen sufficient to make light meals, and a full bath. Coin laundry on premises. Rates from $65; no credit cards or personal checks. For information, write Hanalei Inn, P.O. Box 1373, Hanalei, HI 96714, or call (808) 826-9333. Moderate.

Historic Bed and Breakfast, Hanalei

You can still smell the sweet incense that permeates Historic Bed and Breakfast, Hanalei, 5-5067 Kuhio Hwy., P.O. Box 1662, Hanalei, HI 96714, tel. (808) 826-4622. Housed in Kauai's oldest Buddhist Temple, the simple but elegant structure built in 1901 served the Japanese community until 1985, when it began to fall into disrepair. Neglected and deteriorating, the temple was saved by a consortium of local business people and now has the distinction of being listed in both the National and State Historic Registers. This painstaking and extensive effort refurbished more than 95% of the original structure including the lustrous hardwood floor, polished over the decades by the stockinged tread of devout parishioners. This remarkable B&B is now owned and operated by Jeff and Belle Shepherd, who welcome you to three bright and airy rooms cooled by ceiling fans. Decorated with original art, the two downstairs and one upstairs rooms, priced $55 s, $65 d, are separated by shoji screens and feature beds covered with antique quilts. You are free to relax in the comfortable common area—part of which serves as a dining room for breakfast—or to stroll outdoors to a small garden, perfect for an evening cup of tea. The shared bathrooms have deep Japanese-style *ofuro* tubs where you can soak away to your heart's content. Historic Bed and Breakfast, offering a perfect opportunity to become part of Kauai 's living history, is centrally located, with only a five minute walk to the downtown area or the beach. Moderate.

Bed, Breakfast, and Beach
Bed, Breakfast, and Beach, P.O. Box 748, Hanalei, HI 96714, tel. (808) 826-6111, owned by Caroly Barnes, is a neo-classic trilevel plantation-style home, located in a quiet residential area only a minute's walk from the beach. It gives you a strong feeling that you are part of the community. Upstairs offers a wide, covered lanai, perfect for catching the breeze or listening to the soft patter of a morning shower while eating breakfast—served 8:30-9:30 a.m. and consisting of your choice of piping hot coffee, herbal teas, and fresh island fruits, juices or smoothies, accompanied by muffins, and fresh-baked bread. On the upper levels you'll find plenty of windows from which to enjoy a postcard view of the surrounding mountains scratching the soft bellies of passing clouds causing showers that turn into lace waterfalls cascading from the green luminescent heights. The common area, a casual lounging parlor, is cool and inviting with smooth parquet floors, an open beamed ceiling, and knotty-pine paneling. The decor throughout is a mixture of classic Hawaiian and tasteful New England antique appointed with items like a bent glass china closet, wooden refrigerator, and reclining bamboo chairs and couches covered in floral patterned puff pillows. Nooks and crannies are filled with objets d'art and plenty of reading material. From the common area, a staircase ascends to the Bali Hai Suite. At 700 square feet, it occupies the entire top floor and is divided into a master bedroom, day room/conversation nook, and bath. Off the central area is the Pualani Suite—smaller, but alive, like a living floral arrangement with pastel blooms from ceiling to bedspread. At ground level, two units, called the Garden Lanai and Maki, offer kitchenettes and outdoor showers (Garden Lanai has an indoor

shower as well). The decor in both is island themed, with bamboo or rattan furniture and louvered windows and ceiling fans for catching the breezes. Bed, Breakfast, and Beach is an excellent choice of accommodations for relaxation, a feeling of homeyness, and extremely good value. Rates are $75-90 d; children are welcome except in the Bali Hai Suite. Moderate.

Home Rentals
Private rental homes, generally listed through property and rental agencies, are also available in town (and farther along the coast). For information, contact **Na Pali Properties, Inc.,** P.O. Box 475, Hanalei, HI 96714, tel. (808) 826-7272; **North Shore Properties and Vacation Rentals,** P.O. Box 607, Hanalei, HI 96714, tel. (808) 826-9622; or **Ironwood Rentals,** tel. (808) 826-7533.

FOOD

Hanalei has a number of eating institutions, ranging from excellent restaurants to *kaukau* wagons. The food is great at any time of day, but those in the know time their meals to coincide with sunset. They watch the free show and then go for a great dinner.

The **Hanalei Gourmet,** in the old schoolhouse at the Hanalei Center, tel. (808) 826-2524, open Mon.-Thurs. 10 a.m.-10:30 p.m. for lunch and dinner and Fri.-Sun. 8 a.m.-11:30 p.m., is a born-again-hippie, semi-yuppie, one-stop nouveau cuisine deli, gourmet food shop, and good-time bar. To top it off, it's friendly, the food is exceptionally good, the prices are right, and there's even live entertainment. It is broken into two sections; to the right is the deli, with cases filled with lunch meats, cheeses, salads, and smoked fish, while to the left is the bar/dining area. Here, ceiling fans keep you cool, while blackboards, once used to announce hideous homework assignments, now herald the daily specials. Behind the bar, windows through which reprimanded childhood daydreams once flew now open to frame green-silhouetted mountains. Original hardwood floors, white walls bearing local artworks and hanging plants, two big-screen TVs for sports enthusiasts, and a wide veranda with a few tables for dining alfresco complete the restaurant. Breakfast, served from 8 a.m., offers a half-papaya with other fresh fruit for $4.75; bagels, lox, and cream cheese for $6.95, muesli topped with fresh fruit for $4.25, and huevos Santa Cruz for $6.25. You can also enjoy a cup of Lappert's coffee and a pastry for around $3. Lunch sandwiches, all around $7, are huge wedges filled with pastrami, smoked ham, gourmet cheeses, and more. Lunch and dinner are served 5:30-9:30 p.m. and features specials like Oregon Bay shrimp served open-face on brown bread with melted cheese and remoulade sauce for $7.50, or smoked Alaskan king salmon on a French baguette for $10.50, and fresh catch made in a variety of ways at market price. You can also order a picnic lunch to go, side salads, plenty of baked goods, and even a fine bottle of wine. The Hanalei Gourmet definitely lives up to its name and is the perfect spot for a meal or a social beer.

Bubba Burger, first opened in Kapa'a and now with a branch in Hanalei at the Hanalei Center, open daily 10 a.m.-6 p.m., is still doing what it's always done: serve up double-fisted burgers, individually made, at great prices. Mostly a window restaurant, there is seating on the lanai, with a few tables inside. Bubba's burgers range in price $2.50-4.25, with other offerings on the menu like Italian sausage or a fish burger at $4.50, a Hubba Bubba—rice, a burger patty, and hot dog, all smothered with chili for $5. Try side orders like chili fries or Caesar salad, all light on the wallet but not so light on the waistline.

Papagayo Azul, tel. (808) 826-4494, open 11 a.m.-9 p.m., a north shore institution, features good food at reasonable prices. Before the devastation of Hurricane Iniki, Papagayo Azul was located along the main street, but this spotless *nuevo Mexicano* restaurant has since moved to the back court of the Hanalei Center, where you should definitely seek it out. Inside, the new restaurant boasts an open kitchen, thatched roof, wooden floor, ceiling fans, and the mandatory sombreros, serape, and strung chili peppers of a Mexican restaurant. Lunch brings a regular burrito for $5.95, carnitas burrito at $7.95, fish taco for $4.50, tostadas $6.95, and good old nachos at $4.95. The dinner menu (you can order from the lunch menu at dinner) starts with ceviche at $6.95, quesadilla with a chicken or beef at $4.95, *ensaladas de nopalitos*—a cactus marinated in herbs and spices—at $5.95, and *ensaladas de jicama,* marinated in orange juice for $5.95. Entrees include *pollo borracho,* a boneless breast of chicken grilled in tequila sauce at $9.95, *pescado asado,* charbroiled *ahi* in a light chile wine sauce at $11.95, or beef steak ranchero at $12.95. All items are served à la carte; beans and rice are $1.95 extra. Papagayo Azul has always had a loyal local following and still deserves the distinction of a people's choice restaurant.

If you want a romantic evening, head for the silvery beams of **Cafe Luna,** open daily in the Hanalei Center 5-9:30 p.m. tel. (808) 826-1177, an avant-garde, cosmopolitan restaurant where you can dine alfresco under a wooden pavilion or inside at classically set tables. Begin your meal with seafood bisque for $6, classic Caesar for $7, or polenta with shrimp for $8. Move on to pasta like *aglio e olio* for $11; primavera made with fresh vegetables, sherry, and choice of marinara, white, oglio, or *blu,* a gorgonzola-based sauce with sage, tomato, and cream. The main entrees range in price $14-21 and include choices like filet mignon, grilled fish, and vegetarian lasagna. There is a full selection of pizzas priced $9-12 with a wonderful array of toppings including marinated shrimp, caramelized onions, and sun-dried tomato. To top off your meal, choose a dessert like light and refreshing fresh berries, banana rum crepes, or the Italian standard, tiramisu. Cafe Luna is a fine dining restaurant, offering a perfect mixture of nouvelle and classic dishes that won't cost you the moon.

In a freestanding building in the Hanalei Center follow the aroma of fresh brewed coffee to the **Old Hanalei Coffee Company,** tel. (808) 826-6717, open daily 8 a.m.-5 p.m., where you can revitalize with a cup of espresso, cappuccino, latte, au lait, or an old-fashioned hot chocolate made with Hershey's syrup and milk. If you're in the mood for something else, try a frosted mocha or a flavored Italian soda. The Hanalei Coffee Company serves breakfast and lunch until 2 p.m.; you can eat inside or out on the lanai. The good but limited menu consists of Kauai waffles, three-egg scramble, assorted bagels, homemade soup, and sandwiches like hot cordon bleu or hot turkey, everything priced $2.50-6.50. Smaller items—all made on the premises—include muffins and cheesecake, or you might like to bring home a pound of bulk coffee. Just outside is **Shave Ice Paradise,** which is owned by the same man who owns the Coffee Company (you'll see him scurrying back and forth). Here you can choose from 17 flavors of traditional shave ice including coconut and papaya, with fruit cocktail and adzuki beans thrown in for good measure. There's ice cream and a signature drink called a Summer Breeze, somewhat like an Orange Julius with a special twist. They scoop the ice cream and make the shave ice as if they were doing it for family and friends. Your only problem is to lick faster than these hefty babies can melt.

You've got to stop at the **Tahiti Nui,** tel. (808) 826-6277, if just to look around and have a cool drink. The owner, Louise Marston, a real Tahitian although her name doesn't sound like it, is dedicated to creating a friendly family atmosphere and she succeeds admirably. Inside, it's pure Pacific Island. The decorations are modern Polynesian longhouse, with blowfish lanterns and stools carved from palm tree trunks. The bar, open from noon to midnight, is the center of action and features live music Wed.-Sat. nights. Old-timers drop in to "talk story," and someone is always willing to sing and play a Hawaiian tune. The mai tais are fabulous. Just sit out on the porch, kick back, and sip away. The lunch and dinner menu ($10-21) is limited but includes fresh fish, beef, and chicken—all prepared with an island twist. You sit at long tables and eat family-style. The Tahiti Nui is famous for its luau-style parties Wednesday and Friday at 6:30 p.m. There's singing, dancing, and good cheer all around—a perfect time to mingle with the local people. The food is real Hawaiian, and the show is no glitzy extravaganza or slick production. This luau is very down to earth, casual, Kauaian; everybody has a good time; price is $40 adults, $17 children, free under age five.

Located next to Tahiti Nui, in the Kauhale Center, the **Hanalei Wake-Up Cafe,** tel. (808) 826-5551, open daily 6 a.m.-2:30 p.m., owned and operated by Lani, is the perfect breakfast place in Hanalei. Cubbyhole small, it also has a few tables out on the veranda. The cheery help, the smell of freshly brewed coffee, and the good home cookin' should help start your day off on the right foot. Try a giant muffin for $2, Over the Falls French toast for $4.75, and Hanalei in the Tube, which is a quesadilla with scrambled eggs, onions, and bell peppers in a flour tortilla with rice or hash browns for $6.50. You can also have a veggie tofu sauté of fresh vegetables, served with rice or hash browns for $5.75. Baked goods include bagel with cream cheese for $2, or have a nutritious sunrise smoothie flavored with fresh pineapple, banana, or papaya for $2.75.

Just down the walkway in this group of shops is the **Black Pot Luau Hut** restaurant and bar, tel. (808) 826-9871, serving mostly Hawaiian food. Open on a variable schedule for lunch and dinner, usually 11:30 a.m.-2:30 p.m. and then again 5:30-9 p.m., Black Pot offers saimin for $2.55-4.25, teri chicken or beef sticks at $1, hamburgers for $2.55-3.40, and a selection of sandwiches like fishmelt, crabmelt, teri beef, or teri chicken for under $5. The Hawaiian and local food choices, served with two scoops of rice and potato or macaroni salad, include *kalua* pig for $7.95, stir-fry chicken for $6.50, or a teri chicken plate at $4.95. Downhome basic Black Pot is very friendly, very local, and very good.

At the Hanalei Trader, the first building on the left as you enter town, look for a hanging golden dolphin marking the **Hanalei Dolphin Restaurant,** tel. (808) 826-6113, open daily 5:30-10 p.m., almost hidden in the dense tropical foliage on the banks of the Hanalei River. The interior is casual, with an open beamed ceiling, wood trim, and tapa-like formica tables with blue captain's chairs. Appetizers include ceviche at $5, stuffed mushrooms for $6.50, and seafood cocktails at market price. Seafood, mainly from the owners' fish market around back, includes fresh catch at market price (try the seared teriyaki *ahi*), teriyaki shrimp for $19.50, calamari for $16, fresh fish and chips for $15. Other entrees include Hawaiian chicken for $15, *haole* chicken, a boneless breast of chicken with seasonings and Parmesan for $15, and New York steak at $19.50. Light dinners like broccoli casserole and seafood chowder run $10.50. All entrees are served with family-style salads, steak fries or rice, and hot homemade bread.

The **Hanalei Dolphin Fish Market,** at the Hanalei Trader, open daily 11 a.m.-6 p.m., sells fresh, locally caught fish, perfect for a private dinner or beach luau.

Tropical Taco is a *kaukau* wagon open daily except Monday 11 a.m.-4 p.m. It dispenses great food at cheap prices and is usually parked next to the Hanalei Trader as you enter town. Roger, the owner and an avid surfer, came to the north shore 20 years ago. He's never too busy to "talk story" and is a font of wit and wisdom about Hanalei and the surrounding area. A family man who has proudly sent his daughters off to university through his one-man operation, Roger will take the time—especially with families—to direct you to safe swimming, snorkeling, and hiking areas. Roger has just painted his truck bright green to fit in with the foliage, and from the window dispenses tasty and filling baby burritos for $2, regular tacos for $4, large overstuffed fish tacos for $7, ice cream, and 100% cotton Tropical Taco T-shirts.

A great place to write home about is the covered veranda of the 100-year-old plantation home that was once the Hanalei Museum. The owners of **Postcards**, tel. (808) 826-1191, a cafe and mostly Mexican restaurant, have refurbished the mansion to a condition as close to the original as possible, and today it is listed on the National Register. Breakfast here with a steaming cup of cappuccino and a homemade muffin, or sweet roll, and watch north shore life go by. Postcards is an upbeat, health-conscious vegetarian restaurant that prides itself on using organic ingredients and making every dish from scratch. It roasts all its own peppers, makes its own salsa, and drenches its enchiladas in four different types of sauces simmered from three different types of chili peppers. Dishes are simple but hearty, and the price, especially for the quality, is good. Postcards is wheelchair friendly, while smokers are completely prohibited even from lighting up outside. The food is so pure and the vibes so harmonious that the present owner and staff plan to serve people for at least the next 200 or 300 years.

Zelo's, established in Princeville for seven years, moved to Hanalei in late 1995 after the hurricane, tel. (808) 826-9700. It's open daily 11 a.m.-9:30 p.m. with happy hour 3:30-5:30 p.m. and sometimes music on weekends. The interior of this indoor/outdoor restaurant is distinctive, with a bamboo bar covered with a corrugated roof supported by old beams and tree trunks, and *lau hala* matting on the walls. The lunch menu offers salads ranging from a petite for $3.95 to a Chinese chicken salad for $9.50. Sandwiches include grilled cheese for $4.75, a Philadelphia steak sandwich for $8.95, and turkey and cheese at $6.25. There is a full range of burgers with all the fixings—including teriyaki, pesto, and a Cajun fish burger—priced $5-8. Other items are nachos at $5.95, gourmet onion rings for $4.95, all-you-can-eat spaghetti at $8.95, fettucine Alfredo for $8.95, and linguine with clams and pine nuts at $11.95. The atmosphere is pleasant, the staff friendly, and the prices reasonable.

In the Ching Young Shopping Center, **Pizza Hanalei**, open daily 11 a.m.-9 p.m., tel. (808) 826-9494, serves Hanalei's only pizza, and it's delicious. Made with thin, white, or whole-wheat crust, these pizzas run $8-30 (for the Lizzy Special). There is pizza by the slice 11 a.m.-4 p.m. Green and pasta salads, garlic bread, lasagna, and pizzarittos (pizza filling rolled up in a pizza shell like a burrito) are also on the menu. They also do cholesterol-free tofu pizza using Tofurella.

Next to Pizza Hanalei is **Hanalei Health and Natural Foods,** tel. (808) 826-6990, open daily 8:30 a.m.-8:30 p.m. in summer, 9 a.m.-7 p.m. in winter. Inside are bulk foods, fresh fruits and vegetables, a variety of baked breads, freshly squeezed juices, deli foods, and sandwiches, as well as books and vitamins. They also have a good selection of cosmetics, incense, candles, rolling papers, and massage oils. If you're into natural foods and healthful living, stop in, look around, and chat.

If the little hunger monster gets hold of you and a slab of tofu just won't do, walk across the courtyard to the **Village Snack and Bake Shop.** Open daily 6 a.m.-6 p.m., it serves just what its name implies, along with light breakfasts.

Papa Al's Buffalo Burger and Euro-Asian Mixed Plates, in a freestanding building in the Ching Young Village, serves up burgers, veggie burgers, barbecued steaks, Korean barbecue, and pretzels. They also have unusual items like funnel cakes from New Jersey and fried bologna sandwiches—if burgers of buffalo (raised in Hanalei), $5.65, aren't unusual enough. Papa Al's is basically a window restaurant with outdoor seating where prices are very reasonable, ranging from $2.95 for the fried bologna to $6.75 for stir-fried chicken. Next door is **Zababaz,** where you can refresh yourself with a shave ice or a Lappert's ice cream cone.

Every Tuesday 3-5 p.m., pick up some farm-fresh fruit and vegetables from the **Hawaiian Farmers of Hanalei** farmers' market, located a half-mile west of town, in Waipa, on the road to Haena. Look for the sign along the road on the left.

SHOPPING

The **Hanalei Trader** is the first building as you enter town. Here you'll find **Ola's,** tel. (808) 826-6937, open daily 10 a.m.-9:30 p.m., an "American" craft store with items from all 50 states, like glass work from Oregon, ceramics from California, wood products from Hawaii, and jewelry from New York. Some of the unique items are tiny tots' leather moccasins, wildflower honey bath salts, greeting cards, hairbrushes, wooden hearts, leather purses, cutting boards, and silver and gold jewelry.

Ke Kane Kai, a.k.a. The Water Man, also in the Hanalei Trader, tel. (808) 826-5594, open daily 9 a.m. -9:30 p.m., not only catches your eye but also helps keep the sun out of it with a display of hats for both men and women. It also sells a large selection of alohawear and casual beachwear. Glass cases hold watches and sunglasses, while a canoe fashioned from breadfruit hangs overhead and surfboards line the walls. Although Ke Kane Kai doubles as a clothing shop, its primary function is as a surf shop. Upstairs is filled with surfboards fashioned by legendary shapers like Terry Chung and Billy Hamilton, along with a wide selection of wet suits, leashes, and shorts. Ke Kane Kai does not rent surfboards but does rent top-notch silicone snorkel gear at $5 per day or $20 per week

The **Ching Young Village** in the center of town is a small shopping center. Among its attractions are a Big Save Supermarket, open daily 7 a.m.-9 p.m.; a number of variety and gift stores; public restrooms; a few clothing shops; Flying Fish Film Processing; a Bank of Hawaii; Hanalei Video and Music; the Artists Gallery; and a See Kauai activity and information booth; the post office is next door.

Two shops located just near the Tahiti Nui Restaurant are the **Hanalei Photo Company,** with one-hour developing, cameras, and a fax service; and **Kiki Bikini,** where ladies might want to find that just-right swimsuit.

The **Hanalei Center,** the newest in town, has an excellent assortment of shops and boutiques. Some impressive ones are Rainbow Ducks, specializing in children's wear; Sand People, which offers island casual clothing for men and women; Bamboo Silks, a ladies' shop with elegant and casual dresses; Yellowfish Trading Company, which is stuffed from floor to ceiling with Hawaiiana, antiques, collectibles, hula-doll lamps, classic Hawaiian aloha shirts, kuchi-kuchi dolls, costume and silver jewelry, floral colored day bags, candles, swords, antique hats, Matson Steamship Line posters, and koa carvings and incidentals. Yellowfish is a terrific place to browse and get a taste of classic Hawaii. Here, too, is Whalers General Store, open daily 8 a.m.-8 p.m., selling groceries, liquor, sundries, and souvenirs.

The most distinctive shop, **Kahn Galleries,** in the Hanalei Town Center, tel. (808) 826-6677, open daily 9 a.m.-10 p.m., specializes in original artworks and limited edition prints created by some of the finest artists Hawaii has to offer.

Tropical Tantrum, in the Hanalei Center, tel. (808) 826-6944, open 9 a.m.-9 p.m. and until 7 p.m. in winter, is part of a small chain (others are in Kapa'a and on Maui) that designs its own fabrics, which are then turned into original clothing in Indonesia. At Tropical Tantrum, women can rage in the most vibrant colors of purple, blue, red, green, and yellow, transforming themselves into walking rainforests. Prices for original designs, perfect for either casual or elegant evenings, range $40-120. Complete the ensemble with earrings, necklaces, or bracelets from their selection. Gentlemen may browse through a rack of aloha shirts, priced around $60, stuck off in the corner.

Victor Bailey, a.k.a. **Treasure Chest,** P.O. Box 178, Kealia, HI 96751, tel. (808) 826-1492, offers strings of beads and seashells, mixing in a sprinkling of semiprecious gemstones for color and style. His distinctive creations are affordable—bracelets and anklets at $10, necklaces $20-40. You're going to have to find Victor mostly by chance, since like the wind that bathes Kauai, he's at any beach where the sun shines (although mostly he prefers the north shore).

SPORTS AND RECREATION

Hanalei is alive with outdoor activities. The following is merely a quick list of what's available.

For boat rides up the coast, contact **Na Pali Adventures,** P.O. Box 1017, Hanalei, HI 96714, tel. (808) 826-6804, or (800) 659-6804. They provide environmentally responsible interpretive tours in their specially outfitted catamarans. You can sail, snorkel, or whalewatch in season. Based primarily in Hanalei, they also sail from Nawiliwili or Port Allen, depending on ocean conditions. Rates are $55-80, depending upon which tour you choose, and include a snorkel stop with instructions and equipment, snacks, beverages, and deli sandwiches.

The company to see for a kayaking adventure up the Hanalei River or during summer, along the coast, is **Kayak Kauai,** tel. (808) 826-9844.

A variety of sailing and fishing adventures are available from **Robert McReynolds,** tel. (808) 828-1379, and Captain Andy's **Bluewater Sailing,** tel. (808) 828-1142. The sailboats run only during the summer.

The **Hanalei Surf Co.,** in the Hanalei Center, tel. (808) 826-9000, is a water-sports shop that rents and sells snorkeling equipment, boogie boards, and surfboards. Rental rates are surfboards for $15 per day, boogie boards for $7, snorkel equipment for $5; money-saving weekly rates are available on all rentals. The store is also stocked with a good selection of shirts, shorts, thongs, bathing suits, pareus, incidental bags, sunglasses, sunblock, and dresses.

Pedal and Paddle, in the Ching Young Center, tel. (808) 826-9069, open daily 9 a.m.-5 p.m.

in winter, 9 a.m.-6 p.m. in summer, rents and sells snorkel gear, bikes, boogie boards, and surfboards. Prices are: snorkel gear $7 a day, $20 per week; body board with fins $8 and $25; surfboards $12 and $36; cruiser bikes $10 and $40; mountain bikes $50 and $80 (all bike rentals include lock, helmet, and car rack if desired); two-person dome tents $10 and $30; backpacks $5 and $20; light blankets $3 and $10; day packs $4 and $12. A rental day begins the hour you rent and ends at 5 p.m. the following day. Pedal and Paddle does not sell bikes or kayaks, but has snorkel and camping gear for sale. Kayaks are available for rent, too.

John Sargent's **Bike Doctor,** in Hanalei, tel. (808) 826-7799, open Mon.-Sat. 9 a.m.-5 p.m., is stocked with everything for the casual and serious cyclist. John is also intimately familiar with roads and trails all over the island and is happy to give advice on touring.

SERVICES AND INFORMATION

The North Shore Taxi, tel. (808) 826-6189, not only runs a pickup and delivery service, but also does tours. The ordinary fare from Hanalei to Princeville is under $10, to the end of the road at Ke'e Beach is about $20. Owner Dave Sammann will pick you up and take you to or from the North Shore or to the airport in a taxi, minivan, or station wagon for $63. North Shore Taxi also offers luxury service with one of their Cadillac or Lincoln stretch limos for $135. You must pre-arrange the luxury service and Dave will be waiting, resplendent in his chauffeur's cap and surfing shorts.

ROAD'S END

Past Hanalei you have six miles of pure magic until the road ends at Ke'e Beach. To thrill you further and make your ride even more enjoyable, you'll find historical sites, natural wonders, a resort, restaurant, grocery store, the *heiau* where the hula was born, overlooking a lovely beach, and the trailhead to Kauai's premier hike, the Kalalau Trail.

Sights, Accommodations, and Services

As you drive along, you cross one-lane bridges and pass little beaches and bays, one after another, invariably with a small stream flowing in. Try not to get jaded peering at "just another gorgeous north shore beach."

Over a small white bridge is the village of **Wainiha** (Angry Water), with its tiny **Wainiha Store,** open daily 9:30 a.m.-6:30 p.m., tel. (808) 826-6251, where you can pick up a few supplies and sundries. You can also rent beach equipment like boogie boards ($5 a day), snorkel gear ($6), and surfboards ($12)—a cash deposit is required for any rental. Campers and cyclists heading down the Kalalau Trail can store bags for $2 per bag per day and bikes for $5 a day. A three-day camping equipment package, including tent, lantern, stove, utensils, and a backpack (no sleeping bags), runs $30. Remember that camping permits must be picked up at the DLNR at the State Building way back in Lihue! Talk to Janet if you're looking for a place to stay; people from around the area come to the store to post fliers if they have rooms to rent. You can still get a shack on the beach or in among the banana trees.

Attached to the store are **Wainiha Sandwiches** and a T-shirt and gift shop. Sandwiches, all around $5, include turkey and Swiss, roast beef, ham, or tuna, all with sprouts, tomatoes, mustard, mayonnaise, and veggie salt. It's not hard to find a bunch of local guys hanging around, perhaps listening to Jahawaiian reggae music, who could brighten your day by selling you some of the local produce!

Next up, look for signs to the five-acre **Hanalei Colony Resort**—literally the last resort and the only resort on the beach along the north coast.

You can rent very comfortable, spacious, two-bedroom condos here, each with a full kitchen, shower/tub, and lanai. The brown board-and-batten buildings blend into the surroundings. The resort has a jacuzzi and swimming pool, barbecue grills, coin-operated washers and dryers, Hawaiiana classes, complimentary slide shows, and twice-weekly maid service, but no television or phones. The beach in front of the resort is great for a stroll at sunset, but be very careful swimming during winter months or periods of high surf. Based on single or double occupancy, units cost from $130 for a garden view to $240 for a premium oceanfront, with the seventh night free for a weeklong stay. Car-rental packages are available if arranged before arriving on Kauai. For information, contact Hanalei Colony Resort, P.O. Box 206, Hanalei, HI 96714, tel. (808) 826-6235 or (800) 628-3004, e-mail: hcr @aloha.net, website: www.hcr.com. Premium.

On the premises is **Charo's Restaurant**— yes, *that* Charo! Heavily damaged by Hurricane Iniki, it has reopened and serves lunch and dinner 11:30 a.m.-9 p.m. Next door is **Charo's Gift Shop** where you can buy a T-shirt or poster emblazoned with the famous "hoochi-koochi" girl, as well as cassettes and CDs of Charo's music. Another case displays bangles, bracelets, and beads.

Just past Hanalei Resort, between mile markers 7 and 8 on the highway, look for the entrance to **YMCA Camp Naue.** The turnoff is at the road entrance by the phone booth. Here, several buildings are filled with bunks and a separate toilet area and cooking facilities. The camp caters to large groups but is open to single travelers for the staggering sum of $10 per night. Kauai residents are $9; children are half price; a tent and the first person costs $8; each additional person in the tent is $5. The bunkhouses lie under beachside trees, campers stay in the yard. As with most YMCAs, there are many rules to be followed. You can get full information from YMCA headquarters in Lihue or by writing YMCA of Kauai, P.O. Box 1786, Lihue, HI 96766, tel. (808) 246-9090, 742-1200, or 826-6419 in Haena.

About six-tenths of a mile past YMCA, a driveway turns off the highway to **Tunnels Beach** (look for a two-story house with a green roof). It's superb for snorkeling and scuba, with a host of underwater caves off to the left as you face the sea. Both surfing and windsurfing are great, and so is the swimming if the sea is calm. Watch out for boats that come inside the reef to anchor. Off to the right and down a bit is a nude beach. Be careful not to sunburn delicate parts!

Haena Beach County Park, just before road's end, is a large, flat, fieldlike area, where you carve out your own camping site. For your convenience, the county provides tables, a pavilion, grills, showers, and camping (permit required). The sand on this long crescent beach is rather coarse, and the swimming is good only when the sea is gentle, but in summertime a reef offshore is great for snorkeling. Some Zodiac boats are launched a few hundred yards down the beach to the east. The cold stream running through the park is always good for a dip. Kulei's *kaukau* wagon is usually parked in this lot every day from about 10 a.m.

Tassa Hanalei B&B, P.O. Box 856, Hanalei, HI 96714, tel. (808) 826-7298, owned by Ileah Von Hubbard, is dedicated to the rejuvenation of your body, mind, and spirit. Located along the river in Wainiha Valley, the tranquil surroundings of flowers, foliage, birdlife, and waterfalls create a natural healing balm. Rates, paid in cash or traveler's check only, are $65 s, $85 d for the smaller suite or $105 d, $125 family, and $150 group for the larger. During the last week of every month, Ileah offers a healing retreat. You can also make an appointment between 10 a.m. and 7 p.m. for a variety of therapies including massage, yoga, and colonics. Tassa Hanalei may not be for everyone, but if you have come to Kauai not only to relax but to rejuvenate, it may be perfect for you. Moderate.

Across the road is **Maniniholo dry cave.** Notice the gorgeous grotto of trees, and the jungle wild with vines. You walk in and it feels airy and very conducive as living quarters, but it has never been suggested that the cave was used as a site of permanent habitation. Luckily, even with all the visitors going in and out, it hasn't been trashed. For the past few years, on a night of a full moon, people have gathered in the cave just at sunset for group *sufi* dancing. Unfortunately, there have been communication problems with the local people of the area. The gathering was open to all who wished to join the circle of peaceful humanity, but no one *formally* invited the local people to attend because no one person was the *formal* head of this very independent group. News of the dance spread by word of mouth, and those inclined to come were welcomed. Many of the *sufi* dancers were alternative types and some very misinformed local people believed that some kind of unholy ritual was going on. Most of these feelings have been smoothed over by now, but since the gathering can attract a relatively large crowd, the local constabulary took notice and made their authoritative presence very much felt. It is lamentable that this peaceful and harmonious gathering has caused negative feelings. Perhaps if we all keep dancing in the circle of inner light, the darkness will disappear.

Up the road, just after entering **Haena State Park,** an HVB Warrior points the way to the **wet caves;** right along the road is **Waikanaloa,** and 150 yards up the side of a hill is **Waikapala'e.** Their wide openings are almost like gaping frogs' mouths, and the water is liquid crystal. Amazingly, the dry cave is down by the sea, while Waikapala'e, subject to the tides, is inland and uphill. Look around for ti leaves and a few scraggly guavas. Straight up, different lava that has flowed over the eons has created a stacked pancake effect. The best time to come is in the hour before and the hour after noon, when the sun shoots rays into the water. If azure could bleed, it would be this color.

Limahuli Botanical Garden, in the last valley before the beginning of the Kalalau Trail, a half-mile past mile marker 9, not far from the caves, tel. (808) 828-1053, open Tues.-Fri. and again on Sunday 9:30 a.m.-3 p.m., showcases tropical plants both ancient and modern. Part of the National Tropical Botanical Gardens, the 13 original acres were donated by Juliet Rice Wichman in 1976, later expanded to 17 acres, and an additional 985-acre preserve was donated by her grandson, Chipper Wichman, the garden's curator, in 1994. There are both self-guided ($10) and guided ($15) walking tours of the gardens (wear good shoes; umbrellas are provided). As you walk through this enchanted area you'll pass taro patches, plants introduced to Hawaii by the early Polynesians, living specimens of endangered native Hawaiian species, and post-contact tropicals; your guide treats you to legends of the valley (or you can read them in your brochure) as you follow the three-quarter-mile loop trail. For anyone planning a hiking trip into the interior, or for those who just love the living beauty of plants and flowers, a trip to Limahuli Botanical Garden is well worth the effort.

The road ends at **Ke'e Beach,** a popular spot with restrooms and showers. Here is the beginning of the **Kalalau Trail.** As always, the swimming is mostly good only in the summertime. A reef offshore is also great for snorkeling. If conditions are right and the tide is out, you can walk left around the point to get a dazzling view of the Na Pali cliffs. Don't attempt this when the sea is rough! This path takes you past some hidden beach homes. One was used as the setting for the famous love rendezvous in the miniseries *The Thorn Birds.* Past the homes, another path takes you up the hill to the site of the ancient **Ka Ulu A Paoa Heiau,** birthplace of the hula. The views from up here are remarkable and worth the climb, especially during winter, when the sun drops close to the cliffs and backlight Lehua Island, then sinks into its molten reflection. In the past, after novitiates had graduated from the hula *heiau,* they had to jump into the sea below, swimming around to Ke'e Beach as a sign of dedication. Tourists aren't required to perform this act.

NA PALI COAST

No roads enter the Na Pali Coast area, so your only options are to take a tour with any of the operators listed in the **Hanalei** area or to hike. The road's end at Ke'e beach is also the trailhead for the Kalalau Trail. Other hiking trails along the Na Pali Coast are accessed from the southwest, and are covered in the **Southwest Kauai** chapter.

The Kalalau Trail
The Kalalau Trail not only leads you physically along the Na Pali Coast, but back in time to classic romantic Hawaii. You leave the 20th century further and further behind with every step and reenter a time and place where you can come face to face with your *nature self.*

This hike is *the* premier hike on Kauai and perhaps in the entire state. The Kalalau is a destination in and of itself, and those who have walked these phenomenal 11 miles never forget it. The trail leads down the Na Pali coast—as close as you can get to the Hawaiian paradise of old. Getting there is simple: follow Rt. 56 until it ends and then hike (see **Sightseeing Tours** in the Kauai introduction for alternative rides in or out of Kalalau). But before you start, be aware that the entire area falls under the jurisdiction of the Division of State Parks, and a ranger at Kalalau Valley oversees matters. The trailhead has a box where you sign in. Day-use permits are required beyond Hanakapi'ai (two miles in); camping permits are required to stay overnight at Hanakapi'ai, Hanakoa, or Kalalau. You can camp for five nights, but no two consecutive nights are allowed at either Hanakapi'ai or Hanakoa.

You need a good waterproof tent, sleeping bag, repellent (fierce mosquitoes), first-aid kit, biodegradable soap, food, and toiletries. There are many streams along the trail, but the water can be biologically contaminated and cause horrible stomach distress. Boil it or use purification tablets. Little firewood is available, and you can't cut trees, so take a stove. Don't litter; carry out what you carried in.

The trail is well marked by countless centuries of use, so you won't get lost, but it's rutted, root strewn, and muddy. Remnants of mileage posts are all along the way. Streams become torrents during rains but recede quickly—just wait! Mountain climbing is dangerous because of the crumbly soil, and the swimming along the coast is unpredictable, with many riptides. Summers, when the wave action returns sand to the beach, are usually fine, but stay out of the water Sept.-April. At Hanakapi'ai, a grim reminder reads, "This life-saving equipment was donated by the family and friends of Dr. Rulf Fahleson, a strong swimmer, who drowned at Hanakapi'ai in March 1979." Pay heed! Also, in keeping with the tradition of "Garden of Eden," many people go au naturel at Kalalau Beach. Private parts unaccustomed to sunshine can make you wish you hadn't.

Many people hike in as far as **Hanakapi'ai.** This is a fairly strenuous two-mile hike, the first mile uphill, the last down, ending at the beach. Camp at spots on the far side of the stream up

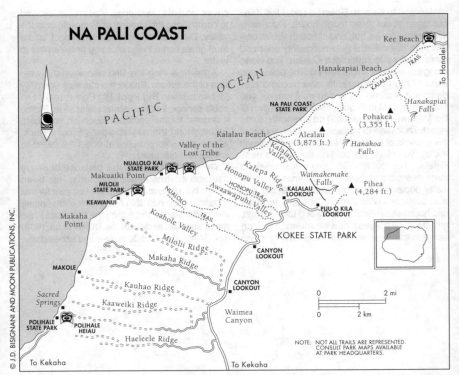

NA PALI COAST

PACIFIC OCEAN

To Hanalei

Kee Beach

Hanakapiai Beach

KALALAU TRAIL

Hanakapiai Falls

NA PALI COAST STATE PARK

Pohakea (3,355 ft.)

Kalalau Beach

Alealau (3,875 ft.)

Hanakoa Falls

Valley of the Lost Tribe

Kalalau Valley

Kalepa Ridge

Waimakemake Falls

Pihea (4,284 ft.)

NUALOLO KAI STATE PARK

Makuaiki Point

Honopu Valley

KALALAU LOOKOUT

MILOLII STATE PARK

HONOPU TRAIL

PIJU-O KILA LOOKOUT

KEAWANUI

Awaawapuhi Valley

NUALOLO TRAIL

Makaha Point

Koahole Valley

KOKEE STATE PARK

Milolii Ridge

CANYON LOOKOUT

Makaha Ridge

MAKOLE

CANYON LOOKOUT

Kauhao Ridge

Sacred Springs

Kaaweiki Ridge

Waimea Canyon

POLIHALE STATE PARK

POLIHALE HEIAU

Haeleele Ridge

0   2 mi

0   2 km

To Kekaha

To Kekaha

NOTE: NOT ALL TRAILS ARE REPRESENTED. CONSULT PARK MAPS AVAILABLE AT PARK HEADQUARTERS.

© J.D. BISIGNANI AND MOON PUBLICATIONS, INC.

from the beach. You can also camp in the caves at the beach, but only during the summer and at low tide. The unmaintained **Hanakapi'ai Trail** leads two miles up the valley to the splendid **Hanakapi'ai Falls,** taking you past some magnificent mango trees and crumbling stone-walled enclosures of ancient taro patches. One mile up you cross the stream. If the stream looks high and is running swiftly, turn back; the trail up ahead is narrow and dangerous during periods of high water. If it's low, keep going—the 300-foot falls and surrounding amphitheater are magnificent. You can swim in the pools away from the falls, but not directly under—rocks and trees can come over at any time.

Hanakapi'ai to **Hanakoa** is two miles of serious hiking (2-3 hours) as the trail climbs steadily, not returning to sea level until reaching Kalalau Beach nine miles away. Switchbacks take you 600 feet out of Hanakapi'ai Valley. Although

heavily traversed, the trail can be very bad in spots. Before arriving at Hanakoa, you must go through **Hoolulu** and **Waiahuakua** hanging valleys. Both are lush with native flora and are parts of a nature preserve. Shortly, Hanakoa comes into view. Its many wide terraces are still intact from when it was a major food-growing area. Coffee plants gone wild can still be seen. You can use the old walls as windbreaks, or you can spend the night in the roofed shelter. Nearby is a Forestry Service trail-crew shack that's open to hikers if the crew isn't using it. Hanakoa is rainy, but the rain is intermittent and the sun always follows. The swimming is fine in the many stream pools. A one-third-mile hike up the east fork of the stream, just after the six-mile marker, takes you past more terraces good for camping before coming to **Hanakoa Falls.** The terraces are wonderful, but the trail is subject to erosion and is treacherous with many steep sections.

Hanakoa to **Kalalau Beach** is under five miles but takes about three tough hours. Start early in the morning; it's hot, and although you're only traveling five miles, it gets noticeably drier and more open as you approach Kalalau. The views along the way are ample reward. The power and spirit of the incomparable *aina* become predominant. Around the seven-mile marker you enter lands that until quite recently were part of the Makaweli cattle ranch. The vegetation turns from lush foliage to lantana and sisal, a sign of the aridness of the land. After crossing Pohakuao Valley, you climb the *pali;* on the other side is Kalalau. The lovely valley, two miles wide and three deep, beckons with its glimmering freshwater pools. It's a beauty among beauties and was cultivated until the 1920s. Many terraces and house sites remain. Plenty of guava, mango, and Java plum trees can be found. You can camp in the trees fronting the beach or in the caves west of the waterfall. You are not allowed to camp along the stream, at its mouth, or in the valley. The waterfall has a freshwater pool, where feral goats come in the morning and evening to water.

A *heiau* is atop the little hillock on the west side of the stream. Follow the trail here up-valley for two miles to **Big Pool.** Big Pool is really two pools connected by a natural water slide. Riding it is great for the spirit but tough on your butt. Enjoy! Along the way you pass Smoke Rock, where *pakalolo* growers at one time came to smoke and talk story.

Note: The Kalalau Trail, because of heavy use and environmental concerns, has been closed from time to time over the last year for trail repairs. There has also been a problem finding the funds needed to perform the trail repairs. So make sure to check with the DLNR at tel. (808) 274-3446 for an update on use and accessibility.

M.G.L. DOMENY DE RIENZI

SOUTHWEST KAUAI

The sometimes turbulent but forever enduring love affair between non-Polynesian travelers and the Hawaiian Islands began in southwest Kauai, when Captain Cook hove to off Waimea Bay and a longboat full of wide-eyed sailors made the beach. Immediately, journals were filled with glowing descriptions of the loveliness of the newly found island and its people, and the liaison has continued unabated ever since.

The Kaumualii (Royal Oven) Highway (Rt. 50) steps west from Lihue, with the Hoary Head Mountains adding a dash of beauty to the south and Queen Victoria's Profile winking down from the heights. Soon, Maluhia (Peaceful) Road branches to the south through an open lei of fragrant eucalyptus trees lining the route to Koloa and Poipu. Quickly come the towns of Omao, Lawai, and Kalaheo, way stations on the road west. Hereabouts, three separate botanical gardens create a living canvas of color in blooms.

After Kalaheo, the road (Rt. 540) dips south again and passes Port Allen, a still-active harbor, and Ele'ele, then goes on to Hanapepe, at the mouth of the Hanapepe River, whose basin has long been known as one of the best taro lands in the islands. You pass tiny "sugar towns" and hidden beaches until you enter Waimea, whose east flank was once dominated by a Russian fort, the last vestige of a dream of island dominance gone sour. Captain Cook landed at Waimea in the midafternoon of January 20, 1778; a small monument in the town center commemorates the great event. A secondary road leading north from Waimea and another from Kekaha farther west converge inland, then meander along Waimea Canyon, the Pacific's most superlative gorge. Kekaha, with its belching sugar stacks, marks the end of civilization, and the hard road gives out just past the Barking Sands Pacific Missile Range. A cane road picks up and carries you to the wide, sun-drenched beach of Polihale (Protected Breast), the end of the line, and the southernmost extremity of the Na Pali coast.

The **Koloa District** starts just west of the Hoary Head Mountains and ends on the east

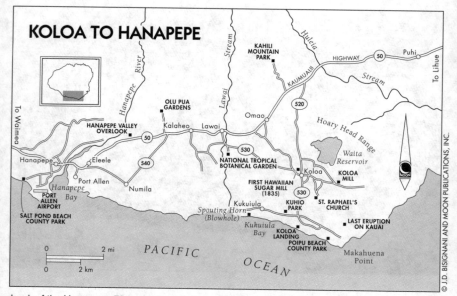

KOLOA TO HANAPEPE

© J.D. BISIGNANI AND MOON PUBLICATIONS, INC.

bank of the Hanapepe River. It mostly incorporates the ancient *ahuapua'a,* a land division shaped like a piece of pie with its pointed end deep in the Alakai Swamp and the broad end along the coast. *Koloa* means "duck"; the area was probably so named because of the preponderance of ponds throughout the district that attract these water-loving fowl. Its villages are strung along Rt. 50, except for Koloa and Poipu, which lie south of the main road.

The adjoining *ahuapua'a* is the **Waimea District,** whose broad end continues from Hanapepe until it terminates about midway up the Na Pali coast. *Waimea* means "Red Waters"; the area was named for the distinctive color of the Waimea River, which bleeds from Mt. Waialeale. It cuts through Waimea Canyon depositing the rich red soil at its mouth.

Poipu/Koloa is the most well-established and developed tourist area on Kauai, but it's now fielding competition from developments in Kapa'a and Princeville. On the site of what was the island's oldest sugar mill—a stone chimney remains to mark the spot—Koloa has been transformed from a tumbledown sugar town to a thriving tourist community where shops, restaurants, and boutiques line its wooden sidewalks. Nearby is the site of Hawaii's first Catholic mission. On the oceanfront in Poipu, luxury accommodations and fine restaurants front the wide beach, the water beckons, and the surf is gentle. Flanking this resort community on the east is Pu'uhi Mount, where the last volcanic eruption occurred on the island; to the west, beyond Prince Kuhio's birthplace, is the Spouting Horn, a plume of water that jets up through an opening in the volcanic rock shore with every incoming wave. Whether you're exploring the sights, cultivating a tan on the beach, combing the shops for your gift list, or sampling island treats, Poipu and Koloa will not fail to provide.

Kauai's southwest underbelly has the best beaches on the island. They're not only lovely to look at and lie in the island's sunbelt; at most of them, the surf is also inviting and cooperative. At some you can camp, at all you can picnic, and a barefoot stroll is easy to come by just about anywhere along these 30 sun-drenched miles.

Practicalities

Lodging in southwest Kauai mostly means staying in the Poipu area. Otherwise, avail yourself of facilities in the county beach parks (for permits and general information, see **Camping and Hik-**

ing), Classic Cottages, the Koke'e Lodge Cabins, the Waimea Plantation Cottages, and at Kahili Mountain Park, which sits at the foot of Mt. Kahili (Tower of Silence) off Rt. 50.

Gasoline is a problem to find after 9 p.m. in this region. The nearest open service station is in Lihue. Make sure not to leave yourself short.

PUHI

This village is technically in Lihue District, but since it's the first settlement you pass heading west, it's included here. Two road signs tip you off that you're in Puhi—one for **Kauai Community College** and the other for the **Queen Victoria's Profile** scenic overlook turnout. It's beneficial to keep abreast of what's happening at the college by reading the local newspaper and free tourist brochures. Oftentimes, workshops

and seminars concerning Hawaiian culture, folk medicine, and various crafts are offered; most are open to the general public and free of charge. Queen Victoria's Profile isn't tremendously remarkable, but a definite resemblance to the double-chinned monarch has been fashioned by nature on the ridge of the Hoary Head Mountains to the south. More importantly, look for the **People's Market** across from the college. Here, you can pick up fruit and vegetables, and they offer excellent prices for freshly strung plumeria lei, an inexpensive way to brighten your day. Next door is the brown-wood Puhi Store, a small sundries shop (built in 1917) that has the feel of bygone days. Also in Puhi is the Grove Farms Co., Inc., office, Lappert's Ice Cream shop, Kauai Sausage shop, the Sea Star store for windsurfing and ocean gear supplies, and a Shell station, with gas slightly cheaper than in either Lihue or Koloa.

KOLOA

Five miles west of Lihue, Maluhia Road (Rt. 520) dips south off Rt. 50 and heads for Koloa. As you head down Maluhia Road, you pass through **Tunnel of Trees,** a stand of rough-bark *Eucalyptus robustus,* sometimes referred to as "swamp mahogany." Brought from Australia, they're now very well established, adding beau-

ty, a heady fragrance, and shade to more than a mile of this narrow country lane.

Koloa Town attracts a large number of tourists and packs them into a small area. There are plenty of shops, restaurants, and water-sport equipment rentals in town. Nearly all the old shops are remodeled plantation buildings.

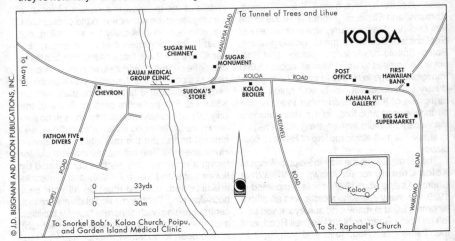

Dressed in red paint and trimmed with white, they are festooned with strings of lights as if decorated for a perpetual Christmas festivity.

The traffic is hectic around 5:30 p.m. and parking is always a problem, but you can easily solve it. Just as you are entering town, look to your right to see a weathered stone chimney standing alone in a little field. Park here and simply walk across the street, avoiding the hassles. This unmarked edifice is what's left of the **Koloa Sugar Plantation,** established in 1835, site of the first successful attempt at refining sugar in the islands. Although of major historical significance, the chimney is in a terrible state of disrepair—many broken beer bottles litter the inside. Notice, too, that shrubs are growing off the top and a nearby banyan has thrown off an aerial root and is engulfing the structure. Unless action is taken soon, this historical site will be lost forever.

On this overgrown corner lot is a circle of more than a dozen varieties of sugarcane, each with a short explanation of its characteristics and where it was grown. A plaque and sculpture have recently been added to this site. Reading the plaque will give you an explanation of and appreciation for the sugar industry on Hawaii, the significance of the Koloa Sugar Plantation, and the people who worked the fields. The bronze sculpture portrays individuals of the seven ethnic groups that provided the greatest manpower for the sugar plantations of Hawaii: Hawaiians, Chinese, Japanese, Portuguese, Puerto Ricans, Koreans, and Filipinos. (From the 1830s to the first decade of this century, smaller numbers of Englishmen, Scots, Germans, Scandinavians, Poles, Spaniards, American blacks, and Russians also arrived to work. All in all, about 35,000 immigrants came to Hawaii to make the sugar industry the success it has been.) Koloa is the birthplace of the Hawaiian sugar industry, the strongest economic force in the state for more than a century. More than anything else, it helped to shape the multiethnic mixture of Hawaii's population.

The tall steeple on the way to Poipu belongs to **Koloa Church,** locally known as the White Church. Dating from 1837, it was remodeled in 1929. For many years the steeple was an official landmark used in many land surveys. If you turn left on Koloa Road, right on Weliweli Road, and then follow Hapa Road to its end, you come to

St. Raphael's Catholic Church, marking the spot where a Roman Catholic mission was first permitted in the islands, in 1841. The stone church itself dates from 1856, when it was built by Friar Robert Walsh. The roof of the church can be seen sticking above the trees from Kiahuna Golf Course in Poipu.

PRACTICALITIES

Most of the accommodations, restaurants, and shopping in the Koloa area are centered around Poipu. Please refer to the **Poipu** section, following, for information.

Accommodations
Kahili Mountain Park is a gem, *if* you enjoy what it has to offer: it's like a camp for big people, at P.O. Box 298, Koloa, HI 96756, tel. (808) 742-9921. To get there, follow Rt. 50 west about one-half mile past the turnoff to Koloa, and look for the sign pointing mountainside up a cane road. Follow it for about one mile to the entranceway. The surroundings are absolutely beautiful, and the only noises, except for singing birds, are from an occasional helicopter flying into Waimea Canyon and the children attending the school on the premises. The high meadow is surrounded by mountains, with the coast visible and Poipu Beach about 15 minutes away. In the middle of the meadow is a cluster of rocks, a mini replica of the mountains in the background. A spring-fed pond is chilly for swimming, but great for catching bass that make a tasty dinner. There are three types of accommodations: cabinettes, cabins, and deluxe cabins. A cabinette is a one-room unit, usually with a double or two twin beds and full kitchen; they rent for $36.95 d, $11 per extra person. A few of the original rustic cabinettes still remain, with no running water, bare wood walls, open ceilings, and cement floors, but the majority didn't survive Hurricane Iniki. The cabinettes are in a cluster facing a meadow, and each is surrounded by flower beds and trees. All dishes and utensils are provided, but you must do all your own housekeeping. Bathrooms and showers are in a central building, with separate laundry facilities available. A relaxing Japanese *ofuro* (hot tub) is also open to guests. The cabins are raised,

wooden-floored houses with full kitchens, bedrooms with chairs, tables, and dressers, private toilets, and outdoor showers, priced reasonably at $49.95 d, plus $11 for an extra person. Deluxe cabins, renting at $59.95 (luxury cabins are available, for $88), are about the same but a bit larger and upgraded with queen-size and two twin beds, indoor showers, and complete kitchens with large refrigerators. The park has been open fo about 25 years and has recently been purchased by the Seventh-Day Adventist Church, which runs the school while retaining the rental units. The grounds and the facility are beautifully kept by the original caretakers, Ralph and Veronica. Inexpensive.

Food

Lappert's Aloha Ice Cream, downtown Koloa, dishes up creamy scoops of delicious Kauai made ice cream. Connoisseurs of the dripping delight consider it among the best in the world. The ice-cream parlor doubles as an espresso bar with pastries thrown in for good measure.

Adjacent to Sueoka's Store in downtown Koloa is a **plate-lunch window** that dishes out hearty, wholesome food until early afternoon. It's difficult to spend more than $5.

Rosie's Kaukau Wagon, parked at the entrance to Koloa's baseball diamond (near the fire station), especially on Monday when the **farmers' market** is operating, dishes up traditional island favorites weighty enough to sink a Boston whaler for only $5.

If you want pampering, keep walking past the **Koloa Broiler,** centrally located on Koloa Rd., tel. (808) 742-9122, but if you want a good meal at an unbeatable price, drop in. The decor is the weatherbeaten, wainscoted building itself with a few neglected potted ferns here and there because someone probably told them they ought to. This cook-it-yourself restaurant is open daily 11 a.m.-10 p.m. for lunch, dinner, and cocktails, 3:30-6 p.m. for happy hour. At the Koloa Broiler, *you* are the chef. Order top sirloin, beef kebab, mahimahi, and barbecued chicken for $10.95-12.95, fresh fish and ribs at $14.95, or a beef burger for $6 until 4 p.m., and $7 after. Your uncooked selection is brought to your table, and you take it to a central grill where a large clock and a poster of cooking times tell you how long your self-made dinner will take. The feeling is like being at a potluck barbecue, and you can't help making friends with the other "chefs." There is a simple salad bar with sticky rice and a huge pot of baked beans to which you can help yourself. Waiters bring fresh-baked bread and a pitcher of ice water. Put your selection on the grill, fix and eat a salad, and it's just about time to turn your meat on the barbecue. Just before it's done, toast some bread on the grill. The Koloa Broiler Bar attracts a good mixture of tourists and local people with its friendly neighborhood atmosphere. After dinner, order a cup of coffee or one of the special house drinks like Mighty Mai Tai, Passionate Margarita, Forbidden Fruit, or the famous Konanut Cooler. The bartenders and patrons are friendly, and you couldn't find a better place for a beer while shooting the breeze.

Follow the raised wooden sidewalk to the **Koloa Cultural Center,** where you will find **Taisho Restaurant,** open Mon.-Sat. for dinner only, from 5 p.m., where you can enjoy a full Japanese meal or pick and choose tidbits from the sushi bar. Classic entrees include tempura at $12.95, chicken *katsu* for $7.95, and mushroom chicken for $8.95. A specialty is Taisho *bento,* a full meal with tempura, sesame chicken, sashimi, gyoza, salad, and rice soup for $13.95. A full menu of *donburi* (a bowl of rice topped with vegetables, egg, tofu, or meat) starts at only $5.50, with the most expensive—10 *donburi*—for $8.95. This intimate restaurant with only a dozen or so tables is very simple with a few strokes of Japanese decor like shoji and wooden partitions.

Shopping

In Koloa, shops and boutiques are strung along the road like flowers on a lei. You can buy everything from original art to beach towels. Jewelry stores, surf shops, gourmet stores, even a specialty shop for sunglasses are just a few examples; Old Koloa Town packs a lot of shopping into a little area. Besides, it's fun just walking the raised sidewalks of what looks very much like an old Western town.

Koloa Town has some fine shops along the main street and for a few hundred yards down Poipu Road. Look for **Island Images,** next to Lappert's Aloha Ice Cream, tel. (808) 742-7447, open daily 9 a.m.-5 p.m., offering fine art prints and posters—posters average $30, with framing and shipping available; **Crazy Shirts,** a Hawaiian firm selling some of the best T-shirts and is-landwear available; **Koloa Gold** and **Koloa Jewelry,** offering rings, necklaces, and scrimshaw; **Progressive Expressions,** for surfboards, surf gear, and islandwear; and **Kahana Ki'i Art Gallery** if you're looking for quality island art.

Along Koloa's elevated walkway, make sure to stop into **Kauai Fine Arts,** open daily 10 a.m.-6 p.m., tel. (808) 742-7608. Owned by Caribbean islander Mona Nicolaus, who operates the original Kauai Fine Arts, in Hanapepe, the boutique specializes in original engravings, antique prints mainly of the Pacific Islands, antique maps, and vintage natural science photos from as far afield as Australia and Egypt, and is also home to a collection of antique bottles. Recently added hand-embroidered pillows and quilts are designed in Hawaii but made on Bali; a smattering of handbags is also on offer, as is tapa imported from Tonga or Fiji. Kauai Fine arts offers framing and worldwide shipping. If not purchasing, at least stop to browse in the museum-like atmosphere, where fine vintage items reach back in time to touch the face of old Hawaii and the Pacific as a whole.

Also along the strip you'll find **Atlantis Gallery and Frames,** featuring prints, posters, and framing. Casual resortwear is available from **Paradise Clothing,** open daily 10 a.m.-7 p.m., where shirts by Tommy Bahama are featured along with a good assortment of bathing suits, beach dresses, men's and women's hats and shorts, and a sampling of clothing for children.

Just before the elevated walkway begins, you'll find **Hula Moon Gifts,** owned by Diana Soong, the proprietress of the Kauai Products store at the Kukui Grove Shopping Center. The shelves at Hula Moon bear mostly arts and crafts made in Hawaii, with some of the gift items fashioned in Indonesia. Featured items include vests imprinted with a tapa design and antique print; lifelike Hawaiian dolls made from resin by Patty Kanaar; tiles, platters, and red-dirt pottery; handmade (and numbered) ukulele made by Jim Adwell; koa bowls by Wayne Jacintho; and less-expensive items like shark-teeth necklaces, barrettes, bracelets, mirror and comb sets, and koa bookmarks.

Kauai One Hour Photo, tel. (808) 742-1719, along Poipu Rd. in Koloa, offers camera needs, film, and processing.

The Blue Orchid at the end of the raised wooden sidewalk in the Koloa Cultural Center, open Mon.-Sat. 9:30 a.m.-5:30 p.m., is a lady's boutique selling dresses, alohawear, earrings, jewelry, and fresh-cut flowers. Arlene, the owner, handpaints the dresses and T-shirts, all of which are made from cotton, rayon, or silk. Prices start at $30 for the dresses and $12 for the T-shirts.

When you see Weliweli Road at the end of the raised wooden sidewalk, look for a sign pointing to St. Raphael's Church and follow it for a minute to **Chang's Tao Wai,** a.k.a. Koloa Variety Store, a discount variety store. Inside is a tangle of touristy junk and nifty items including beach mats, T-shirts, hats, fishing supplies, and inexpensive cotton aloha shirts.

Stuck in a corner near Chang's is **Nileen's Enterprises,** tel. (808) 742-9727, a nutrition center about as large as your average closet. Open Monday, Wednesday, and Friday 12:30-5 p.m. and Saturday 9:30 a.m.-2:30 p.m., Nileen's sells nutritional supplements, vitamins, minerals, homeopathic remedies, and skin-care products.

Food Shopping

In Koloa, a **Big Save Supermarket** is on Koloa Rd., at the junction of Waikomo Road. **Sueoka's Store,** in downtown Koloa, is a local grocery and produce market. Both carry virtually everything that you'll need for condo cooking.

Pick up fresh fruits and vegetables at the **farmers' market** held every Monday at noon at the baseball field in Koloa (turn near the fire station). Depending on what's happening on the farms, you can get everything from coconuts to fresh-cut flowers while enjoying a truly local island experience.

Sports and Recreation

Fathom Five Divers in Koloa, about 100 yards after you make the left-hand turn to Poipu, tel. (808) 742-6991 or (800) 972-3078, open daily 9 a.m.-6 p.m., owned and operated by Karen Long-Olsen, is a complete diving center offering lessons, certification, and rentals. Two-tank boat dives for certified divers, including gear, are $95, or $79 if you have your own equipment. Introductory dives, including lesson and gear, are $129 each; a one-tank shore dive is $64. Certification courses take five days and average about $359 (group). Tank refills are also available.

Fathom Five also does half-day snorkeling cruises that include lessons and gear for $64. Snorkel rental is $5 per day, $15 per week.

Snorkel Bob's, just past Koloa Town along Poipu Rd., tel. (808) 742-2206, rents inexpensive snorkel gear that can be taken inter-island.

The **Koloa Tennis Courts**, in Koloa Town, are open to the public, free, lighted at night, and operate on a first-come, first-served basis.

Health

At the Koloa Clinic, the Kauai Medical Group, tel. (808) 742-1621 (245-6810 after hours), offers medical services Mon.-Fri. 8 a.m.-5 p.m., Saturday 8 a.m.-noon, and after hours by arrangement. This clinic is located by the stream next to the Koloa Sugar Mill chimney. Garden Island Medical Group, Inc., has an office at 3176 Poipu Rd., tel. (808) 742-1677. Hours are the same as those for the Kauau Medical Groups; for after-hours appointments, call (808) 338-9431. The South Shore Pharmacy, is in downtown Koloa, tel. (808) 742-7511, open Mon.-Fri. 9 a.m.-5 p.m. It has not only a prescription service but also first-aid supplies and skin- and health-care products. The Koloa Chiropractic Clinic, at 3176 Poipu Rd., and the HPI Pharmacy, just next door, can also help with medical problems and prescriptions. (If they can't help, the Kauai Mortuary is right down the street.)

Services

Koloa's public restrooms are in the courtyard housing the Koloa History Center, near Crazy Shirts.

The Koloa post office is along Koloa Road, tel. (808) 742-6565. At the end of Koloa Road is First Hawaiian Bank, the area's only bank.

POIPU

Poipu Road continues south from Koloa for two miles until it reaches the coast. En route it passes a cane road (with a traffic signal), which reaches Hanapepe via Numila, and a bit farther passes Lawai Road, which turns right along the coast and terminates at the Spouting Horn and the entrance to the National Tropical Botanical Gardens. Poipu Road itself bends left past a string of condos and hotels, into what might be considered the town, except that nothing in particular makes it so. Both Hoonani and Hoowili Roads lead to different sections of the beach. As you pass the mouth of Waikomo Stream (along Hoonani Road), you're at **Koloa Landing**, once the island's most important port. When whaling was king, dozens of ships anchored here to trade with the natives for provisions. Today nothing remains. Behind Poipu is **Pu'uhi Mount**, believed to be the site of the last eruption to have occurred on Kauai.

Along Poipu Road, look for the driveway into the Kiahuna Plantation Resort on the right across from the Poipu Shopping Village. This is the site of the **Kiahuna Plantation Gardens**, formerly known as the Moir Gardens (the central area still maintains this name). The 35 lovely acres are adorned with more than 3,000 varieties of tropical flowers, trees, and plants, and a lovely lagoon. The gardens were heavily battered by Hurricane Iwa and again by Iniki, but the two dozen full-time gardeners have restored them to their former beauty. These grounds, originally part of the old sugar plantation, were a "cactus patch" started by the manager, Hector Moir, and his wife back in 1938. Over the years, the gardens grew more and more lavish until they became a standard Poipu sight. The Kiahuna Plantation has greatly expanded the original gardens, opening them to the public during daylight hours, free of charge. Many plants are identified.

The **Koloa-Poipu bypass road** has recently been completed and takes you from Koloa Town to Poipu, emerging just near the Hyatt. In Koloa, turn left along the main street, then make a right on Weliweli Road past St. Raphael's Church where you will see signs for the bypass.

The Great Poipu Beaches

Although given a lacing by Hurricane Iniki, **Poipu Beach County Park** is on the mend and is Poipu's best-developed beach park. Located at the eastern end of Poipu, it provides a pavilion, tables, showers, toilets, a playground, and lifeguards. The swimming, snorkeling, and bodysurfing are great. A sheltered pool rimmed by lava boulders is gentle enough for anyone, and going just beyond it provides the more exciting wave action often used by local surfers. Follow the rocks out to Nukumoi Point, where there are a number of tidepools. Following the shoreline around to the east you'll end up at **Brennecke's Beach,** a great spot for boogie boarding and surfing.

At the eastern end of the Hyatt is an access road leading to **Shipwreck Beach,** now improved with a pavilion containing restrooms and showers. The Hyatt Hotel has also developed a nearby walkway affording fantastic seascapes as you amble along. Shipwreck Beach is a long strand of white sand. One of the only beneficiaries of Hurricanes Iwa and Iniki, the beach was broadened and widened with huge deposits of sand making it bigger and better than ever. The swimming and snorkeling are good, but, as always, use caution.

Continue along Poipu Road past the golf course and take a right on the dirt road towards CJM Stables. Park before the hill gets too steep (unless you're in a 4WD vehicle), then walk 10 minutes down to **Mahaulepu Beach,** a wonderful strand with breaks in the reef that make it good for swimming. Remember, however, that beach access is across private land, and the landowner sometimes posts a security guard who asks to see your driver's license and may have you sign a liability release. There is no official camping here, but local people sometimes bivouac in the ironwoods at the east end; beyond is a rocky bluff from which you have a fine view of the coastline east of here. The only people who frequent the beach are fishermen, au naturel sunbathers, and, when the waves are right, surfers.

West End

Turn onto Lawai Road to pass **Kuhio Park,** the birthplace of Prince Kuhio. Loved and respected, Prince Cupid—a nickname by which he was known—was Hawaii's delegate to Congress from the turn of the century until his death in 1922. He often returned to the shores of his birth whenever his duties permitted. Containing a statue and monument, terraced lava walls, palm trees, and a pool, this well-manicured acre faces the sea. Just beyond the park near the beach house is a family-safe snorkeling area. Farther

along is **Kukui'ula Bay.** Before Hurricane Iwa and later Iniki pummeled this shoreline, the bay was an attractive beach park where many small boats anchored. Today, it's coming back, and you can still launch a boat here, but the surrounding area is still recovering from the storm. The pavilion hasn't yet been rebuilt, but there are showers and portable restrooms. The comfort station is slated to be back by now. Sailing cruises leave from this harbor in winter, shore fishermen come to try their luck, and scuba divers explore the coral reef offshore.

In a moment, you arrive at the **Spouting Horn.** A large parking area has many stalls marked for tour buses. (At the flea market here, you can pick up trinkets and souvenirs.) Don't make the mistake of looking just at the Spouting Horn. Have "big eyes" and look around at the full sweep of this remarkable coastline. The Spouting Horn is a lava tube that extends into the sea, with its open mouth on the rocky shore. The wave action causes the spouting phenomenon, which can blow spumes quite high, depending on surf conditions. They say it shot higher in the old days, but when the salt spray damaged the nearby cane fields plantation owners supposedly had the opening made larger so the spray wouldn't carry as far. Photographers wishing to catch the Spouting Horn in action have an ally. Just before it shoots, a hole behind the spout makes a large belch—a second later, the spume flies. Be ready to click.

National Tropical Botanical Garden

The 250 acres of the National Botanical Gardens (formerly the Pacific Tropical Botanical Garden) constitute the only tropical plant research facility in the country. Its primary aims are to preserve, propagate, and dispense knowledge about tropical plants. This is becoming increasingly important as large areas of the world's tropical forests are being destroyed. Chartered by Congress in 1964, this nonprofit botanical and horticultural research and educational organization is supported by private contributions.

Currently, the garden's living collection has more than 6,000 species of tropical plants, and many additional plants are added to the collection each year. The staggering variety flourishing here ranges from common bamboo to romantic orchids. The gardens are separated into individual sections that include plants of nutritional and medicinal value, herbs and spices, and rare and endangered species in need of conservation; other groups include plants of special ethnobotanical interest, plants of unexploited potential, tropical fruits, and ornamentals. Aside from this location, the National Tropical Botanical Gardens also maintains the Limahuli Gardens on the north coast of Kauai, the Kahanu Gardens at Hana, Maui, which contains Piilanihale Heiau, the largest *heiau* in the islands, and one garden in Florida.

These gardens are so enchanting that many visitors regard them as one of the real treats of their trip. The visitors center, with its interpretive displays and small gift shop, open Mon.-Sat. 8:30 a.m.-5:30 p.m., is a restored plantation house. Although it's still being developed, feel free to take a self-guided walking tour of the lawns surrounding the center. This center was opened in 1997, following the total destruction of the former visitors center by Hurricane Iniki. Organized tours of the Lawai Gardens are given on Monday at 9 a.m. and 1 p.m., and of the Allerton Gardens Tues.-Sat. at 9 a.m., 10 a.m., 1 p.m., and 2 p.m. Each tour, led by knowledgeable horticultural staff or a Na Lima Kokua (Helping Hands) volunteer, lasts for about 2.5 hours and costs $25. Wear good walking shoes, carry an umbrella if it looks like showers, and bring mosquito repellent! All tours leave from the visitors center. Reservations are needed and should be made four to five days in advance—longer during the Christmas and Thanksgiving seasons. Call the visitors center at (808) 742-2623, or write well in advance to the reservations secretary at P.O. Box 340, Lawai, HI 96765. Annual membership, from $50 and up, entitles you to many benefits not given casual visitors—write to the membership chairman at the address above or call (808) 332-7324.

Adjoining these gardens is the 100-acre Allerton Garden, started by John Allerton, a member of the Mainland cattle-raising family that founded the First National Bank of Chicago. This garden dates from the 1870s, when Queen Emma made the first plantings here at one of her summer vacation homes. John Allerton (grandson of the original owner), assisting and carrying on the work of his father, Robert, scoured the islands of the South Pacific to bring back their living treasures. Oftentimes, old *kama'aina* families would send cuttings of their rarest plants to be included in the collection. For 20 years, father and son, helped by a host of gardeners, cleared the jungle and planted. The Lawai River runs through the property, and pools and statuary help set the mood. The visitors center is located across from the Spouting Horn, website: www.ntbg.org.

ACCOMMODATIONS

Most of Poipu's available rooms are found in medium- to high-priced condos; however, there are first-class hotels, a handful of cottages, and bed and breakfasts.

Cottages, Cabins, and B&Bs

Koloa Landing Cottages, at 2749 Hoonani Rd., are modern units in a quiet residential area, and some of Poipu's least-expensive accommodations. Two-bedroom, two-bath units for up to five people are available, each with a full kitchen, dishwasher, and color television. Rates are $65 for one or two people, $75 for three or four, and $5 for an additional person beyond that. Studios, also equipped with kitchen and color TVs, run $45 for one or two people. Laundry facilities are on the premises. Reservations are suggested; four nights' deposit is required, 25% for stays longer than 14 days. Contact Sylvia at (808) 742-1470, Hans at (808) 742-6436, or write to Koloa Landing Cottages, RR1, Box 70, Koloa, HI 96756. Moderate.

Garden Isle Cottages are tucked away at the west end along Hoona Road between Poipu Beach and the Spouting Horn. They sit on the beach surrounded by lush foliage, offering privacy. The cottages are operated by artists Robert and Sharon Flynn, whose original works highlight each of the units. All the units are self-contained and fully equipped. Prices range $52-75 for a single or double in a studio with bath and lanai but no kitchen (refrigerator, coffee pot, and toaster only) to $130-135 for a two-bedroom, two-bath unit for up to four people ($6 per additional person in any unit). Weekly maid service is provided for the studios. Four nights' deposit is required, 25% if staying more than 14 days. Write Garden Isle Cottages, 2666 Puuholo Rd., Koloa,

HI 96756, or call (808) 742-6717 or (800) 742-6711 daily 9 a.m.-noon. Moderate.

Poipu Bed and Breakfast Inn and Vacation Rentals is a large and spacious renovated plantation house. Stained in tropical colors, this wooden house has all the comforts of home, plus antiques, art, and crafts from the island. If you have that childlike affection for carousel rides, you'll love this place because there are several carousel horses in the house. The bedrooms are on either side of the large, central sitting room. Each has a color TV, refrigerator, and private bath. The sitting room also has a TV, videotapes, books, and games. There is no smoking allowed inside the house; sit out on the large, comfortable lanai or walk in the garden. Children are welcome. Daily room rates, including a continental breakfast, are $65-100. Rooms combined into two-bedroom, two-bath suites are $140 and $155; the entire house can be rented for $250. An extra $10 is charged for a child or additional person, $5 subtracted for single occupancy. For information and reservations, call (808) 742-1146 or (800) 552-0095, or write to Poipu Bed and Breakfast Inn, 2720 Hoonani

Rd., Koloa, HI 96756. Moderate.

Perched on a cliff and next door to the National Botanical Gardens is **Marjorie's Kauai Inn,** P.O. Box 866, Lawai, Kauai, HI 96765, tel. (808) 332-8838, with a choice of three private accommodations ($78, $80, $88) each with private mini-kitchen, cable TV, radio, and phone. Also included are access to a hot tub, a barbecue, and laundry facilities. Moderate.

Near the mouth of the Waikomo Stream is the **Kauai Cove Cottages,** 2672 Puuholo Rd. #A, Poipu, HI 96756, tel. (808) 742-2562 or (800) 624-9945, e-mail: info@kauaicove.com, website: www.kauaicove.com. Each of the three units has a queen bed, a fully equipped kitchen, ceiling fan, and private lanai; $85 per night. Contact proprietors E.J. and Diane Olsson for additional information. Moderate.

Pua Hale (Flower House), at 2381 Kipuka St., Koloa, HI 96756, tel. (808) 742-1700 or (800) 745-7414, is a lovely, deluxe 750-square-foot house where your privacy and serenity are assured. With a touch of Japan, Pua Hale features shoji screens, cool wooden floors, a relaxing *ofuro,* custom furniture and decorating, and a

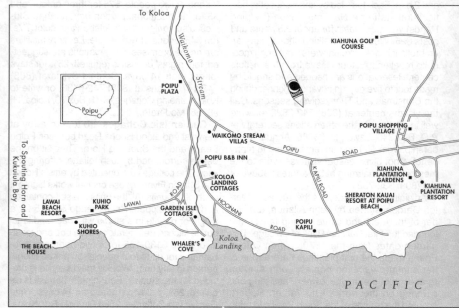

complete kitchen and laundry. This self-contained unit, only minutes from Poipu, is surrounded by a privacy fence and a manicured garden, so you can choose whether you want to socialize or simply enjoy the glorious quietude on your own. Rates are a reasonable $100 per night, or $650 per week. You can't find better. Expensive.

You will find no bedroom closer to the gentle surf than at **Gloria's Spouting Horn Bed and Breakfast.** Leveled by Hurricane Iniki, the one-time humble plantation house has come back as a perfectly designed and highly attractive B&B, with your comfort and privacy assured. Created by Bob and Gloria with the help of a California architect, the stout, hurricane-resistant, natural-wood post-and-beam structure supports a Polynesian longhouse-style roof. None of the three guest rooms share a common wall, and the entire home is designed for maximum exposure to the outdoors. Wide bay windows with louvers underneath bring you as close as possible to the outdoors when opened simultaneously. A nubbed burgundy carpet (all shoes outside, please) massages your feet as you pad the hall to your cross-ventilated suite, which is further cooled by ceiling fans in the main bedroom and in your private bath. Skylights let in the sun or stars as you lie in bed or recline in an easy chair to watch a movie from the extensive video collection on your remote-control color TV. Floral wallpaper and antique tables topped with doilies and cut flowers suggest a Victorian theme. Every suite opens to a private lanai where the rolling surf and dependable whoosh of the Spouting Horn serenade you throughout the evening. All baths are private, spacious, and offer a shower, commode, and Japanese *ofuro* in which you can soak away all cares and worries. Descend a central stairway to a small bar that holds port, brandy, and different liqueurs for your evening enjoyment. Breakfast is a combination of fresh fruits, fresh juices, piping hot coffee and teas, and perhaps a pizza pancake crunchy with macadamia nuts and smothered with homemade banana topping. Contact Gloria's Spouting Horn Bed and Breakfast at 4464 Lawai Beach Rd., Poipu, HI 96756, tel. (808) 742-6995, website: www.best.com/~travel/gloria. Rates are $175-200 per night double occupancy, with long-term discounts offered.

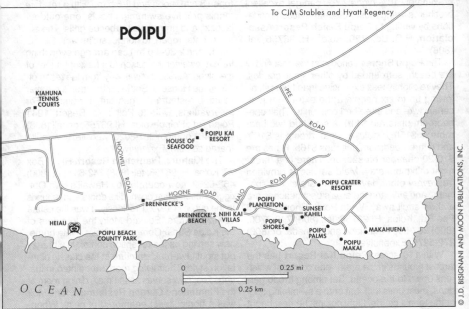

Only a few steps from the Spouting Horn, near the end of this cul-de-sac, traffic disappears at nigh an the quiet settles in at this absolutely excellent accommodation. Luxury.

Condos

Although the prices in Poipu can be a bit higher than elsewhere on Kauai, you get a lot for your money. More than a dozen well-appointed modern condos are lined up along the beach and just off it, with thousands of units available. Most are a variation on the same theme: comfortably furnished, fully equipped, with a tennis court here and there, always a swimming pool, and maid service available. Most require a minimum stay of at least two nights, with discounts for longer visits. The following condos have been chosen to give you a general idea of what to expect and because of their locations. Prices average about $140 s or d for a one-bedroom apartment, up to $200 for a two- or three-bedroom, with extra persons ($10) charged only in groups of more than four or six people in the multiple-bedroom units. Rates during high season (mid-December through mid-April) are approximately 10% higher. You can get excellent brochures listing most Poipu-area accommodations by writing to **Poipu Beach Resort Association,** P.O. Box 730, Koloa, HI 96756, tel. (808) 742-7444.

The **Poipu Shores** condo is at the east end of the beach, surrounded by other small condos. They're slightly less expensive than the rest, allowing up to six people at no extra charge in certain two- and three-bedroom units. Their one-bedroom units run $110; a standard two-bedroom is $150, a deluxe two-bedroom is $160, and a three-bedroom unit runs $165. Rates are $10-20 cheaper off-season. There is a three-night minimum stay. Maid service is provided free every other day. All units are clean, spacious, and airy, and the area's best beaches are a short stroll away. Write Poipu Shores, 1775 Pee Rd., Koloa, HI 96756; tel. (808) 742-7700, (800) 367-5004 Mainland and Canada, or (800) 272-5275. Expensive.

With 110 acres, **Poipu Kai Resort** has the largest grounds in the area—one corner of which runs down to the ocean. Set among broad gardens, most units look out onto a swimming pool or the tennis courts. Light color schemes, bright and airy rooms, wicker furniture, ceiling fans, woven pandanus items decorating walls and tables, and Hawaiian art prints typify the room decorations. Most units have queen-size beds and walk-in closets with chests of drawers; bathrooms have large shower/tubs and double sinks. For your convenience, color TVs, economy washer-and-dryer units, irons and ironing boards, and floor safes are in all units. Daily maid service is provided. Kitchens are fully equipped with electric utilities and sufficient cookware to prepare a full-course meal. Dining rooms adjoin spacious living rooms, which open onto broad lanai. There are one- and two-bedroom units, in 15 different floor plans. Some are Hawaiian in theme; others are Spanish, with stucco and arched entryways; modern units show more glass and chrome; and a few may resemble your own Mainland abode. A handful of three-bedroom homes are also available in the adjacent housing estate. Room rates are $112-198/$92-173 (high/low season) for one-bedroom units, $129-222/$106-194 for two bedrooms and two baths, and $194/$171 for the homes. Facilities on the grounds include nine tennis courts (free for guests), a pro shop (open 8 a.m.-noon and 2-6 p.m.) with a resident tennis pro, five swimming pools, one outdoor jacuzzi, and numerous barbecue grills. The activity center (open, to nonguests as well, 8 a.m.-1 p.m. and 2:30-4 p.m.) can arrange everything from a towel for the beach to a helicopter tour of the island. Across the walkway from the resort office is the House of Seafood, the area's premier seafood restaurant, open only for dinner. For reservations, write to Poipu Kai Resort, 1941 Poipu Rd., Poipu-Koloa, HI 96756, or call (808) 742-6464 or (800) 367-8020, website: www.suite-paradise.com. Expensive.

The **Kiahuna Plantation Resort,** RR 1, Box 73, Koloa, HI 96756; tel. (808) 742-6411 or (800) 462-6262, now operated by Hawaii's own Outrigger Resorts, first opened its doors and grounds to the public in 1972. Previously, it was the estate of Mr. and Mrs. Edward Moir, the founders of the Koloa Sugar Company. Their private home, now serving as the reception center, is a breezy but stout lava-rock structure in the classic plantation style. Their living room, appointed in lustrous koa, now serves as the main dining room of the **Plantations Garden Restaurant.** Mrs. Moir was a horticulturist enamored of cacti. Whenever she went to the Mainland she collected these amazing plants, mainly from Texas and the Southwest, and transported them back to Hawaii to be planted in her cactus garden. However, before planting them she would invite a *kahuna* to bless the land and to pray for their acceptance. The cactus garden flourished, and by magic or mystery was the only thing in the entire area left untouched when Hurricane Iniki swept away everything else in sight like a huge broom. The property, comprising 35 lush acres fronting Poipu Beach, houses just over 300 units, divided into separate buildings. Furniture differs from one unit to another since each is individually owned, but certain standards must be met and in most cases the decor is well above acceptable. You enter the one-bedroom, 800-square-foot apartments through louvered doors. Sliding doors at the other end of the apartment allow breezes to filter through, assisted by ceiling fans in every room. In master bedrooms, most with king- or queen-size beds, you can expect to find rattan furniture, Hawaiian-style quilts, bedside phones, and remote color TVs. Bathrooms feature showers and tubs, dressing areas, and handy hallway closets with complimentary safes. The main living rooms, separated from the kitchens by large dining areas, have their own TVs (video library available), phones, and comfortable furniture perfect for relaxation. The modern full kitchens are complete with garbage disposals, dishwashers, electric ranges, ice-making refrigerators, and all the dinnerware and flatware required for family meals. Each unit has a covered lanai with table, chairs, and lounges overlooking the grounds. With the sea in the distance you'll feel like a transplanted flower in this magnificent garden. The two-bedroom bi-level units—at 1,700 square feet, the size of most homes—are wonderful, easily accommodating up to six guests. In the upstairs area, you will find a sitting room, formal dining area, modern kitchen, bath, and lanai. Like all units on the property, they feature ceiling fans in every room, and cross-ventilation through louvered doors and windows. Downstairs are two bedrooms— one master bedroom, and a smaller but still quite large guest bedroom, each with its own bath, phone, and TV. A ground-level lanai lets you step out into the sunshine. All units are only a minute's walk from the beach, home to the

Hawaiian monk seal March-July. Full beach service is provided including towels, lounge chairs, boogie boards, and snorkel masks. The Kiahuna Plantation also boasts a concierge service that will make arrangements for any activity on the island and tennis courts with their own **Courtside Cafe**, open 7 a.m.-2 p.m. for breakfast and lunch. The units are broken into a number of categories, from a one-bedroom garden view (accommodates up to four) to a two-bedroom oceanfront (up to six). Prices range $155-450, mostly depending on the view. The Kiahuna Plantation Resort is a first-rate condominium, expertly managed, and a terrific value. Luxury.

Poipu Kapili is a three-story condo that looks more like a "back-East" bungalow. Directly across the road from the beach, all units have ocean views. The pool is located in the center of the property. Also on the premises are free, lighted tennis courts, and rackets and balls are provided. The bedrooms are huge, with ceiling fans and wicker headboards; kitchens are spacious with full stoves, dishwashers, and a private lanai for each unit. Rates range $165-225 for a one-bedroom unit to $215-345 for a two-bedroom; monthly and weekly discounts are available. The condo also offers a convenient activities desk, which will book you into any activity that strikes your fancy. Write Poipu Kapili, 2221 Kapili Rd., Koloa, HI 96756, tel. (808) 742-6449 or (800) 443-7714, fax (808) 742-9162, e-mail: kapili@aloha.net, website: www.poipukapili.com. Luxury.

Other condos also stretch along this wonderful shore. The smaller ones generally cluster at the east end of the beach; others are near Koloa Landing and Kuhio Park: **Makahuena** sits on Makahuena Cliff, with the crashing waves below, tel. (808) 742-7555 or (800) 367-8022. **Poipu Crater Resort** snuggles inside a small seaside caldera, tel. (808) 742-7260 or (800) 367-8020. **Poipu Makai,** tel. (808) 245-8841 or (800) 367-5025; **Poipu Palms,** tel. (800) 367-8022; **Sunset Kahili,** tel. (808) 742-7434 or (800) 827-6478; **Poipu Plantation,** tel. (808) 742-6757 or (800) 733-1632; and **Nihi Kai Villas,** tel. (808) 742-7220 or (800) 367-5025, all run in quick succession across the cliff at the east end of Poipu Beach. On the west end, **Grantham Resorts** and **Waikomo Stream Villas** (also managed by Grantham Resorts) are next door to each other along the stream, tel. (800) 325-5701. On the far side of Koloa Landing is **Whaler's Cove,** managed by Village Resorts, at 264 Peuhalo Rd., Koloa, HI 96756, tel. (808) 742-7571 for (800) 225-2683, a deluxe accommodation with only 38 units offering you an excellent sense of privacy and manageability; and at Lawai Beach are **Lawai Beach Resort,** tel. (808) 742-9581 or (800) 777-1700, and **Kuhio Shores,** tel. (808) 742-1391.

Hyatt Regency Kauai

A parade of royal palms lines the grand boulevard that ends at the elegant porte cochere where towering panes of glass open to a roiling sea frothing against the periwinkle sky that fronts the Hyatt Regency Kauai Resort and Spa, 1571 Poipu Rd., Koloa, HI 96756, tel. (808) 742-1234 or (800) 233-1234, website: www.hyatt.com. This magnificent, 600-room hotel, deceptive in size, is architecturally designed so that its five floors rise no taller than the surrounding palms. A bellman pulls the golden frond handles on double doors opening to the main hall, where a floor of green and white marble is covered with an enormous Persian rug bearing a tropical island motif. To left and right, larger-than-life replicas of poi bowls specially fashioned for the royal ali'i mark a formal sitting area illuminated by a magnificent chandelier of cut crystal. Ahead is a central courtyard, tiled to create a sundial effect. As you progress through the heart of the hotel, greenery and flowers, both wild and tamed, compose a living lei of floral beauty. Lustrous koa tables

bear gigantic anthuriums and torch ginger ablaze with color. Artworks, tapa wall hangings, and birdcages filled with flitting plumage and trilling songs line the hallways, while the interplay of marble floors and rich carpets is counterpointed by weathered bronze. Enter the **Stevenson Library,** one of the Hyatt's bars, to find over-stuffed chairs, beveled glass windows, pool and billiard tables, a grand piano, and ornate chess sets waiting for the first move. Outdoors, walking paths scented by tropical blooms lead through acres of pools, both fresh- and saltwater, featuring slides, a rivulet flowing through a "gorge," and the watery massaging fingers of cascading waterfalls and bubbling whirlpools.

Heavy mahogany doors open into guest rooms, all done in soothing pastels with white on tan textured wallpaper. Each room features a full entertainment center with remote-control color TV, private lanai with outdoor furniture, a mini-bar, and double closets. Mahogany furniture, overstuffed chairs and footstools, and Chinese-style lamps insure tasteful relaxation. Spacious bathrooms contain separate commodes with their own telephones, double marble-top sinks, hair dryers, large soaking tubs, and cotton *yukata* (robes). Rates are from $230 for a garden view to $345 for a deluxe oceanfront; $410 Regency Club; and $425 to $1,800 suites.

Restaurants at the Hyatt range from casual to elegant. **Dondero's,** the hotel's signature restaurant, offers superb Italian food, while the **Tidepool Restaurant,** in South Pacific style, offers

Hyatt Regency
Resort and Spa

fresh fish and seafood. The **Ilima Terrace,** at the bottom of a sweeping staircase, is open for breakfast, lunch, and dinner and presents everything from a Philadelphia cheese steak to a children's menu. The **Seaview Terrace,** with its vaulted ceiling, magnificent chandeliers, and carved marble-topped tables is perfect for a sunset drink, while **Kuhio's,** with its sunken parquet dance floor, is perfect for an intimate rendezvous.

In its own facility fronted by a courtyard is the distinctive green tile roof of the horseshoe-shaped **Anara Spa.** The treatment rooms offer ancient Hawaiian remedies for energy and rejuvenation. You begin with *kapu kai* (sacred sea), a steam bath followed by a body scrub with *alae* clay and Hawaiian sea salt. Next you may be immersed in a tub of *limu* and then kneaded by a massage therapist who specializes in *lomi lomi,* the Hawaiian massage favored by the *ali'i.* All therapy rooms are indoor/outdoor, with mini-gardens and the serenade of falling waters to help unjangle nerves. Hibiscus tea and cool water are always available, and once finished you are conducted into the locker rooms, where you can shower and pamper yourself with lotions and potions. The Amara Spa also offers health-conscious cuisine, a lap pool, aerobics room, and complete training equipment including Lifecycles, treadmills, and StairMasters.

Embassy Vacation Resort at Poipu Point

This hotel, 1613 Pee Rd., Kalaheo, HI 96750, tel. (808) 742-1888, (800) 922-7866 Mainland and Canada, and (800) 321-2558 Hawaii, is a marriage of concepts between Embassy Suites, known for their luxury hotels, and Aston Resorts, a Hawaiian company that knows how to deliver the aloha spirit. The property, sitting on 23 manicured, oceanfront acres, further combines the concept of a luxury resort with time-share condominiums. Upon arrival, you enter through a white porte cochere trimmed in light wood framing beveled glass windows offering a view of the landscaping spreading past windswept palms to a reflecting pool fed by a tiny rivulet. In the main lobby you find guest reception, a concierge desk, and a sitting area brightened by immense floral displays framed by arched French doors opening to the gardens below. The grounds are a dramatic combination of water and lava stone

forming a mosaic sculpture reminiscent of both the taro fields of ancient Hawaii and the natural beauty of wild Kauai. The 10 neoclassic plantation-style buildings housing the two-bedroom, 1,200-square-foot units are no taller than a palm tree. They surround a central courtyard where you will discover, fronting a sandy beach, a large pool with one side tiled and the other sand-bottomed. Poolside, you will find complete amenities including lounge chairs, umbrellas, a jacuzzi, and, nearby, a complete fitness center. Mornings bring a complimentary health-conscious breakfast served 8-9:30 a.m. in an outdoor dining area near the pool, complete with coffee, various juices, Hawaiian fruits, bagels, toast, and sweet breads. Late risers can enjoy a more limited buffet in the reception area until 10 a.m., and juice is available throughout the day. Here and there throughout the property you'll find little picnic nooks complete with tables and barbecue grills for your enjoyment. Notice a thick grove of ironwoods completely surrounded by a hedge; these protect the site of an ancient *heiau* that the resort is dedicated to preserving. Guests can look but are not permitted inside—a right reserved for native Hawaiian groups who, on occasion, still come to pray. Just below the pool area lies a stretch of dramatic coastline pounded by heavy wave action, frothing misty azure against the coal-black lava. The area, long known as a productive fishing site, lures local anglers who have embedded pole holders in the rock. From March to July, this coastal area is a favorite lounging spot for Hawaiian monk seals, who arrive just as humpback whales leave the offshore waters for their trek back to the Arctic. These waters are too treacherous for recreational swimming, but a two-minute walk takes you to Shipwreck Beach, one of the premier beaches of Poipu. The two-bedroom units, air conditioned with ceiling fans throughout, are brightened by white tile and textured carpeting and feature full kitchens with marble-topped counters, electric stoves, fridges with ice makers and cold water dispensers, coffee makers, toasters, microwaves, double stainless steel sinks, pine cabinetry, trash compactors, and dishwashers. For added convenience, every room includes a shopping list of basic staples available for *wiki wiki* delivery from a local market. The dining/living room features comfortable bamboo furniture with puff pillows, fold-out couch, distinctive drum-top tables, and floor-to-ceiling glass doors that open to a wraparound lanai. There is a wet bar complete with wine glasses and bar utensils and an entertainment center containing remote-control color TV, CD player, tape deck, and VCR. The master bedroom, large and spacious, offers a queen-size bed with carved headboard, private bedside phone, entertainment center complete with remote-control color TV, and a huge bath with separate commode, hair dryer, extra deep tub, and two-person shower stall. The guest bedroom holds two single beds, a large closet, ceiling fan, and private bath with vanity and shower. Each unit has its own washer and dryer, along with steam iron and board. Room charges, based on double occupancy (no extra charge for up to six) range $275 s for a standard garden view to $590 for an ocean view. The Embassy Resort also offers a discounted "Mini-Vac" for those wishing to consider purchasing a time share on property (call for complete details; professional, no-pressure salespeople guaranteed).

Sheraton Kauai Resort at Poipu Beach

This is the new name for the storm-ravaged Sheraton Kauai Gardens and the Sheraton Kauai Beach, which have been combined into one recently reopened luxury hotel, 2440 Hoonani Rd., Poipu Beach, Koloa, HI 96756, tel. (808) 742-1661 or (800) 325-3535, website: www.sheraton-kauai.com. Rates range from $265 for a garden-view room to $740 for a oceanfront suite. Amenities include two swimming pools and a jacuzzi, a massage and fitness center, tennis courts, and an activity desk with equipment rentals.Guests at this resort can also use the facilities at the Princeville Hotel.

FOOD

Inexpensive

On your right as you approach Poipu from Koloa is a small complex called the Poipu Plaza. There, at **Taqueria Norteños,** you can fill up on Mexican fast food for under $4. They make their tacos and burritos a bit differently from most Mexican food stands: a taco is simply rice and beans in a taco shell. If you want the standard cheese, tomato, and lettuce, you have to ask for it—and

pay an extra charge. The flavorful food is homemade but precooked, waiting in heating trays. Vegetarian meals are also served. Order at the walk-up window and take your tray to one of the picnic tables in the next room; they do takeout as well. Filling and good but nothing special, Taqueria Norteños is open daily except Wednesday 11 a.m.-10:30 p.m.

Shipwreck Subs in the Poipu Shopping Village can fix you up with a sub sandwich like a tuna delight, cheese combo, or vegetarian—$6 for a large and $4.50 for a small.

Brennecke's Snack Bar is located just off Poipu Beach, below Brennecke's restaurant and open 10:30 a.m.-4 p.m. The best deals are takeout hot dogs, burgers, and filling plate lunches. For a bit more sophistication, try one of the hotel's poolside grills and cafes for a light lunch.

Joe Brennecke is a football fanatic from Cleveland, Ohio, who spent many a fall afternoon in that city's "Dog Pound." After the game, Joe and his buddies wanted to wrap their meaty fists around man-size sandwiches and wash them down with cold ones. No froufrou food for these bruisers. So Joe moved to Kauai and opened **Joe's Courtside Cafe,** adjacent to the Kiahuna Tennis Club (look for a sign *mauka* just past the Poipu Shopping Plaza), tel. (808) 742-6363, open for breakfast 7-11 a.m., lunch 11 a.m.-2 p.m., and cocktails daily. Joe serves up his fare on an elevated portico with a brick and tile floor. For breakfast, start with eggs Benedict for $8.75, tofu scramble for $7.50, a croissant breakfast sandwich (okay, nobody's perfect) for $4.95, or French toast at $5.50. You can also create your own omelettes for $6.95 or nosh on a blueberry muffin or cinnamon roll with a steaming mug of coffee. For health conscious "weenies," there's even granola for $1.75. Lunch brings a personalized house salad that you build yourself for $12.50, grilled chicken breast at $7.50, Caesar salad with anchovies at $5.95, or a bowl of Portuguese bean soup for $3.50 (now you're talkin'). Sandwiches, priced $5.50-9, include a tuna melt, turkey breast, a South Shore steak, a Reuben, or fresh island fish. The grill serves a Joe Mama burger for $5.75, a grilled chicken breast for $6.25, or a Dog Named Joe for $4.75, served with a wedge of kosher pickle and authentic stadium mustard imported from Cleveland. Joe takes personal pride in his restaurant and from behind the bar serves drinks like Joe Jones' Juice—a mai tai that includes dark Malibu and 151 rum—a good selection of beers including microbrews like Hawaii's own Kona Pacific, and Chico, California's, Sierra Nevada, along with wine, champagne, and fruit smoothies. Joe's Courtside Cafe is a sleeper, known mostly to local people who come time and again to get a fine breakfast or lunch at a reasonable price.

La Grillia, at the Poipu Shopping Village, tel. (808) 742-2147, open 11 a.m.-10 p.m., offers American standards and Italian dishes directly from Calabria created by owner Cathy Gargalonne. There is a full espresso bar open all day, and breakfast brings omelettes and eggs for around $6. Delicious with a latte or mocha, the homemade cinnamon buns and various muffins sell out quickly. Also available are Hawaiian smoothies made from papaya, lime, banana, and tropical juice, priced around $2.50. For lunch, served 3-5 p.m., you can enjoy a *bambino* burger with pasta for $3.25, rotinni with marinara for $3.25, chop chop salad for $7.95, a blackened burger with Cajun sauce, various *panini* with Italian lunch meats, and a meatball sandwich with marinara and mozzarella for $6.95. An "express lunch," which changes daily, is $6.50. Dinner, served 5-10 p.m., starts with focaccia at $3.95 or stuffed mushrooms or shrimp *crostini* at $5.95. Dinner entrees include meat or spinach lasagna, manicotti, or chicken or eggplant Parmesan for $12.95; pastas including angel hair, linguine, or spaghetti, smothered in a variety of sauces for $10.95. Beside the espresso bar, beverages include wines by the bottle or glass and beer.

Moderate

Located on the terrace of the Kiahuna Plantation Resort (once the plantation manager's home), under towering trees and surrounded by lush greenery, the **Plantation Garden Cafe** emanates a strong Hawaiian atmosphere. *Pu pu* run $3.95-6.95 and just whet your appetite for the meal to come. For a main course, try Hawaiian chicken, shrimp tempura, or the pasta special, each $12.95. Or sample the seafood or vegetable salads or sandwiches. After dinner, have a mouthwatering dessert or walk across the lobby for a tropical drink in the lounge.

Brennecke's Beach Broiler, an open-air, second-story deck directly across from Poipu Beach County Park, tel. (808) 742-7588, offers a view that can't be beat. Seafood is the dinner specialty but pasta and *kiawe*-broiled meat and chicken are also served. Prices range $9.95-22.50. All entrees are served with soup, salad, pasta primavera (instead of regular old potatoes), and garlic bread. Salads and sandwiches are served for lunch, and *pu pu* until dinner starts. There is a children's menu for both lunch and dinner. Lunch is 11:30 a.m.-3 p.m., happy hour 2-4 p.m., and dinner 5-10:30 p.m.

Keoki's Paradise, at the Poipu Shopping Village, tel. (808) 742-7534, is an excellent choice for dinner or a night's entertainment. Enter past a small fountain into the longhouse-style interior with stone floor and thatched roof. Choose a seat at the long bar for a casual evening or at one of the tables overlooking the garden surrounding the restaurant. The varied menu lists savory items including Thai shrimp sticks for $8.95, fresh catch prepared a variety of ways including baked, herb-sautéed, teriyaki-grilled, or in an orange ginger sauce at market price; shrimp and steak $19.95; or beef dishes like top sirloin at $16.95 and prime rib for $23.95. A daily Sunset Special, served 5:30-6:15 p.m., offers items like Balinese chicken and teriyaki sirloin for prices ranging $9.95-14.95. The Cafe Menu (available until closing), includes *pu pu,* burgers, salads, and sandwiches like a Reuben at $6.95, grilled chicken salad for $9.95, chicken quesadilla for $8.95, and buffalo wings for $7.95. "Aloha Fridays" brings food and drink specials 4:30-7 p.m. Margaritas are $2.50, draft beer is $1.50, and all the food on the Cafe Menu more than $5 is $2 off. Desserts are the original Hula Pie, Keoki's Triple Chocolate Cake, or Häagen Dazs Non-Fat Sorbet. A great selection of beer and mixed drinks adds to an enjoyable evening. The seafood and taco bar (a good place for conversation for single travelers) is open 4:30-midnight. Have an island drink before going in to dinner, served 5:30-10 p.m. Live entertainment is offered Thurs.-Sat. by local bands specializing in contemporary Hawaiian music.

An indoor/outdoor cafe, **Pattaya Asian Cafe,** at the Poipu Shopping Village, tel. (808) 742-8818, open 11:30 a.m.-2:30 p.m. for lunch and 5:30-9:30 p.m. for dinner, is a very tasteful, moderately priced restaurant appointed with a flagstone floor, and Thai mahogany tables and chairs. The ornate mahogany bar, covered by a pagoda roof, flashes with mirrors embedded in two gold and blue swans. The exotic menu starts with *mee grop,* a dish of crispy noodles, chicken, bean sprouts, and green onions; Bangkok wings, a concoction of long rice, onion, black mushrooms, carrots, and ground pork served with the house peanut sauce; and delicious fish cakes or sautéed calamari, ranging in price $7.95-9.25. Soups and salads are spicy lemongrass soup for $10.95, a Thai ginger coconut soup with chicken or seafood at $7.25-10.95, and fresh island papaya salad for $5.95. More substantial meals include *pad Thai,* a traditional noodle dish for $9.25; spicy fried rice ranging $6.95-9.25 depending upon ingredients; red, green, and yellow curry made with chicken, pork, beef, or shrimp $7.95-14.95; and plenty of vegetarian selections. Although it is in a shopping center, Pattaya Asian Cafe is a terrific and authentic restaurant with friendly service and good prices.

If you want south-of-the-border food, try the homey **Cantina Flamingo,** on Nalo Rd. in among the condos, tel. (808) 742-9505—follow the pink flamingos! Sizzling fajitas are the specialty of the house and a real treat; other items on the menu are enchiladas tasca, flamingo burritos, taquitos rancheros, flautas Kauai, appetizers, soups, and salads. Chips and salsa are free. Nothing on the menu is more than $9.95. You can't go wrong here. How about deep-fried ice cream for dessert? If not, head to the next room, beyond the wall aquarium, for a cool-down drink at the cantina. There you can choose one of at least nine kinds of fruit margaritas. (Imagine what it's like to peer through the distortion of the aquarium divider after a few of these potent concoctions!) Food is served 3:30-9:30 p.m. daily; *pu pu* is free 3:30-5:30 p.m.; takeout is available for some menu items. Hanging greenery, pink flamingos (of course!), and piñatas lend this eatery its distinctive air.

You can find other mid-priced restaurants at the hotels and clubhouses in Poipu. Try the **Poipu Bay Grill,** in the clubhouse of the Poipu Bay Resort Golf Course, open for breakfast and lunch. This moderately priced restaurant serving American standards has fantastic views of the surrounding mountains and sea.

Fine Dining

Exquisite dining can be enjoyed at various restaurants, some overlooking Poipu's beaches—perfect for catching the setting sun—and others in elegant gardens bathed by tropical breezes. Prices are high, but you definitely get a full measure of what you pay for.

In a freestanding building at the Poipu Shopping Village, culinary magic is created at **Roy's Poipu Bar and Grill,** at 2360 Kiahuna Plantation Dr., tel. (808) 742-5000, open nightly for dinner 5:30-9:30 p.m., reservations recommended. Here, in an open kitchen—one of Roy's trademarks—chef de cuisine Mako Segawa-Gonzales and a superbly trained staff create an array of marvelous dishes from the island's freshest meats, fish, poultry, fruits, and vegetables. Founder Roy Yamaguchi, along with a number of extremely talented chefs throughout Hawaii, is a master of Pacific Rim/Hawaiian regional cuisine. He combines and presents the best recipes of Asia, the Southwest, and the Continent with a flair and creativity that are astounding. The restaurant, easily transformed from indoor to outdoor by huge surrounding glass doors, features marble-topped wooden tables with cushioned chairs. Tropical flowers on each table, muted pink walls, and baby spotlights enhance the atmosphere. The chef's "special sheet" changes nightly, but a sampling of the delectable dishes that you may enjoy includes dim sum appetizers like crispy smoked duck *gyoza,* crispy Asian spring roll, sweet basil-crusted beef sauté, and ravioli with shiitake and spinach, all priced $5.95-7.95. Garden-fresh island greens are the base for spicy Thai beef salad ($6.95), sweet Maui onion salad ($5.95), and crispy calamari Caesar salad ($6.95). *Imu*-baked pizzas range from $4.95 for a child's pie to $6.95 for the deluxe mesquite-grilled-chicken feast. A few entrees usually on the menu are lemongrass-crusted chicken at $14.95, Roy's grilled shrimp at $17.95, and pot roast for $15.95 trimmed with mashed potatoes and old-fashioned apple ginger pineapple sauce. The special sheet always has fresh fish and seafood, like basil-seared *ono* with Thai red curry and lobster sauce, macadamia-nut-crusted *hevi* with a mango and coconut sauce, and sesame-seared *uku* with a shiitake cream sauce, all at market price. Roy's offers a memorable dining experience.

Another superb restaurant recently opened in Poipu is the **Beach House Restaurant**, tel. (808) 742-1424, open daily for dinner 5:30-10 p.m., run under the tutelage of master chef Jean-Marie Josselin, the owner of the Pacific Cafe in Kapa'a. The on-site chef, preparing exquisite Pacific Rim/Hawaiian regional dishes, is Linda Yamada, former executive chef at the Westin Kauai. The menu varies nightly, but expect a blending of East and West with a Mediterranean flair. This is another restaurant where your dining enjoyment is assured.

The **House of Seafood** has windows framing living still-lifes of palm fronds, flower gardens against a background of the distant ocean. It consistently has the largest selection of fresh fish in the area (generally from 8-12 varieties), and its dishes are very creative—baked in puff pastry, sautéed with macadamia nut sauce, or steamed in a ginger sauce, to name a few. Ask the waiter for the best choice of the day. Start your meal off with an appetizer, soup, or salad, and finish with a creamy island-fruit dessert or drink. Entrees run $17-35, a children's menu $9-11. Located at Poipu Kai Resort; call (808) 742-5255 for reservations.

The main dining room at the Hyatt, tel. (808) 742-1234, is the **Ilima Terrace**, open daily for breakfast, lunch, and dinner. Descend a formal staircase and step onto a slate floor covered with an emerald green carpet. The tables, bright with floral-patterned tablecloths, have highback wicker chairs. Floor-to-ceiling beveled glass doors look out onto the lovely grounds, while lighting is provided by massive chandeliers fashioned like flowers. Start your day with a choice of fresh chilled juices and move on to hearty omelettes and servings of eggs accompanied by *paniolo* corned beef or chicken hash for $8.50. Other selections are Belgian waffles or buckwheat or buttermilk pancakes for around $7.50, or simple sides like English muffins, hash browns, and steamed rice for around $3. The Ilima Breakfast Buffet at $14.75 daily, $17 on Sunday, is wonderful and offers specialties like eggs Benedict, stuffed blintzes, freshly made omelettes, fresh fish, and a wide assortment of breakfast meats. The health-conscious can choose homemade muesli, granola, or an assortment of fresh island fruit. Lunch brings

starters like quesadillas, tossed salad, and *ahi* sashimi for $4.25-8. Salads include lemon-barbecued chicken, and niçoise salad with albacore tuna for around $8. Move on to grilled salmon with Bibb lettuce, tomato, and sprouts for $9.25, or you can have a personal pizza topped with mushrooms, pepperoni, and cheese for $12. A daily pasta could be linguine with roasted chicken for $9.75; sandwiches range from a Philly cheese steak to a Reuben for around $9. Dinner offers fresh Hawaiian fish prepared with *hulakoi* pineapple sauce for $19, grilled chicken for $17, and vegetable and shrimp tempura for $18. Desserts include papaya cheesecake, triple chocolate torte, or coconut cream pie. There is a full-service bar, with wines, beers, and cappuccino, and the children's menu is loaded with goodies like alphabet soup, grilled-cheese sandwiches and chips, and hamburgers, all for under $4.

Dondero's, featuring classic Italian cuisine, is the Hyatt's signature restaurant, open for dinner only. To enter, you descend a marble staircase highlighted with green tiles into which have been embedded sea scallop shells. The continental room is formal with high-backed upholstered armchairs and tables covered in white linen and set with crystal and silver. Each has a view through floor-to-ceiling windows facing the manicured gardens. Dinner begins with antipasti, or crepes with porcino mushrooms for $7.50, or sautéed shrimp with lemon and spinach pasta for $9.50. There is open ravioli with seafood, a Caesar salad for $4.50, or fresh buffalo mozzarella with tomato and basil for $5. Soups include minestrone or delicate pasta squares in chicken broth for $4. Entrees are pasta primavera for $18, whole-wheat pizza topped with feta cheese for only $12, and special dishes like spaghettini, gnocchi, farfal, penne, or risotto del giorno for under $22. An excellent dish is cioppino, a heady mixture of sautéed scallops, shrimp, lobster, and clams in a tomato broth, for $26.

Slightly more casual is the hotel's **Tidepool Restaurant,** a mushroom cluster of thatched "huts" supported by huge beams forming an indoor/outdoor restaurant overlooking the tidepools. The Tidepool boasts the island's freshest fish, broiled, seared, grilled, or steamed, with a medley of sauces and toppings to choose from.

ENTERTAINMENT

If, after a sunset dinner and a lovely stroll along the beach, you find yourself with dancing feet or a desire to hear the strains of your favorite tunes, Poipu won't let you down. Many restaurants in the area feature piano music or small combos, often with a Hawaiian flair.

Keoki's, in the Poipu Shopping Village, gently sways with contemporary Hawaiian music Thurs.-Saturday. Come for dinner or a quiet beer and *pu pu,* and let your cares drift away.

SHOPPING

Shopping in Poipu is varied and reasonably extensive for such a small area. The Poipu Shopping Village has the largest concentration of shops, but don't forget Poipu Plaza, the hotel arcades, and the Spouting Horn flea market.

Food Stores

Poipu is home to the generally well-stocked **Kukuiula Store,** at Poipu Plaza, open Mon.-Fri. 8 a.m.-8:30 p.m. and Saturday and Sunday 8 a.m.-6:30 p.m., where you'll find groceries, produce, bakery goods, sundries, and liquor. **Whaler's General Store,** at Poipu Shopping Village, open daily 7:30 a.m.-10 p.m., is a well-stocked convenience store with a good selection of wines and liquors; and **Brennecke's Mini Mart,** heavily hurricane-damaged but coming back, is across from Poipu Beach County Park.

Note: If you're staying in a Poipu condo and are buying large quantities of food, you may save money by making the trip to a larger market in one of the nearby towns such as Koloa.

Poipu Shopping Village

The Poipu Shopping Village offers unique one-stop shopping in a number of shops including **The Ship Store Gallery,** tel. (808) 742-7123, open daily 9 a.m.-9 p.m., for all things nautical including sea-inspired art, especially of the great sailing days of discovery. Some of the nautical artists on display include Raymond Massey and the internationally famous Anthony Cassay, along with Hashiotsuka, who renders colorful Japanese scenes, and sculptor Dale Joseph Evers, who brings dolphins and manta rays up from the deep. **The Black Pearl Collection** sells pearls and jewelry; **Traders of Kauai** features distinctive gifts, children's wear, and alohawear; **Tropical Shirts** puts original airbrush designs on shirts, Red Dirt T-shirts, and sweatshirts; **For Your Eyes Only** carries distinctive sunglasses. Next door to each other you'll find **Onboard,** for men's clothing, and **Overboard,** for women's clothing, both open Mon.-Sat. 9 a.m.-9 p.m. and Sunday until 6 p.m. Both feature casual to elegant alohawear. A freestanding shop named **Pineapples from Paradise,** open Mon.-Sat. 10 a.m.-8 p.m. and Sunday 1-7 p.m., sells food items mostly made from pineapple—salsa, pepper sauce, and various jellies and jams. There's also mango chutney and guava syrup. Besides the food items, they have a wall filled with gold, silver, and crystal jewelry, many pieces fashioned into a pineapple motif. A pewter wine stopper or perhaps some bath lotions and gels make great souvenirs. Notice the juice cans lining the shop; they've been collected from around the world

A perk for those perusing the shops at this center are the free dance shows performed every Monday and Thursday at 5 p.m.

Photo Needs

Poipu Fast Photo, tel. (808) 742-7322, in the Poipu Shopping Village, sells cameras and film and does processing.

SPORTS AND RECREATION

The Koloa/Poipu area has many surf and sailing shops that rent sports equipment and diving gear and sponsor boating excursions. See **Koloa** for outfitters based in that town.

Bicycling and Kayaking

Outfitters Kauai, an ecology-minded sports shop offering kayaking and mountain biking, is owned and operated by Rick and Julie Havilend. Located in the Poipu Plaza, at 2827-A Poipu Rd., P.O. Box 1149, Poipu Beach, HI, 96756, tel. (808) 742-9667, Outfitters Kauai is open Mon.-Sat. 9 a.m.-5 p.m. and Sunday by arrangement. The shop's Poipu "interpretive bike course," self-guided with map and narrative information, is $20-33, $35 tandem, depending upon the grade of bicycle chosen. Mountain-bike rentals, 9 a.m.-5 p.m., helmet and water bottles included, are $20 (multiday discounts). The company also offers mountain "bike and hike" ecotours to Koke'e 7:30 a.m.-1:30 p.m. on Wednesday or by special arrangement. The relaxed-pace 16-mile ride (with a few vigorous climbs) focuses on the natural history of the area and includes cold drinks and a full lunch; $78 per person. Outfitters Kauai retails biking and kayaking incidentals in its shop along with Patagonia clothing—shorts, sweatshirts, shirts, and even hats. Rick and Julie are excellent athletes who know the mountains and seas of Kauai intimately. Their tours are educational as well as highly adventuresome; you couldn't find a better outfit to travel with.

Water Sports

Outfitters Kauai's (listed above) also offers kayak rentals and tours. Their most thrilling adventure is the South Shore Sea Kayaking Tour, offered Thursday or by arrangement; $48 per person; check in at 12:15 p.m., return by 4:30 p.m. Single or double kayaks are available, and the adventure includes snacks and cold drinks. Also offered is the Na Pali Kayak Adventure and the River Kayak Adventure, which takes you up Kauai's navigable rivers; $45 for a double kayak, $30 for a single.

Sea Sports Kauai, at Poipu Plaza, 2827 Poipu Rd., tel. (808) 742-9303, (800) 685-5889, is a full service snorkel/scuba/surf shop. Rentals include snorkel masks, fins, and snorkels at $5 per hour, $15 per day (includes complimentary lesson), $30 for a reef tour; surfboards at $5-10 and $15-20, depending on quality (surfing lessons run $30); two-tank introductory scuba dives for $110; one-tank certified dives for $75, and three-day certification courses for $395 (dive video available for $39.95). Sea Sports Kauai is also a sports boutique with boogie boards, surfboards, underwater equipment, T-shirts, sandals, and unique bags in the form of sharks and colorful reef fish.

Brennecke's Ocean Sports, tel. (808) 742-6570, specializes in snorkel and scuba lessons and also rents surfboards, boogie boards, and windsurfers, and offers canoe rides and charter boats.

World surfing champion Margo Oberg, tel. (808) 742-9533, will teach you how to mount a board and ride gracefully over the shimmering sea.

In Puhi, **Sea Star,** tel. (808) 332-8189, rents windsurfing gear (rack included), but does not offer lessons.

Blue Dolphin Charters, tel. (808) 246-4482, will take you sailing, snorkeling, and scuba diving aboard the *Tropic Bird,* a 56-foot trimaran that's fully licensed and certified. Departing from Kukui'ula Harbor, they give you a good deal for a reasonable price.

Captain Andy's Sailing Adventures runs a catamaran along the lovely, sculpted south coast during winter. Famous are the sunset trips with this jovial seaman; call (808) 822-7833 for information. He also sails the north shore during the summer. **Bass Guides of Kauai,** tel. (808) 822-1405, operates charter tours for two people in 17-foot aluminum boats on the reservoirs near Koloa. All equipment is provided.

Horseback Riding

If you're into horseback riding, try **CJM Country Stables** for any of their three scheduled rides. The one-hour, easy beach ride leaves at 12:30 p.m. and costs $20. Departing at 2:30 p.m., the two-hour ride ($40) is more extensive, wandering along the beach, into the ironwood trees and cane fields, and over sand dunes. Leaving at 8:30 a.m., the beach breakfast ride takes you to a secluded beach girdled by high mountains where you relax while breakfast is prepared for you; $55, three hours. CJM is located two miles past Poipu Kai Resort on the dirt road. For information and reservations, call (808) 742-6096 or 245-6666.

Golf

Designed by Robert Trent Jones Jr., the **Kiahuna Golf Club,** tel. (808) 742-9595, is an 18-hole, par 70 course just up the road from Poipu Shopping Village. Open for play 7 a.m. until sunset, the pro shop hours are 6:30 a.m.-6:30 p.m., with a snack bar available throughout the day. Reservations are requested a week in advance if possible.

The Poipu Bay Resort Golf Course and Pro Shop, tel. (808) 742-8711 or (800) 858-6300, the site of the PGA Grand Slam, is a par-72 Scottish Links-style course also designed by Robert Trent Jones Jr. With 6,499 magnificent yards rolling along the oceanside with the mountains as backdrop, it's noted for stunning views and is described as the Pebble Beach of the Pacific.

SERVICES AND INFORMATION

General Information

The Poipu Beach Resort Association, P.O. Box 730, Koloa, HI 96756, tel. (808) 742-7444 or (888) 357-8020, is an excellent organization that can help you to plan your trip in the Poipu area. It can provide brochures and tips on everything from dining to accommodations; e-mail: info @poipu-beach.org, website: http://poipu-beach .org. See **Koloa** for a wider range of services, including the area's only bank.

WEST TO HANAPEPE

LAWAI

In times past, *ali'i* from throughout the kingdom came to Lawai (along Rt. 50 near the intersection of Rt. 530, which comes up from Koloa) to visit an ancient fishpond in the caldera of an extinct volcano. Legend says that this was the first attempt by Madame Pele to dig herself a fiery home. From more recent times, look into the valley below town to see an abandoned pineapple factory.

Practicalities

Maukalani, 4000 Koloa Rd., Lawai, HI 96756, tel. (808) 742-1700 or (800) 745-7414, is a deluxe, 650-square-foot cottage in a quiet residential area of Lawai. This one-bedroom unit offers a professionally decorated interior, complete kitchen, full bath, and total privacy. Prices are a very reasonable $55 d ($450 weekly). Maukalani is a perfect getaway for those who desire peace and quiet.

At the intersection of Routes 50 and 530 is the Hawaiian Trading Post gift shop and **Mustard's Last Stand** snack shop. Mustard's features more than a dozen varieties of hot dogs and sausages, sandwiches, and delicious scoops of island-flavored Lappert's ice cream. The place lives up to its name—the condiment/mustard table has Dijon, Poupon, horseradish, salsas, and all the other trimmings to flavor your dog. Picnic tables in a pleasant grove of coconut, breadfruit, orange African tulip, and purple Hong Kong orchid trees sit next to a miniature golf course ($1 to play as long as you like). Everything at Mustard's (except the food) is made out of old surfboards. Notice the bottles that have been embedded in the cement floor, and the wave to the rear, fashioned from plaster, where you can stand on a surfboard and have your picture taken. Mustard's is excellent for what they have to offer, and the service is friendly. It is a big hit with the kids and reminds parents of roadside joints of times past.

Mustard's Last Stand features all the trimmings for your dog.

In town next to the post office, at mile marker 10, is the **Lawai Restaurant,** open daily 7 a.m.-9 p.m., a very local restaurant that serves American standard and a smattering of Filipino food at very reasonable prices. Next door is **Matsuura's Store,** a reasonably well-stocked way station open Mon.-Sat. 6 a.m.-6:30 p.m. and Sunday 6 a.m.-5 p.m.

The Hawaiian Trading Post, also at the intersection of Routes 50 and 530, referred to by locals as "the tourist trap," sells a mind-boggling variety of handcrafted items as well as a large selection of souvenirs, treasures, and tourist junk. Featured are goods made from eelskin and other exotic leathers (chicken feet, python, lizard . . .). Other selections include T-shirts, jewelry, carvings, and an excellent display of shells that should be featured but are stuck away on a back counter. For $10 or so, you can treat a lot of people back home with purchases from here.

Lawai General Store, along Koloa Rd. just near Mustard's, sells sundries and groceries.

KALAHEO

The area around Kalaheo is springing up with many new housing subdivisions, and large tracts of coffee, tea, and macadamia nut trees are tinting the hillsides in new shades of green. In town are three gas stations, a liquor store, post office, a medical clinic, restaurants, a mini-mart, and a new office/shopping plaza, all along Rt. 50, making Kalaheo the first sizable town between Lihue and Hanapepe where you can pick up anything you may need before continuing west.

Kukui O Lono Park

Kukui O Lono Park is a personal gift from Walter D. McBryde, the well-known plantation owner who donated the land to the people of Kauai in 1919. Accept it! It's off the beaten track but definitely worth the trip. Turn left in Kalaheo at the Menehune Food Mart and go up Papalina Road for one mile until you come to the second Puu Road (the first skirts the hill below the park). A sharp right turn brings you through the large stone-and-metal-picket gate (open 6:30 a.m.-6:30 p.m.). Inside the park is a golf course and Japanese-style garden. The entrance road leads through a tunnel of eucalyptus trees to a com-

memorative plaque to McBryde. A flock of green parrots that nest in the tall eucalyptus trees on the grounds can be heard in a symphony of sound in the early evening.

For the gardens and McBryde's memorial, head straight ahead to the parking lot; to get to the clubhouse, follow the road to your right for about a half mile. At the clubhouse are a pro shop and snack bar run by a very accommodating man, Mr. Kajitani. He knows a lot about the park and the surrounding area and is willing to chat. A round of golf on the par-36 course is $5; carts and clubs are rented at a similarly reasonable rate. Lessons are $15 a half-hour and must be arranged with the pro.

As it's set on top of a hill, it's great fun, and the sweeping views in all directions are striking. Unfortunately, perfectly placed in the center of one of the nicest views is a microwave antenna and dish. Set amidst a grove of towering trees, the Japanese garden offers peace and tranquillity. A short stone bridge crosses a small pool, around which finely sculpted shrubs and small lanterns have been set; unusually, flowers line the adjoining walks. Many weddings are held here. The whole scene is conducive to Zen-like meditation. Enjoy it.

Accommodations

South Shore Vista B&B, in Kalaheo, tel. (808) 332-9339, offers a completely equipped one-bedroom apartment with an ocean view. The room, with its own private entrance, is almost 600 square feet of living space including a dining/living room, bath, kitchen, and deck. Fresh fruit from the garden, cereal, tea, and coffee are provided. At a rate of only $59 d, South Shore Vista is an excellent choice. Inexpensive.

Classic Cottages, owned and operated by Wynnis and Richard Grow, at 2687 Onu Pl., P.O. Box 901, Kalaheo, HI 96741, tel. (808) 332-9201, are six homey units where you can expect low daily rates while enjoying excellent access to nearby beaches, golf courses, and tennis courts. Rates are $55 for a garden studio and $60 for an ocean view; to include breakfast, add $5; for a third person, add $10; jacuzzi available. Inexpensive.

The restored plantation home of District Judge Jardine in 1926 is now the **Kalaheo Plantation Estates** vacation home. The Magnolia and Orchard suites include private baths, kitchens, and lanai, while the Blue Ginger Room has a kitchenette and bath with shower. Rates run $55-95 a night, or take the whole house for $198. Weekly rates area available, and rental cars can be arranged. Write 4579 Puu Wai Rd., P.O. Box 872, Kalaheo, HI 96741, or call (808) 332-7812 or (888) 332-7812 for additional information and reservations, e-mail: kalaheo1@gte.net, website: www.webbrokers.com/808695/kalaheo.

Food

Local people out for an evening meal at reasonable prices give the nod to **Kalaheo Steak House,** at 4444 Papalina Rd., tel. (808) 332-9780, open daily 5:30-9:30 p.m., where you can get a well-prepared and hearty portion of steak, seafood, pork, or poultry. Make a left at the signal along Rt. 50 in Kalaheo and look for a green building on the left with an awning. The interior, very much in steak house motif, is completely knotty pine—simple, but tasteful, offering seating at a combination of black leatherette booths, and tables with wicker chairs. Hanging ferns, potted plants, and a mural of tropical fish complete the decor. Local lore has it that when you leave Kalaheo Steak house, the *doggie bag* contains more food than you're usually served at most restaurants.

If you're interested in a pizza or sandwich, stop in at **Brick Oven Pizza,** tel. (808) 332-8561, open Tues.-Sun. 11 a.m.-10 p.m. and Sunday noon-10 p.m. (if you're heading to Waimea or Polihale, call ahead to have a pizza ready for you), located mountain side in a brand-new building just as you enter Kalaheo. Pizzas range in price from a 10-inch cheese pizza for $7.35 to a large 15-inch deluxe with all the toppings for $22.85. Brick Oven also prepares vegetarian sandwiches and hot sausage sandwiches for around $5.75, along with pizza bread for $2.35 and a variety of salads $1.70-5.95. Wine, beer, and soft drinks are available. Brick Oven has a well-deserved excellent local reputation.

Grandma "Pomodoro," a native of Salerno, Italy, usually sits in the back room knitting while keeping an eye on the olive oil, garlic, and basil going into the dishes created by her son Tony, the former owner of Casa Italiana in Lihue. After Hurricane Iniki destroyed his restaurant, Tony opened **Pomodoro Restaurant,** along Rt. 50

on the right just before entering Kalaheo, tel. (808) 332-5945, open nightly 5:30-10 p.m. The menu opens with classics like antipasti, with mozzarella, prosciutto, or calamari, ranging in price $6.50-8.50, a mixed green salad at $3.95, and a Caesar for $5.95. Pasta is spaghetti with meatballs or Italian sausage for $11.50, linguine shrimp marinara at $15.95, fettuccine Alfredo for $11.50, and an assortment of ravioli, cannelloni, manicotti, and lasagna in different sauces priced at $13.95. Specialties are veal Parmesan or picatta at $17.95, eggplant Parmesan at $15.95, and chicken cacciatore for $16.95. The wine list, by the bottle or glass, includes wines from California and Italy, with varietals like white zinfandel, merlot, chianti, and cabernet sauvignon. Top off your meal with an espresso and a choice of an Italian dessert made fresh daily. The dining room is small, intimate, and cheery, and the wait staff is professional.

Another option for food is the blue-and-white **Camp House Grill,** across from the Menehune Food Mart along Rt. 50, tel. (808) 332-9755, specializing in burgers, Hawaiian-style barbecued chicken, and box lunches, open for breakfast daily 6:30-10:30 a.m. and for lunch and dinner 11 a.m.-9 p.m. Menu items are basic American standards with a Hawaiian twist and include their famous Camp House breakfasts, like a flour tortilla stuffed with scrambled eggs, sausage, and cheeses, topped with sauce and served with rice or Camp House hash browns at $4.95, a variety of omelettes for around $6.95, and early-bird specials for as little as $2.55. Lunches and dinners start with salad, soup, and chili, a deluxe garden salad at $4.95, chicken à la Eleele at $6.95, and a "quiche of the day" for $2.95. Camp House Grill is famous for its burgers, ranging $3.95-4.95 and topped with items like grilled pineapple and teriyaki sauce. Evening specialties are spaghetti at $8.95, barbecued pork ribs at $9.95, and grilled breast of chicken at $6.95. For a snack, or to top off your meal, notice the pie case filled with luscious homemade beauties like macadamia nut pie, pineapple cream cheese pie, and sour cream apple pie. A nice homey touch is an on-going childrens' place mat-coloring contest. When completed, the entries are pinned to the wall as permanent mementos, and prizes include free meals and coloring sets.

At the signal along Rt. 50 in Kalaheo, you'll find the **Menehune Food Mart** with **Steve's Mini Mart** across the street. Both can supply you with any sundries or light groceries that you may need.

Those in condos or with cooking facilities might even stop in at **Medeiro's Farm,** along Papalina Road toward Kukui O Lono Park, for fresh poultry and eggs. Along Papalina Road you will also find **Horner's Fish Corner,** in a distinctive blue building, where you can purchase fresh fish.

PORT ALLEN AND VICINITY

As you roll along from Kalaheo to Port Allen, you're surrounded by sugarcane fields, and the traditional economy of the area is apparent. About halfway there, an HVB Warrior points to an overlook. Stop. **Hanapepe Valley Overlook** is no farther away than your car door, served up as easily as a fast-food snack at a drive-through window. For no effort, you get a remarkable panorama of a classic Hawaiian valley, much of it still planted in taro.

In a moment, you pass through **Ele'ele** (home of the famous Kauai Kookie Kompany—whose macadamia shortbread, Kona coffee, guava macadamia, and coconut krispies cookies, among others, are now available statewide) and **Port Allen,** separate communities on the east bank of the Hanapepe River, with Hanapepe on the west.

If you're a coffee connoisseur, take a side trip down to the Kauai Coffee Company visitors center and museum at 870 Halewili Rd. in Numila, tel. (808) 335-5471 or (800) 545-8605, open daily 9 a.m.-4 p.m., website: www.kauaicoffee.com. From its historical roots as a product of the Big Island, coffee is now grown on Maui, Molokai, and Kauai as well, and is (relatively) big business here. The Kauai Coffee Company has a 3,400-acre plantation of Hawaiian arabica coffee bean plants, and in 1997 produced more than four million pounds of coffee. Several buildings from the former McBryde Sugar Co. have been refurbished and now hold the gift shop and visitors center. Stop in and learn how coffee is handled at each stage from bush to cup.

Practicalities
Toi's Thai Kitchen, in the shopping center and open weekdays 10:30 a.m.-2:30 p.m. and Saturday 11:30 a.m.-2:30 p.m. for lunch and daily 5:30-9:30 p.m. for dinner, is family operated and one of the best Thai restaurants on Kauai. Prepared by Mom and served by her lovely daughters, the menu offers spicy sour soup with lemongrass and ginger, priced $7.95-10.95 depending upon your choice of pork, beef, or seafood; jasmine rice soup with pork, shrimp, or chicken at $8.95-9.95; and tofu soup for $8.95-9.95. Entrees include stir-fried eggplant and tofu in a spicy sauce with your choice of meat, $8.95-10.95; savory sauté of beef, pork, chicken, shrimp, or tofu with sweet creamy peanut butter priced $7.95-10.95; and basil delight—your choice of meat stir-fried and then enhanced with fresh sweet basil leaves—$8.95-10.95.

At the junction for Rt. 541, at mile marker 16, leading to Port Allen is the **Ele'ele Shopping Center,** marked by McDonald's golden arches. Here, along with various eateries, are a post office, a laundromat, a bank, a Big Save Supermarket (open Mon.-Sat. 7 a.m.-10 p.m.), a service station, and The Garden Isle Medical Group clinic, tel. (808) 335-3107.

What began as a slap from Mother Nature turned **Paradise Sportswear,** located in a large industrial building just before Port Allen Small Boat Harbor, tel. (808) 335-5670, from an obscure tiny company into one of the most famous in the state. After Hurricane Iniki ravaged Kauai in 1994, the staff returned to find the roof of the building completely torn off and the warehouse, containing shirts jobbed from other companies, inundated with red dirt and rendered unsellable—maybe! Amidst the devastation, the future seemed bleak, but as legend would have it, one person said, in effect, "Ah, these shirts actually look pretty cool." Perhaps spurred by desperation, the forlorn faces, after rolling their eyes heavenward, slowly reconsidered and began to smile. Voilà, the **Red Dirt T-Shirt,** now on sale throughout Hawaii and moving onto the Mainland, was born. Dedicated to the community, Paradise Sportswear is a true cottage industry, employing 16 local families who pick up ordinary white shirts, take them home, and repeatedly dip them in vats of Kauai's famous red dirt. After bringing them back, other local people working on the premises apply original silkscreen designs. Since absolutely no chemicals or dyes are used, no two shirts—which range in color from deep copper to burnt orange—are the same. Tour the factory (call for details) to watch the silkscreening process, and make sure to stop in at the retail shop, where you can choose from countless designs and styles, ranging from tiny tank tops for tots to XXXXXXLs for walking Sherman tanks, and take advantage of a 50% discount on factory seconds. Retail outlets featuring Red Dirt Ts are found on every island so far except the Big Island, with innumerable boutiques and shops carrying these very distinctive souvenirs. Mainlanders can even find them in Sedona, Arizona, and Moab, Utah.

HANAPEPE

Hanapepe (Crushed Bay), billing itself as "Kauai's Biggest Little Town," is divided into two sections. One section lies along Rt. 50, the other is Old Hanapepe, a "must-see" along Hanapepe Road, off to the right at the Y-intersection just near the Green Garden Restaurant. In the center of town, along Rt. 50, keep a lookout for the **Soto Zen Temple Zenshuji** on your left. It's quite large and interesting to people who haven't visited a temple before.

Practicalities
The **Green Garden Restaurant,** tel. (808) 335-5422, an old standby, is marked by a tangle of vegetation that almost makes the building look overgrown. It's open daily 7 a.m.-2 p.m. for breakfast and lunch and daily except Tuesday 5-9 p.m. for dinner. This family-owned restaurant offers tourist-quality food in large portions, with *aloha* service. The new section of the restaurant is set up to hold busloads of tourists who arrive for lunch; go a little before or a little after noon. The old room has a few plants, but the name is really held up by the decor—green walls, chairs, tables, place mats, bathrooms. If you see anything on the menu that you might want to mix and match, just ask. Substitutions are made cheerfully. The full-meal selections, including beverage, are mostly under $10. The homemade pies are famous and always delicious.

Immediately past it, look for a tiny white building housing **Susie's Cafe,** tel. (808) 335-3989, an excellent downhome, health-conscious restaurant where you can have everything from a smoothie to Susie's beef stew and rice. Breakfast is particularly scrumptious, with farm-fresh eggs or pancakes made with rice and bananas and topped with macadamia nuts. Almost next door is a **Lappert's Ice Cream** stand. Then on your left is another island institution and oddity, the combination **Conrad's** and **Wong's** restaurants, tel. (808) 335-5066, open daily for breakfast, lunch, and dinner, but closed Monday after 2 p.m. Defying the adage "that two things can't occupy the same space at the same time," the two different restaurants have two different menus in one giant dining room that's reminiscent of a small-town banquet hall that caters to local bowling leagues. Both are very reasonably priced, but they, too, are favorites of the tour buses and can be crowded. When you go into the cafeteria-style dining room, you're handed two separate menus. Feel free to order from either. Conrad's (formerly Mike's—his dad) has standard American fare with a Hawaiian twist. Most sandwiches are under $6, main-course dinners are under $8. Wong's specialties are Chinese and Japanese dishes, all under $10, with many around $7. The service is friendly, the portions large, but the cooking is mediocre—except for the pies. You won't complain, but you won't be impressed, either.

If that isn't enough, next door is **Omoide's Deli and Bakery,** and across the street, in a russet-colored building, is **Kauai Kitchens,** a local coffee shop. Both are open early in the morning for breakfast.

Even if you tried, you couldn't miss **Sinaloa Tacqueria,** open daily for lunch 11 a.m.-5 p.m. and for dinner 5-9 p.m., tel. (808) 335-0006, a huge piñata of a bright turquoise metal building trimmed in yellow and green. The inside is more colorful than a Kauai sunset, with pink, yellow, green, blue, and turquoise chairs and yellow and blue tiles. Dishes include spicy Mexican fare like burritos, *chile verde, carne asada, pollo poblano,* Mazatlán chiles rellenos, eggplant enchiladas, and seafood burritos, all served with extras like chips and salsa, guacamole, and sour cream. These dishes cost $7-12 for lunch, about $2 more for dinner. The bar serves imported beers like

Bohemia, Tecate, and Pacifico, and they also have pitchers of Coors Lite and Fire Gold, a great microbrew from Kona. The house standard is Cuervo Gold Margaritas for $5.50, or by the pitcher for $19.50, with happy-hour prices 4-6 p.m. daily.

Also along the highway in town are the Westside Pharmacy, tel. (808) 335-5342; a library; Bali Hai Helicopter offices, tel. (808) 335-3166; Mariko Mini-Mart; Inter-Island Helicopters, tel. (808) 335-5009; and several gas stations.

As you leave town heading west along Rt. 50, a small gift shop called **The Station** sits on the right. A friendly young woman sells yarn, crochet material, and Hawaiian-style needlepoint designs.

On the western outskirts of town, just past The Station, a sign points *makai* down Rt. 543 to the Kauai Humane Society and Hanapepe Refuse Disposal. Follow the sign to a small Japanese cemetery (there are several others nearby), where an HVB Warrior points to **Salt Pond Beach County Park,** the best beach and windsurfing spot on this end of the island. This beach is at the west end of the runway for the Port Allen Airport, once the major airport for the island but now servicing only a few helicopters and the glider company. The local people from around Hanapepe enjoy this popular beach park with its pavilions, tables, toilets, showers, and camping (with county permit). The swimming and snorkeling are excellent, and a natural breakwater in front of the lifeguard makes a pool safe for tots. Surfers enjoy the breaks here, and a constant gentle breeze makes the area popular with windsurfers. Along the road to Salt Pond Beach, you pass the actual salt ponds, evaporative basins cut into the red earth that have been used for hundreds of years. The sea salt here is still harvested but isn't considered pure enough for commercial use. The local people know better; they make and harvest the salt in the spring and summer and, because of its so-called impurities (which actually add a special flavor), it is a sought-after commodity and an appreciated gift for family and friends. If you see salt in the basins, it belongs to someone, but there won't be any hassles if you take a *small* pinch. Don't scrape it up with your fingers because the sharp crystals can cut you—and you'll rub salt into your own wounds in the process.

OLD HANAPEPE

Much more interesting, Old Hanapepe's is a time-frozen still life of vintage false front buildings housing a palette of art studios, local dry-goods stores, a tavern, and an excellent restaurant/coffee shop that's a must-stop. Old Hanapepe, although tiny, is two sections on each side of "the bridge." Make sure to see it all. At the eastern approach to town, along Rt. 50 just at the Green Garden Restaurant, bear right at the Y-intersection and you'll soon be heading down the main drag. As you approach, look up to your right; if it's early winter, you'll see an entire hillside of bougainvilleas ablaze with a multicolored patchwork of blossoms.

Following in the footsteps of Lahaina, Maui, with its history as an arts center, Hanapepe has established the Hanapepe "Art Night" because of its strong and growing connection with the Hawaiian art community. Every Friday evening, the galleries in town keep their doors open to those who care to look at what the artists of the area have on display. Each week, one of nine participating galleries plays host, where refreshments are often available and performances or demonstrations are usually given. For more information, call (808) 335-0343.

Practicalities

As you come into town, the first shop, housed in a vintage plantation house, is **Uncle Eddie's Aloha Angels,** open Mon.-Sat. 9:30 a.m.-5 p.m. and Sunday from 10 until the mood strikes, tel. (808) 335-0713, featuring angels of all sorts and purposes. If you're unsure of what to expect after your visit from the Grim Reaper, try this tiny shop for a sneak preview of kingdom come.

Along the main street, make sure to stop in at the fine art studio of **Dawn M. Traina,** tel. (808) 335-3993, who, knowing she wanted to be an artist since childhood, pursued an education in art on both coasts, receiving a B.A. in Massachusetts, and an M.A. in California. Working in multimedia with acrylics, pastels, and pencils, Dawn specializes in portraiture ranging from the recognizable actor Tom Selleck to a "Hawaiian Madonna" with suckling babe. She not only captures the feeling of what's current today, working on portraits of passing tourists and celebrities, but somehow, since moving to Hawaii in 1979, has been able to tap into the lore of Hawaii and to visibly render the spirit of ancient chants, dances, legends, and the gentility of the Plantation Days. Dawn says, "It is my hope that the images in my artwork may help in some small way to increase not only the general public's awareness of, but also the respect and concern for, the native Hawaiian people and their rich cultural heritage."

The Village Gallery, on the left as you enter town, tel. (808) 335-0343, open Tues.-Sat. 9:30 a.m.-5 p.m. and Sunday 11 a.m.-4 p.m., offers a collection of art by local artists. Prices are reasonable. A little farther down the road is the **Lele Aka Studio and Gallery,** featuring art ranging from wild mythological creatures to portraits of the children of Kauai.

Another minute's stroll brings you to **Kauai Fine Arts,** at 3848 Hanapepe Rd., P.O. Box 1079, Hanapepe, HI 96716, tel. (808) 335-3778, open Mon.-Fri. 10 a.m.-5 p.m., Saturday and Sunday by appointment only (a monthly catalog costs $8 for a year's subscription). The building is all natural wood, floor to ceiling, and is like walking into a giant treasure chest. The floor is hardwood and the walls and ceiling are all pine imported from Florida. Owned and operated by Caribbean islander Mona Nicolaus, Kauai Fine Arts specializes in original engravings, antique prints mainly of the Pacific Islands, antique maps, and vintage natural science photos from as far afield as Australia and Egypt; it's also home to a collection of antique bottles. Other distinctive and easily transportable items include hand-painted, washable, Hawaiian-theme pillow covers at $18.50 designed by Mona and rendered in Bali, along with matching quilts (single, double, queen, and king) that vary from $90 to $260, all in 100% cotton. Kauai Fine Arts offers framing and worldwide shipping. If not buying, at least stop and browse in this museum-like atmosphere, where fine vintage items touch the face of old Hawaii and the Pacific at large.

Cane Field Clothing, open weekdays 10 a.m.-5 p.m., and until 3 p.m. Saturday, is mainly a ladies' boutique featuring Japanese and island-style print dresses made from either rayon or cotton. A small rack also holds fine aloha shirts for men. Although most dresses have a casual flair, they are quite elegant and perfect for an evening out. Bright with tropical prints, you'll feel as beautiful as a Hawaiian flower. A consignment shop in the rear of the store sells used clothing at bargain prices.

Hanapepe Bookstore Cafe and Espresso Bar, tel. (808) 335-5011, open Tues.-Sat. 8-11 a.m. for breakfast, 11 a.m.-2 p.m. for lunch, and Thurs.-Sat. 6-9 p.m. for dinner with live music, is a fantastic eclectic restaurant for mind and body operated by Chris and Larry, who are still working out the multiple hyphenation possibilities of their last names. Housed in the town's drugstore (circa 1939), the espresso bar/restaurant section is fashioned from the original soda fountain counter tastefully modernized with a black-and-white checkerboard motif. All the food served is health-conscious vegetarian with an attempt at organic and locally grown whenever possible, but always fresh and definitely savory and satisfying. Breakfast is terrific, with homemade pastries and pies washed down with steaming cups of espresso, hot chocolate, cappuccino, caffe latte, and an assortment of herbal teas all priced $1.75-2.75. Lunch brings a garden burger made from rolled oats, low-fat mozzarella cheese, cottage cheese, bulgur wheat, walnuts, the kitchen sink, and sautéed mushrooms for $5.95; Chris's Caesar salad for $3.50 or a large bowl of homemade minestrone soup, all served with fresh bread. Dinner is always vegetarian Italian à la Hawaii and could be baked lasagna al forno, linguine with pesto, or artichokes with cannelloni, all served with soup, salad, and bread for $15.95-17.95. Dinner music is usually provided by a solo local performer playing everything from slack-key to classical flute music. A new "Grazing Menu" is being prepared offering vegetarian *pu pu* that you can munch while enjoying the music. The original wide-board floor and simple shelves in the bookstore/boutique section are reminiscent of an old-time general store. The focus of these articles, including jewelry, hand-crafted tiles, and T-shirts, is mostly on Hawaiiana. Magazines, postcards, and books on Hawaii can also be found. If you are craving a snack, quiet cup of coffee, a full meal, or just a good read, you can't beat the Hanapepe Bookstore Cafe and Espresso Bar.

For local food at moderate prices, try **Linda's Restaurant,** offering breakfast specials for $2.50 and inexpensive dinners; or the **Da Imu Hut Cafe,** open Tues.-Fri. 7 a.m.-2:30 p.m., then

4:30-9 p.m., offering a full assortment of local grinds.

A **farmers' market** operates in the big park right behind the fire station near the post office every Thursday 4-6 p.m. Those in the know are on time; the best pickings are gone in the first hour. The late bird gets the wormy apple! Also lining the main drag is the **Sandbox,** a bar about as local as you can get, the Bank of Hawaii, and a few small grocery stores. At **Uekoa Store** (notice the architecture), you can buy sundries, Kauai coffee, and gifts. For a real treat, visit **Shimonishi Orchid Nursery.** There are hundreds of varieties of this tropical favorite and this is *the* place on the island to buy and ask about orchids.

Over the Bridge
After you meander the two or so blocks of Old Hanapepe, you bear left to rejoin Rt. 50, the main road to Waimea and points west. But before you do, make sure to bear right first and go "over the bridge," to the other half of the town.

In a moment, you'll pass **Kauai Fishing Company,** a great place to purchase fresh fish for an at-home meal or beach cookout.

In 1943, when the entire world was ugly with war, Matsuuki Shimonishi looked for simple beauty, which he found in the delicate blooms of orchids. Until his death in 1989, he worked daily with the flowers, hybridizing many, one of which he named *dandrobum tokiwa shimonishi* for his wife, Tokiwa. **Shimonishi Orchid Nursery,** just over the bridge on the right, tel. (808) 335-5562 or (800) 510-8684, open daily except Sunday and Wednesday 9 a.m. to noon and again 1-4 p.m., is now in the care of his daughter. Born and raised on Kauai, Elsie and her husband, Tom Godbey, returned to the island in 1984 to help restore the nursery after it was ravaged by Hurricane Iwa. After Mr. Shimonishi passed away in 1989, the Godbeys took over the operation and have run the nursery full time since then. You are welcome to tour the nursery to find that perfect flower to take with you or have shipped back to the Mainland. Many are unique hybrids from Mr. Shimonishi's experiments; the "Tokiwa," for instance is a lavender and white cluster orchid modified from a gangly flower that tipped over when put in a vase, to the present, smaller variety perfect as a centerpiece.

Next door, in a commercial space owned by the nursery, you will find the **James Hoyle Gallery,** tel. (808) 335-3582, open daily 9 a.m.-6 p.m. and by appointment. James Hoyle has been able to capture the spirit of Hawaii through fantastic color and movement. The sense that permeates all of Hoyle's work is that in Hawaii, humanity cannot conquer nature but must learn to live in harmony with the *aina*. These fine works range in price from $800 to $40,000. If you can't afford an original, serigraphs finished and embellished in vivid color by the artist go for around $700. Hoyle also plans an artists' workshop that would be located on the main street as you pull into town.

Also in the commercial space you will find **All About Fabrics,** open daily 9 a.m.-5 p.m., featuring custom-sewn classics like aloha shirts and muumuu, made on the premises from aloha cotton, rayon, and 100% cotton Bali prints. They also offer mail-order sales.

The **Bay Town Loft,** a vacation rental owned by the Shimonishi Nursery and originally built as a small hotel in the '40s and closed in the '60s, tel. (808) 335-5562 or (800) 510-8684, has been completely refurbished and reopened as four condo suites renting for $60 nightly, $400 weekly, and $900 monthly. The cross-ventilated units, cooled by ceiling fans, are laid out with a combination dining room, kitchenette, and conversation nook along with a master bedroom and full tiled bath. Fully furnished, the units are appointed with microwaves, toasters, remote-control color TVs, coffee makers, and full refrigerators. Walls are painted in muted tans and pinks and highlighted with natural wood, and the furniture is rattan, made comfortable with puff pillows. The master bedrooms, trimmed in natural wood, feature king-size, double, or twin beds covered by flowered Hawaiian-style quilts; large closets; knotty-pine furniture; and wicker lounging chairs. The shuttered sash windows overlook the orchid nursery. The feeling is totally modern but at the same time homey, reminiscent of when Hanapepe was a sleepy plantation town. Moderate.

WAIMEA DISTRICT

SUGAR TOWNS:
PAST HANAPEPE TO KEKAHA

The road hugs the coast after Hanapepe, by-passing a series of still-working sugar towns until you arrive in Waimea. **Kaumakani,** a small cluster of homes with a few dirt lanes, has a

post office, mini-mart, and the **Niihau Helicopter** office, tel. (808) 335-3500. Put to use mostly for medical emergencies and airlifting supplies to Niihau, the helicopter is scheduled for occasional tours to the island, where the company has the exclusive landing rights and is the only way to get there without a special invitation.

Olokele is another sugar town; when you get

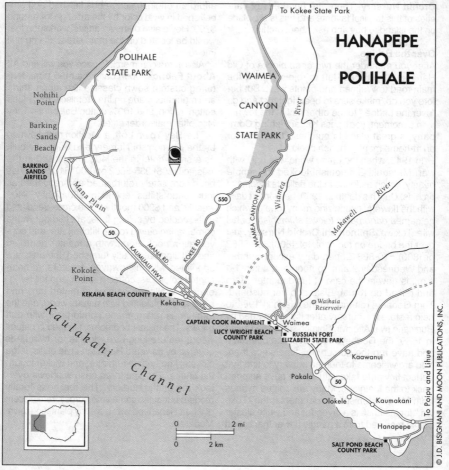

© J.D. BISIGNANI AND MOON PUBLICATIONS, INC.

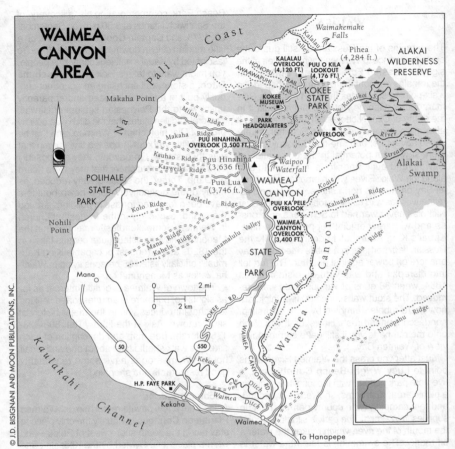

WAIMEA CANYON AREA

here, take a fast drive through, drawing your own conclusions on the quality of life. You'll find small homes that are kept up with obvious pride. The road dips down to the sugar refinery, the focus of the town, while the main street is lined with quaint lampposts giving an air of the last century.

Next is **Pakala,** noted more for its surfing beach than for the town itself. At mile marker 21, a bunch of cars pulled off the road means the surf's up. Follow the pathway to try the waves yourself or just to watch the show. Popular with surfers, this beach is not an official park. Walk down past the bridge to a well-worn pathway leading through a field. In a few minutes is the beach, a 500-yard-long horseshoe of white sand. Off to the left is a rocky promontory popular with local fishermen. The swimming is fair, and the reef provides good snorkeling, but the real go is the surf—the beach is nicknamed "Infinity" because the waves last so long; they come rolling in in graceful arcs to spill upon the beach, then recede in a regular, hypnotic pattern, causing the next wave to break and roll perfectly. Sunset is a wonderful time to come here for a romantic evening picnic.

WAIMEA

The remains of the Russian fort still guard the eastern entrance to Waimea town. Turn left at the sign for **Russian Fort Elizabeth State Park;** the remains are right there. The fort, shaped like a six-pointed star, dates from 1817 when a German doctor, George Anton Scheffer, built it in the name of Czar Nicholas of Russia, naming it after the potentate's daughter. Scheffer, a self-styled adventurer and one-time Moscow policeman, saw great potential in the domination of Hawaii, and built other forts in Honolulu and along the Waioli River, which empties into Hanalei Bay on Kauai's north shore. Due to political maneuverings with other European nations, Czar Nicholas never warmed to Scheffer's enterprises and withdrew official support. For a time, Kauai's King Kaumuali'i continued to fly the Russian flag, perhaps in a subtle attempt to play one foreign power against another. The fort fell into disrepair and was virtually dismantled in 1864, when 38 guns of various sizes were removed. The stout walls, once 30 feet thick, are now mere rubble, humbled by time-encircling, nondescript underbrush. However, if you climb onto the ramparts you'll still get a commanding view of Waimea Bay.

Just after you cross the Waimea River, signs point to **Lucy Wright Beach County Park,** a five-acre park popular with the local folk. There's a picnic area, restrooms, showers, playground, and tent camping (with county permit). Pick up supplies in Waimea. The park is situated around the mouth of the river, which makes the water a bit murky. The swimming is fair if the water is clear, and the surfing is decent around the rivermouth. A few hundred feet to the west of this park is a recreational pier good for fishing. Reach it by walking along the beach or down a back street behind the Waimea Library.

Captain Cook's achievements were surely deserving of more than the uninspiring commemorative markers around Waimea indicate. Whether you revere him as a great explorer or denigrate him as an opportunistic despoiler, his accomplishments in mapping the great Pacific were unparalleled, and changed the course of history. In his memory are **Captain Cook's Landing,** a modest marker near Lucy Wright Beach Park, commemorating his "discovery" of the Sandwich Islands at 3:30 p.m. on September 20, 1778, and **Captain Cook's Monument,** on a little median strip in downtown Waimea. If you're fascinated by Kauai's half-legendary little people, you might want to take a look at the **Menehune Ditch,** a stone wall encasing an aqueduct curiously built in a fashion unused and apparently unknown to the Polynesian settlers of Hawaii. The oral tradition states that the ditch was built by order of Ola, high chief of Waimea, and that he paid his little workers in *opae,* a tiny shrimp that was their staple. On payday, they supposedly sent up such a great cheer that they were heard on Oahu. Today, the site is greatly reduced, as many of the distinctively hand-hewn boulders have been removed for use in buildings around the island, especially in the Protestant church in Waimea. Some steadfastly maintain that the Menehune never existed, but a census taken in the 1820s at the request of capable King Kaumuali'i officially listed 65 persons living in Wainiha Valley as Menehune!

The town of Waimea is of little interest as far as sights go, but there is an unescorted walking tour that introduces you to the major historical sites in town. Ask at the library (tel. 808-338-1738) for the free map and description of each site. The walk should take about one and a half hours. Waimea does have some reasonably good restaurants and shopping.

Accommodations

Aside from a few private rental homes, **Waimea Plantation Cottages** is virtually the only place to stay along the south shore west of Poipu—and what a place it is. Owned by the Kikiaola Land Company, Ltd., and operated by Aston Hotels and Resorts, this oceanfront property is set in a grove of more than 750 coconut palms and a few huge banyan trees at the west end of Waimea. Not victimized by big bucks or modern resort development, workers' and supervisors' cottages and the manager's house from the former Waimea sugar plantation have been renovated and preserved, and the grounds maintained in an old-style way. Here you are treated to a touch from the past. While some modern amenities such as full kitchens, bathrooms, and color cable TVs have been added for comfort and convenience, an effort has been made to keep each unit as much in its original state (1920-30s period) as possible; period furniture and other furnishings add to the feel of that bygone era. Most buildings have bare wood floors and painted wood walls. Nearly all have ceiling fans and lanai. Weekly housekeeping and linen service are included. Complimentary washers and dryers are available on the premises. A swimming pool in the 1930s style has been constructed on the lawn, along with a court and a restaurant. In accordance with this philosophy of preservation, some long-time employees of the plantation (no longer a functioning entity) are still offered low- or no-rent cottages behind the company office rather than being turned out to make way for development of the land.

Presently, there are about 50 units, including 11 cottages moved from the Kekaha Plantation. Rates for the cottages range from a one-bedroom for $195 to a three-bedroom unit for $330; weekly discounts, specials, and kama'aina rates are available, and a $20 decrease applies during low season. The two-story, five-bedroom, two-bath Manager's House is available for $515 a night. The average length of stay is a 7-10 days, with a 35% return rate; make your reservations several months in advance. Low-key and unpretentious, this institution aims to please and offers an opportunity for seclusion and serenity. What could be better than to relax and read a favorite book on your breezy lanai, watch the sunset through the coconut grove, or take a moonlight stroll along the gently lapping shore? The manager or either of the very helpful office workers can provide additional information at tel. (808) 338-1625 or (800) 922-7866, fax (808) 338-2338, daily 7 a.m.-9 p.m., or write Waimea Plantation Cottages, 9600 Kaumualii Hwy., #367, Waimea, HI 96796.

Food

The **Waimea Brewing Company** open daily for breakfast, lunch, and dinner operates on property of Waimea Plantation Cottages. Aside from serving plate lunches and other local foods, the pub brews several beers in a room seen through the glass window behind the bar. Stop for a repast and consider taking away a picnic basket for your journey farther out to the west end.

It's easy to imagine a grizzled paniolo contentedly dangling his spurs over the banister of the distinctive veranda of **The Wrangler Steak House,** in downtown Waimea at 9852 Kamualii, tel. (808) 338-1218, open Mon.-Sat. for lunch 11 a.m.-5 p.m. and for dinner 5-9 p.m. The interior is a large open beamed room with hardwood floors, cooled by ceiling fans. You can choose to dine inside at a private booth, at a table made comfortable with high-backed wicker chairs, or alfresco on the big veranda or in the red blaze-a ginger garden out back. The decor is pure cowboy, with a paniolo whistling his lariat through the air, cowhides and old lanterns for effect, and sculptures of riders and ranch life. A full-service bar stocked with a complete assortment of liquors, wines, and beers complements all meals. The lunch menu begins with Mexican fare such as deluxe nachos or enchiladas at $6.50, a big veggie burrito at $7.75, or an island-inspired crab burrito at $8.50. The sandwich board is loaded with items like breast of chicken, turkey club, or a New York steak sandwich on a French roll, all priced $6.50-7.95. Salads include seafood, taco, or a Caesar chicken, all in the $6.95-8.25 range. Heartier lunches include Japanese-style chicken katsu, Kailua cabbage with pork, or the kaukau tin lunch—a traditional plantation worker's special with soup, rice, beans, teriyaki beef, and shrimp tempura served in a three-tiered pot. From the broiler comes Korean-style kalbi chicken, pepper steak, or a variety of burgers priced $6.75-9.50. The dinner menu appetizers include steak pu pu at $7.25, escargot, or sautéed mushrooms for $6.95. More Mexican favorites are seafood enchiladas stuffed with sautéed shrimp, scallops, fresh fish, and calamari with cream sauce for $11.25, and a (faux crab) crab burrito sautéed with cheese, tomatoes, onions, sliced olives, and green chilies. House specialties are breast of chicken cordon bleu for $11.25, hamburger steak and onions for $10.50, baby back ribs for $14.95, fresh catch at market price, bouillabaisse, and pork Mexicana for $10.95. Steaks sizzling, garlicked, peppered, and capered start at one pound! Wrangler cut, for those tiny appetites, to a platter-filling 20-ounce macho cut complete the menu. The Wrangler Steak House is excellent, friendly, and priced right for what you get.

Other Practicalities

The **Captain's Cargo Company,** 9984 Kaumuali'i Hwy. (Rt. 50), tel. (808) 338-0333, and office of **Liko Kauai Cruises,** is operated by Debra Hookano, wife of Captain Liko. The small but tasteful boutique, open daily 8 a.m.-5 p.m., offers jewelry, fashionable dresses, shorts, T-shirts, and even brocaded vests. The boutique also rents and sells surfboards, boogie boards, and snorkel equipment. Rent boogie boards for $5 per hour and $15 per day, surfboards for $5 and $20, and snorkel gear for $2 and $5.

Along the main road, facing Captain Cook's statue, is **Ishihara's Market,** where you'll find all the necessities. Kitty-corner across the intersection is the police station; the street running inland from there goes to the Menehune Ditch. Across the street is a well-stocked **Big Save Supermarket.** Their lunch counter, believe it or not, features terrific local dishes at very reasonable prices. In town are three gas stations, **Da Booze Shop,** a laundromat, a photography supply shop, a bank, a discount clothing shop, **Kiyoki's Art Gallery,** and **West Side Sporting Goods.** A **Dairy Queen** is at the west end of town, along with the Menehune Pharmacy, and a half-mile up Waimea Canyon Road is Kauai Veterans Memorial Hospital.

West of Town

Heading west out of Waimea, look left to see **Waimea Pizza and Deli,** tel. (808) 338-0009, open Mon.-Sat. 11 a.m.-9 p.m. and Sunday 11 a.m.-8 p.m., offering sandwiches, pizza, espresso, and ice cream, with free delivery throughout this area. Sandwiches like French dip, vegetarian, and tuna are under $5.50, while pizzas range from $8 for a small plain pie to $25 for the Tony Special. Refreshing drinks include Tropical Smoothies with pineapple, mango, or papaya, home-brewed ice tea, and coffee drinks from espresso to latte.

Nearby are **Subway** and **Two Scoops,** an ice-cream parlor featuring Jelly Belly jelly beans. Heading out of town toward Kekaha, look for **Waimea Tropical Tees,** featuring Kauai Red Dirt T-shirts, and **Aloha Oe,** a small shop with Hawaiian Island gifts and pottery made from the red dirt of Kauai.

WAIMEA CANYON STATE PARK

The "Grand Canyon of the Pacific" is an unforgettable part of any trip to Kauai, and you shouldn't miss it for any reason. Waimea Canyon Drive (just near the Dairy Queen) begins in Waimea, heading inland past sugarcane fields for six miles, where it joins Koke'e Road (Rt. 550) coming up from Kekaha town. Either route is worthwhile, and you can catch both by going in on one leg and coming out on the other. In about a mile you enter Waimea Canyon State Park, a ridgetop park that flanks the road to Koke'e. This serpentine route runs along a good but narrow road into Kauai's cool interior, with plenty of fascinating vistas and turnouts along the way. Going up, the passenger gets the better view. Behind you, the coastal towns and their tall refinery stacks fade into the pale blue sea, while the cultivated fields are a study of green on green.

Ever climbing, you feel as though you're entering a mountain fortress. The canyon yawns, devouring clouds washed down by draughts of sunlight. The colors are diffuse, blended strata of grays, royal purples, vibrant reds, russets, jet blacks, and schoolgirl pink. You reach the thrilling spine, where the trees on the red bare earth are gnarled and twisted. The road becomes a roller coaster whipping you past raw beauty, immense and powerful. Drink deeply, contemplate, and move on into the clouds at the 2,000-foot level, where the trees get larger again. As you climb, every lookout demands a photo. At **Waimea Canyon Overlook** (3,400 feet), you have the most expansive view of the canyon and across to valleys that slice down from the lofty peak. From here it's obvious why this canyon was given its nickname. Keep a watch out for soaring birds, mountain goats, and low-flying helicopters.

From **Pu'u Ka Pele Overlook,** Waipoo Waterfall is seen tumbling forcefully off the hanging valley across the canyon. A small rest area with a few picnic tables lies across the road. **Pu'u Hinahina Overlook** (3,500 feet) provides the best views down the canyon toward the ocean. Walk up a short trail behind the restrooms and you have a good view of Niihau adrift in the ocean to the west. A little farther along is a NASA space flight and tracking station, and at turnoff is a track that leads into the valley, from which several trails start. From here, Koke'e's trails come one after another.

KOKE'E STATE PARK

After passing Pu'u Hinahina Overlook, you enter Koke'e State Park and soon reach park headquarters, then the museum and the lodge. At the headquarters, helpful staff (when duties allow them to be present) can provide you with a map of walking trails in the park and some information about the region's flora and fauna. Tempera-

tures here are several degrees cooler than along the coast and can be positively chilly at night, so bring a sweater or jacket. Wild boar hunting and trout fishing are permitted within the park at certain times of the year, but check with the Department of Land and Natural Resources in Lihue (third floor of the state office building) about licenses, limits, season, etc., *before* coming up the mountain. To see wildlife anywhere in the park, it's best to look early in the morning or late in the afternoon when they come out to feed.

Two spectacular lookouts await you farther up the road. At **Kalalau Valley Overlook** (4,120 feet), walk a minute and pray that the clouds are

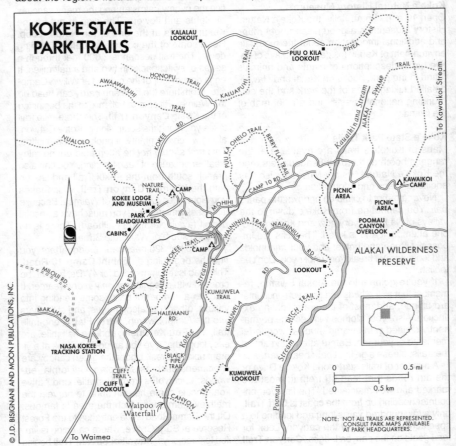

cooperative, allowing lasers of sunlight to illuminate the humpbacked, green-cloaked mountains, silent and tortured, plummeting straight down to the roiling sea far, far below. **Pu'u O Kila Lookout** (4,176 feet) is the end of the road. From here you not only get a wonderful view into the Kalalau Valley—the widest and largest valley along the Na Pali coast—but also up across the Alakai Swamp to Mt. Waialeale—if the clouds permit. One trail starts here and runs along an abandoned road construction project to Pihea, from where others run out to Alealau Point, high above the ocean, and in to the Alakai Swamp.

Koke'e Natural History Museum

Open 10 a.m.-4 p.m. daily, the Koke'e Natural History Museum is a good place to get maps and additional information about the mountain environment of Kauai. Inside are displays of native birds, descriptions of plants and animals found in the park, books on Kauai and Hawaii, detailed hiking maps of the park and the surrounding national forests, and a relief map of the island.

Koke'e State Park Trails

Maps of Koke'e's trails are available at the ranger's booth at the park headquarters, and the Koke'e Natural History Museum also has additional maps and information.

Never attempt to climb up or down the park's *pali*. You *cannot* go from Koke'e down to the valleys of Na Pali. Every now and again someone attempts it and is killed. The cliffs are impossibly steep and brittle, and your handholds and footholds will break from under you. Don't be foolish.

If you're going into the Alakai Swamp, remember that all the birds and flora you encounter are unique, and most of them are fighting extinction. Also, your clothes will become permanently stained with swamp mud—a wonderful memento of your trip. Before attempting any of the trails, please sign in at park headquarters.

A number of trails start along Koke'e Drive or the dirt roads that lead off from it; most are marked and well maintained. The first you encounter heading up from the coast is **Cliff Trail,** only a few hundred yards long and leading to a spectacular overview of the canyon. Look for feral goats on the canyon ledges. **Canyon Trail**

continues off Cliff Trail for one and a half miles. It's a strenuous trail that dips down to Waipoo Waterfall before climbing out of the canyon to Kumuwela Lookout. **Halemanu-Koke'e Trail** begins off a secondary road, from the old ranger station just before the military installation. It travels just more than a mile and is a self-guiding nature trail. With plenty of native plants and trees, it's a favorite area for indigenous birds.

One of the best trails off Koke'e Road is the **Kukui Trail.** The well-marked trailhead is between mile markers 8 and 9. The trail starts with the **Iliau Nature Loop,** an easy, 10-minute, self-guided trail that's great for sunset lovers. Notice the pygmy palms among the many varieties of plants and flowers. The sign-in hut for the Kukui Trail is at the end of the Nature Loop. Read some of the comments before heading down. The trail descends 2,000 feet through a series of switchbacks in two and a half miles. It ends on the floor of the canyon at Wiliwili Campsite. From here the hale and hardy can head up the Waimea River for a half mile to the beginning of the **Koaie Canyon Trail.** This three-mile trail takes you along the south side of Koaie Canyon, along which are plenty of pools and campsites. This trail *should not* be attempted during rainy weather because of flash flooding. You can also branch south from the Kukui Trail and link up with the **Waimea Canyon Trail,** which takes you eight miles to the town of Waimea. Because it crosses private land, you must have a special permit (available at the trailhead). There is no camping south of Waialeale Stream.

At pole no. 320 near park headquarters, you find the beginning of **Mohihi Camp 10 Road.** This road is recommended for 4WDs, but can be crossed with a regular car *only* in dry weather. It leads to a number of trails, some heading into valleys, others out along ridges, and still others into the Alakai Swamp. **Berry Flat,** a one-mile trail, and **Puu Ka Ohelo,** under a half mile, are easy loops that give you an up-close look at a vibrant upland forest. Under the green canopy are specimens such as *sugi* pine, California redwoods, eucalyptus from Australia, and native koa. Locals come here in June to harvest the methley plums, for which the area is famous. Off the Camp Road is the entrance to the Forest Reserve at **Sugi Grove,** where camping is limited to three days. **Kawaikoi Stream Trail** begins three-quarters of a mile past Sugi Grove. This 3.5-mile trail is moderately strenuous and known for its scenic beauty. It follows the south side of the stream (trout), crosses over, and loops back on the north side. Avoid it if the stream is high.

The **Alakai Swamp Trail** is otherworldly, crossing one of the most unusual pieces of real estate in the world. It begins off Camp Road at a parking area a quarter mile north of the Na Pali Forest Reserve entrance sign. The trails descends into the swamp for 3.5 miles and is very strenuous. Because you cross a number of bogs, be prepared to get wet and muddy. Good hiking shoes that won't be sucked off your feet are a must! The trail follows abandoned telephone poles from WW II, and then a series of brown and white (keep an eye out) trail markers. If you smell anise along the way, that's the *mokihana* berry, used with *maile* for fashioning wedding lei. The trail ends at Kilohana, where there's an expansive vista of Wainiha and Hanalei Valley.

One of the most rewarding trails for the time and effort is **Awaawapuhi Trail.** The trailhead is after park headquarters, just past pole no. 152 at the crest of the hill. It's three miles long and takes you out onto a thin finger of *pali,* with the sea and an emerald valley 2,500 feet below. The sun dapples the upland forest that still bears the scars of Hurricane Iniki. Everywhere flowers and fiddlehead ferns delight the eyes, while wild thimbleberries and passion fruit delight the taste buds. The trail is well marked and slightly strenuous. Connecting with the Awaawapuhi at the three-mile marker, the **Nualolo Trail,** which starts near park headquarters, is the easiest trail to the *pali* with an overview of Nualolo Valley.

Pihea Trail begins at the end of the paved road near the Puu O Kila Overlook. It's a good general-interest trail because it gives you a great view of Kalalau Valley, then descends into the Alakai Swamp where it connects with the Alakai Swamp Trail. It also connects with the Kawaikoi Stream Trail, and from each you can return via Camp 10 Rd. for an amazing loop of the area.

Accommodations and Food

Tent camping is allowed at **Koke'e State Park** with a permit, and the **Koke'e Lodge** also provides a dozen self-contained cabins, furnished with stoves, refrigerators, hot showers, cooking and eating utensils, and bedding; wood is available for woodstoves. The cabins cost $35 or $45 per night (five-night maximum; two-night minimum if one of the nights is Friday or Saturday) and vary from one large room (for three people) to two-bedroom units that sleep seven. The cabins are tough to get on holidays, in trout-fishing season (Aug.-Sept.), and during the wild plum harvest in June and July. For reservations, write well in advance (six months perhaps) to Koke'e Lodge, P.O. Box 819, Waimea, HI 96796, tel. (808) 335-6061, website: www.aloha.net /~koke'e. Please include a SASE, number of people, and dates requested. Full payment is required within two weeks of making reservations, with a refund possible (less a $15 service fee) if reservations are canceled *at least one week* before arrival. Check-in is 2 p.m., check-out is 11 a.m. Inexpensive.

The Koke'e Lodge is open Sun.-Thurs. 8:30 a.m.-5:30 p.m. and Friday and Saturday until 10 p.m. Its restaurant serves a full breakfast and lunch daily 8:30 a.m.-3:30 p.m., dinner on Friday and Saturday evenings only, 6-9 p.m. The cool weather calls especially for a slice of homemade pie and a steaming pot of coffee. Drinks can be bought at the lounge. Prices for food and drink are on the high side, but, after all, everything has to be trucked up the mountain. The next nearest restaurant or bar is 15 miles down the road at Kekaha. Also in the lodge is a shop that sells postcards, T-shirts, snacks, sundries, and souvenirs, most of which are island-themed and available nowhere else on Kauai.

KEKAHA

Back on Highway 50 going west, you enter Kekaha, passing the former plantation workers' homes trimmed in neat green lawns and shaded from the baking sun by palm and mango trees. Japanese gardens peek from behind fences. Along the main street are two gas stations—your last chance if heading west or up Waimea Canyon—**Traveler's Den Restaurant,** and the post office. Until 1996, cane trucks, like worker bees returning to the hive, carried their burdens into the ever-hungry jaws of the **Kekaha Sugar Company,** whose smokestack owns the skyline but belches black soot no more. Still, a sweet molasses smell lingers in the air.

Route 550, the western road leading to Waimea Canyon and Koke'e 15 miles away, branches off in the center of town. At this intersection you'll find a small mall with shops like the **Menehune Food Market,** your last chance for snacks and sundries; a **saimin stand** with burgers, *bento,* and plate lunches, open "until midnight unless we close at 10"; **Barbies** and **Emperors Emporium,** side-by-side places to buy postcards, cheap jewelry, outlet alohawear, and souvenirs; and **Lappert's Ice Cream** for a cone, hot dog, or bowl of chili. Every Saturday at noon there is a **farmers' market** where you can pick up fresh produce. As the location changes, ask around for the current spot. Kekaha isn't large, so it shouldn't be hard to find.

Route 50 proceeds along the coast. When still in town, you pass **H.P. Faye Park.** Across the road is **Kekaha Beach County Park** with pavilion, tables, toilets, and grills. Then the golden sands of the beach park stretch for miles, widening as you head west, with pulloffs and shade-tree clusters now and again. The sun always shines, and the swimming and surfing are excellent. Pick your spot anywhere along the beach. The area is good for swimming and snorkeling during calm weather, and fair for surfing, although the reef can be quite shallow in spots. Since there's no tourist development in the area, it's generally quite empty.

BARKING SANDS

The sea sparkles, and the land flattens wide and long, with green cane billowing all around. Dry gulches and red buttes form an impromptu inland wall. In six miles are the gates of Barking Sands Airfield and Pacific Missile Range. Here howl the dogs of war, leashed but on guard. You can use its beach and even arrange to camp for a few days if maneuvers are not in progress by calling (808) 335-4111. The beach is hot, shadeless, and pounded by unfriendly surf, but it affords the best view of Niihau, a purple Rorschach blot on the horizon—and the closest you're likely ever to get to the "Forbidden Island." The Barking Sands beach has the largest sand dunes on Kauai, due to the ocean's shallowness between the two islands. Supposedly, if you slide down the dunes, made from a mixture of sand and

ground coral, the friction will cause a sound like a barking dog, an effect that's most evident during the heat of the day.

The Kauai Educational Association for the Study of Astronomy, a.k.a. **KEASA** welcomes islanders and visitors of all ages to peer through its 14 inch computerized telescope every month on the Saturday nearest the full moon. To get there, turn into the gate at Barking Sands Airfield outside Mana at mile marker 30 and inform the guard of your destination. For a schedule of events, write to KEASA, P.O. Box 161, Waimea, HI 96796.

In late 1996, NASA announced that one of the most advanced studies of the earth's atmosphere will be conducted at the Pacific Missile Range Facility. The research will feature "Pathfinder," an experimental remote-controlled light aircraft that is fueled entirely by solar power. NASA officials chose Kauai because its weather provides 360 clear days, offering perfect flying in virtually unobstructed air space. The program should bring $1 million into the local economy and provide hands-on experience for some lucky students at Kauai's community college.

POLIHALE STATE PARK

Route 50 curves to the right after you pass the missile range, and an HVB Warrior points left to Polihale State Park. You go in by five miles of well-graded dirt cane road. The earth is a definite buff color here, unlike the deep red that predominates throughout the rest of the island. At a stop sign at a crossroads, you're pointed to Polihale (Home of the Spirits). You can day-trip to soak up the sights and you'll find pavilions, showers, toilets, and grills. Both RV and tent camping are allowed with a state park permit. The camping area is on the top of the dune on the left before you get to the pavilions. There are generally no hassles, but the rangers do come around, and you should have a permit with you—it's a long way back to Lihue to get one.

From the parking area at the chain gate, walk over the dune and down to the beach. The swimming can be dangerous, but the hiking is grand. The powdery white sand beach stretches for nearly three miles, pushing up against the Na Pali cliffs to the north and meeting the Mana

Plain to the east. Literally at the end of the road, this beach takes you away from the crowds, but you'll hardly ever be all by yourself. Here the cliffs come down to the sea, brawny and rugged with the Na Pali coast beginning around the far bend. Where the cliffs meet the sea is the ruin of

Polihale Heiau. This is a powerful spot, where the souls of the dead made their leap from land into infinity. The priests of this temple chanted special prayers to speed them on their way, as the waters of life flowed from a sacred spring in the mountainside.

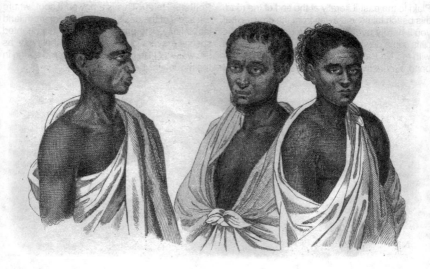

M.G.L. DOMÉNY DE RIENZI

NIIHAU AND THE
NORTHWESTERN ISLANDS
NIIHAU: THE FORBIDDEN ISLAND

The only thing forbidding about Niihau is its nick-name, "The Forbidden Island." Ironically, it's one of the last real havens of peace, tranquillity, and tradition left on the face of the earth. This privately owned island, operating as one large cattle and sheep ranch, is staffed by the last remaining pure Hawaiians in the state. To go there, you must have a personal invitation by the owners or one of the residents. Some people find this situation strange, but it would be no stranger than walking up to an Iowa farmhouse unannounced and expecting to be invited in to dinner. The islanders are free to come and go as they wish and are given the security of knowing that the last real Hawaiian place is not going to be engulfed by the modern world. Niihau is a reservation, but a *free-will* reservation—something you'll admire if you've ever felt that the world was too much with you.

The Land and Climate
The 17-mile **Kaulakahi Channel** separates Niihau from the western tip of Kauai. The island's maximum dimensions are 18 miles long by six miles wide, with a total area of 73 square miles. The highest point on the island, Paniau (1,281 feet), lies on the east-central coast. There are no port facilities on the island, but the occasional boats put in at Kii and Lehua Landings, both on the northern tip. Since Niihau is so low and lies in the rainshadow of Kauai, it receives only 30 inches of precipitation per year, making it rather arid. Oddly enough, low-lying basins, eroded from the single shield volcano that made the island, act as a catchment system. In them are the state's largest naturally occurring lakes, Halalii and the slightly larger 182-acre Lake Halulu. Two uninhabited islets join Niihau as part of Kauai County: Lehua, just off the northern tip

and exceptional for scuba diving, and Kaula, a few miles off the southern tip; each barely covers one-half square mile.

HISTORY

After the goddess Papa returned from Tahiti and discovered that her husband, Wakea, was playing around, she left him. The great Wakea did some squirming, and after these island-parents reconciled, Papa became pregnant and gave birth to Kauai. According to the creation chants found in the *Kumulipo*, Niihau popped out as the afterbirth, along with Lehua and Kaula, the last of the low reef islands.

Niihau was never a very populous island because of the relatively poor soil, so the islanders had to rely on trade with nearby Kauai for many necessities, including poi. Luckily, the fishing grounds off the island's coastal waters are the richest in the area, and Niihauans could always trade fish. The islanders became famous for Niihau mats, a good trade item, made from *makaloa,* a sedge plant that's plentiful on the island. Craftsmen also fashioned *ipu pawehe,* a geometrically designed gourd highly prized in the old days. When Captain Cook arrived and wished to provision his ships, he remarked that the Niihau natives were much more eager to trade than those on Kauai, and he secured potatoes and yams that seemed to be in abundant supply.

Kamehameha IV Sells

Along with Kauai, Niihau became part of the kingdom under Kamehameha. It passed down to his successors, and in the 1860s, Kamehameha IV sold it to the Robinson family for $10,000. This Scottish family, which came to Hawaii via New Zealand, has been the sole proprietor of the island ever since, although they now live on Kauai. They began a sheep and cattle ranch, hiring the island's natives as workers. No one can say exactly why, but it's evident that this family felt a great sense of responsibility and purpose. Tradition passed down over the years dictated that islanders could live on Niihau as long as they pleased, but that visitors were not welcome without a personal invitation. With the native Hawaiian population so devastated, the Robinsons felt that these proud people should have at least one place to call theirs and theirs alone. To keep the race pure, male visitors to the island were generally asked to leave by sundown.

Niihau Invaded

During WW II, Niihau was the only island of Hawaii to be occupied by the Japanese. A Zero pilot developed engine trouble after striking Pearl Harbor and had to ditch on Niihau. At first the islanders took him prisoner, but he somehow managed to escape and commandeer the machine guns from his plane. He terrorized the island, and the residents headed for the hills. One old woman who refused to leave was like a Hawaiian Barbara Fritchie. She told the Japanese prisoner to shoot her if he wished, but to please stop making a nuisance of himself—it wasn't nice! He would have saved himself a lot of trouble if he had only listened. Fed up with hiding, one huge *kanaka,* Benehakaka Kanahele, decided to approach the pilot with *aloha.* He was convinced the intruder would see the error of his ways. This latter-day samurai shot Mr. Kanahele for his trouble. Ben persisted and was shot again. An expression of pain, disgust, and disbelief at the stranger's poor manners spread across Ben's face, but still he tried pleading with the prisoner, who shot him for the third time. Ben had had enough, and grabbed the astonished pilot and flung him headlong against a wall, cracking his skull and killing him instantly. This incident gave rise to a wartime maxim—"Don't shoot a Hawaiian three times or you'll make him mad"—and a song titled, "You Can't Conquer Niihau, Nohow." Mr. Kanahele lived out his life on Niihau and died in the 1960s.

LIFE TODAY

The only reliable connection that the islanders have with the outside world is a WW II-vintage landing craft, which they use to bring in supplies from Kauai, and a new Agusta helicopter used for medical emergencies, supplies, and aerial tours. Until recently, homing pigeons were used to send messages, but they have been replaced by two-way radios. There's no communal electricity on the island, but people do have generators to power refrigerators and TVs. Transistor radios are very popular, and most people get around either on horseback or in pickup trucks. The population numbers around 230 people, 95% of whom are Hawaiian, the other 5% Japanese. There is one elementary school, in which English is used, but most people speak Hawaiian at home. The children go off to Kauai for high school, but after they get a taste of what the world at large has to offer, a surprisingly large number return to Niihau.

After Hurricane Iwa battered the island and Hurricane Iniki followed suit in 1992, the state was very eager to offer aid. The people of Niihau thanked them for their concern but told them not to bother—that they would take care of things themselves. Niihau was the only island to reject statehood in the plebiscite of 1959. In November 1988, when a group of environmentally conscious Kauaians took a boat to Niihau to try to clear some of the beaches of the floating sea junk that had washed up on shore, the Niihauans felt that the island was being trespassed—they didn't want such help in any case—and a few shots were fired, a warning to back off. Still unsettled, the controversy focuses on the question of who owns the beach—all beaches in Hawaii are open to free access, yet the whole island of Niihau is privately owned.

Today, some people accuse the Robinson family of being greedy barons of a medieval fiefdom, holding the Niihauans as virtual slaves. This idea is utter nonsense. Besides the fact that the islanders have an open door, the Robinsons would make immeasurably more money selling the island off to resort developers than running it as a livestock ranch. As if the spirit of old Hawaii was trying to send a sign, it's interesting that Niihau's official lei is fashioned from the *pupu,* a rare shell found only on the island's beaches, and the island's official color is white, the universal symbol of purity.

Niihau Shellwork

The finest shellwork made in Hawaii comes from Niihau, in a tradition passed down over the generations. The shells themselves—tiny and very rare *kahelelani* and *kamoa*—are abundant only in the deep waters off the windward coast. Sometimes, the tides and winds are just right and they are deposited on Niihau's beaches, but rarely more than three times per year. When that does happen, islanders stop everything and head for the shore to painstakingly collect them. The shells are sorted according to size and color, and only the finest are kept: 80% are discarded. The most prized are so tiny that a dozen fit on a thumbnail. Colors are white, yellow, blue, and the very rare gold. The best shells are free from chips or cracks. After being sorted, the shells are drilled. Various pieces of jewelry are fashioned, but the traditional pieces are necklaces and lei. These can be short, single-strand chokers, or the lovely *pikake* pattern—a heavy double strand. The rice motif is always popular; these are usually multistranded with the main shells clipped on the ends with various colored shells strung in as highlights.

A necklace takes long hours to create, with every shell connected by intricate and minute knots. Usually the women of Niihau do this work. Clasps are made from a type of cowrie shell found only on Niihau. No two necklaces are exactly alike. They sell by the inch, and the pure white and golden ones are very expensive—most are handed down as priceless heirlooms. Although Niihau shellwork is available in fine

NIIHAU

Kaulakahi Channel
Kahauna Point
Lehua Island
Keamano Bay
Kaakuu Bay (Lehua Landing)
KII LANDING
Keawanui Bay
KALANAEI
Paniau (1,281 ft.)
Puuwai
Pueo Point
Halawela
Halulu Lake
Halalii Lake
Kalaoa Bay
MAKAHUENA
Poooneone Point
Aliaiki Lake
Oiamoi Point
Niihau
Hawaiian Islands
Leahi Point
Kaumuhonu Bay
Kawaihoa Point
0   4 mi
0   4 km
Kaula 22 Miles

stores all over the state, Kauai, because it's closest, gets the largest selection. If you're after a once-in-a-lifetime purchase, consider Niihau shellwork.

Tours
Niihau Helicopters, P.O. Box 370, Makaweli, HI 96769, tel. (808) 335-3500, offers limited tours to the island. The primary purpose of Niihau Helicopters is to provide medical and emergency treatment for the residents of Niihau. However, to

defray costs, they offer occasional nonscheduled tourist charters on their twin-engine Agusta 109A. Two of their flights last 90 and 110 minutes, each with a 30-minute stop on a secluded beach on Niihau; fares are $185 and $235, respectively. Two other options are an overflight of Niihau for $135 and a tour of the Na Pali coast with a Niihau overflight for $235. Let pilot Tom Mishler show you a bit of this forbidden island.

Hunting expeditions offered by **Niihau Safaris** offer another way to visit the island.

THE NORTHWESTERN ISLANDS

Like tiny gems of a broken necklace, the Northwestern Hawaiian Islands spill across the vast Pacific. Popularly called the **Leewards,** most were discovered last century, oftentimes by hapless ships that ground to a sickening halt on their treacherous, half-submerged reefs. The ship captains left their names: Lisianski, Kure, French Frigate Shoals, Hermes, and Pearl. Even today, craft equipped with the most modern navigational devices must be wary in these waters. They remain among the loneliest outposts on the face of the earth.

Land and Climate
The Leewards are the oldest islands of the Hawaiian chain, believed to have emerged from the sea at least six million years ago; some ex-

perts say 25-30 million years! Slowly they floated northward past the suboceanic hot spot as the other islands were built. Measured from **Nihoa Island,** about 100 miles off the northern tip of Kauai, they stretch for just under 1,100 miles to **Kure Atoll.** There are 13 islets, shoals, and half-submerged reefs in this chain. Most have been eroded flat by the sea and wind, but a few tough volcanic cores endure. Together they make up a landmass of approximately 3,500 acres, the largest being the three Midway islands—taken together—at 1,580 acres, and the smallest the **Gardner Pinnacles** at six acres. The climate is similar to that of the main islands with a slightly larger variance. Temperatures, usually 70-85 degrees, sometimes dip as low as 50 degrees and climb as high as 90 degrees. Rainfall can

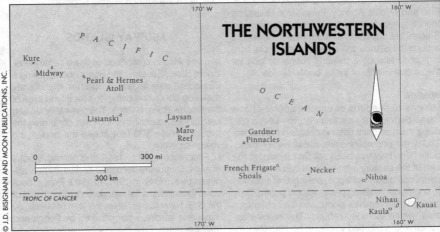

come any month of the year, but is more frequent in the winter. The average annual total is about 40 inches.

Administration and History

Politically, the Leewards are administered by the City and County of Honolulu, except for the Midway Islands, which are under federal jurisdiction. None are permanently inhabited, except for some lonely wildlife field stations on Kure and the French Frigate Shoals. All, except for the Midway Atoll, are part of the **Hawaiian Islands National Wildlife Refuge,** established at the turn of the century by Theodore Roosevelt. In 1996, following the closure of the Naval Air Base on Midway Island, Midway Atoll was turned over to the Department of the Interior and is now administered as the **Midway Atoll National Wildlife Refuge.**

In precontact times, some of the islands supported a Tahitian culture markedly different from the one that emerged on the main Hawaiian islands. Necker Island, for example, was the only island in the entire Hawaiian archipelago on which the inhabitants carved stone figures with a complete head and torso. On many of the others, remains of *heiau* and agricultural terracing allude to their colonization by precontact Hawaiians. Over the years, natives as well as Westerners have exploited the islands for feathers, fertilizer, seals, and fish.

The islands are closely monitored by the U.S. Fish and Wildlife Agency. Permission to land on them is granted only under special circumstances. Studies are underway to determine if the waters around the islands can support commercial fishing, while leaving a plentiful supply of food for the unique wildlife of these lonely islands.

Wildlife

Millions of seabirds of various species have found permanent sanctuary on the Leewards, using them as giant floating nests and rookeries. Today the populations are stable and growing, but it hasn't always been so. On Laysan, at the turn of the century, egg hunters came to gather countless albatross eggs, selling the albumen to companies making photographic paper. They brought their families along, and their children's pets, which included rabbits. The rabbits escaped and multiplied wildly. In no time they invaded the territories of the **Laysan honeycreeper, rail,** and **millerbird,** rendering them extinct. Laysan has recovered and is refuge to more than six million birds, including the rare and indigenous **Laysan teal** and **finch.**

An amazing bird using the rookeries is the **frigate bird.** During mating rituals, the male can inflate its chest like a giant red heart-shaped balloon. Also known as man-o'-war birds, they oftentimes pirate the catches of other birds, devour chicks, and even cannibalize their own offspring.

Some of the most prolific birds of the Leewards are terns, both the delicate all-white **fairy tern** and its darker relative the **sooty tern.** Other distinctive species include a variety of boobies, and the **Laysan albatross,** which has a wingspan of 10-12 feet, the world's largest.

Besides birds, the islands are home to the **Hawaiian monk seal,** one of only two species of indigenous Hawaiian mammals. These beautiful and sleek animals were hunted to near extinction for their skins. Humans encroached on their territory more and more, but now they are protected as an endangered species. About 1,000 individuals still cling to existence on various islands.

The **green turtle** is another species that has found a haven here. They were hunted to near extinction for their meat and leather, and of the few colonies around the world, the largest in the U.S. is on the French Frigate Shoals.

MIDWAY ISLANDS

Midway Atoll is comprised of three separate islands, Sand, Eastern, and Spit, encompassing a 25 square mile lagoon. Together, the islands make up about one half of the total land area of the Northwestern Islands. The three islands and surrounding reef of this atoll are coral growths that rise some 500 feet above the underlying volcanic peak.

First discovered in 1859 and named Brooks Islands, they were renamed Midway when annexed by the U.S. in 1867. In 1903, Pres. Theodore Roosevelt put the islands under the control of the U.S. Navy to help stem the loss of birdlife by Japanese sailors, who gathered bird eggs and feathers there. Employees of a cable company were the first permanent resident on the islands, in the first decade on the 1900s. This communications station was a strategic link between the U.S. and Asia. From 1935 until the early '60s, Midway was a refueling station for most trans-Pacific air routes to the Orient, first used by clipper seaplanes and later by prop and jet planes. With the growing concern about Japanese aggression in Asia, a naval base was begun on Midway in 1940. This installation was bombed on Dec. 7, 1941, after the attack on Pearl Harbor earlier in the day. In June of the following year, the Battle of Midway took place in the ocean off the atoll, and was a turning point in the war of the Pacific. Until 1996, Midway continued to be used as a military base, housing up to 3,000 personnel during the 1960s. With the closure of the naval facility, Midway Atoll has become the **Midway Atoll National Wildlife Refuge,** administered for the Department of the Interior by the U.S. Fish and Wildlife Service. Tourists are allowed to visit the island, but only in strictly limited numbers.

Hawaiian monk seals, green sea turtles, spinner dolphins, and close to 200 varieties of colorful **reef fish** inhabit the lagoon, while more than a dozen species of seabirds live and nest around the atoll. The world's large colony of **Layson albatross** inhabit the island, as do **great frigate birds, red-tailed tropic birds, terns, boobies, petrels,** and **wedge-tailed shearwaters.**

You can visit Midway to birdwatch, snorkel, dive, or fish. Birdwatching and snorkeling are free, but the other activities are run by concessionaires. Transportation to the atoll is provided by Aloha Airlines, which runs a once-weekly charter from Honolulu on Wednesday morning for $750 roundtrip. For more information on Midway Atoll and visiting this far outpost, contact: Midway Ltd., P.O. Box 3028, Lihue, HI 96766, tel. (808) 245-4718 or (888) 574-9000; or the U.S. Fish and Wildlife Service, P.O. Box 50167, Honolulu, HI 96850, tel. (808) 541-1201, website: www.midway-atoll.com.

LOUISE FOOTE

APPENDIX
BOOKLIST

ASTRONOMY

Bryan, E.H. *Stars over Hawaii*. Hilo, HI: Petroglyph Press, 1977. Charts featuring the stars filling the night sky in Hawaii.

Rhoads, Samuel. *The Sky Tonight-A Guided Tour of the Stars over Hawaii*. Honolulu: Bishop Museum, 1993. Four pages per month of star charts-one each for the horizon in every cardinal direction. Exceptional!

COOKING

Alexander, Agnes. *How to Use Hawaiian Fruit*. Hilo, HI: Petroglyph Press, 1984. A full range of recipes using delicious and different Hawaiian fruits.

Beeman, Judy, and Martin Beeman. *Joys of Hawaiian Cooking*. Hilo, HI: Petroglyph Press, 1977. A collection of favorite recipes from Big Island chefs.

Choy, Sam. *Cooking From the Heart with Sam Choy*. Honolulu: Mutual Publishing, 1995. This beautiful, handbound cookbook contains many color photos by Douglas Peebles.

Fukuda, Sachi. *Pupus, An Island Tradition*. Honolulu: Bess Press, 1995.

Margah, Irish, and Elvira Monroe. *Hawaii, Cooking with Aloha*. San Carlos, CA: Wide World, 1984. Island recipes including *kalua* pig and *lomi* salmon, as well as hints on decor.

Rizzuto, Shirley. *Fish Dishes of the Pacific-from the Fishwife*. Honolulu: Hawaii Fishing News, 1986. Features recipes using all the fish commonly caught in Hawaiian waters (husband Jim Rizzuto is the author of *Fishing, Hawaiian Style*).

CULTURE

Hartwell, Jay. *Na Mamo: Hawaiian People Today*. Ai Pohaku Press, 1996. Profiles 12 people practicing Hawaiian traditions in the modern world.

Heyerdahl, Thor. *American Indians in the Pacific*. London: Allen and Unwin Ltd., 1952. Theoretical and anthropological accounts of the influence on Polynesia of the Indians along the Pacific coast of North and South America. Though no longer in print, this book is fascinating reading, presenting unsubstantiated yet intriguing theories.

Kirch, Patrick V. *Feathered Gods and Fishhooks: An Introduction to Hawaiian Archaeology and Prehistory*. Honolulu: University of Hawaii Press, 1985. This scholarly, lavishly illustrated, yet very readable book gives new insight into the development of precontact Hawaiian civilization. It focuses on the sites and major settlements of old Hawaii and chronicles the main cultural developments while weaving in the social climate that contributed to change. A very worthwhile read.

FAUNA

Boom, Robert. *Hawaiian Seashells*. Honolulu: Waikiki Aquarium, 1972. Photos by Jerry Kringle. A collection of 137 seashells found in Hawaiian waters, featuring many found nowhere else on earth. Broken into categories with accompanying text including common and scientific names, physical descriptions, and likely habitats. A must for shell collectors.

Carpenter, Blyth, and Russell Carpenter. *Fish Watching in Hawaii*. San Mateo, CA: Natural World Press, 1981. A color guide to many of the reef fish found in Hawaii and often spotted by snorkelers. If you're interested in the fish that you'll be looking at, this guide will be very helpful.

Fielding, Ann, and Ed Robinson. *An Underwater Guide to Hawaii*. Honolulu: University of Hawaii Press, 1987. If you've ever had a desire to snorkel/scuba the living reef waters of Hawaii and to be familiar with what you're seeing, get this small but fact-packed book. The amazing array of marine life found throughout the archipelago is captured in glossy photos with accompanying informative text. Both the scientific and common names of specimens are given. This book will enrich your underwater experience and serve as an easily understood reference guide for many years.

Goodson, Gar. *The Many-Splendored Fishes of Hawaii*. Stanford, CA: Stanford University Press, 1985. This small but thorough "fish-watchers" book includes entries on some deep-sea fish.

Hobson, Edmend, and E.H. Chave. *Hawaiian Reef Animals*. Honolulu: University of Hawaii Press, 1987. Colorful photos and descriptions of the fish, invertebrates, turtles, and seals that call Hawaiian reefs their home.

Hosaka, Edward. *Shore Fishing in Hawaii*. Hilo, HI: Petroglyph Press, 1984. Known as the best book on Hawaiian fishing since 1944. This book receives the highest praise because it has informed generations of Hawaiian anglers.

Kay, Alison, and Olive Schoenberg-Dole. *Shells of Hawaii*. Honolulu: University of Hawaii Press, 1991. Color photos and tips on where to look for certain shells.

Mahaney, Casey. *Hawaiian Reef Fish, The Identification Book*. 1993. A spiral-bound reference work featuring many color photos and descriptions of common reef fish found in Hawaiian waters.

Nickerson, Roy. *Brother Whale, A Pacific Whalewatcher's Log*. San Francisco: Chronicle Books, 1977. Introduces the average person to the life of earth's greatest mammals. Provides historical accounts, photos, and tips on whalewatching. Well-written, descriptive, and the best "first time" book on whales.

Pratt, H.D., P.L. Bruner, and D.G. Berrett. *The Birds of Hawaii and the Tropical Pacific*. Princeton, N.J.: Princeton University Press, 1987. Useful field guide for novice and expert birdwatchers, covering Hawaii as well as other Pacific Island groups.

van Riper, Charles, and Sandra van Riper. *A Field Guide to the Mammals of Hawaii*. Honolulu: Oriental Publishing. A guide to the surprising number of mammals introduced into Hawaii. Full-color pages document description, uses, tendencies, and habitat. Small and thin, this book makes a worthwhile addition to any serious trekker's backpack.

FLORA

Kepler, Angela. *Exotic Tropicals of Hawaii*. Honolulu: Mutual Publishing, 1989. This small-format book features many color photos of exotic tropical flowers.

Kuck, Lorraine, and Richard Togg. *Hawaiian Flowers and Flowering Trees*. Rutland, VT: Tuttle, 1960. A classic, though no longer in print, field guide to tropical and subtropical flora illustrated in watercolor. A "to the point" description of Hawaiian plants and flowers with a brief history of their places of origin and their introduction to Hawaii.

Merrill, Elmer. *Plant Life of the Pacific World*. Rutland, VT: Tuttle, 1983. The definitive book for anyone planning a botanical tour to the entire Pacific Basin. Originally published in the 1930s, it remains a tremendous work, worth tracking down through the out-of-print book services.

Miyano, Leland. *Hawaii, A Floral Paradise*. Honolulu: Mutual Publishing, 1995. Photographed by Douglas Peebles, this large-format book is filled with informative text and beautiful color shots of tropical flowers commonly seen in Hawaii.

Sohmer, S.H., and R. Gustafson. *Plants and Flowers of Hawaii*. Honolulu: University of Hawaii Press, 1987. Sohmer and Gustafson cover the vegetation zones of Hawaii, from mountains to coast, introducing you to the wide and varied floral biology of the islands. They give a good introduction to the history and unique evolution of Hawaiian plantlife. Beautiful color plates are accompanied by clear and concise plant descriptions, with the scientific and common Hawaiian names listed.

Teho, Fortunato. *Plants of Hawaii-How to grow them.* Hilo, HI: Petroglyph Press, 1992. A small but useful book for those who want their backyards to bloom into tropical paradises.

HEALTH

McBride, L.R. *Practical Folk Medicine of Hawaii.* Hilo, HI: Petroglyph Press, 1975. An illustrated guide to Hawaii's medicinal plants as used by the *kahuna lapa'au* (medical healers). Includes a thorough section on ailments, diagnosis, and the proper folk remedy. Illustrated by the author, a renowned botanical researcher and former ranger at Volcanoes National Park.

Wilkerson, James A., M.D., ed. *Medicine for Mountaineering and Other Wilderness.* 4th ed. Seattle: The Mountaineers, 1992. Don't let the title fool you. Although the book focuses on specific health problems that may be encountered while mountaineering, it is the best first-aid and general health guide available today. Written by doctors for the layperson to use until help arrives, it is jam-packed with easily understandable techniques and procedures. For those intending extended treks, it is a must.

HISTORY

Apple, Russell A. *Trails: From Steppingstones to Kerbstones.* Honolulu: Bishop Museum Press, 1965. This "Special Publication #53" is a special-interest archaeological survey focusing on trails, roadways, footpaths, and highways and how they were designed and maintained throughout the years. Many "royal highways" from pre-contact Hawaii are cited.

Ashdown, Inez MacPhee. *Old Lahaina.* Honolulu: Hawaiian Service Inc., 1976. A small pamphlet-type book listing most of the historical attractions of Lahaina Town, past and present.

Ashdown is a life-long resident of Hawaii and gathered her information firsthand by listening to and recording stories told by ethnic Hawaiians and old *kama'aina* families.

Ashdown, Inez MacPhee. *Ke Alaloa o Maui.* Wailuku, HI: Kama'aina Historians Inc., 1971. A compilation of the history and legends connected to sites on the island of Maui. Ashdown was at one time a "lady in waiting" for Queen Liliuokalani and has since been proclaimed Maui's "Historian Emeritus."

Cameron, Roderick. *The Golden Haze.* New York: World Publishing, 1964. An account of Capt. James Cook's voyages of discovery throughout the South Seas. Uses original diaries and journals for an "on the spot" reconstruction of this great seafaring adventure.

Daws, Gavan. *Shoal of Time, A History of the Hawaiian Islands.* Honolulu: University of Hawaii Press, 1974. A highly readable history of Hawaii dating from its "discovery" by the Western world down to its acceptance as the 50th state. Good insight into the psychological makeup of influential characters who helped form Hawaii's past.

Finney, Ben, and James D. Houston. *Surfing, A History of the Ancient Hawaiian Sport.* Los Angeles: Pomegranate, 1996. Features many early etchings and old photos of Hawaiian surfers practicing their native sport.

Free, David. *Vignettes of Old Hawaii.* Honolulu: Crossroads Press,1994. A collection of short essays on a variety of subjects.

Fuchs, Lawrence. *Hawaii Pono.* New York: Harcourt, Brace and World, 1961. A detailed, scholarly work presenting an overview of Hawaii's history, based upon psychological and sociological interpretations. Encompasses most socio-ethnological groups from native Hawaiians to modern entrepreneurs. A must for social historical background.

Fornander, Abraham. *An Account of the Polynesian Race; Its Origins and Migrations, and the Ancient History of the Hawaiian People to the Times of Kamehameha I.* Rutland, VT: C.E. Tuttle Co., 1969. This is a reprint of a three-volume opus originally published 1878-85. It is still one of the best sources of information on Hawaiian myth and legend.

Handy, E.S., and Elizabeth Handy. *Native Planters in Old Hawaii.* Honolulu: Bishop Museum Press, 1972. A superbly written, easily understood scholarly work on the intimate relationship of precontact Hawaiians and the *aina* (land). Much more than its title implies, this book should be read by anyone seriously interested in Polynesian Hawaii.

Ii, John Papa. *Fragments of Hawaiian History.* Honolulu: Bishop Museum, 1959. Hawaii's history under Kamehameha I as told by a Hawaiian who actually experienced it.

Joesting, Edward. *Hawaii: An Uncommon History.* New York: W.W. Norton Co., 1978. A truly uncommon history told in a series of vignettes relating to the lives and personalities of the first Caucasians in Hawaii, Hawaiian nobility, sea captains, writers, and adventurers. Brings history to life. Absolutely excellent!

Kurisu, Yasushi. *Sugar Town, Hawaiian Plantation Days Remembered.* Honolulu: Watermark Publishing, 1995. Reminiscences of life gowing up on sugar plantations on the Hamakua Coast of the Big Island. Features many old photos.

Liliuokalani. *Hawaii's Story By Hawaii's Queen.* 1964. Reprint, Rutland, VT: Tuttle, 1991. A moving personal account of Hawaii's inevitable move from monarchy to U.S. Territory by its last queen, Liliuokalani. The facts can be found in other histories, but none provides the emotion or point of view expressed by Hawaii's deposed monarch. A "must-read" to get the whole picture.

McBride, Likeke. *Petroglyphs of Hawaii.* Hilo, HI: Petroglyph Press, 1996. A revised and updated guide to petroglyphs found in the Hawaiian Islands.

Nickerson, Roy. *Lahaina, Royal Capital of Hawaii.* Honolulu: Hawaiian Service, 1978. The story of Lahaina from whaling days to present, spiced with ample photographs.

INTRODUCTORY

Cohen, David, and Rick Smolan. *A Day in the Life of Hawaii.* New York: Workman, 1984. On December 2, 1983, 50 of the world's top photojournalists were invited to Hawaii to photograph the variety of daily life on the islands. The photos are excellently reproduced, and accompanied by a minimum of text.

Day, A.G., and C. Stroven. *A Hawaiian Reader.* 1959. Reprint, New York: Appleton, Century, Crofts, 1985. A poignant compilation of essays, diary entries, and fictitious writings that takes you from the death of Captain Cook through the "statehood services."

Department of Geography, University of Hawaii. *Atlas of Hawaii.* 2nd ed. Honolulu: University of Hawaii Press, 1983. Much more than an atlas filled with reference maps, this also contains commentary on the natural environment, culture, and sociology; a gazetteer; and statistical tables. Actually a mini-encyclopedia.

Michener, James A. *Hawaii.* New York: Random House, 1959. Michener's fictionalized historical novel has done more to inform *and* misinform readers about Hawaii than any other book ever written. A great tale with plenty of local color and information, but read it for pleasure, not facts.

Piercy, LaRue. *Hawaii This and That.* Honolulu: Mutual Publishing, 1994. Illustrated by Scot Ebanez. A 60-page book filled with one-sentence facts and oddities about all manner of things Hawaiian. Informative, amazing, and fun to read.

Steele, R. Thomas: *The Hawaiian Shirt: Its Art and History.* Abbeville Press, Inc., 1984

LANGUAGE

Elbert, Samuel, and Mary Pukui. *Hawaiian Dictionary.* Honolulu: University of Hawaii, 1986. The best dictionary available on the Hawaiian language. The *Pocket Hawaiian Dictionary* is a less expensive, condensed version of this dictionary, and adequate for most travelers with a general interest in the language.

Elbert, Samuel. *Spoken Hawaiian*. Honolulu: University of Hawaii Press, 1970. Progressive conversational lessons.

MYTHOLOGY AND LEGENDS

Beckwith, Martha. *Hawaiian Mythology*. 1970. Reprint, Honolulu: University of Hawaii Press, 1977. Nearly 60 years after its original printing in 1940, this work remains the definitive text on Hawaiian mythology. Beckwith compiled this book from many sources, giving exhaustive cross-references to genealogies and legends expressed in the oral tradition. If you are going to read one book on Hawaii's folklore, this should be it.

Colum, Padraic. *Legends of Hawaii*. New Haven: Yale University Press, 1937. Selected legends of old Hawaii, reinterpreted but closely based upon the originals.

Elbert, S., comp. *Hawaiian Antiquities and Folklore*. Honolulu: Univerity of Hawaii Press, 1959. Illustrated by Jean Charlot. A selection of the main legends from Abraham Fornander's great work, *An Account of the Polynesian Race*.

Kalakaua, His Hawaiian Majesty, King David. *The Legends and Myths of Hawaii*. Edited by R.M. Daggett, with a foreword by Glen Grant. Honolulu: Mutual Publishing, 1990. Originally published in 1888, Hawaii's own King Kalakaua draws upon his scholarly and formidable knowledge of the classic oral tradition to bring alive ancient tales from precontact Hawaii. A powerful yet somewhat Victorian voice from Hawaii's past speaks clearly and boldly, especially about the intimate role of pre-Christian religion in the lives of the Hawaiian people.

Melville, Leinanai. *Children of the Rainbow*. Wheaton, IL: Theosophical Publishing, 1969. A book on higher spiritual consciousness attuned to nature, which was the basic belief of pre-Christian Hawaii. The appendix contains illustrations of mystical symbols used by the *kahuna*. An enlightening book in many ways.

Thrum, Thomas. *Hawaiian Folk Tales*. 1907. Reprint, Chicago: McClurg and Co., 1950. A collection of Hawaiian tales from the oral tradition as told to the author from various sources.

Westervelt, W.D. *Hawaiian Legends of Volcanoes*. 1916. Reprint, Boston: Ellis Press, 1991. A small book concerning the volcanic legends of Hawaii and how they related to the fledgling field of volcanism at the turn of the century. The vintage photos alone are worth a look.

NATURAL SCIENCES

Abbott, Agatin, Gordon MacDonald, and Frank Peterson. *Volcanoes in the Sea*. Honolulu: University of Hawaii Press, 1983. A simplified yet comprehensive text covering the geology and volcanism of the Hawaiian Islands. Focuses upon the forces of nature (wind, rain, and surf) that shape the islands.

Carlquist, Sherwin. *Hawaii: A Natural History*, 2nd ed. National Tropical Botany, 1980. Definitive account of Hawaii's natural history.

Hazlett, Richard, and Donald Hyndman. *Roadside Geology of Hawaii*. Missoula, MT: Mountain Press Publishing, 1996. Begins with a general discusion of the geology of the Hawaiian Islands, followed by a road guide to the individual islands offering descriptions of easily seen features.

Hubbard, Douglass, and Gordon MacDonald. *Volcanoes of the National Parks of Hawaii*. 1982. Reprint, Volcanoes, HI: Hawaii Natural History Association, 1989. The volcanology of Hawaii, documenting the major lava flows and their geological effect on the state.

Kay, E. Alison, comp. *A Natural History of the Hawaiian Islands*. Honolulu: University of Hawaii Press, 1994. A selection of concise articles by experts in the fields of volcanism, oceanography, meteorology, and biology. An excellent reference source.

PERIODICALS

Aloha, The Magazine of Hawaii and the Pacific. Davick Publications, P.O. Box 49035, Escondido, CA 92046. This excellent bimonthly magazine is much more than glossy photography. Special features may focus on sports, the arts, history, flora and fauna, or just pure island adventure. *Aloha* is equally useful as a "dream book" for those who wish that they could visit Hawaii and as a current resource for those actually going. One of the best for an overall view of Hawaii, and well worth the subscription price.

Hawaii Magazine. 1400 Kapiolani Blvd., Suite B, Honolulu, HI 96814. This magazine covers the Hawaiian Islands like a tropical breeze. Feature articles on all aspects of life in the islands, with special departments on travel, events, exhibits, and restaurant reviews. Up-to-the-minute information, and a fine read.

Naturist Society Magazine. P.O. Box 132, Oshkosh, WI 54920. This excellent magazine not only *uncovers* bathing-suit-optional beaches throughout the islands, giving tips for naturalists visiting Hawaii, but also reports on local politics, environment, and conservation measures from the health-conscious nudist point of view. A fine publication.

PICTORIALS

La Brucherie, Roger. *Hawaiian World, Hawaiian Heart.* Pine Valley, CA: Imagenes Press, 1989.

Grant, Glenn. *Hawaii The Big Island.* Honolulu: Mutual Publishing, 1988. Includes the historic, social, and nature photos of many photographers.

POLITICAL SCIENCE

Albertini, Jim, et al. *The Dark Side of Paradise, Hawaii in a Nuclear War.* Honolulu: cAtholic Action of Hawaii. Well-documented research outlining Hawaii's role and vulnerability in a nuclear world. This book presents the antinuclear and antimilitary side of the political issue in Hawaii.

Bell, Roger. *Last Among Equals: Hawaiian Statehood and American Politics.* Honolulu: University of Hawaii, 1984. Documents Hawaii's long and rocky road to statehood, tracing political partisanship, racism, and social change.

SPORTS AND RECREATION

Alford, John, D. *Mountain Biking the Hawaiian Islands.* Ohana Pub., 1997. Quite useful.

Ambrose, Greg. *Surfer's Guide to Hawaii.* Honolulu: Bess Press, 1991. Island-by-island guide to surfing spots.

Ball, Stuart. *Hiker's Guide to Oahu.* Honolulu: University of Hawaii Press, 1993. Very excellent.

Cagala, George. *Hawaii: A Camping Guide.* Hunter Pub., 1994. Useful.

Chisholm, Craig. *Hawaiian Hiking Trails.* Lake Oswego, OR: Fernglen Press, 1989.

Lueras, Leonard. *Surfing, the Ultimate Pleasure.* Honolulu: Emphasis International, 1984. One of the most brilliant books ever written on surfing.

McMahon, Richard. *Camping Hawai'i: A Complete Guide.* Honolulu: University of Hawaii Press, 1997. A helpful handbook.

Morey, Kathy. *Oahu Trails.* Berkeley, CA: Wilderness Press, 1993. Morey's books are specialized, detailed trekker's guides to Hawaii's outdoors. Complete with useful maps, historical references, official procedures, and plants and animals encountered along the way. If you're focused on hiking, these are the best to take along. *Maui Trails, Kauai Trails,* and *Hawaii Trails* are also available.

Rosenberg, Steve. *Diving Hawaii.* Locust Valley, NY: Aqua Quest, 1990. Describes diving locations on the major islands as well as the marine life divers are likely to see. Includes many color photos.

Smith, Robert. *Hawaii's Best Hiking Trails*. Huntington Beach, CA: Hawaiian Outdoor Adventures, 1991. Other guides by this author include *Hiking Oahu, Hiking Maui, Hiking Hawaii,* and *Hiking Kauai*.

Thorne, Chuck. *The Diver's Guide to Maui*. Hana, HI: Maui Dive Guide, 1994. A no-nonsense snorkeler's and diver's guide to Maui waters. Extensive maps, descriptions, and "straight from the shoulder" advice by one of Maui's best and most experienced divers. A must for all levels of divers and snorkelers.

Wallin, Doug. *Diving & Snorkeling Guide to the Hawaiian Islands,* 2nd ed. Pisces Books, 1991. A guide offering brief descriptions of diving locations on the four major islands.

TRAVEL

Clark, John. *Beaches of the Big Island*. Honolulu: University of Hawaii Press, 1985. Definitive guide to beaches, including many off the beaten path. Features maps and black-and-white photos.

Riegert, Ray. *Hidden Hawaii*. Berkeley, CA: And/Or Press, 1992. Ray offers a "user-friendly" guide to the islands.

Stanley, David. *South Pacific Handbook*. 7th ed. Chico, CA: Moon Publications, 1999. The model upon which all travel guides should be based. Simply the best book in the world for travel throughout the South Pacific.

Warner, Evie, and Al Davies. *Bed and Breakfast Goes Hawaiian*. Kapa'a, HI: Island Bed and Breakfast, 1990. A combination bed and breakfast directory and guide to sights, activities, events, and restaurants on the six major islands.

GLOSSARY
CAPSULE HAWAIIAN

The list on the following pages gives you a "taste" of Hawaiian and provides a basic vocabulary of words in common usage that you are likely to hear. Becoming familiar with them is not a strict necessity, but they will definitely enhance your experience and make talking with local people more congenial. You'll soon notice that many islanders spice their speech with certain words, especially when they're speaking pidgin, and you too can use them just as soon as you feel comfortable. You might even discover some Hawaiian words that are so perfectly expressive they'll become regular parts of your vocabulary. Many Hawaiian words have been absorbed into English.

Also see the **Language** and **Food and Drink** sections in the Introduction for other applicable Hawaiian words and phrases. The definitions given are not exhaustive, but are generally considered the most common.

Words marked with an asterisk (*) are used commonly throughout the islands.

a'a*—rough clinker lava. A'a has become the correct geological term to describe this type of lava found anywhere in the world.

ae—yes

ahupua'a—pie-shaped land divisions running from mountain to sea that were governed by *konohiki*, local *ali'i* who owed their allegiance to a reigning chief

aikane—male friend; pal; buddy

aina—land; the binding spirit to all Hawaiians. Love of the land is paramount in traditional Hawaiian beliefs.

akamai—smart; clever; wise

akua—a god, or simply "divine." You'll hear people speak of their family or personal *aumakua* (ancestral spirit). Favorites are the shark or the *pueo* (Hawaiian owl).

*ali'i***—a Hawaiian chief or noble

aloha*—the most common greeting in the islands; can mean both hello or goodbye, welcome or farewell. It can also mean romantic love, affection, or best wishes.

aumakua—a personal or family spirit, usually an ancestral spirit

aole—no

auwe—alas; ouch! When a great chief or loved one died, it was a traditional wail of mourning.

'awa—also known as kava, a mildly intoxicating traditional drink made from the juice of chewed 'awa root, spat into a bowl, and used in religious ceremonies

halakahiki—pineapple

*hale***—house or building; often combined with other words to name a specific place, such as Haleakala (House of the Sun), or Hale Pa'i (Printing House)

*hana***—work; combined with *pau* means end of work or quitting time

hanai—literally "to feed." Part of the true *aloha* spirit. A *hanai* is a permanent guest, or an adopted family member, usually an old person or a child. This is an enduring cultural phenomenon in Hawaii, in which a child from one family (perhaps that of a brother or sister, and quite often one's grandchild) is raised as one's own without formal adoption.

*haole***—a word that at one time meant foreigner, but which now means a white person or Caucasian. Many etymological definitions have been put forth, but none satisfies everyone. Some feel that it signified a person without a background, because the first white men could not chant their genealogies as was common to Hawaiians.

*hapa***—half, as in a mixed-blooded person being referred to as *hapa haole*

hapai—pregnant; used by all ethnic groups when a *keiki* is on the way

*haupia***—a coconut custard dessert often served at a luau

heiau*—A platform made of skillfully fitted rocks, upon which temporary structures were built as temples and offerings made to the gods.

holomuu*—an ankle-length dress that is much more fitted than a muumuu, and which is often worn on formal occasions

hono—bay, as in Honolulu (Sheltered Bay)

honu—green sea turtle (endangered)

ho'oilo—traditional Hawaiian winter that began in November

ho'olaule'a—any happy event, but especially a family outing or picnic, street party

hoomalimali*—sweet talk; flattery

huhu*—angry; irritated

hui*—a group; meeting; society. Often used to refer to Chinese businesspeople or family members who pool their money to get businesses started.

hukilau—traditional shoreline fish-gathering in which everyone lends a hand to *huki* (pull) the huge net. Anyone taking part shares in the *lau* (food). It is much more like a party than hard work, and if you're lucky you'll be able to take part in one.

hula*—a native Hawaiian dance in which the rhythm of the islands is captured by swaying hips and stories told by lyrically moving hands. A *halau* is a group or school of hula.

i'a—fish in general. *I'a maka* is raw fish.

imu*—underground oven filled with hot rocks and used for baking. The main cooking method featured at a luau, used to steam-bake pork and other succulent dishes. The tending of the *imu* was traditionally for men only.

ipo—sweetheart; lover; girl- or boyfriend

kahili—a tall pole topped with feathers, resembling a huge feather duster. It was used by an *ali'i* to announce his or her presence.

kahuna*—priest; sorcerer; doctor; skillful person. In old Hawaii *kahuna* had tremendous power, which they used for both good and evil. The *kahuna ana'ana* was a feared individual because he practiced "black magic" and could pray a person to death, while the *kahuna lapa'au* was a medical practitioner bringing aid and comfort to the people.

kai—the sea. Many businesses and hotels employ *kai* as part of their name.

kalua—means roasted underground in an *imu*. A favorite island food is *kalua* pork.

kama'aina*—a child of the land; an old-timer; a longtime island resident of any ethnic background; a resident of Hawaii or native son or daughter. Hotels and airlines often offer discounts called *"kama'aina* rates" to anyone who can prove island residency.

kanaka—man or commoner; later used to distinguish a Hawaiian from other races. Tone of voice can make it a derisive expression.

kane*—means man, but actually used to signify a relationship such as husband or boyfriend. Written on a lavatory door it means "Men's Room."

kaola*—any food that has been broiled or barbecued

kapu*—forbidden; taboo; keep out; do not touch

kapuna—a grandparent or old-timer; usually means someone who has gained wisdom. The statewide school system now invites *kapuna* to talk to the children about the old ways and methods.

kaukau*—slang word meaning food or chow; grub. Some of the best food in Hawaii comes from the *"kaukau* wagons," trucks that sell plate lunches and other morsels.

kauwa—a landless, untouchable caste once confined to living on reservations. Members of this caste were often used as human sacrifices at *heiau*. Calling someone *kauwa* is still considered a grave insult.

kava—also known as *'awa,* a mildly intoxicating traditional drink made from the juice of chewed 'awa root, spat into a bowl, and used in religious ceremonies

keiki*—child or children; used by all ethnic groups. "Have you hugged your *keiki* today?"

kiawe—an algaroba tree from South America commonly found in Hawaii along the shore. It grows a nasty long thorn that can easily puncture a tire. Legend has it that the trees were introduced to the islands by a misguided missionary who hoped the thorns would coerce natives into wearing shoes. Actually, they are good for fuel, as fodder for hogs and cattle, and for reforestation, none of which you'll appreciate if you step on one of their thorns or flatten a tire on your rental car!

kipuka—an area in the midst of a lava flow that was itself never inundated by lava.

kipuupuu—fine mist.

kokua—help. As in "Your *kokua* is needed to keep Hawaii free from litter."

kona wind*—a muggy subtropical wind that blows from the south and hits the leeward side of the islands. It usually brings sticky hot weather and is one of the few times when air-conditioning will be appreciated.

konane—a traditional Hawaiian game, similar to checkers, played with pebbles on a large flat stone used as a board

koolau—windward side of the island

kukui—a candlenut tree whose pods are polished and then strung together to make a beautiful *lei*. Traditionally the oil-rich nuts were strung on the rib of a coconut leaf and used as a candle.

kuleana—homesite; the old homestead; small farms. Especially used to describe the small spreads on Hawaiian Homes Lands on Molokai.

Kumulipo*—ancient Hawaiian genealogical chant that records the pantheon of gods, creation, and the beginning of humankind

kupua—nature spirit

la—the sun. Often combined with other words to be more descriptive, such as Lahaina (Merciless Sun) or Haleakala (House of the Sun).

lanai*—veranda or porch. You'll pay more for a hotel room if it has a lanai with an ocean view.

lani—sky or the heavens

lau hala*—traditional Hawaiian weaving of mats, hats, etc., from the prepared fronds of the pandanus (screw pine)

lei*—a traditional garland of flowers or vines. One of Hawaii's most beautiful customs. Given at any auspicious occasion, but especially when arriving or leaving Hawaii.

lele—the stone altar at a *heiau*

limu—edible seaweed of various types. Gathered from the shoreline, it makes an excellent salad. It's used to garnish many island dishes and is a favorite at luau.

lomi lomi—traditional Hawaiian massage; also, raw salmon made into a vinegared salad with chopped onion and spices

lua*—the toilet; the head; the bathroom

luakini—a human-sacrifice temple. Introduced to Hawaii in the 13th century at Waha'ula Heiau on the Big Island.

luau*—a Hawaiian feast featuring poi, *imu*-baked pork, and other traditional foods. Good ones provide some of the best gastronomical delights in the world.

luna—foreman or overseer in the plantation fields. They were often mounted on horseback and were renowned for either their fairness or their cruelty. Representing the middle class, they served as a buffer between plantation workers and white plantation owners.

mahalo*—thank you. *Mahalo nui* means "big thanks" or "thank you very much."

mahele—division. The "Great Mahele" of 1848 changed Hawaii forever when the traditional common lands were broken up into privately owned plots.

mahimahi*—a favorite eating fish. It's often called a dolphin, but a mahimahi is a true fish, not a cetacean.

mahu—a homosexual; often used derisively like "fag" or "queer"

maile—a fragrant vine used in traditional lei. It looks ordinary but smells delightful.

maka'ainana—a commoner; a person "belonging" to the *aina* (land), who supported the *ali'i* by fishing and farming and as a warrior

makai*—toward the sea; used by most islanders when giving directions

make—dead; deceased

malihini*—what you are if you have just arrived: a newcomer; a tenderfoot; a recent arrival

malo—the native Hawaiian loincloth. Never worn anymore except at festivals or pageants.

mana*—power from the spirit world; innate energy of all things animate or inanimate; the grace of god. Mana could be passed on from one person to another, or even stolen. Great care was taken to protect the *ali'i* from having their mana defiled. Commoners were required to lie flat on the ground and cover their faces whenever a great *ali'i* approached. *Kahuna* were often employed in the regaining or transference of mana.

manuahi—free; gratis; extra

manini—stingy; tight; a Hawaiianized word taken from the name of Don Francisco Marin, who was instrumental in bringing many fruits and plants to Hawaii. He was known for never sharing any of the bounty from his substantial gardens on Vineyard St. in Honolulu, therefore his name came to mean "stingy."

mauka*—toward the mountains; used by most islanders when giving directions

mauna—mountain. Often combined with other words to be more descriptive, such as Mauna Kea (White Mountain).

mele—a song or chant in the Hawaiian oral tradition that records the history and genealogies of the *ali'i*

menehune—the legendary "little people" of Hawaii. Like leprechauns, they are said to shun humans and possess magical powers. Stone walls said to have been completed in one night are often attributed to them. Some historians argue that they actually existed and were the aboriginals of Hawaii, inhabiting the islands before the coming of the Polynesians.

moa—chicken; fowl

moana*—the ocean; the sea. Many businesses and hotels as well as places have *moana* as part of their name.

moe—sleep

moolelo—ancient tales kept alive by the oral tradition and recited only by day

muumuu*—a "Mother Hubbard," an ankle-length dress with a high neckline introduced by the missionaries to cover the nakedness of the Hawaiians. It has become fashionable attire for almost any occasion in Hawaii.

nani—beautiful

nui—big; great; large; as in *mahalo nui* (thank you very much)

ohana—a family; the fundamental social division; extended family. Now used to denote a social organization with grassroots overtones, as in the "Protect Kahoolawe Ohana."

okolehao—literally "iron bottom"; a traditional booze made from ti root. *Okole* means "rear end" and *hao* means "iron," which was descriptive of the huge blubber pots in which *okolehao* was made. Also, if you drink too much it'll surely knock you on your *okole*.

ono*—delicious; delightful; the best. *Ono ono* means "extra or absolutely delicious."

opihi—a shellfish or limpet that clings to rocks and is gathered as one of the islands' favorite *pu pu*. Custom dictates that you never remove all of the *opihi* from a rock; some are always left to grow for future generations.

opu—belly; stomach

pahoehoe*—smooth, ropey lava that looks like burnt pancake batter. It is now the correct geological term used to describe this type of lava found anywhere in the world.

pakalolo—"crazy smoke"; marijuana

pake—a Chinese person. Can be derisive, depending on tone in which it is used. It is a bastardization of the Chinese word meaning "uncle."

pali*—a cliff; precipice. Hawaii's geology makes them quite common. The most famous are the *pali* of Oahu where a major battle was fought.

paniolo*—a Hawaiian cowboy. Derived from the Spanish *española*. The first cowboys brought to Hawaii during the early 19th century were Mexicans from California.

papale—hat. Except for the feathered helmets of the *ali'i* warriors of old Hawaii, hats were generally not worn. However, once the islanders saw their practical uses and how fashionable they were, they began weaving them from various materials and quickly became experts at manufacture and design.

pa'u—long split skirt often worn by women when horseback riding. Last century, an island treat was *pa'u* riders in their beautiful dresses at Kapiolani Park in Honolulu. The tradition is carried on today at many of Hawaii's rodeos.

pau*—finished; done; completed. Often combined into *pau hana*, to mean end of work or quitting time.

pilau—stink; bad smell; stench

pilikia—trouble of any kind, big or small; bad times

poi*—a glutinous paste made from the pounded corm of taro, which ferments slightly and has a light sour taste. Purplish in color, it's a staple at luaus, where it is called "one-, two-, or three-finger" poi, depending upon its thickness.

pono—righteous or excellent

pua—flower

puka*—a hole of any size. *Puka* is used by all island residents, whether talking about a pinhole in a rubber boat or a tunnel through a mountain.

punalua—a traditional practice, before the missionaries arrived, of sharing mates. Western seamen took advantage of it, leading to the spread of contagious diseases and eventually to the ultimate demise of the Hawaiian people.

punee*—bed; narrow couch. Used by all ethnic groups. To recline on a *punee* on a breezy lanai is a true island treat.

pu pu*—an appetizer; a snack; hors d'oeuvres; can be anything from cheese and crackers to sushi. Oftentimes, bars or nightclubs offer them free.

pupule—crazy; nuts; out of your mind

pu'u—hill, as in Pu'u Ulaula (Red Hill)

tapa*—a traditional paper cloth made from beaten bark. Intricate designs were stamped in using beaters, and natural dyes added color. The tradition was lost for many years but is now making a comeback, and provides some of the most beautiful folk art in the islands.

taro*—the staple of old Hawaii. A plant with a distinctive broad leaf that produces a starchy root. It was brought by the first Polynesians and was grown on magnificently irrigated plantations. According to the oral tradition, the lifegiving properties of taro hold mystical significance for Hawaiians, since it was created by the gods at about the same time as humans.

ti—a broad-leafed plant that was used for many purposes, from plates to hula skirts (never grass). Especially used to wrap religious offerings presented at the *heiau*.

tutu*—grandmother; granny; older woman. Used by all as a term of respect and endearment.

ukulele*—*uku* means "flea" and *lele* means "jumping," so literally "jumping flea"—the way the Hawaiians perceived the quick finger movements used on the banjolike Portuguese folk instrument called a *cavaquinho*. The ukulele quickly became synonymous with the islands.

wahine*—young woman; female; girl; wife. Used by all ethnic groups. When written on a lavatory door it means "Women's Room."

wai—fresh water; drinking water

wela—hot. *Wela kahao* is a "hot time" or "making whoopee."

wiki*—quickly; fast; in a hurry. Often seen as *wiki wiki* (very fast), as in "Wiki Wiki Messenger Service."

USEFUL PHRASES

Aloha ahiahi—Good evening.
Aloha au ia oe—I love you
Aloha kakahiaka—Good morning.
Aloha nui loa—Much love; fondest regards
Hauoli la hanau—Happy Birthday
Hauoli makahiki hou—Happy New Year

Komo mai—Please come in; enter; welcome
Mele kalikimaka—Merry Christmas
Okolemaluna—Bottoms up; salute; cheers; kampai

ACCOMMODATIONS INDEX

KAUAI

RESTAURANT INDEX

In addition to the following listings, many towns have fast food restaurants.

MAUI

INDEX

BEACHES

BIRDS/BIRDWATCHING

ECOLOGY

FISH/FISHING

GARDENS

GOLF

general information: 108

BIG ISLAND

MAUI

LANAI

MOLOKAI

OAHU

KAUAI

HEIAU

HIKING TRAILS

MUSEUMS

MYTHS AND LEGENDS

SURFING

ABOUT THE AUTHORS

Robert Nilsen was born and raised in Minnesota. His first major excursion from the Midwest was a two-year stint in South Korea with the Peace Corps. Following that eye-opening service, he stayed on in Korea independently, teaching and traveling for another two years. Setting his sights on other lands and other cultures, he made his way through Asia during 1978-80, first heading south from Seoul to Bali and then west as far as the Kyber Pass before returning home to the United States. Over the intervening years, he has had the good fortune to return five times to various countries in Asia and the Pacific. Robert has written *South Korea Handbook* for Moon Publications, revised *Honolulu-Waikiki Handbook, Kauai Handbook, The Big Island of Hawaii Handbook,* and *Maui Handbook,* and contributed to the *Indonesia Handbook.* Since the passing of his good friend J.D. Bisignani, he has shouldered full responsibility for the revision of the Hawaii series of Moon Travel Handbooks, which also includes *Hawaii Handbook.*

Joe Bisignani was a fortunate man because he made his living doing the two things that he liked best: traveling and writing. He will be greatly missed.

A mainstay of Moon Publications since 1979, he was best known in the travel world for his wildly successful, five-volume Hawaii Handbook series, of which *Maui Handbook* won the Hawaii Visitors Bureau's Best Guidebook Award in 1991, while *Hawaii Handbook* earned Best Guidebook as well as the Grand Award for Excellence in 1988. His *Japan Handbook* won the Lowell Thomas Travel Journalism Gold Award in 1993. Together with founder Bill Dalton and other writers, "Joe Biz" profoundly influenced the company's success in the travel publishing world.

J.D. Bisignani

Robert Nilsen

LOSE YOURSELF IN THE EXPERIENCE, NOT THE CROWD

For more than 25 years, Moon Travel Handbooks have been the guidebooks of choice for adventurous travelers. Our award-winning Handbook series provides focused, comprehensive coverage of distinct destinations all over the world. Each Handbook is like an entire bookcase of cultural insight and introductory information in one portable volume. Our goal at Moon is to give travelers all the background and practical information they'll need for an extraordinary travel experience.

The following pages include a complete list of Handbooks, covering North America and Hawaii, Mexico, Latin America and the Caribbean, and Asia and the Pacific. To purchase Moon Travel Handbooks, check your local bookstore or order C/o Publishers Group West, Attn: Order Department, 1700 Fourth St., Berkeley, CA 94710, or fax to (510) 528-3444.

"An in-depth dunk into the land, the people and their history, arts, and politics."
—*Student Travels*

"I consider these books to be superior to Lonely Planet. When Moon produces a book it is more humorous, incisive, and off-beat."
—*Toronto Sun*

"Outdoor enthusiasts gravitate to the well-written Moon Travel Handbooks. In addition to politically correct historic and cultural features, the series focuses on flora, fauna and outdoor recreation. Maps and meticulous directions also are a trademark of Moon guides."
—*Houston Chronicle*

"Moon [Travel Handbooks] . . . bring a healthy respect to the places they investigate. Best of all, they provide a host of odd nuggets that give a place texture and prod the wary traveler from the beaten path. The finest are written with such care and insight they deserve listing as literature."
—*American Geographical Society*

"Moon Travel Handbooks offer in-depth historical essays and useful maps, enhanced by a sense of humor and a neat, compact format."
—*Swing*

"Perfect for the more adventurous, these are long on history, sightseeing and nitty-gritty information and very price-specific."
—*Columbus Dispatch*

"Moon guides manage to be comprehensive and countercultural at the same time . . . Handbooks are packed with maps, photographs, drawings, and sidebars that constitute a college-level introduction to each country's history, culture, people, and crafts."
—*National Geographic Traveler*

"Few travel guides do a better job helping travelers create their own itineraries than the Moon Travel Handbook series. The authors have a knack for homing in on the essentials."
—**Colorado Springs** *Gazette Telegraph*

MEXICO

"These books will delight the armchair traveler, aid the undecided person in selecting a destination, and guide the seasoned road warrior looking for lesser-known hideaways."
—*Mexican Meanderings* Newsletter

"From tourist traps to off-the-beaten track hideaways, these guides offer consistent, accurate details without pretension."
—*Foreign Service Journal*

Archaeological Mexico	**$19.95**
Andrew Coe	420 pages, 27 maps
Baja Handbook	**$16.95**
Joe Cummings	540 pages, 46 maps
Cabo Handbook	**$14.95**
Joe Cummings	270 pages, 17 maps
Cancún Handbook	**$14.95**
Chicki Mallan	240 pages, 25 maps
Colonial Mexico	**$18.95**
Chicki Mallan	400 pages, 38 maps
Mexico Handbook	**$21.95**
Joe Cummings and Chicki Mallan	1,200 pages, 201 maps
Northern Mexico Handbook	**$17.95**
Joe Cummings	610 pages, 69 maps
Pacific Mexico Handbook	**$17.95**
Bruce Whipperman	580 pages, 68 maps
Puerto Vallarta Handbook	**$14.95**
Bruce Whipperman	330 pages, 36 maps
Yucatán Handbook	**$16.95**
Chicki Mallan	400 pages, 52 maps

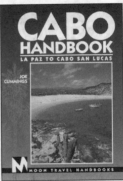

"Beyond question, the most comprehensive Mexican resources available for those who prefer deep travel to shallow tourism. But don't worry, the fiesta-fun stuff's all here too."
—*New York Daily News*

LATIN AMERICA AND THE CARIBBEAN

"Solidly packed with practical information and full of significant cultural asides that will enlighten you on the whys and wherefores of things you might easily see but not easily grasp."

—*Boston Globe*

Belize Handbook	**$15.95**
Chicki Mallan and Patti Lange	390 pages, 45 maps
Caribbean Vacations	**$18.95**
Karl Luntta	910 pages, 64 maps
Costa Rica Handbook	**$19.95**
Christopher P. Baker	780 pages, 73 maps
Cuba Handbook	**$19.95**
Christopher P. Baker	740 pages, 70 maps
Dominican Republic Handbook	**$15.95**
Gaylord Dold	420 pages, 24 maps
Ecuador Handbook	**$16.95**
Julian Smith	450 pages, 43 maps
Honduras Handbook	**$15.95**
Chris Humphrey	330 pages, 40 maps
Jamaica Handbook	**$15.95**
Karl Luntta	330 pages, 17 maps
Virgin Islands Handbook	**$13.95**
Karl Luntta	220 pages, 19 maps

NORTH AMERICA AND HAWAII

"These domestic guides convey the same sense of exoticism that their foreign counterparts do, making home-country travel seem like far-flung adventure."

—*Sierra Magazine*

Alaska-Yukon Handbook	**$17.95**
Deke Castleman and Don Pitcher	530 pages, 92 maps
Alberta and the Northwest Territories Handbook	**$18.95**
Andrew Hempstead	520 pages, 79 maps
Arizona Handbook	**$18.95**
Bill Weir	600 pages, 36 maps
Atlantic Canada Handbook	**$18.95**
Mark Morris	490 pages, 60 maps
Big Island of Hawaii Handbook	**$15.95**
J.D. Bisignani	390 pages, 25 maps
Boston Handbook	**$13.95**
Jeff Perk	200 pages, 20 maps
British Columbia Handbook	**$16.95**
Jane King and Andrew Hempstead	430 pages, 69 maps

Canadian Rockies Handbook	**$14.95**
Andrew Hempstead	220 pages, 22 maps
Colorado Handbook	**$17.95**
Stephen Metzger	480 pages, 46 maps
Georgia Handbook	**$17.95**
Kap Stann	380 pages, 44 maps
Grand Canyon Handbook	**$14.95**
Bill Weir	220 pages, 10 maps
Hawaii Handbook	**$19.95**
J.D. Bisignani	1,030 pages, 88 maps
Honolulu-Waikiki Handbook	**$14.95**
J.D. Bisignani	360 pages, 20 maps
Idaho Handbook	**$18.95**
Don Root	610 pages, 42 maps
Kauai Handbook	**$15.95**
J.D. Bisignani	320 pages, 23 maps
Los Angeles Handbook	**$16.95**
Kim Weir	370 pages, 15 maps
Maine Handbook	**$18.95**
Kathleen M. Brandes	660 pages, 27 maps
Massachusetts Handbook	**$18.95**
Jeff Perk	600 pages, 23 maps
Maui Handbook	**$15.95**
J.D. Bisignani	450 pages, 37 maps
Michigan Handbook	**$15.95**
Tina Lassen	360 pages, 32 maps
Montana Handbook	**$17.95**
Judy Jewell and W.C. McRae	490 pages, 52 maps
Nevada Handbook	**$18.95**
Deke Castleman	530 pages, 40 maps
New Hampshire Handbook	**$18.95**
Steve Lantos	500 pages, 18 maps
New Mexico Handbook	**$15.95**
Stephen Metzger	360 pages, 47 maps
New York Handbook	**$19.95**
Christiane Bird	780 pages, 95 maps
New York City Handbook	**$13.95**
Christiane Bird	300 pages, 20 maps
North Carolina Handbook	**$14.95**
Rob Hirtz and Jenny Daughtry Hirtz	320 pages, 27 maps
Northern California Handbook	**$19.95**
Kim Weir	800 pages, 50 maps
Ohio Handbook	**$15.95**
David K. Wright	340 pages, 18 maps
Oregon Handbook	**$17.95**
Stuart Warren and Ted Long Ishikawa	590 pages, 34 maps

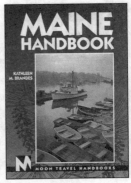

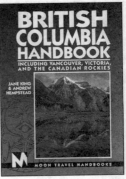

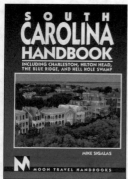

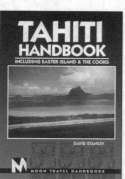

Pennsylvania Handbook	**$18.95**
Joanne Miller	448 pages, 40 maps
Road Trip USA	**$24.00**
Jamie Jensen	940 pages, 175 maps
Road Trip USA Getaways: Chicago	**$9.95**
	60 pages, 1 map
Road Trip USA Getaways: Seattle	**$9.95**
	60 pages, 1 map
Santa Fe-Taos Handbook	**$13.95**
Stephen Metzger	160 pages, 13 maps
South Carolina Handbook	**$16.95**
Mike Sigalas	400 pages, 20 maps
Southern California Handbook	**$19.95**
Kim Weir	720 pages, 26 maps
Tennessee Handbook	**$17.95**
Jeff Bradley	530 pages, 42 maps
Texas Handbook	**$18.95**
Joe Cummings	690 pages, 70 maps
Utah Handbook	**$17.95**
Bill Weir and W.C. McRae	490 pages, 40 maps
Virginia Handbook	**$15.95**
Julian Smith	410 pages, 37 maps
Washington Handbook	**$19.95**
Don Pitcher	840 pages, 111 maps
Wisconsin Handbook	**$18.95**
Thomas Huhti	590 pages, 69 maps
Wyoming Handbook	**$17.95**
Don Pitcher	610 pages, 80 maps

ASIA AND THE PACIFIC

"Scores of maps, detailed practical info down to business hours of small-town libraries. You can't beat the Asian titles for sheer heft. (The) series is sort of an American Lonely Planet, with better writing but fewer titles. (The) individual voice of researchers comes through."

—Travel & Leisure

Australia Handbook	**$21.95**
Marael Johnson, Andrew Hempstead, and Nadina Purdon	940 pages, 141 maps
Bali Handbook	**$19.95**
Bill Dalton	750 pages, 54 maps
Fiji Islands Handbook	**$14.95**
David Stanley	350 pages, 42 maps
Hong Kong Handbook	**$16.95**
Kerry Moran	378 pages, 49 maps

Indonesia Handbook	**$25.00**
Bill Dalton	1,380 pages, 249 maps
Micronesia Handbook	**$16.95**
Neil M. Levy	340 pages, 70 maps
Nepal Handbook	**$18.95**
Kerry Moran	490 pages, 51 maps
New Zealand Handbook	**$19.95**
Jane King	620 pages, 81 maps
Outback Australia Handbook	**$18.95**
Marael Johnson	450 pages, 57 maps
Philippines Handbook	**$17.95**
Peter Harper and Laurie Fullerton	670 pages, 116 maps
Singapore Handbook	**$15.95**
Carl Parkes	350 pages, 29 maps
South Korea Handbook	**$19.95**
Robert Nilsen	820 pages, 141 maps
South Pacific Handbook	**$24.00**
David Stanley	920 pages, 147 maps
Southeast Asia Handbook	**$21.95**
Carl Parkes	1,080 pages, 204 maps
Tahiti Handbook	**$15.95**
David Stanley	450 pages, 51 maps
Thailand Handbook	**$19.95**
Carl Parkes	860 pages, 142 maps
Vietnam, Cambodia & Laos Handbook	**$18.95**
Michael Buckley	760 pages, 116 maps

OTHER GREAT TITLES FROM MOON

"For hardy wanderers, few guides come more highly recommended than the Handbooks. They include good maps, steer clear of fluff and flackery, and offer plenty of money-saving tips. They also give you the kind of information that visitors to strange lands—on any budget—need to survive."

—*US News & World Report*

Moon Handbook	**$10.00**
Carl Koppeschaar	150 pages, 8 maps
The Practical Nomad: How to Travel Around the World	**$17.95**
Edward Hasbrouck	580 pages
Staying Healthy in Asia, Africa, and Latin America	**$11.95**
Dirk Schroeder	230 pages, 4 maps

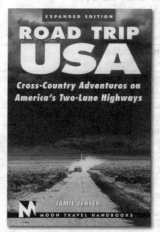

WHERE TO BUY MOON TRAVEL HANDBOOKS

BOOKSTORES AND LIBRARIES: Moon Travel Handbooks are distributed worldwide. Please contact our sales manager at info@moon.com for a list of wholesalers and distributors in your area.

TRAVELERS: We would like to have Moon Travel Handbooks available throughout the world. Please ask your bookstore to contact us for ordering information. If your bookstore will not order our guides for you, please contact us for a free catalog.

> **Moon Travel Handbooks**
> C/o Publishers Group West
> Attn: Order Department
> 1700 Fourth Street
> Berkeley, CA 94710
> fax: (510) 528-3444

IMPORTANT ORDERING INFORMATION

PRICES: All prices are subject to change. We always ship the most current edition. We will let you know if there is a price increase on the book you order.

SHIPPING AND HANDLING OPTIONS: Domestic UPS or USPS priority mail (allow 10 working days for delivery): $6.00 for the first item, $1.00 for each additional item.

UPS 2nd Day Air or Printed Airmail requires a special quote.

International Surface Bookrate 8-12 weeks delivery: $5.00 for the first item, $1.00 for each additional item. Note: We cannot guarantee international surface bookrate shipping. We recommend sending international orders via air mail, which requires a special quote.

FOREIGN ORDERS: Orders that originate outside the U.S.A. must be paid for with an international money order, a check in U.S. currency drawn on a major U.S. bank based in the U.S.A., or Visa, MasterCard, or American Express.

INTERNET ORDERS: Visit our site at: www.moon.com

ORDER FORM

Prices are subject to change without notice. Please check our Web site
at **www.moon.com** for current prices and editions.
(See important ordering information on preceding page.)

Name: _____ Date: _____

Street: _____

City: _____ Daytime Phone: _____

State or Country: _____ Zip Code: _____

QUANTITY	TITLE	PRICE
	Taxable Total	
	Sales Tax in CA and NY	
	Shipping & Handling	
	TOTAL	

Ship: ☐ UPS (no P.O. Boxes) ☐ Priority mail ☐ International surface mail

Ship to: ☐ address above ☐ other _____

_____

Make checks payable to: **PUBLISHERS GROUP WEST**, Attn: Order Department, 1700 Fourth St.,
Berkeley, CA 94710, or fax to (510) 528-3444. We accept Visa, MasterCard, or American Express.
To Order: Fax in your Visa, MasterCard, or American Express number, or send a written order
with your Visa, MasterCard, or American Express number and expiration date clearly written.

Card Number: ☐ **Visa** ☐ **MasterCard** ☐ **American Express**

☐ ☐ ☐ ☐ ☐ ☐ ☐ ☐ ☐ ☐ ☐ ☐ ☐ ☐ ☐ ☐

Exact Name on Card: _____

Expiration date: _____

Signature: _____

Daytime Phone: _____

U.S.~METRIC CONVERSION

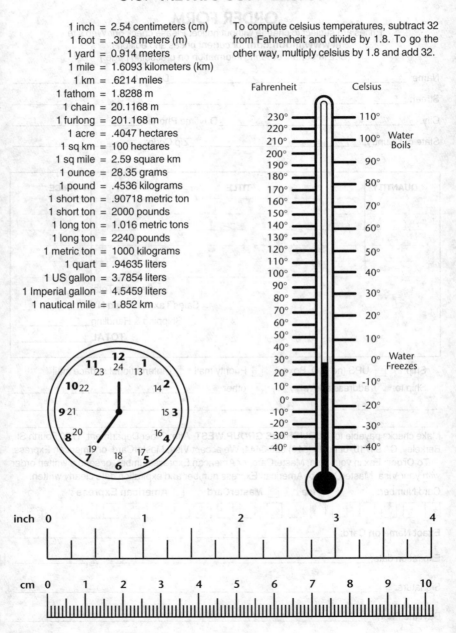

1 inch	= 2.54 centimeters (cm)
1 foot	= .3048 meters (m)
1 yard	= 0.914 meters
1 mile	= 1.6093 kilometers (km)
1 km	= .6214 miles
1 fathom	= 1.8288 m
1 chain	= 20.1168 m
1 furlong	= 201.168 m
1 acre	= .4047 hectares
1 sq km	= 100 hectares
1 sq mile	= 2.59 square km
1 ounce	= 28.35 grams
1 pound	= .4536 kilograms
1 short ton	= .90718 metric ton
1 short ton	= 2000 pounds
1 long ton	= 1.016 metric tons
1 long ton	= 2240 pounds
1 metric ton	= 1000 kilograms
1 quart	= .94635 liters
1 US gallon	= 3.7854 liters
1 Imperial gallon	= 4.5459 liters
1 nautical mile	= 1.852 km

To compute celsius temperatures, subtract 32 from Fahrenheit and divide by 1.8. To go the other way, multiply celsius by 1.8 and add 32.